Pratt's
Guide to Venture Capital Sources

2001
Edition

Sponsored by

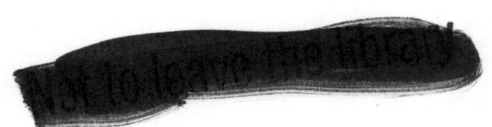

E & A EDWARDS & ANGELL, LLP
Counsellors at Law

THOMSON FINANCIAL
VENTURE ECONOMICS™

Pratt's

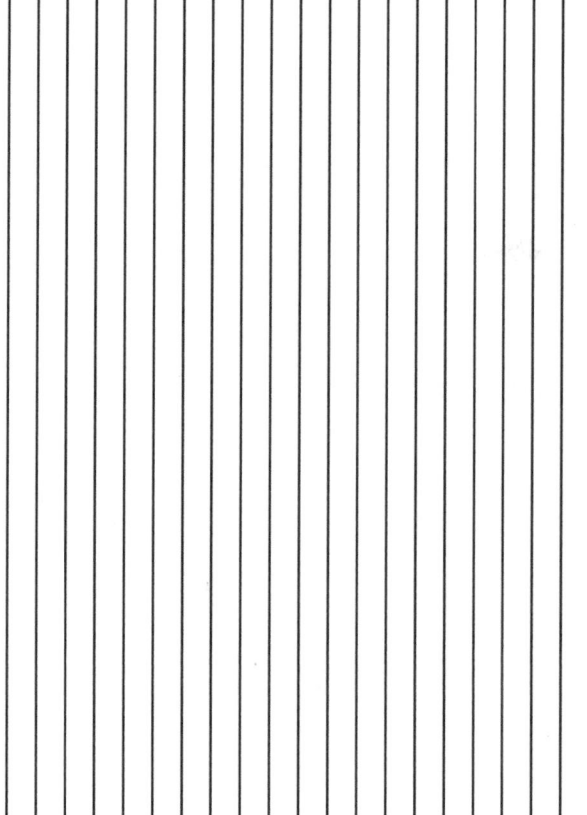

Guide to Venture Capital Sources

2001 Edition

THOMSON FINANCIAL
VENTURE ECONOMICS

195 Broadway • New York, NY 10007
Phone: 1-800-455-5844 or 646-822-2000
Fax: 646-822-4935

For advertising call Albert Guffanti
646-822-3073 or email: albert.guffanti@tfn.com
For book orders call Mark Cialdella
646-822-3046 or email: mark.cialdella@tfn.com

2001 Edition

Printed in the United States of America
ISSN 0884-1616
ISBN 0-914470-09-4
Library of Congress Catalog Card Number 85-644764
Venture Economics, a Thomson Financial Securities Data Company
Two Gateway Center, 11th Floor, Newark, NJ 07102

Preface

The United States was founded and has thrived on the principles of entrepreneurship and individual and collective risk-taking. In many ways, the nation's development has sprung from the willingness to assume the risks inherent in new business development. The imagination, boldness and energy of entrepreneurs and small-business owners combined with the involvement and persistence of experienced venture capital investors have created new industries and new technologies, which in turn have increased the productivity of the nation's economic process and of its workers. In our recovering economy, there should be plenty of opportunities to put those virtues to work.

This book is dedicated to the men and women who are willing to take on the challenges of building new businesses and to those venture capitalists with the skills, fortitude and foresight to participate in new business development. The contributions of the country's entrepreneurs have never seemed more important as we seek to create new jobs and broaden our economic recovery.

A good relationship between the entrepreneur and the venture capitalist is a vital element in a successful venture. Understanding this partnership is a necessary first step for the prospective entrepreneur. The entrepreneur brings fresh ideas, management skills and personal commitment to this relationship, while the venture capitalist adds financial backing and valuable new business development experience. Although the entrepreneur and the management team are usually the most critical elements in the relationship (since venture capitalists cannot perform their roles without entrepreneurs), the partnership of entrepreneurial management and venture investors usually enables a developing business to achieve its objectives faster and more efficiently. In today's dynamic and competitive marketplace such an investor/management partnership is often critical to the survival and success of new business development.

The industry has expanded dramatically in the past year in terms of venture capital fundraising, from $65.4 bil. in 1999 to $98.1 bil. in 2000. While that is a substantial sum, it is a fraction of the asset base of commercial banks and insurance companies. Certain state pension funds control more money than the entire venture capital industry. As a result, the venture capital process involves a personal relationship which can grow and endure or end in frustration and disappointment.

In the last two years, venture capitalists have invested over $163.6 billion in new and growing businesses. The companies that attracted these dollars will require continued financial support to fuel their growth. These follow-on investments, which constitute a large part of current venture capital activity, as well as the commitments to new investment opportunities will absorb the capital currently available in the industry. As these commitments are made, the demand for venture capital intensifies. This book was conceived and has grown over the last 30 years by helping to increase the entrepreneur's chances of success in receiving funding. It provides the most thorough analysis of what each venture capital firm can and will provide to fledgling businesses. It is our hope that by organizing and simplifying this process, we can help you get the right financing for your business idea.

Contents

INTRODUCTION 9

BACKGROUND OF VENTURE CAPITAL

Introduction 13

Venture Capital Market Breaks New Record Despite 4Q Slowdown 15
Jennifer Strauss

Characteristics of a Successful Entrepreneurial Management Team 19
Alexander L.M. Dingee, Brian Haslett and Leonard E. Smollen

HOW TO RAISE VENTURE CAPITAL

Introduction 25

Structuring Venture Capital Investments 27
Jonathan E. Cole, Esq. and Albert L. Sokol, Esq.

Preparing a Business Plan 37
Brian Haslett and Leonard E. Smollen

How to Choose and Approach a Venture Capitalist 47
G. Jackson Tankersley Jr.

Meeting with the Venture Capitalist 51
Wayne B. Kingsley

Venture Capital: More Than Money? 55
Dr. Jeffry A. Timmons and Harry Sapienza

Structuring the Financing 63
Stanley C. Golder

Preliminary Legal Considerations in Forming a New Enterprise 67
Michael P. Ridley, Esq.

SOURCES OF BUSINESS DEVELOPMENT FINANCING

Introduction 73

The Organized Venture Capital Community 75
Stanley E. Pratt

Mezzanine Financing: A Flexible Source of Capital 81
Robert C. Ammerman

Corporate Strategic Partnerships 85
Mark L. Radtke and George W. McKinney

Dealing with the Corporate Strategic Investor 89
Kenneth W. Rind

Non-Traditional Financing Sources 93
Gregory B. Sneddon and Jay K. Turner

PERSPECTIVES

Introduction 99

Relationship Between Venture Capitalist and Entrepreneur 101
Brook H. Byers

An Entrepreneur's Guide to Financing the High Technology Company 105
Thomas H. Bruggere

The SBIC Program: Capital for Entrepreneurs 109
Bruce A. Kinn and Arnold M. Zaff

Managing Deals
Claes E. Larsson *113*

The Geography of Venture Capital Firms
Matthew Zook *119*

DIRECTORIES

United States Venture Capital Firms 125
Non U.S. Venture Capital Firms 723

INDEXES

Index of Venture Capital Professionals 983

Industry Preference Index 1035

Stage Preference Index 1,113

Company Index 1,177

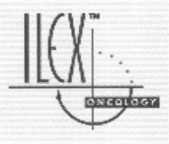

Introduction

This twenty-fifth edition of *Pratt's Guide to Venture Capital Sources* has been enlarged and exhaustively updated to incorporate the most current information on the venture capital investment process and on the individual venture capital firms. The 2001 edition contains substantially more firms than ever before as a result of a change in resources. We are now taking full advantage of both the depth and breadth of the Venture Economics research database to include more domestic and foreign firms.

Pratt's Guide was created as a tool to help entrepreneurs and small-business managers understand the process of raising capital and locating compatible venture capital investors.

Information on the industry and guidelines for companies seeking financing are provided in the articles written by professional venture investors who discuss important aspects of venture financing and describe criteria for investments. The text is divided into four sections: "Background on Venture Capital," "How to Raise Venture Capital," "Sources of Business Development Financing," and "Perspectives."

"Background on Venture Capital" is designed to help prospective entrepreneurs understand the venture investment process. The nature of a venture capitalist's involvement is described as well as the characteristics of successful entrepreneurial management teams. We kick off the section with a look at the state of the industry written by Jennifer Strauss, Editor of the *Venture Capital Journal*.

The articles in "How to Raise Venture Capital" are written by industry professionals whose goal is to expedite the investing process for the investor as well as the entrepreneur by clearly laying out realistic expectations and standard procedures for approaching a venture capitalist.

"Sources of Business Development Financing" describes private- and public-sector financing opportunities. Private venture capital sources include private partnerships and corporations, publicly held venture firms, venture capital funds formed by banks and bank holding companies, divisions of major corporations, affiliates of investment banking firms, venture leasing companies and direct venture investment activity by insurance companies, pension funds or investment advisory firms.

The information in the "Perspectives" portion of the text provides insight into the characteristics venture capitalists look for in their clients, as well as an entrepreneur's view of the venture process. Understanding the different facets of the venture development process will increase the chances of establishing a productive working relationship with a venture capitalist, which can be critical to a venture's success or failure.

At one time, venture capital financing was regarded as the early-stage financing for relatively small, rapidly growing companies. Today, venture investment activity covers a spectrum of interests that encompasses virtually all phases of business growth. In addition to early-stage funding, venture capitalists provide expansion financing for companies that have overcome initial hurdles and require additional capital for growth, but that do not yet have access to public or credit-oriented institutional funding. Venture capitalists, together with entrepreneurs and business managements, also finance leveraged buyouts, which may involve purchasing ailing corporate divisions or absentee-owned private businesses with the objective of revitalizing them.

The directory that follows the text contains detailed information on venture capital companies in the United States and around the world. Four indexes follow the directories: a list of the venture capital companies' personnel, an industry preference index, an investment stage preference index, and a company index.

Since various terms are mentioned throughout the text and in the directories, it is important that these terms are clearly defined.

Early-Stage Financing

- *Seed Financing* is a relatively small amount of capital provided to an inventor or entrepreneur to prove a concept and to qualify for start-up capital. This may involve product development and market research as well as building a management team and developing a business plan, if the initial steps are successful.

- *Research and Development Financing* is a tax-advantaged partnership set up to finance product development for start-ups as well as more mature companies. Investors secure tax write-offs for the investments as well as a later share of the profits if the product development is successful.

- *Start-up Financing* is provided to companies completing product development and initial marketing. Companies may be in the process of organizing or they may already be in business for one year or less, but have not sold their product commercially. Usually such firms will have made market studies, assembled the key management, developed a business plan and are ready to do business.

- *First-Stage Financing* is provided to companies that have expended their initial capital (often in developing and market testing a prototype), and require funds to initiate full-scale manufacturing and sales.

Expansion Financing

- *Second-Stage Financing* is working capital for the initial expansion of a company that is producing and shipping, and has growing accounts receivable and inventories. Although the company has made progress, it may not yet be showing a profit.

- *Third-Stage or Mezzanine Financing* is provided for major expansion of a company whose sales volume is increasing and that is breaking even or profitable. These funds are used for further plant expansion, marketing, working capital, or development of an improved product.

- *Bridge Financing* is needed at times when a company plans to go public within six months to a year. Often bridge financing is structured so that it can be repaid from the proceeds of a public underwriting. It can also involve restructuring of major stockholder positions through secondary transactions. Restructuring is undertaken if there are early investors who want to reduce or liquidate their positions, or if management has changed and the stockholdings of the former management, their relatives and associates are being bought out to relieve a potential oversupply of stock when public.

Acquisition/Buyout Financing

- *Acquisition Financing* provides funds to finance an acquisition of another company.

- *Management/Leveraged Buyout* funds enable an operating management group to acquire a product line or business (which may be at any stage of development) from either a public or private company; often these companies are closely held or family owned. Management/leveraged buyouts usually involve revitalizing an operation, with entrepreneurial management acquiring a significant equity interest.

The type of venture capital firm best suited for a specific situation must be determined by the company seeking financing and by its advisors. Each venture capital firm has particular preferences, methods of investing and selecting investments and its own type of legal investment agreements. Since no two venture firms operate in exactly the same way, it is essential that entrepreneurs and business managers analyze their needs and attempt to match these requirements with the skills and interests of an appropriate venture capital firm. For this reason, *Pratt's Guide* has several indexes, including one listing firms by stage-of-investment preferences, to help speed entrepreneurs to the venture firms that are most likely to be interested in their projects. Two other indexes list venture firms and their personnel alphabetically. Yet another index lists the firms by their industry preferences.

While the venture capital firms included in *Pratt's Guide* have been selected because they are devoted primarily to venture financing, there is no assurance that a specific group will be receptive to an approach or will have immediately available funds. However, many of the firms in the book consider being listed as an excellent marketing opportunity. Even with the current availability of investment capital, the majority of new investment proposals are not financed. Convincing venture capitalists that a potential development is an important investment opportunity is truly a new company's first major sale. Further, a good working relationship must be established and maintained to optimize the benefits of a venture capital investment.

The firms listed have different capacities for servicing client companies, and it is critical for the entrepreneur or business management to understand these capabilities. Some firms can provide a range of financial and managerial services, while others may have specialized talents that would be valuable to some new businesses but relatively unimportant to others.

The nature and extent of active involvement venture capitalists put into their investments varies. Generally, the most successful venturers are actively involved in the companies they finance. While the directories in *Pratt's Guide* attempt to delineate preferences as well as levels of activity and involvement, the entrepreneur and management team must develop a means of evaluating the ongoing role of the venture investor.

Most venture capital firms are not interested in reviewing situations that are clearly not going to meet their stated preferences. Consequently, a careful review of the information in the text and in the directories should help capital seekers begin to develop a productive investment relationship with the firms.

Background of Venture Capital

Venture capital traditionally has been a low profile, private industry. Although the national media has given increased attention to the venture capital process during the 1980s and early 1990s, misconceptions about the industry continue to proliferate, particularly with the reaction of the stock markets to technology stocks in 2000. It is this book's objective to provide a realistic view of what the entrepreneur can expect from venture capital financing and from a long-term relationship with professional venture investors.

The first article in this section, "Venture Capital Market Breaks New Record Despite 4Q Slowdown" examines key trends affecting the venture capital industry today, focusing on the records broken in fund raising and investment in 2000. The article explores how the environment allowed these records to fall and what the implications are for the future.

The qualities of entrepreneurs are examined in "Characteristics of an Entrepreneurial Management Team," which outlines the characteristics needed to create and grow a new venture. Also included are criteria that can be used to judge a new venture's viability and its potential risks.

Understanding the operations of the venture capital industry and the process of new business development, as well as the individual roles involved, is critical to the potential entrepreneur.

Venture Capital Market Breaks New Record Despite 4Q Slowdown

By Jennifer Strauss

Jennifer Strauss is the editor of Venture Capital Journal, a 40-year old monthly publication covering the venture capital/private equity industries.

The venture capital market entered 2000 roaring like a proud lion, following its record-breaking performance during the previous year. Egged on by a most favorable initial public offering market, venture capitalists herded their young portfolio companies into the public market in 1999, and then watched in awe as their valuations shot through the roof. Not wanting to miss out on the opportunity to fund the "next big thing," VCs went into high gear, seemingly investing in almost any business plan with a dotcom.

But in April 2000, the high-speed VC market was forced to slam on the brakes, in the face of a sizeable stock market correction. With IPO investors rethinking their strategies, the venture market's so-called "irrational exuberance" began to subside, and that proud lion starting morphing into a lamb.

However, the April scare wasn't enough to curtail overall investments, as VC investing remained high and steady for the first three quarters of the year. Even with a slowdown in the final quarter, 2000 still finished the year breaking another record, as disbursements exceeded the $100 billion mark for the first time — a feat not likely to be repeated in 2001.

VCs invested a total of $104.2 billion in 2000, an increase of 75% over 1999's $59.4 billion, according to Venture Economics and the National Venture Capital Association (NVCA). The total number of companies receiving VC funding also rose considerably, reaching 5,443, a 37% increase from the 3,968 companies that received funding in 1999.

Disbursements per Company by Industry Minor Group
01/01/2000 to 12/31/2000
Rounds 1 to 99

Company Industry Minor Group	NUM OF COMP	SUM INV $MIL	AVG PER COMP
Internet Specific	2,469	48,282.8	19.6
Communications	572	17,777.0	31.1
Computer Software and Services	974	14,689.2	15.1
Semiconductors/Other Elect.	241	6,172.6	25.6
Other Products	302	5,373.1	17.8
Medical/Health	339	3,665.6	10.8
Biotechnology	182	2,775.2	15.3
Computer Hardware	148	2,313.4	15.6
Consumer Related	142	1,707.4	12.0
Industrial/Energy	74	1,424.4	19.3
TOTAL	5,443	104,180.7	19.1

Source: Venture Economics/NVCA

Despite all the talk of a "dotcom death count" coupled with massive layoffs, Internet-specific companies still managed to attract a overwhelming majority of the venture capital doled out in 2000. According to Venture Economics and the NVCA, Internet-specific companies attracted $48.3 billion for an increase of 91% over 1999, when they received $25.2 billion. These companies also represented a larger share of total funds, receiving 46.3% versus 42.5% in 1999.

The communications and computer software/services sectors were also popular with VCs last year. Communications companies garnered $17.8 billion in 2000, a 78.3% increase from $9.97 billion in 1999, while computer software/services companies raked in $14.7 billion, an 89.7% increase from $7.7 billion the previous year. Meanwhile, the semiconductor sector made the most significant strides, attracting $6.2 billion in 2000, a whopping 163.7% increase over 1999's total of just $2.3 billion.

Disbursements per Company by State Region

1/1/00 to 12/31/00
Rounds 1 to 99

Company State Region	NUM OF COMP	SUM INV $MIL
N. California	1,534	33,913.7
Greater New York	618	12,068.1
New England	607	10,563.5
S. California	500	8,476.7
Southeast	400	6,752.7
Mid-Atlantic	328	6,702.2
Southwest	374	6,484.2
Rocky Mountains	200	5,636.9
Northwest	237	3,840.3
Great Lakes	212	3,494.5
Ohio Valley	199	2,751.7
Great Plains	146	2,227.3
South	67	954.4
Alaska/Hawaii	3	224.5
Unknown	18	90.0

Source: Venture Economics/NVCA

Mega Funds

VC fund raising reached new highs last year, as well, garnering more than $92.6 billion, up 54% from 1999's total of $60 billion, according to Venture Economics. A total of 494 funds were in the market last year, compared with 403 funds in 1999, while the average fund size was $187.5 million versus $148.8 million in 1999. Not surprisingly, the lofty fund-raising totals were helped along by a dramatic increase in the number of mega funds raised.

Indeed, as more and more start-ups requested—and

Commitments per Fund by Fund Raising Year

1/1/1990 to 12/31/2000

Fund Raising Year	NUM OF FUND	SUM RAISED $MIL
1990	82	3,134.0
1991	43	1,747.5
1992	75	5,015.6
1993	94	4,529.9
1994	134	7,623.6
1995	155	9,797.0
1996	163	11,776.2
1997	224	17,026.5
1998	255	29,187.9
1999	403	59,972.2
2000	494	92,612.9

Source: Venture Economics/NVCA

received—larger investments in the first half of 2000, VC firms followed the "bigger is better" philosophy in their fund raising efforts. Some of the large funds of 2000 were: the $2.1 billion Summit Ventures VI, the $2 billion New Enterprise Associates X LP, the $1.77 billion Spectrum Equity Investors IV LP, the $1.25 billion Redpoint Ventures II LP and the $1 billion Battery Venture VI LP.

Toward the end of 2000, some VC firms started to lose confidence in their ability to invest these mega funds. Limited partners were getting more discriminating, and some of the large funds that had already closed in 2000 were holding onto their cash.

In an unprecedented move late in 2000, Crosspoint Venture Partners returned LP commitments after completing fund raising for its latest $1 billion fund citing the current state of market conditions. Only time will tell if Crosspoint's actions are a sign of things to come, or just an extremely cautious firm playing it safe.

IPO Market Sees Ups and Downs

Even with the IPO window shut pretty tight by the end of 2000, it was not that bad a year for venture-backed IPOs. The IPO market enjoyed three robust quarters before trailing off in the final quarter of the year, with venture-backed IPOs accounting for more than half of all IPOs.

The start of 2000 witnessed a good number of VCs ushering their portfolio companies into the public market — in most cases a bit prematurely. But when the bull market began its retreat mid year, culminating in the Nasdaq losing almost half of its value, VCs changed their tune, investing more money and time in their existing portfolio companies.

Data from Venture Economics and the NVCA indicate that following the stock market correction, VCs started to take a harder, longer look at companies before investing, focusing on the long-term viability. That shift resulted in VCs supporting more later-round investments.

All of the above factors help to explain the dropoff in the fourth quarter last year. All told, 230 venture-backed companies went public, raising $21.9 billion and marking a total post-offering valuation of $96.1 billion. In 1999, 258 venture-backed IPOs raised $19.8 billion and marked a post-offering valuation of $126.4 billion.

The average offering size for a venture-backed IPO last year was up 24% from the previous year to $95 million from $76.8 million. However, the average post-offering valuation dipped 14.7% to $417.9 million from $490.2 million.

Even as the IPO window began to close, Chase H&Q reigned supreme by taking 28 of its portfolio companies public. Goldman, Sachs & Co. made a respectable second-place show-

Disbursements per Company by Year

1/1/00 to 12/31/00
Rounds 1 to 99

Company Disbursement Year	NUM OF ROUND	NUM OF COMP	SUM INV $MIL	AVG PER ROUND	AVG PER COMP
1990	1,785	1,317	3,261.6	1.8	2.5
1991	1,528	1,088	2,463.6	1.6	2.3
1992	1,857	1,294	5,058.3	2.7	3.9
1993	1,571	1,150	4,919.2	3.1	4.3
1994	1,648	1,191	5,262.9	3.2	4.4
1995	1,752	1,325	5,471.4	3.1	4.1
1996	2,584	2,001	11,179.4	4.3	5.6
1997	3,564	2,696	17,209.1	4.8	6.4
1998	4,085	3,150	22,101.5	5.4	7.0
1999	5,134	3,968	59,416.1	11.6	15.0
2000	6,933	5,443	104,180.7	15.0	19.1

Source: Venture Economics/NVCA

ing, bringing 19 companies public.

Some of 2000's notable venture-backed IPOs included Corvis Corp., which raised $1.14 billion; TNPC Inc., which raised $504 million; and Mediacom Communications Corp., which raised $380 million.

Regional Breakdown

It should come as no surprise that the largest portion of VC investments went to companies in Silicon Valley and Silicon Alley. VCs invested a total of $33.9 billion in Northern California, a 73.9% increase of the 1999 total of $19.4 billion, and invested $12.1 billion in the Greater New York region, a 61.1% increase from 1999's $7.5 billion. Combined, those areas accounted for 44.1% of all VC disbursements in 2000.

More noteworthy are the areas that recorded the largest percentage gains in 2000. The Rocky Mountains, the Great Plains and New England posted the greatest growth rates last year of 137.6%, 114.3% and 102.6%, respectively. Certainly even with such impressive gains, VCs will not be fleeing Silicon Valley any time soon to head for a more promising land; however they will be keeping close tabs on these vibrant areas.

On the flip side, the South was the only region that posted a loss in 2000, with investments falling off 27.1% to $954.4 million from $1.3 billion.

Venture Economics Information Services
IPO Database Standard Summary Report
IPOs per Company by IPO Year

1/1/00 to 12/31/00

Company IPO Year	NUM OF IPOs	OFFER AMOUNT ($MIL)	POST OFFER VALUE ($MIL)	AVG OFFER AMOUNT ($MIL)	AVG POST VALUE ($MIL)
1990	68	1,398.7	5,472.8	22.9	89.7
1991	151	4,756.7	20,134.2	32.1	136.0
1992	194	7,532.5	32,750.0	40.5	176.1
1993	224	6,780.3	23,236.7	31.5	108.1
1994	167	4,632.8	17,943.9	28.1	108.8
1995	204	8,181.5	32,864.3	40.7	163.5
1996	279	11,903.2	57,886.7	42.7	207.5
1997	137	49,44.3	22,642.6	36.1	165.3
1998	78	38,41.4	17,872.6	49.2	229.1
1999	258	19,819.3	126,466.4	76.8	490.2
2000	230	21,858.9	96,116.5	95.0	417.9

Source: Venture Economics

Characteristics of a Successful Entrepreneurial Management Team

Alexander L. M. Dingee, Brian Haslett and Leonard E. Smollen

Alexander L. M. Dingee *is the Director of the M.I.T. Venture Mentoring Service, which supports innovation and entrepreneurial activity throughout the M.I.T. community by matching prospective entrepreneurs with volunteer mentors. Mr. Dingee is also the Chairman and a founder of Kortec, Inc. (turn-key coinjection molding systems). Previously he served as a Founder, Director and Treasurer of Nexabit Networks, Inc. (terabit switch routers; Nexabit was sold to Lucent in 1999). Mr. Dingee has also been the founding CEO of venture Founders Corporation (start-up venture capital funds), geodyne Corporation (oceanographic instruments) and Massey Dickinson, Inc. (medical instruments). He is a co-author of the textbook New venture Creation (irwin, editions 1-3).*

Brian Haslett *was a cofounder of Venture Founders Corporation and played a lead role in establishing its U.K. subsidiary and in helping many American and British entrepreneurs create and finance their new enterprises. He subsequently was a contributor to* Venture Capital Journal. *Mr. Haslett died in 1985.*

Leonard E. Smollen *was executive vice president and a cofounder of Venture Founders Corporation, a private company that manages venture capital funds. Currently Mr. Smollen provides consulting services to new ventures and venture capital partnerships.*

What are the personal characteristics required to be a successful entrepreneur? Before making the personal sacrifices required to start and build a major enterprise, would-be entrepreneurs should engage in serious soul-searching to be sure they have what it takes to thrive in the toughest jungle of the business world.

To assist in this introspection, the following guidelines have been prepared by principals of Venture Founders Corporation (VFC).

Venture capitalists say they prefer a grade A entrepreneur with a grade B business idea to a grade B entrepreneur with a grade A idea. And it is generally a strong management team not a lone entrepreneur that they back.

With that in mind, there are some initial questions that would-be entrepreneurs must consider: Do I have adequate *commitment, motivation* and *skills* to start and build a major business—to be a successful entrepreneur? Does my management team have the necessary skills to enable us to succeed in building a particular venture? And finally, do I have a viable idea?

If these questions can be answered affirmatively, then it may be wise to consider developing a business plan and beginning a search for venture capital. This, however, is only the first step of the entrepreneurial self-examination process.

Am I an Entrepreneur?

A good way to answer this question is by objectively comparing yourself to a successful entrepreneur. Begin by studying the following characteristics that successful entrepreneurs, venture capitalists and behavioral scientists say are important for success.

Drive and energy level: A successful entrepreneur must have the ability to work long hours for sustained periods with less than the normal amount of sleep.

Self-confidence: A belief in yourself and your ability to achieve your goals and a sense that events in your life are self-determined is essential.

Setting challenging but realistic goals: The ability to set clear goals and objectives that are challenging, yet realistic and attainable.

Long-term involvement: A commitment to projects that will reach completion in four to seven years and to work towards distant goals. This means total dedication to the business and to attaining these goals.

Using money as a performance measure: Money, in the form of salary, profits, or capital gains, should be viewed more as a measure of how the company is doing rather than as an end in itself.

Persistent problem solving: You must have an intense and determined desire to solve problems toward the completion of tasks.

Taking moderate risks: Entrepreneurial success is generally the result of calculated risk-taking that provides a reasonable and challenging chance of success.

Learning from failure: Understanding your role in a failure can be instrumental in avoiding similar problems in the future. A failure may be disappointing, but should not be discouraging.

Using criticism: You need to be able to seek and use criticism of the style and substance of your performance.

Taking initiative and seeking personal responsibility: You need to seize opportunities and put yourself in situations where you are personally responsible for success or failure. You should be able to take the initiative to solve problems or fill leadership vacuums. You should enjoy being involved in situations where your impact on a problem can be measured.

Making good use of resources: Can you identify and use expertise and assistance that is relevant to the accomplishment of your goals? You should not be so involved in the achievement of your goals and in independent accomplishment that you will not let anyone help you.

Competing against self-imposed standards: Do you tend to establish your own standard of performance, which is high yet realistic, and then compete with yourself?

No one individual possesses all these attributes. Weaknesses can be compensated for through other members of your management team. Do remember, though, *you* are the *most* critical risk. Rate yourself on each of these key characteristics "strong," "average," or "weak" compared with others you know and respect. Be as honest and accurate as you can. If you think you are average or weak on most of them, then do yourself, your family, and your would-be business associates a favor—do not start a business.

If you rate yourself high on most traits, this may be unrealistic and therefore you should review these ratings with people who know you well. Spouses, teachers, peers, and professional advisors are all likely to view you differently, both in terms of your past accomplishments and your potential. Take time with each reviewer to explain *why* you rate yourself as you do. Be prepared to alter your ratings in light of their opinions. If people you know tell you that you are likely to fail as an entrepreneur, they may be right. But both of you should be aware that making such an evaluation realistically is no quick-and-dirty task.

Once you believe you have an adequate assessment of yourself, think back on personal experiences that demanded entrepreneurial strengths. Reflect on these incidences and see if you acted in a manner consistent with your rating.

If you are convinced that you have the entrepreneurial wherewithal to start and build a business, you must now evaluate your management skills to determine your abilities and those that your management team must have. To this end, you should systematically audit your managerial experience and accomplishments in marketing and sales; operations; research, development, and engineering; finance and accounting; general management and administration; personnel; and the legal and tax aspects of business. To rate yourself, we suggest the following standards.

Strong	=	Know thoroughly and have proven ability
Average	=	Have limited knowledge and accomplishments and will need backup perhaps part-time
Weak	=	Unfamiliar and need someone's full-time skills

The different nature of each element makes it unlikely for individuals to be equally strong in all elements of these seven functions. For example, a powerful direct salesperson probably will not show equal strength in market research and evaluation.

Before giving yourself an overall rating on each of these functions, we suggest that you break them down to the principal elements and rate yourself on each element. Note that the critical elements of any function may vary with each venture: the marketing and sales function includes market research and evaluation and marketing planning as well as sales management and merchandising, direct selling, service, and distribution. The latter will not be critical if you market through distributors.

A listing and brief description of representative elements of all seven functions is presented at the end of this article.

For a more objective evaluation, you may want to

review your management skills with former and current supervisors, peers and subordinates, who may all see a different side of you. After thoroughly evaluating your entrepreneurial traits and your management skills, you should be able to determine the personal risks you will run if you try to create a business.

If your dream is to build a multimillion-dollar business, it might also be wise to check your evaluation with one or more of the professionals who are active and respected in the fields of career counseling and entrepreneurial behavior. A man with a weak heart may only ask his wife about taking a gentle stroll up a small grassy hill, but he would be wise to consult a doctor before trying to climb a mountain.[1]

Does My Team Have the Necessary Complementary Skills?

Research into successful ventures shows that teams perform better than one individual. Knowing this, venture capitalists always look for a balanced team. So your next task is to analyze the business you are contemplating and determine what abilities and skills are critical to its success in the first two to three years. Then set about building a management team that includes people who are strong where you are weak.

In a new company, you may not need or be able to afford full-time staff to perform all functions. It is, however, important to choose part-time people carefully, since you may want some of them to come on board later. Avoid teaming up with a school friend whom you only know in casual situations or a colleague in the lab or office whose skills match your own. Although these collaborations are tempting, they rarely work out, and venture capitalists may be put off by a team that is made up of all engineers, salespeople or relatives.[2]

Do I Have a Viable Idea?

Imagine yourself a venture capitalist who has just analyzed the few hundred business proposals examined last year. Your analysis shows that you handled the various proposals in these ways.

1. Sixty percent were rejected after a 20-to-30 minute scanning.
2. Another quarter were discarded after a lengthier review.
3. About 15% were investigated in depth and two-thirds of those were dismissed because of serious flaws in the management team or the business plan that could not be easily resolved.
4. Of the 5% that were viable investment opportunities, terms acceptable to the entrepreneur(s) and other existing stock holders were negotiated in only 3%.

The 15% that were investigated in depth were presented by strong, well-balanced management teams who were able to show you relevant accomplishments in marketing, finance and operations and had developed (perhaps with some prodding by you) a comprehensive business plan.

As an entrepreneur, think what that venture capitalist's analysis means to you: there is a three-in-one-hundred chance of securing capital from any one source on terms acceptable to you and the investor and only a 15% chance of being considered seriously for investment, and a comprehensive business plan is usually required to qualify for such consideration.

So if you are really serious about going into business for yourself, you should start to develop a comprehensive business plan. If the plan is done properly and completely, it will probably take you 150 to 300 hours of intense work. Even when it is done, there is no guarantee that you will raise enough investment capital.

Is there any way to avoid going to all this effort only to have your plan rejected after a 20-minute perusal? Try seeing your business idea through the objective, critical eyes of a venture capitalist.

Before developing a business plan, it is important to answer the questions that venture capitalists may have on their minds when they review a plan to determine if it is worth studying and calling a meeting to discuss. The first question: What exactly will be sold to whom? Other key market questions are:

- Why will the customer buy your product?
- Who are the ultimate users and what influences on their purchasing habits are beyond your control?
- Who is the competition? Are they profitable now? Why do you think you can successfully compete with them?
- Is the market large and growing? Does it offer a multi-million-dollar potential for your company?

[1] For a discussion and appraisal of such evaluations, see "Business Leadership Training: A Six-Month Evaluation," a paper by Jeffry A. Timmons, D.B.A., and John L. Hayes.

[2] For further discussion, see "The Entrepreneurial Team: Formation and Development" by Jeffry A. Timmons, D.B.A., a competitive paper presented at the annual Academy of Management meeting in 1973.

- Are you or will you be in a recognized growth indus try?

You should then answer several questions about the other major aspects of the business you contemplate, questions about your team, your financial needs and the risks you are running. Such questions may include:

- What is the *maximum* amount of dollars and length of time that will be needed before your product is ready for market?
- What is the depth of your team's knowledge and extent of their reputations in the types of markets, technologies and operations in which you will be active?
- What are your team's management skills in the three key areas of marketing, finance and operations?
- How many unproven marketing, technical and manufacturing approaches do you contemplate?
- What are the strengths, weaknesses and major risks of your venture?

Careful thought about these areas should enable you to take a reasonable first look at your own venture ideas and to evaluate the potential for success as well as the major risks. The risks in any entrepreneurial venture are you, the entrepreneur, your team and any fundamental flaws in your venture idea. You should then be able to put together a business plan and avoid many of the early errors (for example, team inadequacies; underpricing; weak cash management) that so often cripple new ventures. You should also be able to improve your chances of securing financing and launching a successful venture.

Representative Elements of Seven Management Functions

1. Marketing and sales
   - *a.* *Market research and evaluation:* Ability to design and conduct market research studies and to analyze and interpret study results; familiarity with questionnaire design and sampling techniques.
   - *b.* *Strategic sales:* Experience in developing marketing strategies and establishing forces and then planning appropriate sales, advertising and promotional programs and setting up an effective network distributor or sales representative organization.
   - *c.* *Sales management and merchandising:* Ability in organizing, supervising, motivating and providing merchandising support to a direct sales force; analyzing territory and sales potential; and managing a sales force to obtain a target share of the market.
   - *d.* *Direct sales:* Experience in identifying, meeting and developing new customers, demonstrated success in closing sales.
   - *e.* *Service:* Experience in identifying service needs of particular products and in determining service and spare parts requirements, handling customer complaints, and managing a service organization.
   - *f.* *Distribution management:* Ability to organize and manage the flow of the product from manufacturing through distribution channels to the ultimate customer, including familiarity with shipping costs, scheduling techniques, carriers, etc.
   - *g.* *Overall marketing skills:* Give yourself a combined rating reflecting your skill level across all of the above marketing areas.
2. Operations
   - *a.* *Manufacturing management:* Knowledge of the production processes, machines, manpower, and space requirements to produce the product; experience in managing production to produce products within time, cost, and quality constraints.
   - *b.* *Inventory control:* Familiarity with techniques of controlling inprocess and finished goods inventories of materials.
   - *c.* *Quality control:* Ability to set up inspection systems and standards for effective control of quality in incoming, in-process and finished materials.
   - *d.* *Purchasing:* Ability to identify appropriate sources of supply, the amount of material in inventory, familiarity with economical order quantities and discount advantage.
   - *e.* *Overall operations skills:* Give yourself a combined rating reflecting your skill level across all of the above operations areas.
3. Research, development and engineering
   - *a.* *Direction and management of applied research:* Ability to distinguish and keep a prudent balance between long-range projects at the frontiers of your technology, which attract the most creative individuals, and shorter range research in support of current product development activity.
   - *b.* *Management of development:* Ability to plan and direct work of development engineers and to use time and cost budgets so that perfectionists do

not ruin you and yet product performance, appearance, and production engineering needs can be met; ability to distinguish between bread-board, field and pre-production prototype programs.

- *c.* *Management of engineering:* Ability to plan and direct engineers in the final design of a new product for manufacture and in the engineering and testing of the production process to manufacture that new product.
- *d.* *Technical know-how:* Ability to contribute personally to research, development, and/or engineering because of up-to-date in-depth knowledge of the technologies in which your company is involved.
- *e.* *Overall research, development, and engineering skills:* Give yourself a combined rating reflecting your skill level across the above areas.

4. Financial management
   - *a.* *Raising capital:* Ability to decide how best to acquire funds for start-up and growth; ability to forecast the need for funds and to prepare budgets; familiarity with sources and vehicles of short- and long-term financing.
   - *b.* *Money management:* Ability to design, install, maintain, use financial controls; familiarity with accounting and control systems needed to manage; ability to set up a project cost control system, analyze overhead/contribution/absorption, prepare profit and loss and balance sheets, and manage a bookkeeper.
   - *c.* *Specific skills:* Cash flow analysis; break-even analysis; contribution analysis; budgeting and profit-planning techniques; profit and loss, balance sheet, and present value analysis of return on investment and payback.
   - *d.* *Overall financial skills:* Give yourself a combined rating reflecting your skill level across all of the above financial areas.
5. General management and administration
   - *a.* *Strategic planning and carryout*: Ability to see the big picture complete with a carryout strategy and believably carry this vision to cofounders, staff and employees, customers, financiers, media and pundits.
   - *b.* *Problem solving:* Ability to anticipate potential problems and plan to avoid them; ability to gather facts about problems, analyze them for real causes, and plan effective action to solve problems; thoroughness in dealing with the details of particular problems and in follow-through.
   - *c.* *Communications:* Ability to communicate effectively and clearly, both in speech and in writing, to the media, the public, customers, peers, and subordinates.
   - *d.* *Planning:* Ability to set realistic and attainable goals, identify obstacles to achieving the goals and develop detailed action plans to achieve those goals; ability to schedule own time very systematically.
   - *e.* *Decision making:* Ability to make decisions on your best analysis of incomplete data.
   - *f.* *Project management:* Skill in organizing project teams, setting project goals, defining project tasks, and monitoring task completion in the face of problems and cost/quality constraints.
   - *g.* *Negotiating:* Ability to work effectively in a negotiating situation; ability to quickly balance value given and value received.
   - *h.* *Personnel administration:* Ability to set up payroll, hiring, compensation, and training functions.
   - *i.* *Overall administrative skills:* Give yourself a combined rating reflecting your skill level across all of the above administrative areas.
6. Personnel management
   - *a.* *Leadership:* Ability to understand the relationships between tasks, the leader, and the followers; ability to lead in situations where it is appropriate; willingness to manage actively, supervise, and control activities of others through directions, suggestions, inspiration, and other techniques.
   - *b.* *Listening:* Ability to listen to and understand without interrupting or mentally preparing your own rebuttal at the expense of hearing the message.
   - *c.* *Helping:* Ability to ask for and provide help and to determine situations where assistance is warranted.
   - *d.* *Criticism:* Ability to provide performance and interpersonal criticism to others that they find useful; ability to receive feedback from others without becoming defensive or argumentative.
   - *e.* *Conflict resolution:* Ability to confront differences openly and to deal with them until resolution is obtained.
   - *f.* *Teamwork:* Ability to work well with others in pursuing common goals.
   - *g.* *Selecting and developing subordinates:* Ability to

select and delegate responsibility to subordinates and to coach them in the development of their managerial capabilities.

- *h.* *Climate building:* Ability to create, by the way you manage, a climate and spirit conducive to high performance; ability to press for higher performance while rewarding work well done.
- *i.* *Overall interpersonal skills:* Give yourself a combined rating reflecting your skill level across all of the above personnel management areas.

7. Legal and tax aspects
   - *a.* *Corporate law:* Familiarity with legal issues relating to stock issues, incorporation, distribution agreements, leases, etc.
   - *b.* *Contract law:* Familiarity with contract procedures and requirements (government and commercial), including default, warranty, and incentive provisions; fee structures; overhead, general and administrative expenses allowable, and so forth.
   - *c.* *Patent law:* Experience with preparation and revision of patent applications; ability to recognize a strong patent; familiarity with claim requirements. Familiarity with copyright and trade secret law.
   - *d.* *Tax law:* Familiarity with general state and federal reporting requirements for businesses and with special provisions concerning Subchapter S corporations, tax shelters, fringe benefits, etc.
   - *e.* *Overall legal and tax skills:* Give yourself a combined rating reflecting your skill level across all of the above legal and tax areas.

How to Raise Venture Capital

This section details the steps needed for obtaining venture capital financing. Written by industry veterans, each article explores the practical considerations for dealing with the venture capital process. Included is an outline of a detailed business plan that will facilitate a venture capitalist's investment decision. This information offers entrepreneurs guidance in approaching the venture capitalist and presenting the business plan; anticipating the pricing and structure of the financing; and understanding the legal requirements. The venture capitalists' goals, their expectations from the entrepreneurs, the process of making an investment decision and the situations they would prefer to avoid are also specified. Examining the venture capitalists' objectives and decision-making processes should help the entrepreneur locate the appropriate investor and establish a productive investment relationship.

Structuring Venture Capital Investments

Jonathan E. Cole, Esq. and Albert L. Sokol, Esq.

Jonathan Cole *is Chair of Edwards and Angell's Venture Capital and Emerging Company Group and has been involved in venture capital practice since 1971, first in the Firm's Providence, RI office, and since 1981, in the Palm Beach, Fla. office. He has written and spoken extensively on the venture capital process.*

Albert Sokol *is a partner in the Boston office of Edwards and Angell, and chairs the firm's International Group. He began his venture practice in 1977 and since then, has represented several foreign and U.S. venture capital funds as well as venture-backed foreign and U.S. technology companies. He has written and spoken extensively to both U.S. and foreign groups on the venture capital and capital formation process in domestic and cross-border transactions.*

An entrepreneur raising capital faces a daunting challenge. Keep the R&D, marketing, sales, etc. "show on the road", but also obtain sufficient capital to fund these activities.

This often means running the gauntlet—finding sophisticated venture capitalists (VCs) who like the company's market, business strategy, management team and investment opportunity, and who can be a "value-added" addition to the stockholder group. And, it means dealing with the commonly complex structures that VCs propose for an investment in the company.

For most entrepreneurs who have not been through the process before, such structures often appear confusing, and perhaps overbearing, and involve too much "control" for the VCs and too little appreciation of the sacrifices and contributions of the founders and other management team members. An entrepreneur receiving such a proposal might feel that the structure of the VC's proposed investment sets back his relationship with the VC.

And yet, from the VC's point of view, the basic structure of most investments in entrepreneurial companies is similar, driven largely by the key objectives of the VC fund and its managers. This article seeks to help entrepreneurs understand the link between deal structure and the objectives of the VCs.

The discussion below focuses on the structures used most frequently by the institutional venture capital community, meaning primarily the professionally managed pools of capital listed in *Pratt's Guide to Venture Capital Sources*. In venture capital, as elsewhere, the "golden rule" generally applies ("He who has the Gold makes the Rules"), and a VC's objectives will influence the structure of its investment.

We have not discussed investment structures utilized by so-called "angel investors" (typically private individuals, such as friends and family, wealthy individuals, suppliers or customers, or other industry contacts), or by so-called "strategic partners" (typically operating companies in the same or allied industry or marketplace, including non-U.S. firms). Those types of structures tend to be more diverse and again, are often driven by different objectives than those which drive VCs.

Pre-Investment Considerations

Before approaching the venture capital community for funding, an entrepreneur should expend the resources to assure that his company's legal and organizational structure does not impede an arms-length investment by an institutional VC, and that there are no unusual entangling relationships. Examples of pre-investment considerations are the following:

Business Plan: It is *essential* that the management team has developed a coherent, fairly complete and readable Business Plan with a clear statement of the business strategy that the company intends to pursue and a relatively complete picture of the resources required (including people, plant, intellectual property and money) to achieve the business strategy.

The Business Plan is important to the VC investor not only because it describes the business opportunity, but also because it tangibly demonstrates the ability of the management team to plan for and organize a successful business venture, taking into account the principal factors that can affect the outcome.

For our purposes, however, the Business Plan is important because (a) the investment structure may be largely derived on the basis of the predicted results set forth in the Business Plan; (b) the Business Plan provides the basic set of assumptions on which the entrepreneur and his or her advisors must evaluate the potential impact of the investment structure on the positions of the entrepreneur and the management team; and (c) the important milestones in the company's development identified in the Business Plan may become the benchmarks for important aspects of the investment structure, such as conditions to the release of deferred investment commitments, the vesting of management equity or control of the Board of Directors. The interrelationship of the Business Plan with the investment structure is discussed further below.

Intellectual Property Rights: The company's rights to its primary intellectual property (patents, copyrights, trade secrets or other rights) must be clear and protected. There should be proper assignments to the company of all patents, inventions or other rights acquired from third parties (including the entrepreneur and other founders). Structures that anticipate that the founder or entrepreneur or other related party will retain the rights to the basic patents or other intellectual property under a license and royalty arrangement are not favored by the VC community and will often lead to an investment rejection. Patent or trademark searches or opinions of patent counsel, or other third party evaluations of the basic technology and intellectual property, are often useful.

Key employees should be covered by non-disclosure and invention assignments agreements (protecting the company from any claims by the employees of individual rights to any of the company's technology or other intellectual property), and where appropriate, key employees should also be covered by non-competition agreements. The possibility of entangling relationships between the key employees and their prior employers in relation to the company's intellectual property must also be examined and, where possible, cleared up.

Prior History of the Company: The legal entity to be used as the vehicle for the investment and the conduct of the business should have no unusual prior history. For example, the company should not have been engaged in a prior business that was closed or sold. These situations present too many opportunities for unknown risks or unasserted claims. In particular, the company must not be a "public shell", with the attendant diverse and unrelated stockholder group. In most cases, the equity interests should be held by the entrepreneur and the key management team, and a small group of people who have made investments in the company to support the early development of the business described in its Business Plan.

The company's organizational documents (charter, bylaws and director and shareholder minutes) should be clear, complete and up-to-date, with no unusual provisions granting special rights to any group of stockholders or others. Provisions giving the stockholders, or a particular group of them, "pre-emptive" rights to acquire a pro rata share of new equity issues can be problematical, and in some cases such rights can be implied by law unless specifically denied in the charter documents. If possible, these should be removed.

All prior issuances of equity interests (including not only common or preferred stock, but also options or warrants to acquire stock, or if applicable, partnership interests or limited liability company member interests) must be properly documented and reviewed for compliance with applicable securities laws. In particular, there should be no "exclusive dealing" arrangements with finders, brokers or other financial intermediaries, including arrangements providing for equity interests, options or warrants in the event of a successful financing. These arrangements not only restrict the company's ability to raise capital in the future, but also dilute the ownership percentage of the existing stockholder group and potentially the VC investors.

In most cases, the equity interests held by minority stockholders, including key employees, should be subject to vesting arrangements and to restrictions on transfer and rights of first refusal in favor of the company, as well as rights for the company to acquire the stock held by the employees upon termination of their employment.

Finally, there should be no litigation of any material nature involving the company.

Regulatory Matters: All regulatory filings required by the company should be up-to-date and well documented. Any regulatory or governmental restrictions on the transfer of ownership interests should be analyzed and the impact of a substantial equity financing should be anticipated.

Tax Matters: The impact of federal and state tax on the probable investment structure should be analyzed and understood. For the moment, the institutional VC community appears to continue to favor the "C" corporation as the preferred legal entity for the investee company. "C" corporations present the simplest and perhaps most easily understood legal and capital structures and are the preferred vehicle (in fact, practically the exclusive vehicle) for an initial public offering. Because of the prevalence of the "C" corporation as the investment vehicle for most VC funds, these are the focus of the discussion below.

C corporations can present tricky structuring issues where a substantial net operating loss ("NOL") has been generated from prior operations. While the value of the NOL can be used to "shelter" future profits, its availability will be severely restricted if there is a "change of ownership" under the tax regulations in any three year period. Accordingly, the past and predicted future changes in stock ownership must be considered by the company's tax advisors.

"S" corporations are often used by entrepreneurs during the start-up phase and can provide tax deferral opportunities for the initial investors. Conversion from an "S" to a "C" corporation is feasible (in fact automatic in the case of the issuance of equity interests to non-qualifying investors, such as VC funds), but the tax impact of such conversion must be analyzed. Other structures, principally limited partnerships and limited liability companies, are sometimes utilized. For liability reasons, general partnerships are almost never used.

Of course, all tax returns and other tax filings must be current and well documented.

Cross-border Considerations: For many entrepreneurs and companies, cross-border considerations are significant for at least two reasons.

First, as markets and competition for most products are increasingly global, VCs generally expect every company's business plan to evaluate and discuss how the company will deal with international opportunities and threats. Is there a potential competitor with superior technology in another country? How will the company distribute its products outside its home market? Is it necessary to have different versions of the product to account for regional/geographic variances in markets?

Second, in appropriate cases, a company's global strategy might include arranging that the VCs which invest in the company include one or two VCs from another country. Advantages to be gained for the company include validation of the "international" part of the business plan by the foreign VC, and assistance in certain cross-border matters (for example, access to the foreign VC's business network and to the VC's financial, business and legal expertise in foreign countries). The strategy of arranging a cross-border VC syndicate is not without its problems, however, as some VCs will not do a deal that is more than two hours distance from their home base. Also, such deals do involve some extra planning to account for the cross-border effect of various countries' tax and other laws on VC investments.

Proper attention to these pre-investment structure considerations, as well as to any other unusual aspects of the company or its history, will ease the investment process for VC funds. Inattention may well lead to the rejection of investment interest.

Typical Documentation for a VC Investment

Term Sheet: Typically, the basic terms of the investment structure will be set forth in a Term Sheet prepared by the VC fund and submitted to the entrepreneur and the company as a part of a Letter of Intent. The Letter of Intent and Term Sheet generally are not intended to be binding on the parties, with the exception of certain provisions for the payment of expenses (whether or not the transaction closes) or exclusive dealing rights, which may be included as legally binding agreements. The Term Sheet can be, and often is, negotiated in detail, since it sets forth the fundamental terms of the investment structure as well as the financial terms upon which the investment is proposed to be made.

While some VC funds use their outside counsel to prepare the Term Sheet and Letter of Intent, many do not, and most VCs deliver the Term Sheet directly to the entrepreneur with the expectation that will be discussed and negotiated largely between the business people, without the active participation of counsel on either side. However, because the Term Sheet becomes the "road map" for the preparation of the definitive investment documentation, and since the Term Sheet is only a summary of the principal terms of the investment, the entrepreneur would be wise to consult with experienced counsel and other financial advisors when the Term Sheet is being negotiated. Such advisors can give the entrepreneur a more complete explanation of the ramifications of the summary provisions of the Term Sheet and can suggest negotiating positions that can move the parties toward an agreement relatively quickly and smoothly. Often, this process can minimize the likelihood of unpleasant surprises arising out of the negotiation of the full-blown investment documentation.

Once the Term Sheet has been negotiated and the Letter of Intent executed by the parties, counsel for the VC fund will prepare and circulate drafts of the principal investment documents, based upon the provisions agreed to in the Term Sheet, but set forth in more complete detail, and including other "standard" provisions. This set of documents, including not only agreements among or between the company, some or all of its existing stockholders and, where relevant, its employees, as well as the VC investors, also includes provisions to be included in the company's charter and bylaws. A typical set of investment documents is described further below.

"Standard" Investment Documentation

General: The investment documentation agreed to by the parties at the time the investment is made sets forth the "contract" and legal rights of the parties governing their future relations. While some of the documentation, or at least certain provisions, will be peculiar to each transaction, depending upon the circumstances involved, the venture capital industry has developed a relatively standard set of documentation that the entrepreneur should expect to see.

Since the documentation is prepared by the VC fund in connection with its investment, it is designed largely to protect the rights of the investors. Again, the terms are largely negotiable, although negotiating positions that vary materially from the principal terms set forth in the Term Sheet will typically not be accepted, absent unusual circumstances, and may result in a breakdown of the investment process. Accordingly, the entrepreneur should address the principal terms when the Letter of Intent is executed, even though it may not be legally binding.

The "standard" investment documentation typically includes the following:

- **Securities Purchase Agreement** (also called a Preferred Stock Purchase Agreement or Note and Warrant Purchase Agreement, or similar designation, depending upon the structure of the investment).
- **Form of Investment Security** (including typically the Preferred Stock terms, or the forms of Note and Warrant).
- **Registration Rights Agreement**
- **Exit Rights Agreement** (or alternatively a "Put" Agreement, if such terms are not included in the Stockholders Agreement).
- **Stockholders Agreement.**
- **Employee Agreement** (and Restricted Stock Agreement or similar designation).
- **Non-Compete Agreement.**
- **Inventions and Confidentiality Agreement.**

This set of documentation, taken together, governs the legal rights of the parties relating to the investment and the legal aspects of the company's operations after the investment. The principal terms of these documents are described below.

Securities Purchase Agreement: The Securities Purchase Agreement (or Preferred Stock Purchase Agreement or Note and Warrant Purchase Agreement or similar designation) typically contains the following principal terms:

(i) The financial commitment of the investors to purchase the newly issued securities of the company, which may be common stock, preferred stock, promissory notes (including convertible notes) and stock purchase warrants, or some combination of these securities, which may be purchased in whole at the initial closing, or which may be purchased over time, depending upon the achievement of certain milestones;

(ii) The representations and warranties of the company as to the material facts relating to its organization and business, requiring relatively complete disclosure of any material arrangements;

(iii) The representations and warranties of investors as purchasers of the company's securities;

(iv) Affirmative and negative covenants of the company (the breach of which may give rise to contractual claims for damages, or which may result in other consequences, such as changes in the composition of the Board of Directors, or a default on outstanding indebtedness, or the like), including limitations on debt, mergers and acquisitions, changing the business focus, transactions with affiliates and changes in compensation for the key managers, as well as provision for certain information rights (financial statements, board participation, inspection rights, etc.);

(v) Conditions to the obligations of the VC investors to fund the investment (which will typically include the execution and delivery of the other agreements included in the standard investment documentation);

(vi) Special provisions (covering any special arrangements between the parties); and

(vii) Miscellaneous provisions (often called "legal boilerplate").

Form of Investment Security: The investment security will be either an equity security (i.e., common stock or preferred stock in the case of corporate issuers), or some sort of debt instrument (i.e., promissory notes or debentures, which may be convertible into an equity security), or rights to acquire an equity security (i.e., stock purchase warrants which may cover either preferred or common stock). The principal terms of the security will be contained in the corporate charter for common or preferred stock and in the terms of the instrument itself for promissory notes, debentures or warrants. The terms of equity securities typically cover voting rights, dividends (including preferential and cumulative dividends), liquidation preferences, conversion or exchange rights, redemption or "put" rights (usually in favor of the investors), and special provisions relating to the Board of Directors, including rights to assume control. The terms of debt instruments will include provisions for the payment of interest and principal, default provisions, provision for collateral or guarantees (which will be more completely set forth in separate documents) and, if applicable, conversion or exchange rights.

Special affirmative or negative covenants may also be included in the terms of the equity or debt securities as well as in the Securities Purchase Agreement or Stockholders Agreement.

Convertible securities (e.g., convertible preferred stock or convertible or exchangeable notes) or warrants will also typically contain "anti-dilution" protection, usually giving the investors the right to obtain more common stock, without additional aggregate consideration, in the event the company subsequently issues new common stock (or common stock equivalents) at a price below the effective "as converted" common stock price paid by the investors. The anti-dilution provisions can be quite complex and typically will be based on either the so-called "full ratchet" or "weighted average" formula.

Registration Rights Agreement: The Registration Rights Agreement sets forth the rights of the investors to SEC registration of their equity securities, which will typically include "demand" registration rights and "piggyback" registration rights, as well as related agreements governing the procedures and understandings of the parties as to the implementation of such rights (e.g., so-called "cutback" provisions and indemnity agreements).

Stockholders Agreement: The Stockholders Agreement, which will be entered into among the company, the investors and the principal management stockholders of the company, will often contain provisions that are peculiar to each investment transaction or company, but will typically include restrictions on transfer (e.g., no transfers for a period of time or without the approval of the Board of Directors), rights of first refusal on proposed transfers, voting agreements with respect to the Board of Directors or other matters, and "co-sale" rights (sometimes referred to as "tag-along" or "drag-along" rights). The co-sale rights set forth the rights of the investors and/or others to participate in certain sales of stock by the entrepreneur or other key management stockholders (the "tag-along" right) and the right of the investors to require the management to participate in a sale of stock by the investors (the "drag-along" right). The Stockholders Agreement (or in some cases, the Restricted Stock Agreement with each key stockholder employee) may also include provision for the purchase of the stock held by the entrepreneur or other key management personnel in the event of death or termination of employment (including a "call" in favor of the company, or a "put" in favor of the stockholder or his or her estate, or both), with provision for differing valuations applicable to the purchase, depending upon the circumstances.

Exit Rights Agreement: The Exit Rights Agreement, if there is one, typically replaces the Registration Rights Agreement and may replace the Stockholders Agreement. It will contain the registration rights of the investors as well as any redemption or "put" rights as to common stock or warrants and any "co-sale" rights, all of which provide opportunities for the investors to obtain liquidity for, or "exit", the investment.

Employee Agreement: Typically the investors will want the employment arrangement of the entrepreneur and other key management personnel to be set forth in written agreements, which will provide for duties and responsibilities, compensation (including participation in bonus or other profit sharing or incentive compensation plans or stock option arrangements) and the rights of the company to terminate the employment arrangements, including severance benefits that may be available. Often the VC investors will require that some or all of the common stock or options held by the key management team, or issued to them pursuant to equity incentive plans, be subject to Restricted Stock Agreements, providing for a "vesting" of the rights to the stock or options over a period of three to five years, with restrictions on transfer and "call" or buy-back rights in favor of the company at death or other termination of employment at a price depending on the circumstances of such termination.

Non-Compete Agreement: The investors will typically want the key employees, including the entrepreneur, to enter into non-compete agreements in the event of termination of employment (including termination after the investors have assumed control), the term of which may be related to the severance benefits available.

Inventions and Confidentiality Agreement: The investors may require the key employees to enter into inventions and confidentiality agreements confirming the rights of the company to any intellectual property developed by the key employees, as well as setting forth the obligation of the key employees to maintain confidentiality as to the company's proprietary information and trade secrets.

Achieving Goals through Investment Structure

Four key considerations motivate a VC's investment structure:

- Maximizing financial returns;
- Priority protection against loss;
- Participation in management and potential control; and
- "Exit" rights.

These objectives seem simple enough, but complexities arise when implementing the goals. For example, although a common stock investment will often be a good form for maximizing potential financial returns, common stock will not provide the VC with priority protection against loss or potential control of management, and may provide only limited "exit" (or rights to obtain liquidity) opportunities.

The entrepreneur who understands the key objectives of his or her prospective investors and how the these objectives are reflected in the documentation will be better able to deal with VCs on an efficient, pragmatic and realistic basis.

Financial Returns: The financial returns to the VC investor come primarily in the form of capital appreciation of the equity securities, and occasionally in a current return (i.e., dividends on equity securities or interest on debt securities). In most early stage investments, there will be no current return, since the company's cash flow (if any) will most often be dedicated toward funding future growth of the business. Even in these investments, however, the structure may provide for a "cumulative" dividend on a convertible preferred stock, which will become part of the "liquidation preference" upon sale or redemption. This has the effect of providing a minimum rate of return to the investors on a priority basis before the common stock held by the entrepreneur and others will receive anything.

In later stage and expansion financings, where the company's projected cash flow is strong enough to provide some sort of current return, the structure will often include a so-called "current pay" dividend on preferred stock or current interest payments on debt instruments. Even in those situations, however, the principal financial objective of the VC investors will be capital appreciation of the equity securities associated with the investment.

Standard debt instruments (such as straight promissory notes) or conventional preferred stock provide only for the return of capital through repayment of the principal of the notes or redemption of the preferred stock at its liquidation preference (typically the purchase price plus unpaid cumulative dividends). As a standard debt instrument does not participate in the capital appreciation represented by the company's increase in value, most VC investors will want to obtain their financial return through an equity security that will participate with the common stock in the increased value of the company upon achievement of its business plan.

The most common investment structures that provide the VC investors participation in the common stock value are (a) convertible preferred stock, which is convertible into common stock at the option of the investors or, perhaps, mandatorily upon the occurrence of certain events, such as a public offering; (b) a convertible note, which provides for conversion of the principal amount of the note into common stock at the option of the VC investors or mandatorily upon the Occurrence of certain events; (c) stock purchase warrants (usually issued in conjunction with promissory notes), giving the investors the right to purchase common stock at a fixed price at some future date; and (d) common stock purchased directly at the time of the initial investment, usually in conjunction with the purchase of non-convertible preferred stock or debt instruments.

A key VC consideration is the percentage of the company that the investors will hold on a common stock equivalent basis. Typically, investors will base their investment decision upon an analysis of the risk adjusted projected value of the company, assuming it achieves its business plan, at a fixed time in the future, such that the VC investors will receive an appropriate percentage of the projected value of the company at that time to provide them with their required rates of return on invested capital. This analysis will take into account the projected dilution of the percentage ownership of the VC investors that will arise from anticipated follow-on equity investments, and the investment documentation will typically include both preemptive rights to participate in future equity financings as well as the "anti-dilution" provisions described above.

Protection against Loss: VC investors typically expect that their invested capital will be protected against loss to a greater degree than the capital interests of the founders or other earlier stage stockholders. The investment structure is designed to provide this protection in a number of ways. Of course, with respect to debt securities, the investors have a right to the return of the invested capital through repayment of the debt. This right may be secured through collateral interests in the company's assets or guarantees of others.

The principal "downside" protection for investments in equity securities is typically achieved through the use of preferred stock, which gives the investors the right to receive the liquidation preference (typically the invested capital plus perhaps a guaranteed return through unpaid cumulative dividends) on a priority basis before any distributions can be made on the common stock or junior preferred stock held by the entrepreneur and other stockholders. In the case of multiple rounds of VC investment, the relative priority of each series of preferred stock or note issue must be negotiated among the investors and the company.

VC investors also seek protection against loss through rights to control or liquidate the company in the event the Business Plan is not achieved or other material defaults arise. In the event of such a default, these rights are intended to permit the VC investors to determine the advisability and timing of a sale or liquidation or other material development affecting the company, or a change in management, with maximum flexibility. It is possible that the course of action decided upon may substantially impair the value of the equity securities held by the entrepreneur and other stockholders. The default or "change of control" provisions for equity investments are typically included in the Securities Purchase Agreement or in the preferred stock terms, or both.

In some situations, the investors will invest their funds in installments, depending upon the company's achievement of certain business milestones. This aspect of the structure is intended to reduce the capital commitment of the investors in the event that the company's business does not proceeds anticipated or other developments arise.

Participation in Management and Control: While most VC investors expect that the entrepreneur and management team will control and operate the business without interference from the investors, the investment structure will typically provide for the investors to participate in the management and operation of the company (a) through representation on the Board of Directors, (b) through the restrictions and limitations imposed by the affirmative and negative covenants in the Securities Purchase Agreement or terms of the equity or debt securities, and (c) through stock transfer restrictions on the equity interests held by the management team imposed under the Stockholders Agreement. In addition, the investors will typically insist that the Employee Agreements provide for termination of the employment of the key management upon relatively short notice without cause, but subject to severance and buy-back rights.

In general, the investment structures are designed to permit the entrepreneur and management team to operate the business without substantial participation by the VC investors (except at the board of directors level) so long as the company is operating in accordance with and achieving the objectives set forth in its Business Plan. However, in the event that the company materially fails to achieve its business plan or certain agreed to specific milestones, or the company violates any of the affirmative and negative covenants contained in the Securities Purchase Agreement or the terms of its equity or debt securities, the VC investors may expect the right to either take control of the Board of Directors of the company (including the right to remove existing management), or the right to require the company to purchase the equity securities held by the VC investors, as well as to pay off any debt. These draconian measures are often hotly negotiated. Rights to control the company are typically reserved to situations where the VC investors have acquired a majority ownership position while the "put" rights are typically reserved for those situations where VC investors hold a minority ownership position. In any event, the incidence of the actual exercise of such rights appears to be fairly low, but the availability of such rights in the investment documentation is a useful negotiating tool in the hands of the VC investors in discussions with management in those situations where serious problems have arisen.

"Exit" Rights: As the primary goal of the VC investor is return on investment, VCs favor a structure that provides a means to liquidity (i.e., realization of the return through sale of the investment or sale of the company). VCs use the term "exits" to refer to these paths to liquidity, and a typical structure will provide at least one and often two or more exit mechanisms.

VC funds generally have a limited life (usually 10 years, with a possible extension of up to 2 years). Therefore, VCs will favor structures that provide for an agreed upon exit opportunity within 5 to 7 years, so that an investment made in the third or fourth year of the fund's life will be turned into cash or marketable securities prior to the time when the fund winds up and the fruits of the fund's investments are to be distributed fully to the VC fund's investors. Entrepreneurs seeking capital from institutional VC funds should be aware of these constraints and be prepared to accommodate them. (In this connection, it is advisable for the entrepreneur to inquire about the "age" and investment horizon of the particular investor funds involved so that there are no surprises about the desired timing of an exit.)

The primary paths to liquidity for ventured-backed companies have historically been the public offering and the sale of the company (by merger or otherwise) to another firm, typically an operating company in the same or an allied industry. These tend to produce the highest valuations and accordingly the highest returns to the investors (although their consequences for the entrepreneur and the management team can be markedly diverse). A secondary path for financially successful companies has been the redemption or repurchase of the investment, usually in connection with a refinancing or recapitalization of the company.

The investment structure advances the exit objectives of the investors through the public marketplace by the rights granted in the Registration Rights Agreement, under which the investors can in theory "force" the company to go public through the "demand" registrations rights and can participate in company sponsored registrations though the "piggyback" registration rights. Since most entrepreneurs share the investors' view of the desirability of "going public" — the management stays in control and also obtains liquidity opportunities at a high initial valuation, while the company receives substantial capital to fund future growth — registration rights are typically willingly accepted.

Exits other than through the public market are typically dealt with in the investment structure and documentation by means of a "put", or option to sell, in favor of the investors as to equity securities (generally referred to as a redemption right in the case of preferred stock), usually exercisable after a period of time (five to seven years) if no other liquidity event has occurred (such as a public offering).

The critical issue in the "put" or redemption structure is the pricing formula. Typically the investors will be looking for (a) no less than the minimum return provided for in the liquidation preference of a preferred stock investment (original purchase price plus unpaid cumulative dividends) and (b) if higher, the common stock equivalent value of the investment (e.g., the "as converted value" of the preferred stock as if it had been converted to common stock as shared in the value of the company's common equity on a pro rata basis). Some "put" or redemption pricing formulas determine common stock equivalent value by reference to "fair market value" (FMV), usually fixed by appraisal, while others determine such value by reference to a multiple of earnings (usually EBITDA, or earnings before interest, taxes, depreciation and amortization). In some cases, the "put" or redemption price may be the highest of all three of liquidation preference, FMV, or EBITDA formula value.

Other, more exotic, pricing formulas are also used in appropriate cases. Whatever he formula, however, the ultimate structure will likely contain some form of exit right involving the right of the investors to require the company to "take them out", and entrepreneurs should be prepared to deal with these issues in the Term Sheet and definitive investment documentation.

On a practical basis, however, the "put" may not give the investors the ability to receive cash upon exercise, since many growing companies, especially ones that have experienced bumps in the road to success, will likely not be able to finance a buyout of a significant equity partner. Rather, a "put" gives the VCs the power to force the management to find a practical solution to the exit requirements of the investors, the absence of which will give the investors the right to cause the liquidation and forced sale of the company. Also, the failure of the company to meet a redemption or "put" exercise will likely give rise to a potential shift in control of the Board under the preferred stock terms or Put Agreement or Stockholders' Agreement. The "put" rights set the negotiating table far in advance of the exit date and give a strong incentive to management to plan for a liquidity event for the investors in a timely manner.

Other exit rights that appear in typical investment structures are "tag along" rights, which give the investors the right to join (to "tag along") in any sales of equity securities by management. In cases where the investors control a majority of the company on a common stock equivalent basis, it is not uncommon for the structure to contain "drag-along" rights in favor of the investors. These give the investors the right to require management and other stockholders to sell (to be "dragged along") in the sale of all or substantially all of the company's stock to a third party, providing yet another full exit opportunity to the investors.

With respect to debt oriented investments, of course the repayment of the principal with interest is the primary means to liquidity, but since VC debt investments are typically paired with a convertibility feature or warrants as means of providing for the "upside" financial return, the structure will typically provide for a "put" of the debt or warrants on a formula basis that is the functional equivalent of the redemption pricing structure discussed above.

Conclusion

Entrepreneurs who are new to fundraising efforts may find VC investment structures unduly complex and at times overbearing. However, while the details may vary from one VC fund to another or even from one transaction to another, the investment structures used by the VC community tend to fit common patterns and are designed to achieve of a few basic objectives.

In our experience, the failure of the entrepreneur and the management team to appreciate the objectives of the investors can lead to early breakdowns in what might otherwise be fruitful discussions and negotiations. Entrepreneurs who wish to be successful in dealing with VCs should spend the time and effort to understand the objectives of their potential investors and to expect proposed investment structures that accommodate those objectives. At that point the entrepreneur, together with knowledgeable and experienced counsel and other advisors, should be in a better position to negotiate a fair and rational investment structure which can provide the opportunity for all parties to profit from the arrangement.

— For further information, please contact Mr. Cole at 561-833-7700 or Mr. Sokol at 617-439-4444. —

Preparing a Business Plan*

Brian Haslett and Leonard E. Smollen

See previous background descriptions.

Developing a business plan that will attract professional venture investors' interest as well as their financial commitment is a challenge in itself, and it can be more daunting if it is being done for the first time.

Even those with advanced degrees in business may not have learned how to put together a comprehensive business plan.

Many successful venture capitalists were interviewed and numerous venture proposals were analyzed in order to help the entrepreneur comprehend the scope and the detail required in a business plan. Though entrepreneurs often find the process of building their teams and preparing their plans more arduous than they anticipated, those who complete the course are generally able to raise the capital they need and proceed to successfully move their businesses ahead.

Using These Guidelines

When raising equity capital, a business plan is a vital sales tool. Before committing their funds for what will probably be at least five years, most venture capital investors will want to be certain the plan has been carefully thought through and that management has the appropriate skills and experience in its chosen business area to be able to manage effectively, seize opportunities, solve problems, *and* make profits. These prospective backers will—or should—insist on reviewing the proposal *before* considering any investment seriously. Some will not meet with an entrepreneur without first seeing the business plan. For this reason, the plan must be well-prepared and very persuasive in conveying the company's potential. It should cover all major issues but not be so detailed that it puts the investor-reader off. Fifty pages should suffice for most businesses.

When starting up or expanding a business in a particular industry or market there are certain current critical issues that should be addressed. In the chemical industry, for instance, significant issues may include the following:

- Reduced availability of raw materials and resultant bartering and allocation
- Increasingly strict government regulations covering the use of chemical products and the operation of chemical processes
- Diminishing viability of the high capital cost of special-purpose chemical processing plants that serve narrow markets

Make whatever investigations are needed to develop a list of special issues that are significant to the particular business.

Because these guidelines contain a list of potentially *relevant* issues and are meant to cover a wide variety of manufacturing and service businesses, they will help tailor a list. But it is up to the entrepreneur, while preparing the plan, to determine which issues are significant to future business development.

Professional venture capitalists are not the only people who find business plans invaluable. For the entrepreneur, careful preparation of a plan can be an opportunity to think through all facets of a business expansion or start-up, to examine the consequences of different marketing, operations and financing strategies, and to determine what human, physical and financial resources are required. Much of this can be done effectively on paper without the crippling expense of trial-and-error operation.

In one venture, the discipline of writing the business plan caused the entrepreneur to realize that the major market for his biomedical product was in nursing homes, not in hospital emergency rooms as he had originally thought. He changed the focus of his marketing effort accordingly.

Another successful entrepreneur found that besides using his plan to help raise $650,000 in start-up capital, it helped him monitor his company's performance during its first 18 months. Then, when he needed to increase his company's credit lines and to secure long-term financing for building and equipment, he was able to update his plan in two or three days. Without a plan, it would have taken two to three weeks.

Summary of the Plan

Many investors prefer to read a one- to three-page summary of a business plan that highlights its important features

* Originally published and copyrighted (1972) by the Institute for New Enterprise Development (INED). Revised for this book by the authors.

and opportunities to decide about reviewing the entire plan. The summary should be written after the plan is completed. As each section is drafted, it might be a good idea to circle a few sentences that are important enough to include in the summary.

The summary should be thoughtfully put together since it is probably the first thing about the business that a would-be investor is going to read. Unless it is appealing and convincing, it may also be the last!

The summary should contain *very brief* statements about

1. the company's origins, activities, management and performance
2. any distinguishing features of the product or service
3. the attractiveness of the market
4. a summary of the financial projections
5. the amount of money being sought, in what form (equity or debt or both) and for what purpose

Several people who are not involved in the venture should review the summary while it is still in draft form. Their reactions should be evaluated. Did they quickly grasp the essence of proposal? Were they excited by what they read? This feedback should provide useful indications of how the professional venture capital investor is likely to react.

Description of the Business and Its Industry

This section is an introduction to subsequent sections on the product/service, the market opportunity and the people and plans that will be involved in the venture. The product or service should be described *briefly* as well as the nature and current condition of the industry to show where and how the product will fit in it.

The Company

The business as well as the product or service should be described along with potential customers and regions of operation.

The company's history should also be detailed: when it was formed, how its products/services were chosen and developed, and what role management has played in bringing the business to where it is today.

If the company is already trading and is now seeking further development or expansion financing, the entrepreneur must review its market penetration and its financial performance (sales, profits, return on equity).

If the company has had early setbacks and incurred losses, these need to be described, as well as methods to avoid recurrences. Omission of any reference to past problems can make the proposal appear too good to be true.

The Industry

This section should include the entrepreneur's view of the nature, current status and prospects for the industry in which the business operates; the industry's principal participants and how they are performing; the growth in sales and profits and any published forecasts for the current year; companies that have recently entered or left these markets and why; and what major economic, social, technological, or regulatory trends are affecting your business. This section should not go into too much detail. That is done later. Each topic should be covered summarily in two or three sentences.

Features and Advantages of Products or Services

The potential investor wants to know the entrepreneur's plan: what is going to be sold, what kind of special know-how and protection management has and what its advantages and drawbacks are.

- *Description.* This section should contain detailed information on the products or services and what needs they satisfy. Diagrams and sketches may be used to improve understanding and heighten interest. The product's or service's distinctive features should be emphasized by highlighting the differences between what competitors currently have on the market and what will be offered. Each feature's advantage or disadvantage should be stated candidly.
- *Proprietary Position.* Any patents, trade secrets, or other proprietary features should be discussed as well as any advantage that would achieve a favored or entrenched position in the industry.
- *Potential.* Any opportunities for the logical extension of the existing product line or the development of related products or services should be discussed as well. Investors like to know what entrepreneurs are planning for an encore.

Market Research and Analysis

In this section, the entrepreneur should present enough facts to convince the investor that the market for the product or service is such that sales targets can be met despite competition.

This is probably the most difficult section for entrepreneurs to do well. And because choice of marketing strategies, size of operating work force and facilities and requirements for inventory and receivables financing are all derived from sales forecasts, it is also the most crucial. For these reasons, this section of the business plan should be prepared *first and with the greatest care.*

Customers
Markets should be clearly defined: who are the major purchasers, where are they, and why they buy. The significance of price, quality, service, personal contacts, and political pressures should be detailed in rank order along with the purchasers buying habits and the significance of seasonality—when the buying is done, and how it affects the offering.

List some actual or potential customers who have purchased or expressed an interest in the product or service and indicate why. List any actual or potential customers who have dropped or are uninterested in the product or service, and explain why this was so. The means for counteracting negative customer reaction should also be explained. The absence of frank discussion about the negatives of the offering may precipitate concern about the plan's thoroughness.

Market Size and Trends
The size of the current total market should be described. Discussing the market with potential distributors, dealers, sales representatives, customers and, to some extent, reviewing published data will help define the market. Published information should not be relied on solely since it is often inadequate. The size of the total market in both units and dollars should be provided with care to include only the market that will affect the product. If regional markets are going to be targeted, their sizes should be shown as well.

The potential annual growth of the total market for the product or service must be discussed and market projections should be made for at least three future years. The ways in which major factors such as industry trends, new technical developments, new or changing customer needs are affecting market growth should be thoroughly detailed and previous market trends should be reviewed. Any differences between past and projected future growth rates should be explained. Reasons for the presumed continuation of market trends should be explained. Entrepreneurs tend to overestimate the size of their market. If potential investors become dubious about the market size and growth estimates, they may lose interest in the rest of the proposal.

Competition
Make a realistic assessment of the strengths and weaknesses of competitive products and services and name the companies that supply them. State the data sources used to determine which products are competitive and the strengths of the competition.

The potential products or services should be compared with the competitors' on the basis of price, performance, service, warranties and other pertinent features. A table can be an effective way of presenting these data.

Review competitors' managerial and financial strengths and weaknesses, assessing each competitor's capability in marketing, operations, and finance, and their recent trends in sales, market share, and profitability. If they are not doing well, successful market and sales strategies should be explained.

Entrepreneurs often know less about their competition than they should. Professional investors are very wary of proposals in which competition is treated lightly. Therefore this section should conclude with an explanation of why customers buy from three or four key competitors. Then, if growth is planned by capturing a share of the competitors' business, the reasons why this is feasible should be explained.

Estimated Market Share and Sales
Identify any major customers who have made or are willing to make purchase commitments. Indicate the extent of these commitments.

Estimate the share of the market and the sales in units and dollars that you think that you can achieve. Base this estimate on your assessment of your customers and their acceptance of your product or service, your market size and trends, and the competition, their offerings and their

		Sales and market share data	
		1st year	2nd year
		Q1 Q2 Q3 Q4	Q1 Q2 Q3 Q4
Estimate total market	Units		
	Dollars		
Your estimated sales	Units		
	Dollars		
Your estimated markets share	Units		
	Dollars		

share of sales in prior year. The growth of your sales and your estimated market share should be related to the growth of your industry and customers and the strengths and weaknesses of your competitors. The data should be presented in tabular form, as shown on page 33. If yours is an existing business, also indicate the total market, your market share, and sales for two prior years.

Marketing Plan

Your marketing plan should describe how you will achieve your sales target. The marketing plan should include a description of your sales and service policies and pricing, distribution and advertising strategies that you will use to achieve your goal. The marketing plan should make clear *what is to be done, how it will be done, and who will do it.*

Marketing Strategy

A description of your marketing strategy should include a discussion of the kinds of customers who will be targeted for initial heavy selling effort, customers who will be sought for later selling efforts, method of identifying specific potential customers and of contacting them, and the features of the product or service (quality, price, delivery, warranty) that will be emphasized to generate sales.

If the sales of your product or service are seasonal, discuss this and indicate any ideas you have for obtaining out-of-season sales.

Pricing

Many entrepreneurs, after convincing the investors that they have a superior product, then say they intend to sell it for less than their competitors. This makes a bad impression for two reasons. First, if their product is as good as they say it is, the entrepreneurs can be judged as poor sales people if they have to offer their product at a lower price than the competition. Second, costs do tend to be underestimated. If you start out with low prices, there is little room to maneuver if costs run over budget. Price hikes are tougher to make stick than price cuts.

Your pricing policy is one of the more important decisions you make. Your "price must be right" to penetrate your market, maintain your market position, and produce the profits you project. Devote enough time to considering a number of pricing strategies and convincingly present the one you select.

Discuss the prices to be charged for your product and service and compare your pricing policy with those of your major competitors. Explain how the price you set will enable you to:

- secure/increase acceptance of your offering,
- maintain and desirably increase your market share in the face of competition, and
- produce profits.

Justify any price increases over competitive items on the basis of newness, quality, warranty, and service. If your product is to be priced lower than your competitors' products, explain how you will do this and maintain profitability.

Sales Tactics

Describe how you will sell and distribute your product or service. Do you or will you use your own sales force, sales representatives, and distributors? Are there ready-made manufacturers' sales organizations already selling related products that you already use or can use? If distributors or sales representatives are used, describe how they have been or will be selected, and the areas they will cover. Discuss the margins to be given to retailers, wholesalers, and your commissions to sales representatives, and compare them to those given your competition. Describe any special policies regarding such items as discounts and exclusive distribution rights.

If a direct sales force is being introduced, indicate how it will be organized and at what rate it will be built up. Show the sales expected per salesman per year and what commission incentive and/or salary they will receive. Explain how these figures compare to those of your competition.

Service and Warranty Policies

If your company will offer a product that will require service and warranties, indicate the importance of these to the customer's purchasing decision and discuss your method of handling service problems.

Advertising, Public Relations, and Promotion

Describe the program you will use to bring your product to the attention of prospective customers. Indicate your plans for public relations, trade show participation, trade magazine advertisements, direct mailings, and the preparation of product sheets and promotional literature. If advertising will be a significant part of company expenses, details of how and when these costs will be incurred should be presented.

Design and Development Plans

If any of your products or services require design and development before they are ready to be placed on the market, the nature and extent of this work should be fully discussed. The costs and time required to achieve a marketable product or service should be indicated.

Such design and development might be the engineering work necessary to convert a laboratory prototype to a finished product, the design of special tooling, the work of an industrial designer to make a product more attractive and salable, or the identification and organization of manpower, equipment, and special techniques or to implement a service business, for example, the equipment, new computer software, and skills required for computerized credit checking.

Development Status and Tasks
Describe the current status of the product or service and explain what remains to be done to make it marketable. Describe briefly the competence or expertise that your company has or will acquire to complete this development. Indicate the type and extent of technical assistance that will be required, and state who will supervise this activity within your organization, and give his or her experience in related development work.

Difficulties and Risks
Identify any major anticipated design and development problems and approaches to their solution. Discuss their possible impact on the timing of the market introduction of your product or service and the cost of design and development.

Costs
Present and discuss a design and development budget. The costs should include labor, materials, consulting fees, etc. Design and development costs are often underestimated. This can seriously impact cash flow projections. Accordingly, consider and perhaps show a 10% to 20% cost contingency. These cost data will become an integral part of the financial plan.

Operations Plan
The operations plan should describe the kind of facilities, space requirements, capital equipment, and labor force (part and full time) that are required to deliver the forecast quantities of the company's product or service. For a manufacturing business, discuss your policies regarding purchasing, "make or buy decisions" (which parts of the product will be purchased and which operations will be performed by your work force), inventory control, and production control. A service business should describe the appropriateness of location, and lease of required equipment, and competitive productivity from a skilled or trained labor force.

The discussion guidelines given below are general enough to cover both product and service businesses. Only those that are relevant to your venture—be it product or service—should be used in preparing the business plan.

Geographic Location
Describe the location of the business and discuss any advantages or disadvantages of the site in terms of wage rates, labor unions, labor availability, closeness to customers or suppliers, access to transportation, state and local taxes, state and local laws, utilities, and zoning. For a service business, proximity to customers is generally "a must."

Facilities and Improvements
If yours is an existing business, describe the facilities currently used to conduct the company's business. This should include plant and office space, storage and land areas, machinery, special tooling, and other capital equipment.

If your venture is a start-up, describe how and when the necessary facilities to *start* production will be acquired. Discuss whether equipment and space will be leased or acquired (new or used), and indicate the costs and timing of such actions. Indicate how much of the proposed financings will be devoted to plant and equipment. These cost data will become part of the plan.

Discuss how and when plant space and equipment will be expanded to the capacities required for future sales projections. Discuss any plans to improve or add to existing plant space or to move the facility. Explain future equipment needs and indicate the timing and cost of any acquisitions. A three-year planning period should be used for these projections.

Strategy and Plans
Describe the manufacturing processes involved in your product's production and any decisions with respect to subcontracting component parts rather than manufacturing them in house. The "make or buy" strategy adopted should consider inventory financing, available labor skills and other nontechnical questions as well as purely production, cost, and capability issues. Justify your proposed "make or buy" policy. Discuss any surveys you have completed of potential subcontractors and suppliers and who these are.

Present a production plan that shows cost-volume information at various sales levels of operation with breakdowns of applicable material, labor, purchased components, and factory overhead. Discuss the inventory required at various sales levels. These data will be incorporated into cash flow projections. Explain how any seasonal production loads will be handled without severe dislocation, for example, by building to inventory, using part-time help, or subcontracting the work.

Briefly, describe your approach to quality control, production control, and inventory control. Explain what quality control and inspection procedures the company will use to minimize service problems and associated customer dissatisfaction.

Discuss how you will organize and operate your purchasing function to insure that adequate materials are on hand for production, that the best price and payment terms have been obtained, and that raw materials and in-process inventory, and, hence, working capital have been minimized.

Labor Force

Explain, exclusive of management functions (discussed later), to what extent local labor force has the necessary skills in sufficient quantity and quality (lack of absenteeism, productivity) to manufacture the product or supply the services of your company to whatever quality, time and cost standards you have established. If the skills of the labor force are inadequate for the needs of your company, describe the kinds of training that you will use to upgrade their skills. Discuss how your business can provide and pay for such training and still offer a competitive product both in the short term (first year) and long term (two to five years).

Management Team

The management team is the key to a successful business. Investors look for a committed management team with a balance in marketing operations and financial skills and experience in doing what is proposed.

Accordingly, this section of the business plan will be of primary interest to potential investors and will significantly influence their investment decisions. It should include a description of the key members of the management team and their primary duties, the organizational structure, and the board of directors.

Organization

In a table, present the key management roles in the company and name the person for each position.

Discuss any current or past situations in which the key management people have worked together that indicate how their skills and personalities complement each other and result in an effective management team. If any key individuals will not be on hand at the start of the venture, indicate when they will join the company or what you are doing to locate and secure commitments from such individuals.

In a new business, it may not be possible to fill each executive role with a full-time person without excessively burdening the overhead of the venture. One solution is to use part-time specialists or consultants to perform some functions. If this is your plan, discuss it and indicate who will be used and when they will be replaced by a full-time staff member.

If the company is established and of sufficient size, an organization chart can be appended as an exhibit.

Key Management Personnel

Describe the exact duties and responsibilities of each of the key members of the management team. Include a brief (three or four sentence) statement of the career highlights of each individual to focus on accomplishments that demonstrate ability to perform the assigned role.

Complete resumes for each key management member should be included here or as an exhibit to the business plan. These resumes should stress education, training, experience, and accomplishments of each person in performing functions similar to that person's role in the venture. Accomplishments should be discussed in such concrete terms as profit and sales improvement, labor productivity gains, reduced operating costs, improved product performance, and ability to meet budgets and schedules. When possible, it should be noted who can attest to accomplishments and recognition or rewards received, such as pay increases and promotions.

Management Compensation and Ownership

The likelihood of obtaining financing for a start-up is small when the founding management team is not prepared to accept modest initial salaries. If the founders demand substantial salaries in excess of what they received at their prior employment, the potential investor will conclude that their psychological commitment to the venture is a good deal less than it should be.

State the salary that is to be paid to each key person and compare it with the salary received at his last independent job. Set forth the stock ownership planned for the key management team members, the amount of their equity investment (if any), and any performance-dependent stock option or bonus plans that are contemplated. Mention any loans made to the company by management, indicating on what terms they were made and under what circumstances they can be converted to equity.

Board of Directors

Identify board members and include a one or two sentence statement of the member's background to show how he or she can benefit the company and what investment (if any) has been made.

Management Assistance and Training Needs
Describe candidly the strengths and weaknesses of your management team and board of directors. Discuss the kind, extent, and timing of any management training that will be required to overcome any weaknesses.

Supporting Professional Services
State the legal (including patent-counsel), accounting, public relations, advertising, banking, and other service organizations that you have selected for your venture. Supporting service organizations that are reputable *and* capable (remember reputations often live on after capability diminishes) not only provide professional assistance, but can also add significantly to the credibility of your business. In addition, properly selected professional organizations can help you establish good contacts in the business community, identify potential investors, and help you secure financing.

Overall Schedule
A schedule that shows the timing and interrelationship of the major events necessary to launch the venture and realize its objectives is an essential part of a business plan. In addition to being a planning aid and showing deadlines critical to a venture's success, a well-prepared schedule can be an extremely effective sales tool in raising money from potential investors. A well-prepared and realistic schedule demonstrates the ability of the management team to plan for venture growth in a way that recognizes obstacles and minimizes risk.

Prepare, as a part of this section, a month-by-month schedule that shows the timing of activities such as product development, market planning, sales programs, and operations. Sufficient detail should be included to show the timing of the primary tasks required to accomplish each major goal.

Show on the schedule the deadlines or milestones critical to the venture's success. This should include events as follows:

- Incorporation of the venture (for a new business).
- Completion of prototypes. This is a key date. Its achievement is a tangible measure of the company's ability to perform.
- When sales representatives are obtained.
- Dates of displays at trade shows.
- When distributors and dealers are signed up.
- Order of materials in sufficient quantities for full-time operation.
- Start of operation. This is another key date because it is related to the production of income.
- Receipt of first orders.
- First sales and deliveries. This is a date of maximum interest because it relates directly to the company's credibility and need for capital.
- Payment of first accounts receivable (cash in).

The schedule should also show the following and their relation to the development of the business.

- Number of management personnel
- Number of operations personnel
- Additions to plant or equipment

Discuss in a general way the activities most likely to cause a schedule slippage and what steps you would take to correct such slippages. Discuss the impact of schedule slippages on the venture's operation, especially on its potential viability and capital needs. Keep in mind that the time to do things tends to be underestimated—even more than financing requirements. So be realistic about your schedule.

Critical Risks and Problems
The development of a business has risks and problems, and the business plan invariably contains some implicit assumptions about them. The discovery of any unstated negative factors by potential investors can seriously undermine the credibility of the entrepreneur and his venture and endanger its financing.

On the other hand, identifying and discussing the risks in your venture demonstrates your skill as a manager and increases your credibility with a venture capital investor. Taking the initiative to identify and discuss risks helps you demonstrate to the investor that you have thought about them and can handle them. Risks then tend not to loom as large black clouds in the investor's thinking about your venture.

Accordingly, identify and discuss the major problems and risks that you think you will have to deal with to develop your venture. This should include a description of the risks relating to your industry, your company and its personnel, your product's market appeal, and the timing and financing of your start-up. Among the risks that might require discussion are the following.

- Price cutting by competitors
- Any potentially unfavorable industry-wide trends
- Design or operating costs significantly in excess of estimates

- Development schedule not met
- Sales projections not achieved by target date
- Difficulties or long lead times encountered in the procurement of parts or raw materials
- Difficulties encountered in obtaining needed bank credit line because of tight money
- Larger than expected innovation and development costs to stay competitive
- Lack of availability of trained labor

This list is *not meant to be in any way comprehensive* but only indicative of the kinds of risks and assumptions involved.

Indicate which business plan assumptions or potential problems are most critical to the success of the venture. Describe your plans for minimizing the impact of unfavorable developments in each risk area on the success of your venture.

The Financial Plan

The financial plan is basic to any investor's evaluation of your business and should represent your best estimates of future operations. Its purpose is to indicate the financial potential of your venture and its capital needs. The financial plan should also serve as an operating plan for financial management of your business.

In developing your financial plan, three basic exhibits must be prepared.

- Profit and loss forecasts for three years
- Cash flow projections for three years
- Pro forma balance sheets at start-up, semi-annually in the first year, and at the end of each of the first three years of operation.

In the case of an existing business seeking expansion capital, balance sheets and income statements for the current and two prior years should be presented in addition to these financial projections.

After you have completed the preparation of the financial exhibits, briefly highlight in writing the important conclusions that can be drawn. This might include such items as the maximum cash requirement, the amount to be supplied by equity and debt, the level of profits as a percent of sales, and how fast any debts are repaid.

Profit and Loss Forecast

The preparation of your business' projected income statements is the planning-for-profit part of your financial plan. Crucial to the earnings forecasts, as well as other projections, is the sales forecast. The methods for developing sales forecasts have already been described in these guidelines, and the sales forecasts made there should be used here.

The following list is a group of headings that can be used in drawing up your profit and loss (P&L) forecast for prospective investors. Italics indicate items that should be included in the figures for that heading but not listed separately in the statement.

Sales
Less: Discounts
Less: Bad debt provision
Less: Materials used
Direct labor
Manufacturing overhead
includes rent, utilities, fringe benefits, telephone
Other manufacturing expense
leased equipment, etc.
Depreciation
Total cost of goods sold
Gross profit (or loss)
Less: Sales expense
Engineering expense
General and administrative expense
office supplies, accounting and legal services, management, etc.
Operating profit (or loss)
Less: Other expense
(e.g., interest)
Profit (or loss) before taxes
Income tax provision
Profit (or loss) after taxes

Figures should be projected for three years. The first year should show a breakdown by month for each item. The second and third years should project quarterly figures. Figures for all three years should appear on a single sheet of ruled paper—make sure the paper you use is large enough. Tape two pages together, if necessary.

Once the sales forecasts are in hand, production costs, or operations costs for a service business, should be budgeted. The level of production or operation that is required to meet the sales forecasts and also to fulfill inventory requirements must be determined. The material, labor, service, and manufacturing overhead requirements must be developed and translated into cost data.

Sales expense should include the costs of selling and distribution, storage, discounts, and advertising and promotion. General and administrative expense should include management salaries, secretarial costs, and legal and accounting expenses. Manufacturing or operations overhead includes such items as rent, utilities, fringe benefits, and telephone.

If these earning projections are to be useful, they must represent your realistic and best estimate of probable operating results.

Discussion of Assumptions

Because of the importance of profit and loss projections, you should explain any assumptions that you made in their preparation. Such assumptions could include the amount allowed for bad debts and discounts and sales expenses or general and administrative costs as a fixed percentage of costs or sales.

Cash Flow Forecast

For a new business, the cash flow forecast can be more important than the forecasts of profits because it details the amount and timing of expected cash inflows and outflows. Usually the level of profits, particularly during the start-up years of a venture, will not be sufficient to finance operating cash needs. Moreover, cash inflows do not match the outflows on a short-term basis. The cash flow forecast will indicate these conditions.

The following headings can be used in preparing the pro forma cash flow analysis. Like the income statement, the cash flow analysis should cover three years, with the first year broken down into 12 monthly figures and the second and third year projected by quarters. Again, this analysis should be made on a single large sheet of ruled paper.

Cash balance: Opening
Add: Cash receipts
Collection of accounts receivable
Miscellaneous receipts
Bank loan proceeds
Sale of stock
Total receipts

Less: Disbursements
Trade payables
Direct labor
Manufacturing overhead
Leased equipment
Sales expense
Warranty expense
General and administrative expense
Fixed asset additions
Income tax
Loan interest @ ________%
Loan repayments
Other payments
Total disbursements

Cash increase (or decrease)
Cash balance: Closing

Given a level of projected sales and capital expenditures over a specific period, the cash flow forecast will highlight the need for and timing of additional financing and show you your peak requirements of working capital. You must decide how this additional financing is to be obtained, on what terms, and how it is to be repaid. Part of the needed financing will be supplied by the professional venture capitalists, part by bank loans for one of five years, and the balance by short-term lines of credit from banks. This information becomes part of the final cash flow forecasts.

If the venture is in a seasonal or cyclical industry, in an industry in which suppliers require a new firm to pay cash, or if an inventory buildup occurs before the product can be sold and produce revenues, the cash flow forecast is crucial to the continuing operation of your business. A detailed cash flow forecast that you understand can enable you to direct your attention to operating problems without the distractions caused by periodic cash crises that you should have anticipated.

Discussion of Assumptions

This should include assumptions made on the timing of collection of receivables, trade discounts given, terms of payments to your suppliers, planned salary and wage increases, anticipated increases in any operating expenses, seasonality characteristics of the business as they affect inventory requirements, and capital equipment purchases. Thinking about such assumptions when planning the operation of your business is useful for identifying issues that may later require attention if they are not to become significant problems.

Balance Sheet Forecasts

The balance sheets are used to show the assets required in the operation of your business and, through liabilities, how these assets are to be financed. Investors and bankers look to the projected balance sheets for such information as debt to equity ratios, working capital, current ratios, and inventory turnover. The investor will relate them to the acceptable limits required to justify future financings that are projected for the venture.

The following headings may be used to prepare the balance sheet forecasts.

Assets

Current assets
- Cash
- Marketable securities
- Accounts receivable
- Inventories
  - Raw materials and supplies
  - Work in process
  - Finished goods
    - Total inventory

Prepaid items
- Total current assets

Plant and equipment
- Less: Accumulated depreciation

Net plant and equipment

Deferred charges

Other assets (identify)
- Total assets

Liabilities and Stockholder's Equity

Current liabilities
- Notes payable to banks
- Accounts payable
- Accruals
- Federal and state taxes accrued
- Other
  - Total current liabilities

- Long-term notes
- Other liabilities

- Common stock
- Capital surplus
- Retained earnings

Total liabilities and stockholder's equity

Forecasted balance sheets should be prepared at start-up, semi-annually for the first year, and at the end of each of the first three years of operation.

Cost and Cash Flow Control

Your ability to meet your income and cash flow projections will depend critically on your ability to secure timely reports on, and effectively control, your operating costs. For this reason, investors will want to know what kind of cost and cash control systems you have or will use in your business. The financial plan should include a brief description of how you will design, install, and maintain systems for controlling costs and cash flows appropriate to the nature and size of your business, who will be responsible for getting cost data, how often cost data will be obtained, and how you will take actions to reduce costs that are running higher than you expected.

Proposed Company Offering

The purpose of this section of the plan is to indicate the amount of capital that is being sought and to briefly describe the uses that will be made of the funds raised. The discussion and guidelines given on this page should help you do this.

Desired Financing

Summarize from your cash flow projections how much money you will need over the next three years to carry out the development and expansion of your business that have been described. Indicate how much of this money you expect to obtain now from the sale of stock and how much you think you can borrow from a bank. Describe the kind (common stock, convertible debenture, etc.), unit price, and total amount of securities to be sold in this offering. Also show the percentage of the company that the investors of this offering will hold after the offering is completed or after any exercise of stock conversion or purchase rights.

Capitalization

Show in a table the names of your current shareholders and the number of shares each holds. Also indicate how many shares of your company's common stock will remain authorized but unissued after the offering.

Use of Funds

Investors like to know how their money is going to be spent. Provide a brief description of how the capital raised will be used. Summarize as specifically as possible what amount will be used for such things as product development, capital equipment, marketing, and general working capital needs.

How to Choose and Approach a Venture Capitalist

G. Jackson Tankersley Jr.

G. Jackson Tankersley, Jr. is the founder of Meritage Private Equity Funds, a communications-oriented private equity firm headquartered in Denver, Colorado. Prior to founding Meritage, Mr. Tankersley co-founded The Centennial Funds. Mr. Tankersley received a BA in Economics with high honors from Denison University and an MBA from the Amos Tuck School of Business Administration at Dartmouth College.

Despite the larger flow of capital to the venture capital industry, it continues to be placed in the hands of the more experienced managers. This makes the task of choosing and approaching a venture capitalist absolutely critical. Many proposals are rejected either because management clearly lacks the entrepreneurial skills necessary to build a business or because the venture capitalist does not believe in the market opportunity or the product feasibility. In too many cases, however, turndowns stem from entrepreneurs' lack of familiarity with a particular venture capitalist's tastes, requirements or specializations. It is therefore crucial to know how to choose the right firm and how to approach it.

Choosing the Right Venture Capital Firm

Identifying the most appropriate group of venture capitalists to approach is critical. It is surprising how little research many entrepreneurs conduct before they begin the time-consuming task of raising capital. Two problems can result from approaching venture capitalists unprepared. First, once an investment opportunity is rejected, it is very difficult to get it reconsidered, even with a proper introduction. Second, if an investment opportunity is rejected by a number of firms, it may get an "overshopped" reputation. Venture capitalists frequently share investment information and a turndown by one firm may influence others.

Increased media coverage makes it easier to collect useful snapshots of venture capital. But once you start to focus your search, you need the sort of data on specific venture capital firms that includes amount of capital managed, and their respective geographic, industry and stage of business development investments preferences.

This information is important as it provides five ways of choosing venture capital firms that are most likely to respond to your approach.

The first way is *geographically.* If you are based in an area well served by venture capital, a "local lead" investor is critical. If you cannot attract a "local lead," you will have a more difficult time raising capital. Although there are many firms investing nationwide, the closer the venture capitalist is to the investment, the easier it is to "add value" and to "monitor" the investment, especially in early-stage companies. Today virtually every region of the country is the home of experienced venture capitalists.

Secondly, many venture capitalists have a *stage of development* bias. There are some who prefer the seed capital arena while others are only interested in later-stage investing. Make certain that your company's stage of development meets with the preferred stage of development of the venture firm which you are approaching. One word of caution: many in the venture capital industry invest in "startups" but definitions vary between firms. A start-up for one firm can actually be a later-stage investment for another. So beware of inconsistent uses of stage of development terms.

The third criterion is *amount of capital* needed. There are many firms that have an upper and lower limit to the size of an investment. If your project falls far outside a firm's range, it is better not to approach them. Also, it is unwise to inflate the amount of capital you need to meet their minimum. Some venture capitalists shy away from very large dollar syndications and prefer to invest a smaller amount to give them a meaningful position in a company. These firms may be more appropriate for your initial requirements.

The venture capital industry is witnessing greater *industry specialization* than ever before. There are venture capital firms and individual venture capitalists that specialize their investments in medical technology, communications, consumer products and distribution, for instance. Clearly, if a venture capital firm has a stated investment preference in your industry, not only is it more likely to understand your opportunity, but it will also be in a position to add value to your company. This industry expertise is often acknowledged and respected by other venture capitalists who may provide additional funding. In addition, a number of venture capital firms have excluded certain investment categories such as real estate or oil and gas.

Finally, in every successful venture capital financing, there is a need for *venture capital leadership*. There are a number of funds who are active investors and are willing to lead a financing while others serve as passive investors. In order to complete a syndication, you will need venture capital leadership. It is unwise to approach passive investors until after a lead investor is identified. Therefore, try to identify venture capitalists that take early leadership roles in syndications similar to your opportunity.

Using these five criteria as a basis, prepare a target group of venture capitalists. Make certain that this target group is a reasonable size. (No one likes to receive a business plan that is numbered 128, knowing it has been sent to a mass audience.) A simple matrix may assist this effort. For example, subjectively rate a venture firm's investment orientation as it relates to your firm's needs. Let two (2) represent a good match, one (1) represent an acceptable match and zero (0) represent a poor match. The venture capitalists with the highest ratings should be the initial targets.

	VC #1	VC #2	VC #3
Geography	2	2	1
State of Development	2	2	2
Capital Required	1	0	2
Industry	2	0	2
Leadership	0	1	2
Total	7	5	9

Obvious trade-offs occur. Which is more important, industry focus or geography? In the above example, however, VC #3 is probably the most likely firm to approach, VC #1 should be approached after the lead investor has been identified and there is no apparent reason to contact VC #2.

Before you approach a targeted venture capital firm, you should research it. Most firms have brochures which provide information to entrepreneurs as well as various "deal sources." A phone call can usually get you a copy of the brochure. Information in this literature has been thoughtfully prepared to generate investment opportunities that fit the firm's interests and to discourage opportunities that do not. Today many venture capital firms host a web site. Visit it before you contact the firm.

This background information should help identify what investments the individual venture capitalist has made. Venture capitalists' past successes can be keys to their areas of personal interest and expertise.

Once the target group has been identified and the firms have been researched, it is now time to approach the venture capitalist.

How to Approach the Venture Capitalist

The *best* way to approach a venture capitalist is through a *quality introduction*, because venture capitalists are more likely to turn down an unsolicited business plan. This introduction may be through a banker, a lawyer, an accountant, another entrepreneur or even another venture capitalist. If your banker, lawyer or accountant appear unwilling to provide an introduction, their hesitancy may indicate doubts about the financeability of you and/or your product. If your contact does not know venture capitalists, you may have the wrong banker, lawyer or accountant.

If you are well known by a successful entrepreneur who has received funding from a specific venture capitalist, this is often the best introduction as venture capitalists pay particular attention to such contacts. Be careful with venture capital references, however. If one venture capitalist you ask for an introduction has turned you down, others will want to know why. If a venture capitalist whom you ask is a passive investor, but introduces you to an active investor with the comment "if you invest, we want to do it with you," this could be positive. (The same holds true even if a venture firm is fully invested and is not making new commitments.)

The Purpose of the Initial Contact

The initial contact following the introduction should be by telephone. The purpose of the telephone call should be to get the venture capitalist to request your business plan and to get that business plan read upon receipt. There are a number of articles and books on writing a business plan and a number of service organizations—including accounting firms, consultants and investment bankers—are now making this a specialty. It should be clearly understood that initially *the sole purpose of the business plan sent to a venture capitalist is to get a meeting*. Let the significance of a meeting be clear. If one out of 100 investment opportunities ultimately gets funded by a specific venture capitalist, probably no more than 30 have meetings. Therefore, if you are invited to a meeting with a venture capitalist, you have just increased your odds by a factor of three.

The business plan should be concise and well written and should include a summary that covers at least four points:

(1) What is the business? Many people say their business is building this product or marketing this concept when in fact the fundamental business is something all together different. Understand and articulate your business.

(2) Who are the people on the management team and why or how are they qualified to succeed in this endeavor? Many venture capitalists state that they invest in people before products or markets. Therefore, the people who are responsible for making it happen must be highlighted.

(3) How well has the business done? Any business, even a seed capital entity, has a history. Detail this history and describe what has been done with the time and resources to date.

(4) How well do you expect it to do? Most businesses do not meet a venture capitalist's expectations because of the size or the scope of the potential business. As a rule of thumb, a company should have the potential to be worth at least $100 million within three to five years to be of interest.

Unfortunately, in the initial review venture capitalists generally look for reasons to turn down an investment rather than search for reasons to invite you for a meeting. For example, typographical errors, incomplete or erroneous market information and an ill-conceived organizational structure are all potential negatives.

Meeting the Venture Capitalist

If a meeting has been set up, be prepared to make a formal presentation. However, you should also be prepared and able to deviate from this agenda if necessary. The venture capitalist is using the meeting to learn about the product and market but is primarily focusing on evaluating you and your team. Remember, you may have limited time to make a positive impression and to leave the venture capitalist enthusiastic about your company.

The entrepreneur should also use the meeting to size up the venture capitalist. Do not hesitate to ask a prospective investor for references, especially names of other portfolio entrepreneurs. Call them, find out how well they have worked together from the entrepreneurs' perspectives.

In today's competitive venture capital marketplace you must be even better prepared to successfully compete for the venture capitalists' dollars. It is the task of the entrepreneur to select and approach the venture capitalist. If this is done wisely and systematically, you will improve the odds of finding a professional venture investor.

Meeting with the Venture Capitalist

Wayne B. Kingsley

Wayne B. Kingsley *is a general partner of InterVen Partners, Inc., a venture capital firm with offices in Portland, OR, and Los Angeles. He has 18 years of venture capital experience. Prior to joining InterVen in 1983, Mr. Kingsley was a vice president of Norwest Venture Capital Management, Inc., a Minneapolis-based small business investment company. From 1972 to 1976, he was chief operating officer of Cascade Capital Corporation, which was acquired by Norwest in 1976. Mr. Kingsley is a graduate of Miami University of Ohio and has an M.B.A. from the Darden School at the University of Virginia.*

Obtaining financing for your firm is no different than any other selling task. Every step is important. One of the more critical steps is the first meeting with your customer—the venture capitalist. The impressions formed during this meeting will be the basis for his or her subsequent regard for you and your proposal. Your initial objective is to convince the venture capitalist that your proposal merits further investigation. Your task in this meeting is to present the essence of your plan in a clear, concise manner.

Hopefully, the venture capitalist has studied your plan before meeting with you, but the chances are it was just skimmed. Even worse, the only knowledge of the proposal may be from your telephone conversation or the two page summary you sent. So assume that very little is remembered about your business and that other partners or junior associates totally unfamiliar with your proposal will attend this meeting and will be there to render advice or do subsequent investigation work.

In preparation, you should plan and rehearse a half-hour explanation of your proposal that describes the company's business, the market and external environment in which it operates, the strengths of the management team and similarities to other successful ventures. The presentation should emphasize your proposal's strengths. Weak points as well as remedies for them should also be addressed, to illustrate your recognition of them. You should also state why this will be a profitable investment for the venture capitalist. To do this you have to state your objectives for the company, and how you will attain them. Be reasonable. Even if you firmly believe you will achieve $200 million in sales your first year, revise your projections to something more conservative and consistent with the average, successful venture-backed company.

What image should you convey? First, you should be natural. If you and the venture capitalist want to continue discussions, this will be the first of many meetings. You are going to see each other at the best and worst moments. So a good starting point is the "real you." Beyond this, be confident. You are offering the investor an opportunity to invest in a very promising company, one in which you have decided to risk a part of your life and assets. The venture capitalist may become your partner, so you want to demonstrate your potential as a good partner. Always use reason rather than argument.

When you have concluded your presentation, you want your listeners to have a clear and concise understanding of your business, what is unique about it and how you will achieve your projections. Something they could easily explain to others.

It is most important they understand what is unique about the proposal, if it is not the product then the management team or the location or something else. Very few venture capitalists will invest in something which is a "me-too" product going against established competition.

Using visual aids for your presentation is strictly a matter of preference. Remember, one reason for the meeting is to establish rapport. Overhead projections, slides and videotapes diminish contact and may minimize the interchange of a head-on presentation. Many venture capitalists' offices, however, have equipment to accommodate visual presentations, so do what you think is necessary to present yourself in the best light.

Handling Questions

During and after your presentation, you should be prepared for questions. You may assume the venture capitalist knows something about your business and will ask some obvious questions and some that are more penetrating. Your assumptions may also be challenged. Some of the questions may be blunt and some may expose preconceptions with which you disagree. You may not be questioned at all in these areas. In other words, prepare for any response.

How do you handle this? If you have done your homework and know your business, you should be able to answer most questions in a brief and concise manner. If you do not know the answer or have to prepare an answer, this is an ideal opportunity to arrange another meeting to deliver the necessary information. If you disagree with a statement the venture capitalist makes, explain your reasons and offer to provide additional information on the subject. Do not get sidetracked from your objective by arguing a small point. In the case of an obvious objection which was not raised, you may want to bring it up for discussion so that it does not become a problem if the venture capitalist thinks of it after you have gone.

Even if the person you are talking to is a technological whiz kid in your field, try to keep the meeting focused on the big picture and not get off on details of a technology that he may not be able to fully comprehend in a brief first meeting. Discuss the quality of the management team's technological capabilities and the accomplishments of the technologists. To assess technology, most venture capitalists will hire consultants and check the reputations of the technical people in your company, rather than rely on their own knowledge of the technology. They will probably be more concerned in this first meeting with your ability to demonstrate your overall business acumen.

Maintaining Momentum

If the venture capitalist seems interested, find out what the next step in the process will be. Even the best intentioned people can become involved with a new proposal or with the many flash fires which occur in any portfolio. What you want to do is get a tentative schedule set up with dates and milestones that will hopefully lead to an investment. Once scheduled, you and the prospective investor should keep to these dates religiously. If the venture capitalist starts to fall seriously behind schedule or becomes too distant, this might indicate disinterest in your proposal. If this happens, you will probably have to find a replacement investor who will be more active. Do not be surprised, however, if the first venture capitalist becomes very interested and active again when a deal starts to go together.

Entrepreneurs are always trying to develop a magic money raising strategy. If investors cannot be convinced of the merits of the investment, no amount of intrigue or cosmetics will improve your chances for funding. However, how you present and market your proposal can influence the value investors place on it, as well as their degree of comfort with you and the other members of the management team.

Camp Followers

One common strategy question is whether or not to involve "camp followers" in the project. Camp followers may be of two types. The first is a series of smaller investors who "seed" the deal to establish price and credibility and the second type is the well-known person who becomes an advisor or a director, primarily to establish credibility. This type may also make a small investment to confirm faith in the project.

Do not add camp followers to your project if there is no *operational benefit* from doing so. Small, unsophisticated investors can complicate a larger venture financing by making compliance with securities laws more difficult, by balking at the seemingly onerous terms of the professional financing, by "helping" negotiate the terms and by presenting an unstated but always present risk of suit in the future. New and growing companies often go from crisis to crisis before achieving success. These crises are usually better met by the professionals who deal with them daily. On the other hand, a number of companies start and grow successfully with only the help of smaller investors. If small investors are essential to your company, by all means embrace them. If you plan an institutional venture financing, prepare them for this event.

A number of successful companies have included well-known business people on their boards of directors. Sometimes these people are sought out as advisors or merely passive investors. Far too often these people are included only for cosmetic purposes, similar to an athlete endorsing a brand of running shoe. These people usually add nothing to the company and occasionally they can be detrimental, if they try to become too involved and do not really understand small businesses. On the other hand, a talented person, with proven ability who has worked, and intends to continue working with a business can be an invaluable asset. This decision should be based on whether or not the person will actually take time to work with the company and has the specific talents required to add value.

A few additional helpful hints:

Requiring signed secrecy agreements can be an impediment to obtaining financing. Before you decide to ask for these, make sure that the secret is really worth all the effort. It should also be an easily definable entity—like the formula for Coca-cola..

Investors generally want some rights and information that may not initially appear reasonable. It is perfectly proper to negotiate, but not on every point. Fight only for the issues that seem most important to you. If the investor does the same thing, the chances are neither of you will be left with many substantive areas of disagreement.

Do not become discouraged. Every venture capitalist is

different. Sometimes the same proposal will appeal to a number of them. Often one will be interested in funding a proposal that is of no interest to others. Keep looking until you find the person who likes your company.

The investor will usually negotiate price and terms after the proposal has been investigated. In the beginning, you should talk about price only to ensure the investor's expectations are in a reasonable range. At the end of the process, you and the investor will have considerable time and money invested in each other and will have incentive to strike a deal you each can accept. If you try to negotiate price in the beginning of the relationship, it is much easier to walk away from each other.

For the venture capital relationship to be successful, it has to be built on trust and mutual respect. When negotiating price the relationship is adversarial, when working through problems and facing a competitive world, it must be supportive. If either party suspects such a relationship cannot be perfected, it should be abandoned. Be open and honest with your current and prospective investors and demand the same from them.

Venture Capital: More Than Money?

Dr. Jeffry A. Timmons and Dr. Harry J. Sapienza

Dr. Jeffry A. Timmons *is nationally and internationally recognized for his work in entrepreneurship, new ventures, and venture capital. He is currently the Franklin W. Olin Distinguished Professor at Babson College. In 1989, Dr. Timmons became the first to hold a joint appointment at the Harvard Business School, as the first MBA Class of 1954 Professor of New Ventures, and at Babson College as the Frederic C. Hamilton Professor of Free Enterprise Development. He has authored or co-authored ten books including* New Venture Creation, *5th ed., (McGraw Hill, Irwin, 1999) and* Venture Capital at the Crossroad *(Harvard Business School Press, 1992), and six articles in* Harvard Business Review *on these topics. He was co-founder and director of Boston Communications Group, owners of cellular and telecommunications related ventures, is an advisor to venture funds, and is a Special Advisor to the Board of the Center for Entrepreneurial Leadership at the Ewing Marion Kauffman Foundation, where he created and is dean of the Kauffman Fellows Program.*

Dr. Harry J. Sapienza *is currently the Carlson Chair in Entrepreneurship and Academic Director of the Center for Entrepreneurial Studies in the Carlson School of Management at the University of Minnesota. Dr. Sapienza is nationally and internationally known for his work in venture capitalist-entrepreneur relationships and his work on the internationalization of new high potential ventures. His work has three times won best paper awards in the Entrepreneurship Division of the Academy of Management. His dissertation, "Variations in Venture Capitalist-Entrepreneur Relations: Antecedents and Consequences," conducted with the cooperation of Venture Economics, Inc. won awards as the outstanding dissertation in the entrepreneurship divisions of both the Academy of Management and the Institute of Management Sciences. Dr. Sapienza continues to conduct studies into both private and corporate venture capital.*

You've survived the start-up-thanks to your own sweat equity, help from some friends, your wits, guts and a lot of dedication. Your aspirations and the responses from the marketplace are agreeing more and more: your business can become a substantial one. Your ambitious expansion plans indicate a voracious appetite for cash, and today venture capital is a prime source.

If this is the first time you have sought venture capital, you wonder if it is worth it. You know it can take weeks, months, sometimes a year or more to secure financing, while diverting scarce management's resources away from building and running your fledgling firm. And besides, you wonder if you really want outsiders involved in your company. You ponder a vital question: What real value will the venture capital infuse in your venture beyond money?

To gain some insights into this question, we examined one company in depth, conducted over forty interviews with entrepreneurs and venture capitalists, and surveyed the CEO and the lead investor in 51 venture-backed companies across the U.S. The extensive interviewing and the survey help validate much of what is observed in the case study and highlight the roles of venture capitalist in launching and building businesses. As you will see, excellent personal chemistry developed between the venture capitalist and the management team. The interviews and survey results indicate the importance of this relationship.

Case Study: NBI, Inc.

For our case study, we spoke to the management team of NBI, Inc. (Boulder, Colorado), one of the most successful and rapidly growing firms in the word-processing and office-automation industry. The company was launched in 1973 and in the first year NBI's president, Tom Kavanagh, and his two partners joined the venture, the firm reached sales of $167,000. By 1982, NBI sales had exceeded $100 million, its rapid growth fueled by venture capital and subsequent public offerings. For NBI, the lead investor's main contributions were recruiting management and acting as a sounding board and financier for the long haul. Additionally, the lead investor provided industry expertise, helped foster the necessary entrepreneurial climate, and was a voice of calm and rationality during difficult times.

Tom Kavanagh certainly found significant "added value" in his venture capital partners. Enough so that he succinctly expressed what we call Kavanagh's Law: "It is far more important whose money you get than how much you get or how much you pay for it." The following narrative demonstrates many of the ways a lead investor made contributions the NBI management team deemed to be of great value.

Early Stages: Vital Contributions in Recruiting Key Management

The experience of Kavanagh and his top three vice presidents shows that having the right venture capital partner during the start-up and fragile early stages make a tremendous difference in the odds favoring survival and success. In their minds, there is no doubt that recruiting the top management team was "probably the most indispensable value added" by their venture capital partners. Despite NBI's ambitious and impressive plans, it was very difficult to entice a high-performing executive away from a top-notch company to join the launching of a new venture. The lead investor who played an invaluable role in recruiting two of the three top people was Burton J. McMurtry, then a general partner of Institutional Venture Associates and now of Technology Venture Investors. McMurtry helped bring in Mark Stevenson as vice president of marketing, and David Klein as vice president of new business development; their contribution was central to NBI's explosive growth.

Venture capitalists have developed a specialized network of thousands of contacts, leads and reliable sources of intelligence and verification on personnel. But you can have all that and still wind up with gaps in top management. Locating the right team members is truly an art. McMurtry was always available to assist in searching for and researching top people. The trick, according to Kavanagh, is the ability to convince truly top-notch candidates to give up all they have to take the plunge with you.

Perhaps you're in a situation similar to Tom Kavanagh's in 1975. Your business plan has been well-received by the venture capitalists who have taken the time to get to know you and to review your plan carefully. Further, they have expressed a sincere interest in your venture. But there is one hitch: without an outstanding marketing person with an impressive track record-someone who knows your business inside and out-the investors simply decline to act. You have been pursuing your number-one candidate for over two months, and you hope to celebrate Thanksgiving with the acceptance of your offer.

The call comes; the message is clear: "I like you, your prospective backers, your company, your product and your philosophy. But we've moved eight or nine times, and I'm very happy in what I'm doing. I believe I can achieve income, position, and personal financial goals while being a driving force in the industry right where I am." Now what? You cannot bootstrap it forever. Once your prospective backers find out, and word gets around the industry that your top prospect said "no," well . . .

After hearing Kavanagh's story, McMurtry was convinced that Mark Stevenson-the prime candidate for the marketing position-had "not thought it through completely, particularly the financial consequences," and had thus declined for the wrong reasons. The next day the McMurtry and Kavanagh were on a plane from San Francisco to Dallas to meet with Stevenson. The eyeball-to-eyeball meeting ex tended well into the night. The next day, Stevenson quit his job at Xerox to join NBI.

What had happened? According to Stevenson, "There is no question that without Burt, I would not have done it. His very professional, straightforward manner convinced me. He said that he and Tom wanted to sit down with me and my wife and my two children to talk over the reasons why we should reconsider. He had the sensitivity to know that if my wife also understood the reasons why we might want to change our minds, it would make all the difference. The offer was really not different in terms of salary and stock. What he was able to do was enable me to see the decision in a different context: what it could mean to be in control of my own destiny, while also achieving those other personal goals." Several months later, David Klein, a close colleague from Stevenson's prior job also decided to join NBI, even though he had originally advised Stevenson against moving.

"I would not have joined if it were not for Burt," Klein said. "His understanding of what had to happen to make it a good deal for both of us was key. He was able to convey in a very professional and credible way that he could not get rich unless we did." The advantages of having a top-flight venture capital partner extend far beyond recruiting. Hundreds of times McMurtry played a vital role at NBI, closing with numerous prospective suppliers, dealers and customers.

A Sounding Board

According to Kavanagh, playing devil's advocate was the second major way his lead investor added value to building the venture. Having someone to discuss and critique your plans and ideas before you are firmly committed can help avoid costly mistakes. Ironically, a savvy outsider can provide that insight to a management team. Venture teams come to work together so closely and intimately that they begin to think alike. New product ideas, strategies and directions, can emerge as if out of one mind. The dangers of this tendency are obvious, and the outside investor, because of a reasonably removed and objective view, can better assess the rationale of plans, ideas and initiatives.

At NBI, according to Klein, it was tough to get "tests of reasonableness." In contrast, he found that at an IBM or Xerox you're forced to do so; the "implementors" challenge your innovative decisions. But at NBI, as in most smaller ventures, each member of the top management team has their area of accountability, and they are pretty much on their own. What McMurtry did, was to talk with the individuals of the team, often several times a week. According to the group at NBI, it was extremely valuable to have someone vitally concerned asking constructive questions. One of McMurtry's favorite questions was, "What decisions did you make last week that you were most uncomfortable with?"

Still another example of the kind of immersion NBI experienced centered on the need for longer-range planning, initiating some strategic thinking, even though the immediate pressures of the start-up or expansion seem to be overwhelming. Kavanagh stresses that it was McMurtry who "gets lots of credit for getting us to do it first. He got the process on track and going a good two years earlier than we would have without his prodding, and you never do it soon enough."

In for the Long Haul

For a company with potential and aspirations that are compelling enough to initially attract venture capital investors, it is almost a given that subsequent rounds of financing will be necessary as the venture progresses. Unlike many other sources of finance, professional venture capitalists must possess both the patience and bravery for the longer haul. If you have found the right investors for your company, then you can expect them to be 100% behind you to arrange for subsequent rounds of financing. In doing so, such investors will look out for the best interests of your company, rather than what is most advantageous for the venture capital firm.

In NBI's case, McMurtry was the vital link in attracting two other highly regarded venture capitalists to participate in the later rounds: William Hambrecht, of Hambrecht & Quist, and David Dullum, of Frontenac Venture Capital. According to Kavanagh, Dullum served the company very effectively as a director and member of the audit committee. As an investor and member of NBI's board, Hambrecht served a critical role when it came to determining the most suitable structure and timing of subsequent public offerings. Their contributions complemented McMurtry's and were considered invaluable by the leaders of NBI. They were involved where they could make the greatest contribution.

Other Key Contributions

Securing key customers and accounts is an area where immense help can be contributed. Again, in the fragile start-up period and early stages, every customer can be crucial. Venture capitalists can often articulate the company's case in a more objective manner than the founders. What they add is a sufficient comfort level to enable big-company buyers to cast their fate as customers of a new or small firm. Venture investors can outline by phone why they invested in the venture and the reasons for their confidence. A sense of professional objectivity can shift doubt to confidence. According to the NBI team, McMurtry spent untold hours doing just that. The carefully documented letter he prepared explaining the rationale for investing in NBI was a source of considerable comfort to buyers and vendors alike. AT NBI, "100 times or more" McMurtry played an important role in closing with suppliers, dealers and customers.

Another area that had a lot to do with NBI's success was a sense of clarity about what it takes to create and perpetuate an "entrepreneurial climate and commitment." Kavanagh credits McMurtry's ability in helping create such a climate to his extensive experience working with similar start-up and early-stage ventures. The soul of this spirit appeared to be an incentive system encouraging teamwork rather than only rewarding individual success. "Getting promoted simply did not matter since we did not pay ourselves much anyway," said one NBI vice president. "All the payoffs were based on what was good for NBI." The key executives were convinced that they could all achieve their financial goals, if they could drive NBI to accomplish its business objectives. This spirit continues to permeate the company today.

Roaring cannons are inevitable for most fledgling firms that grow as rapidly as NBI. There are crises, periods of doubt, even some desperation; it's never simple. The fragile process of launching and building such an enterprise requires the qualities of an investor rather than the shirt-sleeve perseverance and uncanny degree of ingenuity of an entrepreneur. Beyond an investor's objectivity and insight, another vital contribution emerged for NBI-support with patience and fortitude.

When a situation takes an unexpected turn-some missed deadlines, a lost key account, a sudden resignation, and the inevitable cash and confidence crisis-nothing is more disturbing than a backer with a weak heart and a weaker pocketbook. "No matter how bad things got at NBI, there was a calmness in Burt. Never once," according to Stevenson, "did he step on your hands when you were lying flat on your back." In short, that kind of professional behavior meant there were no "I told you so's" or threats to withhold future financial backing, or a panicky haste to start changing management, strategies or product. The message was one of concern accompanied by complete confidence in the team and how they were going about the business. For NBI, the involvement was described as "complete immersion, but never any meddling."

The contributions of McMurtry and other venture capitalists in the development of NBI extended well beyond these few examples. Industry savvy, mentoring, strategic insights, and comradery-all these and more played a part in nurturing and building the company.

Our investigation extended across the country to see how the experience here matched those of other entrepreneurs and other venture capitalists. During 1987 through 1988, our research included both questionnaires and in-depth personal interviews to gain a better understanding of the process.

Letters from Our Field Study

We conducted research on over 120 entrepreneurs and venture capitalists on their view of the importance and effectiveness of the lead investor's involvement in developing their current businesses. For each venture, we obtained the view of both the CEO-entrepreneur and the lead venture capital investor. Their perceptions were startlingly similar! While each venture's problems, challenges, and strengths differ from those at NBI, many common themes, however, did emerge-and a few differences were revealed as well.

Our surveys and in-depth interviews revealed the following generalizations: 1) the most intense involvement does indeed occur at the tender early stages of the business; 2) openness of communications and personal chemistry are crucial; 3) venture capitalists add value in a variety of ways, especially through strategic and supportive roles; 4) most of the venture capitalist's key roles become increasingly important as the venture develops.

Lead Investor Importance and Effectiveness: Survey Results

Each entrepreneur-lead investor pair rated the importance and effectiveness of the lead investor's involvement in the venture in eight separate roles. The results of this research is shown on the next page, broken into ratings from early-stage and later-stage ventures.

These ratings show that both entrepreneurs and venture capitalists believe that lead investors make important and effective contributions in a wide variety of value-added roles beyond merely providing capital and sources of additional financing.

The experience of NBI demonstrated how at one company a lead investor could be absolutely crucial to attracting top managers to help launch the new business; at NBI, McMurtry was also viewed as a key strategic adviser who was immersed even in the operating decisions of the venture. Our research indicates that after the initial launching of the business, networking and management recruiting roles are not typically as important as the strategic and supportive roles.

Extent of Involvement

Entrepreneurs often express concern over the extent to which a venture capitalist is involved in the company. The key consideration, of course, is the bottom line effect of such involvement-whether the additional effort and support, in fact, achieves recognized value.

We found a wide fluctuation in terms of the intensity and extent of involvement on the part of venture capitalists. For the most part, however, the quality of the relationship is key. Said one entrepreneur, "Think of it as you would marriage. You don't want to go into it lightly. Think about what it would be like to work with these people day in and day out." Echoing this sentiment, a general partner in a top Boston venture capital firm said, "its like getting married. You've got to ask yourself, 'Can I live with this person when things get really tough?'"

One venture capitalist expressed the value and importance of personal chemistry: "One of the evaluations we make is 'Can you work with this person?' not 'Is this person good?'" For their part, entrepreneurs seem to favor lead investors who are active, involved and interested: "What I like best about Jim's involvement is his enthusiasm for the investment. He really cares, and he's really interested in what we're doing. He is always very positive, helpful and supportive. That's something that, perhaps more than any of the other things, we need most." Another entrepreneur expressed this idea differently: "Experienced venture capitalists are good at listening above and between the lines. They listen real hard."

When things work well, entrepreneurs find themselves seeking a much higher level of involvement than they ever imagined wanting. The CEO of a fast-growing high technology firm said this about his relationship with the lead investor: "It's much more than a professional relationship. We're personal friends . . . I wouldn't change anything-I just wish we had the opportunity to interact more."

Two Sides of the Coin

Needless to say, there are those relationships that fail to develop the special chemistry needed to catapult the venture to bigger and better things. Some venture capitalists are less adept at turning around such situations. As in most relationships, a common complaint when this occurs is the failure to communicate effectively. One entrepreneur complained, "What I can't stand is his

Ratings for Early-Stage Ventures

V.C. Roles	Importance (5 pt. scale) entre.	Importance (5 pt. scale) v.c.	Effectiveness (10 pt. scale) entre.	Effectiveness (10 pt. scale) v.c.
Strategic Roles				
Sounding Board	4.25	4.37	8.05	7.67
Business Consultant	4.17	4.46	8.14	7.83
Financier	4.17	4.42	8.05	8.41
Social/Supportive Roles				
Coach/Mentor	3.63	3.75	6.86	6.79
Friend/Confidant	3.46	3.33	6.71	6.39
Networking Roles				
Management Recruiter	3.17	3.75	5.36	6.17
Professional Contact	3.18	3.33	6.90	6.83
Industry Contact	2.58	3.46	5.52	5.33
Overall effectiveness ratings			***8.04***	***7.39***

Ratings for Late-Stage Ventures

V.C. Roles	Importance (5 pt. scale) entre.	Importance (5 pt. scale) v.c.	Effectiveness (10 pt. scale) entre.	Effectiveness (10 pt. scale) v.c.
Strategic Roles				
Sounding Board	4.29	4.67	8.15	8.13
Business Consultant	3.96	4.42	6.90	7.58
Financier	3.46	2.96	7.22	6.73
Social/Supportive Roles				
Coach/Mentor	3.54	4.08	6.95	7.29
Friend/Confidant	3.25	3.52	6.80	6.50
Networking Roles				
Management Recruiter	2.42	2.33	3.38	3.06
Professional Contact	2.42	2.46	4.94	5.32
Industry Contact	2.04	1.87	2.61	2.55
Overall effectiveness ratings			***7.70***	***7.22***

Summary Ratings

V.C. Roles	Importance Avg. Rating (5 pt. scale)	Effectiveness Avg. Rating (10 pt. scale)
Strategic Roles		
Sounding Board	4.38	8.07
Business Consultant	4.27	7.71
Financier	3.73	7.78
Social/Supportive Roles		
Coach/Mentor	3.76	7.00
Friend/Confidant	2.93	6.73
Networking Roles		
Management Recruiter	2.93	4.74
Professional Contact	2.88	6.17
Industry Contact	2.47	4.07

Ratings for Entire Set of Ventures

V.C. Roles	Importance (5 pt. scale)		Effectiveness (10 pt. scale)	
	entre.	v.c.	entre.	v.c.
Strategic Roles				
Sounding Board	4.27	4.49	8.18	7.96
Business Consultant	4.12	4.41	7.67	7.75
Financier	3.78	3.67	7.73	7.63
Social/Supportive Roles				
Coach/Mentor	3.57	3.94	6.95	7.06
Friend/Confidant	3.37	3.35	6.91	6.55
Networking Roles				
Management Recruiter	2.82	3.04	4.67	4.81
Professional Contact	2.82	2.92	6.17	6.20
Industry Contact	2.26	2.67	4.18	3.96
Overall effectiveness ratings			***7.88***	***7.35***

unwillingness to listen. He has preconceived ideas about a particular topic . . . he just doesn't want to hear the details."

While it has bandied about in the popular press that venture capitalists can be hard-nosed, cutthroat negotiators aiming to take advantage of aspiring entrepreneurs, our interview and survey data paint a much different picture. Every profession will have some who are uncivilized and unscrupulous. An effective venture capitalist, however, generally must have a high level of integrity and interpersonal skills. As one entrepreneur said, "It takes a rare combination of abilities and attributes to make a good venture capitalist. They must have the ability to manage people and to analyze a wide set of diverse information." Our survey ratings show that a surprisingly high percentage of venture capitalists fit the bill.

In Summary

The successful development of a business can be critically impacted by the interaction of the management team and the involved venture capitalists. If a peer relationship can be established, the value-added synergy can be a powerful stimulant for success.

Not all venture capitalists are exactly like those NBI was able to attract, nor will every founder-investor partnership evolve as that one did. Yet many aspiring founders overlook some of the very large "value-added" contributions that professional venture capital investors are accustomed to making and erroneously opt for a "better deal," or a debt backer.

If you have progressed far enough to gain the serious interest of professional venture investors, they will welcome as thorough an examination of their credentials and track record as they will conduct on you, your team and venture. By taking the time to talk to entrepreneurs they have backed, you are likely to discover many of the exceptional qualities that NBI found in their backers. Having just such resources on your team can be the difference in making visions become reality for both the investors and the entrepreneurs.

Structuring the Financing

Stanley C. Golder

Prior to his passing, Stanley C. Golder *was a general partner and consultant in the firm of GTCR Golder Rauner, LLC in Chicago. Founded in 1980, the company currently manages $4.5 billion in seven private equity funds. For the prior nine years, Mr. Golder was president of the Equity Group of First Chicago Corp., one of the largest and most successful bank holding company business development investment affiliates. He was a past chairman of both the National Association of Small Business Investment Companies and the National Venture Capital Association. GTCR Golder Rauner, LLC is an active investor in consolidating fragmented industries.*

The structure of venture capital investments follows no set formula nor does it fit into a perfect structure: the objective is to reconcile the differing needs and concerns of the venture capitalist and the entrepreneur in a way that is satisfactory to both parties. Since each situation is different, structures vary widely.

One issue that relates to the process of formalizing a venture investment is the financial structure; in other words, the form of securities instruments used. These securities instruments have certain advantages and disadvantages and can be used to provide a fair and equitable structure.

Needs and Concerns

The needs of the venture firm and the company will vary based on the company's stage of development, the risk and the ultimate potential as well as the requirements and the philosophy of the individual venture firm. However, there are a number of factors for venture capitalists and entrepreneurs to consider when creating any investment.

Primary considerations for the venture capitalist include:

- Reasonable reward given the level of risk.
- Sufficient influence on the development of the company, usually through board representation.
- Management's relative contribution to capital. (This assures that managers have more at stake than just their egos.)
- Minimization of taxes resulting from the various types of cash flows to investors (dividends versus interest, versus capital gains).
- Future liquidity in the event that the company is successful or stagnates.
- Voting control, which is particularly desirable if performance is substantially below expectations and the management team must be replaced.
- Protection from having any remaining investor dollars split with entrepreneur in the event that the company is unsuccessful and dissolves.
- Current yield in the case of an SBIC (Small Business Investment Company), which has debt to service.

Primary considerations for the typical entrepreneur include:

- Ability to lead the creation of the business that they have conceptualized (operating and strategic control).
- Financial rewards for creating the business.
- Adequate resources needed to achieve their goal.
- Minimization of tax exposure for buying cheap stock.
- Value of substantive contribution from board members.

Common considerations for both sides include:

- Flexibility of structure that will allow room to enable additional investments later, incentives for future management and retention of stock if management leaves.
- Balance sheet attractiveness to suppliers and debt financiers.
- Retention of key employees through adequate equity participation.

The structuring process includes laying out the needs and concerns of both parties; evaluating all the alternatives; and choosing and negotiating a structure that is consistent with the company's financial needs and capabilities and that will provide liquidity and, in extenuating circumstances, control for the investors.

Securities Instruments Commonly Used

The structure of a venture capital financing uses a range of securities instruments, from straight debt to debt with equity features (convertible debt to debt with warrants) to common stock. The following is a summary of the securities that are often used in combination with one another:

- *Senior Debt*—Generally used for long-term financing for low-risk companies or for mezzanine (later stage) financings.

- *Subordinated Debenture*—This is a type of debt that is subordinated to financing from other financial institutions such as banks and may be unsecured. It is usually convertible to common stock or accompanied by warrants to purchase common shares. Senior lenders accept this as equity and therefore allow increased debt from other sources.

- *Preferred Stock*—Generally convertible to common stock, preferred stock gives the venture capitalists "preference" over common shareholders and some rights while from the entrepreneur's perspective it improves the company's debt-to-equity ratio. One disadvantage is that if dividends are attached, they are not tax deductible.

- *Common Stock*—Generally the most expensive in terms of ownership given to the venture capitalist because it has the most risk. But from the venture capitalist's view it is also the least flexible. It affords no protection, allows the least amount of control over management and since there is generally no dividend, provides no return until the stock is sold.

Choosing the "Right" Instruments

The advantage to debt instruments from the venture capitalist's perspective is that they can be designed to provide (1) preference in case of liquidation, (2) some current income and (3) remedies in case of default. An SBIC that has used its leverage and thus has debt to service will prefer an income bearing security. For the company, however, excessive debt can strain its credit standing and make future long-term financing difficult and, in case of default, places the venture capitalist in a position of control. On the other hand, common stock or (as it is often termed) straight equity provides no protection for the venture capitalist and as a result will ultimately be very costly for the entrepreneur in terms of equity give-up.

Entrepreneurs, venture capitalists and their respective attorneys can be creative in modifying traditional securities to meet the needs of a particular situation. Most venture capital financing structures are a combination of debt and equity that satisfies both parties. The often used preferred stock structure is a compromise between common stock and note structures for several reasons. First, preferred stock has more protection than common stock, but less than subordinated notes.

Second, preferred stock usually carries a dividend, but it can only be paid if the company is profitable. Also, preferred stock is a separate class of stock, and accordingly, has certain rights established in the articles of incorporation which are stronger than the rights of common shareholders, but usually not as strong as noteholders. Finally, preferred stock may be redeemable, which would allow investors to obtain a return of principal, assuming that sufficient capital is available for redemption.

Other combinations and unique hybrid structures can often provide preference in sale, liquidation or merger; and current income plus capital gain for the venture capitalist without weighing the balance sheet with too much debt.

A no-load convertible preferred, for example, has no dividend attached; has liquidation preference; converts to common at the option of the holder and automatically at a public offering; votes as if common stock; is considered equity; and requires a board seat, monthly reports, registration rights and a right of first refusal for future financings. This is typically used for start-up and early-stage financings and is attractive to the entrepreneur because there is no dividend obligation.

Common stock may be used in a larger successful company while senior debt with warrants may be more appropriate in a turnaround situation.

Flexibility of Structure

The structure adopted initially affects the ability to take actions subsequently and therefore should be as flexible as possible. Firstly, the rights of initial investors to participate in subsequent financing rounds should be established so as to provide as little obstacle as possible to their being completed. Secondly, there needs to be provision made for providing stock that can motivate key management brought in subsequent to the financing. Thirdly, if management members leave, some or all of their stock should be retained by the company. These last two issues can be dealt with by having a class of stock for management differing from that issued to investors. Reserves can be established for additions to management and stock issued can be escrowed. Care needs to be paid to the tax implications so that members of management are not faced with unexpected liabilities in connection with their holding this stock.

Another point on structure of transactions, which seems obvious, but is often ignored, is that an investor in an early-stage company who puts in considerably more dollars than the entrepreneur should generally not lose money on their investment, while an entrepreneur makes money. This, again, mitigates toward using a senior instrument so as to protect the investor's position.

Obviously, it is in the best interest of both the investor and the entrepreneur that the instruments used be considered equity and be leverageable as the company grows. Preferred stocks should cause no problems as they are clearly equity, even though they may have redemption requirements. These are easily handled by senior lenders if and when the company is capable of acquiring debt. Subordinated debt can be accommodated to this need, but has a few more problems vis-a-vis senior lenders as the company grows. In either case, however, these instruments should be equity as far as any senior creditors are concerned, so that appropriate leverage can be obtained when necessary.

Many venture capitalists prefer not to make outright purchases of common stock except in cases where the majority ownership is in the hands of an investor group. Even then, there are many arguments for preferred stocks. Before taking a common equity position, there can be a waiting period to determine if the company performs as expected and to see if management's objectives are similar to those of the investors and will protect the investors' interest.

The question of ultimate liquidity is also very significant. While there are differences in various parts of the country, an ultimate maturity on investments is preferred, which either provides liquidity or the ability to negotiate toward liquidity when the company has not reached its objectives, but is viable.

In most cases, investments are thought of only in terms of success or failure, but it is very possible that a company will move relatively sideward (sometimes called the living dead) or plateau in its growth and therefore be unable to achieve a public market. Even if companies go public, the market will not usually accept a large amount of stock from inside investors, unless the company makes major progress. The only way out for the venture capitalist is the company's sale or merger. At this point, the goals of the entrepreneurs or managers of the company may differ from the investors' objectives. Consequently, contractual arrangements to achieve liquidity become most important and can be best achieved at the inception of the investment.

Control

Another problem that is handled by appropriate structuring is the very serious aspect of control. Businesspeople approach venture capitalists with the idea that they should control their own business, but history has shown that many entrepreneurs do not have the desire, may not have the ability and certainly do not have the experience to run a business as it grows. Most venture capitalists do not want to run companies, but they feel that it is their basic responsibility to see that the companies in which they invest are well run and if management changes are appropriate, they can be achieved.

Various types of senior instruments can give investors the opportunity to have their interests protected as these types of problems develop. This is not a means to financially disadvantage the equity interest of the entrepreneur. In fact, it is designed to help that interest and to enable a board of directors to make changes in management if they deem appropriate.

There are major differences between investors and not all of the companies in the industry have the same philosophies. Having been involved with many successful companies and having heard many successful entrepreneurs speak who have been backed by venture capitalists, I think entrepreneurs will find that control may be an issue with inexperienced investors and entrepreneurs but not with those who have been successful. De facto day-to-day control needs to be distinguished from voting control.

Keep in mind, appropriate structuring of a transaction cannot make a bad investment good; it can, however, influence the results of investments that are not meeting the initial expectations.

In making every investment, the parties presume a high level of success. Over the years, the record proves that only a small percentage are truly successful. Therefore, achieving liquidity and/or return of capital and the possible remedies available by using instruments other than common stock can be helpful to the investment process and beneficial to both the entrepreneur and venture capitalists.

Avoid inflexible structures. More often than not, an inflexible structure will exaggerate a strategic problem rather than provide a simple solution. For example, there have been situations where an inflexible deal structure enabled one very small player to obstruct an entire round of badly needed financing. Therefore, the best advice for both the entrepreneur and venture capitalist is to keep the structure simple and flexible and to be sure to understand the terms so that they have a good, constructive relationship.

Preliminary Legal Considerations in Forming a New Enterprise

Michael P. Ridley, Esq.

Michael P. Ridley *is a principal of the Orange County office of the law firm of Arter, Hadden, Lawler, Felix & Hall, specializing in venture capital and corporate finance. He and his firm represent numerous venture capital funds and small business investment companies and a large number of companies that have been financed by venture capital sources. Mr. Ridley is a graduate of Stanford University and Yale Law School.*

The following article is a summary of the key legal concerns of the entrepreneur in the planning stages and start-up of a business.

Form of Enterprise

Prior to the Tax Reform Act of 1986, the normal form of business entity would be a corporation. With the repeal of General Utilities, founders should consult with counsel to determine whether S Corp. status, partnership, limited partnership, proprietorship, or a limited liability company may be appropriate during the pre-venture capital period of the entity's existence. If founders operate as a limited partnership or limited liability company, care must be taken to follow statutory formalities to avoid personal liabilities on behalf of limited partners, or to avoid classification as a corporation if a limited liability company is chosen. Unfortunately, S Corp. status, which would be ideal from a liability standpoint and a pass through of income and losses at individual rates without tax at the corporate level, will not be available if venture capital investors are other than individuals or certain trusts (most venture capital funds are limited partnerships) or if there is more than one class of security (most venture capital funds would take preferred stock or convertible debt). In order to minimize out-of-pocket expenses, founders should determine name availability before purchasing stationery, directory listings, brochures, etc.

Relations with Prior Employers

Venture capitalists typically invest in enterprises headed by superior managers with prior track records. It is therefore likely that founders and key employees in a new business will have recently left or are considering leaving their present employment. As such, it will be important during the formation process to ensure that the founders and key employees do not misappropriate the trade secrets of prior employers or otherwise engage in unfair competition with the prior employer.

Trade Secrets

Although employees are free to leave employment and start a competing enterprise, they are not free to utilize their employer's trade secrets or compete while still employed. Most litigation involving the improper use by a departing employee of an employer's trade secrets will center on whether the information used by a departing employee is in fact a trade secret. Definitions of what constitutes a trade secret will vary from state to state. As a general rule, a trade secret means "information, including a formula, pattern, computation, program, device, method, technique or process that (1) derives independent economic value, actual or potential, from not being generally known to the public or to other persons who can obtain economic value from its disclosure or use; and (2) is the subject of efforts that are reasonable under the circumstances to maintain its secrecy." Uniform Trade Secret Act.

It will be important for the new enterprise to avoid situations in which it is involved in the misappropriation of trade secrets of prior employers for several reasons: (a) certain jurisdictions make it a criminal offense to misappropriate trade secrets, e.g., California Penal Code Section 499(c) makes it a misdemeanor punishable by up to one year in prison and up to $5,000 in fines to steal, copy or use without authorization trade secrets; (b) the prior employer has legal recourse to enjoin the new enterprise's use of the employer's trade secrets and to seek damages, including royalties and, where appropriate, punitive damages, which recourse could very well mean the termination of the start-up's activities and, at a minimum, the incurrence in a very short period of time of substantial legal fees and management time diverted from the enterprise; and, last, but not least, (c) venture capitalists, depending upon their respective involvement in formulating the start-up and whether they knew or should have known that the start-up they were financing had misappropriated trade secrets, may themselves be liable for damages to the prior employer.

Although one can never obtain complete assurance that a start-up or a departing employee will not be sued by a prior employer, the departing employees should follow certain steps:

1. Review all nondisclosure and assignment of invention agreements executed by founders and new employees, particularly those sections relating to prior discoveries. Certain jurisdictions provide that inventions developed on an employee's own time not relating to the employer's business constitute the property of the employee. Any work on technology to be utilized by a start-up should be done on the employee's time with the employee's own resources. Employment agreements should be reviewed to determine the existence of and enforceability of covenants not to compete.
2. Prepare the business plan on the employee's individual time.
3. Do not use the prior employer's premises or equipment in preparing the business plan or doing preparatory work in setting up the new venture. Calls to future suppliers, employees and funding sources should be done at home or during the employee's free time. Utilizing E-mail at the employer will leave a trail that is readily discoverable as "deleted".
4. Turn in all customer lists, product specifications, marketing plans, etc. Do not bring copies of proprietary information to the start-up.
5. A problem area will exist where the founder is not merely an employee but rather an officer or director of the former employer. The fiduciary relationship to the former employer may be breached by failing to offer the opportunity to the employer. Corporate opportunity problems may be solved by having the prior employer decline to pursue the opportunity or invention which the start-up is formed to pursue.
6. The safest course of action is for the employee to depart from the employer prior to competing with the employer and to disclose preparations to compete if such failure to disclose preparation would be harmful to the employer. Departing employees should inform the prior employer of plans rather than have the prior employer learn of plans from reference checks of venture capitalists or in a newspaper.

Solicitation of Fellow Employees

The general rule is that, absent unfair or deceptive means, the public interest of the mobility of employees enables the start-up to hire employees, after departure, of former employer. A problem arises if the solicitation occurs while the founders are still employed by the former employer or if the employees are hired not for their skills but rather to obtain the prior employer's trade secrets.

Solicitation of Business of Former Employer

The general rule is that, absent a valid noncompetition agreement, employees may solicit customers of former employers after departing unless proprietary customer lists or confidential information, such as pricing, is used. A problem area is the difficulty of defining what constitutes customer lists. To the extent that the identity of customers, purchasing agents, required terms a vendor must meet, etc., are known to the public, the more likely a customer list will not be found.

Ownership and Protection of Technology

If technology will be important to the success of the start-up, steps should be implemented on formation to acquire and protect the technology. To the extent that technology or intellectual property is being contributed to prior to the raising of funds. There are several alternatives to follow in protecting technology—trade secrets, patents and copyrights. The best method to be used is dependent on the type of technology involved.

Trade Secrets

The general rule is that a trade secret is lost if it is disclosed to the general public or competitors or if the person seeking to protect a trade secret does not take reasonable steps under the circumstances to ensure its confidentiality. A start-up should require that all employees and founders, prior to and as a condition of employment, execute nondisclosure and assignment of invention agreements that (a) set forth recognition of employee of the nature of the importance of trade secrets to the company and contain an agreement to keep all such information in confidence; (b) set forth the prior inventions that are being brought by the employee to the company; (c) represent that no trade secrets of prior employers are being brought to the new enterprise and require that the employee will not disclose to the company trade secrets which may have been obtained as a result of prior employment; and (d) assign all inventions to be used by the company or which are developed during the course of employment, except those inventions which are developed entirely on an employee's own time and do not relate either to the business of the employer or to the employer's actual or anticipated research or development or do not result from any work performed by the employee for the employer; and (e) require such individual to execute and deliver any and all documents necessary to perfect company's ownership rights in and to such intellectual property.

The company should seek a proper balance between the cost to implement certain procedures designed to restrict the flow of information to protect the confidentiality of trade secrets and the necessity for information to flow within the enterprise. At minimum, the company should consider the following:

1. Sensitive areas should be under lock and key with only specified employees having access and that access should be logged. Access to computer files should similarly be controlled. Visitors to the facility should not be shown sensitive areas containing trade secret information, such as a manufacturing process or computer programs. Visitors, consultants or possible purchasers, suppliers or providers of capital should sign nondisclosure and confidentiality agreements. Confidential documents should not be left in open view or unattended in areas in which employees or other persons not authorized to have access to the information would have access. Courts are often impressed with a lock box for blue prints or source and object codes.
2. Proprietary information stored on magnetic or paper media is subject to recovery from such discarded media. Trash should not be an inadvertent conduit of trade secrets to third parties.
3. Proprietary documents and information should be legended as such with restrictions on copying or disseminating the same. Trade secrets and privileged or confidential commercial or financial information disclosed to the federal government should be marked as such to prevent disclosure under the Freedom of Information Act.
4. Departing employees should be interviewed to determine identity of future employer or plans, to ensure no trade secrets are being withdrawn or in the possession of the departing employee and to reiterate the company's claim of trade secrets. Caution should be used in the form of any communications to a departing employee's new employer concerning trade secrets.
5. Employees must be made aware of the fact that they are dealing with trade secrets, that such trade secrets are the property of the employer and are of vital importance to that employer, and that the company will prevent the improper use of the company's trade secrets.
6. To the extent that the company contracts with the federal government and delivers trade secrets such as computer software agreements, it should comply with applicable Federal Acquisition Regulations; Federal Procurement Regulations System, or Defense Federal Acquisition Regulations to limit use.

Patent

A 20-year monopoly created by statute for "new and useful process, machine, manufacture or composition of matter, or any new and useful improvement thereof." The invention must be "new" to be patentable. 35 U.S.C. 102(b) prevents issuance of patent if the invention has been in public use for over a year or if the invention has been described in a publication that has been published for over a year prior to the application. It is important for the company to see patent counsel early to determine patentability, particularly on the issues of (i) when public use has occurred, (ii) whether a patent would be the most appropriate method of protection, (iii) the scope of the license to be granted by the inventor and (iv) whether federal research or contract funds have been utilized in conjunction with the proposed invention. Patent protection extends only to jurisdictions in which it is filed. Major disadvantages relate to the fact that the invention must be disclosed after issued or denied, patent litigation is expensive, and, until recently, most inventors were not successful in patent claims. Patent protection is afforded only in the jurisdiction in which it is issued. In today's global economy advice should be procured with respect to the advisability of filing for patent protection in foreign jurisdictions.

Copyright

A limited monopoly is granted for the term of the individual author's life plus 50 years for an original work of authorship, including computer software, but not ideas, principles, concepts or discoveries. Difficulties will arise in the area of whether "non-employees" are creating copyrightable material and are developing "work for hire" which would grant authorship and copyright protection to the company. New regulations provide that to perfect, an author must deposit a copy of the work with the Library of Congress and the Copyright Office. An author may deposit the first and last 10 or 25 pages of a computer program depending on presence of trade secrets with ability to block out trade secret portions which may prevent disclosure of integral workings of the program. Material must be marked to indicate copyright protection.

Trademark
The company should, at a very early stage after determining its name and the names of its proposed products, conduct name and a trademark availability search. It makes no sense to incur significant advertising, printing and marketing costs only to find that a desired name has been registered by a third party as a trademark. As of November 16, 1989, it is now possible to register a federal trademark prior to consummating a sale in interstate commerce. Evidence of sale must be filed thereafter within six months subject to extensions up to 30 months and affidavits of use must be filed subsequently. Federal registration gives right of holder of trademark to seek damages, including treble damages, for infringement of trademark. Pending registration, a company should not indicate the existence of a trademark on its products. Trademark needs to be renewed every 10 years.

Securities Issues
Shares Issued for Compensation
It will be critical to reduce to writing the proposed ownership split of company by founders. Founders, hopefully, should receive shares in the start-up at a fraction of what the venture capitalists are paying. As such, the company should be organized and shares issued as soon as possible during the formation process. The founders should avoid situations in which the founders are incorporating the enterprise on day one at a low valuation, and capitalists are being issued shares at a much higher valuation.

If shares are issued for services and will be subject to a risk of forfeiture, regardless of whether the founder is paying fair market value, employees and founders should file 83(b) elections with the Internal Revenue Service within 30 days of issuance of such shares to elect to have the value of the securities in excess of the cost to the employee (which should be zero) treated as income in year of issuance. Failure to file will mean that when the risk of forfeiture lapses, the employee will be taxed at the difference between what was paid for the shares and their value at the date the restrictions lapse. If the company is successful, the effect will be disastrous to the founders and employees, since the shares may not then be marketable but may have great value.

An emerging area of the law is wrongful termination of employment. All stock purchase or option agreements should provide that no employment agreement is intended and that the company has the right to terminate employment and repurchase any nonvested shares. Similarly, technology transfer agreements should be independent of ability of company to terminate employee.

Shareholder Agreements
The founders should execute rights of first refusal giving the company and the other founders rights of first refusal in the event of any transfer to a third party. Founders should also consider (i) granting to company and founders rights to purchase in event of founder's death, disability or dissolution of marriage, (ii) imposing restrictions upon transfer by any of the founders during the first years of the enterprise of any significant percentage of shares and (iii) vesting of shares based on length of service with the company and granting to the company of a right to repurchase unvested shares at cost. Venture capitalists will typically insist upon such restrictions and a vesting requirement; it is far better to obtain them while the only value of the company is as perceived in the business plan or in an untested prototype as opposed to after the financing is in place and value is more apparent. Although the founding team, at the onset, may appear quite compatible, as the enterprise grows it is entirely possible that certain elements of that team will not be up to the task and, as such, a portion of those shares should be made available to bring in new people. If the initial funding is from friends and families and includes notes, such persons should be made aware of venture capitalists' typical demands that such notes either should be contributed to capital at closing or subject to deferred pay-out. As such, the founders should ensure that amendments to such notes be made by other than unanimous consent of the note holders. As such, the founders should avoid granting preemptive rights or antidilution rights to such initial funding sources.

Regulatory Compliance
Securities issued to the founders and pre-venture capital sources of funds should be issued in compliance with applicable state blue sky laws and the Securities Act of 1933. Failure to do so gives rights of rescission and may delay and/or hinder a subsequent public offering. The general rule for state purposes is that no securities may be issued without a permit unless an exemption is otherwise available. Exemptions will vary from state to state but will be predicated on the type of security, the qualifications of the purchaser and/or the amount of financing or number of purchasers. Even if an exemption is available for the issuance of securities to sophisticated individuals, the company may wish to issue shares or options to all employees, regardless of their sophistication. In such case, very early in the formation process the company should implement a restricted stock purchase plan or nonqualified or qualified incentive stock option plan (recent tax law changes make qualified incentive stock option plans less desirable for the company) and obtain

permit for the same. Promises to new employees for securities should not be made in absence of permit or exemption.

Under the Securities Act of 1933, securities may not be issued unless registered or unless an exemption from registration is available. The typical exemption would be Regulation D adopted by the SEC on April 15, 1982 which sets forth a means wherein an issuer may issue securities without the need for registering the same.

Rule 504: $1 million limit in 12 months preceding issue, no requirement of disclosure (caveat: fraud rules still applicable), no advertising, restrictions on resale.

Rule 505: $5,000,000 limit in 12 months preceding issue, no more than 35 unaccredited purchasers, no requirement of disclosure to accredited investors but if to nonaccredited investors, Part II of Form 1-A and financial statement information required under Item 310 of SB-2 (only balance sheet) if less than $2 million and the financial information required in Form SB-2 Part 1 of 5-18 if less than $5 million, no advertising, restrictions on resale.

Rule 506: No limit as to dollar size, no more than 35 nonaccredited investors (nonaccredited investor must be able to evaluate merits and risks), no requirement of disclosure to accredited investors but disclosure of information on Part 1 of form SB-2 if nonaccredited and less than $7,500,000 and financial statement as required in a registration statement if over $7,500,000, no advertising, restrictions on resale. The issuer must complete and file Form D with SEC with 15 days of first sale.

Rule 701: Securities issued to employees, directors, consultants or advisers pursuant to written compensatory plan or agreement, shall not exceed in 12 months the greater of $500,000 or 15% of total assets or outstanding securities.

Employment Relationships

Due Diligence

Venture capitalists can be expected to perform extensive reference checks on key people in the company. Misleading or fraudulent resumes may be sufficient grounds for withdrawing a proposed funding. Nondisclosed criminal convictions or existing SEC consent decrees may be disastrous to the company in the future. The chief executive officer should investigate backgrounds of key personnel consistent with statutory and constitutional prohibitions on invasion of privacy.

Wrongful Termination

Ability of employer to terminate at will without "cause" is being eroded in many jurisdictions. Employment agreements, employer handbooks and manuals, personnel files and interview notes should all indicate absence of any implied or oral understanding of continual employment, particularly in cases where new employees are being asked to terminate existing employment and relocate.

Miscellaneous

Insurance: Have in force necessary general liability, casualty, workers' compensation. If certain individuals are key to success of the venture, company should acquire key man life insurance which is usually inexpensive. Venture capitalists will also want it in place.

Permits: Nature of critical governmental permits required to operate business will depend on nature of business and jurisdictions; examples are resale certificate to avoid sales tax on sales, permits to discharge hazardous waste, permits to possess goods, export licenses needed to export high technology products. Company should apply early and have in force prior to obtaining venture capital. Failure to obtain could delay funding or result in fines, penalties or shut down of business.

Conclusion

These are just a few of the potential problem areas to consider prior to commencing a new business and seeking capital. It is wise to consult with an attorney experienced in new company formations very early in the planning process to avoid future difficulties.

Sources of Business Development Financing

Most entrepreneurs are unaware of the myriad of financing sources available to developing businesses. This section describes a variety of sources of capital for potential entrepreneurs.

The venture capital industry has widespread investment interests that run through the entire life of a company, and it has the resources to work with entrepreneurs at any point along the way.

Major corporations also are providing significant amounts of financing to independent business development. One article, "Dealing with the Corporate Strategic Investor," examines the unique problems and opportunities afforded to entrepreneurial companies by venture programs affiliated with major corporations.

Another article, "Non-Traditional Financing Sources," takes a look at sources of entrepreneurial capital outside the venture capital industry.

The Organized Venture Capital Community

Stanley E. Pratt

Stanley E. Pratt *is a managing director of Abbott Capital Management, LLC, an investment management firm specializing in private equity partnership investments for institutional investors. He was formerly president and chairman of Venture Economics, Inc., publisher and editor of the* Venture Capital Journal *and editor of* Pratt's Guide to Venture Capital Sources.

As we view the organized venture capital community in the late 1990s it is important to recognize the diversity of interests and activities that has evolved over the past decade and the unparalleled opportunity for future business development investing. The dramatic growth of venture capital investing in the early 1980s coupled with the predictable problems of the latter half of the decade, in a large part caused by the explosive expansion, brought about a larger and wiser community. After a period of consolidation in the mid-1990s, dramatic growth returned in 1997 and 1998 with a huge influx of new capital as institutional investors increased their allocations to the private equity asset category. The good news is more capital for venture investments, but the bad news is is that there is too much capital for the experienced human resources. Once again, the over exuberance will undoubtedly bring problems over the next few years. As the principal source of long-term capital for business development, however, the organized venture capital community will survive the short-term cycles and be an even stronger contributor to our nation's well being in the near future.

Over the past six or seven years, the differentiation between "classic venture capital" and the overwhelming majority of buyout transactions has been blurred by the realities of successful business development. Many venture capital and buyout firms are employing all the different skills and disciplines that are required in each of the two activities. Venture capitalists have become more creative in their structuring of transactions, pay more attention to mundane operating management requirements and seek to address future exit requirements with pre-planned merger, buyout or recapitalization considerations in addition to hoped for public stock offerings. Buyout managers are recognizing the dangers of over-leveraging and are employing value-added involvement skills to grow and revitalize basic business values. Although this combination of skills and disciplines has made it difficult to separate venture capital and buyout firms in the broader universe of private equity investing, it has benefited two powerful forces for the future health of both venture capitalists and buyout investors.

The universe has been broadened to one of incredible diversity. In addition to some 400 to 600 seed and start-up financings per annum, both venture capitalists and buyout managers are now seeking and developing investments in the vast number of middle-market companies throughout the world. In January 1999, the D&B Market Identifier Database identified more than 156,000 companies in the United States with annual revenues of $10 million or more. Only 22,000 of these are publicly traded and more than 134,000 are private business.

Private Equity Arrives

The combination of this diversity with experienced venture and buyout investment managers is bringing about the recognition by the pension investment world of a rapidly expanding pension asset category—private equity investments. With over $5.6 trillion, pension funds dominate today's capital markets and if venture capital and buyout activity is to survive in the future it must attract ongoing pension investment. While it is clear that the differentiated sector of venture capital will witness some contraction over the next few years as it consolidates from the excesses of the early 1980s, total private investing should continue to expand. The many outstanding investment opportunities in new and developing businesses and in the universe of 121,000 private middle-market U.S. companies will fall outside the reach of institutional investors that limit themselves to marketable securities. Venture capital firms specialize in the unique expertise to develop these opportunities for passive pension investors and consequently serve as the critical bridge between entrepreneurs and the capital markets.

Peter Drucker, in his 1976 book, *The Unseen Revolution: How Pension Fund Socialism Came to America*, discusses the profound changes in U.S. capital markets brought about through the growing domination of investment capital by pension funds. "We are organizing a capital market totally unequipped to supply entrepreneurial capital needs," he said, and further pointed out that "the problems of the small but growing business are dissimilar from those of the established big or fair-sized businesses. They require a different investment policy, different relationships to management and a different understanding of business economics, management and dynamics." As a solution, he proffered that, "What is needed, therefore, are new capital market institutions specifically provided to give these new, young, growing businesses the capital (and the management guidance) they need, and which, at the same time, can act as investment vehicles suited for the fiduciary, the asset manager trustee."

The organized venture capital community has been evolving since the 1960s to perform this role and now serves as an effective vehicle to distribute capital for business development investment. While the total capital committed to professional venture investment management is still a small segment of the nation's economy, a disproportionately large benefit is reaped from its investment.

Charts 1 and 2 indicate the venture capital resources by leading states and the regional distribution of resources.

The major components of the venture industry are independent private firms, corporate industrial groups and venture capital subsidiaries of large financial institutions. Each of these categories includes a number of small business investment companies (SBICs), federally licensed firms that served as pioneers in the development of venture capital investing and today are the principal means of extending venture capital to many diverse small businesses.

Chart 1

Commitments per Fund by State
01/01/2000 to 12/31/2000

Fund State	NUM OF FUND	SUM RAISED $MIL
California	183	41,239.3
New York	62	13,209.4
Massachusetts	51	12,979.2
Texas	27	3,739.9
Maryland	7	3,038.5
Minnesota	7	2,326.5
Pennsylvania	19	2,017.4
Connecticut	13	2,010.0
Illinois	17	1,784.0
Washington	13	1,382.0

Source: Venture Economics/NVCA

Independent Private Venture Capital Firms

The principal institutional source of venture capital is independent private venture capital firms. These include family groups involved with venture investment such as the Rockefeller, Phipps and Whitney organizations, all predecessors of today's industry. Greater emphasis is now placed on professional partnerships funded by pension funds, major corporations, individuals and families, endowments and foundations, insurance companies and foreign investors. According to Venture Economics, there were 620 independent private firms operating in the US at year-end 1999. These firms invest principally in equity, in seed and start-up financings as well as in relatively mature companies and management buyouts. Ranging in size from under $10 million to over $1 billion in capital, each firm usually makes 10 to 15 new investments per year with commitments ranging from $1 million to more than $50 million.

Independent firms are the major source of classic venture developments. The investment orientation of different groups within this sector, however, can be substantially different. Some groups specialize in early stage business developments such as startups and even seed financings, while others prefer expansion financings or management buyout transactions. Management buyouts enable the operating management of a division of a company, whether it is a large corporation or a privately owned business, to purchase significant equity ownership in the business they manage. Also, a number of groups

Chart 2

Commitments per Fund by State Region
01/01/2000 to 12/31/2000

Fund State Region	NUM OF FUND	SUM RAISED $MIL
N. California	155	38,605.2
Greater New York	83	16,090.0
New England	52	13,706.2
Mid-Atlantic	27	5,508.5
Southwest	28	3,814.9
Ohio Valley	27	3,103.7
S. California	27	2,574.1
Great Plains	10	2,424.6
Southeast	30	2,214.2
Great Lakes	23	2,064.6
Northwest	14	1,407.5
Rocky Mountains	9	625.3
South	8	414.1
Unknown	1	60.0
TOTAL	494	92,612.9

Source: Venture Economics/NVCA

operate balanced funds that invest across the entire spectrum of business development investment interests.

Generally, independent venture firms are active investors, working closely with the operating managements to develop a significant business within five to seven years. They are seldom passive investors, and they will provide assistance in such areas as planning, personnel development, marketing, supplier relationships and future financing requirements. Seasoned venture capitalists can bring their experience in prior business development to support new entrepreneurs. Independent venture firms also carefully monitor ongoing operations, serve as a sounding board for problem resolution and are active participants in business development decisions.

Corporate Industrial Groups

In the late 1960s and early 1970s, a number of industrial corporations began investing directly in venture capital situations. In most cases, however, the efforts were misguided and the results were not fruitful. Corporate managers stressed the "window on technology" concept to the exclusion of developing a profitable, independent new business. In the mid-1980s, however, there was a resurgence of industrial corporate venture investment activity, but the activity in this marketplace continues to reflect the ebbs and tides of corporate whims. There has always been a relatively high turnover of firms and individuals in this segment. Chief executive officers and the individuals managing corporate venture operations are constantly moving on and these groups are seldom given the seven to ten years necessary to develop independent new businesses. As venture investors, however, corporations can be very helpful to their portfolio companies. Large corporations in fact develop most new technologies and control most of the distribution channels. What they lack, and what new businesses can bring, is the innovation to develop new products for their distribution channels.

For most industrial corporations, the primary motivation for investing is strategic—using venture capital and the small business innovators to assist in the development of new products or lines of business. As a result, these groups typically invest in new businesses where the product, market, or technology is related to the parent company's operations or where the business is of interest as a diversification opportunity. These "strategic partnering" relationships typically involve large corporations that have a minority equity investment in the small company coupled with a "side business agreement." These side agreements may include a research and development contract, a sales or marketing agreement, a supplier contract, a licensing agreement, a joint product development effort or a creation of joint venture company. In most successful relationships, the large company generally provides more than just capital. They also provide the small company access to their substantial technical, marketing and manufacturing resources. The small company normally provides an innovative product, focused technical expertise and the entrepreneurial zeal required for successful commercialization.

One of the most significant features of the current corporate partnering phenomenon is that both companies are considered equal in the relationship with strategic benefits accruing for each. There are also a number of corporate industrial groups that operate venture capital subsidiaries strictly for financial gain. These corporations operate more autonomously from the parent and may have a wider range of investment interests.

Venture Capital Subsidiaries of Financial Corporations

In the late 1960s a few banks and insurance companies started to participate in venture capital investing. Here again the early results were not encouraging. Banks viewed venture capital as an extension of their lending activities and both banks and insurance companies tried to use their credit-oriented investment-analysis techniques without recognizing the need for specialized skills and ongoing involvement required of equity investments. In the late 1970s, however, a number of financial corporations, most notably commercial bank holding companies, established or redeveloped SBICs and often set up non-SBIC separated subsidiaries to invest in business development situations that do not meet the parent's usual investment or loan criteria, or that would not qualify under SBIC regulations. While these groups do not generally have specific capital restrictions, they are limited to 5% of the parent's capital, which can range from $5 million to more than $200 million. Investments by these groups are most often in later stage business developments and management/leveraged buyouts. These subsidiaries are usually managed by the group's venture investment management team and commitments to individual portfolio companies generally range from $1 million to $5 million.

Small Business Investment Companies

The Small Business Programs Improvement Act of 1996 had a major impact on the Small Business Investment Company (SBIC) segment of the organized venture capital community, primarily by addressing leverage and licensing problems that had plagued the industry. The Small Business Equity Enhancement Act of 1992 created a new financing instrument ("preferred securities") for SBICs that enables SBICs to achieve their own financing in a way that allows them to better serve the needs of their portfolio companies.

Formerly, SBICs generally had to invest with current income producing debentures in order to cover their own debt service requirements. Through the use of "preferred securities" with dividend or interest payments contingent on income, SBICs are now able to invest "patient equity" capital in new and developing businesses without having to require current income payments from their portfolio companies. In addition, the legislation included many structural provisions to make SBICs more attractive investments for institutional investors which should bring about increased private equity capital for this program.

Most of the Standard SBICs licensed by federal government are primarily oriented to venture capital equity related investments. About a third of these firms are lending SBICs that represent the only institutional source of long-term capital for those small businesses that may be successful but clearly lack the potential to become major businesses. Lending SBICs often make numerous small investments, but the venture investment-oriented firms normally make three to fifteen new commitments per year.

The larger venture capital-oriented SBICs, with at least $10 million to $20 million in private capital, operate similarly to the independent private venture capital firms. Larger SBICs operate across a wide range of venture investment interests, including startups, expansion financings and management/leveraged buyouts. SBICs have more diversity in types of investment than other independent firms and can be an excellent source of financing for businesses with more moderate growth prospects and lower potential risks.

Chart 3

Disbursements per Company Location

01/01/2000 to 12/31/2000 Rounds 1 to 99

Company Location	No. of Comp	Avg Per Comp	Sum Inv. ($mil)
California	2,025	20.7	41,923.0
Massachusetts	540	17.4	9,380.0
New York	403	16.9	6,809.8
Texas	312	18.6	5,816.8
Colorado	147	33.5	4,928.0
New Jersey	125	28.6	3,573.5
Virginia	184	15.7	2,883.8
Washington	184	15.0	2,755.7
Georgia	172	14.7	2,532.2
Maryland	106	22.8	2,419.8

Source: Venture Economics/NVCA

While the 1996 legislation repealed the 1958 legislation that created SBICs to invest in minority businesses, the 75 that remain that are privately owned and managed firms licensed that provide financing to small businesses that are at least 51% owned by socially or economically disadvantaged individuals. In 1998, SBIC financing to small businesses involved 639 financings and totaled over $109 million, of which 10% was equity and 89% was debt including debt with equity features.

Industry Investment Patterns

Chart 3 indicates the investment patterns by state in 2000.

Today, venture firms are investing in a broad diversity of manufacturing, distribution and service-oriented companies. The most critical considerations for these investors are a credible management team, an identified market niche for a product with high-growth potential and the resulting possibility of developing a major new business.

Geographic Considerations

Historically, most of the nations' professionally managed venture capital has been concentrated in the Northeast and the San Francisco Bay Area, with secondary centers in Chicago and Minneapolis. In the past decade, however, venture capital has been moving into other areas of the country. Many venture capital firms invest nationally and in other states or regions than their own location. Although most firms still prefer to invest in companies close to their offices, increasing cooperation among venture firms has led to shared responsibilities. When considering an attractive investment opportunity in a distant area, venture capitalists often try to involve another group located within 200 miles of the business opportunity so that the local firm can provide monitoring and ongoing involvement to the portfolio company. Such cooperative relationships permit venture capital firms, even those without branch offices, to operate coast-to-coast. These collaborations have been stimulated by relationships developed through membership in the three major trade associations, the National Venture Capital Association (Arlington, VA), the National Association of Small Business Investment Companies (Washington, DC) and the National Association of Investment Companies (Washington, DC).

Venture Capital in 2001

The organized venture capital community has clearly entered into a watershed period for business development investing. The consolidation of venture capital firms brings the strongest and most experienced to the forefront, and there are now many new firms forming for the wave of the future. The lessons learned from the 1980s have brought about a more realistic environment, given venture capitalists new tools to stimulate successful business development, and provide a far greater understanding of private equity investing. While the decade began with consolidation and retrenchment, the recent explosion of institutional investment has brought more capital into private equity than any of us could have imagined in our wildest dreams at the beginning of the decade. Although there will likely be another consolidation period, there are enough experienced practitioners to waether the downdrafts. Private equity is now a significant factor in global capital structures. Many feel that the privatization and recharging of both domestic and global equity was a hallmark of the 1990s and the organized venture capital community will be a major player in our nation's economic revitalization. In fact, the media is trumpeting this message to the world. Of course this is *both* the good news *and* the bad news. The media's recognition of the enormous benefits of entrepreneurial activity as it fuels innovation, new business development and business revitalization will certainly serve to bring about more investment and developments. On the other hand, whenever the media becomes universally enthusiastic, it generally means that trouble lies ahead.

Mezzanine Financing: A Flexible Source of Capital

Robert C. Ammerman

Robert C. Ammerman is a managing partner of Capital Resource Partners which he founded with Fred Danforth in 1988 to focus on providing mezzanine capital for middle market companies undergoing transitions in their ownership or operations. CRP now manages four investment partnerships, Capital Resource Lenders I, II and III and Capital Resource Partners IV, L.P. The firm has made over 50 investments throughout the United States and manages in excess of $900 million. Capital Resource Partners is one of the oldest independent private mezzanine investment firms in the country. Prior the founding CRP, Mr. Ammerman was a general partner at Advanced Technology Ventures and a Vice President at BT Capital, the SBIC subsidiary of Bankers Trust Company. He is a graduate of Carnegie Mellon University as well as the Graduate School of Industrial Administration at CMU.

Most companies depend on outside capital to fund growth or to execute a change in ownership. Typically, this capital falls into one of three principal categories: equity, senior debt or mezzanine capital. Its name aptly describes its place on the balance sheet and its return/risk perspective: above the ground floor of equity and below the upper floors of senior debt. In a growth financing, equity capital is often used to start a business. As the company grows, creditors become more willing to lend money, financing fixed assets through leases or secured term loans. In addition, banks or finance companies may lend against inventories and receivables. Depending on profitability and capital requirements, additional equity may be necessary to support the balance sheet. At this point, the company has overcome many of the early-stage business risks: it is selling its products or services, and a management team has operated the business for a number of years. Outside venture capital or individual investors may be willing to provide more equity capital but only for significant dilution. In the case of a change of ownership or "buyout" transaction, senior capital is again used to finance part of the purchase prices based upon the working capital and other tangible assets of the business. To increase the leverage, and hence the potential return to the equity investors, a layer of additional junior capital may be sought. In both cases, the frequent solution is mezzanine capital or mezzanine debt, as it is often called, because it is typically structured as long term, unsecured, junior debt with attached equity incentives.

Mezzanine financing then describes capital that is "in between" senior-debt financing and common stock on the balance sheet and hence in between these two in terms of risk of loss of principal and likely target returns. In some cases it takes the form of redeemable preferred stock, but in most cases it is subordinated debt which carries an equity "kicker" consisting of warrants or a conversion feature into common stock. This subordinated-debt capital has many characteristics of debt but also serves as "long term junior capital" to underpin senior debt because its repayment schedule is after the repayment of the senior debt and it is junior in liquidation. Typically unsecured, it will have a fixed coupon, and a maturity of 5 to 10 years. The interest paid will be tax deductible. Other features are the form and amount of equity incentives (options; contingent interest; convertibility); repayment schedule, prepayment penalties, covenants and put or call features. These securities will take a variety of forms to satisfy the needs of the issuer and the goals of the investor/lender. The typical structure results in less dilution than equity capital.

Offsetting this advantage are a few disadvantages to mezzanine capital compared to equity capital. As debt, the interest is payable on a regular basis, and the principal must be repaid, if not converted into equity. This can create a large claim on cash at maturity and may complicate capital planning in a rapidly growing company. On the other hand, its total return objectives and "equity ownership" per dollar invested are often significantly lower than equity because of its current yield and lower risk profile. It represents a real alternative that needs to be evaluated carefully.

Uses of Mezzanine Financing

Mezzanine finance can be used in a number of different situations. While the specifics of each investment opportunity vary greatly, most mezzanine investments fall into one of the following four categories.

Management or Leveraged Buyouts

Management Buyouts ("MBO's") and Leveraged Buyouts ("LBO's") in which most if not all of the ownership changes are the most common mezzanine debt investment opportunities. The lending criteria of senior lenders and the investment criteria of the equity investors who finance these transactions often result in a financing "gap" between the senior debt that the company's assets can support and the equity capital invested in the deal. Mezzanine financing is used to complete the capital structure in such deals.

Growth Financing

Companies presented with the opportunity to grow their business either through internal growth or acquisition are often faced with a difficult financing decisions. Many senior lenders are not willing to provide financing unsecured by assets, and equity financing is often a highly dilutive option especially for growth companies that have established a sales history and are moving rapidly towards profitability where mezzanine capital may also be an option.

Recapitalizations

For a number of reasons, companies often find themselves saddled with unwieldy capital structures as a result of rapid growth, unforeseen business events or changes in senior lending policies. The replacement of part of the senior debt with mezzanine capital may provide more flexibility for expansion or simply a more comfortable level of leverage.

Roll-ups and Incremental Acquisitions

Many companies are presented with the chance to build their business through a series of small acquisitions. In companies with a strong equity base, these acquisitions can often be financed with a combination of mezzanine and senior debt.

Mezzanine capital providers often focus in one area or type of financing more than others. For example, there are many mezzanine debt funds that focus almost exclusively on leveraged buyout financing and other firms that focus on growth financing opportunities for mezzanine capital. But typically, the structural issues and form of the investment are comparable. The risks and return opportunity being pursued will, however, come from different sources: business risk, product risk or financial leverage.

Types of Firms Providing Mezzanine Financing

There are four principal groups that provide mezzanine financing for one or several of the types of transactions described above. They are private investment firms typically organized as partnerships and funded by a broad variety of tax exempt institutional investors or organized as SBIC's; specialized units of commercial banks; the private placement groups of insurance companies; and lastly a wide variety of investment groups focused on mezzanine financing that are affiliated with other corporations. There are also a limited number of pension funds and mutual funds making mezzanine investments. The firms' size and affiliations will impact the types and sizes of their typical investment. Most mezzanine firms are national in scope although there are some groups that have a state focus or investment limitation. Some groups will also provide mezzanine financing for companies located outside the United States.

Historically, mezzanine capital was provided by the insurance companies and banks, typically through specialized units within these institutions. Over the last ten years, the number of independent mezzanine investment firms has grown and a recent survey of mezzanine investment firms conducted by our organization indicated that approximately half of the mezzanine capital today is provided by independent private capital firms. As the market has expanded the variety of investment approaches (styles) has also grown. While this sector has indeed grown, industry data highlight that the amount of capital raised by equity venture capital and buyout firms still dramatically exceeds that managed by mezzanine investment firms.

In a broader market context, public and private high yield debt securities are also considered mezzanine financing.

The market opportunity for mezzanine financing has changed over the last several years as the willingness of senior lenders to be more or less aggressive regarding collateral and cash flow coverage has changed. We've seen fluctuations from a very aggressive senior lending environment in the late 1980's and mid 1990's to much more restrictive approaches by the banks in the early 1990's, and now in late 2000 and early 2001. This environment also affects the pricing parameters used by the mezzanine financing sources.

Investment Criteria

Mezzanine investors generally look for companies that have a demonstrated performance record, with revenues of $10 million or more. Since the financing will involve paying interest, the investor will carefully examine existing and projected cash flow.

Mezzanine financing is utilized in a wide variety of industries ranging from basic manufacturing to retailing, healthcare, business and financial services, distribution, and certain technology areas. Companies that are either very high growth or have high technology/product risk are typically less appropriate candidates given the cash flow dynamics and the greater volatility of sales and profitability. These companies are often better served by venture capital investors.

In reviewing a particular investment, a mezzanine investor will generally focus on the following criteria:

- •An experienced management team with a demonstrated ability to manage their business with both profitability goals and sensitivity to the added risks from leverage
- •A history of steady growth and profitability and increasing cash flow; or a business strategy to achieve these through acquisitions or other business plans financed by the mezzanine capital
- •Proven product success and established market presence with a "defensible" niche as a result of geography, product characteristics or go-to-market strategies.
- •An investment that has both adequate cash flow and equity valuation upside

The mezzanine investor must be convinced that the trade off he is making - lower return than could be achieved from an equity investment offset or compensated for by the reduced risk that comes from a current yield, a repayment schedule and seniority in the balance sheet.

Pricing and Terms

Mezzanine financing are typically structured to yield a return of 18 to 30% given the focus of the firm and the exact type of security used. In some cases a mezzanine financing might be structured as a redeemable preferred stock or as a convertible subordinated debt security which would typically target a higher return. The most important trade off in the structure of a mezzanine financing is the trade off between current yield and fees and the value of the equity participation. In addition, a convertible structure will require a greater equity incentive (hence more dilution) because the repayment of the underlying principal does not still occur. Simply, for the same return; a lower coupon will require more equity incentives; and a convertible security will be more dilutive than a redeemable security with attached warrants or other equity incentives. Given that the typical equity investment targets 30 to 40% returns and is in the form of a convertible security; the dilution or equity ownership required to reach the target return for an equity investor is often 3-4 times that required for a mezzanine investment which is subordinated debt with attached warrants and a lower target return.

The following example illustrate how a typical investment would "payoff":

Most mezzanine investors calculate their total expected return on a discounted cash flow or internal rate of return (IRR). The following mezzanine debt investment, for example, would require a capital gain of approximately $5.3 million in year five to achieve a targeted 25% IRR.

Amount:	$5 million
Coupon:	12%
Years to Maturity:	7 years
Warrants:	For 15% ownership
Repayment Schedule:	$1 million annually beginning at end of year four and $2 million at maturity year

The cash flow assumes interest only during the initial four years, a sinking-fund payment of $1 million at the end of year four and liquidation of the investment early in the fifth year including the exercise of the warrants. The value of the equity (business value less outstanding indebtedness and other redeemable securities) was $35 million, hence our 15% ownership stake is worth $5,250. A simple rule of thumb is that a subordinated debt investment with a 12% coupon needs a future equity value of approximately 1.0x the original investment to yield 25% over a five year period. Obviously, the amount of equity ownership required is a function of the investor's expectations for the growth in equity value, which itself is a function of the growth in sales and profitability and the "exit" multiple the sale achieves.

Year	Principal	Interest	Capital Gain	Total Cash
0	$(5,000)	$-		$(5,000)
1		600		600
2		600		600
3		600		600
4	1,000	600		1,600
5	4,000	480	$5,250	9,730

A change in any of the variables - interest rate, repayment schedule, fees, the exercise amount (if any), or the size of the equity gain - will change the IRR. It is this large number of variables and the ability to offer a potential borrower a variety of structures and trade-offs that provide such great flexibility in mezzanine financing.

In addition to the economic terms, a number of important covenants must be negotiated. Bank and senior lenders will be focused on the subordination agreement and a variety of liquidation preference issues, including in the case of a bankruptcy. There is also a potential tradeoff between return and the level of subordination, including the possibility of a security interest behind the bank. There can be senior-subordinated or junior-subordinated positions, depending on the existing and projected capital structure.

Since most mezzanine investors hope to realize their capital gains in a three-to-seven year time frame, there must also be an agreement on the exit strategy. Two common terms in this area are a registration rights agreement and/or a put/call. These give the investor the right, after a certain period, to force the company to achieve some liquidity for the equity portion of the investment.

Another variable often used in pricing is a performance tradeoff or "claw back." In this provision, the company and the issuer agree that if certain agreed upon performance measurements are met, the equity component will be adjusted. For example, the number of shares or the exercise price might be raised or lowered, resulting in more or less dilution, based on meeting either profitability or valuation objectives during a preset period of time. Thus, if management performs, there is less dilution, and the investor is still happy because the value of the equity is higher. On the other hand, if projections are not met, the investor gets more equity to meet his total return target.

As we have explored from a number of perspectives, mezzanine financing represents a series of trade offs that fit very well in a wide variety of company and balance sheet situations.

Corporate Strategic Partnerships

Mark L. Radtke and George W. McKinney

Mark Radtke *was a vice president with Advent International Corp., a Boston-based venture capital firm. At Advent, Mr. Radtke managed strategic investment programs for 12 major industrial corporations. Prior to Advent, he was a strategic partnering consultant to large and small corporations. Mr. Radtke died in 1994.*

George McKinney *is vice chairman and chief operating officer of Integra LifeSciences Corporation, a medical technology firm in Plainsboro, NJ. He has acted as founding president for several venture-backed firms, including American Superconductor. Dr. McKinney has also been director of planning for Corning and managing partner of ARD, the venture capital firm.*

Industrial corporations have been supporting the development of entrepreneurial companies far longer than the organized venture capital industry has been in existence. Over 70 years ago, DuPont provided funding for a fledgling General Motors Corp. In more recent years, DuPont has formed partnerships with more than 20 young companies.

Today, corporate investors usually fund and support small firms either through a corporate venture capital relationship, in which an individual corporation purchases minority equity positions in smaller firms, or through a strategic partnering relationship.

Strategic partnering, corporate partnering, and strategic alliances all refer to the establishment of long-term collaborative relationships between major corporations and smaller entrepreneurial companies, an activity that has become increasingly popular in recent years. The relationship is initially based on a strategic business agreement—such as a joint technology development program, marketing, or manufacturing agreement—and it may include an equity investment the large company makes in the smaller partner.

Strategic partnerships focus on the business agreement, not the equity position; the long-term relationship; and the fit with the larger corporation's strategic direction. While the business agreement is usually contractual in nature, the relationship differs from a typical contract, since it is expected to be a long-term association, extending beyond the immediate project goals and commitments.

An equity or other financial investment is often part of a strategic partnering relationship because it may be necessary to allow the small company to commit the resources necessary to fulfill the contractual agreement; it may foster a closer working relationship and a more open flow of information; and because the large company may want to share in the increased valuation of the smaller partner resulting from the collaboration.

If an equity investment is part of the relationship, it is usually a minority position of 5% to 20%. The expectation is that the large company will eventually sell out its position when the relationship has run its course. Other typical monetary and non-monetary support for the small company partner includes loans; guaranteed credit lines from suppliers; loans of equipment, facilities, and personnel; market research studies; and beta site testing of new products.

Basic Partnering Strategy for the Small Company

In thinking about strategic planning, the small company should first analyze its business to determine where a corporate relationship can provide the most leverage. The most common partnering relationships center on marketing and product development agreements. If the small company is strong in product development and manufacturing but needs help bringing the new product to market, then a partnership with an established company with a strong market presence makes sense.

The most important strategic partnerships for smaller firms often occur when the smaller firm's technology is broadly "enabling," with a variety of specific market applications. A company developing a new advanced material used in the electronics, medical, aerospace and construction industries, is one example. Here, the small company might be better off forming relationships with larger corporations established in those industries and knowledgeable about product requirements and customer needs, rather than attempting to develop and market a specific product for each industry independently. By giving larger partners the right to pursue the application in a specific market, the smaller company can be funded to develop the basic technology or business concept on a broader basis.

It is important, however, to recognize that large corporations primarily are interested in products, not technologies, and that it is incumbent on the small corporation to define the opportunity for the large company in product terms. If the small company can see product sales within a 24-30 month time frame, then the large corporation becomes a valid partner in managing the product definition and product adoption process. If the small company really needs research or technology development funding, then partnerships are valid only when the opportunity is of major scale and importance to the large corporation.

How to Find Strategic Partners

Successful partnerships almost always involve two elements: direct personal contact with a key executive within the large firm, and a strong fit between the small company's area of product development and the strategic direction of the larger firm. Therefore, in finding large-company partners, a good starting point is developing a list of all the "suspects" : companies that could be reasonably expected to be interested in what you are doing. Think "laterally," some of the best partners can come from industries on the periphery. Many strategic partners of young biotechnology companies, for example, are chemical companies as well as the more obvious pharmaceutical firms.

After preparing the suspect list, run it through two filters: Where do I know a senior executive? (or can get to one through a close friend of the company); and which companies have stated that my technology/market area is one of strategic importance to them? The latter can be determined through annual reports, magazine and newspaper articles and security analyst reports. Compare the list of companies where you have a contact with those that have a strategic interest to yield your best initial list of prospects for partnering.

Strategic partnerships are most likely with a medium-sized corporation ($100-$500M in sales) which has a single technology/market focus or a larger corporation where the partnership is with a division with similar focus. Look for larger corporations where the stated strategy and the smaller company's capabilities are a good match. Experience suggests a need to be realistic in examining the larger corporation's actual strategy rather than its logical strategy.

Corporations with a captive venture capital program are also good initial contacts. The people managing those programs are accustomed to dealing with smaller companies and can usually respond quickly as to whether the parent corporation might have an interest in partnering. In cases where you know that a corporation is interested in your field but you have no contact, ask to speak to someone in the following offices:

- corporate development
- new business development
- mergers and acquisitions
- new ventures
- technology planning/acquisition
- corporate/strategic planning
- licensing

If a company is involved in partnering, these are usually the offices that handle these relationships.

Approaching Potential Corporate Partners

Become an expert on the company before making contact with potential partners. Get their annual report, 10Ks and 10Qs. Use library resources to research their strategy, customers, key executives, etc. Lay out a compelling argument to justify their interest in your company and your interest in them. This should be based on your understanding of their strategic direction, and how the work you are doing helps them achieve their objectives. When explaining your interest in them, do not (repeat, do not!) begin by expressing your desperation for money. While this may be the case, emphasize first that strategically, it is logical (based, for example, on mutual marketing, manufacturing, or technology interests) to work together and that some form of investment might also be considered part of a relationship. This message should be incorporated into a document that includes the following:

- an overview of your company and the business opportunity
- why you are seeking a partner
- your products/technology (do not go into extensive/proprietary details)
- the market you are addressing
- your basic concept for a partnering structure

During your initial meetings with a potential partner, try to meet people from the technical as well as the "business" side of the corporation. Your goal is to try to find a "champion" who sees the strategic logic for working with you and who is willing to put some career capital on the line in selling your cause. That person could come from either the technical or business side of the larger firm, and you should try to expose your company to both. Almost all partnerships require two- or three-tier selling. (In fact, the whole process is like large account selling!) This means you should ideally have a technical sponsor, a line business sponsor and a corporate staff or senior executive sponsor.

Negotiating the Agreement

Beyond the basic decision of whether there is a strategic logic for working with you, the next major decision for the representatives of the large company to make is whether they want to work with you as people and whether they feel you can develop a trusting and open relationship. A recommended approach is to be straightforward about what you can realistically deliver and what your "must haves" may be in the following areas:

- technology/market control
- financial support (equity/non-equity)
- long-term independence

Similarly, try to get the large company to clearly articulate the contribution they will make to the relationship and their "must haves." Based on both sides' objectives and "must haves," design an agreement that meets all the key issues. A common issue for negotiation, for example, is marketing rights to new products developed under the agreement. The large corporation might be willing to co-market or not market the products at all in certain markets if they can have exclusive rights to certain other markets that may be less important to you. The key to arriving at a mutually satisfying and beneficial agreement is frank communication between the two companies and a willingness to explore alternative approaches.

After a proposed agreement is reached, you may still have to help sell the agreement within the large corporation, where the board of directors may have to make the final approval. If your "champion" is high enough in the company, that person can often expedite the process. A good rule of thumb, however, is to expect the process to take as much as two to three times longer than you originally thought. As a consequence, planning for a strategic partner should begin well in advance of the time you will actually need one. One of the most common mistakes seen is a small company deciding to seek a corporate partner when they have only three or four months of cash remaining. Not only does it take longer than that, but large corporations are noticeably reluctant to seriously consider companies, even some very good companies, when they are on the brink of running out of money. Therefore, plan your attack on potential corporate partners 9 to 12 months ahead of your cash needs, perhaps just after a venture financing round.

After the Agreement

Most of the work in making partner relationships successful begins after closing the original agreement. Some advice on making the relationship work includes the following:

- communicate openly and frequently with the partner—
- head off problems early and do not let them become a "surprise"
- perform to plan
- be willing to alter the agreement as objectives or circumstances change
- continually "sell" the strategic logic and value of the relationship within the large company partner—remember, you usually need them more than they need you
- make sure both sides are deriving benefits from the partnership, otherwise they become unstable

Strategic partnering has become an important element of corporate business development and should be part of the strategic thinking of both large and small firms. It takes time and effort, both before and after a deal is struck. As a small company executive, you should consider strategic partnering to be perhaps your highest leverage development tool and should plan for it and make initial approaches to potential partners early in your company's development.

Dealing with the Corporate Strategic Investor

Kenneth W. Rind

Dr. Kenneth W. Rind *has been both a practitioner and a long-time objective observer of corporate strategic investing's ebbs and flows. In addition, he has been a founder/partner in eight venture capital funds, whose L.P.'s included over 25 different corporate strategic investors, with funding from their pension funds as well as from corporate monies. Recently, he formed PEI Corporate Investors, which was organized to extend the activities of corporate programs by purchasing their no-longer-strategic investments in funds and/or portfolio companies.*

Corporate strategic investing (the preferred term to "corporate venturing") generally differs from conventional venture investing because motivations beyond strictly financial rewards are present. Typically, a corporation's goals are to: enhance innovation; gain early exposure to new markets and technologies; generate new products faster and less expensively; identify and assess acquisition candidates; assure a stable source of supply; assist a valued customer; and/or provide access to cooperative, knowledgeable individuals. Corporations may also use venture capital concepts to initiate new ventures internally, or to spin off businesses that are not appropriately kept in-house. Although corporate strategic investors represent only a small part of the venture capital community, their contribution has been considerable, and their dollars invested, particularly in technology-related businesses, have been disproportionate to their number.

Defining Corporate Strategic Investing

Corporate strategic investments are sometimes called strategic alliances or corporate partnerships. However, it is more usual to allow corporate alliances to be the blanket term encompassing joint ventures and outside business arrangements (e.g. technology exchanges, teaming, licensing, etc.), as well as corporate strategic investments.

Typically, strategic investments by corporations are cooperative business arrangements coupled with the provision of financing in the form of: an equity purchase; a loan; a lease/credit guarantee; advance payments; R&D funding; license fees; pre-paid royalties; development contracts; beta-site payments; asset transfers; etc.

These arrangements typically fall into one of three categories:

- *"Corporate strategic partnering"*—a relationship with a less than 24-month time frame, usually to obtain access to a product in order to strengthen the core business. This is most often driven by an operating unit for tactical reasons. An example is a computer manufacturer investing in a software company with the proviso that the software would be ported to the investor's platforms.
- *"Strategically directed venturing"*—characterized by a two-to-seven year time horizon, and used strategically by a corporate development staff that sees a longer-term market opportunity. An example would be an office automation company funding speech recognition with the expectation that it would later add such capabilities to its offerings.
- *"Corporate venturing"*—a long-term (up to 20 year) program driven by a desire to prevent being blindsided by developments from outside. It may be driven by corporate visionaries or others with a desire for a "window" on new technologies. However, it must also provide financial returns, or it will be terminated prematurely. Many examples exist in the pharmaceutical industry.

A number of corporate strategic investors have also funded venture capital partnerships to assist their other programs. Venture capitalists have facilitated this approach by organizing partnerships having just a single corporate strategic investor (a "dedicated fund") and by forming multi-investor partnerships focusing on a particular industry and/or geographic area, including a few partnerships having primarily foreign corporations from a single country.

No matter what form a corporate strategic investment program takes, there are many problems, as well as benefits, of which an entrepreneur must be cognizant when dealing with strategic funds.

History of Corporate Strategic Investing

Probably the first corporate strategic investor was DuPont. When one of its important new customers ran out of funds in 1919, it purchased a 38% equity interest and brought in a new president, Alfred Sloan. General Motors has grown substantially since that investment.

After World War I, AT&T, General Electric and Westinghouse bought out the British interests in American

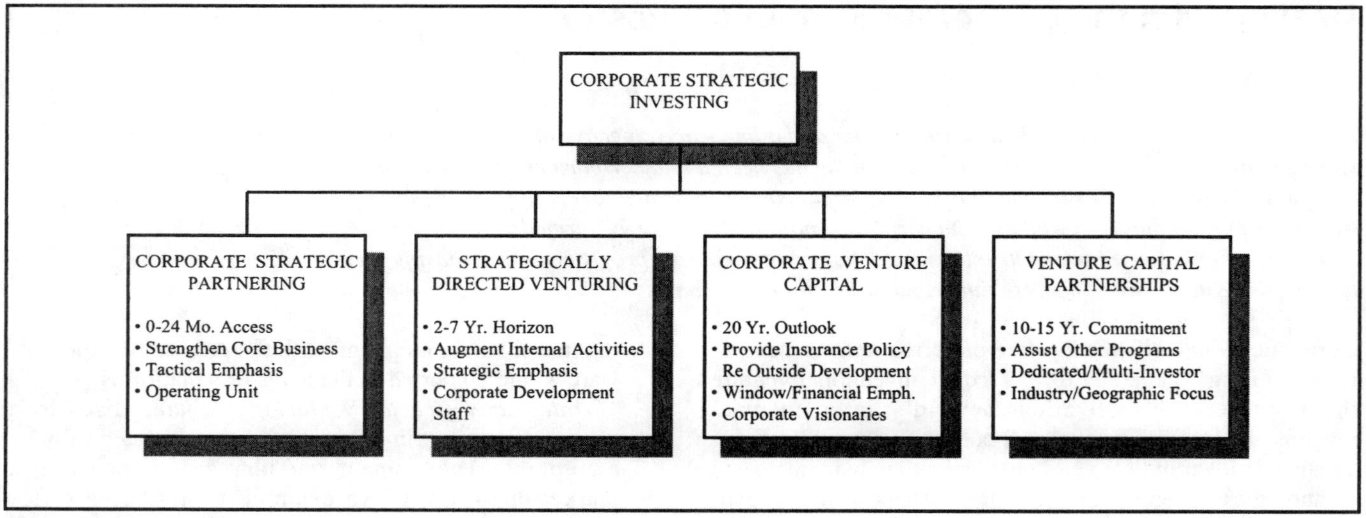

Marconi. They subsequently changed the name of their venture to Radio Corporation of America. Thus GE, in purchasing RCA, acquired a venture it originally helped finance.

Soon after World War II ended, a small company, Haloid Corporation, funded the commercialization of a new technology developed by Chester Carlson and the Battelle Memorial Institute. Haloid later changed its name to Xerox Corporation.

Another corporate strategic investor probably became interested in the activity because its largest stockholder was the son of the venture capitalist behind the formation of IBM. Fairchild Camera and Instrument financed a group of eight technologists who left Shockley Transistor in 1957. They later acquired this venture, Fairchild Semiconductor, the grandparent of many of the companies now populating Silicon Valley, including, of course, Intel.

Many corporations became active investors in the 1960s, seeking a "window on technology". However, the lack of profit orientation and the decline of the stock market in 1970 brought about the exit of most of those established corporate venture capitalists including Alcoa, Bechtel, Dow, DuPont, Firestone, Ford, General Dynamics, GT&E, Mobil, Monsanto, Northrop, Scott, Singer, Sun, Union Carbide and Weyerhaeuser. (Many of these companies have subsequently reentered the field, either directly or through venture partnerships.)

Although the near collapse of the stock market in 1974 and 1975 drove many other corporate venturers from the business, their number has increased dramatically since 1982.

Corporations Become More Active

Between 1982 and 1985, there was substantial growth in the number of corporations investing in venture funds for strategic reasons. However, having learned from these relatively safer investments, and usually investing alongside their investee funds, corporations began to expand their direct investment programs. Some even formed their own partnerships and leveraged internal monies with institutional capital despite the evident conflicts.

The five largest U.S. electronics companies and the 10 largest pharmaceutical companies, for example, have all recently made direct strategic investments. In the last three years, spurred by the Internet, many media companies have entered the field. Foreign corporations have been active as well. However, the dropout rate among companies with direct venture investment programs continues to be very high. Indeed, the number of such groups is believed to have peaked in 1989, and only begun increasing again in the last few years.

Problems of the Corporate Strategic Investor

Although financial rewards are usually a secondary concern, corporate funds that have been run by experienced professionals, even if not primarily for maximum return, have performed well, with reported compound annual returns of 20% to 100%.

Nonetheless, some of the best ones have closed down, usually due to one of the following problems:

- *Lack of appropriately skilled people.* Venture capitalists must be entrepreneurially motivated, patient, realistically optimistic, good at negotiation, persuasive and able to evaluate people as well as businesses. They must also be more than superficially familiar with accounting principles, tax regulations, corporate finance structures, securities analysis and securities law. Good internal people are generally unwilling to leave a company's mainstream activities, even if they possess the appropriate skills. Experienced people from the outside are hard to attract and retain without compensation packages that are sticky to structure and maintain.
- *Contradictory rationales.* A corporate strategic investor may find it difficult to act in the best interests of both the investee company and the parent. For example: if the goal of the corporation is to acquire, then equity financing by others is undesirable; if the rationale is an exclusive marketing arrangement or a preferred supplier role, then the investee's operations may be unduly limited. The parent's desire to have continuous profit increases is also incompatible with the normal results of a venture operation. The entire problem can be exacerbated by an improper reporting structure. For example: if the investment group reports to the vice president of finance, its focus may shift to profitability; if reporting to the vice president of R&D, the focus may be on technology; and if reporting to the vice president of corporate planning, then market information may be the main emphasis.
- *Legal problems.* A corporate investor must be extremely careful to organize its activities so that it will not run afoul of conflict of interest problems, including "fiduciary responsibility" and "corporate opportunity" doctrines. However, several corporations have left the field because they believed, incorrectly, that legal constraints would inhibit the strategic benefits they desired.
- *Inadequate time horizon.* A new strategic investment program usually shows its losses and problems early, with success taking more time to develop than anticipated. Unless a corporation's commitment is at least seven to 10 years, its activities will generally be terminated before any pearls can be harvested.

Selecting a Corporate Partner

In order to assure the viability of a long-term relationship and to avoid the common problems that arise in corporate investment programs, the following points should be considered:

- *Compatibility of goals.* As previously noted, corporations make strategic investments for diverse reasons, including: tactical, strategic, insurance, and also for obtaining a financial return. The business interests of both parties may either reinforce the possibility of success or lead to future conflicts.
- *Longevity.* Many corporate groups have been terminated due to a lack of early success, an inability to set clear objectives or a shift in corporate strategy. Support will probably wane at a time in the economic cycle when raising funds from others is most difficult. A true long-term commitment to the concept must be present.
- *People.* If the corporate group is not managed by experienced, dedicated venture capitalists, unnecessary conflicts may develop. Staff people want to return to a career path inside the corporation, thereby requiring continual efforts at educating new people. The near and long-term goals of the corporate managers should be investigated.
- *Adequate financing.* The corporation must provide appropriate financial resources to enable building and maintaining an independent operation, including adequate rewards to the managers. The likelihood of obtaining additional capital in later rounds and in the IPO must be understood.
- *Flexibility.* The route necessary for decision-making may be uncomplicated or tortuous. It is essential that the investment group have appropriate autonomy so that crises can be confronted expeditiously. Major corporations often measure performance against a yearly plan, whereas entrepreneurs must have the flexibility to react and restructure plans to overcome unexpected problems.
- *Interference.* Unless the relationship is well-structured, the corporation may attempt to require reporting and staff policies that are inappropriate in a venture situation. Curiosity visits may also become an annoyance.
- *Time horizon.* Not all corporate personnel realize the length of time that may be necessary to bring a new business to profitability. If they do not react rationally to unforeseen slippage, then substantial unnecessary difficulties will be created.
- *Style.* Corporate strategic investment groups, like their noncorporate counterparts, differ in attitudes, approaches and interests. A harmonious relationship, which should have developed before the investment, is helpful to a successful alliance and must be fostered in the aftermath.

The most important indicator is the manner in which the program is being managed. If investments are being made by the corporate development/corporate planning staff on a part-time, un-incentivized basis, the situation is fraught with danger of early termination. If the group does well, the people leave. If the group does not do well, the program is ended. Also, several incentivized captive (wholly internal) strategic investing groups have been closed down because their people did too well, and "compensation envy" became an issue. The maximum longevity has been achieved when the corporation outsourced the activity to a new, dedicated fund in which it was the sole investor, and which was managed by people who had been in the corporation teamed with experienced, professional venture capitalists, who were kept on a loose leash by the head of corporate/business development.

Considerations for the Transaction

Before entering into serious discussions it is important to understand what benefits are being sought by the corporate strategic investor. It may be seeking: an acquisition option or right of first refusal; exclusive technology/manufacturing/territorial marketing rights; a modified product; most favored customer status; first deliveries; and/or certain information flows. Some of these requests may be non-negotiable and will make completing a contract problematical.

There are many other issues that need to be addressed at the beginning of a transaction: decision-making and controls; confidentiality; rights to the technology; creation of a potential competitor; ability to work with competing corporations; response to changes in the corporate partner's executive strategies or policies; post-development collaboration; reporting; milestone or performance measurement; and winding down if the arrangement is unsuccessful. Additional details that must be negotiated when relevant include: front-end payments; reimbursements; sharing and payment of economic benefits; quality; quantity; price; delivery terms; other charges; royalties; future product or enhancement rights/procedures; field maintenance; warranty exposure; remedies on default; and rights of first refusal.

Corporate Investors Bring Advantages

Despite the problems cited, many corporations believe they should be preferred investors. In addition to the financial and strategic assistance offered by most venture capitalists, corporate investors can offer many other benefits:

- Assistance in almost all facets of corporate endeavor, such as setting up financial systems, qualifying suppliers, meeting government regulations and adding needed technological/clinical/regulatory skills;
- Credibility with customers, banks and other investors, both from a technical and financial standpoint;
- Relief, if desired, from the full range of corporate activities—for instance, the corporate investor may take on manufacturing and/or marketing responsibilities;
- Immediate income from an R&D or consulting contract;
- Acting as a second source;
- Providing a distribution channel;
- Adding patents to strengthen an existing portfolio;
- A customer interface with an interested party;
- An investor with an infinite lifetime, although the time horizon for profitability will be shorter;
- A merger partner, if and when appropriate;
- A more flexible or lower-cost financing package, since return on investment may not be the only criterion.

Corporate strategic investors can be good partners. Many times, however, parent corporations have terminated their activities despite excellent returns. In fact, in the U.S., with few exceptions, no strategically-oriented corporate venture capital group has succeeded in retaining its key personnel for more than seven years.

Therefore, it is incumbent upon the entrepreneurial team to exercise the same thoroughness in choosing a potential corporate investor as a venture group does in choosing its investments. Indeed, it is likely that several of the most active corporations today will exit the business within the next few years, wreaking havoc as they go, because of their poor organizational structures.

Non-Traditional Financing Sources

Gregory B. Sneddon and Jay K. Turner

Gregory B. Sneddon *is a managing director in the Mergers & Acquisitions Group at FleetBoston Robertson Stephens, Inc., assisting in merger and acquisition transaction advisory and capital-raising activities for middle market companies. Serving as agent or principal, Mr. Sneddon has initiated or participated in more than 50 advisory and financing transactions.*

Jay K. Turner, *a managing director in the Corporate Finance Group of Rauscher Pierce Refsnes, Inc., advises middle market companies on enhancing their shareholder value. Located in Dallas, Mr. Turner focuses on raising capital for rapidly growing companies. Prior to joining RPR, he started and built the Southwest Corporate Finance Group of KPMG Peat Marwick and a lending group to emerging growth companies for a national bank.*

Although the formal venture capital industry provides an important source of capital for a select number of growing companies, the majority of young companies in search of capital are unable to obtain traditional venture capital financing for failure to meet one or more of the criteria sought by professional investors. As a result, such companies may need to explore several financing avenues in order to successfully access the capital needed for their business. In this article, we look at a number of financing options that should be explored by entrepreneurs seeking alternatives to traditional venture capital.

Financing Vehicles and the Company Life-cycle

Most companies require some form of external capital in order to fund their growth. The stage a company is at in its life-cycle has a great influence on the perceived risk of the venture, and therefore on the availability and appropriateness of various types of financing. The table on the following page provides a general sense for the sources of capital most often employed at various stages in a company's development.

It is apparent from the table that the overall cost of capital, and the range of financing alternatives available to a firm depend largely upon the risk characteristics of the enterprise, and, accordingly, the stage of its development. A firm just starting out with minimal levels of bankable assets and little or no operating history will generally find it difficult to obtain bank financing, and must rely principally upon equity financing, typically provided by wealthy individuals or business associates, other owners, family and friends.

As the company grows, resulting in increasing asset levels and a proven product and marketing concept, aggressive banks may be willing to provide loans depending upon the strength of the management team, the overall level and quality of assets available for collateral, and the strength of external credit enhancements, such as personal guarantees or purchase contracts. As the company becomes larger and ultimately matures, the overall risk of business failure decreases markedly, and the public capital markets open up. In addition, bank financing and private placements of debt may become available at competitive rates, lowering the firm's overall cost of capital.

For companies with a solid history of strong and stable cash flows, mezzanine debt financing may also become a viable source of financing beyond conventional bank loans. For most young companies with risk profiles in the start-up or early growth stages, however, equity is generally the predominant financing vehicle.

Assuming the entrepreneur has evaluated the amount and type of financing required, there are a variety of avenues that may be investigated in the pursuit of raising capital. Although venture capital is certainly a popular route for growing companies, only a very small percentage of young companies meet venture capitalists' investment criteria. Discussed below are four alternatives to traditional venture capital.

Informal Venture Capital

The primary source of seed and start-up capital is individual investors. Commonly called business angels, these individuals are far more likely to provide early stage funding than professional venture capitalists. Most venture capitalists favor later-stage investment, where the risks are fewer and the returns are often equal to earlier stage investing.

Stage of Development	Risk Profile and Principal Risk Elements	Financial Characteristics	Typical Financing Instruments
Start-up	Highest: Management, Product, Market, Financial	Losses Minimal assets Negative cash flow	Founders' equity
Growth	Moderate: Management, Financial	Break-even to profitable Rapidly growing assets Negative or modestly positive cash flow	Bank Loans (mid-later growth) Leases (equipment) Private equity (early growth) Public equity (later growth) Strategic alliances
Maturity	Lowest: Competition	Profitable Stable asset levels Positive cash flow	Bank loans (working capital) Leases (equipment) Public & private equity Strategic alliances Mezzanine debt Private & public debt placements
Decline/ Turnaround	High: Financial, Management, Product/market strategy	Losses Declining asset values Cash flow positive or negative (asset liquidation)	Asset-based financing Public equity (dilutive) Turnaround investors

Business angels are individuals able and willing to provide entrepreneurs with enough capital to move their seed or start-up companies to the next phase. There is no standard profile of a typical angel. However, they tend to be successful entrepreneurs, retired corporate executives or professionals (doctors, attorneys or accountants) who meet the Securities and Exchange Commission's standards for "accredited" investors (generally defined as investors with a net worth of $1.0 million or $200,000 in income). Angels represent the only source of capital for many startups.

There are no definitive statistics on the size of capital available through the angel network, but according to William Wetzel, director emeritus of the Center for Venture Research at the University of New Hampshire, the total pool of angel capital is much larger than the institutional venture capital market. Professor Wetzel estimates that 250,000 angels invest a total of more than $10 billion a year in 30,000 to 40,000 companies nationwide. Angels are twice as active as they were five years ago and back 20-to-30 times as many companies as institutional venture capitalists, according to Professor Wetzel.

Angels' typical investments range from $5,000 to several million dollars. They are the predominant source of capital for deals under $500,000.

How do you find angels? Many can be found in traditional high net-worth activities, such as investment clubs, foundations, civic organizations, country clubs and private airports. Historically, angels have been highly fragmented and disorganized. However, recently there have been efforts to organize angel contacts through regional databases. One example is The Capital Network, Inc., which maintains a database of approximately 500 investors' criteria and 1,000 entrepreneurs' capital needs. Since its inception 5 years ago, The Capital Network has been responsible for introducing investors to companies where approximately $70 million has been invested.

A less formal but more traditional network is the entrepreneurs' network—friends, family, business associates, investment and commercial bankers, accounting and law firms, local universities, corporate CEOs and board members, old money families and even prospective employees.

Kiwi International Air Lines found its angels wearing wings—veteran pilots for the defunct Eastern Air Lines. The founders of Kiwi, also former pilots with Eastern, pitched their former colleagues on investing a minimum of $50,000 each in the start-up airline. The result: within six months the founders raised $7.0 million in stock from approximately 140 ex-colleagues, many of whom became employees.

Seeking angels who know something about your market or industry or who have a skill that would allow them to understand your business plan will enhance the likelihood that the investors will get excited about what you're trying to achieve.

Unlike the institutional venture capital market, there are no standard structures, returns or terms sought by angels. Each investment must take into consideration the unique needs, desires and perspectives of the investors. In exchange for high risk and low liquidity, angels typically expect extraordinary returns. Creativity is at a premium when structuring the deals, which often involve debt instruments with warrants attached.

Often the angels expect repayment of the debt within one to two years. Other angel investors prefer equity investments with no immediate cash flow requirements. Still others prefer to invest in order to ensure an opportunity to contribute to the operations of the company.

There is also no standard investment style angels follow. However, they typically make decisions relatively quickly. The time between first meetings with angels and subsequent funding averages about half the time it takes to raise funds from venture capitalists. Angels also typically desire regular meetings, a reason most traditionally prefer to invest within easy travel distance of home. Other investors want a role in running the enterprise that they have chosen to support, based on their experience and skills.

Finally, angels expect to cash out in ways similar to venture funds, through (i) a public offering, (ii) sale of the Company or (iii) a buyout of the angel at a predetermined value/multiple of earnings.

Corporate Investors

Corporate investors are similar to angels in that motivations beyond strictly financial rewards affect their investment criteria.

A typical corporate investor has an established strategic direction and the resources to pursue investments and/or a captive venture capital program.

A typical corporation's investment goals may be to:

- gain exposure to new markets and technologies
- generate new products
- identify and assess acquisition candidates; and
- assure a source of supply/assist a customer

The investment form may fit into one or more of the following structures:

- strategic partnerships/alliances
- minority investments (5%-20%)
- loans or guaranteed credit lines, equipment, facilities, personnel
- market research studies
- beta site testing of new products

The benefits to an emerging growth company able to attract a corporate investor, are many. A few include:

- assistance and resources to address all facets of corporate endeavor (e.g. financial systems, technical skills, regulatory issues, marketing support)
- credibility with customers, suppliers and financial sources
- potential income from R&D or consulting contracts
- access to additional capital, if warranted
- exit vehicle through merger, if and when appropriate
- more flexible or lower cost financing package

However, there are also problems associated with corporate investors. Often personnel responsible for these investments are not qualified. Culture clashes between corporate bureaucracy and entrepreneurial companies are fairly common. Corporate investors also often have different goals from the companies they back and sometimes face legal problems and an inadequate time horizon.

The best way to find a corporate investor or strategic partner is through an organized and methodical approach. Unlike angels, corporate investors aren't difficult to identify. They are often publicly traded companies with annual reports outlining their strategic direction. Once you have identified the companies with the apparent resources and strategic interest in investing in your venture, you must identify and contact the key officers, which generally hold positions in one or more of the following functions:

- corporate development
- new business development
- mergers and acquisitions
- new ventures
- corporate/strategic planning or
- licensing

In summary, corporate investors provide an excellent source of non-traditional financing for those companies who offer a compelling opportunity to meet the corporation's investment goals.

Government Sponsored Financing

SBA Programs

In order to foster the growth of small businesses and the economic development of local communities, federal and state governments have established a number of economic assistance programs for small businesses. Perhaps the best recognized agency in this regard is the federal Small Business

Administration (SBA), which administers a variety of programs and services for the small business owner. The SBA provides information on starting and operating a small business, offers business counseling and sponsors economic assistance programs. The assistance is provided in the form of loan guarantees to assist small businesses that do not yet possess satisfactory credit strength to secure bank financing on their own.

Although SBA programs can often help companies with marginal credit risks to obtain bank financing, a lender's decision to grant a loan is still based upon prudent credit practices. Accordingly, companies that lack adequate collateral or pose significant credit risks in the eyes of a lending institution will generally find it difficult to obtain bank financing with or without SBA assistance. The comparative advantages and disadvantages of SBA loans are discussed in further detail under "Aggressive Bank Financing" on the following page.

The majority of assistance provided by the SBA in recent years has been in the form of loan guarantees. The SBA's principal guarantee program is the 7(a) program under which loans are made by SBA-approved lending institutions for working capital, machinery & equipment and real estate. This program is very flexible and can range in amounts up to $1 million. Loan ceilings have been increased recently in certain instances, so contact your local SBA office for current program details and a list of SBA-approved lenders in your area.

The SBA also provides the 504 program, whereby both the SBA and the lending institution participate in the loan, subject to a minimum contribution of 10% to 20% by the borrower. The 504 program is principally used for real estate and heavy equipment in amounts up to $3 million. For a list of participating 504 lenders, contact your local SBA office.

The SBA also has a number of direct loan programs, but the implementation of these programs has been very limited. As funding under these direct loan programs tends to be sporadic, be sure to contact the SBA for a list of currently available loan programs.

Small Business Innovation Research (SBIR) Program

The SBIR program requires certain federal agencies to allocate a portion of their research and development budgets to qualifying small businesses. This program is intended to foster private development and commercialization of advanced technologies through grants to small businesses with technological proficiency in an area of specific interest to a federal agency.

The program is administered in multiple phases as the project moves from initial validation and concept development through the creation of a product prototype. Program assistance is provided in the form of outright grants which range in amounts, depending upon the stage of research and the nature and complexity work to be performed. Applicants are judged in part by their perceived ability to commercialize the technology developed under the grants, and are expected to access third-party funding sources to finance subsequent development, manufacturing and marketing of technologies developed through grant assistance.

The following federal agencies sponsor SBIR grant programs:

- Department of Agriculture
- Department of Commerce
- Department of Defense
- Department of Education
- Department of Energy
- Department of Health & Human Services
- Department of Transportation
- Environmental Protection Agency
- National Aeronautics & Space Administration
- National Science Foundation

For a current listing of agencies involved in the SBIR program and information on how to apply to such agencies, contact the Office of Innovation Research & Technology at the address listed at the end of this article.

Other Federal Programs

In addition to the SBA and the SBIR, there are a number of other federal agencies that offer financial assistance and provide potential sources of capital for small businesses. A brief summary of these agencies is provided below (a list of agency addresses appears at the end of this article).

The Minority Business Development Agency provides various financial and non-financial assistance programs to women and minority-owned businesses.

The Overseas Company Promotion program provides financing to importers and exporters. Contact the SBA for additional information.

Department of Energy Loans provide financing for businesses engaged in energy-related activities such as product research & development, electric vehicles, geothermal and coal operations.

The Import-Export Bank (EXIM Bank), working in conjunction with the Overseas Private Investment Corporation, provides direct loans and guarantees for importers and exporters of goods between certain countries in an effort to foster greater global competitiveness.

The Department of Housing & Urban Development provides mortgage loans for housing and renewal related construction.

The Department of Commerce, through its Economic Development Administration, provides assistance to businesses in economically declining or redevelopment areas, or areas impacted by foreign competition.

State Programs

Most states offer a variety of additional economic assistance programs. For example, in Massachusetts there are a number of public or quasi-public organizations that provide financial assistance to small businesses including the Community Development Finance Corporation, The Massachusetts Industrial Finance Agency, The Massachusetts Technology Development Corporation, The Massachusetts Business Development Corporation and Massachusetts Capital Resource Corporation.

Such programs vary from state to state, but they generally are oriented to companies conducting business (or planning to conduct business) in a particular state. A comprehensive directory of state assistance programs is available through government bookstores in a publication titled, The States and Small Business.

Aggressive Bank Financing

SBA Guaranteed Loans

If your bank has informed you that you lack sufficient credit strength to qualify for a loan, you may consider exploring SBA-assisted loan programs. As discussed above, the SBA makes available a number of loan guarantee programs to aid small businesses. While an SBA guarantee will generally not cause a bank to extend credit to a client with unacceptably high credit risk, it sometimes will enable a bank to extend loans to a company with only marginally acceptable credit risk. In addition, SBA programs can be quite flexible, and offer the following advantages (and disadvantages) over conventional bank financing:

Advantages:

- Greater eligibility: An SBA guarantee oftentimes makes it possible for a bank to lend to a company that otherwise fails to meet the bank's credit standards.
- Long maturities: up to seven years for working capital, 10 years on equipment and 25 years on real estate.
- Competitive interest rates: Loans backed by an SBA guarantee generally carry lower rates than non-guaranteed loans.
- Greater financing flexibility: SBA guidelines permit substantial borrowings and financial leverage relative to non-SBA guaranteed loans.

Disadvantages

- Collateralization: Like conventional loans, SBA loans are subject to approval by the lending institution and therefore generally will not help a borrower with insufficient collateral to support requested borrowings.
- Time and Paperwork: A borrower applying for an SBA loan must receive two credit approvals, one by the sponsoring bank and a second by the SBA. In addition, SBA loan applications require a significant amount of documentation prior to submission to the SBA, requiring substantial up-front time and effort on the part of the borrower.
- Personal Guarantees & Restrictions: A personal guarantee is almost always required to obtain an SBA loan. In addition, limitations will be imposed on the utilization of loan proceeds as well as other aspects of your business operations (i.e. compensation levels, perks, etc.). Most lenders to small businesses require such guarantees and limitations anyway, so these issues should probably be considered neutral elements when considering SBA assistance.

"Stretch" Lenders

In addition to SBA-assisted loans, there are a number of lenders throughout the country that may be willing to stretch their lending criteria to make loans in situations where most banks would be uncomfortable doing so. Bear in mind, however, that a bank's profit margin is only a couple percent after overhead expenses. Accordingly, a bank's permissible margin of error (i.e. loan write-offs) is very small, generally less than 1% of loans outstanding.

Notwithstanding banks' justifiable conservatism, if you search hard enough, you may be able to uncover bankers who are willing to roll up their sleeves to really get to know and understand your business. In doing so, such bankers may become comfortable enough with the strengths and risks to grant a loan where other banks have formed their decision solely upon financial or other criteria, without a full understanding the unique characteristics of your company.

Therefore, even if you have been turned down for a loan

by one or more lending institutions, it may be worthwhile to contact other institutions with aggressive reputations who may be willing to work hard to understand your business. Given the conservative nature of most institutions however, aggressive lenders are difficult to find.

For loan sizes under a few million dollars, most borrowers should focus on local banks that can cost-effectively administer their loan. Speak with accountants, attorneys, business associates and your local SBA office for ideas as to possible institutions and individuals to contact. As you consider bank sources of capital, keep in mind the following points:

- Finding the appropriate individual within an organization is often more important than selecting the appropriate institution. Seek out senior level individuals who have decision-making authority (or can strongly influence the credit approval process) and who have prior experience in lending to companies in your industry. Keep in mind that lending decisions are made by people, each of whom has unique preconceptions, biases and risk tolerances.
- Do your homework before meeting your banker to discuss your financing needs so you may convey a high level of knowledge and professionalism. Bankers will want to know about industry size and growth, competitive factors, management, historical and projected financial performance (with a focus on cash flow), the value of your personal assets (i.e. for personal guarantees), the nature and quality of collateral available to secure the loan (obtain receivables agings, inventory breakdown and machinery & equipment and real estate listings and appraisals). Accordingly, be sure that you have committed such information to memory, or at least have ready access to answers to all of these questions before you approach an institution for a loan.
- For growing businesses with weak credit characteristics, the availability of capital is far more important than the rate charged on the loan. Many growing companies can generate returns on new investment of 25% to 50% or more. Whether such a company's loan rate is 8% or 12% is unimportant compared with its ability to access capital for growth. In addition, virtually regardless of the interest rate charged on your loan, the after-tax cost to the company is merely a fraction of the investment returns required by providers of alternative forms of capital such as private equity groups. Lastly, as the company flourishes, it always has the option of refinancing into a lower rate loan as warranted by the company's progress.

The amounts and terms of the various SBA programs are subject to periodic change, so check with the SBA for current program requirements.

Resource Directory:

U.S. Small Business Administration
1441 L Street, N.W.
Washington, DC 20416
Phone: 202-606-4000

Office of Innovation Research & Technology
U.S. Small Business Administration
1441 L Street, N.W.
Washington, DC 20416

Minority Business Development Agency
U.S. Department of Commerce
14th Street between Constitution & E Streets, N.W.
Washington, DC 20230
Phone: 202-482-5061

U.S. Department of Energy
1000 Independence Avenue, S.W.
Washington, DC 20585
Phone: 202-586-8800

Export-Import Bank of the U.S.
811 Vermont Avenue, N.W.
Washington, DC 20571
Phone: 202-565-3946 Fax: 202-565-3380
Internet: http://www.exim.gov

U.S. Department of Housing & Urban Development
451 Seventh Street, S.W.
Washington, DC 20410
Phone: 202-708-1422

U.S. Department of Commerce
14th Street & Constitution Avenue, N.W.
Washington, DC 20230
Phone: 202-482-2000

Perspectives

Venture-backed companies such as Intel Corp., Staples, Tandem Computers and Federal Express have achieved notable success as industry leaders and innovators, and in the process they have created new industry sectors. The role of the venture capitalist can be vital to the success of new business development and the character of venture-backed companies and their founders.

Additionally, the relationship between the entrepreneur and the venture capitalist is often a critical factor in the success of a new business. To develop a productive, cohesive working relationship, it is helpful to recognize the biases, prejudices and pressure points that have emerged from the experiences of both venture capitalists and entrepreneurs.

Before making an investment, venture capitalists carefully examine the management team, looking for appropriate skills and disciplines. But they also look for chemistry, a "gut feeling" that gives them the internal go-ahead to invest in the team. This section examines the techniques used by several industry professionals in evaluating management teams and offers some valuable advice for the entrepreneur on early relationships with the venture capitalist.

The views of one entrepreneur are presented. This person has worked with and won the respect of a number of venture capitalists. His insights are valuable as a guide, and they place the entrepreneur-venture capitalist relationship and the money-raising process in a new perspective.

Relationship Between Venture Capitalist and Entrepreneur

Brook H. Byers

Brook H. Byers *is a general partner of Kleiner Perkins Caufield & Byers in Menlo Park, California. He has been a venture capital investor since 1972. Mr. Byers had worked in management positions for two publicly owned, venture-backed companies and has been founding president of four start-up ventures, including Hybritech, Inc. and Ligand Pharmaceuticals, Inc. He received a B.E.E. from Georgia Tech and an M.B.A. from the Stanford Graduate School of Business. KPC&B manages a very large venture capital fund and has helped entrepreneurs build 240 high technology companies in information and life sciences, which today have revenues of $40 billion and employ 120,000 people.*

Venture capital portfolio management might be compared to farming: many different techniques are used between planting the seed and reaping the harvest. No single method is ideal because characteristics, such as the species of plant, the quality of the soil, the ability of the farmer and the condition of the weather are all variable and must be considered in each case.

Similarly, the venture capital investor must decide for each investment what to do in the years between the intense period of analysis and negotiation leading to an investment and the future, the time when the venture capital partnership's stock will be distributed and a return on investment is realized. This decision depends on the type of involvement an investor seeks. Some investors prefer to rely on management reports and periodic company visits, while others prefer to become "working partners" with management.

Our preference at KPC&B is one of "significant involvement"—giving business counsel and emotional support to the company management and receiving enhancement of our investment and personal satisfaction in return.

Factors Affecting Relationship

Each investment requires a different monitoring approach, depending on several key factors affecting our relationship with the company. These factors include the following:

- the length of time to profitability
- the company's need for assistance
- management's willingness to accept advice
- the portion of our total capitalization invested in the company
- our expertise relative to the company's needs
- our time commitments and the company's location
- the competence of co-investors
- the degree of potential influence on the company

Based on such factors, we tailor a method for each investment by using a combination of the chairman of the board or member of the board of directors, interim officer, ad hoc volunteer, founding active entrepreneur, fire extinguisher, project consultant, alliance arranger, strategist, recruiter, fund raiser and counselor. This tailored combination changes significantly over the life of the investment.

Four Examples of this Approach

Venture investment decisions are complex and allow for a variety of entrepreneurial situations to be attractive. Diversity by technology as well as by stage of development is an objective of a well-managed venture investment firm. Described below are four examples of how relationships between our firm and four ventures evolved.

First Example: Tandem Computers, Inc.

Tandem is an example of extreme involvement on the part of the venture capital investors. Our firm recognized a market opportunity for fault-tolerant computers and "incubated" the company internally in 1974. Two of our partners left to become president and vice president of finance, and a third became chairman of the board. All three partners had extensive experience in the computer industry as managers. This opportunity justified the investment of both significant seed capital and partners and resulted in one of the most successful venture capital investments in history. Tandem became a publicly held company in 1977 and continued to grow dramatically, resulting in our stock being worth well over 100 times our investment.

Second Example: Hybritech, Inc.

Hybritech represented a situation where a brilliant scientist saw an opportunity but needed management assistance immediately. In order to capitalize on the lead time provided by the scientist's insight and technology in monoclonal antibodies, one of our partners launched the company in 1978 as acting president to prove the commerciality of the process and to recruit a permanent president with experience in that industry. Our partner then became chairman of the board and continued to advise the management team he helped assemble on strategic and policy matters, leaving operating issues to the team. This process gave the venture a fast start and insured fundamental strategies compatible with our firm's philosophies for high-growth companies. The partner returned to full-time venture capital activity. Hybritech went public in 1981 and the value of the firm's holding appreciated over 100 times our initial investment. Hybritech was subsequently acquired by Eli Lilly for a substantial premium.

Third Example: Caremark (formerly Home Health Care of America, Inc.)

This company is a case where an excellent management team needed capital in 1978 to exploit an unusual market opportunity within a narrow "time window." The strategy for success called for a very rapid build up of the venture and aggressive geographic expansion. We invested with just such an aggressive posture and placed two of our partners on the board of directors to assist in the orderly execution of the plan. This venture encountered difficult periods, including a founder who was not compatible with company goals, emergence of competition and stresses from rapid growth. Our role was to assist in key strategic decisions, to recruit officers and to finance the successful build up. The company went public in 1982 and our firm's holdings have appreciated over 50 times our initial investment. Caremark was subsequently acquired by Baxter International.

Fourth Example: Sun Microsystems, Inc.

Sun was a typical situation where we participated in 1982 in the early financing of an exciting venture along with other venture capital firms. One of our partners joined the Board of Directors, as did another investor. The Company has pioneered the revolution in desktop workstation computing through the creation of novel computation architectures and the establishment of industry software standards. Our involvement has been advisory but intense in nature related to technology choices, new market segment initiatives, recruiting, corporate alliances, and financing. As Sun passed the $2 Billion per year revenue level, two of Sun's executives became partners of KPC&B. Sun went public in 1986 and the value of our firm's holdings have appreciated over 85 times our initial investment.

Benefits of this Approach

We use the significant involvement approach to monitoring primarily because we believe it gives us greater investment success. However, many other benefits are realized as well:

1. greater personal satisfaction in having taken an active role in the growth of a new business
2. further professional training in business and technology from the "scar tissue" of being involved
3. "keeping pace" with the company when business challenges occur and when management seeks well-informed advice
4. intimate familiarity with the investment when later financings or mergers are proposed
5. the ability to attract venture capital investors (and their capital) from other geographical regions, who desire an involved "watchdog" investor

This significant involvement benefits our companies and aids in our investment success because we provide:

1. experience in explosive growth businesses
2. a sounding board for top management on a personal level with non-employees
3. broad contacts for corporate alliances, product line diversification, networking between our portfolio companies, foreign marketing expertise, financing contacts and consultants with special skills
4. independence for specific projects, such as strategic plans, acquisitions, compensation plans, and top management screening
5. arrangements for orderly private equity financings
6. communications with the investment community before and after a public offering
7. assistance in recruiting an excellent top management team

Problems of this Approach

This approach, however, is not without problems:

1. Involvement requires time, which can mean harder work by investors or an increase in staff—usually the former, however, because of the small team nature of the venture capital business.
2. Some managers are slow to accept significant investor involvement, viewing it as an intrusion on their authority.
3. Once trust is established with management and the involvement is mutually satisfying, some entrepreneurs

begin to expect our unlimited support, which makes it difficult to distinguish nonrecurring problems (appropriate for our approach) from recurring problems (the operating responsibilities of management).

4. "Quiet" investment partners sometimes place a de facto responsibility for the investment on active investors.
5. An investor, because of significant involvement, is often obligated to participate in later equity financings, because such participation will determine the success of the offering, even though one might personally prefer not to participate further than a present investment level.
6. An involved investor can lose objectivity about an investment.

Summary

Our investment record has proven that investing capital in venture situations, combined with involved assistance, offers above-average investment returns and better chances for new companies to survive in their difficult early years. The personal satisfaction we have derived, along with the close relationships with outstanding entrepreneurs, makes it a magnificent way to do business.

An Entrepreneur's Guide to Financing the High Technology Company

Thomas H. Bruggere

Thomas H. Bruggere *is founder and former chairman/CEO of Mentor Graphics Corporation, Wilsonville, Oregon. He founded the company in 1981 to manufacture products for the electronics portion of the computer-aided design industry. Mr. Bruggere has extensive management experience including software engineering and product management and development with Tektronix, Inc. from 1977 to 1981, and with Burroughs Corporation from 1972 to 1977. He obtained a B.S. in mathematics from the University of California at Santa Barbara, an M.S. in computer science from the University of Wisconsin, and an M.B.A. from Pepperdine University.*

Raising money for a start-up firm is like getting your first date—it seems like an impossible task, it's hard to take the first step and it's the beginning of an effort you must continue for the rest of your (company's) life in order to be successful. Like that first date, your attitudes, strategies and personal abilities will be instrumental in determining your ultimate degree of success.

The financial guidance a new high technology company may receive will be imprecise and inconsistent. Some successful companies have financed themselves in every imaginable way. Certain details should be attended to in order to maximize a company's chance for success. What follows is one entrepreneur's reflections on where to look for the problems and the opportunities. So let us start at the beginning.

Getting Up the Nerve

Most would-be entrepreneurs worry about one question: what product should I build? The question of raising money is usually not addressed until after the decision is made to strike out on one's own. Because of the entrepreneur's optimism and confidence, it is often assumed that financing will be available.

At this stage, the main concern is leaving the nest of their existing company. A great deal of energy is put into the product technology because, after all, that is the key to success. And, therefore, that is what will bring the financial world to the door, right?

Not necessarily. A good product is certainly important, but it is not the most important detail to consider when starting a company. People are the most important ingredient at this or any other stage. Investors put their money into people first, and then product and market matches. The right people will make a mediocre product successful, while the wrong people for a project will fall short even with a superior product.

Remember, if you really do have a good product idea, you are going to have competition; the bigger the market potential, the tougher the competition. Also, regardless of your experience or success, you will face difficult problems. Your ability to successfully meet the competition and to overcome these problems will depend upon the quality of your people.

So, good people are what will make the company successful, and investors know this. If you want to make it easier to finance the company, pay attention to its people from the beginning. If you are having trouble raising money initially, take a long, introspective look at the people in the company. You may need to make some changes.

Asking the Question

Now that you have your product idea refined and the best people committed, you are almost ready to ask for the money. First, however, you must decide what to ask for, and whom to ask.

What to Ask For

A business plan will be needed that will include pro forma financial statements indicating how much money you will need to make the company profitable. You must decide how much of that money you want to raise now, and how much you are willing to raise later, hopefully at a higher price. A typical financial plan calls for $50 million in sales in five years with 10% after tax earnings.

The general financial stages of a start-up company are prototype development, product development, successful marketing and expansion. Obviously, the farther along your company is, the less business risk an investor is taking, and the greater the price you can charge for your stock. Most high technology companies raise enough money in their initial financing to take them through the product development stage. This strategy allows the company to prove that the product can be built and that someone will buy it.

It is not uncommon for a company to run out of money before the product development is completed. For this reason, you should try to get investors in the first financing who can and will put up more money if things do not go as planned. You should also raise more money than you think you need in order to give yourself a buffer. A good rule is to take 50% more money than you think you need to achieve your plan.

Whom to Ask

The sources of money for the start-up company are almost everywhere. Personal finances, relatives, banks, individuals, investment banks, venture capitalists and many other sources may be available to you if you just know where to look. But, all money is not created equal, so you must know what to look for.

Any time you bring an investor or group of investors into your company, you should ask yourself (and them), "what will they add to the company?" The answer may be guidance, prestige, contacts, high valuation, etc.

Make certain that there is a good match between what your company needs and what the investors bring. And always get the highest quality investors possible. Top quality investors will attract other investors to your company and provide a smooth financing plan.

How can you tell a quality investor? There are some simple tests, and they all attempt to determine how the investors will help you. Ask about their other investments. If they have had a successful track record of investing, they probably can help you be successful too. Find out how well-known they are; the financial community is very close knit, and reputations are often well deserved.

Determine how long they stay invested in a company; you want early investors with "deep pockets" who can continue investing in subsequent financings. You don't, however, want someone with short arms who will not reach down into those pockets to help you in rough times. Finally, ask how they have helped other companies. This will give you some idea how they might help your company.

Next, you should try to match the type of investor to the needs of your company. For example, a start-up company usually requires different types of support from the consultive help of a venture capitalist to adequate lines of credit at the bank. The following priority ranking of what a company needs is broken down by its financial stage.

Prototype/Product Development

Company Need: Active participation in guidance, product strategy, recruiting contacts, management team development

Best Investors: Venture capitalists, knowledgeable individuals

Successful Marketing

Company Need: Customer contacts, prestige, sales strategy, sales recruitment, less price sensitivity

Best Investors: Venture capitalists, investment bankers, large funds

Market Expansion

Company Need: Low price sensitivity, customer contacts, prestige, credibility

Best Investors: Large funds, general public

Venture capital investors are the most popular source of initial capital. Good ones will help nurture a company by providing counseling, insights gained from previous investments, access to potential employees, prestige and often customer contacts. They are, however, often the most price sensitive: a typical initial funding is $1 million to $5 million for 30% to 60% of your company.

Beware of inexperienced venture capitalists. A number of venture capital funds are managed by people who are either inexperienced in helping a company or spread too thin to provide adequate help. Always ask what the venture capitalists will bring to your company besides money, and what other companies they have been involved with—both as investors and as board members.

Investment banking firms can provide a limited private or public offering for your company. This can be an easy way to raise money by selling stock to relatively sophisticated institutional or individual investors who will probably not take an active role in the company. This group of investors will generally pay a higher price than a venture capitalist but will usually contribute minimal operating experience to the company.

For a company's initial financings, this method of financing is less attractive than venture capital, unless the company already has significant operating experience. As with venture capitalists, investment bankers span a wide range of capability, prestige and experience. Always ask about their most recent offerings and be concerned about the type of investors with whom they will try to place your stock. Unsophisticated or impatient investors may not be very supportive if your company stumbles.

Banks will loan you money if you pledge assets as collateral. If the company has assets (inventory, accounts receivable, for example), bank debt is an excellent way to generate cash. If, however, you are just getting started, your only assets may be items like your house. While many companies have gotten started this way, banks are not venture investors (they currently cannot even own stock), and may not be patient when things don't go as planned. In general, it is best not to use banks to finance your start-up, other than traditional leases and debt. It is important, however, to develop a close, supportive relationship with a good bank from the beginning.

Family, friends and personal finances have started many high technology companies. You certainly should plan on a personal investment, however small. If you do finance your company this way, remember two things: growing the company too slowly because of inadequate capital may cost market share and ultimately the long-term viability of your company, and friends and relatives probably won't bring operating experience or accountability to the company. You must, then, get these elsewhere.

One Example

Mentor Graphics is a public company in the fast growing electronic design automation (EDA) industry. It was initially funded in 1981 by three venture capital firms: Venrock Associates, Greylock Management and Sutter Hill Ventures. It received three private rounds of financing totaling $10 million before raising $52 million in a public offering in January 1984. The figure below shows the stages of funding for Mentor Graphics, including the price paid per share by the investors and the total dollars raised.

Building the Relationship

Plan on an ongoing effort to raise money. If your company is successful, you will need capital for expansion. If it is not, you may need it for survival. In any event, you should have a long term financing plan. And don't hesitate to raise money just to have a reserve. These "war chests" have helped many companies to survive rough times while their under capitalized competition has failed.

Also, because financing your company is an ongoing process, you should always be working at it. Don't wait until you need money to go out and tell your company's story. The more investors are informed about what you do, the better able you may be to raise money. (And besides, the best time to raise money is usually when you don't need it.)

For example, there are numerous financing seminars you can participate in whether your company is public or private. And because information on the financial "grapevine" travels quickly, a little exposure goes a long way. Also, always keep in mind that the better you tell your story (form and substance), the more attractive your company may be to an investor.

If the goal is to go public, you should plan your investor strategy accordingly. All else being equal, the strongest initial public offerings will come to companies with the most prestigious backers. (Of course, a strong sales and earnings story will always attract attention in an initial public offering [IPO].)

With either strategy, pay attention to your investors, (especially bankers). Keep them regularly informed of progress (at least quarterly), and treat them as an asset of the company. Their support in subsequent financings will be important to you.

The Marriage

The climax of your financing efforts may be either going public or being acquired. Investors will look for these goals in your plan because that is the way they will get their investment back. This is when it is most important to have a good invest-

Mentor Graphics' Financing History

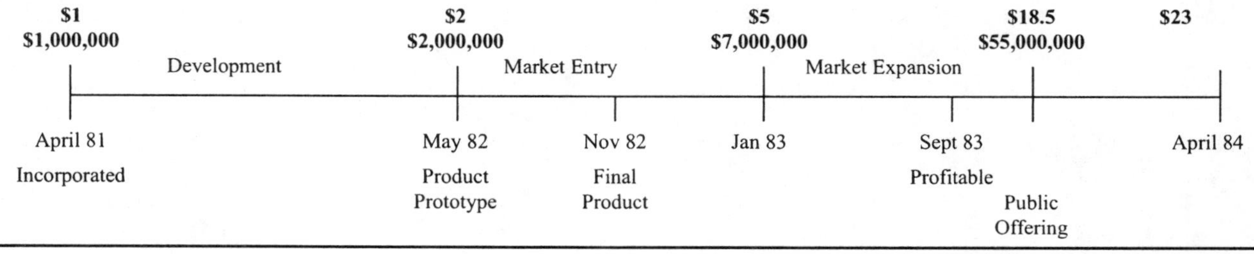

ment banker and a supportive group of previous investors.

There are a variety of reasons why a company should go public. A public offering will provide a significant source of lower-cost capital for the company. It may also enhance the credibility and prestige of your company in the eyes of customers and employees. And it will give early investors and employees some potential liquidity. Besides, the "war chest" of money you raise may give you an important edge over competitors.

On the other hand, being a public company will place new stresses on the company. It will focus you on managing for quarter to quarter increases in earnings, often for the sake of long-term strategy. There will be a significant draw on management's time to deal with the financial community. And you may no longer have inexpensive stock to offer employees. In addition to all these problems, you will also have to begin to do the paperwork required for public reporting results.

So it's very important to evaluate your company before taking it public. Your company should be growing in a market that is growing. It is also best to be at a significant sales level and to be profitable so you will be taken seriously by investors, always try to do an offering when the stock market is strong or you may be in for some disappointments. Most important, be certain you have the infrastructure within your company to manage a public company.

The amount of money you raise during an offering will depend largely on your company's need for cash. You will also want to consider your competitors' resources, since they will probably be trying to outpace you. Also, the price of the stock will be a factor since it will determine the overall dilution of the offering. Finally, listen to your investment bankers since they will have a good measure of what is possible in a given stock market.

If you have done everything right, many of your existing investors, especially the later-stage investors, will show their support by increasing their investment at the public offering. The worst thing you can have is existing investors selling most of their stock at the initial public offering. Potential investors will be unsettled if they see the people who know the most about the company selling out. However, if you have had good investors all along, you will be in good shape at the public offering.

The process of going public may seem so confusing and expensive as to be formidable. But with the right investors, it can be the rewarding pinnacle for your company.

Summary

In summary, there are two lessons that most successful high technology companies have learned about financings:

1. A continuing supply of funds will be needed, so it is important to have a planned investment strategy that brings in investors who will continue to support the company through good and bad times.

2. Investors are mainly backing the people, so it is important to be very introspective about the strengths and weaknesses of the key personnel in the company and to make changes when necessary.

With these lessons in mind, financing a high technology company should be approached with enthusiasm and confidence.

The SBIC Program: Capital for Entrepreneurs

By Bruce A. Kinn and Arnold M. Zaff

The authors are partners in the Boston law firm of Foley, Hoag & Eliot LLP and have been actively involved in development and implementation of the SBIC equity leverage program. Foley, Hoag & Eliot LLP maintains a diverse business practice that includes the representation of start-up and developing companies, leveraged buyout transactions, and the representation of venture capital funds, including SBICs.

Four decades ago, Congress created the small business investment company (SBIC) program to stimulate and supplement the flow of capital to small businesses through privately managed venture capital funds. The program had mixed results, but in 1992 Congress made major improvements that were designed to bring it in line with the practical necessities of venture capital fundraising and investing. The improved program has generated significant interest. Since inception of the new program, the number of SBICs licensed by the Small Business Administration, and the private capital committed to those SBICs, has increased to unprecedented levels, with no sign of abating. When combined with government-backed financing available to SBICs, the result is a significantly increased flow of capital to small businesses. For example, in the fiscal year ended September 30, 2000, SBICs invested nearly $5.5 billion in over 3,000 small businesses, an increase in dollars invested of 30% over the prior year. This article provides an overview of the SBIC program and describes the improvements that benefit entrepreneurs and venture capital funds alike.

The Program

An SBIC is a privately owned and managed venture capital fund that functions, in most respects, like other venture capital funds. The difference is that an SBIC has access to long-term, low-cost, government-backed financing that enables it to supplement the funds it raises from private investors. This government-backed financing may take the form of loans to the SBIC or of equity contributed to the SBIC in exchange for its preferred equity securities. The SBIC is thus able to "leverage" its private capital and (assuming the return on its investments exceeds the cost of the leverage) significantly increase the return to its private investors on the capital they have invested in the SBIC.

The SBIC program is administered by the Small Business Administration, which licenses venture capital funds to participate in the program and issues regulations with which they are required to comply. Those regulations are generally designed to provide that SBICs invest only in small businesses and that SBICs are operated in a reasonably prudent manner.

A key point for both entrepreneurs and venture capital managers is that, although it is a major source of funding, the government is not involved in the management of either the SBIC or its investment portfolio. All investment decisions are made by the venture capitalists who manage the SBIC. They decide in which companies to invest and, together with company management, the terms of the investments; they monitor investments and work with company management; and they, together with company management, determine the timing and method of exiting from investments. The entrepreneur has access to government-backed financing through the SBIC, but deals only with private venture capital professionals.

SBICs are able to provide financing at various stages of a company's development, from seed stage through later stage, and in forms ranging from pure common equity to loans with or without equity "kickers."

Eligible Companies

The managers of each SBIC establish their own investment criteria. The criteria imposed by the SBA are few. Investments in certain types of businesses, such as real estate, finance, and motion picture production companies, are restricted. And, of course, a business must be small, which means meeting one of two tests. First, a company must have a net worth of not more than $18 million and average net after-tax income for the last two years of not more than $6 million (although SBICs are required to allocate a portion of their capital to companies that meet a smaller size test).

Second, for companies unable to meet the net worth/net income test, there is a test that, depending on the nature of a company's business, is based on either the number of employees or total revenues. Employee tests range from 100 to 1,500 employees and total revenue tests range from

$500,000 to $27.5 million, depending on the industry.

Companies with securities that are publicly traded, as well as those with securities that are closely held, are eligible for SBIC financing as long as they meet these criteria.

Funds provided by an SBIC may be used for any valid business purpose, such as working capital, capital expenditures, research and development, and acquisitions, as long as they are used in the United States.

In addition to the foregoing purposes, an entrepreneur who desires to purchase an existing business may be eligible to do so using SBIC financing. SBICs are permitted to finance ownership changes that promote the sound development or preserve the existence of a small business, that result in creation of a small business as the result of a divestiture, or that facilitate ownership in businesses controlled by certain socially or economically disadvantaged persons. If the resulting small business has more than 500 full-time employees, it must also meet a debt-to-equity test.

Increasing Private Equity Capital

The most important improvement that Congress made in 1992 was to allow the SBA to provide funding to an SBIC in the form of preferred equity rather than debt. More specifically, SBA's capital may be provided in exchange for preferred equity interests issued by a limited partnership SBIC (the usual form of organization chosen by venture capital funds). The preferred securities issued by the SBIC to the SBA provide for a preferred return which, although payable before distributions to the SBIC's private investors, is payable only out of the SBIC's profits. This eliminates the problem of mismatching of an SBIC's investment profits and leverage expense, enhancing the SBIC as a vehicle for equity investing in both early stage and later stage companies. In fact, an SBIC is required to invest an amount equal to the preferred equity leverage it obtains in the equity securities of small businesses. This is good news for entrepreneurs, who now find SBICs to be a greatly increased

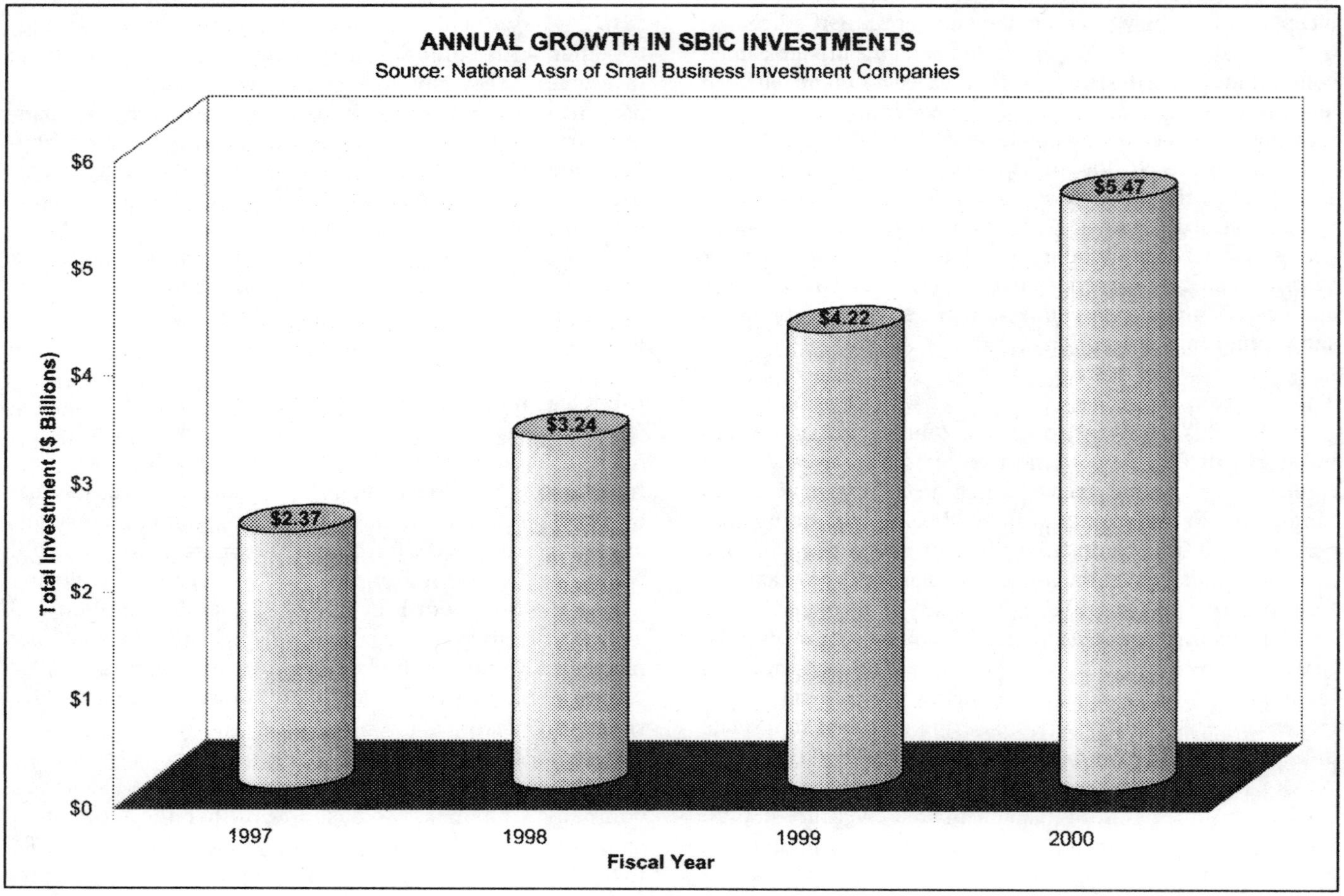

source of equity capital for their businesses.

Just as important is that, unlike leverage in the form of debentures issued by limited partnership SBICs, leverage in the form of preferred equity leverage does not result in taxable income to tax-exempt investors. SBICs are now able to organize as limited partnerships, leverage their private capital, and still attract pension plans and other tax-exempt investors, which now have the prospect of obtaining leveraged investment returns that remain free from taxation. The practical effect is to open the door for pension funds and other tax-exempt institutional investors to participate as a potentially large source of funding for SBICs.

The program also enhances the ability to attract state and local government funds into the SBIC program. Up to 33% of an SBIC's private capital may consist of direct investments by state and local governments, as long as the SBIC is privately managed. State and local governments may act as the lead funding source, and leverage their funds, to promote the growth and development of small businesses in their geographic areas.

Multiplying Available Capital

The SBA pools the preferred equity securities or debentures issued by SBICs and sells interests in the pools to buyers in a secondary market. The SBA enhances the attractiveness of such interests in the secondary market through its guarantee of the current payment of the preferred return or the debenture interest, as the case may be. In the case of the preferred equity pools, the SBA, through payments under its guarantee, "fronts" the current payment of the preferred return and recoups its cost of capital when profits on the SBIC's investments are realized. In exchange for its guarantee support in the secondary market with respect to preferred equity securities, the SBA is entitled to receive a percentage of the SBIC's profits in addition to the preferred return. Access to capital in the secondary market as a result of the SBA's guarantee multiplies the amount of government-backed capital available to SBICs and, ultimately, to the entrepreneurs in whose companies SBICs invest.

An SBIC is eligible to obtain up to $108.8 million in leverage through the SBA, subject to indexing for inflation. The amount of leverage available to an SBIC depends on the amount of its private capital. For example, an SBIC with $20 million in capital raised from investors is eligible to receive up to $40 million of preferred equity leverage, or up to $58.1 million of leverage in the form of debt. The potential increase in funds available for investment in the small business community is thus quite dramatic.

The amounts actually available depend, of course, on annual budget appropriations, which are based on the projected cost (including losses) to the government of providing leverage, net of the return earned by the government on capital previously provided to SBICs. SBICs are now required to pay an increased portion of the program cost to the government, which results in a given budget appropriation yielding greater leverage availability. Although these changes raise slightly the necessary return on equity required by an SBIC for a portfolio investment in order to absorb its slightly higher cost of capital, the long-term benefit should be a program that is less subject to annual Congressional budget politics. Other changes in the program have also facilitated a smooth flow of leveraged funds to SBICs to enable more timely investments in companies. In fact, the SBA is now willing to issue multi-year commitments for leverage capital to SBICs, further demonstrating the increased stability of the program.

For example, for fiscal year 2001, debenture leverage does not require a budget appropriation because the assumed loss rate is zero. Debenture leverage is thus available in the full amount of $1.5 billion contained in the program's statutory authorization. In addition, a subsidy rate of only 1.3% for the preferred equity program means that the relatively meager budget appropriation of $26.2 million will yield $2 billion in preferred equity leverage availability. With so much low cost capital available, it is no surprise that venture capital groups are lining up to apply for SBIC licenses.

The Outlook for Entrepreneurs

The SBIC program provides venture fund managers with an attractive opportunity to multiply capital that is available for equity investment by using long-term, low-cost, government-backed financing, and to attract both public and private pension fund investors as part of the capital base on which leverage can be obtained. As more private and government-backed capital has funneled into the program each year, the ranks of companies that have been funded by SBICs has grown rapidly.

What this means to the small business community is clear: substantial private capital already has been, and should continue to be, drawn into the SBIC program and supplemented by government-backed funds to be invested in small companies. Entrepreneurs, whether in need of seed capital to develop and commercialize their ideas, or later-stage capital to expand their businesses, should not overlook this important source of long-term financing targeted to the small business community.

Managing Problem Deals

Claes E. Larsson

Claes E. Larsson is the founder and president of Point Ledge Associates, which advises venture capital and private equity investors. The firm offers support to improve returns on particular portfolio investments through active, part-time involvement of up to nine months, or more. On behalf of financial owners of smaller companies, Mr. Larsson also acts as a principal, at times taking on active directorships. Prior to establishing this business in 1985, Mr. Larsson was a banking officer with J.P. Morgan and was part of two private equity funds, all in New York. He received his undergraduate degree from Stockholm School of Economics and his MBA from Harvard Business School.

Few venture capital investments are realized without encountering problems that require action on the part of the board or other outsiders. Even good companies have problems and perform poorly at times. In the following article, we will explore issues that may arise and need to be addressed subsequent to the initial investment in a portfolio company.

Poorly performing portfolio companies are very common, but little has been written about how to deal with them. Rapid growth leading to increasing complexity, as well as changes in the competitive environment, requires management to make changes. Sometimes they need to be initiated by the board. Changing the CEO is an obvious, but many times, poor solution. In a small, dynamic environment, the information available to management can easily become inadequate. The financial presentation to the directors may not permit the board to identify the causes for the poor performance or give little direction how it could be improved.

Fundamental problems many times require basic solutions. However, what has worked with other companies, rarely fits the problem "deal" at hand. To tackle problem investments, a new perspective will need to be developed together with management. A great deal of time is required to find the right course of action and to make sure it is properly implemented. With significantly more capital raised by venture capital funds in recent years, venture capitalists' time is increasingly committed to choosing among a finite number of high-potential investment opportunities. Even at a critical juncture for a particular investment, it can prove difficult to find a board member with enough time to address the issues without outside assistance.

Increasingly, the money invested by venture funds goes into well-established companies. We will focus on problems with portfolio companies that have reached at least a few million dollars in sales and where value created over the time of the investment is an important part of generating a superior return.

Underperformance Is the Norm

Less than 10 percent of venture backed portfolio companies reach even the relatively modest target of 25 percent return on investment, according to a study performed for this article with the help of Venture Economics Information Services. The study, which includes more than 3,500 venture portfolio companies, shows that in recent years, more than half, in fact, have negative returns five years after investment. This is true regardless of investment stage. Nevertheless, the same portfolios returned five times the investment due to a few run away successes. Though all the investments passed venture firms' usually rigorous due diligence process, the data show that well over half of the investments that proved viable have not even generated a return to the investors that could have been obtained on a bank CD!

Little Is Written About Problem Investments

A recent review of the literature and research on underperforming portfolio companies showed that this prevalent phenomenon, which has a significant bearing on venture capital returns, is hardly covered at all. How can this be? Two principal reasons come to mind.

The terminology used gives us the first hint. Portfolio companies are commonly referred to by venture capitalists as "deals" or "investments". These terms primarily are used to describe transactions in the investment banking field or in the management of portfolios of public stocks. Critical aspects of managing a private equity/venture capital fund are also transaction oriented, such as fund raising and the acquisition and divestiture of portfolio companies. But just as critical is the management of portfolio companies, and, as the terminology suggests, this aspect of a venture capitalist's job can get short shrift. This is particularly true for the many venture capitalists who have a transactions background. Many entrepreneurs find unexpectedly that few of their venture backers have any real operating experience.

The second reason is more obvious. Talking about the

great successes in one's portfolio is more rewarding than discussing the problem "deals." Specifics about portfolio returns remain a well-kept secret in the industry. This article is thus based on practical experience gained over more than 15 years working with venture capitalists on specific underperforming portfolio companies. It hopes to shed some light on how problems are identified and on the types of problems most often encountered. Managements' need to change and adapt over time to new challenges within their organization and marketplace is being dealt with here. We will also discuss how problems can be addressed. Special emphasis will be given to the role of the board of directors of portfolio companies in solving problem "deals".

Avoiding Problems

Missed projections, operating losses or negative cash flow might indicate problems, but they do not identify the reasons causing them. In some cases, in particular where an operation never gets off the ground because it is not able to deliver a product that can be sold economically, the problem might be obvious. In other cases, especially with more mature companies, the investment could have some fundamental problem that the placement memorandum and the due diligence conducted prior to investment did not reveal. Needless to say, even what appears to be a most exciting investment opportunity warrants careful scrutiny. It should be remembered that the owner willing to sell and the management of the target company know much more about the business than what can be determined in due diligence. Some things can only be found out once on the inside.

A more thorough investigation up front, especially at the operating level, could sometimes have uncovered issues that later became significant problems. An extra effort on due diligence is well spent to avoid having to attempt to turn a "frog into a princess". In addition, not uncovering an existing or potential problem, the investors are likely to have overpaid, further hurting the potential return.

Identifying Problems

What primarily concerns us here are the underperforming "deals" that were good initial investments, but for some reason, maybe a year or two later, are no longer meeting expectations. Portfolio companies that are well established with sales typically in the $5-50 million range are our focus. The company is beyond the "burn rate" associated with the start-up phase. There is no longer a question of the fundamentals (product, market and maybe not even management). However, the board repeatedly is disappointed by shortfalls in sales, margin or cash flow but is unclear as to the real cause. The IPO planned down the line seems ever more distant.

The immediate reaction to this situation from most directors with whom I have worked is that the CEO needs to be replaced. An excellent management team and CEO are almost always the most important factors to getting superior results from a venture investment. However, poor results far less often reflect poor management. In addition, many times the CEO of a company at this stage of its development might have product or market knowledge that is very difficult to replace.

With a good management team and experienced directors on the board, inadequate information is, in my experience, the most common deterrent to identifying the problem. When an operation is small, the CEO is in frequent personal contact with all aspects of the enterprise. As it grows and becomes more complex, the information systems become outmoded. It is not unusual to find a rapidly growing $15 MM company with management systems that barely could support a $5 MM operation. A national rollout of an initially proven successful concept is prone to this type of failure.

Most board packages for small to mid sized companies, at least with financially oriented owners, do not reveal the effect on profitability and cash flow from changes in the customer structure or product mix. In many cases, if the management or the board had a better appreciation for the product and market dynamics and had more timely access to the right information, they would have started to address some of the issues confronting the company with disappointing performance.

A related problem area is the management and board reporting of cost structures. I worked with one investment where, unfortunately, I had to inform the Board that what management reported and what had been accepted by the investors from the time of their investment as fixed costs, in fact, were variable with growth. In other words, with sales increasing, things for this company were not going to get better!

As a venture grows, more emphasis needs to be given to where the margin is generated and less to sales growth. Margin reporting by product or district is something any well-established company takes for granted but something a start-up is not born with. Unless stronger systems are implemented in time, a good investment can become a problem "deal" along the way.

Fundamental problems sometimes cannot be fixed without fundamental changes. As a company develops, management's information needs change. If this is addressed, potential problems often can be identified before the problems become serious. If the company has been subject to a major shift in its circumstances, it might require in-depth work, which is time consuming, just to identify the relationship to the symptoms - weak sales or margins or cost overruns.

Management and the investors might be rutted in an established way of approaching their business, sometimes only relying on information generated by accountants for fiscal reasons. This makes the identification of problems and solutions more difficult. There might be suspicions as to what needs to be changed. The raw data from which the problem can be identified generally are available to management, if not to the board. However, the information needs to be put together in different ways for management to see that they need to redirect their efforts.

Some of the causes of problem deals seem basic in hindsight, so much so that one wonders how they could elude sophisticated, venture-dominated boards. Often, a solution that seems obvious in retrospect, once a new focus has been given to the situation, was very difficult to uncover and has required significant effort to implement.

The Causes of Problem "Deals"

The incidence of the problems I have mentioned so far, in my experience, seems to increase with less industry specialization of the fund and greater geographical distance from the lead investor(s) to the portfolio company. Another issue contributing to problems is a lack of commitment from a particular investor. For example, when there are multiple minority investors or when owners no longer are working with a common objective, problem "deals" seem to appear more often.

Many companies reach $5 or $10 MM in sales on the strength of a superior or novel product offering. The problem initially has been to produce it consistently at an attractive enough cost. It is often at this stage that the venture investors come in, inheriting the management and the sometimes rudimentary organizations and systems the entrepreneur has relied on. I have been surprised to find that companies even beyond this size, as competition has entered for the first time, have to be persuaded to develop something as basic as a sales force and all that comes with it.

For example, a medical service firm had developed a new elective procedure for an indication that previously had not been successfully addressed. It was of great benefit to a major market segment. Business grew rapidly based on patient demand, and the company went public to finance a rollout of its operations nationally. The procedure became well accepted. Then, many physicians started to enter the field providing competition, and the initially pent-up demand was dwindling. The company faced major losses, and the stock price tumbled. The market had fundamentally changed, but the company was too involved in addressing other issues to see it. While the company was marketing directly to consumers, referring physicians were now directing their patients to treatment with specialist colleagues. To address this major change in the marketplace, marketing based on direct sales to referring physicians needed to be developed in place of the previous consumer-oriented efforts. The new customer definition also had major repercussions in terms of the product offering and how the company had to be organized. In the year following the implementation of the new strategy, the stock recovered to more than three times its low.

It is not only the customer definition that can get off track. Once a small company gets the product or service to work well technically, there could be a brief spurt of growing sales that level off later. Based on an intimate understanding of how the market accepts it, the product definition might need to be revamped. The technically skilled entrepreneur sometimes needs support to structure the pricing differently or to aim the product for a different use before sales can successfully take off again.

In some situations, founders have proven unable to learn to manage through delegation, a necessity caused by growth. Others are unable to deal in a more leveraged environment resulting from being bought. Still others chafe at sharing control with new investors. Often, these kinds of problems, one type of which we might call hurdle problems, can be solved by supplementing or temporarily supporting the CEO to get over the hurdle.

There seems always to be the suggestion that more money from the investors will solve the shortfall to expectations. From companies that have gotten beyond the startup phase, a request for more money without a plan for change is more often a sign that there is a problem than an indication of the real cause of it. Buying time rarely makes problems go away. On the other hand, few new game plans can be implemented without the support of additional funds.

How are the Problems Best Addressed?

The best solutions come from management. They know the business. They implement changes and live with them. The issue becomes to get management to accept that often painful change is required and get it focused on addressing it.

Working through a new business plan could be what is called for. To gain perspective, time away from an intense office environment could be productive if thoroughly prepared for beforehand with the help of a neutral outsider. Replacement or addition of certain key management functions, maybe only on a temporary basis, might be a solution. A significant legal problem or real estate-related issues could, for example, become a major distraction for an excellent management team. Relieving management from dealing directly with such issues could be another way a hurdle could be overcome. Finally, while the management team generally is growing with the greater challenge, certain members of it might not be. It is very difficult to realize that this is the case and to take the necessary steps of letting one of the original members of the team go. The board has a big role here as it is, of course, unusual for CEOs to admit their own or their team's shortcomings and ask for help.

Role of the Board in Solving Problem Deals

To optimize the return on a venture portfolio, partners' limited time needs to be spent where major improvements can be obtained. Our study of portfolio returns shows that to get the most out of few very "big winners" is critical. To accept failures and to make the hard decision to cut the losses early preserves time and money for better use elsewhere. However, many excellent investments run into hurdles that management will not overcome by themselves. The investors and the board need to determine if the investment is likely to justify a significant personal commitment and if there is someone available with the necessary capabilities. If that is not the case, and appropriate outside support cannot be found, an early exit might be the best alternative. This it true even though a great return could be achieved if the problems facing the investment could be overcome. Unfortunately, even if there is an opportunity to get back on track, it often is hidden until well into the effort, making a commitment to address a problem investment a very difficult choice for the board.

A management team should be able to deal well with all recurring issues facing the company. If this is not the case, it needs to be permanently strengthened. The role of an effective board should be to guide the strategic development and intervene when objectives are not met.

While problems are sometimes difficult to pinpoint, they are even more difficult for the board to try to take care of itself. Addressing a problem "deal" can also prove quite time consuming, not the least since after one problem is solved, another often surfaces. When a portfolio company underperforms, it is very rare that the problem can be isolated to one particular area that can be addressed by a specialist — for example, a marketing consultant if sales are falling short. A representative of the board, maybe the chairman or a neutral outsider working closely with the board, needs to spend significant time, preferably on location, with several senior management members. Together they must identify the issues and agree on a new direction. An overall approach needs to be taken and agreement needs to be reached as to what financial objectives are realistic in the short term.

Some investors believe that a sudden crisis in a portfolio company can be addressed best by hiring a "crisis manager" to take over the operations. This appears to relieve the board of its immediate responsibility and indicate it has addressed the problem. This course of action might be appropriate for bigger, established companies that have become complacent or where the cost structure is in need of restructuring. It is generally far less beneficial for the small, more delicate venture investment that has hit a rough patch. A more careful approach is called for here to regain the momentum.

Companies that have reached the rollout stage or growth stage have already established a way of operating. It is always difficult for entrepreneurs and their organizations to change from the set course. Once a new plan has been agreed to, the board needs to make sure it gets implemented in a timely fashion. We should remember that small growing companies are perpetually short of resources, not the least of which is qualified management personnel. To find the time to go beyond the issues of the day, to rethink strategic issues and implement new solutions in a demanding operating environment, often requires continuous outside support.

Many managements of small companies are as puzzled about their financial backers' business as the investors are regarding what to do with their investment. Crudely put, fund-raising skills and transaction experience do not always translate into appreciation for operating management problems and the skills required to solve them. There could also be prejudices on both sides. A genuine distrust, not necessarily possible to work through in board meetings, can result in the board being told what management perceives it to want to hear. When directors are distrustful of the CEO, establishing contacts directly with others in the company beyond the CFO, an unhealthy working environment and further problems ensue.

Problems Can Be Overcome

Most of the time, the combination of issues facing an underperforming company at a particular critical time is unique and needs to be addressed as such, keeping in mind the many personalities involved. Thinking you have encountered the same problem earlier and offering a proven solution, rarely, if ever, holds up once all the specific facts are on the table. In the course of advising directors and managements, I have experienced that what I believed were the key issues more than a month into an engagement proved no longer to be the main problems once the board's and management's opinions had been challenged. New assumptions developed from a different perspective and backed up by additional data helped uncover the true issues that needed to be addressed.

As mentioned earlier, having developed a good grasp of the nature of the problem and addressing it early can lead to significant improvements in the investment result. Thinking of the problem, such as a crisis in sales or cash flow, as a sign of a hurdle that needs to be overcome, rather than a reason to undo and redo what has worked well enough up until recently, could permit the investors to unleash a basically great investment and enhance the return of the portfolio. It should be kept in mind that even among the super success stories that make up the lore of the venture capital industry, few had a straight-line experience getting there.

The Geography of Venture Capital Firms

Matthew Zook

Matthew Zook *is a leading researcher on high technology and regional economic development. His research spans topics as diverse as the role of venture capital in regional development, the geography of the Internet industry, and IT training programs for disadvantaged adults. He holds a Master's degree from Cornell University and is currently finishing his Ph.D. at the University of California, Berkeley on the role of venture capital in the development of the Internet industries in the San Francisco Bay and New York regions. He can be reached at zook@socrates.berkeley.edu.*

Introduction

The past several years have been record-breaking in the size of venture funds raised, the amount of money invested, and the number of new companies receiving venture financing. In many ways it seems that there is an unlimited amount of capital available for entrepreneurs to pursue, but in truth, all venture capital is not created equal. Although at the most basic level, capital has unlimited mobility, the importance of human judgement, contacts and frequent face to face interaction can reduce the effective geographic range of venture capital tremendously.

Both venture capitalists and entrepreneurs agree that the actual money in a deal is often the least important aspect of an investment. Entrepreneurs are interested in establishing relationships with people who can help recruit management, provide contacts with other key actors, "legitimize" an enterprise and contribute to overall firm strategy. Venture capitalists also emphasize their non-monetary role in new helping new startups by providing business, management and emotional support in an effort to protect and improve their investment. Thus, rather than the supply of money, the main constraint for many venture investments is the amount of human resources that can be dedicated to evaluating, selecting and shepherding deals. While there has been tremendous growth in the number of venture capital firms and venture capital professionals in the past few years (See Graph 1) it is often the ability for venture capitalists to negotiate deal flow that is most limiting factor.

Venture capitalists, angels and other investors want to have close contact with management because at early stages the risk is quite high. Weekly and even daily phone calls and meetings are not unusual as investors work to protect their investment by providing the support of their experience and contacts. This activity by venture capitalists is only limited by their time and by investing in companies that are closer to them, venture capitalists are able to maximize the return on their time. Therefore, it is common for many venture capitalists to limit their investments to an area which they can easily access. This regional focus also reinforces sectoral and stage preferences among venture capital investments. Although there are advantages in diversification, one sees that venture capital firms in certain regions develop investment tendencies that concentrate on a few specific sectors. Thus, venture capital investing, especially at the seed or startup round, often functions at the regional level within particular sectors.

Graph 1, Number of Venture Capital Offices

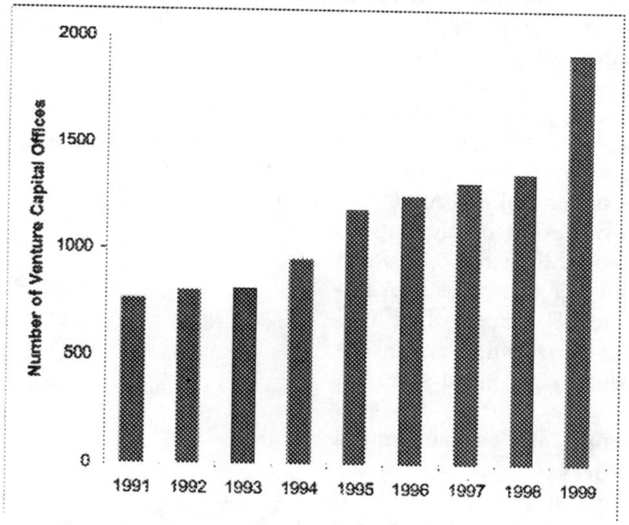

Source: Pratt's Guide to Venture Capital Resources. Various Editions

Although the case of the San Francisco Bay is perhaps the most marked example, other regions in the United States and abroad such as Austin, Texas and Dublin, Ireland also exhibit this local focus. This is not to argue that no venture capital comes from outside a region, but to say that the nature and characteristics of region's venture capital system is important in understanding venture capital investments. Just as each venture capitalist brings different resources to a deal, different regions have various characteristics that they offer which makes certain types of deals more likely to happen. Recognizing this will enable entrepreneurs to understand how and where they might best go to raise venture capital.

Table 1, Number of Venture Capital Offices and Number of Investments, 2000

Metropolitan Area	Total Offices	VC Investments 2000	Ratio of Investments in Region / Total VC Offices
New York Metropolitan Region (*)	356	471	1.32
San Francisco Bay (*)	288	1571	5.45
Boston Metropolitan Region (*)	160	515	3.22
Los Angeles, CA (*)	149	297	1.99
Chicago Metropolitan Region (*)	93	131	1.41
Washington, DC (*)	79	308	3.90
Austin, TX	47	131	2.79
Philadelphia, PA (*)	44	97	2.20
Dallas-Fort Worth, TX (*)	43	111	2.58
Denver, CO (*)	41	129	3.15
Minneapolis-St Paul MN	39	70	1.79
Atlanta GA	33	157	4.76
Pittsburgh PA	29	88	3.03
Seattle, WA (*)	26	165	6.35
San Diego CA	20	148	7.40
United States	1922	5612	2.92

Source: Pratt's Guide to Venture Capital Resources, Online Edition – Aggregated by Zook
*All regions are Metropolitan Statistical Areas (MSA); * Indicates a Consolidated MSA (CMSA). e.g. the San Francisco CMSA consists of several MSAs including San Francisco, San Jose, and Oakland-Berkeley; Number of Venture Capital Investments is based on data from VentureEconomics*

Regional Characteristics of Venture Capital

In order to illustrate how the nature of venture capital firms differs from region this article aggregates the characteristics of venture capital firms given in the various edition of Pratt's guide to the metropolitan level. This level of geography rather than the state level provides a more accurate sense of how venture financing works since it is possible to look at metropolitan regions that cross state boundaries, e.g. New York, and differentiate between regions within the same state, e.g. San Francisco and Los Angeles. This article provides information on the top 15 metropolitan regions which together comprise approximately 80 percent of the venture capital offices and investments in the United States.

Table 2, Percentage of Types of VC Firms in Regions, 2000

Metropolitan Region	Percentage of Firms that are.... Private Venture Capital Firm	Investment banking or merchant banking firm	Consulting firm arranging private placements	SBIC (Small Business Investment Company)	Other
New York Metropolitan Region (*)	57.9	16.9	6.5	5.6	13.2
San Francisco Bay (*)	81.9	6.9	2.8	2.1	6.3
Boston Metropolitan Region (*)	76.9	6.3	5.6	1.9	9.4
Los Angeles, CA (*)	65.1	12.8	4.0	6.7	11.4
Chicago Metropolitan Region (*)	63.4	9.7	5.4	2.2	19.4
Washington, DC (*)	60.8	8.9	5.1	10.1	15.2
Austin, TX	44.7	12.8	2.1	19.1	21.3
Philadelphia, PA (*)	59.1	11.4	2.3	6.8	20.5
Dallas-Fort Worth, TX (*)	74.4	7.0	7.0	4.7	7.0
Denver, CO (*)	56.1	12.2	9.8	7.3	14.6
Minneapolis-St Paul MN	69.2	7.7	0.0	5.1	17.9
Atlanta GA	57.6	18.2	18.2	0.0	6.1
Pittsburgh PA	65.5	6.9	6.9	0.0	20.7
Seattle, WA (*)	80.8	3.8	11.5	0.0	3.8
San Diego CA	80.0	0.0	5.0	0.0	15.0
United States	**63.8**	**10.7**	**5.7**	**6.2**	**13.6**

Source: Pratt's Guide to Venture Capital Resources, Online Edition Aggregated by Zook
*All regions are Metropolitan Statistical Areas (MSA); * Indicates a Consolidated MSA (CMSA). e.g. the San Francisco CMSA consists of several MSAs including San Francisco, San Jose, and Oakland-Berkeley.*

Supply of Venture Capital Offices

The first thing to consider is simply the number of venture capital offices in a metropolitan area. (See Table One) This measure is dominated by the New York and San Francisco Bay regions which together contain thirty-four percent of all venture capital offices.

Another and perhaps better indicator of this intensity is the ratio of investments to offices in the last column. In addition to San Francisco one sees other "hot spots" such as San Diego, Seattle, and Atlanta. New York and Chicago, despite their sizable concentrations of VC offices receive the lowest number of VC investments per office which suggests that these regions likely concentrate on larger deals and/or invest outside of their regions.

Types of Firms

However, understanding the differences in intensity of investment activity between these metropolitan regions involves looking at a number of factors and it is important to understand the types of firms that operate within a metropolitan region. Pratt's Guide identifies several types of venture capital firms, the four most frequently cited of which are outlined in Table Two. As in the previous table, one sees a great deal of variation between regions. The San Francisco Bay region leads the country with the percentage of its firms which are private venture capital firms (the "classic" limited partnership). Other regions such as New York and Atlanta are much more heavily concentrated towards investment banking. This structure provides a good indication of what kind of venture capital firm it would make most sense to pursue given the supply.

Table 3, Preferred Stage of Investment, 2000

Metropolitan Region	Percentage of Firms that prefer the following stages... Seed, R&D, Startup	First and Second	Mezzanine	Leveraged Buyouts	Other**
New York Metropolitan Region (*)	20.5	30.6	10.6	18.1	20.3
San Francisco Bay (*)	40.2	32.9	8.4	8.0	10.4
Boston Metropolitan Region (*)	29.5	36.1	9.7	11.7	13.0
Los Angeles, CA (*)	27.3	25.8	7.6	20.5	18.9
Chicago Metropolitan Region (*)	20.3	33.1	6.8	19.5	20.3
Washington, DC (*)	30.6	36.3	12.9	8.9	11.3
Austin, TX	40.0	28.6	8.6	8.6	14.3
Philadelphia, PA (*)	20.9	35.5	12.7	18.2	12.7
Dallas-Fort Worth, TX (*)	26.6	26.6	10.1	20.3	16.5
Denver, CO (*)	39.7	34.9	7.9	9.5	7.9
Minneapolis-St Paul MN	40.4	31.6	5.3	14.0	8.8
Atlanta GA	17.6	36.5	8.1	20.3	17.6
Pittsburgh PA	22.9	37.1	14.3	17.1	8.6
Seattle, WA (*)	35.9	37.5	12.5	7.8	6.3
San Diego CA	34.4	28.7	8.8	14.1	14.0
United States	**25.9**	**31.1**	**9.2**	**13.8**	**20.0**

Source: Pratt's Guide to Venture Capital Resources, Online Edition Aggregated by Zook
All regions are Metropolitan Statistical Areas (MSA); Indicates a Consolidated MSA (CMSA), e.g. the San Francisco CMSA consists of several MSAs including San Francisco, San Jose, and Oakland-Berkeley.*
***Other includes Special Situations, Control Block Purchases, and Industry Rollups*

Preferred Stage of Investment

Also important in understanding the difference between regions is the stage at which VC firms generally prefer to invest in companies. As outlined in Table Three, companies looking for early stage investment in places such as New York, Philadelphia, and Atlanta may be at a disadvantage since VC firms in these regions tend to concentrate on much later stage investments. Conversely, the venture capital systems in the San Francisco Bay and Austin have a strong focus on the earliest points in a firms lifecycle.

While locating in a region that has a high percentage of VC firms that prefer to invest at the seed or startup round does not guarantee an entrepreneur capital, it does provide a more receptive and insightful audience. Venture capital firms that focus on mezzanine financing or leveraged buyouts are less prepared to access the risks and rewards that early stage companies offer. Moreover, each stage of a company's life brings its own challenges, and a supply of venture capitalists who specialize in certain rounds provide the most value to a firm.

Sectoral Preference

The final preference with which to compare regions are firms' preferences for which sector to invest. Table Four outlines the percentage of firms in a region that prefer to invest in a particular sector with scores that are at least 50 percent more than the national average in each sector marked in bold. Again there are clear differences between regions with both New York and Chicago not exhibiting any particularly strong sectoral preference for investments. Contrasting this are the clear regional preference for investment in particular sectors. From Houston's focus on energy, to Minneapolis's concentration in medical and the San Francisco Bay's strength in communications, computers and electronics, one see connections between the existing industries of a region and the focus of its venture capital activity.

Although it is not possible to assign causality, i.e. do the sectoral preferences of venture capital firms encourage the formation of certain types of firms or does the availability of good firms in a particular sector shape the preferences of venture capital, it does demonstrate the tight connection between venture capital and local firms. Moreover, in many ways this is a chicken-or-the-egg question since causality clearly runs in both directions. What is more important, is recognizing that venture capital systems operate at the regional level and differ tremendously between regions.

Table 4, Sectoral Preference, 1999

Metropolitan Region	Communications	Computer	Consumer	Distribution	Electronics & Instruments	Energy	Genetic Engineering	Industrial	Medical
New York Metropolitan Region*	14.7	22.4	13.6	3.1	2.9	4.2	1.2	9.8	28.0
San Francisco Bay, CA*	**22.9**	**29.5**	9.0	2.2	**8.0**	0.1	2.4	3.3	22.6
Boston, MA Region*	20.0	21.9	7.5,	1.5	6.6	0.9	0.2	4.6	**36.6**
Los Angeles, CA*	8.5	12.3	**49.2**	2.6	6.8	0.1	0.0	9.4	11.0
Chicago, IL Region*	16.4	11.9	18.6	5.1	3.6	4.2	0.4	15.9	23.9
Washington, DC*	**27.8**	10.7	10.5	0.6	1.9	0.9	0.6	12.9	**34.1**
Austin, TX	21.6	12.3	**44.1**	**11.5**	0.0	0.0	0.0	3.5	7.1
Philadelphia, PA*	19.0	**27.4**	12.7	0.0	**8.7**	1.7	**8.3**	4.4	17.8
Dallas-Fort Worth, TX*	**30.0**	20.1	**23.6**	5.1	6.0	0.0	0.0	9.4	5.8
Denver, CO*	**41.0**	19.7	3.5	5.2	**8.0**	0.6	1.5	14.8	5.5
Minneapolis-St Paul MN	16.1	15.7	17.9	3.6	0.2	0.2	0.0	3.4	**42.8**
Atlanta GA	7.1	3.9	1.7	**13.3**	0.5	3.1	0.0	**61.7**	8.6
Pittsburgh PA	19.6	13.1	**20.4**	3.2	2.6	0.0	0.0	**29.7**	11.4
Seattle, WA*	6.8	**25.2**	3.6	0.0	2.1	1.1	0.8	1.8	**58.5**
San Diego CA	11.9	**33.6**	13.0	3.4	2.9	3.0	**7.0**	0.9	24.4
United States	**15.2**	**16.1**	**13.9**	**5.2**	**4.8**	**3.3**	**1.9**	**11.9**	**22.5**

Source: Pratt's Guide to Venture Capital Resources, 1999 Edition Aggregated by Zook
All regions are Metropolitan Statistical Areas (MSA); Indicates a Consolidated MSA (CMSA), e.g. the San Francisco CMSA consists of several MSAs including San Francisco, San Jose, and Oakland-Berkeley*

Conclusion

Clearly despite the mobility of capital, geography remains an important element in the venture capital investment process. The data presented here has demonstrated that regions have specific sectoral, geographical and stage of investment preferences which contributes to the types of firms that become established. However, these tendencies are not written in stone and have evolved over time as regions develop systems that work for them. For example, in the past two years with the advent of electronic commerce, New York's venture system is changing with more emphasis than ever on early round financing.

Entrepreneurs should keep this in mind and while it is not necessary to move to a region that has more advantageous characteristics, they would do well to recognize what seems to work in their region. Not because a firm's location absolutely determines its success or failure but because sources and structures of venture financing vary and thus so must the strategies and techniques that entrepreneurs use to acquire startup capital.

Directories

United States Venture Capital Firms

This directory contains information on over 1,400 venture capital firms. Most of the listees are U.S.-based. They appear in this section. The subsequent section lists venture firms from around the world. Although this information has been compiled on the basis of data received from these companies and without additional verification, we believe that the data accurately represent the interests and structure of these firms.

Names of the managers for the independent venture firms are included, but only appropriate officers are listed for investment banking operations, commercial banks, insurance companies and operating companies with venture activities. Each company has indicated the appropriate people to contact about new financing proposals.

Venture firms have been categorized by type of organization. For instance, if the company is a private venture firm, SBIC, or a subsidiary of an operating company. Differences between these categories are described in the text. "Affiliation" refers to the existence of a parent firm or an involved partner or organization. Describing the venture activities of investment banking firms and specialized consultants is complicated because some firms listed will act as intermediaries to assist in raising capital and will also invest in projects with their own capital or that of selected clients. In most cases, such investment will be made only when the individual firm is instrumental in handling private placement activity.

Membership in a national venture capital trade association is indicated. These associations are the National Association of Investment Companies (NAIC); the National Association of Small Business Investment Companies (NASBIC); the National Venture Capital Association (NVCA); and the Western Association of Venture Capitalists (WAVC). The emergence of these organizations has been a significant development since it has fostered cooperation within a previously individualistic industry. Membership in these associations is generally open to venture capital organizations and individual venture capitalists who invest private capital in young companies on a professional basis. In addition, there are many local venture capital associations, too numerous to list.

Entries in the directory show project preferences and each firm's usual extent of involvement. Most firms indicated their minimum and preferred sizes of investment, although when acting as lead investor, many of the firms will often assist in raising money for larger projects. While specific project financings may total $10 million to $15 million, an individual venture firm may invest only $250,000 to $1 million. Investment bankers and consultants, however, generally described the minimum and preferred size of the total private placement-not the amount the investment banking or consulting firm is interested in investing. In some cases, both of these amounts are indicated.

While many firms have expressed an interest in all types of financing, some prefer to finance either early-stage projects (seed, start-up and first-stage financing) or expansion financing (second- and third-stage financing) or buyout or acquisition financings. Firms that only focus on buyout or acquisition financing usually are interested in situations where the investment group assumes a controlling position in the project. For a detailed description of the types of financing, please see the Introduction. A financing stage preference index is provided at the end of the book.

The venture companies have also indicated their criteria for minimum operating standards of new financing proposals (standards such as annual sales and profit and loss status).

This information is designed to indicate the range of interests of the venture firms, but the minimum does not mean that all of a venture company's financings will be this size. This information only indicates that the venture firm will primarily consider projects that meet these minimum standards, except when firms are exclusively oriented to startups or first-stage projects.

Although companies' geographic preferences are included, this does not necessarily indicate strict adherence to these areas; investment opportunities outside these areas may be considered as well. Many times venture capitalists may participate in financing a geographically distant company if a local venture investor also participates. They may, in fact, attempt to interest a venture capitalist located near the company being considered.

In the portfolio breakdown section, each listee was asked to provide a percentage breakdown of its current investment portfolio by industry, on a cost basis.

The portfolio breakdown may should be used in combination with the industry preferences section, where firms indicate in greater detail the areas they would consider for investment, regardless of whether they have invested in them before. Together, the sections give directory users a sense of where venture firms have investment experience and where they expect to make future investments. An index of industry preferences can be found at the end of the book. While these data should serve as a guide, most companies will range outside these expressed interests if they find a project particularly appealing. These descriptions should not, therefore, be taken as the sole interests of a venture firm. The industries listed in the questionnaire were as follows:

Communications
Cable television
Commercial communications
Data communications
Radio and TV
Satellite and microwave communication
Telephone related

Computer Related
Computer graphics, CAD/CAM and CAE
Computer mainframes
Computer services
Internet related
Memory devices
Micro and minicomputers
Office automation
Scanning-related
Software-applications
Software-artificial intelligence
Software-systems
Specialized turnkey systems
Terminals

Consumer
Computer stores/related services
Consumer products
Consumer services
Food and beverage products
Franchise businesses
Hotels and resort areas
Leisure and recreational products
Restaurants
Retailing

Distribution
Communications equipment
Computer equipment
Consumer products
Electronics equipment
Food products
Industrial products
Medical products

Electronic Components and Instrumentation
Analytical and scientific instrumentation
Circuit boards
Component fabrications and testing equipment
Controllers
Electronic components

Fiber optics
Laser related
Semiconductors

Energy/Natural Resources
Alternative energy
Coal related
Drilling and exploration services
Energy conservation
Minerals
Oil and gas exploration and production
Technology-related products/equipment

Genetic Engineering
Agricultural/animal biotechnology
Biosensors
Biotechnology-related research and other services
Biotechnology-related research and production equipment
Human medical diagnostics
Human medical therapeutics
Industrial biotechnology

Industrial Products and Equipment
Chemicals and materials
Controls and sensors
Equipment and machinery
Other industrial automation
Pollution and waste management systems and services
Robotics/vision systems

Medical/Health Related
Diagnostic and therapeutic services
Diagnostic products
Drug delivery
Hospital and clinical labs
Hospital and other institutional management
Pharmaceuticals
Therapeutic equipment

Other
Agriculture, forestry, fishing
Education related
Finance and insurance
Publishing
Real estate
Specialty consulting
Transportation

A number of companies have not listed industry preferences, while others included industries not specified in the list. Also, some firms noted business areas that they would not consider for investments. Other operating characteristics of a venture firm are noted under the heading "additional information." These characteristics may include the year the firm was founded, the total capital under management, number and dollar amount of investments made in the first half of 1999 and the usual method of compensation. Methods of compensation indicate whether the venture firm charges closing fees, placement fees, contingent fees, and so forth. This information provides insights into the way a firm operates, but such policies usually are not written in stone. Each financing tends to be somewhat different, and the firms like to be flexible enough to suit their compensation to the transaction at hand.

ALABAMA

21ST CENTURY HEALTH VENTURES

One Health South Parkway
Birmingham, AL 35243
Phone: 256-268-6250
Fax: 256-970-8928

Management and Staff
W. Barry McRae
William G. Hicks

Whom to Contact
W. Barry McRae
William G. Hicks

Type of Firm
Private Firm Investing Own Capital

Project Preferences

Role in Financing:
Prefer role as deal originator but will also invest in deals created by others

Type of Financing Preferred:
First Stage Financing
Leveraged Buyout
Second Stage Financing

Geographical Preferences

United States
All U.S.

Industry Preferences

Medical/Health
Diagnostic Services
Drug/Equipmt Delivery
Other Therapeutic
Disposable Med. Products
Hospitals/Clinics/Primary

Additional Information
Name of Most Recent Fund: 21st Century Health Ventures Fund
Most Recent Fund Was Raised: 02/01/1998
Year Founded: 1998
Capital Under Management: $100,000,000
Current Activity Level : Inactive / Unknown
Method of Compensation: Return on investment is of primary concern, do not charge fees

CORDOVA VENTURES (FKA:CORDOVA CAPITAL)

4121 Carmichael Road
Suite 301
Montgomery, AL 36106
Phone: 334-271-6011
Fax: 334-260-0120
Website: www.cordovaventures.com

See Georgia for full listing.

FHL CAPITAL CORP.

600 20th Street North
Suite 350
Birmingham, AL 35203
Phone: 205-328-3098
Fax: 205-323-0001

Management and Staff
Kevin Keck

Whom to Contact
Kevin Keck

Type of Firm
Mgt. Consulting Firm

Project Preferences

Role in Financing:
Prefer role as deal originator but will also invest in deals created by others

Type of Financing Preferred:
Leveraged Buyout
Mezzanine
Special Situation

Size of Investments Considered
Min Size of Investment Considered (000s): $500
Max Size of Investment Considered (000s): $1,000

Geographical Preferences

United States
Southeast

Additional Information
Name of Most Recent Fund: FHL Capital Corp.
Most Recent Fund Was Raised: 02/01/1984
Year Founded: 1984
Current Activity Level : Reducing investment activity
Method of Compensation: Function primarily in service area, receive contingent fee in cash or equity

FJC GROWTH CAPITAL CORP.

200 West Side Square
Suite 340
Huntsville, AL 35801
Phone: 256-922-2918
Fax: 256-922-2909

Management and Staff
William Noojin, President

Whom to Contact
William Noojin

Type of Firm
MESBIC not elsewhere classified

Industry Association Membership
Natl Assoc of Investment Cos. (NAIC)
Natl assoc of Small Bus. Inv. Co (NASBIC)

Project Preferences

Role in Financing:
Prefer role as deal originator but will also invest in deals created by others

Type of Financing Preferred:
Mezzanine
Second Stage Financing

Size of Investments Considered
Min Size of Investment Considered (000s): $300
Max Size of Investment Considered (000s): $500

Geographical Preferences

United States
Southeast

Industry Preferences

Communications and Media
Radio & TV Broadcasting

Semiconductors/Other Elect.
Electronics

Consumer Related
Other Restaurants
Hotels and Resorts

Additional Information
Year Founded: 1989
Capital Under Management: $5,800,000
Current Activity Level : Actively seeking new investments
Method of Compensation: Return on invest. most important, but chg. closing fees, service fees, etc.

HARBERT MANAGEMENT CORP.

One Riverchase Parkway South
Birmingham, AL 35244
Phone: 205-987-5500
Fax: 205-987-5707
Website: www.harbert.net

Management and Staff
Charles Miller, Vice President
Joel Piassick, Vice President

Type of Firm
Private Firm Investing Own Capital

Project Preferences

Role in Financing:
Prefer role as deal originator

Type of Financing Preferred:
Generalist PE

Geographical Preferences

United States
All U.S.
Southeast

Additional Information
Name of Most Recent Fund: Harbinger Private Equity Fund I,LLC
Most Recent Fund Was Raised: 06/30/1999
Capital Under Management: $57,500,000
Current Activity Level : Actively seeking new investments
Method of Compensation: Return on investment is of primary concern, do not charge fees

HICKORY VENTURE CAPITAL CORPORATION

301 Washington St. NW
Suite 301
Huntsville, AL 35801
Phone: 256-539-1931
Fax: 256-539-5130
Website: www.hvcc.com

Other Offices

200 West Court Square
Suite 100
Huntsville, AL 35801
Phone: 205-539-1931
Fax: 205-539-5130

Management and Staff
J. Thomas Noojin, President
John Bise, Vice President
Monro Lanier, Vice President

Type of Firm
SBIC Not elsewhere classified

Project Preferences

Role in Financing:
Prefer role as deal originator but will also invest in deals created by others

Type of Financing Preferred:
First Stage Financing
Later Stage
Leveraged Buyout

Size of Investments Considered
Min Size of Investment Considered (000s): $1,000
Max Size of Investment Considered (000s): $7,000

Geographical Preferences

United States
Midwest
Southeast
Texas

Industry Preferences

(% based on actual investment)

Internet Specific	24.1%
Computer Software and Services	14.4%
Medical/Health	13.8%
Communications and Media	10.9%
Other Products	10.1%
Industrial/Energy	10.0%
Consumer Related	9.5%
Semiconductors/Other Elect.	3.6%
Biotechnology	3.3%
Computer Hardware	0.3%

Additional Information
Year Founded: 1985
Capital Under Management: $12,800,000
Current Activity Level : Actively seeking new investments
Method of Compensation: Return on investment is of primary concern, do not charge fees

JEFFERSON CAPITAL FUND, LTD.

P.O. Box 131329
Birmingham, AL 35213
Phone: 205-324-7709

Type of Firm
Private Firm Investing Own Capital

Project Preferences

Role in Financing:
Prefer role as deal originator but will also invest in deals created by others

Type of Financing Preferred:
Control-block Purchases
Leveraged Buyout
Special Situation

Size of Investments Considered
Min Size of Investment Considered (000s): $1,000
Max Size of Investment Considered: No Limit

Geographical Preferences

United States
Mid Atlantic
Northeast
Southeast

Industry Preferences

Communications and Media
Telecommunications

Semiconductors/Other Elect.
Sensors

Medical/Health
Medical Products
Pharmaceuticals

Consumer Related
Entertainment and Leisure
Consumer Products
Education Related

Industrial/Energy
Industrial Products
Materials
Factory Automation
Environmental Related

Manufact.
Publishing

Additional Information
Year Founded: 1991
Capital Under Management: $10,000,000
Current Activity Level : Actively seeking new investments
Method of Compensation: Return on invest. most important, but chg. closing fees, service fees, etc.

PARADIGM VENTURE PARTNERS I(FKA:EMERGING TECHNOLOGY PARTNERS

500 Beacon Parkway West
Birmingham, AL 35209
Phone: 205-943-5646
Fax: 205-943-8565

Management and Staff
G.Michael Alder, Chief Executive Officer
Philip Hodges, Vice President

Type of Firm
Private Firm Investing Own Capital

Industry Association Membership
National Venture Capital Association (NVCA)

Additional Information
Year Founded: 2000
Current Activity Level : Actively seeking new investments

PRIVATE CAPITAL CORP.

100 Brookwood Place
4th Floor
Birmingham, AL 35209
Phone: 205-879-2722
Fax: 205-879-5121

Other Offices

420 Office Park Drive
Suite 150
Birmingham, AL

Management and Staff
William Acker, Vice President

Type of Firm
Private Firm Investing Own Capital

Project Preferences

Role in Financing:
Prefer role as deal originator but will also invest in deals created by others

Type of Financing Preferred:
First Stage Financing
Leveraged Buyout
Mezzanine
Second Stage Financing
Special Situation
Start-up Financing

Size of Investments Considered
Min Size of Investment Considered (000s): $500
Max Size of Investment Considered (000s): $1,000

Geographical Preferences

United States
Southeast

Industry Preferences

Communications and Media
Commercial Communications
Telecommunications
Data Communications
Other Communication Prod.

Computer Hardware
Computers
Computer Graphics and Dig
Integrated Turnkey System

Computer Software
Computer Services
Systems Software
Applications Software

Internet Specific
Internet

Semiconductors/Other Elect.
Analytic/Scientific

Medical/Health
Drug/Equipmt Delivery
Other Therapeutic
Medical Products
Hospital/Other Instit.

Consumer Related
Retail
Education Related

Industrial/Energy
Industrial Products

Financial Services
Financial Services

Manufact.
Office Automation Equipmt

Additional Information
Name of Most Recent Fund: Private Capital Corporation
Most Recent Fund Was Raised: 05/01/1989
Year Founded: 1973
Capital Under Management: $5,000,000
Current Activity Level : Actively seeking new investments
Method of Compensation: Return on invest. most important, but chg. closing fees, service fees, etc.

SBCA/A.G. BARTHOLOMEW & ASSOCIATES

P.O. Box 231074
Montgomery, AL 36123-1074
Phone: 334-284-3640

Type of Firm
Mgt. Consulting Firm

Project Preferences

Role in Financing:
Prefer role in deals created by others

Type of Financing Preferred:
First Stage Financing
Leveraged Buyout
Second Stage Financing
Special Situation
Start-up Financing

Size of Investments Considered
Min Size of Investment Considered (000s): $2,000
Max Size of Investment Considered: No Limit

Geographical Preferences

United States
Southeast

Industry Preferences

Communications and Media
Commercial Communications
Radio & TV Broadcasting
Data Communications
Satellite Microwave Comm.
Other Communication Prod.

Computer Hardware
Computers
Mainframes / Scientific
Mini and Personal/Desktop
Computer Graphics and Dig
Terminals
Disk Relat. Memory Device

Computer Software
Computer Services
Systems Software
Applications Software
Artificial Intelligence

Semiconductors/Other Elect.
Electronics

Medical/Health
Diagnostic Services
Drug/Equipmt Delivery
Pharmaceuticals

Consumer Related
Retail
Computer Stores
Franchises(NEC)
Food/Beverage
Consumer Products
Consumer Services
Other Restaurants
Education Related

Industrial/Energy
Industrial Products

Transportation
Transportation

Financial Services
Financial Services
Real Estate

Business Serv.
Consulting Services

Manufact.
Office Automation Equipmt

Additional Information
Year Founded: 1990
Current Activity Level : Actively seeking new investments
Method of Compensation: Professional fee required whether or not deal closes

SOUTHEASTERN TECHNOLOGY FUND

7910 South Memorial Parkway
Suite F
Huntsville, AL 35802
Phone: 256-883-8711
Fax: 256-883-8558

Management and Staff
Chris Horgen, Managing Partner
Tina Carley, Chief Financial Officer

Type of Firm
Private Firm Investing Own Capital

Industry Association Membership
Mid-Atlantic Venture Association

Project Preferences

Type of Financing Preferred:
Early Stage
Expansion
First Stage Financing
Second Stage Financing

Size of Investments Considered
Min Size of Investment Considered (000s): $500
Max Size of Investment Considered (000s): $5,000

Geographical Preferences

United States
Southeast

Industry Preferences

(% based on actual investment)

Internet Specific	64.6%
Computer Software and Services	33.2%
Communications and Media	2.2%

Additional Information
Name of Most Recent Fund: Southeastern Technology Fund
Most Recent Fund Was Raised: 09/01/1998
Capital Under Management: $20,000,000
Current Activity Level : Actively seeking new investments

ARIZONA

CNI VENTURES

200 East Van Buren Street
Phoenix, AZ 85004
Website: www.cniventures.com

Other Offices

101 Convention Center Drive
Suite 850
Las Vegas, NV 89109

Management and Staff

Howard Finberg, Vice President
Monte Miller, Partner

Type of Firm

Non-Financial Corp. Affiliate or Subsidiary

Additional Information

Current Activity Level : Actively seeking new investments

COLUMBINE VENTURE FUNDS, THE

9449 North 90th Street
Suite 200
Scottsdale, AZ 85258
Phone: 602-661-9222
Fax: 602-661-6262

See Colorado for full listing.

CORONADO VENTURE FUND

P.O. Box 65420
Tucson, AZ 85728-5420
Phone: 520-577-3764
Fax: 520-299-8491

Other Offices

P.O. Box 65420
Tucson, AZ 85728-5420
Phone: 602-577-3764
Fax: 602-299-8491

Type of Firm

Private Firm Investing Own Capital

Project Preferences

Role in Financing:

Prefer role as deal originator but will also invest in deals created by others

Type of Financing Preferred:

First Stage Financing
Second Stage Financing
Seed
Start-up Financing

Size of Investments Considered

Min Size of Investment Considered (000s): $100
Max Size of Investment Considered (000s): $500

Geographical Preferences

International

No Preference

Industry Preferences

Communications and Media

Telecommunications
Data Communications

Computer Hardware

Computer Graphics and Dig

Computer Software

Systems Software
Applications Software
Artificial Intelligence

Semiconductors/Other Elect.

Electronic Components
Semiconductor
Sensors
Laser Related
Fiber Optics

Biotechnology

Industrial Biotechnology
Biotech Related Research

Medical/Health

Medical Diagnostics
Diagnostic Services
Diagnostic Test Products
Drug/Equipmt Delivery
Disposable Med. Products

Consumer Related

Retail

Industrial/Energy

Robotics

Additional Information

Name of Most Recent Fund: Coronado Venture Fund
Most Recent Fund Was Raised: 02/01/1989
Year Founded: 1986
Capital Under Management: $4,800,000
Current Activity Level : Actively seeking new investments
Method of Compensation: Return on investment is of primary concern, do not charge fees

ESTREETCAPITAL.COM

660 South Mill Avenue
Suite 315
Tempe, AZ 85281
Phone: 480-968-8400
Fax: 480-968-8480
Website: www.estreetcapital.com

Management and Staff

Doug Newell, Chief Financial Officer
Matt Emsley, President

Type of Firm

Private Firm Investing Own Capital

Project Preferences

Role in Financing:

Will function either as deal originator or investor in deals created by others

Geographical Preferences

United States

All U.S.

Additional Information

Capital Under Management: $25,000,000
Current Activity Level : Actively seeking new investments

KOCH VENTURES

17767 N. Perimeter Drive
Suite 101
Scottsdale, AZ 85255
Phone: 480-419-3600
Fax: 480-419-3606
Website: www.kochventures.com

Other Offices

4111 E. 37th Street North
Wichita, KS 67220

Management and Staff
David Duncan, Vice President
David Gibbens, Vice President
David Noble, Managing Director
J.W. "Joe" Moeller, Chief Executive Officer
Jeff Hardesty, Managing Director
Joel Telpner, Managing Director
John Pittenger, President
Matthew Warta, Vice President
Michael Wilkinson, Vice President
Mike Schmidt, Partner
Ray Gary, President
Rob Kennedy, Managing Director & CFO

Type of Firm
Non-Financial Corp. Affiliate or Subsidiary

Project Preferences

Type of Financing Preferred:
Early Stage
Expansion

Size of Investments Considered
Min Size of Investment Considered (000s): $2,000
Max Size of Investment Considered (000s): $10,000

Industry Preferences

(% based on actual investment)

Semiconductors/Other Elect.	53.5%
Internet Specific	33.4%
Computer Software and Services	7.0%
Other Products	2.6%
Communications and Media	1.9%
Industrial/Energy	1.6%

Additional Information
Name of Most Recent Fund: Koch Venture Capital
Most Recent Fund Was Raised: 01/01/1968
Year Founded: 1993
Current Activity Level : Actively seeking new investments

MCKEE & CO.

7702 East Doubletree Ranch Rd
Suite 230
Scottsdale, AZ 85258
Phone: 480-368-0333
Fax: 480-607-7446

Management and Staff
Ed Nicholson
Jan Koontz
Mark Jazwin

Whom to Contact
Ed Nicholson
Jan Koontz
Mark Jazwin

Type of Firm
Mgt. Consulting Firm

Project Preferences

Role in Financing:
Prefer role as deal originator

Type of Financing Preferred:
Leveraged Buyout
Mezzanine
Second Stage Financing

Size of Investments Considered
Min Size of Investment Considered (000s): $1,000
Max Size of Investment Considered: No Limit

Geographical Preferences

United States
All U.S.

Industry Preferences

Communications and Media
Telecommunications
Data Communications
Other Communication Prod.

Computer Hardware
Computer Graphics and Dig

Computer Software
Applications Software

Internet Specific
Internet

Semiconductors/Other Elect.
Electronics
Electronic Components
Laser Related
Fiber Optics

Biotechnology
Biosensors

Medical/Health
Medical Diagnostics
Diagnostic Test Products
Medical Products
Disposable Med. Products

Consumer Related
Entertainment and Leisure
Retail
Food/Beverage
Consumer Products
Consumer Services
Other Restaurants

Industrial/Energy
Oil & Gas Drilling,Explor
Industrial Products
Machinery

Transportation
Transportation

Financial Services
Financial Services

Additional Information
Year Founded: 1987
Current Activity Level : Actively seeking new investments
Method of Compensation: Professional fee required whether or not deal closes

---

MERITA CAPITAL LIMITED

7350 E. Stetson Dr.
Suite 108-A
Scottsdale, AZ 85251
Phone: 480-947-8700
Fax: 480-947-8766

Management and Staff
David Gwynn, President

Type of Firm
Mgt. Consulting Firm

Project Preferences

Role in Financing:
Prefer role as deal originator but will also invest in deals created by others

Type of Financing Preferred:
First Stage Financing
Mezzanine
Second Stage Financing
Special Situation

Geographical Preferences

United States
Midwest
Northwest
Rocky Mountain
Southwest
West Coast

Industry Preferences

Communications and Media
Communications and Media

Computer Hardware
Mainframes / Scientific
Mini and Personal/Desktop
Computer Graphics and Dig
Disk Relat. Memory Device

Computer Software
Computer Services
Systems Software
Applications Software
Artificial Intelligence

Internet Specific
Internet

Semiconductors/Other Elect.
Electronic Components

Biotechnology
Biotech Related Research

Medical/Health
Medical Diagnostics
Drug/Equipmt Delivery
Pharmaceuticals

Consumer Related
Entertainment and Leisure
Computer Stores
Franchises(NEC)
Food/Beverage
Consumer Products
Consumer Services
Other Restaurants
Hotels and Resorts
Education Related

Industrial/Energy
Oil and Gas Exploration
Oil & Gas Drilling,Explor
Robotics
Machinery
Environmental Related

Financial Services
Financial Services

Business Serv.
Distribution

Manufact.
Office Automation Equipmt

Agr/Forestr/Fish
Agriculture related
Mining and Minerals

Additional Information

Name of Most Recent Fund: Profita Fund I Ky
Most Recent Fund Was Raised: 11/25/1996
Year Founded: 1991
Capital Under Management: $17,200,000
Current Activity Level : Actively seeking new investments
Method of Compensation: Return on invest. most important, but chg. closing fees, service fees, etc.

MILLER CAPITAL CORP

4909 East McDowell Rd.
Phoenix, AZ 85008
Phone: 602-225-0504
Fax: 602-225-9024
Website: www.themillergroup.net

Management and Staff

Rudy Miller, President & Chairman

Type of Firm

Mgt. Consulting Firm

Project Preferences

Role in Financing:
Prefer role as deal originator

Type of Financing Preferred:
First Stage Financing
Recapitalizations
Second Stage Financing

Size of Investments Considered
Min Size of Investment Considered (000s): $1,000
Max Size of Investment Considered (000s): $20,000

Geographical Preferences

United States
All U.S.

Industry Preferences

Communications and Media
Communications and Media
Radio & TV Broadcasting
Wireless Communications
Other Communication Prod.

Computer Hardware
Computers

Computer Other
Computer Related

Semiconductors/Other Elect.
Electronics

Consumer Related
Consumer Products
Education Related

Financial Services
Insurance
Real Estate

Business Serv.
Services
Media

Additional Information

Year Founded: 1995
Current Activity Level : Actively seeking new investments
Method of Compensation: Professional fee required whether or not deal closes

---

SILICON VALLEY BANK

4455 E. Camelback Road
Suite E-290
Phoenix, AZ 85018
Phone: 602-381-8722
Fax: 602-667-3556

See California for full listing.

SOLSTICE CAPITAL LLC

13651 East Camino La Cebadilla
Tucson, AZ 85749
Phone: 520-749-5713
Fax: 520-749-4743

See Massachusetts for full listing.

SUNDANCE VENTURE PARTNERS, L.P.

400 East Van Buren
Suite 750
Phoenix, AZ 85004
Phone: 602-252-3441
Fax: 602-252-1450

See California for full listing.

VALLEY VENTURES (FKA: ARIZONA GROWTH PARTNERS, L.P.)

6720 N Scottsdale Rd
280
Paradise Valley, AZ 85253
Phone: 480-661-6600
Fax: 480-661-6262

Management and Staff
Jock Holliman, General Partner
Michael Collins, General Partner

Type of Firm
Private Firm Investing Own Capital

Industry Association Membership
Natl assoc of Small Bus. Inv. Co (NASBIC)

Project Preferences

Role in Financing:
Prefer role as deal originator but will also invest in deals created by others

Type of Financing Preferred:
Leveraged Buyout
Mezzanine
Second Stage Financing

Geographical Preferences

United States
Rocky Mountain
Southwest

Industry Preferences

Communications and Media
Data Communications
Satellite Microwave Comm.

Semiconductors/Other Elect.
Electronic Components
Sensors
Component Testing Equipmt
Laser Related
Analytic/Scientific

Medical/Health
Diagnostic Test Products
Other Therapeutic
Disposable Med. Products

Industrial/Energy
Materials
Machinery

Additional Information
Name of Most Recent Fund: Valley Ventures II
Most Recent Fund Was Raised: 04/01/1999
Year Founded: 1984
Capital Under Management: $12,000,000
Current Activity Level : Actively seeking new investments
Method of Compensation: Return on investment is of primary concern, do not charge fees

ARKANSAS

ALLTEL VENTURES

1 Allied Drive
Little Rock, AR 72202
Phone: 501-905-8970
Fax: 501-905-8589

Type of Firm
Private Firm Investing Own Capital

Industry Association Membership
National Venture Capital Association (NVCA)

Additional Information
Capital Under Management: $50,000,000
Current Activity Level : Actively seeking new investments

ARKANSAS CAPITAL CORPORATION

225 South Pulaski Street
Little Rock, AR 72201
Phone: 501-374-9247
Fax: 501-374-9425
Website: www.arcapital.com

Management and Staff
Joe Hays, President
Larry Carter, Partner
Sam Walls, Chairman & CEO

Type of Firm
Private Firm Investing Own Capital

Project Preferences

Type of Financing Preferred:
Expansion

Additional Information
Name of Most Recent Fund: Diamond State Ventures, L.P.
Most Recent Fund Was Raised: 07/01/1999
Capital Under Management: $56,000,000
Current Activity Level : Actively seeking new investments

STEPHENS GROUP, INC.

21405 Walnut Grove Trail
Little Rock, AR 72223
Phone: 501-821-2885
Fax: 501-218-2512

Management and Staff
Michael Roher, President

Whom to Contact
Michael Roher

Type of Firm
Private Firm Investing Own Capital

Project Preferences

Role in Financing:
Prefer role as deal originator but will also invest in deals created by others

Type of Financing Preferred:
Control-block Purchases
Industry Rollups
Leveraged Buyout
Mezzanine
Second Stage Financing
Special Situation

Size of Investments Considered
Min Size of Investment Considered (000s): $10,000
Max Size of Investment Considered: No Limit

Geographical Preferences

United States
All U.S.

Canada
All Canada

Industry Preferences

(% based on actual investment)

Consumer Related	27.9%
Medical/Health	21.1%
Computer Software and Services	20.9%
Internet Specific	14.1%
Biotechnology	7.6%
Semiconductors/Other Elect.	4.2%
Communications and Media	2.2%
Industrial/Energy	2.0%

Additional Information
Year Founded: 1998
Capital Under Management: $110,000,000
Current Activity Level : Inactive / Unknown
Method of Compensation: Return on invest. most important, but chg. closing fees, service fees, etc.

CALIFORNIA

21ST CENTURY INTERNET MANAGEMENT PARTNERS,LLC

Two South Park
2nd Floor
San Francisco, CA 94107
Phone: 415-512-1221
Fax: 415-512-2650
Website: www.21vc.com

Management and Staff
J. Neil Weintraut, General Partner
Peter Ziebelman, General Partner

Whom to Contact
Shawn Myers

Type of Firm
Private Firm Investing Own Capital

Industry Association Membership
Western Association of Venture Capitalists (WAVC)

Project Preferences

Role in Financing:
Prefer role as deal originator but will also invest in deals created by others

Type of Financing Preferred:
First Stage Financing
Leveraged Buyout
Mezzanine
Research and Development
Second Stage Financing
Seed
Special Situation
Start-up Financing

Size of Investments Considered
Min Size of Investment Considered (000s): $3,000
Max Size of Investment Considered: No Limit

Geographical Preferences

United States
All U.S.

Canada
All Canada

Industry Preferences

(% based on actual investment)

Internet Specific	55.7%
Computer Software and Services	42.7%
Communications and Media	1.5%

Additional Information
Name of Most Recent Fund: 21st Century Internet Venture Partners II
Most Recent Fund Was Raised: 09/30/1996
Year Founded: 1996
Capital Under Management: $55,000,000
Current Activity Level : Actively seeking new investments
Method of Compensation: Return on investment is of primary concern, do not charge fees

2M INVEST, INC.

1875 South Grant Street
Suite 750
San Mateo, CA 94402
Phone: 650-655-3765
Fax: 650-372-9107
Website: www.2minvest.com

Other Offices

Regus House
75 Cannon Street
London, United Kingdom EC4N 5BN
Phone: 44-207-556-7263
Fax: 44-207-556-7824

Strandvejen 100
Hellerup, Denmark DK-2900
Phone: 45 3945 0100
Fax: 45 3945 0107

Suite 705, No. 148 C
Chung Shaio E. Road, Sec 4
Taipei, Taiwan
Phone: 886 2 2773 0132
Fax: 886 2 2778 1314

Management and Staff
Hans Ole Carsen, Chief Financial Officer
Michael Mathiesen, Managing Director
Robert Hsieh, Managing Director
Soren Brumm, Managing Director
Tim Burrow, Partner
William Hipp, Managing Director

Type of Firm
Private Firm Investing Own Capital

Industry Association Membership
Western Association of Venture Capitalists (WAVC)

Project Preferences

Role in Financing:
Prefer role as deal originator

Type of Financing Preferred:
Start-up Financing

Geographical Preferences

United States
West Coast

International
Australia
Bermuda
United Kingdom

Industry Preferences

(% based on actual investment)

Other Products	34.0%
Internet Specific	29.3%
Computer Software and Services	18.6%
Communications and Media	11.9%
Semiconductors/Other Elect.	4.9%
Consumer Related	1.3%

Additional Information
Year Founded: 1993
Capital Under Management: $40,000,000
Current Activity Level : Actively seeking new investments
Method of Compensation: Return on investment is of primary concern, do not charge fees

550 DIGITAL MEDIA VENTURES

190 9th Street
3rd Floor
San Francisco, CA 94103
Website: www.550dmv.com

See New York for full listing.

ABERDARE VENTURES

One Embarcadero Center
Suite 4000
San Francisco, CA 94111
Phone: 415-392-7442
Fax: 415-392-4264
Website: www.aberdare.com

Management and Staff
Brett Battles, General Partner
Jake Odden, Principal
Paul Klingenstein, General Partner

Type of Firm
Private Firm Investing Own Capital

Industry Association Membership
National Venture Capital Association (NVCA)

Project Preferences

Role in Financing:
Will function either as deal originator or investor in deals created by others

Type of Financing Preferred:
First Stage Financing
Second Stage Financing
Startup

Size of Investments Considered
Min Size of Investment Considered (000s): $500
Max Size of Investment Considered (000s): $7,000

Geographical Preferences

United States
All U.S.

Industry Preferences

Communications and Media
Wireless Communications

Computer Software
Software

Internet Specific
E-Commerce Technology
Internet
Web Aggregration/Portals

Biotechnology
Human Biotechnology

Medical/Health
Medical Therapeutics
Drug/Equipmt Delivery

Additional Information
Current Activity Level : Actively seeking new investments
Method of Compensation: Return on investment is of primary concern, do not charge fees

---

ABINGWORTH VENTURE MANAGEMENT LIMITED

2465 East Bayshore Road
Suite 348
Palo Alto, CA 94303
Phone: 650 565 8296
Fax: 650 565 8295
Website: www.abingworth.co.uk

See Foreign Venture Capital Firms for full listing.

ABS VENTURES

1 Market Plaza, Steuart Tower
Suite 2400
San Francisco, CA 94105
Phone: 415-217-4260
Fax: 415-217-4266
Website: www.absventures.com

See Maryland for full listing.

ACACIA VENTURE PARTNERS

101 California Street
Suite 3160
San Francisco, CA 94111
Phone: 415-433-4200
Fax: 415-433-4250
Website: www.acaciavp.com

Management and Staff
Brian Roberts, Managing Director
Bruce Keller, Managing Director
C. Sage Givens, Managing Director
C. Ted Paff, Managing Director
David Heer, Managing Director
P. Christian Hester, Principal

Whom to Contact
Brian Roberts
Bruce Keller

Type of Firm
Private Firm Investing Own Capital

Industry Association Membership
National Venture Capital Association (NVCA)
Western Association of Venture Capitalists (WAVC)

Project Preferences

Role in Financing:
Prefer role as deal originator

Type of Financing Preferred:
First Stage Financing
Leveraged Buyout
Mezzanine
Second Stage Financing
Seed
Start-up Financing

Size of Investments Considered
Min Size of Investment Considered (000s): $5,000
Max Size of Investment Considered: No Limit

Geographical Preferences

United States
All U.S.

Industry Preferences

(% based on actual investment)

Internet Specific	44.1%
Medical/Health	36.0%
Computer Software and Services	18.3%
Communications and Media	1.6%

Additional Information
Name of Most Recent Fund: Acacia Venture Partners II, L.P.
Most Recent Fund Was Raised: 04/01/1999
Year Founded: 1995
Capital Under Management: $200,000,000
Current Activity Level : Actively seeking new investments
Method of Compensation: Return on investment is of primary concern, do not charge fees

---

ACCEL PARTNERS

428 University Avenue
Palo Alto, CA 94301
Phone: 650-614-4800
Fax: 650-614-4880
Website: www.accel.com

Other Offices

One Palmer Square
Princeton, NJ 08542
Phone: 609-683-4500
Fax: 609-683-0384

Management and Staff
Alan Austin, Chief Operating Officer
Arthur Patterson, General Partner
Bill Lanfri, Partner
Bruce Golden, Partner
G. Carter Sednaoui, Chief Financial Officer
James Flach, Partner
James Breyer, Managing Partner
James Swartz, General Partner
Jim Goetz, Partner
Joseph Schoendorf, Partner
Kevin Comolli, Partner
Mitch Kapor, Partner
Peter Wagner, General Partner
Peter Fenton, Principal
Teri McFadden, Partner
Theresia Ranzetta, Partner

Type of Firm
Private Firm Investing Own Capital

Industry Association Membership
National Venture Capital Association (NVCA)
Western Association of Venture Capitalists (WAVC)

Project Preferences

Role in Financing:
Will function either as deal originator or investor in deals created by others

Type of Financing Preferred:
Early Stage
Seed
Startup

Size of Investments Considered
Min Size of Investment Considered (000s): $1,000
Max Size of Investment Considered: No Limit

Geographical Preferences

United States
All U.S.

International
Belgium
France
Germany
Italy
Luxembourg
Netherlands
United Kingdom

Industry Preferences
(% based on actual investment)

Internet Specific	41.4%
Communications and Media	22.8%
Computer Software and Services	20.7%
Medical/Health	4.7%
Other Products	4.2%
Biotechnology	4.1%
Semiconductors/Other Elect.	1.1%
Computer Hardware	0.9%
Industrial/Energy	0.1%

Additional Information
Name of Most Recent Fund: Accel VII L.P.
Most Recent Fund Was Raised: 07/15/1999
Year Founded: 1983
Capital Under Management: $235,000,000
Current Activity Level : Actively seeking new investments
Method of Compensation: Return on investment is of primary concern, do not charge fees

ACCEL-KKR INTERNET CORP.

428 University Avenue
Palo Alto, CA 94301
Phone: 650-614-4800
Fax: 650-614-4880
Website: www.accel-kkr.com

See New Jersey for full listing.

ACCENTURE TECHNOLOGY VENTURES (FKA: AC VENTURES)

1661 Page Mill Road
Palo Alto, CA 94304
Phone: 650-213-2500
Fax: 650-213-2222
Website: www.accenturetechventures.com

Other Offices

17th Flr Menara PJ, AMCORP Trade Center
18, Persiaran Barat, Off Jalan Timur
Petaling Jaya, Selangor Darul , Malaysia 46050
Phone: 60 (3) 752.4800

5215 North O'Connor Blvd
Suite 2100
Irving, TX 75039
Phone: 972-831-4447

60 Queen Victoria Street
London, United Kingdom EC4N 4TW

Kaistrasse 20
Dusseldorf, Germany 40221
Phone: 49 211 9120 30
Fax: 49 211 9120 333

Management and Staff
Barry Cater, Partner
C. Scott Killips, Partner
Carlisle Kirkpatrick, Principal
Cherine Chalaby, Managing Partner
Clifford Jury, Principal
Daniel Schwartmann, Principal
Elizabeth M Steel, Principal
Jackson Wilson, Managing General Partner
Joel Friedman, Partner
John Kunzweiler, Partner
Laureen Palmer, Principal
Leonard Sherman, Partner
Marty Martinson, Principal
Mary Moussa, Principal
Matt Seebaum, Principal
Paul Hasenwinkel, Principal
Paul Walker, Principal
Peter Kurpis, Principal
Thomas Fischer, Partner
Vincent Hui, Principal

Type of Firm
Private Firm Investing Own Capital

Industry Association Membership
National Venture Capital Association (NVCA)
Western Association of Venture Capitalists (WAVC)

Project Preferences

Role in Financing:
Will function either as deal originator or investor in deals created by others

Type of Financing Preferred:
Balanced
Early Stage
Expansion
Later Stage
Mezzanine
Startup

Geographical Preferences

United States
All U.S.

International
China
Europe
France
Germany
Italy
Japan
Latin America
Middle East
Spain
United Kingdom

Industry Preferences
(% based on actual investment)

Internet Specific	54.3%
Computer Software and Services	22.4%
Other Products	13.7%
Computer Hardware	8.5%
Communications and Media	1.0%

Additional Information
Year Founded: 1999
Capital Under Management: $1,000,000,000
Current Activity Level : Actively seeking new investments
Method of Compensation: Return on investment is of primary concern, do not charge fees

ACCESS VENTURE PARTNERS

319 Laidley Street
San Francisco, CA 94131
Phone: 415-586-0132
Fax: 415-392-6310
Website: www.accessventurepartners.com

See Colorado for full listing.

ACER TECHNOLOGY VENTURES(FKA:ACER SOFT CAPITAL INC.)

5201 Great America Parkway
Suite 270
Santa Clara, CA 95054
Phone: 408-894-7900
Fax: 408-894-7939
Website: www.acer.com

Type of Firm
Non-Financial Corp. Affiliate or Subsidiary

Project Preferences

Role in Financing:
Prefer role as deal originator but will also invest in deals created by others

Type of Financing Preferred:
Early Stage
First Stage Financing
Second Stage Financing
Seed
Start-up Financing

Geographical Preferences

United States
All U.S.

Canada
All Canada

Industry Preferences

Communications and Media
CATV & Pay TV Systems
Data Communications

Computer Hardware
Mini and Personal/Desktop
Computer Graphics and Dig
Disk Relat. Memory Device

Computer Software
Systems Software
Applications Software
Artificial Intelligence

Internet Specific
Internet

Semiconductors/Other Elect.
Electronic Components
Semiconductor
Controllers and Sensors
Component Testing Equipmt
Fiber Optics

Consumer Related
Consumer Products

Additional Information
Year Founded: 1998
Capital Under Management: $300,000,000
Current Activity Level : Actively seeking new investments
Method of Compensation: Return on investment is of primary concern, do not charge fees

ACORN VENTURES, INC.

268 Bush Street
Suite 2829
Daly City, CA 94014
Phone: 650-994-7801
Fax: 650-994-3305
Website: www.acornventures.com

Type of Firm
Private Firm Investing Own Capital

Industry Association Membership
Natl assoc of Small Bus. Inv. Co (NASBIC)

Project Preferences

Role in Financing:
Will function either as deal originator or investor in deals created by others

Type of Financing Preferred:
First Stage Financing
Leveraged Buyout
Second Stage Financing
Seed

Size of Investments Considered
Min Size of Investment Considered (000s): $250
Max Size of Investment Considered: No Limit

Geographical Preferences

International
No Preference

Industry Preferences

(% based on actual investment)

Communications and Media	39.9%
Semiconductors/Other Elect.	24.7%
Computer Hardware	12.6%
Internet Specific	11.6%
Industrial/Energy	5.3%
Medical/Health	2.7%
Computer Software and Services	1.9%
Biotechnology	1.3%

Additional Information
Name of Most Recent Fund: Acorn Ventures
Most Recent Fund Was Raised: 01/01/1986
Year Founded: 1986
Capital Under Management: $20,700,000
Current Activity Level : Reducing investment activity
Method of Compensation: Return on investment is of primary concern, do not charge fees

ADLER & CO.

690 Market Street
Suite 702
San Francisco, CA 94104
Phone: 415-398-6352
Fax: 415-398-6355

See New York for full listing.

ADVANCED TECHNOLOGY VENTURES

485 Ramona Street
Suite 200
Palo Alto, CA 94301
Phone: 650-321-8601
Fax: 650-321-0934
Website: www.atvcapital.com

See Massachusetts for full listing.

ADVENT INTERNATIONAL CORP.

2180 Sand Hill Road
Suite 420
Menlo Park, CA 94205
Phone: 650-233-7500
Fax: 650-233-7515
Website: www.adventinternational.com

See Massachusetts for full listing.

AGILENT VENTURES

395 Page Mill Road
Palo Alto, CA 94303
Phone: 650-752-5598
Fax: 650-752-5771
Website: www.agilent.com

Management and Staff
Maximilian Schroeck, Managing Director

Type of Firm
Non-Financial Corp. Affiliate or Subsidiary

Project Preferences

Type of Financing Preferred:
Early Stage
Second Stage Financing

Size of Investments Considered
Min Size of Investment Considered (000s): $2,000
Max Size of Investment Considered (000s): $10,000

Industry Preferences

Communications and Media
Telecommunications
Wireless Communications
Data Communications

Semiconductors/Other Elect.
Semiconductor
Laser Related
Fiber Optics

Biotechnology
Biotech Related Research

Additional Information
Year Founded: 2000
Capital Under Management: $100,000,000
Current Activity Level : Actively seeking new investments

AL SHUGART INTERNATIONAL (ASI)

920 41st Avenue
Santa Cruz, CA 95062
Phone: 831-479-7852
Fax: 831-479-7852
Website: www.alshugart.com

Other Offices

10001 North De Anza Boulevard
Suite 220
Cupertino, CA 95014
Phone: 408-873-2430
Fax: 408-873-2299

Management and Staff
Al Shugart, General Partner

Type of Firm
Mgt. Consulting Firm

Project Preferences

Type of Financing Preferred:
Early Stage
Seed
Startup

Additional Information
Year Founded: 1998
Capital Under Management: $14,000,000
Current Activity Level : Actively seeking new investments

ALCATEL VENTURES

2029 Century Park East
21st Floor
Los Angeles, CA 90067
Phone: 310-229-0922
Fax: 310-229-0220
Website: www.alcatelventures.com

Other Offices

2882 Sand Hill Road
Suite 100
Menlo Park, CA 94025
Phone: 650-926-9447
Fax: 847-589-4197

Anam Tower Suite 1309
702-10 Yeoksam-Dong, Kangnam-Ku
Seoul 135-080, South Korea
Phone: 82-2-2009-31713
Fax: 82-2-2009-3174

Management and Staff
Charles Rim, Chief Financial Officer
David Fogelsong, General Partner
Jay Yang, Partner
Jeff Stevenson, Partner
Steve Kim, Managing Partner
Victor Lee, Partner

Type of Firm
Non-Financial Corp. Affiliate or Subsidiary

Project Preferences

Role in Financing:
Prefer role as deal originator

Type of Financing Preferred:
Early Stage
Seed

Geographical Preferences

United States
All U.S.

Industry Preferences

(% based on actual investment)

Internet Specific	45.5%
Computer Software and Services	36.0%
Computer Hardware	7.9%
Communications and Media	6.7%
Semiconductors/Other Elect.	3.9%

Additional Information
Name of Most Recent Fund: Alcatel Ventures

Most Recent Fund Was Raised: 01/01/2000
Capital Under Management: $125,000,000
Current Activity Level : Actively seeking new investments

ALCE PARTNERS, L.P.

One First Street
Suite 6
Los Altos, CA 94022
Phone: 650-949-3696
Fax: 650-327-9146

Management and Staff
Doug DeVivo, General Partner

Type of Firm
Private Firm Investing Own Capital

Industry Association Membership
National Venture Capital Association (NVCA)
Western Association of Venture Capitalists (WAVC)

Additional Information
Name of Most Recent Fund: Alce Partners, L.P.
Most Recent Fund Was Raised: 01/01/1997
Capital Under Management: $5,000,000
Current Activity Level : Actively seeking new investments

ALIGNMENT CAPITAL PARTNERS, LLC

10600 North De Anza Blvd.
Suite 250
Cupertino, CA 95014
Phone: 408-873-0500
Fax: 408-873-0550
Website: www.alignmentcapital.com

See Texas for full listing.

ALLEGIS CAPITAL (AKA:ALLEGIS MEDIA TECHNOLOGY VENTURES)

One First Street
Suite Two
Los Altos, CA 94022
Phone: 650-917-5900
Fax: 650-917-5901
Website: www.allegiscapital.com

Other Offices

100 Wilshire Boulevard
Suite 1770
Santa Monica, CA 90401
Phone: 310-319-3888
Fax: 310-319-3881

China Basin Landing Building
185 Berry Street, Suite 3600
San Francisco, CA 94107
Phone: 415-977-0500
Fax: 415-977-0502

Management and Staff
Austin Grose, Chief Financial Officer
Barry Weiman, Managing Director
Jim Friedlich, General Partner
Jonathan Funk, General Partner
Leo Hindery, Venture Partner
Natalie Egleston, General Partner
Peter Gardner, General Partner
Phillippe Bouissou, General Partner
Robert Ackerman, Managing Director

Whom to Contact
Robert R. Ackerman Jr.

Type of Firm
Private Firm Investing Own Capital

Industry Association Membership
Western Association of Venture Capitalists (WAVC)

Project Preferences

Role in Financing:
Prefer role as deal originator but will also invest in deals created by others

Type of Financing Preferred:
Early Stage
Seed

Geographical Preferences

United States
D. of Columbia
West Coast

Industry Preferences

(% based on actual investment)

Internet Specific	74.7%
Computer Software and Services	18.7%
Communications and Media	2.3%
Computer Hardware	2.1%
Other Products	2.1%

Additional Information
Name of Most Recent Fund: Media technology Ventures III, L.P. (AKA MTV III)
Most Recent Fund Was Raised: 09/01/1998
Year Founded: 1996
Capital Under Management: $700,000,000
Current Activity Level : Actively seeking new investments

ALLIED CAPITAL CORPORATION

One Market Plaza
Stewart Tower, Suite 2605
San Francisco, CA
Phone: 415-904-4508
Fax: 415-904-4503
Website: www.alliedcapital.com

See D. of Columbia for full listing.

ALLOY VENTURES

480 Cowper Street
Palo Alto, CA 94301
Phone: 650-687-5000
Fax: 650-687-5010
Website: www.alloyventures.com

Management and Staff
Craig Taylor, General Partner
Douglas Kelly, General Partner
Ferrell Sanders, General Partner
John Shoch, General Partner
Peter Loukianoff, Partner
Tony Di Bona, Chief Financial Officer

Type of Firm
Private Firm Investing Own Capital

Industry Association Membership
National Venture Capital Association (NVCA)

Industry Preferences

(% based on actual investment)

Internet Specific	35.8%
Computer Software and Services	18.9%
Biotechnology	14.8%
Communications and Media	12.2%
Medical/Health	8.6%
Computer Hardware	5.6%
Semiconductors/Other Elect.	4.1%

Additional Information
Capital Under Management: $345,000,000
Current Activity Level : Actively seeking new investments

ALPINE TECHNOLOGY VENTURES

20300 Stevens Creek Blvd
Suite 495
Cupertino, CA 95014
Phone: 408-725-1810
Fax: 408-725-1207
Website: www.alpineventures.com

Management and Staff
Chuck Chan, General Partner
David Lane, General Partner

Type of Firm
Private Firm Investing Own Capital

Industry Association Membership
Western Association of Venture Capitalists (WAVC)

Project Preferences

Role in Financing:
Prefer role as deal originator but will also invest in deals created by others

Type of Financing Preferred:
First Stage Financing
Research and Development
Second Stage Financing
Seed
Start-up Financing

Industry Preferences

(% based on actual investment)

Internet Specific	40.4%
Computer Software and Services	24.0%
Communications and Media	18.6%
Semiconductors/Other Elect.	6.6%
Industrial/Energy	5.3%
Other Products	2.8%
Computer Hardware	2.2%

Additional Information
Name of Most Recent Fund: Alpine Technology Ventures II
Most Recent Fund Was Raised: 02/15/1995
Year Founded: 1995
Capital Under Management: $72,000,000
Current Activity Level : Actively seeking new investments
Method of Compensation: Return on investment is of primary concern, do not charge fees

ALTA COMMUNICATIONS

One Embarcadero Center
Suite 4050
San Francisco, CA 94111
Phone: 415-362-4022
Fax: 415-362-6178
Website: www.altacomm.com

See Massachusetts for full listing.

ALTA PARTNERS

One Embarcadero Center
Suite 4050
San Francisco, CA 94111
Phone: 415-362-4022
Fax: 415-362-6178
Website: www.altapartners.com

Management and Staff
Alison De Bord, Partner
Alix Marduel, Managing Director
Daniel Janney, General Partner
Edward Penhoet, Partner
Eugene Chen, General Partner
Farah Champsi, Managing Director
Garrett Gruener, Managing Director
Guy Nohra, Managing Director
Hilary Strain, Chief Financial Officer
Jean Deleage, Managing Director
Marino Polestra, Managing Director
Peter Schwartz, Partner
Ravi Chiruvolu, Principal

Type of Firm
Private Firm Investing Own Capital

Industry Association Membership
National Venture Capital Association (NVCA)
Western Association of Venture Capitalists (WAVC)

Project Preferences

Role in Financing:
Prefer role as deal originator but will also invest in deals created by others

Type of Financing Preferred:
First Stage Financing
Mezzanine
Second Stage Financing
Seed
Start-up Financing

Geographical Preferences

United States
West Coast

International
Bermuda
France
Germany
Italy
Spain
United Kingdom

Industry Preferences

(% based on actual investment)

Biotechnology	40.1%
Medical/Health	33.4%
Internet Specific	14.5%
Communications and Media	5.0%
Computer Software and Services	3.7%
Semiconductors/Other Elect.	1.8%
Computer Hardware	1.4%
Industrial/Energy	0.1%

Additional Information
Name of Most Recent Fund: Alta Biopharma, L.P.
Most Recent Fund Was Raised: 10/01/1998
Year Founded: 1996
Capital Under Management: $728,000,000
Current Activity Level : Actively seeking new investments
Method of Compensation: Return on investment is of primary concern, do not charge fees

ALTOS VENTURES

2882 Sand Hill Road
Suite 100
Menlo Park, CA 94025
Phone: 650-234-9771
Fax: 650-233-9821
Website: www.altosvc.com

Management and Staff
Anthony Lee, Principal
Brendon Kim, General Partner
Han Kim, General Partner
Ho Nam, General Partner

Type of Firm
Private Firm Investing Own Capital

Industry Association Membership
National Venture Capital Association (NVCA)
Western Association of Venture Capitalists (WAVC)

Project Preferences

Type of Financing Preferred:
First Stage Financing
Later Stage
Second Stage Financing
Seed
Start-up Financing

Geographical Preferences

United States
West Coast

Industry Preferences

(% based on actual investment)

Internet Specific	60.2%
Computer Software and Services	29.8%
Computer Hardware	6.7%
Consumer Related	2.0%
Medical/Health	1.2%

Additional Information

Name of Most Recent Fund: Altos Fund I
Most Recent Fund Was Raised: 01/01/1996
Year Founded: 1996
Capital Under Management: $50,000,000
Current Activity Level : Actively seeking new investments

AMERINDO INVESTMENT ADVISORS, INC.

One Embarcadero Center
Suite 2300
San Francisco, CA 94111-3162
Phone: 415-362-0292
Fax: 415-362-0533

See New York for full listing.

AMPERSAND VENTURES

162 South Rancho Santa Fe Rd
Suite 870
Encinitas, CA 92024
Phone: 760-632-0626
Fax: 760-632-0284
Website: www.ampersandventures.com

See Massachusetts for full listing.

ANGEL INVESTORS, LP

1538 Las Positas Road
Santa Barbara, CA 93105
Website: www.svangel.com

Management and Staff

Bob Bozeman, General Partner
Casey McGlynn, General Partner
Emily Andrus, Venture Partner
Fred Grauer, General Partner
Ron Conway, General Partner

Type of Firm

Private Firm Investing Own Capital

Project Preferences

Type of Financing Preferred:
Early Stage

Geographical Preferences

United States
Northern California

Industry Preferences

(% based on actual investment)

Internet Specific	83.9%
Computer Software and Services	14.1%
Communications and Media	2.1%

Additional Information

Year Founded: 2000
Current Activity Level : Actively seeking new investments

ANGELS FORUM MANAGEMENT COMPANY

2452 Embarcadero Way
Palo Alto, CA 94303
Phone: 650-857-0700
Fax: 650-857-0773

Management and Staff

Carol Sands, Managing Director
Eric Walczykowski, Partner

Type of Firm

Private Firm Investing Own Capital

Industry Association Membership

National Venture Capital Association (NVCA)

Additional Information

Year Founded: 1999
Current Activity Level : Actively seeking new investments

ANILA FUND (AKA: ANILA.ORG, LLC)

400 Channing Avenue
Palo Alto, CA 94301
Phone: 650-833-5790
Fax: 650-833-0590
Website: www.anila.com

Other Offices

119 University Avenue
Palo Alto, CA 94301

9973 Valley View Road
Suite 100
Eden Prairie, MN 55344

Management and Staff

Gary Schlageter, Venture Partner
Moses Joseph, Managing Partner
Steven Bowden, Venture Partner

Type of Firm

Incubators

Project Preferences

Role in Financing:
Prefer role as deal originator

Type of Financing Preferred:
Early Stage

Geographical Preferences

United States
All U.S.

Industry Preferences

Communications and Media
Telecommunications

Internet Specific
Internet

Additional Information

Current Activity Level : Actively seeking new investments

APIDC-VENTURE CAPITAL LIMITED

26710 Fond Du Lac Road
Rancho Palos Verdes, CA 90275
Phone: 310-373-8027
Fax: 310-378-5917
Website: www.apidcvc.com

See Foreign Venture Capital Firms for full listing.

APPLIED TECHNOLOGY

1010 ElCamino Real
Suite 300
Menlo Park, CA 94025
Phone: 415-326-8622
Fax: 415-326-8163

See Massachusetts for full listing.

APV TECHNOLOGY PARTNERS

535 Middlefield
Suite 150
Menlo Park, CA 94025
Phone: 650-327-7871
Fax: 650-327-7631
Website: www.apvtp.com

Management and Staff
Elaine Erickson, Chief Financial Officer
James Hinson, General Partner
Peter Bodine, General Partner
Spencer Tall, General Partner
Will Stewart, General Partner

Type of Firm
Private Firm Investing Own Capital

Industry Association Membership
National Venture Capital Association (NVCA)
Western Association of Venture Capitalists (WAVC)

Project Preferences

Role in Financing:
Prefer role as deal originator but will also invest in deals created by others

Type of Financing Preferred:
Early Stage

Size of Investments Considered
Min Size of Investment Considered (000s): $2,000
Max Size of Investment Considered (000s): $10,000

Geographical Preferences

United States
All U.S.

Industry Preferences

(% based on actual investment)

Internet Specific	82.5%
Computer Software and Services	7.1%
Computer Hardware	5.0%
Semiconductors/Other Elect.	3.5%
Communications and Media	1.9%

Additional Information
Name of Most Recent Fund: APV Technology Partners, L.P.
Most Recent Fund Was Raised: 01/01/1996
Year Founded: 1996
Capital Under Management: $212,000,000
Current Activity Level : Actively seeking new investments
Method of Compensation: Return on invest. most important, but chg. closing fees, service fees, etc.

ARTEMIS VENTURES

207 Second St. Suite E
3rd Floor
Sausalito, CA 94965
Phone: 415-289-2500
Fax: 415-289-1789
Website: www.artemisventures.com

Management and Staff
Christine Comaford, Managing Director
Jorg Enge, General Partner
Kimball Atwood, General Partner

Type of Firm
Private Firm Investing Own Capital

Industry Association Membership
National Venture Capital Association (NVCA)

Project Preferences

Role in Financing:
Will function either as deal originator or investor in deals created by others

Type of Financing Preferred:
First Stage Financing
Second Stage Financing
Seed

Geographical Preferences

United States
Northeast
Northern California
Northwest
West Coast

Industry Preferences

(% based on actual investment)

Internet Specific	31.1%
Computer Software and Services	28.1%
Other Products	26.8%
Semiconductors/Other Elect.	14.1%

Additional Information
Name of Most Recent Fund: Artemis Ventures
Most Recent Fund Was Raised: 03/12/1999
Capital Under Management: $22,600,000
Current Activity Level : Actively seeking new investments
Method of Compensation: Return on investment is of primary concern, do not charge fees

ARTHUR ROCK & CO.

One Maritime Plaza
Suite 1220
San Francisco, CA 94111
Phone: 415-981-3921
Fax: 415-981-3924

Type of Firm
Private Firm Investing Own Capital

Project Preferences

Role in Financing:
Prefer role as deal originator but will also invest in deals created by others

Type of Financing Preferred:
First Stage Financing
Leveraged Buyout
Seed
Start-up Financing

Size of Investments Considered
Min Size of Investment Considered (000s): $1,000
Max Size of Investment Considered: No Limit

Geographical Preferences

International
No Preference

Industry Preferences

Communications and Media
Communications and Media

Computer Other
Computer Related

Semiconductors/Other Elect.
Electronic Components

Medical/Health
Medical/Health

Additional Information

Year Founded: 1961
Current Activity Level : Actively seeking new investments
Method of Compensation: Return on investment is of primary concern, do not charge fees

ARTISAN DIGITAL MEDIA

2700 Colorado Ave.
2nd Floor
Santa Monica, CA 90404
Phone: 310-449-9200
Fax: 310-255-3940
Website: www.artisanent.com

Management and Staff

Amir Malin, Chief Executive Officer
Bill Block, President
James Keegan, Chief Financial Officer
Ken Schapiro, Chief Operating Officer

Type of Firm

Affiliate/Subsidary of Oth. Financial. Instit.

Industry Preferences

Internet Specific
Internet

Business Serv.
Media

Additional Information

Year Founded: 2000
Current Activity Level : Actively seeking new investments

ASIATECH INTERNET GROUP (ATIG) (FKA: ASIATECH VENTURES)

1250 Bayhill Drive
Suite 201
San Bruno, CA 94066
Website: www.asiatechv.com

See Foreign Venture Capital Firms for full listing.

ASPEN VENTURES (FORMERLY 3I VENTURES)

1000 Fremont Avenue
Suite 200
Los Altos, CA 94024
Phone: 650-917-5670
Fax: 650-917-5677
Website: www.aspenventures.com

Other Offices

10898 Mora Drive
Los Altos, CA 94024
Phone: 415-948-6833
Fax: 415-941-7764

1198 Jefferson Way
Laguna Beach, CA 92651
Phone: 949-494-2707
Fax: 949-497-3753

3343 Peachtree Road, N.E.
East Tower, Suite 1140
Atlanta, GA 30326
Phone: 404-816-4791
Fax: 404-816-4891

Management and Staff

Alexander Clinton, General Partner
Debra Schilling, Chief Financial Officer
E. David Crockett, General Partner
Thaddeus Whalen, General Partner

Type of Firm

Private Firm Investing Own Capital

Industry Association Membership

National Venture Capital Association (NVCA)
Western Association of Venture Capitalists (WAVC)

Project Preferences

Role in Financing:
Prefer role as deal originator but will also invest in deals created by others

Type of Financing Preferred:
Early Stage
Seed

Size of Investments Considered

Min Size of Investment Considered (000s): $500
Max Size of Investment Considered (000s): $3,300

Geographical Preferences

United States
West Coast

Industry Preferences

(% based on actual investment)

Computer Software and Services	29.1%
Medical/Health	15.6%
Internet Specific	13.7%
Biotechnology	10.8%
Communications and Media	10.3%
Computer Hardware	10.3%
Semiconductors/Other Elect.	4.7%
Industrial/Energy	4.3%
Consumer Related	1.2%

Additional Information

Name of Most Recent Fund: Aspen Ventures III, L.P.
Most Recent Fund Was Raised: 01/01/1999
Year Founded: 1991
Capital Under Management: $140,000,000
Current Activity Level : Actively seeking new investments
Method of Compensation: Return on investment is of primary concern, do not charge fees

ASSET MANAGEMENT COMPANY VENTURE CAPITAL

2275 East Bayshore Road
Suite 150
Palo Alto, CA 94303
Phone: 650-494-7400
Fax: 650-856-1826
Website: www.assetman.com

Management and Staff

Craig Taylor, General Partner
Douglas Kelly, General Partner
Franklin Johnson, Founding Partner
Graham Crooke, Partner
John Shoch, General Partner
Kimberly Koening, Chief Financial Officer
W. Ferrell Sanders, General Partner

Type of Firm
Private Firm Investing Own Capital

Industry Association Membership
National Venture Capital Association (NVCA)
Western Association of Venture Capitalists (WAVC)

Project Preferences

Role in Financing:
Prefer role as deal originator but will also invest in deals created by others

Type of Financing Preferred:
First Stage Financing
Seed
Start-up Financing

Size of Investments Considered
Min Size of Investment Considered (000s): $750
Max Size of Investment Considered: No Limit

Geographical Preferences

United States
Northeast
West Coast

Industry Preferences

(% based on actual investment)

Computer Software and Services	24.6%
Biotechnology	15.1%
Semiconductors/Other Elect.	13.9%
Medical/Health	13.1%
Computer Hardware	12.4%
Internet Specific	11.4%
Communications and Media	4.7%
Consumer Related	2.1%
Other Products	1.5%
Industrial/Energy	1.1%

Additional Information
Name of Most Recent Fund: Asset Management Associates 1998, LLC.
Most Recent Fund Was Raised: 11/01/1998
Year Founded: 1965
Capital Under Management: $180,000,000
Current Activity Level : Actively seeking new investments
Method of Compensation: Return on investment is of primary concern, do not charge fees

ATHENA TECHNOLOGY VENTURES

310 University Avenue
Suite 202
Palo Alto, CA 94301
Phone: 650-470-0370
Fax: 650-470-0378
Website: www.athenatv.com

Management and Staff
Bon Keul Koo, Partner
Karen Ha, Partner
Perry Ha, Partner

Type of Firm
Private Firm Investing Own Capital

Project Preferences

Type of Financing Preferred:
Early Stage
Seed

Geographical Preferences

United States
California

International
All International

Industry Preferences

(% based on actual investment)

Internet Specific	64.1%
Other Products	11.8%
Semiconductors/Other Elect.	10.8%
Computer Hardware	7.2%
Communications and Media	3.5%
Consumer Related	2.6%

Additional Information
Name of Most Recent Fund: Athena Venture Fund
Most Recent Fund Was Raised: 10/01/1997
Year Founded: 1999
Capital Under Management: $50,000,000
Current Activity Level : Actively seeking new investments

ATLAS VENTURE

1600 El Camino Real
Suite 290
Menlo Park, CA 94025
Phone: 650-614-1444
Fax: 650-614-1441
Website: www.atlasventure.com

See Massachusetts for full listing.

ATTRACTOR INVESTMENT MANAGEMENT

1110 Burlingame Ave
#211
Burlingame, CA 94010-4125
Phone: 650-234-0400

Type of Firm
Private Firm Investing Own Capital

Industry Preferences

(% based on actual investment)

Internet Specific	85.7%
Computer Software and Services	8.9%
Other Products	3.7%
Communications and Media	0.8%
Computer Hardware	0.8%

Additional Information
Year Founded: 1999
Current Activity Level : Actively seeking new investments

AUGUST CAPITAL MANAGEMENT

2480 Sand Hill Road
Suite 101
Menlo Park, CA 94025
Phone: 650-234-9900
Fax: 650-234-9910
Website: www.augustcap.com

Management and Staff
Andrew Anker, General Partner
Andrew Rappaport, General Partner
David Marquardt, General Partner
John Johnston, General Partner
Mark Wilson, General Partner
Won Chung, General Partner

Type of Firm
Private Firm Investing Own Capital

Industry Association Membership
Western Association of Venture Capitalists (WAVC)

Project Preferences

Role in Financing:
Prefer role as deal originator but will also invest in deals created by others

Type of Financing Preferred:
First Stage Financing
Special Situation
Start-up Financing

Geographical Preferences
United States
Northwest
Rocky Mountain
Southwest
West Coast

Industry Preferences
(% based on actual investment)

Internet Specific	33.8%
Computer Software and Services	23.2%
Semiconductors/Other Elect.	19.1%
Communications and Media	17.2%
Computer Hardware	6.6%

Additional Information
Name of Most Recent Fund: August Capital II
Most Recent Fund Was Raised: 01/01/1998
Year Founded: 1995
Capital Under Management: $300,000,000
Current Activity Level : Actively seeking new investments
Method of Compensation: Return on investment is of primary concern, do not charge fees

AUTHOSIS

226, Airport Parkway
Suite 405
San Jose, CA 95110
Phone: 650-814-3603
Website: www.authosis.com

Other Offices

2101, 21/F Westlands Centre
20 Westlands Road
Quarry Bay, Hong Kong
Phone: 852-2960-4611
Fax: 852-2960-0185

T02 2300 Century Square, Jalan Usahawan
63000 Cyberjaya, Multimedia Supercorrido
Kuala Lumpur, Malaysia
Phone: 603-8313-3000
Fax: 603-8313-3100

Management and Staff
Danny Lui, Co-Founder

Type of Firm
Affiliate/Subsidary of Oth. Financial. Instit.

Project Preferences

Type of Financing Preferred:
First Stage Financing
Second Stage Financing
Seed

Geographical Preferences
United States
All U.S.

International
Asia

Industry Preferences
Computer Software
Software

Additional Information
Current Activity Level : Actively seeking new investments

AVI CAPITAL, L.P.

One First Street
Suite 2
Los Altos, CA 94022
Phone: 650-949-9862
Fax: 650-949-8510
Website: www.avicapital.com

Management and Staff
Brian Grossi, General Partner

Type of Firm
Private Firm Investing Own Capital

Industry Association Membership
National Venture Capital Association (NVCA)
Natl assoc of Small Bus. Inv. Co (NASBIC)
Western Association of Venture Capitalists (WAVC)

Project Preferences

Role in Financing:
Prefer role as deal originator but will also invest in deals created by others

Type of Financing Preferred:
First Stage Financing
Second Stage Financing
Seed
Special Situation
Start-up Financing

Size of Investments Considered
Min Size of Investment Considered (000s): $1,000
Max Size of Investment Considered (000s): $2,000

Geographical Preferences
United States
West Coast

Industry Preferences
(% based on actual investment)

Computer Hardware	27.6%
Computer Software and Services	27.5%
Internet Specific	21.4%
Communications and Media	10.9%
Semiconductors/Other Elect.	9.1%
Industrial/Energy	1.4%
Medical/Health	1.0%
Consumer Related	1.0%
Other Products	0.1%

Additional Information
Name of Most Recent Fund: Associated Venture Investors
Most Recent Fund Was Raised: 04/01/1982
Year Founded: 1982
Capital Under Management: $300,000,000
Current Activity Level : Actively seeking new investments
Method of Compensation: Return on investment is of primary concern, do not charge fees

AXIOM VENTURE PARTNERS, L.P.

One Post Street
Suite 2525
San Francisco, CA 94104
Phone: 415-434-9999
Fax: 415-434-0505
Website: www.axiomventures.com

See Connecticut for full listing.

AZURE CAPITAL PARTNERS

650 California Street
11th Floor
San Francisco, CA 94108
Phone: 415-276-5500
Fax: 415-276-5590
Website: www.azurecap.com

Management and Staff
Cameron Lester, General Partner
Martin Brusco, Chief Financial Officer
Paul Weinstein, General Partner
Paul Ferris, General Partner

Type of Firm
Private Firm Investing Own Capital

Project Preferences

Type of Financing Preferred:
Balanced
Early Stage
Expansion
Later Stage
Seed

Additional Information
Year Founded: 2000
Capital Under Management: $550,000,000
Current Activity Level : Actively seeking new investments

BA VENTURE PARTNERS (AKA: BANKAMERICA VENTURES)

950 Tower Lane
Suite 700
Foster City, CA 94404
Phone: 650-378-6000
Fax: 650-378-6040
Website: www.baventurepartners.com

Management and Staff
Anchie Kuo, Managing Director
Eric Sigler, Principal
George Rossmann, Principal
James Murphy, Managing Director
Jess Marzak, Venture Partner
John Doughery,Jr., Managing Director
Kate Mitchell, Managing Director
Louis Bock, Managing Director
Mark Brooks, Managing Director
Robert Obuch, Managing Director
Rory O'Driscoll, Managing Director
Stacey Curry, Principal

Whom to Contact
George Rossmann

Type of Firm
SBIC Not elsewhere classified

Industry Association Membership
National Venture Capital Association (NVCA)
Natl assoc of Small Bus. Inv. Co (NASBIC)
Western Association of Venture Capitalists (WAVC)

Project Preferences

Role in Financing:
Prefer role as deal originator but will also invest in deals created by others

Type of Financing Preferred:
First Stage Financing
Second Stage Financing
Startup

Size of Investments Considered
Min Size of Investment Considered (000s): $1,000
Max Size of Investment Considered (000s): $12,000

Geographical Preferences

United States
All U.S.

Industry Preferences

(% based on actual investment)

Internet Specific	43.1%
Medical/Health	13.7%
Computer Software and Services	11.0%
Other Products	9.1%
Industrial/Energy	5.3%
Communications and Media	5.2%
Biotechnology	5.2%
Semiconductors/Other Elect.	3.0%
Consumer Related	2.8%
Computer Hardware	1.6%

Additional Information
Name of Most Recent Fund: BA Venture Partners VI
Most Recent Fund Was Raised: 01/01/1995
Year Founded: 1960
Capital Under Management: $763,000,000
Current Activity Level : Actively seeking new investments
Method of Compensation: Return on investment is of primary concern, do not charge fees

---

BACCHARIS CAPITAL, INC.

2420 Sand Hill Road
Suite 100
Menlo Park, CA 94025
Phone: 650-324-6844
Fax: 650-854-3025

Management and Staff
Michelle von Roedelbronn

Whom to Contact
Michelle von Roedelbronn

Type of Firm
Private Firm Investing Own Capital

Industry Association Membership
Western Association of Venture Capitalists (WAVC)

Project Preferences

Role in Financing:
Prefer role as deal originator but will also invest in deals created by others

Type of Financing Preferred:
Control-block Purchases
First Stage Financing
Leveraged Buyout
Mezzanine
Second Stage Financing
Special Situation
Start-up Financing

Size of Investments Considered
Min Size of Investment Considered (000s): $1,000
Max Size of Investment Considered: No Limit

Geographical Preferences

United States
West Coast

Industry Preferences

Computer Software
Applications Software

Biotechnology
Biotech Related Research

Consumer Related
Entertainment and Leisure
Retail
Food/Beverage
Consumer Products
Consumer Services
Education Related

Industrial/Energy
Alternative Energy
Energy Conservation Relat

Manufact.
Publishing

Agr/Forestr/Fish
Agriculture related

Additional Information
Year Founded: 1990
Capital Under Management: $30,000,000
Current Activity Level : Actively seeking new investments
Method of Compensation: Return on investment is of primary concern, do not charge fees

BANCBOSTON CAPITAL/BANCBOSTON VENTURES

435 Tasso Street
Suite 250
Palo Alto, CA 94305
Phone: 650-470-4100
Website: www.bancbostoncapital.com

See Massachusetts for full listing.

BANCBOSTON/ROBERTSON STEPHENS

555 California Street
26th Floor, Suite 2600
San Francisco, CA 94104
Phone: 415-676-2618
Fax: 415-676-2556
Website: www.robertsonstephens.com

Other Offices

100 Federal Street
Floor 32
Boston, MA 02110
Phone: 617-341-7000

227 West Monroe
Suite 3590
Chicago, IL 60606
Phone: 312-629-3554

39 Victoria Street
London, United Kingdom SW1H 0ED
Phone: 44-207-798-6600

3rd Floor
12 Promenadeplatz
Munich, Germany 80333
Phone: 49.89.25.54.9.0

435 Tasso Street
Suite 250
Palo Alto, CA 94301
Phone: 650-289-7200

590 Madison Avenue
36th Floor
New York, NY 10022
Phone: 212-319-8900

950 East Paces Ferry Road
34th Floor
Atlanta, GA 30326
Phone: 404-442-1100

Milennium Tower
18th Floor, 17 Ha'Arba'a St
Tel Aviv , Israel 64739
Phone: 972.3.6238500

Management and Staff

Madison Wootton, Vice President
Raymond Wong, Principal
Tony Grosso, Managing Director

Type of Firm

Investment/Merchant Bank Investing Own or Client Funds

Project Preferences

Type of Financing Preferred:

Acquisition
Expansion

Geographical Preferences

United States

All U.S.

International

All International

Industry Preferences

(% based on actual investment)

Semiconductors/Other Elect.	24.5%
Internet Specific	23.1%
Medical/Health	15.0%
Computer Software and Services	13.8%
Communications and Media	12.0%
Other Products	8.2%
Consumer Related	1.5%
Industrial/Energy	1.5%
Biotechnology	0.4%

Additional Information

Name of Most Recent Fund: Bayview Investors, Ltd.
Most Recent Fund Was Raised: 01/01/1985
Year Founded: 1999
Capital Under Management: $1,000,000
Current Activity Level : Actively seeking new investments

BAND OF ANGELS

275 Middlefield Road
Suite 1220
Menlo Park, CA 94025
Phone: 650-321-0852
Fax: 650-321-1968
Website: www.bandangels.com

Management and Staff

Hans Severiens, Managing Director
Ian Sobieski, Managing Director

Type of Firm

Investment or Angel network

Industry Association Membership

Western Association of Venture Capitalists (WAVC)

Additional Information

Name of Most Recent Fund: Band of Angels Fund, L.P.
Most Recent Fund Was Raised: 07/01/1999
Year Founded: 1995
Capital Under Management: $50,000,000
Current Activity Level : Actively seeking new investments

BANGERT DAWES READE DAVIS & THOM

220 Montgomery Street
Suite 424
San Francisco, CA 94104
Phone: 415-954-9900
Fax: 415-954-9901

Other Offices

One Madison Avenue
New York, NY 10010
Phone: 212-689-7404

Management and Staff

K. Deane Reade
Lambert Thom

Whom to Contact

K. Deane Reade
Lambert Thom

Type of Firm

Private Firm Investing Own Capital

Project Preferences

Role in Financing:

Prefer role as deal originator but will also invest in deals created by others

Type of Financing Preferred:

Leveraged Buyout
Mezzanine
Second Stage Financing
Special Situation

Size of Investments Considered

Min Size of Investment Considered (000s): $5,000
Max Size of Investment Considered: No Limit

Geographical Preferences

International
No Preference

Industry Preferences

Communications and Media
CATV & Pay TV Systems
Radio & TV Broadcasting

Computer Hardware
Computer Graphics and Dig

Computer Software
Computer Services
Applications Software

Semiconductors/Other Elect.
Sensors
Component Testing Equipmt
Analytic/Scientific

Biotechnology
Industrial Biotechnology
Biosensors
Biotech Related Research
Biotech Related Research

Medical/Health
Medical Diagnostics
Diagnostic Test Products
Medical Products
Disposable Med. Products
Hospitals/Clinics/Primary
Hospital/Other Instit.

Consumer Related
Retail
Food/Beverage
Consumer Products

Industrial/Energy
Industrial Products
Factory Automation
Robotics
Environmental Related

Manufact.
Publishing

Additional Information

Name of Most Recent Fund: Hewlet Packard Corporation
Most Recent Fund Was Raised: 06/01/1985
Year Founded: 1975
Capital Under Management: $100,000,000
Current Activity Level : Actively seeking new investments
Method of Compensation: Return on invest. most important, but chg. closing fees, service fees, etc.

BARKSDALE GROUP

2730 Sand Hill Road
Suite 100
Menlo Park, CA 94025
Phone: 650-234-5200
Fax: 650-234-5201

Type of Firm

Private Firm Investing Own Capital

Industry Preferences

(% based on actual investment)

Internet Specific	78.6%
Computer Software and Services	8.6%
Communications and Media	4.9%
Other Products	4.8%
Semiconductors/Other Elect.	3.1%

Additional Information

Year Founded: 1999
Current Activity Level : Actively seeking new investments

BARRINGTON PARTNERS

1053 Alameda de las Pulgas
Belmont, CA 94002
Phone: 650-637-1902
Fax: 650-637-1917
Website: www.barvc.com

Other Offices

378 Page Street
Suite 3
Stoughton, MA 02072
Fax: 781-297-9933

Management and Staff

James Baker, General Partner
John McDonough, General Partner
Joseph McDonough, General Partner
Patrick Soheili, General Partner
Remy Malan, General Partner
Vance Nahman, Venture Partner
William Nyhan, General Partner

Type of Firm

Private Firm Investing Own Capital

Project Preferences

Type of Financing Preferred:
Seed

Industry Preferences

(% based on actual investment)

Internet Specific	68.5%
Communications and Media	31.5%

Additional Information

Current Activity Level : Actively seeking new investments

BASTION CAPITAL CORP.

1999 Avenue of the Stars
Suite 2960
Los Angeles, CA 90067
Phone: 310-788-5700
Fax: 310-277-7582

Management and Staff

James Villanueva

Whom to Contact

James Villanueva

Type of Firm

Private Firm Investing Own Capital

Project Preferences

Role in Financing:
Prefer role as deal originator but will also invest in deals created by others

Type of Financing Preferred:
Control-block Purchases
Leveraged Buyout
Special Situation

Size of Investments Considered

Min Size of Investment Considered (000s): $10,000
Max Size of Investment Considered: No Limit

Geographical Preferences

United States
All U.S.

Canada
All Canada

Industry Preferences

Communications and Media
Communications and Media
Other Communication Prod.

Semiconductors/Other Elect.
Electronics
Sensors
Analytic/Scientific

Medical/Health
Diagnostic Test Products
Other Therapeutic
Medical Products
Disposable Med. Products
Pharmaceuticals

Consumer Related
Entertainment and Leisure
Retail
Franchises(NEC)
Food/Beverage
Consumer Products
Consumer Services
Other Restaurants
Education Related

Industrial/Energy
Energy Conservation Relat
Industrial Products
Materials
Factory Automation
Machinery
Environmental Related

Transportation
Transportation

Financial Services
Financial Services

Manufact.
Publishing

Additional Information
Name of Most Recent Fund: Bastion Capital Fund, L.P.
Most Recent Fund Was Raised: 06/14/1994
Year Founded: 1990
Capital Under Management: $125,000,000
Current Activity Level : Actively seeking new investments
Method of Compensation: Return on investment is of primary concern, do not charge fees

BATTERY VENTURES, L.P.

901 Mariner's Island Blvd.
Suite 475
San Mateo, CA 94404
Phone: 650-372-3939
Fax: 650-372-3930
Website: www.battery.com

See Massachusetts for full listing.

BAY CITY CAPITAL LLC

750 Battery Street
Suite 600
San Francisco, CA 94111
Phone: 415-676-3830

Type of Firm
Private Firm Investing Own Capital

Industry Preferences
(% based on actual investment)

Biotechnology	45.1%
Medical/Health	24.4%
Internet Specific	19.9%
Communications and Media	5.9%
Other Products	4.7%

Additional Information
Year Founded: 1999
Capital Under Management: $225,000,000
Current Activity Level : Actively seeking new investments

BAY PARTNERS

10600 North De Anza Boulevard
Suite 100
Cupertino, CA 95014-2031
Phone: 408-725-2444
Fax: 408-446-4502
Website: www.baypartners.com

Other Offices

10600 North De Anza Boulevard
Cupertino, CA 95014-2031
Phone: 408-725-2444
Fax: 408-446-4502

Management and Staff
Audrey Vallen, Chief Financial Officer
Chris Noble, General Partner
Dino Vendetti, General Partner
James Wickett, General Partner
John Friedenrich, General Partner
Loring Knoblauch, General Partner
Marcella Yano, General Partner
Neal Dempsey, General Partner
Robert Williams, General Partner

Whom to Contact
Bob Williams

Type of Firm
Private Firm Investing Own Capital

Industry Association Membership
National Venture Capital Association (NVCA)
Natl assoc of Small Bus. Inv. Co (NASBIC)
Western Association of Venture Capitalists (WAVC)

Project Preferences

Role in Financing:
Prefer role as deal originator but will also invest in deals created by others

Type of Financing Preferred:
Seed
Startup

Size of Investments Considered
Min Size of Investment Considered (000s): $500
Max Size of Investment Considered (000s): $15,000

Geographical Preferences

United States
All U.S.

Industry Preferences
(% based on actual investment)

Communications and Media	35.7%
Internet Specific	25.2%
Computer Software and Services	21.2%
Computer Hardware	8.2%
Semiconductors/Other Elect.	4.3%
Industrial/Energy	2.1%
Consumer Related	1.1%
Other Products	1.0%
Medical/Health	0.7%
Biotechnology	0.6%

Additional Information
Name of Most Recent Fund: Bay Partners LS Fund, L.P.
Most Recent Fund Was Raised: 02/01/1999
Year Founded: 1976
Capital Under Management: $1,025,000,000
Current Activity Level : Actively seeking new investments
Method of Compensation: Return on investment is of primary concern, do not charge fees

BEDROCK CAPITAL PARTNERS

One Maritime Plaza
Suite 1100
San Francisco, CA 94111
Phone: 415-274-4453
Fax: 415-434-0395
Website: www.bedrockcapital.com

See Massachusetts for full listing.

BENCHMARK CAPITAL

2480 Sand Hill Road
Suite 200
Menlo Park, CA 94025
Phone: 650-854-8180
Fax: 650-854-8183
Website: www.benchmark.com

Other Offices

Marble Arch Tower
55 Bryston Street
London, United Kingdom W1H 8AA
Phone: 44 20 7868 8590
Fax: 44 20 7868 4280

Management and Staff

Alexandre Balkanski, General Partner
Andy Rachleff, General Partner
Arad Naveh, Partner
Barry Maloney, Partner
Bill Gurley, General Partner
Bob Kagle, General Partner
Bruce Dunlevie, General Partner
David Beirne, General Partner
Eric Archambeau, General Partner
George Coelho, Partner
Kevin Harvey, General Partner
Mark Kremer, Partner
Michael Taylor, Chief Financial Officer
Mike Farmwald, Venture Partner
Nachman Shelef, Partner
Reed Hundt, Partner
Steve Spurlock, Partner

Type of Firm

Private Firm Investing Own Capital

Industry Association Membership

European Venture Capital Association (EVCA)
National Venture Capital Association (NVCA)
Western Association of Venture Capitalists (WAVC)

Project Preferences

Role in Financing:
Prefer role as deal originator but will also invest in deals created by others

Type of Financing Preferred:
Early Stage
First Stage Financing
Research and Development
Second Stage Financing
Seed
Special Situation
Start-up Financing

Geographical Preferences

United States
Southwest
West Coast

Industry Preferences

(% based on actual investment)

Internet Specific	61.8%
Computer Software and Services	11.2%
Other Products	9.9%
Communications and Media	8.2%
Semiconductors/Other Elect.	3.2%
Computer Hardware	2.9%
Consumer Related	2.7%

Additional Information

Name of Most Recent Fund: Benchmark Europe I
Most Recent Fund Was Raised: 09/15/1999
Year Founded: 1995
Capital Under Management: $97,000,000
Current Activity Level : Actively seeking new investments
Method of Compensation: Return on invest. most important, but chg. closing fees, service fees, etc.

BENEFIT CAPITAL COMPANIES, INC., THE

5000 Birch Street
West Tower, Suite 3000
Newport Beach, CA 92660
Phone: 714-833-3767
Fax: 714-752-7569

See Nevada for full listing.

BERKELEY INTERNATIONAL CAPITAL CORP.

650 California Street
Suite 2800
San Francisco, CA 94108-2609
Phone: 415-249-0450
Fax: 415-392-3929
Website: www.berkeleyvc.com

Management and Staff

Arthur I. Trueger

Whom to Contact

Arthur I. Trueger

Type of Firm

Investment/Merchant Bank Investing Own or Client Funds

Project Preferences

Role in Financing:
Prefer role as deal originator but will also invest in deals created by others

Type of Financing Preferred:
Leveraged Buyout
Mezzanine
Second Stage Financing
Special Situation

Size of Investments Considered

Min Size of Investment Considered (000s): $20,000
Max Size of Investment Considered: No Limit

Geographical Preferences

United States
All U.S.

Industry Preferences

(% based on actual investment)

Communications and Media	33.1%
Semiconductors/Other Elect.	25.2%
Computer Software and Services	15.5%
Internet Specific	9.7%
Medical/Health	7.8%
Computer Hardware	5.6%
Biotechnology	2.9%
Industrial/Energy	0.2%

Additional Information
Name of Most Recent Fund: Berkeley International
Most Recent Fund Was Raised: 11/01/1982
Year Founded: 1977
Capital Under Management: $400,000,000
Current Activity Level : Actively seeking new investments
Method of Compensation: Return on investment is of primary concern, do not charge fees

BESSEMER VENTURE PARTNERS

535 Middlefield Road
Suite 245
Menlo Park, CA 94025
Phone: 650-853-7000
Fax: 650-853-7001
Website: www.bvp.com

See Massachusetts for full listing.

BIOASIA INVESTMENTS, LLC

575 High Street
Suite 201
Palo Alto, CA 94301
Phone: 650-688-0818
Fax: 650-688-0815
Website: www.bioasia.com

Management and Staff
Anselm Leung, General Partner
Edgar Engleman, General Partner
Frank Kung, Managing Partner

Type of Firm
Private Firm Investing Own Capital

Industry Preferences
(% based on actual investment)

Biotechnology	57.6%
Medical/Health	32.9%
Communications and Media	3.5%
Industrial/Energy	2.8%
Computer Software and Services	2.4%
Internet Specific	0.8%

Additional Information
Year Founded: 1997
Capital Under Management: $121,700,000
Current Activity Level : Actively seeking new investments

BLUEPRINT VENTURES, LLC

456 Montgomery Street
22nd Floor
San Francisco, CA 94104
Phone: 415-901-4000
Fax: 415-901-4035
Website: www.blueprintventures.com

Management and Staff
Ashley Read, Chief Financial Officer
Bart Schachter, General Partner
Christopher Kersey, Partner
Thomas Unterberg, General Partner

Type of Firm
Private Firm Investing Own Capital

Project Preferences

Type of Financing Preferred:
Early Stage

Size of Investments Considered
Min Size of Investment Considered (000s): $3,000
Max Size of Investment Considered (000s): $10,000

Geographical Preferences

United States
All U.S.

Industry Preferences

Communications and Media
Telecommunications
Wireless Communications
Data Communications
Other Communication Prod.

Internet Specific
Internet

Additional Information
Name of Most Recent Fund: Emerging Communications Fund I, L.P.
Most Recent Fund Was Raised: 02/15/2000
Year Founded: 1999
Capital Under Management: $150,000,000
Current Activity Level : Actively seeking new investments

BLUESTREAM VENTURES

66 Willow Place
Menlo Park, CA 94025
Website: www.bluestreamventures.com

See Minnesota for full listing.

BLUMBERG CAPITAL VENTURES

580 Howard St.
Suite 401
San Francisco, CA 94105
Phone: 415-905-5007
Fax: 415-357-5027
Website: www.blumberg-capital.com

Management and Staff
Bruce Taragin, Principal
David Blumberg, Managing Partner
Mark Pretorius, Principal

Whom to Contact
Mark Pretorius

Type of Firm
Affiliate/Subsidary of Oth. Financial. Instit.

Industry Association Membership
National Venture Capital Association (NVCA)

Project Preferences

Role in Financing:
Will function either as deal originator or investor in deals created by others

Type of Financing Preferred:
Early Stage
Expansion
First Stage Financing
Seed
Startup

Size of Investments Considered
Min Size of Investment Considered (000s): $500
Max Size of Investment Considered (000s): $5,000

Geographical Preferences

United States
All U.S.

International
Australia
India
Israel

Industry Preferences

Communications and Media
Telecommunications
Wireless Communications

Computer Software
Computer Services
Software
Systems Software
Applications Software
Artificial Intelligence

Internet Specific
E-Commerce Technology
Internet

Semiconductors/Other Elect.
Laser Related
Fiber Optics

Additional Information
Name of Most Recent Fund: Blumberg Capital Ventures
Most Recent Fund Was Raised: 03/01/2000
Year Founded: 2000
Capital Under Management: $35,000,000
Current Activity Level : Actively seeking new investments
Method of Compensation: Return on investment is of primary concern, do not charge fees

BOULDER VENTURES, LTD.

44 Montgomery Street
Suite 3800
San Francisco, CA 94104
Phone: 415-617-6201
Fax: 415-617-6239
Website: www.boulderventures.com

See Maryland for full listing.

BOWMAN CAPITAL

1875 South Grant Street
Suite 600
San Mateo, CA 94402
Phone: 650-287-2200
Fax: 650-572-1844
Website: www.bowmancapital.com

Other Offices

5, Park Place, Suite 30
London, United Kingdom SW1A 1LP
Phone: 44 207 898 9027
Fax: 44 207 898 9001

Management and Staff
Hazel Cameron, General Partner
John Hurley, Managing Partner
Kevin Sara, General Partner
Lawrence Bowman, Founder
Matthew Cowan, Partner
William Wiberg, General Partner

Type of Firm
Private Firm Investing Own Capital

Industry Preferences
(% based on actual investment)

Internet Specific	45.3%
Communications and Media	32.0%
Semiconductors/Other Elect.	11.9%
Computer Software and Services	9.4%
Other Products	1.2%
Biotechnology	0.2%

Additional Information
Year Founded: 1995
Capital Under Management: $1,700,000,000
Current Activity Level : Actively seeking new investments

BRAD PEERY CAPITAL

145 Chapel Drive
Mill Valley, CA 94941
Phone: 415-389-0625
Fax: 415-389-1336

Management and Staff
Brad Peery

Whom to Contact
Brad Peery

Type of Firm
Investment/Merchant Bank Subsid/Affil

Project Preferences

Role in Financing:
Prefer role as deal originator but will also invest in deals created by others

Type of Financing Preferred:
Second Stage Financing

Size of Investments Considered
Min Size of Investment Considered (000s): $100
Max Size of Investment Considered (000s): $300

Geographical Preferences

United States
All U.S.

Canada
All Canada

Industry Preferences

Communications and Media
Telecommunications
Data Communications
Satellite Microwave Comm.

Internet Specific
Internet

Additional Information
Year Founded: 1991
Capital Under Management: $50,000,000
Current Activity Level : Actively seeking new investments
Method of Compensation: Return on investment is of primary concern, do not charge fees

BRANTLEY VENTURE PARTNERS

1920 Main Street
Suite 820
Irvine, CA 92614
Phone: 949-475-4242
Fax: 949-475-1950

See Ohio for full listing.

BURR, EGAN, DELEAGE & CO.

One Embarcadero Center
Suite 4050
San Francisco, CA 94111
Phone: 415-362-4022
Fax: 415-362-6178

See Massachusetts for full listing.

BURRILL & COMPANY

120 Montgomery Street
Suite 1370
San Francisco, CA 94104
Phone: 415-591-5400
Fax: 415-591-5401
Website: www.burrillandco.com

Other Offices

595 Madison Avenue
19th Floor
New York, NY

Management and Staff
Charles Dimmler, Managing Director
David Collier, Managing Director
Donna Williams, Chief Financial Officer
G. Steven Burrill, Chief Executive Officer
John Kim, Managing Director
Michael Ullman, Managing Director
Roger Wyse, Managing Director

Type of Firm
Investment/Merchant Bank Investing Own or Client Funds

Industry Association Membership
National Venture Capital Association (NVCA)

Project Preferences

Role in Financing:
Will function either as deal originator or investor in deals created by others

Type of Financing Preferred:
Balanced
Early Stage
Expansion
First Stage Financing
Mezzanine
Second Stage Financing
Seed
Start-up Financing

Geographical Preferences

United States
All U.S.

Canada
All Canada

International
Australia
France
Germany
All International
United Kingdom

Industry Preferences

(% based on actual investment)

Biotechnology	44.5%
Medical/Health	24.3%
Computer Software and Services	14.5%
Internet Specific	14.0%
Industrial/Energy	2.7%

Additional Information
Name of Most Recent Fund: Burrill Agbio Capital Fund
Most Recent Fund Was Raised: 04/01/1998
Year Founded: 1997
Capital Under Management: $250,000,000
Current Activity Level : Actively seeking new investments
Method of Compensation: Return on investment is of primary concern, do not charge fees

BV CAPITAL (FKA BERTELSMANN VENTURES LP)

111 El Paseo
Santa Barbara, CA 93101
Website: www.bvfund.com

Other Offices

Grosse Elbstrasse 145d
Hamburg, Germany D-22767
Phone: 49-40-8222-5550
Fax: 49-40-8222-555999

One Embarcadero Center
Suite 2480
San Francisco, CA 94111

Management and Staff
Jan Buettner, Managing General Partner
Mathias Schilling, Managing Director
Thomas Gieselman, Managing Director
Wolfgang Rose, Managing Director

Type of Firm
Non-Financial Corp. Affiliate or Subsidiary

Project Preferences

Type of Financing Preferred:
Early Stage
Seed

Geographical Preferences

United States
All U.S.

International
Germany
United Kingdom

Industry Preferences

(% based on actual investment)

Internet Specific	83.9%
Computer Hardware	8.2%
Computer Software and Services	6.4%
Other Products	1.5%

Additional Information
Year Founded: 1998
Capital Under Management: $250,000,000
Current Activity Level : Actively seeking new investments

C3 INVESTMENTS, INC.

4966 El Camino Real
Ste. 227
Los Altos, CA 94022
Phone: 1650-428-1688
Fax: 1650-428-1668
E-mail: info@c3investments.com
Website: www.c3investments.com

Management and Staff
Calvin, Jr. Lee, Chief Financial Officer

Type of Firm
Private Firm Investing Own Capital

Project Preferences

Type of Financing Preferred:
Later Stage
Mezzanine

Geographical Preferences

United States
All U.S.

International
Asia

Industry Preferences

Communications and Media
Telecommunications

Internet Specific
Internet

Additional Information
Current Activity Level : Actively seeking new investments

CAMBRIA GROUP, THE

1600 El Camino Real
Suite 155
Menlo Park, CA 94025
Phone: 650-329-8600
Fax: 650-329-8601
Website: www.cambriagroup.com

Management and Staff
Christopher Sekula, Principal
Paul Davies, Principal

Whom to Contact
Paul Davies

Type of Firm
Investment/Merchant Bank Subsid/Affil

Industry Association Membership
National Venture Capital Association (NVCA)

Project Preferences

Role in Financing:
Prefer role as deal originator but will also invest in deals created by others

Type of Financing Preferred:
Control-block Purchases
Leveraged Buyout
Mezzanine
Second Stage Financing
Special Situation

Size of Investments Considered
Min Size of Investment Considered (000s): $3,000
Max Size of Investment Considered: No Limit

Geographical Preferences

United States
All U.S.

Industry Preferences

Communications and Media
Commercial Communications
CATV & Pay TV Systems
Radio & TV Broadcasting
Satellite Microwave Comm.

Semiconductors/Other Elect.
Electronic Components
Component Testing Equipmt
Analytic/Scientific

Medical/Health
Disposable Med. Products

Consumer Related
Entertainment and Leisure
Retail
Franchises(NEC)
Food/Beverage
Consumer Products
Consumer Services
Other Restaurants
Hotels and Resorts
Education Related

Industrial/Energy
Oil and Gas Exploration
Alternative Energy
Coal Related
Energy Conservation Relat
Industrial Products

Transportation
Transportation

Business Serv.
Distribution

Manufact.
Office Automation Equipmt
Publishing

Agr/Forestr/Fish
Mining and Minerals

Additional Information
Year Founded: 1996
Capital Under Management: $6,000,000
Current Activity Level : Actively seeking new investments
Method of Compensation: Return on invest. most important, but chg. closing fees, service fees, etc.

CAMBRIAN VENTURES

201 San Antonio Circle
Suite 235
Mountain View, CA 94040
Phone: 650-917-6630
Fax: 650-917-6636
Website: www.cambrianventures.com

Management and Staff
Anand Rajaraman, Founding Partner
Venky Harinarayan, Founding Partner

Type of Firm
Private Firm Investing Own Capital

Project Preferences

Role in Financing:
Will function either as deal originator or investor in deals created by others

Type of Financing Preferred:
Early Stage
Seed

Geographical Preferences

United States
All U.S.

Industry Preferences

Internet Specific
Internet

Additional Information
Current Activity Level : Actively seeking new investments

CAMBRIDGE SAMSUNG PARTNERS

3655 N.First Street
San Jose, CA 95134
Phone: 408-544-5660
Fax: 408-544-5659

See Massachusetts for full listing.

CANAAN PARTNERS

2884 Sand Hill Road
Suite 115
Menlo Park, CA 94025
Phone: 415-854-8092
Fax: 415-854-8127
Website: www.canaan.com

See Connecticut for full listing.

CAPSTONE VENTURES SBIC, L.P.

3000 Sand Hill Road
Building One, Suite 290
Menlo Park, CA 94025
Phone: 650-854-2523
Fax: 650-854-9010
Website: www.capstonevc.com

Other Offices

Dain Rauscher Plaza
60 South Sixth Street
Minneapolis, MN 55403
Phone: 612-371-7733
Fax: 612-371-2837

Management and Staff
Barbara Santry, General Partner
Brian Johnson, Managing Director
Gene Fischer, General Partner
Richard Capen, General Partner

Whom to Contact
Eugene J. Fischer
Richard Capen

Type of Firm
Private Firm Investing Own Capital

Industry Association Membership
National Venture Capital Association (NVCA)
Natl assoc of Small Bus. Inv. Co (NASBIC)
Western Association of Venture Capitalists (WAVC)

Project Preferences

Role in Financing:
Will function either as deal originator or investor in deals created by others

Type of Financing Preferred:
Early Stage
Expansion
First Stage Financing
Second Stage Financing

Size of Investments Considered
Min Size of Investment Considered (000s): $500
Max Size of Investment Considered (000s): $3,000

Geographical Preferences

United States
All U.S.

Industry Preferences

(% based on actual investment)

Other Products	92.0%
Computer Software and Services	3.5%
Internet Specific	2.3%
Medical/Health	1.0%
Communications and Media	0.5%
Computer Hardware	0.4%
Semiconductors/Other Elect.	0.3%
Biotechnology	0.0%

Additional Information
Name of Most Recent Fund: Capstone Ventures, L.P.
Most Recent Fund Was Raised: 01/01/1996
Year Founded: 1996
Capital Under Management: $54,000,000
Current Activity Level : Actively seeking new investments
Method of Compensation: Return on investment is of primary concern, do not charge fees

---

CARDINAL PARTNERS (FKA: CARDINAL HEALTH PARTNERS)

28202 Cabot Road
suite 200
Laguna Beach, CA 92651
Phone: 949-347-0384
Fax: 973-347-0389
Website: www.cardinalpartners.com

See New Jersey for full listing.

CASCADE COMMUNICATIONS VENTURES, LLC

60 East Sir Francis Drake Blvd
Suite 300
Larkspur, CA 94939
Phone: 415-925-6500
Fax: 415-925-6501

Management and Staff
Dennis Brush, Managing Partner
Greg Kunz, Managing Partner

Whom to Contact
Dennis Brush

Type of Firm
Private Firm Investing Own Capital

Project Preferences

Role in Financing:
Prefer role as deal originator but will also invest in deals created by others

Type of Financing Preferred:
Acquisition
Leveraged Buyout
Mezzanine
Recapitalizations
Turnaround

Geographical Preferences

United States
All U.S.

Canada
All Canada

Industry Preferences

Communications and Media
Commercial Communications
CATV & Pay TV Systems
Radio & TV Broadcasting
Telecommunications
Wireless Communications
Data Communications
Satellite Microwave Comm.
Other Communication Prod.

Consumer Related
Franchises(NEC)

Business Serv.
Media

Additional Information
Year Founded: 1995
Capital Under Management: $100,000,000
Current Activity Level : Actively seeking new investments
Method of Compensation: Return on investment is of primary concern, do not charge fees

---

CE UNTERBERG TOWBIN (FKA:UNTERBERG HARRIS CAPITAL PARTNERS)

275 Battery Street
San Francisco, CA 94111
Phone: 415-399-1500
Website: http://www.unterberg.com

See New York for full listing.

CELTIC HOUSE INTERNATIONAL

2726 Sequoia Way
San Mateo, CA 94402
Phone: 650-759-0933
Fax: 650-594-9227
Website: www.celtic-house.com

See Foreign Venture Capital Firms for full listing.

CHAMPION VENTURES

1031 Middlefield Road
Redwood City, CA 94063

Management and Staff
Harris Barton, Managing Partner
Joe Montana, General Partner
Ronnie Lott, Managing Partner

Type of Firm
Private Firm Investing Own Capital

Project Preferences

Type of Financing Preferred:
Fund of Funds

Geographical Preferences

International
No Preference

Additional Information
Capital Under Management: $190,000,000
Current Activity Level : Actively seeking new investments

CHARLES RIVER VENTURES

2460 Sand Hill Road
Suite 300
Menlo Park, CA 94025
Phone: 650-739-0100
Website: www.crv.com

See Massachusetts for full listing.

CHARTER GROWTH CAPITAL

525 University Avenue
Suite 1400
Palo Alto, CA 94301
Phone: 650-617-0702
Fax: 650-617-0709
Website: www.chartergrowth.com

Management and Staff
Andy Klatt, Chief Financial Officer
David Aronson, General Partner
Erik Lassila, Partner
George Bischof, General Partner
James Boettcher, General Partner
Johnson Cha, Partner
Kevin McQuillan, General Partner
Steven Bird, General Partner

Type of Firm
Private Firm Investing Own Capital

Industry Association Membership
National Venture Capital Association (NVCA)
Western Association of Venture Capitalists (WAVC)

Project Preferences

Type of Financing Preferred:
Later Stage

Geographical Preferences

United States
All U.S.

Industry Preferences

(% based on actual investment)

Internet Specific	55.6%
Communications and Media	18.0%
Computer Software and Services	14.9%
Semiconductors/Other Elect.	7.1%
Medical/Health	3.5%
Biotechnology	0.5%
Other Products	0.2%
Computer Hardware	0.2%

Additional Information
Name of Most Recent Fund: Charter Growth Capital, L.P.
Most Recent Fund Was Raised: 10/30/1997
Year Founded: 1997
Capital Under Management: $571,000,000
Current Activity Level : Actively seeking new investments

CHARTER VENTURES

525 University Avenue
Suite 1400
Palo Alto, CA 94301
Phone: 650-325-6953
Fax: 650-325-4762
Website: www.charterventures.com

Management and Staff
A. Barr Dolan, Partner
Johnson Cha, Partner
Ravi Chiruvolu, Managing Director

Type of Firm
Private Firm Investing Own Capital

Industry Association Membership
National Venture Capital Association (NVCA)

Project Preferences

Role in Financing:
Will function either as deal originator or investor in deals created by others

Type of Financing Preferred:
First Stage Financing
Leveraged Buyout
Mezzanine
Second Stage Financing
Seed
Special Situation
Start-up Financing

Geographical Preferences

United States
All U.S.

Industry Preferences

(% based on actual investment)

Internet Specific	28.5%
Computer Software and Services	19.1%
Medical/Health	14.4%
Biotechnology	11.9%
Communications and Media	9.7%
Computer Hardware	9.3%
Semiconductors/Other Elect.	4.9%
Other Products	1.1%
Industrial/Energy	1.0%

Additional Information
Name of Most Recent Fund: Charter Ventures II
Most Recent Fund Was Raised: 12/31/1994
Year Founded: 1982
Capital Under Management: $70,000,000
Current Activity Level : Actively seeking new investments
Method of Compensation: Return on investment is of primary concern, do not charge fees

CHASE H&Q (FKA HAMBRECHT & QUIST)

50 California Street
29th Floor
San Francisco, CA 94104
Phone: 415-591-1200
Fax: 415-591-1205

Other Offices

50 Rose Wharf
Suite 400
Boston, MA 02110
Phone: 617-310-0507
Fax: 617-310-0562

Management and Staff
Alan Carr, President
Andrew Kahn, Partner
Bruce Crocker, Managing Director
Charles Walker, Managing Partner
Kerri Bisner, Vice President
Michael Beblo, Chief Financial Officer
Nancy Pfund, Partner
Robert Savoy, Chief Financial Officer

Whom to Contact
Aaron Mankovski

Type of Firm
Investment/Merchant Bank Subsid/Affil

Industry Association Membership
Western Association of Venture Capitalists (WAVC)

Project Preferences

Role in Financing:
Prefer role as deal originator but will also invest in deals created by others

Type of Financing Preferred:
Control-block Purchases
First Stage Financing
Leveraged Buyout
Mezzanine
Research and Development
Second Stage Financing
Special Situation
Start-up Financing

Size of Investments Considered
Min Size of Investment Considered (000s): $500
Max Size of Investment Considered: No Limit

Geographical Preferences

United States
All U.S.

Industry Preferences

(% based on actual investment)

Medical/Health	16.0%
Computer Software and Services	15.1%
Internet Specific	14.8%
Computer Hardware	14.8%
Biotechnology	10.2%
Semiconductors/Other Elect.	10.0%
Communications and Media	9.5%
Other Products	5.2%
Industrial/Energy	3.0%
Consumer Related	1.4%

Additional Information
Name of Most Recent Fund: Eucalyptus Ventures LP
Most Recent Fund Was Raised: 04/01/1998
Year Founded: 1997
Capital Under Management: $55,000,000
Current Activity Level : Actively seeking new investments
Method of Compensation: Return on investment is of primary concern, do not charge fees

CIBC CAPITAL PARTNERS (FKA: CIBC WOOD GUNDY CAPITAL)

One Post Street
Suite 3550
San Francisco, CA 94104
Phone: 415-399-5723
Fax: 415-399-1224
Website: www.cibcwm.com

See New York for full listing.

CLEARSTONE VENTURE PARTNERS (FKA: IDEALAB! CAPITAL PARTNERS)

130 West Union Street
Pasadena, CA 91103
Phone: 626-535-2880
Fax: 626-535-2881
Website: www.clearstonevp.com

Other Offices

2500 Sand Hill Road
Suite 205
Menlo Park, CA 94025
Phone: 650-234-0400
Fax: 650-234-0401

Management and Staff
Dana Moraly, Chief Financial Officer
Erik Lassila, Managing Director
Jim Armstrong, Managing Director
Leonid Kazovsky, Venture Partner
William Quigley, Managing Director
William Elkus, Managing Partner

Type of Firm
Private Firm Investing Own Capital

Industry Association Membership
National Venture Capital Association (NVCA)

Project Preferences

Role in Financing:
Prefer role as deal originator but will also invest in deals created by others

Type of Financing Preferred:
Early Stage
Later Stage

Size of Investments Considered
Min Size of Investment Considered (000s): $5,000
Max Size of Investment Considered (000s): $15,000

Geographical Preferences

United States
All U.S.
West Coast

Industry Preferences

(% based on actual investment)

Internet Specific	76.9%
Computer Software and Services	10.9%
Computer Hardware	5.0%
Other Products	5.0%
Communications and Media	2.3%

Additional Information
Name of Most Recent Fund: ICP II
Most Recent Fund Was Raised: 08/01/1999
Year Founded: 1998
Capital Under Management: $469,000,000
Current Activity Level : Actively seeking new investments
Method of Compensation: Return on investment is of primary concern, do not charge fees

CMEA VENTURES (FKA:CHEMICALS & MATERIALS ENTERPRISE ASSOCIA)

235 Montgomery Street
Suite 920
San Francisco, CA 94104
Phone: 415-352-1520
Fax: 415-352-1524
Website: www.cmeaventures.com

Other Offices

One Cleveland Center
1375 East Ninth Street
Cleveland, OH 44114
Phone: 216-861-4800
Fax: 216-621-4543

Management and Staff

Christine Cordaro, General Partner
David Tuckerman, Partner
Gordon Hull, General Partner
Jim Watson, General Partner
Karl Handelsman, General Partner
Thomas Baruch, General Partner
Vlad Dabija, Partner

Type of Firm

Private Firm Investing Own Capital

Industry Association Membership

Mid-Atlantic Venture Association
National Venture Capital Association (NVCA)

Project Preferences

Role in Financing:

Will function either as deal originator or investor in deals created by others

Type of Financing Preferred:

Balanced
Early Stage
First Stage Financing
Later Stage
Mezzanine
Second Stage Financing
Startup

Size of Investments Considered

Min Size of Investment Considered (000s): $250
Max Size of Investment Considered (000s): $10,000

Geographical Preferences

United States

Northwest
West Coast

Industry Preferences

(% based on actual investment)

Biotechnology	20.1%
Semiconductors/Other Elect.	17.0%
Medical/Health	16.4%
Internet Specific	15.7%
Industrial/Energy	11.2%
Communications and Media	10.4%
Computer Software and Services	7.8%
Computer Hardware	1.3%

Additional Information

Name of Most Recent Fund: CMEA Life Sciences Fund, L.P.
Most Recent Fund Was Raised: 06/01/1998
Year Founded: 1989
Capital Under Management: $453,000,000
Current Activity Level : Actively seeking new investments
Method of Compensation: Return on investment is of primary concern, do not charge fees

COMDISCO VENTURES

3000 Sand Hill Road
Building One, Suite 155
Menlo Park, CA 94025
Phone: 650-854-9484
Fax: 650-854-4026

Other Offices

3000 Sand Hill Road
Building 1, Suite 155
Menlo Park, CA 94025
Phone: 650-854-9484
Fax: 650-854-4026

Totten Pond Office Center
400-1 Totten Pond Road; 3rd Floor
Waltham, MA 02451
Phone: 781-672-0250
Fax: 781-398-8099

Management and Staff

Geoffrey Tickner, Managing Director
Jim Labe, Chief Executive Officer
Manuel Henriques, Managing Director

Type of Firm

Non-Financial Corp. Affiliate or Subsidiary

Industry Association Membership

National Venture Capital Association (NVCA)
Western Association of Venture Capitalists (WAVC)

Project Preferences

Role in Financing:

Prefer role as deal originator but will also invest in deals created by others

Type of Financing Preferred:

First Stage Financing
Second Stage Financing
Start-up Financing

Size of Investments Considered

Min Size of Investment Considered (000s): $300
Max Size of Investment Considered (000s): $20,000

Geographical Preferences

United States

All U.S.

Industry Preferences

(% based on actual investment)

Internet Specific	55.0%
Computer Software and Services	16.0%
Communications and Media	10.6%
Semiconductors/Other Elect.	6.1%
Medical/Health	3.3%
Biotechnology	2.7%
Consumer Related	2.6%
Computer Hardware	2.2%
Other Products	1.5%
Industrial/Energy	0.0%

Additional Information

Year Founded: 1987
Capital Under Management: $1,000,000,000
Current Activity Level : Actively seeking new investments
Method of Compensation: Return on invest. most important, but chg. closing fees, service fees, etc.

COMMERCE ONE VENTURES

4440 Rosewood Drive
Pleasanton, CA 94588
Phone: 925-520-6000
Fax: 925-520-6060
Website: www.commerceone.com

Management and Staff

Katie Nittler, Partner

Type of Firm

Non-Financial Corp. Affiliate or Subsidiary

Project Preferences

Type of Financing Preferred:

Expansion

Size of Investments Considered

Min Size of Investment Considered (000s): $3,000
Max Size of Investment Considered (000s): $15,000

Industry Preferences

Internet Specific
Internet

Additional Information

Capital Under Management: $100,000,000
Current Activity Level : Actively seeking new investments

COMMTECH INTERNATIONAL

535 Middlefield Road
Suite 200
Menlo Park, CA 94025
Phone: 650-328-0190
Fax: 650-328-6442

Type of Firm

Private Firm Investing Own Capital

Project Preferences

Role in Financing:
Prefer role as deal originator

Type of Financing Preferred:
Seed
Start-up Financing

Size of Investments Considered

Min Size of Investment Considered (000s): $300
Max Size of Investment Considered (000s): $500

Geographical Preferences

United States
West Coast

Industry Preferences

Communications and Media
Commercial Communications
Telecommunications
Data Communications

Computer Software
Computer Services
Systems Software
Applications Software

Internet Specific
Internet

Semiconductors/Other Elect.
Sensors

Biotechnology
Industrial Biotechnology
Biosensors

Medical/Health
Hospital/Other Instit.

Additional Information

Name of Most Recent Fund: CommTech International
Most Recent Fund Was Raised: 01/01/1983
Year Founded: 1983
Capital Under Management: $40,000,000
Current Activity Level : Making few, if any, new investments
Method of Compensation: Return on invest. most important, but chg. closing fees, service fees, etc.

COMPASS TECHNOLOGY PARTNERS

1550 El Camino Real
Suite 275
Menlo Park, CA 94025-4111
Phone: 650-322-7595
Fax: 650-322-0588
Website: www.compasstechpartners.com

Other Offices

128 East 31st Street
New York, NY 10016-6848
Phone: 212-689-2626
Fax: 212-689-5301

Management and Staff

Alain Harrus, Partner

Whom to Contact

Leon Dulberger

Type of Firm

Private Firm Investing Own Capital

Project Preferences

Role in Financing:
Prefer role as deal originator

Type of Financing Preferred:
Leveraged Buyout
Mezzanine
Special Situation

Geographical Preferences

United States
All U.S.

Industry Preferences

(% based on actual investment)

Computer Software and Services	36.2%
Internet Specific	34.5%
Communications and Media	18.5%
Semiconductors/Other Elect.	10.9%

Additional Information

Year Founded: 1988
Capital Under Management: $50,000,000
Current Activity Level : Actively seeking new investments
Method of Compensation: Return on invest. most important, but chg. closing fees, service fees, etc.

COMVENTURES (AKA: COMMUNICATIONS VENTURES)

505 Hamilton Avenue
Suite 305
Palo Alto, CA 94301
Phone: 650-325-9600
Fax: 650-325-9608
Website: www.comven.com

Other Offices

3000 Sand Hill Road
Building Two, Suite 175
Menlo Park, CA 94025
Phone: 415-854-3098
Fax: 415-854-2276

Management and Staff

Clifford Higgerson, General Partner
David Helfrich, General Partner
Jim McLean, General Partner
Laura Gwosden, Chief Financial Officer
Michael Rolnick, General Partner
Paul Vabakos, Partner
Perry Wu, Venture Partner
Roland Van der Meer, General Partner

Whom to Contact

all of above

Type of Firm

Private Firm Investing Own Capital

Industry Association Membership

National Venture Capital Association (NVCA)
Western Association of Venture Capitalists (WAVC)

Project Preferences

Role in Financing:
Prefer role as deal originator but will also invest in deals created by others

Type of Financing Preferred:
Early Stage
First Stage Financing
Second Stage Financing
Seed
Startup

Size of Investments Considered
Min Size of Investment Considered (000s): $500
Max Size of Investment Considered (000s): $25,000

Geographical Preferences
United States
All U.S.

International
Israel
United Kingdom

Industry Preferences
(% based on actual investment)

Communications and Media	39.8%
Internet Specific	30.2%
Semiconductors/Other Elect.	14.5%
Computer Software and Services	9.5%
Computer Hardware	4.1%
Other Products	1.9%

Additional Information
Name of Most Recent Fund: ComVentures IV
Most Recent Fund Was Raised: 10/01/1999
Year Founded: 1987
Capital Under Management: $1,100,000,000
Current Activity Level : Actively seeking new investments
Method of Compensation: Return on investment is of primary concern, do not charge fees

CONVERGENCE PARTNERS L.P.

3000 Sand Hill Road
Building Two Suite 235
Menlo Park, CA 94025
Phone: 650-854-3010
Fax: 650-854-3015
Website: www.convergencepartners.com

Management and Staff
Chen Tang, Chief Financial Officer
Eric DiBenedetto, General Partner
Robert Selvi, General Partner
Russ Irwin, General Partner

Type of Firm
Private Firm Investing Own Capital

Industry Association Membership
Western Association of Venture Capitalists (WAVC)

Project Preferences
Role in Financing:
Prefer role as deal originator but will also invest in deals created by others

Type of Financing Preferred:
Early Stage
First Stage Financing
Seed

Size of Investments Considered
Min Size of Investment Considered (000s): $2,000
Max Size of Investment Considered (000s): $10,000

Geographical Preferences
United States
All U.S.

Industry Preferences
(% based on actual investment)

Internet Specific	64.0%
Semiconductors/Other Elect.	11.9%
Computer Software and Services	9.9%
Industrial/Energy	5.0%
Other Products	5.0%
Communications and Media	4.2%

Additional Information
Name of Most Recent Fund: Convergence Ventures I, L.P.
Most Recent Fund Was Raised: 09/21/1999
Year Founded: 1997
Capital Under Management: $200,000,000
Current Activity Level : Actively seeking new investments
Method of Compensation: Return on invest. most important, but chg. closing fees, service fees, etc.

CORAL VENTURES

3000 Sand Hill Road
Building 3, Suite 210
Menlo Park, CA 94025
Phone: 650-854-5226
Fax: 650-854-4625
Website: www.coralventures.com

See Minnesota for full listing.

CRESCENDO VENTURE MANAGEMENT LLC (FKA:IAI VENTURES)

480 Cowper Avenue
Suite 300
Palo Alto, CA 94301-2013
Phone: 650-470-1200
Fax: 650-470-1201
Website: www.crescendoventures.com

See Minnesota for full listing.

CROCKER CAPITAL/CROCKER ASSOC.

1 Post Street
Suite 2500
San Francisco, CA 94101
Phone: 415-956-5250
Fax: 415-959-5710

Type of Firm
Investment/Merchant Bank Subsid/Affil

Industry Association Membership
Western Association of Venture Capitalists (WAVC)

Project Preferences
Type of Financing Preferred:
Leveraged Buyout
Second Stage Financing
Startup

Geographical Preferences
United States
West Coast

Industry Preferences
Communications and Media
Communications and Media

Semiconductors/Other Elect.
Laser Related
Fiber Optics

Medical/Health
Medical/Health
Medical Products
Pharmaceuticals

Consumer Related
Consumer
Retail
Food/Beverage
Education Related

Industrial/Energy
Materials

Manufact.
Manufacturing

Other
Environment Responsible

Additional Information
Current Activity Level : Actively seeking new investments

CROSSLINK CAPITAL (FKA: OMEGA VENTURE PARTNERS)

Two Embarcadero Center
Suite 2200
San Francisco, CA 94111
Phone: 415-617-1800
Fax: 415-617-1801
Website: www.crosslinkcapital.com

Management and Staff
Anthony Brenner, Managing Director
Bill Nolan, Managing Director
Dan Dunn, Managing Director
Gerri Holt, Chief Financial Officer
Jason Sanders, Principal
Michael Stark, Managing Director
Sy Kaufman, Managing Director
Thomas Bliska, Managing Director
Tucker Brockhoff, Principal
Vladimir Jacimovic, Managing Director

Type of Firm
Private Firm Investing Own Capital

Industry Association Membership
National Venture Capital Association (NVCA)
Western Association of Venture Capitalists (WAVC)

Project Preferences

Type of Financing Preferred:
Balanced
Later Stage

Size of Investments Considered
Min Size of Investment Considered (000s): $3,000
Max Size of Investment Considered (000s): $10,000

Geographical Preferences

United States
All U.S.
California
All U.S.

International
All International

Industry Preferences
(% based on actual investment)

Internet Specific	52.9%
Computer Software and Services	12.9%
Computer Hardware	9.6%
Semiconductors/Other Elect.	6.7%
Communications and Media	6.4%
Biotechnology	6.2%
Medical/Health	1.9%
Consumer Related	1.8%
Other Products	1.4%
Industrial/Energy	0.2%

Additional Information
Name of Most Recent Fund: Crossover Fund
Most Recent Fund Was Raised: 03/01/1986
Year Founded: 1989
Capital Under Management: $1,000,000,000
Current Activity Level : Actively seeking new investments

CROSSROADS CAPITAL PARTNERS, LLC

1600 Dove Street
Suite 300
Newport Beach, CA 92660
Phone: 949-261-1600

Other Offices

885 3rd Avenue
Suite 2900
New York, NY 10022
Phone: 212-829-5794
Fax: 212-829-5795

Management and Staff
Dennis Simon, Managing Director
James Skelton, Principal
Jim Neidhart, Principal
Mark Barbeau, Principal

Type of Firm
Private Firm Investing Own Capital

Project Preferences

Role in Financing:
Prefer role as deal originator

Size of Investments Considered
Min Size of Investment Considered (000s): $3,000
Max Size of Investment Considered (000s): $25,000

Additional Information
Name of Most Recent Fund: Crossroads Capital Partners
Most Recent Fund Was Raised: 01/01/1997
Year Founded: 1997
Capital Under Management: $200,000,000
Current Activity Level : Actively seeking new investments

CROWN ADVISORS INTERNATIONAL, LTD.

3000 Sand Hill Road
Menlo Park, CA 94025
Phone: 415-854-2215
Website: www.crownadvisors.com

See New York for full listing.

CRYSTAL INTERNET VENTURE FUND, L.P.

361 Lytton Avenue
Palo Alto, CA 94301
Phone: 650-330-3582
Fax: 650-330-3585
Website: www.crystalventure.com

See Ohio for full listing.

CUPERTINO VENTURES PARTNERSHIP, L.P.

20300 Stevens Creek Blvd.
Cupertino, CA 95014
Phone: 408-725-0774

Type of Firm
Private Firm Investing Own Capital

Additional Information
Name of Most Recent Fund: Cupertino Venture Partners III
Most Recent Fund Was Raised: 03/31/1999
Current Activity Level : Actively seeking new investments

CW GROUP, INC.

2187 Newcastle Avenue
Suite 101
Cardiff, CA 92007
Phone: 760-942-4535
Fax: 760-942-4530
Website: www.cwventures.com

See New York for full listing.

DAIMLER CHRYSLER VENTURE GMBH (AKA DCV)

1510 Page Mill Road
Palo Alto, CA 94304
Phone: 650-845-2527
Fax: 650-845-2555
Website: www.dcventure.com

See Foreign Venture Capital Firms for full listing.

DAKOTA GROUP, THE

P.O. Box 1025
Menlo Park, CA 94025
Phone: 650-853-0600
Fax: 650-851-4899

Other Offices

10209 Chastain Drive, N.E.
Atlanta, GA 30342
Phone: 404-851-0100
Fax: 404-851-0100

Type of Firm
Investment/Merchant Bank Subsid/Affil

Project Preferences

Role in Financing:
Prefer role as deal originator but will also invest in deals created by others

Type of Financing Preferred:
First Stage Financing
Recapitalizations
Second Stage Financing
Seed
Special Situation
Start-up Financing

Size of Investments Considered
Min Size of Investment Considered (000s): $300
Max Size of Investment Considered (000s): $500

Geographical Preferences

United States
Northeast
Northwest
Rocky Mountain
Southeast
Southwest

International
Australia
China
France
Germany
Japan
Middle East
Spain
United Kingdom

Industry Preferences

Communications and Media
Commercial Communications
CATV & Pay TV Systems
Telecommunications
Data Communications

Computer Software
Computer Services
Systems Software
Applications Software

Consumer Related
Education Related

Manufact.
Publishing

Additional Information
Year Founded: 1990
Current Activity Level : Actively seeking new investments
Method of Compensation: Return on invest. most important, but chg. closing fees, service fees, etc.

DALI, HOOK PARTNERS (FKA: HOOK PARTNERS)

3000 Sand Hill Road
Building 1, Suite 285
Menlo Park, CA 94025
Phone: 650-926-9820
Fax: 650-926-9825
Website: www.hookpartners.com

See Texas for full listing.

DAVIS GROUP

P.O. Box 69953
Los Angeles, CA 90069-0953
Phone: 310-659-6327

Management and Staff
Roger Davis

Whom to Contact
Roger Davis

Type of Firm
Mgt. Consulting Firm

Project Preferences

Role in Financing:
Prefer role as deal originator but will also invest in deals created by others

Type of Financing Preferred:
First Stage Financing
Leveraged Buyout
Special Situation
Start-up Financing

Geographical Preferences

United States
All U.S.

Canada
All Canada

International
Afghanistan
Australia
Bermuda
China
France
Germany
Italy
Japan
Mexico
South Africa
Spain
United Kingdom

Industry Preferences

Communications and Media
Radio & TV Broadcasting
Satellite Microwave Comm.

Computer Software
Computer Services
Systems Software
Applications Software

Internet Specific
Internet

Biotechnology
Biotechnology

Medical/Health
Diagnostic Services
Other Therapeutic
Medical Products
Hospitals/Clinics/Primary
Hospital/Other Instit.
Pharmaceuticals

Consumer Related
Entertainment and Leisure
Food/Beverage
Consumer Products
Consumer Services
Hotels and Resorts
Education Related

Industrial/Energy
Alternative Energy
Coal Related
Energy Conservation Relat
Machinery
Environmental Related

Transportation
Transportation

Financial Services
Real Estate

Business Serv.
Consulting Services

Manufact.
Publishing

Agr/Forestr/Fish
Agriculture related

Additional Information
Year Founded: 1969
Current Activity Level : Actively seeking new investments
Method of Compensation: Return on invest. most important, but chg. closing fees, service fees, etc.

DAWES INVESTMENT PARTNERS, L.P.

350 Santa Rita Avenue
Palo Alto, CA 94301
Phone: 650-323-1334
Fax: 650-323-4209

Management and Staff
Dexter Dawes, General Partner

Type of Firm
Private Firm Investing Own Capital

Additional Information
Capital Under Management: $3,200,000
Current Activity Level : Actively seeking new investments

DEFTA PARTNERS

Suite 1410
San Francisco, CA 94111-5616
Phone: 415-433-2262
Fax: 415-433-2264
Website: www.deftavc.cc

Other Offices

Greyhound House c/o Pond Venture
23-24 George Street
Richmond, Surrey, United Kingdom TW9 1H
Phone: 0181-940-1001
Fax: 0181-332-6751

Obase-cho 11-19
Tennoji-ku
Osaka 543, Japan
Phone: 81-6-767-4195
Fax: 81-6-765-5532

P.O.B. 2349
Savyon, Israel 56530
Phone: 972-3-5349126
Fax: 972-3-5353615

Sasazuka 2-62-2
Shibuya-ku
Tokyo 151, Japan 151
Phone: 813-5352-2543
Fax: 813-5352-2544

Management and Staff
Akira Ishida, Partner
George Hara, Partner
Kent Hara, Chief Financial Officer

Type of Firm
Private Firm Investing Own Capital

Industry Association Membership
National Venture Capital Association (NVCA)

Project Preferences

Role in Financing:
Prefer role as deal originator but will also invest in deals created by others

Type of Financing Preferred:
Control-block Purchases
First Stage Financing
Mezzanine
Research and Development
Second Stage Financing
Seed
Special Situation
Start-up Financing

Geographical Preferences

United States
Midwest
Northeast
Northwest
Southwest
West Coast

International
China
Japan
United Kingdom

Industry Preferences

(% based on actual investment)

Computer Software and Services	54.7%
Semiconductors/Other Elect.	20.2%
Internet Specific	18.5%
Computer Hardware	3.6%
Communications and Media	2.9%

Additional Information
Name of Most Recent Fund: DEFTA Alliance Fund II
Most Recent Fund Was Raised: 07/01/1999
Year Founded: 1985
Capital Under Management: $25,000,000
Current Activity Level : Actively seeking new investments
Method of Compensation: Return on invest. most important, but chg. closing fees, service fees, etc.

DELPHI VENTURES

3000 Sand Hill Road
Building One, Suite 135
Menlo Park, CA 94025
Phone: 650-854-9650
Fax: 650-854-2961
Website: www.delphiventures.com

Management and Staff
David Douglass, General Partner
Donald Lothrop, General Partner
Doug Roeder, Venture Partner
Erin Alley, Partner
James Bochnowski, General Partner
John Simon, Venture Partner
Kevin Roberg, General Partner
Paul Auerbach, Venture Partner

Type of Firm
Private Firm Investing Own Capital

Industry Association Membership
National Venture Capital Association (NVCA)
Western Association of Venture Capitalists (WAVC)

Project Preferences

Role in Financing:
Prefer role as deal originator but will also invest in deals created by others

Type of Financing Preferred:
First Stage Financing
Second Stage Financing
Seed
Start-up Financing

Size of Investments Considered
Min Size of Investment Considered (000s): $500
Max Size of Investment Considered: No Limit

Geographical Preferences

United States
All U.S.

Industry Preferences

(% based on actual investment)

Medical/Health	51.0%
Internet Specific	20.2%
Biotechnology	12.1%
Computer Software and Services	10.0%
Other Products	2.5%
Computer Hardware	2.5%
Industrial/Energy	1.2%
Communications and Media	0.5%

Additional Information
Name of Most Recent Fund: Delphi Venture V
Most Recent Fund Was Raised: 12/01/1997
Year Founded: 1988
Capital Under Management: $444,000,000
Current Activity Level : Actively seeking new investments
Method of Compensation: Return on investment is of primary concern, do not charge fees

DENALI VENTURE CAPITAL

1925 Woodland Avenue
Santa Clara, CA 95050
Phone: 408-690-4838
Fax: 408-247-6979
E-mail: wael@denaliventurecapital.com
Website: www.denaliventurecapital.com

Type of Firm
Private Equity Advisor or Fund of Fund Mgr

Project Preferences

Type of Financing Preferred:
Early Stage

Size of Investments Considered
Min Size of Investment Considered (000s): $100
Max Size of Investment Considered (000s): $5,000

Geographical Preferences

United States
West Coast

Industry Preferences

Medical/Health
Medical/Health

Additional Information
Year Founded: 1999
Current Activity Level : Actively seeking new investments

DEUCALION VENTURE PARTNERS

19501 Brooklime
Sonoma, CA 95476
Phone: 707-938-4974
Fax: 707-938-8921

Other Offices

19501 Brooklime
Sonoma, CA 95476
Phone: 707-938-4974
Fax: 707-938-8921

Type of Firm
Private Firm Investing Own Capital

Project Preferences

Role in Financing:
Prefer role as deal originator but will also invest in deals created by others

Type of Financing Preferred:
First Stage Financing
Second Stage Financing
Seed
Start-up Financing

Size of Investments Considered
Min Size of Investment Considered (000s): $500
Max Size of Investment Considered: No Limit

Geographical Preferences

United States
West Coast

Industry Preferences

Computer Software
Artificial Intelligence

Biotechnology
Biotech Related Research

Medical/Health
Diagnostic Services
Diagnostic Test Products

Consumer Related
Education Related

Industrial/Energy
Energy Conservation Relat
Machinery

Transportation
Transportation

Financial Services
Financial Services

Manufact.
Publishing

Additional Information
Name of Most Recent Fund: Deucalion Venture Partners
Most Recent Fund Was Raised: 11/01/1987
Year Founded: 1987
Capital Under Management: $5,200,000
Current Activity Level : Actively seeking new investments
Method of Compensation: Return on investment is of primary concern, do not charge fees

DEVELOPERS EQUITY CORP.

1880 Century Park East
Suite 211
Los Angeles, CA 90067
Phone: 213-277-0300

Type of Firm
Private Firm Investing Own Capital

Project Preferences

Role in Financing:
Prefer role as deal originator but will also invest in deals created by others

Type of Financing Preferred:
Leveraged Buyout
Seed
Start-up Financing

Industry Preferences

Industrial/Energy
Industrial Products
Machinery

Transportation
Transportation

Financial Services
Real Estate

Additional Information
Name of Most Recent Fund: Developers Equity Corp.
Most Recent Fund Was Raised: 06/01/1982
Year Founded: 1974
Capital Under Management: $3,000,000
Current Activity Level : Inactive / Unknown
Method of Compensation: Function primarily in service area, receive contingent fee in cash or equity

DIAMONDHEAD VENTURES, L.P.

2460 Sand Hill Road
Suite 301
Sacramento, CA 94205
Phone: 650.233.7526
Fax: 650.233.7527
Website: www.dhven.com

Management and Staff
David Lane, Managing Director
J. Gerry Purdy, Venture Partner
Raman Khanna, Managing Director

Type of Firm
Private Firm Investing Own Capital

Project Preferences

Type of Financing Preferred:
Early Stage

Geographical Preferences

United States
California
All U.S.

Industry Preferences

Internet Specific
Internet

Additional Information
Year Founded: 2000
Capital Under Management: $150,000,000
Current Activity Level : Actively seeking new investments

DIGITAL MEDIA CAMPUS

2221 Park Place
El Segundo, CA 90245
Phone: 310-426-8000
Fax: 310-426-8010
E-mail: info@thecampus.com
Website: www.digitalmediacampus.com

Management and Staff
John Baker, Chief Financial Officer
Leonard Armato, Chairman & CEO

Type of Firm
Incubators

Project Preferences

Role in Financing:
Prefer role as deal originator

Type of Financing Preferred:
Early Stage
Seed

Industry Preferences

Consumer Related
Entertainment and Leisure
Sports

Business Serv.
Media

Additional Information
Year Founded: 2000
Current Activity Level : Actively seeking new investments

DIGITAL VENTURES (FKA DIGITAL TECHNOLOGY PARTNERS, LLC)

50 California Street
8th Floor
San Francisco, CA 94111
Phone: 415-354-6200
Fax: 415-439-5355
Website: wwww.digitalventures.com

Management and Staff
Bashir Wada, Chief Financial Officer
Dean Gardner, Chief Executive Officer
Wendy Paskin-Jordan, Venture Partner

Type of Firm
Private Firm Investing Own Capital

Project Preferences

Role in Financing:
Will function either as deal originator or investor in deals created by others

Industry Preferences

(% based on actual investment)

Computer Software and Services	70.6%
Internet Specific	19.2%
Communications and Media	3.8%
Semiconductors/Other Elect.	2.6%
Medical/Health	2.3%
Biotechnology	1.5%

Additional Information
Name of Most Recent Fund: Digital Technology Partners Seed Fund, L.P.
Most Recent Fund Was Raised: 01/01/1997
Capital Under Management: $105,000,000
Current Activity Level : Actively seeking new investments

DOLL CAPITAL MANAGEMENT

3000 Sand Hill Road
Building Three, Suite 225
Menlo Park, CA 94025
Phone: 650-233-1400
Fax: 650-854-9159
Website: www.dcmvc.com

Management and Staff
David Chao, Managing General Partner
Dixon Doll, Managing General Partner
Eric Gonzales, Partner
Peter Moran, General Partner
Robert Theis, General Partner
Rudolph Rehm, Chief Financial Officer
Thomas Blaisdell, Partner

Type of Firm
Private Firm Investing Own Capital

Industry Association Membership
Western Association of Venture Capitalists (WAVC)

Project Preferences

Role in Financing:
Prefer role as deal originator but will also invest in deals created by others

Type of Financing Preferred:
First Stage Financing
Recapitalizations
Research and Development
Seed
Start-up Financing

Geographical Preferences

United States
Midwest
Northeast
Northwest
Rocky Mountain
Southwest
West Coast

International
Bermuda
China
France
Germany
Japan
United Kingdom

Industry Preferences

(% based on actual investment)

Internet Specific	64.4%
Computer Software and Services	17.9%
Communications and Media	10.5%
Semiconductors/Other Elect.	5.6%
Consumer Related	1.4%
Computer Hardware	0.2%

Additional Information
Name of Most Recent Fund: Doll Capital Management Internet Fund,L.P.
Most Recent Fund Was Raised: 06/04/1999
Year Founded: 1996
Capital Under Management: $650,000,000
Current Activity Level : Actively seeking new investments
Method of Compensation: Return on investment is of primary concern, do not charge fees

DOMAIN ASSOCIATES, L.L.C.

28202 Cabot Road
Suite 200
Laguna Niguel, CA 92677
Phone: 949-347-2446
Fax: 949-347-9720
Website: www.domainvc.com

See New Jersey for full listing.

DOMINION VENTURES, INC.

1656 North California Blvd.
Suite 300
Walnut Creek, CA 94596
Phone: 925-280-6300
Fax: 925-280-6338
Website: www.dominion.com

Other Offices

2400 Sand Hill Road
Building Two, Suite 100
Menlo Park, CA 94025
Phone: 650-854-5932
Fax: 650-854-1957

One Post Office Square
38th Floor, Suite 3820
Boston, MA 02109
Phone: 617-367-8575
Fax: 617-367-0323

Management and Staff
Brian Smith, General Partner
Geoffrey Woolley, Venture Partner
John Kingery, Chief Executive Officer
Kendall Cooper, General Partner
Michael Lee, General Partner
Randolph Werner, General Partner
Renee Baker, Managing Director

Type of Firm
Private Firm Investing Own Capital

Industry Association Membership
Western Association of Venture Capitalists (WAVC)

Project Preferences

Role in Financing:
Prefer role as deal originator but will also invest in deals created by others

Type of Financing Preferred:
Balanced
Early Stage
Expansion
Mezzanine

Size of Investments Considered
Min Size of Investment Considered (000s): $1,000
Max Size of Investment Considered (000s): $6,000

Geographical Preferences

United States
All U.S.

Industry Preferences

(% based on actual investment)

Internet Specific	38.7%
Computer Software and Services	18.5%
Medical/Health	13.6%
Communications and Media	9.9%
Other Products	5.7%
Computer Hardware	4.3%
Consumer Related	3.9%
Semiconductors/Other Elect.	3.7%
Biotechnology	1.6%
Industrial/Energy	0.0%

Additional Information
Name of Most Recent Fund: Dominion Fund V, L.P.
Most Recent Fund Was Raised: 06/28/1996
Year Founded: 1985
Capital Under Management: $383,500,000
Current Activity Level : Actively seeking new investments
Method of Compensation: Return on invest. most important, but chg. closing fees, service fees, etc.

DORSET CAPITAL

Pier 1
Bay 2
San Francisco, CA 94111
Phone: 415-398-7101
Fax: 415-398-7141
Website: www.dorsetcapital.com

Management and Staff
Jeffrey Mills, Principal
John Berg, Managing Partner
Mark Saltzgaber, Principal

Type of Firm
Private Firm Investing Own Capital

Project Preferences

Role in Financing:
Will function either as deal originator or investor in deals created by others

Type of Financing Preferred:
Expansion
Generalist PE
Later Stage
Leveraged Buyout
Management Buyouts
Second Stage Financing

Size of Investments Considered
Min Size of Investment Considered (000s): $1,000
Max Size of Investment Considered (000s): $10,000

Geographical Preferences

United States
All U.S.

Industry Preferences

Consumer Related
Consumer
Retail
Food/Beverage

Business Serv.
Services

Additional Information
Name of Most Recent Fund: Dorset Capital, L.P.
Most Recent Fund Was Raised: 07/01/1999
Year Founded: 1999
Capital Under Management: $70,000,000
Current Activity Level : Actively seeking new investments
Method of Compensation: Return on investment is of primary concern, do not charge fees

---

DOT EDU VENTURES

650 Castro Street
Suite 270
Mountain View, CA 94041
Phone: 650-575-5638
Fax: 650-325-5249
Website: www.doteduventures.com

Management and Staff
Asha Jadeja, Managing Partner
Casey McGlynn, General Partner

Type of Firm
Private Firm Investing Own Capital

Project Preferences

Role in Financing:
Will function either as deal originator or investor in deals created by others

Type of Financing Preferred:
Early Stage
Seed

Geographical Preferences

United States
All U.S.

Industry Preferences

Internet Specific
Internet

Additional Information
Year Founded: 2000
Current Activity Level : Actively seeking new investments

DOTCOM VENTURES L.P.

3945 Freedom Circle
Suite 740
Santa Clara, CA 95054
Phone: 408-919-9855
Fax: 408-919-9857
Website: www.dotcomventuresatl.com

Other Offices

1103 Riverbend Club Drive
Atlanta, GA 30301
Phone: 770-612-9190

Management and Staff
Pauline Duffy, Chief Financial Officer
Sada Chidambaram, General Partner
Stephen Hyndman, General Partner

Type of Firm
Private Firm Investing Own Capital

Industry Association Membership
National Venture Capital Association (NVCA)
Natl assoc of Small Bus. Inv. Co (NASBIC)

Project Preferences

Type of Financing Preferred:
Early Stage
First Stage Financing
Seed

Geographical Preferences

United States
All U.S.

Industry Preferences

Communications and Media
Telecommunications

Internet Specific
Internet

Additional Information
Year Founded: 1999
Current Activity Level : Actively seeking new investments

DOUGERY VENTURES

165 Santa Ana Avenue
San Francisco, CA 94127
Phone: 415-566-5226
Fax: 415-566-5757

Other Offices

155 Bovet Road
Suite 350
San Mateo, CA 94402
Phone: 415-358-8701
Fax: 415-358-8706

Type of Firm
Private Firm Investing Own Capital

Industry Association Membership
National Venture Capital Association (NVCA)
Western Association of Venture Capitalists (WAVC)

Project Preferences

Role in Financing:
Prefer role as deal originator but will also invest in deals created by others

Type of Financing Preferred:
First Stage Financing
Leveraged Buyout
Second Stage Financing
Seed
Start-up Financing

Size of Investments Considered
Min Size of Investment Considered (000s): $1,000
Max Size of Investment Considered: No Limit

Geographical Preferences
United States
West Coast

Industry Preferences
(% based on actual investment)

Communications and Media	20.0%
Computer Hardware	16.9%
Medical/Health	15.1%
Semiconductors/Other Elect.	11.8%
Industrial/Energy	11.7%
Biotechnology	8.3%
Computer Software and Services	7.6%
Other Products	6.2%
Consumer Related	2.4%

Additional Information
Name of Most Recent Fund: D&W III International Investors Partnership
Most Recent Fund Was Raised: 03/01/1988
Year Founded: 1981
Capital Under Management: $130,000,000
Current Activity Level : Actively seeking new investments
Method of Compensation: Return on investment is of primary concern, do not charge fees

DRAPER FISHER JURVETSON (FKA: DRAPER ASSOCIATES)

400 Seaport Court
Suite 250
Redwood City, CA 94063
Phone: 650-599-9000
Fax: 650-599-9726
Website: www.dfj.com

Management and Staff
Jennifer Fonstad, Managing Director
John Fisher, Managing Director
Larry Kubal, Managing Director
Mark Greenstein, Chief Financial Officer
Roderick Thompson, General Partner
Steve Jurvetson, Managing Director
Timothy Draper, Managing Director
Todd Hixon, Managing Director
Warren Packard, Managing Director

Whom to Contact
J.B. Fox
Janelle Durfee

Type of Firm
Private Firm Investing Own Capital

Industry Association Membership
Natl assoc of Small Bus. Inv. Co (NASBIC)
Western Association of Venture Capitalists (WAVC)

Project Preferences
Role in Financing:
Prefer role as deal originator but will also invest in deals created by others

Type of Financing Preferred:
Early Stage
First Stage Financing
Seed
Start-up Financing

Size of Investments Considered
Min Size of Investment Considered (000s): $1,000
Max Size of Investment Considered (000s): $5,000

Geographical Preferences
United States
California
All U.S.
West Coast

International
Europe
All International

Industry Preferences
(% based on actual investment)

Internet Specific	50.1%
Computer Software and Services	20.8%
Communications and Media	12.3%
Semiconductors/Other Elect.	8.2%
Other Products	6.9%
Computer Hardware	1.3%
Industrial/Energy	0.3%
Consumer Related	0.1%
Biotechnology	0.0%

Additional Information
Name of Most Recent Fund: Draper Fisher Jurvetson Gotham Fund
Most Recent Fund Was Raised: 09/01/1999
Year Founded: 1985
Capital Under Management: $1,775,000,000
Current Activity Level : Actively seeking new investments
Method of Compensation: Return on investment is of primary concern, do not charge fees

DRAPER FISHER JURVETSON EPLANET VENTURES, LP

400 Seaport Court
Suite 250
Redwood City, CA 94063
Phone: 650-599-9000
Fax: 650-599-9726
Website: www.dfj.com

Management and Staff
Asad Jamal, Managing Director
Roderick Thomson, Managing Director

Type of Firm
Private Firm Investing Own Capital

Geographical Preferences
International
Europe

Additional Information
Capital Under Management: $690,000,000
Current Activity Level : Actively seeking new investments

DRAPER INTERNATIONAL

50 California Street
Suite 2925
San Francisco, CA 94111
Phone: 415-616-4050
Fax: 415-616-4060
Website: www.draperintl.com

Other Offices

203-204 Prestige Meridian
M.G. Road
Bangalore, India 560001
Phone: 91805550325
Fax: 91805550461

Management and Staff
Abhay Havaldar, Partner
Cynthia Lam, Chief Financial Officer
Kiran Nadkarni, Partner
Robin Donohoe, Partner
William Draper, Managing Director

Type of Firm
Private Firm Investing Own Capital

Industry Association Membership
National Venture Capital Association (NVCA)
Western Association of Venture Capitalists (WAVC)

Project Preferences

Type of Financing Preferred:
Early Stage
Expansion
Second Stage Financing
Seed

Industry Preferences

(% based on actual investment)

Computer Software and Services	42.9%
Internet Specific	33.1%
Computer Hardware	14.7%
Consumer Related	6.2%
Communications and Media	3.1%

Additional Information
Year Founded: 1994
Capital Under Management: $55,000,000
Current Activity Level : Actively seeking new investments

DRAPER RICHARDS

50 California Street
Suite 2925
San Francisco, CA 94111
Phone: 415-616-4050
Fax: 415-616-4060
Website: www.draperrichards.com

Management and Staff
Cynthia Lam, Chief Financial Officer
Robin Donohoe, Vice President
William Draper, President

Type of Firm
Private Firm Investing Own Capital

Industry Association Membership
National Venture Capital Association (NVCA)
Natl assoc of Small Bus. Inv. Co (NASBIC)
Western Association of Venture Capitalists (WAVC)

Project Preferences

Role in Financing:
Will function either as deal originator or investor in deals created by others

Type of Financing Preferred:
Early Stage
First Stage Financing
Second Stage Financing

Geographical Preferences

United States
Mid Atlantic
Northeast
Northern California
West Coast

Industry Preferences

(% based on actual investment)

Internet Specific	62.9%
Computer Software and Services	30.2%
Communications and Media	4.4%
Consumer Related	1.8%
Semiconductors/Other Elect.	0.8%

Additional Information
Name of Most Recent Fund: Draper Richards, L.P.
Most Recent Fund Was Raised: 12/31/1996
Year Founded: 1996
Capital Under Management: $17,000,000
Current Activity Level : Actively seeking new investments
Method of Compensation: Return on investment is of primary concern, do not charge fees

DRYSDALE ENTERPRISES

177 Bovet Road
Suite 600
San Mateo, CA 94402
Phone: 650-341-6336
Fax: 650-341-1329

Other Offices

Marsman Drysdale Building
2246 Pasong Tamo Street
Metro Manila, Philippines
Phone: 632-894-4228
Fax: 632-815-9442

Management and Staff
George Drysdale

Whom to Contact
George Drysdale

Type of Firm
Private Firm Investing Own Capital

Industry Association Membership
Western Association of Venture Capitalists (WAVC)

Project Preferences

Role in Financing:
Prefer role as deal originator but will also invest in deals created by others

Type of Financing Preferred:
First Stage Financing
Leveraged Buyout
Mezzanine
Second Stage Financing
Special Situation

Size of Investments Considered
Min Size of Investment Considered (000s): $3,000
Max Size of Investment Considered: No Limit

Geographical Preferences

United States
West Coast

International
South Africa

Industry Preferences

Communications and Media
Communications and Media

Computer Hardware
Integrated Turnkey System

Computer Software
Computer Services
Systems Software
Applications Software

Semiconductors/Other Elect.
Electronic Components
Semiconductor
Controllers and Sensors
Component Testing Equipmt
Laser Related
Fiber Optics

Biotechnology
Industrial Biotechnology
Biosensors

Medical/Health
Medical/Health
Medical Diagnostics
Medical Therapeutics

Consumer Related
Consumer
Retail

Industrial/Energy
Materials
Factory Automation
Machinery
Environmental Related

Transportation
Transportation

Financial Services
Financial Services
Real Estate

Business Serv.
Distribution

Manufact.
Office Automation Equipmt
Publishing

Agr/Forestr/Fish
Agriculture related
Mining and Minerals

Additional Information
Year Founded: 1991
Capital Under Management: $50,000,000
Current Activity Level : Actively seeking new investments
Method of Compensation: Return on investment is of primary concern, do not charge fees

DYNAFUND VENTURES, L.L.C.

21515 Hawthorne Boulevard
Suite 1200
Torrance, CA 90503
Phone: 310-543-5477
Fax: 310-543-8733
Website: www.dynafundventures.com

Other Offices

1555 Wilson Blvd.
Suite 320
Arlington, VA 22209
Phone: 703-841-0990
Fax: 703-841-8395

525 University Avenue
Suite 610
Taipei, Taiwan 94301
Phone: 650-321-8160
Fax: 650-321-8159

Management and Staff
Danny Yu, Partner
David Lam, Partner
Denny Ko, General Partner
James Liao, General Partner
Peter Lee, Partner
Richard Whiting, General Partner
Scott Walters, Chief Financial Officer
Tony Hung, General Partner
Warren Chao, Principal

Type of Firm
Private Firm Investing Own Capital

Industry Association Membership
Mid-Atlantic Venture Association

Project Preferences

Role in Financing:
Will function either as deal originator or investor in deals created by others

Type of Financing Preferred:
Early Stage
Startup

Size of Investments Considered
Min Size of Investment Considered (000s): $1,000
Max Size of Investment Considered (000s): $4,000

Geographical Preferences

United States
All U.S.

Industry Preferences

(% based on actual investment)

Semiconductors/Other Elect.	29.4%
Internet Specific	27.5%
Computer Software and Services	19.8%
Communications and Media	15.5%
Biotechnology	6.2%
Computer Hardware	1.6%

Additional Information
Year Founded: 1997
Capital Under Management: $210,000,000
Current Activity Level : Actively seeking new investments
Method of Compensation: Return on investment is of primary concern, do not charge fees

E*CAPITAL CORPORATION

1000 Wilshire Boulevard
Los Angeles, CA 90017
Phone: 213-688-8082
Fax: 213-688-8095
Website: www.e-cap.com

Type of Firm
Private Equity Advisor or Fund of Fund Mgr

Industry Association Membership
National Venture Capital Association (NVCA)

Project Preferences

Type of Financing Preferred:
Early Stage

Size of Investments Considered
Min Size of Investment Considered (000s): $500
Max Size of Investment Considered (000s): $1,500

Geographical Preferences

United States
Southern California

Additional Information
Capital Under Management: $20,000,000
Current Activity Level : Actively seeking new investments

E4E INC.

4699 Old Ironsides Drive
Suite 350
Santa Clara, CA 95054
Phone: 408-764-5100
Fax: 408-982-5401
Website: www.e4einc.com

Other Offices

Divyashree Chambers
Langford Road, 3rd Floor
Bangalore , India 560 025
Phone: 91-80-207-2140
Fax: 91-80-207-2186

Management and Staff
Fred Greguras, Vice President
Sridhar Mitta, Managing Director

Type of Firm
Incubators

Project Preferences

Role in Financing:
Will function either as deal originator or investor in deals created by others

Type of Financing Preferred:
Early Stage
Seed
Startup

Geographical Preferences

United States
All U.S.

International
India

Industry Preferences

Internet Specific
Internet

Additional Information

Year Founded: 2000
Capital Under Management: $125,000,000
Current Activity Level : Actively seeking new investments

EARLYBIRD VENTURE CAPITAL

525 University Avenue
Suite 410
Palo Alto, CA 94301
Phone: 650-530-3633
Fax: 650-330-3634
Website: www.earlybird.com

See Foreign Venture Capital Firms for full listing.

EAST WEST VENTURE INVESTORS, L.P.

3000 Sand Hill Road
Building #3, Suite 125
Menlo Park, CA 90001
Phone: 650-234-9721
Fax: 650-234-9722

Management and Staff

Bill Shelander, Managing Director

Type of Firm

Private Firm Investing Own Capital

Additional Information

Name of Most Recent Fund: East West Venture Investors, L.P.
Most Recent Fund Was Raised: 05/31/1998
Year Founded: 1998
Capital Under Management: $2,000,000
Current Activity Level : Actively seeking new investments

EAST/WEST VENTURE GROUP FKA:EAST/WEST CAPITAL ASSOCIATES

10900 Wilshire Blvd.
Suite 950
Los Angeles, CA 90024
Phone: 972-3620-8434
Fax: 310-209-6160
Website: www.eastwestvg.com

Management and Staff

Gary Adelson, Partner
Merv Adelson, Chairman & CEO
Paul Nadel, Managing Partner
Ravin Agrawal, Partner

Type of Firm

Private Firm Investing Own Capital

Project Preferences

Type of Financing Preferred:
Early Stage

Industry Preferences

(% based on actual investment)

Internet Specific	77.6%
Communications and Media	17.4%
Semiconductors/Other Elect.	5.1%

Additional Information

Current Activity Level : Actively seeking new investments

ECOMPANIES-EVERCORE VENTURE PARTNERS (E2VP)

2120 Colorado Avenue
Santa Monica, CA 90404
Phone: 310-586-4000
Fax: 310-586-4425
Website: www.ecompanies.com

Management and Staff

Andrew Greenebaum, Chief Financial Officer
Austin Beutner, Chief Executive Officer
Jacob Winebaum, Co-Founder
Lily Chang, Partner
Sangam Pant, General Partner
Sky Dayton, Co-Founder
Steve Ledger, Managing General Partner
Timothy Spicer, General Partner

Type of Firm

Affiliate/Subsidary of Oth. Financial. Instit.

Project Preferences

Type of Financing Preferred:
Early Stage

Industry Preferences

(% based on actual investment)

Internet Specific	88.6%
Computer Software and Services	11.4%

Additional Information

Name of Most Recent Fund: eCompanies Venture Group, L.P.
Most Recent Fund Was Raised: 09/01/1999
Year Founded: 2000
Capital Under Management: $160,000,000
Current Activity Level : Actively seeking new investments

EDB INVESTMENTS PTE LTD.

210 Twin Dolphin Drive
Redwood City, CA 94065-1402
Phone: 650-591-9102
Fax: 650-591-1328
Website: www.edbi.com

See Foreign Venture Capital Firms for full listing.

EDGE CAPITAL INVESTMENT CO., LLC

268 Bush Street
Suite 4426
San Francisco, CA 94104-3503
Phone: 888-954-0333
Fax: 888-354-4455
E-mail:info@EdgeCapital.net
E-mail:JohnY@EdgeCapital.net
Website: www.EdgeCapital.net

Other Offices

67 Wall Street
22nd Floor
New York, NY 10005
Phone: 212-944-2266
Fax: 212-944-7771
E-mail: info@EdgeCapital.net
E-mail: JohnY@EdgeCapital.net
Website: www.EdgeCapital.net

16 Cardinal Road
Suite 300
Hackettstown, NJ 07840
Phone: 908-684-4444
Fax: 908-684-3333
E-mail: info@EdgeCapital.net
E-mail: JohnY@EdgeCapital.net
Website: www.EdgeCapital.net

1350 East Flamingo Road
Suite 3000
Las Vegas, NV 89119
Phone: 702-438-3343
E-mail: info@EdgeCapital.net
E-mail: JohnY@EdgeCapital.net
Website: www.EdgeCapital.net

Management and Staff
John Yeomans, Managing Director
Pat Romo, Investment Analyst

Whom to Contact
John Yeomans

Type of Firm
Investment/Merchant Bank Investing Own or Client Funds

Industry Association Membership
Natl Assoc of Investment Cos. (NAIC)

Project Preferences

Role in Financing:
Prefer role as deal originator but will also invest in deals created by others

Type of Financing Preferred:
Start-up Financing
Seed
First Stage Financing
Second Stage Financing
Later Stage
Mezzanine
Leveraged Buyout
Special Situation

Size of Investments Considered
Min Size of Investment Considered (000s): $500
Max Size of Investment Considered (000s): $15,000

Geographical Preferences

United States
All U.S.

International
South America
Europe

Canada
All Canada

Industry Preferences

Communications and Media
Commercial Communications
Radio & TV Broadcasting
Telecommunications
Wireless Communications
Satellite Microwave Comm.
Entertainment
Publishing

Computer Hardware
Mini and Personal/Desktop

Computer Software
Computer Services
Software

Internet Specific
Internet
Ecommerce

Computer Other
Computer Related

Semiconductors/Other Elect.
Electronic Components
Laser Related
Fiber Optics

Biotechnology
Genetic Engineering
Agricultural/Animal Bio.
Industrial Biotechnology

Medical/Health
Medical Diagnostics
Medical Therapeutics
Drug/Equipmt Delivery
Medical Products
Pharmaceuticals

Consumer Related
Entertainment and Leisure
Casino/Gambling
Retail
Publishing-Retail
Franchises(NEC)
Food/Beverage
Consumer Products
Consumer Services
Other Restaurants
Hotels and Resorts
Education Related

Industrial/Energy
Alternative Energy
Energy Conservation Relat
Robotics
Environmental Related

Transportation
Transportation

Financial Services
Financial Services
Insurance
Real Estate

Portfolio Breakdown

Communications	25%
Entertainment & Media	25%
Consumer	10%
Medical/Health	10%
Environmental	5%
Computer Related	20%
Transportation	5%

Additional Information
Year Founded: 1990
Current Activity Level : Actively seeking new investments
Method of Compensation: Return on invest. most important, but chg. closing fees, service fees, etc.

EL DORADO VENTURES

2884 Sand Hill Road
Suite 121
Menlo Park, CA 94025
Phone: 650-854-1200
Fax: 650-854-1202
Website: www.eldorado.com

Management and Staff
Charles Beeler, General Partner
Gary Kalbach, General Partner
George Hoyem, Venture Partner
Jim Kunse, Chief Financial Officer
Shanda Bahles, General Partner
Shelley Hebert, Vice President
Thomas Peterson, General Partner

Type of Firm
Private Firm Investing Own Capital

Industry Association Membership
National Venture Capital Association (NVCA)
Natl assoc of Small Bus. Inv. Co (NASBIC)
Western Association of Venture Capitalists (WAVC)

Project Preferences

Role in Financing:
Prefer role as deal originator but will also invest in deals created by others

Type of Financing Preferred:
Early Stage
First Stage Financing
Seed
Startup

Geographical Preferences

United States
West Coast

Industry Preferences

(% based on actual investment)

Internet Specific	42.2%
Computer Software and Services	24.6%
Semiconductors/Other Elect.	12.9%
Communications and Media	12.2%
Computer Hardware	4.2%
Medical/Health	2.5%
Other Products	0.7%
Biotechnology	0.7%

Additional Information
Name of Most Recent Fund: El Dorado Ventures V
Most Recent Fund Was Raised: 09/01/1999
Year Founded: 1986
Capital Under Management: $500,000,000
Current Activity Level : Actively seeking new investments
Method of Compensation: Return on investment is of primary concern, do not charge fees

ELECTRONICS FOR IMAGING (AKA: EFI)

303 Velocity Way
Foster City, CA 94404
Phone: 650-357-3500
Fax: 650-357-3907
Website: www.efi.com

Management and Staff
Guy Gecht, Chief Executive Officer

Type of Firm
Non-Financial Corp. Affiliate or Subsidiary

Project Preferences

Type of Financing Preferred:
Early Stage

Additional Information
Capital Under Management: $20,000,000
Current Activity Level : Actively seeking new investments

EMERALD VENTURE GROUP

12396 World Trade Drive
Suite 116
San Diego, CA 92128
Phone: 858-451-1001
Fax: 858-451-1003
Website: www.emeraldventure.com

Management and Staff
Cherie Simoni, Vice President
Gerry Simoni, President

Whom to Contact
Cherie Simoni
Pamela Taylor

Type of Firm
Mgt. Consulting Firm

Project Preferences

Role in Financing:
Prefer role as deal originator but will also invest in deals created by others

Type of Financing Preferred:
First Stage Financing
Leveraged Buyout
Mezzanine
Research and Development
Second Stage Financing
Seed
Start-up Financing

Size of Investments Considered
Min Size of Investment Considered (000s): $100
Max Size of Investment Considered (000s): $50,000

Geographical Preferences

International
No Preference

Additional Information
Year Founded: 1988
Capital Under Management: $237,500,000
Current Activity Level : Actively seeking new investments
Method of Compensation: Return on invest. most important, but chg. closing fees, service fees, etc.

ENCORE VENTURE PARTNERS, LP

11726 San Vicente
Suite 250
Los Angeles, CA 90049
Phone: 310-820-9955
Fax: 310-820-9775
Website: www.encorevp.com

Other Offices

1901 Ascension Boulevard
Suite 350
Arlington, TX 76006
Phone: 817-436-6052
Fax: 817-436-6053

Management and Staff
Joe Reece, Partner
Rick Beckwitt, Partner
Stephen Perison, Principal
Steve DesJardins, Partner
Todd Temanson, Principal

Type of Firm
Private Firm Investing Own Capital

Project Preferences

Type of Financing Preferred:
Early Stage

Size of Investments Considered
Min Size of Investment Considered (000s): $1,000
Max Size of Investment Considered (000s): $5,000

Geographical Preferences

United States
California

Industry Preferences

(% based on actual investment)

Internet Specific	67.9%
Other Products	14.9%
Computer Software and Services	9.6%
Computer Hardware	7.6%

Additional Information

Name of Most Recent Fund: Encore Venture Partners I
Most Recent Fund Was Raised: 08/01/1999
Year Founded: 1999
Capital Under Management: $200,000
Current Activity Level : Actively seeking new investments

ENDEAVOR CAPITAL MANAGEMENT

35 Linda Vista Avenue
Atherton, CA 94027
Phone: 650-325-3950
Fax: 650-324-3441

See Connecticut for full listing.

ENTERPRISE PARTNERS

979 Ivanhoe Avenue
Suite 550
La Jolla, CA 92037
Phone: 858-454-8833
Fax: 858-454-2489
Website: www.epvc.com

Other Offices

12011 San Vincente Boulevard
Suite 330
Los Angeles, CA 90049
Phone: 310-476-3000
Fax: 310-476-3030

7979 Ivanhoe Avenue
Suite 550
La Jolla, CA 92037
Phone: 619-454-8833
Fax: 619-454-2489

Management and Staff

Andrew Chedrick, Chief Financial Officer
Andrew Senyei, General Partner
Carrie Stone, Venture Partner
Charles Martin, General Partner
James Berglund, General Partner
Naser Partovi, Managing Director
Ronald Taylor, General Partner
Thomas Clancy, Managing Director
William Stensrud, General Partner

Type of Firm

Private Firm Investing Own Capital

Industry Association Membership

National Venture Capital Association (NVCA)
Western Association of Venture Capitalists (WAVC)

Project Preferences

Role in Financing:
Prefer role as deal originator

Type of Financing Preferred:
Early Stage

Size of Investments Considered
Min Size of Investment Considered (000s): $1,000
Max Size of Investment Considered (000s): $20,000

Geographical Preferences

United States
All U.S.
West Coast

Industry Preferences

(% based on actual investment)

Internet Specific	19.6%
Computer Software and Services	17.3%
Medical/Health	14.7%
Communications and Media	14.5%
Semiconductors/Other Elect.	10.5%
Biotechnology	8.1%
Other Products	5.3%
Consumer Related	3.8%
Computer Hardware	3.7%
Industrial/Energy	2.5%

Additional Information

Name of Most Recent Fund: Enterprise Partners V, LLC
Most Recent Fund Was Raised: 10/01/1999
Year Founded: 1985
Capital Under Management: $745,000,000
Current Activity Level : Actively seeking new investments
Method of Compensation: Professional fee required whether or not deal closes

ESSEX WOODLANDS HEALTH VENTURES (FKA:WOODLANDS VENTURE PARTN

43 Balboa Cove
Newport Beach, CA 92663
Phone: 949-500-6220
Website: www.essexwoodlands.com

See Illinois for full listing.

EUROLINK INTERNATIONAL

690 Market Street
Suite 702
San Francisco, CA 94104
Phone: 415-589-6477
Fax: 415-589-3921

Management and Staff

Frederick Adler, General Partner
Jacques Vallee, General Partner
Philip chapman, General Partner

Type of Firm

Private Firm Investing Own Capital

Industry Association Membership

Western Association of Venture Capitalists (WAVC)

Project Preferences

Size of Investments Considered
Min Size of Investment Considered (000s): $300
Max Size of Investment Considered (000s): $1,500

Additional Information

Year Founded: 1987
Capital Under Management: $20,000,000
Current Activity Level : Actively seeking new investments
Method of Compensation: Return on investment is of primary concern, do not charge fees

EVOLUTION GLOBAL PARTNERS

3 Embarcadero Center
Suite 2330
San Francisco, CA 94101
Phone: 1-415-267-3500
Fax: 1-415-267-3501
Website: www.evopartners.com

See Foreign Venture Capital Firms for full listing.

FAR EAST CAPITAL CORP.

350 S. Grand Avenue
Suite 4100
Los Angeles, CA 97001
Phone: 213-687-1361
Fax: 213-617-7939

Type of Firm
Mgt. Consulting Firm

Industry Association Membership
Natl assoc of Small Bus. Inv. Co (NASBIC)

Project Preferences

Role in Financing:
Prefer role as deal originator but will also invest in deals created by others

Type of Financing Preferred:
First Stage Financing
Mezzanine
Second Stage Financing
Special Situation

Size of Investments Considered
Min Size of Investment Considered (000s): $100
Max Size of Investment Considered (000s): $300

Geographical Preferences

United States
West Coast

Industry Preferences

Communications and Media
Commercial Communications
Telecommunications
Data Communications
Satellite Microwave Comm.

Computer Hardware
Computer Graphics and Dig
Disk Relat. Memory Device

Computer Software
Applications Software

Internet Specific
Internet

Semiconductors/Other Elect.
Electronic Components
Semiconductor
Component Testing Equipmt

Medical/Health
Medical Diagnostics
Diagnostic Test Products
Other Therapeutic
Hospital/Other Instit.

Additional Information
Year Founded: 1989
Capital Under Management: $3,500,000
Current Activity Level : Actively seeking new investments
Method of Compensation: Return on invest. most important, but chg. closing fees, service fees, etc.

FINANCIAL TECHNOLOGY RESEARCH CORP.

21724 Ventura Boulevard
Suite 204
Woodland Hills, CA 91364
Phone: 818-710-8600
Fax: 818-999-0533

See New York for full listing.

FINANCIAL TECHNOLOGY VENTURES

601 California Street
Suite 2200
San Francisco, CA 94108
Phone: 415-229-3000
Fax: 415-229-3005
Website: www.ftventures.com

Management and Staff
Charles Ott, Chief Financial Officer
James Hale, General Partner
Richard Garman, General Partner
Robert Huret, General Partner
Scott Wu, General Partner
Tom Lenehan, Principal

Type of Firm
Private Firm Investing Own Capital

Industry Association Membership
National Venture Capital Association (NVCA)

Project Preferences

Role in Financing:
Will function either as deal originator or investor in deals created by others

Type of Financing Preferred:
Generalist PE
Later Stage
Mezzanine
Second Stage Financing

Size of Investments Considered
Min Size of Investment Considered (000s): $2,000
Max Size of Investment Considered (000s): $15,000

Geographical Preferences

United States
All U.S.

Canada
All Canada

International
Europe

Industry Preferences

(% based on actual investment)

Computer Software and Services	72.8%
Internet Specific	19.9%
Computer Hardware	7.3%

Additional Information
Year Founded: 1998
Capital Under Management: $526,000,000
Current Activity Level : Actively seeking new investments
Method of Compensation: Return on investment is of primary concern, do not charge fees

FINOVA MEZZANINE CAPITAL, INC. (FKA: SIRROM CAPITAL CORP)

2 Embarcadero Center
Suite 650
San Francisco, CA 94111
Phone: 415-782-7777
Fax: 415-782-7778
Website: www.finova.com

See Tennessee for full listing.

FLV FUND (AKA FLANDERS LANGUAGE VALLEY FUND)

FLV Management USA, Inc.
23551 Camino Hermoso,
Los Altos Hills, CA 94024
Phone: 16509170935
Fax: 15303259176
Website: www.flvfund.com

See Foreign Venture Capital Firms for full listing.

FLYNN VENTURE, LLC

One Flynn Center
825 Van Ness Avenue
San Francisco, CA 94109
Phone: 415-673-5900
Fax: 415-673-4457
Website: www.flynnventures.com

Other Offices

730 View Street
Suite 800
Victoria, Canada V8W 3Y7

Management and Staff
Barry Lewis, Principal
Bob Downey, Principal
Brian Barnum, Principal
Bruce Bower, Principal
Craig Viehweg, Principal
Donald Flynn, Principal
Gordon Ritter, Principal
Gregory Flynn, Principal
John Mason, Principal
Maurice Werdegar, Principal
Mike Rantz, Principal
Paul Downey, Principal
Rick Garonzik, Principal

Whom to Contact
Gregory Flynn

Type of Firm
Private Firm Investing Own Capital

Industry Association Membership
Canadian Venture Capital Association
National Venture Capital Association (NVCA)

Project Preferences

Role in Financing:
Prefer role in deals created by others

Type of Financing Preferred:
Early Stage

Size of Investments Considered
Min Size of Investment Considered (000s): $250
Max Size of Investment Considered (000s): $5,000

Additional Information
Current Activity Level : Actively seeking new investments

FORREST BINKLEY & BROWN

840 Newport Center Drive
Suite 480
Newport Beach, CA 92660
Phone: 949-729-3222
Fax: 949-729-3226
Website: fbbvc.com

Other Offices

201 Main St, Suite 2302
Fort Worth, TX 76102
Phone: 817-339-7020
Fax: 817-338-2047

265 Santa Helena
Suite 110
Solana Beach, CA 92075
Phone: 619-259-4105
Fax: 619-259-4108

Management and Staff
Christopher Kitching, Principal
Doug Wolter, Partner
Greg Forrest, Partner
Jeff Brown, Partner
Joseph Galligan, Chief Financial Officer
Nick Binkley, Partner

Type of Firm
Private Equity Advisor or Fund of Fund Mgr

Industry Association Membership
National Venture Capital Association (NVCA)
Natl assoc of Small Bus. Inv. Co (NASBIC)

Project Preferences

Role in Financing:
Prefer role as deal originator but will also invest in deals created by others

Type of Financing Preferred:
Balanced
Early Stage
Expansion
First Stage Financing
Generalist PE
Second Stage Financing

Size of Investments Considered
Min Size of Investment Considered (000s): $1,000
Max Size of Investment Considered (000s): $10,000

Geographical Preferences

United States
All U.S.
All U.S.

Industry Preferences

(% based on actual investment)

Internet Specific	30.6%
Computer Software and Services	30.3%
Semiconductors/Other Elect.	16.8%
Biotechnology	11.9%
Communications and Media	6.1%
Consumer Related	4.1%
Medical/Health	0.2%

Additional Information
Name of Most Recent Fund: Forrest Binkley & Brown SBIC Partners L.P.
Most Recent Fund Was Raised: 01/01/1993
Year Founded: 1993
Capital Under Management: $170,000,000
Current Activity Level : Actively seeking new investments
Method of Compensation: Return on invest. most important, but chg. closing fees, service fees, etc.

FORWARD VENTURES

9255 Towne Centre Drive
Suite 300
San Diego, CA 92121
Phone: 858-677-6077
Fax: 858-452-8799
Website: www.forwardventures.com

Management and Staff
Han Chiu, Venture Partner
Ivor Royston, Partner
Jeffrey Sollender, Partner
Maria Walker, Chief Financial Officer
Rose Ignell, Chief Financial Officer
Standish Fleming, Partner

Type of Firm
Private Firm Investing Own Capital

Industry Association Membership
National Venture Capital Association (NVCA)
Western Association of Venture Capitalists (WAVC)

Project Preferences

Role in Financing:
Prefer role as deal originator but will also invest in deals created by others

Type of Financing Preferred:
Early Stage
First Stage Financing
Later Stage
Mezzanine
Private Placement
Second Stage Financing
Seed
Startup

Size of Investments Considered
Min Size of Investment Considered (000s): $500
Max Size of Investment Considered (000s): $10,000

Geographical Preferences

United States
All U.S.

Industry Preferences

(% based on actual investment)

Biotechnology	79.6%
Medical/Health	18.6%
Internet Specific	1.8%

Additional Information
Name of Most Recent Fund: Forward Ventures III Institutional Partners
Most Recent Fund Was Raised: 01/01/1997
Year Founded: 1990
Capital Under Management: $263,500,000
Current Activity Level : Actively seeking new investments
Method of Compensation: Return on investment is of primary concern, do not charge fees

FOUNDATION CAPITAL

70 Willow Road
Suite 200
Menlo Park, CA 94025
Phone: 650-614-0500
Fax: 650-614-0505
Website: www.foundationcapital.com

Management and Staff
Adam Grosser, General Partner
Debra Jones, Venture Partner
Jim Anderson, General Partner
Kathryn Gould, General Partner
Mark Saul, General Partner
Mike Schuh, General Partner
Paul Koontz, General Partner
Ted Meyer, Chief Financial Officer
William Elmore, General Partner

Type of Firm
Private Firm Investing Own Capital

Industry Association Membership
National Venture Capital Association (NVCA)
Western Association of Venture Capitalists (WAVC)

Project Preferences

Role in Financing:
Prefer role as deal originator but will also invest in deals created by others

Type of Financing Preferred:
Balanced
First Stage Financing
Research and Development
Second Stage Financing
Seed
Start-up Financing

Geographical Preferences

United States
All U.S.
West Coast

Industry Preferences

(% based on actual investment)

Internet Specific	35.8%
Computer Software and Services	24.8%
Communications and Media	15.9%
Semiconductors/Other Elect.	13.6%
Other Products	7.6%
Consumer Related	1.3%
Computer Hardware	1.1%

Additional Information
Name of Most Recent Fund: Foundation Capital II
Most Recent Fund Was Raised: 02/01/1998
Year Founded: 1995
Capital Under Management: $200,000,000
Current Activity Level : Actively seeking new investments
Method of Compensation: Return on investment is of primary concern, do not charge fees

FREMONT PARTNERS

199 Fremont Street
Suite 2300
San Francisco, CA 94105
Phone: 415-284-8789
Fax: 415-284-8730
Website: www.fremontgroup.com

Management and Staff
David Lorsch, Principal
Gregory Spivy, Managing Director
James Farrell, Managing Director
Lawrence Ward, Managing Director
Mark Williamson, Managing Director
Robert Jaunich, Managing Director
Suzanne Gagan, Principal
William Lenihan, Principal

Type of Firm
Private Firm Investing Own Capital

Project Preferences

Role in Financing:
Prefer role as deal originator

Type of Financing Preferred:
Leveraged Buyout

Size of Investments Considered
Min Size of Investment Considered (000s): $25,000
Max Size of Investment Considered (000s): $200,000

Geographical Preferences

United States
All U.S.

Canada
All Canada

Industry Preferences

(% based on actual investment)

Other Products	37.7%
Medical/Health	24.5%
Semiconductors/Other Elect.	18.0%
Internet Specific	13.9%

Computer Software and Services	3.1%
Biotechnology	2.2%
Communications and Media	0.6%

Additional Information
Name of Most Recent Fund: Freemont Partners -B, L.P.
Most Recent Fund Was Raised: 08/01/1996
Year Founded: 1980
Capital Under Management: $755,000,000
Current Activity Level : Actively seeking new investments
Method of Compensation: Return on invest. most important, but chg. closing fees, service fees, etc.

FROST CAPITAL PARTNERS

44 Montgomery Street
San Francisco, CA 94104
Phone: 415-274-2400
Fax: 415-274-2444

Management and Staff
Brian Feldman
Ian Berman

Whom to Contact
Brian Feldman
Ian Berman

Type of Firm
Investment/Merchant Bank Subsid/Affil

Project Preferences

Role in Financing:
Prefer role as deal originator

Type of Financing Preferred:
Mezzanine
Second Stage Financing

Size of Investments Considered
Min Size of Investment Considered (000s): $3,000
Max Size of Investment Considered: No Limit

Geographical Preferences

United States
All U.S.

Canada
All Canada

International
Australia
Bermuda
France
Germany
Italy
Spain
United Kingdom

Industry Preferences

Communications and Media
CATV & Pay TV Systems

Computer Software
Systems Software
Applications Software

Internet Specific
Internet

Additional Information
Year Founded: 1991
Current Activity Level : Actively seeking new investments
Method of Compensation: Function primarily in service area, receive contingent fee in cash or equity

FUSIENT VENTURES

940 N. Mansfield Ave.
Los Angeles, CA 90038
Phone: 323-461-9119
Fax: 323-461-9117
E-mail: info@fusient.com
Website: www.fusient.com

See New York for full listing.

GABRIEL VENTURE PARTNERS

350 Marine Parkway
Suite 200
Redwood Shores, CA 94065
Phone: 650-551-5000
Fax: 650-551-5001
Website: www.gabrielvp.com

Other Offices

130 Admiral Cochrane Drive
Suite 102
Annapolis, MD 21401
Phone: 410-571-7800
Fax: 410-571-7801

8000 Towers Crescent Drive
Suite 1350
Vienna, VA 22182
Phone: 703-847-3684
Fax: 703-760-7899

Management and Staff
Alexis Lakes, Chief Financial Officer
B.V. Jagadeesh, Venture Partner
Charles Heller, General Partner
F.W.W.(Rick) Bolander, Managing General Partner
J.Phillip Samper, Managing General Partner
James Ramich, Venture Partner
Joe Roebuck, Venture Partner
Mahesh Kanumury, General Partner
Rudolph Lamone, Venture Partner
Scott Chou, General Partner

Type of Firm
Private Firm Investing Own Capital

Industry Association Membership
Mid-Atlantic Venture Association
National Venture Capital Association (NVCA)
Western Association of Venture Capitalists (WAVC)

Project Preferences

Role in Financing:
Prefer role as deal originator

Type of Financing Preferred:
Early Stage
First Stage Financing
Seed

Size of Investments Considered
Min Size of Investment Considered (000s): $500
Max Size of Investment Considered (000s): $7,000

Geographical Preferences

United States
California
Mid Atlantic
Northeast
Northern California
West Coast

Industry Preferences

(% based on actual investment)

Internet Specific	69.5%
Computer Software and Services	16.9%
Communications and Media	13.0%
Semiconductors/Other Elect.	0.7%

Additional Information
Name of Most Recent Fund: Gabriel Venture Partners
Most Recent Fund Was Raised: 04/30/1999
Year Founded: 1999
Capital Under Management: $250,000,000
Current Activity Level : Actively seeking new investments
Method of Compensation: Return on investment is of primary concern, do not charge fees

---

GATX VENTURES (FKA: MEIER MITCHELL & CO.)

3687 Mount Diablo Boulevard
Suite 200
Lafayette, CA 94549
Phone: 925-258-6000
Fax: 925-258-6020
Website: www.gatxventures.com

Other Offices

16 Munson Road
Fifth Floor
Farmington, CT 06032
Phone: 860-284-4300
Fax: 860-284-4350

Management and Staff
James Mitchell, President

Type of Firm
Private Firm Investing Own Capital

Project Preferences

Type of Financing Preferred:
First Stage Financing
Mezzanine
Research and Development
Second Stage Financing
Seed
Start-up Financing

Size of Investments Considered
Min Size of Investment Considered (000s): $500
Max Size of Investment Considered: No Limit

Geographical Preferences

United States
All U.S.

Industry Preferences

Communications and Media
Commercial Communications
Telecommunications
Data Communications
Satellite Microwave Comm.
Other Communication Prod.

Computer Hardware
Computers
Mainframes / Scientific
Mini and Personal/Desktop
Computer Graphics and Dig
Terminals
Disk Relat. Memory Device

Computer Software
Systems Software
Applications Software
Artificial Intelligence

Semiconductors/Other Elect.
Electronics
Electronic Components

Biotechnology
Biotechnology

Medical/Health
Diagnostic Services
Diagnostic Test Products
Drug/Equipmt Delivery
Other Therapeutic
Medical Products
Disposable Med. Products
Pharmaceuticals

Industrial/Energy
Industrial Products

Manufact.
Office Automation Equipmt

Additional Information
Year Founded: 1984
Capital Under Management: $75,000,000
Current Activity Level : Actively seeking new investments
Method of Compensation: Return on investment is of primary concern, do not charge fees

---

GATX/MM VENTURE PARTNERS

Four Embarcadero Center
Suite 2200
San Francisco, CA 94904
Phone: 415-955-3200
Fax: 415-955-3449

Project Preferences

Role in Financing:
Prefer role as deal originator but will also invest in deals created by others

Type of Financing Preferred:
Expansion
First Stage Financing
Leveraged Buyout
Mezzanine
Second Stage Financing

Size of Investments Considered
Min Size of Investment Considered (000s): $5,000
Max Size of Investment Considered: No Limit

Geographical Preferences

United States
All U.S.

Canada
All Canada

International
United Kingdom

Industry Preferences

Communications and Media
Commercial Communications
CATV & Pay TV Systems
Data Communications
Satellite Microwave Comm.
Other Communication Prod.

Computer Hardware
Computers
Mainframes / Scientific
Computer Graphics and Dig
Terminals
Disk Relat. Memory Device

Computer Software
Systems Software
Applications Software

Internet Specific
Internet

Semiconductors/Other Elect.
Electronics
Electronic Components
Semiconductor
Sensors
Component Testing Equipmt
Laser Related
Fiber Optics
Analytic/Scientific

Biotechnology
Biotechnology

Medical/Health
Diagnostic Services
Diagnostic Test Products
Drug/Equipmt Delivery
Other Therapeutic
Pharmaceuticals

Industrial/Energy
Oil & Gas Drilling,Explor
Materials
Factory Automation
Machinery

Transportation
Transportation

Financial Services
Financial Services

Agr/Forestr/Fish
Agriculture related

Additional Information
Year Founded: 1968
Current Activity Level : Actively seeking new investments
Method of Compensation: Return on investment is of primary concern, do not charge fees

GEMINI CAPITAL FUND MANAGEMENT LTD

2180 Sand Hill Road
Menlo Park, CA 94026
Phone: 650-233-1206
Fax: 650-233-7515
Website: www.gemini.co.il

See Foreign Venture Capital Firms for full listing.

GENERATION CAPITAL PARTNERS

600 Montgomery Street
Suite 3900
San Francisco, CA 94111
Phone: 415-646-8620
Fax: 415-646-8625
Website: www.genpartners.com

See New York for full listing.

GENEVA VENTURE PARTNERS

4 Embarcadero Center
Suite 1400
San Francisco, CA 94111
Phone: 415-732-5672
Fax: 415-433-6635
Website: www.genevaventurepartners.com

Management and Staff
Igor Sill, General Partner
Robert Troy, General Partner

Type of Firm
Private Firm Investing Own Capital

Industry Association Membership
National Venture Capital Association (NVCA)

Project Preferences

Type of Financing Preferred:
Early Stage
Seed

Geographical Preferences

United States
California

International
Eastern Europe

Industry Preferences

(% based on actual investment)

Communications and Media	41.0%
Internet Specific	37.1%
Computer Software and Services	11.1%
Industrial/Energy	6.2%
Computer Hardware	4.6%

Additional Information
Year Founded: 1997
Capital Under Management: $60,000,000
Current Activity Level : Actively seeking new investments

GKM VENTURE PARTNERS, LP

11150 Santa Monica Boulevard
Suite 800
West Los Angeles, CA 90025
Phone: 310-268-2600
Fax: 310-268-0870
Website: www.gkm.com

Other Offices

100 Pine Street
27th Floor, Suite 2785
San Francisco, CA 94110
Phone: 415-591-2100
Fax: 888-456-8081

11150 Santa Monica Boulevard
Suite 800
West Los Angeles, CA 90025
Phone: 310-268-2600
Fax: 888-456-1751

225 Franklin Street
Suite 2940
Boston, MA 02110
Phone: 617-451-0670
Fax: 800-451-7536

28 Bezalel Street
President Tower, 28th Floor
Ramat Gan , Israel 52521
Phone: 972-3-575-4242

311 South Wacker Drive
Suite 2750
Chicago, IL 60606
Phone: 312-697-7180
Fax: 800-697-0005

529 Fifth Avenue
New York, NY 10017
Phone: 212-885-4000
Fax: 888-309-1371

Management and Staff
Jonathan Bloch, Managing Partner
Lance Horn, Managing Partner

Whom to Contact
Nathan Schipper

Type of Firm
Investment/Merchant Bank Subsid/Affil

Project Preferences

Role in Financing:
Will function either as deal originator or investor in deals created by others

Type of Financing Preferred:
Early Stage
Expansion
Later Stage

Size of Investments Considered
Min Size of Investment Considered (000s): $1,000
Max Size of Investment Considered (000s): $5,000

Geographical Preferences

United States
Northeast
Southeast
Southwest
West Coast

International
Israel

Industry Preferences

Communications and Media
Commercial Communications
Telecommunications
Wireless Communications
Data Communications
Satellite Microwave Comm.
Other Communication Prod.

Computer Hardware
Computer Graphics and Dig
Disk Relat. Memory Device

Computer Software
Computer Services
Software
Systems Software
Applications Software

Internet Specific
E-Commerce Technology
Internet

Semiconductors/Other Elect.
Electronic Components
Semiconductor
Micro-Processing
Controllers and Sensors
Sensors
Component Testing Equipmt
Laser Related
Fiber Optics

Additional Information

Year Founded: 2000
Capital Under Management: $20,000,000
Current Activity Level : Actively seeking new investments
Method of Compensation: Return on investment is of primary concern, do not charge fees

GLOBAL CROSSING VENTURES (FKA: FRONTIER VENTURES)

960 Hamlin Court
Sunnyvale, CA 94089
Phone: 408-542-0100
Fax: 408-541-0429
Website: www.gcventures.com

Other Offices

Wessex House
45 Reid Street
Hamilton, Bermuda HM12
Phone: 441-296-8600
Fax: 441-296-8606

Management and Staff

Brian Fink, Vice President
Michael Cohen, Principal
Paul Santinelli, Vice President

Type of Firm

Non-Financial Corp. Affiliate or Subsidiary

Industry Association Membership

National Venture Capital Association (NVCA)

Project Preferences

Role in Financing:
Will function either as deal originator or investor in deals created by others

Type of Financing Preferred:
Early Stage
First Stage Financing
Second Stage Financing

Size of Investments Considered
Min Size of Investment Considered (000s): $2,000
Max Size of Investment Considered (000s): $10,000

Geographical Preferences

United States
All U.S.

Industry Preferences

(% based on actual investment)

Communications and Media	87.6%
Internet Specific	10.0%
Semiconductors/Other Elect.	1.6%
Computer Hardware	0.5%
Computer Software and Services	0.3%

Additional Information

Year Founded: 1999
Capital Under Management: $100,000,000
Current Activity Level : Actively seeking new investments
Method of Compensation: Return on investment is of primary concern, do not charge fees

GLOBAL INTERNET VENTURES (GIV)

4699 Old Ironsides Drive
Suite 430
Santa Clara, CA 95054
Website: www.givinc.com

See Virginia for full listing.

GLOBAL RETAIL PARTNERS (A.K.A. GRP)

2121 Avenue of the Stars
Suite 1630
Los Angeles, CA 90067
Phone: 310-785-5100
Fax: 310-785-5111
Website: www.grpvc.com

Management and Staff

Linda Faynelevinson, Partner
Pierre Morin, Partner
Steven Dietz, Partner
Steven Lebow, Managing Partner
Yves Sisteron, Managing Partner

Type of Firm

Investment/Merchant Bank Subsid/Affil

Project Preferences

Role in Financing:
Prefer role as deal originator but will also invest in deals created by others

Type of Financing Preferred:
Early Stage
First Stage Financing
Second Stage Financing

Geographical Preferences

United States
All U.S.
All U.S.

Canada
All Canada

International
Bermuda
France
Germany
Italy
Spain
United Kingdom

Industry Preferences
(% based on actual investment)

Internet Specific	82.4%
Other Products	6.4%
Consumer Related	6.1%
Computer Software and Services	5.0%

Additional Information
Name of Most Recent Fund: GRP II
Most Recent Fund Was Raised: 12/01/1999
Year Founded: 1996
Capital Under Management: $150,000,000
Current Activity Level : Actively seeking new investments
Method of Compensation: Return on investment is of primary concern, do not charge fees

GLYNN CAPITAL MANAGEMENT

3000 Sand Hill Road
Building 4, Suite 235
Menlo Park, CA 94025
Phone: 650-854-2215
Fax: 650-854-8083

Type of Firm
Private Firm Investing Own Capital

Industry Association Membership
Western Association of Venture Capitalists (WAVC)

Project Preferences

Type of Financing Preferred:
Balanced

Geographical Preferences

United States
Northeast
Northwest
West Coast

Additional Information
Name of Most Recent Fund: Glynn Ventures
Most Recent Fund Was Raised: 01/01/1983
Year Founded: 1983
Current Activity Level : Actively seeking new investments

GLYNN VENTURES

3000 Sand Hill Road
Building Four, Suite 235
Menlo Park, CA 94025
Phone: 650-854-2215

Type of Firm
Private Firm Investing Own Capital

Project Preferences

Role in Financing:
Prefer role as deal originator but will also invest in deals created by others

Type of Financing Preferred:
First Stage Financing
Leveraged Buyout
Mezzanine
Second Stage Financing
Start-up Financing

Size of Investments Considered
Min Size of Investment Considered (000s): $300
Max Size of Investment Considered (000s): $500

Geographical Preferences

United States
Northeast
Northwest
Southeast
West Coast

Industry Preferences
(% based on actual investment)

Internet Specific	48.1%
Computer Software and Services	37.1%
Medical/Health	9.1%
Communications and Media	3.1%
Semiconductors/Other Elect.	2.6%

Additional Information
Year Founded: 1983
Capital Under Management: $25,000,000
Current Activity Level : Actively seeking new investments
Method of Compensation: Return on investment is of primary concern, do not charge fees

GORILLAPARK

576 Folsom Street
San Francisco, CA 94105
Phone: 415 989 900
Website: www.gorillapark.com

See Foreign Venture Capital Firms for full listing.

GRANITE VENTURES LLC (FKA: H & Q VENTURE ASSOCIATES)

One Bush Street
San Francisco, CA 94104
Phone: 415-591-7781
Fax: 415-591-7720
Website: www.granitevc.com

Management and Staff
Chris McKay, Vice President
Chris Hollenbeck, Principal
Eric Zimits, Managing Director
Gene Eidenberg, Principal
Jackie Berterretche, Chief Financial Officer
Rupen Dolasia, Principal
Sam Kingsland, Principal
Standish O'Grady, Managing Director
Tom Furlong, Managing Director
William Hambrecht, Principal

Whom to Contact
Esther Shih

Type of Firm
Investment/Merchant Bank Subsid/Affil

Industry Association Membership
National Venture Capital Association (NVCA)

Project Preferences

Role in Financing:
Prefer role as deal originator but will also invest in deals created by others

Type of Financing Preferred:
Control-block Purchases
Early Stage
First Stage Financing
Leveraged Buyout
Mezzanine
Research and Development
Special Situation
Start-up Financing

Geographical Preferences

United States
All U.S.

Industry Preferences

(% based on actual investment)

Internet Specific	42.1%
Computer Software and Services	35.3%
Communications and Media	11.1%
Semiconductors/Other Elect.	5.0%
Computer Hardware	4.8%
Biotechnology	0.8%
Other Products	0.8%
Consumer Related	0.0%

Additional Information

Name of Most Recent Fund: Adobe Ventures III
Most Recent Fund Was Raised: 07/01/1999
Year Founded: 1968
Capital Under Management: $465,000,000
Current Activity Level : Actively seeking new investments
Method of Compensation: Return on investment is of primary concern, do not charge fees

GREENFIELD TECHNOLOGY VENTURES

3000 Sand Hill Road
Building One, Suite 170
Palo Alto, CA 94025
Phone: 650-566-1565
Fax: 650-853-1748

Management and Staff

David Adams, Managing Director
Jeff Allen, Managing Director

Type of Firm

Private Firm Investing Own Capital

Additional Information

Name of Most Recent Fund: Greenfield Technology Ventures Fund 1
Most Recent Fund Was Raised: 07/01/1999
Capital Under Management: $18,500,000
Current Activity Level : Actively seeking new investments

GREYLOCK

2929 Campus Drive
Suite 400
San Mateo, CA 94401
Phone: 650-493-5525
Fax: 650-493-5575
Website: www.greylock.com

See Massachusetts for full listing.

GROVE STREET ADVISORS, LLC

425 Market St.
Suite 2200
San Francisco, CA 94105
Phone: 415-955-2741
Fax: 415-955-2745
Website: www.grovestreetadvisors.com

See Massachusetts for full listing.

H&Q ASIA PACIFIC, LTD.

156 University Avenue
Palo Alto, CA 94301
Phone: 650-838-8088
Fax: 650-838-0802
Website: www.hamquist.com

Other Offices

1606 Asia Pacific Finance Tower
Citibank Plaza, 3 Garden Rd.
Central, Hong Kong
Phone: 852-2868-4780
Fax: 852-2810-4883

22/F PCI Bank Tower I
Makati Ave & dela Costa St.
Makati City, Manila, Philippines
Phone: 632-819-5776
Fax: 632-815-9217

4-3-20 Toranomon, Kamiya-cho Mori Bldg., Minato-ku
Tokyo, Japan 105-0001
Phone: 813-5425-3470
Fax: 813-5423-3486

79 Anson Road, #11-03
Singapore, Singapore 079906
Phone: 65-221-8144
Fax: 65-222-0729

No. 84-G & 84-1, Jalan 1/76 D
Desa Pandan
Kuala Lumpur, Malaysia 55100
Phone: 65-221-8144
Fax: 65-222-0729

Plaza Bapindo Menara II, 24/F
Jl Jend. Sudirman Kav.54-55
Jakarta, Indonesia 12190
Phone: 62-21-526-6483
Fax: 62-21-526-6487

Rm. 1207 Southern City Tower
175 Sth. Sathorn Road
Bangkok, Thailand 10120
Phone: 662-679-6312
Fax: 662-679-6316

Rm. 709 CCMM Bldg, 12 Yoido-dong
Youngdungpo-ku
Seoul, South Korea 150010
Phone: 822-782-2288
Fax: 822-775-4589

Rm. A2104, Vantone New World Plaza
No. 2 Fuwai Da Jie, Xicheng District
Beijing, China 100037
Phone: 8610-6857-8678
Fax: 8610-6857-8680

Suite 3201, 32F
No. 333 Keelung Road, Sec.1
Taipei, Taiwan 10548
Phone: 8862-2720-9855
Fax: 8862-2722-2106

Management and Staff

Chee Meng Siew, Managing Director
Eduardo David, President
Lee Jae-Woo, Managing Director
Moun-Rong Lin, President
Peter Ko, Managing Director
Purvi Gandhi, Chief Financial Officer
Roger Chiang, Vice President
Stan Sakai, Managing Director
Virapan Pulges, Managing Director
William Chao, Managing Director
Wing Keong Siew, President

Type of Firm

Private Firm Investing Own Capital

Industry Association Membership

Taiwan Venture Capital Association(TVCA)

Project Preferences

Type of Financing Preferred:
Acquisition
Balanced
Early Stage
Expansion
First Stage Financing
Later Stage
Leveraged Buyout
Management Buyouts
Mezzanine
Recapitalizations
Research and Development
Special Situation
Start-up Financing
Startup
Turnaround

Geographical Preferences

United States
All U.S.

International
Asia
Japan
Philippines

Industry Preferences

(% based on actual investment)

Other Products	39.6%
Internet Specific	17.2%
Computer Hardware	14.7%
Semiconductors/Other Elect.	14.5%
Computer Software and Services	4.8%
Industrial/Energy	3.1%
Consumer Related	2.5%
Communications and Media	1.8%
Biotechnology	1.3%
Medical/Health	0.5%

Additional Information
Name of Most Recent Fund: Hantech Venture Capital Corp.(H&Q Taiwan Co., Ltd)
Most Recent Fund Was Raised: 10/01/1986
Year Founded: 1998
Capital Under Management: $1,600,000,000
Current Activity Level : Actively seeking new investments

HALLADOR VENTURE PARTNERS

740 University Avenue
Suite 110
Sacramento, CA 95825-6710
Phone: 916-920-0191
Fax: 916-920-5188

Management and Staff
Chris Branscum, Managing Director
David Hardie, Managing Director

Type of Firm
Private Firm Investing Own Capital

Industry Association Membership
National Venture Capital Association (NVCA)

Project Preferences

Role in Financing:
Prefer role as deal originator but will also invest in deals created by others

Type of Financing Preferred:
First Stage Financing
Research and Development
Second Stage Financing
Seed
Start-up Financing

Size of Investments Considered
Min Size of Investment Considered (000s): $500
Max Size of Investment Considered (000s): $1,000

Geographical Preferences

United States
West Coast

Industry Preferences

Communications and Media
Communications and Media

Computer Software
Systems Software
Applications Software

Internet Specific
Internet

Semiconductors/Other Elect.
Semiconductor

Additional Information
Year Founded: 1979
Capital Under Management: $25,000,000
Current Activity Level : Reducing investment activity
Method of Compensation: Return on investment is of primary concern, do not charge fees

HEALTH CAPITAL GROUP

6371 Royal Grove Drive
Huntington Beach, CA 92648
Phone: 714-536-0367
Fax: 714-536-3056

Type of Firm
Mgt. Consulting Firm

Project Preferences

Role in Financing:
Prefer role as deal originator but will also invest in deals created by others

Type of Financing Preferred:
First Stage Financing
Leveraged Buyout
Mezzanine
Second Stage Financing
Start-up Financing

Size of Investments Considered
Min Size of Investment Considered (000s): $5,000
Max Size of Investment Considered: No Limit

Geographical Preferences

United States
West Coast

Industry Preferences

Communications and Media
Telecommunications
Data Communications
Satellite Microwave Comm.

Computer Hardware
Computer Graphics and Dig

Computer Software
Computer Services
Systems Software
Applications Software
Artificial Intelligence

Semiconductors/Other Elect.
Laser Related

Biotechnology
Biotechnology

Medical/Health
Medical/Health
Medical Products

Consumer Related
Food/Beverage
Consumer Products
Consumer Services

Industrial/Energy
Alternative Energy
Environmental Related

Financial Services
Real Estate

Business Serv.
Consulting Services

Manufact.
Publishing

Additional Information
Year Founded: 1986
Current Activity Level : Actively seeking new investments
Method of Compensation: Return on invest. most important, but chg. closing fees, service fees, etc.

HELLMAN & FRIEDMAN

One Maritime Plaza
12th Floor
San Francisco, CA 94111
Phone: 415-788-5111
Fax: 415-788-0176
Website: www.hf.com

Management and Staff
Brian Powers, Managing Director
Georgia Lee, Managing Director
John Pasquesi, Managing Director
John Bunce, Managing Director
Joseph Niehaus, Managing Director
Kristen Garlinghouse, Principal
Matthew Barger, President
Mick Hellman, Managing Director
Mitch Cohen, Managing Director
Patrick Healy, Managing Director
Philip Hammarskjold, Managing Director
Thomas Steyer, Managing Director

Type of Firm
Private Firm Investing Own Capital

Project Preferences

Role in Financing:
Prefer role as deal originator

Type of Financing Preferred:
Leveraged Buyout
Mezzanine
Second Stage Financing
Special Situation

Geographical Preferences

United States
All U.S.

International
Australia
China
Japan
South Africa

Industry Preferences

(% based on actual investment)

Other Products	68.8%
Communications and Media	14.4%
Consumer Related	9.7%
Medical/Health	5.8%
Internet Specific	1.3%

Additional Information
Name of Most Recent Fund: Hellman & Friedman Capital Partners IV, L.P.
Most Recent Fund Was Raised: 09/01/1999
Year Founded: 1987
Capital Under Management: $4,800,000,000
Current Activity Level : Actively seeking new investments

HENRY & CO.

4370 La Jolla Village Drive
Suite 400
San Diego, CA 92122-1251
Phone: 619-453-1655

See Florida for full listing.

HIGHLAND CAPITAL PARTNERS

555 California Street
Suite 3100
San Francisco, CA 94104
Phone: 415-981-1230
Fax: 415-981-1229
Website: www.hcp.com

See Massachusetts for full listing.

HITACHI AMERICA, LTD.

750 Central Expressway
Santa Clara, CA 95050-2627
Phone: 408-970-7846
Fax: 408-988-0651
Website: www.hitachi.com

Type of Firm
Non-Financial Corp. Affiliate or Subsidiary

Project Preferences

Type of Financing Preferred:
Early Stage

Geographical Preferences

International
All International

Industry Preferences

Internet Specific
Internet

Biotechnology
Biotechnology

Additional Information
Year Founded: 1999
Capital Under Management: $95,000,000
Current Activity Level : Actively seeking new investments

HMS GROUP

2468 Embarcadero Way
Palo Alto, CA 94303-3313
Phone: 650-856-9862
Fax: 650-856-9864

Management and Staff
Richard Grey, General Partner

Type of Firm
Private Firm Investing Own Capital

Industry Preferences

(% based on actual investment)

Communications and Media	62.1%
Computer Software and Services	20.5%
Semiconductors/Other Elect.	7.8%
Internet Specific	7.1%
Consumer Related	0.9%
Industrial/Energy	0.8%
Computer Hardware	0.7%

Additional Information
Name of Most Recent Fund: HMS Capital Partners
Most Recent Fund Was Raised: 07/01/1987
Year Founded: 1987
Current Activity Level : Actively seeking new investments

HMS HAWAII MANAGEMENT PARTNERS

170 Middlefield Road
Suite 150
Menlo Park, CA 94025
Phone: 415-324-4672
Fax: 415-324-4684

See Hawaii for full listing.

HOEBICH VENTURE MANAGEMENT, INC.

5770 Croy Road
Morgan Hill, CA 95037
Phone: 408-778-6271
Fax: 408-779-8691

Type of Firm
Private Firm Investing Own Capital

Project Preferences

Role in Financing:
Prefer role as deal originator but will also invest in deals created by others

Type of Financing Preferred:
Seed
Start-up Financing

Geographical Preferences

International
No Preference

Industry Preferences

Communications and Media
Telecommunications
Data Communications
Satellite Microwave Comm.

Computer Hardware
Mainframes / Scientific
Computer Graphics and Dig
Integrated Turnkey System
Disk Relat. Memory Device

Computer Software
Computer Services
Systems Software
Applications Software
Artificial Intelligence

Biotechnology
Biotech Related Research

Consumer Related
Retail

Manufact.
Office Automation Equipmt

Agr/Forestr/Fish
Agriculture related

Additional Information
Year Founded: 1972
Current Activity Level : Making few, if any, new investments
Method of Compensation: Function primarily in service area, receive contingent fee in cash or equity

HORIZON VENTURES (F.K.A. TECHNOLOGY INVESTMENTS)

Four Main Street
Suite 50
Los Altos, CA 94022
Phone: 650-917-4100
Fax: 650-917-4109
Website: www.horizonvc.com

Management and Staff
Doug Tsui, Managing Director
Jack Carsten, Managing Director
John Hall, Managing Director

Type of Firm
Private Firm Investing Own Capital

Industry Association Membership
Western Association of Venture Capitalists (WAVC)

Project Preferences

Role in Financing:
Prefer role as deal originator but will also invest in deals created by others

Type of Financing Preferred:
First Stage Financing
Second Stage Financing
Start-up Financing

Size of Investments Considered
Min Size of Investment Considered (000s): $500
Max Size of Investment Considered (000s): $5,000

Geographical Preferences

United States
Northern California
All U.S.

Industry Preferences

(% based on actual investment)

Computer Software and Services	52.1%
Internet Specific	28.5%
Communications and Media	8.3%
Computer Hardware	4.2%
Industrial/Energy	3.5%
Medical/Health	3.4%

Additional Information
Name of Most Recent Fund: Horizon Ventures Fund I, L.P.
Most Recent Fund Was Raised: 10/01/1999
Year Founded: 1990
Capital Under Management: $88,000,000
Current Activity Level : Actively seeking new investments
Method of Compensation: Return on investment is of primary concern, do not charge fees

HOUSATONIC PARTNERS

88 Kearny Street
Suite 1610
San Francisco, CA 94108
Phone: 415-955-9020
Fax: 415-955-9053
Website: www.housatonicpartners.com

Other Offices

11 Newbury St.
Suite 500
Boston, MA 02116
Phone: 617-267-4545
Fax: 617-267-5565

Management and Staff
Barry Reynolds, Managing General Partner
Brandon Nixon, General Partner
David Dodson, Venture Partner
David Maney, Venture Partner
Eliot Wadsworth, General Partner
Jill Raimondi, Chief Financial Officer
Karen Liesching, Principal
Michael Jackson, General Partner
William Thorndike, Managing General Partner

Type of Firm
Private Equity Advisor or Fund of Fund Mgr

Industry Association Membership
National Venture Capital Association (NVCA)

Project Preferences

Type of Financing Preferred:
Later Stage

Size of Investments Considered
Min Size of Investment Considered (000s): $2,000
Max Size of Investment Considered (000s): $10,000

Geographical Preferences

United States
All U.S.

Industry Preferences

Communications and Media
Communications and Media

Financial Services
Financial Services

Business Serv.
Media

Additional Information
Year Founded: 2000
Capital Under Management: $200,000,000
Current Activity Level : Actively seeking new investments

HUMMER WINBLAD VENTURE PARTNERS

Two South Park
2nd Floor
San Francisco, CA 94107
Phone: 415-979-9600
Fax: 415-979-9601
Website: www.humwin.com

Management and Staff
Ann Winblad, General Partner
Chuck Robel, Chief Operating Officer
Dan Beldy, General Partner
Deborah Wright, Chief Financial Officer
Hank Barry, General Partner
John Hummer, General Partner
Ken Pereira, Chief Financial Officer
Mark Gorenberg, General Partner

Type of Firm
Private Firm Investing Own Capital

Project Preferences

Role in Financing:
Prefer role as deal originator

Type of Financing Preferred:
Balanced
Early Stage
Expansion
First Stage Financing
Mezzanine
Research and Development
Second Stage Financing
Seed
Start-up Financing

Geographical Preferences

United States
All U.S.

Industry Preferences

(% based on actual investment)

Internet Specific	46.9%
Computer Software and Services	45.3%
Consumer Related	3.9%
Communications and Media	2.3%
Computer Hardware	1.5%

Additional Information
Name of Most Recent Fund: Hummer Winblad Venture Partners IV, L.P.
Most Recent Fund Was Raised: 01/01/1999
Year Founded: 1989
Capital Under Management: $1,000,000,000
Current Activity Level : Actively seeking new investments
Method of Compensation: Return on investment is of primary concern, do not charge fees

IDANTA PARTNERS, LTD.

4660 La Jolla Village Drive
Suite 850
San Diego, CA 92122
Phone: 858-452-9690
Fax: 858-452-2013
Website: www.idanta.com

Other Offices

4660 La Jolla Village Drive
Suite 775
San Diego, CA 92122
Phone: 619-452-9690

Management and Staff
Anita Colmie, Chief Financial Officer
David Dunn, Managing Partner
Jonathan Huberman, General Partner
Mahesh Krishnamarthy, General Partner

Type of Firm
Private Firm Investing Own Capital

Project Preferences

Role in Financing:
Prefer role as deal originator but will also invest in deals created by others

Type of Financing Preferred:
First Stage Financing
Second Stage Financing
Seed
Start-up Financing

Size of Investments Considered
Min Size of Investment Considered (000s): $500
Max Size of Investment Considered: No Limit

Geographical Preferences

United States
All U.S.

Industry Preferences

(% based on actual investment)

Semiconductors/Other Elect.	49.0%
Communications and Media	18.3%
Computer Software and Services	11.2%
Internet Specific	6.8%
Computer Hardware	6.6%
Other Products	4.5%
Medical/Health	1.9%
Consumer Related	1.6%

Additional Information
Year Founded: 1971
Capital Under Management: $400,000,000
Current Activity Level : Actively seeking new investments
Method of Compensation: Return on investment is of primary concern, do not charge fees

IDG TECHNOLOGY VENTURE INVESTMENT INC. (FKA: PTV-CHINA)

Suite 202
1762 Technology Drive
San Jose, CA 95110
Phone: 1-408-437-8880
Fax: 1-408-467-8968
Website: www.ptvchina.com

See Foreign Venture Capital Firms for full listing.

IDG VENTURES

655 Montgomery Street
Suite 1900
San Francisco, CA 94111
Phone: 415-439-4420
Fax: 415-439-4424
Website: www.idgventures.com

Other Offices

17 Cavendish Square
London, United Kingdom W1M 9AA
Phone: 44 20 7665 1800
Fax: 44 20 7665 1232

492 Old Connecticut Path
Framingham, MA 01701
Phone: 508-935-4183
Fax: 508-872-3479

Rm. 616 Tower A, COFCO Plaza,
8 Jianguomen Nei Dajie
Beijing, China 100005
Phone: 8610-6526-2400
Fax: 8610-6526-0700

Management and Staff
Ajay Chowdhury, General Partner
Christopher Smart, General Partner
Kim Davis, General Partner
Kit Gould, General Partner
Pat Kenealy, General Partner
Susan Cheng, General Partner

Type of Firm
Private Firm Investing Own Capital

Industry Association Membership
National Venture Capital Association (NVCA)
Western Association of Venture Capitalists (WAVC)

Project Preferences

Type of Financing Preferred:
First Stage Financing
Later Stage
Seed
Start-up Financing
Startup

Geographical Preferences

United States
All U.S.
All U.S.

International
Asia
China
Europe

Industry Preferences

(% based on actual investment)

Internet Specific	57.9%
Computer Software and Services	31.3%
Biotechnology	5.1%
Computer Hardware	2.9%
Consumer Related	2.8%

Additional Information
Name of Most Recent Fund: Pacific Technology Ventures USA
Most Recent Fund Was Raised: 10/01/1999
Year Founded: 1996
Capital Under Management: $280,000,000
Current Activity Level : Actively seeking new investments
Method of Compensation: Return on investment is of primary concern, do not charge fees

IGNITE ASSOCIATES, LLC

255 Shoreline Drive
Suite 510
Redwood City, CA 94065
Phone: 650-622-2005
Fax: 650-622-2015
Website: www.ignitegroup.com

Other Offices

Tokio Marine New Building 11th Floor
1-2-1 Marinouchi, Chiyoda-Ky
Tokyo, Japan 100-0005
Phone: 81-3-5220-5015
Fax: 81-3-5220-5016

Management and Staff
Deanne Kenneally, General Partner
Jun Kinebuchi, General Partner
Nobuo Mii, Managing Partner
Ray AbuZayyad, General Partner
Steve Payne, General Partner

Type of Firm
Private Firm Investing Own Capital

Industry Association Membership
National Venture Capital Association (NVCA)

Project Preferences

Type of Financing Preferred:
Early Stage
Later Stage

Size of Investments Considered
Min Size of Investment Considered (000s): $2,000
Max Size of Investment Considered (000s): $10,000

Geographical Preferences

United States
All U.S.

International
Japan

Industry Preferences

(% based on actual investment)

Internet Specific	38.4%
Communications and Media	35.4%
Computer Software and Services	26.3%

Additional Information
Name of Most Recent Fund: Ignite Ventures I
Most Recent Fund Was Raised: 01/01/1998
Year Founded: 1998
Capital Under Management: $140,000,000
Current Activity Level : Actively seeking new investments

IMINDS (FKA: INTERACTIVE MINDS)

135 Main Street
Suite 1350
San Francisco, CA 94105
Phone: 415-547-0000
Fax: 415-227-0300
Website: www.iminds.com

Management and Staff

Alan Fisher, General Partner
Carl Nichols, Managing Partner
Greg Stuart, Venture Partner
Howard Goldman, Venture Partner
Randy Haykin, Managing Partner
Steve Bennett, Venture Partner

Type of Firm

Incubators

Project Preferences

Type of Financing Preferred:

Early Stage
Seed
Start-up Financing

Size of Investments Considered

Min Size of Investment Considered (000s): $300
Max Size of Investment Considered (000s): $2,000

Geographical Preferences

United States

California
West Coast

Industry Preferences

(% based on actual investment)

Internet Specific	73.7%
Computer Software and Services	26.3%

Additional Information

Name of Most Recent Fund: Interactive Minds II
Most Recent Fund Was Raised: 07/01/1999
Year Founded: 1995
Capital Under Management: $70,000,000
Current Activity Level : Actively seeking new investments

IMPERIAL VENTURES, INC.

9920 South La Cienega Boulevar
14th Floor
Inglewood, CA 90301
Phone: 310-417-5409
Fax: 310-338-6115

Other Offices

1100 Glendon Avenue
Suite 2020
Westwood, Japan 90024
Phone: 310-481-1001
Fax: 310-481-1099

11512 El Camino Real
Suite 350
San Diego, Japan 92103
Phone: 858-509-2370
Fax: 858-509-2365

211 North Union Street #100
Alexandria, VA 22314
Phone: 703-684-4829
Fax: 703-838-5579

Management and Staff

Chris Hobbs, Vice President
Daniel Styles, Vice President
H. Wayne Snaveley, President
Jeffrey Altman, Vice President

Type of Firm

Non-Financial Corp. Affiliate or Subsidiary

Industry Association Membership

National Venture Capital Association (NVCA)
Natl assoc of Small Bus. Inv. Co (NASBIC)
Western Association of Venture Capitalists (WAVC)

Project Preferences

Role in Financing:

Prefer role as deal originator but will also invest in deals created by others

Type of Financing Preferred:

Leveraged Buyout
Second Stage Financing

Size of Investments Considered

Min Size of Investment Considered (000s): $500
Max Size of Investment Considered (000s): $2,000

Geographical Preferences

International

No Preference

Additional Information

Year Founded: 1979
Capital Under Management: $18,000,000
Current Activity Level : Actively seeking new investments
Method of Compensation: Other

INCORPORATED INVESTORS

P.O. Box 51113
Palo Alto, CA 94303-0688
Phone: 650-938-2320
Fax: 650-938-2324

Other Offices

28, rue de Syren
Alzingen, Luxembourg L-5870
Phone: 352-366-444
Fax: 352-366-441

928 Broadway
Suite 1000
New York, NY 10010
Phone: 212-505-2507
Fax: 212-228-1398

Avenida Reboucas
3534 Pinheiros
Sao Paulo, Brazil 05402-600
Phone: 55-11-870-4481
Fax: 55-11-832-4620

P.O. Box 1336
Crystal Bay, NV 89402-1336
Phone: 702-832-9798
Fax: 702-832-9031

Type of Firm

Mgt. Consulting Firm

Project Preferences

Role in Financing:

Prefer role as deal originator but will also invest in deals created by others

Type of Financing Preferred:

Acquisition
First Stage Financing
Industry Rollups
Leveraged Buyout
Management Buyouts
Recapitalizations
Second Stage Financing
Special Situation
Turnaround

Size of Investments Considered
Min Size of Investment Considered (000s): $2,000
Max Size of Investment Considered (000s): $25,000

Geographical Preferences
United States
All U.S.
West Coast

International
Germany
Latin America

Industry Preferences
Communications and Media
Commercial Communications
CATV & Pay TV Systems
Telecommunications
Wireless Communications
Data Communications
Satellite Microwave Comm.

Computer Hardware
Computer Graphics and Dig

Computer Software
Computer Services
Software
Systems Software
Applications Software
Artificial Intelligence

Semiconductors/Other Elect.
Electronic Components
Semiconductor
Sensors
Circuit Boards
Component Testing Equipmt
Laser Related
Fiber Optics

Consumer Related
Entertainment and Leisure
Food/Beverage

Industrial/Energy
Energy
Oil & Gas Drilling,Explor
Industrial Products
Factory Automation
Process Control
Robotics
Machinery

Manufact.
Office Automation Equipmt

Additional Information
Name of Most Recent Fund: Industrial Investors LLC
Most Recent Fund Was Raised: 12/31/1997
Year Founded: 1991
Capital Under Management: $75,000,000
Current Activity Level : Actively seeking new investments
Method of Compensation: Return on invest. most important, but chg. closing fees, service fees, etc.

INDOSUEZ VENTURES

2180 Sand Hill Road
Suite 450
Menlo Park, CA 94025
Phone: 650-854-0587
Fax: 650-323-5561
Website: www.indosuezventures.com

Type of Firm
Private Firm Investing Own Capital

Industry Association Membership
Western Association of Venture Capitalists (WAVC)

Project Preferences
Role in Financing:
Prefer role as deal originator but will also invest in deals created by others

Type of Financing Preferred:
First Stage Financing
Mezzanine
Second Stage Financing
Start-up Financing

Size of Investments Considered
Min Size of Investment Considered (000s): $250
Max Size of Investment Considered (000s): $1,500

Geographical Preferences
United States
West Coast

Industry Preferences
(% based on actual investment)

Computer Software and Services	32.8%
Medical/Health	17.8%
Computer Hardware	13.9%
Semiconductors/Other Elect.	7.5%
Biotechnology	7.1%
Communications and Media	5.7%
Consumer Related	5.4%
Internet Specific	5.2%
Industrial/Energy	3.4%
Other Products	1.2%

Additional Information
Name of Most Recent Fund: Indosuez Capital Private Equity Partners, L.P.
Most Recent Fund Was Raised: 01/01/1997
Year Founded: 1985
Capital Under Management: $105,000,000
Current Activity Level : Actively seeking new investments
Method of Compensation: Return on investment is of primary concern, do not charge fees

---

INDUSTRY VENTURES

2063 Larkin St
San Francisco, CA 94101
Phone: 415-260-2953
Website: www.industryventures.com

See Massachusetts for full listing.

INFINEON VENTURES

1730 North First Street
San Jose, CA 95112
Website: www.infineon.com/ventures/

See Foreign Venture Capital Firms for full listing.

INFINITY CAPITAL LLC

100 Hamilton Avenue
Suite 400
Palo Alto, CA 94301
Phone: 650-462-8400
Fax: 650-462-8415
Website: www.infinityllc.com

Management and Staff
Atul Kapadia, Managing Director
Bruce Graham, Venture Partner
Eric Chin, Managing Director
George Kitagawa, Chief Financial Officer
John Hershey, Managing Director
Lori Kulvin Crawford, Managing Director
Sam Lee, Managing Director
Virginia Turezyn, Managing Director

Type of Firm
Private Firm Investing Own Capital

Industry Association Membership
Western Association of Venture Capitalists (WAVC)

Project Preferences

Role in Financing:
Prefer role as deal originator but will also invest in deals created by others

Type of Financing Preferred:
Early Stage

Industry Preferences

(% based on actual investment)

Internet Specific	41.9%
Communications and Media	20.8%
Computer Hardware	13.3%
Semiconductors/Other Elect.	11.7%
Computer Software and Services	11.3%
Other Products	1.0%

Additional Information
Name of Most Recent Fund: Infinity Capital VF 1999
Most Recent Fund Was Raised: 09/30/1999
Year Founded: 1999
Capital Under Management: $207,500,000
Current Activity Level : Actively seeking new investments

INFORMATION TECHNOLOGY VENTURES

100 Hamilton Ave.
Suite 400
Palo Alto, CA 94301
Phone: 650-462-8400
Fax: 650-462-8415
Website: www.itventures.com

Management and Staff
Eric Chin, Principal
George Kitagawa, Chief Financial Officer
Lori Kulvin Crawford, Managing Director
Mark Dubovoy, Managing Director
Sam Lee, Managing Director
Virginia Turezyn, Managing Director

Type of Firm
Private Firm Investing Own Capital

Industry Association Membership
Western Association of Venture Capitalists (WAVC)

Project Preferences

Role in Financing:
Prefer role as deal originator but will also invest in deals created by others

Type of Financing Preferred:
Start-up Financing

Geographical Preferences

United States
Northeast
Northwest
West Coast

Industry Preferences

(% based on actual investment)

Internet Specific	42.1%
Computer Software and Services	22.1%
Communications and Media	15.4%
Semiconductors/Other Elect.	12.4%
Computer Hardware	6.4%
Industrial/Energy	0.8%
Other Products	0.7%

Additional Information
Name of Most Recent Fund: Information Technology Ventures II, L.P.
Most Recent Fund Was Raised: 01/01/1998
Year Founded: 1994
Capital Under Management: $213,000,000
Current Activity Level : Actively seeking new investments
Method of Compensation: Return on investment is of primary concern, do not charge fees

INGLEWOOD VENTURES

12526 Highbluff Drive
Suite 300
San Diego, CA 92130
Phone: 858-792-3579
Fax: 858-792-3417

Management and Staff
Blake Ingle, Partner
Daniel Wood, Partner

Type of Firm
Private Firm Investing Own Capital

Additional Information
Name of Most Recent Fund: IngleWood Ventures, L.P.
Most Recent Fund Was Raised: 08/03/1999
Year Founded: 1997
Capital Under Management: $40,000,000
Current Activity Level : Actively seeking new investments

INMAN & BOWMAN

Four Orinda Way
Building D, Suite 150
Orinda, CA 94563
Phone: 925-253-1611
Fax: 925-253-9037

Other Offices

1717 Embarcadero Road
Suite 2000
Palo Alto, CA 94303
Phone: 415-493-8890
Fax: 415-424-8080

Type of Firm
Private Firm Investing Own Capital

Industry Association Membership
Western Association of Venture Capitalists (WAVC)

Project Preferences

Role in Financing:
Prefer role as deal originator but will also invest in deals created by others

Type of Financing Preferred:
First Stage Financing
Leveraged Buyout
Second Stage Financing
Special Situation
Start-up Financing

Size of Investments Considered
Min Size of Investment Considered (000s): $1,000
Max Size of Investment Considered: No Limit

Geographical Preferences

United States
West Coast

Industry Preferences

Computer Hardware
Computer Graphics and Dig
Integrated Turnkey System
Terminals

Computer Software
Computer Services
Systems Software
Applications Software
Artificial Intelligence

Semiconductors/Other Elect.
Electronic Components
Semiconductor
Controllers and Sensors
Circuit Boards
Component Testing Equipmt
Laser Related
Fiber Optics
Analytic/Scientific

Medical/Health
Diagnostic Services
Diagnostic Test Products
Drug/Equipmt Delivery
Other Therapeutic
Disposable Med. Products
Hospitals/Clinics/Primary
Hospital/Other Instit.
Pharmaceuticals

Additional Information
Name of Most Recent Fund: Inman & Bowman
Most Recent Fund Was Raised: 06/01/1985
Year Founded: 1985
Capital Under Management: $44,000,000
Current Activity Level : Making few, if any, new investments
Method of Compensation: Return on investment is of primary concern, do not charge fees

INNOCAL, L.P.

600 Anton Boulevard
Suite 1270
Costa Mesa, CA 92626
Phone: 714-850-6784
Fax: 714-850-6798

Other Offices

Park 80 West
Plaza One
Saddle Brook, NJ 07663
Phone: 201-845-4900
Fax: 201-845-3388

Management and Staff
Eric Harrison
James E. Houlihan III

Whom to Contact
Eric Harrison
James E. Houlihan III

Type of Firm
Private Firm Investing Own Capital

Project Preferences

Role in Financing:
Prefer role as deal originator but will also invest in deals created by others

Type of Financing Preferred:
Early Stage
Expansion
First Stage Financing
Second Stage Financing

Size of Investments Considered
Min Size of Investment Considered (000s): $2,000
Max Size of Investment Considered (000s): $7,000

Geographical Preferences

United States
California

Industry Preferences

(% based on actual investment)

Computer Software and Services	39.2%
Medical/Health	26.4%
Communications and Media	10.5%
Internet Specific	9.1%
Industrial/Energy	7.3%
Biotechnology	4.7%
Computer Hardware	2.6%
Other Products	0.3%

Additional Information
Name of Most Recent Fund: InnoCal II, L.P.
Most Recent Fund Was Raised: 04/01/1993
Year Founded: 1993
Capital Under Management: $175,000,000
Current Activity Level : Actively seeking new investments
Method of Compensation: Return on investment is of primary concern, do not charge fees

INNOVACOM

One Embaradero Centre
Skydeck- 41st Floor
San Francisco, CA 94111
Phone: 415-288-0680
Fax: 415-288-0685
Website: www.innovacomvc.com

See Foreign Venture Capital Firms for full listing.

INSTITUTIONAL VENTURE PARTNERS

3000 Sand Hill Road
Building 2, Suite 290
Menlo Park, CA 94025
Phone: 650-854-0132
Fax: 650-854-5762
Website: www.ivp.com

Management and Staff
Geoff Yang, Partner
John Tillotson, Partner
John McQuillan, Partner
L. James Strand, Partner
Mary Elmore, Partner
Nancy McCroskey, Chief Financial Officer
Norman Fogelsong, Partner
Peter Gotcher, Partner
Peter Thomas, Partner
R. Thomas Dyal, Partner
Rebecca Robertson, Partner
Reid Dennis, Partner
Ruthann Quindlen, Partner
Samuel Colella, Partner
Timothy Haley, General Partner
Todd Chaffee, General Partner
William Tai, Partner

Type of Firm
Private Firm Investing Own Capital

Industry Association Membership
National Venture Capital Association (NVCA)
Western Association of Venture Capitalists (WAVC)

Project Preferences

Role in Financing:
Prefer role as deal originator but will also invest in deals created by others

Type of Financing Preferred:
Early Stage
First Stage Financing
Second Stage Financing
Seed
Special Situation
Start-up Financing

Size of Investments Considered
Min Size of Investment Considered (000s): $500
Max Size of Investment Considered: No Limit

Geographical Preferences

International
Latin America
No Preference

Industry Preferences

(% based on actual investment)

Internet Specific	24.7%
Communications and Media	17.5%
Computer Software and Services	14.6%
Semiconductors/Other Elect.	10.5%
Medical/Health	9.9%
Computer Hardware	9.7%
Biotechnology	7.3%
Consumer Related	2.7%
Other Products	1.7%
Industrial/Energy	1.4%

Additional Information

Name of Most Recent Fund: Institutional Venture Associates
Most Recent Fund Was Raised: 01/01/1974
Year Founded: 1980
Capital Under Management: $750,000,000
Current Activity Level : Actively seeking new investments
Method of Compensation: Return on investment is of primary concern, do not charge fees

INTEGRATED CONSORTIUM, INC.

50 Ridgecrest Road
Kentfield, CA 94904
Phone: 415-925-0386
Fax: 415-461-2726

Type of Firm

Mgt. Consulting Firm

Project Preferences

Role in Financing:

Prefer role as deal originator but will also invest in deals created by others

Type of Financing Preferred:

Control-block Purchases
First Stage Financing
Industry Rollups
Leveraged Buyout
Mezzanine
Second Stage Financing

Size of Investments Considered

Min Size of Investment Considered (000s): $1,000
Max Size of Investment Considered: No Limit

Geographical Preferences

United States

West Coast

Industry Preferences

Consumer Related

Entertainment and Leisure
Retail
Computer Stores
Franchises(NEC)
Food/Beverage
Consumer Products
Consumer Services

Industrial/Energy

Materials

Additional Information

Current Activity Level : Actively seeking new investments
Method of Compensation: Return on invest. most important, but chg. closing fees, service fees, etc.

INTERNET INCUBATOR PLC

Two Embarcadero Inc
Suite 1740
San Francisco, CA 94111
Phone: 1 415 217 6460
Fax: 1 415 217 6464
Website: www.theii.net

See Foreign Venture Capital Firms for full listing.

INTERWEST PARTNERS

3000 Sand Hill Road
Building Three, Suite 255
Menlo Park, CA 94025-7112
Phone: 650-854-8585
Fax: 650-854-4706
Website: www.interwest.com

Other Offices

Two Galleria Tower
13455 Noel Road, Suite 1670
Dallas, TX 75240-6615
Phone: 972-392-7279
Fax: 972-490-6348

Management and Staff

Alan Crites, General Partner
Arnold Oronsky, General Partner
Berry Cash, General Partner
Gilbert Kliman, General Partner
Michael Sweeney, Venture Partner
Philip Gianos, General Partner
Robert Momsen, General Partner
Rodney Ferguson, Venture Partner
Stephen Bowsher, General Partner
Tom Rosch, General Partner
W. Scott Hedrick, General Partner
W. Stephen Holmes, General Partner
Wallace Hawley, General Partner

Whom to Contact

Jeff Hogg
Stephen Cohen

Type of Firm

Private Firm Investing Own Capital

Industry Association Membership

National Venture Capital Association (NVCA)
Western Association of Venture Capitalists (WAVC)

Project Preferences

Role in Financing:

Will function either as deal originator or investor in deals created by others

Type of Financing Preferred:

Early Stage
Expansion
First Stage Financing
Later Stage
Second Stage Financing
Seed
Startup

Size of Investments Considered

Min Size of Investment Considered (000s): $2,000
Max Size of Investment Considered (000s): $25,000

Geographical Preferences

United States

All U.S.

Industry Preferences

(% based on actual investment)

Medical/Health	17.5%
Internet Specific	16.4%
Consumer Related	15.5%
Communications and Media	12.3%
Computer Hardware	9.4%
Semiconductors/Other Elect.	9.4%
Computer Software and Services	7.0%
Biotechnology	6.4%
Other Products	3.8%

Industrial/Energy	2.4%

Additional Information
Name of Most Recent Fund: InterWest Partners VI
Most Recent Fund Was Raised: 02/01/1999
Year Founded: 1979
Capital Under Management: $1,661,700,000
Current Activity Level : Actively seeking new investments
Method of Compensation: Return on investment is of primary concern, do not charge fees

INVENCOR, INC.

P.O. Box 7355
Menlo Park, CA 94026
Phone: 888-292-2999
Fax: 415-945-0646
Website: www.invencor.com

Management and Staff
Debra Guerin, Managing Director
Jim Corzine, General Partner
Kirk Westbrook, Managing Director

Type of Firm
Private Firm Investing Own Capital

Project Preferences

Size of Investments Considered
Min Size of Investment Considered (000s): $500
Max Size of Investment Considered (000s): $3,000

Additional Information
Year Founded: 1997
Capital Under Management: $72,000,000
Current Activity Level : Actively seeking new investments

INVESCO PRIVATE CAPITAL (FKA: CHANCELLOR)

525 University Avenue
Suite 101
Palo Alto, CA 94301
Phone: 650-325-3600
Fax: 650-330-0815
Website: www.privtaecapital.invesco.com

See New York for full listing.

J.F. SHEA & COMPANY

655 Brea Canyon Road
P.O. Box 489
Walnut, CA 91788-0489
Phone: 909-594-9500
Fax: 909-594-0934
Website: www.jfshea.com

Type of Firm
Private Firm Investing Own Capital

Project Preferences

Type of Financing Preferred:
Balanced

Geographical Preferences

International
No Preference

Industry Preferences

(% based on actual investment)

Communications and Media	25.9%
Computer Hardware	21.7%
Internet Specific	17.0%
Computer Software and Services	14.2%
Semiconductors/Other Elect.	10.6%
Biotechnology	3.6%
Other Products	2.9%
Medical/Health	2.1%
Industrial/Energy	1.9%
Consumer Related	0.0%

Additional Information
Year Founded: 1980
Capital Under Management: $50,000,000
Current Activity Level : Inactive / Unknown

J.P. MORGAN CAPITAL CORP.

101 California Street
38th Floor
San Francisco, CA 94111
Phone: 415-954-4735
Website: www.jpmorgan.com

See New York for full listing.

J.P. MORGAN PARTNERS (FKA: CHASE CAPITAL PARTNERS)

50 California Street
Suite 2940
San Francisco, CA 94111
Phone: 415-591-1200
Website: www.chasecapital.com

See New York for full listing.

JAFCO VENTURES, INC.

505 Hamilton Avenue
Suite 310
Palo Alto, CA 94301
Phone: 650-463-8800
Fax: 650-463-8801
Website: www.jafco.com

Other Offices

225 Liberty Street
17th Floor
New York, NY 10281-1196
Phone: 212-667-9001
Fax: 212-667-1004

One Boston Place
Suite 3320
Boston, MA 02108
Phone: 617-367-3510
Fax: 617-367-3532

Management and Staff
Andy Goldfarb, Senior Managing Director
Barry Schiffman, Managing Director
David Polifko, Vice President
David Fachetti, Vice President
Hisashi Washiyama, Principal
Hitoshi Imuta, Chairman & CEO
Lynn Barringer, Chief Financial Officer
Steve Hill, Managing Director
Todd Brooks, Principal
Ullas Naik, Managing Director

Whom to Contact
Andrew P. Goldfarb

Type of Firm
Private Firm Investing Own Capital

Industry Association Membership
Western Association of Venture Capitalists (WAVC)

Project Preferences

Role in Financing:
Prefer role as deal originator but will also invest in deals created by others

Type of Financing Preferred:
Balanced
First Stage Financing
Mezzanine
Second Stage Financing

Size of Investments Considered
Min Size of Investment Considered (000s): $500
Max Size of Investment Considered: No Limit

Geographical Preferences

International
All International

Industry Preferences

(% based on actual investment)

Communications and Media	28.4%
Internet Specific	22.2%
Computer Software and Services	20.7%
Other Products	8.6%
Semiconductors/Other Elect.	6.6%
Biotechnology	4.6%
Medical/Health	4.6%
Computer Hardware	4.2%
Industrial/Energy	0.1%

Additional Information
Name of Most Recent Fund: JAFCO USIT III
Most Recent Fund Was Raised: 09/17/1998
Year Founded: 1984
Capital Under Management: $750,000,000
Current Activity Level : Actively seeking new investments
Method of Compensation: Return on investment is of primary concern, do not charge fees

---

JAMES A. MATZDORFF & CO.

9903 Santa Monica Boulevard
Suite 374
Beverly Hills, CA 90212
Phone: 310-854-4634

Type of Firm
Mgt. Consulting Firm

Project Preferences

Role in Financing:
Prefer role as deal originator but will also invest in deals created by others

Type of Financing Preferred:
Leveraged Buyout
Mezzanine
Second Stage Financing
Special Situation

Size of Investments Considered
Min Size of Investment Considered (000s): $5,000
Max Size of Investment Considered: No Limit

Geographical Preferences

United States
All U.S.

Industry Preferences

Communications and Media
Communications and Media

Computer Other
Computer Related

Semiconductors/Other Elect.
Electronic Components

Biotechnology
Biotechnology

Medical/Health
Medical/Health

Consumer Related
Consumer
Education Related

Industrial/Energy
Energy
Industrial Products

Transportation
Transportation

Financial Services
Financial Services
Real Estate

Business Serv.
Distribution
Consulting Services

Manufact.
Publishing

Agr/Forestr/Fish
Agriculture related

Additional Information
Name of Most Recent Fund: JAM XXIII
Most Recent Fund Was Raised: 01/01/1998
Year Founded: 1977
Capital Under Management: $150,000,000
Current Activity Level : Actively seeking new investments
Method of Compensation: Return on invest. most important, but chg. closing fees, service fees, etc.

JAPAN ASIA INVESTMENT CO LTD

2479 East Bayshore Road
Suite 709
Palo Alto, CA 94303
Phone: 650-213-9011
Fax: 650-213-9012
Website: www.jaic-vc.co.jp

See Foreign Venture Capital Firms for full listing.

JK&B CAPITAL

691 Seale Avenue
Palo Alto, CA 94301-3833
Phone: 650-330-1200
Fax: 650-330-1201
Website: www.jkbcapital.com

See Illinois for full listing.

JUNIPER NETWORKS

P.O. Box 3786
Sunnyvale, CA 94088
Phone: 408-745-2000
Fax: 408-745-2100
Website: www.juniper.net

Management and Staff
Bjorn Liencres, Founder
Dennis Ferguson, Founder
Marcel Gani, Chief Financial Officer
Scott Kriens, Chairman & CEO

Type of Firm
Non-Financial Corp. Affiliate or Subsidiary

Industry Preferences

(% based on actual investment)

Semiconductors/Other Elect.	44.4%
Communications and Media	33.0%

Computer Software and Services	14.5%
Internet Specific	8.0%

Additional Information
Year Founded: 2000
Current Activity Level : Actively seeking new investments

KAISER PERMANENTE (AKA: NATIONAL VENTURE DEVELOPMENT)

1800 Harrison Street
22nd Floor
Oakland, CA 94612
Phone: 510-267-4010
Fax: 510-267-4036
Website: www.kpventures.net

Type of Firm
Non-Financial Corp. Affiliate or Subsidiary

Industry Association Membership
National Venture Capital Association (NVCA)

Project Preferences

Role in Financing:
Prefer role in deals created by others

Type of Financing Preferred:
Balanced
Expansion
First Stage Financing
Joint Ventures
Private Placement
Second Stage Financing

Size of Investments Considered
Min Size of Investment Considered (000s): $500
Max Size of Investment Considered (000s): $2,000

Geographical Preferences

United States
All U.S.

Canada
All Canada

Industry Preferences

Communications and Media
Wireless Communications
Data Communications
Satellite Microwave Comm.

Computer Hardware
Computer Graphics and Dig

Computer Software
Software

Internet Specific
E-Commerce Technology
Internet
Web Aggregration/Portals

Semiconductors/Other Elect.
Analytic/Scientific

Biotechnology
Human Biotechnology
Biosensors
Biotech Related Research

Medical/Health
Medical/Health

Consumer Related
Education Related

Industrial/Energy
Robotics

Additional Information
Capital Under Management: $20,000,000
Current Activity Level : Actively seeking new investments
Method of Compensation: Return on invest. most important, but chg. closing fees, service fees, etc.

KINGSBURY ASSOCIATES

3655 Nobel Drive
Suite 490
San Diego, CA 92122
Phone: 858-677-0600
Fax: 858-677-0800

Management and Staff
Timothy Wollaeger, Partner

Type of Firm
Private Firm Investing Own Capital

Project Preferences

Role in Financing:
Prefer role as deal originator but will also invest in deals created by others

Type of Financing Preferred:
First Stage Financing
Second Stage Financing
Start-up Financing

Size of Investments Considered
Min Size of Investment Considered (000s): $500
Max Size of Investment Considered (000s): $1,000

Geographical Preferences

United States
West Coast

Industry Preferences

(% based on actual investment)

Medical/Health	72.2%
Biotechnology	20.7%
Computer Software and Services	6.4%
Internet Specific	0.7%

Additional Information
Name of Most Recent Fund: Kingsbury Capital Partners LP III
Most Recent Fund Was Raised: 03/01/1998
Year Founded: 1993
Capital Under Management: $88,000,000
Current Activity Level : Actively seeking new investments
Method of Compensation: Return on investment is of primary concern, do not charge fees

KINSHIP PARTNERS

1900 Garvey Avenue
Suite 200
West Covina, CA 91790-2653
Phone: 818-962-3562
Fax: 818-962-0758

See Colorado for full listing.

KLEINER PERKINS CAUFIELD & BYERS

2750 Sand Hill Road
Menlo Park, CA 94025
Phone: 650-233-2750
Fax: 650-233-0300
Website: http://www.kpcb.com

Other Offices

4 Embarcadero Center
Suite 1880
San Francisco, CA 94111
Phone: 415-421-3110
Fax: 415-421-3128

Management and Staff
Bernard Lacroute, Partner
Brook Byers, General Partner
David Schnell, General Partner
Douglas Mackenzie, Partner
E. Floyd Kvamme, Partner
Frank Caufield, Partner
James Lally, Partner
John Doerr, Partner
Joseph Lacob, Partner
Kevin Compton, Partner
Michael Curry, Chief Financial Officer
Peter Neupert, Chief Executive Officer
Ray Lane, General Partner
Russ Siegelman, Partner
Susan Biglieri, Chief Financial Officer
Ted Schlein, Partner
Thomas Perkins, Partner
Thomas Jermoluk, General Partner
Vinod Khosla, Partner
William Hearst, Partner

Type of Firm
Private Firm Investing Own Capital

Industry Association Membership
National Venture Capital Association (NVCA)
Western Association of Venture Capitalists (WAVC)

Project Preferences

Role in Financing:
Prefer role as deal originator but will also invest in deals created by others

Type of Financing Preferred:
First Stage Financing
Second Stage Financing
Seed
Start-up Financing

Size of Investments Considered
Min Size of Investment Considered (000s): $500
Max Size of Investment Considered: No Limit

Geographical Preferences

United States
West Coast

Industry Preferences

(% based on actual investment)

Internet Specific	26.4%
Computer Software and Services	17.7%
Communications and Media	16.3%
Semiconductors/Other Elect.	10.9%
Computer Hardware	9.6%
Medical/Health	7.6%
Biotechnology	6.0%
Other Products	2.6%
Consumer Related	2.3%
Industrial/Energy	0.8%

Additional Information
Name of Most Recent Fund: Kleiner Perkins Caufield & Byers IX - A , L.P.
Most Recent Fund Was Raised: 07/02/1997
Year Founded: 1972
Capital Under Management: $2,700,000,000
Current Activity Level : Actively seeking new investments
Method of Compensation: Return on investment is of primary concern, do not charge fees

KLINE HAWKES & CO.

11726 San Vicente Boulevard
Suite 300
Los Angeles, CA 90049
Phone: 310-442-4700
Fax: 310-442-4707
Website: www.klinehawkes.com

Management and Staff
Frank Kline, Managing Partner
Joseph Ferguson, General Partner
Klaus Koch, Principal
Leslie Shaw, Chief Financial Officer
Nicholas Memmo, General Partner

Whom to Contact
Robert M. Freidland

Type of Firm
Private Firm Investing Own Capital

Industry Association Membership
Natl assoc of Small Bus. Inv. Co (NASBIC)

Project Preferences

Role in Financing:
Will function either as deal originator or investor in deals created by others

Type of Financing Preferred:
Expansion
Later Stage
Private Placement
Second Stage Financing

Size of Investments Considered
Min Size of Investment Considered (000s): $4,000
Max Size of Investment Considered (000s): $10,000

Geographical Preferences

United States
West Coast

Industry Preferences

(% based on actual investment)

Internet Specific	39.4%
Medical/Health	18.9%
Semiconductors/Other Elect.	17.9%
Communications and Media	7.1%
Computer Hardware	5.5%
Biotechnology	4.9%
Computer Software and Services	4.6%
Other Products	1.7%

Additional Information
Name of Most Recent Fund: Kline Hawkes Pacific, L.P.
Most Recent Fund Was Raised: 01/01/1995
Year Founded: 1995
Capital Under Management: $262,000,000
Current Activity Level : Actively seeking new investments
Method of Compensation: Return on investment is of primary concern, do not charge fees

KLM CAPITAL GROUP

Ten Almaden Boulevard
Suite 988
San Jose, CA 95113
Phone: 408-970-8888
Fax: 408-970-8887
Website: www.klmtech.com

Other Offices

10/F, Century Square
1-13, D'Aguilar Street
Central, Hong Kong
Phone: 852-2537-3318
Fax: 852-2537-3138

4516 Seton Center Parkway
Suite 170
Austin, TX 78759
Phone: 512-338-9688
Fax: 512-338-9754

Management and Staff
Alfred Li, Principal
Donald Brooks, Partner
Jerald Shaevitz, Chief Financial Officer
Rick Frasch, President

Type of Firm
Private Firm Investing Own Capital

Project Preferences

Type of Financing Preferred:
Balanced
Early Stage
Later Stage

Geographical Preferences

United States
All U.S.

International
Asia
All International

Industry Preferences

(% based on actual investment)

Semiconductors/Other Elect.	35.4%
Internet Specific	25.5%
Computer Hardware	18.3%
Computer Software and Services	14.1%
Communications and Media	6.7%

Additional Information

Name of Most Recent Fund: Current Ventures II
Most Recent Fund Was Raised: 08/31/1999
Year Founded: 1996
Capital Under Management: $84,000,000
Current Activity Level : Actively seeking new investments

KPE VENTURES

6100 Wilshire Blvd.
Los Angeles, CA 90048
Phone: 323-930-7300

See New York for full listing.

KTB VENTURES (FKA: KTB VENTURE CAPITAL)

720 University Avenue
Suite 100
Palo Alto, CA 94301
Phone: 650-324-4681
Fax: 650-324-4682
Website: www.ktbvc.com

Other Offices

KTB Network Building
826-14
Yeoksam-dong- Kangnam-gu, South Korea 135-080
Phone: 822-3466-2221
Fax: 8222-3466-2380

Management and Staff

JongHo Woo, Managing Director
Sung Yoon, Managing Partner

Type of Firm

Commercial Bank Affiliate or Subsidiary

Project Preferences

Type of Financing Preferred:
Early Stage
First Stage Financing

Geographical Preferences

United States
All U.S.

Industry Preferences

(% based on actual investment)

Communications and Media	56.5%
Internet Specific	21.9%
Computer Software and Services	19.1%
Semiconductors/Other Elect.	2.5%

Additional Information

Year Founded: 1988
Current Activity Level : Actively seeking new investments

KYOCERA INTERNATIONAL, INC.

Corporate Development
8611 Balboa Avenue
San Diego, CA 92123
Phone: 858-576-2600
Fax: 858-492-1456

Other Offices

Corporate Development
8611 Balboa Ave
San Diego, CA 92123
Phone: 619-576-2600

Type of Firm

Non-Financial Corp. Affiliate or Subsidiary

Project Preferences

Role in Financing:
Prefer role in deals created by others

Type of Financing Preferred:
Second Stage Financing

Size of Investments Considered

Min Size of Investment Considered (000s): $300
Max Size of Investment Considered (000s): $500

Geographical Preferences

United States
Northeast
Northwest
West Coast

Industry Preferences

Communications and Media
Communications and Media
Other Communication Prod.

Computer Hardware
Computers
Mini and Personal/Desktop

Internet Specific
Internet

Semiconductors/Other Elect.
Electronics
Electronic Components
Semiconductor
Component Testing Equipmt
Fiber Optics

Manufact.
Office Automation Equipmt

Additional Information

Name of Most Recent Fund: Kyocera Corporation
Most Recent Fund Was Raised: 02/01/1983
Year Founded: 1979
Capital Under Management: $93,000,000
Current Activity Level : Making few, if any, new investments
Method of Compensation: Return on investment is of primary concern, do not charge fees

LAWRENCE FINANCIAL GROUP

701 Teakwood
P.O. Box 491773
Los Angeles, CA 90049
Phone: 310-471-4060
Fax: 310-472-3155

Management and Staff

Larry Hurwitz

Whom to Contact
Larry Hurwitz

Type of Firm
Investment/Merchant Bank Subsid/Affil

Project Preferences

Role in Financing:
Prefer role as deal originator but will also invest in deals created by others

Type of Financing Preferred:
Second Stage Financing

Size of Investments Considered
Min Size of Investment Considered (000s): $500
Max Size of Investment Considered (000s): $1,000

Geographical Preferences

United States
West Coast

Industry Preferences

Communications and Media
Telecommunications
Satellite Microwave Comm.

Computer Other
Computer Related

Semiconductors/Other Elect.
Electronic Components
Circuit Boards
Component Testing Equipmt

Biotechnology
Industrial Biotechnology
Biosensors
Biotech Related Research
Biotech Related Research

Medical/Health
Medical/Health
Medical Diagnostics
Medical Therapeutics

Consumer Related
Consumer
Education Related

Industrial/Energy
Oil and Gas Exploration
Oil & Gas Drilling,Explor
Energy Conservation Relat
Industrial Products

Financial Services
Financial Services

Business Serv.
Distribution

Agr/Forestr/Fish
Agriculture related
Mining and Minerals

Additional Information
Year Founded: 1989
Current Activity Level : Actively seeking new investments
Method of Compensation: Function primarily in service area, receive contingent fee in cash or equity

---

LEONARD GREEN & PARTNERS

11111 Santa Monica Boulevard
Suite 2000
Los Angeles, CA 90025
Phone: 310-954-0444
Fax: 310-954-0404

Management and Staff
Gregory Annick, Partner
Jim Gillette, Chief Financial Officer
John Danhakl, Partner
Jonathan Seiffer, Partner
Jonathan Sokoloff, Partner
Leonard Green, Founding Partner
Peter Nolan, Partner

Whom to Contact
Jonathan Sokoloff

Type of Firm
Private Equity Advisor or Fund of Fund Mgr

Project Preferences

Role in Financing:
Prefer role as deal originator but will also invest in deals created by others

Type of Financing Preferred:
Leveraged Buyout

Size of Investments Considered
Min Size of Investment Considered (000s): $25,000
Max Size of Investment Considered (000s): $300,000

Geographical Preferences

United States
All U.S.
West Coast

Industry Preferences

(% based on actual investment)

Other Products	38.5%
Consumer Related	35.4%
Communications and Media	20.0%
Biotechnology	4.3%
Semiconductors/Other Elect.	1.4%
Computer Software and Services	0.5%

Additional Information
Name of Most Recent Fund: Green Equity Investors III, L.P.
Most Recent Fund Was Raised: 09/01/1998
Year Founded: 1989
Capital Under Management: $1,770,400,000
Current Activity Level : Actively seeking new investments
Method of Compensation: Return on invest. most important, but chg. closing fees, service fees, etc.

LEONARD MAUTNER ASSOCIATES

1434 Sixth Street
Suite 10
Santa Monica, CA 90401
Phone: 213-393-9788
Fax: 310-459-9918

Management and Staff
Leonard Mautner

Whom to Contact
Leonard Mautner

Type of Firm
Mgt. Consulting Firm

Project Preferences

Role in Financing:
Prefer role as deal originator but will also invest in deals created by others

Type of Financing Preferred:
First Stage Financing
Seed
Special Situation
Start-up Financing

Size of Investments Considered
Min Size of Investment Considered (000s): $100
Max Size of Investment Considered (000s): $300

Geographical Preferences

United States
West Coast

Industry Preferences

Communications and Media
Data Communications

Computer Hardware
Mini and Personal/Desktop
Computer Graphics and Dig

Computer Software
Computer Services
Applications Software
Artificial Intelligence

Semiconductors/Other Elect.
Laser Related
Fiber Optics

Medical/Health
Diagnostic Services
Diagnostic Test Products
Disposable Med. Products

Additional Information
Year Founded: 1969
Current Activity Level : Reducing investment activity
Method of Compensation: Return on invest. most important, but chg. closing fees, service fees, etc.

LEVENSOHN CAPITAL MANAGEMENT L.L.C

333 Bush Street
Suite 2580
San Francisco, CA 94104
Phone: 415-217-4710
Fax: 415-217-4727
Website: www.levcap.com

Management and Staff
Frank Brown, General Partner
Pascal Levensohn, President
Richard Slinn, Principal

Type of Firm
Private Firm Investing Own Capital

Industry Association Membership
National Venture Capital Association (NVCA)

Geographical Preferences

United States
All U.S.

Additional Information
Year Founded: 1999
Current Activity Level : Actively seeking new investments

LEVINE LEICHTMAN CAPITAL PARTNERS, INC.

335 North Maple Drive
Suite 240
Beverly Hills, CA 90210
Phone: 310-275-5335
Fax: 310-275-1441
Website: http://www.llcp.com

Management and Staff
Arthur Levine, Co-Founder
Lauren Leichtman, Co-Founder

Whom to Contact
Mark A. Sampson
Robert A. Poletti

Type of Firm
Private Firm Investing Own Capital

Project Preferences

Role in Financing:
Prefer role as deal originator

Type of Financing Preferred:
Industry Rollups
Leveraged Buyout
Special Situation

Geographical Preferences

United States
Rocky Mountain
West Coast

Industry Preferences

Computer Software
Software

Medical/Health
Medical Products

Consumer Related
Food/Beverage

Industrial/Energy
Industrial Products

Transportation
Aerospace

Financial Services
Financial Services

Additional Information
Name of Most Recent Fund: Levine Leichtman Capital Partners II, L.P.
Most Recent Fund Was Raised: 01/01/1998
Year Founded: 1985
Capital Under Management: $417,000,000
Current Activity Level : Actively seeking new investments
Method of Compensation: Return on invest. most important, but chg. closing fees, service fees, etc.

LEXINGTON PARTNERS, INC. (FKA: LPNY ADVISORS, INC.)

2880 Lexington Drive
Suite 205
Santa Clara, CA 95054
Phone: 408-970-0123
Fax: 408-970-0111
Website: ww.lexingtonpartners.com

See New York for full listing.

LF INTERNATIONAL, INC.

360 Post Street
Suite 705
San Francisco, CA 94108
Phone: 415-399-0110
Fax: 415-399-9222
Website: www.lfvc.com

Other Offices

11/F LiFung Tower
888 Cheung Sha Wan Road
Kowloon, Hong Kong
Phone: 852-2300-2322
Fax: 852-2300-2355

360 Post Street
Suite 705
San Francisco, CA 94108
Phone: 415-399-0110

De Bavaylei 66
1800 Vilvoorde, Belgium
Phone: 32-2-251-2604
Fax: 32-2-252-4567

Dukmyung Building
170-9 Samsung-dong
Kangnam-ku, Seoul, South Korea
Phone: 82-2-531-8500
Fax: 82-2-539-6070

Lifung Tower
One Nanking East Road Sec. 4
Taipei, Taiwan
Phone: 886-2-712-4523

No. 1, Lorong 2
Toa Payoh
Singapore, Singapore 1231
Phone: 65-250-2511
Fax: 65-253-3088

Management and Staff
Giles Hefer
Paolo Pellizzari

Whom to Contact
Giles Hefer
Paolo Pellizzari

Type of Firm
Non-Financial Corp. Affiliate or Subsidiary

Industry Association Membership
Hungarian Venture Capital Association

Project Preferences

Role in Financing:
Prefer role as deal originator but will also invest in deals created by others

Type of Financing Preferred:
Control-block Purchases
Early Stage
Expansion
First Stage Financing
Industry Rollups
Management Buyouts
Second Stage Financing
Special Situation

Size of Investments Considered
Min Size of Investment Considered (000s): $500
Max Size of Investment Considered (000s): $1,000

Geographical Preferences

United States
All U.S.

International
Bermuda
Europe
France
Germany
Italy
Spain
United Kingdom

Industry Preferences

Consumer Related
Consumer
Retail
Consumer Products

Additional Information
Name of Most Recent Fund: Golden Horn (III), L.P.
Most Recent Fund Was Raised: 10/01/1997
Year Founded: 1982
Capital Under Management: $45,000,000
Current Activity Level : Actively seeking new investments
Method of Compensation: Return on investment is of primary concern, do not charge fees

LIBERTY ENVIRONMENTAL PARTNERS

220 Montgomery Street
Penthouse 10
San Francisco, CA 94104
Phone: 415-834-1600
Fax: 415-834-1603

Management and Staff
Donald Hichens, General Partner
Tim Woodward, Principal

Type of Firm
Private Firm Investing Own Capital

Project Preferences

Role in Financing:
Prefer role as deal originator but will also invest in deals created by others

Type of Financing Preferred:
First Stage Financing
Second Stage Financing
Start-up Financing

Size of Investments Considered
Min Size of Investment Considered (000s): $300
Max Size of Investment Considered (000s): $500

Geographical Preferences

United States
Rocky Mountain
West Coast

Industry Preferences

(% based on actual investment)

Industrial/Energy	39.2%
Biotechnology	32.7%
Semiconductors/Other Elect.	22.9%
Internet Specific	5.2%

Additional Information
Name of Most Recent Fund: Liberty Environmental Partners
Most Recent Fund Was Raised: 01/01/1997
Year Founded: 1993
Capital Under Management: $5,000,000
Current Activity Level : Actively seeking new investments
Method of Compensation: Return on investment is of primary concern, do not charge fees

LIGHTHOUSE CAPITAL PARTNERS

500 Drake's Landing Road
San Rafael, CA 94904-3011
Phone: 415-464-5911
Fax: 415-925-3387
Website: www.lcpartners.com

Other Offices

16 Fayesweather St
Cambridge, MA 02138
Phone: 617-441-9192
Fax: 617-354-4374

3000 Sand Hill Road
Building Three
Menlo Park, CA 94025
Phone: 650-233-7666
Fax: 650-223-7668

Management and Staff
Edgerton Scott, Managing Director
Gwill York, Managing Director
Ned Hazen, Managing Director
Richard Stubblefield, Managing Director
Thomas Conneely, Vice President

Whom to Contact
Edgerton Scott
Gwill York
Richard Stubblefield
Thomas Conneely

Type of Firm
Private Firm Investing Own Capital

Industry Association Membership
National Venture Capital Association (NVCA)
Western Association of Venture Capitalists (WAVC)

Project Preferences

Role in Financing:
Prefer role in deals created by others

Type of Financing Preferred:
Early Stage
First Stage Financing
Research and Development
Second Stage Financing
Seed
Start-up Financing

Geographical Preferences

United States
All U.S.
All U.S.

Industry Preferences

(% based on actual investment)

Internet Specific	81.1%
Computer Software and Services	13.2%
Other Products	5.3%
Communications and Media	0.4%

Additional Information

Name of Most Recent Fund: Lighthouse Capital Partners, Fund III
Most Recent Fund Was Raised: 07/01/1999
Year Founded: 1994
Capital Under Management: $162,000,000
Current Activity Level : Actively seeking new investments
Method of Compensation: Return on investment is of primary concern, do not charge fees

LIGHTSPEED VENTURE PARTNERS (FKA: WEISS, PECK & GREER)

2882 Sand Hill Road
Suite 106
Menlo Park, CA 94025
Phone: 650-234-8300
Fax: 650-234-8333
Website:
www.lightspeedventurepartners.com

Other Offices

555 California Street
Suite 3130
San Francisco, CA 94104
Phone: 415-622-6864
Fax: 415-989-5108

One New York Plaza
New York, NY 10004
Phone: 212-908-9500
Fax: 212-908-9652

Management and Staff

Amal Johnson, General Partner
Barry Eggers, General Partner
Christopher Schaepe, General Partner
Dave Markland, Chief Financial Officer
Ellen Feeney, General Partner
Gill Cogan, General Partner
Isaac Aplbaum, Venture Partner
Peter Moulds, Partner
Peter Nieh, General Partner
Philip Black, General Partner
Ravi Mhatre, General Partner
Skip Glass, Venture Partner
Tom Barton, Venture Partner

Type of Firm

Private Firm Investing Own Capital

Industry Association Membership

National Venture Capital Association (NVCA)
Western Association of Venture Capitalists (WAVC)

Project Preferences

Role in Financing:
Prefer role as deal originator but will also invest in deals created by others

Type of Financing Preferred:
Balanced
Early Stage
Expansion
Later Stage
Second Stage Financing
Seed

Geographical Preferences

United States
All U.S.
All U.S.

Canada
All Canada

Industry Preferences

(% based on actual investment)

Internet Specific	20.5%
Communications and Media	14.4%
Computer Software and Services	13.0%
Semiconductors/Other Elect.	10.0%
Other Products	8.5%
Medical/Health	8.3%
Computer Hardware	8.1%
Industrial/Energy	6.3%
Consumer Related	5.5%
Biotechnology	5.4%

Additional Information

Name of Most Recent Fund: WPG Venture Associates V & Affiliated Funds
Most Recent Fund Was Raised: 03/01/1997
Year Founded: 2000
Capital Under Management: $700,000,000
Current Activity Level : Actively seeking new investments
Method of Compensation: Return on investment is of primary concern, do not charge fees

LINC CAPITAL PARTNERS, INC.

1176 Nimitz Drive
Broadmark, CA 94015
Phone: 650-994-3503
Fax: 650-994-0244

See Illinois for full listing.

LINCOLNSHIRE MANAGEMENT INC.

1 Sansome Street
Suite 1900
San Francisco, CA 94104
Phone: 415-781-2800
Fax: 415-781-2850
Website: www.lincolnshiremgmt.com

See New York for full listing.

LOMBARD INVESTMENTS, INC.

600 Montgomery Street
36th Floor
San Francisco, CA 94111
Phone: 415-397-5900
Fax: 415-397-5820

Other Offices

901-2 Citibank Tower
3 Garden Road
Central, Hong Kong
Phone: 852-2878-7388
Fax: 852-2878-7288

Management and Staff
Adrian Lam, Managing Director
Daniel Chao, Managing Director
Michael Chan, Vice President
Randall Cox, Managing Director
Scott Sweet, Chief Financial Officer

Whom to Contact
Gregory H. Von Gehr
R. Kenneth Conner

Type of Firm
Investment/Merchant Bank Investing Own or Client Funds

Industry Association Membership
Hungarian Venture Capital Association

Project Preferences

Role in Financing:
Prefer role as deal originator but will also invest in deals created by others

Type of Financing Preferred:
Acquisition
Early Stage
Expansion
Industry Rollups
Leveraged Buyout
Management Buyouts
Recapitalizations
Turnaround

Size of Investments Considered
Min Size of Investment Considered (000s): $5,000
Max Size of Investment Considered: No Limit

Geographical Preferences

United States
All U.S.

International
Asia
China
Hong Kong
India
Indonesia
Korea, South
Malaysia
Philippines
Singapore
Thailand
Vietnam

Industry Preferences

Communications and Media
Communications and Media

Consumer Related
Consumer Products

Industrial/Energy
Industrial Products
Materials
Machinery

Transportation
Transportation

Financial Services
Financial Services

Business Serv.
Services

Manufact.
Manufacturing

Additional Information
Name of Most Recent Fund: Lombard Investments/International Finance Corp.
Most Recent Fund Was Raised: 03/01/1998
Year Founded: 1985
Capital Under Management: $600,000,000
Current Activity Level : Actively seeking new investments
Method of Compensation: Return on investment is of primary concern, do not charge fees

---

LTI VENTURES LEASING CORP.

655 Montgomery St
Suite 800
San Francisco, CA 94121
Phone: 415-834-0773
Website: www.ltileasing.com

See Connecticut for full listing.

LUCENT VENTURE PARTNERS, INC.

3180 Porter Drive
Palo Alto, CA 94304-1226
Phone: 650-565-7400
Fax: 650-565-7401
Website: www.lucentventurepartners.com

Other Offices

600 Mountain Avenue
Room 6A-405
Murray Hill, NJ 07974
Phone: 908-582-8538
Fax: 908-582-6747

950 Winter Street
Suite 2600
Waltham, MA 02453
Phone: 781-926-2222
Fax: 781-890-6901

Management and Staff
Arie Litman, General Partner
Ashton Peery, General Partner
Hassan Parsa, General Partner
John Hanley, Managing Partner
Maureen Lawrence, General Partner
Neil Vasant, General Partner
Samir Balsara, Partner

Type of Firm
Non-Financial Corp. Affiliate or Subsidiary

Industry Association Membership
National Venture Capital Association (NVCA)

Project Preferences

Role in Financing:
Will function either as deal originator or investor in deals created by others

Type of Financing Preferred:
Early Stage
First Stage Financing
Second Stage Financing
Seed
Startup

Industry Preferences

(% based on actual investment)

Communications and Media	29.0%
Semiconductors/Other Elect.	26.4%
Internet Specific	23.0%
Computer Software and Services	17.4%
Computer Hardware	4.2%

Additional Information
Year Founded: 1998
Capital Under Management: $250,000,000
Current Activity Level : Actively seeking new investments
Method of Compensation: Return on investment is of primary concern, do not charge fees

---

M&A WEST INCORPORATED

583 San Mateo Avenue
San Bruno, CA 94066
Phone: 650-588-2678
Fax: 650-827-9508

Management and Staff
Sal Censoprano, Chief Financial Officer
Scott Kelly, Chief Executive Officer

Type of Firm
Investment/Merchant Bank Subsid/Affil

Additional Information
Capital Under Management: $500,000
Current Activity Level : Actively seeking new investments

MACROMEDIA VENTURES

600 Townsend Street
San Francisco, CA 94103
Phone: 415-252-2252
Website: www.macromedia.com/macromedia/ventures

Management and Staff
Norm Meyrowitz, President

Type of Firm
Non-Financial Corp. Affiliate or Subsidiary

Project Preferences

Type of Financing Preferred:
Early Stage
Seed
Startup

Geographical Preferences

International
All International

Industry Preferences

Internet Specific
Internet

Additional Information
Year Founded: 2000
Current Activity Level : Actively seeking new investments

MAGIC VENTURE CAPITAL, LLC

1010 El Camino Real
Suite 300
Menlo Park, CA 94025
Phone: 650-325-4149

Management and Staff
Erin McGurk, Managing Director
Ronald Dieck, Managing Director

Whom to Contact
Patrick Lynn

Type of Firm
Private Firm Investing Own Capital

Project Preferences

Role in Financing:
Prefer role as deal originator but will also invest in deals created by others

Type of Financing Preferred:
First Stage Financing
Seed
Start-up Financing

Size of Investments Considered
Min Size of Investment Considered (000s): $300
Max Size of Investment Considered (000s): $1,000

Geographical Preferences

United States
West Coast

Industry Preferences

Medical/Health
Medical Diagnostics
Diagnostic Services
Diagnostic Test Products
Drug/Equipmt Delivery
Other Therapeutic
Disposable Med. Products

Additional Information
Name of Most Recent Fund: Magic Venture Capital
Most Recent Fund Was Raised: 09/01/1997
Year Founded: 1996
Capital Under Management: $5,000,000
Current Activity Level : Actively seeking new investments
Method of Compensation: Return on investment is of primary concern, do not charge fees

MANAGEMENT RESOURCE PARTNERS

181 Second Avenue
Suite 542
San Mateo, CA 94401
Phone: 650-401-5850
Fax: 650-401-6750

Management and Staff
John Roberts

Whom to Contact
John Roberts

Type of Firm
Investment/Merchant Bank Subsid/Affil

Project Preferences

Role in Financing:
Prefer role as deal originator

Type of Financing Preferred:
Industry Rollups
Leveraged Buyout
Special Situation

Size of Investments Considered
Min Size of Investment Considered (000s): $1,000
Max Size of Investment Considered: No Limit

Geographical Preferences

United States
West Coast

Industry Preferences

Semiconductors/Other Elect.
Electronics
Laser Related
Fiber Optics
Analytic/Scientific

Medical/Health
Medical Products

Consumer Related
Entertainment and Leisure
Franchises(NEC)
Food/Beverage
Consumer Products
Consumer Services

Industrial/Energy
Industrial Products
Factory Automation
Machinery

Additional Information
Year Founded: 1981
Current Activity Level : Actively seeking new investments
Method of Compensation: Return on invest. most important, but chg. closing fees, service fees, etc.

MARWIT CAPITAL LLC

180 Newport Center Drive
Suite 200
Newport Beach, CA 92660
Phone: 949-640-6234
Fax: 949-720-8077
Website: www.marwit.com

Other Offices

180 Newport Center Drive
Suite 200
Newport Beach, CA 92660
Phone: 714-640-6234

Management and Staff
Chris Britt, President
Jeffrey Schaffer, Vice President
Matthew Witte, Chairman & CEO
Thomas Windsor, Vice President

Type of Firm
Private Firm Investing Own Capital

Industry Association Membership
Natl assoc of Small Bus. Inv. Co (NASBIC)

Project Preferences

Role in Financing:
Prefer role as deal originator but will also invest in deals created by others

Type of Financing Preferred:
Acquisition
Control-block Purchases
Leveraged Buyout
Mezzanine

Size of Investments Considered
Min Size of Investment Considered (000s): $250
Max Size of Investment Considered: No Limit

Geographical Preferences

United States
All U.S.

Industry Preferences

Computer Software
Software

Transportation
Transportation

Business Serv.
Distribution

Manufact.
Manufacturing

Additional Information
Year Founded: 1962
Capital Under Management: $42,000,000
Current Activity Level : Actively seeking new investments
Method of Compensation: Return on invest. most important, but chg. closing fees, service fees, etc.

MATON VENTURE

16615 Lark Avenue
Suite 108
Los Gatos, CA 95032
Phone: 408-358-8567
Fax: 408-358-8275
Website: www.maton.com

Management and Staff
Jaff Lin, Partner
Jesse Chen, Partner

Type of Firm
Private Firm Investing Own Capital

Project Preferences

Role in Financing:
Prefer role as deal originator but will also invest in deals created by others

Type of Financing Preferred:
Early Stage
First Stage Financing
Second Stage Financing
Seed

Size of Investments Considered
Min Size of Investment Considered (000s): $200
Max Size of Investment Considered (000s): $2,000

Industry Preferences

Computer Software
Software

Internet Specific
Internet
Ecommerce

Semiconductors/Other Elect.
Semiconductor

Additional Information
Name of Most Recent Fund: Maton Fund I, L.P.
Most Recent Fund Was Raised: 12/31/1997
Year Founded: 1997
Capital Under Management: $23,000,000
Current Activity Level : Actively seeking new investments

MATRIX GROUP

303 Brookside #'s 102/131
P.O. Box 240
Redlands, CA 92373
Phone: 909-793-7153
Fax: 909-793-1715
Website: www.gazellefarm.com

Management and Staff
Thomas Schott, Principal

Whom to Contact
Thomas Schott

Type of Firm
Investment Management/Finance Consulting

Project Preferences

Role in Financing:
Will function either as deal originator or investor in deals created by others

Type of Financing Preferred:
Acquisition
Expansion
Management Buyouts
Mezzanine

Size of Investments Considered
Min Size of Investment Considered (000s): $1,000
Max Size of Investment Considered (000s): $5,000

Geographical Preferences

United States
West Coast

Industry Preferences

Communications and Media
Data Communications

Semiconductors/Other Elect.
Electronic Components
Controllers and Sensors
Circuit Boards
Analytic/Scientific

Medical/Health
Medical Diagnostics
Diagnostic Test Products
Drug/Equipmt Delivery
Medical Products
Disposable Med. Products

Industrial/Energy
Industrial Products
Machinery

Transportation
Aerospace

Manufact.
Manufacturing

Agr/Forestr/Fish
Agriculture related

Additional Information
Year Founded: 1963
Capital Under Management: $10,000,000
Current Activity Level : Actively seeking new investments
Method of Compensation: Return on invest. most important, but chg. closing fees, service fees, etc.

MATRIX PARTNERS

2500 Sand Hill Road
Suite 113
Menlo Park, CA 94025
Phone: 650-854-3131
Fax: 650-854-3296
Website: www.matrixpartners.com

See Massachusetts for full listing.

MAYFIELD FUND

2800 Sand Hill Road
Menlo Park, CA 94025
Phone: 650-854-5560
Fax: 650-854-5712
Website: www.mayfield.com

Other Offices

4233 Hidden Canyon Cove
Austin, TX 78746
Phone: 512-328-0808

Management and Staff
Allen Morgan, General Partner
Dado Banatao, Venture Partner
Dana Settle, Venture Partner
David Ladd, General Partner
George Pavlov, Chief Financial Officer
Gib Myers, Partner
Grant Heidrich, General Partner
James Beck, Chief Financial Officer
Janice Roberts, General Partner
John Stockton, Venture Partner
Kevin Fong, Managing Partner
Michael Levinthal, General Partner
Richard Newton, Venture Partner
Robin Vasan, General Partner
Russell Hirsch, General Partner
Todd Brooks, General Partner
Wende Hutton, Venture Partner
Wendell Van Auken, Partner
William Unger, Partner
Yogen Dalal, Managing Partner

Type of Firm
Private Firm Investing Own Capital

Industry Association Membership
National Venture Capital Association (NVCA)
Western Association of Venture Capitalists (WAVC)

Project Preferences

Role in Financing:
Prefer role as deal originator but will also invest in deals created by others

Type of Financing Preferred:
First Stage Financing
Recapitalizations
Second Stage Financing
Seed
Start-up Financing

Size of Investments Considered
Min Size of Investment Considered (000s): $250
Max Size of Investment Considered: No Limit

Geographical Preferences

United States
Northwest
Rocky Mountain
West Coast

Industry Preferences

(% based on actual investment)

Computer Software and Services	46.2%
Internet Specific	18.5%
Communications and Media	9.9%
Semiconductors/Other Elect.	7.3%
Computer Hardware	6.0%
Medical/Health	4.7%
Biotechnology	4.4%
Consumer Related	1.2%
Other Products	1.1%
Industrial/Energy	0.7%

Additional Information
Name of Most Recent Fund: Mayfield XI
Most Recent Fund Was Raised: 08/01/1999
Year Founded: 1969
Capital Under Management: $700,000,000
Current Activity Level : Actively seeking new investments
Method of Compensation: Return on investment is of primary concern, do not charge fees

---

MBW MANAGEMENT, INC.

350 Second Street
Suite Seven
Los Altos, CA 94022
Phone: 415-941-2392
Fax: 415-941-2865

See New Jersey for full listing.

MCCOWN DE LEEUW & CO.

3000 Sand Hill Road
Building Three, Suite 290
Menlo Park, CA 94025-7111
Phone: 650-854-6000
Fax: 650-854-0853
Website: www.mdcpartners.com

Other Offices

Park Avenue Tower
65 E. 55th Street
New York, NY 10022
Phone: 212-355-5500
Fax: 212-355-6283

Management and Staff
Christopher Crosby, Principal
Elizabeth Crain, Principal
Judy Bornstein, Chief Financial Officer
Phil Collins, Managing Director
Richard Ransom, Chief Financial Officer
Tyler Zachem, Managing Director

Type of Firm
Private Firm Investing Own Capital

Industry Association Membership
Western Association of Venture Capitalists (WAVC)

Project Preferences

Role in Financing:
Prefer role as deal originator

Type of Financing Preferred:
Leveraged Buyout
Special Situation

Size of Investments Considered
Min Size of Investment Considered (000s): $40,000
Max Size of Investment Considered: No Limit

Geographical Preferences

United States
All U.S.

Industry Preferences

(% based on actual investment)

Consumer Related	61.4%
Computer Hardware	18.7%
Other Products	11.7%
Computer Software and Services	4.9%
Internet Specific	2.0%
Semiconductors/Other Elect.	0.9%
Communications and Media	0.3%
Industrial/Energy	0.1%

Additional Information
Name of Most Recent Fund: McCown De Leeuw & Co. IV, L.P
Most Recent Fund Was Raised: 07/07/1997
Year Founded: 1983
Capital Under Management: $800,000,000
Current Activity Level : Actively seeking new investments
Method of Compensation: Return on invest. most important, but chg. closing fees, service fees, etc.

MEDIA VENTURE PARTNERS

111 San Pablo Avenue
San Francisco, CA 94127
Phone: 415-661-3818
Fax: 415-661-2542

Type of Firm
Private Firm Investing Own Capital

Project Preferences

Role in Financing:
Prefer role as deal originator but will also invest in deals created by others

Type of Financing Preferred:
Control-block Purchases
First Stage Financing
Leveraged Buyout
Second Stage Financing
Seed
Special Situation
Start-up Financing

Size of Investments Considered
Min Size of Investment Considered (000s): $500
Max Size of Investment Considered (000s): $1,000

Geographical Preferences

United States
All U.S.

Canada
All Canada

Industry Preferences

Communications and Media
CATV & Pay TV Systems
Radio & TV Broadcasting

Computer Hardware
Mini and Personal/Desktop

Computer Software
Computer Services
Applications Software

Consumer Related
Consumer Products
Education Related

Manufact.
Publishing

Additional Information
Year Founded: 1994
Capital Under Management: $50,000,000
Current Activity Level : Actively seeking new investments
Method of Compensation: Return on investment is of primary concern, do not charge fees

MEDICUS VENTURE PARTNERS

12930 Saratoga Avenue
Suite D8
Saratoga, CA 95070
Phone: 408-447-8600
Fax: 408-447-8599
Website: www.medicusvc.com

Other Offices

800 Airport Boulevard
Suite 508
Burlingame, CA 94010
Phone: 650-375-0200
Fax: 650-375-0230

Management and Staff
Frederick Dotzler, General Partner
John Reher, General Partner

Whom to Contact
Fred Dotzler

Type of Firm
Private Firm Investing Own Capital

Industry Association Membership
Western Association of Venture Capitalists (WAVC)

Project Preferences

Role in Financing:
Prefer role as deal originator but will also invest in deals created by others

Type of Financing Preferred:
Early Stage

Geographical Preferences

United States
Northwest
Rocky Mountain
Southwest
West Coast

Industry Preferences

(% based on actual investment)

Medical/Health	45.7%
Biotechnology	31.6%
Internet Specific	13.1%
Computer Software and Services	5.6%
Computer Hardware	4.0%

Additional Information
Name of Most Recent Fund: Medicus Venture Partners 1998
Most Recent Fund Was Raised: 11/01/1998
Year Founded: 1989
Current Activity Level : Actively seeking new investments
Method of Compensation: Return on investment is of primary concern, do not charge fees

MEDVENTURE ASSOCIATES

Four Orinda Way
Building D, Suite 150
Orinda, CA 94563
Phone: 925-253-0155
Fax: 925-253-0156
Website: www.medven.com

Management and Staff
Annette Campbell-White, General Partner
Gary Stroy, General Partner
George Choi, General Partner

Type of Firm
Private Firm Investing Own Capital

Industry Association Membership
Western Association of Venture Capitalists (WAVC)

Project Preferences

Role in Financing:
Prefer role as deal originator but will also invest in deals created by others

Type of Financing Preferred:
Early Stage
First Stage Financing
Seed
Start-up Financing

Size of Investments Considered
Min Size of Investment Considered (000s): $300
Max Size of Investment Considered (000s): $500

Geographical Preferences

United States
West Coast

Industry Preferences

(% based on actual investment)

Medical/Health	55.5%
Internet Specific	23.8%
Biotechnology	19.2%
Communications and Media	0.7%
Computer Software and Services	0.7%

Additional Information
Name of Most Recent Fund: Medventure Associates III L.P.
Most Recent Fund Was Raised: 06/01/1998
Year Founded: 1986
Capital Under Management: $107,800,000
Current Activity Level : Reducing investment activity
Method of Compensation: Return on investment is of primary concern, do not charge fees

MELLON VENTURES (AKA: MELLON BANK)

400 South Hope Street
5th Floor
Los Angeles, CA 90071-2806
Phone: 213-553-9685
Fax: 213-553-9690
Website: www.mellonventures.com

See Pennsylvania for full listing.

MENLO VENTURES

3000 Sand Hill Road
Building Four, Suite 100
Menlo Park, CA 94025
Phone: 650-854-8540
Fax: 650-854-7059
Website: www.menloventures.com

Management and Staff
Catherine Shaw, Chief Financial Officer
Doug Carlisle, Managing Director
H. DuBose Montgomery, Managing Director
Hal Calhoun, Managing Director
John Jarve, Managing Director
Mark Siegel, Managing Director
Michael Laufer, Managing Director
Sonja Hoel, Managing Director
Thomas Bredt, Managing Director

Type of Firm
Private Firm Investing Own Capital

Industry Association Membership
National Venture Capital Association (NVCA)
Western Association of Venture Capitalists (WAVC)

Project Preferences

Role in Financing:
Will function either as deal originator or investor in deals created by others

Type of Financing Preferred:
Early Stage
Expansion
First Stage Financing
Later Stage
Research and Development
Second Stage Financing
Seed
Startup

Size of Investments Considered
Min Size of Investment Considered (000s): $5,000
Max Size of Investment Considered (000s): $30,000

Geographical Preferences

United States
All U.S.

Industry Preferences

(% based on actual investment)

Communications and Media	26.4%
Internet Specific	26.2%
Computer Software and Services	20.7%
Medical/Health	9.3%
Semiconductors/Other Elect.	6.2%
Computer Hardware	5.0%
Biotechnology	2.4%
Consumer Related	1.7%
Other Products	1.6%
Industrial/Energy	0.3%

Additional Information
Name of Most Recent Fund: Menlo Ventures VIII, L.P.
Most Recent Fund Was Raised: 01/01/1999
Year Founded: 1976
Capital Under Management: $2,820,600,000
Current Activity Level : Actively seeking new investments
Method of Compensation: Return on investment is of primary concern, do not charge fees

MERITECH CAPITAL PARTNERS

285 Hamilton Ave
Suite 200
Palo Alto, CA 94301
Phone: 650-475-2200
Fax: 650-475-2222
Website: www.meritechcapital.com

Management and Staff
Steve Simonian, Chief Financial Officer

Type of Firm
Private Firm Investing Own Capital

Industry Preferences
(% based on actual investment)

Internet Specific	38.0%
Communications and Media	34.3%
Computer Software and Services	13.9%
Semiconductors/Other Elect.	13.2%
Consumer Related	0.6%

Additional Information
Name of Most Recent Fund: Meritech Capital Partners, L.P.
Most Recent Fund Was Raised: 06/21/1999
Year Founded: 1999
Capital Under Management: $1,702,000,000
Current Activity Level : Actively seeking new investments

MERRILL, PICKARD, ANDERSON & EYRE

2480 Sand Hill Road
Suite 200
Menlo Park, CA 94025
Phone: 650-854-8600
Fax: 650-854-0345

Other Offices

2480 Sand Hill Road
Suite 200
Menlo Park, CA 94025
Phone: 415-854-8600

Type of Firm
Private Firm Investing Own Capital

Project Preferences
Role in Financing:
Prefer role as deal originator but will also invest in deals created by others

Type of Financing Preferred:
First Stage Financing
Second Stage Financing
Seed
Start-up Financing

Size of Investments Considered
Min Size of Investment Considered (000s): $1,000
Max Size of Investment Considered: No Limit

Geographical Preferences
International
No Preference

Industry Preferences
(% based on actual investment)

Computer Software and Services	27.4%
Computer Hardware	22.9%
Communications and Media	22.6%
Semiconductors/Other Elect.	14.9%
Internet Specific	4.8%
Medical/Health	2.5%
Consumer Related	1.7%
Industrial/Energy	1.7%
Biotechnology	1.3%
Other Products	0.1%

Additional Information
Year Founded: 1980
Capital Under Management: $200,000,000
Current Activity Level : Actively seeking new investments
Method of Compensation: Return on investment is of primary concern, do not charge fees

MEVC.COM

991 Folsom Street
Suite 301
San Francisco, CA 94107
Phone: 415-977-6150
Fax: 415-977-6160
Website: www.mevc.com

Management and Staff
Andrew Singer, Chief Financial Officer
John Grillos, Managing Partner
Nino Marakovic, Principal
Paul Wozniak, Chief Operating Officer

Type of Firm
Affiliate/Subsidary of Oth. Financial. Instit.

Industry Association Membership
National Venture Capital Association (NVCA)

Project Preferences
Type of Financing Preferred:
Early Stage

Geographical Preferences
United States
All U.S.

Industry Preferences
(% based on actual investment)

Internet Specific	77.5%
Computer Software and Services	17.0%
Communications and Media	5.2%
Other Products	0.2%

Additional Information
Year Founded: 1999
Capital Under Management: $330,000,000
Current Activity Level : Actively seeking new investments

MICROTECHNOLOGY INVESTMENTS, LTD.

46 Red Birch Court
Danville, CA 94506
Phone: 925-866-0111

Other Offices

48 Red Birch Road
Danville, CA 94506
Phone: 612-851-1500

7900 International Drive
Minneapolis, MN 55420
Phone: 612-851-1500

Type of Firm
Private Firm Investing Own Capital

Project Preferences
Role in Financing:
Prefer role as deal originator but will also invest in deals created by others

Type of Financing Preferred:
First Stage Financing
Leveraged Buyout

Size of Investments Considered
Min Size of Investment Considered (000s): $300
Max Size of Investment Considered (000s): $500

Geographical Preferences
United States
Northwest
West Coast

Industry Preferences
Computer Hardware
Mini and Personal/Desktop

Computer Software
Systems Software

Industrial/Energy
Robotics

Manufact.
Publishing

Additional Information
Year Founded: 1982
Current Activity Level : Actively seeking new investments
Method of Compensation: Return on investment is of primary concern, do not charge fees

MISSION VENTURES

11512 El Camino Real
Suite 215
San Diego, CA 92120
Phone: 619-259-0100
Fax: 619-259-0112
Website: www.missionventures.com

Management and Staff
David Ryan, Managing Partner
David Holder, Venture Partner
Jeffrey Starr, General Partner
Leo Spiegel, General Partner
Robert Kibble, Managing Partner
Ted Alexander, General Partner

Type of Firm
Private Firm Investing Own Capital

Project Preferences

Role in Financing:
Prefer role as deal originator but will also invest in deals created by others

Type of Financing Preferred:
First Stage Financing
Later Stage
Seed

Size of Investments Considered
Min Size of Investment Considered (000s): $2,000
Max Size of Investment Considered (000s): $6,000

Geographical Preferences

United States
Southern California

Industry Preferences

(% based on actual investment)

Internet Specific	67.2%
Computer Software and Services	13.6%
Consumer Related	7.9%
Medical/Health	4.8%
Other Products	3.4%
Computer Hardware	3.1%

Additional Information
Name of Most Recent Fund: Mission Ventures II
Most Recent Fund Was Raised: 10/15/0097
Year Founded: 1997
Capital Under Management: $200,000,000
Current Activity Level : Actively seeking new investments
Method of Compensation: Return on investment is of primary concern, do not charge fees

MK GLOBAL VENTURES

2471 East Bayshore Road
Suite 520
Palo Alto, CA 94303
Phone: 650-424-0151
Fax: 650-494-2753

Other Offices

2471 East Bayshore Road
Suite 520
Palo Alto, CA 94303
Phone: 415-424-0151

Type of Firm
Private Firm Investing Own Capital

Industry Association Membership
Western Association of Venture Capitalists (WAVC)

Project Preferences

Role in Financing:
Prefer role as deal originator but will also invest in deals created by others

Type of Financing Preferred:
First Stage Financing
Second Stage Financing
Seed
Start-up Financing

Size of Investments Considered
Min Size of Investment Considered (000s): $1,000
Max Size of Investment Considered: No Limit

Geographical Preferences

International
No Preference

Additional Information
Name of Most Recent Fund: MK Global Ventures
Most Recent Fund Was Raised: 01/01/1987
Year Founded: 1987
Capital Under Management: $80,000,000
Current Activity Level : Actively seeking new investments
Method of Compensation: Return on investment is of primary concern, do not charge fees

MOHR, DAVIDOW VENTURES

2775 Sand Hill Road
Suite 240
Menlo Park, CA 94025
Phone: 650-854-7236
Fax: 650-854-7365
Website: www.mdv.com

Other Offices

1660 International Drive
Suite 400
McLean, VA 22102
Phone: 703-287-4222
Fax: 703-287-4225

505 Fifth Avenue South
Suite 610
Seattle, WA 98104
Phone: 206-344-3800
Fax: 206-344-3388

Management and Staff
Debby Meredith, Venture Partner
Donna Novitsky, Venture Partner
Erik Straser, General Partner
Geoffrey Moore, Venture Partner
George Zachary, General Partner
Jonathan Feiber, Managing Partner
Michael Sheridan, General Partner
Michael Solomon, Venture Partner
Nancy Schoendorf, Managing Partner
Peter Roshko, General Partner
Randy Strahan, Venture Partner
Rob Chaplinsky, General Partner
William Davidow, Partner
William Ericson, General Partner
William Gossman, Venture Partner

Type of Firm
Private Firm Investing Own Capital

Industry Association Membership
Mid-Atlantic Venture Association
National Venture Capital Association (NVCA)
Western Association of Venture Capitalists (WAVC)

Project Preferences

Role in Financing:
Prefer role as deal originator but will also invest in deals created by others

Type of Financing Preferred:
Early Stage

Geographical Preferences

United States
Northwest
Rocky Mountain
Southwest
West Coast

Industry Preferences

(% based on actual investment)

Internet Specific	36.8%
Computer Software and Services	19.1%
Computer Hardware	11.1%
Semiconductors/Other Elect.	10.9%
Communications and Media	8.5%
Other Products	6.0%
Medical/Health	5.8%
Consumer Related	0.7%
Biotechnology	0.5%
Industrial/Energy	0.4%

Additional Information
Name of Most Recent Fund: Mohr, Davidow Ventures V
Most Recent Fund Was Raised: 12/01/1997
Year Founded: 1983
Capital Under Management: $1,500,000,000
Current Activity Level : Actively seeking new investments
Method of Compensation: Return on investment is of primary concern, do not charge fees

---

MONTGOMERY ASSOCIATES, INC.

425 California Street
Suite 200 P.O. Box 2230
San Francisco, CA 94126
Phone: 415-421-4200
Fax: 415-981-3601

Other Offices

550 Montgomery Street
Suite 750
San Francisco, CA 94126
Phone: 415-421-4200

Type of Firm
Private Firm Investing Own Capital

Project Preferences

Role in Financing:
Prefer role as deal originator but will also invest in deals created by others

Type of Financing Preferred:
First Stage Financing
Leveraged Buyout
Research and Development
Second Stage Financing
Seed
Special Situation
Start-up Financing

Size of Investments Considered
Min Size of Investment Considered (000s): $500
Max Size of Investment Considered: No Limit

Geographical Preferences

United States
West Coast

Industry Preferences

Communications and Media
Commercial Communications
Telecommunications
Satellite Microwave Comm.

Semiconductors/Other Elect.
Electronic Components

Medical/Health
Medical/Health

Consumer Related
Entertainment and Leisure
Consumer Products
Consumer Services

Industrial/Energy
Energy
Industrial Products

Transportation
Transportation

Financial Services
Financial Services

Additional Information
Name of Most Recent Fund: Montgomery Associates
Most Recent Fund Was Raised: 12/01/1982
Year Founded: 1978
Capital Under Management: $8,000,000
Current Activity Level : Actively seeking new investments
Method of Compensation: Return on investment is of primary concern, do not charge fees

---

MONTGOMERY MEDICAL VENTURES, L.P.

3645 Grand Ave.
Suite 302
Oakland, CA 94610
Phone: 570-267-9399
Fax: 570-267-9393

Other Offices

600 Montgomery Street
San Francisco, CA 94111
Phone: 415-627-2541

Management and Staff
Steven Weiss

Whom to Contact
Steven Weiss

Type of Firm
Investment/Merchant Bank Subsid/Affil

Project Preferences

Role in Financing:
Prefer role as deal originator but will also invest in deals created by others

Type of Financing Preferred:
First Stage Financing
Seed
Start-up Financing

Size of Investments Considered
Min Size of Investment Considered (000s): $500
Max Size of Investment Considered: No Limit

Geographical Preferences

International
No Preference

Industry Preferences

Biotechnology
Industrial Biotechnology
Biosensors
Biotech Related Research

Medical/Health
Medical/Health
Medical Diagnostics
Medical Therapeutics
Medical Products

Additional Information

Name of Most Recent Fund: Montwest Capital Partners
Most Recent Fund Was Raised: 01/01/1990
Year Founded: 1984
Capital Under Management: $136,000,000
Current Activity Level : Inactive / Unknown
Method of Compensation: Return on investment is of primary concern, do not charge fees

MONTREUX EQUITY PARTNERS

2700 Sand Hill Road
Menlo Park, CA 94025
Phone: 650-234-1200
Fax: 650-234-1250
Website: www.montreuxequity.com

Management and Staff

Daniel Turner, General Partner
Taylor Washbun, Principal
Thomas Fremd, Chief Financial Officer
Tom Soloway, Principal

Whom to Contact

Daniel K. Turner III

Type of Firm

Private Firm Investing Own Capital

Industry Association Membership

National Venture Capital Association (NVCA)
Natl assoc of Small Bus. Inv. Co (NASBIC)
Western Association of Venture Capitalists (WAVC)

Project Preferences

Role in Financing:
Prefer role as deal originator but will also invest in deals created by others

Type of Financing Preferred:
Balanced
Early Stage
First Stage Financing
Second Stage Financing
Seed

Size of Investments Considered

Min Size of Investment Considered (000s): $1,000
Max Size of Investment Considered (000s): $5,000

Geographical Preferences

United States
West Coast

Industry Preferences

(% based on actual investment)

Internet Specific	50.0%
Computer Software and Services	31.1%
Biotechnology	10.7%
Medical/Health	8.1%

Additional Information

Year Founded: 1993
Capital Under Management: $93,000,000
Current Activity Level : Actively seeking new investments
Method of Compensation: Return on invest. most important, but chg. closing fees, service fees, etc.

MORGAN STANLEY VENTURE PARTNERS (AKA: MSDW)

3000 Sand Hill Road
Building 4, Suite 250
Menlo Park, CA 94025
Phone: 650-233-2600
Fax: 650-233-2626
Website: http://www.msvp.com

See New York for full listing.

MORGENTHALER VENTURES

2730 Sand Hill Road
Suite 280
Menlo Park, CA 94025
Phone: 650-233-7600
Fax: 650-233-7606
Website: www.morgenthaler.com

See Ohio for full listing.

MPM CAPITAL (FKA - MPM ASSET MANAGEMENT LLC)

601 Gateway Boulevard
Suite 360
South San Francisco, CA 94080
Phone: 650-829-5820
Fax: 650-829-5828
Website: www.mpmcapital.com

See Massachusetts for full listing.

MUSTANG VENTURES (FKA SIEMENS MUSTANG VENTURES)

4900 Old Ironsides Drive
P.O. Box 58075
Santa Clara, CA 95052
Phone: 408-492-6953
Fax: 408-492-3614
Website: www.mustangventures.com

Other Offices

Hofmannstrasse 51
Munich, Germany 81359
Phone: 49-89-722-61506
Fax: 49-89-722-61831

Management and Staff

Louis Rajczi, Partner
Luis Llovera, Partner
Richard Mattern, Partner
Steffen Schuster, Chief Financial Officer

Type of Firm

Non-Financial Corp. Affiliate or Subsidiary

Project Preferences

Role in Financing:
Will function either as deal originator or investor in deals created by others

Type of Financing Preferred:
Expansion
First Stage Financing
Later Stage
Mezzanine
Second Stage Financing
Startup

Size of Investments Considered
Min Size of Investment Considered (000s): $500
Max Size of Investment Considered (000s): $5,000

Industry Preferences

(% based on actual investment)

Communications and Media	70.1%
Computer Software and Services	15.3%
Internet Specific	9.9%
Semiconductors/Other Elect.	4.7%

Additional Information
Year Founded: 1998
Capital Under Management: $300,000,000
Current Activity Level : Actively seeking new investments
Method of Compensation: Return on investment is of primary concern, do not charge fees

NATIONAL CORPORATE FINANCE, INC.

2082 Southeast Bristol
Suite 203
Newport Beach, CA 92660
Phone: 949-756-2006

Type of Firm
Investment/Merchant Bank Investing Own or Client Funds

Project Preferences

Role in Financing:
Prefer role as deal originator

Type of Financing Preferred:
Control-block Purchases
Leveraged Buyout
Special Situation

Size of Investments Considered
Min Size of Investment Considered (000s): $1,000
Max Size of Investment Considered: No Limit

Geographical Preferences

United States
Northwest
Southwest
West Coast

Industry Preferences

Communications and Media
Commercial Communications
Data Communications
Other Communication Prod.

Computer Hardware
Computers

Semiconductors/Other Elect.
Electronic Components
Controllers and Sensors
Sensors
Circuit Boards
Component Testing Equipmt
Laser Related
Fiber Optics
Analytic/Scientific

Medical/Health
Diagnostic Services
Diagnostic Test Products
Medical Products
Disposable Med. Products
Hospitals/Clinics/Primary
Hospital/Other Instit.
Pharmaceuticals

Consumer Related
Entertainment and Leisure
Computer Stores
Franchises(NEC)
Food/Beverage
Consumer Products
Consumer Services
Other Restaurants
Education Related

Industrial/Energy
Oil and Gas Exploration
Alternative Energy
Energy Conservation Relat
Industrial Products
Materials
Factory Automation
Machinery
Environmental Related

Financial Services
Financial Services

Business Serv.
Consulting Services

Additional Information
Year Founded: 1983
Current Activity Level : Actively seeking new investments
Method of Compensation: Function primarily in service area, receive contingent fee in cash or equity

NATIONAL INVESTMENT MANAGEMENT, INC.

P.O. Box 3095
Palos Verdes Estates, CA 90274
Phone: 310-784-7600

Management and Staff
Richard Robins, President

Type of Firm
Commercial Bank Affiliate or Subsidiary

Project Preferences

Role in Financing:
Prefer role as deal originator

Type of Financing Preferred:
Leveraged Buyout

Size of Investments Considered
Min Size of Investment Considered (000s): $1,000
Max Size of Investment Considered: No Limit

Geographical Preferences

United States
All U.S.

Industry Preferences

(% based on actual investment)

Internet Specific	76.5%
Computer Software and Services	7.8%
Computer Hardware	4.3%
Other Products	3.6%
Consumer Related	3.4%
Industrial/Energy	2.8%
Semiconductors/Other Elect.	1.1%
Communications and Media	0.5%

Additional Information

Name of Most Recent Fund: Spring Street Capital
Most Recent Fund Was Raised: 01/01/1991
Year Founded: 1977
Capital Under Management: $50,000,000
Current Activity Level : Actively seeking new investments
Method of Compensation: Return on investment is of primary concern, do not charge fees

NAZEM & CO.

3000 Sand Hill Road
Building Two, Suite 205
Menlo Park, CA 94025
Phone: 415-854-3010
Fax: 415-854-3015

See New York for full listing.

NEEDHAM & COMPANY, INC.

3000 Sand Hill Road
Building 2, Suite 190
Menlo Park, CA 94025
Phone: 650-854-9111
Fax: 650-854-9853
Website: www.needhamco.com

See New York for full listing.

NEOCARTA VENTURES

Two Embarcadero Center
Suite 460
San Francisco, CA 94111
Phone: 415-277-0230
Fax: 415-277-0240
Website: www.neocarta.com

See Massachusetts for full listing.

NETCATALYST

1119 Colorado Avenue
Suite 21
Santa Monica, CA 90401
Phone: 310-2600-2877
E-mail: admin@netcatalyst.net
Website: www.netcatalyst.com

Management and Staff

Chris Karkenny, Chief Executive Officer
Paul Shapiro, Chief Financial Officer
Riggs Eckelberry, Managing Director

Type of Firm

Private Firm Investing Own Capital

Project Preferences

Type of Financing Preferred:

Early Stage

Geographical Preferences

International

All International

Industry Preferences

Internet Specific

Internet

Additional Information

Year Founded: 1999
Current Activity Level : Actively seeking new investments

NETSCAPE COMMUNICATIONS

501 E. Middlefield Road
Mountain View, CA 94043
Phone: 650-254-1900
Fax: 650-528-4126

Type of Firm

Non-Financial Corp. Affiliate or Subsidiary

Additional Information

Year Founded: 1999
Current Activity Level : Actively seeking new investments

NETWORKS ASSOCIATES, INC.

3965 Freedom Cir
Santa Clara, CA 95054
Phone: 408-988-3832
Fax: 408-970-9727

Management and Staff

Dan McCammon, Chief Financial Officer
Terry Davis, Chief Financial Officer

Type of Firm

Non-Financial Corp. Affiliate or Subsidiary

Additional Information

Year Founded: 1989
Current Activity Level : Actively seeking new investments

NEW ENTERPRISE ASSOCIATES

2490 Sand Hill Road
Menlo Park, CA 94025
Phone: 650-854-9499
Fax: 650-854-9397
Website: www.nea.com

See Maryland for full listing.

NEW MILLENNIUM PARTNERS, LLC

2001 Union Street
Suite 690
San Francisco, CA 94123
Phone: 415-749-2820
Fax: 415-749-2823
Website: www.nmpartners.com

Type of Firm

Private Firm Investing Own Capital

Industry Association Membership

National Venture Capital Association (NVCA)

Industry Preferences

(% based on actual investment)

Internet Specific	80.7%
Computer Hardware	18.0%
Communications and Media	1.1%
Consumer Related	0.2%

Additional Information

Year Founded: 1998
Current Activity Level : Actively seeking new investments

NEW VISTA CAPITAL, LLC

540 Cowper Street
Suite 200
Palo Alto, CA 94301
Phone: 650-329-9333
Fax: 650-328-9434
Website: www.nvcap.com

Management and Staff
Frank Greene, Managing Partner
Roger Barry, Managing Partner

Type of Firm
SBIC Not elsewhere classified

Industry Association Membership
Western Association of Venture Capitalists (WAVC)

Project Preferences

Role in Financing:
Prefer role as deal originator but will also invest in deals created by others

Type of Financing Preferred:
First Stage Financing
Second Stage Financing
Seed
Start-up Financing

Geographical Preferences

United States
Northwest
Rocky Mountain
Southwest
West Coast

Industry Preferences

(% based on actual investment)

Internet Specific	40.5%
Computer Software and Services	36.9%
Semiconductors/Other Elect.	15.4%
Communications and Media	3.4%
Computer Hardware	3.4%
Consumer Related	0.3%

Additional Information
Name of Most Recent Fund: New Vista Capital, L.P.
Most Recent Fund Was Raised: 02/01/1998
Year Founded: 1997
Capital Under Management: $21,000,000
Current Activity Level : Actively seeking new investments
Method of Compensation: Return on investment is of primary concern, do not charge fees

NEWBRIDGE CAPITAL LIMITED

345 California Street
Suite 3300
San Francisco, CA 94104
Phone: 415-743-1500
Fax: 415-743-1507
Website: www.newbridgecapital.com

Other Offices

10/F Marunouchi Mtsui Building
2-2-2 Marunouchi
Chiyoda-ku, Japan 100-0005
Phone: 813-5220-2255
Fax: 813-5220-2256

50 Raffles Place
44-05 Singapore Land Tower
Singapore, Singapore 048623
Phone: 65-435-1866
Fax: 65-532-1866

One International Finance Centre
No. 1 Harbour View Street
Central, Hong Kong
Phone: 852-2530-2652
Fax: 852-2530-9948

Management and Staff
Ashish Shastry, Vice President
Au Ngai, Managing Director
Bien Kiat Tan, Managing Director
Daniel Carroll, Managing Partner
James Chang, Vice President
Paul Chen, Managing Director
Ricky Lau, Vice President
Weijan Shan, Managing Director

Type of Firm
Private Firm Investing Own Capital

Project Preferences

Role in Financing:
Prefer role as deal originator but will also invest in deals created by others

Type of Financing Preferred:
Acquisition
Balanced
Control-block Purchases
Expansion
Joint Ventures
Later Stage
Leveraged Buyout
Management Buyouts
Private Placement
Recapitalizations
Special Situation
Turnaround

Size of Investments Considered
Min Size of Investment Considered (000s): $30,000
Max Size of Investment Considered: No Limit

Geographical Preferences

International
China
Hong Kong
India
Indonesia
Japan
Korea, South
Malaysia
Philippines
Singapore
Taiwan
Thailand

Industry Preferences

Communications and Media
Communications and Media

Computer Software
Computer Services
Data Processing
Software
Systems Software
Applications Software

Internet Specific
Internet
Web Aggregration/Portals

Semiconductors/Other Elect.
Electronic Components
Semiconductor
Circuit Boards
Component Testing Equipmt
Laser Related
Fiber Optics

Biotechnology
Human Biotechnology
Agricultural/Animal Bio.

Consumer Related
Consumer
Entertainment and Leisure
Retail
Food/Beverage
Hotels and Resorts

Transportation
Transportation
Aerospace

Financial Services
Financial Services
Insurance

Business Serv.
Services
Distribution
Consulting Services
Media

Manufact.
Manufacturing

Additional Information
Year Founded: 1994
Capital Under Management: $947,000,000
Current Activity Level : Actively seeking new investments

NEWBURY VENTURES

535 Pacific Avenue
Second Floor
San Francisco, CA 94133
Phone: 415-296-7408
Fax: 415-296-7416
Website: www.newburyven.com

Other Offices

90 Ave Henri Martin
Paris, United Kingdom 75016
Phone: 33 145 04 96 96
Fax: 33 145 04 96 16

One First Street
Suite 12
Los Altos, CA 94022

Management and Staff
Bruce Bauer, General Partner
Colleen Salo, General Partner
Jay Morrison, Managing Partner
Jean-Noel Mereur, Venture Partner
Ossama Hassanein, General Partner
Thao Lane, Venture Partner

Whom to Contact
Colleen E. Young

Type of Firm
Mgt. Consulting Firm

Project Preferences

Role in Financing:
Prefer role as deal originator but will also invest in deals created by others

Type of Financing Preferred:
Early Stage
First Stage Financing
Leveraged Buyout
Mezzanine
Second Stage Financing
Seed
Special Situation
Start-up Financing

Size of Investments Considered
Min Size of Investment Considered (000s): $500
Max Size of Investment Considered (000s): $1,000

Geographical Preferences

United States
Northeast
Northwest
Southwest
All U.S.
West Coast

Canada
All Canada

International
Europe
France
Germany
United Kingdom

Industry Preferences

(% based on actual investment)

Internet Specific	24.6%
Medical/Health	21.4%
Computer Software and Services	20.5%
Semiconductors/Other Elect.	16.4%
Communications and Media	13.8%
Computer Hardware	3.2%

Additional Information
Name of Most Recent Fund: Newbury Ventures, L.P.
Most Recent Fund Was Raised: 01/01/1996
Year Founded: 1992
Capital Under Management: $105,000,000
Current Activity Level : Actively seeking new investments
Method of Compensation: Return on investment is of primary concern, do not charge fees

NEWTEK VENTURES

500 Washington Street
Suite 720
San Francisco, CA 94111
Phone: 415-986-5711
Fax: 415-986-4618
Website: www.newtekventure.com

Other Offices

3000 Sand Hill Road
Building Three, Suite 140
Menlo Park, CA 94025
Phone: 415-854-9744

Type of Firm
Private Firm Investing Own Capital

Industry Association Membership
Western Association of Venture Capitalists (WAVC)

Project Preferences

Role in Financing:
Prefer role as deal originator but will also invest in deals created by others

Type of Financing Preferred:
First Stage Financing
Second Stage Financing
Seed
Start-up Financing

Size of Investments Considered
Min Size of Investment Considered (000s): $1,000
Max Size of Investment Considered: No Limit

Geographical Preferences

United States
Rocky Mountain
Southwest
West Coast

Canada
Western Canada

Industry Preferences

(% based on actual investment)

Computer Software and Services	41.3%
Medical/Health	14.0%
Computer Hardware	13.0%
Industrial/Energy	10.4%
Semiconductors/Other Elect.	9.9%
Biotechnology	9.0%
Internet Specific	1.0%
Communications and Media	0.9%
Other Products	0.4%

Additional Information
Name of Most Recent Fund: Newtek Ventures II-B
Most Recent Fund Was Raised: 01/01/1997
Year Founded: 1983
Capital Under Management: $53,000,000
Current Activity Level : Actively seeking new investments
Method of Compensation: Return on investment is of primary concern, do not charge fees

NEXTGEN PARTNERS LLC

1705 East Valley Road
Santa Barbara, CA 93108
Phone: 805-969-8540
Fax: 805-969-8542
Website: www.nextgenpartners.com

Management and Staff
Alan Heeger, Venture Partner
Anthony Cheetham, Managing Director
Derek Statham, Venture Partner
Edward Kramer, Venture Partner
Jean Frechet, Venture Partner
John Newsam, Venture Partner
Peter Grubstein, Managing Director
Venky Narayanamurti, Venture Partner

Type of Firm
Private Firm Investing Own Capital

Project Preferences

Role in Financing:
Will function either as deal originator or investor in deals created by others

Type of Financing Preferred:
Early Stage
Expansion
First Stage Financing
Research and Development
Second Stage Financing
Seed
Startup

Size of Investments Considered
Min Size of Investment Considered (000s): $100
Max Size of Investment Considered (000s): $3,000

Geographical Preferences

United States
All U.S.

Canada
All Canada

International
Australia
Belgium
France
Germany
India
All International
Italy
Japan
Latin America
Luxembourg
Netherlands
Spain
United Kingdom

Industry Preferences

Communications and Media
Telecommunications
Wireless Communications
Data Communications
Satellite Microwave Comm.

Semiconductors/Other Elect.
Electronic Components
Semiconductor
Controllers and Sensors
Sensors
Laser Related

Biotechnology
Industrial Biotechnology
Biosensors

Industrial/Energy
Energy
Superconductivity
Robotics

Transportation
Aerospace

Other
Environment Responsible

Additional Information
Name of Most Recent Fund: Grubstein Holdings
Most Recent Fund Was Raised: 09/01/1990
Year Founded: 1987
Capital Under Management: $20,000,000
Current Activity Level : Actively seeking new investments
Method of Compensation: Return on investment is of primary concern, do not charge fees

NEXTREME VENTURES

4350 La Jolla Village Drive
Suite 450
San Diego, CA 92122
Phone: 858-623-1331
Fax: 858-623-1333
E-mail: maryann@nextremeventures.com
Website: www.nextremeventures.com

Other Offices

8400 Baltimore Avenue
Suite 301
College Park, MD 20740
Phone: 301-263-9547

Management and Staff
Taher Behbehani, Chief Executive Officer

Type of Firm
Private Firm Investing Own Capital

Project Preferences

Type of Financing Preferred:
Early Stage

Geographical Preferences

United States
All U.S.

Industry Preferences

Communications and Media
Telecommunications
Data Communications

Additional Information
Year Founded: 2000
Current Activity Level : Actively seeking new investments

NEXUS GROUP LLC

201 Spear Street
17th Floor
San Francisco, CA 94105
Phone: 415-836-7621

Management and Staff
David Leyrer, Founder
Robert Horning, Founder
William Weathersby, Founder

Type of Firm
Private Firm Investing Own Capital

Industry Preferences

(% based on actual investment)

Internet Specific	77.0%
Computer Software and Services	14.5%
Communications and Media	5.8%
Semiconductors/Other Elect.	2.7%

Additional Information

Name of Most Recent Fund: Nexus Capital Partners II, LP
Most Recent Fund Was Raised: 10/06/1999
Capital Under Management: $30,000,000
Current Activity Level : Actively seeking new investments

NIF VENTURES USA, INC.(NIPPON INVESTMENT & FINANCE CO., LTD)

5 Palo Alto Square
9th Floor
Palo Alto, CA 94306
Phone: 650-461-5000
Fax: 650-858-0892

Other Offices

DBS Blg.,Tower 2, Suite 21-11
Six Shenton Way
Singapore, Singapore 068809
Phone: 65-227-8121
Fax: 65-224-6153

Daiwa Securities Kabuto-cho Blg.
2nd Fl,1-9 Kayaba-cho
Nihonbashi,Chou-ku, Japan Tokoyo 103
Phone: 81-3-5695-8223
Fax: 81-3-5695-8289

Management and Staff

Jim Timmins, Managing Partner
Nancy Yee, Venture Partner
Shohei Sakazaki, Venture Partner
Yuzuru Miyamoto, Partner

Type of Firm

Private Firm Investing Own Capital

Industry Association Membership

National Venture Capital Association (NVCA)

Project Preferences

Role in Financing:

Prefer role as deal originator but will also invest in deals created by others

Type of Financing Preferred:

First Stage Financing
Mezzanine
Second Stage Financing
Start-up Financing

Geographical Preferences

United States

Northwest
Rocky Mountain
Southwest
West Coast

Industry Preferences

(% based on actual investment)

Internet Specific	27.3%
Computer Software and Services	25.2%
Semiconductors/Other Elect.	20.7%
Communications and Media	18.7%
Other Products	4.0%
Biotechnology	3.1%
Computer Hardware	0.6%
Medical/Health	0.3%
Industrial/Energy	0.2%

Additional Information

Name of Most Recent Fund: Nippon Investment and Finance (Daiwa Securities Group)
Most Recent Fund Was Raised: 10/01/1984
Year Founded: 1996
Capital Under Management: $50,000,000
Current Activity Level : Actively seeking new investments
Method of Compensation: Return on investment is of primary concern, do not charge fees

---

NOKIA VENTURE PARTNERS (AKA: NOKIA OY)

545 Middlefield Road
Suite 210
Menlo Park, CA 94025
Phone: 650-462-7250
Fax: 650-462-7252
Website: www.nokiaventures.com

Other Offices

2121 K Street, NW
Suite 650
Washington, DC 20037
Phone: 202-728-0049

Halahdenkatu 22
Helsinki, Finland 00210
Phone: 358-5116-2030

Marble Arch Tower, 8th Floor
55 Bryanston Street
London, United Kingdom W1H7AA
Phone: 44-207-535-2727
Fax: 44-207-724-7612

Management and Staff

Antti Kokkinen, Partner
David Jaques, Chief Financial Officer
John Gardner, Partner
John Malloy, Managing Partner
John Zeisler, General Partner
Jonathan Ebinger, Principal
Martti Malka, Partner
Thomas Kenney, Principal
W. Peter Buhl, Partner

Type of Firm

Non-Financial Corp. Affiliate or Subsidiary

Industry Association Membership

National Venture Capital Association (NVCA)
Western Association of Venture Capitalists (WAVC)

Project Preferences

Role in Financing:

Prefer role as deal originator but will also invest in deals created by others

Type of Financing Preferred:

First Stage Financing
Second Stage Financing
Seed
Startup

Size of Investments Considered

Min Size of Investment Considered (000s): $1,000
Max Size of Investment Considered (000s): $7,000

Geographical Preferences

United States

All U.S.
West Coast

Canada

All Canada

International

Australia
Bermuda
France
Germany
Italy
Spain
United Kingdom

Industry Preferences

(% based on actual investment)

Internet Specific	46.2%
Communications and Media	30.3%
Computer Software and Services	20.7%
Computer Hardware	2.8%

Additional Information

Name of Most Recent Fund: Nokia Ventures
Most Recent Fund Was Raised: 04/27/1998
Year Founded: 1998
Capital Under Management: $150,000,000
Current Activity Level : Actively seeking new investments
Method of Compensation: Return on investment is of primary concern, do not charge fees

NORTH CAROLINA ENTERPRISE FUND, L.P., THE

10600 N. Pantau Avenue
Cupertino, CA 95014
Phone: 408-777-8817
Fax: 408-777-8617
Website: www.ncef.com

See North Carolina for full listing.

NORWEST EQUITY PARTNERS

245 Lytton Avenue
Suite 250
Palo Alto, CA 94301
Phone: 650-321-8000
Fax: 650-321-8010
Website: ww.norwestvp.com

Other Offices

3600 IDS Center
80 South Eighth Street
Minneapolis, MN 55402
Phone: 612-215-1600
Fax: 612-215-1601

40 William Street
Suite 305
Wellesley, MA 02181-3902
Phone: 781-237-5870
Fax: 781-237-6270

Management and Staff

Blair Whitaker, Partner
Daniel Haggerty, President
Ernest Parizeau, Partner
George Still, Managing General Partner
James Lussier, Venture Partner
John Whaley, Partner
Kevin Hall, Venture Partner
Kurt Betcher, Chief Financial Officer
Matthew Howard, Principal
Promod Haque, Managing General Partner
Robert Abbott, Principal
Vab Goel, Venture Partner
Venkat Mohan, Venture Partner

Whom to Contact

Charles B. Lennin

Type of Firm

Affiliate/Subsidary of Oth. Financial. Instit.

Industry Association Membership

National Venture Capital Association (NVCA)

Project Preferences

Role in Financing:

Prefer role as deal originator but will also invest in deals created by others

Type of Financing Preferred:

Early Stage
Expansion
Later Stage
Seed

Size of Investments Considered

Min Size of Investment Considered (000s): $1,000
Max Size of Investment Considered (000s): $25,000

Geographical Preferences

United States

All U.S.

International

All International

Industry Preferences

(% based on actual investment)

Internet Specific	33.6%
Communications and Media	21.9%
Computer Software and Services	18.1%
Consumer Related	6.3%
Other Products	6.2%
Semiconductors/Other Elect.	6.1%
Industrial/Energy	2.9%
Computer Hardware	2.5%
Medical/Health	1.7%
Biotechnology	0.6%

Additional Information

Name of Most Recent Fund: Norwest Equity Partners VII, L.P.
Most Recent Fund Was Raised: 10/27/1999
Year Founded: 1961
Capital Under Management: $1,490,000,000
Current Activity Level : Actively seeking new investments
Method of Compensation: Return on investment is of primary concern, do not charge fees

NOVUS VENTURES

20111 Stevens Creek Boulevard
Suite 130
Cupertino, CA 95014
Phone: 408-252-3900
Fax: 408-252-1713
Website: www.novusventures.com

Management and Staff

Daniel Tompkins, General Partner
Greg Lahann, General Partner
Randy Hawks, General Partner
Shirley Cerrudo, General Partner

Whom to Contact

Dan Tompkins

Type of Firm

SBIC Not elsewhere classified

Industry Association Membership

Natl assoc of Small Bus. Inv. Co (NASBIC)

Project Preferences

Role in Financing:

Prefer role as deal originator but will also invest in deals created by others

Type of Financing Preferred:

Early Stage
Expansion
First Stage Financing
Management Buyouts
Start-up Financing

Size of Investments Considered

Min Size of Investment Considered (000s): $500
Max Size of Investment Considered (000s): $1,000

Geographical Preferences

United States

Southwest
West Coast

Industry Preferences

(% based on actual investment)

Computer Software and Services	45.7%
Internet Specific	26.8%
Semiconductors/Other Elect.	16.7%
Communications and Media	8.1%
Computer Hardware	1.6%
Other Products	1.0%

Additional Information

Name of Most Recent Fund: Novus Ventures, L.P.
Most Recent Fund Was Raised: 07/01/1994
Year Founded: 1994
Capital Under Management: $120,000,000
Current Activity Level : Actively seeking new investments
Method of Compensation: Return on investment is of primary concern, do not charge fees

NTH POWER TECHNOLOGIES, INC

100 Spear Street
Suite 1450
San Francisco, CA 94105
Phone: 415-974-1668
Fax: 415-974-0608
Website: www.nthfund.com

Management and Staff

Mason Willrich, Principal
Maurice Gunderson, Managing Director
Nancy Floyd, Managing Director
Tim Woodward, Managing Director

Type of Firm

Private Firm Investing Own Capital

Industry Association Membership

National Venture Capital Association (NVCA)
Western Association of Venture Capitalists (WAVC)

Project Preferences

Role in Financing:

Prefer role as deal originator but will also invest in deals created by others

Type of Financing Preferred:

First Stage Financing
Mezzanine
Second Stage Financing
Start-up Financing

Size of Investments Considered

Min Size of Investment Considered (000s): $250
Max Size of Investment Considered: No Limit

Geographical Preferences

International

No Preference

Industry Preferences

(% based on actual investment)

Internet Specific	32.8%
Industrial/Energy	23.9%
Communications and Media	20.5%
Computer Software and Services	14.9%
Other Products	5.4%
Semiconductors/Other Elect.	2.5%

Additional Information

Name of Most Recent Fund: Nth Power Technologies Fund II, L.P.
Most Recent Fund Was Raised: 01/01/1998
Year Founded: 1993
Capital Under Management: $60,000,000
Current Activity Level : Actively seeking new investments
Method of Compensation: Return on investment is of primary concern, do not charge fees

NU CAPITAL ACCESS GROUP, LTD.

7677 Oakport Street
Suite 105
Oakland, CA 94621
Phone: 510-635-7345
Fax: 510-635-7068

Type of Firm

Private Firm Investing Own Capital

Project Preferences

Role in Financing:

Prefer role as deal originator but will also invest in deals created by others

Type of Financing Preferred:

First Stage Financing
Industry Rollups
Leveraged Buyout
Second Stage Financing
Special Situation

Size of Investments Considered

Min Size of Investment Considered (000s): $500
Max Size of Investment Considered (000s): $1,000

Geographical Preferences

United States

Northwest
Southwest
West Coast

Industry Preferences

Consumer Related

Entertainment and Leisure
Franchises(NEC)
Food/Beverage
Consumer Products
Consumer Services

Industrial/Energy

Industrial Products
Factory Automation
Machinery
Environmental Related

Manufact.

Office Automation Equipmt

Additional Information

Year Founded: 1993
Current Activity Level : Actively seeking new investments
Method of Compensation: Return on invest. most important, but chg. closing fees, service fees, etc.

OAK HILL CAPITAL MANAGEMENT, INC.

2775 Sandhill Road
Suite 220
Menlo Park, CA 94025
Phone: 650-234-0500

See New York for full listing.

OAK INVESTMENT PARTNERS

525 University Avenue
Suite 1300
Palo Alto, CA 94301
Phone: 650-614-3700
Fax: 650-328-6345
Website: www.oakvc.com

See Connecticut for full listing.

ODEON CAPITAL PARTNERS, L.P.

10050 North Wolfe Road
Cupertino, CA 95014
Phone: 408-343-0253
Fax: 603-947-9552
Website: www.odeoncapital.com

See New York for full listing.

ONSET VENTURES

2400 Sand Hill Road
Suite 150
Menlo Park, CA 94025
Phone: 650-529-0700
Fax: 650-529-0777
Website: www.onset.com

Other Offices

8911 Capital of Texas Highway
Suite 2310
Austin, TX 78759
Phone: 512-349-2255

Management and Staff

Alexis Lakes, Chief Financial Officer
Darlene Mann, General Partner
David Kelley, Co-Founder
Leslie Bottorff, Partner
Mark Hilderbrand, Partner
Robert Kuhling, General Partner
Susan Mason, General Partner
Terry Opdendyk, General Partner
Thomas Winter, General Partner

Type of Firm

Private Firm Investing Own Capital

Industry Association Membership

National Venture Capital Association (NVCA)
Western Association of Venture Capitalists (WAVC)

Project Preferences

Role in Financing:

Prefer role as deal originator

Type of Financing Preferred:

Early Stage

Size of Investments Considered

Min Size of Investment Considered (000s): $100
Max Size of Investment Considered: No Limit

Geographical Preferences

United States

West Coast

Industry Preferences

(% based on actual investment)

Internet Specific	25.2%
Communications and Media	22.5%
Medical/Health	22.2%
Computer Software and Services	21.1%
Computer Hardware	6.4%
Biotechnology	1.9%
Other Products	0.7%

Additional Information

Name of Most Recent Fund: ONSET III
Most Recent Fund Was Raised: 09/01/1997
Year Founded: 1984
Capital Under Management: $453,600,000
Current Activity Level : Actively seeking new investments
Method of Compensation: Return on investment is of primary concern, do not charge fees

OPPORTUNITY CAPITAL PARTNERS {FKA: THOMPSON CAPITAL MGT)

2201 Walnut Avenue
Suite 210
Fremont, CA 94538
Phone: 510-795-7000
Fax: 510-494-5439
Website: www.ocpcapital.com

Management and Staff

Anita Stephens, Vice President
J. Peter Thompson, Managing Partner
Lewis Byrd, Vice President

Whom to Contact

Peter Thompson

Type of Firm

MESBIC not elsewhere classified

Industry Association Membership

Natl Assoc of Investment Cos. (NAIC)
Natl assoc of Small Bus. Inv. Co (NASBIC)

Project Preferences

Role in Financing:

Prefer role as deal originator but will also invest in deals created by others

Type of Financing Preferred:

Industry Rollups
Later Stage
Leveraged Buyout
Mezzanine
Second Stage Financing

Size of Investments Considered

Min Size of Investment Considered (000s): $100
Max Size of Investment Considered (000s): $1,500

Geographical Preferences

United States

All U.S.
West Coast

Industry Preferences

(% based on actual investment)

Internet Specific	39.5%
Consumer Related	20.0%
Industrial/Energy	10.8%
Communications and Media	9.2%
Computer Software and Services	8.9%
Medical/Health	8.5%
Other Products	2.2%
Computer Hardware	0.8%

Additional Information

Name of Most Recent Fund: Opportunity Capital Partners III, L.P.
Most Recent Fund Was Raised: 12/01/1995
Year Founded: 1970
Capital Under Management: $83,000,000
Current Activity Level : Actively seeking new investments
Method of Compensation: Return on invest. most important, but chg. closing fees, service fees, etc.

OPTICAL CAPITAL GROUP

One Embarcadero Center
Suite 2405
San Francisco, CA 94111
Phone: 415-393-0791
Fax: 415-393-0801
Website: www.opticalcapitalgroup.com

See Maryland for full listing.

ORACLE CORPORATION

500 Oracle Parkway
Redwood Shores, CA 94065
Phone: 650-506-7000
Website: www.oracle.com/corporate/venturefund/index.

Type of Firm
Non-Financial Corp. Affiliate or Subsidiary

Project Preferences

Role in Financing:
Prefer role in deals created by others

Type of Financing Preferred:
Early Stage
Later Stage

Size of Investments Considered
Min Size of Investment Considered (000s): $2,000
Max Size of Investment Considered (000s): $5,000

Geographical Preferences

United States
All U.S.

International
Europe

Industry Preferences

(% based on actual investment)

Internet Specific	58.6%
Computer Software and Services	18.6%
Communications and Media	7.9%
Biotechnology	6.9%
Medical/Health	5.9%
Other Products	2.2%

Additional Information
Year Founded: 1999
Capital Under Management: $500,000,000
Current Activity Level : Actively seeking new investments

ORCHID ASIA HOLDINGS

555 California Street
Suite 5180
San Francisco, CA 94104
Phone: 415-781-2200
Fax: 415-781-2189

Type of Firm
Private Firm Investing Own Capital

Additional Information
Year Founded: 1997
Capital Under Management: $66,000,000
Current Activity Level : Actively seeking new investments

OSPREY VENTURES, L.P.

3000 El Camino Real
5 Palo Alto Square, 9th Floor
Palo Alto, CA 94306
Phone: 650-849-9990
Fax: 650-849-9991
Website: www.ospreyventures.com

Management and Staff
David Stastny, Managing Director
Ken Hausman, Managing Director

Type of Firm
Private Firm Investing Own Capital

Project Preferences

Role in Financing:
Will function either as deal originator or investor in deals created by others

Industry Preferences

(% based on actual investment)

Internet Specific	82.8%
Communications and Media	11.1%
Computer Software and Services	6.0%

Additional Information
Capital Under Management: $92,000,000
Current Activity Level : Actively seeking new investments

OXFORD BIOSCIENCE PARTNERS

650 Town Center Drive
Suite 810
Costa Mesa, CA 92626
Phone: 714-754-5719
Fax: 714-754-6802
Website: www.oxbio.com

See Massachusetts for full listing.

OXFORD FINANCIAL SERVICES CORP.

1055 Torrey Pines Road
Suite 205
La Jolla, CA 92037
Phone: 619-551-0505
Fax: 619-551-0789

See Virginia for full listing.

OXFORD PARTNERS

6809 Shearwater Lane
Malibu, CA 90265
Phone: 310-589-2510
Fax: 310-589-2520

See Connecticut for full listing.

PACIFIC ASSET PARTNERS

222 Kearny Street
San Francisco, CA 94108
Phone: 415-362-6120
Fax: 415-362-3048

Type of Firm
Private Firm Investing Own Capital

Industry Association Membership
Western Association of Venture Capitalists (WAVC)

Project Preferences

Type of Financing Preferred:
Later Stage
Leveraged Buyout

Geographical Preferences

United States
West Coast

Additional Information
Year Founded: 1983
Capital Under Management: $25,000,000
Current Activity Level : Actively seeking new investments

PACIFIC CORPORATE GROUP, INC.

1200 Prospect Street
Suite 200
La Jolla, CA 92037
Phone: 858-456-6000
Fax: 858-456-6018
Website: www.pcgfunds.com

Management and Staff
Adrienne Gaines, Managing Director
Christopher Bower, Chief Executive Officer
Kara King, Vice President
Kelly DePonte, Managing Director
Laura Vossman, Vice President
Lisa Gildred, Vice President
Michael Russell, Managing Director
Michael R. Steed, Managing Director
Philip Posner, Managing Director
Scott Stedman, Managing Director
Tara Blackburn, Managing Director
Walter Fitzsimmons, Managing Director

Type of Firm
Private Equity Advisor or Fund of Fund Mgr

Industry Association Membership
National Venture Capital Association (NVCA)

Project Preferences

Role in Financing:
Will function either as deal originator or investor in deals created by others

Type of Financing Preferred:
Acquisition
Distressed Debt
Early Stage
Expansion
Fund of Funds
Joint Ventures
Later Stage
Leveraged Buyout
Management Buyouts
Mezzanine
Private Placement
Special Situation
Turnaround

Size of Investments Considered
Min Size of Investment Considered (000s): $5,000
Max Size of Investment Considered: No Limit

Geographical Preferences

United States
All U.S.

Canada
All Canada

International
China
France
Germany
Italy
Japan
Latin America
United Kingdom

Industry Preferences

Communications and Media
Commercial Communications
CATV & Pay TV Systems
Radio & TV Broadcasting
Telecommunications
Wireless Communications
Data Communications

Semiconductors/Other Elect.
Semiconductor
Fiber Optics

Medical/Health
Medical Products

Consumer Related
Education Related

Industrial/Energy
Energy

Financial Services
Real Estate

Business Serv.
Media

Utilities
Utilities

Additional Information
Name of Most Recent Fund: Private Market Fund, LP
Most Recent Fund Was Raised: 12/30/1996
Capital Under Management: $1,000,000,000
Current Activity Level : Actively seeking new investments
Method of Compensation: Return on invest. most important, but chg. closing fees, service fees, etc.

PACIFIC VENTURE GROUP

16830 Ventura Boulevard
Suite 244
Encino , CA 91436
Phone: 818-990-4141
Fax: 818-990-6556
Website: www.pacven.com

Other Offices

114 Pacifica
Suite 270
Irvine, CA 92618
Phone: 949-753-0490
Fax: 949-753-8932

202 Twin Dolphin Drive
Suite 600
Redwood City, CA 94065
Phone: 650-610-7930
Fax: 650-610-7930

Management and Staff
William West, Chief Financial Officer

Whom to Contact
Any of the above

Type of Firm
Private Firm Investing Own Capital

Industry Association Membership
National Venture Capital Association (NVCA)
Western Association of Venture Capitalists (WAVC)

Project Preferences

Role in Financing:
Prefer role as deal originator but will also invest in deals created by others

Type of Financing Preferred:
First Stage Financing
Leveraged Buyout
Mezzanine
Research and Development
Second Stage Financing
Seed
Special Situation
Start-up Financing

Size of Investments Considered
Min Size of Investment Considered (000s): $7,000
Max Size of Investment Considered: No Limit

Geographical Preferences

United States
All U.S.

Industry Preferences

(% based on actual investment)

Medical/Health	46.7%
Internet Specific	23.6%
Computer Hardware	9.6%
Computer Software and Services	8.4%
Biotechnology	4.2%
Consumer Related	4.1%
Semiconductors/Other Elect.	2.0%

Communications and Media	1.1%
Other Products	0.5%

Additional Information
Name of Most Recent Fund: Pacific Venture Group II, L.P.
Most Recent Fund Was Raised: 07/01/1998
Year Founded: 1995
Capital Under Management: $209,700,000
Current Activity Level : Actively seeking new investments
Method of Compensation: Return on investment is of primary concern, do not charge fees

PACIFICA FUND

701 Welch Road
Suite 1110
Palo Alto, CA 94304
Phone: 650-233-9571
Fax: 650-365-4661
E-mail: info@pacificafund.com
Website: www.pacificafund.com

Management and Staff
Himanshu Choksi, General Partner
Mochio Umeda, General Partner
Thomas Kuehle, General Partner
Tim Oren, General Partner
Yukio Okamoto, General Partner

Type of Firm
Private Equity Advisor or Fund of Fund Mgr

Project Preferences

Type of Financing Preferred:
Balanced
First Stage Financing
Second Stage Financing

Size of Investments Considered
Min Size of Investment Considered (000s): $500
Max Size of Investment Considered (000s): $1,500

Geographical Preferences

United States
All U.S.
West Coast

Industry Preferences

Communications and Media
Communications and Media

Internet Specific
Internet

Business Serv.
Services

Additional Information
Capital Under Management: $25,000,000
Current Activity Level : Actively seeking new investments

PACRIM VENTURE MANAGEMENT

605 Cowper Street
Palo Alto, CA 94301
Phone: 650-330-0880
Fax: 650-330-0785
Website: www.pacrimpartners.com

Management and Staff
Thomas Toy, Managing Director

Whom to Contact
Huoy-Ming Yeh

Type of Firm
Private Firm Investing Own Capital

Project Preferences

Role in Financing:
Will function either as deal originator or investor in deals created by others

Type of Financing Preferred:
Balanced

Size of Investments Considered
Min Size of Investment Considered (000s): $500
Max Size of Investment Considered (000s): $2,000

Geographical Preferences

United States
All U.S.
Northern California

International
China
Taiwan

Industry Preferences

Communications and Media
Telecommunications
Wireless Communications
Data Communications
Satellite Microwave Comm.
Other Communication Prod.

Computer Software
Software
Systems Software
Applications Software

Internet Specific
E-Commerce Technology
Internet
Web Aggregration/Portals

Semiconductors/Other Elect.
Semiconductor
Micro-Processing
Fiber Optics

Additional Information
Name of Most Recent Fund: PacRim Venture Partners I, L.P.
Most Recent Fund Was Raised: 12/03/1999
Capital Under Management: $25,000,000
Current Activity Level : Actively seeking new investments
Method of Compensation: Return on investment is of primary concern, do not charge fees

PALOMAR VENTURES

100 Wilshire Boulevard
Suite 450
Santa Monica, CA 90401
Phone: 310-260-6050
Fax: 310-656-4150
Website: www.palomarventures.com

Other Offices

18881 Von Karman Avenue
Suite 960
Irvine, CA 92612
Phone: 949-475-9455
Fax: 949-475-9456

Management and Staff
George Abe, Venture Partner
James Gauer, General Partner
John Downing, Venture Partner
Randall Lunn, General Partner
Rick Smith, General Partner

Type of Firm
Private Firm Investing Own Capital

Industry Association Membership
National Venture Capital Association (NVCA)
Western Association of Venture Capitalists (WAVC)

Project Preferences

Role in Financing:
Prefer role as deal originator but will also invest in deals created by others

Type of Financing Preferred:
Early Stage
Expansion
First Stage Financing
Seed
Startup

Size of Investments Considered
Min Size of Investment Considered (000s): $250
Max Size of Investment Considered (000s): $15,000

Geographical Preferences

United States
Northern California
Southwest
West Coast

Industry Preferences

(% based on actual investment)

Communications and Media	46.5%
Internet Specific	35.6%
Computer Software and Services	17.9%

Additional Information
Name of Most Recent Fund: Palomar Ventures I, L.P.
Most Recent Fund Was Raised: 04/07/1999
Year Founded: 1999
Capital Under Management: $300,000,000
Current Activity Level : Actively seeking new investments
Method of Compensation: Return on investment is of primary concern, do not charge fees

PANTHEON VENTURES LIMITED

Suite 906
50 California Street
San Francisco, CA 94111
Phone: 415 291 3100
Fax: 415 291 3132
Website: www.pantheon.co.uk

See Foreign Venture Capital Firms for full listing.

PARAGON VENTURE PARTNERS

3000 Sand Hill Road
Building One, Suite 275
Menlo Park, CA 94025
Phone: 650-854-8000
Fax: 650-854-7260

Other Offices

3000 Sand Hill Road
Suite 906
Menlo Park, CA

Type of Firm
Private Firm Investing Own Capital

Project Preferences

Role in Financing:
Prefer role as deal originator but will also invest in deals created by others

Type of Financing Preferred:
First Stage Financing
Second Stage Financing
Seed
Special Situation
Start-up Financing

Size of Investments Considered
Min Size of Investment Considered (000s): $500
Max Size of Investment Considered (000s): $1,500

Geographical Preferences

International
No Preference

Industry Preferences

(% based on actual investment)

Medical/Health	27.4%
Computer Software and Services	18.0%
Communications and Media	15.9%
Computer Hardware	11.4%
Biotechnology	7.2%
Other Products	5.3%
Consumer Related	4.9%
Industrial/Energy	4.6%
Semiconductors/Other Elect.	4.5%
Internet Specific	0.9%

Additional Information
Name of Most Recent Fund: Paragon Venture Partners III, L.P.
Most Recent Fund Was Raised: 01/01/1997
Year Founded: 1984
Capital Under Management: $70,000,000
Current Activity Level : Inactive / Unknown
Method of Compensation: Return on investment is of primary concern, do not charge fees

PARTECH INTERNATIONAL

50 California Street
Suite 3200
San Francisco, CA 94111
Phone: 415-788-2929
Fax: 415-788-6763
Website: www.partechvc.com

Other Offices

42 Avenue Raymond Poincare
Paris, France 75116
Phone: 33 153.65.65.53
Fax: 33 153.65.65.55

Kamiyacho Tower 45
5-2-5 Toranomon, Minato-Itu
Tokyo, Japan 105
Phone: 813-5470-6495
Fax: 813-5470-6498

Yurakucho Denki Building
North Tower, Room 1903
Tokyo, Japan 100-91
Phone: 81-35-470-6495
Fax: 81-35-470-6498

Management and Staff
David Welsh, General Partner
Glenn Solomon, General Partner
Jean-Marc Patouillaud, General Partner
Matt Wulfstat, Principal
Nicholas El Baze, General Partner
Philippe Collombel, Partner
Philippe Herbert, General Partner
Philippe Cases, General Partner
Scott Matson, Chief Financial Officer
Thomas McKinley, Managing Partner
Vincent Worms, Managing Partner

Whom to Contact
Tadahisa Ota

Type of Firm
Venture Consulting Firm

Industry Association Membership
European Venture Capital Association (EVCA)
Western Association of Venture Capitalists (WAVC)

Project Preferences

Role in Financing:
Will function either as deal originator or investor in deals created by others

Type of Financing Preferred:
Early Stage
First Stage Financing
Later Stage
Mezzanine
Second Stage Financing
Seed
Startup

Size of Investments Considered
Min Size of Investment Considered (000s): $1,000
Max Size of Investment Considered (000s): $15,000

Geographical Preferences

United States
All U.S.

International
Belgium
France
Israel
Japan
Luxembourg
Netherlands
United Kingdom

Industry Preferences

(% based on actual investment)

Internet Specific	44.6%
Computer Software and Services	19.2%
Computer Hardware	9.2%
Medical/Health	8.1%
Communications and Media	6.7%
Semiconductors/Other Elect.	6.1%
Biotechnology	1.9%
Consumer Related	1.5%
Industrial/Energy	1.4%
Other Products	1.3%

Additional Information
Name of Most Recent Fund: Partech International Ventures III
Most Recent Fund Was Raised: 05/01/1996
Year Founded: 1982
Capital Under Management: $1,000,000,000
Current Activity Level : Actively seeking new investments
Method of Compensation: Return on investment is of primary concern, do not charge fees

PATHFINDER VENTURE CAPITAL FUNDS

3000 Sand Hill Road
Building Three, Suite 255
Menlo Park, CA 94025
Phone: 415-854-0650
Fax: 415-854-4706

See Minnesota for full listing.

PATRICOF & CO. VENTURES, INC.

2100 Geng Road
Suite 150
Palo Alto, CA 94303
Phone: 650-494-9944
Fax: 650-494-6751
Website: www.patricof.com

See New York for full listing.

PAUL CAPITAL PARTNERS

10600 N. De Anza Boulevard, Su
Cupertino, CA 95014
Phone: 415-283-4300

Other Offices

99 Park Avenue
8th Floor
New York, NY 10016
Phone: 212-293-2200
Fax: 212-293-2219

Management and Staff
Bryon Sheets, Partner
Carol Archibald, Chief Financial Officer
David deWeese, Partner
Jeff Moelis, Principal
Lionel Leventhal, Principal
Walter Flamenbaum, Partner

Whom to Contact
Bryon Sheets
David de Weese

Type of Firm
Private Firm Investing Own Capital

Industry Association Membership
Western Association of Venture Capitalists (WAVC)

Project Preferences

Role in Financing:
Prefer role as deal originator

Type of Financing Preferred:
Generalist PE

Size of Investments Considered
Min Size of Investment Considered (000s): $1,000
Max Size of Investment Considered: No Limit

Additional Information
Name of Most Recent Fund: Paul Capital Partners VI
Most Recent Fund Was Raised: 01/01/1996
Capital Under Management: $288,000,000
Current Activity Level : Actively seeking new investments
Method of Compensation: Return on investment is of primary concern, do not charge fees

PEQUOT CAPITAL MANAGEMENT INC.

1 Market Plaza
Steuart Tower 22nd Floor
San Francisco, CA 94105
Phone: 415-365-8400
Website: www.pequotcapital.com

See New York for full listing.

PHOENIX GROWTH CAPITAL CORP.

2401 Kerner Boulevard
San Rafael, CA 94901
Phone: 415-485-4569
Fax: 415-485-4663

Other Offices

3000 Sand Hill Road
Building Four, Suite 165
Menlo Park, CA 94025
Phone: 415-854-8404
Fax: 415-854-5732

641 East Morningside Drive, N.E.
Atlanta, GA 30324
Phone: 404-872-2406
Fax: 404-876-1729

Industry Association Membership
Western Association of Venture Capitalists (WAVC)

Project Preferences

Role in Financing:
Prefer role as deal originator but will also invest in deals created by others

Type of Financing Preferred:
First Stage Financing
Mezzanine
Second Stage Financing

Size of Investments Considered
Min Size of Investment Considered (000s): $500
Max Size of Investment Considered (000s): $2,000

Geographical Preferences

United States
All U.S.

Industry Preferences

Communications and Media
Commercial Communications
Telecommunications
Data Communications
Satellite Microwave Comm.

Computer Other
Computer Related

Semiconductors/Other Elect.
Electronic Components

Biotechnology
Biotechnology

Medical/Health
Medical/Health

Consumer Related
Entertainment and Leisure
Retail
Computer Stores
Consumer Products
Consumer Services
Hotels and Resorts
Education Related

Transportation
Transportation

Business Serv.
Distribution

Manufact.
Publishing

Additional Information
Year Founded: 1984
Capital Under Management: $280,000,000
Current Activity Level : Actively seeking new investments
Method of Compensation: Other

POINT WEST VENTURES (FKA: FOURTEEN HILL CAPITAL, L.P.

1700 Montgomery Street
Suite 250
San Francisco, CA 94111
Phone: 415-394-1201
Fax: 415-394-9471
Website: www.pointwestcapital.com

Management and Staff
Alan Perper, President
Bradley Rotter, Chairman & CEO
J. Ward Rotter, Chief Financial Officer

Type of Firm
SBIC Not elsewhere classified

Additional Information
Year Founded: 1997
Capital Under Management: $5,000,000
Current Activity Level : Actively seeking new investments

POLARIS VENTURE CAPITAL

149 Commonwealth Drive
Menlo Park, CA 94025
Phone: 650-688-2800
Fax: 650-688-2848
Website: www.polarisvc.com

See Foreign Venture Capital Firms for full listing.

PREMIER MEDICAL PARTNER FUND L.P.

12225 El Camino Real
San Diego, CA 92130
Phone: 858-509-6550
Fax: 858-481-8919

Management and Staff
Douglas Lee, Managing Director
Palmer Ford, Managing Director
Richard Kuntz, Managing Director

Whom to Contact
Richard Kuntz

Type of Firm
Non-Financial Corp. Affiliate or Subsidiary

Project Preferences

Role in Financing:
Prefer role as deal originator but will also invest in deals created by others

Type of Financing Preferred:
First Stage Financing
Mezzanine
Second Stage Financing

Geographical Preferences

United States
All U.S.

Industry Preferences

Biotechnology
Biosensors

Medical/Health
Medical/Health
Medical Diagnostics
Medical Therapeutics

Additional Information
Name of Most Recent Fund: Premier Medical Partner Fund L.P.
Most Recent Fund Was Raised: 01/01/1995
Year Founded: 1995
Capital Under Management: $36,000,000
Current Activity Level : Actively seeking new investments
Method of Compensation: Return on investment is of primary concern, do not charge fees

PRESCIENT CAPITAL

535 Pacific Avenue
Suite 400
San Francisco, CA 94133
Phone: 415-675-6750
Fax: 415-675-6755
E-mail: eric@prcap.com
Website: www.prcap.com

Management and Staff
Brad Holsworth, Chief Financial Officer
Eric Mathewson, Managing Director

Type of Firm
Private Firm Investing Own Capital

Project Preferences

Role in Financing:
Prefer role as deal originator but will also invest in deals created by others

Type of Financing Preferred:
Early Stage

Geographical Preferences

United States
Colorado
Northern California

Industry Preferences

Communications and Media
Radio & TV Broadcasting

Computer Hardware
Computer Graphics and Dig

Computer Software
Computer Services
Software

Internet Specific
Internet

Consumer Related
Entertainment and Leisure

Additional Information
Year Founded: 1999
Capital Under Management: $100,000,000
Current Activity Level : Actively seeking new investments
Method of Compensation: Return on investment is of primary concern, do not charge fees

PROSPECT VENTURE PARTNERS (FKA: PROSPECT MANAGEMENT, LLC)

435 Tasso
Suite 200
Palo Alto, CA 94301
Phone: 650-327-8800
Fax: 650-324-8838

Management and Staff
Alexander Barkas, Managing Director
Chen Tang, Chief Financial Officer
David Schnell, Managing Director

Type of Firm
Private Firm Investing Own Capital

Industry Preferences

(% based on actual investment)

Biotechnology	70.0%
Medical/Health	17.0%
Computer Software and Services	13.0%

Additional Information
Name of Most Recent Fund: Prospect Venture Partners, L.P.
Most Recent Fund Was Raised: 12/01/1997
Year Founded: 1997
Capital Under Management: $100,000,000
Current Activity Level : Actively seeking new investments

PUTNAM LOVELL CAPITAL PARTNERS, L.P.

501 Deep Valley Dr.
Suite 300
Rolling Hills Estates, CA 90274
Phone: 310-750-3620
Fax: 310-265-1920
E-mail: Info@PutnamLovell.com
Website: www.putnamlovell.com

Other Offices
34 Brook Street
London, United Kingdom W1K 5DN
Phone: 020 7299 8500
Fax: 020 7299 8555

65 East 55th Street
Park Avenue Tower
New York, NY 10022
Phone: 212-546-7500
Fax: 212-644-2271

Four Embarcadero Center
26th Floor
San Francisco, CA 94111
Phone: 415-772-2100
Fax: 415-772-2145

Management and Staff
Cameron Miller, Principal
Donald Putnam, Chief Executive Officer
James Minnick, Managing Director
Jeffery Lovell, Managing Director
Robert Morris, Chief Operating Officer
William Henson, Managing Director

Whom to Contact
Jeffery Lovell

Type of Firm
Investment/Merchant Bank Subsid/Affil

Industry Association Membership
National Venture Capital Association (NVCA)

Project Preferences

Role in Financing:
Prefer role as deal originator but will also invest in deals created by others

Type of Financing Preferred:
Acquisition
Balanced
Early Stage
Expansion
First Stage Financing
Later Stage
Leveraged Buyout
Management Buyouts
Second Stage Financing
Seed
Special Situation
Startup

Size of Investments Considered
Min Size of Investment Considered (000s): $3,000
Max Size of Investment Considered (000s): $50,000

Geographical Preferences

United States
All U.S.

Canada
All Canada

Industry Preferences

Computer Software
Computer Services
Applications Software

Financial Services
Financial Services
Insurance

Business Serv.
Services

Additional Information
Year Founded: 1999
Capital Under Management: $145,000,000
Current Activity Level : Actively seeking new investments
Method of Compensation: Return on invest. most important, but chg. closing fees, service fees, etc.

PYRAMID TECHNOLOGY VENTURES

1000 Chestnut Street
Suite 11A
San Francisco, CA 94109
Phone: 1 415 292 9086

See Foreign Venture Capital Firms for full listing.

QUEST VENTURES

333 Bush Street
Suite 1750
San Francisco, CA 94104
Phone: 415-782-1414
Fax: 415-782-1415

Other Offices

555 California St
Suite 2955
San Francisco, CA

Type of Firm
Private Firm Investing Own Capital

Project Preferences

Role in Financing:
Prefer role as deal originator but will also invest in deals created by others

Type of Financing Preferred:
Early Stage
First Stage Financing
Second Stage Financing
Seed
Special Situation
Start-up Financing

Size of Investments Considered
Min Size of Investment Considered (000s): $300
Max Size of Investment Considered (000s): $1,000

Geographical Preferences

United States
Southwest
West Coast

Industry Preferences

Communications and Media
Commercial Communications
Radio & TV Broadcasting
Telecommunications
Data Communications
Satellite Microwave Comm.
Other Communication Prod.

Computer Hardware
Computers

Computer Other
Computer Related

Semiconductors/Other Elect.
Electronics
Electronic Components
Semiconductor
Controllers and Sensors
Circuit Boards
Component Testing Equipmt
Laser Related
Analytic/Scientific

Biotechnology
Biotechnology

Medical/Health
Medical/Health
Medical Products

Consumer Related
Entertainment and Leisure
Retail
Computer Stores
Food/Beverage
Consumer Products
Consumer Services
Education Related

Industrial/Energy
Alternative Energy
Energy Conservation Relat
Industrial Products

Financial Services
Financial Services

Manufact.
Publishing

Additional Information
Name of Most Recent Fund: Quest Ventures III
Most Recent Fund Was Raised: 09/01/1988
Year Founded: 1986
Capital Under Management: $12,100,000
Current Activity Level : Actively seeking new investments
Method of Compensation: Return on invest. most important, but chg. closing fees, service fees, etc.

RAZA FOUNDRIES

3080 North 1st Street
San Jose, CA 95134
Phone: 408-434-5503
Fax: 408-432-5599
Website: www.razafoundries.com

Management and Staff
Atiq Raza, Managing Partner
Edward Wang, Chief Financial Officer

Type of Firm
Incubators

Project Preferences

Role in Financing:
Prefer role as deal originator

Type of Financing Preferred:
First Stage Financing
Later Stage
Second Stage Financing

Geographical Preferences

United States
California

Industry Preferences

(% based on actual investment)

Communications and Media	31.4%
Semiconductors/Other Elect.	28.5%
Internet Specific	27.5%
Computer Software and Services	7.8%
Computer Hardware	4.8%

Additional Information
Year Founded: 2000
Current Activity Level : Actively seeking new investments

RECOVERY EQUITY INVESTORS, L.P.

901 Mariners Island Boulevard
Suite 465
San Mateo, CA 94404
Phone: 650-578-9752
Fax: 650-578-9842

Type of Firm
Private Firm Investing Own Capital

Project Preferences

Role in Financing:
Prefer role as deal originator but will also invest in deals created by others

Type of Financing Preferred:
Leveraged Buyout
Special Situation

Size of Investments Considered
Min Size of Investment Considered (000s): $10,000
Max Size of Investment Considered: No Limit

Geographical Preferences

United States
All U.S.

Industry Preferences

(% based on actual investment)

Other Products	53.5%
Computer Software and Services	34.4%
Consumer Related	12.1%

Additional Information
Name of Most Recent Fund: Recovery Equity Investors II, L.P.
Most Recent Fund Was Raised: 01/01/1995
Year Founded: 1990
Capital Under Management: $208,000,000
Current Activity Level : Actively seeking new investments
Method of Compensation: Return on invest. most important, but chg. closing fees, service fees, etc.

RED ROCK VENTURES

180 Lytton Avenue
Palo Alto, CA 94301
Phone: 650-325-3111
Fax: 650-853-7044
Website: www.redrockventures.com

Management and Staff
Bob Todd, General Partner
Carol Pereira, Chief Financial Officer
Kip Myers, General Partner
Laura Brege, General Partner
Peter Dumanian, General Partner
Robert Marsh, General Partner

Type of Firm
Private Firm Investing Own Capital

Industry Association Membership
Natl assoc of Small Bus. Inv. Co (NASBIC)
Western Association of Venture Capitalists (WAVC)

Project Preferences

Type of Financing Preferred:
Seed

Size of Investments Considered
Min Size of Investment Considered (000s): $500
Max Size of Investment Considered (000s): $5,000

Geographical Preferences

United States
West Coast

Industry Preferences

(% based on actual investment)

Internet Specific	49.0%
Computer Software and Services	42.4%
Computer Hardware	5.3%
Communications and Media	3.3%

Additional Information
Year Founded: 2000
Capital Under Management: $50,000,000
Current Activity Level : Actively seeking new investments

REDLEAF VENTURE MANAGEMENT

14395 Saratoga Avenue
Suite 130
Saratoga, CA 95070
Phone: 408-868-0800
Fax: 408-868-0810
Website: www.redleaf.com

Other Offices

100 First Avenue
Suite 950
Pittsburgh, PA 15222
Phone: 412-201-5600
Fax: 412-201-5650

1050 Winter Street
Suite 1000
North Waltham, MA 02451
Phone: 781-487-7900
Fax: 781-487-7940

2100 Reston Parkway
Suite 204
Herndon, VA 20191
Phone: 703-860-3000

999 Third Avenue
Suite 2424
Seattle, WA 98104
Phone: 206-447-1350
Fax: 206-4471351

Management and Staff
David Diamond, Managing Director
George Hoyem, Managing Director
J. Gregory Shuk, Managing Director
John Kohler, Chief Executive Officer
Lloyd Mahaffey, Chief Executive Officer
Michael Nelson, Managing Director
Robert von Goeben, Principal
Sherman Baldwin, Managing Director

Whom to Contact
Chris Brookfield

Type of Firm
Private Firm Investing Own Capital

Industry Association Membership
Mid-Atlantic Venture Association

Project Preferences

Role in Financing:
Prefer role as deal originator

Type of Financing Preferred:
First Stage Financing
Second Stage Financing
Seed
Start-up Financing

Geographical Preferences

United States
Northwest
All U.S.

Industry Preferences

(% based on actual investment)

Internet Specific	44.2%
Computer Software and Services	29.3%
Medical/Health	12.4%
Other Products	8.0%
Communications and Media	3.7%
Consumer Related	2.4%

Additional Information
Name of Most Recent Fund: Redleaf Venture II, L.P.
Most Recent Fund Was Raised: 06/07/1999
Year Founded: 1996
Capital Under Management: $250,000,000
Current Activity Level : Actively seeking new investments
Method of Compensation: Return on investment is of primary concern, do not charge fees

REDPOINT VENTURES

3000 Sand Hill Road
Building 2, Suite 290
Menlo Park, CA 94025
Phone: 650-926-5600
Fax: 650-854-5762
Website: www.redpoint.com

Other Offices

11150 Santa Monica Blvd
Suite 1200
West Los Angeles, CA 90025
Phone: 310-477-7678
Fax: 310-312-1868

Management and Staff
Allen Beasley, Principal
Brad Jones, Partner
Geoff Yang, Partner
Jeff Brody, Partner
Jim Mongiello, Venture Partner
John Walecka, Partner
John Hamm, Partner
John McQuillan, Venture Partner
Nancy McCroskey, Chief Financial Officer
Peter Gotcher, Venture Partner
R. Thomas Dyal, Partner
Ross Bott, Partner
Tim Haley, Partner

Type of Firm
Private Firm Investing Own Capital

Industry Association Membership
National Venture Capital Association (NVCA)

Industry Preferences

(% based on actual investment)

Internet Specific	39.1%
Communications and Media	26.2%
Computer Software and Services	22.6%
Semiconductors/Other Elect.	8.0%
Consumer Related	2.8%
Other Products	1.2%

Additional Information
Name of Most Recent Fund: Redpoint Ventures I, L.P.
Most Recent Fund Was Raised: 10/14/1999
Year Founded: 1999
Capital Under Management: $1,850,000,000
Current Activity Level : Actively seeking new investments

REDWOOD CAPITAL CORP.

30 San Diego Road
Building 3 Suite 140
Menlo Park, CA 94025
Phone: 650-854-4949
Fax: 650-854-5440

Type of Firm
Private Firm Investing Own Capital

Project Preferences

Role in Financing:
Prefer role as deal originator but will also invest in deals created by others

Type of Financing Preferred:
First Stage Financing
Leveraged Buyout
Second Stage Financing
Seed
Start-up Financing

Geographical Preferences

United States
West Coast

Industry Preferences

Consumer Related
Entertainment and Leisure
Food/Beverage
Consumer Products
Hotels and Resorts

Additional Information
Year Founded: 1981
Current Activity Level : Actively seeking new investments
Method of Compensation: Return on investment is of primary concern, do not charge fees

REDWOOD VENTURE PARTNERS, LLC.

4984 El Camino Real
Suite 200
Los Altos, CA 94022
Phone: 650-335-1111
Fax: 650-335-1110
Website: www.redwoodvp.com

Management and Staff
Chris Vora, General Partner
Devendra Varma, General Partner
Karim Walji, General Partner
Raj Singh, General Partner
Raj Parekh, General Partner
Sanjiv Ahuja, General Partner

Type of Firm
Non-Financial Corp. Affiliate or Subsidiary

Industry Preferences

(% based on actual investment)

Internet Specific	48.8%
Computer Software and Services	18.9%
Communications and Media	16.4%
Semiconductors/Other Elect.	9.5%
Computer Hardware	6.4%

Additional Information

Year Founded: 1999
Current Activity Level : Actively seeking new investments

REPRISE CAPITAL CORP.

6345 Balboa Boulevard
Encino, CA 91316
Phone: 818-776-2420
Fax: 818-776-2434

See New York for full listing.

RIDGEWOOD CAPITAL MANAGEMENT LLC

540 Cowper Street
Suite 200
Palo Alto, CA 94301
Phone: 650-614-9030
Website: www.ridgewoodcapital.com

See New Jersey for full listing.

RIORDAN, LEWIS & HADEN

300 South Grand Avenue
29th Floor
Los Angeles, CA 90071
Phone: 213-229-8500
Fax: 213-229-8597

Management and Staff

Jonathan Leach

Whom to Contact

Jonathan Leach

Type of Firm

Private Firm Investing Own Capital

Project Preferences

Role in Financing:
Prefer role as deal originator but will also invest in deals created by others

Type of Financing Preferred:
First Stage Financing
Leveraged Buyout
Second Stage Financing
Special Situation
Start-up Financing

Size of Investments Considered

Min Size of Investment Considered (000s): $2,000
Max Size of Investment Considered: No Limit

Geographical Preferences

United States
West Coast

Industry Preferences

Computer Software
Computer Services

Medical/Health
Medical Diagnostics
Medical Therapeutics
Medical Products
Hospital/Other Instit.

Consumer Related
Food/Beverage
Consumer Products
Consumer Services
Other Restaurants
Education Related

Industrial/Energy
Industrial Products
Environmental Related

Transportation
Transportation

Business Serv.
Consulting Services

Manufact.
Publishing

Additional Information

Year Founded: 1974
Capital Under Management: $200,000,000
Current Activity Level : Actively seeking new investments
Method of Compensation: Return on investment is of primary concern, do not charge fees

ROBERTSON STEPHENS & COMPANY, LLC

555 California Street
Suite 2350
San Francisco, CA 94104
Phone: 415-693-3355
Fax: 415-676-2556

Management and Staff

Anthony Brenner, Managing Director
Dan Dunn, Vice President
David Goldsmith, Managing Director
M. Kathleen Behrens, Managing Director
Michael Stark, Managing Director
Seymour Kaufman, Managing Director
Vladimir Jacimovic, Principal

Whom to Contact

Nancy D. Payne

Type of Firm

Private Firm Investing Own Capital

Industry Association Membership

National Venture Capital Association (NVCA)
Western Association of Venture Capitalists (WAVC)

Project Preferences

Role in Financing:
Prefer role as deal originator but will also invest in deals created by others

Type of Financing Preferred:
First Stage Financing
Leveraged Buyout
Mezzanine
Second Stage Financing
Seed
Start-up Financing

Geographical Preferences

United States
All U.S.

International
United Kingdom

Industry Preferences

(% based on actual investment)

Medical/Health	16.7%
Internet Specific	15.2%
Computer Hardware	15.1%
Computer Software and Services	13.5%
Communications and Media	11.3%
Semiconductors/Other Elect.	10.6%
Biotechnology	6.0%
Other Products	5.2%
Industrial/Energy	3.5%
Consumer Related	2.9%

Additional Information
Name of Most Recent Fund: Omega Ventures III
Most Recent Fund Was Raised: 03/01/1998
Year Founded: 1989
Capital Under Management: $400,000,000
Current Activity Level : Actively seeking new investments
Method of Compensation: Return on investment is of primary concern, do not charge fees

ROCKET VENTURES

3000 Sandhill Road
Building 1, Suite 170
Menlo Park, CA 94025
Phone: 650-561-9100
Fax: 650-561-9183
Website: www.rocketventures.com

Management and Staff
David Adams, Managing Director
Grant Dove, Managing Director
Jeff Allen, Managing Director
Larry Roberts, Managing Director
Owen Brown, General Partner
Robert Winter, Managing Director

Type of Firm
Private Firm Investing Own Capital

Industry Association Membership
National Venture Capital Association (NVCA)

Project Preferences

Type of Financing Preferred:
Early Stage
Seed
Start-up Financing

Size of Investments Considered
Min Size of Investment Considered (000s): $100
Max Size of Investment Considered (000s): $5,000

Geographical Preferences

United States
California
West Coast

Industry Preferences

Communications and Media
Communications and Media
Commercial Communications

Computer Software
Software

Internet Specific
Internet

Additional Information
Capital Under Management: $40,000,000
Current Activity Level : Actively seeking new investments

ROSECLIFF

15250 Ventura Boulevard
Suite 520
Sherman Oaks, CA 91403
Phone: 818-981-2210
Fax: 818-981-2223

Management and Staff
Curtice A. Cornell
Stephen W. Testa

Whom to Contact
Curtice A. Cornell
Stephen W. Testa

Type of Firm
Private Firm Investing Own Capital

Project Preferences

Role in Financing:
Prefer role as deal originator but will also invest in deals created by others

Type of Financing Preferred:
Leveraged Buyout
Second Stage Financing

Size of Investments Considered
Min Size of Investment Considered (000s): $10,000
Max Size of Investment Considered: No Limit

Geographical Preferences

United States
All U.S.

Canada
All Canada

Industry Preferences

Communications and Media
Commercial Communications
Data Communications
Other Communication Prod.

Computer Software
Systems Software
Applications Software

Semiconductors/Other Elect.
Electronic Components
Controllers and Sensors
Sensors
Component Testing Equipmt

Medical/Health
Medical Products

Consumer Related
Entertainment and Leisure
Retail
Food/Beverage
Consumer Products
Consumer Services
Other Restaurants

Industrial/Energy
Industrial Products
Factory Automation
Robotics
Machinery

Manufact.
Publishing

Additional Information
Name of Most Recent Fund: Rosecliff
Most Recent Fund Was Raised: 01/01/1994
Year Founded: 1989
Capital Under Management: $150,000,000
Current Activity Level : Actively seeking new investments
Method of Compensation: Return on invest. most important, but chg. closing fees, service fees, etc.

ROSEWOOD CAPITAL, L.P.

One Maritime Plaza
Suite 1330
San Francisco, CA 94111-3503
Phone: 415-362-5526
Fax: 415-362-1192
Website: www.rosewoodvc.com

Other Offices

One Martine Place
Suite 1330
San Francisco, CA 94111
Phone: 415-362-5526

Management and Staff
Chip Adams, Principal
Kevin Reily, Vice President
Kyle Anderson, Principal
Mike Brown, Vice President
Tim Burke, Vice President

Whom to Contact
Byron Adams
Kevin Reilly
Matt Crisp
Tim Burke

Type of Firm
Private Firm Investing Own Capital

Industry Association Membership
National Venture Capital Association (NVCA)
Western Association of Venture Capitalists (WAVC)

Project Preferences

Role in Financing:
Prefer role as deal originator but will also invest in deals created by others

Type of Financing Preferred:
Control-block Purchases
Leveraged Buyout
Mezzanine
Second Stage Financing
Special Situation

Size of Investments Considered
Min Size of Investment Considered (000s): $3,000
Max Size of Investment Considered (000s): $20,000

Geographical Preferences

United States
All U.S.

Industry Preferences

(% based on actual investment)

Other Products	38.1%
Internet Specific	33.0%
Consumer Related	13.7%
Computer Software and Services	12.3%
Communications and Media	2.9%

Additional Information
Name of Most Recent Fund: Rosewood Capital III, L.P.
Most Recent Fund Was Raised: 07/01/1997
Year Founded: 1986
Capital Under Management: $80,000,000
Current Activity Level : Actively seeking new investments
Method of Compensation: Return on investment is of primary concern, do not charge fees

ROSEWOOD STONE GROUP

2320 Marinship Way
Suite 240
Sausalito, CA 94965
Phone: 415-331-4400
Fax: 415-331-4481
Website: www.rosewoodstone.com

Management and Staff
Bruce Katz, Chairman & CEO
Monica Burke, Chief Operating Officer

Type of Firm
Private Firm Investing Own Capital

Additional Information
Year Founded: 1991
Current Activity Level : Actively seeking new investments

RUSSEL MILLER ADVISORS ASIA, LLC

601 California Street
Suite 600
San Francisco, CA 94108
Phone: 415-956-7474
Fax: 415-291-8369
E-mail: info@rmisf.com
Website: www.rmisf.com

Other Offices

4705-06 Central Plaza
18 Harbour Road
Wanchai, Hong Kong
Phone: 852-2534-2600
Fax: 852-2815-5289

Management and Staff
Gang Crist, Managing Director
Russell Miller, Chairman & CEO

Type of Firm
Affiliate/Subsidary of Oth. Financial. Instit.

Project Preferences

Type of Financing Preferred:
Balanced

Geographical Preferences

International
Asia

Industry Preferences

Financial Services
Financial Services
Insurance

Additional Information
Capital Under Management: $56,000,000
Current Activity Level : Actively seeking new investments

RUSTIC CANYON VENTURES (FKA: TMCT VENTURES, L.P.)

2425 Olympic Boulevard
Suite 6050W
Santa Monica, CA 90404
Phone: 310-998-8000
Fax: 310-998-8001
Website: www.rusticcanyon.com

Other Offices

475 Broadway Street
Redwood City, CA 94063
Phone: 650-556-3707
Fax: 650-556-3193

Management and Staff
John Babcock, Partner
Mark Menell, Partner
Michael Song, Partner
Michael Kim, Partner
Renee Labran, Partner
Susanna Lee, Partner
Thomas Unterman, Managing Partner

Type of Firm
Non-Financial Corp. Affiliate or Subsidiary

Industry Preferences

(% based on actual investment)

Internet Specific	80.1%
Communications and Media	10.3%
Computer Software and Services	5.2%
Semiconductors/Other Elect.	4.4%

Additional Information
Capital Under Management: $500,000,000
Current Activity Level : Actively seeking new investments

RWI GROUP, LP

835 Page Mill Road
Palo Alto, CA 94304
Phone: 650-251-1800
Fax: 650-213-8660
Website: www.rwigroup.com

Management and Staff
Donald Lucas, Managing General Partner
Jonathan Barek, Principal
William Baumel, General Partner

Type of Firm
Private Firm Investing Own Capital

Industry Association Membership
National Venture Capital Association (NVCA)
Western Association of Venture Capitalists (WAVC)

Project Preferences

Role in Financing:
Will function either as deal originator or investor in deals created by others

Type of Financing Preferred:
Early Stage
First Stage Financing
Second Stage Financing
Seed
Startup

Size of Investments Considered
Min Size of Investment Considered (000s): $500
Max Size of Investment Considered (000s): $4,000

Geographical Preferences

United States
California
West Coast

Industry Preferences

(% based on actual investment)

Internet Specific	54.9%
Computer Software and Services	20.7%
Communications and Media	11.5%
Semiconductors/Other Elect.	10.4%
Computer Hardware	1.8%
Other Products	0.4%
Industrial/Energy	0.4%

Additional Information
Name of Most Recent Fund: RWI Group, L.P.
Most Recent Fund Was Raised: 12/31/1995
Year Founded: 1994
Capital Under Management: $63,800,000
Current Activity Level : Actively seeking new investments
Method of Compensation: Return on investment is of primary concern, do not charge fees

SAGAPONACK PARTNERS LLC

170 Columbus Avenue
Fifth Floor
San Francisco, CA 94133
Phone: 415-989-7770
Fax: 415-989-8001

Type of Firm
Private Firm Investing Own Capital

Project Preferences

Role in Financing:
Prefer role as deal originator but will also invest in deals created by others

Type of Financing Preferred:
Second Stage Financing
Special Situation

Additional Information
Name of Most Recent Fund: Sagaponack Partners, L.P.
Most Recent Fund Was Raised: 09/01/1996
Year Founded: 1996
Capital Under Management: $100,000,000
Current Activity Level : Actively seeking new investments

SALIX VENTURES, L.P.

350 Townsend Street
Suite 405
San Francisco, CA 94107
Website: www.salixventures.com

See Tennessee for full listing.

SAN FRANCISCO SENTRY INVESTMENT GROUP(AKA: STORIE PARTNERS)

100 Pine Street
Suite 2700
San Francisco, CA 94111
Phone: 415-229-9000
Fax: 415-434-8043

Management and Staff
Richard Dirickson, Chairman & CEO
Timothy Spicer, President & COO

Type of Firm
Private Firm Investing Own Capital

Additional Information
Current Activity Level : Actively seeking new investments

SANDERLING VENTURES

2730 Sand Hill Road
Suite 200
Menlo Park, CA 94025
Phone: 650-854-9855
Fax: 650-854-3648
Website: www.sanderling.com

Management and Staff
Andrea Solari, Chief Financial Officer
Fred Middleton, General Partner
James Healy, Partner
Robert McNeil, General Partner
Tim Mills, General Partner

Whom to Contact
Fred Middleton
James I. Healy, M.D.
Tim Mills
Timothy C. Mills

Type of Firm
Venture Consulting Firm

Industry Association Membership
National Venture Capital Association (NVCA)
Western Association of Venture Capitalists (WAVC)

Project Preferences

Role in Financing:
Prefer role as deal originator but will also invest in deals created by others

Type of Financing Preferred:
Early Stage
Mezzanine
Seed
Startup

Size of Investments Considered
Min Size of Investment Considered (000s): $500
Max Size of Investment Considered (000s): $5,000

Geographical Preferences

United States
All U.S.

Canada
All Canada

International
Italy
Singapore
United Kingdom

Industry Preferences

(% based on actual investment)

Medical/Health	41.4%
Biotechnology	39.0%
Internet Specific	12.3%
Computer Software and Services	5.9%
Computer Hardware	0.6%
Semiconductors/Other Elect.	0.6%
Industrial/Energy	0.1%
Communications and Media	0.1%
Consumer Related	0.1%

Additional Information
Name of Most Recent Fund: Sanderling IV
Most Recent Fund Was Raised: 12/01/1996
Year Founded: 1979
Capital Under Management: $191,000,000
Current Activity Level : Actively seeking new investments
Method of Compensation: Return on investment is of primary concern, do not charge fees

SANDTON FINANCIAL GROUP

21550 Oxnard Street
Suite 300
Woodland Hills, CA 91367
Phone: 818-702-9283

Management and Staff
Lawrence Gaiber, President

Whom to Contact
Lawrence Gaiber

Type of Firm
Private Firm Investing Own Capital

Project Preferences

Role in Financing:
Will function either as deal originator or investor in deals created by others

Type of Financing Preferred:
Early Stage
Expansion
First Stage Financing
Mezzanine
Private Placement
Seed
Special Situation
Start-up Financing
Turnaround

Size of Investments Considered
Min Size of Investment Considered (000s): $250
Max Size of Investment Considered (000s): $10,000

Geographical Preferences

United States
All U.S.

Canada
All Canada

Additional Information
Year Founded: 1979
Current Activity Level : Actively seeking new investments
Method of Compensation: Other

SBV VENTURE PARTNERS (AKA:SIGEFI, BURNETTE & VALLEE)

2880 Lakeside Drive
Suite 224
Santa Clara, CA 95054
Phone: 408-748-0070
Fax: 408-748-0077
Website: www.sbvpartners.com

Management and Staff
Graham Burnette, General Partner
Jacques Vallee, Principal

Type of Firm
Private Firm Investing Own Capital

Industry Association Membership
National Venture Capital Association (NVCA)
Western Association of Venture Capitalists (WAVC)

Project Preferences

Role in Financing:
Prefer role as deal originator but will also invest in deals created by others

Type of Financing Preferred:
Early Stage
First Stage Financing
Research and Development
Second Stage Financing
Seed
Startup

Geographical Preferences

United States
All U.S.
West Coast

International
China
France
Germany
Japan
Middle East
United Kingdom

Industry Preferences

Communications and Media
Telecommunications
Wireless Communications
Data Communications
Other Communication Prod.

Computer Hardware
Mini and Personal/Desktop
Computer Graphics and Dig
Disk Relat. Memory Device

Computer Software
Computer Services
Data Processing
Software
Systems Software
Applications Software
Artificial Intelligence

Internet Specific
E-Commerce Technology
Internet
Web Aggregration/Portals

Semiconductors/Other Elect.
Electronic Components
Laser Related
Fiber Optics

Biotechnology
Human Biotechnology
Industrial Biotechnology
Biotech Related Research

Medical/Health
Medical/Health
Medical Diagnostics

Additional Information
Year Founded: 2000
Capital Under Management: $50,000,000
Current Activity Level : Actively seeking new investments
Method of Compensation: Return on investment is of primary concern, do not charge fees

---

SEACOAST CAPITAL

One Sansome Street
Suite 2100
San Francisco, CA 94104
Phone: 415-956-1400
Fax: 415-956-1459
Website: www.seacoastcapital.com

See Massachusetts for full listing.

SELBY VENTURE PARTNERS

2460 Sand Hill Road
Suite 200
Menlo Park, CA 94025
Phone: 650-854-7399
Fax: 650-854-7039
Website: www.selbyventures.com

Management and Staff
Alice Beukers, Principal
Bob Marshall, Managing Partner
Doug Barry, Partner
Jim Marshall, Partner

Type of Firm
Private Firm Investing Own Capital

Industry Association Membership
National Venture Capital Association (NVCA)
Natl assoc of Small Bus. Inv. Co (NASBIC)

Project Preferences

Role in Financing:
Will function either as deal originator or investor in deals created by others

Type of Financing Preferred:
Early Stage
First Stage Financing
Second Stage Financing
Seed

Size of Investments Considered
Min Size of Investment Considered (000s): $100
Max Size of Investment Considered (000s): $5,000

Geographical Preferences

United States
Northern California
West Coast

Industry Preferences

(% based on actual investment)

Internet Specific	45.3%
Consumer Related	19.4%
Communications and Media	14.1%
Computer Hardware	8.5%
Semiconductors/Other Elect.	7.3%
Computer Software and Services	5.5%

Additional Information
Name of Most Recent Fund: Selby Venture Partners, L.P.
Most Recent Fund Was Raised: 04/01/1998
Year Founded: 1999
Capital Under Management: $135,000,000
Current Activity Level : Actively seeking new investments
Method of Compensation: Return on investment is of primary concern, do not charge fees

---

SEQUOIA CAPITAL

3000 Sand Hill Road
Building Four, Suite 280
Menlo Park, CA 94025
Phone: 650-854-3927
Fax: 650-854-2977
Website: www.sequoiacap.com

Other Offices

3000 Sand Hill Road
4,Suite 280
Menlo Park, CA 94025

Management and Staff
Donald Valentine, Founder
Douglas Leone, General Partner
Gordon Russell, General Partner
Greg McAdoo, Partner
Haim Sadger, General Partner
Mark Stephens, General Partner
Melinda Dunn, Chief Financial Officer
Michael Moritz, General Partner
Sameer Gandhi, General Partner
Shmuel Levy, General Partner
Thomas Stephenson, General Partner

Type of Firm
Private Firm Investing Own Capital

Industry Association Membership
Western Association of Venture Capitalists (WAVC)

Project Preferences

Role in Financing:
Will function either as deal originator or investor in deals created by others

Type of Financing Preferred:
Early Stage
First Stage Financing
Second Stage Financing
Seed
Start-up Financing

Geographical Preferences

United States
West Coast

International
Israel
No Preference

Industry Preferences

(% based on actual investment)

Internet Specific	34.8%
Communications and Media	18.5%
Computer Software and Services	17.0%
Semiconductors/Other Elect.	8.9%
Computer Hardware	7.3%
Medical/Health	4.5%
Consumer Related	4.0%
Biotechnology	2.9%
Other Products	1.6%
Industrial/Energy	0.5%

Additional Information
Name of Most Recent Fund: Sequoia Capital Franchise Fund, L.P.
Most Recent Fund Was Raised: 11/01/1999
Year Founded: 1971
Capital Under Management: $700,000,000
Current Activity Level : Actively seeking new investments
Method of Compensation: Return on investment is of primary concern, do not charge fees

SEVIN ROSEN MANAGEMENT CO.

169 University Avenue
Palo Alto, CA 94301
Phone: 650-326-0550
Fax: 650-326-0707
Website: www.srfunds.com

See Texas for full listing.

SHAD RUN INVESTMENTS, INC.

P.O. Box 470730
San Francisco, CA 94147
Phone: 415-885-6400
Fax: 415-929-6286

Management and Staff
Sara Hendrickson, President

Type of Firm
Private Firm Investing Own Capital

Industry Association Membership
National Venture Capital Association (NVCA)

Project Preferences

Role in Financing:
Prefer role in deals created by others

Type of Financing Preferred:
First Stage Financing
Leveraged Buyout
Second Stage Financing

Size of Investments Considered
Min Size of Investment Considered (000s): $1,000
Max Size of Investment Considered: No Limit

Geographical Preferences

United States
All U.S.

Industry Preferences

Communications and Media
Communications and Media

Internet Specific
Internet

Medical/Health
Medical/Health

Consumer Related
Consumer
Education Related

Financial Services
Financial Services

Business Serv.
Distribution

Manufact.
Publishing

Additional Information
Year Founded: 1992
Capital Under Management: $15,000,000
Current Activity Level : Actively seeking new investments
Method of Compensation: Return on investment is of primary concern, do not charge fees

SHANSBY GROUP/TSG2, L.P., THE

250 Montgomery Street
Suite 1160
San Francisco, CA 94104
Phone: 415-398-2500
Fax: 415-421-5120

Management and Staff
Donald C. Stanners
Mark R. Berwick

Whom to Contact
Donald C. Stanners
Mark R. Berwick

Type of Firm
Investment/Merchant Bank Subsid/Affil

Project Preferences

Role in Financing:
Prefer role as deal originator but will also invest in deals created by others

Type of Financing Preferred:
Leveraged Buyout

Size of Investments Considered
Min Size of Investment Considered (000s): $2,000
Max Size of Investment Considered: No Limit

Geographical Preferences

United States
All U.S.

Industry Preferences

Consumer Related
Entertainment and Leisure
Food/Beverage
Consumer Products
Consumer Services

Industrial/Energy
Materials

Additional Information
Year Founded: 1987
Capital Under Management: $120,000,000
Current Activity Level : Actively seeking new investments
Method of Compensation: Return on investment is of primary concern, do not charge fees

SIEMENS VENTURE CAPITAL GMBH

4900 Old Ironsides Drive
P.O. Box 58075, Mail Stop 104
Santa Clara, CA 95052-8075
Website: www.siemens.de/svc

See Foreign Venture Capital Firms for full listing.

SIENNA VENTURES (FKA: SIENNA HOLDINGS INC.)

2330 Marinship Way
Suite 220
Sausalito, CA 94965
Phone: 415-339-2800
Fax: 415-339-2805
Website: www.siennaventures.com

Management and Staff
Daniel Skaff, Chairman & CEO
Gil Amelio, General Partner

Type of Firm
Private Firm Investing Own Capital

Industry Association Membership
National Venture Capital Association (NVCA)

Project Preferences

Role in Financing:
Prefer role as deal originator but will also invest in deals created by others

Type of Financing Preferred:
Early Stage
First Stage Financing
Second Stage Financing
Start-up Financing

Size of Investments Considered
Min Size of Investment Considered (000s): $35,000
Max Size of Investment Considered: No Limit

Geographical Preferences

United States
All U.S.

Canada
All Canada

Industry Preferences

(% based on actual investment)

Computer Software and Services	27.0%
Internet Specific	22.5%
Communications and Media	16.3%
Consumer Related	15.1%
Other Products	11.3%
Computer Hardware	7.7%

Additional Information
Name of Most Recent Fund: Pon North America
Most Recent Fund Was Raised: 04/01/1998
Year Founded: 1990
Capital Under Management: $180,000,000
Current Activity Level : Actively seeking new investments
Method of Compensation: Return on investment is of primary concern, do not charge fees

SIERRA VENTURES

3000 Sand Hill Road
Building Four, Suite 210
Menlo Park, CA 94025
Phone: 650-854-1000
Fax: 650-854-5593
Website: www.sierraventures.com

Management and Staff
Dave Schwab, General Partner
Jeffrey Drazan, General Partner
Jim Tananbaum, General Partner
Martha Clarke Adamson, Chief Financial Officer
Peter Wendell, General Partner
Petri Vainio, General Partner
Steve Williams, General Partner
Tim Guleri, General Partner
Vincent Tobkin, General Partner

Type of Firm
Private Firm Investing Own Capital

Industry Association Membership
National Venture Capital Association (NVCA)
Western Association of Venture Capitalists (WAVC)

Project Preferences

Role in Financing:
Prefer role as deal originator but will also invest in deals created by others

Type of Financing Preferred:
Early Stage
First Stage Financing
Leveraged Buyout
Recapitalizations
Second Stage Financing
Seed
Start-up Financing

Size of Investments Considered
Min Size of Investment Considered (000s): $100
Max Size of Investment Considered: No Limit

Geographical Preferences

United States
All U.S.
All U.S.
West Coast

International
No Preference

Industry Preferences

(% based on actual investment)

Internet Specific	28.4%
Computer Software and Services	23.5%
Medical/Health	11.9%
Communications and Media	11.5%
Semiconductors/Other Elect.	8.9%
Computer Hardware	5.6%
Biotechnology	4.4%
Other Products	3.5%
Industrial/Energy	2.1%
Consumer Related	0.2%

Additional Information
Name of Most Recent Fund: Sierra Ventures VII
Most Recent Fund Was Raised: 01/01/1999
Year Founded: 1981
Capital Under Management: $650,000,000
Current Activity Level : Actively seeking new investments
Method of Compensation: Return on investment is of primary concern, do not charge fees

SIGMA PARTNERS

2884 Sand Hill Road
Suite 121
Menlo Park, CA 94025
Phone: 650-853-1700
Fax: 650-853-1717
Website: http://www.sigmapartners.com

Other Offices

20 Custom House Street
Suite 830
Boston, MA 02110
Phone: 617-330-7872
Fax: 617-323-7975

Management and Staff
Clifford Haas, Managing Director
John Mandile, Managing Director
Lawrence Finch, Managing Director
Marilyn Stallings, Chief Financial Officer
Robert Davoli, Managing Director
Wade Woodson, Managing Director

Whom to Contact
Gardner C. Hendrie
Lawrence Finch

Type of Firm
Private Firm Investing Own Capital

Industry Association Membership
National Venture Capital Association (NVCA)
Western Association of Venture Capitalists (WAVC)

Project Preferences

Role in Financing:
Prefer role as deal originator but will also invest in deals created by others

Type of Financing Preferred:
Control-block Purchases
First Stage Financing
Leveraged Buyout
Recapitalizations
Second Stage Financing
Seed
Special Situation
Start-up Financing

Geographical Preferences

United States
Midwest
Northeast
Northwest
Rocky Mountain
Southeast
Southwest
West Coast

Industry Preferences
(% based on actual investment)

Internet Specific	48.0%
Computer Software and Services	30.1%
Communications and Media	10.4%
Computer Hardware	6.4%
Semiconductors/Other Elect.	2.7%
Other Products	0.8%
Consumer Related	0.7%
Medical/Health	0.4%
Industrial/Energy	0.4%

Additional Information
Name of Most Recent Fund: Sigma Partners V
Most Recent Fund Was Raised: 10/01/1999
Year Founded: 1984
Capital Under Management: $22,700,000
Current Activity Level : Actively seeking new investments
Method of Compensation: Return on investment is of primary concern, do not charge fees

SIGNIA VENTURES

411 Borel Avenue
Suite 510
San Mateo, CA 94402
Phone: 650-372-1200
Fax: 650-372-1212
E-mail: info@signiaventures.com
Website: www.signiaventures.com

Management and Staff
Dimitri Panasevich, Partner
Lawrence Braitman, Managing Director
Richard Thompson, Managing Director

Type of Firm
Private Firm Investing Own Capital

Industry Association Membership
National Venture Capital Association (NVCA)

Project Preferences

Type of Financing Preferred:
Early Stage

Geographical Preferences

United States
Northern California

Industry Preferences

Internet Specific
Internet

Additional Information
Year Founded: 1999
Current Activity Level : Actively seeking new investments

SILICON VALLEY BANK

3003 Tasman
Santa Clara, CA 95054
Phone: 408-654-7400
Fax: 408-727-8728
Website: www.svb.com

Other Offices

10585 Santa Monica Blvd.
Suite 140
Los Angeles, CA 90025
Phone: 310-234-3556
Fax: 310-234-3569

11000 SW Stratus
Suite 170
Beaverton, OR 97008-7113
Phone: 503-526-1123
Fax: 503-526-0818

1731 Embarcadero
Suite 220
Palo Alto, CA 94303
Phone: 650-812-0799
Fax: 650-812-0640

18872 MacArthur Boulevard
Suite 100
Irvine, CA 92612
Phone: 714-252-1300
Fax: 714-252-0925

2 Palo Alto Square
Suite 110
Palo Alto, CA 94306
Phone: 650-812-0682
Fax: 650-493-5859

3000 Sand Hill Road
Building 1, Suite 240
Menlo Park, CA 94025
Phone: 650-233-7420
Fax: 650-233-9061

3343 Peachtree Road
East Tower, Suite 312
Atlanta, GA 30326
Phone: 404-261-5525
Fax: 404-261-2202

38 Technology drive
Suite 150
Irvine, CA 92612
Phone: 949-790-9000
Fax: 949-789-1928

4430 Arapahoe Avenue
Suite 225
Boulder, CO 80303
Phone: 303-938-0483
Fax: 303-938-0486

4455 E. Camelback Road
Suite E-290
Phoenix, AZ 85018
Phone: 602-381-8722
Fax: 602-667-3556

899 Adams Street
Suite G-2
St Helena, CA 94574
Phone: 707-967-4826
Fax: 707-967-4827

9 East Sand Sage
Santa Fe, NM 87501
Phone: 505-995-9910
Fax: 505-995-9929

9020 Capital of Texas Highway No
Building One Suite
Austin, TX 78759
Phone: 512-372-6750
Fax: 512-794-0855

915 118th Avenue SE
Suite 250
Bellevue, WA 98005
Phone: 206-688-1368
Fax: 206-646-8100

9150 Wilshire Boulevard
Suite 201
Beverly Hills, CA 90212
Phone: 310-786-8640
Fax: 310-786-8657

9645 Scranton Road
Suite 110
San Diego, CA 92121
Phone: 858-784-3300
Fax: 858-622-1269

9701 West Higgins Road
Suite 150
Rosemont, IL 60018
Phone: 847-698-0618
Fax: 847-698-0635

One Central Plaza, Suite 1205
11300 Rockville Pike
Rockville, MD 20852
Phone: 301-984-4977
Fax: 301-984-6282

One Newton Executive Park
2221 Washington Street Suite 200
Newton, MA 02462
Phone: 617-630-4100
Fax: 617-969-4395

Management and Staff
Aaron Gershenberg, Managing Director
Adam Kaufman, Vice President
Douglas Hamilton, Managing Director
Greg Becker, Managing Director
Jim Maynard, Managing Director
Kenneth Wilcox, President
Philip Johnson, Vice President

Whom to Contact
David Fischer
Tim Waterson

Type of Firm
Commercial Bank Affiliate or Subsidiary

Industry Association Membership
National Venture Capital Association (NVCA)

Project Preferences

Role in Financing:
Prefer role as deal originator but will also invest in deals created by others

Type of Financing Preferred:
First Stage Financing
Mezzanine
Second Stage Financing
Start-up Financing

Size of Investments Considered
Min Size of Investment Considered (000s): $500
Max Size of Investment Considered (000s): $1,000

Geographical Preferences

United States
All U.S.

Industry Preferences

(% based on actual investment)

Internet Specific	45.5%
Communications and Media	16.9%
Semiconductors/Other Elect.	16.6%
Computer Software and Services	16.5%
Other Products	1.6%
Computer Hardware	1.5%
Medical/Health	1.4%

Additional Information
Year Founded: 1983
Capital Under Management: $121,000,000
Current Activity Level : Actively seeking new investments
Method of Compensation: Return on invest. most important, but chg. closing fees, service fees, etc.

SIPAREX GROUP (FKA:SIPAREX PROVINCES DE FRANCE)

1835 Franklin ave no 1501
San Francisco, CA 94109
Website: www.siparex.com

See Foreign Venture Capital Firms for full listing.

SIPPL MACDONALD VENTURES I, L.P.

1422 El Camino Real
Menlo Park, CA 94025
Phone: 650-566-6860
Fax: 650-326-4404
Website: www.sipmac.com

Management and Staff
Jacqueline Macdonald, Partner
Roger Sippl, Partner

Type of Firm
Private Firm Investing Own Capital

Industry Association Membership
National Venture Capital Association (NVCA)

Geographical Preferences

United States
West Coast

Industry Preferences

(% based on actual investment)

Computer Software and Services	59.0%
Internet Specific	40.4%
Other Products	0.7%

Additional Information
Year Founded: 1995
Capital Under Management: $18,000,000
Current Activity Level : Actively seeking new investments

SKYLINE VENTURES

125 University Avenue
Palo Alto, CA 94301
Phone: 650-462-5800
Fax: 650-329-1090
Website: www.skylineventures.com

Management and Staff
John Freund, Managing Director
Steve Sullivan, Venture Partner
Yasumori Kaneko, Managing Director

Type of Firm
Private Firm Investing Own Capital

Industry Association Membership
National Venture Capital Association (NVCA)
Western Association of Venture Capitalists (WAVC)

Project Preferences

Type of Financing Preferred:
Balanced
Early Stage

Industry Preferences

(% based on actual investment)

Biotechnology	59.8%
Medical/Health	28.3%
Computer Hardware	11.9%

Additional Information
Name of Most Recent Fund: Skyline Ventures
Most Recent Fund Was Raised: 10/06/1997
Year Founded: 1997
Capital Under Management: $83,000,000
Current Activity Level : Actively seeking new investments

SKYWOOD VENTURES

3000 Sand Hill Road
Building 3 Suite 100
Menlo Park, CA 94025

Management and Staff
Jared Anderson, Managing Director
Jerry Anderson, Founder

Type of Firm
Private Firm Investing Own Capital

Additional Information
Current Activity Level : Actively seeking new investments

SMART TECHNOLOGY VENTURES

1801 Century Park West
5th Floor
Los Angeles, CA 90067
Phone: 310-203-3800
Fax: 310-273-5345
Website: www.smarttechnologyventures.com

Management and Staff
David Nazarian, Managing Director
Joel Balbien, Managing Partner
Joseph Marks, Vice President
Mehran Matloubian, Managing Partner
Michael Holton, Principal
Paula Robins, Chief Financial Officer

Type of Firm
Private Firm Investing Own Capital

Industry Association Membership
Natl assoc of Small Bus. Inv. Co (NASBIC)

Project Preferences

Role in Financing:
Will function either as deal originator or investor in deals created by others

Type of Financing Preferred:
Early Stage
Seed

Size of Investments Considered
Min Size of Investment Considered (000s): $2,000
Max Size of Investment Considered (000s): $5,000

Geographical Preferences

United States
West Coast

Industry Preferences

Communications and Media
Wireless Communications

Computer Hardware
Disk Relat. Memory Device

Computer Software
Systems Software

Semiconductors/Other Elect.
Micro-Processing
Laser Related
Fiber Optics

Additional Information
Year Founded: 2000
Capital Under Management: $175,000,000
Current Activity Level : Actively seeking new investments
Method of Compensation: Return on investment is of primary concern, do not charge fees

SOFINNOVA VENTURES

140 Geary St.
10th Floor
San Francisco, CA 94108
Phone: 415-228-3380
Fax: 415-228-3390
Website: www.sofinnova.com

Other Offices

Sofinnova Partners SA
17 rue de Surene
Paris, France 75008
Phone: 33 153.05.41.00
Fax: 33 153.05.41.29

Management and Staff
Alain Azan, Partner
Bernard Gilly, Partner
Gregory Strikeleather, Partner
James Healy, Partner
Mike Powell, Partner
Nathalie Auber, Chief Financial Officer
Olivier Protard, Partner
Robert Carr, Partner

Type of Firm
Private Firm Investing Own Capital

Industry Association Membership
European Venture Capital Association (EVCA)
French Venture Capital Association
National Venture Capital Association (NVCA)
Western Association of Venture Capitalists (WAVC)

Project Preferences

Role in Financing:
Prefer role as deal originator but will also invest in deals created by others

Type of Financing Preferred:
Early Stage
First Stage Financing
Mezzanine
Second Stage Financing
Seed
Start-up Financing

Geographical Preferences

United States
Northeast
West Coast

International
Bermuda
France
Germany
United Kingdom

Industry Preferences

(% based on actual investment)

Internet Specific	29.9%
Biotechnology	24.0%
Computer Software and Services	19.2%
Medical/Health	13.8%
Communications and Media	7.3%
Computer Hardware	4.7%
Semiconductors/Other Elect.	0.6%
Other Products	0.4%
Industrial/Energy	0.1%

Additional Information
Name of Most Recent Fund: Sofinnova Venture Partners IV
Most Recent Fund Was Raised: 01/01/1998
Year Founded: 1976
Capital Under Management: $300,000,000
Current Activity Level : Actively seeking new investments
Method of Compensation: Return on investment is of primary concern, do not charge fees

SOFTBANK VENTURE CAPITAL (FKA: SOFTBANK TECHNOLOGY VENTURES)

200 West Evelyn Avenue
Suite 200
Mountain View, CA 94041
Phone: 650-962-2000
Fax: 650-962-2030
Website: www.sbvc.com

Other Offices

10 Langley Road
Suite 403
Newton Center, MA 02159-1972
Phone: 617-928-9300
Fax: 617-928-9301

HOTBANK Colorado
100 Superior Plaza Way
Superior, CO 80027

Management and Staff

Bill Burnham, Managing Director
Bradley Feld, Managing Director
Carl Rosendahl, Managing Director
Charles Lax, Managing Director
E. Scott Russell, Managing Director
Gary Rieschel, Managing Director
Greg Prow, Managing Director
Gregory Galanos, Managing Director
Heidi Roizen, Managing Director
Helen MacKenzie, Chief Financial Officer
Matt Ocko, Managing Director
Rayna Brown, Managing Director
Rex Golding, Managing Director
Ryan McIntyre, Venture Partner

Type of Firm

Non-Financial Corp. Affiliate or Subsidiary

Industry Association Membership

National Venture Capital Association (NVCA)

Project Preferences

Role in Financing:
Prefer role as deal originator

Type of Financing Preferred:
Early Stage
First Stage Financing
Seed
Start-up Financing

Size of Investments Considered

Min Size of Investment Considered (000s): $500
Max Size of Investment Considered (000s): $100,000

Geographical Preferences

United States
All U.S.

Industry Preferences

(% based on actual investment)

Internet Specific	59.6%
Consumer Related	11.6%
Computer Software and Services	10.6%
Communications and Media	9.1%
Other Products	6.9%
Computer Hardware	1.7%
Semiconductors/Other Elect.	0.4%

Additional Information

Name of Most Recent Fund: SOFTBANK Technology Ventures IV
Most Recent Fund Was Raised: 03/31/1998
Year Founded: 1981
Capital Under Management: $2,452,300,000
Current Activity Level : Actively seeking new investments
Method of Compensation: Return on investment is of primary concern, do not charge fees

SONERA CORPORATION CORPORATE VENTURE CAPITAL

1620 26th Street South Tower
3rd Floor Suite 15
Santa Monica, CA 90404
Website: www.sonera.fi/english/ventures/

See Foreign Venture Capital Firms for full listing.

SORRENTO ASSOCIATES, INC.

4370 La Jolla Village Drive
Suite 1040
San Diego, CA 92122
Phone: 858-452-3100
Fax: 858-452-7607
Website: www.sorrentoventures.com

Management and Staff

Robert Jaffe, Founder
Vincent Burgess, Vice President

Type of Firm

Mgt. Consulting Firm

Project Preferences

Role in Financing:
Prefer role as deal originator but will also invest in deals created by others

Type of Financing Preferred:
Control-block Purchases
First Stage Financing
Leveraged Buyout
Mezzanine
Second Stage Financing
Special Situation
Start-up Financing

Size of Investments Considered

Min Size of Investment Considered (000s): $250
Max Size of Investment Considered: No Limit

Geographical Preferences

United States
Rocky Mountain
West Coast

Industry Preferences

(% based on actual investment)

Medical/Health	41.5%
Internet Specific	18.9%
Computer Software and Services	15.9%
Biotechnology	12.2%
Communications and Media	7.4%
Consumer Related	3.4%
Semiconductors/Other Elect.	0.7%

Additional Information

Name of Most Recent Fund: Sorrento Ventures IV, L.P.
Most Recent Fund Was Raised: 01/01/1998
Year Founded: 1985
Capital Under Management: $115,000,000
Current Activity Level : Actively seeking new investments
Method of Compensation: Return on investment is of primary concern, do not charge fees

SOUTHERN CALIFORNIA VENTURES

406 Amapola Avenue
Suite 125
Torrance, CA 90501
Phone: 310-787-4381
Fax: 310-787-4382

Other Offices

15303 Ventura Boulevard
Suite 1040
Sherman Oaks, CA 91403
Phone: 818-501-2295
Fax: 818-501-4190

Two Park Plaza
SW 750
Irvine, CA 92714
Phone: 714-251-2785
Fax: 714-251-2781

Type of Firm
Private Firm Investing Own Capital

Project Preferences

Role in Financing:
Prefer role in deals created by others

Type of Financing Preferred:
First Stage Financing
Seed
Start-up Financing

Size of Investments Considered
Min Size of Investment Considered (000s): $300
Max Size of Investment Considered (000s): $1,000

Geographical Preferences

United States
West Coast

Industry Preferences

Communications and Media
Data Communications
Other Communication Prod.

Medical/Health
Other Therapeutic
Medical Products
Disposable Med. Products

Additional Information
Name of Most Recent Fund: Southern California Ventures II
Most Recent Fund Was Raised: 06/01/1986
Year Founded: 1983
Capital Under Management: $45,000,000
Current Activity Level : Making few, if any, new investments
Method of Compensation: Return on investment is of primary concern, do not charge fees

SPECTRUM EQUITY INVESTORS, L.P.

333 Middlefield Road
Suite 200
Menlo Park, CA 94025
Phone: 415-464-4600
Fax: 415-464-4601
Website: www.spectrumequity.com

Other Offices

Berkeley Square House
Suite 3, Sixth Floor
London, United Kingdom W1X 6JP
Phone: 20731817400
Fax: 2073187400

One International Place
29th Floor
Boston, MA 02110
Phone: 617-464-4600
Fax: 617-464-4601

Management and Staff
Benjamin Coughlin, Principal
Brion Applegate, Managing Partner
Drusilla Pratt-Otto, Chief Financial Officer
Kevin Maroni, Managing Partner
Michael Kennealy, General Partner
Neal Douglas, Managing Partner
Randy Henderson, Chief Financial Officer
Robert Nicholson, Managing Partner
Scott Ellison, Principal
Shawn Colo, Principal
Victor Parker, General Partner
William Collatos, Managing Partner
Zev Nijensohn, Principal

Type of Firm
Private Firm Investing Own Capital

Industry Association Membership
Western Association of Venture Capitalists (WAVC)

Project Preferences

Role in Financing:
Prefer role as deal originator but will also invest in deals created by others

Type of Financing Preferred:
Balanced

Size of Investments Considered
Min Size of Investment Considered (000s): $5,000
Max Size of Investment Considered: No Limit

Geographical Preferences

United States
All U.S.

Canada
All Canada

International
Belgium
France
Germany
Italy
Luxembourg
Netherlands
Portugal
Spain
United Kingdom

Industry Preferences

(% based on actual investment)

Communications and Media	41.6%
Internet Specific	34.7%
Computer Software and Services	9.0%
Semiconductors/Other Elect.	5.7%
Other Products	4.5%
Computer Hardware	4.5%

Additional Information
Name of Most Recent Fund: Spectrum Equity Investors, L.P.
Most Recent Fund Was Raised: 04/01/1994
Year Founded: 1994
Capital Under Management: $2,808,300,000
Current Activity Level : Actively seeking new investments
Method of Compensation: Return on investment is of primary concern, do not charge fees

SPENCER TRASK VENTURES, INC. (FKA: SPENCER TRASK SECURITIES)

1299 Ocean Avenue
Suite 900
Santa Monica, CA 90401
Phone: 310-395-5960
Website: www.spencertrask.com

See New York for full listing.

SPINNAKER VENTURES

595 Market Street
21st Floor
San Francisco, CA 94105
Phone: 415-354-5972
Fax: 415-354-5979
Website: www.spinnakerventures.com

Other Offices

Al Santos, 1940-2o
Sao Paulo, SP-01418-200, Brazil
Phone: 55-11-253-2255
Fax: 55-11-253-2437

Management and Staff
Claude Pomper, Principal
Gregorio Schneider, Principal
Marcos Rosenberg, Principal

Type of Firm
Private Firm Investing Own Capital

Project Preferences

Role in Financing:
Prefer role in deals created by others

Type of Financing Preferred:
Expansion

Geographical Preferences

United States
All U.S.

Industry Preferences

Communications and Media
Telecommunications
Other Communication Prod.

Computer Software
Software

Business Serv.
Services

Additional Information
Name of Most Recent Fund: Spinnaker Ventures Fund I, L.P.
Most Recent Fund Was Raised: 02/01/2000
Year Founded: 1999
Capital Under Management: $53,500,000
Current Activity Level : Actively seeking new investments
Method of Compensation: Return on investment is of primary concern, do not charge fees

SPONSORED CONSULTING SERVICES

8929 Wilshire Boulevard
Suite 214
Beverly Hills, CA 90211
Phone: 310-208-1234
Fax: 310-657-4486

Management and Staff
Dick Israel

Whom to Contact
Dick Israel

Type of Firm
Mgt. Consulting Firm

Project Preferences

Role in Financing:
Prefer role as deal originator

Type of Financing Preferred:
First Stage Financing
Leveraged Buyout
Mezzanine
Second Stage Financing
Special Situation

Size of Investments Considered
Min Size of Investment Considered (000s): $10,000
Max Size of Investment Considered: No Limit

Geographical Preferences

International
No Preference

Industry Preferences

Communications and Media
Commercial Communications
Radio & TV Broadcasting

Internet Specific
Internet

Medical/Health
Diagnostic Services
Disposable Med. Products

Consumer Related
Entertainment and Leisure
Retail
Computer Stores
Franchises(NEC)
Food/Beverage
Consumer Products
Consumer Services
Education Related

Industrial/Energy
Factory Automation
Machinery

Financial Services
Financial Services
Real Estate

Business Serv.
Distribution
Consulting Services

Manufact.
Publishing

Agr/Forestr/Fish
Agriculture related

Additional Information
Year Founded: 1974
Current Activity Level : Actively seeking new investments
Method of Compensation: Function primarily in service area, receive contingent fee in cash or equity

SPROUT GROUP

3000 Sand Hill Road
Building 3, Suite 170
Menlo Park, CA 94025
Phone: 650-234-2700
Fax: 650-234-2779
Website: www.sproutgroup.com

See New York for full listing.

ST. PAUL VENTURE CAPITAL, INC.

Three Lagoon Drive
Suite 130
Redwood City, CA 94065-1566
Phone: 650-596-5630
Fax: 650-596-5711
Website: www.stpaulvc.com

See Minnesota for full listing.

STARTER FLUID

633 Battery St
Suite 110
San Francisco, CA 94111
Phone: 415-291-9535
Fax: 415-291-9534
Website: www.starterfluid.com

Management and Staff
Robert von Goeben, Managing Director

Type of Firm
Private Firm Investing Own Capital

Project Preferences

Type of Financing Preferred:
Seed
Startup

Size of Investments Considered
Min Size of Investment Considered (000s): $100
Max Size of Investment Considered (000s): $1,000

Geographical Preferences

United States
Northern California
West Coast

Industry Preferences

Communications and Media
Wireless Communications

Computer Software
Computer Services
Software
Systems Software
Applications Software

Internet Specific
E-Commerce Technology
Internet
Web Aggregration/Portals

Additional Information
Capital Under Management: $32,000,000
Current Activity Level : Actively seeking new investments
Method of Compensation: Return on investment is of primary concern, do not charge fees

STARTING POINT PARTNERS

666 Portofino Lane
Foster City, CA 94404
Phone: 650-722-1035
Website: www.startingpointpartners.com

Other Offices

733 S. Daniel Way
San Jose, CA 95128

Management and Staff
Alex Yu, General Partner
John Chang, General Partner
Karen Ha, General Partner
Mark Armenante, General Partner
Peng Ong, General Partner
Sonia Bhanot, General Partner
Tim Guleri, General Partner
Vivek Mehra, General Partner

Type of Firm
Private Equity Advisor or Fund of Fund Mgr

Project Preferences

Type of Financing Preferred:
Early Stage

Size of Investments Considered
Min Size of Investment Considered (000s): $200
Max Size of Investment Considered (000s): $1,000

Additional Information
Current Activity Level : Actively seeking new investments

STRATOS VENTURES LTD OY

4445 Eastgate Mall
Second Floor
San Diego, CA 92121
Phone: 858 812 20 66
Fax: 858 812 2001
Website: www.stratosventures.com

See Foreign Venture Capital Firms for full listing.

SUMMIT PARTNERS

499 Hamilton Avenue
Suite 200
Palo Alto, CA 94301
Phone: 650-321-1166
Fax: 650-321-1188
Website: www.summitpartners.com

See Massachusetts for full listing.

SUN VALLEY VENTURES

1445 5th Street
Suite A
Santa Monica, CA 90401
Phone: 310-656-1164
Fax: 310-394-2403

Other Offices

160 Second Street
Ketchum, ID 83340
Phone: 208-726-5005
Fax: 208-726-5094

Management and Staff
Daniel Styles

Whom to Contact
Daniel Styles

Type of Firm
Private Firm Investing Own Capital

Project Preferences

Role in Financing:
Prefer role as deal originator but will also invest in deals created by others

Type of Financing Preferred:
Control-block Purchases
Leveraged Buyout
Second Stage Financing
Special Situation

Size of Investments Considered
Min Size of Investment Considered (000s): $5,000
Max Size of Investment Considered: No Limit

Geographical Preferences

United States
All U.S.

Canada
All Canada

Industry Preferences

Computer Software
Computer Services

Internet Specific
Internet

Semiconductors/Other Elect.
Sensors

Medical/Health
Diagnostic Test Products
Disposable Med. Products

Consumer Related
Entertainment and Leisure
Franchises(NEC)
Food/Beverage
Consumer Products
Consumer Services
Hotels and Resorts
Education Related

Industrial/Energy
Materials
Factory Automation
Machinery
Environmental Related

Financial Services
Financial Services
Real Estate

Business Serv.
Distribution

Manufact.
Office Automation Equipmt
Publishing

Additional Information
Year Founded: 1994
Capital Under Management: $10,000,000
Current Activity Level : Actively seeking new investments
Method of Compensation: Return on invest. most important, but chg. closing fees, service fees, etc.

SUNDANCE VENTURE PARTNERS, L.P.

100 Clocktower Place
Suite 130
Carmel, CA 93923
Phone: 831-625-6500
Fax: 831-625-6590

Other Offices

400 East Van Buren
Suite 750
Phoenix, AZ 85004
Phone: 602-252-3441
Fax: 602-252-1450

Management and Staff
Gregory Anderson, General Partner

Type of Firm
SBIC Not elsewhere classified

Industry Association Membership
Natl assoc of Small Bus. Inv. Co (NASBIC)
Western Association of Venture Capitalists (WAVC)

Project Preferences

Role in Financing:
Prefer role as deal originator but will also invest in deals created by others

Type of Financing Preferred:
First Stage Financing
Leveraged Buyout
Mezzanine
Second Stage Financing
Special Situation

Size of Investments Considered
Min Size of Investment Considered (000s): $800
Max Size of Investment Considered: No Limit

Geographical Preferences

United States
Southwest
West Coast

Additional Information
Name of Most Recent Fund: Sundance Ventures
Most Recent Fund Was Raised: 01/01/1993
Year Founded: 1989
Capital Under Management: $25,000,000
Current Activity Level : Actively seeking new investments
Method of Compensation: Return on investment is of primary concern, do not charge fees

---

SUNWESTERN INVESTMENT GROUP

Plaza del Mar
12520 High Bluff Drive
San Diego, CA 92130
Phone: 619-259-8100
Fax: 619-259-0470

See Texas for full listing.

SUTTER HILL VENTURES

755 Page Mill Road
Suite A-200
Palo Alto, CA 94304
Phone: 650-493-5600
Fax: 650-858-1854
Website: www.shv.com

Management and Staff
David Anderson, Managing Director
G. Leonard Baker, Managing Director
Gregory Sands, Managing Director
Jim Gaither, Managing Director
Jim White, Venture Partner
Paul Wythes, Founding Partner
Tench Coxe, Managing Director
William Younger, Managing Director

Type of Firm
Private Firm Investing Own Capital

Industry Association Membership
National Venture Capital Association (NVCA)
Western Association of Venture Capitalists (WAVC)

Project Preferences

Role in Financing:
Prefer role as deal originator but will also invest in deals created by others

Type of Financing Preferred:
First Stage Financing
Second Stage Financing
Seed
Start-up Financing

Size of Investments Considered
Min Size of Investment Considered (000s): $100
Max Size of Investment Considered: No Limit

Geographical Preferences

United States
All U.S.

Industry Preferences

(% based on actual investment)

Computer Software and Services	22.0%
Internet Specific	21.7%
Communications and Media	17.1%
Computer Hardware	10.8%
Biotechnology	8.4%
Medical/Health	8.0%
Semiconductors/Other Elect.	4.7%
Other Products	3.7%

Industrial/Energy	2.0%
Consumer Related	1.5%

Additional Information
Year Founded: 1962
Capital Under Management: $450,000,000
Current Activity Level : Actively seeking new investments
Method of Compensation: Return on investment is of primary concern, do not charge fees

SWANDER PACE CAPITAL

345 California Street
Suite 2500
San Francisco, CA 94104
Phone: 415-477-8500
Fax: 415-477-8510
Website: www.spcap.com

Management and Staff
Andrew Richards, Managing Director
J.B. Handley, Managing Director
Mark Poff, Vice President
Scott Hackenberg, Vice President
Shawn Hecht, Managing Director

Type of Firm
Private Firm Investing Own Capital

Industry Association Membership
National Venture Capital Association (NVCA)

Project Preferences

Role in Financing:
Prefer role as deal originator but will also invest in deals created by others

Type of Financing Preferred:
Leveraged Buyout
Second Stage Financing

Size of Investments Considered
Min Size of Investment Considered (000s): $5,000
Max Size of Investment Considered: No Limit

Geographical Preferences

United States
All U.S.
All U.S.

Industry Preferences

(% based on actual investment)

Internet Specific	67.0%
Consumer Related	19.9%
Computer Software and Services	13.1%

Additional Information
Name of Most Recent Fund: Swander Pace Capital Fund, L.P.
Most Recent Fund Was Raised: 09/30/1997
Year Founded: 1995
Capital Under Management: $85,000,000
Current Activity Level : Actively seeking new investments
Method of Compensation: Return on invest. most important, but chg. closing fees, service fees, etc.

SYBASE, INC.

6475 Christie Avenue
Emeryville, CA 94608
Phone: 510-922-0729
Fax: 510-658-4766
Website: www.sybase.com

Management and Staff
John Chen, Chief Executive Officer
Pieter Vandervorst, Chief Financial Officer

Type of Firm
Non-Financial Corp. Affiliate or Subsidiary

Project Preferences

Role in Financing:
Prefer role in deals created by others

Type of Financing Preferred:
Balanced
Early Stage
Expansion
First Stage Financing
Second Stage Financing

Size of Investments Considered
Min Size of Investment Considered (000s): $1,000
Max Size of Investment Considered (000s): $5,000

Geographical Preferences

United States
All U.S.

Canada
All Canada

International
Australia
France
Germany
Italy
Latin America
Spain
United Kingdom

Industry Preferences

Computer Software
Software
Systems Software
Applications Software
Artificial Intelligence

Internet Specific
E-Commerce Technology
Internet
Web Aggregration/Portals

Additional Information
Year Founded: 1999
Capital Under Management: $50,000,000
Current Activity Level : Actively seeking new investments
Method of Compensation: Return on investment is of primary concern, do not charge fees

SYCAMORE VENTURES

81 Langton Street
Suite 9
San Francisco, CA 94103
Phone: 415-558-8229
Fax: 415-558-8751
Website: www.sycamorevc.com

See New Jersey for full listing.

SYNERGY PARTNERS

535 Middlefield Road
Suite 230
Menlo Park, CA 94025
Phone: 650-322-3475
Fax: 650-326-3735

Management and Staff
Allan Johnston, General Partner
Rob Okun, General Partner

Type of Firm
Private Equity Advisor or Fund of Fund Mgr

Project Preferences

Role in Financing:
Will function either as deal originator or investor in deals created by others

Type of Financing Preferred:
Balanced
Expansion

Size of Investments Considered
Min Size of Investment Considered (000s): $50
Max Size of Investment Considered (000s): $4,000

Geographical Preferences
United States
All U.S.

Industry Preferences
(% based on actual investment)

Medical/Health	93.3%
Internet Specific	2.7%
Biotechnology	2.6%
Industrial/Energy	1.0%
Other Products	0.5%

Additional Information
Year Founded: 1985
Capital Under Management: $28,000,000
Current Activity Level : Actively seeking new investments
Method of Compensation: Return on investment is of primary concern, do not charge fees

SYNOPSYS, INC.

700 East Middlefield Road
MVA-23
Mountain View, CA 94043
Phone: 650-584-1481
Website: www.synopsys.com/corporate/venture.html

Management and Staff
Michael O'Brien, Vice President

Whom to Contact
Harisch Sood

Type of Firm
Business Development Fund

Project Preferences
Type of Financing Preferred:
Early Stage
Expansion
First Stage Financing
Later Stage
Second Stage Financing
Seed
Startup

Size of Investments Considered
Min Size of Investment Considered (000s): $500
Max Size of Investment Considered (000s): $5,000

Industry Preferences
(% based on actual investment)

Semiconductors/Other Elect.	72.3%
Computer Software and Services	20.2%
Computer Hardware	7.4%

Additional Information
Name of Most Recent Fund: Synopsys, Inc. (Corporate Fund)
Most Recent Fund Was Raised: 04/01/1998
Year Founded: 1998
Capital Under Management: $40,000,000
Current Activity Level : Actively seeking new investments
Method of Compensation: Return on investment is of primary concern, do not charge fees

TA ASSOCIATES, INC.

70 Willow Road
Suite 100
Menlo Park, CA 94025
Phone: 650-328-1210
Fax: 650-326-4933
Website: www.ta.com

See Massachusetts for full listing.

TAYLOR & TURNER

220 Montgomery St.
Penthouse 10
San Francisco, CA 94104-3402
Phone: 415-398-6325
Fax: 415-398-3220

Type of Firm
Mgt. Consulting Firm

Project Preferences
Role in Financing:
Prefer role as deal originator

Type of Financing Preferred:
Control-block Purchases
First Stage Financing
Leveraged Buyout
Seed
Special Situation
Start-up Financing

Size of Investments Considered
Min Size of Investment Considered (000s): $300
Max Size of Investment Considered (000s): $500

Geographical Preferences
United States
West Coast

Industry Preferences
Communications and Media
Radio & TV Broadcasting
Telecommunications
Data Communications
Satellite Microwave Comm.

Computer Hardware
Computer Graphics and Dig
Integrated Turnkey System

Computer Software
Systems Software
Applications Software
Artificial Intelligence

Medical/Health
Diagnostic Services
Diagnostic Test Products
Drug/Equipmt Delivery
Other Therapeutic
Disposable Med. Products

Consumer Related
Education Related

Additional Information
Name of Most Recent Fund: Rotan Mosle Tech. Part. - Merge W/ Rotmos
Most Recent Fund Was Raised: 10/01/1983
Year Founded: 1991
Capital Under Management: $18,000,000
Current Activity Level : Reducing investment activity
Method of Compensation: Return on investment is of primary concern, do not charge fees

TECHFARM (AKA:TECHFUND CAPITAL)

200 West Evelyn Avenue
Suite 100
Mountain View, CA 94041
Phone: 650-934-0900
Fax: 650-934-0910
Website: www.techfarm.com

Other Offices

One Bowdoin Square
10th Floor
Boston, MA 02114
Phone: 617-742-7707
Fax: 617-742-7709

Management and Staff

Gordon Cambell, General Partner
James Whims, Partner
Jeffery Grammer, Partner
Koji Morihiro, Partner
Kurt Keilhacker, Partner
Laura Onopchenko, Partner
Mark Louie, Partner
Stephen Meyer, Partner

Type of Firm

Private Firm Investing Own Capital

Project Preferences

Type of Financing Preferred:

Early Stage
Seed

Industry Preferences

(% based on actual investment)

Communications and Media	30.7%
Computer Hardware	26.0%
Internet Specific	25.5%
Computer Software and Services	15.2%
Semiconductors/Other Elect.	2.6%

Additional Information

Year Founded: 1997
Capital Under Management: $93,000,000
Current Activity Level : Actively seeking new investments

TECHNO-VENTURE CO. (JAPAN)

2465 East Bayshore Boulevard
Suite 348
Palo Alto, CA 94303
Phone: 650-565-8296
Fax: 650-565-8295
Website: www.techno-venture.com

See Foreign Venture Capital Firms for full listing.

TECHNOLOGY CROSSOVER VENTURES

575 High Street
Suite 400
Palo Alto, CA 94301
Phone: 650-614-8200
Fax: 650-614-8222
Website: www.tcv.com

Other Offices

160 West 86th Street
Suite 12B
New York, NY 10024
Phone: 212-277-3900
Fax: 212-277-3901

56 Main Street
Suite 210
Millburn, NJ 07041
Phone: 973-476-5320
Fax: 973-476-5323

Management and Staff

A. Brooke Seawell, General Partner
Carla Newell, General Partner
Chris Nawn, General Partner
Donna Smolens, General Partner
Henry Feinberg, Venture Partner
Jake Reynolds, General Partner
Jay Hoag, General Partner
Marc Tesler, Venture Partner
Mike Linnert, General Partner
Rick Kimball, General Partner
Robert Bensky, Chief Financial Officer
Robert Hensley, General Partner
Tom Newby, General Partner

Type of Firm

Private Firm Investing Own Capital

Industry Association Membership

National Venture Capital Association (NVCA)
Western Association of Venture Capitalists (WAVC)

Project Preferences

Role in Financing:

Prefer role as deal originator but will also invest in deals created by others

Type of Financing Preferred:

First Stage Financing
Mezzanine
Second Stage Financing
Start-up Financing

Size of Investments Considered

Min Size of Investment Considered (000s): $5,000
Max Size of Investment Considered (000s): $50,000

Industry Preferences

(% based on actual investment)

Internet Specific	46.4%
Computer Software and Services	26.9%
Communications and Media	14.5%
Computer Hardware	4.7%
Other Products	4.1%
Consumer Related	2.9%
Semiconductors/Other Elect.	0.4%

Additional Information

Name of Most Recent Fund: TCV II, L.P.
Most Recent Fund Was Raised: 10/01/1996
Year Founded: 1995
Capital Under Management: $2,415,900,000
Current Activity Level : Actively seeking new investments
Method of Compensation: Return on investment is of primary concern, do not charge fees

TECHNOLOGY FUNDING

2000 Alameda de las Pulgas
Suite 250
San Mateo, CA 94403
Phone: 650-345-2200
Fax: 650-345-1797

Other Offices

2000 Alameda de las Pulgas
Suite 250
San Mateo, CA 94403
Phone: 415-345-2200

Management and Staff
Charles Kokesh, Managing Partner
Gregory George, General Partner
Peter Bernardoni, Partner
Thomas Toy, Managing Director

Type of Firm
Private Firm Investing Own Capital

Industry Association Membership
Western Association of Venture Capitalists (WAVC)

Project Preferences

Role in Financing:
Prefer role as deal originator but will also invest in deals created by others

Type of Financing Preferred:
First Stage Financing
Mezzanine
Second Stage Financing

Size of Investments Considered
Min Size of Investment Considered (000s): $500
Max Size of Investment Considered (000s): $2,000

Geographical Preferences

United States
All U.S.

Industry Preferences

(% based on actual investment)

Biotechnology	19.7%
Medical/Health	13.9%
Computer Hardware	13.6%
Industrial/Energy	13.6%
Computer Software and Services	10.8%
Internet Specific	10.4%
Semiconductors/Other Elect.	7.9%
Communications and Media	7.7%
Other Products	2.5%

Additional Information
Name of Most Recent Fund: Technology Funding Venture Partners VI, L.P.
Most Recent Fund Was Raised: 01/01/1997
Year Founded: 1979
Capital Under Management: $315,000,000
Current Activity Level : Actively seeking new investments
Method of Compensation: Return on investment is of primary concern, do not charge fees

TECHNOLOGY PARTNERS

550 University Ave.
Palo Alto, CA 94301
Phone: 650-289-9000
Website: www.technologypartners.com

Other Offices

1550 Tiburon Boulevard
Belvedere Tiburon, CA 94920
Phone: 415-435-1935

Management and Staff
Ira Ehrenpreis, General Partner
J.E. Ardell, General Partner
Jason Yoropoulos, Partner
Lisa Buyer, General Partner
Roger Quy, General Partner
Sheila Mutter, Principal
William Hart, General Partner

Type of Firm
Private Firm Investing Own Capital

Industry Association Membership
National Venture Capital Association (NVCA)
Western Association of Venture Capitalists (WAVC)

Project Preferences

Role in Financing:
Prefer role as deal originator

Type of Financing Preferred:
Early Stage
First Stage Financing
Joint Ventures
Later Stage
Mezzanine
Second Stage Financing
Startup

Size of Investments Considered
Min Size of Investment Considered (000s): $1,000
Max Size of Investment Considered (000s): $20,000

Geographical Preferences

United States
West Coast

Industry Preferences

(% based on actual investment)

Medical/Health	22.2%
Internet Specific	21.7%
Communications and Media	16.9%
Consumer Related	14.8%
Computer Hardware	11.1%
Computer Software and Services	9.7%
Biotechnology	2.0%
Semiconductors/Other Elect.	1.7%

Additional Information
Name of Most Recent Fund: Technology Partners Fund VI, L.P.
Most Recent Fund Was Raised: 07/06/1998
Year Founded: 1984
Capital Under Management: $400,000,000
Current Activity Level : Actively seeking new investments
Method of Compensation: Return on investment is of primary concern, do not charge fees

TELECOM ITALIA VENTURES

633 Battery
Suite 640
San Francisco, CA 94111
Phone: 415-399-6558
Fax: 415-399-6565
Website: www.tiventures.com

Management and Staff
Anna Duce, President
Claudia LaRosa, Vice President
Herve Pluche, President
Ian Foley, Vice President

Type of Firm
Non-Financial Corp. Affiliate or Subsidiary

Project Preferences

Type of Financing Preferred:
Balanced

Geographical Preferences

International
All International

Industry Preferences

(% based on actual investment)

Communications and Media	37.0%
Internet Specific	36.8%
Computer Software and Services	26.2%

Additional Information
Year Founded: 2000
Current Activity Level : Actively seeking new investments

TELESOFT PARTNERS

222 Sutter Street
8th Floor
San Francisco, CA 94108
Phone: 415-274-4518
Fax: 415-274-4545
Website: www.telesoftvc.com

Management and Staff
Al Howard, Chief Financial Officer
Arjun Gupta, Chief Executive Officer

Type of Firm
Private Firm Investing Own Capital

Industry Association Membership
Natl assoc of Small Bus. Inv. Co (NASBIC)

Project Preferences

Type of Financing Preferred:
Early Stage
Expansion
Start-up Financing

Size of Investments Considered
Min Size of Investment Considered (000s): $1,000
Max Size of Investment Considered (000s): $5,000

Geographical Preferences

United States
All U.S.

Industry Preferences

(% based on actual investment)

Semiconductors/Other Elect.	28.8%
Communications and Media	28.8%
Internet Specific	27.2%
Computer Software and Services	12.0%
Computer Hardware	3.1%

Additional Information
Name of Most Recent Fund: TeleSoft Partners, L.P.
Most Recent Fund Was Raised: 07/30/1997
Year Founded: 1997
Capital Under Management: $24,000,000
Current Activity Level : Actively seeking new investments

TELIA BUSINESS INNOVATION AB

Building 4, Suit 230
3000 Sand Hill Road
Menlo Park, CA 94025
Phone: 650 854 8070
Fax: 650 854 4961
Website: www.businessinovation.telia.se

See Foreign Venture Capital Firms for full listing.

TELOS VENTURE PARTNERS

2350 Mission College Boulevard
Suite 1070
Santa Clara, CA 95054
Phone: 408-982-5800
Fax: 408-982-5880
Website: www.telosvp.com

Other Offices

Ackerstein Building
103 Medinat Ha'yehudim St.
Herzelia, Israel 46766
Phone: 972-9957-1002
Fax: 972-9957-1675

Management and Staff
Athanasios Kalelos, General Partner
Bruce Bourbon, Managing Partner
Paul Asel, General Partner

Whom to Contact
Paul Asel
Shari Rooney

Type of Firm
Private Firm Investing Own Capital

Industry Association Membership
National Venture Capital Association (NVCA)
Western Association of Venture Capitalists (WAVC)

Project Preferences

Role in Financing:
Prefer role as deal originator but will also invest in deals created by others

Type of Financing Preferred:
First Stage Financing
Research and Development
Second Stage Financing
Start-up Financing

Geographical Preferences

United States
All U.S.

Industry Preferences

(% based on actual investment)

Internet Specific	33.3%
Computer Software and Services	27.5%
Semiconductors/Other Elect.	20.2%
Computer Hardware	9.4%
Communications and Media	7.4%
Other Products	2.2%

Additional Information
Name of Most Recent Fund: TVP1 (AKA: Telos Venture Partners)
Most Recent Fund Was Raised: 02/01/1996
Year Founded: 1996
Capital Under Management: $60,000,000
Current Activity Level : Actively seeking new investments
Method of Compensation: Return on investment is of primary concern, do not charge fees

THIRD MILLENNIUM VENTURE CAPITAL, LTD.

P.O. Box 1123
Los Altos, CA 94023
Phone: 650-941-0336

Other Offices

5733 West Grover Street
Chicago, IL 60630

Management and Staff
John Koza, President
Martin Keane, Vice President

Type of Firm
Private Firm Investing Own Capital

Project Preferences

Role in Financing:
Prefer role as deal originator but will also invest in deals created by others

Type of Financing Preferred:
First Stage Financing
Research and Development
Second Stage Financing
Seed
Start-up Financing

Size of Investments Considered
Min Size of Investment Considered (000s): $300
Max Size of Investment Considered (000s): $500

Geographical Preferences
International
No Preference

Industry Preferences
Computer Other
Computer Related

Industrial/Energy
Factory Automation
Robotics

Additional Information
Name of Most Recent Fund: Third Millennium Venture
Most Recent Fund Was Raised: 01/01/1992
Year Founded: 1987
Capital Under Management: $1,600,000
Current Activity Level : Actively seeking new investments
Method of Compensation: Return on investment is of primary concern, do not charge fees

---

THOMA CRESSEY EQUITY PARTNERS

One Embarcadero Centre
Suite 2930
San Francisco, CA 94111
Phone: 415-263-3660
Fax: 415-392-6480
Website: www.thomacressey.com

See Illinois for full listing.

THOMAS WEISEL PARTNERS, LLC

600 Montgomery Street
34th Floor
San Francisco, CA 94111
Phone: 415-364-2500
Fax: 415-364-2695
Website: www.tweisel.com

Other Offices
390 Park Avenue
17th Floor
New York, NY 10022
Phone: 212-271-3700
Fax: 212-271-3610

Management and Staff
Alan Menkes, Managing Partner
Daniel S. Dross, Partner
Derek Lemke-von Ammon, General Partner
Gregory White, Partner
James Streator, Partner
Keith Oster, Partner
Rick Beatty, Partner
Thomas Nilsson, Partner

Type of Firm
Investment/Merchant Bank Subsid/Affil

Industry Preferences
(% based on actual investment)

Internet Specific	33.9%
Other Products	18.7%
Computer Software and Services	14.9%
Semiconductors/Other Elect.	13.5%
Communications and Media	10.0%
Medical/Health	4.4%
Computer Hardware	4.3%
Consumer Related	0.3%

Additional Information
Year Founded: 1999
Current Activity Level : Actively seeking new investments

THOMPSON CLIVE & PARTNERS LIMITED

3000 Sand Hill Road
Building One Suite 185
Menlo Park, CA 94025
Phone: 650 854-0314
Fax: 650 854-0670
Website: www.tcvc.com

See Foreign Venture Capital Firms for full listing.

THOMPSON CLIVE, INC.

3000 Sand Hill Road
Building #1, Suite 185
Menlo Park, CA 94025-7102
Phone: 650-854-0314
Fax: 650-854-0670
Website: www.tcvc.com

Other Offices
24 Old Bond Street
London, United Kingdom W1X 3DA
Phone: 44-71-491-4809
Fax: 44-71-493-9172

55, rue la Boetie
Paris, France 75008
Phone: 33-1-4413-3606
Fax: 33-1-4413-3746

Management and Staff
Greg Ennis, Managing Director
Michelle Stecklein, Managing Director

Whom to Contact
Nat Hone

Type of Firm
Private Firm Investing Own Capital

Industry Association Membership
Western Association of Venture Capitalists (WAVC)

Project Preferences
Role in Financing:
Prefer role as deal originator but will also invest in deals created by others

Type of Financing Preferred:
First Stage Financing
Leveraged Buyout
Mezzanine
Second Stage Financing
Special Situation
Start-up Financing

Size of Investments Considered
Min Size of Investment Considered (000s): $500
Max Size of Investment Considered (000s): $2,000

Geographical Preferences
United States
All U.S.

Canada
Western Canada

International
Bermuda
France
Germany
Italy
Spain
United Kingdom

Industry Preferences

Communications and Media
Commercial Communications
Telecommunications
Data Communications

Computer Hardware
Computers
Mainframes / Scientific
Mini and Personal/Desktop
Computer Graphics and Dig
Integrated Turnkey System
Disk Relat. Memory Device

Computer Software
Computer Services
Systems Software
Applications Software
Artificial Intelligence

Internet Specific
Internet

Semiconductors/Other Elect.
Electronic Components
Sensors

Biotechnology
Biotechnology

Medical/Health
Medical/Health
Medical Products

Consumer Related
Education Related

Industrial/Energy
Industrial Products
Materials
Robotics
Environmental Related

Manufact.
Office Automation Equipmt

Additional Information
Year Founded: 1977
Capital Under Management: $300,000,000
Current Activity Level : Actively seeking new investments
Method of Compensation: Return on investment is of primary concern, do not charge fees

---

THORNER VENTURES

P.O. Box 830
Larkspur, CA 94977-0830
Phone: 415-925-9304
Fax: 415-461-5855

Management and Staff
Oscar Fuddy, Partner
Tom Thorner, General Partner

Whom to Contact
Tom Thorner

Type of Firm
Private Firm Investing Own Capital

Project Preferences

Role in Financing:
Prefer role as deal originator but will also invest in deals created by others

Type of Financing Preferred:
First Stage Financing
Mezzanine
Second Stage Financing
Seed
Special Situation
Start-up Financing

Size of Investments Considered
Min Size of Investment Considered (000s): $100
Max Size of Investment Considered (000s): $300

Geographical Preferences

International
No Preference

Industry Preferences

Computer Software
Systems Software
Applications Software

Internet Specific
Internet

Semiconductors/Other Elect.
Semiconductor
Laser Related

Biotechnology
Biotechnology

Medical/Health
Diagnostic Services
Diagnostic Test Products
Drug/Equipmt Delivery
Medical Products
Pharmaceuticals

Financial Services
Financial Services

Additional Information
Year Founded: 1981
Capital Under Management: $10,000,000
Current Activity Level : Actively seeking new investments
Method of Compensation: Return on investment is of primary concern, do not charge fees

---

THREE ARCH PARTNERS

2800 Sand Hill Road
Suite 270
Menlo Park, CA 94025
Phone: 650-854-5550
Fax: 650-854-9880
Website: www.threearchpartners.com

Management and Staff
Jeffrey Bird, Partner
Mark Wan, Partner
Michael Kaplan, Partner
Richard Lin, Partner
Thomas Fogarty, Partner
William Harrington, Partner
Wilfred Jaeger, Partner

Type of Firm
Private Firm Investing Own Capital

Project Preferences

Role in Financing:
Prefer role as deal originator but will also invest in deals created by others

Type of Financing Preferred:
First Stage Financing
Seed
Start-up Financing

Geographical Preferences

United States
All U.S.

Industry Preferences

(% based on actual investment)

Medical/Health	69.1%
Internet Specific	14.6%
Biotechnology	8.1%
Communications and Media	5.7%
Computer Software and Services	1.9%
Other Products	0.6%

Additional Information
Name of Most Recent Fund: Three Arch Associates
Most Recent Fund Was Raised: 03/31/2000
Year Founded: 1993
Capital Under Management: $292,000,000
Current Activity Level : Actively seeking new investments
Method of Compensation: Return on investment is of primary concern, do not charge fees

---

TI CAPITAL (AKA: TECHNOLOGY & INTERNET CAPITAL)

9200 Sunset Boulevard
Penthouse 2
Los Angeles, CA 90069
Phone: 310-246-9666
Fax: 310-556-4636
E-mail: infor@ticapital.com
Website: www.ticapital.com

Management and Staff
Aref Mikati, Chief Operating Officer
Ziad Ghandour, President, Founder

Type of Firm
Private Firm Investing Own Capital

Geographical Preferences

International
All International

Industry Preferences

Internet Specific
Internet

Additional Information
Current Activity Level : Actively seeking new investments

TICONDEROGA CAPITAL, INC. (FKA: DILLON READ VENTURE CAPITAL)

555 California Street
Suite 4360
San Francisco, CA 94104
Phone: 415-296-6343
Fax: 415-296-8956
Website: www.ticonderogacap.com

See Massachusetts for full listing.

TIMBERLINE VENTURE PARTNERS

3655 Torrance Ave.
Suite 345
Torrance, CA 90503-4810
Phone: 310-543-0408
Fax: 310-543-0308

See Washington for full listing.

TL VENTURES

The Annex Building
3110 Main Street
Santa Monica, CA 90405
Phone: 310-450-1800
Fax: 310-450-1806
Website: www.tlventures.com

See Pennsylvania for full listing.

TRELLIS HEALTH VENTURES, L.P.

One Sansome Street
Suite 2100
San Francisco, CA 94104
Phone: 415-951-4799
Fax: 415-951-4688

Type of Firm
Private Equity Advisor or Fund of Fund Mgr

Industry Association Membership
National Venture Capital Association (NVCA)

Additional Information
Year Founded: 1998
Capital Under Management: $10,000,000
Current Activity Level : Actively seeking new investments

TRIDENT CAPITAL

505 Hamilton Avenue
Suite 200
Palo Alto, CA 94301
Phone: 650-289-4400
Fax: 650-289-4444
Website: www.tridentcap.com

Other Offices

1001 Pennsylvania Avenue NW
Washington, DC 20004-2505
Phone: 202-347-2626
Fax: 202-393-4568

11150 Santa Monica Blvd.
Suite 320
Los Angeles, CA 90025
Phone: 310-444-3840
Fax: 310-444-3848

190 South LaSalle Street
Suite 2760
Chicago, IL 60603
Phone: 312-630-5500
Fax: 312-630-5501

200 Nyala Farms
Westport, CT 06880
Phone: 203-222-4594

Management and Staff
Bonnie Kennedy, Managing Director
Christopher Marshall, Managing Director
Donald Dixon, Managing Director
John Moragne, Managing Director
Peter Meekin, Managing Director
Robert McCormack, Managing Director
Rockwell Schnabel, Managing Director
Stephen Hall, Managing Director
Stephen Beitler, Managing Director
Talbott Simonds, Vice President
Todd Springer, Managing Director
Venetia Kontogouris, Managing Director

Whom to Contact
Venetia Kontopuris

Type of Firm
Private Firm Investing Own Capital

Industry Association Membership
National Venture Capital Association (NVCA)
Western Association of Venture Capitalists (WAVC)

Project Preferences

Role in Financing:
Prefer role as deal originator but will also invest in deals created by others

Type of Financing Preferred:
Acquisition
Balanced
Early Stage
Expansion
First Stage Financing
Later Stage
Leveraged Buyout
Second Stage Financing
Start-up Financing

Size of Investments Considered
Min Size of Investment Considered (000s): $30,000
Max Size of Investment Considered (000s): $30,000

Geographical Preferences

United States
All U.S.

Canada
All Canada

International
Europe

Industry Preferences

(% based on actual investment)

Internet Specific	51.9%
Computer Software and Services	27.7%
Other Products	9.0%
Communications and Media	7.3%
Semiconductors/Other Elect.	2.2%
Consumer Related	1.8%
Medical/Health	0.1%

Additional Information
Name of Most Recent Fund: Trident Capital Fund - IV
Most Recent Fund Was Raised: 09/01/1999
Year Founded: 1993
Capital Under Management: $1,339,000,000
Current Activity Level : Actively seeking new investments
Method of Compensation: Return on investment is of primary concern, do not charge fees

TRINITY VENTURES

3000 Sand Hill Road
Building Four Suite 160
Menlo Park, CA 94025
Phone: 650-854-9500
Fax: 650-854-9501
Website: www.trinityventures.com

Management and Staff
Augustus Tai, General Partner
Fred Wang, General Partner
James Shennan, General Partner
Kathy Murphy, Chief Financial Officer
Lawrence Orr, Managing Partner
Noel Fenton, General Partner
Timothy McAdam, General Partner
Tod Francis, General Partner

Type of Firm
Private Firm Investing Own Capital

Industry Association Membership
National Venture Capital Association (NVCA)
Western Association of Venture Capitalists (WAVC)

Project Preferences

Role in Financing:
Will function either as deal originator or investor in deals created by others

Type of Financing Preferred:
Early Stage

Size of Investments Considered
Min Size of Investment Considered (000s): $5,000
Max Size of Investment Considered (000s): $20,000

Geographical Preferences

United States
Mid Atlantic
Northeast
Northern California
Northwest
Rocky Mountain
West Coast

Industry Preferences

(% based on actual investment)

Internet Specific	36.2%
Other Products	18.4%
Computer Software and Services	17.8%
Communications and Media	12.0%
Consumer Related	6.7%
Semiconductors/Other Elect.	3.9%
Computer Hardware	3.1%
Medical/Health	1.8%
Industrial/Energy	0.1%

Additional Information
Name of Most Recent Fund: Trinity Ventures VII, LP
Most Recent Fund Was Raised: 10/01/1999
Year Founded: 1986
Capital Under Management: $1,100,000,000
Current Activity Level : Actively seeking new investments
Method of Compensation: Return on invest. most important, but chg. closing fees, service fees, etc.

TRIUNE CAPITAL

19925 Stevens Creek Blvd.
Suite 200
Cupertino, CA 95014
Phone: 310-284-6800
Fax: 310-284-3290

Type of Firm
Mgt. Consulting Firm

Project Preferences

Role in Financing:
Prefer role as deal originator but will also invest in deals created by others

Type of Financing Preferred:
Control-block Purchases
First Stage Financing
Mezzanine
Second Stage Financing
Special Situation
Start-up Financing

Size of Investments Considered
Min Size of Investment Considered (000s): $1,000
Max Size of Investment Considered: No Limit

Geographical Preferences

United States
West Coast

Industry Preferences

Communications and Media
Commercial Communications
Telecommunications
Data Communications

Computer Hardware
Computer Graphics and Dig
Disk Relat. Memory Device

Computer Software
Computer Services
Systems Software
Applications Software
Artificial Intelligence

Internet Specific
Internet

Semiconductors/Other Elect.
Electronics
Electronic Components
Semiconductor
Controllers and Sensors
Sensors
Circuit Boards
Component Testing Equipmt
Fiber Optics
Analytic/Scientific

Biotechnology
Industrial Biotechnology
Biotech Related Research
Biotech Related Research

Medical/Health
Medical/Health
Medical Diagnostics
Medical Therapeutics
Medical Products

Consumer Related
Retail
Computer Stores
Franchises(NEC)
Food/Beverage
Consumer Products
Consumer Services
Other Restaurants

Industrial/Energy
Alternative Energy
Energy Conservation Relat
Industrial Products
Environmental Related

Manufact.
Office Automation Equipmt

Additional Information
Year Founded: 1994
Current Activity Level : Actively seeking new investments
Method of Compensation: Function primarily in service area, receive contingent fee in cash or equity

TVM TECHNO VENTURE MANAGEMENT

100 Spear Street
Suite 1600
San Francisco, CA 94105
Phone: 415-344-0100
Fax: 415-344-0200
Website: www.tvmvc.com

See Foreign Venture Capital Firms for full listing.

TYCO VENTURES

313 Constitution Dr.
Menlo Park, CA 94025
Phone: 650-361-2041
Fax: 650-361-7665
Website: www.tyco.com

Management and Staff
Claude Sandroff, Principal
Mark Maciejewski, Managing Director
Michael Durkin, Managing Director
Richard Kashnow, President

Type of Firm
Non-Financial Corp. Affiliate or Subsidiary

Industry Association Membership
National Venture Capital Association (NVCA)

Additional Information
Current Activity Level : Actively seeking new investments

U.S. BANCORP PIPER JAFFRAY VENTURES, INC.

345 California Street
San Francisco, CA 94104
Phone: 415-984-4628
Fax: 415-984-4633
Website: www.piperjaffrayventures.com

See Minnesota for full listing.

U.S. VENTURE PARTNERS

2180 Sand Hill Road
Suite 300
Menlo Park, CA 94025
Phone: 650-854-9080
Fax: 650-854-3018
Website: www.usvp.com

Other Offices

7900 SE 28th Street
Suite 250,
Mercer Island, WA 98040
Phone: 206-236-5776
Fax: 206-236-5779

Management and Staff
Alan Kaganov, Venture Partner
Arati Prabhakar, Venture Partner
Dale Vogel, Venture Partner
David Liddle, General Partner
Geoffrey Baehr, General Partner
Irwin Federman, General Partner
Jason Green, General Partner
Jonathan Root, General Partner
Lucio Lanza, General Partner
Magdalena Yesil, General Partner
Marc Friend, General Partner
Michael Maher, Chief Financial Officer
Paul Matteucci, Venture Partner
Philip Young, General Partner
Philip Schlein, Venture Partner
Steven Krausz, General Partner
Stuart Phillips, General Partner
William Bowes, Founding Partner
Winston Fu, General Partner

Type of Firm
Private Firm Investing Own Capital

Industry Association Membership
National Venture Capital Association (NVCA)
Western Association of Venture Capitalists (WAVC)

Project Preferences

Type of Financing Preferred:
Early Stage
First Stage Financing
Later Stage
Second Stage Financing
Seed
Startup

Size of Investments Considered
Min Size of Investment Considered (000s): $500
Max Size of Investment Considered: No Limit

Geographical Preferences

United States
Northern California
Northwest
Rocky Mountain
West Coast

Industry Preferences

(% based on actual investment)

Internet Specific	20.9%
Computer Software and Services	18.2%
Communications and Media	15.2%
Consumer Related	12.0%
Semiconductors/Other Elect.	11.9%
Computer Hardware	9.0%
Medical/Health	8.7%
Biotechnology	3.3%

Other Products	0.4%
Industrial/Energy	0.2%

Additional Information
Name of Most Recent Fund: U.S. Venture Partners V, L.P.
Most Recent Fund Was Raised: 01/01/1996
Year Founded: 1981
Capital Under Management: $3,200,000,000
Current Activity Level : Actively seeking new investments
Method of Compensation: Return on invest. most important, but chg. closing fees, service fees, etc.

UNION VENTURE CORP.

445 South Figueroa Street
9th Floor
Los Angeles, CA 90071
Phone: 213-236-4092
Fax: 213-236-6329

Other Offices

445 South Figueroa Street
Los Angeles, CA 90071
Phone: 213-236-4092

Type of Firm
SBIC Not elsewhere classified

Industry Association Membership
Natl assoc of Small Bus. Inv. Co (NASBIC)

Project Preferences

Role in Financing:
Prefer role as deal originator but will also invest in deals created by others

Type of Financing Preferred:
Leveraged Buyout
Mezzanine
Second Stage Financing
Special Situation

Size of Investments Considered
Min Size of Investment Considered (000s): $300
Max Size of Investment Considered (000s): $500

Geographical Preferences

United States
All U.S.

Industry Preferences

Communications and Media
CATV & Pay TV Systems
Radio & TV Broadcasting
Telecommunications

Additional Information
Name of Most Recent Fund: Union Bank
Most Recent Fund Was Raised: 08/01/1987
Year Founded: 1967
Capital Under Management: $50,000,000
Current Activity Level : Reducing investment activity
Method of Compensation: Return on investment is of primary concern, do not charge fees

UTAH VENTURES II, L.P. (A.K.A. UNION VENTURES)

32511 Sea Island Drive
Dana Pt., CA 92629
Phone: 949-661-2861
Website: www.uven.com

See Utah for full listing.

VAN WAGONER CAPITAL MANAGEMENT

345 California Street
Suite 2450
San Francisco, CA 94104
Phone: 415-835-5000
Fax: 415-835-5050

Management and Staff
Bill Minor, Chief Financial Officer

Type of Firm
Private Firm Investing Own Capital

Industry Preferences

(% based on actual investment)

Internet Specific	45.4%
Computer Software and Services	17.4%
Communications and Media	17.4%
Semiconductors/Other Elect.	9.6%
Medical/Health	3.7%
Computer Hardware	3.4%
Other Products	1.9%
Biotechnology	1.3%

Additional Information
Year Founded: 1995
Current Activity Level : Actively seeking new investments

VANGUARD VENTURE PARTNERS

525 University Avenue
Suite 600
Palo Alto, CA 94301
Phone: 650-321-2900
Fax: 650-321-2902
Website: www.vanguardventures.com

Other Offices

1330 Post Oak Boulevard
Suite 1550
Houston, TX 77056
Phone: 713-877-1662
Fax: 713-877-8669

Management and Staff
Daniel Eilers, General Partner
Donald Wood, General Partner
Jack Gill, General Partner
Larry Schwerin, Partner
Laura Gwosden, Chief Financial Officer
Paul Slakey, Partner
Robert Ulrich, General Partner

Type of Firm
Private Firm Investing Own Capital

Industry Association Membership
Western Association of Venture Capitalists (WAVC)

Project Preferences

Role in Financing:
Prefer role as deal originator but will also invest in deals created by others

Type of Financing Preferred:
First Stage Financing
Seed
Start-up Financing

Size of Investments Considered
Min Size of Investment Considered (000s): $500
Max Size of Investment Considered (000s): $1,000

Geographical Preferences

United States
All U.S.

Industry Preferences

(% based on actual investment)

Communications and Media	25.5%
Medical/Health	18.6%
Internet Specific	18.4%
Semiconductors/Other Elect.	12.4%
Computer Hardware	10.3%
Computer Software and Services	9.7%
Biotechnology	3.5%
Other Products	1.1%
Industrial/Energy	0.6%

Additional Information

Name of Most Recent Fund: Vanguard VI
Most Recent Fund Was Raised: 06/01/1998
Year Founded: 1981
Capital Under Management: $15,900,000
Current Activity Level : Actively seeking new investments
Method of Compensation: Return on investment is of primary concern, do not charge fees

VANTAGEPOINT VENTURE PARTNERS

1001 Bayhill Drive
Suite 100
San Bruno, CA 94066
Phone: 650-866-3100
Fax: 650-869-6078
Website: www.vpvp.com

Other Offices

440 Madison Avenue
39th Floor
New York, NY 10022
Phone: 212-750-8220
Fax: 212-750-8223

Management and Staff

Alan Salzman, Founding Partner
Andrew Laszlo, Partner
David Carlick, Partner
J. Stephan Dolezalek, Partner
James Marver, Founding Partner
Jason Strober, Partner
John Kain, Principal
Judie Lucius, Chief Financial Officer
Ken Kharbanda, Partner
Manuel Henriquez, Partner
Matt Ocko, Partner
Paul Sherer, Partner
William Marshall, Partner

Type of Firm

Private Firm Investing Own Capital

Industry Association Membership

Western Association of Venture Capitalists (WAVC)

Project Preferences

Role in Financing:

Prefer role as deal originator but will also invest in deals created by others

Type of Financing Preferred:

Control-block Purchases
First Stage Financing
Mezzanine
Second Stage Financing
Special Situation
Start-up Financing

Geographical Preferences

United States

Northwest
Rocky Mountain
West Coast

Industry Preferences

(% based on actual investment)

Internet Specific	41.4%
Communications and Media	24.7%
Computer Software and Services	20.3%
Semiconductors/Other Elect.	9.3%
Computer Hardware	2.3%
Other Products	1.1%
Medical/Health	0.9%

Additional Information

Name of Most Recent Fund: VantagePoint Venture Partners
Most Recent Fund Was Raised: 08/01/1999
Year Founded: 1996
Capital Under Management: $2,500,000,000
Current Activity Level : Actively seeking new investments
Method of Compensation: Return on investment is of primary concern, do not charge fees

VECTOR CAPITAL

456 Montgomery Street
19th Floor
San Francisco, CA 94104
Phone: 415-293-5000
Fax: 415-293-5100
Website: www.vectorcapital.com

Management and Staff

Alex Frenkel, Chief Financial Officer
Alex Slusky, General Partner
Chris Nicholson, Principal

Type of Firm

Private Firm Investing Own Capital

Industry Association Membership

Western Association of Venture Capitalists (WAVC)

Project Preferences

Size of Investments Considered

Min Size of Investment Considered (000s): $5,000
Max Size of Investment Considered: No Limit

Industry Preferences

(% based on actual investment)

Internet Specific	64.0%
Computer Software and Services	36.0%

Additional Information

Name of Most Recent Fund: Vector Capital I
Most Recent Fund Was Raised: 12/31/1995
Year Founded: 1997
Capital Under Management: $190,000,000
Current Activity Level : Actively seeking new investments

VENCA MANAGEMENT

2295 Washington Street
San Francisco, CA 94115
Phone: 415-885-2100
Fax: 415-885-1410

Other Offices

7-14-11-104 Minami Aoyama
Minato-ku
Tokyo, Japan 108
Phone: 81-3-3486-1807
Fax: 81-3-3486-1068

Type of Firm

Private Firm Investing Own Capital

Project Preferences

Role in Financing:

Prefer role as deal originator but will also invest in deals created by others

Type of Financing Preferred:

First Stage Financing
Recapitalizations
Second Stage Financing
Start-up Financing

Size of Investments Considered
Min Size of Investment Considered (000s): $500
Max Size of Investment Considered (000s): $1,000

Geographical Preferences
United States
West Coast

Industry Preferences
Biotechnology
Biotechnology

Medical/Health
Diagnostic Test Products
Drug/Equipmt Delivery
Other Therapeutic
Pharmaceuticals

Additional Information
Name of Most Recent Fund: Venca II
Most Recent Fund Was Raised: 04/01/1986
Year Founded: 1983
Capital Under Management: $10,000,000
Current Activity Level : Actively seeking new investments
Method of Compensation: Return on investment is of primary concern, do not charge fees

---

VENGLOBAL CAPITAL

5201 Great America Parkway
Suite 320
Santa Clara, CA 95054
Phone: 408-982-2551
Fax: 408-982-2558

Management and Staff
Phil Mak, General Partner

Type of Firm
Private Firm Investing Own Capital

Project Preferences
Role in Financing:
Prefer role as deal originator but will also invest in deals created by others

Type of Financing Preferred:
First Stage Financing
Second Stage Financing
Seed

Geographical Preferences
United States
West Coast

Industry Preferences
(% based on actual investment)

Computer Software and Services	32.3%
Semiconductors/Other Elect.	22.7%
Internet Specific	18.9%
Communications and Media	15.0%
Medical/Health	11.1%

Additional Information
Year Founded: 1997
Capital Under Management: $20,000,000
Current Activity Level : Actively seeking new investments
Method of Compensation: Return on investment is of primary concern, do not charge fees

---

VENROCK ASSOCIATES

2494 SAnd Hill
Suite 200
Menlo Park, CA 94025
Phone: 650-561-9580
Fax: 650-561-9180
Website: www.venrock.com

See New York for full listing.

VENROCK ASSOCIATES

2494 SAnd Hill
Suite 200
Menlo Park, CA 94025
Phone: 650-561-9580
Fax: 650-561-9180
Website: www.venrock.com

See New York for full listing.

VENTANA GLOBAL

18881 Von Karman Avenue
Suite 1150
Irvine, CA 92612
Phone: 949-476-2204
Fax: 949-752-0223
Website: www.ventanaglobal.com

Other Offices

18881 Von Karman Ave
Suite 350
Irvine, CA 92715

Avenida Loma de la Palma 275
Suite Two
Mexico City, Mexico 05100
Phone: 52-5-259-4660
Fax: 52-5-259-5099

Rio Vista Towers
8880 Rio San Diego Drive
San Diego, CA 92108
Phone: 619-291-2757
Fax: 619-295-0189

Management and Staff
F.D. Townsen, Managing Partner
Thomas Gephart, Founder

Whom to Contact
Alvaro Alliende
Carlos de Rivas
Scott A. Burri

Type of Firm
Private Firm Investing Own Capital

Project Preferences
Role in Financing:
Prefer role as deal originator but will also invest in deals created by others

Type of Financing Preferred:
First Stage Financing
Mezzanine
Second Stage Financing
Seed
Special Situation
Start-up Financing

Size of Investments Considered
Min Size of Investment Considered (000s): $1,000
Max Size of Investment Considered: No Limit

Geographical Preferences
United States
Southwest

Industry Preferences
Communications and Media
CATV & Pay TV Systems
Telecommunications
Data Communications
Satellite Microwave Comm.
Other Communication Prod.

Computer Hardware
Computers
Mini and Personal/Desktop
Disk Relat. Memory Device

Internet Specific
Internet

Semiconductors/Other Elect.
Electronics
Electronic Components

Biotechnology
Biotechnology

Medical/Health
Diagnostic Services
Diagnostic Test Products
Other Therapeutic
Disposable Med. Products

Consumer Related
Consumer Products

Industrial/Energy
Alternative Energy
Energy Conservation Relat
Materials
Robotics
Environmental Related

Manufact.
Office Automation Equipmt

Additional Information
Name of Most Recent Fund: Technology Gateway Partnership
Most Recent Fund Was Raised: 01/01/1999
Year Founded: 1974
Capital Under Management: $230,000,000
Current Activity Level : Actively seeking new investments
Method of Compensation: Return on investment is of primary concern, do not charge fees

---

VENTURE CAPITAL FUND OF AMERICA, INC.

211 Fulton Street
Palo Alto, CA 94301
Phone: 650-321-1500
Website: www.vcfa.com

See New York for full listing.

VENTURE CATALYST

16868 Via del Campo Court
Suite 200
San Diego, CA 92127
Phone: 858-385-1000
Fax: 858-385-1001
Website: www.vcat.com

Other Offices

315 Queen Street
Alexandria, VA 22314
Phone: 703-684-1306
Fax: 703-684-1481

3420 Ocean Park Boulevard
Suite 3020
Santa Monica, CA 90405
Phone: 310-399-4059
Fax: 310-399-3431

Management and Staff
Dan Deakin, Chief Operating Officer
Don Speer, Chairman & CEO
Kevin McIntosh, Chief Financial Officer
Sanjay Sabnani, President

Type of Firm
Incubators

Project Preferences

Type of Financing Preferred:
Early Stage

Industry Preferences

Internet Specific
Internet

Additional Information
Current Activity Level : Actively seeking new investments

VENTURE FROGS, LLC

151 Alice B. Toklas Place
Suite 403
San Francisco, CA 94109
Phone: 415-440-7600
Fax: 415-440-9865
Website: www.venturefrogs.com

Management and Staff
Alfred Lin, General Partner
Tony Hsieh, General Partner

Type of Firm
Private Firm Investing Own Capital

Project Preferences

Size of Investments Considered
Min Size of Investment Considered (000s): $100
Max Size of Investment Considered (000s): $3,000

Industry Preferences

(% based on actual investment)

Internet Specific	87.9%
Computer Software and Services	10.4%
Consumer Related	1.7%

Additional Information
Year Founded: 1999
Capital Under Management: $27,000,000
Current Activity Level : Actively seeking new investments

VENTURE GROWTH ASSOCIATES

2479 East Bayshore St.
Suite 710
Palo Alto, CA 94303
Phone: 650-855-9100
Fax: 650-855-9104

Management and Staff
James Berdell
Robert Ledoux

Whom to Contact
James Berdell
Robert Ledoux

Type of Firm
Private Firm Investing Own Capital

Project Preferences

Role in Financing:
Prefer role as deal originator but will also invest in deals created by others

Type of Financing Preferred:
First Stage Financing
Leveraged Buyout
Mezzanine
Second Stage Financing

Size of Investments Considered
Min Size of Investment Considered (000s): $1,000
Max Size of Investment Considered: No Limit

Geographical Preferences

United States
West Coast

Industry Preferences

Communications and Media
Telecommunications
Data Communications

Computer Hardware
Computer Graphics and Dig

Computer Software
Computer Services
Systems Software
Applications Software

Semiconductors/Other Elect.
Electronics
Electronic Components
Semiconductor
Component Testing Equipmt

Biotechnology
Biotech Related Research
Biotech Related Research

Medical/Health
Medical Diagnostics
Diagnostic Services
Diagnostic Test Products
Medical Therapeutics
Other Therapeutic

Consumer Related
Computer Stores

Industrial/Energy
Factory Automation

Financial Services
Financial Services

Additional Information
Name of Most Recent Fund: Venture Growth Associates
Most Recent Fund Was Raised: 10/01/1983
Year Founded: 1982
Capital Under Management: $150,000,000
Current Activity Level : Actively seeking new investments
Method of Compensation: Return on investment is of primary concern, do not charge fees

VENTURE LAW GROUP

2800 Sand Hill Road
Menlo Park, CA 94025
Phone: 650-854-4488
Fax: 650-233-8386
Website: www.vlg.com

Type of Firm
Private Firm Investing Own Capital

Additional Information
Year Founded: 1999
Current Activity Level : Actively seeking new investments

VENTURE SELECT

2550 Hanover Street
Palo Alto, CA 94301
Phone: 408 280 2800
Fax: 408 280 2801
Website: www.venture-select.de

See Foreign Venture Capital Firms for full listing.

VENTURE STRATEGY PARTNERS

655 Third Street
San Francisco, CA 94107
Phone: 415-558-8600
Fax: 415-558-8686
Website: www.vspartners.com

Management and Staff
Anthony Conrad, Partner
Bob Hambrecht, Venture Partner
David Likins, Partner
Joanna Gallanter, Managing Director
Matt Crisp, Partner
Tony Kamin, Venture Partner
William Hambrecht, Venture Partner
William Rosenzweig, Venture Partner

Type of Firm
Private Firm Investing Own Capital

Industry Association Membership
National Venture Capital Association (NVCA)

Project Preferences

Role in Financing:
Prefer role as deal originator but will also invest in deals created by others

Type of Financing Preferred:
First Stage Financing
Seed
Start-up Financing

Geographical Preferences

United States
Northwest
Rocky Mountain
Southwest
West Coast

Industry Preferences

(% based on actual investment)

Internet Specific	89.4%
Computer Hardware	5.9%
Other Products	4.6%

Additional Information
Name of Most Recent Fund: Venture Strategy II (AKA VS-2)
Most Recent Fund Was Raised: 01/01/2000
Year Founded: 1996
Capital Under Management: $3,000,000
Current Activity Level : Actively seeking new investments
Method of Compensation: Return on invest. most important, but chg. closing fees, service fees, etc.

VENTURE TDF PTE LTD.

280 Second Street
Suite #120
Los Altos, CA 94022
Phone: 650-559-9688
Fax: 650-559-9689
Website: www.venturetdf.com

See Foreign Venture Capital Firms for full listing.

VERSANT VENTURES (FKA: PALLADIUM CAPITAL)

11150 Santa Monica Boulevard
Suite 1200
Los Angeles, CA 90025
Phone: 310-477-7678
Fax: 310-312-1868
Website: www.versantventures.com

Other Offices

3000 Sand Hill Road
Bldg 1, Ste 260
Menlo Park, CA 94025
Phone: 650-233-7877
Fax: 650-854-9513

450 Newport Drive Center
Suite 380
Newport Beach, CA 92660
Phone: 949-729-4500
Fax: 949-729-4501

Management and Staff
Erik Engelson, Venture Partner

Type of Firm
Private Firm Investing Own Capital

Industry Association Membership
National Venture Capital Association (NVCA)

Project Preferences

Type of Financing Preferred:
Early Stage

Geographical Preferences

United States
All U.S.
West Coast

International
Utd. Arab Em.

Industry Preferences

(% based on actual investment)

Medical/Health	53.8%
Internet Specific	20.6%
Biotechnology	15.9%
Computer Software and Services	7.5%
Other Products	2.1%

Additional Information

Name of Most Recent Fund: Versant Venture Capital I, L.P.
Most Recent Fund Was Raised: 12/03/1999
Year Founded: 1999
Capital Under Management: $250,000,000
Current Activity Level : Actively seeking new investments

VERTEX MANAGEMENT

Three Lagoon Drive
Suite 220
Redwood City, CA 94065
Phone: 650-591-9300
Fax: 650-591-5926
Website: www.vertexmgt.com

See Foreign Venture Capital Firms for full listing.

VERTICAL GROUP, THE

10600 North Pantau Avenue
Cupertino, CA 95014
Phone: 408-777-8817
Fax: 408-777-8617

See New Jersey for full listing.

VISA INTERNATIONAL

900 Metro Center Blvd.
Foster City, CA 94404-2172
Phone: 650-432-2469

Management and Staff

Todd Chaffe, Managing Director

Type of Firm

Non-Financial Corp. Affiliate or Subsidiary

Project Preferences

Type of Financing Preferred:
Balanced

Size of Investments Considered

Min Size of Investment Considered (000s): $3,000
Max Size of Investment Considered (000s): $5,000

Geographical Preferences

United States
All U.S.

Additional Information

Year Founded: 1999
Current Activity Level : Actively seeking new investments

VISION CAPITAL MANAGEMENT (FKA GLENWOOD CAPITAL)

One Bayshore Plaza; Suite 360
1350 Old Bayshore Hwy
Burlingame, CA 94010
Phone: 650-373-2720
Fax: 650-373-2727
Website: www.visioncap.com

Other Offices

10, Rue du Vieux-College
Geneva, Switzerland 1204
Phone: 41 22 312 3333
Fax: 41 22 312 3366

Management and Staff

Dag Syrrist, General Partner
Dag Tellefsen, Managing Partner
John Turner, General Partner
Sven Lingjaerde, General Partner

Whom to Contact

Sven Lingjaerde

Type of Firm

Investment/Merchant Bank Subsid/Affil

Industry Association Membership

European Venture Capital Association (EVCA)
Western Association of Venture Capitalists (WAVC)

Project Preferences

Role in Financing:
Will function either as deal originator or investor in deals created by others

Type of Financing Preferred:
Expansion
First Stage Financing
Second Stage Financing

Size of Investments Considered

Min Size of Investment Considered (000s): $2,000
Max Size of Investment Considered (000s): $8,000

Geographical Preferences

United States
Northern California

International
France
Germany
Sweden
United Kingdom

Industry Preferences

(% based on actual investment)

Internet Specific	28.5%
Computer Hardware	25.8%
Semiconductors/Other Elect.	25.4%
Computer Software and Services	13.1%
Communications and Media	5.6%
Industrial/Energy	1.6%

Additional Information

Name of Most Recent Fund: Vision Extension L.P.
Most Recent Fund Was Raised: 09/01/1999
Year Founded: 1997
Capital Under Management: $110,000,000
Current Activity Level : Actively seeking new investments
Method of Compensation: Return on investment is of primary concern, do not charge fees

VISTA CAPITAL CORP.

7716 Lookout Drive
La Jolla, CA 92037-3948
Phone: 619-453-0780
Website: www.vistacapital.com

Type of Firm
Private Firm Investing Own Capital

Project Preferences

Role in Financing:
Will function either as deal originator or investor in deals created by others

Type of Financing Preferred:
Control-block Purchases
First Stage Financing
Other
Special Situation

Size of Investments Considered
Min Size of Investment Considered (000s): $350
Max Size of Investment Considered: No Limit

Geographical Preferences

International
No Preference

Additional Information
Year Founded: 1977
Capital Under Management: $600,000
Current Activity Level : Inactive / Unknown
Method of Compensation: Return on invest. most important, but chg. closing fees, service fees, etc.

VITESSE SEMICONDUCTOR CORPORATION

741 Calle Plano
Camarillo, CA 93010
Phone: 805-388-3700
Fax: 805-987-5896
Website: www.vitesse.com

Type of Firm
Non-Financial Corp. Affiliate or Subsidiary

Project Preferences

Type of Financing Preferred:
Early Stage
Startup

Industry Preferences

Communications and Media
Communications and Media

Additional Information
Current Activity Level : Actively seeking new investments

VIVENTURES INC.

66, bovet Road
Suite 318
San Mateo, CA 94420
Phone: 650-356-10-71
Fax: 650-356-10-74
Website: www.viventures.com

See Foreign Venture Capital Firms for full listing.

VK VENTURES

600 California Street
Suite 1700
San Francisco, CA 94111
Phone: 415-391-5600
Fax: 415-397-2744

Other Offices

11661 San Vicente Blvd
Suite 809
San Francisco, CA 94111

11661 San Vicente Boulevard
Suite 709
Los Angeles, CA 90049
Phone: 310-820-2970
Fax: 310-820-5032

Management and Staff
David Horwich

Whom to Contact
David Horwich

Type of Firm
Investment/Merchant Bank Subsid/Affil

Industry Association Membership
Natl assoc of Small Bus. Inv. Co (NASBIC)

Project Preferences

Role in Financing:
Prefer role in deals created by others

Type of Financing Preferred:
Leveraged Buyout
Mezzanine
Second Stage Financing

Size of Investments Considered
Min Size of Investment Considered (000s): $100
Max Size of Investment Considered (000s): $300

Geographical Preferences

United States
West Coast

Industry Preferences

Communications and Media
Telecommunications
Data Communications

Computer Software
Systems Software
Applications Software

Semiconductors/Other Elect.
Semiconductor

Biotechnology
Biotech Related Research

Medical/Health
Medical Diagnostics
Diagnostic Services
Diagnostic Test Products
Medical Therapeutics
Other Therapeutic
Disposable Med. Products

Consumer Related
Food/Beverage
Consumer Products

Industrial/Energy
Industrial Products

Additional Information
Name of Most Recent Fund: V.K. Capital Company
Most Recent Fund Was Raised: 01/01/1997
Year Founded: 1978
Current Activity Level : Making few, if any, new investments
Method of Compensation: Return on invest. most important, but chg. closing fees, service fees, etc.

VOLENDAM CAPITAL ADVISORS,INC.

430 Cowper Street
Suite 222
Palo Alto, CA 94301
Phone: 650-617-4507
Fax: 650-617-4508

Management and Staff
Denis Pomroy, President

Type of Firm
Private Firm Investing Own Capital

Industry Association Membership
Western Association of Venture Capitalists (WAVC)

Project Preferences

Size of Investments Considered
Min Size of Investment Considered (000s): $1,000
Max Size of Investment Considered (000s): $10,000

Additional Information
Year Founded: 1995
Current Activity Level : Actively seeking new investments

VOYAGER CAPITAL

1520 Page Mill Road
Palo Alto, CA 94304
Phone: 650-855-9300
Fax: 650-320-8053
Website: www.voyagercapital.com

See Washington for full listing.

W.R. HAMBRECHT & CO., LLC

539 Bryant Street
Suite 100
San Francisco, CA 94107
Phone: 415-551-8600
Fax: 415-551-8686
Website: www.wrhambrecht.com

Management and Staff
Michael Szeto, Senior Managing Director
William Hambrecht, Co-Founder

Type of Firm
Investment/Merchant Bank Investing Own or Client Funds

Industry Preferences

Internet Specific
Internet

Additional Information
Year Founded: 1998
Current Activity Level : Actively seeking new investments

WALDEN INTERNATIONAL INVESTMENT GROUP (AKA: WALDEN GROUP)

750 Battery Street
Suite 700
San Francisco, CA 94111
Phone: 415-391-7225
Fax: 415-391-7262
Website: www.waldenintl.com

Other Offices

1501 CITIC Tower
1 Tim Mei Avenue
Central, Hong Kong, Hong Kong
Phone: 852-2523-0615
Fax: 852-2521-5778

22nd Floor, 6750 Ayala Avenue
Makati
Metro Manila, Philippines
Phone: 632-813-5253
Fax: 632-812-3996

361 Lytton Avenue
2nd Floor
Palo Alto, CA 94301
Phone: 650-330-3500
Fax: 650-330-3535

396 Alexandra Road, #16-03
BP Tower
Singapore, Singapore 119954
Phone: 65-272-3250
Fax: 65-272-3251

5302 143rd Avenue, S.E.
Bellevue, WA 98006
Phone: 206-643-7572
Fax: 206-649-0241

Level 18, Chung Khiaw Bank Build
Jalan Raja Laut
Kuala Lumpur, Malaysia 50350
Phone: 603-291-7551
Fax: 603-291-0718

No 76 18F/2, Sun Hua South Road
Sec. 2
Taipei, Taiwan
Phone: 886-2704-8018
Fax: 886-2704-2787

One Silverstone
294 Linking Road
Khar (west) Mumbai, India 400052
Phone: 912-2648-5194
Fax: 912-2648-0829

Management and Staff
Amos Barzilay, General Partner
Andrew Kau, General Partner
Arthur Berliner, General Partner
Brian Chiang, General Partner
C. Tang, Managing Director
Charles Hsu, General Partner
Danial Faizullabhoy, General Partner
Daniel Tsai, Vice President
Eric Ramirez, Vice President
George Sarlo, General Partner
Hiroshi Ishiwata, Vice President
Jackson Chen, Vice President
Lip-Bu Tan, Managing General Partner
Nancy Lee, Chief Financial Officer
Paul Chau, General Partner
Peter Mok, Vice President
Rakinder Grover, General Partner
S.C. Mak, Vice President
Somshankar Das, General Partner
Ted Chua, Vice President
Victor Kung, Vice President
William Teo, Vice President
Yong Soo Ping, Vice President

Type of Firm
Private Firm Investing Own Capital

Industry Association Membership
Hungarian Venture Capital Association
National Venture Capital Association (NVCA)
Natl assoc of Small Bus. Inv. Co (NASBIC)
Taiwan Venture Capital Association(TVCA)
Western Association of Venture Capitalists (WAVC)

Project Preferences

Role in Financing:
Prefer role as deal originator

Type of Financing Preferred:
Balanced
Early Stage
First Stage Financing
Mezzanine
Second Stage Financing
Seed
Special Situation
Start-up Financing
Startup

Size of Investments Considered
Min Size of Investment Considered (000s): $500
Max Size of Investment Considered: No Limit

Geographical Preferences
United States
All U.S.
West Coast

International
Asia
China
Hong Kong
Japan
Philippines
Singapore
Vietnam

Industry Preferences
(% based on actual investment)

Internet Specific	26.6%
Communications and Media	24.9%
Semiconductors/Other Elect.	16.5%
Computer Software and Services	12.7%
Computer Hardware	5.5%
Consumer Related	3.2%
Other Products	3.1%
Medical/Health	2.8%
Biotechnology	2.7%
Industrial/Energy	2.0%

Additional Information
Name of Most Recent Fund: O,W&W Investments Limited
Most Recent Fund Was Raised: 09/01/1996
Year Founded: 1991
Capital Under Management: $85,000,000
Current Activity Level : Actively seeking new investments
Method of Compensation: Return on investment is of primary concern, do not charge fees

WALDEN ISRAEL

750 Battery Street
San Francisco, CA CA 94111
Phone: 1-415-391-7225
Fax: 1-415-391-7262
Website: www.walden.co.il

See Foreign Venture Capital Firms for full listing.

WALDENVC

750 Battery Street
Seventh Floor
San Francisco, CA 94111
Phone: 415-391-7225
Fax: 415-391-7262
Website: www.waldenvc.com

Management and Staff
Alex Gove, Vice President
Arthur Berliner, General Partner
George Sarlo, Partner
Larry Marcus, General Partner
Philip Sanderson, General Partner
Rich LeFurgy, General Partner
Steven Eskenazi, General Partner
William McDonagh, Venture Partner

Whom to Contact
Antonio Celis
C.C. Tang
Charles Hsu
Eric Ramirez
K.K. Kuah
Mary Yu
Michael Hilsden
Phil Sanderson
Rahul Chandra
Steve Eskenazi
Tzu-Hwa Hsu
Victor Kung
Visit Tantisunthorn

Type of Firm
Affiliate/Subsidary of Oth. Financial. Instit.

Industry Association Membership
Western Association of Venture Capitalists (WAVC)

Project Preferences
Role in Financing:
Prefer role as deal originator but will also invest in deals created by others

Type of Financing Preferred:
Balanced
Early Stage
Expansion
Later Stage
Mezzanine

Size of Investments Considered
Min Size of Investment Considered (000s): $3,000
Max Size of Investment Considered (000s): $10,000

Geographical Preferences
United States
California
Northern California

Industry Preferences
(% based on actual investment)

Internet Specific	42.8%
Communications and Media	33.3%
Semiconductors/Other Elect.	19.5%
Computer Software and Services	2.6%
Other Products	1.7%

Additional Information
Name of Most Recent Fund: Walden X
Most Recent Fund Was Raised: 08/15/1997
Year Founded: 1974
Capital Under Management: $350,000,000
Current Activity Level : Actively seeking new investments
Method of Compensation: Return on investment is of primary concern, do not charge fees

WARBURG, PINCUS & CO., LLC. (FKA: E.M. WARBURG, PINCUS & CO)

2350 Mission College Blvd.
Suite 300
Santa Clara, CA 95054
Phone: 408-982-8210
Fax: 408-982-5853
Website: www.warburgpincus.com

See New York for full listing.

WASATCH VENTURE FUND (FKA: WASATCH VENTURE CORPORATION)

400 Seaport Court
Suite 250
Redwood City, CA 94059
Phone: 650-599-9000

See Utah for full listing.

WASSERSTEIN, PERELLA & CO., INC.

101 California Street
42nd Floor
San Francisco, CA 94111
Phone: 415-677-4800
Fax: 415-288-3960

See New York for full listing.

WE SIMON & SONS

10990 Wilshire Blvd
Suite 1750
Los Angeles, CA 90024
Phone: 310-575-3174

See New Jersey for full listing.

WEDBUSH CAPITAL PARTNERS

1000 Wilshire Boulevard
Los Angeles, CA 90017
Phone: 213-688-4545
Fax: 213-688-6642
Website: www.wedbush.com

Other Offices

1000 Wilshire Blvd
Suite 900
Los Angeles, CA 90017
Phone: 213-688-4545

Type of Firm
Investment/Merchant Bank Subsid/Affil

Project Preferences

Role in Financing:
Prefer role as deal originator

Type of Financing Preferred:
Leveraged Buyout
Mezzanine
Second Stage Financing

Size of Investments Considered
Min Size of Investment Considered (000s): $500
Max Size of Investment Considered: No Limit

Geographical Preferences

United States
West Coast

Industry Preferences

Computer Hardware
Mainframes / Scientific
Mini and Personal/Desktop
Computer Graphics and Dig
Disk Relat. Memory Device

Computer Software
Computer Services

Internet Specific
Internet

Medical/Health
Medical/Health

Consumer Related
Entertainment and Leisure
Retail
Franchises(NEC)
Food/Beverage
Consumer Products
Consumer Services
Other Restaurants
Hotels and Resorts

Business Serv.
Distribution

Additional Information
Name of Most Recent Fund: Wedbush Ventures
Most Recent Fund Was Raised: 06/01/1987
Year Founded: 1987
Capital Under Management: $20,000,000
Current Activity Level : Reducing investment activity
Method of Compensation: Return on invest. most important, but chg. closing fees, service fees, etc.

WESTAR CAPITAL

949 South Coast Drive
Suite 650
Costa Mesa, CA 92626
Phone: 714-481-5160
Fax: 714-481-5166
E-mail: mailbox@westarcapital.com
Website: www.westarcapital.com

Other Offices

777 Campus Commons Drive
Suite 200
Sacramento, CA 95825
Phone: 916-565-7660
Fax: 916-485-1050

Management and Staff
Frank Do, General Partner

Whom to Contact
Alan Sellers

Type of Firm
Investment/Merchant Bank Subsid/Affil

Project Preferences

Role in Financing:
Prefer role as deal originator but will also invest in deals created by others

Type of Financing Preferred:
Control-block Purchases
Industry Rollups
Leveraged Buyout
Special Situation

Size of Investments Considered
Min Size of Investment Considered (000s): $5,000
Max Size of Investment Considered (000s): $10,000

Geographical Preferences

United States
Northwest
Rocky Mountain
Southwest
West Coast

Industry Preferences

Communications and Media
Communications and Media
Other Communication Prod.

Computer Other
Computer Related

Semiconductors/Other Elect.
Electronics
Electronic Components

Medical/Health
Medical/Health
Medical Products

Consumer Related
Consumer
Food/Beverage
Consumer Products

Industrial/Energy
Energy
Industrial Products

Transportation
Transportation

Financial Services
Financial Services

Manufact.
Publishing

Additional Information
Year Founded: 1987
Capital Under Management: $100,000,000
Current Activity Level : Actively seeking new investments
Method of Compensation: Return on invest. most important, but chg. closing fees, service fees, etc.

WESTERN STATES INVESTMENT GROUP

9191 Towne Centre Drive
Suite 310
San Diego, CA 92122
Phone: 619-678-0800
Fax: 619-678-0900
Website: www.wsig.com

Management and Staff
William Patch, Vice President

Whom to Contact
Scott Pancoast

Type of Firm
Private Firm Investing Own Capital

Project Preferences

Role in Financing:
Prefer role as deal originator but will also invest in deals created by others

Type of Financing Preferred:
First Stage Financing
Leveraged Buyout
Research and Development
Seed
Start-up Financing

Size of Investments Considered
Min Size of Investment Considered (000s): $1,000
Max Size of Investment Considered: No Limit

Geographical Preferences

United States
Southwest
West Coast

Industry Preferences

(% based on actual investment)

Industrial/Energy	25.6%
Communications and Media	24.3%
Computer Software and Services	18.9%
Medical/Health	18.2%
Semiconductors/Other Elect.	13.1%

Additional Information
Year Founded: 1976
Capital Under Management: $35,000,000
Current Activity Level : Actively seeking new investments
Method of Compensation: Return on investment is of primary concern, do not charge fees

WESTERN TECHNOLOGY INVESTMENT

2010 North First Street
Suite 310
San Jose, CA 95131
Phone: 408-436-8577
Fax: 408-436-8625
Website: www.westerntech.com

Management and Staff
Brian Best, Chief Financial Officer
Ronald Swenson, Partner
Salvador Gutierrez, Partner

Type of Firm
Affiliate/Subsidary of Oth. Financial. Instit.

Industry Association Membership
National Venture Capital Association (NVCA)
Western Association of Venture Capitalists (WAVC)

Project Preferences

Role in Financing:
Prefer role in deals created by others

Type of Financing Preferred:
First Stage Financing
Leveraged Buyout
Mezzanine
Research and Development
Second Stage Financing
Seed
Special Situation
Start-up Financing

Geographical Preferences

International
No Preference

Industry Preferences

Communications and Media
Communications and Media

Biotechnology
Biotechnology

Medical/Health
Medical Products

Additional Information
Name of Most Recent Fund: Venture Lending & Leasing II
Most Recent Fund Was Raised: 07/01/1997
Year Founded: 1980
Capital Under Management: $600,000,000
Current Activity Level : Actively seeking new investments
Method of Compensation: Return on investment is of primary concern, do not charge fees

WESTON PRESIDIO CAPITAL MANAGEMENT

343 Sansome Street
Suite 1210
San Francisco, CA 94104-1316
Phone: 415-398-0770
Fax: 415-398-0990
Website: www.westonpresidio.com

See Massachusetts for full listing.

WHITNEY & CO. (FKA: J.H. WHITNEY & CO.)

580 California Street
20th Floor
San Francisco, CA 94104
Phone: 415-229-4000
Fax: 415-229-4001
Website: www.jhwhitney.com

See Connecticut for full listing.

WI HARPER GROUP

50 California Street
Suite 2920
San Francisco, CA 94111
Phone: 415-397-6200
Fax: 415-397-6280
Website: www.wiharper.com

Other Offices

10F-2, No. 76, Tun-Hua
South Road, Section 2
Taipei 106, Taiwan
Phone: 886-2-27556033
Fax: 886-2-27092127

C608, Lufthansa Center
No. 50, Liangmaqiao Road
Beijing, China
Phone: 8610-6264-8556
Fax: 8610-6264-3559

Suite 2914, 29/F,
1 Harbor View Street
Central, Hong Kong
Phone: 852-2836-7878
Fax: 852-2836-7171

Management and Staff

Falton Chao, President
Raymond Ngan, Managing Director
Tom Tsao, Managing Director

Type of Firm

Private Firm Investing Own Capital

Industry Association Membership

Western Association of Venture Capitalists (WAVC)

Project Preferences

Type of Financing Preferred:
Balanced
Expansion
Mezzanine
Seed
Startup

Geographical Preferences

United States
All U.S.

International
China
Hong Kong
All International
Taiwan

Industry Preferences

(% based on actual investment)

Internet Specific	68.1%
Computer Software and Services	14.8%
Computer Hardware	8.2%
Biotechnology	6.1%
Communications and Media	2.8%

Additional Information

Name of Most Recent Fund: International Network Capital Corporation Fund-DIF
Most Recent Fund Was Raised: 08/01/1998
Year Founded: 1989
Capital Under Management: $175,000,000
Current Activity Level : Actively seeking new investments

WILLIAM E. SIMON & SONS (ASIA) LDC

10990 Wilshire Boulevard
Suite 1750
Los Angeles, CA 90024
Phone: 310-914-2410
Fax: 310-575-3174
Website: www.simonasia.com

See Foreign Venture Capital Firms for full listing.

WINDAMERE VENTURE PARTNERS, LLC

12230 El Camino Real
Suite 300
San Diego, CA 92130
Phone: 858-350-7950
Fax: 858-350-7951
Website: www.windamerevp.com

Management and Staff

John Burd, General Partner
Kenneth Widder, General Partner
Scott Glenn, Managing Partner

Type of Firm

Private Firm Investing Own Capital

Project Preferences

Type of Financing Preferred:
Early Stage
Startup

Industry Preferences

Internet Specific
Internet

Medical/Health
Medical/Health
Medical Therapeutics
Pharmaceuticals

Additional Information

Year Founded: 1999
Capital Under Management: $17,000,000
Current Activity Level : Actively seeking new investments

WINDJAMMER CAPITAL INVESTORS (FKA:PACIFIC MEZZANINE INV.)

610 Newport Center Drive
Suite 1100
Newport Beach, CA 92660
Phone: 949-72—4207
Fax: 949-720-4222
Website: www.windjammercapital.com

Other Offices

Damonmill Square
Suite 4A
Concord, MA 01742

Management and Staff
Brett Snyder, Principal
Chris Daniel, Principal
Greg Bondick, Vice President
Jeffrey Dunnigan, Chief Financial Officer
Robert Bartholomew, Principal
Schuyler Lance, Principal

Type of Firm
Private Firm Investing Own Capital

Project Preferences
Role in Financing:
Prefer role as deal originator but will also invest in deals created by others

Type of Financing Preferred:
Leveraged Buyout
Mezzanine

Size of Investments Considered
Min Size of Investment Considered (000s): $50,000
Max Size of Investment Considered: No Limit

Geographical Preferences
United States
All U.S.

Industry Preferences
Semiconductors/Other Elect.
Sensors

Medical/Health
Diagnostic Services
Other Therapeutic
Medical Products
Disposable Med. Products
Hospitals/Clinics/Primary
Hospital/Other Instit.
Pharmaceuticals

Consumer Related
Food/Beverage
Consumer Products
Consumer Services

Industrial/Energy
Industrial Products
Materials
Factory Automation
Machinery

Additional Information
Name of Most Recent Fund: Windjammer Mezzanine & Equity Fund II
Most Recent Fund Was Raised: 01/01/1999
Year Founded: 1990
Capital Under Management: $750,000,000
Current Activity Level : Actively seeking new investments
Method of Compensation: Return on invest. most important, but chg. closing fees, service fees, etc.

WINDWARD VENTURES (FKA: CORONADO CAPITAL)

550 West "C" Street
Suite 2030
San Diego, CA 92101
Phone: 619-234-6800
Fax: 619-234-6886
Website: www.windwardventures.com

Other Offices
P.O. Box 7688
Westlake Village, CA 91359
Phone: 805-497-3222

Management and Staff
James Cole, Managing Partner
M. David Titus, Managing Partner
Neil Rappaport, Venture Partner
Paul Scott, Partner
Peter Shaw, Venture Partner
Rene Massi, Venture Partner

Whom to Contact
M. David Titus

Type of Firm
Private Firm Investing Own Capital

Industry Association Membership
Western Association of Venture Capitalists (WAVC)

Project Preferences
Role in Financing:
Prefer role as deal originator but will also invest in deals created by others

Type of Financing Preferred:
Early Stage

Size of Investments Considered
Min Size of Investment Considered (000s): $2,000
Max Size of Investment Considered (000s): $7,000

Geographical Preferences
United States
Southern California

Industry Preferences
(% based on actual investment)

Internet Specific	45.1%
Computer Software and Services	24.2%
Communications and Media	17.9%
Medical/Health	4.9%
Semiconductors/Other Elect.	4.9%
Other Products	2.9%

Additional Information
Name of Most Recent Fund: Windward Ventures
Most Recent Fund Was Raised: 11/01/1997
Year Founded: 1997
Capital Under Management: $90,000,000
Current Activity Level : Actively seeking new investments
Method of Compensation: Return on investment is of primary concern, do not charge fees

---

WOODSIDE FUND

350 Marine Parkway
Suite 300
Redwood City, CA 94065
Phone: 650-610-8050
Fax: 650-610-8051
Website: www.woodsidefund.com

Other Offices
850 Woodside Drive
Woodside, CA 94062
Phone: 415-368-5545

Management and Staff
Charles Greb, Managing Director
Daniel Ahn, Principal
Gary Tyrrell, Chief Financial Officer
Helen Mackenzie, Chief Financial Officer
John Occhipinti, Principal
Rick Shriner, Venture Partner
Robert Larson, Managing Director
Tom Shields, Venture Partner
Vincent Occhipinti, Managing Director

Type of Firm
Private Firm Investing Own Capital

Industry Association Membership
Western Association of Venture Capitalists (WAVC)

Project Preferences

Role in Financing:
Prefer role as deal originator but will also invest in deals created by others

Type of Financing Preferred:
First Stage Financing
Second Stage Financing
Seed
Special Situation
Startup

Size of Investments Considered
Min Size of Investment Considered (000s): $5,000
Max Size of Investment Considered (000s): $12,000

Geographical Preferences

United States
Northwest
Southwest
West Coast

Industry Preferences

(% based on actual investment)

Biotechnology	25.7%
Computer Software and Services	22.1%
Communications and Media	22.0%
Internet Specific	14.9%
Computer Hardware	11.1%
Consumer Related	1.6%
Industrial/Energy	1.1%
Medical/Health	0.9%
Other Products	0.4%
Semiconductors/Other Elect.	0.2%

Additional Information
Name of Most Recent Fund: Woodside Fund IV
Most Recent Fund Was Raised: 10/01/1999
Year Founded: 1983
Capital Under Management: $209,200,000
Current Activity Level : Actively seeking new investments
Method of Compensation: Return on investment is of primary concern, do not charge fees

WORLDVIEW TECHNOLOGY PARTNERS

435 Tasso Street
Suite 120
Palo Alto, CA 94301
Phone: 650-322-3800
Fax: 650-322-3880
Website: www.worldview.com

Other Offices

16 Raffles Quay
#37-02 Hong Leong Bldg.
, Singapore 048581
Phone: 65-221-7388
Fax: 65-221-7366

6/F Shishido Bldg.1-15-14, Saki
Musashino-Shi
Tokyo, Japan 180
Phone: 814-2255-2007
Fax: 814-2255-2014

Management and Staff
Ajit Shah, General Partner
Colin Savage, General Partner
James Wei, General Partner
John Boyle, General Partner
Michael Orsak, General Partner
Penelope Jackson, Chief Financial Officer
Susumu Tanaka, General Partner
Terence Tan, Managing Director

Whom to Contact
Mike Orsak

Type of Firm
Private Firm Investing Own Capital

Industry Association Membership
Western Association of Venture Capitalists (WAVC)

Project Preferences

Role in Financing:
Prefer role as deal originator but will also invest in deals created by others

Type of Financing Preferred:
Balanced
First Stage Financing
Mezzanine
Research and Development
Second Stage Financing
Seed
Start-up Financing

Geographical Preferences

United States
All U.S.
All U.S.

Industry Preferences

(% based on actual investment)

Internet Specific	34.2%
Communications and Media	29.7%
Semiconductors/Other Elect.	24.4%
Computer Software and Services	10.6%
Other Products	1.1%

Additional Information
Name of Most Recent Fund: Worldview Technology Partners III, L.P.
Most Recent Fund Was Raised: 01/01/1998
Year Founded: 1996
Capital Under Management: $716,100,000
Current Activity Level : Actively seeking new investments
Method of Compensation: Return on investment is of primary concern, do not charge fees

YASUDA ENTERPRISE DEVELOPMENT CO., LTD.(FKA: NIPPON ENT.DEV)

1010 El Camino Real
Suite 350
Menlo Park, CA 94025
Phone: 650-854-8760
Fax: 650-462-9379
Website: www.yedvc.co.jp

Other Offices

19-1, 2-Chame, Shinjuku
RYGS Bldg. 6F
Tokyo, Japan 150
Phone: 813-5367-5260
Fax: 813-3353-4630

Room 602, 6F, No 237
Section 2, Fu-Hsing S. Road
Taipei, Taiwan
Phone: 886-2-2708-2262
Fax: 886-2-2784-5444

Management and Staff
Moto Shimoyamada, Partner

Type of Firm
Insurance Firm Affiliate or Subsidiary

Industry Association Membership
National Venture Capital Association (NVCA)
Western Association of Venture Capitalists (WAVC)

Project Preferences

Role in Financing:
Will function either as deal originator or investor in deals created by others

Type of Financing Preferred:
Early Stage
Expansion
First Stage Financing
Later Stage
Mezzanine
Research and Development
Second Stage Financing
Seed
Startup

Size of Investments Considered
Min Size of Investment Considered (000s): $1,000
Max Size of Investment Considered (000s): $5,000

Geographical Preferences
United States
All U.S.
West Coast

International
China
Japan

Industry Preferences
(% based on actual investment)

Computer Software and Services	22.0%
Semiconductors/Other Elect.	20.5%
Medical/Health	15.0%
Biotechnology	14.8%
Computer Hardware	13.1%
Communications and Media	12.6%
Internet Specific	1.8%
Industrial/Energy	0.3%

Additional Information
Year Founded: 1989
Capital Under Management: $372,000,000
Current Activity Level : Actively seeking new investments
Method of Compensation: Return on investment is of primary concern, do not charge fees

ZERO GRAVITY INTERNET GROUP, INC.

400 Montgomery Street
Third Floor
San Francisco, CA 94104
Phone: 415-391-5335
Fax: 415-391-4884
Website: www.zgigroup.com

Management and Staff
Zara Haimo, Managing Director

Type of Firm
Affiliate/Subsidary of Oth. Financial. Instit.

Project Preferences

Type of Financing Preferred:
Balanced
Early Stage
Expansion

Industry Preferences
Internet Specific
Internet

Additional Information
Year Founded: 2000
Current Activity Level : Actively seeking new investments

ZONE VENTURES

241 S. Figueroa
Suite 340
Los Angeles, CA 90012
Phone: 213-628-2400
Fax: 213-628-2433
Website: www.zonevc.com

Other Offices

1343 Stratford Court
San Diego, CA 92153
Phone: 848-720-6622

Management and Staff
Darius Sankey, Partner
David Cremin, Partner
David Blackburn, Principal
Frank Creer, Managing Director
Timothy Draper, Managing Director

Type of Firm
Private Firm Investing Own Capital

Project Preferences

Role in Financing:
Prefer role as deal originator but will also invest in deals created by others

Type of Financing Preferred:
Early Stage

Size of Investments Considered
Min Size of Investment Considered (000s): $500
Max Size of Investment Considered (000s): $3,000

Geographical Preferences
United States
All U.S.

Industry Preferences
(% based on actual investment)

Internet Specific	87.5%
Computer Software and Services	10.0%
Communications and Media	1.3%
Semiconductors/Other Elect.	1.2%

Additional Information
Name of Most Recent Fund: Zone Ventures I, L.P.
Most Recent Fund Was Raised: 11/01/1998
Year Founded: 1998
Capital Under Management: $135,000,000
Current Activity Level : Actively seeking new investments

COLORADO

ACCESS VENTURE PARTNERS

8787 Turnpike Drive
Suite 260
Westminster, CO 80030
Phone: 303-426-8899
Fax: 303-426-8828
Website: www.accessventurepartners.com

Other Offices

319 Laidley Street
San Francisco, CA 94131
Phone: 415-586-0132
Fax: 415-392-6310

44 East Avenue
Suite 100
Austin, TX 78701
Phone: 512-236-0450
Fax: 512-474-9664

Management and Staff

Frank Mendicino, Managing Director
John Campion, Managing Director
Robert Rees, Managing Director

Type of Firm

Private Firm Investing Own Capital

Project Preferences

Role in Financing:
Prefer role as deal originator but will also invest in deals created by others

Type of Financing Preferred:
First Stage Financing
Seed
Start-up Financing

Geographical Preferences

United States
Rocky Mountain
Southwest

Industry Preferences

(% based on actual investment)

Internet Specific	48.2%
Biotechnology	24.1%
Communications and Media	15.7%
Computer Software and Services	11.9%

Additional Information

Year Founded: 1999
Capital Under Management: $33,400,000
Current Activity Level : Actively seeking new investments
Method of Compensation: Return on investment is of primary concern, do not charge fees

ALTIRA GROUP LLC

1625 Broadway
Suite 2150
Denver, CO 80202
Phone: 303-825-1600
Fax: 303-623-3525
Website: www.altiragroup.com

Management and Staff

Dirk McDermott, Managing Partner
Jim Newell, Chief Financial Officer
Peter Edwards, Vice President

Type of Firm

Private Firm Investing Own Capital

Industry Association Membership

National Venture Capital Association (NVCA)

Additional Information

Capital Under Management: $4,400,000
Current Activity Level : Actively seeking new investments

AWEIDA VENTURES

890 West Cherry Street
Suite 220
Louisville, CO 80027
Phone: 303-664-9520
Fax: 303-664-9530
Website: www.aweida.com

Management and Staff

Daniel Aweida, General Partner
Harry Ross, General Partner
Jesse Aweida, President

Type of Firm

Private Equity Advisor or Fund of Fund Mgr

Project Preferences

Type of Financing Preferred:
First Stage Financing
Second Stage Financing
Seed

Geographical Preferences

United States
All U.S.

Industry Preferences

Computer Software
Software

Internet Specific
Internet

Medical/Health
Medical/Health

Additional Information

Year Founded: 1990
Current Activity Level : Actively seeking new investments

BORANCO MANAGEMENT, L.L.C.

1528 Hillside Drive
Fort Collins, CO 80524-1969
Phone: 970-221-2297

Type of Firm

Private Firm Investing Own Capital

Project Preferences

Role in Financing:
Prefer role as deal originator

Type of Financing Preferred:
First Stage Financing
Research and Development
Second Stage Financing
Seed
Start-up Financing

Geographical Preferences

International
No Preference

Industry Preferences

Consumer Related
Retail

Additional Information

Year Founded: 1994
Current Activity Level : Actively seeking new investments
Method of Compensation: Function primarily in service area, receive contingent fee in cash or equity

BOULDER VENTURES, LTD.

1941 Pearl Street
Suite 300
Boulder, CO 80302
Phone: 303-444-6950
Fax: 303-444-0267
Website: www.boulderventures.com

See Maryland for full listing.

CATALYST PARTNERS INC.

730 North Nevada Avenue
Suite 200
Colorado Springs, CO 80903
Phone: 719-475-0325
Fax: 719-475-0911

Management and Staff

Craig Dawson, General Partner

Type of Firm

Private Firm Investing Own Capital

Industry Preferences

(% based on actual investment)

Biotechnology	40.8%
Computer Software and Services	27.0%
Internet Specific	21.0%
Computer Hardware	11.2%

Additional Information

Name of Most Recent Fund: Catalyst Entrepreneurial Fund
Most Recent Fund Was Raised: 10/15/1996
Year Founded: 1996
Capital Under Management: $10,100,000
Current Activity Level : Actively seeking new investments

CENTENNIAL VENTURES

1428 Fifteenth Street
Denver, CO 80202-1318
Phone: 303-405-7500
Fax: 303-405-7575
Website: www.centennial.com

Other Offices

1330 Post Oak Boulevard
Suite 1525
Houston, TX 77056
Phone: 713-627-9200
Fax: 713-627-9292

600 Congress
Suite 200
Austin, TX 78701
Phone: 512-476-7888
Fax: 512-476-4869

Management and Staff

Adam Goldman, Managing Director
David Hull, Managing Director
Donald Parsons, General Partner
Duncan Butler, Managing Director
Jeffrey Schutz, Managing Director
Robert Keppler, Chief Financial Officer
Sean White, President
Steven Halstedt, Managing Director

Type of Firm

Private Firm Investing Own Capital

Industry Association Membership

National Venture Capital Association (NVCA)
Natl assoc of Small Bus. Inv. Co (NASBIC)

Project Preferences

Role in Financing:

Prefer role as deal originator but will also invest in deals created by others

Type of Financing Preferred:

Early Stage
Seed
Startup

Size of Investments Considered

Min Size of Investment Considered (000s): $250
Max Size of Investment Considered: No Limit

Geographical Preferences

International

No Preference

Industry Preferences

(% based on actual investment)

Communications and Media	45.7%
Internet Specific	29.7%
Computer Hardware	6.8%
Semiconductors/Other Elect.	5.9%
Computer Software and Services	3.2%
Medical/Health	2.6%
Biotechnology	2.5%
Other Products	2.3%
Consumer Related	0.9%
Industrial/Energy	0.5%

Additional Information

Name of Most Recent Fund: Centennial Fund VI
Most Recent Fund Was Raised: 04/01/1999
Year Founded: 1981
Capital Under Management: $753,800,000
Current Activity Level : Actively seeking new investments
Method of Compensation: Return on investment is of primary concern, do not charge fees

CHB CAPITAL PARTNERS

511 Sixteenth Street
Suite 600
Denver, CO 80202
Phone: 303-571-0100
Fax: 303-571-0114
Website: www.chbcapital.com

Management and Staff

Blake Morris, Principal
Grant Clayton, Principal
John Flanigan, General Partner
Sean McClenaghan, Principal
Tad Kelly, General Partner

Type of Firm

Private Firm Investing Own Capital

Additional Information

Name of Most Recent Fund: CHB Capital Partners
Most Recent Fund Was Raised: 07/01/1995
Capital Under Management: $82,000,000
Current Activity Level : Actively seeking new investments

COLORADO VENTURE MANAGEMENT

Suite 300
Boulder, CO 80301
Phone: 303-440-4055
Fax: 303-440-4636

Management and Staff

Gary Bloomer, President & COO
Joe Worden, Partner
Joyce Edwards, Partner
R.D. Peter Bloomer, Chairman & CEO

Type of Firm

Private Firm Investing Own Capital

Project Preferences

Role in Financing:
Will function either as deal originator or investor in deals created by others

Type of Financing Preferred:
Early Stage
First Stage Financing
Second Stage Financing
Seed
Startup

Size of Investments Considered
Min Size of Investment Considered (000s): $250
Max Size of Investment Considered (000s): $1,000

Geographical Preferences

United States
Midwest
Rocky Mountain

Industry Preferences

(% based on actual investment)

Medical/Health	18.7%
Computer Software and Services	17.9%
Computer Hardware	12.0%
Consumer Related	10.4%
Communications and Media	9.8%
Biotechnology	8.1%
Industrial/Energy	7.5%
Semiconductors/Other Elect.	6.4%
Other Products	6.3%
Internet Specific	3.0%

Additional Information
Name of Most Recent Fund: CVM Eqity Fund V. L.L.P.
Most Recent Fund Was Raised: 10/01/1998
Year Founded: 1979
Capital Under Management: $16,600,000
Current Activity Level : Actively seeking new investments
Method of Compensation: Return on invest. most important, but chg. closing fees, service fees, etc.

COLUMBINE VENTURE FUNDS, THE

5460 South Quebec Street
Suite 270
Englewood, CO 80111
Phone: 303-694-3222
Fax: 303-694-9007

Other Offices

3810 Swarthmore
Houston, TX 77005
Phone: 713-661-9260
Fax: 713-661-9269

9449 North 90th Street
Suite 200
Scottsdale, AZ 85258
Phone: 602-661-9222
Fax: 602-661-6262

Management and Staff
Carl Stutts, General Partner
Duane Pearsall, General Partner
Sherman Muller, General Partner
Terry Winters, General Partner

Type of Firm
Private Firm Investing Own Capital

Project Preferences

Role in Financing:
Prefer role as deal originator but will also invest in deals created by others

Type of Financing Preferred:
First Stage Financing
Research and Development
Seed
Start-up Financing

Size of Investments Considered
Min Size of Investment Considered (000s): $300
Max Size of Investment Considered (000s): $800

Geographical Preferences

United States
Rocky Mountain
Southwest
West Coast

Industry Preferences

(% based on actual investment)

Medical/Health	27.8%
Biotechnology	26.6%
Industrial/Energy	14.1%
Semiconductors/Other Elect.	12.5%
Computer Software and Services	12.0%
Computer Hardware	5.5%
Other Products	1.0%
Internet Specific	0.4%
Communications and Media	0.2%

Additional Information
Year Founded: 1983
Capital Under Management: $78,000,000
Current Activity Level : Actively seeking new investments
Method of Compensation: Return on investment is of primary concern, do not charge fees

DEAN & ASSOCIATES

4362 Apple Way
Boulder, CO 80301
Fax: 303-473-9900

Type of Firm
Investment/Merchant Bank Subsid/Affil

Project Preferences

Role in Financing:
Prefer role as deal originator but will also invest in deals created by others

Type of Financing Preferred:
First Stage Financing
Mezzanine
Second Stage Financing

Size of Investments Considered
Min Size of Investment Considered (000s): $5,000
Max Size of Investment Considered (000s): $10,000

Geographical Preferences

United States
West Coast

Industry Preferences

Internet Specific
Internet

Additional Information
Year Founded: 1991
Current Activity Level : Actively seeking new investments
Method of Compensation: Return on investment is of primary concern, do not charge fees

FOREFRONT CAPITAL

2045 Broadway
Suite 200
Boulder, CO 80302
Phone: 303-413-8420
Fax: 303-413-8421

Other Offices

105 W. Madison
Suite 402
Chicago, IL 60602
Phone: 312-782-6235
Fax: 312-782-6236

Type of Firm
Private Firm Investing Own Capital

Additional Information
Current Activity Level : Actively seeking new investments

GRAYSON & ASSOCIATES

1250 17th Street
Suite 1600
Denver, CO 80202
Phone: 303-628-3490
Fax: 303-628-3440

Other Offices

16 East 53rd Street
Seventh Floor
New York, NY 10022
Phone: 212-371-8303
Fax: 212-486-3590

23 Arborwood Drive
Burlington, MA 01803
Phone: 617-229-9205

Management and Staff
Gerald Grayson
Peter J. Leveton

Whom to Contact
Gerald Grayson
Peter J. Leveton

Type of Firm
Mgt. Consulting Firm

Project Preferences

Role in Financing:
Prefer role as deal originator but will also invest in deals created by others

Type of Financing Preferred:
First Stage Financing
Leveraged Buyout
Mezzanine
Second Stage Financing

Size of Investments Considered
Min Size of Investment Considered (000s): $1,000
Max Size of Investment Considered: No Limit

Geographical Preferences

International
No Preference

Industry Preferences

Computer Hardware
Mainframes / Scientific

Computer Software
Computer Services

Biotechnology
Biotechnology

Medical/Health
Medical/Health
Medical Products

Additional Information
Year Founded: 1986
Current Activity Level : Actively seeking new investments
Method of Compensation: Return on invest. most important, but chg. closing fees, service fees, etc.

INVESTMENT SECURITIES OF COLORADO, INC.

4605 Denice Drive
Englewood, CO 80111
Phone: 303-796-9192

Type of Firm
Investment/Merchant Bank Investing Own or Client Funds

Project Preferences

Role in Financing:
Prefer role as deal originator

Type of Financing Preferred:
Seed
Start-up Financing

Geographical Preferences

United States
Rocky Mountain

Industry Preferences

Semiconductors/Other Elect.
Sensors
Analytic/Scientific

Medical/Health
Diagnostic Services
Diagnostic Test Products
Drug/Equipmt Delivery
Other Therapeutic
Disposable Med. Products
Hospitals/Clinics/Primary

Additional Information
Year Founded: 1970
Current Activity Level : Making few, if any, new investments
Method of Compensation: Return on investment is of primary concern, do not charge fees

J.P. MORGAN PARTNERS (FKA: CHASE CAPITAL PARTNERS)

108 South Frontage Road West
Suite 307
Vail, CO 81657
Phone: 970-476-7700
Fax: 970-476-7900
Website: www.chasecapital.com

See New York for full listing.

KINSHIP PARTNERS

6300 S. Syracuse Way
Suite 484
Englewood, CO 80111
Phone: 303-694-0268
Fax: 303-694-1707

Other Offices

1900 Garvey Avenue
Suite 200
West Covina, CA 91790-2653
Phone: 818-962-3562
Fax: 818-962-0758

Type of Firm
Private Firm Investing Own Capital

Project Preferences

Role in Financing:
Prefer role as deal originator but will also invest in deals created by others

Type of Financing Preferred:
First Stage Financing
Seed
Start-up Financing

Size of Investments Considered
Min Size of Investment Considered (000s): $500
Max Size of Investment Considered (000s): $1,000

Geographical Preferences
International
No Preference

Industry Preferences
Communications and Media
Commercial Communications
Telecommunications
Data Communications
Satellite Microwave Comm.

Computer Hardware
Mini and Personal/Desktop
Computer Graphics and Dig
Integrated Turnkey System

Computer Software
Systems Software
Applications Software
Artificial Intelligence

Biotechnology
Biotechnology

Medical/Health
Diagnostic Services
Diagnostic Test Products
Disposable Med. Products
Hospital/Other Instit.
Pharmaceuticals

Additional Information
Year Founded: 1990
Capital Under Management: $30,000,000
Current Activity Level : Actively seeking new investments
Method of Compensation: Return on investment is of primary concern, do not charge fees

---

LIVINGSTON CAPITAL, LTD.

1722 Buffehr Creek Road
Vail, CO 81657
Phone: 970-479-2800
Fax: 970-479-2822

Other Offices
745 Sherman Street
Suite 200
Denver, CO 80203
Phone: 303-866-9850

Management and Staff
Gregory Pusey

Whom to Contact
Gregory Pusey

Type of Firm
Mgt. Consulting Firm

Project Preferences
Role in Financing:
Prefer role as deal originator

Type of Financing Preferred:
First Stage Financing
Industry Rollups
Leveraged Buyout
Second Stage Financing
Special Situation
Start-up Financing

Geographical Preferences
United States
Rocky Mountain
Southwest
West Coast

Additional Information
Year Founded: 1988
Capital Under Management: $5,000,000
Current Activity Level : Actively seeking new investments
Method of Compensation: Return on invest. most important, but chg. closing fees, service fees, etc.

LM CAPITAL CORP.

Republic Plaza
370 17th Street
Denver, CO 80202
Phone: 303-572-5014
Fax: 303-572-5001
Website: www.lmcapitalsecurities.com

See Florida for full listing.

LONETREE CAPITAL PARTNERS

9785 Maroon Circle
Suite 360
Englewood, CO 80112
Phone: 303-645-2020
Fax: 303-645-2099
Website: www.lonetreecapital.com

Management and Staff
Chuck Lillis, Principal
Donnell Heistand, Chief Financial Officer
Frank Eichler, Principal
Rick Post, Principal
Tom Cullen, Principal

Type of Firm
Private Firm Investing Own Capital

Project Preferences
Type of Financing Preferred:
Balanced

Geographical Preferences
United States
All U.S.

International
Asia
Europe

Industry Preferences
Communications and Media
Communications and Media

Additional Information
Current Activity Level : Actively seeking new investments

MERITAGE PRIVATE EQUITY FUND

1600 Wynkoop Street
Suite 300
Denver, CO 80202
Phone: 303-352-2040
Fax: 303-352-2050
Website: www.meritage.net

Management and Staff
Brian Deevy, Principal
Christine Brennet-Morris, Principal
David Solomon, Principal
Jack Tankersley, Principal
James Allen, Principal
John Garrett, Principal
Laura Beller, Principal
Parker Brophy, Principal
Tracy Kerr, Principal

Type of Firm
Private Firm Investing Own Capital

Project Preferences
Role in Financing:
Prefer role as deal originator but will also invest in deals created by others

Type of Financing Preferred:
Balanced
Early Stage
Expansion
First Stage Financing
Later Stage
Seed
Startup

Size of Investments Considered
Min Size of Investment Considered (000s): $1,000
Max Size of Investment Considered (000s): $50,000

Geographical Preferences

United States
All U.S.
All U.S.

Industry Preferences

(% based on actual investment)

Internet Specific	54.0%
Communications and Media	39.2%
Computer Hardware	6.8%

Additional Information
Year Founded: 1998
Capital Under Management: $340,000,000
Current Activity Level : Actively seeking new investments
Method of Compensation: Return on investment is of primary concern, do not charge fees

MURPHREE VENTURE PARTNERS

2005 10th Street
Suite D
Boulder, CO 80302
Phone: 303-413-1264
Fax: 303-413-1266
Website: www.murphreeventures.com

See Texas for full listing.

NEW VENTURE RESOURCES

PMB 342
445C E. Cheyenne Mtn. Blvd.
Colorado Springs, CO 80906-4570
Phone: 719-598-9272
Fax: 719-598-9272

Management and Staff
Jeffrey Cooper

Whom to Contact
Jeffrey Cooper

Type of Firm
Private Firm Investing Own Capital

Project Preferences

Role in Financing:
Prefer role as deal originator but will also invest in deals created by others

Type of Financing Preferred:
Seed
Start-up Financing

Size of Investments Considered
Min Size of Investment Considered (000s): $100
Max Size of Investment Considered (000s): $300

Geographical Preferences

United States
Rocky Mountain
Southwest

Industry Preferences

Communications and Media
Data Communications
Other Communication Prod.

Computer Other
Computer Related

Semiconductors/Other Elect.
Electronics
Electronic Components
Semiconductor
Laser Related
Analytic/Scientific

Biotechnology
Biosensors
Biotech Related Research

Medical/Health
Medical/Health
Medical Diagnostics
Medical Therapeutics
Medical Products

Consumer Related
Retail

Industrial/Energy
Robotics

Additional Information
Current Activity Level : Actively seeking new investments
Method of Compensation: Return on investment is of primary concern, do not charge fees

PHILLIPS-SMITH SPECIALTY RETAIL GROUP

102 South Tejon Street
Suite 1100
Colorado Springs, CO 80903
Phone: 719-578-3301
Fax: 719-578-8869
Website: www.phillips-smith.com

See Texas for full listing.

ROCKMOUNTAIN VENTURES

1840 Deer Creek
Suite 300
Monument, CO 80132
Phone: 714-488-3900
Website: www.rockventures.com

Other Offices

2450 Coyote Run
Suite 700
Rockwall, TX 75087
Phone: 972-772-5350

Management and Staff
Barton Skalla, Managing Director
Don Fairbanks, Chief Financial Officer
Paul Sorenson, Managing Director
Peter Skalla, Managing Director
Robert Edens, Managing Director

Type of Firm
Private Firm Investing Own Capital

Project Preferences

Type of Financing Preferred:
Startup

Geographical Preferences

United States
Colorado
Texas
All U.S.

Industry Preferences

Communications and Media
Communications and Media

Computer Software
Software

Internet Specific
Internet

Semiconductors/Other Elect.
Semiconductor

Additional Information

Year Founded: 1999
Current Activity Level : Actively seeking new investments

ROCKY MOUNTAIN CAPITAL PARTNERS (FKA:HANIFEN IMHOFF CAPITAL)

1125 17th Street
Suite 2260
Denver, CO 80202
Phone: 303-297-1701
Fax: 303-297-1702
Website: www.rockycapital.com

Management and Staff

Edward Brown, Managing Partner
Paul Lyons, Partner
Stephen Sangalis, Partner
William Sullivan, Principal

Type of Firm

SBIC Not elsewhere classified

Industry Association Membership

Natl assoc of Small Bus. Inv. Co (NASBIC)

Project Preferences

Role in Financing:
Prefer role in deals created by others

Type of Financing Preferred:
Management Buyouts
Mezzanine

Size of Investments Considered

Min Size of Investment Considered (000s): $1,000
Max Size of Investment Considered: No Limit

Geographical Preferences

United States
Midwest
Rocky Mountain
Southwest
West Coast

Industry Preferences

(% based on actual investment)

Other Products	38.3%
Consumer Related	23.6%
Industrial/Energy	19.7%
Communications and Media	16.6%
Semiconductors/Other Elect.	1.9%

Additional Information

Name of Most Recent Fund: Rocky Mountain Mezzanine Fund II, L.P.
Most Recent Fund Was Raised: 05/01/1998
Year Founded: 1994
Capital Under Management: $180,000,000
Current Activity Level : Actively seeking new investments
Method of Compensation: Return on invest. most important, but chg. closing fees, service fees, etc.

ROSER VENTURES LLC

1105 Spruce Street
Boulder, CO 80302
Phone: 303-443-6436
Fax: 303-443-1885
Website: www.roserventures.com

Management and Staff

Alan Valenti, Chief Financial Officer
Christopher Roser, Partner
James Roser, Partner
Phillip Dignan, Partner

Type of Firm

Private Firm Investing Own Capital

Industry Association Membership

Natl assoc of Small Bus. Inv. Co (NASBIC)

Project Preferences

Role in Financing:
Prefer role as deal originator but will also invest in deals created by others

Type of Financing Preferred:
Early Stage

Size of Investments Considered

Min Size of Investment Considered (000s): $250
Max Size of Investment Considered (000s): $3,000

Geographical Preferences

United States
Rocky Mountain

Industry Preferences

(% based on actual investment)

Communications and Media	21.1%
Semiconductors/Other Elect.	19.0%
Internet Specific	15.8%
Other Products	12.7%
Industrial/Energy	12.4%
Computer Hardware	8.2%
Computer Software and Services	5.3%
Medical/Health	3.6%
Biotechnology	1.8%
Consumer Related	0.3%

Additional Information

Name of Most Recent Fund: Roser Partnership III - SBIC
Most Recent Fund Was Raised: 06/01/1998
Year Founded: 1987
Capital Under Management: $75,000,000
Current Activity Level : Actively seeking new investments
Method of Compensation: Return on investment is of primary concern, do not charge fees

SANDLOT CAPITAL LLC

600 South Cherry Street
Suite 525
Denver, CO 80246
Phone: 303-893-3400
Fax: 303-893-3403
Website: www.sandlotcapital.com

Type of Firm

Private Firm Investing Own Capital

Industry Association Membership

National Venture Capital Association (NVCA)

Project Preferences

Role in Financing:
Will function either as deal originator or investor in deals created by others

Type of Financing Preferred:
Early Stage
First Stage Financing
Seed
Special Situation
Startup

Size of Investments Considered
Min Size of Investment Considered (000s): $250
Max Size of Investment Considered (000s): $20,000

Industry Preferences

Communications and Media
Commercial Communications
CATV & Pay TV Systems
Radio & TV Broadcasting
Telecommunications
Wireless Communications
Data Communications
Other Communication Prod.

Computer Hardware
Integrated Turnkey System

Computer Software
Software
Systems Software
Applications Software
Artificial Intelligence

Internet Specific
E-Commerce Technology
Internet
Web Aggregration/Portals

Additional Information
Year Founded: 1998
Current Activity Level : Actively seeking new investments
Method of Compensation: Return on investment is of primary concern, do not charge fees

SEQUEL VENTURE PARTNERS

4430 Arapahoe Avenue
Suite 220
Boulder, CO 80303
Phone: 303-546-0400
Fax: 303-546-9728
Website: www.sequelvc.com

Management and Staff
Dan Mitchell, Partner
John Greff, Partner
Kinney Johnson, Partner
Rick Patch, Partner
Tim Connor, Partner
Tom Washing, Partner

Type of Firm
Private Firm Investing Own Capital

Industry Association Membership
National Venture Capital Association (NVCA)

Project Preferences

Role in Financing:
Prefer role as deal originator

Type of Financing Preferred:
Early Stage

Size of Investments Considered
Min Size of Investment Considered (000s): $3,000
Max Size of Investment Considered (000s): $7,000

Geographical Preferences

United States
Colorado
Rocky Mountain

Industry Preferences

(% based on actual investment)

Internet Specific	59.2%
Computer Software and Services	18.1%
Computer Hardware	5.9%
Medical/Health	4.8%
Biotechnology	4.5%
Semiconductors/Other Elect.	3.2%
Other Products	2.6%
Communications and Media	1.6%

Additional Information
Name of Most Recent Fund: Sequel Entrepeneurs Fund II, L.P.
Most Recent Fund Was Raised: 03/02/1999
Year Founded: 1997
Capital Under Management: $224,400,000
Current Activity Level : Actively seeking new investments
Method of Compensation: Return on investment is of primary concern, do not charge fees

SI VENTURES

730 North Nevada
Suite 200
Colorado Springs, CO 80903
Website: www.siventures.com

See Florida for full listing.

SILICON VALLEY BANK

4430 Arapahoe Avenue
Suite 225
Boulder, CO 80303
Phone: 303-938-0483
Fax: 303-938-0486

See California for full listing.

SILVER CREEK TECHNOLOGY INVESTORS (FKA: O'DONNELL & MASUR)

730 17th Street
Suite 690
Denver, CO 80202
Phone: 303-573-3720
Fax: 303-573-3740
Website: www.silvercreekfund.com

See Texas for full listing.

SOFTBANK VENTURE CAPITAL (FKA: SOFTBANK TECHNOLOGY VENTURES)

HOTBANK Colorado
100 Superior Plaza Way
Superior, CO 80027
Website: www.sbvc.com

See California for full listing.

TELECOM PARTNERS (FKA:TELECOM MANAGEMENT, LLC)

4600 S. Syracuse Street
Suite 1000
Denver, CO 80237
Phone: 303-874-1100
Fax: 303-874-1110
Website: www.telecompartners.com

Management and Staff
Mark Adolph, Chief Operating Officer
Teresa Miller, Chief Financial Officer

Type of Firm
Private Firm Investing Own Capital

Project Preferences

Role in Financing:
Prefer role as deal originator but will also invest in deals created by others

Type of Financing Preferred:
Early Stage
Seed

Size of Investments Considered
Min Size of Investment Considered (000s): $1,000
Max Size of Investment Considered (000s): $75,000

Geographical Preferences

United States
All U.S.

International
All International

Industry Preferences

(% based on actual investment)

Communications and Media	47.7%
Internet Specific	25.3%
Semiconductors/Other Elect.	13.4%
Computer Software and Services	13.4%
Consumer Related	0.1%
Other Products	0.1%

Additional Information
Name of Most Recent Fund: Telecom Partners, L.P.
Most Recent Fund Was Raised: 10/24/1995
Year Founded: 1998
Capital Under Management: $640,000,000
Current Activity Level : Actively seeking new investments
Method of Compensation: Return on investment is of primary concern, do not charge fees

THOMA CRESSEY EQUITY PARTNERS

4050 Republic Plaza
370 Seventeenth Street
Denver, CO 80202
Phone: 303-592-4888
Fax: 303-592-4845
Website: www.thomacressey.com

See Illinois for full listing.

UNIROCK MANAGEMENT CORP.

1228 15th Street
Suite 201
Denver, CO 80202
Phone: 303-623-4500
Fax: 303-623-9006

Management and Staff
Scott Maierhofer

Whom to Contact
Scott Maierhofer

Type of Firm
Mgt. Consulting Firm

Project Preferences

Role in Financing:
Prefer role as deal originator but will also invest in deals created by others

Type of Financing Preferred:
Industry Rollups
Leveraged Buyout
Mezzanine
Second Stage Financing

Size of Investments Considered
Min Size of Investment Considered (000s): $1,000
Max Size of Investment Considered: No Limit

Geographical Preferences

United States
Rocky Mountain

Additional Information
Year Founded: 1988
Current Activity Level : Actively seeking new investments
Method of Compensation: Function primarily in service area, receive contingent fee in cash or equity

VENTURE ASSOCIATES, LTD.

4950 East Evans Street
Suite 105
Denver, CO 80222
Phone: 303-758-8710
Fax: 303-758-8747
Website: www.venturea.com

Other Offices

4811 Trailwood Way
Springfield, MO 65804
Phone: 417-882-9218

Management and Staff
James Arkebauer, President

Whom to Contact
James Arkebauer

Project Preferences

Role in Financing:
Prefer role as deal originator but will also invest in deals created by others

Type of Financing Preferred:
Early Stage
Expansion
First Stage Financing
Leveraged Buyout
Private Placement
Second Stage Financing
Seed
Startup

Size of Investments Considered
Min Size of Investment Considered (000s): $100
Max Size of Investment Considered (000s): $10,000

Geographical Preferences

International
No Preference

Industry Preferences

Communications and Media
Communications and Media
Telecommunications
Data Communications
Other Communication Prod.

Internet Specific
Internet

Computer Other
Computer Related

Semiconductors/Other Elect.
Electronic Components

Consumer Related
Consumer Products
Consumer Services

Industrial/Energy
Alternative Energy
Energy Conservation Relat
Industrial Products

Financial Services
Financial Services

Business Serv.
Services
Distribution
Consulting Services

Manufact.
Manufacturing
Publishing

Additional Information
Year Founded: 1982
Capital Under Management: $20,000,000
Current Activity Level : Actively seeking new investments
Method of Compensation: Return on invest. most important, but chg. closing fees, service fees, etc.

WOLF VENTURES (AKA:WOLF ASSET MANAGEMENT CORP.)

1999 Broadway
Suite 3205
Denver, CO 80202
Phone: 303-321-4800
Fax: 303-321-4848
Website: www.wolfventures.com

Management and Staff
Benjamin Kelly, Chief Financial Officer
David Wolf, Managing Partner
Elliot Husney, Principal
James Conboy, Partner
Phillip Dignan, Partner
Steven Joanis, Partner

Whom to Contact
Elliott R. Husney

Type of Firm
Private Firm Investing Own Capital

Industry Association Membership
National Venture Capital Association (NVCA)
Natl assoc of Small Bus. Inv. Co (NASBIC)

Project Preferences

Role in Financing:
Will function either as deal originator or investor in deals created by others

Type of Financing Preferred:
Early Stage
Expansion
First Stage Financing
Later Stage
Management Buyouts
Second Stage Financing

Size of Investments Considered
Min Size of Investment Considered (000s): $500
Max Size of Investment Considered (000s): $2,500

Geographical Preferences

United States
Rocky Mountain
All U.S.

Industry Preferences

(% based on actual investment)

Computer Software and Services	38.8%
Semiconductors/Other Elect.	26.4%
Internet Specific	10.3%
Communications and Media	8.6%
Medical/Health	7.9%
Computer Hardware	2.3%
Other Products	2.1%
Industrial/Energy	1.9%
Consumer Related	1.5%

Additional Information
Name of Most Recent Fund: Wolf Venture III
Most Recent Fund Was Raised: 01/01/1999
Year Founded: 1992
Capital Under Management: $48,000,000
Current Activity Level : Actively seeking new investments
Method of Compensation: Return on investment is of primary concern, do not charge fees

CONNECTICUT

ABP ACQUISITION CORP

115 Maple Avenue
Greenwich, CT 06830
Phone: 203-625-8287
Fax: 520-447-6187

Management and Staff
George Skakel, Chief Executive Officer

Type of Firm
Mgt. Consulting Firm

Project Preferences

Role in Financing:
Prefer role as deal originator

Type of Financing Preferred:
Acquisition
Leveraged Buyout

Size of Investments Considered
Min Size of Investment Considered (000s): $10,000
Max Size of Investment Considered (000s): $30,000

Geographical Preferences

United States
Mid Atlantic
Northeast

Canada
Ontario
Quebec

Industry Preferences

Semiconductors/Other Elect.
Sensors

Consumer Related
Entertainment and Leisure
Education Related

Industrial/Energy
Energy
Industrial Products
Process Control
Machinery

Transportation
Transportation
Aerospace

Financial Services
Financial Services

Business Serv.
Services
Distribution
Consulting Services

Manufact.
Manufacturing

Utilities
Utilities

Additional Information
Year Founded: 1986
Capital Under Management: $25,000,000
Current Activity Level : Actively seeking new investments
Method of Compensation: Return on investment is of primary concern, do not charge fees

ADLER & CO.

100 First Stamford Place
Third Floor
Stamford, CT 06902
Phone: 203-359-9595
Fax: 203-359-0880

See New York for full listing.

ADVANCED MATERIALS PARTNERS, INC.

45 Pine Street
P.O. Box 1022
New Canaan, CT 06840
Phone: 203-966-6415
Fax: 203-966-8448

Project Preferences

Role in Financing:
Prefer role as deal originator but will also invest in deals created by others

Type of Financing Preferred:
First Stage Financing
Leveraged Buyout
Research and Development
Second Stage Financing
Seed
Special Situation
Start-up Financing

Size of Investments Considered
Min Size of Investment Considered (000s): $100
Max Size of Investment Considered (000s): $25,000

Geographical Preferences

Canada
All Canada

Industry Preferences

Computer Hardware
Computer Graphics and Dig
Disk Relat. Memory Device

Semiconductors/Other Elect.
Electronic Components

Biotechnology
Industrial Biotechnology
Biosensors
Biotech Related Research
Biotech Related Research

Medical/Health
Medical Therapeutics
Drug/Equipmt Delivery
Other Therapeutic
Disposable Med. Products
Pharmaceuticals

Consumer Related
Consumer Products

Industrial/Energy
Alternative Energy
Energy Conservation Relat
Industrial Products

Business Serv.
Distribution

Agr/Forestr/Fish
Mining and Minerals

Additional Information
Year Founded: 1987
Current Activity Level : Actively seeking new investments
Method of Compensation: Return on investment is of primary concern, do not charge fees

AO CAPITAL CORP

80 Field Point Road
Greenwich, CT 06830
Phone: 203-622-6600
Fax: 203-622-1292

Management and Staff
Allen Skott, Managing Director
William Cotter, Managing Director
William Zegras, Senior Managing Director

Whom to Contact
Allen Skott
William Zegras

Type of Firm
Private Firm Investing Own Capital

Project Preferences

Type of Financing Preferred:
Acquisition
Leveraged Buyout
Management Buyouts
Turnaround

Size of Investments Considered
Min Size of Investment Considered (000s): $3,000
Max Size of Investment Considered (000s): $25,000

Geographical Preferences

United States
All U.S.

Canada
All Canada

International
Belgium
France
Germany
Italy
Latin America
Luxembourg
Netherlands
Spain
United Kingdom

Industry Preferences

Industrial/Energy
Industrial Products
Process Control
Machinery

Financial Services
Financial Services

Manufact.
Manufacturing

Additional Information
Year Founded: 1972
Capital Under Management: $135,000,000
Current Activity Level : Actively seeking new investments
Method of Compensation: Return on investment is of primary concern, do not charge fees

ATLANTIC COASTAL VENTURES, L.P.(AKA:MULTIMEDIA BROADCAST IN)

777 Summer Street
Suite 30
Stamford, CT 06901
Phone: 203-325-2522
Website: www.atlanticcv.com

See D. of Columbia for full listing.

AXIOM VENTURE PARTNERS, L.P.

CityPlace II, 17th Floor
185 Asylum Street
Hartford, CT 06103
Phone: 860-548-7799
Fax: 860-548-7797
Website: www.axiomventures.com

Other Offices

One Post Street
Suite 2525
San Francisco, CA 94104
Phone: 415-434-9999
Fax: 415-434-0505

Management and Staff
Alan Mendelson, General Partner
Barry Bronfin, General Partner
Linda Sonntag, General Partner
Marc Fogassa, Principal
Martin Chanzit, General Partner
Samuel McKay, General Partner

Type of Firm
Private Firm Investing Own Capital

Industry Association Membership
National Venture Capital Association (NVCA)

Project Preferences

Role in Financing:
Will function either as deal originator or investor in deals created by others

Type of Financing Preferred:
Balanced
Early Stage
Expansion
Later Stage
Seed

Size of Investments Considered
Min Size of Investment Considered (000s): $2,000
Max Size of Investment Considered (000s): $5,000

Geographical Preferences

United States
All U.S.
All U.S.

Industry Preferences

(% based on actual investment)

Computer Software and Services	19.2%
Medical/Health	18.1%
Internet Specific	16.9%
Communications and Media	15.9%
Biotechnology	15.8%
Computer Hardware	6.1%
Other Products	3.0%
Consumer Related	2.7%
Semiconductors/Other Elect.	1.7%
Industrial/Energy	0.5%

Additional Information
Name of Most Recent Fund: Axiom Venture Partners II, L.P.
Most Recent Fund Was Raised: 03/01/1997
Year Founded: 1994
Capital Under Management: $189,000,000
Current Activity Level : Actively seeking new investments
Method of Compensation: Return on investment is of primary concern, do not charge fees

BALLENTINE CAPITAL MANAGEMENT

10 Avon Meadow Lane
Avon, CT 06001
Phone: 860-676-1830
Fax: 860-676-1782
Website: www.ballentine-capital.com

Management and Staff
Steven Ballentine, President

Type of Firm
Private Firm Investing Own Capital

Project Preferences

Type of Financing Preferred:
Balanced

Geographical Preferences

United States
All U.S.

Additional Information
Year Founded: 1989
Current Activity Level : Actively seeking new investments

BAXTER ASSOCIATES, INC.

Post Office Box 1333
Stamford, CT 06904
Phone: 203-323-3143
Fax: 203-348-0622

Type of Firm
Mgt. Consulting Firm

Project Preferences

Role in Financing:
Prefer role as deal originator but will also invest in deals created by others

Type of Financing Preferred:
First Stage Financing
Leveraged Buyout
Research and Development
Seed
Special Situation
Start-up Financing

Size of Investments Considered
Min Size of Investment Considered (000s): $2,000
Max Size of Investment Considered: No Limit

Geographical Preferences

International
No Preference

Industry Preferences

Communications and Media
Radio & TV Broadcasting

Computer Software
Artificial Intelligence

Biotechnology
Industrial Biotechnology
Biosensors
Biotech Related Research
Biotech Related Research

Medical/Health
Drug/Equipmt Delivery
Other Therapeutic
Medical Products

Consumer Related
Retail
Franchises(NEC)

Industrial/Energy
Oil and Gas Exploration
Oil & Gas Drilling,Explor
Alternative Energy
Coal Related
Industrial Products
Materials
Robotics
Environmental Related

Business Serv.
Consulting Services

Agr/Forestr/Fish
Mining and Minerals

Additional Information
Year Founded: 1981
Current Activity Level : Actively seeking new investments
Method of Compensation: Function primarily in service area, receive contingent fee in cash or equity

BCI PARTNERS

760 Hopmeadow Street
P.O. Box 188
Simsbury, CT 06070
Phone: 203-651-9760
Fax: 203-651-8890
Website: www.bcipartners.com

See New Jersey for full listing.

BEACON PARTNERS, INC.

Six Landmark Square
Fourth Floor
Stamford, CT 06901-2792
Phone: 203-359-5776
Fax: 203-359-5876

Type of Firm
Mgt. Consulting Firm

Industry Association Membership
Natl assoc of Small Bus. Inv. Co (NASBIC)

Project Preferences

Role in Financing:
Prefer role as deal originator

Type of Financing Preferred:
First Stage Financing
Leveraged Buyout
Mezzanine
Second Stage Financing

Size of Investments Considered
Min Size of Investment Considered (000s): $300
Max Size of Investment Considered (000s): $1,000

Geographical Preferences

United States
Northeast

Industry Preferences

(% based on actual investment)

Consumer Related	54.0%
Other Products	14.9%
Internet Specific	9.0%
Industrial/Energy	8.8%
Medical/Health	6.2%
Communications and Media	3.9%
Computer Software and Services	2.3%
Semiconductors/Other Elect.	0.9%

Additional Information
Name of Most Recent Fund: Beacon Group Energy Investment Fund II
Most Recent Fund Was Raised: 03/17/1998
Year Founded: 1976
Capital Under Management: $1,000,000
Current Activity Level : Actively seeking new investments

BRAND EQUITY VENTURES

263 Tresser Boulevard
Suite 1600
Stamford, CT 06901
Phone: 203-724-1100
Fax: 203-724-1155
Website: www.brand-equity.com

Management and Staff
Bill Meurer, General Partner
Christopher Kirchen, Managing Partner
David Yarnell, Managing Partner
Marc Singer, General Partner

Type of Firm
Private Firm Investing Own Capital

Project Preferences

Role in Financing:
Prefer role as deal originator but will also invest in deals created by others

Type of Financing Preferred:
First Stage Financing
Leveraged Buyout
Mezzanine
Second Stage Financing
Start-up Financing

Size of Investments Considered
Min Size of Investment Considered (000s): $10,000
Max Size of Investment Considered: No Limit

Geographical Preferences

United States
All U.S.

Industry Preferences

(% based on actual investment)

Internet Specific	62.6%
Consumer Related	29.3%
Computer Software and Services	4.3%
Other Products	3.8%

Additional Information
Name of Most Recent Fund: Brand Equity Ventures I, L.P.
Most Recent Fund Was Raised: 01/01/1997
Year Founded: 1996
Capital Under Management: $95,000,000
Current Activity Level : Actively seeking new investments
Method of Compensation: Return on investment is of primary concern, do not charge fees

CANAAN PARTNERS

105 Rowayton Avenue
Rowayton, CT 06853
Phone: 203-855-0400
Fax: 203-854-9117
Website: www.canaan.com

Other Offices

2884 Sand Hill Road
Suite 115
Menlo Park, CA 94025
Phone: 415-854-8092
Fax: 415-854-8127

Management and Staff
Brent Ahrens, Principal
Deepak Kamra, General Partner
Earl Mix, Partner
Eric Young, General Partner
Gregory Kopchinsky, General Partner
Guy Russo, Chief Financial Officer
Harry Rein, Managing General Partner
James Furnivall, General Partner
James Fitzpatrick, General Partner
John Balen, General Partner
Maha Ibrahim, Principal
Mark Thies, Partner
Robert Migliorino, General Partner
Seth Rudnick, General Partner
Stephan Palfrey, Principal
Stephen Green, General Partner

Type of Firm
Private Firm Investing Own Capital

Industry Association Membership
National Venture Capital Association (NVCA)
Western Association of Venture Capitalists (WAVC)

Project Preferences

Role in Financing:
Prefer role as deal originator but will also invest in deals created by others

Type of Financing Preferred:
Early Stage
Expansion
First Stage Financing
Second Stage Financing

Size of Investments Considered
Min Size of Investment Considered (000s): $5,000
Max Size of Investment Considered (000s): $20,000

Geographical Preferences

United States
All U.S.

Industry Preferences

(% based on actual investment)

Internet Specific	23.7%
Computer Software and Services	19.8%
Communications and Media	13.6%
Other Products	13.3%
Medical/Health	11.0%
Biotechnology	5.9%
Computer Hardware	5.0%
Industrial/Energy	4.1%
Consumer Related	1.9%
Semiconductors/Other Elect.	1.8%

Additional Information
Name of Most Recent Fund: Canaan Equity Partners II, L.P.
Most Recent Fund Was Raised: 01/01/1998
Year Founded: 1987
Capital Under Management: $1,200,000,000
Current Activity Level : Actively seeking new investments
Method of Compensation: Return on investment is of primary concern, do not charge fees

CATTERTON PARTNERS

Nine Greenwich Office Park
Greenwich, CT 06830
Phone: 203-629-4901
Fax: 203-629-4903
Website: www.cpequity.com

Management and Staff
Andrew C. Taub
Stephanie K. Schnabel

Whom to Contact
Andrew C. Taub
Stephanie K. Schnabel

Type of Firm
Investment/Merchant Bank Subsid/Affil

Project Preferences

Role in Financing:
Prefer role as deal originator but will also invest in deals created by others

Type of Financing Preferred:
First Stage Financing
Leveraged Buyout
Second Stage Financing
Special Situation

Size of Investments Considered
Min Size of Investment Considered (000s): $5,000
Max Size of Investment Considered: No Limit

Geographical Preferences

United States
All U.S.

Canada
All Canada

Industry Preferences

(% based on actual investment)

Consumer Related	48.1%
Internet Specific	38.8%
Biotechnology	13.1%

Additional Information
Name of Most Recent Fund: Catterton Partners IV
Most Recent Fund Was Raised: 09/01/1999
Year Founded: 1990
Capital Under Management: $500,000,000
Current Activity Level : Actively seeking new investments
Method of Compensation: Return on invest. most important, but chg. closing fees, service fees, etc.

COLLINSON, HOWE & LENNOX, LLC

1055 Washington Boulevard
Stamford, CT 06901
Phone: 203-324-7700
Fax: 203-324-3636
Website: www.chlmedical.com

Management and Staff
Jeffrey Collinson, Managing Partner
Ronald Lennox, Partner
Timothy Howe, Partner

Type of Firm
Private Firm Investing Own Capital

Industry Association Membership
National Venture Capital Association (NVCA)

Project Preferences

Role in Financing:
Prefer role as deal originator but will also invest in deals created by others

Type of Financing Preferred:
Early Stage
First Stage Financing
Research and Development
Seed
Start-up Financing

Geographical Preferences

United States
All U.S.

Industry Preferences

(% based on actual investment)

Medical/Health	57.5%
Biotechnology	32.6%
Internet Specific	9.8%

Additional Information
Name of Most Recent Fund: CHL Medical Partners LP
Most Recent Fund Was Raised: 04/01/1998
Year Founded: 1990
Capital Under Management: $60,000,000
Current Activity Level : Actively seeking new investments
Method of Compensation: Return on investment is of primary concern, do not charge fees

CONNECTICUT INNOVATIONS, INC.

999 West Street
Rocky Hill, CT 06067
Phone: 860-563-5851
Fax: 860-563-4877
Website: www.ctinnovations.com

Other Offices

Six Landmark Square
Suite 425
Stamford, CT 06901
Phone: 203-359-5616
Fax: 203-359-5816

Management and Staff
Arnold Brandyberry, Chief Operating Officer
Carolyn Kahn, Managing Director
Victor Budnick, President

Type of Firm
State Govt Affiliated NEC

Industry Association Membership
National Venture Capital Association (NVCA)

Project Preferences

Role in Financing:
Will function either as deal originator or investor in deals created by others

Type of Financing Preferred:
First Stage Financing
Joint Ventures
Mezzanine
Second Stage Financing
Startup

Size of Investments Considered
Min Size of Investment Considered (000s): $50
Max Size of Investment Considered (000s): $1,000

Geographical Preferences

United States
Northeast

Industry Preferences

(% based on actual investment)

Internet Specific	25.9%
Computer Software and Services	20.8%
Biotechnology	15.2%
Semiconductors/Other Elect.	12.5%
Industrial/Energy	10.8%
Medical/Health	9.1%
Consumer Related	2.7%
Other Products	1.5%
Communications and Media	1.1%
Computer Hardware	0.5%

Additional Information
Year Founded: 1989
Capital Under Management: $84,000,000
Current Activity Level : Actively seeking new investments
Method of Compensation: Return on investment is of primary concern, do not charge fees

CONNECTICUT-GREENE VENTURES, L.P.

777 Summer Street
Suite 300
Stamford, CT 06905-1022
Phone: 203-325-2522
Fax: 203-325-1064

Other Offices

3101 South Street
Washington, DC 20007
Phone: 202-293-1166
Fax: 202-293-1181

Type of Firm
Private Firm Investing Own Capital

Additional Information
Name of Most Recent Fund: Connecticut-Greene Ventures, L.P.
Most Recent Fund Was Raised: 02/02/1993
Current Activity Level : Reducing investment activity

CONNING CAPITAL PARTNERS

CityPlace II
185 Asylum Street
Hartford, CT 06103-4105
Phone: 860-520-1289
Fax: 860-520-1299
Website: www.conning.com

Management and Staff
Gerard Vecchio, Partner
Gregory Batton, Partner
John Clinton, Managing Partner
Preston Kavanagh, Chief Financial Officer
Stephan Christiansen, Partner
Steven Piaker, Partner

Type of Firm
Insurance Firm Affiliate or Subsidiary

Industry Association Membership
National Venture Capital Association (NVCA)

Project Preferences

Role in Financing:
Prefer role as deal originator

Type of Financing Preferred:
Expansion
Later Stage
Second Stage Financing

Size of Investments Considered
Min Size of Investment Considered (000s): $5,000
Max Size of Investment Considered (000s): $35,000

Geographical Preferences

United States
All U.S.

International
Bermuda
United Kingdom

Industry Preferences

(% based on actual investment)

Other Products	46.9%
Internet Specific	31.5%
Computer Software and Services	9.8%
Consumer Related	6.4%
Medical/Health	5.4%

Additional Information
Name of Most Recent Fund: Conning I nsurance Capital Limited Partnership V
Most Recent Fund Was Raised: 01/01/1997
Year Founded: 1912
Capital Under Management: $596,000,000
Current Activity Level : Actively seeking new investments
Method of Compensation: Return on investment is of primary concern, do not charge fees

CONSUMER VENTURE PARTNERS

Three Pickwick Plaza
Greenwich, CT 06830
Phone: 203-629-8800
Fax: 203-629-2019

Management and Staff
Chris Kirchen, Managing Director
David Yarnell, General Partner
Pearson Cummin, Managing Director

Type of Firm
Private Firm Investing Own Capital

Project Preferences

Role in Financing:
Prefer role as deal originator but will also invest in deals created by others

Type of Financing Preferred:
First Stage Financing
Leveraged Buyout
Second Stage Financing
Start-up Financing

Size of Investments Considered
Min Size of Investment Considered (000s): $10,000
Max Size of Investment Considered: No Limit

Geographical Preferences

United States
All U.S.

Industry Preferences

(% based on actual investment)

Consumer Related	92.8%
Internet Specific	5.9%
Other Products	1.3%

Additional Information
Year Founded: 1986
Capital Under Management: $85,000,000
Current Activity Level : Actively seeking new investments
Method of Compensation: Return on investment is of primary concern, do not charge fees

CRESTVIEW FINANCIAL GROUP, THE

431 Post Road East
Suite One
Westport, CT 06880-4403
Phone: 203-222-0333
Fax: 203-222-0000

Management and Staff
Norman Marland

Whom to Contact
Norman Marland

Type of Firm
Mgt. Consulting Firm

Project Preferences

Role in Financing:
Prefer role as deal originator but will also invest in deals created by others

Type of Financing Preferred:
First Stage Financing
Mezzanine
Research and Development
Second Stage Financing
Seed

Size of Investments Considered
Min Size of Investment Considered (000s): $500
Max Size of Investment Considered (000s): $3,000

Geographical Preferences

United States
All U.S.

Canada
All Canada

International
Australia
Bermuda
China
Eastern Europe
France
Germany
Italy
Mexico
South Africa
Spain
United Kingdom

Industry Preferences

Communications and Media
Communications and Media
Other Communication Prod.

Computer Hardware
Mini and Personal/Desktop
Computer Graphics and Dig
Integrated Turnkey System
Disk Relat. Memory Device

Computer Software
Artificial Intelligence

Internet Specific
Internet

Semiconductors/Other Elect.
Electronics
Electronic Components
Semiconductor
Component Testing Equipmt
Laser Related
Fiber Optics
Analytic/Scientific

Biotechnology
Biotechnology

Medical/Health
Medical/Health
Medical Products

Consumer Related
Consumer
Food/Beverage
Consumer Products
Education Related

Industrial/Energy
Energy
Industrial Products

Financial Services
Financial Services
Real Estate

Business Serv.
Consulting Services

Manufact.
Publishing

Agr/Forestr/Fish
Agriculture related

Additional Information
Year Founded: 1962
Current Activity Level : Actively seeking new investments
Method of Compensation: Return on invest. most important, but chg. closing fees, service fees, etc.

CULLINANE & DONNELLY VENTURE PARTNERS, L.P.

970 Farmington Avenue
West Hartford, CT 06107
Phone: 860-521-7811
Fax: 860-521-7911

Type of Firm
Private Firm Investing Own Capital

Project Preferences

Role in Financing:
Prefer role as deal originator but will also invest in deals created by others

Type of Financing Preferred:
First Stage Financing
Recapitalizations
Second Stage Financing
Seed

Size of Investments Considered
Min Size of Investment Considered (000s): $300
Max Size of Investment Considered (000s): $1,000

Geographical Preferences

United States
Northeast

Industry Preferences

Communications and Media
Data Communications

Computer Hardware
Integrated Turnkey System

Computer Software
Computer Services
Systems Software
Applications Software

Semiconductors/Other Elect.
Sensors
Circuit Boards
Component Testing Equipmt
Laser Related
Fiber Optics

Medical/Health
Diagnostic Services
Diagnostic Test Products

Consumer Related
Education Related

Financial Services
Financial Services

Additional Information
Name of Most Recent Fund: Connecticut Future Fund, L.P.
Most Recent Fund Was Raised: 02/06/1993
Year Founded: 1987
Capital Under Management: $50,000,000
Current Activity Level : Actively seeking new investments
Method of Compensation: Return on investment is of primary concern, do not charge fees

---

ECOM PARTNERS LLC

101 Merritt 7
3rd Floor
Norwalk, CT 06851
Phone: 203-849-6064
Fax: 203-849-5918
Website: www.ecompartners.net

Management and Staff
Bob Bowman, Partner
Gary Mendel, Partner
John Fullmer, Partner
Michael Quinn, Partner
Richard Ward, Partner
Tony Menchaca, Partner

Type of Firm
Private Firm Investing Own Capital

Industry Preferences

(% based on actual investment)

Internet Specific	79.5%
Computer Software and Services	20.5%

Additional Information
Year Founded: 1999
Capital Under Management: $33,000,000
Current Activity Level : Actively seeking new investments

ENDEAVOR CAPITAL MANAGEMENT

830 Post Road East
Westport, CT 06880
Phone: 203-341-7788
Fax: 203-341-7799

Other Offices

317 S Division Street
Suite 49
Ann Arbor, MI 48104
Phone: 313-996-3032
Fax: 313-996-0886

35 Linda Vista Avenue
Atherton, CA 94027
Phone: 650-325-3950
Fax: 650-324-3441

Management and Staff

Anthony Buffa, Managing Partner
David Wisowaty, General Partner
David Miller, Venture Partner
Ed Jones, Venture Partner
Gene Solnick, Chief Financial Officer
Nancy Haar, General Partner
Ron Reed, Partner

Whom to Contact

Nancy Haar

Type of Firm

Private Firm Investing Own Capital

Industry Association Membership

National Venture Capital Association (NVCA)

Project Preferences

Role in Financing:
Prefer role as deal originator but will also invest in deals created by others

Type of Financing Preferred:
Early Stage
Expansion

Size of Investments Considered
Min Size of Investment Considered (000s): $5,000
Max Size of Investment Considered (000s): $20,000

Geographical Preferences

United States
All U.S.

Canada
All Canada

Industry Preferences

(% based on actual investment)

Communications and Media	44.6%
Internet Specific	16.6%
Other Products	15.8%
Consumer Related	14.7%
Computer Hardware	8.4%

Additional Information

Name of Most Recent Fund: Strome Endeavor Partners
Most Recent Fund Was Raised: 01/01/1998
Year Founded: 1998
Capital Under Management: $80,000,000
Current Activity Level : Actively seeking new investments
Method of Compensation: Return on investment is of primary concern, do not charge fees

EQUINOX INVESTMENT PARTNERS

19 Old Kings Highway South
Darien, CT 06820
Phone: 203-656-6080
Fax: 203-656-6085

Management and Staff

Kevin Lynch, Chief Financial Officer

Whom to Contact

Robert Wickey

Type of Firm

Private Equity Advisor or Fund of Fund Mgr

Project Preferences

Role in Financing:
Will function either as deal originator or investor in deals created by others

Type of Financing Preferred:
Acquisition
Balanced
Later Stage
Leveraged Buyout
Mezzanine
Private Placement
Recapitalizations
Special Situation
Turnaround

Size of Investments Considered
Min Size of Investment Considered (000s): $5,000
Max Size of Investment Considered (000s): $25,000

Geographical Preferences

United States
All U.S.

Industry Preferences

Communications and Media
Commercial Communications
CATV & Pay TV Systems
Radio & TV Broadcasting
Telecommunications
Data Communications
Satellite Microwave Comm.
Other Communication Prod.

Computer Other
Computer Related

Semiconductors/Other Elect.
Electronic Components
Semiconductor
Controllers and Sensors
Sensors
Circuit Boards

Medical/Health
Medical/Health
Drug/Equipmt Delivery
Medical Products
Disposable Med. Products
Health Services

Consumer Related
Consumer
Education Related

Industrial/Energy
Energy
Industrial Products
Factory Automation
Process Control
Robotics
Machinery

Transportation
Transportation

Financial Services
Financial Services

Business Serv.
Distribution
Consulting Services
Media

Manufact.
Manufacturing
Publishing

Agr/Forestr/Fish
Agriculture related

Other
Socially Responsible
Environment Responsible

Additional Information
Year Founded: 1989
Capital Under Management: $181,000,000
Current Activity Level : Actively seeking new investments

FERRER FREEMAN THOMPSON & CO

The Mill
10 Glenville Street
Greenwich, CT 06831
Phone: 203-532-8011
Fax: 203-532-8016

Management and Staff
Carlos Ferrer, Co-Founder
David Freeman, Managing Director
Robert Thompson, Managing Director

Whom to Contact
Thomas Flynn

Type of Firm
Private Firm Investing Own Capital

Project Preferences

Role in Financing:
Prefer role as deal originator but will also invest in deals created by others

Type of Financing Preferred:
Industry Rollups
Later Stage
Leveraged Buyout
Second Stage Financing
Special Situation

Geographical Preferences

United States
All U.S.

Canada
All Canada

International
Bermuda
France
Germany
Italy
Spain
United Kingdom
No Preference

Industry Preferences

Medical/Health
Medical/Health
Health Services

Additional Information
Name of Most Recent Fund: Health Care Capital Partners L.P. & Health care Executive Pa
Most Recent Fund Was Raised: 07/01/1996
Year Founded: 1995
Capital Under Management: $220,000,000
Current Activity Level : Actively seeking new investments
Method of Compensation: Return on investment is of primary concern, do not charge fees

FIRST NEW ENGLAND CAPITAL, L.P.

100 Pearl Street
Hartford, CT 06103
Phone: 860-293-3333
Fax: 860-293-3338
Website: www.firstnewenglandcapital.com

Management and Staff
Lawrence Stillman, Vice President

Type of Firm
SBIC Not elsewhere classified

Industry Association Membership
Natl assoc of Small Bus. Inv. Co (NASBIC)

Project Preferences

Role in Financing:
Prefer role as deal originator but will also invest in deals created by others

Type of Financing Preferred:
Expansion
Management Buyouts
Mezzanine

Size of Investments Considered
Min Size of Investment Considered (000s): $100
Max Size of Investment Considered (000s): $1,000

Geographical Preferences

United States
Northeast

Industry Preferences

Communications and Media
Communications and Media

Computer Other
Computer Related

Semiconductors/Other Elect.
Electronics

Medical/Health
Medical/Health

Consumer Related
Consumer

Additional Information
Name of Most Recent Fund: First New England Capital 2, L.P.
Most Recent Fund Was Raised: 09/01/1998
Year Founded: 1988
Capital Under Management: $12,500,000
Current Activity Level : Actively seeking new investments
Method of Compensation: Return on investment is of primary concern, do not charge fees

FLAG VENTURE PARTNERS (FKA FOX VENTURE PARTNERS)

3 Stamford Landing, Suite 330
46 Southfield Avenue
Stamford, CT 06902
Phone: 203-352-0440
Fax: 203-352-0441
Website: www.flagventure.com

Other Offices

10 Post Office Sq.
North Tower, Suite 960
Boston, MA 02109
Phone: 617-426-7756
Fax: 617-426-7765

Management and Staff
Diana Farzier, Managing Partner
Kate O'Neil, General Partner
Louis Sciarretta, Chief Financial Officer
Peter Lawrence, Managing Partner

Type of Firm
Private Firm Investing Own Capital

Additional Information
Name of Most Recent Fund: FOX Venture Partners,L.P. (FKA: Fox Ventures)
Most Recent Fund Was Raised: 01/01/1995
Capital Under Management: $1,585,000,000
Current Activity Level : Inactive / Unknown

GATX VENTURES (FKA: MEIER MITCHELL & CO.)

16 Munson Road
Fifth Floor
Farmington, CT 06032
Phone: 860-284-4300
Fax: 860-284-4350
Website: www.gatxventures.com

See California for full listing.

GREENWICH VENTURE PARTNERS, INC.

Eight Sound Shore Drive
Suite 100
Greenwich, CT 06830
Phone: 203-629-4447
Fax: 203-629-4848

Type of Firm
Private Firm Investing Own Capital

Project Preferences

Role in Financing:
Prefer role as deal originator

Type of Financing Preferred:
First Stage Financing
Leveraged Buyout
Mezzanine
Second Stage Financing
Special Situation

Geographical Preferences

United States
All U.S.

Canada
All Canada

Industry Preferences

Industrial/Energy
Alternative Energy
Energy Conservation Relat

Additional Information
Year Founded: 1984
Current Activity Level : Actively seeking new investments
Method of Compensation: Return on investment is of primary concern, do not charge fees

HAMILTON ROBINSON & CO., INC.

281 Tresser Boulevard
4th Floor
Stamford, CT 06901
Phone: 203-602-0011
Fax: 203-602-2206
Website: www.hrco.com

Management and Staff
Christopher F. Carmel
Mark Riser
Scott Oakford

Whom to Contact
Christopher F. Carmel
Mark Riser
Scott Oakford

Type of Firm
Private Firm Investing Own Capital

Project Preferences

Role in Financing:
Prefer role as deal originator

Type of Financing Preferred:
Leveraged Buyout

Size of Investments Considered
Min Size of Investment Considered (000s): $15,000
Max Size of Investment Considered: No Limit

Geographical Preferences

United States
All U.S.

Canada
All Canada

International
United Kingdom

Industry Preferences

Communications and Media
Other Communication Prod.

Semiconductors/Other Elect.
Electronics
Sensors

Medical/Health
Diagnostic Services
Diagnostic Test Products
Other Therapeutic
Medical Products
Disposable Med. Products
Hospital/Other Instit.

Consumer Related
Entertainment and Leisure
Retail
Food/Beverage
Consumer Products
Consumer Services

Industrial/Energy
Oil and Gas Exploration
Oil & Gas Drilling,Explor
Industrial Products
Materials
Factory Automation
Machinery
Environmental Related

Transportation
Transportation

Financial Services
Financial Services

Manufact.
Publishing

Agr/Forestr/Fish
Agriculture related

Additional Information
Name of Most Recent Fund: Spinnaker Investor Partners II
Most Recent Fund Was Raised: 01/01/1987
Year Founded: 1986
Capital Under Management: $35,000,000
Current Activity Level : Actively seeking new investments
Method of Compensation: Return on invest. most important, but chg. closing fees, service fees, etc.

IFORMATION GROUP

c/o General Atlantic Partners
3 Pickwick Plaza
Greenwich, CT 06830
Phone: 203-629-8624
Fax: 203-622-4143

Management and Staff
Clifton Robbins, Managing Director
David Pecaut, Managing Director
Peter Wheeler, Managing Director
Peter Maillet, Managing Director

Type of Firm
Investment/Merchant Bank Subsid/Affil

Project Preferences

Type of Financing Preferred:
Expansion
Startup

Geographical Preferences

International
All International

Industry Preferences

Internet Specific
Internet

Additional Information

Year Founded: 2000
Capital Under Management: $300,000,000
Current Activity Level : Actively seeking new investments

IMPEX VENTURE MANAGEMENT CO.

300 Ridgefield Road
Wilton, CT 06897

See New York for full listing.

INSURANCE VENTURE PARTNERS, INC.

31 Brookside Drive
Suite 211
Greenwich, CT 06830
Phone: 203-861-0030
Fax: 203-861-2745

Other Offices

23 Old Kings Highway South
P.O. Box 1246
Darien, CT 06820
Phone: 203-656-1000
Fax: 203-656-9526

Management and Staff

Bernard Brown, Managing Director

Type of Firm

Mgt. Consulting Firm

Project Preferences

Role in Financing:
Prefer role as deal originator but will also invest in deals created by others

Type of Financing Preferred:
First Stage Financing
Leveraged Buyout
Second Stage Financing

Size of Investments Considered

Min Size of Investment Considered (000s): $500
Max Size of Investment Considered (000s): $50,000

Geographical Preferences

International
Australia
Bermuda
China
Eastern Europe
France
Germany
Italy
Japan
Mexico
South Africa
Spain
United Kingdom

Industry Preferences

Financial Services
Insurance

Additional Information

Name of Most Recent Fund: Capital Z Financial Services Fund II, LP (FKA:Insurance II)
Most Recent Fund Was Raised: 07/13/1999
Year Founded: 1985
Capital Under Management: $550,000,000
Current Activity Level : Actively seeking new investments
Method of Compensation: Function primarily in service area, receive contingent fee in cash or equity

INTERNET HEALTHCARE GROUP

22 Waterville Road
Avon, CT 06001
Phone: 860-679-5903

Management and Staff

Eric Reimer, Vice President
Rene Lerer, President
Steven Shulman, Chairman & CEO

Type of Firm

Incubators

Project Preferences

Type of Financing Preferred:
Early Stage
Seed
Startup

Industry Preferences

Internet Specific
Internet

Medical/Health
Medical/Health

Additional Information

Capital Under Management: $100,000,000
Current Activity Level : Actively seeking new investments

INTERNET.COM

23 Old Kings Highway South
Darien, CT 06820
Phone: 203-662-2800
Fax: 203-655-4686

Management and Staff

Alan Meckler, Chairman & CEO
Christopher Baudouin, Chief Financial Officer

Type of Firm

Non-Financial Corp. Affiliate or Subsidiary

Project Preferences

Type of Financing Preferred:
Early Stage

Geographical Preferences

International
All International

Industry Preferences

(% based on actual investment)

Internet Specific	98.9%
Computer Software and Services	1.1%

Additional Information

Name of Most Recent Fund: internet.com Venture Fund I LLC
Most Recent Fund Was Raised: 04/12/1999
Year Founded: 2000
Capital Under Management: $5,000,000
Current Activity Level : Actively seeking new investments

JAMES B. KOBAK & CO.

Four Mansfield Place
Darien, CT 06820
Phone: 203-656-3471
Fax: 203-655-2905

Type of Firm
Private Firm Investing Own Capital

Project Preferences

Role in Financing:
Prefer role as deal originator but will also invest in deals created by others

Type of Financing Preferred:
First Stage Financing

Industry Preferences

Manufact.
Publishing

Additional Information
Year Founded: 1971
Current Activity Level : Actively seeking new investments

KIDD, KAMM & COMPANY

Three Pickwick Plaza
Greenwich, CT 06830
Phone: 203-661-0070
Fax: 203-661-1839
Website: www.kiddcompany.com

Type of Firm
Private Firm Investing Own Capital

Project Preferences

Role in Financing:
Prefer role as deal originator but will also invest in deals created by others

Type of Financing Preferred:
First Stage Financing
Leveraged Buyout
Mezzanine
Second Stage Financing

Additional Information
Name of Most Recent Fund: Kidd Kamm Equity Partners
Most Recent Fund Was Raised: 12/23/1991
Year Founded: 1997
Current Activity Level : Inactive / Unknown

LANDMARK PARTNERS, INC.

10 Mill Pond Lane
Simsbury, CT 06070
Phone: 860-651-9760
Fax: 860-651-8890
Website: www.landmarkpartners.com

Other Offices

Portman Square House
43-45 Portman Square
London, United Kingdom W2H 0HN
Phone: 44-207-969-2857

Management and Staff
Anthony Roscigno, Partner
Chad Alfeld, Principal
James McConnell, Partner
John Griner, Managing Partner
Patrick Flanagan, Principal
R. Paul Mehlman, Principal
Richard Maine, Managing Partner
Robert Harvey, Partner
Robert Shanfield, Partner
Scott Conners, Principal
Stanley Alfeld, Managing Partner
Timothy Haviland, Managing Partner

Type of Firm
Private Equity Advisor or Fund of Fund Mgr

Industry Association Membership
National Venture Capital Association (NVCA)

Project Preferences

Role in Financing:
Prefer role as deal originator

Type of Financing Preferred:
First Stage Financing
Fund of Funds
Second Stage Financing
Seed
Special Situation
Start-up Financing

Geographical Preferences

United States
All U.S.

Canada
All Canada

International
All International

Industry Preferences

(% based on actual investment)

Other Products	53.6%
Computer Software and Services	13.3%
Computer Hardware	13.0%
Semiconductors/Other Elect.	5.9%
Medical/Health	5.7%
Consumer Related	3.7%
Internet Specific	2.7%
Biotechnology	1.6%
Industrial/Energy	0.4%

Additional Information
Name of Most Recent Fund: Landmark Private Equity Fund VIII
Most Recent Fund Was Raised: 09/01/1998
Year Founded: 1984
Capital Under Management: $2,900,000,000
Current Activity Level : Actively seeking new investments
Method of Compensation: Other

LTI VENTURES LEASING CORP.

221 Danbury Road
Wilton, CT 06897
Phone: 203-563-1100
Fax: 203-563-1111
Website: www.ltileasing.com

Other Offices

10 Liberty Square
Boston, MA 02109
Phone: 617-426-4116
Fax: 617-482-6475

23 West Park Ave
Suite 1060
Merchantville, NJ 08109
Phone: 856-910-9970

655 Montgomery St
Suite 800
San Francisco, CA 94121
Phone: 415-834-0773

Two Clearfield Road
P.O. Box 447
Ardmore, PA 19003-0447
Phone: 610-446-4479
Fax: 610-446-3771

Management and Staff
F. Jared Sprole, Chief Executive Officer
George Parker, Chief Financial Officer
John Strahley, Vice President
Richard Livingston, Vice President

Whom to Contact
Barbara Hughes
Geoffrey W. Smith
Kenneth R. Maggi

Type of Firm
Private Firm Investing Own Capital

Project Preferences

Role in Financing:
Prefer role as deal originator but will also invest in deals created by others

Type of Financing Preferred:
Early Stage
First Stage Financing
Later Stage
Mezzanine
Second Stage Financing
Special Situation

Size of Investments Considered
Min Size of Investment Considered (000s): $500
Max Size of Investment Considered (000s): $2,000

Geographical Preferences

United States
All U.S.

Industry Preferences

Communications and Media
Commercial Communications
Telecommunications
Data Communications
Satellite Microwave Comm.
Other Communication Prod.

Computer Hardware
Computers
Mini and Personal/Desktop
Computer Graphics and Dig

Computer Software
Systems Software
Applications Software

Internet Specific
Internet

Computer Other
Computer Related

Semiconductors/Other Elect.
Electronics
Electronic Components

Biotechnology
Industrial Biotechnology
Biosensors
Biotech Related Research

Medical/Health
Medical Diagnostics
Diagnostic Services
Diagnostic Test Products
Drug/Equipmt Delivery
Other Therapeutic
Medical Products
Pharmaceuticals

Consumer Related
Retail
Computer Stores
Food/Beverage

Industrial/Energy
Robotics
Machinery

Additional Information
Year Founded: 1983
Capital Under Management: $200,000,000
Current Activity Level : Actively seeking new investments
Method of Compensation: Return on investment is of primary concern, do not charge fees

---

MARKETCORP VENTURES L.P.

274 Riverside Avenue
Westport, CT 06880
Phone: 203-222-3030
Fax: 203-222-3033

Management and Staff
E. Bulkeley Griswold

Whom to Contact
E. Bulkeley Griswold

Type of Firm
Private Firm Investing Own Capital

Project Preferences

Role in Financing:
Prefer role as deal originator but will also invest in deals created by others

Type of Financing Preferred:
First Stage Financing
Leveraged Buyout
Mezzanine
Second Stage Financing

Size of Investments Considered
Min Size of Investment Considered (000s): $500
Max Size of Investment Considered (000s): $1,000

Geographical Preferences

United States
All U.S.

Industry Preferences

Computer Software
Computer Services

Consumer Related
Entertainment and Leisure
Retail
Computer Stores
Food/Beverage
Consumer Products
Consumer Services
Other Restaurants

Additional Information
Name of Most Recent Fund: Marketcorp Venture Associates, L.P.
Most Recent Fund Was Raised: 01/01/1984
Year Founded: 1984
Capital Under Management: $66,000,000
Current Activity Level : Reducing investment activity
Method of Compensation: Return on investment is of primary concern, do not charge fees

---

MEDMAX VENTURES, L.P.

1 Northwestern Drive
Suite 203
Bloomfield, CT 06002
Phone: 860-286-2960
Fax: 860-286-9960

Other Offices

P.O. Box 354
Zichron Yaakov, Israel 30900
Phone: 972-6-396-397
Fax: 972-6-396-133

Management and Staff
Deborah Sopher Matson
Noam Karstaedt

Whom to Contact
Deborah Sopher Matson
Noam Karstaedt

Type of Firm
Private Firm Investing Own Capital

Project Preferences

Role in Financing:
Prefer role as deal originator but will also invest in deals created by others

Type of Financing Preferred:
First Stage Financing
Research and Development
Second Stage Financing
Seed
Start-up Financing

Size of Investments Considered
Min Size of Investment Considered (000s): $500
Max Size of Investment Considered: No Limit

Geographical Preferences
United States
Northeast

Industry Preferences
Biotechnology
Biosensors
Biotech Related Research
Biotech Related Research

Medical/Health
Medical Diagnostics
Diagnostic Services
Diagnostic Test Products
Medical Therapeutics
Drug/Equipmt Delivery
Other Therapeutic
Medical Products
Disposable Med. Products
Pharmaceuticals

Additional Information
Name of Most Recent Fund: Jerome Capital LLC
Most Recent Fund Was Raised: 01/01/1997
Year Founded: 1991
Capital Under Management: $30,000,000
Current Activity Level : Actively seeking new investments
Method of Compensation: Return on investment is of primary concern, do not charge fees

MEMHARD INVESTMENT BANKERS, INC.

P.O. Box 609
Ridgefield, CT 06877
Phone: 203-431-3666
Fax: 203-438-1961

Other Offices
P.O. Box 617
Old Greenwich, CT 06877
Phone: 203-637-5494
Fax: 203-637-9414

Type of Firm
Investment/Merchant Bank Investing Own or Client Funds

Project Preferences
Role in Financing:
Prefer role as deal originator

Type of Financing Preferred:
Control-block Purchases
Leveraged Buyout
Recapitalizations
Second Stage Financing
Special Situation

Size of Investments Considered
Min Size of Investment Considered (000s): $2,000
Max Size of Investment Considered: No Limit

Geographical Preferences
United States
Mid Atlantic
Midwest
Northeast
Northwest
Southeast

Industry Preferences
Communications and Media
Communications and Media

Semiconductors/Other Elect.
Semiconductor
Sensors
Component Testing Equipmt
Laser Related
Fiber Optics
Analytic/Scientific

Medical/Health
Medical Products

Industrial/Energy
Energy Conservation Relat
Industrial Products
Factory Automation
Machinery
Environmental Related

Transportation
Transportation

Financial Services
Real Estate

Manufact.
Office Automation Equipmt

Additional Information
Year Founded: 1973
Capital Under Management: $3,000,000
Current Activity Level : Actively seeking new investments
Method of Compensation: Return on investment is of primary concern, do not charge fees

NATURAL GAS PARTNERS

500 West Putnam Ave.
4th Floor
Greenwich, CT 06830
Phone: 203-629-2440
Fax: 203-629-3334

Management and Staff
David R. Albin
Kenneth A. Hersh

Whom to Contact
David R. Albin
Kenneth A. Hersh

Type of Firm
Private Firm Investing Own Capital

Project Preferences
Role in Financing:
Prefer role as deal originator

Type of Financing Preferred:
First Stage Financing
Leveraged Buyout
Second Stage Financing
Special Situation
Start-up Financing

Size of Investments Considered
Min Size of Investment Considered (000s): $15,000
Max Size of Investment Considered: No Limit

Geographical Preferences
United States
All U.S.

Canada
Central Canada
Western Canada

International
Australia
Mexico
Middle East
South Africa

Industry Preferences

(% based on actual investment)

Industrial/Energy	95.8%
Internet Specific	4.2%

Additional Information

Name of Most Recent Fund: Natural Gas Partners VI, L.P.
Most Recent Fund Was Raised: 05/01/1999
Year Founded: 1988
Capital Under Management: $917,000,000
Current Activity Level : Actively seeking new investments
Method of Compensation: Return on invest. most important, but chg. closing fees, service fees, etc.

NORTHEAST VENTURES

One State Street
Suite 1720
Hartford, CT 06103
Phone: 860-547-1414
Fax: 860-246-8755

Type of Firm

Mgt. Consulting Firm

Project Preferences

Role in Financing:
Prefer role as deal originator

Size of Investments Considered

Min Size of Investment Considered (000s): $1,000
Max Size of Investment Considered: No Limit

Geographical Preferences

United States
All U.S.

Industry Preferences

Communications and Media
Telecommunications
Data Communications
Satellite Microwave Comm.

Computer Hardware
Computer Graphics and Dig
Disk Relat. Memory Device

Computer Software
Systems Software
Applications Software
Artificial Intelligence

Semiconductors/Other Elect.
Electronic Components

Biotechnology
Industrial Biotechnology
Biosensors
Biotech Related Research
Biotech Related Research

Medical/Health
Medical Diagnostics
Diagnostic Test Products
Medical Therapeutics
Other Therapeutic
Hospital/Other Instit.

Consumer Related
Education Related

Industrial/Energy
Oil and Gas Exploration
Oil & Gas Drilling,Explor
Alternative Energy
Energy Conservation Relat
Industrial Products

Additional Information

Year Founded: 1989
Capital Under Management: $10,000,000
Current Activity Level : Actively seeking new investments
Method of Compensation: Return on invest. most important, but chg. closing fees, service fees, etc.

NORTHINGTON PARTNERS

One Northington Place
35 Tower Lane
Avon, CT 06001
Phone: 860-676-1942
Fax: 860-676-1930

Type of Firm

Private Firm Investing Own Capital

Project Preferences

Type of Financing Preferred:
Balanced

Geographical Preferences

United States
All U.S.

Industry Preferences

Financial Services
Insurance

Additional Information

Name of Most Recent Fund: Northington Private Capital L.P.
Most Recent Fund Was Raised: 01/01/1989
Capital Under Management: $142,000,000
Current Activity Level : Actively seeking new investments

NTC GROUP, THE

Three Pickwick Plaza
Suite 200
Greenwich, CT 06830
Phone: 203-862-2800
Fax: 203-622-6538

Type of Firm

Private Firm Investing Own Capital

Project Preferences

Role in Financing:
Prefer role as deal originator but will also invest in deals created by others

Type of Financing Preferred:
Control-block Purchases
First Stage Financing
Leveraged Buyout
Seed

Size of Investments Considered

Min Size of Investment Considered (000s): $1,000
Max Size of Investment Considered: No Limit

Geographical Preferences

United States
All U.S.

Industry Preferences

Semiconductors/Other Elect.
Electronic Components
Sensors

Industrial/Energy
Factory Automation
Machinery

Additional Information

Year Founded: 1985
Capital Under Management: $150,000,000
Current Activity Level : Actively seeking new investments
Method of Compensation: Return on investment is of primary concern, do not charge fees

OAK INVESTMENT PARTNERS

One Gorham Island
Westport, CT 06880
Phone: 203-226-8346
Fax: 203-227-0372
Website: www.oakvc.com

Other Offices

4550 Norwest Center
90 South Seventh Street
Minneapolis, MN 55402
Phone: 612-339-9322
Fax: 612-337-8017

525 University Avenue
Suite 1300
Palo Alto, CA 94301
Phone: 650-614-3700
Fax: 650-328-6345

Management and Staff

Ann Lamont, General Partner
Bandel Carano, General Partner
Basil Horangic, Principal
Catherine Agee, Principal
David Black, Partner
David Walrod, Principal
David Nelson, Chief Financial Officer
David Best, General Partner
Ed Glassmeyer, General Partner
Eileen More, General Partner
Fred Harman, General Partner
Grace Ames, Chief Financial Officer
Jerry Gallagher, General Partner
Michele Cassidy, Chief Financial Officer
Norman Nie, Partner
Seth Harrison, General Partner
Stewart Greenfield, General Partner

Type of Firm

Private Firm Investing Own Capital

Industry Association Membership

National Venture Capital Association (NVCA)
Western Association of Venture Capitalists (WAVC)

Project Preferences

Role in Financing:

Prefer role as deal originator but will also invest in deals created by others

Type of Financing Preferred:

Balanced
Control-block Purchases
Early Stage
First Stage Financing
Generalist PE
Later Stage
Leveraged Buyout
Open Market
Second Stage Financing
Special Situation
Start-up Financing

Geographical Preferences

United States

All U.S.
All U.S.

International

Australia
Bermuda
China
France
Germany
Italy
Japan
Spain
United Kingdom

Industry Preferences

(% based on actual investment)

Internet Specific	25.8%
Communications and Media	19.6%
Computer Software and Services	17.0%
Semiconductors/Other Elect.	13.1%
Computer Hardware	7.9%
Medical/Health	6.3%
Consumer Related	5.5%
Biotechnology	2.3%
Other Products	1.6%
Industrial/Energy	0.8%

Additional Information

Name of Most Recent Fund: Oak Investment Partners IX
Most Recent Fund Was Raised: 09/14/1999
Year Founded: 1978
Capital Under Management: $2,600,000,000
Current Activity Level : Actively seeking new investments
Method of Compensation: Return on investment is of primary concern, do not charge fees

OEM CAPITAL

1071 Post Road East
Westport, CT 06880
Phone: 203-226-7052
Fax: 203-226-5741
Website: www.oemcapital.com

Management and Staff

Ronald Klammer, Managing Director

Whom to Contact

R.J. Klammer

Type of Firm

Investment/Merchant Bank Subsid/Affil

Project Preferences

Role in Financing:

Prefer role as deal originator

Type of Financing Preferred:

Acquisition
Control-block Purchases
Leveraged Buyout
Management Buyouts
Private Placement
Recapitalizations
Special Situation

Size of Investments Considered

Min Size of Investment Considered (000s): $1,000
Max Size of Investment Considered (000s): $5,000

Geographical Preferences

United States

All U.S.

Industry Preferences

Communications and Media

Communications and Media

Computer Hardware

Computers

Semiconductors/Other Elect.

Electronics

Additional Information

Year Founded: 1985
Current Activity Level : Actively seeking new investments
Method of Compensation: Return on invest. most important, but chg. closing fees, service fees, etc.

ORIEN VENTURES

One Post Road
Fairfield, CT 06430
Phone: 203-259-9933
Fax: 203-259-5288

Other Offices

14523 SW Westlake Drive
Lake Oswego, OR 97035
Phone: 503-699-1680
Fax: 503-699-1681

Management and Staff
Anthony Miadich, Managing General Partner
George Kalan, Managing General Partner

Whom to Contact
Anthony Miadich
George Kalan

Type of Firm
Private Firm Investing Own Capital

Project Preferences

Role in Financing:
Will function either as deal originator or investor in deals created by others

Type of Financing Preferred:
Early Stage
First Stage Financing
Seed
Startup

Size of Investments Considered
Min Size of Investment Considered (000s): $500
Max Size of Investment Considered: No Limit

Geographical Preferences

International
No Preference

Industry Preferences

Communications and Media
Telecommunications
Wireless Communications
Data Communications
Other Communication Prod.

Computer Software
Software
Applications Software

Internet Specific
E-Commerce Technology
Internet
Web Aggregration/Portals

Semiconductors/Other Elect.
Component Testing Equipmt
Laser Related
Fiber Optics

Medical/Health
Medical Products

Additional Information
Name of Most Recent Fund: Orien II, L.P.
Most Recent Fund Was Raised: 07/01/1988
Year Founded: 1985
Capital Under Management: $78,000,000
Current Activity Level : Actively seeking new investments
Method of Compensation: Return on investment is of primary concern, do not charge fees

OXFORD BIOSCIENCE PARTNERS

315 Post Road West
Westport, CT 06880
Phone: 203-341-3300
Fax: 617-357-7476
Website: www.oxbio.com

See Massachusetts for full listing.

OXFORD PARTNERS

315 Post Road West
Westport, CT 06880
Phone: 203-341-3300
Fax: 203-341-3309

Other Offices

6809 Shearwater Lane
Malibu, CA 90265
Phone: 310-589-2510
Fax: 310-589-2520

750 Lexington Avenue
New York, NY 10022
Phone: 212446-5230
Fax: 212-446-5290

Type of Firm
Private Firm Investing Own Capital

Industry Association Membership
Natl assoc of Small Bus. Inv. Co (NASBIC)

Project Preferences

Type of Financing Preferred:
Balanced

Geographical Preferences

International
No Preference

Additional Information
Name of Most Recent Fund: Oxford Venture Fund I
Most Recent Fund Was Raised: 10/01/1981
Year Founded: 1981
Capital Under Management: $125,000,000
Current Activity Level : Inactive / Unknown

PEQUOT CAPITAL MANAGEMENT INC.

500 Nyala Farm Road
Westport, CT 06880
Phone: 203-429-2200
Website: www.pequotcapital.com

See New York for full listing.

PHOENIX HOME LIFE MUTUAL INSURANCE CO.

56 Prospect Street
Second Floor P.O. Box 150480
Hartford, CT 06115-0480
Phone: 860-403-5000
Fax: 860-403-5451

Management and Staff
Paul Chute, Managing Director

Whom to Contact
Paul Chute

Type of Firm
Insurance Firm Affiliate or Subsidiary

Project Preferences

Role in Financing:
Other

Type of Financing Preferred:
Control-block Purchases
First Stage Financing
Leveraged Buyout
Mezzanine
Research and Development
Second Stage Financing
Seed
Special Situation
Start-up Financing

Size of Investments Considered
Min Size of Investment Considered (000s): $5,000
Max Size of Investment Considered: No Limit

Geographical Preferences

International
No Preference

Additional Information
Year Founded: 1974
Capital Under Management: $48,000,000
Current Activity Level : Actively seeking new investments
Method of Compensation: Return on investment is of primary concern, do not charge fees

PRIME CAPITAL MANAGEMENT CO., INC.

550 West Avenue
Stamford, CT 06902
Phone: 203-964-0642
Fax: 203-964-0862

Other Offices

1177 Summer St
Stanford, CT

Management and Staff
Dean Fenton

Whom to Contact
Dean Fenton

Type of Firm
Private Firm Investing Own Capital

Project Preferences

Role in Financing:
Prefer role as deal originator but will also invest in deals created by others

Type of Financing Preferred:
First Stage Financing
Recapitalizations
Second Stage Financing

Size of Investments Considered
Min Size of Investment Considered (000s): $300
Max Size of Investment Considered (000s): $800

Geographical Preferences

United States
Northeast

Industry Preferences

Communications and Media
Commercial Communications
Telecommunications
Data Communications
Other Communication Prod.

Computer Hardware
Computers
Mini and Personal/Desktop
Computer Graphics and Dig
Disk Relat. Memory Device

Computer Software
Computer Services
Systems Software
Applications Software
Artificial Intelligence

Semiconductors/Other Elect.
Electronics
Electronic Components
Sensors

Biotechnology
Biosensors
Biotech Related Research
Biotech Related Research

Medical/Health
Diagnostic Services
Diagnostic Test Products
Medical Products
Hospital/Other Instit.

Consumer Related
Retail
Computer Stores
Franchises(NEC)
Consumer Products
Consumer Services

Industrial/Energy
Alternative Energy
Energy Conservation Relat
Industrial Products
Factory Automation
Robotics
Machinery

Financial Services
Financial Services

Business Serv.
Consulting Services

Manufact.
Office Automation Equipmt

Additional Information
Name of Most Recent Fund: Prime Capital III
Most Recent Fund Was Raised: 01/01/1997
Year Founded: 1981
Capital Under Management: $36,200,000
Current Activity Level : Actively seeking new investments
Method of Compensation: Return on investment is of primary concern, do not charge fees

PRINCE VENTURES

25 Ford Road
Westport, CT 06880
Phone: 203-227-8332
Fax: 203-226-5302

See Illinois for full listing.

REGULUS INTERNATIONAL CAPITAL CO., INC.

140 Greenwich Avenue
Greenwich, CT 06830
Phone: 203-625-9700
Fax: 203-625-9706

Type of Firm
Private Firm Investing Own Capital

Project Preferences

Role in Financing:
Prefer role as deal originator

Type of Financing Preferred:
Research and Development
Seed
Start-up Financing

Size of Investments Considered
Min Size of Investment Considered (000s): $100
Max Size of Investment Considered (000s): $500

Geographical Preferences

International
No Preference

Industry Preferences

Computer Software
Artificial Intelligence

Industrial/Energy
Materials
Machinery

Manufact.
Publishing

Additional Information
Year Founded: 1976
Current Activity Level : Actively seeking new investments
Method of Compensation: Return on invest. most important, but chg. closing fees, service fees, etc.

RFE INVESTMENT PARTNERS

36 Grove Street
New Canaan, CT 06840
Phone: 203-966-2800
Fax: 203-966-3109
Website: www.rfeip.com

Other Offices

36 Grove St
New Cannan, CT

Management and Staff
A. Dean Davis, Partner
Andrew Wagner, Partner
Howard Landis, Partner
James Parsons, Partner
Michael Foster, Partner
Robert Williams, Partner

Whom to Contact
A. Dean Davis
Howard Landis
James Parsons

Type of Firm
Private Firm Investing Own Capital

Industry Association Membership
Natl assoc of Small Bus. Inv. Co (NASBIC)

Project Preferences

Role in Financing:
Prefer role as deal originator but will also invest in deals created by others

Type of Financing Preferred:
Industry Rollups
Leveraged Buyout
Mezzanine
Second Stage Financing
Special Situation

Size of Investments Considered
Min Size of Investment Considered (000s): $15,000
Max Size of Investment Considered: No Limit

Geographical Preferences

United States
All U.S.

Industry Preferences

(% based on actual investment)

Other Products	25.1%
Medical/Health	25.1%
Consumer Related	15.3%
Industrial/Energy	15.2%
Computer Hardware	7.5%
Computer Software and Services	5.6%
Communications and Media	3.1%
Semiconductors/Other Elect.	2.5%
Internet Specific	0.5%
Biotechnology	0.2%

Additional Information
Name of Most Recent Fund: RFE Investment Partners VI, L.P.
Most Recent Fund Was Raised: 05/01/1998
Year Founded: 1979
Capital Under Management: $64,000,000
Current Activity Level : Actively seeking new investments
Method of Compensation: Return on investment is of primary concern, do not charge fees

---

RUTLEDGE & CO., INC.

One Greenwich Office Park
51 Weaver Street
Greenwich, CT 06831
Phone: 203-869-8866
Fax: 203-869-7978

Other Offices

One East Putnam Ave
Greenwich, CT

Type of Firm
Private Firm Investing Own Capital

Project Preferences

Role in Financing:
Prefer role as deal originator but will also invest in deals created by others

Type of Financing Preferred:
Control-block Purchases
Industry Rollups
Leveraged Buyout
Special Situation

Size of Investments Considered
Min Size of Investment Considered (000s): $5,000
Max Size of Investment Considered (000s): $10,000

Geographical Preferences

United States
All U.S.

Canada
All Canada

Industry Preferences

Communications and Media
CATV & Pay TV Systems
Radio & TV Broadcasting

Computer Software
Computer Services

Semiconductors/Other Elect.
Component Testing Equipmt
Analytic/Scientific

Medical/Health
Medical/Health

Consumer Related
Consumer
Education Related

Industrial/Energy
Industrial Products

Business Serv.
Distribution

Manufact.
Office Automation Equipmt
Publishing

Agr/Forestr/Fish
Agriculture related

Additional Information
Name of Most Recent Fund: John Rutledge Partners II, L.P.
Most Recent Fund Was Raised: 12/10/1995
Year Founded: 1991
Capital Under Management: $112,000,000
Current Activity Level : Actively seeking new investments
Method of Compensation: Return on invest. most important, but chg. closing fees, service fees, etc.

SAE VENTURES

125 Elm Street
New Canaan, CT 06840
Phone: 203-972-3100
Fax: 203-966-4197

Type of Firm
Mgt. Consulting Firm

Project Preferences

Role in Financing:
Prefer role as deal originator

Type of Financing Preferred:
Control-block Purchases
First Stage Financing
Leveraged Buyout
Mezzanine
Research and Development
Second Stage Financing
Special Situation
Start-up Financing

Size of Investments Considered
Min Size of Investment Considered (000s): $5,000
Max Size of Investment Considered: No Limit

Geographical Preferences

United States
All U.S.

Industry Preferences

Computer Hardware
Integrated Turnkey System

Computer Software
Systems Software
Applications Software
Artificial Intelligence

Internet Specific
Internet

Semiconductors/Other Elect.
Electronic Components

Biotechnology
Biotechnology

Medical/Health
Medical/Health
Medical Products

Additional Information
Year Founded: 1993
Current Activity Level : Actively seeking new investments
Method of Compensation: Return on invest. most important, but chg. closing fees, service fees, etc.

SAUGATUCK CAPITAL COMPANY

One Canterbury Green
Stamford, CT 06901
Phone: 203-348-6669
Fax: 203-324-6995
Website: www.saugatuckcapital.com

Management and Staff
Barbara Parker, Managing Director
Christopher Wright, Managing Director
Christy Sadler, Managing Director
Frank Grzelecki, Principal
Frank Hawley, Managing Director
MArk Allsteadt, Managing Director
Owen Crihfield, Managing Director
Richard Campbell, Managing Director
Stuart Hawley, Managing Director
Thomas Berardino, Managing Director

Type of Firm
Private Firm Investing Own Capital

Industry Association Membership
National Venture Capital Association (NVCA)
Natl assoc of Small Bus. Inv. Co (NASBIC)

Project Preferences

Role in Financing:
Prefer role as deal originator but will also invest in deals created by others

Type of Financing Preferred:
Acquisition
Control-block Purchases
Expansion
Later Stage
Leveraged Buyout
Management Buyouts
Recapitalizations

Size of Investments Considered
Min Size of Investment Considered (000s): $3,000
Max Size of Investment Considered (000s): $25,000

Geographical Preferences

United States
All U.S.

Industry Preferences

(% based on actual investment)

Other Products	38.1%
Medical/Health	19.2%
Communications and Media	13.9%
Consumer Related	13.3%
Industrial/Energy	8.7%
Computer Hardware	3.9%
Computer Software and Services	3.0%

Additional Information
Name of Most Recent Fund: Saugatuck Capital Company L.P. IV
Most Recent Fund Was Raised: 09/15/1999
Year Founded: 1982
Capital Under Management: $190,300,000
Current Activity Level : Actively seeking new investments
Method of Compensation: Return on invest. most important, but chg. closing fees, service fees, etc.

SCHEER & COMPANY

250 W. Main Street
Suite 201
Branford, CT 06405
Phone: 203-481-0767

Management and Staff
David Scheer, Chief Financial Officer

Type of Firm
Investment Management/Finance Consulting

Additional Information
Capital Under Management: $50,000,000
Current Activity Level : Actively seeking new investments

SI VENTURES

56 Top Gallant Road
Stamford, CT 06904
Website: www.siventures.com

See Florida for full listing.

SIGNAL LAKE VENTURE FUND, LP

578 Post Road East
Suite 667
Westport, CT 06880
Phone: 203-454-1133
Fax: 203-454-7142
Website: www.signallake.com

Other Offices

50 Commonwealth Avenue
Suite 504
Boston, MA 02116
Phone: 617-267-5205
Fax: 617-262-7037

Management and Staff
Bart Stuck, Partner
Michael Weingarten, Partner

Type of Firm
Private Firm Investing Own Capital

Project Preferences

Type of Financing Preferred:
Early Stage

Geographical Preferences

United States
Northeast
All U.S.

Industry Preferences

(% based on actual investment)

Internet Specific	40.3%
Semiconductors/Other Elect.	30.5%
Communications and Media	26.5%
Computer Hardware	2.7%

Additional Information
Year Founded: 2000
Capital Under Management: $250,000,000
Current Activity Level : Actively seeking new investments

SOUNDVIEW FINANCIAL GROUP, INC.

22 Gatehouse Road
Stamford, CT 06902
Phone: 203-462-7200
Fax: 203-462-7350
Website: www.sndv.com

Management and Staff
Brian Bristol
Jonathan Meyers
Paul Mejean

Whom to Contact
Brian Bristol
Jonathan Meyers
Paul Mejean

Type of Firm
Investment/Merchant Bank Investing Own or Client Funds

Project Preferences

Role in Financing:
Prefer role in deals created by others

Type of Financing Preferred:
Mezzanine
Second Stage Financing

Geographical Preferences

United States
All U.S.

Canada
All Canada

International
Bermuda
France
Germany
Italy
United Kingdom

Industry Preferences

Communications and Media
Commercial Communications
Telecommunications
Data Communications
Satellite Microwave Comm.

Computer Hardware
Mainframes / Scientific
Mini and Personal/Desktop
Computer Graphics and Dig
Integrated Turnkey System
Disk Relat. Memory Device

Computer Software
Computer Services
Systems Software
Applications Software

Semiconductors/Other Elect.
Electronic Components
Semiconductor
Circuit Boards
Component Testing Equipmt
Laser Related
Fiber Optics
Analytic/Scientific

Manufact.
Office Automation Equipmt

Additional Information
Name of Most Recent Fund: SoundView Venture Partners-I
Most Recent Fund Was Raised: 01/01/1997
Year Founded: 1979
Capital Under Management: $50,000,000
Current Activity Level : Inactive / Unknown
Method of Compensation: Return on investment is of primary concern, do not charge fees

SOUTHPORT PARTNERS

2425 Post Road
Suite 200
Southport, CT 06450
Phone: 203-255-1231
Fax: 203-255-1178

Management and Staff
Dale E. McIvor
Katherine Watts

Whom to Contact
Dale E. McIvor
Katherine Watts

Project Preferences

Role in Financing:
Prefer role as deal originator

Type of Financing Preferred:
Control-block Purchases
Leveraged Buyout
Mezzanine
Second Stage Financing
Special Situation

Size of Investments Considered
Min Size of Investment Considered (000s): $5,000
Max Size of Investment Considered: No Limit

Geographical Preferences

United States
All U.S.

Canada
All Canada

International
South Africa
United Kingdom

Industry Preferences

Communications and Media
Commercial Communications
CATV & Pay TV Systems
Telecommunications
Data Communications
Satellite Microwave Comm.
Other Communication Prod.

Computer Hardware
Computers

Computer Other
Computer Related

Semiconductors/Other Elect.
Semiconductor
Fiber Optics
Analytic/Scientific

Consumer Related
Education Related

Industrial/Energy
Robotics

Manufact.
Publishing

Additional Information

Year Founded: 1986
Current Activity Level : Actively seeking new investments
Method of Compensation: Function primarily in service area, receive contingent fee in cash or equity

SUCSY, FISCHER & CO.

90 State House Square
Hartford, CT 06103-3720
Phone: 203-525-1400
Fax: 203-586-8909
Website: www.sfco.com

See Illinois for full listing.

SWEENEY & CO., INC.

P.O. Box 567
Southport, CT 06490
Phone: 203-255-0220
Fax: 203-255-0220

Type of Firm

Mgt. Consulting Firm

Project Preferences

Role in Financing:
Prefer role as deal originator but will also invest in deals created by others

Type of Financing Preferred:
First Stage Financing
Leveraged Buyout
Mezzanine
Research and Development
Second Stage Financing
Seed
Start-up Financing

Size of Investments Considered

Min Size of Investment Considered (000s): $1,000
Max Size of Investment Considered: No Limit

Geographical Preferences

United States
Mid Atlantic
Northeast

Canada
Eastern Canada
Ontario
Quebec

International
Bermuda
France
Germany
Italy
South Africa
Spain
United Kingdom

Industry Preferences

Communications and Media
Commercial Communications
CATV & Pay TV Systems
Radio & TV Broadcasting
Telecommunications
Satellite Microwave Comm.

Computer Hardware
Computer Graphics and Dig

Computer Software
Computer Services
Systems Software
Applications Software
Artificial Intelligence

Semiconductors/Other Elect.
Electronic Components
Controllers and Sensors
Sensors
Component Testing Equipmt
Laser Related
Analytic/Scientific

Biotechnology
Industrial Biotechnology
Biotech Related Research

Medical/Health
Medical Diagnostics
Diagnostic Services
Medical Therapeutics
Drug/Equipmt Delivery
Other Therapeutic
Medical Products
Disposable Med. Products
Hospitals/Clinics/Primary
Hospital/Other Instit.
Pharmaceuticals

Consumer Related
Entertainment and Leisure
Franchises(NEC)
Food/Beverage
Consumer Products
Consumer Services
Education Related

Industrial/Energy
Alternative Energy
Industrial Products
Materials
Robotics
Machinery
Environmental Related

Financial Services
Financial Services

Business Serv.
Consulting Services

Manufact.
Publishing

Additional Information

Year Founded: 1975
Current Activity Level : Actively seeking new investments
Method of Compensation: Function primarily in service area, receive contingent fee in cash or equity

TRANSAMERICA TECHNOLOGY FINANCE

76 Batterson Park Road
Farmington, CT 06032
Phone: 860-677-6466
Fax: 860-677-6766
Website: www.transamerica.com/techfinance

Management and Staff
Gerald Michaud

Whom to Contact
Gerald Michaud

Type of Firm
Non-Financial Corp. Affiliate or Subsidiary

Project Preferences

Role in Financing:
Prefer role as deal originator but will also invest in deals created by others

Type of Financing Preferred:
First Stage Financing
Mezzanine
Research and Development
Second Stage Financing

Geographical Preferences

United States
All U.S.

Canada
All Canada

Industry Preferences

Communications and Media
Commercial Communications
Telecommunications
Data Communications
Satellite Microwave Comm.

Computer Hardware
Computers
Mainframes / Scientific

Computer Software
Computer Services
Systems Software
Applications Software
Artificial Intelligence

Internet Specific
Internet

Semiconductors/Other Elect.
Electronic Components

Biotechnology
Biotechnology

Medical/Health
Diagnostic Services
Diagnostic Test Products
Drug/Equipmt Delivery
Other Therapeutic
Disposable Med. Products
Pharmaceuticals

Industrial/Energy
Alternative Energy

Additional Information
Year Founded: 1996
Capital Under Management: $600,000,000
Current Activity Level : Actively seeking new investments

TRIAD MEDIA VENTURES

177 Broad St.
15th Floor
Stamford, CT 06901
Phone: 203-328-2341
Fax: 203-323-3540
Website: www.triadmediaventures.com

Management and Staff
Gijs Van Thiel, General Partner
Marc Der Kinderen, General Partner
Steven Rodgers, General Partner
Tom Bartholomew, Partner

Type of Firm
Private Firm Investing Own Capital

Project Preferences

Type of Financing Preferred:
Early Stage

Geographical Preferences

United States
All U.S.

Industry Preferences

Computer Software
Software

Internet Specific
Internet

Consumer Related
Retail

Business Serv.
Media

Additional Information
Capital Under Management: $50,000,000
Current Activity Level : Actively seeking new investments

TRIDENT CAPITAL

200 Nyala Farms
Westport, CT 06880
Phone: 203-222-4594
Website: www.tridentcap.com

See California for full listing.

TSG CAPITAL GROUP, L.L.C.

177 Broad Street
12th Floor
Stamford, CT 06901
Phone: 203-406-1500
Fax: 203-406-1590

Management and Staff
Darryl Thompson
Lauren M. Tyler

Whom to Contact
Darryl Thompson
Lauren M. Tyler

Type of Firm
Private Firm Investing Own Capital

Industry Association Membership
Natl Assoc of Investment Cos. (NAIC)
Natl assoc of Small Bus. Inv. Co (NASBIC)

Project Preferences

Role in Financing:
Prefer role as deal originator but will also invest in deals created by others

Type of Financing Preferred:
Leveraged Buyout
Second Stage Financing

Size of Investments Considered
Min Size of Investment Considered (000s): $30,000
Max Size of Investment Considered: No Limit

Geographical Preferences

United States
All U.S.

Canada
All Canada

Industry Preferences

(% based on actual investment)

Communications and Media	42.7%
Consumer Related	35.3%

Other Products	14.8%
Industrial/Energy	7.2%

Additional Information

Name of Most Recent Fund: TSG Capital Fund III, L.P.
Most Recent Fund Was Raised: 08/01/1998
Year Founded: 1971
Capital Under Management: $740,000,000
Current Activity Level : Actively seeking new investments
Method of Compensation: Return on investment is of primary concern, do not charge fees

VENTURE PARTNERS

Mill Crossing
P.O. Drawer Nine
Kensington, CT 06037
Phone: 860-828-3332
Fax: 860-828-3320

Type of Firm

Mgt. Consulting Firm

Project Preferences

Role in Financing:

Prefer role as deal originator

Type of Financing Preferred:

First Stage Financing
Mezzanine
Recapitalizations
Seed
Special Situation
Start-up Financing

Size of Investments Considered

Min Size of Investment Considered (000s): $300
Max Size of Investment Considered (000s): $500

Geographical Preferences

United States

Northeast

Additional Information

Year Founded: 1985
Current Activity Level : Actively seeking new investments
Method of Compensation: Return on invest. most important, but chg. closing fees, service fees, etc.

WHITNEY & CO. (FKA: J.H. WHITNEY & CO.)

177 Broad Street
Stamford, CT 06901
Phone: 203-973-1400
Fax: 203-973-1422
Website: www.jhwhitney.com

Other Offices

35-01 UOB Plaza 1
80 Raffles Place
Singapore, Singapore
Phone: 011-65-248-4679
Fax: 011-65-248-4966

4 Cork Street
5th Floor
London, United Kingdom W1X 1PB
Phone: 011-44-20-7292-655
Fax: 011-44-20-7292-658

580 California Street
20th Floor
San Francisco, CA 94104
Phone: 415-229-4000
Fax: 415-229-4001

630 Fifth Avenue
Suite 3225
New York, NY 10111
Phone: 212-332-2400
Fax: 212-332-2422

Citibank Tower, Suite 2705
3 Garden Road
Central, Hong Kong
Phone: 011-852-2110-7980
Fax: 011-852-2111-9699

One Liberty Square
12th Floor
Boston, MA 02109
Phone: 617-423-2300
Fax: 617-423-3647

Plaza Mikado 7F
2-14-5 Akaska, Minato-ku
Tokyo, Japan 107-0052
Phone: 011-81-3-3560-6500
Fax: 011-81-3-3560-6510

Management and Staff

Barry Hines, Managing Director
Brian Doyle, Managing Director
Carla Skodinski, Managing Director
Daniel O'Brien, Chief Financial Officer
David Scherl, Managing Director
Dimitri Goulandris, Managing Director
Edward Brogan, Managing Director
Eric Forday, Managing Director
James Matthews, Partner
James Fordyce, Managing Director
James Kastberg, Managing Director
James Pitt, Managing Director
Jeffrey Jay, Managing Director
Jill Kitazaki, Managing Director
Joseph McCullen, Managing Director
Joseph Carrabino, Managing Director
Julian Allen, Managing Director
Lori Gonye, General Partner
Mark Murphy, Managing Director
Masahiro Koshiba, Managing Director
Michael Brooks, Partner
Michael Stone, President & COO
Michael DeFlorio, Managing Director
Ming Siu, Managing Director
Oliver Gardey, Managing Director
Paul Slawson, Managing Director
Peter Castleman, Chairman & CEO
Ray Newton, General Partner
Richard Barkinson, Managing Director
Robert Warden, Vice President
Stephen Hines, Managing Director
Terence Hogan, Managing Director
Tyler Wolfram, Managing Director
William McGlashan, Managing Director
William Dawson, Managing Director
William Bennington, Managing Director

Type of Firm

Private Firm Investing Own Capital

Industry Association Membership

National Venture Capital Association (NVCA)

Project Preferences

Role in Financing:

Prefer role as deal originator but will also invest in deals created by others

Type of Financing Preferred:

Balanced
Expansion
Leveraged Buyout

Size of Investments Considered

Min Size of Investment Considered (000s): $1,000
Max Size of Investment Considered: No Limit

Geographical Preferences

United States
All U.S.

International
All International
No Preference

Industry Preferences

(% based on actual investment)

Internet Specific	20.4%
Other Products	18.1%
Consumer Related	13.7%
Communications and Media	10.0%
Medical/Health	9.3%
Computer Hardware	8.3%
Biotechnology	6.8%
Computer Software and Services	6.2%
Semiconductors/Other Elect.	3.9%
Industrial/Energy	3.4%

Additional Information

Name of Most Recent Fund: J.H. Whitney Mezzanine Fund, L.P.
Most Recent Fund Was Raised: 07/01/1998
Year Founded: 1946
Capital Under Management: $5,000,000,000
Current Activity Level : Actively seeking new investments
Method of Compensation: Return on invest. most important, but chg. closing fees, service fees, etc.

WINDWARD HOLDINGS

38 Sylvan Road
Madison, CT 06443
Phone: 203-245-6870
Fax: 203-245-6865

Project Preferences

Role in Financing:
Prefer role as deal originator but will also invest in deals created by others

Type of Financing Preferred:
Leveraged Buyout
Mezzanine
Recapitalizations
Special Situation

Size of Investments Considered

Min Size of Investment Considered (000s): $300
Max Size of Investment Considered: No Limit

Geographical Preferences

United States
Northeast

Industry Preferences

Semiconductors/Other Elect.
Electronic Components
Controllers and Sensors
Component Testing Equipmt
Analytic/Scientific

Consumer Related
Food/Beverage

Industrial/Energy
Industrial Products

Additional Information

Year Founded: 1992
Capital Under Management: $5,000,000
Current Activity Level : Actively seeking new investments
Method of Compensation: Return on invest. most important, but chg. closing fees, service fees, etc.

ZERO STAGE CAPITAL CO., INC.

195 Church Street
10th Floor
New Haven, CT 06510
Phone: 203-865-7986
Fax: 203-865-7987
Website: www.zerostage.com

See Massachusetts for full listing.

D. OF COLUMBIA

ALIGNMENT CAPITAL PARTNERS, LLC

1667 K. Street, NW
Suite 450
Washington, DC 20006
Phone: 202-857-0850
Fax: 202-857-0869
Website: www.alignmentcapital.com

See Texas for full listing.

ALLIED CAPITAL CORPORATION

1919 Pennsylvania Avenue, NW
3rd Floor
Washington, DC 20006-3434
Phone: 202-331-1122
Fax: 202-659-2053
Website: www.alliedcapital.com

Other Offices

1180 Avenue of the Americas
Suite 1481
New York, NY
Phone: 212-899-5180
Fax: 212-899-5181

401 North Michigan Avenue
Suite 2050
Chicago, IL
Phone: 312-828-0330
Fax: 312-828-0909

One Market Plaza
Stewart Tower, Suite 2605
San Francisco, CA
Phone: 415-904-4508
Fax: 415-904-4503

Zeil 5
Frankfurt 60311, East Germany
Phone: 49-69-2972-4108
Fax: 49-69-2972-4200

Management and Staff

Benjamin Nye, Principal
Cabell Williams, Managing Director
Car Preston, Principal
Joan Sweeney, Chief Operating Officer
John Scheurer, Managing Director
Michael Grisius, Principal
Philip McNeill, Managing Director
Robert Monk, Principal
Robert Corry, Principal
Samuel Guren, Managing Director
Scott Binder, Managing Director
Tom Westbrook, Managing Director
William Walton, Chairman & CEO

Whom to Contact

Biff Barnard
Chris Rushid
G. Cabell Williams III
Rick Fearon
Tricia Daniels

Type of Firm

MESBIC not elsewhere classified

Industry Association Membership

Mid-Atlantic Venture Association
National Venture Capital Association (NVCA)
Natl assoc of Small Bus. Inv. Co (NASBIC)

Project Preferences

Role in Financing:

Will function either as deal originator or investor in deals created by others

Type of Financing Preferred:

Acquisition
Leveraged Buyout
Management Buyouts
Mezzanine
Recapitalizations

Size of Investments Considered

Min Size of Investment Considered (000s): $5,000
Max Size of Investment Considered (000s): $40,000

Geographical Preferences

United States

All U.S.

International

Germany

Industry Preferences

(% based on actual investment)

Other Products	39.9%
Consumer Related	20.6%
Industrial/Energy	11.1%
Communications and Media	9.8%
Medical/Health	7.8%
Internet Specific	6.7%
Computer Software and Services	1.8%
Semiconductors/Other Elect.	1.4%
Computer Hardware	0.5%
Biotechnology	0.5%

Additional Information

Name of Most Recent Fund: Allied Capital Midwest, L.P.
Most Recent Fund Was Raised: 01/07/1997
Year Founded: 1958
Capital Under Management: $1,500,000,000
Current Activity Level : Actively seeking new investments
Method of Compensation: Return on invest. most important, but chg. closing fees, service fees, etc.

ATLANTIC COASTAL VENTURES, L.P.(AKA:MULTIMEDIA BROADCAST IN)

3101 South Street, N.W.
Washington, DC 20007
Phone: 202-293-1166
Fax: 202-293-1181
Website: www.atlanticcv.com

Other Offices

777 Summer Street
Suite 30
Stamford, CT 06901
Phone: 203-325-2522

Management and Staff

Donald Greene, General Partner
Patrick Hall, Partner
Walter Threadgill, General Partner

Type of Firm

Private Firm Investing Own Capital

Project Preferences

Role in Financing:

Prefer role as deal originator but will also invest in deals created by others

Type of Financing Preferred:

Leveraged Buyout
Mezzanine
Special Situation

Size of Investments Considered

Min Size of Investment Considered (000s): $300
Max Size of Investment Considered: No Limit

Industry Preferences

Communications and Media
Commercial Communications
Telecommunications

Computer Hardware
Computer Graphics and Dig

Semiconductors/Other Elect.
Electronics

Additional Information
Name of Most Recent Fund: Atlantic Coastal Ventures
Most Recent Fund Was Raised: 03/01/1997
Year Founded: 1979
Capital Under Management: $19,000,000
Current Activity Level : Actively seeking new investments
Method of Compensation: Return on invest. most important, but chg. closing fees, service fees, etc.

COLUMBIA CAPITAL GROUP, INC.

1660 L Street, N.W.
Suite 308
Washington, DC 20036
Phone: 202-775-8815
Fax: 202-223-0544

Management and Staff
LLoyd Arrington, President
Richard Williams, Jr., Vice President

Whom to Contact
Erica Batie

Type of Firm
Non-Financial Corp. Affiliate or Subsidiary

Industry Association Membership
National Venture Capital Association (NVCA)

Project Preferences

Role in Financing:
Prefer role as deal originator but will also invest in deals created by others

Type of Financing Preferred:
First Stage Financing
Mezzanine
Second Stage Financing

Geographical Preferences

United States
Mid Atlantic

Industry Preferences
(% based on actual investment)

Communications and Media	48.5%
Internet Specific	27.9%
Computer Software and Services	12.8%
Computer Hardware	4.1%
Semiconductors/Other Elect.	3.7%
Biotechnology	3.0%

Additional Information
Name of Most Recent Fund: Columbia Capital Group, Inc. I Fund
Most Recent Fund Was Raised: 08/01/1999
Year Founded: 1988
Capital Under Management: $10,000,000
Current Activity Level : Actively seeking new investments
Method of Compensation: Return on invest. most important, but chg. closing fees, service fees, etc.

CONNECTICUT-GREENE VENTURES, L.P.

3101 South Street
Washington, DC 20007
Phone: 202-293-1166
Fax: 202-293-1181

See Connecticut for full listing.

CORE CAPITAL PARTNERS

901 15th Street, N.W.
9th Floor
Washington, DC 20005
Phone: 202-589-0090
Fax: 202-589-0091
Website: www.core-capital.com

Management and Staff
George George, Vice President
Jonathan Silver, Managing Director
Pascal Luck, Principal
Sandeep Dalal, Vice President
Will Dunbar, Managing Director

Type of Firm
Private Firm Investing Own Capital

Industry Association Membership
Mid-Atlantic Venture Association
National Venture Capital Association (NVCA)
Natl assoc of Small Bus. Inv. Co (NASBIC)

Project Preferences

Role in Financing:
Will function either as deal originator or investor in deals created by others

Type of Financing Preferred:
Early Stage
Expansion
First Stage Financing
Later Stage
Second Stage Financing
Startup

Size of Investments Considered
Min Size of Investment Considered (000s): $1,000
Max Size of Investment Considered (000s): $10,000

Geographical Preferences

United States
Mid Atlantic
Northeast
Southeast

Industry Preferences

Communications and Media
Communications and Media
Telecommunications
Wireless Communications
Data Communications
Other Communication Prod.

Computer Hardware
Disk Relat. Memory Device

Computer Software
Software
Systems Software
Applications Software

Internet Specific
E-Commerce Technology
Internet

Semiconductors/Other Elect.
Electronic Components
Micro-Processing
Controllers and Sensors
Sensors
Circuit Boards
Component Testing Equipmt
Laser Related
Fiber Optics
Analytic/Scientific

Biotechnology
Biotechnology
Biotech Related Research
Biotech Related Research

Industrial/Energy
Energy
Factory Automation
Process Control
Robotics
Machinery

Business Serv.
Media

Utilities
Utilities

Additional Information
Year Founded: 1999
Capital Under Management: $160,000,000
Current Activity Level : Actively seeking new investments
Method of Compensation: Return on investment is of primary concern, do not charge fees

---

EDISON VENTURE FUND

601 13th Street N.W.
10 th Floor
Washington, DC 20005
Phone: 202-661-2279
Fax: 202-661-2295
Website: www.edisonventure.com

See New Jersey for full listing.

EMERGING MARKETS PARTNERSHIP

2001 Pennsylvania Avenue, NW
Suite 1100
Washington, DC 20006
Phone: 202-331-9051
Fax: 202-331-9250
Website: www.empwdc.com

Other Offices

#1201-02 Two Pacific Place
88 Queensway
Hong Kong, Hong Kong
Phone: 852-2918-7999
Fax: 852-2572-3663

#35-01 Singapore Land Tower
50 Raffles Place
Singapore, Singapore 048623
Phone: 65-227-0550
Fax: 65-227-0440

Management and Staff
Paul Applegarth, Managing Director
Rauf Diwan, Managing Director
Scott Glaken, Managing Director

Type of Firm
Private Firm Investing Own Capital

Industry Association Membership
Hong Kong Venture Capital Association (HKVCA)

Project Preferences

Role in Financing:
Will function either as deal originator or investor in deals created by others

Size of Investments Considered
Min Size of Investment Considered (000s): $17,500
Max Size of Investment Considered (000s): $40,000

Additional Information
Name of Most Recent Fund: AIG-GE Capital Latin American Infrastructure, L.P.
Most Recent Fund Was Raised: 01/01/1997
Year Founded: 1996
Capital Under Management: $900,000,000
Current Activity Level : Actively seeking new investments

GCI VENTURE PARTNERS

901 15th Street, NW
Suite 950
Washington, DC 20005
Phone: 202-589-0398
Fax: 202-589-0091
Website: www.gciventures.com

Management and Staff
Christopher Niemczewski, Managing Partner
Edward Marram, Managing Partner
Mark Levine, Managing Partner
Samuel Mitchell, Managing Partner

Type of Firm
Private Firm Investing Own Capital

Industry Association Membership
Mid-Atlantic Venture Association

Project Preferences

Role in Financing:
Will function either as deal originator or investor in deals created by others

Type of Financing Preferred:
Early Stage
First Stage Financing
Research and Development
Seed
Start-up Financing

Size of Investments Considered
Min Size of Investment Considered (000s): $250
Max Size of Investment Considered (000s): $2,000

Geographical Preferences

United States
Mid Atlantic
Northeast
Southeast

Industry Preferences

Communications and Media
Commercial Communications
Telecommunications
Wireless Communications
Data Communications
Other Communication Prod.

Computer Software
Data Processing
Software
Systems Software
Applications Software

Internet Specific
E-Commerce Technology
Internet
Web Aggregration/Portals

Semiconductors/Other Elect.
Electronic Components
Fiber Optics

Biotechnology
Human Biotechnology
Industrial Biotechnology
Biotech Related Research

Medical/Health
Drug/Equipmt Delivery
Disposable Med. Products

Additional Information
Year Founded: 1997
Capital Under Management: $25,000,000
Current Activity Level : Actively seeking new investments
Method of Compensation: Return on investment is of primary concern, do not charge fees

GROSVENOR FUNDS, THE

1808 Eye Street, N.W.
Suite 900
Washington, DC 20006
Phone: 202-861-5650
Fax: 202-861-5653
Website: www.grosvenorfund.com

Management and Staff
Bruce Dunnan, Managing Partner
C. Bowdoin Train, Managing Partner
Douglas Dunnan, Managing Partner
Steven Bottum, Managing Partner

Type of Firm
Private Firm Investing Own Capital

Industry Association Membership
Mid-Atlantic Venture Association

Project Preferences

Type of Financing Preferred:
Early Stage
Later Stage
Seed

Size of Investments Considered
Min Size of Investment Considered (000s): $1,000
Max Size of Investment Considered (000s): $3,000

Industry Preferences

Communications and Media
Telecommunications

Internet Specific
Internet

Semiconductors/Other Elect.
Fiber Optics

Biotechnology
Biotechnology

Additional Information
Year Founded: 1994
Capital Under Management: $40,000,000
Current Activity Level : Actively seeking new investments

LAZARD TECHNOLOGY PARTNERS

5335 Wisconsin Avenue, NW
Suite 410
Washington, DC 20015
Phone: 202-895-1505
Fax: 202-895-1501
Website: www.lazardtp.com

See New York for full listing.

MOTOROLA INC.

1350 I Street NW
Suite 400
Washington, DC 20006
Phone: 202-371-6928
Fax: 202-842-1325

Other Offices

1303 East Algonquin Road
Schaumburg, IL 60196
Phone: 847-576-4929
Fax: 847-538-2250

Management and Staff
James O'Connor, Managing Director

Whom to Contact
Dawn Matthews
James Burke

Type of Firm
Non-Financial Corp. Affiliate or Subsidiary

Industry Association Membership
National Venture Capital Association (NVCA)

Project Preferences

Role in Financing:
Prefer role as deal originator but will also invest in deals created by others

Type of Financing Preferred:
First Stage Financing
Second Stage Financing
Start-up Financing

Industry Preferences

(% based on actual investment)

Internet Specific	36.6%
Communications and Media	26.2%
Computer Software and Services	22.4%
Other Products	6.4%
Computer Hardware	2.9%
Biotechnology	1.9%
Semiconductors/Other Elect.	1.9%
Consumer Related	1.7%

Additional Information
Year Founded: 1999
Current Activity Level : Actively seeking new investments
Method of Compensation: Return on investment is of primary concern, do not charge fees

NEXTPOINT PARTNERS L.P.(FKA: PLAZA STREET)

701 Pennsylvania Avenue NW
Suite 900
Washington, DC 20004
Phone: 202-661-8703
Fax: 202-434-7400
Website: www.nextpointvc.com

Other Offices

One Financial Center
Suite 4100
Boston, MA 02111

Management and Staff
Andrew Quartner, Venture Partner
Johnathan Peskoff, General Partner
Michael Faber, General Partner

Type of Firm
Private Firm Investing Own Capital

Industry Association Membership
Mid-Atlantic Venture Association
National Venture Capital Association (NVCA)

Project Preferences

Role in Financing:
Prefer role as deal originator but will also invest in deals created by others

Type of Financing Preferred:
First Stage Financing
Second Stage Financing

Geographical Preferences

United States
All U.S.

Industry Preferences

Communications and Media
Communications and Media

Computer Other
Computer Related

Semiconductors/Other Elect.
Electronic Components

Additional Information
Year Founded: 2000
Capital Under Management: $55,000,000
Current Activity Level : Actively seeking new investments
Method of Compensation: Return on investment is of primary concern, do not charge fees

NOKIA VENTURE PARTNERS (AKA: NOKIA OY)

2121 K Street, NW
Suite 650
Washington, DC 20037
Phone: 202-728-0049
Website: www.nokiaventures.com

See California for full listing.

PERSEUS LLC

1627 I Street NW
Suite 610
Washington, DC 20006
Phone: 202-452-0101
Fax: 202-439-0588

Management and Staff
Rodd Macklin, Chief Financial Officer

Type of Firm
Private Firm Investing Own Capital

Project Preferences

Type of Financing Preferred:
Acquisition
Balanced
Recapitalizations

Geographical Preferences

United States
All U.S.

Industry Preferences

(% based on actual investment)

Industrial/Energy	31.4%
Semiconductors/Other Elect.	23.4%
Medical/Health	20.2%
Computer Hardware	11.0%
Computer Software and Services	8.0%
Internet Specific	5.9%

Additional Information
Name of Most Recent Fund: Perseus 1996
Most Recent Fund Was Raised: 04/01/1996
Year Founded: 1999
Capital Under Management: $897,700,000
Current Activity Level : Actively seeking new investments

RIGGS CAPITAL PARTNERS

800 17th Street NW
Suite 300
Washington, DC 20006
Phone: 202-835-5048
Fax: 202-835-5506
Website: www.riggsbank.com

Management and Staff
J. Carter Besse, President
Jonathan Cordish, Vice President
Michael Leurdijik, Chief Financial Officer

Type of Firm
Commercial Bank Affiliate or Subsidiary

Industry Association Membership
Mid-Atlantic Venture Association
National Venture Capital Association (NVCA)

Industry Preferences

(% based on actual investment)

Internet Specific	37.3%
Computer Software and Services	30.0%
Communications and Media	24.7%
Medical/Health	5.7%
Biotechnology	2.4%

Additional Information
Year Founded: 1998
Capital Under Management: $100,000,000
Current Activity Level : Actively seeking new investments

TELECOMMUNICATIONS DEVELOPMENT FUND (TDF)

2020 K. Street NW
Suite 375
Washington, DC 20006
Phone: 202-293-8840
Fax: 202-293-8850
Website: www.tdfund.com

Management and Staff
Ginger Lew, Chief Executive Officer
Robert Cerbone, Partner

Type of Firm
Non-Financial Corp. Affiliate or Subsidiary

Industry Association Membership
Mid-Atlantic Venture Association
National Venture Capital Association (NVCA)
Natl Assoc of Investment Cos. (NAIC)
Natl assoc of Small Bus. Inv. Co (NASBIC)

Project Preferences

Role in Financing:
Will function either as deal originator or investor in deals created by others

Type of Financing Preferred:
Early Stage
Expansion
Seed

Size of Investments Considered
Min Size of Investment Considered (000s): $375
Max Size of Investment Considered (000s): $1,000

Geographical Preferences

United States
All U.S.

Industry Preferences

(% based on actual investment)

Internet Specific	37.6%
Computer Software and Services	33.5%
Communications and Media	19.1%
Computer Hardware	9.9%

Additional Information
Capital Under Management: $20,000,000
Current Activity Level : Actively seeking new investments
Method of Compensation: Return on investment is of primary concern, do not charge fees

TRIDENT CAPITAL

1001 Pennsylvania Avenue NW
Washington, DC 20004-2505
Phone: 202-347-2626
Fax: 202-393-4568
Website: www.tridentcap.com

See California for full listing.

WACHTEL & CO., INC.

1101 14th Street, N.W.
Washington, DC 20005-5680
Phone: 202-898-1144

Type of Firm
Mgt. Consulting Firm

Project Preferences

Role in Financing:
Prefer role as deal originator but will also invest in deals created by others

Type of Financing Preferred:
First Stage Financing
Recapitalizations
Second Stage Financing
Start-up Financing

Size of Investments Considered
Min Size of Investment Considered (000s): $100
Max Size of Investment Considered (000s): $300

Industry Preferences

Communications and Media
Commercial Communications
Telecommunications
Data Communications
Satellite Microwave Comm.
Other Communication Prod.

Computer Hardware
Computers
Mini and Personal/Desktop
Computer Graphics and Dig
Integrated Turnkey System

Computer Software
Computer Services
Systems Software
Applications Software
Artificial Intelligence

Semiconductors/Other Elect.
Electronic Components
Semiconductor
Component Testing Equipmt
Laser Related
Fiber Optics
Analytic/Scientific

Medical/Health
Diagnostic Services

Consumer Related
Retail
Computer Stores
Consumer Products
Consumer Services
Education Related

Industrial/Energy
Alternative Energy
Energy Conservation Relat
Robotics

Financial Services
Financial Services

Business Serv.
Consulting Services

Manufact.
Publishing

Additional Information
Year Founded: 1961
Capital Under Management: $15,000,000
Current Activity Level : Actively seeking new investments
Method of Compensation: Function primarily in service area, receive contingent fee in cash or equity

WINSLOW PARTNERS LLC

1300 Connecticut Avenue, NW
Washington, DC 20036-1703
Phone: 202-530-5000
Fax: 202-530-5010

Other Offices

Narodni 41
Prague, Czech Republic
Phone: 4202-2422-1453
Fax: 4202-2421-8463

Management and Staff
Kenneth Brody, Partner
Robert Chartener, Partner

Whom to Contact
Robert Chartener
Shawn Johnson

Type of Firm
Investment/Merchant Bank Subsid/Affil

Project Preferences

Role in Financing:
Prefer role as deal originator

Type of Financing Preferred:
Acquisition
Control-block Purchases
Expansion
Later Stage
Leveraged Buyout
Management Buyouts

Size of Investments Considered
Min Size of Investment Considered (000s): $5,000
Max Size of Investment Considered: No Limit

Geographical Preferences

United States
All U.S.

International
Eastern Europe

Industry Preferences

Communications and Media
Telecommunications

Semiconductors/Other Elect.
Electronics
Electronic Components
Controllers and Sensors
Sensors

Medical/Health
Medical Diagnostics
Diagnostic Services
Medical Products
Disposable Med. Products
Health Services
Hospitals/Clinics/Primary

Consumer Related
Consumer
Education Related

Industrial/Energy
Industrial Products
Factory Automation
Process Control
Machinery

Transportation
Aerospace

Financial Services
Financial Services

Business Serv.
Services
Distribution

Manufact.
Manufacturing

Additional Information

Name of Most Recent Fund: Charles Investment Partners L.P.
Most Recent Fund Was Raised: 09/01/1999
Year Founded: 1996
Capital Under Management: $101,000,000
Current Activity Level : Actively seeking new investments
Method of Compensation: Return on invest. most important, but chg. closing fees, service fees, etc.

WOMEN'S GROWTH CAPITAL FUND

1054 31st Street, North West
Suite 110
Washington, DC 20007
Phone: 202-342-1431
Fax: 202-341-1203
Website: www.wgcf.com

Management and Staff

Ashley Allen, Principal
Patty Abramson, Managing Director
Robert Stein, Managing Director
Wendee Kanarek, Managing Director

Type of Firm

Private Firm Investing Own Capital

Industry Association Membership

Mid-Atlantic Venture Association

Project Preferences

Type of Financing Preferred:

First Stage Financing
Later Stage
Second Stage Financing

Size of Investments Considered

Min Size of Investment Considered (000s): $500
Max Size of Investment Considered (000s): $2,000

Geographical Preferences

United States

Mid Atlantic
Northeast
Southeast
All U.S.

Industry Preferences

(% based on actual investment)

Internet Specific	76.2%
Communications and Media	14.0%
Computer Software and Services	9.8%

Additional Information

Name of Most Recent Fund: Women's Growth Capital Fund I
Most Recent Fund Was Raised: 05/30/1997
Year Founded: 1997
Capital Under Management: $29,000,000
Current Activity Level : Actively seeking new investments

WOMENANGLES.NET

1054 31st Street, NW
Suite 110
Washington, DC 20007
Phone: 202-342-1627
Fax: 202-341-1203
Website: www.womenangels.net

Management and Staff

Ashley Allen, Principal
Kyp Sirinakis, Managing Director
Patty Abramson, Managing Director
Robert Stein, Managing Director
Wendee Kanarek, Managing Director

Type of Firm

Private Firm Investing Own Capital

Industry Association Membership

Mid-Atlantic Venture Association

Project Preferences

Role in Financing:

Prefer role in deals created by others

Type of Financing Preferred:

Balanced
Recapitalizations
Second Stage Financing

Geographical Preferences

United States

Mid Atlantic

Industry Preferences

Communications and Media

Telecommunications
Data Communications
Satellite Microwave Comm.

Computer Software

Applications Software

Internet Specific

Internet

Computer Other

Computer Related

Medical/Health

Medical/Health
Medical Diagnostics
Diagnostic Services
Diagnostic Test Products
Medical Therapeutics
Drug/Equipmt Delivery
Medical Products
Disposable Med. Products
Hospital/Other Instit.
Pharmaceuticals

Consumer Related

Consumer
Entertainment and Leisure
Retail
Computer Stores
Food/Beverage
Consumer Products
Consumer Services
Education Related

Financial Services

Financial Services

Business Serv.

Distribution

Manufact.

Office Automation Equipmt

Other

Women/Minority-Owned Bus.

Additional Information

Name of Most Recent Fund: Womens Growth Capital Fund I
Most Recent Fund Was Raised: 01/01/1998
Year Founded: 1997
Capital Under Management: $6,000,000
Current Activity Level : Actively seeking new investments
Method of Compensation: Return on investment is of primary concern, do not charge fees

DELAWARE

BLUE ROCK CAPITAL

5803 Kennett Pike
Suite A
Wilmington, DE 19807-1135
Phone: 302-426-0981
Fax: 302-426-0982
Website: www.bluerockcapital.com

Other Offices

18004 Calico Circle
Olney, MD 20832

230 Lackawanna Drive
Andover, NJ 07821
Phone: 973-426-1767
Fax: 973-426-0224

Management and Staff
Frank Tower, General Partner
Terry Collison, General Partner
Virginia Bonker, General Partner

Type of Firm
SBIC Not elsewhere classified

Industry Association Membership
Mid-Atlantic Venture Association

Project Preferences

Role in Financing:
Prefer role as deal originator but will also invest in deals created by others

Type of Financing Preferred:
First Stage Financing
Seed
Start-up Financing

Geographical Preferences

United States
Mid Atlantic
Northeast

Industry Preferences

(% based on actual investment)

Internet Specific	35.9%
Computer Software and Services	25.2%
Semiconductors/Other Elect.	23.6%
Communications and Media	7.8%
Consumer Related	7.5%

Additional Information
Name of Most Recent Fund: Blue Rock Capital, L.P.
Most Recent Fund Was Raised: 08/01/1995
Year Founded: 1995
Capital Under Management: $51,000,000
Current Activity Level : Actively seeking new investments
Method of Compensation: Return on investment is of primary concern, do not charge fees

TRIAD INVESTORS CORP

1 Innovation Way
Newark, DE 19711
Phone: 302-452-1120

Management and Staff
Barbara Plantholt-Melera, President
Jeffrey Davison, Vice President

Whom to Contact
Barbara P. Melera

Type of Firm
Private Firm Investing Own Capital

Industry Association Membership
Mid-Atlantic Venture Association

Project Preferences

Role in Financing:
Prefer role as deal originator but will also invest in deals created by others

Type of Financing Preferred:
First Stage Financing
Research and Development
Second Stage Financing
Seed
Start-up Financing

Geographical Preferences

United States
Mid Atlantic

Industry Preferences

(% based on actual investment)

Computer Software and Services	43.8%
Internet Specific	23.7%
Communications and Media	17.8%
Other Products	7.6%
Medical/Health	6.5%
Semiconductors/Other Elect.	0.5%

Additional Information
Name of Most Recent Fund: Tritech Partners, LP
Most Recent Fund Was Raised: 03/31/1994
Year Founded: 1989
Capital Under Management: $11,100,000
Current Activity Level : Actively seeking new investments
Method of Compensation: Return on investment is of primary concern, do not charge fees

FLORIDA

ADLER & CO.

222 Lakeview Avenue
Suite 160-286
West Palm Beach, FL 33401
Phone: 407-837-2220
Fax: 407-837-1010

See New York for full listing.

ADVANTAGE CAPITAL PARTNERS

100 North Tampa
Suite 4100
Tampa, FL 33602
Phone: 813-221-8700
Fax: 813-227-7711
Website: www.advantagecap.com

See Louisiana for full listing.

AMT CAPITAL LTD. (AKA: AMT VENTURE PARTNERS, LTD.)

350 Pensacola Beach Blvd., Suite 3B
P.O. Box 250
Gulf Breeze, FL 32561
Phone: 850-916-7623
Fax: 850-916-7637
Website: www.amtcapital.com

See Texas for full listing.

ANTARES CAPITAL CORPORATION (FKA: HARBOR VENTURES CORP.)

7900 Miami Lakes Drive West
Miami Lakes, FL 33016
Phone: 305-894-2888
Fax: 305-894-3227
Website: www.antarescapital.com

Other Offices

PO Box 410730
Melbourne, FL 32941
Phone: 407-777-4884
Fax: 407-777-5884

Management and Staff

Jonathan Kislak, General Partner
Randall Poliner, General Partner

Type of Firm

Private Firm Investing Own Capital

Industry Association Membership

National Venture Capital Association (NVCA)

Project Preferences

Role in Financing:
Prefer role as deal originator but will also invest in deals created by others

Type of Financing Preferred:
Expansion
Later Stage
Management Buyouts
Second Stage Financing
Special Situation

Size of Investments Considered

Min Size of Investment Considered (000s): $500
Max Size of Investment Considered (000s): $2,000

Geographical Preferences

United States
Southeast
Texas

Industry Preferences

(% based on actual investment)

Consumer Related	49.3%
Medical/Health	11.4%
Semiconductors/Other Elect.	10.7%
Other Products	8.6%
Internet Specific	7.7%
Computer Software and Services	6.8%
Communications and Media	5.3%
Computer Hardware	0.2%

Additional Information

Year Founded: 1993
Capital Under Management: $2,100,000
Current Activity Level : Actively seeking new investments
Method of Compensation: Return on investment is of primary concern, do not charge fees

AVERY BUSINESS DEVELOPMENT SERVICES

2506 St. Michel Court
Ponte Vedra, FL 32082
Phone: 904-285-6033

Type of Firm

Mgt. Consulting Firm

Project Preferences

Role in Financing:
Prefer role as deal originator but will also invest in deals created by others

Type of Financing Preferred:
First Stage Financing
Leveraged Buyout
Research and Development
Seed
Special Situation
Start-up Financing

Size of Investments Considered

Min Size of Investment Considered (000s): $2,000
Max Size of Investment Considered: No Limit

Geographical Preferences

International
No Preference

Industry Preferences

Communications and Media
Radio & TV Broadcasting

Computer Software
Artificial Intelligence

Biotechnology
Industrial Biotechnology
Biosensors
Biotech Related Research
Biotech Related Research

Medical/Health
Drug/Equipmt Delivery
Medical Products
Pharmaceuticals

Consumer Related
Retail
Franchises(NEC)

Industrial/Energy
Oil and Gas Exploration
Oil & Gas Drilling,Explor
Alternative Energy
Coal Related
Industrial Products
Materials
Robotics
Environmental Related

Business Serv.
Consulting Services

Agr/Forestr/Fish
Mining and Minerals

Additional Information
Year Founded: 1981
Current Activity Level : Actively seeking new investments
Method of Compensation: Function primarily in service area, receive contingent fee in cash or equity

BAIRD CAPITAL PARTNERS

401 East Jackson Street
Suite 2900
Tampa, FL 33602
Phone: 888-792-9817
Website: www.rwbaird.com

See Illinois for full listing.

CEO ADVISORS

1061 Maitland Center Commons
Suite 209
Maitland, FL 32751
Phone: 407-660-9327
Fax: 407-660-2109

Type of Firm
Mgt. Consulting Firm

Project Preferences

Role in Financing:
Will function either as deal originator or investor in deals created by others

Type of Financing Preferred:
First Stage Financing
Research and Development
Seed
Start-up Financing

Size of Investments Considered
Min Size of Investment Considered (000s): $300
Max Size of Investment Considered (000s): $500

Geographical Preferences

United States
Southeast

Industry Preferences

Communications and Media
Commercial Communications
Data Communications
Satellite Microwave Comm.

Computer Hardware
Mini and Personal/Desktop
Computer Graphics and Dig
Disk Relat. Memory Device

Computer Software
Systems Software
Applications Software

Internet Specific
Internet

Semiconductors/Other Elect.
Sensors
Laser Related
Fiber Optics
Analytic/Scientific

Biotechnology
Industrial Biotechnology
Biosensors
Biotech Related Research
Biotech Related Research

Medical/Health
Medical Diagnostics
Diagnostic Services
Diagnostic Test Products
Other Therapeutic
Disposable Med. Products

Consumer Related
Consumer Products

Industrial/Energy
Robotics
Machinery

Additional Information
Year Founded: 1989
Current Activity Level : Reducing investment activity
Method of Compensation: Function primarily in service area, receive contingent fee in cash or equity

CHARTWELL CAPITAL MANAGEMENT CO., INC.

One Independent Drive
Suite 3120
Jacksonville, FL 32202
Phone: 904-355-3519
Fax: 904-353-5833

Management and Staff
Mindy Lanigan, Chief Financial Officer

Whom to Contact
Anthony Marinatos
Chris Prentice

Type of Firm
Private Firm Investing Own Capital

Project Preferences

Role in Financing:
Prefer role as deal originator but will also invest in deals created by others

Type of Financing Preferred:
First Stage Financing
Leveraged Buyout
Second Stage Financing

Size of Investments Considered
Min Size of Investment Considered (000s): $5,000
Max Size of Investment Considered: No Limit

Geographical Preferences

United States
Northwest
Southeast

Industry Preferences

(% based on actual investment)

Consumer Related	52.8%
Other Products	30.7%
Computer Software and Services	5.9%
Internet Specific	4.7%
Medical/Health	2.1%
Communications and Media	2.0%
Computer Hardware	1.8%

Additional Information
Name of Most Recent Fund: Chartwell Capital Investors II, L.P.
Most Recent Fund Was Raised: 04/01/1998
Year Founded: 1994
Capital Under Management: $181,100,000
Current Activity Level : Inactive / Unknown
Method of Compensation: Return on invest. most important, but chg. closing fees, service fees, etc.

CMB CAPITAL, LLC (CMBC)

7650 West Courtney Campbell
Suite 1120
Tampa, FL 33607
Phone: 813-387-4087
Fax: 813-835-4197
E-mail: mattinella@cmbcapital.com
Website: www.cmbcapital.com

Management and Staff
Clay Biddinger, Chief Executive Officer
Michael Attinella, Chief Operating Officer

Type of Firm
Private Firm Investing Own Capital

Project Preferences

Type of Financing Preferred:
Early Stage
Expansion
Later Stage

Geographical Preferences

United States
Southeast
All U.S.

Industry Preferences

Communications and Media
Telecommunications

Internet Specific
Internet

Additional Information
Year Founded: 1999
Current Activity Level : Actively seeking new investments

CROSSBOW VENTURES

One North Clematis Street
Suite 510
West Palm Beach, FL 33401-5523
Phone: 561-838-9005
Fax: 561-838-4105
Website: www.cb-ventures.com

Management and Staff
Avi Hersh, Vice President
Bruce Shewmaker, Managing Director
Daniel Braz, Vice President
Dennis Donohue, Chief Financial Officer
Donohue Dennis, Chief Financial Officer
Hank Powell, Managing Director
Leandro Testa, Vice President
Ravi Ugale, Vice President
Rene Eichenberger, Managing Director
Stephen Warner, Managing Director

Type of Firm
Private Firm Investing Own Capital

Industry Association Membership
National Venture Capital Association (NVCA)
Natl assoc of Small Bus. Inv. Co (NASBIC)

Project Preferences

Type of Financing Preferred:
First Stage Financing
Mezzanine
Second Stage Financing

Size of Investments Considered
Min Size of Investment Considered (000s): $2,000
Max Size of Investment Considered (000s): $5,000

Geographical Preferences

United States
All U.S.

Industry Preferences

(% based on actual investment)

Internet Specific	58.4%
Other Products	13.6%
Medical/Health	10.5%
Computer Software and Services	7.3%
Communications and Media	6.7%
Computer Hardware	3.4%

Additional Information
Year Founded: 1999
Capital Under Management: $160,000,000
Current Activity Level : Actively seeking new investments

FLORIDA CAPITAL PARTNERS

601 N. Ashley Drive
Suite 500
Tampa, FL 33602
Phone: 813-222-8000
Fax: 813-222-8001

Management and Staff
David Malizia
Glenn Oken

Whom to Contact
David Malizia
Glenn Oken

Type of Firm
Private Firm Investing Own Capital

Project Preferences

Role in Financing:
Prefer role as deal originator but will also invest in deals created by others

Type of Financing Preferred:
Leveraged Buyout

Size of Investments Considered
Min Size of Investment Considered (000s): $3,000
Max Size of Investment Considered: No Limit

Geographical Preferences

United States
All U.S.

Canada
All Canada

Industry Preferences

(% based on actual investment)

Consumer Related	54.7%
Industrial/Energy	21.0%
Other Products	18.2%
Medical/Health	6.2%

Additional Information
Name of Most Recent Fund: FCP Southeast Investors V
Most Recent Fund Was Raised: 01/01/1996
Year Founded: 1988
Capital Under Management: $214,000,000
Current Activity Level : Inactive / Unknown
Method of Compensation: Return on invest. most important, but chg. closing fees, service fees, etc.

FLORIDA CAPITAL VENTURES, LTD.

325 Florida Bank Plaza
100 West Kennedy Boulevard
Tampa, FL 33602
Phone: 813-229-2294
Fax: 813-229-2028

Other Offices

880 Riverside Plaza
100 West Kennedy Boulevard
Tampa, FL 33602
Phone: 813-229-2294
Fax: 813-229-2028

Management and Staff
Warren Miller

Whom to Contact
Warren Miller

Type of Firm
Private Firm Investing Own Capital

Industry Association Membership
Natl assoc of Small Bus. Inv. Co (NASBIC)

Project Preferences

Role in Financing:
Prefer role as deal originator

Type of Financing Preferred:
First Stage Financing
Leveraged Buyout
Second Stage Financing
Special Situation
Start-up Financing

Size of Investments Considered
Min Size of Investment Considered (000s): $500
Max Size of Investment Considered: No Limit

Geographical Preferences

United States
Southeast

Industry Preferences

Communications and Media
Communications and Media

Computer Other
Computer Related

Semiconductors/Other Elect.
Electronic Components

Biotechnology
Industrial Biotechnology

Medical/Health
Medical/Health
Medical Diagnostics
Medical Therapeutics

Consumer Related
Retail
Food/Beverage
Consumer Products
Education Related

Industrial/Energy
Alternative Energy
Coal Related
Energy Conservation Relat
Industrial Products

Transportation
Transportation

Business Serv.
Distribution

Manufact.
Publishing

Agr/Forestr/Fish
Agriculture related

Additional Information
Year Founded: 1989
Capital Under Management: $7,000,000
Current Activity Level : Actively seeking new investments
Method of Compensation: Return on invest. most important, but chg. closing fees, service fees, etc.

HENRY & CO.

8201 Peters Road
Suite 1000
Plantation, FL 33324
Phone: 954-797-7400

Other Offices

4370 La Jolla Village Drive
Suite 400
San Diego, CA 92122-1251
Phone: 619-453-1655

Management and Staff
June Knaudt

Whom to Contact
June Knaudt

Type of Firm
Private Firm Investing Own Capital

Industry Association Membership
Western Association of Venture Capitalists (WAVC)

Project Preferences

Role in Financing:
Prefer role as deal originator but will also invest in deals created by others

Type of Financing Preferred:
First Stage Financing
Second Stage Financing

Size of Investments Considered
Min Size of Investment Considered (000s): $500
Max Size of Investment Considered (000s): $1,000

Geographical Preferences

United States
West Coast

Industry Preferences

Medical/Health
Diagnostic Services
Diagnostic Test Products
Drug/Equipmt Delivery
Other Therapeutic
Disposable Med. Products

Additional Information
Name of Most Recent Fund: Henry & Co. Venture II Ltd.
Most Recent Fund Was Raised: 11/01/1987
Year Founded: 1983
Capital Under Management: $60,000,000
Current Activity Level : Making few, if any, new investments
Method of Compensation: Return on investment is of primary concern, do not charge fees

INTERPRISE TECHNOLOGY PARTNERS, L.P.

1001 Brickell Avenue
30th Floor
Miami, FL 33131
Phone: 305-374-6808
Fax: 305-374-3317
Website: www.itpvc.com

Management and Staff
Andrew Cohen, Principal
Carlos-Felipe Mejia, Principal
David Parker, Managing Partner
Edmund Miller, Partner
Juan Carlos Campuzano, Principal

Type of Firm
Private Firm Investing Own Capital

Industry Preferences
(% based on actual investment)

Internet Specific	69.4%
Computer Hardware	17.7%
Computer Software and Services	12.5%
Other Products	0.4%

Additional Information
Year Founded: 1999
Capital Under Management: $110,000,000
Current Activity Level : Actively seeking new investments

LEE MUNDER VENTURE PARTNERS

231 Royal Palm Way
Palm Beach, FL 33480
Phone: 561-802-8800
Fax: 561- 802-8801
Website: www.leemunder.com

See Massachusetts for full listing.

LJH GLOBAL INVESTMENTS

801 Laurel Oak Drive
5th Floor
Naples, FL 34108
Phone: 941-593-5000
Fax: 941-593-5001
Website: www.ljh.com

Management and Staff
George Gowdey, Vice President
James Hedges, Managing Director
Willis Williams, Chief Financial Officer

Whom to Contact
Marc Sharpe

Type of Firm
Investment Management/Finance Consulting

Project Preferences
Role in Financing:
Prefer role in deals created by others

Type of Financing Preferred:
First Stage Financing
Second Stage Financing
Special Situation

Geographical Preferences
United States
All U.S.

Industry Preferences
Communications and Media
Communications and Media

Computer Other
Computer Related

Semiconductors/Other Elect.
Electronic Components

Financial Services
Financial Services

Business Serv.
Distribution

Additional Information
Year Founded: 1992
Capital Under Management: $200,000,000
Current Activity Level : Actively seeking new investments
Method of Compensation: Return on investment is of primary concern, do not charge fees

LM CAPITAL CORP.

120 South Olive
Suite 400
West Palm Beach, FL 33401
Phone: 561-833-9700
Fax: 561-655-6587
Website: www.lmcapitalsecurities.com

Other Offices

433 Plaza Real
Suite 365
Boca Raton, FL 33432
Phone: 407-362-4635
Fax: 407-362-4633

Republic Plaza
370 17th Street
Denver, CO 80202
Phone: 303-572-5014
Fax: 303-572-5001

Management and Staff
Leslie Corley, President

Type of Firm
Investment/Merchant Bank Investing Own or Client Funds

Industry Association Membership
Natl Assoc of Investment Cos. (NAIC)

Project Preferences
Role in Financing:
Prefer role as deal originator but will also invest in deals created by others

Type of Financing Preferred:
Leveraged Buyout

Size of Investments Considered
Min Size of Investment Considered (000s): $5,000
Max Size of Investment Considered: No Limit

Geographical Preferences
International
No Preference

Industry Preferences
Computer Hardware
Integrated Turnkey System

Semiconductors/Other Elect.
Sensors

Medical/Health
Diagnostic Test Products
Drug/Equipmt Delivery
Medical Products
Hospitals/Clinics/Primary
Pharmaceuticals

Consumer Related
Food/Beverage
Consumer Products
Consumer Services
Other Restaurants

Industrial/Energy
Materials
Environmental Related

Financial Services
Financial Services

Additional Information
Name of Most Recent Fund: LM Capital Fund II
Most Recent Fund Was Raised: 06/30/1994
Year Founded: 1988
Capital Under Management: $40,000,000
Current Activity Level : Actively seeking new investments
Method of Compensation: Return on invest. most important, but chg. closing fees, service fees, etc.

LOVETT MILLER & CO. INCORPORATED

One Independent Square
Suite 1600
Jacksonville, FL 32202
Phone: 904-634-0077
Fax: 904-634-0633

Other Offices

100 North Tampa Street
Suite 2430
Tampa, FL 33602
Phone: 813-222-1477
Fax: 813-222-1478

Type of Firm
Private Firm Investing Own Capital

Industry Association Membership
National Venture Capital Association (NVCA)

Project Preferences

Type of Financing Preferred:
Early Stage
Later Stage
Leveraged Buyout
Mezzanine
Seed
Startup

Geographical Preferences

United States
All U.S.

Industry Preferences

(% based on actual investment)

Computer Software and Services	53.5%
Internet Specific	24.7%
Medical/Health	10.8%
Consumer Related	8.3%
Other Products	2.7%

Additional Information
Name of Most Recent Fund: Lovett Miller Venture Fund II, Limited Partnership
Most Recent Fund Was Raised: 06/30/1998
Year Founded: 1998
Capital Under Management: $155,000,000
Current Activity Level : Actively seeking new investments

NETJUICE

Waterford Business Center
5200 Blue Lagoon Drive Suite 100
Miami, FL 33126
Website: www.netjuice.com

See Foreign Venture Capital Firms for full listing.

NEW SOUTH VENTURES

5053 Ocean Boulevard
Sarasota, FL 34242
Phone: 941-358-6000
Fax: 941-358-6078
Website: www.newsouthventures.com

Management and Staff
Gary Arnold, Managing Partner
Harvey Vengroff, Partner
John Montelione, Partner
Norman Worthington, Partner
Rob Campbell, Partner

Type of Firm
Private Firm Investing Own Capital

Project Preferences

Type of Financing Preferred:
Early Stage
Seed

Size of Investments Considered
Min Size of Investment Considered (000s): $300
Max Size of Investment Considered (000s): $3,000

Geographical Preferences

United States
Florida
Southeast

Additional Information
Year Founded: 2000
Current Activity Level : Actively seeking new investments

NEWTEK CAPITAL

1201 Brickell Avenue
Miami, FL 33133
Website: www.newtekcapital.com

See New York for full listing.

NORTH AMERICAN BUSINESS DEVELOPMENT CO., L.L.C.

111 East Las Olas Boulevard
Fort Lauderdale, FL 33301
Phone: 305-463-0681
Fax: 305-527-0904
Website: www.northamericanfund.com

See Illinois for full listing.

OSPREY CAPITAL, LLC

4400 Marsh Landing Blvd.
Suite 6
Ponte Vedra Beach, FL 32082
Phone: 904-280-0280
Fax: 904-280-0380
E-mail: rmons@ospreycapital.com
Website: www.ospreycapital.com

Management and Staff
Robert Mons, Managing Partner

Type of Firm
Investment/Merchant Bank Subsid/Affil

Project Preferences

Type of Financing Preferred:
Expansion

Geographical Preferences

United States
All U.S.

Additional Information
Year Founded: 1996
Current Activity Level : Actively seeking new investments
Method of Compensation: Function primarily in service area, receive contingent fee in cash or equity

QUANTUM CAPITAL PARTNERS

339 South Plant Avenue
Tampa, FL 33606
Phone: 813-250-1999
Fax: 813-250-1998
Website: www.quantumcapitalpartners.com

Management and Staff
N.John Simmons, President

Type of Firm
Private Firm Investing Own Capital

Industry Association Membership
National Venture Capital Association (NVCA)

Project Preferences

Role in Financing:
Will function either as deal originator or investor in deals created by others

Type of Financing Preferred:
Expansion
Later Stage
Mezzanine

Size of Investments Considered
Min Size of Investment Considered (000s): $1,000
Max Size of Investment Considered (000s): $5,000

Geographical Preferences

United States
Florida

Industry Preferences

Communications and Media
Commercial Communications
Telecommunications
Wireless Communications
Data Communications

Internet Specific
Internet

Semiconductors/Other Elect.
Electronic Components
Circuit Boards
Component Testing Equipmt
Laser Related
Fiber Optics
Analytic/Scientific

Medical/Health
Medical Diagnostics
Diagnostic Test Products
Medical Therapeutics
Drug/Equipmt Delivery
Medical Products
Disposable Med. Products

Consumer Related
Consumer
Retail

Industrial/Energy
Industrial Products
Factory Automation
Process Control
Machinery

Financial Services
Financial Services

Business Serv.
Services
Distribution
Consulting Services

Manufact.
Manufacturing

Additional Information
Capital Under Management: $10,000,000
Current Activity Level : Actively seeking new investments
Method of Compensation: Return on investment is of primary concern, do not charge fees

ROCK CREEK PARTNERS, L.P.

1200 Riverplace Blvd.
Suite 902
Jacksonville, FL 32207
Phone: 904-393-9020
Fax: 904-393-9003
Website: www.rockcreekpartners.com

Management and Staff
Arthur Cahoon, General Partner
James Dahl, General Partner
John Sites, General Partner
Peter Collins, Managing Director
W. David Shields, Managing Director
William Dahl, Managing Director

Type of Firm
Private Firm Investing Own Capital

Project Preferences

Type of Financing Preferred:
Later Stage

Geographical Preferences

United States
Southeast

Industry Preferences

Financial Services
Financial Services

Additional Information
Capital Under Management: $150,000,000
Current Activity Level : Actively seeking new investments

SI VENTURES

12600 Gateway Boulevard
Ft. Myers, FL 33913
Phone: 941-561-4650
Fax: 941-561-4916
Website: www.siventures.com

Other Offices

56 Top Gallant Road
Stamford, CT 06904

730 North Nevada
Suite 200
Colorado Springs, CO 80903

Management and Staff
Adam Rin, Managing Director
Brian Beach, Principal
John Halligan, Managing Director
Manny Fernandez, Managing Director
Valerie Anderson, Managing Director

Type of Firm
Non-Financial Corp. Affiliate or Subsidiary

Industry Association Membership
National Venture Capital Association (NVCA)

Project Preferences

Role in Financing:
Will function either as deal originator or investor in deals created by others

Type of Financing Preferred:
Balanced
Expansion
Second Stage Financing

Size of Investments Considered
Min Size of Investment Considered (000s): $3,000
Max Size of Investment Considered (000s): $10,000

Geographical Preferences

United States
All U.S.
All U.S.

Industry Preferences

(% based on actual investment)

Internet Specific	59.7%
Computer Software and Services	26.4%
Communications and Media	8.0%
Medical/Health	4.7%
Computer Hardware	1.3%

Additional Information
Year Founded: 1998
Capital Under Management: $122,900,000
Current Activity Level : Actively seeking new investments

SIGMA CAPITAL CORP.

22668 Caravelle Circle
Boca Raton, FL 33433
Phone: 561-368-9783

Type of Firm
Private Firm Investing Own Capital

Project Preferences

Role in Financing:
Prefer role as deal originator but will also invest in deals created by others

Type of Financing Preferred:
Second Stage Financing

Size of Investments Considered
Min Size of Investment Considered (000s): $100
Max Size of Investment Considered (000s): $300

Geographical Preferences

United States
Southeast

Industry Preferences

Communications and Media
CATV & Pay TV Systems
Telecommunications
Data Communications
Other Communication Prod.

Computer Hardware
Mini and Personal/Desktop
Computer Graphics and Dig

Computer Software
Computer Services

Semiconductors/Other Elect.
Electronics
Electronic Components
Sensors
Circuit Boards
Component Testing Equipmt
Laser Related
Fiber Optics
Analytic/Scientific

Biotechnology
Industrial Biotechnology
Biotech Related Research
Biotech Related Research

Medical/Health
Medical Diagnostics
Diagnostic Test Products
Medical Therapeutics
Drug/Equipmt Delivery
Medical Products
Disposable Med. Products

Consumer Related
Food/Beverage
Consumer Products
Consumer Services
Hotels and Resorts

Industrial/Energy
Industrial Products
Materials
Factory Automation
Robotics
Machinery

Financial Services
Financial Services
Real Estate

Manufact.
Office Automation Equipmt

Additional Information
Year Founded: 1988
Current Activity Level : Actively seeking new investments
Method of Compensation: Other

SOUTH ATLANTIC VENTURE FUNDS, L.P.

614 West Bay Street
Tampa, FL 33606-2704
Phone: 813-253-2500
Fax: 813-253-2360
Website: www.southatlantic.com

Other Offices

102 Marseille Place
Cary, NC 27511
Phone: 919-461-0803
Fax: 919-319-0026

1239 O.G. Skinner Drive
West Point, GA 31833
Phone: 706-645-8139
Fax: 706-643-5067

Terremark Center, Suite 1147
2601 South Bayshore Drive
Miami, FL 33133
Phone: 305-250-4681
Fax: 305-250-4682

Management and Staff
Campbell Lanier, Managing Director
Donald Burton, Chairman & Managing Director
Drew Graham, Managing Director
James Davidson, Managing Director
O. Gene Gabbard, Managing Director
Sandra Barber, Managing Director

Type of Firm
Private Firm Investing Own Capital

Industry Association Membership
National Venture Capital Association (NVCA)
Natl assoc of Small Bus. Inv. Co (NASBIC)

Project Preferences

Role in Financing:
Prefer role as deal originator but will also invest in deals created by others

Type of Financing Preferred:
Control-block Purchases
Expansion
First Stage Financing
Second Stage Financing
Special Situation

Size of Investments Considered
Min Size of Investment Considered (000s): $1,500
Max Size of Investment Considered: No Limit

Geographical Preferences

United States
Mid Atlantic
Southeast
Texas

Industry Preferences

(% based on actual investment)

Communications and Media	24.8%
Medical/Health	20.3%
Semiconductors/Other Elect.	14.5%
Other Products	13.8%
Internet Specific	9.0%
Consumer Related	8.0%
Computer Software and Services	5.8%
Computer Hardware	3.3%
Industrial/Energy	0.5%

Additional Information
Name of Most Recent Fund: South Atlantic Private Equity Fund IV, Limited Partnership
Most Recent Fund Was Raised: 07/01/1997
Year Founded: 1983
Capital Under Management: $115,400,000
Current Activity Level : Actively seeking new investments
Method of Compensation: Return on investment is of primary concern, do not charge fees

VENTURE CAPITAL MANAGEMENT CORP.

P.O. Box 2626
Satellite Beach, FL 32937
Phone: 407-777-1969

Type of Firm
Mgt. Consulting Firm

Project Preferences

Role in Financing:
Prefer role as deal originator but will also invest in deals created by others

Type of Financing Preferred:
First Stage Financing
Leveraged Buyout
Second Stage Financing

Size of Investments Considered
Min Size of Investment Considered (000s): $100
Max Size of Investment Considered (000s): $300

Geographical Preferences

International
No Preference

Industry Preferences

Communications and Media
Commercial Communications
Satellite Microwave Comm.

Computer Hardware
Computer Graphics and Dig

Semiconductors/Other Elect.
Analytic/Scientific

Biotechnology
Biotech Related Research
Biotech Related Research

Medical/Health
Diagnostic Services
Diagnostic Test Products
Other Therapeutic
Medical Products
Pharmaceuticals

Consumer Related
Entertainment and Leisure
Retail
Consumer Products
Hotels and Resorts

Industrial/Energy
Alternative Energy
Industrial Products
Materials
Machinery

Transportation
Transportation

Financial Services
Financial Services
Real Estate

Manufact.
Publishing

Agr/Forestr/Fish
Agriculture related

Additional Information
Year Founded: 1974
Current Activity Level : Actively seeking new investments
Method of Compensation: Function primarily in service area, receive contingent fee in cash or equity

VENTURE FIRST ASSOCIATES

1901 South Harbor City Blvd
Suite 501
Melbourne, FL 32901
Phone: 407-952-7750
Fax: 407-952-5787

Other Offices

1901 S. Harbor City Blvd.
Suite 501
Melbourne, FL 32901
Phone: 407-952-7750
Fax: 407-952-5787

4811 Thornwood Drive
Acworth, GA 30101
Phone: 770-928-3733

500 Old Greensboro Road
Chapel Hill, NC 27516
Phone: 919-929-1065
Fax: 919-929-0978

Management and Staff
Brian Williams, Chief Financial Officer
J. Douglass Mullins, Partner

Whom to Contact
J. Douglas Mullins

Type of Firm
Private Firm Investing Own Capital

Industry Association Membership
National Venture Capital Association (NVCA)

Project Preferences

Role in Financing:
Prefer role as deal originator but will also invest in deals created by others

Type of Financing Preferred:
First Stage Financing
Second Stage Financing
Seed
Start-up Financing

Size of Investments Considered
Min Size of Investment Considered (000s): $500
Max Size of Investment Considered (000s): $5,000

Geographical Preferences

United States
Southeast

Industry Preferences

Communications and Media
Commercial Communications
Telecommunications
Wireless Communications
Data Communications
Satellite Microwave Comm.
Other Communication Prod.

Semiconductors/Other Elect.
Electronic Components
Component Testing Equipmt
Laser Related
Analytic/Scientific

Additional Information
Year Founded: 1984
Capital Under Management: $20,000,000
Current Activity Level : Making few, if any, new investments
Method of Compensation: Return on investment is of primary concern, do not charge fees

VENTURE INVESTORS MANAGEMENT LLC

917 Gibbs Road
P.O. Box 1506
Venice, FL 34284
Phone: 941-486-8687
Fax: 941-485-0879
Website: www.ventureinvestors.com

See Wisconsin for full listing.

VENTURE MANAGEMENT ASSOCIATES, INC.

3250 Miami Center
20 South Biscayne Boulevard
Miami, FL 33131
Phone: 305-379-2005

Type of Firm
Private Firm Investing Own Capital

Project Preferences

Type of Financing Preferred:
Early Stage

Geographical Preferences

United States
Southeast

Additional Information
Name of Most Recent Fund: Southeast Sbic (NOW Southeast Venture Capital)
Most Recent Fund Was Raised: 01/01/1973
Year Founded: 1968
Current Activity Level : Inactive / Unknown

XL VISION INC

10315 102nd Terrace
Sebastian, FL 32958
Phone: 561-581-7000
Fax: 561-581-7310
Website: www.xlvision.com

Management and Staff
David Szostak, Chief Financial Officer
John Scott, Chairman & CEO

Type of Firm
Incubators

Project Preferences

Role in Financing:
Prefer role as deal originator

Additional Information
Current Activity Level : Actively seeking new investments

GEORGIA

ADVANCED TECHNOLOGY DEVELOPMENT FUND

1000 Abernathy
Suite 1420
Atlanta, GA 30328-5614
Phone: 404-668-2333
Fax: 404-668-2333

Other Offices

1000 Abernathy Road
Suite 1420
Atlanta, GA 30328
Phone: 404-668-2333
Fax: 404-668-2330

Type of Firm

Private Firm Investing Own Capital

Project Preferences

Role in Financing:

Prefer role as deal originator but will also invest in deals created by others

Type of Financing Preferred:

First Stage Financing
Leveraged Buyout
Second Stage Financing
Seed
Start-up Financing

Size of Investments Considered

Min Size of Investment Considered (000s): $500
Max Size of Investment Considered (000s): $1,500

Geographical Preferences

International

No Preference

Additional Information

Name of Most Recent Fund: Advanced Technology Development Fund
Most Recent Fund Was Raised: 10/01/1983
Year Founded: 1983
Capital Under Management: $27,000,000
Current Activity Level : Actively seeking new investments
Method of Compensation: Return on investment is of primary concern, do not charge fees

ALLIANCE TECHNOLOGY VENTURES

8995 Westside Parkway
Suite 200
Alpharetta, GA 30004
Phone: 678-336-2000
Fax: 678-336-2001
Website: http://www.atv.com

Management and Staff

Connor Seabrook, Chief Financial Officer
Michael Henos, General Partner
Michael Slawson, General Partner
Stephen Fleming, General Partner

Type of Firm

Private Firm Investing Own Capital

Industry Association Membership

National Venture Capital Association (NVCA)

Project Preferences

Role in Financing:

Prefer role as deal originator but will also invest in deals created by others

Type of Financing Preferred:

First Stage Financing
Second Stage Financing
Seed
Start-up Financing
Startup

Geographical Preferences

United States

Southeast

Industry Preferences

(% based on actual investment)

Internet Specific	38.0%
Communications and Media	21.9%
Semiconductors/Other Elect.	14.2%
Computer Software and Services	13.1%
Biotechnology	11.4%
Medical/Health	1.4%

Additional Information

Name of Most Recent Fund: Alliance Technology Ventures III
Most Recent Fund Was Raised: 04/15/1998
Year Founded: 1993
Capital Under Management: $34,000,000
Current Activity Level : Actively seeking new investments
Method of Compensation: Return on investment is of primary concern, do not charge fees

ASPEN VENTURES (FORMERLY 3I VENTURES)

3343 Peachtree Road, N.E.
East Tower, Suite 1140
Atlanta, GA 30326
Phone: 404-816-4791
Fax: 404-816-4891
Website: www.aspenventures.com

See California for full listing.

BLUESHIFT INTERNET VENTURES

3550, Engineering Drive, Suite 140
Technology Park
Norcross, GA 30092
Phone: 1-770-368-1124
Fax: 1-770-368-0998
E-mail: info@blueshift.com
Website: www.ventures.blueshift.com

See Foreign Venture Capital Firms for full listing.

BRAINWORKS VENTURES

4243 Dunwoody Club Drive
Chamblee, GA 30341
Phone: 770-239-7447
Website: www.brainworksvc.com

Management and Staff

John Cayce, President
Marc Wright, Chief Operating Officer
Marc Schwartz, Vice President

Type of Firm

Private Firm Investing Own Capital

Project Preferences

Type of Financing Preferred:

Balanced
Early Stage
Later Stage

Geographical Preferences

United States

Southeast

Industry Preferences

Communications and Media

Telecommunications

Computer Hardware
Computers

Additional Information
Current Activity Level : Actively seeking new investments

CGW SOUTHEAST PARTNERS (AKA: CRAVEY, GREEN, & WAHLEN)

12 Piedmont Center
Suite 210
Atlanta, GA 30305
Phone: 404-816-3255
Fax: 404-816-3258
Website: www.cgwlp.com

Management and Staff
Bart McLean, Partner
Edwin Wahlen, Managing Partner
Gary Kitchen, Partner
Jim O'Donnell, Partner
Michael Long, Partner
Richard Cravey, Principal
Roy Bowman, Partner
William Davies, Partner

Whom to Contact
Garrison M. Kitchen

Type of Firm
Private Firm Investing Own Capital

Project Preferences

Role in Financing:
Prefer role as deal originator but will also invest in deals created by others

Type of Financing Preferred:
Management Buyouts

Size of Investments Considered
Min Size of Investment Considered (000s): $25,000
Max Size of Investment Considered (000s): $200,000

Geographical Preferences

United States
All U.S.

International
Belgium
France
Germany
Luxembourg
Netherlands
Portugal
Spain
United Kingdom

Industry Preferences
(% based on actual investment)

Other Products	39.7%
Industrial/Energy	23.8%
Consumer Related	23.7%
Medical/Health	6.7%
Communications and Media	6.2%

Additional Information
Name of Most Recent Fund: CGW III
Most Recent Fund Was Raised: 04/01/1996
Year Founded: 1984
Capital Under Management: $782,100,000
Current Activity Level : Actively seeking new investments
Method of Compensation: Return on invest. most important, but chg. closing fees, service fees, etc.

CORDOVA VENTURES (FKA:CORDOVA CAPITAL)

2500 North Winds Parkway
Suite 475
Alpharetta, GA 30004
Phone: 678-942-0300
Fax: 678-942-0301
Website: www.cordovaventures.com

Other Offices

4121 Carmichael Road
Suite 301
Montgomery, AL 36106
Phone: 334-271-6011
Fax: 334-260-0120

Management and Staff
Billy Williamson, Principal
Charles Adair, Partner
Chris Valianos, Partner
Don Stout, Partner
Eddie Adair, Partner
Frank Dalton, Partner
Jerry Schmidt, Partner
John Runningen, Partner
Paul DiBella, Partner
Ralph Wright, Partner
T. Forcht Dagi, Partner

Whom to Contact
Teo F. Dagi

Type of Firm
SBIC Not elsewhere classified

Industry Association Membership
National Venture Capital Association (NVCA)
Natl assoc of Small Bus. Inv. Co (NASBIC)

Project Preferences

Role in Financing:
Will function either as deal originator or investor in deals created by others

Type of Financing Preferred:
Balanced
Early Stage
Expansion
Later Stage
Startup

Size of Investments Considered
Min Size of Investment Considered (000s): $250
Max Size of Investment Considered (000s): $4,000

Geographical Preferences

United States
Southeast

Industry Preferences
(% based on actual investment)

Medical/Health	22.8%
Computer Software and Services	21.0%
Internet Specific	16.9%
Communications and Media	11.1%
Biotechnology	10.1%
Other Products	9.7%
Consumer Related	5.1%
Industrial/Energy	2.8%
Semiconductors/Other Elect.	0.4%

Additional Information
Name of Most Recent Fund: Cordova Intellimedia Ventures, L.P.; Industrial Technology V
Most Recent Fund Was Raised: 01/15/1999
Year Founded: 1989
Capital Under Management: $234,500,000
Current Activity Level : Actively seeking new investments
Method of Compensation: Return on invest. most important, but chg. closing fees, service fees, etc.

CYBERSTARTS

1900 Emery Street, NW
3rd Floor
Atlanta, GA 30318
Phone: 404-267-5000
Fax: 404-267-5200
Website: www.cyberstarts.com

Management and Staff
Ashish Bahl, President
Leonard Walker, Chief Operating Officer
Manoj Sharma, Managing Director
Rob Spessard, Managing Director

Type of Firm
Incubators

Project Preferences

Type of Financing Preferred:
Seed
Startup

Geographical Preferences

United States
All U.S.

Industry Preferences

Internet Specific
Internet

Financial Services
Financial Services

Additional Information
Year Founded: 2000
Capital Under Management: $34,000,000
Current Activity Level : Actively seeking new investments

DAKOTA GROUP, THE

10209 Chastain Drive, N.E.
Atlanta, GA 30342
Phone: 404-851-0100
Fax: 404-851-0100

See California for full listing.

DOTCOM VENTURES L.P.

1103 Riverbend Club Drive
Atlanta, GA 30301
Phone: 770-612-9190
Website: www.dotcomventuresatl.com

See California for full listing.

EGL HOLDINGS, INC./NAT WEST VENTURES USA, L.P.

10 Piedmont Center, Suite 412.
3495 Piedmont Road
Atlanta, GA 30305
Phone: 404-949-8300
Fax: 404-949-8311.

Management and Staff
David Ellis, Managing Director
John Festa, Partner
Ronald Wallace, Partner
Salvatore Massaro, Managing Director

Type of Firm
Investment/Merchant Bank Investing Own or Client Funds

Industry Association Membership
National Venture Capital Association (NVCA)
Natl assoc of Small Bus. Inv. Co (NASBIC)

Project Preferences

Role in Financing:
Prefer role as deal originator but will also invest in deals created by others

Type of Financing Preferred:
Industry Rollups
Leveraged Buyout
Mezzanine
Recapitalizations
Second Stage Financing

Size of Investments Considered
Min Size of Investment Considered (000s): $1,000
Max Size of Investment Considered: No Limit

Geographical Preferences

United States
Mid Atlantic
Midwest
Northeast
Southeast

Industry Preferences

Communications and Media
Telecommunications
Data Communications
Satellite Microwave Comm.

Computer Hardware
Mini and Personal/Desktop
Computer Graphics and Dig
Integrated Turnkey System

Computer Software
Computer Services
Systems Software
Applications Software

Internet Specific
Internet

Semiconductors/Other Elect.
Electronic Components
Controllers and Sensors
Sensors
Component Testing Equipmt
Laser Related
Fiber Optics
Analytic/Scientific

Medical/Health
Diagnostic Services
Diagnostic Test Products
Drug/Equipmt Delivery
Other Therapeutic
Disposable Med. Products
Hospital/Other Instit.

Consumer Related
Entertainment and Leisure
Consumer Products
Consumer Services

Industrial/Energy
Industrial Products
Materials
Factory Automation
Machinery
Environmental Related

Manufact.
Office Automation Equipmt
Publishing

Additional Information
Name of Most Recent Fund: EGL Holdings, Inc.
Most Recent Fund Was Raised: 08/01/1988
Year Founded: 1988
Capital Under Management: $50,000,000
Current Activity Level : Actively seeking new investments
Method of Compensation: Return on invest. most important, but chg. closing fees, service fees, etc.

EQUITY-SOUTH (FKA:GRUBB & WILLIAMS LTD.)

1790 The Lenox Building
3399 Peachtree Road, N.E.
Atlanta, GA 30326
Phone: 404-237-6222
Fax: 404-261-1578

Management and Staff
Douglas Diamond

Whom to Contact
Douglas Diamond

Type of Firm
Private Firm Investing Own Capital

Project Preferences

Role in Financing:
Prefer role as deal originator

Type of Financing Preferred:
Control-block Purchases
Leveraged Buyout
Mezzanine
Recapitalizations

Geographical Preferences

United States
Northeast
Southeast
Southwest

Industry Preferences

Communications and Media
Satellite Microwave Comm.

Computer Software
Computer Services
Systems Software
Applications Software

Semiconductors/Other Elect.
Electronic Components
Controllers and Sensors
Sensors
Circuit Boards
Component Testing Equipmt

Medical/Health
Diagnostic Services
Disposable Med. Products
Hospitals/Clinics/Primary
Hospital/Other Instit.

Consumer Related
Entertainment and Leisure
Retail
Computer Stores
Franchises(NEC)
Food/Beverage
Consumer Products
Consumer Services
Other Restaurants

Industrial/Energy
Factory Automation
Machinery
Environmental Related

Business Serv.
Distribution

Manufact.
Office Automation Equipmt

Additional Information
Name of Most Recent Fund: Equity South Partners, L.P.
Most Recent Fund Was Raised: 04/01/1995
Year Founded: 1987
Capital Under Management: $45,000,000
Current Activity Level : Actively seeking new investments
Method of Compensation: Return on investment is of primary concern, do not charge fees

---

FINANCIAL CAPITAL RESOURCES, INC.

21 Eastbrook Bend
Suite 116
Peachtree City, GA 30269
Phone: 404-487-6650

Type of Firm
Mgt. Consulting Firm

Project Preferences

Role in Financing:
Prefer role as deal originator but will also invest in deals created by others

Type of Financing Preferred:
Leveraged Buyout

Size of Investments Considered
Min Size of Investment Considered (000s): $5,000
Max Size of Investment Considered: No Limit

Geographical Preferences

International
No Preference

Industry Preferences

Industrial/Energy
Machinery

Additional Information
Year Founded: 1989
Current Activity Level : Actively seeking new investments
Method of Compensation: Function primarily in service area, receive contingent fee in cash or equity

---

FIRST GROWTH CAPITAL, INC.

Suite 105, Best Western Plaza
P.O. Box 815
Forsyth, GA 31029
Phone: 912-781-7131
Fax: 912-781-0066

Management and Staff
Vidya Patel, Vice President

Type of Firm
MESBIC not elsewhere classified

Industry Association Membership
Natl Assoc of Investment Cos. (NAIC)
Natl assoc of Small Bus. Inv. Co (NASBIC)

Project Preferences

Role in Financing:
Will function either as deal originator or investor in deals created by others

Type of Financing Preferred:
Second Stage Financing
Special Situation

Size of Investments Considered
Min Size of Investment Considered (000s): $100
Max Size of Investment Considered (000s): $300

Geographical Preferences

International
No Preference

Additional Information

Year Founded: 1989
Capital Under Management: $4,100,000
Current Activity Level : Inactive / Unknown
Method of Compensation: Return on invest. most important, but chg. closing fees, service fees, etc.

FIVE PACES VENTURES

3400 Peachtree Road
Suite 200
Atlanta, GA 30326
Phone: 404-439-8300
Fax: 404-439-8301
Website: www.fivepaces.com

Management and Staff

Alan Quarterman, Partner
Mark Mykityshyn, Partner
Michael McChesney, Partner

Type of Firm

Private Firm Investing Own Capital

Project Preferences

Type of Financing Preferred:
Balanced

Geographical Preferences

United States
All U.S.
Southeast

Additional Information

Year Founded: 2000
Current Activity Level : Actively seeking new investments

FRONTLINE CAPITAL, INC.

3475 Lenox Road
Suite 400
Atlanta, GA 30326
Phone: 404-240-7280
Fax: 404-240-7281

Type of Firm

Investment/Merchant Bank Investing Own or Client Funds

Project Preferences

Role in Financing:
Prefer role as deal originator

Type of Financing Preferred:
First Stage Financing

Size of Investments Considered
Min Size of Investment Considered (000s): $1,000
Max Size of Investment Considered: No Limit

Geographical Preferences

United States
Southeast

Industry Preferences

Communications and Media
Communications and Media
Other Communication Prod.

Computer Hardware
Computers

Semiconductors/Other Elect.
Electronics
Controllers and Sensors
Laser Related

Medical/Health
Medical/Health
Medical Products

Consumer Related
Entertainment and Leisure
Retail
Computer Stores
Food/Beverage
Consumer Products
Consumer Services
Other Restaurants
Education Related

Industrial/Energy
Alternative Energy
Energy Conservation Relat
Industrial Products

Transportation
Transportation

Financial Services
Financial Services

Business Serv.
Consulting Services

Manufact.
Publishing

Additional Information

Year Founded: 1994
Current Activity Level : Actively seeking new investments
Method of Compensation: Function primarily in service area, receive contingent fee in cash or equity

FUQUA VENTURES, LLC

1201 W. Peachtree Street NW
Suite 5000
Atlanta, GA 30309
Phone: 404-815-4500
Fax: 404-815-4528
Website: www.fuquaventures.com

Management and Staff

David Guthrie, Partner
J. Rex Fuqua, Managing Director
J. Scott Tapp, Principal
John Huntz, Managing Director

Type of Firm

Private Firm Investing Own Capital

Industry Association Membership

National Venture Capital Association (NVCA)
Natl assoc of Small Bus. Inv. Co (NASBIC)

Project Preferences

Type of Financing Preferred:
Early Stage

Geographical Preferences

United States
All U.S.

Industry Preferences

(% based on actual investment)

Internet Specific	64.0%
Biotechnology	12.4%
Other Products	9.6%
Communications and Media	7.8%
Computer Software and Services	6.2%

Additional Information

Capital Under Management: $10,000,000
Current Activity Level : Actively seeking new investments

GRAY VENTURES

3330 Cumberland Boulevard
Suite 625
Atlanta, GA 30339
Phone: 770-240-1505
Fax: 770-240-1503

Management and Staff

Bernard Gray, President
Chris Rossie, Vice President
Ron Reuss, Vice President

Type of Firm

Private Firm Investing Own Capital

Industry Association Membership

National Venture Capital Association (NVCA)

Project Preferences

Role in Financing:
Prefer role as deal originator

Type of Financing Preferred:
Early Stage

Size of Investments Considered

Min Size of Investment Considered (000s): $1,000
Max Size of Investment Considered (000s): $2,500

Geographical Preferences

United States
Georgia
North Carolina

Industry Preferences

(% based on actual investment)

Internet Specific	53.3%
Computer Software and Services	26.5%
Semiconductors/Other Elect.	10.0%
Communications and Media	9.0%
Computer Hardware	1.2%

Additional Information

Capital Under Management: $30,000,000
Current Activity Level : Actively seeking new investments

IMLAY INVESTMENTS

945 East Paces Ferry Rd.
Suite 2450
Atlanta, GA 30326
Phone: 404-239-1799
Fax: 404-239-1779

Management and Staff

John Imlay, General Partner
Sig Mosley, President

Type of Firm

Private Firm Investing Own Capital

Industry Preferences

(% based on actual investment)

Internet Specific	56.2%
Computer Software and Services	22.0%
Communications and Media	11.7%
Other Products	3.0%
Computer Hardware	2.6%
Biotechnology	1.9%
Consumer Related	1.5%
Semiconductors/Other Elect.	1.2%

Additional Information

Year Founded: 1990
Current Activity Level : Actively seeking new investments

KINETIC VENTURES, INC.

The South Terraces
115 Perimeter Center Plaza
Atlanta, GA 30346
Phone: 770-399-1660
Fax: 770-399-1664
Website: www.kineticventures.com

See Maryland for full listing.

LIVEOAK EQUITY PARTNERS

2500 Northwinds Parkway
Suite 325
Alpharetta, GA 30004
Phone: 678-393-9909
Fax: 678-393-9945
Website: www.liveoakequity.com

Management and Staff

Chad McCall, Managing Partner
Holcombe Green, Managing Director
James Gilbert, Managing Partner
Murali Anantharaman, Managing Partner

Type of Firm

Private Firm Investing Own Capital

Project Preferences

Type of Financing Preferred:
First Stage Financing
Second Stage Financing

Geographical Preferences

United States
Southeast

Industry Preferences

(% based on actual investment)

Internet Specific	41.0%
Computer Software and Services	39.9%
Communications and Media	6.5%
Biotechnology	6.5%
Medical/Health	5.1%
Semiconductors/Other Elect.	1.1%

Additional Information

Name of Most Recent Fund: LiveOak Equity Partners
Most Recent Fund Was Raised: 08/01/1998
Year Founded: 1998
Capital Under Management: $70,000,000
Current Activity Level : Actively seeking new investments

MELLON VENTURES (AKA: MELLON BANK)

One Buckhead Plaza
3060 Peachtree Road, Suite 780
Atlanta, GA 30305-2240
Phone: 404-264-9180
Fax: 404-264-9305
Website: www.mellonventures.com

See Pennsylvania for full listing.

MILLER/ZELL VENTURE GROUP

4715 Frederick Drive, S.W.
Atlanta, GA 30336
Phone: 404-691-7400
Fax: 404-699-2189

Type of Firm

Mgt. Consulting Firm

Project Preferences

Role in Financing:
Prefer role as deal originator but will also invest in deals created by others

Type of Financing Preferred:
Leveraged Buyout
Special Situation

Geographical Preferences

International
No Preference

Industry Preferences

Consumer Related
Retail

Business Serv.
Consulting Services

Additional Information

Year Founded: 1987
Current Activity Level : Actively seeking new investments
Method of Compensation: Return on invest. most important, but chg. closing fees, service fees, etc.

MONARCH CAPITAL PARTNERS, LLC

3414 Peachtree Road NE
Suite 1250
Atlanta, GA 30326
Phone: 404-262-1110
Fax: 404-262-9332
Website: www.monarchpartners.com

Other Offices

3232 McKinney Avenue
Suite 865
Dallas, TX 75204
Phone: 214-871-7784
Fax: 214-740-1792

Management and Staff

Bennie Bray, Managing Partner
Gerry Purdy, General Partner
John Brewer, General Partner
Richard Williams, General Partner
Robert Guyton, Managing Partner

Type of Firm

Private Firm Investing Own Capital

Project Preferences

Type of Financing Preferred:
Early Stage

Geographical Preferences

United States
Southeast
Texas

Industry Preferences

(% based on actual investment)

Internet Specific	65.0%
Computer Software and Services	25.1%
Semiconductors/Other Elect.	6.6%
Communications and Media	3.3%

Additional Information

Year Founded: 1998
Capital Under Management: $30,000,000
Current Activity Level : Actively seeking new investments

NORO-MOSELEY PARTNERS

9 North Parkway Square
4200 Northside Parkway, N.W.
Atlanta, GA 30327
Phone: 404-233-1966
Fax: 404-239-9280
Website: www.noro-moseley.com

Management and Staff

Alan Taetle, Principal
Charles Johnson, General Partner
Charles Moseley, General Partner
Jack Kelly, General Partner
Russell French, Partner
Steve Nussrallah, General Partner
Tripp Rackley, Venture Partner

Type of Firm

Private Firm Investing Own Capital

Project Preferences

Role in Financing:
Prefer role as deal originator but will also invest in deals created by others

Type of Financing Preferred:
Control-block Purchases
First Stage Financing
Leveraged Buyout
Mezzanine
Second Stage Financing
Special Situation
Start-up Financing

Size of Investments Considered

Min Size of Investment Considered (000s): $1,000
Max Size of Investment Considered: No Limit

Geographical Preferences

United States
Florida
Georgia
North Carolina
Southeast

Industry Preferences

(% based on actual investment)

Internet Specific	20.7%
Computer Software and Services	14.7%
Consumer Related	13.2%
Communications and Media	12.3%
Medical/Health	11.6%
Other Products	10.5%
Computer Hardware	8.9%
Industrial/Energy	3.5%
Semiconductors/Other Elect.	3.2%
Biotechnology	1.4%

Additional Information

Name of Most Recent Fund: Noro-Moseley Partners IV, L.P.
Most Recent Fund Was Raised: 03/01/1998
Year Founded: 1983
Capital Under Management: $580,000,000
Current Activity Level : Actively seeking new investments
Method of Compensation: Return on investment is of primary concern, do not charge fees

PHOENIX GROWTH CAPITAL CORP.

641 East Morningside Drive, N.E.
Atlanta, GA 30324
Phone: 404-872-2406
Fax: 404-876-1729

See California for full listing.

PTEK VENTURES

3399 Peachtree Road North East
Suite 600
Atlanta, GA 30326
Phone: 404-262-8400
Fax: 404-504-2347
Website: www.ptekventures.com

Management and Staff
Donald Gasgarth, Partner
Jeffrey Allred, Partner
Jeffrey Zwitter, Partner
Scott Tobin, Partner
Timothy Mann, Managing Director

Type of Firm
Private Equity Advisor or Fund of Fund Mgr

Project Preferences
Type of Financing Preferred:
Early Stage

Geographical Preferences
United States
Southeast

Industry Preferences
(% based on actual investment)

Internet Specific	100.0%

Additional Information
Year Founded: 1999
Capital Under Management: $145,000,000
Current Activity Level : Actively seeking new investments

R-H CAPITAL PARTNERS

3333 Peachtree Road NE
10th floor
Atlanta, GA 30326
Phone: 404-266-6000
Fax: 404-266-5966
Website: www.robinsonhumphrey.com

Management and Staff
Kenneth T. Millar

Whom to Contact
Kenneth T. Millar

Type of Firm
Investment/Merchant Bank Subsid/Affil

Project Preferences
Role in Financing:
Prefer role as deal originator but will also invest in deals created by others

Type of Financing Preferred:
Industry Rollups
Leveraged Buyout
Mezzanine
Second Stage Financing

Geographical Preferences
United States
All U.S.

Industry Preferences
Communications and Media
Communications and Media

Computer Other
Computer Related

Semiconductors/Other Elect.
Component Testing Equipmt
Analytic/Scientific

Medical/Health
Diagnostic Services
Other Therapeutic
Disposable Med. Products
Hospitals/Clinics/Primary
Hospital/Other Instit.

Consumer Related
Entertainment and Leisure
Retail
Computer Stores
Food/Beverage
Consumer Products
Consumer Services
Education Related

Industrial/Energy
Industrial Products

Financial Services
Financial Services

Business Serv.
Distribution

Additional Information
Current Activity Level : Actively seeking new investments
Method of Compensation: Return on investment is of primary concern, do not charge fees

---

RENAISSANCE CAPITAL CORP.

34 Peachtree Street, N.W.
Suite 2230
Atlanta, GA 30303
Phone: 404-658-9061
Fax: 404-658-9064

Management and Staff
Larry Edler

Whom to Contact
Larry Edler

Type of Firm
MESBIC not elsewhere classified

Industry Association Membership
Natl Assoc of Investment Cos. (NAIC)
Natl assoc of Small Bus. Inv. Co (NASBIC)

Project Preferences
Role in Financing:
Prefer role as deal originator but will also invest in deals created by others

Type of Financing Preferred:
Leveraged Buyout
Mezzanine
Second Stage Financing

Size of Investments Considered
Min Size of Investment Considered (000s): $300
Max Size of Investment Considered: No Limit

Geographical Preferences
United States
Southeast

Industry Preferences
Communications and Media
Communications and Media
Other Communication Prod.

Computer Hardware
Integrated Turnkey System

Computer Software
Computer Services
Applications Software

Internet Specific
Internet

Semiconductors/Other Elect.
Electronics
Circuit Boards

Medical/Health
Medical Products
Disposable Med. Products

Consumer Related
Retail
Franchises(NEC)
Food/Beverage
Consumer Products
Consumer Services

Industrial/Energy
Industrial Products
Environmental Related

Financial Services
Real Estate

Manufact.
Publishing

Additional Information
Year Founded: 1986
Capital Under Management: $4,500,000
Current Activity Level : Actively seeking new investments
Method of Compensation: Return on invest. most important, but chg. closing fees, service fees, etc.

RIVER CAPITAL

Two Midtown Plaza
1360 Peachtree St Suite 1430
Atlanta, GA 30309
Phone: 404-873-2166
Fax: 404-873-2158

Other Offices

Two Midtown Plaza
1360 Peachtree St
Atlanta, GA

Management and Staff
Jon Van Tuin, Vice President

Whom to Contact
Jerry Wethington

Type of Firm
Private Firm Investing Own Capital

Project Preferences

Role in Financing:
Prefer role as deal originator but will also invest in deals created by others

Type of Financing Preferred:
Leveraged Buyout
Mezzanine
Recapitalizations

Size of Investments Considered
Min Size of Investment Considered (000s): $3,000
Max Size of Investment Considered: No Limit

Geographical Preferences

United States
Mid Atlantic
Midwest
Southeast
Southwest

Industry Preferences

Semiconductors/Other Elect.
Circuit Boards

Medical/Health
Medical Products
Disposable Med. Products

Consumer Related
Entertainment and Leisure
Franchises(NEC)
Food/Beverage
Consumer Products
Education Related

Industrial/Energy
Industrial Products

Transportation
Transportation

Manufact.
Publishing

Additional Information
Name of Most Recent Fund: River Capital Fund IV
Most Recent Fund Was Raised: 01/01/1997
Year Founded: 1983
Capital Under Management: $50,000,000
Current Activity Level : Actively seeking new investments
Method of Compensation: Return on invest. most important, but chg. closing fees, service fees, etc.

SCIENTIFIC-ATLANTA

One Technology Parkway South
Norcross, GA 30092
Phone: 877-473-2463
Fax: 770-903-4775
Website: www.sciatl.com

Management and Staff
Wallace Haislip, Chief Financial Officer

Type of Firm
Non-Financial Corp. Affiliate or Subsidiary

Additional Information
Year Founded: 1951
Current Activity Level : Actively seeking new investments

SILICON VALLEY BANK

3343 Peachtree Road
East Tower, Suite 312
Atlanta, GA 30326
Phone: 404-261-5525
Fax: 404-261-2202

See California for full listing.

SOUTH ATLANTIC VENTURE FUNDS, L.P.

1239 O.G. Skinner Drive
West Point, GA 31833
Phone: 706-645-8139
Fax: 706-643-5067
Website: www.southatlantic.com

See Florida for full listing.

STATE STREET BANK & TRUST CO.

3414 Peachtree Road, N.E.
Suite 1010
Atlanta, GA 30326
Phone: 404-364-9500
Fax: 404-261-4469

Industry Association Membership
Natl assoc of Small Bus. Inv. Co (NASBIC)

Project Preferences

Role in Financing:
Prefer role as deal originator but will also invest in deals created by others

Type of Financing Preferred:
Leveraged Buyout
Special Situation

Size of Investments Considered
Min Size of Investment Considered (000s): $10,000
Max Size of Investment Considered: No Limit

Geographical Preferences

United States
All U.S.

Industry Preferences

Communications and Media
Commercial Communications
Telecommunications
Data Communications
Satellite Microwave Comm.

Computer Other
Computer Related

Semiconductors/Other Elect.
Electronic Components
Sensors

Biotechnology
Biotechnology

Medical/Health
Diagnostic Services
Diagnostic Test Products
Disposable Med. Products
Pharmaceuticals

Consumer Related
Food/Beverage

Industrial/Energy
Materials
Factory Automation
Robotics
Machinery

Business Serv.
Distribution

Manufact.
Publishing

Additional Information
Year Founded: 1792
Current Activity Level : Actively seeking new investments
Method of Compensation: Return on invest. most important, but chg. closing fees, service fees, etc.

TECHNOLOGY VENTURES, L.L.C.

Two Ravinia Drive
Suite 1000
Atlanta, GA 30346
Phone: 770-522-1800
Fax: 770-390-2899
Website: www.techven.com

Management and Staff
Dave Deiters, Partner
Joe McCall, Managing Partner
Kathy Harris, Partner
Kerry Frederick, Partner
Michelle Kamm, Chief Financial Officer
Richard Currier, Partner

Type of Firm
Private Firm Investing Own Capital

Industry Association Membership
National Venture Capital Association (NVCA)

Project Preferences

Type of Financing Preferred:
Early Stage
Seed
Start-up Financing

Geographical Preferences

United States
Southeast

Industry Preferences

Computer Software
Software

Internet Specific
Internet

Additional Information
Year Founded: 1994
Capital Under Management: $20,000,000
Current Activity Level : Actively seeking new investments

UPS STRATEGIC ENTERPRISE FUND

55 Glenlake Parkway, N.E.
Atlanta, GA 30328
Phone: 404-828-8814
Fax: 404-828-8088
Website: www.ups.com/sef/sef_home

Management and Staff
John Cayce, Managing Director
Nancy Nicodemus, Principal
Raghu Ramachandran, Principal

Type of Firm
Non-Financial Corp. Affiliate or Subsidiary

Industry Association Membership
National Venture Capital Association (NVCA)

Project Preferences

Role in Financing:
Prefer role as deal originator but will also invest in deals created by others

Type of Financing Preferred:
First Stage Financing
Second Stage Financing

Size of Investments Considered
Min Size of Investment Considered (000s): $1,000
Max Size of Investment Considered (000s): $1,000

Geographical Preferences

United States
All U.S.

Canada
All Canada

Industry Preferences

(% based on actual investment)

Internet Specific	51.1%
Computer Software and Services	37.7%
Other Products	8.1%
Computer Hardware	3.1%

Additional Information
Name of Most Recent Fund: UPS Strategic Enterprise Fund
Most Recent Fund Was Raised: 03/01/1998
Year Founded: 1997
Capital Under Management: $50,000,000
Current Activity Level : Actively seeking new investments
Method of Compensation: Return on investment is of primary concern, do not charge fees

---

VENTURE FIRST ASSOCIATES

4811 Thornwood Drive
Acworth, GA 30101
Phone: 770-928-3733

See Florida for full listing.

VERITAS VENTURE CAPITAL MANAGEMENT, LTD.

8240 Newport Bay Passage
Alpharetta, GA 30005
Phone: 770-619-0191
Fax: 770-329-7999
Website: www.veritasvc.com

See Foreign Venture Capital Firms for full listing.

WACHOVIA

191 Peachtree Street, NE
26th Floor
Atlanta, GA 30303
Phone: 404-332-1000
Fax: 404-332-1392
Website: www.wachovia.com/wca

Management and Staff
Andy Rose, Vice President
David Christopher, Vice President
Lawrence DeAngelo, Managing Director
Matthew Sullivan, Managing Director

Type of Firm
Commercial Bank Affiliate or Subsidiary

Project Preferences

Role in Financing:
Prefer role as deal originator but will also invest in deals created by others

Type of Financing Preferred:
Expansion
Later Stage
Management Buyouts
Mezzanine
Private Placement
Recapitalizations

Size of Investments Considered
Min Size of Investment Considered (000s): $5,000
Max Size of Investment Considered (000s): $15,000

Geographical Preferences

United States
Southeast

Industry Preferences

(% based on actual investment)

Other Products	40.8%
Communications and Media	17.2%
Computer Software and Services	15.0%
Industrial/Energy	11.5%
Computer Hardware	8.0%
Consumer Related	5.0%
Semiconductors/Other Elect.	2.5%

Additional Information
Capital Under Management: $150,000,000
Current Activity Level : Actively seeking new investments
Method of Compensation: Return on invest. most important, but chg. closing fees, service fees, etc.

HAWAII

BANCORP HAWAII SBIC, INC.

130 Merchant Street
Honolulu, HI 96813
Phone: 808-537-8286
Fax: 808-521-7602

Management and Staff
Frank Tokioka

Whom to Contact
Frank Tokioka

Type of Firm
SBIC Not elsewhere classified

Industry Association Membership
Natl assoc of Small Bus. Inv. Co (NASBIC)

Project Preferences

Role in Financing:
Prefer role as deal originator but will also invest in deals created by others

Type of Financing Preferred:
Leveraged Buyout
Mezzanine
Second Stage Financing
Special Situation

Size of Investments Considered
Min Size of Investment Considered (000s): $300
Max Size of Investment Considered: No Limit

Geographical Preferences

International
No Preference

Industry Preferences

Communications and Media
Commercial Communications
Telecommunications
Data Communications
Satellite Microwave Comm.

Computer Other
Computer Related

Semiconductors/Other Elect.
Electronic Components

Biotechnology
Biotechnology

Medical/Health
Diagnostic Services
Diagnostic Test Products
Drug/Equipmt Delivery
Other Therapeutic
Disposable Med. Products
Pharmaceuticals

Consumer Related
Entertainment and Leisure
Computer Stores
Franchises(NEC)
Food/Beverage
Consumer Products
Consumer Services

Industrial/Energy
Alternative Energy
Energy Conservation Relat
Industrial Products

Business Serv.
Distribution

Additional Information
Name of Most Recent Fund: Bancorp Hawaii SBIC
Most Recent Fund Was Raised: 01/01/1984
Year Founded: 1984
Capital Under Management: $2,000,000
Current Activity Level : Inactive / Unknown
Method of Compensation: Return on invest. most important, but chg. closing fees, service fees, etc.

HMS HAWAII MANAGEMENT PARTNERS

Davies Pacific Center
841 Bishop St., STe 860
Honolulu, HI 96813
Phone: 808-545-3755
Fax: 808-531-2611

Other Offices

170 Middlefield Road
Suite 150
Menlo Park, CA 94025
Phone: 415-324-4672
Fax: 415-324-4684

Management and Staff
Richard Grey, General Partner

Type of Firm
Private Firm Investing Own Capital

Industry Association Membership
National Venture Capital Association (NVCA)
Western Association of Venture Capitalists (WAVC)

Project Preferences

Role in Financing:
Prefer role as deal originator but will also invest in deals created by others

Type of Financing Preferred:
First Stage Financing
Leveraged Buyout
Seed
Start-up Financing

Size of Investments Considered
Min Size of Investment Considered (000s): $500
Max Size of Investment Considered (000s): $1,500

Geographical Preferences

United States
All U.S.

Industry Preferences

(% based on actual investment)

Internet Specific	55.0%
Communications and Media	37.1%
Consumer Related	5.4%
Other Products	2.5%

Additional Information
Name of Most Recent Fund: HMS Hawaii
Most Recent Fund Was Raised: 01/01/1999
Year Founded: 1982
Capital Under Management: $17,000,000
Current Activity Level : Actively seeking new investments
Method of Compensation: Return on investment is of primary concern, do not charge fees

IDAHO

SUN VALLEY VENTURES

160 Second Street
Ketchum, ID 83340
Phone: 208-726-5005
Fax: 208-726-5094

See California for full listing.

ILLINOIS

ABN AMRO PRIVATE EQUITY (AKA: ABN AMRO CAPITAL (USA) INC.)

208 South LaSalle Street
10th Floor
Chicago, IL 60604
Phone: 312-855-7079
Fax: 312-553-6648
Website: www.abnequity.com

Management and Staff
Brian Hirsch, Vice President
Daniel Foreman, Managing Director
David Bogetz, Managing Director
Donna Williamson, Managing Director
Keith Walz, Managing Director

Type of Firm
Commercial Bank Affiliate or Subsidiary

Industry Association Membership
National Venture Capital Association (NVCA)

Project Preferences

Role in Financing:
Will function either as deal originator or investor in deals created by others

Type of Financing Preferred:
Early Stage
Expansion
Fund of Funds

Size of Investments Considered
Min Size of Investment Considered (000s): $3,000
Max Size of Investment Considered (000s): $10,000

Geographical Preferences

United States
All U.S.

Canada
All Canada

Industry Preferences

(% based on actual investment)

Consumer Related	43.2%
Computer Software and Services	22.5%
Industrial/Energy	10.0%
Internet Specific	9.5%
Communications and Media	7.6%
Other Products	3.2%
Medical/Health	2.0%
Semiconductors/Other Elect.	1.4%
Biotechnology	0.7%

Additional Information
Year Founded: 2000
Capital Under Management: $300,000,000
Current Activity Level : Actively seeking new investments
Method of Compensation: Return on investment is of primary concern, do not charge fees

ADAMS STREET PARTNERS, LLC (FKA: BRINSON PRIVATE EQUITY)

209 South LaSalle Street
Chicago, IL 60604-1295
Phone: 312-553-7890
Fax: 312-553-7891
Website: www.adamsstreetpartners.com

Other Offices

Triton Court
14 Finsbury Square
London, United Kingdom EC2A 1PD
Phone: 020-7567-5388

Management and Staff
A. Bart Holaday, Managing Director
Angela Woodside, Principal
Brian Crawford, Partner
Craig Taylor, Partner
David Timson, Partner
George Spencer, Partner
Gregory Garret, Partner
Hanneke Smits, Partner
Jacqueline Swift, Partner
Jan Persson, Partner
Jeffrey Diehl, Partner
Kathy Wanner, Partner
Kelli Marks, Partner
Marc Sacks, Partner
Molly Meng, Partner
Piau Voon Wang, Partner
Robert DeBolt, Principal
Ronan Cunningham, Principal
Sergey Sheshuryak, Principal
T. Bondurant French, Chief Executive Officer
Terry Gould, Partner
Thomas Dolson, Partner
Thomas Berman, Partner

Type of Firm
Private Equity Advisor or Fund of Fund Mgr

Industry Association Membership
National Venture Capital Association (NVCA)

Project Preferences

Role in Financing:
Will function either as deal originator or investor in deals created by others

Type of Financing Preferred:
Early Stage
Expansion
Fund of Funds
Later Stage
Leveraged Buyout
Other

Size of Investments Considered
Min Size of Investment Considered (000s): $2,000
Max Size of Investment Considered (000s): $10,000

Geographical Preferences

United States
All U.S.
All U.S.

Canada
All Canada

International
All International

Industry Preferences

(% based on actual investment)

Other Products	41.5%
Computer Software and Services	12.7%
Internet Specific	12.0%
Medical/Health	9.1%
Biotechnology	6.2%
Computer Hardware	5.8%
Industrial/Energy	5.1%
Communications and Media	4.3%
Semiconductors/Other Elect.	3.2%
Consumer Related	0.1%

Additional Information
Name of Most Recent Fund: BVCF IV
Most Recent Fund Was Raised: 01/01/1998
Year Founded: 1972
Capital Under Management: $4,600,000,000
Current Activity Level : Actively seeking new investments
Method of Compensation: Return on investment is of primary concern, do not charge fees

ADVANTAGE CAPITAL PARTNERS

1911 Elmore Avenue
Downers Grove, IL 60515
Phone: 630-241-1848
Fax: 630-241-1836
Website: www.advantagecap.com

See Louisiana for full listing.

ALLIED CAPITAL CORPORATION

401 North Michigan Avenue
Suite 2050
Chicago, IL
Phone: 312-828-0330
Fax: 312-828-0909
Website: www.alliedcapital.com

See D. of Columbia for full listing.

ALLSTATE PRIVATE EQUITY

3075 Sanders Road
Suite G5D
Northbrook, IL 60062-7127
Phone: 847-402-8247
Fax: 847-402-0880

Management and Staff
John Goense, Managing Director

Type of Firm
Insurance Firm Affiliate or Subsidiary

Industry Association Membership
Natl assoc of Small Bus. Inv. Co (NASBIC)

Project Preferences

Role in Financing:
Prefer role as deal originator but will also invest in deals created by others

Type of Financing Preferred:
First Stage Financing
Leveraged Buyout
Mezzanine
Second Stage Financing
Special Situation
Start-up Financing

Size of Investments Considered
Min Size of Investment Considered (000s): $5,000
Max Size of Investment Considered: No Limit

Geographical Preferences

United States
All U.S.

Industry Preferences

Communications and Media
Commercial Communications
CATV & Pay TV Systems
Data Communications
Other Communication Prod.

Computer Hardware
Computers
Mini and Personal/Desktop
Computer Graphics and Dig
Terminals

Computer Software
Computer Services
Applications Software

Semiconductors/Other Elect.
Electronics
Electronic Components
Component Testing Equipmt
Laser Related
Fiber Optics
Analytic/Scientific

Biotechnology
Biotechnology

Medical/Health
Medical/Health
Medical Products

Consumer Related
Entertainment and Leisure
Retail
Food/Beverage
Consumer Products
Consumer Services
Other Restaurants

Industrial/Energy
Alternative Energy
Industrial Products

Financial Services
Financial Services

Manufact.
Office Automation Equipmt
Publishing

Additional Information
Name of Most Recent Fund: Allstate Private Equity Fund I
Most Recent Fund Was Raised: 01/01/1997
Year Founded: 1958
Capital Under Management: $700,000,000
Current Activity Level : Inactive / Unknown
Method of Compensation: Return on investment is of primary concern, do not charge fees

ALPHA CAPITAL PARTNERS, INC.

122 South Michigan Avenue
Suite 1700
Chicago, IL 60603
Phone: 312-322-9800
Fax: 312-322-9808

Other Offices

Society Bank Building
32 North Main Street
Dayton, OH 45402
Phone: 513-222-2006
Fax: 513-223-6985

Management and Staff
William Oberholtzer

Whom to Contact
William Oberholtzer

Type of Firm
Private Firm Investing Own Capital

Industry Association Membership
Natl assoc of Small Bus. Inv. Co (NASBIC)

Project Preferences

Role in Financing:
Prefer role as deal originator but will also invest in deals created by others

Type of Financing Preferred:
First Stage Financing
Leveraged Buyout
Second Stage Financing
Special Situation

Size of Investments Considered
Min Size of Investment Considered (000s): $2,000
Max Size of Investment Considered: No Limit

Geographical Preferences

United States
Midwest

Industry Preferences
(% based on actual investment)

Computer Software and Services	53.0%
Communications and Media	12.4%
Other Products	9.2%
Medical/Health	9.1%
Consumer Related	6.2%
Biotechnology	5.3%
Internet Specific	2.7%
Industrial/Energy	1.1%
Semiconductors/Other Elect.	0.5%
Computer Hardware	0.4%

Additional Information
Year Founded: 1985
Capital Under Management: $50,000,000
Current Activity Level : Actively seeking new investments
Method of Compensation: Return on investment is of primary concern, do not charge fees

AMERICAN HEALTHCARE FUND

20 North Wacker Drive
Suite 2200
Chicago, IL 60606
Phone: 312-781-1910

Management and Staff
Rick Blume, General Partner

Type of Firm
Private Firm Investing Own Capital

Project Preferences

Type of Financing Preferred:
Balanced

Geographical Preferences

International
No Preference

Industry Preferences

Biotechnology
Biotechnology

Medical/Health
Medical/Health

Additional Information
Name of Most Recent Fund: American Healthcare Fund
Most Recent Fund Was Raised: 12/01/1986
Year Founded: 1986
Current Activity Level : Inactive / Unknown

AMERITECH DEVELOPMENT CORP.

30 South Wacker Drive
37th Floor
Chicago, IL 60606
Phone: 312-750-5083
Fax: 312-609-0244

Management and Staff
Craig Lee, Managing Director
Darrell Williams, Vice President

Whom to Contact
Darrell Williams

Type of Firm
Non-Financial Corp. Affiliate or Subsidiary

Project Preferences

Role in Financing:
Prefer role as deal originator but will also invest in deals created by others

Type of Financing Preferred:
First Stage Financing
Second Stage Financing
Start-up Financing

Size of Investments Considered
Min Size of Investment Considered (000s): $5,000
Max Size of Investment Considered: No Limit

Geographical Preferences

United States
All U.S.

Industry Preferences

Communications and Media
Commercial Communications
CATV & Pay TV Systems
Telecommunications
Data Communications
Satellite Microwave Comm.

Computer Hardware
Integrated Turnkey System

Computer Software
Systems Software
Applications Software

Semiconductors/Other Elect.
Electronic Components
Semiconductor
Controllers and Sensors
Fiber Optics

Additional Information
Name of Most Recent Fund: Ameritech Development Corporation
Most Recent Fund Was Raised: 01/01/1983
Year Founded: 1983
Current Activity Level : Actively seeking new investments

ANTARES CAPITAL CORP. (FKA: ANTARES LEVERAGED CAPITAL CORP)

311 South Wacker Drive
Suite 2725
Chicago, IL 60694
Phone: 312-697-3999
Fax: 312-697-3998

Management and Staff
Barry Shear, Managing Director
David Brackett, Managing Director

Whom to Contact
Lisa A. Clouse

Type of Firm
Private Firm Investing Own Capital

Project Preferences

Role in Financing:
Prefer role as deal originator but will also invest in deals created by others

Type of Financing Preferred:
First Stage Financing
Leveraged Buyout
Mezzanine
Second Stage Financing
Special Situation

Size of Investments Considered
Min Size of Investment Considered (000s): $10,000
Max Size of Investment Considered (000s): $130,000

Geographical Preferences

United States
Southeast

Industry Preferences

Communications and Media
Commercial Communications
Telecommunications
Data Communications
Satellite Microwave Comm.

Computer Hardware
Mini and Personal/Desktop
Computer Graphics and Dig
Disk Relat. Memory Device

Computer Software
Computer Services
Systems Software
Applications Software
Artificial Intelligence

Internet Specific
Internet

Semiconductors/Other Elect.
Electronic Components
Controllers and Sensors
Sensors
Laser Related
Fiber Optics
Analytic/Scientific

Medical/Health
Diagnostic Services
Diagnostic Test Products
Drug/Equipmt Delivery
Other Therapeutic
Disposable Med. Products
Hospitals/Clinics/Primary
Hospital/Other Instit.

Consumer Related
Retail
Computer Stores
Food/Beverage
Consumer Products
Consumer Services
Other Restaurants

Industrial/Energy
Materials
Factory Automation
Robotics
Machinery

Financial Services
Financial Services

Manufact.
Office Automation Equipmt
Publishing

Additional Information
Name of Most Recent Fund: Antares Capital Fund II, L.P.
Most Recent Fund Was Raised: 02/01/1996
Year Founded: 1993
Capital Under Management: $1,500,000,000
Current Activity Level : Actively seeking new investments
Method of Compensation: Return on investment is of primary concern, do not charge fees

APEX VENTURE PARTNERS

225 West Washington
Suite 1450
Chicago, IL 60606
Phone: 312-857-2800
Fax: 312-857-1800
Website: www.apexvc.com

Management and Staff
Armando Pauker, General Partner
Babu Ranganathan, General Partner
F.W.W.(Rick) Bolander, General Partner
George Middlemas, Managing General Partner
James Johnson, Managing General Partner
Lon Chow, General Partner
Nancy Corrie, Chief Financial Officer
Paul Renze, General Partner
Wayne Boulais, General Partner

Type of Firm
Private Firm Investing Own Capital

Industry Association Membership
National Venture Capital Association (NVCA)

Project Preferences

Role in Financing:
Prefer role as deal originator but will also invest in deals created by others

Type of Financing Preferred:
Early Stage

Size of Investments Considered
Min Size of Investment Considered (000s): $500
Max Size of Investment Considered (000s): $15,000

Geographical Preferences

United States
All U.S.

Industry Preferences

(% based on actual investment)

Internet Specific	28.0%
Computer Software and Services	22.1%
Other Products	15.9%
Communications and Media	14.9%
Industrial/Energy	6.2%
Consumer Related	5.6%
Semiconductors/Other Elect.	3.8%
Medical/Health	1.9%
Computer Hardware	1.1%
Biotechnology	0.4%

Additional Information
Name of Most Recent Fund: Apex IV
Most Recent Fund Was Raised: 06/01/1996
Year Founded: 1988
Capital Under Management: $302,000,000
Current Activity Level : Actively seeking new investments
Method of Compensation: Return on investment is of primary concern, do not charge fees

ARCH VENTURE PARTNERS

8725 West Higgins Road
Suite 290
Chicago, IL 60631
Phone: 773-380-6600
Fax: 773-380-6606
Website: www.archventure.com

Other Offices

1000 Second Avenue
Suite 3700
Seattle, WA 98104
Phone: 206-674-3028
Fax: 206-674-3026

1155 University SE
Albuquerque, NM 87106
Phone: 505-843-4293
Fax: 505-843-4294

561 7th Avenue
11th Floor
New York, NY 10020
Phone: 212-944-2400

6801 N. Capital of Texas Highway
Suite 225
Austin, TX 78731
Phone: 512-795-5830
Fax: 512-795-5831

Management and Staff
Alex Knight, Managing Director
Clinton Bybee, Managing Director
Don Oliverio, Venture Partner
Karen Kerr, Managing Director
Keith Crandell, Managing Director
Keith Rowe, Venture Partner
Kevin Williams, Venture Partner
Mark McDonnell, Chief Financial Officer
Mike Jablo, Venture Partner
Patrick Ennis, Principal
Robert Nelsen, Managing Director
Scott Minick, Venture Partner
Steven Lazarus, Managing Director

Type of Firm
Private Firm Investing Own Capital

Industry Association Membership
National Venture Capital Association (NVCA)

Project Preferences

Role in Financing:
Prefer role as deal originator but will also invest in deals created by others

Type of Financing Preferred:
Early Stage
Seed
Startup

Geographical Preferences

United States
Mid Atlantic
Midwest
Northeast
Northern California
Northwest
Rocky Mountain
All U.S.
West Coast

Industry Preferences

(% based on actual investment)

Internet Specific	42.8%
Computer Software and Services	13.8%
Semiconductors/Other Elect.	12.1%
Medical/Health	12.1%
Biotechnology	8.4%
Communications and Media	6.1%
Industrial/Energy	2.9%
Computer Hardware	1.6%
Other Products	0.2%

Additional Information
Name of Most Recent Fund: ARCH Venture Fund IV, L.P.
Most Recent Fund Was Raised: 04/01/1999
Year Founded: 1986
Capital Under Management: $565,400,000
Current Activity Level : Actively seeking new investments
Method of Compensation: Return on investment is of primary concern, do not charge fees

BAIRD CAPITAL PARTNERS

227 West Monroe Street
Suite 2200
Chicago, IL 60606
Phone: 312-609-4701
Fax: 312-609-4707
Website: www.rwbaird.com

Other Offices

401 East Jackson Street
Suite 2900
Tampa, FL 33602
Phone: 888-792-9817

777 East Wisconsin Avenue
28th Floor
Milwaukee, WI 53202
Phone: 888-761-9641

Management and Staff
Brian Anderson, Partner
C. Andrew Brickman, Partner
David Pelisek, Partner
Paul Carbone, Managing Partner

Whom to Contact
Andrew Brickman

Type of Firm
Investment/Merchant Bank Subsid/Affil

Project Preferences

Role in Financing:
Prefer role as deal originator but will also invest in deals created by others

Type of Financing Preferred:
Acquisition
Generalist PE
Later Stage
Management Buyouts
Recapitalizations

Size of Investments Considered
Min Size of Investment Considered (000s): $5,000
Max Size of Investment Considered (000s): $25,000

Geographical Preferences

United States
Midwest
Southeast
All U.S.

Industry Preferences

(% based on actual investment)

Computer Software and Services	52.3%
Medical/Health	27.3%
Other Products	11.1%
Biotechnology	5.5%
Semiconductors/Other Elect.	3.7%

Additional Information
Name of Most Recent Fund: Baird Capital Partners III
Most Recent Fund Was Raised: 08/01/1999
Year Founded: 1991
Capital Under Management: $250,000,000
Current Activity Level : Actively seeking new investments
Method of Compensation: Return on invest. most important, but chg. closing fees, service fees, etc.

BANK FUNDS, THE

208 South LaSalle Street
Suite 1680
Chicago, IL 60604
Phone: 312-855-6020
Fax: 312-855-8910

Management and Staff
Charles Moore, President

Type of Firm
Private Firm Investing Own Capital

Project Preferences

Role in Financing:
Prefer role as deal originator but will also invest in deals created by others

Type of Financing Preferred:
Control-block Purchases
Later Stage
Leveraged Buyout
Second Stage Financing
Special Situation

Geographical Preferences

United States
All U.S.

International
No Preference

Industry Preferences

(% based on actual investment)

Other Products	99.9%
Communications and Media	0.1%

Additional Information
Name of Most Recent Fund: Banc Fund V
Most Recent Fund Was Raised: 07/15/1998
Year Founded: 1986
Capital Under Management: $350,000,000
Current Activity Level : Inactive / Unknown
Method of Compensation: Return on investment is of primary concern, do not charge fees

BATTERSON VENTURE PARTNERS(AKA:BVP)

303 West Madison
Suite 1110
Chicago, IL 60606-3309
Phone: 312-269-0300
Fax: 312-269-0021
Website: www.battersonvp.com

Other Offices

303 West Madison
Suite 1110
Chicago, IL 60606-3309
Phone: 312-269-0300
Fax: 312-269-0021

Management and Staff
Donald Johnson, Partner
Leonard Batterson, Chairman & CEO
Sona Wang, General Partner

Type of Firm
Private Firm Investing Own Capital

Industry Association Membership
National Venture Capital Association (NVCA)

Project Preferences

Role in Financing:
Will function either as deal originator or investor in deals created by others

Type of Financing Preferred:
Early Stage
First Stage Financing
Second Stage Financing
Seed
Startup

Size of Investments Considered
Min Size of Investment Considered (000s): $500
Max Size of Investment Considered (000s): $3,000

Geographical Preferences

United States
All U.S.

Industry Preferences

(% based on actual investment)

Computer Software and Services	27.2%
Medical/Health	21.7%
Internet Specific	15.5%
Communications and Media	9.9%
Biotechnology	6.0%
Industrial/Energy	5.1%
Other Products	5.0%
Computer Hardware	4.7%
Semiconductors/Other Elect.	3.1%
Consumer Related	1.8%

Additional Information
Name of Most Recent Fund: Batterson, Johnson & Borg
Most Recent Fund Was Raised: 01/01/1991
Year Founded: 1995
Capital Under Management: $72,000,000
Current Activity Level : Actively seeking new investments
Method of Compensation: Return on invest. most important, but chg. closing fees, service fees, etc.

BEECKEN, PETTY & CO. LLC

901 Warrenville Road
Suite 205
Lisle, IL 60532
Phone: 630-435-0300
Fax: 630-435-0370
Website: www.bpcompany.com

Other Offices

208 S. LaSalle St
10th Floor
Chicago, IL 60604
Phone: 312-726-7819

Management and Staff
Dave Beecken, Managing Director
David Cooney, Principal
Greg Moerschel, Managing Director
John Kneen, Managing Director
Ken O'Keefe, Managing Director
Thomas Schlesinger, Principal
William Petty, Managing Director

Whom to Contact
David Beecken
Greg Moerschel

Type of Firm
Private Firm Investing Own Capital

Industry Association Membership
National Venture Capital Association (NVCA)

Project Preferences

Role in Financing:
Will function either as deal originator or investor in deals created by others

Type of Financing Preferred:
Early Stage
Expansion
First Stage Financing
Later Stage
Management Buyouts
Private Placement
Recapitalizations
Second Stage Financing

Size of Investments Considered
Min Size of Investment Considered (000s): $2,000
Max Size of Investment Considered (000s): $12,000

Geographical Preferences

United States
All U.S.

Industry Preferences

(% based on actual investment)

Medical/Health	61.4%
Computer Software and Services	22.1%
Internet Specific	13.1%
Communications and Media	3.4%

Additional Information
Name of Most Recent Fund: Healthcare Equity Partners, L.P.
Most Recent Fund Was Raised: 09/04/1996
Year Founded: 1996
Capital Under Management: $150,000,000
Current Activity Level : Actively seeking new investments
Method of Compensation: Return on investment is of primary concern, do not charge fees

BLUESTAR VENTURES

208 South LaSalle Street
Suite 1020
Chicago, IL 60604
Phone: 312-384-5000
Fax: 312-384-5005
Website: www.bluestarventures.com

Management and Staff
Patrick Pollard, Managing Director
Richard Flynn, Managing Director
William Steinmetz, Managing Director

Type of Firm
Private Firm Investing Own Capital

Industry Association Membership
National Venture Capital Association (NVCA)

Project Preferences

Role in Financing:
Will function either as deal originator or investor in deals created by others

Type of Financing Preferred:
Early Stage
First Stage Financing
Second Stage Financing

Size of Investments Considered
Min Size of Investment Considered (000s): $1,000
Max Size of Investment Considered (000s): $3,000

Geographical Preferences

United States
Midwest

Industry Preferences

Communications and Media
Telecommunications
Wireless Communications
Data Communications

Computer Software
Computer Services
Software
Systems Software
Applications Software

Internet Specific
E-Commerce Technology
Internet
Web Aggregration/Portals

Additional Information
Year Founded: 2000
Capital Under Management: $40,000,000
Current Activity Level : Actively seeking new investments
Method of Compensation: Return on investment is of primary concern, do not charge fees

---

C3 HOLDINGS, LLC

233 South Wacker Drive
Sears Tower, Suite 5330
Chicago, IL 60606
Phone: 312-655-5990
Fax: 312-655-5999

See Missouri for full listing.

CAPITAL FOR BUSINESS, INC.

8770 W. Bryn
Suite 1300
Chicago, IL 60651
Phone: 773-867-8532
Fax: 773-867-8533
Website: www.capitalforbusiness.com

See Missouri for full listing.

CAPITAL STRATEGY MANAGEMENT CO., THE

233 South Wacker Drive
Box 06334
Chicago, IL 60606
Phone: 312-444-1170

Management and Staff
Eric Von Bauer, President

Whom to Contact
Eric Von Bauer

Type of Firm
Business Development Fund

Project Preferences

Role in Financing:
Prefer role as deal originator but will also invest in deals created by others

Type of Financing Preferred:
Acquisition
Control-block Purchases
Early Stage
Expansion
First Stage Financing
Generalist PE
Joint Ventures
Later Stage
Leveraged Buyout
Management Buyouts
Mezzanine
Recapitalizations
Second Stage Financing
Seed
Special Situation
Startup
Turnaround

Size of Investments Considered
Min Size of Investment Considered (000s): $200
Max Size of Investment Considered (000s): $50,000

Geographical Preferences

United States
Mid Atlantic
Midwest
Northwest
Southeast

International
Germany
United Kingdom

Industry Preferences

Communications and Media
Communications and Media

Computer Hardware
Computers

Semiconductors/Other Elect.
Electronics

Biotechnology
Biotech Related Research

Medical/Health
Medical Diagnostics
Diagnostic Test Products
Drug/Equipmt Delivery
Medical Products
Disposable Med. Products

Consumer Related
Consumer
Retail
Franchises(NEC)
Food/Beverage

Industrial/Energy
Energy
Industrial Products
Superconductivity
Factory Automation
Process Control
Robotics
Machinery

Transportation
Transportation
Aerospace

Business Serv.
Services
Distribution
Media

Manufact.
Manufacturing

Utilities
Utilities

Additional Information
Year Founded: 1982
Current Activity Level : Actively seeking new investments
Method of Compensation: Return on invest. most important, but chg. closing fees, service fees, etc.

CERULEAN FUND/WGC ENTERPRISES

1701 East Lake Avenue
Suite 170
Glenview, IL 60025
Phone: 847-657-8002
Fax: 847-657-8168

Other Offices

1701 East Lake Avenue
Suite 275
Glenview, IL 60025
Phone: 708-657-8002
Fax: 708-657-8168

Management and Staff
Brian Dettmann, Partner
George Roe, Partner
Oak Stevens, Partner

Whom to Contact
Walter G. Cornett III

Type of Firm
Private Firm Investing Own Capital

Project Preferences

Role in Financing:
Prefer role as deal originator

Type of Financing Preferred:
Control-block Purchases
Leveraged Buyout
Research and Development
Seed
Special Situation
Start-up Financing

Size of Investments Considered
Min Size of Investment Considered (000s): $5,000
Max Size of Investment Considered: No Limit

Geographical Preferences

United States
Midwest

Industry Preferences

Communications and Media
Commercial Communications
Data Communications
Satellite Microwave Comm.

Computer Hardware
Computer Graphics and Dig
Integrated Turnkey System
Disk Relat. Memory Device

Computer Software
Computer Services
Systems Software
Applications Software

Semiconductors/Other Elect.
Electronic Components
Controllers and Sensors
Circuit Boards
Component Testing Equipmt
Laser Related
Fiber Optics
Analytic/Scientific

Biotechnology
Industrial Biotechnology
Biosensors

Medical/Health
Medical Diagnostics
Diagnostic Services
Diagnostic Test Products
Medical Therapeutics
Other Therapeutic
Disposable Med. Products

Consumer Related
Entertainment and Leisure
Computer Stores
Food/Beverage
Consumer Products
Consumer Services
Education Related

Industrial/Energy
Alternative Energy
Industrial Products

Financial Services
Financial Services

Business Serv.
Distribution
Consulting Services

Manufact.
Office Automation Equipmt
Publishing

Additional Information
Name of Most Recent Fund: Cerulean Fund
Most Recent Fund Was Raised: 06/01/1988
Year Founded: 1988
Capital Under Management: $50,000,000
Current Activity Level : Making few, if any, new investments
Method of Compensation: Return on invest. most important, but chg. closing fees, service fees, etc.

CID EQUITY PARTNERS

Two North Lasalle
Suite 1705
Chicago, IL 60602
Phone: 312-578-5350
Fax: 312-578-5358
Website: www.cidequity.com

See Indiana for full listing.

CIVC PARTNERS (FKA:CONTINENTAL ILLINOIS VENTURE CORP.)

231 South LaSalle Street
Chicago, IL 60697
Phone: 312-828-8021
Fax: 312-987-0763
Website: www.civc.com

Management and Staff
Christopher Perry, Partner
Daniel Helle, Partner
Gregory Wilson, Partner
John Compall, Principal
Keith Yamada, Principal
Marcus Wedner, Partner
Michael Miller, Principal
Sue Rushmore, Partner

Whom to Contact
Gregory Wilson

Type of Firm
Commercial Bank Affiliate or Subsidiary

Industry Association Membership
Natl assoc of Small Bus. Inv. Co (NASBIC)

Project Preferences

Role in Financing:
Prefer role as deal originator but will also invest in deals created by others

Type of Financing Preferred:
Acquisition
Generalist PE
Later Stage
Leveraged Buyout
Management Buyouts
Recapitalizations

Size of Investments Considered
Min Size of Investment Considered (000s): $10,000
Max Size of Investment Considered (000s): $100,000

Geographical Preferences

United States
All U.S.

Canada
All Canada

Industry Preferences

Communications and Media
Commercial Communications
CATV & Pay TV Systems
Radio & TV Broadcasting
Telecommunications
Data Communications
Satellite Microwave Comm.
Other Communication Prod.

Computer Software
Computer Services
Data Processing

Internet Specific
Internet

Semiconductors/Other Elect.
Electronic Components
Controllers and Sensors
Sensors
Circuit Boards
Component Testing Equipmt
Fiber Optics
Analytic/Scientific

Additional Information
Name of Most Recent Fund: CIVC Partners Fund
Most Recent Fund Was Raised: 01/01/1999
Year Founded: 1970
Capital Under Management: $500,000,000
Current Activity Level : Actively seeking new investments
Method of Compensation: Return on invest. most important, but chg. closing fees, service fees, etc.

CODE, HENNESSY & SIMMONS, LLC.

10 South Wacker Drive
Suite 3175
Chicago, IL 60606
Phone: 312-876-1840
Fax: 312-876-3854
Website: www.chsonline.com

Management and Staff
Andrew Code, Partner
Brian Simmons, Partner
Daniel Hennessy, Partner
David Hawkins, Managing Director
Edward Lhee, Vice President
Jon Vesely, Partner
Marcus George, Vice President
Mike Keesey, Chief Financial Officer
Paige Walsh, Vice President
Peter Gotsch, Partner
Richard Lobo, Managing Director
Steven Brown, Managing Director
Thomas Formolo, Partner

Type of Firm
Private Firm Investing Own Capital

Project Preferences

Role in Financing:
Prefer role as deal originator

Type of Financing Preferred:
Leveraged Buyout

Geographical Preferences

United States
All U.S.

Industry Preferences

(% based on actual investment)

Other Products	49.1%
Computer Hardware	36.9%
Semiconductors/Other Elect.	8.1%
Industrial/Energy	3.4%
Consumer Related	2.5%

Additional Information
Name of Most Recent Fund: Code,Hennessy & Simmons IV
Most Recent Fund Was Raised: 09/08/1999
Year Founded: 1988
Capital Under Management: $1,500,000,000
Current Activity Level : Actively seeking new investments
Method of Compensation: Return on invest. most important, but chg. closing fees, service fees, etc.

DIVINE INTERVENTURES (FKA: PLATINUM VENTURE PARTNERS)

3333 Warrenville Road
Suite 800
Lisle, IL 60532
Phone: 630-799-7500
Fax: 630-799-3858
Website: www.divineinterventures.com

Other Offices

7000 MoPac Expressway
2nd Floor
Austin, TX 78731
Phone: 512-514-6297
Fax: 512-514-6499

Management and Staff
Andrea Cunningham, Partner
Andrew Filipowski, Chief Executive Officer
Brian Rowe, Chief Financial Officer
Bryan Kennedy, General Partner
Doug Allen, Managing Partner
James Cowie, Partner
Michael Birck, Partner
Michael Santer, General Partner
Michael Cullinane, Chief Financial Officer
Michael Forster, Partner
Paul Humenansky, Partner
Scott Hartkopf, President

Whom to Contact
Brenda Lee Johnson
David Sick
Mike Santer

Type of Firm
Private Firm Investing Own Capital

Project Preferences

Role in Financing:
Prefer role as deal originator but will also invest in deals created by others

Type of Financing Preferred:
First Stage Financing
Second Stage Financing
Start-up Financing

Geographical Preferences

United States
All U.S.

Industry Preferences

(% based on actual investment)

Computer Software and Services	39.7%
Internet Specific	39.7%

Other Products	10.4%
Consumer Related	7.7%
Medical/Health	2.4%

Additional Information
Name of Most Recent Fund: divine interVentures
Most Recent Fund Was Raised: 01/06/1994
Year Founded: 1992
Capital Under Management: $60,000,000
Current Activity Level : Actively seeking new investments

DN PARTNERS

77 West Wacker Drive
Suite 4550
Chicago, IL 60601
Phone: 312-332-7960
Fax: 312-332-7979

Type of Firm
Private Firm Investing Own Capital

Project Preferences

Role in Financing:
Prefer role as deal originator but will also invest in deals created by others

Type of Financing Preferred:
Leveraged Buyout

Industry Preferences

Communications and Media
Communications and Media
Other Communication Prod.

Computer Hardware
Computer Graphics and Dig
Disk Relat. Memory Device

Internet Specific
Internet

Semiconductors/Other Elect.
Electronics

Medical/Health
Diagnostic Services
Diagnostic Test Products
Medical Products
Disposable Med. Products
Hospitals/Clinics/Primary

Consumer Related
Entertainment and Leisure
Retail
Food/Beverage
Consumer Products
Consumer Services
Other Restaurants
Education Related

Industrial/Energy
Industrial Products
Materials

Transportation
Transportation

Financial Services
Financial Services

Business Serv.
Consulting Services

Manufact.
Office Automation Equipmt
Publishing

Agr/Forestr/Fish
Agriculture related

Additional Information
Year Founded: 1995
Current Activity Level : Actively seeking new investments

DRESDNER KLEINWORT CAPITAL

190 South LaSalle Street
Suite 2700
Chicago, IL 60603
Phone: 312-444-1300
Fax: 312-444-1192
Website: www.dresdnerkb.com

See New York for full listing.

DRESNER CAPITAL RESOURCES, INC.

29 South LaSalle Street
Suite 310
Chicago, IL 60603
Phone: 312-726-3600
Fax: 312-726-7448

Management and Staff
John Riddle
Steven Dresner

Whom to Contact
John Riddle
Steven Dresner

Type of Firm
Investment/Merchant Bank Investing Own or Client Funds

Project Preferences

Role in Financing:
Prefer role as deal originator

Type of Financing Preferred:
Leveraged Buyout
Mezzanine
Second Stage Financing

Size of Investments Considered
Min Size of Investment Considered (000s): $500
Max Size of Investment Considered (000s): $1,000

Geographical Preferences

International
No Preference

Industry Preferences

Communications and Media
Commercial Communications
Telecommunications
Data Communications
Satellite Microwave Comm.

Computer Hardware
Computers
Mini and Personal/Desktop
Computer Graphics and Dig
Disk Relat. Memory Device

Computer Software
Computer Services
Systems Software
Applications Software

Internet Specific
Internet

Semiconductors/Other Elect.
Semiconductor
Sensors
Circuit Boards
Component Testing Equipmt
Laser Related
Fiber Optics
Analytic/Scientific

Medical/Health
Medical/Health
Medical Products

Consumer Related
Entertainment and Leisure
Retail
Computer Stores
Franchises(NEC)
Food/Beverage
Consumer Products
Consumer Services
Other Restaurants

Industrial/Energy
Industrial Products
Materials
Factory Automation
Robotics
Machinery

Financial Services
Financial Services

Business Serv.
Consulting Services

Manufact.
Office Automation Equipmt
Publishing

Additional Information
Year Founded: 1991
Current Activity Level : Actively seeking new investments
Method of Compensation: Return on investment is of primary concern, do not charge fees

---

DUCHOSSOIS TECNOLOGY PARTNERS, LLC

845 Larch Avenue
Elmhurst, IL 60126
Phone: 630-530-6105
Fax: 630-993-8644
Website: www.duchtec.com

Management and Staff
Craig Duchossois, Chairman & CEO
John Riccardi, Vice President
Robert Fealy, Chief Operating Officer

Type of Firm
Non-Financial Corp. Affiliate or Subsidiary

Industry Association Membership
National Venture Capital Association (NVCA)

Project Preferences

Role in Financing:
Will function either as deal originator or investor in deals created by others

Type of Financing Preferred:
Early Stage
First Stage Financing
Second Stage Financing

Size of Investments Considered
Min Size of Investment Considered (000s): $500
Max Size of Investment Considered (000s): $5,000

Geographical Preferences

United States
All U.S.

Industry Preferences

Communications and Media
Telecommunications
Wireless Communications
Data Communications
Other Communication Prod.

Computer Hardware
Terminals

Computer Software
Computer Services
Data Processing
Software
Systems Software

Internet Specific
E-Commerce Technology
Internet

Semiconductors/Other Elect.
Controllers and Sensors
Sensors

Biotechnology
Biotechnology

Consumer Related
Entertainment and Leisure
Sports

Additional Information
Year Founded: 1998
Capital Under Management: $100,000,000
Current Activity Level : Actively seeking new investments

EBLAST VENTURES, LLC

11 South LaSalle
5th Floor
Chicago, IL 60603
Phone: 312-372-2600
Fax: 312-372-5261
Website: www.eblastventures.com

Management and Staff
Pete Georgiadis, Chief Executive Officer

Type of Firm
Private Firm Investing Own Capital

Project Preferences

Role in Financing:
Prefer role as deal originator but will also invest in deals created by others

Type of Financing Preferred:
Early Stage
Seed
Start-up Financing
Turnaround

Size of Investments Considered
Min Size of Investment Considered (000s): $100
Max Size of Investment Considered (000s): $500

Geographical Preferences

United States
Midwest

Industry Preferences

Communications and Media
Wireless Communications

Computer Software
Computer Services
Data Processing
Software
Systems Software
Applications Software
Artificial Intelligence

Internet Specific
E-Commerce Technology
Internet
Web Aggregration/Portals

Medical/Health
Health Services

Consumer Related
Consumer

Industrial/Energy
Industrial Products

Financial Services
Financial Services
Insurance

Business Serv.
Services
Distribution
Consulting Services

Additional Information

Year Founded: 2000
Current Activity Level : Actively seeking new investments
Method of Compensation: Return on investment is of primary concern, do not charge fees

ESSEX WOODLANDS HEALTH VENTURES (FKA:WOODLANDS VENTURE PARTN

190 South LaSalle Street
Suite 2800
Chicago, IL 60603
Phone: 312-444-6040
Fax: 312-444-6034
Website: www.essexwoodlands.com

Other Offices

2170 Buckthorne Place
Suite 170
The Woodlands, TX 77380
Phone: 281-367-9999
Fax: 281-298-1295

43 Balboa Cove
Newport Beach, CA 92663
Phone: 949-500-6220

Management and Staff

Cynthia Doerr, Venture Partner
Don Spyrison, General Partner
Immanuel Thangaraj, Managing Director
J. Douglas Eplett, Managing Director
James Currie, General Partner
Marc Sandroff, General Partner
Martin Sutter, General Partner

Type of Firm

Private Firm Investing Own Capital

Project Preferences

Role in Financing:

Prefer role as deal originator but will also invest in deals created by others

Type of Financing Preferred:

Balanced
Early Stage
First Stage Financing
Mezzanine
Private Placement
Public Companies
Second Stage Financing
Start-up Financing

Geographical Preferences

United States

All U.S.

International

No Preference

Industry Preferences

(% based on actual investment)

Medical/Health	61.2%
Biotechnology	18.9%
Internet Specific	9.9%
Computer Software and Services	9.6%
Communications and Media	0.5%

Additional Information

Name of Most Recent Fund: Essex Woodlands Health Ventures, IV
Most Recent Fund Was Raised: 06/01/1998
Year Founded: 1985
Capital Under Management: $500,000,000
Current Activity Level : Inactive / Unknown
Method of Compensation: Return on investment is of primary concern, do not charge fees

EVANSTON BUSINESS INVESTMENT CORP

1840 Oak Avenue
Evanston, IL 60201
Phone: 847-866-1840
Fax: 847-866-1808
Website: http://www.ebic.com

Type of Firm

Private Firm Investing Own Capital

Project Preferences

Role in Financing:

Prefer role as deal originator but will also invest in deals created by others

Type of Financing Preferred:

First Stage Financing
Seed
Start-up Financing

Industry Preferences

Communications and Media

Telecommunications
Data Communications
Other Communication Prod.

Computer Hardware

Computers
Computer Graphics and Dig
Integrated Turnkey System

Computer Software

Systems Software
Applications Software
Artificial Intelligence

Internet Specific

Internet

Semiconductors/Other Elect.

Electronic Components
Sensors

Medical/Health

Medical Diagnostics
Diagnostic Services
Diagnostic Test Products
Other Therapeutic
Disposable Med. Products

Consumer Related

Food/Beverage
Consumer Products
Consumer Services
Education Related

Industrial/Energy

Energy Conservation Relat
Robotics
Environmental Related

Manufact.

Office Automation Equipmt
Publishing

Additional Information

Name of Most Recent Fund: Evanston Northwestern Univ, Investment Partnership
Most Recent Fund Was Raised: 01/01/1993
Year Founded: 1985
Capital Under Management: $2,000,000
Current Activity Level : Actively seeking new investments
Method of Compensation: Return on investment is of primary concern, do not charge fees

FIRST ANALYSIS VENTURE CAPITAL (FKA:FIRST ANALYSIS CORP)

233 South Wacker Drive
Suite 9500
Chicago, IL 60606
Phone: 312-258-1400
Fax: 312-258-0334
Website: www,firstanalysis.com

Management and Staff
Allen Cohen, Managing Director
Angela Soliz, Principal
Anju Ahuja, Principal
Bret Maxwell, Chief Executive Officer
Brian Boyer, Vice President
Brian Hand, Managing Director
Clement Erbman, Managing Director
David Leshuk, Vice President
Dion Cornett, Vice President
E. Lawrence Hickey, Vice President
F. Oliver Nicklin, President
Howard Smith, Vice President
James Macdonald, Vice President
Joseph Chopp, Chief Financial Officer
Mark Koulogeorge, Managing Director
Nancy Corrie, Chief Financial Officer
Paul Kleinitis, Vice President

Type of Firm
Private Firm Investing Own Capital

Industry Association Membership
National Venture Capital Association (NVCA)

Project Preferences

Role in Financing:
Prefer role as deal originator but will also invest in deals created by others

Type of Financing Preferred:
Early Stage
Expansion
Later Stage

Size of Investments Considered
Min Size of Investment Considered (000s): $3,000
Max Size of Investment Considered (000s): $15,000

Geographical Preferences

United States
All U.S.

Industry Preferences

(% based on actual investment)

Industrial/Energy	49.7%
Internet Specific	18.6%
Computer Software and Services	10.6%
Other Products	7.7%
Communications and Media	6.3%
Consumer Related	2.5%
Semiconductors/Other Elect.	2.1%
Medical/Health	1.5%
Biotechnology	0.7%
Computer Hardware	0.4%

Additional Information
Name of Most Recent Fund: Infrastructure & Environmental Private Equity Fund III, L.P.
Most Recent Fund Was Raised: 01/01/1996
Year Founded: 1981
Capital Under Management: $373,000,000
Current Activity Level : Actively seeking new investments
Method of Compensation: Return on investment is of primary concern, do not charge fees

FOREFRONT CAPITAL

105 W. Madison
Suite 402
Chicago, IL 60602
Phone: 312-782-6235
Fax: 312-782-6236

See Colorado for full listing.

FRONTENAC CO.

135 South LaSalle Street
Suite 3800
Chicago, IL 60603
Phone: 312-368-0044
Fax: 312-368-9520
Website: www.frontenac.com

Management and Staff
David Katz, Partner
James Crawford, Partner
James Cowie, Partner
Jeremy Silverman, Partner
Laura Pearl, Partner
M. Laird Koldyke, Partner
Martin Koldyke, Partner
Patrick Blandford, Vice President
Paul Carbery, Partner
Rodney Goldstein, Managing Partner
Roger McEniry, Partner
Thomas Salentine, Principal
Walter Florence, Vice President

Type of Firm
Private Firm Investing Own Capital

Industry Association Membership
National Venture Capital Association (NVCA)

Project Preferences

Role in Financing:
Prefer role as deal originator but will also invest in deals created by others

Type of Financing Preferred:
First Stage Financing
Industry Rollups
Leveraged Buyout
Second Stage Financing
Special Situation
Start-up Financing

Size of Investments Considered
Min Size of Investment Considered (000s): $500
Max Size of Investment Considered: No Limit

Geographical Preferences

United States
All U.S.

Industry Preferences

(% based on actual investment)

Consumer Related	29.3%
Computer Software and Services	16.4%
Internet Specific	15.9%
Other Products	13.6%
Medical/Health	12.8%
Industrial/Energy	5.0%
Communications and Media	3.8%
Computer Hardware	1.9%
Semiconductors/Other Elect.	0.8%
Biotechnology	0.6%

Additional Information
Name of Most Recent Fund: Frontenac VII Limited Partnership
Most Recent Fund Was Raised: 03/01/1997
Year Founded: 1971
Capital Under Management: $1,237,400,000
Current Activity Level : Actively seeking new investments
Method of Compensation: Other

GKM VENTURE PARTNERS, LP

311 South Wacker Drive
Suite 2750
Chicago, IL 60606
Phone: 312-697-7180
Fax: 800-697-0005
Website: www.gkm.com

See California for full listing.

GLENCOE CAPITAL, LLC (FKA: GLENCOE INVESTMENT CORPORATION)

311 South Wacker Drive
Suite 4990
Chicago, IL 60606
Phone: 312-554-7533
Fax: 312-554-7501

Other Offices

488 Madison Avenue
Suite 1503
New York, NY 10022
Phone: 212-755-2302
Fax: 212-755-2717

Management and Staff
Caroline Williams, Principal
John Cavalaris, Principal
Ronald Wray, Principal
Thomas Berry, Chief Operating Officer

Whom to Contact
Dorn E. Van Cleave III

Type of Firm
Investment/Merchant Bank Subsid/Affil

Project Preferences

Role in Financing:
Prefer role as deal originator but will also invest in deals created by others

Type of Financing Preferred:
Control-block Purchases
Leveraged Buyout
Mezzanine

Size of Investments Considered
Min Size of Investment Considered (000s): $20,000
Max Size of Investment Considered: No Limit

Geographical Preferences

United States
All U.S.

Canada
All Canada

Industry Preferences

Semiconductors/Other Elect.
Sensors
Component Testing Equipmt

Consumer Related
Entertainment and Leisure
Food/Beverage
Consumer Products
Consumer Services

Industrial/Energy
Materials
Factory Automation
Machinery

Transportation
Transportation

Financial Services
Financial Services

Business Serv.
Distribution

Manufact.
Publishing

Additional Information
Name of Most Recent Fund: Glencoe Capital Partners II, L.P.
Most Recent Fund Was Raised: 01/01/1998
Year Founded: 1994
Capital Under Management: $62,000,000
Current Activity Level : Actively seeking new investments
Method of Compensation: Return on invest. most important, but chg. closing fees, service fees, etc.

GRAYSTONE VENTURE PARTNERS, LLC(AKA:PORTAGE VENTURE PARTNERS

One Northfield Plaza
Suite 530
Northfield, IL 60093
Phone: 847-446-9460
Fax: 847-446-9470
Website: www.portageventures.com

Management and Staff
Edward Chandler, Managing Director
Judith Meyer, Managing Director
Judy Dorr, Chief Financial Officer
Matthew McCall, Vice President

Whom to Contact
Eunhee Choi
Mathew B. McCall

Type of Firm
Private Firm Investing Own Capital

Industry Association Membership
National Venture Capital Association (NVCA)

Project Preferences

Role in Financing:
Will function either as deal originator or investor in deals created by others

Type of Financing Preferred:
Early Stage

Geographical Preferences

United States
All U.S.

Industry Preferences

(% based on actual investment)

Computer Software and Services	38.7%
Internet Specific	33.9%
Medical/Health	8.4%
Consumer Related	5.8%
Other Products	5.1%
Communications and Media	4.3%
Biotechnology	3.8%

Additional Information
Name of Most Recent Fund: Portage Founders, L.P.
Most Recent Fund Was Raised: 08/01/1999
Year Founded: 1997
Capital Under Management: $122,000,000
Current Activity Level : Actively seeking new investments
Method of Compensation: Return on investment is of primary concern, do not charge fees

GTCR GOLDER RAUNER, LLC

6100 Sears Tower
Chicago, IL 60606-6402
Phone: 312-382-2200
Fax: 312-382-2201
Website: www.gtcr.com

Management and Staff
Bruce Rauner, Principal
Charles Glew, Vice President
David Donnini, Principal
Donald Edwards, Principal
Edgar Jannotta, Principal
Ethan Budin, Vice President
Joseph Nolan, Principal
Michael Arbour, Vice President
Philip Canfield, Principal
Steven Ross, Chief Financial Officer
Timothy McAdam, Vice President
Vince Hemmer, Vice President
William Kessinger, Principal

Type of Firm
Private Firm Investing Own Capital

Industry Association Membership
National Venture Capital Association (NVCA)

Project Preferences

Role in Financing:
Prefer role as deal originator

Type of Financing Preferred:
Acquisition
Expansion
Leveraged Buyout
Management Buyouts
Recapitalizations

Size of Investments Considered
Min Size of Investment Considered (000s): $10,000
Max Size of Investment Considered (000s): $300,000

Geographical Preferences

United States
All U.S.

Industry Preferences

(% based on actual investment)

Other Products	35.2%
Computer Software and Services	17.4%
Medical/Health	13.1%
Semiconductors/Other Elect.	11.9%
Consumer Related	10.1%
Internet Specific	4.5%
Industrial/Energy	3.9%
Communications and Media	2.3%
Computer Hardware	1.7%

Additional Information
Name of Most Recent Fund: GTCR Capital Partners, L.P.
Most Recent Fund Was Raised: 01/06/2000
Year Founded: 1980
Capital Under Management: $4,448,000,000
Current Activity Level : Actively seeking new investments
Method of Compensation: Return on invest. most important, but chg. closing fees, service fees, etc.

HIGH STREET CAPITAL, LLC

311 South Wacker Drive
Suite 4550
Chicago, IL 60606
Phone: 312-697-4990
Fax: 312-697-4994
Website: www.highstr.com

Management and Staff
Joseph Katcha, Principal

Type of Firm
Private Firm Investing Own Capital

Project Preferences

Role in Financing:
Will function either as deal originator or investor in deals created by others

Type of Financing Preferred:
Acquisition
Control-block Purchases
Expansion
Generalist PE
Leveraged Buyout
Management Buyouts
Recapitalizations
Special Situation

Size of Investments Considered
Min Size of Investment Considered (000s): $2,000
Max Size of Investment Considered (000s): $10,000

Geographical Preferences

United States
All U.S.

Industry Preferences

Communications and Media
Telecommunications
Data Communications
Other Communication Prod.

Computer Software
Computer Services

Internet Specific
E-Commerce Technology

Semiconductors/Other Elect.
Electronics

Medical/Health
Medical Diagnostics
Diagnostic Services
Diagnostic Test Products
Drug/Equipmt Delivery
Medical Products
Disposable Med. Products
Health Services

Consumer Related
Food/Beverage
Education Related

Industrial/Energy
Industrial Products

Business Serv.
Services
Distribution

Manufact.
Manufacturing

Agr/Forestr/Fish
Agriculture related

Additional Information
Name of Most Recent Fund: High Street Capital II, L.L.C.
Most Recent Fund Was Raised: 01/01/1999
Year Founded: 1997
Capital Under Management: $20,000,000
Current Activity Level : Actively seeking new investments
Method of Compensation: Return on investment is of primary concern, do not charge fees

IEG VENTURE MANAGEMENT, INC.

70 West Madison Street
Chicago, IL 60602
Phone: 312-644-0890
Fax: 312-454-0369
Website: www.iegventure.com

Type of Firm
Private Firm Investing Own Capital

Industry Association Membership
National Venture Capital Association (NVCA)

Project Preferences

Role in Financing:
Prefer role as deal originator but will also invest in deals created by others

Type of Financing Preferred:
First Stage Financing
Second Stage Financing
Seed
Start-up Financing

Geographical Preferences

United States
Midwest

Industry Preferences

Communications and Media
Commercial Communications
Telecommunications
Data Communications
Satellite Microwave Comm.
Other Communication Prod.

Computer Hardware
Computers
Mini and Personal/Desktop
Computer Graphics and Dig
Integrated Turnkey System
Disk Relat. Memory Device

Computer Software
Computer Services
Systems Software
Applications Software
Artificial Intelligence

Internet Specific
Internet

Semiconductors/Other Elect.
Electronics
Electronic Components
Sensors
Laser Related
Fiber Optics
Analytic/Scientific

Biotechnology
Industrial Biotechnology
Biosensors

Medical/Health
Medical Diagnostics
Diagnostic Services
Diagnostic Test Products
Drug/Equipmt Delivery
Other Therapeutic
Medical Products
Disposable Med. Products
Hospitals/Clinics/Primary
Hospital/Other Instit.

Industrial/Energy
Alternative Energy
Energy Conservation Relat
Industrial Products
Factory Automation
Robotics
Machinery
Environmental Related

Transportation
Transportation

Manufact.
Office Automation Equipmt

Agr/Forestr/Fish
Agriculture related

Additional Information
Name of Most Recent Fund: LSA Partners
Most Recent Fund Was Raised: 03/01/1984
Year Founded: 1983
Capital Under Management: $10,000,000
Current Activity Level : Actively seeking new investments
Method of Compensation: Return on investment is of primary concern, do not charge fees

---

INROADS CAPITAL PARTNERS, L.P.

1603 Orrington Ave
Suite 2050
Evanston, IL 60201-3841
Phone: 847-864-2000
Fax: 847-864-9692

Management and Staff
Jerrold Carrington, General Partner
Margaret Fisher, General Partner
Sona Wang, General Partner

Type of Firm
Investment/Merchant Bank Subsid/Affil

Project Preferences

Type of Financing Preferred:
Expansion
Later Stage

Size of Investments Considered
Min Size of Investment Considered (000s): $1,000
Max Size of Investment Considered (000s): $5,000

Geographical Preferences

United States
All U.S.

Industry Preferences

(% based on actual investment)

Semiconductors/Other Elect.	36.4%
Internet Specific	32.3%
Computer Software and Services	15.9%
Industrial/Energy	13.3%
Medical/Health	2.0%
Consumer Related	0.1%

Additional Information
Name of Most Recent Fund: Inroads Capital Partners
Most Recent Fund Was Raised: 01/01/1994
Year Founded: 1995
Capital Under Management: $125,000,000
Current Activity Level : Actively seeking new investments

JK&B CAPITAL

180 North Stetson
Suite 4500
Chicago, IL 60601
Phone: 312-946-1200
Fax: 312-946-1103
Website: www.jkbcapital.com

Other Offices

691 Seale Avenue
Palo Alto, CA 94301-3833
Phone: 650-330-1200
Fax: 650-330-1201

Management and Staff
Constance Capone, Principal
David Kronfeld, Founder
Nancy O'Leary, Chief Financial Officer
Tasha Seitz, Principal

Type of Firm
Private Firm Investing Own Capital

Industry Association Membership
National Venture Capital Association (NVCA)

Project Preferences

Role in Financing:
Prefer role as deal originator but will also invest in deals created by others

Type of Financing Preferred:
Early Stage
Expansion
First Stage Financing
Later Stage
Second Stage Financing

Size of Investments Considered
Min Size of Investment Considered (000s): $5,000
Max Size of Investment Considered (000s): $20,000

Geographical Preferences

United States
All U.S.

Industry Preferences

(% based on actual investment)

Internet Specific	35.0%
Computer Software and Services	30.0%
Communications and Media	21.2%
Semiconductors/Other Elect.	10.6%
Computer Hardware	1.6%
Industrial/Energy	1.1%
Consumer Related	0.4%

Additional Information
Name of Most Recent Fund: JK&B Capital I, L.P.
Most Recent Fund Was Raised: 01/01/1996
Year Founded: 1996
Capital Under Management: $597,400,000
Current Activity Level : Actively seeking new investments
Method of Compensation: Return on investment is of primary concern, do not charge fees

KB PARTNERS, LLC

1101 Skokie Blvd.
Suite 260
Northbrook, IL 60062-2856
Phone: 847-714-0444
Fax: 847-714-0445
Website: www.kbpartners.com

Management and Staff
Byron Denenberg, Managing Director
John McBlain, Chief Financial Officer
Keith Bank, Managing Director
Robert Zieserl, Managing Director
Robert Garber, Managing Director

Type of Firm
Private Firm Investing Own Capital

Industry Association Membership
National Venture Capital Association (NVCA)

Project Preferences

Role in Financing:
Will function either as deal originator or investor in deals created by others

Type of Financing Preferred:
Early Stage
First Stage Financing
Second Stage Financing
Seed
Start-up Financing

Size of Investments Considered
Min Size of Investment Considered (000s): $1,000
Max Size of Investment Considered (000s): $5,000

Geographical Preferences

United States
Midwest

Industry Preferences

(% based on actual investment)

Internet Specific	58.1%
Computer Software and Services	24.3%
Industrial/Energy	17.6%

Additional Information
Name of Most Recent Fund: KB Partners Venture Fund I, L.P.
Most Recent Fund Was Raised: 06/01/1998
Year Founded: 2000
Capital Under Management: $95,000,000
Current Activity Level : Actively seeking new investments
Method of Compensation: Return on investment is of primary concern, do not charge fees

KETTLE PARTNERS, L.P.

350 W. Hubbard
Suite 350
Chicago, IL 60610
Phone: 312-329-9300
Fax: 312-527-4519
Website: www.kettlevc.com

Management and Staff
Bruce Beerbower, Chief Financial Officer

Type of Firm
Private Equity Advisor or Fund of Fund Mgr

Project Preferences

Role in Financing:
Prefer role as deal originator but will also invest in deals created by others

Type of Financing Preferred:
Early Stage
First Stage Financing
Second Stage Financing
Seed
Startup

Size of Investments Considered
Min Size of Investment Considered (000s): $1,000
Max Size of Investment Considered (000s): $5,000

Geographical Preferences

United States
All U.S.

Industry Preferences

(% based on actual investment)

Internet Specific	52.6%
Communications and Media	34.0%
Other Products	6.7%
Computer Hardware	3.6%
Computer Software and Services	3.0%

Additional Information
Year Founded: 1988
Capital Under Management: $85,000,000
Current Activity Level : Actively seeking new investments
Method of Compensation: Return on investment is of primary concern, do not charge fees

KEYSTONE VENTURE CAPITAL MANAGEMENT CO.

225 West Washington Street
Suite 1450
Chicago, IL 60606
Phone: 312-857-1400
Fax: 312-857-1800
Website: www.keystonevc.com

See Pennsylvania for full listing.

KOMATSU AMERICA INTERNATIONAL COMPANY (KAIC)

440 North Fairway Drive
Vernon Hills, IL 60061
Phone: 847-970-5773
Fax: 847-970-4183
Website: www.komatsuamerica.com

Management and Staff
James Boyle, Chairman & CEO

Type of Firm
Non-Financial Corp. Affiliate or Subsidiary

Additional Information
Year Founded: 1970
Capital Under Management: $30,000,000
Current Activity Level : Actively seeking new investments

LAKE SHORE CAPITAL PARTNERS, INC.

20 North Wacker Drive
Suite 2807
Chicago, IL 60606
Phone: 312-803-3536
Fax: 312-803-3534

Type of Firm
Mgt. Consulting Firm

Project Preferences

Role in Financing:
Prefer role as deal originator

Type of Financing Preferred:
First Stage Financing
Leveraged Buyout
Mezzanine
Second Stage Financing

Size of Investments Considered
Min Size of Investment Considered (000s): $1,000
Max Size of Investment Considered (000s): $10,000

Geographical Preferences

United States
All U.S.

Industry Preferences

Communications and Media
CATV & Pay TV Systems
Radio & TV Broadcasting
Telecommunications
Data Communications

Computer Hardware
Mini and Personal/Desktop
Computer Graphics and Dig
Integrated Turnkey System
Terminals

Computer Software
Computer Services
Systems Software
Applications Software

Internet Specific
Internet

Semiconductors/Other Elect.
Electronic Components
Circuit Boards
Component Testing Equipmt
Laser Related
Fiber Optics
Analytic/Scientific

Biotechnology
Industrial Biotechnology

Medical/Health
Medical Diagnostics
Diagnostic Services
Diagnostic Test Products
Medical Therapeutics
Other Therapeutic
Disposable Med. Products
Hospitals/Clinics/Primary
Hospital/Other Instit.

Consumer Related
Entertainment and Leisure
Retail
Computer Stores
Franchises(NEC)
Food/Beverage
Consumer Products
Consumer Services
Other Restaurants
Education Related

Industrial/Energy
Industrial Products

Transportation
Transportation

Financial Services
Financial Services

Business Serv.
Distribution
Consulting Services

Manufact.
Office Automation Equipmt
Publishing

Additional Information
Year Founded: 1992
Current Activity Level : Actively seeking new investments
Method of Compensation: Function primarily in service area, receive contingent fee in cash or equity

LASALLE CAPITAL GROUP, INC.

70 West Madison Street
Suite 5710
Chicago, IL 60602
Phone: 312-236-7041
Fax: 312-236-0720

Management and Staff
Anthony Pesavento

Whom to Contact
Anthony Pesavento

Project Preferences

Role in Financing:
Prefer role as deal originator but will also invest in deals created by others

Type of Financing Preferred:
Leveraged Buyout
Special Situation

Size of Investments Considered
Min Size of Investment Considered (000s): $1,000
Max Size of Investment Considered: No Limit

Geographical Preferences

International
No Preference

Industry Preferences

Consumer Related
Entertainment and Leisure
Consumer Products

Industrial/Energy
Industrial Products
Machinery

Additional Information
Year Founded: 1984
Current Activity Level : Actively seeking new investments
Method of Compensation: Return on invest. most important, but chg. closing fees, service fees, etc.

LINC CAPITAL PARTNERS, INC.

303 East Wacker Drive
Suite 1000
Chicago, IL 60601
Phone: 312—346-2670
Fax: 312-938-4290

Other Offices

1176 Nimitz Drive
Broadmark, CA 94015
Phone: 650-994-3503
Fax: 650-994-0244

34 Corte Oriental
Greenbrae, CA 94904
Phone: 415-925-1776
Fax: 415-925-1773

Management and Staff
Allen Palles, Chief Financial Officer
Bert Laing, President
Marty Zimmerman, Chief Executive Officer

Whom to Contact
Dan Wallace
Jonmarie Maloney
Mark Zimmerman
Steve Meeker

Type of Firm
Private Firm Investing Own Capital

Industry Association Membership
Natl assoc of Small Bus. Inv. Co (NASBIC)

Project Preferences

Role in Financing:
Prefer role as deal originator

Type of Financing Preferred:
First Stage Financing
Leveraged Buyout
Mezzanine
Research and Development
Second Stage Financing
Seed
Special Situation
Start-up Financing

Size of Investments Considered
Min Size of Investment Considered (000s): $500
Max Size of Investment Considered (000s): $2,000

Geographical Preferences

United States
All U.S.

International
United Kingdom

Industry Preferences

Communications and Media
Telecommunications
Data Communications
Satellite Microwave Comm.

Computer Other
Computer Related

Semiconductors/Other Elect.
Electronic Components
Sensors

Medical/Health
Medical/Health
Medical Diagnostics
Medical Therapeutics
Medical Products

Industrial/Energy
Robotics
Machinery

Additional Information
Year Founded: 1983
Capital Under Management: $400,000,000
Current Activity Level : Actively seeking new investments
Method of Compensation: Return on invest. most important, but chg. closing fees, service fees, etc.

LINCOLNSHIRE MANAGEMENT INC.

333 W. Wacker Drive
Suite 700
Chicago, IL 60606
Phone: 312-899-9000
Fax: 312-899-9009
Website: www.lincolnshiremgmt.com

See New York for full listing.

MADISON DEARBORN PARTNERS, LLC

Three First National Plaza
Suite 3800
Chicago, IL 60602
Phone: 312-895-1000
Fax: 312-895-1001
Website: www.mdcp.com

Other Offices

One Curzon Street
5th Floor
London, United Kingdom W1J 5RT
Phone: 020-7647-6310
Fax: 020-7647-6311

Management and Staff
Andrew Sinwell, Managing Director
Benjamin Chereskin, Managing Director
David Mosher, Managing Director
Gary Little, Chief Financial Officer
James Perry, Managing Director
James Kirby, Managing Director
John Canning, President
Justin Huscher, Managing Director
Nicholas Alexos, Managing Director
Paul Wood, Managing Director
Paul Finnegan, Managing Director
Robin Selati, Managing Director
Samuel Mencoff, Managing Director
Thomas Souleles, Managing Director
Thomas Reusche, Managing Director
Timothy Hurd, Managing Director
Timothy Sullivan, Managing Director
William Hunckler, Managing Director

Type of Firm
Private Firm Investing Own Capital

Industry Association Membership
National Venture Capital Association (NVCA)

Project Preferences

Role in Financing:
Prefer role as deal originator but will also invest in deals created by others

Type of Financing Preferred:
Acquisition
Early Stage
Expansion
Generalist PE
Later Stage
Leveraged Buyout
Management Buyouts
Special Situation
Startup

Size of Investments Considered
Min Size of Investment Considered (000s): $20,000
Max Size of Investment Considered (000s): $400,000

Geographical Preferences

United States
All U.S.
All U.S.

Canada
All Canada

International
Belgium
Europe
France
Germany
Italy
Latin America
Luxembourg
Mexico
Netherlands
Spain
United Kingdom

Industry Preferences

(% based on actual investment)

Other Products	57.9%
Internet Specific	14.8%
Communications and Media	11.9%
Consumer Related	6.9%
Semiconductors/Other Elect.	3.1%
Industrial/Energy	2.5%
Medical/Health	2.3%
Computer Software and Services	0.5%
Computer Hardware	0.1%

Additional Information
Name of Most Recent Fund: Madison Dearborn Capital Partners III, L.P.
Most Recent Fund Was Raised: 01/01/1999
Year Founded: 1993
Capital Under Management: $7,000,000,000
Current Activity Level : Actively seeking new investments
Method of Compensation: Return on investment is of primary concern, do not charge fees

MARQUETTE VENTURE PARTNERS

520 Lake Cook Road
Suite 450
Deerfield, IL 60015
Phone: 847-940-1700
Fax: 847-940-1724
Website: www.marquetteventures.com

Other Offices

520 Lake Cook Road
Suite 450
Deerfield, IL 60015
Phone: 708-940-1700

Management and Staff
Mark McDonnell, Chief Financial Officer

Type of Firm
Private Firm Investing Own Capital

Project Preferences

Type of Financing Preferred:
First Stage Financing
Second Stage Financing
Start-up Financing

Size of Investments Considered
Min Size of Investment Considered (000s): $1,000
Max Size of Investment Considered (000s): $5,000

Geographical Preferences

United States
Mid Atlantic
Midwest
Rocky Mountain
West Coast

Industry Preferences

(% based on actual investment)

Medical/Health	30.4%
Consumer Related	18.4%
Computer Software and Services	12.8%
Other Products	9.3%
Communications and Media	8.6%
Biotechnology	7.7%
Internet Specific	6.9%
Semiconductors/Other Elect.	3.1%
Industrial/Energy	2.3%
Computer Hardware	0.5%

Additional Information
Name of Most Recent Fund: Marquette Venture Partners III, L.P.
Most Recent Fund Was Raised: 06/01/1997
Year Founded: 1987
Capital Under Management: $227,700,000
Current Activity Level : Actively seeking new investments
Method of Compensation: Return on investment is of primary concern, do not charge fees

MESIROW PRIVATE EQUITY INVESTMENTS, INC.

350 North Clark Street
Chicago, IL 60610
Phone: 312-595-6950
Fax: 312-595-6211

Other Offices

350 North Clark Street
Chicago, IL 60610
Phone: 312-670-6099

Management and Staff
Daniel Howell, Managing Director
Mary Hanevold, Vice President
Michael Barrett, Vice President
William Sutter, Managing Director

Type of Firm
Investment/Merchant Bank Subsid/Affil

Industry Association Membership
Natl assoc of Small Bus. Inv. Co (NASBIC)

Project Preferences

Role in Financing:
Prefer role as deal originator but will also invest in deals created by others

Type of Financing Preferred:
Fund of Funds
Leveraged Buyout
Second Stage Financing
Special Situation

Size of Investments Considered
Min Size of Investment Considered (000s): $4,000
Max Size of Investment Considered (000s): $10,000

Geographical Preferences

United States
All U.S.

Industry Preferences

(% based on actual investment)

Other Products	29.1%
Computer Software and Services	20.0%
Consumer Related	16.5%
Internet Specific	13.0%
Communications and Media	7.2%
Industrial/Energy	5.9%
Medical/Health	3.3%
Biotechnology	2.1%
Semiconductors/Other Elect.	2.0%
Computer Hardware	0.9%

Additional Information
Name of Most Recent Fund: Mesirow Capital Partners VII
Most Recent Fund Was Raised: 04/01/1997
Year Founded: 1981
Capital Under Management: $500,000,000
Current Activity Level : Actively seeking new investments
Method of Compensation: Return on investment is of primary concern, do not charge fees

MINOTAUR CAPITAL MANAGEMENT

150 South Wacker
Suite 470
Chicago, IL 60606
Phone: 312-621-9000
Fax: 312-621-9001
Website: www.minotaurpartners.com

Management and Staff
Ed Finnegan, General Partner
Marc Blum, Vice President
Paul Lapping, General Partner

Type of Firm
Investment/Merchant Bank Subsid/Affil

Additional Information
Year Founded: 1987
Current Activity Level : Actively seeking new investments

MORNINGSIDE GROUP

5225 Main
Downers Grove, IL 60515
Phone: 630-241-3131
Fax: 630-241-0252
Website: www.morningsideusa.com

Management and Staff
David Strosberg, Founder

Type of Firm
Private Firm Investing Own Capital

Project Preferences

Type of Financing Preferred:
Balanced

Geographical Preferences

United States
All U.S.

Additional Information
Current Activity Level : Actively seeking new investments

MOSAIX VENTURES, LLC

1822 North Mohawk
Chicago, IL 60614
Phone: 312-274-0988
Fax: 312-274-0989
Website: www.mosaixventures.com

Management and Staff
Ranjan Lal, Partner

Type of Firm
Private Equity Advisor or Fund of Fund Mgr

Project Preferences

Type of Financing Preferred:
Early Stage
Expansion
Later Stage

Size of Investments Considered
Min Size of Investment Considered (000s): $500
Max Size of Investment Considered (000s): $3,000

Industry Preferences

Medical/Health
Medical/Health

Additional Information
Year Founded: 2000
Capital Under Management: $40,000,000
Current Activity Level : Actively seeking new investments

MOTOROLA INC.

1303 East Algonquin Road
Schaumburg, IL 60196
Phone: 847-576-4929
Fax: 847-538-2250

See D. of Columbia for full listing.

NESBITT BURNS

111 West Monroe Street
20th Fl
Chicago, IL 60603
Phone: 312-461-3855
Fax: 312-765-8000
Website: www.harrisbank.com

Management and Staff
William Morro, President

Whom to Contact
I. David Bird

Type of Firm
Investment/Merchant Bank Subsid/Affil

Project Preferences

Role in Financing:
Prefer role as deal originator but will also invest in deals created by others

Type of Financing Preferred:
Control-block Purchases
Leveraged Buyout
Special Situation

Geographical Preferences

United States
All U.S.

Canada
All Canada

International
South Africa

Industry Preferences

Communications and Media
Communications and Media

Computer Hardware
Mini and Personal/Desktop
Disk Relat. Memory Device

Computer Software
Computer Services
Systems Software

Internet Specific
Internet

Semiconductors/Other Elect.
Electronic Components
Sensors

Biotechnology
Industrial Biotechnology

Medical/Health
Medical Diagnostics
Diagnostic Services
Diagnostic Test Products
Medical Therapeutics
Disposable Med. Products

Consumer Related
Entertainment and Leisure
Retail
Franchises(NEC)
Food/Beverage
Consumer Products
Consumer Services
Hotels and Resorts
Education Related

Industrial/Energy
Energy
Machinery
Environmental Related

Business Serv.
Distribution

Manufact.
Office Automation Equipmt

Agr/Forestr/Fish
Agriculture related

Additional Information
Year Founded: 1996
Capital Under Management: $225,000,000
Current Activity Level : Actively seeking new investments
Method of Compensation: Return on invest. most important, but chg. closing fees, service fees, etc.

NETFUEL VENTURES

350 W. Hubbard Ave
Suite 400
Chicago, IL 60610
Phone: 312-828-9983
E-mail: info@netfuelventures.com
Website: www.netfuelventures.com

Management and Staff
Alicia Eastman, Principal
Chris Quinn, Managing Director
Clay Pew, Managing Director
Forsyth Jennifer, Principal
Kevin Self, Managing Director
Michael Liddell, Managing Director
Waverly Deutsch, Managing Director
Will Garrett, Managing Director

Type of Firm
Incubators

Project Preferences

Type of Financing Preferred:
Seed
Startup

Geographical Preferences

United States
Midwest

Industry Preferences

Internet Specific
Internet

Additional Information
Year Founded: 2000
Capital Under Management: $20,000,000
Current Activity Level : Actively seeking new investments

NEW WORLD VENTURE ADVISORS

1603 Orrington Avenue
Suite 1070
Evanston, IL 60201
Phone: 847-328-0300
Fax: 847-328-8297
Website: www.newworldvc.com

Management and Staff
Adam Schechter, Principal
Christopher Girgenti, Managing Director
J.B. Pritzker, Managing Director
Kathy Smith, Chief Financial Officer
Lisa Flashner, Managing Director

Type of Firm
Private Firm Investing Own Capital

Project Preferences

Type of Financing Preferred:
Early Stage

Geographical Preferences

United States
All U.S.

Industry Preferences

(% based on actual investment)

Internet Specific	98.4%
Computer Software and Services	1.6%

Additional Information
Year Founded: 1996
Capital Under Management: $122,000,000
Current Activity Level : Actively seeking new investments

NORTH AMERICAN BUSINESS DEVELOPMENT CO., L.L.C.

135 South LaSalle Street
Suite 4000
Chicago, IL 60603
Phone: 312-332-4950
Fax: 312-332-1540
Website: www.northamericanfund.com

Other Offices

111 East Las Olas Boulevard
Fort Lauderdale, FL 33301
Phone: 305-463-0681
Fax: 305-527-0904

Management and Staff
R. David Bergonia
Robert Underwood

Whom to Contact
R. David Bergonia
Robert Underwood

Type of Firm
Private Firm Investing Own Capital

Project Preferences

Role in Financing:
Prefer role as deal originator but will also invest in deals created by others

Type of Financing Preferred:
Control-block Purchases
Industry Rollups
Leveraged Buyout
Special Situation

Size of Investments Considered
Min Size of Investment Considered (000s): $10,000
Max Size of Investment Considered: No Limit

Additional Information
Name of Most Recent Fund: North American Fund III
Most Recent Fund Was Raised: 01/01/1996
Year Founded: 1989
Capital Under Management: $115,000,000
Current Activity Level : Actively seeking new investments
Method of Compensation: Return on investment is of primary concern, do not charge fees

OPEN PRAIRIE VENTURES

115 North Neil Street
Suite 209
Champaign, IL 61820
Phone: 217-351-7000
Fax: 217-351-7051
Website: www.openprairie.com

Management and Staff
Andrew Jones, Managing Partner
Dennis Beard, Chief Financial Officer
Dennis Spice, Managing Partner
James Michael Schultz, Managing Partner

Whom to Contact
Andrew S. Jones, Ph.D.

Type of Firm
Private Firm Investing Own Capital

Project Preferences

Role in Financing:
Will function either as deal originator or investor in deals created by others

Type of Financing Preferred:
Early Stage

Size of Investments Considered
Min Size of Investment Considered (000s): $250
Max Size of Investment Considered (000s): $2,500

Geographical Preferences

United States
Midwest

Industry Preferences

Communications and Media
Commercial Communications
Radio & TV Broadcasting
Telecommunications
Wireless Communications
Data Communications
Satellite Microwave Comm.
Other Communication Prod.

Computer Hardware
Computers

Computer Software
Computer Services
Software
Systems Software
Applications Software

Internet Specific
Internet

Computer Other
Computer Related

Semiconductors/Other Elect.
Electronics
Electronic Components
Semiconductor
Micro-Processing
Controllers and Sensors
Sensors
Circuit Boards
Component Testing Equipmt
Laser Related
Fiber Optics

Biotechnology
Biotechnology
Human Biotechnology
Agricultural/Animal Bio.
Industrial Biotechnology
Biosensors
Biotech Related Research
Biotech Related Research

Medical/Health
Diagnostic Services
Diagnostic Test Products
Drug/Equipmt Delivery
Medical Products
Pharmaceuticals

Industrial/Energy
Robotics

Additional Information
Name of Most Recent Fund: Open Prairie Ventures
Most Recent Fund Was Raised: 01/01/1998
Year Founded: 1997
Capital Under Management: $40,000,000
Current Activity Level : Actively seeking new investments
Method of Compensation: Return on invest. most important, but chg. closing fees, service fees, etc.

ORIGIN VENTURES LLC

474 N. Lake Shore Drive
Suite 5804
Chicago, IL 60611
Phone: 312-644-6449
Fax: 312-644-0534
Website: www.originventures.com

Management and Staff
Bruce Barron, Principal
Steven Miller, Principal

Type of Firm
Private Firm Investing Own Capital

Project Preferences

Type of Financing Preferred:
Seed

Geographical Preferences

United States
All U.S.
Midwest

Industry Preferences

Internet Specific
Internet

Additional Information
Year Founded: 2000
Current Activity Level : Actively seeking new investments

PENMAN PARTNERS (FKA PENMAN ASSET MANAGEMENT LP)

333 West Wacker Drive
Suite 700
Chicago, IL 60606
Phone: 312-845-9055
Fax: 312-845-9056

Management and Staff
Kelvin Pennington, General Partner
Lawrence Manson, General Partner

Whom to Contact
Kelvin Pennington

Type of Firm
Mgt. Consulting Firm

Project Preferences

Type of Financing Preferred:
Leveraged Buyout

Size of Investments Considered
Min Size of Investment Considered (000s): $3,000
Max Size of Investment Considered: No Limit

Geographical Preferences

United States
All U.S.

Industry Preferences

Computer Hardware
Disk Relat. Memory Device

Internet Specific
Internet

Medical/Health
Diagnostic Services
Drug/Equipmt Delivery
Medical Products
Disposable Med. Products
Hospitals/Clinics/Primary
Hospital/Other Instit.

Consumer Related
Retail
Computer Stores
Franchises(NEC)
Food/Beverage
Consumer Products
Consumer Services
Other Restaurants
Education Related

Industrial/Energy
Industrial Products
Materials

Transportation
Transportation

Manufact.
Publishing

Additional Information
Name of Most Recent Fund: PENMAN Private Equity and Mezz. Fund, L.P.
Most Recent Fund Was Raised: 10/04/1994
Year Founded: 1992
Capital Under Management: $51,200,000
Current Activity Level : Making few, if any, new investments
Method of Compensation: Return on invest. most important, but chg. closing fees, service fees, etc.

PFINGSTEN PARTNERS, L.P.

520 Lake Cook Road
Suite 375
Deerfield, IL 60015
Phone: 847-374-9140
Fax: 847-374-9150

Other Offices

520 Lake Cook Road
Suite 375
Deerfield, IL

Management and Staff
John McNulty
John H. Underwood
Scott A. Finegan
Thomas Bagley

Whom to Contact
John McNulty
John H. Underwood
Scott A. Finegan
Thomas Bagley

Type of Firm
Private Firm Investing Own Capital

Project Preferences

Role in Financing:
Prefer role as deal originator

Type of Financing Preferred:
Industry Rollups
Leveraged Buyout

Size of Investments Considered
Min Size of Investment Considered (000s): $15,000
Max Size of Investment Considered: No Limit

Geographical Preferences

United States
Midwest

Industry Preferences

Semiconductors/Other Elect.
Electronic Components
Controllers and Sensors
Component Testing Equipmt
Analytic/Scientific

Consumer Related
Food/Beverage
Consumer Products
Education Related

Industrial/Energy
Industrial Products

Business Serv.
Distribution

Manufact.
Publishing

Additional Information
Name of Most Recent Fund: Pfingsten Executive Fund II, L.P.
Most Recent Fund Was Raised: 06/01/1998
Year Founded: 1989
Capital Under Management: $26,300,000
Current Activity Level : Actively seeking new investments
Method of Compensation: Return on investment is of primary concern, do not charge fees

---

POLESTAR CAPITAL, INC.

180 North Michigan Avenue
Suite 1905
Chicago, IL 60601
Phone: 312-984-9090
Fax: 312-984-9877
E-mail: wl@polestarvc.com
Website: www.polestarvc.com

Management and Staff
Wally Lennox, Principal

Type of Firm
Private Firm Investing Own Capital

Industry Association Membership
Natl assoc of Small Bus. Inv. Co (NASBIC)

Project Preferences

Role in Financing:
Prefer role as deal originator but will also invest in deals created by others

Type of Financing Preferred:
First Stage Financing
Second Stage Financing
Start-up Financing

Geographical Preferences

United States
All U.S.

Industry Preferences

Communications and Media
Communications and Media
Commercial Communications
Telecommunications
Data Communications

Computer Software
Systems Software
Applications Software
Artificial Intelligence

Computer Other
Computer Related

Manufact.
Office Automation Equipmt

Additional Information

Year Founded: 1970
Capital Under Management: $40,000,000
Current Activity Level : Actively seeking new investments
Method of Compensation: Return on invest. most important, but chg. closing fees, service fees, etc.

PRINCE VENTURES

10 South Wacker Drive
Suite 2575
Chicago, IL 60606
Phone: 312-454-1408
Fax: 312-454-9125

Other Offices

25 Ford Road
Westport, CT 06880
Phone: 203-227-8332
Fax: 203-226-5302

Type of Firm

Private Firm Investing Own Capital

Project Preferences

Role in Financing:
Prefer role as deal originator but will also invest in deals created by others

Type of Financing Preferred:
First Stage Financing
Leveraged Buyout
Second Stage Financing
Seed
Start-up Financing

Geographical Preferences

International
No Preference

Industry Preferences

(% based on actual investment)

Medical/Health	42.9%
Biotechnology	27.0%
Semiconductors/Other Elect.	7.9%
Computer Software and Services	7.7%
Industrial/Energy	6.4%
Computer Hardware	5.0%
Communications and Media	2.4%
Other Products	0.7%

Additional Information

Year Founded: 1978
Capital Under Management: $90,000,000
Current Activity Level : Actively seeking new investments
Method of Compensation: Return on investment is of primary concern, do not charge fees

PRISM CAPITAL

444 N. Michigan Avenue
Suite 1910
Chicago, IL 60611
Phone: 312-464-7900
Fax: 312-464-7915
Website: www.prismfund.com

Management and Staff

Byron McCann, Principal
Mark Finkel, Principal
Robert Finkel, President
Ted Feierstein, Principal

Type of Firm

SBIC Not elsewhere classified

Industry Association Membership

Natl assoc of Small Bus. Inv. Co (NASBIC)

Project Preferences

Role in Financing:
Prefer role as deal originator but will also invest in deals created by others

Type of Financing Preferred:
First Stage Financing
Leveraged Buyout
Mezzanine
Second Stage Financing
Special Situation

Geographical Preferences

United States
All U.S.

Industry Preferences

(% based on actual investment)

Computer Software and Services	59.2%
Internet Specific	33.2%
Other Products	5.5%
Consumer Related	2.2%

Additional Information

Name of Most Recent Fund: Prism Opportunity Fund
Most Recent Fund Was Raised: 01/01/1995
Capital Under Management: $50,000,000
Current Activity Level : Actively seeking new investments
Method of Compensation: Return on invest. most important, but chg. closing fees, service fees, etc.

PRODUCTIVITY FUND I & II, THE

The Sears Tower
Suite 9500
Chicago, IL 60606
Phone: 312-258-1400
Fax: 312-258-0334

Type of Firm

Private Firm Investing Own Capital

Project Preferences

Role in Financing:
Prefer role as deal originator but will also invest in deals created by others

Type of Financing Preferred:
First Stage Financing
Second Stage Financing

Size of Investments Considered

Min Size of Investment Considered (000s): $500
Max Size of Investment Considered (000s): $1,000

Geographical Preferences

International
No Preference

Industry Preferences

Communications and Media
Commercial Communications
Telecommunications
Data Communications
Satellite Microwave Comm.
Other Communication Prod.

Computer Hardware
Computers
Mini and Personal/Desktop
Computer Graphics and Dig
Integrated Turnkey System
Disk Relat. Memory Device

Computer Software
Computer Services
Systems Software
Applications Software
Artificial Intelligence

Semiconductors/Other Elect.
Electronic Components
Sensors

Consumer Related
Food/Beverage
Consumer Products
Consumer Services

Industrial/Energy
Alternative Energy
Industrial Products
Materials
Robotics
Environmental Related

Manufact.
Office Automation Equipmt

Additional Information

Name of Most Recent Fund: The Productivity Fund III
Most Recent Fund Was Raised: 09/01/1995
Year Founded: 1985
Capital Under Management: $80,000,000
Current Activity Level : Actively seeking new investments
Method of Compensation: Return on investment is of primary concern, do not charge fees

PROSPECT PARTNERS LLC (FKA:KENTER, GLATRIS & TUTTLE, LLC

70 West Madison Street
Suite 2730
Chicago, IL 60602
Phone: 312-782-7400
Fax: 312-782-7410

Type of Firm

Private Firm Investing Own Capital

Project Preferences

Role in Financing:
Prefer role as deal originator

Type of Financing Preferred:
Industry Rollups
Leveraged Buyout
Special Situation

Geographical Preferences

United States
All U.S.

Canada
All Canada

Industry Preferences

Medical/Health
Other Therapeutic
Disposable Med. Products
Hospital/Other Instit.

Consumer Related
Entertainment and Leisure
Food/Beverage
Consumer Products
Education Related

Industrial/Energy
Industrial Products
Machinery

Business Serv.
Consulting Services

Agr/Forestr/Fish
Agriculture related

Additional Information

Name of Most Recent Fund: Prospect Partners, L.P.
Most Recent Fund Was Raised: 08/18/1998
Year Founded: 1996
Capital Under Management: $105,000,000
Current Activity Level : Actively seeking new investments
Method of Compensation: Return on invest. most important, but chg. closing fees, service fees, etc.

RIDGE CAPITAL PARTNERS, L.L.C.

257 East Main Street
Suite 300
Barrington, IL 60010
Phone: 847-381-2510
Fax: 847-381-2599

Management and Staff

J. Bradley Davis
Ross M. Posner

Whom to Contact

J. Bradley Davis
Ross M. Posner

Type of Firm

Investment/Merchant Bank Subsid/Affil

Project Preferences

Role in Financing:
Prefer role as deal originator

Type of Financing Preferred:
Leveraged Buyout
Special Situation

Size of Investments Considered
Min Size of Investment Considered (000s): $6,000
Max Size of Investment Considered: No Limit

Geographical Preferences

United States
All U.S.

Canada
All Canada

Industry Preferences

Communications and Media
Commercial Communications
Satellite Microwave Comm.

Internet Specific
Internet

Semiconductors/Other Elect.
Electronic Components
Sensors
Component Testing Equipmt
Analytic/Scientific

Medical/Health
Diagnostic Test Products
Medical Products
Disposable Med. Products

Consumer Related
Food/Beverage
Consumer Products
Consumer Services

Industrial/Energy
Industrial Products
Materials
Factory Automation
Robotics
Machinery

Transportation
Transportation

Financial Services
Financial Services
Real Estate

Business Serv.
Consulting Services

Manufact.
Office Automation Equipmt

Agr/Forestr/Fish
Agriculture related

Additional Information
Name of Most Recent Fund: Ridge Capital Fund, L.P.
Most Recent Fund Was Raised: 06/01/1998
Year Founded: 1989
Capital Under Management: $70,000,000
Current Activity Level : Inactive / Unknown
Method of Compensation: Return on invest. most important, but chg. closing fees, service fees, etc.

SBC EQUITY PARTNERS, INC.

One South Wacker Drive
Chicago, IL 60606
Phone: 312-782-2649
Fax: 312-853-8753

Type of Firm
Commercial Bank Affiliate or Subsidiary

Industry Association Membership
Natl assoc of Small Bus. Inv. Co (NASBIC)

Project Preferences

Role in Financing:
Prefer role as deal originator but will also invest in deals created by others

Type of Financing Preferred:
Leveraged Buyout
Mezzanine
Second Stage Financing
Special Situation

Size of Investments Considered
Min Size of Investment Considered (000s): $5,000
Max Size of Investment Considered: No Limit

Geographical Preferences

United States
All U.S.

Industry Preferences

Communications and Media
Communications and Media

Computer Other
Computer Related

Semiconductors/Other Elect.
Electronic Components

Biotechnology
Biotechnology

Medical/Health
Medical/Health

Consumer Related
Consumer
Education Related

Industrial/Energy
Industrial Products

Transportation
Transportation

Business Serv.
Distribution
Consulting Services

Manufact.
Publishing

Additional Information
Year Founded: 1997
Capital Under Management: $50,000,000
Current Activity Level : Actively seeking new investments
Method of Compensation: Return on investment is of primary concern, do not charge fees

---

SEIDMAN, JACKSON, FISHER & CO.

233 North Michigan Avenue
Suite 1812
Chicago, IL 60601
Phone: 312-856-1812

Type of Firm
Private Firm Investing Own Capital

Project Preferences

Type of Financing Preferred:
Later Stage
Leveraged Buyout

Geographical Preferences

International
No Preference

Additional Information
Name of Most Recent Fund: North American Private Equity Fund
Most Recent Fund Was Raised: 01/01/1981
Year Founded: 1981
Current Activity Level : Inactive / Unknown

SERVICEMASTER VENTURE FUND,LLC(FKA:SERVICEMASTER CO.LTD PAR)

1 Servicemaster Way
Downers Grove, IL 60515
Phone: 630-271-2052
Fax: 630-271-5933

Management and Staff
Kenneth Hooten, General Partner

Type of Firm
Non-Financial Corp. Affiliate or Subsidiary

Additional Information

Name of Most Recent Fund: ServiceMaster Venture Fund LLC
Most Recent Fund Was Raised: 01/01/1995
Capital Under Management: $25,000,000
Current Activity Level : Actively seeking new investments

SILICON VALLEY BANK

9701 West Higgins Road
Suite 150
Rosemont, IL 60018
Phone: 847-698-0618
Fax: 847-698-0635

See California for full listing.

SPROUT GROUP

520 Lake Cook road
Suite 450
Deerfield, IL 60015
Phone: 847-940-1735
Fax: 847-940-1724
Website: www.sproutgroup.com

See New York for full listing.

STERLING VENTURE PARTNERS

650 Dundee Road
Suite 370
Northbrook, IL 60062
Phone: 847-480-4000
Fax: 847-480-0199
Website: www.sterlingcap.com

See Maryland for full listing.

SUCSY, FISCHER & CO.

311 South Wacker Drive
49th Floor
Chicago, IL 60606-6622
Phone: 312-554-7575
Fax: 312-554-7501
Website: www.sfco.com

Other Offices

90 State House Square
Hartford, CT 06103-3720
Phone: 203-525-1400
Fax: 203-586-8909

Type of Firm

Mgt. Consulting Firm

Project Preferences

Role in Financing:

Prefer role as deal originator

Type of Financing Preferred:

Leveraged Buyout
Mezzanine
Second Stage Financing
Special Situation

Size of Investments Considered

Min Size of Investment Considered (000s): $50,000
Max Size of Investment Considered: No Limit

Geographical Preferences

United States

All U.S.

Industry Preferences

Communications and Media

Commercial Communications
CATV & Pay TV Systems
Radio & TV Broadcasting
Telecommunications
Data Communications
Satellite Microwave Comm.
Other Communication Prod.

Computer Hardware

Mini and Personal/Desktop
Computer Graphics and Dig
Disk Relat. Memory Device

Computer Software

Computer Services
Systems Software
Applications Software

Internet Specific

Internet

Semiconductors/Other Elect.

Electronics
Electronic Components
Sensors
Circuit Boards
Laser Related
Analytic/Scientific

Biotechnology

Biotechnology

Medical/Health

Medical/Health
Medical Products

Consumer Related

Food/Beverage
Consumer Products

Industrial/Energy

Alternative Energy
Industrial Products
Robotics
Machinery
Environmental Related

Financial Services

Financial Services
Real Estate

Manufact.

Office Automation Equipmt
Publishing

Additional Information

Year Founded: 1972
Current Activity Level : Actively seeking new investments
Method of Compensation: Function primarily in service area, receive contingent fee in cash or equity

THIRD COAST CAPITAL

900 North Franklin Street
Suite 700
Chicago, IL 60610
Phone: 312-337-3303
Fax: 312-337-2567
Website: www.thirdcoastcapital.com

Management and Staff

Kathleen Wilkerson, Managing Director
Miroslav Anic, Managing Director

Type of Firm

Private Equity Advisor or Fund of Fund Mgr

Industry Association Membership

National Venture Capital Association (NVCA)

Project Preferences

Type of Financing Preferred:

Balanced

Size of Investments Considered

Min Size of Investment Considered (000s): $2,000
Max Size of Investment Considered (000s): $5,000

Geographical Preferences

United States
All U.S.

Industry Preferences

Communications and Media
Telecommunications

Semiconductors/Other Elect.
Fiber Optics

Additional Information

Year Founded: 1996
Current Activity Level : Actively seeking new investments

THIRD MILLENNIUM VENTURE CAPITAL, LTD.

5733 West Grover Street
Chicago, IL 60630

See California for full listing.

THOMA CRESSEY EQUITY PARTNERS

Sears Tower, 92nd Floor
233 South Wacker Drive
Chicago, IL 60606
Phone: 312-777-4444
Fax: 312-777-4445
Website: www.thomacressey.com

Other Offices

4050 Republic Plaza
370 Seventeenth Street
Denver, CO 80202
Phone: 303-592-4888
Fax: 303-592-4845

One Embarcadero Centre
Suite 2930
San Francisco, CA 94111
Phone: 415-263-3660
Fax: 415-392-6480

Management and Staff

Bryan Cressey, Partner
Carl Thoma, Managing Partner
D. Chris Osborn, Principal
D. Jean Plessinger, Principal
David Mayer, Principal
Lee Mitchell, Partner
Orlando Bravo, Partner
Robert Manning, Partner
Robert Levin, Principal
William Liebeck, Partner

Type of Firm

Private Firm Investing Own Capital

Industry Association Membership

National Venture Capital Association (NVCA)

Project Preferences

Role in Financing:
Prefer role as deal originator

Type of Financing Preferred:
Early Stage
Later Stage
Leveraged Buyout
Recapitalizations

Geographical Preferences

United States
All U.S.
All U.S.

Canada
All Canada

Industry Preferences

(% based on actual investment)

Computer Software and Services	41.4%
Other Products	36.5%
Internet Specific	13.1%
Medical/Health	7.7%
Consumer Related	1.2%

Additional Information

Name of Most Recent Fund: Thoma Cressey Fund VI, L.P.
Most Recent Fund Was Raised: 05/01/1998
Year Founded: 1981
Capital Under Management: $1,000,000,000
Current Activity Level : Actively seeking new investments
Method of Compensation: Return on invest. most important, but chg. closing fees, service fees, etc.

TRANSCAP ASSOCIATES, INC.

900 Skokie Boulevard
Suite 210
Northbrook, IL 60062
Phone: 847-753-9600
Fax: 847-753-9090

Management and Staff

Ira J. Ederson
Paul D. Schuldiner

Whom to Contact

Ira J. Ederson
Paul D. Schuldiner

Type of Firm

Private Firm Investing Own Capital

Project Preferences

Role in Financing:
Prefer role as deal originator but will also invest in deals created by others

Type of Financing Preferred:
Mezzanine
Second Stage Financing
Special Situation

Size of Investments Considered

Min Size of Investment Considered (000s): $500
Max Size of Investment Considered (000s): $5,000

Geographical Preferences

United States
All U.S.

Industry Preferences

Communications and Media
Other Communication Prod.

Computer Hardware
Computers

Semiconductors/Other Elect.
Electronics
Electronic Components
Sensors

Medical/Health
Other Therapeutic
Medical Products
Disposable Med. Products

Consumer Related
Consumer Products

Industrial/Energy
Industrial Products
Factory Automation
Robotics
Machinery

Additional Information
Name of Most Recent Fund: Transcap Associates, Inc.
Most Recent Fund Was Raised: 01/01/1993
Year Founded: 1991
Capital Under Management: $46,000,000
Current Activity Level : Actively seeking new investments
Method of Compensation: Return on invest. most important, but chg. closing fees, service fees, etc.

TRIBUNE VENTURES

435 North Michigan Avenue
Suite 600
Chicago, IL 60611
Phone: 312-527-8797
Fax: 312-222-5993
Website: www.tribuneventures.com

Other Offices

220 East 42nd Street
Suite 400
New York, NY 10017
Phone: 212-210-5902
Fax: 212-210-1057

Management and Staff
Andy Oleszczuk, President
David Kniffin, Vice President
Donn Davis, President
Lisa Wiersma, Vice President
Randy Glein, Vice President

Whom to Contact
Frances McCaughan

Type of Firm
Non-Financial Corp. Affiliate or Subsidiary

Industry Association Membership
National Venture Capital Association (NVCA)

Project Preferences

Role in Financing:
Will function either as deal originator or investor in deals created by others

Type of Financing Preferred:
Early Stage
Expansion
First Stage Financing
Second Stage Financing
Seed
Startup

Size of Investments Considered
Min Size of Investment Considered (000s): $1,000
Max Size of Investment Considered (000s): $10,000

Geographical Preferences

United States
All U.S.

Industry Preferences

(% based on actual investment)

Computer Software and Services	49.4%
Internet Specific	45.6%
Communications and Media	5.0%

Additional Information
Name of Most Recent Fund: Tribune Ventures
Most Recent Fund Was Raised: 01/01/1998
Year Founded: 1992
Capital Under Management: $100,000,000
Current Activity Level : Actively seeking new investments

TRIDENT CAPITAL

190 South LaSalle Street
Suite 2760
Chicago, IL 60603
Phone: 312-630-5500
Fax: 312-630-5501
Website: www.tridentcap.com

See California for full listing.

VECTOR FUND MANAGEMENT, L.P. (FKA: VECTOR SECURITIES)

1751 Lake Cook Road
Third Floor
Deerfield, IL 60015
Phone: 847-374-3946
Fax: 847-374-3899
Website: www.vectorfund.com

Management and Staff
Barclay Phillips, Managing Director
Douglas Reed, Managing Director
James Foght, President
K. Flynn McDonald, Vice President
Mark Flower, Chief Financial Officer
Peter Shagory, Vice President
Ranjan Lal, Managing Director
Theodore Berghorst, Chairman & CEO

Type of Firm
Private Firm Investing Own Capital

Project Preferences

Role in Financing:
Prefer role as deal originator but will also invest in deals created by others

Type of Financing Preferred:
Mezzanine
Special Situation

Geographical Preferences

International
No Preference

Industry Preferences

(% based on actual investment)

Medical/Health	44.7%
Biotechnology	29.9%
Computer Software and Services	19.5%
Consumer Related	3.2%
Internet Specific	2.7%

Additional Information
Year Founded: 1994
Capital Under Management: $240,100,000
Current Activity Level : Actively seeking new investments
Method of Compensation: Return on investment is of primary concern, do not charge fees

VENTANA FINANCIAL RESOURCES, INC.

249 Market Square
Lake Forest, IL 60045
Phone: 847-234-3434

Type of Firm
Mgt. Consulting Firm

Project Preferences

Role in Financing:
Prefer role as deal originator but will also invest in deals created by others

Type of Financing Preferred:
First Stage Financing
Leveraged Buyout
Mezzanine
Research and Development
Second Stage Financing
Seed
Start-up Financing

Size of Investments Considered
Min Size of Investment Considered (000s): $5,000
Max Size of Investment Considered: No Limit

Geographical Preferences

United States
Midwest
Southeast
Southwest

Industry Preferences

Communications and Media
Telecommunications
Data Communications
Satellite Microwave Comm.

Computer Hardware
Computers
Mini and Personal/Desktop
Computer Graphics and Dig
Disk Relat. Memory Device

Computer Software
Computer Services
Systems Software
Applications Software
Artificial Intelligence

Semiconductors/Other Elect.
Electronic Components
Semiconductor
Circuit Boards
Component Testing Equipmt
Laser Related
Fiber Optics
Analytic/Scientific

Biotechnology
Biosensors
Biotech Related Research
Biotech Related Research

Medical/Health
Medical/Health
Medical Diagnostics
Medical Therapeutics
Medical Products

Consumer Related
Entertainment and Leisure
Retail
Franchises(NEC)
Food/Beverage
Consumer Products
Consumer Services
Hotels and Resorts

Industrial/Energy
Alternative Energy
Energy Conservation Relat
Industrial Products
Materials
Factory Automation
Robotics
Machinery
Environmental Related

Manufact.
Office Automation Equipmt

Additional Information
Year Founded: 1984
Current Activity Level : Actively seeking new investments
Method of Compensation: Function primarily in service area, receive contingent fee in cash or equity

---

WALNUT CAPITAL CORP.

333 West Wacker Drive
Suite 2700
Chicago, IL 60606
Phone: 312-984-3100

See Virginia for full listing.

WILLIAM BLAIR CAPITAL PARTNERS

222 West Adams Street
Suite 1300
Chicago, IL 60606
Phone: 312-364-8250
Fax: 312-236-1042
Website: www.wmblair.com

Management and Staff
David Chandler, Managing Director
Edgar Jannotta, Managing Director
Ellen Carnahan-Walsh, Managing Director
Gregg Newmark, Managing Director
Ian Larkin, Managing Director
James Denny, Managing Director
Larry Shagrin, Managing Director
Mio Stojkovich, Vice President
Robert Blank, Managing Director
Thomas Theobald, Managing Director
Timothy Murray, Managing Director

Whom to Contact
Maureen Naddy

Type of Firm
Private Firm Investing Own Capital

Industry Association Membership
Natl assoc of Small Bus. Inv. Co (NASBIC)

Project Preferences

Role in Financing:
Prefer role as deal originator but will also invest in deals created by others

Type of Financing Preferred:
Acquisition
Early Stage
First Stage Financing
Leveraged Buyout

Size of Investments Considered
Min Size of Investment Considered (000s): $5,000
Max Size of Investment Considered: No Limit

Geographical Preferences

United States
Mid Atlantic
Midwest
Northeast

Industry Preferences

(% based on actual investment)

Consumer Related	22.9%
Internet Specific	15.8%
Computer Software and Services	15.1%
Medical/Health	14.4%
Other Products	10.8%
Biotechnology	10.2%
Communications and Media	5.7%
Computer Hardware	4.2%
Industrial/Energy	0.7%
Semiconductors/Other Elect.	0.2%

Additional Information

Name of Most Recent Fund: William Blair Capital Partners fund
Most Recent Fund Was Raised: 07/01/1998
Year Founded: 1981
Capital Under Management: $670,000,000
Current Activity Level : Actively seeking new investments
Method of Compensation: Return on investment is of primary concern, do not charge fees

WILLIS STEIN & PARTNERS

227 West Monroe Street
Suite 4300
Chicago, IL 60606
Phone: 312-422-2400
Fax: 312-422-2424
Website: www.willisstein.com

Management and Staff

Avy Stein, Managing Partner
Beth Johnston, Managing Director
Bradley Shisler, Vice President
Christopher Boehm, Vice President
Daniel Gill, Managing Director
Daniel Blumenthal, Managing Director
Ian Kirson, Vice President
Jeffrey Beyer, Vice President
John Willis, Managing Partner
Mark Michaels, Managing Director
R. Jason Weller, Managing Director
Robert Froetscher, Managing Director
Todd Smith, Chief Financial Officer

Type of Firm

Private Firm Investing Own Capital

Industry Association Membership

National Venture Capital Association (NVCA)

Project Preferences

Role in Financing:

Prefer role as deal originator

Type of Financing Preferred:

Control-block Purchases
Industry Rollups
Leveraged Buyout
Special Situation

Geographical Preferences

United States

All U.S.
All U.S.

Industry Preferences

(% based on actual investment)

Other Products	29.8%
Communications and Media	25.2%
Consumer Related	22.9%
Computer Software and Services	9.5%
Medical/Health	5.4%
Internet Specific	4.3%
Industrial/Energy	2.8%

Additional Information

Name of Most Recent Fund: Willis Stein & Partners II, L.P.
Most Recent Fund Was Raised: 01/01/1998
Year Founded: 1995
Capital Under Management: $2,900,000,000
Current Activity Level : Actively seeking new investments
Method of Compensation: Return on investment is of primary concern, do not charge fees

WIND POINT PARTNERS

676 North Michigan Ave
Suite 330
Chicago, IL 60611
Phone: 312-649-4000
Website: www.wppartners.com

See Michigan for full listing.

INDIANA

1ST SOURCE CAPITAL CORP.

100 North Michigan Street
P.O.Box 1602; South Bend 46634
South Bend, IN 46601
Phone: 219-235-2180
Fax: 219-235-2227
Website: www.1stsource.com

Other Offices

100 North Michigan Street
P.O. Box 1602
South Bend, IN 46634
Phone: 219-235-2180
Fax: 219-235-2719

Management and Staff
Eugene Cavanaugh, Vice President

Whom to Contact
Eugene Cavanaugh

Type of Firm
SBIC Not elsewhere classified

Industry Association Membership
Natl assoc of Small Bus. Inv. Co (NASBIC)

Project Preferences

Role in Financing:
Prefer role in deals created by others

Type of Financing Preferred:
Leveraged Buyout
Mezzanine
Second Stage Financing
Special Situation

Size of Investments Considered
Min Size of Investment Considered (000s): $300
Max Size of Investment Considered (000s): $500

Geographical Preferences

United States
Midwest

Industry Preferences

Communications and Media
Commercial Communications
Telecommunications
Data Communications
Other Communication Prod.

Computer Hardware
Integrated Turnkey System

Computer Software
Systems Software
Applications Software

Semiconductors/Other Elect.
Electronics
Electronic Components
Sensors
Component Testing Equipmt

Medical/Health
Medical Diagnostics
Diagnostic Services
Diagnostic Test Products
Medical Therapeutics
Other Therapeutic
Medical Products
Disposable Med. Products

Consumer Related
Entertainment and Leisure
Consumer Products

Industrial/Energy
Alternative Energy
Industrial Products
Factory Automation
Robotics
Machinery
Environmental Related

Transportation
Transportation

Additional Information
Name of Most Recent Fund: 1ST Source Capital Corporation
Most Recent Fund Was Raised: 06/01/1984
Year Founded: 1983
Capital Under Management: $2,500,000
Current Activity Level : Actively seeking new investments
Method of Compensation: Return on investment is of primary concern, do not charge fees

CAMBRIDGE VENTURE PARTNERS

4181 East 96th Street
Suite 200
Indianapolis, IN 46240
Phone: 317-814-6192
Fax: 317-844-9815

Management and Staff
Carrie Walkup, Partner
Jean Wojtowics, President
Ted Englehart, Partner

Whom to Contact
Carrie Walkup
Jean Wojtowicz

Type of Firm
SBIC Not elsewhere classified

Industry Association Membership
Natl assoc of Small Bus. Inv. Co (NASBIC)

Project Preferences

Role in Financing:
Prefer role as deal originator but will also invest in deals created by others

Type of Financing Preferred:
Leveraged Buyout
Mezzanine
Second Stage Financing

Geographical Preferences

United States
Midwest

Additional Information
Name of Most Recent Fund: Cambridge Venture Partners
Most Recent Fund Was Raised: 01/01/1982
Year Founded: 1991
Capital Under Management: $6,700,000
Current Activity Level : Actively seeking new investments
Method of Compensation: Return on invest. most important, but chg. closing fees, service fees, etc.

CARDINAL VENTURES, L.L.C.

8910 Purdue Road
Suite 690
Indianapolis, IN 46268
Phone: 317-228-5070
Fax: 317-228-5080

Type of Firm
Private Firm Investing Own Capital

Project Preferences

Role in Financing:
Prefer role as deal originator but will also invest in deals created by others

Type of Financing Preferred:
Control-block Purchases
First Stage Financing
Leveraged Buyout
Second Stage Financing
Special Situation
Start-up Financing

Size of Investments Considered
Min Size of Investment Considered (000s): $2,000
Max Size of Investment Considered: No Limit

Geographical Preferences
United States
Midwest

Industry Preferences
Communications and Media
CATV & Pay TV Systems
Radio & TV Broadcasting
Telecommunications
Satellite Microwave Comm.

Semiconductors/Other Elect.
Sensors

Medical/Health
Diagnostic Services
Disposable Med. Products

Consumer Related
Entertainment and Leisure
Retail
Food/Beverage
Consumer Products
Consumer Services
Education Related

Industrial/Energy
Materials
Machinery

Financial Services
Financial Services

Additional Information
Year Founded: 1993
Capital Under Management: $10,000,000
Current Activity Level : Actively seeking new investments
Method of Compensation: Return on investment is of primary concern, do not charge fees

CID EQUITY PARTNERS

One American Square
Suite 2850 Box 82074
Indianapolis, IN 46282
Phone: 317-269-2350
Fax: 317-269-2355
Website: www.cidequity.com

Other Offices

41 South High Street
Suite 3650
Columbus, OH 43215
Phone: 614-222-8185
Fax: 614-222-8190

Two North Lasalle
Suite 1705
Chicago, IL 60602
Phone: 312-578-5350
Fax: 312-578-5358

Management and Staff
G. Cook Jordon, General Partner
Greg Tobin, Principal
James Philipkosky, General Partner
John Aplin, Managing General Partner
John Hackett, Managing General Partner
Kevin Sheehan, General Partner
Robert O'Brien, General Partner
Scot Swerberg, Principal
William Harlan, Principal

Whom to Contact
Chris Gough
Scot Swenberg

Type of Firm
Private Firm Investing Own Capital

Industry Association Membership
Natl assoc of Small Bus. Inv. Co (NASBIC)

Project Preferences
Role in Financing:
Prefer role as deal originator but will also invest in deals created by others

Type of Financing Preferred:
Early Stage
First Stage Financing
Industry Rollups
Leveraged Buyout
Mezzanine
Second Stage Financing
Special Situation
Start-up Financing

Size of Investments Considered
Min Size of Investment Considered (000s): $1,000
Max Size of Investment Considered: No Limit

Geographical Preferences
United States
Midwest
Rocky Mountain

Industry Preferences
(% based on actual investment)

Computer Software and Services	40.7%
Other Products	23.4%
Medical/Health	11.3%
Consumer Related	6.0%
Computer Hardware	4.4%
Industrial/Energy	3.8%
Communications and Media	3.6%
Internet Specific	3.6%
Biotechnology	2.3%
Semiconductors/Other Elect.	1.0%

Additional Information
Name of Most Recent Fund: CID Mezzanine Capital, L.P.
Most Recent Fund Was Raised: 02/01/1998
Year Founded: 1981
Capital Under Management: $96,400,000
Current Activity Level : Actively seeking new investments
Method of Compensation: Return on investment is of primary concern, do not charge fees

CIRCLE VENTURES, INC.

26 North Arsenal Avenue
Indianapolis, IN 46201
Phone: 317-636-7242
Fax: 317-637-7581

Other Offices

26 North Arsenal Avenue
Indianapolis, IN 46201
Phone: 317-636-7242
Fax: 317-637-7581

Management and Staff
Alessandro Piol
Howard Goldstein
John Evans
Parag Saxena

Whom to Contact
Alessandro Piol
Howard Goldstein
John Evans
Parag Saxena

Type of Firm
Private Firm Investing Own Capital

Industry Association Membership
Natl assoc of Small Bus. Inv. Co (NASBIC)

Project Preferences

Role in Financing:
Prefer role as deal originator but will also invest in deals created by others

Type of Financing Preferred:
Leveraged Buyout
Second Stage Financing
Special Situation

Size of Investments Considered
Min Size of Investment Considered (000s): $10,200
Max Size of Investment Considered: No Limit

Geographical Preferences

United States
All U.S.

International
Bermuda
China
France
Germany
Italy
South Africa
Spain
United Kingdom

Industry Preferences

Communications and Media
Data Communications
Satellite Microwave Comm.

Computer Software
Computer Services
Systems Software
Applications Software

Internet Specific
Internet

Semiconductors/Other Elect.
Semiconductor
Analytic/Scientific

Biotechnology
Biotech Related Research
Biotech Related Research

Medical/Health
Diagnostic Services
Medical Therapeutics
Drug/Equipmt Delivery
Medical Products

Consumer Related
Retail
Consumer Products

Industrial/Energy
Industrial Products

Additional Information
Name of Most Recent Fund: Chancellor Private Capital
Most Recent Fund Was Raised: 01/01/1997
Year Founded: 1982
Capital Under Management: $1,500,000,000
Current Activity Level : Actively seeking new investments
Method of Compensation: Return on invest. most important, but chg. closing fees, service fees, etc.

GAZELLE TECHVENTURES

6325 Digital Way
Suite 460
Indianapolis, IN 46278
Phone: 317-275-6800
Fax: 317-275-1101
Website: www.gazellevc.com

Management and Staff
Don Aquilano, Managing Director

Type of Firm
Private Firm Investing Own Capital

Project Preferences

Type of Financing Preferred:
Early Stage
Later Stage

Size of Investments Considered
Min Size of Investment Considered (000s): $2,000
Max Size of Investment Considered (000s): $2,000

Geographical Preferences

United States
Indiana

Additional Information
Year Founded: 2000
Capital Under Management: $60,000,000
Current Activity Level : Actively seeking new investments

IRWIN VENTURES LLC (FKA: IRWIN VENTURES INCORPORATED)

500 Washington Street
Columbus, IN 47202
Phone: 812-373-1434
Fax: 812-376-1709
Website: www.irwinventures.com

Management and Staff
Greg Ehlinger, Chief Financial Officer
Thomas Washburn, President

Type of Firm
Commercial Bank Affiliate or Subsidiary

Industry Association Membership
National Venture Capital Association (NVCA)
Natl assoc of Small Bus. Inv. Co (NASBIC)

Project Preferences

Role in Financing:
Will function either as deal originator or investor in deals created by others

Type of Financing Preferred:
Early Stage
First Stage Financing

Size of Investments Considered
Min Size of Investment Considered (000s): $750
Max Size of Investment Considered (000s): $1,250

Geographical Preferences

United States
Northeast
Northern California
Northwest

Industry Preferences

Internet Specific
Internet

Financial Services
Financial Services

Additional Information
Year Founded: 1999
Capital Under Management: $20,000,000
Current Activity Level : Actively seeking new investments
Method of Compensation: Return on investment is of primary concern, do not charge fees

LINCOLN INVESTMENT MANAGEMENT INC.

200 East Berry Street
Fort Wayne, IN 46802
Phone: 219-455-6275
Fax: 219-455-5499

Management and Staff
David Patch

Whom to Contact
David Patch

Type of Firm
Insurance Firm Affiliate or Subsidiary

Project Preferences

Role in Financing:
Prefer role as deal originator but will also invest in deals created by others

Type of Financing Preferred:
Control-block Purchases
Leveraged Buyout
Mezzanine
Second Stage Financing
Special Situation

Geographical Preferences

United States
All U.S.

Industry Preferences

Communications and Media
CATV & Pay TV Systems
Radio & TV Broadcasting

Semiconductors/Other Elect.
Sensors
Component Testing Equipmt
Analytic/Scientific

Consumer Related
Entertainment and Leisure
Retail
Franchises(NEC)
Food/Beverage
Consumer Products
Consumer Services
Other Restaurants

Industrial/Energy
Alternative Energy
Coal Related
Energy Conservation Relat
Factory Automation
Machinery
Environmental Related

Business Serv.
Distribution

Agr/Forestr/Fish
Mining and Minerals

Additional Information
Name of Most Recent Fund: Lincoln National Mezzanine Funds, L.P.
Most Recent Fund Was Raised: 01/01/1993
Year Founded: 1903
Capital Under Management: $10,000,000
Current Activity Level : Inactive / Unknown
Method of Compensation: Return on invest. most important, but chg. closing fees, service fees, etc.

MONUMENT ADVISORS, INC

BankOne Center/Circle
111 Monument Circle, Suite 600
Indianapolis, IN 46204-5172
Phone: 317-656-5065
Fax: 317-656-5060
Website: www.monumentadv.com

Management and Staff
Bernie Boldt, Managing Director
Joe Schaffer, Managing Director
John Cory, Managing Director
Larry Wechter, Chief Executive Officer

Whom to Contact
Brian S. Williams
Otto N. Freazel IV

Type of Firm
Investment/Merchant Bank Subsid/Affil

Project Preferences

Role in Financing:
Prefer role as deal originator but will also invest in deals created by others

Type of Financing Preferred:
Balanced
Leveraged Buyout
Management Buyouts
Mezzanine

Size of Investments Considered
Min Size of Investment Considered (000s): $500
Max Size of Investment Considered (000s): $7,000

Geographical Preferences

United States
Midwest
Southeast

Industry Preferences

Business Serv.
Services
Distribution

Manufact.
Manufacturing

Additional Information
Name of Most Recent Fund: Monument Capital Partners I
Most Recent Fund Was Raised: 10/01/1997
Year Founded: 1997
Capital Under Management: $35,600,000
Current Activity Level : Actively seeking new investments
Method of Compensation: Return on invest. most important, but chg. closing fees, service fees, etc.

MWV CAPITAL PARTNERS (FKA:MIDDLEWEST VENTURES, L.P.)

201 North Illinois Street
Suite 300
Indianapolis, IN 46204
Phone: 317-237-2323
Fax: 317-237-2325
Website: www.mwvcapital.com

Management and Staff
H. Garth Dickey, Managing Director
Scott Lutzke, Managing Director
Tom Hiatt, Managing Director

Whom to Contact
Garth Dickey
Scott Lutzke
Thomas A. Hiatt

Type of Firm
Private Firm Investing Own Capital

Industry Association Membership
Natl assoc of Small Bus. Inv. Co (NASBIC)

Project Preferences

Role in Financing:
Will function either as deal originator or investor in deals created by others

Type of Financing Preferred:
Balanced
Later Stage
Second Stage Financing

Size of Investments Considered
Min Size of Investment Considered (000s): $1,000
Max Size of Investment Considered (000s): $5,000

Geographical Preferences

United States
Midwest

Industry Preferences

Communications and Media
Commercial Communications
Radio & TV Broadcasting
Telecommunications
Wireless Communications
Data Communications
Satellite Microwave Comm.
Other Communication Prod.

Computer Hardware
Mini and Personal/Desktop
Computer Graphics and Dig

Computer Software
Computer Services
Data Processing
Software
Systems Software
Applications Software
Artificial Intelligence

Internet Specific
E-Commerce Technology
Internet
Web Aggregration/Portals

Semiconductors/Other Elect.
Electronic Components
Controllers and Sensors
Sensors
Component Testing Equipmt
Laser Related
Fiber Optics
Analytic/Scientific

Biotechnology
Human Biotechnology
Industrial Biotechnology
Biosensors
Biotech Related Research
Biotech Related Research

Medical/Health
Medical Diagnostics
Diagnostic Services
Diagnostic Test Products
Medical Therapeutics
Drug/Equipmt Delivery
Medical Products
Disposable Med. Products
Health Services
Hospitals/Clinics/Primary

Industrial/Energy
Industrial Products
Superconductivity
Factory Automation
Process Control

Transportation
Aerospace

Financial Services
Financial Services
Insurance

Business Serv.
Services
Distribution
Media

Manufact.
Manufacturing

Utilities
Utilities

Other
Socially Responsible
Environment Responsible
Women/Minority-Owned Bus.

Additional Information
Name of Most Recent Fund: MWV Capital Partners III, L.P.
Most Recent Fund Was Raised: 01/01/1998
Year Founded: 1985
Capital Under Management: $121,000,000
Current Activity Level : Actively seeking new investments
Method of Compensation: Return on invest. most important, but chg. closing fees, service fees, etc.

IOWA

ALLSOP VENTURE PARTNERS

118 Third Avenue S.E.
Suite 837
Cedar Rapids, IA 52401
Phone: 319-368-6675
Fax: 319-363-9515

Other Offices

2750 First Avenue, N.E.
Suite 210
Cedar Rapids, IA 52402
Phone: 319-363-8971
Fax: 319-363-9519

55 West Port Plaza
Suite 575
St. Louis, MO 63146
Phone: 314-434-1688
Fax: 314-434-6560

7400 College Boulevard
Suite 302
Overland Park, KS 66210
Phone: 913-338-0820
Fax: 913-338-1019

Type of Firm
Private Firm Investing Own Capital

Industry Association Membership
Natl assoc of Small Bus. Inv. Co (NASBIC)

Project Preferences

Role in Financing:
Prefer role as deal originator but will also invest in deals created by others

Type of Financing Preferred:
First Stage Financing
Industry Rollups
Leveraged Buyout
Mezzanine
Second Stage Financing
Special Situation

Size of Investments Considered
Min Size of Investment Considered (000s): $500
Max Size of Investment Considered: No Limit

Geographical Preferences

United States
All U.S.

Industry Preferences

Communications and Media
Commercial Communications
Radio & TV Broadcasting
Telecommunications
Data Communications

Computer Hardware
Computer Graphics and Dig

Computer Software
Computer Services

Semiconductors/Other Elect.
Electronic Components

Medical/Health
Medical/Health

Consumer Related
Entertainment and Leisure
Retail
Food/Beverage
Consumer Products
Consumer Services
Education Related

Industrial/Energy
Industrial Products

Transportation
Transportation

Financial Services
Financial Services

Business Serv.
Distribution

Manufact.
Office Automation Equipmt
Publishing

Additional Information
Name of Most Recent Fund: Marshall
Most Recent Fund Was Raised: 01/01/1997
Year Founded: 1997
Capital Under Management: $5,000,000
Current Activity Level : Actively seeking new investments
Method of Compensation: Return on investment is of primary concern, do not charge fees

BERTHEL FISHER & COMPANY PLANNING, INC.

701 Tama Street
P.O. Box 609
Marion, IA 52302
Phone: 319-497-5700
Fax: 319-497-4244

Management and Staff
Henry Royer, Managing Director
James Thorp, Managing Director

Type of Firm
Investment/Merchant Bank Investing Own or Client Funds

Industry Association Membership
National Venture Capital Association (NVCA)
Natl assoc of Small Bus. Inv. Co (NASBIC)

Project Preferences

Type of Financing Preferred:
Later Stage

Geographical Preferences

United States
Midwest

Additional Information
Name of Most Recent Fund: Berthel Growth & Income Trust
Most Recent Fund Was Raised: 06/30/1997
Capital Under Management: $20,000,000
Current Activity Level : Actively seeking new investments

INVESTAMERICA VENTURE GROUP, INC.

101 Second Street, S.E.
Suite 800
Cedar Rapids, IA 52401
Phone: 319-363-8249
Fax: 319-363-9683

Other Offices

600 East Mason Street
Suite 304
Milwaukee, WI 53202
Phone: 414-276-3839
Fax: 414-276-1885

Commerce Tower
911 Main Street
Kansas City, MO 64105
Phone: 816-842-0114
Fax: 816-471-7339

Management and Staff
David Schroder, President

Whom to Contact
David Schroder
Kevin Mullane
Robert Comey

Type of Firm
Private Firm Investing Own Capital

Industry Association Membership
Natl assoc of Small Bus. Inv. Co (NASBIC)

Project Preferences

Role in Financing:
Prefer role as deal originator but will also invest in deals created by others

Type of Financing Preferred:
First Stage Financing
Leveraged Buyout
Second Stage Financing
Special Situation

Size of Investments Considered
Min Size of Investment Considered (000s): $500
Max Size of Investment Considered (000s): $1,000

Geographical Preferences

United States
All U.S.

Industry Preferences

(% based on actual investment)

Other Products	21.1%
Internet Specific	14.7%
Industrial/Energy	14.4%
Consumer Related	12.4%
Computer Software and Services	8.1%
Computer Hardware	8.0%
Communications and Media	6.0%
Semiconductors/Other Elect.	5.7%
Biotechnology	4.8%
Medical/Health	4.7%

Additional Information
Name of Most Recent Fund: MorAmerica Capital Corporation
Most Recent Fund Was Raised: 01/01/1998
Year Founded: 1959
Capital Under Management: $48,500,000
Current Activity Level : Actively seeking new investments
Method of Compensation: Return on investment is of primary concern, do not charge fees

PAPPAJOHN CAPITAL RESOURCES

2116 Financial Center
Des Moines, IA 50309
Phone: 515-244-5746
Fax: 515-244-2346
Website: pappajohn.com

Other Offices

2116 Financial Center
Des Moines, IA

Management and Staff
Joe Dunham
Matt Kinley

Whom to Contact
Joe Dunham
Matt Kinley

Type of Firm
Mgt. Consulting Firm

Project Preferences

Role in Financing:
Prefer role as deal originator but will also invest in deals created by others

Type of Financing Preferred:
First Stage Financing
Leveraged Buyout
Second Stage Financing
Seed
Special Situation
Start-up Financing

Size of Investments Considered
Min Size of Investment Considered (000s): $500
Max Size of Investment Considered (000s): $1,000

Geographical Preferences

United States
All U.S.

Industry Preferences

(% based on actual investment)

Computer Software and Services	52.6%
Biotechnology	13.6%
Medical/Health	11.8%
Consumer Related	9.9%
Other Products	5.3%
Communications and Media	4.9%
Industrial/Energy	1.2%
Semiconductors/Other Elect.	0.7%

Additional Information
Name of Most Recent Fund: Pappajohn Capital Resources
Most Recent Fund Was Raised: 01/01/1997
Year Founded: 1969
Capital Under Management: $100,000,000
Current Activity Level : Actively seeking new investments
Method of Compensation: Return on investment is of primary concern, do not charge fees

KANSAS

ALLSOP VENTURE PARTNERS

7400 College Boulevard
Suite 302
Overland Park, KS 66210
Phone: 913-338-0820
Fax: 913-338-1019

See Iowa for full listing.

CHILD HEALTH INVESTMENT CORPORATION

6803 W. 64th Street
Suite 208
Shawnee Mission, KS 66202
Phone: 913-262-1436
Fax: 913-262-1575
Website: www.chca.com

Other Offices

541 Main Street
South Weymouth, MA 02190
Phone: 617-337-3449
Fax: 617-337-5938

Management and Staff

Craig Fischer, Chief Financial Officer
Don Black, President

Type of Firm

Non-Financial Corp. Affiliate or Subsidiary

Project Preferences

Role in Financing:
Prefer role in deals created by others

Type of Financing Preferred:
Balanced
Early Stage
First Stage Financing
Seed
Startup

Geographical Preferences

United States
All U.S.

Industry Preferences

(% based on actual investment)

Medical/Health	64.8%
Other Products	12.6%
Internet Specific	8.4%
Biotechnology	8.2%
Computer Software and Services	4.3%
Computer Hardware	1.7%

Additional Information

Name of Most Recent Fund: Child Health Investment I, LLC
Most Recent Fund Was Raised: 01/01/1997
Year Founded: 1992
Capital Under Management: $20,000,000
Current Activity Level : Actively seeking new investments

ENTERPRISE MERCHANT BANK

7400 West 110th Street
Suite 560
Overland Park, KS 66210
Phone: 913-327-8500
Fax: 913-327-8505

Type of Firm

Investment/Merchant Bank Investing Own or Client Funds

Project Preferences

Role in Financing:
Prefer role as deal originator but will also invest in deals created by others

Type of Financing Preferred:
Leveraged Buyout
Mezzanine
Second Stage Financing
Special Situation

Size of Investments Considered

Min Size of Investment Considered (000s): $1,000
Max Size of Investment Considered: No Limit

Geographical Preferences

United States
Midwest

Additional Information

Year Founded: 1995
Capital Under Management: $10,000,000
Current Activity Level : Actively seeking new investments
Method of Compensation: Return on investment is of primary concern, do not charge fees

KANSAS TECHNOLOGY ENTERPRISE CORPORATION

214 SW 6th
First Floor
Topeka, KS 66603-3719
Phone: 785-296-5272
Fax: 785-296-1160
Website: www.ktec.com

Type of Firm

Private Firm Investing Own Capital

Project Preferences

Role in Financing:
Prefer role as deal originator

Type of Financing Preferred:
Research and Development
Seed
Start-up Financing

Size of Investments Considered

Min Size of Investment Considered (000s): $300
Max Size of Investment Considered: No Limit

Industry Preferences

Communications and Media
Communications and Media
Commercial Communications
Telecommunications
Data Communications

Computer Other
Computer Related

Semiconductors/Other Elect.
Electronic Components

Biotechnology
Biotechnology

Medical/Health
Medical/Health

Industrial/Energy
Alternative Energy
Industrial Products

Additional Information

Year Founded: 1987
Capital Under Management: $10,000,000
Current Activity Level : Actively seeking new investments
Method of Compensation: Return on investment is of primary concern, do not charge fees

KANSAS VENTURE CAPITAL, INC.

6700 Antioch Plaza
Suite 460
Overland Park, KS 66204
Phone: 913-262-7117
Fax: 913-262-3509

Management and Staff
John Dalton
Marshall Parker
Thomas Blackburn

Whom to Contact
John Dalton
Marshall Parker
Thomas Blackburn

Type of Firm
SBIC Not elsewhere classified

Industry Association Membership
Natl assoc of Small Bus. Inv. Co (NASBIC)

Project Preferences

Role in Financing:
Prefer role as deal originator but will also invest in deals created by others

Type of Financing Preferred:
First Stage Financing
Leveraged Buyout
Mezzanine
Second Stage Financing

Size of Investments Considered
Min Size of Investment Considered (000s): $1,000
Max Size of Investment Considered: No Limit

Geographical Preferences

United States
Midwest

Industry Preferences

Communications and Media
Communications and Media

Computer Other
Computer Related

Semiconductors/Other Elect.
Electronic Components

Medical/Health
Medical/Health

Consumer Related
Consumer

Industrial/Energy
Industrial Products

Business Serv.
Distribution

Additional Information
Name of Most Recent Fund: Kansas Venture Capital, Inc.
Most Recent Fund Was Raised: 12/10/1999
Year Founded: 1977
Capital Under Management: $15,000,000
Current Activity Level : Actively seeking new investments
Method of Compensation: Return on invest. most important, but chg. closing fees, service fees, etc.

KOCH VENTURES

4111 E. 37th Street North
Wichita, KS 67220
Website: www.kochventures.com

See Arizona for full listing.

KENTUCKY

2ND GENERATION CAPITAL CORP

P.O. Box 1111
Murray, KY 42071
Phone: 270-832-5550
Fax: 615-846-7654
Website: www.2ndgeneration.com

See Tennessee for full listing.

AMT CAPITAL LTD. (AKA: AMT VENTURE PARTNERS, LTD.)

Taylor & Company
1236 Standish Way; P.O. Box 8791
Lexington, KY 40533
Phone: 606-254-9626
Fax: 606- 254-9627
Website: www.amtcapital.com

See Texas for full listing.

CHRYSALIS VENTURES

1650 National City Tower
Louisville, KY 40202
Phone: 502-583-7644
Fax: 502-583-7648
Website: www.chrysalisventures.com

Management and Staff
David Jones, Senior Managing Director
Irving Bailey, Venture Partner
J. David Grissom, Venture Partner
Koleman Karleski, Principal
Michael Gellert, Venture Partner
Robert Saunders, Senior Managing Director

Type of Firm
Private Firm Investing Own Capital

Project Preferences

Role in Financing:
Prefer role as deal originator but will also invest in deals created by others

Type of Financing Preferred:
First Stage Financing
Second Stage Financing
Start-up Financing

Size of Investments Considered
Min Size of Investment Considered (000s): $3,000
Max Size of Investment Considered (000s): $5,000

Geographical Preferences

United States
Midwest
Southeast

Industry Preferences

(% based on actual investment)

Internet Specific	70.9%
Other Products	13.6%
Communications and Media	7.8%
Computer Software and Services	6.8%
Computer Hardware	0.9%

Additional Information
Year Founded: 1994
Capital Under Management: $193,000,000
Current Activity Level : Actively seeking new investments
Method of Compensation: Return on investment is of primary concern, do not charge fees

HUMANA VENTURE CAPITAL

500 West Main Street
Louisville, KY 40202
Phone: 502-580-3922
Fax: 502-580-2051

Other Offices

500 West main Street
Louisville, KY 40202
Phone: 502-580-1663
Fax: 502-580-1690

Management and Staff
George Emont
Thomas Liston

Whom to Contact
George Emont
Thomas Liston

Type of Firm
Private Firm Investing Own Capital

Project Preferences

Role in Financing:
Prefer role as deal originator but will also invest in deals created by others

Type of Financing Preferred:
First Stage Financing
Leveraged Buyout
Mezzanine
Research and Development
Second Stage Financing
Seed
Start-up Financing

Size of Investments Considered
Min Size of Investment Considered (000s): $10,000
Max Size of Investment Considered: No Limit

Geographical Preferences

United States
All U.S.

Industry Preferences

(% based on actual investment)

Medical/Health	44.9%
Internet Specific	20.7%
Computer Hardware	10.6%
Computer Software and Services	9.7%
Biotechnology	8.9%
Other Products	5.0%

Additional Information
Name of Most Recent Fund: Humana Inc.
Most Recent Fund Was Raised: 03/01/1981
Year Founded: 1961
Capital Under Management: $45,000,000
Current Activity Level : Actively seeking new investments
Method of Compensation: Return on investment is of primary concern, do not charge fees

KENTUCKY HIGHLANDS INVESTMENT CORPORATION

362 Old Whitley Road
London, KY 40477
Phone: 606-864-5175
Fax: 606-864-5194
Website: www.khic.org

Type of Firm
Affiliate/Subsidary of Oth. Financial. Instit.

Project Preferences

Type of Financing Preferred:
Second Stage Financing
Special Situation
Start-up Financing

Geographical Preferences

United States
Kentucky

Industry Preferences

Manufact.
Manufacturing

Additional Information

Year Founded: 1968
Capital Under Management: $30,000,000
Current Activity Level : Actively seeking new investments

SUMMIT CAPITAL GROUP

6510 Glenridge Park Place
Suite 8
Louisville, KY 40222
Phone: 713-332-2700
Website: www.summit-cap.com

See Texas for full listing.

LOUISIANA

ADVANTAGE CAPITAL PARTNERS

LLE Tower
909 Poydras Street Suite 2230
New Orleans, LA 70112
Phone: 504-522-4850
Fax: 504-522-4950
Website: www.advantagecap.com

Other Offices

100 North Tampa
Suite 4100
Tampa, FL 33602
Phone: 813-221-8700
Fax: 813-227-7711

1911 Elmore Avenue
Downers Grove, IL 60515
Phone: 630-241-1848
Fax: 630-241-1836

521 Madison Avenue
7th Floor
New York, NY 10119
Phone: 212-893-8600

7733 Forsyth Boulevard
Suite 1850
St. Louis, MO 63105
Phone: 314-725-0800
Fax: 314-725-4265

One Penn Plaza
42nd Floor
New York, NY 10119
Phone: 212-273-7250
Fax: 212-273-7249

Management and Staff
Crichton Brown, Managing Director
David Bergmann, Managing Director
Marc Winthrop, Vice President
Maurice Doyle, Principal
Michael Johnson, Vice President
Scott Zajac, Managing Director
Steven Stull, President
Tate Garrett, Vice President
Tim Cockshutt, Principal

Type of Firm
Private Equity Advisor or Fund of Fund Mgr

Industry Association Membership
National Venture Capital Association (NVCA)

Project Preferences

Role in Financing:
Will function either as deal originator or investor in deals created by others

Type of Financing Preferred:
Early Stage
First Stage Financing
Mezzanine
Second Stage Financing
Seed
Startup

Size of Investments Considered
Min Size of Investment Considered (000s): $1,000
Max Size of Investment Considered (000s): $10,000

Geographical Preferences

United States
Midwest
Northeast
Southeast

Industry Preferences

(% based on actual investment)

Other Products	35.5%
Industrial/Energy	14.5%
Internet Specific	13.7%
Semiconductors/Other Elect.	10.5%
Communications and Media	10.2%
Computer Software and Services	8.4%
Medical/Health	2.9%
Consumer Related	2.5%
Biotechnology	1.8%

Additional Information
Name of Most Recent Fund: Advantage Capital Partners IX Limited Partnership
Most Recent Fund Was Raised: 10/01/1999
Year Founded: 1992
Capital Under Management: $450,000,000
Current Activity Level : Actively seeking new investments
Method of Compensation: Return on invest. most important, but chg. closing fees, service fees, etc.

BANK ONE EQUITY INVESTORS, INC.

451 Florida Street
P.O. Box 1511
Baton Rouge, LA 70821
Phone: 504-332-4421
Fax: 504-332-7377

Management and Staff
Thomas Adamek, President

Whom to Contact
Michael P. Kriby
Philip N. Budd
W. Stephen Keller

Type of Firm
Commercial Bank Affiliate or Subsidiary

Project Preferences

Role in Financing:
Prefer role as deal originator but will also invest in deals created by others

Type of Financing Preferred:
First Stage Financing
Leveraged Buyout
Mezzanine
Second Stage Financing
Special Situation

Size of Investments Considered
Min Size of Investment Considered (000s): $8,000
Max Size of Investment Considered: No Limit

Geographical Preferences

United States
Southeast
Southwest

Industry Preferences

(% based on actual investment)

Computer Software and Services	46.5%
Internet Specific	25.4%
Other Products	16.6%
Consumer Related	4.2%
Medical/Health	3.3%
Industrial/Energy	2.5%
Communications and Media	1.5%

Additional Information
Name of Most Recent Fund: Bank One Equity Investors, Inc.
Most Recent Fund Was Raised: 01/01/1960
Year Founded: 1974
Capital Under Management: $1,200,000,000
Current Activity Level : Actively seeking new investments
Method of Compensation: Return on invest. most important, but chg. closing fees, service fees, etc.

CENTURYTEL INC

100 CenturyTel Drive
Monroe, LA 71203
Phone: 318-388-9000
Website: www.centurytel.com

Management and Staff

R. Stewart Ewing, Jr., Chief Financial Officer

Type of Firm

Private Firm Investing Own Capital

Project Preferences

Type of Financing Preferred:

Balanced

Geographical Preferences

International

All International

Additional Information

Current Activity Level : Actively seeking new investments

NEWTEK CAPITAL

228 St. Charles Avenue
New Orleans, LA 70130
Website: www.newtekcapital.com

See New York for full listing.

MAINE

CEI VENTURES/COASTAL VENTURES LP

2 Portland Fish Pier
Suite 201
Portland, ME 04101
Phone: 207-772-5356
Fax: 207-772-5503
Website: www.ceiventures.com

Management and Staff
Mark Kaplan, Vice President
Nathaniel Henshaw, President

Type of Firm
Non-Financial Corp. Affiliate or Subsidiary

Industry Association Membership
National Venture Capital Association (NVCA)

Project Preferences

Role in Financing:
Will function either as deal originator or investor in deals created by others

Type of Financing Preferred:
Acquisition
Balanced
Early Stage
Expansion
First Stage Financing
Generalist PE
Later Stage
Leveraged Buyout
Management Buyouts
Mezzanine
Private Placement
Recapitalizations
Research and Development
Second Stage Financing
Seed
Special Situation
Startup
Turnaround

Geographical Preferences

United States
Northeast
All U.S.

Industry Preferences

Communications and Media
Communications and Media
Commercial Communications
CATV & Pay TV Systems
Radio & TV Broadcasting
Telecommunications
Data Communications
Satellite Microwave Comm.
Other Communication Prod.

Computer Hardware
Computers
Mainframes / Scientific
Mini and Personal/Desktop
Computer Graphics and Dig
Integrated Turnkey System
Terminals
Disk Relat. Memory Device

Computer Software
Computer Services
Data Processing
Software
Systems Software
Applications Software
Artificial Intelligence

Internet Specific
Internet

Computer Other
Computer Related

Semiconductors/Other Elect.
Electronics
Electronic Components
Semiconductor
Micro-Processing
Controllers and Sensors
Sensors
Circuit Boards
Component Testing Equipmt
Laser Related
Fiber Optics
Analytic/Scientific

Biotechnology
Biotechnology
Industrial Biotechnology
Biosensors
Biotech Related Research
Biotech Related Research

Medical/Health
Medical/Health
Medical Diagnostics
Diagnostic Services
Diagnostic Test Products
Medical Therapeutics
Drug/Equipmt Delivery
Other Therapeutic
Medical Products
Disposable Med. Products
Health Services
Hospitals/Clinics/Primary
Hospital/Other Instit.
Pharmaceuticals

Consumer Related
Consumer
Entertainment and Leisure
Sports
Retail
Computer Stores
Franchises(NEC)
Consumer Products
Consumer Services
Other Restaurants
Hotels and Resorts
Education Related

Industrial/Energy
Energy
Oil and Gas Exploration
Oil & Gas Drilling,Explor
Alternative Energy
Coal Related
Energy Conservation Relat
Industrial Products
Materials
Advanced Materials
Superconductivity
Factory Automation
Process Control
Robotics
Machinery
Environmental Related

Transportation
Transportation
Aerospace

Financial Services
Financial Services
Insurance

Business Serv.
Services
Distribution
Consulting Services
Media

Manufact.
Manufacturing
Office Automation Equipmt
Publishing

Agr/Forestr/Fish
Agribusiness
Agriculture related
Mining and Minerals

Utilities
Utilities

Other
Socially Responsible
Environment Responsible
Women/Minority-Owned Bus.

Additional Information
Name of Most Recent Fund: Coastal Ventures Limited Partnership
Most Recent Fund Was Raised: 06/19/1996
Year Founded: 1994
Capital Under Management: $5,500,000
Current Activity Level : Actively seeking new investments
Method of Compensation: Return on invest. most important, but chg. closing fees, service fees, etc.

COMMONWEALTH BIOVENTURES INC. (CBI)

Four Milk Street
Portland, ME 04101
Phone: 207-780-0904
Fax: 207-780-0913

Other Offices

One Innovation Drive
Worcester, MA 01605
Phone: 508-797-0500

Management and Staff
Gloria Doubleday

Whom to Contact
Gloria Doubleday

Type of Firm
Private Firm Investing Own Capital

Project Preferences

Role in Financing:
Prefer role as deal originator but will also invest in deals created by others

Type of Financing Preferred:
Seed

Geographical Preferences

International
No Preference

Industry Preferences

Biotechnology
Industrial Biotechnology

Medical/Health
Medical Diagnostics
Diagnostic Test Products
Medical Therapeutics
Drug/Equipmt Delivery
Pharmaceuticals

Additional Information
Year Founded: 1987
Capital Under Management: $32,000,000
Current Activity Level : Inactive / Unknown
Method of Compensation: Return on investment is of primary concern, do not charge fees

NORTH ATLANTIC CAPITAL CORP.

Two City Center
Portland, ME 04101
Phone: 207-772-4470
Fax: 207-772-3257
Website: www.northatlanticcapital.com

Other Offices

70 Center Street
Portland, ME 04101
Phone: 207-772-4470

76 St. Paul Street
Suite 600
Burlington, VT 05401
Phone: 802-658-7820
Fax: 802-658-5757

Management and Staff
Albert Coffrin, Vice President
David Coit, President
Gregory Peters, Principal
Kimberley Niles, Chief Financial Officer
Mark Morrissette, Vice President

Type of Firm
Private Firm Investing Own Capital

Industry Association Membership
Natl assoc of Small Bus. Inv. Co (NASBIC)

Project Preferences

Role in Financing:
Prefer role as deal originator but will also invest in deals created by others

Type of Financing Preferred:
First Stage Financing
Leveraged Buyout
Mezzanine
Second Stage Financing

Size of Investments Considered
Min Size of Investment Considered (000s): $1,500
Max Size of Investment Considered: No Limit

Geographical Preferences

United States
Northeast

Industry Preferences

(% based on actual investment)

Other Products	21.6%
Internet Specific	21.1%
Consumer Related	12.4%
Industrial/Energy	11.6%
Communications and Media	10.3%
Medical/Health	9.4%
Computer Software and Services	6.3%
Semiconductors/Other Elect.	4.1%
Computer Hardware	2.0%
Biotechnology	1.3%

Additional Information
Name of Most Recent Fund: North Atlantic Venture Fund II, LP
Most Recent Fund Was Raised: 01/01/1997
Year Founded: 1986
Capital Under Management: $85,000,000
Current Activity Level : Actively seeking new investments
Method of Compensation: Return on invest. most important, but chg. closing fees, service fees, etc.

ZERO STAGE CAPITAL CO., INC.

1 Portland Sqaure
7th Floor
Portland, ME 04112-5480
Phone: 207-879-7868
Fax: 207-761-7085
Website: www.zerostage.com

See Massachusetts for full listing.

MARYLAND

ABELL VENTURE FUND

111 S. Calvert Street
Suite 2300
Baltimore, MD 21202
Phone: 410-547-1300
Fax: 410-539-6579
Website: www.abell.org

Type of Firm
Foundation

Industry Association Membership
Mid-Atlantic Venture Association
National Venture Capital Association (NVCA)

Project Preferences

Role in Financing:
Will function either as deal originator or investor in deals created by others

Type of Financing Preferred:
Early Stage
Expansion
First Stage Financing
Private Placement
Second Stage Financing

Geographical Preferences

United States
Maryland

Industry Preferences

(% based on actual investment)

Internet Specific	52.3%
Semiconductors/Other Elect.	19.5%
Communications and Media	16.9%
Medical/Health	11.3%

Additional Information
Name of Most Recent Fund: Abell Venture Fund
Most Recent Fund Was Raised: 06/01/1998
Year Founded: 1998
Capital Under Management: $25,000,000
Current Activity Level : Actively seeking new investments
Method of Compensation: Return on investment is of primary concern, do not charge fees

ABS VENTURES

One South Street
Suite 2150
Baltimore, MD 21202
Phone: 410-895-3895
Fax: 410-895-3899
Website: www.absventures.com

Other Offices

1 Market Plaza, Steuart Tower
Suite 2400
San Francisco, CA 94105
Phone: 415-217-4260
Fax: 415-217-4266

Management and Staff
Bruns Grayson, Managing Partner
Caley Castelein, Principal
James Shapiro, Partner
Jin Byun, Principal
Philip Black, Partner
Richard Spalding, Partner
Susan Adams, Chief Financial Officer
Virginia Gambale, Partner

Type of Firm
Private Firm Investing Own Capital

Industry Association Membership
Mid-Atlantic Venture Association
National Venture Capital Association (NVCA)

Project Preferences

Role in Financing:
Prefer role as deal originator but will also invest in deals created by others

Type of Financing Preferred:
First Stage Financing
Mezzanine
Second Stage Financing
Start-up Financing

Geographical Preferences

United States
All U.S.

Industry Preferences

(% based on actual investment)

Computer Software and Services	34.0%
Communications and Media	17.0%
Medical/Health	15.6%
Internet Specific	14.1%
Other Products	5.8%
Semiconductors/Other Elect.	3.2%
Biotechnology	3.1%
Computer Hardware	2.6%
Industrial/Energy	2.5%
Consumer Related	2.1%

Additional Information
Name of Most Recent Fund: ABS Ventures IV, L.P.
Most Recent Fund Was Raised: 12/01/1996
Year Founded: 1982
Capital Under Management: $107,000,000
Current Activity Level : Making few, if any, new investments
Method of Compensation: Return on investment is of primary concern, do not charge fees

ADLER & CO.

1122 Kenilworth Drive
Suite 301
Baltimore, MD 21204
Phone: 410-828-6497

See New York for full listing.

AETHER SYSTEMS CAPITAL

11460 Cronridge Drive
Owings Mills, MD 21117
Phone: 410-654-6400
Fax: 410-654-6554
Website: www.aethersystems.com

Management and Staff
David Reymann, Chief Financial Officer
David Oros, Chairman & CEO
George Davis, President
Wayne Jackson, Managing Director

Type of Firm
Non-Financial Corp. Affiliate or Subsidiary

Project Preferences

Type of Financing Preferred:
Balanced

Geographical Preferences

United States
All U.S.

International
All International

Industry Preferences

(% based on actual investment)

Communications and Media	53.4%
Internet Specific	26.7%
Computer Hardware	12.5%
Biotechnology	4.7%

Computer Software and Services 2.7%

Additional Information
Year Founded: 1996
Capital Under Management: $125,000,000
Current Activity Level : Actively seeking new investments

AMERICAN CAPITAL STRATEGIES

2 Bethesda Metro Center
Suite 1400
Bethesda, MD 20814
Phone: 301-951-6122
Fax: 301-654-6714
Website: www.american-capital.com

Management and Staff
Jeffrey MacDowell, Principal
Jen Chang, Chief Financial Officer
Kenneth Jones, Principal
Malon Wilkus, Chairman & CEO

Whom to Contact
John Hoffmire

Type of Firm
Private Firm Investing Own Capital

Project Preferences

Role in Financing:
Prefer role as deal originator but will also invest in deals created by others

Type of Financing Preferred:
Acquisition
Balanced
Control-block Purchases
Industry Rollups
Leveraged Buyout
Recapitalizations
Special Situation

Size of Investments Considered
Min Size of Investment Considered (000s): $20,000
Max Size of Investment Considered: No Limit

Geographical Preferences

United States
All U.S.

Canada
All Canada

International
United Kingdom

Industry Preferences

Communications and Media
CATV & Pay TV Systems
Radio & TV Broadcasting
Telecommunications

Computer Software
Computer Services

Consumer Related
Entertainment and Leisure
Food/Beverage
Consumer Products
Consumer Services

Industrial/Energy
Industrial Products

Business Serv.
Distribution

Manufact.
Office Automation Equipmt

Additional Information
Year Founded: 1986
Capital Under Management: $365,000,000
Current Activity Level : Actively seeking new investments
Method of Compensation: Return on invest. most important, but chg. closing fees, service fees, etc.

ANNAPOLIS VENTURES LLC

151 West St.
Suite 302
Annapolis, MD 21401
Phone: 443-482-9555
Fax: 443-482-9565
Website: www.annapolisventures.com

Management and Staff
Douglas Hickman, President

Type of Firm
Private Firm Investing Own Capital

Industry Association Membership
Mid-Atlantic Venture Association
National Venture Capital Association (NVCA)

Project Preferences

Role in Financing:
Will function either as deal originator or investor in deals created by others

Type of Financing Preferred:
Later Stage

Size of Investments Considered
Min Size of Investment Considered (000s): $2,000
Max Size of Investment Considered (000s): $5,000

Geographical Preferences

United States
Midwest
Northeast
Southeast

Industry Preferences

Communications and Media
Telecommunications
Wireless Communications
Data Communications

Computer Software
Software
Applications Software

Internet Specific
Internet
Web Aggregration/Portals

Biotechnology
Biotech Related Research

Medical/Health
Diagnostic Services
Health Services

Consumer Related
Consumer
Retail
Education Related

Financial Services
Financial Services

Business Serv.
Services

Additional Information
Year Founded: 1999
Capital Under Management: $24,500,000
Current Activity Level : Actively seeking new investments
Method of Compensation: Return on investment is of primary concern, do not charge fees

ANTHEM CAPITAL, L.P.

16 South Calvert Street
Suite 800
Baltimore, MD 21202-1305
Phone: 410-625-1510
Fax: 410-625-1735
Website: www.anthemcapital.com

Other Offices

435 Devon Park Drive
Building 300
Wayne, PA 19087
Phone: 610-254-4164
Fax: 610-975-0355

Management and Staff

C. Edward Spiva, General Partner
Gerald Schaafsma, General Partner
William Gust, Managing Partner
Xander Perry, General Partner

Type of Firm

SBIC Not elsewhere classified

Industry Association Membership

Mid-Atlantic Venture Association
National Venture Capital Association (NVCA)
Natl assoc of Small Bus. Inv. Co (NASBIC)

Project Preferences

Role in Financing:
Prefer role as deal originator but will also invest in deals created by others

Type of Financing Preferred:
First Stage Financing
Mezzanine
Second Stage Financing
Special Situation
Start-up Financing

Size of Investments Considered
Min Size of Investment Considered (000s): $500
Max Size of Investment Considered (000s): $1,000

Geographical Preferences

United States
Mid Atlantic

Industry Preferences

(% based on actual investment)

Computer Software and Services	42.3%
Biotechnology	30.9%
Internet Specific	20.0%
Other Products	3.5%
Industrial/Energy	2.9%
Medical/Health	0.5%

Additional Information

Year Founded: 1994
Capital Under Management: $43,000,000
Current Activity Level : Actively seeking new investments
Method of Compensation: Return on investment is of primary concern, do not charge fees

ARETE CORPORATION

3 Bethesda Metro Centre
Suite 770
Bethesda, MD 20814
Phone: 301-657-6268
Website: www.arete-microgen.com

See New Hampshire for full listing.

BEDFORD CAPITAL CORP.

839 Elkridge Landing Road
Linthicum, MD 21090
Phone: 410-850-0555
Fax: 410-850-0777
Website: www.bedfordnyc.com

See New York for full listing.

BEDROCK CAPITAL PARTNERS

250 West Pratt Street
Suite 1300
Baltimore, MD 21201
Phone: 410-783-4423
Website: www.bedrockcapital.com

See Massachusetts for full listing.

BLUE ROCK CAPITAL

18004 Calico Circle
Olney, MD 20832
Website: www.bluerockcapital.com

See Delaware for full listing.

BOULDER VENTURES, LTD.

4750 Owings Mills Boulevard
Owings Mills, MD 21117
Phone: 410-998-3114
Fax: 410-356-5492
Website: www.boulderventures.com

Other Offices

1941 Pearl Street
Suite 300
Boulder, CO 80302
Phone: 303-444-6950
Fax: 303-444-0267

44 Montgomery Street
Suite 3800
San Francisco, CA 94104
Phone: 415-617-6201
Fax: 415-617-6239

4750 Owings Mills Boulevard
Owings Mills, MD 21117
Phone: 410-998-3114
Fax: 410-356-5492

Management and Staff

Andy Jones, Partner
Josh Fidler, Partner
Kyle Lefkoff, Partner
Larry Macks, Partner
Larry Brenner, Chief Financial Officer
Peter Roshko, Partner

Type of Firm

Private Firm Investing Own Capital

Industry Association Membership

Mid-Atlantic Venture Association
National Venture Capital Association (NVCA)

Project Preferences

Role in Financing:
Will function either as deal originator or investor in deals created by others

Type of Financing Preferred:
Early Stage
Expansion
First Stage Financing
Start-up Financing
Startup

Size of Investments Considered
Min Size of Investment Considered (000s): $2,000
Max Size of Investment Considered (000s): $5,000

Geographical Preferences

United States
All U.S.
Colorado
Mid Atlantic
Northern California

Industry Preferences

(% based on actual investment)

Internet Specific	32.1%
Communications and Media	24.6%
Computer Software and Services	16.3%

Semiconductors/Other Elect.	11.6%
Consumer Related	9.3%
Computer Hardware	3.3%
Medical/Health	1.5%
Other Products	1.4%

Additional Information

Name of Most Recent Fund: Boulder Ventures III
Most Recent Fund Was Raised: 10/19/1999
Year Founded: 1995
Capital Under Management: $242,000,000
Current Activity Level : Actively seeking new investments
Method of Compensation: Return on investment is of primary concern, do not charge fees

BRIDGE PARTNERS, LLC

16 W. Madison Street
Baltimore, MD 21201
Phone: 410-625-0560
Fax: 410-752-2978

Management and Staff

Jim Heerwagen, Managing Partner
O.R. Bengur, Partner

Type of Firm

Private Firm Investing Own Capital

Industry Association Membership

Mid-Atlantic Venture Association

Project Preferences

Type of Financing Preferred:

Early Stage

Geographical Preferences

United States

Mid Atlantic

Industry Preferences

Communications and Media

Communications and Media

Additional Information

Year Founded: 1999
Capital Under Management: $1,000,000
Current Activity Level : Actively seeking new investments

CAMDEN PARTNERS, INC. (FKA: CAHILL, WARNOCK & CO., L.L.C.)

1 South Street
Suite 2150
Baltimore, MD 21202
Phone: 410-895-3800
Fax: 410-895-3805
Website: www.camdenpartners.com

Management and Staff

C. Song, General Partner
Chip Stelljes, Partner
David Warnock, Partner
Edward Cahill, Partner
Richard Johnston, Partner

Type of Firm

Private Firm Investing Own Capital

Project Preferences

Type of Financing Preferred:

Later Stage
Leveraged Buyout

Geographical Preferences

United States

All U.S.

Industry Preferences

(% based on actual investment)

Other Products	30.1%
Medical/Health	29.7%
Internet Specific	18.9%
Computer Software and Services	16.1%
Consumer Related	4.3%
Communications and Media	0.9%

Additional Information

Name of Most Recent Fund: Cahill, Warnock Strategic Partners Fund, L.P.
Most Recent Fund Was Raised: 04/01/1996
Year Founded: 1995
Capital Under Management: $225,000,000
Current Activity Level : Actively seeking new investments

CATALYST VENTURES

1119 St. Paul Street
Baltimore, MD 21202
Phone: 410-244-0123
Fax: 410-752-7721

Other Offices

1119 St. Paul Street
Baltimore, MD 21202
Phone: 410-244-0123
Fax: 410-752-7721

Type of Firm

Private Firm Investing Own Capital

Project Preferences

Role in Financing:

Prefer role as deal originator but will also invest in deals created by others

Type of Financing Preferred:

Research and Development
Seed
Start-up Financing

Size of Investments Considered

Min Size of Investment Considered (000s): $100
Max Size of Investment Considered (000s): $500

Geographical Preferences

United States

Mid Atlantic

Industry Preferences

Communications and Media

Data Communications

Biotechnology

Biosensors
Biotech Related Research
Biotech Related Research

Medical/Health

Medical/Health
Medical Diagnostics
Medical Therapeutics

Additional Information

Name of Most Recent Fund: Catalyst Ventures, Ltd.
Most Recent Fund Was Raised: 09/01/1983
Year Founded: 1988
Capital Under Management: $24,300,000
Current Activity Level : Making few, if any, new investments
Method of Compensation: Return on investment is of primary concern, do not charge fees

DELMAG VENTURES

220 Wardour Drive
Annapolis, MD 21401
Phone: 410-267-8196
Fax: 410-267-8017
Website: www.delmagventures.com

Management and Staff
Denis Seynhaeve, President

Type of Firm
Private Firm Investing Own Capital

Industry Association Membership
Mid-Atlantic Venture Association

Project Preferences

Type of Financing Preferred:
Early Stage
Seed

Size of Investments Considered
Min Size of Investment Considered (000s): $250
Max Size of Investment Considered (000s): $1,000

Geographical Preferences

United States
Mid Atlantic

International
France

Industry Preferences

Communications and Media
Telecommunications
Wireless Communications
Other Communication Prod.

Computer Software
Data Processing
Software
Systems Software
Applications Software

Internet Specific
Internet

Semiconductors/Other Elect.
Fiber Optics

Additional Information
Year Founded: 1994
Capital Under Management: $35,000,000
Current Activity Level : Actively seeking new investments
Method of Compensation: Return on investment is of primary concern, do not charge fees

EMBRYON CAPITAL

7903 Sleaford Place
Bethesda, MD 20814
Phone: 301-656-6837
Fax: 301-656-8056

Management and Staff
Timothy Webb, General Partner

Type of Firm
Private Firm Investing Own Capital

Project Preferences

Role in Financing:
Will function either as deal originator or investor in deals created by others

Size of Investments Considered
Min Size of Investment Considered (000s): $300
Max Size of Investment Considered (000s): $1,000

Additional Information
Year Founded: 1996
Current Activity Level : Actively seeking new investments
Method of Compensation: Return on investment is of primary concern, do not charge fees

GABRIEL VENTURE PARTNERS

130 Admiral Cochrane Drive
Suite 102
Annapolis, MD 21401
Phone: 410-571-7800
Fax: 410-571-7801
Website: www.gabrielvp.com

See California for full listing.

GROTECH CAPITAL GROUP

9690 Deereco Road
Suite 800
Timonium, MD 21093
Phone: 410-560-2000
Fax: 410-560-1910
Website: www.grotech.com

Other Offices

9690 Deereco Road
Suite 800
Timonium, MD 21093
Phone: 410-560-2000
Fax: 410-560-1910

Management and Staff
David Bannister, Managing Director
Deborah Smeltzer, Managing Director
Dennis Shaughnessy, Managing Director
Douglas Schmidt, Partner
Frank Adams, Managing General Partner
Hugh Woltzen, Managing Director
Patrick Kerins, General Partner
Roger Sullivan, Vice President
Stuart Frankel, Managing Director

Type of Firm
Private Firm Investing Own Capital

Industry Association Membership
Mid-Atlantic Venture Association

Project Preferences

Role in Financing:
Prefer role as deal originator but will also invest in deals created by others

Type of Financing Preferred:
Balanced
First Stage Financing
Leveraged Buyout
Mezzanine
Second Stage Financing
Special Situation
Start-up Financing

Geographical Preferences

United States
Mid Atlantic
Southeast

Industry Preferences

(% based on actual investment)

Internet Specific	36.8%
Medical/Health	14.9%
Consumer Related	14.7%
Other Products	13.7%
Computer Software and Services	6.8%
Communications and Media	5.5%
Industrial/Energy	3.5%
Biotechnology	2.6%
Computer Hardware	0.8%
Semiconductors/Other Elect.	0.6%

Additional Information

Name of Most Recent Fund: Grotech Partners V
Most Recent Fund Was Raised: 01/01/1998
Year Founded: 1984
Capital Under Management: $516,000,000
Current Activity Level : Actively seeking new investments
Method of Compensation: Return on invest. most important, but chg. closing fees, service fees, etc.

HRLD VENTURE PARTNERS

7015 Albert Einstein Drive
Columbia, MD 21046
Phone: 443-259-4160

Type of Firm

Private Firm Investing Own Capital

Additional Information

Name of Most Recent Fund: HRLD Venture Partners IV, L.P.
Most Recent Fund Was Raised: 11/09/1999
Capital Under Management: $2,200,000
Current Activity Level : Actively seeking new investments

INTERNET VENTURES SCANDINAVIA A/S

10420 Little Patuxent Parkway
Suite 301
Columbia, MD 21044-3636
Phone: 410 884 1700
Fax: 410 884 6171
Website: www.internetventures.dk

See Foreign Venture Capital Firms for full listing.

KINETIC VENTURES, INC.

Two Wisconsin Circle
Suite 620
Chevy Chase, MD 20815
Phone: 301-652-8066
Fax: 301-652-8310
Website: www.kineticventures.com

Other Offices

The South Terraces
115 Perimeter Center Plaza
Atlanta, GA 30346
Phone: 770-399-1660
Fax: 770-399-1664

Management and Staff

Charles Meyers, Principal
George Levert, Managing Director
Jake Tarr, Managing Director
Nelson Chu, Principal
Todd Klein, Managing Director
William Heflin, Managing Director

Type of Firm

Private Firm Investing Own Capital

Industry Association Membership

Mid-Atlantic Venture Association
National Venture Capital Association (NVCA)

Project Preferences

Role in Financing:

Will function either as deal originator or investor in deals created by others

Type of Financing Preferred:

First Stage Financing
Leveraged Buyout
Second Stage Financing
Start-up Financing

Geographical Preferences

United States

All U.S.

Industry Preferences

(% based on actual investment)

Internet Specific	40.1%
Communications and Media	21.9%
Semiconductors/Other Elect.	19.1%
Industrial/Energy	8.7%
Computer Hardware	4.7%
Computer Software and Services	4.5%
Other Products	0.6%
Medical/Health	0.4%
Biotechnology	0.1%

Additional Information

Name of Most Recent Fund: Kinetic Venture II (FKA: Competitive Advantage Fund II)
Most Recent Fund Was Raised: 12/01/1999
Year Founded: 1983
Capital Under Management: $195,000,000
Current Activity Level : Actively seeking new investments
Method of Compensation: Return on investment is of primary concern, do not charge fees

MARYLAND VENTURE CAPITAL TRUST

217 East Redwood Street
Suite 2200
Baltimore, MD 21202
Phone: 410-767-6361
Fax: 410-333-6931

Other Offices

217 East Redwood Street
Suite 2212
Baltimore, MD 21202
Phone: 410-333-4492
Fax: 410-333-6931

29 West Susquehanna Avenue
Fourth Floor
Baltimore, MD 21204
Phone: 410-828-7292
Fax: 410-828-6084

Type of Firm

Private Firm Investing Own Capital

Industry Association Membership

National Venture Capital Association (NVCA)

Project Preferences

Role in Financing:

Prefer role as deal originator but will also invest in deals created by others

Type of Financing Preferred:

First Stage Financing
Second Stage Financing
Seed
Start-up Financing

Geographical Preferences

United States

Mid Atlantic

Industry Preferences

(% based on actual investment)

Industrial/Energy	30.3%
Medical/Health	18.1%
Other Products	16.2%
Computer Software and Services	16.1%
Semiconductors/Other Elect.	8.8%
Consumer Related	7.0%
Computer Hardware	3.6%

Additional Information
Name of Most Recent Fund: Anthem Capital
Most Recent Fund Was Raised: 09/30/1994
Year Founded: 1990
Capital Under Management: $12,600,000
Current Activity Level : Actively seeking new investments
Method of Compensation: Return on investment is of primary concern, do not charge fees

MATRIX CAPITAL

6701 Democracy Boulevard
Suite 300
Bethesda, MD 20817
Phone: 301-530-0382
Fax: 301-530-3589

See Virginia for full listing.

MMG VENTURES, L.P.

826 East Baltimore Street
Baltimore, MD 21202
Phone: 410-659-7850
Fax: 410-333-2552

Management and Staff
Catherine D. Lockhart

Whom to Contact
Catherine D. Lockhart

Type of Firm
MESBIC not elsewhere classified

Project Preferences

Role in Financing:
Prefer role as deal originator but will also invest in deals created by others

Type of Financing Preferred:
Mezzanine

Geographical Preferences

United States
Mid Atlantic

Industry Preferences

Communications and Media
Commercial Communications
Radio & TV Broadcasting
Telecommunications
Data Communications

Computer Hardware
Computers
Integrated Turnkey System

Computer Software
Computer Services
Systems Software
Applications Software

Internet Specific
Internet

Semiconductors/Other Elect.
Circuit Boards
Fiber Optics

Biotechnology
Biotech Related Research

Medical/Health
Diagnostic Services
Medical Products
Health Services
Hospitals/Clinics/Primary
Hospital/Other Instit.

Consumer Related
Franchises(NEC)
Food/Beverage
Consumer Services
Hotels and Resorts
Education Related

Additional Information
Year Founded: 1996
Capital Under Management: $16,700,000
Current Activity Level : Actively seeking new investments

NEW ENTERPRISE ASSOCIATES

1119 St. Paul Street
Baltimore, MD 21202
Phone: 410-244-0115
Fax: 410-752-7721
Website: www.nea.com

Other Offices

11911 Freedom Drive
One Freedom Square, Suite 1240
Reston, VA 20190
Phone: 703-709-9499
Fax: 703-834-7579

2490 Sand Hill Road
Menlo Park, CA 94025
Phone: 650-854-9499
Fax: 650-854-9397

Management and Staff
Aaron Vermut, Principal
Arno Penzias, Venture Partner
Arthur Marks, General Partner
Arvind Malhan, Principal
C. Richard Kramlich, General Partner
Charles Linehan, Partner
Charles Newhall, General Partner
Eugene Trainor, Partner
Forest Baskett, Venture Partner
Frank Bonsal, Founding Partner
John Nehra, General Partner
Lou Van Dyck, Chief Financial Officer
Mark Perry, General Partner
Nancy Dorman, General Partner
Peter Morris, General Partner
Peter Barris, Managing General Partner
Robert Coneybeer, General Partner
Ronald Kase, General Partner
Ryan Drant, Principal
Scott Sandell, General Partner
Sigrid Van Bladel, Partner
Stewart Alsop, General Partner
Suzanne King, Partner
Thomas McConnell, General Partner

Type of Firm
Private Firm Investing Own Capital

Industry Association Membership
Mid-Atlantic Venture Association
National Venture Capital Association (NVCA)
Natl assoc of Small Bus. Inv. Co (NASBIC)
Western Association of Venture Capitalists (WAVC)

Project Preferences

Role in Financing:
Prefer role as deal originator but will also invest in deals created by others

Type of Financing Preferred:
Early Stage
First Stage Financing
Mezzanine
Second Stage Financing
Seed
Start-up Financing

Size of Investments Considered
Min Size of Investment Considered (000s): $100
Max Size of Investment Considered: No Limit

Geographical Preferences

United States
All U.S.

International
Latin America

Industry Preferences

(% based on actual investment)

Internet Specific	25.3%
Communications and Media	23.2%
Medical/Health	14.9%
Computer Software and Services	13.1%
Semiconductors/Other Elect.	7.0%
Computer Hardware	5.8%
Biotechnology	4.9%
Other Products	2.8%
Consumer Related	2.3%
Industrial/Energy	0.7%

Additional Information

Name of Most Recent Fund: New Enterprise Associates IX
Most Recent Fund Was Raised: 10/01/1999
Year Founded: 1978
Capital Under Management: $4,500,000,000
Current Activity Level : Actively seeking new investments
Method of Compensation: Return on investment is of primary concern, do not charge fees

NEXTREME VENTURES

8400 Baltimore Avenue
Suite 301
College Park, MD 20740
Phone: 301-263-9547
E-mail: maryann@nextremeventures.com
Website: www.nextremeventures.com

See California for full listing.

OPTICAL CAPITAL GROUP

9212 Berger Road
Columbia, MD 21045
Phone: 443-259-0010
Fax: 410-309-4326
Website: www.opticalcapitalgroup.com

Other Offices

One Embarcadero Center
Suite 2405
San Francisco, CA 94111
Phone: 415-393-0791
Fax: 415-393-0801

Management and Staff

Max Straube, President
Michael Joseph, Chief Financial Officer

Type of Firm

Incubators

Project Preferences

Role in Financing:
Will function either as deal originator or investor in deals created by others

Geographical Preferences

United States
All U.S.

International
Asia
Australia
Europe

Industry Preferences

Communications and Media
Telecommunications

Internet Specific
Internet

Additional Information

Current Activity Level : Actively seeking new investments

POTOMAC VENTURES

7920 Norfolk Avenue
Suite 1100
Bethesda, MD 20814
Phone: 301-215-9240
Website: www.potomacventures.com

Management and Staff

John Britti, Partner
Tom Skinner, Partner
Tom Ross, Managing Partner

Type of Firm

Private Firm Investing Own Capital

Industry Association Membership

Mid-Atlantic Venture Association
National Venture Capital Association (NVCA)

Project Preferences

Type of Financing Preferred:
Early Stage

Size of Investments Considered
Min Size of Investment Considered (000s): $400
Max Size of Investment Considered (000s): $1,000

Geographical Preferences

United States
Mid Atlantic

Industry Preferences

Internet Specific
Internet

Additional Information

Capital Under Management: $18,000,000
Current Activity Level : Actively seeking new investments

QUESTMARK PARTNERS, L.P.

One South Street
Suite 800
Baltimore, MD 21202
Phone: 410-895-5800
Fax: 410-895-5808
Website: www.questmarkpartners.com

Management and Staff

Benjamin Schapiro, Partner
Thomas Hitchner, Partner
Timothy Krongard, Chief Financial Officer

Type of Firm

Private Firm Investing Own Capital

Project Preferences

Type of Financing Preferred:
Later Stage
Second Stage Financing

Geographical Preferences

United States
All U.S.

Industry Preferences

(% based on actual investment)

Internet Specific	52.7%
Computer Software and Services	36.4%
Other Products	7.0%
Medical/Health	3.8%

Additional Information

Name of Most Recent Fund: QuestMark Partners L.P.
Most Recent Fund Was Raised: 07/01/1999
Year Founded: 1998
Capital Under Management: $222,000,000
Current Activity Level : Actively seeking new investments

SILICON VALLEY BANK

One Central Plaza, Suite 1205
11300 Rockville Pike
Rockville, MD 20852
Phone: 301-984-4977
Fax: 301-984-6282

See California for full listing.

SPRING CAPITAL PARTNERS, L.P.

16 W. Madison Street
Baltimore, MD 21201
Phone: 410-685-8000
Fax: 410-727-1436
Website: mailbox@springcap.com

Management and Staff
Michael F. Donoghue
Robert M. Stewart

Whom to Contact
Michael F. Donoghue
Robert M. Stewart

Type of Firm
SBIC Not elsewhere classified

Industry Association Membership
Mid-Atlantic Venture Association

Project Preferences

Role in Financing:
Prefer role as deal originator but will also invest in deals created by others

Type of Financing Preferred:
Acquisition
Balanced
Industry Rollups
Later Stage
Leveraged Buyout
Mezzanine
Second Stage Financing

Size of Investments Considered
Min Size of Investment Considered (000s): $2,000
Max Size of Investment Considered: No Limit

Geographical Preferences

United States
Mid Atlantic

Industry Preferences

Communications and Media
Communications and Media
Other Communication Prod.

Computer Other
Computer Related

Semiconductors/Other Elect.
Electronics
Electronic Components

Medical/Health
Medical/Health

Consumer Related
Consumer
Education Related

Industrial/Energy
Industrial Products

Transportation
Transportation

Manufact.
Publishing

Additional Information
Name of Most Recent Fund: Spring Capital Partners, L.P.
Most Recent Fund Was Raised: 08/01/1999
Year Founded: 1999
Capital Under Management: $45,000,000
Current Activity Level : Inactive / Unknown
Method of Compensation: Return on invest. most important, but chg. closing fees, service fees, etc.

STERLING VENTURE PARTNERS

111 South Calvert Street
Suite 2810
Baltimore, MD 21202
Phone: 410-347-2919
Fax: 410-347-3140
Website: www.sterlingcap.com

Other Offices

650 Dundee Road
Suite 370
Northbrook, IL 60062
Phone: 847-480-4000
Fax: 847-480-0199

Management and Staff
Alan Macksey, Principal
Brian Hirsch, Principal
Danny Rosenberg, Principal
Eric Becker, Managing Partner
Michael Bronfein, Managing Partner
Mustafa Chagal, Principal
Sam Beritela, Chief Financial Officer
Scott Schelle, Principal
Stephen Thompson, Principal
Steven Taslitz, Managing Partner

Type of Firm
Affiliate/Subsidary of Oth. Financial. Instit.

Industry Association Membership
Mid-Atlantic Venture Association
National Venture Capital Association (NVCA)

Project Preferences

Type of Financing Preferred:
Early Stage
Leveraged Buyout

Geographical Preferences

United States
Mid Atlantic
Midwest

Industry Preferences

Communications and Media
Telecommunications

Computer Software
Software

Medical/Health
Medical/Health

Consumer Related
Education Related

Business Serv.
Services

Manufact.
Manufacturing

Additional Information
Year Founded: 2000
Capital Under Management: $100,000,000
Current Activity Level : Actively seeking new investments

STEVE WALKER & ASSOCIATES, LLC

3060 Washington Road
Glenwood, MD 21738
Phone: 301-854-6850
Fax: 301-854-6235
Website: ww.stevewalker.com

Management and Staff
Alan Burk, Managing Partner
Gina Dubbe, Managing Partner
Stephen Walker, Principal

Type of Firm
Private Firm Investing Own Capital

Industry Association Membership
Mid-Atlantic Venture Association

Industry Preferences
(% based on actual investment)

Internet Specific	79.5%
Computer Software and Services	9.7%
Other Products	4.5%
Biotechnology	3.2%
Communications and Media	3.1%

Additional Information
Capital Under Management: $50,000,000
Current Activity Level : Actively seeking new investments

T. ROWE PRICE THRESHOLD PARTNERSHIPS

100 East Pratt Street
8th floor
Baltimore, MD 21202
Phone: 410-345-2000
Fax: 410-345-2800

Management and Staff
Al Younger, Chief Financial Officer

Whom to Contact
Terral Jordan

Type of Firm
Affiliate/Subsidary of Oth. Financial. Instit.

Industry Association Membership
Mid-Atlantic Venture Association

Project Preferences
Role in Financing:
Prefer role as deal originator but will also invest in deals created by others

Type of Financing Preferred:
Mezzanine
Special Situation

Size of Investments Considered
Min Size of Investment Considered (000s): $3,000
Max Size of Investment Considered (000s): $5,000

Geographical Preferences
United States
All U.S.

Industry Preferences
(% based on actual investment)

Computer Software and Services	21.8%
Internet Specific	15.3%
Consumer Related	12.9%
Other Products	11.2%
Medical/Health	10.6%
Computer Hardware	8.7%
Communications and Media	6.3%
Semiconductors/Other Elect.	6.3%
Industrial/Energy	4.0%
Biotechnology	2.9%

Additional Information
Name of Most Recent Fund: T. Rowe Price Recovery Fund II
Most Recent Fund Was Raised: 10/18/1996
Year Founded: 1983
Capital Under Management: $245,000,000
Current Activity Level : Actively seeking new investments
Method of Compensation: Return on investment is of primary concern, do not charge fees

TDH

Hampden Square
4800 Montgomery Lane
Bethesda, MD 20814
Phone: 301-718-7353
Fax: 301-913-9615

See Pennsylvania for full listing.

TOUCAN CAPITAL CORP.

3 Bethesda Metro Center
Suite 700
Bethesda, MD 20814
Phone: 301-961-1970
Fax: 301-961-1969
Website: www.toucancapital.com

Other Offices

Warwick House
181/183 Warwick Road
London, United Kingdom W14 8PU
Phone: 44-171-373-8863
Fax: 44-171-373-4626

Management and Staff
Linda Powers, Managing Director
Robert Hemphill, Managing Director

Type of Firm
Private Firm Investing Own Capital

Industry Association Membership
Mid-Atlantic Venture Association
National Venture Capital Association (NVCA)

Project Preferences
Type of Financing Preferred:
Early Stage
Seed
Start-up Financing

Size of Investments Considered
Min Size of Investment Considered (000s): $1,000
Max Size of Investment Considered (000s): $3,000

Geographical Preferences
United States
All U.S.
Northeast

Industry Preferences
Communications and Media
Telecommunications

Internet Specific
Internet

Biotechnology
Biotechnology

Additional Information
Year Founded: 1996
Capital Under Management: $60,000,000
Current Activity Level : Actively seeking new investments

VENTURE MANAGEMENT SERVICES INC. (FKA: AT&T VENTURES)

2 Wisconsin Circle
Suite 610
Chevy Chase, MD 20815-7003
Phone: 301-652-5225
Fax: 301-664-8590
Website: www.vmsgroup.com

See New Jersey for full listing.

MASSACHUSETTS

100 X

880 Winter Street
Suite 300
North Waltham, MA 02451
Phone: 781-529-1000
Fax: 781-529-1098
Website: www.100x.com

Management and Staff
Ken Lang, Chief Executive Officer

Type of Firm
Incubators

Project Preferences

Role in Financing:
Prefer role as deal originator

Type of Financing Preferred:
Early Stage
Seed
Start-up Financing

Industry Preferences

Internet Specific
Internet

Additional Information
Current Activity Level : Actively seeking new investments

3I CAPITAL CORPORATION (US)

99 High Street
Suite 1530
Boston, MA 02110
Phone: 617-542-8560
Fax: 617-542-0394

Type of Firm
Affiliate/Subsidary of Oth. Financial. Instit.

Industry Association Membership
National Venture Capital Association (NVCA)
Natl assoc of Small Bus. Inv. Co (NASBIC)

Project Preferences

Type of Financing Preferred:
Balanced

Geographical Preferences

International
No Preference

Industry Preferences

(% based on actual investment)

Computer Software and Services	20.4%
Semiconductors/Other Elect.	18.6%
Internet Specific	17.5%
Consumer Related	15.2%
Communications and Media	6.9%
Medical/Health	6.1%
Industrial/Energy	5.5%
Computer Hardware	5.0%
Other Products	3.3%
Biotechnology	1.5%

Additional Information
Year Founded: 1982
Capital Under Management: $200,000,000
Current Activity Level : Inactive / Unknown

ADAMS, HARKNESS & HILL, INC.

60 State Street
Boston, MA 02109
Phone: 617-371-3900

Other Offices

One Liberty Square
Boston, MA 02109
Phone: 617-423-6688
Fax: 617-426-8399

Management and Staff
Jay Corscadden, General Partner
Timothy McMahon, President

Whom to Contact
Tim McMahan

Type of Firm
Investment/Merchant Bank Investing Own or Client Funds

Project Preferences

Role in Financing:
Prefer role as deal originator but will also invest in deals created by others

Type of Financing Preferred:
Balanced
Mezzanine
Second Stage Financing
Special Situation

Size of Investments Considered
Min Size of Investment Considered (000s): $1,000
Max Size of Investment Considered: No Limit

Geographical Preferences

United States
Northeast

International
No Preference

Industry Preferences

Communications and Media
Communications and Media

Computer Software
Software

Computer Other
Computer Related

Semiconductors/Other Elect.
Electronic Components

Biotechnology
Biotechnology

Medical/Health
Medical/Health

Consumer Related
Consumer

Industrial/Energy
Industrial Products

Business Serv.
Services

Manufact.
Manufacturing

Additional Information
Year Founded: 1937
Current Activity Level : Inactive / Unknown
Method of Compensation: Function primarily in service area, receive contingent fee in cash or equity

ADVANCED TECHNOLOGY VENTURES

281 Winter Street
Suite 350
Waltham, MA 02451
Phone: 781-290-0707
Fax: 781-684-0045
Website: www.atvcapital.com

Other Offices

485 Ramona Street
Suite 200
Palo Alto, CA 94301
Phone: 650-321-8601
Fax: 650-321-0934

Management and Staff

April Evans, Chief Financial Officer
Jack Harrington, Managing Director
Jos Henkens, Managing Director
Michael Carusi, Managing Director
Michael Frank, Managing Director
Pieter Schiller, Managing Director
Steve Baloff, Managing Director
Wes Raffel, Managing Director

Whom to Contact

Michael Caruci
Steven Baloff

Type of Firm

Private Firm Investing Own Capital

Industry Association Membership

National Venture Capital Association (NVCA)
Western Association of Venture Capitalists (WAVC)

Project Preferences

Role in Financing:

Prefer role as deal originator but will also invest in deals created by others

Type of Financing Preferred:

Balanced
Early Stage
First Stage Financing
Second Stage Financing
Start-up Financing

Size of Investments Considered

Min Size of Investment Considered (000s): $15,000
Max Size of Investment Considered (000s): $35,000

Geographical Preferences

United States

All U.S.

International

Belgium
Israel
Luxembourg
Netherlands

Industry Preferences

(% based on actual investment)

Internet Specific	40.0%
Computer Software and Services	16.6%
Semiconductors/Other Elect.	12.3%
Communications and Media	11.2%
Medical/Health	6.9%
Computer Hardware	5.8%
Biotechnology	4.9%
Industrial/Energy	1.3%
Other Products	1.2%
Consumer Related	0.0%

Additional Information

Name of Most Recent Fund: Advanced Technology Ventures V, L.P.
Most Recent Fund Was Raised: 07/01/1998
Year Founded: 1979
Capital Under Management: $1,500,000,000
Current Activity Level : Actively seeking new investments
Method of Compensation: Return on investment is of primary concern, do not charge fees

---

ADVENT INTERNATIONAL CORP.

75 State Street
29th Floor
Boston, MA 02109
Phone: 617-951-9400
Fax: 617-951-0566
Website: www.adventinternational.com

Other Offices

123 Buckingham Palace Road
London, United Kingdom SW1W 9SL
Phone: 44 20 7333 0800
Fax: 44 20 7333 0801

16th Fl, Unit A, Tower 2
Muang Thai-Phatra, 252/9
Huaykwang, Bangkok, Thailand 10320
Phone: 662-693-2941
Fax: 662-693-2940

2180 Sand Hill Road
Suite 420
Menlo Park, CA 94205
Phone: 650-233-7500
Fax: 650-233-7515

22/F Bapindo Plaza Tower II
Jl. Jend. Sudirman
Kav. 54, Jakarta, Indonesia 12190
Phone: 62-21-526-6845
Fax: 62-21-526-6843

2302D, Philippine Stock Exchange
West Tower, Exchange Rd,
Pasig, Philippines
Phone: 632-638-0403
Fax: 632-638-0408

25 de Mayo 555 24th Floor
1002 Buenos Aires, Argentina
Phone: 541-310-8900
Fax: 541-310-8910

331 North Bridge Road
#05-04/06 Odeon Towers
Singapore, Singapore 188720
Phone: 65-339-9090
Fax: 65-339-8247

55 Avenue Hoche
Paris, France 75008
Phone: 331-5537-2900
Fax: 331-5537-2929

55 Jalan Raja Chulan
15th Floor, Bangunan Ara
Kuala Lumpur, Malaysia 50200
Phone: 603-238-2392
Fax: 603-232-8253

88 Queensway
Suite 1415, 2 Pacific Place
Central, Hong Kong
Phone: 852-2978-9300
Fax: 852-2826-9247

Campos Eliseos 345-4 piso
Col. Polanco, Mexico
Phone: 525-202-6770
Fax: 525-202-7707

Eysseneckstrasse 10
60322
Frankfurt, Germany
Phone: 49-69-955-2700
Fax: 49-69-955-27020

Rua Bandeira Paulista 600, conj.
Sao Paulo, Brazil
Phone: 5511-828-9294
Fax: 5511-820-9610

Via Marina 7
Milan, Italy 20121
Phone: 39 2771.29.81
Fax: 39 277.12.98.88

ul. Emilii Plater 28
Warsaw, Poland 00-688
Phone: 48 22 627-5141
Fax: 48 22 627-5140

Management and Staff
Amos Fleisher, Principal
Andrew Fillat, Managing Director
Ann Capada, Principal
Cheng Guan Loo, Principal
Christopher Pike, Principal
David Mussafer, Managing Director
Derrick Lee, Managing Director
Douglas Kingsley, Managing Director
Ernest Bachrach, Chief Executive Officer
Fawad Zakariya, Principal
Flora Pong, Principal
Francis L.F. Ng, Partner
Gerard Moufflet, Managing Director
Giovanni Galasso, Principal
Greg Smitherman, Principal
Gwendolyn Mogan Phillips, Principal
Hew Chan, Partner
Hoe Kwee, Chief Financial Officer
Jack T.K. Lo, Principal
Jason Fisherman, Partner
Joanna James, Managing Director
John Rockwell, Partner
John Singer, Managing Director
John Brooke, Partner
Juan Zucchini, Principal
Kathleen O'Donnell, Principal
Kevin Chan, Principal
Lawrence McKenna, Partner
Lindsay Jones, Partner
Marcia Hooper, Partner
Massimo Oltramonti, Managing Director
Nicholas Callinan, Managing Director
Olaf Krohg, Partner
Peter Cornetta, Principal
Peter Kucechle, Principal
Raymond Lo, Principal
Robert Byrne, Partner
Robert Taylor, Partner
Shuyi Mo, Principal
Stefano Cassina, Principal
Stephen Kahn, Managing Director
Steven Tadler, Managing Director
Surasawadee Kaewyana, Principal
Tan Boon, Chief Executive Officer
Tom Lauer, Chairman & Managing Director
William Blaz, Vice President
William Schmidt, Managing Director
William Woo, Principal

Whom to Contact
Tan Keng Boon
Will Schmidt

Type of Firm
Private Firm Investing Own Capital

Industry Association Membership
Hungarian Venture Capital Association
National Venture Capital Association (NVCA)
Western Association of Venture Capitalists (WAVC)

Project Preferences

Role in Financing:
Prefer role as deal originator but will also invest in deals created by others

Type of Financing Preferred:
Control-block Purchases
First Stage Financing
Industry Rollups
Leveraged Buyout
Mezzanine
Research and Development
Second Stage Financing
Seed
Special Situation

Size of Investments Considered
Min Size of Investment Considered (000s): $1,000
Max Size of Investment Considered: No Limit

Geographical Preferences

United States
All U.S.
All U.S.

Canada
All Canada

International
All International
South Africa
Western Europe

Industry Preferences

(% based on actual investment)

Other Products	25.1%
Consumer Related	17.4%
Communications and Media	13.3%
Internet Specific	10.4%
Industrial/Energy	8.9%
Medical/Health	8.2%
Semiconductors/Other Elect.	5.7%
Computer Software and Services	5.6%
Biotechnology	3.3%
Computer Hardware	2.2%

Additional Information
Name of Most Recent Fund: Global Private Equity III
Most Recent Fund Was Raised: 01/01/1997
Year Founded: 1984
Capital Under Management: $3,600,000,000
Current Activity Level : Actively seeking new investments
Method of Compensation: Return on investment is of primary concern, do not charge fees

ALTA COMMUNICATIONS

200 Clarendon Street
51st Floor
Boston, MA 02116
Phone: 617-262-7770
Fax: 617-262-9779
Website: www.altacomm.com

Other Offices

One Embarcadero Center
Suite 4050
San Francisco, CA 94111
Phone: 415-362-4022
Fax: 415-362-6178

Management and Staff
Brian McNeill, Managing General Partner
David Retik, General Partner
Eileen McCarthy, Chief Financial Officer
Lane MacDonald, General Partner
Patrick Brubaker, Principal
Phillip Thompson, General Partner
Robert Benbow, General Partner
Robert Emmert, General Partner
Timothy Dibble, Managing General Partner
William Egan, General Partner

Type of Firm
Private Firm Investing Own Capital

Industry Association Membership
National Venture Capital Association (NVCA)

Project Preferences

Role in Financing:
Prefer role as deal originator but will also invest in deals created by others

Type of Financing Preferred:
Acquisition
Early Stage
Expansion
First Stage Financing
Later Stage
Leveraged Buyout
Mezzanine
Recapitalizations
Second Stage Financing
Seed
Special Situation
Startup
Turnaround

Size of Investments Considered
Min Size of Investment Considered (000s): $5,000
Max Size of Investment Considered (000s): $75,000

Geographical Preferences

United States
All U.S.

Canada
All Canada

International
All International

Industry Preferences

(% based on actual investment)

Communications and Media	66.6%
Internet Specific	11.9%
Other Products	7.9%
Computer Software and Services	5.7%
Computer Hardware	2.5%
Biotechnology	1.9%
Consumer Related	1.4%
Semiconductors/Other Elect.	1.3%
Medical/Health	0.9%

Additional Information
Name of Most Recent Fund: Alta Subordinated Debt Partners III
Most Recent Fund Was Raised: 03/15/1993
Year Founded: 1990
Capital Under Management: $1,017,900,000
Current Activity Level : Actively seeking new investments
Method of Compensation: Return on investment is of primary concern, do not charge fees

AMERICAN RESEARCH & DEVELOPMENT CORP.

30 Federal Street
Boston, MA 02110-2508
Phone: 617-423-7500
Fax: 617-423-9655

Other Offices

45 Milk Street
Boston, MA 02109-5173
Phone: 617-423-7500
Fax: 617-423-9655

Management and Staff
Francis Hughes, President

Whom to Contact
Maureen White

Type of Firm
Private Firm Investing Own Capital

Project Preferences

Role in Financing:
Prefer role as deal originator but will also invest in deals created by others

Type of Financing Preferred:
First Stage Financing
Second Stage Financing
Seed
Start-up Financing

Size of Investments Considered
Min Size of Investment Considered (000s): $100
Max Size of Investment Considered: No Limit

Geographical Preferences

United States
Northeast

Industry Preferences

Communications and Media
Telecommunications
Wireless Communications
Data Communications

Computer Hardware
Computer Graphics and Dig

Computer Software
Software

Internet Specific
Internet

Semiconductors/Other Elect.
Electronic Components
Semiconductor
Sensors
Laser Related
Fiber Optics

Additional Information
Name of Most Recent Fund: American Research & Development II
Most Recent Fund Was Raised: 01/01/1988
Year Founded: 1946
Capital Under Management: $25,000,000
Current Activity Level : Actively seeking new investments
Method of Compensation: Return on investment is of primary concern, do not charge fees

AMPERSAND VENTURES

55 William Street
Suite 240
Wellesley, MA 02481
Phone: 781-239-0700
Fax: 781-239-0824
Website: www.ampersandventures.com

Other Offices

162 South Rancho Santa Fe Rd
Suite 870
Encinitas, CA 92024
Phone: 760-632-0626
Fax: 760-632-0284

Management and Staff
Charles Yie, General Partner
David Parker, General Partner
Donald Hawthorne, Chief Financial Officer
K. Kachadurian, General Partner
Paul Zigman, Partner
Peter Parker, General Partner
Richard Charpie, Managing Partner
Samuel Ackerman, General Partner
Stuart Auerbach, General Partner

Type of Firm
Private Firm Investing Own Capital

Industry Association Membership
National Venture Capital Association (NVCA)

Project Preferences

Role in Financing:
Prefer role as deal originator but will also invest in deals created by others

Type of Financing Preferred:
Acquisition
Balanced
Distressed Debt
Early Stage
Expansion
First Stage Financing
Joint Ventures
Later Stage
Leveraged Buyout
Management Buyouts
Recapitalizations
Research and Development
Second Stage Financing
Seed
Startup
Turnaround

Size of Investments Considered
Min Size of Investment Considered (000s): $5,000
Max Size of Investment Considered (000s): $15,000

Geographical Preferences

United States
All U.S.

Canada
All Canada

Industry Preferences

(% based on actual investment)

Semiconductors/Other Elect.	21.2%
Internet Specific	14.3%
Biotechnology	13.8%
Medical/Health	12.3%
Industrial/Energy	9.8%
Other Products	8.7%
Communications and Media	6.9%
Computer Hardware	6.7%
Consumer Related	3.3%
Computer Software and Services	3.2%

Additional Information
Name of Most Recent Fund: AMP-IV
Most Recent Fund Was Raised: 05/01/1999
Year Founded: 1970
Capital Under Management: $308,000,000
Current Activity Level : Actively seeking new investments
Method of Compensation: Return on investment is of primary concern, do not charge fees

APPLIED GENOMIC TECHNOLOGY CAPITAL FUNDS (AGTC)

150 Cambridge Park Drive
10th Floor
Cambridge, MA 02140-2322
Phone: 617-576-7500
Fax: 617-576-5079
Website: www.agtcfunds.com

Management and Staff
Cheryl Goyette, Chief Financial Officer
David Stone, Partner
Leon Palandjian, Principal
Nancy Crowell, Partner
Noubar Afeyan, Managing Partner

Type of Firm
Affiliate/Subsidary of Oth. Financial. Instit.

Project Preferences

Role in Financing:
Prefer role as deal originator

Type of Financing Preferred:
Early Stage
Startup

Size of Investments Considered
Min Size of Investment Considered (000s): $500
Max Size of Investment Considered (000s): $10,000

Geographical Preferences

United States
Northeast
West Coast

Industry Preferences

Computer Software
Software

Biotechnology
Human Biotechnology
Biotech Related Research
Biotech Related Research

Medical/Health
Pharmaceuticals

Additional Information
Name of Most Recent Fund: Applied Genomic Technology Capital Fund, L.P.
Most Recent Fund Was Raised: 05/18/2000
Year Founded: 2000
Capital Under Management: $150,000,000
Current Activity Level : Actively seeking new investments
Method of Compensation: Return on investment is of primary concern, do not charge fees

APPLIED TECHNOLOGY

One Cranberry Hill
Lexington, MA 02421-7397
Phone: 781-862-8622
Fax: 781-862-8367

Other Offices

1001 West Avenue
Austin, TX 78701
Phone: 512-479-8622
Fax: 512-479-5126

1010 ElCamino Real
Suite 300
Menlo Park, CA 94025
Phone: 415-326-8622
Fax: 415-326-8163

Management and Staff
David Boucher, General Partner
Eugene Flath, Partner
Frederick Bamber, General Partner
Nicholas Negroponte, Partner
Thomas Grant, General Partner

Whom to Contact
Ellie McCormack

Type of Firm
Private Firm Investing Own Capital

Industry Association Membership
National Venture Capital Association (NVCA)
Western Association of Venture Capitalists (WAVC)

Project Preferences

Role in Financing:
Prefer role as deal originator but will also invest in deals created by others

Type of Financing Preferred:
First Stage Financing
Leveraged Buyout
Research and Development
Second Stage Financing
Seed
Start-up Financing

Geographical Preferences

United States
All U.S.

Industry Preferences

(% based on actual investment)

Computer Software and Services	28.6%
Internet Specific	27.6%
Computer Hardware	25.1%
Communications and Media	11.6%
Semiconductors/Other Elect.	6.3%
Industrial/Energy	0.7%
Consumer Related	0.1%

Additional Information
Name of Most Recent Fund: Technologies for Information & Entertainment M
Most Recent Fund Was Raised: 01/01/1997
Year Founded: 1983
Capital Under Management: $84,000,000
Current Activity Level : Reducing investment activity
Method of Compensation: Return on investment is of primary concern, do not charge fees

ARGO GLOBAL CAPITAL, INC.

210 Broadway
Suite 101
Lynnfield, MA 01940
Phone: 781-592-5250
Fax: 781-592-5230
Website: www.gsmcapital.com

Other Offices

1000, de La Gauchetiere West
Suite 2500
Montreal, Canada H3B 4W5
Phone: 514-397-8444
Fax: 514-397-8445

2813 One Int'l Finance Centre
1 Harbour View Street
Central, Hong Kong
Phone: 852 2295 2209
Fax: 852 2295 3111

Parkshot House
5 Kew Road, Richmond-Upon-Thames
London, United Kingdom TW9 2PR
Phone: 44 20 8334 8002
Fax: 44 20 8334 8100

Management and Staff
Alan MacIntosh, Partner
Bernice Bradin, Vice President
Flora Pong, Vice President
H.H. Haight, President
Pascal Tremblay, Vice President
Ronald White, Partner
Thomas Wooters, Partner
Vesa Jormakka, Chief Executive Officer

Type of Firm
Private Firm Investing Own Capital

Project Preferences

Type of Financing Preferred:
Balanced
Expansion

Geographical Preferences

International
All International

Industry Preferences

(% based on actual investment)

Communications and Media	58.8%
Internet Specific	24.4%
Computer Software and Services	9.6%
Semiconductors/Other Elect.	7.1%

Additional Information
Year Founded: 2000
Capital Under Management: $437,000,000
Current Activity Level : Actively seeking new investments

ASCENT VENTURE PARTNERS

255 State Street
5th Floor
Boston, MA 02109
Phone: 617-720-9400
Fax: 617-720-9401
Website: www.ascentvp.com

Management and Staff
C.W. Dick, Managing Director
Christopher Lynch, Managing Director
Frank Polestra, Managing Director
Geoffrey Oblak, Principal
Kevin Littlejohn, Chief Financial Officer
Leigh Michl, Managing Director
Tibor Toth, Principal

Type of Firm
Private Firm Investing Own Capital

Industry Association Membership
National Venture Capital Association (NVCA)
Natl assoc of Small Bus. Inv. Co (NASBIC)

Project Preferences

Role in Financing:
Prefer role as deal originator but will also invest in deals created by others

Type of Financing Preferred:
Acquisition
First Stage Financing

Geographical Preferences

United States
Northeast

Industry Preferences

(% based on actual investment)

Internet Specific	25.2%
Computer Software and Services	24.3%
Medical/Health	16.0%
Communications and Media	8.8%
Computer Hardware	8.1%
Other Products	5.6%
Consumer Related	4.8%
Industrial/Energy	4.1%
Semiconductors/Other Elect.	2.7%
Biotechnology	0.3%

Additional Information
Name of Most Recent Fund: Ascent Venture Partners III, L.P.
Most Recent Fund Was Raised: 09/01/1999
Year Founded: 1980
Capital Under Management: $209,000,000
Current Activity Level : Actively seeking new investments
Method of Compensation: Return on investment is of primary concern, do not charge fees

ATLANTIC CAPITAL

164 Cushing Highway
Cohasset, MA 02025
Phone: 617-383-9449
Fax: 617-383-6040

Project Preferences

Role in Financing:
Prefer role as deal originator but will also invest in deals created by others

Type of Financing Preferred:
First Stage Financing
Start-up Financing

Size of Investments Considered
Min Size of Investment Considered (000s): $300
Max Size of Investment Considered (000s): $500

Geographical Preferences

International
No Preference

Industry Preferences

Communications and Media
Telecommunications
Data Communications

Computer Hardware
Mini and Personal/Desktop

Computer Software
Computer Services
Systems Software

Semiconductors/Other Elect.
Electronics
Semiconductor
Circuit Boards

Medical/Health
Diagnostic Services
Medical Products
Disposable Med. Products
Pharmaceuticals

Consumer Related
Retail
Consumer Products

Industrial/Energy
Environmental Related

Financial Services
Financial Services

Manufact.
Office Automation Equipmt

Additional Information
Year Founded: 1986
Capital Under Management: $3,000,000
Current Activity Level : Actively seeking new investments
Method of Compensation: Return on investment is of primary concern, do not charge fees

ATLAS VENTURE

222 Berkeley Street
Suite 1950
Boston, MA 02116
Phone: 617-488-2200
Fax: 617-859-9292
Website: www.atlasventure.com

Other Offices

1201 Third Avenue
Suite 5450
Seattle, WA 98101
Phone: 206-283-9911
Fax: 206-254-9130

1600 El Camino Real
Suite 290
Menlo Park, CA 94025
Phone: 650-614-1444
Fax: 650-614-1441

32 bis, boulevard Haussmann
Paris, France 75009
Phone: 331-4523-4120
Fax: 331-4523-4121

55 Grosvenor Street
London, United Kingdom WIX 9DA
Phone: 44207-529-4444
Fax: 44207 529 4455

Leeuwenveldseweg 16
1382 LX Weesp
, Netherlands
Phone: 31-294-28-06-30
Fax: 31-294-41-84-00

Naarderpoort 1
MA Naarden, Netherlands 1411
Phone: 3135-695-4800
Fax: 3135-695-4888

Widenmayerstrasse 16
Munich, Germany D-80538
Phone: 4989-4587-450
Fax: 4989-4587-4545

Management and Staff
Alexander Bruchl, Principal
Allan Ferguson, General Partner
Axel Bichara, Principal
Barry Fidelman, Principal
Bernard Gautier, Principal
Bill Bryant, Venture Partner
Christopher Spray, Principal
David Perez, Principal
David Rye, Principal
Eric Archambeau, Principal
Gerard Montanus, Principal
Graham O'Keeffe, Principal
Hans Bosman, Principal
Jean-Francois Formela, General Partner
Jeanne Henry, Principal
Joel Besse, Principal
Laura Jennings, Principal
Laura Morse, Principal
Michael Feinstein, Principal
Michiel De Haan, Principal
Philippe Claude, Principal
Rob Zegelaar, Principal
Rolf Guenther, Principal
Ron Nordin, Principal
Rupert Pearce, Principal
Tom Eddy, Principal
Vic Morris, Principal
Werner Dreesbach, Principal

Type of Firm
Private Firm Investing Own Capital

Industry Association Membership
National Venture Capital Association (NVCA)

Project Preferences

Role in Financing:
Prefer role as deal originator but will also invest in deals created by others

Type of Financing Preferred:
Balanced
First Stage Financing
Mezzanine
Research and Development
Second Stage Financing
Seed
Start-up Financing

Size of Investments Considered
Min Size of Investment Considered (000s): $500
Max Size of Investment Considered (000s): $20,000

Geographical Preferences

United States
All U.S.

Canada
All Canada

International
Bermuda
France
Germany
United Kingdom

Industry Preferences

(% based on actual investment)

Internet Specific	43.9%
Computer Software and Services	20.6%
Biotechnology	13.6%
Communications and Media	8.9%
Medical/Health	8.5%
Computer Hardware	2.8%
Semiconductors/Other Elect.	1.2%
Other Products	0.4%
Industrial/Energy	0.1%

Additional Information

Name of Most Recent Fund: Atlas Venture V
Most Recent Fund Was Raised: 02/03/2000
Year Founded: 1980
Capital Under Management: $1,600,000,000
Current Activity Level : Actively seeking new investments
Method of Compensation: Return on investment is of primary concern, do not charge fees

AXXON CAPITAL, INC.

28 State Street
37th Floor
Boston, MA 02109
Phone: 617-722-0980
Fax: 617-557-6014
Website: www.axxoncapital.com

Management and Staff

Paula Groves, Founding Partner
Sheryl Marshall, Founding Partner

Type of Firm

Private Equity Advisor or Fund of Fund Mgr

Project Preferences

Type of Financing Preferred:
Balanced

Size of Investments Considered

Min Size of Investment Considered (000s): $300
Max Size of Investment Considered (000s): $2,500

Geographical Preferences

United States
Northeast

Industry Preferences

Communications and Media
Communications and Media

Business Serv.
Media

Other
Women/Minority-Owned Bus.

Additional Information

Year Founded: 1999
Capital Under Management: $53,000,000
Current Activity Level : Actively seeking new investments

BANCBOSTON CAPITAL/BANCBOSTON VENTURES

175 Federal Street
10th Floor
Boston, MA 02110
Phone: 617-434-2509
Fax: 617-434-6175
Website: www.bancbostoncapital.com

Other Offices

32/F Asian Pacific Finance Tower
Citibank Plaza, 3 Garden Road
Central, Hong Kong
Phone: 852-2878-6200
Fax: 852-2866-3802

39 Victoria Street
Westminster, London, United Kingdom SWIH OED
Phone: 171-932-9053
Fax: 171-932-9117

435 Tasso Street
Suite 250
Palo Alto, CA 94305
Phone: 650-470-4100

8/F Jardine House
1 Connaught Place, Hong Kong
Phone: 852-2687-7687
Fax: 852-2521-0798

Bonchard 547, Piso 14
1106 Buenos Aires, Argentina
Phone: 54-1315-4545
Fax: 54-1315-4816

Rua Pedroso, Alluarengalzzl-7 Fl
0453, 012
San Paolo, SP, Brazil
Phone: 55-11-3061-0611
Fax: 55-11-3064-5545

Management and Staff

Andrew Kellett, Managing Director
Craig Deery, Managing Director
Frederick Fritz, President
John Cullinane, Managing Director
Lee Tesconi, Managing Director
Luiz Fernando Castello, Managing Director
Marcia Bates, Managing Director
Mark Storey, Managing Director
Mark DeBlois, Managing Director
Peter Roberts, Managing Director
Rob Higham, Managing Director
Sanford Anstey, Managing Director
Sebastian Valdez, Vice President
William Gemmell, Managing Director

Type of Firm

Commercial Bank Affiliate or Subsidiary

Industry Association Membership

Hungarian Venture Capital Association
National Venture Capital Association (NVCA)
Natl assoc of Small Bus. Inv. Co (NASBIC)

Project Preferences

Role in Financing:
Will function either as deal originator or investor in deals created by others

Type of Financing Preferred:
Acquisition
Early Stage
Expansion
Generalist PE
Later Stage
Management Buyouts
Mezzanine
Recapitalizations
Seed

Size of Investments Considered

Min Size of Investment Considered (000s): $1,000
Max Size of Investment Considered (000s): $100,000

Geographical Preferences

United States
All U.S.

Canada
Eastern Canada

International
Australia
Bermuda
China
France
Germany
Italy
Mexico
Middle East
South Africa
Spain
United Kingdom

Industry Preferences
(% based on actual investment)

Other Products	19.7%
Communications and Media	18.7%
Internet Specific	17.5%
Consumer Related	14.1%
Computer Software and Services	8.3%
Industrial/Energy	7.4%
Semiconductors/Other Elect.	5.2%
Medical/Health	3.9%
Biotechnology	3.6%
Computer Hardware	1.6%

Additional Information
Name of Most Recent Fund: Private Equity Portfolio Fund II, L.L.C.
Most Recent Fund Was Raised: 01/28/1999
Year Founded: 1959
Capital Under Management: $1,000,000,000
Current Activity Level : Actively seeking new investments
Method of Compensation: Return on invest. most important, but chg. closing fees, service fees, etc.

BARRINGTON PARTNERS

378 Page Street
Suite 3
Stoughton, MA 02072
Fax: 781-297-9933
Website: www.barvc.com

See California for full listing.

BATTERY VENTURES, L.P.

20 William Street
Suite 200
Wellesley, MA 02481
Phone: 781-577-1000
Fax: 781-577-1001
Website: www.battery.com

Other Offices

901 Mariner's Island Blvd.
Suite 475
San Mateo, CA 94404
Phone: 650-372-3939
Fax: 650-372-3930

Management and Staff
Anthony Abate, General Partner
Cornel Faucher, Partner
David Tabors, General Partner
Donald Stanley, Chief Financial Officer
Howard Anderson, Venture Partner
Jim Orlando, Principal
John Abraham, Venture Partner
Kenneth Lawler, General Partner
Mark Sherman, General Partner
Michael Darby, Principal
Morgan Jones, General Partner
Oliver Curme, General Partner
Ravi Mohan, General Partner
Richard Frisbie, General Partner
Richard McGlinchy, Venture Partner
Robert Barrett, General Partner
Scott Tobin, General Partner
Thomas Crotty, General Partner
Todd Dagres, General Partner

Whom to Contact
David A. Hartwig

Type of Firm
Private Firm Investing Own Capital

Industry Association Membership
National Venture Capital Association (NVCA)
Western Association of Venture Capitalists (WAVC)

Project Preferences

Role in Financing:
Prefer role as deal originator but will also invest in deals created by others

Type of Financing Preferred:
Balanced
First Stage Financing
Leveraged Buyout
Mezzanine
Seed
Start-up Financing

Size of Investments Considered
Min Size of Investment Considered (000s): $3,000
Max Size of Investment Considered (000s): $35,000

Geographical Preferences

United States
All U.S.

Canada
All Canada

International
Israel
United Kingdom

Industry Preferences
(% based on actual investment)

Computer Software and Services	26.7%
Internet Specific	26.4%
Communications and Media	22.1%
Semiconductors/Other Elect.	17.2%
Other Products	4.0%
Computer Hardware	3.3%
Industrial/Energy	0.3%
Medical/Health	0.1%

Additional Information
Name of Most Recent Fund: Battery Ventures V, L.P.
Most Recent Fund Was Raised: 04/01/1999
Year Founded: 1983
Capital Under Management: $1,738,400,000
Current Activity Level : Actively seeking new investments
Method of Compensation: Return on invest. most important, but chg. closing fees, service fees, etc.

BEDROCK CAPITAL PARTNERS

One Boston Place
Suite 500
Boston, MA 02108
Phone: 617-305-0660
Fax: 617-305-0700
Website: www.bedrockcapital.com

Other Offices

250 West Pratt Street
Suite 1300
Baltimore, MD 21201
Phone: 410-783-4423

One Maritime Plaza
Suite 1100
San Francisco, CA 94111
Phone: 415-274-4453
Fax: 415-434-0395

Management and Staff
David Duval, Managing Director
James McLean, Managing Director
Jason Rosenbluth, Managing Director
Paul Brown, Managing Director
Thomas Volpe, General Partner

Type of Firm
Private Firm Investing Own Capital

Industry Association Membership
Mid-Atlantic Venture Association

Project Preferences

Type of Financing Preferred:
Early Stage
Seed

Industry Preferences

(% based on actual investment)

Internet Specific	68.4%
Communications and Media	11.2%
Medical/Health	9.4%
Computer Hardware	5.6%
Computer Software and Services	4.9%
Other Products	0.5%

Additional Information
Name of Most Recent Fund: Bedrock Capital Partners I, L.P.
Most Recent Fund Was Raised: 06/01/1998
Year Founded: 1998
Capital Under Management: $120,000,000
Current Activity Level : Actively seeking new investments

BERKSHIRE PARTNERS

One Boston Place
Boston, MA 02108-4401
Phone: 617-227-0050
Fax: 617-227-6105
Website: www.berkshirepartners.com

Management and Staff
Carl Ferenback, Managing Director
Chris Clifford, Managing Director
Randy Peeler, Vice President

Whom to Contact
Jeanine Neumann
Kevin Callaghan

Type of Firm
Private Firm Investing Own Capital

Project Preferences

Role in Financing:
Prefer role as deal originator but will also invest in deals created by others

Type of Financing Preferred:
Leveraged Buyout
Special Situation

Size of Investments Considered
Min Size of Investment Considered (000s): $30,000
Max Size of Investment Considered: No Limit

Geographical Preferences

United States
All U.S.

Canada
All Canada

International
Australia
United Kingdom

Industry Preferences

(% based on actual investment)

Consumer Related	36.6%
Other Products	36.1%
Communications and Media	13.1%
Semiconductors/Other Elect.	6.3%
Internet Specific	4.4%
Industrial/Energy	2.6%
Medical/Health	0.7%
Computer Software and Services	0.2%
Computer Hardware	0.0%

Additional Information
Name of Most Recent Fund: Berkshire Fund V, L.P.
Most Recent Fund Was Raised: 10/01/1998
Year Founded: 1986
Capital Under Management: $1,600,000,000
Current Activity Level : Actively seeking new investments
Method of Compensation: Return on invest. most important, but chg. closing fees, service fees, etc.

BERKSHIRES CAPITAL INVESTORS

296 Main Street
Second Floor
Williamstown, MA 01267
Phone: 413-458-9683
Fax: 413-458-5603
Website: www.berkshirescap.com

Management and Staff
Bradley Svrluga, Principal
George Kennedy, Managing Partner
Matthew Harris, Managing Partner
Robert McGill, Managing Partner
Russell Howard, Managing Director
Taylor Briggs, Managing Partner

Type of Firm
Affiliate/Subsidary of Oth. Financial. Instit.

Project Preferences

Type of Financing Preferred:
Early Stage

Additional Information
Capital Under Management: $20,700,000
Current Activity Level : Actively seeking new investments

BESSEMER VENTURE PARTNERS

83 Walnut Street
Wellesley Hills, MA 02481
Phone: 781-237-6050
Fax: 781-237-7576
Website: www.bvp.com

Other Offices

1400 Old Country Road
Suite 109
Westbury, NY 11590
Phone: 516-997-2300
Fax: 516-997-2371

1865 Palmer Avenue
Suite 104
Larchmont, NY 10538
Phone: 914-833-9100
Fax: 914-833-9200

535 Middlefield Road
Suite 245
Menlo Park, CA 94025
Phone: 650-853-7000
Fax: 650-853-7001

83 Walnut Street
Wellesley, MA 02481
Phone: 781-237-6050
Fax: 781-235-7576

Management and Staff
Bruce Graham, Partner
Christopher Gabrieli, Partner
David Cowan, Managing Partner
G. Felda Hardymon, Partner
Gautam Prakash, Partner
Glenn Falcao, Partner
Joanna Strober, Partner
Judy Sundue, Partner
Ravi Mhatre, Principal
Rob Chandra, Partner
Robert Goodman, Partner
Robert Stavis, Partner
Robert O'Neil, Partner
Robi Soni, Managing Partner
Saurabh Srivastava, Partner
William Burgin, Partner

Whom to Contact
General Address

Type of Firm
Private Firm Investing Own Capital

Industry Association Membership
National Venture Capital Association (NVCA)
Western Association of Venture Capitalists (WAVC)

Project Preferences

Role in Financing:
Will function either as deal originator or investor in deals created by others

Type of Financing Preferred:
Early Stage
Expansion
First Stage Financing
Second Stage Financing
Seed
Startup

Size of Investments Considered
Min Size of Investment Considered (000s): $100
Max Size of Investment Considered (000s): $15,000

Geographical Preferences

United States
All U.S.
All U.S.

International
United Kingdom

Industry Preferences

(% based on actual investment)

Internet Specific	29.4%
Communications and Media	16.7%
Computer Software and Services	16.2%
Semiconductors/Other Elect.	10.0%
Consumer Related	6.5%
Computer Hardware	6.3%
Medical/Health	5.9%
Other Products	4.3%
Industrial/Energy	3.4%
Biotechnology	1.4%

Additional Information
Name of Most Recent Fund: Bessemer Venture Investors L.P.
Most Recent Fund Was Raised: 01/01/1997
Year Founded: 1970
Capital Under Management: $400,000,000
Current Activity Level : Actively seeking new investments
Method of Compensation: Return on investment is of primary concern, do not charge fees

BIOVENTURES INVESTORS, LLC

One Innovation Drive
Worcester, MA 01605
Phone: 508-797-3600

Management and Staff
Marc Goldberg, Partner
Peter Feinstein, Partner
Walter Gilbert, General Partner

Type of Firm
Private Firm Investing Own Capital

Project Preferences

Role in Financing:
Will function either as deal originator or investor in deals created by others

Type of Financing Preferred:
Balanced
Early Stage

Geographical Preferences

United States
Northeast

Industry Preferences

Biotechnology
Human Biotechnology
Biotech Related Research

Medical/Health
Medical Diagnostics
Medical Therapeutics
Drug/Equipmt Delivery
Pharmaceuticals

Additional Information
Name of Most Recent Fund: Bioventures Investors LP
Most Recent Fund Was Raised: 01/01/1999
Year Founded: 1997
Capital Under Management: $18,000,000
Current Activity Level : Actively seeking new investments
Method of Compensation: Return on investment is of primary concern, do not charge fees

BOSTON CAPITAL VENTURES

Old City Hall
45 School Street
Boston, MA 02108
Phone: 617-227-6550
Fax: 617-227-3847
Website: www.bcv.com

Management and Staff
Alex Wilmerding, Principal
Alexander Von der Goltz, Principal
H.J. Von der Goltz, Partner
Jack Shields, Partner

Whom to Contact
Alexander Wilmerding

Type of Firm
Private Firm Investing Own Capital

Industry Association Membership
National Venture Capital Association (NVCA)

Project Preferences

Role in Financing:
Prefer role as deal originator but will also invest in deals created by others

Type of Financing Preferred:
First Stage Financing
Leveraged Buyout
Recapitalizations
Second Stage Financing
Start-up Financing

Geographical Preferences

United States
All U.S.
Mid Atlantic
Midwest
Northeast
Rocky Mountain
Southeast

Industry Preferences

(% based on actual investment)

Internet Specific	36.0%
Communications and Media	22.4%
Medical/Health	11.4%
Computer Software and Services	10.9%
Other Products	8.6%
Computer Hardware	2.7%
Consumer Related	2.3%
Industrial/Energy	1.9%
Semiconductors/Other Elect.	1.9%
Biotechnology	1.8%

Additional Information

Name of Most Recent Fund: BCV IV
Most Recent Fund Was Raised: 05/31/1998
Year Founded: 1982
Capital Under Management: $111,000,000
Current Activity Level : Actively seeking new investments
Method of Compensation: Return on investment is of primary concern, do not charge fees

BOSTON FINANCIAL & EQUITY CORP.

20 Overland Street
P.O. Box 15071
Boston, MA 02215
Phone: 617-267-2900
Fax: 617-437-7601

Management and Staff

Deborah Monosson

Whom to Contact

Deborah Monosson

Project Preferences

Role in Financing:
Prefer role in deals created by others

Type of Financing Preferred:
First Stage Financing
Leveraged Buyout
Mezzanine
Research and Development
Second Stage Financing
Seed
Special Situation
Start-up Financing

Size of Investments Considered

Min Size of Investment Considered (000s): $500
Max Size of Investment Considered (000s): $1,000

Geographical Preferences

United States
All U.S.

Industry Preferences

Communications and Media
Communications and Media

Computer Other
Computer Related

Semiconductors/Other Elect.
Electronic Components

Biotechnology
Biotechnology

Medical/Health
Medical/Health

Consumer Related
Entertainment and Leisure
Consumer Products
Consumer Services
Hotels and Resorts
Education Related

Industrial/Energy
Industrial Products

Financial Services
Financial Services

Business Serv.
Distribution

Manufact.
Publishing

Agr/Forestr/Fish
Agriculture related

Additional Information

Year Founded: 1968
Current Activity Level : Actively seeking new investments

BOSTON MILLENNIA PARTNERS

30 Rowes Wharf
Boston, MA 02110
Phone: 617-428-5150
Fax: 617-428-5160
Website: www.millenniapartners.com

Other Offices

20 Valley Stream Parkway
Malvern, PA 19355-1457
Phone: 610-993-8727
Fax: 610-695-2517

Management and Staff

A.Dana Callow, Managing Partner
Bruce Tiedemann, Chief Financial Officer
Christian Dubiel, Principal
Frank Pinto, Principal
Jean-Yves Lagarde, Partner
Martin Hernon, General Partner
Robert Jevon, Partner
Robert Sherman, General Partner
Robert Edwards, Chief Financial Officer
Stephen Stickells, Principal
Suresh Shanmughan, Partner
Thomas Penn, Principal

Whom to Contact

Dana Callow
Suresh Shanmugham
Tom Penn

Type of Firm

Private Firm Investing Own Capital

Industry Association Membership

National Venture Capital Association (NVCA)

Project Preferences

Role in Financing:
Prefer role as deal originator but will also invest in deals created by others

Type of Financing Preferred:
First Stage Financing
Leveraged Buyout
Mezzanine
Second Stage Financing
Start-up Financing

Size of Investments Considered

Min Size of Investment Considered (000s): $5,000
Max Size of Investment Considered (000s): $25,000

Geographical Preferences

United States
All U.S.

Industry Preferences

(% based on actual investment)

Internet Specific	51.7%
Computer Software and Services	21.4%
Communications and Media	7.3%
Computer Hardware	5.1%
Semiconductors/Other Elect.	4.8%
Biotechnology	4.0%
Consumer Related	2.9%
Other Products	1.9%
Medical/Health	0.9%

Additional Information
Name of Most Recent Fund: Boston Millennia Partners, L.P.
Most Recent Fund Was Raised: 01/01/1998
Year Founded: 1997
Capital Under Management: $650,000,000
Current Activity Level : Actively seeking new investments
Method of Compensation: Return on investment is of primary concern, do not charge fees

BOSTON UNIVERSITY COMMUNITY TECHNOLOGY FUND

108 Bay State Road
Boston, MA 02215
Phone: 617-353-4550
Fax: 617-353-6141
Website: www.bu.edu/ctf

Management and Staff
Matthew Burns, Managing Director

Whom to Contact
Matthew Crowley
Randall Crawford

Type of Firm
University Affiliated Program

Industry Association Membership
National Venture Capital Association (NVCA)

Project Preferences

Role in Financing:
Prefer role in deals created by others

Type of Financing Preferred:
Early Stage
First Stage Financing
Second Stage Financing
Startup

Size of Investments Considered
Min Size of Investment Considered (000s): $250
Max Size of Investment Considered (000s): $2,000

Geographical Preferences

United States
Northeast
All U.S.

Industry Preferences
(% based on actual investment)

Medical/Health	26.8%
Biotechnology	26.6%
Communications and Media	16.2%
Internet Specific	11.5%
Semiconductors/Other Elect.	5.7%
Computer Software and Services	5.6%
Computer Hardware	4.1%
Industrial/Energy	1.4%
Consumer Related	1.1%
Other Products	0.9%

Additional Information
Name of Most Recent Fund: Evergreen
Most Recent Fund Was Raised: 06/01/1982
Year Founded: 1975
Capital Under Management: $53,000,000
Current Activity Level : Actively seeking new investments
Method of Compensation: Return on investment is of primary concern, do not charge fees

BOSTON VENTURES MANAGEMENT, INC.

One Federal Street
23rd Floor
Boston, MA 02110
Phone: 617-350-1500
Fax: 617-350-1509

Management and Staff
Barry Baker, Managing Director

Whom to Contact
Anthony Bolland
John Hunt
Martha Crowninshield
Neil Wallack
Richard Wallace
Roy F. Coppedge III

Type of Firm
Private Firm Investing Own Capital

Project Preferences

Role in Financing:
Prefer role as deal originator but will also invest in deals created by others

Type of Financing Preferred:
Control-block Purchases
Leveraged Buyout
Second Stage Financing
Special Situation

Size of Investments Considered
Min Size of Investment Considered (000s): $30,000
Max Size of Investment Considered (000s): $50,000

Geographical Preferences

United States
All U.S.

Canada
All Canada

International
France
South Africa
Spain
United Kingdom

Industry Preferences
(% based on actual investment)

Communications and Media	44.3%
Other Products	36.5%
Consumer Related	9.5%
Semiconductors/Other Elect.	5.0%
Internet Specific	3.6%
Medical/Health	0.6%
Computer Software and Services	0.5%

Additional Information
Name of Most Recent Fund: Boston Ventures Ltd. Partnership VI
Most Recent Fund Was Raised: 09/30/1996
Year Founded: 1983
Capital Under Management: $5,100,000
Current Activity Level : Actively seeking new investments
Method of Compensation: Return on investment is of primary concern, do not charge fees

BRISTOL INVESTMENT TRUST

842A Beacon Street
Boston, MA 02215-3199
Phone: 617-566-5212
Fax: 617-267-0932

Type of Firm
Private Firm Investing Own Capital

Project Preferences

Role in Financing:
Prefer role as deal originator but will also invest in deals created by others

Type of Financing Preferred:
First Stage Financing
Mezzanine
Second Stage Financing

Geographical Preferences

United States
Northeast

Industry Preferences

Medical/Health
Medical Products
Hospitals/Clinics/Primary
Hospital/Other Instit.

Consumer Related
Entertainment and Leisure
Retail
Franchises(NEC)
Food/Beverage
Consumer Products
Other Restaurants
Hotels and Resorts

Financial Services
Real Estate

Additional Information
Year Founded: 1966
Current Activity Level : Making few, if any, new investments

BROOK VENTURE MANAGEMENT, L.L.C.

50 Federal Street
5th Floor
Boston, MA 02110
Phone: 617-451-8989
Fax: 617-451-2369
Website: www.brookventure.com

Management and Staff
Andrew Clapp, Principal
Edward Williams, Principal
Frederic Morris, Principal
William Ames, Principal

Type of Firm
Investment/Merchant Bank Subsid/Affil

Project Preferences

Role in Financing:
Prefer role as deal originator but will also invest in deals created by others

Type of Financing Preferred:
Early Stage
First Stage Financing

Size of Investments Considered
Min Size of Investment Considered (000s): $500
Max Size of Investment Considered (000s): $2,500

Geographical Preferences

United States
Northeast

Industry Preferences

Communications and Media
Commercial Communications

Computer Software
Software
Systems Software
Applications Software
Artificial Intelligence

Internet Specific
E-Commerce Technology
Internet

Semiconductors/Other Elect.
Electronic Components
Controllers and Sensors
Fiber Optics

Biotechnology
Biotech Related Research
Biotech Related Research

Medical/Health
Medical Products
Disposable Med. Products

Industrial/Energy
Industrial Products

Financial Services
Financial Services

Business Serv.
Services

Additional Information
Name of Most Recent Fund: Brook Venture Fund, LP
Most Recent Fund Was Raised: 07/01/1998
Year Founded: 1998
Capital Under Management: $22,000,000
Current Activity Level : Actively seeking new investments
Method of Compensation: Return on invest. most important, but chg. closing fees, service fees, etc.

BURR, EGAN, DELEAGE & CO.

200 Clarendon Street
Suite 3800
Boston, MA 02116
Phone: 617-262-7770
Fax: 617-262-9779

Other Offices

One Embarcadero Center
Suite 4050
San Francisco, CA 94111
Phone: 415-362-4022
Fax: 415-362-6178

Type of Firm
Private Firm Investing Own Capital

Project Preferences

Role in Financing:
Prefer role as deal originator but will also invest in deals created by others

Type of Financing Preferred:
Control-block Purchases
First Stage Financing
Leveraged Buyout
Mezzanine
Second Stage Financing
Seed
Special Situation
Start-up Financing

Size of Investments Considered
Min Size of Investment Considered (000s): $2,000
Max Size of Investment Considered: No Limit

Geographical Preferences

United States
All U.S.

Industry Preferences

(% based on actual investment)

Communications and Media	46.6%
Medical/Health	12.5%
Computer Software and Services	9.0%
Biotechnology	7.4%
Computer Hardware	6.5%
Semiconductors/Other Elect.	6.5%
Consumer Related	3.6%
Other Products	2.9%
Industrial/Energy	2.5%
Internet Specific	2.4%

Additional Information
Year Founded: 1979
Capital Under Management: $600,000,000
Current Activity Level : Actively seeking new investments
Method of Compensation: Return on investment is of primary concern, do not charge fees

CAMBRIDGE INNOVATIONS (FKA: CAMBRIDGE INCUBATOR)

1 Broadway
14th Floor
Cambridge, MA 02142
Phone: 617-491-8968
Fax: 617-491-8970
Website: www.cambridgeincubator.com

Management and Staff
Bill Hughes, Managing Director
Daniel Oran, Managing Director
Eileen Driscoll, Chief Financial Officer
Geoff Mamlet, Managing Director
Timothy Rowe, Chief Executive Officer

Type of Firm
Incubators

Additional Information
Current Activity Level : Actively seeking new investments

CAMBRIDGE SAMSUNG PARTNERS

One Exeter Plaza
Ninth Floor
Boston, MA 02116
Phone: 617-262-4440
Fax: 617-262-5562

Other Offices

3655 N.First Street
San Jose, CA 95134
Phone: 408-544-5660
Fax: 408-544-5659

Management and Staff
Aashish Kalra
Lee Lambert

Whom to Contact
Aashish Kalra
Lee Lambert

Type of Firm
Private Firm Investing Own Capital

Project Preferences

Role in Financing:
Prefer role as deal originator but will also invest in deals created by others

Type of Financing Preferred:
First Stage Financing

Geographical Preferences

United States
All U.S.

Additional Information
Capital Under Management: $25,000,000
Current Activity Level : Actively seeking new investments

CAMBRIDGE TECHNOLOGY CAPITAL

8 Cambridge Center
Cambridge, MA 02142
Phone: 617-974-8262
Fax: 617-551-5197
Website: www.ctcvc.com

Management and Staff
Barry Rosenbaum, Managing Director
Jack Messman, Managing Director
Ralph Linsalata, Managing Director

Type of Firm
Mgt. Consulting Firm

Industry Association Membership
National Venture Capital Association (NVCA)

Project Preferences

Role in Financing:
Will function either as deal originator or investor in deals created by others

Type of Financing Preferred:
Early Stage
First Stage Financing
Later Stage
Second Stage Financing

Size of Investments Considered
Min Size of Investment Considered (000s): $1,000
Max Size of Investment Considered (000s): $5,000

Geographical Preferences

United States
Mid Atlantic
Northeast
Rocky Mountain
Southeast
Southwest

Canada
Ontario
Quebec

International
Belgium
Europe
Germany
Japan
Luxembourg
Netherlands
United Kingdom

Industry Preferences

(% based on actual investment)

Computer Software and Services	53.7%
Internet Specific	41.1%
Communications and Media	5.3%

Additional Information
Name of Most Recent Fund: Cambridge Technology Capital Fund I L.P.
Most Recent Fund Was Raised: 10/17/1997
Capital Under Management: $25,300,000
Current Activity Level : Actively seeking new investments
Method of Compensation: Return on investment is of primary concern, do not charge fees

CAPITAL RESOURCE PARTNERS

85 Merrimac Street
Suite 200
Boston, MA 02114
Phone: 617-723-9000
Fax: 617-723-9819
Website: www.crp.com

Management and Staff
Alexander McGrath, Partner
Cheryl Walsh, Chief Financial Officer
Christian Michalik, Principal
Fred Danforth, Managing Partner
Jeff Potter, Principal
John Cosentino, Partner
Laura Ketchum, Chief Financial Officer
Robert Ammerman, Managing Partner
Stephen Jenks, Partner
William Holm, Partner

Whom to Contact
David A. Sapp
Jeffrey W. Potter

Type of Firm
Private Firm Investing Own Capital

Industry Association Membership
National Venture Capital Association (NVCA)
Natl assoc of Small Bus. Inv. Co (NASBIC)

Project Preferences

Role in Financing:
Will function either as deal originator or investor in deals created by others

Type of Financing Preferred:
Acquisition
Expansion
Generalist PE
Later Stage
Leveraged Buyout
Management Buyouts
Mezzanine
Recapitalizations
Second Stage Financing

Size of Investments Considered
Min Size of Investment Considered (000s): $5,000
Max Size of Investment Considered (000s): $30,000

Geographical Preferences

United States
All U.S.

Industry Preferences

(% based on actual investment)

Other Products	25.8%
Consumer Related	17.7%
Internet Specific	16.2%
Computer Software and Services	13.0%
Industrial/Energy	8.4%
Medical/Health	8.1%
Communications and Media	6.9%
Semiconductors/Other Elect.	3.9%

Additional Information
Name of Most Recent Fund: Capital Resource Partners IV
Most Recent Fund Was Raised: 12/01/1998
Year Founded: 1987
Capital Under Management: $967,000,000
Current Activity Level : Actively seeking new investments
Method of Compensation: Return on investment is of primary concern, do not charge fees

CASTILE VENTURES

890 Winter Street
Suite 140
Waltham, MA 02451
Phone: 781-890-0060
Fax: 781-890-0065
Website: www.castileventures.com

Management and Staff
Maria Lewis Kussmaul, General Partner
Nina Saberi, General Partner
Roger Walton, Partner
Vernon Ellinger, Chief Financial Officer

Type of Firm
Private Firm Investing Own Capital

Industry Association Membership
National Venture Capital Association (NVCA)

Project Preferences

Role in Financing:
Prefer role as deal originator but will also invest in deals created by others

Type of Financing Preferred:
Early Stage
First Stage Financing
Second Stage Financing
Seed
Startup

Size of Investments Considered
Min Size of Investment Considered (000s): $100
Max Size of Investment Considered (000s): $15,000

Geographical Preferences

United States
Mid Atlantic
Northeast
Southeast

Industry Preferences

Communications and Media
Telecommunications
Wireless Communications
Data Communications

Internet Specific
E-Commerce Technology
Internet

Additional Information
Year Founded: 1999
Capital Under Management: $50,000,000
Current Activity Level : Actively seeking new investments
Method of Compensation: Return on investment is of primary concern, do not charge fees

CB HEALTH VENTURES LLC

One Boston Place
Suite 4010
Boston, MA 02108
Phone: 617-450-9800
Fax: 617-450-9749
Website: www.health-ventures.com

Other Offices

452 Fifth Avenue
25th Floor
New York, NY 10018
Phone: 212-869-5600
Fax: 212-869-6418

Management and Staff
Daniel Cain, General Partner
Enrico Petrillo, General Partner
Frederick Blume, General Partner
Robert Schulz, General Partner

Whom to Contact
Bob Schulz
Rick Blume

Type of Firm
Private Firm Investing Own Capital

Industry Association Membership
National Venture Capital Association (NVCA)

Project Preferences

Role in Financing:
Prefer role as deal originator but will also invest in deals created by others

Type of Financing Preferred:
First Stage Financing
Leveraged Buyout
Mezzanine
Second Stage Financing

Geographical Preferences

United States
All U.S.

Industry Preferences

(% based on actual investment)

Medical/Health	57.3%
Other Products	14.8%
Biotechnology	12.0%
Internet Specific	10.3%
Computer Software and Services	5.6%

Additional Information
Name of Most Recent Fund: CB Healthcare Fund, L.P.
Most Recent Fund Was Raised: 12/13/1997
Year Founded: 1997
Capital Under Management: $76,000,000
Current Activity Level : Actively seeking new investments
Method of Compensation: Return on investment is of primary concern, do not charge fees

CENTURY CAPITAL MANAGEMENT, INC.

1 Liberty Square
Boston, MA 02109
Phone: 617-482-3060
Website: www.centuryfunds.com

Management and Staff
Richard Cook, Chief Financial Officer

Type of Firm
Private Firm Investing Own Capital

Industry Preferences

(% based on actual investment)

Internet Specific	68.2%
Other Products	16.5%
Medical/Health	12.3%
Computer Software and Services	2.4%
Computer Hardware	0.5%
Communications and Media	0.2%

Additional Information
Name of Most Recent Fund: Century Capital
Most Recent Fund Was Raised: 01/01/1983
Year Founded: 1928
Capital Under Management: $300,000,000
Current Activity Level : Inactive / Unknown

CHARLES RIVER VENTURES

1000 Winter Street
Suite 3300
Waltham, MA 02451
Phone: 781-487-7060
Fax: 781-487-7065
Website: www.crv.com

Other Offices

2460 Sand Hill Road
Suite 300
Menlo Park, CA 94025
Phone: 650-739-0100

Management and Staff
Bruce Sachs, Partner
Chris Baldwin, Partner
David Edwards, Partner
Gregory Waldorf, Partner
Izhar Armony, Partner
Jonathan Guerster, Partner
Joseph Pignato, Chief Financial Officer
Michael Zak, Partner
Paul Conway, Chief Financial Officer
Richard Burnes, Partner
Santo Politi, Partner
Ted Dintersmith, Partner

Type of Firm
Private Firm Investing Own Capital

Industry Association Membership
National Venture Capital Association (NVCA)

Project Preferences

Role in Financing:
Prefer role as deal originator but will also invest in deals created by others

Type of Financing Preferred:
Early Stage
First Stage Financing
Seed
Start-up Financing

Size of Investments Considered
Min Size of Investment Considered (000s): $1,000
Max Size of Investment Considered (000s): $20,000

Geographical Preferences

United States
Northeast
All U.S.

Industry Preferences

(% based on actual investment)

Internet Specific	40.5%
Computer Software and Services	18.7%
Communications and Media	18.1%
Computer Hardware	7.1%
Other Products	3.5%
Semiconductors/Other Elect.	3.4%
Medical/Health	3.3%
Industrial/Energy	2.5%
Consumer Related	2.1%
Biotechnology	0.8%

Additional Information
Name of Most Recent Fund: CRP IX
Most Recent Fund Was Raised: 01/01/1999
Year Founded: 1970
Capital Under Management: $676,200,000
Current Activity Level : Actively seeking new investments
Method of Compensation: Return on investment is of primary concern, do not charge fees

CHASE H&Q (FKA HAMBRECHT & QUIST)

50 Rose Wharf
Suite 400
Boston, MA 02110
Phone: 617-310-0507
Fax: 617-310-0562

See California for full listing.

CHESTNUT STREET PARTNERS, INC.

75 State Street, Suite 2500
Boston, MA 02109
Phone: 617-345-7220
Fax: 617-345-7201

Management and Staff
David Croll, Vice President

Whom to Contact
Drew Zalkind
Stephen C. Stickells

Type of Firm
Investment/Merchant Bank Subsid/Affil

Project Preferences

Role in Financing:
Prefer role as deal originator but will also invest in deals created by others

Type of Financing Preferred:
First Stage Financing
Research and Development
Seed
Start-up Financing

Industry Preferences

Communications and Media
Data Communications

Computer Software
Computer Services
Systems Software
Applications Software

Internet Specific
Internet

Semiconductors/Other Elect.
Circuit Boards
Laser Related
Fiber Optics

Medical/Health
Medical Diagnostics
Diagnostic Services
Diagnostic Test Products
Medical Therapeutics
Drug/Equipmt Delivery
Disposable Med. Products
Hospitals/Clinics/Primary

Consumer Related
Consumer Products
Consumer Services

Industrial/Energy
Materials

Additional Information
Year Founded: 1995
Capital Under Management: $10,000,000
Current Activity Level : Actively seeking new investments

CHILD HEALTH INVESTMENT CORPORATION

541 Main Street
South Weymouth, MA 02190
Phone: 617-337-3449
Fax: 617-337-5938
Website: www.chca.com

See Kansas for full listing.

CITIZENS CAPITAL AND CITIZENS VENTURES

28 State Street
38th Floor
Boston, MA 02109
Phone: 617-725-5632
Fax: 617-725-5630
Website: www.citizenscapital.com

Management and Staff
Arthur Sayder, Managing Director
Daniel Corcoran, Managing Director
Gregory Mulligan, Managing Director
Robert Garrow, Managing Director

Type of Firm
Commercial Bank Affiliate or Subsidiary

Industry Association Membership
National Venture Capital Association (NVCA)
Natl assoc of Small Bus. Inv. Co (NASBIC)

Project Preferences

Role in Financing:
Will function either as deal originator or investor in deals created by others

Type of Financing Preferred:
Acquisition
Balanced
Early Stage
Expansion
First Stage Financing
Later Stage
Leveraged Buyout
Management Buyouts
Mezzanine
Recapitalizations
Second Stage Financing
Seed
Startup

Size of Investments Considered
Min Size of Investment Considered (000s): $1,000
Max Size of Investment Considered (000s): $10,000

Geographical Preferences

United States
All U.S.

Industry Preferences

(% based on actual investment)

Communications and Media	54.3%
Internet Specific	18.0%
Computer Software and Services	13.1%
Semiconductors/Other Elect.	8.4%
Consumer Related	4.2%
Industrial/Energy	1.7%
Computer Hardware	0.3%

Additional Information
Name of Most Recent Fund: Citizens Ventures
Most Recent Fund Was Raised: 01/01/1997
Year Founded: 1994
Capital Under Management: $500,000,000
Current Activity Level : Actively seeking new investments
Method of Compensation: Return on investment is of primary concern, do not charge fees

CLAFLIN CAPITAL MANAGEMENT, INC.

10 Liberty Square
Suite 300
Boston, MA 02109
Phone: 617-426-6505
Fax: 617-482-0016
Website: www.claflincapital.com

Other Offices

21 Artema Street
Kiev, Ukraine 254053
Phone: 7044-212-3138
Fax: 7044-212-4972

Management and Staff
William Wilcoxson, General Partner

Whom to Contact
All of above

Type of Firm
Private Firm Investing Own Capital

Industry Association Membership
National Venture Capital Association (NVCA)

Project Preferences

Role in Financing:
Prefer role as deal originator

Type of Financing Preferred:
First Stage Financing
Seed
Start-up Financing

Size of Investments Considered
Min Size of Investment Considered (000s): $100
Max Size of Investment Considered: No Limit

Geographical Preferences

United States
Northeast

Industry Preferences

(% based on actual investment)

Internet Specific	28.2%
Computer Software and Services	26.1%
Communications and Media	8.5%
Semiconductors/Other Elect.	7.2%
Consumer Related	6.3%
Medical/Health	5.8%
Computer Hardware	5.5%
Biotechnology	5.2%
Industrial/Energy	4.2%
Other Products	2.9%

Additional Information
Name of Most Recent Fund: Black Diamond Fund
Most Recent Fund Was Raised: 10/01/1999
Year Founded: 1978
Capital Under Management: $70,000,000
Current Activity Level : Actively seeking new investments
Method of Compensation: Return on investment is of primary concern, do not charge fees

CLARITY CAPITAL

28 State Street
11th Floor
Boston, MA 02109
Phone: 617-573-5020
Fax: 617-573-5041
Website: www.claritycap.com

Type of Firm
Private Firm Investing Own Capital

Project Preferences

Type of Financing Preferred:
Early Stage

Size of Investments Considered
Min Size of Investment Considered (000s): $1,000
Max Size of Investment Considered (000s): $5,000

Geographical Preferences

United States
All U.S.

International
Central Europe
Western Europe

Industry Preferences

Communications and Media
Communications and Media
Telecommunications
Data Communications

Additional Information
Current Activity Level : Actively seeking new investments

COMDISCO VENTURES

Totten Pond Office Center
400-1 Totten Pond Road; 3rd Floor
Waltham, MA 02451
Phone: 781-672-0250
Fax: 781-398-8099

See California for full listing.

COMMONWEALTH BIOVENTURES INC. (CBI)

One Innovation Drive
Worcester, MA 01605
Phone: 508-797-0500

See Maine for full listing.

COMMONWEALTH CAPITAL VENTURES L.P.

20 William Street
Suite 225
Wellesley, MA 02481
Phone: 781-237-7373
Fax: 781-235-8627
Website: www.ccvlp.com

Management and Staff
David Sung, Partner
Jeffrey Hurst, General Partner
Justin Perreault, General Partner
Michael Fitzgerald, General Partner
R. Stephen McCormack, General Partner
Rob Chandra, General Partner

Type of Firm
Private Firm Investing Own Capital

Industry Association Membership
National Venture Capital Association (NVCA)

Project Preferences

Role in Financing:
Prefer role as deal originator but will also invest in deals created by others

Type of Financing Preferred:
First Stage Financing
Leveraged Buyout
Mezzanine
Seed
Special Situation
Start-up Financing

Geographical Preferences

United States
Northeast

Industry Preferences

(% based on actual investment)

Computer Software and Services	41.7%
Internet Specific	21.6%
Communications and Media	15.6%
Consumer Related	14.5%
Medical/Health	5.2%
Semiconductors/Other Elect.	1.3%

Additional Information
Name of Most Recent Fund: Commonwealth Capital Ventures L.P.
Most Recent Fund Was Raised: 01/01/1995
Year Founded: 1995
Capital Under Management: $317,300,000
Current Activity Level : Actively seeking new investments
Method of Compensation: Return on investment is of primary concern, do not charge fees

COPLEY VENTURE PARTNERS

99 Summer Street
Suite 1720
Boston, MA 02110
Phone: 617-737-1253
Fax: 617-439-0699

Type of Firm
Private Firm Investing Own Capital

Project Preferences

Role in Financing:
Will function either as deal originator or investor in deals created by others

Type of Financing Preferred:
First Stage Financing
Second Stage Financing
Start-up Financing

Size of Investments Considered
Min Size of Investment Considered (000s): $1,000
Max Size of Investment Considered: No Limit

Geographical Preferences

International
No Preference

Additional Information
Name of Most Recent Fund: Copley Partners I
Most Recent Fund Was Raised: 01/01/1986
Year Founded: 1983
Capital Under Management: $60,000,000
Current Activity Level : Actively seeking new investments
Method of Compensation: Return on investment is of primary concern, do not charge fees

CORNING CAPITAL (AKA: CORNING TECHNOLOGY VENTURES)

121 High Street
Suite 400
Boston, MA 02110
Phone: 617-338-2656
Fax: 617-261-3864
Website: www.corningventures.com

Management and Staff
Barney Corning, Partner
Sam Foster, Partner

Type of Firm
Private Firm Investing Own Capital

Project Preferences

Role in Financing:
Prefer role in deals created by others

Type of Financing Preferred:
Early Stage

Geographical Preferences

United States
Northeast

Industry Preferences

(% based on actual investment)

Internet Specific	74.1%
Computer Software and Services	19.7%
Medical/Health	3.0%
Semiconductors/Other Elect.	3.0%
Consumer Related	0.2%

Additional Information
Year Founded: 1979
Current Activity Level : Actively seeking new investments

DOMINION VENTURES, INC.

One Post Office Square
38th Floor, Suite 3820
Boston, MA 02109
Phone: 617-367-8575
Fax: 617-367-0323
Website: www.dominion.com

See California for full listing.

DOWNER & CO.

211 Congress Street
Boston, MA 02110
Phone: 617-482-6200
Fax: 617-482-6201
Website: www.downer.com

Other Offices

24, rue du Quatre Septembre
Paris, France 75002
Phone: 33-1-4742-4488
Fax: 33-1-4742-1993

Management and Staff
Ashley Rountree
Charles Downer
John F. Ippolito
Robert Reilly

Whom to Contact
Ashley Rountree
Charles Downer
John F. Ippolito
Robert Reilly

Type of Firm
Investment/Merchant Bank Investing Own or Client Funds

Project Preferences

Role in Financing:
Prefer role as deal originator but will also invest in deals created by others

Type of Financing Preferred:
First Stage Financing
Mezzanine
Second Stage Financing
Start-up Financing

Size of Investments Considered
Min Size of Investment Considered (000s): $300
Max Size of Investment Considered (000s): $500

Geographical Preferences

United States
Northeast

Canada
All Canada

Industry Preferences

Computer Hardware
Mini and Personal/Desktop
Computer Graphics and Dig
Terminals

Computer Software
Computer Services
Applications Software

Semiconductors/Other Elect.
Electronics
Electronic Components
Controllers and Sensors
Sensors
Component Testing Equipmt
Analytic/Scientific

Medical/Health
Diagnostic Test Products
Other Therapeutic
Hospitals/Clinics/Primary
Pharmaceuticals

Consumer Related
Retail
Computer Stores
Food/Beverage
Consumer Products

Industrial/Energy
Industrial Products
Materials
Factory Automation
Machinery
Environmental Related

Manufact.
Office Automation Equipmt

Additional Information
Year Founded: 1975
Capital Under Management: $40,000,000
Current Activity Level : Actively seeking new investments
Method of Compensation: Professional fee required whether or not deal closes

EGAN-MANAGED CAPITAL

30 Federal Street
Boston, MA 02110-2508
Phone: 617-695-2600
Fax: 617-695-2699
Website: www.egancapital.com

Management and Staff
Francis Hughes, Partner
John Egan, Managing Partner
Michael Shanahan, Managing Partner
Robert Creeden, General Partner

Type of Firm
Private Firm Investing Own Capital

Project Preferences

Role in Financing:
Prefer role as deal originator but will also invest in deals created by others

Type of Financing Preferred:
Early Stage

Size of Investments Considered
Min Size of Investment Considered (000s): $2,000
Max Size of Investment Considered (000s): $5,000

Geographical Preferences

United States
Northeast

Industry Preferences

(% based on actual investment)

Computer Software and Services	52.7%
Internet Specific	35.3%
Communications and Media	7.1%
Computer Hardware	4.9%

Additional Information
Name of Most Recent Fund: Egan-Managed Capital
Most Recent Fund Was Raised: 02/01/1997
Year Founded: 1997
Capital Under Management: $110,000,000
Current Activity Level : Actively seeking new investments
Method of Compensation: Return on investment is of primary concern, do not charge fees

ESSEX INVESTMENT MANAGEMENT

125 High Street
Floor 29
Boston, MA 02110-2702
Phone: 617-342-3200

Type of Firm
Private Firm Investing Own Capital

Industry Preferences

(% based on actual investment)

Communications and Media	29.4%
Internet Specific	25.0%
Semiconductors/Other Elect.	20.0%
Computer Software and Services	13.3%
Other Products	5.9%
Biotechnology	3.4%
Medical/Health	3.0%
Computer Hardware	0.0%

Additional Information
Name of Most Recent Fund: Essex Investment Management Fund
Most Recent Fund Was Raised: 07/01/1999
Year Founded: 1999
Capital Under Management: $7,500,000,000
Current Activity Level : Actively seeking new investments

FIDELITY VENTURES (FKA: FIDELITY VENTURE ASSOCIATES)

82 Devonshire Street - R27B
Boston, MA 02109
Phone: 617-563-6370
Fax: 617-476-9023
Website: www.fidelityventures.com

Other Offices

10F, Shiroyama JT Mori Building
3-1 Toranomon, 4-chome
Minato-ku, Tokyo, Japan 105-6019
Phone: 03-5470-9495
Fax: 03-5470-4866

17th Floor One Intl. Finance Center
1 Harbour View Street
Central, Hong Kong
Phone: 852-2629-2830
Fax: 852-2509-0371

25 Lovat Lane
London, United Kingdom EC3R 8LL
Phone: 44-20-7664-2300
Fax: 44-20-7669-2309

Management and Staff
Andrew Flaster, Chief Financial Officer
Anne Mitchell, Principal
Bill Jandovitz, Vice President
Daniel Auerbach, Managing Director
David Milstein, Principal
Douglas Ng, Principal
Eric Lass, Vice President
George Hertz, Managing Director
Jack Conrad, Vice President
James Hynes, Managing Director
Janice Morris-Hatch, Managing Director
John Remondi, Managing Director
Lance Cawley, Vice President
Neal Yanofsky, Vice President
Paul Ciriello, Principal
Peter Mann, Vice President
Robert Ketterson, Managing Director
Simon Davidson, Principal
Simon Clark, Managing Director
Timothy Hilton, President
Warren Morrsion, Vice President

Type of Firm
Private Firm Investing Own Capital

Industry Association Membership
National Venture Capital Association (NVCA)

Project Preferences

Role in Financing:
Prefer role as deal originator but will also invest in deals created by others

Type of Financing Preferred:
Balanced
First Stage Financing
Leveraged Buyout
Second Stage Financing
Special Situation
Start-up Financing

Size of Investments Considered
Min Size of Investment Considered (000s): $1,000
Max Size of Investment Considered (000s): $10,000

Geographical Preferences

United States
Northeast

International
China

Industry Preferences

(% based on actual investment)

Internet Specific	26.4%
Computer Software and Services	25.0%
Communications and Media	13.7%
Other Products	12.3%
Consumer Related	8.3%
Computer Hardware	4.6%
Semiconductors/Other Elect.	3.9%
Medical/Health	3.3%
Industrial/Energy	1.5%
Biotechnology	1.0%

Additional Information
Name of Most Recent Fund: Fidelity Ventures Ltd.
Most Recent Fund Was Raised: 01/01/1996
Year Founded: 1957
Capital Under Management: $475,000,000
Current Activity Level : Actively seeking new investments
Method of Compensation: Return on investment is of primary concern, do not charge fees

---

FLAG VENTURE PARTNERS (FKA FOX VENTURE PARTNERS)

10 Post Office Sq.
North Tower, Suite 960
Boston, MA 02109
Phone: 617-426-7756
Fax: 617-426-7765
Website: www.flagventure.com

See Connecticut for full listing.

FLV FUND (AKA FLANDERS LANGUAGE VALLEY FUND)

52 Third Avenue
Burlington, MA 01803
Phone: 17812035131
Fax: 16172649197
Website: www.flvfund.com

See Foreign Venture Capital Firms for full listing.

FOWLER, ANTHONY & CO.

20 Walnut Street
Wellesley, MA 02481-2041
Phone: 781-237-4201
Fax: 781-237-7718

Management and Staff
John Quagliaroli, President

Type of Firm
Private Firm Investing Own Capital

Project Preferences

Role in Financing:
Prefer role as deal originator but will also invest in deals created by others

Type of Financing Preferred:
Acquisition
Control-block Purchases
Early Stage
Expansion
First Stage Financing
Generalist PE
Later Stage
Management Buyouts
Mezzanine
Private Placement
Recapitalizations
Second Stage Financing
Special Situation
Turnaround

Size of Investments Considered
Min Size of Investment Considered (000s): $4,000
Max Size of Investment Considered (000s): $5,000

Geographical Preferences

United States
All U.S.

Canada
All Canada

International
Italy
United Kingdom

Industry Preferences

Communications and Media
Commercial Communications
CATV & Pay TV Systems
Radio & TV Broadcasting
Telecommunications
Wireless Communications
Data Communications
Satellite Microwave Comm.
Other Communication Prod.

Computer Hardware
Computer Graphics and Dig
Disk Relat. Memory Device

Computer Software
Computer Services
Software
Systems Software
Applications Software
Artificial Intelligence

Internet Specific
E-Commerce Technology
Internet
Web Aggregration/Portals

Semiconductors/Other Elect.
Electronic Components
Semiconductor
Micro-Processing
Controllers and Sensors
Sensors
Circuit Boards
Component Testing Equipmt
Laser Related
Fiber Optics
Analytic/Scientific

Biotechnology
Industrial Biotechnology
Biosensors

Medical/Health
Medical Diagnostics
Diagnostic Services
Diagnostic Test Products
Medical Therapeutics
Drug/Equipmt Delivery
Medical Products
Disposable Med. Products
Health Services
Hospitals/Clinics/Primary
Hospital/Other Instit.
Pharmaceuticals

Consumer Related
Consumer
Entertainment and Leisure
Sports
Retail
Franchises(NEC)
Food/Beverage
Hotels and Resorts
Education Related

Industrial/Energy
Energy Conservation Relat
Industrial Products
Factory Automation
Process Control
Robotics
Machinery

Transportation
Transportation
Aerospace

Financial Services
Financial Services

Business Serv.
Services
Distribution
Consulting Services
Media

Manufact.
Manufacturing

Agr/Forestr/Fish
Agriculture related

Additional Information
Year Founded: 1976
Current Activity Level : Actively seeking new investments
Method of Compensation: Return on invest. most important, but chg. closing fees, service fees, etc.

GEMINI INVESTORS LLC (AKA: GMN INVESTORS)

20 William St.
Wellesley, MA 02181
Phone: 781-237-7001
Fax: 781-237-7233

Management and Staff
David Millet, Managing Director

Whom to Contact
C. Redington Barrett III

Type of Firm
SBIC Not elsewhere classified

Project Preferences

Role in Financing:
Prefer role as deal originator but will also invest in deals created by others

Type of Financing Preferred:
Industry Rollups
Leveraged Buyout
Mezzanine
Second Stage Financing
Special Situation

Geographical Preferences

United States
All U.S.

Industry Preferences

(% based on actual investment)

Internet Specific	31.8%
Consumer Related	20.5%
Communications and Media	19.6%
Computer Hardware	12.3%
Computer Software and Services	8.6%
Other Products	7.1%

Additional Information
Name of Most Recent Fund: GMN Investors II, L.P.
Most Recent Fund Was Raised: 06/05/1997
Year Founded: 1993
Capital Under Management: $125,000,000
Current Activity Level : Actively seeking new investments
Method of Compensation: Return on investment is of primary concern, do not charge fees

GENERAL CATALYST GROUP LLC

800 Boylston Street
Suite 1400
Boston, MA 02199
Phone: 617-585-4900
Fax: 617-247-6266
Website: www.generalcatalyst.com

Management and Staff
Aaron Gowell, Principal
Benjamin Fischman, Venture Partner
David Fialkow, Principal
Joel Cutler, Principal
John Simon, Principal
Kenneth Hubbs, Principal
Lauren Macleod, Principal
Michael Schreck, Principal
Tami Goven, Principal
William Fitzgerald, Principal

Type of Firm
Private Firm Investing Own Capital

Project Preferences

Type of Financing Preferred:
Balanced

Geographical Preferences

United States
All U.S.

Industry Preferences

(% based on actual investment)

Internet Specific	66.8%
Other Products	25.4%
Computer Software and Services	7.8%

Additional Information
Year Founded: 1999
Current Activity Level : Actively seeking new investments

GKM VENTURE PARTNERS, LP

225 Franklin Street
Suite 2940
Boston, MA 02110
Phone: 617-451-0670
Fax: 800-451-7536
Website: www.gkm.com

See California for full listing.

GRACE VENTURE CAPITAL (AKA: GRACE INTERNET CAPITAL)

11 Newbury Street
3rd Floor
Boston, MA 02116
Phone: 617-351-0044
Fax: 617-867-9089

Management and Staff
Christopher Grace, Chief Executive Officer
Gregory Grace, Chief Operating Officer

Type of Firm
Private Firm Investing Own Capital

Industry Association Membership
National Venture Capital Association (NVCA)

Additional Information
Current Activity Level : Actively seeking new investments

GRAYSON & ASSOCIATES

23 Arborwood Drive
Burlington, MA 01803
Phone: 617-229-9205

See Colorado for full listing.

GREAT HILL EQUITY PARTNERS, LLC

One Liberty Square
Swampscott, MA 01907
Phone: 617-790-9400
Fax: 617-790-9401
Website: www.greathillpartners.com

Management and Staff
Bruce Rogoff, Partner
Christopher Gaffney, Managing Partner
John Hayes, Managing Partner
Mark Evans, Principal
Matthew Vettel, Principal
Patrick Curran, Partner
Stephen Gormley, Managing Partner

Type of Firm
Private Firm Investing Own Capital

Industry Association Membership
National Venture Capital Association (NVCA)

Project Preferences

Size of Investments Considered
Min Size of Investment Considered (000s): $5,000
Max Size of Investment Considered (000s): $50,000

Geographical Preferences

United States
All U.S.

Industry Preferences

(% based on actual investment)

Internet Specific	46.0%
Communications and Media	20.4%
Other Products	16.4%
Computer Software and Services	8.9%
Semiconductors/Other Elect.	8.3%

Additional Information
Name of Most Recent Fund: Great Hill Equity Partners L.P.
Most Recent Fund Was Raised: 02/01/1999
Year Founded: 1999
Capital Under Management: $330,000,000
Current Activity Level : Actively seeking new investments

GREYLOCK

One Federal Street
Boston, MA 02110-2065
Phone: 617-423-5525
Fax: 617-482-0059
Website: www.greylock.com

Other Offices

2929 Campus Drive
Suite 400
San Mateo, CA 94401
Phone: 650-493-5525
Fax: 650-493-5575

755 Page Mill Road
Suite A-100
Palo Alto, CA 94304-1018
Phone: 650-493-5525
Fax: 650-493-5575

Management and Staff
Aneel Bhusri, General Partner
Charles Chi, General Partner
Charles Hazard, General Partner
Dan Keshian, Venture Partner
David Aronoff, General Partner
David Sze, General Partner
David Strohm, General Partner
Henry McCance, General Partner
Howard Cox, General Partner
Roger Evans, General Partner
William Helman, General Partner
William Kaiser, General Partner
William Elfers, Founding Partner

Whom to Contact
Chris Surowiec

Type of Firm
Private Firm Investing Own Capital

Industry Association Membership
National Venture Capital Association (NVCA)
Western Association of Venture Capitalists (WAVC)

Project Preferences

Role in Financing:
Prefer role as deal originator but will also invest in deals created by others

Type of Financing Preferred:
Early Stage
Expansion
First Stage Financing
Seed
Start-up Financing

Size of Investments Considered
Min Size of Investment Considered (000s): $250
Max Size of Investment Considered: No Limit

Geographical Preferences

United States
All U.S.
All U.S.

Industry Preferences

(% based on actual investment)

Internet Specific	31.3%
Computer Software and Services	27.6%
Communications and Media	14.0%
Semiconductors/Other Elect.	8.1%
Medical/Health	4.5%

Computer Hardware	3.8%
Other Products	3.7%
Biotechnology	3.4%
Consumer Related	2.6%
Industrial/Energy	1.0%

Additional Information
Name of Most Recent Fund: Greylock X Limited Partnership
Most Recent Fund Was Raised: 02/20/1997
Year Founded: 1965
Capital Under Management: $1,043,200,000
Current Activity Level : Actively seeking new investments
Method of Compensation: Return on investment is of primary concern, do not charge fees

GROVE STREET ADVISORS, LLC

20 William St.
Suite 230
Wellesley, MA 02481
Phone: 781-263-6100
Fax: 781-263-6101
Website: www.grovestreetadvisors.com

Other Offices

425 Market St.
Suite 2200
San Francisco, CA 94105
Phone: 415-955-2741
Fax: 415-955-2745

Management and Staff
Ann St. Germain, Chief Financial Officer
Catherine Crockett, General Partner
Clinton Harris, Managing Partner
David Mazza, Managing Partner

Type of Firm
Private Equity Advisor or Fund of Fund Mgr

Industry Association Membership
National Venture Capital Association (NVCA)

Project Preferences

Role in Financing:
Will function either as deal originator or investor in deals created by others

Type of Financing Preferred:
First Stage Financing
Mezzanine
Second Stage Financing
Special Situation
Startup

Size of Investments Considered
Min Size of Investment Considered (000s): $1,000
Max Size of Investment Considered (000s): $7,500

Industry Preferences

Communications and Media
Commercial Communications
Wireless Communications
Data Communications

Computer Hardware
Integrated Turnkey System

Computer Software
Software
Systems Software
Applications Software
Artificial Intelligence

Internet Specific
Internet

Semiconductors/Other Elect.
Fiber Optics

Consumer Related
Consumer

Industrial/Energy
Industrial Products

Business Serv.
Distribution

Additional Information
Year Founded: 1998
Capital Under Management: $100,000,000
Current Activity Level : Actively seeking new investments
Method of Compensation: Return on investment is of primary concern, do not charge fees

GRYPHON VENTURES

222 Berkeley Street
Suite 1600
Boston, MA 02116
Phone: 617-267-9191
Fax: 617-267-4293

Management and Staff
Andrew Atkinson

Whom to Contact
Andrew Atkinson

Type of Firm
Private Firm Investing Own Capital

Project Preferences

Role in Financing:
Prefer role as deal originator but will also invest in deals created by others

Type of Financing Preferred:
First Stage Financing
Second Stage Financing
Start-up Financing

Size of Investments Considered
Min Size of Investment Considered (000s): $1,000
Max Size of Investment Considered: No Limit

Geographical Preferences

United States
All U.S.

Industry Preferences

Biotechnology
Industrial Biotechnology

Industrial/Energy
Materials
Environmental Related

Additional Information
Name of Most Recent Fund: Gryphon Ventures II
Most Recent Fund Was Raised: 12/01/1989
Year Founded: 1986
Capital Under Management: $40,000,000
Current Activity Level : Actively seeking new investments
Method of Compensation: Return on investment is of primary concern, do not charge fees

HALPERN, DENNY & CO.

500 Boylston Street
Boston, MA 02116
Phone: 617-536-6602
Fax: 617-536-8535

Management and Staff
Barbara Eastman, Vice President
David Malm, Partner
George Denny, Partner
John Halpern, Partner
Terry Chvisuk, Chief Financial Officer
William Nimmo, Partner
William LaPoint, Partner

Type of Firm
Private Firm Investing Own Capital

Project Preferences

Role in Financing:
Prefer role as deal originator but will also invest in deals created by others

Type of Financing Preferred:
Control-block Purchases
First Stage Financing
Leveraged Buyout
Second Stage Financing
Start-up Financing

Size of Investments Considered
Min Size of Investment Considered (000s): $5,000
Max Size of Investment Considered (000s): $40,000

Geographical Preferences

United States
All U.S.

Industry Preferences

(% based on actual investment)

Consumer Related	47.1%
Other Products	21.5%
Internet Specific	12.1%
Industrial/Energy	6.9%
Communications and Media	5.2%
Computer Software and Services	4.6%
Medical/Health	2.6%

Additional Information
Name of Most Recent Fund: HD Fund II L.P.
Most Recent Fund Was Raised: 01/01/1998
Year Founded: 1991
Capital Under Management: $260,000,000
Current Activity Level : Actively seeking new investments
Method of Compensation: Return on invest. most important, but chg. closing fees, service fees, etc.

HARBOUR FINANCIAL CO.

571 Main St.
Hudson, MA 01749
Phone: 978-567-9053
Fax: 978-562-4449

Type of Firm
Mgt. Consulting Firm

Project Preferences

Role in Financing:
Prefer role as deal originator but will also invest in deals created by others

Type of Financing Preferred:
First Stage Financing
Leveraged Buyout
Mezzanine
Second Stage Financing
Special Situation
Start-up Financing

Size of Investments Considered
Min Size of Investment Considered (000s): $5,000
Max Size of Investment Considered: No Limit

Geographical Preferences

United States
Mid Atlantic
Midwest
Northeast

Industry Preferences

Communications and Media
Radio & TV Broadcasting
Data Communications
Satellite Microwave Comm.

Computer Hardware
Mainframes / Scientific
Mini and Personal/Desktop
Computer Graphics and Dig
Integrated Turnkey System
Terminals
Disk Relat. Memory Device

Computer Software
Computer Services
Systems Software
Applications Software
Artificial Intelligence

Semiconductors/Other Elect.
Electronic Components
Controllers and Sensors
Sensors
Fiber Optics
Analytic/Scientific

Biotechnology
Biotechnology

Medical/Health
Diagnostic Services
Other Therapeutic
Disposable Med. Products
Hospital/Other Instit.

Industrial/Energy
Industrial Products
Materials
Factory Automation
Robotics
Machinery

Manufact.
Office Automation Equipmt

Additional Information
Year Founded: 1980
Current Activity Level : Actively seeking new investments
Method of Compensation: Return on invest. most important, but chg. closing fees, service fees, etc.

HARBOURVEST PARTNERS, LLC.

One Financial Center
44th Floor
Boston, MA 02111
Phone: 617-348-3707
Fax: 617-350-0305
Website: www.hvpllc.com

Other Offices

1-11 Hay Hill, 4th Floor
Berkeley Square
London, United Kingdom W1X 7LF
Phone: 44-71-446-7270
Fax: 44-71-446-0146

Suite 1207, Citibank Tower
3 Garden Rd
Central, Hong Kong
Phone: 852-2525-2214
Fax: 852-2525-2241

Management and Staff
D. Brooks Zug, Senior Managing Director
Diane Goodwin, Vice President
Edward Kane, Senior Managing Director
Frederick Maynard, Managing Director
George Anson, Managing Director
Gregory Stento, Principal
Hemal Mirani, Vice President
John Morris, Principal
John Begg, Managing Director
Julie Eiermann, Vice President
Kathleen Bacon, Principal
Kevin Delbridge, Managing Director
Martha Vorlicek, Managing Director
Mary Traer, Vice President
Michael Taylor, Principal
Ofer Nemirovsky, Managing Director
Peter Wilson, Principal
Philip Bilden, Managing Director
Robert Wadsworth, Managing Director
Theodore Clark, Managing Director
William Johnston, Managing Director

Type of Firm
Private Equity Advisor or Fund of Fund Mgr

Industry Association Membership
Hungarian Venture Capital Association
National Venture Capital Association (NVCA)

Project Preferences

Role in Financing:
Prefer role as deal originator but will also invest in deals created by others

Type of Financing Preferred:
Acquisition
Balanced
Early Stage
Expansion
First Stage Financing
Fund of Funds
Generalist PE
Joint Ventures
Later Stage
Leveraged Buyout
Management Buyouts
Mezzanine
Recapitalizations
Second Stage Financing
Special Situation
Startup

Size of Investments Considered
Min Size of Investment Considered (000s): $5,000
Max Size of Investment Considered (000s): $100,000

Geographical Preferences

United States
All U.S.

Canada
All Canada

International
Europe
France
Germany
All International
Italy
United Kingdom

Industry Preferences

(% based on actual investment)

Internet Specific	26.5%
Communications and Media	16.6%
Other Products	14.8%
Computer Software and Services	13.8%
Computer Hardware	8.0%
Industrial/Energy	5.9%
Consumer Related	4.7%
Semiconductors/Other Elect.	3.7%
Biotechnology	3.3%
Medical/Health	2.7%

Additional Information
Name of Most Recent Fund: HarbourVest Partners VI
Most Recent Fund Was Raised: 10/06/1999
Year Founded: 1982
Capital Under Management: $11,500,000,000
Current Activity Level : Actively seeking new investments
Method of Compensation: Return on invest. most important, but chg. closing fees, service fees, etc.

HEALTHCARE VENTURES LLC (FKA: HEALTHCARE INVESTMENTS)

One Kendall Square
Bldg. 300
Cambridge, MA 02139
Phone: 617-252-4343
Fax: 617-252-4342
Website: www.hcven.com

See New Jersey for full listing.

HERITAGE PARTNERS

30 Rowes Wharf
Suite 300
Boston, MA 02110
Phone: 617-439-0688
Fax: 617-439-0689
Website: www.heritagepartnersinc.com

Management and Staff
Brook Parker, Vice President
Mark Jrolf, Vice President
Mark Sullivan, General Partner
Michael Gilligan, General Partner
Michel Reichert, Managing Partner
Peter Herman, General Partner

Whom to Contact
Peter Jeton
Peter Z. Hermann

Type of Firm
Private Firm Investing Own Capital

Project Preferences

Role in Financing:
Prefer role as deal originator

Type of Financing Preferred:
Industry Rollups
Leveraged Buyout

Size of Investments Considered
Min Size of Investment Considered (000s): $60,000
Max Size of Investment Considered: No Limit

Geographical Preferences

United States
All U.S.

Industry Preferences

(% based on actual investment)

Other Products	54.4%
Medical/Health	32.8%
Consumer Related	12.8%

Additional Information
Name of Most Recent Fund: Heritage Fund III
Most Recent Fund Was Raised: 06/01/1999
Year Founded: 1994
Capital Under Management: $1,433,000,000
Current Activity Level : Reducing investment activity
Method of Compensation: Return on investment is of primary concern, do not charge fees

HIGHLAND CAPITAL PARTNERS

Two International Place
Boston, MA 02110
Phone: 617-531-1500
Fax: 617-531-1550
Website: www.hcp.com

Other Offices

555 California Street
Suite 3100
San Francisco, CA 94104
Phone: 415-981-1230
Fax: 415-981-1229

Management and Staff
Bob Davis, Venture Partner
Burton Hurlock, Partner
Daniel Nova, Managing General Partner
Jo Tango, General Partner
Jon Auerbach, Principal
Keith Benjamin, General Partner
Lee Wrubel, Principal
Paul Maeder, Managing General Partner
Robert Higgins, Partner
Sean Dalton, General Partner
Stephen Harrick, Principal
Wycliffe Grousbeck, General Partner

Whom to Contact
any of above

Type of Firm
Private Equity Advisor or Fund of Fund Mgr

Industry Association Membership
National Venture Capital Association (NVCA)

Project Preferences

Role in Financing:
Prefer role as deal originator but will also invest in deals created by others

Type of Financing Preferred:
Early Stage
First Stage Financing
Second Stage Financing
Seed
Startup

Geographical Preferences

United States
All U.S.

Canada
All Canada

International
Belgium
France
Germany
Italy
Luxembourg
Netherlands
Spain
United Kingdom

Industry Preferences

(% based on actual investment)

Internet Specific	51.0%
Computer Software and Services	15.4%
Communications and Media	8.4%
Medical/Health	7.9%
Other Products	5.4%
Computer Hardware	4.8%
Biotechnology	4.7%
Semiconductors/Other Elect.	2.0%
Consumer Related	0.3%

Additional Information
Name of Most Recent Fund: Highland Capital Partners IV Limited Partnership
Most Recent Fund Was Raised: 09/01/1998
Year Founded: 1988
Capital Under Management: $969,800,000
Current Activity Level : Actively seeking new investments
Method of Compensation: Return on investment is of primary concern, do not charge fees

HOUSATONIC PARTNERS

11 Newbury St.
Suite 500
Boston, MA 02116
Phone: 617-267-4545
Fax: 617-267-5565
Website: www.housatonicpartners.com

See California for full listing.

IDG TECHNOLOGY VENTURE INVESTMENT INC. (FKA: PTV-CHINA)

15/F Penthouse Suite
One Exeter Plaza
Boston, MA 02116
Phone: 1-617-534-1243
Fax: 1-617-527-5256
Website: www.ptvchina.com

See Foreign Venture Capital Firms for full listing.

IDG VENTURES

492 Old Connecticut Path
Framingham, MA 01701
Phone: 508-935-4183
Fax: 508-872-3479
Website: www.idgventures.com

See California for full listing.

IMPEX VENTURE MANAGEMENT CO.

36 Parker Street
Cambridge, MA 02138-2244

See New York for full listing.

INDUSTRY VENTURES

6 Bayne Lane
Newburyport, MA 01950
Phone: 978-499-7606
Fax: 978-499-0686
Website: www.industryventures.com

Other Offices

2063 Larkin St
San Francisco, CA 94101
Phone: 415-260-2953

Management and Staff
Hans Swildens, Managing Director
Norman Villarina, Managing Director
Thomas Litle, Managing Director

Type of Firm
Private Firm Investing Own Capital

Project Preferences

Role in Financing:
Will function either as deal originator or investor in deals created by others

Type of Financing Preferred:
Early Stage
First Stage Financing
Second Stage Financing
Seed
Startup

Size of Investments Considered
Min Size of Investment Considered (000s): $250
Max Size of Investment Considered (000s): $2,000

Geographical Preferences

United States
Mid Atlantic
Northeast
Northern California
West Coast

Industry Preferences

Communications and Media
Wireless Communications

Computer Software
Data Processing
Software

Internet Specific
E-Commerce Technology
Internet

Consumer Related
Retail

Business Serv.
Media

Additional Information
Year Founded: 1999
Capital Under Management: $36,000,000
Current Activity Level : Actively seeking new investments
Method of Compensation: Return on investment is of primary concern, do not charge fees

---

IRONSIDE VENTURES, LLC (FKA: MF PRIVATE CAPITAL)

45 Milk Street
Suite 600
Boston, MA 02109
Phone: 617-451-5647
Fax: 617-451-5601
Website: www.ironsideventures.com

Management and Staff
David Alpert, Managing Director
Myles Gilbert, Managing Director
Raymond Britt, Managing Director
Stephen Brackett, Managing Director
William Sheehan, Managing Director

Type of Firm
Insurance Firm Affiliate or Subsidiary

Project Preferences

Type of Financing Preferred:
Balanced

Industry Preferences

Communications and Media
Communications and Media

Internet Specific
Internet

Medical/Health
Medical Products

Additional Information
Capital Under Management: $25,000,000
Current Activity Level : Actively seeking new investments

JAFCO VENTURES, INC.

One Boston Place
Suite 3320
Boston, MA 02108
Phone: 617-367-3510
Fax: 617-367-3532
Website: www.jafco.com

See California for full listing.

JT VENTURE PARTNERS, LLC

47 Commonwealth Ave
Suite 12
Boston, MA 02116
Phone: 617-536-0577
Fax: 240-208-6309
Website: www.jtventures.com

See New Jersey for full listing.

KESTREL VENTURE MANAGEMENT (FKA:CORNING VENTURE MANAGEMENT)

31 Milk Street
Boston, MA 02109
Phone: 617-451-6722
Fax: 617-451-3322
Website: www.kestrelvm.com

Other Offices

100 Venture Way
Third Floor
Hadley, MA 01035
Phone: 413-587-2150
Fax: 413-587-2156

Management and Staff
Edward Stewart, Partner
Nuri Wissa, Partner
R. Gregg Stone, Partner
Tripp Peake, Partner

Type of Firm
Private Firm Investing Own Capital

Project Preferences

Role in Financing:
Prefer role as deal originator but will also invest in deals created by others

Type of Financing Preferred:
Early Stage

Size of Investments Considered
Min Size of Investment Considered (000s): $250
Max Size of Investment Considered: No Limit

Geographical Preferences

United States
Northeast

Industry Preferences
(% based on actual investment)

Internet Specific	26.5%
Biotechnology	25.2%
Semiconductors/Other Elect.	9.5%
Computer Software and Services	9.0%
Medical/Health	7.4%
Consumer Related	5.1%
Computer Hardware	4.9%
Communications and Media	4.8%
Other Products	4.6%
Industrial/Energy	2.9%

Additional Information
Name of Most Recent Fund: Kestrel Venture Partners, LP
Most Recent Fund Was Raised: 06/01/1996
Year Founded: 1995
Capital Under Management: $45,000,000
Current Activity Level : Actively seeking new investments
Method of Compensation: Return on investment is of primary concern, do not charge fees

---

LANCET CAPITAL PARTNER(FKA:CADUCEUS CAPITAL PARTNERS)

124 Mount Auburn Street
Suite 200 N
Cambridge, MA 02138
Phone: 617-330-9345
Fax: 617-330-9349

Other Offices

45 Rockefeller Plaza
20th Floor
New York, NY 10111
Phone: 212-332-3220
Fax: 212-332-3221

Management and Staff
George Sing, Managing Director
William Golden, Managing Director

Type of Firm
SBIC Not elsewhere classified

Industry Association Membership
National Venture Capital Association (NVCA)
Natl assoc of Small Bus. Inv. Co (NASBIC)

Project Preferences

Type of Financing Preferred:
Early Stage
Seed

Geographical Preferences

United States
All U.S.

Industry Preferences

Medical/Health
Medical/Health
Pharmaceuticals

Additional Information

Name of Most Recent Fund: Lancet Capital Health Ventures (FKA: Caduceus Capital Healt)
Most Recent Fund Was Raised: 07/31/1998
Year Founded: 1998
Capital Under Management: $60,000,000
Current Activity Level : Actively seeking new investments

LEE MUNDER VENTURE PARTNERS

John Hancock Tower T-53
200 Clarendon Street
Boston, MA 02103
Phone: 617-380-5600
Fax: 617-380-5601
Website: www.leemunder.com

Other Offices

231 Royal Palm Way
Palm Beach, FL 33480
Phone: 561-802-8800
Fax: 561- 802-8801

Management and Staff

Murray Metcalfe, Managing Director
Randall Crawford, Managing Director
Robert Deziel, Managing Director
Roger Kitterman, Managing Director
Terry Gardner, Chief Financial Officer

Type of Firm

Affiliate/Subsidary of Oth. Financial. Instit.

Project Preferences

Role in Financing:
Will function either as deal originator or investor in deals created by others

Type of Financing Preferred:
Early Stage
Expansion
First Stage Financing
Later Stage
Mezzanine
Second Stage Financing
Seed
Special Situation
Startup

Geographical Preferences

United States
East Coast
Mid Atlantic
Northeast
Southeast

Canada
All Canada
Ontario
Quebec

Industry Preferences

Communications and Media
Commercial Communications
Telecommunications
Wireless Communications
Data Communications

Computer Software
Computer Services
Data Processing
Software
Systems Software
Applications Software

Internet Specific
E-Commerce Technology
Internet

Semiconductors/Other Elect.
Electronics
Semiconductor

Additional Information

Year Founded: 2000
Capital Under Management: $30,000,000
Current Activity Level : Actively seeking new investments
Method of Compensation: Return on investment is of primary concern, do not charge fees

LIGHTHOUSE CAPITAL PARTNERS

16 Fayesweather St
Cambridge, MA 02138
Phone: 617-441-9192
Fax: 617-354-4374
Website: www.lcpartners.com

See California for full listing.

LONGWORTH VENTURE PARTNERS, L.P.

1050 Winter Street
Suite 2600
Waltham, MA 02451
Phone: 781-663-3600
Fax: 781-663-3619
Website: www.longworth.com

Type of Firm

Private Firm Investing Own Capital

Industry Association Membership

National Venture Capital Association (NVCA)

Geographical Preferences

United States
East Coast

Additional Information

Name of Most Recent Fund: Longworth Venture Partners
Most Recent Fund Was Raised: 06/18/1999
Year Founded: 2000
Capital Under Management: $55,000,000
Current Activity Level : Actively seeking new investments

LTI VENTURES LEASING CORP.

10 Liberty Square
Boston, MA 02109
Phone: 617-426-4116
Fax: 617-482-6475
Website: www.ltileasing.com

See Connecticut for full listing.

LUCENT VENTURE PARTNERS, INC.

950 Winter Street
Suite 2600
Waltham, MA 02453
Phone: 781-926-2222
Fax: 781-890-6901
Website: www.lucentventurepartners.com

See California for full listing.

M/C VENTURE PARTNERS

75 State Street
Suite 2500
Boston, MA 02109
Phone: 617-345-7200
Fax: 617-345-7201
Website: www.mcventurepartners.com

Management and Staff

David Croll, General Partner
James Wade, Managing Partner
John Ward, Partner
Joseph Monaco, Chief Financial Officer
Matthew Rubins, General Partner
Neil Sheth, Partner
Peter Schober, Partner
Peter Claudy, General Partner
Russell Pyle, Vice President

Type of Firm

Private Firm Investing Own Capital

Project Preferences

Role in Financing:

Prefer role as deal originator but will also invest in deals created by others

Type of Financing Preferred:

Early Stage

Size of Investments Considered

Min Size of Investment Considered (000s): $5,000
Max Size of Investment Considered (000s): $20,000

Geographical Preferences

United States

All U.S.

Canada

All Canada

International

Mexico
South Africa

Industry Preferences

(% based on actual investment)

Communications and Media	43.1%
Internet Specific	35.3%
Computer Software and Services	20.5%
Semiconductors/Other Elect.	1.2%

Additional Information

Year Founded: 1976
Capital Under Management: $500,000,000
Current Activity Level : Actively seeking new investments
Method of Compensation: Return on investment is of primary concern, do not charge fees

MARCONI VENTURES

890 Winter Street
Suite 310
Waltham, MA 02451
Phone: 781-839-7177
Fax: 781-522-7477
Website: www.marconi.com

Other Offices

One Bruton Street
London , United Kingdom W1X 8AQ
Phone: 44-20-7493-8484
Fax: 44-20-7493-1974

Management and Staff

Mark Aslett, Managing General Partner
Philip Wilson, Chief Financial Officer

Type of Firm

Non-Financial Corp. Affiliate or Subsidiary

Industry Association Membership

National Venture Capital Association (NVCA)

Project Preferences

Role in Financing:

Will function either as deal originator or investor in deals created by others

Type of Financing Preferred:

Balanced
First Stage Financing
Later Stage
Second Stage Financing
Startup

Size of Investments Considered

Min Size of Investment Considered (000s): $1,000
Max Size of Investment Considered (000s): $10,000

Geographical Preferences

United States

All U.S.

Canada

All Canada

International

Italy
Middle East
United Kingdom

Industry Preferences

Communications and Media

Communications and Media
Wireless Communications
Data Communications

Computer Software

Software
Applications Software

Internet Specific

E-Commerce Technology
Internet

Semiconductors/Other Elect.

Semiconductor
Circuit Boards
Fiber Optics

Medical/Health

Medical/Health

Additional Information

Year Founded: 2000
Capital Under Management: $100,000,000
Current Activity Level : Actively seeking new investments

MARLBOROUGH CAPITAL ADVISORS

9 Newbvry Street
Boston, MA 02116
Phone: 617-236-8281
Fax: 617-421-9631

Management and Staff

Gayle Slattery, Partner
Margaret Lanoix, Partner

Whom to Contact

Margaret Lanoix

Type of Firm
Private Firm Investing Own Capital

Project Preferences

Role in Financing:
Prefer role as deal originator but will also invest in deals created by others

Type of Financing Preferred:
Expansion
Leveraged Buyout
Mezzanine
Private Placement

Size of Investments Considered
Min Size of Investment Considered (000s): $3,000
Max Size of Investment Considered (000s): $6,000

Geographical Preferences

United States
All U.S.

Industry Preferences

(% based on actual investment)

Other Products	38.6%
Industrial/Energy	30.1%
Consumer Related	27.3%
Medical/Health	3.9%

Additional Information
Name of Most Recent Fund: Marlborough Capital Investment Fund III
Most Recent Fund Was Raised: 12/18/1997
Capital Under Management: $170,000,000
Current Activity Level : Actively seeking new investments
Method of Compensation: Return on invest. most important, but chg. closing fees, service fees, etc.

MARLEAU, LEMIRE, INC.

793 Washington Street
Suite One
Brookline, MA 02146-2121

See Foreign Venture Capital Firms for full listing.

MASSACHUSETTS CAPITAL RESOURCE CO.

420 Boylston Street
Boston, MA 02116
Phone: 617-536-3900
Fax: 617-536-7930

Other Offices

420 Boylston Street
Boston, MA 02116
Phone: 617-536-3900

Management and Staff
William J. Torpey Jr.

Whom to Contact
William J. Torpey Jr.

Type of Firm
Private Firm Investing Own Capital

Project Preferences

Role in Financing:
Prefer role as deal originator but will also invest in deals created by others

Type of Financing Preferred:
Leveraged Buyout
Mezzanine
Second Stage Financing

Size of Investments Considered
Min Size of Investment Considered (000s): $500
Max Size of Investment Considered (000s): $1,000

Geographical Preferences

United States
Northeast

Industry Preferences

(% based on actual investment)

Consumer Related	21.5%
Industrial/Energy	18.5%
Other Products	18.2%
Semiconductors/Other Elect.	14.3%
Computer Hardware	9.8%
Communications and Media	6.3%
Computer Software and Services	6.0%
Medical/Health	2.9%
Internet Specific	2.6%

Additional Information
Name of Most Recent Fund: Massachusetts Capital Resource Company
Most Recent Fund Was Raised: 01/01/1978
Year Founded: 1977
Capital Under Management: $100,000,000
Current Activity Level : Inactive / Unknown
Method of Compensation: Return on investment is of primary concern, do not charge fees

MASSACHUSETTS INSTITUTE OF TECHNOLOGY

238 Main Street, Suite 200
Cambridge, MA 02142
Phone: 617-253-1000
Fax: 617-258-6676

Type of Firm
Endowment

Industry Preferences

(% based on actual investment)

Medical/Health	21.4%
Internet Specific	20.8%
Computer Software and Services	18.4%
Communications and Media	15.1%
Consumer Related	13.3%
Industrial/Energy	9.0%
Biotechnology	2.0%

Additional Information
Current Activity Level : Inactive / Unknown

MASSACHUSETTS TECHNOLOGY DEVELOPMENT CORP. (MTDC)

148 State Street
Boston, MA 02109
Phone: 617-723-4920
Fax: 617-723-5983
Website: www.mtdc.com

Other Offices

148 State Street
Boston, MA 02109
Phone: 617-723-4920

Management and Staff
John Hodgman, President
Karin Gregory, Vice President
Robert Creeden, Vice President

Type of Firm
State Govt Affiliated NEC

Industry Association Membership
Natl assoc of Small Bus. Inv. Co (NASBIC)

Project Preferences

Role in Financing:
Will function either as deal originator or investor in deals created by others

Type of Financing Preferred:
Early Stage
Seed
Startup

Size of Investments Considered
Min Size of Investment Considered (000s): $200
Max Size of Investment Considered (000s): $1,000

Geographical Preferences

United States
Massachusetts

Industry Preferences

(% based on actual investment)

Computer Software and Services	30.8%
Internet Specific	14.5%
Semiconductors/Other Elect.	13.7%
Computer Hardware	12.9%
Biotechnology	10.1%
Medical/Health	7.9%
Industrial/Energy	5.6%
Communications and Media	2.9%
Other Products	1.7%

Additional Information
Name of Most Recent Fund: MTDC Commonwealth Fund
Most Recent Fund Was Raised: 06/01/1995
Year Founded: 1978
Capital Under Management: $45,000,000
Current Activity Level : Actively seeking new investments
Method of Compensation: Return on investment is of primary concern, do not charge fees

MATRIX PARTNERS

Bay Colony Corporate Center
1000 Winter Street Suite 4500
Waltham, MA 02451
Phone: 781-890-2244
Fax: 781-890-2288
Website: www.matrixpartners.com

Other Offices

2500 Sand Hill Road
Suite 113
Menlo Park, CA 94025
Phone: 650-854-3131
Fax: 650-854-3296

Management and Staff
Andrew Marcuvitz, General Partner
Andrew Verhalen, General Partner
David Skok, Partner
David Schantz, General Partner
Edgar Masri, Partner
Frederick Fluegel, General Partner
Joseph Rizzi, General Partner
Mark Vershel, General Partner
Michael Humphreys, General Partner
Paul Ferri, General Partner
Timothy Barrows, General Partner

Type of Firm
Private Firm Investing Own Capital

Industry Association Membership
National Venture Capital Association (NVCA)
Western Association of Venture Capitalists (WAVC)

Project Preferences

Role in Financing:
Prefer role as deal originator but will also invest in deals created by others

Type of Financing Preferred:
Early Stage
First Stage Financing
Leveraged Buyout
Second Stage Financing
Start-up Financing

Size of Investments Considered
Min Size of Investment Considered (000s): $500
Max Size of Investment Considered (000s): $1,000

Geographical Preferences

United States
All U.S.
Northeast

Industry Preferences

(% based on actual investment)

Communications and Media	34.3%
Internet Specific	28.8%
Computer Software and Services	17.9%
Computer Hardware	6.0%
Semiconductors/Other Elect.	5.9%
Consumer Related	3.2%
Medical/Health	2.6%
Industrial/Energy	0.7%
Other Products	0.5%
Biotechnology	0.1%

Additional Information
Name of Most Recent Fund: Matrix Partners VI, L.P.
Most Recent Fund Was Raised: 01/08/1998
Year Founded: 1982
Capital Under Management: $926,300,000
Current Activity Level : Actively seeking new investments
Method of Compensation: Return on investment is of primary concern, do not charge fees

MDT ADVISERS, INC.

125 Cambridge Park Drive
Cambridge, MA 02140
Phone: 617-234-2200
Fax: 617-234-2210
Website: www.mdtai.com

Management and Staff
Charles Levin, Chief Financial Officer
Jay Senerchia, Principal
Kenneth Revis, Principal
Lawrence Kernan, Principal
Michael O'Malley, Principal

Type of Firm
Private Firm Investing Own Capital

Industry Association Membership
National Venture Capital Association (NVCA)

Project Preferences

Role in Financing:
Will function either as deal originator or investor in deals created by others

Type of Financing Preferred:
Early Stage
Expansion

Size of Investments Considered
Min Size of Investment Considered (000s): $500
Max Size of Investment Considered (000s): $5,000

Geographical Preferences
United States
Northeast

Industry Preferences
(% based on actual investment)

Consumer Related	23.6%
Internet Specific	19.1%
Other Products	17.9%
Communications and Media	15.3%
Computer Software and Services	11.2%
Semiconductors/Other Elect.	6.4%
Medical/Health	3.8%
Industrial/Energy	1.6%
Computer Hardware	0.8%
Biotechnology	0.4%

Additional Information
Name of Most Recent Fund: MDT Venture III
Most Recent Fund Was Raised: 06/01/1998
Year Founded: 1951
Capital Under Management: $80,000,000
Current Activity Level : Actively seeking new investments
Method of Compensation: Return on investment is of primary concern, do not charge fees

MEDEQUITY INVESTORS LLC

36 Washington Street
Suite 170
Wellesley, MA 02481
Phone: 781-237-6910
Fax: 781-237-6911
Website: www.medequity.com

Management and Staff
Jeffrey Ward, Principal
Peter Gares, Managing Director
Robert Daly, Managing Director
W. Brandon Ingersoll, Principal

Type of Firm
Private Firm Investing Own Capital

Additional Information
Name of Most Recent Fund: MedEquity Direct Investment Program
Most Recent Fund Was Raised: 08/01/1999
Year Founded: 1998
Capital Under Management: $100,000,000
Current Activity Level : Actively seeking new investments

MEDICAL IMAGING INNOVATION & INVESTMENTS, L.P (AKA: MI3)

One Hollis Street
Suite 232
Wellesley, MA 02482
Phone: 781-707-5050
Fax: 781-607-1760

Management and Staff
William McPhee, General Partner

Type of Firm
Private Firm Investing Own Capital

Project Preferences
Role in Financing:
Prefer role as deal originator but will also invest in deals created by others

Size of Investments Considered
Min Size of Investment Considered (000s): $2,000
Max Size of Investment Considered (000s): $3,000

Additional Information
Name of Most Recent Fund: Medical Imaging Innovation & Investments, L.P.
Most Recent Fund Was Raised: 11/30/1998
Year Founded: 1998
Capital Under Management: $35,000,000
Current Activity Level : Actively seeking new investments
Method of Compensation: Return on investment is of primary concern, do not charge fees

MEDICAL SCIENCE PARTNERS

161 Wister Rd.
Suite 301
Framingham, MA 01701
Phone: 508-620-9250
Fax: 508-670-9251

Management and Staff
Andre Lamotte, Managing Partner
Joseph Lovett, General Partner
Kim Oakley, Chief Financial Officer

Type of Firm
Private Firm Investing Own Capital

Project Preferences
Role in Financing:
Prefer role as deal originator

Type of Financing Preferred:
First Stage Financing
Second Stage Financing
Seed
Start-up Financing

Size of Investments Considered
Min Size of Investment Considered (000s): $300
Max Size of Investment Considered (000s): $2,500

Geographical Preferences
International
No Preference

Industry Preferences
(% based on actual investment)

Biotechnology	68.3%
Medical/Health	31.3%
Industrial/Energy	0.4%

Additional Information
Year Founded: 1989
Capital Under Management: $80,000,000
Current Activity Level : Actively seeking new investments

MEDIPHASE VENTURE PARTNERS (FKA: EHEALTH TECHNOLOGY FUND)

150 Coolidge Avenue
East Watertown, MA 02472
Phone: 617-924-1256
Fax: 617-972-8587
Website: www.mediphaseventure.com

Management and Staff
Lawrence Miller, General Partner
Paul Howard, General Partner
Peter Svennilson, Venture Partner

Type of Firm
Private Firm Investing Own Capital

Project Preferences

Type of Financing Preferred:
Early Stage

Geographical Preferences

United States
All U.S.

Industry Preferences

Internet Specific
Internet

Medical/Health
Medical/Health
Drug/Equipmt Delivery

Additional Information
Year Founded: 2000
Capital Under Management: $55,000,000
Current Activity Level : Actively seeking new investments

MEES PIERSON INVESTERINGSMAAT. B.V.

20 William Street
Suite 210
Wellesley, MA 02181
Phone: 781-239-7600
Fax: 781-239-0377

Management and Staff
Dennis P. Cameron
Kevin Stadtler

Whom to Contact
Dennis P. Cameron
Kevin Stadtler

Type of Firm
Investment/Merchant Bank Subsid/Affil

Project Preferences

Role in Financing:
Prefer role in deals created by others

Type of Financing Preferred:
First Stage Financing
Second Stage Financing
Start-up Financing

Geographical Preferences

United States
All U.S.

Canada
All Canada

International
Bermuda
Germany
Middle East
United Kingdom

Industry Preferences

Communications and Media
Commercial Communications
Telecommunications
Data Communications
Satellite Microwave Comm.

Internet Specific
Internet

Semiconductors/Other Elect.
Fiber Optics

Additional Information
Year Founded: 1991
Capital Under Management: $115,000,000
Current Activity Level : Actively seeking new investments

MEGUNTICOOK MANAGEMENT

137 Newberry Street
Floor 2
Boston, MA 02116
Phone: 617-986-3000
Fax: 617-986-3100
Website: www.megunticook.com

Management and Staff
Heberden Ryan, Partner
James Houghton, Partner
Lynne Anderson, Chief Financial Officer
Matthew Lorentzen, Partner
Thomas Matlack, Managing Director

Type of Firm
Private Firm Investing Own Capital

Project Preferences

Type of Financing Preferred:
Early Stage

Industry Preferences

(% based on actual investment)

Internet Specific	47.8%
Communications and Media	26.0%
Computer Software and Services	17.7%
Consumer Related	8.5%

Additional Information
Name of Most Recent Fund: Megunticook Fund I L.P.
Most Recent Fund Was Raised: 05/01/1999
Year Founded: 2000
Capital Under Management: $96,000,000
Current Activity Level : Actively seeking new investments

METAPOINT PARTNERS

Three Centennial Drive
Peabody, MA 01960
Phone: 978-531-4444
Fax: 978-531-6662

Management and Staff
Keith Shaughnessy, President
Luke McInnis, Vice President

Whom to Contact
Keith Shaughnessy
Stuart Mathews

Type of Firm
Private Firm Investing Own Capital

Project Preferences

Role in Financing:
Prefer role as deal originator but will also invest in deals created by others

Type of Financing Preferred:
Leveraged Buyout
Recapitalizations

Size of Investments Considered
Min Size of Investment Considered (000s): $5,000
Max Size of Investment Considered: No Limit

Geographical Preferences

United States
Midwest
Northeast
Southeast

Industry Preferences

Semiconductors/Other Elect.
Sensors

Industrial/Energy
Materials
Machinery
Environmental Related

Additional Information
Name of Most Recent Fund: Metapoint Partners Fund III, L.P.
Most Recent Fund Was Raised: 06/01/1997
Year Founded: 1988
Capital Under Management: $32,000,000
Current Activity Level : Actively seeking new investments
Method of Compensation: Return on investment is of primary concern, do not charge fees

MORGAN STANLEY VENTURE PARTNERS (AKA: MSDW)

Two International Place
Boston, MA 02110
Phone: 617-856-8000
Fax: 617-856-8022
Website: http://www.msvp.com

See New York for full listing.

MPM CAPITAL (FKA - MPM ASSET MANAGEMENT LLC)

One Cambridge Center
9th Floor
Cambridge, MA 02142
Phone: 617-225-7054
Fax: 617-225-2210
Website: www.mpmcapital.com

Other Offices

601 Gateway Boulevard
Suite 360
South San Francisco, CA 94080
Phone: 650-829-5820
Fax: 650-829-5828

Weissfrauenstrasse 10
60311
Frankfurt, Germany 94080
Phone: 49-691-33-8980
Fax: 49-691-33-898-29

Management and Staff
Ansbert Gadicke, Managing Director
Elline Hildebrandt, Vice President
Joachim Rothe, Principal
Kurt Wheeler, Venture Partner
Luke Evnin, General Partner
Michael Steinmetz, Managing Director
Nicholas Galakatos, General Partner

Type of Firm
Private Firm Investing Own Capital

Industry Association Membership
National Venture Capital Association (NVCA)

Project Preferences

Type of Financing Preferred:
Early Stage
First Stage Financing

Industry Preferences

(% based on actual investment)

Biotechnology	51.0%
Medical/Health	43.9%
Computer Software and Services	2.6%
Internet Specific	2.5%

Additional Information
Name of Most Recent Fund: BB Bioventures L.P./MPM Bioventures Parallel Fund L.P.
Most Recent Fund Was Raised: 11/01/1997
Year Founded: 1997
Capital Under Management: $830,000,000
Current Activity Level : Actively seeking new investments
Method of Compensation: Return on investment is of primary concern, do not charge fees

MVP VENTURES (AKA: MILK STREET VENTURES)

9 Harcourt
Suite 206
Boston, MA 20116
Phone: 617-345-7228
Fax: 617-345-7201

Type of Firm
Private Firm Investing Own Capital

Project Preferences

Role in Financing:
Prefer role as deal originator but will also invest in deals created by others

Type of Financing Preferred:
First Stage Financing
Mezzanine
Second Stage Financing
Start-up Financing

Size of Investments Considered
Min Size of Investment Considered (000s): $500
Max Size of Investment Considered (000s): $3,000

Geographical Preferences

International
No Preference

Industry Preferences

Communications and Media
Communications and Media

Computer Other
Computer Related

Semiconductors/Other Elect.
Electronic Components

Additional Information
Name of Most Recent Fund: MVP Ventures
Most Recent Fund Was Raised: 01/01/1992
Year Founded: 1997
Capital Under Management: $124,000,000
Current Activity Level : Actively seeking new investments
Method of Compensation: Return on investment is of primary concern, do not charge fees

NAVIS PARTNERS (FKA:FLEET EQUITY PARTNERS)

1740 Massachusetts Avenue
Boxborough, MA 01719
Phone: 508-263-0177
Website: www.navispartners.com

See Rhode Island for full listing.

NEEDHAM & COMPANY, INC.

One Post Office Square
Suite 3710
Boston, MA 02109
Phone: 617-457-0900
Fax: 617-457-5777
Website: www.needhamco.com

See New York for full listing.

NEOCARTA VENTURES

45 Fairfield St.
4th Floor
Boston, MA 02116
Phone: 617-239-9000
Fax: 617-266-4107
Website: www.neocarta.com

Other Offices

1350 Avenue of the Americas
32nd Floor
New York, NY 10019
Phone: 212-931-8050
Fax: 212-931-8001

Two Embarcadero Center
Suite 460
San Francisco, CA 94111
Phone: 415-277-0230
Fax: 415-277-0240

Management and Staff

Jarrett Collins, Managing Director
Karen Kassine, Managing Director
Tom Naughton, Managing Director
Tony Pantuso, Managing Director

Type of Firm

Private Firm Investing Own Capital

Industry Preferences

(% based on actual investment)

Internet Specific	81.8%
Computer Hardware	7.6%
Communications and Media	6.8%
Other Products	3.1%
Computer Software and Services	0.8%

Additional Information

Capital Under Management: $300,000,000
Current Activity Level : Actively seeking new investments

NEW ENGLAND PARTNERS

One Boston Place
Suite 2100
Boston, MA 02108
Phone: 617-624-8400
Fax: 617-624-8999
Website: www.nepartners.com

Management and Staff

Chris Young, General Partner
David Dullum, General Partner
Edwin Snape, General Partner
John Rousseau, General Partner
Robert Hanks, General Partner

Whom to Contact

Christopher P. Young

Type of Firm

SBIC Not elsewhere classified

Industry Association Membership

National Venture Capital Association (NVCA)
Natl assoc of Small Bus. Inv. Co (NASBIC)

Project Preferences

Role in Financing:

Will function either as deal originator or investor in deals created by others

Type of Financing Preferred:

Balanced
Early Stage
First Stage Financing
Second Stage Financing

Size of Investments Considered

Min Size of Investment Considered (000s): $1,000
Max Size of Investment Considered (000s): $5,000

Geographical Preferences

United States

All U.S.

Industry Preferences

(% based on actual investment)

Biotechnology	47.6%
Consumer Related	15.1%
Communications and Media	12.1%
Computer Software and Services	11.3%
Internet Specific	8.7%
Medical/Health	2.6%
Semiconductors/Other Elect.	2.0%
Other Products	0.5%

Additional Information

Name of Most Recent Fund: New England Growth Fund III
Most Recent Fund Was Raised: 10/01/1999
Year Founded: 1992
Capital Under Management: $200,000,000
Current Activity Level : Actively seeking new investments
Method of Compensation: Return on investment is of primary concern, do not charge fees

NEWBURY, PIRET & CO., INC.

One Boston Place
26th Floor
Boston, MA 02108
Phone: 617-367-7300
Fax: 617-367-7301

Management and Staff

John J. Piret

Whom to Contact

John J. Piret

Type of Firm

Mgt. Consulting Firm

Project Preferences

Role in Financing:

Prefer role as deal originator but will also invest in deals created by others

Type of Financing Preferred:

Industry Rollups
Leveraged Buyout
Mezzanine
Second Stage Financing
Special Situation

Size of Investments Considered

Min Size of Investment Considered (000s): $3,000
Max Size of Investment Considered: No Limit

Geographical Preferences

United States

All U.S.

Canada

All Canada

International

Bermuda
China
France
Germany
Italy
Japan
Spain
United Kingdom

Industry Preferences

Communications and Media

Communications and Media

Computer Other

Computer Related

Semiconductors/Other Elect.
Electronic Components

Biotechnology
Biotechnology

Medical/Health
Medical/Health

Consumer Related
Food/Beverage
Consumer Products
Education Related

Industrial/Energy
Alternative Energy
Industrial Products

Financial Services
Financial Services

Business Serv.
Distribution

Manufact.
Publishing

Additional Information
Year Founded: 1981
Current Activity Level : Actively seeking new investments
Method of Compensation: Function primarily in service area, receive contingent fee in cash or equity

NEXTPOINT PARTNERS L.P.(FKA: PLAZA STREET)

One Financial Center
Suite 4100
Boston, MA 02111
Website: www.nextpointvc.com

See D. of Columbia for full listing.

NORTH BRIDGE VENTURE PARTNERS

950 Winter Street
Suite 4600
Waltham, MA 02451
Phone: 781-290-0004
Fax: 781-290-0999

Management and Staff
Angelo Santinelli, Principal
Edward Anderson, General Partner
Richard D'Amore, General Partner
Robert Walkingshaw, General Partner
William Geary, General Partner

Type of Firm
Private Firm Investing Own Capital

Industry Association Membership
National Venture Capital Association (NVCA)

Project Preferences

Role in Financing:
Prefer role as deal originator but will also invest in deals created by others

Type of Financing Preferred:
First Stage Financing
Research and Development
Second Stage Financing
Seed
Start-up Financing

Size of Investments Considered
Min Size of Investment Considered (000s): $2,000
Max Size of Investment Considered (000s): $3,000

Geographical Preferences

United States
All U.S.

Canada
All Canada

International
Middle East

Industry Preferences

(% based on actual investment)

Communications and Media	37.2%
Internet Specific	27.8%
Computer Software and Services	26.0%
Computer Hardware	4.0%
Medical/Health	2.0%
Semiconductors/Other Elect.	1.1%
Other Products	1.0%
Biotechnology	0.9%

Additional Information
Name of Most Recent Fund: North Bridge Venture Partners IV, L.P.
Most Recent Fund Was Raised: 09/01/1999
Year Founded: 1994
Capital Under Management: $585,000,000
Current Activity Level : Actively seeking new investments
Method of Compensation: Return on investment is of primary concern, do not charge fees

NORTH HILL VENTURES

Ten Post Office Square
11th Floor
Boston, MA 02109
Phone: 617-788-2112
Fax: 617-788-2152
Website: www.northhillventures.com

Management and Staff
Benjamin Malka, Principal
Brett Rome, General Partner
Shamez Kanji, General Partner

Type of Firm
Non-Financial Corp. Affiliate or Subsidiary

Industry Association Membership
National Venture Capital Association (NVCA)

Project Preferences

Role in Financing:
Will function either as deal originator or investor in deals created by others

Type of Financing Preferred:
Balanced
Expansion
Later Stage
Second Stage Financing

Size of Investments Considered
Min Size of Investment Considered (000s): $1,500
Max Size of Investment Considered (000s): $7,000

Geographical Preferences

United States
All U.S.

International
United Kingdom

Industry Preferences

Communications and Media
Telecommunications
Wireless Communications

Computer Software
Computer Services
Data Processing
Software
Systems Software
Applications Software

Internet Specific
E-Commerce Technology
Internet

Consumer Related
Consumer
Retail

Financial Services
Financial Services
Insurance

Business Serv.
Services

Additional Information
Year Founded: 1999
Capital Under Management: $100,000,000
Current Activity Level : Actively seeking new investments
Method of Compensation: Return on investment is of primary concern, do not charge fees

NORWEST EQUITY PARTNERS

40 William Street
Suite 305
Wellesley, MA 02181-3902
Phone: 781-237-5870
Fax: 781-237-6270
Website: ww.norwestvp.com

See California for full listing.

NUCON CAPITAL CORP.

225 Franklin Street
Boston, MA 02110
Phone: 617-423-2301
Fax: 617-338-2150

Management and Staff
Dave Weener, Chief Financial Officer

Type of Firm
Private Firm Investing Own Capital

Additional Information
Current Activity Level : Actively seeking new investments

ONELIBERTY VENTURES (FKA: MORGAN, HOLLAND VENTURES CORP.)

150 CambridgePark Drive
Cambridge, MA 02140-2322
Phone: 617-492-7280
Fax: 617-492-7290
Website: www.oneliberty.com

Management and Staff
Cheryl Goyette, Chief Financial Officer
Daniel Holland, Venture Partner
David Flaschen, General Partner
Duncan McCallum, General Partner
E. Langley Steinert, Venture Partner
Edwin Kania, Managing General Partner
Joseph McCullen, General Partner
Stephen Ricci, General Partner

Whom to Contact
Stephen J. McCullen

Type of Firm
Private Firm Investing Own Capital

Industry Association Membership
National Venture Capital Association (NVCA)

Project Preferences

Role in Financing:
Prefer role as deal originator but will also invest in deals created by others

Type of Financing Preferred:
Early Stage

Size of Investments Considered
Min Size of Investment Considered (000s): $1,000
Max Size of Investment Considered (000s): $8,000

Geographical Preferences

United States
Northeast

Industry Preferences

(% based on actual investment)

Communications and Media	27.4%
Internet Specific	20.1%
Computer Software and Services	18.3%
Semiconductors/Other Elect.	9.5%
Medical/Health	8.1%
Other Products	5.3%
Computer Hardware	5.1%
Biotechnology	4.3%
Industrial/Energy	1.9%

Additional Information
Name of Most Recent Fund: Oneliberty Fund IV L.P.
Most Recent Fund Was Raised: 12/01/1997
Year Founded: 1995
Capital Under Management: $404,400,000
Current Activity Level : Actively seeking new investments
Method of Compensation: Return on investment is of primary concern, do not charge fees

ORION PARTNERS, L.P.

20 William Street
Suite 145
Wellesley, MA 02481
Phone: 781-235-1904
Fax: 781-235-8822
Website: www.orionlp.com

Management and Staff
Jefferey R. Ackerman

Whom to Contact
Jefferey R. Ackerman

Type of Firm
Private Firm Investing Own Capital

Project Preferences

Role in Financing:
Prefer role as deal originator but will also invest in deals created by others

Type of Financing Preferred:
First Stage Financing
Leveraged Buyout
Second Stage Financing
Special Situation

Size of Investments Considered
Min Size of Investment Considered (000s): $5,000
Max Size of Investment Considered: No Limit

Geographical Preferences

United States
Northeast
Southeast

Canada
Quebec

Industry Preferences

Communications and Media
Data Communications

Computer Hardware
Computer Graphics and Dig
Integrated Turnkey System

Computer Software
Computer Services
Applications Software

Semiconductors/Other Elect.
Electronic Components
Sensors

Medical/Health
Medical/Health

Consumer Related
Entertainment and Leisure
Retail
Food/Beverage
Consumer Products
Consumer Services

Industrial/Energy
Materials

Financial Services
Financial Services

Business Serv.
Distribution
Consulting Services

Manufact.
Publishing

Additional Information
Name of Most Recent Fund: Orion Capital Holdings, L.P.
Most Recent Fund Was Raised: 04/01/1993
Year Founded: 1993
Capital Under Management: $51,000,000
Current Activity Level : Inactive / Unknown
Method of Compensation: Return on investment is of primary concern, do not charge fees

---

OSBORN CAPITAL LLC

171 Grove Street
Lexington, MA 02420
Phone: 781-402-1790
Fax: 781-402-1793
Website: www.osborncapital.com

Other Offices

41582 Spring Valley Lane
Leesburg, VA 20175
Phone: 703-748-8462
Fax: 703-748-8463

Management and Staff
Eric Janszen, Managing Director
Jeffrey Osborn, Principal

Type of Firm
Private Firm Investing Own Capital

Industry Association Membership
Mid-Atlantic Venture Association

Project Preferences

Type of Financing Preferred:
Seed
Startup

Additional Information
Year Founded: 1998
Current Activity Level : Actively seeking new investments

OXFORD BIOSCIENCE PARTNERS

31 St. James Avenue
Suite 905
Boston, MA 02116
Phone: 617-357-7474
Fax: 617-357-7476
Website: www.oxbio.com

Other Offices

315 Post Road West
Westport, CT 06880
Phone: 203-341-3300
Fax: 617-357-7476

650 Town Center Drive
Suite 810
Costa Mesa, CA 92626
Phone: 714-754-5719
Fax: 714-754-6802

Management and Staff
Alan Walton, General Partner
Douglas Fambrough, Principal
Edmund Olivier, General Partner
Jeffrey Barnes, General Partner
Jonathan Fleming, Managing General Partner
Mark Carthy, Venture Partner
Martin Vogelbaum, General Partner
Matthew Gibbs, Venture Partner
Michael Brennan, General Partner
Michelle O'Grady, Chief Financial Officer
Neil Ryan, General Partner
Ray Charest, Chief Financial Officer
Richard Hamilton, Principal
Stella Sung, General Partner

Whom to Contact
Matt Gibbs
William Greenman

Type of Firm
Investment Management/Finance Consulting

Industry Association Membership
National Venture Capital Association (NVCA)

Project Preferences

Role in Financing:
Prefer role as deal originator but will also invest in deals created by others

Type of Financing Preferred:
Early Stage
First Stage Financing
Research and Development

Geographical Preferences

United States
All U.S.

Canada
All Canada

International
Bermuda
France
Germany
Japan
United Kingdom

Industry Preferences

(% based on actual investment)

Biotechnology	49.9%
Medical/Health	31.3%
Internet Specific	8.1%
Computer Software and Services	6.2%
Consumer Related	2.5%
Computer Hardware	1.1%
Semiconductors/Other Elect.	0.9%

Additional Information
Name of Most Recent Fund: Oxford Bioscience Partners II
Most Recent Fund Was Raised: 04/01/1997
Year Founded: 1992
Capital Under Management: $397,000,000
Current Activity Level : Actively seeking new investments
Method of Compensation: Return on investment is of primary concern, do not charge fees

PALMER PARTNERS, L.P.

200 Unicorn Park Drive
Woburn, MA 01801
Phone: 781-933-5445
Fax: 781-933-0698

Management and Staff
John Shane

Whom to Contact
John Shane

Type of Firm
Private Firm Investing Own Capital

Project Preferences

Role in Financing:
Prefer role as deal originator but will also invest in deals created by others

Type of Financing Preferred:
First Stage Financing
Recapitalizations
Second Stage Financing
Special Situation
Start-up Financing

Geographical Preferences

United States
Mid Atlantic
Midwest
Northeast
Southeast
Southwest

Canada
Central Canada
Eastern Canada

Industry Preferences

Communications and Media
Communications and Media

Computer Other
Computer Related

Consumer Related
Education Related

Industrial/Energy
Industrial Products

Financial Services
Financial Services

Manufact.
Publishing

Additional Information
Name of Most Recent Fund: The Palmer Organization III L.P.
Most Recent Fund Was Raised: 01/01/1996
Year Founded: 1972
Capital Under Management: $53,000,000
Current Activity Level : Actively seeking new investments
Method of Compensation: Return on investment is of primary concern, do not charge fees

POLARIS VENTURE PARTNERS

Bay Colony Corporate Center
1000 Winter Street, Suite 3350
Waltham, MA 02451
Phone: 781-290-0770
Fax: 781-290-0880
Website: www.polarisventures.com

Other Offices

804 Las Cimas Parkway
Building One, Suite 140
Austin, TX 78746
Phone: 512-225-5400
Fax: 512-225-5444

Bank of America Tower
701 Fifth Avenue; Suite 6850
Seattle, WA 98104
Phone: 206-652-4555
Fax: 206-652-4666

Management and Staff
Alan Spoon, Managing Partner
Brian Chee, Partner
Christoph Westphal, Principal
Dave Barrett, Venture Partner
George Conrades, Venture Partner
James Brown, Partner
John Gannon, Partner
Jonathan Flint, Managing Partner
Michael Hirshland, Partner
Robert Metcalf, Venture Partner
Steven Arnold, Managing Partner
Terry McGuire, Managing Partner
Thomas Herring, Partner

Type of Firm
Private Firm Investing Own Capital

Industry Association Membership
Mid-Atlantic Venture Association
National Venture Capital Association (NVCA)

Project Preferences

Role in Financing:
Prefer role as deal originator but will also invest in deals created by others

Type of Financing Preferred:
Early Stage
First Stage Financing
Second Stage Financing
Seed
Startup

Size of Investments Considered
Min Size of Investment Considered (000s): $250
Max Size of Investment Considered (000s): $15,000

Industry Preferences

(% based on actual investment)

Internet Specific	49.9%
Computer Software and Services	23.6%
Medical/Health	11.2%
Communications and Media	8.0%
Biotechnology	6.2%
Other Products	0.6%
Computer Hardware	0.5%
Industrial/Energy	0.0%

Additional Information
Name of Most Recent Fund: Polaris Venture Partners II
Most Recent Fund Was Raised: 04/01/1998
Year Founded: 1995
Capital Under Management: $1,080,000,000
Current Activity Level : Actively seeking new investments
Method of Compensation: Return on investment is of primary concern, do not charge fees

PRISM VENTURE PARTNERS

100 Lowder Brook Drive
Suite 2500
Westwood, MA 02090
Phone: 781-302-4000
Fax: 781-302-4040
Website: www.prismventure.com

Management and Staff
Daniel Wright, Chief Financial Officer
David Baum, General Partner
Duane Mason, General Partner
John Brooks, General Partner
Laurie Thomsen, Venture Partner
Michael Baum, Venture Partner
Robert Fleming, General Partner
William Seifert, General Partner

Type of Firm
Private Firm Investing Own Capital

Industry Association Membership
National Venture Capital Association (NVCA)

Project Preferences

Role in Financing:
Prefer role as deal originator but will also invest in deals created by others

Type of Financing Preferred:
Early Stage

Size of Investments Considered
Min Size of Investment Considered (000s): $2,000
Max Size of Investment Considered (000s): $10,000

Geographical Preferences

United States
All U.S.

Canada
All Canada

Industry Preferences

(% based on actual investment)

Internet Specific	38.1%
Medical/Health	23.7%
Computer Software and Services	14.4%
Biotechnology	8.1%
Communications and Media	6.4%
Computer Hardware	6.3%
Semiconductors/Other Elect.	2.9%

Additional Information
Name of Most Recent Fund: PVP II, L.P.
Most Recent Fund Was Raised: 10/01/1998
Year Founded: 1997
Capital Under Management: $559,500,000
Current Activity Level : Actively seeking new investments
Method of Compensation: Return on investment is of primary concern, do not charge fees

---

PROSPECT STREET VENTURES (FKA:PROSPECT STREET INVEST. MGMT)

Exchange Place
37th Floor
Boston, MA 02109
Phone: 617-742-3800
Fax: 617-742-9455
Website: www.prospectstreet.com

See New York for full listing.

PSILOS GROUP MANAGERS LLC

152 West 57th Street
33rd Floor
New York, MA 10019
Phone: 212-399-2070
Fax: 212-399-2081
Website: www.psilos.com

See New York for full listing.

RCT BIOVENTURES NE (RESEARCH CORPORATION TECHNOLOGIES)

30 Monument Square
Suite 215
Concord, MA 01742-1858
Phone: 978-371-7100
Fax: 978-371-2371
Website: www.rctbvne.com

Management and Staff
Debra Peattie, President

Whom to Contact
Robert Robb

Type of Firm
Private Firm Investing Own Capital

Project Preferences

Role in Financing:
Prefer role as deal originator but will also invest in deals created by others

Type of Financing Preferred:
Research and Development
Seed
Start-up Financing

Geographical Preferences

United States
West Coast

Industry Preferences

Biotechnology
Biotechnology

Medical/Health
Medical/Health
Diagnostic Services
Diagnostic Test Products
Drug/Equipmt Delivery
Other Therapeutic
Disposable Med. Products
Pharmaceuticals

Industrial/Energy
Materials
Robotics

Additional Information
Year Founded: 1987
Capital Under Management: $30,000,000
Current Activity Level : Actively seeking new investments
Method of Compensation: Return on investment is of primary concern, do not charge fees

---

REACH INCUBATOR

Oliver Street Tower, 8th Floor
125 High Street
Boston, MA 02110
Phone: 617-948-7200
Fax: 617-948-7201
Website: www.reachincubator.com

Management and Staff
Frank Selldorff, Co-Founder
Mike Kinkead, Chief Executive Officer
Peter Cowie, Co-Founder
Voula Kanellias, Chief Financial Officer

Type of Firm
Incubators

Project Preferences

Role in Financing:
Prefer role as deal originator

Type of Financing Preferred:
Early Stage

Geographical Preferences

United States
Massachusetts
All U.S.

Additional Information
Year Founded: 1999
Current Activity Level : Actively seeking new investments

REDLEAF VENTURE MANAGEMENT

1050 Winter Street
Suite 1000
North Waltham, MA 02451
Phone: 781-487-7900
Fax: 781-487-7940
Website: www.redleaf.com

See California for full listing.

ROYALTY CAPITAL FUND, L.P. I/ROYALTY CAPITAL MANAGEMENT, INC

Five Downing Road
Lexington, MA 02421-6918
Phone: 781-861-8490

Other Offices

12 Brady Loop
Andover, MA 01810-3224
Phone: 978-474-9112
Fax: 978-474-9112

Type of Firm
Private Firm Investing Own Capital

Project Preferences

Role in Financing:
Prefer role as deal originator but will also invest in deals created by others

Type of Financing Preferred:
First Stage Financing
Leveraged Buyout
Second Stage Financing
Seed
Special Situation
Start-up Financing

Size of Investments Considered
Min Size of Investment Considered (000s): $100
Max Size of Investment Considered (000s): $300

Geographical Preferences

United States
Northeast

Industry Preferences

Communications and Media
Telecommunications
Data Communications
Satellite Microwave Comm.

Computer Hardware
Computer Graphics and Dig
Integrated Turnkey System

Computer Software
Systems Software
Applications Software
Artificial Intelligence

Internet Specific
Internet

Semiconductors/Other Elect.
Semiconductor
Sensors
Laser Related
Fiber Optics
Analytic/Scientific

Biotechnology
Industrial Biotechnology
Biosensors
Biotech Related Research

Medical/Health
Medical Diagnostics
Diagnostic Services
Diagnostic Test Products
Medical Therapeutics
Other Therapeutic
Disposable Med. Products
Pharmaceuticals

Consumer Related
Retail
Food/Beverage
Education Related

Industrial/Energy
Alternative Energy
Factory Automation
Robotics
Machinery
Environmental Related

Manufact.
Office Automation Equipmt

Additional Information
Name of Most Recent Fund: Royalty Capital Fund L.P. I
Most Recent Fund Was Raised: 01/01/1995
Year Founded: 1994
Capital Under Management: $3,000,000
Current Activity Level : Actively seeking new investments
Method of Compensation: Return on investment is of primary concern, do not charge fees

RSA VENTURES

20 Crosby Drive
Bedford, MA 01730
Phone: 781-301-5000
Fax: 781-301-5170
Website: www.rsasecurity.com

Management and Staff
Barry Rosenbaum, Managing Director
David Clark, Partner
Fergal Mullen, Partner

Type of Firm
Affiliate/Subsidary of Oth. Financial. Instit.

Project Preferences

Type of Financing Preferred:
Balanced
Early Stage

Size of Investments Considered
Min Size of Investment Considered (000s): $2,000
Max Size of Investment Considered (000s): $5,000

Geographical Preferences

United States
All U.S.

International
Europe

Industry Preferences

Communications and Media
Telecommunications

Internet Specific
Internet

Additional Information
Current Activity Level : Actively seeking new investments

SAGE MANAGEMENT GROUP

44 South Street
P.O. Box 2026
East Dennis, MA 02641
Phone: 508-385-7172
Fax: 508-385-7272

Management and Staff
Charles Bauer

Whom to Contact
Charles Bauer

Type of Firm
Mgt. Consulting Firm

Project Preferences

Role in Financing:
Prefer role as deal originator but will also invest in deals created by others

Type of Financing Preferred:
First Stage Financing
Leveraged Buyout
Mezzanine
Second Stage Financing
Special Situation

Size of Investments Considered
Min Size of Investment Considered (000s): $500
Max Size of Investment Considered (000s): $1,000

Geographical Preferences

United States
All U.S.

Industry Preferences

Communications and Media
CATV & Pay TV Systems
Telecommunications
Data Communications
Satellite Microwave Comm.

Computer Hardware
Computer Graphics and Dig

Computer Software
Applications Software

Internet Specific
Internet

Semiconductors/Other Elect.
Electronic Components
Sensors

Medical/Health
Diagnostic Test Products
Drug/Equipmt Delivery
Other Therapeutic

Industrial/Energy
Materials
Factory Automation
Robotics
Machinery

Manufact.
Office Automation Equipmt

Additional Information
Name of Most Recent Fund: Sage Management Partners
Most Recent Fund Was Raised: 01/01/1997
Year Founded: 1989
Current Activity Level : Actively seeking new investments
Method of Compensation: Function primarily in service area, receive contingent fee in cash or equity

SCHOONER CAPITAL INTERNATIONAL, L.P.

745 Atlantic Avenue
Boston, MA 02111
Phone: 617-357-9031
Fax: 617-357-5545

Other Offices

346 Jybek Jolust
Kuartira 1, Podyezd 1
Bishkek, Kyrgyzstan
Phone: 7-3312-222730
Fax: 7-3312-222730

Plac Powstancow Warszawy 1
Pokoj 256
00-950 Warsaw, Poland
Phone: 48-22-269142
Fax: 48-22-269136

Management and Staff
Cristina Fernandez-Haegg

Whom to Contact
Cristina Fernandez-Haegg

Type of Firm
Investment/Merchant Bank Subsid/Affil

Project Preferences

Role in Financing:
Prefer role as deal originator

Type of Financing Preferred:
Control-block Purchases
First Stage Financing
Second Stage Financing
Special Situation
Start-up Financing

Size of Investments Considered
Min Size of Investment Considered (000s): $10,000
Max Size of Investment Considered: No Limit

Geographical Preferences

United States
All U.S.

Industry Preferences

Communications and Media
Communications and Media
Commercial Communications
CATV & Pay TV Systems
Radio & TV Broadcasting
Telecommunications
Data Communications
Satellite Microwave Comm.

Computer Software
Computer Services
Systems Software

Medical/Health
Medical Therapeutics
Medical Products

Consumer Related
Food/Beverage
Consumer Products

Industrial/Energy
Alternative Energy

Financial Services
Financial Services

Additional Information
Name of Most Recent Fund: Schooner Capital Corp.
Most Recent Fund Was Raised: 01/01/1969
Year Founded: 1971
Capital Under Management: $300,000,000
Current Activity Level : Actively seeking new investments

SCHRODER VENTURES

Life Sciences
60 State Street Suite 3650
Boston, MA 02109
Phone: 617-367-8100
Fax: 617-367-1590
Website: www.schroderventures.com

Other Offices

20 Southampton Street
London, United Kingdom WC2E 7QG
Phone: 44 207 632 1000
Fax: 44 207 497 2174

Atlas Building, 5 Ichiban-cho
Chiyoda-Ku
Tokyo, Japan 102-0082
Phone: 813-5275-2640
Fax: 813-5275-2655

Republic Plaza Tower One
9 Raffles Place
Singapore, Singapore 048619
Phone: 65-536-6177
Fax: 65-536-6077

Suite 1103, St. George's Bldg.
2 Ice House Street
Central, Hong Kong
Phone: 852-2801-6199
Fax: 852-2801-7979

Management and Staff
Damon Buffini, Managing Partner
David LaRue, Partner
Don Nelson, Chief Financial Officer
Hingge Hsu, Principal
Jeffrey Ferrell, Principal
Jonathan Gertler, Partner
Ken Kato, Partner
Masayuki Noguchi, General Partner
Michael Carter, Partner
Nobuo Matsuki, Managing General Partner
Sanjay Sehgal, Partner
Shoko Matsui, Partner

Type of Firm
Private Firm Investing Own Capital

Industry Association Membership
British Venture Capital Association
European Venture Capital Association (EVCA)

Project Preferences

Role in Financing:
Prefer role as deal originator but will also invest in deals created by others

Type of Financing Preferred:
Balanced
First Stage Financing
Leveraged Buyout
Mezzanine
Second Stage Financing
Special Situation
Start-up Financing

Size of Investments Considered
Min Size of Investment Considered (000s): $250
Max Size of Investment Considered: No Limit

Geographical Preferences

United States
All U.S.

Canada
All Canada

International
Bermuda
China
France
Germany
India
Italy
Japan
Spain
United Kingdom

Industry Preferences

(% based on actual investment)

Other Products	57.3%
Medical/Health	12.9%
Computer Software and Services	8.3%
Biotechnology	6.2%
Internet Specific	6.1%
Consumer Related	4.3%
Semiconductors/Other Elect.	2.3%
Communications and Media	1.4%
Industrial/Energy	0.6%
Computer Hardware	0.6%

Additional Information
Name of Most Recent Fund: ILSF II
Most Recent Fund Was Raised: 01/01/1998
Year Founded: 1983
Capital Under Management: $410,000,000
Current Activity Level : Actively seeking new investments
Method of Compensation: Return on invest. most important, but chg. closing fees, service fees, etc.

SCHRODER VENTURES INTERNATIONAL LIFE SCIENCES

60 State Street
Suite 3650
Boston, MA 02109QG
Phone: 617-367-8100
Fax: 617-367-1590

Other Offices

20 Southhampton Street
Convent Garden
London, Hong Kong WC2E7QG
Phone: 44-171-632-1000
Fax: 44-171-240-5346

Management and Staff
Charles Warden, Principal
Don Nelson, Chief Financial Officer
Eugene Hill, Partner
Hsu Hingge, Partner
James M. Garvey, Managing Partner
Jeffrey Ferrell, Principal
John Cheesmond, Partner
Kate Bingham, Partner
Tom Daniel, Partner

Type of Firm
Private Firm Investing Own Capital

Industry Association Membership
National Venture Capital Association (NVCA)

Project Preferences

Role in Financing:
Prefer role as deal originator

Industry Preferences

(% based on actual investment)

Biotechnology	50.6%
Medical/Health	37.5%
Computer Hardware	6.1%
Internet Specific	3.9%
Semiconductors/Other Elect.	2.0%

Additional Information
Name of Most Recent Fund: Schroder International Life Science Fund
Most Recent Fund Was Raised: 04/29/1994
Year Founded: 1994
Capital Under Management: $410,600,000
Current Activity Level : Actively seeking new investments
Method of Compensation: Return on investment is of primary concern, do not charge fees

SEACOAST CAPITAL

55 Ferncroft Road
Danvers, MA 01923
Phone: 978-750-1300
Fax: 978-750-1301
Website: www.seacoastcapital.com

Other Offices

One Sansome Street
Suite 2100
San Francisco, CA 94104
Phone: 415-956-1400
Fax: 415-956-1459

Management and Staff

Eben Moulton, Senior Managing Director
Jeffrey Holland, Managing Director
Paul Giovacchini, Managing Director
Thomas Gorman, Managing Director
Walter Leonard, Chief Financial Officer

Whom to Contact

Gregory A. Hulecki
Paul Giovacchini

Type of Firm

Private Firm Investing Own Capital

Industry Association Membership

Natl assoc of Small Bus. Inv. Co (NASBIC)

Project Preferences

Role in Financing:

Prefer role as deal originator but will also invest in deals created by others

Type of Financing Preferred:

Industry Rollups
Leveraged Buyout
Mezzanine
Second Stage Financing
Special Situation

Size of Investments Considered

Min Size of Investment Considered (000s): $3,000
Max Size of Investment Considered: No Limit

Geographical Preferences

United States

All U.S.

Industry Preferences

(% based on actual investment)

Other Products	28.7%
Internet Specific	22.6%
Consumer Related	16.6%
Industrial/Energy	12.1%
Medical/Health	10.7%
Semiconductors/Other Elect.	7.4%
Computer Software and Services	1.9%

Additional Information

Name of Most Recent Fund: Seacoast Capital Partners
Most Recent Fund Was Raised: 01/01/1995
Year Founded: 1989
Capital Under Management: $250,000,000
Current Activity Level : Actively seeking new investments
Method of Compensation: Return on invest. most important, but chg. closing fees, service fees, etc.

SEAFLOWER VENTURES

Bay Colony Corporate Center
1000 Winter Street Suite 1000
Waltham, MA 02451
Phone: 781-466-9552
Fax: 781-466-9553
Website: www.seaflower.com

Other Offices

5170 Nicholson Road
P.O. Box 474
Fowlerville, MI 48836
Phone: 517-223-3335
Fax: 517-223-3337

Management and Staff

Alex Moot, General Partner
James Sherblom, President
M. Christine Gibbons, Partner

Whom to Contact

Alexander Moot
M. Christine Gibbons

Type of Firm

Private Firm Investing Own Capital

Industry Association Membership

National Venture Capital Association (NVCA)

Project Preferences

Role in Financing:

Prefer role as deal originator but will also invest in deals created by others

Type of Financing Preferred:

First Stage Financing
Recapitalizations
Research and Development
Second Stage Financing
Seed
Start-up Financing
Strategic Alliances

Geographical Preferences

United States

Mid Atlantic
Midwest
Northeast

Industry Preferences

(% based on actual investment)

Medical/Health	42.6%
Internet Specific	33.1%
Biotechnology	16.3%
Industrial/Energy	6.2%
Other Products	1.2%
Computer Hardware	0.7%

Additional Information

Name of Most Recent Fund: Seaflower BioVenture Fund VI
Most Recent Fund Was Raised: 07/01/1998
Year Founded: 1993
Capital Under Management: $17,000,000
Current Activity Level : Actively seeking new investments
Method of Compensation: Return on investment is of primary concern, do not charge fees

SHALOR VENTURES, INC.

65 East India Row
Suite 16F
Boston, MA 02110
Phone: 617-367-1077

Type of Firm

Private Firm Investing Own Capital

Project Preferences

Role in Financing:

Prefer role as deal originator but will also invest in deals created by others

Type of Financing Preferred:

First Stage Financing
Leveraged Buyout
Mezzanine
Recapitalizations
Second Stage Financing

Size of Investments Considered
Min Size of Investment Considered (000s): $1,000
Max Size of Investment Considered (000s): $5,000

Geographical Preferences

United States
Northeast

Industry Preferences

Consumer Related
Retail
Consumer Products

Additional Information
Year Founded: 1986
Current Activity Level : Actively seeking new investments
Method of Compensation: Return on investment is of primary concern, do not charge fees

---

SHAWMUT CAPITAL PARTNERS

75 Federal Street
18th Floor
Boston, MA 02110
Phone: 617-368-4900
Fax: 617-368-4910
Website: www.shawmutcapital.com

Management and Staff
Daniel Doyle, Managing Director
Glenn Dixon, Managing Director
Joel Alvord, Managing Director

Whom to Contact
Daniel Doyle
Jon A. Bernstein
Peter J. Grondin

Type of Firm
Private Firm Investing Own Capital

Project Preferences

Role in Financing:
Prefer role as deal originator but will also invest in deals created by others

Type of Financing Preferred:
Control-block Purchases
First Stage Financing
Industry Rollups
Leveraged Buyout
Mezzanine
Second Stage Financing
Special Situation
Start-up Financing

Size of Investments Considered
Min Size of Investment Considered (000s): $5,000
Max Size of Investment Considered: No Limit

Geographical Preferences

United States
All U.S.

Canada
All Canada

Industry Preferences

Financial Services
Financial Services

Additional Information
Name of Most Recent Fund: Shawmut Equity Partners, L.P.
Most Recent Fund Was Raised: 07/01/1997
Year Founded: 1997
Capital Under Management: $108,000,000
Current Activity Level : Actively seeking new investments
Method of Compensation: Return on investment is of primary concern, do not charge fees

---

SHEPHERD GROUP LLC, THE

636 Great Road
Stow, MA 01775
Phone: 978-461-9900
Website: www.tsgequity.com

Management and Staff
Sean Marsh, Vice President
T. Nathanael Shepherd, President

Whom to Contact
T. Nathanael Shepherd

Type of Firm
Private Firm Investing Own Capital

Industry Association Membership
National Venture Capital Association (NVCA)

Project Preferences

Role in Financing:
Prefer role as deal originator but will also invest in deals created by others

Type of Financing Preferred:
First Stage Financing
Leveraged Buyout
Recapitalizations
Second Stage Financing
Special Situation

Geographical Preferences

United States
Mid Atlantic
Northeast

Industry Preferences

Communications and Media
Commercial Communications
Telecommunications
Data Communications
Satellite Microwave Comm.

Computer Hardware
Mini and Personal/Desktop
Computer Graphics and Dig
Integrated Turnkey System
Disk Relat. Memory Device

Computer Software
Computer Services
Systems Software
Applications Software

Internet Specific
Internet

Semiconductors/Other Elect.
Electronic Components
Semiconductor
Circuit Boards
Laser Related
Analytic/Scientific

Medical/Health
Diagnostic Services
Diagnostic Test Products
Hospital/Other Instit.

Consumer Related
Entertainment and Leisure
Retail
Franchises(NEC)
Food/Beverage
Consumer Products
Consumer Services
Other Restaurants
Education Related

Industrial/Energy
Materials
Robotics

Business Serv.
Distribution

Manufact.
Office Automation Equipmt
Publishing

Additional Information
Name of Most Recent Fund: Shepherd Group Equity Fund, L.P.
Most Recent Fund Was Raised: 04/23/1999
Year Founded: 1996
Capital Under Management: $26,000,000
Current Activity Level : Actively seeking new investments
Method of Compensation: Return on invest. most important, but chg. closing fees, service fees, etc.

SHERBROOKE CAPITAL PARTNERS

2344 Washington Street
Newton Lower Falls, MA 02462
Phone: 617-332-7227
Fax: 617-332-3113
Website: www.sherbrookecapital.com

Management and Staff
Carol Bramson, General Partner
Christopher J. Carter, Principal
Joel L. Uchenick, General Partner
John K. Giannuzzi, Managing Director
Robert A. Stringer Jr., General Partner

Whom to Contact
Chris Carter
John K. Gianuzzi

Type of Firm
Private Firm Investing Own Capital

Project Preferences

Role in Financing:
Prefer role as deal originator but will also invest in deals created by others

Type of Financing Preferred:
Balanced
First Stage Financing
Industry Rollups
Leveraged Buyout
Second Stage Financing

Geographical Preferences

United States
All U.S.

Industry Preferences

Medical/Health
Medical/Health
Medical Diagnostics
Diagnostic Test Products
Pharmaceuticals

Consumer Related
Retail
Food/Beverage
Consumer Products
Other Restaurants

Additional Information
Year Founded: 1998
Capital Under Management: $85,000,000
Current Activity Level : Actively seeking new investments

SIGMA PARTNERS

20 Custom House Street
Suite 830
Boston, MA 02110
Phone: 617-330-7872
Fax: 617-323-7975
Website: http://www.sigmapartners.com

See California for full listing.

SIGNAL LAKE VENTURE FUND, LP

50 Commonwealth Avenue
Suite 504
Boston, MA 02116
Phone: 617-267-5205
Fax: 617-262-7037
Website: www.signallake.com

See Connecticut for full listing.

SILICON VALLEY BANK

One Newton Executive Park
2221 Washington Street Suite 200
Newton, MA 02462
Phone: 617-630-4100
Fax: 617-969-4395

See California for full listing.

SOFTBANK CAPITAL PARTNERS

10 Langley Road
Suite 202
Newton Center, MA 02459
Phone: 617-928-9300
Fax: 617-928-9305

Management and Staff
Charles Lax, General Partner
Michael Perlis, Venture Partner
Ronald Fisher, General Partner

Whom to Contact
Gary Rieschel
Ryan Moore

Type of Firm
Non-Financial Corp. Affiliate or Subsidiary

Project Preferences

Role in Financing:
Prefer role as deal originator but will also invest in deals created by others

Type of Financing Preferred:
First Stage Financing
Leveraged Buyout
Mezzanine
Second Stage Financing
Seed
Special Situation
Start-up Financing

Geographical Preferences

United States
All U.S.

Canada
All Canada

International
Middle East

Industry Preferences

(% based on actual investment)

Internet Specific	63.5%
Computer Software and Services	15.6%
Other Products	12.5%
Communications and Media	8.5%

Additional Information
Name of Most Recent Fund: SOFTBANK Capital Partners I, L.P.
Most Recent Fund Was Raised: 07/01/1999
Year Founded: 1994
Capital Under Management: $3,300,000,000
Current Activity Level : Actively seeking new investments
Method of Compensation: Return on investment is of primary concern, do not charge fees

SOFTBANK VENTURE CAPITAL (FKA: SOFTBANK TECHNOLOGY VENTURES)

10 Langley Road
Suite 403
Newton Center, MA 02159-1972
Phone: 617-928-9300
Fax: 617-928-9301
Website: www.sbvc.com

See California for full listing.

SOLSTICE CAPITAL LLC

15 Broad Street
Floor #3
Boston, MA 02109-4216
Phone: 617-523-7733
Fax: 617-523-5827

Other Offices

13651 East Camino La Cebadilla
Tucson, AZ 85749
Phone: 520-749-5713
Fax: 520-749-4743

Management and Staff
Harry George, Managing Partner
Henry Newman, General Partner

Type of Firm
Private Firm Investing Own Capital

Industry Association Membership
National Venture Capital Association (NVCA)

Project Preferences

Role in Financing:
Will function either as deal originator or investor in deals created by others

Type of Financing Preferred:
Early Stage
Seed

Size of Investments Considered
Min Size of Investment Considered (000s): $250
Max Size of Investment Considered (000s): $1,000

Geographical Preferences

United States
Northeast
Rocky Mountain
Southwest
West Coast

Industry Preferences

(% based on actual investment)

Computer Software and Services	51.7%
Industrial/Energy	25.6%
Biotechnology	8.4%
Internet Specific	5.1%
Computer Hardware	3.8%
Medical/Health	2.6%
Communications and Media	1.4%
Consumer Related	1.1%
Other Products	0.4%

Additional Information
Name of Most Recent Fund: Solstice Capital L.P.
Most Recent Fund Was Raised: 10/06/1995
Year Founded: 1995
Capital Under Management: $22,800,000
Current Activity Level : Actively seeking new investments
Method of Compensation: Return on invest. most important, but chg. closing fees, service fees, etc.

SONERA CORPORATION CORPORATE VENTURE CAPITAL

890 Winter Street
Suite 310
North Waltham, MA 02451
Website: www.sonera.fi/english/ventures/

See Foreign Venture Capital Firms for full listing.

SPARKVENTURES, LLC

44 Pleasant Street
Suite 210
Watertown, MA 02472
Phone: 617-923-3640
Fax: 617-923-0798
Website: www.sparkventures.com

Management and Staff
Andrew Robbins, Managing Director
Matt D'Arbeloff, Managing Director

Type of Firm
Private Firm Investing Own Capital

Project Preferences

Type of Financing Preferred:
Early Stage

Geographical Preferences

United States
Northeast

Industry Preferences

Computer Software
Software

Internet Specific
Internet

Additional Information
Year Founded: 2000
Current Activity Level : Actively seeking new investments

SPECTRUM EQUITY INVESTORS, L.P.

One International Place
29th Floor
Boston, MA 02110
Phone: 617-464-4600
Fax: 617-464-4601
Website: www.spectrumequity.com

See California for full listing.

SPRAY VENTURE PARTNERS

One Walnut St.
Boston, MA 02108
Phone: 617-305-4140
Fax: 617-305-4144
Website: www.sprayventure.com

Management and Staff
Dale Spencer, Venture Partner
Dan Sachs, Partner
J. Daniel Cole, General Partner
Joe Ciffolillo, Venture Partner
Kevin Connors, General Partner
Paul Gisholt, General Partner

Type of Firm
Private Firm Investing Own Capital

Industry Association Membership
National Venture Capital Association (NVCA)

Project Preferences

Role in Financing:
Prefer role as deal originator but will also invest in deals created by others

Type of Financing Preferred:
First Stage Financing
Research and Development
Second Stage Financing
Seed
Start-up Financing

Industry Preferences

(% based on actual investment)

Medical/Health	91.3%
Internet Specific	4.8%
Biotechnology	3.9%

Additional Information
Name of Most Recent Fund: The Spray Venture Fund
Most Recent Fund Was Raised: 04/01/1998
Year Founded: 1996
Capital Under Management: $52,000,000
Current Activity Level : Actively seeking new investments
Method of Compensation: Return on investment is of primary concern, do not charge fees

ST. PAUL VENTURE CAPITAL, INC.

138 River Road
Andover, MA 01810
Phone: 978-837-3198
Fax: 978-837-3199
Website: www.stpaulvc.com

See Minnesota for full listing.

STILL RIVER FUND, THE

100 Federal Street
29th Floor
Boston, MA 02110
Phone: 617-348-2327
Fax: 617-348-2371
Website: www.stillriverfund.com

Management and Staff
James Saalfield, General Partner
Joseph Tischler, General Partner
Steven Susel, Vice President

Type of Firm
Private Firm Investing Own Capital

Industry Association Membership
Natl assoc of Small Bus. Inv. Co (NASBIC)

Project Preferences

Role in Financing:
Prefer role as deal originator but will also invest in deals created by others

Type of Financing Preferred:
Early Stage
Expansion
First Stage Financing
Second Stage Financing
Seed
Startup

Size of Investments Considered
Min Size of Investment Considered (000s): $300
Max Size of Investment Considered (000s): $4,000

Geographical Preferences

United States
Northeast
All U.S.

Industry Preferences

(% based on actual investment)

Other Products	25.2%
Internet Specific	24.1%
Communications and Media	22.5%
Semiconductors/Other Elect.	12.2%
Biotechnology	8.0%
Computer Software and Services	5.5%
Consumer Related	2.5%

Additional Information
Name of Most Recent Fund: Still River Fund II
Most Recent Fund Was Raised: 01/01/1999
Year Founded: 1996
Capital Under Management: $62,000,000
Current Activity Level : Actively seeking new investments
Method of Compensation: Return on investment is of primary concern, do not charge fees

STONEGATE PARTNERS, L.L.C.

45 Milk Street
7th Floor
Boston, MA 02109
Phone: 617-330-9009
Fax: 617-330-9010
Website: www.stonegatepartners.com

Management and Staff
Brian Bernier, Managing Director
Richard Lodewick, Managing Director

Whom to Contact
C. Roger Kendrick
Jennifer R. Hutchins

Type of Firm
Investment/Merchant Bank Subsid/Affil

Project Preferences

Type of Financing Preferred:
Expansion

Size of Investments Considered
Min Size of Investment Considered (000s): $3,000
Max Size of Investment Considered (000s): $5,000

Geographical Preferences

United States
Northeast
All U.S.

Industry Preferences

Communications and Media
Telecommunications

Medical/Health
Medical/Health

Additional Information
Year Founded: 1997
Current Activity Level : Actively seeking new investments
Method of Compensation: Return on invest. most important, but chg. closing fees, service fees, etc.

SUMMIT PARTNERS

600 Atlantic Avenue
Suite 2800
Boston, MA 02210-2227
Phone: 617-824-1000
Fax: 617-824-1159
Website: www.summitpartners.com

Other Offices

499 Hamilton Avenue
Suite 200
Palo Alto, CA 94301
Phone: 650-321-1166
Fax: 650-321-1188

Management and Staff
Bruce Evans, General Partner
E. Roe Stamps, Managing Partner
Gregory Avis, Managing Partner
James Atwell, General Partner
John Partridge, Partner
John Carroll, Vice President
Joseph Trustey, General Partner
Kevin Mohan, General Partner
Kip Sheeline, General Partner
Martin Mannion, General Partner
Michael Balmuth, General Partner
Peter Chung, General Partner
Scott Collins, Principal
Stephen Woodsum, Managing Partner
Steven Casper, Vice President
Steven Tagtmeier, Vice President
Thomas Farb, General Partner
Thomas Roberts, General Partner
Walter Kortschak, Managing Partner
Will Chou, Vice President

Whom to Contact
Christopher W. Sheeline

Type of Firm
Private Firm Investing Own Capital

Industry Association Membership
National Venture Capital Association (NVCA)
Western Association of Venture Capitalists (WAVC)

Project Preferences

Role in Financing:
Prefer role as deal originator but will also invest in deals created by others

Type of Financing Preferred:
Control-block Purchases
Early Stage
First Stage Financing
Leveraged Buyout
Mezzanine
Second Stage Financing
Special Situation

Size of Investments Considered
Min Size of Investment Considered (000s): $1,500
Max Size of Investment Considered: No Limit

Geographical Preferences

United States
All U.S.
All U.S.

Canada
All Canada

International
Bermuda
Europe
France
Germany
Israel
Italy
Spain
United Kingdom

Industry Preferences

(% based on actual investment)

Computer Software and Services	18.6%
Communications and Media	16.3%
Other Products	14.3%
Computer Hardware	11.5%
Internet Specific	10.7%
Semiconductors/Other Elect.	9.0%
Consumer Related	7.6%
Medical/Health	7.2%
Industrial/Energy	3.1%
Biotechnology	1.7%

Additional Information
Name of Most Recent Fund: Summit Accelerator Fund, L.P.
Most Recent Fund Was Raised: 03/03/1998
Year Founded: 1984
Capital Under Management: $3,566,900,000
Current Activity Level : Actively seeking new investments
Method of Compensation: Return on investment is of primary concern, do not charge fees

---

TA ASSOCIATES, INC.

High Street Tower
125 High Street Suite 2500
Boston, MA 02110
Phone: 617-574-6700
Fax: 617-574-6728
Website: www.ta.com

Other Offices

70 Willow Road
Suite 100
Menlo Park, CA 94025
Phone: 650-328-1210
Fax: 650-326-4933

One Oxford Center
Suite 4260
Pittsburgh, PA 15219-1407
Phone: 412-441-4949
Fax: 412-441-5784

Management and Staff

A. Bruce Johnston, Principal
Ajit Nedungadi, Vice President
Benjamin Ball, Vice President
Brian Conway, Managing Director
C. Kevin Landry, CEO & Managing Director
David Lang, Principal
Gregory White, Vice President
Jacqueline Morby, Managing Director
Jamie McJunkin, Vice President
Jeffrey Chambers, Managing Director
Jonathan Meeks, Vice President
Jonathan Goldstein, Managing Director
Katherine Cromwell, Managing Director & CFO
Kenneth Schiciano, Managing Director
Kurt Jaggers, Managing Director
Laura Kim, Vice President
Michael Wilson, Principal
Michael Child, Managing Director
P. Andrews McLane, Senior Managing Director
Philip Rueppel, Principal
Richard Tadler, Managing Director
Roger Kafker, Managing Director
Thomas Alber, Chief Financial Officer
Todd Crockett, Vice President

Type of Firm

Private Firm Investing Own Capital

Industry Association Membership

National Venture Capital Association (NVCA)
Western Association of Venture Capitalists (WAVC)

Project Preferences

Role in Financing:

Prefer role as deal originator but will also invest in deals created by others

Type of Financing Preferred:

Control-block Purchases
Leveraged Buyout
Special Situation

Size of Investments Considered

Min Size of Investment Considered (000s): $20,000
Max Size of Investment Considered (000s): $60,000

Geographical Preferences

International

No Preference

Industry Preferences

(% based on actual investment)

Computer Software and Services	21.2%
Communications and Media	18.4%
Internet Specific	14.2%
Other Products	12.7%
Medical/Health	11.3%
Semiconductors/Other Elect.	7.9%
Consumer Related	5.2%
Computer Hardware	5.0%
Industrial/Energy	2.6%
Biotechnology	1.7%

Additional Information

Name of Most Recent Fund: TA Advent VIII
Most Recent Fund Was Raised: 12/01/1996
Year Founded: 1968
Capital Under Management: $5,000,000,000
Current Activity Level : Actively seeking new investments
Method of Compensation: Return on investment is of primary concern, do not charge fees

TECHFARM (AKA:TECHFUND CAPITAL)

One Bowdoin Square
10th Floor
Boston, MA 02114
Phone: 617-742-7707
Fax: 617-742-7709
Website: www.techfarm.com

See California for full listing.

TICONDEROGA CAPITAL, INC. (FKA: DILLON READ VENTURE CAPITAL)

20 William Street
Suite G-40
Wellesley, MA 02481
Phone: 781-416-3400
Fax: 781-416-9868
Website: www.ticonderogacap.com

Other Offices

535 Madison Avenue
36th Floor
New York, NY 10022
Phone: 212-906-7100
Fax: 212-906-8690

555 California Street
Suite 4360
San Francisco, CA 94104
Phone: 415-296-6343
Fax: 415-296-8956

Management and Staff

Craig Jones, Managing Partner
Gene Solnick, Chief Financial Officer
Graham Crooke, Partner
James Vandervelden, Partner
Michael Mills, Partner
Peter Leidel, Partner
Robert Hannon, Vice President
Tyler Wick, Vice President

Whom to Contact

Fawad Zakariya

Type of Firm

Private Equity Advisor or Fund of Fund Mgr

Industry Association Membership

National Venture Capital Association (NVCA)

Project Preferences

Role in Financing:

Prefer role as deal originator

Type of Financing Preferred:

Later Stage

Size of Investments Considered

Min Size of Investment Considered (000s): $3,000
Max Size of Investment Considered (000s): $10,000

Geographical Preferences

United States

All U.S.

Canada

All Canada

Industry Preferences

(% based on actual investment)

Other Products	23.0%
Computer Software and Services	16.8%
Industrial/Energy	14.5%
Biotechnology	10.4%
Medical/Health	9.7%
Consumer Related	6.2%
Communications and Media	5.4%
Semiconductors/Other Elect.	5.2%
Computer Hardware	4.7%
Internet Specific	4.0%

Additional Information
Name of Most Recent Fund: Ticonderoga Partners IV, L.P.
Most Recent Fund Was Raised: 05/01/1998
Year Founded: 1982
Capital Under Management: $180,000,000
Current Activity Level : Actively seeking new investments
Method of Compensation: Return on investment is of primary concern, do not charge fees

TTC VENTURES

One Main Street
6th Floor
Cambridge, MA 02142
Phone: 617-528-3137
Fax: 617-577-1715

Type of Firm
Non-Financial Corp. Affiliate or Subsidiary

Project Preferences

Role in Financing:
Prefer role as deal originator but will also invest in deals created by others

Type of Financing Preferred:
First Stage Financing
Mezzanine
Second Stage Financing
Seed
Start-up Financing

Geographical Preferences

United States
All U.S.

Industry Preferences

(% based on actual investment)

Internet Specific	74.5%
Computer Software and Services	18.9%
Computer Hardware	6.6%

Additional Information
Name of Most Recent Fund: TTC Ventures
Most Recent Fund Was Raised: 01/01/1997
Year Founded: 1995
Capital Under Management: $2,500,000
Current Activity Level : Actively seeking new investments
Method of Compensation: Return on investment is of primary concern, do not charge fees

TVM TECHNO VENTURE MANAGEMENT

101 Arch Street
Suite 1950
Boston, MA 02110
Phone: 617-345-9320
Fax: 617-345-9377
Website: www.tvmvc.com

See Foreign Venture Capital Firms for full listing.

ULIN & HOLLAND, INC.

176 Federal Street
Boston, MA 02110
Phone: 617-261-6360
Fax: 617-261-6442

Type of Firm
Mgt. Consulting Firm

Project Preferences

Role in Financing:
Other

Type of Financing Preferred:
Leveraged Buyout
Mezzanine
Recapitalizations
Second Stage Financing

Size of Investments Considered
Min Size of Investment Considered (000s): $5,000
Max Size of Investment Considered: No Limit

Geographical Preferences

United States
Midwest
Northeast
Southeast

Industry Preferences

Medical/Health
Diagnostic Services
Diagnostic Test Products
Other Therapeutic
Medical Products
Disposable Med. Products

Consumer Related
Retail
Computer Stores
Food/Beverage
Consumer Products
Consumer Services
Other Restaurants

Additional Information
Year Founded: 1992
Current Activity Level : Actively seeking new investments
Method of Compensation: Other

UNC VENTURES

64 Burough Street
Boston, MA 02130-4017
Phone: 617-482-7070
Fax: 617-522-2176

Type of Firm
Private Firm Investing Own Capital

Project Preferences

Role in Financing:
Prefer role as deal originator but will also invest in deals created by others

Type of Financing Preferred:
Leveraged Buyout
Mezzanine
Second Stage Financing

Size of Investments Considered
Min Size of Investment Considered (000s): $500
Max Size of Investment Considered (000s): $1,000

Geographical Preferences

United States
All U.S.

Industry Preferences

Communications and Media
Radio & TV Broadcasting

Industrial/Energy
Environmental Related

Financial Services
Financial Services

Additional Information
Year Founded: 1971
Capital Under Management: $28,600,000
Current Activity Level : Making few, if any, new investments

UST CAPITAL CORP.

40 Court Street
Boston, MA 02108
Phone: 617-726-7138
Fax: 617-695-4185

Other Offices

40 Court Street
Boston, MA 02108
Phone: 617-726-7171

Management and Staff
A.F.F. Snyder, President & Chairman

Type of Firm
SBIC Not elsewhere classified

Industry Association Membership
Natl assoc of Small Bus. Inv. Co (NASBIC)

Project Preferences

Role in Financing:
Will function either as deal originator or investor in deals created by others

Type of Financing Preferred:
First Stage Financing
Mezzanine
Seed
Start-up Financing

Size of Investments Considered
Min Size of Investment Considered (000s): $100
Max Size of Investment Considered (000s): $3,100

Geographical Preferences

International
No Preference

Additional Information
Year Founded: 1961
Capital Under Management: $4,500,000
Current Activity Level : Inactive / Unknown
Method of Compensation: Return on investment is of primary concern, do not charge fees

VENROCK ASSOCIATES

101 Federal Street
Suite 190
Boston, MA 02110
Phone: 617-204-5710
Fax: 617-204-6190
Website: www.venrock.com

See New York for full listing.

VENTURE CAPITAL FUND OF NEW ENGLAND, THE

70 Walnut St.
Suite 120
Wellesley Hills, MA 02481-2175
Phone: 781-239-8262
Fax: 781-239-8263

Management and Staff
Harry Healer, General Partner
Karen McWade, Chief Financial Officer
Kevin Dougherty, General Partner
Richard Farrell, General Partner
William Mills, General Partner

Type of Firm
Private Firm Investing Own Capital

Industry Association Membership
National Venture Capital Association (NVCA)
Natl assoc of Small Bus. Inv. Co (NASBIC)

Project Preferences

Role in Financing:
Prefer role as deal originator

Type of Financing Preferred:
First Stage Financing
Second Stage Financing
Start-up Financing

Size of Investments Considered
Min Size of Investment Considered (000s): $750
Max Size of Investment Considered (000s): $3,000

Geographical Preferences

United States
Northeast

Industry Preferences

(% based on actual investment)

Communications and Media	17.2%
Medical/Health	17.0%
Computer Software and Services	16.6%
Industrial/Energy	14.5%
Semiconductors/Other Elect.	11.0%
Computer Hardware	8.4%
Biotechnology	4.6%
Consumer Related	4.3%
Internet Specific	4.2%
Other Products	2.2%

Additional Information
Name of Most Recent Fund: VCFNE III
Most Recent Fund Was Raised: 06/01/1992
Year Founded: 1981
Capital Under Management: $30,700,000
Current Activity Level : Actively seeking new investments
Method of Compensation: Return on investment is of primary concern, do not charge fees

VENTURE INVESTMENT MANAGEMENT COMPANY LLC (AKA: VIMAC)

177 Milk Street
Boston, MA 02109-3410
Phone: 617-292-3300
Fax: 617-292-7979
Website: www.vimac.com

Management and Staff
John Evans, Managing Director
Neal Hill, Managing Director
Robert Roeper, Managing Director

Type of Firm
Private Firm Investing Own Capital

Industry Association Membership
National Venture Capital Association (NVCA)

Project Preferences

Role in Financing:
Prefer role as deal originator but will also invest in deals created by others

Type of Financing Preferred:
Balanced
Early Stage
First Stage Financing
Second Stage Financing
Seed
Start-up Financing

Size of Investments Considered
Min Size of Investment Considered (000s): $1,000
Max Size of Investment Considered (000s): $7,000

Geographical Preferences

United States
Northeast

Canada
Eastern Canada

Industry Preferences

(% based on actual investment)

Internet Specific	50.7%
Computer Software and Services	23.2%
Communications and Media	13.2%
Medical/Health	4.2%
Consumer Related	3.3%
Computer Hardware	2.3%
Semiconductors/Other Elect.	2.2%
Industrial/Energy	0.8%

Additional Information

Year Founded: 1996
Capital Under Management: $118,000,000
Current Activity Level : Actively seeking new investments
Method of Compensation: Return on investment is of primary concern, do not charge fees

WATERMILL EVENTURES

Watermill Center
800 South Street
South Waltham, MA 02453-1435
Phone: 781-891-6660
Fax: 781-891-9712
E-mail: info@Watermill.com
Website: www.watermill.com

Management and Staff

Benjamin Procter, Partner
Dale Okonow, Managing Partner
Jeffrey Stein, Partner
Steven Karol, Managing Partner

Type of Firm

Affiliate/Subsidary of Oth. Financial. Instit.

Project Preferences

Type of Financing Preferred:

Seed

Industry Preferences

Internet Specific

Internet

Additional Information

Year Founded: 2000
Current Activity Level : Actively seeking new investments

WESTON PRESIDIO CAPITAL MANAGEMENT

One Federal Street
21st Floor
Boston, MA 02110-2004
Phone: 617-988-2500
Fax: 617-988-2515
Website: www.westonpresidio.com

Other Offices

343 Sansome Street
Suite 1210
San Francisco, CA 94104-1316
Phone: 415-398-0770
Fax: 415-398-0990

Management and Staff

Alan Stein, Venture Partner
Carlo Von Schroeter, General Partner
Courtney Russell, Principal
Daphne Dufresne, Principal
Dianne Hillyard, Chief Financial Officer
James McElwee, General Partner
Kevin Hayes, General Partner
Mark Bono, General Partner
Mathew Janopaul, Principal
Michael Cronin, Managing Partner
Michael Lazarus, Managing Partner
Philip Halperin, General Partner
Rick Friedman, Principal
Sean Honey, Principal
Therese Mrozek, Chief Operating Officer
Thomas Patterson, General Partner

Type of Firm

Private Firm Investing Own Capital

Industry Association Membership

National Venture Capital Association (NVCA)
Western Association of Venture Capitalists (WAVC)

Project Preferences

Role in Financing:

Prefer role as deal originator but will also invest in deals created by others

Type of Financing Preferred:

Balanced
Early Stage
Later Stage
Leveraged Buyout

Size of Investments Considered

Min Size of Investment Considered (000s): $5,000
Max Size of Investment Considered (000s): $50,000

Geographical Preferences

United States

All U.S.

Canada

All Canada

International

Europe

Industry Preferences

(% based on actual investment)

Internet Specific	31.4%
Consumer Related	25.8%
Communications and Media	21.8%
Computer Software and Services	6.6%
Medical/Health	5.9%
Other Products	3.7%
Industrial/Energy	2.8%
Semiconductors/Other Elect.	1.6%
Computer Hardware	0.4%

Additional Information

Name of Most Recent Fund: Weston Presidio Capital III
Most Recent Fund Was Raised: 06/30/1995
Year Founded: 1991
Capital Under Management: $2,279,200,000
Current Activity Level : Actively seeking new investments
Method of Compensation: Return on investment is of primary concern, do not charge fees

WHITNEY & CO. (FKA: J.H. WHITNEY & CO.)

One Liberty Square
12th Floor
Boston, MA 02109
Phone: 617-423-2300
Fax: 617-423-3647
Website: www.jhwhitney.com

See Connecticut for full listing.

WINDJAMMER CAPITAL INVESTORS (FKA:PACIFIC MEZZANINE INV.)

Damonmill Square
Suite 4A
Concord, MA 01742
Website: www.windjammercapital.com

See California for full listing.

YANKEETEK VENTURES

One Memorial Drive
12th Floor
Cambridge, MA 02142
Phone: 617-250-0500
Fax: 617-250-0501
Website: www.yankeetek.com

Management and Staff
Burt Rubenstein, Managing Director
Howard Anderson, Senior Managing Director
John Genest, Managing Director
Timothy Kraskey, Managing Director

Type of Firm
Private Equity Advisor or Fund of Fund Mgr

Industry Association Membership
National Venture Capital Association (NVCA)

Project Preferences

Role in Financing:
Prefer role as deal originator but will also invest in deals created by others

Type of Financing Preferred:
Early Stage
First Stage Financing
Research and Development
Seed
Startup

Size of Investments Considered
Min Size of Investment Considered (000s): $500
Max Size of Investment Considered (000s): $5,000

Geographical Preferences

United States
Northeast

Industry Preferences

Communications and Media
Telecommunications
Wireless Communications

Computer Software
Software

Internet Specific
Internet

Semiconductors/Other Elect.
Semiconductor
Fiber Optics

Additional Information
Capital Under Management: $60,000,000
Current Activity Level : Actively seeking new investments
Method of Compensation: Return on investment is of primary concern, do not charge fees

ZERO STAGE CAPITAL CO., INC.

101 Main Street
17th Floor
Cambridge, MA 02142-1519
Phone: 617-876-5355
Fax: 617-876-1248
Website: www.zerostage.com

Other Offices

1 Portland Sqaure
7th Floor
Portland, ME 04112-5480
Phone: 207-879-7868
Fax: 207-761-7085

195 Church Street
10th Floor
New Haven, CT 06510
Phone: 203-865-7986
Fax: 203-865-7987

40 Westminster Street
Suite 702
Providence, RI 02903
Phone: 401-351-3036
Fax: 401-351-3056

Management and Staff
G. Bickley Stevens, Managing Director
Mark Thaller, Vice President
Paul Kelley, President
Stanley Fung, General Partner

Type of Firm
Private Firm Investing Own Capital

Industry Association Membership
National Venture Capital Association (NVCA)

Project Preferences

Role in Financing:
Prefer role as deal originator but will also invest in deals created by others

Type of Financing Preferred:
Early Stage
First Stage Financing
Second Stage Financing
Seed
Start-up Financing

Size of Investments Considered
Min Size of Investment Considered (000s): $10,000
Max Size of Investment Considered (000s): $15,000

Geographical Preferences

United States
All U.S.
Mid Atlantic
Northeast

Industry Preferences

(% based on actual investment)

Internet Specific	29.6%
Computer Software and Services	17.2%
Communications and Media	8.9%
Semiconductors/Other Elect.	8.0%
Biotechnology	7.0%
Medical/Health	6.9%
Other Products	6.5%
Computer Hardware	6.3%
Consumer Related	5.2%
Industrial/Energy	4.2%

Additional Information
Name of Most Recent Fund: Zero Stage Capital VI, L.P.
Most Recent Fund Was Raised: 08/01/1998
Year Founded: 1982
Capital Under Management: $250,000,000
Current Activity Level : Actively seeking new investments
Method of Compensation: Return on investment is of primary concern, do not charge fees

MICHIGAN

ARBOR PARTNERS LLC

130 South First Street
Ann Arbor, MI 48104
Phone: 734-668-9000
Fax: 734-669-4195
Website: www.arborpartners.com

Management and Staff
Donald Walker, Managing Director
Richard Crandall, Managing Director
Richard Eidswick, Managing Director
Stephen Swanson, Managing Director

Type of Firm
Private Firm Investing Own Capital

Industry Association Membership
National Venture Capital Association (NVCA)

Project Preferences

Role in Financing:
Will function either as deal originator or investor in deals created by others

Type of Financing Preferred:
Early Stage
Expansion

Size of Investments Considered
Min Size of Investment Considered (000s): $250
Max Size of Investment Considered: No Limit

Geographical Preferences

United States
Midwest

Industry Preferences

(% based on actual investment)

Internet Specific	51.0%
Computer Software and Services	44.1%
Computer Hardware	3.5%
Consumer Related	1.0%
Other Products	0.3%

Additional Information
Name of Most Recent Fund: AVP II, The E Fund (Arbor Partners)
Most Recent Fund Was Raised: 10/29/1999
Year Founded: 1996
Capital Under Management: $38,200,000
Current Activity Level : Actively seeking new investments
Method of Compensation: Return on invest. most important, but chg. closing fees, service fees, etc.

AVALON INVESTMENTS INC.

201 South Main Street
First National Bank-10th Floor
Ann Arbor, MI 48104
Phone: 734-994-7000
Fax: 734-994-4302

Management and Staff
Chris Rizik, Managing Director
Richard Snyder, President
Stephen Jaqua, Managing Director
William Woodward, Managing Director

Type of Firm
Private Firm Investing Own Capital

Industry Preferences

(% based on actual investment)

Internet Specific	63.5%
Computer Software and Services	22.6%
Medical/Health	13.2%
Other Products	0.7%

Additional Information
Year Founded: 1999
Current Activity Level : Actively seeking new investments

BLUE WATER CAPITAL, LLC

260 E. Brown Street
Suite 310
Birmingham, MI 48009
Phone: 248-647-2010
Fax: 248-647-1130
Website: www.bluewatercapital.com

See Virginia for full listing.

CAMELOT VENTURES

100 Galleria Officentre
Suite 419
Southfield, MI 48034
Phone: 248-827-7799
Fax: 248-352-5973
Website: www.camelotventures.com

Management and Staff
Allan Bittker, Partner
Daniel Gilbert, Partner
David Katzman, Managing Partner
Gilbert Silverman, Partner
Joe Golden, Partner
Nathan Forbes, Partner
Nicholas Pyett, Chief Financial Officer

Type of Firm
Investment Management/Finance Consulting

Industry Association Membership
Natl assoc of Small Bus. Inv. Co (NASBIC)

Project Preferences

Role in Financing:
Will function either as deal originator or investor in deals created by others

Type of Financing Preferred:
Balanced
Early Stage
Expansion
Generalist PE
Later Stage
Mezzanine
Private Placement
Second Stage Financing

Size of Investments Considered
Min Size of Investment Considered (000s): $5,000
Max Size of Investment Considered (000s): $150,000

Geographical Preferences

United States
All U.S.

Canada
All Canada

Industry Preferences

Communications and Media
Telecommunications
Wireless Communications
Data Communications
Other Communication Prod.

Computer Hardware
Mainframes / Scientific
Integrated Turnkey System
Disk Relat. Memory Device

Computer Software
Computer Services
Data Processing
Software
Systems Software
Applications Software

Internet Specific
E-Commerce Technology
Internet
Web Aggregration/Portals

Semiconductors/Other Elect.
Micro-Processing
Fiber Optics

Consumer Related
Retail

Financial Services
Financial Services

Business Serv.
Services
Consulting Services

Additional Information
Year Founded: 2000
Current Activity Level : Making few, if any, new investments
Method of Compensation: Return on investment is of primary concern, do not charge fees

DOW CHEMICAL CO.

2030 Dow Center
Midland, MI 48674
Phone: 517-636-5692
Fax: 517-636-8127

Other Offices

Europe Headquarters
Admin & R&D
Horgen, Switzerland
Phone: 41-1-728-2468
Fax: 41-1-728-2097

Type of Firm
Non-Financial Corp. Affiliate or Subsidiary

Industry Association Membership
National Venture Capital Association (NVCA)

Project Preferences

Role in Financing:
Prefer role in deals created by others

Type of Financing Preferred:
First Stage Financing
Leveraged Buyout
Mezzanine
Second Stage Financing
Start-up Financing

Size of Investments Considered
Min Size of Investment Considered (000s): $5,000
Max Size of Investment Considered: No Limit

Geographical Preferences

United States
All U.S.

Canada
All Canada

International
Bermuda
France
Germany
Italy
Middle East
United Kingdom

Industry Preferences

(% based on actual investment)

Biotechnology	38.1%
Internet Specific	29.4%
Communications and Media	11.2%
Semiconductors/Other Elect.	11.0%
Computer Software and Services	7.7%
Other Products	1.9%
Consumer Related	0.6%

Additional Information
Year Founded: 1970
Current Activity Level : Actively seeking new investments
Method of Compensation: Return on investment is of primary concern, do not charge fees

EDF VENTURES (F.K.A. ENTERPRISE DEVELOPMENT FUND)

425 North Main Street
Ann Arbor, MI 48104
Phone: 734-663-3213
Fax: 734-663-7358
Website: www.edfvc.com

Management and Staff
Beau Laskey, Partner
Hayden Harris, General Partner
James Adox, Partner
Mary Campbell, General Partner
Thomas Porter, General Partner

Type of Firm
SBIC Not elsewhere classified

Industry Association Membership
National Venture Capital Association (NVCA)
Natl assoc of Small Bus. Inv. Co (NASBIC)

Project Preferences

Role in Financing:
Will function either as deal originator or investor in deals created by others

Type of Financing Preferred:
Early Stage
Expansion
First Stage Financing
Later Stage
Research and Development
Second Stage Financing
Seed
Startup

Size of Investments Considered
Min Size of Investment Considered (000s): $500
Max Size of Investment Considered (000s): $10,000

Geographical Preferences

United States
Midwest

Industry Preferences

(% based on actual investment)

Internet Specific	20.8%
Semiconductors/Other Elect.	19.3%
Biotechnology	18.4%
Medical/Health	16.8%
Computer Software and Services	14.6%
Communications and Media	4.3%
Consumer Related	2.8%
Other Products	1.6%
Computer Hardware	1.4%

Additional Information
Name of Most Recent Fund: EDF Ventures
Most Recent Fund Was Raised: 01/01/1999
Year Founded: 1987
Capital Under Management: $123,000,000
Current Activity Level : Actively seeking new investments
Method of Compensation: Return on investment is of primary concern, do not charge fees

ENDEAVOR CAPITAL MANAGEMENT

317 S Division Street
Suite 49
Ann Arbor, MI 48104
Phone: 313-996-3032
Fax: 313-996-0886

See Connecticut for full listing.

GMA CAPITAL LLC (AKA: INVESTCARE PARTNERS, L.P.)

32330 West Twelve Mile Road
Farmington Hills, MI 48334
Phone: 248-489-9000
Fax: 248-489-8819
Website: www.gmacapital.com

Management and Staff
Charles Rothstein, Managing Director
David Eberly, Managing Director
Malcolm Moss, Managing Director

Type of Firm
SBIC Not elsewhere classified

Industry Association Membership
National Venture Capital Association (NVCA)

Additional Information
Name of Most Recent Fund: Investcare Partners L.P.
Most Recent Fund Was Raised: 02/01/1999
Year Founded: 1999
Capital Under Management: $65,000,000
Current Activity Level : Actively seeking new investments

INNOVATION CAPITAL ASSOCIATES LTD

2401 Plymouth Road
Suite B
Ann Arbor, MI
Phone: 734-747-9401
Fax: 734-747-9704
Website: www.innovationcapital.net

See Foreign Venture Capital Firms for full listing.

LIBERTY BIDCO INVESTMENT CORPORATION

30833 Northwestern Highway
Suite 211
Farmington Hills, MI 48334
Phone: 248-626-6070
Fax: 248-626-6072

Management and Staff
Jim Zabriskie, Vice President

Whom to Contact
James C. Zabriskie

Type of Firm
Investment/Merchant Bank Investing Own or Client Funds

Project Preferences

Role in Financing:
Prefer role as deal originator but will also invest in deals created by others

Type of Financing Preferred:
Leveraged Buyout
Mezzanine
Second Stage Financing
Special Situation

Size of Investments Considered
Min Size of Investment Considered (000s): $500
Max Size of Investment Considered: No Limit

Geographical Preferences

United States
All U.S.
Midwest

Canada
Ontario

Industry Preferences
(% based on actual investment)

Other Products	50.9%
Consumer Related	29.4%
Industrial/Energy	11.2%
Communications and Media	8.6%

Additional Information
Year Founded: 1988
Capital Under Management: $20,000,000
Current Activity Level : Inactive / Unknown
Method of Compensation: Return on invest. most important, but chg. closing fees, service fees, etc.

MBW MANAGEMENT, INC.

2929 Plymouth Road
Suite 210
Ann Arbor, MI 48105
Phone: 313-747-9401
Fax: 313-747-9704

See New Jersey for full listing.

NANTUCKET CAPITAL MANAGEMENT

40950 Woodward
Suite 307
Bloomfield Hills, MI 48304
Phone: 248-723-9286
Fax: 248-723-9289
Website: www.nantucketfunds.com

Management and Staff
Beth Duff, Managing Director
Libby Greenstone, Managing Director
William Goldsmith, Managing Director

Type of Firm
Private Equity Advisor or Fund of Fund Mgr

Project Preferences

Type of Financing Preferred:
Fund of Funds

Additional Information
Name of Most Recent Fund: Nantucket Private Equity Fund
Most Recent Fund Was Raised: 01/18/2000
Year Founded: 2000
Capital Under Management: $7,500,000
Current Activity Level : Actively seeking new investments

NORTH COAST TECHNOLOGY INVESTORS, L.P.

300 Rodd Street
Suite 201
Midland, MI 48640
Phone: 517-832-2300
Fax: 517-832-2301

Type of Firm
Private Firm Investing Own Capital

Industry Association Membership
National Venture Capital Association (NVCA)

Additional Information
Current Activity Level : Actively seeking new investments

PENINSULA CAPITAL PARTNERS, L.L.C

The Buhl Building
535 Griswold Suite 2050
Detroit, MI 48226
Phone: 313-237-5100
Fax: 313-237-5111

Management and Staff
Jon Krempel, Vice President
Scott Reilly, President

Whom to Contact
Chris J. Moye
Hector A. Bultynck
Karl E. LaPeer
Steven S. Beckett

Type of Firm
Private Firm Investing Own Capital

Project Preferences

Role in Financing:
Prefer role in deals created by others

Type of Financing Preferred:
Industry Rollups
Leveraged Buyout
Mezzanine
Second Stage Financing
Special Situation

Size of Investments Considered
Min Size of Investment Considered (000s): $15,000
Max Size of Investment Considered: No Limit

Geographical Preferences

United States
All U.S.

Canada
All Canada

Industry Preferences

(% based on actual investment)

Industrial/Energy	34.8%
Other Products	27.0%
Consumer Related	20.2%
Semiconductors/Other Elect.	12.5%
Computer Hardware	4.7%
Internet Specific	0.7%

Additional Information
Name of Most Recent Fund: The Peninsula Fund II, L.P.
Most Recent Fund Was Raised: 08/01/1999
Year Founded: 1995
Capital Under Management: $347,800,000
Current Activity Level : Actively seeking new investments
Method of Compensation: Return on invest. most important, but chg. closing fees, service fees, etc.

RALPH WILSON EQUITY FUND, L.L.C.

15400 E. Jefferson Ave.
Grosse Pointe Park, MI 48230
Phone: 313-821-9122
Fax: 313-821-9101
Website: www.RalphWilsonEquityFund.com

Management and Staff
J.Skip Simms, President

Whom to Contact
J.Skip Simms

Type of Firm
Private Equity Advisor or Fund of Fund Mgr

Industry Association Membership
National Venture Capital Association (NVCA)

Project Preferences

Role in Financing:
Prefer role in deals created by others

Type of Financing Preferred:
Balanced
Early Stage
Expansion
First Stage Financing
Second Stage Financing

Size of Investments Considered
Min Size of Investment Considered (000s): $200
Max Size of Investment Considered (000s): $1,000

Geographical Preferences

United States
All U.S.
Midwest

Industry Preferences

Communications and Media
Commercial Communications
Telecommunications
Wireless Communications
Data Communications

Computer Software
Data Processing
Software
Systems Software
Applications Software
Artificial Intelligence

Internet Specific
E-Commerce Technology
Internet

Semiconductors/Other Elect.
Electronic Components
Semiconductor
Micro-Processing
Controllers and Sensors
Sensors

Biotechnology
Industrial Biotechnology
Biosensors
Biotech Related Research

Medical/Health
Medical Diagnostics
Drug/Equipmt Delivery

Consumer Related
Sports

Industrial/Energy
Industrial Products
Superconductivity
Factory Automation
Process Control
Robotics
Machinery

Business Serv.
Distribution

Additional Information
Year Founded: 1999
Capital Under Management: $28,000,000
Current Activity Level : Actively seeking new investments
Method of Compensation: Return on investment is of primary concern, do not charge fees

SEAFLOWER VENTURES

5170 Nicholson Road
P.O. Box 474
Fowlerville, MI 48836
Phone: 517-223-3335
Fax: 517-223-3337
Website: www.seaflower.com

See Massachusetts for full listing.

SYNTEL INC. WEB INCUBATOR PROGRAM

2800 Livernois
Troy, MI 48083
Phone: 248 619-2800
E-mail: jonathan_james@syntelinc.com
Website: www.syntelinc.com

Management and Staff
Bharat Desai, Chairman & CEO

Type of Firm
Non-Financial Corp. Affiliate or Subsidiary

Project Preferences

Type of Financing Preferred:
Early Stage
Expansion
Startup

Industry Preferences

Internet Specific
Internet

Business Serv.
Services

Additional Information
Year Founded: 2000
Current Activity Level : Actively seeking new investments

VENTURE FUNDING, LTD.

Fisher Building
3011 West Grand Blvd Ste 321
Detroit, MI 48202
Phone: 313-871-3606
Fax: 313-873-4935

Management and Staff
Caron Harte
Monis Schuster

Whom to Contact
Caron Harte
Monis Schuster

Type of Firm
Mgt. Consulting Firm

Project Preferences

Role in Financing:
Prefer role as deal originator but will also invest in deals created by others

Type of Financing Preferred:
Leveraged Buyout
Research and Development
Seed
Special Situation
Start-up Financing

Size of Investments Considered
Min Size of Investment Considered (000s): $1,000
Max Size of Investment Considered: No Limit

Geographical Preferences

United States
All U.S.

Industry Preferences

Biotechnology
Biotech Related Research
Biotech Related Research

Medical/Health
Medical Diagnostics
Diagnostic Services
Medical Therapeutics
Drug/Equipmt Delivery
Disposable Med. Products
Hospitals/Clinics/Primary
Pharmaceuticals

Consumer Related
Consumer Products

Additional Information
Year Founded: 1983
Current Activity Level : Making few, if any, new investments
Method of Compensation: Return on investment is of primary concern, do not charge fees

WELLMAX, INC.

3541 Bendway Blvd.
Suite 100
Bloomfield Hills, MI 48301
Phone: 248-646-3554
Fax: 248-646-6220

Type of Firm
Mgt. Consulting Firm

Project Preferences

Role in Financing:
Prefer role as deal originator

Type of Financing Preferred:
First Stage Financing
Leveraged Buyout
Second Stage Financing
Special Situation
Start-up Financing

Size of Investments Considered
Min Size of Investment Considered (000s): $100
Max Size of Investment Considered (000s): $1,000

Geographical Preferences

United States
Midwest
Southeast

Industry Preferences

Semiconductors/Other Elect.
Electronics
Circuit Boards
Laser Related

Medical/Health
Medical Diagnostics
Diagnostic Services
Diagnostic Test Products
Medical Therapeutics
Other Therapeutic
Medical Products

Consumer Related
Consumer Products
Education Related

Industrial/Energy
Industrial Products
Machinery
Environmental Related

Agr/Forestr/Fish
Agriculture related

Additional Information
Year Founded: 1976
Current Activity Level : Actively seeking new investments

WHITE PINES MANAGEMENT, L.L.C.

2401 Plymouth Road
Suite B
Ann Arbor, MI 48105
Phone: 734-747-9401
Fax: 734-747-9704
Website: www.whitepines.com

Management and Staff
Ian Bund, President
Michael Williams, Vice President
Ron Kalish, Partner
Tony Grover, Vice President

Whom to Contact
Daniel Boyle
Lois Marler

Type of Firm
Mgt. Consulting Firm

Industry Association Membership
Natl assoc of Small Bus. Inv. Co (NASBIC)

Project Preferences

Role in Financing:
Prefer role as deal originator but will also invest in deals created by others

Type of Financing Preferred:
Expansion
Mezzanine
Second Stage Financing
Special Situation

Size of Investments Considered
Min Size of Investment Considered (000s): $1,000
Max Size of Investment Considered (000s): $4,000

Geographical Preferences

United States
All U.S.
Midwest
Southeast

Industry Preferences

(% based on actual investment)

Internet Specific	38.3%
Communications and Media	15.3%
Other Products	13.8%
Biotechnology	10.4%
Medical/Health	9.0%
Consumer Related	7.6%
Computer Software and Services	5.6%

Additional Information
Year Founded: 1995
Capital Under Management: $100,000,000
Current Activity Level : Actively seeking new investments
Method of Compensation: Return on invest. most important, but chg. closing fees, service fees, etc.

WIND POINT PARTNERS

One Town Square
Suite 780
South Field, MI 48076
Phone: 248-945-7200
Fax: 248-945-7220
Website: www.wppartners.com

Other Offices

676 North Michigan Ave
Suite 330
Chicago, IL 60611
Phone: 312-649-4000

Management and Staff
James TenBroek, Managing Director
James Forrest, Managing Director
Jeffrey Gonyo, Managing Director
Michael Mahoney, Chief Financial Officer
Richard Kracum, Managing Director
Robert Cummings, Managing Director

Type of Firm
Private Firm Investing Own Capital

Project Preferences

Role in Financing:
Prefer role as deal originator but will also invest in deals created by others

Type of Financing Preferred:
Acquisition
Balanced
Expansion
Generalist PE
Later Stage
Leveraged Buyout
Management Buyouts
Recapitalizations

Size of Investments Considered
Min Size of Investment Considered (000s): $10,000
Max Size of Investment Considered (000s): $60,000

Geographical Preferences

United States
All U.S.
All U.S.

Industry Preferences

(% based on actual investment)

Industrial/Energy	30.1%
Communications and Media	21.8%
Consumer Related	15.4%
Other Products	14.7%
Internet Specific	7.5%
Medical/Health	5.3%
Biotechnology	2.0%
Computer Hardware	1.5%
Semiconductors/Other Elect.	1.3%
Computer Software and Services	0.5%

Additional Information
Name of Most Recent Fund: Wind Point Partners IV, L.P.
Most Recent Fund Was Raised: 07/30/1999
Year Founded: 1983
Capital Under Management: $711,500,000
Current Activity Level : Making few, if any, new investments
Method of Compensation: Return on invest. most important, but chg. closing fees, service fees, etc.

MINNESOTA

ADC VENTURES

12501 Whitewater Dr.
Minnetonka, MN 55343
Phone: 612-946-3293

Management and Staff
Robert Switz, Chief Financial Officer

Type of Firm
Non-Financial Corp. Affiliate or Subsidiary

Additional Information
Current Activity Level : Actively seeking new investments

AFFINITY CAPITAL MANAGEMENT(FKA:PETERSON-SPENCER-FANSLER CO)

901Marquette Ave
Suite 1810
Minneapolis, MN 55402
Phone: 612-252-9900
Fax: 612-252-9911
Website: www.affinitycapital.net

Management and Staff
Edson Spencer, General Partner
Kristine Johnson, General Partner
Robin Dowdle, Chief Financial Officer

Whom to Contact
Edson W. Spencer

Type of Firm
Private Firm Investing Own Capital

Industry Association Membership
National Venture Capital Association (NVCA)
Natl assoc of Small Bus. Inv. Co (NASBIC)

Project Preferences

Role in Financing:
Will function either as deal originator or investor in deals created by others

Type of Financing Preferred:
Early Stage
First Stage Financing
Second Stage Financing
Seed
Startup

Geographical Preferences

United States
Midwest

Industry Preferences

(% based on actual investment)

Medical/Health	45.1%
Internet Specific	38.6%
Computer Software and Services	10.5%
Semiconductors/Other Elect.	3.1%
Biotechnology	2.1%
Other Products	0.7%

Additional Information
Name of Most Recent Fund: Affinity Ventures II, LLC
Most Recent Fund Was Raised: 04/01/1997
Year Founded: 1991
Capital Under Management: $65,000,000
Current Activity Level : Actively seeking new investments
Method of Compensation: Return on investment is of primary concern, do not charge fees

AGIO CAPITAL PARTNERS I, L.P.

US Bank Place, Suite 4600
601 Second Avenue South
Minneapolis, MN 55402
Phone: 612-339-8408
Fax: 612-349-4232
Website: www.agio-capital.com

Management and Staff
Donald Haas, Managing Director

Whom to Contact
Kenneth Gudorf

Type of Firm
SBIC Not elsewhere classified

Industry Association Membership
Natl assoc of Small Bus. Inv. Co (NASBIC)

Project Preferences

Role in Financing:
Prefer role as deal originator but will also invest in deals created by others

Type of Financing Preferred:
Industry Rollups
Leveraged Buyout
Second Stage Financing

Size of Investments Considered
Min Size of Investment Considered (000s): $3,000
Max Size of Investment Considered: No Limit

Geographical Preferences

United States
Midwest

Industry Preferences

Semiconductors/Other Elect.
Electronics
Sensors
Component Testing Equipmt
Analytic/Scientific

Medical/Health
Diagnostic Test Products
Medical Products
Disposable Med. Products

Consumer Related
Entertainment and Leisure
Consumer Services

Industrial/Energy
Energy Conservation Relat
Industrial Products
Machinery

Financial Services
Financial Services

Additional Information
Name of Most Recent Fund: Agio Capital Partners I, L.P.
Most Recent Fund Was Raised: 01/30/1996
Year Founded: 1996
Capital Under Management: $42,000,000
Current Activity Level : Actively seeking new investments
Method of Compensation: Return on investment is of primary concern, do not charge fees

ANILA FUND (AKA: ANILA.ORG, LLC)

9973 Valley View Road
Suite 100
Eden Prairie, MN 55344
Website: www.anila.com

See California for full listing.

ARTESIAN CAPITAL

1700 Foshay Tower
821 Marquette Avenue South
Minneapolis, MN 55402
Phone: 612-334-5600
Fax: 612-334-5601

Other Offices

1700 Foshay Tower
821 Marquette Avenue South
Minneapolis, MN 55402
Phone: 612334-5600
Fax: 612-334-5601

Management and Staff
Frank Bennett, President

Type of Firm
Private Firm Investing Own Capital

Project Preferences

Role in Financing:
Prefer role as deal originator but will also invest in deals created by others

Type of Financing Preferred:
Leveraged Buyout
Research and Development
Second Stage Financing
Seed
Start-up Financing

Size of Investments Considered
Min Size of Investment Considered (000s): $300
Max Size of Investment Considered (000s): $500

Geographical Preferences

United States
Midwest

Industry Preferences

Communications and Media
Communications and Media

Biotechnology
Biosensors
Biotech Related Research

Medical/Health
Medical/Health
Medical Diagnostics
Medical Therapeutics

Industrial/Energy
Environmental Related

Additional Information
Year Founded: 1989
Capital Under Management: $2,500,000
Current Activity Level : Actively seeking new investments
Method of Compensation: Return on investment is of primary concern, do not charge fees

BLUESTREAM VENTURES

601 Carlson Parkway
Suite 650
Minnetonka, MN 55305
Phone: 952-745-4515
Website: www.bluestreamventures.com

Other Offices

66 Willow Place
Menlo Park, CA 94025

Management and Staff
John Vander Vort, Principal
Raj Gollamudi, Principal
Tom Erickson, Principal
Travis Winkey, Principal

Type of Firm
Private Firm Investing Own Capital

Project Preferences

Size of Investments Considered
Min Size of Investment Considered (000s): $3,000
Max Size of Investment Considered (000s): $12,000

Additional Information
Capital Under Management: $250,000,000
Current Activity Level : Actively seeking new investments

CAPSTONE VENTURES SBIC, L.P.

Dain Rauscher Plaza
60 South Sixth Street
Minneapolis, MN 55403
Phone: 612-371-7733
Fax: 612-371-2837
Website: www.capstonevc.com

See California for full listing.

CHERRY TREE INVESTMENTS, INC.

7601 France Ave. S.
Suite 150
Edina, MN 55435
Phone: 952-893-9012
Fax: 952-893-9036
Website: www.cherrytree.com

Management and Staff
Gordon Stofer, Managing Partner
Tony Christianson, Managing Partner

Whom to Contact
Sandy Trump

Type of Firm
Private Firm Investing Own Capital

Industry Association Membership
National Venture Capital Association (NVCA)

Project Preferences

Role in Financing:
Will function either as deal originator or investor in deals created by others

Type of Financing Preferred:
Balanced
Early Stage

Size of Investments Considered
Min Size of Investment Considered (000s): $100
Max Size of Investment Considered: No Limit

Geographical Preferences

United States
Midwest

Industry Preferences

Communications and Media
Commercial Communications
Telecommunications
Data Communications

Computer Hardware
Computer Graphics and Dig

Computer Software
Computer Services
Systems Software
Applications Software
Artificial Intelligence

Internet Specific
Internet

Consumer Related
Entertainment and Leisure
Retail
Computer Stores
Food/Beverage
Consumer Products
Consumer Services
Other Restaurants
Education Related

Financial Services
Financial Services

Business Serv.
Distribution

Manufact.
Office Automation Equipmt
Publishing

Additional Information
Name of Most Recent Fund: Cherry Tree Ventures IV
Most Recent Fund Was Raised: 04/01/1991
Year Founded: 1980
Capital Under Management: $16,200,000
Current Activity Level : Actively seeking new investments
Method of Compensation: Return on investment is of primary concern, do not charge fees

CHURCHILL CAPITAL, INC.

2400 Metropolitan Centre
333 South Seventh Street
Minneapolis, MN 55402-2435
Phone: 612-673-6633
Fax: 612-673-6630
Website: www.churchillnet.com

Other Offices

590 Madison Avenue
38th Floor
New York, NY 10022
Phone: 212-832-3300
Fax: 212-832-4270

Management and Staff
David Wakefield, Principal
Michael Hahn, Chief Executive Officer
Michael McHugh, Principal
Thomas Kreimer, Chief Financial Officer

Type of Firm
Private Firm Investing Own Capital

Project Preferences

Role in Financing:
Prefer role as deal originator but will also invest in deals created by others

Type of Financing Preferred:
Acquisition
Leveraged Buyout
Management Buyouts
Mezzanine
Recapitalizations

Size of Investments Considered
Min Size of Investment Considered (000s): $5,000
Max Size of Investment Considered (000s): $25,000

Geographical Preferences

United States
All U.S.
All U.S.

Canada
All Canada

Industry Preferences

(% based on actual investment)

Industrial/Energy	53.7%
Consumer Related	18.6%
Other Products	14.0%
Medical/Health	6.9%
Semiconductors/Other Elect.	6.2%
Computer Software and Services	0.5%

Additional Information
Name of Most Recent Fund: Churchill Environmental & Industrial Equity Partners
Most Recent Fund Was Raised: 01/21/1999
Year Founded: 1987
Capital Under Management: $1,064,800,000
Current Activity Level : Actively seeking new investments
Method of Compensation: Return on invest. most important, but chg. closing fees, service fees, etc.

CORAL VENTURES

60 South Sixth Street
Suite 3510
Minneapolis, MN 55402
Phone: 612-335-8666
Fax: 612-335-8668
Website: www.coralventures.com

Other Offices

3000 Sand Hill Road
Building 3, Suite 210
Menlo Park, CA 94025
Phone: 650-854-5226
Fax: 650-854-4625

Management and Staff
Karen Boezi, General Partner
Linda Watchmaker, Chief Financial Officer
Peter McNerney, Managing Partner
William Baumel, General Partner
Yuval Almog, Managing Partner

Type of Firm
Private Firm Investing Own Capital

Project Preferences

Role in Financing:
Will function either as deal originator or investor in deals created by others

Type of Financing Preferred:
Early Stage
Later Stage
Seed
Startup

Size of Investments Considered
Min Size of Investment Considered (000s): $1,000
Max Size of Investment Considered (000s): $11,000

Geographical Preferences

United States
All U.S.

International
Israel

Industry Preferences

(% based on actual investment)

Communications and Media	25.9%
Medical/Health	25.1%
Internet Specific	17.8%
Computer Software and Services	10.9%
Biotechnology	6.9%
Semiconductors/Other Elect.	6.2%
Industrial/Energy	2.5%
Other Products	2.4%
Computer Hardware	2.1%
Consumer Related	0.2%

Additional Information
Name of Most Recent Fund: Coral Partners V
Most Recent Fund Was Raised: 06/01/1998
Year Founded: 1983
Capital Under Management: $253,100,000
Current Activity Level : Actively seeking new investments
Method of Compensation: Return on investment is of primary concern, do not charge fees

CRESCENDO VENTURE MANAGEMENT LLC (FKA:IAI VENTURES)

800 LaSalle Avenue
Suite 2250
Minneapolis, MN 55402
Phone: 612-607-2800
Fax: 612-607-2801
Website: www.crescendoventures.com

Other Offices

36 Dover Street
Mayfair
London, United Kingdom W1X 3RB
Phone: 44-20-7529-6300
Fax: 44-20-7529-6301

480 Cowper Avenue
Suite 300
Palo Alto, CA 94301-2013
Phone: 650-470-1200
Fax: 650-470-1201

Management and Staff
Anthony Daffer, Partner
Christopher Chu, Principal
David Spreng, Managing Partner
Doug Robertson, Principal
James Behnke, Principal
Jay Schmelter, Principal
Jeff Hinck, Partner
Jeff Yu, Principal
Jeffrey Tollefson, Partner
John Borchers, Partner
Kevin Spreng, Principal
Kristi Buxell, Principal
Lorraine Fox, Partner
Richard Grogan-Crane, Partner
Roeland Boonstoppel, Partner
Subra Narayan, Principal

Type of Firm
Private Firm Investing Own Capital

Industry Association Membership
European Venture Capital Association (EVCA)
National Venture Capital Association (NVCA)
Western Association of Venture Capitalists (WAVC)

Project Preferences

Role in Financing:
Will function either as deal originator or investor in deals created by others

Type of Financing Preferred:
Early Stage
First Stage Financing
Second Stage Financing
Seed
Startup

Size of Investments Considered
Min Size of Investment Considered (000s): $1,000
Max Size of Investment Considered (000s): $5,000

Geographical Preferences

United States
All U.S.

Canada
All Canada

International
Belgium
China
France
Germany
India
Italy
Japan
Luxembourg
Netherlands
Spain
United Kingdom

Industry Preferences

(% based on actual investment)

Internet Specific	31.4%
Communications and Media	25.6%
Semiconductors/Other Elect.	16.2%
Computer Software and Services	13.7%
Medical/Health	7.3%
Other Products	3.3%
Biotechnology	1.7%
Computer Hardware	0.8%

Additional Information
Name of Most Recent Fund: Crescendo III Executive Fund
Most Recent Fund Was Raised: 11/05/1998
Year Founded: 1995
Capital Under Management: $1,132,600,000
Current Activity Level : Actively seeking new investments
Method of Compensation: Return on investment is of primary concern, do not charge fees

DAIN RAUCHER WESSELS

60 South Sixth Street
Dain Rauscher Plaza
Minneapolis, MN 55402-4422
Phone: 612-371-7676
Fax: 612-371-2763

Other Offices

1201 Third Street
Suite 2500
Seattle, WA 98101-3044
Phone: 206-621-3110
Fax: 206-621-3047

Management and Staff
Ian Berman, Managing Director
Jeffrey Greiner, Managing Director
Mary Zimmer, Managing Director
Peter Grant, Managing Director
Robert Reynolds, Managing Director
Suzanne Bookstein, Managing Director
Travis Winkey, Managing Director

Type of Firm
Bank Group

Industry Association Membership
National Venture Capital Association (NVCA)

Project Preferences

Industry Preferences

(% based on actual investment)

Internet Specific	42.0%
Computer Software and Services	29.3%
Communications and Media	12.5%
Semiconductors/Other Elect.	11.6%
Medical/Health	3.2%
Consumer Related	1.3%

Additional Information
Year Founded: 1999
Capital Under Management: $23,000,000
Current Activity Level : Actively seeking new investments

DEVELOPMENT CORP. OF AUSTIN

1900 Eighth Avenue, N.W.
Austin, MN 55912
Phone: 507-433-0346
Fax: 507-433-0361
Website: www.spamtownusa.com

Project Preferences

Role in Financing:
Prefer role as deal originator but will also invest in deals created by others

Type of Financing Preferred:
First Stage Financing
Seed
Start-up Financing

Geographical Preferences

International
No Preference

Industry Preferences

Computer Hardware
Mini and Personal/Desktop
Computer Graphics and Dig
Terminals
Disk Relat. Memory Device

Computer Software
Systems Software
Applications Software

Semiconductors/Other Elect.
Electronic Components

Biotechnology
Biotechnology

Medical/Health
Diagnostic Services
Diagnostic Test Products
Other Therapeutic
Disposable Med. Products
Hospitals/Clinics/Primary
Pharmaceuticals

Consumer Related
Food/Beverage
Education Related

Industrial/Energy
Alternative Energy
Energy Conservation Relat
Industrial Products

Business Serv.
Consulting Services

Additional Information

Year Founded: 1986
Capital Under Management: $1,300,000
Current Activity Level : Actively seeking new investments
Method of Compensation: Return on investment is of primary concern, do not charge fees

FOOD FUND LTD. PARTNERSHIP, THE

5720 Smetana Drive
Suite 300
Minnetonka, MN 55343
Phone: 612-939-3950
Fax: 612-939-8106

Management and Staff

John Trucano, General Partner

Whom to Contact

John Trucano

Type of Firm

Private Firm Investing Own Capital

Project Preferences

Role in Financing:
Prefer role as deal originator but will also invest in deals created by others

Type of Financing Preferred:
First Stage Financing
Leveraged Buyout
Second Stage Financing
Special Situation
Start-up Financing

Size of Investments Considered

Min Size of Investment Considered (000s): $800
Max Size of Investment Considered: No Limit

Geographical Preferences

United States
All U.S.

Industry Preferences

(% based on actual investment)

Consumer Related	91.8%
Industrial/Energy	7.1%
Semiconductors/Other Elect.	1.1%

Additional Information

Year Founded: 1990
Capital Under Management: $9,500,000
Current Activity Level : Actively seeking new investments
Method of Compensation: Return on investment is of primary concern, do not charge fees

GIDEON HIXON FUND

1900 Foshay Tower
821 Marquette Avenue
Minneapolis, MN 55402
Phone: 612-904-2314
Fax: 612-204-0913

Management and Staff

Benson Whitney, Managing Partner

Type of Firm

Private Firm Investing Own Capital

Project Preferences

Role in Financing:
Prefer role as deal originator but will also invest in deals created by others

Type of Financing Preferred:
First Stage Financing
Second Stage Financing
Seed
Start-up Financing

Size of Investments Considered

Min Size of Investment Considered (000s): $300
Max Size of Investment Considered (000s): $500

Geographical Preferences

United States
West Coast

Industry Preferences

(% based on actual investment)

Internet Specific	43.0%
Medical/Health	26.0%
Semiconductors/Other Elect.	24.3%
Computer Software and Services	6.8%

Additional Information
Year Founded: 1989
Capital Under Management: $30,000,000
Current Activity Level : Actively seeking new investments
Method of Compensation: Return on investment is of primary concern, do not charge fees

GMAC-RESIDENTIAL FUNDING

8400 Normandale Lake Blvd
Minneapolis, MN 55437
Phone: 952-832-7000
Fax: 612-832-7086
Website: www.rfc.com

Management and Staff
Nathan Kornfeld, Managing Partner

Type of Firm
Non-Financial Corp. Affiliate or Subsidiary

Project Preferences

Size of Investments Considered
Min Size of Investment Considered (000s): $5,000
Max Size of Investment Considered (000s): $15,000

Additional Information
Year Founded: 1982
Current Activity Level : Actively seeking new investments

GOLDNER HAWN JOHNSON & MORRISON INCORPORATED

5250 Norwest Center
90 South Seventh Street
Minneapolis, MN 55402
Phone: 612-338-5912
Fax: 612-338-2860

Management and Staff
Edward J. Rieckelman

Whom to Contact
Edward J. Rieckelman

Type of Firm
Investment/Merchant Bank Subsid/Affil

Project Preferences

Role in Financing:
Prefer role as deal originator

Type of Financing Preferred:
Leveraged Buyout

Geographical Preferences

United States
Midwest
Northwest
Rocky Mountain

Industry Preferences

Semiconductors/Other Elect.
Sensors

Consumer Related
Entertainment and Leisure
Food/Beverage
Consumer Products
Consumer Services

Industrial/Energy
Industrial Products
Materials
Machinery

Manufact.
Publishing

Additional Information
Name of Most Recent Fund: Marathon Fund IV
Most Recent Fund Was Raised: 10/01/1998
Capital Under Management: $325,000,000
Current Activity Level : Inactive / Unknown
Method of Compensation: Return on invest. most important, but chg. closing fees, service fees, etc.

IAI VENTURES, INC.(AKA: INVESTMENT ADVISORS)

601 2nd Avenue South
3800 First Bank Place
Minneapolis, MN 55402
Phone: 612-376-2800
Fax: 612-376-2824

Type of Firm
Affiliate/Subsidary of Oth. Financial. Instit.

Project Preferences

Role in Financing:
Will function either as deal originator or investor in deals created by others

Industry Preferences

(% based on actual investment)

Computer Software and Services	36.0%
Communications and Media	20.1%
Medical/Health	17.1%
Consumer Related	8.4%
Industrial/Energy	7.2%
Other Products	6.4%
Biotechnology	3.6%
Internet Specific	1.1%

Additional Information
Name of Most Recent Fund: Superior Ventures
Most Recent Fund Was Raised: 06/01/1986
Year Founded: 1982
Capital Under Management: $79,600,000
Current Activity Level : Actively seeking new investments

MAYO MEDICAL VENTURES

200 First Street SW
Rochester, MN 55905
Phone: 507-266-4586
Fax: 507-284-5410
Website: www.mayo.edu

Type of Firm
Other NEC

Industry Association Membership
National Venture Capital Association (NVCA)

Project Preferences

Role in Financing:
Prefer role in deals created by others

Type of Financing Preferred:
Early Stage

Size of Investments Considered
Min Size of Investment Considered (000s): $1,000
Max Size of Investment Considered (000s): $1,000

Geographical Preferences

United States
All U.S.

Industry Preferences

(% based on actual investment)

Biotechnology	45.7%
Medical/Health	42.3%
Internet Specific	6.3%
Industrial/Energy	3.0%
Semiconductors/Other Elect.	2.7%

Additional Information

Year Founded: 1998
Capital Under Management: $25,000,000
Current Activity Level : Actively seeking new investments

MEDICAL INNOVATION PARTNERS

6450 City West Parkway
Eden Prairie, MN 55344-3245
Phone: 952-828-9616
Fax: 952-828-9596

Other Offices

Opus Center
9900 Bren Road,Suite 421
Minneapolis, MN 55343
Phone: 612-931-0154

Management and Staff

Mark Knudson, Managing Partner
Robert Nickoloff, General Partner

Type of Firm

Private Firm Investing Own Capital

Project Preferences

Role in Financing:

Prefer role as deal originator

Type of Financing Preferred:

First Stage Financing
Seed
Start-up Financing

Geographical Preferences

United States

Midwest
Northwest

Industry Preferences

(% based on actual investment)

Medical/Health	37.2%
Communications and Media	33.7%
Biotechnology	26.6%
Other Products	2.3%
Computer Software and Services	0.1%

Additional Information

Year Founded: 1982
Capital Under Management: $61,000,000
Current Activity Level : Actively seeking new investments
Method of Compensation: Return on investment is of primary concern, do not charge fees

MICROTECHNOLOGY INVESTMENTS, LTD.

7900 International Drive
Minneapolis, MN 55420
Phone: 612-851-1500

See California for full listing.

MINNESOTA MANAGEMENT PARTNERS

539 East Lake Street
Wayzata, MN 55391
Phone: 612-943-1517
Fax: 612-943-1965

Management and Staff

C. McKenzie Lewis, General Partner
Dennis Anderson, General Partner
Scott Drill, General Partner

Type of Firm

Private Firm Investing Own Capital

Additional Information

Year Founded: 1997
Current Activity Level : Actively seeking new investments

NORTHEAST VENTURES CORP.

802 Alworth Building
Duluth, MN 55802
Phone: 218-722-9915
Fax: 218-722-9871

Management and Staff

Nick Smith, Chief Executive Officer
Tom Van Hale, Vice President

Whom to Contact

Greg Sandbulte
Mark Phillips
Tom Van Hale

Type of Firm

Private Firm Investing Own Capital

Industry Association Membership

Natl assoc of Small Bus. Inv. Co (NASBIC)

Project Preferences

Role in Financing:

Prefer role as deal originator but will also invest in deals created by others

Type of Financing Preferred:

First Stage Financing
Leveraged Buyout
Mezzanine
Research and Development
Second Stage Financing
Seed
Start-up Financing

Size of Investments Considered

Min Size of Investment Considered (000s): $100
Max Size of Investment Considered (000s): $500

Geographical Preferences

United States

Midwest

Industry Preferences

(% based on actual investment)

Other Products	44.8%
Semiconductors/Other Elect.	33.9%
Medical/Health	12.8%
Communications and Media	5.2%
Computer Software and Services	2.6%
Consumer Related	0.7%

Additional Information

Year Founded: 1989
Capital Under Management: $10,200,000
Current Activity Level : Actively seeking new investments
Method of Compensation: Return on invest. most important, but chg. closing fees, service fees, etc.

NORWEST EQUITY PARTNERS

3600 IDS Center
80 South Eighth Street
Minneapolis, MN 55402
Phone: 612-215-1600
Fax: 612-215-1601
Website: ww.norwestvp.com

See California for full listing.

OAK INVESTMENT PARTNERS

4550 Norwest Center
90 South Seventh Street
Minneapolis, MN 55402
Phone: 612-339-9322
Fax: 612-337-8017
Website: www.oakvc.com

See Connecticut for full listing.

PATHFINDER VENTURE CAPITAL FUNDS

7300 Metro Boulevard
Suite 585
Minneapolis, MN 55439
Phone: 952-835-1121
Fax: 952-835-8389

Other Offices

3000 Sand Hill Road
Building Three, Suite 255
Menlo Park, CA 94025
Phone: 415-854-0650
Fax: 415-854-4706

7300 Metro Blvd
Suite 585
Minneapolis, MN

Management and Staff
Jack K. Ahrens II

Whom to Contact
Jack K. Ahrens II

Type of Firm
Private Firm Investing Own Capital

Industry Association Membership
Natl assoc of Small Bus. Inv. Co (NASBIC)

Project Preferences

Role in Financing:
Prefer role as deal originator but will also invest in deals created by others

Type of Financing Preferred:
First Stage Financing
Leveraged Buyout
Mezzanine
Second Stage Financing
Seed
Special Situation
Start-up Financing

Size of Investments Considered
Min Size of Investment Considered (000s): $2,000
Max Size of Investment Considered: No Limit

Geographical Preferences

United States
All U.S.

Canada
All Canada

Industry Preferences

(% based on actual investment)

Medical/Health	42.0%
Computer Hardware	16.6%
Semiconductors/Other Elect.	8.9%
Other Products	7.4%
Communications and Media	7.0%
Computer Software and Services	6.8%
Biotechnology	5.8%
Industrial/Energy	4.9%
Consumer Related	0.7%

Additional Information
Name of Most Recent Fund: Pathfinder Venture Capital Fund III, A Limited Partership
Most Recent Fund Was Raised: 12/01/1999
Year Founded: 1980
Capital Under Management: $25,100,000
Current Activity Level : Actively seeking new investments
Method of Compensation: Return on investment is of primary concern, do not charge fees

SHARED VENTURES, INC.

6550 York Avenue South
Edina, MN 55435
Phone: 612-925-3411

Other Offices

6550 York Avenue South
Edina, MN

Management and Staff
Howard Weiner

Whom to Contact
Howard Weiner

Type of Firm
Private Firm Investing Own Capital

Industry Association Membership
Natl assoc of Small Bus. Inv. Co (NASBIC)

Project Preferences

Role in Financing:
Prefer role as deal originator but will also invest in deals created by others

Type of Financing Preferred:
Control-block Purchases
First Stage Financing
Leveraged Buyout
Second Stage Financing
Special Situation
Start-up Financing

Size of Investments Considered
Min Size of Investment Considered (000s): $100
Max Size of Investment Considered (000s): $300

Geographical Preferences

United States
Midwest

Industry Preferences

Semiconductors/Other Elect.
Electronics

Medical/Health
Diagnostic Test Products
Drug/Equipmt Delivery
Other Therapeutic
Medical Products
Disposable Med. Products

Consumer Related
Entertainment and Leisure
Franchises(NEC)
Food/Beverage
Consumer Products

Industrial/Energy
Energy Conservation Relat
Industrial Products

Agr/Forestr/Fish
Agriculture related

Additional Information
Name of Most Recent Fund: Shared Ventures, Inc.
Most Recent Fund Was Raised: 08/01/1982
Year Founded: 1981
Capital Under Management: $15,000,000
Current Activity Level : Making few, if any, new investments
Method of Compensation: Return on investment is of primary concern, do not charge fees

SHERPA PARTNERS, LLC

5050 Lincoln Drive
Suite 490
Edina, MN 55436
Phone: 952-942-1070
Fax: 952-942-1071
Website: www.sherpapartners.com

Management and Staff
C. McKenzie Lewis, Managing Partner
Richard Brimacomb, Partner
Steven Pederson, Partner

Type of Firm
Private Firm Investing Own Capital

Project Preferences

Type of Financing Preferred:
Early Stage

Size of Investments Considered
Min Size of Investment Considered (000s): $250
Max Size of Investment Considered (000s): $5,000

Geographical Preferences

United States
Midwest

Industry Preferences

Communications and Media
Telecommunications

Computer Software
Software

Internet Specific
Internet

Additional Information
Year Founded: 2000
Capital Under Management: $15,000,000
Current Activity Level : Actively seeking new investments

SQUARE ONE VENTURES (AKA: SMABY GROUP)

1315 Foshay Tower
Minneapolis, MN 55402
Phone: 612-333-0002
Fax: 612-333-0204
E-mail: info@smaby.com
Website: www.smaby.com

Management and Staff
Gary Smaby, Principal

Type of Firm
Investment Management/Finance Consulting

Project Preferences

Type of Financing Preferred:
Seed
Startup

Geographical Preferences

United States
Midwest

Industry Preferences

Internet Specific
Internet

Additional Information
Current Activity Level : Actively seeking new investments

ST. PAUL VENTURE CAPITAL, INC.

10400 Viking Drive
Suite 550
Eden Prairie, MN 55344
Phone: 952-995-7474
Fax: 952-995-7475
Website: www.stpaulvc.com

Other Offices

138 River Road
Andover, MA 01810
Phone: 978-837-3198
Fax: 978-837-3199

Three Lagoon Drive
Suite 130
Redwood City, CA 94065-1566
Phone: 650-596-5630
Fax: 650-596-5711

Management and Staff
Brian Jacobs, General Partner
Carl Witonsky, Partner
David Stassen, General Partner
Everett Cox, General Partner
Fredrick Boswell, General Partner
James Simons, General Partner
John Rollwagon, Venture Partner
Katherine Carney, Chief Financial Officer
Kurt Winters, Principal
Mary Jeffries, General Partner
Michael Gorman, General Partner
Nancy Olson, General Partner
Patrick Hopf, Managing General Partner
Raj Alur, Principal
Rick Boswell, General Partner
Roderick Randall, General Partner
Staffan Ericsson, Venture Partner
Steven Goldstein, Venture Partner
Tom Simonson, Partner
Tom Rowbotham, Venture Partner
William Cadogan, General Partner
Zenas Hutcheson, General Partner

Type of Firm
Insurance Firm Affiliate or Subsidiary

Industry Association Membership
National Venture Capital Association (NVCA)

Project Preferences

Role in Financing:
Prefer role as deal originator but will also invest in deals created by others

Type of Financing Preferred:
Early Stage

Size of Investments Considered
Min Size of Investment Considered (000s): $500
Max Size of Investment Considered: No Limit

Geographical Preferences

United States
California
Massachusetts
Minnesota

Industry Preferences

(% based on actual investment)

Computer Software and Services	25.8%
Internet Specific	23.9%
Communications and Media	13.3%
Medical/Health	13.3%
Consumer Related	11.4%
Semiconductors/Other Elect.	5.6%
Computer Hardware	3.0%
Biotechnology	2.8%
Other Products	0.5%
Industrial/Energy	0.4%

Additional Information
Year Founded: 1988
Capital Under Management: $3,000,000,000
Current Activity Level : Actively seeking new investments
Method of Compensation: Return on investment is of primary concern, do not charge fees

U.S. BANCORP CAPITAL CORPORATION

U.S. Bank Place
601 Second Avenue South
Minneapolis, MN 55402
Phone: 503-275-4705

Type of Firm
SBIC Not elsewhere classified

Additional Information
Current Activity Level : Actively seeking new investments

U.S. BANCORP PIPER JAFFRAY VENTURES, INC.

800 Nicollet Mall
Suite 800
Minneapolis, MN 55402
Phone: 612-303-5686
Fax: 612-303-1350
Website: www.piperjaffrayventures.com

Other Offices

345 California Street
San Francisco, CA 94104
Phone: 415-984-4628
Fax: 415-984-4633

Management and Staff
Arden Koontz, Vice President
Buzz Benson, Managing Director
Charles Beeler, Vice President
David Geisler, Vice President
Gary Blauer, Managing Director
Heath Lukatch, Managing Director
Ken Higgins, Managing Director
Marco DeMiroz, Managing Director
Maureen Harder, Chief Financial Officer
Mike Severson, Managing Director
Ned Scheetz, Managing Director

Type of Firm
Investment/Merchant Bank Investing Own or Client Funds

Industry Association Membership
National Venture Capital Association (NVCA)
Natl assoc of Small Bus. Inv. Co (NASBIC)

Project Preferences

Role in Financing:
Prefer role as deal originator but will also invest in deals created by others

Type of Financing Preferred:
Early Stage
Expansion
Later Stage

Size of Investments Considered
Min Size of Investment Considered (000s): $250
Max Size of Investment Considered: No Limit

Geographical Preferences

United States
All U.S.

Industry Preferences

(% based on actual investment)

Medical/Health	39.5%
Internet Specific	25.6%
Computer Software and Services	10.2%
Communications and Media	9.7%
Semiconductors/Other Elect.	4.2%
Biotechnology	3.3%
Other Products	3.3%
Consumer Related	2.0%
Computer Hardware	1.6%
Industrial/Energy	0.7%

Additional Information
Name of Most Recent Fund: Piper Jaffray Health Care Fund III, L.P.
Most Recent Fund Was Raised: 01/21/1999
Year Founded: 1982
Capital Under Management: $228,100,000
Current Activity Level : Actively seeking new investments
Method of Compensation: Return on investment is of primary concern, do not charge fees

UPPER LAKE GROWTH CAPITAL

10400 Viking Drive
Suite 530
Eden Prairie, MN 55344
Phone: 612-995-7496
Fax: 612-995-7499

Management and Staff
David Stassen, Managing Director
Keith Eastman, Managing Director

Type of Firm
Private Firm Investing Own Capital

Industry Preferences

(% based on actual investment)

Internet Specific	50.0%
Semiconductors/Other Elect.	21.0%
Medical/Health	17.7%
Computer Software and Services	11.3%

Additional Information
Current Activity Level : Actively seeking new investments

MISSOURI

A.G. EDWARDS CAPITAL INC

One North Jefferson
Saint Louis, MO 63103
Phone: 314-955-3000

Management and Staff
Chris Redmond, Managing Director
Patricia Dahl, Vice President

Type of Firm
Investment/Merchant Bank Subsid/Affil

Additional Information
Current Activity Level : Actively seeking new investments

ADVANTAGE CAPITAL PARTNERS

7733 Forsyth Boulevard
Suite 1850
St. Louis, MO 63105
Phone: 314-725-0800
Fax: 314-725-4265
Website: www.advantagecap.com

See Louisiana for full listing.

ALLSOP VENTURE PARTNERS

55 West Port Plaza
Suite 575
St. Louis, MO 63146
Phone: 314-434-1688
Fax: 314-434-6560

See Iowa for full listing.

AMERICAN CENTURY VENTURES

4500 Main Street
Tower 1, 9th Floor
Kansas City, MO 64111
Phone: 816-340-4054
Fax: 816-340-3278
Website: www.americancenturyventures.com

Management and Staff
Diane Mulcahy, Partner
Harold Bradley, President
Sheila Davis, Partner

Type of Firm
Affiliate/Subsidary of Oth. Financial. Instit.

Project Preferences

Type of Financing Preferred:
Early Stage

Industry Preferences

Communications and Media
Telecommunications

Financial Services
Financial Services

Additional Information
Current Activity Level : Actively seeking new investments

BANKERS CAPITAL CORP.

3100 Gillham Road
Kansas City, MO 64109
Phone: 816-531-1600
Fax: 816-531-1334

Management and Staff
Lee Glasnapp

Whom to Contact
Lee Glasnapp

Type of Firm
SBIC Not elsewhere classified

Industry Association Membership
Natl assoc of Small Bus. Inv. Co (NASBIC)

Project Preferences

Role in Financing:
Prefer role as deal originator but will also invest in deals created by others

Type of Financing Preferred:
Leveraged Buyout

Size of Investments Considered
Min Size of Investment Considered (000s): $100
Max Size of Investment Considered: No Limit

Geographical Preferences

United States
Midwest

Industry Preferences

Semiconductors/Other Elect.
Electronics

Consumer Related
Consumer Products

Industrial/Energy
Machinery

Additional Information
Year Founded: 1975
Current Activity Level : Actively seeking new investments
Method of Compensation: Return on invest. most important, but chg. closing fees, service fees, etc.

BARING PRIVATE EQUITY PARTNERS (FKA:BARING VENTURE PARTNERS)

P.O. Box 12491
St. Louis, MO 63132
Phone: 314-993-0007
Fax: 314-993-0464
Website: www.bpep.com

See Foreign Venture Capital Firms for full listing.

BOME INVESTORS, INC.

8000 Maryland Avenue
Suite 1190
St. Louis, MO 63105
Phone: 314-721-5707
Fax: 314-721-5135
Website: www.gatewayventures.com

Type of Firm
SBIC Not elsewhere classified

Project Preferences

Role in Financing:
Prefer role as deal originator but will also invest in deals created by others

Type of Financing Preferred:
First Stage Financing
Second Stage Financing
Start-up Financing

Geographical Preferences

United States
Midwest

Industry Preferences

Communications and Media
Commercial Communications
CATV & Pay TV Systems
Telecommunications
Data Communications
Satellite Microwave Comm.
Other Communication Prod.

Computer Hardware
Computers
Computer Graphics and Dig

Computer Software
Computer Services

Internet Specific
Internet

Semiconductors/Other Elect.
Electronics
Electronic Components
Controllers and Sensors
Laser Related
Fiber Optics
Analytic/Scientific

Biotechnology
Biotechnology

Medical/Health
Medical/Health
Medical Products

Industrial/Energy
Industrial Products
Materials
Environmental Related

Additional Information

Year Founded: 1997
Capital Under Management: $3,000,000
Current Activity Level : Actively seeking new investments
Method of Compensation: Return on investment is of primary concern, do not charge fees

C3 HOLDINGS, LLC

4520 Main Street
Suite 1600
Kansas City, MO 64111
Phone: 816-756-2225
Fax: 816-756-5552

Other Offices

2100 McKinney Avenue
Suite 1550
Dallas, TX 75201
Phone: 214-292-2000

233 South Wacker Drive
Sears Tower, Suite 5330
Chicago, IL 60606
Phone: 312-655-5990
Fax: 312-655-5999

5005 LBJ Freeway
LB 119
Dallas, TX 75244
Phone: 972-233-8778
Fax: 972-233-0112

Management and Staff

A.Baron Cass, Principal
Barton Cohen, Principal
D. Patrick Curran, Principal
Patrick Healy, Principal

Whom to Contact

Gregg Herman

Type of Firm

Investment/Merchant Bank Subsid/Affil

Project Preferences

Role in Financing:
Prefer role as deal originator

Type of Financing Preferred:
Acquisition
Expansion
Generalist PE
Later Stage
Leveraged Buyout
Management Buyouts
Recapitalizations

Size of Investments Considered
Min Size of Investment Considered (000s): $5,000
Max Size of Investment Considered (000s): $100,000

Geographical Preferences

United States
All U.S.

Industry Preferences

Computer Hardware
Computer Graphics and Dig

Computer Software
Computer Services
Artificial Intelligence

Internet Specific
Internet

Semiconductors/Other Elect.
Electronic Components
Controllers and Sensors
Circuit Boards
Component Testing Equipmt
Fiber Optics
Analytic/Scientific

Biotechnology
Industrial Biotechnology
Biosensors
Biotech Related Research

Medical/Health
Medical Diagnostics
Diagnostic Services
Diagnostic Test Products
Other Therapeutic
Disposable Med. Products

Consumer Related
Entertainment and Leisure
Retail
Food/Beverage
Consumer Products
Consumer Services
Education Related

Industrial/Energy
Industrial Products

Manufact.
Office Automation Equipmt
Publishing

Additional Information

Year Founded: 1996
Capital Under Management: $750,000,000
Current Activity Level : Actively seeking new investments
Method of Compensation: Return on invest. most important, but chg. closing fees, service fees, etc.

CAPITAL FOR BUSINESS, INC.

11 South Meramec Street
Suite 1430
St. Louis, MO 63105
Phone: 314-746-7427
Fax: 314-746-8739
Website: www.capitalforbusiness.com

Other Offices

1000 Walnut Street
18th Floor
Kansas City, MO 64106
Phone: 816-234-2357
Fax: 816-234-2952

8770 W. Bryn
Suite 1300
Chicago, IL 60651
Phone: 773-867-8532
Fax: 773-867-8533

Management and Staff
Bart Bergman, President
James O'Donnell, Chairman & CEO
William Witzofsky, Vice President

Whom to Contact
Hollis A. Huels
S. Wesley Hampp

Type of Firm
Commercial Bank Affiliate or Subsidiary

Industry Association Membership
National Venture Capital Association (NVCA)
Natl assoc of Small Bus. Inv. Co (NASBIC)

Project Preferences

Role in Financing:
Prefer role as deal originator but will also invest in deals created by others

Type of Financing Preferred:
Expansion
Later Stage
Leveraged Buyout
Management Buyouts

Size of Investments Considered
Min Size of Investment Considered (000s): $500
Max Size of Investment Considered (000s): $5,000

Geographical Preferences

United States
Midwest

Industry Preferences

(% based on actual investment)

Industrial/Energy	31.0%
Other Products	15.6%
Consumer Related	12.7%
Internet Specific	11.6%
Medical/Health	9.0%
Semiconductors/Other Elect.	6.8%
Computer Hardware	5.0%
Communications and Media	4.7%
Biotechnology	3.6%

Additional Information
Name of Most Recent Fund: CFB Emerging Business Fund
Most Recent Fund Was Raised: 07/01/1998
Year Founded: 1959
Capital Under Management: $43,100,000
Current Activity Level : Actively seeking new investments

CROWN CAPITAL CORP

540 Maryville Centre Drive
Suite 120
Saint Louis, MO 63141
Phone: 314-576-1201
Fax: 314-576-1525
Website: www.crown-cap.com

Management and Staff
Gary Barohn, Managing Director
Harry Rich, Managing Director
Paul Sabo, Managing Director
R. William Breece, Managing Director
Robert Mohrmann, Managing Director

Type of Firm
Investment/Merchant Bank Investing Own or Client Funds

Project Preferences

Role in Financing:
Prefer role as deal originator but will also invest in deals created by others

Type of Financing Preferred:
Control-block Purchases
First Stage Financing
Leveraged Buyout
Mezzanine
Second Stage Financing
Special Situation

Geographical Preferences

United States
All U.S.

Canada
All Canada

International
Australia
Bermuda
China
France
Germany
Italy
Japan
Spain
United Kingdom

Industry Preferences

Communications and Media
Communications and Media

Computer Software
Computer Services

Semiconductors/Other Elect.
Electronic Components
Sensors

Biotechnology
Industrial Biotechnology

Medical/Health
Medical/Health
Medical Diagnostics
Medical Therapeutics

Consumer Related
Entertainment and Leisure
Retail
Franchises(NEC)
Food/Beverage
Consumer Products
Consumer Services
Other Restaurants
Hotels and Resorts
Education Related

Industrial/Energy
Oil and Gas Exploration
Oil & Gas Drilling,Explor
Energy Conservation Relat
Materials
Factory Automation
Machinery
Environmental Related

Transportation
Transportation

Financial Services
Financial Services
Real Estate

Business Serv.
Distribution

Manufact.
Office Automation Equipmt
Publishing

Agr/Forestr/Fish
Mining and Minerals

Additional Information
Year Founded: 1985
Capital Under Management: $120,000,000
Current Activity Level : Actively seeking new investments
Method of Compensation: Return on invest. most important, but chg. closing fees, service fees, etc.

DE VRIES & CO., INC.

800 West 47th Street
Kansas City, MO 64112
Phone: 816-756-0055
Fax: 816-756-0061

Management and Staff
Robert De Vries, President

Whom to Contact
Rex Wiggins

Type of Firm
Placement Agent

Project Preferences

Role in Financing:
Prefer role as deal originator

Type of Financing Preferred:
Acquisition
Expansion
Later Stage
Leveraged Buyout
Management Buyouts
Mezzanine
Private Placement
Recapitalizations
Second Stage Financing

Size of Investments Considered
Min Size of Investment Considered (000s): $500
Max Size of Investment Considered: No Limit

Geographical Preferences

International
No Preference

Industry Preferences

Communications and Media
Communications and Media
Commercial Communications
Telecommunications
Wireless Communications
Data Communications
Other Communication Prod.

Computer Hardware
Mainframes / Scientific
Mini and Personal/Desktop
Computer Graphics and Dig

Computer Software
Data Processing
Software
Systems Software
Applications Software

Internet Specific
Internet

Semiconductors/Other Elect.
Electronic Components
Micro-Processing
Sensors
Circuit Boards
Component Testing Equipmt
Fiber Optics
Analytic/Scientific

Biotechnology
Human Biotechnology

Medical/Health
Medical Diagnostics
Diagnostic Services
Medical Therapeutics
Drug/Equipmt Delivery
Disposable Med. Products
Pharmaceuticals

Consumer Related
Consumer
Computer Stores
Food/Beverage
Consumer Products
Consumer Services
Education Related

Industrial/Energy
Industrial Products
Process Control
Robotics
Machinery

Business Serv.
Services
Distribution
Media

Manufact.
Manufacturing
Office Automation Equipmt
Publishing

Agr/Forestr/Fish
Agriculture related
Mining and Minerals

Additional Information
Name of Most Recent Fund: De Vries & Company
Most Recent Fund Was Raised: 01/01/1996
Year Founded: 1984
Current Activity Level : Actively seeking new investments
Method of Compensation: Function primarily in service area, receive contingent fee in cash or equity

GATEWAY ASSOCIATES, L.P.

8000 Maryland Avenue
Suite 1190
St. Louis, MO 63105
Phone: 314-721-5707
Fax: 314-721-5135

Management and Staff
Charles Dill, General Partner
Gregory Johnson, General Partner
John McCarthy, General Partner
Richard Ford, General Partner

Type of Firm
SBIC Not elsewhere classified

Project Preferences

Role in Financing:
Prefer role as deal originator but will also invest in deals created by others

Type of Financing Preferred:
Control-block Purchases
First Stage Financing
Leveraged Buyout
Mezzanine
Second Stage Financing
Special Situation
Start-up Financing

Size of Investments Considered
Min Size of Investment Considered (000s): $1,000
Max Size of Investment Considered: No Limit

Geographical Preferences

United States
All U.S.

Industry Preferences

(% based on actual investment)

Biotechnology	15.9%
Communications and Media	15.2%
Computer Software and Services	13.1%
Semiconductors/Other Elect.	12.0%
Internet Specific	11.5%
Medical/Health	10.8%
Computer Hardware	10.7%
Other Products	6.8%
Industrial/Energy	3.4%
Consumer Related	0.7%

Additional Information
Year Founded: 1984
Capital Under Management: $30,000,000
Current Activity Level : Reducing investment activity
Method of Compensation: Return on investment is of primary concern, do not charge fees

HARBISON CORPORATION

8112 Maryland Avenue
Suite 250
St. Louis, MO 63105
Phone: 314-727-8200
Fax: 314-727-0249

Management and Staff
Keith Harbison

Whom to Contact
Keith Harbison

Project Preferences

Role in Financing:
Prefer role as deal originator

Type of Financing Preferred:
Control-block Purchases
Leveraged Buyout
Special Situation

Size of Investments Considered
Min Size of Investment Considered (000s): $500
Max Size of Investment Considered: No Limit

Geographical Preferences

United States
Mid Atlantic
Southeast

Canada
Ontario
Quebec

International
Bermuda
United Kingdom

Additional Information
Year Founded: 1992
Capital Under Management: $10,000,000
Current Activity Level : Actively seeking new investments
Method of Compensation: Return on invest. most important, but chg. closing fees, service fees, etc.

IEMERGE VENTURES

1700 Wyandotte Street
Kansas City, MO 64108
Phone: 816-960-3456
E-mail: info@iemerge.com
Website: www.iemerge.com

Type of Firm
Incubators

Project Preferences

Type of Financing Preferred:
Seed

Size of Investments Considered
Min Size of Investment Considered (000s): $300
Max Size of Investment Considered (000s): $500

Additional Information
Year Founded: 2000
Current Activity Level : Actively seeking new investments

INVESTAMERICA VENTURE GROUP, INC.

Commerce Tower
911 Main Street
Kansas City, MO 64105
Phone: 816-842-0114
Fax: 816-471-7339

See Iowa for full listing.

KANSAS CITY EQUITY PARTNERS

233 West 47th Street
Kansas City, MO 64112
Phone: 816-960-1771
Fax: 816-960-1777
Website: www.kcep.com

Management and Staff
Abel Mojica, Principal
Bill Reisler, Managing Partner
Dave Schulte, Partner
Jack Claire, Vice President
Jeffrey Teeven, Vice President
Terry Matlack, Partner
Thomas Palmer, Managing Director

Type of Firm
Private Firm Investing Own Capital

Industry Association Membership
National Venture Capital Association (NVCA)
Natl assoc of Small Bus. Inv. Co (NASBIC)

Project Preferences

Role in Financing:
Will function either as deal originator or investor in deals created by others

Type of Financing Preferred:
Early Stage
Expansion
Joint Ventures
Startup

Size of Investments Considered
Min Size of Investment Considered (000s): $2,000
Max Size of Investment Considered (000s): $8,000

Geographical Preferences

United States
Midwest

Industry Preferences
(% based on actual investment)

Internet Specific	43.9%
Communications and Media	21.7%
Industrial/Energy	9.4%
Semiconductors/Other Elect.	7.8%
Consumer Related	6.7%
Other Products	6.5%
Computer Software and Services	3.9%

Additional Information
Name of Most Recent Fund: KCEP Ventures II L.P.
Most Recent Fund Was Raised: 03/01/1999
Year Founded: 1993
Capital Under Management: $75,000,000
Current Activity Level : Actively seeking new investments
Method of Compensation: Return on invest. most important, but chg. closing fees, service fees, etc.

PAULI & CO., INC.

7733 Forsyth Boulevard
Suite 2000
St. Louis, MO 63105
Phone: 314-863-3300
Fax: 314-862-0544

Management and Staff
Edward P. Russell

Whom to Contact
Edward P. Russell

Type of Firm
Mgt. Consulting Firm

Project Preferences

Role in Financing:
Prefer role as deal originator but will also invest in deals created by others

Type of Financing Preferred:
Control-block Purchases
Leveraged Buyout
Mezzanine
Second Stage Financing
Special Situation

Size of Investments Considered
Min Size of Investment Considered (000s): $5,000
Max Size of Investment Considered: No Limit

Geographical Preferences

United States
All U.S.

Industry Preferences

Computer Hardware
Integrated Turnkey System

Computer Software
Systems Software
Applications Software

Semiconductors/Other Elect.
Laser Related

Medical/Health
Medical Products
Pharmaceuticals

Consumer Related
Retail
Food/Beverage
Consumer Products
Other Restaurants

Industrial/Energy
Industrial Products
Materials
Machinery

Manufact.
Office Automation Equipmt
Publishing

Additional Information
Year Founded: 1969
Capital Under Management: $63,000,000
Current Activity Level : Actively seeking new investments
Method of Compensation: Professional fee required whether or not deal closes

RIVERVEST VENTURE PARTNERS

7733 Forsyth Boulevard
Suite 1650
Saint Louis, MO 63105
Phone: 314-726-6700
Fax: 314-726-6715
Website: www.rivervest.com

Management and Staff
Andrew Craig, Managing Director
Jay Schmelter, Managing Director
Mark Mendel, Managing Director
Thomas Melzer, Managing Director

Type of Firm
Private Firm Investing Own Capital

Industry Association Membership
National Venture Capital Association (NVCA)

Project Preferences

Type of Financing Preferred:
Early Stage

Geographical Preferences

United States
Midwest
All U.S.

Industry Preferences

Biotechnology
Biotechnology
Human Biotechnology

Medical/Health
Medical Therapeutics
Drug/Equipmt Delivery
Medical Products
Disposable Med. Products
Pharmaceuticals

Additional Information
Year Founded: 2000
Capital Under Management: $28,500,000
Current Activity Level : Actively seeking new investments

VENTURE ASSOCIATES, LTD.

4811 Trailwood Way
Springfield, MO 65804
Phone: 417-882-9218
Website: www.venturea.com

See Colorado for full listing.

NEBRASKA

AGRIBUSINESS PARTNERS INTERNATIONAL PARTNERS

1004 Farnam Street
Suite 400
Omaha, NE 68102
Phone: 402-444-1630
Fax: 402-930-3007
Website: am1st.com

Management and Staff
André Tikhomirov
Gregory Berenstein
Robert Peyton
Steven Crosby

Whom to Contact
André Tikhomirov
Gregory Berenstein
Robert Peyton
Steven Crosby

Type of Firm
Investment/Merchant Bank Subsid/Affil

Project Preferences

Role in Financing:
Prefer role in deals created by others

Type of Financing Preferred:
First Stage Financing
Mezzanine
Second Stage Financing

Industry Preferences

Consumer Related
Food/Beverage
Consumer Products

Agr/Forestr/Fish
Agriculture related

Additional Information
Name of Most Recent Fund: Agribusiness Partners International, L.P.
Most Recent Fund Was Raised: 12/01/1995
Year Founded: 1995
Capital Under Management: $100,000,000
Current Activity Level : Actively seeking new investments
Method of Compensation: Return on investment is of primary concern, do not charge fees

HEARTLAND CAPITAL FUND, LTD.

PO Box 642117
Omaha, NE 68164
Phone: 402-778-5124
Fax: 402-445-2370
Website: www.heartlandcapitalfund.com

Management and Staff
Bradley Edwards, General Partner
John Gustafson, Vice President
Patrick Rivelli, General Partner

Type of Firm
Private Firm Investing Own Capital

Industry Association Membership
National Venture Capital Association (NVCA)

Project Preferences

Role in Financing:
Will function either as deal originator or investor in deals created by others

Type of Financing Preferred:
Expansion
First Stage Financing
Second Stage Financing

Size of Investments Considered
Min Size of Investment Considered (000s): $500
Max Size of Investment Considered (000s): $3,000

Geographical Preferences

United States
Midwest
Southwest

Industry Preferences

Communications and Media
Telecommunications
Data Communications

Computer Software
Computer Services
Data Processing
Software

Internet Specific
E-Commerce Technology
Internet

Medical/Health
Health Services

Additional Information
Name of Most Recent Fund: Heartland Capital Fund, Ltd.
Most Recent Fund Was Raised: 12/01/1993
Year Founded: 1993
Capital Under Management: $11,000,000
Current Activity Level : Actively seeking new investments
Method of Compensation: Return on investment is of primary concern, do not charge fees

ODIN CAPITAL GROUP

1625 Farnam Street
Suite 700
Omaha, NE 68102
Phone: 402-346-6200
Fax: 402-342-9311
Website: www.odincapital.com

Management and Staff
David McLeese, Partner
Donna Walsh, Partner
Thompson Rogers, Partner

Type of Firm
Private Equity Advisor or Fund of Fund Mgr

Project Preferences

Type of Financing Preferred:
Early Stage
Expansion
First Stage Financing
Second Stage Financing

Size of Investments Considered
Min Size of Investment Considered (000s): $1,000
Max Size of Investment Considered (000s): $5,000

Industry Preferences

Internet Specific
E-Commerce Technology
Internet

Financial Services
Financial Services

Additional Information
Year Founded: 1999
Capital Under Management: $40,000,000
Current Activity Level : Actively seeking new investments

NEVADA

BENEFIT CAPITAL COMPANIES, INC., THE

P.O. Box 542
Logandale, NV 89021
Phone: 702-398-3222
Fax: 702-398-3700

Other Offices

5000 Birch Street
West Tower, Suite 3000
Newport Beach, CA 92660
Phone: 714-833-3767
Fax: 714-752-7569

Management and Staff
Robert Smiley

Whom to Contact
Robert Smiley

Type of Firm
Investment/Merchant Bank Investing Own or Client Funds

Project Preferences

Role in Financing:
Prefer role as deal originator but will also invest in deals created by others

Type of Financing Preferred:
Leveraged Buyout
Mezzanine

Size of Investments Considered
Min Size of Investment Considered (000s): $2,500
Max Size of Investment Considered: No Limit

Geographical Preferences

United States
All U.S.

Industry Preferences

Communications and Media
Telecommunications

Computer Software
Computer Services
Applications Software

Semiconductors/Other Elect.
Sensors

Consumer Related
Retail
Food/Beverage
Consumer Products
Consumer Services

Industrial/Energy
Materials
Factory Automation
Machinery

Transportation
Transportation

Financial Services
Financial Services

Business Serv.
Distribution
Consulting Services

Additional Information
Name of Most Recent Fund: Benefit Capital Companies
Most Recent Fund Was Raised: 10/01/1991
Year Founded: 1984
Capital Under Management: $15,000,000
Current Activity Level : Reducing investment activity
Method of Compensation: Return on invest. most important, but chg. closing fees, service fees, etc.

CNI VENTURES

101 Convention Center Drive
Suite 850
Las Vegas, NV 89109
Website: www.cniventures.com

See Arizona for full listing.

EDGE CAPITAL INVESTMENT CO., LLC

1350 East Flamingo Road
Suite 3000
Las Vegas, NV 89119
Phone: 702-438-3343
E-mail:info@EdgeCapital.net
E-mail:JohnY@EdgeCapital.net
Wesbite: www.EdgeCapital.net

See California for full listing.

HOMESEEKERS.COM

6490 S. McCarran, Suite D-28
Reno, NV 89509
Phone: 827-6886
Fax: 827-8182
Website: www.homeseekers.com

Management and Staff
Greg Costley, Chairman & CEO
John Giaimo, President & COO

Type of Firm
Private Firm Investing Own Capital

Project Preferences

Type of Financing Preferred:
Balanced

Geographical Preferences

International
All International

Additional Information
Current Activity Level : Actively seeking new investments

INCORPORATED INVESTORS

P.O. Box 1336
Crystal Bay, NV 89402-1336
Phone: 702-832-9798
Fax: 702-832-9031

See California for full listing.

MILLENNIUM THREE VENTURE GROUP, L.L.C.

6880 South McCarran Boulevard
Suite A-11
Reno, NV 89509
Phone: 775-954-2020
Fax: 775-954-2023
Website: www.m3vg.com

Type of Firm
Private Firm Investing Own Capital

Industry Association Membership
National Venture Capital Association (NVCA)

Project Preferences

Type of Financing Preferred:
Early Stage
Expansion
First Stage Financing
Mezzanine
Second Stage Financing
Seed

Size of Investments Considered
Min Size of Investment Considered (000s): $500
Max Size of Investment Considered (000s): $2,000

Geographical Preferences

United States
West Coast

Additional Information
Capital Under Management: $10,000,000
Current Activity Level : Actively seeking new investments
Method of Compensation: Return on invest. most important, but chg. closing fees, service fees, etc.

NEW HAMPSHIRE

ARETE CORPORATION

P.O. Box 1299
Center Harbor, NH 03226
Phone: 603-253-9797
Fax: 603-253-9799
Website: www.arete-microgen.com

Other Offices

3 Bethesda Metro Centre
Suite 770
Bethesda, MD 20814
Phone: 301-657-6268

Management and Staff
Robert Shaw, President

Whom to Contact
Jill S. Wilmoth

Type of Firm
Private Firm Investing Own Capital

Industry Association Membership
National Venture Capital Association (NVCA)

Project Preferences

Role in Financing:
Prefer role as deal originator but will also invest in deals created by others

Type of Financing Preferred:
First Stage Financing
Research and Development
Seed
Start-up Financing

Geographical Preferences

United States
All U.S.

Canada
All Canada

International
Australia
France
United Kingdom

Industry Preferences

Industrial/Energy
Alternative Energy

Additional Information
Year Founded: 1997
Capital Under Management: $40,000,000
Current Activity Level : Actively seeking new investments

NEW JERSEY

ABERLYN CAPITAL MANAGEMENT CO., INC.

18 Winter Place
Matawan, NJ 07747
Phone: 908-583-5108
Fax: 908-583-8499

See New York for full listing.

ACCEL PARTNERS

One Palmer Square
Princeton, NJ 08542
Phone: 609-683-4500
Fax: 609-683-0384
Website: www.accel.com

See California for full listing.

ACCEL-KKR INTERNET CORP.

One Palmer Square
Princeton, NJ 08542
Phone: 609-683-4500
Fax: 609-683-0389
Website: www.accel-kkr.com

Other Offices

428 University Avenue
Palo Alto, CA 94301
Phone: 650-614-4800
Fax: 650-614-4880

Management and Staff
Carter Sednaoui, Chief Operating Officer
James Breyer, General Partner

Type of Firm
Private Firm Investing Own Capital

Additional Information
Year Founded: 2000
Capital Under Management: $50,000,000
Current Activity Level : Actively seeking new investments

ALAN I. GOLDMAN & ASSOCIATES

497 Ridgewood Avenue
Glen Ridge, NJ 07028
Phone: 973-857-5680
Fax: 973-509-8856

Management and Staff
Alan Goldman

Whom to Contact
Alan Goldman

Type of Firm
Mgt. Consulting Firm

Project Preferences

Role in Financing:
Prefer role as deal originator

Type of Financing Preferred:
Control-block Purchases
Leveraged Buyout
Mezzanine
Second Stage Financing
Special Situation

Size of Investments Considered
Min Size of Investment Considered (000s): $500
Max Size of Investment Considered: No Limit

Geographical Preferences

United States
All U.S.

Canada
All Canada

International
United Kingdom

Industry Preferences

Communications and Media
Communications and Media

Computer Other
Computer Related

Semiconductors/Other Elect.
Electronic Components

Biotechnology
Biotechnology

Medical/Health
Medical/Health

Consumer Related
Entertainment and Leisure
Retail
Franchises(NEC)
Food/Beverage
Consumer Products
Consumer Services
Hotels and Resorts
Education Related

Industrial/Energy
Oil and Gas Exploration
Oil & Gas Drilling,Explor
Energy Conservation Relat
Industrial Products

Transportation
Transportation

Financial Services
Financial Services

Business Serv.
Distribution
Consulting Services

Manufact.
Publishing

Agr/Forestr/Fish
Agriculture related

Additional Information
Year Founded: 1990
Current Activity Level : Actively seeking new investments
Method of Compensation: Function primarily in service area, receive contingent fee in cash or equity

AMERICAN ACQUISITION PARTNERS

175 South Street
Morristown, NJ 07960
Phone: 973-267-7800
Fax: 973-267-7695

Management and Staff
Ted Bustany

Whom to Contact
Ted Bustany

Type of Firm
Investment/Merchant Bank Subsid/Affil

Project Preferences

Role in Financing:
Prefer role as deal originator but will also invest in deals created by others

Type of Financing Preferred:
Leveraged Buyout
Recapitalizations

Size of Investments Considered
Min Size of Investment Considered (000s): $1,000
Max Size of Investment Considered (000s): $5,000

Geographical Preferences

United States
Mid Atlantic
Midwest
Northeast
Southeast

Industry Preferences

Consumer Related
Consumer Products

Industrial/Energy
Industrial Products
Materials
Factory Automation
Machinery

Additional Information
Name of Most Recent Fund: American Acquisition Partners
Most Recent Fund Was Raised: 06/19/1987
Year Founded: 1987
Capital Under Management: $40,000,000
Current Activity Level : Actively seeking new investments
Method of Compensation: Return on investment is of primary concern, do not charge fees

BCI PARTNERS

Glenpointe Centre West
Teaneck, NJ 07666
Phone: 201-836-3900
Fax: 201-836-6368
Website: www.bcipartners.com

Other Offices

760 Hopmeadow Street
P.O. Box 188
Simsbury, CT 06070
Phone: 203-651-9760
Fax: 203-651-8890

Management and Staff
Donald Remey, General Partner
Hoyt Goodrich, General Partner
J. Barton Goodwin, General Partner
Lorelei Koran, Chief Financial Officer
Mark Hastings, General Partner
Peter Wilde, General Partner
Stephen Eley, General Partner
Theodore Horton, General Partner
Thomas Cusick III, General Partner

Whom to Contact
Peter O'Wilde
Thomas J. Cusick

Type of Firm
Private Firm Investing Own Capital

Project Preferences

Role in Financing:
Prefer role as deal originator but will also invest in deals created by others

Type of Financing Preferred:
Expansion

Size of Investments Considered
Min Size of Investment Considered (000s): $5,000
Max Size of Investment Considered (000s): $25,000

Geographical Preferences

United States
All U.S.

Industry Preferences

(% based on actual investment)

Communications and Media	36.4%
Internet Specific	16.0%
Other Products	13.6%
Consumer Related	9.8%
Computer Software and Services	8.1%
Medical/Health	6.5%
Industrial/Energy	3.9%
Semiconductors/Other Elect.	2.7%
Computer Hardware	1.7%
Biotechnology	1.3%

Additional Information
Name of Most Recent Fund: BCI Growth V
Most Recent Fund Was Raised: 10/01/1998
Year Founded: 1982
Capital Under Management: $820,500,000
Current Activity Level : Actively seeking new investments
Method of Compensation: Return on invest. most important, but chg. closing fees, service fees, etc.

BECTON, DICKINSON & CO. (AKA: BD VENTURES)

1 Becton Drive
Franklin Lakes, NJ 07417
Phone: 201-847-5643
Fax: 201-847-4874

Management and Staff
Clateo Castellini, Chairman & CEO

Type of Firm
Non-Financial Corp. Affiliate or Subsidiary

Project Preferences

Type of Financing Preferred:
Early Stage

Industry Preferences

Biotechnology
Biotechnology

Additional Information
Name of Most Recent Fund: Becton, Dickinson & Co.
Most Recent Fund Was Raised: 09/01/1981
Year Founded: 1998
Capital Under Management: $40,000,000
Current Activity Level : Actively seeking new investments

BLUE ROCK CAPITAL

230 Lackawanna Drive
Andover, NJ 07821
Phone: 973-426-1767
Fax: 973-426-0224
Website: www.bluerockcapital.com

See Delaware for full listing.

CAPITAL EXPRESS, L.L.C.

1100 Valleybrook Avenue
Lyndhurst, NJ 07071
Phone: 201-438-8228
Fax: 201-438-5131
Website: niles@capitalexpress.com

Management and Staff
Niles Cohen

Whom to Contact
Niles Cohen

Type of Firm
Investment/Merchant Bank Investing Own or Client Funds

Project Preferences

Role in Financing:
Prefer role as deal originator but will also invest in deals created by others

Type of Financing Preferred:
First Stage Financing
Recapitalizations
Second Stage Financing
Start-up Financing

Size of Investments Considered
Min Size of Investment Considered (000s): $300
Max Size of Investment Considered (000s): $500

Industry Preferences

Internet Specific
Internet

Consumer Related
Entertainment and Leisure
Retail
Food/Beverage
Consumer Services
Other Restaurants
Education Related

Manufact.
Publishing

Additional Information
Year Founded: 1994
Current Activity Level : Actively seeking new investments
Method of Compensation: Return on investment is of primary concern, do not charge fees

---

CARDINAL PARTNERS (FKA: CARDINAL HEALTH PARTNERS)

221 Nassau Street
Princeton, NJ 08542
Phone: 609-924-6452
Fax: 609-683-0174
Website: www.cardinalpartners.com

Other Offices
28202 Cabot Road
suite 200
Laguna Beach, CA 92651
Phone: 949-347-0384
Fax: 973-347-0389

Management and Staff
Brandon Hull, General Partner
John Park, Chief Financial Officer
John Clarke, Managing General Partner
Lisa Skeete Tatum, Partner

Whom to Contact
John L. Parke
Lisa Skeete Tatum

Type of Firm
Private Firm Investing Own Capital

Industry Association Membership
National Venture Capital Association (NVCA)

Project Preferences

Role in Financing:
Prefer role as deal originator but will also invest in deals created by others

Type of Financing Preferred:
Early Stage
First Stage Financing
Second Stage Financing
Seed
Startup

Size of Investments Considered
Min Size of Investment Considered (000s): $1,000
Max Size of Investment Considered (000s): $8,000

Geographical Preferences

United States
All U.S.

Canada
All Canada

Industry Preferences

(% based on actual investment)

Internet Specific	19.9%
Computer Hardware	17.6%
Computer Software and Services	13.5%
Biotechnology	12.7%
Medical/Health	11.2%
Semiconductors/Other Elect.	10.7%
Industrial/Energy	5.3%
Communications and Media	4.8%
Other Products	4.0%
Consumer Related	0.2%

Additional Information
Name of Most Recent Fund: Cardinal Health Partners
Most Recent Fund Was Raised: 01/01/1997
Year Founded: 1997
Capital Under Management: $188,000,000
Current Activity Level : Actively seeking new investments
Method of Compensation: Return on investment is of primary concern, do not charge fees

---

CIT GROUP/VENTURE CAPITAL, INC., THE

650 CIT Drive
Livingston, NJ 07039
Phone: 973-740-5429
Fax: 973-740-5555
Website: www.cit.com

Management and Staff
Kenneth Walters, Vice President
Mark Veen, Vice President
Paul Laud, President
Scott Schneiderman, Vice President

Whom to Contact
Bruce Schackman
Colby Collier
Janice Beckmen

Type of Firm
SBIC Not elsewhere classified

Industry Association Membership
Natl assoc of Small Bus. Inv. Co (NASBIC)

Project Preferences

Role in Financing:
Prefer role as deal originator but will also invest in deals created by others

Type of Financing Preferred:
First Stage Financing
Leveraged Buyout
Mezzanine
Second Stage Financing

Size of Investments Considered
Min Size of Investment Considered (000s): $3,000
Max Size of Investment Considered: No Limit

Geographical Preferences

United States
All U.S.

Industry Preferences

(% based on actual investment)

Internet Specific	37.0%
Communications and Media	23.9%
Computer Software and Services	19.6%
Other Products	5.7%
Medical/Health	4.9%
Industrial/Energy	4.0%
Semiconductors/Other Elect.	3.3%
Biotechnology	1.4%

Additional Information

Year Founded: 1992
Capital Under Management: $15,000,000
Current Activity Level : Actively seeking new investments
Method of Compensation: Return on invest. most important, but chg. closing fees, service fees, etc.

CS CAPITAL PARTNERS, LLC

328 Second Street
Suite 200
Lakewood, NJ 08701
Phone: 732-901-1111
Fax: 212-202-5071
Website: www.cs-capital.com

Management and Staff

Charles Nebenzahl, Principal
Solomon Lax, Principal

Type of Firm

Private Firm Investing Own Capital

Project Preferences

Role in Financing:
Prefer role as deal originator

Type of Financing Preferred:
Distressed Debt
Early Stage
Expansion
First Stage Financing
Second Stage Financing
Turnaround

Size of Investments Considered

Min Size of Investment Considered (000s): $500
Max Size of Investment Considered (000s): $3,000

Geographical Preferences

United States
Mid Atlantic
Midwest
Northeast
Southeast
Southwest
All U.S.

Canada
Ontario
Quebec

Industry Preferences

(% based on actual investment)

Internet Specific	64.3%
Computer Software and Services	26.4%
Communications and Media	7.3%
Medical/Health	2.0%

Additional Information

Name of Most Recent Fund: CS Private Equity Fund, L.P.
Most Recent Fund Was Raised: 12/31/1998
Year Founded: 1998
Capital Under Management: $18,000,000
Current Activity Level : Actively seeking new investments
Method of Compensation: Return on investment is of primary concern, do not charge fees

DFW CAPITAL PARTNERS (AKA:DEMUTH, FOLGER & WETHERILL)

Glenpointe Centre East- 5th Fl
300 Frank W. Burr Boulevard
Teaneck, NJ 07666
Phone: 201-836-2233
Fax: 201-836-5666
Website: www.dfwcapital.com

Management and Staff

David Wetherill, General Partner
Donald DeMuth, General Partner
Keith Pennell, General Partner
Lisa Roumell, General Partner
Thomas Folger, General Partner

Type of Firm

Private Firm Investing Own Capital

Industry Association Membership

National Venture Capital Association (NVCA)

Project Preferences

Role in Financing:
Prefer role as deal originator but will also invest in deals created by others

Type of Financing Preferred:
Acquisition
Control-block Purchases
Later Stage
Leveraged Buyout
Management Buyouts
Recapitalizations
Special Situation

Size of Investments Considered

Min Size of Investment Considered (000s): $500
Max Size of Investment Considered: No Limit

Geographical Preferences

United States
All U.S.

Industry Preferences

(% based on actual investment)

Medical/Health	29.6%
Consumer Related	16.6%
Communications and Media	15.0%
Computer Hardware	10.0%
Internet Specific	9.3%
Semiconductors/Other Elect.	9.3%
Other Products	5.3%
Industrial/Energy	2.6%
Computer Software and Services	2.4%

Additional Information

Name of Most Recent Fund: DeMuth, Folger & Wetherill II
Most Recent Fund Was Raised: 05/31/1996
Year Founded: 1983
Capital Under Management: $40,000,000
Current Activity Level : Actively seeking new investments
Method of Compensation: Return on investment is of primary concern, do not charge fees

DOMAIN ASSOCIATES, L.L.C.

One Palmer Square
Suite 515
Princeton, NJ 08542
Phone: 609-683-5656
Fax: 609-683-9789
Website: www.domainvc.com

Other Offices

28202 Cabot Road
Suite 200
Laguna Niguel, CA 92677
Phone: 949-347-2446
Fax: 949-347-9720

Management and Staff
Arthur Klausner, General Partner
Brian Dovey, General Partner
Eckard Weber, Venture Partner
James Blair, General Partner
Jesse I. Treu, General Partner
Kathleen Schoemaker, Chief Financial Officer
Nicole Vitullo, Managing Director
Olav Bergheim, Venture Partner
Richard Schneider, General Partner
Robert More, General Partner
Sharon Stevenson, Principal

Type of Firm
Private Firm Investing Own Capital

Industry Association Membership
National Venture Capital Association (NVCA)

Project Preferences

Role in Financing:
Will function either as deal originator or investor in deals created by others

Type of Financing Preferred:
Balanced
Early Stage
Expansion
First Stage Financing
Later Stage
Mezzanine
Private Placement
Research and Development
Second Stage Financing
Seed
Startup

Size of Investments Considered
Min Size of Investment Considered (000s): $1,000
Max Size of Investment Considered (000s): $20,000

Geographical Preferences

United States
All U.S.
All U.S.

Industry Preferences

(% based on actual investment)

Biotechnology	47.3%
Medical/Health	39.1%
Internet Specific	6.4%
Computer Software and Services	2.8%
Industrial/Energy	2.7%
Computer Hardware	1.2%
Semiconductors/Other Elect.	0.4%
Consumer Related	0.2%

Additional Information
Name of Most Recent Fund: Domain Partners IV, L.P.
Most Recent Fund Was Raised: 08/01/1998
Year Founded: 1985
Capital Under Management: $445,000,000
Current Activity Level : Actively seeking new investments
Method of Compensation: Return on investment is of primary concern, do not charge fees

EARLY STAGE ENTERPRISES, L.P.

995 Route 518
Skillman, NJ 08558
Phone: 609-921-8896
Fax: 609-921-8703
Website: www.esevc.com

Management and Staff
James Millar, General Partner
Kef Kasdin, General Partner
Ronald Hahn, General Partner

Type of Firm
SBIC Not elsewhere classified

Industry Association Membership
Mid-Atlantic Venture Association
National Venture Capital Association (NVCA)
Natl assoc of Small Bus. Inv. Co (NASBIC)

Project Preferences

Role in Financing:
Prefer role as deal originator but will also invest in deals created by others

Type of Financing Preferred:
Early Stage
Seed
Start-up Financing

Size of Investments Considered
Min Size of Investment Considered (000s): $250
Max Size of Investment Considered (000s): $1,000

Geographical Preferences

United States
Mid Atlantic

Industry Preferences

(% based on actual investment)

Internet Specific	35.6%
Computer Software and Services	25.5%
Communications and Media	21.3%
Medical/Health	9.2%
Other Products	8.4%

Additional Information
Name of Most Recent Fund: Early Stage Enterprises
Most Recent Fund Was Raised: 07/01/1996
Year Founded: 1996
Capital Under Management: $44,000,000
Current Activity Level : Actively seeking new investments
Method of Compensation: Return on investment is of primary concern, do not charge fees

EDELSON TECHNOLOGY PARTNERS

300 Tice Boulevard
Woodcliff Lake, NJ 07675
Phone: 201-930-9898
Fax: 201-930-8899
Website: www.edelsontech.com

Management and Staff
Harry Edelson, General Partner
Jack Fox, General Partner

Type of Firm
Private Firm Investing Own Capital

Industry Association Membership
National Venture Capital Association (NVCA)

Project Preferences

Role in Financing:
Prefer role as deal originator but will also invest in deals created by others

Type of Financing Preferred:
First Stage Financing
Leveraged Buyout
Mezzanine
Second Stage Financing
Seed
Start-up Financing

Size of Investments Considered
Min Size of Investment Considered (000s): $500
Max Size of Investment Considered (000s): $1,000

Geographical Preferences

International
No Preference

Industry Preferences

(% based on actual investment)

Communications and Media	25.5%
Industrial/Energy	18.8%
Computer Software and Services	16.5%
Computer Hardware	13.9%
Consumer Related	10.6%
Semiconductors/Other Elect.	7.2%
Medical/Health	5.2%
Internet Specific	1.1%
Other Products	0.9%
Biotechnology	0.4%

Additional Information

Name of Most Recent Fund: Edelson IV
Most Recent Fund Was Raised: 06/01/1997
Year Founded: 1984
Capital Under Management: $125,000,000
Current Activity Level : Actively seeking new investments
Method of Compensation: Return on investment is of primary concern, do not charge fees

EDGE CAPITAL INVESTMENT CO., LLC

16 Cardinal Road
Suite 300
Hackettstown, NJ 07840
Phone: 908-684-4444
Fax: 908-684-3333
E-mail:info@EdgeCapital.net
E-mail:JohnY@EdgeCapital.net
Wesbite: www.EdgeCapital.net

See California for full listing.

EDISON VENTURE FUND

1009 Lenox Drive #4
Lawrenceville, NJ 08648
Phone: 609-896-1900
Fax: 609-896-0066
Website: www.edisonventure.com

Other Offices

1420 Spring Hill Road
Suite 420
McLean, VA 22102
Phone: 703-903-9546
Fax: 703-903-9528

1950 Old Gallows Road
Suite 440
Vienna, VA 22182
Phone: 703-847-8823
Fax: 703-847-1848

213 Market Street
Ninth Floor
Harrisburg, PA 17108-0749
Phone: 717-237-3069
Fax: 717-236-377

3 Bala Plaza East
Suite 502
Bala Cynwyd, PA 19004
Phone: 610-771-2140
Fax: 610-660-5202

601 13th Street N.W.
10 th Floor
Washington, DC 20005
Phone: 202-661-2279
Fax: 202-661-2295

Management and Staff

Bruce Luehrs, General Partner
Dan McLaughlin, Vice President
Gary Golding, General Partner
Gustav Koven, General Partner
James Gunton, Vice President
John Shin, Vice President
John Martinson, Managing Partner
Larry Hollin, Vice President
Richard Defieux, General Partner
Ross Martinson, General Partner
Thomas Smith, General Partner

Type of Firm

Private Firm Investing Own Capital

Industry Association Membership

Mid-Atlantic Venture Association
National Venture Capital Association (NVCA)
Natl assoc of Small Bus. Inv. Co (NASBIC)

Project Preferences

Role in Financing:
Prefer role as deal originator but will also invest in deals created by others

Type of Financing Preferred:
Early Stage
Expansion
Later Stage
Management Buyouts

Size of Investments Considered

Min Size of Investment Considered (000s): $1,000
Max Size of Investment Considered (000s): $6,000

Geographical Preferences

United States
Mid Atlantic
Northeast

Industry Preferences

(% based on actual investment)

Computer Software and Services	37.6%
Internet Specific	13.1%
Industrial/Energy	12.6%
Communications and Media	12.2%
Medical/Health	11.8%
Other Products	4.4%
Semiconductors/Other Elect.	3.7%
Computer Hardware	2.3%
Consumer Related	2.3%

Additional Information

Name of Most Recent Fund: Edison IV
Most Recent Fund Was Raised: 10/01/1999
Year Founded: 1986
Capital Under Management: $238,500,000
Current Activity Level : Actively seeking new investments
Method of Compensation: Return on investment is of primary concern, do not charge fees

FIREMARK ADVISORS, INC.

67 Park Place
Morristown, NJ 07960
Phone: 973-538-7259
Fax: 973-538-0484

Management and Staff

Bart T. Zanelli
Joshua H. Landau

Whom to Contact

Bart T. Zanelli
Joshua H. Landau

Type of Firm

Private Firm Investing Own Capital

Project Preferences

Role in Financing:
Prefer role as deal originator but will also invest in deals created by others

Type of Financing Preferred:
First Stage Financing
Second Stage Financing

Industry Preferences

(% based on actual investment)

Internet Specific	36.6%
Computer Software and Services	24.8%
Medical/Health	24.3%
Computer Hardware	14.3%

Additional Information

Name of Most Recent Fund: Firemark Insurance Fund III
Most Recent Fund Was Raised: 04/01/1998
Year Founded: 1983
Capital Under Management: $200,000,000
Current Activity Level : Actively seeking new investments
Method of Compensation: Return on investment is of primary concern, do not charge fees

FIRST PRINCETON CAPITAL CORP.

189 Berdan Avenue #131
Wayne, NJ 07470-3233
Phone: 973-278-3233
Fax: 973-278-4290
Website: www.lytellcatt.net

Other Offices

One Garret Mountain Plaza
Ninth Floor
West Paterson, NJ 07424
Phone: 201-278-8111
Fax: 201-278-4290

Management and Staff

Michael Lytell

Whom to Contact

Michael Lytell

Type of Firm

SBIC Not elsewhere classified

Industry Association Membership

Natl assoc of Small Bus. Inv. Co (NASBIC)

Project Preferences

Role in Financing:
Prefer role as deal originator but will also invest in deals created by others

Type of Financing Preferred:
Control-block Purchases
First Stage Financing
Leveraged Buyout
Mezzanine
Recapitalizations
Second Stage Financing

Size of Investments Considered

Min Size of Investment Considered (000s): $200
Max Size of Investment Considered: No Limit

Geographical Preferences

United States
Northeast

Industry Preferences

Computer Hardware
Computer Graphics and Dig

Medical/Health
Medical/Health

Consumer Related
Entertainment and Leisure
Franchises(NEC)
Food/Beverage
Consumer Products
Consumer Services
Other Restaurants
Education Related

Industrial/Energy
Industrial Products

Financial Services
Financial Services
Real Estate

Business Serv.
Distribution
Consulting Services

Manufact.
Office Automation Equipmt

Additional Information

Year Founded: 1983
Capital Under Management: $5,000,000
Current Activity Level : Actively seeking new investments
Method of Compensation: Return on invest. most important, but chg. closing fees, service fees, etc.

GEOCAPITAL PARTNERS, L.L.C.

2 Executive Drive
Fort Lee, NJ 07024
Phone: 201-461-7793
Fax: 201-461-7793
Website: www.geocapital.com

Other Offices

Pollen House
10-12 Cork Street
London, United Kingdom WIX IPD
Phone: 44-20-7851-2800
Fax: 44-20-7851-2801

Management and Staff

Colin Amies, General Partner
Daniel Cahillane, Chief Financial Officer
Henry Allen, General Partner
Irwin Leiber, General Partner
Judith Benardete, Principal
Judy Bolger, Principal
Kimberly Eads, General Partner
Lawrence Lepard, Managing General Partner
Nic Humphries, General Partner
Stephen Clearman, Managing General Partner
Whitney Bower, General Partner

Type of Firm

Investment/Merchant Bank Subsid/Affil

Industry Association Membership

National Venture Capital Association (NVCA)

Project Preferences

Role in Financing:
Prefer role as deal originator

Type of Financing Preferred:
Early Stage
First Stage Financing
Private Placement
Seed

Size of Investments Considered

Min Size of Investment Considered (000s): $5,000
Max Size of Investment Considered (000s): $25,000

Geographical Preferences

United States
All U.S.

Canada
All Canada

International
Belgium
East Germany
France
Luxembourg
Netherlands
Portugal
Spain
Western Europe

Industry Preferences

(% based on actual investment)

Computer Software and Services	40.1%
Internet Specific	39.5%
Other Products	8.2%
Communications and Media	6.9%
Consumer Related	3.0%
Computer Hardware	1.6%
Medical/Health	0.5%
Industrial/Energy	0.3%

Additional Information
Name of Most Recent Fund: Geocapital Advisors
Most Recent Fund Was Raised: 12/24/1998
Year Founded: 1984
Capital Under Management: $490,300,000
Current Activity Level : Actively seeking new investments
Method of Compensation: Return on investment is of primary concern, do not charge fees

GLENMEDE TRUST COMPANY

16 Chambers Street
Princeton, NJ 08542
Phone: 609-683-1005
Fax: 609-252-0082
Website: www.glenmede.com

Management and Staff
Al Piscopo, Chief Operating Officer

Type of Firm
Affiliate/Subsidary of Oth. Financial. Instit.

Project Preferences

Type of Financing Preferred:
Fund of Funds of Second

Geographical Preferences

United States
All U.S.

Additional Information
Name of Most Recent Fund: Glenmede Private Equity Fund, LLC.
Most Recent Fund Was Raised: 09/01/1998
Capital Under Management: $31,000,000
Current Activity Level : Actively seeking new investments

HEALTHCARE VENTURES LLC (FKA: HEALTHCARE INVESTMENTS)

44 Nassau Street
Princeton, NJ 08542-4506
Phone: 609-430-3900
Fax: 609-430-9525
Website: www.hcven.com

Other Offices

One Kendall Square
Bldg. 300
Cambridge, MA 02139
Phone: 617-252-4343
Fax: 617-252-4342

Management and Staff
Augustine Lawlor, General Partner
Christopher Mirabelli, General Partner
Harold Werner, General Partner
James Cavanaugh, General Partner
John Littlechild, General Partner
Mark Leschly, Managing Director
William Crouse, General Partner

Type of Firm
Private Firm Investing Own Capital

Industry Association Membership
Mid-Atlantic Venture Association
National Venture Capital Association (NVCA)

Project Preferences

Role in Financing:
Will function either as deal originator or investor in deals created by others

Type of Financing Preferred:
Early Stage
Expansion
First Stage Financing
Later Stage
Mezzanine
Open Market
Private Placement
Second Stage Financing
Seed
Startup

Size of Investments Considered
Min Size of Investment Considered (000s): $500
Max Size of Investment Considered (000s): $15,000

Geographical Preferences

United States
Mid Atlantic
Northeast
West Coast

Industry Preferences

(% based on actual investment)

Biotechnology	49.7%
Medical/Health	47.8%
Internet Specific	1.8%
Consumer Related	0.7%

Additional Information
Name of Most Recent Fund: HealthCare Ventures VI
Most Recent Fund Was Raised: 06/01/1997
Year Founded: 1986
Capital Under Management: $60,300,000
Current Activity Level : Actively seeking new investments
Method of Compensation: Return on investment is of primary concern, do not charge fees

INNOCAL, L.P.

Park 80 West
Plaza One
Saddle Brook, NJ 07663
Phone: 201-845-4900
Fax: 201-845-3388

See California for full listing.

JOHNSTON ASSOCIATES, INC.

181 Cherry Valley Road
Princeton, NJ 08540
Phone: 609-924-3131
Fax: 609-683-7524

Management and Staff
Lynn Johnston, Vice President
Robert Johnston, President
Robert Stockman, Vice President

Type of Firm
Private Firm Investing Own Capital

Industry Association Membership
National Venture Capital Association (NVCA)

Project Preferences

Role in Financing:
Will function either as deal originator or investor in deals created by others

Type of Financing Preferred:
Early Stage
Start-up Financing

Size of Investments Considered
Min Size of Investment Considered (000s): $500
Max Size of Investment Considered (000s): $5,000

Geographical Preferences

United States
Northeast

Industry Preferences

Biotechnology
Human Biotechnology
Industrial Biotechnology

Medical/Health
Medical Diagnostics
Pharmaceuticals

Additional Information
Name of Most Recent Fund: Johnston Associates, Inc.
Most Recent Fund Was Raised: 07/01/1978
Year Founded: 1967
Capital Under Management: $40,000,000
Current Activity Level : Reducing investment activity
Method of Compensation: Return on investment is of primary concern, do not charge fees

---

JT VENTURE PARTNERS, LLC

7 Rosewood Lane
Suite 2B
Denville, NJ 07834
Phone: 973-442-2999
Fax: 503-213-7294
Website: www.jtventures.com

Other Offices
47 Commonwealth Ave
Suite 12
Boston, MA 02116
Phone: 617-536-0577
Fax: 240-208-6309

Management and Staff
Shaji John, Managing Partner
Thomas Thekkethala, Managing Partner

Type of Firm
Private Firm Investing Own Capital

Project Preferences

Type of Financing Preferred:
Balanced
Early Stage
Expansion
Startup

Geographical Preferences

United States
California
Northern California
All U.S.

Industry Preferences

Communications and Media
Telecommunications

Computer Software
Software

Internet Specific
Internet

Additional Information
Current Activity Level : Actively seeking new investments

KEMPER VENTURES

Princeton Forrestal Village
155 Village Boulevard
Princeton, NJ 08540
Phone: 609-936-3035
Fax: 609-936-3051

Management and Staff
John Reynolds, Managing Partner
Rick Secchia, Partner

Whom to Contact
Richard F. Secchia

Type of Firm
Private Firm Investing Own Capital

Industry Association Membership
National Venture Capital Association (NVCA)

Project Preferences

Role in Financing:
Prefer role as deal originator but will also invest in deals created by others

Type of Financing Preferred:
First Stage Financing
Research and Development
Second Stage Financing
Seed
Start-up Financing

Industry Preferences

Computer Hardware
Integrated Turnkey System

Computer Software
Computer Services
Systems Software
Applications Software
Artificial Intelligence

Internet Specific
Internet

Medical/Health
Diagnostic Services
Diagnostic Test Products
Hospitals/Clinics/Primary
Pharmaceuticals

Industrial/Energy
Environmental Related

Financial Services
Financial Services

Manufact.
Office Automation Equipmt

Additional Information
Year Founded: 1999
Capital Under Management: $100,000,000
Current Activity Level : Actively seeking new investments
Method of Compensation: Return on investment is of primary concern, do not charge fees

---

LTI VENTURES LEASING CORP.

23 West Park Ave
Suite 1060
Merchantville, NJ 08109
Phone: 856-910-9970
Website: www.ltileasing.com

See Connecticut for full listing.

LUCENT VENTURE PARTNERS, INC.

600 Mountain Avenue
Room 6A-405
Murray Hill, NJ 07974
Phone: 908-582-8538
Fax: 908-582-6747
Website: www.lucentventurepartners.com

See California for full listing.

MAYFAIR CAPITAL PARTNERS, INC.

158 Mount Olivet Avenue
Newark, NJ 07114
Phone: 201-621-2802
Fax: 201-621-2816

See New York for full listing.

MBW MANAGEMENT, INC.

1 Springfield Avenue
Summit, NJ 07901
Phone: 908-273-4060
Fax: 908-273-4430

Other Offices

2929 Plymouth Road
Suite 210
Ann Arbor, MI 48105
Phone: 313-747-9401
Fax: 313-747-9704

350 Second Street
Suite Seven
Los Altos, CA 94022
Phone: 415-941-2392
Fax: 415-941-2865

365 South St
2nd Floor
Morristown, NJ 07960
Phone: 201-285-5533

Type of Firm
Private Firm Investing Own Capital

Industry Association Membership
Natl assoc of Small Bus. Inv. Co (NASBIC)

Project Preferences

Role in Financing:
Will function either as deal originator or investor in deals created by others

Type of Financing Preferred:
First Stage Financing
Leveraged Buyout
Second Stage Financing
Special Situation
Start-up Financing

Size of Investments Considered
Min Size of Investment Considered (000s): $1,000
Max Size of Investment Considered: No Limit

Geographical Preferences

International
No Preference

Additional Information
Name of Most Recent Fund: Michigan Investment Fund
Most Recent Fund Was Raised: 01/01/1983
Year Founded: 1984
Capital Under Management: $105,000,000
Current Activity Level : Making few, if any, new investments
Method of Compensation: Return on investment is of primary concern, do not charge fees

MED-TECH VENTURES, INC.

201 Tabor Road
Morris Plains, NJ 07950
Phone: 973-540-6780
Fax: 973-540-6485

Management and Staff
Richard B. Van Duyne

Whom to Contact
Richard B. Van Duyne

Type of Firm
Non-Financial Corp. Affiliate or Subsidiary

Project Preferences

Role in Financing:
Prefer role as deal originator but will also invest in deals created by others

Type of Financing Preferred:
First Stage Financing
Research and Development
Second Stage Financing
Start-up Financing

Size of Investments Considered
Min Size of Investment Considered (000s): $500
Max Size of Investment Considered (000s): $1,000

Geographical Preferences

International
No Preference

Industry Preferences

Medical/Health
Pharmaceuticals

Additional Information
Name of Most Recent Fund: Med-Tech Ventures, Inc. (Warner Lambert)
Most Recent Fund Was Raised: 04/01/1983
Year Founded: 1983
Capital Under Management: $25,000,000
Current Activity Level : Actively seeking new investments
Method of Compensation: Return on investment is of primary concern, do not charge fees

NASSAU CAPITAL, L.L.C.

22 Chambers Street
Princeton, NJ 08542
Phone: 609-924-3555
Fax: 609-924-8887

Management and Staff
Curtis Glovier, Managing Director
Jonathan Sweemer, Managing Director
Lisa McGovern, Chief Financial Officer
Thomas Barnds, Managing Director
William Stewart, Managing Director

Whom to Contact
John Quigley

Type of Firm
Private Firm Investing Own Capital

Project Preferences

Role in Financing:
Prefer role as deal originator but will also invest in deals created by others

Type of Financing Preferred:
Leveraged Buyout
Second Stage Financing
Special Situation

Size of Investments Considered
Min Size of Investment Considered (000s): $25,000
Max Size of Investment Considered: No Limit

Geographical Preferences
United States
All U.S.

Industry Preferences
(% based on actual investment)

Medical/Health	65.0%
Communications and Media	17.2%
Internet Specific	8.1%
Computer Software and Services	6.3%
Semiconductors/Other Elect.	2.1%
Industrial/Energy	1.1%

Additional Information
Name of Most Recent Fund: Nassau Capital L.P.
Most Recent Fund Was Raised: 01/01/1996
Year Founded: 1994
Capital Under Management: $1,500,000,000
Current Activity Level : Actively seeking new investments
Method of Compensation: Return on investment is of primary concern, do not charge fees

NEW JERSEY TECHNOLOGY COUNCIL (AKA:NJTC)

500 College Road
Suite 200
Princeton, NJ 08540
Phone: 609-452-1010
Fax: 609-452-1007

Management and Staff
James Gunton, General Partner

Type of Firm
State Govt Affiliated NEC

Project Preferences
Type of Financing Preferred:
Early Stage
Startup

Size of Investments Considered
Min Size of Investment Considered (000s): $500
Max Size of Investment Considered (000s): $3,000

Geographical Preferences
United States
New Jersey

Additional Information
Capital Under Management: $20,000,000
Current Activity Level : Actively seeking new investments

OMEGA PARTNERS L.P.

113 Hervontown Lane
Princeton, NJ 08540
Phone: 609-683-8848
Fax: 609-683-8123

Management and Staff
Jason Duckworth, Vice President
Michael Myers, General Partner

Type of Firm
Private Firm Investing Own Capital

Additional Information
Year Founded: 1999
Capital Under Management: $2,000,000
Current Activity Level : Actively seeking new investments

PENNY LANE PARTNERS

One Palmer Square
Suite 309
Princeton, NJ 08542
Phone: 609-497-4646
Fax: 609-497-0611

Other Offices

767 Fifth Avenue
New York, NY 10153
Phone: 212-980-4292
Fax: 212-319-6046

Management and Staff
William Denslow, President

Type of Firm
Private Firm Investing Own Capital

Industry Association Membership
Natl assoc of Small Bus. Inv. Co (NASBIC)

Project Preferences
Role in Financing:
Prefer role as deal originator but will also invest in deals created by others

Type of Financing Preferred:
Leveraged Buyout
Recapitalizations
Second Stage Financing

Size of Investments Considered
Min Size of Investment Considered (000s): $1,000
Max Size of Investment Considered: No Limit

Geographical Preferences
United States
Mid Atlantic
Northeast

Industry Preferences
(% based on actual investment)

Other Products	24.1%
Internet Specific	20.8%
Biotechnology	15.3%
Medical/Health	14.2%
Semiconductors/Other Elect.	9.1%
Communications and Media	8.0%
Computer Hardware	7.9%
Computer Software and Services	0.7%

Additional Information
Name of Most Recent Fund: Penny Lane Partners L.P.
Most Recent Fund Was Raised: 11/01/1996
Year Founded: 1996
Capital Under Management: $30,000,000
Current Activity Level : Actively seeking new investments
Method of Compensation: Return on invest. most important, but chg. closing fees, service fees, etc.

PROQUEST INVESTMENTS, L.P.

600 Alexander Park
Suite 204
Princeton, NJ 08540
Phone: 609-919-3567
Fax: 609-919-3570
Website: www.proquestvc.com

Management and Staff
Alain Schreiber, Partner
Jay Moorin, Partner
Jeremy Goldberg, Partner
Joyce Tsang, Principal
Pasquale DeAngelis, Chief Financial Officer

Type of Firm
Private Firm Investing Own Capital

Project Preferences

Role in Financing:
Will function either as deal originator or investor in deals created by others

Type of Financing Preferred:
Balanced
Early Stage
Expansion
First Stage Financing
Later Stage
Mezzanine
Private Placement
Research and Development
Second Stage Financing
Seed
Start-up Financing

Size of Investments Considered
Min Size of Investment Considered (000s): $2,000
Max Size of Investment Considered (000s): $15,000

Geographical Preferences

United States
All U.S.

Canada
All Canada

International
East Germany
France
Italy
United Kingdom

Industry Preferences

(% based on actual investment)

Medical/Health	40.4%
Biotechnology	39.4%
Internet Specific	20.2%

Additional Information
Name of Most Recent Fund: ProQuest Investments I, L.P.
Most Recent Fund Was Raised: 08/13/1998
Year Founded: 1998
Capital Under Management: $206,000,000
Current Activity Level : Actively seeking new investments
Method of Compensation: Return on investment is of primary concern, do not charge fees

REIN CAPITAL

150 Airport Road
Suite 800
Lakewood, NJ 08701
Phone: 732-367-3300
Fax: 732-367-8948
Website: www.reincapital.com

Management and Staff
David Rein, Chairman & CEO
Steve Rein, President & COO

Type of Firm
Private Firm Investing Own Capital

Industry Association Membership
National Venture Capital Association (NVCA)

Additional Information
Current Activity Level : Actively seeking new investments

RIDGEWOOD CAPITAL MANAGEMENT LLC

Ridgewood Commons
947 Linwood Avenue
Ridgewood, NJ 07450
Phone: 201-447-9000
Fax: 201-447-0474
Website: www.ridgewoodcapital.com

Other Offices

540 Cowper Street
Suite 200
Palo Alto, CA 94301
Phone: 650-614-9030

Management and Staff
Cate Cavanagh, Venture Partner
Douglas Wilson, Managing Director
Elton Sherwin, Senior Managing Director
Joerg Sperling, Managing Director
Warren Majek, Chief Financial Officer

Type of Firm
Private Firm Investing Own Capital

Industry Association Membership
National Venture Capital Association (NVCA)

Project Preferences

Role in Financing:
Prefer role as deal originator but will also invest in deals created by others

Type of Financing Preferred:
Early Stage
First Stage Financing
Startup

Size of Investments Considered
Min Size of Investment Considered (000s): $1,000
Max Size of Investment Considered (000s): $10,000

Geographical Preferences

United States
All U.S.
All U.S.

Industry Preferences

(% based on actual investment)

Internet Specific	68.6%
Semiconductors/Other Elect.	18.2%
Computer Hardware	5.0%
Other Products	3.2%
Communications and Media	3.1%
Medical/Health	1.5%
Computer Software and Services	0.4%

Additional Information
Name of Most Recent Fund: Ridgewood Capital Venture Partners, LLC
Most Recent Fund Was Raised: 12/01/1998
Year Founded: 1982
Capital Under Management: $216,000,000
Current Activity Level : Actively seeking new investments
Method of Compensation: Return on investment is of primary concern, do not charge fees

SYCAMORE VENTURES

989 Lenox Drive
Suite 208
Lawrenceville, NJ 08648
Phone: 609-219-0100
Fax: 609-219-0101
Website: www.sycamorevc.com

Other Offices

40/F Citibank Tower, Citibank Plaza
3 Garden Road
Central, Hong Kong
Phone: 852-2248-2600
Fax: 852-2248-2018

81 Langton Street
Suite 9
San Francisco, CA 94103
Phone: 415-558-8229
Fax: 415-558-8751

B1, 52, Sec 4
Ming Sheng E. Rd.
Taipei, Taiwan
Phone: 8862-2526-2484
Fax: 8862-2545-9271

Management and Staff

Jerry Sze, Principal
John Whitman, Managing Partner
Joseph Shue, Principal
Kilin To, Managing Partner
Kit Wong, Partner
Peter Gerry, Managing Partner
Richard Chong, Partner
Richard Goodwyn, Principal
Simon Wong, Partner
William Morton, Principal

Type of Firm

Private Firm Investing Own Capital

Project Preferences

Role in Financing:

Prefer role as deal originator but will also invest in deals created by others

Type of Financing Preferred:

Balanced
Control-block Purchases
Expansion
First Stage Financing
Industry Rollups
Leveraged Buyout
Mezzanine
Second Stage Financing
Special Situation

Geographical Preferences

United States

All U.S.

Canada

All Canada

International

China
All International
United Kingdom

Industry Preferences

(% based on actual investment)

Internet Specific	79.1%
Communications and Media	13.9%
Computer Software and Services	4.5%
Other Products	2.5%

Additional Information

Name of Most Recent Fund: CG Asia Development Fund
Most Recent Fund Was Raised: 02/01/1998
Year Founded: 1995
Capital Under Management: $550,000,000
Current Activity Level : Actively seeking new investments
Method of Compensation: Return on investment is of primary concern, do not charge fees

TAPPAN ZEE CAPITAL CORP.

201 Lower Notch Road
P.O. Box 416
Little Falls, NJ 07424
Phone: 973-256-8280
Fax: 973-256-2841

Management and Staff

Jeffrey Birnberg, President

Whom to Contact

Jeffrey Birnberg

Type of Firm

SBIC Not elsewhere classified

Industry Association Membership

Natl assoc of Small Bus. Inv. Co (NASBIC)

Project Preferences

Role in Financing:

Prefer role as deal originator but will also invest in deals created by others

Type of Financing Preferred:

Leveraged Buyout

Geographical Preferences

International

No Preference

Industry Preferences

Communications and Media

Other Communication Prod.

Semiconductors/Other Elect.

Electronics

Consumer Related

Franchises(NEC)
Food/Beverage
Consumer Products
Other Restaurants

Industrial/Energy

Industrial Products

Additional Information

Year Founded: 1962
Capital Under Management: $4,000,000
Current Activity Level : Actively seeking new investments
Method of Compensation: Return on invest. most important, but chg. closing fees, service fees, etc.

TECHNOLOGY CROSSOVER VENTURES

56 Main Street
Suite 210
Millburn, NJ 07041
Phone: 973-476-5320
Fax: 973-476-5323
Website: www.tcv.com

See California for full listing.

UPDATA VENTURE PARTNERS

125 Half Mile Road
Suite 202
Red Bank, NJ 07701
Phone: 732-945-1010
Fax: 732-945-1025
Website: www.updataventures.com

See Virginia for full listing.

VENTURE INVESTMENT ASSOCIATES

1300 Mt. Kemble Avenue
Morristown, NJ 07962
Phone: 973-425-0400

Type of Firm

Private Equity Advisor or Fund of Fund Mgr

Project Preferences

Type of Financing Preferred:

Fund of Funds

Additional Information

Name of Most Recent Fund: Venture Investment Associates L.P.
Most Recent Fund Was Raised: 01/01/1993
Capital Under Management: $550,000,000
Current Activity Level : Actively seeking new investments

VENTURE MANAGEMENT SERVICES INC. (FKA: AT&T VENTURES)

295 North Maple Avenue
Room 3354B3
Basking Ridge, NJ 07920
Phone: 908-221-3893
Fax: 908-630-1455
Website: www.vmsgroup.com

Other Offices

2 Wisconsin Circle
Suite 610
Chevy Chase, MD 20815-7003
Phone: 301-652-5225
Fax: 301-664-8590

Management and Staff

Dominick Turiano, Chief Financial Officer
James Pastoriza, Partner
Neal Douglas, General Partner
R. Bradford Burnham, General Partner
Richard Bodman, Managing Partner
Tom Rosch, Partner

Whom to Contact

Any of the officers

Type of Firm

Non-Financial Corp. Affiliate or Subsidiary

Project Preferences

Role in Financing:

Prefer role as deal originator but will also invest in deals created by others

Type of Financing Preferred:

First Stage Financing
Mezzanine
Second Stage Financing
Seed
Start-up Financing

Size of Investments Considered

Min Size of Investment Considered (000s): $1,000
Max Size of Investment Considered (000s): $2,000

Geographical Preferences

International

No Preference

Industry Preferences

(% based on actual investment)

Communications and Media	39.4%
Computer Software and Services	25.3%
Internet Specific	25.0%
Computer Hardware	7.3%
Semiconductors/Other Elect.	2.4%
Consumer Related	0.4%
Other Products	0.1%

Additional Information

Name of Most Recent Fund: AT&T Venture Fund II
Most Recent Fund Was Raised: 01/01/1996
Year Founded: 1991
Capital Under Management: $350,000,000
Current Activity Level : Actively seeking new investments
Method of Compensation: Return on investment is of primary concern, do not charge fees

VERTICAL GROUP, THE

18 Bank Street
Summit, NJ 07901
Phone: 908-277-3737
Fax: 908-273-9434

Other Offices

10600 North Pantau Avenue
Cupertino, CA 95014
Phone: 408-777-8817
Fax: 408-777-8617

173 Constitution Drive
Menlo Park, CA 94025
Phone: 408-777-8817
Fax: 408-777-8716

Management and Staff

Jack Lasersohn, General Partner
John Runnells, General Partner
Richard Emmitt, General Partner
Stephen Baksa, General Partner

Type of Firm

Private Firm Investing Own Capital

Industry Association Membership

National Venture Capital Association (NVCA)

Project Preferences

Role in Financing:

Prefer role as deal originator but will also invest in deals created by others

Type of Financing Preferred:

Control-block Purchases
First Stage Financing
Leveraged Buyout
Mezzanine
Research and Development
Second Stage Financing
Seed
Special Situation
Start-up Financing

Industry Preferences

(% based on actual investment)

Medical/Health	77.0%
Biotechnology	23.0%

Additional Information

Name of Most Recent Fund: Vertical Group, The
Most Recent Fund Was Raised: 01/01/1993
Year Founded: 1993
Capital Under Management: $100,000,000
Current Activity Level : Actively seeking new investments
Method of Compensation: Return on investment is of primary concern, do not charge fees

WE SIMON & SONS

Morristown, NJ 07960

Other Offices

10990 Wilshire Blvd
Suite 1750
Los Angeles, CA 90024
Phone: 310-575-3174

310 South Street
PO Box 1913
Morristown, NJ 07962
Phone: 201-898-0290

Type of Firm

Private Firm Investing Own Capital

Project Preferences

Type of Financing Preferred:

Balanced

Geographical Preferences

International

No Preference

Additional Information
Year Founded: 1985
Current Activity Level : Inactive / Unknown

WESTFORD TECHNOLOGY VENTURES, L.P.

17 Academy Street
Newark, NJ 07102
Phone: 973-624-2131
Fax: 973-624-2008

Management and Staff
Jeffrey Hamilton, General Partner

Type of Firm
Private Firm Investing Own Capital

Industry Association Membership
National Venture Capital Association (NVCA)

Project Preferences

Role in Financing:
Prefer role as deal originator but will also invest in deals created by others

Type of Financing Preferred:
First Stage Financing
Second Stage Financing
Start-up Financing

Size of Investments Considered
Min Size of Investment Considered (000s): $300
Max Size of Investment Considered (000s): $500

Geographical Preferences

International
No Preference

Industry Preferences

Communications and Media
Data Communications
Satellite Microwave Comm.
Other Communication Prod.

Computer Hardware
Disk Relat. Memory Device

Computer Software
Systems Software
Applications Software

Semiconductors/Other Elect.
Semiconductor
Sensors
Laser Related
Fiber Optics

Industrial/Energy
Factory Automation
Machinery

Manufact.
Office Automation Equipmt

Additional Information
Name of Most Recent Fund: Westford Technology Ventures
Most Recent Fund Was Raised: 01/01/1989
Year Founded: 1987
Capital Under Management: $10,000,000
Current Activity Level : Actively seeking new investments
Method of Compensation: Return on investment is of primary concern, do not charge fees

NEW MEXICO

ARCH VENTURE PARTNERS

1155 University SE
Albuquerque, NM 87106
Phone: 505-843-4293
Fax: 505-843-4294
Website: www.archventure.com

See Illinois for full listing.

BRUCE F. GLASPELL & ASSOCIATES

10400 Academy Road, N.E.
Suite 313
Albuquerque, NM 87111
Phone: 505-292-4505
Fax: 505-292-4258

Management and Staff
Bruce Glaspell, Managing Director

Whom to Contact
Bruce Glaspell

Type of Firm
Investment Management/Finance Consulting

Project Preferences

Role in Financing:
Will function either as deal originator or investor in deals created by others

Type of Financing Preferred:
Early Stage
Expansion
First Stage Financing
Later Stage
Private Placement
Second Stage Financing
Seed
Start-up Financing

Size of Investments Considered
Min Size of Investment Considered (000s): $100
Max Size of Investment Considered (000s): $5,000

Geographical Preferences

United States
All U.S.

Canada
All Canada

International
Australia
Bermuda
France
Germany
Italy
South Africa
Spain
United Kingdom

Industry Preferences

Communications and Media
Data Communications
Satellite Microwave Comm.

Computer Hardware
Mainframes / Scientific
Mini and Personal/Desktop
Computer Graphics and Dig
Integrated Turnkey System
Terminals
Disk Relat. Memory Device

Computer Software
Computer Services
Data Processing
Software
Systems Software
Applications Software
Artificial Intelligence

Internet Specific
E-Commerce Technology
Internet
Web Aggregration/Portals

Semiconductors/Other Elect.
Electronic Components
Semiconductor
Micro-Processing
Controllers and Sensors
Sensors
Laser Related
Fiber Optics
Analytic/Scientific

Biotechnology
Biotechnology
Human Biotechnology
Agricultural/Animal Bio.
Industrial Biotechnology
Biosensors
Biotech Related Research

Medical/Health
Medical/Health
Medical Diagnostics
Diagnostic Services
Diagnostic Test Products
Medical Therapeutics
Drug/Equipmt Delivery
Medical Products
Disposable Med. Products
Health Services
Hospitals/Clinics/Primary
Pharmaceuticals

Consumer Related
Entertainment and Leisure
Retail
Franchises(NEC)
Food/Beverage
Consumer Products
Consumer Services
Hotels and Resorts
Education Related

Industrial/Energy
Energy
Oil and Gas Exploration
Oil & Gas Drilling,Explor
Alternative Energy
Energy Conservation Relat
Industrial Products
Materials
Factory Automation
Machinery
Environmental Related

Transportation
Transportation
Aerospace

Financial Services
Financial Services

Business Serv.
Media

Manufact.
Office Automation Equipmt
Publishing

Agr/Forestr/Fish
Agriculture related
Mining and Minerals

Other
Socially Responsible
Environment Responsible
Women/Minority-Owned Bus.

Additional Information
Name of Most Recent Fund: Bruce Glaspell & Assoc.
Most Recent Fund Was Raised: 02/01/1983
Year Founded: 1979
Current Activity Level : Actively seeking new investments
Method of Compensation: Return on invest. most important, but chg. closing fees, service fees, etc.

HIGH DESERT VENTURES INC

6101 Imperata Street, N.E.
Suite 1721
Albuquerque, NM 87111
Phone: 505-797-3330
Fax: 505-338-5147
E-mail: zilenziger@aol

Management and Staff
David Zilenziger, President

Type of Firm
Investment/Merchant Bank Subsid/Affil

Project Preferences

Role in Financing:
Prefer role as deal originator

Type of Financing Preferred:
First Stage Financing
Start-up Financing

Geographical Preferences

United States
Northeast
Southwest

International
Australia

Industry Preferences

Communications and Media
Communications and Media

Internet Specific
Internet

Semiconductors/Other Elect.
Laser Related
Fiber Optics
Analytic/Scientific

Biotechnology
Biotechnology

Medical/Health
Medical/Health
Medical Products

Consumer Related
Food/Beverage

Manufact.
Publishing

Additional Information
Year Founded: 1997
Current Activity Level : Actively seeking new investments
Method of Compensation: Return on invest. most important, but chg. closing fees, service fees, etc.

MURPHREE VENTURE PARTNERS

1155 University Blvd. SE
Albuquerque, NM 87106
Phone: 505-843-4277
Fax: 505-843-4278
Website: www.murphreeventures.com

See Texas for full listing.

NEW BUSINESS CAPITAL FUND LTD.

5805 Torreon, N.E.
Albuquerque, NM 87109
Phone: 505-822-8445

Other Offices

5805 Torreon NE
Albuquerque, NM 87109
Phone: 505-822-8445

Type of Firm
Private Firm Investing Own Capital

Project Preferences

Role in Financing:
Prefer role as deal originator but will also invest in deals created by others

Type of Financing Preferred:
First Stage Financing
Seed
Start-up Financing

Geographical Preferences

International
No Preference

Industry Preferences

Computer Hardware
Integrated Turnkey System

Semiconductors/Other Elect.
Component Testing Equipmt

Medical/Health
Medical Products
Disposable Med. Products

Consumer Related
Franchises(NEC)
Consumer Products
Consumer Services
Other Restaurants

Industrial/Energy
Alternative Energy
Energy Conservation Relat
Industrial Products
Machinery

Manufact.
Office Automation Equipmt

Additional Information
Year Founded: 1987
Capital Under Management: $1,500,000
Current Activity Level : Inactive / Unknown
Method of Compensation: Return on investment is of primary concern, do not charge fees

RED RIVER VENTURES

1155 University Blvd SE
Albuquerque, NM 87101
Phone: 505-843-4275
Fax: 505-843-4273
Website: www.redriverventures.com

See Texas for full listing.

SBC VENTURES

10400 Academy Road, NE
Suite 313
Albuquerque, NM 87111
Phone: 505-292-4505
Fax: 505-292-4258

Management and Staff
David Stevens, General Partner
Ronald Brakke, General Partner
Viviana Cloninger, General Partner

Whom to Contact
Viviana Cloninger

Type of Firm
Private Firm Investing Own Capital

Project Preferences

Role in Financing:
Prefer role as deal originator but will also invest in deals created by others

Type of Financing Preferred:
First Stage Financing
Research and Development
Seed
Start-up Financing

Size of Investments Considered
Min Size of Investment Considered (000s): $300
Max Size of Investment Considered (000s): $3,000

Geographical Preferences

United States
All U.S.

Canada
All Canada

International
Australia
Bermuda
France
Germany
Mexico
Middle East
South Africa
Spain
United Kingdom

Industry Preferences

Communications and Media
Communications and Media

Computer Other
Computer Related

Semiconductors/Other Elect.
Electronic Components
Semiconductor

Biotechnology
Industrial Biotechnology
Biosensors
Biotech Related Research
Biotech Related Research

Medical/Health
Medical Diagnostics
Diagnostic Test Products
Medical Therapeutics

Consumer Related
Consumer
Food/Beverage
Education Related

Industrial/Energy
Alternative Energy
Environmental Related

Transportation
Transportation

Financial Services
Financial Services

Manufact.
Publishing

Agr/Forestr/Fish
Agriculture related

Additional Information
Name of Most Recent Fund: SRI Ventures
Most Recent Fund Was Raised: 01/01/1998
Year Founded: 1998
Capital Under Management: $100,000,000
Current Activity Level : Inactive / Unknown
Method of Compensation: Return on investment is of primary concern, do not charge fees

SILICON VALLEY BANK

9 East Sand Sage
Santa Fe, NM 87501
Phone: 505-995-9910
Fax: 505-995-9929

See California for full listing.

TECHNOLOGY VENTURES CORP.

1155 University Blvd, S.E.
Albuquerque, NM 87106
Phone: 505-246-2882
Fax: 505-246-2891

Management and Staff
Beverly Bendicksen

Whom to Contact
Beverly Bendicksen

Project Preferences

Role in Financing:
Prefer role in deals created by others

Type of Financing Preferred:
First Stage Financing
Second Stage Financing
Seed
Start-up Financing

Geographical Preferences

United States
Southwest

Additional Information
Year Founded: 1993
Current Activity Level : Actively seeking new investments
Method of Compensation: Return on investment is of primary concern, do not charge fees

NEW YORK

4C VENTURES (FKA: OLIVETTI HOLDING, N.V.)

237 Park Avenue
Suite 801
New York, NY 10017
Phone: 212-692-3680
Fax: 212-692-3685
Website: www.4cventures.com

Management and Staff
Alexandra Ghirgini, General Partner
Elserino Piol, General Partner
Ghiliano Raviola, General Partner
Ted Hobart, General Partner

Whom to Contact
Alexandra Giurgiu
Ted Hobart

Type of Firm
Private Firm Investing Own Capital

Project Preferences

Role in Financing:
Prefer role as deal originator but will also invest in deals created by others

Type of Financing Preferred:
First Stage Financing
Research and Development
Second Stage Financing
Seed
Start-up Financing

Size of Investments Considered
Min Size of Investment Considered (000s): $500
Max Size of Investment Considered (000s): $1,000

Geographical Preferences

United States
All U.S.

Canada
All Canada

International
Bermuda
France
Germany
Italy
Spain
United Kingdom

Industry Preferences

(% based on actual investment)

Computer Software and Services	49.4%
Computer Hardware	28.8%
Internet Specific	20.8%
Communications and Media	1.1%

Additional Information
Name of Most Recent Fund: 4C Ventures II, L.P.
Most Recent Fund Was Raised: 01/01/1995
Year Founded: 1985
Capital Under Management: $60,000,000
Current Activity Level : Actively seeking new investments
Method of Compensation: Return on investment is of primary concern, do not charge fees

550 DIGITAL MEDIA VENTURES

555 Madison Avenue
10th Floor
New York, NY 10022
Website: www.550dmv.com

Other Offices

1 Undershaft
CGU Tower
London, United Kingdom EC3A 8NP

190 9th Street
3rd Floor
San Francisco, CA 94103

640 North Sepulveda Boulevard
Los Angeles, CA 90049

Type of Firm
Incubators

Project Preferences

Role in Financing:
Prefer role as deal originator

Type of Financing Preferred:
Early Stage

Geographical Preferences

United States
All U.S.

Industry Preferences

Consumer Related
Entertainment and Leisure

Business Serv.
Media

Additional Information
Current Activity Level : Actively seeking new investments

ABBOTT CAPITAL MANAGEMENT

1330 Avenue of the Americas
Suite 2800
New York, NY 10019
Phone: 212-757-2700
Fax: 212-757-0835

Management and Staff
Jonathan Roth, Managing Director
Kathryn Stokel, Managing Director
Lauren Massey, Managing Director
Raymond Held, Managing Director
Stanley Pratt, Managing Director
Thaddeus Gray, Managing Director

Type of Firm
Private Equity Advisor or Fund of Fund Mgr

Project Preferences

Role in Financing:
Prefer role in deals created by others

Type of Financing Preferred:
Fund of Funds
Generalist PE

Additional Information
Name of Most Recent Fund: Abbott Capital Management
Most Recent Fund Was Raised: 06/01/1986
Capital Under Management: $5,360,700,000
Current Activity Level : Actively seeking new investments
Method of Compensation: Return on invest. most important, but chg. closing fees, service fees, etc.

ABERLYN CAPITAL MANAGEMENT CO., INC.

500 Fifth Avenue
New York, NY 10110
Phone: 212-391-7750
Fax: 212-391-7762

Other Offices

18 Winter Place
Matawan, NJ 07747
Phone: 908-583-5108
Fax: 908-583-8499

Management and Staff
Lawrence Hoffman

Whom to Contact
Lawrence Hoffman

Type of Firm
Investment/Merchant Bank Investing Own or Client Funds

Project Preferences

Role in Financing:
Prefer role as deal originator

Type of Financing Preferred:
First Stage Financing
Leveraged Buyout
Second Stage Financing
Special Situation
Start-up Financing

Size of Investments Considered
Min Size of Investment Considered (000s): $25,000
Max Size of Investment Considered: No Limit

Geographical Preferences

International
No Preference

Industry Preferences

Computer Software
Systems Software
Applications Software
Artificial Intelligence

Semiconductors/Other Elect.
Laser Related
Fiber Optics

Biotechnology
Industrial Biotechnology
Biotech Related Research
Biotech Related Research

Medical/Health
Medical/Health
Medical Diagnostics
Medical Therapeutics
Medical Products

Consumer Related
Food/Beverage

Additional Information
Name of Most Recent Fund: ConQuest I
Most Recent Fund Was Raised: 03/01/1995
Year Founded: 1992
Capital Under Management: $90,000,000
Current Activity Level : Actively seeking new investments
Method of Compensation: Return on invest. most important, but chg. closing fees, service fees, etc.

ADLER & CO.

342 Madison Ave. Suite 807
New York, NY 10173
Phone: 212-599-2535
Fax: 212-599-2526

Other Offices

100 First Stamford Place
Third Floor
Stamford, CT 06902
Phone: 203-359-9595
Fax: 203-359-0880

1122 Kenilworth Drive
Suite 301
Baltimore, MD 21204
Phone: 410-828-6497

222 Lakeview Avenue
Suite 160-286
West Palm Beach, FL 33401
Phone: 407-837-2220
Fax: 407-837-1010

690 Market Street
Suite 702
San Francisco, CA 94104
Phone: 415-398-6352
Fax: 415-398-6355

Management and Staff
Frederick Adler, General Partner
Jay Nickse, Chief Financial Officer
Mark Beaudoin, General Partner

Whom to Contact
Jay Nickse

Type of Firm
Private Firm Investing Own Capital

Project Preferences

Role in Financing:
Prefer role as deal originator but will also invest in deals created by others

Type of Financing Preferred:
Control-block Purchases
First Stage Financing
Leveraged Buyout
Second Stage Financing
Start-up Financing

Size of Investments Considered
Min Size of Investment Considered (000s): $1,000
Max Size of Investment Considered: No Limit

Geographical Preferences

United States
All U.S.

Industry Preferences

(% based on actual investment)

Computer Software and Services	22.4%
Semiconductors/Other Elect.	20.1%
Computer Hardware	16.2%
Medical/Health	8.6%
Communications and Media	8.6%
Biotechnology	7.9%
Other Products	6.5%
Industrial/Energy	4.3%
Consumer Related	2.7%
Internet Specific	2.5%

Additional Information
Name of Most Recent Fund: Port Authority Fund
Most Recent Fund Was Raised: 10/01/1984
Year Founded: 1965
Capital Under Management: $200,000,000
Current Activity Level : Reducing investment activity
Method of Compensation: Return on invest. most important, but chg. closing fees, service fees, etc.

ADLER & SHAYKIN

599 Lexington Avenue
Suite 2300
New York, NY 10022
Phone: 212-319-2800
Fax: 212-319-2808

Management and Staff
Leonard Shaykin

Whom to Contact
Leonard Shaykin

Type of Firm
Private Firm Investing Own Capital

Project Preferences

Role in Financing:
Prefer role as deal originator but will also invest in deals created by others

Type of Financing Preferred:
First Stage Financing
Leveraged Buyout
Second Stage Financing
Special Situation
Start-up Financing

Size of Investments Considered
Min Size of Investment Considered (000s): $15,000
Max Size of Investment Considered (000s): $50,000

Geographical Preferences

United States
All U.S.

Canada
All Canada

International
Australia
Japan
United Kingdom

Industry Preferences

Internet Specific
Internet

Biotechnology
Biotech Related Research
Biotech Related Research

Medical/Health
Pharmaceuticals

Additional Information
Name of Most Recent Fund: Adler & Shaykin Fund II
Most Recent Fund Was Raised: 03/01/1989
Year Founded: 1983
Capital Under Management: $300,000,000
Current Activity Level : Inactive / Unknown
Method of Compensation: Return on invest. most important, but chg. closing fees, service fees, etc.

ADVANTA PARTNERS, L.P.

712 Fifth Avenue
28th Floor
New York, NY 10019-4102
Phone: 212-649-6900
Fax: 212-956-3301
Website: www.advantapartnerslp.com

See Pennsylvania for full listing.

ADVANTAGE CAPITAL PARTNERS

521 Madison Avenue
7th Floor
New York, NY 10119
Phone: 212-893-8600
Website: www.advantagecap.com

See Louisiana for full listing.

AIG CAPITAL PARTNERS INC.

175 Water Street
24th Floor
New York, NY 10038
Phone: 212-770-7971
Fax: 212-458-2250
Website: www.aig.com

Other Offices

AIG Private Equity
Baarerstrasse 8
Zug, Switzerland CH - 6300
Phone: 41 41710 7060
Fax: 41 41710 7064

AIG Private Equity (Bermuda) Ltd.
29 Richmond Road
Pembroke, Bermuda HM 08

AIG-CET Capital Management Sp.
Skorupki 5 5th Floor
Warsaw, Poland PL - 00-54
Phone: 48 22-583-7000
Fax: 48 22-583-6969

Str. Gen. Berthelot 57
Bucharest, Romania 70747
Phone: 40 1311 05 71
Fax: 40 1311 33 52

Management and Staff
David Pinkerton, Managing Director
Klaus Hermann, Partner
Pierre Mellinger, Partner
Rocco Sgobbo, Managing Director
Steven Costabile, Partner
Val Ionescu, Partner

Type of Firm
Insurance Firm Affiliate or Subsidiary

Industry Association Membership
European Venture Capital Association (EVCA)

Project Preferences

Type of Financing Preferred:
Balanced
Early Stage
Expansion
Fund of Funds
Generalist PE
Management Buyouts
Mezzanine
Recapitalizations

Geographical Preferences

United States
All U.S.

International
Asia
Europe
Israel
Latin America

Industry Preferences

(% based on actual investment)

Internet Specific	43.6%
Consumer Related	21.2%
Communications and Media	14.9%
Computer Software and Services	14.2%
Medical/Health	6.1%

Additional Information
Year Founded: 1999
Capital Under Management: $2,838,000,000
Current Activity Level : Actively seeking new investments

AKIN GUMP INVESTMENT PARTNERS 2000, LP

590 Madison Avenue
New York, NY 10022
Phone: 212-872-1000
Fax: 212-872-1002
Website: www.akingump.com

See Texas for full listing.

ALIMANSKY CAPITAL GROUP, INC.

605 Madison Avenue
Suite 300
New York, NY 10022-1901
Phone: 212-832-7300
Fax: 212-832-7338

Management and Staff
Burt Alimansky, Managing Director

Whom to Contact
Howard D. Duby

Type of Firm
Mgt. Consulting Firm

Industry Association Membership
Natl assoc of Small Bus. Inv. Co (NASBIC)

Project Preferences

Role in Financing:
Prefer role as deal originator but will also invest in deals created by others

Type of Financing Preferred:
First Stage Financing
Leveraged Buyout
Mezzanine
Second Stage Financing
Special Situation

Size of Investments Considered
Min Size of Investment Considered (000s): $2,000
Max Size of Investment Considered: No Limit

Geographical Preferences

United States
All U.S.

Canada
All Canada

Industry Preferences

Communications and Media
Communications and Media

Computer Other
Computer Related

Semiconductors/Other Elect.
Electronic Components

Biotechnology
Biotechnology

Medical/Health
Medical/Health

Consumer Related
Consumer
Education Related

Industrial/Energy
Alternative Energy
Energy Conservation Relat
Industrial Products

Transportation
Transportation

Financial Services
Financial Services

Business Serv.
Distribution
Consulting Services

Manufact.
Publishing

Agr/Forestr/Fish
Agriculture related

Additional Information
Name of Most Recent Fund: Alimansky Capital Group
Most Recent Fund Was Raised: 01/01/1992
Year Founded: 1980
Capital Under Management: $2,000,000
Current Activity Level : Actively seeking new investments
Method of Compensation: Return on invest. most important, but chg. closing fees, service fees, etc.

ALLEGRA PARTNERS (FKA: LAWRENCE, SMITH & HOREY)

515 Madison Avenue
29th Floor
New York, NY 10022
Phone: 212-826-9080
Fax: 212-759-2561

Management and Staff
Larry Lawrence, General Partner
Richard Defieux, General Partner
Richard Lefebvre, General Partner
Richard Smith, General Partner

Type of Firm
Private Firm Investing Own Capital

Project Preferences

Role in Financing:
Prefer role as deal originator

Type of Financing Preferred:
First Stage Financing
Leveraged Buyout
Recapitalizations
Second Stage Financing
Special Situation

Size of Investments Considered
Min Size of Investment Considered (000s): $1,000
Max Size of Investment Considered: No Limit

Geographical Preferences

United States
Mid Atlantic
Midwest
Northeast
Southeast
Southwest

Industry Preferences

(% based on actual investment)

Communications and Media	39.5%
Computer Software and Services	34.6%
Other Products	20.4%
Consumer Related	5.5%

Additional Information
Name of Most Recent Fund: Allegra Capital Partners IV
Most Recent Fund Was Raised: 01/01/1999
Year Founded: 1981
Capital Under Management: $42,300,000
Current Activity Level : Actively seeking new investments
Method of Compensation: Return on investment is of primary concern, do not charge fees

ALLEN & CO., INC.

711 Fifth Ave
New York, NY 10022
Phone: 212-832-8000

Type of Firm
Investment/Merchant Bank Investing Own or Client Funds

Industry Preferences

(% based on actual investment)

Internet Specific	48.2%
Communications and Media	10.4%
Medical/Health	10.0%
Other Products	10.0%
Computer Software and Services	6.0%
Industrial/Energy	4.7%

Biotechnology	3.9%
Computer Hardware	3.6%
Consumer Related	2.2%
Semiconductors/Other Elect.	1.0%

Additional Information
Name of Most Recent Fund: Allen & Co., Inc.
Most Recent Fund Was Raised: 08/01/1983
Year Founded: 1983
Current Activity Level : Inactive / Unknown

ALLIED CAPITAL CORPORATION

1180 Avenue of the Americas
Suite 1481
New York, NY
Phone: 212-899-5180
Fax: 212-899-5181
Website: www.alliedcapital.com

See D. of Columbia for full listing.

AMERICAN SECURITIES, L.P.

Chrysler Center
666 Third Avenue, 29th Floor
New York, NY 10017-4011
Phone: 212-476-8000
Fax: 212-697-5524
Website: www.american-securities.com

Management and Staff
Charles Klein, Managing Director
David Horing, Managing Director
Glenn Kaufman, Principal
Joseph Mancuso, Chief Financial Officer
Matthew LeBaron, Principal
Michael Fisch, President
Paul Rossetti, Managing Director
Robert Klein, Principal

Type of Firm
Investment/Merchant Bank Subsid/Affil

Project Preferences

Role in Financing:
Prefer role as deal originator but will also invest in deals created by others

Type of Financing Preferred:
Control-block Purchases
Industry Rollups
Leveraged Buyout
Second Stage Financing
Special Situation

Size of Investments Considered
Min Size of Investment Considered (000s): $75,000
Max Size of Investment Considered: No Limit

Geographical Preferences

United States
All U.S.

Canada
All Canada

Industry Preferences

Communications and Media
Communications and Media

Computer Hardware
Mainframes / Scientific
Mini and Personal/Desktop
Computer Graphics and Dig
Integrated Turnkey System
Disk Relat. Memory Device

Computer Software
Computer Services
Systems Software
Applications Software
Artificial Intelligence

Computer Other
Computer Related

Semiconductors/Other Elect.
Electronic Components
Sensors

Medical/Health
Diagnostic Services
Diagnostic Test Products
Other Therapeutic
Disposable Med. Products

Consumer Related
Entertainment and Leisure
Retail
Franchises(NEC)
Food/Beverage
Consumer Products
Consumer Services
Other Restaurants

Industrial/Energy
Factory Automation
Robotics
Machinery
Environmental Related

Transportation
Transportation

Business Serv.
Distribution
Consulting Services

Manufact.
Office Automation Equipmt

Agr/Forestr/Fish
Agriculture related

Additional Information
Name of Most Recent Fund: American Securities Partners II, LP
Most Recent Fund Was Raised: 06/01/1998
Capital Under Management: $1,000,000,000
Current Activity Level : Inactive / Unknown
Method of Compensation: Return on invest. most important, but chg. closing fees, service fees, etc.

AMERINDO INVESTMENT ADVISORS, INC.

399 Park Avenue
22th Floor
New York, NY 10022
Phone: 212-371-6360
Fax: 212-371-6988

Other Offices

43 Upper Grove Street
London, United Kingdom WIX 9PG
Phone: 44-171-629-2349
Fax: 44-171-493-5158

One Embarcadero Center
Suite 2300
San Francisco, CA 94111-3162
Phone: 415-362-0292
Fax: 415-362-0533

Management and Staff
Alberto Vilar

Whom to Contact
Alberto Vilar

Type of Firm
Private Firm Investing Own Capital

Project Preferences

Role in Financing:
Prefer role as deal originator but will also invest in deals created by others

Type of Financing Preferred:
Mezzanine
Second Stage Financing

Geographical Preferences

United States
All U.S.

Canada
All Canada

Industry Preferences

(% based on actual investment)

Internet Specific	47.1%
Communications and Media	24.7%
Computer Software and Services	12.5%
Semiconductors/Other Elect.	7.8%
Computer Hardware	3.2%
Biotechnology	2.1%
Medical/Health	1.2%
Other Products	1.2%
Consumer Related	0.3%

Additional Information

Year Founded: 1979
Capital Under Management: $30,000,000
Current Activity Level : Actively seeking new investments

AMPHION VENTURES L.P.(FKA: WOLFENSOHN ASSOCIATES, L.P.)

590 Madison Avenue
32nd Floor
New York, NY 10022
Phone: 212-849-8120
Fax: 212-849-8171

Management and Staff

Richard Morgan, Partner
Robert Bertoldi, Partner

Whom to Contact

Jonathan E. Gold

Type of Firm

Private Firm Investing Own Capital

Project Preferences

Role in Financing:
Prefer role as deal originator but will also invest in deals created by others

Type of Financing Preferred:
First Stage Financing
Research and Development
Second Stage Financing
Seed
Special Situation
Start-up Financing

Size of Investments Considered

Min Size of Investment Considered (000s): $1,000
Max Size of Investment Considered: No Limit

Geographical Preferences

International
No Preference

Industry Preferences

Communications and Media
Communications and Media

Computer Other
Computer Related

Semiconductors/Other Elect.
Electronic Components
Sensors

Biotechnology
Biotechnology

Medical/Health
Medical/Health

Consumer Related
Entertainment and Leisure
Retail
Computer Stores
Food/Beverage
Consumer Products
Consumer Services
Education Related

Industrial/Energy
Materials
Factory Automation
Robotics
Machinery

Transportation
Transportation

Business Serv.
Distribution

Manufact.
Publishing

Additional Information

Name of Most Recent Fund: Wolfensohn Associates LP
Most Recent Fund Was Raised: 01/01/1984
Year Founded: 1984
Capital Under Management: $70,000,000
Current Activity Level : Reducing investment activity
Method of Compensation: Return on investment is of primary concern, do not charge fees

ARCH VENTURE PARTNERS

561 7th Avenue
11th Floor
New York, NY 10020
Phone: 212-944-2400
Website: www.archventure.com

See Illinois for full listing.

ARDSHEIL, INC.

230 Park Avenue
Suite 2527
New York, NY 10169
Phone: 212-697-8570
Fax: 212-972-1809

Management and Staff

Daniel T. Morley
James G. Turner

Whom to Contact

Daniel T. Morley
James G. Turner

Type of Firm

Investment/Merchant Bank Investing Own or Client Funds

Project Preferences

Role in Financing:
Prefer role as deal originator but will also invest in deals created by others

Type of Financing Preferred:
Control-block Purchases
Industry Rollups
Leveraged Buyout
Second Stage Financing

Size of Investments Considered

Min Size of Investment Considered (000s): $50,000
Max Size of Investment Considered: No Limit

Geographical Preferences

United States
All U.S.

Canada
All Canada

International
Australia
Bermuda
France
Germany
Italy
Japan
South Africa
United Kingdom

Industry Preferences

Communications and Media
Communications and Media

Computer Other
Computer Related

Semiconductors/Other Elect.
Electronic Components

Biotechnology
Biotechnology

Medical/Health
Medical/Health

Consumer Related
Consumer
Education Related

Industrial/Energy
Oil and Gas Exploration
Oil & Gas Drilling,Explor
Industrial Products

Transportation
Transportation

Financial Services
Financial Services

Business Serv.
Distribution

Manufact.
Publishing

Agr/Forestr/Fish
Agriculture related

Additional Information
Name of Most Recent Fund: Ardshiel Associates
Most Recent Fund Was Raised: 12/01/1982
Year Founded: 1975
Capital Under Management: $250,000,000
Current Activity Level : Inactive / Unknown
Method of Compensation: Return on invest. most important, but chg. closing fees, service fees, etc.

ARENA CAPITAL PARTNERS

540 Madison Avenue
25th Floor
New York, NY 10022
Phone: 212-735-8510
Fax: 212-735-8585

Management and Staff
Jerry Armstrong, Partner

Type of Firm
Private Firm Investing Own Capital

Additional Information
Year Founded: 2000
Current Activity Level : Actively seeking new investments

ARGENTUM GROUP, THE

The Chrysler Building
405 Lexington Avenue, 54th Fl
New York, NY 10174
Phone: 212-949-6262
Fax: 212-949-8294
Website: www.argentumgroup.com

Type of Firm
Private Firm Investing Own Capital

Industry Association Membership
Natl assoc of Small Bus. Inv. Co (NASBIC)

Project Preferences

Role in Financing:
Prefer role as deal originator but will also invest in deals created by others

Type of Financing Preferred:
Leveraged Buyout
Mezzanine
Second Stage Financing
Special Situation

Size of Investments Considered
Min Size of Investment Considered (000s): $10,000
Max Size of Investment Considered: No Limit

Geographical Preferences

United States
All U.S.

Industry Preferences

(% based on actual investment)

Internet Specific	29.4%
Other Products	20.7%
Medical/Health	14.5%
Communications and Media	11.9%
Computer Software and Services	10.9%
Industrial/Energy	8.0%
Semiconductors/Other Elect.	4.7%

Additional Information
Name of Most Recent Fund: Argentum Capital Partners II, L.P.
Most Recent Fund Was Raised: 03/15/1997
Year Founded: 1988
Capital Under Management: $250,000,000
Current Activity Level : Actively seeking new investments
Method of Compensation: Return on invest. most important, but chg. closing fees, service fees, etc.

ARTHUR P. GOULD & CO.

One Wilshire Drive
Lake Success, NY 11020
Phone: 516-773-3000
Fax: 516-773-3289

Management and Staff
Andrew Gould

Whom to Contact
Andrew Gould

Type of Firm
Mgt. Consulting Firm

Project Preferences

Role in Financing:
Prefer role as deal originator but will also invest in deals created by others

Type of Financing Preferred:
First Stage Financing
Leveraged Buyout
Mezzanine
Research and Development
Second Stage Financing
Seed
Start-up Financing

Size of Investments Considered
Min Size of Investment Considered (000s): $5,000
Max Size of Investment Considered: No Limit

Geographical Preferences

International
No Preference

Industry Preferences

Communications and Media
Telecommunications
Data Communications
Satellite Microwave Comm.
Other Communication Prod.

Computer Hardware
Computers
Computer Graphics and Dig
Integrated Turnkey System
Terminals
Disk Relat. Memory Device

Computer Software
Applications Software
Artificial Intelligence

Semiconductors/Other Elect.
Electronics
Electronic Components

Biotechnology
Biotechnology

Medical/Health
Medical/Health

Consumer Related
Entertainment and Leisure
Retail
Computer Stores
Food/Beverage
Consumer Products
Other Restaurants
Education Related

Industrial/Energy
Energy
Industrial Products

Transportation
Transportation

Financial Services
Financial Services
Real Estate

Manufact.
Office Automation Equipmt
Publishing

Agr/Forestr/Fish
Agriculture related

Additional Information
Year Founded: 1968
Current Activity Level : Actively seeking new investments
Method of Compensation: Return on invest. most important, but chg. closing fees, service fees, etc.

ARTS ALLIANCE

565 Fifth Avenue, 22nd Floor
New York, NY 10017
Phone: 212-687-4820
Fax: 212-687-9266
Website: www.artsalliance.com

See Foreign Venture Capital Firms for full listing.

ATLANTIC MEDICAL MANAGEMENT, LLC

156 West 56th Street
Suite 1605
New York, NY 10019
Phone: 212-307-3580
Fax: 212-957-1586
Website: www.atlanticmedcap.com

Management and Staff
H. Tomkins O'Connor, Partner
J. Andrew Cowherd, Partner
Michael Sinclair, Partner

Whom to Contact
H. Tomkins O'Connor
Michael Sinclair

Type of Firm
Investment/Merchant Bank Subsid/Affil

Project Preferences

Role in Financing:
Prefer role as deal originator but will also invest in deals created by others

Type of Financing Preferred:
Control-block Purchases
Leveraged Buyout
Second Stage Financing
Special Situation

Size of Investments Considered
Min Size of Investment Considered (000s): $4,000
Max Size of Investment Considered: No Limit

Geographical Preferences

United States
All U.S.

Canada
All Canada

International
Bermuda
France
Germany
Italy
Spain
United Kingdom

Industry Preferences
(% based on actual investment)

Medical/Health	71.4%
Internet Specific	15.8%
Other Products	12.8%

Additional Information
Name of Most Recent Fund: Atlantic Medical Capital, L.P.
Most Recent Fund Was Raised: 07/09/1996
Year Founded: 1993
Capital Under Management: $81,000,000
Current Activity Level : Actively seeking new investments
Method of Compensation: Return on invest. most important, but chg. closing fees, service fees, etc.

AUGUST PARTNERS

555 Fifth Avenue
17th Floor
New York, NY 10017
Phone: 212-599-5000
Fax: 212-986-5316

Management and Staff
Gregory T. Camp

Whom to Contact
Gregory T. Camp

Type of Firm
Investment/Merchant Bank Subsid/Affil

Project Preferences

Role in Financing:
Prefer role as deal originator but will also invest in deals created by others

Type of Financing Preferred:
Industry Rollups
Leveraged Buyout
Special Situation

Size of Investments Considered
Min Size of Investment Considered (000s): $5,000
Max Size of Investment Considered: No Limit

Geographical Preferences

United States
All U.S.

Canada
All Canada

International
France
Germany
South Africa
United Kingdom

Industry Preferences

Communications and Media
CATV & Pay TV Systems
Telecommunications

Internet Specific
Internet

Computer Other
Computer Related

Biotechnology
Biotechnology

Medical/Health
Medical Diagnostics
Diagnostic Services
Diagnostic Test Products
Medical Therapeutics
Drug/Equipmt Delivery
Other Therapeutic
Disposable Med. Products
Pharmaceuticals

Consumer Related
Entertainment and Leisure
Retail
Food/Beverage
Consumer Products
Consumer Services
Other Restaurants
Hotels and Resorts
Education Related

Transportation
Transportation

Financial Services
Financial Services
Real Estate

Manufact.
Publishing

Additional Information

Year Founded: 1991
Current Activity Level : Actively seeking new investments
Method of Compensation: Return on invest. most important, but chg. closing fees, service fees, etc.

AXA INVESTMENT MANAGERS

600 Fifth Avenue
24th Floor
New York, NY 10020
Phone: 212-218-2001
Fax: 212-218-2040

Other Offices

7 Newgate Street
London, United Kingdom ECIA7NY

Management and Staff

Barry Miller, Vice President
Charles Flynn, Managing Director
Philippe Franceries, Managing Director
Sasha Vandewater, Managing Director

Whom to Contact

Charles Flynn

Type of Firm

Private Equity Advisor or Fund of Fund Mgr

Industry Association Membership

National Venture Capital Association (NVCA)

Project Preferences

Role in Financing:
Prefer role as deal originator

Type of Financing Preferred:
Fund of Funds

Geographical Preferences

International
Asia
Eastern Europe
Western Europe

Additional Information

Name of Most Recent Fund: AXA Capital
Most Recent Fund Was Raised: 10/01/1975
Year Founded: 1998
Capital Under Management: $855,000,000
Current Activity Level : Actively seeking new investments
Method of Compensation: Return on investment is of primary concern, do not charge fees

---

AXAVISION, INC.

14 Wall Street
26th Floor
New York, NY 10005
Phone: 212-619-4000
Fax: 212-619-7202

Type of Firm

Private Firm Investing Own Capital

Project Preferences

Role in Financing:
Prefer role as deal originator

Type of Financing Preferred:
Seed
Start-up Financing

Size of Investments Considered
Min Size of Investment Considered (000s): $100
Max Size of Investment Considered (000s): $300

Geographical Preferences

International
No Preference

Industry Preferences

Computer Software
Computer Services
Systems Software
Applications Software

Internet Specific
Internet

Financial Services
Financial Services

Additional Information

Year Founded: 1992
Capital Under Management: $5,000,000
Current Activity Level : Actively seeking new investments
Method of Compensation: Return on invest. most important, but chg. closing fees, service fees, etc.

B2B-HIVE, LLC

821 Broadway
New York, NY 10003
Phone: 212-677-6300
Fax: 212-777-1172
Website: www.b2b-hive.com

Management and Staff
Bruce Tully, Co-Founder
George Israel, Principal
Jennifer Airo, Vice President
Mark Mahan, Vice President
Rich Marin, Co-Founder
Sam Alfstad, Co-Founder
Shivan Govindan, Vice President
Terry Chabrowe, Co-Founder

Type of Firm
Private Firm Investing Own Capital

Project Preferences

Role in Financing:
Prefer role as deal originator

Type of Financing Preferred:
Early Stage
Seed
Startup

Size of Investments Considered
Min Size of Investment Considered (000s): $1,000
Max Size of Investment Considered (000s): $5,000

Geographical Preferences

United States
New York

Industry Preferences

Financial Services
Insurance
Real Estate

Business Serv.
Media

Additional Information
Year Founded: 2000
Capital Under Management: $37,500,000
Current Activity Level : Actively seeking new investments

BAKER CAPITAL CORP.

540 Madison Avenue
29th Floor
New York, NY 10022
Phone: 212-848-2000
Fax: 212-486-0660
Website: www.bakercapital.com

Management and Staff
Ashley Leeds, Co-Founder
Ed Scott, Co-Founder
Faisal Nisar, Partner
Henry Baker, Co-Founder
James Cosgrove, Chief Executive Officer
John Baker, Co-Founder
Jonathon Grabel, Partner
Joseph Saviano, Chief Financial Officer
Lawrence Bettino, Co-Founder
Simon Lee, Partner
Tracy Chadwell, Partner

Type of Firm
Private Firm Investing Own Capital

Industry Association Membership
National Venture Capital Association (NVCA)

Project Preferences

Type of Financing Preferred:
Early Stage
Expansion

Geographical Preferences

United States
All U.S.

International
Western Europe

Industry Preferences

(% based on actual investment)

Internet Specific	57.6%
Computer Software and Services	22.4%
Communications and Media	16.3%
Semiconductors/Other Elect.	3.7%

Additional Information
Name of Most Recent Fund: Baker Communications Fund, L.P.
Most Recent Fund Was Raised: 04/01/1997
Year Founded: 1995
Capital Under Management: $1,506,000,000
Current Activity Level : Actively seeking new investments

BANGERT DAWES READE DAVIS & THOM

One Madison Avenue
New York, NY 10010
Phone: 212-689-7404

See California for full listing.

BANKERS TRUST (AKA:BT TECHNOLOGY PARTNERS)

130 Liberty Street
MS 2243
New York, NY 10006
Phone: 212-250-3572
Fax: 212-250-9347

Management and Staff
Peter Scutt, Managing Director

Type of Firm
Commercial Bank Affiliate or Subsidiary

Project Preferences

Size of Investments Considered
Min Size of Investment Considered (000s): $300
Max Size of Investment Considered (000s): $3,000

Additional Information
Year Founded: 1996
Capital Under Management: $25,000,000
Current Activity Level : Actively seeking new investments

BANKERS TRUST NEW YORK CORP./DEUTSCHE BANC ALEX BROWN

130 Liberty Street
25th Floor
New York, NY 10006
Phone: 212-250-4648
Fax: 212-669-1749

Management and Staff
Richard Berkeley, Managing Director

Whom to Contact
Charlie Ayres
Frank Nash
Jeff Ott
Manjit Dale

Type of Firm
Investment/Merchant Bank Investing Own or Client Funds

Project Preferences

Role in Financing:
Prefer role as deal originator but will also invest in deals created by others

Type of Financing Preferred:
Leveraged Buyout
Mezzanine
Second Stage Financing
Special Situation

Industry Preferences

(% based on actual investment)

Communications and Media	37.6%
Internet Specific	37.1%
Computer Software and Services	8.1%
Other Products	7.1%
Semiconductors/Other Elect.	4.8%
Consumer Related	2.1%
Medical/Health	1.6%
Computer Hardware	1.1%
Industrial/Energy	0.4%

Additional Information
Name of Most Recent Fund: BT Real Estate Mezzanine Investment Fund
Most Recent Fund Was Raised: 11/30/1998
Year Founded: 1972
Capital Under Management: $1,200,000,000
Current Activity Level : Actively seeking new investments
Method of Compensation: Return on invest. most important, but chg. closing fees, service fees, etc.

BARNARD & COMPANY

535 Madison Avenue
Floor 25
New York, NY 10022
Phone: 212-734-7884
Website: www.barnardco.com

Management and Staff
Steven Chang, Principal

Type of Firm
Private Firm Investing Own Capital

Geographical Preferences

International
All International

Industry Preferences

Communications and Media
Telecommunications

Internet Specific
Internet

Additional Information
Year Founded: 2000
Current Activity Level : Actively seeking new investments

BATAVIA GROUP, LTD., THE

38 East 57th Street
New York, NY 10022
Phone: 212-308-1100
Fax: 212-308-1565

Type of Firm
Mgt. Consulting Firm

Project Preferences

Role in Financing:
Prefer role as deal originator but will also invest in deals created by others

Type of Financing Preferred:
Leveraged Buyout
Recapitalizations
Second Stage Financing
Special Situation

Size of Investments Considered
Min Size of Investment Considered (000s): $5,000
Max Size of Investment Considered: No Limit

Geographical Preferences

United States
Mid Atlantic
Southeast
West Coast

Industry Preferences

Communications and Media
Data Communications

Semiconductors/Other Elect.
Sensors

Consumer Related
Food/Beverage
Consumer Products

Industrial/Energy
Oil & Gas Drilling,Explor
Industrial Products
Materials
Machinery

Additional Information
Year Founded: 1988
Capital Under Management: $57,200,000
Current Activity Level : Actively seeking new investments

BAUSCH & LOMB, INC.

One Bausch Place
Rochester, NY 14604-2701
Phone: 716-338-5830
Fax: 716-338-5043

Type of Firm
Non-Financial Corp. Affiliate or Subsidiary

Project Preferences

Role in Financing:
Prefer role as deal originator but will also invest in deals created by others

Type of Financing Preferred:
Control-block Purchases
Research and Development

Geographical Preferences

International
No Preference

Industry Preferences

Biotechnology
Biotech Related Research

Medical/Health
Diagnostic Test Products
Drug/Equipmt Delivery
Medical Products
Pharmaceuticals

Consumer Related
Retail

Additional Information
Year Founded: 1853
Current Activity Level : Actively seeking new investments
Method of Compensation: Return on investment is of primary concern, do not charge fees

BEAR VENTURES

524 Broadway
Suite 206
New York, NY 10012
Phone: 212-226-5503
Fax: 212-226-5504

Management and Staff
Philip Erdoes, President

Type of Firm
Private Firm Investing Own Capital

Additional Information
Year Founded: 1999
Current Activity Level : Actively seeking new investments

BEDFORD CAPITAL CORP.

18 East 48th Street
Suite 1800
New York, NY 10017
Phone: 212-688-5700
Fax: 212-754-4699
Website: www.bedfordnyc.com

Other Offices

839 Elkridge Landing Road
Linthicum, MD 21090
Phone: 410-850-0555
Fax: 410-850-0777

Management and Staff
Nathan Bernstein
Neal Ochsner

Whom to Contact
Nathan Bernstein
Neal Ochsner

Type of Firm
Investment/Merchant Bank Investing Own or Client Funds

Project Preferences

Role in Financing:
Prefer role as deal originator but will also invest in deals created by others

Type of Financing Preferred:
First Stage Financing
Industry Rollups
Leveraged Buyout
Recapitalizations
Second Stage Financing

Size of Investments Considered
Min Size of Investment Considered (000s): $100
Max Size of Investment Considered (000s): $300

Geographical Preferences

United States
Midwest

Industry Preferences

Internet Specific
Internet

Medical/Health
Disposable Med. Products

Consumer Related
Consumer Products

Industrial/Energy
Energy Conservation Relat
Environmental Related

Financial Services
Real Estate

Manufact.
Publishing

Additional Information
Year Founded: 1992
Current Activity Level : Actively seeking new investments
Method of Compensation: Return on invest. most important, but chg. closing fees, service fees, etc.

BEHRMAN CAPITAL

126 East 56th Street
New York, NY 10022
Phone: 212-980-6500
Fax: 212-980-7024
Website: www.behrmancap.com

Management and Staff
Bob Byrnes, Partner
Darryl Behrman, Managing Partner
Elliot Maluth, Partner
Grant Behrman, Managing Partner
Mark Visser, Principal
Milan Mandaric, Partner
Neal Sandler, Partner
William Matthes, Managing Partner

Type of Firm
Private Firm Investing Own Capital

Project Preferences

Role in Financing:
Prefer role as deal originator but will also invest in deals created by others

Type of Financing Preferred:
Leveraged Buyout
Second Stage Financing

Size of Investments Considered
Min Size of Investment Considered (000s): $2,000
Max Size of Investment Considered: No Limit

Geographical Preferences

United States
All U.S.

Canada
All Canada

Industry Preferences

(% based on actual investment)

Other Products	35.8%
Internet Specific	35.4%
Communications and Media	14.9%
Computer Software and Services	8.0%
Medical/Health	4.7%
Semiconductors/Other Elect.	1.3%

Additional Information
Name of Most Recent Fund: Behrman Capital III, L.P.
Most Recent Fund Was Raised: 07/01/1997
Year Founded: 1992
Capital Under Management: $423,000,000
Current Activity Level : Actively seeking new investments
Method of Compensation: Return on invest. most important, but chg. closing fees, service fees, etc.

BESSEMER VENTURE PARTNERS

1400 Old Country Road
Suite 109
Westbury, NY 11590
Phone: 516-997-2300
Fax: 516-997-2371
Website: www.bvp.com

See Massachusetts for full listing.

BLOOM & CO.

950 Third Avenue
New York, NY 10022
Phone: 212-838-1858
Fax: 212-838-1843

Management and Staff
Jack Bloom

Whom to Contact
Jack Bloom

Type of Firm
Mgt. Consulting Firm

Project Preferences

Role in Financing:
Prefer role as deal originator

Type of Financing Preferred:
Control-block Purchases
First Stage Financing
Leveraged Buyout
Mezzanine
Second Stage Financing
Seed
Special Situation
Start-up Financing

Size of Investments Considered
Min Size of Investment Considered (000s): $3,000
Max Size of Investment Considered: No Limit

Geographical Preferences

International
No Preference

Additional Information
Year Founded: 1983
Current Activity Level : Actively seeking new investments
Method of Compensation: Function primarily in service area, receive contingent fee in cash or equity

---

BRADFORD EQUITIES FUND, LLC

1 Rockefeller Plaza
Suite 1722
New York, NY 10020
Phone: 212-218-6900
Fax: 212-218-6901
Website: www.bradfordequities.com

Management and Staff
Neil Taylor, Chief Financial Officer
Noel Wilens, Managing Director
Richard Rudolph, Principal
Robert Simon, Managing Director
Thomas Ferguson, Managing Director

Type of Firm
Investment/Merchant Bank Subsid/Affil

Project Preferences

Type of Financing Preferred:
Acquisition

Size of Investments Considered
Min Size of Investment Considered (000s): $10,000
Max Size of Investment Considered (000s): $50,000

Geographical Preferences

United States
Mid Atlantic
Northeast
Southeast
Southwest
West Coast

Industry Preferences

Consumer Related
Food/Beverage

Industrial/Energy
Industrial Products
Machinery

Business Serv.
Services
Distribution

Manufact.
Manufacturing

Additional Information
Name of Most Recent Fund: Bradford Equities Fund III, L.P.
Most Recent Fund Was Raised: 10/01/1997
Year Founded: 1974
Capital Under Management: $120,000,000
Current Activity Level : Actively seeking new investments
Method of Compensation: Return on investment is of primary concern, do not charge fees

---

BRISTOL CAPITAL MANAGEMENT

300 Park Avenue
17th Floor
New York, NY 10022
Phone: 212-572-6306
Fax: 212-705-4292

Management and Staff
Alan Donenfeld, President

Type of Firm
Private Firm Investing Own Capital

Project Preferences

Role in Financing:
Prefer role as deal originator

Type of Financing Preferred:
Leveraged Buyout
Mezzanine
Second Stage Financing
Special Situation

Geographical Preferences

United States
All U.S.

Industry Preferences

Communications and Media
Communications and Media

Computer Other
Computer Related

Semiconductors/Other Elect.
Electronic Components
Sensors

Medical/Health
Medical/Health

Consumer Related
Entertainment and Leisure
Retail
Food/Beverage
Consumer Services
Other Restaurants

Industrial/Energy
Machinery
Environmental Related

Manufact.
Publishing

Additional Information
Year Founded: 1990
Capital Under Management: $25,000,000
Current Activity Level : Actively seeking new investments
Method of Compensation: Return on investment is of primary concern, do not charge fees

---

BURRILL & COMPANY

595 Madison Avenue
19th Floor
New York, NY
Website: www.burrillandco.com

See California for full listing.

CALGARY ENTERPRISES, INC.

Four Park Avenue
Suite 12G
New York, NY 10016-5310
Phone: 212-683-0119
Fax: 212-683-3119
Website: www.calgaryenterprises.com

Management and Staff
Steven Insalaco

Whom to Contact
Steven Insalaco

Type of Firm
Investment Management/Finance Consulting

Project Preferences

Role in Financing:
Prefer role as deal originator

Type of Financing Preferred:
Acquisition
Early Stage
Expansion
First Stage Financing
Later Stage
Leveraged Buyout
Management Buyouts
Mezzanine
Private Placement
Recapitalizations
Second Stage Financing
Special Situation
Start-up Financing
Turnaround

Size of Investments Considered
Min Size of Investment Considered (000s): $5,000
Max Size of Investment Considered: No Limit

Geographical Preferences

United States
All U.S.

Canada
All Canada

Additional Information
Year Founded: 1988
Current Activity Level : Actively seeking new investments
Method of Compensation: Professional fee required whether or not deal closes

CANTERBURY CAPITAL L.L.C.(AKA: CANTERBURY DETROIT PARTNERS)

600 Fifth Avenue
23rd Floor
New York, NY 10020
Phone: 212-332-1565
Fax: 212-332-1584

Management and Staff
David Buttolph, Principal

Whom to Contact
David Buttolph

Type of Firm
Private Firm Investing Own Capital

Project Preferences

Role in Financing:
Prefer role in deals created by others

Type of Financing Preferred:
Leveraged Buyout
Mezzanine

Size of Investments Considered
Min Size of Investment Considered (000s): $10,000
Max Size of Investment Considered: No Limit

Geographical Preferences

United States
All U.S.

Canada
All Canada

Industry Preferences

Communications and Media
Other Communication Prod.

Semiconductors/Other Elect.
Electronic Components
Controllers and Sensors
Sensors
Circuit Boards
Component Testing Equipmt
Analytic/Scientific

Medical/Health
Diagnostic Test Products
Medical Products
Disposable Med. Products

Consumer Related
Entertainment and Leisure
Retail
Food/Beverage
Consumer Products
Consumer Services
Other Restaurants

Industrial/Energy
Industrial Products
Materials
Factory Automation
Machinery
Environmental Related

Business Serv.
Consulting Services

Manufact.
Publishing

Additional Information
Name of Most Recent Fund: Canterbury Mezzanine Capital II, LP
Most Recent Fund Was Raised: 07/01/1999
Year Founded: 1989
Capital Under Management: $160,000,000
Current Activity Level : Actively seeking new investments
Method of Compensation: Return on investment is of primary concern, do not charge fees

CARLIN VENTURES LLC

445 Park Avenue,
9th Floor
New York, NY 10022
Phone: 212-753-6431
Website: www.carlinventures.com

Management and Staff
Dillon Cohen, President
Greg Scholl, Chief Financial Officer

Type of Firm
Private Firm Investing Own Capital

Project Preferences

Type of Financing Preferred:
Early Stage

Geographical Preferences

United States
All U.S.

Industry Preferences

Internet Specific
Internet

Additional Information

Year Founded: 1999
Current Activity Level : Actively seeking new investments

CASTLE GROUP, LTD., THE

787 Seventh Avenue
48th Floor
New York, NY 10019
Phone: 212-554-4300
Fax: 212-554-4488

Type of Firm

Investment/Merchant Bank Investing Own or Client Funds

Project Preferences

Role in Financing:

Prefer role as deal originator

Type of Financing Preferred:

Control-block Purchases
First Stage Financing
Research and Development
Second Stage Financing
Seed
Start-up Financing

Size of Investments Considered

Min Size of Investment Considered (000s): $3,000
Max Size of Investment Considered (000s): $20,000

Geographical Preferences

International

No Preference

Industry Preferences

Medical/Health

Medical Therapeutics
Pharmaceuticals

Additional Information

Year Founded: 1990
Current Activity Level : Actively seeking new investments
Method of Compensation: Return on invest. most important, but chg. closing fees, service fees, etc.

CB CAPITAL INVESTORS, L.P.

380 Madison Avenue
12th Floor
New York, NY 10017
Phone: 212-622-3100
Fax: 212-622-3799

Management and Staff

George Kelts, Managing Director

Type of Firm

Investment/Merchant Bank Subsid/Affil

Industry Preferences

(% based on actual investment)

Internet Specific	68.4%
Communications and Media	10.6%
Computer Software and Services	10.2%
Medical/Health	7.2%
Other Products	3.5%

Additional Information

Year Founded: 1986
Capital Under Management: $122,800,000
Current Activity Level : Actively seeking new investments

CB HEALTH VENTURES LLC

452 Fifth Avenue
25th Floor
New York, NY 10018
Phone: 212-869-5600
Fax: 212-869-6418
Website: www.health-ventures.com

See Massachusetts for full listing.

CE UNTERBERG TOWBIN (FKA:UNTERBERG HARRIS CAPITAL PARTNERS)

10 East 50th Street
22nd Floor
New York, NY 10022
Phone: 212-572-8000
Fax: 212-888-8611
Website: http://www.unterberg.com

Other Offices

275 Battery Street
San Francisco, CA 94111
Phone: 415-399-1500

Management and Staff

Robert Kahan, President
Thomas Unterberg, Chairman & CEO
Vered Sharon, Managing Director

Whom to Contact

Brett Wallace
David S. Wachter

Type of Firm

Investment/Merchant Bank Subsid/Affil

Project Preferences

Role in Financing:

Prefer role as deal originator but will also invest in deals created by others

Type of Financing Preferred:

Mezzanine
Second Stage Financing

Industry Preferences

(% based on actual investment)

Internet Specific	51.1%
Computer Software and Services	21.7%
Communications and Media	13.7%
Consumer Related	9.6%
Medical/Health	1.8%
Semiconductors/Other Elect.	1.2%
Computer Hardware	0.7%

Additional Information

Name of Most Recent Fund: Unterberg Towbin Capital Partners I (FKA Unterberg Harris I)
Most Recent Fund Was Raised: 01/01/1995
Year Founded: 1989
Capital Under Management: $75,000,000
Current Activity Level : Inactive / Unknown
Method of Compensation: Return on investment is of primary concern, do not charge fees

CHARLES STREET SECURITIES, INC.

212 East 48th Street
Suite 9C
New York, NY 10017
Phone: 212-588-9411
Fax: 212-486-6595

Other Offices

One Wilton Crescent
London, United Kingdom SW1X 8RN
Phone: 44-171-235-7642
Fax: 44-171-235-7647

Type of Firm
Investment/Merchant Bank Investing Own or Client Funds

Project Preferences

Role in Financing:
Prefer role as deal originator but will also invest in deals created by others

Type of Financing Preferred:
Leveraged Buyout

Geographical Preferences

International
No Preference

Additional Information
Year Founded: 1983
Current Activity Level : Actively seeking new investments

CHURCHILL CAPITAL, INC.

590 Madison Avenue
38th Floor
New York, NY 10022
Phone: 212-832-3300
Fax: 212-832-4270
Website: www.churchillnet.com

See Minnesota for full listing.

CIBC CAPITAL PARTNERS (FKA: CIBC WOOD GUNDY CAPITAL)

200 Liberty Street
1 World Financial Center
New York, NY 10281
Phone: 416-594-7443
Fax: 416-594-8037
Website: www.cibcwm.com

Other Offices

161 Bay Street
8th Floor
Toronto, Canada M5J 2S8
Phone: 416-594-8021
Fax: 416-594-8037

One Post Street
Suite 3550
San Francisco, CA 94104
Phone: 415-399-5723
Fax: 415-399-1224

Management and Staff
Ann Fusco, Managing Director
Richard White, Managing Director
Robi Blumenstein, Managing Director

Whom to Contact
Kimberley Benoit
Tim Whiltaker

Type of Firm
Investment/Merchant Bank Subsid/Affil

Industry Association Membership
Canadian Venture Capital Association
Natl assoc of Small Bus. Inv. Co (NASBIC)
Western Association of Venture Capitalists (WAVC)

Project Preferences

Role in Financing:
Prefer role as deal originator but will also invest in deals created by others

Type of Financing Preferred:
Leveraged Buyout
Mezzanine
Other
Second Stage Financing
Special Situation

Size of Investments Considered
Min Size of Investment Considered (000s): $2,000
Max Size of Investment Considered: No Limit

Geographical Preferences

United States
All U.S.

Canada
All Canada

International
United Kingdom

Industry Preferences

(% based on actual investment)

Internet Specific	33.2%
Communications and Media	24.7%
Semiconductors/Other Elect.	13.5%
Computer Software and Services	9.9%
Other Products	7.2%
Medical/Health	5.7%
Consumer Related	2.2%
Industrial/Energy	1.9%
Biotechnology	1.7%
Computer Hardware	0.1%

Additional Information
Name of Most Recent Fund: CIBC Wood Gundy Ventures Fund
Most Recent Fund Was Raised: 01/01/1993
Year Founded: 1996
Capital Under Management: $75,000,000
Current Activity Level : Actively seeking new investments
Method of Compensation: Return on invest. most important, but chg. closing fees, service fees, etc.

CIBC OPPENHEIMER & CO., INC.

Oppenheimer Tower
World Financial Ctr 31st Floor
New York, NY 10281
Phone: 212-667-7640
Fax: 212-667-4468

Type of Firm
Investment/Merchant Bank Investing Own or Client Funds

Project Preferences

Type of Financing Preferred:
First Stage Financing
Fund of Funds
Leveraged Buyout

Geographical Preferences

United States
All U.S.

Industry Preferences

(% based on actual investment)

Other Products	26.1%
Medical/Health	18.0%
Internet Specific	17.5%
Communications and Media	16.9%
Consumer Related	16.2%
Computer Hardware	2.8%
Semiconductors/Other Elect.	2.2%
Industrial/Energy	0.4%

Additional Information
Name of Most Recent Fund: CIBC Oppenheimer Private Equity Partners, L.P.
Most Recent Fund Was Raised: 01/01/1995
Year Founded: 1950
Capital Under Management: $590,000,000
Current Activity Level : Actively seeking new investments

CITIBANK GLOBAL ASSET MANAGEMENT

599 Lexington Avenue
New York, NY 10043
Phone: 212-559-0079

Type of Firm
Commercial Bank Affiliate or Subsidiary

Additional Information
Name of Most Recent Fund: Citibank Participating Mortgage Liquidating Fund (PMF)
Most Recent Fund Was Raised: 05/01/1980
Year Founded: 1998
Capital Under Management: $257,000,000
Current Activity Level : Actively seeking new investments

CITICORP VENTURE CAPITAL, LTD.

399 Park Avenue
14th Floor, Zone Four
New York, NY 10043
Phone: 212-559-1127
Fax: 212-888-2940

Other Offices

399 Park Avenue
14th Floor
New York, NY 10043
Phone: 212-559-1127
Fax: 212-888-2940

Type of Firm
Commercial Bank Affiliate or Subsidiary

Industry Association Membership
Natl assoc of Small Bus. Inv. Co (NASBIC)

Project Preferences

Role in Financing:
Prefer role as deal originator

Type of Financing Preferred:
Leveraged Buyout
Second Stage Financing
Special Situation

Size of Investments Considered
Min Size of Investment Considered (000s): $50,000
Max Size of Investment Considered: No Limit

Geographical Preferences

United States
All U.S.

International
Bermuda
France
Germany
United Kingdom

Industry Preferences

(% based on actual investment)

Computer Hardware	17.8%
Industrial/Energy	15.9%
Communications and Media	15.3%
Internet Specific	10.9%
Other Products	8.9%
Consumer Related	8.2%
Computer Software and Services	7.7%
Semiconductors/Other Elect.	7.0%
Medical/Health	6.4%
Biotechnology	1.9%

Additional Information
Name of Most Recent Fund: CG Asian American Fund, L.P.
Most Recent Fund Was Raised: 01/01/1996
Year Founded: 1968
Capital Under Management: $250,000,000
Current Activity Level : Actively seeking new investments
Method of Compensation: Return on investment is of primary concern, do not charge fees

CM EQUITY PARTNERS

135 East 57th Street
New York, NY 10022
Phone: 212-909-8428
Fax: 212-980-2630

Management and Staff
Carlos Signoret, Partner
Daniel Colon, Partner
Joel Jacks, Managing Partner
Joel Levy, Managing Partner
Peter Schulte, Managing Partner
Robert Hopkins, Partner

Type of Firm
Investment/Merchant Bank Subsid/Affil

Industry Association Membership
Natl assoc of Small Bus. Inv. Co (NASBIC)

Project Preferences

Role in Financing:
Prefer role as deal originator but will also invest in deals created by others

Type of Financing Preferred:
First Stage Financing
Industry Rollups
Leveraged Buyout
Mezzanine
Second Stage Financing
Special Situation
Start-up Financing

Size of Investments Considered
Min Size of Investment Considered (000s): $2,000
Max Size of Investment Considered: No Limit

Geographical Preferences

United States
All U.S.

Canada
All Canada

Industry Preferences

(% based on actual investment)

Consumer Related	42.8%
Other Products	24.5%
Communications and Media	10.0%
Semiconductors/Other Elect.	7.8%
Industrial/Energy	4.8%
Computer Software and Services	4.0%
Biotechnology	2.7%
Computer Hardware	2.5%
Internet Specific	0.7%

Additional Information
Name of Most Recent Fund: Carl Marks Distressed Debt Fund
Most Recent Fund Was Raised: 04/16/1997
Year Founded: 1925
Capital Under Management: $100,000,000
Current Activity Level : Actively seeking new investments
Method of Compensation: Return on investment is of primary concern, do not charge fees

COHEN & CO., L.L.C.

800 Third Avenue
New York, NY 10022
Phone: 212-317-2250
Fax: 212-317-2255

Other Offices

1100 Franklin Avenue
Garden City, NY 11530

Type of Firm
Investment/Merchant Bank Investing Own or Client Funds

Project Preferences

Role in Financing:
Prefer role as deal originator but will also invest in deals created by others

Type of Financing Preferred:
Control-block Purchases
First Stage Financing
Leveraged Buyout
Mezzanine
Second Stage Financing
Seed
Special Situation
Start-up Financing

Size of Investments Considered
Min Size of Investment Considered (000s): $10,000
Max Size of Investment Considered: No Limit

Geographical Preferences

International
No Preference

Industry Preferences

Communications and Media
Communications and Media

Computer Software
Applications Software

Semiconductors/Other Elect.
Electronic Components

Medical/Health
Medical/Health

Consumer Related
Consumer

Industrial/Energy
Energy
Industrial Products

Business Serv.
Distribution

Additional Information
Year Founded: 1994
Current Activity Level : Actively seeking new investments
Method of Compensation: Return on invest. most important, but chg. closing fees, service fees, etc.

COLEMAN VENTURE GROUP

5909 Northern Boulevard
P.O. Box 244
East Norwich, NY 11732
Phone: 516-626-3642
Fax: 516-626-9722

Other Offices

5909 Northern Boulevard
P.O. Box 244
East Norwich, NY 11732
Phone: 516-626-3642
Fax: 516-626-9722

Type of Firm
Mgt. Consulting Firm

Project Preferences

Role in Financing:
Prefer role as deal originator but will also invest in deals created by others

Type of Financing Preferred:
First Stage Financing
Recapitalizations
Seed
Special Situation
Start-up Financing

Size of Investments Considered
Min Size of Investment Considered (000s): $100
Max Size of Investment Considered (000s): $1,000

Geographical Preferences

United States
Northeast
West Coast

Canada
All Canada

Industry Preferences

Semiconductors/Other Elect.
Electronic Components
Semiconductor

Consumer Related
Consumer Products

Industrial/Energy
Alternative Energy

Additional Information
Year Founded: 1965
Capital Under Management: $9,000,000
Current Activity Level : Actively seeking new investments
Method of Compensation: Return on investment is of primary concern, do not charge fees

---

COMPASS TECHNOLOGY PARTNERS

128 East 31st Street
New York, NY 10016-6848
Phone: 212-689-2626
Fax: 212-689-5301
Website: www.compasstechpartners.com

See California for full listing.

CONSTELLATION VENTURES

575 Lexington Avenue
10th Floor
New York, NY 10022
Phone: 212-272-3814
Fax: 212-272-9256
Website: www.constellationventures.com

Management and Staff
Angela Danielson, Principal
Clifford Friedman, Managing Partner
Dennis Miller, General Partner
Kathryn Wortsman, Principal
Melissa Blau, General Partner
Ronald Celmer, General Partner
Ross Miyamoto, General Partner

Type of Firm
Investment/Merchant Bank Subsid/Affil

Project Preferences

Type of Financing Preferred:
Early Stage
Expansion

Size of Investments Considered
Min Size of Investment Considered (000s): $5,000
Max Size of Investment Considered (000s): $10,000

Geographical Preferences

United States
All U.S.

International
Japan

Industry Preferences

(% based on actual investment)

Internet Specific	62.8%
Computer Software and Services	36.0%
Semiconductors/Other Elect.	1.2%

Additional Information

Name of Most Recent Fund: Constellation Ventures
Most Recent Fund Was Raised: 12/23/1998
Year Founded: 1998
Capital Under Management: $451,000,000
Current Activity Level : Actively seeking new investments

CORNERSTONE EQUITY INVESTORS, LLC

717 Fifth Avenue
Suite 1100
New York, NY 10022
Phone: 212-753-0901
Fax: 212-826-6798
Website: www.cornerstone-equity.com

Management and Staff

Dana O'Brien, Senior Managing Director
David Haddad, Principal
Derek Jones, Managing Director
John Downer, Managing Director
Mark Rossi, Senior Managing Director
Martha Robinson, Managing Director
Michael Najjar, Managing Director
Paul Hirschbiel, Managing Director
Robert Getz, Managing Director
Robert Knox, Senior Managing Director
Stephen Larson, Managing Director
Tyler Wolfram, Managing Director
William Austin, Chief Financial Officer

Type of Firm

Affiliate/Subsidary of Oth. Financial. Instit.

Industry Association Membership

National Venture Capital Association (NVCA)

Project Preferences

Role in Financing:
Prefer role as deal originator but will also invest in deals created by others

Type of Financing Preferred:
Leveraged Buyout
Special Situation

Size of Investments Considered

Min Size of Investment Considered (000s): $50,000
Max Size of Investment Considered: No Limit

Geographical Preferences

International
No Preference

Industry Preferences

(% based on actual investment)

Consumer Related	26.8%
Semiconductors/Other Elect.	17.8%
Medical/Health	16.4%
Communications and Media	11.2%
Internet Specific	9.0%
Other Products	6.3%
Computer Software and Services	6.1%
Computer Hardware	4.2%
Industrial/Energy	1.9%
Biotechnology	0.2%

Additional Information

Name of Most Recent Fund: Cornerstone Equity Investors IV, L.P.
Most Recent Fund Was Raised: 01/01/1996
Year Founded: 1982
Capital Under Management: $960,100,000
Current Activity Level : Actively seeking new investments
Method of Compensation: Return on investment is of primary concern, do not charge fees

CORPORATE VENTURE PARTNERS, L.P.

200 Sunset Park
Ithaca, NY 14850
Phone: 607-257-6323
Fax: 607-257-6128

Type of Firm

Private Firm Investing Own Capital

Project Preferences

Role in Financing:
Prefer role as deal originator but will also invest in deals created by others

Type of Financing Preferred:
First Stage Financing

Size of Investments Considered

Min Size of Investment Considered (000s): $500
Max Size of Investment Considered (000s): $1,000

Geographical Preferences

United States
Northeast

Industry Preferences

Communications and Media
Data Communications

Computer Hardware
Computer Graphics and Dig

Computer Software
Computer Services
Systems Software
Applications Software
Artificial Intelligence

Semiconductors/Other Elect.
Electronic Components
Sensors
Laser Related
Fiber Optics
Analytic/Scientific

Biotechnology
Biotech Related Research
Biotech Related Research

Medical/Health
Medical Diagnostics
Diagnostic Services
Pharmaceuticals

Consumer Related
Retail

Industrial/Energy
Robotics
Machinery
Environmental Related

Manufact.
Office Automation Equipmt
Publishing

Additional Information

Year Founded: 1988
Capital Under Management: $26,000,000
Current Activity Level : Reducing investment activity
Method of Compensation: Return on investment is of primary concern, do not charge fees

COWEN & CO.

Financial Square
28th Floor
New York, NY 10005
Phone: 212-495-6000

Management and Staff
Jarrod Cohen
Ronald Rich

Whom to Contact
Jarrod Cohen
Ronald Rich

Type of Firm
Investment/Merchant Bank Investing Own or Client Funds

Project Preferences

Role in Financing:
Prefer role in deals created by others

Type of Financing Preferred:
Second Stage Financing

Industry Preferences

Communications and Media
Communications and Media

Computer Other
Computer Related

Semiconductors/Other Elect.
Electronic Components

Biotechnology
Industrial Biotechnology
Biotech Related Research
Biotech Related Research

Medical/Health
Medical/Health
Medical Diagnostics
Medical Therapeutics

Additional Information
Name of Most Recent Fund: Cowen & Co.
Most Recent Fund Was Raised: 01/01/1983
Capital Under Management: $4,000,000
Current Activity Level : Inactive / Unknown
Method of Compensation: Return on investment is of primary concern, do not charge fees

CRAMER ROSENTHAL MCGLYNN, LLC

707 Westchester Avenue
White Plains, NY 10604
Phone: 212-326-5325
Website: www.CRMLLC.com

Other Offices

520 Madison Avenue
New York, NY 10022

Management and Staff
Adam Starr, Vice President
Christopher Fox, Principal
Edward Rosenthal, Co-Founder
Gerald Cramer, Co-Founder
Kevin Chin, Principal
Lena Khatcherian, Principal
Michael Marrone, Principal
Michael Prober, Principal
Scott Geller, Principal
Scott Scher, Principal
William Cline, Principal

Type of Firm
Private Equity Advisor or Fund of Fund Mgr

Additional Information
Year Founded: 1973
Capital Under Management: $50,000,000
Current Activity Level : Actively seeking new investments

CREST COMMUNICATIONS HOLDINGS LLC

320 Park Avenue
17th Floor
New York, NY 10022
Phone: 212-317-2700
Fax: 212-317-2710
Website: www.crestholdings.com

Management and Staff
William Sprague, Partner

Whom to Contact
Gregg A. Mockenhaupt
James Kuster
Matthew O'Connell

Type of Firm
Private Firm Investing Own Capital

Project Preferences

Role in Financing:
Prefer role as deal originator but will also invest in deals created by others

Type of Financing Preferred:
Balanced
Early Stage
Expansion
First Stage Financing
Industry Rollups
Later Stage
Leveraged Buyout
Second Stage Financing
Special Situation
Startup

Geographical Preferences

United States
All U.S.
All U.S.

Canada
All Canada

International
South Africa

Industry Preferences

(% based on actual investment)

Communications and Media	68.2%
Internet Specific	19.7%
Computer Software and Services	6.8%
Computer Hardware	5.3%

Additional Information
Name of Most Recent Fund: Crest Communications Partners
Most Recent Fund Was Raised: 08/01/1999
Year Founded: 1996
Capital Under Management: $150,000,000
Current Activity Level : Actively seeking new investments
Method of Compensation: Return on invest. most important, but chg. closing fees, service fees, etc.

CROSSROADS CAPITAL PARTNERS, LLC

885 3rd Avenue
Suite 2900
New York, NY 10022
Phone: 212-829-5794
Fax: 212-829-5795

See California for full listing.

CROWN ADVISORS INTERNATIONAL, LTD.

The Lincoln Building
60 East 42nd St Suite 3405
New York, NY 10165
Phone: 212-808-5278
Fax: 212-808-9073
Website: www.crownadvisors.com

Other Offices

3000 Sand Hill Road
Menlo Park, CA 94025
Phone: 415-854-2215

60 East 42nd Street
Suite 3405
New York, NY 10165
Phone: 212-808-5278
Fax: 212-619-5073

Management and Staff
Geoffrey Block, Partner
Randy Huyser, Partner

Type of Firm
Private Firm Investing Own Capital

Project Preferences

Role in Financing:
Prefer role in deals created by others

Type of Financing Preferred:
Balanced
Industry Rollups
Leveraged Buyout
Mezzanine
Second Stage Financing
Special Situation

Size of Investments Considered
Min Size of Investment Considered (000s): $500
Max Size of Investment Considered (000s): $1,000

Geographical Preferences

United States
All U.S.

Industry Preferences

(% based on actual investment)

Communications and Media	25.0%
Computer Hardware	15.3%
Computer Software and Services	13.7%
Internet Specific	13.7%
Medical/Health	11.7%
Semiconductors/Other Elect.	10.7%
Other Products	7.0%
Consumer Related	2.6%
Biotechnology	0.3%

Additional Information
Name of Most Recent Fund: Crown Growth Partners
Most Recent Fund Was Raised: 01/01/1995
Year Founded: 1980
Capital Under Management: $600,000,000
Current Activity Level : Actively seeking new investments
Method of Compensation: Return on investment is of primary concern, do not charge fees

CW GROUP, INC.

1041 Third Avenue
Second Floor
New York, NY 10021
Phone: 212-308-5266
Fax: 212-644-0354
Website: www.cwventures.com

Other Offices

2187 Newcastle Avenue
Suite 101
Cardiff, CA 92007
Phone: 760-942-4535
Fax: 760-942-4530

Management and Staff
Andrea Olenik, Chief Financial Officer
Barry Weinberg, General Partner
Charles Hartman, General Partner
Douglass Levy, Chief Financial Officer
John Stuelpnagel, General Partner
Lawrence Bock, General Partner
Walter Channing, General Partner

Whom to Contact
Christopher Fenimore

Type of Firm
Private Firm Investing Own Capital

Industry Association Membership
National Venture Capital Association (NVCA)

Project Preferences

Role in Financing:
Prefer role as deal originator but will also invest in deals created by others

Type of Financing Preferred:
Control-block Purchases
First Stage Financing
Leveraged Buyout
Research and Development
Second Stage Financing
Seed
Special Situation
Start-up Financing

Geographical Preferences

United States
All U.S.

Industry Preferences

(% based on actual investment)

Medical/Health	43.3%
Biotechnology	29.0%
Internet Specific	8.9%
Computer Software and Services	5.7%
Other Products	4.4%
Industrial/Energy	4.1%
Computer Hardware	2.5%
Semiconductors/Other Elect.	2.3%

Additional Information
Name of Most Recent Fund: CW Ventures III
Most Recent Fund Was Raised: 03/31/1998
Year Founded: 1982
Capital Under Management: $200,000,000
Current Activity Level : Actively seeking new investments
Method of Compensation: Return on invest. most important, but chg. closing fees, service fees, etc.

D.H. BLAIR INVESTMENT BANKING CORP.

44 Wall Street
Second Floor
New York, NY 10005
Phone: 212-495-5000
Fax: 212-269-1438

Type of Firm
Investment/Merchant Bank Investing Own or Client Funds

Project Preferences

Role in Financing:
Prefer role as deal originator but will also invest in deals created by others

Type of Financing Preferred:
First Stage Financing
Leveraged Buyout
Research and Development
Start-up Financing

Size of Investments Considered
Min Size of Investment Considered (000s): $100
Max Size of Investment Considered: No Limit

Geographical Preferences

International
No Preference

Industry Preferences

Communications and Media
Commercial Communications
Radio & TV Broadcasting
Telecommunications
Data Communications
Satellite Microwave Comm.

Computer Hardware
Computer Graphics and Dig

Computer Software
Computer Services
Systems Software
Applications Software
Artificial Intelligence

Semiconductors/Other Elect.
Component Testing Equipmt
Laser Related
Analytic/Scientific

Biotechnology
Biosensors
Biotech Related Research
Biotech Related Research

Medical/Health
Medical Diagnostics
Diagnostic Services
Medical Therapeutics
Drug/Equipmt Delivery
Other Therapeutic
Medical Products
Pharmaceuticals

Consumer Related
Entertainment and Leisure
Retail
Food/Beverage
Consumer Products
Consumer Services

Industrial/Energy
Alternative Energy
Materials
Environmental Related

Financial Services
Real Estate

Manufact.
Office Automation Equipmt
Publishing

Additional Information
Year Founded: 1904
Capital Under Management: $100,000,000
Current Activity Level : Actively seeking new investments
Method of Compensation: Return on investment is of primary concern, do not charge fees

---

DAUPHIN CAPITAL PARTNERS

108 Forest Avenue
Locust Valley, NY 11560
Phone: 516-759-3339
Fax: 516-759-3322
Website: www.dauphincapital.com

Management and Staff
Austin Broadhaust, Managing Partner
James Hoover, Managing Partner

Type of Firm
Private Firm Investing Own Capital

Project Preferences

Role in Financing:
Will function either as deal originator or investor in deals created by others

Type of Financing Preferred:
Balanced
Early Stage
First Stage Financing
Later Stage
Second Stage Financing

Size of Investments Considered
Min Size of Investment Considered (000s): $1,000
Max Size of Investment Considered (000s): $3,000

Geographical Preferences

United States
All U.S.

Industry Preferences

Internet Specific
Internet

Biotechnology
Biotech Related Research
Biotech Related Research

Medical/Health
Medical Diagnostics
Diagnostic Services
Diagnostic Test Products
Medical Therapeutics
Drug/Equipmt Delivery
Medical Products
Health Services
Hospitals/Clinics/Primary
Hospital/Other Instit.
Pharmaceuticals

Consumer Related
Education Related

Business Serv.
Services

Additional Information
Name of Most Recent Fund: Dauphin Capital Partners I, L.P.
Most Recent Fund Was Raised: 03/19/1998
Year Founded: 1998
Capital Under Management: $30,000,000
Current Activity Level : Actively seeking new investments
Method of Compensation: Return on investment is of primary concern, do not charge fees

---

DESAI CAPITAL MANAGEMENT INC.

540 Madison Avenue
36th Floor
New York, NY 10022
Phone: 212-838-9191
Fax: 212-838-9807
Website: www.desaicapital.com

Management and Staff
Rohit Desai, President
Tom Perlmutter, Vice President

Type of Firm
Investment/Merchant Bank Investing Own or Client Funds

Project Preferences

Role in Financing:
Prefer role as deal originator

Type of Financing Preferred:
Generalist PE

Size of Investments Considered
Min Size of Investment Considered (000s): $25,000
Max Size of Investment Considered: No Limit

Geographical Preferences

United States
All U.S.

Canada
All Canada

Industry Preferences

(% based on actual investment)

Communications and Media	59.6%
Other Products	23.5%
Consumer Related	11.1%
Internet Specific	3.3%
Industrial/Energy	2.0%
Medical/Health	0.4%

Additional Information
Name of Most Recent Fund: Desai Capital
Most Recent Fund Was Raised: 07/01/1985
Year Founded: 1984
Capital Under Management: $1,000,000,000
Current Activity Level : Inactive / Unknown
Method of Compensation: Return on invest. most important, but chg. closing fees, service fees, etc.

DILLON READ & CO.

535 Madison Ave
New York, NY 10022
Phone: 212-906-7000

Management and Staff
Gene Solnick, Chief Financial Officer

Type of Firm
Investment/Merchant Bank Investing Own or Client Funds

Additional Information
Name of Most Recent Fund: Dillon Read & Co.
Most Recent Fund Was Raised: 01/01/1979
Current Activity Level : Inactive / Unknown

DOLPHIN COMMUNICATIONS

750 Lexington Avenue
16th Floor
New York, NY 10022
Phone: 212-446-1604
Fax: 212-446-1638
Website: www.dolphinfund.com

Management and Staff
Barry Stewart, Managing Director
Dennis O'Connell, Venture Partner
Donald Kraftson, Managing Director
Mark Brooks, Chief Financial Officer
Richard Brekka, Managing Director
Salvatore Tirabassi, Principal

Type of Firm
Private Firm Investing Own Capital

Industry Association Membership
National Venture Capital Association (NVCA)

Project Preferences

Type of Financing Preferred:
Expansion
Later Stage

Size of Investments Considered
Min Size of Investment Considered (000s): $10,000
Max Size of Investment Considered (000s): $75,000

Geographical Preferences

United States
All U.S.

International
All International

Industry Preferences

(% based on actual investment)

Communications and Media	56.6%
Internet Specific	41.4%
Computer Hardware	2.0%

Additional Information
Name of Most Recent Fund: Dolphin Communication Fund, L.P.
Most Recent Fund Was Raised: 06/16/1998
Year Founded: 1999
Capital Under Management: $73,000,000
Current Activity Level : Actively seeking new investments

DRAPER FISHER JURVETSON GOTHAM VENTURE PARTNERS

132 West 31st Street
Suite 1102
New York, NY 10001
Phone: 212-279-3980
Fax: 212-279-3825
Website: www.dfjgotham.com

Management and Staff
Chip Meakem, Principal
Daniel Schultz, Managing Partner
Ross Goldstein, Managing Partner
Timothy Draper, Managing Director

Type of Firm
Affiliate/Subsidary of Oth. Financial. Instit.

Project Preferences

Type of Financing Preferred:
Early Stage

Size of Investments Considered
Min Size of Investment Considered (000s): $1,000
Max Size of Investment Considered (000s): $5,000

Geographical Preferences

United States
New York
Northeast

Industry Preferences

Communications and Media
Communications and Media

Computer Software
Software

Internet Specific
Internet

Additional Information
Capital Under Management: $107,000,000
Current Activity Level : Actively seeking new investments

DRESDNER KLEINWORT CAPITAL

75 Wall Street
24th Floor
New York, NY 10005
Phone: 212-429-3131
Fax: 212-429-3139
Website: www.dresdnerkb.com

Other Offices

190 South LaSalle Street
Suite 2700
Chicago, IL 60603
Phone: 312-444-1300
Fax: 312-444-1192

33/F, Jardine House
1 Connaught Place
Central, Hong Kong
Phone: 852-2521-5331
Fax: 852-2525-8077

PO Box 18075 Riverbank House
2 Swan Lane
London, United Kingdom EC4R 3UX

Suite 1700, Exchange Tower
130 King Street West
Toronto, Canada M5X 1E3
Phone: 416-369-8300
Fax: 416-369-8362

Management and Staff
Alexander Coleman, Partner
Christopher Wright, President
Christopher Hammond, Vice President
Richard Wolf, Partner
Volkert Doeksen, Partner

Type of Firm
Investment/Merchant Bank Subsid/Affil

Industry Association Membership
British Venture Capital Association
Natl assoc of Small Bus. Inv. Co (NASBIC)

Project Preferences

Role in Financing:
Prefer role as deal originator but will also invest in deals created by others

Type of Financing Preferred:
Early Stage
Expansion
Leveraged Buyout
Mezzanine
Second Stage Financing

Size of Investments Considered
Min Size of Investment Considered (000s): $5,000
Max Size of Investment Considered: No Limit

Geographical Preferences

United States
All U.S.

International
All International

Industry Preferences

(% based on actual investment)

Communications and Media	28.7%
Computer Software and Services	20.6%
Medical/Health	18.8%
Internet Specific	17.7%
Biotechnology	7.0%
Other Products	6.2%
Consumer Related	0.6%
Semiconductors/Other Elect.	0.4%

Additional Information
Name of Most Recent Fund: China Investment and Development Fund Limited, The
Most Recent Fund Was Raised: 10/01/1992
Year Founded: 1997
Capital Under Management: $200,000,000
Current Activity Level : Actively seeking new investments
Method of Compensation: Return on invest. most important, but chg. closing fees, service fees, etc.

EARLYBIRDCAPITAL.COM INC.

One State Street Plaza
New York, NY 10004
Phone: 212-792-8100
Fax: 212-269-3787
E-mail: info@earlybirdcapital.com
Website: www.EarlyBirdCapital.com

Management and Staff
Peter Kent, President

Type of Firm
Incubators

Project Preferences

Role in Financing:
Prefer role as deal originator

Type of Financing Preferred:
Early Stage

Industry Preferences

Communications and Media
Telecommunications

Internet Specific
Internet

Medical/Health
Medical/Health

Business Serv.
Media

Additional Information
Current Activity Level : Actively seeking new investments

EAST RIVER VENTURES, L.P.

645 Madison Avenue
22nd Floor
New York, NY 10022
Phone: 212-644-2322
Fax: 212-644-5498

Management and Staff
Montague H. Hackett

Whom to Contact
Montague H. Hackett

Type of Firm
SBIC Not elsewhere classified

Project Preferences

Role in Financing:
Prefer role as deal originator but will also invest in deals created by others

Type of Financing Preferred:
First Stage Financing
Mezzanine
Second Stage Financing

Geographical Preferences

United States
All U.S.

Canada
All Canada

International
Bermuda
France
Germany
Italy
Spain
United Kingdom

Industry Preferences
(% based on actual investment)

Internet Specific	25.7%
Computer Software and Services	20.2%
Medical/Health	19.8%
Biotechnology	9.4%
Computer Hardware	9.0%
Communications and Media	7.9%
Other Products	6.4%
Semiconductors/Other Elect.	1.6%

Additional Information
Name of Most Recent Fund: EVR II
Most Recent Fund Was Raised: 08/01/1999
Year Founded: 1997
Capital Under Management: $42,000,000
Current Activity Level : Actively seeking new investments
Method of Compensation: Return on investment is of primary concern, do not charge fees

EASTON HUNT CAPITAL PARTNERS

641 Lexington Avenue
21st Floor
New York, NY 10022
Phone: 212-702-0950
Fax: 212-702-0952
Website: www.eastoncapital.com

Management and Staff
Ed Meyer, Vice President
Francisco Garcia, Managing Director
John Friedman, Managing Director
Livio Borghese, Managing Director
Mark Chen, Principal
Richard Schneider, Managing Director

Whom to Contact
Easton Capital

Type of Firm
Private Firm Investing Own Capital

Industry Association Membership
Natl assoc of Small Bus. Inv. Co (NASBIC)

Project Preferences
Role in Financing:
Prefer role as deal originator but will also invest in deals created by others

Type of Financing Preferred:
First Stage Financing
Mezzanine
Special Situation

Geographical Preferences
United States
All U.S.

Industry Preferences
Communications and Media
Communications and Media

Internet Specific
Internet

Computer Other
Computer Related

Semiconductors/Other Elect.
Electronic Components

Medical/Health
Medical/Health
Medical Diagnostics
Medical Therapeutics

Consumer Related
Consumer
Education Related

Business Serv.
Distribution

Manufact.
Publishing

Additional Information
Current Activity Level : Actively seeking new investments
Method of Compensation: Return on invest. most important, but chg. closing fees, service fees, etc.

EDGE CAPITAL INVESTMENT CO., LLC

67 Wall Street
22nd Floor
New York, NY 10005
Phone: 212-944-2266
Fax: 212-944-7771
E-mail:info@EdgeCapital.net
E-mail:JohnY@EdgeCapital.net
Wesbite: www.EdgeCapital.net

See California for full listing.

ELDON CAPITAL, INC

200 Park Avenue
New York, NY 10166
Phone: 212-490-3385

Management and Staff
Terry Temescu, Managing Director

Type of Firm
Private Firm Investing Own Capital

Additional Information
Capital Under Management: $69,400,000
Current Activity Level : Actively seeking new investments

ELECTRA FLEMING LIMITED

320 Park Avenue
28th Floor
New York, NY 10022
Phone: 212-319-0081
Fax: 212-319-3069

Other Offices

320 Park Avenue
28th Floor
New York, NY 10022
Phone: 212-319-0081
Fax: 212-319-3069

Management and Staff
Carl C. Cordova
Scott D. Steele

Whom to Contact
Carl C. Cordova
Scott D. Steele

Type of Firm
Private Firm Investing Own Capital

Project Preferences
Role in Financing:
Prefer role as deal originator but will also invest in deals created by others

Type of Financing Preferred:
Industry Rollups
Leveraged Buyout
Mezzanine
Special Situation

Size of Investments Considered
Min Size of Investment Considered (000s): $15,000
Max Size of Investment Considered: No Limit

Geographical Preferences
United States
All U.S.

Canada
All Canada

International
China
India
South Africa

Industry Preferences
Communications and Media
Communications and Media
Other Communication Prod.

Medical/Health
Medical/Health
Medical Products

Consumer Related
Consumer
Food/Beverage
Consumer Products
Education Related

Industrial/Energy
Industrial Products

Transportation
Transportation

Financial Services
Financial Services

Business Serv.
Consulting Services

Manufact.
Publishing

Additional Information
Name of Most Recent Fund: Patagonia Fund, L.P.
Most Recent Fund Was Raised: 01/01/1997
Year Founded: 1988
Capital Under Management: $350,000,000
Current Activity Level : Actively seeking new investments
Method of Compensation: Return on invest. most important, but chg. closing fees, service fees, etc.

ELK ASSOCIATES FUNDING CORP.

747 Third Avenue
Suite 4C
New York, NY 10017
Phone: 212-355-2449
Fax: 212-759-3338

Management and Staff
Gary Granoff, President

Whom to Contact
Gary Granoff

Type of Firm
SBIC Not elsewhere classified

Industry Association Membership
Natl Assoc of Investment Cos. (NAIC)
Natl assoc of Small Bus. Inv. Co (NASBIC)

Project Preferences
Role in Financing:
Prefer role as deal originator but will also invest in deals created by others

Type of Financing Preferred:
Leveraged Buyout
Second Stage Financing

Size of Investments Considered
Min Size of Investment Considered (000s): $100
Max Size of Investment Considered (000s): $300

Geographical Preferences
United States
Midwest
Southeast

Industry Preferences
Communications and Media
Radio & TV Broadcasting

Consumer Related
Franchises(NEC)
Hotels and Resorts

Transportation
Transportation

Additional Information
Year Founded: 1979
Capital Under Management: $45,000,000
Current Activity Level : Actively seeking new investments
Method of Compensation: Return on invest. most important, but chg. closing fees, service fees, etc.

ENTERPRISE INVESTORS

375 Park Avenue
Suite 1902
New York, NY 10152
Phone: 212-339-8330
Fax: 212-339-8359
Website: www.ei.com.pl

Other Offices

Atrium Tower
Al. Jana Pawla II 25
Warsaw, Poland 00-854
Phone: 22 653-4500
Fax: 22 653-4555

ul. Nowy Swiat 6/12
00-400 Warsaw, Poland
Phone: 48-2-625-1921
Fax: 48-2-625-7933

Management and Staff
Dariusz Pronczuk, Vice President
Robert Faris, President
Robert Manz, Vice President

Whom to Contact
Robert Manz

Type of Firm
Private Firm Investing Own Capital

Project Preferences
Role in Financing:
Prefer role as deal originator but will also invest in deals created by others

Type of Financing Preferred:
First Stage Financing
Leveraged Buyout
Mezzanine
Second Stage Financing
Special Situation

Geographical Preferences
International
Eastern Europe
Poland
Romania

Industry Preferences
Communications and Media
Communications and Media

Computer Hardware
Integrated Turnkey System

Computer Software
Computer Services
Systems Software
Applications Software

Internet Specific
Internet

Semiconductors/Other Elect.
Electronic Components
Sensors
Component Testing Equipmt
Analytic/Scientific

Biotechnology
Industrial Biotechnology

Medical/Health
Medical/Health
Medical Diagnostics
Medical Therapeutics

Consumer Related
Entertainment and Leisure
Retail
Computer Stores
Franchises(NEC)
Food/Beverage
Consumer Products
Consumer Services
Education Related

Industrial/Energy
Energy Conservation Relat
Materials
Factory Automation
Machinery
Environmental Related

Transportation
Transportation

Financial Services
Financial Services

Business Serv.
Distribution
Media

Manufact.
Office Automation Equipmt
Publishing

Agr/Forestr/Fish
Agriculture related
Mining and Minerals

Additional Information
Name of Most Recent Fund: Polish Enterprise Fund
Most Recent Fund Was Raised: 04/01/1997
Year Founded: 1990
Capital Under Management: $505,000,000
Current Activity Level : Actively seeking new investments
Method of Compensation: Return on investment is of primary concern, do not charge fees

EOS PARTNERS, L.P.

320 Park Avenue
22nd Floor
New York, NY 10022
Phone: 212-832-5800
Fax: 212-832-5815
Website: www.eospartners.com

Management and Staff
Beth Berstein, Chief Financial Officer
David Lee, Principal
Doug Korn, Managing Director
Mark First, Managing Director

Whom to Contact
Douglas R. Korn
Mark First

Type of Firm
Private Firm Investing Own Capital

Project Preferences

Role in Financing:
Prefer role as deal originator but will also invest in deals created by others

Type of Financing Preferred:
Industry Rollups
Leveraged Buyout
Mezzanine
Second Stage Financing
Special Situation

Size of Investments Considered
Min Size of Investment Considered (000s): $3,000
Max Size of Investment Considered: No Limit

Geographical Preferences

United States
All U.S.

Canada
All Canada

International
South Africa

Industry Preferences
(% based on actual investment)

Consumer Related	24.0%
Semiconductors/Other Elect.	18.9%
Computer Software and Services	17.0%
Medical/Health	16.5%
Communications and Media	13.7%
Other Products	6.3%
Industrial/Energy	3.6%

Additional Information
Name of Most Recent Fund: Eos Partners SBIC
Most Recent Fund Was Raised: 01/01/1994
Year Founded: 1994
Capital Under Management: $300,000,000
Current Activity Level : Making few, if any, new investments
Method of Compensation: Return on investment is of primary concern, do not charge fees

ETF GROUP

230 Park Avenue
Suite 814
New York, NY 10169
Phone: 1-212-983-7003
Fax: 1-212-983-7002
Website: www.etfgroup.com

See Foreign Venture Capital Firms for full listing.

EUCLIDSR PARTNERS

45 Rockefeller Plaza
Suite 3240
New York, NY 10111
Phone: 212-218-6880
Fax: 212-218-6877
Website: www.euclidsr.com

Other Offices

200 Barr Harbor Drive, Suite 250
Four Tower Bridge
Conshohocken, PA 19428-2977
Phone: 610-567-1000
Fax: 610-567-1039

Management and Staff
Barbara Dalton, General Partner
Bliss McCrum, Partner
Elaine Jones, General Partner
Graham Anderson, Partner
John Braca, General Partner
Milton Pappas, Partner
Raymond Whitaker, General Partner
Stephen Reidy, Partner

Type of Firm
Private Firm Investing Own Capital

Project Preferences

Role in Financing:
Prefer role as deal originator but will also invest in deals created by others

Type of Financing Preferred:
Balanced
First Stage Financing
Second Stage Financing
Start-up Financing

Geographical Preferences

International
No Preference

Industry Preferences

(% based on actual investment)

Computer Software and Services	31.6%
Internet Specific	30.3%
Medical/Health	15.4%
Biotechnology	8.0%
Computer Hardware	5.5%
Industrial/Energy	4.3%
Communications and Media	2.4%
Semiconductors/Other Elect.	1.2%
Other Products	1.0%
Consumer Related	0.2%

Additional Information
Name of Most Recent Fund: Euclid Partners V, L.P.
Most Recent Fund Was Raised: 09/11/1998
Year Founded: 1970
Capital Under Management: $25,300,000
Current Activity Level : Actively seeking new investments
Method of Compensation: Return on investment is of primary concern, do not charge fees

EVERGER ASSOCIATES

E.M. Warburg, Pincus & Co., LLC
466 Lexington Avenue
New York, NY 10017-3147
Phone: 212 878 0794
Website: www.everger.co.uk

See Foreign Venture Capital Firms for full listing.

EVERGREEN CAPITAL PARTNERS INC

150 East 58th St.
New York, NY 10155
Phone: 212-813-0758
Fax: 212-813-0754

Management and Staff
Richard Smith, President

Whom to Contact
Richard Smith

Type of Firm
Placement Agent

Project Preferences

Role in Financing:
Prefer role as deal originator but will also invest in deals created by others

Type of Financing Preferred:
Acquisition
Balanced
First Stage Financing
Generalist PE
Later Stage
Leveraged Buyout
Management Buyouts
Private Placement
Recapitalizations
Second Stage Financing
Special Situation
Turnaround

Size of Investments Considered
Min Size of Investment Considered (000s): $1,000
Max Size of Investment Considered (000s): $300,000

Geographical Preferences

United States
All U.S.

Canada
All Canada
Ontario

Industry Preferences

Communications and Media
Communications and Media

Computer Other
Computer Related

Semiconductors/Other Elect.
Laser Related
Analytic/Scientific

Biotechnology
Biotechnology

Medical/Health
Medical/Health

Consumer Related
Consumer
Education Related

Industrial/Energy
Alternative Energy
Energy Conservation Relat
Industrial Products

Transportation
Transportation

Financial Services
Financial Services

Business Serv.
Distribution

Manufact.
Publishing

Additional Information
Year Founded: 1993
Current Activity Level : Actively seeking new investments
Method of Compensation: Professional fee required whether or not deal closes

EXETER CAPITAL, L.P.

10 East 53rd Street
32nd Floor
New York, NY 10022
Phone: 212-872-1172
Fax: 212-872-1198

Management and Staff
Keith Fox, General Partner
Robin Patterson, Chief Financial Officer

Whom to Contact
Karen J. Watai

Type of Firm
Private Firm Investing Own Capital

Industry Association Membership
Natl assoc of Small Bus. Inv. Co (NASBIC)

Project Preferences

Role in Financing:
Prefer role as deal originator but will also invest in deals created by others

Type of Financing Preferred:
Leveraged Buyout
Mezzanine
Second Stage Financing
Special Situation

Size of Investments Considered
Min Size of Investment Considered (000s): $1,000
Max Size of Investment Considered: No Limit

Geographical Preferences

United States
All U.S.

Industry Preferences

(% based on actual investment)

Consumer Related	25.8%
Other Products	23.8%
Computer Software and Services	16.2%
Internet Specific	15.3%
Computer Hardware	8.1%
Medical/Health	7.2%
Communications and Media	3.7%

Additional Information
Name of Most Recent Fund: Exeter Venture Lenders
Most Recent Fund Was Raised: 01/01/1994
Year Founded: 1986
Capital Under Management: $135,000,000
Current Activity Level : Actively seeking new investments
Method of Compensation: Other

EXPONENTIAL BUSINESS DEVELOPMENT CO.

216 Walton Street
Syracuse, NY 13202-1227
Phone: 315-474-4500
Fax: 315-474-4682
Website: www.exponential-ny.com

Management and Staff
Dirk Sonneborn, Managing Partner

Type of Firm
Private Firm Investing Own Capital

Project Preferences

Role in Financing:
Prefer role as deal originator

Type of Financing Preferred:
Early Stage
First Stage Financing

Size of Investments Considered
Min Size of Investment Considered (000s): $100
Max Size of Investment Considered (000s): $600

Geographical Preferences

United States
New York

Additional Information
Year Founded: 1993
Capital Under Management: $10,000,000
Current Activity Level : Actively seeking new investments
Method of Compensation: Return on invest. most important, but chg. closing fees, service fees, etc.

FINANCIAL TECHNOLOGY RESEARCH CORP.

518 Broadway
Penthouse
New York, NY 10012
Phone: 212-625-9100
Fax: 212-431-0300

Other Offices

21724 Ventura Boulevard
Suite 204
Woodland Hills, CA 91364
Phone: 818-710-8600
Fax: 818-999-0533

Management and Staff
Neal Bruckman
Simon Weinberger

Whom to Contact
Neal Bruckman
Simon Weinberger

Type of Firm
Investment/Merchant Bank Investing Own or Client Funds

Project Preferences

Role in Financing:
Prefer role as deal originator but will also invest in deals created by others

Type of Financing Preferred:
First Stage Financing
Research and Development
Second Stage Financing
Seed
Special Situation
Start-up Financing

Size of Investments Considered
Min Size of Investment Considered (000s): $300
Max Size of Investment Considered (000s): $500

Geographical Preferences

United States
All U.S.

Canada
All Canada

International
Afghanistan
Australia
Bermuda
China
France
Germany
Italy
Japan
Middle East
South Africa
Spain
United Kingdom

Industry Preferences

Communications and Media
Communications and Media

Computer Other
Computer Related

Semiconductors/Other Elect.
Electronic Components

Biotechnology
Biotechnology

Medical/Health
Medical/Health

Consumer Related
Entertainment and Leisure
Retail
Computer Stores
Franchises(NEC)
Food/Beverage
Consumer Products
Consumer Services
Other Restaurants
Education Related

Industrial/Energy
Energy
Industrial Products

Transportation
Transportation

Financial Services
Financial Services

Business Serv.
Distribution
Consulting Services

Manufact.
Publishing

Agr/Forestr/Fish
Agriculture related

Additional Information
Year Founded: 1983
Current Activity Level : Inactive / Unknown
Method of Compensation: Return on investment is of primary concern, do not charge fees

---

FIRST ATLANTIC CAPITAL, LTD.

135 East 57th Street
29th Floor
New York, NY 10022
Phone: 212-207-0300
Fax: 212-750-0954

Management and Staff
Joseph Haviv, Managing Director
Mahesh Saladi, Chief Financial Officer

Whom to Contact
Joseph S. Levy

Type of Firm
Investment/Merchant Bank Investing Own or Client Funds

Project Preferences

Type of Financing Preferred:
Leveraged Buyout
Special Situation

Geographical Preferences

United States
All U.S.

Industry Preferences

Consumer Related
Food/Beverage
Consumer Products

Industrial/Energy
Industrial Products
Materials

Business Serv.
Services

Additional Information
Name of Most Recent Fund: Atlantic Equity Partners III LP
Most Recent Fund Was Raised: 10/14/1999
Year Founded: 1989
Capital Under Management: $435,000,000
Current Activity Level : Inactive / Unknown

FLATIRON PARTNERS

257 Park Avenue South
15th Floor
New York, NY 10010
Phone: 212-228-3800
Fax: 212-228-0552
Website: www.flatironpartners.com

Management and Staff
Dan Malvern, Principal
Fred Wilson, Managing Partner
I. Robert Greene, Managing Partner
Jerry Colonna, Managing Partner
Michael Connor, Chief Financial Officer
Philip Summe, Principal
Seth Goldstein, Principal

Type of Firm
Private Firm Investing Own Capital

Industry Association Membership
National Venture Capital Association (NVCA)

Project Preferences

Type of Financing Preferred:
Early Stage

Geographical Preferences

United States
New York
Northeast

Industry Preferences

(% based on actual investment)

Internet Specific	82.4%
Computer Software and Services	7.9%
Communications and Media	3.9%
Other Products	3.5%
Consumer Related	2.3%

Additional Information
Name of Most Recent Fund: Flatiron Fund, LLC
Most Recent Fund Was Raised: 08/26/1996
Year Founded: 1996
Capital Under Management: $757,300,000
Current Activity Level : Actively seeking new investments

FOUNDERS EQUITY, INC.

711 Fifth Avenue
14th Floor
New York, NY 10022
Phone: 212-829-0900
Fax: 212-223-2490

Management and Staff
John Teeger

Whom to Contact
John Teeger

Type of Firm
Investment/Merchant Bank Investing Own or Client Funds

Project Preferences

Role in Financing:
Prefer role as deal originator

Type of Financing Preferred:
Leveraged Buyout
Special Situation

Size of Investments Considered
Min Size of Investment Considered (000s): $2,000
Max Size of Investment Considered: No Limit

Geographical Preferences

United States
All U.S.

Industry Preferences

Medical/Health
Medical Products

Consumer Related
Entertainment and Leisure
Retail
Franchises(NEC)
Consumer Products
Other Restaurants

Industrial/Energy
Industrial Products
Factory Automation
Machinery

Financial Services
Real Estate

Manufact.
Publishing

Additional Information
Year Founded: 1969
Current Activity Level : Actively seeking new investments
Method of Compensation: Return on invest. most important, but chg. closing fees, service fees, etc.

FRONTLINE CAPITAL GROUP, INC.

1350 Avenue of the Americas
32nd Floor
New York, NY 10019
Phone: 212-931-8024
Website: www.frontlinecapital.com

Management and Staff
Erik Froelich, Vice President
Matthew Esh, Vice President
Robert Vialardi, Vice President
Sasha Grutman, Vice President
Timothy Hall, Vice President
Timothy Lemmon, Vice President

Type of Firm
Incubators

Additional Information
Current Activity Level : Actively seeking new investments

FUSIENT VENTURES

99 Park Avenue
20th Floor
New York, NY 10016
Phone: 212-972-8999
Fax: 212-972-9876
E-mail: info@fusient.com
Website: www.fusient.com

Other Offices

940 N. Mansfield Ave.
Los Angeles, CA 90038
Phone: 323-461-9119
Fax: 323-461-9117

Management and Staff
Tom Lassally, President

Type of Firm
Incubators

Project Preferences

Role in Financing:
Prefer role as deal originator

Type of Financing Preferred:
Early Stage
First Stage Financing
Seed

Size of Investments Considered
Min Size of Investment Considered (000s): $500
Max Size of Investment Considered (000s): $3,000

Industry Preferences

Internet Specific
Internet

Consumer Related
Entertainment and Leisure

Business Serv.
Media

Additional Information
Current Activity Level : Actively seeking new investments

GABELLI MULTIMEDIA PARTNERS

One Corporate Center
Rye, NY 10580
Phone: 914-921-5395
Fax: 914-921-5031

Management and Staff
Robert Zuccaro, Chief Financial Officer

Type of Firm
Private Firm Investing Own Capital

Project Preferences

Role in Financing:
Prefer role as deal originator but will also invest in deals created by others

Type of Financing Preferred:
First Stage Financing
Second Stage Financing
Seed
Start-up Financing

Geographical Preferences

United States
Northeast

Industry Preferences

Communications and Media
Commercial Communications
CATV & Pay TV Systems
Radio & TV Broadcasting
Telecommunications
Satellite Microwave Comm.

Additional Information
Current Activity Level : Inactive / Unknown

GABELLI SECURITIES INC.

One Corporate Center
Rye, NY 10580
Phone: 914-921-5100

Management and Staff
Gus Coutsouros, Chief Financial Officer

Type of Firm
Private Firm Investing Own Capital

Additional Information
Current Activity Level : Actively seeking new investments

GALEN ASSOCIATES (FKA:GALEN PARTNERS)

610 Fifth Avenue
Fifth Fl Rockefeller Center
New York, NY 10020
Phone: 212-218-4990
Fax: 212-218-4999

Management and Staff
David Jahns
Zubeen Shroff

Whom to Contact
David Jahns
Zubeen Shroff

Type of Firm
Private Firm Investing Own Capital

Project Preferences

Role in Financing:
Prefer role as deal originator but will also invest in deals created by others

Type of Financing Preferred:
Second Stage Financing

Size of Investments Considered
Min Size of Investment Considered (000s): $20,000
Max Size of Investment Considered: No Limit

Geographical Preferences

United States
All U.S.

Industry Preferences

(% based on actual investment)

Medical/Health	46.9%
Internet Specific	16.6%
Computer Software and Services	15.9%
Communications and Media	10.5%
Computer Hardware	5.2%
Consumer Related	3.6%
Other Products	1.3%

Additional Information
Name of Most Recent Fund: Galen Partners III
Most Recent Fund Was Raised: 01/01/1997
Year Founded: 1990
Capital Under Management: $397,000,000
Current Activity Level : Actively seeking new investments
Method of Compensation: Return on investment is of primary concern, do not charge fees

GENERATION CAPITAL PARTNERS

551 Fifth Avenue
Suite 3100
New York, NY 10176
Phone: 212-450-8507
Fax: 212-450-8550
Website: www.genpartners.com

Other Offices

600 Montgomery Street
Suite 3900
San Francisco, CA 94111
Phone: 415-646-8620
Fax: 415-646-8625

Management and Staff
Erich Vaden, Vice President
John Hawkins, Managing Partner
Lloyd Mandell, Partner
Mark Jennings, Managing Partner
Robert Pflieger, Partner

Type of Firm
Private Firm Investing Own Capital

Industry Association Membership
Western Association of Venture Capitalists (WAVC)

Project Preferences

Role in Financing:
Prefer role as deal originator but will also invest in deals created by others

Type of Financing Preferred:
First Stage Financing
Leveraged Buyout
Second Stage Financing
Start-up Financing

Size of Investments Considered
Min Size of Investment Considered (000s): $5,000
Max Size of Investment Considered: No Limit

Geographical Preferences

United States
All U.S.

Canada
All Canada

Industry Preferences

(% based on actual investment)

Internet Specific	47.0%
Computer Software and Services	23.4%
Communications and Media	17.5%
Consumer Related	12.0%

Additional Information
Name of Most Recent Fund: Generation Capital Partners, L.P.
Most Recent Fund Was Raised: 09/15/1996
Year Founded: 1995
Capital Under Management: $165,000,000
Current Activity Level : Actively seeking new investments
Method of Compensation: Return on invest. most important, but chg. closing fees, service fees, etc.

GENESEE FUNDING, INC.

70 Linden Oaks
Third Floor
Rochester, NY 14625
Phone: 716-383-5550
Fax: 716-383-5305

Other Offices

70 Linden Oaks
Third Floor
Rochester, NY 14625
Phone: 716-383-5550

Type of Firm
Private Firm Investing Own Capital

Industry Association Membership
Natl assoc of Small Bus. Inv. Co (NASBIC)

Project Preferences

Role in Financing:
Prefer role as deal originator but will also invest in deals created by others

Type of Financing Preferred:
Leveraged Buyout
Mezzanine
Second Stage Financing

Size of Investments Considered
Min Size of Investment Considered (000s): $200
Max Size of Investment Considered: No Limit

Geographical Preferences

United States
Northeast

Industry Preferences

Communications and Media
Commercial Communications
CATV & Pay TV Systems
Telecommunications
Data Communications

Computer Hardware
Computer Graphics and Dig

Semiconductors/Other Elect.
Laser Related
Analytic/Scientific

Medical/Health
Diagnostic Services
Diagnostic Test Products
Drug/Equipmt Delivery
Other Therapeutic
Disposable Med. Products

Consumer Related
Entertainment and Leisure
Food/Beverage
Consumer Products
Consumer Services

Industrial/Energy
Materials
Factory Automation
Robotics
Machinery
Environmental Related

Business Serv.
Distribution

Manufact.
Office Automation Equipmt
Publishing

Additional Information
Year Founded: 1986
Capital Under Management: $1,600,000
Current Activity Level : Actively seeking new investments
Method of Compensation: Return on invest. most important, but chg. closing fees, service fees, etc.

GENESIS CAPITAL, INC.

230 Park Avenue
Suite 903
New York, NY 10169
Phone: 212-682-3603
Fax: 212-682-4025

Other Offices
230 Park Avenue
Suite 903
New York, NY 10169
Phone: 212-682-3603
Fax: 212-682-4025

Type of Firm
Investment/Merchant Bank Investing Own or Client Funds

Project Preferences

Role in Financing:
Prefer role as deal originator but will also invest in deals created by others

Type of Financing Preferred:
Leveraged Buyout
Second Stage Financing
Special Situation

Size of Investments Considered
Min Size of Investment Considered (000s): $10,000
Max Size of Investment Considered: No Limit

Geographical Preferences

International
No Preference

Industry Preferences

Communications and Media
Commercial Communications
CATV & Pay TV Systems
Radio & TV Broadcasting
Telecommunications
Data Communications

Computer Hardware
Computer Graphics and Dig
Integrated Turnkey System

Computer Software
Computer Services
Systems Software
Applications Software
Artificial Intelligence

Semiconductors/Other Elect.
Electronic Components
Semiconductor
Component Testing Equipmt
Laser Related
Fiber Optics
Analytic/Scientific

Biotechnology
Biotech Related Research
Biotech Related Research

Medical/Health
Medical/Health
Medical Diagnostics
Medical Therapeutics

Consumer Related
Retail
Food/Beverage
Consumer Products
Education Related

Industrial/Energy
Alternative Energy
Environmental Related

Financial Services
Real Estate

Business Serv.
Consulting Services

Manufact.
Office Automation Equipmt
Publishing

Agr/Forestr/Fish
Agriculture related

Additional Information
Name of Most Recent Fund: Genesis Capital
Most Recent Fund Was Raised: 05/01/1982
Year Founded: 1991
Current Activity Level : Actively seeking new investments
Method of Compensation: Return on invest. most important, but chg. closing fees, service fees, etc.

GENESYS PARTNERS

310 West 86 Street
New York, NY 10024
Phone: 212-388-0397
Fax: 212-873-2146
Website: www.genesyspartners.com

Management and Staff
Daniel Summa, Partner
James Kollegger, Chief Executive Officer
Paul Sagan, Partner

Type of Firm
Private Firm Investing Own Capital

Project Preferences

Type of Financing Preferred:
Early Stage

Geographical Preferences

United States
All U.S.

Industry Preferences

Internet Specific
Internet

Additional Information

Capital Under Management: $40,000,000
Current Activity Level : Actively seeking new investments

GKM VENTURE PARTNERS, LP

529 Fifth Avenue
New York, NY 10017
Phone: 212-885-4000
Fax: 888-309-1371
Website: www.gkm.com

See California for full listing.

GLEACHER & CO.

660 Madison Avenue
19th Floor
New York, NY 10021
Phone: 212-418-4516
Fax: 212-752-3201
Website: www.gleacher.com

Management and Staff

Alton F Irby, Partner
Charles Phillips, President
David Mills, Managing Director
Emil Henry, Managing Director
Eric Gleacher, Chairman & CEO
Jeffrey Tepper, Managing Director
John Craven, Partner
Robert A. Engel, Managing Director

Type of Firm

Private Firm Investing Own Capital

Project Preferences

Type of Financing Preferred:
Balanced

Geographical Preferences

United States
All U.S.

Industry Preferences

(% based on actual investment)

Other Products	56.7%
Internet Specific	17.3%
Consumer Related	15.1%
Communications and Media	6.5%
Computer Hardware	2.2%
Semiconductors/Other Elect.	2.2%

Additional Information

Year Founded: 1990
Current Activity Level : Actively seeking new investments

GLENCOE CAPITAL, LLC (FKA: GLENCOE INVESTMENT CORPORATION)

488 Madison Avenue
Suite 1503
New York, NY 10022
Phone: 212-755-2302
Fax: 212-755-2717

See Illinois for full listing.

GMS CAPITAL

405 Park Avenue
16th Floor
New York, NY 10022
Phone: 212-832-4013

Management and Staff

Joachim Gfoeller, Partner

Type of Firm

Private Firm Investing Own Capital

Project Preferences

Type of Financing Preferred:
Early Stage

Industry Preferences

Internet Specific
Internet

Additional Information

Current Activity Level : Actively seeking new investments

GOLUB ASSOCIATES

555 Madison Avenue
New York, NY 10022
Phone: 212-750-6060
Fax: 212-750-5505

Management and Staff

Evelyn Mordechai, Vice President
Greg Cashman, Vice President
Lawrence Golub, President

Type of Firm

Private Firm Investing Own Capital

Project Preferences

Role in Financing:
Prefer role as deal originator but will also invest in deals created by others

Type of Financing Preferred:
Leveraged Buyout
Mezzanine
Recapitalizations
Second Stage Financing
Special Situation

Size of Investments Considered

Min Size of Investment Considered (000s): $1,000
Max Size of Investment Considered (000s): $10,000

Geographical Preferences

United States
Mid Atlantic
Northeast
Southeast

Industry Preferences

Communications and Media
Commercial Communications
CATV & Pay TV Systems
Radio & TV Broadcasting
Telecommunications
Data Communications

Semiconductors/Other Elect.
Electronic Components
Controllers and Sensors
Sensors
Circuit Boards
Component Testing Equipmt
Analytic/Scientific

Medical/Health
Diagnostic Services
Diagnostic Test Products
Drug/Equipmt Delivery
Other Therapeutic
Disposable Med. Products
Hospitals/Clinics/Primary
Hospital/Other Instit.

Consumer Related
Entertainment and Leisure
Retail
Computer Stores
Franchises(NEC)
Food/Beverage
Consumer Products
Consumer Services
Other Restaurants
Education Related

Industrial/Energy
Materials
Factory Automation
Machinery
Environmental Related

Business Serv.
Distribution

Manufact.
Publishing

Additional Information
Name of Most Recent Fund: LEG Partners III, L.P.
Most Recent Fund Was Raised: 01/01/1999
Year Founded: 1994
Capital Under Management: $313,000,000
Current Activity Level : Actively seeking new investments
Method of Compensation: Return on investment is of primary concern, do not charge fees

GRAND CENTRAL HOLDINGS

250 Lafayette Street
Fourth Floor
New York, NY 10012
Phone: 212-625-9710
Fax: 212-625-9711

Management and Staff
Gregory Belmont, Chief Financial Officer

Type of Firm
Private Firm Investing Own Capital

Additional Information
Current Activity Level : Actively seeking new investments

GRAYSON & ASSOCIATES

16 East 53rd Street
Seventh Floor
New York, NY 10022
Phone: 212-371-8303
Fax: 212-486-3590

See Colorado for full listing.

HAMBRO AMERICA BIOSCIENCES, INC.

650 Madison Avenue
21st Floor
New York, NY 10022
Phone: 212-223-7400
Fax: 212-223-0305

Type of Firm
Private Firm Investing Own Capital

Project Preferences

Role in Financing:
Prefer role as deal originator but will also invest in deals created by others

Type of Financing Preferred:
First Stage Financing
Second Stage Financing
Special Situation

Geographical Preferences

United States
All U.S.

Industry Preferences

Biotechnology
Biosensors
Biotech Related Research
Biotech Related Research

Medical/Health
Diagnostic Services
Medical Therapeutics
Drug/Equipmt Delivery
Pharmaceuticals

Industrial/Energy
Materials

Additional Information
Year Founded: 1982
Capital Under Management: $150,000,000
Current Activity Level : Actively seeking new investments
Method of Compensation: Return on investment is of primary concern, do not charge fees

HAMBROS BANK

650 Madison Avenue
New York, NY 10022
Phone: 212-288-7778

Type of Firm
Investment/Merchant Bank Investing Own or Client Funds

Additional Information
Name of Most Recent Fund: Hambros Bank
Most Recent Fund Was Raised: 01/01/1977
Capital Under Management: $400,000,000
Current Activity Level : Inactive / Unknown

HANOVER CAPITAL CORP.

505 Park Avenue
15th Floor
New York, NY 10022
Phone: 212-755-1222
Fax: 212-935-1787

Other Offices

505 Park Avenue
New York, NY 10022
Phone: 212-838-5893

Management and Staff
Michael Wainstein

Whom to Contact
Michael Wainstein

Type of Firm
Investment/Merchant Bank Investing Own or Client Funds

Project Preferences

Role in Financing:
Prefer role as deal originator

Type of Financing Preferred:
Leveraged Buyout
Mezzanine
Second Stage Financing

Size of Investments Considered
Min Size of Investment Considered (000s): $500
Max Size of Investment Considered: No Limit

Geographical Preferences
United States
All U.S.

Industry Preferences
Communications and Media
Telecommunications
Data Communications

Computer Hardware
Integrated Turnkey System

Computer Software
Applications Software

Medical/Health
Diagnostic Services
Hospitals/Clinics/Primary

Industrial/Energy
Machinery
Environmental Related

Transportation
Transportation

Financial Services
Financial Services

Business Serv.
Distribution

Manufact.
Office Automation Equipmt

Additional Information
Name of Most Recent Fund: Hanover Capital Corporation
Most Recent Fund Was Raised: 09/01/1981
Year Founded: 1983
Capital Under Management: $5,000,000
Current Activity Level : Inactive / Unknown
Method of Compensation: Return on invest. most important, but chg. closing fees, service fees, etc.

HARVEST PARTNERS, INC.

280 Park Avenue
33rd Floor
New York, NY 10017
Phone: 212-599-6300
Fax: 212-812-0100
Website: www.harvpart.com

Management and Staff
Harvey Mallement, General Partner
Harvey Wertheim, General Partner
Ira Kleinman, General Partner
Robert Jackowitz, Chief Financial Officer
Stephen Eisenstein, General Partner
Tom Arenz, General Partner
William Kane, General Partner

Whom to Contact
Harvey Mallement
Ira Kleinman
William Kane

Type of Firm
Investment/Merchant Bank Subsid/Affil

Industry Association Membership
Natl assoc of Small Bus. Inv. Co (NASBIC)

Project Preferences
Role in Financing:
Will function either as deal originator or investor in deals created by others

Type of Financing Preferred:
Acquisition
Leveraged Buyout
Management Buyouts
Private Placement
Special Situation
Turnaround

Size of Investments Considered
Min Size of Investment Considered (000s): $15,000
Max Size of Investment Considered (000s): $100,000

Geographical Preferences
United States
All U.S.

Canada
All Canada

International
Belgium
France
Germany
Italy
Luxembourg
Netherlands
Portugal
Spain
United Kingdom

Industry Preferences
(% based on actual investment)

Other Products	65.3%
Communications and Media	19.5%
Industrial/Energy	9.8%
Consumer Related	5.3%

Additional Information
Name of Most Recent Fund: Harvest Partners III, L.P.
Most Recent Fund Was Raised: 11/23/1997
Year Founded: 1976
Capital Under Management: $600,000,000
Current Activity Level : Actively seeking new investments
Method of Compensation: Return on invest. most important, but chg. closing fees, service fees, etc.

HERBERT YOUNG SECURITIES, INC.

98 Cuttermill Road
Great Neck, NY 11021
Phone: 516-487-8300
Fax: 516-487-8319

Management and Staff
Herbert Levine

Whom to Contact
Herbert Levine

Type of Firm
Mgt. Consulting Firm

Project Preferences
Role in Financing:
Prefer role as deal originator but will also invest in deals created by others

Type of Financing Preferred:
First Stage Financing
Leveraged Buyout
Mezzanine
Second Stage Financing
Special Situation

Size of Investments Considered
Min Size of Investment Considered (000s): $1,000
Max Size of Investment Considered: No Limit

Geographical Preferences
International
No Preference

Industry Preferences

Communications and Media
Commercial Communications
Radio & TV Broadcasting
Telecommunications
Data Communications
Satellite Microwave Comm.

Computer Hardware
Computer Graphics and Dig
Integrated Turnkey System
Disk Relat. Memory Device

Computer Software
Computer Services
Systems Software
Applications Software
Artificial Intelligence

Internet Specific
Internet

Semiconductors/Other Elect.
Electronic Components
Semiconductor
Component Testing Equipmt
Laser Related
Fiber Optics
Analytic/Scientific

Biotechnology
Biotechnology

Medical/Health
Medical/Health

Consumer Related
Entertainment and Leisure
Franchises(NEC)
Food/Beverage
Consumer Products
Consumer Services
Other Restaurants

Industrial/Energy
Alternative Energy
Energy Conservation Relat
Industrial Products

Financial Services
Real Estate

Business Serv.
Distribution
Consulting Services

Manufact.
Office Automation Equipmt

Agr/Forestr/Fish
Mining and Minerals

Additional Information
Year Founded: 1959
Current Activity Level : Actively seeking new investments
Method of Compensation: Function primarily in service area, receive contingent fee in cash or equity

HFTP INVESTMENT LLC

750 Lexington Avenue
22nd Floor
New York, NY 10022
Phone: 212-702-5200
Fax: 212-758-9334

Management and Staff
Jamie O'Brien, Chief Financial Officer

Type of Firm
Private Firm Investing Own Capital

Additional Information
Current Activity Level : Actively seeking new investments

HOLDING CAPITAL GROUP, INC.

10 E. 53rd St.
30th Floor
New York, NY 10022
Phone: 212-486-6670
Fax: 212-486-0843

Other Offices

1301 Fifth Avenue
Suite 3410
Seattle, WA 98101

4018 Wingren Drive
Irving, TX 75062
Phone: 214-717-1920
Fax: 214-717-9113

Management and Staff
James Donaghy
Karl Dillon

Whom to Contact
James Donaghy
Karl Dillon

Type of Firm
Private Firm Investing Own Capital

Project Preferences

Role in Financing:
Prefer role as deal originator but will also invest in deals created by others

Type of Financing Preferred:
Leveraged Buyout

Size of Investments Considered
Min Size of Investment Considered (000s): $5,000
Max Size of Investment Considered: No Limit

Geographical Preferences

United States
All U.S.

International
Australia
China

Additional Information
Year Founded: 1975
Capital Under Management: $100,000,000
Current Activity Level : Actively seeking new investments
Method of Compensation: Return on invest. most important, but chg. closing fees, service fees, etc.

HOLLINGER CAPITAL (FKA: HOLLINGER VENTURES)

270 Lafayette St.
Suite 600
New York, NY 10012
Phone: 212-334-5944
Fax: 212-334-5957
Website: www.hollingercapital.com

Other Offices

2225 Sheppard Ave. East
15th Floor
Toronto, Canada M2J 5C2
Phone: 416-642-6215
Fax: 416-642-6207

Management and Staff
Doug Lamb, Partner
Matthew Doull, Partner
Michael Pilmer, Partner

Type of Firm
Non-Financial Corp. Affiliate or Subsidiary

Industry Association Membership
Canadian Venture Capital Association
National Venture Capital Association (NVCA)

Project Preferences

Role in Financing:
Will function either as deal originator or investor in deals created by others

Type of Financing Preferred:
Early Stage
Expansion
First Stage Financing
Later Stage
Second Stage Financing

Size of Investments Considered
Min Size of Investment Considered (000s): $2,000
Max Size of Investment Considered (000s): $15,000

Geographical Preferences

United States
Northeast

Canada
All Canada

International
United Kingdom

Industry Preferences

Communications and Media
Wireless Communications
Data Communications

Computer Software
Software
Applications Software

Internet Specific
E-Commerce Technology
Internet
Web Aggregration/Portals

Business Serv.
Media

Additional Information

Year Founded: 1997
Capital Under Management: $100,000,000
Current Activity Level : Actively seeking new investments
Method of Compensation: Return on investment is of primary concern, do not charge fees

HT CAPITAL ADVISORS, LLC

437 Madison Avenue
New York, NY 10022
Phone: 212-759-9080
Fax: 212-759-0299
Website: www.htcapital.com

Management and Staff

C.A. Burkhardt, Senior Managing Director
Eric Lomas, President

Type of Firm

Investment/Merchant Bank Subsid/Affil

Industry Association Membership

National Venture Capital Association (NVCA)

Project Preferences

Role in Financing:
Will function either as deal originator or investor in deals created by others

Type of Financing Preferred:
Acquisition
Control-block Purchases
Early Stage
First Stage Financing
Leveraged Buyout
Management Buyouts
Private Placement
Second Stage Financing

Geographical Preferences

United States
All U.S.

Canada
All Canada

International
France
Germany
Italy
United Kingdom

Industry Preferences

Computer Software
Software
Applications Software

Internet Specific
Internet

Semiconductors/Other Elect.
Electronic Components
Controllers and Sensors
Sensors
Fiber Optics
Analytic/Scientific

Biotechnology
Industrial Biotechnology

Medical/Health
Medical Diagnostics
Diagnostic Test Products

Consumer Related
Consumer
Food/Beverage
Education Related

Industrial/Energy
Industrial Products
Process Control
Machinery

Transportation
Transportation
Aerospace

Financial Services
Financial Services

Business Serv.
Distribution

Manufact.
Manufacturing

Agr/Forestr/Fish
Agriculture related

Additional Information

Year Founded: 1932
Current Activity Level : Actively seeking new investments
Method of Compensation: Return on invest. most important, but chg. closing fees, service fees, etc.

HUDSON VENTURE PARTNERS

660 Madison Avenue
14th Floor
New York, NY 10021
Phone: 212-644-9797
Fax: 212-644-7430
Website: www.hudsonptr.com

Management and Staff

Arnon Steinhart, Chief Financial Officer
Doug Chertok, Managing Director
Glen Lewy, Senior Managing Director
Jay Goldberg, Managing Director
Kim Groh, Senior Managing Director
Lawrence Howard, Managing Director
Marilyn Adler, Managing Director
Michael Gartenberg, Managing Director
Richard Glaser, Managing Director

Type of Firm
SBIC Not elsewhere classified

Industry Association Membership
Natl assoc of Small Bus. Inv. Co (NASBIC)

Project Preferences

Role in Financing:
Prefer role as deal originator but will also invest in deals created by others

Type of Financing Preferred:
Early Stage
Expansion
First Stage Financing
Seed
Start-up Financing

Size of Investments Considered
Min Size of Investment Considered (000s): $500
Max Size of Investment Considered (000s): $2,800

Geographical Preferences

United States
All U.S.
Mid Atlantic
Northeast

Industry Preferences

(% based on actual investment)

Computer Software and Services	37.8%
Internet Specific	25.8%
Computer Hardware	9.5%
Biotechnology	8.5%
Communications and Media	8.5%
Medical/Health	4.2%
Other Products	4.1%
Semiconductors/Other Elect.	1.7%

Additional Information
Year Founded: 1997
Capital Under Management: $170,000,000
Current Activity Level : Actively seeking new investments
Method of Compensation: Return on investment is of primary concern, do not charge fees

I-HATCH VENTURES, LLC

599 Broadway
11th Floor
New York, NY 10166
Phone: 212-651-1750
Fax: 212-208-2576
Website: www.i-hatch.com

Management and Staff
Andrew Sutton, Chief Financial Officer
Brad Farkas, Principal
Chip Austin, Principal
Derek Reisfield, Principal

Type of Firm
Private Firm Investing Own Capital

Project Preferences

Type of Financing Preferred:
Early Stage

Geographical Preferences

United States
Northeast

Industry Preferences

(% based on actual investment)

Internet Specific	93.4%
Computer Software and Services	3.9%
Computer Hardware	2.7%

Additional Information
Name of Most Recent Fund: i-Hatch Ventures, LLC
Most Recent Fund Was Raised: 01/19/2000
Year Founded: 1999
Capital Under Management: $80,000,000
Current Activity Level : Actively seeking new investments

IBJS CAPITAL CORP.

One State Street
9th Floor
New York, NY 10004
Phone: 212-858-2018
Fax: 212-858-2768

Management and Staff
George Zombek, Chief Operating Officer

Whom to Contact
George Zombek

Type of Firm
Private Firm Investing Own Capital

Industry Association Membership
Natl assoc of Small Bus. Inv. Co (NASBIC)

Project Preferences

Role in Financing:
Prefer role as deal originator but will also invest in deals created by others

Type of Financing Preferred:
Leveraged Buyout
Mezzanine
Special Situation

Size of Investments Considered
Min Size of Investment Considered (000s): $2,000
Max Size of Investment Considered: No Limit

Geographical Preferences

United States
All U.S.
Midwest
Northeast
Southwest

Industry Preferences

Semiconductors/Other Elect.
Sensors

Consumer Related
Food/Beverage
Consumer Products
Consumer Services

Industrial/Energy
Materials
Machinery

Additional Information
Year Founded: 1990
Current Activity Level : Actively seeking new investments
Method of Compensation: Return on invest. most important, but chg. closing fees, service fees, etc.

IMPACT VENTURE PARTNERS

599 Broadway
11th Floor
New York, NY 10019
Phone: 212-219-3931
Fax: 212-214-0909
Website: www.impactvp.com

Management and Staff
Adam Dell, General Partner
Jay Brichke, Chief Financial Officer
Michael Rosenfelt, Venture Partner
Rene Benedetto, General Partner

Type of Firm
Private Firm Investing Own Capital

Project Preferences

Type of Financing Preferred:
Early Stage

Size of Investments Considered
Min Size of Investment Considered (000s): $3,000
Max Size of Investment Considered (000s): $5,000

Geographical Preferences

United States
Northeast
Texas

Industry Preferences

(% based on actual investment)

Internet Specific	56.0%
Computer Hardware	17.4%
Consumer Related	17.2%
Computer Software and Services	9.4%

Additional Information
Year Founded: 1999
Capital Under Management: $100,000,000
Current Activity Level : Actively seeking new investments

IMPEX VENTURE MANAGEMENT CO.

P.O. Box 1570
Green Island, NY 12183
Phone: 518-271-8008
Fax: 518-271-9101

Other Offices

300 Ridgefield Road
Wilton, CT 06897

36 Parker Street
Cambridge, MA 02138-2244

Management and Staff
Jay Banker

Whom to Contact
Jay Banker

Type of Firm
Investment/Merchant Bank Investing Own or Client Funds

Project Preferences

Role in Financing:
Prefer role as deal originator

Type of Financing Preferred:
First Stage Financing
Leveraged Buyout
Second Stage Financing
Special Situation
Start-up Financing

Size of Investments Considered
Min Size of Investment Considered (000s): $1,000
Max Size of Investment Considered: No Limit

Geographical Preferences

United States
Mid Atlantic
Northeast

Canada
Quebec

Industry Preferences

Communications and Media
Satellite Microwave Comm.

Computer Hardware
Computer Graphics and Dig

Internet Specific
Internet

Semiconductors/Other Elect.
Laser Related
Fiber Optics

Biotechnology
Industrial Biotechnology

Consumer Related
Retail

Industrial/Energy
Alternative Energy
Energy Conservation Relat
Industrial Products
Materials
Robotics
Environmental Related

Financial Services
Financial Services

Additional Information
Year Founded: 1980
Current Activity Level : Actively seeking new investments
Method of Compensation: Return on invest. most important, but chg. closing fees, service fees, etc.

INCORPORATED INVESTORS

928 Broadway
Suite 1000
New York, NY 10010
Phone: 212-505-2507
Fax: 212-228-1398

See California for full listing.

INSIGHT CAPITAL PARTNERS LLC

527 Madison Avenue
Tenth Floor
New York, NY 10168
Phone: 212-230-9200
Fax: 212-230-9272
Website: www.insightcapital.com

Other Offices

Villa Rodestein
Mollaan la
2061 CR Bloemendaal, Netherlands
Phone: 31-23-541-1222
Fax: 31-23-541-1200

Management and Staff
Deven Parekh, Managing Director
Jeff Lieberman, Principal
Jeff Horing, Managing Director
Jerry Murdock, Managing Director
John Losier, Partner
Mike Triplett, Principal
Peter Sobiloff, Managing Director
Ramnan Raghavenvran, Partner
Roel Pieper, Managing Director
Scott Maxwell, Managing Director
Tom Cheung, Principal
William Doyle, Managing Director
William Conroy, Venture Partner

Type of Firm
Private Firm Investing Own Capital

Project Preferences

Type of Financing Preferred:
Balanced

Geographical Preferences

United States
All U.S.

International
Europe

Industry Preferences

(% based on actual investment)

Internet Specific	52.5%
Computer Software and Services	31.5%
Communications and Media	9.8%
Other Products	6.1%

Additional Information

Name of Most Recent Fund: Insight Capital Partners II, L.P.
Most Recent Fund Was Raised: 01/01/1997
Year Founded: 1995
Capital Under Management: $1,385,000,000
Current Activity Level : Actively seeking new investments

INTEREQUITY CAPITAL PARTNERS, L.P.

220 Fifth Avenue
12th Fl
New York, NY 10001
Phone: 212-779-2022
Fax: 212-779-2103
Website: http://www.interequity-capital.com

Management and Staff

Irwin Schlass, President

Type of Firm

Private Firm Investing Own Capital

Industry Association Membership

Natl assoc of Small Bus. Inv. Co (NASBIC)

Project Preferences

Role in Financing:

Prefer role as deal originator but will also invest in deals created by others

Type of Financing Preferred:

First Stage Financing
Leveraged Buyout
Mezzanine
Second Stage Financing
Special Situation

Size of Investments Considered

Min Size of Investment Considered (000s): $1,000
Max Size of Investment Considered (000s): $3,000

Geographical Preferences

United States

All U.S.

Industry Preferences

(% based on actual investment)

Medical/Health	34.1%
Internet Specific	27.9%
Computer Software and Services	25.9%
Consumer Related	4.3%
Other Products	4.0%
Industrial/Energy	3.2%
Communications and Media	0.6%

Additional Information

Name of Most Recent Fund: InterEquity Capital Partners, LP
Most Recent Fund Was Raised: 01/01/1996
Year Founded: 1990
Capital Under Management: $2,400,000
Current Activity Level : Actively seeking new investments
Method of Compensation: Return on invest. most important, but chg. closing fees, service fees, etc.

INVESCO PRIVATE CAPITAL (FKA: CHANCELLOR)

1166 Avenue of the Americas
27th Floor
New York, NY 10036
Phone: 212-278-9680
Fax: 212-278-9884
Website: www.privtaecapital.invesco.com

Other Offices

11 Devonshire Squre
London, United Kingdom EC2M 4YR
Phone: 44-207-454-3066
Fax: 44-207-623-3339

525 University Avenue
Suite 101
Palo Alto, CA 94301
Phone: 650-325-3600
Fax: 650-330-0815

Management and Staff

Alessandro Piol, Managing Director
Andrew Dworkin, Managing Director
Damian Witkowski, Vice President
Esfandiar Lohrasbpar, Managing Director
Howard Goldstein, Managing Director
Johnston Evans, Managing Director
Kathleen Loonam, Vice President
Leigh Ann Poggio, Vice President
Louise Neville, Managing Director
Mark Radovanovich, Vice President
Parag Saxena, President
Phil Shaw, Managing Director
Ray Maxwell, Managing Director

Type of Firm

Private Equity Advisor or Fund of Fund Mgr

Industry Association Membership

National Venture Capital Association (NVCA)

Project Preferences

Role in Financing:

Prefer role as deal originator but will also invest in deals created by others

Type of Financing Preferred:

Balanced
Early Stage
Expansion

Geographical Preferences

United States

All U.S.

Industry Preferences

(% based on actual investment)

Internet Specific	19.0%
Computer Software and Services	17.3%
Medical/Health	15.1%
Communications and Media	13.0%
Consumer Related	10.0%
Biotechnology	9.0%
Semiconductors/Other Elect.	7.7%
Other Products	7.4%
Computer Hardware	0.8%
Industrial/Energy	0.7%

Additional Information

Name of Most Recent Fund: Chancellor Venture Capital
Most Recent Fund Was Raised: 08/20/1991
Year Founded: 1993
Capital Under Management: $2,600,000
Current Activity Level : Actively seeking new investments

ITOCHU TECHNOLOGY

335 Madison Avenue
New York, NY 10017
Phone: 212-818-8000
Fax: 212-818-8378
Website: www.itochu.com

Type of Firm
Incubators

Project Preferences

Role in Financing:
Prefer role as deal originator

Type of Financing Preferred:
Second Stage Financing

Size of Investments Considered
Min Size of Investment Considered (000s): $500
Max Size of Investment Considered (000s): $1,000

Geographical Preferences

International
No Preference

Industry Preferences

(% based on actual investment)

Internet Specific	45.1%
Computer Software and Services	35.2%
Communications and Media	11.0%
Computer Hardware	8.7%

Additional Information
Current Activity Level : Actively seeking new investments
Method of Compensation: Return on investment is of primary concern, do not charge fees

J&W SELIGMAN & COMPANY

100 Park Avenue
7th Floor
New York, NY 10017
Phone: 212-850-1642
Fax: 212-682-4225
Website: www.jwseligman.com

Management and Staff
Chris Boova, Vice President
Gregory Cote, Vice President
Thomas Hirschfeld, Managing Director

Type of Firm
Investment/Merchant Bank Investing Own or Client Funds

Industry Preferences

(% based on actual investment)

Internet Specific	53.3%
Computer Software and Services	14.5%
Semiconductors/Other Elect.	9.5%
Communications and Media	9.4%
Other Products	5.0%
Consumer Related	3.5%
Computer Hardware	2.9%
Industrial/Energy	1.3%
Medical/Health	0.7%

Additional Information
Year Founded: 1989
Capital Under Management: $1,750,000,000
Current Activity Level : Actively seeking new investments

J.E. MANN & CO.

10 Old Road Lane
Mt. Kisco, NY 10549
Phone: 914-241-0297
Fax: 914-241-0726

Type of Firm
Investment/Merchant Bank Investing Own or Client Funds

Project Preferences

Role in Financing:
Prefer role as deal originator but will also invest in deals created by others

Type of Financing Preferred:
First Stage Financing

Size of Investments Considered
Min Size of Investment Considered (000s): $100
Max Size of Investment Considered (000s): $500

Geographical Preferences

United States
Northeast

Industry Preferences

Communications and Media
Data Communications

Computer Hardware
Computers
Integrated Turnkey System

Computer Software
Applications Software

Semiconductors/Other Elect.
Electronics
Electronic Components
Component Testing Equipmt

Industrial/Energy
Industrial Products
Machinery
Environmental Related

Manufact.
Publishing

Additional Information
Year Founded: 1983
Capital Under Management: $5,000,000
Current Activity Level : Reducing investment activity
Method of Compensation: Other

J.P. MORGAN CAPITAL CORP.

60 Wall Street
New York, NY 10260-0060
Phone: 212-648-9000
Fax: 212-648-5002
Website: www.jpmorgan.com

Other Offices

101 California Street
38th Floor
San Francisco, CA 94111
Phone: 415-954-4735

333 South Hope Street
35th Floor
Los Angeles, CA 90071
Phone: 213-437-9278
Fax: 213-437-9365

522 5th Avenue
New York, NY 10036
Phone: 212-837-2151
Fax: 212-837-2695

Edinburgh Tower, 15 Queen's Road
Central, Hong Kong
Phone: 852-2841-1168
Fax: 852-2973-5471

One International Finance Center
22/F No. 1 Harbour View St.
Central, Hong Kong
Phone: 852-2231-1000
Fax: 852-2231-1918

Management and Staff
Cheryl Eustace, Vice President
John Mayer, Chief Executive Officer
Karl Fooks, Vice President
Kevin Alger, Managing Director
Martin O'Neill, Managing Director
Monty Cerf, Managing Director
Sanjay Jain, Vice President
T. Lynne Seden, Vice President
Tim Purcell, Managing Director

Whom to Contact
Lincoln E. Frank

Type of Firm
Investment/Merchant Bank Investing Own or Client Funds

Industry Association Membership
Hungarian Venture Capital Association
National Venture Capital Association (NVCA)
Natl assoc of Small Bus. Inv. Co (NASBIC)

Project Preferences

Role in Financing:
Prefer role as deal originator but will also invest in deals created by others

Type of Financing Preferred:
Second Stage Financing
Special Situation

Size of Investments Considered
Min Size of Investment Considered (000s): $10,000
Max Size of Investment Considered (000s): $20,000

Geographical Preferences

United States
All U.S.

Canada
All Canada

International
Australia
Bermuda
China
France
Germany
Italy
Japan
South Africa
Spain
United Kingdom

Industry Preferences

(% based on actual investment)

Internet Specific	35.1%
Consumer Related	24.0%
Other Products	13.4%
Communications and Media	12.3%
Computer Software and Services	6.3%
Semiconductors/Other Elect.	5.5%
Medical/Health	1.3%
Computer Hardware	0.8%
Biotechnology	0.7%
Industrial/Energy	0.6%

Additional Information
Name of Most Recent Fund: J.P. Morgan Direct Corporate Finance Institutional Investors
Most Recent Fund Was Raised: 12/31/1998
Year Founded: 1985
Capital Under Management: $800,000,000
Current Activity Level : Actively seeking new investments
Method of Compensation: Return on investment is of primary concern, do not charge fees

---

J.P. MORGAN PARTNERS (FKA: CHASE CAPITAL PARTNERS)

1221 Ave. of the Americas
39th Floor
New York, NY 10020-1080
Phone: 212-899-3400
Fax: 212899-3401
Website: www.chasecapital.com

Other Offices

108 South Frontage Road West
Suite 307
Vail, CO 81657
Phone: 970-476-7700
Fax: 970-476-7900

125 London Wall
London, United Kingdom EC2Y 5AJ
Phone: 44171-777-3365
Fax: 44171-777-4731

150 Beach Road
Gateway West
, Singapore 189720
Phone: 65-290-1651

50 California Street
Suite 2940
San Francisco, CA 94111
Phone: 415-591-1200

840 Apollo Street
Suite 223
El Segundo, CA 90245
Phone: 310-335-1955
Fax: 310-335-1965

One International Finance Centre
Central, Hong Kong
Phone: 852-2533-1818
Fax: 852-2868-5551

df
dfds
df, Congo, Dem Rep of the(DRC) f

Management and Staff
Andrew Kahn, Partner
Brian Richmond, General Partner
Christopher Behrens, General Partner
Damion Wicker, General Partner
David Ferguson, Partner
David Britts, General Partner
Donald Hofmann, General Partner
H. Scott McKinley, Managing Director
James Roberts, Principal
Jeffrey Walker, Managing Partner
John Baron, General Partner
John Lewis, Managing Director
Jonathan Lynch, Partner
Jonathan Meggs, General Partner
Kelly Shackelford, Partner
Lindsay Stuart, General Partner
Michael Hannon, General Partner
Miguel Ferro, Principal
Richard Waters, Partner
Risa Stack, General Partner
Sean Epps, Principal
Shahan Soghikian, General Partner
Stephen Murray, General Partner
Stephen McKenna, Principal
Timothy Walsh, General Partner
W. Brett Ingersoll, Partner
Yu-Seng Ting, General Partner

Type of Firm
Investment/Merchant Bank Subsid/Affil

Industry Association Membership
National Venture Capital Association (NVCA)
Natl assoc of Small Bus. Inv. Co (NASBIC)

Project Preferences

Role in Financing:
Will function either as deal originator or investor in deals created by others

Type of Financing Preferred:
Acquisition
Early Stage
Expansion
Later Stage
Leveraged Buyout
Management Buyouts
Mezzanine
Recapitalizations
Second Stage Financing

Size of Investments Considered
Min Size of Investment Considered (000s): $5,000
Max Size of Investment Considered (000s): $200,000

Geographical Preferences

United States
All U.S.

Canada
Alberta

International
Australia
China
Eastern Europe
France
Germany
Hong Kong
Italy
Japan
Latin America
Mexico
New Zealand
Portugal
Spain
United Kingdom

Industry Preferences

(% based on actual investment)

Internet Specific	29.0%
Other Products	23.2%
Industrial/Energy	10.5%
Communications and Media	10.3%
Consumer Related	7.3%
Computer Software and Services	7.2%
Semiconductors/Other Elect.	4.4%
Biotechnology	3.7%
Medical/Health	3.2%
Computer Hardware	1.2%

Additional Information
Name of Most Recent Fund: Chase 1999/2000 Partnership
Most Recent Fund Was Raised: 07/01/1999
Year Founded: 1984
Capital Under Management: $24,000,000,000
Current Activity Level : Actively seeking new investments
Method of Compensation: Return on investment is of primary concern, do not charge fees

JAFCO VENTURES, INC.

225 Liberty Street
17th Floor
New York, NY 10281-1196
Phone: 212-667-9001
Fax: 212-667-1004
Website: www.jafco.com

See California for full listing.

JAPAN/AMERICA VENTURES, INC.

180 Maiden Lane
21st Floor
New York, NY 10038-4939
Phone: 212-269-8900

Type of Firm
Private Firm Investing Own Capital

Industry Association Membership
Natl assoc of Small Bus. Inv. Co (NASBIC)

Project Preferences

Type of Financing Preferred:
Balanced

Geographical Preferences

International
Japan

Industry Preferences

(% based on actual investment)

Consumer Related	56.3%
Other Products	15.9%
Semiconductors/Other Elect.	9.5%
Industrial/Energy	5.4%
Computer Hardware	3.4%
Medical/Health	2.9%
Biotechnology	2.2%
Computer Software and Services	2.2%
Communications and Media	2.1%

Additional Information
Name of Most Recent Fund: Japan/America Venture Partners
Most Recent Fund Was Raised: 08/01/1985
Year Founded: 1986
Current Activity Level : Inactive / Unknown

JAVVA PARTNERS LLC

75 Montebello Road
Suite T-104
Suffern, NY 10901
Phone: 845-369-8100
Website: www.javva.com

Management and Staff
Alan Brandfon, Principal
Howard Katz, Managing Partner

Type of Firm
Private Firm Investing Own Capital

Project Preferences

Type of Financing Preferred:
Balanced

Geographical Preferences

United States
All U.S.

Industry Preferences

Communications and Media
Telecommunications

Additional Information
Year Founded: 1999
Current Activity Level : Actively seeking new investments

JERUSALEM VENTURE PARTNERS (AKA: JVP)

888 Seventh Avenue
33rd Floor
New York, NY 10106
Phone: 212-603-2692
Fax: 212-765-3203
Website: www.jvpvc.com

See Foreign Venture Capital Firms for full listing.

JNET VENTURES

498 7th Avenue
New York, NY 10021
Phone: 212-502-6236
Website: www.jnettech.com

Management and Staff
Allan Tessler, Chairman & CEO
Steven Korby, Chief Financial Officer

Type of Firm
Non-Financial Corp. Affiliate or Subsidiary

Additional Information
Capital Under Management: $100,000,000
Current Activity Level : Actively seeking new investments

Industry Preferences

Manufact.
Publishing

Additional Information
Year Founded: 1987
Current Activity Level : Actively seeking new investments
Method of Compensation: Function primarily in service area, receive contingent fee in cash or equity

JORDAN, EDMISTON GROUP, INC., THE

150 East 52nd Street
18th Floor
New York, NY 10022
Phone: 212-754-0710
Fax: 212-754-0337

Management and Staff
Scott Peters
Wilma Jordan

Whom to Contact
Scott Peters
Wilma Jordan

Type of Firm
Investment/Merchant Bank Investing Own or Client Funds

Project Preferences

Role in Financing:
Prefer role as deal originator

Type of Financing Preferred:
Leveraged Buyout
Mezzanine
Second Stage Financing
Special Situation

Size of Investments Considered
Min Size of Investment Considered (000s): $1,000
Max Size of Investment Considered: No Limit

Geographical Preferences

International
No Preference

JOSEPHBERG GROSZ & CO., INC.

633 3rd Avenue
13th Floor
New York, NY 10017
Phone: 212-974-9926
Fax: 212-397-5832

Management and Staff
Richard Josephberg

Whom to Contact
Richard Josephberg

Type of Firm
Investment Management/Finance Consulting

Project Preferences

Role in Financing:
Prefer role as deal originator

Type of Financing Preferred:
Acquisition
Balanced
Control-block Purchases
Early Stage
Expansion
First Stage Financing
Generalist PE
Joint Ventures
Later Stage
Leveraged Buyout
Management Buyouts
Open Market
Private Placement
Recapitalizations
Research and Development
Second Stage Financing
Special Situation
Turnaround

Size of Investments Considered
Min Size of Investment Considered (000s): $1,000
Max Size of Investment Considered (000s): $30,000

Geographical Preferences

United States
All U.S.

International
Bermuda
France
Germany
Italy
Japan
Spain
United Kingdom

Industry Preferences

Communications and Media
Communications and Media
Commercial Communications
CATV & Pay TV Systems
Radio & TV Broadcasting
Telecommunications
Wireless Communications
Data Communications
Satellite Microwave Comm.
Other Communication Prod.

Computer Hardware
Computer Graphics and Dig

Computer Software
Systems Software
Applications Software
Artificial Intelligence

Internet Specific
Internet

Semiconductors/Other Elect.
Electronic Components

Biotechnology
Biotechnology
Human Biotechnology

Medical/Health
Medical/Health

Consumer Related
Consumer

Industrial/Energy
Alternative Energy
Coal Related
Energy Conservation Relat
Industrial Products

Business Serv.
Distribution

Manufact.
Office Automation Equipmt

Additional Information
Name of Most Recent Fund: Josephberg, Grosz & Co., Inc.
Most Recent Fund Was Raised: 01/01/1994
Year Founded: 1986
Capital Under Management: $50,000,000
Current Activity Level : Actively seeking new investments
Method of Compensation: Return on invest. most important, but chg. closing fees, service fees, etc.

KATALYST LLC

405 Lexington Avenue
Suite 480
New York, NY 10174
Phone: 917-592-8852
Fax: 212-504-8118
Website: www.katalyst.com

See Pennsylvania for full listing.

KAUFMANN FUND, INC., THE

140 East 45th Street
43rd Floor
New York, NY 10017
Phone: 212-922-0123
Website: www.kaufmann.com

Type of Firm
Investment Management/Finance Consulting

Project Preferences

Type of Financing Preferred:
Balanced

Geographical Preferences

International
All International

Additional Information
Year Founded: 1967
Current Activity Level : Actively seeking new investments

KBL HEALTHCARE VENTURES

645 Madison Avenue
14th Floor
New York, NY 10022
Phone: 212-319-5555
Fax: 212-319-5591
Website: www.kblhealthcare.com

Management and Staff
Marlene Krauss, Managing Director
Mike Kaswan, Vice President
Zachary Berk, Managing Director

Whom to Contact
Marlene R. Krauss, M.D.

Type of Firm
Private Firm Investing Own Capital

Industry Association Membership
National Venture Capital Association (NVCA)
Natl assoc of Small Bus. Inv. Co (NASBIC)

Project Preferences

Role in Financing:
Prefer role as deal originator but will also invest in deals created by others

Type of Financing Preferred:
Early Stage
Expansion
First Stage Financing
Later Stage
Mezzanine
Second Stage Financing
Seed
Start-up Financing

Size of Investments Considered
Min Size of Investment Considered (000s): $500
Max Size of Investment Considered (000s): $5,000

Geographical Preferences

United States
All U.S.

Industry Preferences

(% based on actual investment)

Medical/Health	40.3%
Internet Specific	22.7%
Biotechnology	20.8%
Communications and Media	15.1%
Computer Software and Services	1.1%

Additional Information
Name of Most Recent Fund: KBL Healthcare Ventures
Most Recent Fund Was Raised: 08/06/1999
Year Founded: 1991
Capital Under Management: $100,000,000
Current Activity Level : Actively seeking new investments
Method of Compensation: Return on investment is of primary concern, do not charge fees

KPE VENTURES

860 Broadway
New York, NY 10003
Phone: 212-652-9600
Fax: 212-652-9696

Other Offices

6100 Wilshire Blvd.
Los Angeles, CA 90048
Phone: 323-930-7300

860 Broadway
New York, NY 10003
Phone: 212-652-9600
Fax: 212-652-9696

95 New Cavendish Street
London, United Kingdom W1M7FR
Phone: 0171-526-1170

Management and Staff
Charles Wood, Chief Financial Officer

Type of Firm
Incubators

Additional Information
Current Activity Level : Actively seeking new investments

LAMBDA FUNDS, THE

380 Lexington Avenue
54th Floor
New York, NY 10168
Phone: 212-682-3454
Fax: 212-682-9231

Management and Staff
Anthony Lamport, General Partner
Richard Dumler, General Partner

Type of Firm
Private Firm Investing Own Capital

Industry Association Membership
National Venture Capital Association (NVCA)

Project Preferences

Role in Financing:
Will function either as deal originator or investor in deals created by others

Type of Financing Preferred:
Early Stage
Expansion
First Stage Financing
Management Buyouts
Second Stage Financing

Size of Investments Considered
Min Size of Investment Considered (000s): $200
Max Size of Investment Considered (000s): $500

Geographical Preferences

United States
Mid Atlantic
Northeast
West Coast

Industry Preferences

(% based on actual investment)

Biotechnology	27.9%
Computer Hardware	16.6%
Industrial/Energy	10.6%
Other Products	9.1%
Semiconductors/Other Elect.	8.8%
Computer Software and Services	8.4%
Consumer Related	5.7%
Communications and Media	4.4%
Medical/Health	4.4%
Internet Specific	4.1%

Additional Information
Name of Most Recent Fund: LAMBDA IV
Most Recent Fund Was Raised: 01/01/1996
Year Founded: 1979
Capital Under Management: $5,000,000
Current Activity Level : Actively seeking new investments
Method of Compensation: Return on investment is of primary concern, do not charge fees

LANCET CAPITAL PARTNER(FKA:CADUCEUS CAPITAL PARTNERS)

45 Rockefeller Plaza
20th Floor
New York, NY 10111
Phone: 212-332-3220
Fax: 212-332-3221

See Massachusetts for full listing.

LAUNCH CENTER 39

609 Greenwich Street
5th Floor
New York, NY 10014
Phone: 212-905-1639
Fax: 212-905-1539
Website: www.lc39.com

Management and Staff
Albert Wenger, Chief Executive Officer
Bradley Muro, Managing Director
Etienne Boillot, Chief Financial Officer
Jim Butterworth, Chief Executive Officer
Kristin Brown, Managing Director
Phil Granof, Managing Director

Type of Firm
Incubators

Project Preferences

Type of Financing Preferred:
Early Stage

Geographical Preferences

United States
All U.S.

Industry Preferences

Internet Specific
Internet

Additional Information
Year Founded: 2000
Current Activity Level : Actively seeking new investments

LAZARD TECHNOLOGY PARTNERS

30 Rockefeller Plaza
61st Floor
New York, NY 10020
Phone: 212-632-6819
Fax: 212-656-1662
Website: www.lazardtp.com

Other Offices
5335 Wisconsin Avenue, NW
Suite 410
Washington, DC 20015
Phone: 202-895-1505
Fax: 202-895-1501

Management and Staff
Gene Lowe, Principal
Gerry McClure, Vice President
Kevin Burns, Principal
Manu Rana, Vice President
Russell Planitzer, Principal
Tom Marler, Vice President

Type of Firm
Investment/Merchant Bank Subsid/Affil

Industry Association Membership
Mid-Atlantic Venture Association

Project Preferences

Type of Financing Preferred:
Early Stage
First Stage Financing
Second Stage Financing
Seed
Startup

Geographical Preferences

United States
East Coast
Mid Atlantic
Northeast

International
Europe
United Kingdom

Industry Preferences

(% based on actual investment)

Internet Specific	43.5%
Computer Software and Services	37.0%
Communications and Media	19.5%

Additional Information
Year Founded: 1998
Capital Under Management: $190,000,000
Current Activity Level : Actively seeking new investments

LEPERCQ CAPITAL MANAGEMENT, INC.(AKA:LEPERCQ,DE NEUFLIZE IN)

1675 Broadway
New York, NY 10019
Phone: 212-698-0795
Fax: 212-262-0155

Management and Staff
Michael J. Connelly

Whom to Contact
Michael J. Connelly

Type of Firm
Mgt. Consulting Firm

Project Preferences

Role in Financing:
Prefer role as deal originator but will also invest in deals created by others

Type of Financing Preferred:
Control-block Purchases
Leveraged Buyout
Second Stage Financing

Size of Investments Considered
Min Size of Investment Considered (000s): $1,000
Max Size of Investment Considered (000s): $10,000

Geographical Preferences

International
No Preference

Industry Preferences

Communications and Media
Radio & TV Broadcasting

Computer Hardware
Integrated Turnkey System

Computer Software
Applications Software

Internet Specific
Internet

Consumer Related
Consumer Services
Education Related

Additional Information
Name of Most Recent Fund: LN Investment Capital Limited Partnership II
Most Recent Fund Was Raised: 06/01/1990
Year Founded: 1987
Capital Under Management: $32,000,000
Current Activity Level : Making few, if any, new investments
Method of Compensation: Return on invest. most important, but chg. closing fees, service fees, etc.

LEXINGTON PARTNERS, INC. (FKA: LPNY ADVISORS, INC.)

660 Madison Avenue
23rd Floor
New York, NY 10021
Phone: 212-754-0411
Fax: 212-754-1494
Website: ww.lexingtonpartners.com

Other Offices

2880 Lexington Drive
Suite 205
Santa Clara, CA 95054
Phone: 408-970-0123
Fax: 408-970-0111

Management and Staff
Marshall Parke, Managing Director
Nick Harris, General Partner

Type of Firm
Private Firm Investing Own Capital

Geographical Preferences

International
All International

Additional Information
Year Founded: 1999
Capital Under Management: $2,800,000,000
Current Activity Level : Actively seeking new investments

LIGHTSPEED VENTURE PARTNERS (FKA: WEISS, PECK & GREER)

One New York Plaza
New York, NY 10004
Phone: 212-908-9500
Fax: 212-908-9652
Website: www.lightspeedventurepartners.com

See California for full listing.

LINCOLNSHIRE MANAGEMENT INC.

780 Third Avenue
40th Floor
New York, NY 10017
Phone: 212-319-3633
Fax: 212-755-5457
Website: www.lincolnshiremgmt.com

Other Offices

1 Sansome Street
Suite 1900
San Francisco, CA 94104
Phone: 415-781-2800
Fax: 415-781-2850

333 W. Wacker Drive
Suite 700
Chicago, IL 60606
Phone: 312-899-9000
Fax: 312-899-9009

8300 Boone Blvd
Suite 500
McLean, VA 22102
Phone: 703-761-6730
Fax: 703-848-4586

Management and Staff
Jeffrey Muti, Managing Director
Peter Van Raalte, Managing Director
T.J. Maloney, President

Whom to Contact
John Camp
Thomas R. Ley

Type of Firm
Private Equity Advisor or Fund of Fund Mgr

Project Preferences

Role in Financing:
Prefer role as deal originator

Type of Financing Preferred:
Acquisition
Management Buyouts
Recapitalizations

Size of Investments Considered
Min Size of Investment Considered (000s): $25,000
Max Size of Investment Considered (000s): $150,000

Geographical Preferences

United States
All U.S.

Canada
All Canada

Industry Preferences

Semiconductors/Other Elect.
Electronic Components
Component Testing Equipmt

Medical/Health
Diagnostic Test Products

Industrial/Energy
Industrial Products
Factory Automation
Machinery

Business Serv.
Distribution

Manufact.
Manufacturing

Additional Information
Name of Most Recent Fund: Lincolnshire Equity Fund II, L.P.
Most Recent Fund Was Raised: 09/01/1999
Year Founded: 1985
Capital Under Management: $400,000,000
Current Activity Level : Actively seeking new investments
Method of Compensation: Return on invest. most important, but chg. closing fees, service fees, etc.

LOEB PARTNERS CORP.

61 Broadway
Suite 2400
New York, NY 10006
Phone: 212-483-7000
Fax: 212-574-2001

Type of Firm
Investment/Merchant Bank Subsid/Affil

Project Preferences

Role in Financing:
Prefer role as deal originator but will also invest in deals created by others

Type of Financing Preferred:
Acquisition
Early Stage
Expansion
Leveraged Buyout
Management Buyouts

Size of Investments Considered
Min Size of Investment Considered (000s): $100
Max Size of Investment Considered: No Limit

Geographical Preferences

United States
All U.S.

Industry Preferences

(% based on actual investment)

Biotechnology	50.2%
Medical/Health	23.6%
Internet Specific	23.4%
Semiconductors/Other Elect.	2.8%

Additional Information
Year Founded: 1931
Capital Under Management: $150,000,000
Current Activity Level : Actively seeking new investments
Method of Compensation: Return on invest. most important, but chg. closing fees, service fees, etc.

LONG ISLAND VENTURE FUND L.P.

123 Hofstra University,Ste 213
Business Development Center
Hempstead, NY 11550-1090
Phone: 516-463-3662
Fax: 516-463-3667

Type of Firm
Endowment

Industry Association Membership
National Venture Capital Association (NVCA)

Industry Preferences

(% based on actual investment)

Semiconductors/Other Elect.	40.0%
Communications and Media	35.0%
Industrial/Energy	15.0%
Internet Specific	10.0%

Additional Information
Name of Most Recent Fund: Long Island Venture Fund, LP
Most Recent Fund Was Raised: 12/31/1994
Year Founded: 1994
Capital Under Management: $20,000,000
Current Activity Level : Actively seeking new investments

M&F ASSOCIATES, L.P.

45 Rockefeller Plaza
Suite 1960
New York, NY 10111
Phone: 212-332-2929
Fax: 212-332-2920
Website: www.murphy-partners.com

Management and Staff
John Murphy, Managing General Partner
Philip Giordano, Chief Financial Officer
Stuart Agranoff, Partner
Thomas Keane, Partner

Type of Firm
Private Firm Investing Own Capital

Project Preferences

Role in Financing:
Prefer role as deal originator

Type of Financing Preferred:
Acquisition
Balanced
Control-block Purchases
Early Stage
Expansion
First Stage Financing
Leveraged Buyout
Management Buyouts
Private Placement
Second Stage Financing
Startup

Size of Investments Considered
Min Size of Investment Considered (000s): $1,000
Max Size of Investment Considered (000s): $7,000

Geographical Preferences

United States
All U.S.

Industry Preferences

Communications and Media
Radio & TV Broadcasting

Medical/Health
Health Services

Business Serv.
Media

Additional Information

Name of Most Recent Fund: Murphy & Partners Fund II, L.P.
Most Recent Fund Was Raised: 03/31/1998
Year Founded: 1988
Capital Under Management: $254,000,000
Current Activity Level : Actively seeking new investments
Method of Compensation: Return on invest. most important, but chg. closing fees, service fees, etc.

M31 VENTURES, LLC

712 Fifth Avenue
22nd Floor
New York, NY 10019
Phone: 212-581-3143
Fax: 212-581-2433
Website: www.m31ventures.com

Management and Staff

Adam Pelzman, Managing Partner

Type of Firm

Private Firm Investing Own Capital

Project Preferences

Role in Financing:
Prefer role as deal originator but will also invest in deals created by others

Type of Financing Preferred:
Early Stage
Expansion
Later Stage

Geographical Preferences

United States
All U.S.

Industry Preferences

Internet Specific
Internet

Financial Services
Financial Services

Additional Information

Name of Most Recent Fund: M31 Venture Fund, LP
Most Recent Fund Was Raised: 06/01/1999
Year Founded: 1999
Capital Under Management: $10,000,000
Current Activity Level : Inactive / Unknown
Method of Compensation: Return on investment is of primary concern, do not charge fees

---

MADISON INVESTMENT PARTNERS, INC.

660 Madison Avenue
New York, NY 10021
Phone: 212-223-2600
Fax: 212-223-8208

Management and Staff

B. Martha Cassidy, Managing Director
Emile Geisenheimer, President
Susan Goodrich, Managing Director

Type of Firm

SBIC Not elsewhere classified

Industry Association Membership

National Venture Capital Association (NVCA)

Project Preferences

Role in Financing:
Prefer role as deal originator but will also invest in deals created by others

Type of Financing Preferred:
Industry Rollups
Leveraged Buyout
Second Stage Financing

Size of Investments Considered
Min Size of Investment Considered (000s): $5,000
Max Size of Investment Considered: No Limit

Geographical Preferences

United States
All U.S.

Industry Preferences

Communications and Media
Communications and Media
Other Communication Prod.

Semiconductors/Other Elect.
Electronics
Electronic Components
Controllers and Sensors
Circuit Boards
Component Testing Equipmt
Laser Related
Fiber Optics
Analytic/Scientific

Medical/Health
Diagnostic Services
Diagnostic Test Products
Other Therapeutic
Medical Products
Disposable Med. Products
Hospitals/Clinics/Primary
Hospital/Other Instit.

Consumer Related
Entertainment and Leisure
Retail
Franchises(NEC)
Consumer Products
Consumer Services

Industrial/Energy
Industrial Products

Financial Services
Financial Services

Manufact.
Publishing

Additional Information

Name of Most Recent Fund: Madison Investment Partners II, L.P.
Most Recent Fund Was Raised: 12/16/1997
Year Founded: 1993
Capital Under Management: $5,000,000
Current Activity Level : Inactive / Unknown

MANHATTAN VENTURE CO., INC.

340 East 57th Street
New York, NY 10022
Phone: 212-688-4445
Fax: 212-486-3138

Project Preferences

Type of Financing Preferred:
First Stage Financing
Leveraged Buyout
Second Stage Financing
Start-up Financing

Size of Investments Considered
Min Size of Investment Considered (000s): $2,000
Max Size of Investment Considered (000s): $100,000

Geographical Preferences
United States
All U.S.

Canada
All Canada

Industry Preferences
Communications and Media
Communications and Media

Computer Other
Computer Related

Semiconductors/Other Elect.
Electronic Components

Biotechnology
Biotechnology

Medical/Health
Medical/Health

Consumer Related
Consumer

Industrial/Energy
Industrial Products

Financial Services
Financial Services

Business Serv.
Distribution

Manufact.
Publishing

Additional Information
Year Founded: 1968
Current Activity Level : Actively seeking new investments
Method of Compensation: Function primarily in service area, receive contingent fee in cash or equity

MAYFAIR CAPITAL PARTNERS, INC.

P.O. Box 30
New York, NY 10021
Phone: 212-288-0500
Fax: 212-737-0039

Other Offices
158 Mount Olivet Avenue
Newark, NJ 07114
Phone: 201-621-2802
Fax: 201-621-2816

45, quai Wilson
CH-1201 Geneva, Switzerland
Phone: 41-22-732-2527
Fax: 41-22-732-2673

Type of Firm
Mgt. Consulting Firm

Project Preferences
Role in Financing:
Prefer role as deal originator but will also invest in deals created by others

Type of Financing Preferred:
Leveraged Buyout
Mezzanine
Special Situation

Size of Investments Considered
Min Size of Investment Considered (000s): $1,000
Max Size of Investment Considered: No Limit

Geographical Preferences
International
No Preference

Industry Preferences
Semiconductors/Other Elect.
Analytic/Scientific

Biotechnology
Industrial Biotechnology
Biosensors

Medical/Health
Diagnostic Test Products
Other Therapeutic
Medical Products
Disposable Med. Products
Pharmaceuticals

Consumer Related
Retail
Food/Beverage
Consumer Products

Industrial/Energy
Industrial Products
Materials
Environmental Related

Business Serv.
Consulting Services

Additional Information
Year Founded: 1980
Current Activity Level : Actively seeking new investments
Method of Compensation: Return on invest. most important, but chg. closing fees, service fees, etc.

MC CAPITAL, INC.

520 Madison Avenue
16th Floor
New York, NY 10022
Phone: 212-644-0841
Fax: 212-644-2926

Management and Staff
Katsuhiko Oba, Chief Financial Officer

Whom to Contact
Shunichi Maeda

Type of Firm
Non-Financial Corp. Affiliate or Subsidiary

Project Preferences
Role in Financing:
Prefer role in deals created by others

Type of Financing Preferred:
Acquisition
Expansion
First Stage Financing
Fund of Funds
Generalist PE
Joint Ventures
Later Stage
Leveraged Buyout
Private Placement
Second Stage Financing
Special Situation
Turnaround

Size of Investments Considered
Min Size of Investment Considered (000s): $1,000
Max Size of Investment Considered (000s): $30,000

Geographical Preferences
United States
All U.S.

Canada
All Canada

International
All International

Industry Preferences

Communications and Media
Communications and Media

Computer Hardware
Computers

Semiconductors/Other Elect.
Electronics

Biotechnology
Biotechnology

Medical/Health
Medical/Health

Additional Information
Year Founded: 1991
Capital Under Management: $200,000,000
Current Activity Level : Actively seeking new investments
Method of Compensation: Return on investment is of primary concern, do not charge fees

MCCOWN DE LEEUW & CO.

Park Avenue Tower
65 E. 55th Street
New York, NY 10022
Phone: 212-355-5500
Fax: 212-355-6283
Website: www.mdcpartners.com

See California for full listing.

MCGRAW-HILL VENTURES

1221 Avenue of the Americas
47th Floor
New York, NY 10020-1095
Phone: 212-512-3916
Fax: 212-512-4729
Website: www.mcgraw-hill.com

Management and Staff
Michael Hehir, President

Type of Firm
Non-Financial Corp. Affiliate or Subsidiary

Project Preferences

Role in Financing:
Prefer role in deals created by others

Type of Financing Preferred:
Early Stage
Expansion
Later Stage
Second Stage Financing

Size of Investments Considered
Min Size of Investment Considered (000s): $500
Max Size of Investment Considered (000s): $5,000

Geographical Preferences

United States
All U.S.

International
All International

Industry Preferences

Communications and Media
Wireless Communications

Computer Software
Software
Applications Software
Artificial Intelligence

Internet Specific
E-Commerce Technology
Internet
Web Aggregration/Portals

Business Serv.
Media

Additional Information
Name of Most Recent Fund: McGraw Hill Capital Corporation
Most Recent Fund Was Raised: 07/01/1995
Year Founded: 1995
Capital Under Management: $125,000,000
Current Activity Level : Actively seeking new investments
Method of Compensation: Return on investment is of primary concern, do not charge fees

MEDICAL VENTURE HOLDINGS, INC.

c/o CIBC-Openheimer, Inc.
200 Liberty Street
New York, NY 10281
Phone: 212-667-5053
Fax: 212-667-8148

Type of Firm
Non-Financial Corp. Affiliate or Subsidiary

Project Preferences

Role in Financing:
Prefer role as deal originator but will also invest in deals created by others

Type of Financing Preferred:
First Stage Financing
Mezzanine
Second Stage Financing
Seed
Start-up Financing

Size of Investments Considered
Min Size of Investment Considered (000s): $1,000
Max Size of Investment Considered: No Limit

Geographical Preferences

United States
All U.S.

Industry Preferences

Biotechnology
Biotechnology

Medical/Health
Medical/Health

Additional Information
Name of Most Recent Fund: WestMed Ventures
Most Recent Fund Was Raised: 01/01/1991
Year Founded: 1987
Capital Under Management: $52,000,000
Current Activity Level : Reducing investment activity
Method of Compensation: Return on investment is of primary concern, do not charge fees

MELLON VENTURES (AKA: MELLON BANK)

1114 Avenue of the Americas
31st Floor
New York, NY 10036-7701
Phone: 212-389-2700
Fax: 212-389-2755
Website: www.mellonventures.com

See Pennsylvania for full listing.

MERIFIN CAPITAL GROUP

75 Wall Street
35th Floor
New York, NY 10005
Phone: 212-429-3123
Fax: 212-429-3139

See Foreign Venture Capital Firms for full listing.

METROPOLITAN VENTURE PARTNERS (METVP)

Two World Financial Center
27th Floor
New York, NY 10281-2700
Phone: 212-566-6280
Fax: 212-566-9385
Website: www.metvp.com

Other Offices

Sugar Quay
Lower Thames Street
London, United Kingdom EC3R 6DU
Phone: 44 (0) 207-285-590
Fax: 44 (0) 207-285-371

Management and Staff
Adrian Blumfield, Chief Executive Officer
Michael Levin, Managing Director
Nick Wood, Managing Director
Paul Lisiak, Managing Director

Type of Firm
Private Firm Investing Own Capital

Project Preferences

Type of Financing Preferred:
Early Stage

Geographical Preferences

United States
All U.S.

International
Europe

Industry Preferences

Computer Software
Software

Internet Specific
Internet

Additional Information
Current Activity Level : Actively seeking new investments

MEYER, DUFFY & ASSOCIATES

780 Third Avenue
15th Floor
New York, NY 10017
Phone: 646-282-9260
Fax: 646-282-9279
Website: www.meyerduffy.com

Management and Staff
Donald Duffy, Partner
Eric Meyer, Partner
John Mills, Partner
Ray Gavin, Partner
Teddy Kaplan, Vice President
Thomas Hess, Vice President

Whom to Contact
Kier Kleinknecht

Type of Firm
Private Firm Investing Own Capital

Project Preferences

Role in Financing:
Prefer role as deal originator but will also invest in deals created by others

Type of Financing Preferred:
First Stage Financing
Second Stage Financing

Industry Preferences

(% based on actual investment)

Computer Software and Services	60.8%
Communications and Media	15.2%
Internet Specific	14.1%
Other Products	9.9%

Additional Information
Year Founded: 1994
Capital Under Management: $40,000,000
Current Activity Level : Actively seeking new investments
Method of Compensation: Return on invest. most important, but chg. closing fees, service fees, etc.

MILESTONE VENTURE PARTNERS

650 Madison Avenue
21st Floor
New York, NY 10022
Phone: 212-223-7400
Website: www.milestonevp.com

Management and Staff
Edwin Goodman, Partner
Todd Pietri, Partner

Type of Firm
Private Firm Investing Own Capital

Project Preferences

Type of Financing Preferred:
Early Stage

Geographical Preferences

United States
Northeast
All U.S.

Industry Preferences

Internet Specific
Internet

Additional Information
Year Founded: 2000
Current Activity Level : Actively seeking new investments

MITSUI & CO., LTD.

200 Park Avenue
36th Floor
New York, NY 10166-0130
Phone: 212-878-4044
Fax: 212-878-4070
Website: www.mitsuipe.com

Management and Staff
Ted Yamamoto

Whom to Contact
Ted Yamamoto

Type of Firm
Non-Financial Corp. Affiliate or Subsidiary

Industry Association Membership
National Venture Capital Association (NVCA)

Project Preferences

Role in Financing:
Prefer role as deal originator but will also invest in deals created by others

Type of Financing Preferred:
First Stage Financing
Research and Development
Second Stage Financing
Seed
Start-up Financing

Geographical Preferences

United States
All U.S.

Canada
All Canada

Industry Preferences

(% based on actual investment)

Internet Specific	38.7%
Communications and Media	25.2%
Computer Software and Services	13.4%
Semiconductors/Other Elect.	8.8%
Other Products	6.3%
Medical/Health	5.1%
Computer Hardware	2.6%

Additional Information

Year Founded: 1997
Capital Under Management: $40,000,000
Current Activity Level : Actively seeking new investments
Method of Compensation: Return on investment is of primary concern, do not charge fees

MOORE CAPITAL MANAGEMENT INC.

1251 Avenue of the Americas
New York, NY 10020
Phone: 212-782-7080
Fax: 212-782-7576
Website: www.moorecap.com

Management and Staff

James Caccavo, Managing Director
Louis Moore Bacon, Managing Director

Type of Firm

Investment/Merchant Bank Investing Own or Client Funds

Project Preferences

Role in Financing:
Will function either as deal originator or investor in deals created by others

Type of Financing Preferred:
First Stage Financing
Leveraged Buyout
Research and Development
Second Stage Financing
Start-up Financing

Size of Investments Considered

Min Size of Investment Considered (000s): $100
Max Size of Investment Considered: No Limit

Geographical Preferences

International
No Preference

Industry Preferences

(% based on actual investment)

Internet Specific	67.6%
Communications and Media	14.8%
Computer Software and Services	9.6%
Medical/Health	6.1%
Other Products	1.8%

Additional Information

Year Founded: 1989
Capital Under Management: $500,000
Current Activity Level : Inactive / Unknown
Method of Compensation: Return on invest. most important, but chg. closing fees, service fees, etc.

MORGAN STANLEY VENTURE PARTNERS (AKA: MSDW)

1221 Avenue of the Americas
33rd Floor
New York, NY 10020
Phone: 212-762-7900
Fax: 212-762-8424
Website: http://www.msvp.com

Other Offices

3000 Sand Hill Road
Building 4, Suite 250
Menlo Park, CA 94025
Phone: 650-233-2600
Fax: 650-233-2626

Two International Place
Boston, MA 02110
Phone: 617-856-8000
Fax: 617-856-8022

Management and Staff

Aaron Broad, Venture Partner
Debra Abramovitz, Chief Operating Officer
Gary Stein, Vice President
Ghassan Bejjani, General Partner
Grace Voorhis, Vice President
Guy De Chazal, General Partner
Howard Hoffen, Chairman & CEO
Jeff Booth, Principal
M. Fazle Husain, General Partner
Noah Walley, General Partner
Pete Chung, Vice President
Philip R. Dur, Venture Partner
Robert Loarie, General Partner
Scott Halsted, General Partner
William Harding, General Partner

Type of Firm

Investment/Merchant Bank Subsid/Affil

Industry Association Membership

Natl assoc of Small Bus. Inv. Co (NASBIC)
Western Association of Venture Capitalists (WAVC)

Project Preferences

Role in Financing:
Prefer role as deal originator but will also invest in deals created by others

Type of Financing Preferred:
Industry Rollups
Leveraged Buyout
Mezzanine
Second Stage Financing

Size of Investments Considered

Min Size of Investment Considered (000s): $2,000
Max Size of Investment Considered: No Limit

Geographical Preferences

United States
All U.S.

Canada
All Canada

Industry Preferences

(% based on actual investment)

Computer Software and Services	34.4%
Internet Specific	27.7%
Communications and Media	11.6%
Semiconductors/Other Elect.	8.9%
Medical/Health	7.4%
Computer Hardware	5.2%

Biotechnology	3.9%
Other Products	0.4%
Industrial/Energy	0.4%

Additional Information
Name of Most Recent Fund: Morgan Stanley Venture Partners III, L.P.
Most Recent Fund Was Raised: 01/01/1997
Year Founded: 1985
Capital Under Management: $864,900,000
Current Activity Level : Actively seeking new investments
Method of Compensation: Return on investment is of primary concern, do not charge fees

MST PARTNERS

841 Broadway
Suite 504
New York, NY 10003
Phone: 212-674-1900
Fax: 212-674-6821

Type of Firm
Private Firm Investing Own Capital

Project Preferences

Role in Financing:
Prefer role as deal originator but will also invest in deals created by others

Type of Financing Preferred:
Leveraged Buyout
Special Situation

Size of Investments Considered
Min Size of Investment Considered (000s): $3,000
Max Size of Investment Considered (000s): $7,000

Geographical Preferences

United States
All U.S.

Industry Preferences

Semiconductors/Other Elect.
Sensors

Medical/Health
Disposable Med. Products

Industrial/Energy
Materials
Factory Automation
Machinery

Additional Information
Name of Most Recent Fund: MST Partners
Most Recent Fund Was Raised: 01/01/1989
Year Founded: 1989
Capital Under Management: $76,000,000
Current Activity Level : Actively seeking new investments
Method of Compensation: Return on invest. most important, but chg. closing fees, service fees, etc.

NATIONAL BANK OF KUWAIT

299 Park Avenue
17th Floor
New York, NY 10171
Phone: 212-303-9828
Fax: 212-838-1805

Other Offices

20 Collyer Hex 20-00
Tong Center
Singapore, Singapore 0104
Phone: 65-222-5348
Fax: 65-224-5438

Management and Staff
Jason Bross, Managing Director

Whom to Contact
Gordon Hargraves
Nadim Barakat
Richard McKegney

Type of Firm
Commercial Bank Affiliate or Subsidiary

Project Preferences

Role in Financing:
Prefer role as deal originator but will also invest in deals created by others

Type of Financing Preferred:
Early Stage
Expansion
First Stage Financing
Fund of Funds
Generalist PE
Later Stage
Leveraged Buyout
Management Buyouts
Mezzanine
Private Placement
Second Stage Financing

Size of Investments Considered
Min Size of Investment Considered (000s): $5,000
Max Size of Investment Considered (000s): $10,000

Geographical Preferences

United States
All U.S.

International
Eastern Europe
India
Italy
Japan
Latin America
Middle East
South Africa
Spain
United Kingdom

Industry Preferences

Communications and Media
Commercial Communications
CATV & Pay TV Systems
Radio & TV Broadcasting
Telecommunications
Wireless Communications
Data Communications
Satellite Microwave Comm.
Other Communication Prod.

Computer Software
Software

Internet Specific
E-Commerce Technology

Semiconductors/Other Elect.
Fiber Optics

Industrial/Energy
Energy

Business Serv.
Media

Additional Information
Year Founded: 1995
Capital Under Management: $175,000,000
Current Activity Level : Actively seeking new investments
Method of Compensation: Return on investment is of primary concern, do not charge fees

NATIONAL FINANCIAL COS. LLC

375 Park Ave.
#1606
New York, NY 10022-6006
Phone: 212-399-2500
Fax: 212-399-9199

Management and Staff
Michael Zarriello
Robert Barron

Whom to Contact
Michael Zarriello
Robert Barron

Type of Firm
Investment/Merchant Bank Subsid/Affil

Project Preferences

Role in Financing:
Prefer role as deal originator

Type of Financing Preferred:
Leveraged Buyout
Special Situation

Size of Investments Considered
Min Size of Investment Considered (000s): $5,000
Max Size of Investment Considered: No Limit

Geographical Preferences

United States
All U.S.

Canada
Eastern Canada

Industry Preferences

Communications and Media
Other Communication Prod.

Semiconductors/Other Elect.
Sensors
Circuit Boards
Component Testing Equipmt
Analytic/Scientific

Medical/Health
Disposable Med. Products

Consumer Related
Franchises(NEC)
Consumer Products

Industrial/Energy
Industrial Products
Materials
Factory Automation
Machinery
Environmental Related

Financial Services
Financial Services

Additional Information
Year Founded: 1980
Capital Under Management: $50,000,000
Current Activity Level : Actively seeking new investments
Method of Compensation: Return on invest. most important, but chg. closing fees, service fees, etc.

NAZEM & CO.

645 Madison Avenue
12th Floor
New York, NY 10022
Phone: 212-371-7900
Fax: 212-371-2150

Other Offices

3000 Sand Hill Road
Building Two, Suite 205
Menlo Park, CA 94025
Phone: 415-854-3010
Fax: 415-854-3015

600 Madison Ave
14th Floor
New York, NY 10022
Phone: 212-644-6433

Management and Staff
Fred Nazem, Managing Partner
Jeffrey Krauss, General Partner
Lynn Amato Madonna, Partner
Philip Barak, General Partner
Richard Racine, General Partner

Type of Firm
Private Firm Investing Own Capital

Project Preferences

Role in Financing:
Prefer role as deal originator but will also invest in deals created by others

Type of Financing Preferred:
First Stage Financing
Leveraged Buyout
Mezzanine
Second Stage Financing
Seed
Special Situation
Start-up Financing

Size of Investments Considered
Min Size of Investment Considered (000s): $1,000
Max Size of Investment Considered: No Limit

Geographical Preferences

United States
All U.S.

Industry Preferences

(% based on actual investment)

Medical/Health	23.6%
Computer Hardware	20.2%
Computer Software and Services	12.7%
Communications and Media	12.2%
Semiconductors/Other Elect.	10.2%
Biotechnology	6.9%
Internet Specific	5.5%
Industrial/Energy	4.0%
Other Products	3.7%
Consumer Related	0.9%

Additional Information
Year Founded: 1976
Capital Under Management: $152,000,000
Current Activity Level : Actively seeking new investments
Method of Compensation: Return on investment is of primary concern, do not charge fees

NEEDHAM & COMPANY, INC.

445 Park Avenue
New York, NY 10022-4406
Phone: 212-371-8300
Fax: 212-705-0299
Website: www.needhamco.com

Other Offices

1000 S.W. Broadway
Suite 960
Portland, OR 97205
Phone: 503-221-7000
Fax: 503-221-3906

3000 Sand Hill Road
Building 2, Suite 190
Menlo Park, CA 94025
Phone: 650-854-9111
Fax: 650-854-9853

Balance Capital Markets
3a Jabotinsky Street
GanDiamond Tower Ramat, Israel 52520
Phone: 03-57556274
Fax: 03-57556272

One Post Office Square
Suite 3710
Boston, MA 02109
Phone: 617-457-0900
Fax: 617-457-5777

Management and Staff
Chad Keck, Managing Director
George Needham, General Partner
Glen Albanese, Chief Financial Officer
Jack Iacovone, Vice President
John Prior, General Partner
John Michaelson, General Partner
Margaret Johns, Managing Director

Whom to Contact
Joseph Abramoff

Type of Firm
Investment/Merchant Bank Investing Own or Client Funds

Industry Association Membership
National Venture Capital Association (NVCA)
Natl assoc of Small Bus. Inv. Co (NASBIC)

Project Preferences

Role in Financing:
Will function either as deal originator or investor in deals created by others

Type of Financing Preferred:
Expansion
Later Stage
Leveraged Buyout
Management Buyouts
Mezzanine

Size of Investments Considered
Min Size of Investment Considered (000s): $1,000
Max Size of Investment Considered (000s): $10,000

Geographical Preferences

United States
All U.S.

International
United Kingdom

Industry Preferences
(% based on actual investment)

Computer Software and Services	28.7%
Communications and Media	21.0%
Internet Specific	16.9%
Semiconductors/Other Elect.	14.5%
Computer Hardware	9.4%
Consumer Related	7.0%
Other Products	1.3%
Medical/Health	1.1%

Additional Information
Name of Most Recent Fund: Needham Capital International
Most Recent Fund Was Raised: 04/01/1998
Year Founded: 1985
Capital Under Management: $750,000,000
Current Activity Level : Actively seeking new investments
Method of Compensation: Return on investment is of primary concern, do not charge fees

NEOCARTA VENTURES

1350 Avenue of the Americas
32nd Floor
New York, NY 10019
Phone: 212-931-8050
Fax: 212-931-8001
Website: www.neocarta.com

See Massachusetts for full listing.

NEOMED MANAGEMENT AS (FKA MEDICAL VENTURE MANAGEMENT)

565 Fifth Avenue
22nd Floor
New York, NY 10017
Website: www.neomed.com

See Foreign Venture Capital Firms for full listing.

NEW THINGS, LLC

35 West 35th Street
3rd Floor
New York, NY 10001
Phone: 212-967-1066
Fax: 917-591-3126
Website: www.newthingsvc.com

Management and Staff
David Bennahum, Partner
Martin Puris, Partner

Type of Firm
Private Firm Investing Own Capital

Project Preferences

Type of Financing Preferred:
Early Stage
First Stage Financing

Size of Investments Considered
Min Size of Investment Considered (000s): $1,000
Max Size of Investment Considered (000s): $4,000

Geographical Preferences

United States
All U.S.

Industry Preferences

Communications and Media
Wireless Communications

Business Serv.
Services
Media

Additional Information
Year Founded: 2001
Current Activity Level : Actively seeking new investments

NEW YORK LIFE VENTURE CAPITAL GROUP

51 Madison Avenue
New York, NY 10010
Phone: 212-576-7000
Fax: 212-576-8080

Type of Firm
Insurance Firm Affiliate or Subsidiary

Project Preferences

Role in Financing:
Prefer role in deals created by others

Type of Financing Preferred:
First Stage Financing
Second Stage Financing
Start-up Financing

Size of Investments Considered
Min Size of Investment Considered (000s): $500
Max Size of Investment Considered (000s): $1,000

Geographical Preferences

United States
All U.S.

Canada
All Canada

Industry Preferences

(% based on actual investment)

Biotechnology	33.3%
Communications and Media	17.5%
Computer Hardware	14.1%
Computer Software and Services	8.0%
Medical/Health	6.9%
Other Products	6.3%
Internet Specific	6.2%
Semiconductors/Other Elect.	2.9%
Industrial/Energy	2.8%
Consumer Related	2.0%

Additional Information
Name of Most Recent Fund: New York Life Venture Capital
Most Recent Fund Was Raised: 01/01/1996
Year Founded: 1982
Capital Under Management: $312,000,000
Current Activity Level : Actively seeking new investments
Method of Compensation: Return on invest. most important, but chg. closing fees, service fees, etc.

NEW YORK STATE SCIENCE & TECHNOLOGY FOUNDATION

99 Washington Ave Suite 1731
Albany, NY 12210
Phone: 518-473-9741
Fax: 518-473-6876

Type of Firm
Private Firm Investing Own Capital

Project Preferences

Role in Financing:
Prefer role as deal originator but will also invest in deals created by others

Type of Financing Preferred:
First Stage Financing
Second Stage Financing
Seed
Start-up Financing

Size of Investments Considered
Min Size of Investment Considered (000s): $100
Max Size of Investment Considered (000s): $300

Geographical Preferences

United States
Northeast

Industry Preferences

Communications and Media
Commercial Communications
Telecommunications
Data Communications
Satellite Microwave Comm.

Computer Other
Computer Related

Semiconductors/Other Elect.
Electronic Components

Biotechnology
Biotechnology

Medical/Health
Diagnostic Services
Diagnostic Test Products
Other Therapeutic
Disposable Med. Products
Pharmaceuticals

Consumer Related
Education Related

Industrial/Energy
Alternative Energy
Energy Conservation Relat
Industrial Products

Agr/Forestr/Fish
Agriculture related

Additional Information
Year Founded: 1982
Capital Under Management: $20,000,000
Current Activity Level : Actively seeking new investments
Method of Compensation: Other

NEWTEK CAPITAL

845 Third Avenue
8th Floor
New York, NY 10022
Website: www.newtekcapital.com

Other Offices

1201 Brickell Avenue
Miami, FL 33133

1330 West Towne Square Road
Thiensville, WI 53092

1500 Hempstead Turnpike
East Meadow, NY 11554

228 St. Charles Avenue
New Orleans, LA 70130

845 Third Avenue
8th Floor
New York, NY 10022

Management and Staff
Barry Sloane, Chairman & CEO
Brian Wasserman, Chief Financial Officer
Jeffrey Rubin, President

Type of Firm
Private Firm Investing Own Capital

Project Preferences

Type of Financing Preferred:
Early Stage

Geographical Preferences

United States
New York
All U.S.
Wisconsin

Industry Preferences

Internet Specific
Internet

Additional Information
Capital Under Management: $35,000,000
Current Activity Level : Actively seeking new investments

NIB CAPITAL PRIVATE EQUITY N.V. (FKA: PARNIB HOLDING NV)

712 Fifth Avenue
19th Floor
New York, NY 10019
Phone: 1-212-271-8410
Fax: 1-212-271-8480
Website: www.nibcapital.com

See Foreign Venture Capital Firms for full listing.

NORTH AMERICAN CAPITAL CORP.

510 Broad Hollow Road
Suite 205
Melville, NY 11747
Phone: 516-752-9600
Fax: 516-752-9618

Type of Firm
Mgt. Consulting Firm

Industry Association Membership
Natl assoc of Small Bus. Inv. Co (NASBIC)

Project Preferences

Role in Financing:
Prefer role as deal originator but will also invest in deals created by others

Type of Financing Preferred:
Leveraged Buyout
Mezzanine
Second Stage Financing

Size of Investments Considered
Min Size of Investment Considered (000s): $1,000
Max Size of Investment Considered: No Limit

Geographical Preferences

International
No Preference

Additional Information
Year Founded: 1976
Current Activity Level : Actively seeking new investments
Method of Compensation: Professional fee required whether or not deal closes

NORTHWOOD VENTURES

485 Underhill Boulevard
Suite 205
Syosset, NY 11791
Phone: 516-364-5544
Fax: 516-364-0879
Website: www.northwoodventures.com

Other Offices

485 Madison Avenue
20th Floor
New York, NY 10022
Phone: 212-935-4595
Fax: 212-826-1093

Management and Staff
Henry Wilson, Managing Director
Peter Schiff, President

Type of Firm
Private Firm Investing Own Capital

Industry Association Membership
National Venture Capital Association (NVCA)

Project Preferences

Role in Financing:
Will function either as deal originator or investor in deals created by others

Type of Financing Preferred:
Acquisition
Balanced
Early Stage
Expansion
First Stage Financing
Generalist PE
Later Stage
Leveraged Buyout
Management Buyouts
Private Placement
Recapitalizations
Second Stage Financing
Special Situation

Size of Investments Considered
Min Size of Investment Considered (000s): $1,000
Max Size of Investment Considered (000s): $10,000

Geographical Preferences

United States
All U.S.

Canada
All Canada

Industry Preferences

(% based on actual investment)

Communications and Media	60.2%
Internet Specific	15.3%
Consumer Related	9.4%
Industrial/Energy	4.6%
Biotechnology	4.0%
Other Products	3.0%
Semiconductors/Other Elect.	1.9%
Computer Hardware	0.8%
Computer Software and Services	0.6%

Additional Information
Year Founded: 1983
Capital Under Management: $200,000,000
Current Activity Level : Actively seeking new investments
Method of Compensation: Return on investment is of primary concern, do not charge fees

NORWOOD VENTURE CORP.

1430 Broadway
Suite 1607
New York, NY 10018
Phone: 212-869-5075
Fax: 212-869-5331
Website: www.norven.com

Management and Staff
Mark Littell

Whom to Contact
Mark Littell

Type of Firm
Private Firm Investing Own Capital

Industry Association Membership
Natl assoc of Small Bus. Inv. Co (NASBIC)

Project Preferences

Role in Financing:
Prefer role as deal originator but will also invest in deals created by others

Type of Financing Preferred:
Balanced
Leveraged Buyout
Mezzanine
Special Situation

Size of Investments Considered
Min Size of Investment Considered (000s): $500
Max Size of Investment Considered (000s): $1,000

Geographical Preferences

United States
All U.S.

Additional Information

Name of Most Recent Fund: Norwood Venture Corporation
Most Recent Fund Was Raised: 07/01/1989
Year Founded: 1980
Capital Under Management: $17,000,000
Current Activity Level : Actively seeking new investments
Method of Compensation: Return on invest. most important, but chg. closing fees, service fees, etc.

NOVELTEK VENTURE CORP.

521 Fifth Avenue
Suite 1700
New York, NY 10175
Phone: 212-286-1963

Type of Firm

Investment/Merchant Bank Subsid/Affil

Project Preferences

Role in Financing:
Prefer role as deal originator but will also invest in deals created by others

Type of Financing Preferred:
Control-block Purchases
First Stage Financing
Mezzanine
Second Stage Financing
Special Situation
Start-up Financing

Size of Investments Considered

Min Size of Investment Considered (000s): $1,000
Max Size of Investment Considered: No Limit

Geographical Preferences

United States
All U.S.

Canada
All Canada

International
Bermuda
France
Germany
United Kingdom

Industry Preferences

Communications and Media
Communications and Media
Other Communication Prod.

Computer Hardware
Computers

Computer Other
Computer Related

Semiconductors/Other Elect.
Electronics
Electronic Components
Semiconductor
Controllers and Sensors
Sensors
Component Testing Equipmt
Laser Related
Fiber Optics
Analytic/Scientific

Biotechnology
Biotechnology

Medical/Health
Medical/Health
Medical Products

Consumer Related
Entertainment and Leisure
Retail
Computer Stores
Franchises(NEC)
Consumer Products

Industrial/Energy
Alternative Energy
Energy Conservation Relat
Industrial Products
Factory Automation
Robotics
Machinery
Environmental Related

Additional Information

Year Founded: 1983
Current Activity Level : Actively seeking new investments
Method of Compensation: Return on invest. most important, but chg. closing fees, service fees, etc.

NOVO NETWORKS (FKA: EVENTURES GROUP, INC.)

520 Madison Avenue
Suite 3820
New York, NY 10022
Phone: 646-658-1700
Fax: 646-658-1717
Website: www.evnt.com

See Texas for full listing.

NPV CAPITAL PARTNERS, LLC

1 Rockefeller Plaza
Suite 920
New York, NY 10020
Phone: 212-897-7778
Fax: 212-397-2656
Website: http://www.radiusventures.com

Management and Staff

Jordan Davis, Chief Financial Officer

Whom to Contact

Daniel C. Lubin
Peter A. Origenes

Type of Firm

Private Firm Investing Own Capital

Project Preferences

Role in Financing:
Prefer role as deal originator but will also invest in deals created by others

Type of Financing Preferred:
First Stage Financing
Research and Development
Seed
Start-up Financing

Size of Investments Considered

Min Size of Investment Considered (000s): $100
Max Size of Investment Considered: No Limit

Geographical Preferences

United States
All U.S.

Industry Preferences

Computer Software
Systems Software
Applications Software
Artificial Intelligence

Internet Specific
Internet

Semiconductors/Other Elect.
Laser Related
Analytic/Scientific

Biotechnology
Biotechnology

Medical/Health
Medical/Health
Medical Products

Additional Information
Name of Most Recent Fund: Radius Venture Partners I, L.P.
Most Recent Fund Was Raised: 01/01/1997
Year Founded: 1996
Capital Under Management: $25,000,000
Current Activity Level : Actively seeking new investments
Method of Compensation: Return on investment is of primary concern, do not charge fees

OAK HILL CAPITAL MANAGEMENT, INC.

65 East 55th Street
32nd Floor
New York, NY 10022
Phone: 212-326-1500
Fax: 212-838-8411

Other Offices

2775 Sandhill Road
Suite 220
Menlo Park, CA 94025
Phone: 650-234-0500

Management and Staff
Andrew Nathanson, Managing Partner
Brad Henske, Partner
J Crandall, Managing Director
James Alexander, Partner
Mark Wolfson, Managing Director
Ying Blake, Chief Operating Officer

Whom to Contact
Bradford Bernstein

Type of Firm
Investment/Merchant Bank Investing Own or Client Funds

Project Preferences

Role in Financing:
Prefer role as deal originator but will also invest in deals created by others

Type of Financing Preferred:
Control-block Purchases
Leveraged Buyout
Special Situation

Size of Investments Considered
Min Size of Investment Considered (000s): $75,000
Max Size of Investment Considered (000s): $125,000

Geographical Preferences

United States
All U.S.

International
South Africa
United Kingdom
No Preference

Industry Preferences

(% based on actual investment)

Consumer Related	82.2%
Other Products	5.1%
Internet Specific	5.0%
Medical/Health	3.9%
Communications and Media	2.2%
Computer Software and Services	1.2%
Industrial/Energy	0.3%

Additional Information
Name of Most Recent Fund: Oak Hill Capital Partners, L.P.
Most Recent Fund Was Raised: 02/25/1999
Year Founded: 1992
Capital Under Management: $1,800,000,000
Current Activity Level : Actively seeking new investments
Method of Compensation: Return on invest. most important, but chg. closing fees, service fees, etc.

ODEON CAPITAL PARTNERS, L.P.

One State Street Plaza
29th Floor
New York, NY 10004
Phone: 212-785-1300
Fax: 212-785-3159
Website: www.odeoncapital.com

Other Offices

10050 North Wolfe Road
Cupertino, CA 95014
Phone: 408-343-0253
Fax: 603-947-9552

Management and Staff
Ira Machefsky, Partner
Jeffrey Finkle, General Partner
Matthew Smith, Managing Partner

Type of Firm
Private Firm Investing Own Capital

Industry Preferences

(% based on actual investment)

Internet Specific	85.2%
Communications and Media	10.7%
Computer Software and Services	4.1%

Additional Information
Name of Most Recent Fund: Odeon Capital Partners I
Most Recent Fund Was Raised: 08/01/1999
Year Founded: 2000
Capital Under Management: $115,000,000
Current Activity Level : Actively seeking new investments

OLYMPUS CAPITAL HOLDINGS ASIA

153 East 53rd Street, 45/F
New York, NY 10022
Phone: 212-292-6633
Fax: 212-292-6644
Website: www.olympuscap.com

See Foreign Venture Capital Firms for full listing.

ONEX CORP.

712 Fifth Avenue
New York, NY 10019
Phone: 212-582-2211
Fax: 212-582-0909

See Foreign Venture Capital Firms for full listing.

ONONDAGA VENTURE CAPITAL FUND, INC.

714 State Tower Building
Syracuse, NY 13202
Phone: 315-478-0157
Fax: 315-478-0158

Management and Staff
Irving Schwartz, President

Whom to Contact
Irving Schwartz

Type of Firm
Private Firm Investing Own Capital

Project Preferences

Role in Financing:
Will function either as deal originator or investor in deals created by others

Type of Financing Preferred:
Expansion
Later Stage
Mezzanine

Size of Investments Considered
Min Size of Investment Considered (000s): $100
Max Size of Investment Considered (000s): $250

Geographical Preferences

United States
Mid Atlantic
Northeast

Industry Preferences

Communications and Media
Telecommunications

Computer Hardware
Computer Graphics and Dig
Integrated Turnkey System
Disk Relat. Memory Device

Computer Software
Applications Software

Internet Specific
Internet

Semiconductors/Other Elect.
Controllers and Sensors
Sensors
Laser Related
Fiber Optics
Analytic/Scientific

Medical/Health
Medical/Health
Medical Diagnostics
Medical Therapeutics

Consumer Related
Retail
Food/Beverage
Consumer Products

Industrial/Energy
Energy Conservation Relat
Factory Automation
Machinery
Environmental Related

Business Serv.
Distribution

Manufact.
Publishing

Additional Information
Name of Most Recent Fund: Onondaga Venture Capital
Most Recent Fund Was Raised: 06/01/1985
Year Founded: 1985
Capital Under Management: $2,500,000
Current Activity Level : Actively seeking new investments
Method of Compensation: Return on investment is of primary concern, do not charge fees

OVATION CAPITAL PARTNERS (FKA:ICENTENNIAL VENTURES LLC)

120 Bloomingdale Road
4th Floor
White Plains, NY 10605
Phone: 914-258-0011
Fax: 914-684-0848
Website: www.ovationcapital.com

Other Offices
34 John Street
London, United Kingdom WCIN 2EU
Phone: 44-20-7841-1828
Fax: 44-20-7841-1861

Management and Staff
Adam Rosenberg, Principal
Alan Clingman, General Partner
Greg Frank, Managing General Partner
Henry Schachar, General Partner
Kevin Arenson, General Partner
Steven Blend, General Partner
Todd Squilanti, Partner

Type of Firm
Incubators

Industry Association Membership
National Venture Capital Association (NVCA)

Project Preferences

Role in Financing:
Prefer role as deal originator

Type of Financing Preferred:
Early Stage

Size of Investments Considered
Min Size of Investment Considered (000s): $500
Max Size of Investment Considered (000s): $4,000

Geographical Preferences

United States
Northeast

International
Western Europe

Industry Preferences

Internet Specific
Internet

Additional Information
Year Founded: 2000
Capital Under Management: $50,000,000
Current Activity Level : Actively seeking new investments

OXFORD PARTNERS

750 Lexington Avenue
New York, NY 10022
Phone: 212446-5230
Fax: 212-446-5290

See Connecticut for full listing.

PARIBAS PRINCIPAL, INC.

787 Seventh Avenue
32 Fl
New York, NY 10019
Phone: 212-841-2005
Fax: 212-841-3558
Website: www.bnpparibas.com

Management and Staff
Miles Alexander, President

Whom to Contact
Gary Binning
Miles Alexander
Stephen Eisenstein

Type of Firm
Investment/Merchant Bank Investing Own or Client Funds

Industry Association Membership
Natl assoc of Small Bus. Inv. Co (NASBIC)

Project Preferences

Role in Financing:
Prefer role as deal originator but will also invest in deals created by others

Type of Financing Preferred:
Control-block Purchases
Leveraged Buyout
Special Situation

Size of Investments Considered
Min Size of Investment Considered (000s): $50,000
Max Size of Investment Considered: No Limit

Geographical Preferences

United States
All U.S.

Industry Preferences

Communications and Media
Commercial Communications
Radio & TV Broadcasting
Satellite Microwave Comm.

Computer Software
Computer Services

Semiconductors/Other Elect.
Electronic Components
Sensors
Component Testing Equipmt
Analytic/Scientific

Medical/Health
Medical Diagnostics
Diagnostic Services
Diagnostic Test Products
Medical Therapeutics
Drug/Equipmt Delivery
Other Therapeutic
Disposable Med. Products
Hospitals/Clinics/Primary
Hospital/Other Instit.

Consumer Related
Entertainment and Leisure
Retail
Franchises(NEC)
Food/Beverage
Consumer Products
Consumer Services
Other Restaurants

Industrial/Energy
Materials
Machinery
Environmental Related

Transportation
Transportation

Business Serv.
Distribution

Manufact.
Office Automation Equipmt
Publishing

Additional Information
Year Founded: 1989
Capital Under Management: $250,000,000
Current Activity Level : Actively seeking new investments
Method of Compensation: Return on invest. most important, but chg. closing fees, service fees, etc.

PATRICOF & CO. VENTURES, INC.

445 Park Avenue
New York, NY 10022
Phone: 212-753-6300
Fax: 212-319-6155
Website: www.patricof.com

Other Offices

15 Portland Place
London, United Kingdom WIN 3AA
Phone: 44-171-872-6300
Fax: 44-171-666-6441

2 Weizmann St.,IBM Bldg, 10th Fl
P.O. Box 33031
Tel Aviv, Israel 61330
Phone: 9723-696-5990
Fax: 9723-696-5977

2100 Geng Road
Suite 150
Palo Alto, CA 94303
Phone: 650-494-9944
Fax: 650-494-6751

4 Park Square East
Leeds, United Kingdom LS1 2NE
Phone: 44-113-242-3040
Fax: 44-113-242-3047

45, Avenue Kleber
Cedex 16
Paris, France 75784
Phone: 331-5365-0100
Fax: 331-5365-0101

455 South Gulph Road
Suite 410
King of Prussia, PA 19406
Phone: 610-265-0286
Fax: 610-265-4959

Bahnhofstrasse 17
Zollikon/Zurich, Switzerland Ch-8702
Phone: 411-391-5268
Fax: 411-391-5935

Mohlstrasse 22
Munich, Germany 81675
Phone: 4989-998-9090
Fax: 4989-998-90932

Management and Staff
Adele Oliva, Principal
David Landau, Managing Director
Evangelos Simoudis, Venture Partner
F.E. Weissman, Venture Partner
George Jenkins, Managing Director
George Phipps, Managing Director
Gregory Case, Managing Director
Janet Effland, Managing Director
Lori Rafield, General Partner
Paul Vais, Managing Director
Robert Chefitz, Managing Director
Ron Weissman, Venture Partner
Salem Shuchman, Managing Director
Theodore Schell, General Partner
Thomas Hirschfeld, Managing Director

Type of Firm
Private Firm Investing Own Capital

Industry Association Membership
National Venture Capital Association (NVCA)
Western Association of Venture Capitalists (WAVC)

Project Preferences

Role in Financing:
Prefer role as deal originator

Type of Financing Preferred:
First Stage Financing
Leveraged Buyout
Second Stage Financing
Seed
Start-up Financing

Size of Investments Considered
Min Size of Investment Considered (000s): $500
Max Size of Investment Considered: No Limit

Geographical Preferences

United States
All U.S.

International
All International
Japan

Industry Preferences

(% based on actual investment)

Industrial/Energy	27.2%
Internet Specific	15.0%
Other Products	11.0%
Consumer Related	10.8%
Communications and Media	8.3%
Computer Software and Services	7.5%
Medical/Health	6.3%
Computer Hardware	5.0%
Biotechnology	4.9%
Semiconductors/Other Elect.	4.0%

Additional Information
Name of Most Recent Fund: APA Excelsior V, L.P.
Most Recent Fund Was Raised: 10/01/1998
Year Founded: 1969
Capital Under Management: $5,500,000,000
Current Activity Level : Actively seeking new investments
Method of Compensation: Return on investment is of primary concern, do not charge fees

PAUL CAPITAL PARTNERS

99 Park Avenue
8th Floor
New York, NY 10016
Phone: 212-293-2200
Fax: 212-293-2219

See California for full listing.

PECKS MANAGEMENT PARTNERS, LTD.

One Rockefeller Plaza
New York, NY 10020
Phone: 212-332-1333
Fax: 212-332-1334
Website: http://www.pecks.com

Management and Staff
Elaine Healy
Robert Cresci

Whom to Contact
Elaine Healy
Robert Cresci

Type of Firm
Private Firm Investing Own Capital

Project Preferences

Role in Financing:
Prefer role as deal originator but will also invest in deals created by others

Type of Financing Preferred:
Mezzanine
Special Situation

Size of Investments Considered
Min Size of Investment Considered (000s): $6,000
Max Size of Investment Considered: No Limit

Geographical Preferences

United States
All U.S.

Additional Information
Year Founded: 1990
Capital Under Management: $1,100,000,000
Current Activity Level : Actively seeking new investments
Method of Compensation: Return on invest. most important, but chg. closing fees, service fees, etc.

PENNELL VENTURE PARTNERS

55 Broad Street
11th Floor
New York, NY 10004
Phone: 212-378-4996
Fax: 212-378-4990

Type of Firm
Private Firm Investing Own Capital

Industry Association Membership
National Venture Capital Association (NVCA)

Additional Information
Year Founded: 1999
Current Activity Level : Actively seeking new investments

PENNY LANE PARTNERS

767 Fifth Avenue
New York, NY 10153
Phone: 212-980-4292
Fax: 212-319-6046

See New Jersey for full listing.

PEQUOT CAPITAL MANAGEMENT INC.

153 East 53rd Street
35th Street
New York, NY 10022
Phone: 212-702-4400
Fax: 212-655-0174
Website: www.pequotcapital.com

Other Offices

1 Market Plaza
Steuart Tower 22nd Floor
San Francisco, CA 94105
Phone: 415-365-8400

500 Nyala Farm Road
Westport, CT 06880
Phone: 203-429-2200

Management and Staff
Arthur Samberg, Chairman & CEO
Deborah Bernstein, Vice President
Erik Jansen, Principal
Gerald Poch, Managing Director
Greg Rossmann, Principal
Jeff Martin, Vice President
Jim McNiel, Principal
Karen White, Principal
Lawrence Lenihan, Managing Director
Michael Karfopoulos, Principal
Nicholas Romano, Principal
Rick Heitzmann, Vice President
Zev Scherl, Vice President

Type of Firm
Private Firm Investing Own Capital

Project Preferences

Role in Financing:
Prefer role as deal originator but will also invest in deals created by others

Type of Financing Preferred:
Early Stage
Expansion
First Stage Financing
Later Stage
Mezzanine
Open Market
Private Placement
Recapitalizations
Second Stage Financing
Seed
Startup

Size of Investments Considered
Min Size of Investment Considered (000s): $2,000
Max Size of Investment Considered (000s): $50,000

Geographical Preferences

United States
All U.S.

Canada
All Canada

International
Belgium
Eastern Europe
France
Germany
Italy
Luxembourg
Netherlands
Spain
United Kingdom

Industry Preferences

(% based on actual investment)

Internet Specific	42.3%
Communications and Media	19.8%
Computer Software and Services	14.5%
Semiconductors/Other Elect.	6.4%
Other Products	6.0%
Medical/Health	5.2%
Consumer Related	2.3%
Computer Hardware	2.1%
Biotechnology	1.4%

Additional Information
Year Founded: 1999
Capital Under Management: $1,692,000,000
Current Activity Level : Actively seeking new investments

PHILLIPS-SMITH SPECIALTY RETAIL GROUP

Seven Locust Lane
Bronxville, NY 10708
Phone: 914-961-0407
Fax: 914-961-0407
Website: www.phillips-smith.com

See Texas for full listing.

PITTSFORD GROUP, INC., THE

Eight Lodge Pole Road
Pittsford, NY 14534
Phone: 716-223-3523

Type of Firm
Private Firm Investing Own Capital

Project Preferences

Role in Financing:
Prefer role as deal originator but will also invest in deals created by others

Type of Financing Preferred:
Control-block Purchases
First Stage Financing
Second Stage Financing
Start-up Financing

Size of Investments Considered
Min Size of Investment Considered (000s): $100
Max Size of Investment Considered (000s): $300

Geographical Preferences

United States
Northeast
Southeast

Canada
Central Canada
Eastern Canada
Ontario
Quebec

Industry Preferences

Communications and Media
Telecommunications
Other Communication Prod.

Computer Software
Applications Software

Internet Specific
Internet

Semiconductors/Other Elect.
Semiconductor
Sensors
Laser Related

Biotechnology
Biosensors

Consumer Related
Retail

Industrial/Energy
Materials

Additional Information
Name of Most Recent Fund: Pittsford Capital Partners
Most Recent Fund Was Raised: 07/01/1985
Year Founded: 1975
Capital Under Management: $175,000,000
Current Activity Level : Actively seeking new investments
Method of Compensation: Return on invest. most important, but chg. closing fees, service fees, etc.

PLATINUM GROUP, INC., THE

350 Fifth Avenue
Suite 7113
New York, NY 10118
Phone: 212-736-4300
Fax: 212-736-6086
Website: www.platinumgroup.com

Management and Staff
Daniel Nevadovic
Harold Mintz
Michael Grant
Rohit Mehrotta

Whom to Contact
Daniel Nevadovic
Harold Mintz
Michael Grant
Rohit Mehrotta

Type of Firm
Mgt. Consulting Firm

Project Preferences

Role in Financing:
Prefer role as deal originator but will also invest in deals created by others

Type of Financing Preferred:
First Stage Financing
Leveraged Buyout
Second Stage Financing
Start-up Financing

Geographical Preferences

United States
All U.S.

Industry Preferences

Communications and Media
CATV & Pay TV Systems
Radio & TV Broadcasting
Telecommunications
Data Communications
Other Communication Prod.

Computer Hardware
Computers
Mainframes / Scientific
Computer Graphics and Dig
Integrated Turnkey System
Terminals
Disk Relat. Memory Device

Computer Software
Computer Services
Systems Software
Applications Software
Artificial Intelligence

Internet Specific
Internet

Semiconductors/Other Elect.
Semiconductor
Circuit Boards
Laser Related
Fiber Optics

Biotechnology
Industrial Biotechnology
Biotech Related Research

Medical/Health
Medical Diagnostics
Diagnostic Test Products
Hospitals/Clinics/Primary

Consumer Related
Consumer Products
Consumer Services
Education Related

Industrial/Energy
Oil & Gas Drilling,Explor
Robotics

Manufact.
Office Automation Equipmt
Publishing

Additional Information

Year Founded: 1990
Current Activity Level : Actively seeking new investments
Method of Compensation: Return on invest. most important, but chg. closing fees, service fees, etc.

POLY VENTURES

901 Route 110
Farmingdale, NY 11735
Phone: 631-249-4710
Fax: 631-249-4713

Other Offices

901 Route 110
Farmingdale, NY

Type of Firm

Private Firm Investing Own Capital

Project Preferences

Role in Financing:
Other

Type of Financing Preferred:
First Stage Financing
Second Stage Financing
Seed
Start-up Financing

Size of Investments Considered
Min Size of Investment Considered (000s): $500
Max Size of Investment Considered (000s): $1,000

Geographical Preferences

International
No Preference

Industry Preferences

(% based on actual investment)

Computer Software and Services	42.4%
Computer Hardware	25.9%
Industrial/Energy	20.7%
Semiconductors/Other Elect.	7.2%
Communications and Media	3.8%

Additional Information

Year Founded: 1987
Capital Under Management: $53,000,000
Current Activity Level : Actively seeking new investments
Method of Compensation: Return on investment is of primary concern, do not charge fees

POMONA CAPITAL

780 Third Avenue
28th Floor
New York, NY 10017
Phone: 212-593-3639
Fax: 212-593-3987
Website: www.pomonacapital.com

Other Offices

16 Hanover Square
London, United Kingdom W1R 9AJ
Phone: 44-171-408-9433
Fax: 44-171-408-9434

Management and Staff

Brian Wright, Partner
Frances Janis, Partner
Julie Cochran, Partner
Mark Maruszewski, Vice President
Marshall Parke, General Partner
Michael Granoff, Chief Executive Officer
Stephen Futrell, Chief Financial Officer
Thomas Bradley, Partner

Whom to Contact

Karen Macleod

Type of Firm

Private Firm Investing Own Capital

Project Preferences

Role in Financing:
Prefer role as deal originator but will also invest in deals created by others

Type of Financing Preferred:
Balanced
Fund of Funds
Later Stage
Leveraged Buyout
Mezzanine
Other
Second Stage Financing
Special Situation

Size of Investments Considered
Min Size of Investment Considered (000s): $1,000
Max Size of Investment Considered: No Limit

Geographical Preferences

United States
All U.S.
All U.S.

International
Europe
All International
Western Europe

Industry Preferences

Communications and Media
Communications and Media

Computer Hardware
Computer Graphics and Dig

Computer Software
Computer Services
Systems Software
Applications Software

Biotechnology
Biotechnology

Medical/Health
Medical/Health
Medical Diagnostics
Diagnostic Services
Diagnostic Test Products
Medical Therapeutics
Drug/Equipmt Delivery
Medical Products
Pharmaceuticals

Consumer Related
Retail
Food/Beverage
Consumer Products

Industrial/Energy
Oil & Gas Drilling,Explor
Materials

Financial Services
Financial Services

Manufact.
Publishing

Additional Information
Name of Most Recent Fund: Pomona Capital IV
Most Recent Fund Was Raised: 09/01/1998
Year Founded: 1999
Capital Under Management: $650,000,000
Current Activity Level : Actively seeking new investments
Method of Compensation: Return on investment is of primary concern, do not charge fees

PRIMEDIA VENTURES

745 Fifth Avenue
New York, NY 10151
Phone: 212-745-0100
Fax: 212-610-9422
Website: www.primediaventures.com

Management and Staff
Andrew Thompson, Managing Director
James Carlisle, Venture Partner
Jason Chervokas, Venture Partner
Lawrence Phillips, Managing Director

Whom to Contact
Andy Thompson
Larry Phillips

Type of Firm
Non-Financial Corp. Affiliate or Subsidiary

Industry Association Membership
National Venture Capital Association (NVCA)

Project Preferences

Type of Financing Preferred:
Early Stage
First Stage Financing
Seed
Start-up Financing

Geographical Preferences

United States
All U.S.

Industry Preferences

(% based on actual investment)

Internet Specific	91.1%
Consumer Related	5.5%
Computer Software and Services	1.8%
Communications and Media	1.6%

Additional Information
Name of Most Recent Fund: PRIMEDIA Ventures
Most Recent Fund Was Raised: 10/01/1998
Year Founded: 1998
Capital Under Management: $70,000,000
Current Activity Level : Actively seeking new investments

PRIVATE EQUITY INVESTORS, INC.

115 East 62nd Street
New York, NY 10021
Phone: 212-750-1228
Fax: 212-750-2685
Website: www.peifunds.com

Management and Staff
Charles Stetson, Managing Director
David Parshall, Managing Director
Gunnar Fremuth, Vice President
John Wiencek, Chief Financial Officer

Type of Firm
Private Firm Investing Own Capital

Project Preferences

Role in Financing:
Prefer role as deal originator but will also invest in deals created by others

Type of Financing Preferred:
Leveraged Buyout
Mezzanine
Second Stage Financing
Special Situation

Geographical Preferences

United States
All U.S.

Additional Information
Name of Most Recent Fund: Private Equity Investors III, L.P.
Most Recent Fund Was Raised: 05/01/1997
Year Founded: 1995
Capital Under Management: $110,000,000
Current Activity Level : Actively seeking new investments
Method of Compensation: Return on investment is of primary concern, do not charge fees

PROSPECT STREET VENTURES (FKA:PROSPECT STREET INVEST. MGMT)

10 East 40th Street
44th Floor
New York, NY 10016
Phone: 212-448-0702
Fax: 212-448-9652
Website: www.prospectstreet.com

Other Offices

Exchange Place
37th Floor
Boston, MA 02109
Phone: 617-742-3800
Fax: 617-742-9455

Management and Staff
John Barry, General Partner
Joseph Cote, Chief Operating Officer
Ronald Celmer, General Partner
Russell Hirsch, Partner

Whom to Contact
Edward Ryeom

Type of Firm
SBIC Not elsewhere classified

Industry Association Membership
Natl assoc of Small Bus. Inv. Co (NASBIC)

Project Preferences

Role in Financing:
Prefer role as deal originator but will also invest in deals created by others

Type of Financing Preferred:
Control-block Purchases
First Stage Financing
Recapitalizations
Second Stage Financing
Special Situation
Start-up Financing

Size of Investments Considered
Min Size of Investment Considered (000s): $1,000
Max Size of Investment Considered: No Limit

Geographical Preferences

United States
Mid Atlantic
Northeast
West Coast

Canada
Eastern Canada

Industry Preferences

(% based on actual investment)

Internet Specific	62.8%
Computer Software and Services	22.9%
Computer Hardware	5.6%
Communications and Media	4.9%
Other Products	3.9%

Additional Information
Year Founded: 1993
Capital Under Management: $126,000,000
Current Activity Level : Actively seeking new investments
Method of Compensation: Return on investment is of primary concern, do not charge fees

PROVEN PRIVATE EQUITY (FKA:GUINNESS MAHON DEVELOPMENT CAP.)

335 Madison Avenue
11th Floor
New York, NY 10017
Phone: 212 922 2391
Fax: 212 922 2358
Website: www.proven.co.uk

See Foreign Venture Capital Firms for full listing.

PSILOS GROUP MANAGERS LLC

625 Avenue of the Americas
4th Floor
New York, NY 10011
Phone: 212-242-8844
Fax: 212-242-8855
Website: www.psilos.com

Other Offices

152 West 57th Street
33rd Floor
New York, MA 10019
Phone: 212-399-2070
Fax: 212-399-2081

Management and Staff
Albert Waxman, Managing Director
Curt Mondale, Principal
David Eichler, Principal
Deborah Friedland, Principal
Jeffrey Krauss, Managing Director
Joseph Riley, Principal
Lisa Suennen, Managing Director
Samuel Bain, Managing Director
Steven Krupa, Managing Director
Thomas Armstrong, Managing Director

Type of Firm
Private Firm Investing Own Capital

Industry Association Membership
National Venture Capital Association (NVCA)

Project Preferences

Type of Financing Preferred:
Balanced

Industry Preferences

(% based on actual investment)

Internet Specific	55.2%
Medical/Health	36.7%
Computer Software and Services	8.0%

Additional Information
Name of Most Recent Fund: Psilos Group Ventures (AKA: Psilos Partners, L.P.)
Most Recent Fund Was Raised: 01/01/1998
Year Founded: 1998
Capital Under Management: $178,000,000
Current Activity Level : Actively seeking new investments

PUTNAM LOVELL CAPITAL PARTNERS, L.P.

65 East 55th Street
Park Avenue Tower
New York, NY 10022
Phone: 212-546-7500
Fax: 212-644-2271
E-mail: Info@PutnamLovell.com
Website: www.putnamlovell.com

See California for full listing.

RAND CAPITAL CORPORATION

2200 Rand Building
Buffalo, NY 14203
Phone: 716-853-0802
Fax: 716-854-8480
Website: www.randcapital.com

Management and Staff
Allen Grum, President
Daniel Penberthy, Chief Financial Officer

Whom to Contact
Allen Grum
Daniel Penberthy

Type of Firm
Private Firm Investing Own Capital

Industry Association Membership
National Venture Capital Association (NVCA)

Project Preferences

Role in Financing:
Will function either as deal originator or investor in deals created by others

Type of Financing Preferred:
Second Stage Financing

Size of Investments Considered
Min Size of Investment Considered (000s): $25
Max Size of Investment Considered (000s): $500

Geographical Preferences

United States
Northeast

Canada
Ontario

Industry Preferences

(% based on actual investment)

Other Products	23.9%
Communications and Media	14.2%
Computer Hardware	12.6%
Computer Software and Services	12.0%
Industrial/Energy	10.0%
Consumer Related	9.7%
Semiconductors/Other Elect.	7.5%
Medical/Health	4.7%
Internet Specific	3.7%
Biotechnology	1.8%

Additional Information
Name of Most Recent Fund: Rand Capital Corporation
Most Recent Fund Was Raised: 06/01/1969
Year Founded: 1969
Capital Under Management: $8,000,000
Current Activity Level : Actively seeking new investments
Method of Compensation: Return on investment is of primary concern, do not charge fees

---

RARE VENTURES

565 Fifth Avenue
New York, NY 10017
Phone: 212-883-6940
Fax: 212-856-9081

Management and Staff
Derrick Chen, Managing Director

Type of Firm
Non-Financial Corp. Affiliate or Subsidiary

Industry Preferences

(% based on actual investment)

Internet Specific	100.0%

Additional Information
Year Founded: 1999
Current Activity Level : Actively seeking new investments

RBC DOMINION SECURITIES CORPORATION

One Liberty Plaza
New York, NY 10002
Phone: 212-428-3035
Fax: 212-858-7678

Type of Firm
Private Firm Investing Own Capital

Additional Information
Year Founded: 1999
Current Activity Level : Actively seeking new investments

REGENT CAPITAL MANAGEMENT

505 Park Avenue
Suite 1700
New York, NY 10022
Phone: 212-735-9900
Fax: 212-735-9908

Management and Staff
J. Oliver Maggard, Managing Director
Nina McLemore, Managing Director
Richard Hochman, Managing Director

Whom to Contact
Richard Hochman

Type of Firm
Private Firm Investing Own Capital

Project Preferences

Role in Financing:
Prefer role as deal originator but will also invest in deals created by others

Type of Financing Preferred:
Leveraged Buyout
Mezzanine
Second Stage Financing

Size of Investments Considered
Min Size of Investment Considered (000s): $3,500
Max Size of Investment Considered: No Limit

Geographical Preferences

United States
All U.S.

Industry Preferences

(% based on actual investment)

Consumer Related	62.9%
Communications and Media	30.0%
Other Products	7.2%

Additional Information
Name of Most Recent Fund: Regent Capital Partners
Most Recent Fund Was Raised: 01/01/1996
Year Founded: 1995
Capital Under Management: $28,000,000
Current Activity Level : Actively seeking new investments
Method of Compensation: Return on invest. most important, but chg. closing fees, service fees, etc.

REPRISE CAPITAL CORP.

400 Post Avenue
Westbury, NY 11590
Phone: 516-997-2400
Fax: 516-338-2808

Other Offices

400 Post Ave
Westbury, NY

6345 Balboa Boulevard
Encino, CA 91316
Phone: 818-776-2420
Fax: 818-776-2434

Type of Firm
Private Firm Investing Own Capital

Project Preferences

Role in Financing:
Prefer role as deal originator

Size of Investments Considered
Min Size of Investment Considered (000s): $2,000
Max Size of Investment Considered: No Limit

Geographical Preferences
United States
All U.S.

Industry Preferences
Semiconductors/Other Elect.
Electronic Components
Sensors

Medical/Health
Medical/Health

Consumer Related
Entertainment and Leisure
Retail
Computer Stores
Franchises(NEC)
Food/Beverage
Consumer Products
Consumer Services
Other Restaurants

Industrial/Energy
Materials
Factory Automation
Machinery
Environmental Related

Transportation
Transportation

Financial Services
Financial Services

Business Serv.
Distribution

Manufact.
Publishing

Additional Information
Name of Most Recent Fund: Reprise Special Situation Venture Fund II
Most Recent Fund Was Raised: 06/01/1987
Year Founded: 1985
Capital Under Management: $22,000,000
Current Activity Level : Actively seeking new investments
Method of Compensation: Return on investment is of primary concern, do not charge fees

RHO MANAGEMENT

152 West 57th Street
23rd Floor
New York, NY 10019
Phone: 212-751-6677
Fax: 212-731-3613
Website: www.rhomanagement.com

Management and Staff
Ben Terk, Principal
Gordon Hargraves, Vice President
Habib Kairouz, Managing Director
Mark Leschly, Managing Director
Martin Kahn, Partner
Peter Kalkanis, Chief Financial Officer
Yag Patel, Principal

Type of Firm
Affiliate/Subsidary of Oth. Financial. Instit.

Industry Association Membership
National Venture Capital Association (NVCA)

Project Preferences
Type of Financing Preferred:
Early Stage
Later Stage
Seed

Size of Investments Considered
Min Size of Investment Considered (000s): $3,500
Max Size of Investment Considered: No Limit

Industry Preferences
(% based on actual investment)

Internet Specific	28.4%
Industrial/Energy	21.5%
Communications and Media	17.6%
Medical/Health	7.9%
Computer Software and Services	7.4%
Semiconductors/Other Elect.	5.9%
Computer Hardware	5.2%
Biotechnology	5.0%
Other Products	1.1%

Additional Information
Year Founded: 1981
Capital Under Management: $181,000,000
Current Activity Level : Actively seeking new investments

RIVERSIDE MANAGEMENT GROUP

757 Third Avenue
27th Floor
New York, NY 10017
Phone: 212-230-1880
Fax: 212-230-1057
Website: www.rmginvestments.com

Other Offices
Stranveien 50
Lysaker, Norway 1366
Phone: 476-712-3900
Fax: 476-710-4990

Management and Staff
Christopher Patyk, General Partner
Christopher Wood, General Partner
D. Jim Carpenter, Managing Partner
Kenneth Rand, General Partner
Mark Bernegger, General Partner
Robert Hoguet, General Partner

Type of Firm
Private Firm Investing Own Capital

Industry Preferences
(% based on actual investment)

Internet Specific	62.9%
Communications and Media	21.0%
Computer Software and Services	9.4%
Industrial/Energy	4.5%
Other Products	2.2%

Additional Information
Year Founded: 1996
Capital Under Management: $84,000,000
Current Activity Level : Actively seeking new investments

ROTHSCHILD VENTURES, INC.

1251 Avenue of the Americas
51st Floor
New York, NY 10020
Phone: 212-403-3500
Fax: 212-403-3652
Website: www.nmrothschild.com

Other Offices

1251 Avenue of the Americas
51st Floor
New York, NY

Management and Staff
Bob Andrew, Chief Financial Officer
Paul Jenssen, Chief Financial Officer

Type of Firm
Investment/Merchant Bank Investing Own or Client Funds

Project Preferences

Role in Financing:
Prefer role as deal originator but will also invest in deals created by others

Type of Financing Preferred:
First Stage Financing
Leveraged Buyout
Mezzanine
Research and Development
Second Stage Financing
Seed
Start-up Financing

Geographical Preferences

United States
All U.S.

Canada
All Canada

Industry Preferences

(% based on actual investment)

Computer Hardware	22.6%
Industrial/Energy	18.3%
Communications and Media	17.2%
Medical/Health	9.6%
Other Products	7.4%
Biotechnology	6.9%
Consumer Related	6.1%
Semiconductors/Other Elect.	5.6%
Computer Software and Services	5.5%
Internet Specific	0.8%

Additional Information
Name of Most Recent Fund: Resource Capital Fund L.P.
Most Recent Fund Was Raised: 05/29/1998
Year Founded: 1949
Capital Under Management: $59,500,000
Current Activity Level : Inactive / Unknown
Method of Compensation: Return on investment is of primary concern, do not charge fees

RRE VENTURES LLC

126 East 56th Street
New York, NY 10022
Phone: 212-418-5100
Fax: 212-355-0330
Website: www.rre.com

Management and Staff
Andrew Zalasin, Chief Financial Officer
James Robinson, General Partner
Ken Ross, Partner
M. Michel Orban, Venture Partner
Sreedhar Menon, Venture Partner
Stuart Ellman, General Partner

Whom to Contact
James D. Robinson IV

Type of Firm
Private Firm Investing Own Capital

Industry Association Membership
National Venture Capital Association (NVCA)

Project Preferences

Role in Financing:
Prefer role as deal originator but will also invest in deals created by others

Type of Financing Preferred:
First Stage Financing
Mezzanine
Second Stage Financing

Geographical Preferences

United States
All U.S.

Industry Preferences

(% based on actual investment)

Internet Specific	61.5%
Computer Software and Services	21.2%
Computer Hardware	7.2%
Communications and Media	5.7%
Other Products	3.2%
Consumer Related	1.3%

Additional Information
Name of Most Recent Fund: RRE Ventures II, L.P.
Most Recent Fund Was Raised: 08/01/1999
Year Founded: 1994
Capital Under Management: $250,000,000
Current Activity Level : Actively seeking new investments
Method of Compensation: Return on investment is of primary concern, do not charge fees

SALOMON SMITH BARNEY VENTURE SERVICES LLC

Seven World Trade Center
New York, NY 10048
Phone: 212-816-6000
Fax: 212-816-7040
Website: www.salomonsmithbarney.com

Management and Staff
Andy Chase, President
Darren Friedman, Vice President

Type of Firm
Investment/Merchant Bank Subsid/Affil

Project Preferences

Type of Financing Preferred:
Fund of Funds

Geographical Preferences

United States
All U.S.

International
Europe

Additional Information
Name of Most Recent Fund: Salomon Smith Barney Private Selection Fund I, L.L.C.
Most Recent Fund Was Raised: 01/01/1998
Capital Under Management: $708,000,000
Current Activity Level : Actively seeking new investments

SANDLER CAPITAL MANAGEMENT

767 Fifth Avenue
45th Floor
New York, NY 10153
Phone: 212-754-8100
Fax: 212-826-0280

Type of Firm
Private Firm Investing Own Capital

Project Preferences

Role in Financing:
Prefer role as deal originator but will also invest in deals created by others

Type of Financing Preferred:
Control-block Purchases
First Stage Financing
Leveraged Buyout
Mezzanine
Research and Development
Second Stage Financing
Seed
Special Situation
Start-up Financing

Size of Investments Considered
Min Size of Investment Considered (000s): $20,000
Max Size of Investment Considered: No Limit

Geographical Preferences

United States
All U.S.

Canada
All Canada

International
Australia
Bermuda
France
Germany
Italy
Middle East
South Africa
Spain
United Kingdom

Industry Preferences

(% based on actual investment)

Internet Specific	37.8%
Communications and Media	31.9%
Computer Software and Services	20.0%
Other Products	6.2%
Semiconductors/Other Elect.	4.0%

Additional Information
Name of Most Recent Fund: Sandler Partners Capital IV
Most Recent Fund Was Raised: 12/31/1997
Year Founded: 1980
Capital Under Management: $1,000,000,000
Current Activity Level : Inactive / Unknown
Method of Compensation: Return on investment is of primary concern, do not charge fees

SCRIPPS VENTURES

200 Madison Avenue
4th Floor
New York, NY 10010
Phone: 212-293-8709
Fax: 212-293-8716
Website: www.scrippsventures.com

Management and Staff
Doug Stern

Whom to Contact
Doug Stern

Type of Firm
Non-Financial Corp. Affiliate or Subsidiary

Project Preferences

Role in Financing:
Prefer role as deal originator but will also invest in deals created by others

Type of Financing Preferred:
First Stage Financing
Second Stage Financing

Size of Investments Considered
Min Size of Investment Considered (000s): $5,000
Max Size of Investment Considered: No Limit

Geographical Preferences

United States
All U.S.

Canada
All Canada

Industry Preferences

(% based on actual investment)

Internet Specific	61.9%
Computer Software and Services	14.0%
Consumer Related	10.4%
Other Products	7.9%
Computer Hardware	5.8%

Additional Information
Name of Most Recent Fund: Scripps Ventures II
Most Recent Fund Was Raised: 09/01/1999
Year Founded: 1996
Capital Under Management: $150,000,000
Current Activity Level : Actively seeking new investments
Method of Compensation: Return on investment is of primary concern, do not charge fees

SEAPORT CAPITAL

199 Water Street
20th Floor
New York, NY 10038
Phone: 212-425-1400
Fax: 212-425-1420
Website: www.seaportcapital.com

Other Offices

1235 Westlakes Drive
Suite 140
Berwyn, PA 19312
Phone: 215-251-0650
Fax: 215-251-9180

375 Park Avenue
Suite 3808
New York, NY 10152
Phone: 212-319-1968
Fax: 212-319-4203

Stradttor 1
Dusseldorf, Germany 40219
Phone: 49 211 60042100
Fax: 49 211 60042200

Management and Staff
Alison Mulhern, Partner
George Pollack, Chief Financial Officer
James Collis, Partner
Kevin Brandon, Principal
Stephen Baker, Vice President
Steven McCall, Principal
William Luby, Managing Partner

Whom to Contact
Stephen Baker
Steven McCall

Type of Firm
Private Firm Investing Own Capital

Industry Association Membership
National Venture Capital Association (NVCA)

Project Preferences

Role in Financing:
Prefer role as deal originator but will also invest in deals created by others

Type of Financing Preferred:
Acquisition
Early Stage
Expansion
Later Stage
Leveraged Buyout
Management Buyouts
Recapitalizations
Second Stage Financing

Size of Investments Considered
Min Size of Investment Considered (000s): $5,000
Max Size of Investment Considered (000s): $25,000

Geographical Preferences
United States
All U.S.

Canada
All Canada

Industry Preferences
(% based on actual investment)

Communications and Media	67.8%
Internet Specific	12.9%
Other Products	10.0%
Consumer Related	7.9%
Computer Software and Services	1.4%

Additional Information
Name of Most Recent Fund: CEA Capital Partners USA, L.P.
Most Recent Fund Was Raised: 02/01/1997
Year Founded: 1996
Capital Under Management: $410,000,000
Current Activity Level : Actively seeking new investments
Method of Compensation: Return on investment is of primary concern, do not charge fees

SEED CAPITAL PARTNERS

620 Main Street
Buffalo, NY 14202
Phone: 716-845-7520
Fax: 716-845-7539
Website: www.seedcp.com

Management and Staff
Gary Crosby, Partner
Jordan Levy, Partner
Ronald Schreiber, Partner

Type of Firm
Affiliate/Subsidary of Oth. Financial. Instit.

Project Preferences
Type of Financing Preferred:
Early Stage

Geographical Preferences
United States
Northeast

Industry Preferences
(% based on actual investment)

Computer Software and Services	51.9%
Internet Specific	24.3%
Communications and Media	15.4%
Semiconductors/Other Elect.	5.2%
Other Products	3.3%

Additional Information
Year Founded: 2000
Current Activity Level : Actively seeking new investments

SENTINEL CAPITAL PARTNERS

777 Third Avenue
32nd Floor
New York, NY 10017
Phone: 212-688-3100
Fax: 212-688-6513
Website: www.sentinelpartners.com

Management and Staff
Christopher Weiler, Principal
David Lobel, Managing Partner
Eric Bommer, Principal
James Coady, Vice President
John McCormack, Partner
Paul Murphy, Principal

Type of Firm
Private Firm Investing Own Capital

Project Preferences
Role in Financing:
Prefer role as deal originator but will also invest in deals created by others

Type of Financing Preferred:
Control-block Purchases
Industry Rollups
Leveraged Buyout
Mezzanine
Special Situation

Size of Investments Considered
Min Size of Investment Considered (000s): $17,500
Max Size of Investment Considered: No Limit

Geographical Preferences
United States
All U.S.

Canada
All Canada

Industry Preferences
(% based on actual investment)

Consumer Related	75.8%
Internet Specific	10.6%
Communications and Media	7.2%
Other Products	6.4%

Additional Information
Name of Most Recent Fund: Sentinel Capital Partners II, L.P.
Most Recent Fund Was Raised: 01/01/1999
Year Founded: 1995
Capital Under Management: $176,000,000
Current Activity Level : Actively seeking new investments
Method of Compensation: Return on investment is of primary concern, do not charge fees

SGI CAPITAL L.L.C

1221 Avenue of the Americas
New York, NY 10020
Phone: 212-278-5400
Fax: 212-278-5454
Website: www.sgicapital.com

Management and Staff
Andrew Howley, President
Gary DiLella, Vice President
Richard Stewart, Vice President
Thomas Balderston, President

Whom to Contact
Christopher M. Neenan
Elan A. Schultz

Type of Firm
Investment/Merchant Bank Subsid/Affil

Industry Association Membership
National Venture Capital Association (NVCA)

Project Preferences
Role in Financing:
Prefer role as deal originator but will also invest in deals created by others

Type of Financing Preferred:
Industry Rollups
Leveraged Buyout
Mezzanine
Second Stage Financing
Special Situation

Geographical Preferences
United States
All U.S.

Canada
All Canada

International
South Africa

Industry Preferences

Industrial/Energy
Industrial Products

Business Serv.
Services

Manufact.
Manufacturing

Additional Information

Year Founded: 1997
Capital Under Management: $20,000,000
Current Activity Level : Actively seeking new investments

SHATTAN GROUP, THE

590 Madison Avenue
18th Floor
New York, NY 10022
Phone: 212-308-9200
Fax: 212-308-5205
E-mail: postmaster@shattan.com
Website: www.shattan.com

Management and Staff

Craig Staub, Vice President
Gregory Mendel, Managing Director
James Mattutat, Chief Financial Officer
Kevin Fechtmeyer, Managing Director
Thomas Shattan, Managing Director

Whom to Contact

Thomas Shattan

Type of Firm

Placement Agent

Project Preferences

Role in Financing:
Prefer role in deals created by others

Type of Financing Preferred:
Expansion
Leveraged Buyout
Management Buyouts
Mezzanine
Private Placement
Second Stage Financing
Special Situation

Size of Investments Considered
Min Size of Investment Considered (000s): $10,000
Max Size of Investment Considered (000s): $100,000

Geographical Preferences

United States
All U.S.

Canada
All Canada

International
Belgium
France
Germany
Italy
Latin America
Luxembourg
Netherlands
Spain
United Kingdom

Industry Preferences

Communications and Media
Communications and Media

Computer Hardware
Integrated Turnkey System

Computer Software
Computer Services
Data Processing
Software
Systems Software
Applications Software

Internet Specific
E-Commerce Technology
Internet

Semiconductors/Other Elect.
Fiber Optics

Medical/Health
Medical/Health

Consumer Related
Consumer
Entertainment and Leisure
Retail
Franchises(NEC)
Food/Beverage
Consumer Products
Education Related

Industrial/Energy
Energy
Industrial Products
Factory Automation
Machinery
Environmental Related

Transportation
Transportation
Aerospace

Financial Services
Financial Services
Insurance

Business Serv.
Services
Distribution
Consulting Services
Media

Manufact.
Manufacturing

Agr/Forestr/Fish
Agriculture related

Utilities
Utilities

Other
Environment Responsible
Women/Minority-Owned Bus.

Additional Information

Year Founded: 1996
Current Activity Level : Actively seeking new investments
Method of Compensation: Function primarily in service area, receive contingent fee in cash or equity

SHOTT CAPITAL MANAGEMENT

19 West 34th Street
Suite 1013
New York, NY 10001
Phone: 212-947-8610
Fax: 212-947-8641

Management and Staff

Webb Trammell

Whom to Contact

Webb Trammell

Type of Firm

Private Firm Investing Own Capital

Project Preferences

Type of Financing Preferred:
First Stage Financing
Leveraged Buyout
Mezzanine
Research and Development
Second Stage Financing
Seed
Start-up Financing

Geographical Preferences

United States
All U.S.

Canada
All Canada

International
Australia
France
Germany
Japan
South Africa
Spain
United Kingdom

Additional Information
Current Activity Level : Inactive / Unknown
Method of Compensation: Return on investment is of primary concern, do not charge fees

SIGNATURE CAPITAL, LLC.

712 Fifth Avenue
11th Floor
New York, NY 10019
Phone: 212-765-4700
Fax: 212-765-3843

Management and Staff
LouAnne Flanders-Stec, Chief Financial Officer
Wilson Allen, President

Type of Firm
Private Firm Investing Own Capital

Industry Association Membership
National Venture Capital Association (NVCA)

Project Preferences

Additional Information
Current Activity Level : Actively seeking new investments

SIGULER GUFF & COMPANY, LLC

Rockefeller Center
630 Fifth Avenue, 16th Floor
New York, NY 10111
Phone: 212-332-5100
Fax: 212-332-5120

Type of Firm
Private Firm Investing Own Capital

Project Preferences

Role in Financing:
Prefer role as deal originator but will also invest in deals created by others

Type of Financing Preferred:
Balanced
Control-block Purchases
First Stage Financing
Leveraged Buyout
Mezzanine
Second Stage Financing
Special Situation
Start-up Financing

Geographical Preferences

United States
All U.S.

International
Middle East
Soviet Union

Industry Preferences

Communications and Media
Commercial Communications
CATV & Pay TV Systems
Radio & TV Broadcasting
Telecommunications
Data Communications

Computer Hardware
Mainframes / Scientific
Mini and Personal/Desktop
Computer Graphics and Dig
Disk Relat. Memory Device

Computer Software
Computer Services
Systems Software
Applications Software

Internet Specific
Internet

Semiconductors/Other Elect.
Electronic Components
Semiconductor
Sensors
Component Testing Equipmt
Laser Related
Fiber Optics
Analytic/Scientific

Biotechnology
Biosensors
Biotech Related Research
Biotech Related Research

Medical/Health
Medical/Health
Medical Diagnostics
Medical Therapeutics

Consumer Related
Retail
Food/Beverage
Consumer Products
Consumer Services
Education Related

Industrial/Energy
Oil and Gas Exploration
Oil & Gas Drilling,Explor
Coal Related
Energy Conservation Relat
Factory Automation
Robotics

Transportation
Transportation

Financial Services
Financial Services
Real Estate

Business Serv.
Distribution

Manufact.
Office Automation Equipmt
Publishing

Agr/Forestr/Fish
Agriculture related
Mining and Minerals

Additional Information
Name of Most Recent Fund: Middle East/North Africa Fund
Most Recent Fund Was Raised: 03/31/1998
Year Founded: 1994
Capital Under Management: $850,000,000
Current Activity Level : Actively seeking new investments
Method of Compensation: Return on investment is of primary concern, do not charge fees

SILICON ALLEY VENTURE PARTNERS LLC (AKA SAVP)

224 West 30th Street
Suite 1206
New York, NY 10001
Phone: 212-967-6545
Fax: 212-898-9044
Website: www.savp.com

Other Offices

1010 Northern Blvd
Suite 310
Great Neck, NY 11021
Phone: 516-773-6200
Fax: 516-773-6228

Management and Staff

David Montoya, Principal
Steve Brotman, Managing Director
Todd Pines, Principal

Type of Firm

Private Firm Investing Own Capital

Project Preferences

Type of Financing Preferred:
Early Stage
Seed
Startup

Size of Investments Considered

Min Size of Investment Considered (000s): $200
Max Size of Investment Considered (000s): $1,500

Geographical Preferences

United States
All U.S.
New York
All U.S.

Industry Preferences

Internet Specific
Internet

Additional Information

Year Founded: 1998
Capital Under Management: $14,000,000
Current Activity Level : Actively seeking new investments

SIXTY WALL STREET SBIC FUND

60 Wall Street
New York, NY 10260
Phone: 212-648-7778
Fax: 212-648-5032

Management and Staff

Brian Watson, Managing Director
John Mayer, Managing Director

Type of Firm

Private Firm Investing Own Capital

Additional Information

Year Founded: 1995
Capital Under Management: $5,200,000
Current Activity Level : Actively seeking new investments

SOLERA CAPITAL LLC

590 Madison Avenue
21st Floor
New York, NY 10022
Phone: 212-521-4081
Fax: 212-521-4428
Website: www.soleracapital.com

Management and Staff

Amy Wildstein, Principal
Karen Mills, Managing Director
Lori Koffman, Managing Director
Mary Hennessy-Jones, Managing Director
Molly Ashby, Chief Executive Officer

Type of Firm

Private Firm Investing Own Capital

Project Preferences

Type of Financing Preferred:
Later Stage
Mezzanine

Size of Investments Considered

Min Size of Investment Considered (000s): $10,000
Max Size of Investment Considered (000s): $40,000

Additional Information

Capital Under Management: $100,000,000
Current Activity Level : Actively seeking new investments

SPENCER TRASK VENTURES, INC. (FKA: SPENCER TRASK SECURITIES)

535 Madison Avenue
New York, NY 10022
Phone: 212-355-5565
Fax: 212-751-3362
Website: www.spencertrask.com

Other Offices

12030 Sunrise Valley Drive
Suite 300
Reston, VA 20191
Phone: 703-860-6870
Fax: 703-834-0919

1299 Ocean Avenue
Suite 900
Santa Monica, CA 90401
Phone: 310-395-5960

Management and Staff

George Egan, Managing Director
Larry Zeller, Vice President
Ron Luken, Chief Operating Officer
Thomas McClain, Chief Executive Officer
Thomas Hutzel, Chief Financial Officer
William Dioguardi, President

Whom to Contact

A. Emerson Martin

Type of Firm

Private Firm Investing Own Capital

Project Preferences

Role in Financing:
Prefer role as deal originator

Type of Financing Preferred:
Balanced
Early Stage
First Stage Financing
Industry Rollups
Second Stage Financing
Special Situation
Start-up Financing

Size of Investments Considered

Min Size of Investment Considered (000s): $3,000
Max Size of Investment Considered: No Limit

Geographical Preferences

United States
All U.S.

Industry Preferences

Communications and Media
Communications and Media
Telecommunications

Computer Hardware
Computer Graphics and Dig
Disk Relat. Memory Device

Computer Software
Computer Services
Systems Software
Applications Software

Internet Specific
Internet

Semiconductors/Other Elect.
Electronic Components
Semiconductor
Controllers and Sensors
Circuit Boards
Fiber Optics

Biotechnology
Biotechnology
Biosensors
Biotech Related Research

Medical/Health
Diagnostic Services
Diagnostic Test Products
Drug/Equipmt Delivery
Hospitals/Clinics/Primary
Hospital/Other Instit.
Pharmaceuticals

Consumer Related
Consumer Products
Other Restaurants
Education Related

Industrial/Energy
Alternative Energy
Materials
Robotics
Machinery

Financial Services
Financial Services

Manufact.
Office Automation Equipmt
Publishing

Additional Information

Year Founded: 1991
Current Activity Level : Actively seeking new investments
Method of Compensation: Function primarily in service area, receive contingent fee in cash or equity

SPIRE CAPITAL (FKA: WALLER CAPITAL CORP.)

30 Rockefeller Plaza
Suite 4200
New York, NY 10112
Phone: 212-218-5454
Fax: 212-218-5455
Website: www.spirecapital.com

Management and Staff

Andrew Armstrong, Partner
Bruce Hernandez, Partner
Joel Goldblatt, Partner
Pilar Lorente, Chief Financial Officer
Richard Patterson, Partner
Sean White, Principal
Thomas Savage, Principal

Type of Firm

Investment/Merchant Bank Investing Own or Client Funds

Industry Association Membership

National Venture Capital Association (NVCA)

Project Preferences

Role in Financing:
Prefer role as deal originator but will also invest in deals created by others

Type of Financing Preferred:
Early Stage
First Stage Financing
Leveraged Buyout
Second Stage Financing
Start-up Financing

Size of Investments Considered
Min Size of Investment Considered (000s): $5,000
Max Size of Investment Considered: No Limit

Geographical Preferences

United States
All U.S.
All U.S.

Canada
All Canada

International
Australia
Bermuda
China
Europe
France
Germany
Italy
Japan
Middle East
South Africa
Spain
United Kingdom

Industry Preferences

(% based on actual investment)

Internet Specific	77.3%
Communications and Media	16.2%
Consumer Related	6.4%

Additional Information

Name of Most Recent Fund: Waller-Sutton Media Partners, L.P.
Most Recent Fund Was Raised: 09/09/1997
Year Founded: 1997
Capital Under Management: $260,000,000
Current Activity Level : Actively seeking new investments
Method of Compensation: Return on investment is of primary concern, do not charge fees

SPORTS CAPITAL PARTNERS

65 East 55th Street
18th Floor
New York, NY 10022
Phone: 212-634-3304
Fax: 212-634-3374
Website: www.sportscapital.com

Management and Staff

Charles Lelon, Principal
David Moross, Managing Partner
Desiree DeStefano, Chief Financial Officer
Paul Behrman, Principal

Type of Firm

Private Firm Investing Own Capital

Project Preferences

Role in Financing:
Prefer role as deal originator but will also invest in deals created by others

Type of Financing Preferred:
Generalist PE
Leveraged Buyout

Size of Investments Considered
Min Size of Investment Considered (000s): $5,000
Max Size of Investment Considered (000s): $25,000

Geographical Preferences

United States
All U.S.

International
United Kingdom

Industry Preferences

Internet Specific
Internet

Consumer Related
Entertainment and Leisure
Sports
Hotels and Resorts

Business Serv.
Media

Additional Information
Name of Most Recent Fund: IMG/Chase Sports Capital
Most Recent Fund Was Raised: 07/01/1999
Capital Under Management: $170,000,000
Current Activity Level : Actively seeking new investments
Method of Compensation: Return on invest. most important, but chg. closing fees, service fees, etc.

SPROUT GROUP

277 Park Avenue
42nd Floor
New York, NY 10172
Phone: 212-892-3600
Fax: 212-892-3444
Website: www.sproutgroup.com

Other Offices

3000 Sand Hill Road
Building 3, Suite 170
Menlo Park, CA 94025
Phone: 650-234-2700
Fax: 650-234-2779

520 Lake Cook road
Suite 450
Deerfield, IL 60015
Phone: 847-940-1735
Fax: 847-940-1724

Management and Staff
Alexander Rosen, Vice President
Arthur Zuckerman, General Partner
Farrokh Billimoria, General Partner
Janet Hickey, General Partner
Jeani Delagardelle, General Partner
Kathleen LaPorte, General Partner
Keith Geeslin, Managing Partner
Michael Arbour, Vice President
Neil Hammer, Venture Partner
Patrick Boroian, General Partner
Phillippe Chambon, General Partner
Rakesh Sood, General Partner
Robert Finzi, General Partner
Robert Curry, General Partner
Scott Meadow, Venture Partner
Semir Sirazi, Partner
Simon Guenzl, Vice President
Stephen Diamond, General Partner

Type of Firm
Investment/Merchant Bank Subsid/Affil

Industry Association Membership
National Venture Capital Association (NVCA)
Western Association of Venture Capitalists (WAVC)

Project Preferences

Role in Financing:
Will function either as deal originator or investor in deals created by others

Type of Financing Preferred:
Early Stage
Expansion
Later Stage
Leveraged Buyout
Management Buyouts
Startup

Size of Investments Considered
Min Size of Investment Considered (000s): $5,000
Max Size of Investment Considered (000s): $50,000

Geographical Preferences

United States
All U.S.

International
France
Germany
Italy
Spain
United Kingdom

Industry Preferences
(% based on actual investment)

Internet Specific	20.7%
Medical/Health	19.9%
Consumer Related	13.5%
Communications and Media	12.5%
Computer Software and Services	8.6%
Other Products	7.4%
Biotechnology	6.4%
Computer Hardware	4.4%
Semiconductors/Other Elect.	4.4%
Industrial/Energy	2.2%

Additional Information
Name of Most Recent Fund: Sprout Capital VIII, LP
Most Recent Fund Was Raised: 01/01/1998
Year Founded: 1969
Capital Under Management: $2,615,100,000
Current Activity Level : Actively seeking new investments

SRK MANAGEMENT CO.

126 East 56th Street
New York, NY 10022
Phone: 212-371-0900
Fax: 212-371-1549

Management and Staff
Sidney Knafel

Whom to Contact
Sidney Knafel

Type of Firm
Private Firm Investing Own Capital

Project Preferences

Role in Financing:
Prefer role as deal originator but will also invest in deals created by others

Type of Financing Preferred:
First Stage Financing
Second Stage Financing
Seed
Start-up Financing

Size of Investments Considered
Min Size of Investment Considered (000s): $300
Max Size of Investment Considered (000s): $1,000

Geographical Preferences

International
No Preference

Industry Preferences

Communications and Media
Communications and Media
Other Communication Prod.

Semiconductors/Other Elect.
Electronics
Laser Related
Fiber Optics
Analytic/Scientific

Biotechnology
Industrial Biotechnology
Biosensors
Biotech Related Research
Biotech Related Research

Medical/Health
Diagnostic Services
Diagnostic Test Products
Medical Therapeutics
Other Therapeutic
Medical Products
Disposable Med. Products
Hospitals/Clinics/Primary
Hospital/Other Instit.

Consumer Related
Retail

Industrial/Energy
Industrial Products
Materials

Additional Information
Name of Most Recent Fund: SRK Management Company
Most Recent Fund Was Raised: 01/01/1990
Year Founded: 1981
Current Activity Level : Reducing investment activity
Method of Compensation: Return on investment is of primary concern, do not charge fees

---

STAMFORD FINANCIAL

108 Main Street
Stamford, NY 12167
Phone: 607-652-3311
Fax: 607-652-6301
E-mail: dcre@wpe.com
Website: www.stamfordfinancial.com

Other Offices

86-19 88th Avenue
Woodhaven, NY 11421
Phone: 718-847-6878
Fax: 718-847-6994

Management and Staff
Alexander C. Brosda
George Bergleitner

Whom to Contact
Alexander C. Brosda
George Bergleitner

Type of Firm
Mgt. Consulting Firm

Industry Association Membership
National Venture Capital Association (NVCA)

Project Preferences

Role in Financing:
Prefer role as deal originator

Type of Financing Preferred:
Expansion
Mezzanine

Size of Investments Considered
Min Size of Investment Considered (000s): $1,000
Max Size of Investment Considered (000s): $2,500

Geographical Preferences

United States
Northeast
All U.S.

International
Germany
United Kingdom

Industry Preferences

Communications and Media
Telecommunications

Semiconductors/Other Elect.
Semiconductor

Consumer Related
Franchises(NEC)

Industrial/Energy
Industrial Products

Financial Services
Financial Services

Manufact.
Manufacturing

Additional Information
Year Founded: 1973
Capital Under Management: $2,000,000
Current Activity Level : Actively seeking new investments
Method of Compensation: Professional fee required whether or not deal closes

---

STERLING GRACE CAPITAL MANAGEMENT, L.P.

55 Brookville Road
P.O. Box 163
Glen Head, NY 11545
Phone: 516-686-2201

Other Offices

515 Madison Avenue
Suite 2000
New York, NY 10022

Management and Staff
Davis Stowell

Whom to Contact
Davis Stowell

Type of Firm
Private Firm Investing Own Capital

Project Preferences

Role in Financing:
Prefer role as deal originator but will also invest in deals created by others

Type of Financing Preferred:
Control-block Purchases
First Stage Financing
Leveraged Buyout
Mezzanine
Second Stage Financing
Special Situation

Size of Investments Considered
Min Size of Investment Considered (000s): $300
Max Size of Investment Considered: No Limit

Geographical Preferences

United States
All U.S.

International
Australia
France
Germany
United Kingdom

Industry Preferences

Communications and Media
CATV & Pay TV Systems
Radio & TV Broadcasting
Telecommunications
Data Communications

Computer Software
Applications Software

Internet Specific
Internet

Consumer Related
Entertainment and Leisure
Food/Beverage
Consumer Products
Consumer Services
Hotels and Resorts

Industrial/Energy
Oil & Gas Drilling,Explor
Alternative Energy

Financial Services
Financial Services
Real Estate

Agr/Forestr/Fish
Agriculture related

Additional Information
Year Founded: 1983
Capital Under Management: $100,000,000
Current Activity Level : Actively seeking new investments
Method of Compensation: Return on investment is of primary concern, do not charge fees

STERLING/CARL MARKS CAPITAL {FKA - STERLING COMMERCIAL

175 Great Neck Road
Suite 408
Great Neck, NY 11021
Phone: 516-482-7374
Fax: 516-487-0781
Website: www.sterlingcarlmarks.com

Management and Staff
Debra Glickman, Vice President
Harvey Granat, President, CEO, Director
Howard Davidoff, Managing Director
Robert Davidoff, Managing Director

Type of Firm
Private Firm Investing Own Capital

Industry Association Membership
Natl assoc of Small Bus. Inv. Co (NASBIC)

Project Preferences

Role in Financing:
Prefer role as deal originator but will also invest in deals created by others

Type of Financing Preferred:
Expansion
Management Buyouts
Mezzanine
Second Stage Financing

Size of Investments Considered
Min Size of Investment Considered (000s): $1,000
Max Size of Investment Considered (000s): $2,000

Geographical Preferences

United States
New York
Northeast

Industry Preferences

(% based on actual investment)

Internet Specific	31.6%
Computer Software and Services	28.2%
Other Products	23.4%
Consumer Related	15.7%
Medical/Health	1.0%

Additional Information
Year Founded: 1988
Capital Under Management: $20,000,000
Current Activity Level : Actively seeking new investments
Method of Compensation: Return on investment is of primary concern, do not charge fees

STOLBERG PARTNERS

767 Third Avenue
32nd Floor
New York, NY 10017
Phone: 212-826-1110
Fax: 212-826-0371

Other Offices

445 Park Ave
19th Floor
New York, NY 10022
Phone: 212-826-1110

Management and Staff
E. Theodore Stolberg, Partner
Robert Geiger, Partner

Whom to Contact
Matthew Meehan

Type of Firm
Private Firm Investing Own Capital

Project Preferences

Role in Financing:
Prefer role as deal originator but will also invest in deals created by others

Type of Financing Preferred:
Control-block Purchases
Leveraged Buyout
Second Stage Financing
Special Situation

Size of Investments Considered
Min Size of Investment Considered (000s): $100,000
Max Size of Investment Considered: No Limit

Geographical Preferences

United States
All U.S.

Industry Preferences

(% based on actual investment)

Communications and Media	29.8%
Internet Specific	18.3%
Consumer Related	17.8%
Medical/Health	16.1%
Other Products	13.4%
Computer Software and Services	4.6%

Additional Information
Name of Most Recent Fund: Stolberg, Meehan & Scano II, L.P.
Most Recent Fund Was Raised: 11/01/1997
Year Founded: 1993
Capital Under Management: $70,000,000
Current Activity Level : Actively seeking new investments
Method of Compensation: Return on invest. most important, but chg. closing fees, service fees, etc.

STONEBRIDGE PARTNERS

50 Main Street
9th Floor
White Plains, NY 10606
Phone: 914-682-2700
Fax: 914-682-0834
Website: www.stonebridgepartners.com

Other Offices

P.O. Box 512
Washington, PA 15301
Phone: 412-223-0707

Management and Staff
Andrew Thomas, Partner
Harrison Wilson, Partner
Michael Bruno, Partner
Robert Raziano, Partner

Whom to Contact
Michael S. Bruno Jr.
Scott L. Rodman

Type of Firm
Private Firm Investing Own Capital

Project Preferences

Role in Financing:
Prefer role as deal originator

Type of Financing Preferred:
Leveraged Buyout

Size of Investments Considered
Min Size of Investment Considered (000s): $20,000
Max Size of Investment Considered: No Limit

Geographical Preferences

United States
All U.S.

Industry Preferences

Semiconductors/Other Elect.
Electronic Components
Controllers and Sensors
Sensors
Component Testing Equipmt
Analytic/Scientific

Medical/Health
Diagnostic Test Products
Other Therapeutic
Disposable Med. Products

Consumer Related
Food/Beverage
Consumer Products

Industrial/Energy
Factory Automation
Machinery

Additional Information
Name of Most Recent Fund: Stonebridge Private Equity Partners II
Most Recent Fund Was Raised: 06/30/1997
Year Founded: 1986
Capital Under Management: $250,000,000
Current Activity Level : Actively seeking new investments
Method of Compensation: Return on invest. most important, but chg. closing fees, service fees, etc.

STRATEGIC INVESTMENTS & HOLDINGS, INC.

Cyclorama Building
369 Franklin Street
Buffalo, NY 14202
Phone: 716-857-6000
Fax: 716-857-6490

Management and Staff
David Zebro, Principal
Gary Brost, Principal
John Dunbar, Principal
William Joyce, Principal

Whom to Contact
David Zebro
Gary Brost
John Dunbar

Type of Firm
Investment/Merchant Bank Investing Own or Client Funds

Project Preferences

Role in Financing:
Prefer role as deal originator

Type of Financing Preferred:
Leveraged Buyout
Management Buyouts

Size of Investments Considered
Min Size of Investment Considered (000s): $1,000
Max Size of Investment Considered (000s): $5,000

Geographical Preferences

United States
All U.S.

Industry Preferences

Communications and Media
Other Communication Prod.

Semiconductors/Other Elect.
Electronics
Electronic Components
Controllers and Sensors
Sensors
Circuit Boards
Component Testing Equipmt
Fiber Optics
Analytic/Scientific

Medical/Health
Diagnostic Test Products
Medical Products
Disposable Med. Products

Consumer Related
Consumer
Food/Beverage
Consumer Products

Industrial/Energy
Industrial Products
Materials
Factory Automation
Process Control
Machinery

Manufact.
Manufacturing

Additional Information
Year Founded: 1983
Capital Under Management: $50,000,000
Current Activity Level : Actively seeking new investments
Method of Compensation: Return on invest. most important, but chg. closing fees, service fees, etc.

SUMMIT CAPITAL ASSOCIATES, INC.

750 Lexington Avenue
24th Floor
New York, NY 10022
Phone: 212-308-4155
Fax: 212-223-7363

Management and Staff
Richard Messina, Managing Director

Type of Firm
Investment/Merchant Bank Investing Own or Client Funds

Project Preferences

Role in Financing:
Prefer role as deal originator but will also invest in deals created by others

Type of Financing Preferred:
First Stage Financing
Industry Rollups
Leveraged Buyout
Mezzanine
Second Stage Financing

Size of Investments Considered
Min Size of Investment Considered (000s): $5,000
Max Size of Investment Considered: No Limit

Geographical Preferences

International
No Preference

Industry Preferences

Communications and Media
Communications and Media

Computer Other
Computer Related

Semiconductors/Other Elect.
Electronic Components

Biotechnology
Biotechnology

Medical/Health
Medical/Health

Consumer Related
Consumer

Industrial/Energy
Alternative Energy
Energy Conservation Relat
Industrial Products

Business Serv.
Distribution

Additional Information

Name of Most Recent Fund: Enervest
Most Recent Fund Was Raised: 01/01/1978
Year Founded: 1987
Capital Under Management: $20,000,000
Current Activity Level : Actively seeking new investments
Method of Compensation: Return on invest. most important, but chg. closing fees, service fees, etc.

SUNRISE CAPITAL PARTNERS

685 Third Ave.
15th Floor
New York, NY 10017-4024
Phone: 212-497-4100
Fax: 212-661-3070

Type of Firm

Private Firm Investing Own Capital

Additional Information

Year Founded: 1999
Current Activity Level : Actively seeking new investments

SYNERGY VENTURES

Suite 40N Carnegie Hall Tower
152W 57th Street
New York, NY 10019
Phone: 212-245-0100
Fax: 212-586-9600
Website: www.synergyventures.com

Management and Staff

Geva Perry, General Partner
Idan Ofer, General Partner
Yariv Zghoul, General Partner

Type of Firm

Private Firm Investing Own Capital

Geographical Preferences

United States
All U.S.
Southeast

Industry Preferences

Internet Specific
Internet

Additional Information

Current Activity Level : Actively seeking new investments

TECHNOLOGY CROSSOVER VENTURES

160 West 86th Street
Suite 12B
New York, NY 10024
Phone: 212-277-3900
Fax: 212-277-3901
Website: www.tcv.com

See California for full listing.

TECHSPACE XCHANGE LLC (TSX)

41 East 11th Street
University Place
New York, NY 10003
Phone: 212-699-3725
Fax: 212-331-1248
Website: www.techspace.com

Management and Staff

Stephen Nordal, Managing Director

Type of Firm

Incubators

Project Preferences

Size of Investments Considered
Min Size of Investment Considered (000s): $500
Max Size of Investment Considered (000s): $2,000

Industry Preferences

Internet Specific
Internet

Additional Information

Year Founded: 1997
Current Activity Level : Actively seeking new investments

THCG INC.

512 Seventh Avenue
17th Floor
New York, NY 10019
Phone: 212-223-0440
Fax: 212-223-0161
Website: www.thcg.com

Management and Staff

Adi Raviv, Chief Executive Officer
Ed Tedeschi, Senior Managing Director
Evan Marks, Senior Managing Director
Gary Antsey, Senior Managing Director
Joseph Mark, Chief Executive Officer
Larry Smith, President
Michael Gegenheimer, Senior Managing Director
Shai Novik, Chief Financial Officer
Ziad Abdelnour, Managing Director

Type of Firm

Incubators

Project Preferences

Type of Financing Preferred:
First Stage Financing
Second Stage Financing

Geographical Preferences

United States
All U.S.

Industry Preferences

Communications and Media
Communications and Media

Semiconductors/Other Elect.
Electronics

Business Serv.
Services

Additional Information
Year Founded: 1999
Capital Under Management: $20,000,000
Current Activity Level : Actively seeking new investments

THOMAS WEISEL PARTNERS, LLC

390 Park Avenue
17th Floor
New York, NY 10022
Phone: 212-271-3700
Fax: 212-271-3610
Website: www.tweisel.com

See California for full listing.

THREE CITIES RESEARCH, INC.

650 Madison Ave.
24th Floor
New York, NY 10022-1029
Phone: 212-838-9660
Fax: 212-980-1142
Website: www.tcr-ny.com

Other Offices

229, boulevard Saint-Germain
Paris, France 75007
Phone: 33-1-4705-7154
Fax: 33-1-4705-7173

Velasquez 83
28006 Madrid, Spain
Phone: 34-1-577-2869
Fax: 34-1-435-9558

Viale Maino 3
20129 Milan, Italy
Phone: 39-2-76004711
Fax: 39-2-76009016

Management and Staff
Karen Kochevar, Principal

Type of Firm
Investment/Merchant Bank Investing Own or Client Funds

Project Preferences

Role in Financing:
Prefer role as deal originator

Type of Financing Preferred:
Leveraged Buyout
Special Situation

Size of Investments Considered
Min Size of Investment Considered (000s): $10,000
Max Size of Investment Considered: No Limit

Geographical Preferences

United States
All U.S.

Industry Preferences

Consumer Related
Retail
Food/Beverage
Consumer Products

Industrial/Energy
Industrial Products
Machinery

Additional Information
Name of Most Recent Fund: Three Cities Fund III, L.P.
Most Recent Fund Was Raised: 08/01/1999
Year Founded: 1976
Capital Under Management: $400,000,000
Current Activity Level : Actively seeking new investments
Method of Compensation: Return on invest. most important, but chg. closing fees, service fees, etc.

TICONDEROGA CAPITAL, INC. (FKA: DILLON READ VENTURE CAPITAL)

535 Madison Avenue
36th Floor
New York, NY 10022
Phone: 212-906-7100
Fax: 212-906-8690
Website: www.ticonderogacap.com

See Massachusetts for full listing.

TRIBUNE VENTURES

220 East 42nd Street
Suite 400
New York, NY 10017
Phone: 212-210-5902
Fax: 212-210-1057
Website: www.tribuneventures.com

See Illinois for full listing.

TRUE NORTH PARTNERS LLC

464 Neptune Avenue
Brooklyn, NY 11224
Website: www.truenorthpartners.com

Management and Staff
Alex Charlton, Managing Director
Jeff Zucker, Managing Director
Michael Bittan, Managing Director
Vince Aurentz, Managing Director

Type of Firm
Private Firm Investing Own Capital

Project Preferences

Type of Financing Preferred:
Balanced

Geographical Preferences

United States
All U.S.

Industry Preferences

Internet Specific
Internet

Medical/Health
Medical/Health

Additional Information
Year Founded: 2000
Capital Under Management: $8,000,000
Current Activity Level : Actively seeking new investments

TUDOR INVESTMENT CORPORATION

One Liberty Plaza
Floor 51
New York, NY 10006
Phone: 212-602-6700

Management and Staff
Carmen Scarpa, Managing Partner
Richard Ganong, Managing Partner
Robert Forlenza, Managing Partner

Type of Firm
Private Firm Investing Own Capital

Industry Preferences

(% based on actual investment)

Internet Specific	33.3%
Communications and Media	18.8%
Computer Software and Services	15.8%
Semiconductors/Other Elect.	10.8%
Consumer Related	8.8%
Computer Hardware	6.2%
Other Products	5.3%
Medical/Health	1.0%

Additional Information

Capital Under Management: $101,000,000
Current Activity Level : Actively seeking new investments

UBS CAPITAL

299 Park Avenue
New York, NY 10171
Phone: 1-212-821-6303
Website: www.ubs.com

See Foreign Venture Capital Firms for full listing.

UNIVERSITYANGELS.COM

50 Main Street
Suite 1000
White Plains, NY 10606
Phone: 914-682-2028
E-mail: info@universityangels.com
Website: www.UniversityAngels.com

Management and Staff

Charles Sanford, President
James Marcus, Chief Executive Officer

Type of Firm

Private Equity Advisor or Fund of Fund Mgr

Project Preferences

Type of Financing Preferred:
Seed
Start-up Financing

Geographical Preferences

United States
All U.S.

Additional Information

Year Founded: 2000
Current Activity Level : Actively seeking new investments

US TRUST PRIVATE EQUITY

114 West 47th Street
New York, NY 10036
Phone: 212-852-3949
Fax: 212-852-3759
Website: www.ustrust.com/privateequity

Management and Staff

Alan Braverman, Managing Director
David Fann, Managing Director
Douglas Lindgren, Managing Director
James Dorment, Vice President
James Rorer, Vice President
Lee Gardella, Vice President
Pamela Jacobson, Vice President
Raghav Nandagopal, Vice President

Whom to Contact

Doug Lindgren
Jim Dorment
Jim Ruler

Type of Firm

Investment/Merchant Bank Subsid/Affil

Industry Association Membership

National Venture Capital Association (NVCA)

Project Preferences

Role in Financing:
Will function either as deal originator or investor in deals created by others

Type of Financing Preferred:
Early Stage
First Stage Financing
Second Stage Financing

Size of Investments Considered
Min Size of Investment Considered (000s): $5,000
Max Size of Investment Considered: No Limit

Geographical Preferences

United States
All U.S.

Industry Preferences

(% based on actual investment)

Internet Specific	21.6%
Computer Software and Services	19.8%
Medical/Health	17.2%
Other Products	14.8%
Communications and Media	10.6%
Consumer Related	8.4%
Semiconductors/Other Elect.	6.0%
Biotechnology	1.6%

Additional Information

Name of Most Recent Fund: Excelsior Private Equity Fund II, Inc.
Most Recent Fund Was Raised: 10/01/1997
Year Founded: 1995
Capital Under Management: $236,500,000
Current Activity Level : Actively seeking new investments
Method of Compensation: Return on investment is of primary concern, do not charge fees

VANTAGE PARTNERS L.L.C

610 Fifth Ave
7th Floor
New York, NY 10020
Phone: 212-218-8130
Fax: 212-218-8133

Type of Firm

Private Firm Investing Own Capital

Industry Association Membership

National Venture Capital Association (NVCA)

Additional Information

Current Activity Level : Actively seeking new investments

VANTAGEPOINT VENTURE PARTNERS

440 Madison Avenue
39th Floor
New York, NY 10022
Phone: 212-750-8220
Fax: 212-750-8223
Website: www.vpvp.com

See California for full listing.

VEGA CAPITAL CORP.

45 Knollwood Road
Elmsford, NY 10523
Phone: 914-345-9500
Fax: 914-345-9505

Other Offices

80 Business Park Drive
Armonk, NY 10504
Phone: 914-273-1025

Management and Staff
Ronald Linden

Whom to Contact
Ronald Linden

Type of Firm
SBIC Not elsewhere classified

Industry Association Membership
Natl assoc of Small Bus. Inv. Co (NASBIC)

Project Preferences

Role in Financing:
Prefer role as deal originator but will also invest in deals created by others

Type of Financing Preferred:
Leveraged Buyout
Mezzanine
Second Stage Financing
Special Situation

Size of Investments Considered
Min Size of Investment Considered (000s): $300
Max Size of Investment Considered: No Limit

Geographical Preferences

United States
Mid Atlantic
Northeast
Southeast

Industry Preferences

Communications and Media
Commercial Communications
CATV & Pay TV Systems
Data Communications
Satellite Microwave Comm.
Other Communication Prod.

Computer Hardware
Computers
Mainframes / Scientific
Mini and Personal/Desktop
Computer Graphics and Dig
Disk Relat. Memory Device

Semiconductors/Other Elect.
Electronics
Electronic Components

Medical/Health
Medical/Health
Medical Products

Consumer Related
Entertainment and Leisure
Retail
Food/Beverage
Consumer Products
Other Restaurants
Hotels and Resorts
Education Related

Industrial/Energy
Alternative Energy
Industrial Products

Transportation
Transportation

Financial Services
Real Estate

Manufact.
Office Automation Equipmt

Agr/Forestr/Fish
Agriculture related

Additional Information
Name of Most Recent Fund: Vega Capital Corporation
Most Recent Fund Was Raised: 04/01/1982
Year Founded: 1968
Capital Under Management: $10,000,000
Current Activity Level : Actively seeking new investments
Method of Compensation: Return on invest. most important, but chg. closing fees, service fees, etc.

VENCON MANAGEMENT, INC.

301 West 53rd Street
Suite 10F
New York, NY 10019
Phone: 212-581-8787
Fax: 212-397-4126
E-mail: vencon@worldnet.att.net
Website: www.venconinc.com

Management and Staff
Ingrid Yang

Whom to Contact
Ingrid Yang

Type of Firm
Private Firm Investing Own Capital

Project Preferences

Role in Financing:
Prefer role as deal originator but will also invest in deals created by others

Type of Financing Preferred:
First Stage Financing
Leveraged Buyout
Second Stage Financing
Seed
Special Situation
Start-up Financing

Size of Investments Considered
Min Size of Investment Considered (000s): $500
Max Size of Investment Considered (000s): $10,000

Geographical Preferences

United States
All U.S.

Canada
All Canada

International
China
Hong Kong
Middle East

Industry Preferences

Communications and Media
Telecommunications
Wireless Communications
Satellite Microwave Comm.
Other Communication Prod.

Computer Software
Artificial Intelligence

Internet Specific
E-Commerce Technology
Internet

Semiconductors/Other Elect.
Electronic Components
Semiconductor
Sensors
Laser Related
Fiber Optics
Analytic/Scientific

Biotechnology
Industrial Biotechnology
Biosensors
Biotech Related Research
Biotech Related Research

Medical/Health
Medical Diagnostics
Diagnostic Services
Diagnostic Test Products
Medical Therapeutics
Drug/Equipmt Delivery
Medical Products
Disposable Med. Products
Health Services
Pharmaceuticals

Additional Information
Year Founded: 1973
Current Activity Level : Actively seeking new investments
Method of Compensation: Return on invest. most important, but chg. closing fees, service fees, etc.

VENKOL VENTURES

444 Madison Avenue, #2201
New York, NY 10005
Phone: 212-759-9094

Type of Firm
Private Firm Investing Own Capital

Additional Information
Name of Most Recent Fund: Venkol Ventures
Most Recent Fund Was Raised: 05/01/1987
Year Founded: 1987
Current Activity Level : Inactive / Unknown

VENNWORKS (FKA: INCUVEST LLC)

590 Madison Avenue
32nd Floor
New York, NY 10022
Phone: 212-849-8160
Fax: 212-849-8171
Website: www.vennworks.com

Other Offices

Manfield House 2nd Floor
1 Southampton Street
London, United Kingdom WC2R OLR
Phone: 44 207 245 8551
Fax: 44 207 245 8559

Management and Staff
Gregory Haskell, Managing Director
Henry Pan, Managing Director
Jonathon Gold, Managing Director
Richard Morgan, Chairman & CEO
Robert Bertoldi, President
Roger Baumann, Managing Director
Tim Duffy, Managing Director

Type of Firm
Incubators

Project Preferences

Role in Financing:
Prefer role as deal originator

Type of Financing Preferred:
Early Stage

Additional Information
Current Activity Level : Actively seeking new investments

VENROCK ASSOCIATES

30 Rockefeller Plaza
Suite 5508
New York, NY 10112
Phone: 212-649-5600
Fax: 212-649-5788
Website: www.venrock.com

Other Offices

101 Federal Street
Suite 190
Boston, MA 02110
Phone: 617-204-5710
Fax: 617-204-6190

2494 SAnd Hill
Suite 200
Menlo Park, CA 94025
Phone: 650-561-9580
Fax: 650-561-9180

66 Catalpa Drive
Atherton, CA 94027
Phone: 650-321-1500
Fax: 650-321-1501

755 Page Mill Road
Suite A230
Palo Alto, CA 94304
Phone: 650-493-5577
Fax: 650-493-6443

Management and Staff
Anthony Sun, Managing General Partner
Anthony Evnin, Managing General Partner
Bryan Roberts, General Partner
David Hathaway, Managing General Partner
Eric Copeland, General Partner
Joseph Casey, General Partner
Kim Rummelsburg, General Partner
Michael Tyrrell, General Partner
Michael Brooks, General Partner
Patrick Latterell, General Partner
Ray Rothrock, General Partner
Ted McCourtney, General Partner
Terence Garnett, Venture Partner
Thomas Frederick, General Partner

Type of Firm
Private Firm Investing Own Capital

Industry Association Membership
National Venture Capital Association (NVCA)
Western Association of Venture Capitalists (WAVC)

Project Preferences

Role in Financing:
Prefer role as deal originator but will also invest in deals created by others

Type of Financing Preferred:
First Stage Financing
Research and Development
Second Stage Financing
Seed
Start-up Financing

Size of Investments Considered
Min Size of Investment Considered (000s): $500
Max Size of Investment Considered: No Limit

Geographical Preferences

United States
All U.S.

Industry Preferences
(% based on actual investment)

Biotechnology	31.9%
Internet Specific	21.4%
Communications and Media	13.5%
Computer Software and Services	12.2%
Medical/Health	7.4%
Computer Hardware	5.3%
Semiconductors/Other Elect.	5.0%
Industrial/Energy	1.7%
Other Products	0.9%
Consumer Related	0.7%

Additional Information
Name of Most Recent Fund: Venrock Entrepreneurs Fund
Most Recent Fund Was Raised: 10/01/1999
Year Founded: 1969
Capital Under Management: $2,000,000,000
Current Activity Level : Actively seeking new investments
Method of Compensation: Return on investment is of primary concern, do not charge fees

VENTURE CAPITAL FUND OF AMERICA, INC.

509 Madison Avenue
Suite 812
New York, NY 10022
Phone: 212-838-5577
Fax: 212-838-7614
Website: www.vcfa.com

Other Offices

211 Fulton Street
Palo Alto, CA 94301
Phone: 650-321-1500

One Sansome Street
Suite 2100
San Francisco, CA 94104
Phone: 415-765-5585
Fax: 415-986-1169

Management and Staff
Arnaud Isnard, General Partner
Brett Byers, General Partner
Dayton Carr, General Partner
Stephen Dondero, General Partner

Type of Firm
Private Firm Investing Own Capital

Industry Association Membership
National Venture Capital Association (NVCA)

Project Preferences

Type of Financing Preferred:
Other

Size of Investments Considered
Min Size of Investment Considered (000s): $500
Max Size of Investment Considered (000s): $100,000

Geographical Preferences

United States
All U.S.

International
China
India
Japan
Middle East

Additional Information
Name of Most Recent Fund: VCFA Venture Partners III, L.P.
Most Recent Fund Was Raised: 01/01/1999
Year Founded: 1983
Capital Under Management: $180,000,000
Current Activity Level : Actively seeking new investments
Method of Compensation: Return on investment is of primary concern, do not charge fees

VENTURE FUNDING GROUP INTERNATIONAL

49 West 12th Street
Executive Suite
New York, NY 10011
Phone: 212-691-9895

Management and Staff
Allan Skora

Whom to Contact
Allan Skora

Type of Firm
Mgt. Consulting Firm

Project Preferences

Role in Financing:
Prefer role as deal originator but will also invest in deals created by others

Type of Financing Preferred:
First Stage Financing
Industry Rollups
Leveraged Buyout
Mezzanine
Research and Development
Second Stage Financing
Seed
Special Situation
Start-up Financing

Size of Investments Considered
Min Size of Investment Considered (000s): $1,000
Max Size of Investment Considered: No Limit

Geographical Preferences

United States
All U.S.

Canada
All Canada

International
Afghanistan
Australia
Bermuda
China
Eastern Europe
France
Germany
India
Italy
Japan
Mexico
Middle East
South Africa
Spain
United Kingdom

Industry Preferences

Communications and Media
Communications and Media

Computer Other
Computer Related

Semiconductors/Other Elect.
Electronic Components

Biotechnology
Biotechnology

Medical/Health
Medical/Health

Consumer Related
Consumer
Education Related

Industrial/Energy
Energy
Industrial Products

Transportation
Transportation

Financial Services
Financial Services
Real Estate

Business Serv.
Distribution
Consulting Services

Manufact.
Publishing

Agr/Forestr/Fish
Agriculture related

Additional Information
Year Founded: 1976
Current Activity Level : Actively seeking new investments
Method of Compensation: Return on investment is of primary concern, do not charge fees

VENTURE OPPORTUNITIES CORP.

150 E. 58th St.
New York, NY 10155
Phone: 212-832-3737
Fax: 212-980-6603

Management and Staff
A. Fred March, President

Whom to Contact
Jerry March

Type of Firm
SBIC Not elsewhere classified

Industry Association Membership
Natl Assoc of Investment Cos. (NAIC)
Natl assoc of Small Bus. Inv. Co (NASBIC)

Project Preferences

Role in Financing:
Prefer role as deal originator but will also invest in deals created by others

Type of Financing Preferred:
First Stage Financing
Leveraged Buyout
Mezzanine
Second Stage Financing
Special Situation
Start-up Financing

Size of Investments Considered
Min Size of Investment Considered (000s): $2,000
Max Size of Investment Considered: No Limit

Geographical Preferences

United States
All U.S.

Industry Preferences

Communications and Media
Communications and Media
Other Communication Prod.

Computer Other
Computer Related

Semiconductors/Other Elect.
Electronic Components

Biotechnology
Biotechnology

Medical/Health
Medical/Health
Medical Products

Consumer Related
Entertainment and Leisure
Franchises(NEC)
Food/Beverage
Consumer Products
Consumer Services
Other Restaurants
Education Related

Industrial/Energy
Alternative Energy
Industrial Products
Factory Automation
Robotics
Machinery
Environmental Related

Transportation
Transportation

Manufact.
Publishing

Additional Information
Year Founded: 1978
Capital Under Management: $12,000,000
Current Activity Level : Actively seeking new investments
Method of Compensation: Return on investment is of primary concern, do not charge fees

VICTORY VENTURES L.L.C.

645 Madison Avenue
22nd Floor
New York, NY 10022
Phone: 212-644-6211
Fax: 212-644-5498

Management and Staff
Alicia Lindgren, Managing Director
Walter Carozza, President

Whom to Contact
Alicia Lindgren

Type of Firm
Private Firm Investing Own Capital

Project Preferences

Role in Financing:
Prefer role as deal originator but will also invest in deals created by others

Type of Financing Preferred:
First Stage Financing
Mezzanine
Second Stage Financing
Special Situation

Geographical Preferences

United States
All U.S.

Industry Preferences

(% based on actual investment)

Industrial/Energy	34.4%
Other Products	26.8%
Communications and Media	12.1%
Consumer Related	10.9%
Computer Hardware	9.3%
Internet Specific	3.7%
Computer Software and Services	2.7%
Medical/Health	0.1%

Additional Information
Year Founded: 1996
Capital Under Management: $80,000,000
Current Activity Level : Actively seeking new investments
Method of Compensation: Return on investment is of primary concern, do not charge fees

VITAL CAPITAL LIMITED

Suite 800, 529 Fifth Avenue
New York, NY 10017
Website: www.vitalcapital.com

See Foreign Venture Capital Firms for full listing.

VS&A COMMUNICATIONS PARTNERS, L.P.

350 Park Avenue
New York, NY 10022
Phone: 212-935-4990
Fax: 212-935-0877
Website: www.veronissuhler.com

Management and Staff
George Coles, Principal
Jeffrey Stevenson, Managing General Partner
Scott Troeller, General Partner

Whom to Contact
Jeffrey Stevenson

Type of Firm
Investment/Merchant Bank Subsid/Affil

Project Preferences

Role in Financing:
Prefer role as deal originator but will also invest in deals created by others

Type of Financing Preferred:
Leveraged Buyout
Special Situation

Size of Investments Considered
Min Size of Investment Considered (000s): $75,000
Max Size of Investment Considered: No Limit

Geographical Preferences

International
All International

Industry Preferences

Communications and Media
Communications and Media
CATV & Pay TV Systems
Radio & TV Broadcasting

Additional Information
Year Founded: 1987
Capital Under Management: $330,000,000
Current Activity Level : Actively seeking new investments

WALDEN CAPITAL MANAGEMENT CORPORATION

708 Third Avenue
21st Floor
New York, NY 10017
Phone: 212-355-0090
Fax: 212-755-8894
Website: www.waldencapital.com

Management and Staff
Allen Greenberg, Principal
Anne Anquillare, Principal
John Costantino, Principal
Martin Boorstein, Principal

Type of Firm
Investment Management/Finance Consulting

Industry Association Membership
National Venture Capital Association (NVCA)
Natl assoc of Small Bus. Inv. Co (NASBIC)

Project Preferences

Role in Financing:
Will function either as deal originator or investor in deals created by others

Type of Financing Preferred:
Acquisition
Balanced
Early Stage
Expansion
Generalist PE
Management Buyouts

Size of Investments Considered
Min Size of Investment Considered (000s): $1,000
Max Size of Investment Considered (000s): $4,000

Geographical Preferences

United States
Mid Atlantic
Northeast
All U.S.

Industry Preferences

(% based on actual investment)

Communications and Media	27.5%
Other Products	22.7%
Internet Specific	20.1%
Semiconductors/Other Elect.	18.0%
Computer Software and Services	10.9%
Biotechnology	0.8%

Additional Information
Name of Most Recent Fund: Walden Capital Partners, L.P.
Most Recent Fund Was Raised: 07/26/1996
Year Founded: 1996
Capital Under Management: $60,000,000
Current Activity Level : Actively seeking new investments
Method of Compensation: Return on invest. most important, but chg. closing fees, service fees, etc.

WAND PARTNERS

630 Fifth Avenue
Suite 2435
New York, NY 10111
Phone: 212-632-3795
Fax: 212-307-5599

Management and Staff
David J. Callard
Malcolm P. Appelbaum

Whom to Contact
David J. Callard
Malcolm P. Appelbaum

Type of Firm
Investment/Merchant Bank Subsid/Affil

Project Preferences

Role in Financing:
Prefer role as deal originator but will also invest in deals created by others

Type of Financing Preferred:
Leveraged Buyout

Geographical Preferences

United States
All U.S.

Canada
All Canada

International
United Kingdom

Industry Preferences

(% based on actual investment)

Internet Specific	42.4%
Computer Software and Services	24.2%
Consumer Related	13.1%
Other Products	10.3%
Industrial/Energy	9.0%
Semiconductors/Other Elect.	0.9%

Additional Information
Name of Most Recent Fund: Wand Equity Portfolio II
Most Recent Fund Was Raised: 04/01/1997
Year Founded: 1985
Capital Under Management: $250,000,000
Current Activity Level : Inactive / Unknown
Method of Compensation: Return on invest. most important, but chg. closing fees, service fees, etc.

WARBURG, PINCUS & CO., LLC. (FKA: E.M. WARBURG, PINCUS & CO)

466 Lexington Avenue
11th Floor
New York, NY 10017
Phone: 212-878-9309
Fax: 212-878-9200
Website: www.warburgpincus.com

Other Offices

12/F, St. George's Building
2 Ice House Street
Central, Hong Kong
Phone: 852-2521-3183
Fax: 852-2521-3869

20th Floor Seoul Finance Center
63 Mookyo-Dong, Chung-ku
Seoul, South Korea 100-768
Phone: 822-316-7900
Fax: 822-316-7999

2350 Mission College Blvd.
Suite 300
Santa Clara, CA 95054
Phone: 408-982-8210
Fax: 408-982-5853

80 Raffles Place
#17-01 UOB Plaza 1
, Singapore
Phone: 65-532-1838
Fax: 65-532-7678

Almack House
28 King Street
St. James's, London, United Kingdom SW1Y 1QW
Phone: 44-207-306-0306
Fax: 44-207-321-0881

Kishimoto Building, Marunouchi
2-2-1 Chiyoda-ku
Tokyo, Japan
Phone: 813-3287-5037
Fax: 813-5288-6262

Palais am Lenbachplatz
Ottostrasse 8
D-80333 Munchen, Germany
Phone: 49-89-55-155500
Fax: 49-89-55-155555

Rua Alexandre Dumas, 1711
Ed. Birmann 11, 4th Floor
Sao Paulo, Brazil 04717-004
Phone: 5-11-538-3980
Fax: 55-11-538-3715

Management and Staff

Alfred Grunwald, Partner
Barry Taylor, Managing Director
Cary Davis, Partner
Chang Sun, Managing Director
Charles Kaye, Partner
Dalip Pathak, Partner
David Libowitz, Partner
Dominic Shorthouse, Partner
Douglas Karp, Partner
Edward McKinley, Partner
Ernest Pomerantz, Managing Director
Gary Nusbaum, Partner
Henry Kressel, Partner
Howard Newman, Partner
James McNaught-Davis, Partner
Jeffrey Harris, Partner
Jeremy Young, Partner
Joel Ackerman, Partner
John Macintosh, Partner
John Santoleri, Partner
Jonathan Leff, Managing Director
Joseph Landy, Partner
Kewsong Lee, Partner
Lionel Pincus, Chairman & CEO
Melchior Stahl, Partner
Nancy Martin, Partner
Nicholas Lowcock, Partner
Patrick Hackett, Partner
Reuben Leibowitz, Partner
Roberto Italia, Partner
Rodman Moorhead, Partner
Sidney Lapidus, Partner
Steven Schneider, Managing Director
Stewart Gross, Partner
Sung-Jin Hwang, Managing Director
Tetsuya Fukagawa, Partner
W. Bowman Cutter, Managing Director
William Janeway, Partner

Type of Firm

Private Firm Investing Own Capital

Industry Association Membership

Hong Kong Venture Capital Association (HKVCA)
National Venture Capital Association (NVCA)

Project Preferences

Role in Financing:

Will function either as deal originator or investor in deals created by others

Type of Financing Preferred:

Acquisition
Balanced
Early Stage
Expansion
First Stage Financing
Generalist PE
Later Stage
Leveraged Buyout
Management Buyouts
Mezzanine
Private Placement
Recapitalizations
Second Stage Financing
Seed
Special Situation
Startup

Size of Investments Considered

Min Size of Investment Considered (000s): $1,000
Max Size of Investment Considered (000s): $500,000

Geographical Preferences

United States

All U.S.

Canada

All Canada

International

China
Eastern Europe
France
Germany
India
Italy
Japan
Latin America
Spain
United Kingdom

Industry Preferences

(% based on actual investment)

Other Products	30.5%
Communications and Media	13.9%
Medical/Health	13.2%
Consumer Related	10.5%
Computer Software and Services	9.9%
Internet Specific	8.4%
Industrial/Energy	5.7%
Biotechnology	4.4%
Computer Hardware	2.3%
Semiconductors/Other Elect.	1.2%

Additional Information
Name of Most Recent Fund: Warburg, Pincas Equity Partners, L.P.
Most Recent Fund Was Raised: 09/01/1998
Year Founded: 1966
Capital Under Management: $9,500,000,000
Current Activity Level : Actively seeking new investments
Method of Compensation: Return on investment is of primary concern, do not charge fees

WASSERSTEIN, PERELLA & CO., INC.

31 West 52nd Street
27th Floor
New York, NY 10019
Phone: 212-702-5691
Fax: 212-969-7879

Other Offices

101 California Street
42nd Floor
San Francisco, CA 94111
Phone: 415-677-4800
Fax: 415-288-3960

Management and Staff
Anup Bagaria, Partner
Bruce Wasserstein, Partner
Ellis Jones, Partner
George Majoros, Partner
W. Townsend Ziebold, President

Whom to Contact
Perry W. Steiner
W. Townsend Ziebold

Type of Firm
SBIC Not elsewhere classified

Project Preferences

Role in Financing:
Prefer role as deal originator but will also invest in deals created by others

Type of Financing Preferred:
Leveraged Buyout

Geographical Preferences

United States
All U.S.

Industry Preferences

(% based on actual investment)

Internet Specific	47.6%
Communications and Media	14.5%
Other Products	13.2%
Semiconductors/Other Elect.	10.6%
Computer Software and Services	4.5%
Medical/Health	4.1%
Consumer Related	3.1%
Computer Hardware	2.3%

Additional Information
Name of Most Recent Fund: U.S. Equity Partners, L.P.
Most Recent Fund Was Raised: 04/01/1998
Year Founded: 1996
Capital Under Management: $135,000,000
Current Activity Level : Actively seeking new investments
Method of Compensation: Return on investment is of primary concern, do not charge fees

WELSH, CARSON, ANDERSON & STOWE

320 Park Avenue
Suite 2500
New York, NY 10022-6815
Phone: 212-893-9500
Fax: 212-893-9575
Website: www.welshcarson.com

Management and Staff
Andrew Paul, General Partner
Anthony De Nicola, General Partner
Bruce Anderson, Co-Founder
Charles Moore, General Partner
D. Scott Mackesy, Principal
James Matthews, Principal
John Rather, Chief Financial Officer
John Clark, Principal
Larry Sorrell, General Partner
Laura Van Buren, General Partner
Patrick Welsh, Co-Founder
Paul Qucally, General Partner
Robert Minicucci, General Partner
Rudolph Rupert, General Partner
Russell Carson, General Partner
Sanjay Swani, Principal
Thomas McInerney, General Partner

Type of Firm
Private Firm Investing Own Capital

Industry Association Membership
National Venture Capital Association (NVCA)

Project Preferences

Role in Financing:
Prefer role as deal originator

Type of Financing Preferred:
Leveraged Buyout
Special Situation

Size of Investments Considered
Min Size of Investment Considered (000s): $25,000
Max Size of Investment Considered: No Limit

Geographical Preferences

United States
All U.S.
All U.S.

International
All International

Industry Preferences

(% based on actual investment)

Medical/Health	28.9%
Communications and Media	22.1%
Internet Specific	17.6%
Other Products	13.3%
Computer Software and Services	9.2%
Computer Hardware	6.3%
Consumer Related	2.2%
Semiconductors/Other Elect.	0.2%
Industrial/Energy	0.2%

Additional Information
Name of Most Recent Fund: Welsh, Carson, Anderson & Stowe VIII
Most Recent Fund Was Raised: 07/01/1998
Year Founded: 1979
Capital Under Management: $10,857,300,000
Current Activity Level : Actively seeking new investments
Method of Compensation: Return on invest. most important, but chg. closing fees, service fees, etc.

WESTBRIDGE CAPITAL ADVISORS (INDIA) PVT. LTD.

54 Thomson Street
New York, NY 10012
Phone: 1-212-965-2474
Fax: 1-212-965-2365
Website: www.wbcapital.com

See Foreign Venture Capital Firms for full listing.

WESTBURY PARTNERS

1400 Old Country Road
Suite 313
Westbury, NY 11590
Phone: 516-333-0218
Fax: 516-333-2724

Management and Staff
Brett Rome
James Schubaur
Richard Sicoli

Whom to Contact
Brett Rome
James Schubaur
Richard Sicoli

Type of Firm
Investment/Merchant Bank Investing Own or Client Funds

Project Preferences

Role in Financing:
Prefer role as deal originator but will also invest in deals created by others

Type of Financing Preferred:
Leveraged Buyout
Mezzanine
Second Stage Financing
Special Situation

Size of Investments Considered
Min Size of Investment Considered (000s): $50,000
Max Size of Investment Considered: No Limit

Geographical Preferences

United States
All U.S.

Canada
All Canada

International
South Africa

Industry Preferences

(% based on actual investment)

Communications and Media	38.7%
Internet Specific	21.0%
Computer Software and Services	14.7%
Computer Hardware	10.3%
Other Products	9.8%
Medical/Health	5.5%

Additional Information
Name of Most Recent Fund: Westbury Equity Partners L.P.
Most Recent Fund Was Raised: 01/01/1996
Year Founded: 1993
Capital Under Management: $25,000,000
Current Activity Level : Actively seeking new investments
Method of Compensation: Return on investment is of primary concern, do not charge fees

WESTSPHERE EQUITY INVESTORS, LP

55 East 59th Street
13th Floor
New York, NY 10022
Phone: 212-317-3600
Fax: 212-317-0739

Management and Staff
Joseph J. Vadapalas
Thomas R. Donohue

Whom to Contact
Joseph J. Vadapalas
Thomas R. Donohue

Type of Firm
Investment/Merchant Bank Subsid/Affil

Project Preferences

Role in Financing:
Prefer role as deal originator but will also invest in deals created by others

Type of Financing Preferred:
Leveraged Buyout

Geographical Preferences

International
Mexico
South Africa

Industry Preferences

Computer Software
Software

Semiconductors/Other Elect.
Fiber Optics

Medical/Health
Medical Products

Consumer Related
Entertainment and Leisure
Food/Beverage
Consumer Products
Consumer Services

Industrial/Energy
Industrial Products
Factory Automation
Environmental Related

Financial Services
Financial Services

Manufact.
Publishing

Additional Information
Name of Most Recent Fund: WestSphere Latin America Private Equity Growth Fund II
Most Recent Fund Was Raised: 08/02/1998
Year Founded: 1989
Capital Under Management: $429,000,000
Current Activity Level : Actively seeking new investments
Method of Compensation: Return on invest. most important, but chg. closing fees, service fees, etc.

WHEATLEY PARTNERS

80 Cutter Mill Road
Suite 311
Great Neck, NY 11021
Phone: 516-773-1024
Fax: 516-773-0996

Other Offices

767 Fifth Avenue
New York, NY 10153-4590
Phone: 212-486-4455
Fax: 212-486-4469

Management and Staff
Barry Fingerhut, General Partner
Barry Rubenstein, General Partner
Irwin Lieber, General Partner
Jonathan Leiber, General Partner
Seth Lieber, General Partner

Type of Firm
Private Firm Investing Own Capital

Project Preferences

Role in Financing:
Will function either as deal originator or investor in deals created by others

Size of Investments Considered
Min Size of Investment Considered (000s): $2,000
Max Size of Investment Considered (000s): $3,000

Industry Preferences
(% based on actual investment)

Internet Specific	39.5%
Computer Software and Services	26.0%
Communications and Media	21.2%
Semiconductors/Other Elect.	7.0%
Biotechnology	3.4%
Other Products	1.7%
Medical/Health	1.1%

Additional Information
Year Founded: 1992
Capital Under Management: $200,000,000
Current Activity Level : Actively seeking new investments
Method of Compensation: Return on investment is of primary concern, do not charge fees

WHITNEY & CO. (FKA: J.H. WHITNEY & CO.)

630 Fifth Avenue
Suite 3225
New York, NY 10111
Phone: 212-332-2400
Fax: 212-332-2422
Website: www.jhwhitney.com

See Connecticut for full listing.

WILLIAM A.M. BURDEN & CO.

10 East 53rd Street
32nd Floor
New York, NY 10022
Phone: 212-872-1133
Fax: 212-872-1199

Type of Firm
Private Firm Investing Own Capital

Project Preferences

Role in Financing:
Prefer role as deal originator but will also invest in deals created by others

Type of Financing Preferred:
Control-block Purchases
Leveraged Buyout
Mezzanine
Special Situation

Size of Investments Considered
Min Size of Investment Considered (000s): $2,000
Max Size of Investment Considered: No Limit

Geographical Preferences

International
No Preference

Industry Preferences

Communications and Media
Communications and Media
Other Communication Prod.

Semiconductors/Other Elect.
Electronics
Electronic Components
Sensors

Medical/Health
Other Therapeutic
Medical Products
Hospitals/Clinics/Primary
Hospital/Other Instit.

Consumer Related
Entertainment and Leisure
Retail
Franchises(NEC)
Food/Beverage
Consumer Products
Consumer Services
Other Restaurants
Hotels and Resorts
Education Related

Industrial/Energy
Oil and Gas Exploration
Oil & Gas Drilling,Explor
Coal Related
Energy Conservation Relat
Industrial Products
Materials
Factory Automation
Machinery
Environmental Related

Financial Services
Financial Services
Real Estate

Manufact.
Publishing

Agr/Forestr/Fish
Mining and Minerals

Additional Information
Name of Most Recent Fund: William A.M. Burden & CO
Most Recent Fund Was Raised: 07/01/1971
Year Founded: 1949
Current Activity Level : Actively seeking new investments
Method of Compensation: Return on investment is of primary concern, do not charge fees

WINTHROP VENTURES

74 Trinity Place
Suite 600
New York, NY 10006
Phone: 212-422-0100

Management and Staff
Cyrus Brown

Whom to Contact
Cyrus Brown

Type of Firm
Investment/Merchant Bank Subsid/Affil

Project Preferences

Role in Financing:
Prefer role as deal originator

Type of Financing Preferred:
First Stage Financing
Leveraged Buyout
Second Stage Financing
Start-up Financing

Size of Investments Considered
Min Size of Investment Considered (000s): $1,000
Max Size of Investment Considered: No Limit

Geographical Preferences

International
No Preference

Industry Preferences

Communications and Media
Commercial Communications
CATV & Pay TV Systems
Telecommunications
Data Communications
Satellite Microwave Comm.
Other Communication Prod.

Computer Hardware
Computers
Computer Graphics and Dig
Integrated Turnkey System
Terminals
Disk Relat. Memory Device

Computer Software
Computer Services
Systems Software
Applications Software

Semiconductors/Other Elect.
Electronics
Electronic Components
Semiconductor
Laser Related
Analytic/Scientific

Biotechnology
Industrial Biotechnology
Biosensors
Biotech Related Research
Biotech Related Research

Medical/Health
Medical Diagnostics
Diagnostic Test Products
Drug/Equipmt Delivery
Other Therapeutic
Medical Products
Disposable Med. Products
Hospitals/Clinics/Primary
Hospital/Other Instit.
Pharmaceuticals

Consumer Related
Entertainment and Leisure
Retail
Computer Stores
Food/Beverage
Consumer Products
Consumer Services
Education Related

Industrial/Energy
Alternative Energy
Energy Conservation Relat
Industrial Products

Transportation
Transportation

Financial Services
Financial Services

Manufact.
Office Automation Equipmt
Publishing

Additional Information
Year Founded: 1972
Current Activity Level : Actively seeking new investments
Method of Compensation: Return on invest. most important, but chg. closing fees, service fees, etc.

WIT CAPITAL CORPORATION

826 Broadway
New York, NY 10003
Phone: 212-253-4400
Fax: 212-253-4467

Management and Staff
Robert Lessin, Chairman & CEO

Whom to Contact
Michael Benedek
Ronald Drake

Type of Firm
Mgt. Consulting Firm

Project Preferences

Type of Financing Preferred:
Second Stage Financing

Industry Preferences

Computer Other
Computer Related

Consumer Related
Consumer Products
Consumer Services

Additional Information
Capital Under Management: $10,000,000
Current Activity Level : Actively seeking new investments

WITSOUNDVIEW VENTURES-DAWNTREADER FUNDS

826 Broadway
8th Floor
New York, NY 10003
Phone: 646-654-2600
Fax: 646-654-2654
Website: www.witcapital.com

Management and Staff
Andrew Weissman, Managing Director
Daniel DeWolf, Managing Director
Edward Sim, Managing Director
Robert Lessin, President
Stephen Klein, Managing Director

Type of Firm
Private Firm Investing Own Capital

Industry Preferences

(% based on actual investment)

Internet Specific	80.2%
Semiconductors/Other Elect.	10.8%
Computer Software and Services	9.0%

Additional Information
Name of Most Recent Fund: Dawntreader Fund I
Most Recent Fund Was Raised: 01/01/1998
Year Founded: 1996
Capital Under Management: $325,000,000
Current Activity Level : Actively seeking new investments

WORMS CAPITAL MANAGEMENT

900 Third Avenue
New York, NY 10022
Phone: 212-418-6508
Fax: 212-418-6510

Management and Staff
Robert DiGeronimo
Thomas M. DeLitlo

Whom to Contact
Robert DiGeronimo
Thomas M. DeLitlo

Type of Firm
Investment/Merchant Bank Subsid/Affil

Project Preferences

Role in Financing:
Prefer role as deal originator but will also invest in deals created by others

Type of Financing Preferred:
Control-block Purchases
Leveraged Buyout
Mezzanine
Second Stage Financing
Special Situation

Size of Investments Considered
Min Size of Investment Considered (000s): $1,000
Max Size of Investment Considered: No Limit

Geographical Preferences
International
No Preference

Industry Preferences
Communications and Media
Communications and Media

Computer Other
Computer Related

Semiconductors/Other Elect.
Electronic Components

Medical/Health
Medical/Health

Consumer Related
Entertainment and Leisure
Retail
Computer Stores
Franchises(NEC)
Food/Beverage
Consumer Products
Consumer Services
Other Restaurants
Education Related

Industrial/Energy
Industrial Products

Transportation
Transportation

Financial Services
Financial Services

Business Serv.
Distribution
Consulting Services

Manufact.
Publishing

Additional Information
Name of Most Recent Fund: Permal Private Equity Holdings, LP
Most Recent Fund Was Raised: 01/01/1995
Year Founded: 1964
Capital Under Management: $100,000,000
Current Activity Level : Actively seeking new investments
Method of Compensation: Return on investment is of primary concern, do not charge fees

WSI HOLDING CORPORATION

126 Newmarket Road
Garden City, NY 11530
Phone: 516-873-8948
Fax: 516-873-1229

Management and Staff
William Leone, President

Type of Firm
Non-Financial Corp. Affiliate or Subsidiary

Industry Association Membership
National Venture Capital Association (NVCA)

Project Preferences
Type of Financing Preferred:
Seed
Startup

Geographical Preferences
United States
Northeast

Industry Preferences
Communications and Media
Wireless Communications

Internet Specific
Internet

Other
Environment Responsible

Additional Information
Capital Under Management: $3,000,000
Current Activity Level : Actively seeking new investments
Method of Compensation: Professional fee required whether or not deal closes

ZEPHYR INTERNET PARTNERS

320 Park Ave.
Suite 4A
New York, NY 10022
Phone: 212-508-9430
Fax: 212-508-9440
Website: www.zephyrmanagement.com

Management and Staff
Corbett Leo, Managing Partner

Type of Firm
Private Equity Advisor or Fund of Fund Mgr

Industry Association Membership
National Venture Capital Association (NVCA)

Project Preferences
Type of Financing Preferred:
Seed

Industry Preferences
Internet Specific
Internet

Additional Information
Year Founded: 2000
Capital Under Management: $6,000,000
Current Activity Level : Actively seeking new investments

ZS FUND, L.P.

120 West 45th Street
Suite 2600
New York, NY 10036
Phone: 212-398-6200
Fax: 212-398-1808

Management and Staff
Jeffery A. Oyster

Whom to Contact
Jeffery A. Oyster

Type of Firm
Private Firm Investing Own Capital

Project Preferences
Role in Financing:
Prefer role as deal originator but will also invest in deals created by others

Type of Financing Preferred:
Leveraged Buyout

Size of Investments Considered
Min Size of Investment Considered (000s): $90,000
Max Size of Investment Considered: No Limit

Geographical Preferences
United States
All U.S.

Canada
All Canada

International
Bermuda
China
France
United Kingdom

Industry Preferences

Communications and Media
Communications and Media

Semiconductors/Other Elect.
Electronics
Electronic Components
Sensors

Medical/Health
Disposable Med. Products

Consumer Related
Entertainment and Leisure
Retail
Food/Beverage
Consumer Products
Consumer Services
Other Restaurants
Education Related

Industrial/Energy
Industrial Products
Materials
Factory Automation
Machinery

Manufact.
Office Automation Equipmt
Publishing

Additional Information
Name of Most Recent Fund: ZS Investment Fund
Most Recent Fund Was Raised: 10/01/1985
Year Founded: 1985
Capital Under Management: $150,000,000
Current Activity Level : Actively seeking new investments
Method of Compensation: Return on invest. most important, but chg. closing fees, service fees, etc.

ZURICH SCUDDER INVESTMENTS (FKA: SCUDDER KEMPER INVESTMENTS)

345 Park Avenue
New York, NY 10154
Phone: 212-326-6612
Fax: 212-751-3660

Management and Staff
J. Scott Swensen, Managing Director

Type of Firm
Investment Management/Finance Consulting

Project Preferences

Role in Financing:
Will function either as deal originator or investor in deals created by others

Type of Financing Preferred:
Fund of Funds
Later Stage

Size of Investments Considered
Min Size of Investment Considered (000s): $5,000
Max Size of Investment Considered: No Limit

Geographical Preferences

United States
All U.S.

Industry Preferences

Medical/Health
Medical/Health

Additional Information
Year Founded: 1919
Capital Under Management: $2,250,000,000
Current Activity Level : Actively seeking new investments
Method of Compensation: Return on invest. most important, but chg. closing fees, service fees, etc.

NORTH CAROLINA

A.M. PAPPAS & ASSOCIATES

Beta Building, Suite 402
2222 Chapel Hill Nelsons Hwy
Durham, NC 27713
Phone: 919-361-4990
Fax: 919-361-0497

Management and Staff
Art Pappas, President
Ford Worthy, Vice President
Russ Saure, Chief Financial Officer

Whom to Contact
Charlie Turner
William Wight

Type of Firm
Venture Consulting Firm

Project Preferences

Role in Financing:
Will function either as deal originator or investor in deals created by others

Type of Financing Preferred:
Balanced
Early Stage
Expansion
First Stage Financing
Later Stage
Leveraged Buyout
Mezzanine
Open Market
Second Stage Financing
Seed
Startup

Size of Investments Considered
Min Size of Investment Considered (000s): $2,000
Max Size of Investment Considered (000s): $7,000

Geographical Preferences

United States
All U.S.
Northeast
Northern California
Southeast
West Coast

Canada
All Canada
Ontario
Quebec

International
Belgium
China
France
Germany
Hong Kong
Italy
Luxembourg
Netherlands
United Kingdom

Industry Preferences

(% based on actual investment)

Biotechnology	54.4%
Medical/Health	26.5%
Computer Software and Services	19.1%

Additional Information
Name of Most Recent Fund: Techamp International
Most Recent Fund Was Raised: 11/17/1998
Year Founded: 1994
Capital Under Management: $130,000,000
Current Activity Level : Actively seeking new investments
Method of Compensation: Return on invest. most important, but chg. closing fees, service fees, etc.

ACADEMY FUNDS (FKA: LONGLEAF VENTURE FUND LLC)

101 North Chestnut Street
Suite 103
Winston Salem, NC 27101
Phone: 336-748-9991
Fax: 336-748-9909
Website: www.academyfunds.com

Other Offices

11540 N. Community Howe Rd
Suite 150
Charlotte, NC 28277
Phone: 704-540-9379

920 Main Campus Drive
Suite 400
Raleigh, NC 27606
Phone: 919-424-3799

Management and Staff
Gregory Johnson, Managing Director
Matt Crawford, Managing Director

Type of Firm
Private Firm Investing Own Capital

Project Preferences

Role in Financing:
Prefer role as deal originator but will also invest in deals created by others

Type of Financing Preferred:
Early Stage
First Stage Financing
Research and Development
Seed
Startup

Geographical Preferences

United States
North Carolina
South Carolina

Industry Preferences

Communications and Media
Commercial Communications
Telecommunications
Wireless Communications
Data Communications
Satellite Microwave Comm.
Other Communication Prod.

Computer Hardware
Computer Graphics and Dig
Disk Relat. Memory Device

Computer Software
Software
Systems Software
Applications Software
Artificial Intelligence

Internet Specific
E-Commerce Technology
Internet
Web Aggregration/Portals

Semiconductors/Other Elect.
Electronics

Biotechnology
Human Biotechnology
Agricultural/Animal Bio.
Industrial Biotechnology
Biosensors
Biotech Related Research
Biotech Related Research

Medical/Health
Medical Diagnostics
Diagnostic Services
Diagnostic Test Products
Medical Therapeutics
Drug/Equipmt Delivery
Medical Products
Disposable Med. Products
Pharmaceuticals

Consumer Related
Education Related

Industrial/Energy
Energy
Superconductivity
Factory Automation
Process Control
Robotics

Transportation
Aerospace

Additional Information
Capital Under Management: $30,000,000
Current Activity Level : Actively seeking new investments
Method of Compensation: Return on investment is of primary concern, do not charge fees

ATLANTIS GROUP LLC

2530 Meridian Parkway
Third Floor
Durham, NC 27713
Phone: 919.806.4340
Fax: 919.806.4840
Website: www.theatlantisgroup.net

Type of Firm
Private Firm Investing Own Capital

Project Preferences

Type of Financing Preferred:
Seed

Geographical Preferences

United States
All U.S.

Additional Information
Year Founded: 2000
Capital Under Management: $6,000,000
Current Activity Level : Actively seeking new investments

AURORA FUNDS, INC.

2525 Meridian Parkway
Suite 220
Durham, NC 27713
Phone: 919-484-0400
Fax: 919-484-0444
Website: www.aurorafunds.com

Management and Staff
B. Jefferson Clark, General Partner
Erik Rasmussen, Principal
M. Scott Albert, General Partner
Richard Brown, Principal
V. Tobin Geatz, General Partner
William Brooke, Chief Operating Officer

Type of Firm
Private Firm Investing Own Capital

Industry Association Membership
National Venture Capital Association (NVCA)

Project Preferences

Role in Financing:
Will function either as deal originator or investor in deals created by others

Type of Financing Preferred:
Early Stage
First Stage Financing
Seed
Startup

Size of Investments Considered
Min Size of Investment Considered (000s): $250
Max Size of Investment Considered (000s): $1,500

Geographical Preferences

United States
Mid Atlantic
Southeast

Industry Preferences

(% based on actual investment)

Medical/Health	36.0%
Internet Specific	27.0%
Computer Software and Services	21.9%
Biotechnology	6.2%
Semiconductors/Other Elect.	4.5%
Communications and Media	4.1%
Industrial/Energy	0.4%

Additional Information
Name of Most Recent Fund: Harbinger/Aurora Venture Fund LLC
Most Recent Fund Was Raised: 10/15/1999
Year Founded: 1994
Capital Under Management: $90,000,000
Current Activity Level : Actively seeking new investments
Method of Compensation: Return on investment is of primary concern, do not charge fees

BANCAMERICA CAPITAL INVESTORS (FKA:NATIONSBANC CAPITAL CORP)

100 North Tryon Street
25th Floor
Charlotte, NC 28255
Phone: 704-386-8063
Fax: 704-386-6432

Management and Staff
W. Walker, Managing Director

Whom to Contact
Doug Williamson

Type of Firm
SBIC Not elsewhere classified

Industry Association Membership
Natl assoc of Small Bus. Inv. Co (NASBIC)

Project Preferences

Role in Financing:
Prefer role as deal originator but will also invest in deals created by others

Type of Financing Preferred:
Generalist PE
Leveraged Buyout
Mezzanine
Recapitalizations
Second Stage Financing
Special Situation

Size of Investments Considered
Min Size of Investment Considered (000s): $30,000
Max Size of Investment Considered: No Limit

Geographical Preferences

United States
All U.S.

Industry Preferences

(% based on actual investment)

Communications and Media	46.6%
Consumer Related	10.7%
Other Products	10.1%
Computer Software and Services	8.9%
Internet Specific	7.9%
Semiconductors/Other Elect.	7.0%
Industrial/Energy	4.9%
Medical/Health	3.8%

Additional Information
Year Founded: 1993
Capital Under Management: $1,900,000
Current Activity Level : Actively seeking new investments
Method of Compensation: Return on invest. most important, but chg. closing fees, service fees, etc.

CAPITALSOUTH PARTNERS, L.L.C.

1228 East Morehead St.
Suite 102
Charlotte, NC 28204
Phone: 704-376-5502
Fax: 704-376-5877
Website: www.capitalsouthpartners.com

Management and Staff
Elyn Dortch, Managing Director
Hunt Broyhill, Managing Director
Joseph Alala, President

Type of Firm
Private Equity Advisor or Fund of Fund Mgr

Industry Association Membership
Mid-Atlantic Venture Association
National Venture Capital Association (NVCA)
Natl assoc of Small Bus. Inv. Co (NASBIC)

Project Preferences

Role in Financing:
Will function either as deal originator or investor in deals created by others

Size of Investments Considered
Min Size of Investment Considered (000s): $1,000
Max Size of Investment Considered (000s): $5,000

Additional Information
Year Founded: 1998
Capital Under Management: $30,000,000
Current Activity Level : Actively seeking new investments
Method of Compensation: Return on investment is of primary concern, do not charge fees

CAROLINAS CAPITAL INVESTMENT CORP.

1408 Biltmore Dr.
Charlotte, NC 28207
Phone: 704-375-3888
Fax: 704-375-6226

Other Offices

6337 Morrison Boulevard
Charlotte, NC 28211
Phone: 704-362-8222
Fax: 704-362-8221

Management and Staff
Edward Goode

Whom to Contact
Edward Goode

Type of Firm
Private Firm Investing Own Capital

Industry Association Membership
Natl assoc of Small Bus. Inv. Co (NASBIC)

Project Preferences

Role in Financing:
Prefer role as deal originator but will also invest in deals created by others

Type of Financing Preferred:
First Stage Financing
Leveraged Buyout
Research and Development
Second Stage Financing
Seed
Start-up Financing

Size of Investments Considered
Min Size of Investment Considered (000s): $200
Max Size of Investment Considered (000s): $1,000

Geographical Preferences

International
No Preference

Industry Preferences

Communications and Media
Communications and Media

Semiconductors/Other Elect.
Electronic Components

Additional Information
Name of Most Recent Fund: Carolinas Capital
Most Recent Fund Was Raised: 10/01/1989
Year Founded: 1988
Current Activity Level : Actively seeking new investments
Method of Compensation: Return on investment is of primary concern, do not charge fees

CAROUSEL CAPITAL PARTNERS

201 North Tryon Street
Suite 2450
Charlotte, NC 28202
Phone: 704-372-2040
Fax: 704-372-1040
Website: www.carouselcap.com

Management and Staff
Brian Bailey, Managing Director
Erskine Bowles, Managing Director
Nelson Schwab, Managing Director

Type of Firm
Private Firm Investing Own Capital

Project Preferences

Role in Financing:
Will function either as deal originator or investor in deals created by others

Type of Financing Preferred:
Expansion
Later Stage
Leveraged Buyout

Size of Investments Considered
Min Size of Investment Considered (000s): $10,000
Max Size of Investment Considered (000s): $20,000

Geographical Preferences

United States
Southeast

Industry Preferences

(% based on actual investment)

Communications and Media	49.3%
Medical/Health	27.6%
Industrial/Energy	11.8%
Internet Specific	10.7%
Consumer Related	0.6%

Additional Information
Name of Most Recent Fund: Carousel Capital Partners I
Most Recent Fund Was Raised: 04/18/1996
Capital Under Management: $163,500,000
Current Activity Level : Actively seeking new investments
Method of Compensation: Return on invest. most important, but chg. closing fees, service fees, etc.

ENO RIVER CAPITAL

905 West Main Street
Box 44, Suite 25-B
Durham, NC 27701
Phone: 919-680-4511
Fax: 919-680-3282

Management and Staff
Daniel Egger, Managing Director
Greg Davis, Principal
Harlan Boyles, Venture Partner
Paul Jones, Managing Director

Type of Firm
Private Firm Investing Own Capital

Industry Association Membership
National Venture Capital Association (NVCA)

Industry Preferences
(% based on actual investment)

Computer Software and Services	34.1%
Internet Specific	28.1%
Biotechnology	17.8%
Medical/Health	12.5%
Other Products	7.4%

Additional Information
Name of Most Recent Fund: North Carolina Bioscience Investment Fund
Most Recent Fund Was Raised: 09/01/1998
Year Founded: 1997
Capital Under Management: $26,000,000
Current Activity Level : Actively seeking new investments

FIRST UNION CAPITAL PARTNERS

One First Union Center, 12th F
301 South College Street
Charlotte, NC 28288-0732
Phone: 704-383-0000
Fax: 704-374-6711
Website: www.fucp.com

Management and Staff
Arthur Roselle, Partner
David Scanlan, Principal
Frederick Eubank, Partner
George Hashbarger, Partner
James Cook, Partner
L. Watts Hamrick, Partner
Matt Soule, Principal
Neal Morrison, Partner
Pearce Landry, Partner
Robert Calton, Partner
Scott Perper, Managing Partner
Ted Gardner, Managing Partner
Tracey Chaffin, Chief Financial Officer
Walker Simmons, Principal
Wellford Tabor, Partner

Whom to Contact
L. Watts Hamrick III

Type of Firm
Commercial Bank Affiliate or Subsidiary

Industry Association Membership
Natl assoc of Small Bus. Inv. Co (NASBIC)

Project Preferences

Role in Financing:
Will function either as deal originator or investor in deals created by others

Type of Financing Preferred:
Acquisition
Early Stage
Expansion
First Stage Financing
Later Stage
Leveraged Buyout
Mezzanine
Recapitalizations
Second Stage Financing
Seed
Special Situation
Startup

Size of Investments Considered
Min Size of Investment Considered (000s): $5,000
Max Size of Investment Considered: No Limit

Geographical Preferences

United States
All U.S.

International
Latin America
Western Europe

Industry Preferences
(% based on actual investment)

Internet Specific	32.0%
Other Products	24.7%
Communications and Media	17.8%
Consumer Related	8.9%
Computer Software and Services	8.9%
Medical/Health	3.8%
Industrial/Energy	2.4%
Biotechnology	1.4%
Semiconductors/Other Elect.	0.1%

Additional Information
Name of Most Recent Fund: First Union Capital Partners
Most Recent Fund Was Raised: 01/01/1988
Year Founded: 1988
Capital Under Management: $900,000,000
Current Activity Level : Actively seeking new investments
Method of Compensation: Return on investment is of primary concern, do not charge fees

FRONTIER CAPITAL, LLC

525 North Tryon Street
Suite 1700
Charlotte, NC 28202
Phone: 704-414-2880
Fax: 704-414-2881
Website: www.frontierfunds.com

Management and Staff
Andrew Lindner, Partner
Paul Stackhouse, Partner
Richard Maclean, Partner

Type of Firm
Private Firm Investing Own Capital

Industry Association Membership
National Venture Capital Association (NVCA)

Project Preferences

Role in Financing:
Will function either as deal originator or investor in deals created by others

Type of Financing Preferred:
Early Stage
Expansion

Size of Investments Considered
Min Size of Investment Considered (000s): $500
Max Size of Investment Considered (000s): $3,000

Geographical Preferences
United States
Mid Atlantic
Southeast

Industry Preferences
Communications and Media
Telecommunications
Other Communication Prod.

Computer Software
Computer Services
Software

Semiconductors/Other Elect.
Electronic Components

Industrial/Energy
Energy

Additional Information
Year Founded: 1999
Capital Under Management: $46,000,000
Current Activity Level : Actively seeking new investments
Method of Compensation: Return on investment is of primary concern, do not charge fees

FUSION VENTURES

112 South Duke Street
Suite Four
Durham, NC 27701
Phone: 919-688-7744
Fax: 919-688-3366

Management and Staff
David Reed, Partner
Sue Harnett, Vice President

Type of Firm
Incubators

Additional Information
Current Activity Level : Actively seeking new investments

GENEVA MERCHANT BANKING PARTNERS

P.O. Box 21962
Greensboro, NC 27420
Phone: 336-275-7002
Fax: 336-275-9155
Website: www.genevamerchantbank.com

Other Offices

380 Knollwood Street
Suite 600
Winston-Salem, NC 27103
Phone: 910-727-4211
Fax: 910-725-4356

Management and Staff
H. Michael Weaver, General Partner

Type of Firm
Private Firm Investing Own Capital

Industry Association Membership
Natl assoc of Small Bus. Inv. Co (NASBIC)

Project Preferences
Role in Financing:
Prefer role as deal originator but will also invest in deals created by others

Type of Financing Preferred:
Balanced
Distressed Debt
Expansion
Leveraged Buyout
Management Buyouts
Mezzanine
Second Stage Financing
Special Situation

Size of Investments Considered
Min Size of Investment Considered (000s): $1,000
Max Size of Investment Considered (000s): $7,000

Geographical Preferences
United States
Mid Atlantic
Midwest
Southeast

Industry Preferences
(% based on actual investment)

Communications and Media	39.0%
Computer Hardware	16.2%
Internet Specific	15.0%
Consumer Related	8.1%
Medical/Health	7.5%
Computer Software and Services	6.8%
Industrial/Energy	6.1%
Semiconductors/Other Elect.	1.5%

Additional Information
Name of Most Recent Fund: Blue Ridge Investors, L.P.
Most Recent Fund Was Raised: 10/01/1994
Year Founded: 1999
Capital Under Management: $68,000,000
Current Activity Level : Actively seeking new investments
Method of Compensation: Return on invest. most important, but chg. closing fees, service fees, etc.

INTERSOUTH PARTNERS

3211 Shannon Road
Suite 610
Durham, NC 27707
Phone: 919-493-6640
Fax: 919-493-6649
Website: www.intersouth.com

Other Offices

1000 Park Forty Plaza
Suite 290
Durham, NC 27713
Phone: 919-544-6173
Fax: 919-544-6645

3001 United Founders Boulevard
Oklahoma City, OK 73112
Phone: 405-843-7890
Fax: 405-843-8048

The Presidio, Suite 220
6907 North Capital of Texas Hwy
Austin, TX 78731
Phone: 512-372-8843
Fax: 512-372-3844

Management and Staff
Bonnie Layman, Chief Financial Officer
Dennis Dougherty, General Partner
Donald Rainey, Venture Partner
Jonathon Perl, Partner
Kip Frey, Venture Partner
Mitch Mumma, General Partner
Philip Tracy, Venture Partner
Robert Bell, Venture Partner
Sallie Russell, General Partner
Selby Wellman, Venture Partner

Whom to Contact
Jonathan Perl

Type of Firm
Private Firm Investing Own Capital

Industry Association Membership
Mid-Atlantic Venture Association
National Venture Capital Association (NVCA)

Project Preferences

Role in Financing:
Prefer role as deal originator but will also invest in deals created by others

Type of Financing Preferred:
Early Stage
First Stage Financing
Seed
Startup

Size of Investments Considered
Min Size of Investment Considered (000s): $2,000
Max Size of Investment Considered (000s): $10,000

Geographical Preferences

United States
Southeast

Industry Preferences

(% based on actual investment)

Internet Specific	25.4%
Medical/Health	25.0%
Biotechnology	23.0%
Computer Software and Services	14.9%
Communications and Media	4.2%
Semiconductors/Other Elect.	3.1%
Industrial/Energy	1.6%
Consumer Related	1.2%
Other Products	0.8%
Computer Hardware	0.7%

Additional Information
Name of Most Recent Fund: Intersouth Partners IV
Most Recent Fund Was Raised: 02/01/1998
Year Founded: 1984
Capital Under Management: $298,800,000
Current Activity Level : Actively seeking new investments
Method of Compensation: Return on investment is of primary concern, do not charge fees

KITTY HAWK CAPITAL

2700 Coltsgate Road
Suite 202
Charlotte, NC 28211
Phone: 704-362-3909
Fax: 704-362-2774
Website: www.kittyhawkcapital.com

Management and Staff
Lawrence Gladstone, General Partner
Stephen Buchanan, General Partner
W. Chris Hegele, General Partner
Walter Wilkinson, General Partner

Type of Firm
Investment Management/Finance Consulting

Industry Association Membership
Mid-Atlantic Venture Association
National Venture Capital Association (NVCA)
Natl assoc of Small Bus. Inv. Co (NASBIC)

Project Preferences

Role in Financing:
Will function either as deal originator or investor in deals created by others

Type of Financing Preferred:
Early Stage
Expansion
First Stage Financing

Size of Investments Considered
Min Size of Investment Considered (000s): $1,000
Max Size of Investment Considered (000s): $7,000

Geographical Preferences

United States
Southeast

Industry Preferences

(% based on actual investment)

Medical/Health	27.8%
Biotechnology	13.7%
Internet Specific	12.9%
Industrial/Energy	11.9%
Computer Software and Services	10.7%
Other Products	10.7%
Consumer Related	5.4%
Semiconductors/Other Elect.	3.4%
Communications and Media	2.2%
Computer Hardware	1.1%

Additional Information
Name of Most Recent Fund: Kitty Hawk Capital Limited Partnership IV
Most Recent Fund Was Raised: 01/01/1998
Year Founded: 1980
Capital Under Management: $69,300,000
Current Activity Level : Actively seeking new investments
Method of Compensation: Return on investment is of primary concern, do not charge fees

MASSEY BURCH CAPITAL CORP.

1000 Park Forty Plaza
Suite 300
Durham, NC 27713
Phone: 919-544-6162
Fax: 919-544-6667

See Tennessee for full listing.

MATRIX CAPITAL

318 Holland Street
P.O. Box 1328
Durham, NC 27702-1328
Phone: 919-688-6060
Fax: 919-682-9083

See Virginia for full listing.

MATRIX CAPITAL

318 Holland Street
P.O. Box 1328
Durham, NC 27702-1328
Phone: 919-688-6060
Fax: 919-682-9083

See Virginia for full listing.

NORTH CAROLINA ENTERPRISE FUND, L.P., THE

3600 Glenwood Avenue
Suite 107
Raleigh, NC 27612
Phone: 919-781-2691
Fax: 919-783-9195
Website: www.ncef.com

Other Offices

10600 N. Pantau Avenue
Cupertino, CA 95014
Phone: 408-777-8817
Fax: 408-777-8617

Management and Staff
Charles Closson
Joseph Velk

Whom to Contact
Charles Closson
Joseph Velk

Type of Firm
Private Firm Investing Own Capital

Industry Association Membership
National Venture Capital Association (NVCA)

Project Preferences

Role in Financing:
Prefer role as deal originator but will also invest in deals created by others

Type of Financing Preferred:
First Stage Financing
Mezzanine
Start-up Financing

Size of Investments Considered
Min Size of Investment Considered (000s): $2,000
Max Size of Investment Considered: No Limit

Geographical Preferences

United States
North Carolina
Southeast

Industry Preferences

(% based on actual investment)

Communications and Media	31.2%
Medical/Health	22.6%
Computer Software and Services	15.3%
Internet Specific	11.2%
Semiconductors/Other Elect.	8.1%
Computer Hardware	5.4%
Consumer Related	2.9%
Biotechnology	1.8%
Other Products	1.4%

Additional Information
Name of Most Recent Fund: North Carolina Enterprise Fund, L.P., The
Most Recent Fund Was Raised: 04/01/1989
Year Founded: 1989
Capital Under Management: $30,000,000
Current Activity Level : Actively seeking new investments
Method of Compensation: Return on investment is of primary concern, do not charge fees

NORTH CAROLINA TECHNOLOGICAL DEVELOPMENT AUTHORITY, INC.

Two Davis Drive
P.O. Box 13169
Res. Triangle Park, NC 27709-3169
Phone: 919-990-8558
Fax: 919-558-0156

Management and Staff
David L. Emmett

Whom to Contact
David L. Emmett

Type of Firm
State Govt Affiliated NEC

Project Preferences

Role in Financing:
Prefer role as deal originator but will also invest in deals created by others

Type of Financing Preferred:
First Stage Financing
Research and Development
Second Stage Financing
Seed
Start-up Financing

Geographical Preferences

United States
Southeast

Industry Preferences

Communications and Media
Commercial Communications
Telecommunications
Data Communications
Satellite Microwave Comm.

Computer Hardware
Mini and Personal/Desktop
Computer Graphics and Dig
Disk Relat. Memory Device

Computer Software
Systems Software
Applications Software
Artificial Intelligence

Internet Specific
Internet

Semiconductors/Other Elect.
Electronic Components

Biotechnology
Biotechnology

Medical/Health
Diagnostic Services
Diagnostic Test Products
Drug/Equipmt Delivery
Other Therapeutic
Disposable Med. Products
Pharmaceuticals

Industrial/Energy
Alternative Energy
Energy Conservation Relat
Industrial Products
Materials

Additional Information
Year Founded: 1983
Capital Under Management: $3,000,000
Current Activity Level : Actively seeking new investments
Method of Compensation: Return on investment is of primary concern, do not charge fees

OBERLIN CAPITAL, L.P.

702 Oberlin Road
Suite 150
Raleigh, NC 27605
Phone: 919-743-2544
Fax: 919-743-2501
Website: www.oberlincapital.com

Management and Staff
Randall Mountcastle, Vice President
Shepley Robert, Managing Partner

Type of Firm
Private Firm Investing Own Capital

Industry Association Membership
Natl assoc of Small Bus. Inv. Co (NASBIC)

Project Preferences

Type of Financing Preferred:
Balanced
Expansion
Later Stage
Leveraged Buyout
Management Buyouts

Size of Investments Considered
Min Size of Investment Considered (000s): $1,000
Max Size of Investment Considered (000s): $2,000

Geographical Preferences

United States
Mid Atlantic
Southeast

Additional Information

Capital Under Management: $35,000,000
Current Activity Level : Actively seeking new investments

PIEDMONT VENTURE PARTNERS

One Morrocroft Centre
6805 Morrison Blvd Suite 380
Charlotte, NC 28211
Phone: 704-731-5200
Fax: 704-365-9733
Website: www.piedmontvp.com

Management and Staff

Chris Lyford, Chief Financial Officer
Minor Hinson, Managing Partner
Stacy Anderson, Managing Partner
William Neal, Managing Partner

Type of Firm

Private Firm Investing Own Capital

Industry Association Membership

National Venture Capital Association (NVCA)
Natl assoc of Small Bus. Inv. Co (NASBIC)

Project Preferences

Role in Financing:
Will function either as deal originator or investor in deals created by others

Type of Financing Preferred:
Early Stage

Size of Investments Considered

Min Size of Investment Considered (000s): $250
Max Size of Investment Considered (000s): $5,000

Geographical Preferences

United States
Southeast

Industry Preferences

(% based on actual investment)

Internet Specific	64.6%
Biotechnology	13.4%
Computer Software and Services	7.9%
Medical/Health	6.9%
Computer Hardware	5.9%
Other Products	1.3%

Additional Information

Name of Most Recent Fund: Piedmont Venture Partners II, L.P.
Most Recent Fund Was Raised: 11/16/1998
Year Founded: 1996
Capital Under Management: $45,000,000
Current Activity Level : Actively seeking new investments
Method of Compensation: Return on invest. most important, but chg. closing fees, service fees, etc.

RED HAT VENTURES

2600 Meridian Parkway
Durham, NC 27713
Phone: 919-547-0012
Fax: 919-547-0024
Website: ww.redhat.com

Management and Staff

Harold Covert, Chief Financial Officer
Robert Young, Chairman & CEO

Type of Firm

Non-Financial Corp. Affiliate or Subsidiary

Project Preferences

Role in Financing:
Prefer role in deals created by others

Size of Investments Considered

Min Size of Investment Considered (000s): $500
Max Size of Investment Considered (000s): $2,000

Geographical Preferences

International
All International

Industry Preferences

Computer Software
Software

Internet Specific
Internet

Additional Information

Current Activity Level : Actively seeking new investments

RUDDICK INVESTMENT CO.

1800 Two First Union Center
Charlotte, NC 28282
Phone: 704-372-5404
Fax: 704-372-6409

Management and Staff

Richard Brigden

Whom to Contact

Richard Brigden

Type of Firm

Non-Financial Corp. Affiliate or Subsidiary

Project Preferences

Role in Financing:
Prefer role as deal originator but will also invest in deals created by others

Type of Financing Preferred:
First Stage Financing
Mezzanine
Second Stage Financing

Size of Investments Considered

Min Size of Investment Considered (000s): $500
Max Size of Investment Considered (000s): $1,000

Geographical Preferences

United States
Southeast

Additional Information

Year Founded: 1977
Capital Under Management: $11,000,000
Current Activity Level : Actively seeking new investments
Method of Compensation: Return on investment is of primary concern, do not charge fees

SHELTON COMPANIES, INC., THE

3600 One First Union Center
301 South College Street
Charlotte, NC 28202
Phone: 704-348-2200
Fax: 704-348-2260

Type of Firm

Investment/Merchant Bank Investing Own or Client Funds

Project Preferences

Role in Financing:
Prefer role as deal originator but will also invest in deals created by others

Type of Financing Preferred:
Control-block Purchases
Leveraged Buyout
Recapitalizations
Second Stage Financing

Size of Investments Considered
Min Size of Investment Considered (000s): $1,000
Max Size of Investment Considered (000s): $10,000

Geographical Preferences

United States
Mid Atlantic
Midwest
Southeast
Southwest

Industry Preferences

Communications and Media
Radio & TV Broadcasting

Semiconductors/Other Elect.
Sensors

Medical/Health
Diagnostic Test Products
Disposable Med. Products

Consumer Related
Entertainment and Leisure
Food/Beverage
Consumer Products
Consumer Services
Education Related

Industrial/Energy
Materials
Machinery
Environmental Related

Transportation
Transportation

Financial Services
Financial Services

Business Serv.
Distribution

Manufact.
Publishing

Additional Information
Year Founded: 1991
Capital Under Management: $50,000,000
Current Activity Level : Actively seeking new investments
Method of Compensation: Return on invest. most important, but chg. closing fees, service fees, etc.

SOUTH ATLANTIC VENTURE FUNDS, L.P.

102 Marseille Place
Cary, NC 27511
Phone: 919-461-0803
Fax: 919-319-0026
Website: www.southatlantic.com

See Florida for full listing.

SOUTHEAST INTERACTIVE TECHNOLOGY FUNDS

630 Davis Drive
Suite 220
Morrisville, NC 27560
Phone: 919-558-8324
Fax: 919-558-2025
Website: www.se-interactive.com

Management and Staff
Chris Horgen, Managing Partner
Christopher Austen, Partner
David Blivin, Managing Director
Lee Bryan, General Partner
Mark Dunkel, Partner
Mike Preston, Principal
Norvell Miller, Managing Director
Ruth Taylor, Principal
Steven Rakes, Chief Financial Officer
Suresh Arora, Partner
Thomas Tull, Principal

Type of Firm
Private Firm Investing Own Capital

Industry Association Membership
National Venture Capital Association (NVCA)

Project Preferences

Type of Financing Preferred:
First Stage Financing
Seed

Size of Investments Considered
Min Size of Investment Considered (000s): $1,000
Max Size of Investment Considered (000s): $4,000

Geographical Preferences

United States
Southeast

Industry Preferences

(% based on actual investment)

Internet Specific	53.3%
Computer Software and Services	25.8%
Other Products	8.0%
Communications and Media	6.9%
Semiconductors/Other Elect.	3.7%
Computer Hardware	2.4%

Additional Information
Name of Most Recent Fund: Southeast Interactive Technology Fund II, LLC
Most Recent Fund Was Raised: 06/30/1996
Year Founded: 1995
Capital Under Management: $177,100,000
Current Activity Level : Actively seeking new investments

SOUTHERN CAPITOL VENTURES

1201 Edwards Mill Road
Suite 111-A
Raleigh, NC 27607
Phone: 919-858-7580
Fax: 919-858-7932
Website: www.southerncapitolventures.com

Management and Staff
Benjamin Brooks, Managing Partner
Dan Wilson, Partner
Dave Murray, Partner
Jane De Giacomo, Partner
Jason Caplain, Partner

Type of Firm
Private Firm Investing Own Capital

Project Preferences

Type of Financing Preferred:
Balanced
Early Stage
Expansion
Later Stage

Geographical Preferences

United States
Southeast

Additional Information

Year Founded: 2000
Current Activity Level : Actively seeking new investments

STANFORD KEENE

2850 One First Union Center
Charlotte, NC 28202
Phone: 704-347-0700
Fax: 704-347-0701

Management and Staff

Brian Boscheman, Chief Financial Officer

Type of Firm

Investment/Merchant Bank Subsid/Affil

Additional Information

Name of Most Recent Fund: Stanford Keene Internet One
Most Recent Fund Was Raised: 09/30/1997
Capital Under Management: $250,000,000
Current Activity Level : Actively seeking new investments

SUSTAINABLE JOBS FUND (SJF), THE

115 Market Street
Suite 211
Durham, NC 27701
Phone: 919-530-1177
Fax: 919-530-1178
Website: www.sjfund.com

Other Offices

620 Chestnut Street
Suite 560
Philadelphia, PA 19106
Phone: 215-923-8870
Fax: 215-923-8871

Management and Staff

Dan Hoversten, Managing Director
David Kirkpatrick, Managing Director
Richard Defieux, Co-Founder

Type of Firm

Private Firm Investing Own Capital

Project Preferences

Type of Financing Preferred:
Early Stage
Expansion
Seed

Geographical Preferences

United States
East Coast

Industry Preferences

Manufact.
Manufacturing

Other
Environment Responsible

Additional Information

Capital Under Management: $17,000,000
Current Activity Level : Actively seeking new investments

TRUEPILOT, LLC

2530 Meridian Parkway
3rd Floor
Durham, NC 27713
Phone: 919-806-4930
Fax: 919-806-4845
Website: www.truepilot.com

Management and Staff

Michael Brader-Araje, Chief Executive Officer

Type of Firm

Private Firm Investing Own Capital

Project Preferences

Type of Financing Preferred:
Early Stage

Size of Investments Considered
Min Size of Investment Considered (000s): $50
Max Size of Investment Considered (000s): $500

Geographical Preferences

United States
North Carolina

Industry Preferences

Internet Specific
Internet

Additional Information

Year Founded: 2000
Current Activity Level : Actively seeking new investments

VENTURE FIRST ASSOCIATES

500 Old Greensboro Road
Chapel Hill, NC 27516
Phone: 919-929-1065
Fax: 919-929-0978

See Florida for full listing.

VIRIDIAN CAPITAL LLC

6100 Fairview Road
Suite 770
Charlotte, NC 28210
Phone: 704-556-1950
Fax: 704-556-0556

Management and Staff

Frank Backinsky, President
Frank Bachinsky, Chief Executive Officer
Jeff Sampson, Managing Director
Scheline Moore, Vice President
Scott Holmes, President

Type of Firm

Private Firm Investing Own Capital

Industry Association Membership

National Venture Capital Association (NVCA)

Industry Preferences

(% based on actual investment)

Computer Software and Services	53.3%
Biotechnology	17.1%
Internet Specific	10.7%
Communications and Media	10.2%
Medical/Health	8.7%

Additional Information

Year Founded: 1998
Capital Under Management: $6,000,000
Current Activity Level : Actively seeking new investments

VIRIDIAN CAPITAL PARTNERS (FKA: AURORA VENTURE PARTNERS)

6100 Fairview Road
Suite 770
Charlotte, NC 28210
Phone: 704-550-1950
Fax: 704-556-0556
Website: www.viridiancapital.com

Management and Staff
Christine Cordaro, General Partner
Frank Bachinsky, Managing Partner
Jeff Sampson, Managing Partner
Mark Jensen, General Partner
Willa Seldon, General Partner

Type of Firm
SBIC Not elsewhere classified

Industry Preferences

Internet Specific
Internet

Business Serv.
Media

Additional Information
Name of Most Recent Fund: Viridian Capital, L.P.
Most Recent Fund Was Raised: 12/31/1998
Year Founded: 1999
Capital Under Management: $54,600,000
Current Activity Level : Actively seeking new investments

WAKEFIELD GROUP

1110 East Morehead Street
P.O. Box 36329
Charlotte, NC 28236
Phone: 704-372-0355
Fax: 704-372-8216
Website: www.wakefieldgroup.com

Other Offices

2530 Meridian Parkway
3rd Floor
Durham, NC 27713
Phone: 919-806-4224
Fax: 919-806-4824

Management and Staff
Anna Nelson, Partner
David Gilroy, Vice President
L. Steve Nelson, Partner
Michael Elliot, Managing Director
Thomas Nelson, Partner

Whom to Contact
Anna Nelson
Michael Elliot

Type of Firm
Private Firm Investing Own Capital

Industry Association Membership
National Venture Capital Association (NVCA)

Project Preferences

Role in Financing:
Prefer role as deal originator but will also invest in deals created by others

Type of Financing Preferred:
Early Stage

Size of Investments Considered
Min Size of Investment Considered (000s): $1,000
Max Size of Investment Considered (000s): $5,000

Geographical Preferences

United States
Southeast

Industry Preferences

(% based on actual investment)

Internet Specific	36.4%
Computer Software and Services	15.7%
Medical/Health	10.7%
Semiconductors/Other Elect.	10.4%
Biotechnology	9.2%
Computer Hardware	5.9%
Other Products	5.8%
Communications and Media	4.5%
Consumer Related	1.3%

Additional Information
Name of Most Recent Fund: Wakefield Group
Most Recent Fund Was Raised: 01/01/1994
Year Founded: 1988
Capital Under Management: $100,000,000
Current Activity Level : Actively seeking new investments
Method of Compensation: Return on investment is of primary concern, do not charge fees

OHIO

ALPHA CAPITAL PARTNERS, INC.

Society Bank Building
32 North Main Street
Dayton, OH 45402
Phone: 513-222-2006
Fax: 513-223-6985

See Illinois for full listing.

ATHENIAN VENTURES (FKA: OHIO VALLEY VENTURE FUND)

20 East Circle Drive
Suite 190
Athens, OH 45701
Phone: 740-593-9393
Fax: 740-593-9311
Website: www.athenianvp.com

Management and Staff
Karl Elderkin, Managing Partner

Type of Firm
Private Firm Investing Own Capital

Additional Information
Year Founded: 1997
Current Activity Level : Actively seeking new investments

BANC ONE CAPITAL PARTNERS

150 East Gay Street
24th Floor
Columbus, OH 43215
Phone: 614-217-1100
Fax: 614-217-1217

Other Offices

150 East Gay
Suite 400
Columbus, OH 43215
Phone: 614-224-6900
Fax: 614-224-7675

Management and Staff
all of the above

Whom to Contact
all of the above

Type of Firm
SBIC Not elsewhere classified

Industry Association Membership
Natl assoc of Small Bus. Inv. Co (NASBIC)

Project Preferences

Role in Financing:
Prefer role as deal originator but will also invest in deals created by others

Type of Financing Preferred:
Industry Rollups
Leveraged Buyout
Mezzanine
Second Stage Financing
Special Situation

Size of Investments Considered
Min Size of Investment Considered (000s): $1,000
Max Size of Investment Considered: No Limit

Geographical Preferences

United States
All U.S.

Industry Preferences

Communications and Media
Communications and Media
Telecommunications
Satellite Microwave Comm.

Computer Hardware
Integrated Turnkey System

Computer Software
Computer Services
Systems Software
Applications Software

Semiconductors/Other Elect.
Electronic Components
Sensors

Medical/Health
Diagnostic Services
Drug/Equipmt Delivery
Disposable Med. Products
Hospital/Other Instit.

Consumer Related
Food/Beverage
Consumer Services
Education Related

Industrial/Energy
Oil and Gas Exploration
Factory Automation
Machinery
Environmental Related

Financial Services
Financial Services

Business Serv.
Distribution
Consulting Services

Manufact.
Office Automation Equipmt
Publishing

Additional Information
Name of Most Recent Fund: Banc ONE Capital Corp.
Most Recent Fund Was Raised: 09/01/1979
Year Founded: 1999
Capital Under Management: $250,000,000
Current Activity Level : Inactive / Unknown
Method of Compensation: Return on invest. most important, but chg. closing fees, service fees, etc.

BATTELLE VENTURE PARTNERS (SCIENTIFIC ADVANCES)

505 King Avenue
Columbus, OH 43201
Phone: 614-424-7005
Fax: 614-424-4874

Type of Firm
Non-Financial Corp. Affiliate or Subsidiary

Industry Association Membership
Natl assoc of Small Bus. Inv. Co (NASBIC)

Project Preferences

Role in Financing:
Prefer role as deal originator but will also invest in deals created by others

Type of Financing Preferred:
First Stage Financing
Second Stage Financing
Start-up Financing

Size of Investments Considered
Min Size of Investment Considered (000s): $500
Max Size of Investment Considered (000s): $1,000

Geographical Preferences

United States
All U.S.

Industry Preferences

Semiconductors/Other Elect.
Sensors

Industrial/Energy
Environmental Related

Additional Information

Year Founded: 1981
Capital Under Management: $25,000,000
Current Activity Level : Actively seeking new investments
Method of Compensation: Return on investment is of primary concern, do not charge fees

BLUE CHIP VENTURE COMPANY

1100 Chiquita Ctr.
250 East Fifth St.
Cincinnati, OH 45202
Phone: 513-723-2300
Fax: 513-723-2306
Website: www.bcvc.com

Other Offices

First National Plaza
130 W. Second St.,Ste.1818
Dayton, OH 45402
Phone: 937-222-1480
Fax: 937-222-1323

Management and Staff

Jack Wyant, General Partner
John Wyant, Managing Director
John McIlwraith, Managing Director
Z. David Patterson, Managing Director

Type of Firm

Private Firm Investing Own Capital

Industry Association Membership

National Venture Capital Association (NVCA)
Natl Assoc of Investment Cos. (NAIC)

Project Preferences

Role in Financing:
Will function either as deal originator or investor in deals created by others

Type of Financing Preferred:
Early Stage
Expansion
First Stage Financing
Second Stage Financing
Startup

Size of Investments Considered

Min Size of Investment Considered (000s): $2,000
Max Size of Investment Considered (000s): $6,000

Geographical Preferences

United States
Midwest
All U.S.

Industry Preferences

(% based on actual investment)

Internet Specific	43.4%
Computer Software and Services	19.8%
Medical/Health	10.4%
Communications and Media	6.6%
Consumer Related	6.1%
Semiconductors/Other Elect.	5.4%
Industrial/Energy	3.6%
Other Products	2.8%
Biotechnology	1.4%
Computer Hardware	0.5%

Additional Information

Name of Most Recent Fund: Blue Chip Capital Fund II
Most Recent Fund Was Raised: 01/01/1997
Year Founded: 1990
Capital Under Management: $600,000,000
Current Activity Level : Actively seeking new investments
Method of Compensation: Return on investment is of primary concern, do not charge fees

BRANTLEY VENTURE PARTNERS

20600 Chagrin Boulevard
Suite 1150
Cleveland, OH 44122
Phone: 216-283-4800
Fax: 216-283-5324

Other Offices

1920 Main Street
Suite 820
Irvine, CA 92614
Phone: 949-475-4242
Fax: 949-475-1950

Management and Staff

James Bergman, General Partner
Michael Finn, General Partner
Paul Cascio, General Partner
Robert Pinkas, General Partner
Tab Keplinger, Chief Financial Officer

Whom to Contact

Kevin Cook

Type of Firm

Private Firm Investing Own Capital

Industry Association Membership

National Venture Capital Association (NVCA)

Project Preferences

Role in Financing:
Prefer role as deal originator

Type of Financing Preferred:
First Stage Financing
Industry Rollups
Seed
Start-up Financing

Geographical Preferences

United States
All U.S.

Industry Preferences

(% based on actual investment)

Other Products	29.3%
Industrial/Energy	28.0%
Biotechnology	11.3%
Medical/Health	7.7%
Consumer Related	7.4%
Semiconductors/Other Elect.	6.0%
Computer Software and Services	5.5%
Communications and Media	3.3%
Internet Specific	1.4%

Additional Information

Name of Most Recent Fund: Brantley Partners IV, L.P.
Most Recent Fund Was Raised: 01/01/1999
Year Founded: 1987
Capital Under Management: $300,000,000
Current Activity Level : Actively seeking new investments
Method of Compensation: Return on investment is of primary concern, do not charge fees

CAPITAL TECHNOLOGY GROUP, LLC

400 MetroPlace N.
Suite 300
Dublin, OH 43017
Phone: 614-792-6066
Fax: 614-792-6036
Website: www.capitaltech.com

Management and Staff
Lance Schneier, Chairman & CEO

Type of Firm
Investment/Merchant Bank Subsid/Affil

Project Preferences

Role in Financing:
Will function either as deal originator or investor in deals created by others

Type of Financing Preferred:
Early Stage
Seed
Startup

Industry Preferences

Communications and Media
Wireless Communications
Data Communications

Internet Specific
E-Commerce Technology
Internet
Web Aggregration/Portals

Additional Information
Name of Most Recent Fund: Capital Technology Group
Most Recent Fund Was Raised: 10/01/1982
Current Activity Level : Inactive / Unknown
Method of Compensation: Return on investment is of primary concern, do not charge fees

CARILLON CAPITAL, INC.

Kettering Tower
40 North Main St Suite 1480
Dayton, OH 45423-1480
Phone: 937-228-7920
Fax: 937-496-4055

Management and Staff
C. Ronald McSwiney, Managing Director
William Sherk, Managing Director

Type of Firm
Private Firm Investing Own Capital

Project Preferences

Role in Financing:
Prefer role as deal originator but will also invest in deals created by others

Type of Financing Preferred:
Control-block Purchases
Leveraged Buyout
Mezzanine
Second Stage Financing
Special Situation

Size of Investments Considered
Min Size of Investment Considered (000s): $1,500
Max Size of Investment Considered: No Limit

Geographical Preferences

United States
All U.S.

Industry Preferences

Communications and Media
Communications and Media

Computer Hardware
Mini and Personal/Desktop
Computer Graphics and Dig
Integrated Turnkey System
Terminals
Disk Relat. Memory Device

Computer Software
Computer Services
Systems Software
Applications Software
Artificial Intelligence

Internet Specific
Internet

Semiconductors/Other Elect.
Electronic Components

Medical/Health
Medical/Health

Consumer Related
Consumer
Education Related

Industrial/Energy
Alternative Energy
Energy Conservation Relat
Industrial Products

Transportation
Transportation

Financial Services
Financial Services

Business Serv.
Distribution
Consulting Services

Manufact.
Office Automation Equipmt
Publishing

Agr/Forestr/Fish
Agriculture related

Additional Information
Year Founded: 1992
Capital Under Management: $15,000,000
Current Activity Level : Actively seeking new investments
Method of Compensation: Return on invest. most important, but chg. closing fees, service fees, etc.

CID EQUITY PARTNERS

41 South High Street
Suite 3650
Columbus, OH 43215
Phone: 614-222-8185
Fax: 614-222-8190
Website: www.cidequity.com

See Indiana for full listing.

CLARION CAPITAL CORP.

1801 East Ninth Street
Suite 1120
Cleveland, OH 44114
Phone: 216-687-1096
Fax: 216-694-3545

Other Offices

1801 East Ninth Street
Suite 510
Cleveland, OH 44114
Phone: 216-687-1096
Fax: 216-694-3545

Management and Staff
Morris Wheeler, Vice President
Thomas Niehaus, Chief Financial Officer

Type of Firm
Private Firm Investing Own Capital

Industry Association Membership
Natl assoc of Small Bus. Inv. Co (NASBIC)

Project Preferences

Role in Financing:
Prefer role as deal originator but will also invest in deals created by others

Type of Financing Preferred:
Early Stage
First Stage Financing
Second Stage Financing

Geographical Preferences

United States
Midwest
Northeast
West Coast

Industry Preferences

(% based on actual investment)

Biotechnology	24.1%
Other Products	20.9%
Medical/Health	15.3%
Communications and Media	12.2%
Computer Software and Services	8.8%
Semiconductors/Other Elect.	7.6%
Consumer Related	5.9%
Industrial/Energy	3.1%
Computer Hardware	2.1%

Additional Information

Year Founded: 1968
Capital Under Management: $50,000,000
Current Activity Level : Actively seeking new investments
Method of Compensation: Return on investment is of primary concern, do not charge fees

CMEA VENTURES (FKA:CHEMICALS & MATERIALS ENTERPRISE ASSOCIA)

One Cleveland Center
1375 East Ninth Street
Cleveland, OH 44114
Phone: 216-861-4800
Fax: 216-621-4543
Website: www.cmeaventures.com

See California for full listing.

CRYSTAL INTERNET VENTURE FUND, L.P.

1120 Chester Avenue
Suite 418
Cleveland, OH 44114
Phone: 216-263-5515
Fax: 216-263-5518
Website: www.crystalventure.com

Other Offices

361 Lytton Avenue
Palo Alto, CA 94301
Phone: 650-330-3582
Fax: 650-330-3585

Management and Staff

Brain Goncher, Partner
Dan Kellogg, Partner
Howard Lee, Partner
John Hsin, Principal
Joseph Tzeng, Managing Director
Rick Kovach, Chief Financial Officer

Whom to Contact

Daniel Kellog

Type of Firm

Private Firm Investing Own Capital

Project Preferences

Role in Financing:
Will function either as deal originator or investor in deals created by others

Type of Financing Preferred:
Balanced
Early Stage

Size of Investments Considered

Min Size of Investment Considered (000s): $1,000
Max Size of Investment Considered (000s): $6,000

Geographical Preferences

United States
All U.S.

International
Asia
Belgium
China
Europe
France
Germany
India
Italy
Latin America
Luxembourg
Mexico
Middle East
Netherlands
Spain
United Kingdom

Industry Preferences

(% based on actual investment)

Internet Specific	77.6%
Computer Software and Services	11.6%
Communications and Media	7.3%
Computer Hardware	2.8%
Semiconductors/Other Elect.	0.8%

Additional Information

Name of Most Recent Fund: Crystal Internet Venture Fund II
Most Recent Fund Was Raised: 10/01/1999
Year Founded: 1997
Capital Under Management: $240,000,000
Current Activity Level : Actively seeking new investments
Method of Compensation: Return on investment is of primary concern, do not charge fees

FORT WASHINGTON CAPITAL PARTNERS, LLC

420 East Fourth Street
P.O. Box 2388
Cincinnati, OH 45201-2388
Phone: 513-361-7670
Fax: 513-361-7689
Website: www.fortwashington.com

Management and Staff

Augustine Long, Managing Director

Type of Firm

Private Equity Advisor or Fund of Fund Mgr

Project Preferences

Role in Financing:
Will function either as deal originator or investor in deals created by others

Type of Financing Preferred:
Fund of Funds

Size of Investments Considered
Min Size of Investment Considered (000s): $1,000
Max Size of Investment Considered: No Limit

Geographical Preferences

United States
All U.S.
All U.S.

Canada
All Canada

International
Asia
Europe
France
Germany
Hong Kong
Japan
United Kingdom
No Preference

Industry Preferences

Communications and Media
Commercial Communications
CATV & Pay TV Systems
Radio & TV Broadcasting
Telecommunications
Wireless Communications
Data Communications
Satellite Microwave Comm.

Computer Software
Data Processing
Software

Internet Specific
Internet
Web Aggregration/Portals

Semiconductors/Other Elect.
Electronics
Semiconductor
Sensors
Circuit Boards
Component Testing Equipmt
Laser Related
Fiber Optics

Biotechnology
Biotechnology
Human Biotechnology
Agricultural/Animal Bio.
Industrial Biotechnology
Biotech Related Research

Medical/Health
Medical Therapeutics
Drug/Equipmt Delivery
Medical Products
Pharmaceuticals

Consumer Related
Retail
Education Related

Industrial/Energy
Superconductivity
Process Control

Utilities
Utilities

Additional Information
Year Founded: 1990
Capital Under Management: $550,000,000
Current Activity Level : Actively seeking new investments
Method of Compensation: Return on investment is of primary concern, do not charge fees

---

FREDERIC H. MAYERSON GROUP, THE

420 East Fourth Street
P.O. Box 2388
Cincinnati, OH 45201-2388
Phone: 513-361-7670
Fax: 513-361-7689

Management and Staff
Lawrence H. Horwitz

Whom to Contact
Lawrence H. Horwitz

Project Preferences

Type of Financing Preferred:
First Stage Financing
Leveraged Buyout
Mezzanine
Second Stage Financing
Special Situation

Geographical Preferences

United States
All U.S.

Canada
All Canada

Industry Preferences

Communications and Media
Commercial Communications
Telecommunications

Consumer Related
Entertainment and Leisure
Food/Beverage
Consumer Products
Consumer Services

Financial Services
Financial Services

Manufact.
Publishing

HILLSTREET CAPITAL, INC.

300 Main Street
Cincinnati, OH 45202
Phone: 513-241-8716
Fax: 513-421-3602

Management and Staff
John C. Kern Jr.

Whom to Contact
John C. Kern Jr.

Type of Firm
Investment/Merchant Bank Investing Own or Client Funds

Project Preferences

Role in Financing:
Prefer role as deal originator but will also invest in deals created by others

Type of Financing Preferred:
First Stage Financing
Leveraged Buyout
Second Stage Financing

Size of Investments Considered
Min Size of Investment Considered (000s): $10,000
Max Size of Investment Considered: No Limit

Geographical Preferences

United States
All U.S.

Canada
All Canada

International
United Kingdom

Industry Preferences

Communications and Media
Commercial Communications
Telecommunications
Data Communications
Satellite Microwave Comm.

Computer Hardware
Integrated Turnkey System

Computer Software
Computer Services
Systems Software
Applications Software

Internet Specific
Internet

Semiconductors/Other Elect.
Sensors

Medical/Health
Hospital/Other Instit.
Pharmaceuticals

Consumer Related
Consumer

Industrial/Energy
Oil & Gas Drilling,Explor
Materials
Factory Automation
Machinery

Financial Services
Financial Services
Real Estate

Business Serv.
Distribution
Consulting Services

Manufact.
Office Automation Equipmt
Publishing

Additional Information
Name of Most Recent Fund: HillStreet Fund, L.P.
Most Recent Fund Was Raised: 07/01/1997
Year Founded: 1979
Capital Under Management: $1,500,000,000
Current Activity Level : Actively seeking new investments
Method of Compensation: Return on invest. most important, but chg. closing fees, service fees, etc.

ISABELLA CAPITAL LLC

312 Walnut Street
Suite 3540
Cincinnati, OH 45202
Phone: 513-721-7110
Fax: 513-721-7115

Management and Staff
Margaret H. Wyant, Managing Director

Type of Firm
Private Firm Investing Own Capital

Project Preferences

Size of Investments Considered
Min Size of Investment Considered (000s): $200
Max Size of Investment Considered (000s): $2,000

Additional Information
Name of Most Recent Fund: Fund Isabella, L.P.
Most Recent Fund Was Raised: 10/01/1999
Capital Under Management: $5,000,000
Current Activity Level : Actively seeking new investments

KEY EQUITY CAPITAL CORP.(AKA:KEY COMMUNITY DEVELOPMENT CORP)

127 Public Square
28th Floor
Cleveland, OH 44114
Phone: 216-689-3000
Fax: 216-689-3204
Website: www.keybank.com

Other Offices

700 5th Avenue
48th Floor
Seattle, WA 98111
Phone: 206-684-6480
Fax: 206-689-5450

Management and Staff
James Marra, Vice President
John Kirby, Vice President
Sean Ward, Vice President
Stephen Haynes, Vice President

Whom to Contact
Cindy J. Babitt
Gregory B. Davis
John A. LeMay
Jon D. Kleinke
Julianne Marley
Shawn R. Ely
William H. Lehr

Type of Firm
Commercial Bank Affiliate or Subsidiary

Industry Association Membership
Natl assoc of Small Bus. Inv. Co (NASBIC)

Project Preferences

Role in Financing:
Prefer role as deal originator but will also invest in deals created by others

Type of Financing Preferred:
Expansion
Industry Rollups
Leveraged Buyout
Second Stage Financing
Special Situation

Size of Investments Considered
Min Size of Investment Considered (000s): $1,000
Max Size of Investment Considered: No Limit

Geographical Preferences

United States
All U.S.
Northeast
Northwest
Rocky Mountain

Industry Preferences

Communications and Media
Commercial Communications
CATV & Pay TV Systems
Radio & TV Broadcasting
Telecommunications
Data Communications

Computer Hardware
Computer Graphics and Dig
Integrated Turnkey System
Disk Relat. Memory Device

Computer Software
Systems Software

Semiconductors/Other Elect.
Sensors

Biotechnology
Industrial Biotechnology
Biosensors

Medical/Health
Medical Diagnostics
Diagnostic Services
Medical Therapeutics
Medical Products
Hospital/Other Instit.
Pharmaceuticals

Consumer Related
Consumer Products
Consumer Services

Industrial/Energy
Industrial Products
Materials
Factory Automation
Environmental Related

Manufact.
Manufacturing
Office Automation Equipmt
Publishing

Additional Information
Capital Under Management: $150,000,000
Current Activity Level : Actively seeking new investments
Method of Compensation: Return on invest. most important, but chg. closing fees, service fees, etc.

MORGENTHALER VENTURES

Terminal Tower
50 Public Square Suite 2700
Cleveland, OH 44113
Phone: 216-416-7500
Fax: 216-416-7501
Website: www.morgenthaler.com

Other Offices

2730 Sand Hill Road
Suite 280
Menlo Park, CA 94025
Phone: 650-233-7600
Fax: 650-233-7606

Management and Staff
David Morgenthaler, Partner
Drew Lanza, Venture Partner
G. Gary Shaffer, Partner
Gary Little, Partner
Gary Morgenthaler, Partner
Greg Blonder, Venture Partner
James Broderick, Partner
John Lutsi, Partner
Keith Kerman, Partner
Paul Brentlinger, Partner
Paul Levine, Venture Partner
Peter Taft, Partner
Randy Brown, Venture Partner
Robert Bellas, Partner
Robert Pavey, Partner
Robin Bellas, General Partner
Scott Fine, Venture Partner
Theodore Laufik, Chief Financial Officer

Whom to Contact
Keith M. Kerman, M.D.
Robert C. Bellas Jr.

Type of Firm
Private Firm Investing Own Capital

Industry Association Membership
National Venture Capital Association (NVCA)
Western Association of Venture Capitalists (WAVC)

Project Preferences

Role in Financing:
Prefer role as deal originator but will also invest in deals created by others

Type of Financing Preferred:
Acquisition
Early Stage
Expansion
First Stage Financing
Leveraged Buyout
Management Buyouts
Second Stage Financing

Size of Investments Considered
Min Size of Investment Considered (000s): $500
Max Size of Investment Considered: No Limit

Geographical Preferences

United States
All U.S.

Canada
Ontario

Industry Preferences

(% based on actual investment)

Semiconductors/Other Elect.	25.5%
Communications and Media	16.2%
Internet Specific	12.8%
Medical/Health	12.6%
Computer Software and Services	10.3%
Other Products	5.9%
Biotechnology	5.9%
Computer Hardware	5.3%
Industrial/Energy	4.9%
Consumer Related	0.5%

Additional Information
Name of Most Recent Fund: Morgenthaler Venture Partners V
Most Recent Fund Was Raised: 07/01/1998
Year Founded: 1968
Capital Under Management: $1,083,700,000
Current Activity Level : Actively seeking new investments
Method of Compensation: Return on investment is of primary concern, do not charge fees

NATIONAL CITY EQUITY PARTNERS, INC

1965 East Sixth Street
Suite 1010
Cleveland, OH 44114
Phone: 216-575-2491
Fax: 216-575-9965
Website: www.nccapital.com

Other Offices

1965 East 6th St
Cleveland, OH 44114
Phone: 216-575-2491

Management and Staff
Carl Baldassarre, Managing Director
Edward Pentecost, Managing Director
Oliver Kimberly, Vice President
Richard Martinko, Managing Director
Todd McCuaig, Managing Director
William Schecter, President

Whom to Contact
Carl Baldassarre
Jay Freund
Todd McCuaig

Type of Firm
Commercial Bank Affiliate or Subsidiary

Industry Association Membership
Natl assoc of Small Bus. Inv. Co (NASBIC)

Project Preferences

Role in Financing:
Will function either as deal originator or investor in deals created by others

Type of Financing Preferred:
Acquisition
Expansion
Generalist PE
Later Stage
Leveraged Buyout
Management Buyouts
Mezzanine
Recapitalizations
Second Stage Financing

Size of Investments Considered
Min Size of Investment Considered (000s): $1,000
Max Size of Investment Considered (000s): $20,000

Geographical Preferences

United States
All U.S.

Industry Preferences

(% based on actual investment)

Other Products	26.7%
Internet Specific	18.6%
Industrial/Energy	17.7%
Communications and Media	14.6%
Consumer Related	10.7%
Medical/Health	8.3%
Semiconductors/Other Elect.	3.1%
Computer Hardware	0.3%

Additional Information

Year Founded: 1979
Capital Under Management: $700,000,000
Current Activity Level : Actively seeking new investments
Method of Compensation: Return on invest. most important, but chg. closing fees, service fees, etc.

NORTHWEST OHIO VENTURE FUND

4159 Holland-Sylvania Rd.
Suite 202
Toledo, OH 43623
Phone: 419-824-8144
Fax: 419-882-2035

Management and Staff

Barry Walsh, Managing Partner

Whom to Contact

Barry Walsh

Type of Firm

Private Firm Investing Own Capital

Industry Association Membership

National Venture Capital Association (NVCA)

Project Preferences

Role in Financing:

Prefer role as deal originator but will also invest in deals created by others

Type of Financing Preferred:

First Stage Financing
Leveraged Buyout
Mezzanine
Research and Development
Second Stage Financing
Seed
Start-up Financing

Size of Investments Considered

Min Size of Investment Considered (000s): $250
Max Size of Investment Considered: No Limit

Geographical Preferences

United States

Midwest

Industry Preferences

(% based on actual investment)

Medical/Health	37.8%
Biotechnology	21.4%
Semiconductors/Other Elect.	11.8%
Other Products	9.9%
Computer Software and Services	9.8%
Industrial/Energy	9.3%

Additional Information

Name of Most Recent Fund: Northwest Ohio Venture Fund
Most Recent Fund Was Raised: 01/01/1992
Year Founded: 1992
Capital Under Management: $15,000,000
Current Activity Level : Inactive / Unknown
Method of Compensation: Return on invest. most important, but chg. closing fees, service fees, etc.

OHANA VENTURES, LLC

1228 Euclid Avenue
Suite 840
Cleveland, OH 44140
Phone: 216-621-4621
Fax: 216-621-5381
Website: www.ohanaventures.com

Management and Staff

Jeffery Ambrosio, Managing Director

Whom to Contact

Diane Pruchinsky

Type of Firm

Investment Management/Finance Consulting

Industry Association Membership

National Venture Capital Association (NVCA)

Project Preferences

Role in Financing:

Will function either as deal originator or investor in deals created by others

Type of Financing Preferred:

Early Stage
Expansion
First Stage Financing
Second Stage Financing

Size of Investments Considered

Min Size of Investment Considered (000s): $250
Max Size of Investment Considered (000s): $3,000

Geographical Preferences

United States

Midwest

Industry Preferences

Communications and Media

Telecommunications

Computer Software

Software
Systems Software

Internet Specific

Internet

Semiconductors/Other Elect.

Micro-Processing
Laser Related
Fiber Optics

Additional Information

Year Founded: 1999
Capital Under Management: $5,300,000
Current Activity Level : Actively seeking new investments
Method of Compensation: Return on invest. most important, but chg. closing fees, service fees, etc.

OHIO PARTNERS

62 East Broad Street
Third Floor
Columbus, OH 43215
Phone: 614-621-1210
Fax: 614-621-1240

Management and Staff

Mark Butterworth, Vice President
Maury Cox, President

Type of Firm

Private Firm Investing Own Capital

Project Preferences

Role in Financing:

Prefer role as deal originator but will also invest in deals created by others

Type of Financing Preferred:
First Stage Financing
Second Stage Financing
Start-up Financing

Geographical Preferences

United States
Midwest
Northwest
West Coast

Industry Preferences

(% based on actual investment)

Computer Software and Services	60.9%
Internet Specific	39.1%

Additional Information

Name of Most Recent Fund: Ohio Partners, The
Most Recent Fund Was Raised: 01/01/1995
Year Founded: 1995
Capital Under Management: $40,000,000
Current Activity Level : Actively seeking new investments
Method of Compensation: Return on investment is of primary concern, do not charge fees

PRIMUS VENTURE PARTNERS, INC.

5900 Landerbrook Dr.
Suite 2000
Cleveland, OH 44124-4020
Phone: 440-684-7300
Fax: 440-684-7342
Website: www.primusventure.com

Management and Staff

Craig Milius, Principal
James Bartlett, Managing Director
Jeffery Milius, Principal
Loyal Wilson, Managing Director
Scott Harper, Principal
Steven Rothman, Chief Financial Officer
William Mulligan, Managing Director

Whom to Contact

Jeffrey J. Milius
Shati Mittra

Type of Firm

Private Firm Investing Own Capital

Industry Association Membership

National Venture Capital Association (NVCA)

Project Preferences

Role in Financing:
Prefer role as deal originator but will also invest in deals created by others

Type of Financing Preferred:
Balanced
Early Stage
Expansion
Start-up Financing
Startup

Size of Investments Considered

Min Size of Investment Considered (000s): $5,000
Max Size of Investment Considered: No Limit

Geographical Preferences

International
All International
No Preference

Industry Preferences

(% based on actual investment)

Internet Specific	22.0%
Other Products	17.7%
Consumer Related	14.0%
Communications and Media	13.5%
Medical/Health	8.7%
Biotechnology	8.6%
Industrial/Energy	7.8%
Computer Software and Services	3.7%
Semiconductors/Other Elect.	2.5%
Computer Hardware	1.6%

Additional Information

Name of Most Recent Fund: Primus Capital Fund IV
Most Recent Fund Was Raised: 08/01/1997
Year Founded: 1984
Capital Under Management: $502,800,000
Current Activity Level : Actively seeking new investments
Method of Compensation: Return on investment is of primary concern, do not charge fees

SENMED MEDICAL VENTURES

4445 Lake Forest Drive
Suite 600
Cincinnati, OH 45242
Phone: 513-563-3264
Fax: 513-563-3261

Type of Firm

Non-Financial Corp. Affiliate or Subsidiary

Industry Association Membership

National Venture Capital Association (NVCA)
Natl assoc of Small Bus. Inv. Co (NASBIC)

Project Preferences

Role in Financing:
Prefer role as deal originator but will also invest in deals created by others

Type of Financing Preferred:
Mezzanine
Second Stage Financing

Size of Investments Considered

Min Size of Investment Considered (000s): $500
Max Size of Investment Considered (000s): $1,000

Geographical Preferences

International
No Preference

Industry Preferences

(% based on actual investment)

Medical/Health	54.6%
Biotechnology	33.6%
Communications and Media	5.6%
Internet Specific	3.7%
Semiconductors/Other Elect.	2.5%

Additional Information

Year Founded: 1986
Capital Under Management: $12,000,000
Current Activity Level : Actively seeking new investments
Method of Compensation: Return on investment is of primary concern, do not charge fees

U.S. MEDICAL RESOURCES CORP.

188 Lafayette Circle
Cincinnati, OH 45220-1105
Phone: 513-751-8926
Fax: 513-751-8926

Type of Firm

Mgt. Consulting Firm

Project Preferences

Role in Financing:
Prefer role as deal originator

Type of Financing Preferred:
First Stage Financing
Leveraged Buyout
Second Stage Financing
Special Situation
Start-up Financing

Size of Investments Considered
Min Size of Investment Considered (000s): $500
Max Size of Investment Considered: No Limit

Geographical Preferences

United States
Midwest

International
Mexico

Industry Preferences

Medical/Health
Medical Diagnostics
Diagnostic Test Products
Medical Products
Disposable Med. Products

Additional Information
Year Founded: 1988
Current Activity Level : Actively seeking new investments
Method of Compensation: Return on invest. most important, but chg. closing fees, service fees, etc.

WALNUT GROUP, THE

312 Walnut Street
Suite 1151
Cincinnati, OH 45202
Phone: 513-651-3300
Fax: 513-929-4441
Website: www.thewalnutgroup.com

Management and Staff
Daniel Staton, Partner
Frederic Mayerson, Partner
James Gould, Partner

Type of Firm
Private Equity Advisor or Fund of Fund Mgr

Project Preferences

Type of Financing Preferred:
Balanced

Geographical Preferences

United States
Northeast

Additional Information
Name of Most Recent Fund: Walnut Venture Fund I
Most Recent Fund Was Raised: 01/01/1995
Year Founded: 1995
Capital Under Management: $155,000,000
Current Activity Level : Actively seeking new investments

OKLAHOMA

CHISHOLM PRIVATE CAPITAL PARTNERS

100 West 5th Street
Suite 805
Tulsa, OK 74103
Phone: 918-584-0440
Fax: 918-584-0441
Website: www.chisholmvc.com

Other Offices

211 North Robinson
Suite 1910
Oklahoma City, OK 73102
Phone: 405-848-8014
Fax: 405-416-1035

Management and Staff

C. James Bode, General Partner
Greg Main, General Partner
John Frick, General Partner
William Palva, Partner

Whom to Contact

James Bode

Type of Firm

Investment/Merchant Bank Subsid/Affil

Industry Association Membership

National Venture Capital Association (NVCA)

Project Preferences

Role in Financing:
Prefer role as deal originator but will also invest in deals created by others

Type of Financing Preferred:
Balanced
First Stage Financing
Second Stage Financing
Seed

Size of Investments Considered

Min Size of Investment Considered (000s): $1,000
Max Size of Investment Considered (000s): $4,000

Geographical Preferences

United States
Midwest
Texas
All U.S.

Industry Preferences

(% based on actual investment)

Communications and Media	36.7%
Computer Software and Services	14.0%
Other Products	13.6%
Semiconductors/Other Elect.	10.3%
Internet Specific	9.6%
Medical/Health	9.5%
Consumer Related	3.1%
Industrial/Energy	2.5%
Computer Hardware	0.7%

Additional Information

Name of Most Recent Fund: Chisholm Partners IV
Most Recent Fund Was Raised: 09/29/1999
Year Founded: 1989
Capital Under Management: $100,000,000
Current Activity Level : Actively seeking new investments
Method of Compensation: Return on investment is of primary concern, do not charge fees

DAVIS, TUTTLE VENTURE PARTNERS, L.P.(FKA:DAVIS VENTURE)

320 South Boston
Suite 1000
Tulsa, OK 74103-3703
Phone: 918-584-7272
Fax: 918-582-3404
Website: www.davistuttle.com

Other Offices

8 Greenway Plaza
Suite 1020
Houston, TX 77046
Phone: 713-993-0440
Fax: 713-621-2297

Management and Staff

Barry Davis, Managing General Partner
David Humphrey, Principal
Elmer Wilkening, General Partner
Philip Tuttle, General Partner

Type of Firm

Private Firm Investing Own Capital

Industry Association Membership

National Venture Capital Association (NVCA)
Natl assoc of Small Bus. Inv. Co (NASBIC)

Project Preferences

Role in Financing:
Prefer role as deal originator but will also invest in deals created by others

Type of Financing Preferred:
First Stage Financing
Leveraged Buyout
Mezzanine
Second Stage Financing

Size of Investments Considered

Min Size of Investment Considered (000s): $5,000
Max Size of Investment Considered: No Limit

Geographical Preferences

United States
Southwest

Industry Preferences

(% based on actual investment)

Consumer Related	31.8%
Medical/Health	27.9%
Industrial/Energy	15.3%
Other Products	7.7%
Semiconductors/Other Elect.	6.4%
Internet Specific	5.6%
Communications and Media	5.3%

Additional Information

Name of Most Recent Fund: Davis, Tuttle Venture Partners, L.P.
Most Recent Fund Was Raised: 02/01/1998
Year Founded: 1985
Capital Under Management: $45,300,000
Current Activity Level : Actively seeking new investments
Method of Compensation: Return on investment is of primary concern, do not charge fees

INTERSOUTH PARTNERS

3001 United Founders Boulevard
Oklahoma City, OK 73112
Phone: 405-843-7890
Fax: 405-843-8048
Website: www.intersouth.com

See North Carolina for full listing.

MOORE & ASSOCIATES

1000 W. Wilshire Blvd.
Suite 370
Oklahoma City, OK 73116
Phone: 405-842-3660
Fax: 405-842-3763

Management and Staff
Guerry Moore

Whom to Contact
Guerry Moore

Type of Firm
Investment/Merchant Bank Subsid/Affil

Industry Association Membership
Natl assoc of Small Bus. Inv. Co (NASBIC)

Project Preferences

Role in Financing:
Prefer role as deal originator but will also invest in deals created by others

Type of Financing Preferred:
First Stage Financing
Leveraged Buyout
Mezzanine
Second Stage Financing
Start-up Financing

Size of Investments Considered
Min Size of Investment Considered (000s): $500
Max Size of Investment Considered: No Limit

Geographical Preferences

United States
All U.S.

Industry Preferences

Semiconductors/Other Elect.
Electronic Components
Semiconductor
Controllers and Sensors
Laser Related
Fiber Optics

Medical/Health
Other Therapeutic
Pharmaceuticals

Consumer Related
Franchises(NEC)
Food/Beverage
Consumer Products
Consumer Services

Industrial/Energy
Industrial Products

Transportation
Transportation

Financial Services
Financial Services
Real Estate

Business Serv.
Distribution

Manufact.
Publishing

Additional Information
Year Founded: 1987
Capital Under Management: $100,000,000
Current Activity Level : Actively seeking new investments
Method of Compensation: Function primarily in service area, receive contingent fee in cash or equity

RBC VENTURES, INC.

2627 East 21st Street
Tulsa, OK 74114
Phone: 918-744-5607
Fax: 918-743-8630

Management and Staff
K.Y. Vargas

Whom to Contact
K.Y. Vargas

Type of Firm
Private Firm Investing Own Capital

Project Preferences

Role in Financing:
Prefer role as deal originator but will also invest in deals created by others

Type of Financing Preferred:
Control-block Purchases
Leveraged Buyout
Mezzanine
Second Stage Financing
Special Situation

Size of Investments Considered
Min Size of Investment Considered (000s): $2,000
Max Size of Investment Considered: No Limit

Geographical Preferences

United States
Southwest

Industry Preferences

Transportation
Transportation

Additional Information
Year Founded: 1989
Current Activity Level : Actively seeking new investments
Method of Compensation: Return on investment is of primary concern, do not charge fees

OREGON

EMPIRE VENTURES

1020 SW Taylor Street
Suite 415
Portland, OR 97205
Phone: 503-222-1556
Fax: 503-222-1607
Website: www.empireventures.com

Management and Staff
Alan Rand, Venture Partner
Steven Brunk, General Partner
Wade Bradley, Managing Partner

Type of Firm
Private Firm Investing Own Capital

Project Preferences

Type of Financing Preferred:
Balanced

Additional Information
Capital Under Management: $10,000,000
Current Activity Level : Actively seeking new investments

FBR COMOTION VENTURE CAPITAL

208 S.W. First Ave
Suite 300
Portland, OR 97204
Phone: 503-221-0200
Fax: 503-478-0559
Website: www.comotionvc.com

See Washington for full listing.

MADRONA VENTURE GROUP

121 SW Morrison Street
Suite 450
Portland, OR 97204
Website: www.madrona.com

See Washington for full listing.

NEEDHAM & COMPANY, INC.

1000 S.W. Broadway
Suite 960
Portland, OR 97205
Phone: 503-221-7000
Fax: 503-221-3906
Website: www.needhamco.com

See New York for full listing.

OREGON RESOURCE AND TECHNOLOGY DEVELOPMENT FUND

4370 N.E. Halsey St.
Suite 233
Portland, OR 97213-1566
Phone: 503-282-4462
Fax: 503-282-2976

Other Offices

4370 NE Halsey
Suite 233
Portland, OR

Type of Firm
Private Firm Investing Own Capital

Project Preferences

Role in Financing:
Prefer role as deal originator but will also invest in deals created by others

Type of Financing Preferred:
Research and Development
Seed
Start-up Financing

Size of Investments Considered
Min Size of Investment Considered (000s): $100
Max Size of Investment Considered (000s): $300

Geographical Preferences

United States
West Coast

Industry Preferences

(% based on actual investment)

Biotechnology	34.5%
Semiconductors/Other Elect.	11.7%
Computer Software and Services	11.3%
Medical/Health	10.9%
Other Products	9.5%
Computer Hardware	9.1%
Consumer Related	7.3%
Industrial/Energy	5.6%

Additional Information
Year Founded: 1986
Capital Under Management: $20,000,000
Current Activity Level : Actively seeking new investments
Method of Compensation: Return on investment is of primary concern, do not charge fees

ORIEN VENTURES

14523 SW Westlake Drive
Lake Oswego, OR 97035
Phone: 503-699-1680
Fax: 503-699-1681

See Connecticut for full listing.

OVP VENTURE PARTNERS (FKA: OLYMPIC VENTURE PARTNERS)

340 Oswego Pointe Drive
Suite 200
Lake Oswego, OR 97034
Phone: 503-697-8766
Fax: 503-697-8863
Website: www.ovp.com

See Washington for full listing.

ROSENFELD & CO.

1211 S.W. Sixth Avenue
Portland, OR 97204
Phone: 503-228-3255

Management and Staff
William Rosenfeld

Whom to Contact
William Rosenfeld

Type of Firm
Investment/Merchant Bank Investing Own or Client Funds

Project Preferences

Role in Financing:
Prefer role as deal originator

Type of Financing Preferred:
Industry Rollups
Leveraged Buyout
Mezzanine
Second Stage Financing
Special Situation

Size of Investments Considered
Min Size of Investment Considered (000s): $20,000
Max Size of Investment Considered: No Limit

Geographical Preferences

United States
Northwest

Industry Preferences

Communications and Media
Telecommunications

Semiconductors/Other Elect.
Component Testing Equipmt
Laser Related
Analytic/Scientific

Biotechnology
Industrial Biotechnology

Medical/Health
Medical/Health
Medical Diagnostics
Medical Therapeutics

Consumer Related
Entertainment and Leisure
Retail
Food/Beverage
Consumer Products
Consumer Services
Education Related

Industrial/Energy
Energy Conservation Relat
Industrial Products

Transportation
Transportation

Financial Services
Financial Services

Business Serv.
Distribution

Manufact.
Publishing

Agr/Forestr/Fish
Agriculture related
Mining and Minerals

Additional Information
Year Founded: 1977
Current Activity Level : Actively seeking new investments
Method of Compensation: Function primarily in service area, receive contingent fee in cash or equity

SHAW VENTURE PARTNERS (FKA: SHAW GLASGOW PARTNERS)

400 S.W. Sixth Avenue
Suite 1100
Portland, OR 97204-1636
Phone: 503-228-4884
Fax: 503-227-2471
Website: www.shawventures.com

Management and Staff
Gayle Kovacs, Chief Financial Officer
Ralph Shaw, General Partner

Type of Firm
SBIC Not elsewhere classified

Project Preferences

Role in Financing:
Will function either as deal originator or investor in deals created by others

Type of Financing Preferred:
Balanced
First Stage Financing
Leveraged Buyout
Second Stage Financing
Seed
Special Situation
Start-up Financing

Size of Investments Considered
Min Size of Investment Considered (000s): $250
Max Size of Investment Considered (000s): $3,000

Geographical Preferences

United States
Northwest

Industry Preferences

(% based on actual investment)

Communications and Media	35.8%
Internet Specific	21.2%
Semiconductors/Other Elect.	12.3%
Consumer Related	9.2%
Computer Hardware	7.5%
Industrial/Energy	5.5%
Computer Software and Services	3.5%
Medical/Health	2.4%
Biotechnology	1.9%
Other Products	0.7%

Additional Information
Name of Most Recent Fund: Shaw Venture Partners III
Most Recent Fund Was Raised: 01/01/1994
Year Founded: 1983
Capital Under Management: $80,000,000
Current Activity Level : Making few, if any, new investments
Method of Compensation: Return on investment is of primary concern, do not charge fees

SILICON VALLEY BANK

11000 SW Stratus
Suite 170
Beaverton, OR 97008-7113
Phone: 503-526-1123
Fax: 503-526-0818

See California for full listing.

UTAH VENTURES II, L.P. (A.K.A. UNION VENTURES)

10700 SW Beaverton
Hillsdale Hwy 548
Beaverton, OR 97005
Phone: 503-574-4125
Website: www.uven.com

See Utah for full listing.

PENNSYLVANIA

ADAMS CAPITAL MANAGEMENT, INC.

500 Blackburn Avenue
Sewickley, PA 15143
Phone: 412-749-9454
Fax: 412-749-9459
Website: www.acm.com

Other Offices

107 Ranch Road 620 S
Suite 5B
Austin, TX 78734
Phone: 512-266-1741
Fax: 512-266-2093

668 Stoney Hill Road
Suite 155
Yardley, PA 19067
Phone: 215-321-0929

Management and Staff
Andrea Joseph, General Partner
Anthony Warren, Partner
George Ugras, General Partner
Jerry Sullivan, Partner
Joel Adams, Managing Partner
William Hulley, General Partner

Type of Firm
Private Firm Investing Own Capital

Industry Association Membership
National Venture Capital Association (NVCA)

Project Preferences

Role in Financing:
Prefer role as deal originator but will also invest in deals created by others

Type of Financing Preferred:
Early Stage
First Stage Financing

Geographical Preferences

United States
All U.S.

Industry Preferences

(% based on actual investment)

Internet Specific	67.5%
Computer Hardware	10.1%
Semiconductors/Other Elect.	7.9%
Computer Software and Services	7.6%
Communications and Media	3.7%
Medical/Health	3.2%

Additional Information
Name of Most Recent Fund: Adams Capital Management, II, L.P.
Most Recent Fund Was Raised: 10/08/1999
Year Founded: 1994
Capital Under Management: $700,000,000
Current Activity Level : Actively seeking new investments
Method of Compensation: Return on investment is of primary concern, do not charge fees

ADVANTA PARTNERS, L.P.

Welsh & McKean Roads
P.O. Box 844
Spring House, PA 19477-0844
Phone: 215-444-6450
Fax: 215-444-6499
Website: www.advantapartnerslp.com

Other Offices

712 Fifth Avenue
28th Floor
New York, NY 10019-4102
Phone: 212-649-6900
Fax: 212-956-3301

Management and Staff
Gary Neems, Managing Director
Mitchell Hollin, Managing Director

Whom to Contact
Gary Neems

Type of Firm
Private Firm Investing Own Capital

Project Preferences

Role in Financing:
Prefer role as deal originator but will also invest in deals created by others

Type of Financing Preferred:
Leveraged Buyout
Mezzanine
Second Stage Financing
Special Situation

Size of Investments Considered
Min Size of Investment Considered (000s): $20,000
Max Size of Investment Considered: No Limit

Geographical Preferences

United States
All U.S.

Industry Preferences

(% based on actual investment)

Internet Specific	48.7%
Other Products	34.9%
Communications and Media	6.7%
Computer Software and Services	5.3%
Consumer Related	4.3%

Additional Information
Name of Most Recent Fund: Advanta Partners, L.P.
Most Recent Fund Was Raised: 01/01/1994
Year Founded: 1994
Capital Under Management: $100,000,000
Current Activity Level : Inactive / Unknown
Method of Compensation: Return on investment is of primary concern, do not charge fees

ALPHA CAPITAL CORPORATION, L.L.C.

529 Favette Street
Conshohocken, PA 19428
Phone: 610-828-8301
Fax: 610-828-1995

Management and Staff
Edward Bachurski, Principal
Robert Ventresca, Principal

Type of Firm
Private Firm Investing Own Capital

Industry Association Membership
National Venture Capital Association (NVCA)

Additional Information
Capital Under Management: $15,000,000
Current Activity Level : Actively seeking new investments

ANTHEM CAPITAL, L.P.

435 Devon Park Drive
Building 300
Wayne, PA 19087
Phone: 610-254-4164
Fax: 610-975-0355
Website: www.anthemcapital.com

See Maryland for full listing.

ARGOSY PARTNERS

950 West Valley Road
Suite 2902
Wayne, PA 19087
Phone: 610-971-9685
Fax: 610-964-9524
Website: www.argosycapital.com

Management and Staff
John Kirwin, Partner
Kirk Griswold, Partner
Knute Albrecht, Partner

Type of Firm
Private Firm Investing Own Capital

Industry Association Membership
Natl assoc of Small Bus. Inv. Co (NASBIC)

Project Preferences

Role in Financing:
Will function either as deal originator or investor in deals created by others

Type of Financing Preferred:
Later Stage
Leveraged Buyout
Management Buyouts
Recapitalizations

Size of Investments Considered
Min Size of Investment Considered (000s): $1,000
Max Size of Investment Considered (000s): $2,500

Geographical Preferences

United States
All U.S.
Rocky Mountain

Industry Preferences

Business Serv.
Services
Distribution

Manufact.
Manufacturing

Additional Information
Year Founded: 1996
Capital Under Management: $95,000,000
Current Activity Level : Actively seeking new investments

BACHOW & ASSOCIATES, INC.

Three Bala Plaza East
Suite 502
Bala Cynwyd, PA 19004
Phone: 610-660-4900
Fax: 610-660-4930
Website: http://www.bachow.com

Management and Staff
Frank Novaczek, Managing Director
Jay Seid, Managing Director
Noah Walley, Vice President
Paul Bachow, Senior Managing Director
Robert Ivanoff, Vice President
Salvatore Grasso, Chief Financial Officer
Sam Schwartz, Vice President
Steve Fisher, Managing Director

Type of Firm
Private Firm Investing Own Capital

Project Preferences

Role in Financing:
Prefer role as deal originator but will also invest in deals created by others

Type of Financing Preferred:
Control-block Purchases
Leveraged Buyout
Recapitalizations
Second Stage Financing
Special Situation

Size of Investments Considered
Min Size of Investment Considered (000s): $8,000
Max Size of Investment Considered: No Limit

Geographical Preferences

United States
Mid Atlantic
Midwest
Northeast
Southeast

Industry Preferences

(% based on actual investment)

Communications and Media	42.0%
Internet Specific	29.1%
Computer Software and Services	19.7%
Other Products	7.7%
Semiconductors/Other Elect.	1.5%

Additional Information
Name of Most Recent Fund: Bachow Investment Partners IV, L.P.
Most Recent Fund Was Raised: 01/01/1997
Year Founded: 1985
Capital Under Management: $185,000,000
Current Activity Level : Actively seeking new investments
Method of Compensation: Return on investment is of primary concern, do not charge fees

BEN FRANKLIN TECHNOLOGY CENTER, THE

3625 Market Street
Philadelphia, PA 19104
Phone: 215-382-0380
Fax: 215-387-6050

Type of Firm
State Govt Affiliated NEC

Industry Preferences

(% based on actual investment)

Internet Specific	29.7%
Medical/Health	21.6%
Biotechnology	12.6%
Industrial/Energy	8.3%
Computer Software and Services	8.2%
Other Products	7.7%
Consumer Related	3.8%
Computer Hardware	3.8%
Semiconductors/Other Elect.	3.4%
Communications and Media	1.0%

Additional Information
Name of Most Recent Fund: Ben Franklin/Progress Capital Fund, L.P.
Most Recent Fund Was Raised: 02/28/1997
Capital Under Management: $8,800,000
Current Activity Level : Actively seeking new investments

BERWIND FINANCIAL GROUP, L.P.

3000 Centre Square West
1500 Market Street
Philadelphia, PA 19102
Phone: 215-575-2400
Fax: 215-564-5402
Website: www.berwindfinancial.com

Management and Staff
Christine Jones, Principal
Christopher Hanssens, Vice President
Jeffrey Davison, Principal
Linda DeJure, Principal
Marc Chesen, Managing Director
Michael O'Malley, Partner
Peter Gould, President
Peter Askey, Principal
Ray Baran, Chief Financial Officer
Thomas Calibeo, Vice President
Timothy Webb, Partner

Whom to Contact
Graeme Fraizer
Peter Gould

Type of Firm
Investment/Merchant Bank Subsid/Affil

Project Preferences

Role in Financing:
Prefer role as deal originator but will also invest in deals created by others

Type of Financing Preferred:
Control-block Purchases
First Stage Financing
Industry Rollups
Leveraged Buyout
Mezzanine
Recapitalizations
Research and Development
Second Stage Financing
Special Situation
Start-up Financing

Size of Investments Considered
Min Size of Investment Considered (000s): $2,000
Max Size of Investment Considered: No Limit

Geographical Preferences

United States
Mid Atlantic
Midwest
Northeast
Southeast

Canada
Ontario

Industry Preferences

Communications and Media
Commercial Communications
CATV & Pay TV Systems
Telecommunications
Data Communications

Semiconductors/Other Elect.
Controllers and Sensors
Sensors
Component Testing Equipmt
Analytic/Scientific

Medical/Health
Medical Products
Disposable Med. Products
Hospitals/Clinics/Primary
Hospital/Other Instit.

Consumer Related
Entertainment and Leisure
Consumer Products
Consumer Services
Education Related

Industrial/Energy
Industrial Products
Materials
Factory Automation
Machinery
Environmental Related

Transportation
Transportation

Financial Services
Financial Services

Manufact.
Publishing

Additional Information
Name of Most Recent Fund: Eureka I, L.P.
Most Recent Fund Was Raised: 01/01/1999
Year Founded: 1992
Capital Under Management: $150,000,000
Current Activity Level : Actively seeking new investments
Method of Compensation: Return on invest. most important, but chg. closing fees, service fees, etc.

BIRCHMERE VENTURES, INC.(FKA:BIRCHMERE INVESTMENTS)

2000 Technology Drive
Pittsburgh, PA 15219-3109
Phone: 412-803-8000
Fax: 412-687-8139
Website: www.birchmerevc.com

Management and Staff
Gary Glausser, Partner
John Isherwood, Principal
Ned Renzi, Partner
Rajiv Enand, Venture Partner
Sean Sebastian, Partner

Type of Firm
Private Firm Investing Own Capital

Industry Association Membership
Mid-Atlantic Venture Association

Project Preferences

Role in Financing:
Prefer role as deal originator but will also invest in deals created by others

Type of Financing Preferred:
Early Stage
Expansion
First Stage Financing
Later Stage
Second Stage Financing
Startup

Geographical Preferences

United States
Mid Atlantic

Industry Preferences

(% based on actual investment)

Internet Specific	34.4%
Computer Software and Services	30.3%
Biotechnology	14.7%
Computer Hardware	14.3%
Industrial/Energy	4.8%
Other Products	1.5%

Additional Information
Year Founded: 1996
Capital Under Management: $95,000,000
Current Activity Level : Actively seeking new investments
Method of Compensation: Return on investment is of primary concern, do not charge fees

---

BOSTON MILLENNIA PARTNERS

20 Valley Stream Parkway
Malvern, PA 19355-1457
Phone: 610-993-8727
Fax: 610-695-2517
Website: www.millenniapartners.com

See Massachusetts for full listing.

CEO VENTURE FUND

2000 Technology Drive
Suite 160
Pittsburgh, PA 15219-3109
Phone: 412-687-3451
Fax: 412-687-8139
Website: www.ceoventurefund.com

Other Offices

1950 Old Gallows Road
Suite 440
Vienna, VA 22182
Phone: 703-847-8823
Fax: 703-847-1848

4516 Henry Street
Pittsburgh, PA 15213
Phone: 412-687-3451
Fax: 412-687-2791

Management and Staff

Gary Glausser, Chief Financial Officer
Gene Yost, General Partner
Glen Chatfield, General Partner
John Boles, Partner
Ned Renzi, General Partner
Thomas McConomy, Partner
Timothy Parks, Partner
William Newlin, General Partner

Type of Firm

Private Firm Investing Own Capital

Industry Association Membership

Mid-Atlantic Venture Association
Natl assoc of Small Bus. Inv. Co (NASBIC)

Project Preferences

Role in Financing:

Prefer role as deal originator but will also invest in deals created by others

Type of Financing Preferred:

First Stage Financing
Leveraged Buyout
Second Stage Financing
Special Situation
Start-up Financing

Size of Investments Considered

Min Size of Investment Considered (000s): $1,000
Max Size of Investment Considered (000s): $2,000

Geographical Preferences

United States

Mid Atlantic

Industry Preferences

(% based on actual investment)

Computer Software and Services	51.1%
Biotechnology	14.4%
Computer Hardware	10.3%
Semiconductors/Other Elect.	4.6%
Other Products	4.5%
Internet Specific	4.2%
Medical/Health	3.8%
Industrial/Energy	3.3%
Communications and Media	1.9%
Consumer Related	1.8%

Additional Information

Name of Most Recent Fund: CEO Venture Fund III
Most Recent Fund Was Raised: 03/10/1997
Year Founded: 1985
Capital Under Management: $5,900,000
Current Activity Level : Actively seeking new investments
Method of Compensation: Return on invest. most important, but chg. closing fees, service fees, etc.

CROSS ATLANTIC CAPITAL PARTNERS

5 Radnor Corporate Center
Suite 555
Radnor, PA 19087
Phone: 610-995-2650
Fax: 610-971-2062
Website: www.xacp.com

Other Offices

3006 Lake Drive
Citywest
Dublin, Ireland, Republic of
Phone: 011-35-31-241-6100
Fax: 011-35-31-466-0170

7 Carendish Square
London, Ireland, Republic of WC2B 6AA
Phone: 011-44-20-7681-652
Fax: 011-44-20-7681-661

Management and Staff

Brian Adamsky, Chief Financial Officer
Donald Caldwell, General Partner
Gerry McCrory, General Partner
Glenn Rieger, General Partner
Justin Rea, Principal
Richard Fox, General Partner
Sheryl Daniels-Young, General Partner

Type of Firm

Private Firm Investing Own Capital

Industry Association Membership

Mid-Atlantic Venture Association
National Venture Capital Association (NVCA)

Project Preferences

Role in Financing:

Will function either as deal originator or investor in deals created by others

Type of Financing Preferred:

Balanced
Early Stage
Expansion
Seed
Startup

Size of Investments Considered

Min Size of Investment Considered (000s): $1,000
Max Size of Investment Considered (000s): $10,000

Geographical Preferences

United States

All U.S.

International

All International
Ireland
United Kingdom

Industry Preferences

(% based on actual investment)

Internet Specific	48.5%
Communications and Media	14.5%
Other Products	12.9%
Computer Software and Services	8.4%
Computer Hardware	6.4%
Semiconductors/Other Elect.	5.7%
Industrial/Energy	3.6%

Additional Information

Name of Most Recent Fund: Crucible I Fund
Most Recent Fund Was Raised: 01/02/1999
Year Founded: 1999
Capital Under Management: $278,600,000
Current Activity Level : Actively seeking new investments
Method of Compensation: Return on investment is of primary concern, do not charge fees

DELAWARE VALLEY COMMUNITY REINVESTMENT FUND (DVCRF)

718 Arch Street
Suite 300 North
Philadelphia, PA 19106
Phone: 215-925-1130
Fax: 215-923-4764
Website: www.trfund.com

Management and Staff
John Freyhof, Managing Director
Joseph Killackey, Managing Director

Type of Firm
Business Development Fund

Industry Preferences
(% based on actual investment)

Medical/Health	35.6%
Internet Specific	33.1%
Industrial/Energy	14.8%
Consumer Related	9.7%
Computer Software and Services	6.8%

Additional Information
Year Founded: 1985
Capital Under Management: $22,000,000
Current Activity Level : Actively seeking new investments

DRAPER TRIANGLE VENTURES LP

2 Gateway Center
20th Floor
Pittsburgh, PA 15222
Phone: 412-288-9800
Fax: 412-288-9799
Website: www.dtvc.com

Management and Staff
Donald Jones, Managing Director
Joseph Katariacic, Principal
Michael Stubler, Principal
Tom Jones, Principal

Type of Firm
Private Firm Investing Own Capital

Project Preferences
Type of Financing Preferred:
Early Stage

Size of Investments Considered
Min Size of Investment Considered (000s): $500
Max Size of Investment Considered (000s): $3,000

Geographical Preferences
United States
Mid Atlantic
Midwest

Industry Preferences
Communications and Media
Telecommunications
Wireless Communications

Computer Software
Software
Systems Software

Internet Specific
E-Commerce Technology
Internet

Medical/Health
Medical Products

Industrial/Energy
Factory Automation
Robotics

Additional Information
Year Founded: 1999
Capital Under Management: $53,000,000
Current Activity Level : Actively seeking new investments

EDISON VENTURE FUND

213 Market Street
Ninth Floor
Harrisburg, PA 17108-0749
Phone: 717-237-3069
Fax: 717-236-377
Website: www.edisonventure.com

See New Jersey for full listing.

ENERTECH CAPITAL PARTNERS, L.P.

435 Devon Park Dr
700 Building
Wayne, PA 19087
Phone: 610-254-4141
Fax: 610-254-4188
Website: www.enertechcapital.com

Management and Staff
David Lincoln, Managing Director
James Biddle, Vice President
Kenneth Kazmer, Venture Partner
Michael DeRosa, Principal
Rahul Gujral, Principal
Scott Ungerer, Managing Director
William Kingsley, Managing Director

Type of Firm
Private Firm Investing Own Capital

Industry Association Membership
Mid-Atlantic Venture Association
National Venture Capital Association (NVCA)

Project Preferences
Role in Financing:
Prefer role as deal originator but will also invest in deals created by others

Type of Financing Preferred:
Early Stage
First Stage Financing
Later Stage
Second Stage Financing
Seed

Size of Investments Considered
Min Size of Investment Considered (000s): $3,000
Max Size of Investment Considered (000s): $20,000

Geographical Preferences
United States
All U.S.

Industry Preferences
(% based on actual investment)

Internet Specific	66.6%
Computer Software and Services	16.0%
Other Products	6.4%
Semiconductors/Other Elect.	4.1%
Communications and Media	3.4%
Industrial/Energy	2.3%
Computer Hardware	1.3%

Additional Information
Name of Most Recent Fund: Enertech Capital I
Most Recent Fund Was Raised: 08/01/1996
Year Founded: 1996
Capital Under Management: $284,000,000
Current Activity Level : Actively seeking new investments
Method of Compensation: Return on invest. most important, but chg. closing fees, service fees, etc.

EUCLIDSR PARTNERS

200 Barr Harbor Drive, Suite 250
Four Tower Bridge
Conshohocken, PA 19428-2977
Phone: 610-567-1000
Fax: 610-567-1039
Website: www.euclidsr.com

See New York for full listing.

EXELON CAPITAL PARTNERS

2301 Market Street
Suite S8-5
Philadelphia, PA 19101
Phone: 215-841-5690
Fax: 215-841-5581

Management and Staff
Gregory Cucchi, President
Kimberly Roerig, Chief Financial Officer
Robert Shinn, Vice President

Type of Firm
Private Firm Investing Own Capital

Industry Association Membership
National Venture Capital Association (NVCA)

Additional Information
Current Activity Level : Actively seeking new investments

FOSTER MANAGEMENT COMPANY

1018 W Ninth Ave
King Of Prussia, PA 19406
Phone: 610-992-7650

Type of Firm
Private Firm Investing Own Capital

Project Preferences

Type of Financing Preferred:
Balanced

Geographical Preferences

International
No Preference

Additional Information
Name of Most Recent Fund: Foster Management Company
Most Recent Fund Was Raised: 01/01/1978
Year Founded: 1972
Capital Under Management: $64,000,000
Current Activity Level : Actively seeking new investments

FUTURE FUND, THE

945 Liberty Avenue
Suite 3
Pittsburgh, PA 15222
Phone: 412-467-8370
Fax: 412-467-8377
Website: www.future-fund.com

Management and Staff
Esther Dormer, Founder
Richard Madden, Founder

Type of Firm
Private Firm Investing Own Capital

Industry Association Membership
National Venture Capital Association (NVCA)

Additional Information
Year Founded: 1999
Current Activity Level : Actively seeking new investments

GAMMA INVESTORS LLC

555 Croton Road
Suite 111
King of Prussia, PA 19406
Phone: 610-265-8116
Fax: 610-265-7245
Website: www.gammainvestors.com

Management and Staff
Alec Petro, Managing Director
Christopher Nuevillar, Managing Director

Type of Firm
Private Firm Investing Own Capital

Project Preferences

Type of Financing Preferred:
Early Stage
First Stage Financing
Second Stage Financing

Size of Investments Considered
Min Size of Investment Considered (000s): $500
Max Size of Investment Considered (000s): $2,000

Geographical Preferences

United States
All U.S.

Industry Preferences

Internet Specific
Internet

Additional Information
Year Founded: 1998
Capital Under Management: $15,000,000
Current Activity Level : Actively seeking new investments

GREATER PHILADELPHIA VENTURE CAPITAL CORP.

351 East Conestoga Road
Wayne, PA 19087
Phone: 610-688-6829
Fax: 610-254-8958

Management and Staff
Fred Choate

Whom to Contact
Fred Choate

Type of Firm
MESBIC not elsewhere classified

Industry Association Membership
Natl assoc of Small Bus. Inv. Co (NASBIC)

Project Preferences

Role in Financing:
Prefer role as deal originator but will also invest in deals created by others

Type of Financing Preferred:
First Stage Financing
Leveraged Buyout
Mezzanine
Second Stage Financing
Special Situation

Size of Investments Considered
Min Size of Investment Considered (000s): $100
Max Size of Investment Considered (000s): $300

Geographical Preferences

United States
Mid Atlantic

Industry Preferences

Communications and Media
CATV & Pay TV Systems
Data Communications
Satellite Microwave Comm.

Computer Hardware
Computer Graphics and Dig

Computer Software
Computer Services

Medical/Health
Medical Products

Consumer Related
Franchises(NEC)

Additional Information

Year Founded: 1971
Capital Under Management: $2,500,000
Current Activity Level : Actively seeking new investments
Method of Compensation: Return on investment is of primary concern, do not charge fees

HOWARD, LAWSON & CO.

Two Penn Center Plaza
Philadelphia, PA 19102
Phone: 215-988-0010
Fax: 215-568-0029

Management and Staff

Michael Cuneo

Whom to Contact

Michael Cuneo

Type of Firm

Investment/Merchant Bank Investing Own or Client Funds

Project Preferences

Role in Financing:
Prefer role as deal originator

Type of Financing Preferred:
Leveraged Buyout
Mezzanine
Recapitalizations
Second Stage Financing

Size of Investments Considered

Min Size of Investment Considered (000s): $1,000
Max Size of Investment Considered: No Limit

Geographical Preferences

United States
Mid Atlantic
Midwest

Industry Preferences

Communications and Media
Other Communication Prod.

Semiconductors/Other Elect.
Electronics
Electronic Components
Controllers and Sensors
Component Testing Equipmt
Laser Related
Fiber Optics
Analytic/Scientific

Medical/Health
Diagnostic Services
Diagnostic Test Products
Medical Products
Disposable Med. Products

Consumer Related
Entertainment and Leisure
Food/Beverage
Consumer Products

Industrial/Energy
Oil and Gas Exploration
Industrial Products

Manufact.
Office Automation Equipmt

Additional Information

Year Founded: 1972
Current Activity Level : Actively seeking new investments
Method of Compensation: Return on invest. most important, but chg. closing fees, service fees, etc.

INNOVATION WORKS, INC.

2000 Technology Drive
Suite 250
Pittsburgh, PA 15219
Phone: 412-681-1520
Fax: 412-681-2625
Website: www.innovationworks.org

Type of Firm

Private Firm Investing Own Capital

Industry Association Membership

National Venture Capital Association (NVCA)

Project Preferences

Role in Financing:
Prefer role as deal originator

Type of Financing Preferred:
Early Stage
First Stage Financing
Seed
Startup

Size of Investments Considered

Min Size of Investment Considered (000s): $100
Max Size of Investment Considered (000s): $500

Geographical Preferences

United States
Pennsylvania

Industry Preferences

Communications and Media
Telecommunications
Wireless Communications

Computer Hardware
Mainframes / Scientific
Mini and Personal/Desktop
Computer Graphics and Dig
Integrated Turnkey System
Terminals
Disk Relat. Memory Device

Computer Software
Computer Services
Data Processing
Software
Systems Software
Applications Software
Artificial Intelligence

Internet Specific
E-Commerce Technology
Internet
Web Aggregration/Portals

Semiconductors/Other Elect.
Electronic Components
Semiconductor
Micro-Processing
Controllers and Sensors
Sensors
Circuit Boards
Component Testing Equipmt
Laser Related
Fiber Optics

Biotechnology
Human Biotechnology
Industrial Biotechnology

Medical/Health
Medical Diagnostics
Diagnostic Services
Diagnostic Test Products
Medical Therapeutics
Drug/Equipmt Delivery
Medical Products
Disposable Med. Products
Health Services
Pharmaceuticals

Industrial/Energy
Superconductivity
Robotics

Additional Information
Name of Most Recent Fund: Innovation Investment Fund
Most Recent Fund Was Raised: 07/01/1999
Year Founded: 1999
Capital Under Management: $35,000,000
Current Activity Level : Actively seeking new investments
Method of Compensation: Return on investment is of primary concern, do not charge fees

INNOVEST GROUP, INC.

2000 Market Street
Suite 1400
Philadelphia, PA 19103
Phone: 215-564-3960
Fax: 215-569-3272

Management and Staff
Richard Woosnam

Whom to Contact
Richard Woosnam

Type of Firm
Investment/Merchant Bank Investing Own or Client Funds

Project Preferences

Role in Financing:
Prefer role as deal originator but will also invest in deals created by others

Type of Financing Preferred:
First Stage Financing
Leveraged Buyout
Recapitalizations
Second Stage Financing
Special Situation
Start-up Financing

Size of Investments Considered
Min Size of Investment Considered (000s): $500
Max Size of Investment Considered (000s): $1,000

Geographical Preferences

United States
Mid Atlantic
Midwest
Northeast
Southeast

Industry Preferences

Communications and Media
Commercial Communications
CATV & Pay TV Systems
Radio & TV Broadcasting
Telecommunications
Data Communications
Satellite Microwave Comm.
Other Communication Prod.

Computer Hardware
Computer Graphics and Dig
Integrated Turnkey System
Disk Relat. Memory Device

Computer Software
Computer Services
Applications Software

Semiconductors/Other Elect.
Sensors
Component Testing Equipmt
Laser Related
Fiber Optics

Medical/Health
Other Therapeutic
Medical Products
Hospital/Other Instit.

Consumer Related
Franchises(NEC)
Education Related

Industrial/Energy
Industrial Products
Factory Automation
Robotics
Machinery
Environmental Related

Transportation
Transportation

Financial Services
Financial Services

Manufact.
Office Automation Equipmt
Publishing

Additional Information
Year Founded: 1971
Capital Under Management: $20,000,000
Current Activity Level : Actively seeking new investments
Method of Compensation: Return on invest. most important, but chg. closing fees, service fees, etc.

JUSTSYSTEM, INC.

5301 5th Ave.
Pittsburgh, PA 15232-2124
Phone: 650-233-9890
Fax: 650-233-9896

Management and Staff
Yoshihiko Morimoto, President & COO

Whom to Contact
Eric Stetzler

Type of Firm
Non-Financial Corp. Affiliate or Subsidiary

Industry Association Membership
Western Association of Venture Capitalists (WAVC)

Project Preferences

Role in Financing:
Prefer role in deals created by others

Type of Financing Preferred:
First Stage Financing
Second Stage Financing

Size of Investments Considered
Min Size of Investment Considered (000s): $500
Max Size of Investment Considered (000s): $2,000

Geographical Preferences

United States
Northwest
West Coast

Industry Preferences

Computer Hardware
Computer Graphics and Dig

Computer Software
Computer Services
Systems Software
Applications Software
Artificial Intelligence

Internet Specific
Internet

Manufact.
Office Automation Equipmt

Additional Information
Year Founded: 1996
Current Activity Level : Actively seeking new investments

KATALYST LLC

5 Radnor Corporate Center
Suite 560, 100 Matsonford Road
Radnor, PA 19087
Phone: 610-975-0640
Fax: 610-975-9579
Website: www.katalyst.com

Other Offices

405 Lexington Avenue
Suite 480
New York, NY 10174
Phone: 917-592-8852
Fax: 212-504-8118

8133 Leesburg Pike
Suite 220
Vienna, VA 22182
Phone: 703-568-7413

Management and Staff
Douglas Epstein, Managing Director
John Fitzgerald, President
Jonathan Kalman, Chairman & CEO
Joseph Worth, Chief Financial Officer
Kathy Boden, Chief Operating Officer
Neil Heller, General Partner
Richard Tuley, Principal
Tucker Twitmyer, Managing Director

Type of Firm
Incubators

Industry Association Membership
Mid-Atlantic Venture Association

Additional Information
Year Founded: 1999
Current Activity Level : Actively seeking new investments

KEYSTONE MINORITY CAPITAL FUND, L.P.

1801 Centre Avenue
Suite 201 Williams Square
Pittsburgh, PA 15219
Phone: 412-338-2230
Fax: 412-338-2224

Management and Staff
Earl Hord, General Partner

Whom to Contact
Earl Hord

Type of Firm
Private Firm Investing Own Capital

Industry Association Membership
Natl Assoc of Investment Cos. (NAIC)

Project Preferences

Role in Financing:
Prefer role as deal originator but will also invest in deals created by others

Type of Financing Preferred:
First Stage Financing
Leveraged Buyout
Mezzanine
Second Stage Financing
Start-up Financing

Size of Investments Considered
Min Size of Investment Considered (000s): $500
Max Size of Investment Considered: No Limit

Geographical Preferences

United States
Mid Atlantic

Industry Preferences

Communications and Media
Communications and Media

Computer Other
Computer Related

Semiconductors/Other Elect.
Electronic Components

Biotechnology
Industrial Biotechnology
Biosensors
Biotech Related Research

Medical/Health
Medical/Health
Medical Diagnostics
Medical Therapeutics

Consumer Related
Entertainment and Leisure
Retail
Computer Stores
Franchises(NEC)
Food/Beverage
Consumer Products
Consumer Services
Education Related

Industrial/Energy
Industrial Products

Business Serv.
Distribution

Manufact.
Publishing

Additional Information
Name of Most Recent Fund: Keystone Minority Capital Fund
Most Recent Fund Was Raised: 12/01/1994
Year Founded: 1994
Capital Under Management: $5,200,000
Current Activity Level : Actively seeking new investments
Method of Compensation: Return on investment is of primary concern, do not charge fees

KEYSTONE VENTURE CAPITAL MANAGEMENT CO.

1601 Market Street
Suite 2500
Philadelphia, PA 19103
Phone: 215-241-1200
Fax: 215-241-1211
Website: www.keystonevc.com

Other Offices

2034 Eisenhower Ave
Suite 290
Philadelphia, PA 22314
Phone: 703-519-6400
Fax: 703-684-4523

225 West Washington Street
Suite 1450
Chicago, IL 60606
Phone: 312-857-1400
Fax: 312-857-1800

Management and Staff
Atlee Brown, Chief Executive Officer
Atull Madahar, Vice President
John Regan, General Partner
Kerry Dale, General Partner
Peter Ligeti, General Partner
Robert Pace, Vice President

Type of Firm
Private Firm Investing Own Capital

Industry Association Membership
Mid-Atlantic Venture Association
National Venture Capital Association (NVCA)

Project Preferences

Role in Financing:
Prefer role as deal originator but will also invest in deals created by others

Type of Financing Preferred:
Balanced
Expansion
First Stage Financing
Second Stage Financing

Size of Investments Considered
Min Size of Investment Considered (000s): $2,000
Max Size of Investment Considered (000s): $5,000

Geographical Preferences

United States
Mid Atlantic

Industry Preferences

(% based on actual investment)

Internet Specific	33.0%
Computer Software and Services	14.6%
Medical/Health	13.2%
Communications and Media	10.9%
Other Products	9.3%
Consumer Related	9.1%
Industrial/Energy	4.0%
Computer Hardware	3.2%
Semiconductors/Other Elect.	2.7%

Additional Information
Name of Most Recent Fund: Keystone Venture V, L. P.
Most Recent Fund Was Raised: 12/26/1997
Year Founded: 1983
Capital Under Management: $170,000,000
Current Activity Level : Actively seeking new investments
Method of Compensation: Return on investment is of primary concern, do not charge fees

LIBERTY VENTURE PARTNERS, INC.

One Commerce Square
2005 Market St., Suite 200
Philadelphia, PA 19103-7058
Phone: 215-282-4484
Fax: 215-282-4485
Website: www.libertyvp.com

Management and Staff
David Robkin, Principal
Karen Griffith Gryga, Principal
Maria Hahn, Principal
Thomas Morse, Principal

Type of Firm
Private Firm Investing Own Capital

Project Preferences

Type of Financing Preferred:
Early Stage
Expansion

Size of Investments Considered
Min Size of Investment Considered (000s): $3,000
Max Size of Investment Considered (000s): $7,000

Industry Preferences

(% based on actual investment)

Computer Software and Services	57.9%
Communications and Media	27.3%
Internet Specific	14.7%

Additional Information
Capital Under Management: $85,000,000
Current Activity Level : Actively seeking new investments

LLR EQUITY PARTNERS

1811 Chestnut Street
Suite 210
Philadelphia, PA 19103
Phone: 215-717-2900
Fax: 215-717-2270
Website: www.llrpartners.com

Other Offices

1150 First Avenue
Suite 100
Norristown, PA 19406

Management and Staff
Howard Ross, Partner
Ira Lubert, Partner
Joseph Keller, Chief Financial Officer
Mitchell Hollin, Partner
Seth Lehr, Partner

Type of Firm
Private Firm Investing Own Capital

Project Preferences

Type of Financing Preferred:
Balanced
Expansion

Geographical Preferences

United States
Mid Atlantic

Industry Preferences

Communications and Media
Telecommunications

Computer Software
Software

Internet Specific
Internet

Medical/Health
Medical/Health
Pharmaceuticals

Consumer Related
Education Related

Manufact.
Manufacturing

Additional Information
Capital Under Management: $260,000,000
Current Activity Level : Actively seeking new investments

LOYALHANNA VENTURE FUND

527 Cedar Way
Suite 104
Oakmont, PA 15139
Phone: 412-820-7035
Fax: 412-820-7036

Other Offices

P.O. Box 36
Ligonier, PA 15658
Phone: 412-928-1440
Fax: 412-238-6508

Management and Staff
James Knowles

Whom to Contact
James Knowles

Type of Firm
Private Firm Investing Own Capital

Project Preferences

Role in Financing:
Prefer role as deal originator but will also invest in deals created by others

Type of Financing Preferred:
First Stage Financing
Leveraged Buyout
Second Stage Financing

Size of Investments Considered
Min Size of Investment Considered (000s): $300
Max Size of Investment Considered (000s): $1,000

Geographical Preferences

International
No Preference

Additional Information
Year Founded: 1984
Capital Under Management: $10,000,000
Current Activity Level : Making few, if any, new investments
Method of Compensation: Return on investment is of primary concern, do not charge fees

LTI VENTURES LEASING CORP.

Two Clearfield Road
P.O. Box 447
Ardmore, PA 19003-0447
Phone: 610-446-4479
Fax: 610-446-3771
Website: www.ltileasing.com

See Connecticut for full listing.

LYCOS VENTURES

Two Gateway Center
20th Floor
Pittsburgh, PA 15222
Phone: 412-338-8600
Fax: 412-338-8699
Website: www.lycosventures.com

Management and Staff
David Hart, Principal
Dennis Ciccone, Managing Director
Joseph Katarincic, Principal
Michael Stubler, Principal

Type of Firm
Non-Financial Corp. Affiliate or Subsidiary

Industry Association Membership
Mid-Atlantic Venture Association
National Venture Capital Association (NVCA)

Project Preferences

Role in Financing:
Will function either as deal originator or investor in deals created by others

Type of Financing Preferred:
Early Stage
First Stage Financing
Second Stage Financing

Industry Preferences

(% based on actual investment)

Internet Specific	63.5%
Computer Software and Services	24.7%
Computer Hardware	11.0%
Communications and Media	0.8%

Additional Information
Year Founded: 1999
Capital Under Management: $75,000,000
Current Activity Level : Actively seeking new investments

MELLON VENTURES (AKA: MELLON BANK)

One Mellon Center
Room 5300
Pittsburgh, PA 15258-0001
Phone: 412-236-3594
Fax: 412-236-3593
Website: www.mellonventures.com

Other Offices

1114 Avenue of the Americas
31st Floor
New York, NY 10036-7701
Phone: 212-389-2700
Fax: 212-389-2755

400 South Hope Street
5th Floor
Los Angeles, CA 90071-2806
Phone: 213-553-9685
Fax: 213-553-9690

Five Radnor Corporate Center
100 Matsonford Road, Suite 170
Wayne, PA 19087-4515
Phone: 610-688-4600
Fax: 610-688-3930

One Buckhead Plaza
3060 Peachtree Road, Suite 780
Atlanta, GA 30305-2240
Phone: 404-264-9180
Fax: 404-264-9305

Management and Staff
Burton Goldstein, Venture Partner
Chuck Billerbeck, Managing Director
Jeff Anderson, Managing Director
John Geer, Partner
John Adams, Vice President
John Shoemaker, Vice President
John Richardson, Managing Director
Mark Patton, Vice President
Mark Downs, Vice President
Max Chee, Vice President
Paul Cohn, Principal
Paul Morrison, Principal
Robert Driscoll, Vice President
Ron Coombs, Principal
Ryan Busch, Vice President

Type of Firm
Commercial Bank Affiliate or Subsidiary

Industry Association Membership
Natl assoc of Small Bus. Inv. Co (NASBIC)

Project Preferences

Role in Financing:
Prefer role as deal originator but will also invest in deals created by others

Type of Financing Preferred:
Balanced
Leveraged Buyout
Mezzanine
Special Situation

Size of Investments Considered
Min Size of Investment Considered (000s): $2,000
Max Size of Investment Considered (000s): $25,000

Geographical Preferences

United States
All U.S.

Industry Preferences

(% based on actual investment)

Internet Specific	36.4%
Other Products	26.7%
Computer Software and Services	14.3%
Communications and Media	10.6%

Computer Hardware	3.8%
Consumer Related	3.4%
Semiconductors/Other Elect.	3.3%
Industrial/Energy	1.5%

Additional Information
Name of Most Recent Fund: netWorth Partners
Most Recent Fund Was Raised: 01/01/1997
Year Founded: 2001
Capital Under Management: $500,000,000
Current Activity Level : Actively seeking new investments
Method of Compensation: Return on investment is of primary concern, do not charge fees

MENTOR CAPITAL PARTNERS

P.O. Box 560
Yardley, PA 19067
Phone: 215-736-8882
Website: www.mentorcapitalpartners.com

Management and Staff
Edward Sager, General Partner
George Stasen, Partner

Type of Firm
Investment/Merchant Bank Subsid/Affil

Industry Association Membership
National Venture Capital Association (NVCA)

Project Preferences

Role in Financing:
Prefer role as deal originator but will also invest in deals created by others

Type of Financing Preferred:
Acquisition
Balanced
Expansion
Generalist PE
Later Stage
Leveraged Buyout
Management Buyouts
Mezzanine
Recapitalizations
Special Situation

Geographical Preferences

United States
Mid Atlantic

Industry Preferences

Communications and Media
Commercial Communications
CATV & Pay TV Systems
Telecommunications
Data Communications
Satellite Microwave Comm.

Computer Software
Software
Systems Software
Applications Software
Artificial Intelligence

Internet Specific
Internet

Semiconductors/Other Elect.
Electronic Components
Sensors
Component Testing Equipmt
Laser Related
Fiber Optics
Analytic/Scientific

Medical/Health
Medical Diagnostics
Diagnostic Services
Diagnostic Test Products
Health Services

Consumer Related
Consumer
Education Related

Industrial/Energy
Industrial Products
Factory Automation
Process Control
Machinery

Transportation
Aerospace

Financial Services
Financial Services

Business Serv.
Services
Distribution
Consulting Services

Manufact.
Manufacturing

Additional Information
Name of Most Recent Fund: Mentor Special Situation Fund, L.P.
Most Recent Fund Was Raised: 01/01/1996
Year Founded: 1996
Capital Under Management: $5,000,000
Current Activity Level : Actively seeking new investments
Method of Compensation: Return on invest. most important, but chg. closing fees, service fees, etc.

MERIDIAN VENTURE PARTNERS (MVP)

The Radnor Court Building
Ste 140 259 Radnor-Chester Rd
Radnor, PA 19087
Phone: 610-254-2999
Fax: 610-254-2996

Management and Staff
Bernard Markey, General Partner
Elam Hitchner, General Partner
Joseph Hawke, Vice President
Kenneth Jones, General Partner
Raymond Rafferty, General Partner
Robert Brown, General Partner

Type of Firm
SBIC Not elsewhere classified

Industry Association Membership
National Venture Capital Association (NVCA)
Natl assoc of Small Bus. Inv. Co (NASBIC)

Project Preferences

Role in Financing:
Other

Type of Financing Preferred:
Leveraged Buyout
Second Stage Financing
Special Situation

Size of Investments Considered
Min Size of Investment Considered (000s): $1,000
Max Size of Investment Considered (000s): $2,000

Geographical Preferences

United States
All U.S.
Midwest
Northeast
Southeast

Industry Preferences

(% based on actual investment)

Internet Specific	32.4%
Computer Software and Services	28.3%
Other Products	14.2%
Medical/Health	12.1%
Consumer Related	4.3%
Industrial/Energy	3.7%
Computer Hardware	2.7%
Communications and Media	2.3%

Additional Information

Name of Most Recent Fund: Meridian Venture Partners II
Most Recent Fund Was Raised: 11/01/1999
Year Founded: 1987
Capital Under Management: $55,000,000
Current Activity Level : Actively seeking new investments
Method of Compensation: Return on invest. most important, but chg. closing fees, service fees, etc.

MID-ATLANTIC VENTURE FUNDS (FKA: NEPA MANAGEMENT CORP.)

125 Goodman Drive
Bethlehem, PA 18015
Phone: 610-865-6550
Fax: 610-865-6427
Website: www.mavf.com

Other Offices

11710 Plaza America Drive
Suite 120
Reston, VA 20190
Phone: 703-904-4120
Fax: 703-904-4124

Management and Staff

Frederick Beste, Partner
Glen Bressner, Partner
Marc Benson, Partner
Mike Long, Chief Financial Officer

Whom to Contact

Thomas A. Smith

Type of Firm

Private Firm Investing Own Capital

Industry Association Membership

Mid-Atlantic Venture Association
Natl assoc of Small Bus. Inv. Co (NASBIC)

Project Preferences

Role in Financing:

Prefer role as deal originator but will also invest in deals created by others

Type of Financing Preferred:

First Stage Financing
Leveraged Buyout
Research and Development
Second Stage Financing
Seed

Size of Investments Considered

Min Size of Investment Considered (000s): $500
Max Size of Investment Considered (000s): $8,000

Geographical Preferences

United States

Mid Atlantic
Northeast

Industry Preferences

(% based on actual investment)

Internet Specific	32.9%
Computer Software and Services	23.3%
Medical/Health	19.2%
Semiconductors/Other Elect.	7.1%
Other Products	6.6%
Industrial/Energy	5.4%
Communications and Media	5.0%
Consumer Related	0.3%
Biotechnology	0.2%
Computer Hardware	0.1%

Additional Information

Name of Most Recent Fund: Mid-Atlantic Venture Fund III, L.P.
Most Recent Fund Was Raised: 04/01/1997
Year Founded: 1984
Capital Under Management: $200,000,000
Current Activity Level : Inactive / Unknown
Method of Compensation: Return on investment is of primary concern, do not charge fees

NEWSPRING VENTURES

100 West Elm Street
Suite 101
Conshohocken, PA 19428
Phone: 610-567-2380
Fax: 610-567-2388
Website: www.newspringventures.com

Management and Staff

Janet Paroo, Managing Partner
Joseph Hawke, Partner
Michael DiPiano, Partner
Steven Hobman, Partner
W. Kirk Wycoff, Partner

Type of Firm

Affiliate/Subsidary of Oth. Financial. Instit.

Industry Association Membership

Natl assoc of Small Bus. Inv. Co (NASBIC)

Project Preferences

Role in Financing:

Will function either as deal originator or investor in deals created by others

Type of Financing Preferred:

Early Stage
Expansion

Size of Investments Considered

Min Size of Investment Considered (000s): $1,000
Max Size of Investment Considered: No Limit

Geographical Preferences

United States

Mid Atlantic

Industry Preferences

Communications and Media

Telecommunications
Wireless Communications
Data Communications

Computer Software

Software
Applications Software

Medical/Health

Medical Products

Industrial/Energy

Industrial Products

Business Serv.

Services
Media

Additional Information

Year Founded: 1999
Capital Under Management: $90,000,000
Current Activity Level : Actively seeking new investments
Method of Compensation: Return on investment is of primary concern, do not charge fees

PA EARLY STAGE (AKA:PENNSYLVANIA EARLY STAGE PARTNERS)

435 Devon Park Drive
Bldg. 500, Suite 510
Wayne, PA 19087
Phone: 610-293-4075
Fax: 610-254-4240
Website: www.paearlystage.com

Management and Staff
Dean Miller, Principal
Matt Rieke, Principal
Michael Bolton, CEO & Managing Director
Paul Schmitt, Managing Director
Rob McCord, Managing Director
Scott Nissenbaum, Principal
Stephen Barnes, Chief Financial Officer
Stephen Amsterdam, Principal

Type of Firm
Non-Financial Corp. Affiliate or Subsidiary

Industry Association Membership
Mid-Atlantic Venture Association
National Venture Capital Association (NVCA)

Project Preferences

Role in Financing:
Prefer role as deal originator but will also invest in deals created by others

Type of Financing Preferred:
Early Stage
First Stage Financing
Second Stage Financing
Seed
Startup

Size of Investments Considered
Min Size of Investment Considered (000s): $100
Max Size of Investment Considered (000s): $10,000

Geographical Preferences

United States
Mid Atlantic

Industry Preferences

(% based on actual investment)

Internet Specific	61.1%
Computer Software and Services	13.1%
Other Products	8.8%
Semiconductors/Other Elect.	7.0%
Biotechnology	6.2%
Consumer Related	2.5%
Industrial/Energy	1.2%
Communications and Media	0.2%

Additional Information
Name of Most Recent Fund: Pennsylvania Early Stage Partners, LP
Most Recent Fund Was Raised: 01/20/1998
Year Founded: 1998
Capital Under Management: $151,500,000
Current Activity Level : Actively seeking new investments
Method of Compensation: Return on investment is of primary concern, do not charge fees

PATRICOF & CO. VENTURES, INC.

455 South Gulph Road
Suite 410
King of Prussia, PA 19406
Phone: 610-265-0286
Fax: 610-265-4959
Website: www.patricof.com

See New York for full listing.

PENN-JANNEY FUND, INC., THE

1801 Market Street
11th Floor
Philadelphia, PA 19103
Phone: 215-665-4447
Fax: 215-557-0820

Management and Staff
William Rulon-Miller

Whom to Contact
William Rulon-Miller

Type of Firm
Insurance Firm Affiliate or Subsidiary

Project Preferences

Role in Financing:
Prefer role as deal originator but will also invest in deals created by others

Type of Financing Preferred:
Leveraged Buyout
Mezzanine
Second Stage Financing
Special Situation

Size of Investments Considered
Min Size of Investment Considered (000s): $1,000
Max Size of Investment Considered: No Limit

Geographical Preferences

United States
Mid Atlantic
Northeast
West Coast

Industry Preferences

Communications and Media
Commercial Communications
Satellite Microwave Comm.

Computer Hardware
Mini and Personal/Desktop
Computer Graphics and Dig
Disk Relat. Memory Device

Computer Software
Computer Services
Systems Software
Applications Software
Artificial Intelligence

Semiconductors/Other Elect.
Analytic/Scientific

Biotechnology
Industrial Biotechnology
Biosensors
Biotech Related Research

Medical/Health
Medical Diagnostics
Diagnostic Services
Diagnostic Test Products
Medical Therapeutics
Drug/Equipmt Delivery
Other Therapeutic
Disposable Med. Products
Hospital/Other Instit.
Pharmaceuticals

Consumer Related
Consumer
Retail

Industrial/Energy
Alternative Energy
Energy Conservation Relat
Industrial Products

Business Serv.
Distribution

Manufact.
Office Automation Equipmt

Additional Information
Year Founded: 1990
Capital Under Management: $20,000,000
Current Activity Level : Actively seeking new investments
Method of Compensation: Return on invest. most important, but chg. closing fees, service fees, etc.

PENNSYLVANIA GROWTH FUND

5850 Ellsworth Avenue
Suite 303
Pittsburgh, PA 15232
Phone: 412-661-1000
Fax: 412-361-0676

Management and Staff
Barry Lhormer
Hal Mendlowitz

Whom to Contact
Barry Lhormer
Hal Mendlowitz

Type of Firm
Private Firm Investing Own Capital

Project Preferences

Role in Financing:
Prefer role as deal originator

Type of Financing Preferred:
Leveraged Buyout
Mezzanine
Second Stage Financing
Special Situation

Size of Investments Considered
Min Size of Investment Considered (000s): $500
Max Size of Investment Considered: No Limit

Geographical Preferences

United States
Mid Atlantic
Midwest
Northeast
Southeast

Industry Preferences

Computer Software
Applications Software

Semiconductors/Other Elect.
Electronic Components

Medical/Health
Drug/Equipmt Delivery
Medical Products
Pharmaceuticals

Consumer Related
Retail
Franchises(NEC)
Consumer Products
Consumer Services
Education Related

Industrial/Energy
Industrial Products
Materials
Factory Automation
Machinery
Environmental Related

Financial Services
Real Estate

Additional Information
Year Founded: 1992
Capital Under Management: $3,000,000
Current Activity Level : Actively seeking new investments
Method of Compensation: Return on invest. most important, but chg. closing fees, service fees, etc.

PHILADELPHIA VENTURES, INC.

The Bellevue
200 South Broad Street
Philadelphia, PA 19102
Phone: 215-732-4445
Fax: 215-732-4644

Management and Staff
Charles Burton, Managing Director
David Robkin, Vice President
Karen Griffith Gryga, Managing Director
Maria Hahn, Chief Financial Officer
Thomas Morse, Managing Director

Whom to Contact
Walter Aikman

Type of Firm
Private Firm Investing Own Capital

Industry Association Membership
National Venture Capital Association (NVCA)

Project Preferences

Role in Financing:
Prefer role as deal originator but will also invest in deals created by others

Type of Financing Preferred:
First Stage Financing
Leveraged Buyout
Mezzanine
Second Stage Financing
Start-up Financing

Geographical Preferences

United States
All U.S.

Industry Preferences

(% based on actual investment)

Communications and Media	18.9%
Computer Software and Services	18.5%
Medical/Health	15.9%
Biotechnology	12.1%
Industrial/Energy	8.4%
Computer Hardware	8.1%
Internet Specific	7.1%
Semiconductors/Other Elect.	7.0%
Other Products	3.6%
Consumer Related	0.4%

Additional Information
Name of Most Recent Fund: Philadelphia Ventures III
Most Recent Fund Was Raised: 01/01/1996
Year Founded: 1983
Capital Under Management: $123,000,000
Current Activity Level : Actively seeking new investments
Method of Compensation: Return on investment is of primary concern, do not charge fees

POINT VENTURE PARTNERS

The Century Building
130 Seventh Street, 7th Floor
Pittsburgh, PA 15222
Phone: 412-261-1966
Fax: 412-261-1718

Other Offices

2970 USX Tower
600 Grant St
Pittsburgh, PA

Management and Staff
Kent Engelmeier

Whom to Contact
Kent Engelmeier

Type of Firm
Mgt. Consulting Firm

Project Preferences

Role in Financing:
Prefer role as deal originator but will also invest in deals created by others

Type of Financing Preferred:
First Stage Financing
Leveraged Buyout
Mezzanine
Recapitalizations
Second Stage Financing
Start-up Financing

Size of Investments Considered
Min Size of Investment Considered (000s): $2,000
Max Size of Investment Considered: No Limit

Geographical Preferences

United States
Mid Atlantic
Midwest
Northeast
Southeast

Industry Preferences

Communications and Media
Commercial Communications
Telecommunications
Data Communications

Computer Hardware
Mini and Personal/Desktop
Computer Graphics and Dig
Integrated Turnkey System
Disk Relat. Memory Device

Computer Software
Computer Services
Systems Software
Applications Software
Artificial Intelligence

Semiconductors/Other Elect.
Electronic Components

Biotechnology
Biotechnology

Medical/Health
Medical/Health

Consumer Related
Entertainment and Leisure
Retail
Food/Beverage
Consumer Products
Consumer Services
Education Related

Industrial/Energy
Alternative Energy
Coal Related
Energy Conservation Relat
Industrial Products

Transportation
Transportation

Financial Services
Financial Services

Business Serv.
Distribution

Manufact.
Office Automation Equipmt

Additional Information
Year Founded: 1989
Capital Under Management: $19,300,000
Current Activity Level : Actively seeking new investments
Method of Compensation: Return on investment is of primary concern, do not charge fees

PROVCO GROUP, THE

Two Radnor Station
290 King of Prussia Rd Ste 314
Radnor, PA 19087
Phone: 610-964-1642
Fax: 610-964-1647

Type of Firm
Private Firm Investing Own Capital

Project Preferences

Role in Financing:
Prefer role as deal originator but will also invest in deals created by others

Type of Financing Preferred:
First Stage Financing
Second Stage Financing

Size of Investments Considered
Min Size of Investment Considered (000s): $500
Max Size of Investment Considered: No Limit

Geographical Preferences

United States
Northeast

International
United Kingdom

Industry Preferences

Communications and Media
Telecommunications

Semiconductors/Other Elect.
Fiber Optics

Biotechnology
Biotech Related Research

Medical/Health
Medical Therapeutics
Drug/Equipmt Delivery
Medical Products
Pharmaceuticals

Consumer Related
Retail
Other Restaurants

Financial Services
Real Estate

Additional Information
Capital Under Management: $100,000,000
Current Activity Level : Actively seeking new investments
Method of Compensation: Return on investment is of primary concern, do not charge fees

RAF VENTURES

165 Township Line Road
Suite 2100
Jenkintown, PA 19046
Phone: 215-572-0738
Fax: 215-576-1640
Website: www.rafind.com

Management and Staff
James Coane, Managing Director

Type of Firm
Private Firm Investing Own Capital

Project Preferences

Role in Financing:
Prefer role as deal originator

Type of Financing Preferred:
First Stage Financing
Leveraged Buyout
Second Stage Financing
Seed
Start-up Financing

Size of Investments Considered
Min Size of Investment Considered (000s): $37,000
Max Size of Investment Considered: No Limit

Geographical Preferences

United States
Northeast

Industry Preferences

(% based on actual investment)

Internet Specific	91.0%
Computer Hardware	5.5%
Medical/Health	2.3%
Computer Software and Services	1.3%

Additional Information
Year Founded: 1979
Current Activity Level : Actively seeking new investments
Method of Compensation: Return on investment is of primary concern, do not charge fees

REDLEAF VENTURE MANAGEMENT

100 First Avenue
Suite 950
Pittsburgh, PA 15222
Phone: 412-201-5600
Fax: 412-201-5650
Website: www.redleaf.com

See California for full listing.

ROCK HILL VENTURES INC.(FKA:HILLMAN MEDICAL VENTURES,INC.)

100 Front Street
Suite 1350
West Conshohocken, PA 19428
Phone: 610-940-0300
Fax: 610-940-0301
Website: chuck@rockhillventures.com

Type of Firm
Private Firm Investing Own Capital

Project Preferences

Role in Financing:
Prefer role as deal originator but will also invest in deals created by others

Type of Financing Preferred:
First Stage Financing
Leveraged Buyout
Recapitalizations
Research and Development
Second Stage Financing
Seed
Start-up Financing

Size of Investments Considered
Min Size of Investment Considered (000s): $1,000
Max Size of Investment Considered (000s): $2,000

Geographical Preferences

United States
Mid Atlantic
Northeast
Southeast

Industry Preferences

(% based on actual investment)

Medical/Health	91.3%
Biotechnology	8.7%

Additional Information
Name of Most Recent Fund: Hillman Medical Ventures
Most Recent Fund Was Raised: 01/01/1996
Year Founded: 1996
Capital Under Management: $9,600,000
Current Activity Level : Actively seeking new investments
Method of Compensation: Return on investment is of primary concern, do not charge fees

RRZ CAPITAL

625 Liberty Ave
Pittsburgh, PA 15222
Phone: 412-562-1000
Fax: 412-562-0222

Type of Firm
Private Firm Investing Own Capital

Additional Information
Name of Most Recent Fund: RRZ Private Equity Fund, L.P.
Most Recent Fund Was Raised: 01/01/1995
Year Founded: 1995
Capital Under Management: $20,000,000
Current Activity Level : Actively seeking new investments

S.R. ONE, LIMITED

Four Tower Bridge
200 Barr Harbor Drive Ste 250
West Conshohocken, PA 19428
Phone: 610-567-1000
Fax: 610-567-1039

Management and Staff
Barbara Dalton, Vice President
Brenda Gavin, President
John Braca, Chief Financial Officer
Raymond Whitaker, Vice President

Whom to Contact
Any of above

Type of Firm
Non-Financial Corp. Affiliate or Subsidiary

Industry Association Membership
National Venture Capital Association (NVCA)

Project Preferences

Role in Financing:
Prefer role as deal originator but will also invest in deals created by others

Type of Financing Preferred:
Early Stage
First Stage Financing
Later Stage
Second Stage Financing
Startup

Size of Investments Considered
Min Size of Investment Considered (000s): $500
Max Size of Investment Considered (000s): $5,000

Geographical Preferences

International
No Preference

Industry Preferences

(% based on actual investment)

Biotechnology	55.4%
Medical/Health	27.2%
Computer Software and Services	13.2%
Internet Specific	3.4%
Other Products	0.8%

Additional Information
Name of Most Recent Fund: Evergreen Fund
Most Recent Fund Was Raised: 01/01/1996
Year Founded: 1985
Capital Under Management: $100,000,000
Current Activity Level : Actively seeking new investments
Method of Compensation: Return on investment is of primary concern, do not charge fees

SANDHURST VENTURE FUND, L.P., THE

351 East Conestoga Road
Wayne, PA 19087
Phone: 610-254-8900
Fax: 610-254-8958

Other Offices

351 East Conestoga Road
Wayne, PA 19087
Phone: 610-254-8900

Type of Firm
Private Firm Investing Own Capital

Project Preferences

Role in Financing:
Prefer role as deal originator but will also invest in deals created by others

Type of Financing Preferred:
Leveraged Buyout
Recapitalizations
Second Stage Financing

Size of Investments Considered
Min Size of Investment Considered (000s): $500
Max Size of Investment Considered (000s): $1,000

Geographical Preferences

United States
Mid Atlantic

Industry Preferences

Semiconductors/Other Elect.
Sensors

Medical/Health
Disposable Med. Products

Consumer Related
Computer Stores

Industrial/Energy
Factory Automation

Additional Information
Year Founded: 1987
Capital Under Management: $8,000,000
Current Activity Level : Actively seeking new investments
Method of Compensation: Return on investment is of primary concern, do not charge fees

SCHOFFSTALL VENTURES

5790 Devnonshire Road
Harrisburg, PA 17112
Phone: 717-671-3208
Website: www.schoffstallventures.com

Management and Staff
Dennis Fingers, Vice President
Martin Schoffstall, General Partner
Marvin Schoffstall, General Partner

Type of Firm
Private Firm Investing Own Capital

Industry Association Membership
Mid-Atlantic Venture Association

Project Preferences

Type of Financing Preferred:
Early Stage
Expansion

Geographical Preferences

United States
All U.S.

Industry Preferences

Communications and Media
Communications and Media

Internet Specific
Internet

Additional Information
Year Founded: 2000
Current Activity Level : Actively seeking new investments

SEAPORT CAPITAL

1235 Westlakes Drive
Suite 140
Berwyn, PA 19312
Phone: 215-251-0650
Fax: 215-251-9180
Website: www.seaportcapital.com

See New York for full listing.

STONEBRIDGE PARTNERS

P.O. Box 512
Washington, PA 15301
Phone: 412-223-0707
Website: www.stonebridgepartners.com

See New York for full listing.

SUSTAINABLE JOBS FUND (SJF), THE

620 Chestnut Street
Suite 560
Philadelphia, PA 19106
Phone: 215-923-8870
Fax: 215-923-8871
Website: www.sjfund.com

See North Carolina for full listing.

TA ASSOCIATES, INC.

One Oxford Center
Suite 4260
Pittsburgh, PA 15219-1407
Phone: 412-441-4949
Fax: 412-441-5784
Website: www.ta.com

See Massachusetts for full listing.

TDH

919 Conestoga Road
Building One, Suite 301
Rosemont, PA 19010
Phone: 610-526-9970
Fax: 610-526-9971

Other Offices

Hampden Square
4800 Montgomery Lane
Bethesda, MD 20814
Phone: 301-718-7353
Fax: 301-913-9615

Management and Staff
J.B. Doherty
James M. Buck III
Stephen Harris

Whom to Contact
J.B. Doherty
James M. Buck III
Stephen Harris

Type of Firm
Private Firm Investing Own Capital

Project Preferences

Role in Financing:
Prefer role as deal originator but will also invest in deals created by others

Type of Financing Preferred:
First Stage Financing
Leveraged Buyout
Mezzanine
Recapitalizations
Second Stage Financing
Start-up Financing

Size of Investments Considered
Min Size of Investment Considered (000s): $1,500
Max Size of Investment Considered: No Limit

Geographical Preferences

United States
Mid Atlantic
Midwest
Northeast
Southeast

Industry Preferences

Communications and Media
Communications and Media

Computer Hardware
Integrated Turnkey System

Computer Software
Computer Services
Systems Software

Semiconductors/Other Elect.
Electronic Components

Biotechnology
Industrial Biotechnology

Medical/Health
Medical/Health
Medical Diagnostics
Medical Therapeutics

Consumer Related
Retail
Computer Stores
Food/Beverage
Consumer Products
Education Related

Industrial/Energy
Industrial Products

Transportation
Transportation

Financial Services
Financial Services

Business Serv.
Distribution

Manufact.
Office Automation Equipmt
Publishing

Additional Information
Name of Most Recent Fund: TDH III, L.P.
Most Recent Fund Was Raised: 09/01/1993
Year Founded: 1971
Capital Under Management: $70,000,000
Current Activity Level : Actively seeking new investments
Method of Compensation: Return on investment is of primary concern, do not charge fees

---

TDH CAPITAL

259 Radnor-Chester Road
Suite 200
Radnor, PA 19087
Phone: 610-293-9787
Fax: 610-971-2154

Type of Firm
Private Firm Investing Own Capital

Additional Information
Name of Most Recent Fund: TDH II
Most Recent Fund Was Raised: 10/01/1983
Year Founded: 1971
Current Activity Level : Inactive / Unknown

TL VENTURES

435 Devon Park Drive
700 Building
Wayne, PA 19087-1990
Phone: 610-975-3765
Fax: 610-254-4210
Website: www.tlventures.com

Other Offices

15305 Dallas Parkway
Suite 300 Colonnade III
Addison, TX 75001
Phone: 310-914-0783
Fax: 602-922-0787

600 Congress Avenue
Suite 1700
Austin, TX 78701
Phone: 512-391-2850
Fax: 512-391-2875

The Annex Building
3110 Main Street
Santa Monica, CA 90405
Phone: 310-450-1800
Fax: 310-450-1806

Management and Staff
Adam Green, Principal
Andrew Morozov, Principal
Carolyn Harkins, Principal
Christopher Moller, Managing Director
Dev Kantesaria, Principal
Doug Petillo, Principal
Gary Anderson, Managing Director
Guy Hoffman, Partner
John Boyd, Principal
M. Ira Lubert, Managing Director
Mark DeNino, Managing Director
Massoud Entekhabi, Managing Director
Michael Barker, Venture Partner
Neil Malik, Principal
Peter Norwood, Venture Partner
Robert Repass, Partner
Robert Fabbio, General Partner
Robert Adams, Venture Partner
Robert Keith, Managing Director
Robert Verratti, Managing Director
Skip Maner, Vice President
Stanley Tims, Managing Director
Stephen Andriole, Principal
Steve Yeich, Partner
Sujit Banerjee, Principal
Sydney Edwards, Principal
Tami Frans, Vice President
Valerie Brown, Principal

Whom to Contact
Pam Strisofsky
Stan Tims

Type of Firm
Private Firm Investing Own Capital

Project Preferences

Role in Financing:
Prefer role as deal originator but will also invest in deals created by others

Type of Financing Preferred:
Early Stage
Seed

Size of Investments Considered
Min Size of Investment Considered (000s): $2,000
Max Size of Investment Considered: No Limit

Geographical Preferences

United States
Massachusetts
Mid Atlantic
Northeast
Southwest
All U.S.
Virginia
West Coast

Industry Preferences

(% based on actual investment)

Internet Specific	32.9%
Computer Software and Services	32.4%
Communications and Media	11.0%
Other Products	7.8%
Medical/Health	5.5%
Biotechnology	5.0%
Semiconductors/Other Elect.	2.5%
Computer Hardware	2.0%
Consumer Related	0.9%

Additional Information
Name of Most Recent Fund: TL Ventures IV, L .P.
Most Recent Fund Was Raised: 04/08/1999
Year Founded: 1988
Capital Under Management: $1,436,800,000
Current Activity Level : Actively seeking new investments
Method of Compensation: Return on investment is of primary concern, do not charge fees

YABLON ENTERPRISES, INC.

720 South Second Street
P.O. Box 7475
Steelton, PA 17113-7475
Phone: 717-939-4545
Fax: 717-939-4545

Management and Staff
Leonard F. Yablon, J.D.

Whom to Contact
Leonard F. Yablon, J.D.

Type of Firm
Mgt. Consulting Firm

Project Preferences

Role in Financing:
Prefer role as deal originator but will also invest in deals created by others

Type of Financing Preferred:
Leveraged Buyout
Second Stage Financing
Special Situation

Size of Investments Considered
Min Size of Investment Considered (000s): $1,000
Max Size of Investment Considered: No Limit

Geographical Preferences

Canada
All Canada

International
Australia
Eastern Europe
Italy
Mexico
South Africa

Industry Preferences

Consumer Related
Hotels and Resorts

Financial Services
Financial Services
Real Estate

Additional Information
Year Founded: 1971
Capital Under Management: $7,500,000
Current Activity Level : Actively seeking new investments
Method of Compensation: Function primarily in service area, receive contingent fee in cash or equity

RHODE ISLAND

CARIAD CAPITAL, INC.

One Turks Head Place
Suite 1550
Providence, RI 02903-2215
Phone: 401-751-8111
Fax: 401-751-8222
Website: www.cariadcapital.com

Management and Staff
Roger Vandenberg

Whom to Contact
Roger Vandenberg

Type of Firm
Private Firm Investing Own Capital

Project Preferences

Role in Financing:
Prefer role as deal originator

Type of Financing Preferred:
Control-block Purchases
Leveraged Buyout
Recapitalizations

Size of Investments Considered
Min Size of Investment Considered (000s): $2,000
Max Size of Investment Considered (000s): $10,000

Geographical Preferences

United States
Mid Atlantic
Midwest
Northeast
Southeast

Industry Preferences

Semiconductors/Other Elect.
Sensors

Industrial/Energy
Industrial Products
Materials
Factory Automation
Machinery
Environmental Related

Additional Information
Name of Most Recent Fund: Cariad Capital, Inc.
Most Recent Fund Was Raised: 01/01/1993
Year Founded: 1992
Current Activity Level : Actively seeking new investments
Method of Compensation: Return on invest. most important, but chg. closing fees, service fees, etc.

MANCHESTER HUMPHREYS, INC.

40 Westminster Street
Suite 900
Providence, RI 02903
Phone: 401-454-0400
Fax: 401-454-0403

Management and Staff
Raymond Desrocher, Vice President
Robert Manchester, President

Whom to Contact
James Rudgers

Type of Firm
Private Firm Investing Own Capital

Industry Association Membership
Natl assoc of Small Bus. Inv. Co (NASBIC)

Project Preferences

Role in Financing:
Prefer role as deal originator but will also invest in deals created by others

Type of Financing Preferred:
Leveraged Buyout
Management Buyouts

Size of Investments Considered
Min Size of Investment Considered (000s): $500
Max Size of Investment Considered: No Limit

Geographical Preferences

United States
Mid Atlantic
Midwest
Northeast
Southeast
Southwest

Industry Preferences

Computer Hardware
Computer Graphics and Dig

Computer Software
Systems Software
Applications Software

Internet Specific
Internet

Semiconductors/Other Elect.
Electronic Components
Controllers and Sensors
Sensors
Circuit Boards
Component Testing Equipmt
Laser Related
Fiber Optics
Analytic/Scientific

Medical/Health
Diagnostic Test Products
Drug/Equipmt Delivery
Other Therapeutic
Disposable Med. Products

Consumer Related
Food/Beverage

Industrial/Energy
Industrial Products
Materials
Factory Automation
Process Control
Robotics
Machinery

Business Serv.
Distribution

Manufact.
Manufacturing
Office Automation Equipmt

Additional Information
Name of Most Recent Fund: Manchester Humphreys Equity Partners
Most Recent Fund Was Raised: 01/01/1998
Year Founded: 1992
Capital Under Management: $250,000,000
Current Activity Level : Actively seeking new investments
Method of Compensation: Return on investment is of primary concern, do not charge fees

NAVIS PARTNERS (FKA:FLEET EQUITY PARTNERS)

50 Kennedy Plaza
12th Floor
Providence, RI 02903
Phone: 401-278-6770
Fax: 401-278-6387
Website: www.navispartners.com

Other Offices

111 Westminster Street
Providence, RI 02903
Phone: 401-278-6770

1740 Massachusetts Avenue
Boxborough, MA 01719
Phone: 508-263-0177

Management and Staff

Bernard Buonanno, Managing Director
Brad Wightman, Vice President
Christopher Crosby, Vice President
Cynthia Balasco, Chief Financial Officer
Cynthia Halasen, Chief Financial Officer
Demetriouse Russell, Vice President
Donald Bates, Partner
Donald Barez, Partner
Glenn Dixon, Partner
Gregory Barr, Managing Director
Habib Gorgi, Managing Director
Michael Gorman, Managing Director
Michael Joe, Managing Director
Riordon Smith, Managing Director
Robert Van Degna, Managing Director
Scott Hilinski, Managing Director
Ted Mocarski, Managing Director

Whom to Contact

Rory B. Smith

Type of Firm

Commercial Bank Affiliate or Subsidiary

Industry Association Membership

National Venture Capital Association (NVCA)
Natl assoc of Small Bus. Inv. Co (NASBIC)

Project Preferences

Role in Financing:

Will function either as deal originator or investor in deals created by others

Type of Financing Preferred:

Acquisition
Early Stage
Expansion
Later Stage
Leveraged Buyout
Management Buyouts
Recapitalizations
Second Stage Financing

Size of Investments Considered

Min Size of Investment Considered (000s): $20,000
Max Size of Investment Considered (000s): $75,000

Geographical Preferences

United States

All U.S.

Canada

All Canada

International

Belgium
France
Germany
Italy
Luxembourg
Netherlands
Spain
United Kingdom

Industry Preferences

(% based on actual investment)

Communications and Media	43.2%
Internet Specific	23.6%
Consumer Related	9.4%
Medical/Health	8.4%
Other Products	3.9%
Industrial/Energy	3.9%
Semiconductors/Other Elect.	3.4%
Computer Software and Services	2.1%
Biotechnology	1.2%
Computer Hardware	1.1%

Additional Information

Name of Most Recent Fund: Chisholm Fund Partners
Most Recent Fund Was Raised: 11/01/1998
Year Founded: 1986
Capital Under Management: $1,200,000,000
Current Activity Level : Actively seeking new investments
Method of Compensation: Return on invest. most important, but chg. closing fees, service fees, etc.

PROVIDENCE EQUITY PARTNERS, INC.(FKA: PROVIDENCE VENTURES)

50 Kennedy Plaza
Providence, RI 02903
Phone: 401-751-1700
Fax: 401-751-1790
Website: www.provequity.com

Other Offices

78 Brook Street
1st Floor
London, United Kingdom W1Y 1YD
Phone: 44 207 514 8800
Fax: 44 207 629 2778

Management and Staff

Al Dobron, Vice President
Alexander Evans, Principal
Anne Farlow, Principal
Carolyn Katz, Principal
Glenn Creamer, Managing Director
John Hahn, Managing Director
Jonathan Nelson, President
Julie Fisher, Vice President
Malcolm Stewart, Vice President
Mark Masiello, Managing Director
Mark Pelson, Managing Director
Michael Dominguez, Vice President
Michael Angelakis, Managing Director
Paul Salem, Managing Director
Raymond Mathieu, Chief Financial Officer

Whom to Contact

Albert J. Dobron
Michael J. Dominguez
Michael J. Patton
Roy N. Merritt

Type of Firm

Private Firm Investing Own Capital

Project Preferences

Role in Financing:

Prefer role as deal originator

Type of Financing Preferred:

Generalist PE
Leveraged Buyout

Size of Investments Considered

Min Size of Investment Considered (000s): $5,000
Max Size of Investment Considered (000s): $300,000

Geographical Preferences

United States
All U.S.

Canada
All Canada

International
Bermuda
Eastern Europe
France
Germany
India
Italy
South Africa
Spain
United Kingdom
No Preference

Industry Preferences

(% based on actual investment)

Communications and Media	42.3%
Internet Specific	27.1%
Semiconductors/Other Elect.	13.3%
Other Products	12.5%
Computer Software and Services	2.4%
Consumer Related	1.4%
Computer Hardware	1.0%

Additional Information
Name of Most Recent Fund: Providence Media Partners, L.P,
Most Recent Fund Was Raised: 01/01/1994
Year Founded: 1991
Capital Under Management: $4,600,000,000
Current Activity Level : Actively seeking new investments

ZERO STAGE CAPITAL CO., INC.

40 Westminster Street
Suite 702
Providence, RI 02903
Phone: 401-351-3036
Fax: 401-351-3056
Website: www.zerostage.com

See Massachusetts for full listing.

SOUTH CAROLINA

CAPITAL INSIGHTS, L.L.C.

P.O. Box 27162
Greenville, SC 27162-2162
Phone: 864-242-6832
Fax: 864-242-6755
Website: www.capitalinsights.com

Management and Staff
Charles Duke, Vice President
John Warner, President

Type of Firm
Private Firm Investing Own Capital

Project Preferences

Role in Financing:
Prefer role as deal originator but will also invest in deals created by others

Type of Financing Preferred:
First Stage Financing
Second Stage Financing

Geographical Preferences

United States
Southeast

Industry Preferences

(% based on actual investment)

Communications and Media	58.2%
Other Products	25.7%
Consumer Related	10.5%
Industrial/Energy	5.6%

Additional Information
Name of Most Recent Fund: Capital Insights Growth Investors
Most Recent Fund Was Raised: 10/01/1995
Year Founded: 1992
Capital Under Management: $14,000,000
Current Activity Level : Actively seeking new investments
Method of Compensation: Return on invest. most important, but chg. closing fees, service fees, etc.

PALMETTO SEED CAPITAL CORP.

7 N. Laurens St.
Suite 603
Greenville, SC 29601
Phone: 864-232-6198
Fax: 864-241-4444

Other Offices

PO Box 17526
Greenville, SC

Type of Firm
Private Firm Investing Own Capital

Industry Association Membership
Natl assoc of Small Bus. Inv. Co (NASBIC)

Project Preferences

Role in Financing:
Prefer role as deal originator

Type of Financing Preferred:
First Stage Financing
Research and Development
Seed
Start-up Financing

Size of Investments Considered
Min Size of Investment Considered (000s): $1,000
Max Size of Investment Considered: No Limit

Geographical Preferences

International
No Preference

Additional Information
Name of Most Recent Fund: Palmetto Seed Capital Corp.
Most Recent Fund Was Raised: 11/01/1989
Year Founded: 1989
Capital Under Management: $20,000,000
Current Activity Level : Actively seeking new investments
Method of Compensation: Return on investment is of primary concern, do not charge fees

TRANSAMERICA MEZZANINE FINANCING

Seven North Laurens Street
Suite 603
Greenville, SC 29601
Phone: 864-232-6198
Fax: 864-241-4444

Management and Staff
Capers Easterby, President
Edward Stein, Vice President
Roger Brook, Vice President
William Litchfield, Vice President

Whom to Contact
J. Phillip Falls
Roger Brook

Type of Firm
Private Firm Investing Own Capital

Project Preferences

Role in Financing:
Prefer role as deal originator but will also invest in deals created by others

Type of Financing Preferred:
First Stage Financing
Mezzanine
Second Stage Financing
Seed
Start-up Financing

Geographical Preferences

United States
Southeast

Industry Preferences

Communications and Media
Communications and Media

Computer Software
Computer Services
Applications Software

Semiconductors/Other Elect.
Controllers and Sensors
Laser Related
Fiber Optics

Medical/Health
Hospital/Other Instit.

Industrial/Energy
Industrial Products

Additional Information
Year Founded: 1981
Capital Under Management: $55,000,000
Current Activity Level : Actively seeking new investments
Method of Compensation: Return on invest. most important, but chg. closing fees, service fees, etc.

SOUTH DAKOTA

BLUESTEM CAPITAL PARTNERS

122 South Phillips Avenue
Suite 300
Sioux Falls, SD 57104-6706
Phone: 605-331-0091
Fax: 605-334-1218
Website: www.bluestemcapital.com

Management and Staff
Sandy Horst, Chief Financial Officer

Type of Firm
Private Firm Investing Own Capital

Industry Association Membership
Natl assoc of Small Bus. Inv. Co (NASBIC)

Industry Preferences

(% based on actual investment)

Internet Specific	30.0%
Consumer Related	22.1%
Computer Software and Services	20.1%
Communications and Media	16.0%
Other Products	6.9%
Industrial/Energy	3.3%
Medical/Health	1.7%

Additional Information
Name of Most Recent Fund: Bluestem Capital Partners I, LLC
Most Recent Fund Was Raised: 12/31/1996
Year Founded: 1991
Capital Under Management: $76,000,000
Current Activity Level : Actively seeking new investments

TENNESSEE

2ND GENERATION CAPITAL CORP

618 Church Street
Nashville, TN 37219
Phone: 615-846-7650
Fax: 615-782-4225
Website: www.2ndgeneration.com

Other Offices

P.O. Box 1111
Murray, KY 42071
Phone: 270-832-5550
Fax: 615-846-7654

Management and Staff

Michael Collins, President
Thomas Roady, Principal

Type of Firm

Investment/Merchant Bank Investing Own or Client Funds

Project Preferences

Role in Financing:
Prefer role as deal originator but will also invest in deals created by others

Type of Financing Preferred:
First Stage Financing
Industry Rollups
Leveraged Buyout
Research and Development
Second Stage Financing
Seed

Size of Investments Considered

Min Size of Investment Considered (000s): $1,000
Max Size of Investment Considered: No Limit

Geographical Preferences

United States
Southeast

Industry Preferences

Biotechnology
Biotech Related Research

Medical/Health
Medical Diagnostics
Diagnostic Services
Diagnostic Test Products
Medical Therapeutics
Drug/Equipmt Delivery
Other Therapeutic
Disposable Med. Products
Pharmaceuticals

Consumer Related
Consumer Products

Industrial/Energy
Industrial Products
Machinery

Financial Services
Financial Services

Manufact.
Publishing

Additional Information

Year Founded: 1994
Current Activity Level : Actively seeking new investments
Method of Compensation: Return on invest. most important, but chg. closing fees, service fees, etc.

CAPITAL ACROSS AMERICA, L.P.

501 Union Street
Suite 201
Nashville, TN 37219
Phone: 615-254-1414
Fax: 615-254-1856
Website: www.capitalacrossamerica.com

Management and Staff

Chris Brown, President
Whitney Johns, Chief Executive Officer

Type of Firm

Private Firm Investing Own Capital

Industry Association Membership

Natl assoc of Small Bus. Inv. Co (NASBIC)

Project Preferences

Type of Financing Preferred:
Balanced

Geographical Preferences

United States
All U.S.
Mid Atlantic
Midwest
Southeast

Industry Preferences

Other
Women/Minority-Owned Bus.

Additional Information

Current Activity Level : Actively seeking new investments

CAPITAL SERVICES & RESOURCES, INC.

5159 Wheelis Drive
Suite 106
Memphis, TN 38117
Phone: 901-761-2156
Fax: 901-767-0060

Management and Staff

Charles Bancroft

Whom to Contact

Charles Bancroft

Type of Firm

Investment/Merchant Bank Investing Own or Client Funds

Industry Association Membership

Natl assoc of Small Bus. Inv. Co (NASBIC)

Project Preferences

Role in Financing:
Prefer role as deal originator but will also invest in deals created by others

Type of Financing Preferred:
Leveraged Buyout
Second Stage Financing
Special Situation

Size of Investments Considered

Min Size of Investment Considered (000s): $300
Max Size of Investment Considered: No Limit

Geographical Preferences

United States
All U.S.

Canada
All Canada

International
Germany
South Africa
United Kingdom

Industry Preferences

Communications and Media
Communications and Media
Other Communication Prod.

Computer Other
Computer Related

Semiconductors/Other Elect.
Electronics
Controllers and Sensors
Component Testing Equipmt
Laser Related
Analytic/Scientific

Biotechnology
Biotech Related Research

Medical/Health
Diagnostic Test Products
Medical Products
Hospitals/Clinics/Primary

Consumer Related
Franchises(NEC)
Food/Beverage
Hotels and Resorts

Industrial/Energy
Alternative Energy
Energy Conservation Relat
Industrial Products
Robotics
Machinery
Environmental Related

Transportation
Transportation

Manufact.
Publishing

Agr/Forestr/Fish
Agriculture related

Additional Information
Year Founded: 1977
Current Activity Level : Actively seeking new investments
Method of Compensation: Return on invest. most important, but chg. closing fees, service fees, etc.

CHANCELLOR FUND

Vanderbilt University
3401 West End Ave, Suite 500
Nashville, TN 37203
Phone: 615-250-1655
Fax: 615-250-1677
Website: www.vanderbilt.edu

Type of Firm
University Affiliated Program

Industry Association Membership
National Venture Capital Association (NVCA)

Additional Information
Current Activity Level : Actively seeking new investments

COLEMAN SWENSON BOOTH INC.(FKA:COLEMAN SWENSON HOFFMAN BOOTH

237 Second Avenue South
Franklin, TN 37064-2649
Phone: 615-791-9462
Fax: 615-791-9636
Website: www.colemanswenson.com

Management and Staff
Cornelia Holland, Chief Financial Officer
James Hoffman, General Partner
John Booth, General Partner
Larry Coleman, Managing General Partner
W.David Swenson, General Partner

Whom to Contact
W. David Swenson

Type of Firm
Private Firm Investing Own Capital

Project Preferences

Role in Financing:
Prefer role as deal originator but will also invest in deals created by others

Type of Financing Preferred:
First Stage Financing
Mezzanine
Second Stage Financing
Seed
Special Situation
Start-up Financing

Size of Investments Considered
Min Size of Investment Considered (000s): $1,000
Max Size of Investment Considered (000s): $7,000

Geographical Preferences

United States
All U.S.

Industry Preferences

(% based on actual investment)

Medical/Health	63.1%
Internet Specific	19.3%
Computer Software and Services	10.7%
Consumer Related	3.7%
Biotechnology	1.8%
Other Products	1.4%

Additional Information
Name of Most Recent Fund: Coleman Swenson Hoffman Booth IV L.P.
Most Recent Fund Was Raised: 04/01/1998
Year Founded: 1986
Capital Under Management: $188,400,000
Current Activity Level : Actively seeking new investments
Method of Compensation: Return on investment is of primary concern, do not charge fees

EQUITAS, L.P.

2000 Glen Echo Road
Suite 100 P.O. Box 158838
Nashville, TN 37215-8838
Phone: 615-383-8673
Fax: 615-383-8693

Management and Staff
Bill Nutter, Principal
D. Shannon LeRoy, President

Type of Firm
Private Firm Investing Own Capital

Project Preferences

Role in Financing:
Prefer role as deal originator but will also invest in deals created by others

Type of Financing Preferred:
Leveraged Buyout
Mezzanine
Recapitalizations
Second Stage Financing
Special Situation

Geographical Preferences

United States
Midwest
Southeast

Industry Preferences

Communications and Media
CATV & Pay TV Systems
Telecommunications
Satellite Microwave Comm.

Medical/Health
Diagnostic Services
Medical Products
Hospitals/Clinics/Primary
Hospital/Other Instit.

Consumer Related
Franchises(NEC)
Food/Beverage
Consumer Products
Other Restaurants
Education Related

Industrial/Energy
Industrial Products
Factory Automation
Machinery

Additional Information

Name of Most Recent Fund: Equitas, L.P.
Most Recent Fund Was Raised: 01/01/1997
Year Founded: 1992
Capital Under Management: $11,500,000
Current Activity Level : Actively seeking new investments
Method of Compensation: Return on invest. most important, but chg. closing fees, service fees, etc.

FINOVA MEZZANINE CAPITAL, INC. (FKA: SIRROM CAPITAL CORP)

500 Church Street
Suite 200
Nashville, TN 37203
Phone: 615-329-9448
Fax: 615-329-2937
Website: www.finova.com

Other Offices

2 Embarcadero Center
Suite 650
San Francisco, CA 94111
Phone: 415-782-7777
Fax: 415-782-7778

500 Church Street
Suite 200
Nashville, TN 37219
Phone: 615-256-0701
Fax: 615-726-1208

Management and Staff

Kathy Harris

Whom to Contact

Kathy Harris

Type of Firm

SBIC Not elsewhere classified

Industry Association Membership

Western Association of Venture Capitalists (WAVC)

Project Preferences

Role in Financing:
Prefer role as deal originator

Type of Financing Preferred:
Leveraged Buyout
Mezzanine

Size of Investments Considered
Min Size of Investment Considered (000s): $5,000
Max Size of Investment Considered: No Limit

Geographical Preferences

United States
All U.S.

Canada
Central Canada

International
United Kingdom

Industry Preferences

(% based on actual investment)

Internet Specific	25.9%
Consumer Related	22.5%
Other Products	21.8%
Computer Hardware	10.9%
Medical/Health	9.4%
Communications and Media	6.5%
Industrial/Energy	2.9%

Additional Information

Year Founded: 1992
Capital Under Management: $600,000,000
Current Activity Level : Actively seeking new investments
Method of Compensation: Return on invest. most important, but chg. closing fees, service fees, etc.

FIRST AVENUE PARTNERS

4117 Hillsboro Road
Suite 103254
Nashville, TN 37215
Phone: 615-370-0056
Fax: 615-376-6310

Type of Firm

Private Firm Investing Own Capital

Project Preferences

Size of Investments Considered
Min Size of Investment Considered (000s): $3,000
Max Size of Investment Considered (000s): $4,000

Additional Information

Name of Most Recent Fund: First Avenue Partners
Most Recent Fund Was Raised: 12/31/1998
Year Founded: 1998
Capital Under Management: $39,000,000
Current Activity Level : Actively seeking new investments

MASSEY BURCH CAPITAL CORP.

One Burton Hills Blvd.
Suite 350
Nashville, TN 37215
Phone: 615-665-3221
Fax: 615-665-3240

Other Offices

1000 Park Forty Plaza
Suite 300
Durham, NC 27713
Phone: 919-544-6162
Fax: 919-544-6667

310 25th Ave North
Suite 103
Nashville, TN 37203
Phone: 615-329-9448

Management and Staff

Lucious E. Burch

Whom to Contact

Lucious E. Burch

Type of Firm

Venture Consulting Firm

Project Preferences

Role in Financing:
Prefer role as deal originator

Type of Financing Preferred:
Early Stage
First Stage Financing
Seed
Start-up Financing

Size of Investments Considered

Min Size of Investment Considered (000s): $1,000
Max Size of Investment Considered (000s): $5,000

Geographical Preferences

United States
Southeast

Industry Preferences

(% based on actual investment)

Other Products	29.2%
Medical/Health	17.8%
Internet Specific	10.8%
Communications and Media	9.8%
Biotechnology	6.5%
Industrial/Energy	6.4%
Computer Hardware	5.6%
Consumer Related	5.3%
Computer Software and Services	4.8%
Semiconductors/Other Elect.	3.8%

Additional Information

Name of Most Recent Fund: Southern Venture Fund II
Most Recent Fund Was Raised: 03/01/1994
Year Founded: 1994
Capital Under Management: $126,000,000
Current Activity Level : Actively seeking new investments
Method of Compensation: Return on investment is of primary concern, do not charge fees

NELSON CAPITAL CORP.

3401 West End Avenue
Suite 300
Nashville, TN 37203
Phone: 615-292-8787
Fax: 615-385-3150

Management and Staff

John Harrington, Vice President

Whom to Contact

John Harrington

Type of Firm

Investment/Merchant Bank Investing Own or Client Funds

Project Preferences

Role in Financing:
Prefer role as deal originator but will also invest in deals created by others

Type of Financing Preferred:
First Stage Financing
Leveraged Buyout
Mezzanine
Second Stage Financing

Size of Investments Considered

Min Size of Investment Considered (000s): $500
Max Size of Investment Considered: No Limit

Geographical Preferences

United States
Southeast

Industry Preferences

Communications and Media
Commercial Communications
Data Communications

Computer Other
Computer Related

Medical/Health
Diagnostic Services
Diagnostic Test Products
Drug/Equipmt Delivery
Other Therapeutic
Medical Products
Disposable Med. Products
Hospitals/Clinics/Primary
Hospital/Other Instit.

Consumer Related
Consumer Products
Education Related

Industrial/Energy
Machinery

Financial Services
Financial Services

Manufact.
Publishing

Additional Information

Name of Most Recent Fund: Nelson Capital Corporation
Most Recent Fund Was Raised: 01/01/1979
Year Founded: 1985
Capital Under Management: $25,000,000
Current Activity Level : Actively seeking new investments
Method of Compensation: Return on invest. most important, but chg. closing fees, service fees, etc.

PARADIGM CAPITAL PARTNERS LLC

6410 Poplar Avenue
Suite 395
Memphis, TN 38119
Phone: 901-682-6060
Fax: 901-328-3061
Website: www.paradigmcp.com

Management and Staff

Frank McGrew, Managing Director
Jon Peters, Chief Financial Officer
Robert Blow, Managing Director
William Razzouk, Managing Director

Type of Firm

Private Firm Investing Own Capital

Project Preferences

Role in Financing:
Will function either as deal originator or investor in deals created by others

Type of Financing Preferred:
First Stage Financing
Second Stage Financing
Seed

Size of Investments Considered

Min Size of Investment Considered (000s): $500
Max Size of Investment Considered (000s): $6,000

Geographical Preferences

United States
Southeast

Industry Preferences

Communications and Media
Telecommunications
Wireless Communications
Data Communications

Computer Software
Computer Services
Applications Software

Internet Specific
E-Commerce Technology
Internet
Web Aggregration/Portals

Semiconductors/Other Elect.
Fiber Optics

Consumer Related
Retail

Industrial/Energy
Process Control

Business Serv.
Consulting Services

Manufact.
Manufacturing

Agr/Forestr/Fish
Agriculture related

Additional Information
Year Founded: 1999
Capital Under Management: $25,000,000
Current Activity Level : Actively seeking new investments
Method of Compensation: Return on investment is of primary concern, do not charge fees

PETRA CAPITAL PARTNERS LLC

172 Second Avenue North
Suite 112
Nashville, TN 37201
Phone: 615-313-5999
Fax: 615-313-5990
Website: www.petracapital.com

Management and Staff
Joe O'Brian, General Partner
Mike Blackburn, General Partner
Robert Smith, Vice President

Whom to Contact
Michael Blackburn

Type of Firm
Private Firm Investing Own Capital

Industry Association Membership
Mid-Atlantic Venture Association
National Venture Capital Association (NVCA)
Natl assoc of Small Bus. Inv. Co (NASBIC)

Project Preferences

Role in Financing:
Will function either as deal originator or investor in deals created by others

Type of Financing Preferred:
Expansion
Later Stage
Mezzanine

Size of Investments Considered
Min Size of Investment Considered (000s): $1,000
Max Size of Investment Considered (000s): $4,000

Geographical Preferences

United States
All U.S.

Industry Preferences

(% based on actual investment)

Computer Software and Services	33.7%
Medical/Health	18.8%
Other Products	15.8%
Industrial/Energy	13.8%
Consumer Related	11.9%
Computer Hardware	5.9%

Additional Information
Name of Most Recent Fund: Petra Mezzanine Fund
Most Recent Fund Was Raised: 06/01/1999
Year Founded: 1996
Capital Under Management: $150,000,000
Current Activity Level : Actively seeking new investments
Method of Compensation: Return on invest. most important, but chg. closing fees, service fees, etc.

RICHLAND VENTURES

200 31st Avenue North
Suite 200
Nashville, TN 37203
Phone: 615-383-8030
Fax: 615-269-0463
Website: www.richlandventures.com

Other Offices

3100 West End Ave
Suite 400
Nashville, TN

Management and Staff
Jack Tyrrell, Partner
John Chadwick, Partner
W. Patrick Ortale, Partner

Type of Firm
Private Firm Investing Own Capital

Project Preferences

Role in Financing:
Will function either as deal originator or investor in deals created by others

Type of Financing Preferred:
Expansion
First Stage Financing
Second Stage Financing

Size of Investments Considered
Min Size of Investment Considered (000s): $5,000
Max Size of Investment Considered (000s): $15,000

Geographical Preferences

United States
All U.S.

Industry Preferences

(% based on actual investment)

Medical/Health	27.3%
Internet Specific	24.4%
Other Products	12.4%
Computer Software and Services	12.1%
Communications and Media	10.2%
Consumer Related	5.5%
Computer Hardware	4.4%
Industrial/Energy	2.1%
Biotechnology	0.9%
Semiconductors/Other Elect.	0.7%

Additional Information
Name of Most Recent Fund: Richland Ventures III
Most Recent Fund Was Raised: 10/01/1996
Year Founded: 1994
Capital Under Management: $456,000,000
Current Activity Level : Actively seeking new investments
Method of Compensation: Return on investment is of primary concern, do not charge fees

RIVER ASSOCIATES, LLC

633 Chestnut Street
Suite 1640
Chattanooga, TN 37450
Phone: 423-755-0888
Fax: 423-755-0870
Website: www.riverassociatesllc.com

Management and Staff
Mark Jones, Partner

Whom to Contact
J. Mark Jones

Type of Firm
Private Firm Investing Own Capital

Project Preferences

Role in Financing:
Will function either as deal originator or investor in deals created by others

Type of Financing Preferred:
Acquisition
Generalist PE
Leveraged Buyout
Management Buyouts
Recapitalizations

Size of Investments Considered
Min Size of Investment Considered (000s): $5,000
Max Size of Investment Considered (000s): $50,000

Geographical Preferences

United States
All U.S.

Canada
Ontario

Industry Preferences

Consumer Related
Consumer
Food/Beverage

Industrial/Energy
Industrial Products
Factory Automation
Process Control
Robotics
Machinery

Business Serv.
Distribution

Manufact.
Manufacturing

Additional Information
Name of Most Recent Fund: River III, L.P.
Most Recent Fund Was Raised: 01/01/1996
Year Founded: 1989
Capital Under Management: $64,500,000
Current Activity Level : Actively seeking new investments
Method of Compensation: Return on invest. most important, but chg. closing fees, service fees, etc.

SALIX VENTURES, L.P.

30 Burton Hills Blvd.
Suite 370
Nashville, TN 37215
Phone: 615-665-1409
Fax: 615-665-2912
Website: www.salixventures.com

Other Offices

350 Townsend Street
Suite 405
San Francisco, CA 94107

Management and Staff
Christopher Grant, General Partner
David Ward, General Partner
Mark Donovan, Principal
Martin Felsenthal, General Partner
Robert Ivy, Chief Financial Officer

Type of Firm
Private Firm Investing Own Capital

Industry Association Membership
National Venture Capital Association (NVCA)

Project Preferences

Role in Financing:
Will function either as deal originator or investor in deals created by others

Type of Financing Preferred:
Early Stage

Geographical Preferences

United States
All U.S.

Industry Preferences

(% based on actual investment)

Medical/Health	40.7%
Internet Specific	34.3%
Computer Software and Services	15.3%
Computer Hardware	7.6%
Biotechnology	2.1%

Additional Information
Name of Most Recent Fund: Salix Ventures, L.P.
Most Recent Fund Was Raised: 11/01/1997
Year Founded: 1999
Capital Under Management: $184,500,000
Current Activity Level : Actively seeking new investments
Method of Compensation: Return on investment is of primary concern, do not charge fees

SSM VENTURES

845 Crossover Lane
Suite 140
Memphis, TN 38117
Phone: 901-767-1131
Fax: 901-767-1135
Website: www.ssmventures.com

Other Offices

110 Wild Basin Road
Suite 280
Austin, TX 78746
Phone: 512-437-7900
Fax: 512-437-7925

Management and Staff
Bill Henagan, General Partner
C. Barham Ray, Partner
Dick Moeller, Partner
Eric Jones, Partner
James Witherington, General Partner
Marsha Hefner, Chief Financial Officer
R. Wilson Orr, General Partner
William Harrison, Partner

Whom to Contact
R. Wilson Orr III

Type of Firm
Private Firm Investing Own Capital

Project Preferences

Role in Financing:
Prefer role as deal originator but will also invest in deals created by others

Type of Financing Preferred:
Expansion
Leveraged Buyout
Start-up Financing

Size of Investments Considered
Min Size of Investment Considered (000s): $2,000
Max Size of Investment Considered (000s): $10,000

Geographical Preferences

United States
Southeast
Texas

Industry Preferences

(% based on actual investment)

Internet Specific	34.5%
Computer Software and Services	30.9%
Medical/Health	13.0%
Communications and Media	6.8%
Semiconductors/Other Elect.	6.4%
Computer Hardware	4.2%
Consumer Related	3.9%
Other Products	0.5%

Additional Information

Name of Most Recent Fund: SSM Venture Partners II, L.P.
Most Recent Fund Was Raised: 06/01/1998
Year Founded: 1973
Capital Under Management: $156,500,000
Current Activity Level : Actively seeking new investments
Method of Compensation: Return on investment is of primary concern, do not charge fees

VALLEY CAPITAL CORP.

Suite 212, Krystal Building
Chattanooga, TN 37402
Phone: 423-265-1557
Fax: 423-265-1588

Management and Staff

Lamar Partridge, President

Whom to Contact

Faye Robinson

Industry Association Membership

Natl Assoc of Investment Cos. (NAIC)
Natl assoc of Small Bus. Inv. Co (NASBIC)

Project Preferences

Role in Financing:
Prefer role as deal originator but will also invest in deals created by others

Type of Financing Preferred:
Leveraged Buyout
Mezzanine
Second Stage Financing

Size of Investments Considered

Min Size of Investment Considered (000s): $200
Max Size of Investment Considered: No Limit

Geographical Preferences

United States
Southeast

Industry Preferences

Communications and Media
Communications and Media

Semiconductors/Other Elect.
Electronic Components

Medical/Health
Diagnostic Test Products
Other Therapeutic
Disposable Med. Products

Consumer Related
Consumer

Industrial/Energy
Alternative Energy
Energy Conservation Relat
Materials
Machinery
Environmental Related

Transportation
Transportation

Business Serv.
Distribution

Additional Information

Year Founded: 1982
Capital Under Management: $2,000,000
Current Activity Level : Actively seeking new investments
Method of Compensation: Return on invest. most important, but chg. closing fees, service fees, etc.

VENTURE ASSOCIATES PARTNERS, LLC

355 Sweetbriar Road
Memphis, TN 38120
Phone: 901-763-1434
Fax: 901-763-1428
E-mail: email@venture-associates.com
Website: www.venture-associates.com

Management and Staff

Burton Weil

Whom to Contact

Burton Weil

Type of Firm

Private Firm Investing Own Capital

Project Preferences

Role in Financing:
Prefer role as deal originator

Type of Financing Preferred:
Acquisition
Leveraged Buyout
Turnaround

Size of Investments Considered

Min Size of Investment Considered (000s): $20,000
Max Size of Investment Considered (000s): $200,000

Geographical Preferences

United States
All U.S.

Canada
Central Canada
Quebec

Industry Preferences

Semiconductors/Other Elect.
Circuit Boards

Industrial/Energy
Industrial Products

Transportation
Aerospace

Manufact.
Manufacturing

Additional Information

Year Founded: 1985
Current Activity Level : Actively seeking new investments
Method of Compensation: Return on investment is of primary concern, do not charge fees

TEXAS

ACCENTURE TECHNOLOGY VENTURES (FKA: AC VENTURES)

5215 North O'Connor Blvd
Suite 2100
Irving, TX 75039
Phone: 972-831-4447
Website: www.accenturetechventures.com

See California for full listing.

ACCESS VENTURE PARTNERS

44 East Avenue
Suite 100
Austin, TX 78701
Phone: 512-236-0450
Fax: 512-474-9664
Website: www.accessventurepartners.com

See Colorado for full listing.

ADAMS CAPITAL MANAGEMENT, INC.

107 Ranch Road 620 S
Suite 5B
Austin, TX 78734
Phone: 512-266-1741
Fax: 512-266-2093
Website: www.acm.com

See Pennsylvania for full listing.

AKIN GUMP INVESTMENT PARTNERS 2000, LP

1700 Pacific Avenue
Suite 4100
Dallas, TX 75201
Phone: 214-969-2800
Fax: 214-969-4343
Website: www.akingump.com

Other Offices

590 Madison Avenue
New York, NY 10022
Phone: 212-872-1000
Fax: 212-872-1002

816 Congress Avenue
Suite 1900
Austin, TX 78701
Phone: 512-499-6200
Fax: 512-499-6290

Management and Staff
Craig Comeaux, Partner
Eliot Raffkind, Partner
Mike Tarski, Partner
Terry Schpok, Partner
William Dennis, Partner

Type of Firm
Profit Sharing Fund

Project Preferences

Type of Financing Preferred:
Early Stage

Industry Preferences

Computer Software
Software

Internet Specific
Internet

Biotechnology
Biotechnology

Additional Information
Capital Under Management: $5,000,000
Current Activity Level : Actively seeking new investments

ALIGNMENT CAPITAL PARTNERS, LLC

701 Brazos Street
Suite 500
Austin, TX 78701
Phone: 512-320-9177
Fax: 512-320-7331
Website: www.alignmentcapital.com

Other Offices

10600 North De Anza Blvd.
Suite 250
Cupertino, CA 95014
Phone: 408-873-0500
Fax: 408-873-0550

1667 K. Street, NW
Suite 450
Washington, DC 20006
Phone: 202-857-0850
Fax: 202-857-0869

Management and Staff
Austin Long, Managing Director
Charles Preston, Managing Director
Craig Nickels, Managing Director
James Griffin, Managing Director

Type of Firm
Investment/Merchant Bank Subsid/Affil

Project Preferences

Role in Financing:
Will function either as deal originator or investor in deals created by others

Type of Financing Preferred:
First Stage Financing
Fund of Funds
Second Stage Financing

Size of Investments Considered
Min Size of Investment Considered (000s): $5,000
Max Size of Investment Considered (000s): $20,000

Industry Preferences

Communications and Media
Telecommunications

Computer Software
Software

Medical/Health
Medical/Health

Additional Information
Current Activity Level : Actively seeking new investments

ALLIANCE FINANCIAL OF HOUSTON

218 Heather Lane
Conroe, TX 77385-9013
Phone: 281-447-3300
Fax: 281-447-4222

Type of Firm
MESBIC not elsewhere classified

Industry Association Membership
Natl Assoc of Investment Cos. (NAIC)

Project Preferences

Role in Financing:
Prefer role as deal originator but will also invest in deals created by others

Type of Financing Preferred:
First Stage Financing
Leveraged Buyout
Mezzanine
Second Stage Financing
Special Situation

Size of Investments Considered
Min Size of Investment Considered (000s): $300
Max Size of Investment Considered (000s): $500

Additional Information
Year Founded: 1993
Capital Under Management: $15,000,000
Current Activity Level : Actively seeking new investments
Method of Compensation: Return on invest. most important, but chg. closing fees, service fees, etc.

AMERIMARK CAPITAL GROUP

1111 West Mockingbird
Suite 1111
Dallas, TX 75247
Phone: 214-638-7878
Fax: 214-638-7612
Website: www.amcapital.com

Type of Firm
Mgt. Consulting Firm

Project Preferences

Role in Financing:
Prefer role as deal originator

Type of Financing Preferred:
Leveraged Buyout
Mezzanine
Second Stage Financing

Size of Investments Considered
Min Size of Investment Considered (000s): $500
Max Size of Investment Considered: No Limit

Geographical Preferences

United States
All U.S.

Industry Preferences

Communications and Media
Radio & TV Broadcasting
Telecommunications
Data Communications

Computer Hardware
Integrated Turnkey System

Internet Specific
Internet

Consumer Related
Entertainment and Leisure
Retail
Food/Beverage
Consumer Products
Consumer Services

Industrial/Energy
Materials
Machinery
Environmental Related

Financial Services
Financial Services

Business Serv.
Distribution
Consulting Services

Additional Information
Year Founded: 1989
Capital Under Management: $32,000,000
Current Activity Level : Actively seeking new investments
Method of Compensation: Return on invest. most important, but chg. closing fees, service fees, etc.

AMT CAPITAL LTD. (AKA: AMT VENTURE PARTNERS, LTD.)

5220 Spring Valley Road
Suite 600
Dallas, TX 75240
Phone: 214-905-9757
Fax: 214-905-9761
Website: www.amtcapital.com

Other Offices

350 Pensacola Beach Blvd., Suite 3B
P.O. Box 250
Gulf Breeze, FL 32561
Phone: 850-916-7623
Fax: 850-916-7637

Taylor & Company
1236 Standish Way; P.O. Box 8791
Lexington, KY 40533
Phone: 606-254-9626
Fax: 606- 254-9627

Management and Staff
Peter Walmsley, General Partner
Tom Delimitros, General Partner

Type of Firm
Private Firm Investing Own Capital

Industry Association Membership
Natl assoc of Small Bus. Inv. Co (NASBIC)

Project Preferences

Role in Financing:
Prefer role as deal originator but will also invest in deals created by others

Type of Financing Preferred:
Early Stage
Expansion
First Stage Financing
Second Stage Financing

Size of Investments Considered
Min Size of Investment Considered (000s): $100
Max Size of Investment Considered (000s): $500

Geographical Preferences

United States
All U.S.

Industry Preferences

Semiconductors/Other Elect.
Electronic Components
Analytic/Scientific

Industrial/Energy
Alternative Energy
Materials
Robotics

Additional Information
Name of Most Recent Fund: AMT Associates, Ltd.
Most Recent Fund Was Raised: 01/01/1996
Year Founded: 1989
Capital Under Management: $26,000,000
Current Activity Level : Actively seeking new investments
Method of Compensation: Return on investment is of primary concern, do not charge fees

APPLIED TECHNOLOGY

1001 West Avenue
Austin, TX 78701
Phone: 512-479-8622
Fax: 512-479-5126

See Massachusetts for full listing.

ARCH VENTURE PARTNERS

6801 N. Capital of Texas Highway
Suite 225
Austin, TX 78731
Phone: 512-795-5830
Fax: 512-795-5831
Website: www.archventure.com

See Illinois for full listing.

ARKOMA VENTURE PARTNERS

5950 Berkshire Lane
Suite 1400
Dallas, TX 75225
Phone: 214-739-3515
Fax: 214-739-3572
Website: www.arkomavp.com

Management and Staff
Bob Roth, Managing Partner
Joel Fontenot, Managing Director
Michael McCoy, President

Type of Firm
Private Firm Investing Own Capital

Project Preferences

Role in Financing:
Will function either as deal originator or investor in deals created by others

Type of Financing Preferred:
Early Stage
Expansion
First Stage Financing
Second Stage Financing
Seed
Startup

Size of Investments Considered
Min Size of Investment Considered (000s): $250
Max Size of Investment Considered (000s): $2,500

Geographical Preferences

United States
Southwest

Industry Preferences

Communications and Media
Communications and Media

Computer Hardware
Computers

Semiconductors/Other Elect.
Electronics

Additional Information
Year Founded: 1997
Capital Under Management: $20,000,000
Current Activity Level : Actively seeking new investments
Method of Compensation: Return on investment is of primary concern, do not charge fees

ARTHUR ANDERSEN VENTURES LLC

711 Louisiana
Suite 1300
Houston, TX 77002
Phone: 713-237-5119
Fax: 713-237-2167
Website: www.arthurandersen.com

Type of Firm
Affiliate/Subsidary of Oth. Financial. Instit.

Additional Information
Capital Under Management: $500,000,000
Current Activity Level : Actively seeking new investments

AUSTIN VENTURES, L.P.

701 Brazos Street
Suite 1400
Austin, TX 78701
Phone: 512-485-1900
Fax: 512-476-3952
Website: www.austinventures.com

Other Offices

2001 N. Lamar Street
Suite 400
Dallas, TX 75201
Phone: 214-561-6600
Fax: 214-561-6601

800 E. Campbell Road
Suite 100
Richardson, TX 75081
Phone: 972-892-3700
Fax: 972-892-3701

Management and Staff
Basil Horangic, Partner
Blaine Wesner, General Partner
Brian Goffman, Principal
Chris Grafft, Venture Partner
Christopher Pacitti, General Partner
Daniel Shimer, Venture Partner
Edward Olkkola, General Partner
James Treybig, Venture Partner
James Clardy, Venture Partner
Jeffrey Garvey, General Partner
John Dirvin, Partner
John Nicholson, Chief Financial Officer
John Thornton, General Partner
John McHale, Venture Partner
Joseph Aragona, General Partner
Kenneth DeAngelis, General Partner
Mark Feighner, Venture Partner
Michael Bennet, Venture Partner
Peter Huff, Partner
Robert Kornblum, Principal
Ross Cockrell, General Partner
Shelby Carter, Venture Partner
Stephen Straus, General Partner
Venu Shamapant, Partner

Type of Firm
Private Firm Investing Own Capital

Industry Association Membership
National Venture Capital Association (NVCA)

Project Preferences

Role in Financing:
Prefer role as deal originator but will also invest in deals created by others

Type of Financing Preferred:
Early Stage
First Stage Financing
Leveraged Buyout
Second Stage Financing
Seed
Special Situation
Start-up Financing

Size of Investments Considered
Min Size of Investment Considered (000s): $1,000
Max Size of Investment Considered (000s): $15,000

Geographical Preferences

United States
Southwest
Texas

International
No Preference

Industry Preferences

(% based on actual investment)

Internet Specific	25.8%
Computer Software and Services	21.6%
Communications and Media	17.8%
Other Products	10.8%
Semiconductors/Other Elect.	9.6%
Consumer Related	5.7%
Computer Hardware	4.9%
Medical/Health	2.6%
Industrial/Energy	1.1%
Biotechnology	0.0%

Additional Information
Name of Most Recent Fund: Fund VII
Most Recent Fund Was Raised: 10/12/1999
Year Founded: 1980
Capital Under Management: $3,100,000,000
Current Activity Level : Actively seeking new investments
Method of Compensation: Return on investment is of primary concern, do not charge fees

AV LABS

720 Bavos Street
Suite 900
Austin, TX 78701
Phone: 512-651-3200
Fax: 512-651-3201
Website: www.avlabs.com

Management and Staff
Edward Perry, Venture Partner
Eric Loeffel, Venture Partner
Robert Adams, Managing Director

Type of Firm
Private Firm Investing Own Capital

Industry Association Membership
National Venture Capital Association (NVCA)

Project Preferences

Type of Financing Preferred:
Early Stage
First Stage Financing
Seed

Geographical Preferences

United States
Texas

Industry Preferences

(% based on actual investment)

Computer Software and Services	51.1%
Internet Specific	31.7%
Other Products	11.7%
Computer Hardware	5.5%

Additional Information
Year Founded: 1999
Capital Under Management: $185,000,000
Current Activity Level : Actively seeking new investments

BANCHEM FINANCIAL SERVICES, INC.

One Omni Plaza
409 North Loop 336 Suite Six
Conroe, TX 77301
Phone: 409-788-8282
Fax: 409-788-8289

Type of Firm
Mgt. Consulting Firm

Project Preferences

Role in Financing:
Prefer role as deal originator but will also invest in deals created by others

Type of Financing Preferred:
Leveraged Buyout
Mezzanine

Size of Investments Considered
Min Size of Investment Considered (000s): $1,000
Max Size of Investment Considered: No Limit

Geographical Preferences

United States
Southwest

Industry Preferences

Semiconductors/Other Elect.
Electronics
Analytic/Scientific

Biotechnology
Industrial Biotechnology
Biotech Related Research

Industrial/Energy
Alternative Energy
Energy Conservation Relat
Materials
Machinery
Environmental Related

Financial Services
Financial Services

Agr/Forestr/Fish
Agriculture related

Additional Information
Year Founded: 1987
Capital Under Management: $750,000,000
Current Activity Level : Actively seeking new investments
Method of Compensation: Function primarily in service area, receive contingent fee in cash or equity

BCM TECHNOLOGIES, INC.

Medical Towers Building
1709 Dryden Road Suite 901
Houston, TX 77030
Phone: 713-795-0105
Website: www.bcm.tmc.edu/bcmt

Management and Staff
Christine Powaser, Chief Financial Officer
Lynne Schaefer, Vice President
Stephen Banks, President

Type of Firm
Non-Financial Corp. Affiliate or Subsidiary

Industry Association Membership
National Venture Capital Association (NVCA)

Project Preferences

Role in Financing:
Prefer role as deal originator

Type of Financing Preferred:
Seed

Geographical Preferences

International
No Preference

Industry Preferences

Biotechnology
Biotechnology

Medical/Health
Diagnostic Services
Diagnostic Test Products
Drug/Equipmt Delivery
Other Therapeutic
Disposable Med. Products
Hospitals/Clinics/Primary
Pharmaceuticals

Additional Information
Name of Most Recent Fund: BCM Technologies Fund
Most Recent Fund Was Raised: 01/01/1987
Year Founded: 1984
Capital Under Management: $5,000,000
Current Activity Level : Actively seeking new investments
Method of Compensation: Return on invest. most important, but chg. closing fees, service fees, etc.

BUENA VENTURE ASSOCIATES

201 Main Street
32nd Floor
Fort Worth, TX 76102
Phone: 817-339-7400
Fax: 817-390-8408
Website: www.buenaventure.com

Management and Staff
John Pergande, Partner
Sid Bass, Partner

Type of Firm
Private Firm Investing Own Capital

Project Preferences

Role in Financing:
Will function either as deal originator or investor in deals created by others

Type of Financing Preferred:
Early Stage
First Stage Financing
Second Stage Financing
Seed
Startup

Size of Investments Considered
Min Size of Investment Considered (000s): $1,000
Max Size of Investment Considered (000s): $50,000

Geographical Preferences

United States
All U.S.

Industry Preferences

Communications and Media
Wireless Communications
Data Communications

Computer Software
Computer Services
Software
Systems Software

Internet Specific
Internet

Medical/Health
Health Services

Additional Information
Year Founded: 1998
Current Activity Level : Actively seeking new investments
Method of Compensation: Return on investment is of primary concern, do not charge fees

C3 HOLDINGS, LLC

2100 McKinney Avenue
Suite 1550
Dallas, TX 75201
Phone: 214-292-2000

See Missouri for full listing.

CAPITAL NETWORK, THE (AKA: TEXAS CAPITAL NETWORK)

3925 West Braker Lane
Suite 406
Austin, TX 78759-5321
Phone: 512-305-0826
Fax: 512-305-0836

Management and Staff
David Gerhardt, President

Type of Firm
Mgt. Consulting Firm

Project Preferences

Role in Financing:
Prefer role as deal originator but will also invest in deals created by others

Type of Financing Preferred:
First Stage Financing
Leveraged Buyout
Mezzanine
Research and Development
Second Stage Financing
Seed
Special Situation
Start-up Financing

Size of Investments Considered
Min Size of Investment Considered (000s): $100
Max Size of Investment Considered (000s): $500

Geographical Preferences

United States
All U.S.

Canada
All Canada

Industry Preferences

Communications and Media
Commercial Communications
CATV & Pay TV Systems
Telecommunications
Data Communications
Satellite Microwave Comm.

Computer Other
Computer Related

Semiconductors/Other Elect.
Electronic Components

Biotechnology
Biotechnology

Medical/Health
Medical/Health

Consumer Related
Entertainment and Leisure
Retail
Computer Stores
Food/Beverage
Consumer Products
Consumer Services
Education Related

Industrial/Energy
Oil and Gas Exploration
Oil & Gas Drilling,Explor
Alternative Energy
Energy Conservation Relat
Industrial Products

Financial Services
Financial Services

Business Serv.
Distribution

Manufact.
Publishing

Agr/Forestr/Fish
Mining and Minerals

Additional Information
Year Founded: 1989
Capital Under Management: $100,000,000
Current Activity Level : Actively seeking new investments
Method of Compensation: Professional fee required whether or not deal closes

CAPITAL SOUTHWEST CORPORATION

12900 Preston Road
Suite 700
Dallas, TX 75230
Phone: 972-233-8242
Fax: 972-233-7362
Website: www.capitalsouthwest.com

Management and Staff
D. Scott Collier, Vice President
J. Bruce Duty, Vice President
Patrick Hamner, Vice President
Tim Smith, Vice President
William Thomas, President & Chairman

Whom to Contact
Howard Thomas
Patrick Hamner

Type of Firm
Business Development Fund

Industry Association Membership
National Venture Capital Association (NVCA)
Natl assoc of Small Bus. Inv. Co (NASBIC)

Project Preferences

Role in Financing:
Will function either as deal originator or investor in deals created by others

Type of Financing Preferred:
Acquisition
Early Stage
Expansion
First Stage Financing
Later Stage
Leveraged Buyout
Management Buyouts
Mezzanine
Second Stage Financing

Size of Investments Considered
Min Size of Investment Considered (000s): $1,000
Max Size of Investment Considered (000s): $6,000

Geographical Preferences

United States
All U.S.

Industry Preferences

(% based on actual investment)

Consumer Related	30.2%
Other Products	21.5%
Industrial/Energy	20.7%
Communications and Media	12.4%
Internet Specific	3.5%
Computer Hardware	3.4%
Medical/Health	3.4%
Biotechnology	2.3%
Semiconductors/Other Elect.	2.0%
Computer Software and Services	0.6%

Additional Information
Name of Most Recent Fund: CSC Capital Corporation
Most Recent Fund Was Raised: 06/01/1983
Year Founded: 1961
Capital Under Management: $313,000,000
Current Activity Level : Actively seeking new investments
Method of Compensation: Return on investment is of primary concern, do not charge fees

CARDINAL INVESTMENT COMPANY, INC.

500 Crescent Court
Suite 250
Dallas, TX 75201
Phone: 214-871-6807
Fax: 214-871-6801
Website: www.cardinalinvestment.com

Management and Staff
Drew Johnson, Principal
Rusty Rose, Principal

Type of Firm
Private Firm Investing Own Capital

Additional Information
Current Activity Level : Actively seeking new investments

CATALYST GROUP, THE

Three Riverway
Suite 770
Houston, TX 77056
Phone: 713-623-8133
Fax: 713-623-0473
Website: www.thecatalystgroup.net

Management and Staff
Rick Herrman, Partner
Roger Linn, Partner
Ron Nixon, Partner

Whom to Contact
Rick Herrman
Ron Nixon

Type of Firm
Private Firm Investing Own Capital

Industry Association Membership
Natl assoc of Small Bus. Inv. Co (NASBIC)

Project Preferences

Role in Financing:
Prefer role as deal originator but will also invest in deals created by others

Type of Financing Preferred:
Control-block Purchases
Leveraged Buyout
Mezzanine
Second Stage Financing

Size of Investments Considered
Min Size of Investment Considered (000s): $1,000
Max Size of Investment Considered: No Limit

Geographical Preferences

International
No Preference

Industry Preferences

Communications and Media
Radio & TV Broadcasting

Semiconductors/Other Elect.
Sensors
Circuit Boards
Analytic/Scientific

Medical/Health
Medical Products
Hospitals/Clinics/Primary

Consumer Related
Other Restaurants

Industrial/Energy
Oil and Gas Exploration
Industrial Products
Materials
Factory Automation
Machinery
Environmental Related

Additional Information
Name of Most Recent Fund: Southwest/Catalyst Capital
Most Recent Fund Was Raised: 06/01/1997
Year Founded: 1990
Capital Under Management: $51,000,000
Current Activity Level : Actively seeking new investments
Method of Compensation: Return on invest. most important, but chg. closing fees, service fees, etc.

CCG VENTURE PARTNERS, LLC

504 West 24th Street
Suite F
Austin, TX 78705
Phone: 512-477-1235
Fax: 512-477-4652
Website: www.ccgvp.com

Other Offices

504 West 24th Street
Suite F
Austin, TX 78705
Phone: 512-477-1235
Fax: 512-477-4652

Management and Staff
John Kiltz, Partner
Rick Davis, Chief Executive Officer
Sam Loughlin, Partner

Type of Firm
Private Firm Investing Own Capital

Additional Information
Current Activity Level : Actively seeking new investments

CENTENNIAL VENTURES

1330 Post Oak Boulevard
Suite 1525
Houston, TX 77056
Phone: 713-627-9200
Fax: 713-627-9292
Website: www.centennial.com

See Colorado for full listing.

CENTERPOINT VENTURE PARTNERS

13455 Noel Road
Two Galleria Tower, Suite 1670
Dallas, TX 75240
Phone: 972-702-1101
Fax: 972-702-1103
Website: www.cpventures.com

Other Offices

6801 N. Capital of Texas Highway
Building 2, Suite 225
Austin, TX 78731
Phone: 512-795-5800
Fax: 512-795-5849

Management and Staff
Cameron McMartin, General Partner
Kent Fuka, Partner
Robert Paluck, General Partner
Terry Rock, General Partner

Type of Firm
Private Firm Investing Own Capital

Industry Association Membership
National Venture Capital Association (NVCA)

Project Preferences

Type of Financing Preferred:
Early Stage

Geographical Preferences

United States
Southwest

Industry Preferences

(% based on actual investment)

Communications and Media	21.8%
Internet Specific	17.4%
Computer Software and Services	15.7%
Semiconductors/Other Elect.	14.3%
Medical/Health	12.0%
Computer Hardware	10.5%
Other Products	7.8%
Biotechnology	0.6%

Additional Information
Name of Most Recent Fund: CenterPoint Venture Partners
Most Recent Fund Was Raised: 11/15/1996
Year Founded: 1996
Capital Under Management: $50,000,000
Current Activity Level : Actively seeking new investments

COLUMBINE VENTURE FUNDS, THE

3810 Swarthmore
Houston, TX 77005
Phone: 713-661-9260
Fax: 713-661-9269

See Colorado for full listing.

CT HOLDINGS

3811 Turtle Creek Boulevard
Suite 770
Dallas, TX 75219
Phone: 214-520-9292
Fax: 214-520-9293
E-mail: invest@citadel.com
Website: www.ct-holdings.com

Management and Staff
Carl Banzhof, General Partner
Lester Sideropoulos, General Partner
Steven Solomon, Chief Executive Officer
Victor Kiam, General Partner

Type of Firm
Incubators

Project Preferences

Type of Financing Preferred:
Early Stage

Industry Preferences

Internet Specific
Internet

Additional Information
Year Founded: 1999
Current Activity Level : Actively seeking new investments

CURETON & CO., INC.

1100 Louisiana
Suite 3250
Houston, TX 77002
Phone: 713-658-9806
Fax: 713-658-0476

Management and Staff
Stewart Cureton, President

Whom to Contact
Robert Antonoff
Stewart Cureton

Type of Firm
Investment/Merchant Bank Investing Own or Client Funds

Project Preferences

Role in Financing:
Prefer role as deal originator but will also invest in deals created by others

Type of Financing Preferred:
First Stage Financing
Leveraged Buyout
Second Stage Financing
Special Situation

Size of Investments Considered
Min Size of Investment Considered (000s): $10,000
Max Size of Investment Considered: No Limit

Geographical Preferences

United States
Southwest

Industry Preferences

Communications and Media
Commercial Communications
CATV & Pay TV Systems
Telecommunications
Data Communications
Satellite Microwave Comm.
Other Communication Prod.

Computer Hardware
Computers
Mainframes / Scientific
Mini and Personal/Desktop
Computer Graphics and Dig
Disk Relat. Memory Device

Computer Software
Computer Services
Applications Software

Internet Specific
Internet

Semiconductors/Other Elect.
Electronics
Semiconductor
Sensors
Laser Related

Medical/Health
Diagnostic Services
Diagnostic Test Products
Disposable Med. Products

Consumer Related
Consumer Products
Consumer Services
Education Related

Industrial/Energy
Alternative Energy
Industrial Products
Materials
Factory Automation
Machinery
Environmental Related

Financial Services
Financial Services

Additional Information
Year Founded: 1974
Current Activity Level : Inactive / Unknown
Method of Compensation: Return on invest. most important, but chg. closing fees, service fees, etc.

DALI, HOOK PARTNERS (FKA: HOOK PARTNERS)

One Lincoln Centre, Suite 1550
5400 LBJ Freeway
Dallas, TX 75240
Phone: 972-991-5457
Fax: 972-991-5458
Website: www.hookpartners.com

Other Offices

3000 Sand Hill Road
Building 1, Suite 285
Menlo Park, CA 94025
Phone: 650-926-9820
Fax: 650-926-9825

Management and Staff
David Hook, General Partner
George Chase, General Partner
John Hook, General Partner
Paul Dali, General Partner

Type of Firm
Private Firm Investing Own Capital

Project Preferences

Role in Financing:
Prefer role as deal originator but will also invest in deals created by others

Type of Financing Preferred:
Balanced
First Stage Financing
Second Stage Financing

Size of Investments Considered
Min Size of Investment Considered (000s): $100
Max Size of Investment Considered (000s): $5,000

Geographical Preferences

United States
Southwest
West Coast

Industry Preferences

(% based on actual investment)

Computer Software and Services	32.6%
Communications and Media	25.4%
Semiconductors/Other Elect.	18.0%
Computer Hardware	11.6%
Internet Specific	10.3%
Consumer Related	1.0%
Biotechnology	0.5%
Industrial/Energy	0.2%
Medical/Health	0.2%
Other Products	0.2%

Additional Information
Name of Most Recent Fund: Hook Communications Partners
Most Recent Fund Was Raised: 04/01/1999
Year Founded: 1978
Capital Under Management: $155,000,000
Current Activity Level : Actively seeking new investments
Method of Compensation: Return on investment is of primary concern, do not charge fees

DAVIS, TUTTLE VENTURE PARTNERS, L.P.(FKA:DAVIS VENTURE)

8 Greenway Plaza
Suite 1020
Houston, TX 77046
Phone: 713-993-0440
Fax: 713-621-2297
Website: www.davistuttle.com

See Oklahoma for full listing.

DIVINE INTERVENTURES (FKA: PLATINUM VENTURE PARTNERS)

7000 MoPac Expressway
2nd Floor
Austin, TX 78731
Phone: 512-514-6297
Fax: 512-514-6499
Website: www.divineinterventures.com

See Illinois for full listing.

ENCORE VENTURE PARTNERS, LP

1901 Ascension Boulevard
Suite 350
Arlington, TX 76006
Phone: 817-436-6052
Fax: 817-436-6053
Website: www.encorevp.com

See California for full listing.

ENRON BROADBAND VENTURES

1400 Smith Street
Houston, TX 77002
Phone: 713-853-6161
Fax: 713-646-8010
Website: www.enron.com

Other Offices

40 Grosvenor Place
London, United Kingdom SW1X 7EN
Phone: 44-20-7783-0000

Management and Staff

Andrew Marsden, Partner
Christian Hackett, Partner
Jon Thomsen, Vice President
Kevin Garland, Vice President
Patrick Hickey, Vice President
Paul Rodseth, Partner
Steven Sheldon, Managing Director

Type of Firm

Non-Financial Corp. Affiliate or Subsidiary

Project Preferences

Type of Financing Preferred:
Balanced

Geographical Preferences

International
All International

Industry Preferences

Communications and Media
Communications and Media

Additional Information

Year Founded: 1999
Current Activity Level : Actively seeking new investments

EQUUS CAPITAL CORP.

2929 Allen Parkway
25th Floor
Houston, TX 77019
Phone: 713-529-0900
Fax: 713-529-9545
Website: http://www.equuscap.com

Management and Staff

Gary Forbes, Vice President
Patrick Cahill, Chief Financial Officer
Randall Hall, Vice President

Whom to Contact

Gary Forbes
Patrick Cahill
Randall B. Hale

Type of Firm

Private Firm Investing Own Capital

Project Preferences

Role in Financing:
Prefer role as deal originator but will also invest in deals created by others

Type of Financing Preferred:
Leveraged Buyout
Special Situation

Size of Investments Considered

Min Size of Investment Considered (000s): $2,000
Max Size of Investment Considered (000s): $5,000

Geographical Preferences

United States
All U.S.

Industry Preferences

(% based on actual investment)

Other Products	38.9%
Consumer Related	23.2%
Industrial/Energy	18.1%
Medical/Health	11.2%
Communications and Media	6.7%
Biotechnology	1.8%
Computer Software and Services	0.1%
Internet Specific	0.1%

Additional Information

Name of Most Recent Fund: Equus Equity Appreciation Fund, L.P.
Most Recent Fund Was Raised: 06/01/1992
Year Founded: 1983
Capital Under Management: $150,000,000
Current Activity Level : Actively seeking new investments
Method of Compensation: Return on invest. most important, but chg. closing fees, service fees, etc.

ESSEX WOODLANDS HEALTH VENTURES (FKA:WOODLANDS VENTURE PARTN

2170 Buckthorne Place
Suite 170
The Woodlands, TX 77380
Phone: 281-367-9999
Fax: 281-298-1295
Website: www.essexwoodlands.com

See Illinois for full listing.

EXCEL COMMUNICATIONS

16675 Addison Road
Dallas, TX 75248
Phone: 972-738-1000
Website: www.excel.com

Type of Firm
Non-Financial Corp. Affiliate or Subsidiary

Industry Preferences

Communications and Media
Telecommunications

Additional Information
Current Activity Level : Actively seeking new investments

FIRST CAPITAL MANAGEMENT CO.

750 East Mulberry Street
Suite 305 P.O. Box 15616
San Antonio, TX 78212
Phone: 210-736-4233
Fax: 210-736-5449

Management and Staff
Jeffrey Blanchard

Whom to Contact
Jeffrey Blanchard

Type of Firm
Private Firm Investing Own Capital

Industry Association Membership
Natl assoc of Small Bus. Inv. Co (NASBIC)

Project Preferences

Role in Financing:
Prefer role as deal originator but will also invest in deals created by others

Type of Financing Preferred:
First Stage Financing
Leveraged Buyout
Mezzanine
Second Stage Financing
Special Situation

Size of Investments Considered
Min Size of Investment Considered (000s): $1,000
Max Size of Investment Considered: No Limit

Geographical Preferences

United States
Southwest

Industry Preferences

Communications and Media
Telecommunications
Data Communications

Biotechnology
Industrial Biotechnology
Biosensors

Medical/Health
Medical Diagnostics
Medical Therapeutics

Transportation
Transportation

Additional Information
Name of Most Recent Fund: First Capital Group of Texas, II
Most Recent Fund Was Raised: 10/01/1995
Year Founded: 1984
Capital Under Management: $31,200,000
Current Activity Level : Actively seeking new investments
Method of Compensation: Return on investment is of primary concern, do not charge fees

---

FIRST CHARTER PARTNERS, INC.

The Towers of Williams Square
5215 N. O'Connor, 2nd Floor
Irving, TX 75039
Phone: 817-481-8116
Fax: 817-488-1818

Management and Staff
Eric Gilchrest

Whom to Contact
Eric Gilchrest

Type of Firm
Investment/Merchant Bank Subsid/Affil

Project Preferences

Role in Financing:
Prefer role as deal originator but will also invest in deals created by others

Type of Financing Preferred:
Leveraged Buyout
Second Stage Financing
Special Situation

Size of Investments Considered
Min Size of Investment Considered (000s): $3,000
Max Size of Investment Considered: No Limit

Geographical Preferences

United States
All U.S.

Industry Preferences

Semiconductors/Other Elect.
Electronics
Sensors

Medical/Health
Drug/Equipmt Delivery
Medical Products
Disposable Med. Products
Pharmaceuticals

Consumer Related
Entertainment and Leisure
Franchises(NEC)
Food/Beverage
Consumer Products
Consumer Services
Hotels and Resorts

Industrial/Energy
Industrial Products
Materials
Factory Automation
Machinery
Environmental Related

Financial Services
Financial Services

Manufact.
Publishing

Additional Information
Year Founded: 1993
Capital Under Management: $10,000,000
Current Activity Level : Actively seeking new investments
Method of Compensation: Return on invest. most important, but chg. closing fees, service fees, etc.

FORREST BINKLEY & BROWN

201 Main St, Suite 2302
Fort Worth, TX 76102
Phone: 817-339-7020
Fax: 817-338-2047
Website: fbbvc.com

See California for full listing.

G-51 CAPITAL LLC

304 Las Cimas Parkway
Suite 140 B
Austin, TX 78746
Phone: 512-929-5151
Fax: 512-932-0886
Website: www.g51.com

Management and Staff
Frank Reeves, Partner
N. Rudy Garza, President

Type of Firm
Investment/Merchant Bank Subsid/Affil

Project Preferences

Role in Financing:
Prefer role as deal originator but will also invest in deals created by others

Type of Financing Preferred:
Early Stage
First Stage Financing
Mezzanine
Second Stage Financing
Seed
Start-up Financing

Geographical Preferences

United States
Southwest
Texas
All U.S.

Industry Preferences

(% based on actual investment)

Computer Hardware	49.2%
Internet Specific	44.6%
Computer Software and Services	6.2%

Additional Information
Year Founded: 1997
Capital Under Management: $9,000,000
Current Activity Level : Actively seeking new investments
Method of Compensation: Return on invest. most important, but chg. closing fees, service fees, etc.

HEARTLAND CAPITAL PARTNERS, L.P.

2200 Ross Avenue
Suite 4300 West
Dallas, TX 75201
Phone: 214-665-4300
Fax: 214-665-4333
Website: www.heartlandfund.com

Type of Firm
Private Firm Investing Own Capital

Project Preferences

Role in Financing:
Prefer role as deal originator

Type of Financing Preferred:
Second Stage Financing

Size of Investments Considered
Min Size of Investment Considered (000s): $1,000
Max Size of Investment Considered: No Limit

Geographical Preferences

International
No Preference

Industry Preferences

Medical/Health
Medical Products
Disposable Med. Products

Consumer Related
Entertainment and Leisure
Retail
Food/Beverage
Consumer Products
Consumer Services
Education Related

Industrial/Energy
Industrial Products
Environmental Related

Transportation
Transportation

Manufact.
Publishing

Additional Information
Name of Most Recent Fund: Heartland Capital Partners III
Most Recent Fund Was Raised: 01/01/1995
Year Founded: 1994
Capital Under Management: $52,000,000
Current Activity Level : Actively seeking new investments
Method of Compensation: Return on investment is of primary concern, do not charge fees

HO2 PARTNERS LLC

Two Galleria Tower
13455 Noel Rd. Suite 1670
Dallas, TX 75240
Phone: 972-702-1144
Fax: 972-702-8234
Website: www.ho2.com

Management and Staff
Charles B. Humphreyson, General Partner
Daniel T. Owen, General Partner
Zachary Aills, Chief Financial Officer

Type of Firm
Private Firm Investing Own Capital

Project Preferences

Role in Financing:
Prefer role as deal originator but will also invest in deals created by others

Type of Financing Preferred:
First Stage Financing
Seed
Start-up Financing

Size of Investments Considered
Min Size of Investment Considered (000s): $750
Max Size of Investment Considered (000s): $3,000

Geographical Preferences

United States
Texas

Industry Preferences

Communications and Media
Telecommunications
Wireless Communications

Computer Software
Software
Applications Software

Internet Specific
Internet
Web Aggregration/Portals

Additional Information
Name of Most Recent Fund: HO2.1 Fund
Most Recent Fund Was Raised: 12/01/1999
Year Founded: 1997
Capital Under Management: $34,000,000
Current Activity Level : Actively seeking new investments
Method of Compensation: Return on investment is of primary concern, do not charge fees

HOAK CAPITAL CORP.

13355 Noel Road
Suite 1050
Dallas, TX 75240
Phone: 972-960-4848
Fax: 972-960-4899

Management and Staff
James Harrison, Principal
James Hoak, Principal
Laura Robinson, Chief Financial Officer
Robert Sussman, Vice President

Type of Firm
Private Firm Investing Own Capital

Project Preferences

Role in Financing:
Prefer role as deal originator but will also invest in deals created by others

Type of Financing Preferred:
Control-block Purchases
Industry Rollups
Leveraged Buyout
Special Situation

Size of Investments Considered
Min Size of Investment Considered (000s): $35,000
Max Size of Investment Considered: No Limit

Geographical Preferences

United States
All U.S.

Industry Preferences

(% based on actual investment)

Communications and Media	40.3%
Consumer Related	31.2%
Semiconductors/Other Elect.	15.8%
Industrial/Energy	4.2%
Internet Specific	3.7%
Other Products	2.7%
Computer Software and Services	1.9%

Additional Information
Name of Most Recent Fund: Hoak Communications Partners, LP
Most Recent Fund Was Raised: 04/01/1996
Year Founded: 1991
Capital Under Management: $174,000,000
Current Activity Level : Actively seeking new investments
Method of Compensation: Return on investment is of primary concern, do not charge fees

HOLDING CAPITAL GROUP, INC.

4018 Wingren Drive
Irving, TX 75062
Phone: 214-717-1920
Fax: 214-717-9113

See New York for full listing.

HOUSTON VENTURE PARTNERS (AKA: HOUSTON PARTNERS)

401 Louisiana, 8th Fl
Houston, TX 77002
Phone: 713-222-8600
Fax: 713-222-8932
Website: 73313.1571@compuserve.com

Management and Staff
Glenda Overbeck, President

Type of Firm
Private Firm Investing Own Capital

Industry Association Membership
National Venture Capital Association (NVCA)
Natl assoc of Small Bus. Inv. Co (NASBIC)

Project Preferences

Role in Financing:
Prefer role as deal originator but will also invest in deals created by others

Type of Financing Preferred:
Expansion
First Stage Financing
Second Stage Financing
Start-up Financing

Size of Investments Considered
Min Size of Investment Considered (000s): $500
Max Size of Investment Considered (000s): $1,000

Geographical Preferences

United States
All U.S.
Southeast
Southwest
West Coast

Industry Preferences

Computer Hardware
Mini and Personal/Desktop
Computer Graphics and Dig

Computer Software
Systems Software
Applications Software

Semiconductors/Other Elect.
Electronic Components
Analytic/Scientific

Biotechnology
Biosensors
Biotech Related Research
Biotech Related Research

Medical/Health
Medical Diagnostics
Diagnostic Services
Diagnostic Test Products
Medical Therapeutics
Drug/Equipmt Delivery
Other Therapeutic
Disposable Med. Products
Pharmaceuticals

Additional Information
Name of Most Recent Fund: Houston Venture Partners
Most Recent Fund Was Raised: 07/01/1987
Year Founded: 1986
Capital Under Management: $27,000,000
Current Activity Level : Actively seeking new investments
Method of Compensation: Return on investment is of primary concern, do not charge fees

HUNT CAPITAL GROUP

1601 Elm Street
Suite 4000
Dallas, TX 75201
Phone: 214-720-1600
Fax: 214-720-1662
Website: www.huntcapital.com

Other Offices

132492 Research Boulevard
Suite 120
Austin, TX 78750
Phone: 512-258-0001
Fax: 512-258-0009

Management and Staff

J.R. Holland, President
Peter Stein, Partner
R.Brad Oldham, Partner
Scott Colvert, Partner

Type of Firm

Private Firm Investing Own Capital

Project Preferences

Role in Financing:
Will function either as deal originator or investor in deals created by others

Type of Financing Preferred:
Acquisition
Early Stage
Expansion
First Stage Financing
Generalist PE
Later Stage
Management Buyouts
Second Stage Financing

Size of Investments Considered

Min Size of Investment Considered (000s): $3,000
Max Size of Investment Considered (000s): $8,000

Geographical Preferences

United States
All U.S.

Canada
All Canada

Industry Preferences

(% based on actual investment)

Other Products	43.1%
Internet Specific	27.0%
Computer Software and Services	13.5%
Medical/Health	10.8%
Communications and Media	3.9%
Consumer Related	1.7%

Additional Information

Year Founded: 1993
Capital Under Management: $120,000,000
Current Activity Level : Actively seeking new investments
Method of Compensation: Return on investment is of primary concern, do not charge fees

HUNT VENTURES, LP

816 Congress Avenue
Suite 1550
Austin, TX 78701
Phone: 512-482-0714
Fax: 512-482-8308
Website: www.huntventures.com

Other Offices

1445 Ross At Field
Dallas, TX 75202
Phone: 214-978-8956
Fax: 214-978-8858

Management and Staff

Christopher Kleinert, Managing Director
Fulton Murray, Managing Director
Mike Bierman, Managing Director
Scott Segell, Managing Director
Steve Coffey, Managing Director
Tom Meurer, Managing Director

Type of Firm

Affiliate/Subsidary of Oth. Financial. Instit.

Project Preferences

Type of Financing Preferred:
Early Stage

Geographical Preferences

International
All International

Industry Preferences

Biotechnology
Agricultural/Animal Bio.

Industrial/Energy
Energy
Oil and Gas Exploration

Financial Services
Real Estate

Additional Information

Year Founded: 1999
Current Activity Level : Actively seeking new investments

I2B VENTURES

200 Crescent Court
Suite 600
Dallas, TX 75201
Phone: 214-661-7600
Fax: 214-661-7606
E-mail: contact@i2b.com
Website: www.i2b.com

Management and Staff

Daniel Chu, Partner
Jeff Smith, Partner
Stan Woodward, Partner
Sunny Vanderbeck, Partner

Type of Firm

Incubators

Project Preferences

Type of Financing Preferred:
Early Stage

Geographical Preferences

United States
Texas

Additional Information

Capital Under Management: $20,000,000
Current Activity Level : Actively seeking new investments

INTERFASE CAPITAL PARTNERS LP

1301 Capital of Texas Highway
Suite A300
Austin, TX 78746
Phone: 512-328-8113
Fax: 512-328-9662
E-mail: info@interfase-capital.com
Website: www.interfasecapital.com

Management and Staff

Melissa Hamilton, Principal
Richard Salwen, Partner
Ronald Carroll, Partner
Scott Hyten, Managing Partner

Type of Firm

Private Firm Investing Own Capital

Project Preferences

Type of Financing Preferred:
Early Stage

Geographical Preferences

United States
All U.S.

Industry Preferences

Internet Specific
Internet

Additional Information

Year Founded: 1999
Current Activity Level : Actively seeking new investments

INTERSOUTH PARTNERS

The Presidio, Suite 220
6907 North Capital of Texas Hwy
Austin, TX 78731
Phone: 512-372-8843
Fax: 512-372-3844
Website: www.intersouth.com

See North Carolina for full listing.

INTERWEST PARTNERS

Two Galleria Tower
13455 Noel Road, Suite 1670
Dallas, TX 75240-6615
Phone: 972-392-7279
Fax: 972-490-6348
Website: www.interwest.com

See California for full listing.

JATOTECH MANAGEMENT LLC

301 Congress
Suite 2050
Austin, TX 78701
Phone: 512-236 - 6950
Fax: 512-236-6959
Website: www.jatotech.com

Management and Staff

Daniel Ray, Partner
Molly Pieroni, Partner
Walter Thirion, Partner

Type of Firm

Private Firm Investing Own Capital

Project Preferences

Role in Financing:
Prefer role as deal originator

Type of Financing Preferred:
Early Stage

Size of Investments Considered
Min Size of Investment Considered (000s): $500
Max Size of Investment Considered (000s): $5,000

Industry Preferences

Communications and Media
Data Communications

Internet Specific
Internet

Additional Information

Year Founded: 2000
Capital Under Management: $55,000,000
Current Activity Level : Actively seeking new investments

JUMP.NET VENTURES

7218 McNeil Drive
Suite 303
Austin, TX 78729
Phone: 512-532-2235
Website: www.jumpnetventures.com

Type of Firm

Non-Financial Corp. Affiliate or Subsidiary

Project Preferences

Type of Financing Preferred:
Seed
Startup

Geographical Preferences

United States
Southwest

Industry Preferences

Internet Specific
Internet

Additional Information

Capital Under Management: $25,000,000
Current Activity Level : Actively seeking new investments

KAHALA INVESTMENTS, INC.

8214 Westchester Drive
Suite 715
Dallas, TX 75225
Phone: 214-987-0077
Fax: 214-987-2332

Management and Staff

Lee Slaughter

Whom to Contact

Lee Slaughter

Type of Firm

Mgt. Consulting Firm

Project Preferences

Role in Financing:
Prefer role as deal originator but will also invest in deals created by others

Type of Financing Preferred:
Control-block Purchases
Industry Rollups
Leveraged Buyout
Mezzanine
Special Situation

Size of Investments Considered
Min Size of Investment Considered (000s): $10,000
Max Size of Investment Considered: No Limit

Geographical Preferences

United States
Southeast
Southwest

Industry Preferences

Consumer Related
Entertainment and Leisure
Retail
Franchises(NEC)
Food/Beverage
Consumer Products
Consumer Services

Industrial/Energy
Industrial Products
Machinery

Additional Information
Year Founded: 1978
Capital Under Management: $5,000,000
Current Activity Level : Actively seeking new investments
Method of Compensation: Return on invest. most important, but chg. closing fees, service fees, etc.

KLM CAPITAL GROUP

4516 Seton Center Parkway
Suite 170
Austin, TX 78759
Phone: 512-338-9688
Fax: 512-338-9754
Website: www.klmtech.com

See California for full listing.

LEWIS HOLLINGSWORTH

2210 Galleria Tower
13355 Noel Road
Dallas, TX 75240
Phone: 972-702-7390
Fax: 972-702-7391
Website: www.lhequity.com

Management and Staff
Arthur Hollingsworth, General Partner
John Lewis, General Partner
Luke Sweetser, General Partner

Type of Firm
Private Firm Investing Own Capital

Industry Association Membership
National Venture Capital Association (NVCA)

Additional Information
Capital Under Management: $25,000,000
Current Activity Level : Actively seeking new investments

MAIN STREET EQUITY ADVISORS, LLC

1360 Post Oak Boulevard
Suite 800
Houston, TX 77056
Phone: 713-350-6000
Website: www.mainstreethouston.com

Management and Staff
C. Byron Synder, Senior Managing Director
Gregory Sangalis, Managing Director
James Cohen, Managing Director
Todd Reppert, Managing Director
Vincent Foster, Senior Managing Director

Type of Firm
Private Equity Advisor or Fund of Fund Mgr

Additional Information
Capital Under Management: $30,000,000
Current Activity Level : Actively seeking new investments

MAPLELEAF CAPITAL CORP.

Three Forrest Plaza, Suite 935
12221 Merit Drive
Dallas, TX 75251
Phone: 972-239-5650
Fax: 972-701-0024

Type of Firm
Private Firm Investing Own Capital

Industry Association Membership
Natl assoc of Small Bus. Inv. Co (NASBIC)

Project Preferences

Type of Financing Preferred:
Balanced

Geographical Preferences

International
No Preference

Additional Information
Year Founded: 1980
Capital Under Management: $8,000,000
Current Activity Level : Inactive / Unknown

MAYFIELD FUND

4233 Hidden Canyon Cove
Austin, TX 78746
Phone: 512-328-0808
Website: www.mayfield.com

See California for full listing.

MBA VENTURE GROUP

1004 Olde Towne Road
Suite 102
Irving, TX 75061
Phone: 972-986-6703

Management and Staff
John Mason

Whom to Contact
John Mason

Type of Firm
Private Firm Investing Own Capital

Project Preferences

Role in Financing:
Prefer role as deal originator but will also invest in deals created by others

Type of Financing Preferred:
First Stage Financing
Leveraged Buyout
Mezzanine
Research and Development
Second Stage Financing
Seed
Start-up Financing

Size of Investments Considered
Min Size of Investment Considered (000s): $1,000
Max Size of Investment Considered: No Limit

Geographical Preferences

United States
All U.S.

Industry Preferences

Communications and Media
Communications and Media

Computer Other
Computer Related

Semiconductors/Other Elect.
Electronic Components

Medical/Health
Medical/Health

Consumer Related
Consumer
Education Related

Industrial/Energy
Industrial Products

Transportation
Transportation

Business Serv.
Distribution

Manufact.
Publishing

Additional Information
Year Founded: 1990
Current Activity Level : Actively seeking new investments
Method of Compensation: Return on invest. most important, but chg. closing fees, service fees, etc.

MCGUIRE CAPITAL CORP.

8700 Crewenbull Blvd.
San Antonio, TX 78216
Phone: 210-821-6755
Fax: 210-821-6859

Type of Firm
Investment/Merchant Bank Investing Own or Client Funds

Project Preferences

Role in Financing:
Prefer role as deal originator

Type of Financing Preferred:
Leveraged Buyout
Mezzanine
Second Stage Financing

Size of Investments Considered
Min Size of Investment Considered (000s): $10,000
Max Size of Investment Considered: No Limit

Geographical Preferences

United States
Southwest

Industry Preferences

Consumer Related
Food/Beverage

Transportation
Transportation

Agr/Forestr/Fish
Agriculture related

Additional Information
Year Founded: 1988
Current Activity Level : Actively seeking new investments
Method of Compensation: Return on invest. most important, but chg. closing fees, service fees, etc.

MEDTECH INTERNATIONAL, INC.

1742 Carriageway
Sugarland, TX 77478
Phone: 713-980-8474
Fax: 713-980-6343

Management and Staff
Dave Banker

Whom to Contact
Dave Banker

Type of Firm
Mgt. Consulting Firm

Project Preferences

Role in Financing:
Prefer role as deal originator but will also invest in deals created by others

Type of Financing Preferred:
First Stage Financing
Leveraged Buyout
Mezzanine
Research and Development
Second Stage Financing
Seed
Special Situation
Start-up Financing

Size of Investments Considered
Min Size of Investment Considered (000s): $100
Max Size of Investment Considered (000s): $500

Geographical Preferences

International
No Preference

Industry Preferences

Communications and Media
Communications and Media
Other Communication Prod.

Computer Hardware
Computers

Computer Software
Computer Services
Systems Software
Applications Software
Artificial Intelligence

Semiconductors/Other Elect.
Electronics
Electronic Components
Semiconductor
Sensors
Laser Related
Fiber Optics
Analytic/Scientific

Biotechnology
Biotechnology

Medical/Health
Diagnostic Services
Diagnostic Test Products
Drug/Equipmt Delivery
Other Therapeutic
Medical Products
Hospitals/Clinics/Primary
Hospital/Other Instit.
Pharmaceuticals

Consumer Related
Entertainment and Leisure
Retail
Franchises(NEC)
Consumer Products
Consumer Services
Education Related

Industrial/Energy
Oil and Gas Exploration
Oil & Gas Drilling,Explor
Alternative Energy
Energy Conservation Relat
Industrial Products
Materials
Environmental Related

Financial Services
Financial Services

Manufact.
Office Automation Equipmt

Additional Information
Year Founded: 1991
Capital Under Management: $15,000,000
Current Activity Level : Actively seeking new investments
Method of Compensation: Return on invest. most important, but chg. closing fees, service fees, etc.

MERCURY VENTURES LTD.

17950 Preston
Suite 800
Dallas, TX 75252
Phone: 972-931-6814
Fax: 972-248-0226

Management and Staff
Don Goodwin, Partner
Kevin Howe, Partner

Type of Firm
Private Firm Investing Own Capital

Project Preferences

Industry Preferences

(% based on actual investment)

Internet Specific	80.8%
Other Products	9.7%
Computer Software and Services	9.5%

Additional Information
Year Founded: 1999
Current Activity Level : Actively seeking new investments

MESBIC VENTURES HOLDING CO. (AKA PACESETTER GROWTH FUND, L.P

2435 North Central Expressway
Suite 200
Richardson, TX 75080
Phone: 972-991-1597
Fax: 972-991-4770
Website: www.mvhc.com

Management and Staff
Divakar Kamath, Managing Director
Thomas Gerron, Managing Director

Whom to Contact
Jeff Schaefer
Verncen Russell

Type of Firm
MESBIC not elsewhere classified

Industry Association Membership
Natl Assoc of Investment Cos. (NAIC)
Natl assoc of Small Bus. Inv. Co (NASBIC)

Project Preferences

Role in Financing:
Prefer role as deal originator but will also invest in deals created by others

Type of Financing Preferred:
Leveraged Buyout
Mezzanine
Second Stage Financing

Size of Investments Considered
Min Size of Investment Considered (000s): $1,000
Max Size of Investment Considered: No Limit

Geographical Preferences

United States
Southeast
Southwest

Industry Preferences

(% based on actual investment)

Communications and Media	28.0%
Computer Software and Services	27.8%
Consumer Related	16.8%
Semiconductors/Other Elect.	11.1%
Medical/Health	6.2%
Computer Hardware	4.0%
Other Products	3.9%
Internet Specific	1.7%
Industrial/Energy	0.3%

Additional Information
Name of Most Recent Fund: Pacesetter Growth Fund, L.P.
Most Recent Fund Was Raised: 05/31/1997
Year Founded: 1970
Capital Under Management: $130,000,000
Current Activity Level : Actively seeking new investments
Method of Compensation: Return on invest. most important, but chg. closing fees, service fees, etc.

MONARCH CAPITAL PARTNERS, LLC

3232 McKinney Avenue
Suite 865
Dallas, TX 75204
Phone: 214-871-7784
Fax: 214-740-1792
Website: www.monarchpartners.com

See Georgia for full listing.

MURPHREE VENTURE PARTNERS

1100 Louisiana
Suite 5005
Houston, TX 77002
Phone: 713-655-8500
Fax: 713-655-8503
Website: www.murphreeventures.com

Other Offices

111 Congress Avenue
Suite 1600
Austin, TX 78701
Phone: 512-397-3800
Fax: 512-477-6524

1155 University Blvd. SE
Albuquerque, NM 87106
Phone: 505-843-4277
Fax: 505-843-4278

2005 10th Street
Suite D
Boulder, CO 80302
Phone: 303-413-1264
Fax: 303-413-1266

Management and Staff
Alan Moore, Partner
David Lee, Partner
Dennis Murphree, Managing General Partner
Elliott Boullion, Venture Partner
Geoffrey Tudor, Venture Partner
John Dennis, Venture Partner
L. Murphree, Partner
Marty Fluke, Venture Partner
Thomas Stephenson, Partner
William Rice, Venture Partner

Type of Firm
Private Firm Investing Own Capital

Project Preferences

Role in Financing:
Will function either as deal originator or investor in deals created by others

Type of Financing Preferred:
Balanced
Early Stage
First Stage Financing
Second Stage Financing
Seed
Startup

Size of Investments Considered
Min Size of Investment Considered (000s): $250
Max Size of Investment Considered (000s): $10,000

Geographical Preferences

United States
Rocky Mountain
Southeast
Southwest

Industry Preferences

(% based on actual investment)

Computer Software and Services	54.4%
Internet Specific	34.4%
Medical/Health	5.0%
Consumer Related	2.4%
Semiconductors/Other Elect.	1.8%
Computer Hardware	1.2%
Communications and Media	0.6%
Industrial/Energy	0.2%

Additional Information

Name of Most Recent Fund: Murphree Venture Partners IV
Most Recent Fund Was Raised: 06/30/1999
Year Founded: 1987
Capital Under Management: $35,100,000
Current Activity Level : Actively seeking new investments
Method of Compensation: Return on investment is of primary concern, do not charge fees

NORTH TEXAS MESBIC, INC.

9500 Forest Lane
Suite 430
Dallas, TX 75243
Phone: 214-221-3565
Fax: 214-221-3566

Management and Staff

Allan Lee, President

Type of Firm

Private Firm Investing Own Capital

Industry Association Membership

Natl Assoc of Investment Cos. (NAIC)
Natl assoc of Small Bus. Inv. Co (NASBIC)

Project Preferences

Role in Financing:

Prefer role as deal originator but will also invest in deals created by others

Type of Financing Preferred:

Leveraged Buyout
Mezzanine
Second Stage Financing

Size of Investments Considered

Min Size of Investment Considered (000s): $300
Max Size of Investment Considered: No Limit

Geographical Preferences

United States

Southwest
Texas

Industry Preferences

Consumer Related

Entertainment and Leisure
Retail
Food/Beverage
Consumer Products

Additional Information

Year Founded: 1991
Capital Under Management: $4,500,000
Current Activity Level : Actively seeking new investments
Method of Compensation: Return on invest. most important, but chg. closing fees, service fees, etc.

NORTH TEXAS OPPORTUNITY FUND

13355 Noel Road
Suite 2210
Dallas, TX 75240
Phone: 972-702-7390
Fax: 972-702-7391
E-mail: lms@ntofund.com
Website: www.ntofund.com

Management and Staff

Arthur Hollingsworth, Principal
Gregory Campbell, Principal
Luke Sweetser, Principal

Type of Firm

Private Firm Investing Own Capital

Project Preferences

Type of Financing Preferred:

Balanced

Geographical Preferences

United States

Texas

Industry Preferences

Other

Women/Minority-Owned Bus.

Additional Information

Year Founded: 2000
Capital Under Management: $20,500,000
Current Activity Level : Actively seeking new investments

NOTRE CAPITAL VENTURES

Three Riverway
Suite 630
Houston, TX 77056
Phone: 713-965-0331
Fax: 713-965-0579
Website: www.notrecap.com

Management and Staff

Kenneth Garcia, Managing Director
Richard Howell, Vice President
Shellie LePori, Vice President
Steve Harter, President

Type of Firm

Private Firm Investing Own Capital

Additional Information

Year Founded: 2000
Current Activity Level : Actively seeking new investments

NOVO NETWORKS (FKA: EVENTURES GROUP, INC.)

300 Crescent Court
Suite 800
Dallas, TX 75201
Phone: 972-386-8907
Fax: 972-239-8581
Website: www.evnt.com

Other Offices

520 Madison Avenue
Suite 3820
New York, NY 10022
Phone: 646-658-1700
Fax: 646-658-1717

Management and Staff

Barrett Wissman, President
Jeffrey Marcus, Chairman & CEO

Type of Firm

Private Firm Investing Own Capital

Additional Information

Current Activity Level : Actively seeking new investments

OMNIMED CORP.

4611 Montrose Boulevard
Suite 201
Houston, TX 77006
Phone: 713-524-7373
Fax: 713-524-0987

Other Offices

5430 LBJ Freeway
Suite 1500
Dallas, TX 75240
Phone: 214-661-2024
Fax: 214-701-0530

Management and Staff
Ralph Weaver

Whom to Contact
Ralph Weaver

Type of Firm
Private Firm Investing Own Capital

Project Preferences

Role in Financing:
Prefer role as deal originator but will also invest in deals created by others

Type of Financing Preferred:
First Stage Financing
Second Stage Financing
Start-up Financing

Size of Investments Considered
Min Size of Investment Considered (000s): $500
Max Size of Investment Considered (000s): $1,000

Geographical Preferences

United States
Southwest

Industry Preferences

Biotechnology
Biotech Related Research
Biotech Related Research

Medical/Health
Diagnostic Services
Diagnostic Test Products
Disposable Med. Products
Hospitals/Clinics/Primary

Additional Information
Year Founded: 1986
Current Activity Level : Actively seeking new investments
Method of Compensation: Return on invest. most important, but chg. closing fees, service fees, etc.

ONSET VENTURES

8911 Capital of Texas Highway
Suite 2310
Austin, TX 78759
Phone: 512-349-2255
Website: www.onset.com

See California for full listing.

PHILLIPS-SMITH SPECIALTY RETAIL GROUP

5080 Spectrum Drive
Suite 805 West
Addison, TX 75001
Phone: 972-387-0725
Fax: 972-458-2560
Website: www.phillips-smith.com

Other Offices

102 South Tejon Street
Suite 1100
Colorado Springs, CO 80903
Phone: 719-578-3301
Fax: 719-578-8869

5080 Spectrum Drive
Suite 700 West
Dallas, TX

Seven Locust Lane
Bronxville, NY 10708
Phone: 914-961-0407
Fax: 914-961-0407

Management and Staff
Cece Smith, General Partner
Craig Foley, Principal
Erik Anderson, Chief Financial Officer
G. Michael Machens, General Partner
James Rothe, Principal

Type of Firm
Private Firm Investing Own Capital

Project Preferences

Role in Financing:
Prefer role as deal originator but will also invest in deals created by others

Type of Financing Preferred:
First Stage Financing
Industry Rollups
Leveraged Buyout
Mezzanine
Second Stage Financing
Seed
Start-up Financing

Size of Investments Considered
Min Size of Investment Considered (000s): $1,000
Max Size of Investment Considered: No Limit

Geographical Preferences

United States
All U.S.

Industry Preferences

(% based on actual investment)

Consumer Related	82.3%
Internet Specific	8.6%
Other Products	4.7%
Computer Software and Services	4.5%

Additional Information
Name of Most Recent Fund: Phillips-Smith Specialty Retail Group III, LP
Most Recent Fund Was Raised: 01/01/1993
Year Founded: 1986
Capital Under Management: $140,400,000
Current Activity Level : Actively seeking new investments
Method of Compensation: Return on investment is of primary concern, do not charge fees

POLARIS VENTURE PARTNERS

804 Las Cimas Parkway
Building One, Suite 140
Austin, TX 78746
Phone: 512-225-5400
Fax: 512-225-5444
Website: www.polarisventures.com

See Massachusetts for full listing.

POWERSHIFT GROUP

7600 B N.Capital of Texas
Highway Suite 220
Austin, TX 78731
Phone: 512-306-7330
Fax: 512-306-7331

Management and Staff
Frank Moss, Partner

Type of Firm
Non-Financial Corp. Affiliate or Subsidiary

Additional Information
Current Activity Level : Actively seeking new investments

PRIME NEW VENTURES

600 Congress Avenue
Suite 3000
Austin, TX 78701
Phone: 512-476-7888
Fax: 512-476-4869

Management and Staff
Dean Greenwood, Managing Director
Duncan Butler, Managing Director
Gregory Marchbanks, Managing Partner
Robert Hughes, Managing Director
William Glasgow, Managing Director

Type of Firm
Private Firm Investing Own Capital

Industry Preferences
(% based on actual investment)

Internet Specific	38.5%
Communications and Media	35.1%
Computer Software and Services	13.3%
Semiconductors/Other Elect.	13.1%

Additional Information
Year Founded: 1997
Capital Under Management: $123,200,000
Current Activity Level : Actively seeking new investments

PRIVATE EQUITY PARTNERS

301 Commerce Street
Suite 1600
Fort Worth, TX 76102
Phone: 817-332-1600
Fax: 817-336-7523

Management and Staff
Jeff Alexander, Vice President
Scott Kleberg, President

Whom to Contact
Jeff Alexander
Scott Kleberg

Type of Firm
Private Firm Investing Own Capital

Project Preferences

Role in Financing:
Prefer role as deal originator but will also invest in deals created by others

Type of Financing Preferred:
Industry Rollups
Leveraged Buyout
Second Stage Financing

Geographical Preferences

United States
Southeast
Southwest

Additional Information
Name of Most Recent Fund: Private Equity Partners I, L.P.
Most Recent Fund Was Raised: 07/01/1997
Year Founded: 1996
Capital Under Management: $65,000,000
Current Activity Level : Actively seeking new investments
Method of Compensation: Return on investment is of primary concern, do not charge fees

Q VENTURES

301 Commerce Street
Suite 2975
Fort Worth, TX 76102
Phone: 817-332-5572
E-mail: slett@acmewidget.com
Website: www.qventures.com

Management and Staff
Russ Miron, Managing Director

Type of Firm
Incubators

Project Preferences

Type of Financing Preferred:
Early Stage

Industry Preferences

Internet Specific
Internet

Additional Information
Current Activity Level : Actively seeking new investments

R. CHANEY & CO., INC.

909 Fannin
Suite 1275
Houston, TX 77010-0006
Phone: 713-356-7555
Fax: 713-750-0021

Management and Staff
Curtis F. Harrell
Jason Whitley

Whom to Contact
Curtis F. Harrell
Jason Whitley

Type of Firm
Private Firm Investing Own Capital

Project Preferences

Role in Financing:
Prefer role as deal originator but will also invest in deals created by others

Type of Financing Preferred:
Mezzanine
Second Stage Financing

Geographical Preferences

United States
Rocky Mountain
Southwest

Canada
Western Canada

Industry Preferences

Industrial/Energy
Oil and Gas Exploration
Oil & Gas Drilling,Explor
Alternative Energy
Energy Conservation Relat

Additional Information

Name of Most Recent Fund: R. Chaney & Partners IV L.P.
Most Recent Fund Was Raised: 02/01/1998
Year Founded: 1993
Capital Under Management: $381,000,000
Current Activity Level : Inactive / Unknown
Method of Compensation: Return on investment is of primary concern, do not charge fees

RED RIVER VENTURES

15301 Dallas Parkway
Suite 820
Addison, TX 75001
Phone: 972-687-7770
Fax: 972-687-7760
Website: www.redriverventures.com

Other Offices

1155 University Blvd SE
Albuquerque, NM 87101
Phone: 505-843-4275
Fax: 505-843-4273

Management and Staff

Bruce Duty, Partner
Robert Korman, Partner

Type of Firm

Private Firm Investing Own Capital

Project Preferences

Role in Financing:

Will function either as deal originator or investor in deals created by others

Type of Financing Preferred:

Expansion
Management Buyouts
Second Stage Financing

Size of Investments Considered

Min Size of Investment Considered (000s): $3,000
Max Size of Investment Considered (000s): $5,000

Geographical Preferences

United States

Southwest

Industry Preferences

Communications and Media

Telecommunications
Wireless Communications
Data Communications
Other Communication Prod.

Computer Hardware

Mainframes / Scientific
Mini and Personal/Desktop
Computer Graphics and Dig

Computer Software

Computer Services
Software
Systems Software
Applications Software

Internet Specific

Internet

Semiconductors/Other Elect.

Electronics

Medical/Health

Medical Diagnostics
Diagnostic Services
Diagnostic Test Products
Medical Therapeutics
Drug/Equipmt Delivery
Medical Products
Disposable Med. Products
Pharmaceuticals

Consumer Related

Consumer
Retail
Food/Beverage

Industrial/Energy

Energy
Industrial Products
Factory Automation
Process Control
Robotics
Machinery

Transportation

Transportation

Financial Services

Financial Services

Business Serv.

Services
Distribution
Consulting Services

Manufact.

Manufacturing

Additional Information

Name of Most Recent Fund: Red River Ventures
Most Recent Fund Was Raised: 06/07/2000
Year Founded: 2000
Capital Under Management: $86,000,000
Current Activity Level : Actively seeking new investments
Method of Compensation: Return on investment is of primary concern, do not charge fees

RICE, SANGALIS, TOOLE & WILSON (FKA: RICE CAPITAL PARTNERS)

5847 San Felipe
Suite 4350
Houston, TX 77057
Phone: 713-783-7770
Fax: 713-783-9750
Website: www.rstw.com

Management and Staff

Darl Petty, Managing Director
Don Rice, Managing Partner
Gregory Houghtaling, Managing Director
James Wilson, Managing Partner
Jeffrey Sangalis, Managing Partner
Jeffrey Toole, Managing Partner
Kurt Keene, Managing Director
M. Duyen Le, Chief Financial Officer
Phillip Davidson, Managing Director

Whom to Contact

Don Rice
Jeffrey Sangalis
Jeffrey Toole

Type of Firm

Private Firm Investing Own Capital

Project Preferences

Role in Financing:

Prefer role as deal originator but will also invest in deals created by others

Type of Financing Preferred:

Industry Rollups
Leveraged Buyout
Mezzanine

Size of Investments Considered

Min Size of Investment Considered (000s): $5,000
Max Size of Investment Considered: No Limit

Geographical Preferences

United States

All U.S.

Industry Preferences

(% based on actual investment)

Consumer Related	46.0%
Other Products	34.2%
Industrial/Energy	10.7%
Semiconductors/Other Elect.	5.7%
Communications and Media	2.6%
Computer Hardware	0.8%

Additional Information
Name of Most Recent Fund: RSTW Partners III, L.P.
Most Recent Fund Was Raised: 06/16/1997
Year Founded: 1989
Capital Under Management: $875,000,000
Current Activity Level : Actively seeking new investments
Method of Compensation: Return on invest. most important, but chg. closing fees, service fees, etc.

RICHARD JAFFE & CO., INC.

7318 Royal Circle
Dallas, TX 75230
Phone: 214-265-9397
Fax: 214-739-1845

Management and Staff
Richard Jaffe

Whom to Contact
Richard Jaffe

Type of Firm
Private Firm Investing Own Capital

Project Preferences

Role in Financing:
Prefer role as deal originator but will also invest in deals created by others

Type of Financing Preferred:
First Stage Financing
Leveraged Buyout
Special Situation
Start-up Financing

Size of Investments Considered
Min Size of Investment Considered (000s): $100
Max Size of Investment Considered (000s): $300

Geographical Preferences

United States
Southwest

Industry Preferences

Communications and Media
Commercial Communications
Telecommunications
Satellite Microwave Comm.
Other Communication Prod.

Computer Hardware
Computers
Computer Graphics and Dig

Computer Software
Computer Services

Semiconductors/Other Elect.
Electronics

Medical/Health
Medical Products

Consumer Related
Consumer Products
Consumer Services

Industrial/Energy
Industrial Products
Factory Automation

Financial Services
Real Estate

Business Serv.
Consulting Services

Manufact.
Office Automation Equipmt

Additional Information
Year Founded: 1962
Capital Under Management: $4,000,000
Current Activity Level : Actively seeking new investments
Method of Compensation: Return on invest. most important, but chg. closing fees, service fees, etc.

ROCKMOUNTAIN VENTURES

2450 Coyote Run
Suite 700
Rockwall, TX 75087
Phone: 972-772-5350
Website: www.rockventures.com

See Colorado for full listing.

SAGEBROOK TECHNOLOGY

3811 Turtle Creek Blvd.
Suite 1300
Dallas, TX 75219
Phone: 214-252-0088
Fax: 214-526-9728
E-mail: info@sagebrook.com
Website: www.sagebrook.com

Other Offices
106 East 6th Street
Suite 900
Austin, TX 78701
Phone: 512-322-5350
Fax: 512-349-7900

Management and Staff
Jack Baum, President
Paul Gerling, Partner
Steve Winter, Chief Executive Officer

Type of Firm
Private Firm Investing Own Capital

Additional Information
Current Activity Level : Actively seeking new investments

SBC COMMUNICATIONS

175 East Houston
11th Floor
San Antonio, TX 78205
Phone: 210-351-2575
Fax: 210-351-2547
Website: www.sbc.com

Management and Staff
Keli Flynn, Vice President

Type of Firm
Non-Financial Corp. Affiliate or Subsidiary

Additional Information
Year Founded: 2000
Current Activity Level : Actively seeking new investments

SEED COMPANY PARTNERS

15301 Dallas Parkway
Suite 840
Dallas, TX 75248
Phone: 972-458-5505
Fax: 972-458-5515
Website: www.seedco.com

Management and Staff
Allen Fleener, General Partner
Lawrence Goldstein, General Partner

Type of Firm
Private Firm Investing Own Capital

Project Preferences

Role in Financing:
Prefer role as deal originator but will also invest in deals created by others

Type of Financing Preferred:
First Stage Financing
Seed
Start-up Financing

Size of Investments Considered
Min Size of Investment Considered (000s): $500
Max Size of Investment Considered (000s): $1,000

Geographical Preferences

United States
All U.S.

Industry Preferences

Computer Software
Software

Internet Specific
Internet

Additional Information
Year Founded: 1992
Capital Under Management: $20,000,000
Current Activity Level : Actively seeking new investments
Method of Compensation: Return on investment is of primary concern, do not charge fees

SEVIN ROSEN MANAGEMENT CO.

13455 Noel Road
Suite 1670
Dallas, TX 75240
Phone: 972-702-1100
Fax: 972-702-1103
Website: www.srfunds.com

Other Offices

169 University Avenue
Palo Alto, CA 94301
Phone: 650-326-0550
Fax: 650-326-0707

402 Broadway
Suite 2050
San Diego, CA 92101

6801 N. Capital of Texas Highway
Building 2, Suite 225
Austin, TX 78731
Phone: 512-795-5810
Fax: 512-795-5849

Management and Staff
Al Schuele, General Partner
Amra Tareen, Partner
Charles Phipps, General Partner
David Shrigley, General Partner
Jackie Kimzey, General Partner
Jennifer Roberts, General Partner
John Jaggers, General Partner
John Oxaal, Venture Partner
Jon Bayless, General Partner
Murray Freeman, Venture Partner
Robert Miles, Venture Partner
Rosemary Remacle, Venture Partner
Stephen Domenik, General Partner
Stephen Dow, General Partner
Victor Liu, General Partner

Type of Firm
Private Firm Investing Own Capital

Industry Association Membership
National Venture Capital Association (NVCA)
Western Association of Venture Capitalists (WAVC)

Project Preferences

Role in Financing:
Prefer role in deals created by others

Type of Financing Preferred:
Early Stage
First Stage Financing
Start-up Financing

Size of Investments Considered
Min Size of Investment Considered (000s): $500
Max Size of Investment Considered: No Limit

Geographical Preferences

United States
All U.S.

International
All International

Industry Preferences

(% based on actual investment)

Communications and Media	27.3%
Internet Specific	22.1%
Semiconductors/Other Elect.	17.5%
Computer Software and Services	16.2%
Computer Hardware	9.2%
Industrial/Energy	3.0%
Biotechnology	2.0%
Other Products	1.2%
Medical/Health	1.1%
Consumer Related	0.4%

Additional Information
Name of Most Recent Fund: Sevin Rosen Partners Ltd.
Most Recent Fund Was Raised: 01/01/1981
Year Founded: 1981
Capital Under Management: $1,776,000,000
Current Activity Level : Actively seeking new investments
Method of Compensation: Return on investment is of primary concern, do not charge fees

SILICON VALLEY BANK

9020 Capital of Texas Highway No
Building One Suite
Austin, TX 78759
Phone: 512-372-6750
Fax: 512-794-0855

See California for full listing.

SILVER CREEK TECHNOLOGY INVESTORS (FKA: O'DONNELL & MASUR)

5949 Sherry Lane
Suite 1450
Dallas, TX 75225
Phone: 214-265-2020
Fax: 214-692-6233
Website: www.silvercreekfund.com

Other Offices

730 17th Street
Suite 690
Denver, CO 80202
Phone: 303-573-3720
Fax: 303-573-3740

Management and Staff
Barry Cox, Venture Partner
Barton Burstein, Venture Partner
Mark Masur, General Partner
Martin Silver, Venture Partner
Michael Segrest, General Partner
Russ Silvestri, Venture Partner
Stephen Hamilton, Chief Financial Officer
Terrence Schmid, Venture Partner
Wes Patterson, Venture Partner
William Stanfill, General Partner

Type of Firm
Private Firm Investing Own Capital

Industry Association Membership
National Venture Capital Association (NVCA)

Project Preferences

Role in Financing:
Prefer role as deal originator but will also invest in deals created by others

Type of Financing Preferred:
First Stage Financing
Second Stage Financing

Geographical Preferences

United States
Rocky Mountain
Southwest
West Coast

Industry Preferences

(% based on actual investment)

Communications and Media	63.3%
Semiconductors/Other Elect.	29.3%
Consumer Related	4.8%
Internet Specific	1.4%
Other Products	1.2%

Additional Information
Year Founded: 1995
Capital Under Management: $40,000,000
Current Activity Level : Actively seeking new investments

SOUTHWEST VENTURE GROUP

10878 Westheimer
Suite 178
Houston, TX 77042
Phone: 713-827-8947
Fax: 713-461-1470

Management and Staff
David Klausmeyer

Whom to Contact
David Klausmeyer

Type of Firm
Mgt. Consulting Firm

Project Preferences

Role in Financing:
Prefer role as deal originator but will also invest in deals created by others

Type of Financing Preferred:
Control-block Purchases
First Stage Financing
Leveraged Buyout
Mezzanine
Research and Development
Second Stage Financing
Seed
Special Situation
Start-up Financing

Size of Investments Considered
Min Size of Investment Considered (000s): $50,000
Max Size of Investment Considered: No Limit

Geographical Preferences

United States
All U.S.

Canada
All Canada

International
Australia
Bermuda
China
France
Germany
Italy
Japan
Middle East
South Africa
Spain
United Kingdom

Industry Preferences

Communications and Media
Commercial Communications
Telecommunications
Data Communications
Satellite Microwave Comm.

Computer Hardware
Disk Relat. Memory Device

Computer Software
Computer Services
Systems Software
Applications Software
Artificial Intelligence

Internet Specific
Internet

Semiconductors/Other Elect.
Electronics
Electronic Components
Sensors

Biotechnology
Biotechnology

Medical/Health
Medical/Health
Medical Products

Consumer Related
Food/Beverage
Consumer Products
Consumer Services
Other Restaurants
Education Related

Industrial/Energy
Industrial Products
Materials
Factory Automation
Robotics
Environmental Related

Financial Services
Financial Services

Agr/Forestr/Fish
Mining and Minerals

Additional Information
Year Founded: 1970
Capital Under Management: $120,000,000
Current Activity Level : Actively seeking new investments
Method of Compensation: Return on investment is of primary concern, do not charge fees

SOUTHWEST VENTURE PARTNERSHIPS, THE

16414 San Pedro
Suite 345
San Antonio, TX 78232
Phone: 210-402-1200
Fax: 210-402-1221

Management and Staff
C.R. Tucker, General Partner

Type of Firm
Private Firm Investing Own Capital

Project Preferences

Role in Financing:
Prefer role as deal originator but will also invest in deals created by others

Type of Financing Preferred:
First Stage Financing
Leveraged Buyout
Second Stage Financing
Start-up Financing

Geographical Preferences

United States
Southwest

Industry Preferences

Communications and Media
Communications and Media

Computer Hardware
Computers
Mini and Personal/Desktop
Computer Graphics and Dig

Computer Software
Computer Services
Applications Software

Medical/Health
Diagnostic Services
Diagnostic Test Products
Other Therapeutic
Medical Products
Disposable Med. Products
Hospitals/Clinics/Primary
Pharmaceuticals

Industrial/Energy
Environmental Related

Additional Information

Name of Most Recent Fund: Bioven Partners
Most Recent Fund Was Raised: 01/01/1998
Year Founded: 1975
Capital Under Management: $20,000,000
Current Activity Level : Inactive / Unknown
Method of Compensation: Return on investment is of primary concern, do not charge fees

SSM VENTURES

110 Wild Basin Road
Suite 280
Austin, TX 78746
Phone: 512-437-7900
Fax: 512-437-7925
Website: www.ssmventures.com

See Tennessee for full listing.

STARTECH

1225 N Alma Road, Suite 110
Building 412, P.O. Box 832047
Richardson, TX 75083-2047
Phone: 214-576-9800
Fax: 214-576-9849
Website: www.startech.org

Other Offices

6801 North Capital of Texas Highway
Building 2, Suite 225
Austin, TX 78731
Phone: 512-795-5814
Fax: 512-795-5849

Management and Staff

Frank Gerome, Partner
George Hillhouse, Partner
Matt Blanton, Managing Partner
Paul Nichols, Principal
Robert Carruthers, Managing Partner
Roger Hughes, Partner
Sejal Desai, Principal
Will Tubb, Principal

Type of Firm

University Affiliated Program

Project Preferences

Type of Financing Preferred:
Seed
Startup

Size of Investments Considered
Min Size of Investment Considered (000s): $500
Max Size of Investment Considered (000s): $900

Geographical Preferences

United States
Texas

Industry Preferences

Computer Software
Software

Internet Specific
Internet

Additional Information

Year Founded: 1998
Capital Under Management: $36,000,000
Current Activity Level : Actively seeking new investments

STERNHILL PARTNERS

777 Post Oak Boulevard
Suite 250
Houston, TX 77056
Phone: 713-622-2727
Fax: 713-622-3529
Website: www.sternhillpartners.com

Other Offices

8911 Capital of Texas Highway
Suite 2310
Austin, TX 78759
Phone: 512-349-0240
Fax: 512-349-2888

Management and Staff

David Cabello, Venture Partner
Mansoor Ghori, Principal
Marc Geller, Managing Director
Robert Stearns, Managing Director

Type of Firm

Private Firm Investing Own Capital

Industry Preferences

(% based on actual investment)

Internet Specific	55.0%
Computer Software and Services	18.3%
Communications and Media	18.2%
Semiconductors/Other Elect.	8.5%

Additional Information

Name of Most Recent Fund: Sternhill Partners I, LP
Most Recent Fund Was Raised: 12/20/2000
Year Founded: 1999
Capital Under Management: $100,000,000
Current Activity Level : Actively seeking new investments

STRATFORD EQUITY PARTNERS, L.P.

300 Crescent Court
Suite 500
Dallas, TX 75201
Phone: 214-740-7377
Fax: 214-720-7393

Management and Staff

John Farmer, Managing Partner
Michael Brown, Managing Partner

Type of Firm

Private Firm Investing Own Capital

Industry Association Membership

Natl assoc of Small Bus. Inv. Co (NASBIC)

Project Preferences

Role in Financing:
Prefer role as deal originator but will also invest in deals created by others

Type of Financing Preferred:
Acquisition
Balanced
Expansion
Later Stage
Leveraged Buyout
Management Buyouts
Mezzanine
Recapitalizations

Size of Investments Considered
Min Size of Investment Considered (000s): $1,000
Max Size of Investment Considered: No Limit

Geographical Preferences

United States
All U.S.
All U.S.

Industry Preferences

(% based on actual investment)

Consumer Related	39.2%
Other Products	17.5%
Computer Software and Services	14.8%
Communications and Media	14.0%
Computer Hardware	11.0%
Industrial/Energy	3.5%

Additional Information
Name of Most Recent Fund: Stratford Equity Partners, L.P.
Most Recent Fund Was Raised: 08/30/1995
Year Founded: 1995
Capital Under Management: $110,000,000
Current Activity Level : Actively seeking new investments
Method of Compensation: Return on invest. most important, but chg. closing fees, service fees, etc.

SUMMIT CAPITAL GROUP

600 Travis
Suite 6110
Houston, TX 77002
Phone: 713-332-2700
Fax: 713-332-2722
Website: www.summit-cap.com

Other Offices

6510 Glenridge Park Place
Suite 8
Louisville, KY 40222
Phone: 713-332-2700

Management and Staff
David Graham, Principal
Fred Brazelton, Partner
Fred Lummis, Principal
George Kelly, Principal
Greg Elliott, Partner
Monica Benton, Managing Director

Type of Firm
Investment/Merchant Bank Subsid/Affil

Project Preferences

Role in Financing:
Prefer role as deal originator but will also invest in deals created by others

Type of Financing Preferred:
Control-block Purchases
Expansion
Generalist PE
Leveraged Buyout
Management Buyouts

Size of Investments Considered
Min Size of Investment Considered (000s): $10,000
Max Size of Investment Considered (000s): $40,000

Geographical Preferences

United States
Southeast
Southwest

Industry Preferences

(% based on actual investment)

Computer Software and Services	33.1%
Industrial/Energy	26.9%
Communications and Media	18.0%
Biotechnology	13.9%
Consumer Related	8.2%

Additional Information
Year Founded: 1994
Capital Under Management: $370,000,000
Current Activity Level : Actively seeking new investments
Method of Compensation: Professional fee required whether or not deal closes

SUNWESTERN INVESTMENT GROUP

12221 Merit Drive
Suite 935
Dallas, TX 75251
Phone: 972-239-5650
Fax: 972-701-0024

Other Offices

12221 Merit Drive
Suite 1300
Dallas, TX 75251
Phone: 214-239-5650

Plaza del Mar
12520 High Bluff Drive
San Diego, CA 92130
Phone: 619-259-8100
Fax: 619-259-0470

Type of Firm
Private Firm Investing Own Capital

Industry Association Membership
Natl assoc of Small Bus. Inv. Co (NASBIC)

Project Preferences

Role in Financing:
Prefer role as deal originator but will also invest in deals created by others

Type of Financing Preferred:
Leveraged Buyout
Second Stage Financing
Special Situation

Size of Investments Considered
Min Size of Investment Considered (000s): $500
Max Size of Investment Considered (000s): $1,000

Geographical Preferences

United States
Southwest
West Coast

Industry Preferences

Communications and Media
Data Communications
Satellite Microwave Comm.
Other Communication Prod.

Computer Hardware
Computers
Computer Graphics and Dig
Disk Relat. Memory Device

Computer Software
Computer Services
Systems Software
Applications Software

Semiconductors/Other Elect.
Electronics
Electronic Components
Semiconductor
Component Testing Equipmt
Laser Related
Fiber Optics

Medical/Health
Diagnostic Services
Drug/Equipmt Delivery
Other Therapeutic
Medical Products
Disposable Med. Products
Pharmaceuticals

Additional Information
Year Founded: 1982
Capital Under Management: $33,600,000
Current Activity Level : Actively seeking new investments
Method of Compensation: Return on invest. most important, but chg. closing fees, service fees, etc.

TECHXAS VENTURES, LLC

5000 Plaza on the Lake
Suite 275
Austin, TX 78746
Phone: 512-343-0118
Fax: 512-343-1879
Website: www.techxas.com

Management and Staff
Bruce Ezell, General Partner
James Schellhase, General Partner
Michael LaVigna, General Partner
Steve Vandergraft, General Partner

Type of Firm
Venture Consulting Firm

Industry Association Membership
National Venture Capital Association (NVCA)

Project Preferences

Role in Financing:
Will function either as deal originator or investor in deals created by others

Type of Financing Preferred:
Balanced
Early Stage
First Stage Financing
Joint Ventures
Second Stage Financing
Seed
Startup

Size of Investments Considered
Min Size of Investment Considered (000s): $500
Max Size of Investment Considered (000s): $5,000

Geographical Preferences

United States
Texas

Industry Preferences

(% based on actual investment)

Computer Software and Services	55.5%
Computer Hardware	18.7%
Semiconductors/Other Elect.	13.7%
Internet Specific	12.0%
Other Products	0.1%

Additional Information
Name of Most Recent Fund: Techxas Fund v 1.0, L.P.
Most Recent Fund Was Raised: 10/01/1998
Year Founded: 1998
Capital Under Management: $75,000,000
Current Activity Level : Actively seeking new investments
Method of Compensation: Return on investment is of primary concern, do not charge fees

TEXAS GROWTH FUND MANAGEMENT

111 Congress Avenue
Suite 2900
Austin, TX 78701
Phone: 512-322-3100
Fax: 512-322-3101
Website: www.texasgrowthfund.com

Management and Staff
Barry Twomey, Principal
Brent Humphries, Principal
James Kozlowski, Principal
Janet Waldeier, Chief Financial Officer
Stephen Soileau, Principal

Whom to Contact
J. Brent Humphries

Type of Firm
Private Firm Investing Own Capital

Project Preferences

Role in Financing:
Prefer role as deal originator but will also invest in deals created by others

Type of Financing Preferred:
Acquisition
Later Stage
Leveraged Buyout
Management Buyouts
Mezzanine
Recapitalizations
Second Stage Financing

Size of Investments Considered
Min Size of Investment Considered (000s): $7,500
Max Size of Investment Considered (000s): $40,000

Geographical Preferences

United States
Texas
All U.S.

Industry Preferences

(% based on actual investment)

Other Products	37.2%
Communications and Media	18.1%
Industrial/Energy	13.3%
Computer Software and Services	10.4%
Consumer Related	10.0%
Internet Specific	7.2%
Medical/Health	2.6%
Computer Hardware	1.2%

Additional Information
Name of Most Recent Fund: Texas Growth Fund II-1998 Trust
Most Recent Fund Was Raised: 12/22/1998
Year Founded: 1992
Capital Under Management: $577,000,000
Current Activity Level : Actively seeking new investments
Method of Compensation: Return on investment is of primary concern, do not charge fees

TL VENTURES

15305 Dallas Parkway
Suite 300 Colonnade III
Addison, TX 75001
Phone: 310-914-0783
Fax: 602-922-0787
Website: www.tlventures.com

See Pennsylvania for full listing.

TRELLIS PARTNERS

2600 Via Fortuna
Suite 150
Austin, TX 78746
Phone: 512-330-9200
Fax: 512-330-9400
Website: www.trellispartners.com

Management and Staff
Alex Broeker, General Partner
H. Leland Murphy, Founding Partner
John Long, Founding Partner
Sonja Eagle, Partner

Type of Firm
Private Firm Investing Own Capital

Industry Association Membership
National Venture Capital Association (NVCA)

Project Preferences

Role in Financing:
Will function either as deal originator or investor in deals created by others

Type of Financing Preferred:
Early Stage
First Stage Financing
Second Stage Financing
Seed
Start-up Financing

Geographical Preferences

United States
Southwest

Industry Preferences

(% based on actual investment)

Internet Specific	40.1%
Computer Software and Services	31.4%
Communications and Media	17.9%
Semiconductors/Other Elect.	10.5%

Additional Information
Year Founded: 1997
Capital Under Management: $67,000,000
Current Activity Level : Actively seeking new investments
Method of Compensation: Return on investment is of primary concern, do not charge fees

TRIAD VENTURES, LTD.

4600 Post Oak Place
Suite 100
Houston, TX 77027
Phone: 713-627-9111
Fax: 713-627-9119

Other Offices

1716 Briarcrest
Suite 507
Bryan, TX 77802
Phone: 409-846-6072
Fax: 409-846-9172

4600 Post Oak PLace
Suite 100
Houston, TX 77027
Phone: 713-627-9111
Fax: 713-627-9119

8911 Capital of Texas Highway
Westech 360, Suite 2310
Austin, TX 78759
Phone: 512-342-2024
Fax: 512-342-1993

Management and Staff
David Mueller

Whom to Contact
David Mueller

Type of Firm
Private Firm Investing Own Capital

Project Preferences

Role in Financing:
Prefer role as deal originator but will also invest in deals created by others

Type of Financing Preferred:
First Stage Financing
Mezzanine
Second Stage Financing

Size of Investments Considered
Min Size of Investment Considered (000s): $300
Max Size of Investment Considered (000s): $800

Geographical Preferences

United States
Southwest

Industry Preferences

(% based on actual investment)

Semiconductors/Other Elect.	24.0%
Computer Software and Services	16.3%
Biotechnology	15.7%
Medical/Health	15.0%
Internet Specific	12.8%
Industrial/Energy	6.8%
Communications and Media	5.2%
Other Products	3.5%
Consumer Related	0.8%

Additional Information
Year Founded: 1984
Capital Under Management: $50,000,000
Current Activity Level : Actively seeking new investments
Method of Compensation: Return on investment is of primary concern, do not charge fees

TRITON VENTURES

6801 N. Capital of Texas Hwy.
Building 2, Suite 225
Austin, TX 78731
Phone: 512-795-5820
Fax: 512-795-5828
Website: www.tritonventures.com

Management and Staff
D. Scott Collier, Managing Director
Laura Kilcrease, Managing Director

Type of Firm
Private Firm Investing Own Capital

Industry Association Membership
National Venture Capital Association (NVCA)

Project Preferences

Type of Financing Preferred:
Early Stage

Size of Investments Considered
Min Size of Investment Considered (000s): $500
Max Size of Investment Considered (000s): $4,000

Geographical Preferences

United States
All U.S.

Industry Preferences

Communications and Media
Communications and Media

Internet Specific
Internet

Additional Information
Current Activity Level : Actively seeking new investments

VANGUARD VENTURE PARTNERS

1330 Post Oak Boulevard
Suite 1550
Houston, TX 77056
Phone: 713-877-1662
Fax: 713-877-8669
Website: www.vanguardventures.com

See California for full listing.

VENTEX MANAGEMENT, INC.

3417 Milam St.
Houston, TX 77002-9531
Phone: 713-659-7870
Fax: 713-659-7855

Type of Firm
Private Firm Investing Own Capital

Industry Association Membership
Natl assoc of Small Bus. Inv. Co (NASBIC)

Project Preferences

Role in Financing:
Prefer role as deal originator but will also invest in deals created by others

Type of Financing Preferred:
Leveraged Buyout
Mezzanine
Second Stage Financing
Special Situation

Size of Investments Considered
Min Size of Investment Considered (000s): $2,000
Max Size of Investment Considered: No Limit

Geographical Preferences

United States
Southwest

Industry Preferences

Communications and Media
Commercial Communications
Data Communications
Other Communication Prod.

Computer Hardware
Integrated Turnkey System

Computer Software
Computer Services
Applications Software

Semiconductors/Other Elect.
Sensors
Fiber Optics
Analytic/Scientific

Biotechnology
Industrial Biotechnology
Biotech Related Research

Medical/Health
Medical Diagnostics
Diagnostic Services
Diagnostic Test Products
Drug/Equipmt Delivery
Medical Products
Disposable Med. Products
Hospitals/Clinics/Primary

Consumer Related
Retail
Food/Beverage
Consumer Products
Consumer Services
Education Related

Industrial/Energy
Alternative Energy
Industrial Products
Materials
Machinery
Environmental Related

Transportation
Transportation

Manufact.
Publishing

Agr/Forestr/Fish
Agriculture related

Additional Information
Name of Most Recent Fund: Smith Miller Partners II
Most Recent Fund Was Raised: 01/01/1991
Year Founded: 1978
Capital Under Management: $43,000,000
Current Activity Level : Actively seeking new investments
Method of Compensation: Return on investment is of primary concern, do not charge fees

VENTURELINK HOLDINGS

Two Galleria Centre
13455 Noel Road, Suite 1710
Dallas, TX 75240
Phone: 972-720-1993
Fax: 972-720-1893
Website: www.venturelinkholdings.com

Management and Staff
Bobby Hashaway, Chief Operating Officer

Type of Firm
Private Firm Investing Own Capital

Project Preferences

Type of Financing Preferred:
Balanced

Industry Preferences

Internet Specific
Internet

Additional Information
Current Activity Level : Actively seeking new investments

VENTURES MEDICAL ASSOCIATES

7 Switchbud Place
Suite 192
Spring, TX 77380
Phone: 281-364-1003
Fax: 281-364-1082

Other Offices

16945 Northchase Dr
Suite 2150
Houston, TX 77060
Phone: 713-873-5748

Management and Staff
Stanley Appel, Partner
William Mullaney, Managing Partner

Whom to Contact
Cyndi Alvarado

Type of Firm
Private Firm Investing Own Capital

Project Preferences

Role in Financing:
Will function either as deal originator or investor in deals created by others

Type of Financing Preferred:
Early Stage
Start-up Financing

Size of Investments Considered
Min Size of Investment Considered (000s): $500
Max Size of Investment Considered (000s): $2,000

Geographical Preferences

United States
Southwest
West Coast

Industry Preferences

(% based on actual investment)

Medical/Health	65.5%
Biotechnology	27.8%
Computer Software and Services	6.7%

Additional Information
Name of Most Recent Fund: Ventures Medical
Most Recent Fund Was Raised: 09/01/1992
Year Founded: 1987
Capital Under Management: $33,900,000
Current Activity Level : Actively seeking new investments
Method of Compensation: Return on investment is of primary concern, do not charge fees

VERO GROUP PLC

811 Dallas Street
Suite 1025
Houston, TX 77002
Phone: 713-655-0071
Fax: 713-655-0072

Type of Firm
Private Firm Investing Own Capital

Project Preferences

Role in Financing:
Prefer role as deal originator but will also invest in deals created by others

Type of Financing Preferred:
Control-block Purchases
Leveraged Buyout
Mezzanine
Second Stage Financing
Special Situation

Size of Investments Considered
Min Size of Investment Considered (000s): $50,000
Max Size of Investment Considered: No Limit

Geographical Preferences

United States
All U.S.

Canada
All Canada

International
Afghanistan
Australia
Bermuda
China
Eastern Europe
France
Germany
Italy
Middle East
South Africa
Spain
United Kingdom

Industry Preferences

Communications and Media
Commercial Communications
Telecommunications
Data Communications

Computer Other
Computer Related

Semiconductors/Other Elect.
Electronic Components

Medical/Health
Medical/Health

Consumer Related
Consumer

Industrial/Energy
Industrial Products

Additional Information
Year Founded: 1986
Capital Under Management: $1,000,000,000
Current Activity Level : Actively seeking new investments
Method of Compensation: Return on investment is of primary concern, do not charge fees

WEST CENTRAL CAPITAL CORP.

9533 Ferndale Road
Suite 103
Dallas, TX 75238-4424
Phone: 214-348-3969

Management and Staff
Howard Jacob

Whom to Contact
Howard Jacob

Type of Firm
Private Firm Investing Own Capital

Project Preferences

Role in Financing:
Prefer role as deal originator

Type of Financing Preferred:
Second Stage Financing

Geographical Preferences

International
No Preference

Industry Preferences

Medical/Health
Hospital/Other Instit.

Consumer Related
Franchises(NEC)
Consumer Products
Consumer Services

Industrial/Energy
Industrial Products
Machinery

Financial Services
Real Estate

Additional Information
Year Founded: 1964
Current Activity Level : Actively seeking new investments
Method of Compensation: Return on invest. most important, but chg. closing fees, service fees, etc.

WINGATE PARTNERS, L.P.

750 North St. Paul
Suite 1200
Dallas, TX 75201
Phone: 214-720-1313
Fax: 214-871-8799

Other Offices

750 North St. Paul
Suite 1200
Dallas, TX

950 Echo Lane
Suite 335
Houston, TX 77024
Phone: 713-973-7722
Fax: 713-973-8237

Type of Firm
Private Firm Investing Own Capital

Project Preferences

Role in Financing:
Prefer role as deal originator but will also invest in deals created by others

Type of Financing Preferred:
Control-block Purchases
Leveraged Buyout

Size of Investments Considered
Min Size of Investment Considered (000s): $20,000
Max Size of Investment Considered: No Limit

Geographical Preferences

United States
All U.S.

Canada
All Canada

Industry Preferences

Semiconductors/Other Elect.
Electronic Components
Controllers and Sensors
Sensors
Component Testing Equipmt
Analytic/Scientific

Medical/Health
Diagnostic Test Products
Other Therapeutic
Disposable Med. Products

Consumer Related
Retail
Consumer Products

Industrial/Energy
Materials
Factory Automation
Machinery
Environmental Related

Business Serv.
Distribution

Additional Information
Name of Most Recent Fund: Wingate Partners II, L.P.
Most Recent Fund Was Raised: 12/01/1994
Year Founded: 1987
Capital Under Management: $12,900,000
Current Activity Level : Actively seeking new investments
Method of Compensation: Return on invest. most important, but chg. closing fees, service fees, etc.

UTAH

EVERGREEN VENTURES

588 East Quail Road
Orem, UT 84057
Phone: 801-225-7999
Fax: 801-225-8542

Management and Staff
any of above

Whom to Contact
any of above

Type of Firm
Private Firm Investing Own Capital

Project Preferences

Role in Financing:
Prefer role as deal originator but will also invest in deals created by others

Type of Financing Preferred:
Leveraged Buyout
Mezzanine
Second Stage Financing

Size of Investments Considered
Min Size of Investment Considered (000s): $10,000
Max Size of Investment Considered: No Limit

Industry Preferences

(% based on actual investment)

Computer Software and Services	53.6%
Internet Specific	22.5%
Medical/Health	14.6%
Computer Hardware	4.5%
Semiconductors/Other Elect.	4.3%
Communications and Media	0.5%

Additional Information
Name of Most Recent Fund: Evergreen Ventures
Most Recent Fund Was Raised: 03/01/1985
Year Founded: 1994
Current Activity Level : Inactive / Unknown
Method of Compensation: Return on invest. most important, but chg. closing fees, service fees, etc.

FIRST SECURITY BUSINESS INVESTMENT CORP.

15 East 100 South
Suite 100
Salt Lake City, UT 84111
Phone: 801-246-5737
Fax: 801-246-5740

Type of Firm
SBIC Not elsewhere classified

Industry Association Membership
Natl assoc of Small Bus. Inv. Co (NASBIC)

Project Preferences

Role in Financing:
Prefer role as deal originator but will also invest in deals created by others

Type of Financing Preferred:
Leveraged Buyout
Mezzanine
Second Stage Financing

Size of Investments Considered
Min Size of Investment Considered (000s): $300
Max Size of Investment Considered (000s): $800

Geographical Preferences

United States
Rocky Mountain
West Coast

Industry Preferences

Communications and Media
Other Communication Prod.

Computer Hardware
Computers

Semiconductors/Other Elect.
Electronics

Medical/Health
Medical Products

Consumer Related
Consumer Products

Industrial/Energy
Industrial Products

Additional Information
Name of Most Recent Fund: First Security Business Investment - Unkown
Most Recent Fund Was Raised: 01/01/1995
Year Founded: 1993
Capital Under Management: $5,000,000
Current Activity Level : Actively seeking new investments
Method of Compensation: Return on invest. most important, but chg. closing fees, service fees, etc.

NOVELL VENTURES

1800 South Novell Place
Provo, UT 84606
Phone: 801-861-1644
Fax: 801-861-1677
Website: www.novell.com

Management and Staff
Blake Modersitzki, Vice President
Christopher Andrews, Principal
Rob Kain, Principal

Type of Firm
Non-Financial Corp. Affiliate or Subsidiary

Industry Association Membership
National Venture Capital Association (NVCA)

Project Preferences

Role in Financing:
Will function either as deal originator or investor in deals created by others

Type of Financing Preferred:
Early Stage

Size of Investments Considered
Min Size of Investment Considered (000s): $1,000
Max Size of Investment Considered (000s): $5,000

Industry Preferences

(% based on actual investment)

Internet Specific	54.6%
Computer Software and Services	43.7%
Communications and Media	1.6%

Additional Information
Year Founded: 1997
Capital Under Management: $220,000,000
Current Activity Level : Actively seeking new investments

RED ROCK CAPITAL

5252 N. Edgewood Drive
Suite 300
Provo, UT 84604
Phone: 801-222-9414
Fax: 801-222-9914
E-mail: admin@redrockcapital.com
Website: www.redrockcapital.com

Management and Staff
Kirby Cochran, Managing Partner
William Sadleir, Managing Partner
William Davidson, Managing Partner

Type of Firm
Incubators

Industry Association Membership
National Venture Capital Association (NVCA)

Additional Information
Current Activity Level : Actively seeking new investments

UTAH VENTURES II, L.P. (A.K.A. UNION VENTURES)

423 Wakara Way
Suite 206
Salt Lake City, UT 84108
Phone: 801-583-5922
Fax: 801-583-4105
Website: www.uven.com

Other Offices

10700 SW Beaverton
Hillsdale Hwy 548
Beaverton, OR 97005
Phone: 503-574-4125

32511 Sea Island Drive
Dana Pt., CA 92629
Phone: 949-661-2861

400 Lincoln Center Tower
10260 SW Greenburg Road
Portland, OR 97223
Phone: 503-293-3588
Fax: 503-293-3527

Management and Staff
Alan Dishlip, General Partner
Allan Wolfe, General Partner
James Dreyfous, Managing General Partner
Steve Borst, Partner

Type of Firm
SBIC Not elsewhere classified

Industry Association Membership
National Venture Capital Association (NVCA)
Natl assoc of Small Bus. Inv. Co (NASBIC)

Project Preferences

Role in Financing:
Prefer role as deal originator but will also invest in deals created by others

Type of Financing Preferred:
Early Stage

Size of Investments Considered
Min Size of Investment Considered (000s): $1,000
Max Size of Investment Considered (000s): $7,000

Geographical Preferences

United States
Northwest
Rocky Mountain

Industry Preferences

(% based on actual investment)

Internet Specific	54.9%
Biotechnology	20.4%
Medical/Health	16.4%
Computer Software and Services	6.3%
Industrial/Energy	1.1%
Computer Hardware	0.6%
Semiconductors/Other Elect.	0.3%
Communications and Media	0.2%

Additional Information
Name of Most Recent Fund: Utah Ventures II, L.P.
Most Recent Fund Was Raised: 04/01/1998
Year Founded: 1986
Capital Under Management: $67,000,000
Current Activity Level : Actively seeking new investments
Method of Compensation: Return on investment is of primary concern, do not charge fees

WASATCH VENTURE FUND (FKA: WASATCH VENTURE CORPORATION)

One South Main Street
Suite 1660
Salt Lake City, UT 84133
Phone: 801-524-8939
Fax: 801-524-8941

Other Offices

400 Seaport Court
Suite 250
Redwood City, CA 94059
Phone: 650-599-9000

Management and Staff
Kent Madsen, Partner
Nick Efstratis, Partner
Todd Stevens, Managing Director

Whom to Contact
Todd Stevens

Type of Firm
SBIC Not elsewhere classified

Industry Association Membership
National Venture Capital Association (NVCA)
Natl assoc of Small Bus. Inv. Co (NASBIC)

Project Preferences

Role in Financing:
Prefer role as deal originator but will also invest in deals created by others

Type of Financing Preferred:
Early Stage

Size of Investments Considered
Min Size of Investment Considered (000s): $500
Max Size of Investment Considered (000s): $2,000

Geographical Preferences

United States
Rocky Mountain
West Coast

Industry Preferences

(% based on actual investment)

Internet Specific	56.5%
Computer Software and Services	19.6%
Communications and Media	11.9%
Semiconductors/Other Elect.	4.7%
Other Products	3.5%
Computer Hardware	1.8%
Biotechnology	1.0%
Consumer Related	0.6%
Medical/Health	0.4%

Additional Information

Name of Most Recent Fund: Wasatch Venture Fund II, LLC
Most Recent Fund Was Raised: 12/01/1998
Year Founded: 1994
Capital Under Management: $160,000,000
Current Activity Level : Actively seeking new investments
Method of Compensation: Return on investment is of primary concern, do not charge fees

VERMONT

GREEN MOUNTAIN ADVISORS, INC.

PO Box 1230
Clubhouse Road
Quechee, VT 05059
Phone: 802-296-7800
Fax: 802-296-6012

Management and Staff
Richard Egan, Vice President
Sarah Martel, Vice President
Timothy Briglin, Vice President

Whom to Contact
Michael Sweatman

Type of Firm
Private Firm Investing Own Capital

Industry Association Membership
Natl assoc of Small Bus. Inv. Co (NASBIC)

Project Preferences

Role in Financing:
Prefer role as deal originator but will also invest in deals created by others

Type of Financing Preferred:
Expansion
Mezzanine
Second Stage Financing

Size of Investments Considered
Min Size of Investment Considered (000s): $100
Max Size of Investment Considered (000s): $500

Geographical Preferences

United States
All U.S.
Northeast

Industry Preferences

(% based on actual investment)

Industrial/Energy	91.0%
Other Products	4.7%
Computer Software and Services	2.7%
Medical/Health	0.5%
Computer Hardware	0.5%
Communications and Media	0.3%
Consumer Related	0.3%
Biotechnology	0.0%

Additional Information
Name of Most Recent Fund: Green Mountain Partners II, L.P.
Most Recent Fund Was Raised: 12/21/1998
Year Founded: 1993
Capital Under Management: $432,000,000
Current Activity Level : Actively seeking new investments
Method of Compensation: Return on invest. most important, but chg. closing fees, service fees, etc.

NORTH ATLANTIC CAPITAL CORP.

76 St. Paul Street
Suite 600
Burlington, VT 05401
Phone: 802-658-7820
Fax: 802-658-5757
Website: www.northatlanticcapital.com

See Maine for full listing.

VIRGINIA

BLUE WATER CAPITAL, LLC

1420 Beverly Road
Suite 300
McLean, VA 22101
Phone: 703-790-8821
Fax: 703-443-1849
Website: www.bluewatercapital.com

Other Offices

260 E. Brown Street
Suite 310
Birmingham, MI 48009
Phone: 248-647-2010
Fax: 248-647-1130

Management and Staff
Eugene Weber, President
Henry Barratt, Managing Director
Kim Cooke, Managing Director
Michael Acheson, Managing Director
Reid Miles, Managing Director
Wilbur Priester, Chief Financial Officer

Whom to Contact
Kim Daniel Cooke

Type of Firm
Private Firm Investing Own Capital

Industry Association Membership
Mid-Atlantic Venture Association
Western Association of Venture Capitalists (WAVC)

Project Preferences

Role in Financing:
Prefer role as deal originator but will also invest in deals created by others

Type of Financing Preferred:
Expansion

Size of Investments Considered
Min Size of Investment Considered (000s): $5,000
Max Size of Investment Considered (000s): $7,000

Geographical Preferences

United States
All U.S.
East Coast

Canada
All Canada

Industry Preferences

(% based on actual investment)

Internet Specific	44.2%
Computer Software and Services	42.2%
Communications and Media	9.4%
Biotechnology	2.2%
Medical/Health	1.2%
Semiconductors/Other Elect.	0.8%

Additional Information
Name of Most Recent Fund: Blue Water Venture Fund II, L.L.C.
Most Recent Fund Was Raised: 09/01/1998
Year Founded: 1996
Capital Under Management: $76,000,000
Current Activity Level : Actively seeking new investments
Method of Compensation: Return on investment is of primary concern, do not charge fees

CALVERT SOCIAL VENTURE PARTNERS, L.P.

402 Maple Avenue West
Vienna, VA 22180
Phone: 703-255-4930
Fax: 703-255-4931

Management and Staff
D. Wayne Silby, Managing Director
John May, Managing Director
Steve Graubart, Managing Director

Type of Firm
Private Firm Investing Own Capital

Industry Association Membership
Mid-Atlantic Venture Association
National Venture Capital Association (NVCA)

Project Preferences

Role in Financing:
Will function either as deal originator or investor in deals created by others

Type of Financing Preferred:
First Stage Financing

Size of Investments Considered
Min Size of Investment Considered (000s): $100
Max Size of Investment Considered (000s): $750

Geographical Preferences

United States
Mid Atlantic

Industry Preferences

Semiconductors/Other Elect.
Sensors

Biotechnology
Biosensors
Biotech Related Research

Medical/Health
Medical Diagnostics
Diagnostic Services
Medical Therapeutics
Other Therapeutic

Consumer Related
Retail
Consumer Products
Consumer Services
Education Related

Industrial/Energy
Alternative Energy
Energy Conservation Relat
Environmental Related

Business Serv.
Consulting Services

Additional Information
Name of Most Recent Fund: Public Venture Fund
Most Recent Fund Was Raised: 05/01/1998
Year Founded: 1989
Capital Under Management: $10,000,000
Current Activity Level : Actively seeking new investments
Method of Compensation: Return on investment is of primary concern, do not charge fees

CAPITAL INVESTORS

1001 Nineteenth Street North
Arlington, VA 22209
Phone: 703-469-1082
Fax: 703-469-1063
Website: www.capitalinvestors.com

Management and Staff
Andrew Sachs, President
Jeff Tonkel, President

Type of Firm
Investment or Angel network

Industry Association Membership
Mid-Atlantic Venture Association

Project Preferences

Role in Financing:
Prefer role in deals created by others

Type of Financing Preferred:
Early Stage
First Stage Financing
Second Stage Financing
Seed

Size of Investments Considered
Min Size of Investment Considered (000s): $50
Max Size of Investment Considered (000s): $1,000

Geographical Preferences
United States
D. of Columbia

Industry Preferences
Communications and Media
Telecommunications

Computer Software
Software

Internet Specific
Internet

Additional Information
Year Founded: 1998
Current Activity Level : Actively seeking new investments
Method of Compensation: Return on investment is of primary concern, do not charge fees

CEO VENTURE FUND

1950 Old Gallows Road
Suite 440
Vienna, VA 22182
Phone: 703-847-8823
Fax: 703-847-1848
Website: www.ceoventurefund.com

See Pennsylvania for full listing.

COLONNADE CAPITAL L.L.C.

901 East Byrd Street
Suite 1300
Richmond, VA 23219
Phone: 804-782-3501
Fax: 804-782-6606

Type of Firm
Private Firm Investing Own Capital

Project Preferences
Role in Financing:
Prefer role as deal originator but will also invest in deals created by others

Type of Financing Preferred:
Leveraged Buyout

Geographical Preferences
United States
All U.S.

Canada
All Canada

International
Australia
Bermuda
China
France
Germany
Italy
South Africa
Spain
United Kingdom

Industry Preferences
Communications and Media
Radio & TV Broadcasting
Data Communications

Semiconductors/Other Elect.
Sensors

Medical/Health
Diagnostic Services
Diagnostic Test Products
Other Therapeutic
Medical Products
Disposable Med. Products

Consumer Related
Entertainment and Leisure
Retail
Food/Beverage
Consumer Products
Consumer Services
Other Restaurants

Industrial/Energy
Industrial Products
Factory Automation
Machinery
Environmental Related

Manufact.
Publishing

Additional Information
Name of Most Recent Fund: Commonwealth Investors II, L.P.
Most Recent Fund Was Raised: 07/03/1996
Year Founded: 1996
Capital Under Management: $60,000,000
Current Activity Level : Actively seeking new investments
Method of Compensation: Return on invest. most important, but chg. closing fees, service fees, etc.

CONTINENTAL S.B.I.C.

4141 N. Henderson Road
Suite #8
Arlington, VA 22203
Phone: 703-527-5200
Fax: 703-527-3700

Management and Staff
Arthur Walters, President
Mark Walters, Vice President
Thomas Goodfellow, Chief Financial Officer

Whom to Contact
Michael W. Jones

Type of Firm
Investment/Merchant Bank Subsid/Affil

Industry Association Membership
Mid-Atlantic Venture Association
National Venture Capital Association (NVCA)
Natl assoc of Small Bus. Inv. Co (NASBIC)

Project Preferences
Role in Financing:
Will function either as deal originator or investor in deals created by others

Type of Financing Preferred:
Early Stage
Expansion
First Stage Financing
Fund of Funds
Joint Ventures
Leveraged Buyout
Management Buyouts
Mezzanine
Private Placement
Second Stage Financing
Seed
Special Situation
Startup

Size of Investments Considered
Min Size of Investment Considered (000s): $300
Max Size of Investment Considered (000s): $5,000

Geographical Preferences

United States
Mid Atlantic
Northeast
Southeast
Southwest

Canada
Central Canada
Ontario
Quebec

International
Belgium
China
Eastern Europe
Germany
Latin America
Luxembourg
Mexico
Netherlands
Spain
United Kingdom

Industry Preferences

Communications and Media
Radio & TV Broadcasting
Telecommunications
Wireless Communications
Satellite Microwave Comm.

Computer Software
Computer Services
Data Processing
Software
Systems Software
Applications Software
Artificial Intelligence

Internet Specific
Internet

Semiconductors/Other Elect.
Laser Related
Fiber Optics

Medical/Health
Medical Products

Consumer Related
Hotels and Resorts
Education Related

Industrial/Energy
Energy
Robotics

Transportation
Aerospace

Financial Services
Financial Services
Insurance
Real Estate

Business Serv.
Distribution

Utilities
Utilities

Additional Information
Year Founded: 1990
Capital Under Management: $2,000,000
Current Activity Level : Actively seeking new investments
Method of Compensation: Return on invest. most important, but chg. closing fees, service fees, etc.

DINNER CLUB, LLC, THE

402 Maple Avenue West
Vienna, VA 22180
Phone: 703-255-4930
Fax: 703-255-4931
Website: www.thedinnerclub.com

Management and Staff
John May

Whom to Contact
John May

Type of Firm
Private Firm Investing Own Capital

Industry Association Membership
Mid-Atlantic Venture Association

Project Preferences

Role in Financing:
Will function either as deal originator or investor in deals created by others

Type of Financing Preferred:
Early Stage

Size of Investments Considered
Min Size of Investment Considered (000s): $250
Max Size of Investment Considered (000s): $1,000

Geographical Preferences

United States
Mid Atlantic

Additional Information
Year Founded: 1999
Current Activity Level : Actively seeking new investments
Method of Compensation: Return on investment is of primary concern, do not charge fees

DRAPER ATLANTIC MANAGEMENT CO., LLC

11600 Sunrise Valley Drive
Suite 380
Reston, VA 20191
Phone: 703-995-3600
Fax: 703-995-3588
Website: www.draperatlantic.com

Management and Staff
Chris Miller, Principal
Dan Rua, Partner
James Lynch, Founder
John Backus, Managing Partner
Thanasis Delistathis, Principal
Timothy Draper, Founder

Type of Firm
Private Firm Investing Own Capital

Industry Association Membership
Mid-Atlantic Venture Association

Project Preferences

Type of Financing Preferred:
Start-up Financing

Geographical Preferences

United States
Mid Atlantic
Southeast
All U.S.

Industry Preferences

(% based on actual investment)

Internet Specific	73.6%
Communications and Media	12.3%
Other Products	7.0%
Computer Software and Services	3.9%
Computer Hardware	3.2%

Additional Information
Name of Most Recent Fund: Draper Atlantic Venture Fund
Most Recent Fund Was Raised: 07/01/1999
Year Founded: 1999
Capital Under Management: $372,000,000
Current Activity Level : Actively seeking new investments

DYNAFUND VENTURES, L.L.C.

1555 Wilson Blvd.
Suite 320
Arlington, VA 22209
Phone: 703-841-0990
Fax: 703-841-8395
Website: www.dynafundventures.com

See California for full listing.

EDISON VENTURE FUND

1420 Spring Hill Road
Suite 420
McLean, VA 22102
Phone: 703-903-9546
Fax: 703-903-9528
Website: www.edisonventure.com

See New Jersey for full listing.

FAIRFAX PARTNERS

8000 Towers Crescent Drive
Suite 940
Vienna, VA 22182
Phone: 703-847-9486
Fax: 703-847-0911

Management and Staff
Raymond List, Managing Partner

Whom to Contact
Bruce K. Gouldey
Stephen Ritterbush

Type of Firm
Mgt. Consulting Firm

Project Preferences

Role in Financing:
Prefer role as deal originator

Type of Financing Preferred:
First Stage Financing
Industry Rollups
Leveraged Buyout
Second Stage Financing
Start-up Financing

Geographical Preferences

United States
Mid Atlantic

Industry Preferences

Communications and Media
Commercial Communications

Computer Software
Computer Services

Internet Specific
Internet

Medical/Health
Medical/Health

Additional Information
Name of Most Recent Fund: Fairfax Partners I/Venture Fund of Washington
Most Recent Fund Was Raised: 01/01/1989
Year Founded: 1989
Capital Under Management: $15,000,000
Current Activity Level : Actively seeking new investments
Method of Compensation: Return on invest. most important, but chg. closing fees, service fees, etc.

FBR TECHNOLOGY VENTURE PARTNERS,L.P.(AKA:FRIEDMAN,BILLINGS)

11600 Sunrise Valley Dr
Suite 460
Reston, VA 20191
Phone: 703-312-9500
Fax: 703-312-9676
Website: www.fbrtvp.com

Management and Staff
Gene Riechers, Managing Director
Harry Weller, Principal
Hooks Johnston, Managing Director
Philip Facchina, Senior Managing Director
Scott Frederick, Principal
Todd Headley, Chief Financial Officer

Type of Firm
Private Firm Investing Own Capital

Industry Association Membership
Mid-Atlantic Venture Association
National Venture Capital Association (NVCA)

Project Preferences

Type of Financing Preferred:
Early Stage
First Stage Financing

Geographical Preferences

United States
All U.S.
Mid Atlantic

Industry Preferences

(% based on actual investment)

Internet Specific	60.3%
Computer Software and Services	22.1%
Other Products	9.2%
Communications and Media	5.9%
Computer Hardware	2.5%

Additional Information
Year Founded: 1997
Capital Under Management: $50,000,000
Current Activity Level : Actively seeking new investments

GABRIEL VENTURE PARTNERS

8000 Towers Crescent Drive
Suite 1350
Vienna, VA 22182
Phone: 703-847-3684
Fax: 703-760-7899
Website: www.gabrielvp.com

See California for full listing.

GLOBAL INTERNET VENTURES (GIV)

8150 Leesburg Pike
Suite 1210
Vienna, VA 22182
Phone: 703-442-3300
Fax: 703-442-3388
Website: www.givinc.com

Other Offices

4699 Old Ironsides Drive
Suite 430
Santa Clara, CA 95054

No. 714 Carlton Towers
No. 1 Airport Road
Bangalore, India
Phone: 9180-521-6066
Fax: 9180-521-6077

Suite 11, 3/F Beijing Kerry Center
1 Guanghua Road, Chaoyand District
Beijing , China
Phone: 8610-8529-8905
Fax: 8610-8529-8866

Management and Staff
Jeff Tonkel, Managing Director
Jeong Kim, Co-Founder
Jim McGregor, Managing Director
Naresh Malhotra, Managing Director
Rajesh Subramaniam, Vice President

Type of Firm
Private Firm Investing Own Capital

Project Preferences

Role in Financing:
Will function either as deal originator or investor in deals created by others

Type of Financing Preferred:
Early Stage

Size of Investments Considered
Min Size of Investment Considered (000s): $500
Max Size of Investment Considered (000s): $3,000

Geographical Preferences

International
China
India

Industry Preferences

Communications and Media
Telecommunications
Data Communications

Computer Software
Computer Services
Data Processing
Software
Systems Software
Applications Software

Internet Specific
Internet

Additional Information
Year Founded: 2000
Capital Under Management: $140,000,000
Current Activity Level : Actively seeking new investments

GLOBAL PARTNER VENTURES

6630 West Broad Street
Suite 100
Richmond, VA 23230-1702
Phone: 804-673-6230
Fax: 804-281-0708

Other Offices

2 Fontanka Naberezhnaya
Suite 331
St. Petersburg, Russian Federation 191187
Phone: 7-812-311-3936
Fax: 7-812-327-3268

52/4 Kosmodamianskaya Naberezhna
14th Floor
Moscow, Russian Federation 113054
Phone: 7-501-961-3040
Fax: 7-501-961-3041

Martirosyana Street
Office A
Kyiv, Ukraine 252180
Phone: 380-44-243-7300
Fax: 380-44-243-7298

Management and Staff
Elizabeth Ames, Vice President
Karen Westergaard, Vice President

Type of Firm
Private Firm Investing Own Capital

Project Preferences

Role in Financing:
Prefer role as deal originator but will also invest in deals created by others

Type of Financing Preferred:
First Stage Financing
Research and Development
Second Stage Financing
Seed
Start-up Financing

Industry Preferences

Communications and Media
Communications and Media

Computer Other
Computer Related

Semiconductors/Other Elect.
Electronic Components
Semiconductor
Controllers and Sensors
Circuit Boards
Component Testing Equipmt
Laser Related
Fiber Optics

Biotechnology
Industrial Biotechnology
Biosensors
Biotech Related Research
Biotech Related Research

Medical/Health
Diagnostic Services
Diagnostic Test Products
Pharmaceuticals

Industrial/Energy
Oil and Gas Exploration
Oil & Gas Drilling,Explor
Energy Conservation Relat
Industrial Products

Financial Services
Financial Services

Business Serv.
Consulting Services

Additional Information
Year Founded: 1994
Capital Under Management: $67,000,000
Current Activity Level : Actively seeking new investments
Method of Compensation: Return on invest. most important, but chg. closing fees, service fees, etc.

HFS CAPITAL (AKA: HOFFMAN, FITZGERALD & SNYDER)

7926 Jones Branch Drive
Suite 330
McLean, VA 22102
Phone: 703-847-4600
Fax: 703-356-4821
Website: www.hfscpa.com

Management and Staff
Larry Hoffman, Chief Executive Officer

Type of Firm
Affiliate/Subsidary of Oth. Financial. Instit.

Project Preferences

Type of Financing Preferred:
Early Stage

Geographical Preferences

United States
Mid Atlantic
All U.S.

Industry Preferences

Medical/Health
Medical/Health
Medical Products

Consumer Related
Food/Beverage
Consumer Products

Business Serv.
Services

Additional Information

Capital Under Management: $5,000,000
Current Activity Level : Actively seeking new investments

IMPERIAL VENTURES, INC.

211 North Union Street #100
Alexandria, VA 22314
Phone: 703-684-4829
Fax: 703-838-5579

See California for full listing.

JEFFERSON CAPITAL PARTNERS, LTD.

901 E. Cary Street
Suite 1600
Richmond, VA 23219
Phone: 804-643-0100
Website: www.jeffersoncapital.com

Management and Staff

Chip Moelchert, Partner
Palmer Garson, Partner
R. Timothy O'Donnell, Partner

Type of Firm

Private Firm Investing Own Capital

Industry Preferences

(% based on actual investment)

Internet Specific	26.5%
Consumer Related	21.9%
Computer Software and Services	20.6%
Other Products	20.6%
Computer Hardware	10.5%

Additional Information

Name of Most Recent Fund: Jefferson Capital Partners I, L.P.
Most Recent Fund Was Raised: 01/01/1998
Capital Under Management: $51,000,000
Current Activity Level : Actively seeking new investments

KATALYST LLC

8133 Leesburg Pike
Suite 220
Vienna, VA 22182
Phone: 703-568-7413
Website: www.katalyst.com

See Pennsylvania for full listing.

LEACHMAN STEINBERG VENTURE PARTNERS

P.O. Box 316
Markham, VA 22643
Phone: 540-364-4830
Fax: 540-364-4932

Management and Staff

W Leachman, Partner

Type of Firm

Private Firm Investing Own Capital

Project Preferences

Role in Financing:
Prefer role as deal originator

Additional Information

Year Founded: 1994
Capital Under Management: $25,000,000
Current Activity Level : Actively seeking new investments
Method of Compensation: Return on invest. most important, but chg. closing fees, service fees, etc.

LINCOLNSHIRE MANAGEMENT INC.

8300 Boone Blvd
Suite 500
McLean, VA 22102
Phone: 703-761-6730
Fax: 703-848-4586
Website: www.lincolnshiremgmt.com

See New York for full listing.

MATRIX CAPITAL

11 South 12th St, 3rd Floor
Richmond, VA 23219
Phone: 804-780-0060
Fax: 804-780-0158

Other Offices

2108 Cricket Court
Virginia Beach, VA 23454
Phone: 804-481-4210
Fax: 804-496-9280

318 Holland Street
P.O. Box 1328
Durham, NC 27702-1328
Phone: 919-688-6060
Fax: 919-682-9083

4400 Silas Creek Parkway
Suite 200
Winston-Salem, NC 27104
Phone: 910-768-6608
Fax: 910-768-7666

6701 Democracy Boulevard
Suite 300
Bethesda, MD 20817
Phone: 301-530-0382
Fax: 301-530-3589

Two First Union Center
301 South Tyron Street
Charlotte, NC 27702-1328
Phone: 704-552-5000
Fax: 704-344-0098

Management and Staff

Jeffrey Moore

Whom to Contact

Jeffrey Moore

Type of Firm

Investment/Merchant Bank Subsid/Affil

Project Preferences

Role in Financing:
Prefer role as deal originator but will also invest in deals created by others

Type of Financing Preferred:
First Stage Financing
Leveraged Buyout
Mezzanine
Research and Development
Second Stage Financing
Start-up Financing

Size of Investments Considered
Min Size of Investment Considered (000s): $10,000
Max Size of Investment Considered: No Limit

Geographical Preferences

United States
All U.S.

Industry Preferences

Semiconductors/Other Elect.
Electronic Components

Medical/Health
Diagnostic Test Products
Other Therapeutic
Disposable Med. Products

Consumer Related
Retail
Food/Beverage
Consumer Products

Industrial/Energy
Industrial Products

Business Serv.
Distribution

Additional Information
Year Founded: 1988
Capital Under Management: $100,000,000
Current Activity Level : Actively seeking new investments
Method of Compensation: Return on invest. most important, but chg. closing fees, service fees, etc.

MCG VENTURES

1100 Wilson Boulevard
Suite 800
Arlington, VA 22209
Phone: 703-247-7500
Fax: 703-247-7505
Website: www.mcgcapital.com

Type of Firm
Affiliate/Subsidary of Oth. Financial. Instit.

Industry Preferences

Communications and Media
Communications and Media

Business Serv.
Media

Additional Information
Year Founded: 2000
Current Activity Level : Actively seeking new investments

MERCATOR BROADBAND PARTNERS, L.P.

11911 Freedom Drive
Suite 1080
Reston, VA 20190
Phone: 703-995-5520
Fax: 703-995-5535
Website: www.mercatorbroadband.com

Management and Staff
Charles Cozean, Partner
David Ballarini, Partner
Guillame Girard, Vice President
John Baring, Managing Partner
Lior Samuelson, Managing Partner
Michael Smith, Vice President
Rhodric Hackman, Managing Partner

Type of Firm
Private Firm Investing Own Capital

Industry Association Membership
Mid-Atlantic Venture Association

Project Preferences

Type of Financing Preferred:
Balanced

Geographical Preferences

United States
All U.S.

Industry Preferences

Communications and Media
Data Communications

Internet Specific
Internet

Additional Information
Year Founded: 2000
Capital Under Management: $75,000,000
Current Activity Level : Actively seeking new investments

MID-ATLANTIC VENTURE FUNDS (FKA: NEPA MANAGEMENT CORP.)

11710 Plaza America Drive
Suite 120
Reston, VA 20190
Phone: 703-904-4120
Fax: 703-904-4124
Website: www.mavf.com

See Pennsylvania for full listing.

MOHR, DAVIDOW VENTURES

1660 International Drive
Suite 400
McLean, VA 22102
Phone: 703-287-4222
Fax: 703-287-4225
Website: www.mdv.com

See California for full listing.

MONUMENTAL VENTURE PARTNERS, LLC

8150 Leesburg Pike
Suite 600
Vienna, VA 22182
Phone: 703-748-4800
Website: www.mvpfunds.com

Management and Staff
Jeff Friedman, Managing Director
Marco Rubin, Managing Director
Roland Oliver, President & Chairman

Type of Firm
Private Firm Investing Own Capital

Project Preferences

Role in Financing:
Will function either as deal originator or investor in deals created by others

Type of Financing Preferred:
Early Stage
Seed

Size of Investments Considered
Min Size of Investment Considered (000s): $250
Max Size of Investment Considered (000s): $3,000

Geographical Preferences

United States
Mid Atlantic
Northwest

Industry Preferences

Communications and Media
Telecommunications
Wireless Communications
Data Communications
Other Communication Prod.

Internet Specific
Internet

Additional Information
Year Founded: 1999
Capital Under Management: $13,000,000
Current Activity Level : Actively seeking new investments

NEW ENTERPRISE ASSOCIATES

11911 Freedom Drive
One Freedom Square, Suite 1240
Reston, VA 20190
Phone: 703-709-9499
Fax: 703-834-7579
Website: www.nea.com

See Maryland for full listing.

NEW HORIZONS VENTURE CAPITAL

1000 Wilson Boulevard
Suite 2700
Arlington, VA 22209
Phone: 703-807-1900
Fax: 703-807-1950
Website: www.newhorizonsvc.com

Management and Staff
Amy Klein, Principal
T.J. Jubeir, Managing Partner

Type of Firm
Private Firm Investing Own Capital

Industry Association Membership
Mid-Atlantic Venture Association

Industry Preferences

(% based on actual investment)

Internet Specific	84.3%
Computer Software and Services	15.7%

Additional Information
Year Founded: 1999
Capital Under Management: $200,000,000
Current Activity Level : Actively seeking new investments

NEXTGEN CAPITAL LLC

12701 Fair Lakes Circle
Suite 690
Fairfax, VA 22033
Phone: 703-803-0544
Fax: 703-803-0543
Website: www.nextgencapital.com

Management and Staff
Jeffrey Lombardi, Managing Director
Zimri Putney, Managing Director

Type of Firm
Private Firm Investing Own Capital

Industry Association Membership
Mid-Atlantic Venture Association

Project Preferences

Role in Financing:
Prefer role in deals created by others

Type of Financing Preferred:
First Stage Financing
Second Stage Financing
Start-up Financing

Geographical Preferences

United States
Mid Atlantic

Industry Preferences

(% based on actual investment)

Internet Specific	52.9%
Communications and Media	28.0%
Computer Software and Services	13.1%
Consumer Related	4.0%
Semiconductors/Other Elect.	2.0%

Additional Information
Year Founded: 1997
Capital Under Management: $28,400,000
Current Activity Level : Actively seeking new investments
Method of Compensation: Return on investment is of primary concern, do not charge fees

NOVAK BIDDLE VENTURE PARTNERS, L.P.

1750 Tysons Blvd
Suite1190
McLean, VA 22102
Phone: 703-847-3770
Fax: 703-847-3771
Website: www.novakbiddle.com

Management and Staff
Jack Biddle, General Partner
Joy Binford, Chief Financial Officer
Roger Novak, General Partner
Steve Fredrick, General Partner

Type of Firm
Private Firm Investing Own Capital

Industry Association Membership
Mid-Atlantic Venture Association
National Venture Capital Association (NVCA)

Project Preferences

Role in Financing:
Will function either as deal originator or investor in deals created by others

Type of Financing Preferred:
Early Stage
Seed

Size of Investments Considered
Min Size of Investment Considered (000s): $1,000
Max Size of Investment Considered (000s): $5,000

Geographical Preferences

United States
Mid Atlantic
Northeast
Southeast

Industry Preferences

(% based on actual investment)

Communications and Media	44.1%
Internet Specific	34.2%
Computer Software and Services	14.7%
Semiconductors/Other Elect.	3.7%

Other Products	3.3%

Additional Information
Name of Most Recent Fund: Novak Biddle Venture Partners II, LP
Most Recent Fund Was Raised: 04/01/1999
Year Founded: 1997
Capital Under Management: $90,000,000
Current Activity Level : Actively seeking new investments
Method of Compensation: Return on investment is of primary concern, do not charge fees

OSBORN CAPITAL LLC

41582 Spring Valley Lane
Leesburg, VA 20175
Phone: 703-748-8462
Fax: 703-748-8463
Website: www.osborncapital.com

See Massachusetts for full listing.

OXFORD FINANCIAL SERVICES CORP.

133 North Fairfax Street
Alexandria, VA 22314
Phone: 703-519-4900
Fax: 703-519-4910

Other Offices

1055 Torrey Pines Road
Suite 205
La Jolla, CA 92037
Phone: 619-551-0505
Fax: 619-551-0789

9171 Towne Centre Drive
Suite 425
San Diego, CA 92122
Phone: 619-457-5400
Fax: 619-457-5443

Management and Staff
J. Alden Philbrick

Whom to Contact
J. Alden Philbrick

Type of Firm
Bank Group

Project Preferences

Role in Financing:
Prefer role as deal originator but will also invest in deals created by others

Type of Financing Preferred:
First Stage Financing
Mezzanine
Research and Development
Second Stage Financing
Seed
Start-up Financing

Size of Investments Considered
Min Size of Investment Considered (000s): $1,000
Max Size of Investment Considered: No Limit

Geographical Preferences

United States
All U.S.

Industry Preferences

Communications and Media
Communications and Media
Other Communication Prod.

Computer Hardware
Computers

Computer Other
Computer Related

Semiconductors/Other Elect.
Electronics
Electronic Components

Biotechnology
Industrial Biotechnology
Biotech Related Research
Biotech Related Research

Medical/Health
Medical/Health
Medical Diagnostics
Medical Therapeutics

Consumer Related
Retail

Industrial/Energy
Factory Automation
Robotics
Machinery

Transportation
Transportation

Additional Information
Year Founded: 1987
Capital Under Management: $180,000,000
Current Activity Level : Actively seeking new investments
Method of Compensation: Return on invest. most important, but chg. closing fees, service fees, etc.

PERENNIAL VENTURES (FKA: TREDEGAR INVESTMENTS)

1100 Boulders Parkway
Richmond, VA 23225
Phone: 804-330-1062
Fax: 804-330-1777
Website: www.perennialventures.com

See Washington for full listing.

PIERCE FINANCIAL CORPORATION(FKA:PIERC E INVESTMENT BANKING)

2385 N. Vernon Street
Arlington, VA 22207
Phone: 703-516-7002
Fax: 703-243-0756

Management and Staff
David Gregg, Managing Director
John Clark, President

Whom to Contact
David Gregg
Ted Leigh

Type of Firm
Investment/Merchant Bank Investing Own or Client Funds

Industry Association Membership
Mid-Atlantic Venture Association

Project Preferences

Role in Financing:
Prefer role as deal originator but will also invest in deals created by others

Type of Financing Preferred:
Leveraged Buyout
Mezzanine
Recapitalizations
Second Stage Financing

Size of Investments Considered
Min Size of Investment Considered (000s): $5,000
Max Size of Investment Considered: No Limit

Geographical Preferences
United States
Mid Atlantic

International
Mexico

Industry Preferences
Communications and Media
Communications and Media

Computer Hardware
Computer Graphics and Dig
Integrated Turnkey System

Computer Software
Computer Services
Systems Software
Applications Software
Artificial Intelligence

Internet Specific
Internet

Semiconductors/Other Elect.
Analytic/Scientific

Biotechnology
Industrial Biotechnology
Biotech Related Research

Medical/Health
Medical Diagnostics
Diagnostic Services
Diagnostic Test Products
Medical Therapeutics
Drug/Equipmt Delivery
Other Therapeutic
Medical Products
Disposable Med. Products
Pharmaceuticals

Consumer Related
Entertainment and Leisure
Retail
Franchises(NEC)
Food/Beverage
Consumer Products

Industrial/Energy
Alternative Energy
Energy Conservation Relat
Industrial Products
Robotics
Environmental Related

Transportation
Transportation

Financial Services
Financial Services

Business Serv.
Consulting Services

Manufact.
Publishing

Agr/Forestr/Fish
Agriculture related

Additional Information
Year Founded: 1978
Capital Under Management: $12,000,000
Current Activity Level : Actively seeking new investments
Method of Compensation: Return on invest. most important, but chg. closing fees, service fees, etc.

PSINET VENTURES

44983 Knoll Square
Ashburn, VA 20147
Phone: 703-726-4100
Fax: 703-726-4200
Website: www.psinetventures.com

Management and Staff
Ed Frankenberg, Vice President
Jeffrey Shapard, Vice President

Type of Firm
Non-Financial Corp. Affiliate or Subsidiary

Industry Preferences
(% based on actual investment)

Internet Specific	48.9%
Communications and Media	42.8%
Computer Software and Services	5.9%
Computer Hardware	2.3%

Additional Information
Current Activity Level : Making few, if any, new investments

REDLEAF VENTURE MANAGEMENT

2100 Reston Parkway
Suite 204
Herndon, VA 20191
Phone: 703-860-3000
Website: www.redleaf.com

See California for full listing.

RENAISSANCE VENTURES

33 S. 13th St., 3rd Floor
Richmond, VA 23219
Phone: 804-643-5500
Fax: 804-643-5322

Management and Staff
Herbert Jackson, General Partner
Michael Grow, General Partner

Type of Firm
Private Firm Investing Own Capital

Project Preferences
Type of Financing Preferred:
Early Stage

Geographical Preferences
International
Europe

Industry Preferences
Biotechnology
Biotechnology

Additional Information
Year Founded: 1995
Capital Under Management: $12,000,000
Current Activity Level : Actively seeking new investments

SPACEVEST

11911 Freedom Drive
Suite 500
Reston, VA 20190
Phone: 703-904-9800
Fax: 703-904-0571
Website: www.spacevest.com

Management and Staff
Frank DiBello, Managing Director
Ransom Parker, Managing Director
Richard Harris, Vice President
Roger Widing, Managing Director
Sheila Gindes, Vice President
Stephen Rochereau, Managing Director

Type of Firm
Private Firm Investing Own Capital

Industry Association Membership
Mid-Atlantic Venture Association
National Venture Capital Association (NVCA)

Project Preferences

Role in Financing:
Prefer role as deal originator but will also invest in deals created by others

Type of Financing Preferred:
Expansion
First Stage Financing
Later Stage
Mezzanine
Second Stage Financing

Size of Investments Considered
Min Size of Investment Considered (000s): $250
Max Size of Investment Considered (000s): $10,000

Geographical Preferences

United States
All U.S.

Canada
All Canada

International
United Kingdom

Industry Preferences

(% based on actual investment)

Communications and Media	30.4%
Internet Specific	28.0%
Computer Software and Services	23.3%
Semiconductors/Other Elect.	12.4%
Industrial/Energy	3.3%
Other Products	2.6%

Additional Information
Name of Most Recent Fund: Spacevest Fund, L.P.
Most Recent Fund Was Raised: 06/01/1995
Year Founded: 1991
Capital Under Management: $187,900,000
Current Activity Level : Actively seeking new investments
Method of Compensation: Return on invest. most important, but chg. closing fees, service fees, etc.

SPENCER TRASK VENTURES, INC. (FKA: SPENCER TRASK SECURITIES)

12030 Sunrise Valley Drive
Suite 300
Reston, VA 20191
Phone: 703-860-6870
Fax: 703-834-0919
Website: www.spencertrask.com

See New York for full listing.

STRATEGIC INVESTMENT MANAGEMENT

1001 19th Street North
16th Floor
Arlington, VA 22209-1722
Phone: 703-243-4433
Fax: 703-243-2266

Type of Firm
Private Firm Investing Own Capital

Project Preferences

Type of Financing Preferred:
Fund of Funds

Additional Information
Name of Most Recent Fund: SIG Private Equity Vintage Funds 2001
Most Recent Fund Was Raised: 04/16/2001
Year Founded: 2001
Capital Under Management: $100,000,000
Current Activity Level : Actively seeking new investments

UPDATA VENTURE PARTNERS

11600 Sunrise Valley Drive
Suite 450
Herndon, VA 20191
Phone: 703-736-0020
Fax: 703-736-0022
Website: www.updataventures.com

Other Offices

125 Half Mile Road
Suite 202
Red Bank, NJ 07701
Phone: 732-945-1010
Fax: 732-945-1025

Management and Staff
Barry Goldsmith, General Partner
Conor Mullett, General Partner
David Wetmore, Venture Partner
Ira Cohen, Venture Partner
John Burton, Managing General Partner
Tim Meyers, General Partner

Type of Firm
Investment/Merchant Bank Subsid/Affil

Project Preferences

Type of Financing Preferred:
Balanced
Early Stage

Industry Preferences

Communications and Media
Communications and Media

Computer Software
Software

Internet Specific
Internet

Additional Information
Year Founded: 2000
Capital Under Management: $92,000,000
Current Activity Level : Actively seeking new investments

VENTURE CATALYST

315 Queen Street
Alexandria, VA 22314
Phone: 703-684-1306
Fax: 703-684-1481
Website: www.vcat.com

See California for full listing.

VIRGINIA CAPITAL

1801 Libbie Avenue
Suite 201
Richmond, VA 23226
Phone: 804-648-4802
Fax: 804-648-4809
Website: www.vacapital.com

Management and Staff
Fred Russell, Managing Director
Justin Marriott, Principal
Robert Louthan, General Partner
Tom Deardorff, Vice President

Whom to Contact
Thomas E. Deardorff

Type of Firm
Private Firm Investing Own Capital

Industry Association Membership
Mid-Atlantic Venture Association
Natl assoc of Small Bus. Inv. Co (NASBIC)

Project Preferences

Role in Financing:
Will function either as deal originator or investor in deals created by others

Type of Financing Preferred:
Acquisition
Balanced
Expansion
Leveraged Buyout
Management Buyouts

Size of Investments Considered
Min Size of Investment Considered (000s): $1,000
Max Size of Investment Considered (000s): $5,000

Geographical Preferences

United States
Mid Atlantic

Industry Preferences

Medical/Health
Health Services

Consumer Related
Entertainment and Leisure

Financial Services
Insurance
Real Estate

Business Serv.
Services
Media

Additional Information
Name of Most Recent Fund: Virginia Capital SBIC, L.P.
Most Recent Fund Was Raised: 01/01/1998
Year Founded: 1991
Capital Under Management: $62,000,000
Current Activity Level : Actively seeking new investments
Method of Compensation: Return on investment is of primary concern, do not charge fees

WALNUT CAPITAL CORP.

8000 Towers Crescent Drive
Suite 1070
Vienna, VA 22182
Phone: 703-448-3771
Fax: 703-448-7751

Other Offices

333 West Wacker Drive
Suite 2700
Chicago, IL 60606
Phone: 312-984-3100

Management and Staff
Joel Kanter, General Partner
Robert Mauer, General Partner

Type of Firm
SBIC Not elsewhere classified

Industry Association Membership
Natl assoc of Small Bus. Inv. Co (NASBIC)

Project Preferences

Role in Financing:
Prefer role as deal originator but will also invest in deals created by others

Type of Financing Preferred:
First Stage Financing
Leveraged Buyout
Mezzanine
Second Stage Financing
Start-up Financing

Size of Investments Considered
Min Size of Investment Considered (000s): $300
Max Size of Investment Considered (000s): $500

Geographical Preferences

International
No Preference

Industry Preferences

(% based on actual investment)

Consumer Related	29.7%
Biotechnology	29.2%
Medical/Health	17.7%
Computer Software and Services	15.4%
Semiconductors/Other Elect.	4.7%
Computer Hardware	1.9%
Other Products	0.8%
Internet Specific	0.5%
Industrial/Energy	0.1%

Additional Information
Year Founded: 1983
Capital Under Management: $40,000,000
Current Activity Level : Inactive / Unknown
Method of Compensation: Return on investment is of primary concern, do not charge fees

WASHINGTON

ALEXANDER HUTTON, INC.

999 Third Avenue
Suite 3700
Seattle, WA 98104
Phone: 206-341-9800
Fax: 206-341-9810
Website: www.alexanderhutton.com

Other Offices

2626 North Pearl
Tacoma, WA 98407
Phone: 253-752-3612
Fax: 253-752-3676

Management and Staff
Jerry Keppler, Principal
Kent Johnson, Managing Director
Mark Klebanoff, Managing Director
Tom Johnston, Managing Director

Type of Firm
Investment/Merchant Bank Investing Own or Client Funds

Project Preferences

Type of Financing Preferred:
Early Stage
First Stage Financing
Second Stage Financing

Size of Investments Considered
Min Size of Investment Considered (000s): $300
Max Size of Investment Considered (000s): $7,000

Geographical Preferences

United States
Northwest

Industry Preferences

Communications and Media
Data Communications

Computer Software
Software

Internet Specific
Internet

Additional Information
Name of Most Recent Fund: Alexander Hutton Venture Partners, LP
Most Recent Fund Was Raised: 12/31/1999
Year Founded: 1999
Capital Under Management: $90,000,000
Current Activity Level : Actively seeking new investments

ARCH VENTURE PARTNERS

1000 Second Avenue
Suite 3700
Seattle, WA 98104
Phone: 206-674-3028
Fax: 206-674-3026
Website: www.archventure.com

See Illinois for full listing.

ATLAS VENTURE

1201 Third Avenue
Suite 5450
Seattle, WA 98101
Phone: 206-283-9911
Fax: 206-254-9130
Website: www.atlasventure.com

See Massachusetts for full listing.

BROADMARK CAPITAL CORP.

3030 U.S. Bank Centre
1420 Fifth Avenue
Seattle, WA 98101-2333
Phone: 206-623-1200
Fax: 206-623-2213

Other Offices

20, avenue Kleber
Second Floor
Paris, France 75116
Phone: 33-1-4500-2425
Fax: 33-1-4500-9020

Management and Staff
James Ahlstedt
Joseph Schocken
Steve DeGroat

Whom to Contact
James Ahlstedt
Joseph Schocken
Steve DeGroat

Type of Firm
Mgt. Consulting Firm

Project Preferences

Role in Financing:
Prefer role as deal originator but will also invest in deals created by others

Type of Financing Preferred:
First Stage Financing
Leveraged Buyout
Mezzanine
Second Stage Financing

Size of Investments Considered
Min Size of Investment Considered (000s): $10,000
Max Size of Investment Considered: No Limit

Geographical Preferences

United States
West Coast

International
Bermuda
France
Germany
Italy
Spain
United Kingdom

Industry Preferences

Communications and Media
Communications and Media

Computer Hardware
Computer Graphics and Dig
Integrated Turnkey System

Computer Software
Systems Software
Applications Software

Semiconductors/Other Elect.
Electronic Components
Controllers and Sensors
Component Testing Equipmt
Laser Related
Fiber Optics
Analytic/Scientific

Biotechnology
Biotechnology

Medical/Health
Diagnostic Test Products
Drug/Equipmt Delivery
Medical Products
Disposable Med. Products
Pharmaceuticals

Consumer Related
Entertainment and Leisure
Retail
Franchises(NEC)
Food/Beverage
Consumer Products
Consumer Services
Other Restaurants
Education Related

Industrial/Energy
Energy Conservation Relat
Industrial Products

Manufact.
Office Automation Equipmt
Publishing

Additional Information
Year Founded: 1986
Capital Under Management: $20,000,000
Current Activity Level : Actively seeking new investments
Method of Compensation: Function primarily in service area, receive contingent fee in cash or equity

---

CABLE & HOWSE VENTURES

10210 NE Pints Drive
Suite 200
Kirkland, WA 98033
Phone: 425-576-7067
Fax: 425-576-7103

Type of Firm
Private Firm Investing Own Capital

Project Preferences

Role in Financing:
Prefer role as deal originator but will also invest in deals created by others

Type of Financing Preferred:
First Stage Financing
Second Stage Financing
Seed
Special Situation
Start-up Financing

Size of Investments Considered
Min Size of Investment Considered (000s): $1,000
Max Size of Investment Considered: No Limit

Geographical Preferences

International
No Preference

Additional Information
Name of Most Recent Fund: CH Partners
Most Recent Fund Was Raised: 10/01/1980
Year Founded: 1977
Capital Under Management: $162,000,000
Current Activity Level : Inactive / Unknown
Method of Compensation: Return on investment is of primary concern, do not charge fees

---

CHANEN, PAINTER & CO., LTD.

1420 Fifth Avenue
Suite 2975
Seattle, WA 98101
Phone: 206-386-5656
Fax: 206-386-5376

Management and Staff
Gordon Chanen

Whom to Contact
Gordon Chanen

Type of Firm
Mgt. Consulting Firm

Project Preferences

Role in Financing:
Prefer role as deal originator

Type of Financing Preferred:
First Stage Financing
Leveraged Buyout
Mezzanine
Second Stage Financing
Special Situation

Size of Investments Considered
Min Size of Investment Considered (000s): $20,000
Max Size of Investment Considered: No Limit

Geographical Preferences

United States
Rocky Mountain
West Coast

Canada
Western Canada

Industry Preferences

Communications and Media
Commercial Communications
Radio & TV Broadcasting
Telecommunications
Data Communications
Satellite Microwave Comm.

Computer Hardware
Mainframes / Scientific

Computer Software
Computer Services
Systems Software
Applications Software

Internet Specific
Internet

Semiconductors/Other Elect.
Fiber Optics

Medical/Health
Medical/Health

Consumer Related
Entertainment and Leisure
Retail
Food/Beverage
Consumer Products
Hotels and Resorts
Education Related

Industrial/Energy
Machinery

Financial Services
Real Estate

Additional Information
Year Founded: 1988
Current Activity Level : Actively seeking new investments
Method of Compensation: Function primarily in service area, receive contingent fee in cash or equity

---

DAIN RAUCHER WESSELS

1201 Third Street
Suite 2500
Seattle, WA 98101-3044
Phone: 206-621-3110
Fax: 206-621-3047

See Minnesota for full listing.

DIGITAL PARTNERS

999 3rd Avenue
Suite 1610
Seattle, WA 98104
Phone: 206-405-3607
Fax: 206-405-3617
Website: www.digitalpartnersvc.com

Management and Staff
Bill Tenneson, President
Dan Regis, Managing Director
Pamela Gaspers, Managing Director

Type of Firm
Private Firm Investing Own Capital

Industry Association Membership
Western Association of Venture Capitalists (WAVC)

Project Preferences

Role in Financing:
Will function either as deal originator or investor in deals created by others

Type of Financing Preferred:
Early Stage
First Stage Financing
Second Stage Financing
Seed

Size of Investments Considered
Min Size of Investment Considered (000s): $250
Max Size of Investment Considered (000s): $3,000

Geographical Preferences

United States
Northwest

Canada
Western Canada

Industry Preferences

Communications and Media
Telecommunications
Wireless Communications
Data Communications

Computer Software
Software
Systems Software
Applications Software

Internet Specific
Internet

Additional Information
Name of Most Recent Fund: Digital Partners III
Most Recent Fund Was Raised: 01/28/2000
Year Founded: 1999
Capital Under Management: $36,000,000
Current Activity Level : Actively seeking new investments
Method of Compensation: Return on investment is of primary concern, do not charge fees

EFUND, LLC

5350 NE Carillon Point
Kirkland, WA 98033
Phone: 206-389-4901
Fax: 206-389-4901
Website: www.efundllc.com

Management and Staff
Dan Kranzler, Managing Partner
George Lightbody, Partner
Jeff Canin, Partner
Joe Tanous, Partner

Type of Firm
Private Firm Investing Own Capital

Project Preferences

Type of Financing Preferred:
Early Stage

Geographical Preferences

United States
All U.S.

Industry Preferences

Communications and Media
Communications and Media

Internet Specific
Internet

Additional Information
Year Founded: 2000
Current Activity Level : Actively seeking new investments

ENCOMPASS VENTURES

777 108th Avenue NE
Suite 2300
Bellevue, WA 98004
Phone: 425-468-3900
Fax: 425-468-3901
Website: www.encompassventures.com

Management and Staff
James Geddes, Managing Director
Kiyoyuki Kubota, Managing Director
Scot Land, Managing Director
Wayne Wager, Managing Director
Yasuki Matsumoto, Managing Director

Type of Firm
Non-Financial Corp. Affiliate or Subsidiary

Project Preferences

Role in Financing:
Prefer role as deal originator but will also invest in deals created by others

Type of Financing Preferred:
First Stage Financing
Research and Development
Second Stage Financing
Start-up Financing

Size of Investments Considered
Min Size of Investment Considered (000s): $100
Max Size of Investment Considered (000s): $3,000

Geographical Preferences

United States
Northwest
West Coast

Canada
Western Canada

Industry Preferences

(% based on actual investment)

Internet Specific	47.1%
Computer Software and Services	37.1%
Computer Hardware	6.1%
Medical/Health	5.2%
Biotechnology	2.5%
Communications and Media	2.0%

Additional Information
Name of Most Recent Fund: EVP II
Most Recent Fund Was Raised: 10/01/1999
Year Founded: 1997
Capital Under Management: $85,000,000
Current Activity Level : Actively seeking new investments
Method of Compensation: Return on investment is of primary concern, do not charge fees

FBR COMOTION VENTURE CAPITAL

1111 Third Avenue
Suite 2400
Seattle, WA 98101
Phone: 206-382-9191
Fax: 206-342-9077
Website: www.comotionvc.com

Other Offices

208 S.W. First Ave
Suite 300
Portland, OR 97204
Phone: 503-221-0200
Fax: 503-478-0559

Management and Staff
David Billstrom, Managing Partner
Will Neuhauser, Managing Director

Type of Firm
Private Equity Advisor or Fund of Fund Mgr

Project Preferences

Role in Financing:
Will function either as deal originator or investor in deals created by others

Type of Financing Preferred:
Early Stage
First Stage Financing
Seed

Geographical Preferences

United States
Northwest

Industry Preferences

(% based on actual investment)

Internet Specific	54.0%
Computer Software and Services	46.0%

Additional Information
Year Founded: 2000
Capital Under Management: $50,000,000
Current Activity Level : Actively seeking new investments
Method of Compensation: Return on investment is of primary concern, do not charge fees

FLUKE VENTURE PARTNERS.

11400 S.E. Sixth Street
Suite 230
Bellevue, WA 98004
Phone: 425-453-4590
Fax: 425-453-4675
Website: www.flukeventures.com

Management and Staff
Dennis Weston, Senior Managing Director
Kevin Gabelein, Managing Director
Kirsten Morbeck, Managing Director

Whom to Contact
Dennis Weston

Type of Firm
Private Firm Investing Own Capital

Project Preferences

Role in Financing:
Will function either as deal originator or investor in deals created by others

Type of Financing Preferred:
Early Stage
Expansion
First Stage Financing
Later Stage
Second Stage Financing
Seed
Start-up Financing

Size of Investments Considered
Min Size of Investment Considered (000s): $250
Max Size of Investment Considered (000s): $2,500

Geographical Preferences

United States
Northwest

Industry Preferences

(% based on actual investment)

Computer Software and Services	32.0%
Internet Specific	26.4%
Medical/Health	12.7%
Consumer Related	6.0%
Communications and Media	5.5%
Industrial/Energy	5.5%
Other Products	4.8%
Biotechnology	3.7%
Computer Hardware	2.9%
Semiconductors/Other Elect.	0.5%

Additional Information
Year Founded: 1977
Capital Under Management: $100,000,000
Current Activity Level : Inactive / Unknown
Method of Compensation: Return on investment is of primary concern, do not charge fees

FRAZIER & COMPANY

601 Union Street
Suite 3300
Seattle, WA 98101
Phone: 206-621-7200
Fax: 206-621-1848

Management and Staff
Alan Frazier, Managing Partner
Bob Overell, General Partner
Carol Lokey, Chief Financial Officer
Charles Blanchard, General Partner
Fred Silverstein, General Partner
Jon Gilbert, General Partner
Nader Naini, General Partner
Nathan Every, Vice President
Thomas Hodges, Chief Operating Officer
Trevor Moody, Vice President

Type of Firm
Private Firm Investing Own Capital

Industry Association Membership
National Venture Capital Association (NVCA)

Project Preferences

Role in Financing:
Prefer role as deal originator but will also invest in deals created by others

Type of Financing Preferred:
Control-block Purchases
First Stage Financing
Industry Rollups
Leveraged Buyout
Mezzanine
Research and Development
Second Stage Financing
Seed
Special Situation
Start-up Financing
Startup

Size of Investments Considered
Min Size of Investment Considered (000s): $2,000
Max Size of Investment Considered (000s): $3,000

Geographical Preferences

International
No Preference

Industry Preferences

(% based on actual investment)

Medical/Health	38.3%
Biotechnology	29.2%
Internet Specific	13.5%
Computer Hardware	6.4%
Computer Software and Services	5.6%
Consumer Related	5.0%
Industrial/Energy	1.9%

Additional Information

Name of Most Recent Fund: Frazier Healthcare III, L.P.
Most Recent Fund Was Raised: 10/20/1998
Year Founded: 1991
Capital Under Management: $550,000,000
Current Activity Level : Actively seeking new investments
Method of Compensation: Return on investment is of primary concern, do not charge fees

GUIDE VENTURES

999 3rd Avenue
Suite 2424
Seattle, WA 98104
Phone: 206-447-1350
Fax: 206-447-1351
Website: www.guideventures.com

Management and Staff

James Thornton, Managing Director
Michael Templeman, Principal
Russ Aldrich, Managing Director

Type of Firm

Private Firm Investing Own Capital

Industry Association Membership

National Venture Capital Association (NVCA)

Project Preferences

Role in Financing:
Prefer role as deal originator but will also invest in deals created by others

Type of Financing Preferred:
Early Stage

Geographical Preferences

United States
Northwest

Industry Preferences

Communications and Media
Telecommunications
Wireless Communications
Data Communications

Computer Software
Computer Services
Data Processing
Software
Systems Software
Applications Software
Artificial Intelligence

Internet Specific
E-Commerce Technology
Internet
Web Aggregration/Portals

Additional Information

Name of Most Recent Fund: Guide Ventures II, LP
Most Recent Fund Was Raised: 06/01/1999
Year Founded: 1999
Capital Under Management: $21,000,000
Current Activity Level : Actively seeking new investments
Method of Compensation: Return on investment is of primary concern, do not charge fees

HOLDING CAPITAL GROUP, INC.

1301 Fifth Avenue
Suite 3410
Seattle, WA 98101

See New York for full listing.

IGNITION CORPORATION

PO Box 580
Bellevue, WA 98009
Phone: 425-709-0772
Fax: 425-709-0798
Website: www.ignitioncorp.com

Management and Staff

Brad Silverberg, Chairman & CEO
Carolyn Duffy, Vice President
John Zagula, Vice President
Jon Anderson, Chief Financial Officer
Robert Headley, Vice President
Steve Hooper, Founder

Type of Firm

Incubators

Industry Preferences

Communications and Media
Telecommunications

Internet Specific
Internet

Additional Information

Year Founded: 2000
Current Activity Level : Actively seeking new investments

INCEPTA LLC

999 Third Avenue
Suite 2500
Seattle, WA 98104
Phone: 206-336-6500
Fax: 206-336-6501
Website: www.inceptagroup.com

Management and Staff

John Stachowiak, Managing Director & CFO
William Cortes, Managing Director

Type of Firm

Affiliate/Subsidary of Oth. Financial. Instit.

Project Preferences

Type of Financing Preferred:
Early Stage

Industry Preferences

Communications and Media
Telecommunications

Additional Information

Current Activity Level : Actively seeking new investments

INTEGRA VENTURES (F.K.A. INTEGRA BIO-HEALTH INC.)

1114 21st Avenue, East
Seattle, WA 98112
Phone: 206-329-5009
Fax: 206-329-5105
Website: www.integraventures.net

Management and Staff

Hans Lundin, Managing Partner
Johannes Koch, Partner
Joseph Piper, Managing Partner
Luciana Simoncini, Partner
Tim Black, Partner

Type of Firm
Private Firm Investing Own Capital

Project Preferences

Type of Financing Preferred:
Early Stage

Size of Investments Considered
Min Size of Investment Considered (000s): $500
Max Size of Investment Considered (000s): $5,000

Geographical Preferences

United States
All U.S.

Industry Preferences

Medical/Health
Medical/Health

Additional Information
Name of Most Recent Fund: IBH II
Most Recent Fund Was Raised: 12/01/1998
Year Founded: 1998
Capital Under Management: $8,500,000
Current Activity Level : Actively seeking new investments

KEY EQUITY CAPITAL CORP.(AKA:KEY COMMUNITY DEVELOPMENT CORP)

700 5th Avenue
48th Floor
Seattle, WA 98111
Phone: 206-684-6480
Fax: 206-689-5450
Website: www.keybank.com

See Ohio for full listing.

KIRLAN VENTURE CAPITAL, INC.

221 First Avenue West
Suite 108
Seattle, WA 98119-4223
Phone: 206-281-8610
Fax: 206-285-3451

Management and Staff
Bill Tenneson, President

Type of Firm
Private Firm Investing Own Capital

Project Preferences

Role in Financing:
Prefer role in deals created by others

Type of Financing Preferred:
First Stage Financing
Mezzanine
Second Stage Financing

Size of Investments Considered
Min Size of Investment Considered (000s): $300
Max Size of Investment Considered (000s): $500

Geographical Preferences

United States
West Coast

Canada
Western Canada

Industry Preferences

(% based on actual investment)

Communications and Media	36.8%
Computer Software and Services	27.5%
Medical/Health	19.4%
Internet Specific	7.2%
Consumer Related	7.2%
Industrial/Energy	2.1%

Additional Information
Name of Most Recent Fund: Kirlan Venture Partners II, L.P.
Most Recent Fund Was Raised: 10/01/1997
Year Founded: 1993
Capital Under Management: $20,000,000
Current Activity Level : Actively seeking new investments
Method of Compensation: Return on investment is of primary concern, do not charge fees

MADRONA VENTURE GROUP

1000 Second Avenue
Suite 3700
Seattle, WA 98104
Phone: 206-674-3000
Fax: 206-674-3012
Website: www.madrona.com

Other Offices
121 SW Morrison Street
Suite 450
Portland, OR 97204

Management and Staff
Greg Gottesman, Managing Director
Paul Goodrich, Principal
Paul Goodrich, Managing Director
Tom Alberg, Managing Director
Troy Cichos, Chief Financial Officer
William Glasgow, Managing Director

Type of Firm
Private Firm Investing Own Capital

Project Preferences

Role in Financing:
Will function either as deal originator or investor in deals created by others

Type of Financing Preferred:
Early Stage

Geographical Preferences

United States
Northwest
West Coast

Industry Preferences

(% based on actual investment)

Internet Specific	67.6%
Computer Software and Services	12.4%
Communications and Media	11.8%
Other Products	6.9%
Computer Hardware	1.5%

Additional Information
Year Founded: 1999
Current Activity Level : Actively seeking new investments

MARISTETH VENTURES, L.L.C.

1201 Pacific Avenue
Suite 1702
Tacoma, WA 98401
Phone: 253-272-1636
Fax: 253-272-1482
Website: www.carlsongroup.com

Management and Staff
Jan Tonning, Chief Financial Officer
Kim Pederson, Principal

Type of Firm
Affiliate/Subsidary of Oth. Financial. Instit.

Industry Association Membership
National Venture Capital Association (NVCA)

Project Preferences

Type of Financing Preferred:
Early Stage
Expansion
First Stage Financing
Second Stage Financing
Seed
Special Situation
Startup

Size of Investments Considered
Min Size of Investment Considered (000s): $250
Max Size of Investment Considered (000s): $10,000

Geographical Preferences

United States
Midwest
Northwest
Rocky Mountain
West Coast

Industry Preferences

Communications and Media
Telecommunications
Wireless Communications
Data Communications

Computer Hardware
Mainframes / Scientific

Computer Software
Data Processing
Software
Systems Software
Applications Software

Internet Specific
E-Commerce Technology
Internet
Web Aggregration/Portals

Semiconductors/Other Elect.
Electronics

Industrial/Energy
Superconductivity
Process Control

Financial Services
Financial Services

Utilities
Utilities

Additional Information
Year Founded: 1997
Capital Under Management: $20,000,000
Current Activity Level : Actively seeking new investments
Method of Compensation: Return on invest. most important, but chg. closing fees, service fees, etc.

MATERIA VENTURES ASSOCIATES,L.P. (FKA:PIERCE NORDQUIST ASSO)

3435 Carillon Point
Kirkland, WA 98033-7354
Phone: 425-822-4100
Fax: 425-827-4086

Other Offices

5350 Carillon Point
Kirkland, WA 98033
Phone: 206-822-4100
Fax: 206-827-4086

Type of Firm
Private Firm Investing Own Capital

Project Preferences

Role in Financing:
Prefer role as deal originator but will also invest in deals created by others

Type of Financing Preferred:
First Stage Financing
Mezzanine
Second Stage Financing
Start-up Financing

Size of Investments Considered
Min Size of Investment Considered (000s): $500
Max Size of Investment Considered (000s): $1,000

Geographical Preferences

United States
All U.S.

Additional Information
Name of Most Recent Fund: PNP II (Pierce Nordquist)
Most Recent Fund Was Raised: 05/01/1986
Year Founded: 1986
Capital Under Management: $18,000,000
Current Activity Level : Actively seeking new investments
Method of Compensation: Return on investment is of primary concern, do not charge fees

---

MAVERON LLC.

505 5th Avenue South
Suite 600
Seattle, WA 98104
Phone: 206-447-1300
Fax: 206-470-1150
Website: www.maveron.com

Management and Staff
Dan Levitan, Managing Partner
Debra Somberg, Managing Partner
Howard Schultz, Managing Partner
Jody Miller, Venture Partner
Mary Ryan, Venture Partner
Zachary Herlick, Managing Partner

Type of Firm
Private Firm Investing Own Capital

Industry Association Membership
National Venture Capital Association (NVCA)

Industry Preferences

(% based on actual investment)

Internet Specific	88.3%
Consumer Related	6.7%
Other Products	2.6%
Communications and Media	2.4%

Additional Information
Name of Most Recent Fund: Maveron Equity Partners, L.P.
Most Recent Fund Was Raised: 06/11/1998
Year Founded: 1998
Capital Under Management: $415,000,000
Current Activity Level : Actively seeking new investments

MDS HEALTH VENTURES, INC. (AKA: MDS CAPITAL CORP.)

11804 North Creek Parkway South
Bothell, WA
Phone: 425-487-8229
Website: www.mdscapital.com

See Foreign Venture Capital Firms for full listing.

MOHR, DAVIDOW VENTURES

505 Fifth Avenue South
Suite 610
Seattle, WA 98104
Phone: 206-344-3800
Fax: 206-344-3388
Website: www.mdv.com

See California for full listing.

NORTHERN STREAM CAPITAL

P.O. Box 676
Medina, WA 98039-0676
Phone: 206-691-1511
Website: www.northernstreamcapital.com

Management and Staff
Nordstrom Jim, Managing Director

Type of Firm
Private Equity Advisor or Fund of Fund Mgr

Project Preferences

Type of Financing Preferred:
Early Stage
Later Stage

Industry Preferences

Internet Specific
Internet

Additional Information
Current Activity Level : Actively seeking new investments

NORTHWEST VENTURE ASSOCIATES, INC.(FKA:SPOKANE CAPITAL MGMT)

221 North Wall Street
Suite 628
Spokane, WA 99201
Phone: 509-747-0728
Fax: 509-747-0758
Website: www.nwva.com

Other Offices

505 Fifth Avenue South
Suite 630
Seattle, WA 98104
Phone: 206-826-6982

Management and Staff
Chris Brookfield, Managing Director
Jean Balek-Miner, Managing Director
Joe Herzog, Managing Director
Mark Mecham, Managing Director
Tom Simpson, Managing Partner

Whom to Contact
Christopher Brookfield
Thomas C. Simpson

Type of Firm
Private Firm Investing Own Capital

Industry Association Membership
Natl assoc of Small Bus. Inv. Co (NASBIC)

Project Preferences

Role in Financing:
Prefer role as deal originator but will also invest in deals created by others

Type of Financing Preferred:
Balanced
Expansion
First Stage Financing
Mezzanine
Research and Development
Second Stage Financing
Seed
Start-up Financing

Size of Investments Considered
Min Size of Investment Considered (000s): $1,000
Max Size of Investment Considered (000s): $2,000

Geographical Preferences

United States
Northwest
Rocky Mountain

Canada
Western Canada

Industry Preferences

(% based on actual investment)

Internet Specific	37.0%
Communications and Media	23.0%
Computer Software and Services	18.9%
Consumer Related	10.8%
Medical/Health	6.8%
Industrial/Energy	3.4%

Additional Information
Name of Most Recent Fund: Northwest Venture Partners III, L.P.
Most Recent Fund Was Raised: 12/01/1999
Year Founded: 1988
Capital Under Management: $174,600,000
Current Activity Level : Actively seeking new investments
Method of Compensation: Return on investment is of primary concern, do not charge fees

OVP VENTURE PARTNERS (FKA: OLYMPIC VENTURE PARTNERS)

2420 Carillon Point
Kirkland, WA 98033
Phone: 425-889-9192
Fax: 425-889-0152
Website: www.ovp.com

Other Offices

340 Oswego Pointe Drive
Suite 200
Lake Oswego, OR 97034
Phone: 503-697-8766
Fax: 503-697-8863

Management and Staff
Bill Funcannon, Chief Financial Officer
Bill Miller, General Partner
Chad Waite, General Partner
David Chen, General Partner
George Clute, General Partner
Gerard Langeler, General Partner

Type of Firm
Venture Consulting Firm

Industry Association Membership
European Venture Capital Association (EVCA)
Western Association of Venture Capitalists (WAVC)

Project Preferences

Role in Financing:
Prefer role as deal originator

Type of Financing Preferred:
Early Stage
Seed
Startup

Size of Investments Considered
Min Size of Investment Considered (000s): $1,000
Max Size of Investment Considered (000s): $10,000

Geographical Preferences

United States
Northwest
West Coast

Canada
Western Canada

Industry Preferences

(% based on actual investment)

Internet Specific	33.4%
Computer Software and Services	25.7%
Medical/Health	11.1%
Communications and Media	7.4%
Semiconductors/Other Elect.	6.7%
Biotechnology	4.8%
Computer Hardware	3.7%
Other Products	3.5%
Consumer Related	1.9%
Industrial/Energy	1.8%

Additional Information
Name of Most Recent Fund: OVP IV
Most Recent Fund Was Raised: 12/01/1997
Year Founded: 1982
Capital Under Management: $317,000,000
Current Activity Level : Actively seeking new investments
Method of Compensation: Return on investment is of primary concern, do not charge fees

PACIFIC HORIZON VENTURES LLC

1001 Fourth Avenue Plaza
Suite 4105
Seattle, WA 98154
Phone: 206-682-1181
Fax: 206-682-8077
Website: www.pacifichorizon.com

Management and Staff
Bruce Jackson, General Partner
Donald Elmer, Managing General Partner
Gene Rowland, Chief Financial Officer
J. Douglas Eplett, General Partner
Richard Carone, General Partner

Type of Firm
Private Firm Investing Own Capital

Industry Association Membership
National Venture Capital Association (NVCA)

Project Preferences

Role in Financing:
Prefer role as deal originator but will also invest in deals created by others

Type of Financing Preferred:
Early Stage

Geographical Preferences

United States
All U.S.
Northwest

Industry Preferences

(% based on actual investment)

Biotechnology	49.9%
Medical/Health	16.5%
Internet Specific	16.3%
Industrial/Energy	12.1%
Computer Software and Services	5.3%

Additional Information
Name of Most Recent Fund: Pacific Horizon Partners III, L.P.
Most Recent Fund Was Raised: 09/01/1998
Year Founded: 1993
Capital Under Management: $35,000,000
Current Activity Level : Actively seeking new investments
Method of Compensation: Return on investment is of primary concern, do not charge fees

PACIFIC NORTHWEST PARTNERS SBIC, L.P.

15352 SE 53rd. Street
Bellevue, WA 98006
Phone: 425-455-9967
Fax: 425-455-9404

Management and Staff
Louis Kertesz, General Partner
Nancy Isely-Fletcher, Vice President
Theodore Wight, General Partner

Type of Firm
Private Firm Investing Own Capital

Industry Association Membership
Natl assoc of Small Bus. Inv. Co (NASBIC)

Project Preferences

Role in Financing:
Prefer role as deal originator but will also invest in deals created by others

Type of Financing Preferred:
Early Stage
First Stage Financing
Seed
Start-up Financing

Size of Investments Considered
Min Size of Investment Considered (000s): $500
Max Size of Investment Considered: No Limit

Geographical Preferences

United States
All U.S.
Northwest
West Coast

Industry Preferences

(% based on actual investment)

Internet Specific	45.5%
Medical/Health	30.0%
Consumer Related	19.5%
Other Products	2.8%
Computer Software and Services	2.3%

Additional Information
Name of Most Recent Fund: Pacific Northwest Partners SBIC, L.P.
Most Recent Fund Was Raised: 01/01/1994
Year Founded: 1994
Capital Under Management: $31,500,000
Current Activity Level : Actively seeking new investments
Method of Compensation: Return on investment is of primary concern, do not charge fees

PALADIN PARTNERS

1644 10th Street
Kirkland, WA 98033
Phone: 425-739-0978
Fax: 425-739-0980
Website: www.paladinpartners.com

Management and Staff
Doug Brown, Partner
Elaine Kong, Partner
Janis Machala, Managing Partner
Susan Harker, Partner

Type of Firm
Mgt. Consulting Firm

Project Preferences

Role in Financing:
Will function either as deal originator or investor in deals created by others

Type of Financing Preferred:
Early Stage
First Stage Financing
Seed
Startup

Geographical Preferences

United States
West Coast

Industry Preferences

Communications and Media
Wireless Communications

Computer Software
Software
Systems Software
Applications Software

Internet Specific
E-Commerce Technology
Internet
Web Aggregration/Portals

Business Serv.
Consulting Services
Media

Additional Information
Year Founded: 1995
Current Activity Level : Actively seeking new investments
Method of Compensation: Professional fee required whether or not deal closes

PERENNIAL VENTURES (FKA: TREDEGAR INVESTMENTS)

701 Fifth Avenue
Suite 6600
Seattle, WA 98104
Phone: 206-652-9240
Fax: 206-652-9250
Website: www.perennialventures.com

Other Offices

1100 Boulders Parkway
Richmond, VA 23225
Phone: 804-330-1062
Fax: 804-330-1777

Management and Staff
Steven Johnson, Partner

Type of Firm
Private Firm Investing Own Capital

Industry Association Membership
National Venture Capital Association (NVCA)

Project Preferences

Role in Financing:
Prefer role as deal originator but will also invest in deals created by others

Type of Financing Preferred:
Balanced
First Stage Financing
Research and Development
Second Stage Financing
Seed
Start-up Financing

Size of Investments Considered
Min Size of Investment Considered (000s): $500
Max Size of Investment Considered (000s): $4,000

Geographical Preferences

United States
All U.S.

Industry Preferences
(% based on actual investment)

Internet Specific	28.6%
Medical/Health	23.0%
Communications and Media	12.5%
Biotechnology	11.1%
Semiconductors/Other Elect.	10.3%
Computer Software and Services	9.7%
Other Products	2.6%
Industrial/Energy	1.7%
Computer Hardware	0.4%

Additional Information
Year Founded: 1990
Capital Under Management: $136,000,000
Current Activity Level : Actively seeking new investments
Method of Compensation: Return on investment is of primary concern, do not charge fees

PHOENIX PARTNERS, THE

1000 Second Avenue
Suite 3600
Seattle, WA 98104
Phone: 206-624-8968
Fax: 206-624-1907

Management and Staff
Will Horne, Chief Financial Officer

Whom to Contact
William B. Horne

Type of Firm
Private Firm Investing Own Capital

Project Preferences

Role in Financing:
Prefer role as deal originator but will also invest in deals created by others

Type of Financing Preferred:
First Stage Financing
Mezzanine
Research and Development
Second Stage Financing
Seed
Start-up Financing

Size of Investments Considered
Min Size of Investment Considered (000s): $2,000
Max Size of Investment Considered (000s): $3,000

Geographical Preferences

International
No Preference

Industry Preferences

(% based on actual investment)

Internet Specific	38.8%
Biotechnology	31.5%
Computer Software and Services	11.1%
Computer Hardware	7.6%
Consumer Related	4.8%
Medical/Health	3.6%
Semiconductors/Other Elect.	1.5%
Communications and Media	0.7%
Other Products	0.4%

Additional Information

Name of Most Recent Fund: Phoenix Partners IV, L.P.
Most Recent Fund Was Raised: 01/01/1996
Year Founded: 1982
Capital Under Management: $170,000,000
Current Activity Level : Actively seeking new investments
Method of Compensation: Return on investment is of primary concern, do not charge fees

POLARIS VENTURE PARTNERS

Bank of America Tower
701 Fifth Avenue; Suite 6850
Seattle, WA 98104
Phone: 206-652-4555
Fax: 206-652-4666
Website: www.polarisventures.com

See Massachusetts for full listing.

REDLEAF VENTURE MANAGEMENT

999 Third Avenue
Suite 2424
Seattle, WA 98104
Phone: 206-447-1350
Fax: 206-4471351
Website: www.redleaf.com

See California for full listing.

ROANOKE CAPITAL, LTD.

1111 Third Avenue
Suite 2220
Seattle, WA 98101
Phone: 206-628-0606
Fax: 206-628-0479

Other Offices

111 Third Ave
Suite 2220
Seattle, WA

Type of Firm

Private Firm Investing Own Capital

Project Preferences

Role in Financing:
Prefer role as deal originator but will also invest in deals created by others

Type of Financing Preferred:
Leveraged Buyout
Mezzanine
Second Stage Financing

Size of Investments Considered

Min Size of Investment Considered (000s): $300
Max Size of Investment Considered (000s): $1,000

Geographical Preferences

United States
Northwest

Industry Preferences

Communications and Media
Communications and Media

Computer Hardware
Mainframes / Scientific
Mini and Personal/Desktop
Computer Graphics and Dig
Integrated Turnkey System
Disk Relat. Memory Device

Computer Software
Computer Services
Systems Software
Applications Software
Artificial Intelligence

Semiconductors/Other Elect.
Electronic Components

Biotechnology
Industrial Biotechnology
Biosensors
Biotech Related Research

Medical/Health
Medical Diagnostics
Diagnostic Services
Diagnostic Test Products
Medical Therapeutics
Drug/Equipmt Delivery
Other Therapeutic
Disposable Med. Products
Hospital/Other Instit.
Pharmaceuticals

Consumer Related
Entertainment and Leisure
Retail
Computer Stores
Food/Beverage
Consumer Products
Consumer Services
Education Related

Industrial/Energy
Alternative Energy
Energy Conservation Relat
Industrial Products

Financial Services
Financial Services

Business Serv.
Distribution

Manufact.
Office Automation Equipmt
Publishing

Additional Information

Name of Most Recent Fund: Roanoke Investors' Limited Partners
Most Recent Fund Was Raised: 05/01/1988
Year Founded: 1982
Capital Under Management: $29,600,000
Current Activity Level : Actively seeking new investments
Method of Compensation: Return on investment is of primary concern, do not charge fees

SEAPOINT VENTURES

777 108th Ave NE
Suite 1895
Bellevue, WA 98004
Phone: 425-455-0879
Fax: 425-455-1093
Website: www.seapointventures.com

Management and Staff

Cliff Beer, Chief Financial Officer
Robert Hart, General Partner
Susan Sigl, Partner
Thomas Huseby, Managing Partner

Type of Firm
Private Firm Investing Own Capital

Project Preferences

Type of Financing Preferred:
Early Stage

Geographical Preferences

United States
Northwest

Industry Preferences

(% based on actual investment)

Internet Specific	57.4%
Computer Software and Services	19.0%
Communications and Media	13.9%
Medical/Health	6.6%
Biotechnology	3.1%

Additional Information
Year Founded: 1997
Current Activity Level : Actively seeking new investments

SILICON VALLEY BANK

915 118th Avenue SE
Suite 250
Bellevue, WA 98005
Phone: 206-688-1368
Fax: 206-646-8100

See California for full listing.

STAENBERG PRIVATE CAPITAL, LLC

2000 1st Ave
Suite 1001
Seattle, WA 98121
Phone: 206-374-0234
Fax: 708-575-1324
Website: www.staenberg.com

Management and Staff
Jon Staenberg, Managing Partner

Type of Firm
Private Equity Advisor or Fund of Fund Mgr

Project Preferences

Type of Financing Preferred:
Balanced

Size of Investments Considered
Min Size of Investment Considered (000s): $100
Max Size of Investment Considered (000s): $3,000

Geographical Preferences

United States
Northern California
Northwest

Industry Preferences

(% based on actual investment)

Internet Specific	73.6%
Computer Software and Services	21.3%
Consumer Related	5.1%

Additional Information
Year Founded: 1998
Current Activity Level : Actively seeking new investments

TIMBERLINE VENTURE PARTNERS

8000 Northeast
Parkway Drive 300
Vancouver, WA 98668
Phone: 360-882-9577
Fax: 360-882-9590

Other Offices

3655 Torrance Ave.
Suite 345
Torrance, CA 90503-4810
Phone: 310-543-0408
Fax: 310-543-0308

Management and Staff
Jeffrey Tung, Managing Partner
Tim Draper, General Partner
William Kallman, Managing Partner

Type of Firm
Private Firm Investing Own Capital

Industry Association Membership
National Venture Capital Association (NVCA)

Additional Information
Name of Most Recent Fund: Timberline Venture Partners
Most Recent Fund Was Raised: 07/01/1999
Year Founded: 1997
Capital Under Management: $31,000,000
Current Activity Level : Actively seeking new investments
Method of Compensation: Return on investment is of primary concern, do not charge fees

U.S. VENTURE PARTNERS

7900 SE 28th Street
Suite 250,
Mercer Island, WA 98040
Phone: 206-236-5776
Fax: 206-236-5779
Website: www.usvp.com

See California for full listing.

UNION STREET CAPITAL CORP.

P.O. Box 219
Mercer Island, WA 98040
Phone: 206-232-2272
Fax: 206-232-2272

Management and Staff
Stanton Barnes

Whom to Contact
Stanton Barnes

Type of Firm
Mgt. Consulting Firm

Project Preferences

Role in Financing:
Prefer role as deal originator but will also invest in deals created by others

Type of Financing Preferred:
Leveraged Buyout
Second Stage Financing

Size of Investments Considered
Min Size of Investment Considered (000s): $600
Max Size of Investment Considered: No Limit

Geographical Preferences

United States
Northwest

Canada
Western Canada

Industry Preferences

Communications and Media
CATV & Pay TV Systems
Radio & TV Broadcasting
Data Communications
Other Communication Prod.

Computer Software
Applications Software

Internet Specific
Internet

Semiconductors/Other Elect.
Sensors
Component Testing Equipmt
Fiber Optics
Analytic/Scientific

Medical/Health
Diagnostic Services
Diagnostic Test Products
Disposable Med. Products
Hospital/Other Instit.

Consumer Related
Entertainment and Leisure
Franchises(NEC)
Food/Beverage
Hotels and Resorts

Industrial/Energy
Energy Conservation Relat
Industrial Products
Factory Automation
Robotics

Business Serv.
Consulting Services

Manufact.
Publishing

Additional Information
Year Founded: 1983
Capital Under Management: $4,000,000
Current Activity Level : Actively seeking new investments
Method of Compensation: Return on invest. most important, but chg. closing fees, service fees, etc.

VAULT CAPITAL

Smith Tower; 506 Second Avenue
Suite 3200
Seattle, WA 98104
Phone: 206-625-1700
Fax: 206-625-2381
Website: www.vaultcapital.com

Management and Staff
Petra Franklin, Chief Executive Officer

Type of Firm
Private Firm Investing Own Capital

Project Preferences

Type of Financing Preferred:
Early Stage

Additional Information
Current Activity Level : Actively seeking new investments

VOYAGER CAPITAL

800 Fifth Avenue
Suite 4100
Seattle, WA 98104
Phone: 206-470-1180
Fax: 206-470-1185
Website: www.voyagercapital.com

Other Offices

1520 Page Mill Road
Palo Alto, CA 94304
Phone: 650-855-9300
Fax: 650-320-8053

Management and Staff
Antonio Audino, Managing Director
Bill Hughlett, Chief Financial Officer
Brian Hilgendorf, Venture Partner
Curtis Feeny, Managing Director
Enrique Godreau, Managing Director
Erik Benson, Principal
William McAleer, Managing Director

Type of Firm
Private Firm Investing Own Capital

Industry Association Membership
European Venture Capital Association (EVCA)
Western Association of Venture Capitalists (WAVC)

Project Preferences

Role in Financing:
Prefer role as deal originator but will also invest in deals created by others

Type of Financing Preferred:
Early Stage
First Stage Financing
Second Stage Financing
Seed

Size of Investments Considered
Min Size of Investment Considered (000s): $5,000
Max Size of Investment Considered (000s): $10,000

Geographical Preferences

United States
Northern California
Northwest
Texas
West Coast

Canada
Western Canada

Industry Preferences

(% based on actual investment)

Internet Specific	63.8%
Computer Software and Services	34.9%
Communications and Media	1.3%

Additional Information
Name of Most Recent Fund: Voyager Capital
Most Recent Fund Was Raised: 11/01/1997
Year Founded: 1997
Capital Under Management: $264,100,000
Current Activity Level : Actively seeking new investments
Method of Compensation: Return on investment is of primary concern, do not charge fees

VULCAN VENTURES, INC.

Communications, Vulcan NW
110 110th Ave NE, Suite 550
Bellevue, WA 98004
Phone: 425-453-1940
Fax: 425-453-1985
Website: www.paulallen.com

Management and Staff
William Savoy, President

Type of Firm
Private Firm Investing Own Capital

Industry Preferences

(% based on actual investment)

Internet Specific	53.1%
Communications and Media	23.8%
Other Products	11.4%
Biotechnology	4.4%
Medical/Health	2.3%
Computer Hardware	1.9%
Computer Software and Services	1.8%
Semiconductors/Other Elect.	1.3%

Additional Information

Year Founded: 1986

Current Activity Level : Actively seeking new investments

WALDEN INTERNATIONAL INVESTMENT GROUP (AKA: WALDEN GROUP)

5302 143rd Avenue, S.E.
Bellevue, WA 98006
Phone: 206-643-7572
Fax: 206-649-0241
Website: www.waldenintl.com

See California for full listing.

WRF CAPITAL

2815 Eastlake Avenue E
Suite 300
Seattle, WA 98102
Phone: 206-336-5600
Fax: 206-336-5615

Management and Staff

John Reagh, Managing Director
Lortetta Little, Managing Director
Ronald Howell, Managing Director

Type of Firm

Non-Financial Corp. Affiliate or Subsidiary

Industry Association Membership

National Venture Capital Association (NVCA)

Additional Information

Current Activity Level : Actively seeking new investments

WEST VIRGINIA

MOUNTAINEER CAPITAL LP

107 Capital Street
Suite 300
Charleston, WV 25301
Phone: 304-347-7525
Fax: 304-347-2252
Website: www.mountaineercapital.com

Management and Staff
F. Eric Nelson, General Partner
J. Rudy Henley, Partner
Patrick Bond, Partner
William Taylor, Managing General Partner

Type of Firm
SBIC Not elsewhere classified

Industry Association Membership
Natl assoc of Small Bus. Inv. Co (NASBIC)

Project Preferences

Role in Financing:
Will function either as deal originator or investor in deals created by others

Type of Financing Preferred:
Balanced
Early Stage
Expansion
First Stage Financing
Later Stage
Management Buyouts
Second Stage Financing
Special Situation
Start-up Financing

Size of Investments Considered
Min Size of Investment Considered (000s): $250
Max Size of Investment Considered (000s): $1,500

Geographical Preferences

United States
Mid Atlantic
West Virginia

Industry Preferences

Communications and Media
Telecommunications
Data Communications

Internet Specific
E-Commerce Technology
Internet
Web Aggregration/Portals

Semiconductors/Other Elect.
Electronic Components
Sensors

Medical/Health
Medical Diagnostics
Diagnostic Services
Diagnostic Test Products
Medical Products
Disposable Med. Products

Consumer Related
Consumer
Education Related

Industrial/Energy
Energy
Industrial Products
Factory Automation
Process Control
Machinery

Transportation
Transportation

Business Serv.
Services
Distribution

Manufact.
Manufacturing

Agr/Forestr/Fish
Agriculture related

Additional Information
Year Founded: 2000
Capital Under Management: $5,500,000
Current Activity Level : Actively seeking new investments
Method of Compensation: Return on invest. most important, but chg. closing fees, service fees, etc.

WISCONSIN

BAIRD CAPITAL PARTNERS

777 East Wisconsin Avenue
28th Floor
Milwaukee, WI 53202
Phone: 888-761-9641
Website: www.rwbaird.com

See Illinois for full listing.

CAPITAL INVESTMENTS, INC.

1009 West Glen Oaks Lane
Suite 103
Mequon, WI 53092
Phone: 262-241-0303
Fax: 262-241-8451
Website: www.capitalinvesmentsinc.com

Other Offices

744 North Fourth Street
Suite 540
Milwaukee, WI 53203
Phone: 414-273-6560
Fax: 414-273-0530

Type of Firm
SBIC Not elsewhere classified

Industry Association Membership
Natl assoc of Small Bus. Inv. Co (NASBIC)

Project Preferences

Role in Financing:
Prefer role as deal originator but will also invest in deals created by others

Type of Financing Preferred:
Leveraged Buyout
Mezzanine
Second Stage Financing

Size of Investments Considered
Min Size of Investment Considered (000s): $500
Max Size of Investment Considered (000s): $1,000

Geographical Preferences

United States
Midwest
Southwest

Industry Preferences
(% based on actual investment)

Industrial/Energy	28.1%
Computer Software and Services	24.3%
Other Products	16.8%
Computer Hardware	16.4%
Medical/Health	6.9%
Consumer Related	4.1%
Communications and Media	3.5%

Additional Information
Year Founded: 1959
Capital Under Management: $20,000,000
Current Activity Level : Actively seeking new investments
Method of Compensation: Return on invest. most important, but chg. closing fees, service fees, etc.

CEDAR CREEK PARTNERS, LLC

111 East Kilbourn Avenue
Suite 1600
Milwaukee, WI 53202
Phone: 414-272-5500
Fax: 414-272-1029
Website: www.cedarllc.com

Management and Staff
Daniel Jagla, Managing Director
Ellie Berg, Vice President
H. Wayne Foreman, Managing Director
Robert Cook, Managing Director

Whom to Contact
Ellie Berg

Type of Firm
Private Firm Investing Own Capital

Project Preferences

Role in Financing:
Prefer role as deal originator but will also invest in deals created by others

Type of Financing Preferred:
Industry Rollups
Leveraged Buyout

Size of Investments Considered
Min Size of Investment Considered (000s): $8,000
Max Size of Investment Considered: No Limit

Geographical Preferences

United States
All U.S.

Industry Preferences

Communications and Media
Other Communication Prod.

Semiconductors/Other Elect.
Electronics
Electronic Components
Controllers and Sensors
Sensors
Component Testing Equipmt
Analytic/Scientific

Medical/Health
Other Therapeutic
Medical Products
Disposable Med. Products

Consumer Related
Entertainment and Leisure
Food/Beverage
Consumer Products
Education Related

Industrial/Energy
Industrial Products
Materials
Machinery
Environmental Related

Transportation
Transportation

Manufact.
Publishing

Additional Information
Name of Most Recent Fund: CCP Limited Partnership
Most Recent Fund Was Raised: 01/01/1997
Year Founded: 1997
Capital Under Management: $125,000,000
Current Activity Level : Actively seeking new investments
Method of Compensation: Return on invest. most important, but chg. closing fees, service fees, etc.

FUTURE VALUE VENTURES, INC.

2745 N Martin Luther King Dr
Suite 204
Milwaukee, WI 53212-2300
Phone: 414-264-2252
Fax: 414-264-2253
Website: fvvventures@aol.com

Management and Staff
William Beckett, President

Whom to Contact
William Beckett

Type of Firm
MESBIC not elsewhere classified

Industry Association Membership
Natl Assoc of Investment Cos. (NAIC)
Natl assoc of Small Bus. Inv. Co (NASBIC)

Project Preferences

Role in Financing:
Prefer role as deal originator but will also invest in deals created by others

Type of Financing Preferred:
First Stage Financing
Mezzanine
Second Stage Financing
Start-up Financing

Size of Investments Considered
Min Size of Investment Considered (000s): $100
Max Size of Investment Considered (000s): $300

Geographical Preferences

United States
All U.S.

Additional Information
Year Founded: 1984
Capital Under Management: $3,500,000
Current Activity Level : Actively seeking new investments
Method of Compensation: Return on invest. most important, but chg. closing fees, service fees, etc.

GCI

20875 Crossroads Circle
Suite 100
Waukesha, WI 53186
Phone: 262-798-5080
Fax: 262-798-5087

Other Offices

5404A West 115th Street
Milwaukee, WI 53225
Phone: 414-464-9333
Fax: 414-464-1321

Type of Firm
Private Firm Investing Own Capital

Project Preferences

Role in Financing:
Prefer role as deal originator but will also invest in deals created by others

Type of Financing Preferred:
First Stage Financing
Leveraged Buyout
Second Stage Financing

Size of Investments Considered
Min Size of Investment Considered (000s): $2,000
Max Size of Investment Considered: No Limit

Geographical Preferences

United States
All U.S.

Industry Preferences

Communications and Media
Other Communication Prod.

Computer Hardware
Computer Graphics and Dig
Integrated Turnkey System

Computer Software
Systems Software
Applications Software
Artificial Intelligence

Semiconductors/Other Elect.
Electronics
Electronic Components
Laser Related
Analytic/Scientific

Consumer Related
Consumer Products

Industrial/Energy
Materials

Business Serv.
Consulting Services

Additional Information
Name of Most Recent Fund: Global Capital Investors, L.P.
Most Recent Fund Was Raised: 01/01/1997
Year Founded: 1990
Capital Under Management: $20,000,000
Current Activity Level : Actively seeking new investments
Method of Compensation: Return on invest. most important, but chg. closing fees, service fees, etc.

GRANVILLE BAIRD CAPITAL PARTNERS (FKA:GRANVILLE PR EQ MNGRS)

Robert W. Baird & Co.
777 East Wisconsin Avenue
Milwaukee, WI 53202
Phone: 414 765 3758
Website: www.granvillebaird.com

See Foreign Venture Capital Firms for full listing.

INVESTAMERICA VENTURE GROUP, INC.

600 East Mason Street
Suite 304
Milwaukee, WI 53202
Phone: 414-276-3839
Fax: 414-276-1885

See Iowa for full listing.

LUBAR & CO.

700 North Water
Suite 1200
Milwaukee, WI 53202
Phone: 414-291-9000
Fax: 414-291-9061

Other Offices

3380 Firstar Center
Milwaukee, WI 53202
Phone: 414-276-3839

Management and Staff
David Lubar
Gus Taylor

Whom to Contact
David Lubar
Gus Taylor

Type of Firm
Investment/Merchant Bank Investing Own or Client Funds

Project Preferences

Role in Financing:
Prefer role as deal originator but will also invest in deals created by others

Type of Financing Preferred:
Control-block Purchases
Leveraged Buyout
Second Stage Financing
Special Situation

Size of Investments Considered
Min Size of Investment Considered (000s): $10,000
Max Size of Investment Considered: No Limit

Geographical Preferences

United States
Midwest

Industry Preferences

Communications and Media
Commercial Communications

Computer Hardware
Integrated Turnkey System

Computer Software
Computer Services
Systems Software

Semiconductors/Other Elect.
Electronics

Medical/Health
Diagnostic Services
Diagnostic Test Products
Other Therapeutic
Medical Products
Disposable Med. Products
Hospitals/Clinics/Primary

Consumer Related
Entertainment and Leisure
Retail
Food/Beverage
Consumer Products
Consumer Services
Education Related

Industrial/Energy
Industrial Products

Transportation
Transportation

Financial Services
Financial Services

Manufact.
Publishing

Agr/Forestr/Fish
Agriculture related

Additional Information
Name of Most Recent Fund: Lubar & Company
Most Recent Fund Was Raised: 01/01/1981
Year Founded: 1977
Capital Under Management: $80,000,000
Current Activity Level : Actively seeking new investments
Method of Compensation: Return on investment is of primary concern, do not charge fees

---

NEWTEK CAPITAL

1330 West Towne Square Road
Thiensville, WI 53092
Website: www.newtekcapital.com

See New York for full listing.

PANGAEA PARTNERS

402 Laurel Lane
Madison, WI 53704-6053
Phone: 608-242-1801
Fax: 608-242-1606

Type of Firm
Investment/Merchant Bank Subsid/Affil

Additional Information
Current Activity Level : Actively seeking new investments

QUAESTUS & CO. INC. (FKA: QUAESTUS MANAGEMENT CORP..)

400 East Wisconsin Ave
4th Floor
Milwaukee, WI 53202
Phone: 414-615-4600
Fax: 414-615-4640

Management and Staff
Barbara Miller, Vice President
John Riley, General Partner
Richard Weening, Chief Executive Officer
Stephen Getsy, General Partner

Type of Firm
Private Firm Investing Own Capital

Industry Association Membership
National Venture Capital Association (NVCA)

Project Preferences

Role in Financing:
Will function either as deal originator or investor in deals created by others

Type of Financing Preferred:
Acquisition
Fund of Funds
Joint Ventures
Recapitalizations
Seed
Start-up Financing
Turnaround

Size of Investments Considered
Min Size of Investment Considered (000s): $500
Max Size of Investment Considered: No Limit

Geographical Preferences

United States
All U.S.

International
France
India
United Kingdom

Industry Preferences

Communications and Media
Radio & TV Broadcasting
Wireless Communications

Computer Hardware
Mini and Personal/Desktop

Computer Software
Computer Services
Data Processing
Software
Systems Software
Applications Software

Internet Specific
E-Commerce Technology
Internet

Biotechnology
Human Biotechnology

Business Serv.
Consulting Services
Media

Additional Information

Name of Most Recent Fund: Quaestus III
Most Recent Fund Was Raised: 01/01/1994
Year Founded: 1989
Capital Under Management: $125,000,000
Current Activity Level : Actively seeking new investments
Method of Compensation: Return on invest. most important, but chg. closing fees, service fees, etc.

VENTURE INVESTORS MANAGEMENT LLC

University Research Park
505 S. Rosa Road
Madison, WI 53719
Phone: 608-441-2700
Fax: 608-441-2727
Website: www.ventureinvestors.com

Other Offices

917 Gibbs Road
P.O. Box 1506
Venice, FL 34284
Phone: 941-486-8687
Fax: 941-485-0879

Management and Staff

John Neis, Managing Partner
Roger Ganser, Managing Partner
Scott Button, Partner

Type of Firm

Private Firm Investing Own Capital

Industry Association Membership

National Venture Capital Association (NVCA)
Natl assoc of Small Bus. Inv. Co (NASBIC)

Project Preferences

Role in Financing:

Prefer role as deal originator but will also invest in deals created by others

Type of Financing Preferred:

First Stage Financing
Mezzanine
Second Stage Financing
Seed
Special Situation
Start-up Financing

Geographical Preferences

United States

Midwest
Southeast

Industry Preferences

(% based on actual investment)

Other Products	33.2%
Medical/Health	16.0%
Computer Software and Services	16.0%
Biotechnology	15.7%
Consumer Related	6.0%
Internet Specific	5.6%
Semiconductors/Other Elect.	3.8%
Computer Hardware	3.3%
Communications and Media	0.3%

Additional Information

Name of Most Recent Fund: Venture Investors Early Stage Fund II LP
Most Recent Fund Was Raised: 05/01/1997
Year Founded: 1982
Capital Under Management: $69,000,000
Current Activity Level : Actively seeking new investments
Method of Compensation: Return on investment is of primary concern, do not charge fees

WYOMING

SAPIENT CAPITAL

P.O. Box 1590
Wilson, WY 83014
Phone: 307-733-3806
Fax: 307-733-4630
Website: www.sapientcapital.com

Management and Staff
Mitchell Dann, Principal

Type of Firm
Private Firm Investing Own Capital

Industry Association Membership
National Venture Capital Association (NVCA)

Project Preferences

Role in Financing:
Will function either as deal originator or investor in deals created by others

Type of Financing Preferred:
Early Stage
First Stage Financing
Research and Development
Seed
Startup

Geographical Preferences

United States
Midwest
Northern California
Northwest
Rocky Mountain
West Coast

Industry Preferences

Biotechnology
Human Biotechnology
Biosensors

Medical/Health
Medical/Health
Medical Diagnostics
Diagnostic Services
Diagnostic Test Products
Medical Therapeutics
Drug/Equipmt Delivery
Medical Products
Disposable Med. Products
Health Services
Hospitals/Clinics/Primary
Hospital/Other Instit.
Pharmaceuticals

Additional Information
Year Founded: 2000
Capital Under Management: $26,000,000
Current Activity Level : Actively seeking new investments
Method of Compensation: Return on investment is of primary concern, do not charge fees

Non-US Venture Capital Firms

Private equity across the world has grown tremendously in the last few years. Both limited and general partners have been more eager to diversify their investments by looking outside their domestic locales. To best represent the expanding market of venture capital worldwide, *Pratt's Guide to Venture Capital Sources* includes listings of venture capital firms listed outside the United States. There are approximately 754 firms outside the United States that are listed in this section, not including foreign branch offices of firms headquartered in the United States. As an example of the breadth of coverage, venture capital firms from the United Kingdom, the Czech Republic, Finland, France, Sweden, Hong Kong, Australia, Singapore, Taiwan, and Israel are listed.

2M INVEST, INC.

Suite 705, No. 148 C
Chung Shaio E. Road, Sec 4
Taipei, Taiwan
Phone: 886 2 2773 0132
Fax: 886 2 2778 1314

See California for full listing.

3I AUSTRIA (FKA BANK AUSTRIA TFV HIGH TECH -UB GMBH)

Wallnerstarsse 8
Wien, Austria A-1010
Phone: 431-532-1960
Fax: 431-532-1960-19
Website: www.ba-tfv.at

Management and Staff

Heinz Rieder, Managing Director
Reinhard Jonke, Managing Director

Type of Firm

Private Firm Investing Own Capital

Industry Association Membership

European Venture Capital Association (EVCA)

Project Preferences

Type of Financing Preferred:

Early Stage
Seed
Start-up Financing

Geographical Preferences

International

Austria
Germany

Industry Preferences

(% based on actual investment)

Computer Software and Services	75.5%
Other Products	13.3%
Industrial/Energy	11.3%

Additional Information

Name of Most Recent Fund: 3i Austria (FKA:Bank Austria TFV High Tech - UB GmbH)
Most Recent Fund Was Raised: 02/01/1997
Year Founded: 1996
Capital Under Management: $22,100,000
Current Activity Level : Actively seeking new investments

3I FINLAND OY (FKA SFK FINANCE)

Mikonkatu 25
P.O. Box 247
Helsinki, Finland FIN-00101
Phone: 358 9 6815 4100
Fax: 358 9 6815 4451
Website: www.sfk.fi

Management and Staff

Hannu Isohaaro, Partner
Jarkko Virtanen, Partner
Matti Vanhanen, Partner
Mikko-Jussi Suonenlahti, Partner
Vesa Sadeharju, Partner

Type of Firm

Private Firm Investing Own Capital

Industry Association Membership

European Venture Capital Association (EVCA)
Finnish Venture Capital Association

Project Preferences

Role in Financing:

Prefer role as deal originator but will also invest in deals created by others

Type of Financing Preferred:

Expansion
First Stage Financing
Management Buyouts
Mezzanine
Second Stage Financing
Seed
Start-up Financing

Geographical Preferences

International

Europe
Finland
Scandanavia/Nordic Region

Industry Preferences

(% based on actual investment)

Communications and Media	48.0%
Industrial/Energy	26.4%
Computer Software and Services	10.7%
Other Products	6.5%
Consumer Related	4.7%
Internet Specific	3.7%

Additional Information

Name of Most Recent Fund: Telecomia Venture I & Forenvia Venture I
Most Recent Fund Was Raised: 01/01/1996
Year Founded: 1990
Capital Under Management: $90,500,000
Current Activity Level : Actively seeking new investments
Method of Compensation: Return on investment is of primary concern, do not charge fees

3I GESTION SA

168, av Charles de Gaulle
Neuilly-sur-Seine Cedex
Paris, France 92573
Phone: 33 14 715 1100
Fax: 33 14 745 3124
Website: www.3i.com

Other Offices

2 rue Crebillon
Nantes, France 44000
Phone: 33 25 117 3300
Fax: 33 25 117 3301

Tour Societe Suisse
1 Boulevard Vivier Merle
Lyon, France 69443
Phone: 33 47 233 1672
Fax: 33 47 233 9864

Management and Staff

Bertrand Fesneau, Partner
Clement Cordier, Partner
Frederic De Broglie, Partner

Type of Firm

Private Firm Investing Own Capital

Industry Association Membership

European Venture Capital Association (EVCA)

Project Preferences

Type of Financing Preferred:

Balanced
Leveraged Buyout

Geographical Preferences

International

France

Industry Preferences

(% based on actual investment)

Other Products	53.0%
Computer Software and Services	32.0%
Internet Specific	11.1%
Industrial/Energy	3.8%

Additional Information

Year Founded: 1998
Capital Under Management: $906,300,000
Current Activity Level : Actively seeking new investments

3I GROUP PLC

91 Waterloo Road
London, United Kingdom SE1 8XP
Phone: 44-20-7928-3131
Fax: 44-20-7928-0058
Website: www.3i.com

Other Offices

2-2-3 Uchisaiwaicho
Chiyoda-ku, Tokyo, Japan 100-0011
Phone: 813-5251-4131
Fax: 813-5251-4141

168 av Charles de Gaulle
F - 92573
Neuilly-sur-Seine Cedex, France
Phone: 33 1/47.15.11.00
Fax: 33 1/47.45.31.24

20 Cecil Street
#08/04 The Exchange
Singapore, Singapore 049705
Phone: 65-438-3131
Fax: 65-536-2429

227 West George Street
Glasgow, United Kingdom G2 2ND
Phone: 44 141 248 4456
Fax: 44 141 248 3245

3 The Embankment
Sovereign Street
Leeds, United Kingdom LS1 4BP
Phone: 44 113 243 0511
Fax: 44 113 244 5800

38 Carden Place
Aberdeen, United Kingdom AB10 1UP
Phone: 44 1224 638 666
Fax: 44 1224 641 460

3i Niederlassung Schweiz
Othmarstrasse 8
Zurich, Switzerland CH-8008
Phone: 41 1 250 44 00
Fax: 41 1 250 44 10

40 Queen Square
Bristol, United Kingdom BS1 4LE
Phone: 44 870 243 3131
Fax: 44 117 927 9433

47 City Plaza
Cannon Street
Birmingham, United Kingdom
Phone: 44-121-633-3131
Fax: 44-121-633-9999

51 Grey Street
Newcastle-Upon-Tyne, United Kingdom NE1 6EF
Phone: 44 191 222 1966
Fax: 44 191 261 4701

Apex Plaza
Forbury Road
Reading, United Kingdom RG1 1AX
Phone: 44 118 958 4344
Fax: 44 118 958 4340

Bancho Kaikan 5/F
12-2 Gobancho Chiyoda-Ku
Tokyo, Japan 102
Phone: 813-3239-5670
Fax: 813-3239-6828

Bockenheimer Landstrasse 55
Frankfurt, Germany 60325
Phone: 49 69 710 0000
Fax: 49 69 719 00039

Burggrafenstrasse 5
Dusseldorf, Germany D-40545
Phone: 49 211 95444-0
Fax: 49 211 9544449

Calle Ruiz de Alarcon 12
Madrid, Spain 28014
Phone: 34 91/521.44.19
Fax: 34 91/521.98.19

Cambridge Science Park
Milton Road
Cambridge, United Kingdom CB4 0FZ
Phone: 44 1223 420 031
Fax: 44 1223 420 459

Cornelis Schuytstraat 72
Amsterdam, Netherlands 1071 JL
Phone: 31-20-3057-444
Fax: 31-20-3057-455

Friedrichstrasse 60
Berlin, Germany 10117
Phone: 49 30 767153-0
Fax: 49 30 76715319

Kronprinzstrasse 11
Stuttgart, Germany 70173
Phone: 49 711 2229220
Fax: 49 71122292229

Lock House
2 Castle Meadow Road
Nottingham, United Kingdom NG2 1AG
Phone: 44 115 941 2766
Fax: 44 115 941 9152

Neuer Wall 71
Hamburg, Germany 20354
Phone: 49 40 374767-0
Fax: 49 40 37476767

Nikolaistrasse 55
Leipzig, Germany 04109
Phone: 49 341 98445-0
Fax: 49 341 9845599

Romanstrasse 35
Munich, Germany 80639
Phone: 49 89 54862-0
Fax: 49 8954862299

Saltire Court
20 Castle Terrace
Edinburgh, United Kingdom EH1 2EN
Phone: 44 131 459 3131
Fax: 44 131 459 3140

Silkhouse Court
Tithebarn Street
Liverpool, United Kingdom L2 2LZ
Phone: 44 151 236 2944
Fax: 44 151 236 6252

Vig Gaetano Negri 8
Milan, Italy 20123
Phone: 39 02 880 841

Management and Staff
Andrew Garside, Partner
Antony Ross, Partner
Brian Larcombe, Chief Executive Officer
Carlo Michero, Partner
Carlos Mallo, Partner
Jamie Paton, Partner
Jane Crawford, Managing Director
Kevin Lyon, Managing Director
Lawrence Ross, Partner
Mark Heappey, Partner
Martin Green, Partner
Mike Robins, Partner
Pietro Lifonti, Partner
Roberto Ranera, Partner
Robin Jones, Partner
Rupert Lyle, Partner
Russ Cummings, Partner
Sergio Sambonet, Partner

Whom to Contact
Gabriel Gutiérrez Ugalde
Martin Gagen
Peter Williams

Type of Firm
Investment/Merchant Bank Subsid/Affil

Industry Association Membership
British Venture Capital Association
European Venture Capital Association (EVCA)
German Venture Capital Association
Hungarian Venture Capital Association

Project Preferences

Role in Financing:
Prefer role as deal originator but will also invest in deals created by others

Type of Financing Preferred:
Expansion
First Stage Financing
Leveraged Buyout
Management Buyouts
Recapitalizations
Second Stage Financing
Start-up Financing
Turnaround

Geographical Preferences

International
Belgium
France
Germany
Italy
Japan
Luxembourg
Netherlands
Spain
United Kingdom
No Preference

Industry Preferences

(% based on actual investment)

Other Products	25.4%
Internet Specific	18.6%
Consumer Related	16.7%
Computer Software and Services	10.8%
Communications and Media	8.2%
Industrial/Energy	5.6%
Semiconductors/Other Elect.	5.2%
Medical/Health	4.7%
Biotechnology	4.4%
Computer Hardware	0.3%

Additional Information
Name of Most Recent Fund: 3i Eurofund III
Most Recent Fund Was Raised: 10/06/1999
Year Founded: 1945
Capital Under Management: $7,000,000,000
Current Activity Level : Actively seeking new investments
Method of Compensation: Return on invest. most important, but chg. closing fees, service fees, etc.

3K DIGITAL

32 - 34 Gordon House Road
London, United Kingdom NW5 1LP
Phone: 44 20-7692 5319
Fax: 44 20-7692 5301
Website: www.3kdigital.com

Management and Staff
Rob Keve, Managing Director
Robin Klein, Principal
Ted Kalborg, Co-Founder

Type of Firm
Private Firm Investing Own Capital

Industry Association Membership
British Venture Capital Association

Project Preferences

Type of Financing Preferred:
Early Stage
First Stage Financing
Seed
Startup

Geographical Preferences

United States
All U.S.

International
Europe
Portugal
Scandanavia/Nordic Region
Spain
United Kingdom

Industry Preferences

Communications and Media
Communications and Media
Telecommunications

Internet Specific
Internet

Business Serv.
Media

Additional Information
Year Founded: 1999
Capital Under Management: $15,000,000
Current Activity Level : Actively seeking new investments

3TS VENTURE PARTNERS AG

Vaclavske 12
Manes House 2nd Floor
Prague, Czech Republic 12000
Phone: 4202 2146 0130
Fax: 4202 2146 0137

Other Offices

Andrassy ut. 11
Budapest, Hungary 1065
Phone: 36 1 411 2310
Fax: 36 1 411 2319

Warsaw Sheraton Plaza
ul. Prusa 2
Warsaw, Poland 00 493
Phone: 48 22 657 0475
Fax: 48 22 657 0158

Management and Staff
Michael White, Chief Executive Officer

Type of Firm
Private Equity Advisor or Fund of Fund Mgr

Project Preferences

Type of Financing Preferred:
Early Stage
Expansion
Startup

Size of Investments Considered
Min Size of Investment Considered (000s): $500
Max Size of Investment Considered (000s): $500,000

Geographical Preferences

International
Central Europe
Eastern Europe

Industry Preferences

Communications and Media
Communications and Media

Computer Software
Software

Internet Specific
Internet

Semiconductors/Other Elect.
Electronics

Additional Information
Year Founded: 2001
Capital Under Management: $70,000,000
Current Activity Level : Actively seeking new investments

550 DIGITAL MEDIA VENTURES

1 Undershaft
CGU Tower
London, United Kingdom EC3A 8NP

See New York for full listing.

ABERDEEN ASSET MANAGERS

One Albyn Place
Aberdeen, United Kingdom AB10 1YG
Phone: 44-1224-631999
Fax: 44-1224-425916
Website: www.aberdeen-asset.com

Management and Staff
Hugh Little

Whom to Contact
Hugh Little

Type of Firm
Private Firm Investing Own Capital

Project Preferences

Role in Financing:
Prefer role in deals created by others

Type of Financing Preferred:
Expansion
Leveraged Buyout
Second Stage Financing

Geographical Preferences

International
United Kingdom

Industry Preferences

(% based on actual investment)

Internet Specific	40.3%
Computer Software and Services	29.8%
Other Products	14.3%
Consumer Related	13.6%
Industrial/Energy	2.0%

Additional Information
Year Founded: 1986
Capital Under Management: $150,000,000
Current Activity Level : Actively seeking new investments
Method of Compensation: Return on invest. most important, but chg. closing fees, service fees, etc.

ABERDEEN MURRAY JOHNSTONE PRIVATE EQUITY

7 West Nile Street
Glasgow, United Kingdom G1 2PX
Phone: 44-141-226-3131
Fax: 44-141-248-5636
Website: www.murrayjohnstone.com

Other Offices

1 Albyn Place
Aberdeen, United Kingdom AB10 1YG
Phone: 44 1224 631 999
Fax: 44 1224 647 010

1 Cornwall Street
Birmingham, United Kingdom B3 2JN
Phone: 0121-236-1222
Fax: 0121-233-4628

3 The Embankment
Sovereign Street
Leeds, United Kingdom LS1 4BA
Phone: 0113-242-2644
Fax: 0113-242-2640

30 Coleman Street
London, United Kingdom EC2R 5AN
Phone: 020-7606-6969
Fax: 020-7606-5818

55 Spring Gardens
Manchester, United Kingdom M2 2BY
Phone: 0161-236-2288
Fax: 0161-236-5539

Ballantyne House, 4th Floor
84 Academy Street
Inverness, United Kingdom IV1 1LU
Phone: 44 1463 717 214
Fax: 44 1463 717 211

Management and Staff
Jonathan Diggines, Managing Director

Whom to Contact
Neil MacFayden

Type of Firm
Affiliate/Subsidary of Oth. Financial. Instit.

Industry Association Membership
British Venture Capital Association

Project Preferences

Role in Financing:
Prefer role as deal originator but will also invest in deals created by others

Type of Financing Preferred:
Acquisition
Balanced
Early Stage
Expansion
Fund of Funds
Generalist PE
Leveraged Buyout
Management Buyouts
Recapitalizations
Second Stage Financing
Startup
Turnaround

Geographical Preferences

International
Europe
United Kingdom

Industry Preferences

(% based on actual investment)

Other Products	28.6%
Consumer Related	13.8%

Computer Software and Services	10.4%
Computer Hardware	9.5%
Semiconductors/Other Elect.	9.4%
Internet Specific	8.2%
Medical/Health	8.2%
Industrial/Energy	7.1%
Communications and Media	4.4%
Biotechnology	0.3%

Additional Information

Name of Most Recent Fund: Murray Johnstone Private Acquisitions Partnership II (MJPAP

Most Recent Fund Was Raised: 08/01/1997

Year Founded: 1981

Capital Under Management: $637,300,000

Current Activity Level : Actively seeking new investments

ABINGWORTH VENTURE MANAGEMENT LIMITED

5th Floor, Princes House
38 Jermyn Street
London, United Kingdom SW1Y 6DN
Phone: 207-534-1500
Fax: 44-207-287-0480
Website: www.abingworth.co.uk

Other Offices

2465 East Bayshore Road
Suite 348
Palo Alto, United States of America 94303
Phone: 650 565 8296
Fax: 650 565 8295

Management and Staff

James Abell, Chief Financial Officer

Whom to Contact

Jonathan Macquitby

Type of Firm

Private Firm Investing Own Capital

Project Preferences

Role in Financing:

Prefer role as deal originator but will also invest in deals created by others

Type of Financing Preferred:

First Stage Financing
Second Stage Financing
Seed
Special Situation
Start-up Financing

Size of Investments Considered

Min Size of Investment Considered (000s): $500

Max Size of Investment Considered: No Limit

Geographical Preferences

United States

All U.S.
All U.S.

International

Bermuda
Europe
France
Germany
United Kingdom

Industry Preferences

(% based on actual investment)

Biotechnology	44.5%
Medical/Health	11.8%
Computer Software and Services	11.6%
Computer Hardware	8.0%
Communications and Media	7.1%
Other Products	5.2%
Internet Specific	5.0%
Industrial/Energy	3.0%
Semiconductors/Other Elect.	2.4%
Consumer Related	1.3%

Additional Information

Name of Most Recent Fund: Abingworth Bioventures II

Most Recent Fund Was Raised: 01/01/1997

Year Founded: 1973

Capital Under Management: $230,000,000

Current Activity Level : Actively seeking new investments

Method of Compensation: Return on investment is of primary concern, do not charge fees

ABN-AMRO CORPORATE INVESTMENTS

Foppingadreef 22
BS Amsterdam, Netherlands NL - 1102
Phone: 3120-629-5568
Fax: 31-20-628-7822
Website: www.abnamro.com

Other Offices

199 Bishopsgate
London, United Kingdom EC2M 3XW
Phone: 44 20 7678 0092
Fax: 44 20 7678 2050

23 Rue Balzac
Paris, France F-75008
Phone: 33-15-393-6900
Fax: 33-15-393-6925

31/F Edinburgh Tower
15 Queen's Road
Central, Hong Kong
Phone: 852-2102-2335
Fax: 852-2525-9115

Bockenheimer Landstrasse 99
Frankfurt, Germany D-60325
Phone: 49-69-972-0690
Fax: 49-69-972-09529

Csorsz Utca 3
Budapest, Hungary H-1123
Phone: 36-1-155-1367
Fax: 36-1-212-1978

European Renaissance Capital
Blanicka 28
Prague, Czech Republic 120 00
Phone: 420-2-2225-2407
Fax: 420-2-2225-1791

Ilka ut 47
Budapest, Hungary
Phone: 36-1-343-1627
Fax: 36-1-343-1629

Ul. Lowicka 44
Warsaw, Poland PL-02 551
Phone: 48-22-480-773
Fax: 48-3912-2416

Via Principessa Clotilde 7
Rome, Italy 00196
Phone: 39-06 32476 320
Fax: 39-06 3219949

Management and Staff

Bob Kramer, Partner
Cor Van 't Spijker, Partner
Francesco Panfilo, Partner
Herve Claquin, Chief Executive Officer
Ian Taylor, Chief Executive Officer
Jan Stolker, Partner
Marc Staal, Chief Executive Officer
Roger Marshall, Managing Director

Whom to Contact

Carolyn Maddox
Tim Lawrence

Type of Firm

Investment/Merchant Bank Investing Own or Client Funds

Industry Association Membership
Belgium Venture Capital Association
British Venture Capital Association
Dutch Venture Capital Associaton
European Venture Capital Association (EVCA)
German Venture Capital Association
Hungarian Venture Capital Association
Italian Venture Capital Association

Project Preferences

Role in Financing:
Prefer role as deal originator

Type of Financing Preferred:
Balanced
Early Stage
Expansion
Leveraged Buyout
Management Buyouts
Mezzanine
Recapitalizations

Size of Investments Considered
Min Size of Investment Considered (000s): $300
Max Size of Investment Considered (000s): $100,000

Geographical Preferences

United States
All U.S.

International
Asia
Central Europe
Eastern Europe
Europe
France
Hungary
All International

Industry Preferences

(% based on actual investment)

Industrial/Energy	32.9%
Other Products	22.1%
Consumer Related	13.5%
Communications and Media	13.0%
Internet Specific	8.3%
Computer Software and Services	3.4%
Semiconductors/Other Elect.	2.7%
Computer Hardware	2.4%
Biotechnology	0.9%
Medical/Health	0.8%

Additional Information
Name of Most Recent Fund: ABN AMRO Causeway Mezzanine Partnership
Most Recent Fund Was Raised: 04/01/1998
Year Founded: 1980
Capital Under Management: $400,000,000
Current Activity Level : Actively seeking new investments
Method of Compensation: Return on investment is of primary concern, do not charge fees

ACCELERATOR MEDIA (UK), LTD

30 St. James' Square
London, United Kingdom SW1Y 4JH
Phone: 44 20 7968 4288
Fax: 44 20 7968 4298
Website: www.acceleratormedia.com

Management and Staff
Philip McDanell, Chief Executive Officer

Type of Firm
Affiliate/Subsidary of Oth. Financial. Instit.

Project Preferences

Type of Financing Preferred:
Early Stage

Geographical Preferences

International
Europe
United Kingdom

Industry Preferences

Communications and Media
Communications and Media

Internet Specific
Internet

Computer Other
Computer Related

Semiconductors/Other Elect.
Electronics

Business Serv.
Media

Additional Information
Name of Most Recent Fund: Accelerator Media (AKA Gold-Zack AG)
Most Recent Fund Was Raised: 08/29/2000
Year Founded: 2000
Capital Under Management: $52,400,000
Current Activity Level : Actively seeking new investments

ACCENTURE TECHNOLOGY VENTURES (FKA: AC VENTURES)

Kaistrasse 20
Dusseldorf, Germany 40221
Phone: 49 211 9120 30
Fax: 49 211 9120 333

See California for full listing.

ACCESS CAPITAL PARTNERS

19 avenue de Messine
Paris, France F - 75008
Phone: 33 156.43.61.00
Fax: 33 156.43.61.01
Website: www.access-capital-partners.com

Other Offices

PO Box 431 13-15 Victoria Road
St Peter Port Guernsey
Channel Islands, United Kingdom GY1 3ZD
Phone: 44 1481 728 782

Management and Staff
Agnes Nahum, Partner
Dominique Peninon, Partner
Marie Annick Tomlinson, Chief Financial Officer
Philippe Poggioli, Partner

Type of Firm
Private Firm Investing Own Capital

Industry Association Membership
European Venture Capital Association (EVCA)

Project Preferences

Type of Financing Preferred:
Early Stage
Expansion
Fund of Funds
Later Stage
Leveraged Buyout

Size of Investments Considered
Min Size of Investment Considered (000s): $4,700
Max Size of Investment Considered: No Limit

Geographical Preferences

International
Europe
Western Europe

Industry Preferences

(% based on actual investment)

Other Products	100.0%

Additional Information

Year Founded: 1999
Capital Under Management: $434,400,000
Current Activity Level : Actively seeking new investments

ACCESS2NET

28 Boulevard Haussmann
Paris, France 75009
Phone: 33 144 7135 59
Fax: 33 153 2417 23
Website: www.access2net.com

Management and Staff

Pierre-Yves Dargaud, Chairman & CEO

Type of Firm

Non-Financial Corp. Affiliate or Subsidiary

Project Preferences

Type of Financing Preferred:
Early Stage

Geographical Preferences

International
Europe

Industry Preferences

Internet Specific
Internet

Additional Information

Year Founded: 2000
Capital Under Management: $9,700,000
Current Activity Level : Actively seeking new investments

ACE MANAGEMENT

48 Rue de Lisbonne
Paris, France F-75008
Phone: 33 1 58 562 562
Fax: 33 1 58 562 563
Website: www.acemanagement.fr

Other Offices

Financiere de Brienne
2 place Rio de Janeiro
Paris Cedex 08, France F-75362
Phone: 33 144.95.29.60
Fax: 33 144.95.29.69

Type of Firm

Private Firm Investing Own Capital

Project Preferences

Type of Financing Preferred:
Expansion
Startup

Geographical Preferences

International
Europe
France

Industry Preferences

Internet Specific
Internet

Semiconductors/Other Elect.
Electronics

Additional Information

Year Founded: 1993
Capital Under Management: $105,700,000
Current Activity Level : Actively seeking new investments

ACF EQUITY ATLANTIC, INC

Purdy's Wharf Tower II
Suite 2106
Halifax, Canada B3J 3R7
Phone: 902-421-1965
Fax: 902-421-1808

Management and Staff

David Wilson
Jeff Norman

Whom to Contact

David Wilson
Jeff Norman

Type of Firm

Private Firm Investing Own Capital

Project Preferences

Role in Financing:
Prefer role as deal originator but will also invest in deals created by others

Type of Financing Preferred:
Balanced
First Stage Financing
Leveraged Buyout
Mezzanine
Second Stage Financing
Seed
Start-up Financing

Geographical Preferences

Canada
All Canada

Industry Preferences

Communications and Media
Commercial Communications
Telecommunications
Data Communications
Satellite Microwave Comm.

Computer Hardware
Computer Graphics and Dig
Integrated Turnkey System
Disk Relat. Memory Device

Computer Software
Computer Services
Systems Software
Applications Software
Artificial Intelligence

Internet Specific
Internet

Semiconductors/Other Elect.
Electronic Components
Component Testing Equipmt
Laser Related
Fiber Optics
Analytic/Scientific

Biotechnology
Industrial Biotechnology
Biotech Related Research

Medical/Health
Medical Diagnostics
Diagnostic Services
Diagnostic Test Products
Medical Therapeutics
Drug/Equipmt Delivery
Other Therapeutic
Disposable Med. Products
Pharmaceuticals

Consumer Related
Retail
Consumer Products
Consumer Services
Education Related

Industrial/Energy
Industrial Products

Agr/Forestr/Fish
Agriculture related

Additional Information
Year Founded: 1997
Capital Under Management: $22,000,000
Current Activity Level : Actively seeking new investments
Method of Compensation: Return on investment is of primary concern, do not charge fees

ACR VENTURE MANAGEMENT AB (AKA: ACR CAPITAL AB)

Biblioteksgatan 6
Stockholm, Sweden 111 46
Phone: 46-8-456-8880
Fax: 46-8-456-8898
Website: www.slottsbacken.com

Other Offices

Mannerheimintie 12 B, 5th floor
Helsinki, Finland FIN-00100
Phone: 358-9-260-0066
Fax: 358-9-2516-6100

Niels Juels gade 5
Copenhagen, Denmark 1059
Phone: 45-33-38-2040
Fax: 45-33-38-2010

Management and Staff
Claes Ander, Partner
Erkki Hietalahti, Partner
Hakan Claesson, Partner
Leif Rylander, Partner
Ulf Svensson, Managing Director

Type of Firm
Investment Management/Finance Consulting

Project Preferences

Type of Financing Preferred:
Balanced

Geographical Preferences

International
Europe
Scandanavia/Nordic Region

Additional Information
Name of Most Recent Fund: Slottsbacken Fund I
Most Recent Fund Was Raised: 11/12/1996
Year Founded: 1996
Capital Under Management: $108,500,000
Current Activity Level : Actively seeking new investments

ACT VENTURE CAPITAL LTD.

Windsor Business Centre
58 Howard Street
Belfast, Ireland, Republic of BT1 6PJ
Phone: 44 28 9024 7266
Fax: 44 28 9024 7372
Website: www.actvc.ie

Management and Staff
Aiden Byrnes, Partner
Niall V.G. Carol, Managing Director
Owen Murphy, Partner
Walter Hobbs, Partner

Whom to Contact
Niall V.G. Carroll

Type of Firm
Private Firm Investing Own Capital

Industry Association Membership
European Venture Capital Association (EVCA)

Project Preferences

Role in Financing:
Prefer role as deal originator but will also invest in deals created by others

Type of Financing Preferred:
Early Stage
Expansion
Leveraged Buyout
Recapitalizations
Second Stage Financing

Size of Investments Considered
Min Size of Investment Considered (000s): $500
Max Size of Investment Considered (000s): $500,000

Geographical Preferences

International
Ireland
United Kingdom

Industry Preferences
(% based on actual investment)

Computer Software and Services	34.4%
Consumer Related	16.5%
Semiconductors/Other Elect.	16.0%
Internet Specific	14.9%
Communications and Media	9.6%
Other Products	6.3%
Computer Hardware	1.7%
Industrial/Energy	0.5%

Additional Information
Name of Most Recent Fund: ACT 1999 Polnate Equity Limited Partnership
Most Recent Fund Was Raised: 01/01/1999
Year Founded: 1994
Capital Under Management: $200,000,000
Current Activity Level : Actively seeking new investments

ADAMS STREET PARTNERS, LLC (FKA: BRINSON PRIVATE EQUITY)

Triton Court
14 Finsbury Square
London, United Kingdom EC2A 1PD
Phone: 020-7567-5388

See Illinois for full listing.

ADCAPITAL AG (FKA BERLINER ELEKTRO HOLDING AG)

Kurfurstendamm 36
Berlin, Germany D-10719
Phone: 49 3088 5751-0
Fax: 49 3088 5751-27
Website: www.adcapital.de

Management and Staff
Christoph Schug, Chief Executive Officer

Type of Firm
Private Firm Investing Own Capital

Project Preferences

Type of Financing Preferred:
Balanced
Early Stage
Management Buyouts
Recapitalizations

Size of Investments Considered
Min Size of Investment Considered (000s): $14,400
Max Size of Investment Considered (000s): $119,800

Geographical Preferences

International
Germany

Industry Preferences

Communications and Media
Communications and Media

Internet Specific
Internet

Semiconductors/Other Elect.
Electronics

Financial Services
Financial Services

Business Serv.
Media

Additional Information
Year Founded: 1979
Current Activity Level : Actively seeking new investments

ADD PARTNERS

118 Picadilly
Mayfair
London, United Kingdom W1V 9FJ
Phone: 44 20 7569 6765
Fax: 44 20 7569 6768
E-mail: catherine-web@addpartners.com
Website: www.addpartners.com

Management and Staff
Jim Martin, Managing Partner
Maisy Ng, Managing Partner
Sebastien de Lafond, Managing Partner

Type of Firm
Private Firm Investing Own Capital

Industry Association Membership
European Venture Capital Association (EVCA)

Project Preferences

Role in Financing:
Prefer role as deal originator but will also invest in deals created by others

Type of Financing Preferred:
Early Stage
Later Stage
Startup

Geographical Preferences

International
Europe

Additional Information
Year Founded: 2000
Capital Under Management: $130,200,000
Current Activity Level : Actively seeking new investments

ADVENT INTERNATIONAL CORP.

123 Buckingham Palace Road
London, United Kingdom SW1W 9SL
Phone: 44 20 7333 0800
Fax: 44 20 7333 0801

See Massachusetts for full listing.

ADVENT MANAGEMENT N.V.

Industriepark Keiberg
Zaventem, Belgium B-1930
Phone: 32 2 720 7007
Fax: 32 2 721 4352

Other Offices

Park Hill
Emiel Mommaertslaan 18B
Diegem, Belgium B 1831
Phone: 32 2 720 7007
Fax: 32 2 721 4352

Type of Firm
Private Firm Investing Own Capital

Industry Association Membership
Belgium Venture Capital Association

Project Preferences

Role in Financing:
Prefer role as deal originator but will also invest in deals created by others

Type of Financing Preferred:
Control-block Purchases
Leveraged Buyout
Special Situation

Size of Investments Considered
Min Size of Investment Considered (000s): $200
Max Size of Investment Considered (000s): $200,000

Geographical Preferences

International
Belgium
Europe

Additional Information
Year Founded: 1983
Capital Under Management: $50,000,000
Current Activity Level : Actively seeking new investments
Method of Compensation: Return on investment is of primary concern, do not charge fees

---

ADVENT VENTURE PARTNERS (FKA ADVENT LIMITED)

25 Buckingham Gate
London, United Kingdom SW1E 6LD
Phone: 44-20-7630-9811
Fax: 44-20-7828-1474
Website: www.adventventures.com

Type of Firm
Private Firm Investing Own Capital

Industry Association Membership
British Venture Capital Association
European Venture Capital Association (EVCA)

Project Preferences

Role in Financing:
Prefer role as deal originator but will also invest in deals created by others

Type of Financing Preferred:
Early Stage
Expansion
Management Buyouts
Startup

Geographical Preferences

United States
All U.S.

International
United Kingdom
Western Europe

Industry Preferences

(% based on actual investment)

Computer Software and Services	21.0%
Internet Specific	19.1%
Biotechnology	18.5%
Medical/Health	12.3%
Other Products	9.0%
Communications and Media	8.9%
Semiconductors/Other Elect.	7.8%
Industrial/Energy	1.8%
Computer Hardware	1.7%

Additional Information

Name of Most Recent Fund: Advent Technology
Most Recent Fund Was Raised: 01/01/1981
Year Founded: 1981
Capital Under Management: $683,500,000
Current Activity Level : Actively seeking new investments

ADVENT-MORRO EQUITY PARTNERS

Banco Popular Building
206 Tetuan Street Suite 903
San Juan, Puerto Rico 902
Phone: 787-725-5285
Fax: 787-721-1735

Management and Staff

Cyril Meduna, President
Ricaardo Fishman, Principal

Whom to Contact

Carmen E. Rocafort
Cyril Meduna
Javier Jaramillo
Ricardo Fishman
Zoilo Mendez

Type of Firm

Private Equity Advisor or Fund of Fund Mgr

Project Preferences

Role in Financing:
Will function either as deal originator or investor in deals created by others

Type of Financing Preferred:
Acquisition
Early Stage
Expansion
First Stage Financing
Generalist PE
Later Stage
Leveraged Buyout
Management Buyouts
Recapitalizations
Second Stage Financing
Turnaround

Size of Investments Considered

Min Size of Investment Considered (000s): $500
Max Size of Investment Considered (000s): $3,000

Geographical Preferences

International
Puerto Rico

Industry Preferences

Communications and Media
Commercial Communications
Telecommunications
Wireless Communications
Data Communications

Computer Hardware
Integrated Turnkey System

Computer Software
Computer Services
Systems Software
Applications Software

Internet Specific
E-Commerce Technology
Internet
Web Aggregration/Portals

Medical/Health
Health Services

Consumer Related
Consumer
Retail
Food/Beverage
Hotels and Resorts
Education Related

Financial Services
Financial Services

Business Serv.
Distribution

Manufact.
Manufacturing

Additional Information

Year Founded: 1989
Capital Under Management: $52,000,000
Current Activity Level : Actively seeking new investments
Method of Compensation: Return on invest. most important, but chg. closing fees, service fees, etc.

ADVEQ MANAGEMENT AG (FKA ADVISERS ON PRIVATE EQUITY AG)

Stampfenbachstrasse 40
Zurich, Switzerland 8035
Phone: 41-1-365 32 00
Fax: 41-1-365 32 10
Website: www.adveq.com

Management and Staff

Andre Jaeggi, Managing Director
Bruno Raschle, Founder
Peter Kessel, Managing Director
Peter Laib, Managing Director

Type of Firm

Private Equity Advisor or Fund of Fund Mgr

Industry Association Membership

European Venture Capital Association (EVCA)

Project Preferences

Type of Financing Preferred:
Early Stage
Expansion
Fund of Funds
Management Buyouts
Startup

Geographical Preferences

United States
All U.S.

International
Europe

Additional Information

Year Founded: 1997
Capital Under Management: $700,000,000
Current Activity Level : Actively seeking new investments

AGF PRIVATE EQUITY

26 rue du 4 Septembre
Paris, France 75002
Phone: 33 1 4312 5547
Fax: 33 1 4312 5545
Website: www.agfprivatequity.com

Management and Staff
Antoine Valdes, Chief Executive Officer
Jean-Francois Paumelle, Managing Director

Type of Firm
Insurance Firm Affiliate or Subsidiary

Industry Association Membership
European Venture Capital Association (EVCA)

Project Preferences

Type of Financing Preferred:
Balanced

Geographical Preferences

International
Europe
France

Additional Information
Year Founded: 1999
Capital Under Management: $151,100,000
Current Activity Level : Actively seeking new investments

AIB WBK FUND MANAGEMENT SP.ZOO

3 Biala Str.
Warsaw, Poland 00-895
Phone: 48226204183
Fax: 48226204184
Website: www.magnapolonia.com.pl

Management and Staff
Jerzy Bujko, President
Marzena Tomecka, Chief Financial Officer
Witold Radwanski, Chief Executive Officer

Type of Firm
Investment/Merchant Bank Subsid/Affil

Industry Association Membership
European Venture Capital Association (EVCA)

Project Preferences

Type of Financing Preferred:
Expansion
Turnaround

Geographical Preferences

International
Poland

Additional Information
Name of Most Recent Fund: National Investment Fund Magna Polonia
Most Recent Fund Was Raised: 01/01/1995
Year Founded: 1995
Capital Under Management: $60,400,000
Current Activity Level : Actively seeking new investments

AIG CAPITAL PARTNERS INC.

Str. Gen. Berthelot 57
Bucharest, Romania 70747
Phone: 40 1311 05 71
Fax: 40 1311 33 52

See New York for full listing.

AIG INVESTMENT CORPORATION (ASIA) LIMITED

31/F NatWest Tower
Times Square
Causeway Bay, Hong Kong
Phone: 852-2143-1300
Fax: 852-2893-9530

Other Offices

Hanil Bldg., Suite 910, 9/F, 64-5
Chungmu-Ro 2-GA, Chung-Ku
Seoul, South Korea
Phone: 822-752-3876
Fax: 822-752-3877

Philamlife Bldg., 4/F UN Avenue,
Manila, Philippines
Phone: 632-521-6300
Fax: 632-522-2868

Type of Firm
Insurance Firm Affiliate or Subsidiary

Industry Association Membership
Hungarian Venture Capital Association

Project Preferences

Type of Financing Preferred:
Expansion

Size of Investments Considered
Min Size of Investment Considered (000s): $5,000
Max Size of Investment Considered: No Limit

Geographical Preferences

International
Asia

Industry Preferences

Communications and Media
Commercial Communications
Telecommunications

Transportation
Transportation

Manufact.
Manufacturing

Additional Information
Name of Most Recent Fund: AIG Asian Infrastructure Fund, L.P.
Most Recent Fund Was Raised: 04/28/1994
Year Founded: 1989
Capital Under Management: $5,000,000,000
Current Activity Level : Actively seeking new investments

ALBEMARLE PRIVATE EQUITY LTD

1 Albemarle Street
London, United Kingdom W1X 3HF
Phone: 44-207-491-9555
Fax: 44-207-491-7245

Management and Staff
Mark Hallala

Whom to Contact
Mark Hallala

Type of Firm
Private Firm Investing Own Capital

Industry Association Membership
British Venture Capital Association

Project Preferences

Role in Financing:
Prefer role as deal originator but will also invest in deals created by others

Type of Financing Preferred:
Leveraged Buyout
Second Stage Financing

Size of Investments Considered
Min Size of Investment Considered (000s): $1,500
Max Size of Investment Considered: No Limit

Geographical Preferences

International
Bermuda
France
Germany
Italy
Spain
United Kingdom

Industry Preferences

Communications and Media
Commercial Communications
Telecommunications
Data Communications

Computer Software
Computer Services
Systems Software
Applications Software

Semiconductors/Other Elect.
Electronic Components
Sensors

Medical/Health
Pharmaceuticals

Consumer Related
Consumer
Education Related

Industrial/Energy
Materials
Factory Automation
Machinery
Environmental Related

Transportation
Transportation

Financial Services
Financial Services

Business Serv.
Distribution

Manufact.
Office Automation Equipmt
Publishing

Additional Information
Name of Most Recent Fund: Third (Brown Shipley) Private Equity Fund
Most Recent Fund Was Raised: 01/01/1996
Year Founded: 1987
Capital Under Management: $158,500,000
Current Activity Level : Actively seeking new investments
Method of Compensation: Return on invest. most important, but chg. closing fees, service fees, etc.

ALCATEL VENTURES

Anam Tower Suite 1309
702-10 Yeoksam-Dong, Kangnam-Ku
Seoul 135-080, South Korea
Phone: 82-2-2009-31713
Fax: 82-2-2009-3174

See California for full listing.

ALCHEMY PARTNERS

20 Bedfordbury
London, United Kingdom WC2N 4BL
Phone: 44 20 7240 9596
Fax: 44 20 7240 9594
Website: www.alchemypartners.com

Other Offices

TOPAS 2
Mergenthaleralle 79-81
Eschborn, Germany 65760
Phone: 49 6196 47 550
Fax: 49 6196 47 5529

Management and Staff
Dominic Slade, Partner
Eric Walters, Partner
Graham Hallworth, Partner
Jon Moulton, Managing Partner
Martin Bolland, Partner
Paul Bridges, Partner
Peter Asbach, Managing Director
Robert Barnes, Partner
Scott Greenhalgh, Partner

Type of Firm
Private Equity Advisor or Fund of Fund Mgr

Industry Association Membership
British Venture Capital Association
European Venture Capital Association (EVCA)

Project Preferences

Role in Financing:
Prefer role as deal originator

Type of Financing Preferred:
Leveraged Buyout
Second Stage Financing
Special Situation
Turnaround

Size of Investments Considered
Min Size of Investment Considered (000s): $8,250
Max Size of Investment Considered (000s): $100,000

Geographical Preferences

International
Austria
Germany
United Kingdom

Industry Preferences

(% based on actual investment)

Consumer Related	39.0%
Other Products	20.9%
Industrial/Energy	15.8%
Communications and Media	14.0%
Computer Software and Services	6.4%
Computer Hardware	3.8%

Additional Information
Year Founded: 1997
Capital Under Management: $873,700,000
Current Activity Level : Actively seeking new investments
Method of Compensation: Return on invest. most important, but chg. closing fees, service fees, etc.

ALICE VENTURES

Piazzale Baracca 1
Milan, Italy 20123
Phone: 39 2499.81.71
Fax: 39 248.51.75.83
Website: www.aliceventures.it

Management and Staff
David Kuller, Partner
Edoardo Lecaldano, Partner
John Gonzalez, Partner
Piergiorgio Calanchi, Partner

Type of Firm
Private Firm Investing Own Capital

Industry Association Membership
European Venture Capital Association (EVCA)

Project Preferences

Type of Financing Preferred:
Early Stage
Seed
Startup

Size of Investments Considered
Min Size of Investment Considered (000s): $900
Max Size of Investment Considered: No Limit

Geographical Preferences

International
Europe
Israel

Industry Preferences

Communications and Media
Communications and Media

Internet Specific
Internet

Business Serv.
Media

Additional Information
Name of Most Recent Fund: MB Venture Capital Fund I
Most Recent Fund Was Raised: 06/18/1999
Capital Under Management: $131,500,000
Current Activity Level : Actively seeking new investments

ALL ASIA PARTNERS

7F-5,No.148
Chung-Hsiao E. Road, Section 4
Taipei, Taiwan
Phone: 8862-2778-7552
Fax: 8862-2778-1314

Management and Staff
Benjamin Feng, President & Chairman

Type of Firm
Private Firm Investing Own Capital

Industry Association Membership
Taiwan Venture Capital Association(TVCA)

Project Preferences

Type of Financing Preferred:
Expansion
Mezzanine
Startup

Geographical Preferences

International
Taiwan

Industry Preferences

Communications and Media
Telecommunications

Computer Software
Software

Semiconductors/Other Elect.
Electronics
Electronic Components
Semiconductor

Industrial/Energy
Factory Automation
Machinery

Additional Information
Year Founded: 1997
Capital Under Management: $32,300,000
Current Activity Level : Actively seeking new investments

ALLEN & BUCKERIDGE PTY LTD

18 Bulletin Place
Sydney, Australia 02000
Phone: 61-2-9252-3600
Fax: 61-2-9251-9808
Website: www.a-b.com.au

Management and Staff
Bob Nagel, Chief Operating Officer

Whom to Contact
Jack Hennessy

Type of Firm
Affiliate/Subsidary of Oth. Financial. Instit.

Industry Association Membership
Australian Venture Capital Association (AVCAL)

Project Preferences

Role in Financing:
Prefer role as deal originator but will also invest in deals created by others

Type of Financing Preferred:
Early Stage

Size of Investments Considered
Min Size of Investment Considered (000s): $1,300
Max Size of Investment Considered (000s): $3,300

Geographical Preferences

International
Australia

Industry Preferences

(% based on actual investment)

Internet Specific	54.6%
Computer Software and Services	29.9%
Computer Hardware	9.1%
Semiconductors/Other Elect.	4.2%
Communications and Media	2.3%

Additional Information
Name of Most Recent Fund: Allen & Buckeridge II
Most Recent Fund Was Raised: 05/01/1998
Year Founded: 1996
Capital Under Management: $101,700,000
Current Activity Level : Actively seeking new investments
Method of Compensation: Return on invest. most important, but chg. closing fees, service fees, etc.

ALLIANCE INVESTMENT CAPITAL

CFI House
Clonskeagh Square
Dublin, Ireland, Republic of 14
Phone: 353 1 283 7656
Fax: 353 1 283 7256
Website: www.allinv.com

Type of Firm
Investment/Merchant Bank Subsid/Affil

Project Preferences

Type of Financing Preferred:
Later Stage

Geographical Preferences

International
Ireland

Industry Preferences

Business Serv.
Services
Distribution

Manufact.
Manufacturing

Additional Information

Capital Under Management: $8,700,000
Current Activity Level : Actively seeking new investments

ALLIANCE VENTURE CAPITAL ADVISORS LIMITED

607, Raheja Chambers
213 Free Press Journal Rd.
Mumbai, India 400021
Phone: 9122-283-4016
Fax: 9122-204-5702

Other Offices

11 Lake Avenue
Calcutta, India 700 026
Phone: 9133-464-8555
Fax: 9133-464-8884

Management and Staff

P.D. Shedde, President

Type of Firm

Private Firm Investing Own Capital

Project Preferences

Type of Financing Preferred:
Expansion
Startup

Geographical Preferences

International
India

Industry Preferences

Computer Software
Software

Medical/Health
Pharmaceuticals

Consumer Related
Food/Beverage

Business Serv.
Services

Manufact.
Manufacturing

Additional Information

Year Founded: 1997
Capital Under Management: $25,000,000
Current Activity Level : Actively seeking new investments

ALPHA GROUP (FKA:ALPHA ASSOCIATES MANAGEMENT, LTD.)

89 rue Taitbout
Paris, France F 75009
Phone: 33-1-5321-8888
Fax: 33-1-4016-4323
Website: www.groupealpha.com

Other Offices

Niedenau 78
Frankfurt, Germany D-60325
Phone: 49-69971-4940
Fax: 49-69971-42422

Management and Staff

Alain Blanc-Brude, Managing General Partner
Florence Fesneau, General Partner
Harald Ronn, General Partner
Herve Hautin, Chief Financial Officer
Nicolas Hulst, General Partner
Thomas Schlytter-Henrichsen, Managing General Partner

Type of Firm

Private Firm Investing Own Capital

Industry Association Membership

European Venture Capital Association (EVCA)

Project Preferences

Role in Financing:
Prefer role as deal originator but will also invest in deals created by others

Type of Financing Preferred:
Balanced
Expansion
Leveraged Buyout

Size of Investments Considered

Min Size of Investment Considered (000s): $5,000
Max Size of Investment Considered: No Limit

Geographical Preferences

International
Belgium
Europe
France
Germany
Luxembourg
Netherlands
Switzerland
United Kingdom

Industry Preferences

(% based on actual investment)

Other Products	66.3%
Internet Specific	9.9%
Consumer Related	7.7%
Biotechnology	6.3%
Communications and Media	5.1%
Computer Software and Services	3.2%
Medical/Health	0.9%
Industrial/Energy	0.6%

Additional Information

Name of Most Recent Fund: Alpha Private Equity Fund III
Most Recent Fund Was Raised: 08/01/1999
Year Founded: 1985
Capital Under Management: $567,400,000
Current Activity Level : Actively seeking new investments
Method of Compensation: Return on investment is of primary concern, do not charge fees

---

ALPHA VENTURES SA

8 Merlin Street
Athens, Greece 106 71
Phone: 30-1-362-7710
Fax: 30-1-361-9532
E-mail: mail@alphavc.gr
Website: www.alpha.gr/eventures.htm

Type of Firm

Private Firm Investing Own Capital

Additional Information

Name of Most Recent Fund: Alpha Ventures
Most Recent Fund Was Raised: 01/01/1991
Capital Under Management: $18,400,000
Current Activity Level : Actively seeking new investments

ALPINVEST HOLDING NV (AKA NIB CAPITAL PRIVATE EQUITY NV)

Gooimeer 3
P.O. Box 5073
Naarden, Netherlands NL-1410 AB
Phone: 31-35-695-2600
Fax: 31-35-694-7525
Website: www.alpinvest.nl

Type of Firm
Private Firm Investing Own Capital

Industry Association Membership
European Venture Capital Association (EVCA)

Project Preferences

Role in Financing:
Prefer role as deal originator but will also invest in deals created by others

Type of Financing Preferred:
Leveraged Buyout
Mezzanine
Second Stage Financing

Size of Investments Considered
Min Size of Investment Considered (000s): $5,000
Max Size of Investment Considered: No Limit

Geographical Preferences

International
Bermuda
France
Germany
Italy
Spain
United Kingdom

Industry Preferences

(% based on actual investment)

Other Products	87.5%
Consumer Related	6.7%
Medical/Health	3.9%
Internet Specific	1.2%
Computer Software and Services	0.7%

Additional Information
Name of Most Recent Fund: Alpinvest Private Equity Fund
Most Recent Fund Was Raised: 01/01/1993
Year Founded: 1991
Capital Under Management: $750,000,000
Current Activity Level : Inactive / Unknown
Method of Compensation: Return on invest. most important, but chg. closing fees, service fees, etc.

ALTA BERKELEY VENTURE PARTNERS

9-10 Savile Row
London, United Kingdom W1X 1AF
Phone: 44-20-7440-0200
Fax: 44-20-7734-6711
Website: www.alta-berkeley.com

Other Offices

Rue de la Pelisserie 16
Geneva , Switzerland CH-1204
Phone: 41-22-311-5533
Fax: 41-22-311-5536

Management and Staff
Bryan Wood, Founder
Hugh Smith, Chief Financial Officer

Whom to Contact
Guus Keder
Tim Brown

Type of Firm
Private Firm Investing Own Capital

Industry Association Membership
British Venture Capital Association
European Venture Capital Association (EVCA)

Project Preferences

Role in Financing:
Prefer role as deal originator but will also invest in deals created by others

Type of Financing Preferred:
Early Stage
Expansion
Seed
Start-up Financing

Size of Investments Considered
Min Size of Investment Considered (000s): $2,000
Max Size of Investment Considered: No Limit

Geographical Preferences

International
Bermuda
France
Germany
Italy
Spain
United Kingdom
Western Europe

Industry Preferences

(% based on actual investment)

Medical/Health	23.8%
Biotechnology	19.6%
Communications and Media	17.8%
Other Products	9.7%
Computer Software and Services	7.7%
Semiconductors/Other Elect.	6.7%
Computer Hardware	5.6%
Internet Specific	4.8%
Industrial/Energy	3.3%
Consumer Related	0.8%

Additional Information
Name of Most Recent Fund: Alta-Berkeley V C.V.
Most Recent Fund Was Raised: 11/01/1996
Year Founded: 1982
Capital Under Management: $170,000,000
Current Activity Level : Actively seeking new investments
Method of Compensation: Return on investment is of primary concern, do not charge fees

ALTAMIRA CAPITAL CORP.

2020 University
Niveau de Maisoneuve, Bur. 201
Montreal, Canada H3A 2A5
Phone: 514-499-1656
Fax: 514-499-9570

Other Offices

250 Bloor Street East
Suite 301
, Canada
Phone: 416-925-4274

475 Dumont Avenue
, Canada
Phone: 514-631-2682

Type of Firm
Affiliate/Subsidary of Oth. Financial. Instit.

Industry Association Membership
Canadian Venture Capital Association

Project Preferences

Role in Financing:
Prefer role as deal originator

Type of Financing Preferred:
First Stage Financing

Size of Investments Considered
Min Size of Investment Considered (000s): $1,000
Max Size of Investment Considered: No Limit

Geographical Preferences

International
No Preference

Additional Information

Year Founded: 1992
Capital Under Management: $114,000,000
Current Activity Level : Inactive / Unknown
Method of Compensation: Return on investment is of primary concern, do not charge fees

AMADEUS CAPITAL PARTNERS

5 Shaftesbury Road
Cambridge, United Kingdom CB2 2BW
Phone: 44 1223 707 000
Fax: 44 1223 707 070
Website: www.amadeus1.com

Other Offices

19 Hanover Square
London, United Kingdom W1S 1HY
Phone: 44 20 7298 6800
Fax: 44 20 7495 6536

Management and Staff

Andrea Traversone, Partner
Anne Glover, Managing Partner
Badri Nathan, Partner
Herman Hauser, Partner
Hitesh Mehta, Partner
Peter Wynn, Partner
Richard Anton, Partner

Whom to Contact

Sam Joffe
Vicky Beaulah

Type of Firm

Private Firm Investing Own Capital

Industry Association Membership

British Venture Capital Association
European Venture Capital Association (EVCA)

Project Preferences

Role in Financing:
Prefer role as deal originator but will also invest in deals created by others

Type of Financing Preferred:
First Stage Financing
Research and Development
Second Stage Financing
Seed
Start-up Financing

Size of Investments Considered
Min Size of Investment Considered (000s): $700
Max Size of Investment Considered: No Limit

Geographical Preferences

International
United Kingdom

Industry Preferences

(% based on actual investment)

Internet Specific	35.6%
Communications and Media	23.6%
Semiconductors/Other Elect.	15.1%
Computer Software and Services	14.4%
Biotechnology	10.1%
Industrial/Energy	1.2%

Additional Information

Name of Most Recent Fund: Amadeus I, L.P.
Most Recent Fund Was Raised: 12/01/1998
Year Founded: 1997
Capital Under Management: $217,400,000
Current Activity Level : Actively seeking new investments
Method of Compensation: Return on investment is of primary concern, do not charge fees

AMERINDO INVESTMENT ADVISORS, INC.

43 Upper Grove Street
London, United Kingdom WIX 9PG
Phone: 44-171-629-2349
Fax: 44-171-493-5158

See New York for full listing.

AMP ASSET MANAGEMENT LIMITED - DEVELOPMENT CAPITAL

Level 20, 33 Alfred Street
Sydney, Australia 02000
Phone: 612-9257-9344
Fax: 612-9257-7989

Other Offices

Level 5 City Tower
95 Customhouse Quay
Wellington, New Zealand
Phone: 644-494-2200
Fax: 644-494-2100

Management and Staff

Murray Gribben, Managing Director

Type of Firm

Insurance Firm Affiliate or Subsidiary

Industry Association Membership

Australian Venture Capital Association (AVCAL)

Project Preferences

Role in Financing:
Prefer role as deal originator

Type of Financing Preferred:
Expansion
Management Buyouts

Size of Investments Considered
Min Size of Investment Considered (000s): $5,000
Max Size of Investment Considered (000s): $50,000

Geographical Preferences

International
Australia

Industry Preferences

(% based on actual investment)

Other Products	65.2%
Internet Specific	26.9%
Industrial/Energy	4.4%
Computer Software and Services	1.8%
Communications and Media	1.6%

Additional Information
Year Founded: 1993
Capital Under Management: $269,800,000
Current Activity Level : Actively seeking new investments
Method of Compensation: Return on invest. most important, but chg. closing fees, service fees, etc.

AMWIN MANAGEMENT PTY LTD

Level 2, The Terrace
155 George Street
Sydney, Australia 02000
Phone: 61-2-9251-9655
Fax: 61-2-9251-7655
Website: www.amil.com.au

Management and Staff
Paul Riley, Chief Executive Officer

Type of Firm
Investment/Merchant Bank Investing Own or Client Funds

Industry Association Membership
Australian Venture Capital Association (AVCAL)

Project Preferences

Type of Financing Preferred:
Early Stage
Seed

Geographical Preferences

International
Oceania/Australasia

Industry Preferences

(% based on actual investment)

Internet Specific	73.1%
Biotechnology	15.0%
Computer Hardware	6.3%
Industrial/Energy	5.6%

Additional Information
Year Founded: 1998
Capital Under Management: $26,800,000
Current Activity Level : Actively seeking new investments

ANGEL-INVEST

31 rue Daru
Paris, France F-75008
Phone: 33-144-298-888
Fax: 33-144-298-880
Website: www.angel-invest.com

Type of Firm
Incubators

Project Preferences

Type of Financing Preferred:
Early Stage

Size of Investments Considered
Min Size of Investment Considered (000s): $100
Max Size of Investment Considered (000s): $100,000

Geographical Preferences

International
Europe
France

Industry Preferences

Internet Specific
Internet

Additional Information
Year Founded: 2000
Capital Under Management: $9,900,000
Current Activity Level : Actively seeking new investments

ANTFACTORY

Prospect House
80-100 New Oxford Street
London, United Kingdom WC1A 1HB
Phone: 44-207-947-5000
Fax: 44-207-947-5001
Website: www.antfactory.com

Management and Staff
Angelos Papadimitriou, Chief Operating Officer
Charles Murphy, Chief Financial Officer
David Turnbull, Chief Operating Officer
Harpal Randhawa, Chairman & CEO

Type of Firm
Private Firm Investing Own Capital

Project Preferences

Type of Financing Preferred:
Joint Ventures
Startup

Geographical Preferences

International
All International

Industry Preferences

Computer Software
Software

Internet Specific
Internet

Consumer Related
Retail

Business Serv.
Media

Additional Information
Year Founded: 1999
Capital Under Management: $550,000,000
Current Activity Level : Actively seeking new investments

APAX GLOBIS PARTNERS & CO. (APAX JAPAN)

Sumitomofudosan Building 4F
11-7 Nibancho, Chiyoda-ku
Tokyo, Japan 102-0084
Phone: 813-5275-3939
Fax: 813-5275-3825
Website: www.globis.co.jp

Type of Firm
Private Equity Advisor or Fund of Fund Mgr

Project Preferences

Type of Financing Preferred:
Balanced

Geographical Preferences

International
Japan

Industry Preferences

Communications and Media
Telecommunications

Computer Software
Software

Semiconductors/Other Elect.
Semiconductor

Additional Information
Year Founded: 1999
Capital Under Management: $180,000,000
Current Activity Level : Actively seeking new investments

APAX PARTNERS & CIE (AKA: APAX FRANCE)

45 Avenue Kleber
Paris, Cedex 16, France 75784
Phone: 33-1-53-650-141
Fax: 33-1-53-650-106
Website: www.apax.com

Type of Firm
Private Firm Investing Own Capital

Industry Association Membership
European Venture Capital Association (EVCA)

Project Preferences

Type of Financing Preferred:
Early Stage
Expansion
Leveraged Buyout
Other
Start-up Financing
Turnaround

Size of Investments Considered
Min Size of Investment Considered (000s): $3,000
Max Size of Investment Considered (000s): $201,400

Geographical Preferences

United States
All U.S.

International
France
Germany
Ireland
Israel
Japan
Spain
Switzerland
United Kingdom

Industry Preferences

(% based on actual investment)

Computer Software and Services	31.2%
Other Products	18.2%
Internet Specific	15.5%
Industrial/Energy	13.5%
Consumer Related	8.5%
Biotechnology	6.6%
Communications and Media	4.0%
Medical/Health	1.7%
Computer Hardware	0.8%

Additional Information
Name of Most Recent Fund: APAX Capital Risque
Most Recent Fund Was Raised: 01/01/1983
Year Founded: 1987
Capital Under Management: $1,160,300,000
Current Activity Level : Actively seeking new investments

APAX PARTNERS & CO. VENTURES LTD (AKA: APAX UK)

15 Portland Place
London, United Kingdom W1B 1PT
Phone: 44-207-872-6300
Fax: 44-207-636-6475
Website: www.apax.com

Other Offices

1 City Square
Leeds, United Kingdom LS1 2AL
Phone: 44-113-388-9200
Fax: 44-113-388-9222

10 Fitzwilliam Square
Dublin 2, Ireland, Republic of
Phone: 353-1-661-2671
Fax: 353-1-661-3057

Velazquez 10-5 izq
Madrid, Spain 28001
Phone: 34 91 423 1000
Fax: 34 91 423 1010

Type of Firm
Private Firm Investing Own Capital

Industry Association Membership
British Venture Capital Association
European Venture Capital Association (EVCA)

Project Preferences

Type of Financing Preferred:
Balanced
Early Stage
Expansion
Generalist PE
Leveraged Buyout
Startup
Turnaround

Size of Investments Considered
Min Size of Investment Considered (000s): $4,000
Max Size of Investment Considered (000s): $151,100

Geographical Preferences

International
Europe
United Kingdom

Industry Preferences

(% based on actual investment)

Computer Software and Services	31.6%
Internet Specific	21.8%
Other Products	17.3%
Communications and Media	11.9%
Biotechnology	9.4%
Semiconductors/Other Elect.	4.5%
Consumer Related	1.6%
Medical/Health	0.9%
Computer Hardware	0.5%
Industrial/Energy	0.3%

Additional Information
Name of Most Recent Fund: APAX Venture Capital Fund
Most Recent Fund Was Raised: 09/01/1981
Year Founded: 1997
Capital Under Management: $5,600,000
Current Activity Level : Actively seeking new investments

APAX PARTNERS & CO.BETEILIGUNGSBERAT UNG AG

Possartstrasse 11
Munchen, Germany 81679
Phone: 49-89-998-9090
Fax: 49-89-998-90932
Website: www.apax.de

Other Offices

Bahnhofstrasse 17
Zollikon, Switzerland CH-8702
Phone: 41 1 391 52 68
Fax: 41 1 391 59 35

Management and Staff
Christian Wipf, Partner
Martin Halusa, Partner
Michael Hinderer, Partner
Sabina Van Den Brandt, Partner

Type of Firm
Private Firm Investing Own Capital

Industry Association Membership
Swiss Venture Capital Association

Project Preferences

Type of Financing Preferred:
Early Stage
Expansion
Management Buyouts
Seed
Startup

Geographical Preferences

International
Europe

Industry Preferences

Communications and Media
Communications and Media

Computer Other
Computer Related

Biotechnology
Biotechnology

Medical/Health
Medical/Health

Consumer Related
Consumer

Financial Services
Financial Services

Business Serv.
Media

Additional Information
Name of Most Recent Fund: APA German European Ventures L.P.
Most Recent Fund Was Raised: 03/01/1991
Year Founded: 1990
Capital Under Management: $221,600,000
Current Activity Level : Actively seeking new investments

APC ASSET MANAGEMENT

605B Peregrine Tower
Lippo Center, 89 Queensway
Admiralty, Hong Kong
Phone: 852-2801-5993
Fax: 852-2530-5527

Type of Firm
Non-Financial Corp. Affiliate or Subsidiary

Project Preferences

Type of Financing Preferred:
Expansion
Later Stage

Geographical Preferences

International
Asia

Additional Information
Name of Most Recent Fund: GE Asia Pacific Technology Fund Limited
Most Recent Fund Was Raised: 03/01/2000
Capital Under Management: $140,000,000
Current Activity Level : Actively seeking new investments

APEX VENTURES BV

Velmolenweg 52 - 54
PO Box 461
Uden, Netherlands 5400 AL
Phone: 31 413 24 34 44
Fax: 31 413 25 57 38
E-mail: interactive@apex.nl
Website: www.apex.nl

Management and Staff
Dick van Druten, Managing Partner

Type of Firm
Incubators

Project Preferences

Type of Financing Preferred:
Early Stage
Seed
Startup

Geographical Preferences

International
Western Europe

Industry Preferences

Communications and Media
Communications and Media

Computer Software
Software

Internet Specific
Internet

Computer Other
Computer Related

Additional Information
Capital Under Management: $8,400,000
Current Activity Level : Actively seeking new investments

APIDC-VENTURE CAPITAL LIMITED

1102 Block A, 11/F
Babukhan Estate, Basheerbagh
Hyderabad, India 500 001
Phone: 9140-329-9951
Fax: 9140-329-7449
Website: www.apidcvc.com

Other Offices

26710 Fond Du Lac Road
Rancho Palos Verdes, United States of America 90275
Phone: 310-373-8027
Fax: 310-378-5917

Management and Staff
A. Ramesh, Vice President
Sarath Naru, Managing Director

Whom to Contact
A. Ramesh
Sarath Naru

Type of Firm
Non-Financial Corp. Affiliate or Subsidiary

Project Preferences

Role in Financing:
Prefer role as deal originator but will also invest in deals created by others

Type of Financing Preferred:
Early Stage
Expansion
First Stage Financing
Second Stage Financing
Seed
Start-up Financing
Startup

Geographical Preferences

International
India

Industry Preferences

Communications and Media
Communications and Media
Telecommunications

Computer Other
Computer Related

Semiconductors/Other Elect.
Electronic Components

Biotechnology
Biotechnology

Medical/Health
Medical/Health
Pharmaceuticals

Industrial/Energy
Energy
Industrial Products
Materials

Transportation
Transportation

Additional Information
Name of Most Recent Fund: APIDC-Venture Capital Fund 1990
Most Recent Fund Was Raised: 12/01/1999
Year Founded: 1990
Capital Under Management: $4,400,000
Current Activity Level : Actively seeking new investments
Method of Compensation: Return on invest. most important, but chg. closing fees, service fees, etc.

APOLLO INVEST

231 rue Saint-honore
Paris, France F-75001
Phone: 33 1 4296 4242
Fax: 33 1 4296 4244
Website: www.apolloinvest.com

Management and Staff
Herve Giaoui, Co-Founder
Laurent Asscher, Co-Founder

Type of Firm
Private Firm Investing Own Capital

Project Preferences

Type of Financing Preferred:
Early Stage

Geographical Preferences

International
France
All International

Industry Preferences

Communications and Media
Telecommunications

Internet Specific
Internet

Additional Information
Year Founded: 1999
Capital Under Management: $18,100,000
Current Activity Level : Actively seeking new investments

ARGNOR WIRELESS VENTURES

Smidesvagen 10, 4tr
Solna, Sweden SE-171 41
Phone: 46 8 564 84 735
Fax: 46 8 754 00 02
Website: www.argnor.com

Management and Staff
Anders Bjorkman, President

Type of Firm
Affiliate/Subsidary of Oth. Financial. Instit.

Project Preferences

Type of Financing Preferred:
Early Stage

Size of Investments Considered
Min Size of Investment Considered (000s): $1,000
Max Size of Investment Considered (000s): $5,000

Geographical Preferences

International
Sweden

Industry Preferences

Communications and Media
Telecommunications

Additional Information
Capital Under Management: $50,000,000
Current Activity Level : Actively seeking new investments

ARGO GLOBAL CAPITAL, INC.

1000, de La Gauchetiere West
Suite 2500
Montreal, Canada H3B 4W5
Phone: 514-397-8444
Fax: 514-397-8445

See Massachusetts for full listing.

ARGOS SODITIC SA

118 rue du Rhone
Geneva, Switzerland CH-1204
Phone: 41-22-849-6633
Fax: 41-22-849-6627
Website: www.argos-soditic.com

Other Offices

14, rue Bassano
Paris, France 75116
Phone: 33-1-5367-2050
Fax: 33-1-5367-2055

Espiga Capital Gestion Prim, 19
Madrid, Spain ESP-28004
Phone: 34 91 531 7277
Fax: 34 91 531 2552

Rua Rosa Araujo no2-9.Andar
Lisbon, Portugal 1250
Phone: 351 21/355.29.10
Fax: 351 21/355.29.20

Via Cerva 28
Milan, Italy 20122
Phone: 390 2/774.93.30
Fax: 390 2/78.11.75

Management and Staff
Matteo Carlotti, Partner

Whom to Contact
Guy Simmons

Type of Firm
Private Firm Investing Own Capital

Industry Association Membership
European Venture Capital Association (EVCA)
Swiss Venture Capital Association

Project Preferences

Role in Financing:
Prefer role as deal originator but will also invest in deals created by others

Type of Financing Preferred:
Early Stage
Expansion
Later Stage
Leveraged Buyout
Management Buyouts
Recapitalizations
Second Stage Financing
Special Situation
Turnaround

Geographical Preferences

International
Europe
France
Italy
Portugal
Spain
Switzerland

Industry Preferences

(% based on actual investment)

Consumer Related	46.7%
Communications and Media	24.3%
Other Products	20.4%
Industrial/Energy	8.6%

Additional Information

Name of Most Recent Fund: Euroknights III
Most Recent Fund Was Raised: 03/01/1996
Year Founded: 1989
Capital Under Management: $238,000,000
Current Activity Level : Actively seeking new investments
Method of Compensation: Return on invest. most important, but chg. closing fees, service fees, etc.

ARGOSY PARTNERS, INC.

8/F Pacific Star Building
Makati Avenue, Makati
Manila, Philippines
Phone: 632-811-5551
Fax: 632-886-0145

Management and Staff

Aloysius Colayco, Founder
Eduardo Cuyegkeng, Managing Director
Gloria Tan Climaco, Founder
Rufo Colayco, Founder

Type of Firm

Private Firm Investing Own Capital

Project Preferences

Type of Financing Preferred:
Expansion
Leveraged Buyout
Mezzanine

Size of Investments Considered
Min Size of Investment Considered (000s): $10,000
Max Size of Investment Considered (000s): $100,000

Geographical Preferences

International
Philippines

Additional Information

Year Founded: 1998
Capital Under Management: $175,000,000
Current Activity Level : Actively seeking new investments

ARGUS CAPITAL GROUP

4th Floor, Cutlers Court
115 Houndsditch
London, United Kingdom EC3A 7BR
Phone: 44-20-7398-2001
Fax: 44-20-7398-2003
Website: www.arguscapitalgroup.co.uk

Other Offices

Istenhegyi ut 40-a
Budapest, Hungary 1126
Phone: 361-391-0231
Fax: 361-391-0234

Skretova 12
Prague, Czech Republic 120 00
Phone: 420-22-142-4214
Fax: 420-22-142-4210

ul. Emilii Plater 28
Warsaw, Poland 00-688
Phone: 48-22-630-3031
Fax: 48-22-630-3033

Management and Staff

Ali Artunkal, Managing Director

Type of Firm

Insurance Firm Affiliate or Subsidiary

Industry Association Membership

European Venture Capital Association (EVCA)

Project Preferences

Type of Financing Preferred:
Expansion
Industry Rollups
Joint Ventures
Leveraged Buyout
Management Buyouts
Recapitalizations
Turnaround

Geographical Preferences

International
Bulgaria
Central Europe
Croatia
Czech Republic
Eastern Europe
Estonia
Hungary
Latvia
Lithuania
Poland
Romania
Slovak Repub.
Slovenia
Turkey

Additional Information

Name of Most Recent Fund: Argus Capital Partners
Most Recent Fund Was Raised: 03/01/1999
Year Founded: 1998
Capital Under Management: $172,000,000
Current Activity Level : Actively seeking new investments

ARIA VENTURES LTD.

85 Medinat Hayehudim
P.O. Box 12245
Herzliya, Israel 46733
Phone: 9729-956-7484
Fax: 9729-951-4152
E-mail: amit@ariaventures.com
Website: www.ariaventures.com

Management and Staff

Boaz Dotan, Partner

Type of Firm

Private Firm Investing Own Capital

Project Preferences

Type of Financing Preferred:
Early Stage
Seed

Geographical Preferences

International
Israel

Industry Preferences

Computer Software
Software

Additional Information

Current Activity Level : Actively seeking new investments

ARMADA ASSET MANAGEMENT

Lagiewnicka 54/56
Lodz, Poland 91456
Phone: 48426563242
Fax: 48426563309
Website: www.armada.pl

Management and Staff
Janusz Skrzypkowski, Partner
Marek Bernatek, Partner
Michal Mackiewicz, Partner
Pawel Gierynski, Partner
Piotr Miller, Partner

Type of Firm
Private Firm Investing Own Capital

Industry Association Membership
European Venture Capital Association (EVCA)

Project Preferences

Type of Financing Preferred:
Early Stage
Expansion
Mezzanine
Turnaround

Geographical Preferences

International
Europe
Poland

Industry Preferences

Computer Other
Computer Related

Consumer Related
Consumer
Retail

Business Serv.
Services

Additional Information
Capital Under Management: $9,500,000
Current Activity Level : Actively seeking new investments

ARTS ALLIANCE

60 Sloane Avenue
London, United Kingdom SW3 3DD
Phone: 44-207-594-4062
Website: www.artsalliance.com

Other Offices

565 Fifth Avenue, 22nd Floor
New York, United States of America 10017
Phone: 212-687-4820
Fax: 212-687-9266

Management and Staff
Adam Valkin, Principal
David Eun, Partner
Hillary Hedges, Principal
Laurent Laffy, General Partner
Martine Vice Holter, Chief Operating Officer
Thomas Hoegh, Founder
Victoria Hackett, General Partner

Type of Firm
Private Firm Investing Own Capital

Project Preferences

Type of Financing Preferred:
Early Stage

Geographical Preferences

United States
All U.S.
All U.S.

International
Europe
Western Europe

Industry Preferences

(% based on actual investment)

Internet Specific	70.3%
Consumer Related	10.2%
Communications and Media	7.6%
Computer Software and Services	7.4%
Other Products	4.5%

Additional Information
Name of Most Recent Fund: Digital Ventures II
Most Recent Fund Was Raised: 01/01/1999
Year Founded: 1996
Capital Under Management: $165,000,000
Current Activity Level : Actively seeking new investments

AS VENTURE GMBH

Mangerstrasse 26
Potsdam, Germany D-14467
Phone: 49331 601068000
Fax: 49331 601068003
Website: www.asventure.com

Management and Staff
Jens Mueffelmann, Managing Director

Type of Firm
Non-Financial Corp. Affiliate or Subsidiary

Industry Association Membership
European Venture Capital Association (EVCA)

Project Preferences

Type of Financing Preferred:
Expansion
Startup

Geographical Preferences

International
Europe
Germany
All International

Industry Preferences

Internet Specific
Internet

Business Serv.
Media

Additional Information
Year Founded: 2000
Capital Under Management: $135,100,000
Current Activity Level : Actively seeking new investments

ASC GROUP

24 Raffles Place
#17-04 Clifford Centre
Singapore, Singapore 48621
Phone: 65-535-8066
Fax: 65-535-6629

Other Offices

25/F, Hang Lung Centre
2-20 Patterson St., Causeway Bay
, Hong Kong
Phone: 852-2894-9800
Fax: 852-2577-3509

Management and Staff
Cheong Seng Lee, Managing Director

Type of Firm
Private Firm Investing Own Capital

Project Preferences

Type of Financing Preferred:
Early Stage
Expansion
Mezzanine
Second Stage Financing
Special Situation

Size of Investments Considered
Min Size of Investment Considered (000s): $4,000
Max Size of Investment Considered (000s): $8,000

Geographical Preferences

International
Asia

Industry Preferences

Communications and Media
Commercial Communications
Telecommunications
Data Communications
Satellite Microwave Comm.
Other Communication Prod.

Computer Hardware
Integrated Turnkey System

Computer Software
Systems Software
Applications Software
Artificial Intelligence

Semiconductors/Other Elect.
Electronic Components
Sensors
Component Testing Equipmt
Laser Related
Fiber Optics

Medical/Health
Medical Diagnostics
Diagnostic Test Products
Medical Therapeutics
Medical Products
Hospitals/Clinics/Primary

Consumer Related
Entertainment and Leisure
Retail
Franchises(NEC)
Food/Beverage
Education Related

Industrial/Energy
Alternative Energy
Factory Automation
Robotics
Environmental Related

Transportation
Transportation

Financial Services
Financial Services

Additional Information

Name of Most Recent Fund: ASC Asian Equity, Ltd.
Most Recent Fund Was Raised: 06/01/1995
Year Founded: 1989
Capital Under Management: $150,000,000
Current Activity Level : Actively seeking new investments
Method of Compensation: Return on investment is of primary concern, do not charge fees

ASCEND TECHNOLOGY VENTURES

14A Achimeir Street
Ramat Gan, Israel
Phone: 972-3-751-3707
Fax: 972-3-751-3706
Website: www.ascendvc.com

Management and Staff

Avner Shelem, Principal
Liora Lev, Principal
Moshe Bar-Niv, Principal

Type of Firm

Private Firm Investing Own Capital

Project Preferences

Type of Financing Preferred:
Early Stage
Seed
Startup

Geographical Preferences

International
Israel

Industry Preferences

Communications and Media
Communications and Media

Medical/Health
Medical/Health

Additional Information

Year Founded: 1999
Capital Under Management: $100,000,000
Current Activity Level : Actively seeking new investments

ASIAN DIRECT CAPITAL MANAGEMENT

48/F Bank of China Tower
1 Garden Road
Central, Hong Kong
Phone: 852-2103-0276
Fax: 852-2103-0279

Type of Firm

Investment/Merchant Bank Subsid/Affil

Industry Association Membership

Hungarian Venture Capital Association

Project Preferences

Type of Financing Preferred:
Balanced
Early Stage
Expansion
Management Buyouts
Recapitalizations
Seed
Startup
Turnaround

Geographical Preferences

International
China
Hong Kong
India
Korea, South
Malaysia
Philippines
Singapore
Thailand

Industry Preferences

Consumer Related
Consumer

Business Serv.
Distribution

Manufact.
Manufacturing

Additional Information

Name of Most Recent Fund: Arirang Fund
Most Recent Fund Was Raised: 11/01/1998
Year Founded: 1996
Capital Under Management: $300,000,000
Current Activity Level : Actively seeking new investments

ASIAN INFRASTRUCTURE FUND ADVISERS LIMITED

Suite 2302-03
Nine Queen's Road
Central, Hong Kong
Phone: 852-2912-7888
Fax: 852-2845-0786

Management and Staff
Bruce Allen, Managing Director
Ted Rule, Managing Director

Type of Firm
Private Equity Advisor or Fund of Fund Mgr

Project Preferences

Type of Financing Preferred:
Early Stage

Size of Investments Considered
Min Size of Investment Considered (000s): $3,000
Max Size of Investment Considered (000s): $75,000

Geographical Preferences

International
Asia
China
Hong Kong
India
Indonesia
Philippines

Industry Preferences

Communications and Media
Telecommunications

Industrial/Energy
Energy

Transportation
Transportation

Additional Information
Year Founded: 1994
Capital Under Management: $780,000,000
Current Activity Level : Actively seeking new investments
Method of Compensation: Professional fee required whether or not deal closes

ASIATECH INTERNET GROUP (ATIG) (FKA: ASIATECH VENTURES)

2308 Alexandra House
18 Chater Road
Central, Hong Kong
Phone: 852-2116-6868
Fax: 852-2116-0000
Website: www.asiatechv.com

Other Offices

1250 Bayhill Drive
Suite 201
San Bruno, United States of America 94066

12F, No. 285, Sec. 3,
Nan-King East Road,
Taipei, Taiwan
Phone: 8862-8712-1010
Fax: 8862-8712-2020

535 Cowper Street
2nd Floor
Palo Alto, United States of America 94301
Phone: 1650-321-0688
Fax: 1650-321-6188

70 Club Street
Singapore, Singapore 069443
Phone: 65-327-1800
Fax: 65-327-1877

C311, Beijing Lufthansa Center
50 Liangmaqiao Road Chaoyang District
Beijing, China 100016
Phone: 8610-6465-1303
Fax: 8610-6465-1802

Management and Staff
Anthony Fan, Managing Director
Peter Chu, Managing Director

Type of Firm
Private Firm Investing Own Capital

Project Preferences

Type of Financing Preferred:
Early Stage
Seed

Geographical Preferences

United States
All U.S.

International
Asia
China
Hong Kong
Taiwan

Industry Preferences

(% based on actual investment)

Internet Specific	65.1%
Computer Software and Services	11.4%
Computer Hardware	9.2%
Communications and Media	6.9%
Consumer Related	5.0%
Other Products	2.3%

Additional Information
Name of Most Recent Fund: Applied Research Fund
Most Recent Fund Was Raised: 11/04/1998
Year Founded: 1997
Capital Under Management: $96,800,000
Current Activity Level : Actively seeking new investments

ASPIRO VENTURES

Grabrodersgatan 2
P.O Box 118
Malmo, Sweden SE-20121
Phone: 46-709-91-8001
Website: www.aspiro.com

Management and Staff
Christer Mansson, Chief Executive Officer

Type of Firm
Private Firm Investing Own Capital

Project Preferences

Type of Financing Preferred:
Balanced

Geographical Preferences

International
Europe

Industry Preferences

Internet Specific
Internet

Additional Information
Year Founded: 2000
Current Activity Level : Actively seeking new investments

AT INDIA MANAGEMENT SERVICES PVT. LTD.

5 Crescent Road
Highgrounds
Bangalore, India 560 001
Phone: 9180-228-2092
Fax: 9180-226-6858
E-mail: contact@atindiainc.com
Website: www.atindiainc.com

Management and Staff
N. Narasimhan, Chief Financial Officer
Ramesh Vangal, Founder
Vivek Gour, Chief Operating Officer

Type of Firm
Affiliate/Subsidary of Oth. Financial. Instit.

Project Preferences

Type of Financing Preferred:
Balanced

Geographical Preferences

International
All International

Additional Information
Capital Under Management: $50,000,000
Current Activity Level : Actively seeking new investments

ATILA VENTURE PARTNERS LTD.

Cedar House
41 Cedar Avenue
Hamilton, Bermuda
Phone: 44 1 295 2244
Fax: 44 1 292 8666

Other Offices

Landsberger Str. 155
Munchen, Germany 80687
Phone: 49.172-671 0955
Fax: 49.6173-929984

Type of Firm
Private Firm Investing Own Capital

Industry Association Membership
European Venture Capital Association (EVCA)

Project Preferences

Type of Financing Preferred:
Early Stage
Expansion
Later Stage
Mezzanine
Special Situation

Geographical Preferences

International
Austria
Germany
Italy
Switzerland

Additional Information
Capital Under Management: $151,300,000
Current Activity Level : Actively seeking new investments

ATLAS VENTURE

Widenmayerstrasse 16
Munich, Germany D-80538
Phone: 4989-4587-450
Fax: 4989-4587-4545

See Massachusetts for full listing.

ATLE FORETAGSKAPITAL AB (FKA FORETAGSKAPITAL AB)

Norra Kungstornet
Kungsgatan 30, 15 tr POB 1301
Stockholm, Sweden S-111 83
Phone: 46-8-441-9140
Fax: 46-8-219310
Website: www.fkapital.se

Management and Staff
Gunnar Huss, Managing Director
Hans Dirtoft, Managing Director
Lars Gardo, Managing Director

Type of Firm
Private Firm Investing Own Capital

Project Preferences

Role in Financing:
Prefer role as deal originator but will also invest in deals created by others

Type of Financing Preferred:
Leveraged Buyout
Second Stage Financing
Special Situation

Geographical Preferences

International
Europe

Additional Information
Year Founded: 1973
Capital Under Management: $55,000,000
Current Activity Level : Actively seeking new investments
Method of Compensation: Return on investment is of primary concern, do not charge fees

ATLE VENTURES (FKA TEKNOLOGIPARKERNAS UTVECKLING AB)

Norra Kungsgatan
Kungsgatan 30, 15 tr POB 1301
Stockholm, Sweden 111 83
Phone: 46 08 5451 2100
Fax: 46 08 21 9310
Website: www.fkapital.se/tuab

Management and Staff
Christer Nilsson, Chief Executive Officer

Type of Firm
Affiliate/Subsidary of Oth. Financial. Instit.

Project Preferences

Type of Financing Preferred:
Early Stage
Startup

Geographical Preferences

International
Europe

Additional Information
Year Founded: 2000
Current Activity Level : Actively seeking new investments

AUGUSTA VENTURE GMBH

Wilhelm-Leuschner-Strasse 9-11
Frankfut am Main, Germany D-60329
Phone: 49 69 2426 69-0
Fax: 49 69 2426 6940
Website: www.augusta-venture.de

Management and Staff
Axel Haas, Chief Executive Officer
Dominik Kramer, Managing Director

Type of Firm
Non-Financial Corp. Affiliate or Subsidiary

Project Preferences

Type of Financing Preferred:
Startup

Geographical Preferences

United States
All U.S.

International
Europe

Industry Preferences

Communications and Media
Communications and Media

Computer Software
Software

Semiconductors/Other Elect.
Sensors

Additional Information
Year Founded: 2000
Current Activity Level : Actively seeking new investments

AURIC ASSET MANAGEMENT PTE. LTD.

9 Temasek Boulevard #38-002
Suntec Tower Two
Singapore, Singapore 038989
Phone: 65-333-4138
Fax: 65-333-4398
Website: www.aurictech.com.sg

Management and Staff
Boh-Soon Lim, Chief Executive Officer

Type of Firm
Non-Financial Corp. Affiliate or Subsidiary

Project Preferences

Type of Financing Preferred:
Expansion
Mezzanine
Seed
Startup

Geographical Preferences

International
Asia

Industry Preferences

Internet Specific
Internet

Semiconductors/Other Elect.
Semiconductor

Biotechnology
Biotechnology

Additional Information
Capital Under Management: $58,000,000
Current Activity Level : Actively seeking new investments

AUSTRALIAN TECHNOLOGY GROUP LTD

Level 7, Bligh House
4-6 Bligh Street
Sydney, Australia 02107
Phone: 612-9223-1014
Fax: 612-9223-1015
Website: www.ozemail.com.au/~atgaus

Management and Staff
Ken Roberts, Managing Director

Type of Firm
Govt Program NEC

Industry Association Membership
Australian Venture Capital Association (AVCAL)

Project Preferences

Role in Financing:
Prefer role as deal originator but will also invest in deals created by others

Type of Financing Preferred:
First Stage Financing
Second Stage Financing
Seed

Size of Investments Considered
Min Size of Investment Considered (000s): $650
Max Size of Investment Considered (000s): $1,950

Geographical Preferences

International
Asia
Oceania/Australasia

Industry Preferences

(% based on actual investment)

Computer Software and Services	54.2%
Internet Specific	22.1%
Biotechnology	16.6%
Industrial/Energy	7.0%

Additional Information
Year Founded: 1994
Capital Under Management: $19,700,000
Current Activity Level : Actively seeking new investments
Method of Compensation: Return on investment is of primary concern, do not charge fees

AUTHOSIS

T02 2300 Century Square, Jalan Usahawan
63000 Cyberjaya, Multimedia Supercorrido
Kuala Lumpur, Malaysia
Phone: 603-8313-3000
Fax: 603-8313-3100

See California for full listing.

AVENTIC PARTNERS AG

Geisshubelstrasse 4
Postfach
Zurich, Switzerland 8027
Phone: 41 1 285 1585
Fax: 41 1 285 1586
Website: www.aventic.ch

Management and Staff
Alan Frei, Partner
Christof Wolfer, Partner
Jean-Claude Rebetez, Chief Financial Officer

Type of Firm
Investment/Merchant Bank Subsid/Affil

Industry Association Membership
Swiss Venture Capital Association

Project Preferences

Type of Financing Preferred:
Acquisition
Early Stage
Expansion
Mezzanine
Turnaround

Geographical Preferences

International
Austria
France
Germany
Italy
Switzerland

Additional Information
Year Founded: 2000
Capital Under Management: $157,000,000
Current Activity Level : Actively seeking new investments

AXA INVESTMENT MANAGERS

7 Newgate Street
London, United Kingdom ECIA7NY

See New York for full listing.

AXA INVESTMENT MANAGERS PRIVATE EQUITY EUROPE

20 Place Vendome
Paris, France 75001
Phone: 33 1 5537 4385
Fax: 33 1 5537 4761
Website: www.axa-im.fr

Management and Staff
Dominique Senequier, Chief Executive Officer
Vincent Gombault, Partner

Type of Firm
Affiliate/Subsidary of Oth. Financial. Instit.

Industry Association Membership
European Venture Capital Association (EVCA)

Project Preferences

Type of Financing Preferred:
Expansion
Leveraged Buyout
Recapitalizations
Start-up Financing
Turnaround

Geographical Preferences

International
Europe

Additional Information
Year Founded: 1999
Capital Under Management: $913,200,000
Current Activity Level : Actively seeking new investments

AXIOMLAB PLC

40 Princess Street
Manchester, United Kingdom M1 6DE
Phone: 44 870 909 6333
Fax: 44 870 909 733
Website: www.axiomlab.com

Other Offices

One St Colme Street
Edinburgh, United Kingdom EH3 6AA
Phone: 44 131 220 8293
Fax: 44 131 220 8393

Wellington Building
28-32 Wellington Road
London, United Kingdom NW8 9SP
Phone: 44 870 909 6333
Fax: 44 870 909 7333

Management and Staff
Andrew Mayhew, Partner
Gavin Maitland, Partner
Nick Perrett, Partner
Steve Durnan, Partner

Type of Firm
Incubators

Project Preferences

Type of Financing Preferred:
Early Stage

Geographical Preferences

International
United Kingdom

Industry Preferences

Communications and Media
Communications and Media

Internet Specific
Internet

Additional Information
Year Founded: 2000
Capital Under Management: $25,500,000
Current Activity Level : Actively seeking new investments

AYALA INTERNET VENTURE PARTNERS

412 Makati Stock Exchange Bldg
Ayala Avenue
Makati, Philippines 1254
Phone: 632-752-5943
Fax: 632-752-5944
Website: www.aivp.com.ph

Management and Staff
Jack Madrid, President
Maite Cunanan, Chief Financial Officer

Type of Firm
Affiliate/Subsidary of Oth. Financial. Instit.

Project Preferences

Role in Financing:
Will function either as deal originator or investor in deals created by others

Type of Financing Preferred:
Early Stage
First Stage Financing
Later Stage
Second Stage Financing

Geographical Preferences

United States
All U.S.

International
Asia

Industry Preferences

Communications and Media
Telecommunications

Computer Software
Applications Software

Additional Information
Year Founded: 2000
Capital Under Management: $10,000,000
Current Activity Level : Actively seeking new investments
Method of Compensation: Return on investment is of primary concern, do not charge fees

B-BUSINESS PARTNERS

Strawinskylaan 1159
D-Tower
Amsterdam, Netherlands 1077
Phone: 31 20 577 6640
Fax: 31 20 577 6609
Website: www.b-bp.com

Other Offices

10 Hill Street
London, United Kingdom W1J 5NQ
Phone: 44 20 7514 1220
Fax: 44 20 7514 1229

Arsenalsgatan 8c
Stockholm, Sweden SE-103 32
Phone: 46 8 614 2000
Fax: 46 8 614 2824

Sporerstrasse 2
Munich, Germany D-80331
Phone: 49 8925 54 990
Fax: 49 8925 54 9999

Management and Staff

Anders Gruden, Managing Director
Andreas Beaucamp, Managing Director
Hans-Dieter Koch, Chief Executive Officer
Simon Edwards, Chief Financial Officer
Stephen Campe, Chief Operating Officer

Type of Firm

Non-Financial Corp. Affiliate or Subsidiary

Project Preferences

Type of Financing Preferred:

Early Stage
Startup

Geographical Preferences

International

Europe

Industry Preferences

Computer Software

Software

Internet Specific

Internet

Computer Other

Computer Related

Additional Information

Capital Under Management: $900,000,000
Current Activity Level : Actively seeking new investments

BAILEY & CO. INC.

594 Spadina Avenue
Toronto, Canada M5S 2H4
Phone: 416-921-6930
Fax: 416-925-4670

Type of Firm

Mgt. Consulting Firm

Project Preferences

Role in Financing:

Prefer role as deal originator but will also invest in deals created by others

Type of Financing Preferred:

First Stage Financing
Mezzanine
Research and Development
Special Situation

Size of Investments Considered

Min Size of Investment Considered (000s): $500
Max Size of Investment Considered (000s): $1,000

Geographical Preferences

International

No Preference

Industry Preferences

Communications and Media

Telecommunications

Semiconductors/Other Elect.

Laser Related
Fiber Optics

Biotechnology

Biotech Related Research

Medical/Health

Drug/Equipmt Delivery
Pharmaceuticals

Industrial/Energy

Materials

Additional Information

Year Founded: 1987
Current Activity Level : Actively seeking new investments
Method of Compensation: Function primarily in service area, receive contingent fee in cash or equity

BAINLAB

40 Strand
London, United Kingdom WC2N 5HZ
Phone: 44 207 484 9477
Fax: 44 207 484 9498
Website: www.bainlab.com

Other Offices

Karlsplatz 1
Muncih, Germany 80335
Phone: 49 89 51 23 0
Fax: 49 89 51 23 1113

Via Crocefisso n. 10
Milan, Italy 20122
Phone: 39 2 582881
Fax: 39 2 583 14070

Management and Staff

Nick Greenspan, Co-Founder
Stan Miranda, Co-Founder

Type of Firm

Incubators

Project Preferences

Type of Financing Preferred:

Early Stage
Seed
Startup

Geographical Preferences

United States

All U.S.

International

Germany
Hong Kong
United Kingdom

Industry Preferences

Internet Specific

Internet

Additional Information

Year Founded: 1999
Capital Under Management: $40,000,000
Current Activity Level : Actively seeking new investments

BALTCAP MANAGEMENT, LTD

Aleksanterinkatu 48B
7th Floor
Helsinki, Finland 00100
Phone: 358 9 6226 900
Fax: 358 9 6226 9040
Website: www.baltcap.com

Other Offices

Gostauto 40
Vilnius, Lithuania 2009
Phone: 370 236 2783
Fax: 370 236 2784

Parnu mnt 10
Tallinn, Estonia 10148
Phone: 372 6 405 710
Fax: 372 6 405 730

Management and Staff

Jarmo Rautiainen, Managing Partner
Kristjan Kalda, Partner
Ruth Laatre, Partner
Sari Grenman, Partner

Type of Firm

Private Firm Investing Own Capital

Project Preferences

Type of Financing Preferred:

Early Stage
Expansion
Later Stage

Size of Investments Considered

Min Size of Investment Considered (000s): $500
Max Size of Investment Considered (000s): $500,000

Geographical Preferences

International

Eastern Europe
Estonia
Latvia
Lithuania

Additional Information

Name of Most Recent Fund: Baltic Investment Fund, L.P.
Most Recent Fund Was Raised: 01/01/1995
Capital Under Management: $65,000,000
Current Activity Level : Actively seeking new investments

BAMBOO INVESTMENTS PLC (FKA RAILIKE LIMITED)

7 Old Park Lane
London, United Kingdom W1Y 3LJ
Phone: 44 20 7514 8917
Fax: 44 20 7409 0302
Website: www.bamboo-investments.com

Type of Firm

Non-Financial Corp. Affiliate or Subsidiary

Project Preferences

Type of Financing Preferred:

Early Stage
Seed

Geographical Preferences

International

United Kingdom

Additional Information

Year Founded: 1962
Capital Under Management: $24,000,000
Current Activity Level : Actively seeking new investments

BANCAMERICA EQUITY PARTNERS (ASIA)

17/F Dixon House
979 Kings Road
Central, Hong Kong
Phone: 852-2597-3308
Fax: 852-2597-3311

Other Offices

22/F Express Towers
Mumbai, India
Phone: 9122-287-6343
Fax: 9122-287-6350

Suite 07-01A
78 Shenton Way, Singapore
Phone: 65-320-2902
Fax: 65-320-2920

Management and Staff

Dharma Bajpai, Managing Director
Kayu Mehta, Managing Director

Type of Firm

Private Firm Investing Own Capital

Project Preferences

Role in Financing:

Prefer role in deals created by others

Size of Investments Considered

Min Size of Investment Considered (000s): $10,000
Max Size of Investment Considered (000s): $25,000

Additional Information

Year Founded: 1995
Capital Under Management: $20,000,000
Current Activity Level : Actively seeking new investments

BANCBOSTON CAPITAL/BANCBOSTON VENTURES

Rua Pedroso, Alluarengalzzl-7 Fl
0453, 012
San Paolo, SP, Brazil
Phone: 55-11-3061-0611
Fax: 55-11-3064-5545

See Massachusetts for full listing.

BANEXI CORP.

12, rue Chauchat
Paris, France 75009
Phone: 33-1-4014-6413
Fax: 33-1-4014-9119

Other Offices

12, rue Chauchat
Paris, France 75009
Phone: 33-1-4014-6413
Fax: 33-1-4014-9119

Type of Firm

Investment/Merchant Bank Investing Own or Client Funds

Project Preferences

Role in Financing:

Prefer role as deal originator but will also invest in deals created by others

Type of Financing Preferred:

First Stage Financing
Leveraged Buyout
Mezzanine
Second Stage Financing
Start-up Financing

Size of Investments Considered
Min Size of Investment Considered (000s): $1,500
Max Size of Investment Considered: No Limit

Geographical Preferences
United States
All U.S.

Canada
All Canada

International
Bermuda
France
Germany
Italy
Spain
United Kingdom

Industry Preferences
(% based on actual investment)

Semiconductors/Other Elect.	33.0%
Biotechnology	31.7%
Internet Specific	11.2%
Computer Software and Services	11.0%
Other Products	7.3%
Computer Hardware	3.2%
Consumer Related	1.4%
Industrial/Energy	1.2%

Additional Information
Name of Most Recent Fund: BNP Central European Partnership Fund
Most Recent Fund Was Raised: 07/01/1998
Year Founded: 1969
Capital Under Management: $900,000,000
Current Activity Level : Actively seeking new investments
Method of Compensation: Return on investment is of primary concern, do not charge fees

BANKINVEST GROUP AS

Toldbodgade 33
Kobenhavn, Denmark 1023
Phone: 45-773-090-00
Fax: 45-773-091-00
Website: www.bankinvest.dk

Other Offices

New York, United States of America

Type of Firm
Investment/Merchant Bank Investing Own or Client Funds

Project Preferences
Type of Financing Preferred:
Early Stage
Expansion

Geographical Preferences
International
Denmark
Europe
Sweden

Industry Preferences
Computer Software
Software

Internet Specific
Internet

Biotechnology
Biotechnology

Medical/Health
Health Services
Pharmaceuticals

Additional Information
Capital Under Management: $429,400,000
Current Activity Level : Actively seeking new investments

BANQUE BRUXELLES LAMBERT (ING GROUP)

24 Avenue Marnix
Brussels, Belgium 1000
Phone: 32 2 547 3589
Fax: 32 2 547 8482
Website: www.bbl.be

Type of Firm
Investment/Merchant Bank Investing Own or Client Funds

Industry Association Membership
Belgium Venture Capital Association

Project Preferences
Type of Financing Preferred:
Expansion

Geographical Preferences
International
No Preference

Additional Information
Capital Under Management: $60,000,000
Current Activity Level : Actively seeking new investments

BANQUE DE VIZILLE

Espace Cordeliers
2 rue President Carnot
Lyon, France 69002
Phone: 33-4-7256-9100
Fax: 33-4-7277-58-55
Website: www.banquedevizille.fr

Management and Staff
Dominique Minvielle
Michel Cotte

Whom to Contact
Dominique Minvielle
Michel Cotte

Type of Firm
Investment/Merchant Bank Investing Own or Client Funds

Project Preferences
Role in Financing:
Prefer role as deal originator but will also invest in deals created by others

Type of Financing Preferred:
Leveraged Buyout
Second Stage Financing

Geographical Preferences
International
France

Industry Preferences
Biotechnology
Industrial Biotechnology

Medical/Health
Diagnostic Services

Consumer Related
Food/Beverage
Consumer Products
Consumer Services

Industrial/Energy
Industrial Products
Materials
Factory Automation
Machinery

Transportation
Transportation

Financial Services
Financial Services

Additional Information
Year Founded: 1988
Capital Under Management: $170,000,000
Current Activity Level : Actively seeking new investments
Method of Compensation: Return on invest. most important, but chg. closing fees, service fees, etc.

BARCLAYS VENTURES

Ground Floor Charles House
5-11 Regent Street
London, United Kingdom SW1Y 4LR
Phone: 44 20 7445 5900
Fax: 44 20 7445 5909
Website: www.barclaysventures.com

Other Offices

4th Floor Bank House
8 Cherry Street
Birmingham, United Kingdom B2 5AL
Phone: 44 121-633 4469
Fax: 44 121-631 1071

50 Fountain Street
Manchester, United Kingdom M2 2AS
Phone: 44 161-252 2400
Fax: 44161-833 9374

PO Box 1 Barclays House
6 East Parade
Leeds, United Kingdom LS1 1HA
Phone: 44 113-296 3340
Fax: 44 113-296 3341

Type of Firm
Investment/Merchant Bank Subsid/Affil

Industry Association Membership
British Venture Capital Association

Project Preferences

Type of Financing Preferred:
Expansion
Management Buyouts
Recapitalizations

Geographical Preferences

International
United Kingdom

Industry Preferences

(% based on actual investment)

Internet Specific	36.8%
Consumer Related	28.1%
Computer Software and Services	19.5%
Computer Hardware	9.6%
Industrial/Energy	6.0%

Additional Information
Year Founded: 2000
Capital Under Management: $65,300,000
Current Activity Level : Actively seeking new investments

BARING COMMUNICATIONS EQUITY

33 Cavendish Square
London, United Kingdom W1M OBQ
Phone: 44-207-290-5000
Fax: 44-207-290-5025
Website: www.bpep.com

Other Offices

Chocimska 28
Room 531
Warsaw, Poland 00-791
Phone: 48 22 627 4156
Fax: 48 22 849 2784

Parizska 11
Prague 1, Czech Republic
Phone: 42 02 2481 7694
Fax: 42 02 2481 4292

Management and Staff
Brian Wardrop, Principal
David French, Partner
David Huckfield, Partner
Heather Potters, Managing Partner
Markus Pedriks, Managing Director
Richard Onians, Managing Partner
Terrence Tehranian, Partner
Tim Green, Partner
Victor Serrato, Managing Director

Type of Firm
Private Equity Advisor or Fund of Fund Mgr

Project Preferences

Role in Financing:
Prefer role as deal originator but will also invest in deals created by others

Type of Financing Preferred:
Early Stage
Startup

Geographical Preferences

International
Central Europe
Eastern Europe

Industry Preferences

Communications and Media
Telecommunications

Business Serv.
Media

Additional Information
Name of Most Recent Fund: Baring Communications Equity Emerging Europe
Most Recent Fund Was Raised: 09/30/1997
Year Founded: 1992
Capital Under Management: $750,000,000
Current Activity Level : Actively seeking new investments
Method of Compensation: Return on investment is of primary concern, do not charge fees

BARING PRIVATE EQUITY PARTNERS (FKA:BARING VENTURE PARTNERS)

33 Cavendish Square
London, United Kingdom W1M 0BQ
Phone: 44-20-7290-5000
Fax: 44-20-7290-5020
Website: www.bpep.com

Other Offices

#34-03 Singapore Land Tower
50 Raffles Place
Singapore, Singapore 048623
Phone: 65-533-2002
Fax: 65-532-2002

10 Uspenski Pereulok, 5th Floor
Moscow, Russian Federation 103006
Phone: 007-501-967-1307
Fax: 007-501-967-1308

23 rue Vernet
Paris, France F - 75008
Phone: 33 147.20.44.40
Fax: 33 147.20.44.42

39/F One International Finance
1 Harbour View Street
Central, Hong Kong
Phone: 852-2846-3080
Fax: 852-2501-0609

6-A Bolshaya Zhitomirskaya Str
Kiev, Ukraine 254025

Darro 22, portal A, bajo izqda
Madrid, Spain E-28002
Phone: 34-91-563-7149
Fax: 34-91-563-7089

Flat No. 502, Mercantile House
15 Kasturba Gandhi Marg
New Delhi, India 110001
Phone: 9111-373-9663
Fax: 9111-335-0863

Friedrichstrasse 59
Frankfurt am Main, Germany 60323
Phone: 49 6971 4070
Fax: 49 6917 3980

P.O. Box 12491
St. Louis, United States of America 63132
Phone: 314-993-0007
Fax: 314-993-0464

Management and Staff

Christopher Brotchie, Partner
Dick Kwan, Managing Director
Gordon Shaw, Partner
Jean Eric Salata, Managing Partner
Jean-Charles Guillou, Partner
N Subramanian, Partner
Peter Chan, Partner
Pierre-Michel Piccino, Partner
Rahul Bhasin, Partner
T.S. Yong, Partner

Type of Firm

Investment/Merchant Bank Subsid/Affil

Industry Association Membership

Hong Kong Venture Capital Association (HKVCA)

Project Preferences

Role in Financing:

Will function either as deal originator or investor in deals created by others

Type of Financing Preferred:

Expansion
First Stage Financing
Mezzanine
Second Stage Financing
Seed
Start-up Financing
Turnaround

Size of Investments Considered

Min Size of Investment Considered (000s): $100
Max Size of Investment Considered: No Limit

Geographical Preferences

International

Brazil
China
Hong Kong
Hungary
India
Mexico
Poland
Russia
Ukraine

Industry Preferences

(% based on actual investment)

Biotechnology	55.5%
Internet Specific	19.3%
Other Products	9.9%
Semiconductors/Other Elect.	5.6%
Computer Software and Services	3.2%
Communications and Media	3.1%
Industrial/Energy	2.0%
Computer Hardware	1.4%

Additional Information

Name of Most Recent Fund: Baring Hambrecht Alpine Ltd
Most Recent Fund Was Raised: 01/01/1986
Year Founded: 1984
Capital Under Management: $300,000,000
Current Activity Level : Actively seeking new investments
Method of Compensation: Return on investment is of primary concern, do not charge fees

BATAVIA INVESTMENT MANAGEMENT LTD

12/F, Plaza Bapindo
Jl. Jendral Sudirman Kav.54-55
Jakarta, Indonesia 12190
Phone: 6221-524-6006
Fax: 6221-526-7516
E-mail: batavia@bataviafund.com
Website: www.bataviafund.com

Management and Staff

Patrick Alexander, Managing Director

Type of Firm

Private Firm Investing Own Capital

Project Preferences

Role in Financing:

Prefer role as deal originator but will also invest in deals created by others

Type of Financing Preferred:

Mezzanine
Second Stage Financing
Special Situation

Geographical Preferences

International

Asia

Industry Preferences

Communications and Media

CATV & Pay TV Systems
Radio & TV Broadcasting
Telecommunications
Satellite Microwave Comm.

Computer Software

Computer Services

Internet Specific

Internet

Medical/Health

Medical Products
Hospitals/Clinics/Primary
Hospital/Other Instit.
Pharmaceuticals

Consumer Related

Entertainment and Leisure
Retail
Franchises(NEC)
Food/Beverage
Consumer Products
Consumer Services
Other Restaurants
Hotels and Resorts

Industrial/Energy

Oil & Gas Drilling,Explor
Coal Related
Industrial Products
Materials
Machinery
Environmental Related

Transportation

Transportation

Financial Services

Financial Services

Agr/Forestr/Fish

Agriculture related
Mining and Minerals

Additional Information

Capital Under Management: $224,500,000
Current Activity Level : Actively seeking new investments
Method of Compensation: Return on investment is of primary concern, do not charge fees

BAYBG BAYERISCHE BETEILIGUNGSGESELLSC HAFT MBH

Bruderstrasse 7
Munich, Germany D-80538
Phone: 49 89 2198-02
Fax: 49 89 2198-2555
Website: www.baybg.de

Type of Firm
Bank Group

Industry Association Membership
German Venture Capital Association

Project Preferences

Role in Financing:
Prefer role as deal originator

Type of Financing Preferred:
Expansion
Management Buyouts
Mezzanine
Recapitalizations
Startup
Turnaround

Geographical Preferences

International
Germany

Industry Preferences

Consumer Related
Entertainment and Leisure

Manufact.
Manufacturing

Additional Information
Year Founded: 1994
Capital Under Management: $230,000,000
Current Activity Level : Actively seeking new investments

BAYERN KAPITAL RISIKOKAPITALBETEILIGU NGS GMBH

Altstadt 72
Landshut, Germany D-84028
Phone: 49 871 92325-0
Fax: 49 871 92325-55
Website: www.bayernkapital.de

Management and Staff
Alexander Garnreiter, Partner
Brigitte Linseis, Partner
Georg Reid, Partner
Heinz Michael Meier, Managing Director
Joseph Martin Schuster, Managing Director
Klaus Loschner, Partner
Markus Baumgartner, Partner
Markus Mrachacz, Partner
Monika Steger, Partner
Stefan Gotz, Partner

Type of Firm
Affiliate/Subsidary of Oth. Financial. Instit.

Industry Association Membership
German Venture Capital Association

Project Preferences

Type of Financing Preferred:
Early Stage
Seed
Startup

Size of Investments Considered
Min Size of Investment Considered (000s): $1,000
Max Size of Investment Considered: No Limit

Geographical Preferences

International
Germany

Industry Preferences

Communications and Media
Communications and Media

Semiconductors/Other Elect.
Electronics

Biotechnology
Biotechnology

Industrial/Energy
Environmental Related

Other
Environment Responsible

Additional Information
Year Founded: 1995
Capital Under Management: $95,000,000
Current Activity Level : Actively seeking new investments

BBS FINANCE

33 rue de Niromesnil
Paris, France F-75008
Phone: 33 1 4312 9999
Fax: 33 1 4312 9990

Management and Staff
B. Nallol, Partner

Type of Firm
Private Firm Investing Own Capital

Project Preferences

Type of Financing Preferred:
Early Stage
Expansion
Leveraged Buyout

Geographical Preferences

International
Europe

Industry Preferences

Communications and Media
Telecommunications

Transportation
Transportation

Business Serv.
Services

Additional Information
Year Founded: 1998
Capital Under Management: $60,000,000
Current Activity Level : Actively seeking new investments

BC PARTNERS

105 Piccadilly
London, United Kingdom W1J 7NJ
Phone: 44-20-7408-1282
Fax: 44-20-7493-1368
Website: www.bcpartners.com

Other Offices

148, boulevard Haussmann
Paris, France 75008
Phone: 33-1-4359-0366
Fax: 33-1-4359-5059

Heimhuderstrasse 72
D-2000 Hamburg, Germany 13
Phone: 49-40-449690
Fax: 49-40-458364

Via Brera 3
20121 Milan, Italy
Phone: 39-2-7200-3101
Fax: 39-2-876929

Management and Staff
Ian Riley, Partner
Kevin O'Donohue, Partner
Otto Van der Wyck, Partner
Simon Palley, Partner

Type of Firm
Private Firm Investing Own Capital

Industry Association Membership
British Venture Capital Association

Project Preferences

Role in Financing:
Prefer role as deal originator but will also invest in deals created by others

Type of Financing Preferred:
Leveraged Buyout

Size of Investments Considered
Min Size of Investment Considered (000s): $150,000
Max Size of Investment Considered: No Limit

Geographical Preferences

International
France
Germany
Italy
United Kingdom

Industry Preferences

(% based on actual investment)

Other Products	57.3%
Consumer Related	24.0%
Industrial/Energy	11.3%
Communications and Media	7.4%

Additional Information
Name of Most Recent Fund: BC European Capital VI
Most Recent Fund Was Raised: 09/01/1997
Year Founded: 1986
Capital Under Management: $4,631,000,000
Current Activity Level : Actively seeking new investments
Method of Compensation: Return on invest. most important, but chg. closing fees, service fees, etc.

BCE CAPITAL

200 Bay Street
Suite 3120, South Tower
Toronto, Canada M5J 2J2
Phone: 416-815-0078
Fax: 416-941-1073
Website: www.bcecapital.com

Other Offices

Suite 412
1545 Carling Avenue
Ottawa, Canada K1Z 8P9
Phone: 613-725-1939
Fax: 613-725-9040

Management and Staff
David McCarthy, Managing Director
Paul Cataford, Managing Director

Type of Firm
Investment Management/Finance Consulting

Industry Association Membership
Canadian Venture Capital Association

Project Preferences

Role in Financing:
Prefer role as deal originator but will also invest in deals created by others

Type of Financing Preferred:
Early Stage
Expansion
Research and Development
Seed
Startup

Size of Investments Considered
Min Size of Investment Considered (000s): $350
Max Size of Investment Considered (000s): $2,000

Geographical Preferences

Canada
Ontario
Western Canada

Industry Preferences

(% based on actual investment)

Communications and Media	52.7%
Internet Specific	20.2%
Semiconductors/Other Elect.	18.3%
Computer Software and Services	8.8%

Additional Information
Year Founded: 1995
Capital Under Management: $135,000,000
Current Activity Level : Actively seeking new investments
Method of Compensation: Return on invest. most important, but chg. closing fees, service fees, etc.

BCR ASSET MANAGEMENT PTY LTD.

Level 13, 499 St. Kilda Road
Melbourne, Australia 3004
Phone: 613-9820-0654
Fax: 613-9820-0656

Other Offices

Level 12, 86 Collins Street
Hobart, Australia 7000
Phone: 613-6231-4114
Fax: 613-6231-4113

Level 5, 12 Pirie Street
Adelaide, Australia 5000
Phone: 618-8212-8197
Fax: 618-8231-1647

Management and Staff
Ronald Bassett, Chairman & CEO

Type of Firm
Private Firm Investing Own Capital

Project Preferences

Role in Financing:
Prefer role as deal originator but will also invest in deals created by others

Type of Financing Preferred:
Acquisition
Balanced
Early Stage
Expansion
First Stage Financing
Later Stage
Leveraged Buyout
Management Buyouts
Mezzanine
Second Stage Financing
Start-up Financing
Startup
Turnaround

Size of Investments Considered
Min Size of Investment Considered (000s): $150
Max Size of Investment Considered (000s): $6,000

Geographical Preferences

International
Australia
Oceania/Australasia

Industry Preferences

Communications and Media
Communications and Media
Radio & TV Broadcasting
Telecommunications

Computer Software
Computer Services
Software

Internet Specific
Internet

Computer Other
Computer Related

Semiconductors/Other Elect.
Electronics
Electronic Components

Biotechnology
Biotechnology

Medical/Health
Medical/Health
Medical Products
Health Services
Pharmaceuticals

Consumer Related
Consumer
Entertainment and Leisure
Retail
Food/Beverage
Consumer Services
Education Related

Industrial/Energy
Industrial Products
Materials

Transportation
Transportation
Aerospace

Financial Services
Financial Services
Insurance
Real Estate

Business Serv.
Services
Distribution
Media

Manufact.
Manufacturing
Publishing

Agr/Forestr/Fish
Agriculture related

Other
Environment Responsible

Additional Information

Year Founded: 1989
Capital Under Management: $88,600,000
Current Activity Level : Actively seeking new investments
Method of Compensation: Return on investment is of primary concern, do not charge fees

---

BENCHMARK CAPITAL

Marble Arch Tower
55 Bryston Street
London, United Kingdom W1H 8AA
Phone: 44 20 7868 8590
Fax: 44 20 7868 4280

See California for full listing.

BERENBERG PRIVATE EQUITY GMBH

Neuer Jungfernstieg 20
Hamburg, Germany 20354
Phone: 49 40 3510 6080
Fax: 49 40 3506 0326
Website: www.berenberg.com

Type of Firm

Investment/Merchant Bank Subsid/Affil

Industry Association Membership

German Venture Capital Association

Project Preferences

Type of Financing Preferred:
Expansion
Generalist PE
Leveraged Buyout

Geographical Preferences

International
Germany

Additional Information

Capital Under Management: $55,200,000
Current Activity Level : Actively seeking new investments

BERLIN CAPITAL FUND (FKA LBB BETEILIGUNGSGESELLSC HAFT GMBH)

Hauptstrasse 65
Berlin, Germany D - 12159
Phone: 49-30-8595-4319
Fax: 49-30-8595-4320
Website: www.berlin-capitalfund.de

Management and Staff

Andreas Noth, Managing Director
Bettina Strube, Vice President
Markus Muller von Blumencron, Managing Director
Martin Dolling, Managing Director
Wolfgang Radszuweit, Managing Director

Type of Firm

Investment/Merchant Bank Subsid/Affil

Industry Association Membership

European Venture Capital Association (EVCA)
German Venture Capital Association

Project Preferences

Type of Financing Preferred:
Early Stage
Expansion
Management Buyouts
Mezzanine
Recapitalizations
Turnaround

Geographical Preferences

International
Europe
Germany
Russia
Switzerland

Industry Preferences

Communications and Media
Communications and Media
Telecommunications

Computer Other
Computer Related

Medical/Health
Medical/Health

Consumer Related
Consumer
Retail

Industrial/Energy
Industrial Products
Materials

Business Serv.
Media

Additional Information
Year Founded: 1983
Capital Under Management: $49,000,000
Current Activity Level : Actively seeking new investments

BETWIN INVESTMENTS, INC.

Box 23110
Sault Ste. Marie, Canada P6A 6W6
Phone: 705-253-0744
Fax: 705-253-0744

Management and Staff
D.B. Stinson

Whom to Contact
D.B. Stinson

Type of Firm
Mgt. Consulting Firm

Industry Association Membership
Canadian Venture Capital Association

Project Preferences

Role in Financing:
Prefer role as deal originator but will also invest in deals created by others

Type of Financing Preferred:
Second Stage Financing

Size of Investments Considered
Min Size of Investment Considered (000s): $500
Max Size of Investment Considered (000s): $1,000

Geographical Preferences

United States
All U.S.

Canada
All Canada

International
United Kingdom

Industry Preferences

Computer Other
Computer Related

Semiconductors/Other Elect.
Electronic Components
Circuit Boards
Fiber Optics

Medical/Health
Hospitals/Clinics/Primary
Pharmaceuticals

Consumer Related
Food/Beverage
Hotels and Resorts
Education Related

Industrial/Energy
Oil and Gas Exploration
Oil & Gas Drilling,Explor
Industrial Products
Machinery
Environmental Related

Financial Services
Real Estate

Additional Information
Year Founded: 1983
Capital Under Management: $2,000,000,000
Current Activity Level : Actively seeking new investments
Method of Compensation: Function primarily in service area, receive contingent fee in cash or equity

---

BIG BANG VENTURES

Antwerpsesteenweg 19
Lochristi, Belgium 9080
Phone: 32 477 20 17 82
Fax: 32 2 70 65 812
Website: www.bbv.be

Management and Staff
Barend Van den Brande, Founder
Frank Maene, Managing Partner

Type of Firm
Incubators

Project Preferences

Type of Financing Preferred:
Early Stage
Seed
Startup

Geographical Preferences

International
Europe

Industry Preferences

Communications and Media
Telecommunications

Internet Specific
Internet

Additional Information
Year Founded: 2000
Capital Under Management: $8,900,000
Current Activity Level : Actively seeking new investments

BLUE RIBBON AG

Endresstrasse 9
Munich, Germany 80807
Phone: 49-89-21589-550
Fax: 49-89-21589-580
Website: www.blueribbon.de

Management and Staff
Anna Otto, Founder
Marco Janezic, Chief Executive Officer
Sven Hauch, Chief Financial Officer

Type of Firm
Incubators

Project Preferences

Type of Financing Preferred:
Early Stage
Seed
Startup

Geographical Preferences

United States
All U.S.

International
Eastern Europe
Germany

Industry Preferences

Communications and Media
Communications and Media

Computer Software
Software

Internet Specific
Internet

Business Serv.
Media

Additional Information
Year Founded: 2000
Capital Under Management: $3,000,000
Current Activity Level : Actively seeking new investments

BLUESHIFT INTERNET VENTURES

Dignity Center, 21
Abdul Razack St., Saidapet
Chennai, India 600015
Phone: 9144-431-3211
Fax: 9144-431-3210
E-mail: info@blueshift.com
Website: www.ventures.blueshift.com

Other Offices

3550, Engineering Drive, Suite 140
Technology Park
Norcross, United States of America 30092
Phone: 1-770-368-1124
Fax: 1-770-368-0998

Management and Staff
S.P. Raghunathan, Founder

Type of Firm
Incubators

Project Preferences

Type of Financing Preferred:
Seed

Geographical Preferences

International
India

Industry Preferences

Computer Software
Software

Internet Specific
Internet

Additional Information
Year Founded: 1999
Current Activity Level : Actively seeking new investments

BMP AKTIENGESELLSCHAFT AG

Charlottenstrasse 16
Berlin, Germany D 10117
Phone: 49-30-2030-50
Fax: 49-30-2030-5555
Website: www.bmp.com

Type of Firm
Private Firm Investing Own Capital

Industry Association Membership
European Venture Capital Association (EVCA)
German Venture Capital Association

Project Preferences

Type of Financing Preferred:
Early Stage
Expansion
Seed
Startup

Size of Investments Considered
Min Size of Investment Considered (000s): $300
Max Size of Investment Considered (000s): $300,000

Geographical Preferences

International
Europe

Industry Preferences

(% based on actual investment)

Internet Specific	35.3%
Medical/Health	28.6%
Computer Software and Services	11.2%
Biotechnology	7.5%
Computer Hardware	7.2%
Communications and Media	5.3%
Other Products	5.0%

Additional Information
Year Founded: 1997
Capital Under Management: $93,800,000
Current Activity Level : Actively seeking new investments

BOSTON VENTURE PARTNERS, LTD.

1-4-12 Hirawaka-Cho
Chiyoda-ku
Tokyo, Japan 102-0093
Phone: 03-5213-6710
Fax: 03-3288-0362
Website: www.ventureboston.com

Type of Firm
Private Firm Investing Own Capital

Project Preferences

Type of Financing Preferred:
Balanced

Geographical Preferences

International
Japan

Additional Information
Year Founded: 1999
Capital Under Management: $6,200,000
Current Activity Level : Actively seeking new investments

BOTTICELLI VENTURE FUNDS (AKA: BOTTICELLI INVESTMENTS)

3 Abba Hillel Street
Harel Building, 11th Floor
Ramat Gan, Israel 52522
Phone: 9723-576-5795
Fax: 9723-575-1948
Website: www.botticelli-vc.com

Management and Staff
Amir Goldstein, Chief Executive Officer

Type of Firm
Non-Financial Corp. Affiliate or Subsidiary

Project Preferences

Type of Financing Preferred:
Startup

Geographical Preferences

International
Israel

Industry Preferences

Internet Specific
Internet

Additional Information

Year Founded: 2000
Capital Under Management: $15,000,000
Current Activity Level : Actively seeking new investments

BOTTS & CO.

Lintas House
15-19 New Fetter Lane
London, United Kingdom EC4A 1BA
Phone: 0-20-7427-6300
Fax: 0-20-7427-6301
Website: www.bottscompany.com

Management and Staff

Andrew Haining, General Partner
Robin Black, General Partner

Type of Firm

Private Firm Investing Own Capital

Industry Association Membership

British Venture Capital Association
European Venture Capital Association (EVCA)

Project Preferences

Role in Financing:

Will function either as deal originator or investor in deals created by others

Type of Financing Preferred:

Acquisition
Expansion
First Stage Financing
Generalist PE
Leveraged Buyout
Mezzanine
Second Stage Financing

Size of Investments Considered

Min Size of Investment Considered (000s): $4,478
Max Size of Investment Considered (000s): $44,781

Geographical Preferences

International

Belgium
Europe
France
Germany
Italy
Luxembourg
Netherlands
Portugal
Spain
United Kingdom

Industry Preferences

(% based on actual investment)

Internet Specific	40.0%
Other Products	33.4%
Communications and Media	23.8%
Consumer Related	2.9%

Additional Information

Name of Most Recent Fund: Botts Capital Partners L.P.
Most Recent Fund Was Raised: 12/10/1998
Year Founded: 1987
Capital Under Management: $373,200,000
Current Activity Level : Actively seeking new investments
Method of Compensation: Return on invest. most important, but chg. closing fees, service fees, etc.

BOWMAN CAPITAL

5, Park Place, Suite 30
London, United Kingdom SW1A 1LP
Phone: 44 207 898 9027
Fax: 44 207 898 9001

See California for full listing.

BRAINHEART CAPITAL AB

Skeppsbron 44
PO Box 1238
Stockholm, Sweden 111 82
Phone: 46 733 77 9900
Fax: 46 733 77 9901
Website: www.brainheart.com

Management and Staff

Magnus Melander, Partner
Sigrun Hjelmquist, Partner
Ulf Jonstromer, Founding Partner

Type of Firm

Private Firm Investing Own Capital

Project Preferences

Type of Financing Preferred:

Early Stage
Expansion
Leveraged Buyout
Seed
Startup

Geographical Preferences

International

Europe
Scandanavia/Nordic Region

Industry Preferences

Communications and Media

Telecommunications

Computer Software

Software

Internet Specific

Internet

Additional Information

Capital Under Management: $223,300,000
Current Activity Level : Actively seeking new investments

BRAIT CAPITAL PARTNERS

9 Fricker Road
Illovo Boulevard Illovo
Sandton, South Africa
Phone: 27 11 507-1000
Fax: 27 11 507-1001
Website: www.brait.com

Other Offices

Suite 1 C NAUTICA
The Water Club Beach Road
Mouille Point, South Africa
Phone: 27 21 425-5262
Fax: 27 21 425-6262

Suite 305 3rd Floor
Caudan Waterfront
Port Louis, Mauritius
Phone: 09230) 210-6909
Fax: (09230) 210-6913

Management and Staff

Anthony Ball, Chief Executive Officer

Type of Firm

Private Firm Investing Own Capital

Project Preferences

Type of Financing Preferred:

Early Stage
Later Stage
Startup

Geographical Preferences

International

Israel
South Africa

Industry Preferences

Communications and Media
Communications and Media

Semiconductors/Other Elect.
Electronics

Medical/Health
Medical/Health

Consumer Related
Retail
Food/Beverage

Transportation
Transportation

Business Serv.
Distribution
Media

Manufact.
Manufacturing
Publishing

Additional Information

Year Founded: 1998
Capital Under Management: $650,000,000
Current Activity Level : Actively seeking new investments

BRIDGEPOINT CAPITAL LTD (FKA: NWEP & NATWEST VENTURES LTD)

101 Finsbury Pavement
London, United Kingdom EC2A 1EJ
Phone: 44-20-7374-3500
Fax: 44-20-7374-3636
Website: www.bridgepoint-capital.com

Other Offices

18 Blythswood Square
Glasgow, United Kingdom G2 4BG
Phone: 44-141-248-8281
Fax: 44-141-248-8425

4 St Davids Street
David Street
Leeds, United Kingdom LS11 5QA
Phone: 44-113-224-3444
Fax: 44-113-242-9848

9 rue de Phalsbourg
Paris Cedex 17, France 75854
Phone: 33-1-4429-2100
Fax: 33-1-4429-2110

Berliner Allee 42
Dusseldorf, Germany 40212
Phone: 49-211-139080
Fax: 49-211-1390855

Clarence House
Clarence Street
Manchester, United Kingdom M2 4DN
Phone: 44-161-838-3700
Fax: 44-161-832-3158

Edificio Torre Europa
Paseo de la Castellana, 95-Planta 19
Madrid, Spain 28046
Phone: 34-91-555-1390
Fax: 34-91-555-1350

Platz der Einheit 1
Frankfurt, Germany 60327
Phone: 49-6997-503145
Fax: 49-6997-503315

Via Brera 3
Milan, Italy 20121
Phone: 39-02-806-951
Fax: 39-02-861-52424

Wellesway House
37 Waterloo Street
Birmingham, United Kingdom B2 5TJ
Phone: 44-121-236-1641
Fax: 44-121-236-2089

Management and Staff

Alan Lewis, Managing Director
Alastair Gibbons, Managing Director
Benoit Bassi, Managing Director
David Shaw, Chairman & CEO
Graham Dewhirst, Managing Director
Guido Belli, Managing Director
Jose Maria Maldonado, Managing Director
Juan Lopez-Quesada, Managing Director
Keith Churchman, Managing Director
Mark Foulds, Partner
Rod Selkirk, Managing Director
Tony Bunker, Managing Director
Wolfgang Lenoir, Managing Director

Type of Firm

Private Firm Investing Own Capital

Industry Association Membership

British Venture Capital Association
European Venture Capital Association (EVCA)
Italian Venture Capital Association

Project Preferences

Type of Financing Preferred:
Balanced
Expansion
Generalist PE
Leveraged Buyout
Recapitalizations
Second Stage Financing
Turnaround

Geographical Preferences

International
All International
United Kingdom
Western Europe

Industry Preferences

(% based on actual investment)

Other Products	41.9%
Industrial/Energy	26.6%
Consumer Related	14.6%
Computer Software and Services	5.6%
Semiconductors/Other Elect.	3.7%
Communications and Media	2.6%
Medical/Health	1.9%
Internet Specific	1.3%
Computer Hardware	1.2%
Biotechnology	0.7%

Additional Information

Name of Most Recent Fund: Gartmore 1990 Limited
Most Recent Fund Was Raised: 01/01/1990
Year Founded: 1994
Capital Under Management: $2,752,500,000
Current Activity Level : Actively seeking new investments

BRIGHTSTAR

BT ACT Centre, Adastral Park
Martlesham Heath
Ipswich, United Kingdom IP5 3RE
Phone: 44 1473 647434
Fax: 44 1473 648707
Website: www.btbrightstar.com

Management and Staff

Harry Berry, Chief Executive Officer

Type of Firm

Incubators

Project Preferences

Type of Financing Preferred:
Startup

Geographical Preferences

International
Europe

Industry Preferences

Communications and Media
Communications and Media
Telecommunications

Internet Specific
Internet

Additional Information

Year Founded: 2000
Current Activity Level : Actively seeking new investments

BRITISH STEEL LTD.

Bridge House
Bridge Street
Sheffield, United Kingdom S3 8NS
Phone: 44 114 273 1612
Fax: 44 114 270 1390

Other Offices

Grovewood Business Centre
Stathclyde Business Park
Bellshill, Lanarkshire, United Kingdom ML4 3NQ
Phone: 44 1698 845 045
Fax: 44 1698 845 123

The Innovation Centre
Vienna Court, Kirkleatham Business Park
Redcar, United Kingdom TS10 5SH
Phone: 44 1642 777 888
Fax: 44 1642 777 999

Titan House, Cardiff Bay Business Centre
Ocean Park, Lewis Road
Cardiff, United Kingdom CF24 5BS
Phone: 44 29 2047 1122
Fax: 44 29 2049 2622

Management and Staff

Stuart Green, Managing Director

Whom to Contact

Keith Williams
Mary Broadhead
Nigel Feirn

Type of Firm

Non-Financial Corp. Affiliate or Subsidiary

Project Preferences

Role in Financing:
Prefer role as deal originator but will also invest in deals created by others

Type of Financing Preferred:
First Stage Financing
Later Stage
Leveraged Buyout
Second Stage Financing
Start-up Financing
Startup

Geographical Preferences

International
United Kingdom

Additional Information

Year Founded: 1975
Capital Under Management: $17,000,000
Current Activity Level : Actively seeking new investments
Method of Compensation: Return on investment is of primary concern, do not charge fees

---

BROADMARK CAPITAL CORP.

20, avenue Kleber
Second Floor
Paris, France 75116
Phone: 33-1-4500-2425
Fax: 33-1-4500-9020

See Washington for full listing.

BULLDOG PARTNERS LIMITED

3rd Floor Albemarle House
1 Albemarle Street
London, United Kingdom W1X 3HF
Phone: 44 20 7529 7800
Fax: 44 20 7529 7801
Website: www.bulldogpartners.co.uk

Management and Staff

Howard Mundy, Partner
Jeremy Brassington, Partner

Type of Firm

Private Firm Investing Own Capital

Industry Association Membership

British Venture Capital Association

Project Preferences

Type of Financing Preferred:
Early Stage
Expansion
Management Buyouts
Mezzanine
Recapitalizations
Startup
Turnaround

Size of Investments Considered

Min Size of Investment Considered (000s): $700
Max Size of Investment Considered: No Limit

Geographical Preferences

International
Austria
Belgium
France
Germany
Greece
Ireland
Italy
Netherlands
Portugal
Spain
Switzerland
United Kingdom

Industry Preferences

Communications and Media
Communications and Media

Computer Other
Computer Related

Semiconductors/Other Elect.
Electronics

Biotechnology
Biotechnology

Medical/Health
Medical/Health

Consumer Related
Consumer

Industrial/Energy
Energy
Industrial Products

Transportation
Transportation

Manufact.
Manufacturing

Additional Information
Capital Under Management: $37,600,000
Current Activity Level : Actively seeking new investments

BURE EQUITY

Box 5419
Gothenburg, Sweden SE 402 29
Phone: 46 31 335 76 35
Fax: 46 31 778 58 38
Website: www.bure.se

Other Offices

Sodra Kungstornet
Kungsgatan 33
Stockholm, Sweden 111 56
Phone: 46 8 791 7700
Fax: 46 8 791 7775

Management and Staff
Hans Ljungkvist, Chief Financial Officer

Type of Firm
Investment Management/Finance Consulting

Project Preferences

Type of Financing Preferred:
Balanced

Geographical Preferences

International
Europe

Industry Preferences

Communications and Media
Telecommunications

Internet Specific
Internet

Medical/Health
Medical/Health

Consumer Related
Entertainment and Leisure

Business Serv.
Media

Additional Information
Year Founded: 1992
Current Activity Level : Actively seeking new investments

BUSINESS LINK DONCASTER

White Rose Way
Doncastle, United Kingdom DN4 5ND
Phone: 44-1302-761000
Fax: 44-1302-739999

Type of Firm
SBIC Not elsewhere classified

Project Preferences

Role in Financing:
Prefer role as deal originator but will also invest in deals created by others

Type of Financing Preferred:
First Stage Financing
Mezzanine
Research and Development
Second Stage Financing
Seed
Start-up Financing

Geographical Preferences

International
United Kingdom

Industry Preferences

Communications and Media
Commercial Communications

Computer Hardware
Computer Graphics and Dig

Computer Software
Computer Services

Semiconductors/Other Elect.
Electronic Components

Biotechnology
Industrial Biotechnology
Biotech Related Research
Biotech Related Research

Medical/Health
Diagnostic Services

Consumer Related
Retail
Other Restaurants
Hotels and Resorts

Industrial/Energy
Industrial Products

Business Serv.
Distribution
Consulting Services

Manufact.
Office Automation Equipmt

Agr/Forestr/Fish
Agriculture related

Additional Information
Name of Most Recent Fund: Doncaster Venture Capital, Plc.
Most Recent Fund Was Raised: 01/01/1989
Year Founded: 1986
Capital Under Management: $4,000,000
Current Activity Level : Actively seeking new investments
Method of Compensation: Return on invest. most important, but chg. closing fees, service fees, etc.

BUTLER CAPITAL PARTNERS FRANCE

30 Cours Albert 1er.
Paris, France F - 75008
Phone: 33 145.61.55.80
Fax: 33 145.61.97.94

Management and Staff
Karine Jacquemart-Pernod, Partner
Laurent Parquet, Partner
Michel Vedrines, Partner
Sophie Teissedre, Chief Financial Officer

Type of Firm
Private Firm Investing Own Capital

Industry Association Membership
European Venture Capital Association (EVCA)
French Venture Capital Association

Project Preferences

Role in Financing:
Prefer role as deal originator

Type of Financing Preferred:
Leveraged Buyout
Second Stage Financing
Special Situation
Start-up Financing

Size of Investments Considered
Min Size of Investment Considered (000s): $40,000
Max Size of Investment Considered: No Limit

Geographical Preferences

International
Belgium
Europe
France
Switzerland

Industry Preferences

Communications and Media
Communications and Media

Computer Other
Computer Related

Consumer Related
Consumer

Financial Services
Financial Services

Business Serv.
Distribution

Manufact.
Publishing

Additional Information

Name of Most Recent Fund: France Private Equity II
Most Recent Fund Was Raised: 04/01/1998
Year Founded: 1990
Capital Under Management: $234,300,000
Current Activity Level : Actively seeking new investments
Method of Compensation: Return on invest. most important, but chg. closing fees, service fees, etc.

BV CAPITAL (FKA BERTELSMANN VENTURES LP)

Grosse Elbstrasse 145d
Hamburg, Germany D-22767
Phone: 49-40-8222-5550
Fax: 49-40-8222-555999

See California for full listing.

CAIRNSFORD ASSOCIATES LTD.

Hillsdown House
32 Hampstead High Street
London, United Kingdom NW3 1JQ
Phone: 44 20-7435 9100
Fax: 44 20-7435 7377
Website: www.globalfinanceonline.com

Management and Staff

Joel Jervis, Partner
Paddy Walker, Partner

Whom to Contact

Vincent R. Smith

Type of Firm

Affiliate/Subsidary of Oth. Financial. Instit.

Industry Association Membership

British Venture Capital Association

Project Preferences

Role in Financing:
Prefer role as deal originator but will also invest in deals created by others

Type of Financing Preferred:
Expansion
Leveraged Buyout
Management Buyouts
Mezzanine
Recapitalizations
Startup
Strategic Alliances
Turnaround

Geographical Preferences

International
United Kingdom

Industry Preferences

Communications and Media
Commercial Communications
Data Communications

Computer Hardware
Computers
Computer Graphics and Dig

Computer Software
Computer Services
Systems Software
Applications Software

Manufact.
Office Automation Equipmt

Additional Information

Year Founded: 1992
Capital Under Management: $32,800,000
Current Activity Level : Actively seeking new investments
Method of Compensation: Return on invest. most important, but chg. closing fees, service fees, etc.

CALTECH CAPITAL PARTNERS LTD.

Level 8, Kensington Swan Bldg.
22 Fanshawe St.
Auckland, New Zealand 1035
Phone: 649-303-3488
Fax: 649-303-1772
Website: www.caltechvc.com

Management and Staff

Wendie Hall, Managing Director

Type of Firm

Private Firm Investing Own Capital

Project Preferences

Role in Financing:
Prefer role as deal originator

Type of Financing Preferred:
Early Stage
Expansion
Start-up Financing

Size of Investments Considered
Min Size of Investment Considered (000s): $264
Max Size of Investment Considered (000s): $528

Geographical Preferences

International
Oceania/Australasia
Pacific Rim

Industry Preferences

Communications and Media
Telecommunications

Computer Software
Software

Internet Specific
Internet

Semiconductors/Other Elect.
Electronics

Biotechnology
Biotechnology

Industrial/Energy
Industrial Products

Additional Information
Year Founded: 1996
Capital Under Management: $1,000,000
Current Activity Level : Actively seeking new investments
Method of Compensation: Return on invest. most important, but chg. closing fees, service fees, etc.

CAMBRIDGE RESEARCH & INNOVATION LTD (AKA CRIL)

13 Station Road
Cambridge, United Kingdom CB1 2JB
Phone: 44-1223-312856
Fax: 44-1223-365704
Website: www.cril.co.uk

Management and Staff
Tony Diment, Chief Executive Officer

Type of Firm
Private Firm Investing Own Capital

Industry Association Membership
British Venture Capital Association

Project Preferences

Role in Financing:
Will function either as deal originator or investor in deals created by others

Type of Financing Preferred:
Seed
Startup

Size of Investments Considered
Min Size of Investment Considered (000s): $75
Max Size of Investment Considered (000s): $746

Geographical Preferences

International
United Kingdom

Industry Preferences

Communications and Media
Communications and Media
Commercial Communications
Telecommunications
Wireless Communications
Data Communications
Other Communication Prod.

Computer Hardware
Mainframes / Scientific
Mini and Personal/Desktop
Computer Graphics and Dig
Disk Relat. Memory Device

Internet Specific
Internet

Computer Other
Computer Related

Semiconductors/Other Elect.
Electronics
Electronic Components
Semiconductor
Micro-Processing
Controllers and Sensors
Sensors
Circuit Boards
Component Testing Equipmt
Laser Related
Fiber Optics
Analytic/Scientific

Biotechnology
Human Biotechnology
Agricultural/Animal Bio.
Industrial Biotechnology
Biosensors
Biotech Related Research
Biotech Related Research

Medical/Health
Medical/Health
Medical Diagnostics
Diagnostic Test Products
Medical Therapeutics
Drug/Equipmt Delivery
Other Therapeutic
Medical Products
Disposable Med. Products
Pharmaceuticals

Consumer Related
Retail

Industrial/Energy
Alternative Energy
Energy Conservation Relat
Industrial Products

Manufact.
Office Automation Equipmt

Additional Information
Name of Most Recent Fund: Cambridge Research and Innovation Fund
Most Recent Fund Was Raised: 01/01/1988
Year Founded: 1987
Capital Under Management: $20,600,000
Current Activity Level : Actively seeking new investments
Method of Compensation: Return on investment is of primary concern, do not charge fees

---

CAMELOT ENTERPRISES PRIVATE LIMITED

1110, Prasad Chanbers
Opera House
Mumbai, India
Phone: 9122-368-0310
Fax: 9122-363-6888

Type of Firm
Private Firm Investing Own Capital

Project Preferences

Type of Financing Preferred:
Balanced

Geographical Preferences

International
India

Additional Information
Current Activity Level : Actively seeking new investments

CANBANK VENTURE CAPITAL FUND LTD

Kareem Towers, II Floor
19/5 & 19/6, Cunningham Road
Bangalore, India 560052
Phone: 9180-226-4390
Fax: 9180-225-1165
Website: www.canbankindia.com

Other Offices

P.O. Box 174, Longbow House
14/20 Chiswell St.
London, United Kingdom EC1Y4TW
Phone: 0171-628-2187
Fax: 0171-374-2468

Management and Staff
M.R. Nagarajan, Managing Director
T. Bhagwandas, Managing Director

Whom to Contact
T. Bhagawandas

Type of Firm
Commercial Bank Affiliate or Subsidiary

Project Preferences

Role in Financing:
Prefer role as deal originator but will also invest in deals created by others

Type of Financing Preferred:
First Stage Financing
Later Stage
Mezzanine
Second Stage Financing
Start-up Financing

Size of Investments Considered
Min Size of Investment Considered (000s): $300
Max Size of Investment Considered (000s): $300,000

Geographical Preferences

International
India

Industry Preferences

Communications and Media
Communications and Media
Satellite Microwave Comm.

Computer Software
Software

Semiconductors/Other Elect.
Electronics
Semiconductor

Biotechnology
Industrial Biotechnology

Medical/Health
Medical Diagnostics
Medical Therapeutics
Pharmaceuticals

Consumer Related
Consumer

Industrial/Energy
Alternative Energy
Materials
Factory Automation
Environmental Related

Business Serv.
Distribution

Manufact.
Manufacturing

Additional Information
Name of Most Recent Fund: CVCF II
Most Recent Fund Was Raised: 05/01/1998
Year Founded: 1995
Capital Under Management: $6,000,000
Current Activity Level : Actively seeking new investments
Method of Compensation: Return on invest. most important, but chg. closing fees, service fees, etc.

CANDOVER INVESTMENTS PLC

20 Old Bailey
London, United Kingdom EC4M 7LN
Phone: 44-207-489-9848
Fax: 44-207-248-5483
Website: www.candover.com

Management and Staff
Stephen Curran, Chief Executive Officer

Type of Firm
Other NEC

Industry Association Membership
British Venture Capital Association

Project Preferences

Role in Financing:
Prefer role as deal originator

Type of Financing Preferred:
Industry Rollups
Leveraged Buyout

Size of Investments Considered
Min Size of Investment Considered (000s): $25,000
Max Size of Investment Considered: No Limit

Geographical Preferences

International
Bermuda
Europe
France
Germany
United Kingdom
No Preference

Industry Preferences

(% based on actual investment)

Other Products	51.2%
Consumer Related	20.4%
Industrial/Energy	20.1%
Biotechnology	4.3%
Communications and Media	3.3%
Computer Software and Services	0.3%
Medical/Health	0.3%
Semiconductors/Other Elect.	0.1%
Computer Hardware	0.1%

Additional Information
Name of Most Recent Fund: The Candover 1997 Fund
Most Recent Fund Was Raised: 12/01/1997
Year Founded: 1980
Capital Under Management: $2,800,000,000
Current Activity Level : Actively seeking new investments
Method of Compensation: Return on invest. most important, but chg. closing fees, service fees, etc.

CAPITAL DEVELOPMENT & INVESTMENT CO. LTD.

7/F 65C Dharamapala Mawatha
Colombo, Sri Lanka 07
Phone: 94-1-327189
Fax: 94-1-423126

Management and Staff
Tennyson Rodrigo, Managing Director

Type of Firm
Private Firm Investing Own Capital

Project Preferences

Role in Financing:
Prefer role as deal originator but will also invest in deals created by others

Type of Financing Preferred:
First Stage Financing
Mezzanine
Second Stage Financing
Start-up Financing

Size of Investments Considered
Min Size of Investment Considered (000s): $300
Max Size of Investment Considered (000s): $500

Geographical Preferences

International
Pacific Rim

Industry Preferences

Communications and Media
Communications and Media
Telecommunications

Computer Software
Computer Services
Systems Software

Internet Specific
Internet

Semiconductors/Other Elect.
Electronic Components

Biotechnology
Biotechnology

Medical/Health
Health Services

Consumer Related
Consumer Services
Education Related

Industrial/Energy
Energy
Industrial Products
Materials
Environmental Related

Business Serv.
Media

Manufact.
Manufacturing

Additional Information
Year Founded: 1983
Capital Under Management: $8,100,000
Current Activity Level : Actively seeking new investments
Method of Compensation: Return on investment is of primary concern, do not charge fees

CAPITAL FOR COMPANIES (CFC)

Quayside House
Canal Wharf
Leeds, United Kingdom LS11 5PU
Phone: 44 113-243-8043
Fax: 44 113-245-1777
Website: www.cfc-vct.co.uk

Other Offices

100 Old Hall Street
Liverpool, United Kingdom L3 9AB
Phone: 44 151 227 2030
Fax: 44 151 227 2444

Type of Firm
Private Firm Investing Own Capital

Industry Association Membership
British Venture Capital Association

Project Preferences

Type of Financing Preferred:
Early Stage
Later Stage
Leveraged Buyout
Turnaround

Geographical Preferences

International
United Kingdom

Additional Information
Year Founded: 1983
Capital Under Management: $59,700,000
Current Activity Level : Actively seeking new investments

CAPITAL PARTNERS LLC

P.O. Box 653088
Benmore, South Africa 2068
Phone: 27-11-784-4152
Fax: 27-11-784-9070

Management and Staff
Peter Manos, Managing Director
T.J. Jubier, Managing Director

Type of Firm
Investment/Merchant Bank Subsid/Affil

Project Preferences

Role in Financing:
Prefer role as deal originator but will also invest in deals created by others

Type of Financing Preferred:
Leveraged Buyout
Mezzanine

Size of Investments Considered
Min Size of Investment Considered (000s): $20,000
Max Size of Investment Considered: No Limit

Geographical Preferences

United States
All U.S.

International
Afghanistan

Industry Preferences

Medical/Health
Medical/Health

Financial Services
Financial Services

Business Serv.
Services

Additional Information
Name of Most Recent Fund: Capital Partners I, L.P.
Most Recent Fund Was Raised: 01/01/1999
Year Founded: 1991
Capital Under Management: $150,000,000
Current Activity Level : Actively seeking new investments
Method of Compensation: Return on invest. most important, but chg. closing fees, service fees, etc.

CAPITAL PRIVE (FKA NATWEST EQUITY PARTNERS, FRANCE)

9, rue de Phalsbourg
Paris, France 75017
Phone: 33 1 5396 7967
Fax: 33 1 4225 0904
Website: www.capitalprive.fr

Management and Staff
Jean-Louis De Bernady, Chief Executive Officer

Type of Firm
Private Firm Investing Own Capital

Industry Association Membership
European Venture Capital Association (EVCA)
French Venture Capital Association

Project Preferences

Role in Financing:
Prefer role as deal originator but will also invest in deals created by others

Type of Financing Preferred:
Acquisition
Expansion
Leveraged Buyout
Management Buyouts
Second Stage Financing
Special Situation

Geographical Preferences

International
Europe
France

Additional Information
Name of Most Recent Fund: Capital Prive
Most Recent Fund Was Raised: 01/01/1990
Year Founded: 1990
Capital Under Management: $10,900,000
Current Activity Level : Actively seeking new investments
Method of Compensation: Return on invest. most important, but chg. closing fees, service fees, etc.

CAPITAL RIESGO INTERNET SCR SA (BSCH)

C/Sevilla 3
3a Planta
Madrid, Spain 28014
Phone: 34-915-582-012
Fax: 34-915-218-477
Website: www.cr-internet.com

Management and Staff
Nicolas Merigo, Managing Director

Type of Firm
Investment/Merchant Bank Subsid/Affil

Project Preferences
Type of Financing Preferred:
Early Stage

Geographical Preferences
International
Europe
Latin America

Industry Preferences
Internet Specific
Internet

Additional Information
Year Founded: 1999
Capital Under Management: $56,200,000
Current Activity Level : Actively seeking new investments

CAPITAL Z ASIA

38/F, Tower One, Lippo Centre
89 Queensway
Central, Hong Kong
Phone: 852-2230-9800
Fax: 852-2230-9898
Website: www.capitalzasia.com

Type of Firm
Private Firm Investing Own Capital

Project Preferences
Type of Financing Preferred:
Expansion
Later Stage

Geographical Preferences
International
Asia
Australia
China
Hong Kong
Indonesia
North Korea
Thailand

Industry Preferences
Communications and Media
Telecommunications

Consumer Related
Consumer Services

Financial Services
Financial Services

Business Serv.
Media

Additional Information
Name of Most Recent Fund: Capital Z Asia Partners I, L.P.
Most Recent Fund Was Raised: 12/01/1998
Year Founded: 1998
Capital Under Management: $235,000,000
Current Activity Level : Actively seeking new investments

CAPMAN MANAGEMENT GMBH

Lenbachplatz 4
Munich, Germany D - 80333
Phone: 49-89-2555-0610
Fax: 49-89-2555-0620
Website: www.capman.de

Management and Staff
Felix Hick, Managing Director
Jorg Muschiol, Partner

Type of Firm
Private Firm Investing Own Capital

Industry Association Membership
European Venture Capital Association (EVCA)

Project Preferences
Type of Financing Preferred:
Early Stage
Expansion
Seed
Startup

Geographical Preferences
United States
All U.S.

International
Germany
Western Europe

Industry Preferences
Communications and Media
Communications and Media

Internet Specific
Internet

Computer Other
Computer Related

Biotechnology
Biotechnology

Medical/Health
Medical/Health

Business Serv.
Media

Additional Information
Year Founded: 1999
Capital Under Management: $26,100,000
Current Activity Level : Actively seeking new investments
Method of Compensation: Return on invest. most important, but chg. closing fees, service fees, etc.

CAPRICORN VENTURES INTERNATIONAL

St Mary's House
42 Vicarage Crescent
London, United Kingdom SW11 3LD
Phone: 44 20 7223 9130
Fax: 44 20 7326 8457

Management and Staff
Faisal Rahmatallah, Managing Director

Type of Firm
Private Firm Investing Own Capital

Industry Association Membership
British Venture Capital Association

Project Preferences

Type of Financing Preferred:
Early Stage
Expansion
Later Stage

Size of Investments Considered
Min Size of Investment Considered (000s): $800
Max Size of Investment Considered: No Limit

Geographical Preferences

International
Europe
Pacific Rim
South Africa

Additional Information
Year Founded: 1995
Capital Under Management: $808,800,000
Current Activity Level : Actively seeking new investments
Method of Compensation: Return on investment is of primary concern, do not charge fees

CAPVEST MANAGEMENT, LTD

100 Pall Mall
London, United Kingdom SW1Y 5NQ
Phone: 44-20-73897940
Fax: 44-20-73897901
Website: www.capvest.co.uk

Management and Staff
Alberto Cairo, Principal
Doug Evans, Partner
Kate Briant, Principal
Lemy Gresh, Partner
Randl Shure, Managing Partner
Santiago Corral, Principal
Scott Paton, Partner
Seamus FitzPatrick, Partner
Stephen Mostyn-Williams, Partner

Type of Firm
Private Firm Investing Own Capital

Project Preferences

Type of Financing Preferred:
Expansion
Later Stage
Mezzanine

Size of Investments Considered
Min Size of Investment Considered (000s): $13,400
Max Size of Investment Considered: No Limit

Geographical Preferences

International
Scandanavia/Nordic Region
United Kingdom
Western Europe

Industry Preferences

Communications and Media
Telecommunications

Business Serv.
Services

Additional Information
Year Founded: 1999
Capital Under Management: $50,000,000
Current Activity Level : Actively seeking new investments

CAPVIS EQUITY PARTNERS AG

Walchestrasse 9
Zurich, Switzerland 80098
Phone: 41 1 239 8500
Fax: 41 1 239 5811
Website: www.capvis.com

Type of Firm
Investment/Merchant Bank Subsid/Affil

Industry Association Membership
European Venture Capital Association (EVCA)
Swiss Venture Capital Association

Project Preferences

Role in Financing:
Prefer role as deal originator but will also invest in deals created by others

Type of Financing Preferred:
Expansion
Leveraged Buyout
Management Buyouts
Recapitalizations

Geographical Preferences

International
Austria
Switzerland

Industry Preferences

Communications and Media
Commercial Communications
Telecommunications
Data Communications

Computer Software
Computer Services
Systems Software

Semiconductors/Other Elect.
Electronic Components

Medical/Health
Medical Diagnostics
Diagnostic Services
Diagnostic Test Products
Medical Therapeutics
Drug/Equipmt Delivery
Other Therapeutic
Disposable Med. Products

Consumer Related
Entertainment and Leisure
Retail
Computer Stores
Franchises(NEC)
Food/Beverage
Consumer Products
Consumer Services
Education Related

Industrial/Energy
Factory Automation
Machinery
Environmental Related

Business Serv.
Distribution
Consulting Services

Manufact.
Office Automation Equipmt
Publishing

Additional Information
Name of Most Recent Fund: CapVis Equity L.P.
Most Recent Fund Was Raised: 01/01/1999
Year Founded: 1995
Capital Under Management: $218,500,000
Current Activity Level : Actively seeking new investments
Method of Compensation: Return on invest. most important, but chg. closing fees, service fees, etc.

CARMEL VENTURES

16 Hagalim Avenue
Delta House
Herzeliya 46725, Israel
Phone: 972-9-959-4894
Fax: 972-9-959-4898
Website: www.carmelventures.com

Other Offices

Munich, Germany

Management and Staff

Avi Zeevi, Principal
Daniel Chertoff, Principal
Rina Shainski, Principal
Sam Burshtein, Principal
Shlomo Dovrat, Principal

Type of Firm

Private Firm Investing Own Capital

Project Preferences

Type of Financing Preferred:
Balanced

Geographical Preferences

United States
All U.S.

International
Europe
Israel

Industry Preferences

Computer Software
Software

Internet Specific
Internet

Additional Information

Year Founded: 2000
Capital Under Management: $170,000,000
Current Activity Level : Actively seeking new investments

CASTLE HARLAN AUSTRALIAN MEZZANINE PARTNERS PTY. LTD.

Level 2, The Terrace
155 George Street
Sydney, Australia 02000
Phone: 612-9241-4444
Fax: 612-9247-5551
Website: www.amil.com.au

Other Offices

Playford Centre, Hospitality House
60 Hindmarsh Square
Adelaide, Australia 5000
Phone: 618-8226-7369
Fax: 618-8226-7399

Management and Staff

Joseph Skrzynski, Managing Director

Whom to Contact

A. Savage
J. Skrzynski
P.K. Riley
W.D. Ferris

Type of Firm

Investment Management/Finance Consulting

Industry Association Membership

Australian Venture Capital Association (AVCAL)

Project Preferences

Role in Financing:
Prefer role as deal originator but will also invest in deals created by others

Type of Financing Preferred:
Balanced
Expansion
Leveraged Buyout
Mezzanine
Special Situation

Size of Investments Considered

Min Size of Investment Considered (000s): $6,500
Max Size of Investment Considered (000s): $9,750

Geographical Preferences

International
Asia
Australia
China
Europe
Hong Kong

Industry Preferences

(% based on actual investment)

Consumer Related	69.4%
Other Products	17.9%
Industrial/Energy	4.6%
Biotechnology	3.2%
Internet Specific	2.5%
Computer Hardware	2.3%

Additional Information

Name of Most Recent Fund: AMWIN
Most Recent Fund Was Raised: 03/01/1998
Year Founded: 1987
Capital Under Management: $410,800,000
Current Activity Level : Actively seeking new investments
Method of Compensation: Return on invest. most important, but chg. closing fees, service fees, etc.

CASTLEHILL VENTURES

55 University Avenue
Suite 500
Toronto, Canada M5J 2H7
Phone: 416-862-8574
Fax: 416-862-8875

Type of Firm

Private Firm Investing Own Capital

Project Preferences

Type of Financing Preferred:
Startup

Geographical Preferences

Canada
Ontario

Industry Preferences

Communications and Media
Telecommunications

Computer Other
Computer Related

Additional Information

Capital Under Management: $10,000,000
Current Activity Level : Actively seeking new investments

CATALYST FUND MANAGEMENT & RESEARCH LTD

15 Whitcomb Street
London, United Kingdom WC2 H7HA
Phone: 44 20 7747 8600
Fax: 44 20 7930 2688
Website: www.catfund.com

Management and Staff
Rodney Schwartz, Founder

Type of Firm
Private Firm Investing Own Capital

Industry Association Membership
British Venture Capital Association

Project Preferences

Type of Financing Preferred:
Early Stage
Expansion
Later Stage
Seed
Startup

Geographical Preferences

International
Europe

Industry Preferences

Internet Specific
E-Commerce Technology

Business Serv.
Services

Additional Information
Name of Most Recent Fund: European Financial Services Venture Fund
Most Recent Fund Was Raised: 06/01/1999
Year Founded: 1997
Capital Under Management: $64,700,000
Current Activity Level : Actively seeking new investments

CATALYST VENTURE CAPITAL FIRM

12/F,No. 13,Fu-Hsin S. Road
Section 2
Taipei, Taiwan
Phone: 8862-2706-5750
Fax: 8862-2706-5800

Management and Staff
Timothy Lin, President & Chairman

Type of Firm
Private Firm Investing Own Capital

Industry Association Membership
Taiwan Venture Capital Association(TVCA)

Project Preferences

Type of Financing Preferred:
Expansion
Mezzanine
Startup

Geographical Preferences

International
Taiwan

Industry Preferences

(% based on actual investment)

Computer Hardware	22.4%
Semiconductors/Other Elect.	22.3%
Internet Specific	19.3%
Computer Software and Services	18.8%
Communications and Media	13.2%
Other Products	4.0%

Additional Information
Year Founded: 1996
Capital Under Management: $18,600,000
Current Activity Level : Actively seeking new investments

CATELLA IT AB

Box 5894
Birger Jarlsgatan 6
Stockholm, Sweden 102 40
Phone: 46 8 463 3300
Fax: 46 8 463 3399
Website: www.catella.se

Management and Staff
Urban Lindskog, Managing Director

Type of Firm
Affiliate/Subsidary of Oth. Financial. Instit.

Industry Association Membership
European Venture Capital Association (EVCA)
Swedish Venture Capital Association

Project Preferences

Type of Financing Preferred:
Expansion
Startup

Geographical Preferences

International
Europe

Industry Preferences

Communications and Media
Communications and Media

Internet Specific
Internet

Additional Information
Year Founded: 1998
Capital Under Management: $18,800,000
Current Activity Level : Actively seeking new investments

CAZENOVE PRIVATE EQUITY

12 Tokenhouse Yard
London, United Kingdom EC2R 7AN
Phone: 44 20 7588 2828

Management and Staff
Tod Bensen, Partner

Type of Firm
Investment/Merchant Bank Subsid/Affil

Project Preferences

Type of Financing Preferred:
Expansion
Later Stage
Second Stage Financing

Geographical Preferences

International
Europe

Industry Preferences

Communications and Media
Telecommunications

Internet Specific
Internet

Business Serv.
Media

Additional Information
Year Founded: 2000
Capital Under Management: $310,600,000
Current Activity Level : Actively seeking new investments

CCFL MEZZANINE PARTNERS OF CANADA

70 University Avenue
Suite 1450
Toronto, Canada M5J 2M4
Phone: 416-977-1450
Fax: 416-977-6764
E-mail: info@ccfl.com
Website: www.ccfl.com

Other Offices

1010 Sherbrooke Street West
Suite 2210
Montreal, Canada H3A 2R7
Phone: 514-287-9884
Fax: 514-287-9030

Management and Staff
Nagib Premji, Vice President
Richard Kinlough, President
Robert Olsen, President

Whom to Contact
Paul Benson

Type of Firm
Investment/Merchant Bank Subsid/Affil

Industry Association Membership
Canadian Venture Capital Association

Project Preferences

Role in Financing:
Prefer role as deal originator but will also invest in deals created by others

Type of Financing Preferred:
Generalist PE

Size of Investments Considered
Min Size of Investment Considered (000s): $10,000
Max Size of Investment Considered: No Limit

Geographical Preferences

United States
All U.S.

Canada
All Canada

Industry Preferences

Communications and Media
Communications and Media
Telecommunications

Computer Other
Computer Related

Semiconductors/Other Elect.
Electronic Components
Component Testing Equipmt
Fiber Optics
Analytic/Scientific

Medical/Health
Medical/Health
Disposable Med. Products
Hospitals/Clinics/Primary

Consumer Related
Franchises(NEC)
Food/Beverage
Consumer Products

Industrial/Energy
Industrial Products

Transportation
Transportation

Business Serv.
Distribution

Additional Information
Name of Most Recent Fund: CCFL High Yield Fund & Co. L.P.
Most Recent Fund Was Raised: 01/01/1990
Year Founded: 1979
Capital Under Management: $200,000,000
Current Activity Level : Actively seeking new investments
Method of Compensation: Return on invest. most important, but chg. closing fees, service fees, etc.

CD TECHNICOM S.A.

Avenue Destenay 13
Liege, Belgium B-4000
Phone: 32-4-221-9823
Fax: 32-4-221-9999

Management and Staff
Philippe Deville, Chief Executive Officer

Type of Firm
Private Firm Investing Own Capital

Industry Association Membership
Belgium Venture Capital Association
European Venture Capital Association (EVCA)

Project Preferences

Role in Financing:
Will function either as deal originator or investor in deals created by others

Type of Financing Preferred:
Expansion
First Stage Financing
Second Stage Financing
Seed

Size of Investments Considered
Min Size of Investment Considered (000s): $100
Max Size of Investment Considered (000s): $100,000

Geographical Preferences

International
Belgium
Europe
Luxembourg
Netherlands

Industry Preferences

Communications and Media
Communications and Media
Telecommunications
Wireless Communications
Data Communications
Satellite Microwave Comm.
Other Communication Prod.

Computer Hardware
Mainframes / Scientific
Mini and Personal/Desktop

Computer Software
Software
Applications Software
Artificial Intelligence

Internet Specific
E-Commerce Technology
Internet
Web Aggregration/Portals

Computer Other
Computer Related

Semiconductors/Other Elect.
Electronics

Business Serv.
Media

Additional Information
Year Founded: 1988
Capital Under Management: $30,000,000
Current Activity Level : Actively seeking new investments
Method of Compensation: Return on investment is of primary concern, do not charge fees

CDC ADVISORS PRIVATE LTD.

11 Golf Links
New Delhi, India 110003
Phone: 9111-469-1691
Fax: 9111-469-1693
E-mail: info@cdc.com

Type of Firm
Private Firm Investing Own Capital

Project Preferences

Type of Financing Preferred:
Balanced

Geographical Preferences

International
India

Additional Information
Capital Under Management: $30,000,000
Current Activity Level : Actively seeking new investments

CDC INNOVATION PARTNERS

Tour Maine Montparnasse
33 av. du Maine
Paris, France 75755
Phone: 33 1 4064 2000
Fax: 33 1 4064 2200
Website: www.cdcinnov.com

Management and Staff
Christophe Talon, General Partner
Jean-Francois Bru, General Partner
Raffy Kazandjian, Managing Partner
Stephane Boudon, General Partner
Thierry Laugel, Partner

Type of Firm
Investment/Merchant Bank Subsid/Affil

Project Preferences

Type of Financing Preferred:
Early Stage
Expansion
Seed
Startup

Geographical Preferences

International
France

Industry Preferences

(% based on actual investment)

Internet Specific	52.3%
Other Products	12.7%
Medical/Health	10.9%
Computer Software and Services	9.0%
Communications and Media	8.2%
Computer Hardware	5.6%
Biotechnology	1.3%

Additional Information
Name of Most Recent Fund: CDC Innovation 2000
Most Recent Fund Was Raised: 01/13/2000
Year Founded: 1996
Capital Under Management: $195,000,000
Current Activity Level : Actively seeking new investments

CDC SERVICES INDUSTRIES GESTION (CDC IXIS PRIVATE EQUITY)

Tour Maine-Montparnasse
33 avenue du Maine
Paris Cedex 15, France F-75755
Phone: 33 1 4064 2200
Fax: 33 1 4064 2222
Website: www.cdcpart.com

Type of Firm
Investment/Merchant Bank Subsid/Affil

Project Preferences

Type of Financing Preferred:
Expansion
Turnaround

Geographical Preferences

International
Europe
France

Industry Preferences

Industrial/Energy
Industrial Products

Business Serv.
Services

Manufact.
Manufacturing

Additional Information
Capital Under Management: $242,000,000
Current Activity Level : Actively seeking new investments

CELTIC HOUSE INTERNATIONAL

555 Legget Drive
Suite 211
Kanata, Canada K2K 2X3
Phone: 613-271-2020
Fax: 613-271-2025
Website: www.celtic-house.com

Other Offices

100 Simcoe Street
Suite 100
Toronto, Canada M5H 3G2
Phone: 416-542-2436
Fax: 416-542-2435

2726 Sequoia Way
San Mateo, United States of America 94402
Phone: 650-759-0933
Fax: 650-594-9227

Michelin House
81 Fulham Road
London, United Kingdom SW3 6RD
Phone: 020-7808-8540

Management and Staff
Alo D'Arcy, General Partner
Andrew Waitman, Managing General Partner
Brian Antonen, General Partner
Debi Rosati, General Partner
Jose Medeiros, Chief Financial Officer
Michele Dundas Macpherson, General Partner
Roger Maggs, General Partner
Ron Dizy, General Partner
Terry Matthews, Principal
Tom Valis, General Partner

Type of Firm
Private Firm Investing Own Capital

Project Preferences

Type of Financing Preferred:
Early Stage

Geographical Preferences

United States
All U.S.

Canada
All Canada

Industry Preferences

(% based on actual investment)

Computer Software and Services	48.4%
Semiconductors/Other Elect.	29.6%

Internet Specific	12.3%
Communications and Media	7.0%
Computer Hardware	2.7%

Additional Information
Current Activity Level : Actively seeking new investments

CENTRAL AMERICA INVESTMENT MANAGERS

Apdo 721-1000
San Jose, Costa Rica
Phone: 506-290-5200
Fax: 506-290-5220

Type of Firm
Private Firm Investing Own Capital

Additional Information
Capital Under Management: $26,000,000
Current Activity Level : Actively seeking new investments

CHALLENGER INTERNATIONAL LTD.

Level 43, AMP Tower
50 Bridge Street
Sydney, Australia 2000
Phone: 612-9930-7058
Fax: 612-9231-6191
Website: www.challengergroup.com

Type of Firm
Investment Management/Finance Consulting

Project Preferences

Type of Financing Preferred:
Early Stage
Expansion
Mezzanine

Geographical Preferences

International
Australia

Industry Preferences

Biotechnology
Biotechnology

Additional Information
Year Founded: 2000
Capital Under Management: $21,800,000
Current Activity Level : Actively seeking new investments

CHAMPION CONSULTING GROUP, INCORPORATED

12F-B, No. 138, Min Sheng Road
Section 3
Taipei, Taiwan
Phone: 8862-2546-0889
Fax: 8862-2546-0738

Management and Staff
Ding-Hua Hu, President & Chairman

Type of Firm
Private Firm Investing Own Capital

Industry Association Membership
Taiwan Venture Capital Association(TVCA)

Project Preferences

Type of Financing Preferred:
Balanced
Expansion
Mezzanine
Seed
Startup

Geographical Preferences

International
Taiwan

Industry Preferences

Communications and Media
Telecommunications

Computer Software
Software

Semiconductors/Other Elect.
Electronics
Semiconductor

Additional Information
Year Founded: 1990
Capital Under Management: $37,100,000
Current Activity Level : Actively seeking new investments

CHARLES STREET SECURITIES, INC.

One Wilton Crescent
London, United Kingdom SW1X 8RN
Phone: 44-171-235-7642
Fax: 44-171-235-7647

See New York for full listing.

CHENG XIN TECHNOLOGY DEVELOPMENT CORP. (FKA:FIDELITY VC CORP

5F, No. 143
Ming-Sheng East Road
Taipei, Taiwan
Phone: 8862-2507-2960
Fax: 8862-2500-6908

Management and Staff
Cheng-Ming Lee, President & Chairman
Jerry Chen, Managing Director

Type of Firm
Private Firm Investing Own Capital

Industry Association Membership
Taiwan Venture Capital Association(TVCA)

Project Preferences

Type of Financing Preferred:
Early Stage

Size of Investments Considered
Min Size of Investment Considered (000s): $1,000
Max Size of Investment Considered (000s): $2,000

Geographical Preferences

United States
All U.S.

International
Taiwan

Industry Preferences

Biotechnology
Biotechnology

Additional Information
Year Founded: 1990
Capital Under Management: $79,900,000
Current Activity Level : Actively seeking new investments

CHIAO TUNG BANK

5F, No.91, Heng Yang Road
Taipei, Taiwan
Phone: 8862-2361-3000
Fax: 8862-2331-0549
Website: www.ctnbank.com.tw

Management and Staff
Edward Chi, President

Type of Firm
Business Development Fund

Industry Association Membership
Taiwan Venture Capital Association(TVCA)

Project Preferences

Type of Financing Preferred:
Expansion
Mezzanine
Seed

Geographical Preferences

International
Taiwan

Industry Preferences

Communications and Media
Telecommunications

Semiconductors/Other Elect.
Electronics
Electronic Components
Semiconductor

Biotechnology
Biotechnology

Industrial/Energy
Machinery

Additional Information
Year Founded: 1906
Capital Under Management: $37,400,000
Current Activity Level : Actively seeking new investments

CHINA DEVELOPMENT CORP.

125 Nanking East Rd
Sec 5
Taipei, China
Phone: 023-931-122
Fax: 023-215-954

Type of Firm
Non-Financial Corp. Affiliate or Subsidiary

Industry Preferences

(% based on actual investment)

Biotechnology	34.4%
Semiconductors/Other Elect.	25.6%
Computer Hardware	14.2%
Medical/Health	9.3%
Computer Software and Services	7.6%
Communications and Media	4.7%
Industrial/Energy	4.3%

Additional Information
Year Founded: 1998
Capital Under Management: $400,000,000
Current Activity Level : Actively seeking new investments

CHINA ENTERPRISE INVESTMENT MANAGEMENT LIMITED

11/F, 19 Des Voeux Road
World Wide House
Kowloon, Hong Kong
Phone: 852-2521-0078
Fax: 852-2537-1075

Management and Staff
Peter Au, Managing Director
Raymond Lee, Chief Financial Officer

Type of Firm
Private Firm Investing Own Capital

Industry Association Membership
Hungarian Venture Capital Association

Additional Information
Year Founded: 1994
Capital Under Management: $40,000,000
Current Activity Level : Actively seeking new investments

CHINA VENTURE MANAGEMENT, INC.

99, Tunhwa South Road Sec. 2
27th Floor
Taipei, Taiwan
Phone: 8862-2705-1006
Fax: 8862-2705-1008

Other Offices

12F, No.125,Nan-King East Road
Section 5
Taipei, Taiwan
Phone: 886-2-7051006
Fax: 886-2-7051008

15F, No.376, Jen-Ai Road
Section 4
Taipei, Taiwan
Phone: 886-2-27845589
Fax: 886-27544926

Management and Staff
Chin Lin, President
James Liang, Vice President
Jeng-Ming Pai, Vice President
Wayne Lo, Vice President

Whom to Contact
Kevin Chan
Tom Wong

Type of Firm
Private Firm Investing Own Capital

Industry Association Membership
Taiwan Venture Capital Association(TVCA)

Project Preferences

Role in Financing:
Prefer role as deal originator but will also invest in deals created by others

Type of Financing Preferred:
First Stage Financing
Leveraged Buyout
Mezzanine
Research and Development
Second Stage Financing
Seed
Start-up Financing

Size of Investments Considered
Min Size of Investment Considered (000s): $1,000
Max Size of Investment Considered (000s): $5,000

Geographical Preferences

United States
All U.S.

Canada
All Canada

International
Australia
Bermuda
China
France
Germany
Italy
Japan
Spain
United Kingdom

Industry Preferences

(% based on actual investment)

Computer Software and Services	30.2%
Communications and Media	29.7%
Internet Specific	27.5%
Semiconductors/Other Elect.	9.2%
Industrial/Energy	3.5%

Additional Information
Year Founded: 1986
Capital Under Management: $200,000,000
Current Activity Level : Actively seeking new investments
Method of Compensation: Return on invest. most important, but chg. closing fees, service fees, etc.

CHINAVEST

160 Sansome Street
Suite 1800
San Francisco, Taiwan 94104
Phone: 415-276-8888
Fax: 415-276-8885
Website: www.chinavest.com

Other Offices

19/F Dina House
11 Duddell Street
Hong Kong, Hong Kong
Phone: 852-2810-7081
Fax: 852-2845-2949

Suite 2505 OOCL Building
841 Yanan Road Central
Shanghai, China
Phone: 8621-6289-5128
Fax: 8621-6289-5127

Suite 706 7/F Beijing China Resources Building, 8 Jian Guo Men Bei Avenue
Beijing, China 100005
Phone: 8610-8519-1535
Fax: 8610-8519-1530

Worldwide House, Suite 602
129 Ming Sheng East Road, Section 3
Taipei, Taiwan
Phone: 8862-719-9255
Fax: 8862-719-9219

Management and Staff
Monique Lau, Chief Operating Officer
Peter Chen, Vice President

Type of Firm
Private Firm Investing Own Capital

Project Preferences

Type of Financing Preferred:
Expansion

Geographical Preferences

International
China

Additional Information
Name of Most Recent Fund: ChinaVest IV
Most Recent Fund Was Raised: 03/01/1993
Year Founded: 1993
Capital Under Management: $100,000,000
Current Activity Level : Actively seeking new investments

CHRYSALEAD

23 rue Taitbout
Paris, France F 75009
Phone: 33 1 4483 6710
Fax: 33 1 4483 0855
Website: www.chrysalead.net

Management and Staff
Daniel Pinto, Chief Executive Officer
Eric Clairefond, Founding Partner
Jacques Le Gendre, Founding Partner

Type of Firm
Bank Group

Project Preferences

Type of Financing Preferred:
Early Stage

Geographical Preferences

International
No Preference

Industry Preferences

Internet Specific
Internet

Additional Information
Year Founded: 2000
Capital Under Management: $53,600,000
Current Activity Level : Actively seeking new investments

CHRYSALIS CAPITAL

Poddar Chambers, D2 Mathuradas
Mills Compound, Lower Parel
Mumbai, India 400-013
Phone: 9122-460-6100
Fax: 9122-460-5100
Website: www.chrysaliscapital.com

Management and Staff
Luis Miranda, Chief Financial Officer

Type of Firm
Private Firm Investing Own Capital

Project Preferences

Type of Financing Preferred:
Balanced

Geographical Preferences

International
India

Industry Preferences

(% based on actual investment)

Internet Specific	86.6%
Computer Software and Services	13.4%

Additional Information
Name of Most Recent Fund: Chrysalis Capital Fund
Most Recent Fund Was Raised: 10/01/1999
Year Founded: 1999
Capital Under Management: $65,000,000
Current Activity Level : Actively seeking new investments

CIBC CAPITAL PARTNERS (FKA: CIBC WOOD GUNDY CAPITAL)

161 Bay Street
8th Floor
Toronto, Canada M5J 2S8
Phone: 416-594-8021
Fax: 416-594-8037

See New York for full listing.

CICLAD

8 avenue Franklin D. Roosevelt
Paris, France 75008
Phone: 33 1 5659 7733
Fax: 33 1 5376 2210
Website: www.ciclad.com

Management and Staff
Jean-Francois Vaury, Founding Partner
Lionel Lambert, Founding Partner
Thierry Thomann, Founding Partner

Whom to Contact
Jean François Vaury

Type of Firm
Private Firm Investing Own Capital

Project Preferences

Role in Financing:
Prefer role as deal originator but will also invest in deals created by others

Type of Financing Preferred:
Leveraged Buyout
Management Buyouts
Special Situation

Size of Investments Considered
Min Size of Investment Considered (000s): $4,000
Max Size of Investment Considered: No Limit

Geographical Preferences

International
France

Additional Information
Name of Most Recent Fund: CICLAD 2 FCPR
Most Recent Fund Was Raised: 12/01/1995
Year Founded: 1988
Capital Under Management: $115,700,000
Current Activity Level : Actively seeking new investments
Method of Compensation: Return on invest. most important, but chg. closing fees, service fees, etc.

CINVEN LTD

Pinners Hall
105-108 Old Broad Street
London, United Kingdom EC2N 1EH
Phone: 44-207-661-3333
Fax: 44-207-256-2225
Website: www.cinven.com

Other Offices

Edouard VII
26 Boulevard des Capucines
Paris, France 75009
Phone: 33 14 471 4444
Fax: 33 14 471 4499

Main Tower
Neue Mainzer Strasse 52
Frankfurt am Main, Germany 60311
Phone: 49 69 900 27-0
Fax: 49 69 900 27-100

Management and Staff
Robin Hall, Managing Director

Type of Firm
Private Firm Investing Own Capital

Industry Association Membership
British Venture Capital Association
European Venture Capital Association (EVCA)

Project Preferences

Role in Financing:
Prefer role as deal originator but will also invest in deals created by others

Type of Financing Preferred:
Acquisition
Leveraged Buyout
Management Buyouts

Size of Investments Considered
Min Size of Investment Considered (000s): $150,000
Max Size of Investment Considered: No Limit

Geographical Preferences

International
France
Germany
Italy
Spain
United Kingdom
Western Europe

Industry Preferences

(% based on actual investment)

Consumer Related	41.9%
Other Products	34.1%
Biotechnology	14.3%
Industrial/Energy	9.6%
Internet Specific	0.1%

Additional Information
Name of Most Recent Fund: Second Cinven Fund
Most Recent Fund Was Raised: 01/01/1996
Year Founded: 1977
Capital Under Management: $2,200,000,000
Current Activity Level : Actively seeking new investments
Method of Compensation: Return on invest. most important, but chg. closing fees, service fees, etc.

CIRLAB!

Via Brera 5
Milan, Italy 20121
Phone: 39-02-806168
Fax: 3902 806168.624
Website: www.cirlab.com

Type of Firm
Private Firm Investing Own Capital

Project Preferences

Type of Financing Preferred:
Startup

Geographical Preferences

International
Europe

Industry Preferences

Communications and Media
Communications and Media

Internet Specific
Internet

Business Serv.
Media

Additional Information
Year Founded: 1999
Current Activity Level : Actively seeking new investments

CITADEL POOLED DEVELOPMENT LTD.

Level 10, 379 Collins Street
Melbourne, Australia 3000
Phone: 613-9614-4086
Fax: 613-9614-4069
Website: www.citadel-pdl.com.au

Type of Firm
Private Firm Investing Own Capital

Project Preferences

Role in Financing:
Prefer role as deal originator

Type of Financing Preferred:
Expansion
Leveraged Buyout
Management Buyouts

Size of Investments Considered
Min Size of Investment Considered (000s): $309
Max Size of Investment Considered (000s): $1,540

Geographical Preferences

International
Australia

Industry Preferences

Communications and Media
Radio & TV Broadcasting
Telecommunications

Computer Software
Software

Internet Specific
Internet

Consumer Related
Food/Beverage

Financial Services
Financial Services

Other
Environment Responsible

Additional Information

Year Founded: 1996
Capital Under Management: $6,500,000
Current Activity Level : Actively seeking new investments
Method of Compensation: Return on investment is of primary concern, do not charge fees

CITICORP CAPITAL ASIA (AKA: CITIC PACIFIC LTD.)

32/F, CITIC Tower
1 Tim Mei Avenue
Central, Hong Kong
Website: www.citicpacific.com

Other Offices

47/F, Citibank Tower, Citibank Plaza,
3 Garden Rd.
Central, Hong Kong
Phone: 852-2868-6677
Fax: 852-2868-6549

Management and Staff

Henry Fan Hung Ling, Managing Director
John McLean, Chief Executive Officer
K.S. Butalia, Managing Director
Vincent Fan, Chief Executive Officer

Type of Firm

Commercial Bank Affiliate or Subsidiary

Project Preferences

Type of Financing Preferred:
Expansion
Leveraged Buyout
Mezzanine
Public Companies

Geographical Preferences

International
Asia
Philippines

Industry Preferences

Communications and Media
Telecommunications

Computer Other
Computer Related

Semiconductors/Other Elect.
Electronic Components
Fiber Optics

Biotechnology
Biotechnology

Medical/Health
Medical/Health
Pharmaceuticals

Consumer Related
Entertainment and Leisure

Industrial/Energy
Energy
Industrial Products

Transportation
Transportation

Financial Services
Financial Services

Business Serv.
Services
Distribution
Media

Manufact.
Manufacturing

Additional Information

Year Founded: 1972
Capital Under Management: $600,000,000
Current Activity Level : Actively seeking new investments

CLAFLIN CAPITAL MANAGEMENT, INC.

21 Artema Street
Kiev, Ukraine 254053
Phone: 7044-212-3138
Fax: 7044-212-4972

See Massachusetts for full listing.

CLAIRVEST GROUP, INC.

22 St. Clair Avenue East
Suite 1700
Toronto, Canada M4T 2S3
Phone: 416-925-9270
Fax: 416-925-5753

Management and Staff

Jeff Parr
Ken B. Rotman

Whom to Contact

Jeff Parr
Ken B. Rotman

Type of Firm

Investment/Merchant Bank Investing Own or Client Funds

Project Preferences

Role in Financing:
Prefer role as deal originator

Type of Financing Preferred:
Balanced
Control-block Purchases
Later Stage
Leveraged Buyout
Special Situation

Size of Investments Considered
Min Size of Investment Considered (000s): $5,000
Max Size of Investment Considered: No Limit

Geographical Preferences

United States
All U.S.
All U.S.

Canada
All Canada

International
All International

Industry Preferences

Communications and Media
CATV & Pay TV Systems

Computer Hardware
Integrated Turnkey System

Computer Software
Systems Software
Applications Software

Semiconductors/Other Elect.
Sensors

Medical/Health
Medical Diagnostics
Diagnostic Services
Diagnostic Test Products
Medical Therapeutics

Consumer Related
Food/Beverage
Consumer Products
Consumer Services
Other Restaurants
Education Related

Industrial/Energy
Materials
Factory Automation
Machinery
Environmental Related

Transportation
Transportation

Additional Information
Year Founded: 1987
Capital Under Management: $160,000,000
Current Activity Level : Actively seeking new investments
Method of Compensation: Return on invest. most important, but chg. closing fees, service fees, etc.

CLAL VENTURE CAPITAL MANAGEMENT LTD (AKA CVC MANAGEMENT)

Clal Atidim Tower, 16th Floor
Atidim High-Tech Ind. Park
Tel Aviv, Israel 61581
Phone: 972 3 765 0302
Fax: 972 3 765 0303
Website: www.clal.co.il

Management and Staff
Hillel Milo, Partner
Ophir Shahaf, Partner

Type of Firm
Non-Financial Corp. Affiliate or Subsidiary

Project Preferences

Type of Financing Preferred:
Early Stage
Expansion
Startup

Geographical Preferences

International
Israel
Middle East

Industry Preferences

Computer Software
Software

Medical/Health
Medical/Health

Additional Information
Capital Under Management: $36,000,000
Current Activity Level : Actively seeking new investments

CLASSIC FUND MANAGEMENT, LTD.

Marble Arch Tower
55 Bryanston Street
London, United Kingdom W1H 8AA
Phone: 44 20 7868 8883
Fax: 44 20 7868 8629
Website: www.classicfunds.co.uk

Management and Staff
Anthony Stacey, Partner
Bill Cunningham, Partner
Graham Spooner, Partner
Nick Lewis, Partner
Richard Hargreaves, Partner

Type of Firm
Investment Management/Finance Consulting

Industry Association Membership
British Venture Capital Association

Project Preferences

Type of Financing Preferred:
Early Stage
Expansion
Later Stage
Seed
Startup

Geographical Preferences

International
United Kingdom

Industry Preferences

Communications and Media
Communications and Media
Telecommunications

Computer Software
Software

Internet Specific
Internet

Computer Other
Computer Related

Additional Information
Name of Most Recent Fund: Downing Classic Venture Capital Trust, PLC
Most Recent Fund Was Raised: 04/01/1999
Year Founded: 1998
Capital Under Management: $28,100,000
Current Activity Level : Actively seeking new investments

CLEMENTE CAPITAL (ASIA) LTD.

8/F, The World Centre Bldg.
330 Puyat Ave.
Makati, Philippines 1259
Phone: 632-867-8945
Fax: 632-867-8950

Management and Staff
Federico Macaranas, President
Oscar Barerra, Managing Director

Type of Firm
Private Firm Investing Own Capital

Project Preferences

Type of Financing Preferred:
Balanced
Expansion
Mezzanine

Size of Investments Considered
Min Size of Investment Considered (000s): $1,000
Max Size of Investment Considered: No Limit

Geographical Preferences

International
Philippines

Industry Preferences

Communications and Media
Telecommunications

Medical/Health
Medical/Health

Consumer Related
Retail
Hotels and Resorts

Manufact.
Manufacturing

Additional Information
Name of Most Recent Fund: Philippine Strategic Investment Limited (PSIL)
Most Recent Fund Was Raised: 03/31/1993
Year Founded: 1993
Capital Under Management: $9,000,000
Current Activity Level : Actively seeking new investments

CLOSE BROTHERS INVESTMENT LIMITED

12 Appold Street
London, United Kingdom EC2A 2AW
Phone: 44 20 7426 4000
Fax: 44 20 7426 4040
Website: www.cbil.com

Management and Staff
C.V. Reader, Managing Director

Type of Firm
Investment/Merchant Bank Investing Own or Client Funds

Project Preferences

Type of Financing Preferred:
Balanced

Geographical Preferences

International
United Kingdom
No Preference

Additional Information
Year Founded: 1991
Capital Under Management: $205,700,000
Current Activity Level : Actively seeking new investments

CLOSE BROTHERS PRIVATE EQUITY

12 Appold Street
London, United Kingdom EC2A 2AW
Phone: 44 20 7426-4000
Fax: 44 20 7426-4004
Website: www.cbpel.com

Type of Firm
Investment/Merchant Bank Subsid/Affil

Industry Association Membership
British Venture Capital Association

Project Preferences

Type of Financing Preferred:
Expansion
Later Stage
Management Buyouts
Turnaround

Geographical Preferences

International
United Kingdom

Industry Preferences

Consumer Related
Entertainment and Leisure

Industrial/Energy
Industrial Products

Transportation
Transportation

Business Serv.
Services

Manufact.
Manufacturing

Additional Information
Name of Most Recent Fund: Close Investment 1986 Fund
Most Recent Fund Was Raised: 01/01/1986
Year Founded: 1984
Capital Under Management: $330,200,000
Current Activity Level : Actively seeking new investments

COATES MYER & CO. PTY LTD. (AKA: CM CAPITAL INVESTMENTS)

Level 2 Telstra House
167 Eagle Street
Brisbane, Australia 04000
Phone: 617-3221-5922
Fax: 617-3221-5933
E-mail: info@cmcapital.com
Website: www.cmcapital.com

Management and Staff
Carrie Hillyard, General Partner
Michael Begun, Managing Partner

Type of Firm
Private Firm Investing Own Capital

Industry Association Membership
Australian Venture Capital Association (AVCAL)

Project Preferences

Type of Financing Preferred:
Expansion
Seed
Startup

Geographical Preferences

International
Oceania/Australasia

Industry Preferences

Communications and Media
Telecommunications

Biotechnology
Biotechnology

Additional Information
Year Founded: 1998
Capital Under Management: $41,300,000
Current Activity Level : Actively seeking new investments

COLONIAL FIRST STATE PRIVATE EQUITY LTD (FKA: HAMBRO-G MGMT)

Level 14, AMP Centre
50 Bridge Street
Sydney, Australia 02000
Phone: 612-9221-4311
Fax: 612-9221-7094
Website: www.colonialfirststate.com.au/privateequity

Management and Staff
Alex Zaininger, Chief Operating Officer

Whom to Contact
Guy Manson

Type of Firm
Private Firm Investing Own Capital

Industry Association Membership
Australian Venture Capital Association (AVCAL)

Project Preferences

Role in Financing:
Prefer role as deal originator but will also invest in deals created by others

Type of Financing Preferred:
Early Stage
Expansion
Management Buyouts

Size of Investments Considered

Min Size of Investment Considered (000s): $1,300

Max Size of Investment Considered (000s): $6,500

Geographical Preferences

International

Oceania/Australasia

Industry Preferences

(% based on actual investment)

Computer Software and Services	36.4%
Other Products	20.8%
Medical/Health	18.7%
Consumer Related	11.0%
Internet Specific	6.3%
Communications and Media	4.3%
Semiconductors/Other Elect.	1.5%
Computer Hardware	1.1%

Additional Information

Name of Most Recent Fund: Hambro-Grantham Fund 5

Most Recent Fund Was Raised: 07/01/1997

Year Founded: 1984

Capital Under Management: $118,200,000

Current Activity Level : Actively seeking new investments

Method of Compensation: Return on investment is of primary concern, do not charge fees

COMMERZ BETEILIGUNGSGESELLSCHAFT MBH (CBG)

Kaiserstrasse 16
Frankfurtam Main, Germany 60311
Phone: 49 69-136-44494
Fax: 49 69-136-29876
Website: www.cbg.commerzbank.com

Management and Staff

Armin Schuler, Managing Director
Dieter Firmenich, Managing Director
Gert Schorradt, Managing Director

Type of Firm

Investment/Merchant Bank Investing Own or Client Funds

Industry Association Membership

European Venture Capital Association (EVCA)
German Venture Capital Association

Project Preferences

Role in Financing:

Prefer role as deal originator

Type of Financing Preferred:

Early Stage
Expansion
Fund of Funds
Management Buyouts
Mezzanine
Recapitalizations
Startup

Size of Investments Considered

Min Size of Investment Considered (000s): $1,000

Max Size of Investment Considered (000s): $100,000

Geographical Preferences

International

Germany
Western Europe

Industry Preferences

Communications and Media

Communications and Media

Computer Other

Computer Related

Semiconductors/Other Elect.

Electronics

Biotechnology

Biotechnology

Medical/Health

Medical/Health

Consumer Related

Consumer

Industrial/Energy

Industrial Products
Factory Automation

Additional Information

Year Founded: 1987

Capital Under Management: $174,200,000

Current Activity Level : Actively seeking new investments

Method of Compensation: Return on investment is of primary concern, do not charge fees

COMPASS INVESTMENT MANAGEMENT LTD.

33 Cork Street
London, United Kingdom W1X 1HB
Phone: 44 20 74343488
Fax: 44 20 74343155

Management and Staff

Dennis Hallahane, Partner
Peter Dale, Partner

Type of Firm

Investment/Merchant Bank Investing Own or Client Funds

Industry Association Membership

British Venture Capital Association

Project Preferences

Role in Financing:

Prefer role as deal originator but will also invest in deals created by others

Type of Financing Preferred:

Early Stage
Expansion
Leveraged Buyout
Recapitalizations
Second Stage Financing
Special Situation

Geographical Preferences

United States

All U.S.

Canada

All Canada

International

United Kingdom
Western Europe

Industry Preferences

Communications and Media

Telecommunications
Data Communications

Semiconductors/Other Elect.

Electronic Components
Sensors
Component Testing Equipmt

Medical/Health

Drug/Equipmt Delivery
Other Therapeutic
Medical Products
Disposable Med. Products
Pharmaceuticals

Consumer Related
Entertainment and Leisure
Food/Beverage
Consumer Products
Other Restaurants

Industrial/Energy
Industrial Products
Materials
Factory Automation
Machinery
Environmental Related

Additional Information
Year Founded: 1986
Capital Under Management: $5,900,000
Current Activity Level : Actively seeking new investments
Method of Compensation: Return on invest. most important, but chg. closing fees, service fees, etc.

CONCORD VENTURE MANAGEMENT (FKA:NITZANIM)

85 Medinat Hayehudim St
P.O.Box 4011
Herzelia, Israel 46140
Phone: 972-9-960-2020
Fax: 972-9-960-2022
Website: www.concord-ventures.co.il

Management and Staff
Avi Domoshevizki, General Partner
Batsheva Elran, General Partner
Matty Karp, Managing Partner
Shlomo Kalish, Venture Partner
Yair Safrai, General Partner
Yaron Rosenboim, Chief Financial Officer

Type of Firm
Investment Management/Finance Consulting

Project Preferences

Role in Financing:
Prefer role as deal originator but will also invest in deals created by others

Type of Financing Preferred:
Early Stage
First Stage Financing
Leveraged Buyout
Private Placement
Second Stage Financing
Seed
Startup

Size of Investments Considered
Min Size of Investment Considered (000s): $100
Max Size of Investment Considered (000s): $15,000

Geographical Preferences

United States
All U.S.

International
Israel
Middle East

Industry Preferences

Communications and Media
Telecommunications
Wireless Communications
Data Communications

Computer Hardware
Integrated Turnkey System

Computer Software
Data Processing
Software
Systems Software
Applications Software
Artificial Intelligence

Internet Specific
Internet

Semiconductors/Other Elect.
Semiconductor
Micro-Processing
Controllers and Sensors
Circuit Boards
Component Testing Equipmt
Fiber Optics

Biotechnology
Human Biotechnology
Biosensors
Biotech Related Research

Medical/Health
Medical Diagnostics
Diagnostic Test Products
Drug/Equipmt Delivery
Medical Products

Industrial/Energy
Robotics

Additional Information
Year Founded: 1993
Capital Under Management: $260,000,000
Current Activity Level : Actively seeking new investments
Method of Compensation: Return on investment is of primary concern, do not charge fees

CONCORDIA CAPITAL

Etelaesplanadi 22 A
Helsinki, Finland 00130
Phone: 358 9 612 6471
Fax: 358 9 647 814
E-mail: ulf.rosenlof@concordia-capital.fi
Website: www.concordia-capital.fi

Management and Staff
Ulf Rosenlof, President

Type of Firm
Private Firm Investing Own Capital

Project Preferences

Type of Financing Preferred:
Expansion

Geographical Preferences

International
Europe
Scandanavia/Nordic Region

Industry Preferences

Communications and Media
Telecommunications

Business Serv.
Media

Additional Information
Year Founded: 1999
Capital Under Management: $21,900,000
Current Activity Level : Actively seeking new investments

CONTINENTAL VENTURE CAPITAL

Level 40, AMP Centre
50 Bridge Street
Sydney, Australia 2000
Phone: 612-9223-8800
Fax: 612-9223-9808
Website: www.cvcltd.com.au

Management and Staff
John Leaver, Managing Director

Whom to Contact
Johanna Plumndge

Type of Firm
Private Firm Investing Own Capital

Industry Association Membership
Australian Venture Capital Association (AVCAL)

Project Preferences

Role in Financing:
Will function either as deal originator or investor in deals created by others

Type of Financing Preferred:
Acquisition
Distressed Debt
Early Stage
Expansion
First Stage Financing
Generalist PE
Later Stage
Leveraged Buyout
Management Buyouts
Mezzanine
Private Placement
Recapitalizations
Second Stage Financing
Seed
Special Situation
Start-up Financing
Turnaround

Size of Investments Considered
Min Size of Investment Considered (000s): $1,000
Max Size of Investment Considered (000s): $5,000

Geographical Preferences

International
Asia
Australia
Europe
Oceania/Australasia

Industry Preferences

(% based on actual investment)

Other Products	48.8%
Medical/Health	20.9%
Consumer Related	15.8%
Industrial/Energy	9.5%
Semiconductors/Other Elect.	3.0%
Internet Specific	1.4%
Computer Hardware	0.5%
Computer Software and Services	0.1%

Additional Information
Year Founded: 1985
Capital Under Management: $31,400,000
Current Activity Level : Actively seeking new investments
Method of Compensation: Return on invest. most important, but chg. closing fees, service fees, etc.

CONTINUUM GROUP LIMITED

118 Piccadilly
London, United Kingdom W1V 9FJ
Phone: 44 207 569 6771
Fax: 44 207 569 6772
Website: www.continuumgroup.co.uk

Management and Staff
Andrew S Frey, Vice President
Ehren B. Stenzler, Vice President
Jean-Francois Astier, Co-Founder
Jorg Mohaupt, Co-Founder
Nicolas Massard, Vice President

Type of Firm
Private Firm Investing Own Capital

Project Preferences

Type of Financing Preferred:
Early Stage

Geographical Preferences

International
Europe

Industry Preferences

Communications and Media
Telecommunications

Internet Specific
Internet

Additional Information
Year Founded: 2000
Capital Under Management: $80,000,000
Current Activity Level : Actively seeking new investments

COPERNICUS CAPITAL MANAGEMENT LTD

ul. Krakowskie Przedmiescie 79
Second Floor
Warsaw, Poland 00-079
Phone: 48-22-826-8580
Fax: 48-22-826-4462
Website: www.copernicus-capital.com

Management and Staff
Greg Stangl, Partner
Neil Milne, Managing Director
Piotr Wypych, Partner
Steve Richmond, Partner

Type of Firm
Private Equity Advisor or Fund of Fund Mgr

Industry Association Membership
European Venture Capital Association (EVCA)

Project Preferences

Role in Financing:
Will function either as deal originator or investor in deals created by others

Type of Financing Preferred:
Acquisition
Early Stage
Expansion
Leveraged Buyout

Size of Investments Considered
Min Size of Investment Considered (000s): $1,000
Max Size of Investment Considered (000s): $2,500

Geographical Preferences

International
Central Europe
Poland

Industry Preferences

Communications and Media
CATV & Pay TV Systems
Radio & TV Broadcasting

Computer Hardware
Integrated Turnkey System

Computer Software
Software

Internet Specific
Internet

Consumer Related
Consumer
Entertainment and Leisure
Retail

Business Serv.
Distribution
Media

Manufact.
Manufacturing

Additional Information
Name of Most Recent Fund: Poland Investment Fund L.P., The
Most Recent Fund Was Raised: 12/01/1994
Year Founded: 1994
Capital Under Management: $25,000,000
Current Activity Level : Actively seeking new investments
Method of Compensation: Return on investment is of primary concern, do not charge fees

CORE PACIFIC CONSULTING COMPANY

8/F,No. 12,Tung-Hsin Road
Taipei, Taiwan
Phone: 8862-2748-1807
Fax: 8862-2748-1820

Management and Staff
Wu Ting, President

Type of Firm
Private Firm Investing Own Capital

Industry Association Membership
Taiwan Venture Capital Association(TVCA)

Project Preferences

Type of Financing Preferred:
Balanced
Mezzanine
Seed
Startup

Geographical Preferences

International
Taiwan

Industry Preferences

Computer Software
Software

Semiconductors/Other Elect.
Electronic Components
Semiconductor

Biotechnology
Biotechnology

Industrial/Energy
Machinery

Additional Information
Year Founded: 1997
Capital Under Management: $20,200,000
Current Activity Level : Actively seeking new investments

CORPFIN CAPITAL S.A.

Marqués de Villamejor 3
Madrid, Spain E-28006
Phone: 34-91-577-8581
Fax: 34-91-577-8583

Management and Staff
Juan Cuesta
Paola DeCegama
Patrick Gandarias

Whom to Contact
Juan Cuesta
Paola DeCegama
Patrick Gandarias

Type of Firm
Private Firm Investing Own Capital

Project Preferences

Role in Financing:
Prefer role as deal originator but will also invest in deals created by others

Type of Financing Preferred:
Leveraged Buyout

Size of Investments Considered
Min Size of Investment Considered (000s): $5,000
Max Size of Investment Considered: No Limit

Geographical Preferences

International
Spain

Industry Preferences

Semiconductors/Other Elect.
Electronic Components

Medical/Health
Medical/Health

Consumer Related
Consumer
Education Related

Industrial/Energy
Industrial Products

Transportation
Transportation

Manufact.
Publishing

Additional Information
Name of Most Recent Fund: Corpfin Capital Fund
Most Recent Fund Was Raised: 12/01/1996
Year Founded: 1990
Capital Under Management: $34,000,000
Current Activity Level : Actively seeking new investments
Method of Compensation: Return on invest. most important, but chg. closing fees, service fees, etc.

CORPORATE GROWTH ASSISTANCE, LTD.

19 York Ridge Road
North York, Canada M2P 1R8
Phone: 416-222-7772
Fax: 416-222-6091

Other Offices

Boden's Ride House
Boden's Ride, Swinley Forest
Berkshire, United Kingdom SL5 9LE
Phone: 44-344-20738
Fax: 44-344-25130

Management and Staff
Bob McBean

Whom to Contact
Bob McBean

Type of Firm
Investment/Merchant Bank Investing Own or Client Funds

Industry Association Membership
Canadian Venture Capital Association

Project Preferences

Role in Financing:
Prefer role as deal originator but will also invest in deals created by others

Type of Financing Preferred:
Leveraged Buyout
Mezzanine
Recapitalizations
Second Stage Financing

Size of Investments Considered
Min Size of Investment Considered (000s): $1,000
Max Size of Investment Considered: No Limit

Geographical Preferences

United States
Midwest
Northwest

Canada
Ontario
Western Canada

Industry Preferences

Communications and Media
CATV & Pay TV Systems
Data Communications
Other Communication Prod.

Computer Software
Computer Services
Applications Software

Semiconductors/Other Elect.
Component Testing Equipmt

Medical/Health
Disposable Med. Products
Hospital/Other Instit.
Pharmaceuticals

Consumer Related
Food/Beverage
Consumer Products
Consumer Services

Industrial/Energy
Energy Conservation Relat
Industrial Products
Materials
Machinery

Manufact.
Publishing

Additional Information

Year Founded: 1967
Current Activity Level : Actively seeking new investments
Method of Compensation: Return on invest. most important, but chg. closing fees, service fees, etc.

COVENT INDUSTRIAL CAPITAL INVESTMENT CO LTD

Maros u. 27
Budapest, Hungary H-1122
Phone: 36-1-355-2493
Fax: 36-1-202-2381

Management and Staff

Janos Bolyky, Chief Executive Officer

Whom to Contact

Géza Popovics

Type of Firm

Private Firm Investing Own Capital

Industry Association Membership

Hungarian Venture Capital Association

Project Preferences

Role in Financing:
Prefer role as deal originator but will also invest in deals created by others

Type of Financing Preferred:
Expansion
Startup
Turnaround

Geographical Preferences

International
Hungary
Scandanavia/Nordic Region
Sweden

Industry Preferences

Financial Services
Real Estate

Business Serv.
Consulting Services

Additional Information

Year Founded: 1990
Capital Under Management: $4,000,000
Current Activity Level : Actively seeking new investments

CPH INVESTMENT CORP.

14 Argyle Place
Sydney, Australia 2000
Phone: 612-9247-5066
Fax: 612-9247-9798
Website: www.cph.com.au

Type of Firm

Affiliate/Subsidary of Oth. Financial. Instit.

Project Preferences

Role in Financing:
Will function either as deal originator or investor in deals created by others

Type of Financing Preferred:
Balanced

Geographical Preferences

International
Asia
Australia

Additional Information

Current Activity Level : Actively seeking new investments
Method of Compensation: Return on investment is of primary concern, do not charge fees

---

CR&T VENTURES AB

Stora Badhusgatan 18-20
Goteborg, Sweden SE - 411 2
Phone: 46-31-701 42 00
Fax: 46-31-10 19 87
Website: www.crtventures.com

Management and Staff

Hans Jacobsson, General Partner
Staffan Hillberg, General Partner

Type of Firm

Incubators

Industry Association Membership

European Venture Capital Association (EVCA)
Swedish Venture Capital Association

Project Preferences

Type of Financing Preferred:
Early Stage
Seed
Startup

Geographical Preferences

International
Scandanavia/Nordic Region

Industry Preferences

Communications and Media
Telecommunications

Computer Software
Software

Internet Specific
Internet

Computer Other
Computer Related

Semiconductors/Other Elect.
Electronics
Fiber Optics

Additional Information
Year Founded: 2000
Capital Under Management: $10,000,000
Current Activity Level : Actively seeking new investments

CREAFUND CVBA

Clintonpark
Ter Reigerie 9
Roeselare, Belgium 8800
Phone: 32-51-262042
Fax: 32-51-252979
Website: www.creafund.be

Type of Firm
Private Firm Investing Own Capital

Industry Association Membership
Belgium Venture Capital Association

Project Preferences

Type of Financing Preferred:
Early Stage
Fund of Funds
Seed

Geographical Preferences

International
Belgium

Industry Preferences

Communications and Media
Telecommunications

Computer Software
Software

Biotechnology
Biotechnology

Transportation
Transportation

Business Serv.
Media

Manufact.
Manufacturing

Additional Information
Year Founded: 1997
Capital Under Management: $2,100,000
Current Activity Level : Actively seeking new investments

CREDIT LYONNAIS SECURITIES ASIA PVT EQUITY LIMITED (CLSA)

33/F Lippo Centre, Tower 2
89 Queensway
Admiralty, Hong Kong
Phone: 852-2600-8888
Fax: 852-2868-0189
Website: www.clsagem.com

Other Offices

9 Raffles Place, #19-20/21
Republic Plaza II
Singapore, Singapore 048619
Phone: 65-534-3268
Fax: 65-533-8922

9/F Youone Building
75-95 Seosomun-Dong, Chung-ku
Seoul, South Korea
Phone: 82-23708-7300
Fax: 82-2771-8583

Suite 15-2 Level 15, Menara PanGlobal
8 Lorong P. Ramlee, Off Jalan P Ramlee
Kuala Lumpur, Malaysia 50250
Phone: 603-232-42888
Fax: 603-238-4868

Torre Bouchard
Bouchard 547, Piso 11
Buenos Aires, Argentina
Phone: 541-311-9949
Fax: 541-311-9926

Type of Firm
Private Firm Investing Own Capital

Additional Information
Name of Most Recent Fund: ARIA Investment Holdings Limited
Most Recent Fund Was Raised: 05/01/2000
Year Founded: 1999
Capital Under Management: $70,000,000
Current Activity Level : Actively seeking new investments

CRESCENDO VENTURE MANAGEMENT LLC (FKA:IAI VENTURES)

36 Dover Street
Mayfair
London, United Kingdom W1X 3RB
Phone: 44-20-7529-6300
Fax: 44-20-7529-6301

See Minnesota for full listing.

CRESCENT CAPITAL NI LTD (FKA HAMBRO NORTHERN IRELAND)

5 Crescent Gardens
Belfast, United Kingdom BT7 INS
Phone: 44-28-9023-3633
Fax: 44-28-9032-9525

Type of Firm
Private Firm Investing Own Capital

Industry Association Membership
British Venture Capital Association

Project Preferences

Type of Financing Preferred:
Balanced

Geographical Preferences

International
United Kingdom

Industry Preferences

Communications and Media
Communications and Media

Computer Other
Computer Related

Semiconductors/Other Elect.
Electronics

Biotechnology
Biotechnology

Medical/Health
Medical/Health

Industrial/Energy
Industrial Products
Materials
Factory Automation

Manufact.
Manufacturing

Additional Information
Name of Most Recent Fund: Hambro Northen Ireland Ventures L.P.
Most Recent Fund Was Raised: 01/01/1995
Capital Under Management: $20,500,000
Current Activity Level : Actively seeking new investments

CROSBIE & CO INC

One First Canadian Place
9th Floor, P.O. Box 116
Toronto, Canada M5X 1A4
Phone: 416-362-7726
Fax: 416-362-3447
E-mail: info@crosbieco.com
Website: www.crosbieco.com

Management and Staff
Allan Crosbie, Managing Partner
Brad Cherniak, Partner
Colin Walker, Partner
Ian MacDonell, Partner

Type of Firm
Investment/Merchant Bank Subsid/Affil

Project Preferences

Role in Financing:
Prefer role as deal originator but will also invest in deals created by others

Type of Financing Preferred:
Acquisition
Distressed Debt
Expansion
Generalist PE
Later Stage
Leveraged Buyout
Management Buyouts
Mezzanine
Private Placement
Recapitalizations
Special Situation
Turnaround

Geographical Preferences

Canada
Ontario

Industry Preferences

Communications and Media
Telecommunications
Wireless Communications
Satellite Microwave Comm.

Computer Software
Software

Semiconductors/Other Elect.
Electronic Components
Semiconductor
Circuit Boards
Component Testing Equipmt
Analytic/Scientific

Medical/Health
Medical Diagnostics
Diagnostic Test Products
Medical Products

Consumer Related
Consumer
Food/Beverage

Industrial/Energy
Industrial Products
Factory Automation
Machinery

Business Serv.
Services
Distribution
Media

Manufact.
Manufacturing

Agr/Forestr/Fish
Agriculture related

Additional Information
Year Founded: 1991
Capital Under Management: $15,000,000
Current Activity Level : Actively seeking new investments
Method of Compensation: Return on invest. most important, but chg. closing fees, service fees, etc.

CROSS ATLANTIC CAPITAL PARTNERS

3006 Lake Drive
Citywest
Dublin, Ireland, Republic of
Phone: 011-35-31-241-6100
Fax: 011-35-31-466-0170

See Pennsylvania for full listing.

CSK VENTURE CAPITAL CO., LTD.

Kenchiku Kaikan, 7/F
26-20 Shiba, 5-chome Minato-ku
Tokyo, Japan 108-0014
Phone: 813-3457-5588
Fax: 813-3547-7070
Website: www.cskvc.co.jp

Management and Staff
Kinya Nakagome, Managing Director
Masahiro Aozono, President
Satoru Iino, Senior Managing Director

Whom to Contact
Kenji Suzuki

Type of Firm
Private Firm Investing Own Capital

Project Preferences

Role in Financing:
Prefer role in deals created by others

Type of Financing Preferred:
Early Stage
First Stage Financing
Second Stage Financing
Seed
Start-up Financing

Size of Investments Considered
Min Size of Investment Considered (000s): $500
Max Size of Investment Considered (000s): $3,000

Geographical Preferences

United States
Northeast
West Coast

International
Israel
Japan

Industry Preferences

(% based on actual investment)

Internet Specific	52.1%
Computer Software and Services	18.3%
Semiconductors/Other Elect.	13.1%
Other Products	7.4%
Computer Hardware	3.5%
Consumer Related	2.3%
Biotechnology	1.7%
Communications and Media	1.5%

Additional Information

Name of Most Recent Fund: CSK Ventures
Most Recent Fund Was Raised: 08/01/1988
Year Founded: 1991
Capital Under Management: $200,000,000
Current Activity Level : Actively seeking new investments
Method of Compensation: Return on investment is of primary concern, do not charge fees

CVC CAPITAL PARTNERS

Hudson House
8-10 Tavistock Street
London, United Kingdom WC2E7PP
Phone: 44-20-7420-4240
Fax: 44-20-7420-4233
Website: www.cvceurope.com

Other Offices

40 Rue La Perouse
Paris, France 75116
Phone: 01 45 02 2300
Fax: 01 45 02 2301

47/F Citibank Tower
Citibank Plaza, 3 Garden Rd
Central Hong Kong, Hong Kong
Phone: 852-2868-6628
Fax: 852-2868-6510

Bahnhofstrasse 94
Zurich, Switzerland 8001
Phone: 41 1 252 6990
Fax: 41 01 252 6993

Chausse de la Hulpe 166
Brussels, Belgium B - 1170
Phone: 32 2/663.80.90
Fax: 32 2/663.80 99

HC Andersens Boulevard 12
Copenhagen V, Denmark DK - 1553
Phone: 45/33.12.00.10
Fax: 45/33.12.00.15

Jose Ortegay Gasset 29
Madrid, Spain 28006
Phone: 34 91 436 4280
Fax: 34 91 436 4282

Maser Samuelsgatan 10
Box 7625
Stockholm, Sweden 10394
Phone: 46 8/54.50.01.50
Fax: 46 8/611.05.65

MesseTurm
Friedrich - Ebert - Anlage 49
Frankfurt am Main, Germany D 60308
Phone: 49 69 975 835 0
Fax: 49 69 975 835 11

Via Brera 7
Milan, Italy 20121
Phone: 390 2/806.81.71
Fax: 390 2/80.68.17.40

World Trade Centre Schiphol Airport
Tower B 6th Floor Schiphol Boulevard 285
Luchthaven Schiphol, Netherlands 1118BH
Phone: 31 20 6514 213
Fax: 31 20 6514 251

Management and Staff

Christian Wildmoser, Managing Director
David Seto, Managing Director
Geert Duyck, Managing Director
Heinz Hasler, Partner
Luigi Lanari, Partner
Philippe Gleize, Managing Director
Rolly Van Rappard, Managing Director
Vincent Fan, Chief Executive Officer

Whom to Contact

Donald Mackenzie
Javier de Jaime
Soren Vestergaard-Poulsen
Steven Koltes

Type of Firm

Private Firm Investing Own Capital

Industry Association Membership

British Venture Capital Association
European Venture Capital Association (EVCA)

Project Preferences

Role in Financing:

Prefer role as deal originator but will also invest in deals created by others

Type of Financing Preferred:

Leveraged Buyout

Geographical Preferences

International

Australia
Belgium
China
France
Germany
Italy
Luxembourg
Netherlands
Scandanavia/Nordic Region
Spain
United Kingdom

Industry Preferences

(% based on actual investment)

Industrial/Energy	33.1%
Other Products	31.4%
Communications and Media	21.2%
Consumer Related	9.6%
Semiconductors/Other Elect.	2.2%
Internet Specific	1.7%
Computer Hardware	0.6%
Computer Software and Services	0.1%

Additional Information

Name of Most Recent Fund: CVC European Equity Partners II L.P.
Most Recent Fund Was Raised: 07/01/1998
Year Founded: 1981
Capital Under Management: $2,200,000
Current Activity Level : Actively seeking new investments
Method of Compensation: Return on investment is of primary concern, do not charge fees

CYBERWORKS VENTURES

38/F Citibank Tower, Citibank
Plaza, 3 Garden Rd.
Central, Hong Kong
Phone: 852-2514-8888
Fax: 852-2524-4375
Website: www.pcg-group.com

Management and Staff

Alexander Arena, Managing Director
John Chen, Managing Director
Richard Li, Chairman & CEO

Type of Firm

Non-Financial Corp. Affiliate or Subsidiary

Project Preferences

Type of Financing Preferred:

Early Stage

Geographical Preferences

International

Hong Kong

Industry Preferences

Internet Specific

Internet

Additional Information

Current Activity Level : Actively seeking new investments

CYCLE & CARRIAGE INDUSTRIES PTE LTD

239 Alexandra Road
Singapore, Singapore 159930
Phone: 65-470-8113
Fax: 65-475-3881
Website: www.cyclecarriage.com.sg

Type of Firm
Non-Financial Corp. Affiliate or Subsidiary

Project Preferences

Type of Financing Preferred:
Balanced

Geographical Preferences

International
Singapore

Industry Preferences

Transportation
Transportation

Additional Information
Current Activity Level : Actively seeking new investments

CYGNUS VENTURE PARTNERS

4-10 Guildford Road
Chertsey
Surrey, United Kingdom KT16 9HH
Phone: 44-1932-562563
Fax: 44-1932-563041
E-mail: 101602.120@compuserve.com

Management and Staff
Bill Birkett, General Partner
Colin Pearce, General Partner

Whom to Contact
Nigel Keen

Type of Firm
Private Firm Investing Own Capital

Industry Association Membership
European Venture Capital Association (EVCA)

Project Preferences

Role in Financing:
Prefer role as deal originator

Type of Financing Preferred:
First Stage Financing
Research and Development
Second Stage Financing
Seed
Start-up Financing

Geographical Preferences

International
United Kingdom

Industry Preferences

(% based on actual investment)

Computer Hardware	50.7%
Medical/Health	32.1%
Other Products	10.1%
Consumer Related	3.6%
Biotechnology	2.6%
Computer Software and Services	0.9%

Additional Information
Name of Most Recent Fund: CIDC
Most Recent Fund Was Raised: 01/01/1997
Capital Under Management: $50,000,000
Current Activity Level : Inactive / Unknown
Method of Compensation: Return on invest. most important, but chg. closing fees, service fees, etc.

CZECH VENTURE PARTNERS SRO

Jureckova 1
Ostrava, Czech Republic CZ - 70100
Phone: 420-69-616-3500
Fax: 420-69-616-3501
E-mail: cvp@cvp.cz
Website: www.cvp.cz

Other Offices

Parizska 11
Prague, Czech Republic 11000
Phone: 42 0224 817 694
Fax: 42 0224 814 292

Management and Staff
Gijs Boot, Chief Executive Officer
Pavel Zabransky, Partner

Whom to Contact
L. Palata
P. Zabránsky

Type of Firm
Private Firm Investing Own Capital

Industry Association Membership
European Venture Capital Association (EVCA)

Project Preferences

Role in Financing:
Will function either as deal originator or investor in deals created by others

Type of Financing Preferred:
First Stage Financing
Leveraged Buyout
Second Stage Financing

Geographical Preferences

International
Czech Republic

Additional Information
Year Founded: 1997
Capital Under Management: $35,000,000
Current Activity Level : Actively seeking new investments
Method of Compensation: Return on invest. most important, but chg. closing fees, service fees, etc.

D. BRAIN CAPITAL COMPANY, LTD.

3-5-4 Shiba Koen
Minato-ku
Tokyo, Japan
Phone: 03-3435-8854
Fax: 03-3435-8787
Website: www.d-brain.co.jp

Type of Firm
Private Firm Investing Own Capital

Project Preferences

Type of Financing Preferred:
Balanced

Geographical Preferences

International
Japan

Industry Preferences

(% based on actual investment)

Consumer Related	46.8%
Internet Specific	30.5%
Other Products	11.3%
Communications and Media	8.8%
Computer Software and Services	2.2%
Medical/Health	0.4%

Additional Information
Capital Under Management: $10,800,000
Current Activity Level : Actively seeking new investments

DAEWOO VENTURE CAPITAL CO LTD

541, 5-ga, Namdaemun-ro
Chung-gu
Seoul, South Korea
Phone: 822-757-1291
Fax: 822-757-1297

Management and Staff
Sik Eui Park, President

Whom to Contact
Sang-Hyuk Lee

Type of Firm
Non-Financial Corp. Affiliate or Subsidiary

Project Preferences

Role in Financing:
Prefer role as deal originator but will also invest in deals created by others

Type of Financing Preferred:
First Stage Financing
Leveraged Buyout
Mezzanine

Size of Investments Considered
Min Size of Investment Considered (000s): $300
Max Size of Investment Considered: No Limit

Geographical Preferences

United States
All U.S.

International
Philippines
Thailand

Industry Preferences

Communications and Media
Commercial Communications
Data Communications
Other Communication Prod.

Computer Hardware
Computer Graphics and Dig

Internet Specific
Internet

Semiconductors/Other Elect.
Electronics
Sensors
Component Testing Equipmt
Analytic/Scientific

Biotechnology
Biosensors

Medical/Health
Diagnostic Services
Diagnostic Test Products
Medical Therapeutics

Consumer Related
Franchises(NEC)
Consumer Services
Education Related

Industrial/Energy
Alternative Energy
Environmental Related

Manufact.
Publishing

Additional Information
Name of Most Recent Fund: Daewoo No. 1 Venture
Most Recent Fund Was Raised: 09/01/1998
Year Founded: 1996
Capital Under Management: $33,300,000
Current Activity Level : Actively seeking new investments
Method of Compensation: Return on invest. most important, but chg. closing fees, service fees, etc.

DAIMLER CHRYSLER VENTURE GMBH (AKA DCV)

Epplestrasse 225
Stuttgart, Germany 70567
Phone: 49 711-17-92144
Fax: 49 711-17-97957
Website: www.dcventure.com

Other Offices

1510 Page Mill Road
Palo Alto, United States of America 94304
Phone: 650-845-2527
Fax: 650-845-2555

Management and Staff
Marianne Tumpen, Managing Director

Whom to Contact
Marianne Tuemper

Type of Firm
Non-Financial Corp. Affiliate or Subsidiary

Industry Association Membership
German Venture Capital Association

Project Preferences

Role in Financing:
Prefer role as deal originator but will also invest in deals created by others

Type of Financing Preferred:
Expansion
First Stage Financing
Management Buyouts
Second Stage Financing
Seed
Start-up Financing

Geographical Preferences

United States
All U.S.

International
Germany

Industry Preferences

Communications and Media
Commercial Communications
Telecommunications
Data Communications

Computer Hardware
Computer Graphics and Dig

Computer Software
Systems Software
Applications Software
Artificial Intelligence

Internet Specific
Internet

Semiconductors/Other Elect.
Electronic Components
Semiconductor
Sensors
Laser Related
Fiber Optics

Industrial/Energy
Robotics

Manufact.
Office Automation Equipmt

Additional Information
Year Founded: 1997
Capital Under Management: $20,000,000
Current Activity Level : Actively seeking new investments
Method of Compensation: Return on investment is of primary concern, do not charge fees

DAIWA BUSINESS INVESTMENT CO LTD, THE

Okura Honkan Bldg., 3/F
6-12, Ginza 2-chome, Chuo-ku
Tokyo, Japan 104
Phone: 813-3562-1851
Fax: 813-3562-1850

Other Offices

2-1-1, Bingo-machi 2-chome, Chuo-ku
Osaka, Japan 541
Phone: 06-6232-0052
Fax: 06-6232-0300

Management and Staff
Hirokazu Nagata, President

Type of Firm
Private Firm Investing Own Capital

Project Preferences

Role in Financing:
Prefer role as deal originator but will also invest in deals created by others

Type of Financing Preferred:
Mezzanine
Second Stage Financing

Size of Investments Considered
Min Size of Investment Considered (000s): $100
Max Size of Investment Considered (000s): $500

Geographical Preferences

International
Asia
Pacific Rim

Additional Information
Year Founded: 1986
Capital Under Management: $128,000,000
Current Activity Level : Actively seeking new investments
Method of Compensation: Return on investment is of primary concern, do not charge fees

DANISH DEVELOPMENT FINANCE CORP.

Gladsaxevej 376
Soborg, Denmark DK-2860
Phone: 45-39-660400
Fax: 45-39-661311
Website: www.danishventure.dk

Type of Firm
Private Firm Investing Own Capital

Project Preferences

Role in Financing:
Prefer role as deal originator but will also invest in deals created by others

Type of Financing Preferred:
First Stage Financing
Research and Development
Seed
Start-up Financing

Geographical Preferences

United States
All U.S.

International
Bermuda
United Kingdom

Industry Preferences

Communications and Media
Telecommunications
Data Communications
Satellite Microwave Comm.

Computer Hardware
Computer Graphics and Dig

Computer Software
Systems Software
Applications Software
Artificial Intelligence

Internet Specific
Internet

Semiconductors/Other Elect.
Electronic Components

Biotechnology
Industrial Biotechnology
Biotech Related Research
Biotech Related Research

Medical/Health
Medical Diagnostics
Diagnostic Services
Diagnostic Test Products
Medical Therapeutics
Disposable Med. Products

Consumer Related
Retail

Industrial/Energy
Factory Automation
Robotics

Additional Information
Year Founded: 1988
Capital Under Management: $90,000,000
Current Activity Level : Actively seeking new investments
Method of Compensation: Return on investment is of primary concern, do not charge fees

DANSK UDVIKLINGSFINANSIERIN G A/S

Gladsaxejev 376
Sxborg DK-2860, Denmark
Phone: 45-39-66-04-00
Fax: 45-39-66-13-11
Website: www.danishventure.dk

Management and Staff
Frede Morck, Partner
Kent Hansen, Managing Director
Linda Sjostrom, Partner
Ole Christensen, Partner
Peter Ibsen, Partner
Steen Helde Hemmingsen, Partner

Type of Firm
Private Firm Investing Own Capital

Industry Association Membership
European Venture Capital Association (EVCA)

Project Preferences

Type of Financing Preferred:
Early Stage
Seed
Startup

Geographical Preferences

United States
All U.S.

International
Denmark
Europe

Industry Preferences

Computer Software
Software

Computer Other
Computer Related

Semiconductors/Other Elect.
Electronics

Biotechnology
Biotechnology

Medical/Health
Medical/Health

Additional Information

Name of Most Recent Fund: Danish Venture Finance (FKA:Danish Development Finance Corp)
Most Recent Fund Was Raised: 01/01/1989
Year Founded: 1988
Capital Under Management: $66,700,000
Current Activity Level : Actively seeking new investments

DANSKE EVENTURES

Lyngbyvej 20
Copenhagen, Denmark 2100
Phone: 45-70-26-66-86
Fax: 45-70-26-66-96
Website: www.danskeeventures.com

Management and Staff

Claus Hojbjerg Andersen, Partner
Eva Reman, Partner
Hendrik Albertsen, Managing Director
Lars Jorgensen, Partner
Peter Tottrup, Partner
Soren Jessen Nielsen, Partner

Type of Firm

Investment/Merchant Bank Subsid/Affil

Industry Association Membership

European Venture Capital Association (EVCA)

Project Preferences

Type of Financing Preferred:
Balanced

Geographical Preferences

International
Scandanavia/Nordic Region

Industry Preferences

Communications and Media
Telecommunications

Computer Software
Software

Internet Specific
Internet

Business Serv.
Media

Additional Information

Year Founded: 2000
Capital Under Management: $170,000,000
Current Activity Level : Actively seeking new investments

DASSAULT DEVELOPPMENT

8 avenue Franklin Roosevelt
Paris, France F-75008
Phone: 33-1-5688-3200
Fax: 33-1-5688-3209
Website: www.dassault-developpement.fr

Management and Staff

Benoit Habert, Partner
Jean-Claude Leveque, Partner
Jean-Marie Chauvet, Partner
Luc Lechelle, Partner

Type of Firm

Non-Financial Corp. Affiliate or Subsidiary

Industry Association Membership

European Venture Capital Association (EVCA)

Project Preferences

Type of Financing Preferred:
Early Stage
Expansion
Start-up Financing

Geographical Preferences

United States
All U.S.

International
Europe

Industry Preferences

(% based on actual investment)

Internet Specific	44.5%
Semiconductors/Other Elect.	23.4%
Other Products	10.6%
Computer Software and Services	7.9%
Consumer Related	7.3%
Communications and Media	4.6%
Biotechnology	1.7%

Additional Information

Year Founded: 1995
Capital Under Management: $46,900,000
Current Activity Level : Actively seeking new investments

DB VENTURE PARTNERS

Tower 42 Level 40
25 Old Broad Street
London, United Kingdom EC2N 1HQ
Phone: 44-207-9717000
Fax: 44-207-9717455
Website: www.db.com

Management and Staff

Maggie Abrahams, Vice President
Michael Patton, Managing Director
Roy Merritt, Managing Director

Type of Firm

Investment/Merchant Bank Subsid/Affil

Project Preferences

Type of Financing Preferred:
Balanced
Early Stage
Startup

Geographical Preferences

International
Europe
Israel

Industry Preferences

Communications and Media
Telecommunications

Internet Specific
Internet

Additional Information

Year Founded: 2000
Capital Under Management: $915,600,000
Current Activity Level : Actively seeking new investments

DEFTA PARTNERS

Greyhound House c/o Pond Venture
23-24 George Street
Richmond, Surrey, United Kingdom TW9 1H
Phone: 0181-940-1001
Fax: 0181-332-6751

See California for full listing.

DELTA PARTNERS

South County Business Park
Leopardstown
Dublin, Ireland, Republic of 18
Phone: 353-1-294-0870
Fax: 353-1-294-0877
Website: www.delta.ie

Management and Staff
Dermot Berkery, General Partner
Maurice Roche, General Partner
Shay Garvey, General Partner

Whom to Contact
Dermot Bekery

Type of Firm
Private Firm Investing Own Capital

Industry Association Membership
European Venture Capital Association (EVCA)

Project Preferences

Role in Financing:
Prefer role as deal originator but will also invest in deals created by others

Type of Financing Preferred:
Second Stage Financing

Geographical Preferences

International
France
Germany
United Kingdom

Industry Preferences

(% based on actual investment)

Internet Specific	61.1%
Computer Software and Services	22.6%
Biotechnology	5.9%
Semiconductors/Other Elect.	5.3%
Communications and Media	5.1%

Additional Information
Name of Most Recent Fund: Bank of Ireland Entrepreneurs Fund, L.P.
Most Recent Fund Was Raised: 04/01/1997
Year Founded: 1994
Capital Under Management: $37,000,000
Current Activity Level : Actively seeking new investments
Method of Compensation: Return on investment is of primary concern, do not charge fees

DELTA VENTURES

85 Medinat Hayeudim st.
14th Floor
Hertzelia Pituach, Israel 46766
Phone: 972-9-951-7755
Fax: 972-9-951-7799
Website: www.delta-ventures.com

Management and Staff
Ben Harel, General Partner
Lilach Pe'er, Chief Financial Officer
Ofer Timor, General Partner

Type of Firm
Private Firm Investing Own Capital

Project Preferences

Type of Financing Preferred:
Early Stage
Seed

Geographical Preferences

International
Asia
Israel
Philippines

Industry Preferences

Communications and Media
Communications and Media

Computer Software
Software

Internet Specific
Internet

Semiconductors/Other Elect.
Electronics
Semiconductor

Additional Information
Name of Most Recent Fund: Delta Fund I
Most Recent Fund Was Raised: 02/02/2000
Capital Under Management: $60,000,000
Current Activity Level : Actively seeking new investments

DEUTSCHE ASSET MANAGEMENT (AUSTRALIA) LIMITED

85 Clarence Street
Level 21
Sydney, Australia 2000
Phone: 612-9249-9000
Fax: 612-9249-9795
Website: www.db.com/dam/australia

Type of Firm
Investment/Merchant Bank Investing Own or Client Funds

Industry Association Membership
Australian Venture Capital Association (AVCAL)

Project Preferences

Type of Financing Preferred:
Expansion
Management Buyouts
Mezzanine

Geographical Preferences

International
Australia
New Zealand

Industry Preferences

(% based on actual investment)

Industrial/Energy	54.5%
Other Products	35.2%
Internet Specific	10.3%

Additional Information
Year Founded: 1994
Capital Under Management: $520,100,000
Current Activity Level : Actively seeking new investments

DEUTSCHE BANK EVENTURES (AKA DB EVENTURES)

1 Great Winchester Street
London, United Kingdom EC2N 2DB
Phone: 44 20 7545 8836
Fax: 44 20 7545 4314
Website: www.dbeventures.com

Management and Staff
Scott Moeller, Managing Director

Type of Firm
Investment/Merchant Bank Investing Own or Client Funds

Project Preferences

Type of Financing Preferred:
First Stage Financing
Mezzanine
Second Stage Financing

Geographical Preferences

International
All International

Industry Preferences

(% based on actual investment)

Computer Software and Services	58.9%
Internet Specific	31.7%
Communications and Media	6.4%
Computer Hardware	3.0%

Additional Information
Year Founded: 2000
Current Activity Level : Actively seeking new investments

DEUTSCHE BETEILIGUNGS AG

Emil-von-Behring-Strasse 2
Frankfurt, Germany D-60349
Phone: 49-69-957-8701
Fax: 49-69-957-87390
Website: www.deutsche-beteiligung.de

Type of Firm
Private Firm Investing Own Capital

Industry Association Membership
European Venture Capital Association (EVCA)
German Venture Capital Association

Project Preferences

Role in Financing:
Prefer role as deal originator but will also invest in deals created by others

Type of Financing Preferred:
Balanced
Expansion
Leveraged Buyout
Management Buyouts
Recapitalizations

Geographical Preferences

United States
All U.S.

International
Asia
France
Germany
Italy
United Kingdom

Additional Information
Year Founded: 1965
Capital Under Management: $453,500,000
Current Activity Level : Actively seeking new investments

DEUTSCHE EFFECTEN UND WECHSEL-BETEILIGUNGS GESELLSCHAFT AG

Carl-Zeiss-Strasse 1
Jena, Germany 07743
Phone: 49 3641-65-2230
Fax: 49 3641-65-2486
Website: www.dewb-vc.com

Management and Staff
Dietmar Kubis, Chief Executive Officer

Type of Firm
Private Firm Investing Own Capital

Industry Association Membership
German Venture Capital Association

Project Preferences

Type of Financing Preferred:
Expansion
Seed
Startup

Geographical Preferences

International
Europe
Germany

Industry Preferences

Communications and Media
Telecommunications

Semiconductors/Other Elect.
Fiber Optics

Biotechnology
Biotechnology

Additional Information
Year Founded: 1872
Current Activity Level : Actively seeking new investments

DEUTSCHE VENTURE CAPITAL GMBH (DVCG)

Emil von Behring Strasse 2
Frankfurt, Germany 60439
Phone: 49-6-957-0060
Fax: 49-69-570-6200
Website: www.dvcg.de

Other Offices

Charlottenstrasse 65
Berlin, Germany 10117
Phone: 49-302-062-9440
Fax: 49-302-062-9450

Innere Wiener Strasse 13
Munich, Germany 81667
Phone: 49-894-580-8330
Fax: 49-894-580-8353

Menlo Park, United States of America

Management and Staff
Dirk Meurer, Partner
Frank Schuhardt, Partner
Hansjoerg Thomas, General Partner
Joachim Von Lohr, Partner
Jorg Neermann, Partner
Kai Brandes, Partner
Stephan Uhlmann, Partner
Werner Schauerte, Managing Director

Type of Firm
Private Firm Investing Own Capital

Industry Association Membership
European Venture Capital Association (EVCA)

Project Preferences

Type of Financing Preferred:
Early Stage
Expansion
Seed
Startup

Size of Investments Considered
Min Size of Investment Considered (000s): $500
Max Size of Investment Considered (000s): $500,000

Geographical Preferences

International
Austria
Germany
Switzerland

Industry Preferences

(% based on actual investment)

Biotechnology	50.4%
Internet Specific	31.0%
Computer Software and Services	18.6%

Additional Information

Name of Most Recent Fund: Deutsche Venture Capital GmbH Fund II
Most Recent Fund Was Raised: 06/01/1998
Year Founded: 1998
Capital Under Management: $288,700,000
Current Activity Level : Actively seeking new investments

DIRECT CAPITAL PRIVATE EQUITY

6/F, 2 Kitchener Street
Auckland, New Zealand 6466
Phone: 649-307-2562
Fax: 649-307-2349
Website: www.directcapital.co.nz

Management and Staff

Ross George, Managing Director

Type of Firm

Private Firm Investing Own Capital

Industry Association Membership

Australian Venture Capital Association (AVCAL)

Project Preferences

Role in Financing:
Prefer role as deal originator but will also invest in deals created by others

Type of Financing Preferred:
Acquisition
Expansion
Management Buyouts

Size of Investments Considered

Min Size of Investment Considered (000s): $3,000
Max Size of Investment Considered (000s): $13,000

Geographical Preferences

International
Asia
Australia
Oceania/Australasia

Industry Preferences

Computer Software
Computer Services

Semiconductors/Other Elect.
Electronic Components

Biotechnology
Biotechnology

Medical/Health
Medical/Health

Consumer Related
Entertainment and Leisure
Food/Beverage

Transportation
Transportation
Aerospace

Manufact.
Manufacturing

Additional Information

Year Founded: 1994
Capital Under Management: $23,400,000
Current Activity Level : Actively seeking new investments
Method of Compensation: Return on invest. most important, but chg. closing fees, service fees, etc.

DISCOVERY CAPITAL

5th Floor
1199 West Hastings
Vancouver, Canada V6E 3T5
Phone: 604-683-3000
Fax: 604-662-3457
E-mail: info@discoverycapital.com
Website: www.discoverycapital.com

Management and Staff

Randy Garg, Chief Financial Officer

Type of Firm

Incubators

Project Preferences

Role in Financing:
Prefer role as deal originator

Type of Financing Preferred:
Early Stage
Startup

Geographical Preferences

Canada
British Columbia
All Canada

Industry Preferences

Internet Specific
Internet

Additional Information

Year Founded: 1986
Current Activity Level : Actively seeking new investments

DONGBU VENTURE CAPITAL CO LTD

36-5 Yoido-dong
Yongdungpo-gu
Seoul, South Korea
Phone: 822-784-8250/4
Fax: 822-784-8350
Website: www.dongbu.com.kr

Management and Staff

Byung-Hwa Oh, President
Jae Ku Wooh, President
Tark Won Chung, President

Whom to Contact

Jae-Joon Yoo

Type of Firm

Private Firm Investing Own Capital

Project Preferences

Role in Financing:
Prefer role as deal originator but will also invest in deals created by others

Type of Financing Preferred:
First Stage Financing
Research and Development
Second Stage Financing

Size of Investments Considered

Min Size of Investment Considered (000s): $100
Max Size of Investment Considered (000s): $500

Geographical Preferences

United States
All U.S.

International
Asia

Industry Preferences

Communications and Media
Commercial Communications
CATV & Pay TV Systems

Computer Hardware
Mainframes / Scientific

Computer Software
Systems Software

Semiconductors/Other Elect.
Electronic Components
Semiconductor
Analytic/Scientific

Medical/Health
Diagnostic Test Products

Consumer Related
Retail
Food/Beverage
Consumer Products

Industrial/Energy
Energy Conservation Relat
Machinery
Environmental Related

Business Serv.
Consulting Services

Additional Information
Year Founded: 1989
Capital Under Management: $20,000,000
Current Activity Level : Actively seeking new investments
Method of Compensation: Return on invest. most important, but chg. closing fees, service fees, etc.

DOR VENTURES

16 Hagalim Ave.
Delta House, 2nd Floor
Herzliya, Israel
Phone: 09-959-4990
Fax: 09-959-4898
Website: www.dorventures.com

Management and Staff
Arie Rosenfeld, Managing Director
Ilan Neugarten, Managing Director

Type of Firm
Private Firm Investing Own Capital

Project Preferences

Type of Financing Preferred:
Early Stage

Geographical Preferences

United States
All U.S.

International
Europe
Israel

Additional Information
Current Activity Level : Actively seeking new investments

DOW CHEMICAL CO.

Europe Headquarters
Admin & R&D
Horgen, Switzerland
Phone: 41-1-728-2468
Fax: 41-1-728-2097

See Michigan for full listing.

DOWNER & CO.

24, rue du Quatre Septembre
Paris, France 75002
Phone: 33-1-4742-4488
Fax: 33-1-4742-1993

See Massachusetts for full listing.

DRAPER INTERNATIONAL

203-204 Prestige Meridian
M.G. Road
Bangalore, India 560001
Phone: 91805550325
Fax: 91805550461

See California for full listing.

DRESDNER KLEINWORT CAPITAL

PO Box 18075 Riverbank House
2 Swan Lane
London, United Kingdom EC4R 3UX

See New York for full listing.

DRUG ROYALTY CORP., INC.

Eight King Street East
Suite 202
Toronto, Canada M5C 1B5
Phone: 416-863-1865
Fax: 416-863-5161

Management and Staff
Harry K. Loveys
James Webster

Whom to Contact
Harry K. Loveys
James Webster

Project Preferences

Role in Financing:
Prefer role as deal originator

Type of Financing Preferred:
Research and Development
Special Situation

Size of Investments Considered
Min Size of Investment Considered (000s): $3,000
Max Size of Investment Considered (000s): $4,000

Geographical Preferences

International
No Preference

Industry Preferences

Biotechnology
Biotechnology

Medical/Health
Medical/Health

Additional Information
Year Founded: 1989
Capital Under Management: $60,000,000
Current Activity Level : Actively seeking new investments
Method of Compensation: Return on investment is of primary concern, do not charge fees

DRYSDALE ENTERPRISES

Marsman Drysdale Building
2246 Pasong Tamo Street
Metro Manila, Philippines
Phone: 632-894-4228
Fax: 632-815-9442

See California for full listing.

DSE INVESTMENT SERVICES LIMITED

38/F Dah Sing Financial Ctr
108 Gloucester Road
Wanchai, Hong Kong
Phone: 852-2845-7420
Fax: 852-2598-8941

Management and Staff
Nicholas Mayhew, Managing Director

Whom to Contact
Roger Perrin

Type of Firm
Investment/Merchant Bank Subsid/Affil

Industry Association Membership
Hungarian Venture Capital Association

Project Preferences

Role in Financing:
Prefer role as deal originator but will also invest in deals created by others

Type of Financing Preferred:
Balanced
Early Stage
Expansion
Later Stage
Mezzanine
Turnaround

Geographical Preferences

International
China
Hong Kong

Industry Preferences

Communications and Media
Telecommunications

Semiconductors/Other Elect.
Electronic Components

Medical/Health
Pharmaceuticals

Consumer Related
Entertainment and Leisure
Food/Beverage
Consumer Products
Consumer Services

Industrial/Energy
Machinery

Financial Services
Financial Services

Business Serv.
Distribution

Additional Information
Year Founded: 1995
Capital Under Management: $60,000,000
Current Activity Level : Actively seeking new investments
Method of Compensation: Return on invest. most important, but chg. closing fees, service fees, etc.

DUNEDIN CAPITAL PARTNERS LTD (FKA:DUNEDIN VENTURES LIMITED)

Napier House
27 Thistle Street
Edinburgh, United Kingdom EH2 1BT
Phone: 44-131-225-6699
Fax: 44-131-624-1234
Website: www.dunedin-capital.com

Management and Staff
Brian Finlayson, Partner
Dougal Bennett, Partner
Mark Ligertwood, Partner
Ross Marshall, Managing Director
Shaun Middleton, Partner
Simon Miller, Partner

Type of Firm
Private Firm Investing Own Capital

Industry Association Membership
British Venture Capital Association

Project Preferences

Role in Financing:
Prefer role as deal originator but will also invest in deals created by others

Type of Financing Preferred:
Leveraged Buyout

Geographical Preferences

International
United Kingdom

Industry Preferences

Communications and Media
Communications and Media

Semiconductors/Other Elect.
Electronic Components

Consumer Related
Consumer

Industrial/Energy
Energy
Industrial Products

Business Serv.
Distribution

Additional Information
Name of Most Recent Fund: Dunedin Enterprise Investment Trust PLC
Most Recent Fund Was Raised: 01/01/1987
Year Founded: 1987
Capital Under Management: $146,100,000
Current Activity Level : Actively seeking new investments
Method of Compensation: Return on invest. most important, but chg. closing fees, service fees, etc.

DURLACHER LIMITED

4 Chiswell Street
London, United Kingdom EC1Y 4UP
Phone: 44 20 7628 4306
Fax: 44 20 7638 8848
Website: www.durlacher.com

Management and Staff
Geoffrey Chamberlain, Chairman & CEO

Type of Firm
Affiliate/Subsidary of Oth. Financial. Instit.

Project Preferences

Type of Financing Preferred:
Balanced
Early Stage
Startup

Geographical Preferences

International
United Kingdom
No Preference

Industry Preferences

Internet Specific
Internet

Biotechnology
Biotechnology

Medical/Health
Medical/Health

Additional Information

Current Activity Level : Actively seeking new investments

DYNAFUND VENTURES, L.L.C.

525 University Avenue
Suite 610
Taipei, Taiwan 94301
Phone: 650-321-8160
Fax: 650-321-8159

See California for full listing.

E-MERGE

rue de la Technologie 35
Bruxelles, Belgium 1082
Phone: 32 2 464 28 44
Fax: 32 2 465 08 30
Website: www.e-merge.be

Management and Staff

Laurent Drion, Chief Executive Officer

Type of Firm

Incubators

Project Preferences

Type of Financing Preferred:
Early Stage
Startup

Geographical Preferences

International
Belgium

Industry Preferences

(% based on actual investment)

Additional Information

Year Founded: 1998
Current Activity Level : Actively seeking new investments

E4E INC.

Divyashree Chambers
Langford Road, 3rd Floor
Bangalore , India 560 025
Phone: 91-80-207-2140
Fax: 91-80-207-2186

See California for full listing.

EARLYBIRD VENTURE CAPITAL

Van-der-Smissen Strasse 3
Hamburg, Germany 22767
Phone: 49-40-432-9410
Fax: 49-40-432-94129
Website: www.earlybird.com

Other Offices

525 University Avenue
Suite 410
Palo Alto, United States of America 94301
Phone: 650-530-3633
Fax: 650-330-3634

Maximilianstrasse 14
Munich, Germany 80539
Phone: 49-89-2907-020
Fax: 49-89-2907-0222

Management and Staff

Christian Nagel, Partner
Hendrik Brandis, Partner
Roland Manger, Partner
Rolf Mathies, Partner
Steven Ciesinski, Partner
Vera Kallmeyer, Partner

Type of Firm

Private Firm Investing Own Capital

Industry Association Membership

European Venture Capital Association (EVCA)
National Venture Capital Association (NVCA)

Project Preferences

Type of Financing Preferred:
Early Stage
Expansion
Later Stage
Seed
Startup

Size of Investments Considered

Min Size of Investment Considered (000s): $500
Max Size of Investment Considered (000s): $500,000

Geographical Preferences

United States
All U.S.
All U.S.

International
Europe
Germany
Israel

Industry Preferences

(% based on actual investment)

Internet Specific	74.9%
Computer Software and Services	8.8%
Medical/Health	6.4%
Biotechnology	3.8%
Computer Hardware	2.7%
Semiconductors/Other Elect.	2.4%
Communications and Media	1.1%

Additional Information

Year Founded: 1997
Capital Under Management: $300,000,000
Current Activity Level : Actively seeking new investments

EBM SOCIEDAD GESTORA DE ENTIDADES DE CAPITAL RIESGO SA

Almagro 46
Madrid, Spain 28010
Phone: 34 91 700 9800
Fax: 34 91 700 9829
E-mail: capitalriesgo@bnbanco.com

Type of Firm

Investment/Merchant Bank Subsid/Affil

Industry Association Membership

Spanish Venture Capital Association

Project Preferences

Type of Financing Preferred:
Unknown

Geographical Preferences

International
Spain

Additional Information

Year Founded: 1999
Capital Under Management: $62,600,000
Current Activity Level : Actively seeking new investments

ECAT DEVELOPMENT CAPITAL LIMITED

Level 13, The Forrest Centre,
221 St George's Terrace
Perth, Australia 6000
Phone: 618-9481-3733
Fax: 618-9321-1523
Website: www.ecatdc.com.au

Management and Staff

Adam Rankine-Wilson, Managing Director

Type of Firm

Private Firm Investing Own Capital

Project Preferences

Type of Financing Preferred:

Mezzanine
Seed

Geographical Preferences

International

Australia

Industry Preferences

(% based on actual investment)

Other Products	46.2%
Internet Specific	23.0%
Computer Software and Services	16.0%
Industrial/Energy	7.6%
Biotechnology	7.2%

Additional Information

Year Founded: 1999
Capital Under Management: $6,300,000
Current Activity Level : Actively seeking new investments

ECI VENTURES LTD

Brettenham House
Lancaster Place
London, United Kingdom WC2E 7EN
Phone: 44-20-7606-1000
Fax: 44-20-7240-5050
Website: www.eciv.co.uk

Other Offices

Royal House
Sovereign Street
Leeds, United Kingdom LS1 4BJ
Phone: 44 113- 234 3401
Fax: 44 113- 234 3402

St Andrews Chambers
20 Albert Square
Manchester, United Kingdom M2 5PE
Phone: 44 161-831 3200
Fax: 44 161-831 3201

Management and Staff

Janet Brooks

Whom to Contact

Janet Brooks

Type of Firm

Private Firm Investing Own Capital

Industry Association Membership

British Venture Capital Association

Project Preferences

Role in Financing:

Prefer role as deal originator but will also invest in deals created by others

Type of Financing Preferred:

Control-block Purchases
Expansion
Industry Rollups
Leveraged Buyout
Management Buyouts
Recapitalizations
Second Stage Financing
Special Situation

Size of Investments Considered

Min Size of Investment Considered (000s): $1,500
Max Size of Investment Considered: No Limit

Geographical Preferences

International

United Kingdom

Industry Preferences

(% based on actual investment)

Industrial/Energy	30.8%
Consumer Related	30.4%
Other Products	22.4%
Computer Software and Services	8.9%
Communications and Media	6.1%
Biotechnology	0.7%
Medical/Health	0.7%
Internet Specific	0.1%

Additional Information

Name of Most Recent Fund: ECI 6
Most Recent Fund Was Raised: 01/01/1997
Year Founded: 1976
Capital Under Management: $499,700,000
Current Activity Level : Actively seeking new investments
Method of Compensation: Return on invest. most important, but chg. closing fees, service fees, etc.

ECICS VENTURES PTE LTD.

7 Temasek Blvd. #11-01
Suntec, Tower One
Singapore, Singapore 038987
Phone: 65-337-4780
Fax: 65-338-9778

Management and Staff

Patrick Yang, Vice President

Type of Firm

Non-Financial Corp. Affiliate or Subsidiary

Project Preferences

Role in Financing:

Prefer role in deals created by others

Type of Financing Preferred:

Balanced
First Stage Financing
Mezzanine
Research and Development
Second Stage Financing
Seed
Special Situation
Startup

Geographical Preferences

United States

All U.S.
California

International

Asia
Eastern Europe
All International
Pacific Rim

Industry Preferences

Communications and Media

Communications and Media
Radio & TV Broadcasting
Telecommunications

Internet Specific

Internet

Computer Other
Computer Related

Semiconductors/Other Elect.
Electronic Components

Biotechnology
Biotechnology

Medical/Health
Medical/Health
Pharmaceuticals

Consumer Related
Entertainment and Leisure
Food/Beverage
Consumer Services

Transportation
Transportation

Financial Services
Financial Services

Additional Information
Year Founded: 1993
Capital Under Management: $30,200,000
Current Activity Level : Actively seeking new investments
Method of Compensation: Return on investment is of primary concern, do not charge fees

ECM EQUITY CAPITAL MANAGEMENT GMBH

Oberlindau 80
Frankfurt/Main, Germany 60323
Phone: 49 69 971020
Fax: 49 69 9710224
E-mail: info@ecm-ffm.de
Website: www.ecm-gmbh.de

Management and Staff
Stefan Rebmann, Managing Director

Type of Firm
Private Firm Investing Own Capital

Industry Association Membership
German Venture Capital Association

Project Preferences

Type of Financing Preferred:
Expansion
Management Buyouts
Mezzanine
Turnaround

Geographical Preferences

International
Germany

Additional Information
Capital Under Management: $175,500,000
Current Activity Level : Actively seeking new investments

EDB INVESTMENTS PTE LTD.

250 North Bridge Rd.
#27-04 Raffles City Tower
Singapore, Singapore 179101
Phone: 65-832-6597
Fax: 65-336-2503
Website: www.edbi.com

Other Offices

210 Twin Dolphin Drive
Redwood City, United States of America 94065-1402
Phone: 650-591-9102
Fax: 650-591-1328

Management and Staff
Heng Soon Pang, Vice President
Leok Yeen Loh, Vice President
Natasha Foong, Vice President

Type of Firm
State Govt Affiliated NEC

Industry Association Membership
Singapore Venture Capital Association

Project Preferences

Type of Financing Preferred:
Early Stage
Expansion
Seed
Startup

Geographical Preferences

United States
All U.S.

International
Asia
Israel
Singapore
Western Europe

Industry Preferences

Communications and Media
Communications and Media
Telecommunications
Wireless Communications

Internet Specific
E-Commerce Technology

Computer Other
Computer Related

Semiconductors/Other Elect.
Electronic Components

Biotechnology
Biotechnology

Consumer Related
Retail
Consumer Services

Industrial/Energy
Industrial Products

Financial Services
Financial Services

Additional Information
Year Founded: 1991
Capital Under Management: $120,800,000
Current Activity Level : Actively seeking new investments
Method of Compensation: Return on investment is of primary concern, do not charge fees

EDMOND DE ROTHSCHILD VENTURE CAPITAL MANAGEMENT

The Technology Park
Building 8
Manhat, Jerusalem, Israel 96251
Phone: 972-2-649-0670
Fax: 972-2-649-0680
Website: www.rothschild.co.il

Management and Staff
Samuel Katz, Vice President

Type of Firm
Private Firm Investing Own Capital

Project Preferences

Type of Financing Preferred:
Balanced

Geographical Preferences

International
Israel

Additional Information
Year Founded: 2000
Capital Under Management: $30,000,000
Current Activity Level : Actively seeking new investments

EFICOR OYJ

Kalevankatu 4
Helsinki, Finland 00101
Phone: 358-9-686-280
Fax: 358-9-6862-8203
Website: www.eficor.com

Management and Staff
Jouko Virta, Chief Financial Officer
Kai Luotonen, Managing Director
Pekka Pere, Managing Director
Terho Mussalo, Managing Director
Villie Haataja, Chief Executive Officer

Type of Firm
Private Firm Investing Own Capital

Project Preferences

Type of Financing Preferred:
Later Stage
Startup

Geographical Preferences

International
Finland

Industry Preferences

Internet Specific
Internet

Additional Information
Year Founded: 2000
Capital Under Management: $7,700,000
Current Activity Level : Actively seeking new investments

EIRCOM ENTERPRISE FUND LTD.

114 St. Stephen's Green West
Dublin, Ireland, Republic of 2
Phone: 353 1/701.51.30
Fax: 353 1/679.72.53
Website: www.eircom-enterprise-fund.ie

Type of Firm
Non-Financial Corp. Affiliate or Subsidiary

Industry Association Membership
European Venture Capital Association (EVCA)

Project Preferences

Type of Financing Preferred:
Early Stage
Seed
Start-up Financing

Geographical Preferences

International
Ireland

Industry Preferences

Communications and Media
Communications and Media
Telecommunications

Business Serv.
Media

Additional Information
Year Founded: 1998
Capital Under Management: $2,400,000
Current Activity Level : Actively seeking new investments

ELDERSTREET INVESTMENTS LTD

32 Bedford Row
London, United Kingdom WC1R 4HE
Phone: 44-207-831-5088
Fax: 44-207-831-5077
Website: www.elderstreet.com

Management and Staff
Chris Kay, Managing Director
Michael Jackson, Founder
Paul Frew, Managing Director

Type of Firm
Private Firm Investing Own Capital

Industry Association Membership
British Venture Capital Association

Project Preferences

Type of Financing Preferred:
Early Stage
Expansion
Management Buyouts
Recapitalizations
Turnaround

Geographical Preferences

International
Europe
United Kingdom
Western Europe

Industry Preferences

(% based on actual investment)

Internet Specific	61.6%
Computer Software and Services	29.3%
Communications and Media	6.3%
Consumer Related	1.7%
Semiconductors/Other Elect.	1.1%

Additional Information
Name of Most Recent Fund: Elderstreet Investor Club
Most Recent Fund Was Raised: 12/31/1999
Year Founded: 1990
Capital Under Management: $158,800,000
Current Activity Level : Actively seeking new investments

ELECTRA PARTNERS ASIA [FKA: JF ELECTRA LIMITED]

46/F Jardine House
1 Connaught Place
Central, Hong Kong
Phone: 852-2530-8700
Fax: 852-2530-5525
Website: www.jfleming.com

Other Offices

Amerchand Mansion
16 Madame Cama Road
Mumbai, India 400001
Phone: 92-2283-5841
Fax: 912-2288-3284

Management and Staff
Andrew Russell
Anne Farlow

Whom to Contact
Andrew Russell
Anne Farlow

Type of Firm
Investment/Merchant Bank Subsid/Affil

Project Preferences

Role in Financing:
Prefer role as deal originator but will also invest in deals created by others

Type of Financing Preferred:
Acquisition
Distressed Debt
Leveraged Buyout
Management Buyouts
Mezzanine
Recapitalizations
Second Stage Financing
Special Situation

Geographical Preferences

International
Australia
China
Hong Kong
India
Korea, South
Malaysia
Philippines
Singapore
Thailand

Industry Preferences

(% based on actual investment)

Communications and Media	29.9%
Other Products	24.3%
Computer Hardware	15.0%
Computer Software and Services	14.0%
Internet Specific	9.3%
Industrial/Energy	5.6%
Semiconductors/Other Elect.	1.9%

Additional Information
Name of Most Recent Fund: Swiss Life Private Equity China Fund, The
Most Recent Fund Was Raised: 09/01/1999
Year Founded: 1995
Capital Under Management: $50,000,000
Current Activity Level : Actively seeking new investments
Method of Compensation: Return on invest. most important, but chg. closing fees, service fees, etc.

EMERGING MARKETS PARTNERSHIP

#35-01 Singapore Land Tower
50 Raffles Place
Singapore, Singapore 048623
Phone: 65-227-0550
Fax: 65-227-0440

See D. of Columbia for full listing.

EMERGING TECHNOLOGIES

Biblioteksgatan 29
P.O. Box 5754
Stockholm, Sweden SE-114 87
Phone: 08-555 220 00
Fax: 08-555 220 99
Website: www.emergingtechnologies.se

Management and Staff
Alf Blomqvist, Partner
Anders Barsk, Venture Partner
Bernt Andersson, Chief Financial Officer
Bjorn Algkvist, Venture Partner
Fredrik Fredrik, Partner
Jim Blomgren, Partner
Lars Ahlman, Venture Partner
Lennart Johansson, Partner
Per Wassen, Partner
Peter Sandberg, President
Stefan Wigren, Venture Partner

Type of Firm
Private Equity Advisor or Fund of Fund Mgr

Industry Association Membership
Swedish Venture Capital Association

Project Preferences

Type of Financing Preferred:
Early Stage
Expansion
Seed
Startup

Geographical Preferences

International
All International

Industry Preferences

Communications and Media
Telecommunications

Internet Specific
Internet

Additional Information
Year Founded: 2000
Capital Under Management: $276,100,000
Current Activity Level : Actively seeking new investments

ENDEAVOUR CAPITAL PTY LTD

Level 4, 280 George Street
Sydney, Australia 2001
Phone: 612-9223-1131
Fax: 612-9223-7329
Website: www.endeavourcapital.com.au

Management and Staff
Peter Wallace, Managing Director

Type of Firm
Private Firm Investing Own Capital

Industry Association Membership
Australian Venture Capital Association (AVCAL)

Project Preferences

Type of Financing Preferred:
Early Stage
Expansion
Management Buyouts

Size of Investments Considered
Min Size of Investment Considered (000s): $700
Max Size of Investment Considered (000s): $3,300

Geographical Preferences

International
Oceania/Australasia

Industry Preferences

(% based on actual investment)

Consumer Related	42.9%
Communications and Media	22.0%
Semiconductors/Other Elect.	17.3%
Other Products	10.1%
Biotechnology	7.6%

Additional Information
Year Founded: 1998
Capital Under Management: $18,100,000
Current Activity Level : Actively seeking new investments

ENRON BROADBAND VENTURES

40 Grosvenor Place
London, United Kingdom SW1X 7EN
Phone: 44-20-7783-0000

See Texas for full listing.

ENTERPRISE EQUITY (NI) LIMITED

78a Dublin Road
Belfast, N. Ireland, United Kingdom BT2 7HP
Phone: 44 1232-242500
Fax: 44-1232-242487
Website: www.eeni.com

Other Offices

Enterprise Equity Ireland Ltd
Dublin Road
Dundalk County Louth, Ireland, Republic of
Phone: 353 42/933.31.67
Fax: 353 42/933.48.57

Management and Staff

Bob McGowan-Smyth, Chief Executive Officer
Conor O'Connor, Chief Executive Officer

Type of Firm

Private Firm Investing Own Capital

Industry Association Membership

British Venture Capital Association
European Venture Capital Association (EVCA)

Project Preferences

Role in Financing:

Prefer role as deal originator but will also invest in deals created by others

Type of Financing Preferred:

First Stage Financing
Leveraged Buyout
Second Stage Financing
Start-up Financing

Size of Investments Considered

Min Size of Investment Considered (000s): $100
Max Size of Investment Considered (000s): $100,000

Geographical Preferences

International

Ireland
United Kingdom

Industry Preferences

Communications and Media

Data Communications

Computer Software

Computer Services
Applications Software

Internet Specific

Internet

Semiconductors/Other Elect.

Semiconductor
Sensors
Component Testing Equipmt
Analytic/Scientific

Biotechnology

Industrial Biotechnology
Biosensors

Medical/Health

Medical Diagnostics
Diagnostic Services
Diagnostic Test Products
Drug/Equipmt Delivery
Medical Products

Consumer Related

Entertainment and Leisure
Food/Beverage
Consumer Products

Industrial/Energy

Alternative Energy
Industrial Products
Factory Automation

Manufact.

Publishing

Agr/Forestr/Fish

Agriculture related

Additional Information

Year Founded: 1987
Capital Under Management: $20,000,000
Current Activity Level : Actively seeking new investments
Method of Compensation: Return on invest. most important, but chg. closing fees, service fees, etc.

ENTERPRISE INVESTORS

Atrium Tower
Al. Jana Pawla II 25
Warsaw, Poland 00-854
Phone: 22 653-4500
Fax: 22 653-4555

See New York for full listing.

ENTERPRISEASIA.COM

Room 5707, 57/F, The Center
99 Queen's Road, Central
Hong Kong, Hong Kong
Phone: 852-2116-5900
Website: www.enterpriseasia.com.hk

Other Offices

Parkland Business Centre
Greengates
Bradford, United Kingdom BD10 9TQ

Management and Staff

Benjamin Ng, Chief Executive Officer

Type of Firm

Incubators

Project Preferences

Type of Financing Preferred:

Early Stage

Geographical Preferences

International

Asia

Additional Information

Current Activity Level : Actively seeking new investments

EPICEA

166 rue du Faubourg
Saint-Honore
Paris, France F - 75008
Phone: 33 153.93.02.20
Fax: 33 153.93.02.30
E-mail: ptholly@siparex.com

Management and Staff

Marc Rispal, Partner
Pascal Demichel, Managing Director
Paul Tholly, Partner
Serge Bindel, Partner

Type of Firm

Govt Program NEC

Industry Association Membership

European Venture Capital Association (EVCA)

Project Preferences

Type of Financing Preferred:
Early Stage
Expansion
Leveraged Buyout
Start-up Financing

Geographical Preferences

International
Europe
France

Industry Preferences

Communications and Media
Communications and Media

Computer Software
Software

Computer Other
Computer Related

Semiconductors/Other Elect.
Electronics

Medical/Health
Medical/Health

Industrial/Energy
Industrial Products

Additional Information

Year Founded: 1980
Capital Under Management: $9,600,000
Current Activity Level : Actively seeking new investments

EPISODE-1 PARTNERS

1 Hinde Street
London, United Kingdom W1M 5RH
Phone: 44 20 7486 4841
Fax: 44 20 7935 7963
Website: www.episode-1.com

Management and Staff

Perry Blacher, Founding Partner
Richard Tahta, Founding Partner
Simon Murdoch, Founding Partner

Type of Firm

Private Firm Investing Own Capital

Project Preferences

Type of Financing Preferred:
Early Stage
Seed
Startup

Geographical Preferences

International
Europe
United Kingdom

Industry Preferences

Internet Specific
Internet

Additional Information

Year Founded: 2000
Capital Under Management: $100,000,000
Current Activity Level : Actively seeking new investments

EPS FINANZ AG

Bahnhofstrasse 46
Zurich, Switzerland 8001
Phone: 41 1 212 74 74
Fax: 41 1 212 74 84
Website: www.eps-finanz.ch

Other Offices

26 rue Adrian Lachenal
Geneva, Switzerland 1207
Phone: 41 22 700 24 88
Fax: 41 22 786 04 49

Management and Staff

Rolf Wagli, Chief Executive Officer

Type of Firm

Private Firm Investing Own Capital

Industry Association Membership

Swiss Venture Capital Association

Project Preferences

Type of Financing Preferred:
Balanced

Geographical Preferences

United States
All U.S.

International
Europe
Switzerland

Industry Preferences

Other
Socially Responsible
Environment Responsible

Additional Information

Year Founded: 2000
Capital Under Management: $17,200,000
Current Activity Level : Actively seeking new investments

EQUINET VENTURE PARTNERS AG

Emilstrasse 21
Damstadt, Germany D 64293
Phone: 49 615196.59.50
Fax: 49 615196.59.49
Website: www.equinet-ag.de

Management and Staff

Gerald Worner, Partner
Gerrit Imsieke, Partner
Gert Purkert, Partner
Thomas Hoch, Partner

Type of Firm

Private Equity Advisor or Fund of Fund Mgr

Industry Association Membership

European Venture Capital Association (EVCA)
German Venture Capital Association

Project Preferences

Type of Financing Preferred:
Early Stage
Expansion
Mezzanine
Seed
Start-up Financing

Geographical Preferences

International
Europe
Germany

Industry Preferences

Computer Software
Software

Internet Specific
Internet

Medical/Health
Medical/Health

Additional Information

Capital Under Management: $2,300,000
Current Activity Level : Actively seeking new investments

EQUITY PARTNERS MANAGEMENT PTY LTD

Level 9, 34 Hunter Street
Sydney, Australia 02000
Phone: 612-9223-9348
Fax: 612-9223-0464
Website: www.equitypartners.com.au

Management and Staff

Peter Johnson, Managing Director
Richard Gregson, Managing Director

Type of Firm

Private Firm Investing Own Capital

Industry Association Membership

Australian Venture Capital Association (AVCAL)

Project Preferences

Role in Financing:

Prefer role as deal originator but will also invest in deals created by others

Type of Financing Preferred:

Expansion
First Stage Financing
Management Buyouts
Recapitalizations
Second Stage Financing
Special Situation
Startup

Size of Investments Considered

Min Size of Investment Considered (000s): $1,300
Max Size of Investment Considered (000s): $3,300

Geographical Preferences

International

Oceania/Australasia

Industry Preferences

(% based on actual investment)

Computer Software and Services	56.3%
Internet Specific	29.6%
Consumer Related	14.0%

Additional Information

Year Founded: 1995
Capital Under Management: $23,000,000
Current Activity Level : Actively seeking new investments
Method of Compensation: Return on investment is of primary concern, do not charge fees

EQUITY VENTURES, LTD

28 Grosvenor Street
London, United Kingdom W1X 9FE
Phone: 44-171-917-9611
Fax: 44-171-917-6002
Website: www.equityventures.co.uk

Other Offices

Du Pont House
Bristol Business Park
Bristol, United Kingdom BS16 1QD
Phone: 44 117 931 1318
Fax: 44 117 969 5421

Management and Staff

David Tallboys, Partner

Type of Firm

Mgt. Consulting Firm

Industry Association Membership

British Venture Capital Association

Project Preferences

Role in Financing:

Prefer role as deal originator but will also invest in deals created by others

Type of Financing Preferred:

First Stage Financing
Leveraged Buyout
Second Stage Financing

Size of Investments Considered

Min Size of Investment Considered (000s): $500
Max Size of Investment Considered: No Limit

Geographical Preferences

International

United Kingdom

Industry Preferences

(% based on actual investment)

Semiconductors/Other Elect.	53.6%
Communications and Media	35.5%
Computer Software and Services	3.9%
Computer Hardware	3.3%
Biotechnology	2.5%
Industrial/Energy	0.8%
Other Products	0.5%

Additional Information

Name of Most Recent Fund: Equity Ventures
Most Recent Fund Was Raised: 11/01/1983
Capital Under Management: $10,000,000
Current Activity Level : Inactive / Unknown
Method of Compensation: Return on invest. most important, but chg. closing fees, service fees, etc.

EQUITY4LIFE AG

Muhlebachstrasse 54
Zurich, Switzerland 8034
Phone: 41-1-265-3970
Fax: 41-1-265-3980
Website: www.equity4life.com

Management and Staff

Pascal Moura, Managing Director

Type of Firm

Private Firm Investing Own Capital

Project Preferences

Type of Financing Preferred:

Balanced
Early Stage

Geographical Preferences

International

All International

Industry Preferences

Biotechnology

Biotechnology

Medical/Health

Medical/Health

Additional Information

Year Founded: 2000
Capital Under Management: $89,500,000
Current Activity Level : Actively seeking new investments

EQVITEC PARTNERS OY

Mannerheimintie 8
Helsinki, Finland 00100
Phone: 358-9689-4551
Fax: 358-9689-45595
Website: www.eqvitec.fi

Management and Staff
Jari Mieskonen, Partner
Juha Mikkola, Partner
Jukka Hayrynen, Partner
Jukka Makinen, Partner
Markku Puskala, Partner
Matti Turunen, Managing Director

Type of Firm
Private Firm Investing Own Capital

Industry Association Membership
European Venture Capital Association (EVCA)

Project Preferences

Type of Financing Preferred:
Early Stage
Expansion
Leveraged Buyout
Mezzanine
Startup

Size of Investments Considered
Min Size of Investment Considered (000s): $200
Max Size of Investment Considered (000s): $200,000

Geographical Preferences

United States
All U.S.

International
Europe
Finland
Scandanavia/Nordic Region

Industry Preferences

Communications and Media
Communications and Media
Wireless Communications

Computer Other
Computer Related

Semiconductors/Other Elect.
Electronics

Industrial/Energy
Industrial Products
Materials

Additional Information
Year Founded: 1997
Capital Under Management: $102,200,000
Current Activity Level : Actively seeking new investments

ESPIRITO SANTO DEVELOPMENT

Amoreiras
Tower 3, 12th Floor
Lisbon, Portugal P-1070
Phone: 351-1-383-1529
Fax: 351-1-385-9237

Type of Firm
Commercial Bank Affiliate or Subsidiary

Project Preferences

Role in Financing:
Prefer role as deal originator

Type of Financing Preferred:
Control-block Purchases
Leveraged Buyout
Special Situation

Size of Investments Considered
Min Size of Investment Considered (000s): $100,000
Max Size of Investment Considered: No Limit

Industry Preferences

Communications and Media
CATV & Pay TV Systems

Medical/Health
Other Therapeutic

Consumer Related
Food/Beverage
Consumer Products

Industrial/Energy
Materials

Additional Information
Name of Most Recent Fund: Espirito Santo Development Capital Investors, Ltd.
Most Recent Fund Was Raised: 12/01/1993
Year Founded: 1993
Capital Under Management: $96,000,000
Current Activity Level : Actively seeking new investments
Method of Compensation: Return on invest. most important, but chg. closing fees, service fees, etc.

ETCAPITAL LTD (AKA: EGAN & TALBOT CAPITAL LTD)

St. John's Innovation Centre
Cowley Road
Cambridge, United Kingdom CB4 4W5
Phone: 44-1223-422010
Fax: 44-1223-422011
Website: www.etcapital.com

Management and Staff
Martin Rigby, Managing Director

Type of Firm
Investment/Merchant Bank Investing Own or Client Funds

Project Preferences

Role in Financing:
Prefer role as deal originator but will also invest in deals created by others

Type of Financing Preferred:
First Stage Financing
Second Stage Financing
Start-up Financing

Geographical Preferences

International
United Kingdom

Additional Information
Name of Most Recent Fund: QTP
Most Recent Fund Was Raised: 01/01/1999
Year Founded: 1990
Capital Under Management: $5,000,000
Current Activity Level : Actively seeking new investments
Method of Compensation: Return on invest. most important, but chg. closing fees, service fees, etc.

ETF GROUP

Via Cantonale
The Fantastic Building
Manno, Switzerland 6928
Phone: 41-91-610-7111
Fax: 41-91-610-7166
Website: www.etfgroup.com

Other Offices

10 Place Vendome
Paris, France F-75001
Phone: 33 1 5345 5446
Fax: 33 1 5345 5455

100 Walker Street
Suite 15 Level 9
North Sydney, Australia NSW 2060
Phone: 61-2-9922-4256
Fax: 61-2-9954-3583

230 Park Avenue
Suite 814
New York, United States of America 10169
Phone: 1-212-983-7003
Fax: 1-212-983-7002

28 Saville Row
London, United Kingdom W1S 2EU
Phone: 44 20 7440 5300
Fax: 44 20 7440 5333

Largo Quinto Alpini 12
Milan, Italy 20145
Phone: 39 02 4804 8401
Fax: 39 02 4802 4885

Ms Building 6F
2-4 Mita, 3-Chrome
Minato-ku Tokyo, Japan 108-0074
Phone: 81 3 5439 5601
Fax: 81 3 5439 5603

Pilotystrasse 4
Munich, Germany 80538
Phone: 49-89-2303-5175
Fax: 49-89-2303-5298

Management and Staff
Aldo Monteforte, Managing Director
Chris Pelly, Chief Financial Officer
Giorgio Ronchi, Chairman & CEO
Jens Bodenkamp, Managing Director
Lorcan Burke, Vice President
Maurice Khawam, Managing Director
Michael Sheldon, President
Olav Ostin, Managing Director
Peter Thompson, President
Stefano Devescovi, Managing Director
Sven Lung, Partner
Tetsushi Yamada, President

Type of Firm
Private Firm Investing Own Capital

Project Preferences

Type of Financing Preferred:
Early Stage
Expansion
Startup

Geographical Preferences

International
France
Germany
Italy
Sweden
United Kingdom

Industry Preferences

(% based on actual investment)

Internet Specific	89.6%
Communications and Media	10.4%

Additional Information
Year Founded: 1999
Capital Under Management: $800,000,000
Current Activity Level : Actively seeking new investments

EURAZEO (FKA GAZ-ET-EAUX & AZEO)

3 rue Jacques Bingen
Paris, France 75017
Phone: 33-14-415-1798
Fax: 33-14-267-8825
Website: www.azeo.com

Management and Staff
Bruno Keller, Chief Executive Officer
Philippe Franchet, Partner

Type of Firm
Non-Financial Corp. Affiliate or Subsidiary

Industry Association Membership
European Venture Capital Association (EVCA)

Project Preferences

Type of Financing Preferred:
Expansion
Leveraged Buyout

Geographical Preferences

United States
All U.S.

International
Asia
Europe
France

Industry Preferences

Communications and Media
Communications and Media

Internet Specific
Internet

Semiconductors/Other Elect.
Electronics

Consumer Related
Consumer

Industrial/Energy
Industrial Products

Business Serv.
Media

Additional Information
Year Founded: 2000
Capital Under Management: $2,201,800,000
Current Activity Level : Actively seeking new investments

EUROC VENTURE CAPITAL CORPORATION

22, Aikuo East Road
11th Floor
Taipei, Taiwan
Phone: 8862-395-2588
Fax: 8862-394-7170

Management and Staff
Mary Tsai, President

Whom to Contact
Mary Tsai
Michael Leray

Type of Firm
Private Firm Investing Own Capital

Industry Association Membership
Taiwan Venture Capital Association(TVCA)

Project Preferences

Role in Financing:
Prefer role as deal originator but will also invest in deals created by others

Type of Financing Preferred:
Second Stage Financing
Startup

Geographical Preferences

International
Taiwan

Industry Preferences

Communications and Media
Telecommunications
Data Communications

Computer Hardware
Computer Graphics and Dig
Disk Relat. Memory Device

Semiconductors/Other Elect.
Electronic Components
Semiconductor
Circuit Boards

Medical/Health
Medical Diagnostics
Diagnostic Test Products
Medical Therapeutics
Other Therapeutic
Pharmaceuticals

Industrial/Energy
Materials
Machinery

Manufact.
Manufacturing
Office Automation Equipmt

Additional Information
Year Founded: 1990
Capital Under Management: $68,000,000
Current Activity Level : Actively seeking new investments
Method of Compensation: Return on investment is of primary concern, do not charge fees

EUROFUND LP

99 Hayarkon Street
Tel Aviv, Israel 63432
Phone: 972 3 520 2447
Fax: 972 3 527 0041

Type of Firm
Private Firm Investing Own Capital

Project Preferences

Type of Financing Preferred:
Early Stage

Geographical Preferences

International
Europe

Industry Preferences

Communications and Media
Communications and Media

Internet Specific
Internet

Additional Information
Year Founded: 1994
Capital Under Management: $72,000,000
Current Activity Level : Actively seeking new investments

EUROPEAN ACQUISITION CAPITAL LTD.

26 Finsbury Square
London, United Kingdom EC2A 1DS
Phone: 171-382-1700
Fax: 44-171-588-3401

Management and Staff
A.E.B. Wiegman
C.W. Robinson
E. Rinner
J.C. Cotta
J.L. Heathcote
P.W.E. Downes
R.S. Mason

Whom to Contact
A.E.B. Wiegman
C.W. Robinson
E. Rinner
J.C. Cotta
J.L. Heathcote
P.W.E. Downes
R.S. Mason

Type of Firm
Private Firm Investing Own Capital

Project Preferences

Role in Financing:
Prefer role as deal originator but will also invest in deals created by others

Type of Financing Preferred:
First Stage Financing
Leveraged Buyout
Second Stage Financing

Size of Investments Considered
Min Size of Investment Considered (000s): $5,000
Max Size of Investment Considered: No Limit

Geographical Preferences

International
Bermuda
France
Germany
United Kingdom

Industry Preferences

Communications and Media
Communications and Media

Semiconductors/Other Elect.
Electronic Components

Consumer Related
Consumer
Education Related

Industrial/Energy
Energy
Industrial Products

Transportation
Transportation

Financial Services
Financial Services

Business Serv.
Distribution

Manufact.
Publishing

Additional Information
Name of Most Recent Fund: EAC Fund II
Most Recent Fund Was Raised: 03/01/1998
Year Founded: 1991
Capital Under Management: $350,000,000
Current Activity Level : Actively seeking new investments
Method of Compensation: Return on invest. most important, but chg. closing fees, service fees, etc.

EUROPEAN EQUITY PARTNERS

76 Brook Street
London , United Kingdom W1Y 1YF
Phone: 442-07629-9992
Fax: 442-07629 2072
Website: www.eeplp.com

Management and Staff
Hans Blomberg, Founder

Type of Firm
Private Firm Investing Own Capital

Project Preferences

Type of Financing Preferred:
Early Stage
Later Stage

Geographical Preferences

International
Europe

Industry Preferences

Communications and Media
Communications and Media

Internet Specific
Internet

Financial Services
Financial Services

Additional Information

Year Founded: 2000
Current Activity Level : Actively seeking new investments

EUROPEAN INVESTMENT BANK, THE

100, boulevard Konrad Adenauer
Luxembourg, Luxembourg L - 2950
Phone: 352 43 79 31 22
Fax: 352 43 79 31 89
Website: www.eib.org

Type of Firm

Investment/Merchant Bank Investing Own or Client Funds

Project Preferences

Type of Financing Preferred:
Unknown

Geographical Preferences

International
Europe

Additional Information

Current Activity Level : Actively seeking new investments

EUROPEAN WEBGROUP

Baarerstrasse 37
Zug, Switzerland 6304
Phone: 41 41 727 8585
Fax: 41 41 727 8558
Website: www.e-webgroup.com

Management and Staff

Beat Naf, Partner
George Schmidt, Chairman & CEO
Jean-Marc Chevre, Partner
Marc Erzberger, Partner
Marcel Erni, Chief Financial Officer

Type of Firm

Affiliate/Subsidary of Oth. Financial. Instit.

Industry Association Membership

European Venture Capital Association (EVCA)

Project Preferences

Type of Financing Preferred:
Early Stage

Geographical Preferences

United States
All U.S.

International
Europe

Industry Preferences

Communications and Media
Communications and Media

Internet Specific
Internet

Additional Information

Year Founded: 1999
Capital Under Management: $6,500,000
Current Activity Level : Actively seeking new investments

EUROVENTURES BENELUX TEAM B.V.

H. Henneaulann 366
Zaventem, Belgium B-1930
Phone: 32-2-725-1838
Fax: 32-2-721-4435

Management and Staff

Frits Van der Have, Partner
Paul Verdurme, Partner
Roger Claes, Partner

Type of Firm

Private Firm Investing Own Capital

Industry Association Membership

European Venture Capital Association (EVCA)

Project Preferences

Type of Financing Preferred:
Expansion
Management Buyouts
Start-up Financing
Startup

Geographical Preferences

International
Belgium
France
Luxembourg
Netherlands

Industry Preferences

Biotechnology
Biotechnology

Medical/Health
Medical/Health

Additional Information

Name of Most Recent Fund: Euroventures Benelux I B.V. (1985)
Most Recent Fund Was Raised: 01/01/1985
Year Founded: 1985
Capital Under Management: $81,300,000
Current Activity Level : Actively seeking new investments

EUROVENTURES MANAGEMENT AB

Birger Jarlsgatan 27
Box 7210
Stockholm, Sweden 10388
Phone: 46-854-513130
Fax: 46-820-8997
Website: www.euroventures.se

Other Offices

Elleparken 17
Vedbaek, Denmark 2950
Phone: 45-214-632-06
Fax: 45-45-66-34-30

Kiiltokallionkuja 9
Espoo, Finland 02180
Phone: 358-950-22-756
Fax: 358-952-37-16

Management and Staff

Per Wahlstom, Founder

Type of Firm

Private Firm Investing Own Capital

Industry Association Membership
European Venture Capital Association (EVCA)
Swedish Venture Capital Association

Project Preferences

Type of Financing Preferred:
Early Stage
Expansion
Leveraged Buyout
Turnaround

Size of Investments Considered
Min Size of Investment Considered (000s): $942
Max Size of Investment Considered (000s): $9,416

Geographical Preferences

International
Denmark
Europe
Finland
Norway
Scandanavia/Nordic Region
Sweden

Industry Preferences

Communications and Media
Communications and Media

Semiconductors/Other Elect.
Electronics

Medical/Health
Medical/Health

Industrial/Energy
Industrial Products

Additional Information
Name of Most Recent Fund: Euroventures Nordica A/S (Euroventures Nordica I BV)
Most Recent Fund Was Raised: 01/01/1986
Year Founded: 1985
Capital Under Management: $81,000,000
Current Activity Level : Actively seeking new investments

EVC CHRISTOWS PLC (FKA: EVESTMENT COMPANY PLC)

223a Kensington High Street
London, United Kingdom W8 6SG
Phone: 44 207 937 4445
Fax: 44-207-937-4446
Website: www.evestment.co.uk

Management and Staff
Alex Snow, Chief Executive Officer
Chris Roberts, Chief Executive Officer
Oliver Vaughan, Founder

Type of Firm
Private Firm Investing Own Capital

Project Preferences

Role in Financing:
Prefer role as deal originator

Type of Financing Preferred:
Early Stage
Startup

Geographical Preferences

United States
All U.S.

International
Europe
United Kingdom

Industry Preferences

Communications and Media
Communications and Media

Internet Specific
Internet

Additional Information
Capital Under Management: $87,400,000
Current Activity Level : Actively seeking new investments
Method of Compensation: Return on invest. most important, but chg. closing fees, service fees, etc.

EVERGER ASSOCIATES

Parker Tower
43-49 Parker Street
London, United Kingdom WC2B 5P
Phone: 44 20 7550 3231
Fax: 44 20 7405 1059
Website: www.everger.co.uk

Other Offices

E.M. Warburg, Pincus & Co., LLC
466 Lexington Avenue
New York, United States of America 10017-3147
Phone: 212 878 0794

Management and Staff
Andrew Burke, Chief Executive Officer
Andrew Harwood, Partner

Type of Firm
Private Firm Investing Own Capital

Project Preferences

Type of Financing Preferred:
Early Stage
First Stage Financing
Second Stage Financing
Seed

Geographical Preferences

United States
All U.S.

International
Europe
United Kingdom

Industry Preferences

Internet Specific
Internet

Additional Information
Year Founded: 2000
Capital Under Management: $100,000,000
Current Activity Level : Actively seeking new investments

EVERGREEN CANADA ISRAEL INVESTMENTS LTD

90 Rothschild Boulevard
P.O. Box 14111
Tel Aviv, Israel 65224
Phone: 972-3-710-8282
Fax: 972-3-710-8210
Website: www.evergreen-invest.com

Management and Staff
Moty Hoss, Chief Financial Officer

Whom to Contact
Iftach Atir

Type of Firm
Private Firm Investing Own Capital

Project Preferences

Role in Financing:
Prefer role as deal originator but will also invest in deals created by others

Type of Financing Preferred:
First Stage Financing
Leveraged Buyout
Mezzanine
Research and Development
Second Stage Financing
Seed
Start-up Financing

Size of Investments Considered
Min Size of Investment Considered (000s): $300
Max Size of Investment Considered: No Limit

Geographical Preferences

International
Middle East

Industry Preferences

Communications and Media
CATV & Pay TV Systems
Telecommunications
Data Communications
Satellite Microwave Comm.
Other Communication Prod.

Computer Hardware
Computers

Computer Software
Computer Services
Systems Software
Applications Software

Internet Specific
Internet

Semiconductors/Other Elect.
Semiconductor
Laser Related
Fiber Optics

Medical/Health
Diagnostic Test Products

Consumer Related
Computer Stores

Additional Information
Name of Most Recent Fund: Peace Technology Fund Ltd.
Most Recent Fund Was Raised: 01/01/1999
Year Founded: 2000
Capital Under Management: $500,000,000
Current Activity Level : Actively seeking new investments
Method of Compensation: Return on investment is of primary concern, do not charge fees

EVOLUTION GLOBAL PARTNERS

40 Strand
7th Floor
London, United Kingdom WC2N 5HZ
Phone: 44-20-7969-4800
Fax: 44-20-7969-4888
Website: www.evopartners.com

Other Offices

3 Embarcadero Center
Suite 2330
San Francisco, United States of America 94101
Phone: 1-415-267-3500
Fax: 1-415-267-3501

Karlsplatz
Munich, Germany 80335
Phone: 49-89-5123-1001
Fax: 49-89-5123-1002

Management and Staff
David Sanderson, Managing Director
David Siegel, Managing Director
Graham Elton, Managing Director
James Allen, Chief Executive Officer

Type of Firm
Private Firm Investing Own Capital

Project Preferences

Type of Financing Preferred:
Early Stage

Geographical Preferences

United States
All U.S.

International
Asia
Europe

Industry Preferences

Internet Specific
Internet

Additional Information
Year Founded: 2000
Capital Under Management: $500,000,000
Current Activity Level : Actively seeking new investments

EXPANSO CAPITAL

25 cours du Marechal Foch
Bordeaux Cedex, France F-33076
Phone: 33 556 00 86 10
Fax: 33 556 81 57 15
Website: www.expanso.com

Type of Firm
Private Firm Investing Own Capital

Project Preferences

Type of Financing Preferred:
Expansion
Leveraged Buyout
Management Buyouts
Startup

Geographical Preferences

International
France

Industry Preferences

Industrial/Energy
Industrial Products

Business Serv.
Services

Additional Information
Capital Under Management: $13,100,000
Current Activity Level : Actively seeking new investments

EXSEED

6 Wissotzky Street
Tel Aviv, Israel 62338
Phone: 972 3544 2518
Fax: 972 3605 9990
Website: www.ex-seed.com

Management and Staff
Ariella Zochovitzky, Partner
Eyal Weinstein, Partner
Ziv Dascalu, Partner

Type of Firm
Incubators

Project Preferences

Type of Financing Preferred:
Seed
Startup

Geographical Preferences

International
All International

Industry Preferences

Communications and Media
Communications and Media

Computer Software
Software

Internet Specific
Internet

Additional Information

Year Founded: 2000
Current Activity Level : Actively seeking new investments

F. TURISMO-CAPITAL DE RISCO SA

Rua Ivone Silva
lote 6-3o Esq.
Lisbon, Portugal 1050-124
Phone: 351-21-781-5900
Fax: 351-21-781-5809

Type of Firm

Govt Program NEC

Industry Association Membership

European Venture Capital Association (EVCA)
Portuguese Venture Capital Association

Project Preferences

Role in Financing:
Prefer role in deals created by others

Type of Financing Preferred:
Early Stage
Expansion
Recapitalizations
Turnaround

Geographical Preferences

International
Brazil
Cape Verde
Portugal

Industry Preferences

Consumer Related
Hotels and Resorts

Business Serv.
Services

Additional Information

Year Founded: 1991
Capital Under Management: $27,400,000
Current Activity Level : Actively seeking new investments
Method of Compensation: Return on invest. most important, but chg. closing fees, service fees, etc.

FAIRGILL INVESTMENTS PROPERTY LIMITED

Suite 15, 201 New South Head
Edgecliff
Sydney, Australia 2027
Phone: 612-9327-7613
Fax: 612-9326-1258

Type of Firm

Private Firm Investing Own Capital

Project Preferences

Type of Financing Preferred:
Early Stage
Expansion
Management Buyouts
Seed
Startup

Geographical Preferences

International
Australia
Europe
All International

Industry Preferences

Business Serv.
Services

Manufact.
Manufacturing

Additional Information

Year Founded: 1989
Capital Under Management: $59,800,000
Current Activity Level : Actively seeking new investments

FAR BLUE

1 Marble Quay
London, United Kingdom E1W 1UH
Phone: 44 20 7481 8002
Fax: 44 20 7481 8003
Website: www.farblue.com

Other Offices

The Beacon
176 St Vincent Street
Glasgow, United Kingdom G2 5SG
Phone: 44 141 249 6630
Fax: 44 141 249 6634

Management and Staff

Matthew Hudson, Chief Executive Officer

Type of Firm

Private Firm Investing Own Capital

Industry Association Membership

British Venture Capital Association

Project Preferences

Type of Financing Preferred:
Early Stage
Seed

Geographical Preferences

International
Europe
United Kingdom

Industry Preferences

Medical/Health
Medical/Health

Additional Information

Year Founded: 2000
Capital Under Management: $15,000,000
Current Activity Level : Actively seeking new investments

FASTVENTURES

BECSI UT 126-128
Budapest, Hungary 1034
Phone: 36 309 429 000
Website: www.fast-ventures.hu

Management and Staff

Peter Fodor, Managing Director

Type of Firm

Incubators

Project Preferences

Type of Financing Preferred:
Startup

Geographical Preferences

International
Eastern Europe
Hungary

Industry Preferences

Internet Specific
Internet

Biotechnology
Biotechnology

Business Serv.
Media

Additional Information

Year Founded: 2000
Capital Under Management: $1,700,000
Current Activity Level : Actively seeking new investments

FEDERAL BUSINESS DEVELOPMENT BANK

Venture Capital Division
Five Place Ville Marie Ste 600
Montreal, Canada H3B 5E7
Phone: 514-283-1896
Fax: 514-283-5455

Other Offices

601 West Hastings Street
Suite 700
Vancouver, Canada V6B 5G9
Phone: 604-666-7815
Fax: 604-666-7650

777 Bay Street
29th Floor
Toronto, Canada M5G 2C8
Phone: 416-973-0034
Fax: 416-973-5529

Type of Firm

Affiliate/Subsidary of Oth. Financial. Instit.

Industry Association Membership

Canadian Venture Capital Association

Project Preferences

Role in Financing:
Prefer role as deal originator but will also invest in deals created by others

Type of Financing Preferred:
First Stage Financing
Leveraged Buyout
Mezzanine
Research and Development
Second Stage Financing
Seed
Start-up Financing

Size of Investments Considered

Min Size of Investment Considered (000s): $1,000
Max Size of Investment Considered: No Limit

Geographical Preferences

Canada
All Canada

Industry Preferences

(% based on actual investment)

Biotechnology	40.6%
Internet Specific	31.0%
Computer Software and Services	18.4%
Computer Hardware	10.0%

Additional Information

Year Founded: 1983
Capital Under Management: $90,000,000
Current Activity Level : Actively seeking new investments
Method of Compensation: Return on investment is of primary concern, do not charge fees

---

FEO VENTURES PTE. LTD.

14 Scotts Road
#06-00 Far East Plaza
Singapore, Singapore 228213
Phone: 65-830-6469
Fax: 65-733-8781
Website: www.fareast.com.sg

Other Offices

1 Tanglin Road
#04-18 Orchard Parade Hotel
Singapore, Singapore 247905
Phone: 65-833-6666
Fax: 75-736-2043

Type of Firm

Non-Financial Corp. Affiliate or Subsidiary

Project Preferences

Role in Financing:
Will function either as deal originator or investor in deals created by others

Type of Financing Preferred:
Expansion
Start-up Financing

Geographical Preferences

International
Asia

Industry Preferences

Internet Specific
Internet

Additional Information

Name of Most Recent Fund: UOB Venture Investments Ltd.
Most Recent Fund Was Raised: 01/01/1995
Year Founded: 2000
Capital Under Management: $1,700,000
Current Activity Level : Actively seeking new investments
Method of Compensation: Return on investment is of primary concern, do not charge fees

---

FIDELITY VENTURES (FKA: FIDELITY VENTURE ASSOCIATES)

25 Lovat Lane
London, United Kingdom EC3R 8LL
Phone: 44-20-7664-2300
Fax: 44-20-7669-2309

See Massachusetts for full listing.

FINADVANCE S.A.

"Le Derby"
570 Avenue du Club Hippique
Aix en Provence, France F-13090
Phone: 33-442-529-130
Fax: 33-442-529-139
Website: www.finadvance.fr

Management and Staff

Gillot or Legoupil

Whom to Contact

Gillot or Legoupil

Type of Firm

Private Firm Investing Own Capital

Project Preferences

Role in Financing:
Prefer role as deal originator but will also invest in deals created by others

Type of Financing Preferred:
Acquisition
Expansion
Leveraged Buyout
Management Buyouts

Geographical Preferences

International
France

Industry Preferences

Industrial/Energy
Industrial Products

Business Serv.
Services

Additional Information

Name of Most Recent Fund: Financial Capital II
Most Recent Fund Was Raised: 07/01/1998
Year Founded: 1988
Capital Under Management: $41,000,000
Current Activity Level : Actively seeking new investments
Method of Compensation: Return on invest. most important, but chg. closing fees, service fees, etc.

FINANSA CAPITAL LIMITED

8/F, TISCO Tower
No. 48 North Sathorn Road
Bangkok, Thailand 10500
Phone: 662-266-6677
Fax: 662-266-6688
Website: www.finansa.com

Other Offices

3/F Metropolitan Tower
235 Dong Khoi, District 1
Ho Chi Minh, Vietnam
Phone: 848-825-0168
Fax: 848-825-0167

Suite 16, 27 Ly Thai To
Hanoi, Vietnam
Phone: 84-48-247-607
Fax: 84-48-247-608

Management and Staff

Eugene Davis, Managing Director
Jake Vigoda, Vice President
Teera Kankirawatano, Vice President

Whom to Contact

G. Davis

Type of Firm

Investment/Merchant Bank Investing Own or Client Funds

Project Preferences

Role in Financing:
Prefer role as deal originator but will also invest in deals created by others

Type of Financing Preferred:
Acquisition
Balanced
Distressed Debt
Management Buyouts
Recapitalizations
Special Situation
Turnaround

Size of Investments Considered

Min Size of Investment Considered (000s): $3,000
Max Size of Investment Considered (000s): $5,000

Geographical Preferences

International
Asia
Thailand

Industry Preferences

Communications and Media
Radio & TV Broadcasting

Semiconductors/Other Elect.
Electronic Components

Medical/Health
Pharmaceuticals

Consumer Related
Entertainment and Leisure
Retail
Food/Beverage
Consumer Services
Education Related

Industrial/Energy
Energy
Materials

Financial Services
Financial Services
Real Estate

Manufact.
Manufacturing
Publishing

Other
Environment Responsible

Additional Information

Name of Most Recent Fund: Siam Investment Fund II L.P.
Most Recent Fund Was Raised: 10/01/1999
Year Founded: 1992
Capital Under Management: $100,000,000
Current Activity Level : Actively seeking new investments
Method of Compensation: Return on invest. most important, but chg. closing fees, service fees, etc.

FINORPA

23 rue du 11 novembre
BP 351
Lens Cedex, France 62334
Phone: 33 3 2128 5555
Fax: 33 3 2143 0652
Website: www.finorpa.fr

Other Offices

17 rue Capron
Valenciennes, France 59300
Phone: 33 3 2747 4707
Fax: 33 3 2733 5177

21 avenue Le Corbusier
Lille, France 59800
Phone: 33 3 2031 5954
Fax: 33 3 2031 2265

50 Boulevard Jacquard
Calais, France 62100
Phone: 33 3 2185 5460
Fax: 33 3 2185 0758

Management and Staff

Jean-Marie Duvivier, President

Type of Firm

Business Development Fund

Project Preferences

Type of Financing Preferred:
Expansion
Management Buyouts
Startup
Turnaround

Geographical Preferences

International
France

Industry Preferences

Semiconductors/Other Elect.
Electronics

Consumer Related
Food/Beverage

Industrial/Energy
Industrial Products
Materials

Manufact.
Manufacturing
Publishing

Additional Information
Year Founded: 1984
Current Activity Level : Actively seeking new investments

FINOVELEC

4, rue Ancelle
Neuilly-sur-Seine, France 92521
Phone: 33-1-5561-5156
Fax: 33-1-4640-7938

Management and Staff
Jacques Chatain
Jean Jacquin

Whom to Contact
Jacques Chatain
Jean Jacquin

Type of Firm
Private Firm Investing Own Capital

Project Preferences

Role in Financing:
Prefer role in deals created by others

Type of Financing Preferred:
Balanced
Start-up Financing

Geographical Preferences

United States
All U.S.

Canada
All Canada

International
Bermuda
France
Germany
All International
Italy
Japan
Middle East
United Kingdom

Industry Preferences

Communications and Media
Data Communications

Computer Hardware
Mainframes / Scientific
Computer Graphics and Dig
Disk Relat. Memory Device

Computer Software
Computer Services
Systems Software
Applications Software

Semiconductors/Other Elect.
Electronic Components
Semiconductor
Component Testing Equipmt
Laser Related
Fiber Optics
Analytic/Scientific

Biotechnology
Industrial Biotechnology
Biotech Related Research
Biotech Related Research

Medical/Health
Medical Diagnostics
Diagnostic Test Products
Medical Therapeutics
Drug/Equipmt Delivery
Other Therapeutic

Industrial/Energy
Factory Automation
Robotics
Machinery
Environmental Related

Additional Information
Year Founded: 1981
Capital Under Management: $100,000,000
Current Activity Level : Actively seeking new investments
Method of Compensation: Return on investment is of primary concern, do not charge fees

FIRST FLOOR CAPITAL SDN. BHD.

Level 7, Plaza Kelanamas
19 Lorong Dungun, Damansara
Kuala Lumpur, Malaysia 50490
Phone: 603-253-4044
Fax: 603-253-8244
E-mail: climb@firstfloorcapital.com
Website: www.firstfloorcapital.com

Management and Staff
Ismael Fariz Ali, Managing Director

Type of Firm
Private Firm Investing Own Capital

Project Preferences

Type of Financing Preferred:
Distressed Debt
Early Stage

Geographical Preferences

International
Asia

Additional Information
Year Founded: 2000
Capital Under Management: $1,300,000
Current Activity Level : Actively seeking new investments

FIRST GEN-E INVESTMENTS

c/o Gesfid via Adamini 10
Lugano, Switzerland 6900
Phone: 41 91 985 7539
Fax: 41 91 993 0970

Management and Staff
Domenico Grassi, Partner
Gianfranco Pitzolu, Partner
Giovanni Saladino, Partner
Guilio Carmignato, Partner
Luca Duranti, Partner

Type of Firm
Private Firm Investing Own Capital

Industry Association Membership
Italian Venture Capital Association

Project Preferences

Type of Financing Preferred:
Early Stage
Expansion
Seed
Startup

Geographical Preferences

United States
All U.S.

International
Europe
Italy

Industry Preferences

Communications and Media
Communications and Media

Computer Software
Software

Semiconductors/Other Elect.
Electronics

Additional Information
Year Founded: 2000
Capital Under Management: $55,500,000
Current Activity Level : Actively seeking new investments

FJ BENJAMIN HOLDINGS PTE LTD

6B Orange Grove Rd.
FJ Benjamin Bldg.
Singapore, Singapore 258332
Phone: 65-737-0155
Fax: 65-733-7398
E-mail: enquiry@hld.fjb.com.sg
Website: www.fjben.com.sg

Management and Staff
Frank Benjamin, Chairman & CEO

Type of Firm
Private Firm Investing Own Capital

Project Preferences

Role in Financing:
Will function either as deal originator or investor in deals created by others

Type of Financing Preferred:
Balanced

Geographical Preferences

International
Asia

Additional Information
Year Founded: 1959
Current Activity Level : Actively seeking new investments
Method of Compensation: Return on investment is of primary concern, do not charge fees

---

FLINDERS CAPITAL LIMITED

Level 3, 350 Collins Street
Melbourne, Australia 03000
Phone: 613-9642-5299
Fax: 613-9642-5266
Website: www.flinderscap.com.au

Management and Staff
Jeremy Ingall, Managing Director

Type of Firm
Investment/Merchant Bank Investing Own or Client Funds

Project Preferences

Type of Financing Preferred:
Expansion
Later Stage
Management Buyouts
Mezzanine

Geographical Preferences

International
Australia

Industry Preferences

Computer Software
Software

Internet Specific
Internet

Medical/Health
Medical/Health

Consumer Related
Food/Beverage

Financial Services
Financial Services

Additional Information
Year Founded: 1997
Capital Under Management: $15,000,000
Current Activity Level : Actively seeking new investments

FLV FUND (AKA FLANDERS LANGUAGE VALLEY FUND)

Flanders Language Valley 63
Ieper, Belgium 8903
Phone: 3257229430
Fax: 3257206842
Website: www.flvfund.com

Other Offices

29 International Business Park
08-06 Acer Tower B
Singapore, Singapore 609923
Phone: 657998908
Fax: 652346516

52 Third Avenue
Burlington, United States of America 01803
Phone: 17812035131
Fax: 16172649197

FLV Management USA, Inc.
23551 Camino Hermoso,
Los Altos Hills, United States of America 94024
Phone: 16509170935
Fax: 15303259176

Management and Staff
Jan Leys, Chief Executive Officer
Philip Vermeulen, Managing Director
Tanja Michiels, Partner

Type of Firm
Private Firm Investing Own Capital

Industry Association Membership
Belgium Venture Capital Association
European Venture Capital Association (EVCA)

Project Preferences

Type of Financing Preferred:
Early Stage
Expansion
Seed
Startup

Size of Investments Considered
Min Size of Investment Considered (000s): $1,000
Max Size of Investment Considered: No Limit

Geographical Preferences

United States
All U.S.

International
Asia
Europe
Middle East

Industry Preferences

(% based on actual investment)

Computer Software and Services	57.5%
Internet Specific	17.2%
Communications and Media	9.9%
Computer Hardware	7.8%
Semiconductors/Other Elect.	3.9%
Other Products	1.9%
Consumer Related	1.8%
Medical/Health	0.1%

Additional Information
Name of Most Recent Fund: Flanders Language Valley Fund
Most Recent Fund Was Raised: 12/24/1995
Year Founded: 1995
Capital Under Management: $120,000,000
Current Activity Level : Actively seeking new investments

FLYNN VENTURE, LLC

730 View Street
Suite 800
Victoria, Canada V8W 3Y7

See California for full listing.

FOND RIZIVEHO KAPITALU SRO

Na Stahlavce 1555/2
Prague 6, Czech Republic CZ-16000
Phone: 420 2 3332 6330
Fax: 420 2 3332 6295
Website: www.frk.cz

Management and Staff
Stanislav Sràmek

Whom to Contact
Stanislav Sràmek

Type of Firm
SBIC Not elsewhere classified

Industry Association Membership
European Venture Capital Association (EVCA)

Project Preferences

Role in Financing:
Prefer role as deal originator

Type of Financing Preferred:
Early Stage
First Stage Financing
Second Stage Financing
Start-up Financing

Geographical Preferences

International
Czech Republic

Additional Information
Name of Most Recent Fund: Fond Riziveho Kapitalu SRO
Most Recent Fund Was Raised: 01/01/1996
Year Founded: 1995
Capital Under Management: $2,800,000
Current Activity Level : Actively seeking new investments
Method of Compensation: Return on invest. most important, but chg. closing fees, service fees, etc.

FONDINVEST (GRP. CAISSE DE DEPOTS)

33 rue de la Baume
Paris, France F 75008
Phone: 33 1 5836 4800
Fax: 33 1 8838 4828
Website: www.cdcpart.com/fond.htm

Management and Staff
Charles Soulignac, Chief Executive Officer

Type of Firm
Affiliate/Subsidary of Oth. Financial. Instit.

Industry Association Membership
European Venture Capital Association (EVCA)

Project Preferences

Role in Financing:
Prefer role as deal originator but will also invest in deals created by others

Type of Financing Preferred:
Fund of Funds
Fund of Funds of Second

Geographical Preferences

United States
All U.S.

International
Asia
Europe

Additional Information
Name of Most Recent Fund: Fondinvest III
Most Recent Fund Was Raised: 01/01/1999
Year Founded: 1994
Capital Under Management: $320,000,000
Current Activity Level : Actively seeking new investments
Method of Compensation: Return on invest. most important, but chg. closing fees, service fees, etc.

FONDS D'INVESTISSEMENTS R.T.V.L.

Centre Mercure
445, boulevard Gambetta
Tourcoing, France 59200
Phone: 33-3-2024-9787
Fax: 33-3-2027-1804
E-mail: rtvl@nordnet.fr

Management and Staff
Eric Grimonprez, Chief Executive Officer

Type of Firm
Business Development Fund

Project Preferences

Role in Financing:
Prefer role as deal originator but will also invest in deals created by others

Type of Financing Preferred:
First Stage Financing
Second Stage Financing
Start-up Financing

Geographical Preferences

International
France

Industry Preferences

Communications and Media
Telecommunications

Computer Hardware
Computer Graphics and Dig

Biotechnology
Industrial Biotechnology

Medical/Health
Medical Therapeutics
Hospitals/Clinics/Primary

Consumer Related
Food/Beverage

Industrial/Energy
Environmental Related

Additional Information
Year Founded: 1991
Capital Under Management: $5,000,000
Current Activity Level : Actively seeking new investments
Method of Compensation: Return on investment is of primary concern, do not charge fees

FONDS DE SOLIDARITE@' DES TRAVAILLEURS DU QUE@'BEC (F.T.Q.)

8717 Berri Street
Montreal, Canada H2M 2T9
Phone: 514-383-8383
Fax: 514-383-2502
Website: www.fondsftq.com

Management and Staff
Daniel Laporte, Vice President
Jacques Simoneau, Vice President
Maurice Prudhomme, Vice President
Raymond Bachand, President
Richard Cloutier, Principal

Whom to Contact
Daniel Laporte
Luc Charron
Maurice Prud'homme
Raymond Bachand
Roger Giraldeau
Sylvie Jacques
Yves Lamarre

Type of Firm
Private Firm Investing Own Capital

Industry Association Membership
Canadian Venture Capital Association

Project Preferences

Role in Financing:
Will function either as deal originator or investor in deals created by others

Type of Financing Preferred:
Acquisition
Control-block Purchases
Distressed Debt
Early Stage
Expansion
First Stage Financing
Generalist PE
Joint Ventures
Later Stage
Leveraged Buyout
Management Buyouts
Mezzanine
Open Market
Private Placement
Recapitalizations
Research and Development
Second Stage Financing
Seed
Special Situation
Startup
Turnaround

Size of Investments Considered
Min Size of Investment Considered (000s): $750
Max Size of Investment Considered: No Limit

Geographical Preferences

Canada
Quebec

Industry Preferences

Communications and Media
Telecommunications
Wireless Communications
Data Communications
Satellite Microwave Comm.
Other Communication Prod.

Internet Specific
Internet

Semiconductors/Other Elect.
Electronic Components

Biotechnology
Agricultural/Animal Bio.
Industrial Biotechnology
Biotech Related Research
Biotech Related Research

Medical/Health
Medical Diagnostics
Diagnostic Services
Diagnostic Test Products
Medical Therapeutics
Drug/Equipmt Delivery
Medical Products
Disposable Med. Products
Health Services

Consumer Related
Entertainment and Leisure
Food/Beverage
Hotels and Resorts

Industrial/Energy
Industrial Products
Factory Automation
Process Control
Robotics
Machinery

Transportation
Transportation

Financial Services
Financial Services
Insurance
Real Estate

Business Serv.
Services
Distribution

Manufact.
Manufacturing

Agr/Forestr/Fish
Agriculture related

Other
Socially Responsible
Environment Responsible
Women/Minority-Owned Bus.

Additional Information
Year Founded: 1983
Capital Under Management: $2,600,000,000
Current Activity Level : Actively seeking new investments
Method of Compensation: Return on invest. most important, but chg. closing fees, service fees, etc.

FORESIGHT

Levinstein Tower
23 Petach Tikva Road
Tel Aviv, Israel 66182
Phone: 972 3 5666 626
Fax: 972 3 5666 630
Website: www.foresight.co.il

Management and Staff
Shalom Tshuva, Managing Director

Type of Firm
Investment/Merchant Bank Subsid/Affil

Project Preferences

Type of Financing Preferred:
Early Stage
Seed
Startup

Geographical Preferences

International
Israel

Industry Preferences

Communications and Media
Telecommunications

Internet Specific
Internet

Additional Information
Name of Most Recent Fund: Golden Gate Bridge Fund
Most Recent Fund Was Raised: 06/30/2000
Year Founded: 1993
Capital Under Management: $12,000,000
Current Activity Level : Actively seeking new investments

FORETAGSBYGGARNA AB

Norrmalmstorg 14
Stockholm, Sweden S-111 46
Phone: 46-8-678-1450
Fax: 46-8-678-1460

Management and Staff
Hennrietta Stiernberg

Whom to Contact
Hennrietta Stiernberg

Type of Firm
Private Firm Investing Own Capital

Project Preferences

Role in Financing:
Prefer role as deal originator

Type of Financing Preferred:
First Stage Financing
Start-up Financing

Industry Preferences

Communications and Media
Commercial Communications
Telecommunications
Data Communications

Computer Software
Computer Services

Medical/Health
Diagnostic Test Products
Drug/Equipmt Delivery
Pharmaceuticals

Additional Information
Name of Most Recent Fund: ForetagsByggarna AB
Most Recent Fund Was Raised: 01/01/1993
Year Founded: 1990
Capital Under Management: $7,000,000
Current Activity Level : Actively seeking new investments
Method of Compensation: Return on invest. most important, but chg. closing fees, service fees, etc.

FORTKNOX-VENTURE AG

Horbeller Strasse 10-14
Koln, Germany 50858
Phone: 49 2234 249541
Fax: 49 2234 249551
Website: www.fortknox-venture.de

Type of Firm
Private Firm Investing Own Capital

Project Preferences

Type of Financing Preferred:
Expansion
Mezzanine
Seed
Startup

Geographical Preferences

International
Europe
Germany
United Kingdom

Industry Preferences

Communications and Media
Telecommunications

Computer Software
Software

Internet Specific
Internet

Semiconductors/Other Elect.
Electronics
Sensors
Laser Related

Medical/Health
Medical/Health

Industrial/Energy
Industrial Products

Additional Information
Year Founded: 1999
Capital Under Management: $22,500,000
Current Activity Level : Actively seeking new investments

FORTUNE CONSULTING GROUP INCORPORATED

13F-1, No. 128
Min Sheng East Road, Section 3
Taipei, Taiwan
Phone: 8862-2718-2330
Fax: 8862-2546-7182

Management and Staff
James Chew, Chief Executive Officer
Y. C. Li, President

Type of Firm
Private Firm Investing Own Capital

Industry Association Membership
Taiwan Venture Capital Association(TVCA)

Project Preferences

Type of Financing Preferred:
Early Stage
Expansion
Later Stage
Mezzanine
Seed

Geographical Preferences

United States
All U.S.
All U.S.

International
China
Hong Kong
Singapore
Taiwan

Industry Preferences

Communications and Media
Telecommunications

Computer Software
Software

Internet Specific
Internet
Ecommerce

Semiconductors/Other Elect.
Electronics
Semiconductor
Fiber Optics

Biotechnology
Biotechnology

Additional Information
Year Founded: 1995
Capital Under Management: $372,000,000
Current Activity Level : Actively seeking new investments

FORTUNE INTERNATIONAL LIMITED

18/F One International Finance Centre, 1 Harbour View Street
Central, Hong Kong
E-mail: info@fortune-int.com
Website: www.fortune-int.com

Other Offices

2111 Wing On House
71 Des Voeux Rd.
Central, Hong Kong

31/F Jin Mao Tower
2 Centenary Blvd. Pudong
Shanghai, China 200720

Level 15 Prudential Tower
30 Cecil St.
Singapore, Singapore 049712

Level 9, AIG Bldg.
1-1-3 Maninouchi
Tokyo, Japan

Management and Staff
Jonathan Marshal, Chairman & CEO
Katherine Hamnett, Chief Financial Officer
Michael Lockwood, Managing Director

Type of Firm
Affiliate/Subsidary of Oth. Financial. Instit.

Project Preferences

Role in Financing:
Will function either as deal originator or investor in deals created by others

Type of Financing Preferred:
Balanced

Geographical Preferences

International
Asia
Hong Kong

Industry Preferences

Internet Specific
Internet

Medical/Health
Health Services
Pharmaceuticals

Consumer Related
Consumer

Additional Information
Year Founded: 1978
Current Activity Level : Actively seeking new investments
Method of Compensation: Return on investment is of primary concern, do not charge fees

---

FORTUNE VENTURE CAPITAL INCORPORATED

2F, No. 76, Tun-Hwa South Road
Section 2
Taipei, Taiwan
Phone: 8862-2718-2330
Fax: 8862-2546-7182

Management and Staff
Robert Tsao, President & Chairman

Type of Firm
Private Firm Investing Own Capital

Industry Association Membership
Taiwan Venture Capital Association(TVCA)

Project Preferences

Type of Financing Preferred:
Balanced
Expansion
Seed
Start-up Financing
Turnaround

Geographical Preferences

International
Taiwan

Industry Preferences

Communications and Media
Telecommunications

Computer Software
Software

Semiconductors/Other Elect.
Semiconductor

Additional Information
Name of Most Recent Fund: Fortune Venture Capital Incorporated
Most Recent Fund Was Raised: 01/01/1997
Year Founded: 1993
Capital Under Management: $62,100,000
Current Activity Level : Actively seeking new investments

FORTUNE VENTURE MANAGEMENT PTE LTD.

No. 05-04 Goldbell Towers
47 Scotts Road
Singapore, Singapore 228233
Phone: 65-238-1911
Fax: 65-738-1511

Management and Staff
James Chew, Chief Executive Officer

Type of Firm
Private Firm Investing Own Capital

Project Preferences

Type of Financing Preferred:
Balanced
Early Stage
Expansion
Later Stage

Geographical Preferences

United States
California
All U.S.

International
China
Singapore

Industry Preferences

Communications and Media
Data Communications

Computer Software
Software

Internet Specific
Internet

Semiconductors/Other Elect.
Electronics
Semiconductor

Biotechnology
Biotechnology

Additional Information
Year Founded: 1999
Capital Under Management: $80,000,000
Current Activity Level : Actively seeking new investments

FOUNDATION CAPITAL LIMITED

Level 12, 225 St. George's Terrace
Perth, Australia 6009
Phone: 618-9322-2360
Fax: 618-9322-1148
Website: www.foundationcap.com.au

Management and Staff
Ian Murchison, Managing Director

Type of Firm
Private Firm Investing Own Capital

Industry Association Membership
Australian Venture Capital Association (AVCAL)

Project Preferences

Role in Financing:
Prefer role in deals created by others

Type of Financing Preferred:
Early Stage
Expansion
First Stage Financing
Mezzanine
Second Stage Financing
Startup

Size of Investments Considered
Min Size of Investment Considered (000s): $2,000
Max Size of Investment Considered: No Limit

Geographical Preferences

International
Asia
Oceania/Australasia

Industry Preferences

Communications and Media
Communications and Media
Telecommunications

Computer Software
Software

Computer Other
Computer Related

Semiconductors/Other Elect.
Electronic Components

Biotechnology
Biotechnology

Industrial/Energy
Energy
Materials

Transportation
Transportation

Financial Services
Financial Services

Business Serv.
Services
Distribution

Manufact.
Manufacturing

Additional Information
Year Founded: 1994
Capital Under Management: $18,100,000
Current Activity Level : Actively seeking new investments

FOUNTAINHEAD CAPITAL LTD.

1 Beach Queen, J.P. Rd.
Versova Andheri (W)
Mumbai, India
Phone: 9122-633-0688
Fax: 9122-629-0914

Management and Staff
Chiranjit Banerjee, Managing Director

Type of Firm
Private Equity Advisor or Fund of Fund Mgr

Project Preferences

Role in Financing:
Prefer role in deals created by others

Type of Financing Preferred:
Mezzanine

Geographical Preferences

International
India

Industry Preferences

Communications and Media
Communications and Media

Consumer Related
Consumer

Additional Information
Year Founded: 1995
Current Activity Level : Actively seeking new investments

FRASER & NEAVE LIMITED

#21-00 Alexandra Point
438 Alexandra Road
Singapore, Singapore 119958
Phone: 65-272-9488
Fax: 65-271-0811
Website: www.fraserandneave.com.sg

Management and Staff
Lai Seck Khui, Chief Operating Officer

Type of Firm
Non-Financial Corp. Affiliate or Subsidiary

Project Preferences

Type of Financing Preferred:
Balanced

Geographical Preferences

International
Asia

Additional Information
Year Founded: 1883
Current Activity Level : Actively seeking new investments

FRIEDLI CORPORATE FINANCE AG

Freigutstrasse 5
Zurich, Switzerland 8002
Phone: 41 1283 2900
Fax: 41 1283 2901
Website: www.friedlicorp.com

Management and Staff
Peter Friedli, President

Type of Firm
Private Firm Investing Own Capital

Project Preferences

Type of Financing Preferred:
Early Stage
Startup

Geographical Preferences

United States
All U.S.

Additional Information
Name of Most Recent Fund: InVenture, Inc.
Most Recent Fund Was Raised: 01/01/1999
Year Founded: 1986
Capital Under Management: $900,000,000
Current Activity Level : Actively seeking new investments

FRIENDS IVORY & SIME PRIVATE EQUITY (IVORY &SIME BARONSMEAD)

100 Wood Street
London, United Kingdom EC2V 87N
Phone: 44-20-7853-6900
Fax: 44-20-7853-6970

Other Offices

Bank House
8 Cherry Street
Birmingham, United Kingdom B2 5AN
Phone: 44-121-253-1600
Fax: 44-121-253-1616

Management and Staff

David Thorp, Managing Director
Wol Kolade, Managing Director

Whom to Contact

Adam Attwood
Dominic Ely
Mark Advani
Robin Lincoln
Shani Zindel

Type of Firm

Private Firm Investing Own Capital

Industry Association Membership

British Venture Capital Association

Project Preferences

Role in Financing:

Prefer role as deal originator but will also invest in deals created by others

Type of Financing Preferred:

Balanced
Expansion
Leveraged Buyout

Geographical Preferences

International

Europe
Germany
Netherlands
United Kingdom

Industry Preferences

(% based on actual investment)

Other Products	32.0%
Internet Specific	16.9%
Computer Software and Services	15.3%
Communications and Media	13.3%
Biotechnology	9.1%
Consumer Related	8.3%
Medical/Health	5.2%

Additional Information

Name of Most Recent Fund: Institutional Annual Partnership
Most Recent Fund Was Raised: 12/01/1998
Year Founded: 1983
Capital Under Management: $209,000,000
Current Activity Level : Actively seeking new investments

FRIULIA SPA FIN.REG.FRIULI-VENEZIA

Via Locchi N. 19
Trieste, Italy 34123
Phone: 39-040-31971
Fax: 39-40-3197400
Website: www.friulia.it

Management and Staff

Franco Asquini, Partner
Giorgio Frassini, Chief Executive Officer

Type of Firm

State Govt Affiliated NEC

Industry Association Membership

European Venture Capital Association (EVCA)
Italian Venture Capital Association

Project Preferences

Role in Financing:

Prefer role as deal originator but will also invest in deals created by others

Type of Financing Preferred:

Early Stage
Expansion
First Stage Financing
Leveraged Buyout
Mezzanine
Second Stage Financing

Geographical Preferences

International

Italy

Industry Preferences

Computer Software

Computer Services
Systems Software

Medical/Health

Medical Diagnostics

Consumer Related

Food/Beverage

Industrial/Energy

Industrial Products
Factory Automation
Machinery

Additional Information

Year Founded: 1967
Capital Under Management: $31,000,000
Current Activity Level : Actively seeking new investments
Method of Compensation: Professional fee required whether or not deal closes

FUTURE VENTURE CAPITAL CO., LTD.

Itoko Apparel Bldg 5F, 314
Oikeno-cho, Muramachi-dori
Kyoto, Japan
Phone: 075-257-6656
Fax: 075-211-6965
Website: www.fvc.co.jp

Type of Firm

Private Firm Investing Own Capital

Project Preferences

Type of Financing Preferred:

Balanced
Early Stage

Geographical Preferences

International

Japan

Industry Preferences

(% based on actual investment)

Consumer Related	23.8%
Other Products	22.2%
Medical/Health	17.6%
Internet Specific	16.2%
Computer Software and Services	7.2%
Semiconductors/Other Elect.	6.6%
Industrial/Energy	4.0%
Communications and Media	2.5%

Additional Information

Capital Under Management: $7,000,000
Current Activity Level : Actively seeking new investments

GALILEO PARTNERS

89 rue Taitbout
Paris, France 75009
Phone: 33-1-5635-0550
Fax: 33-1-5635-0514
Website: www.galileo.fr

Management and Staff
Bernard Maitre, Partner
Joel Flichy, Partner
Michel Angue, Partner

Type of Firm
Private Firm Investing Own Capital

Industry Association Membership
European Venture Capital Association (EVCA)

Geographical Preferences

International
Europe

Industry Preferences

Internet Specific
Internet

Additional Information
Name of Most Recent Fund: Galileo II FCPR
Most Recent Fund Was Raised: 09/01/1998
Year Founded: 1989
Capital Under Management: $95,200,000
Current Activity Level : Actively seeking new investments

GAON ASSET MANAGEMENT

11 Tuval Street
Ramat Gan, Israel 52522
Phone: 972 3 795 4100
Fax: 972 3 612 3305

Management and Staff
Dan Gilat, Partner

Type of Firm
Private Equity Advisor or Fund of Fund Mgr

Project Preferences

Type of Financing Preferred:
Balanced

Geographical Preferences

International
Israel

Industry Preferences

Medical/Health
Medical/Health

Additional Information
Capital Under Management: $75,000,000
Current Activity Level : Actively seeking new investments

GAP FUND MANAGERS LTD

90 Main Street
Rutherglen
Glasgow, United Kingdom G73 2HX
Phone: 44-141-647-7646
Fax: 44-141-647-7647

Management and Staff
Nelson Gray, Chief Executive Officer

Type of Firm
Private Equity Advisor or Fund of Fund Mgr

Project Preferences

Type of Financing Preferred:
Early Stage
Expansion
Startup

Geographical Preferences

International
United Kingdom

Additional Information
Year Founded: 2000
Capital Under Management: $23,000,000
Current Activity Level : Actively seeking new investments

GEMINI CAPITAL FUND MANAGEMENT LTD

11 Galgaley Haplada Street
P.O. Box 12548
Herzliya Pituach, Israel 46733
Phone: 972-9-958-3596
Fax: 972-9-958-4842
Website: www.gemini.co.il

Other Offices

2180 Sand Hill Road
Menlo Park, United States of America 94026
Phone: 650-233-1206
Fax: 650-233-7515

Management and Staff
Adi Pundak-Mintz, Partner
David Cohen, Chief Executive Officer
Ed Mlavsky, Chairman & Managing Director
Lior Berger, Partner
Tali Aben, General Partner
Yossi Sela, Managing Partner

Whom to Contact
Steve Kahn

Type of Firm
Private Equity Advisor or Fund of Fund Mgr

Project Preferences

Role in Financing:
Prefer role as deal originator but will also invest in deals created by others

Type of Financing Preferred:
Early Stage
Expansion
Seed
Startup

Size of Investments Considered
Min Size of Investment Considered (000s): $500
Max Size of Investment Considered (000s): $5,000

Geographical Preferences

International
Israel

Industry Preferences

(% based on actual investment)

Communications and Media	23.5%
Computer Software and Services	23.4%
Internet Specific	15.8%
Medical/Health	13.8%
Computer Hardware	10.0%
Other Products	9.2%
Biotechnology	3.7%
Semiconductors/Other Elect.	0.4%
Consumer Related	0.3%

Additional Information
Name of Most Recent Fund: Gimini Israel II
Most Recent Fund Was Raised: 11/01/1997
Year Founded: 1993
Capital Under Management: $350,000,000
Current Activity Level : Actively seeking new investments
Method of Compensation: Return on investment is of primary concern, do not charge fees

GENERAL ENTERPRISE MANAGEMENT SERVICES LTD (AKA: GEMS)

2108 Gloucester Tower
The Landmark, 11 Pedder Street
Central, Hong Kong
Phone: 852-2838-0093
Fax: 852-2838-0292

Management and Staff
Geoff Spender, Chief Executive Officer

Type of Firm
Private Firm Investing Own Capital

Industry Association Membership
Hungarian Venture Capital Association

Project Preferences

Type of Financing Preferred:
Expansion

Geographical Preferences

International
Asia

Industry Preferences

Communications and Media
Telecommunications

Consumer Related
Retail

Industrial/Energy
Energy

Transportation
Transportation

Financial Services
Financial Services

Business Serv.
Media

Manufact.
Manufacturing

Additional Information
Name of Most Recent Fund: GEMS Oriental & General Fund Limited
Most Recent Fund Was Raised: 07/01/1998
Year Founded: 1998
Capital Under Management: $250,000,000
Current Activity Level : Actively seeking new investments

GENES GMBH VENTURE SERVICES

Koelner Strasse 27
Frechen, Germany D-50226
Phone: 49-2234-955460
Fax: 49-2234-955464
Website: www.genes-vc.com

Other Offices
Porsestrasse 19
Magdeburg, Germany D-39104

Management and Staff
Eckart Bohm, Partner
Joerg Kreisel, Partner
Klaus Nathusius, Partner

Whom to Contact
Joerg Kreisel
Klaus Nathusius

Type of Firm
Mgt. Consulting Firm

Industry Association Membership
European Venture Capital Association (EVCA)
German Venture Capital Association

Project Preferences

Role in Financing:
Prefer role as deal originator

Type of Financing Preferred:
Early Stage
Expansion
First Stage Financing
Fund of Funds
Later Stage
Leveraged Buyout
Management Buyouts
Second Stage Financing
Special Situation
Start-up Financing
Unknown

Size of Investments Considered
Min Size of Investment Considered (000s): $500
Max Size of Investment Considered (000s): $500,000

Geographical Preferences

International
Europe
France
Germany

Industry Preferences

Communications and Media
Communications and Media

Internet Specific
E-Commerce Technology

Industrial/Energy
Alternative Energy
Materials
Factory Automation
Machinery
Environmental Related

Additional Information
Year Founded: 1978
Capital Under Management: $23,800,000
Current Activity Level : Actively seeking new investments
Method of Compensation: Return on invest. most important, but chg. closing fees, service fees, etc.

GENESIS PARTNERS

Top Tower, 50 Dizengoff
P.O. Box 23722
Tel Aviv, Israel
Phone: 972-3-526-2644
Fax: 972-3-526-2696
Website: www.genesispartners.co.il

Management and Staff
Eddie Shalev, General Partner
Eyal Kishon, Managing Partner
Vered Assulin, Partner
Yair Shoham, Partner

Type of Firm
Private Firm Investing Own Capital

Project Preferences

Type of Financing Preferred:
Balanced
Early Stage
Expansion
Later Stage
Seed
Startup

Geographical Preferences

International
Israel

Industry Preferences

(% based on actual investment)

Communications and Media	49.7%
Computer Software and Services	38.8%
Semiconductors/Other Elect.	7.5%
Internet Specific	4.0%

Additional Information
Year Founded: 1997
Capital Under Management: $350,000,000
Current Activity Level : Actively seeking new investments

GENEVEST CONSULTING GROUP, S.A.

10, rue du Vieux-College
Geneva, Switzerland CH-1204
Phone: 41-22-312-3333
Fax: 41-22-312-3366

Management and Staff
Jean-Louis Fatio, Partner
Sven Lingjaerde, Managing Director

Type of Firm
Mgt. Consulting Firm

Industry Association Membership
European Venture Capital Association (EVCA)

Project Preferences

Role in Financing:
Prefer role as deal originator but will also invest in deals created by others

Type of Financing Preferred:
Early Stage
Expansion
Startup
Unknown

Geographical Preferences

United States
All U.S.

International
Europe
Switzerland

Industry Preferences

Computer Software
Software

Computer Other
Computer Related

Semiconductors/Other Elect.
Electronics

Business Serv.
Media

Additional Information
Name of Most Recent Fund: Genevest Group of Switzerland
Most Recent Fund Was Raised: 02/01/1984
Year Founded: 1983
Capital Under Management: $60,400,000
Current Activity Level : Actively seeking new investments
Method of Compensation: Return on invest. most important, but chg. closing fees, service fees, etc.

GEOCAPITAL PARTNERS, L.L.C.

Pollen House
10-12 Cork Street
London, United Kingdom WIX IPD
Phone: 44-20-7851-2800
Fax: 44-20-7851-2801

See New Jersey for full listing.

GILDE INVESTMENT MANAGEMENT

Newtonlaan 91
P.O. Box 85067
Utrecht, Netherlands 3508 AB
Phone: 31-30-219-2525
Fax: 31-30-254-0004
Website: www.gilde.nl

Other Offices

69 Boulevard Haussmann
Paris, France F-75008

Management and Staff
Albert Bolema
Gerhard Nordemann
Michael van Olerbeek
Toon den Heijer
Tor Gardeniers

Whom to Contact
Albert Bolema
Gerhard Nordemann
Michael van Olerbeek
Toon den Heijer
Tor Gardeniers

Type of Firm
Investment/Merchant Bank Subsid/Affil

Industry Association Membership
European Venture Capital Association (EVCA)

Project Preferences

Role in Financing:
Prefer role as deal originator but will also invest in deals created by others

Type of Financing Preferred:
First Stage Financing
Leveraged Buyout
Management Buyouts
Second Stage Financing

Size of Investments Considered
Min Size of Investment Considered (000s): $100,000
Max Size of Investment Considered: No Limit

Geographical Preferences

United States
All U.S.

Canada
All Canada

International
Australia
Bermuda
Europe
France
Germany
Italy
Middle East
Spain
United Kingdom

Industry Preferences

(% based on actual investment)

Industrial/Energy	49.9%
Communications and Media	18.5%
Computer Software and Services	12.5%
Internet Specific	11.5%
Computer Hardware	3.6%
Biotechnology	1.8%
Medical/Health	1.5%
Semiconductors/Other Elect.	0.4%
Other Products	0.4%

Additional Information
Name of Most Recent Fund: Gilde IT Fund
Most Recent Fund Was Raised: 01/01/1998
Year Founded: 1982
Capital Under Management: $685,400,000
Current Activity Level : Actively seeking new investments
Method of Compensation: Return on invest. most important, but chg. closing fees, service fees, etc.

GIMVINDUS NV

Matenstraat 214
Niel, Belgium B-2845
Phone: 32-3-880-8120
Fax: 32-3-844-7508

Management and Staff
Roger Maleve, Partner

Type of Firm
Private Firm Investing Own Capital

Industry Association Membership
European Venture Capital Association (EVCA)

Project Preferences

Type of Financing Preferred:
Expansion
Fund of Funds
Leveraged Buyout
Management Buyouts
Turnaround

Geographical Preferences

International
Belgium
Europe

Industry Preferences

Industrial/Energy
Industrial Products

Financial Services
Financial Services
Insurance
Real Estate

Additional Information
Capital Under Management: $985,500,000
Current Activity Level : Actively seeking new investments

GIZA VENTURE CAPITAL (FKA GIZA INVESTMENT MANAGEMENT)

Ramat Aviv Tower, 12th Floor
40 Einstein Street
Tel Aviv 61172, Israel
Phone: 972-3-640-2323
Fax: 972-3-640-2300
Website: www.giza.co.il

Management and Staff
Ezer Soref, Vice President
Giora Bitan, Managing Director
Zeev Holzman, Chairman & CEO
Zvi Shechter, Managing Director

Type of Firm
Investment/Merchant Bank Subsid/Affil

Project Preferences

Role in Financing:
Prefer role as deal originator

Type of Financing Preferred:
First Stage Financing
Second Stage Financing
Start-up Financing

Size of Investments Considered
Min Size of Investment Considered (000s): $3,000
Max Size of Investment Considered (000s): $5,000

Geographical Preferences

International
Israel

Industry Preferences

(% based on actual investment)

Communications and Media	35.2%
Internet Specific	32.5%
Biotechnology	12.4%
Computer Software and Services	10.7%
Medical/Health	9.2%

Additional Information
Year Founded: 1992
Capital Under Management: $270,000,000
Current Activity Level : Actively seeking new investments
Method of Compensation: Return on investment is of primary concern, do not charge fees

GKM VENTURE PARTNERS, LP

28 Bezalel Street
President Tower, 28th Floor
Ramat Gan , Israel 52521
Phone: 972-3-575-4242

See California for full listing.

GLOBAL CROSSING VENTURES (FKA: FRONTIER VENTURES)

Wessex House
45 Reid Street
Hamilton, Bermuda HM12
Phone: 441-296-8600
Fax: 441-296-8606

See California for full listing.

GLOBAL FINANCE SA

14 Philikis Eterias Square
Athens, Greece 10673
Phone: 30-1-729-2640
Fax: 30-1-729-2643

Other Offices

39 Vitosha Blvd.
1st Floor
Sofia, France 1000
Phone: 359-2-9801619
Fax: 359-2-980-8245

Bdul Unirii nr. 19
Bl. 4B Sc.1
Bucharast, France
Phone: 40-1-336-3365
Fax: 40-1-336-3518

Management and Staff
Angelos Plakopitas, Managing Director

Whom to Contact
Angelos Plakopitas
Aurelian Trifa
Mirolub Voutov

Type of Firm
Mgt. Consulting Firm

Project Preferences

Role in Financing:
Prefer role as deal originator but will also invest in deals created by others

Type of Financing Preferred:
Leveraged Buyout
Mezzanine

Size of Investments Considered
Min Size of Investment Considered (000s): $1,000
Max Size of Investment Considered: No Limit

Geographical Preferences

International
Cyprus
Greece

Additional Information

Name of Most Recent Fund: Black Sea Fund
Most Recent Fund Was Raised: 01/01/1998
Year Founded: 1991
Capital Under Management: $154,000,000
Current Activity Level : Actively seeking new investments
Method of Compensation: Return on invest. most important, but chg. closing fees, service fees, etc.

GLOBAL INTERNET VENTURES (GIV)

No. 714 Carlton Towers
No. 1 Airport Road
Bangalore, India
Phone: 9180-521-6066
Fax: 9180-521-6077

See Virginia for full listing.

GLOBAL PARTNER VENTURES

Martirosyana Street
Office A
Kyiv, Ukraine 252180
Phone: 380-44-243-7300
Fax: 380-44-243-7298

See Virginia for full listing.

GLOBAL TECHNOLOGY VENTURES (GTV)

321 Raheja Chambers
12 Musuem Road
Bangalore, India 560001
Phone: 9180-559-4648/9
Fax: 9180-559-8990
Website: www.gtvltd.com

Type of Firm

Incubators

Project Preferences

Type of Financing Preferred:
Early Stage
Later Stage
Startup

Geographical Preferences

International
India

Additional Information

Capital Under Management: $5,000,000
Current Activity Level : Actively seeking new investments

GLOBAL VENTURE CAPITAL CORPORATION

4/F,No. 2,Hsin-Sheng S. Road
Section 2
Taipei, Taiwan
Phone: 8862-2393-3851
Fax: 8862-2394-3622

Type of Firm

Private Firm Investing Own Capital

Industry Association Membership

Taiwan Venture Capital Association(TVCA)

Project Preferences

Type of Financing Preferred:
Early Stage
Seed

Geographical Preferences

International
Taiwan

Industry Preferences

Biotechnology
Biotechnology

Additional Information

Year Founded: 1998
Capital Under Management: $15,500,000
Current Activity Level : Actively seeking new investments

GO CAPITAL

Amsterdamsestraatweg 47
Baarn, Netherlands 3744 MA
Phone: 31 35 5485070
Fax: 31 35 5485079
E-mail: Ron.Belt@go-capital.nl
Website: www.go-capital.nl

Management and Staff

Corneille Couwenberg, Partner
Frans Van Schaik, Partner
Ron Belt, Partner

Type of Firm

Private Firm Investing Own Capital

Project Preferences

Type of Financing Preferred:
Early Stage
Startup

Geographical Preferences

International
Europe

Industry Preferences

Computer Software
Software

Additional Information

Capital Under Management: $17,100,000
Current Activity Level : Actively seeking new investments

GO EQUITY GMBH

Hoyosgasse 5
Vienna, Austria A - 1040
Phone: 431-503-5980
Fax: 431-503-5980 30
Website: www.goequity.at

Type of Firm

Private Firm Investing Own Capital

Industry Association Membership

European Venture Capital Association (EVCA)

Project Preferences

Type of Financing Preferred:
Early Stage
Expansion
Management Buyouts
Mezzanine
Start-up Financing

Size of Investments Considered

Min Size of Investment Considered (000s): $1,400
Max Size of Investment Considered: No Limit

Geographical Preferences

International
Asia
Austria
Europe

Industry Preferences

(% based on actual investment)

Communications and Media	37.4%
Other Products	29.6%
Biotechnology	14.9%
Computer Hardware	9.8%
Internet Specific	4.8%
Industrial/Energy	3.4%

Additional Information

Name of Most Recent Fund: Go Asia
Most Recent Fund Was Raised: 12/01/1998
Year Founded: 1993
Capital Under Management: $37,000,000
Current Activity Level : Actively seeking new investments

GOODWILL COMMUNICATION, INC.

Kyocera-Harajuku Bldg., 6-27-8
Jigumae, Japan
Phone: 81-03-5766-7111
Fax: 81-03-5766-7112
Website: www.gcm.co.jp/en/company/index.shtml

Type of Firm

Private Equity Advisor or Fund of Fund Mgr

Project Preferences

Type of Financing Preferred:
Balanced

Geographical Preferences

International
No Preference

Additional Information

Year Founded: 1992
Current Activity Level : Actively seeking new investments

GORILLAPARK

Stephensonstraat 19
Amsterdam, Netherlands 1097 BA
Phone: 31 20 750 7300
Fax: 31 20 750 7301
Website: www.gorillapark.com

Other Offices

112 Avenue Kleber
Paris, France 75116
Phone: 33 147 557 407
Fax: 33 147 557 463

42-46 Princelet Street
London, United Kingdom E1 5LP
Phone: 44 207 920 2500
Fax: 44 207 920 2501

576 Folsom Street
San Francisco, United States of America 94105
Phone: 415 989 900

Cuvilliestrasse 14a
Munich, Germany 81679
Phone: 49 8999 888 2100

Riddargatan 7a, 6tr
Stockholm, Sweden 11435
Phone: 46-8-555 194 70
Fax: 46-8-555 194 75

Management and Staff

Jerome Mol, Chairman & CEO
Paul Sturrock, Managing Director
Peter van Oorschot, Chief Operating Officer
Richard Farr, Chief Financial Officer

Type of Firm

Incubators

Project Preferences

Type of Financing Preferred:
Early Stage

Geographical Preferences

International
Europe

Industry Preferences

Internet Specific
Internet

Additional Information

Year Founded: 1999
Capital Under Management: $81,800,000
Current Activity Level : Actively seeking new investments

GRAND PACIFIC VENTURE CAPITAL COMPANY LTD.

11/F,No. 3 Sung Shou Road
Taipei, Taiwan
Phone: 8862-2345-8998
Fax: 8862-2345-5382

Management and Staff

Daniel Wu, President & Chairman

Type of Firm

Private Firm Investing Own Capital

Industry Association Membership

Taiwan Venture Capital Association(TVCA)

Project Preferences

Type of Financing Preferred:
Expansion
Mezzanine
Seed
Startup

Geographical Preferences

International
Taiwan

Industry Preferences

Semiconductors/Other Elect.
Electronics
Electronic Components

Biotechnology
Biotechnology

Medical/Health
Pharmaceuticals

Additional Information

Year Founded: 1996
Capital Under Management: $15,500,000
Current Activity Level : Actively seeking new investments

GRANVILLE BAIRD CAPITAL PARTNERS (FKA:GRANVILLE PR EQ MNGRS)

Mint House
77 Mansell Street
London, United Kingdom E1 8AF
Phone: 44-207-488-1212
Fax: 44-207-481-3911
Website: www.granvillebaird.com

Other Offices

16 Avenue Hoche
Paris, France 75008
Phone: 33 140.76.04.01
Fax: 33 140.76.04.02

Aintree House
1 York Place
Leeds, United Kingdom LS1 2DR
Phone: 44 113 280 3500
Fax: 44 113 280 3501

Castle Chambers
Fourth Floor
Liverpool, United Kingdom LS1 9SH
Phone: 44-51-258-1859
Fax: 44-51-258-1860

Cheshire House
18-20 Booth Street
Manchester , United Kingdom M2 4AN
Phone: 44 161 236 6600
Fax: 44 161 236 6650

Edificio El Dau
Avda Diagonal 615, 8oE
Barcelona, Spain 08028
Phone: 34 93 494 9400
Fax: 34 93 494 9401

Haus am Hafen
Steinhoeft 5-7
Hamburg, Germany 20459
Phone: 49 40 3748 0210
Fax: 49 40 3748 0223

Palais Liechtenstein
Alserbachstrasse 14-16
Vienna, Austria 1090
Phone: 43 1 31 05 73 0
Fax: 43 1 31 05 73 3

Robert W. Baird & Co.
777 East Wisconsin Avenue
Milwaukee, United States of America 53202
Phone: 414 765 3758

Management and Staff
Gary Solomon, Chief Executive Officer
Jacques Paquin, Partner
Michael Fell, Managing Director

Whom to Contact
C.J. Harper
D.G. Martin
J. Berge
M.S. Fuller

Type of Firm
Private Firm Investing Own Capital

Industry Association Membership
European Venture Capital Association (EVCA)
German Venture Capital Association

Project Preferences

Role in Financing:
Prefer role as deal originator but will also invest in deals created by others

Type of Financing Preferred:
Expansion
Leveraged Buyout
Management Buyouts
Recapitalizations
Turnaround

Size of Investments Considered
Min Size of Investment Considered (000s): $8,000
Max Size of Investment Considered: No Limit

Geographical Preferences

International
France
Germany
Italy
Spain
United Kingdom

Industry Preferences

(% based on actual investment)

Other Products	42.9%
Internet Specific	21.4%
Computer Software and Services	19.7%
Industrial/Energy	7.4%
Medical/Health	5.0%
Computer Hardware	2.4%
Biotechnology	1.3%

Additional Information
Name of Most Recent Fund: Granville Private Equity Managers (UK) Fund VI
Most Recent Fund Was Raised: 02/10/1999
Year Founded: 1973
Capital Under Management: $750,000,000
Current Activity Level : Actively seeking new investments
Method of Compensation: Return on invest. most important, but chg. closing fees, service fees, etc.

GRANVILLE PRIVATE EQUITY SPAIN

Avenida Diagonal 615
Barcelona, Spain 08028
Phone: 34-93494-9400
Fax: 34-93494-9401
E-mail: j.berge@granvillebaird.com
Website: www.granvillebaird.com

Management and Staff
Jaume Berge, Managing Director

Type of Firm
Private Firm Investing Own Capital

Industry Association Membership
European Venture Capital Association (EVCA)

Additional Information
Capital Under Management: $28,600,000
Current Activity Level : Actively seeking new investments

GRAPHITE CAPITAL (FKA: F&C VENTURES LTD)

Berkeley Square House
Berkeley Square
London, United Kingdom W1X 5PA
Phone: 44-207-825-5300
Fax: 44-207-825-5399
Website: www.graphitecapital.com

Management and Staff
A. Gray
S. Fitch
S. Cavell

Whom to Contact
A. Gray
S. Fitch
S. Cavell

Type of Firm
Private Firm Investing Own Capital

Industry Association Membership
British Venture Capital Association

Project Preferences

Role in Financing:
Prefer role as deal originator but will also invest in deals created by others

Type of Financing Preferred:
Leveraged Buyout
Second Stage Financing
Special Situation

Geographical Preferences

International
Bermuda
France
Germany
Italy
Spain
United Kingdom
Western Europe

Industry Preferences

(% based on actual investment)

Industrial/Energy	58.4%
Communications and Media	15.8%
Consumer Related	12.2%
Other Products	12.0%
Medical/Health	1.6%
Semiconductors/Other Elect.	0.1%

Additional Information

Name of Most Recent Fund: F&C Ventures Private Equity Fund
Most Recent Fund Was Raised: 06/15/1994
Year Founded: 1981
Capital Under Management: $750,000,000
Current Activity Level : Actively seeking new investments
Method of Compensation: Return on invest. most important, but chg. closing fees, service fees, etc.

GREENSTONE VENTURE PARTNERS

1177 West Hastings Street
Suite 400
Vancouver, Canada V6E 2K3
Phone: 604-717-1977
Fax: 604-717-1976
Website: www.greenstonevc.com

Management and Staff

Brent Holliday, General Partner
Livia Mahler, General Partner
Richard Osborn, General Partner

Type of Firm

Private Firm Investing Own Capital

Additional Information

Year Founded: 2000
Capital Under Management: $35,000,000
Current Activity Level : Actively seeking new investments

GRESHAM CEA MANAGEMENT LIMITED

175 Macquarie Street
Level 6
Sydney, Australia 02000
Phone: 612-9235-1100
Fax: 612-9235-1144
Website: www.gresham.com.au/live/special_fr.html

Management and Staff

Tim Downing, Managing Director

Type of Firm

Investment/Merchant Bank Investing Own or Client Funds

Industry Association Membership

Australian Venture Capital Association (AVCAL)

Project Preferences

Role in Financing:
Prefer role as deal originator but will also invest in deals created by others

Type of Financing Preferred:
Early Stage
Expansion

Size of Investments Considered
Min Size of Investment Considered (000s): $3,300
Max Size of Investment Considered (000s): $6,500

Geographical Preferences

International
Oceania/Australasia

Industry Preferences

(% based on actual investment)

Internet Specific	50.7%
Communications and Media	29.0%
Consumer Related	20.3%

Additional Information

Year Founded: 1996
Capital Under Management: $34,300,000
Current Activity Level : Actively seeking new investments
Method of Compensation: Professional fee required whether or not deal closes

GRESHAM RABO MANAGEMENT LIMITED

175 Macquarie Street
Level 6
Sydney, Australia 02000
Phone: 612-9221-4133
Fax: 612-9232-3352
Website: www.gresham.com.au

Management and Staff

Brian Hanley, Managing Director
Roger Casey, Managing Director

Type of Firm

Investment/Merchant Bank Investing Own or Client Funds

Industry Association Membership

Australian Venture Capital Association (AVCAL)

Project Preferences

Type of Financing Preferred:
Acquisition
Expansion
First Stage Financing
Leveraged Buyout
Management Buyouts
Recapitalizations
Second Stage Financing
Special Situation
Startup
Turnaround

Geographical Preferences

International
Oceania/Australasia

Industry Preferences

Biotechnology
Biotechnology

Consumer Related
Food/Beverage

Agr/Forestr/Fish
Agribusiness

Additional Information
Name of Most Recent Fund: Food and Agribusiness Investment Fund (FAIF)
Most Recent Fund Was Raised: 07/01/1998
Year Founded: 1997
Capital Under Management: $41,700,000
Current Activity Level : Actively seeking new investments

GRIEVE, HORNER, BROWN & ASCULAI

Eight King Street East
Suite 1704
Toronto, Canada M5C 1B5
Phone: 416-362-7668
Fax: 416-362-7660

Type of Firm
Private Firm Investing Own Capital

Industry Association Membership
Canadian Venture Capital Association

Project Preferences

Role in Financing:
Prefer role as deal originator but will also invest in deals created by others

Type of Financing Preferred:
First Stage Financing
Second Stage Financing
Start-up Financing

Size of Investments Considered
Min Size of Investment Considered (000s): $300
Max Size of Investment Considered (000s): $500

Geographical Preferences

United States
All U.S.

Canada
All Canada

Industry Preferences

Communications and Media
Communications and Media

Computer Software
Systems Software
Applications Software
Artificial Intelligence

Internet Specific
Internet

Medical/Health
Drug/Equipmt Delivery
Pharmaceuticals

Consumer Related
Consumer Products
Consumer Services
Education Related

Manufact.
Publishing

Additional Information
Name of Most Recent Fund: Grieve Horner & Associates
Most Recent Fund Was Raised: 07/01/1981
Year Founded: 1976
Capital Under Management: $10,000,000
Current Activity Level : Actively seeking new investments
Method of Compensation: Return on investment is of primary concern, do not charge fees

GROWTH FACTORY, THE

Molleparken 6
Oslo, Norway 0458
Phone: 47 22 80 77 70
Fax: 47 22 80 79 01
E-mail: investors@thegrowthfactory.com
Website: www.tgfactory.com

Other Offices

Amaliegade 39
Copenhagen, Denmark 1256
Phone: 45 33 14 79 15
Fax: 45 33 14 08 24

Birger Jarlsgatan 26
4 tr Box 7224
Stockholm, Sweden 103 89
Phone: 46 8 679 79 97
Fax: 46 8 440 50 90

Management and Staff
Alexander Woxen, Founder
Colin Bartel, Founder
Fredrik Mowill, Founder
Rein Inge Hoff, Founder

Type of Firm
Incubators

Project Preferences

Type of Financing Preferred:
Seed
Startup

Geographical Preferences

International
Scandanavia/Nordic Region

Industry Preferences

Communications and Media
Communications and Media

Computer Software
Software

Internet Specific
Internet

Additional Information
Capital Under Management: $4,700,000
Current Activity Level : Actively seeking new investments

GROWTH VENTURE GROUP PTY LTD.

390 Beach Road
Beaumaris, Australia 3193
Phone: 613-9589-0655
Fax: 613-9589-0677

Type of Firm
Private Firm Investing Own Capital

Project Preferences

Role in Financing:
Prefer role in deals created by others

Type of Financing Preferred:
Acquisition
Expansion
Leveraged Buyout
Management Buyouts
Turnaround

Size of Investments Considered
Min Size of Investment Considered (000s): $62,000
Max Size of Investment Considered (000s): $617,000

Geographical Preferences

International
Australia

Industry Preferences

Communications and Media
Telecommunications

Consumer Related
Retail
Food/Beverage

Industrial/Energy
Industrial Products

Business Serv.
Distribution

Manufact.
Manufacturing

Additional Information
Year Founded: 1995
Capital Under Management: $49,400,000
Current Activity Level : Actively seeking new investments
Method of Compensation: Return on investment is of primary concern, do not charge fees

GROWTHWORKS CAPITAL

2600-1055 West Georgia Street
Box 11170 Royal Centre
Vancouver, Canada V6E 3R5
Phone: 604-895-7259
Fax: 604-669-7605
Website: www.wofund.com

Management and Staff
Mike Phillips

Whom to Contact
Mike Phillips

Type of Firm
Private Firm Investing Own Capital

Industry Association Membership
Canadian Venture Capital Association

Project Preferences

Role in Financing:
Will function either as deal originator or investor in deals created by others

Type of Financing Preferred:
Balanced
Early Stage
First Stage Financing
Joint Ventures
Later Stage
Management Buyouts
Mezzanine
Private Placement
Research and Development
Second Stage Financing
Seed
Startup

Size of Investments Considered
Min Size of Investment Considered (000s): $330
Max Size of Investment Considered (000s): $3,300

Geographical Preferences

Canada
British Columbia

Industry Preferences

Communications and Media
Commercial Communications
Telecommunications
Wireless Communications
Data Communications
Satellite Microwave Comm.
Other Communication Prod.

Internet Specific
Internet

Computer Other
Computer Related

Semiconductors/Other Elect.
Electronics

Biotechnology
Human Biotechnology
Agricultural/Animal Bio.
Industrial Biotechnology
Biosensors

Medical/Health
Medical/Health

Consumer Related
Entertainment and Leisure
Education Related

Industrial/Energy
Energy
Industrial Products
Superconductivity
Factory Automation
Process Control
Robotics
Machinery

Transportation
Transportation

Manufact.
Manufacturing

Agr/Forestr/Fish
Agriculture related

Other
Socially Responsible
Environment Responsible

Additional Information
Year Founded: 1999
Capital Under Management: $520,000,000
Current Activity Level : Actively seeking new investments
Method of Compensation: Return on investment is of primary concern, do not charge fees

GUJARAT VENTURE FINANCE LIMITED

1/F Premchand House Annex
Ashram Road
Ahmedabad, India 380 009
Phone: 9179-658-0704
Fax: 9179-658-5226
Website: www.gvfl.com

Other Offices

#45 Trade Centre
Bangalore, India 560042
Phone: 9180-559-9955
Fax: 9180-558-1354

Management and Staff
Rajeev Pai, Vice President
Vinodkumar Chopra, Vice President
Vipul Mankad, Vice President

Whom to Contact
Vishnu Varshney

Type of Firm
Private Firm Investing Own Capital

Project Preferences

Role in Financing:
Prefer role as deal originator but will also invest in deals created by others

Type of Financing Preferred:
Early Stage
Expansion
Startup

Geographical Preferences

International
India

Industry Preferences

(% based on actual investment)

Industrial/Energy	27.9%
Other Products	22.2%
Computer Software and Services	16.8%
Communications and Media	12.9%
Internet Specific	9.5%
Consumer Related	4.7%

Computer Hardware	3.5%
Medical/Health	1.8%
Biotechnology	0.7%

Additional Information
Name of Most Recent Fund: GVCF-97 Software
Most Recent Fund Was Raised: 10/01/1997
Year Founded: 1990
Capital Under Management: $30,000,000
Current Activity Level : Actively seeking new investments
Method of Compensation: Return on investment is of primary concern, do not charge fees

H&Q ASIA PACIFIC, LTD.

Rm. 709 CCMM Bldg, 12 Yoido-dong
Youngdungpo-ku
Seoul, South Korea 150010
Phone: 822-782-2288
Fax: 822-775-4589

See California for full listing.

HALDER HOLDINGS B.V.

Lange Voorhout 9
The Hague, Netherlands 2514 EA
Phone: 31-70-361-8618
Fax: 31-70-361-8616
Website: www.halder.nl

Other Offices

Bockenheimer Landstrasse 23
Frankfurt, Germany D-60325
Phone: 49-69-24-25330
Fax: 49-69-23-6866

Mechelsesteenweg 267
Antwerp, Bermuda B-2018
Phone: 32-3-239-3600
Fax: 32-3-281-6152

Management and Staff
Joachim Kramer, Managing Director
Lieven Cuvelier, Managing Director
Paul De Ridder, Managing Director
Paul Deiters, Managing Director
Rene Smits, Managing Director
Sam Alleman, Managing Director

Whom to Contact
Antoine van den Abeele

Type of Firm
Private Firm Investing Own Capital

Industry Association Membership
Belgium Venture Capital Association
European Venture Capital Association (EVCA)
German Venture Capital Association

Project Preferences

Role in Financing:
Prefer role as deal originator but will also invest in deals created by others

Type of Financing Preferred:
Expansion
Leveraged Buyout
Management Buyouts
Recapitalizations

Size of Investments Considered
Min Size of Investment Considered (000s): $8,000
Max Size of Investment Considered: No Limit

Geographical Preferences

International
Belgium
Germany
Netherlands

Industry Preferences

(% based on actual investment)

Industrial/Energy	67.7%
Other Products	14.0%
Medical/Health	9.4%
Consumer Related	7.1%
Computer Software and Services	1.3%
Biotechnology	0.3%

Additional Information
Name of Most Recent Fund: Halder Investments IV, L.P.
Most Recent Fund Was Raised: 12/01/1996
Year Founded: 1984
Capital Under Management: $225,000,000
Current Activity Level : Actively seeking new investments
Method of Compensation: Return on investment is of primary concern, do not charge fees

HAMBRO EUROPEAN VENTURES (HAMBROS PLC)

41 Tower Hill
London, United Kingdom EC3N 4HA
Phone: 171-702-3593
Fax: 44-171-338-9264

Management and Staff
Alex Cooper-Evans
Giles Cheek
Iain Kennedy

Whom to Contact
Alex Cooper-Evans
Giles Cheek
Iain Kennedy

Type of Firm
Investment/Merchant Bank Subsid/Affil

Project Preferences

Role in Financing:
Prefer role as deal originator but will also invest in deals created by others

Type of Financing Preferred:
Leveraged Buyout
Special Situation

Geographical Preferences

International
Bermuda
France
Germany
Italy
Spain
United Kingdom

Industry Preferences

Communications and Media
CATV & Pay TV Systems
Data Communications
Satellite Microwave Comm.

Semiconductors/Other Elect.
Electronic Components

Consumer Related
Entertainment and Leisure
Retail
Consumer Products
Consumer Services
Other Restaurants
Hotels and Resorts

Industrial/Energy
Industrial Products

Business Serv.
Distribution

Manufact.
Publishing

Agr/Forestr/Fish
Agriculture related

Additional Information
Year Founded: 1988
Capital Under Management: $550,000,000
Current Activity Level : Actively seeking new investments
Method of Compensation: Return on invest. most important, but chg. closing fees, service fees, etc.

HAMILTON PORTFOLIO, LTD.

Standard Buildings
94 Hope Street
Glasgow, United Kingdom G2 6PH

Management and Staff
Andrew Lapping, Chief Executive Officer
John Boyle, Founder

Type of Firm
Private Firm Investing Own Capital

Project Preferences

Type of Financing Preferred:
Later Stage

Size of Investments Considered
Min Size of Investment Considered (000s): $400
Max Size of Investment Considered (000s): $400,000

Geographical Preferences

International
Europe
United Kingdom

Additional Information
Year Founded: 1999
Capital Under Management: $7,400,000
Current Activity Level : Actively seeking new investments

HAMON INVESTMENT CORPORATION

Room 2701
1 Harbour View Street
Central, Hong Kong
Phone: 852-2526-4268
Fax: 852-2526-7277
Website: www.hamon.com.hk

Type of Firm
Private Firm Investing Own Capital

Industry Association Membership
Hungarian Venture Capital Association

Additional Information
Year Founded: 1989
Capital Under Management: $400,000,000
Current Activity Level : Actively seeking new investments

HANBYUCK INVESTMENT CO LTD

Wonlim Building, 10th Floor
1422-6 Seocho-dong, Seocho-gu
Seoul, South Korea 137-070
Phone: 822-521-7141/2
Fax: 822-521-7144
E-mail: hic3494@hitel.net

Other Offices

81-11, 4-ga, Joongang-dong
Jung-gu
Pusan, South Korea 600-014

Management and Staff
Young Joo Woo, President

Whom to Contact
Jeong-Ryul Kim
Jeong-Soo Lee

Type of Firm
Non-Financial Corp. Affiliate or Subsidiary

Project Preferences

Role in Financing:
Prefer role as deal originator but will also invest in deals created by others

Type of Financing Preferred:
First Stage Financing
Leveraged Buyout
Second Stage Financing
Seed
Start-up Financing

Size of Investments Considered
Min Size of Investment Considered (000s): $1,000
Max Size of Investment Considered: No Limit

Geographical Preferences

United States
All U.S.

Canada
All Canada

International
Australia
Bermuda
France
Germany
Japan
Korea, South
Middle East
South Africa
United Kingdom

Industry Preferences

Communications and Media
Telecommunications
Data Communications
Satellite Microwave Comm.
Other Communication Prod.

Computer Hardware
Computers
Mainframes / Scientific
Mini and Personal/Desktop
Disk Relat. Memory Device

Computer Software
Systems Software
Applications Software
Artificial Intelligence

Internet Specific
Internet

Semiconductors/Other Elect.
Electronics
Electronic Components
Semiconductor
Controllers and Sensors
Sensors
Analytic/Scientific

Biotechnology
Industrial Biotechnology
Biotech Related Research

Medical/Health
Medical Diagnostics
Diagnostic Services
Diagnostic Test Products
Medical Products

Consumer Related
Franchises(NEC)
Consumer Products
Education Related

Industrial/Energy
Alternative Energy
Materials
Robotics
Environmental Related

Transportation
Transportation

Financial Services
Real Estate

Business Serv.
Consulting Services

Manufact.
Office Automation Equipmt

Additional Information
Year Founded: 1983
Capital Under Management: $1,000,000
Current Activity Level : Actively seeking new investments
Method of Compensation: Return on invest. most important, but chg. closing fees, service fees, etc.

HANNOVER FINANZ GMBH

Gunther-Wagner-Allee 13
Hannover, Germany 30177
Phone: 49 511 280 0701
Fax: 49 511 280 0737
Website: www.hannoverfinanz.de

Type of Firm
Private Firm Investing Own Capital

Industry Association Membership
European Venture Capital Association (EVCA)
German Venture Capital Association

Project Preferences

Type of Financing Preferred:
Expansion
Management Buyouts
Mezzanine
Recapitalizations
Startup
Turnaround

Geographical Preferences

International
Europe
Germany

Additional Information
Name of Most Recent Fund: Hannover Finanz GmbH
Most Recent Fund Was Raised: 01/01/1980
Year Founded: 1979
Capital Under Management: $366,400,000
Current Activity Level : Actively seeking new investments

HANSOL INVESTMENT INC.

1321-11 Seocho-dong
Seocho-gu
Seoul, South Korea
Phone: 822-3474-1080
Fax: 822-3474-6152

Management and Staff
Do Youn Kim, President

Type of Firm
Private Firm Investing Own Capital

Project Preferences

Type of Financing Preferred:
Balanced

Geographical Preferences

International
Korea, South

Additional Information
Current Activity Level : Actively seeking new investments

HARBOURVEST PARTNERS, LLC.

Suite 1207, Citibank Tower
3 Garden Rd
Central, Hong Kong
Phone: 852-2525-2214
Fax: 852-2525-2241

See Massachusetts for full listing.

HEIDELBERG INNOVATION GMBH

Im Neuenheimer Feld 515
Heidelberg, Germany 69120
Phone: 49-6221-64680
Fax: 49-6221-646864
Website: www.hd-innovation.de

Type of Firm
Private Firm Investing Own Capital

Industry Association Membership
European Venture Capital Association (EVCA)
German Venture Capital Association

Project Preferences

Type of Financing Preferred:
Early Stage
Expansion
Mezzanine
Seed
Startup

Size of Investments Considered
Min Size of Investment Considered (000s): $500
Max Size of Investment Considered (000s): $500,000

Geographical Preferences

International
Germany

Industry Preferences

Biotechnology
Biotechnology

Medical/Health
Medical/Health

Additional Information
Year Founded: 1997
Capital Under Management: $58,600,000
Current Activity Level : Actively seeking new investments

HIBERNIA CAPITAL PARTNERS

88 St Stephens Green
Dublin, Ireland, Republic of 2
Phone: 353-1-475-4725
Fax: 353-1-475-4728
Website: www.hcp.ie

Management and Staff
Charles K Ortel, Co-Founder
David Gavagan, Managing Partner
Luke Crosbie, Principal
Niall McFadden, Partner
Shane Reihill, Co-Founder

Type of Firm
Private Firm Investing Own Capital

Industry Association Membership
European Venture Capital Association (EVCA)

Project Preferences
Type of Financing Preferred:
Expansion
Leveraged Buyout
Recapitalizations
Turnaround

Geographical Preferences
International
Ireland
United Kingdom

Industry Preferences
Communications and Media
Communications and Media

Medical/Health
Medical/Health

Consumer Related
Consumer

Industrial/Energy
Industrial Products

Manufact.
Manufacturing

Additional Information
Name of Most Recent Fund: Hibernia Development Capital Partners
Most Recent Fund Was Raised: 07/01/1997
Year Founded: 1998
Capital Under Management: $73,000,000
Current Activity Level : Actively seeking new investments

HIGIN VENTURE CAPITAL CO., LTD.

9-6 Koya Machi
Kumamoto City, Japan
Phone: 096-311-5922
Fax: 096-311-5130

Type of Firm
Private Firm Investing Own Capital

Project Preferences
Type of Financing Preferred:
Balanced

Geographical Preferences
International
Japan

Industry Preferences
Internet Specific
Internet

Semiconductors/Other Elect.
Semiconductor

Additional Information
Capital Under Management: $4,800,000
Current Activity Level : Actively seeking new investments

HIKARI TSUSHIN CAPITAL, INC.

Libiera Minamiaoyama Bldg. A-6
3-3-3 Minamiaoyama, Minato-ku
Tokyo, Japan 107-0062
Phone: 03-3402-2211
Fax: 03-3402-2269
Website: www.hikaritsushin-capital.com

Type of Firm
Non-Financial Corp. Affiliate or Subsidiary

Project Preferences
Type of Financing Preferred:
Balanced

Geographical Preferences
United States
All U.S.

International
Asia
Europe
Japan

Industry Preferences
Internet Specific
Internet

Additional Information
Year Founded: 1999
Capital Under Management: $528,400,000
Current Activity Level : Actively seeking new investments

HMS HOLTRON MANAGEMENT SERVICES, LTD

Erottiajankatu 11 A
4th Floor
Helsinki, Finland 00130
Phone: 358 96 126 0430
Fax: 358 96 126 0410
Website: www.holtron.fi

Management and Staff
Ari Torpo, Partner
Jani Hursti, Partner
Tom Henriksson, Partner

Type of Firm
Non-Financial Corp. Affiliate or Subsidiary

Industry Association Membership
European Venture Capital Association (EVCA)

Project Preferences
Type of Financing Preferred:
Early Stage
Seed
Startup

Size of Investments Considered
Min Size of Investment Considered (000s): $300
Max Size of Investment Considered (000s): $300,000

Geographical Preferences
International
Finland

Industry Preferences
Communications and Media
Communications and Media

Computer Software
Software

Internet Specific
Internet

Computer Other
Computer Related

Additional Information
Year Founded: 1993
Capital Under Management: $4,800,000
Current Activity Level : Actively seeking new investments

HODGSON MARTIN, LTD.

36 George Street
Edinburgh, United Kingdom EH2 2LE
Phone: 131-226-7644
Fax: 44-131-226-7647

Management and Staff
Allan Hodgson
David Walker
Martin Greig
Yvonne Savage

Whom to Contact
Allan Hodgson
David Walker
Martin Greig
Yvonne Savage

Project Preferences

Role in Financing:
Prefer role as deal originator but will also invest in deals created by others

Type of Financing Preferred:
First Stage Financing
Second Stage Financing

Size of Investments Considered
Min Size of Investment Considered (000s): $500
Max Size of Investment Considered (000s): $1,000

Geographical Preferences

International
United Kingdom

Industry Preferences

Financial Services
Financial Services

Additional Information
Year Founded: 1980
Capital Under Management: $205,000,000
Current Activity Level : Actively seeking new investments
Method of Compensation: Return on invest. most important, but chg. closing fees, service fees, etc.

HOLLAND VENTURE B.V. (FKA: HOLLAND VENTURE HOLDING C.V.)

Dreeftoren 14e etage
Haaksbergweg 55
Amsterdam ZO, Netherlands NL- 101BR
Phone: 31-20-69-76-841
Fax: 31-20-69-73-326
Website: info@hollandventure.com

Management and Staff
Carl Kamper, Founder
David Sharir, Partner
Michael Okrouhlik, Partner
Rolf Deves, Founder
Steven Tan, Partner

Type of Firm
Private Firm Investing Own Capital

Industry Association Membership
European Venture Capital Association (EVCA)

Project Preferences

Type of Financing Preferred:
Early Stage
Expansion
Startup

Geographical Preferences

International
Europe
Israel
Netherlands
Scandanavia/Nordic Region

Industry Preferences

(% based on actual investment)

Computer Software and Services	40.5%
Internet Specific	38.7%
Communications and Media	20.8%

Additional Information
Name of Most Recent Fund: Holland Venture BV (FKA: Holland Venture Holdings II, C.V)
Most Recent Fund Was Raised: 01/01/1986
Year Founded: 1981
Capital Under Management: $135,900,000
Current Activity Level : Actively seeking new investments

HOLLINGER CAPITAL (FKA: HOLLINGER VENTURES)

2225 Sheppard Ave. East
15th Floor
Toronto, Canada M2J 5C2
Phone: 416-642-6215
Fax: 416-642-6207

See New York for full listing.

HONHO CONSULTING COMPANY LIMITED

17F, 106, Sec. 1
Hsin Tai Wu Rd.
Taipei, Taiwan
Phone: 8862-2696-1666
Fax: 8862-2696-1216

Management and Staff
Steven Cheng, President

Type of Firm
Private Firm Investing Own Capital

Industry Association Membership
Taiwan Venture Capital Association(TVCA)

Project Preferences

Type of Financing Preferred:
Balanced

Geographical Preferences

International
Taiwan

Industry Preferences

Computer Software
Software

Semiconductors/Other Elect.
Electronics
Electronic Components

Additional Information
Year Founded: 1998
Capital Under Management: $26,100,000
Current Activity Level : Actively seeking new investments

HORIZONTE VENTURE MANAGEMENT GMBH

Bauernmarkt 6
Vienna, Austria A-1010
Phone: 43-1-533-5601
Fax: 43-1-533-56014
Website: www.horizonte.at

Other Offices

Teslova 30
Ljubliana, Slovak Republic SLO - 1000
Phone: 386-611261440
Fax: 386-611259446

ul. Ferhadija br. II
Sarajevo, Bosnia and Herzegovina BIH - 7100
Phone: 387 7120 7087
Fax: 387 7120 7463

Management and Staff
Alfred Matzka, Managing Partner
Franz Krejs, Managing Partner

Type of Firm
Private Firm Investing Own Capital

Industry Association Membership
European Venture Capital Association (EVCA)

Project Preferences

Role in Financing:
Prefer role as deal originator but will also invest in deals created by others

Type of Financing Preferred:
Balanced
Early Stage
Expansion
Mezzanine
Startup

Size of Investments Considered
Min Size of Investment Considered (000s): $200
Max Size of Investment Considered (000s): $200,000

Geographical Preferences

International
Austria
Bosnia
Eastern Europe
Europe
Slovenia

Industry Preferences

Communications and Media
Communications and Media
CATV & Pay TV Systems
Wireless Communications

Computer Software
Software
Systems Software

Computer Other
Computer Related

Semiconductors/Other Elect.
Semiconductor

Biotechnology
Biotechnology
Human Biotechnology
Agricultural/Animal Bio.
Industrial Biotechnology
Biosensors
Biotech Related Research

Medical/Health
Medical/Health
Drug/Equipmt Delivery

Industrial/Energy
Industrial Products

Business Serv.
Services

Other
Environment Responsible

Additional Information
Name of Most Recent Fund: Horizonte Austrian Technology Fund
Most Recent Fund Was Raised: 08/01/1998
Year Founded: 1985
Capital Under Management: $44,500,000
Current Activity Level : Actively seeking new investments
Method of Compensation: Return on investment is of primary concern, do not charge fees

HOTUNG INTERNATIONAL COMPANY, LTD.

261 Sungkiang Road
10th Floor
Taipei, Taiwan
Phone: 8862-2500-6700
Fax: 8862-2502-9716
Website: www.hotung.com.tw

Other Offices

13F, No. 261, Sung-chiang Road
Taipei, Taiwan
Phone: 886-2-25006700
Fax: 886-2-2509716

Management and Staff
S.C. Hong, President

Whom to Contact
Phina Lin

Type of Firm
Mgt. Consulting Firm

Industry Association Membership
Taiwan Venture Capital Association(TVCA)

Project Preferences

Role in Financing:
Prefer role as deal originator

Type of Financing Preferred:
Expansion
Mezzanine
Second Stage Financing
Seed
Startup

Geographical Preferences

United States
All U.S.
West Coast

Canada
Quebec
Western Canada

International
France
Germany
Japan
Middle East
Taiwan
United Kingdom

Industry Preferences

Communications and Media
Telecommunications
Data Communications
Satellite Microwave Comm.

Semiconductors/Other Elect.
Electronic Components
Semiconductor
Circuit Boards

Biotechnology
Biosensors
Biotech Related Research

Medical/Health
Diagnostic Services
Other Therapeutic
Pharmaceuticals

Consumer Related
Retail

Industrial/Energy
Machinery
Environmental Related

Additional Information
Name of Most Recent Fund: Chiatung, Kuotung, Chung-Shan VC
Most Recent Fund Was Raised: 01/01/1987
Year Founded: 1978
Capital Under Management: $114,700,000
Current Activity Level : Actively seeking new investments
Method of Compensation: Return on investment is of primary concern, do not charge fees

---

HPI HOLDING SA

Rue Perdtemp 5
Nyon, Switzerland 1260
Phone: 41229947020
Fax: 41229947021
Website: www.hpi.ch

Management and Staff
Stephane Crettex, Partner

Type of Firm
Private Firm Investing Own Capital

Industry Association Membership
European Venture Capital Association (EVCA)

Project Preferences
Type of Financing Preferred:
Expansion
Mezzanine
Startup

Size of Investments Considered
Min Size of Investment Considered (000s): $300
Max Size of Investment Considered (000s): $300,000

Geographical Preferences
United States
All U.S.

International
Australia
Europe

Industry Preferences
Computer Software
Software

Computer Other
Computer Related

Additional Information
Year Founded: 1991
Capital Under Management: $40,300,000
Current Activity Level : Actively seeking new investments

HSBC PRIVATE EQUITY (ASIA), LTD. (FKA: HSBC PE MANAGEMENT)

Level 17, One Queens Road
Central
Hong Kong, Hong Kong
Phone: 852-2845-7688
Fax: 852-2845-9992

Other Offices
India Liason Office, 3/F Ashoka Estate
24, Barakhamba Road
New Delhi, India 110001
Phone: 911-1372-1234
Fax: 911-1332-8501

Management and Staff
George Raffini, Managing Director

Whom to Contact
Jonathan R.A. Bond

Type of Firm
Private Firm Investing Own Capital

Project Preferences
Role in Financing:
Prefer role as deal originator but will also invest in deals created by others

Type of Financing Preferred:
Control-block Purchases
Early Stage
Leveraged Buyout
Mezzanine
Second Stage Financing
Special Situation

Size of Investments Considered
Min Size of Investment Considered (000s): $20,000
Max Size of Investment Considered: No Limit

Geographical Preferences
International
Asia
China
Japan
Oceania/Australasia

Industry Preferences
(% based on actual investment)

Other Products	56.6%
Industrial/Energy	13.5%
Consumer Related	10.4%
Semiconductors/Other Elect.	6.9%
Medical/Health	6.5%
Internet Specific	5.3%
Computer Software and Services	1.0%

Additional Information
Name of Most Recent Fund: HSBC Partnership Scheme
Most Recent Fund Was Raised: 05/01/1997
Year Founded: 1989
Capital Under Management: $1,000,000,000
Current Activity Level : Actively seeking new investments
Method of Compensation: Return on investment is of primary concern, do not charge fees

---

HSBC PRIVATE EQUITY LTD (FKA MONTAGU PRIVATE EQUITY LTD)

Vintners Place
68 Upper Thames Street
London, United Kingdom EC4V 3BJ
Phone: 44 20 7336 9955
Fax: 44 20 7336 9961
Website: www.privateequity.hsbc.com

Other Offices
20 bis avenue Rapp
07 Cedex
Paris, France 75332
Phone: 33 1 44 42 72 55
Fax: 33 1 44 42 72 46

56 Spring Gardens
Manchester, United Kingdom M60 2RX
Phone: 44 161 910 222

Steinstrabe 1-3/Konigsallee
Dusseldorf, Germany 40212
Phone: 49 211 867 6930
Fax: 49 211 867 6939

Management and Staff
George Raffini, Managing Director
Ian Forrest, Managing Director
Max Von Drechsel, Managing Director

Whom to Contact
John Brandon

Type of Firm
Commercial Bank Affiliate or Subsidiary

Industry Association Membership
British Venture Capital Association
European Venture Capital Association (EVCA)

Project Preferences

Role in Financing:
Prefer role as deal originator but will also invest in deals created by others

Type of Financing Preferred:
Acquisition
Balanced
Expansion
Leveraged Buyout
Mezzanine
Recapitalizations
Special Situation

Size of Investments Considered
Min Size of Investment Considered (000s): $1,400
Max Size of Investment Considered (000s): $139,600

Geographical Preferences

International
France
Germany
All International
Italy
Spain
United Kingdom

Industry Preferences

Communications and Media
Telecommunications

Semiconductors/Other Elect.
Electronics

Medical/Health
Medical/Health
Pharmaceuticals

Industrial/Energy
Materials

Transportation
Transportation

Business Serv.
Media

Additional Information
Year Founded: 1968
Capital Under Management: $843,400,000
Current Activity Level : Actively seeking new investments
Method of Compensation: Return on invest. most important, but chg. closing fees, service fees, etc.

HSBC VENTURES (UK) LTD

36 Poultry
London, United Kingdom EC2R 8JA
Phone: 44-207-260-7935
Fax: 44-207-260-6767

Management and Staff
John Brandon, Managing Director

Type of Firm
Investment/Merchant Bank Subsid/Affil

Industry Association Membership
British Venture Capital Association

Project Preferences

Type of Financing Preferred:
Expansion
Leveraged Buyout

Size of Investments Considered
Min Size of Investment Considered (000s): $400
Max Size of Investment Considered (000s): $400,000

Geographical Preferences

International
United Kingdom

Additional Information
Year Founded: 1992
Capital Under Management: $37,200,000
Current Activity Level : Actively seeking new investments

HUNGARIAN-AMERICAN ENTERPRISE FUND, THE (HAEF)

Tartsay Vilmos u.14
Budapest, Hungary H-1126
Phone: 36-1-214-8160
Fax: 36-1-214-8159

Other Offices

21 Bedford Street
Flat 7
London, United Kingdom WCZE 0EQ
Fax: 44 207 240 9644

Romer Floris 57
Budapest, Hungary 1023
Phone: 36 1 315 0887
Fax: 36 1 346 0056

Management and Staff
Francis Skrobiszewski, Managing Director
Jozsef Berecz, Managing Director
Laszlo Hradszki, Managing Director

Type of Firm
Private Firm Investing Own Capital

Project Preferences

Role in Financing:
Prefer role as deal originator but will also invest in deals created by others

Type of Financing Preferred:
Control-block Purchases
Leveraged Buyout
Second Stage Financing

Size of Investments Considered
Min Size of Investment Considered (000s): $5,000
Max Size of Investment Considered: No Limit

Geographical Preferences

International
Hungary

Industry Preferences

Computer Hardware
Computer Graphics and Dig

Computer Software
Systems Software
Applications Software
Artificial Intelligence

Semiconductors/Other Elect.
Semiconductor
Fiber Optics
Analytic/Scientific

Consumer Related
Retail
Food/Beverage
Consumer Products

Industrial/Energy
Alternative Energy
Energy Conservation Relat
Robotics
Machinery
Environmental Related

Manufact.
Office Automation Equipmt

Agr/Forestr/Fish
Agriculture related

Additional Information
Year Founded: 1990
Capital Under Management: $70,000,000
Current Activity Level : Actively seeking new investments
Method of Compensation: Return on investment is of primary concern, do not charge fees

HYDRO-QUEBEC CAPITECH INC.

75 Boul. Rene Levesque Ouest
22e etage
Montreal, Canada H2Z 1A4
Phone: 514-289-4783
Fax: 514-289-5420
Website: www.hqcapitech.com

Management and Staff
Michel DeBroux, Vice President

Type of Firm
Non-Financial Corp. Affiliate or Subsidiary

Industry Association Membership
Canadian Venture Capital Association

Project Preferences

Type of Financing Preferred:
Balanced
Early Stage
Expansion
First Stage Financing
Mezzanine
Second Stage Financing
Seed
Startup

Geographical Preferences

United States
All U.S.

Canada
All Canada

Industry Preferences

Communications and Media
Wireless Communications
Data Communications
Other Communication Prod.

Internet Specific
Internet

Semiconductors/Other Elect.
Electronic Components
Semiconductor

Industrial/Energy
Energy
Superconductivity

Utilities
Utilities

Additional Information
Year Founded: 1998
Capital Under Management: $320,000,000
Current Activity Level : Actively seeking new investments

HYUNDAI VENTURE CAPITAL CO., LTD.

14/F, Sisa (ELS) Building
Jongno 2-ga, 48-1 Chongro-gu
Seoul, South Korea
Phone: 822-268-6177
Fax: 822-271-3980

Other Offices

566-8 Mojong-dong
Asan-si
Chungcheongnam-do, South Korea
Phone: 82-418-44-6546
Fax: 82-418-44-6548

Management and Staff
Young Chung, President

Type of Firm
Non-Financial Corp. Affiliate or Subsidiary

Project Preferences

Type of Financing Preferred:
Balanced

Geographical Preferences

International
Korea, South

Additional Information
Current Activity Level : Actively seeking new investments

I2I VENTURE

Kungsgatan 48
Box3216
Stockholm, Sweden 103 64
Phone: 46 8 412 30 00
Fax: 46 8 412 30 01

Management and Staff
Ole Oftedal, Chief Executive Officer

Type of Firm
Affiliate/Subsidary of Oth. Financial. Instit.

Project Preferences

Type of Financing Preferred:
Early Stage
Startup

Geographical Preferences

International
Europe
Scandanavia/Nordic Region

Industry Preferences

Internet Specific
Internet

Additional Information
Year Founded: 2000
Capital Under Management: $4,300,000
Current Activity Level : Actively seeking new investments

I2S PLC (FKA: TARPAN PLC)

3rd Floor, Commonwealth House
2 Chalk Hill Road
London, United Kingdom W6 8DW
Phone: 44 208 846 2703
Fax: 44 208 748 9817
E-mail: enquiries@i2s.co.uk
Website: www.i2s.co.uk

Type of Firm
Private Firm Investing Own Capital

Project Preferences

Type of Financing Preferred:
Later Stage

Geographical Preferences

International
Europe
United Kingdom

Industry Preferences

Communications and Media
Communications and Media

Internet Specific
Internet

Business Serv.
Media

Additional Information

Year Founded: 1999
Capital Under Management: $9,800,000
Current Activity Level : Actively seeking new investments

IASIA ALLIANCE CAPITAL

80 Raffles Place
#17-01 UOB Plaza 1
Singapore, Singapore 048624
Phone: 65-532-1838
Fax: 65-532-7678

Management and Staff

Thomas Yeoh, Managing Director

Type of Firm

Affiliate/Subsidary of Oth. Financial. Instit.

Project Preferences

Type of Financing Preferred:
Early Stage
Seed
Startup

Geographical Preferences

International
Asia
Singapore

Industry Preferences

Communications and Media
Communications and Media

Computer Software
Software

Internet Specific
Internet

Additional Information

Capital Under Management: $25,000,000
Current Activity Level : Actively seeking new investments

IBB BETEILIGUNGSGESELLSCHAFT MBH

Bundesallee 210
Berlin, Germany 10719
Phone: 49 30-2125-3201
Fax: 49 30-2125-3202
Website: www.ibb-bet.de

Management and Staff

Marco Zeller, Managing Director

Type of Firm

Private Firm Investing Own Capital

Industry Association Membership

European Venture Capital Association (EVCA)
German Venture Capital Association

Project Preferences

Type of Financing Preferred:
Early Stage
Startup

Geographical Preferences

International
Germany

Industry Preferences

Communications and Media
Communications and Media

Computer Hardware
Computers

Semiconductors/Other Elect.
Electronics

Biotechnology
Biotechnology

Industrial/Energy
Energy

Additional Information

Name of Most Recent Fund: IBB Beteilgungsgesellschaft
Most Recent Fund Was Raised: 10/01/1997
Year Founded: 1997
Capital Under Management: $25,500,000
Current Activity Level : Actively seeking new investments

IBK CAPITAL CORPORATION

6-8/F, Yoosung Building
702-22 Yoksam-dong, Kangnam-gu
Seoul, South Korea
Phone: 822-554-3131
Fax: 822-568-3533
Website: www.ibkfinance.co.kr

Management and Staff

Taek Joo Lee, President

Whom to Contact

Jong-Soo Min

Type of Firm

Commercial Bank Affiliate or Subsidiary

Project Preferences

Role in Financing:
Prefer role as deal originator but will also invest in deals created by others

Type of Financing Preferred:
Balanced
Leveraged Buyout
Mezzanine
Research and Development
Second Stage Financing

Size of Investments Considered

Min Size of Investment Considered (000s): $5,000
Max Size of Investment Considered: No Limit

Geographical Preferences

United States
All U.S.
West Coast

Canada
All Canada

International
France
Germany
Japan
Korea, South
United Kingdom
No Preference

Industry Preferences

Communications and Media
Telecommunications
Data Communications
Satellite Microwave Comm.
Other Communication Prod.

Computer Hardware
Integrated Turnkey System
Disk Relat. Memory Device

Computer Software
Systems Software
Applications Software

Internet Specific
Internet

Semiconductors/Other Elect.
Electronics
Electronic Components
Semiconductor
Fiber Optics

Biotechnology
Industrial Biotechnology
Biotech Related Research

Medical/Health
Medical Diagnostics
Diagnostic Test Products
Medical Products

Consumer Related
Franchises(NEC)
Hotels and Resorts

Industrial/Energy
Alternative Energy
Industrial Products
Materials
Machinery
Environmental Related

Agr/Forestr/Fish
Mining and Minerals

Additional Information
Year Founded: 1986
Capital Under Management: $166,000,000
Current Activity Level : Actively seeking new investments
Method of Compensation: Return on investment is of primary concern, do not charge fees

ICC VENTURE CAPITAL

72-74 Harcourt Street
Dublin, Ireland, Republic of 2
Phone: 353-1-415-5555
Fax: 353-1-475-0437
Website: www.icc.ie

Management and Staff
Anne Bannon, Partner
David Fassbender, Managing Director
Martin O'Brian, Partner
Maurice McHenry, Partner
Pat McGrath, Partner
Prisca Grady, Partner
Tom Kirwan, Partner

Whom to Contact
John Tracey

Type of Firm
Commercial Bank Affiliate or Subsidiary

Industry Association Membership
European Venture Capital Association (EVCA)

Project Preferences

Role in Financing:
Prefer role as deal originator

Type of Financing Preferred:
Expansion
Leveraged Buyout
Mezzanine
Recapitalizations
Second Stage Financing

Size of Investments Considered
Min Size of Investment Considered (000s): $700
Max Size of Investment Considered: No Limit

Geographical Preferences

International
Ireland
Western Europe

Industry Preferences

(% based on actual investment)

Computer Software and Services	37.5%
Other Products	25.1%
Communications and Media	11.2%
Consumer Related	6.2%
Computer Hardware	5.4%
Semiconductors/Other Elect.	4.1%
Industrial/Energy	3.0%
Internet Specific	2.6%
Medical/Health	2.5%
Biotechnology	2.2%

Additional Information
Name of Most Recent Fund: ICC Bank PLC
Most Recent Fund Was Raised: 04/01/1996
Year Founded: 1987
Capital Under Management: $354,400,000
Current Activity Level : Actively seeking new investments
Method of Compensation: Return on invest. most important, but chg. closing fees, service fees, etc.

ICF VENTURES PRIVATE LTD.

DBS Corporate Centre
26 Cunningham Road
Bangalore, India 560052
Phone: 9180-208-8210
Fax: 9180-509-5236
Website: www.icfventures.com

Management and Staff
Amit Kulkarni, Managing Director
Norman Prouty, Managing Director
Vijay Angadi, Managing Director

Type of Firm
Private Firm Investing Own Capital

Project Preferences

Role in Financing:
Prefer role as deal originator

Type of Financing Preferred:
Early Stage
Expansion
Startup

Geographical Preferences

International
India

Industry Preferences

Biotechnology
Biotechnology

Medical/Health
Medical/Health

Additional Information
Year Founded: 1998
Capital Under Management: $20,000,000
Current Activity Level : Actively seeking new investments

ICICI VENTURE FUNDS MNGT. CO. LTD.

IV Floor, 17 Commisariat Rd
D'Souza Circle
Bangalore, India 560025
Phone: 9180-558-3681
Fax: 9180-558-0741
Website: www.icici.com

Other Offices

Ground Floor, Scindia House
N.M.Marg, Ballard Estate
Mumbai, India 400 038
Phone: 9122-266-4767
Fax: 9122-266-4769

ICICI Towers
Bandra Kurla Complex
Mumbai, India 400051
Phone: 9122-653-8818

Management and Staff
Renuka Ramnath, Managing Director

Type of Firm
Investment/Merchant Bank Investing Own or Client Funds

Project Preferences

Role in Financing:
Prefer role as deal originator but will also invest in deals created by others

Type of Financing Preferred:
Balanced
Expansion
Leveraged Buyout
Management Buyouts
Mezzanine
Startup
Turnaround

Geographical Preferences

United States
All U.S.

International
India

Industry Preferences

(% based on actual investment)

Internet Specific	37.3%
Consumer Related	22.1%
Computer Software and Services	15.6%
Computer Hardware	5.8%
Communications and Media	5.2%
Industrial/Energy	3.7%
Other Products	3.7%
Medical/Health	3.6%
Biotechnology	2.1%
Semiconductors/Other Elect.	0.8%

Additional Information
Year Founded: 1988
Capital Under Management: $252,000,000
Current Activity Level : Actively seeking new investments

IDG TECHNOLOGY VENTURE INVESTMENT INC. (FKA: PTV-CHINA)

Rm. 616 Tower A, COFCO Plaza,
8 Jianguomen Nei Dajie
Beijing, China 100005
Phone: 8610-6526-2400
Fax: 8610-6526-0700
Website: www.ptvchina.com

Other Offices

12/F Suite A Ketou Building
#285 West Jianguo Rd.
Shanghai, China 200031
Phone: 8621-6415-6627
Fax: 8621-6467-6662

15/F Penthouse Suite
One Exeter Plaza
Boston, United States of America 02116
Phone: 1-617-534-1243
Fax: 1-617-527-5256

3-303 Bldg.3, Keyuan Apartment
126 Xiquing Rd., Hongqiao District
Tianjin, China 300122
Phone: 8622-2771-7369
Fax: 8622-2771-7369

98-A Beilishi Rd.
Xicheng District
Beijing, China 100037
Phone: 8610-6831-4160
Fax: 8610-6834-4320

Rm 1615, Wuyang New City Plaza
111-115 Siyou New Road
Guangzhou, China 510600
Phone: 8620-8737-7435
Fax: 8620-8737-7597

Suite 202
1762 Technology Drive
San Jose, United States of America 95110
Phone: 1-408-437-8880
Fax: 1-408-467-8968

Management and Staff
Dongliang Lin, Vice President
Juanguang Li, Vice President
Quan Zhou, Managing Director
Shu Wang, Vice President
Suyang Zhang, Vice President
Young Guo, Partner

Type of Firm
Private Firm Investing Own Capital

Project Preferences

Role in Financing:
Prefer role in deals created by others

Type of Financing Preferred:
Balanced

Size of Investments Considered
Min Size of Investment Considered (000s): $500
Max Size of Investment Considered (000s): $2,000

Geographical Preferences

International
China

Industry Preferences

Communications and Media
Communications and Media
Telecommunications

Computer Software
Computer Services
Software

Internet Specific
Internet

Computer Other
Computer Related

Biotechnology
Biotechnology

Medical/Health
Pharmaceuticals

Manufact.
Publishing

Additional Information
Year Founded: 1992
Capital Under Management: $100,000,000
Current Activity Level : Actively seeking new investments
Method of Compensation: Return on investment is of primary concern, do not charge fees

IDG VENTURES

Rm. 616 Tower A, COFCO Plaza,
8 Jianguomen Nei Dajie
Beijing, China 100005
Phone: 8610-6526-2400
Fax: 8610-6526-0700

See California for full listing.

IDI-KAIROS

18 avenue Matignon
Paris, France F-75008
Phone: 33 1 5527 8000
Fax: 33 1 4017 0444

Management and Staff
Jacques Halperin, Chief Executive Officer

Type of Firm
Unknown

Project Preferences

Type of Financing Preferred:
Early Stage

Geographical Preferences

International
No Preference

Additional Information
Year Founded: 1999
Capital Under Management: $284,400,000
Current Activity Level : Actively seeking new investments

IFCI VENTURE CAP. FUNDS (FORMERLY RISK CAPITAL & TECH.)

E-216, 3/F, East of Kailash
New Delhi, India 110 003
Phone: 9111-645-3343
Fax: 9111-645-3348
Website: www.ifciventure.com

Management and Staff
S.P. Lavakara, Chief Executive Officer

Whom to Contact
Dinesh Sharma
S.P. Lavakare

Type of Firm
Affiliate/Subsidary of Oth. Financial. Instit.

Project Preferences

Role in Financing:
Prefer role as deal originator but will also invest in deals created by others

Type of Financing Preferred:
Early Stage
Expansion
First Stage Financing
Mezzanine
Start-up Financing

Geographical Preferences

International
India

Industry Preferences

Communications and Media
Commercial Communications
Data Communications

Computer Hardware
Computer Graphics and Dig

Computer Software
Systems Software
Applications Software

Semiconductors/Other Elect.
Electronic Components
Component Testing Equipmt
Laser Related
Analytic/Scientific

Biotechnology
Industrial Biotechnology
Biotech Related Research
Biotech Related Research

Medical/Health
Diagnostic Test Products
Disposable Med. Products
Pharmaceuticals

Consumer Related
Retail
Food/Beverage
Consumer Products

Industrial/Energy
Alternative Energy
Industrial Products
Materials
Robotics
Machinery

Agr/Forestr/Fish
Agriculture related

Additional Information
Name of Most Recent Fund: VECAUS-III
Most Recent Fund Was Raised: 01/01/1994
Year Founded: 1988
Capital Under Management: $34,000,000
Current Activity Level : Actively seeking new investments
Method of Compensation: Return on invest. most important, but chg. closing fees, service fees, etc.

IGLOBE PARTNERS LIMITED

435 Orchard Road
#19-03 Wisma Atria
Singapore, Singapore 238877
Phone: 65-462-4292
Fax: 65-836-9119
Website: www.iglobepartners.com

Management and Staff
Koh Soo Boon, Managing Partner

Type of Firm
Private Firm Investing Own Capital

Project Preferences

Type of Financing Preferred:
Early Stage
Mezzanine

Geographical Preferences

United States
All U.S.

International
Asia
Europe
Singapore

Industry Preferences

Communications and Media
Communications and Media

Internet Specific
Internet

Additional Information
Capital Under Management: $200,000,000
Current Activity Level : Actively seeking new investments

IGNITE ASSOCIATES, LLC

Tokio Marine New Building 11th Floor
1-2-1 Marinouchi, Chiyoda-Ky
Tokyo, Japan 100-0005
Phone: 81-3-5220-5015
Fax: 81-3-5220-5016

See California for full listing.

IKB VENTURE CAPITAL GMBH (AKA IKB BETEILIGUNGSGESELLSC HAFT

Wilhelm-Botzkes-Strasse 1
Dusseldorf, Germany 40474
Phone: 49 211 822116
Fax: 49 211 82212749
Website: www.ikb-venture-capital.de

Management and Staff
Anne Osthaus, Managing Director

Type of Firm
Investment/Merchant Bank Subsid/Affil

Industry Association Membership
European Venture Capital Association (EVCA)
German Venture Capital Association

Project Preferences

Type of Financing Preferred:
Early Stage
Expansion
Management Buyouts
Mezzanine
Recapitalizations
Seed
Startup

Geographical Preferences

International
Germany

Industry Preferences

Communications and Media
Communications and Media
Telecommunications

Semiconductors/Other Elect.
Electronics

Biotechnology
Biotechnology

Additional Information
Year Founded: 2000
Current Activity Level : Actively seeking new investments

IL&FS VENTURE CORPORATION (FKA. CREDITCAPITAL VENTURE FUND)

5/F HDFC House
51 Kasturba Road
Bangalore, India 560-001
Phone: 9180-227-2950
Fax: 9180-224-5564
Website: www.ivcindia.com

Other Offices

4/F Mahindra Towers, Road No. 13
GM Bhosle Marg Worli
Mumbai, India 400 018
Phone: 9122-496-2411
Fax: 9122-493-0080

USI Complex
Rao Tula Ram Marg
New Delhi, India 110 010
Phone: 9111-614-8100
Fax: 9111-614-7217

Management and Staff
Hetal Gandhi, Managing Director

Type of Firm
Affiliate/Subsidary of Oth. Financial. Instit.

Project Preferences

Role in Financing:
Prefer role as deal originator but will also invest in deals created by others

Type of Financing Preferred:
Early Stage
Expansion
Turnaround

Geographical Preferences

International
India

Industry Preferences

(% based on actual investment)

Consumer Related	36.2%
Internet Specific	16.4%
Other Products	15.9%
Computer Software and Services	12.4%
Communications and Media	10.9%
Biotechnology	8.2%

Additional Information
Year Founded: 1986
Capital Under Management: $45,600,000
Current Activity Level : Actively seeking new investments
Method of Compensation: Professional fee required whether or not deal closes

IMGO (AKA: INVESTOR MOBILE GO; FKA: GUOCO LAND LTD.)

11/F The Centre
99 Queen's Road
Central, Hong Kong
Phone: 852-2218-8618
Website: www.imGOasia.com

Management and Staff
Lim Heng Tan, Managing Director

Type of Firm
Non-Financial Corp. Affiliate or Subsidiary

Project Preferences

Type of Financing Preferred:
Balanced

Geographical Preferences

International
Asia

Industry Preferences

Communications and Media
Wireless Communications

Additional Information
Current Activity Level : Actively seeking new investments

IMH INDUSTRIE MANAGEMENT HOLDING GMBH

Blucherstrasse 37 A
Berlin, Germany D-10961
Phone: 49-3069-8030
Fax: 49-3069-803333
Website: www.imhventure.de

Other Offices

Schiffgraben 13
Hannover, Germany 30159
Phone: 49-511-3579-140
Fax: 49-511-3579-1414

Management and Staff
Erich Mayer, Managing Partner
Florian Volk, Managing Partner
Johannes Gross, Managing Partner

Type of Firm
Private Firm Investing Own Capital

Industry Association Membership
European Venture Capital Association (EVCA)
German Venture Capital Association

Project Preferences

Type of Financing Preferred:
Early Stage
Expansion
Startup
Turnaround

Size of Investments Considered
Min Size of Investment Considered (000s): $300
Max Size of Investment Considered (000s): $300,000

Geographical Preferences

International
Germany
Western Europe

Industry Preferences

Communications and Media
Communications and Media

Computer Other
Computer Related

Semiconductors/Other Elect.
Electronics

Biotechnology
Biotechnology

Medical/Health
Medical/Health

Additional Information
Year Founded: 1998
Capital Under Management: $68,800,000
Current Activity Level : Actively seeking new investments

INCORPORATED INVESTORS

Avenida Reboucas
3534 Pinheiros
Sao Paulo, Brazil 05402-600
Phone: 55-11-870-4481
Fax: 55-11-832-4620

See California for full listing.

INDASIA FUND ADVISORS PRIVATE LIMITED

3, Scheherazade, Justice Vyas Road, Colaba
Mumbai, India
Phone: 9122-288-1301
Fax: 9122-283-0376
Website: www.indasiafund.com

Type of Firm
Private Equity Advisor or Fund of Fund Mgr

Project Preferences

Role in Financing:
Prefer role as deal originator

Type of Financing Preferred:
Expansion
Turnaround

Geographical Preferences

International
India

Industry Preferences

Communications and Media
Telecommunications

Computer Other
Computer Related

Semiconductors/Other Elect.
Electronics

Medical/Health
Medical/Health

Consumer Related
Entertainment and Leisure

Financial Services
Financial Services

Business Serv.
Services
Media

Manufact.
Manufacturing

Additional Information
Year Founded: 1994
Capital Under Management: $40,000,000
Current Activity Level : Actively seeking new investments

INDEKON MANAGEMENT OY

Tekniikantie 12
Espoo, Finland FIN-02150
Phone: 358 9 2517 3100
Fax: 358 9 2517 3118

Other Offices

PO Box 293
Snellmaninkatu 10
Lappeenranta, Finland FIN-53101
Phone: 358-5-621-9100
Fax: 358-5-621-9190

Management and Staff
Toivo Koski

Whom to Contact
Toivo Koski

Type of Firm
Private Firm Investing Own Capital

Project Preferences

Role in Financing:
Prefer role as deal originator but will also invest in deals created by others

Type of Financing Preferred:
First Stage Financing
Second Stage Financing
Special Situation
Start-up Financing

Geographical Preferences

International
Finland

Industry Preferences

Communications and Media
Telecommunications
Data Communications
Other Communication Prod.

Computer Hardware
Mainframes / Scientific
Computer Graphics and Dig

Computer Software
Systems Software
Applications Software
Artificial Intelligence

Internet Specific
Internet

Semiconductors/Other Elect.
Electronics
Electronic Components
Controllers and Sensors
Component Testing Equipmt
Analytic/Scientific

Medical/Health
Diagnostic Test Products

Industrial/Energy
Alternative Energy
Energy Conservation Relat
Industrial Products

Transportation
Transportation

Additional Information
Name of Most Recent Fund: Lahden Alueen Paaomarahasto Ky
Most Recent Fund Was Raised: 02/11/1997
Year Founded: 1993
Capital Under Management: $10,000,000
Current Activity Level : Actively seeking new investments
Method of Compensation: Return on invest. most important, but chg. closing fees, service fees, etc.

INDEX VENTURES

2, rue de Jargonnant
Geneva, Switzerland 1207
Phone: 41-227-37-0000
Fax: 41-227-37-0099
Website: www.indexventures.com

Management and Staff
Bernard Dalle, Partner
David Rimer, Chief Financial Officer
Francesco De Rubertis, Partner
Giuseppe Zocco, General Partner
Herve Lebret, Principal
Neil Rimer, General Partner

Type of Firm
Investment/Merchant Bank Subsid/Affil

Industry Association Membership
European Venture Capital Association (EVCA)

Project Preferences

Type of Financing Preferred:
Balanced
Early Stage
Expansion
Later Stage

Size of Investments Considered
Min Size of Investment Considered (000s): $3,000
Max Size of Investment Considered: No Limit

Geographical Preferences

United States
All U.S.

International
Europe
Israel
No Preference

Industry Preferences

(% based on actual investment)

Internet Specific	50.6%
Biotechnology	30.6%
Computer Software and Services	14.7%
Medical/Health	2.1%
Communications and Media	2.0%

Additional Information
Name of Most Recent Fund: Index Ventures I, L.P.
Most Recent Fund Was Raised: 11/30/1998
Year Founded: 1992
Capital Under Management: $550,000,000
Current Activity Level : Actively seeking new investments

INDIAN DIRECT EQUITY ADVISORS PVT. LTD

1007 Raheja Centre
Nariman Point
Mumbai, India 400021
Phone: 9122-204-1140
Fax: 9122-281-8156
Website: www.ideaequity.com

Management and Staff
Nimesh Grover, Vice President
Sanjaya Kulkarni, Managing Director

Type of Firm
Affiliate/Subsidary of Oth. Financial. Instit.

Project Preferences

Type of Financing Preferred:
First Stage Financing
Second Stage Financing

Geographical Preferences

United States
All U.S.

International
India

Industry Preferences

(% based on actual investment)

Other Products	31.9%
Industrial/Energy	26.5%
Internet Specific	13.3%
Consumer Related	11.8%
Computer Hardware	10.5%
Communications and Media	6.0%

Additional Information
Year Founded: 1999
Capital Under Management: $60,000,000
Current Activity Level : Actively seeking new investments

INDOCEAN CHASE CAPITAL ADVISORS

15/F, Nirmal Building
Nariman Point
Mumbai, India 400021
Phone: 9122-283-8040
Fax: 9122-283-8010
Website: www.indocean.com

Management and Staff
Bharat Kewalramani, Managing Director

Type of Firm
Affiliate/Subsidary of Oth. Financial. Instit.

Project Preferences

Role in Financing:
Will function either as deal originator or investor in deals created by others

Type of Financing Preferred:
Acquisition
Expansion

Geographical Preferences

International
India

Industry Preferences

(% based on actual investment)

Internet Specific	31.6%
Other Products	29.7%
Semiconductors/Other Elect.	9.5%
Consumer Related	8.5%
Industrial/Energy	7.9%
Communications and Media	7.0%
Computer Software and Services	5.9%

Additional Information

Year Founded: 1994
Capital Under Management: $255,000,000
Current Activity Level : Actively seeking new investments

INDUS VENTURE MANAGEMENT LTD.

12/F Mafatlal Centre
Nariman Point
Mumbai, India 400021
Phone: 9122-202-4692
Fax: 9122-232-4028

Management and Staff

Anil Chopra, Vice President

Type of Firm

Private Firm Investing Own Capital

Project Preferences

Type of Financing Preferred:
Early Stage
Expansion
Startup

Geographical Preferences

International
India

Industry Preferences

Communications and Media
Communications and Media

Computer Other
Computer Related

Semiconductors/Other Elect.
Electronics

Industrial/Energy
Industrial Products

Additional Information

Year Founded: 1989
Capital Under Management: $56,000,000
Current Activity Level : Actively seeking new investments

INDUSTRIAL TECHNOLOGY INVESTMENT CORPORATION

6/F, No. 106
Ho-Ping E. Road, Section 2
Taipei, Taiwan
Phone: 8862-2737-7069
Fax: 8862-2737-7386

Management and Staff

Shirley Chang, President

Type of Firm

Private Firm Investing Own Capital

Industry Association Membership

Taiwan Venture Capital Association(TVCA)

Project Preferences

Type of Financing Preferred:
Seed
Startup

Geographical Preferences

International
Taiwan

Additional Information

Year Founded: 1979
Capital Under Management: $12,400,000
Current Activity Level : Actively seeking new investments

INDUSTRIAL TECHNOLOGY SECURITIES LTD

Surrey Technology Centre
Surrey Research Park
Guildford, United Kingdom GU2 5YG
Phone: 44-1483-457-398
Fax: 44-1483-568-710
Website: www.indtechsec.com

Management and Staff

Bruce Smith, Partner
Chris Elliot, Partner

Whom to Contact

Jan E. Berglund

Type of Firm

MESBIC not elsewhere classified

Industry Association Membership

British Venture Capital Association

Project Preferences

Role in Financing:
Prefer role as deal originator

Type of Financing Preferred:
First Stage Financing
Mezzanine
Research and Development
Second Stage Financing
Seed
Start-up Financing
Startup

Geographical Preferences

International
United Kingdom

Industry Preferences

Communications and Media
Telecommunications
Data Communications
Satellite Microwave Comm.
Other Communication Prod.

Computer Hardware
Computers
Computer Graphics and Dig
Terminals

Computer Software
Applications Software

Internet Specific
Internet

Semiconductors/Other Elect.
Laser Related
Fiber Optics
Analytic/Scientific

Manufact.
Office Automation Equipmt

Additional Information

Year Founded: 1984
Capital Under Management: $5,000,000
Current Activity Level : Actively seeking new investments
Method of Compensation: Return on invest. most important, but chg. closing fees, service fees, etc.

INFINEON VENTURES

St.-Martin-Strasse 53
Munich, Germany 81541
Phone: 49 89-234-26359
Fax: 49 89-234-27483
Website: www.infineon.com/ventures/

Other Offices

1730 North First Street
San Jose, United States of America 95112

Type of Firm
Non-Financial Corp. Affiliate or Subsidiary

Project Preferences

Type of Financing Preferred:
Balanced
Seed
Startup

Geographical Preferences

United States
All U.S.

International
Australia
Germany
Israel
United Kingdom

Industry Preferences

Internet Specific
Internet

Additional Information
Year Founded: 1998
Capital Under Management: $64,000,000
Current Activity Level : Actively seeking new investments

INFINITY TECHNOLOGY INVESTMENTS PVT. LTD.

119-A Mittal Chambers
Nariman Point
Mumbai, India 400021
Phone: 9122-498-1856
Fax: 9122-495-2075

Type of Firm
Private Firm Investing Own Capital

Project Preferences

Type of Financing Preferred:
Early Stage

Geographical Preferences

International
India

Additional Information
Capital Under Management: $35,000,000
Current Activity Level : Actively seeking new investments

INFLEXION PLC

9-13 St Andrews Street
London, United Kingdom EC4A 3AF
Phone: 44 20 7955 1421
E-mail: yasmin.fahiya@inflexion.com
Website: www.inflexion.com

Management and Staff
John Hartz, Chief Executive Officer
Simon Turner, Chief Executive Officer

Type of Firm
Private Firm Investing Own Capital

Project Preferences

Type of Financing Preferred:
Expansion

Geographical Preferences

International
Europe

Industry Preferences

Communications and Media
Communications and Media

Internet Specific
Internet

Additional Information
Current Activity Level : Actively seeking new investments

INFOCOMM INVESTMENTS PTE LTD (IIPL)

8 Temasek Boulevard
#14-00 Suntec Tower Three
Singapore, Singapore
Phone: 65-211-0888
Fax: 65-211-2203
Website: www.ida.gov.sg

Management and Staff
Lee Fook Chiew, Chief Executive Officer

Type of Firm
Govt Program NEC

Project Preferences

Type of Financing Preferred:
Expansion

Geographical Preferences

International
Asia

Industry Preferences

Communications and Media
Communications and Media

Additional Information
Capital Under Management: $57,700,000
Current Activity Level : Actively seeking new investments

INNOFINANCE OY (FKA CULMINATUM OY)

Tekniikantie 12
Espoo, Finland FIN-02150
Phone: 358 9 2517 3100
Fax: 358 9 2517 3118
Website: www.innofinance.fi

Management and Staff
Martti Hintikka, Managing Director

Type of Firm
Business Development Fund

Industry Association Membership
Finnish Venture Capital Association

Project Preferences

Type of Financing Preferred:
Seed
Startup

Geographical Preferences

International
Finland

Additional Information
Name of Most Recent Fund: Spinno-seed Oy
Most Recent Fund Was Raised: 08/31/1994
Year Founded: 1994
Capital Under Management: $9,400,000
Current Activity Level : Actively seeking new investments

INNOVA CAPITAL (FKA: POLAND PARTNERS MANAGEMENT COMPANY)

Aurum Building, 4th Floor
Walicow 11
Warsaw, Poland 00 685
Phone: 48 22 583 9400
Fax: 48 22 583 9420
Website: www.innovacap.com

Management and Staff
Artur Cakata, Managing Director
David Fisher, Managing Director
Rafat Nowakowski, Managing Director
Robert Conn, Partner
Steven Buckley, Partner

Type of Firm
Private Firm Investing Own Capital

Industry Association Membership
European Venture Capital Association (EVCA)

Project Preferences

Role in Financing:
Prefer role as deal originator but will also invest in deals created by others

Type of Financing Preferred:
Control-block Purchases
First Stage Financing
Industry Rollups
Leveraged Buyout
Mezzanine
Second Stage Financing
Special Situation

Geographical Preferences

International
Eastern Europe

Industry Preferences

Communications and Media
Communications and Media

Internet Specific
Internet

Consumer Related
Consumer

Additional Information
Name of Most Recent Fund: Innova/98, L.P.
Most Recent Fund Was Raised: 06/01/1998
Year Founded: 1994
Capital Under Management: $200,000,000
Current Activity Level : Actively seeking new investments

INNOVACOM

23, rue Royale
Paris, France 75008
Phone: 33-1-4494-1500
Fax: 33-1-4494-1515
Website: www.innovacomvc.com

Other Offices

One Embaradero Centre
Skydeck- 41st Floor
San Francisco, United States of America 94111
Phone: 415-288-0680
Fax: 415-288-0685

Management and Staff
Aymerik Renard, Managing Director
Denis Champenois, Managing Director
Denis Barrier, Managing Director
Frederic Veyssiere, Managing Director
Frederic Humbert, Managing Director
Geoffroy Dubus, Managing Director
Jacques Meheut, Managing Director
Jerome Lecoeur, Managing Director

Type of Firm
Non-Financial Corp. Affiliate or Subsidiary

Industry Association Membership
European Venture Capital Association (EVCA)

Project Preferences

Type of Financing Preferred:
First Stage Financing
Second Stage Financing
Seed
Start-up Financing

Geographical Preferences

United States
West Coast

Canada
Quebec

International
Austria
France
Germany
All International
United Kingdom

Industry Preferences

(% based on actual investment)

Internet Specific	46.4%
Computer Software and Services	18.0%
Semiconductors/Other Elect.	16.2%
Communications and Media	14.7%
Other Products	2.4%
Computer Hardware	2.3%

Additional Information
Year Founded: 1988
Capital Under Management: $200,000,000
Current Activity Level : Actively seeking new investments
Method of Compensation: Return on investment is of primary concern, do not charge fees

INNOVATION CAPITAL ASSOCIATES LTD

11/32 Macquarie Place
Sydney, Australia 48105
Phone: 612-9252-4844
Fax: 612-9252-4855
Website: www.innovationcapital.net

Other Offices

2401 Plymouth Road
Suite B
Ann Arbor, United States of America
Phone: 734-747-9401
Fax: 734-747-9704

Level 1, 117 Stirling Highway
Nedlands
Perth, Australia 6000
Phone: 618-9389-7911
Fax: 618-9389-6788

Type of Firm
Private Firm Investing Own Capital

Industry Association Membership
Australian Venture Capital Association (AVCAL)

Project Preferences

Type of Financing Preferred:
Early Stage

Geographical Preferences

United States
All U.S.

International
Australia

Additional Information
Name of Most Recent Fund: Innovation Capital, L.L.C
Most Recent Fund Was Raised: 09/01/1999
Year Founded: 1999
Capital Under Management: $14,700,000
Current Activity Level : Actively seeking new investments

INNOVATIONSAGENTUR GESMBH

Taborstrasse 10
Vienna, Austria A-1020
Phone: 431-216-5293-10
Fax: 431-216-5293-99
E-mail: innov@innovation.co.at
Website: www.innovation.co.at

Management and Staff
Christian Laurer, Partner
Helmut Dorn, Partner
Markus Lenotti, Partner

Type of Firm
Govt Program NEC

Industry Association Membership
European Venture Capital Association (EVCA)

Project Preferences

Role in Financing:
Prefer role as deal originator

Type of Financing Preferred:
First Stage Financing
Second Stage Financing
Seed
Start-up Financing

Geographical Preferences

International
Austria

Industry Preferences

Communications and Media
Communications and Media

Computer Other
Computer Related

Semiconductors/Other Elect.
Electronic Components

Biotechnology
Biotechnology

Medical/Health
Other Therapeutic

Industrial/Energy
Industrial Products

Additional Information
Year Founded: 1989
Capital Under Management: $12,800,000
Current Activity Level : Actively seeking new investments

INNOVATIONSKAPITAL MANAGEMENT GOTEBORG AB

Kungsportsplatson 1
Guteborg, Sweden SE-411-10
Phone: 46-31-60-9190
Fax: 46-31-609199
Website: www.innkap.se

Other Offices

Sveavagen 17
4th floor
Stockholm, Sweden 10387

Teknikringen 1E
Linkoping, Sweden 58330

Management and Staff
Gunnar Fernstrom, Managing General Partner
Robert Gothner, General Partner
Staffan Ingeborn, Managing General Partner

Whom to Contact
all of the above

Type of Firm
Private Firm Investing Own Capital

Industry Association Membership
European Venture Capital Association (EVCA)
Swedish Venture Capital Association

Project Preferences

Role in Financing:
Prefer role as deal originator but will also invest in deals created by others

Type of Financing Preferred:
Early Stage
First Stage Financing
Research and Development
Second Stage Financing
Seed
Start-up Financing
Startup

Geographical Preferences

International
Scandanavia/Nordic Region

Industry Preferences

(% based on actual investment)

Semiconductors/Other Elect.	31.1%
Communications and Media	18.9%
Medical/Health	18.5%
Computer Software and Services	18.0%
Internet Specific	13.4%

Additional Information
Name of Most Recent Fund: Innkap 2
Most Recent Fund Was Raised: 09/01/1999
Year Founded: 1994
Capital Under Management: $65,000,000
Current Activity Level : Actively seeking new investments
Method of Compensation: Return on investment is of primary concern, do not charge fees

INNVOTEC LTD

1 Castle Lane
London, United Kingdom SW1E 6DN
Phone: 44-20-7630-6990
Fax: 44-20-7828-8232
Website: www.innvotec.co.uk

Other Offices

Business Link House
Salford UBP, 35 Winders Way
Salford, United Kingdom M6 6AR
Phone: 44 161 278 2600
Fax: 44 161 278 2610

MSIF, 5th Floor
Cunard Building, Pier Head
Liverpool, United Kingdom L3 1DS
Phone: 44 151 236 4040
Fax: 44 151 236 3060

Management and Staff
David Hall, Partner
Jeremy Mobbs, Partner

Whom to Contact
Alan Mawson

Type of Firm
Private Firm Investing Own Capital

Industry Association Membership
British Venture Capital Association

Project Preferences

Role in Financing:
Prefer role as deal originator but will also invest in deals created by others

Type of Financing Preferred:
Balanced
First Stage Financing
Leveraged Buyout
Second Stage Financing
Seed
Start-up Financing

Size of Investments Considered
Min Size of Investment Considered (000s): $800
Max Size of Investment Considered: No Limit

Geographical Preferences

International
United Kingdom

Industry Preferences

Communications and Media
Commercial Communications
Radio & TV Broadcasting
Telecommunications
Data Communications
Satellite Microwave Comm.

Computer Hardware
Mini and Personal/Desktop
Computer Graphics and Dig
Disk Relat. Memory Device

Computer Software
Computer Services
Systems Software
Applications Software
Artificial Intelligence

Internet Specific
Internet

Semiconductors/Other Elect.
Electronics
Electronic Components

Biotechnology
Biotechnology

Medical/Health
Diagnostic Services
Diagnostic Test Products
Drug/Equipmt Delivery
Other Therapeutic
Disposable Med. Products
Pharmaceuticals

Consumer Related
Food/Beverage
Consumer Products

Industrial/Energy
Alternative Energy
Energy Conservation Relat
Industrial Products

Additional Information
Name of Most Recent Fund: Electra Private Equity Partners
Most Recent Fund Was Raised: 01/01/1989
Year Founded: 1987
Capital Under Management: $50,100,000
Current Activity Level : Actively seeking new investments
Method of Compensation: Return on investment is of primary concern, do not charge fees

INOVA CAPITAL SCR

Marques de Villamagna 3
5th floor
Madrid, Spain 28001
Phone: 34 91 426 25 90
Fax: 34 91 431 32 67
Website: www.inovacapital.com

Management and Staff
Jorge Calvet, President

Type of Firm
Private Firm Investing Own Capital

Project Preferences

Type of Financing Preferred:
Early Stage

Geographical Preferences

International
No Preference

Industry Preferences

Communications and Media
Telecommunications

Internet Specific
E-Commerce Technology
Internet

Additional Information
Year Founded: 2000
Capital Under Management: $85,600,000
Current Activity Level : Actively seeking new investments

INSIGHT CAPITAL PARTNERS LLC

Villa Rodestein
Mollaan la
2061 CR Bloemendaal, Netherlands
Phone: 31-23-541-1222
Fax: 31-23-541-1200

See New York for full listing.

INTERMEDIATE CAPITAL GROUP PLC

62-63 Threadneedle Street
London, United Kingdom EC2R 8HE
Phone: 44-20-7628-9898
Fax: 44-20-7628-2268
Website: www.intermediatecapital.co.uk

Other Offices

38 Avenue Hoche
Paris, France 75008
Phone: 33-1-4495-8686
Fax: 33-1-4495-8687

Management and Staff
Andrew Jackson, Managing Partner
Christopher Evain, Managing Partner
Jean Loup de Gersigny, Managing Partner
Paul Piper, Managing Partner
Tom Attwood, General Partner
Tom Bartlam, Managing Partner

Type of Firm
Investment/Merchant Bank Subsid/Affil

Industry Association Membership
British Venture Capital Association
European Venture Capital Association (EVCA)

Project Preferences

Role in Financing:
Prefer role in deals created by others

Type of Financing Preferred:
Expansion
Leveraged Buyout
Management Buyouts
Mezzanine
Public Companies
Recapitalizations

Geographical Preferences

International
Belgium
France
Germany
Italy
Spain
United Kingdom

Additional Information

Year Founded: 1989
Capital Under Management: $731,200,000
Current Activity Level : Actively seeking new investments
Method of Compensation: Return on invest. most important, but chg. closing fees, service fees, etc.

INTERNET INCUBATOR PLC

22 Soho Square
London, United Kingdom W1D 4NS
Phone: 44 20 7070 7070
Fax: 44 20 7070 7077
Website: www.theii.net

Other Offices

Kronhusgatan 11
Gothenburg, Sweden 411 055
Phone: 46 31 107 461
Fax: 46 31 135 329

Schuttershofstraat 9
Antwerp, Belgium 2000
Phone: 33 3 234 1644

Two Embarcadero Inc
Suite 1740
San Francisco, United States of America 94111
Phone: 1 415 217 6460
Fax: 1 415 217 6464

Management and Staff

Jennifer Moore, Partner
Nigel Drummond, Chief Executive Officer

Type of Firm

Incubators

Project Preferences

Type of Financing Preferred:
Startup

Geographical Preferences

International
Europe

Industry Preferences

Communications and Media
Communications and Media

Internet Specific
Internet

Computer Other
Computer Related

Semiconductors/Other Elect.
Electronics

Additional Information

Year Founded: 2000
Capital Under Management: $19,200,000
Current Activity Level : Actively seeking new investments

INTERNET VENTURES SCANDINAVIA A/S

Dr. Neergaards vej 5A
Horsholm, Denmark 2970
Phone: 45 70 220 228
Fax: 45 70 220 227
Website: www.internetventures.dk

Other Offices

10420 Little Patuxent Parkway
Suite 301
Columbia, United States of America 21044-3636
Phone: 410 884 1700
Fax: 410 884 6171

6 Arosa Road
Richmond Bridge, East Twickenham
Middlesex, United Kingdom TW1 2TL
Phone: 44 181 408 2041

Surenweg 6
Walchwil, Switzerland 6318
Phone: 41 417 581 422
Fax: 41 417 581 588

Management and Staff

Benny Guld, Founder
Steen Louis Reinholdt, Founder

Type of Firm

Private Firm Investing Own Capital

Project Preferences

Type of Financing Preferred:
Early Stage

Industry Preferences

Internet Specific
Internet

Additional Information

Year Founded: 1999
Current Activity Level : Actively seeking new investments

INTERPACIFIC VENTURE GROUP INCORPORATED

3F, No. 57
Fu-Hsing North Road
Taipei, Taiwan
Phone: 8862-2771-0168
Fax: 8862-2773-3342

Type of Firm

Private Firm Investing Own Capital

Industry Association Membership

Taiwan Venture Capital Association(TVCA)

Project Preferences

Type of Financing Preferred:
Expansion
Mezzanine
Seed

Geographical Preferences

International
Taiwan

Additional Information

Year Founded: 1999
Capital Under Management: $9,600,000
Current Activity Level : Actively seeking new investments

INTERREGNUM

22/23 Old Burlington Street
London, United Kingdom W1S 2JJ
Phone: 44 20 7494 3080
Fax: 44 20 7494 3090
Website: www.interregnum.com

Management and Staff

Karen Whiteley, President
Ken Olisa, Managing Director
Linda Church, Chief Financial Officer
Sherry Madera, Principal
Simon Davies, Principal
Stuart Keeler, Principal

Type of Firm
Private Equity Advisor or Fund of Fund Mgr

Project Preferences

Type of Financing Preferred:
Early Stage
Industry Rollups
Seed
Start-up Financing
Turnaround

Size of Investments Considered
Min Size of Investment Considered (000s): $300
Max Size of Investment Considered (000s): $300,000

Geographical Preferences

United States
All U.S.

International
Europe

Industry Preferences

Computer Software
Software
Applications Software

Internet Specific
Internet

Additional Information
Year Founded: 1992
Current Activity Level : Actively seeking new investments

INVENTURES MANAGEMENT LTD

12 Leadenhall Street
London, United Kingdom EC3V 1LP
Phone: 44 20 7816 6300
Fax: 44 20 7816 6350
Website: www.inventures-europe.com

Other Offices

Strowinskylaan 3105
Amsterdam, Netherlands 1077 ZX

Type of Firm
Private Firm Investing Own Capital

Project Preferences

Type of Financing Preferred:
Seed
Startup

Geographical Preferences

International
Europe

Industry Preferences

Internet Specific
Internet

Additional Information
Capital Under Management: $25,000,000
Current Activity Level : Actively seeking new investments

INVESCO PRIVATE CAPITAL (FKA: CHANCELLOR)

11 Devonshire Squre
London, United Kingdom EC2M 4YR
Phone: 44-207-454-3066
Fax: 44-207-623-3339

See New York for full listing.

INVESTAR CAPITAL, INC.

Room 1201,12/F,No. 333
Kee-Lung Road, Section 1
Taipei, Taiwan
Phone: 8862-2757-9585
Fax: 8862-2757-9586

Type of Firm
Private Firm Investing Own Capital

Industry Association Membership
Taiwan Venture Capital Association(TVCA)

Project Preferences

Type of Financing Preferred:
Expansion
Mezzanine
Seed
Startup

Geographical Preferences

International
Taiwan

Industry Preferences

(% based on actual investment)

Semiconductors/Other Elect.	50.7%
Internet Specific	15.9%
Communications and Media	13.9%
Computer Hardware	11.4%
Computer Software and Services	8.1%

Additional Information
Name of Most Recent Fund: InveStar Dayspring Venture Capital, Inc.
Most Recent Fund Was Raised: 01/01/1997
Year Founded: 1996
Capital Under Management: $18,600,000
Current Activity Level : Actively seeking new investments

INVESTISSEMENT DESJARDINS

2, complexe Desjardins
C.P. 760
Montreal, Canada H5B 1B8
Phone: 514-281-7131
Fax: 514-281-7808
Website: www.desjardins.com/id

Type of Firm
Commercial Bank Affiliate or Subsidiary

Industry Association Membership
Canadian Venture Capital Association

Project Preferences

Role in Financing:
Prefer role as deal originator but will also invest in deals created by others

Type of Financing Preferred:
Control-block Purchases
First Stage Financing
Leveraged Buyout
Mezzanine
Second Stage Financing
Start-up Financing

Size of Investments Considered
Min Size of Investment Considered (000s): $5,000
Max Size of Investment Considered: No Limit

Geographical Preferences

Canada
Quebec

Industry Preferences

Communications and Media
Communications and Media

Computer Other
Computer Related

Semiconductors/Other Elect.
Electronic Components
Controllers and Sensors
Sensors
Component Testing Equipmt
Laser Related
Fiber Optics
Analytic/Scientific

Biotechnology
Biotechnology

Medical/Health
Medical/Health

Consumer Related
Entertainment and Leisure
Computer Stores
Food/Beverage
Consumer Products

Industrial/Energy
Materials
Factory Automation
Machinery
Environmental Related

Additional Information
Year Founded: 1974
Capital Under Management: $150,000,000
Current Activity Level : Actively seeking new investments
Method of Compensation: Return on invest. most important, but chg. closing fees, service fees, etc.

INVESTISSEMENTS NOVACAP (AKA:NOVACAP INVESTMENTS, INC.)

375 Boulevard Roland Therrien
Bureau 210
Longueuil, Canada J4H 4A6
Phone: 450-651-5000
Fax: 450-651-7585
Website: www.novacap-inc.com

Management and Staff
Marc Beauchamp, President
Marc Paiement, Vice President

Whom to Contact
any/all of above

Type of Firm
Venture Consulting Firm

Industry Association Membership
Canadian Venture Capital Association

Project Preferences

Role in Financing:
Prefer role as deal originator but will also invest in deals created by others

Type of Financing Preferred:
Control-block Purchases
Early Stage
Expansion
First Stage Financing
Leveraged Buyout
Management Buyouts
Turnaround

Size of Investments Considered
Min Size of Investment Considered (000s): $1,000
Max Size of Investment Considered: No Limit

Geographical Preferences

United States
Northeast

Canada
New Brunswick
Newfoundland
Ontario
Prince Edward Island
Quebec

Industry Preferences

Communications and Media
Telecommunications
Wireless Communications
Data Communications
Satellite Microwave Comm.
Other Communication Prod.

Computer Software
Applications Software

Internet Specific
Internet

Semiconductors/Other Elect.
Electronic Components
Semiconductor
Micro-Processing
Controllers and Sensors
Sensors
Circuit Boards
Component Testing Equipmt
Laser Related
Fiber Optics

Biotechnology
Human Biotechnology

Medical/Health
Medical Therapeutics
Medical Products

Consumer Related
Entertainment and Leisure

Industrial/Energy
Industrial Products
Robotics
Machinery

Transportation
Aerospace

Manufact.
Manufacturing

Additional Information
Name of Most Recent Fund: Novacap Investments, Inc
Most Recent Fund Was Raised: 04/01/1985
Year Founded: 1981
Capital Under Management: $220,000,000
Current Activity Level : Actively seeking new investments
Method of Compensation: Return on investment is of primary concern, do not charge fees

---

INVISION AG (FKA AUREUS PRIVATE EQUITY AG)

Industriestrasse 24
Zug, Switzerland CH-6300
Phone: 41 41 729 0101
Fax: 41 41 729 0100
Website: www.invision.ch

Management and Staff
Frederic Martel, Partner
Martin Staub, Partner
Peter Titz, President

Type of Firm
Private Firm Investing Own Capital

Industry Association Membership
European Venture Capital Association (EVCA)
Swiss Venture Capital Association

Project Preferences

Type of Financing Preferred:
Early Stage
Expansion
Generalist PE
Seed
Startup

Geographical Preferences

United States
All U.S.

International
China
Europe
France
Germany
Ireland
Israel
Switzerland

Industry Preferences

(% based on actual investment)

Internet Specific	54.8%
Computer Software and Services	41.6%
Communications and Media	2.4%
Other Products	1.2%

Additional Information
Year Founded: 1998
Capital Under Management: $41,900,000
Current Activity Level : Actively seeking new investments

IPE CAPITAL-SOC.DE CAP.DE RISOC SA

Av. Julio Dinis, 9-1
Lisbon, Portugal P-1050
Phone: 351-1-795-0022
Fax: 351-1-795-0027
Website: www.ipecapital.pt

Management and Staff
Filomena Pastor, Partner
Fraga Figueiredo, Partner
Pimenta Da Silva, Partner
Rui Goncalves Soares, Partner

Type of Firm
Non-Financial Corp. Affiliate or Subsidiary

Industry Association Membership
European Venture Capital Association (EVCA)
Portuguese Venture Capital Association

Project Preferences

Role in Financing:
Prefer role as deal originator but will also invest in deals created by others

Type of Financing Preferred:
Early Stage
Expansion
Leveraged Buyout
Mezzanine
Startup

Size of Investments Considered
Min Size of Investment Considered (000s): $1,500
Max Size of Investment Considered: No Limit

Geographical Preferences

International
Afghanistan
Asia
Bermuda
Brazil
France
Germany
Italy
Latin America
South Africa
Spain
United Kingdom

Industry Preferences

Consumer Related
Education Related

Financial Services
Financial Services
Real Estate

Additional Information
Year Founded: 1988
Capital Under Management: $59,700,000
Current Activity Level : Actively seeking new investments
Method of Compensation: Return on invest. most important, but chg. closing fees, service fees, etc.

IPS INDUSTRIAL PROMOTION SERVICES, LTD.

60 Columbia Way
Suite 720
Markham, Canada L3R 0C9
Phone: 905-475-9400
Fax: 905-475-5003

Management and Staff
Azim Lalani
Nizar Alibhai
Shamsh Dhala

Whom to Contact
Azim Lalani
Nizar Alibhai
Shamsh Dhala

Type of Firm
Private Firm Investing Own Capital

Industry Association Membership
Canadian Venture Capital Association

Project Preferences

Role in Financing:
Prefer role as deal originator but will also invest in deals created by others

Type of Financing Preferred:
Control-block Purchases
Leveraged Buyout
Second Stage Financing
Special Situation

Size of Investments Considered
Min Size of Investment Considered (000s): $500
Max Size of Investment Considered: No Limit

Geographical Preferences

United States
All U.S.

Canada
All Canada

Industry Preferences

Communications and Media
Telecommunications

Computer Hardware
Mini and Personal/Desktop

Semiconductors/Other Elect.
Electronics
Laser Related
Fiber Optics

Biotechnology
Industrial Biotechnology

Medical/Health
Drug/Equipmt Delivery
Medical Products
Pharmaceuticals

Consumer Related
Food/Beverage
Consumer Products

Industrial/Energy
Energy Conservation Relat
Industrial Products
Environmental Related

Transportation
Transportation

Additional Information
Year Founded: 1979
Capital Under Management: $25,000,000
Current Activity Level : Actively seeking new investments
Method of Compensation: Return on invest. most important, but chg. closing fees, service fees, etc.

IREKA VENTURE CAPITAL LIMITED

32-34 Medan Setia Dua
Bukit Damansara
Kuala Lumpur, Malaysia 50490
Phone: 603-254-0133
Fax: 603-255-2096
Website: www.ireka.com.my

Management and Staff
Lai Siew Wah, Managing Director

Type of Firm
Non-Financial Corp. Affiliate or Subsidiary

Project Preferences

Type of Financing Preferred:
Balanced

Geographical Preferences

International
Asia

Industry Preferences

Internet Specific
Internet

Computer Other
Computer Related

Consumer Related
Hotels and Resorts

Additional Information
Current Activity Level : Actively seeking new investments

ISEP NV

Bruul 81
Mechelen, Belgium B-2800
Phone: 32-15-202662
Fax: 32-15-203709

Management and Staff
Tony Van Wesel, Managing Director

Type of Firm
Commercial Bank Affiliate or Subsidiary

Project Preferences

Role in Financing:
Prefer role as deal originator but will also invest in deals created by others

Type of Financing Preferred:
First Stage Financing
Leveraged Buyout
Research and Development
Second Stage Financing
Seed
Start-up Financing

Size of Investments Considered
Min Size of Investment Considered (000s): $1,000
Max Size of Investment Considered: No Limit

Geographical Preferences

International
Belgium
France
Germany
Italy
Spain
United Kingdom

Industry Preferences

Communications and Media
Telecommunications
Data Communications

Computer Hardware
Computer Graphics and Dig
Disk Relat. Memory Device

Computer Software
Computer Services
Applications Software

Internet Specific
Internet

Semiconductors/Other Elect.
Electronics
Electronic Components
Sensors
Component Testing Equipmt
Analytic/Scientific

Biotechnology
Biotech Related Research

Medical/Health
Medical Diagnostics
Diagnostic Services
Diagnostic Test Products
Medical Therapeutics
Medical Products

Consumer Related
Franchises(NEC)
Consumer Products
Consumer Services

Industrial/Energy
Industrial Products
Robotics
Machinery

Additional Information
Year Founded: 1983
Capital Under Management: $20,000,000
Current Activity Level : Inactive / Unknown
Method of Compensation: Return on invest. most important, but chg. closing fees, service fees, etc.

ISRAEL SEED PARTNERS

64 Emek Refaim
Jerusalem, Israel
Phone: 972-2-561-2090
Fax: 972-2-561-1955
Website: www.israelseed.com

Management and Staff
Alan Feld, General Partner
Daphna Pearl, Chief Financial Officer
Jonathan Medved, General Partner
Michael Eisenberg, General Partner
Neil Cohen, General Partner

Type of Firm
Private Firm Investing Own Capital

Project Preferences

Type of Financing Preferred:
Early Stage
Seed

Size of Investments Considered
Min Size of Investment Considered (000s): $2,500
Max Size of Investment Considered: No Limit

Geographical Preferences

International
All International

Industry Preferences

(% based on actual investment)

Internet Specific	52.0%
Computer Software and Services	23.4%
Communications and Media	15.5%
Semiconductors/Other Elect.	6.6%
Computer Hardware	2.5%

Additional Information
Year Founded: 1995
Capital Under Management: $258,000,000
Current Activity Level : Actively seeking new investments

IT PROVIDER ADVISOR

Hamngaten 13
Stockholm, Sweden 11147
Phone: 46-8-614-0000
Fax: 46-8-611-3959
Website: www.it-provider.com

Management and Staff
Carl Bildt, Partner
Johan Hernmarck, Managing Director
Lars Irstad, Chief Executive Officer

Type of Firm
Private Firm Investing Own Capital

Project Preferences

Type of Financing Preferred:
Early Stage
Expansion
Seed
Startup

Geographical Preferences

International
Europe

Industry Preferences

Computer Hardware
Computers

Computer Software
Software

Additional Information
Year Founded: 1998
Current Activity Level : Actively seeking new investments

ITACT

Biblioteksgatan 12
Stockholm, Sweden S-111 46
Phone: 46 8-611 63 50
Fax: 46 8-611 50 03
Website: www.itact.com

Other Offices

Stora Sodergatan 3
Lund, Sweden S-222 23
Phone: 46 46-32 88 60
Fax: 46 46-211 35 70

Management and Staff
Alex Molvin, Partner
Erica Franzen, Partner
Eva Helgesen, Partner
Fredric Gunnarson, Partner
Jonas Lundhagen, Partner
Martin Gren, Co-Founder
Stefan Lindskog, Partner

Type of Firm
Incubators

Project Preferences

Type of Financing Preferred:
Early Stage
Startup

Geographical Preferences

International
Sweden

Industry Preferences

Communications and Media
Telecommunications

Additional Information
Year Founded: 1999
Capital Under Management: $32,800,000
Current Activity Level : Actively seeking new investments

ITP-MANAGEMENT N.V.

Excelsiorlaan 13
Zaventum, Belgium B-1930
Phone: 32-2-725-1838
Fax: 32-2-721-4435
Website: www.it-partners.be

Management and Staff
Paul Verdurme, General Partner
Stefaan Nicolay, General Partner

Type of Firm
Private Firm Investing Own Capital

Industry Association Membership
Belgium Venture Capital Association
European Venture Capital Association (EVCA)

Project Preferences

Type of Financing Preferred:
Early Stage

Geographical Preferences

United States
All U.S.

International
Belgium
Europe
Israel
Luxembourg
Netherlands

Industry Preferences

Communications and Media
Communications and Media

Additional Information
Year Founded: 1997
Capital Under Management: $70,000,000
Current Activity Level : Actively seeking new investments

J.L. ALBRIGHT VENTURE PARTNERS

Suite 4440, P.O. Box 215
Canada Trust Tower, 161 Bay St
Toronto, Canada M5J 2S1
Phone: 416-367-2440
Fax: 416-367-4604
Website: www.jlaventures.com

Management and Staff
Gary Rubinoff, Partner
John Albright, Partner
Osama Arafat, Partner
Rick Segal, Partner
Stuart Lombard, Partner

Whom to Contact
Jon Prosser

Type of Firm
Private Firm Investing Own Capital

Industry Association Membership
Canadian Venture Capital Association

Project Preferences

Role in Financing:
Prefer role as deal originator

Type of Financing Preferred:
First Stage Financing
Second Stage Financing

Geographical Preferences

United States
All U.S.
Northeast

Canada
All Canada
Ontario
Quebec

Industry Preferences

(% based on actual investment)

Internet Specific	76.5%
Other Products	10.5%
Communications and Media	5.8%
Computer Hardware	4.1%
Computer Software and Services	3.1%

Additional Information

Year Founded: 1996
Capital Under Management: $168,900,000
Current Activity Level : Actively seeking new investments
Method of Compensation: Return on invest. most important, but chg. closing fees, service fees, etc.

J.P. MORGAN CAPITAL CORP.

Edinburgh Tower, 15 Queen's Road
Central, Hong Kong
Phone: 852-2841-1168
Fax: 852-2973-5471

See New York for full listing.

J.P. MORGAN PARTNERS (FKA: CHASE CAPITAL PARTNERS)

One International Finance Centre
Central, Hong Kong
Phone: 852-2533-1818
Fax: 852-2868-5551

See New York for full listing.

JAFCO CO. LTD.

Daini Tekko Building
1-8-2 Marunouchi, Chiyoda-ku
Tokyo, Japan 100-0005
Phone: 03-5223-7073
Fax: 03-5223-7561
Website: www.jafco.co.jp

Management and Staff

Hitoshi Imuta, President
Mitsumasa Murase, President

Type of Firm

Private Firm Investing Own Capital

Industry Association Membership

Natl assoc of Small Bus. Inv. Co (NASBIC)

Project Preferences

Role in Financing:
Will function either as deal originator or investor in deals created by others

Type of Financing Preferred:
Early Stage
Management Buyouts
Mezzanine
Startup

Geographical Preferences

United States
All U.S.

International
Australia
China
Germany
Japan
Middle East
United Kingdom

Industry Preferences

(% based on actual investment)

Consumer Related	42.4%
Industrial/Energy	33.7%
Internet Specific	15.0%
Medical/Health	4.6%
Communications and Media	3.1%
Semiconductors/Other Elect.	0.9%
Computer Hardware	0.3%

Additional Information

Year Founded: 1973
Capital Under Management: $1,926,800,000
Current Activity Level : Actively seeking new investments
Method of Compensation: Return on investment is of primary concern, do not charge fees

JAFCO INVESTMENT (FKA:NOMURA/JAFCO INVESTMENT (ASIA) LIMITED

6 Battery Road #42-01
Singapore, Singapore 049909
Phone: 65-224-6383
Fax: 65-221-3690
Website: www.jafcoasia.com

Other Offices

Level 42, ANZ Tower
55 Collins Street
Melbourne, Australia 3000
Phone: 613-9654-2121
Fax: 613-9650-9098

Management and Staff

John Tan Teck Shoon, Vice President

Type of Firm

Commercial Bank Affiliate or Subsidiary

Industry Association Membership

Australian Venture Capital Association (AVCAL)

Project Preferences

Type of Financing Preferred:
Early Stage
Expansion
Startup

Geographical Preferences

International
Asia

Industry Preferences

(% based on actual investment)

Internet Specific	37.2%
Computer Software and Services	17.1%
Computer Hardware	15.4%
Biotechnology	9.6%
Medical/Health	9.6%
Consumer Related	5.5%
Semiconductors/Other Elect.	3.4%
Communications and Media	2.2%

Additional Information
Year Founded: 1995
Capital Under Management: $660,900,000
Current Activity Level : Actively seeking new investments

JAPAN ASIA INVESTMENT CO LTD

Kojimachi Tsuruyahachiman Bldg
2-4 Kojimachi, Chiyoda-ku
Tokyo, Japan 102-8518
Phone: 03-3238-1461
Fax: 03-3238-1460
Website: www.jaic-vc.co.jp

Other Offices

14/F C Room Grand Amarin
Tower 1550 New Petchburi Rd., Makasan
Bangkok, Thailand 10310
Phone: 662-207-0216
Fax: 662-207-0215

2/F Sakura Hiroshima Bldg.
2-26 Kamiyacho 1-Chome, Naka-ku
Hiroshima, Japan 730-0031
Phone: 818-2504-6920
Fax: 818-2504-6921

2479 East Bayshore Road
Suite 709
Palo Alto, United States of America 94303
Phone: 650-213-9011
Fax: 650-213-9012

3/F, Mitsuikaijo Okayama Bldg.
12-1 Yanagimachi 1-Chome
Okayama, Japan 700-0904
Phone: 818-6224-0048
Fax: 818-6224-0040

4/F, Taiyo Twin Bldg. TWIN-2,
13-22 Honcho 1-Chome, Aoba-ku
Sendai, Japan 980-0014
Phone: 812-2216-8551
Fax: 812-2216-8550

50 Raffles Place #24-03
Singapore Land Tower
Singapore, Singapore 048623
Phone: 65-557-0559
Fax: 65-557-0332

6/F Kanazawa Fukokuseimei-ekimae
11-7 Honmachi 2-Chome
Kanazawa, Japan 920-0853
Phone: 817-6232-5040
Fax: 817-6232-5043

6/F, Kabutodecom 92 Bldg.
1000-2 Minami 2-jo Nishi 10-Chome Chuo-k
Sapporo, Japan 060-0062
Phone: 811-1232-3550
Fax: 811-1232-3556

8/F Nichijukin Kakaku Bldg.
8-36 Tenjin 2-Chome, Chuo-ku
Fukuoka, Japan 810-0001
Phone: 819-2725-5733
Fax: 819-2725-5717

8/F, Kitahama Seiyukaikan Bldg.
1-3, Kitahama 2-Chome, Chuo-ku
Osaka, Japan 541-0041
Phone: 816-232-2881
Fax: 816-232-2880

9/F, Ikko Fushimi Bldg.
20-10 Nishiki 1-Chome, Naka-ku
Nagoya, Japan 460-0003
Phone: 815-2211-2921
Fax: 815-2211-2920

Mayban Ventures Sdn.Bhd.-20/F W. Wing,
Menera Maybank 100 Jalan Tun Perak
Kuala Lumpur, Malaysia 50050
Phone: 603-202-2188
Fax: 603-201-2188

Suite 2511, Two Pacific Place
88 Queensway Admiralty
Hong Kong, Hong Kong
Phone: 852-2509-3011
Fax: 852-2509-3025

Unit 707, Antel 2000 Corp. Center
121 Valero St., Salcedo Vill.
Makati, Philippines
Phone: 632-751-0000
Fax: 632-751-1560

Management and Staff
Eizou Akashi, Senior Managing Director
Hidetaka Fukuzawa, Managing Director
Jiro Uno, Senior Managing Director
Yoshiki Sasaki, Managing Director

Whom to Contact
Mami Katagawa

Type of Firm
Investment/Merchant Bank Investing Own or Client Funds

Project Preferences

Role in Financing:
Prefer role as deal originator but will also invest in deals created by others

Type of Financing Preferred:
Balanced

Geographical Preferences

United States
All U.S.

International
China
India
Indonesia
Japan
Singapore
Thailand

Additional Information
Year Founded: 1981
Capital Under Management: $736,800,000
Current Activity Level : Actively seeking new investments
Method of Compensation: Return on invest. most important, but chg. closing fees, service fees, etc.

JEFFERSON PARTNERS

77 King Street West
Suite 4010, P.O. Box 136
Toronto, Canada M5K 1H1
Phone: 416-367-1533
Fax: 416-367-5827
Website: www.jefferson.com

Management and Staff
David Folk, Managing General Partner
David Harris Kolada, Venture Partner
Ian Locke, General Partner
Jack Kiervin, Managing General Partner
Jonathan Black, Venture Partner

Type of Firm
Private Firm Investing Own Capital

Project Preferences

Role in Financing:
Prefer role as deal originator but will also invest in deals created by others

Type of Financing Preferred:
Expansion
Seed

Size of Investments Considered
Min Size of Investment Considered (000s): $3,000
Max Size of Investment Considered (000s): $10,000

Geographical Preferences

United States
Northeast

Canada
All Canada

Industry Preferences

Communications and Media
Communications and Media

Computer Software
Software

Internet Specific
Internet

Additional Information

Year Founded: 1994
Capital Under Management: $110,000,000
Current Activity Level : Actively seeking new investments
Method of Compensation: Return on invest. most important, but chg. closing fees, service fees, etc.

JERUSALEM GLOBAL VENTURES

House, Har Hotzvim
PO Box 45129
Jerusalem, Israel 91450
Phone: 972 2 572 2222
Fax: 972 2572 2255
Website: www.jgventures.com

Management and Staff

Joel Weiss, Chief Operating Officer
Shlomo Kalish, Founding Partner

Whom to Contact

Glen Schwaber
Mark Lesnick

Type of Firm

Private Firm Investing Own Capital

Project Preferences

Role in Financing:
Prefer role as deal originator

Type of Financing Preferred:
Seed
Startup

Geographical Preferences

United States
All U.S.

Canada
All Canada

International
Israel
Middle East

Industry Preferences

Communications and Media
Communications and Media
Telecommunications

Computer Software
Software

Internet Specific
Internet

Computer Other
Computer Related

Semiconductors/Other Elect.
Electronics
Electronic Components

Biotechnology
Biotechnology

Medical/Health
Medical Diagnostics
Diagnostic Services
Diagnostic Test Products
Medical Therapeutics
Other Therapeutic
Medical Products

Industrial/Energy
Robotics

Manufact.
Publishing

Additional Information

Year Founded: 1998
Capital Under Management: $200,000,000
Current Activity Level : Actively seeking new investments

JERUSALEM VENTURE PARTNERS (AKA: JVP)

Jerusalem Technology Park
Building One
Jerusalem, Jordan 91487
Phone: 972-2-679-7270
Fax: 972-2-679-7273
Website: www.jvpvc.com

Other Offices

10 Stratton Street
London, United Kingdom WIX 5FD
Phone: 44-20-7544-6835
Fax: 44-20-7544-6870

888 Seventh Avenue
33rd Floor
New York, United States of America 10106
Phone: 212-603-2692
Fax: 212-765-3203

East Tower, 4th Floor
Otemachi First Square
Tokyo, Japan 100-0004
Phone: 81 3 5219 1509
Fax: 81 3 5219 1201

Management and Staff

Dan Isenberg, Venture Partner
Erel Margalit, Managing Partner
Glen Schwaber, General Partner
Yuval Cohen, General Partner

Type of Firm

Private Firm Investing Own Capital

Project Preferences

Type of Financing Preferred:
Early Stage

Geographical Preferences

International
All International

Industry Preferences

(% based on actual investment)

Communications and Media	40.9%
Internet Specific	24.0%
Semiconductors/Other Elect.	15.4%
Computer Software and Services	12.9%
Computer Hardware	6.8%

Additional Information

Year Founded: 1993
Capital Under Management: $245,000,000
Current Activity Level : Actively seeking new investments

JUMPSTARTUP FUND ADVISORS PVT. LTD.

206 Raheja Plaza
17 Commissariat Road
Bangalore, India 560 025
Phone: 9180-556-4829
Fax: 9180-556-4897
Website: www.jumpstartup.net

Management and Staff

KGanapathy Subramanian, Principal
Kiran Nadkarni, Principal
Sanjay Anandaram, Principal

Type of Firm
Private Firm Investing Own Capital

Project Preferences
Type of Financing Preferred:
Early Stage
Seed

Geographical Preferences
International
India

Industry Preferences
Computer Software
Software

Internet Specific
Internet

Semiconductors/Other Elect.
Semiconductor

Additional Information
Year Founded: 2000
Capital Under Management: $45,000,000
Current Activity Level : Actively seeking new investments

KANGAROO VILLAGE

6, rue d'Argenson
Paris, France F-75008
Phone: 33 1 5330 2050
Fax: 33 1 5330 2051
E-mail: info@kangaroovillage.com
Website: www.kangaroovillage.com

Management and Staff
Anne Lalou, Partner
Fabrice Grinda, Founder
Gael Duval, Founder
Maurizio Arrigo, Partner
Patrick Robin, Founder
Phillippe Hayat, Chief Executive Officer
Serge Cohen, Partner
Xavier Lorphelin, Partner

Type of Firm
Incubators

Project Preferences
Type of Financing Preferred:
Seed
Startup

Geographical Preferences
International
Europe
All International

Industry Preferences
Internet Specific
Internet

Additional Information
Capital Under Management: $2,200,000
Current Activity Level : Actively seeking new investments

KANKAKU INVESTMENT CO LTD

Kankaku Honcho Building, 3-3-3
Honcho Nihonbashi, Chuo-ku
Tokyo, Japan 101-0052
Phone: 81-3-3246-5821
Fax: 81-3-3246-5881
Website: www.mydome.or.jp/ord/data/2018.html

Other Offices

1-2-2-100 Umeda, Kita-Ku
Osaka, Japan 530-0001
Phone: 816-3430-298
Fax: 816-3430-492

Type of Firm
Investment/Merchant Bank Investing Own or Client Funds

Project Preferences
Role in Financing:
Prefer role in deals created by others

Type of Financing Preferred:
First Stage Financing
Mezzanine
Second Stage Financing

Size of Investments Considered
Min Size of Investment Considered (000s): $500
Max Size of Investment Considered (000s): $1,000

Geographical Preferences
United States
All U.S.

International
Asia
Pacific Rim
Western Europe

Industry Preferences
Communications and Media
Telecommunications
Data Communications

Computer Software
Computer Services
Applications Software

Internet Specific
Internet

Computer Other
Computer Related

Semiconductors/Other Elect.
Electronic Components
Semiconductor

Consumer Related
Consumer Services

Industrial/Energy
Industrial Products

Transportation
Transportation

Financial Services
Real Estate

Manufact.
Manufacturing
Publishing

Additional Information
Name of Most Recent Fund: KIC- 3 Investment Partners
Most Recent Fund Was Raised: 12/01/1996
Year Founded: 1984
Capital Under Management: $180,000,000
Current Activity Level : Actively seeking new investments
Method of Compensation: Return on invest. most important, but chg. closing fees, service fees, etc.

KAPPA-IT VENTURES

Residenzstrasse 3
Munich, Germany D - 80333
Phone: 49-89-242-37-00
Fax: 49-89-2423-7070
Website: www.kappa-it.com

Other Offices

Hohe Strasse 73
53119
Bonn, Germany
Phone: 49-89-87-97-30
Fax: 49-89-87-97-44

Management and Staff
Alexander Lewald, Founding Partner
Bettina Strube, Principal
Hans Botho von Portatius, Managing Director
Keith Gruen, Founding Partner
Marc Breitfeld, Principal

Type of Firm
Private Firm Investing Own Capital

Industry Association Membership
European Venture Capital Association (EVCA)

Project Preferences

Type of Financing Preferred:
Early Stage
Expansion
Seed
Startup

Size of Investments Considered
Min Size of Investment Considered (000s): $500
Max Size of Investment Considered (000s): $500,000

Geographical Preferences

United States
All U.S.

International
France
Germany
Israel
Scandanavia/Nordic Region
United Kingdom

Industry Preferences

Communications and Media
Communications and Media

Internet Specific
Internet

Additional Information
Year Founded: 1998
Capital Under Management: $35,000,000
Current Activity Level : Actively seeking new investments

KENNET CAPITAL LTD

St James's House
London, United Kingdom SW1Y 6QY
Phone: 44-20-7839-8020
Fax: 44-20-7839-8485
Website: www.kennetcapital.com

Management and Staff
Michael Elias, Managing Director

Whom to Contact
Martin Poulsen

Type of Firm
Private Firm Investing Own Capital

Industry Association Membership
British Venture Capital Association
European Venture Capital Association (EVCA)

Project Preferences

Role in Financing:
Prefer role as deal originator but will also invest in deals created by others

Type of Financing Preferred:
Early Stage
Expansion
Startup

Geographical Preferences

International
Bermuda
France
Germany
United Kingdom

Industry Preferences

(% based on actual investment)

Internet Specific	49.5%
Computer Software and Services	28.4%
Communications and Media	19.1%
Semiconductors/Other Elect.	3.0%

Additional Information
Name of Most Recent Fund: Kennet I L.P.
Most Recent Fund Was Raised: 01/01/1998
Year Founded: 1997
Capital Under Management: $320,000,000
Current Activity Level : Actively seeking new investments
Method of Compensation: Return on investment is of primary concern, do not charge fees

KICK-START VENTURES

4th Floor
2 Caxton Street
London, United Kingdom SW1H 0QE
Phone: 44-20-7233-2211
Fax: 44-20-8668-2023
E-mail: info@kickstartventures.com
Website: www.kickstartventures.com

Other Offices

4e Binnenvestgracht 26
Leiden, Netherlands 2311
Phone: 31 71 51 400 55
Fax: 31 71 6 5333 49 69

Management and Staff
Dominique Megret, Chief Executive Officer
Erik Vasquez, Partner
Goetz Otto, Partner
Harry MacMillan, Managing Partner
Jacques Putzeys, Partner
Laurent Bignier, Chief Executive Officer
Oliver Gorter, Partner

Type of Firm
Incubators

Project Preferences

Type of Financing Preferred:
Early Stage
Expansion
Startup

Geographical Preferences

International
Belgium
France
Italy
Luxembourg
Netherlands
South Africa
United Kingdom

Industry Preferences

Communications and Media
Telecommunications

Additional Information
Year Founded: 1999
Capital Under Management: $90,800,000
Current Activity Level : Actively seeking new investments

KLB INVESTMENT CO., LTD.

KLB Financial Plaza, 14th Fl
648-19, Yoksam-dong Gangnam-gu
Seoul, South Korea 135-080
Phone: 82-2-508-2677
Fax: 82-2-508-2678

Type of Firm
Commercial Bank Affiliate or Subsidiary

Project Preferences

Role in Financing:
Prefer role as deal originator but will also invest in deals created by others

Type of Financing Preferred:
Leveraged Buyout
Mezzanine
Second Stage Financing

Size of Investments Considered
Min Size of Investment Considered (000s): $1,000
Max Size of Investment Considered: No Limit

Geographical Preferences

United States
All U.S.

International
Asia

Industry Preferences

Communications and Media
CATV & Pay TV Systems
Telecommunications
Data Communications
Satellite Microwave Comm.

Computer Hardware
Computer Graphics and Dig
Disk Relat. Memory Device

Computer Software
Computer Services
Systems Software
Applications Software
Artificial Intelligence

Internet Specific
Internet

Semiconductors/Other Elect.
Electronic Components
Semiconductor
Controllers and Sensors
Laser Related
Fiber Optics
Analytic/Scientific

Biotechnology
Industrial Biotechnology

Medical/Health
Other Therapeutic
Disposable Med. Products
Pharmaceuticals

Consumer Related
Food/Beverage
Consumer Products

Industrial/Energy
Alternative Energy
Energy Conservation Relat
Industrial Products

Manufact.
Office Automation Equipmt

Additional Information

Year Founded: 1990
Capital Under Management: $45,000,000
Current Activity Level : Actively seeking new investments
Method of Compensation: Return on invest. most important, but chg. closing fees, service fees, etc.

KLM CAPITAL GROUP

10/F, Century Square
1-13, D'Aguilar Street
Central, Hong Kong
Phone: 852-2537-3318
Fax: 852-2537-3138

See California for full listing.

KOKUSAI FINANCE CO., LTD.

1-7-2 Nihonbashi Kayaba-cho
Chuo-ku
Tokyo, Japan
Phone: 03-3668-6456
Fax: 03-3668-6214
Website: www.kokusaifinance.co.jp

Type of Firm

Private Firm Investing Own Capital

Project Preferences

Type of Financing Preferred:
Balanced

Geographical Preferences

International
Japan
No Preference

Additional Information

Year Founded: 1989
Capital Under Management: $160,700,000
Current Activity Level : Actively seeking new investments

KOOKMIN VENTURE CAPITAL CO LTD

KPC Building, 1st-2nd Fl.
122-1 Jeoksun-dong, Jongro-gu
Seoul, South Korea 110-052
Phone: 822-736-0190
Fax: 822-730-3401

Management and Staff

Chong Rhee, President

Whom to Contact

Sae-Ho Song
Sun-Jai Lee

Type of Firm

Commercial Bank Affiliate or Subsidiary

Project Preferences

Role in Financing:
Prefer role as deal originator but will also invest in deals created by others

Type of Financing Preferred:
Second Stage Financing

Size of Investments Considered
Min Size of Investment Considered (000s): $500
Max Size of Investment Considered (000s): $1,000

Geographical Preferences

International
Korea, South

Industry Preferences

Communications and Media
Commercial Communications
CATV & Pay TV Systems
Satellite Microwave Comm.
Other Communication Prod.

Computer Hardware
Computers
Mainframes / Scientific

Internet Specific
Internet

Semiconductors/Other Elect.
Electronic Components
Controllers and Sensors
Sensors
Circuit Boards
Component Testing Equipmt
Analytic/Scientific

Biotechnology
Biotech Related Research
Biotech Related Research

Medical/Health
Medical Diagnostics
Diagnostic Services
Diagnostic Test Products
Medical Therapeutics

Consumer Related
Franchises(NEC)
Food/Beverage
Consumer Products

Industrial/Energy
Materials
Factory Automation
Environmental Related

Transportation
Transportation

Business Serv.
Consulting Services

Additional Information
Year Founded: 1986
Capital Under Management: $400,000,000
Current Activity Level : Actively seeking new investments
Method of Compensation: Return on invest. most important, but chg. closing fees, service fees, etc.

KOOR CORPORATE VENTURE CAPITAL

Platinum House
21 Ha'arba'a Street
Tel Aviv, Israel 64739
Phone: 972 3 623 333
Fax: 972 3 623 8334
Website: www.koorcvc.com

Management and Staff
Einat Wilf, General Partner
Yiftach Atir, Managing Director

Type of Firm
Affiliate/Subsidary of Oth. Financial. Instit.

Project Preferences

Type of Financing Preferred:
Early Stage
Fund of Funds
Startup

Geographical Preferences

International
Israel

Industry Preferences

Communications and Media
Telecommunications

Internet Specific
Internet

Biotechnology
Biotechnology

Additional Information
Year Founded: 2000
Capital Under Management: $250,000,000
Current Activity Level : Actively seeking new investments

KORDA & CO.

The Studio
11 Bath Road
London, United Kingdom W4 1LJ
Phone: 0181-987-0220
Fax: 0181-994-3012

Type of Firm
Private Firm Investing Own Capital

Project Preferences

Role in Financing:
Prefer role as deal originator

Type of Financing Preferred:
First Stage Financing
Research and Development
Seed
Start-up Financing

Size of Investments Considered
Min Size of Investment Considered (000s): $300
Max Size of Investment Considered (000s): $500

Geographical Preferences

International
No Preference

Additional Information
Name of Most Recent Fund: Korda Seed Capital Fund
Most Recent Fund Was Raised: 01/01/1995
Year Founded: 1982
Capital Under Management: $7,000,000
Current Activity Level : Actively seeking new investments
Method of Compensation: Return on investment is of primary concern, do not charge fees

---

KOREA DEVELOPMENT INVESTMENT CORP.

A-Ju Building, 8th Floor
679-5, Yeoksam Gangnam-Gu
Seoul, South Korea 135-081
Phone: 82-2-538-2411
Fax: 82-2-538-1583
Website: www.tgventures.co.kr

Management and Staff
Hyun-Suk Chai

Whom to Contact
Hyun-Suk Chai

Type of Firm
Non-Financial Corp. Affiliate or Subsidiary

Project Preferences

Role in Financing:
Prefer role as deal originator but will also invest in deals created by others

Type of Financing Preferred:
First Stage Financing
Mezzanine
Second Stage Financing

Size of Investments Considered
Min Size of Investment Considered (000s): $500
Max Size of Investment Considered (000s): $5,000

Industry Preferences

Communications and Media
Communications and Media

Computer Other
Computer Related

Semiconductors/Other Elect.
Electronic Components

Biotechnology
Biotechnology

Medical/Health
Medical/Health

Consumer Related
Consumer

Industrial/Energy
Energy
Industrial Products
Materials
Factory Automation
Machinery

Business Serv.
Distribution

Additional Information
Name of Most Recent Fund: KODICO
Most Recent Fund Was Raised: 07/01/1990
Year Founded: 1982
Capital Under Management: $96,000,000
Current Activity Level : Actively seeking new investments
Method of Compensation: Return on investment is of primary concern, do not charge fees

KOREA TECHNOLOGY FINANCE CORP.

43 Insa-dong
Chongro-ku
Seoul, South Korea 110-290
Phone: 82-2-3700-1114
Fax: 82-2-3700-1113
E-mail: webmst@ktfc.co.kr
Website: http://www.ktfc.co.kr

Other Offices

133, 5-ga, Keumnam-ro
Dong-gu
Kwangju, South Korea 501-025
Phone: 82-62-226-5410
Fax: 82-62-228-5402

190-5 Pumo-dong
Susung-gu
Taegu, South Korea 706-010
Phone: 82-53-743-8863
Fax: 82-53-743-8862

44-1, 2-ga, Jungang-dong
Jung-gu
Pusan, South Korea 600-012
Phone: 82-51-245-1375
Fax: 82-51-242-5459

467-1 Shinbu-dong
Chunan
Chungnam-do, South Korea 330-160
Phone: 82-417-62-9087
Fax: 82-417-62-9086

523-8 Kozan-dong
Ansan
Kyungi-do, South Korea 425-020
Phone: 82-345-80-5700
Fax: 82-345-80-5729

Management and Staff
Bum-Pyo Hong, Vice President
Yul Chung, Vice President

Whom to Contact
Joong-sun Koh

Type of Firm
Commercial Bank Affiliate or Subsidiary

Project Preferences

Role in Financing:
Prefer role as deal originator but will also invest in deals created by others

Type of Financing Preferred:
Mezzanine
Research and Development

Size of Investments Considered
Min Size of Investment Considered (000s): $500
Max Size of Investment Considered (000s): $1,000

Industry Preferences

Communications and Media
Commercial Communications
CATV & Pay TV Systems
Telecommunications
Data Communications
Satellite Microwave Comm.
Other Communication Prod.

Computer Hardware
Computers
Terminals
Disk Relat. Memory Device

Computer Software
Computer Services
Systems Software
Applications Software
Artificial Intelligence

Internet Specific
Internet

Semiconductors/Other Elect.
Electronics
Semiconductor
Sensors
Circuit Boards
Component Testing Equipmt
Laser Related
Analytic/Scientific

Biotechnology
Industrial Biotechnology
Biosensors
Biotech Related Research
Biotech Related Research

Medical/Health
Diagnostic Test Products
Other Therapeutic
Medical Products
Hospitals/Clinics/Primary
Pharmaceuticals

Consumer Related
Computer Stores
Consumer Products

Industrial/Energy
Robotics
Environmental Related

Financial Services
Financial Services

Additional Information
Year Founded: 1984
Capital Under Management: $1,000,000,000
Current Activity Level : Actively seeking new investments
Method of Compensation: Return on investment is of primary concern, do not charge fees

KPE VENTURES

95 New Cavendish Street
London, United Kingdom W1M7FR
Phone: 0171-526-1170

See New York for full listing.

KPMG ADVENT MANAGEMENT GROUP (FKA:ADVENT WESTERN PACIFIC)

6/F 410 Collins Street
Melbourne, Australia 03000
Phone: 613-9670-0599
Fax: 613-9760-0561
Website: www.adventgroup.com.au

Type of Firm
Affiliate/Subsidary of Oth. Financial. Instit.

Industry Association Membership
Australian Venture Capital Association (AVCAL)

Project Preferences

Type of Financing Preferred:
Expansion
Management Buyouts
Mezzanine
Turnaround

Geographical Preferences

International
Australia
Oceania/Australasia

Industry Preferences

Communications and Media
Communications and Media

Internet Specific
Internet

Consumer Related
Entertainment and Leisure
Hotels and Resorts

Business Serv.
Services

Additional Information
Name of Most Recent Fund: Advent Limited
Most Recent Fund Was Raised: 08/01/1986
Year Founded: 1984
Capital Under Management: $58,700,000
Current Activity Level : Actively seeking new investments

KREDITANSTALT FUR WIEDERAUFBAU (KFW)

Palmengartenstrasse 5-9
Frankfurt, Germany 60325
Phone: 49 69 7431 3536
Fax: 49 69 7431 3608
Website: www.kfw.de

Other Offices

Charlottenstrasse 33/33a
Berlin, Germany D-10117
Phone: 49-30-20264-0
Fax: 49-30-20264-188

Type of Firm
Bank Group

Industry Association Membership
European Venture Capital Association (EVCA)
German Venture Capital Association

Project Preferences

Type of Financing Preferred:
Fund of Funds

Geographical Preferences

International
Europe

Additional Information
Capital Under Management: $971,300,000
Current Activity Level : Actively seeking new investments

KTB VENTURES (FKA: KTB VENTURE CAPITAL)

KTB Network Building
826-14
Yeoksam-dong- Kangnam-gu, South Korea 135-080
Phone: 822-3466-2221
Fax: 8222-3466-2380

See California for full listing.

KYORITSU CAPITAL COMPANY, LTD.

3-98 Kuruwa-machi
Ohgaki City, Japan
Phone: 0584-74-2251
Fax:.0584-74-2204
E-mail: capital@okbnet.ne.jp

Type of Firm
Private Firm Investing Own Capital

Project Preferences

Type of Financing Preferred:
Balanced

Geographical Preferences

International
Japan

Industry Preferences

Consumer Related
Consumer Services

Additional Information
Capital Under Management: $9,800,000
Current Activity Level : Actively seeking new investments

LADYBIRD TECHNOLOGIES, LTD.

Greener House
66-68 The Haymarket
London, United Kingdom SW1Y 4RF
Phone: 44-207-925-2543
Fax: 44-207-925-2549
E-mail: contact@lbird.com
Website: www.ladybird.com

Management and Staff
Emre Oral, Managing Director
Ilker Kara, Chief Operating Officer

Type of Firm
Private Firm Investing Own Capital

Project Preferences

Type of Financing Preferred:
Early Stage
Seed
Startup

Geographical Preferences

United States
All U.S.

International
Israel
Netherlands
United Kingdom

Industry Preferences

Internet Specific
Internet

Additional Information

Year Founded: 1999
Current Activity Level : Actively seeking new investments

LANDMARK PARTNERS, INC.

Portman Square House
43-45 Portman Square
London, United Kingdom W2H 0HN
Phone: 44-207-969-2857

See Connecticut for full listing.

LAS AMERICAS ADMINISTRADORA

Miraflores No. 222
21st Floor
Santiago, Chile
Phone: 56-2-633-7812
Fax: 56-2-639-3748

Management and Staff

Alfredo Enrione, Ph.D.
Pamela Gómez Schindler

Whom to Contact

Alfredo Enrione, Ph.D.
Pamela Gómez Schindler

Type of Firm

Endowment

Project Preferences

Role in Financing:
Prefer role as deal originator but will also invest in deals created by others

Type of Financing Preferred:
First Stage Financing
Second Stage Financing
Special Situation
Start-up Financing

Geographical Preferences

International
South Africa

Industry Preferences

Communications and Media
Communications and Media

Computer Hardware
Mini and Personal/Desktop

Computer Software
Computer Services
Systems Software

Semiconductors/Other Elect.
Electronic Components

Biotechnology
Biotechnology

Medical/Health
Medical/Health

Consumer Related
Consumer

Industrial/Energy
Energy
Industrial Products

Transportation
Transportation

Financial Services
Financial Services
Real Estate

Business Serv.
Distribution

Manufact.
Publishing

Agr/Forestr/Fish
Agriculture related

Additional Information

Year Founded: 1992
Capital Under Management: $220,000,000
Current Activity Level : Actively seeking new investments
Method of Compensation: Function primarily in service area, receive contingent fee in cash or equity

LAUNCHWORKS INC.

1902J - 11th Street, S.E.
Calgary, Canada T2G 3G2
Phone: 403-269-1119
Fax: 403-269-1141
Website: www.launchworks.com

Management and Staff

Byron Osing, Chief Executive Officer
Keith Steeves, Chief Financial Officer
Stephen Kenny, President

Type of Firm

Incubators

Project Preferences

Type of Financing Preferred:
Startup

Geographical Preferences

Canada
All Canada

Additional Information

Current Activity Level : Actively seeking new investments

LAZARD ASIA INVESTMENT MANAGEMENT (PRIVATE) LIMITED

Room 2601, Henley Building
5 Queen's Road
Central, Hong Kong
Phone: 852-2522-8187
Fax: 852-2522-8581
Website: www.lazard.com

Management and Staff

Clarence Chung, Vice President
David Anderson, Managing Director

Type of Firm

Affiliate/Subsidary of Oth. Financial. Instit.

Project Preferences

Type of Financing Preferred:
Balanced

Geographical Preferences

International
Asia

Additional Information
Year Founded: 1998
Current Activity Level : Actively seeking new investments

LEGAL & GENERAL VENTURES LTD

Bucklersbury House
3 Queen Victoria Street
London, United Kingdom EC4N 8NH
Phone: 44-207-528-6456
Fax: 44-207-528-6444
Website: www.legalandgeneralventures.com

Other Offices

28 Boulevard Malesherbes
Paris, France 75008
Phone: 33-1-4312-9110
Fax: 33-1-4312-9111

Dunedin Capital Partners Ltd
Napier House 27 Thistle Street
Edinburgh, United Kingdom EH2 1BT
Phone: 44 131 225 6699
Fax: 44 131 624 1234

Kaiserstrasse 10
Frankfurt am Main, Germany 60311
Phone: 49-69-2998-770
Fax: 49-69-2998-7777

Management and Staff
Adrian Johnson, Chief Executive Officer
Andrew Cole, Managing Director
Brian Phillips, Managing Director
Christian Schlesiger, Managing Director
Christophe Fercocq, Managing Director
Eric Cooper, Managing Director
Herve Franc, Managing Director
Roger Charlesworth, Managing Director

Type of Firm
Insurance Firm Affiliate or Subsidiary

Industry Association Membership
British Venture Capital Association

Project Preferences

Role in Financing:
Prefer role as deal originator

Type of Financing Preferred:
Balanced
Early Stage
Expansion
Leveraged Buyout
Management Buyouts
Mezzanine

Size of Investments Considered
Min Size of Investment Considered (000s): $15,000
Max Size of Investment Considered (000s): $298,540

Geographical Preferences

International
Europe
France
Germany
United Kingdom
Western Europe

Industry Preferences

Communications and Media
Communications and Media

Computer Other
Computer Related

Semiconductors/Other Elect.
Electronics

Medical/Health
Medical/Health

Consumer Related
Consumer
Entertainment and Leisure
Food/Beverage

Industrial/Energy
Energy
Industrial Products
Factory Automation

Transportation
Transportation

Financial Services
Financial Services

Business Serv.
Services

Manufact.
Manufacturing

Agr/Forestr/Fish
Agriculture related

Additional Information
Name of Most Recent Fund: Legal & General Ventures 1998 Unquoted Equity Fund, L.P.
Most Recent Fund Was Raised: 02/01/1998
Year Founded: 1988
Capital Under Management: $935,700,000
Current Activity Level : Actively seeking new investments
Method of Compensation: Return on invest. most important, but chg. closing fees, service fees, etc.

LEGENDARY INVESTMENTS PLC

4th Floor
1 Harrow Road
Wembley, United Kingdom HA9 6DE
Phone: 44 89039037
Fax: 44 161 833 4342

Management and Staff
Michael Fry, Co-Founder
Shami Ahmed, Chief Executive Officer
Smit Berry, Co-Founder

Type of Firm
Private Firm Investing Own Capital

Project Preferences

Type of Financing Preferred:
Unknown

Geographical Preferences

International
No Preference

Industry Preferences

Internet Specific
Internet

Additional Information
Year Founded: 2000
Current Activity Level : Actively seeking new investments

LEVENTURE KAPITALBETEILIGUNGSGESELLSCHAFT MBH & CO.KG

Friedrich-Ebert-Strasse 39
Leverkusen, Germany 51373
Phone: 49 214 355 3195
Fax: 49 214 355 1789
E-mail: info@leventure.de
Website: www.leventure.de

Management and Staff
Christian Hein, Partner

Type of Firm
Private Firm Investing Own Capital

Industry Association Membership
German Venture Capital Association

Project Preferences

Type of Financing Preferred:
Seed
Startup

Geographical Preferences

International
Europe

Industry Preferences

Biotechnology
Biotechnology

Industrial/Energy
Materials

Business Serv.
Media

Additional Information

Capital Under Management: $8,900,000
Current Activity Level : Actively seeking new investments

LF INTERNATIONAL, INC.

De Bavaylei 66
1800 Vilvoorde, Belgium
Phone: 32-2-251-2604
Fax: 32-2-252-4567

See California for full listing.

LG VENTURE INVESTMENT INC.

891 Daechi-dong
Kangnam-gu
Seoul, South Korea
Phone: 822-3467-0500
Fax: 822-3467-0530
Website: www.lginvest.co.kr

Management and Staff

Hee-gyoo Lee, Partner
Hong-Chae Kim, Partner
Mahn-Joon Jang, Partner
Young Kim, President

Type of Firm

Non-Financial Corp. Affiliate or Subsidiary

Project Preferences

Type of Financing Preferred:
Early Stage

Geographical Preferences

International
Korea, South

Industry Preferences

Communications and Media
Communications and Media
Telecommunications

Internet Specific
Internet

Semiconductors/Other Elect.
Semiconductor

Biotechnology
Biotechnology

Additional Information

Year Founded: 1996
Capital Under Management: $35,000,000
Current Activity Level : Actively seeking new investments

LIBON CAPITAL MANAGEMENT LIMITED

4F, No. 508, Section 5
Chun Hsiao East Road
Taipei, Taiwan
Phone: 8862-2759-7279
Fax: 8862-2759-6859

Type of Firm

Private Firm Investing Own Capital

Industry Association Membership

Taiwan Venture Capital Association(TVCA)

Project Preferences

Type of Financing Preferred:
Balanced
Expansion
Mezzanine
Seed
Startup

Geographical Preferences

International
Taiwan

Industry Preferences

Communications and Media
Telecommunications

Computer Software
Software

Semiconductors/Other Elect.
Electronic Components
Semiconductor

Additional Information

Year Founded: 1997
Capital Under Management: $12,400,000
Current Activity Level : Actively seeking new investments

LIFE SCIENCE VENTURES

Von-der-Tann-Strasse 3
Munchen , Germany D-80539
Phone: 49-89-288-1510
Fax: 49-89-288-15130
Website: www.life-science-ventures.de

Management and Staff

Hanns-Peter Wiese, Managing Director
Hans Kupper, Managing Director
Peter Reinisch, Partner
Philip Morgan, Partner

Type of Firm

Private Firm Investing Own Capital

Industry Association Membership

European Venture Capital Association (EVCA)
German Venture Capital Association

Project Preferences

Type of Financing Preferred:
Early Stage
Expansion
Management Buyouts
Recapitalizations
Seed
Startup

Geographical Preferences

United States
All U.S.

International
Asia
Europe
Germany

Industry Preferences

(% based on actual investment)

Biotechnology	61.8%
Medical/Health	36.2%
Internet Specific	2.1%

Additional Information
Name of Most Recent Fund: Global Life Science LP
Most Recent Fund Was Raised: 10/01/1996
Year Founded: 1996
Capital Under Management: $58,400,000
Current Activity Level : Actively seeking new investments

LIFE SCIENCES PARTNERS BV

Johannes Vermeerplein 9
Amsterdam, Netherlands 1071 DV
Phone: 31-20-664-55-00
Fax: 31-20-676-88-10
Website: www.lsp.nl

Management and Staff
Frits Van Der Have, Partner
Martijn Kleijwegt, Partner
Tom Schwarz, Partner

Type of Firm
Private Firm Investing Own Capital

Industry Association Membership
Dutch Venture Capital Associaton
European Venture Capital Association (EVCA)

Project Preferences

Type of Financing Preferred:
Early Stage
Expansion
Later Stage
Management Buyouts
Seed
Startup

Size of Investments Considered
Min Size of Investment Considered (000s): $600
Max Size of Investment Considered: No Limit

Geographical Preferences

United States
All U.S.

International
Europe
Israel

Industry Preferences

Biotechnology
Biotechnology
Human Biotechnology

Medical/Health
Medical/Health
Medical Products

Additional Information
Capital Under Management: $155,000,000
Current Activity Level : Actively seeking new investments

LIPPO GROUP

9th floor Lippo Centre Jl.
Gatot Subroto Kav. 35-36
Jakarta, Indonesia 12920
Phone: 6221-520-0541
Fax: 6221-520-5619

Management and Staff
James Riady, Chairman & CEO
Tjokro Libianto, Vice President

Type of Firm
Private Firm Investing Own Capital

Project Preferences

Type of Financing Preferred:
Balanced

Geographical Preferences

International
Asia

Additional Information
Current Activity Level : Actively seeking new investments
Method of Compensation: Return on investment is of primary concern, do not charge fees

LN MITTAL

London, United Kingdom 400051

Type of Firm
Private Firm Investing Own Capital

Project Preferences

Type of Financing Preferred:
Balanced

Geographical Preferences

United States
All U.S.

International
Asia
Europe
India

Industry Preferences

Communications and Media
Communications and Media

Internet Specific
Internet

Financial Services
Financial Services

Additional Information
Capital Under Management: $50,000,000
Current Activity Level : Actively seeking new investments

LOMBARD INVESTMENTS, INC.

901-2 Citibank Tower
3 Garden Road
Central, Hong Kong
Phone: 852-2878-7388
Fax: 852-2878-7288

See California for full listing.

LONDON MERCHANT SECURITY (AKA LMS)

Carlton House
33 Robert Adam Street
London, United Kingdom W1U 3HR
Phone: 44 20 7935 3555
Fax: 44 20 7935 3737
Website: www.lms-plc.com

Management and Staff
Robert Rayne, Managing Director

Whom to Contact
Adam L. Rothstein

Type of Firm
Affiliate/Subsidary of Oth. Financial. Instit.

Project Preferences

Role in Financing:
Prefer role in deals created by others

Type of Financing Preferred:
Early Stage

Geographical Preferences

United States
All U.S.

International
United Kingdom

Industry Preferences

Communications and Media
Communications and Media

Computer Software
Software

Internet Specific
Internet

Additional Information

Capital Under Management: $200,000,000
Current Activity Level : Actively seeking new investments
Method of Compensation: Return on investment is of primary concern, do not charge fees

LONDON VENTURES (FUND MANAGERS) LTD.

17 Golden Square
3rd Floor
London, United Kingdom W1R 3AG
Phone: 44-20-7434-2425
Fax: 44-20-7434-2426
Website: www.londonventures.co.uk

Management and Staff

James Orman, Partner

Type of Firm

Private Firm Investing Own Capital

Industry Association Membership

British Venture Capital Association

Project Preferences

Type of Financing Preferred:
Early Stage
Expansion
Management Buyouts
Seed
Startup

Geographical Preferences

International
United Kingdom

Industry Preferences

(% based on actual investment)

Consumer Related	66.1%
Other Products	22.7%
Computer Software and Services	7.6%
Internet Specific	2.8%
Semiconductors/Other Elect.	0.9%

Additional Information

Name of Most Recent Fund: HSBC UK Enterprise Fund for Greater London
Most Recent Fund Was Raised: 01/01/1993
Year Founded: 1993
Capital Under Management: $10,200,000
Current Activity Level : Actively seeking new investments

LONG-TERM PARTNERS LIMITED

Suite 908 B, Tower II
Lippo Centre, 88 Queensway
Central, Hong Kong
Phone: 852-2521-7218
Fax: 852-2521-2626

Type of Firm

Private Firm Investing Own Capital

Industry Association Membership

Hungarian Venture Capital Association

Additional Information

Year Founded: 1995
Current Activity Level : Actively seeking new investments

LOST BOYS INCUBATOR

Olympisch Stadion 11
Amsterdam, Netherlands 1076 DE
Phone: 31 20 422 7422
Fax: 31 20 626 6665
Website: www.incubator.nl

Type of Firm

Incubators

Project Preferences

Type of Financing Preferred:
Seed
Startup

Geographical Preferences

International
Europe

Industry Preferences

Communications and Media
Communications and Media

Internet Specific
Internet

Additional Information

Year Founded: 2000
Capital Under Management: $5,600,000
Current Activity Level : Actively seeking new investments

LRM INVESTERINGSMAATSCHAPPIJ VOOR LIMBURG

Havermarket 22
Hasselt, Belgium B - 3500
Phone: 32 11/24.68.49
Fax: 32 11/24.68.59
Website: www.lrm.be

Type of Firm

Govt Program NEC

Industry Association Membership

Belgium Venture Capital Association
European Venture Capital Association (EVCA)

Project Preferences

Type of Financing Preferred:
Balanced
Expansion
Leveraged Buyout
Mezzanine
Recapitalizations
Start-up Financing

Size of Investments Considered

Min Size of Investment Considered (000s): $500
Max Size of Investment Considered (000s): $500,000

Geographical Preferences

International
Belgium

Additional Information

Capital Under Management: $2,842,200,000
Current Activity Level : Actively seeking new investments

LV CAPITAL (AKA LVMH/GROUP ARNAULT)

30 avenue Hoche
Paris, France 75008
Phone: 331-4413-2222
Fax: 331-4413-2119

Management and Staff
Daniel Piette, President

Type of Firm
Non-Financial Corp. Affiliate or Subsidiary

Project Preferences

Type of Financing Preferred:
Unknown

Geographical Preferences

International
No Preference

Industry Preferences

(% based on actual investment)

Internet Specific	36.8%
Other Products	35.9%
Communications and Media	17.5%
Consumer Related	9.9%

Additional Information
Year Founded: 1998
Current Activity Level : Actively seeking new investments

MACQUARIE DIRECT INVESTMENT LIMITED

Level 13
No. 1 Martin Place
Sydney, Australia 02000
Phone: 02-8232-3333
Fax: 02-8232-4111
Website:
www.macquarie.com.au/directinvestment

Management and Staff
Sandy Lockhart, Managing Director

Whom to Contact
Sandy Lockhart

Type of Firm
Investment/Merchant Bank Investing Own or Client Funds

Industry Association Membership
Australian Venture Capital Association (AVCAL)
National Venture Capital Association (NVCA)

Project Preferences

Role in Financing:
Prefer role as deal originator but will also invest in deals created by others

Type of Financing Preferred:
Expansion
Later Stage
Management Buyouts
Mezzanine
Recapitalizations

Size of Investments Considered
Min Size of Investment Considered (000s): $4,000
Max Size of Investment Considered (000s): $15,000

Geographical Preferences

International
Oceania/Australasia

Industry Preferences

(% based on actual investment)

Other Products	30.7%
Communications and Media	17.6%
Computer Software and Services	16.3%
Internet Specific	14.3%
Industrial/Energy	12.0%
Consumer Related	9.1%

Additional Information
Year Founded: 1982
Capital Under Management: $225,100,000
Current Activity Level : Actively seeking new investments
Method of Compensation: Return on invest. most important, but chg. closing fees, service fees, etc.

MACQUARIE INVESTMENT MANAGEMENT LTD (MIML)

Level 27, 20 Bond Street
Sydney, Australia 02000
Phone: 612-8232-3929
Fax: 612-8232-4730
Website:
www.macquarie.com.au/whole_funds

Management and Staff
A. McGill
David Jones
Michael Taranto
Patrick Elliot

Whom to Contact
A. McGill
David Jones
Michael Taranto
Patrick Elliot

Type of Firm
Investment/Merchant Bank Investing Own or Client Funds

Project Preferences

Role in Financing:
Prefer role as deal originator but will also invest in deals created by others

Type of Financing Preferred:
Fund of Funds

Geographical Preferences

International
Australia
New Zealand

Industry Preferences

(% based on actual investment)

Other Products	100.0%

Additional Information
Year Founded: 1980
Capital Under Management: $11,437,800,000
Current Activity Level : Actively seeking new investments
Method of Compensation: Return on investment is of primary concern, do not charge fees

MACQUARIE TECHNOLOGY FUNDS MANAGEMENT

No. 1 Martin Place
Sydney, Australia 2000
Phone: 612-8232-4988
Fax: 612-8232-4713

Type of Firm
Investment/Merchant Bank Subsid/Affil

Project Preferences

Type of Financing Preferred:
Expansion
Startup

Geographical Preferences

International
Oceania/Australasia

Additional Information

Name of Most Recent Fund: Acer Technology Partners Fund
Most Recent Fund Was Raised: 06/30/1999
Year Founded: 1999
Capital Under Management: $30,000,000
Current Activity Level : Actively seeking new investments

MADISON DEARBORN PARTNERS, LLC

One Curzon Street
5th Floor
London, United Kingdom W1J 5RT
Phone: 020-7647-6310
Fax: 020-7647-6311

See Illinois for full listing.

MAGNUM COMMUNICATIONS (AKA: MCF ADVISORY SERVICES LTD)

Azrieli Center 1
35th Floor
Tel Aviv, Israel 67021
Phone: 972 3 696 7285
Fax: 972 3 695 5960
Website: www.magnum-comm.com

Management and Staff

Modi Rosen, Managing Partner
Yahal Zilka, Managing Partner

Type of Firm

Private Firm Investing Own Capital

Project Preferences

Type of Financing Preferred:
Early Stage
Later Stage

Geographical Preferences

International
Israel

Industry Preferences

Communications and Media
Communications and Media

Internet Specific
Internet

Additional Information

Year Founded: 1999
Capital Under Management: $70,000,000
Current Activity Level : Actively seeking new investments

MALMOHUS INVEST AB

Storgatan 22 A
Malmo, Sweden 211 42
Phone: 46 040 330 280
Fax: 46 040 6111 843
Website: www.mhusinvest.se

Management and Staff

Hakan Nelson

Whom to Contact

Hakan Nelson

Type of Firm

Private Firm Investing Own Capital

Industry Association Membership

Swedish Venture Capital Association

Project Preferences

Role in Financing:
Prefer role as deal originator but will also invest in deals created by others

Type of Financing Preferred:
Expansion
First Stage Financing
Mezzanine
Second Stage Financing
Seed
Special Situation
Startup

Size of Investments Considered

Min Size of Investment Considered (000s): $300
Max Size of Investment Considered (000s): $300,000

Geographical Preferences

International
Scandanavia/Nordic Region
Sweden

Industry Preferences

Communications and Media
Telecommunications
Data Communications
Satellite Microwave Comm.

Computer Hardware
Mini and Personal/Desktop
Computer Graphics and Dig
Disk Relat. Memory Device

Computer Software
Systems Software
Applications Software
Artificial Intelligence

Internet Specific
Internet

Semiconductors/Other Elect.
Electronic Components
Controllers and Sensors
Component Testing Equipmt
Laser Related
Fiber Optics
Analytic/Scientific

Biotechnology
Biotechnology

Medical/Health
Disposable Med. Products
Hospitals/Clinics/Primary
Hospital/Other Instit.

Industrial/Energy
Energy
Industrial Products

Additional Information

Year Founded: 1979
Capital Under Management: $19,100,000
Current Activity Level : Actively seeking new investments
Method of Compensation: Return on invest. most important, but chg. closing fees, service fees, etc.

MANGROVE CAPITAL PARTNERS SA

4 rue Jos Felten
Howald, Luxembourg 1508
Phone: 352 91 185 884
Fax: 352 33 4283
Website: www.mangrove-vc.com

Other Offices

39 allee Scheffer
Luxembourg, Luxembourg 2520
Phone: 352 40 116 2331
Fax: 352 40 116 2331

Type of Firm
Private Firm Investing Own Capital

Project Preferences

Type of Financing Preferred:
Early Stage
Seed
Startup

Geographical Preferences

United States
All U.S.

International
Belgium
Europe
France
Germany
Italy
Luxembourg
Netherlands
Spain

Industry Preferences

Internet Specific
Internet

Additional Information
Capital Under Management: $4,000,000
Current Activity Level : Actively seeking new investments

MARCH.FIFTEEN AG (FKA PETERP@N)

Tuchlauben 12
Vienna, Austria 1010
Phone: 431 512 3917
Fax: 431 512 39 1720
E-mail: office@marchfifteen.at
Website: www.marchfifteen.at

Other Offices

Corex House 10
Zarchin Street
Ra'anana, Israel
Phone: 972 9 741 8560
Fax: 972 9 741 8565

ilmet building
ul pawla II
Warsaw, Poland 00-828
Phone: 48 602 255 515
Fax: 48 602 245 510

Management and Staff
Alexander Grunwald, Chief Operating Officer
Christian Wolf, Chief Executive Officer
Rainer Leu, Chief Financial Officer

Type of Firm
Incubators

Project Preferences

Type of Financing Preferred:
Early Stage
Seed
Startup

Geographical Preferences

International
Central Europe
Eastern Europe

Industry Preferences

Internet Specific
Internet

Additional Information
Year Founded: 1999
Current Activity Level : Actively seeking new investments

MARCONI VENTURES

One Bruton Street
London , United Kingdom W1X 8AQ
Phone: 44-20-7493-8484
Fax: 44-20-7493-1974

See Massachusetts for full listing.

MARKS AND SPENCER VENTURES LTD

Michael House
Baker Street
London, United Kingdom W1A 1DN
Phone: 44 20 7268 4362
Fax: 44 20 7268 2690

Type of Firm
Non-Financial Corp. Affiliate or Subsidiary

Industry Association Membership
British Venture Capital Association

Project Preferences

Type of Financing Preferred:
Expansion

Geographical Preferences

International
United Kingdom

Industry Preferences

Internet Specific
Internet

Additional Information
Year Founded: 1999
Capital Under Management: $83,300,000
Current Activity Level : Actively seeking new investments

MARLEAU, LEMIRE, INC.

One Place Ville-Marie
Suite 3601
Montreal, Canada H3B 3P2
Phone: 514-877-3800
Fax: 514-875-6415

Other Offices

150 King Street West
Suite 2400, Box 62
Toronto, Canada M5H 1J9
Phone: 416-595-5500
Fax: 416-595-1487

793 Washington Street
Suite One
Brookline, United States of America 02146-2121

999 West Hastings Street
Suite 500
Vancouver, Canada V6C 2W2
Phone: 604-668-7900
Fax: 604-668-7965

Management and Staff
Jean-François Perrault

Whom to Contact
Jean-François Perrault

Type of Firm
Investment/Merchant Bank Investing Own or Client Funds

Project Preferences

Role in Financing:
Prefer role as deal originator but will also invest in deals created by others

Type of Financing Preferred:
Leveraged Buyout
Mezzanine
Second Stage Financing
Special Situation

Size of Investments Considered
Min Size of Investment Considered (000s): $3,000
Max Size of Investment Considered: No Limit

Geographical Preferences

Canada
All Canada

International
France
United Kingdom

Industry Preferences

Communications and Media
Commercial Communications
Telecommunications
Data Communications
Satellite Microwave Comm.

Computer Hardware
Mainframes / Scientific
Mini and Personal/Desktop
Computer Graphics and Dig
Integrated Turnkey System
Disk Relat. Memory Device

Computer Software
Computer Services
Systems Software
Applications Software
Artificial Intelligence

Internet Specific
Internet

Semiconductors/Other Elect.
Electronic Components
Sensors

Medical/Health
Diagnostic Test Products
Drug/Equipmt Delivery
Other Therapeutic
Disposable Med. Products
Pharmaceuticals

Consumer Related
Entertainment and Leisure
Retail
Franchises(NEC)
Food/Beverage
Consumer Products

Industrial/Energy
Factory Automation
Robotics
Machinery
Environmental Related

Business Serv.
Distribution

Manufact.
Office Automation Equipmt

Agr/Forestr/Fish
Agriculture related
Mining and Minerals

Additional Information
Year Founded: 1989
Capital Under Management: $51,000,000
Current Activity Level : Actively seeking new investments
Method of Compensation: Return on invest. most important, but chg. closing fees, service fees, etc.

MATRIX PRIVATE EQUITY

9-10 Saville Row
London, United Kingdom W1S 3PF
Phone: 44-20-7439-6050
Fax: 44-20-7287-2312
Website: www.matrixgroup.co.uk

Type of Firm
Affiliate/Subsidary of Oth. Financial. Instit.

Industry Association Membership
British Venture Capital Association

Project Preferences

Type of Financing Preferred:
Early Stage
Expansion
Special Situation
Startup

Geographical Preferences

International
United Kingdom

Industry Preferences

Communications and Media
Commercial Communications

Internet Specific
Internet

Computer Other
Computer Related

Semiconductors/Other Elect.
Electronics

Industrial/Energy
Industrial Products

Financial Services
Financial Services

Business Serv.
Services
Media

Additional Information
Year Founded: 2000
Capital Under Management: $20,000,000
Current Activity Level : Actively seeking new investments

MAVA INVESTMENT MANAGEMENT KFT (AKA: HUNGARIAN-AMERICAN ENT)

Romer Floris u.57
Budapest, Hungary 1025
Phone: 36-1-315-0644
Fax: 36-1-315-0444
Website: www.mava.hu

Management and Staff
Geza Tatrallyay, General Partner
Zoltan Szemerey, Managing Partner
Zsuzsa Fekete, General Partner

Type of Firm
Investment Management/Finance Consulting

Industry Association Membership
European Venture Capital Association (EVCA)

Project Preferences

Type of Financing Preferred:
Expansion
Recapitalizations

Geographical Preferences

International
Central Europe
Hungary

Industry Preferences

Communications and Media
Communications and Media

Computer Other
Computer Related

Consumer Related
Consumer

Industrial/Energy
Industrial Products

Manufact.
Manufacturing

Additional Information
Name of Most Recent Fund: Hungarian Equity Partners, L.P.
Most Recent Fund Was Raised: 01/01/1997
Year Founded: 1997
Capital Under Management: $110,000,000
Current Activity Level : Actively seeking new investments

MAYFAIR CAPITAL PARTNERS, INC.

45, quai Wilson
CH-1201 Geneva, Switzerland
Phone: 41-22-732-2527
Fax: 41-22-732-2673

See New York for full listing.

MC CAPITAL ASIA PRIVATE LIMITED

1 Temasek Avenue
#20-02A Millenia Tower
Singapore, Singapore 039192
Phone: 65-434-4247
Fax: 65-434-4246
Website: www.mitsubishi.com.sg/csfi.html

Other Offices

1002 C/D, 10/F, Tower 1 Admiralty Centre
No. 18 Harcourt Road
, Hong Kong
Phone: 852-2866-3393
Fax: 852-2866-2693

Management and Staff
Taro Ikeba, Vice President
Yuji Komiya, Managing Director

Type of Firm
Non-Financial Corp. Affiliate or Subsidiary

Industry Association Membership
Hong Kong Venture Capital Association (HKVCA)

Project Preferences

Type of Financing Preferred:
Early Stage
Expansion

Geographical Preferences

International
Australia
Indonesia
Malaysia
Philippines
Singapore
Thailand

Industry Preferences

Communications and Media
Telecommunications

Consumer Related
Retail
Food/Beverage

Business Serv.
Media

Additional Information
Year Founded: 1995
Capital Under Management: $80,000,000
Current Activity Level : Actively seeking new investments

MCH PRIVATE EQUITY SA

Serrano 59-5 izda
Madrid, Spain 28006
Phone: 34 91 426 4444
Fax: 34 91 426 4440
Website: www.mch.es

Management and Staff
Andres Pelaez, Partner
Jaime Hernandez Soto, Partner
Jose Munoz, Partner

Type of Firm
Private Equity Advisor or Fund of Fund Mgr

Industry Association Membership
Spanish Venture Capital Association

Project Preferences

Type of Financing Preferred:
Generalist PE
Leveraged Buyout
Seed

Geographical Preferences

International
Spain

Additional Information
Year Founded: 1998
Current Activity Level : Actively seeking new investments

MCLEAN WATSON CAPITAL INC.

One First Canadian Place
Suite 1410 P.O. Box 129
Toronto, Canada M5X 1A4
Phone: 416-363-2000
Fax: 416-363-2010
Website: www.mcleanwatson.com

Management and Staff
Matt H. Lawton

Whom to Contact
Matt H. Lawton

Type of Firm
Private Firm Investing Own Capital

Project Preferences

Role in Financing:
Prefer role as deal originator but will also invest in deals created by others

Type of Financing Preferred:
First Stage Financing
Second Stage Financing

Geographical Preferences

United States
All U.S.

Canada
All Canada

Industry Preferences

Communications and Media
Commercial Communications
Telecommunications
Data Communications
Satellite Microwave Comm.

Computer Other
Computer Related

Semiconductors/Other Elect.
Semiconductor
Laser Related
Fiber Optics

Additional Information
Name of Most Recent Fund: McLean Watson Ventures II Limited Partnership
Most Recent Fund Was Raised: 01/01/1999
Year Founded: 1993
Capital Under Management: $150,000,000
Current Activity Level : Actively seeking new investments
Method of Compensation: Return on investment is of primary concern, do not charge fees

MDS DISCOVERY VENTURE MANAGEMENT, INC.

555 West Eighth Avenue
Suite 305
Vancouver, Canada V5Z 1C6
Phone: 604-872-8464
Fax: 604-872-2977

Management and Staff
Bob Rieder, Vice President
David Scott, President

Type of Firm
Non-Financial Corp. Affiliate or Subsidiary

Industry Association Membership
Canadian Venture Capital Association

Project Preferences

Role in Financing:
Prefer role as deal originator but will also invest in deals created by others

Type of Financing Preferred:
First Stage Financing
Research and Development
Second Stage Financing
Seed
Start-up Financing

Size of Investments Considered
Min Size of Investment Considered (000s): $500
Max Size of Investment Considered (000s): $1,000

Geographical Preferences

United States
Northwest

Canada
Western Canada

Industry Preferences

(% based on actual investment)

Biotechnology	78.7%
Communications and Media	15.3%
Computer Software and Services	6.0%

Additional Information
Year Founded: 1994
Capital Under Management: $27,000,000
Current Activity Level : Actively seeking new investments
Method of Compensation: Return on investment is of primary concern, do not charge fees

MDS HEALTH VENTURES, INC. (AKA: MDS CAPITAL CORP.)

100 International Boulevard
Toronto, Canada M9W 6J6
Phone: 416-675-7661
Fax: 416-213-4232
Website: www.mdscapital.com

Other Offices

1095 West Pender Street
Suite 1120
Vancouver, Canada
Phone: 604-872-8464

11804 North Creek Parkway South
Bothell, United States of America
Phone: 425-487-8229

1550 Metcalfe Street
Suite 602
Montreal, Canada
Phone: 514-844-3637

Management and Staff
all of the above

Whom to Contact
all of the above

Type of Firm
Venture Consulting Firm

Industry Association Membership
Canadian Venture Capital Association
National Venture Capital Association (NVCA)

Project Preferences

Role in Financing:
Will function either as deal originator or investor in deals created by others

Type of Financing Preferred:
Balanced
Early Stage
Expansion
Later Stage
Mezzanine
Seed
Startup

Size of Investments Considered
Min Size of Investment Considered (000s): $1,000
Max Size of Investment Considered: No Limit

Geographical Preferences

United States
All U.S.

Canada
All Canada

Industry Preferences

(% based on actual investment)

Biotechnology	54.6%
Internet Specific	33.0%
Medical/Health	5.0%
Communications and Media	3.7%
Computer Software and Services	3.7%

Additional Information
Name of Most Recent Fund: MDS Life Science Technology Fund
Most Recent Fund Was Raised: 12/16/1997
Year Founded: 1988
Capital Under Management: $600,000,000
Current Activity Level : Actively seeking new investments
Method of Compensation: Return on investment is of primary concern, do not charge fees

MEDIAVENTURE CAPITAL AG & CO. KGAA

Hansaring 61
Koln, Germany D-50670
Phone: 49 70007000404
Fax: 49 70007000505
Website: www.mediaventure.net

Type of Firm
Private Firm Investing Own Capital

Industry Association Membership
German Venture Capital Association

Project Preferences

Type of Financing Preferred:
Expansion
Seed
Startup

Geographical Preferences

International
Germany

Industry Preferences

Communications and Media
Telecommunications

Consumer Related
Entertainment and Leisure

Business Serv.
Media

Additional Information
Capital Under Management: $16,500,000
Current Activity Level : Actively seeking new investments

MEDICIS AG

Rueckerstrasse 1
Munich, Germany Lombard Od
Phone: 49-89-544-79-20
Fax: 4989-5447-92240
Website: www.medicis.de

Management and Staff
Kai Deusch, Partner
Matthias Ackermann, Partner
Michael Muth, Partner
Michael Steiner, Partner

Type of Firm
Private Firm Investing Own Capital

Industry Association Membership
European Venture Capital Association (EVCA)

Project Preferences

Type of Financing Preferred:
Early Stage
Expansion
Seed
Startup

Geographical Preferences

International
Europe
Israel

Industry Preferences

Internet Specific
Internet

Biotechnology
Biotechnology

Medical/Health
Medical/Health

Other
Environment Responsible

Additional Information
Year Founded: 1999
Capital Under Management: $15,200,000
Current Activity Level : Actively seeking new investments

MEDICON VALLEY CAPITAL

Strandvejen 82
Hellerup, Denmark 2900
Phone: 45 3961 8101
Fax: 45 3961 8102
Website: www.mvc.dk

Other Offices

Stortorget 29
Malmo, Sweden 211 34
Phone: 46 40 978 880
Fax: 46 40 978 865

Type of Firm
Private Equity Advisor or Fund of Fund Mgr

Project Preferences

Type of Financing Preferred:
Expansion
Later Stage

Geographical Preferences

International
Denmark
Sweden

Industry Preferences

Biotechnology
Biotechnology

Medical/Health
Medical/Health
Pharmaceuticals

Additional Information
Year Founded: 2000
Capital Under Management: $51,000,000
Current Activity Level : Actively seeking new investments

MEDMAX VENTURES, L.P.

P.O. Box 354
Zichron Yaakov, Israel 30900
Phone: 972-6-396-397
Fax: 972-6-396-133

See Connecticut for full listing.

MERCANTILE MUTUAL INVESTMENT MANAGEMENT LIMITED

Level 11, 347 Kent Street
Sydney, Australia 2000
Phone: 612-9234-8111
Fax: 612-9234-8018
Website: www.mercantilemutual.com.au

Other Offices

Level 19, Central Park
152-155 St. Georges Terrace
Perth, Australia 6000
Phone: 618-9278-5888
Fax: 618-9322-3058

Level 9, 486 Albert Street
East Melbourne, Australia 3002
Phone: 613-9230-3444
Fax: 613-9663-2202

Type of Firm
Insurance Firm Affiliate or Subsidiary

Project Preferences

Type of Financing Preferred:
Fund of Funds

Geographical Preferences

International
Australia

Industry Preferences

(% based on actual investment)

Other Products	100.0%

Additional Information
Year Founded: 1998
Capital Under Management: $43,400,000
Current Activity Level : Actively seeking new investments

MERCURY PRIVATE EQUITY

33 King William Street
London, United Kingdom EC4R 9AS
Phone: 44 20 7280 2800
Fax: 44 20 7743 1121
Website: www.mam.com/pe

Other Offices

Neue Mainzer Strasse 52
Frankfurt, Germany 60311
Phone: 49 69 5899 2202
Fax: 49 69 5899 4024

Management and Staff
Ian Armitage, Chief Executive Officer
Jeremy Sharman, Managing Director
Trevor Bayley, Managing Director

Type of Firm
Private Firm Investing Own Capital

Industry Association Membership
British Venture Capital Association
European Venture Capital Association (EVCA)

Project Preferences

Type of Financing Preferred:
Leveraged Buyout
Second Stage Financing
Special Situation

Geographical Preferences

International
Germany
Ireland
United Kingdom
Western Europe

Industry Preferences

Communications and Media
Telecommunications

Semiconductors/Other Elect.
Electronics

Medical/Health
Medical/Health

Business Serv.
Services

Additional Information
Name of Most Recent Fund: MUST 3 (FKA: Third Mercury Unquoted Securities Trust)
Most Recent Fund Was Raised: 01/07/1997
Year Founded: 1996
Capital Under Management: $970,300,000
Current Activity Level : Actively seeking new investments

MERIFIN CAPITAL GROUP

Avenue Lloyd George 6
8th Floor
Brussels, Belgium B-1000
Phone: 32-2-646-2580
Fax: 32-2-646-3036

Other Offices

75 Wall Street
35th Floor
New York, United States of America 10005
Phone: 212-429-3123
Fax: 212-429-3139

Type of Firm
Private Firm Investing Own Capital

Industry Association Membership
European Venture Capital Association (EVCA)

Project Preferences

Role in Financing:
Will function either as deal originator or investor in deals created by others

Type of Financing Preferred:
Control-block Purchases
Early Stage
Expansion
Generalist PE
Leveraged Buyout
Management Buyouts
Mezzanine
Private Placement
Second Stage Financing
Special Situation
Turnaround

Size of Investments Considered
Min Size of Investment Considered (000s): $250
Max Size of Investment Considered (000s): $3,000

Geographical Preferences

United States
All U.S.

Canada
All Canada

International
Asia
Australia
Bermuda
China
Eastern Europe
Europe
France
Germany
Italy
Latin America
South Africa
Spain
United Kingdom

Additional Information
Year Founded: 1980
Current Activity Level : Actively seeking new investments
Method of Compensation: Return on invest. most important, but chg. closing fees, service fees, etc.

MERITA CAPITAL LTD

Mikonkatu 13a
Helsinki, Finland 00020
Phone: 358 9 165 42784
Fax: 358 9 625 878
Website: www.merita.fi

Management and Staff
Jouko Helomaa, Managing Director

Type of Firm
Investment/Merchant Bank Investing Own or Client Funds

Industry Association Membership
European Venture Capital Association (EVCA)
Finnish Venture Capital Association

Project Preferences

Type of Financing Preferred:
Expansion
Generalist PE
Management Buyouts

Geographical Preferences

International
Finland
Scandanavia/Nordic Region

Additional Information
Name of Most Recent Fund: Merita Capital
Most Recent Fund Was Raised: 10/01/1994
Capital Under Management: $55,000,000
Current Activity Level : Actively seeking new investments

MERLIN BIOSCIENCES (AKA MERLIN VENTURES)

12 St. James's Square
London, United Kingdom SW1Y 4RB
Phone: 44 20 7849 6003
Fax: 44 20 7976 1444
Website: www.merlin-biosciences.com

Other Offices
Unit 329 Cambridge Science Park
Milton Road
Cambridge, United Kingdom CB4 4WG
Phone: 44 1223 437800
Fax: 44 1223 226166

Management and Staff
Peter Keen, Co-Founder

Type of Firm
Private Firm Investing Own Capital

Industry Association Membership
British Venture Capital Association

Project Preferences

Role in Financing:
Prefer role as deal originator

Type of Financing Preferred:
Early Stage
Expansion
Seed
Startup

Geographical Preferences

International
Europe
United Kingdom

Industry Preferences

(% based on actual investment)

Biotechnology	50.3%
Medical/Health	49.7%

Additional Information
Name of Most Recent Fund: Merlin Fund, The
Most Recent Fund Was Raised: 02/14/1997
Year Founded: 1996
Capital Under Management: $216,700,000
Current Activity Level : Actively seeking new investments

MERRILL LYNCH INVESTMENT MANAGERS FKA MERCURY ASSET MGMT

33 King William Street
London, United Kingdom EC4R 9AS
Phone: 44 20 7280 2800
Fax: 44 20 7203 5833
Website: www.mlim.co.uk

Other Offices
Platz der Einhert 1
Frankfurt am Main, Germany 60327
Phone: 49 69 975 03234
Fax: 49 69 975 03305

Ropemaker Place
25 Ropemaker Street
London, United Kingdom EC2Y 9LY
Phone: 44 20 7628 1000
Fax: 44 20 7867 2867

Management and Staff
Ian Armitage, Chief Executive Officer
Jeremy Sharman, Managing Director
Linda Wilding, Managing Director
Trevor Bayley, Managing Director

Whom to Contact
Helen Lewis

Type of Firm
Private Firm Investing Own Capital

Project Preferences

Role in Financing:
Prefer role as deal originator but will also invest in deals created by others

Type of Financing Preferred:
Leveraged Buyout
Second Stage Financing
Special Situation

Geographical Preferences

International
Germany
United Kingdom

Industry Preferences

(% based on actual investment)

Semiconductors/Other Elect.	75.7%
Computer Software and Services	13.8%
Communications and Media	6.9%
Biotechnology	3.0%
Other Products	0.5%

Additional Information
Name of Most Recent Fund: MUST 3 (FKA: Third Mercury Unquoted Securities Trust)
Most Recent Fund Was Raised: 01/07/1997
Year Founded: 1985
Capital Under Management: $1,000,000,000
Current Activity Level : Actively seeking new investments
Method of Compensation: Return on invest. most important, but chg. closing fees, service fees, etc.

METROPOLITAN VENTURE PARTNERS (METVP)

Sugar Quay
Lower Thames Street
London, United Kingdom EC3R 6DU
Phone: 44 (0) 207-285-590
Fax: 44 (0) 207-285-371

See New York for full listing.

MEZZANINE MANAGEMENT UK LIMITED

Manfield House
1 Southampton Street
London, United Kingdom WC2R 0LR
Phone: 44 20-7665 5000
Fax: 44 20-7665 5001
Website: www.mezzanine-management.com

Management and Staff
Rory Brooks, Managing Director

Whom to Contact
Angus Penman
Martin P. Dineen
Steffen Lehmann
Valerie Lebreton

Type of Firm
Investment/Merchant Bank Investing Own or Client Funds

Industry Association Membership
British Venture Capital Association
European Venture Capital Association (EVCA)

Project Preferences

Role in Financing:
Prefer role as deal originator but will also invest in deals created by others

Type of Financing Preferred:
Expansion
Industry Rollups
Leveraged Buyout
Mezzanine
Recapitalizations
Special Situation

Size of Investments Considered
Min Size of Investment Considered (000s): $7,500
Max Size of Investment Considered (000s): $150,400

Geographical Preferences

United States
All U.S.

Canada
All Canada

International
Bermuda
France
Germany
Italy
Spain
United Kingdom

Industry Preferences

Communications and Media
Communications and Media

Computer Other
Computer Related

Semiconductors/Other Elect.
Electronics

Medical/Health
Medical/Health

Consumer Related
Consumer

Industrial/Energy
Energy
Industrial Products
Materials
Factory Automation

Transportation
Transportation

Business Serv.
Services

Manufact.
Manufacturing

Additional Information
Name of Most Recent Fund: Mezzanine Management Fund III
Most Recent Fund Was Raised: 11/12/1999
Capital Under Management: $2,256,600,000
Current Activity Level : Actively seeking new investments
Method of Compensation: Return on invest. most important, but chg. closing fees, service fees, etc.

MIDDLEFIELD CAPITAL FUND

One First Canadian Place
58th Floor P.O. Box 192
Toronto, Canada M5X 1A6
Phone: 416-362-0714
Fax: 416-362-7925
Website: www.middlefield.com

Other Offices

199 Bishopsgate
London, United Kingdom EC2M 3T4
Phone: 44-207-814-6644
Fax: 44-207-600-5127

Management and Staff
Garth Jestley, President & COO
M.J. Brasseur, Chairman & CEO

Whom to Contact
David Roode
Dean Orrico
Garth Jestley
M.J. Brasseur

Type of Firm
Investment/Merchant Bank Subsid/Affil

Industry Association Membership
Canadian Venture Capital Association

Project Preferences

Role in Financing:
Prefer role as deal originator but will also invest in deals created by others

Type of Financing Preferred:
Control-block Purchases
Industry Rollups
Leveraged Buyout
Mezzanine
Second Stage Financing

Size of Investments Considered
Min Size of Investment Considered (000s): $3,000
Max Size of Investment Considered: No Limit

Geographical Preferences

United States
All U.S.

Canada
All Canada

International
France
Germany
Spain
United Kingdom

Industry Preferences

Communications and Media
Commercial Communications
CATV & Pay TV Systems
Telecommunications
Other Communication Prod.

Computer Hardware
Computers

Semiconductors/Other Elect.
Electronics
Electronic Components
Sensors
Laser Related
Fiber Optics

Medical/Health
Other Therapeutic
Medical Products
Pharmaceuticals

Consumer Related
Food/Beverage

Industrial/Energy
Oil and Gas Exploration
Oil & Gas Drilling,Explor
Alternative Energy
Energy Conservation Relat
Industrial Products
Materials
Robotics
Machinery

Transportation
Transportation

Financial Services
Financial Services
Real Estate

Agr/Forestr/Fish
Mining and Minerals

Additional Information
Name of Most Recent Fund: Middlefield Capital
Most Recent Fund Was Raised: 04/01/1984
Year Founded: 1979
Capital Under Management: $110,000,000
Current Activity Level : Actively seeking new investments
Method of Compensation: Return on invest. most important, but chg. closing fees, service fees, etc.

MIDINVEST OY

P.O. Box 27
Survontie 9
Jyvaskyla, Finland 40101
Phone: 358-14-650-100
Fax: 358-14-650-120

Type of Firm
Business Development Fund

Industry Association Membership
Finnish Venture Capital Association

Project Preferences

Type of Financing Preferred:
Expansion
Management Buyouts
Startup

Geographical Preferences

International
Finland

Industry Preferences

(% based on actual investment)

Internet Specific	55.0%
Communications and Media	27.8%
Semiconductors/Other Elect.	6.8%
Industrial/Energy	4.5%
Medical/Health	3.0%
Computer Software and Services	2.8%

Additional Information
Name of Most Recent Fund: Midinvest Oy
Most Recent Fund Was Raised: 12/31/1994
Capital Under Management: $3,900,000
Current Activity Level : Actively seeking new investments

MIDLANDS VENTURE FUND MANAGERS LTD. (AKA: MIDVEN LTD)

PO Box 66
33 Bennetts Hill
Birmingham, United Kingdom B2 5RJ
Phone: 44-121-616-1133
Fax: 44-121-616-2223

Other Offices
The Square
Beeston
Nottingham, United Kingdom NG9 2JG
Phone: 44-115-967-8400
Fax: 44-115-967-8687

Management and Staff
John O'Neill, Managing Director
Terry Swainbank, Partner
Tony Scott, Partner

Whom to Contact
T. Stott

Type of Firm
Private Firm Investing Own Capital

Industry Association Membership
British Venture Capital Association

Project Preferences

Role in Financing:
Prefer role as deal originator but will also invest in deals created by others

Type of Financing Preferred:
Early Stage
Expansion
Leveraged Buyout
Recapitalizations
Second Stage Financing
Seed
Startup
Turnaround

Geographical Preferences

International
United Kingdom

Industry Preferences

Communications and Media
Communications and Media

Computer Other
Computer Related

Biotechnology
Biotechnology

Medical/Health
Medical/Health

Consumer Related
Consumer

Industrial/Energy
Energy
Industrial Products
Materials

Transportation
Transportation

Manufact.
Manufacturing

Additional Information
Name of Most Recent Fund: Midlands Enterprise Fund
Most Recent Fund Was Raised: 01/01/1997
Year Founded: 1992
Capital Under Management: $12,900,000
Current Activity Level : Actively seeking new investments
Method of Compensation: Return on invest. most important, but chg. closing fees, service fees, etc.

MIRALTA CAPITAL, INC.

4445 Calgary Trail South
888 Terrace Plaza Alberta
Edmonton, Canada T6H 5R7
Phone: 780-438-3535
Fax: 780-438-3129

Other Offices

250 Bloor Street East
Suite 301
Toronto, Canada M4W 1E6
Phone: 416-925-4274

Management and Staff
Michael Welsh

Whom to Contact
Michael Welsh

Type of Firm
Private Firm Investing Own Capital

Industry Association Membership
Canadian Venture Capital Association

Project Preferences

Role in Financing:
Prefer role as deal originator

Type of Financing Preferred:
First Stage Financing
Leveraged Buyout
Second Stage Financing

Size of Investments Considered
Min Size of Investment Considered (000s): $1,000
Max Size of Investment Considered: No Limit

Geographical Preferences

Canada
All Canada

Industry Preferences

Communications and Media
Data Communications

Computer Hardware
Computer Graphics and Dig
Integrated Turnkey System

Computer Software
Computer Services
Systems Software
Applications Software

Semiconductors/Other Elect.
Electronics
Electronic Components
Sensors
Analytic/Scientific

Consumer Related
Consumer Products

Industrial/Energy
Industrial Products
Materials
Factory Automation
Robotics
Machinery

Manufact.
Office Automation Equipmt

Additional Information
Year Founded: 1997
Capital Under Management: $28,000,000
Current Activity Level : Actively seeking new investments
Method of Compensation: Return on investment is of primary concern, do not charge fees

MITISKA NV

Industrielaan 24
Ternat, Belgium 1740
Phone: 32-2-583-1946
Fax: 32-2-583-1964
Website: www.netfundeurope.com

Management and Staff
Michiel Deturck, Managing Partner

Type of Firm
Private Firm Investing Own Capital

Project Preferences

Type of Financing Preferred:
Early Stage
Expansion
Seed
Startup

Geographical Preferences

International
Europe

Industry Preferences

(% based on actual investment)

Other Products	87.3%
Internet Specific	10.4%
Computer Software and Services	2.3%

Additional Information
Year Founded: 1999
Capital Under Management: $66,800,000
Current Activity Level : Actively seeking new investments

MITSUI MARINE CAPITAL CO., LTD.

3-9 Kanda Surugadai
Chiyoda-ku
Tokyo, Japan
Phone: 03-3259-3066
Fax: 03-3292-9105
Website: www.mitsuimarine.co.jp

Type of Firm
Insurance Firm Affiliate or Subsidiary

Project Preferences

Type of Financing Preferred:
Balanced

Geographical Preferences

International
Japan

Industry Preferences

(% based on actual investment)

Other Products	28.6%
Consumer Related	27.1%
Semiconductors/Other Elect.	26.5%
Computer Software and Services	10.4%
Internet Specific	2.7%
Industrial/Energy	2.4%
Communications and Media	1.2%
Computer Hardware	1.2%

Additional Information
Capital Under Management: $31,000,000
Current Activity Level : Actively seeking new investments

MMC ADVENTURES LTD

Braywick House
Gregory Place
London, United Kingdom W8 4NG
Phone: 44-20-938-2220
Fax: 44-20-7938-2259
Website: www.mmcadventures.com

Type of Firm
Private Firm Investing Own Capital

Industry Association Membership
British Venture Capital Association

Project Preferences

Type of Financing Preferred:
Early Stage
Seed
Startup

Size of Investments Considered
Min Size of Investment Considered (000s): $300
Max Size of Investment Considered (000s): $300,000

Geographical Preferences

International
Central Europe
Eastern Europe
United Kingdom
Western Europe

Industry Preferences

Computer Other
Computer Related

Additional Information
Year Founded: 2000
Capital Under Management: $19,400,000
Current Activity Level : Actively seeking new investments

MOFET VENTURE CAPITAL

11 Galgalei Haplacha Street
PO Box 12896
Herzliya Piuah, Israel 46733
Phone: 972 9 956 1290
Fax: 972 9 956 1293
Website: www.mofet.co.il

Management and Staff
Elie Barr, Managing Partner
Iris Shapira, Chief Financial Officer
Rani Cohen, Managing Partner

Type of Firm
Private Firm Investing Own Capital

Industry Association Membership
European Venture Capital Association (EVCA)

Project Preferences

Role in Financing:
Will function either as deal originator or investor in deals created by others

Type of Financing Preferred:
Early Stage
Expansion

Geographical Preferences

International
Israel

Industry Preferences

Communications and Media
Telecommunications

Internet Specific
Internet

Medical/Health
Medical/Health

Additional Information
Year Founded: 1997
Current Activity Level : Actively seeking new investments

MONTGOMERIE, HUCK & CO.

146 Bluenose Drive
P.O. Box 538
Lunenburg, Canada B0J 2C0
Phone: 902-634-7125
Fax: 902-634-7130

Management and Staff
Christopher Huck

Whom to Contact
Christopher Huck

Type of Firm
Mgt. Consulting Firm

Project Preferences

Role in Financing:
Prefer role in deals created by others

Type of Financing Preferred:
First Stage Financing
Leveraged Buyout
Mezzanine
Second Stage Financing
Special Situation

Size of Investments Considered
Min Size of Investment Considered (000s): $300
Max Size of Investment Considered (000s): $500

Geographical Preferences

United States
Northeast

Canada
All Canada

Industry Preferences

Communications and Media
Communications and Media

Computer Software
Systems Software
Applications Software

Industrial/Energy
Machinery

Additional Information
Year Founded: 1989
Current Activity Level : Actively seeking new investments
Method of Compensation: Professional fee required whether or not deal closes

MOREL VENTURES LIMITED

Level 9, Wool House
10 Brandon Street
Wellington, New Zealand
Phone: 644-499-2029
Fax: 644-471-1612
Website: www.no8ventures.co.nz

Type of Firm
Investment/Merchant Bank Subsid/Affil

Project Preferences

Role in Financing:
Will function either as deal originator or investor in deals created by others

Type of Financing Preferred:
Balanced
Start-up Financing

Geographical Preferences

International
New Zealand

Industry Preferences

Communications and Media
Communications and Media

Semiconductors/Other Elect.
Electronics

Biotechnology
Biotechnology

Additional Information

Year Founded: 1999
Capital Under Management: $12,200,000
Current Activity Level : Actively seeking new investments
Method of Compensation: Return on investment is of primary concern, do not charge fees

---

MORGAN GRENFELL PRIVATE EQUITY LIMITED

23 Great Winchester Street
London, United Kingdom EC2P 2AX
Phone: 44-207-545-8000
Fax: 44-207-545-5282

Other Offices

35 St. Andrew Square
Edinburgh, United Kingdom EH2 2AD
Phone: 44-131-557-8600
Fax: 44-131-557-8306

Management and Staff

Andy Macfie

Whom to Contact

Andy Macfie

Type of Firm

Investment/Merchant Bank Subsid/Affil

Project Preferences

Role in Financing:
Prefer role as deal originator but will also invest in deals created by others

Type of Financing Preferred:
Industry Rollups
Leveraged Buyout
Second Stage Financing

Size of Investments Considered

Min Size of Investment Considered (000s): $30,000
Max Size of Investment Considered: No Limit

Geographical Preferences

International
Bermuda
France
Germany
Italy
Spain
United Kingdom

Industry Preferences

Communications and Media
Communications and Media

Semiconductors/Other Elect.
Electronic Components

Medical/Health
Medical/Health

Consumer Related
Consumer

Industrial/Energy
Energy
Industrial Products

Transportation
Transportation

Financial Services
Financial Services

Business Serv.
Distribution
Consulting Services

Manufact.
Publishing

Agr/Forestr/Fish
Agriculture related

Additional Information

Name of Most Recent Fund: Morgan Grenfell Equity Partners
Most Recent Fund Was Raised: 05/01/1995
Year Founded: 1989
Capital Under Management: $1,000,000,000
Current Activity Level : Actively seeking new investments
Method of Compensation: Return on invest. most important, but chg. closing fees, service fees, etc.

MOSAIC VENTURE PARTNERS

24 Duncan Street
Suite 300
Toronto, Canada M5V 3M6
Phone: 416-597-8889
Fax: 416-597-2345

Management and Staff

David Samuel, Managing Director

Type of Firm

Incubators

Project Preferences

Type of Financing Preferred:
Early Stage

Geographical Preferences

United States
All U.S.

Canada
All Canada

Industry Preferences

Internet Specific
Internet

Additional Information

Current Activity Level : Actively seeking new investments

MPM CAPITAL (FKA - MPM ASSET MANAGEMENT LLC)

Weissfrauenstrasse 10
60311
Frankfurt, Germany 94080
Phone: 49-691-33-8980
Fax: 49-691-33-898-29

See Massachusetts for full listing.

MSC VENTURE CORPORATION SDN. BHD.

1/F Raja Wali Block, Cyberview
Garden Villas, Cyberjaya
Selangor Darul Ehsan, Malaysia 63000
Phone: 603-8312-7260
Fax: 603-8312-7290
Website: www.mdc.com.my/mscvc/index.html

Management and Staff

Sarina Karim, Chief Executive Officer

Type of Firm

Non-Financial Corp. Affiliate or Subsidiary

Project Preferences

Type of Financing Preferred:
Early Stage
Expansion
Mezzanine
Startup

Geographical Preferences

International
Malaysia

Industry Preferences

Communications and Media
Communications and Media
Telecommunications

Computer Software
Software

Internet Specific
Internet

Business Serv.
Media

Additional Information

Year Founded: 1999
Capital Under Management: $32,000,000
Current Activity Level : Actively seeking new investments

MTI PARTNERS LTD

Langley Place
99 Langley Road
Watford, Herts., United Kingdom WD1 3PE
Phone: 44 1923-250244
Fax: 44-1923-247783
Website: www.mtifirms.com

Other Offices

Woodvale House
Woodvale Road
Brighouse, West Yorkshire, United Kingdom HD6 4AB
Phone: 44 1484 400481
Fax: 44 1484 400491

Management and Staff

John Polden, Partner
Paul Castle, Chief Executive Officer

Type of Firm

Private Firm Investing Own Capital

Industry Association Membership

British Venture Capital Association
European Venture Capital Association (EVCA)

Project Preferences

Role in Financing:
Prefer role as deal originator but will also invest in deals created by others

Type of Financing Preferred:
Early Stage
Expansion
First Stage Financing
Second Stage Financing
Start-up Financing

Size of Investments Considered
Min Size of Investment Considered (000s): $400
Max Size of Investment Considered (000s): $7,500

Geographical Preferences

International
United Kingdom

Industry Preferences

(% based on actual investment)

Industrial/Energy	40.9%
Computer Software and Services	35.2%
Internet Specific	8.9%
Semiconductors/Other Elect.	8.2%
Communications and Media	4.6%
Consumer Related	2.1%
Other Products	0.0%

Additional Information

Name of Most Recent Fund: MTI 3
Most Recent Fund Was Raised: 04/01/1998
Year Founded: 1983
Capital Under Management: $218,100,000
Current Activity Level : Actively seeking new investments
Method of Compensation: Return on invest. most important, but chg. closing fees, service fees, etc.

MULTIVENTURE INVESTMENT, INC.

21F, No. 88, Hsin-Tai Wu Road
1, His-Chih
Taipei, Taiwan
Phone: 8862-8691-1072
Fax: 8862-8691-2397

Management and Staff

Stan Shih, President & Chairman

Type of Firm

Private Firm Investing Own Capital

Industry Association Membership

Taiwan Venture Capital Association(TVCA)

Project Preferences

Type of Financing Preferred:
Early Stage
Expansion
Research and Development
Seed
Startup

Geographical Preferences

United States
South Carolina

International
Taiwan

Industry Preferences

Communications and Media
Communications and Media

Computer Other
Computer Related

Semiconductors/Other Elect.
Electronics

Additional Information

Name of Most Recent Fund: Multiventure Capital Corporation
Most Recent Fund Was Raised: 11/01/1984
Year Founded: 1984
Capital Under Management: $7,800,000
Current Activity Level : Actively seeking new investments

MUSTANG VENTURES (FKA SIEMENS MUSTANG VENTURES)

Hofmannstrasse 51
Munich, Germany 81359
Phone: 49-89-722-61506
Fax: 49-89-722-61831

See California for full listing.

MUTUAL FUND PUBLIC COMPANY LTD.

30-32/Flrs., Lake Rajada Bldg.
193-195 Ratchadaphisek Rd.
Khlong-Toey, Thailand 10110
Phone: 662-661-9000
Fax: 662-661-9100
Website: www.mfcfund.com

Type of Firm
Investment Management/Finance Consulting

Project Preferences

Type of Financing Preferred:
Expansion

Geographical Preferences

International
Asia
Thailand

Industry Preferences

Medical/Health
Medical/Health

Consumer Related
Food/Beverage
Hotels and Resorts

Additional Information
Year Founded: 1975
Capital Under Management: $1,000,000
Current Activity Level : Actively seeking new investments

MVC AG (AKA MITTELDEUTSCHE VENTURE CAPITAL AG)

Friedrich-List-Strasse 28
Leipzig, Germany 04103
Phone: 49 341 9886 245
Fax: 49 341 9886 250
Website: www.mvcag.de

Type of Firm
Non-Financial Corp. Affiliate or Subsidiary

Industry Association Membership
German Venture Capital Association

Project Preferences

Type of Financing Preferred:
Expansion
Management Buyouts
Mezzanine
Recapitalizations
Seed
Startup

Geographical Preferences

International
Germany

Industry Preferences

Communications and Media
Communications and Media

Semiconductors/Other Elect.
Electronics

Biotechnology
Biotechnology

Financial Services
Financial Services

Additional Information
Year Founded: 1999
Capital Under Management: $22,400,000
Current Activity Level : Actively seeking new investments

MVI SVERIGE AB

Norrlandsg 15
Stockholm, Sweden 11143
Phone: 46 8 22 00 90
Fax: 46 8 22 00 92
Website: www.mvigroup.com

Other Offices

MVI (UK) Ltd.
17 Waterloo Place
London, United Kingdom SW1Y 4AR
Phone: 44 171 878 2222
Fax: 44 171 878 2200

MVI A/S
Holmensgate 3, 4 etg.
Oslo, Norway 0250
Phone: 47 22 01 7320
Fax: 47 22 01 7322

MVI Oy
Runeberginkatu 5B, 7th Floor
Helsinki, Finland 00100
Phone: 358 9 6869 2250
Fax: 358 9 6869 2251

Type of Firm
Private Firm Investing Own Capital

Industry Association Membership
Swedish Venture Capital Association

Project Preferences

Type of Financing Preferred:
Expansion
Management Buyouts

Geographical Preferences

International
No Preference

Additional Information
Current Activity Level : Actively seeking new investments

MVM LTD

6 Henrietta Street
London, United Kingdom WC2E 8LA
Phone: 44 20 7557 7500
Fax: 44 20 7557 7501

Management and Staff
Stephen Reeders, Chief Executive Officer

Type of Firm
Private Firm Investing Own Capital

Project Preferences

Type of Financing Preferred:
Early Stage
Seed

Geographical Preferences

United States
All U.S.

International
Europe
Scandanavia/Nordic Region
United Kingdom

Industry Preferences

Biotechnology
Biotechnology

Additional Information
Year Founded: 1998
Capital Under Management: $57,700,000
Current Activity Level : Actively seeking new investments

NANYANG VENTURES PTY LTD (AKA: NANYANG MANAGEMENT PTY LTD)

Level 5, 255 George Street
Sydney, Australia 02000
Phone: 612-9247-4866
Fax: 612-9241-1087
Website: www.nanyang.com.au

Management and Staff
Ian Neal, Managing Director

Type of Firm
Private Firm Investing Own Capital

Industry Association Membership
Australian Venture Capital Association (AVCAL)

Project Preferences

Type of Financing Preferred:
Expansion

Size of Investments Considered
Min Size of Investment Considered (000s): $1,300
Max Size of Investment Considered (000s): $3,300

Geographical Preferences

International
Oceania/Australasia

Industry Preferences

(% based on actual investment)

Consumer Related	31.8%
Computer Software and Services	22.6%
Semiconductors/Other Elect.	17.4%
Internet Specific	9.6%
Medical/Health	5.7%
Communications and Media	5.4%
Other Products	4.0%
Industrial/Energy	3.5%

Additional Information
Name of Most Recent Fund: St.George Development Capital
Most Recent Fund Was Raised: 04/16/1996
Year Founded: 1993
Capital Under Management: $50,700,000
Current Activity Level : Actively seeking new investments

NATIONAL AUSTRALIA INVESTMENT CAPITAL LIMITED

Level 3, 500 Bourke Street
Melbourne, Australia 03000
Phone: 613-8641-4604
Fax: 613-8641-3459

Management and Staff
Russell Hayes, Managing Director

Type of Firm
Affiliate/Subsidary of Oth. Financial. Instit.

Industry Association Membership
Australian Venture Capital Association (AVCAL)

Project Preferences

Type of Financing Preferred:
Expansion
Management Buyouts

Size of Investments Considered
Min Size of Investment Considered (000s): $3,300
Max Size of Investment Considered (000s): $6,500

Geographical Preferences

International
Oceania/Australasia

Industry Preferences

(% based on actual investment)

Other Products	44.0%
Internet Specific	21.0%
Semiconductors/Other Elect.	17.7%
Consumer Related	17.2%

Additional Information
Year Founded: 1996
Capital Under Management: $26,000,000
Current Activity Level : Actively seeking new investments

NATIONAL BANK OF KUWAIT

20 Collyer Hex 20-00
Tong Center
Singapore, Singapore 0104
Phone: 65-222-5348
Fax: 65-224-5438

See New York for full listing.

NATIONAL ENTERPRISE COMPANY, LTD.

2-4-9 Kayaba-cho
Chuo-ku
Tokyo, Japan
Phone: 03-3664-5958
Fax: 03-5695-2498

Other Offices

1-6-8 Koraibashi
Chuo-ku
Osaka, Japan

Type of Firm
Private Firm Investing Own Capital

Project Preferences

Type of Financing Preferred:
Balanced

Geographical Preferences

International
Japan

Industry Preferences

(% based on actual investment)

Other Products	25.2%
Consumer Related	24.5%
Communications and Media	14.2%
Computer Hardware	9.8%
Industrial/Energy	8.7%
Biotechnology	6.3%
Internet Specific	4.4%
Semiconductors/Other Elect.	3.7%
Computer Software and Services	3.2%

Additional Information
Capital Under Management: $24,500,000
Current Activity Level : Actively seeking new investments

NATIVE VENTURE CAPITAL CO., LTD.

21 Artist View Pointe, Box 7
Site 25, RR12
Calgary, Canada T3E 6W3
Phone: 903-208-5380

Management and Staff
Milt Pahl

Whom to Contact
Milt Pahl

Industry Association Membership
Canadian Venture Capital Association

Project Preferences

Role in Financing:
Prefer role as deal originator but will also invest in deals created by others

Type of Financing Preferred:
First Stage Financing
Leveraged Buyout
Second Stage Financing
Seed
Start-up Financing

Size of Investments Considered
Min Size of Investment Considered (000s): $300
Max Size of Investment Considered: No Limit

Geographical Preferences

Canada
Western Canada

Additional Information
Year Founded: 1981
Capital Under Management: $10,000,000
Current Activity Level : Actively seeking new investments
Method of Compensation: Return on invest. most important, but chg. closing fees, service fees, etc.

NAVIS INVESTMENT PARTNERS (ASIA) LIMITED

9/F MNI Building, Power 2
11-Gelan Pinang
Kuala Lumpur, Malaysia
Phone: 603-2166-8770
Fax: 603-2166-8773
Website: www.navis.com.my

Management and Staff
Richard Foyston, Managing Director

Type of Firm
Private Firm Investing Own Capital

Project Preferences

Type of Financing Preferred:
Expansion

Geographical Preferences

International
Malaysia

Additional Information
Name of Most Recent Fund: Navis Asia Fund
Most Recent Fund Was Raised: 03/01/1999
Year Founded: 1998
Capital Under Management: $55,000,000
Current Activity Level : Actively seeking new investments

NCB VENTURES LIMITED

3 George's Dock
IFSC
Dublin 1, Ireland, Republic of
Phone: 353-1-6115611
Fax: 353-1-6115987
Website: www.ncb.ie

Type of Firm
Affiliate/Subsidary of Oth. Financial. Instit.

Project Preferences

Type of Financing Preferred:
Balanced
Expansion

Geographical Preferences

International
Europe
Ireland
No Preference

Additional Information
Year Founded: 2001
Capital Under Management: $24,100,000
Current Activity Level : Actively seeking new investments

NCOTEC VENTURES LTD

40 Portman Square
London, United Kingdom W1H 9HB
Phone: 44-20-7947-8800
Fax: 44-20-7947-8801
Website: www.ncotec.com

Other Offices

Stureplan 4C
4th Floor
Stockholm, Sweden 114 35

Management and Staff
Alasdair Warren, Managing Director
Sanjay Jawa, Chief Financial Officer
Tim Horlick, Managing Director

Type of Firm
Private Firm Investing Own Capital

Industry Association Membership
British Venture Capital Association

Project Preferences

Type of Financing Preferred:
Early Stage
Expansion
Seed
Startup

Geographical Preferences

International
Europe
Germany
Ireland
Scandanavia/Nordic Region
United Kingdom
Western Europe

Industry Preferences

Communications and Media
Communications and Media

Internet Specific
Internet

Additional Information
Year Founded: 2000
Capital Under Management: $17,600,000
Current Activity Level : Actively seeking new investments

NCP ADVISORS PHILIPPINES, INC.

22/F Ayala Tower One
Ayala Triangle, Ayala Ave.
Makati City, Philippines 1200
Phone: 632-813-4678
Fax: 632-848-6741
E-mail: ncp@nextpartners.com
Website: www.nextpartners.com

Other Offices

Asia Insurance Bldg. #17-03
2 Finlayson Green
Singapore, Singapore 049247
Phone: 65-222-7500
Fax: 65-222-7577

Barfield Hse., St. Julian's Ave.
St. Peter Port, Guernsey
Channel Islands, Guernsey GY13QL
Phone: 441-481-710-651
Fax: 441-481-710-284

Management and Staff

Patrick Go, Managing Director
Vincent Perez, Managing Director

Type of Firm

Private Firm Investing Own Capital

Project Preferences

Role in Financing:
Prefer role as deal originator but will also invest in deals created by others

Type of Financing Preferred:
Balanced
Startup

Size of Investments Considered

Min Size of Investment Considered (000s): $10,000
Max Size of Investment Considered (000s): $25,000

Geographical Preferences

International
Asia
Pacific Rim

Industry Preferences

Communications and Media
Radio & TV Broadcasting

Semiconductors/Other Elect.
Electronics

Medical/Health
Medical/Health

Consumer Related
Entertainment and Leisure
Retail
Food/Beverage

Business Serv.
Distribution

Manufact.
Manufacturing

Additional Information

Year Founded: 1996
Capital Under Management: $94,000,000
Current Activity Level : Actively seeking new investments
Method of Compensation: Return on investment is of primary concern, do not charge fees

NEEDHAM & COMPANY, INC.

Balance Capital Markets
3a Jabotinsky Street
GanDiamond Tower Ramat, Israel 52520
Phone: 03-57556274
Fax: 03-57556272

See New York for full listing.

NEOMED MANAGEMENT AS (FKA MEDICAL VENTURE MANAGEMENT)

Parkveien 55
Oslo, Norway N-0256
Phone: 47-22-54-5940
Fax: 47-22-54-5941
Website: www.neomed.com

Other Offices

565 Fifth Avenue
22nd Floor
New York, United States of America 10017

Management and Staff

Carl Christian Gilhuus-Moe, Partner
Erik Amble, Partner

Type of Firm

Private Firm Investing Own Capital

Industry Association Membership

National Venture Capital Association (NVCA)

Project Preferences

Role in Financing:
Will function either as deal originator or investor in deals created by others

Type of Financing Preferred:
Early Stage
Expansion
Mezzanine
Open Market
Private Placement
Second Stage Financing
Seed

Size of Investments Considered

Min Size of Investment Considered (000s): $500
Max Size of Investment Considered (000s): $2,000

Geographical Preferences

International
Europe
All International

Industry Preferences

Biotechnology
Biotechnology

Medical/Health
Medical/Health
Medical Diagnostics
Diagnostic Services
Diagnostic Test Products
Medical Therapeutics
Drug/Equipmt Delivery
Medical Products
Disposable Med. Products
Health Services
Pharmaceuticals

Additional Information

Name of Most Recent Fund: Pomona Partnership Holdings II
Most Recent Fund Was Raised: 02/01/2000
Year Founded: 1989
Capital Under Management: $83,000,000
Current Activity Level : Actively seeking new investments
Method of Compensation: Return on investment is of primary concern, do not charge fees

NET PARTNERS

Avenue Franklin Roosevelt 83
Brussels, Belgium 1050
Phone: 32 2 644 2900
Fax: 32 2 644 1669
Website: www.net-partners.com

Other Offices

Marble Arch Tower
55 Bryanston Street
London, United Kingdom W1H 8AA
Phone: 44 207 868 8044
Fax: 44 207 868 8785

Via Sant'Orsola 3
Milan, Italy 20122
Phone: 39 02 880 7731
Fax: 39 02 880 7735

Management and Staff
Danielle Bodor, Managing Director
Fausto Boni, Managing Director
Michele Appendino, Managing Director

Type of Firm
Private Firm Investing Own Capital

Industry Association Membership
European Venture Capital Association (EVCA)

Project Preferences

Type of Financing Preferred:
Balanced
Early Stage
Seed

Geographical Preferences

International
France
Germany
Israel
Italy
Scandanavia/Nordic Region
Spain
United Kingdom

Industry Preferences

Communications and Media
Telecommunications

Computer Software
Software

Internet Specific
Internet

Additional Information
Year Founded: 1997
Capital Under Management: $173,300,000
Current Activity Level : Actively seeking new investments

NETALONE.COM LTD

68/F 99 Queen's Road
The Centre
Central, Hong Kong
Phone: 852-2330-0336
Fax: 852-2296-6966
E-mail: info@netalone.com
Website: www.netalone.com

Type of Firm
Incubators

Project Preferences

Type of Financing Preferred:
Startup

Geographical Preferences

International
China

Industry Preferences

Internet Specific
Internet

Additional Information
Current Activity Level : Actively seeking new investments

NETJUICE

95 J Miniparc Empresarial III
El Soto Alcobendas
Madrid, Spain 28109
Phone: 34-91-229-4700
Fax: 34-91-229-4747
Website: www.netjuice.com

Other Offices

Avenue del Libertador 6250
8o Piso Cp
Capital Federal, Argentina 1428

Ed. Atrium V Rua Federico Ramos 195
2o andar Vila Olimpia
Sao Paulo, Brazil 21/23/25

Edificio Omega
Campos Eliseos 345 Piso 5o
Mexico, Mexico DF 11560

Waterford Business Center
5200 Blue Lagoon Drive Suite 100
Miami, United States of America 33126

Management and Staff
Fernando de Nunez, Chief Operating Officer
Jesus Gomez, Chief Executive Officer
Silvia Garcia Alonso, Chief Operating Officer

Type of Firm
Incubators

Project Preferences

Type of Financing Preferred:
Early Stage
Expansion
Seed
Startup

Geographical Preferences

United States
All U.S.

International
Argentina
Brazil
Mexico
Portugal
Spain

Industry Preferences

Internet Specific
Internet

Additional Information
Year Founded: 1996
Capital Under Management: $53,400,000
Current Activity Level : Actively seeking new investments

NETSPARK VENTURES N.V.

Koninginnegracht 58
The Hague, Netherlands 2514
Phone: 31 70 362 8134
Fax: 31 70 362 8135
Website: www.netsparkventures.com

Management and Staff
Alexander Van Rossum, General Partner
Sander Zondag, General Partner

Type of Firm
Private Firm Investing Own Capital

Project Preferences

Type of Financing Preferred:
Expansion
Startup

Geographical Preferences

United States
All U.S.

Canada
All Canada

International
Europe

Industry Preferences

Internet Specific
Internet

Computer Other
Computer Related

Additional Information

Current Activity Level : Actively seeking new investments

NETWORKASIA

One International Finance
Centre,1 Harbour View St.
Hong Kong, Hong Kong 2701-2
Phone: 852-2973-5311
Fax: 852-2526-7277
Website: www.nwkasia.com

Management and Staff

Alfredo Lobo, Chief Executive Officer
Jason Cornell, Vice President
Tomoyuki Oe, Vice President

Type of Firm

Private Firm Investing Own Capital

Project Preferences

Role in Financing:
Will function either as deal originator or investor in deals created by others

Type of Financing Preferred:
Balanced

Geographical Preferences

International
Asia

Industry Preferences

Computer Software
Software

Internet Specific
Internet

Additional Information

Current Activity Level : Actively seeking new investments
Method of Compensation: Return on investment is of primary concern, do not charge fees

---

NEURONE VENTURE CAPITAL

2A Habarzel Street
PO Box 58151
Tel Aviv, Israel 61580
Phone: 972-3-765-7260
Fax: 972-3-765-7255
Website: www.neurone.co.il

Management and Staff

Yigal Livne, Managing Partner

Type of Firm

Private Firm Investing Own Capital

Project Preferences

Type of Financing Preferred:
Seed

Geographical Preferences

International
All International
Israel

Industry Preferences

Communications and Media
Commercial Communications
Telecommunications

Internet Specific
Internet

Additional Information

Year Founded: 1997
Capital Under Management: $75,000,000
Current Activity Level : Actively seeking new investments

NEW WORLD INFRASTRUCTURE LIMITED

33/F, New World Tower
18 Queen's Road
Central, Hong Kong
Phone: 852-2844-3197
Fax: 852-2525-9530
Website: www.nw-infra.com.hk

Management and Staff

Cheng Yu-tung, Managing Director

Type of Firm

Non-Financial Corp. Affiliate or Subsidiary

Project Preferences

Type of Financing Preferred:
Balanced

Geographical Preferences

International
Asia

Industry Preferences

Communications and Media
Telecommunications

Consumer Related
Hotels and Resorts

Financial Services
Real Estate

Additional Information

Year Founded: 1970
Current Activity Level : Actively seeking new investments

NEWBRIDGE CAPITAL LIMITED

10/F Marunouchi Mtsui Building
2-2-2 Marunouchi
Chiyoda-ku, Japan 100-0005
Phone: 813-5220-2255
Fax: 813-5220-2256

See California for full listing.

NEWBURY VENTURES

90 Ave Henri Martin
Paris, United Kingdom 75016
Phone: 33 145 04 96 96
Fax: 33 145 04 96 16

See California for full listing.

NEWMARGIN VENTURE CAPITAL

Shanghai Central Plaza 2201
Shanghai, China 200020
Phone: 8621-5383-2000
Fax: 8621-5383-1000
Website: www.newmargin.com

Other Offices

Jian Yie Bldg. 415, South Yi Tiao
Zhong Guan Cun
Beijing, China 100080
Phone: 8610-6257-5185
Fax: 8610-6257-3220

Management and Staff
Feng Tao, General Partner
Winston Zheng, Principal
Yu Xiaomin, Principal

Type of Firm
Private Firm Investing Own Capital

Project Preferences

Type of Financing Preferred:
Early Stage
Expansion

Geographical Preferences

International
Asia

Industry Preferences

Biotechnology
Biotechnology

Medical/Health
Medical/Health

Other
Environment Responsible

Additional Information
Year Founded: 1999
Capital Under Management: $110,000,000
Current Activity Level : Actively seeking new investments

NEWPORT CAPITAL GROUP PTY LTD

Level 3, 170 Pacific Highway
St. Leonards
Sydney, Australia 2065
Phone: 612-9438-3388
Fax: 612-9438-5808
Website: www.newportcapital.com.au

Management and Staff
Stuart Mitchell, Chief Executive Officer

Type of Firm
Private Firm Investing Own Capital

Project Preferences

Type of Financing Preferred:
Later Stage
Mezzanine

Geographical Preferences

International
Australia

Industry Preferences

Communications and Media
Telecommunications

Computer Software
Software

Internet Specific
Internet

Medical/Health
Medical/Health

Manufact.
Manufacturing

Additional Information
Name of Most Recent Fund: Newport CDIB Funds Management (AKA: Newport Technology Fund)
Most Recent Fund Was Raised: 03/01/2000
Year Founded: 1989
Capital Under Management: $55,000,000
Current Activity Level : Actively seeking new investments

NEXIT VENTURES OY

Kaisaniemenkatu 2b
Helsinki, Finland 00100
Phone: 358 9 6874 0600
Fax: 358 9 6874 0610
Website: www.nexitventures.com

Management and Staff
Antti Hannula, General Partner
Artturi Tarjanne, General Partner
Tarja Jyrkas, Chief Financial Officer

Type of Firm
Private Equity Advisor or Fund of Fund Mgr

Industry Association Membership
European Venture Capital Association (EVCA)
Finnish Venture Capital Association

Project Preferences

Type of Financing Preferred:
Early Stage
Startup

Geographical Preferences

International
Scandanavia/Nordic Region

Industry Preferences

Communications and Media
Communications and Media

Internet Specific
Internet

Additional Information
Year Founded: 2000
Capital Under Management: $90,000,000
Current Activity Level : Actively seeking new investments

NEXT VENTURES LIMITED

32-34/Flrs., Alexandra House
16 Chater Road
Central, Hong Kong
Phone: 852-2896-8688
Fax: 852-2556-1627

Type of Firm
Non-Financial Corp. Affiliate or Subsidiary

Project Preferences

Type of Financing Preferred:
Early Stage

Geographical Preferences

International
Hong Kong

Industry Preferences

Internet Specific
Internet

Additional Information
Current Activity Level : Actively seeking new investments

NIB CAPITAL PRIVATE EQUITY N.V. (FKA: PARNIB HOLDING NV)

Van Karnebeeklaan 8
P.O. Box 674
The Hague, Netherlands 2501 CR
Phone: 31-70-302-2800
Fax: 31-70-345-2598
Website: www.nibcapital.com

Other Offices

7 Bishopsgate
London, United Kingdom EC2N 3BX
Phone: 44-20-7375-8080
Fax: 44-20-7588-6483

712 Fifth Avenue
19th Floor
New York, United States of America 10019
Phone: 1-212-271-8410
Fax: 1-212-271-8480

Fentener van Vlissingenkade 1
Utrecht, Netherlands 3521 AA
Phone: 31-30-290-8100
Fax: 31-30-290-6199

Uitbreidingstraat 10-16
Antwerpen, Belgium B - 2600
Phone: 32 3/286.91.40
Fax: 32 3/286.91.50

Westendstrasse 16
Frankfurt am Main, Germany 60325
Phone: 49-699-720-830
Fax: 49-699-720-8320

Management and Staff
C.M. Vermeulen, Managing Director
E.J. Van Der Burg, Managing Director
G.V.H. Doekson, Chairman & Managing Director
Hilde Famaey, Partner
J.H. Vermeulen, Managing Director
Joris De Meester, Partner
Piet Serrure, Partner
W. Borgdorff, Managing Director

Type of Firm
Commercial Bank Affiliate or Subsidiary

Industry Association Membership
European Venture Capital Association (EVCA)
Natl Assoc of Investment Cos. (NAIC)

Project Preferences

Role in Financing:
Prefer role as deal originator but will also invest in deals created by others

Type of Financing Preferred:
Leveraged Buyout
Mezzanine
Second Stage Financing
Special Situation

Geographical Preferences

International
Bermuda
France
Germany
United Kingdom

Industry Preferences

(% based on actual investment)

Biotechnology	32.1%
Computer Software and Services	20.9%
Internet Specific	20.0%
Other Products	16.4%
Medical/Health	8.4%
Communications and Media	2.3%

Additional Information
Name of Most Recent Fund: Alpinvest
Most Recent Fund Was Raised: 01/01/1993
Year Founded: 1994
Capital Under Management: $12,117,600,000
Current Activity Level : Actively seeking new investments
Method of Compensation: Return on investment is of primary concern, do not charge fees

NIF VENTURES CO., LTD.

Daiwa Yaesu Building 1-2-1
Kyobashi, Chuo-ku
Tokyo, Japan
Phone: 813-5201-1530
Fax: 813-5201-1513
Website: www.nif.co.jp

Other Offices

6 Shenton Way, #21-11
DBS Building Tower Two
Singapore, Singapore 068809
Phone: 65-227-8121
Fax: 65-224-6153

Type of Firm
Private Firm Investing Own Capital

Project Preferences

Type of Financing Preferred:
Balanced

Geographical Preferences

International
Asia
Japan

Industry Preferences

Communications and Media
Communications and Media

Semiconductors/Other Elect.
Electronics

Biotechnology
Biotechnology

Additional Information
Year Founded: 1983
Capital Under Management: $683,800,000
Current Activity Level : Actively seeking new investments

NIF VENTURES USA, INC.(NIPPON INVESTMENT & FINANCE CO., LTD)

DBS Blg.,Tower 2, Suite 21-11
Six Shenton Way
Singapore, Singapore 068809
Phone: 65-227-8121
Fax: 65-224-6153

See California for full listing.

NIIT VENTURES

8 Balaji Estate
Sudarshan Munjal Marg, Kalkaji
New Delhi, India 110019
Phone: 9111-620-3434
Fax: 9111-620-3333
Website: www.e-mahamillionaire.com

Type of Firm
Non-Financial Corp. Affiliate or Subsidiary

Project Preferences

Type of Financing Preferred:
Startup

Geographical Preferences

United States
All U.S.

International
India

Industry Preferences

Internet Specific
Internet

Additional Information

Current Activity Level : Actively seeking new investments

NIKKO CAPITAL CO LTD

Tanaka Kougyo Bldg. 4F, 7-2
Nihombashi-kabutocho, Chuo-ku
Tokyo, Japan 103-0026
Phone: 813-3667-7250
Fax: 813-3667-7271
Website: www.nikko-capital.co.jp

Management and Staff

Shigeki Tsujikawa, President

Whom to Contact

Masanobu Okabe

Type of Firm

Affiliate/Subsidary of Oth. Financial. Instit.

Project Preferences

Role in Financing:
Prefer role as deal originator but will also invest in deals created by others

Type of Financing Preferred:
First Stage Financing
Mezzanine
Second Stage Financing
Start-up Financing

Geographical Preferences

United States
West Coast

International
China
Japan

Industry Preferences

Communications and Media
Commercial Communications
Telecommunications
Data Communications
Satellite Microwave Comm.
Other Communication Prod.

Computer Hardware
Computers
Computer Graphics and Dig
Integrated Turnkey System
Disk Relat. Memory Device

Computer Software
Computer Services
Systems Software
Applications Software
Artificial Intelligence

Internet Specific
Internet

Semiconductors/Other Elect.
Electronics
Controllers and Sensors
Laser Related
Fiber Optics
Analytic/Scientific

Biotechnology
Biotech Related Research

Medical/Health
Diagnostic Services
Diagnostic Test Products
Drug/Equipmt Delivery
Other Therapeutic
Medical Products

Consumer Related
Computer Stores
Consumer Products

Industrial/Energy
Industrial Products
Robotics
Environmental Related

Additional Information

Year Founded: 1983
Capital Under Management: $640,000,000
Current Activity Level : Actively seeking new investments
Method of Compensation: Return on investment is of primary concern, do not charge fees

NIPPON TECHNOLOGY VENTURE PARTNERS LTD.

4-1-11 Hongo
Bunkyo-ku
Tokyo, Japan 113-0033
Phone: 813-3815-8641
Fax: 813-3815-8642
Website: www.ntvp.com

Other Offices

3-5-9 Chidori, Ohta-ku
Tokyo, Japan 146-0083
Phone: 813-3756-3965

Management and Staff

Kazutaka Muraguchi, Chief Executive Officer

Type of Firm

Private Firm Investing Own Capital

Project Preferences

Type of Financing Preferred:
Early Stage

Geographical Preferences

International
Japan

Industry Preferences

Computer Hardware
Computers

Internet Specific
Internet

Semiconductors/Other Elect.
Semiconductor

Financial Services
Financial Services

Additional Information

Year Founded: 2000
Capital Under Management: $26,400,000
Current Activity Level : Actively seeking new investments

NIPPON VENTURE CAPITAL CO., LTD.

Nissei Akasaka Building 2, 7F
7-1-16 Akasaka, Minato-ku
Tokyo, Japan
Phone: 03-5413-2680
Fax: 03-5413-2688
Website: plaza12mbn.or.jp/nvcc/

Type of Firm
Private Firm Investing Own Capital

Project Preferences

Type of Financing Preferred:
Balanced

Geographical Preferences

International
Japan

Additional Information
Year Founded: 2000
Capital Under Management: $242,300,000
Current Activity Level : Actively seeking new investments

NMAS1 ELECTRA CAPITAL PRIVADO , S.G.E.C.R., S.A.

Plaza de la Lealtad 3
Madrid, Spain 28014
Phone: 34-91-412-1242
Fax: 34-91-521-8886
Website: www.dinamia.es

Management and Staff
Adolfo Anton, Chief Executive Officer
Joaquin Suarez, Partner
Jorge Mataix, Partner

Type of Firm
Private Firm Investing Own Capital

Industry Association Membership
Spanish Venture Capital Association

Project Preferences

Type of Financing Preferred:
Expansion
Generalist PE
Leveraged Buyout

Geographical Preferences

International
Europe

Industry Preferences

Industrial/Energy
Industrial Products

Business Serv.
Services

Additional Information
Year Founded: 1997
Capital Under Management: $140,000,000
Current Activity Level : Actively seeking new investments

NMT NEW MEDICAL TECHNOLOGIES

Elisabethenstrasse 23
Basel, Switzerland CH-4051
Phone: 41 61 270 35 35
Fax: 41 61 270 35 00
Website: www.nmt.ch

Management and Staff
Lukas R Alioth, Chief Financial Officer

Type of Firm
Private Firm Investing Own Capital

Project Preferences

Type of Financing Preferred:
Early Stage
Expansion
Startup

Geographical Preferences

International
Austria
France
Germany
All International
Italy
Switzerland

Industry Preferences

Biotechnology
Biotechnology

Medical/Health
Medical/Health
Medical Products
Pharmaceuticals

Additional Information
Year Founded: 1997
Capital Under Management: $84,800,000
Current Activity Level : Actively seeking new investments

NOKIA VENTURE PARTNERS (AKA: NOKIA OY)

Marble Arch Tower, 8th Floor
55 Bryanston Street
London, United Kingdom W1H7AA
Phone: 44-207-535-2727
Fax: 44-207-724-7612

See California for full listing.

NOMURA INTERNATIONAL, PLC.

Nomura House
1 St Martin's-Le-Grand
London, United Kingdom ED1A 4NP
Phone: 44 20 7521 2000
Fax: 44 20 7521 2121
Website: www.nomura.com

Type of Firm
Investment/Merchant Bank Subsid/Affil

Project Preferences

Type of Financing Preferred:
Fund of Funds
Later Stage

Geographical Preferences

United States
All U.S.

International
Asia
Europe
Israel

Industry Preferences

(% based on actual investment)

Internet Specific	35.1%
Biotechnology	31.3%
Medical/Health	14.8%
Communications and Media	12.4%
Computer Software and Services	6.4%

Additional Information
Capital Under Management: $102,000,000
Current Activity Level : Actively seeking new investments

NOMURA/JAFCO INVESTMENT (HK) LIMITED

20/F, Asia Pacific Finance Twr
Citibank Plaza, 3 Garden Road
Central, Hong Kong
Phone: 852-2536-1960
Fax: 852-2536-1979

Other Offices

17/F, The Peak Bldg.
Alfaro St. Salcedo Vill.
Makati, Philippines
Phone: 632-848-5251
Fax: 632-848-5254

7/F, Bank Perdania Bldg. Jl. Jend.
Sudirman Kav. 40-41
Jakarta, Indonesia 10210
Phone: 6221-570-73-21
Fax: 6221-570-73-18

Management and Staff

Hironori Hozoji
Hiroshi Ikegaya

Whom to Contact

Hironori Hozoji
Hiroshi Ikegaya

Type of Firm

Investment/Merchant Bank Investing Own or Client Funds

Project Preferences

Role in Financing:

Prefer role as deal originator but will also invest in deals created by others

Type of Financing Preferred:

Early Stage
Expansion
First Stage Financing
Mezzanine
Second Stage Financing
Seed
Start-up Financing
Startup

Geographical Preferences

United States

All U.S.

International

Australia
Bermuda
China
France
Germany
Hong Kong
Italy
Japan
Korea, South
Philippines
Spain
United Kingdom
Vietnam

Industry Preferences

Communications and Media

Commercial Communications
CATV & Pay TV Systems
Telecommunications
Data Communications
Satellite Microwave Comm.

Computer Hardware

Computer Graphics and Dig
Disk Relat. Memory Device

Computer Software

Computer Services
Systems Software
Applications Software
Artificial Intelligence

Internet Specific

Internet

Semiconductors/Other Elect.

Electronics
Semiconductor
Circuit Boards
Laser Related
Fiber Optics

Biotechnology

Biosensors
Biotech Related Research
Biotech Related Research

Medical/Health

Medical Diagnostics
Diagnostic Services
Diagnostic Test Products
Medical Therapeutics
Drug/Equipmt Delivery
Other Therapeutic
Disposable Med. Products
Pharmaceuticals

Consumer Related

Consumer
Retail
Education Related

Industrial/Energy

Energy
Industrial Products

Transportation

Transportation

Business Serv.

Distribution

Manufact.

Publishing

Agr/Forestr/Fish

Agriculture related

Additional Information

Name of Most Recent Fund: JAFCO USIT III, L.P.
Most Recent Fund Was Raised: 03/01/1999
Year Founded: 1999
Capital Under Management: $748,500,000
Current Activity Level : Actively seeking new investments
Method of Compensation: Return on investment is of primary concern, do not charge fees

NORD INNOVATION

40 rue Eugene Jacquet
SP 15
Marcq en Baroeul cedex, France F 59708
Phone: 33 3 2063 0326
Website: www.nordfinancement.com

Type of Firm

Private Firm Investing Own Capital

Project Preferences

Type of Financing Preferred:

Seed

Geographical Preferences

International

France

Industry Preferences

Internet Specific

Internet

Additional Information

Year Founded: 1999
Capital Under Management: $2,200,000
Current Activity Level : Actively seeking new investments

NORTH AMERICA INVESTMENT CORP.

Mercantil Plaza, Suite 813
P.O. Box 1831 Hato Rey Sta.
San Juan, Puerto Rico 00919
Phone: 787-754-6178
Fax: 787-754-6181

Management and Staff
Marcelino Torres, President

Whom to Contact
Marcelino D. Pastrana-Torres

Type of Firm
Private Firm Investing Own Capital

Industry Association Membership
Natl Assoc of Investment Cos. (NAIC)
Natl assoc of Small Bus. Inv. Co (NASBIC)

Project Preferences

Role in Financing:
Will function either as deal originator or investor in deals created by others

Type of Financing Preferred:
Early Stage
Expansion

Size of Investments Considered
Min Size of Investment Considered (000s): $25
Max Size of Investment Considered (000s): $250

Geographical Preferences

International
Puerto Rico

Industry Preferences

Communications and Media
Telecommunications

Consumer Related
Consumer
Retail

Financial Services
Real Estate

Business Serv.
Services

Additional Information
Year Founded: 1974
Current Activity Level : Actively seeking new investments
Method of Compensation: Return on investment is of primary concern, do not charge fees

NORTHERN VENTURE MANAGERS LIMITED

Northumberland House
Princess Square
Newcastle upon Tyne, United Kingdom NE1 8ER
Phone: 191-244-6000
Fax: 44-191-244-6001
Website: www.nvm.co.uk

Other Offices

30-31 Friar Street
Reading, United Kingdom RG1 1DX
Phone: 0118 951 7000
Fax: 0118 951 7001

50 Moray Place
Edinburgh, United Kingdom EH3 6BQ
Phone: 44-131-220-4110
Fax: 44-131-220-4132

Enterprise House
Ocean Village
Southampton, United Kingdom SO14 3XB
Phone: 44-170-323-8111
Fax: 44-170-323-8112

Management and Staff
Alastair Conn, Managing Director

Type of Firm
Affiliate/Subsidary of Oth. Financial. Instit.

Industry Association Membership
British Venture Capital Association
European Venture Capital Association (EVCA)

Project Preferences

Role in Financing:
Prefer role as deal originator but will also invest in deals created by others

Type of Financing Preferred:
Early Stage
First Stage Financing
Leveraged Buyout
Second Stage Financing
Startup
Turnaround

Size of Investments Considered
Min Size of Investment Considered (000s): $1,000
Max Size of Investment Considered: No Limit

Geographical Preferences

International
United Kingdom

Industry Preferences

(% based on actual investment)

Other Products	27.4%
Computer Software and Services	24.5%
Biotechnology	15.8%
Industrial/Energy	12.9%
Consumer Related	8.6%
Internet Specific	6.6%
Medical/Health	4.2%

Additional Information
Name of Most Recent Fund: Northern 2 VCT
Most Recent Fund Was Raised: 01/01/1989
Year Founded: 1988
Capital Under Management: $212,400,000
Current Activity Level : Actively seeking new investments
Method of Compensation: Return on invest. most important, but chg. closing fees, service fees, etc.

NORTHZONE VENTURES (FKA VENTURE PARTNERS AS)

Molleparken 6
Oslo, Norway N-0459
Phone: 47 22 87 16 00
Fax: 47 22 87 16 01
Website: www.northzoneventures.com

Other Offices

HighTech Building
Sveav 9-11
Stockholm, Sweden 101 52
Phone: 46 8 566 150 78
Fax: 46 8 566 150 01

Management and Staff
Bjorn Stray, Partner
Ingar Ostby, Partner
Jorgen H Bladh, Partner
Karl-Christian Agerup, Partner
Tellef Torleifsson, Partner

Type of Firm
Private Firm Investing Own Capital

Project Preferences

Type of Financing Preferred:
Seed
Startup

Geographical Preferences

International
Scandanavia/Nordic Region

Industry Preferences

Communications and Media
Telecommunications

Computer Software
Software

Internet Specific
Internet

Business Serv.
Services

Additional Information

Year Founded: 1995
Capital Under Management: $76,300,000
Current Activity Level : Actively seeking new investments

NOVARTIS AG

Novartis International AG
WSJ-200.220 P.O. Box
Basel , Switzerland CH 4010
Website: www.venturefund.novartis.com

Type of Firm

Non-Financial Corp. Affiliate or Subsidiary

Project Preferences

Type of Financing Preferred:
Early Stage
Startup

Geographical Preferences

International
Europe

Industry Preferences

(% based on actual investment)

Biotechnology	71.4%
Internet Specific	18.1%
Medical/Health	10.5%

Additional Information

Capital Under Management: $72,500,000
Current Activity Level : Actively seeking new investments

NPE INVESTMENT ADVISORS (AKA:NORDIC PRIVATE EQUITY PARTNERS)

Stockholmsgade 41
Copenhagen OE, Denmark DK 2100
Phone: 45 35 26 02 12
Fax: 45 35 26 02 14
Website: www.npep.dk

Management and Staff

Leif Jensen, Managing Director
Robert Andreen, Managing Director

Type of Firm

Affiliate/Subsidary of Oth. Financial. Instit.

Industry Association Membership

European Venture Capital Association (EVCA)

Project Preferences

Type of Financing Preferred:
Expansion
Leveraged Buyout
Mezzanine
Recapitalizations

Geographical Preferences

International
Scandanavia/Nordic Region

Additional Information

Name of Most Recent Fund: Nordic Private Equity Partners II, Ltd.
Most Recent Fund Was Raised: 12/31/1984
Year Founded: 1991
Capital Under Management: $32,800,000
Current Activity Level : Actively seeking new investments

NPM CAPITAL (AKA NEDERLANDSE PARTICIPATIE MIJ NV)

Breitnerstraat 1-3
P.O. Box 7224
Amsterdam, Netherlands 1007 JE
Phone: 31-20-570-5555
Fax: 31-20-671-0855
Website: www.npm-capital.com

Other Offices

NPM Capital Beteiligungsberatung GmbH
Prinzenallee 7
Dusseldorf , Germany D-40549
Phone: 49-21152391122
Fax: 49-21152391200

Management and Staff

M.W. Dekker

Whom to Contact

M.W. Dekker

Type of Firm

Private Firm Investing Own Capital

Industry Association Membership

Dutch Venture Capital Associaton
European Venture Capital Association (EVCA)
German Venture Capital Association

Project Preferences

Role in Financing:
Prefer role as deal originator but will also invest in deals created by others

Type of Financing Preferred:
Expansion
Leveraged Buyout
Management Buyouts
Mezzanine
Recapitalizations
Special Situation

Geographical Preferences

International
Belgium
France
Germany
Ireland
Netherlands

Industry Preferences

(% based on actual investment)

Computer Software and Services	29.6%
Semiconductors/Other Elect.	22.9%
Internet Specific	20.8%
Computer Hardware	11.0%
Other Products	8.5%
Biotechnology	7.3%

Additional Information

Year Founded: 1948
Capital Under Management: $900,000,000
Current Activity Level : Actively seeking new investments
Method of Compensation: Return on invest. most important, but chg. closing fees, service fees, etc.

NTUC CLUB INVESTMENTS PTE LTD (NCI)

627 Aljunied Road
#06-00 Pacific Building
Singapore, Singapore 389837
Phone: 65-848-6299
Fax: 65-848-4523
Website: www.nci.com.sg

Management and Staff
Chng Hee Kok, Chief Executive Officer

Type of Firm
Non-Financial Corp. Affiliate or Subsidiary

Project Preferences

Role in Financing:
Will function either as deal originator or investor in deals created by others

Type of Financing Preferred:
Balanced

Geographical Preferences

International
Singapore

Industry Preferences

Consumer Related
Entertainment and Leisure
Hotels and Resorts

Additional Information
Year Founded: 1994
Current Activity Level : Actively seeking new investments

OBELISK CAPITAL PTY LTD

Level 3, Suite 3, 144 - 148
Pacific Highway
North Sydney, Australia 2060
Phone: 612-9409-1350
Fax: 612-9966-1440
Website: www.obeliskcapital.com.au

Management and Staff
Andrew Randall, Managing Director

Type of Firm
Private Firm Investing Own Capital

Project Preferences

Role in Financing:
Prefer role as deal originator

Type of Financing Preferred:
Early Stage
Expansion
Research and Development
Seed
Startup

Geographical Preferences

International
Asia
Australia

Industry Preferences

Communications and Media
Communications and Media
Telecommunications

Computer Software
Software

Medical/Health
Medical/Health
Pharmaceuticals

Industrial/Energy
Energy

Financial Services
Financial Services
Real Estate

Other
Environment Responsible

Additional Information
Year Founded: 1990
Current Activity Level : Actively seeking new investments
Method of Compensation: Return on invest. most important, but chg. closing fees, service fees, etc.

OCBC, WEARNES & WALDEN INVESTMENTS (S), LTD.

65 Chulia Street
#39-01 OCBC Centre
Singapore, Singapore 049513
Phone: 65-538-1220
Fax: 65-538-0544

Management and Staff
J Chong, Vice President

Type of Firm
Commercial Bank Affiliate or Subsidiary

Industry Association Membership
Singapore Venture Capital Association

Project Preferences

Type of Financing Preferred:
Balanced

Geographical Preferences

United States
All U.S.

International
Asia
China

Additional Information
Year Founded: 2000
Current Activity Level : Actively seeking new investments

ODLANDER FREDRIKSON & CO

Sturengatan 34
Stockholm, Sweden 11436
Phone: 46 8 442 5850
Fax: 46 8 442 5879
Website: www.healthcap.se

Management and Staff
Anki Forsberg, Partner
Bjorn Odlander, Founding Partner
Fredrik Buch, Partner
Magnus Persson, Partner
Peder Fredrikson, Founding Partner
Per Samuelsson, Partner
Staffan Lindstrand, Partner

Type of Firm
Private Equity Advisor or Fund of Fund Mgr

Project Preferences

Type of Financing Preferred:
Early Stage
Later Stage

Geographical Preferences

International
Scandanavia/Nordic Region

Industry Preferences

Biotechnology
Biotechnology

Additional Information
Year Founded: 1998
Capital Under Management: $270,500,000
Current Activity Level : Actively seeking new investments

OLYMPUS CAPITAL HOLDINGS ASIA

Suite 3406 One Exchange Square
Central, Hong Kong
Phone: 852-2140-0500
Fax: 852-2140-0555
Website: www.olympuscap.com

Other Offices

15/F The Tokyo Sankei Building
1-7-2 Ohtemachi, Chiyoda-ku
Tokyo, Japan 100-0004
Phone: 813-3516-7681
Fax: 813-5200-977

153 East 53rd Street, 45/F
New York, United States of America 10022
Phone: 212-292-6633
Fax: 212-292-6644

Young Poong Building, 14/F
Suhrin-Dong, Jongro-Ku
Seoul, South Korea
Phone: 822-399-5100
Fax: 822-399-5555

Management and Staff

Daniel Mintz, Managing Director
Dirk Long, Managing Director
Ha-Ouk Lee, Managing Director
Larry Miao, Managing Director

Type of Firm

Private Firm Investing Own Capital

Project Preferences

Type of Financing Preferred:
Balanced
Early Stage
Expansion
Management Buyouts
Mezzanine
Seed
Startup
Turnaround

Geographical Preferences

International
Asia
Australia
China
Hong Kong
India
Indonesia
Japan
Korea, South
Malaysia
Philippines
Singapore
Thailand
Vietnam

Additional Information

Year Founded: 1997
Capital Under Management: $275,000,000
Current Activity Level : Actively seeking new investments

ONEX CORP.

161 Bay Street
P.O. Box 700
Toronto, Canada M5J 2S1
Phone: 416-362-7711
Fax: 416-362-5765

Other Offices

712 Fifth Avenue
New York, United States of America 10019
Phone: 212-582-2211
Fax: 212-582-0909

Management and Staff

Anthony Munk
Eric Rosen
Ewout Heersink
Seth Mersky

Whom to Contact

Anthony Munk
Eric Rosen
Ewout Heersink
Seth Mersky

Type of Firm

Investment/Merchant Bank Investing Own or Client Funds

Project Preferences

Role in Financing:
Prefer role as deal originator but will also invest in deals created by others

Type of Financing Preferred:
Control-block Purchases
Leveraged Buyout
Special Situation

Size of Investments Considered

Min Size of Investment Considered (000s): $10,000
Max Size of Investment Considered: No Limit

Geographical Preferences

United States
All U.S.

Canada
All Canada

International
Australia
China
France
Germany
Italy
Mexico
Spain
United Kingdom

Additional Information

Name of Most Recent Fund: Onex Corporation
Most Recent Fund Was Raised: 06/01/1986
Year Founded: 1983
Capital Under Management: $420,000,000
Current Activity Level : Actively seeking new investments
Method of Compensation: Return on invest. most important, but chg. closing fees, service fees, etc.

ORANGE VENTURES

50 George Street
London, United Kingdom W1H 5RF
Phone: 44 207 984 1600

Management and Staff

Alison Hancock, Partner
Kenny Hirschhorn, Partner

Type of Firm

Non-Financial Corp. Affiliate or Subsidiary

Project Preferences

Type of Financing Preferred:
Balanced

Geographical Preferences

International
No Preference

Industry Preferences

Communications and Media
Communications and Media

Additional Information

Year Founded: 2000
Capital Under Management: $450,600,000
Current Activity Level : Actively seeking new investments

ORESA VENTURES, S.A.

Waterloo Office Park
Building O Drève Richelle 161
Waterloo, Belgium B-1410
Phone: 32-2-357-5500
Fax: 32-2-357-5505
Website: www.oresaventures.com

Other Offices

24 Popa Savu Street
Bucharest, Romania
Phone: 401 2234245
Fax: 401 222 1807

Avenue Pasteur 3
Luxembourg, Luxembourg L-2311

ul. Sapiezynska 10
Warsaw, Poland 00-215
Phone: 48 22 531-4100
Fax: 48 22 531-4111

Management and Staff

Erik Hallgren, Partner

Whom to Contact

all of above

Type of Firm

Private Firm Investing Own Capital

Industry Association Membership

European Venture Capital Association (EVCA)

Project Preferences

Role in Financing:
Prefer role as deal originator but will also invest in deals created by others

Type of Financing Preferred:
First Stage Financing
Second Stage Financing
Start-up Financing
Startup

Size of Investments Considered

Min Size of Investment Considered (000s): $4,800
Max Size of Investment Considered: No Limit

Geographical Preferences

International
Central Europe
Eastern Europe
Poland
Romania

Industry Preferences

Biotechnology
Biotechnology

Medical/Health
Medical/Health
Medical Diagnostics

Consumer Related
Consumer
Consumer Products
Education Related

Financial Services
Financial Services

Business Serv.
Distribution

Additional Information

Year Founded: 1996
Capital Under Management: $75,000,000
Current Activity Level : Making few, if any, new investments
Method of Compensation: Return on investment is of primary concern, do not charge fees

---

ORIX CAPITAL CORPORATION

32/F, World Trade Center Bldg.
2-4-1 Hamamatsu-cho
Tokyo, Japan 105-6132
Phone: 813-3435-3341
Fax: 813-3435-3349
Website: www.orixcapital.co.jp

Type of Firm

Affiliate/Subsidary of Oth. Financial. Instit.

Project Preferences

Type of Financing Preferred:
Mezzanine

Geographical Preferences

International
Asia
No Preference

Industry Preferences

Semiconductors/Other Elect.
Electronics

Biotechnology
Biotechnology

Other
Environment Responsible

Additional Information

Year Founded: 1983
Current Activity Level : Actively seeking new investments

OVATION CAPITAL PARTNERS (FKA:ICENTENNIAL VENTURES LLC)

34 John Street
London, United Kingdom WCIN 2EU
Phone: 44-20-7841-1828
Fax: 44-20-7841-1861

See New York for full listing.

PAC-LINK MANAGEMENT CORPORATION

16F, No.2
Tun-Hwa South Road, Section 2
Taipei, Taiwan
Phone: 8862-2755-5000
Fax: 8862-2755-2000
Website: www.paclink.com.tw

Type of Firm

Private Firm Investing Own Capital

Industry Association Membership

Taiwan Venture Capital Association(TVCA)

Project Preferences

Type of Financing Preferred:
Balanced
Expansion
Mezzanine
Seed
Startup

Geographical Preferences

International
Taiwan

Industry Preferences

Communications and Media
Telecommunications

Computer Software
Software

Semiconductors/Other Elect.
Semiconductor

Industrial/Energy
Factory Automation
Process Control
Machinery
Environmental Related

Additional Information
Year Founded: 1998
Capital Under Management: $31,100,000
Current Activity Level : Actively seeking new investments

PACIFIC CAPITAL PARTNERS

5/F,No.420 Fu-Hsin N. Road
Taipei, Taiwan
Phone: 8862-2509-3533
Fax: 8862-2509-9358

Management and Staff
Walter Wang, President

Type of Firm
Private Firm Investing Own Capital

Industry Association Membership
Taiwan Venture Capital Association(TVCA)

Project Preferences

Type of Financing Preferred:
Early Stage
Expansion
Mezzanine
Seed
Startup

Geographical Preferences

International
Taiwan

Industry Preferences

Computer Software
Software

Semiconductors/Other Elect.
Electronics
Electronic Components
Semiconductor

Biotechnology
Biotechnology

Industrial/Energy
Factory Automation
Machinery

Additional Information
Year Founded: 1997
Capital Under Management: $53,700,000
Current Activity Level : Actively seeking new investments

PACIFIC CENTURY GROUP VENTURES LTD.

525 Wheelhouse Square
Suite 405
Vancouver, Canada V5Z 4L8
Phone: 604-871-0452
Fax: 604-871-0451
Website: www.pcentury.com

Management and Staff
Harish Consul, President, Founder

Type of Firm
Private Firm Investing Own Capital

Additional Information
Year Founded: 1998
Current Activity Level : Actively seeking new investments

PACIFIC EQUITY PARTNERS

Level 36 The Chifley Tower
2 Chifley Square
Sydney, Australia 02000
Phone: 612-9229-1400
Fax: 612-9231-2804
Website: www.pep.com.au

Management and Staff
Adrian Warner, Vice President
Anthony Kerwick, Vice President
Paul McCullagh, Managing Director
Rickard Gardell, Managing Director
Rob Koczkar, Vice President
Simon Pillar, Managing Director
Steve Zide, Managing Director
Tim Sims, Managing Director

Type of Firm
Private Firm Investing Own Capital

Industry Association Membership
Australian Venture Capital Association (AVCAL)

Project Preferences

Type of Financing Preferred:
Expansion
Later Stage
Management Buyouts

Geographical Preferences

International
Oceania/Australasia

Additional Information
Year Founded: 1998
Capital Under Management: $29,900,000
Current Activity Level : Actively seeking new investments

PACIFIC VENTURE PARTNERS

5/F, No.420, Fu-Hsin N. Road
Taipei, Taiwan
Phone: 8862-2509-3533
Fax: 8862-2509-9358
Website: www.pacificventuregroup.com

Management and Staff
Ben Yang, President
David Chow, Managing Director

Type of Firm
Private Firm Investing Own Capital

Industry Association Membership
Taiwan Venture Capital Association(TVCA)

Project Preferences

Type of Financing Preferred:
Expansion
Mezzanine
Seed

Geographical Preferences

International
Asia

Industry Preferences

Communications and Media
Telecommunications

Internet Specific
Internet

Semiconductors/Other Elect.
Electronics
Semiconductor

Biotechnology
Biotechnology

Industrial/Energy
Machinery

Manufact.
Manufacturing

Additional Information
Year Founded: 1997
Capital Under Management: $111,500,000
Current Activity Level : Actively seeking new investments

PAMA GROUP INC. (FKA:PRUDENTIAL ASSET MANAGEMENT ASIA)

Alexandra House, 32nd Floor
18 Chater Road
Central, Hong Kong
Phone: 852-2844-1900
Fax: 852-2877-3748

Other Offices

20 Collyer Quay
#21-02 Tung Centre
Singapore, Singapore 049319
Phone: 65-326-1800
Fax: 65-225-7829

22 Jalan Imbi
Amoda 01-08
Kuala Lumpur, Malaysia 55100
Phone: 603-241-0318
Fax: 603-241-0818

Maneeya Centre Bldg., 10/F, 518/5
Ploenchit Road
Bangkok, Thailand 10330
Phone: 662-255-6816
Fax: 662-253-9110

Shinwa Building, 5/F
2-9-11,Toranomon, Minato-ku
Tokyo, Japan 105
Phone: 813-3597-0051
Fax: 813-3597-0053

Walsin Lihwa Building, 8F
117 Min Sheng,E. Road Sec 3
Taipei, Taiwan
Phone: 8862-718-8136
Fax: 8862-718-8135

Wisma Rajawali,12A Floor,
Jl Jend.Sudirman Kav.34
Jakarta, Indonesia 10220
Phone: 622-1573-6650
Fax: 622-1573-3184

Management and Staff
Douglas Fergusson, Co-Founder
Michael Kwee, Chairman & CEO
Tan Yong-Nang, Managing Director
Timothy Chia, President
Yong Nam Tan, Managing Director

Whom to Contact
Tan Yong Nang

Type of Firm
Non-Financial Corp. Affiliate or Subsidiary

Project Preferences

Role in Financing:
Prefer role as deal originator but will also invest in deals created by others

Type of Financing Preferred:
Acquisition
Control-block Purchases
Early Stage
Expansion
Generalist PE
Later Stage
Leveraged Buyout
Management Buyouts
Private Placement
Recapitalizations
Special Situation
Turnaround

Size of Investments Considered
Min Size of Investment Considered (000s): $10,000
Max Size of Investment Considered (000s): $80,000

Geographical Preferences

International
Asia
Australia
China
Hong Kong
Indonesia
Japan
Korea, South
Malaysia
Philippines
Singapore
Thailand

Industry Preferences

(% based on actual investment)

Other Products	36.0%
Consumer Related	33.9%
Communications and Media	13.5%
Semiconductors/Other Elect.	8.4%
Computer Hardware	4.2%
Internet Specific	4.1%

Additional Information
Name of Most Recent Fund: Prudential Asia Private Equity Limited Partnership II
Most Recent Fund Was Raised: 01/01/1998
Year Founded: 1986
Capital Under Management: $1,300,000,000
Current Activity Level : Actively seeking new investments
Method of Compensation: Return on invest. most important, but chg. closing fees, service fees, etc.

PANTHEON VENTURES LIMITED

Charles House
5-11 Regent Street
London, United Kingdom SW1Y 4LR
Phone: 44-20-7484-6200
Fax: 44-20-7484-6201
Website: www.pantheon.co.uk

Other Offices

Suite 1606, 16th Floor
2Exchange Sq. 8Connaught Pl
Central, Hong Kong
Phone: 852-2810-8063
Fax: 852-2526-0218

Suite 906
50 California Street
San Francisco, United States of America 94111
Phone: 415 291 3100
Fax: 415 291 3132

Waterloo Office Park
161 Dreve de Richelle
Waterloo, Belgium B - 1410
Phone: 32-2-352-8797
Fax: 32-2-352-8889

Management and Staff
Colin Wimsett, Managing Director
Gary Hiatt, Vice President
Ian Deas, Partner
J. Jay Pierrepont, Managing Director
John Lance, Managing Director
Richard Bowley, Chief Executive Officer
Roar Storebaug, Vice President
Serge Raicher, Managing Director

Type of Firm
Private Equity Advisor or Fund of Fund Mgr

Industry Association Membership
European Venture Capital Association (EVCA)

Project Preferences

Role in Financing:
Prefer role in deals created by others

Type of Financing Preferred:
Early Stage
Expansion
Fund of Funds
Leveraged Buyout
Recapitalizations
Turnaround

Geographical Preferences

United States
All U.S.

International
Asia
Europe

Additional Information
Name of Most Recent Fund: Pantheon European Europe Fund II, Limited
Most Recent Fund Was Raised: 12/01/1999
Year Founded: 2000
Capital Under Management: $4,800,000,000
Current Activity Level : Actively seeking new investments
Method of Compensation: Return on investment is of primary concern, do not charge fees

PARCOM VENTURES BV

P.O. Box 434
Hilversum, Netherlands 1200 AK
Phone: 31 35 646 44 40
Fax: 31 35 685 85 85
Website: www.parcomventures.nl

Management and Staff
Aris Wateler, Managing Director

Type of Firm
Non-Financial Corp. Affiliate or Subsidiary

Industry Association Membership
European Venture Capital Association (EVCA)

Project Preferences

Type of Financing Preferred:
Expansion
Fund of Funds
Leveraged Buyout
Management Buyouts

Geographical Preferences

International
Europe
Netherlands

Industry Preferences

Computer Software
Software

Consumer Related
Consumer

Industrial/Energy
Industrial Products

Business Serv.
Services

Additional Information
Year Founded: 1982
Capital Under Management: $704,900,000
Current Activity Level : Actively seeking new investments

PARI CAPITAL AG

Muthmannstrasse 1
Munich, Germany 80939
Phone: 49 89 99 8480-0
Fax: 49 89 998480-10
E-mail: info@paricapital.com
Website: www.paricapital.com

Management and Staff
Wolfgang Klemm, Managing Director

Type of Firm
Incubators

Project Preferences

Type of Financing Preferred:
Early Stage
Seed
Startup

Industry Preferences

Computer Software
Software

Internet Specific
Internet

Additional Information
Year Founded: 1999
Current Activity Level : Actively seeking new investments

PART'COM

Tour Maine de Montparnasse
33 av de Maine BP 178
Paris Cedex 15, France F-75755
Phone: 33-1-4064-2312
Fax: 33-1-4064-2334
Website: www.partcom.com

Management and Staff
Antoine Garrigues, Managing Partner
Pierre Chevallier, Partner
Pierre de Fouquet, Managing Partner
Serge Desvignes, Partner

Type of Firm
Commercial Bank Affiliate or Subsidiary

Industry Association Membership
European Venture Capital Association (EVCA)

Project Preferences

Type of Financing Preferred:
Early Stage
Expansion
Startup

Size of Investments Considered
Min Size of Investment Considered (000s): $881
Max Size of Investment Considered (000s): $22,030

Geographical Preferences

United States
All U.S.

International
Europe

Industry Preferences

Communications and Media
Telecommunications

Internet Specific
Internet

Business Serv.
Media

Additional Information
Year Founded: 1986
Capital Under Management: $458,200,000
Current Activity Level : Actively seeking new investments

PARTECH INTERNATIONAL

Kamiyacho Tower 45
5-2-5 Toranomon, Minato-Itu
Tokyo, Japan 105
Phone: 813-5470-6495
Fax: 813-5470-6498

See California for full listing.

PARTNERS GROUP

Baarerstrasse 37
Zug, Switzerland 6304
Phone: 41 41 726 8585
Fax: 41 41 726 8558
Website: www.partnersgroup.ch

Management and Staff
Christoph Rubeli, Partner
Franz Aatz, Partner
Fredy Gantner, Partner
Hans Ulrich Muller, Partner
Marcel Erni, Partner
Urs Wietlisbach, Partner

Type of Firm
Private Firm Investing Own Capital

Industry Association Membership
European Venture Capital Association (EVCA)

Project Preferences

Type of Financing Preferred:
Early Stage
Expansion
Fund of Funds
Leveraged Buyout
Management Buyouts

Geographical Preferences

International
All International
No Preference

Industry Preferences

Communications and Media
Communications and Media

Internet Specific
E-Commerce Technology

Biotechnology
Biotechnology

Consumer Related
Consumer

Industrial/Energy
Materials
Machinery

Additional Information
Year Founded: 1998
Capital Under Management: $3,000,000,000
Current Activity Level : Actively seeking new investments

PATHFINDER INVESTMENT CO PVT LTD

2/F Varun Complex
153A Law College Road
Pune, India 411004
Phone: 9120-565-1851
Fax: 9120-565-1846

Management and Staff
Sujay Joshi

Whom to Contact
Sujay Joshi

Type of Firm
Private Firm Investing Own Capital

Project Preferences

Role in Financing:
Prefer role as deal originator but will also invest in deals created by others

Type of Financing Preferred:
Expansion
Mezzanine
Second Stage Financing
Special Situation

Geographical Preferences

International
India

Industry Preferences

Communications and Media
Commercial Communications
Telecommunications

Computer Hardware
Integrated Turnkey System

Computer Software
Computer Services
Systems Software
Applications Software

Computer Other
Computer Related

Semiconductors/Other Elect.
Electronic Components
Analytic/Scientific

Medical/Health
Medical/Health
Diagnostic Services
Medical Products
Disposable Med. Products
Hospital/Other Instit.
Pharmaceuticals

Consumer Related
Consumer
Franchises(NEC)
Food/Beverage
Consumer Products
Consumer Services
Hotels and Resorts
Education Related

Industrial/Energy
Alternative Energy
Energy Conservation Relat
Industrial Products
Materials
Factory Automation
Machinery
Environmental Related

Financial Services
Financial Services

Business Serv.
Services
Consulting Services

Manufact.
Manufacturing
Publishing

Additional Information
Year Founded: 1991
Current Activity Level : Actively seeking new investments
Method of Compensation: Return on investment is of primary concern, do not charge fees

PATRICOF & CO. VENTURES, INC.

2 Weizmann St.,IBM Bldg, 10th Fl
P.O. Box 33031
Tel Aviv, Israel 61330
Phone: 9723-696-5990
Fax: 9723-696-5977

See New York for full listing.

PENFUND PARTNERS, INC.

145 King Street West
Suite 1920
Toronto, Canada M5H 1J8
Phone: 416-865-0300
Fax: 416-364-6912
Website: www.penfund.com

Other Offices

770 Sherbrooke Street West
Suite 1215
Montreal, Canada H3A 1G1
Phone: 514-499-9670
Fax: 514-499-9673

Management and Staff
David Collins

Whom to Contact
David Collins

Type of Firm
Investment/Merchant Bank Subsid/Affil

Industry Association Membership
Canadian Venture Capital Association

Project Preferences

Role in Financing:
Will function either as deal originator or investor in deals created by others

Type of Financing Preferred:
Generalist PE
Leveraged Buyout
Management Buyouts
Mezzanine

Size of Investments Considered
Min Size of Investment Considered (000s): $667
Max Size of Investment Considered (000s): $4,670

Geographical Preferences

Canada
All Canada

Industry Preferences

Communications and Media
Communications and Media

Computer Hardware
Computer Graphics and Dig
Integrated Turnkey System

Computer Software
Systems Software
Applications Software
Artificial Intelligence

Medical/Health
Medical/Health

Consumer Related
Consumer
Entertainment and Leisure
Food/Beverage
Consumer Products
Consumer Services

Industrial/Energy
Alternative Energy
Industrial Products
Machinery

Transportation
Transportation

Financial Services
Financial Services

Business Serv.
Distribution

Manufact.
Manufacturing
Office Automation Equipmt

Utilities
Utilities

Additional Information
Year Founded: 1978
Capital Under Management: $700,000,000
Current Activity Level : Actively seeking new investments
Method of Compensation: Return on investment is of primary concern, do not charge fees

PENTA CAPITAL PARTNERS LTD

150 St. Vincent Street
Glasgow, United Kingdom G2 5NE
Phone: 44 141 572 7300
Fax: 44 141 572 7310
Website: www.pentacapital.com

Management and Staff
David Calder, Partner
Mark Phillips, Partner
Steven Scott, Partner
Torquil MacNaughton, Partner

Type of Firm
Private Firm Investing Own Capital

Industry Association Membership
British Venture Capital Association

Project Preferences

Type of Financing Preferred:
Expansion
Later Stage
Leveraged Buyout
Management Buyouts
Mezzanine
Recapitalizations

Geographical Preferences

International
Ireland
United Kingdom

Industry Preferences

Communications and Media
Communications and Media

Consumer Related
Entertainment and Leisure

Business Serv.
Services

Additional Information
Name of Most Recent Fund: Penta Fund 1
Most Recent Fund Was Raised: 05/04/2000
Year Founded: 1999
Capital Under Management: $187,100,000
Current Activity Level : Actively seeking new investments

PHOENIX EQUITY PARTNERS (FKA: DLJ EUROPEAN PRIVATE EQUITY)

99 Bishopsgate
London, United Kingdom EC2M 3YF
Phone: 44-207-655-7600
Fax: 44-207-655-7683

Other Offices

111 Broad Street
London, United Kingdom EC1N 1AP
Phone: 44 20 7888 8888
Fax: 44 20 7883 5980

Management and Staff
David Gregson, Managing Director
James Thomas, Managing Director

Type of Firm
Private Firm Investing Own Capital

Industry Association Membership
British Venture Capital Association
European Venture Capital Association (EVCA)

Project Preferences

Role in Financing:
Prefer role as deal originator but will also invest in deals created by others

Type of Financing Preferred:
Leveraged Buyout
Mezzanine
Second Stage Financing
Special Situation
Turnaround

Size of Investments Considered
Min Size of Investment Considered (000s): $16,200
Max Size of Investment Considered (000s): $151,100

Geographical Preferences

International
Bermuda
France
Germany
Italy
Spain
United Kingdom

Industry Preferences

(% based on actual investment)

Consumer Related	40.7%
Communications and Media	24.6%
Other Products	14.3%
Internet Specific	10.6%
Biotechnology	7.1%
Medical/Health	2.6%
Industrial/Energy	0.1%

Additional Information
Name of Most Recent Fund: Phoenix Equity Partners II
Most Recent Fund Was Raised: 11/01/1996
Year Founded: 1997
Capital Under Management: $925,300,000
Current Activity Level : Actively seeking new investments
Method of Compensation: Return on invest. most important, but chg. closing fees, service fees, etc.

PILOTBIRD

Michelin House
81 Fulham Road
London, United Kingdom SW3 6RD
Phone: 44 870 870 4546
Fax: 44 870 870 4547
Website: www.pilotbird.com

Management and Staff
Andrew Shortis, Chief Operating Officer
Tim Murray, Chief Executive Officer

Type of Firm
Private Firm Investing Own Capital

Project Preferences

Type of Financing Preferred:
Early Stage
Seed
Startup

Geographical Preferences

International
Europe

Industry Preferences

Communications and Media
Telecommunications
Wireless Communications

Additional Information
Year Founded: 1999
Current Activity Level : Actively seeking new investments

PINO VENTURE PARTNERS

Piazza Duse 3
Milan, Italy 20121
Phone: 39-277-12-18-1
Fax: 39-276-01-16-63
Website: www.pino.it

Other Offices

47, Esplanade
St. Helier
Jersey, United Kingdom JE1 0BD
Phone: 44-1534-832202
Fax: 44-1534-832203

7 Val Ste Croix
B.P. 522
, Luxembourg L-2015
Phone: 352-455-858
Fax: 352-455-859

Management and Staff
Elserino Piol, President
Oliver Novick, Partner

Type of Firm
Investment Management/Finance Consulting

Industry Association Membership
European Venture Capital Association (EVCA)
Italian Venture Capital Association

Project Preferences

Type of Financing Preferred:
Early Stage
Seed
Startup

Geographical Preferences

United States
All U.S.

International
Italy
Western Europe

Industry Preferences

Communications and Media
Communications and Media
Telecommunications

Additional Information
Year Founded: 2000
Capital Under Management: $103,100,000
Current Activity Level : Actively seeking new investments

PME CAPITAL

Av. Dr Antunes Guimaraes 103
Porto, Portugal 4100-079
Phone: 351-22-616-5390
Fax: 351-22-610-2089
Website: www.pmecapital.pt

Type of Firm
Private Firm Investing Own Capital

Industry Association Membership
European Venture Capital Association (EVCA)
Portuguese Venture Capital Association

Project Preferences

Type of Financing Preferred:
Expansion
Leveraged Buyout
Seed
Startup

Geographical Preferences

International
Africa
Portugal

Industry Preferences

Communications and Media
Communications and Media

Internet Specific
Internet

Computer Other
Computer Related

Semiconductors/Other Elect.
Electronics

Biotechnology
Biotechnology

Industrial/Energy
Energy
Materials

Business Serv.
Media

Additional Information

Year Founded: 1989
Capital Under Management: $89,900,000
Current Activity Level : Actively seeking new investments

POALIM CAPITAL MARKETS TECHNOLOGIES, LTD.

Al-Rov Tower
46 Rothschild Blvd.
Tel Aviv, Israel 66883
Phone: 972 3 567 5333
Fax: 972 3 567 5740
Website: www.pcm.co.il

Management and Staff

Avi Geffen, Managing Director
Eran Auerbach-Gersht, Managing Director
Yoav Levy, Chief Executive Officer

Type of Firm

Investment/Merchant Bank Investing Own or Client Funds

Project Preferences

Type of Financing Preferred:
Fund of Funds

Geographical Preferences

International
Israel

Industry Preferences

Communications and Media
Telecommunications

Computer Software
Software

Internet Specific
Internet

Additional Information

Capital Under Management: $64,000,000
Current Activity Level : Actively seeking new investments

POLARIS VENTURE CAPITAL

Europe House
37 Shaul Hamelech Ave.
Tel-Aviv, Israel 61333
Phone: 972-3-609-0790
Fax: 972-3-609-0791
Website: www.polarisvc.com

Other Offices

149 Commonwealth Drive
Menlo Park, United States of America 94025
Phone: 650-688-2800
Fax: 650-688-2848

Management and Staff

Chemi Peres, Managing Partner
Isaac Hillel, General Partner
Moshe Levin, Vice President
Rami Beracha, Partner
Rami Kalish, Managing Partner
Ruth Alon, Managing Director
Zeev Binman, Chief Financial Officer

Type of Firm

Private Firm Investing Own Capital

Project Preferences

Type of Financing Preferred:
Balanced
Early Stage
Later Stage
Seed
Startup

Geographical Preferences

United States
All U.S.

International
Europe
Israel

Industry Preferences

(% based on actual investment)

Communications and Media	36.3%
Internet Specific	19.9%
Computer Software and Services	19.9%
Semiconductors/Other Elect.	9.1%
Medical/Health	8.3%
Computer Hardware	3.4%
Biotechnology	3.1%

Additional Information

Year Founded: 2000
Capital Under Management: $700,000,000
Current Activity Level : Actively seeking new investments

POLYTECHNOS VENTURE PARTNERS GMBH

Promenadeplatz 12
Munich, Germany D-80333
Phone: 49-89-2422-6210
Fax: 49-89-2422-6221
Website: www.polytechnos.com

Other Offices

13-15 Victoria Road
St. Peter Port
Guernsey, Channel Islands, United Kingdom

Avenue Brassine 72
Rhode St Genese, Belgium B-1640
Phone: 32-2-358-3703
Fax: 32-2-358-6069

Friedrichstrasse 59
Frankfurt, Gabon 60323
Phone: 49-69-714-0710
Fax: 49-69-173980

Management and Staff

Dirk Kanngiesser, Managing Partner
Eric Achtmann, Partner
Hasso Von Falkenhausen, Managing Partner
Knut Heitmann, Managing Partner
Pierre Hochuli, Managing Partner
Simon Waddington, Partner

Type of Firm

Private Firm Investing Own Capital

Industry Association Membership

European Venture Capital Association (EVCA)

Project Preferences

Type of Financing Preferred:
Early Stage
Expansion
Startup

Geographical Preferences

United States
All U.S.

International
Europe
Middle East

Industry Preferences

(% based on actual investment)

Internet Specific	50.6%
Biotechnology	36.6%
Medical/Health	12.8%

Additional Information
Year Founded: 1998
Capital Under Management: $54,300,000
Current Activity Level : Actively seeking new investments

POMONA CAPITAL

16 Hanover Square
London, United Kingdom W1R 9AJ
Phone: 44-171-408-9433
Fax: 44-171-408-9434

See New York for full listing.

PORTVIEW COMMUNICATIONS PARTNERS

10 Hayetsira Street, POB 2197
Post Office Box 2197
Ra'anana, Israel 43650
Phone: 972-9-741-3140
Fax: 972-9-741-3240
Website: www.portviewcommunications.com

Other Offices

Grand Pavilion Commercial Center
Bougainvillea Way, 802 West Bay Road
Grand Cayman, Cayman Islands
Phone: 345-949-7942
Fax: 345-949-8340

Management and Staff
Julie Kunstler, Founder
Robin Hacke, Founder

Type of Firm
Private Firm Investing Own Capital

Project Preferences

Type of Financing Preferred:
Balanced

Size of Investments Considered
Min Size of Investment Considered (000s): $2,000
Max Size of Investment Considered (000s): $7,000

Geographical Preferences

United States
All U.S.

International
All International
Israel
Sweden
United Kingdom

Industry Preferences

Communications and Media
Communications and Media

Additional Information
Capital Under Management: $61,000,000
Current Activity Level : Actively seeking new investments

POWERWORD CAPITAL MANAGEMENT, INC.

8/F, No.70 Nan-King E. Road
Section 3
Taipei, Taiwan
Phone: 8862-2517-6896
Fax: 8862-2517-9208

Management and Staff
Jeffrey Lee, President

Type of Firm
Private Firm Investing Own Capital

Industry Association Membership
Taiwan Venture Capital Association(TVCA)

Project Preferences

Type of Financing Preferred:
Balanced
Expansion
Mezzanine
Seed
Startup
Turnaround

Geographical Preferences

International
Taiwan

Industry Preferences

Communications and Media
Telecommunications

Computer Software
Software

Semiconductors/Other Elect.
Electronic Components
Semiconductor

Biotechnology
Biotechnology

Additional Information
Year Founded: 1996
Capital Under Management: $79,500,000
Current Activity Level : Actively seeking new investments

PPM VENTURES LTD (FKA: PRUDENTIAL VENTURE MANAGERS LTD)

1 Waterhouse Square
Holborn Bars
London, United Kingdom ECIN 2TL
Phone: 44-207-831-7747
Fax: 44-207-831-9528
Website: www.ppmventures.com

Other Offices

11/F Yurakucho Bldg. (Business Center)
1-10-1 Yurakucho, Chiyoda-ku
Tokyo, Japan 100-0006
Phone: 813-5219-2024
Fax: 813-5219-2025

95 Avenue des Champs-Elysees
Paris, France 75008
Phone: 33-1-5689-1414
Fax: 33-1-5689-1429

Level 38, Tower Building
Australia Square
Sydney, Australia NSW 2000
Phone: 61-02-9252-5200
Fax: 61-02-9252-5255

Schafflerhof
Maffeistrasse 3
Munich, Germany D-80333
Phone: 49-089-238896-0
Fax: 49-89 25558-517

Suites 1213-19 Two Pacific Place
88 Queensway
Central, Hong Kong
Phone: 852-2868-5330
Fax: 852-2868-3809

Management and Staff
Jonathan Morgan, Managing Director

Type of Firm
Insurance Firm Affiliate or Subsidiary

Industry Association Membership
British Venture Capital Association
Hungarian Venture Capital Association

Project Preferences

Role in Financing:
Prefer role as deal originator but will also invest in deals created by others

Type of Financing Preferred:
Expansion
Leveraged Buyout
Management Buyouts
Special Situation
Turnaround

Size of Investments Considered
Min Size of Investment Considered (000s): $46,855
Max Size of Investment Considered (000s): $468,550

Geographical Preferences

International
Australia
Belgium
China
France
Germany
Japan
Luxembourg
Netherlands
United Kingdom

Industry Preferences

(% based on actual investment)

Other Products	96.4%
Internet Specific	3.2%
Consumer Related	0.4%
Biotechnology	0.0%

Additional Information
Name of Most Recent Fund: Prudential Life Funds
Most Recent Fund Was Raised: 01/01/1989
Year Founded: 1986
Capital Under Management: $874,600,000
Current Activity Level : Actively seeking new investments
Method of Compensation: Return on invest. most important, but chg. closing fees, service fees, etc.

PRE-IPO AKTIENGESELLSCHAFT

Am Sandtorkai 75
Hamburg, Germany 20457
Phone: 49 40/374834-0
Fax: 49 40/374834-10
Website: www.pre-ipo.de

Management and Staff
Felix Goedhart, Chief Executive Officer

Type of Firm
Private Firm Investing Own Capital

Industry Association Membership
German Venture Capital Association

Project Preferences

Type of Financing Preferred:
Early Stage
Expansion
Later Stage

Size of Investments Considered
Min Size of Investment Considered (000s): $1,400
Max Size of Investment Considered: No Limit

Geographical Preferences

United States
All U.S.

International
Europe
Germany
All International
Israel
Netherlands

Industry Preferences

Communications and Media
Telecommunications

Computer Software
Software

Internet Specific
Internet

Biotechnology
Biotechnology

Medical/Health
Medical/Health

Consumer Related
Entertainment and Leisure

Business Serv.
Media

Additional Information
Year Founded: 1999
Capital Under Management: $31,400,000
Current Activity Level : Actively seeking new investments

PRELUDE TECHNOLOGY INVESTMENTS LTD

Sycamore Studios
New Road, Over
Cambridge, United Kingdom CB4 5PJ
Phone: 44-1954-288-090
Fax: 44-1954-288-099
Website: www.prelude-technology.co.uk

Type of Firm
Private Firm Investing Own Capital

Industry Association Membership
British Venture Capital Association
European Venture Capital Association (EVCA)

Project Preferences

Role in Financing:
Prefer role as deal originator but will also invest in deals created by others

Type of Financing Preferred:
Early Stage
First Stage Financing
Seed
Start-up Financing

Size of Investments Considered
Min Size of Investment Considered (000s): $500
Max Size of Investment Considered (000s): $1,000

Geographical Preferences

International
Bermuda
Europe
France
Germany
Italy
Spain
United Kingdom

Industry Preferences

(% based on actual investment)

Biotechnology	43.2%
Communications and Media	16.2%
Medical/Health	16.0%
Semiconductors/Other Elect.	11.0%
Industrial/Energy	8.2%
Computer Software and Services	5.4%

Additional Information

Name of Most Recent Fund: Prelude Technology Fund II, Ltd.
Most Recent Fund Was Raised: 01/01/1989
Year Founded: 1984
Capital Under Management: $96,700,000
Current Activity Level : Actively seeking new investments
Method of Compensation: Return on invest. most important, but chg. closing fees, service fees, etc.

PRIMAXIS TECHNOLOGY VENTURES INC.

1 Richmond Street W.
8th Floor
Toronto, Canada M5H 3W4
Phone: 416-313-5210
Fax: 416-313-5218
Website: www.primaxis.com

Management and Staff

Joel Liederman, Vice President
Kerri Golden, Vice President
Tony Redpath, Vice President

Type of Firm

Private Firm Investing Own Capital

Project Preferences

Type of Financing Preferred:
Early Stage
Seed

Industry Preferences

Communications and Media
Telecommunications

Semiconductors/Other Elect.
Electronics
Semiconductor

Manufact.
Manufacturing

Additional Information

Year Founded: 2000
Capital Under Management: $55,000,000
Current Activity Level : Actively seeking new investments

PRIME TECHNOLOGY VENTURES NV

Entrada 102
Amsterdam, Netherlands 1096 EA
Phone: 31-20-330-06-50
Fax: 31-20-330-06-51
Website: www.ptventures.com

Management and Staff

Dolf Gransberg, Chief Financial Officer
Ilja Bobbert, Managing Partner
Pekka Roine, General Partner
Sake Bosch, Managing Partner

Type of Firm

Private Firm Investing Own Capital

Industry Association Membership

Dutch Venture Capital Associaton
European Venture Capital Association (EVCA)

Project Preferences

Type of Financing Preferred:
Early Stage
Expansion
Seed
Startup

Geographical Preferences

International
Europe
Israel

Industry Preferences

Communications and Media
Communications and Media

Computer Other
Computer Related

Semiconductors/Other Elect.
Electronics

Medical/Health
Medical/Health

Additional Information

Year Founded: 1999
Capital Under Management: $70,500,000
Current Activity Level : Actively seeking new investments

PRIMEPARTNERS ASSET MANAGEMENT PTE. LTD.

30 Raffles Place
#21-02 Caltex House
Singapore, Singapore 048622
Phone: 65-534-3766
Fax: 65-534-3266
Website: www.primepartners.com.sg

Other Offices

1201 Nine Queen's Road
Central, Hong Kong
Phone: 852-2537-5822
Fax: 852-2537-3475

15/F Jakarta Stock Exchange II
Jl. Jendel Sundiman Kav 52-53
Jakarta, Indonesia 12190
Phone: 62-21-515-4825
Fax: 62-21-515-4829

Management and Staff

Teo Ek Tor, Managing Partner
Toh Yiu Joe, Partner

Type of Firm

Private Firm Investing Own Capital

Project Preferences

Role in Financing:
Will function either as deal originator or investor in deals created by others

Type of Financing Preferred:
Expansion

Geographical Preferences

International
China
Hong Kong
Japan
Malaysia
North Korea
Singapore
Taiwan
Thailand

Industry Preferences

Communications and Media
Communications and Media

Semiconductors/Other Elect.
Electronics

Biotechnology
Biotechnology

Consumer Related
Consumer
Consumer Products
Consumer Services

Business Serv.
Media

Additional Information
Year Founded: 2000
Capital Under Management: $119,000,000
Current Activity Level : Actively seeking new investments

PRIVEQ CAPITAL FUNDS

240 Duncan Mill Road
Suite 602
Toronto, Canada M3B 3P1
Phone: 416-447-3330
Fax: 416-447-3331
E-mail: priveq@sympatico.ca

Type of Firm
Private Firm Investing Own Capital

Project Preferences

Role in Financing:
Prefer role as deal originator but will also invest in deals created by others

Type of Financing Preferred:
Industry Rollups
Leveraged Buyout
Mezzanine
Recapitalizations
Second Stage Financing
Special Situation

Size of Investments Considered
Min Size of Investment Considered (000s): $1,000
Max Size of Investment Considered: No Limit

Geographical Preferences

United States
Mid Atlantic
Midwest
Northeast
Northwest
Southeast

Canada
All Canada

Industry Preferences

Communications and Media
Communications and Media
Commercial Communications

Semiconductors/Other Elect.
Electronic Components

Medical/Health
Diagnostic Test Products
Disposable Med. Products

Consumer Related
Entertainment and Leisure
Retail
Food/Beverage
Consumer Products
Consumer Services

Industrial/Energy
Industrial Products

Business Serv.
Distribution

Manufact.
Publishing

Additional Information
Name of Most Recent Fund: Priveq II Limited Partnership
Most Recent Fund Was Raised: 01/01/1999
Year Founded: 1994
Capital Under Management: $37,000,000
Current Activity Level : Actively seeking new investments

PROCURITAS PARTNERS KB

Skeppsbron 20
Stockholm, Sweden SE-111 30
Phone: 46-8-50-614300
Fax: 46-8-50-614344
Website: www.procuritas.se

Other Offices

NY Ostergade 9
2.sal
Copenhagen, Denmark DK-1101
Phone: 45-3391-8700
Fax: 45-3391-8786

Management and Staff
Hans Karlander, Managing Director
Mikael Ahlstrom, Partner

Type of Firm
Private Equity Advisor or Fund of Fund Mgr

Project Preferences

Role in Financing:
Prefer role as deal originator

Type of Financing Preferred:
Management Buyouts

Size of Investments Considered
Min Size of Investment Considered (000s): $5,000
Max Size of Investment Considered (000s): $250,000

Geographical Preferences

International
Denmark
Finland
Sweden

Additional Information
Name of Most Recent Fund: Procuritas Capital Partners II
Most Recent Fund Was Raised: 03/01/1997
Year Founded: 1986
Capital Under Management: $100,000,000
Current Activity Level : Actively seeking new investments
Method of Compensation: Return on invest. most important, but chg. closing fees, service fees, etc.

PROSEED CAPITAL HOLDINGS CVA

De Broquevillelaan 162
Brussels, Belgium 1200
Phone: 32 2 772 1876
Fax: 32 2 772 3189
Website: www.proseedcapital.com

Management and Staff
Benjamin Van Oudenhove, Chairman & CEO
David Katsnelson, Vice President
Ori Shilo, Vice President
Pascal Weerts, Vice President

Type of Firm
Private Firm Investing Own Capital

Project Preferences

Type of Financing Preferred:
Early Stage
Seed
Startup

Geographical Preferences

United States
All U.S.

Canada
All Canada

International
Europe
India
Israel

Industry Preferences

Internet Specific
Internet

Additional Information

Year Founded: 1999
Current Activity Level : Actively seeking new investments

PROVEN PRIVATE EQUITY (FKA:GUINNESS MAHON DEVELOPMENT CAP.)

42 Craven Street
London, United Kingdom WC2N 5NG
Phone: 44 20 7451 6500
Fax: 44 20 7839 8349
Website: www.proven.co.uk

Other Offices

335 Madison Avenue
11th Floor
New York, United States of America 10017
Phone: 212 922 2391
Fax: 212 922 2358

Management and Staff

Gordon Power, Chief Executive Officer
Malcolm Moss, Founder
Stephen Edwards, Managing Director

Type of Firm

Private Firm Investing Own Capital

Industry Association Membership

British Venture Capital Association

Project Preferences

Role in Financing:
Prefer role as deal originator but will also invest in deals created by others

Type of Financing Preferred:
Early Stage
Expansion
Management Buyouts
Second Stage Financing
Startup
Unknown

Size of Investments Considered

Min Size of Investment Considered (000s): $600
Max Size of Investment Considered: No Limit

Geographical Preferences

United States
All U.S.

International
Europe
United Kingdom

Industry Preferences

Medical/Health
Medical/Health

Consumer Related
Entertainment and Leisure

Business Serv.
Media

Manufact.
Publishing

Additional Information

Name of Most Recent Fund: Global Rights Fund II, L.P.
Most Recent Fund Was Raised: 01/01/1997
Year Founded: 1984
Capital Under Management: $209,600,000
Current Activity Level : Actively seeking new investments
Method of Compensation: Return on invest. most important, but chg. closing fees, service fees, etc.

PROVIDENCE EQUITY PARTNERS, INC.(FKA: PROVIDENCE VENTURES)

78 Brook Street
1st Floor
London, United Kingdom W1Y 1YD
Phone: 44 207 514 8800
Fax: 44 207 629 2778

See Rhode Island for full listing.

PROXIMITAS AG VENTURE CAPITAL

Lotzingstrasse, 9
Munich, Germany D-81241
Phone: 49 89 896 6636
Fax: 49 89 896 66377
Website: www.proximitas.com

Management and Staff

Jan Porschmann, Managing Director

Type of Firm

Private Firm Investing Own Capital

Industry Association Membership

German Venture Capital Association

Project Preferences

Type of Financing Preferred:
Early Stage
Expansion
Seed
Startup

Size of Investments Considered

Min Size of Investment Considered (000s): $200
Max Size of Investment Considered (000s): $200,000

Geographical Preferences

International
Europe
Germany

Industry Preferences

Communications and Media
Telecommunications

Semiconductors/Other Elect.
Electronics

Industrial/Energy
Robotics

Additional Information

Year Founded: 1999
Capital Under Management: $9,000,000
Current Activity Level : Actively seeking new investments

PUTNAM LOVELL CAPITAL PARTNERS, L.P.

34 Brook Street
London, United Kingdom W1K 5DN
Phone: 020 7299 8500
Fax: 020 7299 8555

See California for full listing.

PYRAMID TECHNOLOGY VENTURES

42 rue de Bassano
Paris, France 75008
Phone: 33 1 56 892 892
Fax: 33 1 56 892 893

Other Offices

1000 Chestnut Street
Suite 11A
San Francisco, United States of America 94109
Phone: 1 415 292 9086

Management and Staff
Marc Cellier, Founding Partner

Type of Firm
Private Firm Investing Own Capital

Project Preferences

Type of Financing Preferred:
Balanced

Geographical Preferences

United States
All U.S.

International
Europe

Additional Information
Year Founded: 2000
Capital Under Management: $150,000,000
Current Activity Level : Actively seeking new investments

PYTHAGORAS NV

Ijzerlaan 54-56
Antwerp, Belgium 2060
Phone: 32-32211-441
Fax: 32-32133-544
Website: www.pythagoras.be

Management and Staff
Johan Koning, General Partner
Marc Van Rompaey, Founder
Mark Hoet, Partner
Stefaan Top, General Partner

Type of Firm
Private Firm Investing Own Capital

Industry Association Membership
European Venture Capital Association (EVCA)

Project Preferences

Type of Financing Preferred:
Early Stage
First Stage Financing
Second Stage Financing
Seed

Geographical Preferences

United States
All U.S.

International
Europe

Industry Preferences

Computer Software
Software

Additional Information
Year Founded: 1998
Capital Under Management: $44,700,000
Current Activity Level : Actively seeking new investments

QUADRIGA CAPITAL MANAGEMENT GMBH

Hamburger Allee 2-10
Frankfurt, Germany D-60486
Phone: 49-69-7950000
Fax: 49-69-795000-60
Website: www.quadriga-capital.de

Other Offices

Deputatskay St. 1
Yarozlavl, Russian Federation RF-150000
Phone: 7/0852/328789
Fax: 7/0852/329183

Nevski Prospekt
30 - Office No. 3.3
St. Petersburg, Russian Federation RF-191011
Phone: 7/812/3258474
Fax: 7/812/3258477

Osharskaya St. 52
Nizhny Novgorod , Russian Federation RF-603600
Phone: 7/8312/773255
Fax: 7/8312/773252

Management and Staff
Andreas Fendel
Max W. Roemer

Whom to Contact
Andreas Fendel
Max W. Roemer

Type of Firm
Private Equity Advisor or Fund of Fund Mgr

Industry Association Membership
European Venture Capital Association (EVCA)
German Venture Capital Association
National Venture Capital Association (NVCA)

Project Preferences

Role in Financing:
Prefer role as deal originator

Type of Financing Preferred:
Expansion
Generalist PE
Leveraged Buyout
Management Buyouts
Special Situation

Size of Investments Considered
Min Size of Investment Considered (000s): $15,000
Max Size of Investment Considered: No Limit

Geographical Preferences

International
Belgium
Eastern Europe
France
Germany
Luxembourg
Netherlands
Scandanavia/Nordic Region
Switzerland

Additional Information
Year Founded: 1994
Capital Under Management: $200,000,000
Current Activity Level : Actively seeking new investments
Method of Compensation: Return on invest. most important, but chg. closing fees, service fees, etc.

QUANTUM FUND, LTD.

TT Centre, Alrick Building
Mayfield Road
Edinburgh, United Kingdom EH9 3JL
Phone: 44 131 472 4719
Fax: 44 131 472 4776

Management and Staff
Alastair Macpherson, Partner
Mike Weber, Partner

Type of Firm
University Affiliated Program

Project Preferences

Type of Financing Preferred:
Seed

Geographical Preferences

International
United Kingdom

Additional Information
Capital Under Management: $900,000
Current Activity Level : Actively seeking new investments

QUESTER CAPITAL MANAGEMENT LTD

29 Queen Anne's Gate
London, United Kingdom SW1H 9BU
Phone: 44-171-222-5472
Fax: 44-171-222-5250
Website: www.quester.co.uk

Management and Staff
Andrew Holmes, Managing Director
John Spooner, Founder
Richard Drover, Chief Financial Officer

Type of Firm
Private Firm Investing Own Capital

Industry Association Membership
British Venture Capital Association

Project Preferences

Role in Financing:
Prefer role as deal originator but will also invest in deals created by others

Type of Financing Preferred:
First Stage Financing
Leveraged Buyout
Second Stage Financing
Special Situation
Start-up Financing

Size of Investments Considered
Min Size of Investment Considered (000s): $700
Max Size of Investment Considered: No Limit

Geographical Preferences

International
United Kingdom

Industry Preferences

(% based on actual investment)

Internet Specific	28.1%
Computer Software and Services	19.2%
Other Products	15.1%
Semiconductors/Other Elect.	14.5%
Biotechnology	14.5%
Consumer Related	3.1%
Communications and Media	2.9%
Industrial/Energy	2.6%

Additional Information
Name of Most Recent Fund: Quester VCT 2 PLC
Most Recent Fund Was Raised: 01/01/1999
Year Founded: 1984
Capital Under Management: $198,000,000
Current Activity Level : Actively seeking new investments
Method of Compensation: Return on invest. most important, but chg. closing fees, service fees, etc.

RED-STARS.COM

Ignaz Kock-Strasse 3
Vienna, Austria 1210
Phone: 43 1272 0272
Fax: 43 1272 0272-20
Website: www.red-stars.com

Other Offices
Bld. 2, 13, Nikoloyamskaya Str.
Moscow, Russian Federation 109240
Phone: 7 095 363 60 90
Fax: 7 095 363 60 99

red-stars.com Sp. z o.o.
Al. Jerozolimskie 133/113
Wasaw, Poland 02-304
Phone: 48/22 /822 0008
Fax: 48/22 /822 0108

Management and Staff
Peter Schonhofer, Chief Financial Officer
Thomas Huber, Chief Executive Officer
Thomas Streimelweger, Founder

Type of Firm
Incubators

Project Preferences

Type of Financing Preferred:
Startup

Geographical Preferences

International
Central Europe
Eastern Europe
Russia
Turkey

Industry Preferences

Internet Specific
Internet

Additional Information
Year Founded: 2000
Capital Under Management: $2,900,000
Current Activity Level : Actively seeking new investments

REGENT PACIFIC PRIVATE EQUITY

904-906 Asia Pacific Finance
Tower, 3 Garden Road
Central, Hong Kong
Phone: 852-2514-6111
Fax: 852-2810-4396
Website: www.regentpac.com

Management and Staff
Jim Mellon, Chief Executive Officer

Type of Firm
Private Firm Investing Own Capital

Additional Information
Year Founded: 1999
Capital Under Management: $100,000,000
Current Activity Level : Actively seeking new investments

REITEN & CO STRATEGIC INVESTMENTS AS

Haakon VII's gate 1
PO Box 1531
Oslo, Norway 0117
Phone: 47 23 11 37 20
Fax: 47 23 11 37 21
Website: www.reitenco.no

Management and Staff
Bard Brath Ingero, Partner
John Bjerkan, Partner
Kathryn Baker Pettersen, Partner
Morten Bosterud, Partner
Narve Reiten, Partner
Thorstein Bostad, Partner

Type of Firm
Private Firm Investing Own Capital

Industry Association Membership
European Venture Capital Association (EVCA)

Project Preferences

Type of Financing Preferred:
Expansion
Management Buyouts

Geographical Preferences

United States
All U.S.

International
Denmark
Finland
Norway
Sweden

Industry Preferences

Computer Other
Computer Related

Medical/Health
Medical/Health

Consumer Related
Consumer

Industrial/Energy
Energy

Financial Services
Financial Services
Insurance
Real Estate

Business Serv.
Services

Additional Information
Capital Under Management: $9,100,000
Current Activity Level : Actively seeking new investments

RENAISSANCE PARTNERS

Blanicka 28
Prague 2, Czech Republic 12000
Phone: 420-2-2225-2407
Fax: 420-2-225-1791
Website: www.rp.cz

Other Offices

ul Lowicka 44
Warsaw, Poland 02-551
Phone: 48-22-480773
Fax: 48-39-122416

Management and Staff
Alois Strnad, Managing Partner
Dalibor Jerabek, Partner

Type of Firm
Private Firm Investing Own Capital

Industry Association Membership
Czech Venture Capital Association
European Venture Capital Association (EVCA)

Project Preferences

Type of Financing Preferred:
Balanced

Geographical Preferences

International
Czech Republic
Eastern Europe
Poland
Slovak Repub.

Additional Information
Year Founded: 1993
Capital Under Management: $89,000,000
Current Activity Level : Actively seeking new investments

RIVERSIDE MANAGEMENT GROUP

Stranveien 50
Lysaker, Norway 1366
Phone: 476-712-3900
Fax: 476-710-4990

See New York for full listing.

RMB VENTURES LIMITED

Level 5, Underwood House
37-49 Pitt Street
Sydney, Australia 02000
Phone: 612-9256-6245
Fax: 612-9251-5957
Website: www.rmb.com.au

Management and Staff
Philip Latham, Managing Director

Type of Firm
Investment/Merchant Bank Subsid/Affil

Industry Association Membership
Australian Venture Capital Association (AVCAL)

Project Preferences

Type of Financing Preferred:
Expansion
Management Buyouts

Size of Investments Considered
Min Size of Investment Considered (000s): $6,500
Max Size of Investment Considered (000s): $13,000

Geographical Preferences

International
Oceania/Australasia

Additional Information
Year Founded: 1998
Capital Under Management: $65,000,000
Current Activity Level : Actively seeking new investments

ROTHSCHILD BIOSCIENCE UNIT

Five Arrows House
St. Swithin's Lane
London, United Kingdom EC4N 8NR
Phone: 171-623-1000
Fax: 44-171-623-6261

Type of Firm
Commercial Bank Affiliate or Subsidiary

Project Preferences

Role in Financing:
Prefer role as deal originator but will also invest in deals created by others

Type of Financing Preferred:
First Stage Financing
Second Stage Financing
Seed
Start-up Financing

Geographical Preferences

United States
All U.S.

Canada
All Canada

Industry Preferences
(% based on actual investment)

Communications and Media	49.1%
Medical/Health	17.5%
Industrial/Energy	15.1%
Biotechnology	12.7%
Computer Software and Services	3.5%
Computer Hardware	2.1%

Additional Information
Name of Most Recent Fund: International Biotechnology Trust
Most Recent Fund Was Raised: 12/31/1994
Year Founded: 1987
Capital Under Management: $400,000,000
Current Activity Level : Inactive / Unknown
Method of Compensation: Return on investment is of primary concern, do not charge fees

ROTHSCHILD VENTURES ASIA PTE LTD.

The Exchange
20 Cecil Street Suite 09-00
Singapore, Singapore 49705
Phone: 65-535-8311
Fax: 65-538-1935
E-mail: rva@pacific.net.sg
Website: www.nmrothschild.com.sg

Management and Staff
Benjamin Yeo, Managing Director

Whom to Contact
Benjamin Yeo
Boey Sek Onn
Sek Onn Boey

Type of Firm
Investment/Merchant Bank Subsid/Affil

Industry Association Membership
Singapore Venture Capital Association

Project Preferences

Role in Financing:
Prefer role as deal originator but will also invest in deals created by others

Type of Financing Preferred:
First Stage Financing
Leveraged Buyout
Mezzanine
Seed
Special Situation
Start-up Financing

Size of Investments Considered
Min Size of Investment Considered (000s): $250
Max Size of Investment Considered (000s): $5,000

Geographical Preferences

International
Asia
India

Industry Preferences

Communications and Media
Commercial Communications
Data Communications
Satellite Microwave Comm.

Computer Software
Computer Services
Systems Software
Applications Software
Artificial Intelligence

Semiconductors/Other Elect.
Electronic Components
Laser Related
Fiber Optics
Analytic/Scientific

Medical/Health
Diagnostic Services
Drug/Equipmt Delivery
Disposable Med. Products
Hospitals/Clinics/Primary
Hospital/Other Instit.
Pharmaceuticals

Consumer Related
Education Related

Transportation
Transportation

Agr/Forestr/Fish
Agriculture related

Additional Information
Year Founded: 1990
Capital Under Management: $58,000,000
Current Activity Level : Actively seeking new investments
Method of Compensation: Return on investment is of primary concern, do not charge fees

ROYAL BANK PRIVATE EQUITY (FKA: ROYAL BANK DEVELOPMENT CAP)

26 St. Andrew Square
Edinburgh, United Kingdom EH2 1AF
Phone: 44-131-524-8300
Fax: 44-131-557-2900
Website: www.rbs.co.uk

Other Offices

62 Threadneedle Street
London, United Kingdom EC2R 8HP
Phone: 44 20 7842 0130

75-77 Colmore Row
Birmingham, United Kingdom B3 2AP
Phone: 44 121-236 5656
Fax: 44 121-237 5636

Moncrieff House
69 West Nile Street
Glasgow, United Kingdom G1 2LT
Phone: 44 141-353 8300
Fax: 44 141-353 2060

Waterhouse Square
138-142 Holborn
London, United Kingdom EC1N 2TH
Phone: 44 20 7842 0130
Fax: 44 20 7427 9973

Management and Staff
Bill Troup, Partner
Mark Nicholls, Managing Director

Whom to Contact
Douglas Kearney

Type of Firm
Commercial Bank Affiliate or Subsidiary

Industry Association Membership
British Venture Capital Association

Project Preferences

Role in Financing:
Prefer role as deal originator but will also invest in deals created by others

Type of Financing Preferred:
Balanced
Early Stage
Expansion
Later Stage
Leveraged Buyout
Management Buyouts
Recapitalizations
Second Stage Financing
Turnaround

Size of Investments Considered
Min Size of Investment Considered (000s): $7,200
Max Size of Investment Considered (000s): $108,300

Geographical Preferences

International
Europe
France
Spain
United Kingdom

Industry Preferences

(% based on actual investment)

Other Products	66.1%
Consumer Related	15.9%
Communications and Media	6.5%
Computer Software and Services	6.2%
Semiconductors/Other Elect.	3.0%
Internet Specific	2.2%

Additional Information
Year Founded: 1993
Capital Under Management: $678,600,000
Current Activity Level : Actively seeking new investments
Method of Compensation: Return on invest. most important, but chg. closing fees, service fees, etc.

ROYNAT VENTURES

40 King Street West
26th Floor
Toronto, Canada M5H 1H1
Phone: 416-933-2667
Fax: 416-933-2783
Website: www.roynatcapital.com

Other Offices

1800 McGill College
Suite 1800
Montreal, Canada H8A 3J6
Phone: 514-987-4900
Fax: 514-987-4905

Canterra Tower
400 Third Avenue
Calgary, Canada T2P 4H2
Phone: 403-269-7755
Fax: 403-269-7701

Purdy's Wharf Tower II
1969 Upper Water Street
Halifax, Canada B3J 3R7
Phone: 902-429-3500
Fax: 902-423-5607

Management and Staff
Bob Roy
Earl Lande
James Webster
Mark Gardhouse
Robert Théoret
Wray Stannard

Whom to Contact
Bob Roy
Earl Lande
James Webster
Mark Gardhouse
Robert Théoret
Wray Stannard

Type of Firm
Investment/Merchant Bank Subsid/Affil

Industry Association Membership
Canadian Venture Capital Association

Project Preferences

Role in Financing:
Prefer role as deal originator but will also invest in deals created by others

Type of Financing Preferred:
Early Stage
Expansion

Size of Investments Considered
Min Size of Investment Considered (000s): $3,000
Max Size of Investment Considered: No Limit

Geographical Preferences

Canada
All Canada

Additional Information
Year Founded: 1962
Capital Under Management: $78,000,000
Current Activity Level : Actively seeking new investments
Method of Compensation: Return on invest. most important, but chg. closing fees, service fees, etc.

RUSSEL MILLER ADVISORS ASIA, LLC

4705-06 Central Plaza
18 Harbour Road
Wanchai, Hong Kong
Phone: 852-2534-2600
Fax: 852-2815-5289

See California for full listing.

S-REFIT GMBH & CO KG

Sedanstrasse 15
Regensburg, Germany D-93055
Phone: 49 941 695 560
Fax: 49 941 695 5611
Website: www.s-refit.de

Type of Firm
Bank Group

Industry Association Membership
German Venture Capital Association

Project Preferences

Type of Financing Preferred:
Expansion
Leveraged Buyout
Seed
Startup

Geographical Preferences

International
Germany

Additional Information

Year Founded: 1990
Capital Under Management: $9,400,000
Current Activity Level : Actively seeking new investments

SAARLANDISCHE WAGNISFINANZIERUNGSGESELLSCHAFT MBH (AKA SWG)

Johannisstrasse 2
Saarbrucken, Germany D-66111
Phone: 49 681 37958-0
Fax: 49 681 37958-29
Website: www.swgmbh.de

Management and Staff

Lutz Schroter, Partner

Type of Firm

Bank Group

Industry Association Membership

German Venture Capital Association

Project Preferences

Type of Financing Preferred:
Early Stage
Expansion
Startup

Geographical Preferences

International
Germany

Industry Preferences

Communications and Media
Communications and Media

Biotechnology
Biotechnology

Medical/Health
Medical/Health

Industrial/Energy
Materials

Additional Information

Year Founded: 1998
Current Activity Level : Actively seeking new investments

SADOT VENTURE CAPITAL MANAGEMENT (1992) LTD

Levenstein Tower
23 Petach Tikva Road
Tel Aviv, Israel 61361
Phone: 972 3 560 6005
Fax: 972 3 560 6004
Website: www.sadot.co.il

Management and Staff

Abraham Radzinski, Partner
Ben-Zion Israel, Partner
Jack Elaad, Managing Partner
Roy Segev, Partner

Type of Firm

Private Firm Investing Own Capital

Project Preferences

Type of Financing Preferred:
Early Stage
Startup

Size of Investments Considered

Min Size of Investment Considered (000s): $500
Max Size of Investment Considered (000s): $500,000

Geographical Preferences

International
Israel

Additional Information

Year Founded: 1992
Capital Under Management: $40,000,000
Current Activity Level : Actively seeking new investments

SAFFRON HILL VENTURES (FKA LOOTLAB LTD.)

Clerkenwell House
67 Clerkenwell Road
London, United Kingdom EC1R 5BL
Phone: 44-207-693-8300
Website: www.lootlab.com

Management and Staff

Ranjeet Bhatia, Chief Executive Officer
Shawn Luetchens, Chief Executive Officer

Type of Firm

Incubators

Project Preferences

Type of Financing Preferred:
Early Stage
First Stage Financing
Seed
Startup

Size of Investments Considered

Min Size of Investment Considered (000s): $700
Max Size of Investment Considered: No Limit

Geographical Preferences

International
Europe
United Kingdom

Industry Preferences

Internet Specific
Internet

Additional Information

Capital Under Management: $20,000,000
Current Activity Level : Actively seeking new investments

SAND AIRE PRIVATE EQUITY LTD

101 Wigmore Street
London, United Kingdom W1U 1QU
Phone: 44 20 7290 5200
Fax: 44 20 7495 0204
Website: www.sandaire.co.uk

Management and Staff

David Williams, Managing Director

Type of Firm

Private Firm Investing Own Capital

Industry Association Membership

British Venture Capital Association

Project Preferences

Type of Financing Preferred:
Expansion
Leveraged Buyout
Mezzanine
Turnaround

Geographical Preferences

International
United Kingdom

Additional Information

Year Founded: 1997
Capital Under Management: $75,000,000
Current Activity Level : Actively seeking new investments

SANPAOLO IMI PRIVATE EQUITY S.P.A.

Viale dell'Arte, 25
Rome, Italy 00144
Phone: 39-659-593-211
Fax: 39-335-775-1389
Website: www.spipe.it

Other Offices

Via Brera, 19
Milan, Italy 20121
Phone: 39-272-383-150
Fax: 39-272-383-169

Management and Staff

Carlo Viola, Managing Director
Claudio Montanari, Managing Director

Type of Firm

Investment/Merchant Bank Subsid/Affil

Project Preferences

Role in Financing:
Prefer role as deal originator but will also invest in deals created by others

Type of Financing Preferred:
Balanced
Early Stage
Expansion
Generalist PE
Leveraged Buyout
Management Buyouts

Size of Investments Considered
Min Size of Investment Considered (000s): $2,000
Max Size of Investment Considered (000s): $20,000

Geographical Preferences

International
Italy

Industry Preferences

Communications and Media
Radio & TV Broadcasting
Wireless Communications

Computer Software
Software

Internet Specific
E-Commerce Technology
Internet
Web Aggregration/Portals

Semiconductors/Other Elect.
Electronic Components
Fiber Optics

Medical/Health
Medical Products
Pharmaceuticals

Consumer Related
Consumer
Entertainment and Leisure
Retail
Food/Beverage

Industrial/Energy
Industrial Products
Machinery

Business Serv.
Services
Media

Manufact.
Manufacturing

Additional Information

Year Founded: 1987
Capital Under Management: $111,500,000
Current Activity Level : Making few, if any, new investments
Method of Compensation: Return on investment is of primary concern, do not charge fees

SASKATCHEWAN GOVERNMENT GROWTH FUND

1810 Hamilton St., Suite 1210
Canada Trust Tower
Regina, Canada S4P 4B4
Phone:

Management and Staff

Rob Duguid, Vice President

Whom to Contact

Gary K. Benson

Type of Firm

Private Firm Investing Own Capital

Project Preferences

Role in Financing:
Prefer role as deal originator but will also invest in deals created by others

Type of Financing Preferred:
First Stage Financing
Mezzanine
Second Stage Financing
Start-up Financing

Geographical Preferences

Canada
Western Canada

Additional Information

Name of Most Recent Fund: SGGF VIII Ltd.
Most Recent Fund Was Raised: 03/01/1999
Year Founded: 1989
Capital Under Management: $160,600,000
Current Activity Level : Actively seeking new investments
Method of Compensation: Return on invest. most important, but chg. closing fees, service fees, etc.

SAVOY/SOCIOS FONDOS DE FINANCIACON MANAGEMENT

Paseao Caftellana 31
1st Floor
Madrid, Spain 28046
Phone: 34 91 308 30 37
Fax: 34 91 310 50 11

Management and Staff

Jaime Carbo, Partner
Jose De Santiago, Partner

Type of Firm

Private Firm Investing Own Capital

Project Preferences

Type of Financing Preferred:
Balanced

Geographical Preferences

International
Europe
All International

Additional Information
Capital Under Management: $30,000,000
Current Activity Level : Actively seeking new investments

SCHNEIDER ELECTRIC VENTURES

58 avenue d'iena
Paris, France F-75116
Phone: 33 1 5367 8060
Fax: 33 1 5367 8070
Website: ventures.schneider-electric.com/index_frameset.htm

Management and Staff
Christelle Trinh, Partner
Eric Pilaud, Vice President
Jean-Marc Bally, Partner

Type of Firm
Non-Financial Corp. Affiliate or Subsidiary

Project Preferences

Type of Financing Preferred:
First Stage Financing
Second Stage Financing
Startup

Size of Investments Considered
Min Size of Investment Considered (000s): $500
Max Size of Investment Considered (000s): $500,000

Geographical Preferences

United States
All U.S.

International
Europe
All International

Industry Preferences

Communications and Media
Communications and Media

Internet Specific
Internet

Semiconductors/Other Elect.
Electronics

Industrial/Energy
Industrial Products
Factory Automation

Additional Information
Year Founded: 2000
Capital Under Management: $46,900,000
Current Activity Level : Actively seeking new investments

SCHOONER CAPITAL INTERNATIONAL, L.P.

Plac Powstancow Warszawy 1
Pokoj 256
00-950 Warsaw, Poland
Phone: 48-22-269142
Fax: 48-22-269136

See Massachusetts for full listing.

SCHRODER CAPITAL PARTNERS (ASIA) PTE LTD

#10-02 Republic Plaza Tower 1
9 Raffles Place
Singapore, Singapore 048619
Phone: 65-536-6177
Fax: 65-536-6077

Other Offices

906 Maker Chambers V
Nariman Point
Mumbai, India 400 021
Phone: 9122-288-2763
Fax: 9122-288-2766

Suite 1103, St. George's Bldg.
2 Ice House Street
Central, Hong Kong
Phone: 852-2801-6199
Fax: 852-2801-7979

Management and Staff
Deepak Vaidya, Partner
Sanjay Sehgal, Partner

Type of Firm
Affiliate/Subsidary of Oth. Financial. Instit.

Project Preferences

Role in Financing:
Prefer role as deal originator

Type of Financing Preferred:
Expansion
Leveraged Buyout

Geographical Preferences

International
Australia
Hong Kong
India
Japan
New Zealand
Singapore
Taiwan
Thailand

Industry Preferences

Medical/Health
Medical/Health

Consumer Related
Consumer Products
Consumer Services

Manufact.
Manufacturing

Additional Information
Capital Under Management: $723,300,000
Current Activity Level : Actively seeking new investments

SCHRODER VENTURES

Suite 1103, St. George's Bldg.
2 Ice House Street
Central, Hong Kong
Phone: 852-2801-6199
Fax: 852-2801-7979

See Massachusetts for full listing.

SCOOT.COM PLC

Beaufort House
Cricketfield Road
Uxbridge, Middlesex, United Kingdom UB8 1QG
Phone: 44 1895 520 000
Fax: 44 1895 520 001
Website: www.scoot.com/plc

Management and Staff
Robert Bonnier, Chief Executive Officer
Ronald Dorjee, Chief Financial Officer

Type of Firm
Private Firm Investing Own Capital

Project Preferences

Type of Financing Preferred:
Balanced
Expansion

Geographical Preferences

United States
All U.S.

International
Europe
United Kingdom

Industry Preferences

Internet Specific
Internet

Additional Information

Year Founded: 1995
Current Activity Level : Actively seeking new investments

SCOTTISH DEVELOPMENT FINANCE (SDF)

120 Bothwell Street
Glasgow, United Kingdom G2 7JP
Phone: 44-141-248-2700
Fax: 44-141-204-3648
E-mail: calum.peterson@scotent.co.uk
Website: www.scotent.co.uk

Management and Staff

Robert Crawford, Chief Executive Officer

Type of Firm

State Govt Affiliated NEC

Industry Association Membership

British Venture Capital Association
European Venture Capital Association (EVCA)

Project Preferences

Type of Financing Preferred:
Expansion
Startup

Geographical Preferences

International
United Kingdom

Additional Information

Year Founded: 1991
Capital Under Management: $101,500,000
Current Activity Level : Actively seeking new investments

SCOTTISH EQUITY PARTNERS LIMITED

17 Blythswood Square
Glasgow, United Kingdom G2 4AD
Phone: 44 141 273 4000
Fax: 44 141 273 4001
Website: www.sepl.co.uk

Management and Staff

Calum Paterson, Managing Director

Type of Firm

Private Firm Investing Own Capital

Project Preferences

Type of Financing Preferred:
Early Stage
Expansion
Seed
Startup

Geographical Preferences

International
United Kingdom

Industry Preferences

(% based on actual investment)

Computer Software and Services	54.5%
Semiconductors/Other Elect.	15.5%
Biotechnology	10.3%
Internet Specific	10.2%
Communications and Media	9.5%

Additional Information

Year Founded: 2000
Capital Under Management: $189,000,000
Current Activity Level : Actively seeking new investments

SEAPORT CAPITAL

Stradttor 1
Dusseldorf, Germany 40219
Phone: 49 211 60042100
Fax: 49 211 60042200

See New York for full listing.

SEB E-INVEST

Kungstradgardsgatan 8
Stockholm, Sweden 106 40
Phone: 46 8 763 8000
Fax: 46 8 763 9080
E-mail: sebeinvest@seb.se
Website: www.seb.se

Type of Firm

Affiliate/Subsidary of Oth. Financial. Instit.

Industry Association Membership

Swedish Venture Capital Association

Project Preferences

Type of Financing Preferred:
Early Stage
Expansion

Geographical Preferences

International
Scandanavia/Nordic Region
Sweden

Industry Preferences

Communications and Media
Communications and Media

Additional Information

Capital Under Management: $115,200,000
Current Activity Level : Actively seeking new investments

SEB FORETAGSINVEST

Hamngatan 24
Stockholm, Sweden 10640
Phone: 46-8/763-79-00
Fax: 46-8/763-79-09
Website: www.foretagsinvest.seb.se

Management and Staff

Bjorn Osterlund, Partner
Dan Peterson, Partner
Frederick Johansson, Partner
Hans Engblom, Partner
Jan Sundberg, Chief Executive Officer
Thomas Sjostrom, Partner
Ulf Lewander, Partner

Type of Firm

Investment/Merchant Bank Subsid/Affil

Industry Association Membership

European Venture Capital Association (EVCA)
Swedish Venture Capital Association

Project Preferences

Type of Financing Preferred:
Early Stage
Expansion
Generalist PE
Leveraged Buyout

Geographical Preferences

International
Eastern Europe
Scandanavia/Nordic Region

Industry Preferences

Communications and Media
Telecommunications

Computer Other
Computer Related

Semiconductors/Other Elect.
Electronics

Biotechnology
Biotechnology

Medical/Health
Medical/Health

Industrial/Energy
Industrial Products

Additional Information

Year Founded: 1999
Capital Under Management: $52,000,000
Current Activity Level : Actively seeking new investments

SEED CAPITAL INVESTMENTS

Bernadottelaan 15
P.O. Box 8323
Utrecht, Netherlands 3503 RH
Phone: 31-30-296-5347
Fax: 31-30-294-1526

Management and Staff

G.A. Monaster
H.J. Grande

Whom to Contact

G.A. Monaster
H.J. Grande

Type of Firm

Private Firm Investing Own Capital

Industry Association Membership

European Venture Capital Association (EVCA)

Project Preferences

Role in Financing:
Prefer role in deals created by others

Type of Financing Preferred:
Seed

Geographical Preferences

International
Bermuda
Netherlands

Industry Preferences

Biotechnology
Biotechnology

Medical/Health
Diagnostic Services
Diagnostic Test Products
Drug/Equipmt Delivery
Medical Products
Pharmaceuticals

Consumer Related
Food/Beverage

Industrial/Energy
Industrial Products

Agr/Forestr/Fish
Agriculture related

Additional Information

Year Founded: 1994
Capital Under Management: $1,500,000
Current Activity Level : Actively seeking new investments
Method of Compensation: Return on invest. most important, but chg. closing fees, service fees, etc.

SEED CAPITAL LTD

The Magdalen Centre
The Oxford Science Park
Oxford, United Kingdom OX4 4GA
Phone: 44-1865-784466
Fax: 44-1865-784430
Website: www.oxfordtechnology.com

Management and Staff

Lucius Cary, Managing Director

Type of Firm

Private Firm Investing Own Capital

Industry Association Membership

British Venture Capital Association

Project Preferences

Role in Financing:
Prefer role as deal originator but will also invest in deals created by others

Type of Financing Preferred:
Early Stage
Seed
Startup

Geographical Preferences

International
United Kingdom

Industry Preferences

(% based on actual investment)

Medical/Health	26.9%
Industrial/Energy	18.1%
Biotechnology	15.5%
Semiconductors/Other Elect.	12.7%
Computer Software and Services	11.4%
Communications and Media	6.7%
Computer Hardware	5.6%
Internet Specific	3.0%

Additional Information

Name of Most Recent Fund: Oxford Technology Venture Capital Trust
Most Recent Fund Was Raised: 04/01/1997
Year Founded: 1983
Capital Under Management: $7,700,000
Current Activity Level : Actively seeking new investments
Method of Compensation: Return on invest. most important, but chg. closing fees, service fees, etc.

SHANGHAI INFORMATION INVESTMENT (SII)

1318 Beijing Rd. (W)
Shanghai, China 200040
Phone: 8621-6207-7004
Fax: 8621-6207-7001
Website: www.sii.com.cn

Management and Staff

Cai Xiaohong, President

Type of Firm

Non-Financial Corp. Affiliate or Subsidiary

Project Preferences

Type of Financing Preferred:
Balanced

Geographical Preferences

International
China

Additional Information

Current Activity Level : Actively seeking new investments

SHANGHAI INTERNATIONAL ASSET MANAGEMENT (HK) COMPANY LTD

Room 1608 Jardine House
Central, Hong Kong
Phone: 852-2840-1608
Fax: 852-2840-1286

Management and Staff

Qu Cheng Kang, Vice President
Song Wee Tan, President

Type of Firm

Private Firm Investing Own Capital

Industry Association Membership

Hungarian Venture Capital Association

Additional Information

Year Founded: 1993
Capital Under Management: $96,000,000
Current Activity Level : Actively seeking new investments

SHANNON DEVELOPMENT COMPANY

Park House
National Technology Park
Castleroy, Limerick, Ireland, Republic of
Phone: 353 61/33.65.55
Fax: 353 61/33.65.45
E-mail: investments@shannon-dev.ie
Website: www.shannon-dev.ie/investments

Management and Staff

Geoff McMullen, Partner
Michael Halpin, Partner
Michelle O'Grady, Partner

Type of Firm

SBIC Not elsewhere classified

Industry Association Membership

European Venture Capital Association (EVCA)

Project Preferences

Role in Financing:
Prefer role as deal originator but will also invest in deals created by others

Type of Financing Preferred:
First Stage Financing
Second Stage Financing
Seed
Start-up Financing

Size of Investments Considered

Min Size of Investment Considered (000s): $100
Max Size of Investment Considered (000s): $5,000

Geographical Preferences

International
Ireland

Industry Preferences

Communications and Media
Telecommunications
Wireless Communications

Computer Hardware
Integrated Turnkey System

Computer Software
Computer Services
Systems Software
Applications Software

Internet Specific
Internet

Semiconductors/Other Elect.
Electronic Components
Component Testing Equipmt
Analytic/Scientific

Biotechnology
Agricultural/Animal Bio.

Medical/Health
Medical Products
Pharmaceuticals

Consumer Related
Consumer
Food/Beverage

Transportation
Aerospace

Agr/Forestr/Fish
Agriculture related

Additional Information

Year Founded: 1959
Capital Under Management: $17,000,000
Current Activity Level : Actively seeking new investments
Method of Compensation: Return on invest. most important, but chg. closing fees, service fees, etc.

SHAW, KWEI & PARTNERS LIMITED

#1810 Hutchison House
10 Harcourt Road
Central, Hong Kong
Phone: 852-2868-5883
Fax: 852-2523-4142
Website: www.shawkwei.com

Management and Staff

John Pinkel, Partner
Kyle Shaw, Managing Director
Randy Kwei, Partner

Type of Firm

Private Firm Investing Own Capital

Project Preferences

Type of Financing Preferred:
Early Stage
Expansion
Later Stage
Management Buyouts
Mezzanine

Geographical Preferences

International
China
Hong Kong
Indonesia
Korea, South
Malaysia
Philippines
Singapore
Taiwan
Thailand

Additional Information

Name of Most Recent Fund: Asian Value Investment Fund
Most Recent Fund Was Raised: 04/01/2000
Year Founded: 1998
Capital Under Management: $26,000,000
Current Activity Level : Actively seeking new investments

SHIGAGIN CAPITAL CO., LTD.

4-28 Hama-machi, Ohtsu City
Shiga Prefecture
Ohtsu, Japan
Phone: 077-521-2070
Fax: 077-521-2878

Type of Firm
Private Firm Investing Own Capital

Project Preferences

Type of Financing Preferred:
Balanced

Geographical Preferences

International
Japan

Additional Information
Year Founded: 1996
Capital Under Management: $14,700,000
Current Activity Level : Actively seeking new investments

SHREM FUDIM KELNER TECHNOLOGIES LTD.

21 Haarbah St.
Tel Aviv, Israel 64739
Phone: 9723-684-5555
Fax: 9723-684-5554
Website: www.sfk.co.il

Management and Staff
Yair Fudim, Chief Executive Officer

Type of Firm
Affiliate/Subsidary of Oth. Financial. Instit.

Project Preferences

Type of Financing Preferred:
Seed

Geographical Preferences

International
Israel

Industry Preferences

Communications and Media
Telecommunications

Internet Specific
Internet

Additional Information
Year Founded: 1991
Capital Under Management: $74,000,000
Current Activity Level : Actively seeking new investments

SIEMENS VENTURE CAPITAL GMBH

Wittelsbacherplatz 2
Munich, Germany 80333
Phone: 49-89-636-33585
Fax: 49-89-636-34884
Website: www.siemens.de/svc

Other Offices

2, Kaufman Street
P.O. Box 50043
Tel Aviv, Israel 61500
Phone: 972-3-5163-431
Fax: 972-3-5163-433

4900 Old Ironsides Drive
P.O. Box 58075, Mail Stop 104
Santa Clara, United States of America 95052-8075

Management and Staff
Bjorn Christensen, President
Louis Rajczi, Vice President
Penne Stockinger, President
Steffen Schuster, Vice President
Thomas Kolbinger, Chief Financial Officer
Vesa Jormakka, Vice President

Type of Firm
Non-Financial Corp. Affiliate or Subsidiary

Industry Association Membership
European Venture Capital Association (EVCA)
German Venture Capital Association
National Venture Capital Association (NVCA)

Project Preferences

Type of Financing Preferred:
Early Stage
Mezzanine
Seed
Startup

Geographical Preferences

United States
All U.S.

International
Asia
Europe
Germany
Israel

Industry Preferences

(% based on actual investment)

Other Products	75.8%
Communications and Media	8.7%
Internet Specific	7.5%
Computer Hardware	3.9%
Computer Software and Services	3.6%
Semiconductors/Other Elect.	0.5%

Additional Information
Year Founded: 1999
Capital Under Management: $200,000,000
Current Activity Level : Actively seeking new investments

SILKROUTE CAPITAL LIMITED

371 Beach Road
#25-01 Keypoint
Singapore, Singapore 199597
Phone: 65-298-4664
Fax: 65-298-4994
E-mail: info@silkroute.com
Website: www.silkroute.com

Management and Staff
Felix Tan, Managing Director

Type of Firm
Affiliate/Subsidary of Oth. Financial. Instit.

Project Preferences

Type of Financing Preferred:
Early Stage
Startup

Geographical Preferences

International
Asia
Singapore

Industry Preferences

Internet Specific
Internet

Additional Information
Year Founded: 1994
Capital Under Management: $15,000,000
Current Activity Level : Actively seeking new investments

SINGAPORE TECHNOLOGIES TELEMEDIA (AKA: ST TELEMEDIA)

51 Cuppage Road
#10-11/17 StarHub Centre
Singapore, Singapore 229 469
Phone: 65-723-8777
Fax: 65-835-0200
E-mail: tanmelinda@stt.st.com.sg
Website: www.sttcomms.com

Management and Staff
Irene Lum, Chief Financial Officer
Lee Theng Kiat, President

Type of Firm
Non-Financial Corp. Affiliate or Subsidiary

Project Preferences
Type of Financing Preferred:
Balanced

Geographical Preferences
International
Singapore

Industry Preferences
Communications and Media
Telecommunications
Data Communications

Internet Specific
Internet

Additional Information
Year Founded: 1994
Current Activity Level : Actively seeking new investments

SINGTEL VENTURES

31 Exeter Road
Comcentre
Singapore, Singapore 239732
Phone: 65-838-3388
Fax: 65-738-3769
Website: www.singtel.com

Management and Staff
Wai-Leong Kong, Managing Director

Type of Firm
Non-Financial Corp. Affiliate or Subsidiary

Project Preferences
Type of Financing Preferred:
Early Stage
Seed
Start-up Financing

Geographical Preferences
International
Singapore

Industry Preferences
Communications and Media
Telecommunications

Business Serv.
Media

Additional Information
Year Founded: 1999
Capital Under Management: $50,000,000
Current Activity Level : Actively seeking new investments

SIPAREX GROUP (FKA:SIPAREX PROVINCES DE FRANCE)

139, rue Vendome
Lyon, France F - 69006
Phone: 33-4-7283-2323
Fax: 33-4-7283-2300
Website: www.siparex.com

Other Offices

15 rue de Belleville
Nantes, France F - 44100
Phone: 33 02 40 69 38 38
Fax: 33 02 40 69 01 50

166 rue du Faubourg Saint-Honore
Paris, France F - 75008
Phone: 33 01 53 93 02 20
Fax: 33 01 53 93 02 30

17 rue Vorobiov
Smolensk, Russian Federation 214006
Phone: 7 081 00 34 789

1835 Franklin ave no 1501
San Francisco, United States of America 94109

28 rue de la republique
BP 56087
Besancon cedex 6 , France 25013
Phone: 33 03 81 25 06 14
Fax: 33 03 21 25 06 13

Management and Staff
Benoit Metais, Managing Director
Denis Rodarie, Managing Director
Dominique Nouvellet, Chief Executive Officer
Jean-Francois Puech, Managing Director
Paul Tholly, Managing Director
Pierre Rispoli, Managing Director
Rene Maury, Senior Managing Director
Tanguy Hoffmann, Managing Director
William Higgons, Managing Director

Type of Firm
Private Firm Investing Own Capital

Industry Association Membership
European Venture Capital Association (EVCA)

Project Preferences
Type of Financing Preferred:
Early Stage
Expansion
Leveraged Buyout
Recapitalizations
Startup

Geographical Preferences
United States
All U.S.

International
France

Industry Preferences
(% based on actual investment)

Computer Software and Services	59.0%
Internet Specific	15.0%
Other Products	8.7%
Consumer Related	6.5%
Communications and Media	4.3%
Industrial/Energy	4.2%
Medical/Health	1.9%
Semiconductors/Other Elect.	0.4%

Additional Information
Name of Most Recent Fund: Siparex Provinces de France
Most Recent Fund Was Raised: 06/01/1993
Year Founded: 1977
Capital Under Management: $439,900,000
Current Activity Level : Actively seeking new investments

SISIR INTERNATIONAL PTE LTD.

3 Science Park Drive, #01-05
Singapore, Singapore 118223
Phone: 65-772-9661
Fax: 65-778-0437
Website: www.sisirint.com

Type of Firm
Non-Financial Corp. Affiliate or Subsidiary

Project Preferences

Role in Financing:
Prefer role as deal originator

Type of Financing Preferred:
Expansion

Size of Investments Considered
Min Size of Investment Considered (000s): $100
Max Size of Investment Considered (000s): $600

Geographical Preferences

United States
All U.S.

International
Asia
All International

Industry Preferences

Computer Software
Software

Computer Other
Computer Related

Semiconductors/Other Elect.
Electronics

Consumer Related
Food/Beverage

Industrial/Energy
Industrial Products

Business Serv.
Services

Other
Environment Responsible

Additional Information
Year Founded: 1988
Capital Under Management: $6,000,000
Current Activity Level : Actively seeking new investments
Method of Compensation: Return on investment is of primary concern, do not charge fees

SITRA (AKA FINNISH NATIONAL FUND FOR RESEARCH AND DEV.)

Itamerentori 2
P.O. Box 160
Helsinki, Finland 00181
Phone: 358-9-618-991
Fax: 358-9-645-072
Website: www.sitra.fi

Management and Staff
Olli Lindblad, Vice President

Type of Firm
Endowment

Industry Association Membership
European Venture Capital Association (EVCA)
Finnish Venture Capital Association
National Venture Capital Association (NVCA)

Project Preferences

Role in Financing:
Will function either as deal originator or investor in deals created by others

Type of Financing Preferred:
Early Stage
First Stage Financing
Research and Development
Seed
Startup

Size of Investments Considered
Min Size of Investment Considered (000s): $100
Max Size of Investment Considered (000s): $5,000

Geographical Preferences

United States
All U.S.

International
Europe
Finland

Industry Preferences

(% based on actual investment)

Semiconductors/Other Elect.	35.3%
Communications and Media	31.1%
Computer Software and Services	30.3%
Industrial/Energy	3.2%

Additional Information
Name of Most Recent Fund: SITRA
Most Recent Fund Was Raised: 01/01/1987
Year Founded: 1967
Capital Under Management: $166,400,000
Current Activity Level : Actively seeking new investments
Method of Compensation: Return on investment is of primary concern, do not charge fees

SK GLOBAL CO., LTD.

226 Sinmunno 1-ga
Jongno-gu
Seoul, South Korea 110-061
Phone: 822-2221-2114
Fax: 822-754-9414
E-mail: webmaster@skglobal.com
Website: www.skglobal.com

Type of Firm
Non-Financial Corp. Affiliate or Subsidiary

Project Preferences

Type of Financing Preferred:
Startup

Geographical Preferences

International
Korea, South

Industry Preferences

Communications and Media
Communications and Media

Semiconductors/Other Elect.
Electronics

Manufact.
Manufacturing

Additional Information
Year Founded: 1953
Capital Under Management: $16,000,000
Current Activity Level : Actively seeking new investments

SMALL INDUSTRIES DEVELOPMENT BANK OF INDIA (SIDBI), THE

10/10 Madan Mohan
Malviya Marg
Lucknow, India 226001
Phone: 9122-204-3065
Fax: 9122-204-3078
Website: www.sidbi.com

Other Offices

11 Dr. U.N. Brahmachari Street, 8/F
Calcutta , India 700 017
Phone: 9133-247-9809
Fax: 9133-240-4093

IDBI Building, G.S. Road
Guwahati, India 781 005
Phone: 91361-563-922
Fax: 91361-562-545

Temple Tower, 5/F, 476 Anna Salai
Nandanam
Chennai, India 600 035
Phone: 9111-433-0286
Fax: 9111-434-0348

YMCA Cultural Centre
1 Jai Singh Road
New Delhi, India 110 001
Phone: 9111-336-4037
Fax: 9111-374-7120

Management and Staff
Rakesh Rewari, Chief Executive Officer
Sailendra Narain, Managing Director

Type of Firm
Govt Program NEC

Project Preferences

Type of Financing Preferred:
Balanced
Early Stage
Expansion

Geographical Preferences

International
India

Industry Preferences

Computer Software
Software

Additional Information
Year Founded: 1990
Capital Under Management: $21,700,000
Current Activity Level : Actively seeking new investments

SMIFS VENTURE CAPITAL LIMITED

5/F Vaibhav
4 Lee Road
Calcutta, India 700001
Phone: 9133-247-0362
Fax: 9133-240-4052
E-mail: smifscap@hd1.vsnl.net.in

Type of Firm
Affiliate/Subsidary of Oth. Financial. Instit.

Project Preferences

Type of Financing Preferred:
Balanced

Geographical Preferences

International
Asia
India

Industry Preferences

Communications and Media
Communications and Media
Data Communications

Computer Software
Software

Consumer Related
Entertainment and Leisure

Business Serv.
Media

Additional Information
Capital Under Management: $10,900,000
Current Activity Level : Actively seeking new investments

SOCIETE GENERALE-PRIVATE EQUITY ACTIVITY

Tour Societe Generale
17 Cours Valmy
Paris, France F - 92972

Type of Firm
Commercial Bank Affiliate or Subsidiary

Industry Association Membership
European Venture Capital Association (EVCA)

Project Preferences

Type of Financing Preferred:
Early Stage
Expansion
Leveraged Buyout
Recapitalizations

Geographical Preferences

United States
All U.S.

International
Europe

Additional Information
Capital Under Management: $620,300,000
Current Activity Level : Actively seeking new investments

SOCIETE REGIONALE D'INVESTISSEMENT DE BRUXELLES (SRIB/GIMB)

Rue de Stassart 32
Brussels, Belgium B-1050
Phone: 32-2-548-2211
Fax: 32-2-511-9074
Website: www.srib.be

Management and Staff
E Gelder, Partner

Type of Firm
SBIC Not elsewhere classified

Industry Association Membership
Belgium Venture Capital Association
European Venture Capital Association (EVCA)

Project Preferences

Role in Financing:
Prefer role as deal originator but will also invest in deals created by others

Type of Financing Preferred:
Expansion
First Stage Financing
Leveraged Buyout
Mezzanine
Second Stage Financing
Startup

Geographical Preferences

International
Belgium

Industry Preferences

Communications and Media
Commercial Communications
CATV & Pay TV Systems
Telecommunications
Data Communications
Satellite Microwave Comm.

Computer Hardware
Computer Graphics and Dig

Computer Software
Systems Software
Applications Software
Artificial Intelligence

Semiconductors/Other Elect.
Electronic Components

Biotechnology
Industrial Biotechnology
Biotech Related Research

Medical/Health
Medical Diagnostics
Medical Therapeutics
Hospitals/Clinics/Primary
Hospital/Other Instit.

Consumer Related
Food/Beverage
Consumer Products

Industrial/Energy
Industrial Products
Factory Automation
Machinery
Environmental Related

Financial Services
Financial Services

Additional Information

Year Founded: 1984
Capital Under Management: $63,900,000
Current Activity Level : Actively seeking new investments
Method of Compensation: Return on investment is of primary concern, do not charge fees

SOFINNOVA PARTNERS

17 rue de Surene
Paris, Zambia 75008
Phone: 33-153-05-41-00
Fax: 33-153-05-41-29
Website: www.sofinnova.fr

Management and Staff

Alain Rodermann, General Partner
Antoine Papiernik, General Partner
Bernard Gilly, Partner
Denis Lucquin, General Partner
Franck Delorme, General Partner
Jean-Bernard Schmidt, General Partner
Monique Saulnier, Chief Financial Officer
Olivier Protard, General Partner

Type of Firm

Private Firm Investing Own Capital

Industry Association Membership

European Venture Capital Association (EVCA)

Project Preferences

Type of Financing Preferred:
Early Stage
Startup

Size of Investments Considered
Min Size of Investment Considered (000s): $400
Max Size of Investment Considered (000s): $400,000

Geographical Preferences

International
Europe

Industry Preferences

Communications and Media
Telecommunications

Computer Software
Software

Internet Specific
Internet

Biotechnology
Biotechnology

Medical/Health
Medical/Health
Medical Products
Pharmaceuticals

Business Serv.
Media

Additional Information

Year Founded: 1972
Capital Under Management: $193,700,000
Current Activity Level : Actively seeking new investments

SOFINNOVA VENTURES

Sofinnova Partners SA
17 rue de Surene
Paris, France 75008
Phone: 33 153.05.41.00
Fax: 33 153.05.41.29

See California for full listing.

SOFINOV (AKA:CAISSE DE DEPOT ET PLACEMENT DU QUEBEC)

1981 avenue McGill College
Room 650
Montreal, Canada H3A 3C7
Phone: 514-842-3261
Fax: 514-847-2498
Website: www.lacaisse.com

Management and Staff

Jean-Claude Scraire, Chairman & CEO

Type of Firm

Private Equity Advisor or Fund of Fund Mgr

Project Preferences

Type of Financing Preferred:
Balanced

Geographical Preferences

United States
All U.S.

Canada
All Canada

International
Asia
Europe

Industry Preferences

Biotechnology
Biotechnology

Industrial/Energy
Industrial Products

Transportation
Aerospace

Additional Information
Year Founded: 1995
Current Activity Level : Actively seeking new investments

SOFTBANK CHINA VENTURE CAPITAL

28F, Zhoa Feng W.T. Building
369 Jian Su Road
Shanghai, China 200050
Phone: 8621-3212-4666
Website: www.sbcvc.com

Other Offices

11F Beihai-Wantai Building
6, North Zhoa Yang Men Street
Beijing, China
Phone: 8610-6554-2058

Type of Firm
Non-Financial Corp. Affiliate or Subsidiary

Project Preferences

Type of Financing Preferred:
Balanced
Early Stage

Size of Investments Considered
Min Size of Investment Considered (000s): $500
Max Size of Investment Considered (000s): $500,000

Geographical Preferences

International
Hong Kong
Macau
Taiwan

Additional Information
Year Founded: 2000
Capital Under Management: $30,000,000
Current Activity Level : Actively seeking new investments

SOFTBANK CORP.

24-1 Hihonbashi Hakozaki Cho
Chuo Ku
Tokyo, Japan 103
Phone: 813-5642-8005
Fax: 813-5641-3401
Website: www.softbank.co.jp

Type of Firm
Non-Financial Corp. Affiliate or Subsidiary

Project Preferences

Type of Financing Preferred:
Balanced
Early Stage
Startup
Unknown

Geographical Preferences

United States
All U.S.

International
Asia
China
Europe
Japan
Korea, South
United Kingdom

Industry Preferences

(% based on actual investment)

Other Products	64.4%
Internet Specific	30.9%
Communications and Media	2.0%
Medical/Health	1.8%
Computer Software and Services	0.9%

Additional Information
Year Founded: 2000
Capital Under Management: $2,600,000,000
Current Activity Level : Actively seeking new investments

SOFTCAPITAL, INC.

1-8-1-5F
1-8-1 Ginza, Chuo-ku
Tokyo, Japan
Phone: 03-3563-0505
Fax: 03-3561-7535
Website: www.softcapital.co.jp

Type of Firm
Private Firm Investing Own Capital

Project Preferences

Type of Financing Preferred:
Balanced

Geographical Preferences

International
Japan

Additional Information
Current Activity Level : Actively seeking new investments

SONERA CORPORATION CORPORATE VENTURE CAPITAL

Elimaenkatu 5
P.O. Box 190 Sonera
Helsinki, Finland 00051
Phone: 358 20 404 092
Fax: 358 20 405 950
Website: www.sonera.fi/english/ventures/

Other Offices

1620 26th Street South Tower
3rd Floor Suite 15
Santa Monica, United States of America 90404

1875 Charleston Road
Mountain View, United States of America 94043
Phone: 650-316-3820
Fax: 650-316-3829

8 The Square
Stockely Park Uxbridge
Middlesex, United Kingdom UB11 1FW

890 Winter Street
Suite 310
North Waltham, United States of America 02451

Elsenheimer Strasse 50
Munich, Germany D-80687

Harel House 3 Abba Hillel
Silver Street 8th floor
Ramat Gan Tel Aviv, Israel 52522

Sonera Japan KK AKABISHI-II
Akasaka 4-1-30 Manato-Ku
Tokyo, Japan 107-0052

Type of Firm
Non-Financial Corp. Affiliate or Subsidiary

Industry Association Membership
Finnish Venture Capital Association
National Venture Capital Association (NVCA)

Project Preferences

Type of Financing Preferred:
Early Stage
Expansion
Fund of Funds
Joint Ventures
Startup

Geographical Preferences

United States
Massachusetts
Northern California

International
Belgium
Germany
Israel
Japan
Luxembourg
Netherlands
Scandanavia/Nordic Region
United Kingdom

Industry Preferences

Communications and Media
Telecommunications

Additional Information

Year Founded: 1999
Current Activity Level : Actively seeking new investments

SOPARTEC SA

Place des Sciences 4
Louvain-la-Neuve, Belgium B - 1328
Phone: 32 10 479 054
Fax: 32 10 479 053

Management and Staff

F Lagae, Partner
H Bultot, Partner
O Witmeur, Partner

Type of Firm

University Affiliated Program

Industry Association Membership

European Venture Capital Association (EVCA)

Project Preferences

Type of Financing Preferred:
Early Stage
Expansion
Seed
Start-up Financing

Geographical Preferences

United States
All U.S.

International
Europe

Industry Preferences

Communications and Media
Communications and Media

Computer Other
Computer Related

Biotechnology
Biotechnology

Medical/Health
Medical/Health

Industrial/Energy
Energy
Materials

Additional Information

Year Founded: 1990
Capital Under Management: $34,000,000
Current Activity Level : Actively seeking new investments

SOVEREIGN CAPITAL (FKA:NASH, SELLS & PARTNERS LIMITED)

25 Buckingham Gate
London, United Kingdom SW1E 6LD
Phone: 44 207 828 6944
Fax: 44 207 828 9958
Website: www.sovereigncapital.co.uk

Management and Staff

Andrew Sells, Managing Director
Michael Needley, Chief Financial Officer

Type of Firm

Private Firm Investing Own Capital

Industry Association Membership

British Venture Capital Association

Project Preferences

Role in Financing:
Prefer role as deal originator but will also invest in deals created by others

Type of Financing Preferred:
Early Stage
Expansion
First Stage Financing
Later Stage
Leveraged Buyout
Recapitalizations
Second Stage Financing
Start-up Financing

Size of Investments Considered
Min Size of Investment Considered (000s): $2,900
Max Size of Investment Considered: No Limit

Geographical Preferences

International
United Kingdom

Industry Preferences

Communications and Media
Communications and Media
Telecommunications

Computer Software
Computer Services

Internet Specific
Internet

Computer Other
Computer Related

Semiconductors/Other Elect.
Electronics

Medical/Health
Medical/Health
Hospital/Other Instit.

Consumer Related
Entertainment and Leisure
Food/Beverage
Consumer Services
Other Restaurants
Hotels and Resorts

Industrial/Energy
Energy
Energy Conservation Relat
Industrial Products
Materials
Factory Automation
Environmental Related

Transportation
Transportation

Financial Services
Real Estate

Business Serv.
Services
Distribution

Other
Environment Responsible

Additional Information
Name of Most Recent Fund: Nash, Sells Limited Partnership II
Most Recent Fund Was Raised: 12/01/1995
Year Founded: 1988
Capital Under Management: $165,000,000
Current Activity Level : Actively seeking new investments
Method of Compensation: Return on invest. most important, but chg. closing fees, service fees, etc.

SPECTRUM EQUITY INVESTORS, L.P.

Berkeley Square House
Suite 3, Sixth Floor
London, United Kingdom W1X 6JP
Phone: 20731817400
Fax: 2073187400

See California for full listing.

SPECTRUM VENTURE MANAGEMENT

Greencoat House
Francis Street
London, United Kingdom SW1P 1DH
Phone: 44 20 7630 1400
Fax: 44 20 7630 7011
Website: www.spectrumsc.com

Management and Staff
Ross Fitzgerald, Managing Director

Type of Firm
Mgt. Consulting Firm

Project Preferences

Type of Financing Preferred:
Startup

Geographical Preferences

International
United Kingdom

Industry Preferences

Internet Specific
Internet

Additional Information
Capital Under Management: $14,700,000
Current Activity Level : Actively seeking new investments

SPEED VENTURES

Tegeluddsvagen 64
Stockholm, Sweden 11528
Phone: 46-8555-43660
Fax: 46-8555-43661
Website: www.speedventures.com

Other Offices

Centennial Tower, 21/F
3 Temasek Avenue
Singapore, Singapore 039190
Phone: 65-549-7107
Fax: 65-549-7101

Keizersgracht 363
Amsterdam, Netherlands 1017 EJ
Phone: 31 20 33 03 911
Fax: 31 20 33 03 912

Mikonkatu 8
5th Floor
Helsinki, Finland 00100
Phone: 358 (0)9 681 494 8
Fax: 358 (0)9 681 494 8

One Pacific Place, 39/F
88 Queensway
Admiralty, Hong Kong
Phone: 852-2273-5070
Fax: 852-2273-5479

Management and Staff
Anders Frisk, Chief Executive Officer
Gustaf Ohrn, Managing Director
Jesper Jos Olsson, Co-Founder
Mikael Bragd, Chief Operating Officer
Petteri Terho, Managing Director

Type of Firm
Incubators

Project Preferences

Type of Financing Preferred:
Early Stage
Startup

Geographical Preferences

International
Asia
Europe

Industry Preferences

Internet Specific
Internet

Additional Information
Year Founded: 1998
Capital Under Management: $90,300,000
Current Activity Level : Actively seeking new investments

SPEF BANQUES POPULAIRES

Le Ponant de Paris
11, rue Leblanc
Paris, France 75513
Phone: 33-1-4039-6085
Fax: 33-1-4039-6066
Website: www.spef.banquepopulaire.fr

Other Offices

1 rue de la Republique
Lyon, France 69001
Phone: 33-4-7210-6999
Fax: 33-7827-8672

14 boulevard Winston Churchill
Nantes, France 44040
Phone: 33-2-4046-0808
Fax: 33-2-5180-9960

2 boulevard de Strasbourg
Toulouse, France 31000
Phone: 33-5-3441-3141
Fax: 33-5-6162-6863

3 rue Francois de Curel
BP 40124
Metz Cedex 1, Faroe Islands 57024
Phone: 33 387 37.70.65
Fax: 33 387 63.14.30

Management and Staff
Daniel Foin, Managing Director
Marc Wouthoz, Managing Director

Type of Firm
Investment/Merchant Bank Investing Own or Client Funds

Industry Association Membership
European Venture Capital Association (EVCA)

Project Preferences

Type of Financing Preferred:
Early Stage
Expansion
Leveraged Buyout

Geographical Preferences

International
Europe
France

Industry Preferences

Communications and Media
Communications and Media

Consumer Related
Consumer

Industrial/Energy
Industrial Products
Materials
Factory Automation

Other
Environment Responsible

Additional Information

Year Founded: 1982
Capital Under Management: $399,600,000
Current Activity Level : Actively seeking new investments

SPEIRS CONSULTANTS, INC.

365 Stanstead
Montreal, Canada H3R 1X5
Phone: 514-342-3858
Fax: 514-342-1977

Management and Staff

Derek Speirs

Whom to Contact

Derek Speirs

Type of Firm

Mgt. Consulting Firm

Project Preferences

Role in Financing:
Prefer role as deal originator

Type of Financing Preferred:
Control-block Purchases
First Stage Financing
Industry Rollups
Leveraged Buyout
Mezzanine
Research and Development
Second Stage Financing
Seed
Special Situation
Start-up Financing

Size of Investments Considered

Min Size of Investment Considered (000s): $1,000
Max Size of Investment Considered: No Limit

Additional Information

Year Founded: 1991
Current Activity Level : Actively seeking new investments
Method of Compensation: Function primarily in service area, receive contingent fee in cash or equity

SPRINGBOARD VENTURE MANAGERS PLC

82 King Street
Manchester, United Kingdom M2 4WQ
Phone: 0161-935-8100
Fax: 0161-935-8185

Management and Staff

Alasdair Culshaw, Managing Director
Geoff Spink, Managing Director
Hugh Hoather, Managing Director
John Young, Managing Director
Stephen Ross, Chief Executive Officer

Type of Firm

Private Firm Investing Own Capital

Additional Information

Year Founded: 1998
Current Activity Level : Actively seeking new investments

SPRINGBOARD-HARPER INVESTMENT PTE. LTD.

Unit 12, 29/F, International
Plaza, 10 Anson Road
Singapore, Singapore 079-903
Phone: 65-227-3054
Fax: 65-227-6045
E-mail: info@sbharper.com
Website: www.sbharper.com

Management and Staff

Song-How Ng, Managing Director

Type of Firm

Non-Financial Corp. Affiliate or Subsidiary

Project Preferences

Type of Financing Preferred:
Early Stage
Mezzanine

Geographical Preferences

United States
All U.S.

International
Asia
Europe

Industry Preferences

Communications and Media
Communications and Media

Semiconductors/Other Elect.
Semiconductor

Biotechnology
Biotechnology

Additional Information

Year Founded: 2000
Capital Under Management: $55,000,000
Current Activity Level : Actively seeking new investments

SPUTNIK TECHNOLOGY VENTURES

Usadba Centre
22 Voznesensky pereulok
Moscow, Russian Federation 103009
Phone: 7 095 725 5000
Fax: 7 095 725 5001
E-mail: DAlimov@sputniktech.com
Website: www.sputniktech.com

Management and Staff

Anton Kudriashov, Managing Director
Dmitry Alimov, Vice President
Sergei Riabtsov, Managing Director

Type of Firm

Affiliate/Subsidary of Oth. Financial. Instit.

Project Preferences

Type of Financing Preferred:
Balanced

Geographical Preferences

International
Russia

Industry Preferences

Communications and Media
Communications and Media

Internet Specific
Internet

Business Serv.
Media

Additional Information
Year Founded: 2000
Capital Under Management: $50,000,000
Current Activity Level : Actively seeking new investments

SSANGYONG CEMENT (SINGAPORE) LTD

17 Pioneer Crescent
Jurong Town
Singapore, Singapore 628552
Phone: 65-265-4588
Fax: 65-264-0371

Management and Staff
Cheng Gay Tan, Managing Director

Whom to Contact
Wong Toon Hong

Type of Firm
Private Firm Investing Own Capital

Project Preferences

Role in Financing:
Prefer role as deal originator but will also invest in deals created by others

Type of Financing Preferred:
Expansion
First Stage Financing
Second Stage Financing
Seed
Start-up Financing

Geographical Preferences

United States
All U.S.

Canada
All Canada

International
Eastern Europe
Pacific Rim
Western Europe

Industry Preferences

Communications and Media
Telecommunications
Data Communications
Other Communication Prod.

Computer Hardware
Computers

Computer Software
Computer Services
Systems Software
Applications Software

Internet Specific
Internet

Semiconductors/Other Elect.
Electronics
Electronic Components
Semiconductor
Laser Related
Fiber Optics

Consumer Related
Entertainment and Leisure
Computer Stores
Consumer Products

Manufact.
Office Automation Equipmt

Additional Information
Year Founded: 1973
Capital Under Management: $18,000,000
Current Activity Level : Actively seeking new investments
Method of Compensation: Return on investment is of primary concern, do not charge fees

---

STANDARD LIFE INVESTMENTS (PRIVATE EQUITY) LTD

2nd Floor
1 George Street
Edinburgh, United Kingdom EH2 2LL
Phone: 44-131-245-0055
Fax: 44-131-245-6105
Website: www.standardlifeinvestments.com

Management and Staff
Graeme Gunn

Whom to Contact
Graeme Gunn

Type of Firm
Insurance Firm Affiliate or Subsidiary

Industry Association Membership
British Venture Capital Association
European Venture Capital Association (EVCA)

Project Preferences

Role in Financing:
Prefer role as deal originator but will also invest in deals created by others

Type of Financing Preferred:
Expansion
Fund of Funds
Leveraged Buyout
Second Stage Financing
Turnaround

Size of Investments Considered
Min Size of Investment Considered (000s): $4,100
Max Size of Investment Considered: No Limit

Geographical Preferences

United States
All U.S.

International
Bermuda
Central Europe
Eastern Europe
Europe
France
Germany
All International
Italy
Spain
United Kingdom
Western Europe

Additional Information
Name of Most Recent Fund: European Strategic Partners
Most Recent Fund Was Raised: 01/01/1999
Year Founded: 1998
Capital Under Management: $700,000,000
Current Activity Level : Actively seeking new investments
Method of Compensation: Return on investment is of primary concern, do not charge fees

---

STAR CAPITAL GROUP, INC.

17F-1,No.105, Tun-Hun S.Road
Section 2
Taipei, Taiwan
Phone: 8862-2754-0168
Fax: 8862-2754-0169

Type of Firm
Private Firm Investing Own Capital

Industry Association Membership
Taiwan Venture Capital Association(TVCA)

Project Preferences

Type of Financing Preferred:
Expansion
Startup
Turnaround

Geographical Preferences

International
Taiwan

Industry Preferences

Communications and Media
Telecommunications

Semiconductors/Other Elect.
Electronics
Semiconductor

Additional Information

Year Founded: 1998
Capital Under Management: $55,900,000
Current Activity Level : Actively seeking new investments

STAR-VENTURES MANAGEMENT GMBH (SVM)

9 Possartstrasse
Munich, Germany D-81679
Phone: 49-89-419-4300
Fax: 49-89-419-43030
Website: www.star-ventures.com

Other Offices

11 Galgaley Haplada Street
P.O.Box 12600
Herzliya Pituah, Israel 46733
Phone: 972-9951-2888
Fax: 972-9951-2889

Management and Staff

Andreas Hofbauer, Chief Financial Officer
Benny Hanigal, Partner
Christina Moehrle, Partner
Meir Barel, Managing Director
Yaffa Krindel, Managing Director

Whom to Contact

Rolf Nagel
Wolfgang Hanrieder
Yaffa Krindel

Type of Firm

Private Firm Investing Own Capital

Industry Association Membership

European Venture Capital Association (EVCA)

Project Preferences

Role in Financing:
Prefer role as deal originator but will also invest in deals created by others

Type of Financing Preferred:
Early Stage
Later Stage

Size of Investments Considered

Min Size of Investment Considered (000s): $500
Max Size of Investment Considered (000s): $500,000

Geographical Preferences

United States
All U.S.
All U.S.

International
Europe
All International
Israel

Industry Preferences

(% based on actual investment)

Communications and Media	29.0%
Internet Specific	21.6%
Computer Software and Services	17.8%
Semiconductors/Other Elect.	12.2%
Medical/Health	6.9%
Computer Hardware	6.0%
Industrial/Energy	3.8%
Other Products	2.1%
Biotechnology	0.6%

Additional Information

Name of Most Recent Fund: Star Growth
Most Recent Fund Was Raised: 01/01/1999
Year Founded: 1991
Capital Under Management: $850,000,000
Current Activity Level : Actively seeking new investments
Method of Compensation: Return on investment is of primary concern, do not charge fees

START-UP AUSTRALIA PTY LIMITED

Level 5, 15 Castlereagh Street
Sydney, Australia 02000
Phone: 612-9235-1140
Fax: 612-9233-8129
Website: www.start-up.com.au

Management and Staff

George Jessup, Managing Director

Type of Firm

Private Firm Investing Own Capital

Industry Association Membership

Australian Venture Capital Association (AVCAL)

Project Preferences

Role in Financing:
Prefer role as deal originator but will also invest in deals created by others

Type of Financing Preferred:
Expansion
Seed
Startup

Size of Investments Considered

Min Size of Investment Considered (000s): $700
Max Size of Investment Considered (000s): $3,300

Geographical Preferences

International
Australia

Industry Preferences

Medical/Health
Medical/Health

Consumer Related
Food/Beverage

Agr/Forestr/Fish
Agribusiness

Other
Environment Responsible

Additional Information

Name of Most Recent Fund: BioVentures Australia
Most Recent Fund Was Raised: 01/01/1999
Year Founded: 1996
Capital Under Management: $12,000,000
Current Activity Level : Actively seeking new investments
Method of Compensation: Return on investment is of primary concern, do not charge fees

---

STARTECH PARTNERS, LTD.

4 Woodside Place
Glasgow, United Kingdom G3 7QF
Phone: 44 141 353 5230
Fax: 44 141 332 2928
Website: www.startech.co.uk

Management and Staff

Jim Mather, Managing Director

Type of Firm

Private Firm Investing Own Capital

Project Preferences

Type of Financing Preferred:

Seed

Geographical Preferences

International

United Kingdom

Additional Information

Current Activity Level : Actively seeking new investments

STONEPATH EUROPE

Hantverkargatan 22
Stockholm, Sweden SE-112 21
Phone: 46-8-545-554-30
Fax: 46-8-545-554-39
E-mail: info.europe@stonepath.com
Website: www.stonepatheurope.com

Other Offices

Stortorget 6
Karlskrona, Sweden 371 34
Phone: 46-455-840-67
Fax: 46-455-844-67

Management and Staff

Svante Carlsson, Chief Executive Officer

Type of Firm

Mgt. Consulting Firm

Project Preferences

Role in Financing:

Will function either as deal originator or investor in deals created by others

Type of Financing Preferred:

Early Stage
Startup

Geographical Preferences

International

Europe

Industry Preferences

Communications and Media

Telecommunications

Computer Software

Software

Internet Specific

Internet

Additional Information

Year Founded: 2000
Current Activity Level : Actively seeking new investments

STRATEGIC CAPITAL GROUP HONG KONG LIMITED

6/F, Landmark East
12 Ice House St.
Central, Hong Kong
Phone: 852-2526-9665
Fax: 852-2526-6904
E-mail: scg@strategicgroup.com
Website: www.strategicgroup.com

Management and Staff

Eric Solberg, Chief Executive Officer
Selina Ip, Vice President

Type of Firm

Private Equity Advisor or Fund of Fund Mgr

Project Preferences

Type of Financing Preferred:

Balanced

Geographical Preferences

International

Asia

Additional Information

Current Activity Level : Actively seeking new investments

STRATEGIC CAPITAL MANAGEMENT

9E-F Cindic Tower
128 Gloucester Road
Wanchai, Hong Kong
Phone: 852-2877-0156
Fax: 852-2511-3479

Management and Staff

Daniel Souza, Managing Director

Type of Firm

Private Firm Investing Own Capital

Project Preferences

Role in Financing:

Prefer role as deal originator but will also invest in deals created by others

Type of Financing Preferred:

Acquisition
Later Stage
Management Buyouts
Mezzanine
Second Stage Financing
Special Situation

Geographical Preferences

International

Asia

Industry Preferences

Communications and Media

Communications and Media
Radio & TV Broadcasting
Telecommunications

Semiconductors/Other Elect.

Electronic Components

Medical/Health

Medical/Health
Pharmaceuticals

Consumer Related

Retail

Industrial/Energy

Industrial Products

Transportation

Transportation

Financial Services

Financial Services

Business Serv.
Services
Distribution

Manufact.
Manufacturing
Publishing

Additional Information
Year Founded: 1994
Capital Under Management: $100,000,000
Current Activity Level : Actively seeking new investments
Method of Compensation: Return on invest. most important, but chg. closing fees, service fees, etc.

STRATHDON INVESTMENTS LTD

14-15 Jewry Street
Winchester
Hants, United Kingdom SO23 8RZ
Phone: 44-1962-870492
Fax: 44-1962-843413
Website: www.strathdon.com

Management and Staff
Hugh Stewert, Chief Executive Officer

Type of Firm
Private Firm Investing Own Capital

Industry Association Membership
British Venture Capital Association

Project Preferences

Type of Financing Preferred:
Early Stage
Expansion
Seed
Startup
Turnaround

Size of Investments Considered
Min Size of Investment Considered (000s): $100
Max Size of Investment Considered (000s): $100,000

Geographical Preferences

United States
All U.S.

International
United Kingdom
Western Europe

Industry Preferences

Communications and Media
Communications and Media

Computer Other
Computer Related

Semiconductors/Other Elect.
Electronics

Medical/Health
Medical/Health

Industrial/Energy
Energy

Financial Services
Financial Services

Additional Information
Year Founded: 1999
Capital Under Management: $25,000,000
Current Activity Level : Actively seeking new investments

STRATOS VENTURES LTD OY

Kapteeninkatu 7
Helsinki, Finland 00140
Phone: 358 9 4243 2500
Fax: 358 9 626 507
Website: www.stratosventures.com

Other Offices

41 Dover Street
London, United Kingdom W1X 3RB
Phone: 44 20 7408 0765
Fax: 44 20 7491 2855

4445 Eastgate Mall
Second Floor
San Diego, United States of America 92121
Phone: 858 812 20 66
Fax: 858 812 2001

Management and Staff
Anton Mayr, Managing Partner
Kai Karttunen, Managing Partner
Sami Sarkamies, Chief Operating Officer

Type of Firm
Private Firm Investing Own Capital

Industry Association Membership
European Venture Capital Association (EVCA)
Finnish Venture Capital Association

Project Preferences

Type of Financing Preferred:
Expansion
Seed
Startup

Geographical Preferences

United States
All U.S.

International
Europe

Additional Information
Capital Under Management: $56,500,000
Current Activity Level : Actively seeking new investments

SUDKB & SUDVC

Am Hauptbahnhof 2
Stuttgart, Germany D-70173
Phone: 49 711-127-7067
Fax: 49 711-127-3040
Website: www.suedvc.de

Other Offices

Friedrichstrasse 24
Stuttgart, Germany D-70174
Phone: 49 711 122-4854
Fax: 49 711 124-4855

Kronenstrasse 20
(Abt. 3760 Z)
Stuttgart, Germany D-70173

c/o Landesbank Baden-Wurttemberg
Augustaanlage 33
Mannheim, Germany D-68165
Phone: 49-621-428-2156
Fax: 49-621-428-2616

Type of Firm
Commercial Bank Affiliate or Subsidiary

Industry Association Membership
German Venture Capital Association

Project Preferences

Type of Financing Preferred:
Early Stage
Expansion
Later Stage
Management Buyouts
Recapitalizations
Seed
Startup
Turnaround

Geographical Preferences

United States
All U.S.

International
Europe
Germany

Industry Preferences

Communications and Media
Communications and Media

Biotechnology
Biotechnology

Medical/Health
Medical/Health
Pharmaceuticals

Industrial/Energy
Materials

Business Serv.
Media

Additional Information

Year Founded: 1998
Capital Under Management: $21,000,000
Current Activity Level : Actively seeking new investments

SUEZ ASIA HOLDINGS PTE LTD.

6 Raffles Quay
#10-07 John Hancock
Singapore, Singapore 048580
Phone: 65-538-5383
Fax: 65-538-5382

Other Offices

One Exchange Square, 45/F
Central, Hong Kong
Phone: 852-2847-5140
Fax: 852-2521-7054

Management and Staff

Andrey Berzins, Chief Financial Officer
Douglas Li, Managing Director
Janine Tran, Managing Director

Type of Firm

Investment/Merchant Bank Investing Own or Client Funds

Project Preferences

Role in Financing:
Prefer role in deals created by others

Type of Financing Preferred:
Acquisition
First Stage Financing
Management Buyouts
Mezzanine
Recapitalizations
Second Stage Financing
Special Situation

Geographical Preferences

International
Asia

Industry Preferences

Communications and Media
Telecommunications

Semiconductors/Other Elect.
Electronic Components

Medical/Health
Medical/Health
Pharmaceuticals

Consumer Related
Retail
Food/Beverage
Consumer Services

Industrial/Energy
Materials
Machinery

Transportation
Transportation

Business Serv.
Distribution

Manufact.
Manufacturing

Additional Information

Year Founded: 1995
Capital Under Management: $400,000,000
Current Activity Level : Actively seeking new investments
Method of Compensation: Return on invest. most important, but chg. closing fees, service fees, etc.

SUMMIT GROUP LTD, THE

The Pavilion
3 Broadgate
London, United Kingdom EC2M 2QS
Phone: 44 20 7614 0000
Fax: 44 20 7614 0044
Website: www.summit-group.co.uk

Type of Firm

Private Firm Investing Own Capital

Industry Association Membership

British Venture Capital Association

Project Preferences

Type of Financing Preferred:
Early Stage
Expansion
Seed
Startup

Geographical Preferences

United States
All U.S.

Canada
All Canada

International
Europe
United Kingdom

Industry Preferences

Communications and Media
Commercial Communications

Computer Other
Computer Related

Medical/Health
Medical/Health

Industrial/Energy
Energy

Financial Services
Financial Services

Additional Information

Year Founded: 2000
Capital Under Management: $30,000,000
Current Activity Level : Actively seeking new investments

SUN HUNG KAI PROPERTIES LIMITED

45/F Sun Hung Kai Center
30 Harbour Road
Wan Chai, Hong Kong
Phone: 852-2827-8111
Fax: 852-2827-2862
E-mail: shkp@shkp.com.hk
Website: www.shkp.com.hk

Management and Staff
Raymond Kwok Ping-luen, Managing Director
Thomas Kwok Ping-kwong, Managing Director
Walter Kwok Ping-sheung, Chairman & CEO

Type of Firm
Non-Financial Corp. Affiliate or Subsidiary

Project Preferences

Type of Financing Preferred:
Balanced

Geographical Preferences

International
Asia

Industry Preferences

Communications and Media
Telecommunications

Consumer Related
Hotels and Resorts

Financial Services
Financial Services
Real Estate

Additional Information
Current Activity Level : Actively seeking new investments

SUNEVISION HOLDINGS LTD

21/F Sun Hung Kai Centre
30 Harbour Rd.
Wanchai, Hong Kong
Phone: 852-2627-9000
Fax: 852-2802-0022
Website: www.sunevision.com

Management and Staff
Raymond Kwok, Chairman & CEO

Type of Firm
Non-Financial Corp. Affiliate or Subsidiary

Project Preferences

Role in Financing:
Will function either as deal originator or investor in deals created by others

Type of Financing Preferred:
Early Stage

Geographical Preferences

International
Asia
Hong Kong

Industry Preferences

Communications and Media
Communications and Media

Computer Software
Applications Software

Internet Specific
Internet

Additional Information
Year Founded: 2000
Current Activity Level : Actively seeking new investments
Method of Compensation: Return on investment is of primary concern, do not charge fees

---

SUNSINO DEVELOPMENT ASSOCIATE INC.

7/F,No.184 Hsin-Yi Road
Section 4
Taipei, Taiwan
Phone: 8862-2706-6627
Fax: 8862-2707-9751

Management and Staff
Cheng Sang Huang, President
Freemand Chang, Vice President

Type of Firm
Private Firm Investing Own Capital

Industry Association Membership
Taiwan Venture Capital Association(TVCA)

Project Preferences

Role in Financing:
Prefer role as deal originator but will also invest in deals created by others

Type of Financing Preferred:
Expansion
Mezzanine
Startup

Geographical Preferences

United States
All U.S.

International
Taiwan

Industry Preferences

Communications and Media
Telecommunications

Computer Software
Software

Semiconductors/Other Elect.
Electronics
Semiconductor

Biotechnology
Biotechnology

Medical/Health
Pharmaceuticals

Industrial/Energy
Advanced Materials
Factory Automation
Machinery

Additional Information
Year Founded: 1993
Capital Under Management: $46,600,000
Current Activity Level : Actively seeking new investments

SWEDESTART MANAGEMENT AB

Nybrogatan 16
PO Box 5745
Stockholm, Sweden 11487
Phone: 46 854 51 31 30
Fax: 46 854 58 54 89
E-mail: info@swedestart.se
Website: www.swedestart.se

Management and Staff
Jan Lundahl, Partner
Lars Hagdahl, Partner
Lennart Jacobsson, Partner

Type of Firm
Private Firm Investing Own Capital

Industry Association Membership
European Venture Capital Association (EVCA)
Swedish Venture Capital Association

Project Preferences

Type of Financing Preferred:
Early Stage
Seed
Startup

Geographical Preferences

International
Sweden

Industry Preferences

Communications and Media
Communications and Media

Computer Other
Computer Related

Semiconductors/Other Elect.
Electronics

Biotechnology
Biotechnology

Medical/Health
Medical/Health

Additional Information
Name of Most Recent Fund: Swedestart AB
Most Recent Fund Was Raised: 01/01/1995
Year Founded: 1995
Capital Under Management: $34,200,000
Current Activity Level : Actively seeking new investments

SWEDISH INDUSTRIAL DEVELOPMENT FUND (AKA INDUSTRIFONDEN)

PO Box 1163
Stockholm, Sweden 11191
Phone: 46 858.79.19.00
Fax: 46 858.79.19.50
Website: www.industrifonden.se

Type of Firm
Govt Program NEC

Industry Association Membership
European Venture Capital Association (EVCA)
Swedish Venture Capital Association

Project Preferences

Type of Financing Preferred:
Early Stage
Expansion

Geographical Preferences

International
Sweden

Industry Preferences

Semiconductors/Other Elect.
Electronics

Biotechnology
Biotechnology

Medical/Health
Medical/Health

Industrial/Energy
Industrial Products
Factory Automation

Manufact.
Manufacturing

Additional Information
Year Founded: 1979
Capital Under Management: $372,600,000
Current Activity Level : Actively seeking new investments

SYNERFI S.A.

Boulevard du Souverain 288
Brussels, Belgium B - 1160
Phone: 32-2-675-5757
Fax: 32-2-675-5800
Website: www.viv.be

Management and Staff
Leo Thielemans, Chief Executive Officer

Whom to Contact
Hugues Bullot
Natalie Silé

Type of Firm
Commercial Bank Affiliate or Subsidiary

Industry Association Membership
Belgium Venture Capital Association
European Venture Capital Association (EVCA)

Project Preferences

Role in Financing:
Prefer role as deal originator but will also invest in deals created by others

Type of Financing Preferred:
Leveraged Buyout
Mezzanine
Recapitalizations
Second Stage Financing
Turnaround

Size of Investments Considered
Min Size of Investment Considered (000s): $500
Max Size of Investment Considered: No Limit

Geographical Preferences

International
Belgium
France
Germany
Luxembourg
Western Europe

Industry Preferences

Communications and Media
Telecommunications
Data Communications

Computer Software
Computer Services
Applications Software

Semiconductors/Other Elect.
Electronics
Electronic Components
Circuit Boards
Component Testing Equipmt
Analytic/Scientific

Biotechnology
Industrial Biotechnology
Biosensors
Biotech Related Research
Biotech Related Research

Medical/Health
Medical Diagnostics
Diagnostic Services
Diagnostic Test Products
Drug/Equipmt Delivery
Medical Products
Disposable Med. Products

Consumer Related
Entertainment and Leisure
Franchises(NEC)
Food/Beverage
Consumer Products
Consumer Services

Industrial/Energy
Industrial Products

Business Serv.
Consulting Services

Manufact.
Publishing

Additional Information
Year Founded: 1987
Capital Under Management: $15,000,000
Current Activity Level : Actively seeking new investments
Method of Compensation: Return on invest. most important, but chg. closing fees, service fees, etc.

TAILINK VENTURE PARTNERS

One Nanking East Road Sec. 4
12th Floor
Taipei, Taiwan
Phone: 8862-718-4318
Fax: 8862-717-3073

Management and Staff
Conrad Hsueh, President & Chairman

Type of Firm
Non-Financial Corp. Affiliate or Subsidiary

Industry Association Membership
Taiwan Venture Capital Association(TVCA)

Project Preferences

Role in Financing:
Prefer role as deal originator but will also invest in deals created by others

Type of Financing Preferred:
Expansion
First Stage Financing
Mezzanine
Second Stage Financing
Seed
Startup

Geographical Preferences

United States
West Coast

International
China
Taiwan

Industry Preferences

Communications and Media
CATV & Pay TV Systems
Telecommunications
Data Communications

Computer Hardware
Disk Relat. Memory Device

Computer Software
Software
Systems Software

Semiconductors/Other Elect.
Semiconductor
Sensors
Component Testing Equipmt
Fiber Optics

Consumer Related
Retail
Consumer Products

Industrial/Energy
Factory Automation
Machinery

Additional Information
Year Founded: 1989
Capital Under Management: $30,000,000
Current Activity Level : Actively seeking new investments
Method of Compensation: Return on investment is of primary concern, do not charge fees

TAIWAN UNITED VENTURE MANAGEMENT CORPORATION

9F
No. 212, Chung-Hsiao East Road
Taipei, Taiwan
Phone: 8862-2721-6511
Fax: 8862-2773-4203

Management and Staff
Der-Chang Yeh, President

Type of Firm
Private Firm Investing Own Capital

Industry Association Membership
Taiwan Venture Capital Association(TVCA)

Project Preferences

Type of Financing Preferred:
Expansion
Mezzanine
Startup

Geographical Preferences

International
Taiwan

Industry Preferences

Communications and Media
Telecommunications

Industrial/Energy
Factory Automation
Machinery

Additional Information
Year Founded: 1987
Capital Under Management: $18,600,000
Current Activity Level : Actively seeking new investments

TAIWAN W&S FINANCIAL MANAGEMENT INCORPORATED

14F, No. 117
Min-Sheng East Road
Taipei, Taiwan
Phone: 8862-2546-5155
Fax: 8862-2719-5365
Website: www.concord.com

Type of Firm
Private Firm Investing Own Capital

Industry Association Membership
Taiwan Venture Capital Association(TVCA)

Project Preferences

Type of Financing Preferred:
Expansion
Mezzanine
Startup

Geographical Preferences

International
Taiwan

Additional Information
Year Founded: 1997
Capital Under Management: $100,400,000
Current Activity Level : Actively seeking new investments

TAMIR FISHMAN VENTURES

46 Rothschild Blvd.
Alrov Tower, 11th Floor
Tel Aviv, Israel 66883
Phone: 972 3 560 3888
Fax: 972 3 560 5010
Website: www.tfventures.com

Management and Staff
Danny Fishman, Chief Executive Officer
Eldad Tamir, Chief Executive Officer
Oren Ahr, Partner
Shai Saul, Founding Partner

Type of Firm
Investment/Merchant Bank Subsid/Affil

Project Preferences

Type of Financing Preferred:
Early Stage
Later Stage
Seed

Geographical Preferences

International
Israel

Industry Preferences

(% based on actual investment)

Computer Software and Services	31.6%
Internet Specific	27.3%
Semiconductors/Other Elect.	17.9%
Communications and Media	13.0%
Computer Hardware	10.3%

Additional Information

Name of Most Recent Fund: Eucalyptus Ventures, L.P. (FKA: Discovery Ventures)
Most Recent Fund Was Raised: 04/01/1998
Year Founded: 2000
Capital Under Management: $280,000,000
Current Activity Level : Actively seeking new investments

TARGET PARTNERS

Maffeistrasse 3
Munich, Germany 80333
Phone: 89-255 58-500
Fax: 89-255-58-511
E-mail: info@targetpartners.de
Website: www.targetpartners.de

Management and Staff

Berthold Von Freyburg, Founding Partner
Kurt Muller, Founding Partner
Waldemar Jantz, Founding Partner

Type of Firm

Private Firm Investing Own Capital

Industry Association Membership

European Venture Capital Association (EVCA)

Project Preferences

Type of Financing Preferred:
Early Stage

Geographical Preferences

United States
All U.S.

International
Germany
Western Europe

Industry Preferences

Communications and Media
Telecommunications

Computer Software
Software

Internet Specific
Internet

Additional Information

Capital Under Management: $105,700,000
Current Activity Level : Actively seeking new investments

TBG TECHNOLOGIE-BETEILIGUNGSGESELLSCHAFT MBH

Ludwig-Erhard-Platz 3
Bonn, Germany 53179
Phone: 49 228 831 2290
Fax: 49 228 831 2493
Website: www.tbgbonn.de

Other Offices

Sarrazinstrasse 11-15
Berlin, Germany D-12159
Phone: 49-30-85085-423
Fax: 49-30-85085-4314

Management and Staff

Ernst G Mayer, Managing Director
Hansgeorg Rasch, Managing Director
JWolfgang Posselt, Managing Director

Type of Firm

Private Firm Investing Own Capital

Industry Association Membership

European Venture Capital Association (EVCA)
German Venture Capital Association

Project Preferences

Role in Financing:
Prefer role in deals created by others

Type of Financing Preferred:
Early Stage
Expansion
Management Buyouts
Mezzanine
Seed
Startup

Geographical Preferences

International
Germany

Industry Preferences

(% based on actual investment)

Biotechnology	43.7%
Medical/Health	22.7%
Internet Specific	12.4%
Computer Software and Services	9.4%
Communications and Media	7.3%
Computer Hardware	4.5%

Additional Information

Year Founded: 1989
Capital Under Management: $347,000,000
Current Activity Level : Actively seeking new investments

TCR EUROPE SA

55 Avenue Hoche
Paris, France 75008
Phone: 33-1-5381-7781
Fax: 33-1-5381-7799

Management and Staff

Marco De Alfaro, Partner

Whom to Contact

Vivian de Mesquita

Type of Firm

Private Firm Investing Own Capital

Project Preferences

Role in Financing:
Prefer role as deal originator

Type of Financing Preferred:
Leveraged Buyout
Second Stage Financing

Size of Investments Considered

Min Size of Investment Considered (000s): $10,000
Max Size of Investment Considered: No Limit

Geographical Preferences

International
France
Italy
Spain

Industry Preferences

Communications and Media
Commercial Communications
Other Communication Prod.

Semiconductors/Other Elect.
Sensors
Component Testing Equipmt

Medical/Health
Diagnostic Services
Diagnostic Test Products
Medical Products
Disposable Med. Products

Consumer Related
Food/Beverage
Consumer Products

Industrial/Energy
Industrial Products
Materials
Machinery
Environmental Related

Transportation
Transportation

Additional Information
Name of Most Recent Fund: TCRE Fund
Most Recent Fund Was Raised: 10/01/1996
Year Founded: 1988
Capital Under Management: $100,000,000
Current Activity Level : Actively seeking new investments
Method of Compensation: Return on invest. most important, but chg. closing fees, service fees, etc.

TEAK INVESTMENT PARTNERS I LIMITED

Graha Irama 3/F, Blk. X-1
HR Rasuna Said, Kav 1-2
Jakarta, Indonesia 12950
Phone: 6221-526-1420
Fax: 6221-526-1425

Management and Staff
Kelly Knight, Managing Director

Whom to Contact
Budi Widjaja
Cahyono Halim
Kelly Knight

Type of Firm
Affiliate/Subsidary of Oth. Financial. Instit.

Project Preferences

Role in Financing:
Prefer role as deal originator but will also invest in deals created by others

Type of Financing Preferred:
Expansion
Mezzanine
Second Stage Financing

Geographical Preferences

International
Indonesia

Industry Preferences

Medical/Health
Diagnostic Services
Medical Products
Hospitals/Clinics/Primary
Hospital/Other Instit.
Pharmaceuticals

Consumer Related
Entertainment and Leisure
Retail
Franchises(NEC)
Food/Beverage
Consumer Products
Consumer Services

Industrial/Energy
Industrial Products
Materials
Machinery

Financial Services
Financial Services

Additional Information
Year Founded: 1994
Capital Under Management: $25,000,000
Current Activity Level : Actively seeking new investments

TEAK INVESTMENT PARTNERS II LIMITED

Graha Irama 3/F, Blk. X-1
HR Rasuna Said, Kav 1-2
Jakarta, Indonesia 12950
Phone: 6221-526-1420
Fax: 6221-526-1425

Management and Staff
Kelly Knight, Managing Director

Type of Firm
Affiliate/Subsidary of Oth. Financial. Instit.

Project Preferences

Type of Financing Preferred:
Acquisition
Balanced
Expansion
Turnaround

Geographical Preferences

International
Indonesia

Additional Information
Name of Most Recent Fund: Nusantara Investment Fund II
Most Recent Fund Was Raised: 12/01/1998
Year Founded: 1998
Capital Under Management: $38,000,000
Current Activity Level : Actively seeking new investments

TEAK INVESTMENT PARTNERS III LTD.

Graha Irama 3/F, Blk X-1
Jl. H.R. Rasuna Said Kav.1-2
Jakarta, Indonesia 12950
Phone: 6221-526-1420
Fax: 6221-526-1425

Type of Firm
Affiliate/Subsidary of Oth. Financial. Instit.

Project Preferences

Type of Financing Preferred:
Balanced

Geographical Preferences

International
Indonesia

Additional Information
Capital Under Management: $20,000,000
Current Activity Level : Actively seeking new investments

TECHNO NORD VC GMBH

Jungfernstieg 30
Hamburg, Germany 20354
Phone: 49-40-355-28-20
Fax: 49-40-3552-8239
Website: www.technonord.de

Management and Staff
Gottfried Neuhaus, Partner

Type of Firm
Private Firm Investing Own Capital

Industry Association Membership
European Venture Capital Association (EVCA)

Project Preferences

Type of Financing Preferred:
Early Stage
Expansion
Seed
Startup

Geographical Preferences

International
Europe
Germany
Scandanavia/Nordic Region

Industry Preferences

Communications and Media
Communications and Media

Computer Other
Computer Related

Semiconductors/Other Elect.
Electronics

Additional Information

Name of Most Recent Fund: INCOM GbRmbH
Most Recent Fund Was Raised: 01/01/1999
Capital Under Management: $18,000,000
Current Activity Level : Actively seeking new investments

TECHNO-VENTURE CO. (JAPAN)

Ichibancho NN Building
15-5, Ichiban-cho Chiyoda-ku
Tokyo, Japan 102-0082
Phone: 81-3-3262-3131
Fax: 81-3-3262-3372
Website: www.techno-venture.com

Other Offices

2465 East Bayshore Boulevard
Suite 348
Palo Alto, United States of America 94303
Phone: 650-565-8296
Fax: 650-565-8295

855 Oak Grove Avenue
Suite 202
Menlo Park, United States of America 94025
Phone: 650-323-2561
Fax: 650-323-5825

Management and Staff

Jonathan MacQuitty, Chief Executive Officer
Junta Ayukawa, Chairman & CEO

Whom to Contact

Jonathan J. MacQuitty, Ph.D.
Junta Ayukawa
Masanobu Kaneyoshi

Type of Firm

Private Firm Investing Own Capital

Project Preferences

Role in Financing:
Prefer role as deal originator but will also invest in deals created by others

Type of Financing Preferred:
First Stage Financing
Mezzanine
Second Stage Financing
Start-up Financing

Size of Investments Considered

Min Size of Investment Considered (000s): $2,000
Max Size of Investment Considered: No Limit

Geographical Preferences

United States
All U.S.
California

Industry Preferences

(% based on actual investment)

Internet Specific	65.3%
Semiconductors/Other Elect.	8.5%
Medical/Health	6.6%
Industrial/Energy	5.9%
Other Products	5.9%
Biotechnology	4.9%
Communications and Media	2.9%

Additional Information

Name of Most Recent Fund: Techno-VIII L.P.
Most Recent Fund Was Raised: 04/01/1997
Year Founded: 1997
Capital Under Management: $70,000,000
Current Activity Level : Actively seeking new investments
Method of Compensation: Return on investment is of primary concern, do not charge fees

TECHNOCAP INC

4028 Marlowe
Montreal, Canada H4A-3M2
Phone: 514-483-6009
Fax: 514-483-6045
Website: www.tecnocap.com

Management and Staff

Richard Prytula, President

Type of Firm

Venture Consulting Firm

Industry Association Membership

Canadian Venture Capital Association

Project Preferences

Role in Financing:
Will function either as deal originator or investor in deals created by others

Type of Financing Preferred:
Early Stage
Expansion

Size of Investments Considered

Min Size of Investment Considered (000s): $1,000
Max Size of Investment Considered: No Limit

Geographical Preferences

United States
Northeast
Southwest

Canada
Central Canada
Ontario
Quebec

Industry Preferences

Communications and Media
Communications and Media
Other Communication Prod.

Computer Hardware
Computers

Computer Other
Computer Related

Semiconductors/Other Elect.
Electronic Components

Consumer Related
Entertainment and Leisure
Computer Stores
Consumer Services

Additional Information

Name of Most Recent Fund: TechnoCap
Most Recent Fund Was Raised: 01/01/1994
Year Founded: 1993
Capital Under Management: $250,000,000
Current Activity Level : Actively seeking new investments
Method of Compensation: Return on investment is of primary concern, do not charge fees

TECHNOLOGIEHOLDING VC GMBH

Lenbachplatz 3
Munich, Germany D-80333
Phone: 49 895 4862-0
Fax: 49 895 4862-299
Website: www.technologieholding.de

Other Offices

AM Eschenhorst 20
Friedrichsd, Germany D-61381
Phone: 49-6175-3549
Fax: 49-6175-3726

Bockenheimer
Landstrasse 55
Frankfurt, Germany 60325
Phone: 49 697100000
Fax: 49 6971000059

Friedrichstrasse 60
Berlin, Germany 10117
Phone: 49 30767153-0
Fax: 49 30767153-19

Kronprinzstrasse 11
Stuttgart, Germany 70173
Phone: 49 711222922-0
Fax: 49 71122292229

Neuer Wall 71
Hamburg, Germany 20354
Phone: 49 40374767-0
Fax: 49 40374767-67

Nikolaistrasse 55
Leipzig, Germany 04109
Phone: 49 34198445-0
Fax: 49 34198445-99

Management and Staff
Holger Specht, Partner
Rudolf Franz, Partner
Stefan Friese, Partner
Stefan Elsser, Partner
Stefano Wulf, Partner

Type of Firm
Private Firm Investing Own Capital

Industry Association Membership
European Venture Capital Association (EVCA)
German Venture Capital Association

Project Preferences

Role in Financing:
Prefer role as deal originator

Type of Financing Preferred:
Early Stage
First Stage Financing
Second Stage Financing
Seed
Start-up Financing

Size of Investments Considered
Min Size of Investment Considered (000s): $300
Max Size of Investment Considered (000s): $300,000

Geographical Preferences

United States
All U.S.

International
Austria
France
Germany
Italy
Switzerland

Industry Preferences

(% based on actual investment)

Computer Software and Services	33.5%
Internet Specific	25.4%
Medical/Health	11.4%
Biotechnology	9.3%
Communications and Media	7.2%
Computer Hardware	6.7%
Industrial/Energy	4.2%
Semiconductors/Other Elect.	1.8%
Consumer Related	0.5%

Additional Information
Name of Most Recent Fund: Strategic European Technologies N.V.
Most Recent Fund Was Raised: 08/28/1997
Year Founded: 1987
Capital Under Management: $250,000,000
Current Activity Level : Actively seeking new investments
Method of Compensation: Return on invest. most important, but chg. closing fees, service fees, etc.

TECHNOLOGY ASSOCIATES MANAGEMENT CORPORATION

9/F,No.108 Nan-King East Road
Section 5
Taipei, Taiwan 105
Phone: 8862-2747-0030
Fax: 8862-2747-2177

Management and Staff
Emery Hsia, President

Type of Firm
Private Firm Investing Own Capital

Industry Association Membership
Taiwan Venture Capital Association(TVCA)

Project Preferences

Type of Financing Preferred:
Early Stage
Expansion
Mezzanine
Seed
Startup
Turnaround

Geographical Preferences

International
Taiwan

Industry Preferences

(% based on actual investment)

Semiconductors/Other Elect.	49.4%
Communications and Media	34.2%
Internet Specific	12.5%
Computer Software and Services	3.8%

Additional Information
Year Founded: 1990
Capital Under Management: $25,500,000
Current Activity Level : Actively seeking new investments

TECHNOLOGY VENTURE PARTNERS PTY LTD

4-6 Bligh Street
Level 7
Sydney, Australia 02000
Phone: 612-9234-3600
Fax: 612-9234-3601
Website: www.tvp.com.au

Type of Firm
Private Firm Investing Own Capital

Industry Association Membership
Australian Venture Capital Association (AVCAL)

Project Preferences

Role in Financing:
Prefer role as deal originator

Type of Financing Preferred:
Early Stage
Expansion
First Stage Financing
Second Stage Financing
Seed
Startup

Size of Investments Considered
Min Size of Investment Considered (000s): $1,300
Max Size of Investment Considered (000s): $3,300

Geographical Preferences

United States
All U.S.

International
Australia

Industry Preferences

(% based on actual investment)

Internet Specific	56.5%
Computer Software and Services	28.0%
Communications and Media	10.9%
Other Products	4.6%

Additional Information
Year Founded: 1998
Capital Under Management: $39,100,000
Current Activity Level : Actively seeking new investments
Method of Compensation: Return on investment is of primary concern, do not charge fees

TECHNOPLUS VENTURES

24 Raul Wallenberg Street
Tel Aviv, Israel 69719
Phone: 972 3 766 6555
Fax: 972 3 766 6556
Website: www.technoplusvc.com

Management and Staff
Dror Gad, Chief Executive Officer

Type of Firm
Private Firm Investing Own Capital

Project Preferences

Type of Financing Preferred:
Seed
Startup

Size of Investments Considered
Min Size of Investment Considered (000s): $200
Max Size of Investment Considered (000s): $200,000

Geographical Preferences

United States
All U.S.

International
Israel

Industry Preferences

Communications and Media
Communications and Media
Telecommunications

Medical/Health
Medical/Health

Additional Information
Year Founded: 1997
Capital Under Management: $50,000,000
Current Activity Level : Actively seeking new investments

TECHNOSTART GMBH

Frisonistrasse 4
Ludwigsburg, Germany D - 71636
Phone: 49-7141-971590
Fax: 49-71419715910
Website: www.technostart.com

Management and Staff
Michael Rheinnecker, Partner
Michael Mayer, Founder

Type of Firm
Private Firm Investing Own Capital

Industry Association Membership
European Venture Capital Association (EVCA)
German Venture Capital Association

Project Preferences

Type of Financing Preferred:
Early Stage
Seed
Startup

Size of Investments Considered
Min Size of Investment Considered (000s): $300
Max Size of Investment Considered (000s): $300,000

Geographical Preferences

International
Europe
Germany

Industry Preferences

(% based on actual investment)

Biotechnology	45.4%
Medical/Health	26.8%
Computer Software and Services	12.2%
Internet Specific	8.0%
Semiconductors/Other Elect.	4.2%
Communications and Media	3.4%

Additional Information
Year Founded: 1991
Capital Under Management: $30,000,000
Current Activity Level : Actively seeking new investments

TECHPACIFIC.COM LTD.

1505, The Center
99 Queen's Road
Central, Hong Kong
Phone: 852-2169-2800
Fax: 852-2169-0008
Website: www.techpacific.com

Management and Staff
Chris Leahy, Chief Financial Officer
Johnny Chan, Chief Executive Officer

Type of Firm
Private Firm Investing Own Capital

Industry Association Membership
Hong Kong Venture Capital Association (HKVCA)

Project Preferences

Type of Financing Preferred:
Early Stage
Expansion
Startup

Geographical Preferences

United States
All U.S.

International
Australia
China
Hong Kong
India
Indonesia
Korea, South
Malaysia
Philippines
Singapore
Thailand
Vietnam

Additional Information
Year Founded: 1999
Capital Under Management: $98,000,000
Current Activity Level : Actively seeking new investments

TECVENTURE PARTNERS GMBH

Leopold Strasse 18
Munich, Germany D-80802
Phone: 49 89 3854 7750
Fax: 4989 3854 7752
Website: www.tec-venture.com

Management and Staff
Edward M Stadum, Managing Partner
Klaus-Jurgen Werner, Chief Financial Officer

Type of Firm
Private Firm Investing Own Capital

Industry Association Membership
German Venture Capital Association

Project Preferences

Type of Financing Preferred:
Early Stage
Expansion
Startup

Geographical Preferences

International
Europe
Germany

Industry Preferences

Communications and Media
Telecommunications

Computer Software
Software

Internet Specific
E-Commerce Technology
Internet

Biotechnology
Biotechnology

Medical/Health
Medical/Health

Industrial/Energy
Factory Automation

Additional Information
Year Founded: 1999
Capital Under Management: $24,000,000
Current Activity Level : Actively seeking new investments

TEKNIA INVEST OY

P.O. Box 1750
Kuopio, Finland 70211
Phone: 358-71-240-240
Fax: 358-71-240-241
Website: www.tekniainvest.fi

Other Offices

Kauppakatu 23 b B 19
Joensuu, Finland 80100
Phone: 358 013 126 983
Fax: 358 013 225 243

Linnankatu 5
Mikkeli, Finland 50100
Phone: 358 015 3370 365
Fax: 358 015 3370 366

Management and Staff
Eero Rasa, Partner

Type of Firm
Private Firm Investing Own Capital

Industry Association Membership
Finnish Venture Capital Association

Project Preferences

Type of Financing Preferred:
Expansion
Leveraged Buyout
Seed
Startup
Turnaround

Geographical Preferences

International
Finland

Additional Information
Year Founded: 1999
Capital Under Management: $18,600,000
Current Activity Level : Actively seeking new investments

TEKNOINVEST MANAGEMENT AS

Grev Wedels plass 5
P.O. Box 556 Sentrum
Oslo, Norway N-0105
Phone: 47-22-82-2390
Fax: 47-22-82-2391
Website: www.teknoinvest.com

Other Offices

Radhusgt 5B
N-0151 Oslo, Norway
Phone: 47-2-2330020
Fax: 47-2-2421041

Management and Staff
Andreas Mollatt, Partner
Steinar Engelsen, Partner
Tore Mengshoel, Partner

Whom to Contact
Bjorn Bjora

Type of Firm
Private Firm Investing Own Capital

Project Preferences

Role in Financing:
Will function either as deal originator or investor in deals created by others

Type of Financing Preferred:
First Stage Financing
Second Stage Financing
Start-up Financing

Size of Investments Considered
Min Size of Investment Considered (000s): $500
Max Size of Investment Considered (000s): $5,000

Geographical Preferences

United States
All U.S.

International
Norway
Sweden

Industry Preferences

Communications and Media
Communications and Media

Computer Other
Computer Related

Semiconductors/Other Elect.
Electronics

Biotechnology
Biotechnology

Medical/Health
Medical Diagnostics
Diagnostic Services
Diagnostic Test Products
Medical Therapeutics
Drug/Equipmt Delivery
Medical Products
Pharmaceuticals

Additional Information
Name of Most Recent Fund: KS Teknoinvest VI
Most Recent Fund Was Raised: 01/01/1998
Year Founded: 1984
Capital Under Management: $100,000,000
Current Activity Level : Actively seeking new investments
Method of Compensation: Return on investment is of primary concern, do not charge fees

---

TELECOM VENTURE GROUP LTD. (TVG)

Suite 3810 Jardine House
1 Connaught Place
Central, Hong Kong
Phone: 852-2801-3982
Fax: 852-2147-3320
Website: www.tvgfunds.com

Management and Staff
John Troy, Managing Director
Varun Bery, Managing Director

Type of Firm
Private Firm Investing Own Capital

Project Preferences

Type of Financing Preferred:
Early Stage
Expansion
Turnaround

Size of Investments Considered
Min Size of Investment Considered (000s): $5,000
Max Size of Investment Considered: No Limit

Geographical Preferences

International
Asia
Australia
Hong Kong
India
Indonesia
Philippines

Industry Preferences

(% based on actual investment)

Internet Specific	46.6%
Communications and Media	41.9%
Computer Software and Services	11.5%

Additional Information
Year Founded: 1998
Capital Under Management: $600,000,000
Current Activity Level : Actively seeking new investments

TELIA BUSINESS INNOVATION AB

Augustendalsvagen 70-72
Box 1208
Nacka Strand, Sweden SE-131 27
Phone: 46 8 601 30 10
Fax: 46 8 601 30 20
Website: www.businessinovation.telia.se

Other Offices

Building 4, Suit 230
3000 Sand Hill Road
Menlo Park, United States of America 94025
Phone: 650 854 8070
Fax: 650 854 4961

Management and Staff
Ylva Hambraeus Bjorling, President

Type of Firm
Non-Financial Corp. Affiliate or Subsidiary

Industry Association Membership
Swedish Venture Capital Association

Project Preferences

Type of Financing Preferred:
Early Stage
Expansion
Seed
Startup

Size of Investments Considered
Min Size of Investment Considered (000s): $100
Max Size of Investment Considered (000s): $100,000

Geographical Preferences

United States
All U.S.

International
Europe
Scandanavia/Nordic Region

Industry Preferences

Communications and Media
Telecommunications

Internet Specific
Internet

Additional Information
Year Founded: 1999
Capital Under Management: $51,200,000
Current Activity Level : Actively seeking new investments

TELOS VENTURE PARTNERS

Ackerstein Building
103 Medinat Ha'yehudim St.
Herzelia, Israel 46766
Phone: 972-9957-1002
Fax: 972-9957-1675

See California for full listing.

TELSOFT VENTURES

1000, Rue De La Gauchetiere
Ouest, 25eme Etage
Montreal, Canada H3B 4W5
Phone: 514-397-8450
Fax: 514-397-8451

Type of Firm
Private Firm Investing Own Capital

Project Preferences

Role in Financing:
Prefer role as deal originator but will also invest in deals created by others

Type of Financing Preferred:
First Stage Financing
Mezzanine
Second Stage Financing

Geographical Preferences

United States
West Coast

Canada
Ontario
Quebec
Western Canada

Industry Preferences

Computer Software
Systems Software
Applications Software
Artificial Intelligence

Additional Information
Year Founded: 1995
Capital Under Management: $78,200,000
Current Activity Level : Actively seeking new investments
Method of Compensation: Return on investment is of primary concern, do not charge fees

---

TEMASEK CAPITAL

8 Shenton Way #38-03
Temasek Tower
Singapore, Singapore 068811
Phone: 65-220-4981
Fax: 65-324-5983
Website: www.temasekholdings.com.sg

Other Offices

3010-3012 One Pacific Place
Queensway
Admiralty, Hong Kong
Phone: 852-2524-7711
Fax: 852-2877-2699

Type of Firm
State Govt Affiliated NEC

Project Preferences

Type of Financing Preferred:
Early Stage
Expansion
Management Buyouts
Mezzanine
Seed
Startup

Geographical Preferences

International
China
Hong Kong
Singapore
Taiwan

Additional Information
Year Founded: 1999
Current Activity Level : Actively seeking new investments

TERA CAPITAL CORPORATION

366 Adelaide Street East
Suite 337
Toronto, Canada M5A 3X9
Phone: 416-368-1024
Fax: 416-368-1427

Type of Firm
Private Firm Investing Own Capital

Project Preferences

Type of Financing Preferred:
Balanced

Geographical Preferences

United States
All U.S.

Canada
All Canada

Industry Preferences

Computer Other
Computer Related

Biotechnology
Biotechnology

Additional Information
Capital Under Management: $22,600,000
Current Activity Level : Actively seeking new investments

TG ASIA VENTURES LIMITED

3501, Two Exchange Square,
8 Connaught Place,
Central, Hong Kong
Phone: 852-2297-0155
Fax: 852-2297-0369
Website: www.tgasiaventures.com

Other Offices

20/F Thrunet Bldg., 1337-20,
Seocho 2-Dong, Seocho-Ku,
Seoul, South Korea 137072
Phone: 822-3019-4625
Fax: 822-598-8668

Rm. 2510, 25/F, North Tower,
Kerry Center, 1 Guang Hua Road,
Chao Yang District, Beijing, China 100020
Phone: 8610-6539-1070
Fax: 8610-6539-1060

Management and Staff
Jason Kim, Managing Director

Type of Firm
Non-Financial Corp. Affiliate or Subsidiary

Project Preferences

Type of Financing Preferred:
Early Stage
Expansion

Geographical Preferences

International
Asia
China
Hong Kong
Korea, South

Industry Preferences

Internet Specific
Internet

Computer Other
Computer Related

Consumer Related
Education Related

Additional Information
Year Founded: 2000
Capital Under Management: $50,000,000
Current Activity Level : Actively seeking new investments

THINKVENTURES.COM LTD

Lansdowne House
Berkeley Square
London, United Kingdom W1X 6HJ
Phone: 44-207-306-2222
Fax: 44-207-306-2345
Website: www.thinkventures.com

Management and Staff
Andy Evans, Chief Financial Officer
John Morris, Chief Executive Officer
Mark Danby, Chief Operating Officer

Type of Firm
Private Firm Investing Own Capital

Project Preferences

Type of Financing Preferred:
Early Stage
Startup

Geographical Preferences

International
Europe

Industry Preferences

Internet Specific
Internet

Additional Information
Capital Under Management: $80,000,000
Current Activity Level : Actively seeking new investments

THOMPSON CLIVE & PARTNERS LIMITED

24 Old Bond Street
London, United Kingdom WIX 4JD
Phone: 44-20-491-4809
Fax: 44-20-493-9172
Website: www.tcvc.com

Other Offices

3000 Sand Hill Road
Building One Suite 185
Menlo Park, United States of America 94025
Phone: 650 854-0314
Fax: 650 854-0670

49 rue Francois 1er
Paris, France 75008
Phone: 33 1 1 4720 040
Fax: 33 1 4720 6568

Management and Staff
Colin Clive, Co-Founder
Greg Ennis, Principal
Jonathan Morgan, Managing Director
Richard Thompson, Co-Founder

Type of Firm
Affiliate/Subsidary of Oth. Financial. Instit.

Industry Association Membership
British Venture Capital Association

Project Preferences

Type of Financing Preferred:
Early Stage
Expansion
Management Buyouts
Recapitalizations
Turnaround

Geographical Preferences

United States
All U.S.

International
Austria
Belgium
Denmark
Finland
France
Germany
Ireland
Netherlands
Norway
Sweden
Switzerland
United Kingdom

Industry Preferences

(% based on actual investment)

Computer Software and Services	66.8%
Communications and Media	8.9%
Semiconductors/Other Elect.	6.7%
Biotechnology	5.0%
Medical/Health	4.7%
Computer Hardware	4.5%
Internet Specific	3.5%

Additional Information
Name of Most Recent Fund: Thompson Clive Growth Companies Fund
Most Recent Fund Was Raised: 01/01/1983
Year Founded: 1977
Capital Under Management: $264,000,000
Current Activity Level : Actively seeking new investments

THOMPSON CLIVE, INC.

55, rue la Boetie
Paris, France 75008
Phone: 33-1-4413-3606
Fax: 33-1-4413-3746

See California for full listing.

THREE CITIES RESEARCH, INC.

Velasquez 83
28006 Madrid, Spain
Phone: 34-1-577-2869
Fax: 34-1-435-9558

See New York for full listing.

THROUNARFELAG ISLANDS PLC(AKA:THE ICELANDIC FINANCE&INVEST.)

Sudurlandsbraut 22
Reykjavik, Iceland 108
Phone: 354-568-8266
Fax: 354-568-0191

Management and Staff
Andri Teitsson, Managing Director
Hulda Sigurford, Chief Financial Officer

Whom to Contact
Andri Teitsson

Type of Firm
Private Firm Investing Own Capital

Project Preferences

Role in Financing:
Prefer role as deal originator but will also invest in deals created by others

Type of Financing Preferred:
Leveraged Buyout
Second Stage Financing

Size of Investments Considered
Min Size of Investment Considered (000s): $200
Max Size of Investment Considered: No Limit

Geographical Preferences

United States
All U.S.

Canada
All Canada

International
Bermuda
China
France
Germany
Japan
United Kingdom

Industry Preferences

Communications and Media
CATV & Pay TV Systems
Telecommunications
Data Communications
Other Communication Prod.

Computer Hardware
Computers

Computer Software
Computer Services
Systems Software
Applications Software

Internet Specific
Internet

Semiconductors/Other Elect.
Electronics
Electronic Components
Semiconductor
Sensors
Analytic/Scientific

Biotechnology
Industrial Biotechnology

Medical/Health
Diagnostic Test Products
Pharmaceuticals

Consumer Related
Retail
Computer Stores
Hotels and Resorts
Education Related

Industrial/Energy
Materials
Environmental Related

Financial Services
Financial Services

Manufact.
Publishing

Additional Information
Name of Most Recent Fund: Throunarfelag Islands Plc.
Most Recent Fund Was Raised: 07/14/1987
Year Founded: 1985
Capital Under Management: $50,000,000
Current Activity Level : Actively seeking new investments
Method of Compensation: Return on investment is of primary concern, do not charge fees

---

TIANGUIS LTD

5 Edwardes Place
London, United Kingdom W8 6LR
Phone: 44 20 7603 7788
Fax: 44 20 7603 7667
E-mail: info@tianguis-ltd.com
Website: www.tianguis-ltd.com

Type of Firm
Private Firm Investing Own Capital

Industry Association Membership
European Venture Capital Association (EVCA)

Project Preferences

Role in Financing:
Prefer role as deal originator but will also invest in deals created by others

Type of Financing Preferred:
Acquisition
First Stage Financing
Leveraged Buyout
Management Buyouts
Recapitalizations
Second Stage Financing
Turnaround

Size of Investments Considered
Min Size of Investment Considered (000s): $500
Max Size of Investment Considered (000s): $10,000

Geographical Preferences

United States
All U.S.

Canada
All Canada

International
Australia
All International
Italy
Spain
United Kingdom

Industry Preferences

Biotechnology
Agricultural/Animal Bio.

Industrial/Energy
Industrial Products

Additional Information
Year Founded: 1985
Capital Under Management: $10,100,000
Current Activity Level : Actively seeking new investments
Method of Compensation: Return on invest. most important, but chg. closing fees, service fees, etc.

TOKYO MARINE CAPITAL COMPANY

Tokyo Marine Bldg. New 6F,
1-2-1 Marunouchi, Chiyoda-ku
Tokyo, Japan
Phone: 03-5223-3516
Fax: 03-5223-3547

Type of Firm
Private Firm Investing Own Capital

Project Preferences

Type of Financing Preferred:
Balanced

Geographical Preferences

International
Japan

Additional Information
Capital Under Management: $316,600,000
Current Activity Level : Actively seeking new investments

TOKYO SMALL & MEDIUM BUSINESS INVESTMENT & CONSULTATION CO.

3-29-22 Shibuya
Shibuya-ku
Tokyo, Japan 150-0002
Phone: 813-5469-1811
Fax: 813-5469-5875

Other Offices

1-2-6 Tajimahama
Kita-Ku
Osaka, Japan
Phone: 06-6341-5479
Fax: 06-6341-7687

Asahi Seimei Sendai Honcho Bldg.
2-3-10 Hon-cho, Aoba-ku
Sendai, Japan 980-0014
Phone: 812-2213-7966
Fax: 812-2213-7997

Nagoya, Japan

Management and Staff
Akira Watanabe, Managing Director
Hideaki Kumano, President
Isao Usami, Managing Director

Whom to Contact
Masanori Takemoto

Type of Firm
SBIC Not elsewhere classified

Project Preferences

Role in Financing:
Prefer role as deal originator

Type of Financing Preferred:
First Stage Financing
Mezzanine
Second Stage Financing
Start-up Financing

Size of Investments Considered
Min Size of Investment Considered (000s): $500
Max Size of Investment Considered (000s): $1,000

Geographical Preferences

International
Asia

Industry Preferences

(% based on actual investment)

Internet Specific	42.9%
Semiconductors/Other Elect.	12.8%
Other Products	12.5%
Biotechnology	12.2%
Computer Software and Services	9.1%
Medical/Health	6.8%
Industrial/Energy	3.0%
Communications and Media	0.8%

Additional Information
Year Founded: 1963
Capital Under Management: $350,000,000
Current Activity Level : Actively seeking new investments
Method of Compensation: Return on investment is of primary concern, do not charge fees

TOKYO VENTURE CAPITAL CO., LTD.

1-6-10 Nihonbashi Yaibucho
Chuo-ku
Tokyo, Japan
Phone: 03-3662-8961
Fax: 03-3662-9739

Type of Firm
Private Firm Investing Own Capital

Additional Information
Current Activity Level : Actively seeking new investments

TOLL TECHNOLOGIES

Level I, 3IT
St. Kilda Road
Melbourne, Australia 03704
Phone: 613-9694-2807
Fax: 613-9694-2880

Management and Staff
Mark Rowsthorn, Chief Executive Officer

Type of Firm
Non-Financial Corp. Affiliate or Subsidiary

Project Preferences

Type of Financing Preferred:
Expansion
Mezzanine
Seed
Startup

Geographical Preferences

International
Oceania/Australasia

Industry Preferences

Communications and Media
Telecommunications

Computer Software
Software

Internet Specific
Internet

Additional Information
Capital Under Management: $29,000,000
Current Activity Level : Actively seeking new investments

TOP TAIWAN VENTURE CAPITAL COMPANY, LTD.

19F, No.17, Hsu Chang Street
Taipei, Taiwan
Phone: 8862-2331-8113
Fax: 8862-2375-6460

Management and Staff
Andy Chiu, President

Type of Firm
Private Firm Investing Own Capital

Industry Association Membership
Taiwan Venture Capital Association(TVCA)

Project Preferences

Type of Financing Preferred:
Expansion
Mezzanine
Startup

Geographical Preferences

International
Taiwan

Industry Preferences

Semiconductors/Other Elect.
Electronics
Electronic Components
Semiconductor

Biotechnology
Biotechnology

Industrial/Energy
Advanced Materials
Machinery

Additional Information
Year Founded: 1996
Capital Under Management: $9,300,000
Current Activity Level : Actively seeking new investments

TOP TECHNOLOGY LIMITED (AKA:HAMBROS-ADVANCED TECHNOLOGY TRU)

20-21 Tooks Court
Cursitor Street
London, United Kingdom EC4A 1LB
Phone: 44 207-242-9900
Fax: 44 207-405-2863
Website: www.toptechnology.co.uk

Management and Staff
Harry Fitzgibbons, Managing Director

Type of Firm
Investment/Merchant Bank Investing Own or Client Funds

Industry Association Membership
British Venture Capital Association

Project Preferences
Type of Financing Preferred:
Early Stage

Geographical Preferences
International
United Kingdom

Industry Preferences
(% based on actual investment)

Computer Software and Services	38.0%
Internet Specific	28.4%
Other Products	20.6%
Communications and Media	4.6%
Semiconductors/Other Elect.	4.2%
Computer Hardware	2.3%
Consumer Related	1.8%

Additional Information
Name of Most Recent Fund: Hambros Advanced Technology Trust, PLC.
Most Recent Fund Was Raised: 02/01/1982
Capital Under Management: $64,700,000
Current Activity Level : Actively seeking new investments

TOSHIBA CORPORATION

1-1, Shibaura 1-chome
Minato-ku
Tokyo, Japan 105-8001
Phone: 813-3457-4511
Fax: 813-3456-1631
Website: www.toshiba.co.jp

Type of Firm
Non-Financial Corp. Affiliate or Subsidiary

Project Preferences
Type of Financing Preferred:
Balanced

Geographical Preferences
International
Japan

Additional Information
Current Activity Level : Actively seeking new investments

TOUCAN CAPITAL CORP.

Warwick House
181/183 Warwick Road
London, United Kingdom W14 8PU
Phone: 44-171-373-8863
Fax: 44-171-373-4626

See Maryland for full listing.

TRANSATLANTIC CAPITAL LTD.

17 Devonshire Street
London, United Kingdom W1N 2EY
Phone: 44-207-436-1216
Fax: 44-207-436-1226

Management and Staff
Fred H. Offer

Whom to Contact
Fred H. Offer

Type of Firm
Private Firm Investing Own Capital

Project Preferences
Role in Financing:
Prefer role as deal originator but will also invest in deals created by others

Type of Financing Preferred:
First Stage Financing
Second Stage Financing

Geographical Preferences
United States
All U.S.

Canada
All Canada

International
Bermuda
France
Germany
Italy
Spain
United Kingdom

Industry Preferences
Biotechnology
Biotechnology

Medical/Health
Diagnostic Services
Diagnostic Test Products
Drug/Equipmt Delivery
Other Therapeutic
Disposable Med. Products
Hospitals/Clinics/Primary
Pharmaceuticals

Industrial/Energy
Materials

Additional Information
Name of Most Recent Fund: Transatlantic Capital Bio-Sciences Fund C
Most Recent Fund Was Raised: 01/01/1985
Year Founded: 1985
Capital Under Management: $13,000,000
Current Activity Level : Actively seeking new investments
Method of Compensation: Return on invest. most important, but chg. closing fees, service fees, etc.

TRANSPAC CAPITAL PTE, LTD.

Suite 20-09 6 Shenton Way
Singapore, Singapore 68809
Phone: 65-224-1211
Fax: 65-225-5538

Other Offices

19/F Gedung Bank Artha Graha Sudirman
Central Business District Jl. Jend.
Jakarta, Indonesia 12190
Phone: 6221-515-2888
Fax: 6221-515-2828

51, Nanking East Road Sec. 4
Fifth Floor
Taipei, Taiwan
Phone: 886-2-719-1293
Fax: 886-2-719-4416

Hotel Landmark Canton
Room 817
Guangzhou, Guangdon, China 510115
Phone: 86-20-335-5988x817
Fax: 86-20-333-5988x817

Maneeya Centre Building
Eighth Floor
Bangkok, Thailand 10330
Phone: 66-2-652-0791
Fax: 66-2-652-0793

Secondary Tower Block, Sixth Floor
Wisma MCIS, Jalan Barat
Selangor, Malaysia
Phone: 60-3-756-0560
Fax: 60-3-755-4205

Shanghai Int'l Business Center
Room 408
Shanghai, China 200040
Phone: 86-21-248-3040x408
Fax: 86-21-248-4607x408

Suite 606-607, 6/F Tower One and
Exchange Plaza, Ayala Ave.
Makati, Philippines
Phone: 632-759-4889
Fax: 632-891-9459

Two Pacific Place
88 Queensway
Central, Hong Kong
Phone: 852-525-2661
Fax: 852-877-6612

Wisma Rajawali
14th Floor
Jakarta, Indonesia 10220
Phone: 62-21-570-0669
Fax: 62-21-573-4684

Type of Firm
Investment/Merchant Bank Investing Own or Client Funds

Project Preferences

Role in Financing:
Prefer role as deal originator

Type of Financing Preferred:
Early Stage
Expansion
Management Buyouts
Mezzanine
Seed
Startup
Turnaround

Size of Investments Considered
Min Size of Investment Considered (000s): $5,000
Max Size of Investment Considered: No Limit

Geographical Preferences

International
Australia
China
Hong Kong
Indonesia
Malaysia
Philippines
Singapore
Thailand

Industry Preferences

(% based on actual investment)

Computer Software and Services	32.0%
Internet Specific	24.4%
Other Products	18.2%
Industrial/Energy	9.7%
Communications and Media	8.1%
Semiconductors/Other Elect.	5.3%
Consumer Related	1.3%
Medical/Health	1.1%
Unknown	0.0%

Additional Information
Name of Most Recent Fund: Transpac Capital 1996
Most Recent Fund Was Raised: 02/01/1997
Year Founded: 1989
Capital Under Management: $820,000,000
Current Activity Level : Actively seeking new investments

TRIANGLE VENTURE CAPITAL GROUP

Talstrasse 27 e
Breckenridge, Germany 64625
Phone: 49 6251 800830
Fax: 49 6251 800839
E-mail: b.geiger@triangle-venture.com
Website: www.triangle-venture.com

Management and Staff
Bernd Geiger, Managing Partner
James Moses, Managing Partner
Karl Ebetshuber, Managing Partner
Malte Kollner, Managing Partner
Uli Fricke, Managing Partner

Type of Firm
Private Firm Investing Own Capital

Project Preferences

Type of Financing Preferred:
Balanced

Geographical Preferences

International
Europe

Additional Information
Capital Under Management: $43,400,000
Current Activity Level : Actively seeking new investments

TRINOVA

17 Avenue Charles de Gaulle
Saint Didier au Mont d'Or, France 69771
Phone: 33-478-643-150
Fax: 33-478-643-122
Website: www.trinova.fr

Type of Firm
Non-Financial Corp. Affiliate or Subsidiary

Project Preferences

Type of Financing Preferred:
Early Stage

Geographical Preferences

International
Europe

Industry Preferences

Communications and Media
Telecommunications

Computer Software
Software

Internet Specific
Internet

Semiconductors/Other Elect.
Electronics

Additional Information
Capital Under Management: $13,900,000
Current Activity Level : Actively seeking new investments

TRUSTCAPITAL PARTNERS NV

Ter Bede Business Centre
Kapel ter Bede
Kortrijk, Belgium 8500
Phone: 32 56 26 4311
Fax: 32 56 26 4310
Website: www.trustcapitalpartners.be

Management and Staff
Ignace Gheysens, Partner
Katrien Mattelaer, Chief Financial Officer
Martin Hinoul, Partner
Michel Delloye, Partner
Ronald Everaert, Partner
Wim Dejonghe, Partner

Type of Firm
Private Firm Investing Own Capital

Industry Association Membership
Belgium Venture Capital Association

Project Preferences

Type of Financing Preferred:
Balanced
Later Stage
Seed

Geographical Preferences

International
Belgium

Industry Preferences

(% based on actual investment)

Medical/Health	43.8%
Internet Specific	41.0%
Biotechnology	8.8%
Other Products	2.4%
Computer Hardware	2.0%
Computer Software and Services	1.9%

Additional Information
Year Founded: 1998
Capital Under Management: $131,100,000
Current Activity Level : Actively seeking new investments

TTP VENTURE MANAGERS (FKA: THE TECHNOLOGY PARTNERSHIP)

Melbourn Science Park
Cambridge Road
Melbourn, United Kingdom SG8 6EE
Phone: 44-1763-266900
Fax: 44-1763-261582
Website: www.ttpventures.com

Management and Staff
David Connell, Chief Executive Officer

Type of Firm
Private Firm Investing Own Capital

Industry Association Membership
British Venture Capital Association
European Venture Capital Association (EVCA)

Project Preferences

Type of Financing Preferred:
Early Stage
Expansion
Seed
Startup

Size of Investments Considered
Min Size of Investment Considered (000s): $1,000
Max Size of Investment Considered (000s): $2,000

Geographical Preferences

United States
All U.S.

International
Europe

Industry Preferences

Communications and Media
Communications and Media

Computer Other
Computer Related

Semiconductors/Other Elect.
Electronics

Medical/Health
Medical/Health

Industrial/Energy
Industrial Products
Materials

Additional Information
Name of Most Recent Fund: TTP Venture Fund
Most Recent Fund Was Raised: 02/11/1999
Year Founded: 1998
Capital Under Management: $51,700,000
Current Activity Level : Actively seeking new investments

TVI INVESTMENTS BV

Kastanie Laan 4
P.O. Box 1030
Ridderkerk, Netherlands
Phone: 0180-460412
Fax: 0180-487218

Management and Staff
Chris Melisse, President

Whom to Contact
Chris Melisse

Type of Firm
Private Firm Investing Own Capital

Project Preferences

Role in Financing:
Prefer role as deal originator but will also invest in deals created by others

Type of Financing Preferred:
Control-block Purchases
Leveraged Buyout
Turnaround

Size of Investments Considered
Min Size of Investment Considered (000s): $100
Max Size of Investment Considered (000s): $1,000

Geographical Preferences

United States
Northeast

International
Belgium
Luxembourg
Netherlands

Industry Preferences

Computer Hardware
Computer Graphics and Dig

Computer Software
Computer Services

Internet Specific
E-Commerce Technology
Internet

Consumer Related
Consumer Products

Industrial/Energy
Industrial Products

Additional Information
Year Founded: 1996
Capital Under Management: $20,000,000
Current Activity Level : Actively seeking new investments
Method of Compensation: Return on invest. most important, but chg. closing fees, service fees, etc.

TVM TECHNO VENTURE MANAGEMENT

Maximilianstrasse 35
Munich, Germany 80395
Phone: 49-89-9989920
Fax: 49-89-99899255
Website: www.tvmvc.com

Other Offices

100 Spear Street
Suite 1600
San Francisco, United States of America 94105
Phone: 415-344-0100
Fax: 415-344-0200

101 Arch Street
Suite 1950
Boston, United States of America 02110
Phone: 617-345-9320
Fax: 617-345-9377

650 Town Center Drive
Suite 1350
Costa Mesa, United States of America 92626

Phone: 714-545-6400
Fax: 714-545-0106

Management and Staff

Alexandra Goll, Partner
Christian Claussen, Partner
Devon Giacalone, Principal
Friedrich Bornikoel, Managing Partner
Gert Caspritz, Partner
Hans Schreck, Partner
Helmut Schuhsler, Managing Partner
John Chapman, Partner
John Downing, Partner
Nola Masterson, Principal
Peter Levin, Partner
Peter Kaleschke, Managing Partner
Robert Lamkin, Venture Partner

Whom to Contact

Helmut Schuehsler

Type of Firm

Private Firm Investing Own Capital

Industry Association Membership

German Venture Capital Association
National Venture Capital Association (NVCA)

Project Preferences

Role in Financing:

Prefer role as deal originator but will also invest in deals created by others

Type of Financing Preferred:

Early Stage
First Stage Financing
Seed
Start-up Financing

Geographical Preferences

United States

All U.S.

International

Asia
Australia
Belgium
Bermuda
France
Germany
Luxembourg
Netherlands
United Kingdom

Industry Preferences

(% based on actual investment)

Biotechnology	38.2%
Medical/Health	27.6%
Computer Software and Services	11.8%
Internet Specific	8.6%
Communications and Media	5.8%
Computer Hardware	3.6%
Semiconductors/Other Elect.	2.0%
Other Products	0.9%
Consumer Related	0.7%
Industrial/Energy	0.7%

Additional Information

Name of Most Recent Fund: TVM Medical Ventures
Most Recent Fund Was Raised: 05/15/1998
Year Founded: 1983
Capital Under Management: $600,000,000
Current Activity Level : Actively seeking new investments
Method of Compensation: Return on investment is of primary concern, do not charge fees

TVS FINANCE LTD.

Jayalakshmi Estates 8
Haddows Road
Chennai, India 600 006
Phone: 9144-827-7155
Fax: 9144-823-2296

Type of Firm

Non-Financial Corp. Affiliate or Subsidiary

Project Preferences

Type of Financing Preferred:

Balanced

Geographical Preferences

International

India

Industry Preferences

Medical/Health

Medical/Health

Consumer Related

Consumer

Additional Information

Year Founded: 1998
Capital Under Management: $2,800,000
Current Activity Level : Actively seeking new investments

TWINNING VENTURES

Kruislaan 400
1098 SM
Amsterdam, Netherlands
Phone: 310208884000
Fax: 310208884311
Website: www.twinning.com

Management and Staff

Han De Ronde, Partner
Lucas Wildervanck, Partner
Nita Studen Kiliaan, Partner

Type of Firm

Business Development Fund

Industry Association Membership

European Venture Capital Association (EVCA)

Project Preferences

Type of Financing Preferred:

Early Stage
Expansion
Seed
Start-up Financing

Geographical Preferences

International

Netherlands

Industry Preferences

(% based on actual investment)

Internet Specific	83.6%
Computer Hardware	16.4%

Additional Information
Year Founded: 1998
Capital Under Management: $10,000,000
Current Activity Level : Actively seeking new investments

TWINWOOD ENGINEERING LTD

10 Penjuru Close
Singapore, Singapore 608618
Phone: 65-264-6688
Fax: 65-264-2268
Website: www.twindyno.com.sg

Type of Firm
Affiliate/Subsidary of Oth. Financial. Instit.

Project Preferences

Type of Financing Preferred:
Balanced

Geographical Preferences

International
Singapore

Additional Information
Current Activity Level : Actively seeking new investments

UBF MITTELSTANDSFUNANZIERUNGS AG

Hohenstaufengasse 6
Postfach 85
Vienna, Austria A 1013
Phone: 43 1 532 89790
Fax: 431532897946280
Website: www.ubf.at

Type of Firm
Investment/Merchant Bank Investing Own or Client Funds

Industry Association Membership
European Venture Capital Association (EVCA)

Project Preferences

Type of Financing Preferred:
Expansion
Later Stage
Management Buyouts
Recapitalizations
Turnaround

Geographical Preferences

International
Austria

Additional Information
Year Founded: 2000
Capital Under Management: $35,000,000
Current Activity Level : Actively seeking new investments

UBS CAPITAL

Bahnhofstrasse 45
Zurich, Switzerland CH-8098
Phone: 41-1-234 3970
Website: www.ubs.com

Other Offices

25/F, One Exchange Square
8 Connaught Place
Central, Hong Kong
Phone: 852-2971-8618

299 Park Avenue
New York, United States of America 10171
Phone: 1-212-821-6303

5 Temasek Boulevard
Suntec City Tower #18-00
Singapore , Singapore 038895
Phone: 65-836 5132

69, Boulevard Haussmann
Paris, France F-75008
Phone: 33-1-4456 4311

Av. Juscelino Kubitschek, 50
6 andar
Sao Paulo, Brazil 04543-000
Phone: 55-11-820 1922

EIBA
Bleicherweg 30
Zurich, Switzerland 8002
Phone: 41-1-208-51-11
Fax: 41-1-208-53-86

L25, Governor Phillip Tower
1 Farrer Place
Sydney, Australia 2000
Phone: 612-9324-2297
Fax: 612-9324-2331

Maximilianstrasse 43
Munich, Germany D—80538
Phone: 49-89-212 6750

Phildrew Ventures
100 Liverpool Street
London, United Kingdom EC2M 2RH
Phone: 44-20-7568 7025

Tucuman 1
Piso 16
Buenos Aires, Argentina 1049
Phone: 54-1-316 0213

Via Salvini, 10
Milan, Italy I-20122
Phone: 39-02-760 98210

Management and Staff
Pierre De Weck, Chairman & CEO

Type of Firm
Investment/Merchant Bank Subsid/Affil

Industry Association Membership
Australian Venture Capital Association (AVCAL)
European Venture Capital Association (EVCA)

Project Preferences

Type of Financing Preferred:
Early Stage
Expansion
Later Stage
Management Buyouts
Second Stage Financing
Seed
Turnaround

Geographical Preferences

United States
All U.S.

International
Asia
Europe
Oceania/Australasia

Industry Preferences

(% based on actual investment)

Internet Specific	21.3%
Medical/Health	20.7%
Semiconductors/Other Elect.	17.7%
Other Products	10.0%
Consumer Related	8.9%
Communications and Media	8.2%
Computer Software and Services	7.4%
Industrial/Energy	5.7%

Additional Information
Year Founded: 1999
Capital Under Management: $97,500,000
Current Activity Level : Actively seeking new investments

UBS CAPITAL (AKA PHILDREW VENTURES)

100 Liverpool St.
London, United Kingdom EC2M 2RH
Phone: 44 20 7568 9000
Fax: 44 20 7568 9022
Website: www.phildrewventures.com

Management and Staff
Adrian Yurkwich, Partner
Antony Fraser, Partner
Chris Tennant, Partner
Frank Neale, Partner
Ian Hawkins, Partner
Manekesh Dattai, Partner
Robert Jenkins, Partner
Ruth Storm, Partner
Simon Jennings, Partner

Type of Firm
Private Firm Investing Own Capital

Industry Association Membership
British Venture Capital Association

Project Preferences

Role in Financing:
Prefer role as deal originator

Type of Financing Preferred:
Early Stage
Expansion
Leveraged Buyout
Management Buyouts
Recapitalizations
Second Stage Financing
Startup
Turnaround

Size of Investments Considered
Min Size of Investment Considered (000s): $4,400
Max Size of Investment Considered (000s): $148,300

Geographical Preferences

International
United Kingdom

Industry Preferences

(% based on actual investment)

Other Products	82.6%
Consumer Related	4.9%
Internet Specific	4.6%
Industrial/Energy	3.6%
Medical/Health	3.5%
Semiconductors/Other Elect.	0.8%

Additional Information
Name of Most Recent Fund: Phildrew Ventures Fifth Fund
Most Recent Fund Was Raised: 03/01/1999
Year Founded: 1985
Capital Under Management: $800,000,000
Current Activity Level : Actively seeking new investments

ULSTER DEVELOPMENT CAPITAL, LTD.

Lesley Buildings
16 Howard Street
Belfast, N. Ireland, United Kingdom BT1 6PA
Phone: 1232-238744
Fax: 44-1232-232982

Management and Staff
Tom McStraw

Whom to Contact
Tom McStraw

Type of Firm
Private Firm Investing Own Capital

Project Preferences

Role in Financing:
Prefer role as deal originator but will also invest in deals created by others

Type of Financing Preferred:
Leveraged Buyout
Mezzanine
Second Stage Financing

Size of Investments Considered
Min Size of Investment Considered (000s): $500
Max Size of Investment Considered: No Limit

Geographical Preferences

International
United Kingdom

Industry Preferences

Semiconductors/Other Elect.
Sensors

Medical/Health
Drug/Equipmt Delivery
Medical Products
Disposable Med. Products
Pharmaceuticals

Consumer Related
Entertainment and Leisure
Franchises(NEC)
Food/Beverage
Consumer Products
Consumer Services

Industrial/Energy
Industrial Products
Materials
Factory Automation
Machinery
Environmental Related

Manufact.
Publishing

Additional Information
Name of Most Recent Fund: Ulster Development Capital Limited
Most Recent Fund Was Raised: 01/01/1985
Year Founded: 1985
Capital Under Management: $7,000,000
Current Activity Level : Actively seeking new investments
Method of Compensation: Return on invest. most important, but chg. closing fees, service fees, etc.

UNION VENTURE CAPITAL CORPORATION

8F, No. 69, Ming-Sheng
East Road, Section 3
Taipei, Taiwan
Phone: 8862-2501-8350
Fax: 8862-2507-4943

Management and Staff
Lander Liu, President

Type of Firm
Private Firm Investing Own Capital

Industry Association Membership
Taiwan Venture Capital Association(TVCA)

Project Preferences

Type of Financing Preferred:
Balanced
Expansion
Mezzanine
Seed
Startup

Geographical Preferences

International
Taiwan

Industry Preferences

Semiconductors/Other Elect.
Electronic Components

Biotechnology
Biotechnology

Medical/Health
Pharmaceuticals

Additional Information
Year Founded: 1995
Capital Under Management: $7,800,000
Current Activity Level : Actively seeking new investments

UNIT TRUST OF INDIA (UTI)

13, Sir Vithaldas Thakersey
Marg, New Marine Lines
Mumbai, India 400 020
Phone: 9122-218-1982
Website: www.unittrustofindia.com

Type of Firm
Govt Program NEC

Project Preferences

Type of Financing Preferred:
Startup

Geographical Preferences

International
India

Industry Preferences

Communications and Media
Telecommunications

Internet Specific
Internet

Biotechnology
Biotechnology

Medical/Health
Health Services
Pharmaceuticals

Consumer Related
Entertainment and Leisure

Business Serv.
Media

Additional Information
Year Founded: 1964
Capital Under Management: $16,713,300,000
Current Activity Level : Actively seeking new investments

UOB VENTURE MANAGEMENT PTE LTD.

80 Raffles Place, 30th Storey
UOB Plaza 2
Singapore, Singapore 048624
Phone: 65-533-9898
Fax: 65-534-2334
Website: www.uob.com.sg

Management and Staff
Cher Teck Quek, Managing Director

Type of Firm
Investment/Merchant Bank Subsid/Affil

Industry Association Membership
Singapore Venture Capital Association

Project Preferences

Role in Financing:
Prefer role in deals created by others

Type of Financing Preferred:
Early Stage
Expansion
Mezzanine
Startup

Size of Investments Considered
Min Size of Investment Considered (000s): $1,000
Max Size of Investment Considered: No Limit

Geographical Preferences

United States
All U.S.

International
Asia
Singapore

Industry Preferences

Communications and Media
Communications and Media

Computer Software
Software

Internet Specific
Internet

Computer Other
Computer Related

Semiconductors/Other Elect.
Electronic Components

Biotechnology
Biotechnology

Medical/Health
Medical/Health
Pharmaceuticals

Consumer Related
Food/Beverage
Consumer Services

Transportation
Transportation

Business Serv.
Services
Consulting Services

Manufact.
Manufacturing
Publishing

Agr/Forestr/Fish
Agriculture related

Additional Information
Name of Most Recent Fund: UOB Venture Investments II Ltd.
Most Recent Fund Was Raised: 01/01/1995
Year Founded: 1991
Capital Under Management: $150,000,000
Current Activity Level : Actively seeking new investments
Method of Compensation: Return on investment is of primary concern, do not charge fees

VALEO VENTURES

43 rue Bayen
Paris, France 75848
Phone: 33 1 4055 2020
Fax: 33 1 4055 2171
Website: www.valeo.com

Management and Staff
Philippe Gire, President

Type of Firm
Non-Financial Corp. Affiliate or Subsidiary

Project Preferences

Type of Financing Preferred:
Startup

Geographical Preferences

United States
All U.S.

International
Germany

Industry Preferences

Transportation
Transportation

Manufact.
Manufacturing

Additional Information

Capital Under Management: $97,000,000
Current Activity Level : Actively seeking new investments

VALUE MANAGEMENT & RESEARCH AG (VMR)

Am Kronberger Hang 5
Schwalbach am Taunus, Germany D-65824
Phone: 49 61 968800444
Fax: 49 61 968800449
Website: www.vmr.de

Management and Staff

Florian Homm, Managing Partner
Kevin Devine, Chief Executive Officer

Type of Firm

Investment Management/Finance Consulting

Project Preferences

Type of Financing Preferred:
Early Stage
Expansion

Geographical Preferences

United States
All U.S.

International
Germany
United Kingdom

Industry Preferences

Communications and Media
Telecommunications

Computer Software
Software

Internet Specific
Internet

Biotechnology
Biotechnology

Business Serv.
Media

Additional Information

Year Founded: 1993
Current Activity Level : Actively seeking new investments

VANENBURG GROUP

P.O. Box 231
3880 AE Putten
The Netherlands, Netherlands
Phone: 31-34137-5555
Fax: 31-34137-5500
Website: www.vanenburg.com

Management and Staff

Erik Biekart, Chief Financial Officer
Jan Baan, Chief Executive Officer
Wim Heijting, Chief Operating Officer

Type of Firm

Private Firm Investing Own Capital

Project Preferences

Type of Financing Preferred:
Startup

Additional Information

Year Founded: 1978
Current Activity Level : Actively seeking new investments

VCF PARTNERS

5 The Old Yard
Rectory Lane
Brasted KENT, United Kingdom TN16 1JP
Phone: 44-1959-563443
Fax: 44-1959-563562
Website: www.vcf.co.uk

Management and Staff

Bernard Fairman, Partner
Peter English, Partner

Type of Firm

Private Firm Investing Own Capital

Industry Association Membership

British Venture Capital Association

Project Preferences

Type of Financing Preferred:
Early Stage
Expansion
Management Buyouts

Geographical Preferences

International
United Kingdom

Industry Preferences

Communications and Media
Communications and Media
Telecommunications

Computer Software
Software

Internet Specific
Internet

Computer Other
Computer Related

Semiconductors/Other Elect.
Electronics

Biotechnology
Biotechnology

Industrial/Energy
Industrial Products

Additional Information

Year Founded: 1984
Capital Under Management: $75,100,000
Current Activity Level : Actively seeking new investments

VCM VENTURE CAPITAL MANAGEMENT

Max-Joseph-Str. 7
Munchen, Germany D-80333
Phone: 89-549-0858-0
Fax: 89-549-0858-55

Management and Staff

Stefan Herzog

Whom to Contact

Stefan Herzog

Type of Firm

Mgt. Consulting Firm

Project Preferences

Type of Financing Preferred:
First Stage Financing
Leveraged Buyout
Mezzanine
Second Stage Financing
Special Situation
Start-up Financing

Size of Investments Considered
Min Size of Investment Considered (000s): $100
Max Size of Investment Considered (000s): $300

Geographical Preferences

United States
All U.S.

International
Bermuda
France
Germany
Italy
Spain
United Kingdom

Additional Information
Year Founded: 1991
Capital Under Management: $400,000,000
Current Activity Level : Actively seeking new investments
Method of Compensation: Return on invest. most important, but chg. closing fees, service fees, etc.

VENCA MANAGEMENT

7-14-11-104 Minami Aoyama
Minato-ku
Tokyo, Japan 108
Phone: 81-3-3486-1807
Fax: 81-3-3486-1068

See California for full listing.

VENCAP EQUITIES ALBERTA, LTD.

10180-101st Street
Suite 1980
Edmonton, Canada T5J 3S4
Phone: 403-420-1171
Fax: 403-429-2451

Other Offices
800 Fifth Avenue, S.W.
Suite 2000
Calgary, Canada T2P 3T6
Phone: 403-237-8101
Fax: 403-264-0324

Type of Firm
Private Firm Investing Own Capital

Industry Association Membership
Canadian Venture Capital Association
Natl assoc of Small Bus. Inv. Co (NASBIC)

Project Preferences

Role in Financing:
Prefer role as deal originator but will also invest in deals created by others

Type of Financing Preferred:
Control-block Purchases
First Stage Financing
Leveraged Buyout
Mezzanine
Second Stage Financing
Start-up Financing

Size of Investments Considered
Min Size of Investment Considered (000s): $1,000
Max Size of Investment Considered: No Limit

Geographical Preferences

United States
Northwest
Rocky Mountain

Canada
Western Canada

Industry Preferences

Communications and Media
Communications and Media

Computer Other
Computer Related

Semiconductors/Other Elect.
Electronics
Electronic Components

Medical/Health
Diagnostic Services
Diagnostic Test Products
Medical Products
Disposable Med. Products

Consumer Related
Entertainment and Leisure
Retail
Computer Stores
Franchises(NEC)
Food/Beverage
Consumer Products
Consumer Services
Education Related

Industrial/Energy
Oil and Gas Exploration
Alternative Energy
Coal Related
Energy Conservation Relat
Industrial Products

Transportation
Transportation

Manufact.
Publishing

Agr/Forestr/Fish
Agriculture related
Mining and Minerals

Additional Information
Name of Most Recent Fund: Vencap Equities Alberta Ltd.
Most Recent Fund Was Raised: 01/01/1984
Year Founded: 1983
Capital Under Management: $100,000,000
Current Activity Level : Actively seeking new investments
Method of Compensation: Return on investment is of primary concern, do not charge fees

VENETO SVILUPPO S.P.A

Via Ca Marcello 67/2
Mestre
Venezia, Italy 30172
Phone: 39 41/2573911
Fax: 39 41/5310033
Website: www.venetossviluppo.it

Type of Firm
Business Development Fund

Industry Association Membership
Italian Venture Capital Association

Project Preferences

Type of Financing Preferred:
Expansion

Geographical Preferences

International
Italy

Additional Information
Capital Under Management: $10,700,000
Current Activity Level : Actively seeking new investments

VENNWORKS (FKA: INCUVEST LLC)

Manfield House 2nd Floor
1 Southampton Street
London, United Kingdom WC2R OLR
Phone: 44 207 245 8551
Fax: 44 207 245 8559

See New York for full listing.

VENTANA GLOBAL

Avenida Loma de la Palma 275
Suite Two
Mexico City, Mexico 05100
Phone: 52-5-259-4660
Fax: 52-5-259-5099

See California for full listing.

VENTECH

48 bis rue Fabert
Paris, France 75340
Phone: 33 1 4955 7000
Fax: 33 1 4955 7085

Management and Staff
Alain Caffi, General Partner

Type of Firm
Affiliate/Subsidary of Oth. Financial. Instit.

Geographical Preferences

United States
All U.S.

International
Europe
Germany
Israel

Industry Preferences

Biotechnology
Biotechnology

Additional Information
Capital Under Management: $181,000,000
Current Activity Level : Actively seeking new investments

VENTURE CAPITAL FUND MANAGERS (PTY), LTD., THE

24 Napier Road
Richmond P.O. Box 2993
Johannesburg, South Africa 2000
Phone: 27-11-359-5000
Fax: 27-11-359-5001

Management and Staff
G.C. Swanepoel

Whom to Contact
G.C. Swanepoel

Type of Firm
Private Firm Investing Own Capital

Project Preferences

Role in Financing:
Prefer role as deal originator but will also invest in deals created by others

Type of Financing Preferred:
Second Stage Financing
Special Situation

Size of Investments Considered
Min Size of Investment Considered (000s): $500
Max Size of Investment Considered (000s): $1,000

Geographical Preferences

International
Afghanistan

Industry Preferences

Communications and Media
Telecommunications

Computer Hardware
Computer Graphics and Dig

Computer Software
Computer Services

Semiconductors/Other Elect.
Fiber Optics

Medical/Health
Medical Products

Consumer Related
Franchises(NEC)
Education Related

Financial Services
Financial Services

Additional Information
Year Founded: 1992
Capital Under Management: $2,500,000
Current Activity Level : Actively seeking new investments
Method of Compensation: Return on invest. most important, but chg. closing fees, service fees, etc.

VENTURE CAPITAL PARTNERS PTY LIMITED

Level 23 Aon Tower
201 Kent Street
Sydney, Australia 02001
Phone: 612-9251-8877
Fax: 612-9251-9787
Website: www.ventures.com.au

Other Offices

40 City Road Southbank
Level 21 HWT Tower Southgate
Melbourne, Australia 3006
Phone: 613-9284-3146
Fax: 613-9284-3210

Management and Staff
David Gemmell, Managing Director
John O'Farrell, Managing Director

Type of Firm
Private Firm Investing Own Capital

Industry Association Membership
Australian Venture Capital Association (AVCAL)

Project Preferences

Role in Financing:
Will function either as deal originator or investor in deals created by others

Type of Financing Preferred:
Acquisition
Distressed Debt
Expansion
First Stage Financing
Management Buyouts
Recapitalizations
Second Stage Financing
Special Situation

Size of Investments Considered
Min Size of Investment Considered (000s): $1,300
Max Size of Investment Considered (000s): $2,000

Geographical Preferences

International
Australia

Additional Information
Name of Most Recent Fund: Venture Capital Partners Number 1 Fund
Most Recent Fund Was Raised: 06/01/2000
Year Founded: 1997
Capital Under Management: $18,400,000
Current Activity Level : Actively seeking new investments
Method of Compensation: Return on investment is of primary concern, do not charge fees

VENTURE PARTNERS AG

Bodmerstrasse 7
PO Box 406
Zurich, Switzerland 8027
Phone: 41 1 206 5080
Fax: 41 1 206 5090
Website: www.venturepartners.ch

Management and Staff
Benedikt Gotte, Partner
Francesco Badaracco, Partner
Hans Van Den Berg, Partner
Massimo Lattmann, Partner
Olivier Tavel, Partner

Type of Firm
Private Firm Investing Own Capital

Industry Association Membership
European Venture Capital Association (EVCA)
Swiss Venture Capital Association

Project Preferences

Type of Financing Preferred:
Early Stage
Expansion
Seed
Start-up Financing

Size of Investments Considered
Min Size of Investment Considered (000s): $500
Max Size of Investment Considered (000s): $500,000

Geographical Preferences

United States
All U.S.

International
Europe

Industry Preferences

(% based on actual investment)

Internet Specific	55.6%
Industrial/Energy	16.0%
Computer Software and Services	14.9%
Communications and Media	11.2%
Computer Hardware	1.6%
Other Products	0.7%

Additional Information
Name of Most Recent Fund: MiniCap Technology Investment AG
Most Recent Fund Was Raised: 01/01/1997
Year Founded: 1998
Capital Under Management: $107,600,000
Current Activity Level : Actively seeking new investments

VENTURE SELECT

Hesseloher Strasse 9
Munich, Germany 80802
Phone: 49 89 7400 9233
Fax: 49 89 7400 9155
Website: www.venture-select.de

Other Offices

1842 avenue des Templiers
Vence/Sophia-Antipolis, France 06140
Phone: 33 4 9358 8558
Fax: 33 4 9358 6830

2550 Hanover Street
Palo Alto, United States of America 94301
Phone: 408 280 2800
Fax: 408 280 2801

Management and Staff
Stefan Ostermaier, Chief Operating Officer

Type of Firm
Private Firm Investing Own Capital

Project Preferences

Type of Financing Preferred:
Early Stage
Expansion
First Stage Financing
Later Stage
Second Stage Financing
Seed
Startup

Geographical Preferences

International
All International

Industry Preferences

Communications and Media
Telecommunications

Computer Software
Software

Internet Specific
Internet

Medical/Health
Medical/Health

Business Serv.
Media

Additional Information
Year Founded: 1998
Current Activity Level : Actively seeking new investments

VENTURE TDF PTE LTD.

9 Scotts Road
#06-01 Pacific Plaza
Singapore, Singapore 228210
Phone: 65-735-9339
Fax: 65-887-0535
Website: www.venturetdf.com

Other Offices

280 Second Street
Suite #120
Los Altos, United States of America 94022
Phone: 650-559-9688
Fax: 650-559-9689

Management and Staff
Thomas Ng, Managing Director

Type of Firm
Private Firm Investing Own Capital

Industry Association Membership
National Venture Capital Association (NVCA)

Project Preferences

Type of Financing Preferred:
Early Stage
Seed
Start-up Financing

Geographical Preferences

United States
All U.S.

International
Asia
China
Hong Kong
Israel
Singapore

Industry Preferences

Internet Specific
Internet

Computer Other
Computer Related

Semiconductors/Other Elect.
Electronics
Semiconductor

Medical/Health
Medical/Health

Additional Information

Year Founded: 1995
Capital Under Management: $350,000,000
Current Activity Level : Actively seeking new investments

VENTURECAP MANAGEMENT GMBH (AKA VCH EQUITY GROUP AG)

Wittelsbacherring 3
Bayreuth, Germany D-95444
Phone: 49 921 87110820
Fax: 49 921 87110821
Website: www.venturecap.de

Other Offices

Friedrichstrasse 15
Frankfurt / Main, Germany D-60323
Phone: 49 69 7137588 20
Fax: 49 69 7137588 11

Maximiliansstrasse 35
Munich, Germany D-80539
Phone: 49 89 24218 221
Fax: 49 89 24218 200

Management and Staff

Lutz Michalski, Partner
Michael Gruner, Partner
Michael H Schulz, Partner
Peter Brumm, Partner

Type of Firm

Venture Consulting Firm

Industry Association Membership

German Venture Capital Association

Project Preferences

Type of Financing Preferred:
Early Stage
Expansion
Mezzanine
Startup

Size of Investments Considered
Min Size of Investment Considered (000s): $500
Max Size of Investment Considered (000s): $500,000

Geographical Preferences

International
Germany

Industry Preferences

Communications and Media
Communications and Media
Telecommunications

Computer Software
Software

Internet Specific
E-Commerce Technology
Internet

Computer Other
Computer Related

Semiconductors/Other Elect.
Electronics
Semiconductor
Laser Related
Fiber Optics

Biotechnology
Biotechnology

Medical/Health
Medical/Health
Pharmaceuticals

Industrial/Energy
Energy
Alternative Energy
Environmental Related

Business Serv.
Media

Additional Information

Year Founded: 1998
Capital Under Management: $13,000,000
Current Activity Level : Actively seeking new investments

VENTUREPARK INCUBATOR (FKA GRIZZLYFARM AG)

Ehrenbergstrasse 11-14
Berlin, Germany D-10245
Phone: 4930 7262 66200
Fax: 4930 7262 66299
Website: www.venturepark.com

Other Offices

Bayerstrasse 21
Munich, Germany D-80335
Phone: 49 89599444400
Fax: 49 89599444402

Venturepark France
42 Avenue Montaigne
Paris, France 75008
Phone: 33 153 67 59 65
Fax: 33 153 67 53 53

Venturepark Spain
Ayala 15
Madrid, Spain 28001
Phone: 34 91 426 1915
Fax: 34 91 426 1916

Type of Firm

Private Firm Investing Own Capital

Project Preferences

Type of Financing Preferred:
Early Stage
Startup

Geographical Preferences

International
Europe

Industry Preferences

Communications and Media
Telecommunications

Internet Specific
Internet

Business Serv.
Media

Additional Information
Year Founded: 2000
Capital Under Management: $30,600,000
Current Activity Level : Actively seeking new investments

VENTURES WEST MANAGEMENT, INC.

1285 West Pender Street
Suite 280
Vancouver, Canada V6E 4B1
Phone: 604-688-9495
Fax: 604-687-2145
Website: www.ventureswest.com

Other Offices

36 Toronto Street
Suite 850
Toronto, Canada M5C 2C5
Phone: 416-861-0700

880-410 22nd Street East
Saskatoon, Canada S7K 5T6
Phone: 306-653-8887
Fax: 306-653-8886

Type of Firm
Investment/Merchant Bank Investing Own or Client Funds

Industry Association Membership
Canadian Venture Capital Association

Project Preferences

Role in Financing:
Prefer role as deal originator but will also invest in deals created by others

Type of Financing Preferred:
First Stage Financing
Research and Development
Second Stage Financing
Seed
Start-up Financing

Size of Investments Considered
Min Size of Investment Considered (000s): $1,000
Max Size of Investment Considered: No Limit

Geographical Preferences

United States
Northeast
Northwest
Southwest
West Coast

Canada
All Canada

Industry Preferences

(% based on actual investment)

Computer Software and Services	32.5%
Biotechnology	29.8%
Communications and Media	14.0%
Internet Specific	10.5%
Medical/Health	8.9%
Computer Hardware	3.1%
Industrial/Energy	0.6%
Semiconductors/Other Elect.	0.6%

Additional Information
Name of Most Recent Fund: Ventures West VII
Most Recent Fund Was Raised: 03/14/2000
Year Founded: 1973
Capital Under Management: $300,000,000
Current Activity Level : Actively seeking new investments
Method of Compensation: Return on investment is of primary concern, do not charge fees

VERITAS VENTURE CAPITAL MANAGEMENT, LTD.

91 Medinat HaYehudim Street
P.O. Box 2074
Herzliya Pituach, Israel 46120
Phone: 972-9-956-1621
Fax: 972-9-956-1619
Website: www.veritasvc.com

Other Offices

8240 Newport Bay Passage
Alpharetta, United States of America 30005
Phone: 770-619-0191
Fax: 770-329-7999

Management and Staff
Gideon Tolkowsky, Co-Founder
Gill Zaphrir, Venture Partner
Laurie Olivier, Partner
Rann Marom, Partner
Yadin Kaufmann, Co-Founder

Type of Firm
Investment Management/Finance Consulting

Project Preferences

Role in Financing:
Prefer role as deal originator but will also invest in deals created by others

Type of Financing Preferred:
Balanced
Early Stage
Seed
Startup

Size of Investments Considered
Min Size of Investment Considered (000s): $100
Max Size of Investment Considered: No Limit

Geographical Preferences

United States
Southeast
All U.S.

International
Israel

Industry Preferences

Communications and Media
CATV & Pay TV Systems
Telecommunications
Wireless Communications
Data Communications
Satellite Microwave Comm.

Computer Software
Software
Systems Software
Applications Software

Internet Specific
E-Commerce Technology
Internet

Semiconductors/Other Elect.
Fiber Optics

Medical/Health
Medical/Health
Medical Diagnostics
Diagnostic Test Products
Medical Therapeutics
Drug/Equipmt Delivery
Medical Products
Disposable Med. Products

Additional Information

Year Founded: 1990
Capital Under Management: $60,000,000
Current Activity Level : Actively seeking new investments
Method of Compensation: Return on investment is of primary concern, do not charge fees

VERTEX MANAGEMENT

77 Science Park Drive
#02-15 Cintech III
Singapore, Singapore 118256
Phone: 65-777-0122
Fax: 65-777-1878
Website: www.vertexmgt.com

Other Offices

1 HaShikma
P.O.B 144
Savyou, Israel 56530
Phone: 97-235-357-621
Fax: 97-235-357-622

12F, No.1 Sec 4 Nan-King East Road
Taipei, Taiwan
Phone: 886-2-2715-2996
Fax: 886-2-2715-2718

20 Berkeley Square
London, United Kingdom W1X 5HD
Phone: 44-20-762-988-38
Fax: 44-20-762-988-38

63/FB, Bank of China Tower
1 Garden Road Central
Hong Kong, Hong Kong
Phone: 852-252-36133
Fax: 852-252-37233

Room 2512/15 Beijing Silver Tower
2 Dong San Huan Bei Road
Chao Yang District Beijing, China 100027
Phone: 86-10-6410-8033/35
Fax: 86-10-6410-8038

Three Lagoon Drive
Suite 220
Redwood City, United States of America 94065
Phone: 650-591-9300
Fax: 650-591-5926

Management and Staff

Alan Feld, Vice President
Christina Lim, Vice President
Kheng Nam Lee, President
Kum Tho Wan, Vice President
Yip Loi Lee, Vice President

Type of Firm

Non-Financial Corp. Affiliate or Subsidiary

Project Preferences

Role in Financing:

Prefer role as deal originator but will also invest in deals created by others

Type of Financing Preferred:

Early Stage
First Stage Financing
Later Stage
Mezzanine
Second Stage Financing
Seed

Size of Investments Considered

Min Size of Investment Considered (000s): $500
Max Size of Investment Considered (000s): $10,000

Geographical Preferences

United States

All U.S.

International

China
Europe
All International
Israel
Singapore
Taiwan

Industry Preferences

(% based on actual investment)

Internet Specific	38.1%
Computer Software and Services	37.3%
Communications and Media	14.7%
Semiconductors/Other Elect.	4.7%
Computer Hardware	3.1%
Biotechnology	2.2%

Additional Information

Name of Most Recent Fund: Vertex Investment Pte Ltd.
Most Recent Fund Was Raised: 01/01/1998
Year Founded: 1988
Capital Under Management: $905,000,000
Current Activity Level : Actively seeking new investments
Method of Compensation: Return on investment is of primary concern, do not charge fees

VERTEX MANAGEMENT ISRAEL (AKA: VERTEX MANAGEMENT III LTD.)

1 Hashikau Street
Savyou, Israel 56530
Phone: 97-235-357-621
Fax: 97-235-357-622
Website: www.vertexisrael.co.il

Management and Staff

David Heller, Vice President
Gideon Shichman, Vice President
Ran Gartenberg, Chief Financial Officer
Yoram Oron, President

Type of Firm

Non-Financial Corp. Affiliate or Subsidiary

Project Preferences

Type of Financing Preferred:

Balanced
Early Stage
Seed

Geographical Preferences

United States

All U.S.

International

Israel

Industry Preferences

Communications and Media

Communications and Media

Internet Specific

Internet

Additional Information

Capital Under Management: $280,000,000
Current Activity Level : Actively seeking new investments

VESTA CAPITAL PARTNERS (AKA: VESTA GROUP, THE)

1st Floor, Knightway House
20 Soho Square
London, United Kingdom W1V 5FD
Phone: 44-20-7440-5420
Fax: 44-20-7440-5421
Website: www.vesta.eu.com

Management and Staff
Ann Wingerstrand, Managing Director
Chris Jackson, Chief Executive Officer
Fields Wicker-Miurin, Chief Financial Officer
Jamie Mitchell, Managing Director

Type of Firm
Affiliate/Subsidary of Oth. Financial. Instit.

Project Preferences

Type of Financing Preferred:
Startup

Geographical Preferences

United States
All U.S.

International
Europe

Industry Preferences

Communications and Media
Telecommunications

Internet Specific
Internet

Business Serv.
Media

Additional Information
Year Founded: 1999
Capital Under Management: $300,000,000
Current Activity Level : Actively seeking new investments

VICKERS BALLAS ASSET MANAGEMENT PTE LTD.

30 Raffles Place
#07-00 Caltex House
Singapore, Singapore 048622
Phone: 65-439-3989
Fax: 65-533-0175
E-mail: wtan@vickersballas.com.sg

Other Offices

5/F, Ayala Tower & Exchange Plaza
Ayala Ave. Cor. Paseo De Roxas
Makati, Philippines
Phone: 632-848-6631
Fax: 632-759-4555

B-1 Qutab Hotel
Shaheed Jeet Singh Marg
New Delhi, India 110016
Phone: 9111-686-4531
Fax: 9111-651-1697

Jalan Jendral Sudirman Kav 24
3/F, Tamara Centre
Jakarta, Indonesia 12920
Phone: 6221-520-6328
Fax: 6221-520-3701

Management and Staff
Rajeev Thakore, Managing Director

Type of Firm
Affiliate/Subsidary of Oth. Financial. Instit.

Project Preferences

Role in Financing:
Prefer role as deal originator but will also invest in deals created by others

Type of Financing Preferred:
Balanced

Geographical Preferences

International
Asia

Additional Information
Year Founded: 1995
Capital Under Management: $100,000,000
Current Activity Level : Actively seeking new investments

VIGECOM LIMITED

Viglen House
368 Alperton
Middlesex, United Kingdom HA0 1DX
E-mail: investments@vigecom.com
Website: www.viglen.co.uk

Management and Staff
Rajv Bhatia, Managing Director

Type of Firm
Non-Financial Corp. Affiliate or Subsidiary

Project Preferences

Type of Financing Preferred:
Startup

Geographical Preferences

International
No Preference

Industry Preferences

Internet Specific
Internet

Additional Information
Current Activity Level : Actively seeking new investments

VISION CAPITAL MANAGEMENT (FKA GLENWOOD CAPITAL)

10, Rue du Vieux-College
Geneva, Switzerland 1204
Phone: 41 22 312 3333
Fax: 41 22 312 3366

See California for full listing.

VISTA CAPITAL DE EXPANSION S.A.

Plaza Marqués de Salamanca 2
Madrid, Spain E-28006
Phone: 34-1-436-0606
Fax: 34-1-578-2915

Management and Staff
Carlos Guerrero
Mariano Olaso-Yohn

Whom to Contact
Carlos Guerrero
Mariano Olaso-Yohn

Type of Firm
Commercial Bank Affiliate or Subsidiary

Project Preferences

Role in Financing:
Prefer role as deal originator

Type of Financing Preferred:
Leveraged Buyout
Second Stage Financing

Size of Investments Considered
Min Size of Investment Considered (000s): $5,000
Max Size of Investment Considered: No Limit

Geographical Preferences

International
Spain

Industry Preferences

Communications and Media
Data Communications

Consumer Related
Entertainment and Leisure
Retail
Food/Beverage
Consumer Products

Industrial/Energy
Alternative Energy
Industrial Products
Environmental Related

Additional Information
Name of Most Recent Fund: Vista Expansion
Most Recent Fund Was Raised: 01/01/1989
Year Founded: 1990
Capital Under Management: $127,000,000
Current Activity Level : Actively seeking new investments
Method of Compensation: Return on invest. most important, but chg. closing fees, service fees, etc.

VITAL CAPITAL LIMITED

Level 2, 90 William Street
Melbourne, Australia 3000
Phone: 613-9605-5900
Fax: 613-9605-5999
Website: www.vitalcapital.com

Other Offices

Suite 800, 529 Fifth Avenue
New York, United States of America 10017

Management and Staff
Steven Korman, Chief Executive Officer

Type of Firm
Business Development Fund

Project Preferences

Role in Financing:
Will function either as deal originator or investor in deals created by others

Type of Financing Preferred:
Expansion

Geographical Preferences

International
Australia

Additional Information
Year Founded: 1999
Capital Under Management: $9,000,000
Current Activity Level : Actively seeking new investments
Method of Compensation: Return on investment is of primary concern, do not charge fees

VIV NV (AKA VLAAMSE INVESTERINGVENNOOTSCHAP NV)

Bollebergen 2a
Zwijnaarde
Gent, Belgium B - 9052
Phone: 32 9 221 33 64
Fax: 32 9 221 34 69
Website: www.viv.be

Management and Staff
Frank Claeys, Partner
Julien Smets, Managing Director
Raf Moons, Partner

Type of Firm
Commercial Bank Affiliate or Subsidiary

Industry Association Membership
Belgium Venture Capital Association
European Venture Capital Association (EVCA)

Project Preferences

Role in Financing:
Prefer role as deal originator but will also invest in deals created by others

Type of Financing Preferred:
Early Stage
Expansion
Fund of Funds
Leveraged Buyout
Management Buyouts
Recapitalizations

Geographical Preferences

International
Belgium
France
Germany
Luxembourg
Netherlands

Industry Preferences

Communications and Media
Communications and Media

Internet Specific
Internet

Business Serv.
Services
Media

Manufact.
Manufacturing

Additional Information
Year Founded: 1987
Capital Under Management: $71,100,000
Current Activity Level : Actively seeking new investments
Method of Compensation: Return on invest. most important, but chg. closing fees, service fees, etc.

VIVENTURES INC.

Tour Cedre - 20e etage
7, allee de l'Arche
Courbevoie Cedex, France F-92677
Phone: 33-1-7177-0010
Fax: 33-1-7177-0030
Website: www.viventures.com

Other Offices

66, bovet Road
Suite 318
San Mateo, United States of America 94420
Phone: 650-356-10-71
Fax: 650-356-10-74

Management and Staff
Alain Vandenborre, Partner
Benoist Grossmann, General Partner
Edward Colby, General Partner
Jean-Pascal Tranie, Managing Partner
Slim Shekar, Partner

Type of Firm
Private Firm Investing Own Capital

Industry Association Membership
European Venture Capital Association (EVCA)

Project Preferences

Type of Financing Preferred:
Early Stage
Expansion
Mezzanine
Seed
Startup

Size of Investments Considered
Min Size of Investment Considered (000s): $1,000
Max Size of Investment Considered (000s): $4,000

Geographical Preferences

United States
All U.S.

International
Asia
Europe

Industry Preferences
(% based on actual investment)

Internet Specific	55.4%
Computer Software and Services	15.9%
Communications and Media	14.0%
Consumer Related	9.9%
Semiconductors/Other Elect.	3.6%
Computer Hardware	1.1%

Additional Information
Name of Most Recent Fund: Viventures
Most Recent Fund Was Raised: 03/01/1999
Year Founded: 1998
Capital Under Management: $669,900,000
Current Activity Level : Actively seeking new investments

VLAAMSE INVESTERINGVENNOOTSCHAP NV

Bollebergen 2A
Zwijnaarde, Belgium B-9052
Phone: 32-9-221-3364
Fax: 32-9-221-3469

Management and Staff
Frank Claeys
Luc J. de Clippele

Whom to Contact
Frank Claeys
Luc J. de Clippele

Type of Firm
Commercial Bank Affiliate or Subsidiary

Project Preferences

Role in Financing:
Prefer role as deal originator but will also invest in deals created by others

Type of Financing Preferred:
First Stage Financing
Leveraged Buyout
Mezzanine
Second Stage Financing

Geographical Preferences

International
Bermuda
France

Additional Information
Year Founded: 1981
Capital Under Management: $80,000,000
Current Activity Level : Actively seeking new investments
Method of Compensation: Return on invest. most important, but chg. closing fees, service fees, etc.

VLINK GLOBAL LIMITED

40/F New World Tower
16-18 Queen's Road
Central, Hong Kong
Phone: 852-2544-8000
Fax: 852-2544-8004
Website: www.vlinkglobal.com

Management and Staff
Alec Chan, Partner
Fan Look, Partner
Henry Fong, Partner
Jimmy Wong, Chief Executive Officer
Michael Tsang, Managing Director
Steven Yang, Partner

Type of Firm
Non-Financial Corp. Affiliate or Subsidiary

Project Preferences

Type of Financing Preferred:
Balanced

Geographical Preferences

International
Hong Kong

Additional Information
Year Founded: 2000
Current Activity Level : Actively seeking new investments

VP PRIVATE EQUITY LIMITED

608 Bank of America Tower
12 Harcourt Road
Central, Hong Kong
Phone: 852-2111-2028
Fax: 852-2111-9688

Type of Firm
Private Firm Investing Own Capital

Additional Information
Year Founded: 1996
Capital Under Management: $240,000,000
Current Activity Level : Actively seeking new investments

VTC PARTNERS GMBH

Karolinenstrasse 4
Munich, Germany 80538
Phone: 49 89 21025 60
Fax: 49 89 21025 660
Website: www.vtc-partners.com

Management and Staff
Jurgen Max Leuze, Managing Director
Richard G. Ramsauer, Managing Director
Stefan Leuze, Managing Director
Stefan C. Heilmann, Managing Director
Thomas Robl, Managing Director

Type of Firm
Private Firm Investing Own Capital

Project Preferences

Type of Financing Preferred:
Early Stage
Industry Rollups
Seed
Startup

Geographical Preferences

United States
All U.S.

International
Austria
Europe
Germany

Industry Preferences

Computer Software
Software

Internet Specific
Internet

Additional Information
Year Founded: 1992
Capital Under Management: $31,300,000
Current Activity Level : Actively seeking new investments

WALDEN INTERNATIONAL INVESTMENT GROUP (AKA: WALDEN GROUP)

One Silverstone
294 Linking Road
Khar (west) Mumbai, India 400052
Phone: 912-2648-5194
Fax: 912-2648-0829

See California for full listing.

WALDEN ISRAEL

11 Galgaley Haplada St.
Bld Three, Third Fl POB 12057
Herzliya Pituach, Israel 46733
Phone: 972-9-951-3460
Fax: 972-9-951-3461
Website: www.walden.co.il

Other Offices

750 Battery Street
San Francisco, United States of America CA 94111
Phone: 1-415-391-7225
Fax: 1-415-391-7262

Management and Staff

Eyal Kaplan, General Partner
Gabi Heller, Chief Financial Officer
Oded Rose, Partner
Roni Hefetz, General Partner

Type of Firm

Affiliate/Subsidary of Oth. Financial. Instit.

Project Preferences

Role in Financing:

Prefer role as deal originator but will also invest in deals created by others

Type of Financing Preferred:

Early Stage
Expansion
First Stage Financing
Mezzanine
Research and Development
Second Stage Financing
Seed
Start-up Financing
Startup

Geographical Preferences

United States

Northeast
Southwest

International

China
Israel
Japan
Middle East

Industry Preferences

Communications and Media

Communications and Media
Telecommunications

Computer Software

Software

Internet Specific

Internet

Computer Other

Computer Related

Semiconductors/Other Elect.

Electronics

Biotechnology

Biotechnology

Medical/Health

Medical/Health
Pharmaceuticals

Consumer Related

Computer Stores
Consumer Products
Consumer Services
Other Restaurants

Industrial/Energy

Industrial Products

Additional Information

Year Founded: 1993
Capital Under Management: $200,000,000
Current Activity Level : Actively seeking new investments
Method of Compensation: Return on investment is of primary concern, do not charge fees

WARBURG, PINCUS & CO., LLC. (FKA: E.M. WARBURG, PINCUS & CO)

Kishimoto Building, Marunouchi
2-2-1 Chiyoda-ku
Tokyo, Japan
Phone: 813-3287-5037
Fax: 813-5288-6262

See New York for full listing.

WELLINGTON PARTNERS VENTURE CAPITAL GMBH

Pacellistrasse 14
Munich, Germany 80333
Phone: 49-89-219-9410
Fax: 49-89-219-94198
Website: www.wellington.de

Management and Staff

Frank Boehnke, Partner
Harold Keller, Chief Financial Officer
Ingo Krocke, Partner
Rolf Dienst, Founding Partner

Type of Firm

Private Firm Investing Own Capital

Industry Association Membership

European Venture Capital Association (EVCA)
German Venture Capital Association

Project Preferences

Type of Financing Preferred:

Early Stage
Expansion
Seed
Startup

Geographical Preferences

International

Austria
Germany
Switzerland

Industry Preferences

(% based on actual investment)

Communications and Media	41.4%
Internet Specific	38.5%
Industrial/Energy	16.8%
Computer Software and Services	3.3%

Additional Information
Year Founded: 1991
Capital Under Management: $45,300,000
Current Activity Level : Actively seeking new investments

WEST MIDLANDS ENTERPRISE LTD

Wellington House
31-34 Waterloo Street
Birmingham, United Kingdom B2 5TJ
Phone: 44-121-236-8855
Fax: 44-121-233-3942
Website: www.wm-enterprise.co.uk

Management and Staff
Andrew Henton

Whom to Contact
Andrew Henton

Type of Firm
Private Firm Investing Own Capital

Industry Association Membership
British Venture Capital Association

Project Preferences

Role in Financing:
Prefer role as deal originator but will also invest in deals created by others

Type of Financing Preferred:
Expansion
Management Buyouts
Recapitalizations

Size of Investments Considered
Min Size of Investment Considered (000s): $746
Max Size of Investment Considered (000s): $11,942

Geographical Preferences

International
United Kingdom

Industry Preferences

Communications and Media
Commercial Communications
Telecommunications
Data Communications
Other Communication Prod.

Computer Hardware
Computers
Integrated Turnkey System

Computer Software
Computer Services
Systems Software
Applications Software

Computer Other
Computer Related

Semiconductors/Other Elect.
Electronics
Electronic Components

Medical/Health
Medical/Health
Drug/Equipmt Delivery
Other Therapeutic
Disposable Med. Products

Consumer Related
Entertainment and Leisure
Computer Stores
Food/Beverage
Consumer Products
Consumer Services
Education Related

Industrial/Energy
Energy
Industrial Products

Transportation
Transportation

Financial Services
Financial Services

Manufact.
Manufacturing
Office Automation Equipmt

Additional Information
Year Founded: 1982
Capital Under Management: $60,000,000
Current Activity Level : Actively seeking new investments
Method of Compensation: Return on invest. most important, but chg. closing fees, service fees, etc.

WESTBRIDGE CAPITAL ADVISORS (INDIA) PVT. LTD.

World Trade Centre
19/5, Centre 1 Cuffe Parade
Mumbai, India 400 005
Phone: 9122-218-5180
Fax: 9122-218-7125
Website: www.wbcapital.com

Other Offices
54 Thomson Street
New York, United States of America 10012
Phone: 1-212-965-2474
Fax: 1-212-965-2365

Management and Staff
KP Balaraj, Partner
Raj Dugar, Partner
Sumir Chadha, Partner

Type of Firm
Affiliate/Subsidary of Oth. Financial. Instit.

Project Preferences

Role in Financing:
Prefer role as deal originator but will also invest in deals created by others

Type of Financing Preferred:
Early Stage
Expansion
Later Stage
Mezzanine

Geographical Preferences

United States
All U.S.

International
India
All International

Industry Preferences

Communications and Media
Telecommunications

Computer Software
Software

Internet Specific
Internet

Additional Information
Capital Under Management: $140,000,000
Current Activity Level : Actively seeking new investments
Method of Compensation: Return on investment is of primary concern, do not charge fees

WHITNEY & CO. (FKA: J.H. WHITNEY & CO.)

Citibank Tower, Suite 2705
3 Garden Road
Central, Hong Kong
Phone: 011-852-2110-7980
Fax: 011-852-2111-9699

See Connecticut for full listing.

WI HARPER GROUP

Suite 2914, 29/F,
1 Harbor View Street
Central, Hong Kong
Phone: 852-2836-7878
Fax: 852-2836-7171

See California for full listing.

WILLIAM E. SIMON & SONS (ASIA) LDC

1809 Harbour Centre
25 Harbour Road
Wan Chai, Hong Kong 07962-1913
Phone: 973-682-2683
Fax: 973-829-0840
Website: www.simonasia.com

Other Offices

10990 Wilshire Boulevard
Suite 1750
Los Angeles, United States of America 90024

Phone: 310-914-2410
Fax: 310-575-3174

1809 Harbour Centre
25 Harbour Road
Wanchai, Hong Kong
Phone: 852-511-1668
Fax: 852-588-1328

Management and Staff
Conor Mullet, Vice President
Michael Lenard, Managing Director
Richard Roque, Principal
Robert MacDonald, Managing Director

Whom to Contact
Henry J. Brandon
Mark C. Sellon

Type of Firm
Private Firm Investing Own Capital

Industry Association Membership
Hong Kong Venture Capital Association (HKVCA)

Project Preferences

Role in Financing:
Prefer role as deal originator but will also invest in deals created by others

Type of Financing Preferred:
Leveraged Buyout
Mezzanine
Second Stage Financing

Size of Investments Considered
Min Size of Investment Considered (000s): $20,000
Max Size of Investment Considered: No Limit

Geographical Preferences

United States
All U.S.

Industry Preferences

(% based on actual investment)

Computer Software and Services	46.1%
Internet Specific	35.7%
Other Products	10.7%
Consumer Related	6.3%
Communications and Media	0.6%
Industrial/Energy	0.6%

Additional Information
Name of Most Recent Fund: William E. Simon & Sons
Most Recent Fund Was Raised: 01/01/1995
Year Founded: 1994
Capital Under Management: $50,500,000
Current Activity Level : Actively seeking new investments
Method of Compensation: Return on invest. most important, but chg. closing fees, service fees, etc.

WINSLOW PARTNERS LLC

Narodni 41
Prague, Czech Republic
Phone: 4202-2422-1453
Fax: 4202-2421-8463

See D. of Columbia for full listing.

WIT JAPAN INVESTMENT, INC.

Shin Aoyama Building 12F
1-1-1 Minami Aoyama, Minato-ku
Tokyo, Japan
Phone: 03-5772-5472
Website: www.witcapital.ne.jp

Type of Firm
Private Firm Investing Own Capital

Project Preferences

Type of Financing Preferred:
Balanced

Geographical Preferences

International
Japan

Industry Preferences

Internet Specific
Internet

Additional Information
Capital Under Management: $23,200,000
Current Activity Level : Actively seeking new investments

WK ASSOCIATES

10/F,No.115 Ming-Sheng E. Road
Section 3
Taipei, Taiwan
Phone: 8862-2719-1010
Fax: 8862-2719-1019

Management and Staff
Wen Ko, President

Type of Firm
Private Firm Investing Own Capital

Industry Association Membership
Taiwan Venture Capital Association(TVCA)

Project Preferences

Type of Financing Preferred:
Expansion
Later Stage
Mezzanine

Geographical Preferences

International
Taiwan

Industry Preferences

(% based on actual investment)

Internet Specific	53.2%
Semiconductors/Other Elect.	23.6%
Communications and Media	17.0%
Computer Software and Services	6.3%

Additional Information
Year Founded: 1990
Capital Under Management: $217,400,000
Current Activity Level : Actively seeking new investments

WL VENTURES (FKA:LOTHIAN ENTERPRISE LTD.)

Geddes House
Kirkton North
Livingston, United Kingdom EH54 6G4
Phone: 44 1506-415144
Fax: 44 1506-415145
Website: www.wlventures.co.uk

Management and Staff
Kathy Greenwood

Whom to Contact
Kathy Greenwood

Type of Firm
Private Firm Investing Own Capital

Industry Association Membership
British Venture Capital Association

Project Preferences

Role in Financing:
Prefer role as deal originator but will also invest in deals created by others

Type of Financing Preferred:
Early Stage
Expansion
Management Buyouts
Seed
Startup

Size of Investments Considered
Min Size of Investment Considered (000s): $100
Max Size of Investment Considered (000s): $100,000

Geographical Preferences

International
United Kingdom

Additional Information
Name of Most Recent Fund: West Lothian Venture Fund
Most Recent Fund Was Raised: 08/01/1997
Year Founded: 1988
Capital Under Management: $2,900,000
Current Activity Level : Actively seeking new investments
Method of Compensation: Return on invest. most important, but chg. closing fees, service fees, etc.

WOOSHIN DEVELOPMENT FINANCE CORP

Asia Tower, 1/F, 726,
Yuksam-Dong, Kangnam-Ku
Seoul, South Korea
Phone: 822-538-5906
Fax: 822-567-3184
Website: www.wooshinv.co.kr

Management and Staff
Chang Hi Jeong, President
Yong Seop Kim, Managing Director

Whom to Contact
Seok-Ho Kim

Type of Firm
Non-Financial Corp. Affiliate or Subsidiary

Industry Association Membership
Korean Venture Capital Association

Project Preferences

Role in Financing:
Prefer role as deal originator

Type of Financing Preferred:
Early Stage
Expansion

Size of Investments Considered
Min Size of Investment Considered (000s): $500
Max Size of Investment Considered (000s): $5,000

Geographical Preferences

International
Korea, South

Industry Preferences

Communications and Media
CATV & Pay TV Systems
Data Communications
Satellite Microwave Comm.

Computer Other
Computer Related

Semiconductors/Other Elect.
Electronic Components

Biotechnology
Biotechnology

Medical/Health
Medical/Health

Consumer Related
Consumer Products

Industrial/Energy
Industrial Products

Additional Information
Year Founded: 1986
Capital Under Management: $15,000,000
Current Activity Level : Making few, if any, new investments
Method of Compensation: Return on investment is of primary concern, do not charge fees

WORKING VENTURES CANADIAN FUND, INC.

250 Bloor Street East
Suite 1600
Toronto, Canada M4W 1E6
Phone: 416-934-7718
Fax: 416-929-0901
Website: www.workingventures.ca

Other Offices

830-410 22nd Street East
Saskatoon, Canada S7K 5T6
Phone: 306-242-1023
Fax: 306-242-9959

Type of Firm
Private Firm Investing Own Capital

Industry Association Membership
Canadian Venture Capital Association

Project Preferences

Role in Financing:
Will function either as deal originator or investor in deals created by others

Type of Financing Preferred:
Acquisition
Balanced
Early Stage
Expansion
First Stage Financing
Later Stage
Leveraged Buyout
Management Buyouts
Mezzanine
Private Placement
Recapitalizations
Research and Development
Second Stage Financing
Seed
Special Situation
Start-up Financing

Size of Investments Considered

Min Size of Investment Considered (000s): $334
Max Size of Investment Considered (000s): $10,008

Geographical Preferences

Canada

Ontario
Western Canada

Industry Preferences

(% based on actual investment)

Consumer Related	18.1%
Other Products	13.4%
Computer Software and Services	12.8%
Internet Specific	12.6%
Industrial/Energy	11.0%
Semiconductors/Other Elect.	9.5%
Communications and Media	9.2%
Biotechnology	5.4%
Medical/Health	5.0%
Computer Hardware	3.0%

Additional Information

Name of Most Recent Fund: WVCF
Most Recent Fund Was Raised: 03/01/1999
Year Founded: 1989
Capital Under Management: $483,700,000
Current Activity Level : Actively seeking new investments
Method of Compensation: Return on investment is of primary concern, do not charge fees

WORLDVIEW TECHNOLOGY PARTNERS

16 Raffles Quay
#37-02 Hong Leong Bldg.
, Singapore 048581
Phone: 65-221-7388
Fax: 65-221-7366

See California for full listing.

XDL INTERVEST CAPITAL CORP. (FKA: XDL CAPITAL CORPORATION)

40 Sheppard Avenue West
Suite 606
Toronto, Canada M2N 6K9
Phone: 416-250-6500
Fax: 416-250-6330
Website: www.xdl.com

Management and Staff

Cindy Gordon, Principal
David Latner, Principal
Dennis Bennie, Principal
Michael Bregman, Principal
Tony Van Marken, Principal

Type of Firm

Private Firm Investing Own Capital

Additional Information

Year Founded: 1997
Capital Under Management: $17,500,000
Current Activity Level : Actively seeking new investments

YASUDA ENTERPRISE DEVELOPMENT CO., LTD.(FKA: NIPPON ENT.DEV)

Room 602, 6F, No 237
Section 2, Fu-Hsing S. Road
Taipei, Taiwan
Phone: 886-2-2708-2262
Fax: 886-2-2784-5444

See California for full listing.

YORKSHIRE FUND MANAGERS LTD.

Saint Martin's House
210/212 Chapeltown Road
Leeds, United Kingdom LS7 4HZ
Phone: 44-113-294-5050
Fax: 44-113-254-5002
Website: www.yorkshire-enterprise.co.uk

Type of Firm

Investment/Merchant Bank Subsid/Affil

Industry Association Membership

British Venture Capital Association

Project Preferences

Role in Financing:

Prefer role as deal originator but will also invest in deals created by others

Type of Financing Preferred:

Balanced
Early Stage
Later Stage
Leveraged Buyout
Second Stage Financing
Special Situation
Start-up Financing

Size of Investments Considered

Min Size of Investment Considered (000s): $250
Max Size of Investment Considered: No Limit

Geographical Preferences

International

United Kingdom

Industry Preferences

(% based on actual investment)

Communications and Media	30.0%
Consumer Related	22.5%
Computer Software and Services	12.6%
Semiconductors/Other Elect.	6.5%
Medical/Health	6.4%
Other Products	6.1%
Biotechnology	5.4%
Internet Specific	4.6%
Industrial/Energy	3.1%
Computer Hardware	2.9%

Additional Information

Name of Most Recent Fund: Yorkshire Fund Pool 4
Most Recent Fund Was Raised: 01/01/1994
Year Founded: 1987
Capital Under Management: $111,800,000
Current Activity Level : Actively seeking new investments
Method of Compensation: Return on invest. most important, but chg. closing fees, service fees, etc.

YOUNG ASSOCIATES LIMITED

Harcourt Hosue
19 Cavendish Square
London, United Kingdom W1M 9AB
Phone: 44 20 7447 8800
Fax: 44 20 7447 8849
E-mail: info@youngassoc.com
Website: www.youngassoc.com

Management and Staff
David Young, Lord of Graffham, Founder

Type of Firm
Private Firm Investing Own Capital

Project Preferences

Type of Financing Preferred:
Early Stage

Geographical Preferences

International
United Kingdom

Industry Preferences

Communications and Media
Communications and Media

Additional Information
Year Founded: 1996
Current Activity Level : Actively seeking new investments

YOZMA VENTURE CAPITAL LTD

Ramat Aviv Tower
40 Einstein Street
Tel Aviv, Israel 69102
Phone: 972-3-643-7766
Fax: 972-3-643-7888
Website: www.yozma.com

Management and Staff
Chen Schor, Chief Financial Officer
Yoav Sebba, Principal

Type of Firm
Private Firm Investing Own Capital

Project Preferences

Type of Financing Preferred:
Early Stage
Later Stage

Size of Investments Considered
Min Size of Investment Considered (000s): $500
Max Size of Investment Considered (000s): $500,000

Geographical Preferences

International
Israel

Industry Preferences

Communications and Media
Communications and Media

Additional Information
Capital Under Management: $200,000,000
Current Activity Level : Actively seeking new investments

ZODIAC VENTURE CAPITAL KB

Norrmalmstorg 14
PO Box 7030
Stockholm, Sweden 103 86
Phone: 46 8 407 1300
Fax: 46 8 407 1350
E-mail: zodiak@brummer.se
Website: www.brummer.se

Type of Firm
Affiliate/Subsidary of Oth. Financial. Instit.

Industry Association Membership
Swedish Venture Capital Association

Project Preferences

Type of Financing Preferred:
Expansion
Startup

Geographical Preferences

International
Europe
Sweden

Industry Preferences

Communications and Media
Communications and Media
Telecommunications

Business Serv.
Media

Additional Information
Capital Under Management: $48,500,000
Current Activity Level : Actively seeking new investments

ZOUK VENTURES

1b Portland Place
London, United Kingdom W1N 3AA
Phone: 44 20 7947 3400
Fax: 44 20 7947 3449
Website: www.zouk.com

Management and Staff
Felix von Schubert, Founding Partner
Samer Salty, Founder

Type of Firm
Private Firm Investing Own Capital

Project Preferences

Type of Financing Preferred:
Balanced

Geographical Preferences

International
Europe

Industry Preferences

Internet Specific
Internet

Additional Information
Name of Most Recent Fund: European E-Commerce Fund, L.P.
Most Recent Fund Was Raised: 01/01/1999
Capital Under Management: $81,800,000
Current Activity Level : Actively seeking new investments

Indexes

Index of Venture Capital Professionals

A
Aatz, Franz, 910
Abate, Anthony, 409
Abbott, Robert, 223
Abdelnour, Ziad, 582
Abe, George, 228
Abell, James, 729
Aben, Tali, 825
Abraham, John, 409
Abramovitz, Debra, 554
Abramson, Patty, 318
Abramson, Patty, 318
AbuZayyad, Ray, 192
Acheson, Michael, 690
Achtmann, Eric, 913
Ackerman, Jefferey R., 439
Ackerman, Joel, 590
Ackerman, Robert, 143
Ackerman, Samuel, 404
Ackermann, Matthias, 882
Adair, Charles, 331
Adair, Eddie, 331
Adamek, Thomas, 386
Adams, Chip, 237
Adams, David, 187
Adams, David, 237
Adams, Frank, 394
Adams, Joel, 622
Adams, Robert, 640
Adams, Robert, 658
Adams, Susan, 390
Adamsky, Brian, 625
Adelson, Gary, 175
Adelson, Merv, 175
Adler, Frederick, 502
Adler, Frederick, 178
Adler, Marilyn, 538
Adolph, Mark, 285
Adox, James, 458
Afeyan, Noubar, 405
Agee, Catherine, 302
Agerup, Karl-Christian, 902
Agranoff, Stuart, 549
Agrawal, Ravin, 175
Ahlman, Lars, 804
Ahlstedt, James, 702
Ahlstrom, Mikael, 917
Ahmed, Shami, 872
Ahn, Daniel, 274
Ahr, Oren, 946
Ahrens, Brent, 290
Ahrens II, Jack K., 470
Ahuja, Anju, 354
Ahuja, Sanjiv, 235
Aills, Zachary, 665
Akashi, Eizou, 863
Alala, Joseph, 599
Albanese, Glen, 556
Alber, Thomas, 451
Alberg, Tom, 707
Albert, M. Scott, 598
Albertsen, Hendrik, 794

Albin, David R., 300
Albrecht, Knute, 623
Albright, John, 861
Alder, G.Michael, 131
Aldrich, Russ, 706
Alexander, James, 561
Alexander, Miles, 563
Alexander, Patrick, 756
Alexander, Ted, 214
Alexos, Nicholas, 361
Alfeld, Chad, 298
Alfeld, Stanley, 298
Alfstad, Sam, 509
Alger, Kevin, 542
Algkvist, Bjorn, 804
Ali, Ismael Fariz, 817
Alibhai, Nizar, 859
Alimansky, Burt, 504
Alioth, Lukas R, 900
Alleman, Sam, 835
Allen, Ashley, 318
Allen, Ashley, 318
Allen, Bruce, 748
Allen, Doug, 351
Allen, Henry, 489
Allen, James, 281
Allen, James, 813
Allen, Jeff, 187
Allen, Jeff, 237
Allen, Julian, 310
Allen, Wilson, 575
Alley, Erin, 167
Allred, Jeffrey, 336
Allsteadt, MArk, 306
Almog, Yuval, 465
Alon, Ruth, 913
Alonso, Silvia Garcia, 895
Alpert, David, 429
Alsop, Stewart, 396
Alur, Raj, 471
Alvord, Joel, 447
Amble, Erik, 894
Ambrosio, Jeffery, 615
Amelio, Gil, 242
Ames, Grace, 302
Ames, William, 414
Amies, Colin, 489
Ammerman, Robert, 415
Amsterdam, Stephen, 635
Anandaram, Sanjay, 864
Anantharaman, Murali, 335
Ander, Claes, 732
Andersen, Claus Hojbjerg, 794
Anderson, Brian, 347
Anderson, Bruce, 591
Anderson, David, 251
Anderson, David, 871
Anderson, Dennis, 469
Anderson, Edward, 438
Anderson, Erik, 673
Anderson, Gary, 640
Anderson, Graham, 527
Anderson, Gregory, 251
Anderson, Howard, 409
Anderson, Howard, 456
Anderson, Jared, 246
Anderson, Jeff, 632
Anderson, Jerry, 246
Anderson, Jim, 181
Anderson, Jon, 706
Anderson, Kyle, 237
Anderson, Lynne, 435
Anderson, Stacy, 604
Anderson, Valerie, 326
Andersson, Bernt, 804
Andreen, Robert, 903
Andrew, Bob, 570
Andrews, Christopher, 686
Andriole, Stephen, 640
Andrus, Emily, 145
Angadi, Vijay, 845
Angelakis, Michael, 643
Angue, Michel, 824
Anic, Miroslav, 370
Anker, Andrew, 148
Annick, Gregory, 203
Annick Tomlinson, Marie, 730
Anquillare, Anne, 589
Anson, George, 426
Anstey, Sanford, 408
Anton, Adolfo, 900
Anton, Richard, 740
Antonen, Brian, 775
Antsey, Gary, 582
Aozono, Masahiro, 789
Aplin, John, 376
Appel, Stanley, 683
Appelbaum, Malcolm P., 589
Appendino, Michele, 895
Applegarth, Paul, 314
Applegate, Brion, 248
Aquilano, Don, 377
Arafat, Osama, 861
Aragona, Joseph, 657
Archambeau, Eric, 407
Archambeau, Eric, 154
Archibald, Carol, 230
Ardell, J.E., 255
Arena, Alexander, 790
Arenson, Kevin, 562
Arenz, Tom, 536
Arkebauer, James, 285
Armato, Leonard, 169
Armenante, Mark, 250
Armitage, Ian, 884
Armitage, Ian, 883
Armony, Izhar, 417
Armstrong, Andrew, 577
Armstrong, Jerry, 507
Armstrong, Jim, 161
Armstrong, Thomas, 568
Arnold, Gary, 325
Arnold, Steven, 441
Aronoff, David, 424

Aronson, David, 160
Arora, Suresh, 605
Arrigo, Maurizio, 865
Arrington, LLoyd, 313
Artunkal, Ali, 745
Asbach, Peter, 736
Asel, Paul, 256
Ashby, Molly, 576
Askey, Peter, 623
Aslett, Mark, 431
Asquini, Franco, 824
Asscher, Laurent, 744
Assulin, Vered, 826
Astier, Jean-Francois, 785
Atir, Yiftach, 868
Atkinson, Andrew, 425
Attinella, Michael, 322
Attwood, Tom, 855
Atwell, James, 451
Atwood, Kimball, 146
Au, Peter, 777
Auber, Nathalie, 246
Audino, Antonio, 714
Auerbach, Daniel, 421
Auerbach, Jon, 427
Auerbach, Paul, 167
Auerbach, Stuart, 404
Auerbach-Gersht, Eran, 913
Aurentz, Vince, 583
Austen, Christopher, 605
Austin, Alan, 139
Austin, Chip, 539
Austin, William, 519
Avis, Gregory, 451
Aweida, Daniel, 277
Aweida, Jesse, 277
Ayukawa, Junta, 949
Azan, Alain, 246

B

Baan, Jan, 965
Babcock, John, 238
Babitt, Cindy J., 613
Bachand, Raymond, 820
Bachinsky, Frank, 606
Bachinsky, Frank, 607
Bachow, Paul, 623
Bachrach, Ernest, 402
Bachurski, Edward, 622
Backinsky, Frank, 606
Backus, John, 692
Bacon, Kathleen, 426
Bacon, Louis Moore, 554
Badaracco, Francesco, 968
Baelir, Geoffrey, 261
Bagley, Thomas, 366
Bahl, Ashish, 332
Bahles, Shanda, 176
Bailey, Brian, 599
Bailey, Irving, 384
Bain, Samuel, 568
Bajpai, Dharma, 753
Baker, Barry, 413
Baker, G. Leonard, 251
Baker, Henry, 510
Baker, James, 152
Baker, John, 169
Baker, John, 510
Baker, Renee, 170
Baker Pettersen, Kathryn, 921
Baksa, Stephen, 496
Balaraj, KP, 976
Balasco, Cynthia, 643
Balbien, Joel, 246
Baldassarre, Carl, 614
Balderston, Thomas, 573
Baldwin, Chris, 417
Baldwin, Sherman, 234
Balek-Miner, Jean, 709
Balen, John, 290
Balkanski, Alexandre, 154
Ball, Anthony, 762
Ballarini, David, 696
Ballentine, Steven, 288
Bally, Jean-Marc, 926
Balmuth, Michael, 451
Baloff, Steve, 401
Balsara, Samir, 207
Bamber, Frederick, 405
Banatao, Dado, 210
Bancroft, Charles, 648
Banerjee, Chiranjit, 823
Banerjee, Sujit, 640
Bank, Keith, 359
Banker, Dave, 670
Banker, Jay, 540
Banks, Stephen, 658
Bannister, David, 394
Bannon, Anne, 845
Banzhof, Carl, 661
Bar-Niv, Moshe, 747
Barak, Philip, 556
Baran, Ray, 623
Barbeau, Mark, 165
Barber, Sandra, 327
Barek, Jonathan, 239
Barel, Meir, 940
Barerra, Oscar, 781
Barez, Donald, 643
Barger, Matthew, 189
Baring, John, 696
Barkas, Alexander, 232
Barker, Michael, 640
Barkinson, Richard, 310
Barnds, Thomas, 492
Barnes, Jeffrey, 440
Barnes, Robert, 736
Barnes, Stanton, 713
Barnes, Stephen, 635
Barnum, Brian, 180
Barohn, Gary, 475
Baron, John, 543
Barr, Elie, 888

Barr, Gregory, 643
Barratt, Henry, 690
Barrett, Dave, 441
Barrett, Robert, 409
Barrier, Denis, 853
Barringer, Lynn, 198
Barris, Peter, 396
Barron, Bruce, 365
Barron, Robert, 556
Barrows, Timothy, 433
Barry, Doug, 241
Barry, Hank, 191
Barry, John, 567
Barry, Roger, 218
Barsk, Anders, 804
Bartel, Colin, 833
Bartholomew, Robert, 273
Bartholomew, Tom, 309
Bartlam, Tom, 855
Bartlett, James, 616
Barton, Harris, 159
Barton, Tom, 206
Baruch, Thomas, 161
Barzilay, Amos, 269
Baskett, Forest, 396
Bass, Sid, 659
Bassett, Ronald, 758
Bassi, Benoit, 763
Bates, Donald, 643
Bates, Marcia, 408
Batterson, Leonard, 348
Battles, Brett, 138
Batton, Gregory, 292
Baudouin, Christopher, 297
Bauer, Bruce, 220
Bauer, Charles, 444
Baum, David, 441
Baum, Jack, 676
Baum, Michael, 441
Baumann, Roger, 586
Baumel, William, 465
Baumel, William, 239
Baumgartner, Markus, 757
Bayless, Jon, 677
Bayley, Trevor, 884
Bayley, Trevor, 883
Beach, Brian, 326
Beard, Dennis, 365
Beasley, Allen, 235
Beatty, Rick, 257
Beaucamp, Andreas, 752
Beauchamp, Marc, 858
Beaudoin, Mark, 502
Beblo, Michael, 160
Beck, James, 210
Becker, Eric, 398
Becker, Greg, 244
Beckett, William, 717
Beckwitt, Rick, 177
Beecken, Dave, 348
Beeler, Charles, 176
Beer, Cliff, 712
Beerbower, Bruce, 359
Begg, John, 426
Begun, Michael, 782
Behbehani, Taher, 221
Behnke, James, 466
Behrens, Christopher, 543
Behrens, M. Kathleen, 236
Behrman, Darryl, 512
Behrman, Grant, 512
Behrman, Paul, 577
Beirne, David, 154
Beitler, Stephen, 259
Bejjani, Ghassan, 554
Beldy, Dan, 191
Bell, Robert, 601
Bellas, Robert, 614
Bellas, Robin, 614
Beller, Laura, 281
Belli, Guido, 763
Belmont, Gregory, 535
Belt, Ron, 829
Benardete, Judith, 489
Benbow, Robert, 403
Bendicksen, Beverly, 500
Benedetto, Rene, 539
Bengur, O.R., 393
Benjamin, Frank, 818
Benjamin, Keith, 427
Bennahum, David, 557
Bennet, Michael, 657
Bennett, Dougal, 799
Bennett, Frank, 464
Bennett, Steve, 193
Bennie, Dennis, 979
Bennington, William, 310
Bensen, Tod, 773
Bensky, Robert, 254
Benson, Buzz, 472
Benson, Erik, 714
Benson, Gary K., 925
Benson, Marc, 634
Benton, Monica, 680
Beracha, Rami, 913
Berardino, Thomas, 306
Berdell, James, 265
Berecz, Jozsef, 842
Berenstein, Gregory, 479
Berg, John, 170
Berge, Jaume, 831
Berger, Lior, 825
Bergheim, Olav, 486
Berghorst, Theodore, 372
Bergleitner, George, 579
Berglund, James, 178
Bergman, Bart, 474
Bergman, James, 609
Bergmann, David, 386
Bergonia, R. David, 364
Beritela, Sam, 398
Berk, Zachary, 546
Berkeley, Richard, 510
Berkery, Dermot, 795

Berliner, Arthur, 269
Berliner, Arthur, 270
Berman, Ian, 182
Berman, Ian, 466
Berman, Thomas, 343
Bernardoni, Peter, 254
Bernatek, Marek, 746
Bernegger, Mark, 570
Bernier, Brian, 450
Bernstein, Nathan, 512
Berry, Harry, 763
Berry, Smit, 872
Berry, Thomas, 356
Berstein, Beth, 527
Berterretche, Jackie, 186
Bertoldi, Robert, 506
Bertoldi, Robert, 586
Berwick, Mark R., 242
Bery, Varun, 953
Berzins, Andrey, 943
Besse, J. Carter, 316
Besse, Joel, 407
Best, Brian, 272
Best, David, 302
Beste, Frederick, 634
Betcher, Kurt, 223
Bettino, Lawrence, 510
Beukers, Alice, 241
Beutner, Austin, 175
Bhagwandas, T., 767
Bhanot, Sonia, 250
Bhasin, Rahul, 755
Bhatia, Rajv, 972
Bhatia, Ranjeet, 924
Bhusri, Aneel, 424
Bichara, Axel, 407
Biddinger, Clay, 322
Biddle, Jack, 697
Biekart, Erik, 965
Bierman, Mike, 667
Biglieri, Susan, 200
Bignier, Laurent, 866
Bilden, Philip, 426
Bildt, Carl, 861
Billerbeck, Chuck, 632
Billimoria, Farrokh, 578
Billstrom, David, 705
Bindel, Serge, 805
Binder, Scott, 312
Binford, Joy, 697
Bingham, Kate, 445
Binkley, Nick, 180
Binman, Zeev, 913
Birck, Michael, 351
Bird, Jeffrey, 258
Bird, Steven, 160
Birkett, Bill, 791
Birnberg, Jeffrey, 495
Bischof, George, 160
Bitan, Giora, 828
Bittan, Michael, 583
Bittker, Allan, 457
Bjerkan, John, 921
Bjorkman, Anders, 744
Bjorling, Ylva Hambraeus, 953
Blacher, Perry, 806
Black, David, 302
Black, Don, 382
Black, Jonathan, 863
Black, Philip, 390
Black, Philip, 206
Black, Robin, 762
Black, Tim, 706
Blackburn, David, 276
Blackburn, Mike, 652
Blackburn, Tara, 227
Blackburn, Thomas, 383
Bladh, Jorgen H, 902
Blair, James, 486
Blaisdell, Thomas, 169
Blake, Ying, 561
Blanc-Brude, Alain, 738
Blanchard, Charles, 705
Blanchard, Jeffrey, 664
Blank, Robert, 373
Blanton, Matt, 679
Blau, Melissa, 518
Blauer, Gary, 472
Blend, Steven, 562
Bliska, Thomas, 165
Blivin, David, 605
Bloch, Jonathan, 184
Block, Bill, 147
Block, Geoffrey, 521
Blomberg, Hans, 810
Blomgren, Jim, 804
Blomqvist, Alf, 804
Blonder, Greg, 614
Bloom, Jack, 512
Bloomer, Gary, 278
Bloomer, R.D. Peter, 278
Blow, Robert, 651
Blumberg, David, 155
Blume, Frederick, 416
Blume, Rick, 345
Blumenstein, Robi, 516
Blumenthal, Daniel, 374
Blumfield, Adrian, 553
Bobbert, Ilja, 916
Bochnowski, James, 167
Bock, Lawrence, 521
Bock, Louis, 150
Bode, C. James, 618
Boden, Kathy, 630
Bodenkamp, Jens, 808
Bodine, Peter, 146
Bodman, Richard, 496
Bodor, Danielle, 895
Boehnke, Frank, 975
Boettcher, James, 160
Boezi, Karen, 465
Bogetz, David, 343
Bohm, Eckart, 826
Boillot, Etienne, 547

Bolander, F.W.W.(Rick), 346
Bolander, F.W.W.(Rick), 182
Boldt, Bernie, 378
Bolema, Albert, 827
Boles, John, 625
Bolger, Judy, 489
Bolland, Martin, 736
Bolton, Michael, 635
Bolyky, Janos, 787
Bommer, Eric, 573
Bond, Patrick, 716
Boni, Fausto, 895
Bonker, Virginia, 319
Bonnier, Robert, 926
Bono, Mark, 455
Bonsal, Frank, 396
Bookstein, Suzanne, 466
Boon, Koh Soo, 847
Boon, Tan, 402
Boonstoppel, Roeland, 466
Boorstein, Martin, 589
Boot, Gijs, 791
Booth, Jeff, 554
Booth, John, 649
Borchers, John, 466
Borgdorff, W., 898
Borghese, Livio, 525
Bornikoel, Friedrich, 961
Bornstein, Judy, 210
Boroian, Patrick, 578
Borst, Steve, 687
Bosch, Sake, 916
Boscheman, Brian, 606
Bosman, Hans, 407
Bostad, Thorstein, 921
Bosterud, Morten, 921
Boswell, Fredrick, 471
Boswell, Rick, 471
Botho von Portatius, Hans, 865
Bott, Ross, 235
Bottorff, Leslie, 225
Bottum, Steven, 315
Boucher, David, 405
Boudon, Stephane, 775
Bouissou, Phillippe, 143
Boulais, Wayne, 346
Boullion, Elliott, 671
Bourbon, Bruce, 256
Bowden, Steven, 145
Bower, Bruce, 180
Bower, Christopher, 227
Bower, Whitney, 489
Bowes, William, 261
Bowles, Erskine, 599
Bowley, Richard, 908
Bowman, Bob, 293
Bowman, Lawrence, 156
Bowman, Roy, 331
Bowsher, Stephen, 197
Boyd, John, 640
Boyle, James, 360
Boyle, John, 836
Boyle, John, 275
Boyles, Harlan, 600
Bozeman, Bob, 145
Braca, John, 527
Braca, John, 638
Brackett, David, 345
Brackett, Stephen, 429
Brader-Araje, Michael, 606
Bradley, Harold, 473
Bradley, Thomas, 566
Bradley, Wade, 620
Bragd, Mikael, 937
Braitman, Lawrence, 244
Brakke, Ronald, 499
Bramson, Carol, 448
Brandes, Kai, 796
Brandfon, Alan, 544
Brandis, Hendrik, 800
Brandon, John, 842
Brandon, Kevin, 572
Brandyberry, Arnold, 291
Branscum, Chris, 188
Brasseur, M.J., 885
Brassington, Jeremy, 764
Brath Ingero, Bard, 921
Braverman, Alan, 584
Bravo, Orlando, 371
Bray, Bennie, 336
Brazelton, Fred, 680
Bredt, Thomas, 212
Breece, R. William, 475
Brege, Laura, 234
Bregman, Michael, 979
Breitfeld, Marc, 865
Brekka, Richard, 523
Brennan, Michael, 440
Brenner, Anthony, 236
Brenner, Anthony, 165
Brenner, Larry, 392
Brennet-Morris, Christine, 281
Brentlinger, Paul, 614
Bressner, Glen, 634
Brewer, John, 336
Breyer, James, 139
Breyer, James, 483
Briant, Kate, 771
Brichke, Jay, 539
Brickman, C. Andrew, 347
Bridges, Paul, 736
Brigden, Richard, 604
Briggs, Taylor, 410
Brimacomb, Richard, 471
Bristol, Brian, 307
Britt, Chris, 209
Britt, Raymond, 429
Britti, John, 397
Britts, David, 543
Broad, Aaron, 554
Broadhaust, Austin, 522
Brockhoff, Tucker, 165
Broderick, James, 614
Brody, Jeff, 235

Brody, Kenneth, 317
Broeker, Alex, 682
Brogan, Edward, 310
Bronfein, Michael, 398
Bronfin, Barry, 288
Brooke, John, 402
Brooke, William, 598
Brookfield, Chris, 709
Brooks, Benjamin, 605
Brooks, Donald, 201
Brooks, Janet, 801
Brooks, John, 441
Brooks, Mark, 150
Brooks, Mark, 523
Brooks, Michael, 310
Brooks, Michael, 586
Brooks, Rory, 885
Brooks, Todd, 210
Brooks, Todd, 198
Brophy, Parker, 281
Brosda, Alexander C., 579
Bross, Jason, 555
Brost, Gary, 581
Brotchie, Christopher, 755
Brotman, Steve, 576
Brown, Atlee, 630
Brown, Bernard, 297
Brown, Chris, 648
Brown, Crichton, 386
Brown, Cyrus, 593
Brown, Doug, 711
Brown, Edward, 283
Brown, Frank, 204
Brown, James, 441
Brown, Jeff, 180
Brown, Kristin, 547
Brown, Michael, 679
Brown, Owen, 237
Brown, Paul, 409
Brown, Randy, 614
Brown, Rayna, 247
Brown, Richard, 598
Brown, Robert, 633
Brown, Steven, 351
Brown, Valerie, 640
Broyhill, Hunt, 599
Bru, Jean-Francois, 775
Brubaker, Patrick, 403
Bruchl, Alexander, 407
Bruckman, Neal, 529
Brumm, Peter, 969
Brumm, Soren, 138
Brunk, Steven, 620
Bruno, Michael, 580
Brusco, Martin, 149
Brush, Dennis, 159
Bryan, Lee, 605
Buch, Fredrik, 904
Buchanan, Stephen, 602
Buck III, James M., 639
Buckley, Steven, 853
Budnick, Victor, 291
Buettner, Jan, 157
Buffa, Anthony, 294
Buffini, Damon, 445
Buhl, W. Peter, 222
Bujko, Jerzy, 735
Bultot, H, 936
Bunce, John, 189
Bund, Ian, 462
Bunker, Tony, 763
Buonanno, Bernard, 643
Burch, Lucious E., 650
Burd, John, 273
Burgin, William, 410
Burk, Alan, 399
Burke, Andrew, 812
Burke, Monica, 238
Burkhardt, C.A., 538
Burnes, Richard, 417
Burnette, Graham, 240
Burnham, Bill, 247
Burnham, R. Bradford, 496
Burns, Kevin, 547
Burns, Matthew, 413
Burrill, G. Steven, 156
Burrow, Tim, 138
Burshtein, Sam, 772
Burstein, Barton, 677
Burton, Charles, 636
Burton, Donald, 327
Burton, John, 700
Bustany, Ted, 483
Butalia, K.S., 780
Butler, Duncan, 278
Butler, Duncan, 674
Butterworth, Jim, 547
Buttolph, David, 514
Button, Scott, 720
Buxell, Kristi, 466
Buyer, Lisa, 255
Bybee, Clinton, 346
Byers, Brett, 587
Byers, Brook, 200
Byrne, Robert, 402
Byrnes, Aiden, 732
Byrnes, Bob, 512
Byun, Jin, 390

C

Cabello, David, 679
Caccavo, James, 554
Cadogan, William, 471
Caffi, Alain, 967
Cahill, Edward, 393
Cahill, Patrick, 663
Cahillane, Daniel, 489
Cahoon, Arthur, 326
Cain, Daniel, 416
Cairo, Alberto, 771
Cakata, Artur, 853
Calanchi, Piergiorgio, 736
Calder, David, 911

Caldwell, Donald, 625
Calhoun, Hal, 212
Callard, David J., 589
Callinan, Nicholas, 402
Callow, A.Dana, 412
Calton, Robert, 600
Calvet, Jorge, 855
Cambell, Gordon, 254
Cameron, Dennis P., 435
Cameron, Hazel, 156
Camp, Gregory T., 508
Campbell, Gregory, 672
Campbell, Mary, 458
Campbell, Richard, 306
Campbell, Rob, 325
Campbell-White, Annette, 212
Campe, Stephen, 752
Campion, John, 277
Campuzano, Juan Carlos, 323
Canfield, Philip, 356
Canin, Jeff, 704
Canning, John, 361
Capada, Ann, 402
Capen, Richard, 158
Caplain, Jason, 605
Capone, Constance, 358
Carano, Bandel, 302
Carbery, Paul, 355
Carbo, Jaime, 925
Carbone, Paul, 347
Carley, Tina, 132
Carlick, David, 263
Carlisle, Doug, 212
Carlisle, James, 567
Carlotti, Matteo, 744
Carlsson, Svante, 941
Carmel, Christopher F., 296
Carmignato, Guilio, 817
Carnahan-Walsh, Ellen, 373
Carney, Katherine, 471
Carol, Niall V.G., 732
Carone, Richard, 710
Carozza, Walter, 588
Carpenter, D. Jim, 570
Carr, Alan, 160
Carr, Dayton, 587
Carr, Robert, 246
Carrabino, Joseph, 310
Carrington, Jerrold, 358
Carroll, Daniel, 219
Carroll, Ronald, 667
Carruthers, Robert, 679
Carson, Russell, 591
Carsten, Jack, 190
Carter, Christopher J., 448
Carter, Larry, 137
Carter, Michael, 445
Carter, Shelby, 657
Carthy, Mark, 440
Carusi, Michael, 401
Cary, Lucius, 928
Cascio, Paul, 609
Case, Gregory, 563
Cases, Philippe, 229
Casey, Joseph, 586
Casey, Roger, 832
Cash, Berry, 197
Caspritz, Gert, 961
Cass, A.Baron, 474
Cassidy, B. Martha, 550
Cassidy, Michele, 302
Cassina, Stefano, 402
Castelein, Caley, 390
Castellini, Clateo, 484
Castello, Luiz Fernando, 408
Castle, Paul, 890
Castleman, Peter, 310
Cataford, Paul, 758
Cater, Barry, 140
Caufield, Frank, 200
Cavalaris, John, 356
Cavanagh, Cate, 494
Cavanaugh, Eugene, 375
Cavanaugh, James, 490
Cavell, S., 831
Cayce, John, 339
Cayce, John, 330
Cellier, Marc, 919
Celmer, Ronald, 567
Celmer, Ronald, 518
Censoprano, Sal, 207
Cerbone, Robert, 316
Cerf, Monty, 542
Cerrudo, Shirley, 223
Cha, Johnson, 160
Cha, Johnson, 160
Chabrowe, Terry, 509
Chadha, Sumir, 976
Chadwell, Tracy, 510
Chadwick, John, 652
Chaffe, Todd, 267
Chaffee, Todd, 196
Chaffin, Tracey, 600
Chagal, Mustafa, 398
Chai, Hyun-Suk, 868
Chalaby, Cherine, 140
Chamberlain, Geoffrey, 799
Chambers, Jeffrey, 451
Chambon, Phillippe, 578
Champenois, Denis, 853
Champsi, Farah, 144
Chan, Alec, 974
Chan, Chuck, 144
Chan, Hew, 402
Chan, Johnny, 951
Chan, Kevin, 402
Chan, Peter, 755
Chandler, David, 373
Chandler, Edward, 356
Chandra, Rob, 410
Chandra, Rob, 419
Chanen, Gordon, 703
Chang, Jen, 391
Chang, John, 250

Chang, Shirley, 851
Chang, Steven, 511
Channing, Walter, 521
Chanzit, Martin, 288
Chao, Daniel, 206
Chao, David, 169
Chao, Falton, 273
Chao, Warren, 174
Chao, William, 187
Chaplinsky, Rob, 214
Chapman, John, 961
chapman, Philip, 178
Charest, Ray, 440
Charlesworth, Roger, 872
Charlton, Alex, 583
Charpie, Richard, 404
Chartener, Robert, 317
Chase, Andy, 571
Chase, George, 662
Chatain, Jacques, 817
Chatfield, Glen, 625
Chau, Paul, 269
Chauvet, Jean-Marie, 794
Chedrick, Andrew, 178
Chee, Brian, 441
Cheek, Giles, 835
Cheesmond, John, 445
Cheetham, Anthony, 221
Chefitz, Robert, 563
Chen, David, 709
Chen, Derrick, 569
Chen, Eugene, 144
Chen, Jerry, 776
Chen, Jesse, 209
Chen, John, 252
Chen, John, 790
Chen, Mark, 525
Chen, Paul, 219
Cheng, Steven, 839
Cheng, Susan, 192
Chereskin, Benjamin, 361
Cherniak, Brad, 789
Chertoff, Daniel, 772
Chertok, Doug, 538
Chervokas, Jason, 567
Chesen, Marc, 623
Cheung, Cliff, 908
Cheung, Tom, 540
Chevallier, Pierre, 909
Chevre, Jean-Marc, 811
Chew, James, 821
Chew, James, 822
Chi, Charles, 424
Chi, Edward, 776
Chia, Timothy, 908
Chiang, Brian, 269
Chidambaram, Sada, 171
Chiew, Lee Fook, 852
Child, Michael, 451
Chin, Eric, 195
Chin, Eric, 194
Chin, Kevin, 520
Chiruvolu, Ravi, 160
Chiruvolu, Ravi, 144
Chiu, Andy, 957
Chiu, Han, 180
Choate, Fred, 627
Choi, George, 212
Choksi, Himanshu, 228
Chong, Richard, 494
Chopp, Joseph, 354
Chou, Scott, 182
Chow, David, 907
Chow, Lon, 346
Chowdhury, Ajay, 192
Christensen, Bjorn, 930
Christensen, Ole, 793
Christiansen, Stephan, 292
Christianson, Tony, 464
Chu, Christopher, 466
Chu, Daniel, 667
Chu, Nelson, 395
Chu, Peter, 748
Chung, Peter, 451
Chung, Tark Won, 797
Chung, Won, 148
Chung, Young, 843
Church, Linda, 856
Churchman, Keith, 763
Chute, Paul, 303
Chvisuk, Terry, 425
Ciccone, Dennis, 632
Cichos, Troy, 707
Ciesinski, Steven, 800
Ciffolillo, Joe, 450
Ciriello, Paul, 421
Claes, Roger, 811
Claesson, Hakan, 732
Claeys, Frank, 974
Claeys, Frank, 973
Clairefond, Eric, 778
Clancy, Thomas, 178
Clapp, Andrew, 414
Claquin, Herve, 729
Clardy, James, 657
Clark, B. Jefferson, 598
Clark, David, 443
Clark, John, 591
Clark, John, 698
Clark, Simon, 421
Clark, Theodore, 426
Clarke, John, 485
Clarke Adamson, Martha, 243
Claude, Philippe, 407
Claudy, Peter, 431
Claussen, Christian, 961
Clayton, Grant, 278
Clearman, Stephen, 489
Clifford, Chris, 410
Cline, William, 520
Clingman, Alan, 562
Clinton, Alexander, 147
Clinton, John, 292
Clive, Colin, 955

Cloninger, Viviana, 499
Closson, Charles, 602
Cloutier, Richard, 820
Clute, George, 709
Coane, James, 637
Cochran, Julie, 566
Cochran, Kirby, 687
Cockrell, Ross, 657
Cockshutt, Tim, 386
Code, Andrew, 351
Coelho, George, 154
Coffey, Steve, 667
Cogan, Gill, 206
Cohen, Allen, 354
Cohen, Andrew, 323
Cohen, Barton, 474
Cohen, David, 825
Cohen, Dillon, 514
Cohen, Ira, 700
Cohen, James, 669
Cohen, Jarrod, 520
Cohen, Michael, 185
Cohen, Mitch, 189
Cohen, Neil, 860
Cohen, Niles, 484
Cohen, Rani, 888
Cohen, Serge, 865
Cohen, Yuval, 864
Cohn, Paul, 632
Coit, David, 389
Colayco, Aloysius, 745
Colayco, Rufo, 745
Colby, Edward, 973
Cole, Andrew, 872
Cole, J. Daniel, 450
Cole, James, 274
Colella, Samuel, 196
Coleman, Alexander, 524
Coleman, Larry, 649
Coles, George, 588
Collatos, William, 248
Collier, D. Scott, 682
Collier, David, 156
Collins, David, 911
Collins, Jarrett, 437
Collins, Michael, 136
Collins, Michael, 648
Collins, Peter, 326
Collins, Phil, 210
Collins, Scott, 451
Collinson, Jeffrey, 291
Collis, James, 572
Collison, Terry, 319
Collombel, Philippe, 229
Colmie, Anita, 191
Colo, Shawn, 248
Colon, Daniel, 517
Colonna, Jerry, 530
Colvert, Scott, 667
Comaford, Christine, 146
Comeaux, Craig, 655
Comolli, Kevin, 139
Compall, John, 350
Compton, Kevin, 200
Conboy, James, 286
Coneybeer, Robert, 396
Conn, Alastair, 902
Conn, Robert, 853
Connell, David, 960
Connelly, Michael J., 548
Conners, Scott, 298
Connor, Michael, 530
Connor, Tim, 284
Connors, Kevin, 450
Conrad, Anthony, 266
Conrades, George, 441
Conroy, William, 540
Consul, Harish, 907
Conway, Brian, 451
Conway, Paul, 417
Conway, Ron, 145
Cook, James, 600
Cook, Richard, 417
Cook, Robert, 717
Cooke, Kim, 690
Coombs, Ron, 632
Cooney, David, 348
Cooper, Eric, 872
Cooper, Jeffrey, 282
Cooper, Kendall, 170
Cooper-Evans, Alex, 835
Copeland, Eric, 586
Corcoran, Daniel, 418
Cordaro, Christine, 161
Cordaro, Christine, 607
Cordier, Clement, 725
Cordova, Carl C., 525
Corley, Leslie, 324
Cornell, Curtice A., 237
Cornetta, Peter, 402
Corning, Barney, 420
Corral, Santiago, 771
Corrie, Nancy, 346
Corrie, Nancy, 354
Corry, Robert, 312
Corscadden, Jay, 401
Cortes, William, 706
Cory, John, 378
Corzine, Jim, 198
Cosentino, John, 415
Cosgrove, James, 510
Costabile, Steven, 503
Costantino, John, 589
Costley, Greg, 480
Cote, Joseph, 567
Cotta, J.C., 810
Cotte, Michel, 754
Cotter, William, 287
Coughlin, Benjamin, 248
Coutsouros, Gus, 531
Couwenberg, Corneille, 829
Covert, Harold, 604
Cowan, David, 410
Cowan, Matthew, 156

Cowherd, J. Andrew, 508
Cowie, James, 355
Cowie, James, 351
Cowie, Peter, 442
Cox, Barry, 677
Cox, Everett, 471
Cox, Howard, 424
Cox, Maury, 615
Cox, Randall, 206
Coxe, Tench, 251
Cozean, Charles, 696
Craig, Andrew, 478
Crain, Elizabeth, 210
Cramer, Gerald, 520
Crandall, J, 561
Crandall, Richard, 457
Crandell, Keith, 346
Craven, John, 534
Cravey, Richard, 331
Crawford, Brian, 343
Crawford, James, 355
Crawford, Jane, 726
Crawford, Matt, 597
Crawford, Randall, 430
Crawford, Robert, 927
Creamer, Glenn, 643
Creeden, Robert, 421
Creer, Frank, 276
Cremin, David, 276
Cresci, Robert, 564
Cressey, Bryan, 371
Crettex, Stephane, 841
Crihfield, Owen, 306
Crisp, Matt, 266
Crist, Gang, 238
Crites, Alan, 197
Crocker, Bruce, 160
Crockett, Catherine, 425
Crockett, E. David, 147
Croll, David, 431
Cromwell, Katherine, 451
Cronin, Michael, 455
Crooke, Graham, 452
Crosbie, Allan, 789
Crosbie, Luke, 837
Crosby, Christopher, 210
Crosby, Gary, 573
Crosby, Steven, 479
Crotty, Thomas, 409
Crouse, William, 490
Crowell, Nancy, 405
Cucchi, Gregory, 627
Cuesta, Juan, 786
Cullen, Tom, 281
Cullinane, John, 408
Cullinane, Michael, 351
Culshaw, Alasdair, 938
Cummin, Pearson, 292
Cummings, Robert, 462
Cummings, Russ, 726
Cunanan, Maite, 751
Cuneo, Michael, 628
Cunningham, Andrea, 351
Cunningham, Bill, 781
Cunningham, Ronan, 343
Cureton, Stewart, 662
Curme, Oliver, 409
Curran, D. Patrick, 474
Curran, Patrick, 424
Curran, Stephen, 768
Currie, James, 354
Currier, Richard, 339
Curry, Michael, 200
Curry, Robert, 578
Curry, Stacey, 150
Cusick III, Thomas, 484
Cutler, Joel, 423
Cutter, W. Bowman, 590
Cuvelier, Lieven, 835
Cuyegkeng, Eduardo, 745

D

D'Amore, Richard, 438
D'Arbeloff, Matt, 449
D'Arcy, Alo, 775
Da Silva, Pimenta, 859
Dabija, Vlad, 161
Daffer, Anthony, 466
Dagi, T. Forcht, 331
Dagres, Todd, 409
Dahl, James, 326
Dahl, William, 326
Dalal, Yogen, 210
Dale, Kerry, 630
Dale, Peter, 783
Dali, Paul, 662
Dalle, Bernard, 850
Dalton, Barbara, 527
Dalton, Frank, 331
Dalton, John, 383
Dalton, Sean, 427
Daly, Robert, 434
Danby, Mark, 954
Danforth, Fred, 415
Danhakl, John, 203
Daniel, Chris, 273
Daniel, Tom, 445
Daniels-Young, Sheryl, 625
Danielson, Angela, 518
Dann, Mitchell, 721
Darby, Michael, 409
Dargaud, Pierre-Yves, 731
Das, Somshankar, 269
Dascalu, Ziv, 813
Dattai, Manekesh, 963
David, Eduardo, 187
Davidoff, Howard, 580
Davidoff, Robert, 580
Davidow, William, 214
Davidson, James, 327
Davidson, Phillip, 675
Davidson, Simon, 421
Davidson, William, 687

Davies, Paul, 157
Davies, Simon, 856
Davies, William, 331
Davis, A. Dean, 305
Davis, Barry, 618
Davis, Bob, 427
Davis, Cary, 590
Davis, Donn, 372
Davis, Eugene, 816
Davis, George, 390
Davis, Greg, 600
Davis, Gregory B., 613
Davis, J. Bradley, 368
Davis, Jordan, 560
Davis, Kim, 192
Davis, Rick, 661
Davis, Roger, 166
Davis, Sheila, 473
Davis, Terry, 218
Davison, Jeffrey, 623
Davoli, Robert, 243
Dawes, Dexter, 167
Dawson, Craig, 278
Dawson, William, 310
Dayton, Sky, 175
De Alfaro, Marco, 947
De Bernady, Jean-Louis, 769
De Bord, Alison, 144
De Broglie, Frederic, 725
De Chazal, Guy, 554
de Clippele, Luc J., 974
De Giacomo, Jane, 605
De Haan, Michiel, 407
De Meester, Joris, 898
De Nicola, Anthony, 591
De Ridder, Paul, 835
De Ronde, Han, 961
De Rubertis, Francesco, 850
De Santiago, Jose, 925
De Vries, Robert, 476
De Weck, Pierre, 962
Deakin, Dan, 265
DeAngelis, Kenneth, 657
DeAngelis, Pasquale, 493
DeAngelo, Lawrence, 340
Deas, Ian, 908
DeBlois, Mark, 408
DeBolt, Robert, 343
DeCegama, Paola, 786
Deery, Craig, 408
Deevy, Brian, 281
Defieux, Richard, 504
Defieux, Richard, 488
Defieux, Richard, 606
DeFlorio, Michael, 310
DeGroat, Steve, 702
Deiters, Dave, 339
Deiters, Paul, 835
Dejonghe, Wim, 959
DeJure, Linda, 623
Dekker, M.W., 903
Delagardelle, Jeani, 578
Delbridge, Kevin, 426
Deleage, Jean, 144
Delimitros, Tom, 656
Delistathis, Thanasis, 692
DeLitlo, Thomas M., 594
Dell, Adam, 539
Delloye, Michel, 959
Delorme, Franck, 934
Demichel, Pascal, 805
DeMiroz, Marco, 472
Dempsey, Neal, 153
DeMuth, Donald, 486
den Heijer, Toon, 827
Denenberg, Byron, 359
DeNino, Mark, 640
Dennis, Donohue, 322
Dennis, John, 671
Dennis, Reid, 196
Dennis, William, 655
Denny, George, 425
Denny, James, 373
Denslow, William, 493
DePonte, Kelly, 227
Der Kinderen, Marc, 309
DeRosa, Michael, 626
Desai, Bharat, 461
Desai, Rohit, 522
Desai, Sejal, 679
DesJardins, Steve, 177
DeStefano, Desiree, 577
Desvignes, Serge, 909
Dettmann, Brian, 350
Deturck, Michiel, 887
Deusch, Kai, 882
Deutsch, Waverly, 364
Deves, Rolf, 839
Devescovi, Stefano, 808
Deville, Philippe, 774
Devine, Kevin, 965
DeVivo, Doug, 143
deWeese, David, 230
Dewhirst, Graham, 763
DeWolf, Daniel, 594
Deziel, Robert, 430
Dhala, Shamsh, 859
Di Bona, Tony, 143
Diamond, David, 234
Diamond, Douglas, 333
Diamond, Stephen, 578
Dibble, Timothy, 403
DiBella, Paul, 331
DiBello, Frank, 699
DiBenedetto, Eric, 164
Dick, C.W., 406
Dickey, H. Garth, 378
Dieck, Ronald, 208
Diehl, Jeffrey, 343
Dienst, Rolf, 975
Dietz, Steven, 185
DiGeronimo, Robert, 594
Diggines, Jonathan, 728
Dignan, Phillip, 283

Dignan, Phillip, 286
Dill, Charles, 476
Dillon, Karl, 537
Diment, Tony, 767
Dimmler, Charles, 156
Dintersmith, Ted, 417
Dioguardi, William, 576
DiPiano, Michael, 634
Dirickson, Richard, 239
Dirtoft, Hans, 749
Dirvin, John, 657
Dishlip, Alan, 687
Diwan, Rauf, 314
Dixon, Donald, 259
Dixon, Glenn, 643
Dixon, Glenn, 447
Dizy, Ron, 775
Do, Frank, 271
Dodson, David, 190
Doeksen, Volkert, 524
Doekson, G.V.H., 898
Doerr, Cynthia, 354
Doerr, John, 200
Doherty, J.B., 639
Dolan, A. Barr, 160
Dolasia, Rupen, 186
Dolezalek, J. Stephan, 263
Doll, Dixon, 169
Dolling, Martin, 759
Dolson, Thomas, 343
Domenik, Stephen, 677
Domoshevizki, Avi, 784
Donaghy, James, 537
Dondero, Stephen, 587
Donenfeld, Alan, 513
Donnini, David, 356
Donoghue, Michael F., 398
Donohoe, Robin, 172
Donohue, Dennis, 322
Donohue, Thomas R., 592
Donovan, Mark, 653
Dorjee, Ronald, 926
Dorman, Nancy, 396
Dormer, Esther, 627
Dorn, Helmut, 854
Dorr, Judy, 356
Dortch, Elyn, 599
Dotan, Boaz, 745
Dotzler, Frederick, 211
Doubleday, Gloria, 389
Dougherty, Dennis, 601
Dougherty, Kevin, 454
Doughery,Jr., John, 150
Douglas, Neal, 496
Douglas, Neal, 248
Douglass, David, 167
Doull, Matthew, 537
Dove, Grant, 237
Dovey, Brian, 486
Dovrat, Shlomo, 772
Dow, Stephen, 677
Dowdle, Robin, 463
Downer, Charles, 420
Downer, John, 519
Downes, P.W.E., 810
Downey, Bob, 180
Downey, Paul, 180
Downing, John, 961
Downing, John, 228
Downing, Tim, 832
Doyle, Brian, 310
Doyle, Daniel, 447
Doyle, Maurice, 386
Doyle, William, 540
Drant, Ryan, 396
Draper, Tim, 713
Draper, Timothy, 172
Draper, Timothy, 276
Draper, Timothy, 692
Draper, Timothy, 523
Draper, William, 172
Draper, William, 173
Drazan, Jeffrey, 243
Dreesbach, Werner, 407
Dresner, Steven, 352
Dreyfous, James, 687
Drill, Scott, 469
Drion, Laurent, 800
Driscoll, Eileen, 415
Dross, Daniel S., 257
Drover, Richard, 920
Drummond, Nigel, 856
Druten, Dick van, 743
Drysdale, George, 173
Dubbe, Gina, 399
Dubiel, Christian, 412
Dubovoy, Mark, 195
Dubus, Geoffroy, 853
Duce, Anna, 255
Duchossois, Craig, 353
Duff, Beth, 459
Duffy, Donald, 553
Duffy, Pauline, 171
Duffy, Tim, 586
Dufresne, Daphne, 455
Dugar, Raj, 976
Dullum, David, 437
Dumanian, Peter, 234
Dumler, Richard, 546
Dunbar, John, 581
Dunbar, Will, 313
Dunham, Joe, 381
Dunkel, Mark, 605
Dunlevie, Bruce, 154
Dunn, Dan, 165
Dunn, David, 191
Dunn, Melinda, 241
Dunnan, Bruce, 315
Dunnan, Douglas, 315
Dunnigan, Jeffrey, 273
Dur, Philip R., 554
Duranti, Luca, 817
Durkin, Michael, 261
Durnan, Steve, 751

Duty, Bruce, 675
Duval, David, 409
Duval, Gael, 865
Duvivier, Jean-Marie, 816
Duyck, Geert, 790
Dworkin, Andrew, 541
Dyal, R. Thomas, 196
Dyal, R. Thomas, 235

E

Eads, Kimberly, 489
Eagle, Sonja, 682
Easterby, Capers, 645
Eastman, Alicia, 364
Eastman, Keith, 472
Eberly, David, 459
Ebetshuber, Karl, 959
Ebinger, Jonathan, 222
Eckelberry, Riggs, 218
Eddy, Tom, 407
Edelson, Harry, 487
Edens, Robert, 282
Ederson, Ira J., 371
Edler, Larry, 337
Edwards, Bradley, 479
Edwards, David, 417
Edwards, Donald, 356
Edwards, Joyce, 278
Edwards, Robert, 412
Edwards, Simon, 752
Edwards, Stephen, 918
Edwards, Sydney, 640
Effland, Janet, 563
Efstratis, Nick, 687
Egan, George, 576
Egan, John, 421
Egan, William, 403
Egger, Daniel, 600
Eggers, Barry, 206
Egleston, Natalie, 143
Ehlinger, Greg, 377
Ehrenpreis, Ira, 255
Eichenberger, Rene, 322
Eichler, David, 568
Eichler, Frank, 281
Eidenberg, Gene, 186
Eidswick, Richard, 457
Eilers, Daniel, 262
Eisenberg, Michael, 860
Eisenstein, Stephen, 536
El Baze, Nicholas, 229
Elaad, Jack, 924
Elderkin, Karl, 608
Eley, Stephen, 484
Elfers, William, 424
Elias, Michael, 866
Elkus, William, 161
Ellinger, Vernon, 416
Elliot, Chris, 851
Elliot, Michael, 607
Elliot, Patrick, 876
Elliott, Greg, 680
Ellis, David, 332
Ellison, Scott, 248
Ellman, Stuart, 571
Elmer, Donald, 710
Elmore, Mary, 196
Elmore, William, 181
Elran, Batsheva, 784
Elsser, Stefan, 950
Elton, Graham, 813
Ely, Shawn R., 613
Emmert, Robert, 403
Emmett, David L., 603
Emmitt, Richard, 496
Emont, George, 384
Emsley, Matt, 133
Enand, Rajiv, 624
Engblom, Hans, 927
Enge, Jorg, 146
Engel, Robert A., 534
Engelmeier, Kent, 636
Engelsen, Steinar, 952
Engelson, Erik, 266
Englehart, Ted, 375
Engleman, Edgar, 155
English, Peter, 965
Ennis, Greg, 257
Ennis, Greg, 955
Ennis, Patrick, 346
Enrione, Ph.D., Alfredo, 871
Entekhabi, Massoud, 640
Eplett, J. Douglas, 354
Eplett, J. Douglas, 710
Epps, Sean, 543
Epstein, Douglas, 630
Erbman, Clement, 354
Erdoes, Philip, 511
Erickson, Elaine, 146
Erickson, Tom, 464
Ericson, William, 214
Ericsson, Staffan, 471
Erni, Marcel, 910
Erni, Marcel, 811
Erzberger, Marc, 811
Eskenazi, Steven, 270
Eubank, Frederick, 600
Eun, David, 746
Evain, Christopher, 855
Evans, Alexander, 643
Evans, Andy, 954
Evans, April, 401
Evans, Bruce, 451
Evans, Doug, 771
Evans, John, 376
Evans, John, 454
Evans, Johnston, 541
Evans, Mark, 424
Evans, Roger, 424
Everaert, Ronald, 959
Evnin, Anthony, 586
Evnin, Luke, 436
Ewing, Jr., R. Stewart, 387

Ezell, Bruce, 681

F
Fabbio, Robert, 640
Faber, Michael, 315
Facchina, Philip, 693
Fairbanks, Don, 282
Fairman, Bernard, 965
Faizullabhoy, Danial, 269
Falcao, Glenn, 410
Famaey, Hilde, 898
Fambrough, Douglas, 440
Fan, Anthony, 748
Fan, Vincent, 790
Fan, Vincent, 780
Fann, David, 584
Farb, Thomas, 451
Faris, Robert, 526
Farkas, Brad, 539
Farlow, Anne, 643
Farlow, Anne, 803
Farmer, John, 679
Farmwald, Mike, 154
Farr, Richard, 830
Farrell, James, 181
Farrell, Richard, 454
Farzier, Diana, 295
Fassbender, David, 845
Fatio, Jean-Louis, 827
Faucher, Cornel, 409
Fayneleviinson, Linda, 185
Fealy, Robert, 353
Fechtmeyer, Kevin, 574
Federman, Irwin, 261
Feeney, Ellen, 206
Feeny, Curtis, 714
Feiber, Jonathan, 214
Feierstein, Ted, 367
Feighner, Mark, 657
Feinberg, Henry, 254
Feinstein, Michael, 407
Feinstein, Peter, 411
Fekete, Zsuzsa, 879
Feld, Alan, 860
Feld, Bradley, 247
Feldman, Brian, 182
Fell, Michael, 830
Felsenthal, Martin, 653
Fendel, Andreas, 919
Feng, Benjamin, 737
Fenton, Dean, 304
Fenton, Noel, 260
Fenton, Peter, 139
Fercocq, Christophe, 872
Ferenback, Carl, 410
Ferguson, Allan, 407
Ferguson, David, 543
Ferguson, Dennis, 199
Ferguson, Joseph, 201
Ferguson, Rodney, 197
Ferguson, Thomas, 513
Fergusson, Douglas, 908
Fernandez, Manny, 326
Fernandez-Haegg, Cristina, 444
Fernstrom, Gunnar, 854
Ferrell, Jeffrey, 445
Ferrell, Jeffrey, 445
Ferrer, Carlos, 295
Ferri, Paul, 433
Ferris, Paul, 149
Ferro, Miguel, 543
Fesneau, Bertrand, 725
Fesneau, Florence, 738
Festa, John, 332
Fialkow, David, 423
Fidelman, Barry, 407
Fidler, Josh, 392
Figueiredo, Fraga, 859
Filipowski, Andrew, 351
Fillat, Andrew, 402
Finch, Lawrence, 243
Fine, Scott, 614
Finegan, Scott A., 366
Fingerhut, Barry, 592
Finkel, Mark, 367
Finkel, Robert, 367
Finkle, Jeffrey, 561
Finlayson, Brian, 799
Finn, Michael, 609
Finnegan, Ed, 363
Finnegan, Paul, 361
Finzi, Robert, 578
Firmenich, Dieter, 783
First, Mark, 527
Fisch, Michael, 505
Fischer, Craig, 382
Fischer, Gene, 158
Fischer, Thomas, 140
Fischman, Benjamin, 423
Fisher, Alan, 193
Fisher, David, 853
Fisher, John, 172
Fisher, Margaret, 358
Fisher, Ronald, 448
Fisher, Steve, 623
Fisherman, Jason, 402
Fishman, Danny, 946
Fishman, Ricaardo, 734
Fitch, S., 831
Fitzgerald, John, 630
Fitzgerald, Michael, 419
Fitzgerald, Ross, 937
Fitzgerald, William, 423
Fitzgibbons, Harry, 957
Fitzpatrick, James, 290
FitzPatrick, Seamus, 771
Fitzsimmons, Walter, 227
Flach, James, 139
Flamenbaum, Walter, 230
Flanagan, Patrick, 298
Flanders-Stec, LouAnne, 575
Flanigan, John, 278
Flaschen, David, 439

Flashner, Lisa, 364
Flaster, Andrew, 421
Flath, Eugene, 405
Fleener, Allen, 676
Fleisher, Amos, 402
Fleming, Jonathan, 440
Fleming, Robert, 441
Fleming, Standish, 180
Fleming, Stephen, 330
Flichy, Joel, 824
Flint, Jonathan, 441
Flower, Mark, 372
Floyd, Nancy, 224
Fluegel, Frederick, 433
Fluke, Marty, 671
Flynn, Charles, 509
Flynn, Donald, 180
Flynn, Gregory, 180
Flynn, Richard, 348
Fodor, Peter, 814
Fogarty, Thomas, 258
Fogassa, Marc, 288
Fogelsong, David, 142
Fogelsong, Norman, 196
Foght, James, 372
Foin, Daniel, 937
Foley, Craig, 673
Folger, Thomas, 486
Folk, David, 863
Fong, Henry, 974
Fong, Kevin, 210
Fonstad, Jennifer, 172
Fontenot, Joel, 657
Forbes, Nathan, 457
Ford, Palmer, 231
Ford, Richard, 476
Forday, Eric, 310
Fordyce, James, 310
Foreman, Daniel, 343
Foreman, H. Wayne, 717
Forlenza, Robert, 583
Formela, Jean-Francois, 407
Formolo, Thomas, 351
Forrest, Greg, 180
Forrest, Ian, 841
Forrest, James, 462
Forsberg, Anki, 904
Forster, Michael, 351
Foster, Michael, 305
Foster, Sam, 420
Foster, Vincent, 669
Foulds, Mark, 763
Fouquet, Pierre de, 909
Fox, Christopher, 520
Fox, Jack, 487
Fox, Keith, 528
Fox, Lorraine, 466
Fox, Richard, 625
Foyston, Richard, 893
Franc, Herve, 872
Franceries, Philippe, 509
Franchet, Philippe, 809
Francis, Tod, 260
Frank, Greg, 562
Frank, Michael, 401
Frankel, Stuart, 394
Franklin, Petra, 714
Franz, Rudolf, 950
Franzen, Erica, 861
Frasch, Rick, 201
Fraser, Antony, 963
Frassini, Giorgio, 824
Frazier, Alan, 705
Frechet, Jean, 221
Frederick, Kerry, 339
Frederick, Scott, 693
Frederick, Thomas, 586
Fredrick, Steve, 697
Fredrik, Fredrik, 804
Fredrikson, Peder, 904
Freeman, David, 295
Freeman, Murray, 677
Frei, Alan, 750
Fremd, Thomas, 216
French, David, 755
French, Russell, 336
French, T. Bondurant, 343
Frenkel, Alex, 263
Freund, John, 245
Frew, Paul, 803
Frey, Kip, 601
Freyhof, John, 626
Frick, John, 618
Fricke, Uli, 959
Friedenrich, John, 153
Friedland, Deborah, 568
Friedli, Peter, 823
Friedlich, Jim, 143
Friedman, Clifford, 518
Friedman, Jeff, 696
Friedman, Joel, 140
Friedman, John, 525
Friedman, Rick, 455
Friend, Marc, 261
Friese, Stefan, 950
Frisbie, Richard, 409
Frisk, Anders, 937
Fritz, Frederick, 408
Froetscher, Robert, 374
Fry, Michael, 872
Fu, Winston, 261
Fuddy, Oscar, 258
Fudim, Yair, 930
Fuka, Kent, 661
Fukagawa, Tetsuya, 590
Fukuzawa, Hidetaka, 863
Fullmer, John, 293
Funcannon, Bill, 709
Fung, Stanley, 456
Funk, Jonathan, 143
Fuqua, J. Rex, 334
Furlong, Tom, 186
Furnivall, James, 290
Fusco, Ann, 516

Futrell, Stephen, 566

G
Gabbard, O. Gene, 327
Gabelein, Kevin, 705
Gabrieli, Christopher, 410
Gad, Dror, 951
Gadicke, Ansbert, 436
Gaffney, Christopher, 424
Gagan, Suzanne, 181
Gaiber, Lawrence, 240
Gaines, Adrienne, 227
Gaither, Jim, 251
Galakatos, Nicholas, 436
Galanos, Gregory, 247
Galasso, Giovanni, 402
Gallagher, Jerry, 302
Gallanter, Joanna, 266
Galligan, Joseph, 180
Gambale, Virginia, 390
Gandarias, Patrick, 786
Gandhi, Hetal, 848
Gandhi, Purvi, 187
Gandhi, Sameer, 241
Gani, Marcel, 199
Gannon, John, 441
Ganong, Richard, 583
Ganser, Roger, 720
Gantner, Fredy, 910
Garber, Robert, 359
Garcia, Francisco, 525
Garcia, Kenneth, 672
Gardell, Rickard, 907
Gardeniers, Tor, 827
Gardey, Oliver, 310
Gardhouse, Mark, 923
Gardner, Dean, 169
Gardner, John, 222
Gardner, Peter, 143
Gardner, Ted, 600
Gardner, Terry, 430
Gardo, Lars, 749
Gares, Peter, 434
Garg, Randy, 797
Garlinghouse, Kristen, 189
Garman, Richard, 179
Garnett, Terence, 586
Garnreiter, Alexander, 757
Garonzik, Rick, 180
Garret, Gregory, 343
Garrett, John, 281
Garrett, Will, 364
Garrigues, Antoine, 909
Garrow, Robert, 418
Garside, Andrew, 726
Garson, Palmer, 695
Gartenberg, Michael, 538
Gartenberg, Ran, 971
Garvey, James M., 445
Garvey, Jeffrey, 657
Garvey, Shay, 795
Gary, Ray, 133
Garza, N. Rudy, 665
Gasgarth, Donald, 336
Gaspers, Pamela, 704
Gauer, James, 228
Gautier, Bernard, 407
Gavagan, David, 837
Gavin, Brenda, 638
Gavin, Ray, 553
Geary, William, 438
Geatz, V. Tobin, 598
Gecht, Guy, 177
Geddes, James, 704
Geer, John, 632
Geeslin, Keith, 578
Geffen, Avi, 913
Gegenheimer, Michael, 582
Geiger, Bernd, 959
Geiger, Robert, 580
Geisenheimer, Emile, 550
Gelder, E, 933
Geller, Marc, 679
Geller, Scott, 520
Gellert, Michael, 384
Gemmell, David, 967
Gemmell, William, 408
Genest, John, 456
George, Gregory, 254
George, Harry, 449
George, Ross, 797
Georgiadis, Pete, 353
Gephart, Thomas, 264
Gerhardt, David, 659
Gerling, Paul, 676
Germain, Ann St., 425
Gerome, Frank, 679
Gerron, Thomas, 671
Gerry, Peter, 494
Gershenberg, Aaron, 244
Gertler, Jonathan, 445
Getsy, Stephen, 719
Getz, Robert, 519
Gfoeller, Joachim, 534
Ghandour, Ziad, 259
Gheysens, Ignace, 959
Ghirgini, Alexandra, 501
Ghori, Mansoor, 679
Giacalone, Devon, 961
Giaimo, John, 480
Giannuzzi, John K., 448
Gianos, Philip, 197
Giaoui, Herve, 744
Gibbons, Alastair, 763
Gibbons, M. Christine, 446
Gibbs, Matthew, 440
Gierynski, Pawel, 746
Gieselman, Thomas, 157
Gilat, Dan, 825
Gilbert, Daniel, 457
Gilbert, James, 335
Gilbert, Jon, 705
Gilbert, Myles, 429

Gilbert, Walter, 411
Gilchrest, Eric, 664
Gilhuus-Moe, Carl Christian, 894
Gill, Daniel, 374
Gill, Jack, 262
Gillette, Jim, 203
Gilligan, Michael, 427
Gilly, Bernard, 246
Gilly, Bernard, 934
Giordano, Philip, 549
Giovacchini, Paul, 446
Gire, Philippe, 964
Girgenti, Christopher, 364
Gisholt, Paul, 450
Givens, C. Sage, 139
Gladstone, Lawrence, 602
Glaken, Scott, 314
Glaser, Richard, 538
Glasgow, William, 674
Glasgow, William, 707
Glasnapp, Lee, 473
Glaspell, Bruce, 498
Glass, Skip, 206
Glassmeyer, Ed, 302
Glausser, Gary, 625
Glausser, Gary, 624
Gleacher, Eric, 534
Gleize, Philippe, 790
Glenn, Scott, 273
Glover, Anne, 740
Glovier, Curtis, 492
Go, Patrick, 894
Godreau, Enrique, 714
Goedhart, Felix, 915
Goel, Vab, 223
Goense, John, 344
Goetz, Jim, 139
Goffman, Brian, 657
Gold, Jonathon, 586
Goldberg, Jay, 538
Goldberg, Jeremy, 493
Goldberg, Marc, 411
Goldblatt, Joel, 577
Golden, Bruce, 139
Golden, Joe, 457
Golden, William, 429
Goldfarb, Andy, 198
Golding, Gary, 488
Golding, Rex, 247
Goldman, Adam, 278
Goldman, Alan, 483
Goldman, Howard, 193
Goldsmith, Barry, 700
Goldsmith, David, 236
Goldsmith, William, 459
Goldstein, Amir, 761
Goldstein, Burton, 632
Goldstein, Howard, 541
Goldstein, Howard, 376
Goldstein, Jonathan, 451
Goldstein, Lawrence, 676
Goldstein, Rodney, 355
Goldstein, Ross, 523
Goldstein, Seth, 530
Goldstein, Steven, 471
Goll, Alexandra, 961
Gollamudi, Raj, 464
Golub, Lawrence, 534
Gombault, Vincent, 751
Gomez, Jesus, 895
Goncalves Soares, Rui, 859
Goncher, Brain, 611
Gonye, Lori, 310
Gonyo, Jeffrey, 462
Gonzales, Eric, 169
Gonzalez, John, 736
Goode, Edward, 599
Goodfellow, Thomas, 691
Goodman, Edwin, 553
Goodman, Robert, 410
Goodrich, Hoyt, 484
Goodrich, Paul, 707
Goodrich, Susan, 550
Goodwin, Don, 670
Goodwin, J. Barton, 484
Goodwyn, Richard, 494
Gordon, Cindy, 979
Gorenberg, Mark, 191
Gorgi, Habib, 643
Gorman, Michael, 643
Gorman, Michael, 471
Gorman, Thomas, 446
Gormley, Stephen, 424
Gorter, Oliver, 866
Gossman, William, 214
Gotcher, Peter, 196
Gotcher, Peter, 235
Gothner, Robert, 854
Gotsch, Peter, 351
Gotte, Benedikt, 968
Gottesman, Greg, 707
Gotz, Stefan, 757
Goulandris, Dimitri, 310
Gould, Andrew, 507
Gould, James, 617
Gould, Kathryn, 181
Gould, Kit, 192
Gould, Peter, 623
Gould, Terry, 343
Gour, Vivek, 749
Goven, Tami, 423
Gowell, Aaron, 423
Goyette, Cheryl, 405
Goyette, Cheryl, 439
Grabel, Jonathon, 510
Grace, Christopher, 424
Grace, Gregory, 424
Grady, Prisca, 845
Grafft, Chris, 657
Graham, Bruce, 410
Graham, Bruce, 194
Graham, David, 680
Graham, Drew, 327
Grammer, Jeffery, 254

Granat, Harvey, 580
Grande, H.J., 928
Granof, Phil, 547
Granoff, Gary, 526
Granoff, Michael, 566
Gransberg, Dolf, 916
Grant, Christopher, 653
Grant, Michael, 565
Grant, Peter, 466
Grant, Thomas, 405
Grassi, Domenico, 817
Grasso, Salvatore, 623
Graubart, Steve, 690
Grauer, Fred, 145
Gray, A., 831
Gray, Bernard, 335
Gray, Nelson, 825
Gray, Thaddeus, 501
Grayson, Bruns, 390
Grayson, Gerald, 280
Greb, Charles, 274
Green, Adam, 640
Green, Holcombe, 335
Green, Jason, 261
Green, Leonard, 203
Green, Martin, 726
Green, Stephen, 290
Green, Stuart, 764
Green, Tim, 755
Greenberg, Allen, 589
Greene, Donald, 312
Greene, Frank, 218
Greene, I. Robert, 530
Greenebaum, Andrew, 175
Greenfield, Stewart, 302
Greenhalgh, Scott, 736
Greenspan, Nick, 752
Greenstein, Mark, 172
Greenstone, Libby, 459
Greenwood, Dean, 674
Greenwood, Kathy, 978
Greff, John, 284
Gregg, David, 698
Gregson, David, 911
Gregson, Richard, 807
Greig, Martin, 839
Greiner, Jeffrey, 466
Gren, Martin, 861
Grenman, Sari, 753
Gresh, Lemy, 771
Grey, Richard, 341
Grey, Richard, 189
Gribben, Murray, 740
Griffin, James, 655
Griffith Gryga, Karen, 636
Griffith Gryga, Karen, 631
Grillos, John, 213
Grimonprez, Eric, 819
Grinda, Fabrice, 865
Griner, John, 298
Grisius, Michael, 312
Grissom, J. David, 384
Griswold, E. Bulkeley, 299
Griswold, Kirk, 623
Grogan-Crane, Richard, 466
Groh, Kim, 538
Grose, Austin, 143
Gross, Johannes, 848
Gross, Stewart, 590
Grosser, Adam, 181
Grossi, Brian, 149
Grossmann, Benoist, 973
Grousbeck, Wycliffe, 427
Grover, Rakinder, 269
Groves, Paula, 408
Grow, Michael, 699
Grubstein, Peter, 221
Gruden, Anders, 752
Gruen, Keith, 865
Gruener, Garrett, 144
Grum, Allen, 568
Gruner, Michael, 969
Grunwald, Alexander, 878
Grunwald, Alfred, 590
Grzelecki, Frank, 306
Gómez Schindler, Pamela, 871
Guenther, Rolf, 407
Guerin, Debra, 198
Guerrero, Carlos, 972
Guerster, Jonathan, 417
Guillou, Jean-Charles, 755
Gujral, Rahul, 626
Guld, Benny, 856
Guleri, Tim, 250
Guleri, Tim, 243
Gunderson, Maurice, 224
Gunn, Graeme, 939
Gunnarson, Fredric, 861
Gunton, James, 493
Guo, Young, 846
Gupta, Arjun, 256
Guren, Samuel, 312
Gurley, Bill, 154
Gust, William, 391
Guthrie, David, 334
Gutierrez, Salvador, 272
Guyton, Robert, 336
Gwosden, Laura, 163
Gwosden, Laura, 262
Gwynn, David, 134

H

Ha, Karen, 148
Ha, Karen, 250
Ha, Perry, 148
Haar, Nancy, 294
Haas, Axel, 749
Haas, Clifford, 243
Haas, Donald, 463
Haataja, Villie, 803
Habert, Benoit, 794
Hacke, Robin, 914
Hackett, Christian, 663

Hackett, John, 376
Hackett, Montague H., 524
Hackett, Patrick, 590
Hackett, Victoria, 746
Hackman, Rhodric, 696
Haddad, David, 519
Hagdahl, Lars, 944
Haggerty, Daniel, 223
Hahn, John, 643
Hahn, Maria, 636
Hahn, Maria, 631
Hahn, Michael, 465
Hahn, Ronald, 487
Haight, H.H., 406
Haimo, Zara, 276
Haining, Andrew, 762
Haislip, Wallace, 338
Halasen, Cynthia, 643
Hale, James, 179
Haley, Tim, 235
Haley, Timothy, 196
Hall, David, 854
Hall, John, 190
Hall, Kevin, 223
Hall, Patrick, 312
Hall, Robin, 779
Hall, Stephen, 259
Hall, Wendie, 766
Hallahane, Dennis, 783
Hallala, Mark, 735
Hallgren, Erik, 906
Halligan, John, 326
Hallworth, Graham, 736
Halperin, Jacques, 847
Halperin, Philip, 455
Halpern, John, 425
Halpin, Michael, 929
Halsted, Scott, 554
Halstedt, Steven, 278
Halusa, Martin, 742
Hambrecht, Bob, 266
Hambrecht, William, 266
Hambrecht, William, 186
Hambrecht, William, 269
Hamilton, Douglas, 244
Hamilton, Jeffrey, 497
Hamilton, Melissa, 667
Hamilton, Richard, 440
Hamilton, Stephen, 677
Hamm, John, 235
Hammarskjold, Philip, 189
Hammer, Neil, 578
Hamnett, Katherine, 821
Hamrick, L. Watts, 600
Hancock, Alison, 905
Hand, Brian, 354
Handelsman, Karl, 161
Handley, J.B., 252
Hanigal, Benny, 940
Hanks, Robert, 437
Hanley, Brian, 832
Hanley, John, 207
Hannon, Michael, 543
Hannula, Antti, 897
Hansen, Kent, 793
Haque, Promod, 223
Hara, George, 167
Hara, Kent, 167
Harbison, Keith, 477
Harder, Maureen, 472
Hardesty, Jeff, 133
Hardie, David, 188
Harding, William, 554
Hardymon, G. Felda, 410
Harel, Ben, 795
Hargreaves, Richard, 781
Harinarayan, Venky, 158
Harker, Susan, 711
Harkins, Carolyn, 640
Harlan, William, 376
Harman, Fred, 302
Harper, Scott, 616
Harrell, Curtis F., 674
Harrick, Stephen, 427
Harrington, Jack, 401
Harrington, John, 651
Harrington, WIlliam, 258
Harris, Clinton, 425
Harris, Hayden, 458
Harris, Jeffrey, 590
Harris, Kathy, 650
Harris, Kathy, 339
Harris, Matthew, 410
Harris, Nick, 548
Harris, Stephen, 639
Harrison, Eric, 196
Harrison, James, 666
Harrison, Seth, 302
Harrison, William, 653
Harrus, Alain, 163
Hart, David, 632
Hart, Robert, 712
Hart, William, 255
Harte, Caron, 461
Harter, Steve, 672
Hartkopf, Scott, 351
Hartman, Charles, 521
Hartz, John, 852
Harvey, Kevin, 154
Harvey, Robert, 298
Harwood, Andrew, 812
Hasenwinkel, Paul, 140
Hashaway, Bobby, 683
Hashbarger, George, 600
Haskell, Gregory, 586
Hasler, Heinz, 790
Hassanein, Ossama, 220
Hastings, Mark, 484
Hathaway, David, 586
Hauch, Sven, 760
Hauser, Herman, 740
Hausman, Ken, 226
Hautin, Herve, 738
Havaldar, Abhay, 172

Haviland, Timothy, 298
Haviv, Joseph, 530
Hawke, Joseph, 634
Hawkins, David, 351
Hawkins, Ian, 963
Hawkins, John, 532
Hawks, Randy, 223
Hawley, Frank, 306
Hawley, Stuart, 306
Hawiey, Wallace, 197
Hawthorne, Donald, 404
Hayat, Phillippe, 865
Hayes, John, 424
Hayes, Kevin, 455
Hayes, Russell, 892
Haykin, Randy, 193
Hayrynen, Jukka, 807
Hays, Joe, 137
Hazard, Charles, 424
Hazen, Ned, 205
Headley, Todd, 693
Healer, Harry, 454
Healy, Elaine, 564
Healy, James, 239
Healy, James, 246
Healy, Patrick, 189
Healy, Patrick, 474
Heappey, Mark, 726
Hearst, William, 200
Heathcote, J.L., 810
Hecht, Shawn, 252
Hedges, Hillary, 746
Hedges, James, 324
Hedrick, W. Scott, 197
Heeger, Alan, 221
Heer, David, 139
Heersink, Ewout, 905
Heerwagen, Jim, 393
Hefer, Giles, 204
Hefetz, Roni, 975
Heflin, William, 395
Hefner, Marsha, 653
Hegele, W. Chris, 602
Hehir, Michael, 552
Heidrich, Grant, 210
Heijting, Wim, 965
Heilmann, Stefan C., 974
Hein, Christian, 872
Heistand, Donnell, 281
Heitmann, Knut, 913
Held, Raymond, 501
Helde Hemmingsen, Steen, 793
Helfrich, David, 163
Helgesen, Eva, 861
Helle, Daniel, 350
Heller, Charles, 182
Heller, Gabi, 975
Heller, Neil, 630
Hellman, Mick, 189
Helman, William, 424
Helomaa, Jouko, 884
Hemphill, Robert, 399
Henagan, Bill, 653
Henderson, Randy, 248
Hendrickson, Sara, 242
Henkens, Jos, 401
Henley, J. Rudy, 716
Hennessy, Daniel, 351
Hennessy-Jones, Mary, 576
Henos, Michael, 330
Henriksson, Tom, 838
Henriques, Manuel, 162
Henriquez, Manuel, 263
Henry, Emil, 534
Henry, Jeanne, 407
Henshaw, Nathaniel, 388
Henske, Brad, 561
Hensley, Robert, 254
Henson, William, 232
Henton, Andrew, 976
Herbert, Philippe, 229
Herlick, Zachary, 708
Herman, Peter, 427
Hermann, Klaus, 503
Hernandez, Bruce, 577
Hernmarck, Johan, 861
Hernon, Martin, 412
Herring, Thomas, 441
Herrman, Rick, 660
Hersh, Kenneth A., 300
Hershey, John, 194
Hertz, George, 421
Herzog, Joe, 709
Herzog, Stefan, 965
Hester, P. Christian, 139
Hiatt, Tom, 378
Hichens, Donald, 205
Hick, Felix, 770
Hickey, Janet, 578
Hickman, Douglas, 391
Hicks, William G., 129
Hietalahti, Erkki, 732
Higgerson, Clifford, 163
Higgins, Ken, 472
Higgins, Robert, 427
Higgons, William, 931
Higham, Rob, 408
Hilderbrand, Mark, 225
Hilgendorf, Brian, 714
Hilinski, Scott, 643
Hill, Eugene, 445
Hill, Neal, 454
Hill, Steve, 198
Hillberg, Staffan, 787
Hillel, Isaac, 913
Hillhouse, George, 679
Hillyard, Carrie, 782
Hillyard, Dianne, 455
Hilton, Timothy, 421
Hinck, Jeff, 466
Hinderer, Michael, 742
Hindery, Leo, 143
Hines, Barry, 310
Hines, Stephen, 310

Hingge, Hsu, 445
Hinoul, Martin, 959
Hinson, James, 146
Hinson, Minor, 604
Hintikka, Martti, 852
Hipp, William, 138
Hirsch, Brian, 398
Hirsch, Russell, 210
Hirsch, Russell, 567
Hirschbiel, Paul, 519
Hirschfeld, Thomas, 563
Hirschfeld, Thomas, 542
Hirschhorn, Kenny, 905
Hirshland, Michael, 441
Hitchner, Elam, 633
Hitchner, Thomas, 397
Hixon, Todd, 172
Hjelmquist, Sigrun, 762
Hoag, Jay, 254
Hoak, James, 666
Hoather, Hugh, 938
Hobart, Ted, 501
Hobbs, Walter, 732
Hobman, Steven, 634
Hoch, Thomas, 806
Hochman, Richard, 569
Hochuli, Pierre, 913
Hodgman, John, 432
Hodgson, Allan, 839
Hoegh, Thomas, 746
Hoel, Sonja, 212
Hoet, Mark, 919
Hofbauer, Andreas, 940
Hoff, Rein Inge, 833
Hoffen, Howard, 554
Hoffman, Guy, 640
Hoffman, James, 649
Hoffman, Larry, 694
Hoffman, Lawrence, 501
Hoffmann, Tanguy, 931
Hofmann, Donald, 543
Hogan, Terence, 310
Hoguet, Robert, 570
Holaday, A. Bart, 343
Holder, David, 214
Holland, Cornelia, 649
Holland, Daniel, 439
Holland, J.R., 667
Holland, Jeffrey, 446
Hollenbeck, Chris, 186
Holliday, Brent, 832
Holliman, Jock, 136
Hollin, Mitchell, 622
Hollin, Mitchell, 631
Hollingsworth, Arthur, 672
Hollingsworth, Arthur, 669
Holm, William, 415
Holmes, Andrew, 920
Holmes, Scott, 606
Holmes, W. Stephen, 197
Holsworth, Brad, 232
Holt, Gerri, 165
Holton, Michael, 246
Holzman, Zeev, 828
Homm, Florian, 965
Honey, Sean, 455
Hong, S.C., 840
Hook, David, 662
Hook, John, 662
Hooper, Marcia, 402
Hooper, Steve, 706
Hooten, Kenneth, 369
Hoover, James, 522
Hopf, Patrick, 471
Hopkins, Robert, 517
Horangic, Basil, 302
Horangic, Basil, 657
Hord, Earl, 630
Horgen, Chris, 132
Horgen, Chris, 605
Horing, David, 505
Horing, Jeff, 540
Horlick, Tim, 893
Horn, Lance, 184
Horne, Will, 711
Horning, Robert, 221
Horst, Sandy, 647
Horton, Theodore, 484
Horwich, David, 268
Horwitz, Lawrence H., 612
Hoss, Moty, 812
Houghtaling, Gregory, 675
Houghton, James, 435
Houlihan III, James E., 196
Hoversten, Dan, 606
Howard, Al, 256
Howard, Lawrence, 538
Howard, Matthew, 223
Howard, Paul, 434
Howard, Russell, 410
Howe, Kevin, 670
Howe, Timothy, 291
Howell, Daniel, 362
Howell, Ronald, 715
Howley, Andrew, 573
Hoyem, George, 176
Hoyem, George, 234
Hozoji, Hironori, 901
Hradszki, Laszlo, 842
Hsia, Emery, 950
Hsieh, Robert, 138
Hsieh, Tony, 265
Hsin, John, 611
Hsu, Charles, 269
Hsu, Hingge, 445
Hsueh, Conrad, 946
Hu, Ding-Hua, 776
Huang, Cheng Sang, 944
Hubbs, Kenneth, 423
Huber, Thomas, 920
Huberman, Jonathan, 191
Huck, Christopher, 888
Huckfield, David, 755
Hudson, Matthew, 814

Huff, Peter, 657
Hughes, Bill, 415
Hughes, Francis, 404
Hughes, Francis, 421
Hughes, Robert, 674
Hughes, Roger, 679
Hughlett, Bill, 714
Hui, Vincent, 140
Hull, Brandon, 485
Hull, David, 278
Hull, Gordon, 161
Hulley, William, 622
Hulst, Nicolas, 738
Humbert, Frederic, 853
Humenansky, Paul, 351
Hummer, John, 191
Humphrey, David, 618
Humphreys, Michael, 433
Humphreyson, Charles B., 665
Humphries, Brent, 681
Humphries, Nic, 489
Hunckler, William, 361
Hundt, Reed, 154
Hung, Tony, 174
Hung Ling, Henry Fan, 780
Huntz, John, 334
Hurd, Timothy, 361
Huret, Robert, 179
Hurley, John, 156
Hurlock, Burton, 427
Hurst, Jeffrey, 419
Hursti, Jani, 838
Hurwitz, Larry, 202
Husain, M. Fazle, 554
Huscher, Justin, 361
Huseby, Thomas, 712
Husney, Elliot, 286
Huss, Gunnar, 749
Hutcheson, Zenas, 471
Hutton, Wende, 210
Hutzel, Thomas, 576
Huyser, Randy, 521
Hwang, Sung-Jin, 590
Hyndman, Stephen, 171
Hynes, James, 421
Hyten, Scott, 667

I
Ibrahim, Maha, 290
Ibsen, Peter, 793
Ignell, Rose, 180
Iino, Satoru, 789
Ikegaya, Hiroshi, 901
Imlay, John, 335
Imsieke, Gerrit, 806
Imuta, Hitoshi, 198
Imuta, Hitoshi, 862
Ingall, Jeremy, 818
Ingeborn, Staffan, 854
Ingersoll, W. Brandon, 434
Ingersoll, W. Brett, 543
Ingle, Blake, 195
Insalaco, Steven, 514
Ionescu, Val, 503
Ippolito, John F., 420
Irby, Alton F, 534
Irstad, Lars, 861
Irwin, Russ, 164
Isenberg, Dan, 864
Isherwood, John, 624
Ishida, Akira, 167
Isnard, Arnaud, 587
Isohaaro, Hannu, 725
Israel, Ben-Zion, 924
Israel, Dick, 249
Israel, George, 509
Italia, Roberto, 590
Ivy, Robert, 653

J
Jablo, Mike, 346
Jacimovic, Vladimir, 236
Jacimovic, Vladimir, 165
Jackowitz, Robert, 536
Jacks, Joel, 517
Jackson, Andrew, 855
Jackson, Bruce, 710
Jackson, Chris, 971
Jackson, Herbert, 699
Jackson, Michael, 803
Jackson, Michael, 190
Jackson, Penelope, 275
Jackson, Wayne, 390
Jacob, Howard, 684
Jacobs, Brian, 471
Jacobsson, Hans, 787
Jacobsson, Lennart, 944
Jacquemart-Pernod, Karine, 765
Jacquin, Jean, 817
Jadeja, Asha, 171
Jae-Woo, Lee, 187
Jaeger, Wilfred, 258
Jaeggi, Andre, 734
Jaffe, Richard, 676
Jaffe, Robert, 247
Jagadeesh, B.V., 182
Jaggers, John, 677
Jaggers, Kurt, 451
Jagla, Daniel, 717
Jahns, David, 531
Jamal, Asad, 172
James, Joanna, 402
Janeway, William, 590
Janezic, Marco, 760
Jang, Mahn-Joon, 873
Janis, Frances, 566
Janney, Daniel, 144
Jannotta, Edgar, 373
Jannotta, Edgar, 356
Janopaul, Mathew, 455
Jansen, Erik, 564
Janszen, Eric, 440

Jantz, Waldemar, 947
Jaqua, Stephen, 457
Jaques, David, 222
Jarve, John, 212
Jaunich, Robert, 181
Jawa, Sanjay, 893
Jay, Jeffrey, 310
Jazwin, Mark, 134
Jeffries, Mary, 471
Jenkins, George, 563
Jenkins, Robert, 963
Jenks, Stephen, 415
Jennifer, Forsyth, 364
Jennings, Laura, 407
Jennings, Mark, 532
Jennings, Simon, 963
Jensen, Leif, 903
Jensen, Mark, 607
Jenssen, Paul, 570
Jeong, Chang Hi, 978
Jerabek, Dalibor, 921
Jermoluk, Thomas, 200
Jervis, Joel, 766
Jessup, George, 940
Jestley, Garth, 885
Jevon, Robert, 412
Jim, Nordstrom, 709
Joanis, Steven, 286
Joe, Michael, 643
Joe, Toh Yiu, 916
Johansson, Frederick, 927
Johansson, Lennart, 804
John, Shaji, 491
Johns, Margaret, 556
Johns, Whitney, 648
Johnson, Adrian, 872
Johnson, Amal, 206
Johnson, Brian, 158
Johnson, Charles, 336
Johnson, Donald, 348
Johnson, Drew, 660
Johnson, Franklin, 147
Johnson, Gregory, 476
Johnson, Gregory, 597
Johnson, James, 346
Johnson, Kent, 702
Johnson, Kinney, 284
Johnson, Kristine, 463
Johnson, Peter, 807
Johnson, Steven, 711
Johnston, A. Bruce, 451
Johnston, Allan, 252
Johnston, Beth, 374
Johnston, Hooks, 693
Johnston, John, 148
Johnston, Richard, 393
Johnston, Robert, 490
Johnston, Tom, 702
Johnston, William, 426
Jones, Andrew, 365
Jones, Andy, 392
Jones, Brad, 235
Jones, Christine, 623
Jones, Craig, 452
Jones, David, 384
Jones, David, 876
Jones, Debra, 181
Jones, Derek, 519
Jones, Donald, 626
Jones, Ed, 294
Jones, Elaine, 527
Jones, Eric, 653
Jones, Kenneth, 633
Jones, Kenneth, 391
Jones, Lindsay, 402
Jones, Mark, 653
Jones, Morgan, 409
Jones, Paul, 600
Jones, Robin, 726
Jones, Tom, 626
Jonke, Reinhard, 725
Jonstromer, Ulf, 762
Jordan, Wilma, 545
Jordon, G. Cook, 376
Jorgensen, Lars, 794
Jormakka, Vesa, 406
Joseph, Andrea, 622
Joseph, Michael, 397
Joseph, Moses, 145
Josephberg, Richard, 545
Joshi, Sujay, 910
Joyce, William, 581
Jubeir, T.J., 697
Jubier, T.J., 769
Jurvetson, Steve, 172
Jury, Clifford, 140
Jyrkas, Tarja, 897

K

Kachadurian, K., 404
Kaewyana, Surasawadee, 402
Kafker, Roger, 451
Kaganov, Alan, 261
Kagle, Bob, 154
Kahan, Robert, 515
Kahn, Andrew, 160
Kahn, Andrew, 543
Kahn, Carolyn, 291
Kahn, Martin, 570
Kahn, Stephen, 402
Kain, John, 263
Kain, Rob, 686
Kairouz, Habib, 570
Kaiser, William, 424
Kalan, George, 303
Kalbach, Gary, 176
Kalborg, Ted, 727
Kalda, Kristjan, 753
Kalelos, Athanasios, 256
Kaleschke, Peter, 961
Kalish, Rami, 913
Kalish, Ron, 462
Kalish, Shlomo, 784

Kalish, Shlomo, 864
Kalkanis, Peter, 570
Kallman, William, 713
Kallmeyer, Vera, 800
Kalman, Jonathan, 630
Kalra, Aashish, 415
Kamath, Divakar, 671
Kamin, Tony, 266
Kamm, Michelle, 339
Kamper, Carl, 839
Kamra, Deepak, 290
Kanarek, Wendee, 318
Kanarek, Wendee, 318
Kane, Edward, 426
Kane, William, 536
Kaneko, Yasumori, 245
Kanellias, Voula, 442
Kania, Edwin, 439
Kanji, Shamez, 438
Kanngiesser, Dirk, 913
Kanter, Joel, 701
Kantesaria, Dev, 640
Kanumury, Mahesh, 182
Kapadia, Atul, 194
Kaplan, Eyal, 975
Kaplan, Michael, 258
Kapor, Mitch, 139
Kara, Ilker, 870
Karfopoulos, Michael, 564
Karim, Sarina, 890
Karkenny, Chris, 218
Karlander, Hans, 917
Karleski, Koleman, 384
Karol, Steven, 455
Karp, Douglas, 590
Karp, Matty, 784
Karstaedt, Noam, 299
Karttunen, Kai, 942
Kasdin, Kef, 487
Kase, Ronald, 396
Kashnow, Richard, 261
Kassine, Karen, 437
Kastberg, James, 310
Katariacic, Joseph, 626
Katarincic, Joseph, 632
Katcha, Joseph, 357
Kato, Ken, 445
Katz, Bruce, 238
Katz, Carolyn, 643
Katz, David, 355
Katz, Howard, 544
Katzman, David, 457
Kau, Andrew, 269
Kaufman, Glenn, 505
Kaufman, Seymour, 236
Kaufman, Sy, 165
Kaufmann, Yadin, 970
Kavanagh, Preston, 292
Kay, Chris, 803
Kaye, Charles, 590
Kazandjian, Raffy, 775
Kazmer, Kenneth, 626
Kazovsky, Leonid, 161
Keane, Thomas, 549
Keck, Chad, 556
Keck, Kevin, 129
Keegan, James, 147
Keeler, Stuart, 856
Keen, Peter, 884
Keene, Kurt, 675
Keesey, Mike, 351
Keilhacker, Kurt, 254
Keith, Robert, 640
Keller, Bruce, 139
Keller, Bruno, 809
Keller, Harold, 975
Keller, Joseph, 631
Kellett, Andrew, 408
Kelley, David, 225
Kelley, Paul, 456
Kellogg, Dan, 611
Kelly, Benjamin, 286
Kelly, Douglas, 147
Kelly, Douglas, 143
Kelly, George, 680
Kelly, Jack, 336
Kelly, Scott, 207
Kelly, Tad, 278
Kelts, George, 515
Kenealy, Pat, 192
Kenneally, Deanne, 192
Kennealy, Michael, 248
Kennedy, Bonnie, 259
Kennedy, Bryan, 351
Kennedy, George, 410
Kennedy, Iain, 835
Kennedy, Rob, 133
Kenney, Thomas, 222
Kenny, Stephen, 871
Kent, Peter, 524
Keplinger, Tab, 609
Keppler, Jerry, 702
Keppler, Robert, 278
Kerins, Patrick, 394
Kerman, Keith, 614
Kern Jr., John C., 612
Kernan, Lawrence, 433
Kerr, Karen, 346
Kerr, Tracy, 281
Kersey, Christopher, 155
Kertesz, Louis, 710
Keshian, Dan, 424
Kessel, Peter, 734
Kessinger, William, 356
Ketchum, Laura, 415
Ketterson, Robert, 421
Keve, Rob, 727
Kewalramani, Bharat, 850
Khanna, Raman, 169
Kharbanda, Ken, 263
Khatcherian, Lena, 520
Khawam, Maurice, 808
Khosla, Vinod, 200
Khui, Lai Seck, 823

Kiam, Victor, 661
Kiat, Lee Theng, 931
Kibble, Robert, 214
Kiervin, Jack, 863
Kilcrease, Laura, 682
Killackey, Joseph, 626
Killips, C. Scott, 140
Kiltz, John, 661
Kim, Brendon, 144
Kim, Do Youn, 837
Kim, Han, 144
Kim, Hong-Chae, 873
Kim, Jason, 954
Kim, Jeong, 693
Kim, John, 156
Kim, Michael, 238
Kim, Steve, 142
Kim, Yong Seop, 978
Kim, Young, 873
Kimball, Rick, 254
Kimzey, Jackie, 677
Kinebuchi, Jun, 192
King, Suzanne, 396
Kingery, John, 170
Kingsland, Sam, 186
Kingsley, Douglas, 402
Kingsley, William, 626
Kinkead, Mike, 442
Kinley, Matt, 381
Kinlough, Richard, 774
Kirby, James, 361
Kirchen, Chris, 292
Kirchen, Christopher, 289
Kirkpatrick, Carlisle, 140
Kirkpatrick, David, 606
Kirwan, Tom, 845
Kirwin, John, 623
Kishon, Eyal, 826
Kislak, Jonathan, 320
Kitagawa, George, 195
Kitagawa, George, 194
Kitazaki, Jill, 310
Kitchen, Gary, 331
Kitching, Christopher, 180
Kitterman, Roger, 430
Klammer, Ronald, 302
Klatt, Andy, 160
Klausmeyer, David, 678
Klausner, Arthur, 486
Klebanoff, Mark, 702
Kleberg, Scott, 674
Kleijwegt, Martijn, 874
Klein, Amy, 697
Klein, Charles, 505
Klein, Robert, 505
Klein, Robin, 727
Klein, Stephen, 594
Klein, Todd, 395
Kleinert, Christopher, 667
Kleinke, Jon D., 613
Kleinman, Ira, 536
Klemm, Wolfgang, 909
Kliman, Gilbert, 197
Kline, Frank, 201
Klingenstein, Paul, 138
Knafel, Sidney, 578
Knaudt, June, 323
Kneen, John, 348
Knight, Alex, 346
Knight, Kelly, 948
Knight, Kelly, 948
Knoblauch, Loring, 153
Knowles, James, 631
Knox, Robert, 519
Knudson, Mark, 469
Ko, Denny, 174
Ko, Peter, 187
Ko, Wen, 977
Koch, Hans-Dieter, 752
Koch, Johannes, 706
Koch, Klaus, 201
Kochevar, Karen, 583
Koening, Kimberly, 147
Koffman, Lori, 576
Koh, Joong-sun, 869
Kohler, John, 234
Kok, Chng Hee, 904
Kokesh, Charles, 254
Kokkinen, Antti, 222
Kolada, David Harris, 863
Kolade, Wol, 823
Kolbinger, Thomas, 930
Koldyke, M. Laird, 355
Koldyke, Martin, 355
Kollegger, James, 533
Kollner, Malte, 959
Komiya, Yuji, 880
Kong, Elaine, 711
Kong, Wai-Leong, 931
Koning, Johan, 919
Kontogouris, Venetia, 259
Koo, Bon Keul, 148
Koontz, Jan, 134
Koontz, Paul, 181
Kopchinsky, Gregory, 290
Koran, Lorelei, 484
Korby, Steven, 545
Korman, Robert, 675
Korman, Steven, 973
Korn, Doug, 527
Kornblum, Robert, 657
Kornfeld, Nathan, 468
Kortschak, Walter, 451
Koshiba, Masahiro, 310
Koski, Toivo, 849
Koulogeorge, Mark, 354
Kovach, Rick, 611
Kovacs, Gayle, 621
Koven, Gustav, 488
Koza, John, 256
Kozlowski, James, 681
Kracum, Richard, 462
Kraftson, Donald, 523
Kramer, Bob, 729

Kramer, Dominik, 749
Kramer, Edward, 221
Kramer, Joachim, 835
Kramlich, C. Richard, 396
Kranzler, Dan, 704
Kraskey, Timothy, 456
Krauss, Jeffrey, 556
Krauss, Jeffrey, 568
Krauss, Marlene, 546
Krausz, Steven, 261
Kreimer, Thomas, 465
Kreisel, Joerg, 826
Krejs, Franz, 840
Kremer, Mark, 154
Kressel, Henry, 590
Kriens, Scott, 199
Krindel, Yaffa, 940
Krishnamarthy, Mahesh, 191
Krocke, Ingo, 975
Krohg, Olaf, 402
Kronfeld, David, 358
Krongard, Timothy, 397
Krupa, Steven, 568
Kubal, Larry, 172
Kubis, Dietmar, 796
Kubota, Kiyoyuki, 704
Kucechle, Peter, 402
Kudriashov, Anton, 938
Kuehle, Thomas, 228
Kuhling, Robert, 225
Kulkarni, Amit, 845
Kulkarni, Sanjaya, 850
Kuller, David, 736
Kulvin Crawford, Lori, 195
Kulvin Crawford, Lori, 194
Kumano, Hideaki, 956
Kung, Frank, 155
Kunse, Jim, 176
Kunstler, Julie, 914
Kuntz, Richard, 231
Kunz, Greg, 159
Kunzweiler, John, 140
Kuo, Anchie, 150
Kupper, Hans, 873
Kurpis, Peter, 140
Kvamme, E. Floyd, 200
Kwan, Dick, 755
Kwee, Hoe, 402
Kwee, Michael, 908
Kwei, Randy, 929
Kwok, Raymond, 944

L

Laatre, Ruth, 753
Labe, Jim, 162
Labran, Renee, 238
Lacob, Joseph, 200
Lacroute, Bernard, 200
Ladd, David, 210
Laffy, Laurent, 746
Lafond, Sebastien de, 733
Lagae, F, 936
Lagarde, Jean-Yves, 412
Lahann, Greg, 223
Laib, Peter, 734
Laing, Bert, 361
Lakes, Alexis, 225
Lakes, Alexis, 182
Lal, Ranjan, 372
Lal, Ranjan, 363
Lalani, Azim, 859
Lally, James, 200
Lalou, Anne, 865
Lam, Adrian, 206
Lam, Cynthia, 172
Lam, Cynthia, 173
Lam, David, 174
Lamb, Doug, 537
Lambert, Lee, 415
Lambert, Lionel, 778
Lamkin, Robert, 961
Lamone, Rudolph, 182
Lamont, Ann, 302
Lamotte, Andre, 434
Lamport, Anthony, 546
Lanari, Luigi, 790
Lance, John, 908
Lance, Schuyler, 273
Land, Scot, 704
Landau, David, 563
Landau, Joshua H., 488
Lande, Earl, 923
Landis, Howard, 305
Landry, C. Kevin, 451
Landry, Pearce, 600
Landy, Joseph, 590
Lane, David, 144
Lane, David, 169
Lane, Ray, 200
Lane, Thao, 220
Lanfri, Bill, 139
Lang, David, 451
Lang, Ken, 401
Langeler, Gerard, 709
Lanier, Campbell, 327
Lanigan, Mindy, 321
Lanoix, Margaret, 431
Lanza, Drew, 614
Lanza, Lucio, 261
Lapidus, Sidney, 590
LaPoint, William, 425
LaPorte, Kathleen, 578
Lapping, Andrew, 836
Lapping, Paul, 363
Larcombe, Brian, 726
Larkin, Ian, 373
Larson, Robert, 274
Larson, Stephen, 519
LaRue, David, 445
Lasersohn, Jack, 496
Laskey, Beau, 458
Lassally, Tom, 531
Lassila, Erik, 160

Lassila, Erik, 161
Laszlo, Andrew, 263
Latham, Philip, 921
Latner, David, 979
Latterell, Patrick, 586
Lattmann, Massimo, 968
Laud, Paul, 485
Lauer, Tom, 402
Laufer, Michael, 212
Laufik, Theodore, 614
Laugel, Thierry, 775
Laurer, Christian, 854
Lavakara, S.P., 847
LaVigna, Michael, 681
Lawler, Kenneth, 409
Lawlor, Augustine, 490
Lawrence, Larry, 504
Lawrence, Maureen, 207
Lawrence, Peter, 295
Lawton, Matt H., 880
Lax, Charles, 247
Lax, Charles, 448
Lax, Solomon, 486
Layman, Bonnie, 601
Lazarus, Michael, 455
Lazarus, Steven, 346
Le, M. Duyen, 675
Le Gendre, Jacques, 778
Leach, Jonathan, 236
Leachman, W, 695
Leahy, Chris, 951
Leaver, John, 784
LeBaron, Matthew, 505
Lebow, Steven, 185
Lebret, Herve, 850
Lecaldano, Edoardo, 736
Lechelle, Luc, 794
Lecoeur, Jerome, 853
Ledger, Steve, 175
Ledoux, Robert, 265
Lee, Allan, 672
Lee, Anthony, 144
Lee, Calvin, Jr., 157
Lee, Cheng-Ming, 776
Lee, Craig, 345
Lee, David, 527
Lee, David, 671
Lee, Derrick, 402
Lee, Douglas, 231
Lee, Georgia, 189
Lee, Ha-Ouk, 905
Lee, Hee-gyoo, 873
Lee, Howard, 611
Lee, Jeffrey, 914
Lee, Kewsong, 590
Lee, Kheng Nam, 971
Lee, Michael, 170
Lee, Nancy, 269
Lee, Peter, 174
Lee, Raymond, 777
Lee, Sam, 195
Lee, Sam, 194
Lee, Simon, 510
Lee, Susanna, 238
Lee, Taek Joo, 844
Lee, Victor, 142
Leeds, Ashley, 510
Lefebvre, Richard, 504
Leff, Jonathan, 590
Lefkoff, Kyle, 392
LeFurgy, Rich, 270
Legoupil, Gillot or, 815
Lehr, Seth, 631
Lehr, William H., 613
Leiber, Irwin, 489
Leiber, Jonathan, 592
Leibowitz, Reuben, 590
Leichtman, Lauren, 204
Leidel, Peter, 452
Lelon, Charles, 577
LeMay, John A., 613
Lemke-von Ammon, Derek, 257
Lenard, Michael, 977
Lenehan, Tom, 179
Lenihan, Lawrence, 564
Lenihan, William, 181
Lennox, Ronald, 291
Lennox, Wally, 366
Lenoir, Wolfgang, 763
Lenotti, Markus, 854
Leo, Corbett, 595
Leonard, Walter, 446
Leone, Douglas, 241
Leone, William, 595
Lepard, Lawrence, 489
Lerer, Rene, 297
LeRoy, D. Shannon, 649
Leschly, Mark, 570
Leschly, Mark, 490
Lessin, Robert, 594
Lessin, Robert, 594
Lester, Cameron, 149
Leu, Rainer, 878
Leung, Anselm, 155
Leurdijik, Michael, 316
Leuze, Jurgen Max, 974
Leuze, Stefan, 974
Lev, Liora, 747
Levensohn, Pascal, 204
Leventhal, Lionel, 230
Leveque, Jean-Claude, 794
Levert, George, 395
Leveton, Peter J., 280
Levin, Charles, 433
Levin, Michael, 553
Levin, Peter, 961
Levin, Robert, 371
Levine, Arthur, 204
Levine, Herbert, 536
Levine, Mark, 314
Levine, Paul, 614
Levinthal, Michael, 210
Levitan, Dan, 708
Levy, Douglass, 521

Levy, Ellen, 437
Levy, Joel, 517
Levy, Jordan, 573
Levy, Shmuel, 241
Levy, Yoav, 913
Lew, Ginger, 316
Lewald, Alexander, 865
Lewander, Ulf, 927
Lewis, Alan, 763
Lewis, Barry, 180
Lewis, C. McKenzie, 469
Lewis, C. McKenzie, 471
Lewis, John, 543
Lewis, John, 669
Lewis, Nick, 781
Lewis Kussmaul, Maria, 416
Lewy, Glen, 538
Leyrer, David, 221
Leys, Jan, 818
Lhormer, Barry, 636
Li, Alfred, 201
Li, Douglas, 943
Li, Richard, 790
Li, Y. C., 821
Liao, James, 174
Libowitz, David, 590
Liddell, Michael, 364
Liddle, David, 261
Liebeck, William, 371
Lieber, Irwin, 592
Lieber, Seth, 592
Lieberman, Jeff, 540
Liencres, Bjorn, 199
Liesching, Karen, 190
Lifonti, Pietro, 726
Ligertwood, Mark, 799
Ligeti, Peter, 630
Lightbody, George, 704
Likins, David, 266
Lillis, Chuck, 281
Lim, Boh-Soon, 750
Lin, Alfred, 265
Lin, Chin, 777
Lin, Jaff, 209
Lin, Moun-Rong, 187
Lin, Richard, 258
Lin, Timothy, 773
Lincoln, David, 626
Linden, Ronald, 584
Lindgren, Alicia, 588
Lindgren, Douglas, 584
Lindner, Andrew, 600
Lindskog, Stefan, 861
Lindskog, Urban, 773
Lindstrand, Staffan, 904
Linehan, Charles, 396
Lingjaerde, Sven, 827
Lingjaerde, Sven, 267
Linn, Roger, 660
Linnert, Mike, 254
Linsalata, Ralph, 415
Linseis, Brigitte, 757
Lisiak, Paul, 553
List, Raymond, 693
Liston, Thomas, 384
Litle, Thomas, 428
Litman, Arie, 207
Littell, Mark, 559
Little, Gary, 614
Little, Gary, 361
Little, Hugh, 728
Little, Lortetta, 715
Littlechild, John, 490
Littlejohn, Kevin, 406
Liu, Lander, 963
Liu, Victor, 677
Livne, Yigal, 896
Ljungkvist, Hans, 765
Llovera, Luis, 216
Lo, Jack T.K., 402
Lo, Raymond, 402
Loarie, Robert, 554
Lobel, David, 573
Lobo, Alfredo, 896
Lobo, Richard, 351
Locke, Ian, 863
Lockhart, Catherine D., 396
Lockhart, Sandy, 876
Lockwood, Michael, 821
Lodewick, Richard, 450
Loeffel, Eric, 658
Lohrasbpar, Esfandiar, 541
Lokey, Carol, 705
Lomas, Eric, 538
Lombard, Stuart, 861
Lombardi, Jeffrey, 697
Long, Augustine, 611
Long, Austin, 655
Long, Dirk, 905
Long, John, 682
Long, Michael, 331
Long, Mike, 634
Loo, Cheng Guan, 402
Look, Fan, 974
Lopez-Quesada, Juan, 763
Lorente, Pilar, 577
Lorentzen, Matthew, 435
Lorphelin, Xavier, 865
Lorsch, David, 181
Loschner, Klaus, 757
Losier, John, 540
Lothrop, Donald, 167
Lott, Ronnie, 159
Loughlin, Sam, 661
Louie, Mark, 254
Loukianoff, Peter, 143
Loup de Gersigny, Jean, 855
Louthan, Robert, 701
Lovell, Jeffery, 232
Lovett, Joseph, 434
Loveys, Harry K., 798
Lowcock, Nicholas, 590
Lowe, Gene, 547
Lubar, David, 718

Lubert, Ira, 631
Lubert, M. Ira, 640
Luby, William, 572
Lucas, Donald, 239
Lucius, Judie, 263
Luck, Pascal, 313
Lucquin, Denis, 934
Luehrs, Bruce, 488
Luetchens, Shawn, 924
Lui, Danny, 149
Lukatch, Heath, 472
Luken, Ron, 576
Lum, Irene, 931
Lummis, Fred, 680
Lundahl, Jan, 944
Lundhagen, Jonas, 861
Lundin, Hans, 706
Lung, Sven, 808
Lunn, Randall, 228
Luotonen, Kai, 803
Lussier, James, 223
Lutsi, John, 614
Lutzke, Scott, 378
Lyford, Chris, 604
Lyle, Rupert, 726
Lynch, Christopher, 406
Lynch, James, 692
Lynch, Jonathan, 543
Lynch, Kevin, 294
Lyon, Kevin, 726
Lyons, Paul, 283
Lytell, Michael, 489

M

Macaranas, Federico, 781
Macdonald, Jacqueline, 245
MacDonald, Lane, 403
MacDonald, Robert, 977
MacDonell, Ian, 789
Macfie, Andy, 889
Machala, Janis, 711
Machefsky, Ira, 561
Machens, G. Michael, 673
Maciejewski, Mark, 261
MacIntosh, Alan, 406
Macintosh, John, 590
Mackenzie, Douglas, 200
Mackenzie, Helen, 274
MacKenzie, Helen, 247
Mackesy, D. Scott, 591
Mackiewicz, Michal, 746
Macklin, Rodd, 316
Macks, Larry, 392
Macksey, Alan, 398
Maclean, Richard, 600
Macleod, Lauren, 423
MacMillan, Harry, 866
MacNaughton, Torquil, 911
Macpherson, Alastair, 920
Macpherson, Michele Dundas, 775
MacQuitty, Jonathan, 949
Madden, Richard, 627
Madera, Sherry, 856
Madonna, Lynn Amato, 556
Madrid, Jack, 751
Madsen, Kent, 687
Maeder, Paul, 427
Maene, Frank, 760
Maggard, J. Oliver, 569
Maggs, Roger, 775
Mahaffey, Lloyd, 234
Maher, Michael, 261
Mahler, Livia, 832
Mahoney, Michael, 462
Maierhofer, Scott, 285
Maillet, Peter, 296
Main, Greg, 618
Maine, Richard, 298
Maitland, Gavin, 751
Maitre, Bernard, 824
Majek, Warren, 494
Mak, Phil, 264
Makinen, Jukka, 807
Malan, Remy, 152
Maldonado, Jose Maria, 763
Maleve, Roger, 828
Malhan, Arvind, 396
Malhotra, Naresh, 693
Malik, Neil, 640
Malin, Amir, 147
Malizia, David, 322
Malka, Benjamin, 438
Malka, Martti, 222
Mallement, Harvey, 536
Mallo, Carlos, 726
Malloy, John, 222
Malm, David, 425
Maloney, Barry, 154
Maloney, T.J., 548
Maluth, Elliot, 512
Malvern, Dan, 530
Mamlet, Geoff, 415
Manchester, Robert, 642
Mancuso, Joseph, 505
Mandaric, Milan, 512
Mandell, Lloyd, 532
Mandile, John, 243
Maney, David, 190
Manger, Roland, 800
Mann, Darlene, 225
Mann, Timothy, 336
Manning, Robert, 371
Mannion, Martin, 451
Manos, Peter, 769
Manson, Lawrence, 365
Mansson, Christer, 748
Marakovic, Nino, 213
March, A. Fred, 588
Marchbanks, Gregory, 674
Marcus, James, 584
Marcus, Jeffrey, 672
Marcus, Larry, 270
Marcuvitz, Andrew, 433

Marduel, Alix, 144
Margalit, Erel, 864
Marin, Rich, 509
Mark, Joseph, 582
Markey, Bernard, 633
Markland, Dave, 206
Marks, Arthur, 396
Marks, Evan, 582
Marks, Kelli, 343
Marland, Norman, 292
Marley, Julianne, 613
Marom, Rann, 970
Maroni, Kevin, 248
Marquardt, David, 148
Marram, Edward, 314
Marriott, Justin, 701
Marrone, Michael, 520
Marsden, Andrew, 663
Marsh, Robert, 234
Marshal, Jonathan, 821
Marshall, Bob, 241
Marshall, Christopher, 259
Marshall, Jim, 241
Marshall, Roger, 729
Marshall, Ross, 799
Marshall, Sheryl, 408
Marshall, William, 263
Martel, Frederic, 858
Martin, Charles, 178
Martin, Jim, 733
Martin, Nancy, 590
Martinko, Richard, 614
Martinson, John, 488
Martinson, Marty, 140
Martinson, Ross, 488
Marver, James, 263
Marzak, Jess, 150
Masiello, Mark, 643
Mason, Duane, 441
Mason, John, 669
Mason, John, 180
Mason, R.S., 810
Mason, Susan, 225
Masri, Edgar, 433
Massaro, Salvatore, 332
Massey, Lauren, 501
Massi, Rene, 274
Masterson, Nola, 961
Masur, Mark, 677
Mataix, Jorge, 900
Mather, Jim, 941
Mathewson, Eric, 232
Mathies, Rolf, 800
Mathiesen, Michael, 138
Mathieu, Raymond, 643
Matlack, Terry, 477
Matlack, Thomas, 435
Matloubian, Mehran, 246
Matson, Deborah Sopher, 299
Matson, Scott, 229
Matsui, Shoko, 445
Matsuki, Nobuo, 445
Matsumoto, Yasuki, 704
Mattelaer, Katrien, 959
Mattern, Richard, 216
Matteucci, Paul, 261
Matthes, William, 512
Matthews, James, 310
Matthews, James, 591
Matthews, Terry, 775
Mattutat, James, 574
Matzka, Alfred, 840
Mauer, Robert, 701
Maury, Rene, 931
Mautner, Leonard, 203
Maxwell, Bret, 354
Maxwell, Ray, 541
Maxwell, Scott, 540
May, John, 690
May, John, 692
Mayer, David, 371
Mayer, Erich, 848
Mayer, Ernst G, 947
Mayer, John, 542
Mayer, John, 576
Mayer, Michael, 951
Mayerson, Frederic, 617
Mayhew, Andrew, 751
Mayhew, Nicholas, 799
Maynard, Frederick, 426
Maynard, Jim, 244
Mayr, Anton, 942
Mazza, David, 425
McAdam, Timothy, 260
McAdoo, Greg, 241
McAleer, William, 714
McBean, Bob, 786
McBlain, John, 359
McCall, Chad, 335
McCall, Joe, 339
McCall, Steven, 572
McCallum, Duncan, 439
McCammon, Dan, 218
McCance, Henry, 424
McCann, Byron, 367
McCarthy, David, 758
McCarthy, Eileen, 403
McCarthy, John, 476
McChesney, Michael, 334
McClain, Thomas, 576
McClenaghan, Sean, 278
McConnell, James, 298
McConnell, Thomas, 396
McConomy, Thomas, 625
McCord, Rob, 635
McCormack, John, 573
McCormack, R. Stephen, 419
McCormack, Robert, 259
McCourtney, Ted, 586
McCoy, Michael, 657
McCrory, Gerry, 625
McCroskey, Nancy, 196
McCroskey, Nancy, 235
McCrum, Bliss, 527

McCuaig, Todd, 614
McCullagh, Paul, 907
McCullen, Joseph, 310
McCullen, Joseph, 439
McDanell, Philip, 730
McDermott, Dirk, 277
McDonagh, William, 270
McDonnell, Mark, 346
McDonnell, Mark, 362
McDonough, John, 152
McDonough, Joseph, 152
McElwee, James, 455
McEniry, Roger, 355
McFadden, Niall, 837
McFadden, Teri, 139
McGill, A., 876
McGill, Robert, 410
McGlashan, William, 310
McGlinchy, Richard, 409
McGlynn, Casey, 145
McGlynn, Casey, 171
McGovern, Lisa, 492
McGowan-Smyth, Bob, 805
McGrath, Alexander, 415
McGrath, Pat, 845
McGregor, Jim, 693
McGrew, Frank, 651
McGuire, Terry, 441
McGurk, Erin, 208
McHale, John, 657
McHenry, Maurice, 845
McHugh, Michael, 465
McIlwraith, John, 609
McInerney, Thomas, 591
McIntosh, Kevin, 265
McIntyre, Ryan, 247
McIvor, Dale E., 307
McKay, Samuel, 288
McKenna, Lawrence, 402
McKenna, Stephen, 543
McKinley, Edward, 590
McKinley, H. Scott, 543
McKinley, Thomas, 229
McLane, P. Andrews, 451
McLean, Bart, 331
McLean, James, 409
McLean, Jim, 163
McLean, John, 780
McLeese, David, 479
McLemore, Nina, 569
McMahon, Timothy, 401
McMartin, Cameron, 661
McMullen, Geoff, 929
McNaught-Davis, James, 590
McNeil, Robert, 239
McNeill, Brian, 403
McNeill, Philip, 312
McNerney, Peter, 465
McNiel, Jim, 564
McNulty, John, 366
McPhee, William, 434
McQuillan, John, 196
McQuillan, John, 235
McQuillan, Kevin, 160
McRae, W. Barry, 129
McStraw, Tom, 963
McSwiney, C. Ronald, 610
McWade, Karen, 454
Meadow, Scott, 578
Meakem, Chip, 523
Mecham, Mark, 709
Meckler, Alan, 297
Medeiros, Jose, 775
Meduna, Cyril, 734
Medved, Jonathan, 860
Meekin, Peter, 259
Meggs, Jonathan, 543
Megret, Dominique, 866
Meheut, Jacques, 853
Mehlman, R. Paul, 298
Mehra, Vivek, 250
Mehrotta, Rohit, 565
Mehta, Hitesh, 740
Mehta, Kayu, 753
Meier, Heinz Michael, 757
Mejean, Paul, 307
Mejia, Carlos-Felipe, 323
Melander, Magnus, 762
Melisse, Chris, 960
Mellinger, Pierre, 503
Mellon, Jim, 920
Melzer, Thomas, 478
Memmo, Nicholas, 201
Menchaca, Tony, 293
Mencoff, Samuel, 361
Mendel, Gary, 293
Mendel, Gregory, 574
Mendel, Mark, 478
Mendelson, Alan, 288
Mendicino, Frank, 277
Mendlowitz, Hal, 636
Menell, Mark, 238
Meng, Molly, 343
Mengshoel, Tore, 952
Menkes, Alan, 257
Menon, Sreedhar, 571
Meredith, Debby, 214
Mereur, Jean-Noel, 220
Merigo, Nicolas, 770
Merritt, Roy, 794
Mersky, Seth, 905
Messina, Richard, 581
Messman, Jack, 415
Metais, Benoit, 931
Metcalf, Robert, 441
Metcalfe, Murray, 430
Meurer, Bill, 289
Meurer, Dirk, 796
Meurer, Tom, 667
Meyer, Eric, 553
Meyer, Judith, 356
Meyer, Stephen, 254
Meyer, Ted, 181
Meyers, Charles, 395

Meyers, Jonathan, 307
Meyers, Tim, 700
Meyrowitz, Norm, 208
Mhatre, Ravi, 410
Mhatre, Ravi, 206
Miadich, Anthony, 303
Miao, Larry, 905
Michaels, Mark, 374
Michaelson, John, 556
Michalik, Christian, 415
Michalski, Lutz, 969
Michaud, Gerald, 309
Michero, Carlo, 726
Michiels, Tanja, 818
Michl, Leigh, 406
Middlemas, George, 346
Middleton, Fred, 239
Middleton, Shaun, 799
Mieskonen, Jari, 807
Migliorino, Robert, 290
Mii, Nobuo, 192
Mikati, Aref, 259
Mikkola, Juha, 807
Miles, Reid, 690
Miles, Robert, 677
Milius, Craig, 616
Milius, Jeffery, 616
Millar, James, 487
Millar, Kenneth T., 337
Miller, Bill, 709
Miller, Cameron, 232
Miller, Chris, 692
Miller, David, 294
Miller, Dean, 635
Miller, Dennis, 518
Miller, Edmund, 323
Miller, Jody, 708
Miller, Lawrence, 434
Miller, Michael, 350
Miller, Monte, 133
Miller, Norvell, 605
Miller, Piotr, 746
Miller, Rudy, 135
Miller, Russell, 238
Miller, Simon, 799
Miller, Steven, 365
Miller, Teresa, 285
Miller, Warren, 323
Millet, David, 423
Mills, David, 534
Mills, Jeffrey, 170
Mills, John, 553
Mills, Karen, 576
Mills, Michael, 452
Mills, Tim, 239
Mills, William, 454
Milne, Neil, 785
Milo, Hillel, 781
Milstein, David, 421
Minick, Scott, 346
Minicucci, Robert, 591
Minnick, James, 232
Minor, Bill, 262
Mintz, Daniel, 905
Mintz, Harold, 565
Minvielle, Dominique, 754
Mirabelli, Christopher, 490
Miranda, Luis, 778
Miranda, Stan, 752
Miron, Russ, 674
Mitchell, Anne, 421
Mitchell, Dan, 284
Mitchell, James, 183
Mitchell, Jamie, 971
Mitchell, Kate, 150
Mitchell, Lee, 371
Mitchell, Samuel, 314
Mitchell, Stuart, 897
Mitta, Sridhar, 174
Mix, Earl, 290
Miyamoto, Ross, 518
Miyamoto, Yuzuru, 222
Mlavsky, Ed, 825
Mo, Shuyi, 402
Mobbs, Jeremy, 854
Mocarski, Ted, 643
Moehrle, Christina, 940
Moelchert, Chip, 695
Moelis, Jeff, 230
Moeller, Dick, 653
Moeller, J.W. "Joe", 133
Moeller, Scott, 795
Moerschel, Greg, 348
Mogan Phillips, Gwendolyn, 402
Mohan, Kevin, 451
Mohan, Ravi, 409
Mohan, Venkat, 223
Mohaupt, Jorg, 785
Mohrmann, Robert, 475
Mojica, Abel, 477
Mol, Jerome, 830
Mollatt, Andreas, 952
Moller, Christopher, 640
Molvin, Alex, 861
Momsen, Robert, 197
Monaco, Joseph, 431
Monaster, G.A., 928
Mondale, Curt, 568
Mongiello, Jim, 235
Monk, Robert, 312
Monosson, Deborah, 412
Mons, Robert, 325
Montana, Joe, 159
Montanari, Claudio, 925
Montanus, Gerard, 407
Monteforte, Aldo, 808
Montelione, John, 325
Montgomery, H. DuBose, 212
Montoya, David, 576
Moons, Raf, 973
Moore, Alan, 671
Moore, Charles, 591
Moore, Charles, 347
Moore, Geoffrey, 214

Moore, Guerry, 619
Moore, Jeffrey, 695
Moore, Jennifer, 856
Moorhead, Rodman, 590
Moorin, Jay, 493
Moot, Alex, 446
Moragne, John, 259
Moraly, Dana, 161
Moran, Peter, 169
Morbeck, Kirsten, 705
Morby, Jacqueline, 451
Morck, Frede, 793
More, Eileen, 302
More, Robert, 486
Morgan, Allen, 210
Morgan, Jonathan, 914
Morgan, Jonathan, 955
Morgan, Philip, 873
Morgan, Richard, 506
Morgan, Richard, 586
Morgenthaler, David, 614
Morgenthaler, Gary, 614
Morihiro, Koji, 254
Morimoto, Yoshihiko, 629
Morin, Pierre, 185
Moritz, Michael, 241
Morley, Daniel T., 506
Moross, David, 577
Morozov, Andrew, 640
Morris, Blake, 278
Morris, Frederic, 414
Morris, John, 426
Morris, John, 954
Morris, Peter, 396
Morris, Robert, 232
Morris, Vic, 407
Morris-Hatch, Janice, 421
Morrison, Jay, 220
Morrison, Neal, 600
Morrison, Paul, 632
Morro, William, 363
Morse, Laura, 407
Morse, Thomas, 636
Morse, Thomas, 631
Morton, William, 494
Moseley, Charles, 336
Moses, James, 959
Mosher, David, 361
Mosley, Sig, 335
Moss, Frank, 674
Moss, Malcolm, 918
Moss, Malcolm, 459
Mostyn-Williams, Stephen, 771
Moufflet, Gerard, 402
Moulton, Eben, 446
Moulton, Jon, 736
Moura, Pascal, 807
Moussa, Mary, 140
Mowill, Fredrik, 833
Mrachacz, Markus, 757
Mrozek, Therese, 455
Mueffelmann, Jens, 746
Mueller, David, 682
Mulcahy, Diane, 473
Mulhern, Alison, 572
Mullaney, William, 683
Mullen, Fergal, 443
Muller, Kurt, 947
Muller, Sherman, 279
Muller von Blumencron, Markus, 759
Mullett, Conor, 700
Mulligan, Gregory, 418
Mulligan, William, 616
Mullins, J. Douglass, 328
Mumma, Mitch, 601
Mundy, Howard, 764
Munk, Anthony, 905
Munoz, Jose, 880
Muraguchi, Kazutaka, 899
Murase, Mitsumasa, 862
Murchison, Ian, 822
Murdoch, Simon, 806
Murdock, Jerry, 540
Muro, Bradley, 547
Murphree, Dennis, 671
Murphree, L., 671
Murphy, Charles, 741
Murphy, H. Leland, 682
Murphy, James, 150
Murphy, John, 549
Murphy, Kathy, 260
Murphy, Mark, 310
Murphy, Owen, 732
Murphy, Paul, 573
Murphy, Peg, 437
Murray, Dave, 605
Murray, Fulton, 667
Murray, Stephen, 543
Murray, Tim, 912
Murray, Timothy, 373
Muschiol, Jorg, 770
Mussafer, David, 402
Mussalo, Terho, 803
Muth, Michael, 882
Muti, Jeffrey, 548
Mutter, Sheila, 255
Myers, Gib, 210
Myers, Kip, 234
Myers, Michael, 493
Mykityshyn, Mark, 334

N

Nadel, Paul, 175
Nadkarni, Kiran, 172
Nadkarni, Kiran, 864
Naf, Beat, 811
Nagarajan, M.R., 767
Nagata, Hirokazu, 793
Nagel, Bob, 737
Nagel, Christian, 800
Nahman, Vance, 152
Nahum, Agnes, 730
Naik, Ullas, 198

Naini, Nader, 705
Najjar, Michael, 519
Nakagome, Kinya, 789
Nallol, B., 757
Nam, Ho, 144
Narain, Sailendra, 933
Narasimhan, N., 749
Narayan, Subra, 466
Narayanamurti, Venky, 221
Naru, Sarath, 743
Nathan, Badri, 740
Nathanson, Andrew, 561
Nathusius, Klaus, 826
Naughton, Tom, 437
Naveh, Arad, 154
Nawn, Chris, 254
Nazarian, David, 246
Nazem, Fred, 556
Neal, Ian, 892
Neal, William, 604
Neale, Frank, 963
Nebenzahl, Charles, 486
Needham, George, 556
Needley, Michael, 936
Neems, Gary, 622
Neermann, Jorg, 796
Negroponte, Nicholas, 405
Nehra, John, 396
Neidhart, Jim, 165
Neis, John, 720
Nelsen, Robert, 346
Nelson, Anna, 607
Nelson, David, 302
Nelson, Don, 445
Nelson, Don, 445
Nelson, F. Eric, 716
Nelson, Hakan, 877
Nelson, Jonathan, 643
Nelson, L. Steve, 607
Nelson, Michael, 234
Nelson, Thomas, 607
Nemirovsky, Ofer, 426
Neugarten, Ilan, 798
Neuhaus, Gottfried, 948
Neuhauser, Will, 705
Neupert, Peter, 200
Nevadovic, Daniel, 565
Neville, Louise, 541
Newby, Tom, 254
Newell, Carla, 254
Newell, Doug, 133
Newell, Jim, 277
Newhall, Charles, 396
Newlin, William, 625
Newman, Henry, 449
Newman, Howard, 590
Newmark, Gregg, 373
Newsam, John, 221
Newton, Ray, 310
Newton, Richard, 210
Ng, Benjamin, 805
Ng, Douglas, 421
Ng, Francis L.F., 402
Ng, Maisy, 733
Ng, Song-How, 938
Ng, Thomas, 968
Ngai, Au, 219
Ngan, Raymond, 273
Nicholls, Mark, 922
Nichols, Carl, 193
Nichols, Paul, 679
Nicholson, Chris, 263
Nicholson, Ed, 134
Nicholson, John, 657
Nicholson, Robert, 248
Nickels, Craig, 655
Nicklin, F. Oliver, 354
Nickoloff, Robert, 469
Nickse, Jay, 502
Nicodemus, Nancy, 339
Nicolay, Stefaan, 861
Nie, Norman, 302
Nieh, Peter, 206
Niehaus, Joseph, 189
Niehaus, Thomas, 610
Nielsen, Soren Jessen, 794
Niemczewski, Christopher, 314
Nijensohn, Zev, 248
Niles, Kimberley, 389
Nilsson, Christer, 749
Nilsson, Thomas, 257
Nimmo, William, 425
Nisar, Faisal, 510
Nissenbaum, Scott, 635
Nittler, Katie, 162
Nixon, Brandon, 190
Nixon, Ron, 660
Noble, Chris, 153
Noble, David, 133
Noguchi, Masayuki, 445
Nohra, Guy, 144
Nolan, Bill, 165
Nolan, Joseph, 356
Nolan, Peter, 203
Noojin, J. Thomas, 130
Noojin, William, 129
Nordal, Stephen, 582
Nordemann, Gerhard, 827
Nordin, Ron, 407
Norman, Jeff, 731
Norwood, Peter, 640
Noth, Andreas, 759
Nouvellet, Dominique, 931
Nova, Daniel, 427
Novaczek, Frank, 623
Novak, Roger, 697
Novick, Oliver, 912
Novik, Shai, 582
Novitsky, Donna, 214
Nowakowski, Rafat, 853
Nuevillar, Christopher, 627
Nunez, Fernando de, 895
Nusbaum, Gary, 590
Nussrallah, Steve, 336

Nutter, Bill, 649
Nye, Benjamin, 312
Nyhan, William, 152

O

O'Brian, Joe, 652
O'Brian, Martin, 845
O'Brien, Dana, 519
O'Brien, Daniel, 310
O'Brien, Jamie, 537
O'Brien, Robert, 376
O'Connell, Dennis, 523
O'Connor, Conor, 805
O'Connor, H. Tomkins, 508
O'Connor, James, 315
O'Donnell, James, 474
O'Donnell, Jim, 331
O'Donnell, Kathleen, 402
O'Donnell, R. Timothy, 695
O'Donohue, Kevin, 757
O'Driscoll, Rory, 150
O'Farrell, John, 967
O'Grady, Michelle, 440
O'Grady, Michelle, 929
O'Grady, Standish, 186
O'Keefe, Ken, 348
O'Keeffe, Graham, 407
O'Leary, Nancy, 358
O'Malley, Michael, 433
O'Malley, Michael, 623
O'Neil, Kate, 295
O'Neil, Robert, 410
O'Neill, John, 886
O'Neill, Martin, 542
Oakford, Scott, 296
Oakley, Kim, 434
Oba, Katsuhiko, 551
Oberholtzer, William, 344
Oblak, Geoffrey, 406
Obuch, Robert, 150
Occhipinti, John, 274
Occhipinti, Vincent, 274
Ochsner, Neal, 512
Ocko, Matt, 263
Ocko, Matt, 247
Odden, Jake, 138
Odlander, Bjorn, 904
Ofer, Idan, 582
Offer, Fred H., 958
Oftedal, Ole, 843
Oh, Byung-Hwa, 797
Ohrn, Gustaf, 937
Okamoto, Yukio, 228
Oken, Glenn, 322
Okonow, Dale, 455
Okrouhlik, Michael, 839
Okun, Rob, 252
Olaso-Yohn, Mariano, 972
Oldham, R.Brad, 667
Ole Carsen, Hans, 138
Olenik, Andrea, 521
Oleszczuk, Andy, 372
Olisa, Ken, 856
Oliva, Adele, 563
Oliver, Roland, 696
Oliverio, Don, 346
Olivier, Edmund, 440
Olivier, Laurie, 970
Olkkola, Edward, 657
Olsen, Robert, 774
Olson, Nancy, 471
Olsson, Jesper Jos, 937
Oltramonti, Massimo, 402
Ong, Peng, 250
Onians, Richard, 755
Onopchenko, Laura, 254
Oorschot, Peter van, 830
Opdendyk, Terry, 225
Oral, Emre, 870
Oran, Daniel, 415
Orban, M. Michel, 571
Oren, Tim, 228
Orlando, Jim, 409
Orman, James, 875
Oron, Yoram, 971
Oronsky, Arnold, 197
Oros, David, 390
Orr, Lawrence, 260
Orr, R. Wilson, 653
Orsak, Michael, 275
Ortale, W. Patrick, 652
Ortel, Charles K, 837
Osborn, D. Chris, 371
Osborn, Jeffrey, 440
Osborn, Richard, 832
Osing, Byron, 871
Ostby, Ingar, 902
Oster, Keith, 257
Osterlund, Bjorn, 927
Ostermaier, Stefan, 968
Osthaus, Anne, 848
Ostin, Olav, 808
Ott, Charles, 179
Otto, Anna, 760
Otto, Goetz, 866
Overbeck, Glenda, 666
Overell, Bob, 705
Owen, Daniel T., 665
Oxaal, John, 677
Oyster, Jeffery A., 595

P

Pacitti, Christopher, 657
Packard, Warren, 172
Paff, C. Ted, 139
Pahl, Milt, 893
Palandjian, Leon, 405
Palfrey, Stephan, 290
Palles, Allen, 361
Palley, Simon, 757
Palmer, Laureen, 140
Palmer, Thomas, 477

Paluck, Robert, 661
Palva, William, 618
Pan, Henry, 586
Panasevich, Dimitri, 244
Pancoast, Scott, 272
Panfilo, Francesco, 729
Pant, Sangam, 175
Pantuso, Tony, 437
Papadimitriou, Angelos, 741
Papiernik, Antoine, 934
Pappas, Art, 597
Pappas, Milton, 527
Paquin, Jacques, 830
Parekh, Deven, 540
Parekh, Raj, 235
Parizeau, Ernest, 223
Park, John, 485
Park, Sik Eui, 792
Parke, Marshall, 566
Parke, Marshall, 548
Parker, Barbara, 306
Parker, David, 404
Parker, David, 323
Parker, George, 298
Parker, Marshall, 383
Parker, Peter, 404
Parker, Ransom, 699
Parker, Victor, 248
Parks, Timothy, 625
Paroo, Janet, 634
Parquet, Laurent, 765
Parr, Jeff, 780
Parsa, Hassan, 207
Parshall, David, 567
Parsons, Donald, 278
Parsons, James, 305
Partovi, Naser, 178
Partridge, John, 451
Partridge, Lamar, 654
Paskin-Jordan, Wendy, 169
Pasquesi, John, 189
Pastor, Filomena, 859
Pastoriza, James, 496
Patch, David, 378
Patch, Rick, 284
Patel, Yag, 570
Paterson, Calum, 927
Pathak, Dalip, 590
Paton, Jamie, 726
Paton, Scott, 771
Patouillaud, Jean-Marc, 229
Patterson, Arthur, 139
Patterson, Richard, 577
Patterson, Robin, 528
Patterson, Thomas, 455
Patterson, Wes, 677
Patterson, Z. David, 609
Patton, Michael, 794
Patyk, Christopher, 570
Pauker, Armando, 346
Paul, Andrew, 591
Paumelle, Jean-Francois, 735
Pavey, Robert, 614
Pavlov, George, 210
Payne, Steve, 192
Pe'er, Lilach, 795
Peake, Tripp, 429
Pearce, Colin, 791
Pearce, Rupert, 407
Pearl, Daphna, 860
Pearl, Laura, 355
Pearsall, Duane, 279
Peattie, Debra, 442
Pecaut, David, 296
Pederson, Kim, 707
Pederson, Steven, 471
Pedriks, Markus, 755
Peery, Ashton, 207
Peery, Brad, 156
Pelaez, Andres, 880
Pelisek, David, 347
Pellizzari, Paolo, 204
Pelly, Chris, 808
Pelson, Mark, 643
Pelzman, Adam, 550
Penberthy, Daniel, 568
Penhoet, Edward, 144
Peninon, Dominique, 730
Penn, Thomas, 412
Pennell, Keith, 486
Pennington, Kelvin, 365
Pentecost, Edward, 614
Penzias, Arno, 396
Pere, Pekka, 803
Pereira, Carol, 234
Pereira, Ken, 191
Peres, Chemi, 913
Perez, David, 407
Perez, Vincent, 894
Pergande, John, 659
Perison, Stephen, 177
Perkins, Thomas, 200
Perl, Jonathon, 601
Perlis, Michael, 448
Perper, Alan, 231
Perper, Scott, 600
Perrault, Jean-François, 878
Perreault, Justin, 419
Perrett, Nick, 751
Perry, Christopher, 350
Perry, Edward, 658
Perry, Geva, 582
Perry, James, 361
Perry, Mark, 396
Perry, Xander, 391
Persson, Jan, 343
Persson, Magnus, 904
Pesavento, Anthony, 360
Peskoff, Johnathan, 315
Peters, Gregory, 389
Peters, Jon, 651
Peters, Scott, 545
Peterson, Dan, 927
Peterson, Thomas, 176

Petillo, Doug, 640
Petrillo, Enrico, 416
Petro, Alec, 627
Petty, Darl, 675
Petty, William, 348
Pew, Clay, 364
Peyton, Robert, 479
Pflieger, Robert, 532
Pfund, Nancy, 160
Philbrick, J. Alden, 698
Philipkosky, James, 376
Phillips, Barclay, 372
Phillips, Brian, 872
Phillips, Charles, 534
Phillips, Lawrence, 567
Phillips, Mark, 911
Phillips, Mike, 834
Phillips, Stuart, 261
Phipps, Charles, 677
Phipps, George, 563
Piaker, Steven, 292
Piccino, Pierre-Michel, 755
Pieper, Roel, 540
Pieroni, Molly, 668
Pierrepont, J. Jay, 908
Pietri, Todd, 553
Piette, Daniel, 876
Pignato, Joseph, 417
Pike, Christopher, 402
Pillar, Simon, 907
Pilmer, Michael, 537
Pincus, Lionel, 590
Pines, Todd, 576
Ping-kwong, Thomas Kwok, 943
Ping-luen, Raymond Kwok, 943
Ping-sheung, Walter Kwok, 943
Pinkas, Robert, 609
Pinkel, John, 929
Pinkerton, David, 503
Pinto, Daniel, 778
Pinto, Frank, 412
Piol, Alessandro, 541
Piol, Alessandro, 376
Piol, Elserino, 501
Piol, Elserino, 912
Piper, Joseph, 706
Piper, Paul, 855
Piret, John J., 437
Piscopo, Al, 490
Pitt, James, 310
Pittenger, John, 133
Pitzolu, Gianfranco, 817
Plakopitas, Angelos, 828
Planitzer, Russell, 547
Plantholt-Melera, Barbara, 319
Plessinger, D. Jean, 371
Pluche, Herve, 255
Poch, Gerald, 564
Poggioli, Philippe, 730
Polden, John, 890
Polestra, Frank, 406
Polestra, Marino, 144
Poliner, Randall, 320
Politi, Santo, 417
Pollack, George, 572
Pollard, Patrick, 348
Pomerantz, Ernest, 590
Pomper, Claude, 249
Pomroy, Denis, 269
Pong, Flora, 402
Porschmann, Jan, 918
Porter, Thomas, 458
Posner, Philip, 227
Posner, Ross M., 368
Posselt, JWolfgang, 947
Post, Rick, 281
Potter, Jeff, 415
Potters, Heather, 755
Powaser, Christine, 658
Powell, Hank, 322
Powell, Mike, 246
Power, Gordon, 918
Powers, Brian, 189
Powers, Linda, 399
Prabhakarar, Arati, 261
Prakash, Gautam, 410
Pratt, Stanley, 501
Pratt-Otto, Drusilla, 248
Preston, Car, 312
Preston, Charles, 655
Preston, Mike, 605
Pretorius, Mark, 155
Priester, Wilbur, 690
Prior, John, 556
Pritzker, J.B., 364
Prober, Michael, 520
Procter, Benjamin, 455
Protard, Olivier, 934
Protard, Olivier, 246
Prouty, Norman, 845
Prow, Greg, 247
Prytula, Richard, 949
Puech, Jean-Francois, 931
Pulges, Virapan, 187
Pundak-Mintz, Adi, 825
Purcell, Tim, 542
Purdy, Gerry, 336
Purdy, J. Gerry, 169
Puris, Martin, 557
Purkert, Gert, 806
Pusey, Gregory, 281
Puskala, Markku, 807
Putnam, Donald, 232
Putney, Zimri, 697
Putzeys, Jacques, 866
Pyett, Nicholas, 457

Q

Quagliaroli, John, 422
Quarterman, Alan, 334
Quartner, Andrew, 315
Qucally, Paul, 591
Quek, Cher Teck, 964

Quigley, William, 161
Quindlen, Ruthann, 196
Quinn, Chris, 364
Quinn, Michael, 293
Quy, Roger, 255

R
Rachleff, Andy, 154
Racine, Richard, 556
Rackley, Tripp, 336
Radszuweit, Wolfgang, 759
Radwanski, Witold, 735
Radzinski, Abraham, 924
Raffel, Wes, 401
Rafferty, Raymond, 633
Raffini, George, 841
Raffini, George, 841
Raffkind, Eliot, 655
Rafield, Lori, 563
Raghavenvran, Ramnan, 540
Raghunathan, S.P., 761
Rahmatallah, Faisal, 770
Raicher, Serge, 908
Raimondi, Jill, 190
Rainey, Donald, 601
Rajaraman, Anand, 158
Rajczi, Louis, 216
Rakes, Steven, 605
Ramachandran, Raghu, 339
Ramich, James, 182
Ramnath, Renuka, 846
Ramsauer, Richard G., 974
Rand, Alan, 620
Rand, Kenneth, 570
Randall, Andrew, 904
Randall, Roderick, 471
Randhawa, Harpal, 741
Ranera, Roberto, 726
Ranganathan, Babu, 346
Rankine-Wilson, Adam, 801
Ransom, Richard, 210
Rantz, Mike, 180
Ranzetta, Theresia, 139
Rappaport, Andrew, 148
Rappaport, Neil, 274
Rasa, Eero, 952
Rasch, Hansgeorg, 947
Raschle, Bruno, 734
Rasmussen, Erik, 598
Rather, John, 591
Rauner, Bruce, 356
Rautiainen, Jarmo, 753
Raviola, Ghiliano, 501
Raviv, Adi, 582
Ray, C. Barham, 653
Ray, Daniel, 668
Rayne, Robert, 874
Raza, Atiq, 233
Raziano, Robert, 580
Razzouk, William, 651
Rea, Justin, 625
Read, Ashley, 155
Reade, K. Deane, 151
Reader, C.V., 782
Reagh, John, 715
Rebetez, Jean-Claude, 750
Rebmann, Stefan, 802
Redmond, Chris, 473
Reece, Joe, 177
Reed, David, 601
Reed, Douglas, 372
Reed, Ron, 294
Reeders, Stephen, 891
Rees, Robert, 277
Reeves, Frank, 665
Regan, John, 630
Regis, Dan, 704
Reher, John, 211
Rehm, Rudolph, 169
Reichert, Michel, 427
Reid, Georg, 757
Reidy, Stephen, 527
Reihill, Shane, 837
Reilly, Robert, 420
Reilly, Scott, 460
Rein, David, 494
Rein, Harry, 290
Rein, Steve, 494
Reinholdt, Steen Louis, 856
Reinisch, Peter, 873
Reisfield, Derek, 539
Reisler, Bill, 477
Reiten, Narve, 921
Remacle, Rosemary, 677
Reman, Eva, 794
Remey, Donald, 484
Remondi, John, 421
Renard, Aymerik, 853
Renze, Paul, 346
Renzi, Ned, 625
Renzi, Ned, 624
Repass, Robert, 640
Reppert, Todd, 669
Retik, David, 403
Reusche, Thomas, 361
Revis, Kenneth, 433
Rewari, Rakesh, 933
Reymann, David, 390
Reynolds, Barry, 190
Reynolds, Jake, 254
Reynolds, John, 491
Reynolds, Robert, 466
Rhee, Chong, 867
Rheinnecker, Michael, 951
Riabtsov, Sergei, 938
Riady, James, 874
Ricci, Stephen, 439
Rice, Don, 675
Rice, William, 671
Rich, Harry, 475
Rich, Ronald, 520
Richards, Andrew, 252
Richardson, John, 632

Richmand, Brian, 543
Richmond, Steve, 785
Riddle, John, 352
Riechers, Gene, 693
Rieckelman, Edward J., 468
Rieder, Heinz, 725
Rieger, Glenn, 625
Rieke, Matt, 635
Rieschel, Gary, 247
Rigby, Martin, 808
Riley, Ian, 757
Riley, John, 719
Riley, Joseph, 568
Riley, Paul, 741
Rim, Charles, 142
Rimer, David, 850
Rimer, Neil, 850
Rin, Adam, 326
Rinner, E., 810
Riser, Mark, 296
Rispal, Marc, 805
Rispoli, Pierre, 931
Ritter, Gordon, 180
Rivelli, Patrick, 479
Rizik, Chris, 457
Rizzi, Joseph, 433
Roady, Thomas, 648
Robbins, Andrew, 449
Robbins, Clifton, 296
Robel, Chuck, 191
Roberg, Kevin, 167
Robert, Shepley, 603
Roberts, Brian, 139
Roberts, Bryan, 586
Roberts, Chris, 812
Roberts, James, 543
Roberts, Janice, 210
Roberts, Jennifer, 677
Roberts, John, 208
Roberts, Ken, 750
Roberts, Larry, 237
Roberts, Peter, 408
Roberts, Thomas, 451
Robertson, Doug, 466
Robertson, Rebecca, 196
Robin, Patrick, 865
Robins, Mike, 726
Robins, Paula, 246
Robins, Richard, 217
Robinson, C.W., 810
Robinson, James, 571
Robinson, Laura, 666
Robinson, Martha, 519
Robkin, David, 631
Robl, Thomas, 974
Roche, Maurice, 795
Rochereau, Stephen, 699
Rock, Terry, 661
Rockwell, John, 402
Rodarie, Denis, 931
Rodermann, Alain, 934
Rodgers, Steven, 309
Rodrigo, Tennyson, 768
Rodseth, Paul, 663
Roe, George, 350
Roebuck, Joe, 182
Roeder, Doug, 167
Roemer, Max W., 919
Roeper, Robert, 454
Roerig, Kimberly, 627
Rogers, Thompson, 479
Rogoff, Bruce, 424
Roher, Michael, 137
Roine, Pekka, 916
Roizen, Heidi, 247
Rollwagon, John, 471
Rolnick, Michael, 163
Romano, Nicholas, 564
Rome, Brett, 592
Rome, Brett, 438
Ronchi, Giorgio, 808
Ronn, Harald, 738
Root, Jonathan, 261
Roque, Richard, 977
Rosati, Debi, 775
Rosch, Tom, 197
Rosch, Tom, 496
Roscigno, Anthony, 298
Rose, Oded, 975
Rose, Rusty, 660
Rose, Wolfgang, 157
Roselle, Arthur, 600
Rosen, Eric, 905
Rosen, Modi, 877
Rosenbaum, Barry, 443
Rosenbaum, Barry, 415
Rosenberg, Adam, 562
Rosenberg, Danny, 398
Rosenberg, Marcos, 249
Rosenbluth, Jason, 409
Rosenboim, Yaron, 784
Rosendahl, Carl, 247
Rosenfeld, Arie, 798
Rosenfeld, William, 620
Rosenfelt, Michael, 539
Rosenlof, Ulf, 784
Rosenthal, Edward, 520
Rosenzweig, William, 266
Roser, Christopher, 283
Roser, James, 283
Roshko, Peter, 214
Roshko, Peter, 392
Ross, Antony, 726
Ross, Harry, 277
Ross, Howard, 631
Ross, Ken, 571
Ross, Lawrence, 726
Ross, Stephen, 938
Ross, Steven, 356
Ross, Tom, 397
Rossetti, Paul, 505
Rossi, Mark, 519
Rossmann, George, 150
Rossmann, Greg, 564

Roth, Bob, 657
Roth, Jonathan, 501
Rothe, James, 673
Rothe, Joachim, 436
Rothman, Steven, 616
Rothrock, Ray, 586
Rothstein, Charles, 459
Rotman, Ken B., 780
Rotter, Bradley, 231
Rotter, J. Ward, 231
Roumell, Lisa, 486
Rountree, Ashley, 420
Rousseau, John, 437
Rowbotham, Tom, 471
Rowe, Brian, 351
Rowe, Keith, 346
Rowe, Timothy, 415
Rowland, Gene, 710
Rowsthorn, Mark, 957
Roy, Bob, 923
Royer, Henry, 380
Royston, Ivor, 180
Rua, Dan, 692
Rubeli, Christoph, 910
Rubenstein, Barry, 592
Rubenstein, Burt, 456
Rubin, Jeffrey, 558
Rubin, Marco, 696
Rubinoff, Gary, 861
Rubins, Matthew, 431
Rudnick, Seth, 290
Rudolph, Richard, 513
Rueppel, Philip, 451
Rule, Ted, 748
Rulon-Miller, William, 635
Rummelsburg, Kim, 586
Runnells, John, 496
Runningen, John, 331
Rupert, Rudolph, 591
Rushmore, Sue, 350
Russell, Andrew, 803
Russell, Courtney, 455
Russell, E. Scott, 247
Russell, Edward P., 477
Russell, Fred, 701
Russell, Gordon, 241
Russell, Michael, 227
Russell, Sallie, 601
Russo, Guy, 290
Ryan, David, 214
Ryan, Heberden, 435
Ryan, Mary, 708
Ryan, Neil, 440
Rye, David, 407
Rylander, Leif, 732

S

Saalfield, James, 450
Saberi, Nina, 416
Sabnani, Sanjay, 265
Sabo, Paul, 475
Sachs, Andrew, 690
Sachs, Bruce, 417
Sachs, Dan, 450
Sacks, Marc, 343
Sadeharju, Vesa, 725
Sadger, Haim, 241
Sadleir, William, 687
Sadler, Christy, 306
Safrai, Yair, 784
Sagan, Paul, 533
Sager, Edward, 633
Sakai, Stan, 187
Sakazaki, Shohei, 222
Saladi, Mahesh, 530
Saladino, Giovanni, 817
Salata, Jean Eric, 755
Salem, Paul, 643
Salentine, Thomas, 355
Salo, Colleen, 220
Salty, Samer, 980
Saltzgaber, Mark, 170
Salwen, Richard, 667
Salzman, Alan, 263
Samberg, Arthur, 564
Sambonet, Sergio, 726
Samper, J.Phillip, 182
Sampson, Jeff, 606
Sampson, Jeff, 607
Samuel, David, 889
Samuelson, Lior, 696
Samuelsson, Per, 904
Sandberg, Peter, 804
Sandell, Scott, 396
Sanders, Ferrell, 143
Sanders, Jason, 165
Sanders, W. Ferrell, 147
Sanderson, David, 813
Sanderson, Philip, 270
Sandler, Neal, 512
Sandroff, Claude, 261
Sandroff, Marc, 354
Sands, Carol, 145
Sands, Gregory, 251
Sanford, Charles, 584
Sangalis, Gregory, 669
Sangalis, Jeffrey, 675
Sangalis, Stephen, 283
Sankey, Darius, 276
Santer, Michael, 351
Santinelli, Angelo, 438
Santoleri, John, 590
Santry, Barbara, 158
Sara, Kevin, 156
Sarkamies, Sami, 942
Sarlo, George, 269
Sarlo, George, 270
Sasaki, Yoshiki, 863
Saul, Mark, 181
Saul, Shai, 946
Saulnier, Monique, 934
Saunders, Robert, 384
Saure, Russ, 597

Savage, Colin, 275
Savage, Thomas, 577
Savage, Yvonne, 839
Saviano, Joseph, 510
Savoy, Robert, 160
Savoy, William, 714
Saxena, Parag, 541
Saxena, Parag, 376
Sayder, Arthur, 418
Scanlan, David, 600
Scarpa, Carmen, 583
Schaafsma, Gerald, 391
Schachar, Henry, 562
Schachter, Bart, 155
Schaepe, Christopher, 206
Schaffer, Joe, 378
Schantz, David, 433
Schapiro, Benjamin, 397
Schapiro, Ken, 147
Schauerte, Werner, 796
Schechter, Adam, 364
Schecter, William, 614
Scheer, David, 306
Scheetz, Ned, 472
Schell, Theodore, 563
Schelle, Scott, 398
Schellhase, James, 681
Scher, Scott, 520
Scherl, David, 310
Scheurer, John, 312
Schiciano, Kenneth, 451
Schiff, Peter, 559
Schiffman, Barry, 198
Schiller, Pieter, 401
Schilling, Debra, 147
Schilling, Mathias, 157
Schlageter, Gary, 145
Schlass, Irwin, 541
Schlein, Philip, 261
Schlein, Ted, 200
Schlesiger, Christian, 872
Schlesinger, Thomas, 348
Schlytter-Henrichsen, Thomas, 738
Schmelter, Jay, 466
Schmelter, Jay, 478
Schmid, Terrence, 677
Schmidt, Douglas, 394
Schmidt, George, 811
Schmidt, Jean-Bernard, 934
Schmidt, Jerry, 331
Schmidt, Mike, 133
Schmidt, William, 402
Schmitt, Paul, 635
Schnabel, Rockwell, 259
Schnabel, Stephanie K., 290
Schneider, Gregorio, 249
Schneider, Richard, 486
Schneider, Richard, 525
Schneider, Steven, 590
Schneier, Lance, 610
Schnell, David, 200
Schnell, David, 232
Schober, Peter, 431
Schocken, Joseph, 702
Schoemaker, Kathleen, 486
Schoendorf, Joseph, 139
Schoendorf, Nancy, 214
Schoffstall, Martin, 639
Schoffstall, Marvin, 639
Scholl, Greg, 514
Schonhofer, Peter, 920
Schor, Chen, 980
Schorradt, Gert, 783
Schott, Thomas, 209
Schpok, Terry, 655
Schreck, Hans, 961
Schreck, Michael, 423
Schreiber, Alain, 493
Schreiber, Ronald, 573
Schroder, David, 380
Schroeck, Maximilian, 142
Schroter, Lutz, 924
Schubaur, James, 592
Schubert, Felix von, 980
Schuele, Al, 677
Schug, Christoph, 732
Schuh, Mike, 181
Schuhardt, Frank, 796
Schuhsler, Helmut, 961
Schuldiner, Paul D., 371
Schuler, Armin, 783
Schulte, Dave, 477
Schulte, Peter, 517
Schultz, Daniel, 523
Schultz, Howard, 708
Schultz, James Michael, 365
Schulz, Michael H, 969
Schulz, Robert, 416
Schuster, Joseph Martin, 757
Schuster, Monis, 461
Schuster, Steffen, 216
Schutz, Jeffrey, 278
Schwab, Dave, 243
Schwab, Nelson, 599
Schwaber, Glen, 864
Schwartmann, Daniel, 140
Schwartz, Irving, 562
Schwartz, Peter, 144
Schwartz, Rodney, 773
Schwarz, Tom, 874
Schwerin, Larry, 262
Sciarretta, Louis, 295
Scott, David, 881
Scott, Ed, 510
Scott, Edgerton, 205
Scott, John, 329
Scott, Paul, 274
Scott, Steven, 911
Scott, Tony, 886
Scraire, Jean-Claude, 934
Scutt, Peter, 510
Seabrook, Connor, 330
Seawell, A. Brooke, 254
Sebastian, Sean, 624

Sebba, Yoav, 980
Secchia, Rick, 491
Sednaoui, Carter, 483
Sednaoui, G. Carter, 139
Seebaum, Matt, 140
Segal, Rick, 861
Segell, Scott, 667
Segev, Roy, 924
Segrest, Michael, 677
Sehgal, Sanjay, 445
Sehgal, Sanjay, 926
Seid, Jay, 623
Seifert, William, 441
Seiffer, Jonathan, 203
Seitz, Tasha, 358
Sekula, Christopher, 157
Sela, Yossi, 825
Selati, Robin, 361
Seldon, Willa, 607
Self, Kevin, 364
Selkirk, Rod, 763
Selldorff, Frank, 442
Sells, Andrew, 936
Selvi, Robert, 164
Senequier, Dominique, 751
Senerchia, Jay, 433
Seng Lee, Cheong, 746
Senyei, Andrew, 178
Serrato, Victor, 755
Serrure, Piet, 898
Seto, David, 790
Settle, Dana, 210
Severiens, Hans, 151
Severson, Mike, 472
Seynhaeve, Denis, 394
Sgobbo, Rocco, 503
Shackelford, Kelly, 543
Shaevitz, Jerald, 201
Shaffer, G. Gary, 614
Shagrin, Larry, 373
Shah, Ajit, 275
Shahaf, Ophir, 781
Shainski, Rina, 772
Shalev, Eddie, 826
Shamapant, Venu, 657
Shan, Weijan, 219
Shanahan, Michael, 421
Shane, John, 441
Shanfield, Robert, 298
Shanmughan, Suresh, 412
Shapira, Iris, 888
Shapiro, James, 390
Shapiro, Paul, 218
Sharir, David, 839
Sharma, Manoj, 332
Sharman, Jeremy, 884
Sharman, Jeremy, 883
Sharon, Vered, 515
Shattan, Thomas, 574
Shaughnessy, Dennis, 394
Shaughnessy, Keith, 435
Shaw, Catherine, 212
Shaw, David, 763
Shaw, Gordon, 755
Shaw, Kyle, 929
Shaw, Leslie, 201
Shaw, Peter, 274
Shaw, Phil, 541
Shaw, Ralph, 621
Shaw, Robert, 482
Shaykin, Leonard, 502
Shear, Barry, 345
Shechter, Zvi, 828
Shedde, P.D., 738
Sheehan, Kevin, 376
Sheehan, William, 429
Sheeline, Kip, 451
Sheets, Bryon, 230
Shekar, Slim, 973
Shelander, Bill, 175
Sheldon, Michael, 808
Sheldon, Steven, 663
Shelef, Nachman, 154
Shelem, Avner, 747
Shennan, James, 260
Shepherd, T. Nathanael, 447
Sherblom, James, 446
Sherer, Paul, 263
Sheridan, Michael, 214
Sherk, William, 610
Sherman, Leonard, 140
Sherman, Mark, 409
Sherman, Robert, 412
Sherwin, Elton, 494
Sheshuryak, Sergey, 343
Sheth, Neil, 431
Shewmaker, Bruce, 322
Shields, Jack, 411
Shields, Tom, 274
Shields, W. David, 326
Shih, Stan, 890
Shimer, Daniel, 657
Shimoyamada, Moto, 275
Shoch, John, 147
Shoch, John, 143
Shoham, Yair, 826
Shorthouse, Dominic, 590
Shortis, Andrew, 912
Shrigley, David, 677
Shriner, Rick, 274
Shroff, Zubeen, 531
Shuchman, Salem, 563
Shue, Joseph, 494
Shugart, Al, 142
Shuk, J. Gregory, 234
Shulman, Steven, 297
Shure, Randl, 771
Sicoli, Richard, 592
Sideropoulos, Lester, 661
Siegel, David, 813
Siegel, Mark, 212
Siegelman, Russ, 200
Siew, Chee Meng, 187
Siew, Wing Keong, 187

Siew Wah, Lai, 860
Sigl, Susan, 712
Sigler, Eric, 150
Signoret, Carlos, 517
Sigurford, Hulda, 955
Silby, D. Wayne, 690
Sill, Igor, 184
Silver, Jonathan, 313
Silver, Martin, 677
Silverberg, Brad, 706
Silverman, Gilbert, 457
Silverman, Jeremy, 355
Silverstein, Fred, 705
Silvestri, Russ, 677
Sim, Edward, 594
Simmons, Brian, 351
Simmons, N.John, 325
Simmons, Walker, 600
Simms, J.Skip, 460
Simon, Dennis, 165
Simon, John, 167
Simon, John, 423
Simon, Robert, 513
Simoncini, Luciana, 706
Simoni, Gerry, 177
Simonian, Steve, 212
Simons, James, 471
Simonson, Tom, 471
Simoudis, Evangelos, 563
Simpson, Tom, 709
Sims, Tim, 907
Sinclair, Michael, 508
Sing, George, 429
Singer, Andrew, 213
Singer, John, 402
Singer, Marc, 289
Singh, Raj, 235
Sinwell, Andrew, 361
Sippl, Roger, 245
Sirazi, Semir, 578
Sirinakis, Kyp, 318
Sisteron, Yves, 185
Sites, John, 326
Siu, Ming, 310
Sjostrom, Linda, 793
Sjostrom, Thomas, 927
Skaff, Daniel, 242
Skakel, George, 287
Skalla, Barton, 282
Skalla, Peter, 282
Skeete Tatum, Lisa, 485
Skelton, James, 165
Skinner, Tom, 397
Skodinski, Carla, 310
Skok, David, 433
Skora, Allan, 587
Skott, Allen, 287
Skrobiszewski, Francis, 842
Skrzynski, Joseph, 772
Skrzypkowski, Janusz, 746
Slade, Dominic, 736
Slakey, Paul, 262
Slattery, Gayle, 431
Slaughter, Lee, 668
Slawson, Michael, 330
Slawson, Paul, 310
Slinn, Richard, 204
Sloane, Barry, 558
Slusky, Alex, 263
Smaby, Gary, 471
Smart, Christopher, 192
Smeltzer, Deborah, 394
Smets, Julien, 973
Smiley, Robert, 480
Smith, Brian, 170
Smith, Bruce, 851
Smith, Cece, 673
Smith, Hugh, 739
Smith, Jeff, 667
Smith, Kathy, 364
Smith, Larry, 582
Smith, Matthew, 561
Smith, Nick, 469
Smith, Richard, 504
Smith, Richard, 528
Smith, Rick, 228
Smith, Riordon, 643
Smith, Thomas, 488
Smith, Todd, 374
Smitherman, Greg, 402
Smits, Hanneke, 343
Smits, Rene, 835
Smolens, Donna, 254
Snape, Edwin, 437
Snaveley, H. Wayne, 193
Snow, Alex, 812
Snyder, A.F.F., 454
Snyder, Brett, 273
Snyder, Richard, 457
Sobieski, Ian, 151
Sobiloff, Peter, 540
Soghikian, Shahan, 543
Soheili, Patrick, 152
Soileau, Stephen, 681
Sokoloff, Jonathan, 203
Solari, Andrea, 239
Solberg, Eric, 941
Soliz, Angela, 354
Sollender, Jeffrey, 180
Solnick, Gene, 452
Solnick, Gene, 294
Solnick, Gene, 523
Soloman, Michael, 214
Solomon, David, 281
Solomon, Gary, 830
Solomon, Glenn, 229
Solomon, Steven, 661
Soloway, Tom, 216
Somberg, Debra, 708
Song, C., 393
Song, Michael, 238
Soni, Robi, 410
Sonneborn, Dirk, 529
Sonntag, Linda, 288

Sood, Harisch, 253
Sood, Rakesh, 578
Sorenson, Paul, 282
Sorrell, Larry, 591
Soto, Jaime Hernandez, 880
Soule, Matt, 600
Souleles, Thomas, 361
Soulignac, Charles, 819
Souza, Daniel, 941
Spalding, Richard, 390
Specht, Holger, 950
Speer, Don, 265
Speirs, Derek, 938
Spencer, Dale, 450
Spencer, Edson, 463
Spencer, George, 343
Spender, Geoff, 825
Sperling, Joerg, 494
Spessard, Rob, 332
Spice, Dennis, 365
Spicer, Timothy, 239
Spicer, Timothy, 175
Spiegel, Leo, 214
Spink, Geoff, 938
Spiva, C. Edward, 391
Spivy, Gregory, 181
Spoon, Alan, 441
Spooner, Graham, 781
Spooner, John, 920
Sprague, William, 520
Spray, Christopher, 407
Spreng, David, 466
Spreng, Kevin, 466
Springer, Todd, 259
Sprole, F. Jared, 298
Spurlock, Steve, 154
Spyrison, Don, 354
Squilanti, Todd, 562
Srivastava, Saurabh, 410
Sràmek, Stanislav, 819
Staal, Marc, 729
Stacey, Anthony, 781
Stachowiak, John, 706
Stack, Risa, 543
Stackhouse, Paul, 600
Stadtler, Kevin, 435
Stadum, Edward M, 952
Staenberg, Jon, 713
Stahl, Melchior, 590
Stallings, Marilyn, 243
Stamps, E. Roe, 451
Stanfill, William, 677
Stangl, Greg, 785
Stanley, Donald, 409
Stannard, Wray, 923
Stanners, Donald C., 242
Stark, Michael, 236
Stark, Michael, 165
Starr, Jeffrey, 214
Stasen, George, 633
Stassen, David, 471
Stassen, David, 472
Stastny, David, 226
Statham, Derek, 221
Staton, Daniel, 617
Staub, Martin, 858
Stavis, Robert, 410
Stearns, Robert, 679
Stecklein, Michelle, 257
Stedman, Scott, 227
Steed, Michael R., 227
Steel, Elizabeth M, 140
Steele, Scott D., 525
Steeves, Keith, 871
Steger, Monika, 757
Stein, Alan, 455
Stein, Avy, 374
Stein, Jeffrey, 455
Stein, Peter, 667
Stein, Robert, 318
Stein, Robert, 318
Steiner, Michael, 882
Steinert, E. Langley, 439
Steinhart, Arnon, 538
Steinmetz, Michael, 436
Steinmetz, William, 348
Stelljes, Chip, 393
Stensrud, William, 178
Stento, Gregory, 426
Stephens, Mark, 241
Stephenson, Thomas, 241
Stephenson, Thomas, 671
Stern, Doug, 572
Stetson, Charles, 567
Stevens, David, 499
Stevens, G. Bickley, 456
Stevens, Oak, 350
Stevens, Todd, 687
Stevenson, Jeff, 142
Stevenson, Jeffrey, 588
Stevenson, Sharon, 486
Stewart, Barry, 523
Stewart, Edward, 429
Stewart, Robert M., 398
Stewart, Will, 146
Stewart, William, 492
Stewert, Hugh, 942
Steyer, Thomas, 189
Stickells, Stephen, 412
Stickells, Stephen C., 417
Stiernberg, Hennrietta, 821
Still, George, 223
Stinson, D.B., 760
Stockinger, Penne, 930
Stockton, John, 210
Stofer, Gordon, 464
Stokel, Kathryn, 501
Stolberg, E. Theodore, 580
Stolker, Jan, 729
Stone, Carrie, 178
Stone, David, 405
Stone, Michael, 310
Stone, R. Gregg, 429
Storey, Mark, 408

Storm, Ruth, 963
Stout, Don, 331
Stowell, Davis, 579
Strahan, Randy, 214
Strain, Hilary, 144
Strand, L. James, 196
Straser, Erik, 214
Straube, Max, 397
Straus, Stephen, 657
Stray, Bjorn, 902
Streator, James, 257
Streimelweger, Thomas, 920
Strikeleather, Gregory, 246
Stringer Jr., Robert A., 448
Strnad, Alois, 921
Strober, Jason, 263
Strober, Joanna, 410
Strohm, David, 424
Strosberg, David, 363
Stroy, Gary, 212
Strube, Bettina, 865
Stuart, Greg, 193
Stuart, Lindsay, 543
Stubblefield, Richard, 205
Stubler, Michael, 632
Stubler, Michael, 626
Stuck, Bart, 307
Studen Kiliaan, Nita, 961
Stuelpnagel, John, 521
Stull, Steven, 386
Sturrock, Paul, 830
Stutts, Carl, 279
Styles, Daniel, 250
Suarez, Joaquin, 900
Subramanian, KGanapathy, 864
Subramanian, N, 755
Suennen, Lisa, 568
Sullivan, Jerry, 622
Sullivan, Mark, 427
Sullivan, Matthew, 340
Sullivan, Steve, 245
Sullivan, Timothy, 361
Sullivan, William, 283
Summa, Daniel, 533
Summe, Philip, 530
Sun, Anthony, 586
Sun, Chang, 590
Sundberg, Jan, 927
Sundue, Judy, 410
Sung, David, 419
Sung, Stella, 440
Suonenlahti, Mikko-Jussi, 725
Sutter, Martin, 354
Sutter, William, 362
Sutton, Andrew, 539
Svennilson, Peter, 434
Svensson, Ulf, 732
Svrluga, Bradley, 410
Swainbank, Terry, 886
Swanepoel, G.C., 967
Swani, Sanjay, 591
Swanson, Stephen, 457
Swartz, James, 139
Sweatman, Michael, 689
Sweemer, Jonathan, 492
Sweeney, Joan, 312
Sweeney, Michael, 197
Sweet, Scott, 206
Sweetser, Luke, 669
Sweetser, Luke, 672
Swensen, J. Scott, 596
Swenson, Ronald, 272
Swenson, W.David, 649
Swerberg, Scot, 376
Swift, Jacqueline, 343
Swildens, Hans, 428
Switz, Robert, 463
Synder, C. Byron, 669
Syrrist, Dag, 267
Sze, David, 424
Sze, Jerry, 494
Szemerey, Zoltan, 879
Szeto, Michael, 269
Szostak, David, 329

T

Tabor, Wellford, 600
Tabors, David, 409
Tadler, Richard, 451
Tadler, Steven, 402
Taetle, Alan, 336
Taft, Peter, 614
Tahta, Richard, 806
Tai, Augustus, 260
Tai, William, 196
Tall, Spencer, 146
Tallboys, David, 807
Talon, Christophe, 775
Tamir, Eldad, 946
Tan, Bien Kiat, 219
Tan, Cheng Gay, 939
Tan, Felix, 930
Tan, Lim Heng, 848
Tan, Lip-Bu, 269
Tan, Song Wee, 929
Tan, Steven, 839
Tan, Terence, 275
Tan, Yong Nam, 908
Tan Climaco, Gloria, 745
Tanaka, Susumu, 275
Tananbaum, Jim, 243
Tang, C., 269
Tang, Chen, 164
Tang, Chen, 232
Tango, Jo, 427
Tankersley, Jack, 281
Tanous, Joe, 704
Tao, Feng, 897
Tapp, J. Scott, 334
Taragin, Bruce, 155
Taranto, Michael, 876
Tareen, Amra, 677
Tarjanne, Artturi, 897

Tarr, Jake, 395
Tarski, Mike, 655
Taslitz, Steven, 398
Tatrallyay, Geza, 879
Taub, Andrew C., 290
Tavel, Olivier, 968
Taylor, Barry, 590
Taylor, Craig, 147
Taylor, Craig, 343
Taylor, Craig, 143
Taylor, Gus, 718
Taylor, Ian, 729
Taylor, Michael, 426
Taylor, Michael, 154
Taylor, Neil, 513
Taylor, Robert, 402
Taylor, Ronald, 178
Taylor, Ruth, 605
Taylor, William, 716
Tedeschi, Ed, 582
Teeger, John, 530
Tehranian, Terrence, 755
Teissedre, Sophie, 765
Teitsson, Andri, 955
Tellefsen, Dag, 267
Telpner, Joel, 133
Temanson, Todd, 177
Temescu, Terry, 525
Templeman, Michael, 706
TenBroek, James, 462
Tennant, Chris, 963
Tenneson, Bill, 707
Tenneson, Bill, 704
Tepper, Jeffrey, 534
Terho, Petteri, 937
Terk, Ben, 570
Tesconi, Lee, 408
Tesler, Marc, 254
Tessler, Allan, 545
Testa, Stephen W., 237
Thakore, Rajeev, 972
Thangaraj, Immanuel, 354
Theis, Robert, 169
Thekkethala, Thomas, 491
Theobald, Thomas, 373
Thielemans, Leo, 945
Thies, Mark, 290
Théoret, Robert, 923
Thirion, Walter, 668
Tholly, Paul, 931
Tholly, Paul, 805
Thom, Lambert, 151
Thoma, Carl, 371
Thomann, Thierry, 778
Thomas, Andrew, 580
Thomas, Hansjoerg, 796
Thomas, James, 911
Thomas, Peter, 196
Thomas, William, 660
Thompson, Andrew, 567
Thompson, Darryl, 309
Thompson, J. Peter, 225
Thompson, Peter, 808
Thompson, Phillip, 403
Thompson, Richard, 955
Thompson, Richard, 244
Thompson, Robert, 295
Thompson, Roderick, 172
Thompson, Stephen, 398
Thomsen, Laurie, 441
Thomson, Roderick, 172
Thorndike, William, 190
Thorner, Tom, 258
Thornton, James, 706
Thornton, John, 657
Thorp, David, 823
Thorp, James, 380
Threadgill, Walter, 312
Tickner, Geoffrey, 162
Tiedemann, Bruce, 412
Tikhomirov, André, 479
Tillotson, John, 196
Timmins, Jim, 222
Timor, Ofer, 795
Tims, Stanley, 640
Timson, David, 343
Ting, Wu, 786
Ting, Yu-Seng, 543
Tirabassi, Salvatore, 523
Tischler, Joseph, 450
Titus, M. David, 274
Titz, Peter, 858
To, Kilin, 494
Tobin, Greg, 376
Tobin, Scott, 409
Tobin, Scott, 336
Tobkin, Vincent, 243
Todd, Bob, 234
Tokioka, Frank, 341
Tolkowsky, Gideon, 970
Tollefson, Jeffrey, 466
Tomecka, Marzena, 735
Tompkins, Daniel, 223
Tonkel, Jeff, 690
Tonkel, Jeff, 693
Tonning, Jan, 707
Toole, Jeffrey, 675
Top, Stefaan, 919
Tor, Teo Ek, 916
Torleifsson, Tellef, 902
Torpey Jr., William J., 432
Torpo, Ari, 838
Torres, Marcelino, 902
Toth, Tibor, 406
Tottrup, Peter, 794
Tower, Frank, 319
Townsen, F.D., 264
Toy, Thomas, 254
Toy, Thomas, 228
Tracy, Philip, 601
Train, C. Bowdoin, 315
Trainor, Eugene, 396
Trammell, Webb, 574
Tran, Janine, 943

Tranie, Jean-Pascal, 973
Traversone, Andrea, 740
Treu, Jesse I., 486
Treybig, James, 657
Trinh, Christelle, 926
Triplett, Mike, 540
Troeller, Scott, 588
Troup, Bill, 922
Troy, John, 953
Troy, Robert, 184
Trucano, John, 467
Trueger, Arthur I., 154
Trustey, Joseph, 451
Tsai, Mary, 809
Tsang, Joyce, 493
Tsang, Michael, 974
Tsao, Robert, 822
Tsao, Tom, 273
Tshuva, Shalom, 820
Tsui, Doug, 190
Tsujikawa, Shigeki, 899
Tubb, Will, 679
Tucker, C.R., 678
Tuckerman, David, 161
Tudor, Geoffrey, 671
Tuley, Richard, 630
Tull, Thomas, 605
Tully, Bruce, 509
Tumpen, Marianne, 792
Tung, Jeffrey, 713
Turezyn, Virginia, 195
Turezyn, Virginia, 194
Turiano, Dominick, 496
Turnbull, David, 741
Turner, Daniel, 216
Turner, James G., 506
Turner, John, 267
Turner, Simon, 852
Turunen, Matti, 807
Tuttle, Philip, 618
Twitmyer, Tucker, 630
Twomey, Barry, 681
Tyler, Lauren M., 309
Tyrrell, Gary, 274
Tyrrell, Jack, 652
Tyrrell, Michael, 586
Tzeng, Joseph, 611

U

Uchenick, Joel L., 448
Ugras, George, 622
Uhlmann, Stephan, 796
Ullman, Michael, 156
Ulrich, Robert, 262
Ulrich Muller, Hans, 910
Umeda, Mochio, 228
Underwood, John H., 366
Underwood, Robert, 364
Unger, William, 210
Ungerer, Scott, 626
Uno, Jiro, 863
Unterberg, Thomas, 515
Unterberg, Thomas, 155
Unterman, Thomas, 238
Usami, Isao, 956

V

Vabakos, Paul, 163
Vadapalas, Joseph J., 592
Vaidya, Deepak, 926
Vainio, Petri, 243
Vais, Paul, 563
Valdes, Antoine, 735
Valenti, Alan, 283
Valentine, Donald, 241
Valianos, Chris, 331
Valis, Tom, 775
Valkin, Adam, 746
Vallee, Jacques, 178
Vallee, Jacques, 240
Vallen, Audrey, 153
Van 't Spijker, Cor, 729
Van Auken, Wendell, 210
Van Bladel, Sigrid, 396
Van Buren, Laura, 591
Van Degna, Robert, 643
Van Den Berg, Hans, 968
Van den Brande, Barend, 760
Van Den Brandt, Sabina, 742
Van Der Burg, E.J., 898
Van der Have, Frits, 811
Van Der Have, Frits, 874
Van der Meer, Roland, 163
Van der Wyck, Otto, 757
Van Duyne, Richard B., 492
Van Dyck, Lou, 396
Van Marken, Tony, 979
van Olerbeek, Michael, 827
Van Oudenhove, Benjamin, 917
Van Raalte, Peter, 548
Van Rappard, Rolly, 790
Van Rompaey, Marc, 919
Van Rossum, Alexander, 895
Van Schaik, Frans, 829
Van Thiel, Gijs, 309
Van Wesel, Tony, 860
Vandenberg, Roger, 642
Vandenborre, Alain, 973
Vander Vort, John, 464
Vanderbeck, Sunny, 667
Vandergraft, Steve, 681
Vandervelden, James, 452
Vandervorst, Pieter, 252
Vandewater, Sasha, 509
Vangal, Ramesh, 749
Vanhanen, Matti, 725
Vargas, K.Y., 619
Varma, Devendra, 235
Varshney, Vishnu, 834
Vasan, Robin, 210
Vasant, Neil, 207
Vasquez, Erik, 866

Vaughan, Oliver, 812
Vaury, Jean-Francois, 778
Vecchio, Gerard, 292
Vedrines, Michel, 765
Velk, Joseph, 602
Vendetti, Dino, 153
Vengroff, Harvey, 325
Ventresca, Robert, 622
Verdurme, Paul, 811
Verdurme, Paul, 861
Verhalen, Andrew, 433
Vermeulen, C.M., 898
Vermeulen, J.H., 898
Vermeulen, Philip, 818
Vermut, Aaron, 396
Verratti, Robert, 640
Vershel, Mark, 433
Vesely, Jon, 351
Vettel, Matthew, 424
Veyssiere, Frederic, 853
Vice Holter, Martine, 746
Viehweg, Craig, 180
Vilar, Alberto, 505
Villanueva, James, 152
Villarina, Norman, 428
Viola, Carlo, 925
Virta, Jouko, 803
Virtanen, Jarkko, 725
Visser, Mark, 512
Vitullo, Nicole, 486
Vogel, Dale, 261
Vogelbaum, Martin, 440
Volk, Florian, 848
Volpe, Thomas, 409
Von Bauer, Eric, 349
Von der Goltz, Alexander, 411
Von der Goltz, H.J., 411
Von Drechsel, Max, 841
Von Falkenhausen, Hasso, 913
Von Freyburg, Berthold, 947
von Goeben, Robert, 234
von Goeben, Robert, 250
Von Lohr, Joachim, 796
von Roedelbronn, Michelle, 150
Von Schroeter, Carlo, 455
Voon Wang, Piau, 343
Vora, Chris, 235
Vorlicek, Martha, 426

W

Wada, Bashir, 169
Waddington, Simon, 913
Wade, James, 431
Wadsworth, Eliot, 190
Wadsworth, Robert, 426
Wager, Wayne, 704
Wagli, Rolf, 806
Wagner, Andrew, 305
Wagner, Peter, 139
Wahlen, Edwin, 331
Wahlstom, Per, 811
Wainstein, Michael, 535
Waite, Chad, 709
Waitman, Andrew, 775
Wakefield, David, 465
Walczykowski, Eric, 145
Waldeier, Janet, 681
Waldorf, Gregory, 417
Walecka, John, 235
Walji, Karim, 235
Walker, Charles, 160
Walker, Colin, 789
Walker, David, 839
Walker, Donald, 457
Walker, Jeffrey, 543
Walker, Leonard, 332
Walker, Maria, 180
Walker, Paddy, 766
Walker, Paul, 140
Walker, Stephen, 399
Walker, W., 598
Walkingshaw, Robert, 438
Walkup, Carrie, 375
Wallace, Peter, 804
Wallace, Ronald, 332
Walley, Noah, 554
Walls, Sam, 137
Walmsley, Peter, 656
Walrod, David, 302
Walsh, Barry, 615
Walsh, Cheryl, 415
Walsh, Donna, 479
Walsh, Timothy, 543
Walters, Arthur, 691
Walters, Eric, 736
Walters, Scott, 174
Walton, Alan, 440
Walton, Roger, 416
Walton, William, 312
Walz, Keith, 343
Wan, Mark, 258
Wang, Edward, 233
Wang, Fred, 260
Wang, Sona, 348
Wang, Sona, 358
Wang, Walter, 907
Wanner, Kathy, 343
Ward, David, 653
Ward, Jeffrey, 434
Ward, John, 431
Ward, Lawrence, 181
Ward, Richard, 293
Warden, Charles, 445
Wardrop, Brian, 755
Warner, John, 645
Warner, Stephen, 322
Warnock, David, 393
Warren, Alasdair, 893
Warren, Anthony, 622
Washbun, Taylor, 216
Washburn, Thomas, 377
Washing, Tom, 284
Washiyama, Hisashi, 198

Wassen, Per, 804
Wasserman, Brian, 558
Watanabe, Akira, 956
Watchmaker, Linda, 465
Wateler, Aris, 909
Waters, Richard, 543
Watson, Brian, 576
Watson, Jim, 161
Watts, Katherine, 307
Waxman, Albert, 568
Weathersby, William, 221
Weaver, H. Michael, 601
Weaver, Ralph, 673
Webb, Timothy, 394
Webb, Timothy, 623
Weber, Eckard, 486
Weber, Eugene, 690
Weber, Mike, 920
Webster, James, 923
Webster, James, 798
Wechter, Larry, 378
Wedner, Marcus, 350
Weener, Dave, 439
Weening, Richard, 719
Wei, James, 275
Weil, Burton, 654
Weiler, Christopher, 573
Weiman, Barry, 143
Weinberg, Barry, 521
Weinberger, Simon, 529
Weiner, Howard, 470
Weingarten, Michael, 307
Weinstein, Eyal, 813
Weinstein, Paul, 149
Weintraut, J. Neil, 138
Weiss, Joel, 864
Weiss, Steven, 215
Weissman, Andrew, 594
Weissman, F.E., 563
Weissman, Ron, 563
Weller, Harry, 693
Weller, R. Jason, 374
Wellman, Selby, 601
Welsh, David, 229
Welsh, Michael, 887
Welsh, Patrick, 591
Wendell, Peter, 243
Wenger, Albert, 547
Werdegar, Maurice, 180
Werner, Harold, 490
Werner, Klaus-Jurgen, 952
Werner, Randolph, 170
Wertheim, Harvey, 536
Wesner, Blaine, 657
West, William, 227
Westbrook, Kirk, 198
Westbrook, Tom, 312
Weston, Dennis, 705
Westphal, Christoph, 441
Wetherill, David, 486
Wethington, Jerry, 338
Wetmore, David, 700
Whalen, Thaddeus, 147
Whaley, John, 223
Wheeler, Kurt, 436
Whims, James, 254
Whitaker, Blair, 223
Whitaker, Raymond, 527
White, Gregory, 257
White, Jim, 251
White, Karen, 564
White, Michael, 727
White, Richard, 516
White, Ronald, 406
White, Sean, 278
White, Sean, 577
Whiteley, Karen, 856
Whiting, Richard, 174
Whitley, Jason, 674
Whitman, John, 494
Whitney, Benson, 467
Wiberg, William, 156
Wicker, Damion, 543
Wicker-Miurin, Fields, 971
Wickett, James, 153
Widder, Kenneth, 273
Widing, Roger, 699
Wiegman, A.E.B., 810
Wiencek, John, 567
Wietlisbach, Urs, 910
Wight, Theodore, 710
Wigren, Stefan, 804
Wilcox, Kenneth, 244
Wilcoxson, William, 418
Wilde, Peter, 484
Wildervanck, Lucas, 961
Wilding, Linda, 884
Wildmoser, Christian, 790
Wildstein, Amy, 576
Wilens, Noel, 513
Wilf, Einat, 868
Wilkening, Elmer, 618
Wilkerson, Kathleen, 370
Wilkinson, Walter, 602
Wilkus, Malon, 391
Williams, Brian, 328
Williams, Cabell, 312
Williams, Caroline, 356
Williams, David, 924
Williams, Donna, 156
Williams, Edward, 414
Williams, Kevin, 346
Williams, Richard, 336
Williams, Robert, 153
Williams, Robert, 305
Williams, Steve, 243
Williams, Willis, 324
Williamson, Billy, 331
Williamson, Donna, 343
Williamson, Mark, 181
Willis, John, 374
Willrich, Mason, 224
Wilmerding, Alex, 411
Wilson, Dan, 605

Wilson, David, 731
Wilson, Douglas, 494
Wilson, Fred, 530
Wilson, Gregory, 350
Wilson, Harrison, 580
Wilson, Henry, 559
Wilson, Jackson , 140
Wilson, James, 675
Wilson, Loyal, 616
Wilson, Mark, 148
Wilson, Michael, 451
Wilson, Peter, 426
Wilson, Philip, 431
Wimsett, Colin, 908
Winblad, Ann, 191
Winebaum, Jacob, 175
Wingerstrand, Ann, 971
Winkey, Travis, 464
Winkey, Travis, 466
Winter, Robert, 237
Winter, Steve, 676
Winter, Thomas, 225
Winters, Kurt, 471
Winters, Terry, 279
Wipf, Christian, 742
Wisowaty, David, 294
Wissa, Nuri, 429
Wissman, Barrett, 672
Witherington, James, 653
Witmeur, O, 936
Witonsky, Carl, 471
Witte, Matthew, 209
Wojtowics, Jean, 375
Wolf, Christian, 878
Wolf, David, 286
Wolf, Richard, 524
Wolfe, Allan, 687
Wolfer, Christof, 750
Wolfram, Tyler, 310
Wolfram, Tyler, 519
Wolfson, Mark, 561
Wollaeger, Timothy, 200
Wolter, Doug, 180
Woltzen, Hugh, 394
Wong, Jimmy, 974
Wong, Kit, 494
Wong, Simon, 494
Woo, JongHo, 202
Woo, William, 402
Woo, Young Joo, 836
Wood, Bryan, 739
Wood, Charles, 546
Wood, Christopher, 570
Wood, Daniel, 195
Wood, Donald, 262
Wood, Nick, 553
Wood, Paul, 361
Woodside, Angela, 343
Woodson, Wade, 243
Woodsum, Stephen, 451
Woodward, Stan, 667
Woodward, Tim, 205
Woodward, Tim, 224
Woodward, William, 457
Wooh, Jae Ku, 797
Woolley, Geoffrey, 170
Woosnam, Richard, 629
Wooters, Thomas, 406
Worden, Joe, 278
Worms, Vincent, 229
Worner, Gerald, 806
Worth, Joseph, 630
Worthington, Norman, 325
Wortsman, Kathryn, 518
Wouthoz, Marc, 937
Woxen, Alexander, 833
Wozniak, Paul, 213
Wray, Ronald, 356
Wright, Christopher, 306
Wright, Christopher, 524
Wright, Daniel, 441
Wright, Deborah, 191
Wright, Marc, 330
Wright, Ralph, 331
Wrubel, Lee, 427
Wu, Daniel, 830
Wu, Perry, 163
Wu, Scott, 179
Wulf, Stefano, 950
Wulfstat, Matt, 229
Wyant, Jack, 609
Wyant, John, 609
Wyant, Margaret H., 613
Wycoff, W. Kirk, 634
Wynn, Peter, 740
Wypych, Piotr, 785
Wyse, Roger, 156
Wythes, Paul, 251

X

Xiaohong, Cai, 928
Xiaomin, Yu, 897

Y

Yablon, J.D., Leonard F., 641
Yamada, Keith, 350
Yamada, Tetsushi, 808
Yamamoto, Ted, 553
Yang, Ben, 907
Yang, Geoff, 196
Yang, Geoff, 235
Yang, Ingrid, 585
Yang, Jay, 142
Yang, Steven, 974
Yano, Marcella, 153
Yarnell, David, 292
Yarnell, David, 289
Yee, Nancy, 222
Yeh, Der-Chang, 946
Yeich, Steve, 640
Yeo, Benjamin, 922
Yeoh, Thomas, 844

Yeomans, John, 175
Yesil, Magdalena, 261
Yie, Charles, 404
Yong, T.S., 755
Yong-Nang, Tan, 908
Yoon, Sung, 202
York, Gwill, 205
Yoropoulos, Jason, 255
Yost, Gene, 625
Young, Chris, 437
Young, Eric, 290
Young, Jeremy, 590
Young, John, 938
Young, Philip, 261
Young, Robert, 604
Young, Lord of Graffham, David, 980
Younger, Al, 399
Younger, William, 251
Yu, Alex, 250
Yu, Danny, 174
Yu, Jeff, 466
Yu-tung, Cheng, 896
Yurkwich, Adrian, 963

Z
Zabransky, Pavel, 791
Zabriskie, James C., 459
Zachary, George, 214
Zachem, Tyler, 210
Zaininger, Alex, 782
Zajac, Scott, 386
Zak, Michael, 417
Zakariya, Fawad, 402
Zalasin, Andrew, 571
Zalkind, Drew, 417
Zanelli, Bart T., 488
Zaphrir, Gill, 970
Zarriello, Michael, 556
Zebro, David, 581
Zeevi, Avi, 772
Zegelaar, Rob, 407
Zegras, William, 287
Zeisler, John, 222
Zeller, Marco, 844
Zghoul, Yariv, 582
Zheng, Winston, 897
Zhou, Quan, 846
Zide, Steve, 907
Ziebelman, Peter, 138
Ziebold, W. Townsend, 591
Zieserl, Robert, 359
Zigman, Paul, 404
Zilka, Yahal, 877
Zimits, Eric, 186
Zimmer, Mary, 466
Zimmerman, Marty, 361
Zocco, Giuseppe, 850
Zochovitzky, Ariella, 813
Zombek, George, 539
Zondag, Sander, 895
Zuccaro, Robert, 531
Zucchini, Juan, 402
Zucker, Jeff, 583
Zuckerman, Arthur, 578
Zug, D. Brooks, 426
Zwitter, Jeffrey, 336

Industry Preference Index

Agriculture/Forestry/Fishing
Aberdeen Asset Managers, 728
ACF Equity Atlantic, Inc, 731
ACT Venture Capital Ltd., 732
Advanced Materials Partners, Inc., 287
Agribusiness Partners International Partners, 479
Alan I. Goldman & Associates, 483
Alimansky Capital Group, Inc., 504
American Securities, L.P., 505
Ardsheil, Inc., 506
Arthur P. Gould & Co., 507
Australian Technology Group Ltd, 750
Avery Business Development Services, 320
Baccharis Capital, Inc., 150
BanChem Financial Services, Inc., 658
Bankers Trust New York Corp./Deutsche Banc Alex Brown, 510
Baring Private Equity Partners (FKA:Baring Venture Partners), 755
Batavia Investment Management Ltd, 756
Baxter Associates, Inc., 289
BCR Asset Management Pty Ltd., 758
Boston Financial & Equity Corp., 412
Bruce F. Glaspell & Associates, 498
Business Link Doncaster, 765
Cambria Group, The, 157
Capital Network, The (AKA: Texas Capital Network), 659
Capital Services & Resources, Inc., 648
Carillon Capital, Inc., 610
CEI Ventures/Coastal Ventures LP, 388
Chisholm Private Capital Partners, 618
CIBC Capital Partners (FKA: CIBC Wood Gundy Capital), 516
CID Equity Partners, 376
Crestview Financial Group, The , 292
Crosbie & Co Inc, 789
Crown Capital Corp, 475
Davis Group, 166
Davis, Tuttle Venture Partners, L.P.(FKA:Davis Venture), 618
De Vries & Co., Inc., 476
DN Partners, 352
Dow Chemical Co., 458
Drysdale Enterprises, 173
Enterprise Equity (NI) Limited, 805
Enterprise Investors, 526
Equinox Investment Partners, 294
Federal Business Development Bank, 815
Financial Technology Research Corp., 529
Florida Capital Ventures, Ltd., 323
Fonds de Solidarité des Travailleurs du Québec (F.T.Q.), 820
Fowler, Anthony & Co., 422
GATX/MM Venture Partners, 183
Genesis Capital, Inc., 533
Gresham Rabo Management Limited, 832
GrowthWorks Capital, 834
Gujarat Venture Finance Limited, 834
Hambro European Ventures (Hambros PLC), 835
Hamilton Robinson & Co., Inc., 296
Herbert Young Securities, Inc., 536
Heritage Partners, 427
High Street Capital, LLC, 357
Hoebich Venture Management, Inc., 190
HSBC Private Equity (Asia), Ltd. (FKA: HSBC PE Management), 841

HT Capital Advisors, LLC, 538
Hungarian-American Enterprise Fund, The (HAEF), 842
IBK Capital Corporation, 844
IEG Venture Management, Inc., 357
IFCI Venture Cap. Funds (Formerly Risk Capital & Tech.), 847
InvestAmerica Venture Group, Inc., 380
Itochu Technology, 542
JAFCO Co. Ltd., 862
James A. Matzdorff & Co., 199
Las Americas Administradora, 871
Lawrence Financial Group, 202
Legal & General Ventures Ltd, 872
Lincoln Investment Management Inc., 378
Lubar & Co., 718
Marleau, Lemire, Inc., 878
Matrix Group, 209
McGuire Capital Corp., 670
MDT Advisers, Inc., 433
Merita Capital Limited, 134
Middlefield Capital Fund, 885
Morgan Grenfell Private Equity Limited, 889
Mountaineer Capital LP, 716
Nassau Capital, L.L.C., 492
Natural Gas Partners, 300
Nesbitt Burns, 363
New York State Science & Technology Foundation, 558
Nomura/JAFCO Investment (HK) Limited, 901
North Atlantic Capital Corp., 389
Northwest Ohio Venture Fund, 615
Nth Power Technologies, Inc, 224
Oregon Resource and Technology Development Fund, 620
Paradigm Capital Partners LLC, 651
Patricof & Co. Ventures, Inc., 563
Pierce Financial Corporation(FKA:Pierce Investment Banking), 698
Prospect Partners LLC (FKA:Kenter, Glatris & Tuttle, LLC, 368
Ridge Capital Partners, L.L.C., 368
Rosenfeld & Co., 620
Rothschild Bioscience Unit, 922
Rothschild Ventures Asia Pte Ltd., 922
Rutledge & Co., Inc., 305
SBC Ventures, 499
Seed Capital Investments, 928
Shannon Development Company, 929
Shared Ventures, Inc., 470
Shattan Group, The, 574
Shaw Venture Partners (FKA: Shaw Glasgow Partners), 621
Siguler Guff & Company, LLC, 575
Southwest Venture Group, 678
Sponsored Consulting Services, 249
Start-up Australia Pty Limited, 940
Sterling Grace Capital Management, L.P., 579
Stolberg Partners, 580
UOB Venture Management Pte Ltd., 964
Vega Capital Corp., 584
Vencap Equities Alberta, Ltd., 966
Ventex Management, Inc., 683
Venture Capital Management Corp., 328
Venture Funding Group International, 587
Venture Investors Management LLC, 720
Walden Capital Management Corporation, 589
Wellmax, Inc., 461
William A.M. Burden & Co., 593
Zero Stage Capital Co., Inc., 456

Biotechnology

2nd Generation Capital Corp, 648
A.M. Pappas & Associates, 597
Aberdare Ventures, 138
Aberlyn Capital Management Co., Inc., 501
Abingworth Venture Management Limited, 729
ABS Ventures, 390
Academy Funds (FKA: Longleaf Venture Fund LLC), 597
Accenture Technology Ventures (FKA: AC Ventures), 140
ACF Equity Atlantic, Inc, 731
ACT Venture Capital Ltd., 732
Adams Street Partners, LLC (FKA: Brinson Private Equity), 343
Adams, Harkness & Hill, Inc., 401
Adler & Co., 502
Adler & Shaykin, 502
Advanced Materials Partners, Inc., 287
Advanced Technology Ventures, 401
Advantage Capital Partners, 386
Advent International Corp., 402
Advent Venture Partners (FKA Advent Limited), 733
Agilent Ventures, 142
Akin Gump Investment Partners 2000, LP, 655
Alan I. Goldman & Associates, 483
Alimansky Capital Group, Inc., 504
Alliance Technology Ventures, 330
Allstate Private Equity, 344
Alpha Capital Partners, Inc., 344
Alta Berkeley Venture Partners, 739
Alta Partners, 144
Amadeus Capital Partners, 740
American Healthcare Fund, 345
Amerindo Investment Advisors, Inc., 505
Ampersand Ventures, 404
Amphion Ventures L.P.(FKA: Wolfensohn Associates, L.P.), 506
Annapolis Ventures LLC, 391
Anthem Capital, L.P., 391
Apax Partners & Cie (AKA: Apax France), 742
Apax Partners & Co.Beteiligungsberatung AG, 742
APIDC-Venture Capital Limited, 743
Applied Genomic Technology Capital Funds (AGTC), 405
ARCH Venture Partners, 346
Ardsheil, Inc., 506
Argos Soditic SA, 744
Artesian Capital, 464
Arthur P. Gould & Co., 507
Asset Management Company Venture Capital, 147
Atlas Venture, 407
August Partners, 508
Auric Asset Management Pte. Ltd., 750
Aurora Funds, Inc., 598
Australian Technology Group Ltd, 750
Avery Business Development Services, 320
Axiom Venture Partners, L.P., 288
Baccharis Capital, Inc., 150
Bachow & Associates, Inc., 623
Bailey & Co. Inc., 752
BancAmerica Capital Investors (FKA:NationsBanc Capital Corp), 598

BancBoston Capital/BancBoston Ventures, 408
BanChem Financial Services, Inc., 658
Bancorp Hawaii SBIC, Inc., 341
Bangert Dawes Reade Davis & Thom, 151
Bank One Equity Investors, Inc., 386
BankInvest Group AS, 754
Banque De Vizille, 754
Batterson Venture Partners(AKA:BVP), 348
Bausch & Lomb, Inc., 511
Baxter Associates, Inc., 289
Bayern Kapital Risikokapitalbeteiligungs GmbH, 757
BCM Technologies, Inc., 658
BCR Asset Management Pty Ltd., 758
Beacon Partners, Inc., 289
Becton, Dickinson & Co. (AKA: BD Ventures), 484
BioVentures Investors, LLC, 411
Birchmere Ventures, Inc.(FKA:Birchmere Investments), 624
bmp Aktiengesellschaft AG, 761
BOME Investors, Inc., 473
Boston Financial & Equity Corp., 412
Boston University Community Technology Fund , 413
Boulder Ventures, Ltd., 392
Broadmark Capital Corp., 702
Brook Venture Management, L.L.C., 414
Bruce F. Glaspell & Associates, 498
Bulldog Partners Limited, 764
Burr, Egan, Deleage & Co., 414
Burrill & Company, 156
Business Link Doncaster, 765
C3 Holdings, LLC, 474
Caltech Capital Partners Ltd., 766
Calvert Social Venture Partners, L.P., 690
Cambridge Research & Innovation Ltd (AKA CRIL), 767
Canaan Partners, 290
Canbank Venture Capital Fund Ltd, 767
Capital Development & Investment Co. Ltd., 768
Capital Investments, Inc., 717
Capital Network, The (AKA: Texas Capital Network), 659
Capital Services & Resources, Inc., 648
Capital Strategy Management Co., The, 349
Capman Management GmbH, 770
Capstone Ventures SBIC, L.P., 158
Cardinal Partners (FKA: Cardinal Health Partners), 485
Castle Harlan Australian Mezzanine Partners Pty. Ltd. , 772
Catalyst Venture Capital Firm, 773
Catalyst Ventures, 393
CB Health Ventures LLC, 416
CDC Innovation Partners, 775
CEI Ventures/Coastal Ventures LP, 388
CEO Advisors, 321
CEO Venture Fund, 625
Cerulean Fund/WGC Enterprises, 350
Challenger International Ltd., 776
Charter Ventures, 160
Cheng Xin Technology Development Corp. (FKA:Fidelity VC Corp, 776
Chiao Tung Bank, 776
China Venture Management, Inc., 777
CID Equity Partners, 376
Circle Ventures, Inc., 376
CIT Group/Venture Capital, Inc., The, 485
Citicorp Capital Asia (AKA: CITIC Pacific Ltd.), 780
Citizens Capital and Citizens Ventures, 418
Clarion Capital Corp., 610
CMEA Ventures (FKA:Chemicals & Materials Enterprise Associa), 161
Coates Myer & Co. Pty Ltd. (AKA: CM Capital Investments), 782
Coleman Swenson Booth Inc.(FKA:Coleman Swenson Hoffman Booth, 649
Collinson, Howe & Lennox, LLC, 291
Colorado Venture Management, 278
Columbine Venture Funds, The , 279
Comdisco Ventures, 162
Commerz Beteiligungsgesellschaft mbH (CBG), 783
Commonwealth BioVentures Inc. (CBI), 389
CommTech International, 163
Compass Technology Partners, 163
Concord Venture Management (FKA:Nitzanim), 784
Connecticut Innovations, Inc., 291
Continental Venture Capital , 784
CORAL Ventures, 465
Cordova Ventures (FKA:Cordova Capital), 331
Core Capital Partners, 313
Core Pacific Consulting Company, 786
Cornerstone Equity Investors, LLC, 519
Coronado Venture Fund, 133
Corporate Venture Partners, L.P., 519
Cowen & Co., 520
Creafund CVBA, 788
Crescent Capital NI Ltd (FKA Hambro Northern Ireland), 788
Crestview Financial Group, The , 292
CrossBow Ventures, 322
Crown Capital Corp, 475
CSK Venture Capital Co., Ltd., 789
CW Group, Inc., 521
D.H. Blair Investment Banking Corp., 521
Daewoo Venture Capital Co Ltd, 792
Danish Development Finance Corp., 793
DANSK Udviklingsfinansiering A/S, 793
Dauphin Capital Partners, 522
Davis Group, 166
De Vries & Co., Inc., 476
Delphi Ventures, 167
Deucalion Venture Partners, 168
Deutsche Effecten und Wechsel-Beteiligungsgesellschaft AG, 796
Deutsche Venture Capital GmbH (DVCG), 796
Development Corp. of Austin, 467
Direct Capital Private Equity, 797
Domain Associates, L.L.C., 486
Dougery Ventures, 171
Dow Chemical Co., 458
Drug Royalty Corp., Inc., 798
Drysdale Enterprises, 173
Duchossois TECnology Partners, LLC, 353
Durlacher Limited, 799
Early Stage Enterprises, L.P., 487
Earlybird Venture Capital, 800
ECICS Ventures Pte Ltd., 801
EDB Investments Pte Ltd., 802
EDF Ventures (F.K.A. Enterprise Development Fund), 458
Edge Capital Investment Co., LLC, 175
Electra Partners Asia [FKA: JF Electra Limited], 803
Enterprise Equity (NI) Limited, 805
Enterprise Investors, 526

Enterprise Partners, 178
Equity Partners Management Pty Ltd, 807
equity4life AG, 807
Essex Woodlands Health Ventures (FKA:Woodlands Venture Partn, 354
EuclidSR Partners , 527
Euroventures Benelux Team B.V., 811
Evergreen Capital Partners Inc, 528
FastVentures, 814
Federal Business Development Bank, 815
Financial Technology Research Corp., 529
Finovelec, 817
First Analysis Venture Capital (FKA:First Analysis Corp), 354
First Capital Management Co., 664
Florida Capital Ventures, Ltd., 323
Fluke Venture Partners., 705
Fonds D'Investissements R.T.V.L., 819
Fonds de Solidarité des Travailleurs du Québec (F.T.Q.), 820
Fort Washington Capital Partners, LLC, 611
Fortune Consulting Group Incorporated, 821
Fortune Venture Management Pte Ltd., 822
Forward Ventures, 180
Foundation Capital Limited, 822
Fowler, Anthony & Co., 422
Frazier & Company, 705
Friends Ivory & Sime Private Equity (Ivory &Sime Baronsmead), 823
GATX Ventures (FKA: Meier Mitchell & Co.), 183
GATX/MM Venture Partners, 183
GCI Venture Partners, 314
Genesis Capital, Inc., 533
Genesis Partners, 826
Global Partner Ventures, 694
Global Venture Capital Corporation, 829
Glynn Ventures, 186
Go Equity GmbH, 829
Grand Pacific Venture Capital Company Ltd., 830
Granite Ventures LLC (FKA: H & Q Venture Associates), 186
Grayson & Associates, 280
Graystone Venture Partners, LLC(AKA:Portage Venture Partners, 356
Gresham Rabo Management Limited, 832
Grosvenor Funds, The, 315
GrowthWorks Capital, 834
Gryphon Ventures, 425
H&Q Asia Pacific, Ltd., 187
Hambro America Biosciences, Inc., 535
Hanbyuck Investment Co Ltd, 836
Harbour Financial Co., 426
Health Capital Group, 188
Healthcare Ventures LLC (FKA: Healthcare Investments), 490
Heidelberg Innovation GmbH, 837
Herbert Young Securities, Inc., 536
Highland Capital Partners, 427
Hitachi America, Ltd., 189
Hoebich Venture Management, Inc., 190
Horizonte Venture Management GmbH, 840
Hotung International Company, Ltd., 840
Houston Venture Partners (AKA: Houston Partners), 666
HSBC Private Equity (Asia), Ltd. (FKA: HSBC PE Management), 841
HT Capital Advisors, LLC, 538
Hudson Venture Partners, 538
Hunt Ventures, LP, 667
IBB Beteiligungsgesellschaft mbH, 844
IBK Capital Corporation, 844
ICF Ventures Private Ltd., 845
ICICI Venture Funds Mngt. Co. Ltd., 846
IDG Technology Venture Investment Inc. (FKA: PTV-China), 846
IEG Venture Management, Inc., 357
IFCI Venture Cap. Funds (Formerly Risk Capital & Tech.), 847
IKB Venture Capital GmbH (AKA IKB Beteiligungsgesellschaft , 848
IMH Industrie Management Holding GmbH, 848
Impex Venture Management Co., 540
Index Ventures, 850
Indosuez Ventures, 194
Innovation Works, Inc., 628
Innovationsagentur Gesmbh, 854
InnovationsKapital Management Goteborg AB , 854
Innvotec Ltd, 854
Intersouth Partners, 601
InterWest Partners, 197
InvestAmerica Venture Group, Inc., 380
Investissement Desjardins, 857
Investissements Novacap (AKA:Novacap Investments, Inc.), 858
IPS Industrial Promotion Services, Ltd., 859
ISEP NV, 860
J.P. Morgan Capital Corp., 542
J.P. Morgan Partners (FKA: Chase Capital Partners), 543
JAFCO Co. Ltd., 862
James A. Matzdorff & Co., 199
Jerusalem Global Ventures, 864
Johnston Associates, Inc., 490
Josephberg Grosz & Co., Inc., 545
Kaiser Permanente (AKA: National Venture Development), 200
Kansas Technology Enterprise Corporation, 382
KB Partners, LLC, 359
KBL Healthcare Ventures, 546
Key Equity Capital Corp.(AKA:Key Community Development Corp), 613
Keystone Minority Capital Fund, L.P., 630
Kingsbury Associates, 200
Kinship Partners, 280
Kitty Hawk Capital, 602
KLB Investment Co., Ltd., 866
Kleiner Perkins Caufield & Byers, 200
Kookmin Venture Capital Co Ltd, 867
Koor Corporate Venture Capital, 868
Korea Development Investment Corp., 868
Korea Technology Finance Corp., 869
Lake Shore Capital Partners, Inc., 360
Lambda Funds, The, 546
Las Americas Administradora, 871
Lawrence Financial Group, 202
LeVenture Kapitalbeteiligungsgesellschaft mbH & Co.KG, 872
LG Venture Investment Inc., 873
Life Science Ventures, 873
Life Sciences Partners BV, 874
Lighthouse Capital Partners, 205
LTI Ventures Leasing Corp., 298
Macquarie Direct Investment Limited, 876
Malmohus Invest AB, 877
Manhattan Venture Co., Inc., 550

Maryland Venture Capital Trust, 395
Mayfair Capital Partners, Inc., 551
Mayfield Fund, 210
Mayo Medical Ventures, 468
MC Capital, Inc., 551
McKee & Co., 134
MDS Discovery Venture Management, Inc., 881
MDS Health Ventures, Inc. (AKA: MDS Capital Corp.), 881
MDT Advisers, Inc., 433
Medical Innovation Partners, 469
Medical Science Partners, 434
Medical Venture Holdings, Inc., 552
Medicis AG, 882
Medicon Valley Capital, 882
Medicus Venture Partners, 211
Medmax Ventures, L.P., 299
MedTech International, Inc., 670
MedVenture Associates, 212
Merita Capital Limited, 134
Merlin Biosciences (AKA Merlin Ventures), 884
Mid-Atlantic Venture Funds (FKA: NEPA Management Corp.), 634
Midlands Venture Fund Managers Ltd. (AKA: Midven Ltd), 886
Mitsui & Co., Ltd., 553
MMG Ventures, L.P., 396
Montgomery Medical Ventures, L.P., 215
Montreux Equity Partners, 216
Morel Ventures Limited, 888
Motorola Inc., 315
MPM Capital (FKA - MPM Asset Management LLC), 436
MTI Partners Ltd, 890
MVC AG (AKA Mitteldeutsche Venture Capital AG), 891
MVM Ltd, 891
MWV Capital Partners (FKA:Middlewest Ventures, L.P.), 378
Navis Partners (FKA:Fleet Equity Partners), 643
Nazem & Co., 556
Needham & Company, Inc., 556
NeoMed Management AS (FKA Medical Venture Management), 894
Nesbitt Burns, 363
New England Partners, 437
New Venture Resources, 282
New York Life Venture Capital Group, 557
New York State Science & Technology Foundation, 558
Newbridge Capital Limited, 219
Newbury Ventures, 220
Newbury, Piret & Co., Inc., 437
NewMargin Venture Capital, 897
Newtek Ventures, 220
NextGen Partners LLC, 221
NIB Capital Private Equity N.V. (FKA: Parnib Holding NV) , 898
NIF Ventures Co., Ltd., 898
Nikko Capital Co Ltd, 899
NMT New Medical Technologies, 900
Nomura International, Plc., 900
Nomura/JAFCO Investment (HK) Limited, 901
North Atlantic Capital Corp., 389
North Carolina Technological Development Authority, Inc., 603
NorthEast Ventures, 301
Northern Venture Managers Limited, 902
Northwest Ohio Venture Fund, 615
Northwood Ventures, 559
Novartis AG, 903
Noveltek Venture Corp., 560
NPM Capital (AKA Nederlandse Participatie MIJ NV), 903
NPV Capital Partners, LLC, 560
Oak Investment Partners, 302
Odlander Fredrikson & Co, 904
OmniMed Corp., 673
OneLiberty Ventures (FKA: Morgan, Holland Ventures Corp.), 439
Open Prairie Ventures, 365
Oregon Resource and Technology Development Fund, 620
Oresa Ventures, S.A., 906
Orix Capital Corporation, 906
OVP Venture Partners (FKA: Olympic Venture Partners), 709
Oxford Bioscience Partners, 440
Oxford Financial Services Corp., 698
PA Early Stage (AKA:Pennsylvania Early Stage Partners), 635
Pacific Capital Partners, 907
Pacific Horizon Ventures LLC, 710
Pacific Venture Partners, 907
Pappajohn Capital Resources, 381
Partners Group, 910
Pathfinder Venture Capital Funds, 470
Patricof & Co. Ventures, Inc., 563
Peninsula Capital Partners, L.L.C, 460
Penn-Janney Fund, Inc., The, 635
Penny Lane Partners, 493
Perennial Ventures (FKA: Tredegar Investments), 711
Philadelphia Ventures, Inc., 636
Phoenix Equity Partners (FKA: DLJ European Private Equity), 911
Phoenix Growth Capital Corp., 231
Phoenix Partners, The , 711
Piedmont Venture Partners, 604
Pierce Financial Corporation(FKA:Pierce Investment Banking), 698
Pittsford Group, Inc., The , 565
Platinum Group, Inc., The , 565
PME Capital, 912
Point Venture Partners, 636
Polaris Venture Capital, 913
Polaris Venture Partners, 441
PolyTechnos Venture Partners GmbH, 913
Pomona Capital, 566
PowerWord Capital Management, Inc., 914
pre-IPO Aktiengesellschaft, 915
Prelude Technology Investments Ltd, 915
Premier Medical Partner Fund L.P., 231
Prime Capital Management Co., Inc., 304
PrimePartners Asset Management Pte. Ltd., 916
Prince Ventures, 367
Provco Group, The , 637
Quaestus & Co. Inc. (FKA: Quaestus Management Corp..), 719
Quest Ventures, 233
Quester Capital Management Ltd, 920
Ralph Wilson Equity Fund, L.L.C., 460
RCT BioVentures NE (Research Corporation Technologies), 442
RiverVest Venture Partners , 478
Roanoke Capital, Ltd., 712
Robertson Stephens & Company, LLC, 236
Rock Hill Ventures Inc.(FKA:Hillman Medical Ventures,Inc.), 638
Rosenfeld & Co., 620
Roser Ventures LLC, 283

Rothschild Bioscience Unit, 922
Rothschild Ventures, Inc., 570
Royal Bank Private Equity (FKA: Royal Bank Development Cap), 922
Royalty Capital Fund, L.P. I/Royalty Capital Management, Inc, 443
S.R. One, Limited, 638
Saarlandische Wagnisfinanzierungsgesellschaft mbh (AKA SWG), 924
SAE Ventures, 306
Sanderling Ventures, 239
Sapient Capital, 721
SBC Equity Partners, Inc., 369
SBC Ventures, 499
SBV Venture Partners (AKA:Sigefi, Burnette & Vallee), 240
Schroder Ventures, 445
Seaflower Ventures, 446
SEB Foretagsinvest, 927
Seed Capital Investments, 928
Seed Capital Ltd, 928
SENMED Medical Ventures, 616
Sequel Venture Partners, 284
Sequoia Capital, 241
Shannon Development Company, 929
Shaw Venture Partners (FKA: Shaw Glasgow Partners), 621
Sigma Capital Corp., 327
Siguler Guff & Company, LLC, 575
Silicon Valley Bank, 244
Sitra (AKA Finnish National Fund for Research and Dev.), 932
Skyline Ventures, 245
Societe Regionale d'Investissement de Bruxelles (SRIB/GIMB), 933
Sofinnova Partners, 934
Sofinov (AKA:Caisse de depot et placement du Quebec), 934
Softbank Corp., 935
Solstice Capital LLC, 449
Sopartec SA, 936
Sorrento Associates, Inc., 247
Southwest Venture Group, 678
Spencer Trask Ventures, Inc. (FKA: Spencer Trask Securities), 576
Spray Venture Partners, 450
Springboard-Harper Investment Pte. Ltd., 938
Sprout Group, 578
SRK Management Co., 578
State Street Bank & Trust Co., 338
Still River Fund, The, 450
Sucsy, Fischer & Co., 370
SudKB & SudVC, 942
Summit Capital Associates, Inc., 581
Sunsino Development Associate Inc., 944
Sutter Hill Ventures, 251
Swedestart Management AB, 944
Swedish Industrial Development Fund (AKA Industrifonden), 945
Sweeney & Co., Inc., 308
Synerfi S.A., 945
T. Rowe Price Threshold Partnerships, 399
TA Associates, Inc., 451
tbg Technologie-Beteiligungsgesellschaft mbH, 947
TDH, 639
Techno-Venture Co. (Japan), 949
Technologieholding VC GmbH, 950
Technology Funding, 254
Technostart GmbH, 951
TecVenture Partners GmbH, 952
Teknoinvest Management As, 952
Tera Capital Corporation, 954
Thoma Cressey Equity Partners, 371
Thompson Clive, Inc., 257
Thorner Ventures, 258
Throunarfelag Islands Plc(AKA:The Icelandic Finance&Invest.), 955
Tianguis Ltd, 956
TL Ventures, 640
Top Taiwan Venture Capital Company, Ltd., 957
Top Technology Limited (AKA:Hambros-Advanced Technology Tru), 957
Toucan Capital Corp., 399
Transamerica Technology Finance, 309
Transatlantic Capital Ltd., 958
Triad Investors Corp, 319
Triune Capital, 260
TrustCapital Partners NV, 959
TVM Techno Venture Management, 961
U.S. Venture Partners, 261
UBS Capital (AKA Phildrew Ventures), 963
Union Venture Capital Corporation, 963
Unit Trust of India (UTI), 964
UOB Venture Management Pte Ltd., 964
US Trust Private Equity, 584
Utah Ventures II, L.P. (A.K.A. Union Ventures), 687
Value Management & Research AG (VMR), 965
Vanguard Venture Partners, 262
VantagePoint Venture Partners, 263
VCF Partners, 965
Vector Fund Management, L.P. (FKA: Vector Securities), 372
Venca Management, 263
Vencon Management, Inc., 585
Venrock Associates, 586
Ventana Financial Resources, Inc., 372
Ventana Global, 264
Ventech, 967
Ventex Management, Inc., 683
Venture Capital Management Corp., 328
Venture Funding Group International, 587
Venture Funding, Ltd., 461
Venture Growth Associates, 265
Venture Investment Management Company LLC (AKA: VIMAC), 454
Venture Investors Management LLC, 720
Venture Opportunities Corp., 588
VentureCap Management GmbH (AKA VCH Equity Group AG), 969
Ventures West Management, Inc., 970
Victory Ventures L.L.C., 588
VK Ventures, 268
Wakefield Group, 607
Walden International Investment Group (AKA: Walden Group), 269
Walden Israel, 975
WaldenVC, 270
Walnut Capital Corp., 701
Warburg, Pincus & Co., LLC. (FKA: E.M. Warburg, Pincus & Co), 590
Wasatch Venture Fund (FKA: Wasatch Venture Corporation), 687

Western Technology Investment, 272
Weston Presidio Capital Management, 455
White Pines Management, L.L.C., 462
Winthrop Ventures, 593
Wolf Ventures (AKA:Wolf Asset Management Corp.), 286
Wooshin Development Finance Corp, 978
Working Ventures Canadian Fund, Inc., 978
Yasuda Enterprise Development Co., Ltd.(FKA: Nippon Ent.Dev), 275
Zero Stage Capital Co., Inc., 456
Zone Ventures, 276

Business Services

3K Digital, 727
550 Digital Media Ventures , 501
Aberdeen Asset Managers, 728
ABN AMRO Private Equity (AKA: ABN AMRO Capital (USA) Inc.) , 343
ABN-AMRO Corporate Investments, 729
ABP Acquisition Corp, 287
Accelerator Media (UK), Ltd, 730
Accenture Technology Ventures (FKA: AC Ventures), 140
ACT Venture Capital Ltd., 732
Adams Street Partners, LLC (FKA: Brinson Private Equity), 343
Adams, Harkness & Hill, Inc., 401
AdCapital AG (FKA Berliner Elektro Holding AG), 732
Advanced Materials Partners, Inc., 287
Advent International Corp., 402
Advent-Morro Equity Partners, 734
Alan I. Goldman & Associates, 483
Albemarle Private Equity Ltd, 735
Alchemy Partners, 736
Alice Ventures, 736
Alimansky Capital Group, Inc., 504
Alliance Investment Capital, 737
Alliance Venture Capital Advisors Limited, 738
Allied Capital Corporation, 312
Allsop Venture Partners, 380
Alta Communications, 403
American Capital Strategies, 391
American Securities, L.P., 505
Amerimark Capital Group, 656
AMP Asset Management Limited - Development Capital, 740
Amphion Ventures L.P.(FKA: Wolfensohn Associates, L.P.), 506
Annapolis Ventures LLC, 391
Antares Capital Corporation (FKA: Harbor Ventures Corp.), 320
antfactory, 741
Apax Partners & Cie (AKA: Apax France), 742
Apax Partners & Co. Ventures Ltd (AKA: Apax UK), 742
Apax Partners & Co.Beteiligungsberatung AG, 742
Ardsheil, Inc., 506
Argentum Group, The , 507
Argosy Partners, 623
Armada Asset Management, 746
Artisan Digital Media, 147
AS Venture GmbH, 746
Asian Direct Capital Management, 747
Austin Ventures, L.P., 657
Australian Technology Group Ltd, 750
Avery Business Development Services, 320
Axxon Capital, Inc., 408
B2B-Hive, LLC, 509
Baird Capital Partners, 347
Banc One Capital Partners, 608
BancAmerica Capital Investors (FKA:NationsBanc Capital Corp), 598
BancBoston Capital/BancBoston Ventures, 408
Bancorp Hawaii SBIC, Inc., 341
Bankers Trust New York Corp./Deutsche Banc Alex Brown, 510
Baring Communications Equity, 755
Baxter Associates, Inc., 289
BBS Finance, 757
BCI Partners, 484
BCR Asset Management Pty Ltd., 758
Beacon Partners, Inc., 289
Benefit Capital Companies, Inc., The, 480
Berlin Capital Fund (FKA LBB Beteiligungsgesellschaft GmbH), 759
Bessemer Venture Partners, 410
Blue Ribbon AG, 760
Boston Capital Ventures, 411
Boston Financial & Equity Corp., 412
Botts & Co., 762
Bradford Equities Fund, LLC, 513
Brait Capital Partners, 762
Brand Equity Ventures, 289
Brantley Venture Partners, 609
Brook Venture Management, L.L.C., 414
Bruce F. Glaspell & Associates, 498
Bure Equity, 765
Business Link Doncaster, 765
Butler Capital Partners France, 765
BV Capital (FKA Bertelsmann Ventures LP), 157
Calvert Social Venture Partners, L.P., 690
Cambria Group, The, 157
Cambridge Technology Capital, 415
Camelot Ventures, 457
Canbank Venture Capital Fund Ltd, 767
Candover Investments PLC, 768
Canterbury Capital L.L.C.(AKA: Canterbury Detroit Partners), 514
Capital Development & Investment Co. Ltd., 768
Capital For Business, Inc., 474
Capital Investments, Inc., 717
Capital Network, The (AKA: Texas Capital Network), 659
Capital Partners LLC, 769
Capital Resource Partners, 415
Capital Southwest Corporation, 660
Capital Strategy Management Co., The, 349
Capital Z Asia, 770
Capman Management GmbH, 770
Capstone Ventures SBIC, L.P., 158
CapVest Management, Ltd, 771
CapVis Equity Partners AG, 771
Carillon Capital, Inc., 610
Carousel Capital Partners, 599
Cascade Communications Ventures, LLC, 159
Castle Harlan Australian Mezzanine Partners Pty. Ltd. , 772
Catalyst Fund Management & Research Ltd, 773
Catterton Partners, 290
Cazenove Private Equity, 773
CCFL Mezzanine Partners of Canada , 774
CD Technicom S.A., 774
CDC Services Industries Gestion (CDC IXIS Private Equity), 775

CE Unterberg Towbin (FKA:Unterberg Harris Capital Partners), 515
CEI Ventures/Coastal Ventures LP, 388
Cerulean Fund/WGC Enterprises, 350
CGW Southeast Partners (AKA: Cravey, Green, & Wahlen), 331
Chartwell Capital Management Co., Inc., 321
Cherry Tree Investments, Inc., 464
Chrysalis Ventures, 384
Churchill Capital, Inc., 465
CID Equity Partners, 376
cirlab!, 779
Citicorp Capital Asia (AKA: CITIC Pacific Ltd.), 780
Citizens Capital and Citizens Ventures, 418
Close Brothers Private Equity, 782
CM Equity Partners, 517
Cohen & Co., L.L.C., 517
Colonial First State Private Equity Ltd (FKA: Hambro-G Mgmt), 782
Concordia Capital, 784
Conning Capital Partners, 292
Constellation Ventures, 518
Continental S.B.I.C., 691
Continental Venture Capital , 784
Convergence Partners L.P., 164
Copernicus Capital Management Ltd, 785
Cordova Ventures (FKA:Cordova Capital), 331
Core Capital Partners, 313
Cornerstone Equity Investors, LLC, 519
Covent Industrial Capital Investment Co Ltd, 787
Creafund CVBA, 788
Crestview Financial Group, The , 292
Crosbie & Co Inc, 789
Crosslink Capital (FKA: Omega Venture Partners), 165
Crown Capital Corp, 475
CS Capital Partners, LLC, 486
CSK Venture Capital Co., Ltd., 789
CVC Capital Partners, 790
Cygnus Venture Partners, 791
Danske eVentures, 794
Dauphin Capital Partners, 522
Davis Group, 166
De Vries & Co., Inc., 476
Desai Capital Management Inc., 522
Development Corp. of Austin, 467
Digital Media Campus, 169
DN Partners, 352
Dongbu Venture Capital Co Ltd, 797
Dorset Capital, 170
Dresdner Kleinwort Capital , 524
Dresner Capital Resources, Inc., 352
Drysdale Enterprises, 173
DSE Investment Services Limited, 799
Dunedin Capital Partners Ltd (FKA:Dunedin Ventures Limited), 799
EarlyBirdCapital.com Inc., 524
Easton Hunt Capital Partners, 525
eBlast Ventures, LLC, 353
ECI Ventures Ltd, 801
EDF Ventures (F.K.A. Enterprise Development Fund), 458
Edison Venture Fund, 488
Eircom Enterprise Fund Ltd., 803
Elderstreet Investments Ltd, 803
Electra Fleming Limited, 525
Electra Partners Asia [FKA: JF Electra Limited], 803
Endeavour Capital Pty Ltd, 804
EnerTech Capital Partners, L.P., 626
Enterprise Investors, 526
Eos Partners, L.P., 527
Equinox Investment Partners, 294
Equity Partners Management Pty Ltd, 807
Equity Ventures, Ltd, 807
Equity-South (FKA:Grubb & Williams Ltd.), 333
ETF Group, 808
EURAZEO (FKA Gaz-et-Eaux & AZEO), 809
European Acquisition Capital Ltd., 810
Evergreen Capital Partners Inc, 528
Evergreen Ventures, 686
Exeter Capital, L.P., 528
Expanso Capital, 813
F. Turismo-Capital De Risco SA, 814
Fairgill Investments Property Limited, 814
FastVentures, 814
FINADVANCE S.A., 815
Financial Technology Research Corp., 529
FINOVA Mezzanine Capital, Inc. (FKA: Sirrom Capital Corp), 650
First Analysis Venture Capital (FKA:First Analysis Corp), 354
First Atlantic Capital, Ltd., 530
First Princeton Capital Corp., 489
First Union Capital Partners, 600
Florida Capital Partners, 322
Florida Capital Ventures, Ltd., 323
Fluke Venture Partners., 705
FLV Fund (AKA Flanders Language Valley Fund), 818
Fonds de Solidarité des Travailleurs du Québec (F.T.Q.), 820
Foundation Capital, 181
Foundation Capital Limited, 822
Fowler, Anthony & Co., 422
Fremont Partners, 181
Friends Ivory & Sime Private Equity (Ivory &Sime Baronsmead), 823
Frontenac Co., 355
Frontline Capital, Inc., 334
Fusient Ventures, 531
GCI, 718
Genesee Funding, Inc., 532
Genesis Capital, Inc., 533
Geneva Merchant Banking Partners, 601
Genevest Consulting Group, S.A., 827
Glencoe Capital, LLC (FKA: Glencoe Investment Corporation), 356
Global Partner Ventures, 694
Golub Associates, 534
Granville Baird Capital Partners (FKA:Granville Pr Eq Mngrs), 830
Graystone Venture Partners, LLC(AKA:Portage Venture Partners, 356
Great Hill Equity Partners, LLC, 424
Gresham CEA Management Limited, 832
Greylock, 424
Grotech Capital Group, 394
Grove Street Advisors, LLC, 425
Growth Venture Group Pty Ltd., 833
GTCR Golder Rauner, LLC, 356

Gujarat Venture Finance Limited, 834
H&Q Asia Pacific, Ltd., 187
Halder Holdings B.V., 835
Hambro European Ventures (Hambros PLC), 835
Hanbyuck Investment Co Ltd, 836
Hanover Capital Corp., 535
Harvest Partners, Inc., 536
Health Capital Group, 188
Hellman & Friedman, 189
Herbert Young Securities, Inc., 536
HFS Capital (AKA: Hoffman, Fitzgerald & Snyder), 694
High Street Capital, LLC, 357
HillStreet Capital, Inc., 612
Hollinger Capital (FKA: Hollinger Ventures), 537
Horizon Ventures (F.K.A. Technology Investments), 190
Horizonte Venture Management GmbH, 840
Housatonic Partners, 190
HSBC Private Equity (Asia), Ltd. (FKA: HSBC PE Management), 841
HSBC Private Equity Ltd (FKA Montagu Private Equity Ltd), 841
HT Capital Advisors, LLC, 538
Hudson Venture Partners, 538
Hunt Capital Group, 667
i2s PLC (FKA: Tarpan PLC), 843
ICICI Venture Funds Mngt. Co. Ltd., 846
Impact Venture Partners, 539
IndAsia Fund Advisors Private Limited, 849
Indocean Chase Capital Advisors, 850
Indosuez Ventures, 194
Industry Ventures , 428
InnovationsKapital Management Goteborg AB , 854
InvestAmerica Venture Group, Inc., 380
Invision AG (FKA Aureus Private Equity AG), 858
J.P. Morgan Partners (FKA: Chase Capital Partners), 543
JAFCO Co. Ltd., 862
James A. Matzdorff & Co., 199
Josephberg Grosz & Co., Inc., 545
Kansas City Equity Partners, 477
Kansas Venture Capital, Inc., 383
KB Partners, LLC, 359
Keystone Minority Capital Fund, L.P., 630
Kookmin Venture Capital Co Ltd, 867
Korea Development Investment Corp., 868
KPMG Advent Management Group (FKA:Advent Western Pacific), 870
Lake Shore Capital Partners, Inc., 360
Las Americas Administradora, 871
Lawrence Financial Group, 202
Legal & General Ventures Ltd, 872
Leonard Green & Partners, 203
LeVenture Kapitalbeteiligungsgesellschaft mbH & Co.KG, 872
Lincoln Investment Management Inc., 378
Lincolnshire Management Inc., 548
LJH Global Investments , 324
Lombard Investments, Inc., 206
London Ventures (Fund Managers) Ltd., 875
M&F Associates, L.P., 549
Madison Dearborn Partners, LLC, 361
Manchester Humphreys, Inc., 642
Manhattan Venture Co., Inc., 550
Marleau, Lemire, Inc., 878
Marquette Venture Partners, 362
Marwit Capital LLC, 209
Matrix Capital, 695
Matrix Private Equity, 879
Mayfair Capital Partners, Inc., 551
MBA Venture Group, 669
MC Capital Asia Private Limited, 880
MCG Ventures, 696
McGraw-Hill Ventures, 552
MediaVenture Capital AG & Co. KGaA, 882
Mentor Capital Partners, 633
Mercury Private Equity, 883
Meridian Venture Partners (MVP), 633
Merita Capital Limited, 134
Merrill Lynch Investment Managers FKA Mercury Asset Mgmt, 884
Mesirow Private Equity Investments, Inc., 362
Mezzanine Management UK Limited, 885
Miller Capital Corp, 135
Miller/Zell Venture Group, 335
Monument Advisors, Inc, 378
Moore & Associates, 619
Morgan Grenfell Private Equity Limited, 889
Mountaineer Capital LP, 716
MSC Venture Corporation Sdn. Bhd., 890
MWV Capital Partners (FKA:Middlewest Ventures, L.P.), 378
Nanyang Ventures Pty Ltd (AKA: Nanyang Management Pty Ltd), 892
Nassau Capital, L.L.C., 492
National Bank Of Kuwait, 555
National City Equity Partners, Inc, 614
National Corporate Finance, Inc., 217
Navis Partners (FKA:Fleet Equity Partners), 643
NCP Advisors Philippines, Inc., 894
Nesbitt Burns, 363
New Things, LLC, 557
Newbridge Capital Limited, 219
Newbury, Piret & Co., Inc., 437
NewSpring Ventures, 634
Nmas1 Electra Capital Privado , S.G.E.C.R., S.A., 900
Nomura International, Plc., 900
Nomura/JAFCO Investment (HK) Limited, 901
North America Investment Corp., 902
North Atlantic Capital Corp., 389
North Hill Ventures, 438
Northern Venture Managers Limited, 902
Northwest Ohio Venture Fund, 615
Northwest Venture Associates, Inc.(FKA:Spokane Capital Mgmt), 709
Northwood Ventures, 559
Northzone Ventures (FKA Venture Partners AS), 902
NPM Capital (AKA Nederlandse Participatie MIJ NV), 903
Oak Investment Partners, 302
Onondaga Venture Capital Fund, Inc., 562
Oresa Ventures, S.A., 906
Orion Partners, L.P., 439
PA Early Stage (AKA:Pennsylvania Early Stage Partners), 635
Pacific Corporate Group, Inc., 227
Pacifica Fund , 228
Paladin Partners, 711
Paradigm Capital Partners LLC, 651
Parcom Ventures BV, 909
Paribas Principal, Inc., 563

Part'com, 909
Pathfinder Investment Co Pvt Ltd, 910
Patricof & Co. Ventures, Inc., 563
Penfund Partners, Inc., 911
Peninsula Capital Partners, L.L.C, 460
Penn-Janney Fund, Inc., The, 635
Penny Lane Partners, 493
Penta Capital Partners Ltd, 911
Petra Capital Partners LLC, 652
Pfingsten Partners, L.P., 366
Philadelphia Ventures, Inc., 636
Phoenix Equity Partners (FKA: DLJ European Private Equity), 911
Phoenix Growth Capital Corp., 231
Phoenix Partners, The , 711
Pierce Financial Corporation(FKA:Pierce Investment Banking), 698
PME Capital, 912
Point Venture Partners, 636
Polaris Venture Partners, 441
PPM Ventures Ltd (FKA: Prudential Venture Managers Ltd), 914
pre-IPO Aktiengesellschaft, 915
Prime Capital Management Co., Inc., 304
PrimePartners Asset Management Pte. Ltd., 916
Priveq Capital Funds, 917
Prospect Partners LLC (FKA:Kenter, Glatris & Tuttle, LLC, 368
ProVen Private Equity (FKA:Guinness Mahon Development Cap.), 918
Providence Equity Partners, Inc.(FKA: Providence Ventures), 643
Putnam Lovell Capital Partners, L.P., 232
Quaestus & Co. Inc. (FKA: Quaestus Management Corp..), 719
Quantum Capital Partners, 325
Quester Capital Management Ltd, 920
QuestMark Partners, L.P., 397
R-H Capital Partners, 337
Ralph Wilson Equity Fund, L.L.C., 460
Recovery Equity Investors, L.P., 234
Red River Ventures, 675
Redpoint Ventures, 235
Reiten & Co Strategic Investments AS, 921
Reprise Capital Corp., 569
Richard Jaffe & Co., Inc., 676
Ridge Capital Partners, L.L.C., 368
Ridgewood Capital Management LLC, 494
Riordan, Lewis & Haden, 236
River Associates, LLC, 653
Roanoke Capital, Ltd., 712
Rosenfeld & Co., 620
Rothschild Ventures, Inc., 570
Royal Bank Private Equity (FKA: Royal Bank Development Cap), 922
Rutledge & Co., Inc., 305
Sanpaolo IMI Private Equity S.p.A., 925
Saugatuck Capital Company, 306
SBC Equity Partners, Inc., 369
SBCA/A.G. Bartholomew & Associates, 131
Seacoast Capital, 446
Seaport Capital, 572
SGI Capital L.L.C, 573
Shad Run Investments, Inc., 242
Shattan Group, The, 574
Shaw Venture Partners (FKA: Shaw Glasgow Partners), 621
Shelton Companies, Inc., The , 604
Shepherd Group LLC, The, 447
Siguler Guff & Company, LLC, 575
SingTel Ventures, 931
SISIR International Pte Ltd., 932
SMIFS Venture Capital Limited, 933
Sofinnova Partners, 934
SOFTBANK Venture Capital (FKA: SOFTBANK Technology Ventures), 247
South Atlantic Venture Funds, L.P., 327
Sovereign Capital (FKA:Nash, Sells & Partners Limited), 936
Spectrum Equity Investors, L.P., 248
Spinnaker Ventures, 249
Sponsored Consulting Services, 249
Sports Capital Partners, 577
Sprout Group, 578
Sputnik Technology Ventures, 938
SSM Ventures, 653
State Street Bank & Trust Co., 338
Stephens Group, Inc., 137
Sterling Venture Partners, 398
Still River Fund, The, 450
Stolberg Partners, 580
Strategic Capital Management, 941
Stratford Equity Partners, L.P., 679
SudKB & SudVC, 942
Suez Asia Holdings Pte Ltd., 943
Summit Capital Associates, Inc., 581
Summit Partners, 451
Sun Valley Ventures, 250
Sweeney & Co., Inc., 308
Sycamore Ventures, 494
Synerfi S.A., 945
Syntel Inc. Web Incubator Program, 461
tbg Technologie-Beteiligungsgesellschaft mbH, 947
TDH, 639
Texas Growth Fund Management, 681
THCG Inc., 582
Thoma Cressey Equity Partners, 371
Thompson Clive & Partners Limited, 955
Tokyo Small & Medium Business Investment & Consultation Co., 956
Triad Media Ventures, 309
Tribune Ventures, 372
UBS Capital (AKA Phildrew Ventures), 963
Union Street Capital Corp., 713
Unit Trust of India (UTI), 964
UOB Venture Management Pte Ltd., 964
Valley Capital Corp., 654
Value Management & Research AG (VMR), 965
Venture Associates, Ltd., 285
Venture Funding Group International, 587
Venture Select, 968
Venture Strategy Partners, 266
VentureCap Management GmbH (AKA VCH Equity Group AG), 969
Venturepark Incubator (FKA grizzlyfarm AG), 969
Vesta Capital Partners (AKA: Vesta Group, The), 971
Virginia Capital , 701
Viridian Capital Partners (FKA: Aurora Venture Partners), 607
VIV NV (AKA Vlaamse Investeringvennootschap NV), 973
Viventures Inc., 973
Wachovia, 340

Wachtel & Co., Inc., 317
Wakefield Group, 607
Walden Capital Management Corporation, 589
Warburg, Pincus & Co., LLC. (FKA: E.M. Warburg, Pincus & Co), 590
Wedbush Capital Partners, 271
Westbury Partners, 592
Western States Investment Group, 272
Weston Presidio Capital Management, 455
White Pines Management, L.L.C., 462
William Blair Capital Partners, 373
Willis Stein & Partners, 374
Wind Point Partners, 462
Wingate Partners, L.P., 685
Winslow Partners LLC, 317
WomenAngles.net, 318
Worms Capital Management, 594
Zero Stage Capital Co., Inc., 456
Zodiac Venture Capital KB, 980
Zone Ventures, 276

Communications and Media

1st Source Capital Corp., 375
21st Century Internet Management Partners,LLC, 138
2M Invest, Inc., 138
3i Austria (FKA Bank Austria TFV High Tech -UB GmbH), 725
3i Finland Oy (FKA SFK Finance), 725
3K Digital, 727
3TS Venture Partners AG, 727
4C Ventures (FKA: Olivetti Holding, N.V.), 501
Abell Venture Fund, 390
Aberdare Ventures, 138
Aberdeen Asset Managers, 728
ABN AMRO Private Equity (AKA: ABN AMRO Capital (USA) Inc.) , 343
ABN-AMRO Corporate Investments, 729
ABS Ventures, 390
Academy Funds (FKA: Longleaf Venture Fund LLC), 597
Accel Partners, 139
Accelerator Media (UK), Ltd, 730
Accenture Technology Ventures (FKA: AC Ventures), 140
Access Venture Partners, 277
Acer Technology Ventures(FKA:Acer Soft Capital Inc.), 141
ACF Equity Atlantic, Inc, 731
ACT Venture Capital Ltd., 732
Adams Capital Management, Inc., 622
Adams Street Partners, LLC (FKA: Brinson Private Equity), 343
Adams, Harkness & Hill, Inc., 401
AdCapital AG (FKA Berliner Elektro Holding AG), 732
Adler & Co., 502
Advanced Technology Ventures, 401
Advanta Partners, L.P., 622
Advantage Capital Partners, 386
Advent International Corp., 402
Advent Venture Partners (FKA Advent Limited), 733
Advent-Morro Equity Partners, 734
Aether Systems Capital, 390
Agilent Ventures, 142
AIG Investment Corporation (Asia) Limited, 735
Alan I. Goldman & Associates, 483
Albemarle Private Equity Ltd, 735
Alcatel Ventures, 142
Alchemy Partners, 736
Alexander Hutton, Inc., 702
Alice Ventures, 736
Alignment Capital Partners, LLC, 655
Alimansky Capital Group, Inc., 504
All Asia Partners, 737
Allegis Capital (AKA:Allegis Media Technology Ventures), 143
Allegra Partners (FKA: Lawrence, Smith & Horey), 504
Alliance Technology Ventures, 330
Allied Capital Corporation, 312
Allsop Venture Partners, 380
Allstate Private Equity, 344
Alpha Capital Partners, Inc., 344
Alpine Technology Ventures, 144
Alta Berkeley Venture Partners, 739
Alta Communications, 403
Alta Partners, 144
Altos Ventures, 144
Amadeus Capital Partners, 740
American Capital Strategies, 391
American Century Ventures, 473
American Research & Development Corp., 404
American Securities, L.P., 505
Amerimark Capital Group, 656
Amerindo Investment Advisors, Inc., 505
Ameritech Development Corp., 345
AMP Asset Management Limited - Development Capital, 740
Amphion Ventures L.P.(FKA: Wolfensohn Associates, L.P.), 506
Anila Fund (AKA: Anila.org, LLC), 145
Annapolis Ventures LLC, 391
Antares Capital Corp. (FKA: Antares Leveraged Capital Corp), 345
Antares Capital Corporation (FKA: Harbor Ventures Corp.), 320
Anthem Capital, L.P., 391
Apax Globis Partners & Co. (APAX Japan), 741
Apax Partners & Cie (AKA: Apax France), 742
Apax Partners & Co. Ventures Ltd (AKA: Apax UK), 742
Apax Partners & Co.Beteiligungsberatung AG, 742
Apex Venture Partners, 346
Apex Ventures BV, 743
APIDC-Venture Capital Limited, 743
Apollo Invest , 744
Applied Technology, 405
APV Technology Partners, 146
ARCH Venture Partners, 346
Ardsheil, Inc., 506
Argentum Group, The , 507
ArgNor Wireless Ventures, 744
Argo Global Capital, Inc., 406
Argos Soditic SA, 744
Arkoma Venture Partners, 657
Artemis Ventures, 146
Artesian Capital, 464
Arthur P. Gould & Co., 507
Arthur Rock & Co., 146
Arts Alliance, 746
ASC Group, 746
Ascend Technology Ventures, 747
Ascent Venture Partners, 406
Asian Infrastructure Fund Advisers Limited, 748
AsiaTech Internet Group (ATIG) (FKA: AsiaTech Ventures), 748

Aspen Ventures (formerly 3i Ventures), 147
Asset Management Company Venture Capital, 147
Athena Technology Ventures, 148
Atlantic Capital, 407
Atlantic Coastal Ventures, L.P.(AKA:Multimedia Broadcast In), 312
Atlas Venture, 407
August Capital Management, 148
August Partners, 508
AUGUSTA Venture GmbH, 749
Aurora Funds, Inc., 598
Austin Ventures, L.P., 657
Australian Technology Group Ltd, 750
Avery Business Development Services, 320
AVI Capital, L.P., 149
Axiom Venture Partners, L.P., 288
Axiomlab PLC, 751
Axxon Capital, Inc., 408
Ayala Internet Venture Partners, 751
Bachow & Associates, Inc., 623
Bailey & Co. Inc., 752
Baird Capital Partners, 347
Baker Capital Corp., 510
Banc One Capital Partners, 608
BancAmerica Capital Investors (FKA:NationsBanc Capital Corp), 598
BancBoston Capital/BancBoston Ventures, 408
Bancorp Hawaii SBIC, Inc., 341
BANEXI Corp., 753
Bangert Dawes Reade Davis & Thom, 151
Bank One Equity Investors, Inc., 386
Bankers Trust New York Corp./Deutsche Banc Alex Brown, 510
Baring Communications Equity, 755
Baring Private Equity Partners (FKA:Baring Venture Partners), 755
Barnard & Company, 511
Bastion Capital Corp., 152
Batavia Group, Ltd., The , 511
Batavia Investment Management Ltd, 756
Battery Ventures, L.P., 409
Baxter Associates, Inc., 289
Bay Partners, 153
Bayern Kapital Risikokapitalbeteiligungs GmbH, 757
BBS Finance, 757
BCE Capital, 758
BCI Partners, 484
BCR Asset Management Pty Ltd., 758
Beacon Partners, Inc., 289
Bedrock Capital Partners, 409
Behrman Capital, 512
Benchmark Capital, 154
Benefit Capital Companies, Inc., The, 480
Berkeley International Capital Corp., 154
Berkshire Partners, 410
Berlin Capital Fund (FKA LBB Beteiligungsgesellschaft GmbH), 759
Berwind Financial Group, L.P., 623
Bessemer Venture Partners, 410
Big Bang Ventures, 760
Birchmere Ventures, Inc.(FKA:Birchmere Investments), 624
Blue Chip Venture Company, 609
Blue Ribbon AG, 760
Blue Rock Capital, 319
Blue Water Capital, LLC, 690
Blueprint Ventures, LLC, 155
BlueStar Ventures, 348
Blumberg Capital Ventures, 155
BOME Investors, Inc., 473
Boston Capital Ventures, 411
Boston Financial & Equity Corp., 412
Boston Millennia Partners, 412
Boston University Community Technology Fund , 413
Boston Ventures Management, Inc., 413
Botts & Co., 762
Boulder Ventures, Ltd., 392
Brad Peery Capital, 156
BrainHeart Capital AB, 762
BrainWorks Ventures, 330
Brait Capital Partners, 762
Brantley Venture Partners, 609
Bridge Partners, LLC, 393
Brightstar, 763
Bristol Capital Management, 513
Broadmark Capital Corp., 702
Brook Venture Management, L.L.C., 414
Bruce F. Glaspell & Associates, 498
Buena Venture Associates, 659
Bulldog Partners Limited, 764
Bure Equity, 765
Burr, Egan, Deleage & Co., 414
Business Link Doncaster, 765
Butler Capital Partners France, 765
BV Capital (FKA Bertelsmann Ventures LP), 157
C3 Investments, Inc., 157
Cairnsford Associates Ltd., 766
Caltech Capital Partners Ltd., 766
Cambria Group, The, 157
Cambridge Research & Innovation Ltd (AKA CRIL), 767
Cambridge Technology Capital, 415
Camelot Ventures, 457
Canaan Partners, 290
Canbank Venture Capital Fund Ltd, 767
Candover Investments PLC, 768
Canterbury Capital L.L.C.(AKA: Canterbury Detroit Partners), 514
Capital Development & Investment Co. Ltd., 768
Capital For Business, Inc., 474
Capital Insights, L.L.C., 645
Capital Investments, Inc., 717
Capital Investors, 690
Capital Network, The (AKA: Texas Capital Network), 659
Capital Resource Partners, 415
Capital Services & Resources, Inc., 648
Capital Southwest Corporation, 660
Capital Strategy Management Co., The, 349
Capital Technology Group, LLC, 610
Capital Z Asia, 770
Capman Management GmbH, 770
CapVest Management, Ltd, 771
CapVis Equity Partners AG, 771
Cardinal Ventures, L.L.C., 375
Carillon Capital, Inc., 610
Carolinas Capital Investment Corp., 599
Carousel Capital Partners, 599
Cascade Communications Ventures, LLC, 159
Castile Ventures, 416

Castle Harlan Australian Mezzanine Partners Pty. Ltd. , 772
CastleHill Ventures , 772
Catalyst Group, The , 660
Catalyst Venture Capital Firm, 773
Catalyst Ventures, 393
Catella IT AB, 773
Cazenove Private Equity, 773
CCFL Mezzanine Partners of Canada , 774
CD Technicom S.A., 774
CDC Innovation Partners, 775
CE Unterberg Towbin (FKA:Unterberg Harris Capital Partners), 515
Cedar Creek Partners, LLC, 717
CEI Ventures/Coastal Ventures LP, 388
Celtic House International, 775
Centennial Ventures, 278
CenterPoint Venture Partners, 661
CEO Advisors, 321
CEO Venture Fund, 625
Cerulean Fund/WGC Enterprises, 350
Champion Consulting Group, Incorporated, 776
Chanen, Painter & Co., Ltd., 703
Charles River Ventures, 417
Charter Growth Capital, 160
Charter Ventures, 160
Chartwell Capital Management Co., Inc., 321
Chase H&Q (FKA Hambrecht & Quist), 160
Cherry Tree Investments, Inc., 464
Chestnut Street Partners, Inc., 417
Chiao Tung Bank, 776
China Venture Management, Inc., 777
Chisholm Private Capital Partners, 618
Chrysalis Ventures, 384
CIBC Capital Partners (FKA: CIBC Wood Gundy Capital), 516
CID Equity Partners, 376
Circle Ventures, Inc., 376
cirlab!, 779
CIT Group/Venture Capital, Inc., The, 485
Citadel Pooled Development Ltd. , 779
Citicorp Capital Asia (AKA: CITIC Pacific Ltd.), 780
Citicorp Venture Capital, Ltd., 517
Citizens Capital and Citizens Ventures, 418
CIVC Partners (FKA:Continental Illinois Venture Corp.), 350
Claflin Capital Management, Inc., 418
Clairvest Group, Inc., 780
Clarion Capital Corp., 610
Clarity Capital, 419
Classic Fund Management, Ltd., 781
Clearstone Venture Partners (FKA: idealab! Capital Partners), 161
Clemente Capital (Asia) Ltd., 781
CM Equity Partners, 517
CMB Capital, LLC (CMBC), 322
CMEA Ventures (FKA:Chemicals & Materials Enterprise Associa), 161
Coates Myer & Co. Pty Ltd. (AKA: CM Capital Investments), 782
Cohen & Co., L.L.C., 517
Colonial First State Private Equity Ltd (FKA: Hambro-G Mgmt), 782
Colonnade Capital L.L.C., 691
Colorado Venture Management, 278
Columbia Capital Group, Inc., 313
Comdisco Ventures, 162
Commerz Beteiligungsgesellschaft mbH (CBG), 783
Commonwealth Capital Ventures L.P., 419
CommTech International, 163
Compass Investment Management Ltd., 783
Compass Technology Partners, 163
ComVentures (AKA: Communications Ventures), 163
Concord Venture Management (FKA:Nitzanim), 784
Concordia Capital, 784
Connecticut Innovations, Inc., 291
Constellation Ventures, 518
Continental S.B.I.C., 691
Continental Venture Capital , 784
Continuum Group Limited, 785
Convergence Partners L.P., 164
Copernicus Capital Management Ltd, 785
CORAL Ventures, 465
Cordova Ventures (FKA:Cordova Capital), 331
Core Capital Partners, 313
Cornerstone Equity Investors, LLC, 519
Coronado Venture Fund, 133
Corporate Growth Assistance, Ltd., 786
Corporate Venture Partners, L.P., 519
Cowen & Co., 520
CR&T Ventures AB, 787
Creafund CVBA, 788
Crescendo Venture Management LLC (FKA:IAI Ventures), 466
Crescent Capital NI Ltd (FKA Hambro Northern Ireland), 788
Crest Communications Holdings LLC, 520
Crestview Financial Group, The , 292
Crocker Capital/Crocker Assoc., 164
Crosbie & Co Inc, 789
Cross Atlantic Capital Partners, 625
CrossBow Ventures, 322
Crosslink Capital (FKA: Omega Venture Partners), 165
Crown Advisors International, Ltd., 521
Crown Capital Corp, 475
Crystal Internet Venture Fund, L.P., 611
CS Capital Partners, LLC, 486
CSK Venture Capital Co., Ltd., 789
Cullinane & Donnelly Venture Partners, L.P., 293
Cureton & Co., Inc., 662
CVC Capital Partners, 790
Cygnus Venture Partners, 791
D.H. Blair Investment Banking Corp., 521
Daewoo Venture Capital Co Ltd, 792
Daimler Chrysler Venture Gmbh (AKA DCV), 792
Dakota Group, The , 166
Dali, Hook Partners (FKA: Hook Partners), 662
Danish Development Finance Corp., 793
Danske eVentures, 794
Dassault Developpment, 794
Davis Group, 166
Davis, Tuttle Venture Partners, L.P.(FKA:Davis Venture), 618
DB Venture Partners, 794
De Vries & Co., Inc., 476
Defta Partners, 167
Delmag Ventures, 394
Delta Partners, 795
Delta Ventures, 795
Desai Capital Management Inc., 522
Deutsche Effecten und Wechsel-Beteiligungsgesellschaft AG, 796
Deutsche Venture Capital GmbH (DVCG), 796

DFW Capital Partners (AKA:DeMuth, Folger & Wetherill), 486
Digital Partners, 704
Divine interVentures (FKA: Platinum Venture Partners), 351
DN Partners, 352
Doll Capital Management, 169
Dolphin Communications, 523
Dominion Ventures, Inc., 170
Dongbu Venture Capital Co Ltd, 797
DotCom Ventures L.P., 171
Dougery Ventures, 171
Dow Chemical Co., 458
Draper Atlantic Management Co., LLC, 692
Draper Fisher Jurvetson (FKA: Draper Associates), 172
Draper Fisher Jurvetson Gotham Venture Partners, 523
Draper International, 172
Draper Richards, 173
Draper Triangle Ventures LP, 626
Dresdner Kleinwort Capital , 524
Dresner Capital Resources, Inc., 352
Drysdale Enterprises, 173
DSE Investment Services Limited, 799
Duchossois TECnology Partners, LLC, 353
Dunedin Capital Partners Ltd (FKA:Dunedin Ventures Limited), 799
DynaFund Ventures, L.L.C., 174
Early Stage Enterprises, L.P., 487
EarlyBirdCapital.com Inc., 524
East River Ventures, L.P., 524
Easton Hunt Capital Partners, 525
eBlast Ventures, LLC, 353
ECI Ventures Ltd, 801
ECICS Ventures Pte Ltd., 801
EDB Investments Pte Ltd., 802
Edelson Technology Partners, 487
EDF Ventures (F.K.A. Enterprise Development Fund), 458
Edge Capital Investment Co., LLC, 175
Edison Venture Fund, 488
eFund, LLC, 704
Egan-Managed Capital, 421
EGL Holdings, Inc./Nat West Ventures USA, L.P., 332
Eircom Enterprise Fund Ltd., 803
El Dorado Ventures, 176
Elderstreet Investments Ltd, 803
Electra Fleming Limited, 525
Electra Partners Asia [FKA: JF Electra Limited], 803
Elk Associates Funding Corp., 526
Emerging Technologies , 804
EnCompass Ventures, 704
Encore Venture Partners, LP, 177
Endeavor Capital Management, 294
EnerTech Capital Partners, L.P., 626
Enron Broadband Ventures, 663
Enterprise Equity (NI) Limited, 805
Enterprise Investors, 526
Enterprise Partners, 178
Eos Partners, L.P., 527
Epicea, 805
Equinox Investment Partners, 294
Equitas, L.P., 649
Equity Partners Management Pty Ltd, 807
Equity Ventures, Ltd, 807
Equity-South (FKA:Grubb & Williams Ltd.), 333
Equus Capital Corp., 663
Eqvitec Partners Oy, 807
Espirito Santo Development, 808
EuclidSR Partners , 527
EURAZEO (FKA Gaz-et-Eaux & AZEO), 809
Euroc Venture Capital Corporation, 809
Eurofund LP, 810
European Acquisition Capital Ltd., 810
European Equity Partners , 810
European Webgroup, 811
Euroventures Management AB , 811
Evanston Business Investment Corp, 354
EVC Christows PLC (FKA: eVestment Company PLC), 812
Evergreen Canada Israel Investments Ltd, 812
Evergreen Capital Partners Inc, 528
Evergreen Ventures, 686
Excel Communications, 663
Exeter Capital, L.P., 528
eXseed, 813
Fairfax Partners, 693
Far East Capital Corp., 179
FBR CoMotion Venture Capital, 705
FBR Technology Venture Partners,L.P.(AKA:Friedman,Billings), 693
Federal Business Development Bank, 815
Fidelity Ventures (FKA: Fidelity Venture Associates), 421
Financial Technology Research Corp., 529
Financial Technology Ventures, 179
Finansa Capital Limited, 816
FINOVA Mezzanine Capital, Inc. (FKA: Sirrom Capital Corp), 650
Finovelec, 817
First Analysis Venture Capital (FKA:First Analysis Corp), 354
First Capital Management Co., 664
First Gen-e Investments, 817
First New England Capital, L.P., 295
First Security Business Investment Corp., 686
First Union Capital Partners, 600
FJC Growth Capital Corp., 129
Florida Capital Ventures, Ltd., 323
Fluke Venture Partners., 705
FLV Fund (AKA Flanders Language Valley Fund), 818
Fonds D'Investissements R.T.V.L., 819
Fonds de Solidarité des Travailleurs du Québec (F.T.Q.), 820
Foresight, 820
ForetagsByggarna AB, 821
Forrest Binkley & Brown, 180
Fort Washington Capital Partners, LLC, 611
FORTKNOX-VENTURE AG, 821
Fortune Consulting Group Incorporated, 821
Fortune Venture Capital Incorporated, 822
Fortune Venture Management Pte Ltd., 822
Foundation Capital, 181
Foundation Capital Limited, 822
Fountainhead Capital Ltd., 823
Fowler, Anthony & Co., 422
Frazier & Company, 705
Frederic H. Mayerson Group, The, 612
Fremont Partners, 181
Friends Ivory & Sime Private Equity (Ivory &Sime Baronsmead), 823
Frontenac Co., 355

Frontier Capital, LLC, 600
Frontline Capital, Inc., 334
Frost Capital Partners, 182
Fuqua Ventures, LLC, 334
G-51 Capital LLC, 665
Gabelli Multimedia Partners, 531
Gabriel Venture Partners, 182
Gateway Associates, L.P., 476
GATX Ventures (FKA: Meier Mitchell & Co.), 183
GATX/MM Venture Partners, 183
GCI, 718
GCI Venture Partners, 314
Gemini Capital Fund Management Ltd, 825
Generation Capital Partners, 532
GENES GmbH Venture Services, 826
Genesee Funding, Inc., 532
Genesis Capital, Inc., 533
Genesis Partners, 826
Geneva Merchant Banking Partners, 601
Geneva Venture Partners, 184
Geocapital Partners, L.L.C., 489
Gideon Hixon Fund, 467
Gilde Investment Management, 827
GKM Venture Partners, LP, 184
Global Crossing Ventures (FKA: Frontier Ventures), 185
Global Internet Ventures (GIV), 693
Global Partner Ventures, 694
Glynn Ventures, 186
Go Equity GmbH, 829
Golub Associates, 534
Granite Ventures LLC (FKA: H & Q Venture Associates), 186
Granville Baird Capital Partners (FKA:Granville Pr Eq Mngrs), 830
Gray Ventures, 335
Graystone Venture Partners, LLC(AKA:Portage Venture Partners, 356
Great Hill Equity Partners, LLC, 424
Greater Philadelphia Venture Capital Corp., 627
Gresham CEA Management Limited, 832
Greylock, 424
Grieve, Horner, Brown & Asculai, 833
Grosvenor Funds, The, 315
Grotech Capital Group, 394
Grove Street Advisors, LLC, 425
Growth Factory, The, 833
Growth Venture Group Pty Ltd., 833
GrowthWorks Capital, 834
GTCR Golder Rauner, LLC, 356
Guide Ventures, 706
Gujarat Venture Finance Limited, 834
H&Q Asia Pacific, Ltd., 187
Hallador Venture Partners, 188
Halpern, Denny & Co., 425
Hambro European Ventures (Hambros PLC), 835
Hamilton Robinson & Co., Inc., 296
Hanbyuck Investment Co Ltd, 836
Hanover Capital Corp., 535
Harbour Financial Co., 426
HarbourVest Partners, LLC., 426
Health Capital Group, 188
Heartland Capital Fund, Ltd., 479
Hellman & Friedman, 189
Herbert Young Securities, Inc., 536
Heritage Partners, 427
Hibernia Capital Partners, 837
Hickory Venture Capital Corporation, 130
High Street Capital, LLC, 357
Highland Capital Partners, 427
HillStreet Capital, Inc., 612
HMS Hawaii Management Partners, 341
HMS Holtron Management Services, Ltd, 838
HO2 Partners LLC, 665
Hoak Capital Corp., 666
Hoebich Venture Management, Inc., 190
Holland Venture B.V. (FKA: Holland Venture Holding C.V.), 839
Hollinger Capital (FKA: Hollinger Ventures), 537
Horizon Ventures (F.K.A. Technology Investments), 190
Horizonte Venture Management GmbH, 840
Hotung International Company, Ltd., 840
Housatonic Partners, 190
Howard, Lawson & Co., 628
HSBC Private Equity (Asia), Ltd. (FKA: HSBC PE Management), 841
HSBC Private Equity Ltd (FKA Montagu Private Equity Ltd), 841
Hummer Winblad Venture Partners, 191
Hunt Capital Group, 667
Hydro-Quebec CapiTech Inc., 843
i2s PLC (FKA: Tarpan PLC), 843
iAsia Alliance Capital, 844
IBB Beteiligungsgesellschaft mbH, 844
IBK Capital Corporation, 844
ICC Venture Capital, 845
ICICI Venture Funds Mngt. Co. Ltd., 846
Idanta Partners, Ltd., 191
IDG Technology Venture Investment Inc. (FKA: PTV-China), 846
IDG Ventures, 192
IEG Venture Management, Inc., 357
IFCI Venture Cap. Funds (Formerly Risk Capital & Tech.), 847
iGlobe Partners Limited, 847
Ignite Associates, LLC, 192
Ignition Corporation, 706
IKB Venture Capital GmbH (AKA IKB Beteiligungsgesellschaft , 848
IL&FS Venture Corporation (FKA. CreditCapital Venture Fund), 848
imGO (AKA: Investor Mobile GO; FKA: Guoco Land Ltd.), 848
IMH Industrie Management Holding GmbH, 848
iMinds (FKA: Interactive Minds), 193
Impact Venture Partners, 539
Impex Venture Management Co., 540
Incepta LLC, 706
Incorporated Investors, 193
IndAsia Fund Advisors Private Limited, 849
Indekon Management Oy, 849
Index Ventures, 850
Indian Direct Equity Advisors Pvt. Ltd, 850
Indocean Chase Capital Advisors, 850
Indosuez Ventures, 194
Indus Venture Management Ltd., 851
Industrial Technology Securities Ltd, 851
Industry Ventures , 428
Infinity Capital LLC, 194
Inflexion plc, 852
Infocomm Investments Pte Ltd (IIPL), 852

Information Technology Ventures, 195
InnoCal, L.P., 196
Innova Capital (FKA: Poland Partners Management Company), 853
Innovacom, 853
Innovation Works, Inc., 628
Innovationsagentur Gesmbh, 854
InnovationsKapital Management Goteborg AB , 854
Innovest Group, Inc., 629
Innvotec Ltd, 854
Inova Capital SCR, 855
InterEquity Capital Partners, L.P., 541
Internet Incubator PLC, 856
Intersouth Partners, 601
InterWest Partners, 197
InvestAmerica Venture Group, Inc., 380
InveStar Capital, Inc., 857
Investissement Desjardins, 857
Investissements Novacap (AKA:Novacap Investments, Inc.), 858
Invision AG (FKA Aureus Private Equity AG), 858
IPS Industrial Promotion Services, Ltd., 859
Ironside Ventures, LLC (FKA: MF Private Capital), 429
ISEP NV, 860
Israel Seed Partners, 860
ITACT, 861
ITP-Management N.V., 861
J.E. Mann & Co., 542
J.L. Albright Venture Partners, 861
J.P. Morgan Capital Corp., 542
J.P. Morgan Partners (FKA: Chase Capital Partners), 543
JAFCO Co. Ltd., 862
JAFCO Investment (FKA:Nomura/JAFCO Investment (Asia) Limited, 862
JAFCO Ventures, Inc., 198
James A. Matzdorff & Co., 199
JatoTech Management LLC, 668
Javva Partners LLC, 544
Jefferson Capital Fund, Ltd., 130
Jefferson Partners , 863
Jerusalem Global Ventures, 864
Jerusalem Venture Partners (AKA: JVP), 864
JK&B Capital, 358
Josephberg Grosz & Co., Inc., 545
JT Venture Partners, LLC, 491
Kaiser Permanente (AKA: National Venture Development), 200
Kankaku Investment Co Ltd, 865
Kansas City Equity Partners, 477
Kansas Technology Enterprise Corporation, 382
Kansas Venture Capital, Inc., 383
Kappa-IT Ventures, 865
KB Partners, LLC, 359
Kennet Capital Ltd, 866
Kettle Partners, L.P., 359
Key Equity Capital Corp.(AKA:Key Community Development Corp), 613
Keystone Minority Capital Fund, L.P., 630
Keystone Venture Capital Management Co., 630
Kick-Start Ventures, 866
Kinship Partners, 280
Kirlan Venture Capital, Inc., 707
Kitty Hawk Capital, 602
KLB Investment Co., Ltd., 866
Kleiner Perkins Caufield & Byers, 200
Kline Hawkes & Co., 201
KLM Capital Group, 201
Koch Ventures, 133
Kookmin Venture Capital Co Ltd, 867
Koor Corporate Venture Capital, 868
Korea Development Investment Corp., 868
Korea Technology Finance Corp., 869
KPMG Advent Management Group (FKA:Advent Western Pacific), 870
KTB Ventures (FKA: KTB Venture Capital), 202
Kyocera International, Inc., 202
Lake Shore Capital Partners, Inc., 360
Lambda Funds, The, 546
Las Americas Administradora, 871
Lawrence Financial Group, 202
Lazard Technology Partners, 547
Lee Munder Venture Partners, 430
Legal & General Ventures Ltd, 872
Leonard Green & Partners, 203
Leonard Mautner Associates, 203
Lepercq Capital Management, Inc.(AKA:Lepercq,de Neuflize In), 548
LG Venture Investment Inc., 873
Liberty Venture Partners, Inc., 631
Libon Capital Management Limited, 873
Lighthouse Capital Partners, 205
Lightspeed Venture Partners (FKA: Weiss, Peck & Greer), 206
LINC Capital Partners, Inc., 361
Lincoln Investment Management Inc., 378
LJH Global Investments , 324
LLR Equity Partners, 631
LN Mittal, 874
Lombard Investments, Inc., 206
London Merchant Security (AKA LMS), 874
London Ventures (Fund Managers) Ltd., 875
LoneTree Capital Partners, 281
Lost Boys Incubator, 875
LTI Ventures Leasing Corp., 298
Lubar & Co., 718
Lucent Venture Partners, Inc., 207
Lycos Ventures, 632
M&F Associates, L.P., 549
M/C Venture Partners, 431
Macquarie Direct Investment Limited, 876
Madison Dearborn Partners, LLC, 361
Madison Investment Partners, Inc., 550
Madrona Venture Group, 707
Magnum Communications (AKA: MCF Advisory Services Ltd), 877
Malmohus Invest AB, 877
Manhattan Venture Co., Inc., 550
Marconi Ventures, 431
Maristeth Ventures, L.L.C., 707
Marlborough Capital Advisors, 431
Marleau, Lemire, Inc., 878
Marquette Venture Partners, 362
Maryland Venture Capital Trust, 395
Massachusetts Technology Development Corp. (MTDC), 432
Massey Burch Capital Corp., 650
Matrix Group, 209
Matrix Partners, 433

Matrix Private Equity, 879
MAVA Investment Management kft (AKA: Hungarian-American Ent), 879
Mayfield Fund, 210
MBA Venture Group, 669
MC Capital Asia Private Limited, 880
MC Capital, Inc., 551
McCown De Leeuw & Co., 210
MCG Ventures, 696
McGraw-Hill Ventures, 552
McKee & Co., 134
McLean Watson Capital Inc., 880
MDT Advisers, Inc., 433
Media Venture Partners, 211
MediaVenture Capital AG & Co. KGaA, 882
MedTech International, Inc., 670
Mees Pierson Investeringsmaat. B.V., 435
Mellon Ventures (AKA: Mellon Bank), 632
Memhard Investment Bankers, Inc., 300
Menlo Ventures, 212
Mentor Capital Partners, 633
Mercator Broadband Partners, L.P., 696
Mercury Private Equity, 883
Meridian Venture Partners (MVP), 633
Merita Capital Limited, 134
Meritage Private Equity Fund, 281
Meritech Capital Partners, 212
Merrill Lynch Investment Managers FKA Mercury Asset Mgmt, 884
Merrill, Pickard, Anderson & Eyre, 213
MESBIC Ventures Holding Co. (AKA Pacesetter Growth Fund, L.P, 671
Mesirow Private Equity Investments, Inc., 362
meVC.com, 213
Meyer, Duffy & Associates, 553
Mezzanine Management UK Limited, 885
Mid-Atlantic Venture Funds (FKA: NEPA Management Corp.), 634
Middlefield Capital Fund, 885
Midlands Venture Fund Managers Ltd. (AKA: Midven Ltd), 886
Miller Capital Corp, 135
Miralta Capital, Inc., 887
Mission Ventures, 214
Mitsui & Co., Ltd., 553
MMG Ventures, L.P., 396
Mofet Venture Capital , 888
Mohr, Davidow Ventures, 214
Montgomerie, Huck & Co., 888
Montgomery Associates, Inc., 215
Montreux Equity Partners, 216
Monumental Venture Partners, LLC, 696
Morel Ventures Limited, 888
Morgan Grenfell Private Equity Limited, 889
Morgan Stanley Venture Partners (AKA: MSDW), 554
Morgenthaler Ventures, 614
Motorola Inc., 315
Mountaineer Capital LP, 716
MSC Venture Corporation Sdn. Bhd., 890
MTI Partners Ltd, 890
Multiventure Investment, Inc., 890
Murphree Venture Partners, 671
Mustang Ventures (FKA Siemens Mustang Ventures), 216
MVC AG (AKA Mitteldeutsche Venture Capital AG), 891
MVP Ventures (AKA: Milk Street Ventures), 436
MWV Capital Partners (FKA:Middlewest Ventures, L.P.), 378
Nanyang Ventures Pty Ltd (AKA: Nanyang Management Pty Ltd), 892
Nassau Capital, L.L.C., 492
National Australia Investment Capital Limited, 892
National Bank Of Kuwait, 555
National City Equity Partners, Inc, 614
National Corporate Finance, Inc., 217
National Financial Cos. LLC, 556
Navis Partners (FKA:Fleet Equity Partners), 643
Nazem & Co., 556
nCoTec Ventures Ltd, 893
NCP Advisors Philippines, Inc., 894
Needham & Company, Inc., 556
Nelson Capital Corp., 651
Nesbitt Burns, 363
Net Partners, 895
Neurone Venture Capital, 896
New England Partners, 437
New Things, LLC, 557
New Venture Resources, 282
New Vista Capital, LLC, 218
New World Infrastructure Limited, 896
New World Venture Advisors, 364
New York Life Venture Capital Group, 557
New York State Science & Technology Foundation, 558
Newbridge Capital Limited, 219
Newbury Ventures, 220
Newbury, Piret & Co., Inc., 437
Newport Capital Group Pty Ltd, 897
NewSpring Ventures, 634
Newtek Ventures, 220
Nexit Ventures Oy, 897
NextGen Capital LLC, 697
NextGen Partners LLC, 221
NextPoint Partners L.P.(FKA: Plaza Street), 315
Nextreme Ventures, 221
NIB Capital Private Equity N.V. (FKA: Parnib Holding NV) , 898
NIF Ventures Co., Ltd., 898
NIF Ventures USA, Inc.(Nippon Investment & Finance Co., Ltd), 222
Nikko Capital Co Ltd, 899
Nokia Venture Partners (AKA: Nokia Oy), 222
Nomura International, Plc., 900
Nomura/JAFCO Investment (HK) Limited, 901
North America Investment Corp., 902
North Atlantic Capital Corp., 389
North Bridge Venture Partners, 438
North Carolina Technological Development Authority, Inc., 603
North Hill Ventures, 438
NorthEast Ventures, 301
Northern Venture Managers Limited, 902
Northwest Ohio Venture Fund, 615
Northwest Venture Associates, Inc.(FKA:Spokane Capital Mgmt), 709
Northwood Ventures, 559
Northzone Ventures (FKA Venture Partners AS), 902
Norwest Equity Partners, 223
Novak Biddle Venture Partners, L.P., 697
Noveltek Venture Corp., 560

Novus Ventures, 223
NPM Capital (AKA Nederlandse Participatie MIJ NV), 903
Nth Power Technologies, Inc, 224
Oak Hill Capital Management, Inc., 561
Oak Investment Partners, 302
Obelisk Capital Pty Ltd, 904
Oem Capital, 302
Ohana Ventures, LLC, 615
Ohio Partners, 615
OneLiberty Ventures (FKA: Morgan, Holland Ventures Corp.), 439
Onondaga Venture Capital Fund, Inc., 562
Onset Ventures, 225
Open Prairie Ventures, 365
Opportunity Capital Partners {FKA: Thompson Capital Mgt), 225
Optical Capital Group , 397
Orange Ventures, 905
Oregon Resource and Technology Development Fund, 620
Orien Ventures, 303
Orion Partners, L.P., 439
OVP Venture Partners (FKA: Olympic Venture Partners), 709
Oxford Financial Services Corp., 698
PA Early Stage (AKA:Pennsylvania Early Stage Partners), 635
Pac-Link Management Corporation, 906
Pacific Corporate Group, Inc., 227
Pacific Northwest Partners SBIC, L.P., 710
Pacific Venture Partners, 907
Pacifica Fund , 228
PacRim Venture Management , 228
Paladin Partners, 711
Palmer Partners, L.P., 441
Palomar Ventures, 228
Pappajohn Capital Resources, 381
Paradigm Capital Partners LLC, 651
Paribas Principal, Inc., 563
Part'com, 909
Partech International, 229
Partners Group, 910
Pathfinder Investment Co Pvt Ltd, 910
Pathfinder Venture Capital Funds, 470
Patricof & Co. Ventures, Inc., 563
Penfund Partners, Inc., 911
Peninsula Capital Partners, L.L.C, 460
Penn-Janney Fund, Inc., The, 635
Penny Lane Partners, 493
Penta Capital Partners Ltd, 911
Pequot Capital Management Inc., 564
Perennial Ventures (FKA: Tredegar Investments), 711
Petra Capital Partners LLC, 652
Philadelphia Ventures, Inc., 636
Phoenix Equity Partners (FKA: DLJ European Private Equity), 911
Phoenix Growth Capital Corp., 231
Phoenix Partners, The , 711
Piedmont Venture Partners, 604
Pierce Financial Corporation(FKA:Pierce Investment Banking), 698
Pilotbird, 912
Pino Venture Partners, 912
Pittsford Group, Inc., The , 565
Platinum Group, Inc., The , 565
PME Capital, 912
Poalim Capital Markets Technologies, Ltd., 913
Point Venture Partners, 636
Polaris Venture Capital, 913
Polaris Venture Partners, 441
Polestar Capital, Inc., 366
Poly Ventures, 566
PolyTechnos Venture Partners GmbH, 913
Pomona Capital, 566
Portview Communications Partners, 914
PowerWord Capital Management, Inc., 914
pre-IPO Aktiengesellschaft, 915
Prelude Technology Investments Ltd, 915
Prescient Capital, 232
Primaxis Technology Ventures Inc. , 916
Prime Capital Management Co., Inc., 304
Prime Technology Ventures NV, 916
Primedia Ventures, 567
PrimePartners Asset Management Pte. Ltd., 916
Primus Venture Partners, Inc., 616
Prism Capital, 367
Prism Venture Partners, 441
Private Capital Corp., 131
Priveq Capital Funds, 917
Productivity Fund I & II, The, 367
Prospect Street Ventures (FKA:Prospect Street Invest. Mgmt), 567
Provco Group, The , 637
Providence Equity Partners, Inc.(FKA: Providence Ventures), 643
Proximitas AG Venture Capital, 918
Ptek Ventures , 336
Quaestus & Co. Inc. (FKA: Quaestus Management Corp..), 719
Quantum Capital Partners, 325
Quest Ventures, 233
Quester Capital Management Ltd, 920
QuestMark Partners, L.P., 397
R-H Capital Partners, 337
Ralph Wilson Equity Fund, L.L.C., 460
Rand Capital Corporation, 568
Raza Foundries, 233
Recovery Equity Investors, L.P., 234
Red River Ventures, 675
Redleaf Venture Management, 234
Regent Capital Management, 569
Renaissance Capital Corp., 337
RFE Investment Partners, 305
Richard Jaffe & Co., Inc., 676
Richland Ventures, 652
Ridge Capital Partners, L.L.C., 368
Ridgewood Capital Management LLC, 494
Roanoke Capital, Ltd., 712
Robertson Stephens & Company, LLC, 236
Rocket Ventures, 237
RockMountain Ventures, 282
Rocky Mountain Capital Partners (FKA:Hanifen Imhoff Capital), 283
Rosecliff, 237
Rosenfeld & Co., 620
Roser Ventures LLC, 283
Rothschild Ventures Asia Pte Ltd., 922
Rothschild Ventures, Inc., 570
Royal Bank Private Equity (FKA: Royal Bank Development Cap), 922
Royalty Capital Fund, L.P. I/Royalty Capital Management, Inc, 443
RRE Ventures LLC, 571

RSA Ventures, 443
Rutledge & Co., Inc., 305
RWI Group, LP, 239
Saarlandische Wagnisfinanzierungsgesellschaft mbh (AKA SWG), 924
Sage Management Group, 444
Sandler Capital Management, 571
Sandlot Capital LLC, 283
Sanpaolo IMI Private Equity S.p.A., 925
Saugatuck Capital Company, 306
SBC Equity Partners, Inc., 369
SBC Ventures, 499
SBCA/A.G. Bartholomew & Associates, 131
SBV Venture Partners (AKA:Sigefi, Burnette & Vallee), 240
Schneider Electric Ventures, 926
Schoffstall Ventures , 639
Schooner Capital International, L.P., 444
Scottish Equity Partners Limited, 927
Seacoast Capital, 446
Seaport Capital, 572
SEB e-invest, 927
SEB Foretagsinvest, 927
Seed Capital Ltd, 928
Selby Venture Partners, 241
Sentinel Capital Partners, 573
Sequel Venture Partners, 284
Sequoia Capital, 241
Sevin Rosen Management Co., 677
Shad Run Investments, Inc., 242
Shannon Development Company, 929
Shattan Group, The, 574
Shaw Venture Partners (FKA: Shaw Glasgow Partners), 621
Shelton Companies, Inc., The , 604
Shepherd Group LLC, The, 447
Sherpa Partners, LLC, 471
Shrem Fudim Kelner Technologies Ltd. , 930
SI Ventures, 326
Siemens Venture Capital GmbH, 930
Sienna Ventures (FKA: Sienna Holdings Inc.), 242
Sierra Ventures, 243
Sigma Capital Corp., 327
Sigma Partners, 243
Signal Lake Venture Fund, LP, 307
Siguler Guff & Company, LLC, 575
Silicon Valley Bank, 244
Silver Creek Technology Investors (FKA: O'Donnell & Masur), 677
Singapore Technologies Telemedia (AKA: ST Telemedia), 931
SingTel Ventures, 931
Sitra (AKA Finnish National Fund for Research and Dev.), 932
SK Global Co., Ltd., 932
Smart Technology Ventures, 246
SMIFS Venture Capital Limited, 933
Societe Regionale d'Investissement de Bruxelles (SRIB/GIMB), 933
Sofinnova Partners, 934
Sofinnova Ventures, 246
SOFTBANK Capital Partners, 448
Softbank Corp., 935
SOFTBANK Venture Capital (FKA: SOFTBANK Technology Ventures), 247
Sonera Corporation Corporate Venture Capital, 935
Sopartec SA, 936
Sorrento Associates, Inc., 247
SoundView Financial Group, Inc., 307
South Atlantic Venture Funds, L.P., 327
Southeastern Technology Fund, 132
Southern California Ventures, 247
Southport Partners, 307
Southwest Venture Group, 678
Southwest Venture Partnerships, The, 678
Sovereign Capital (FKA:Nash, Sells & Partners Limited), 936
SpaceVest, 699
Spectrum Equity Investors, L.P., 248
SPEF Banques Populaires, 937
Spencer Trask Ventures, Inc. (FKA: Spencer Trask Securities), 576
Spinnaker Ventures, 249
Spire Capital (FKA: Waller Capital Corp.), 577
Sponsored Consulting Services, 249
Spring Capital Partners, L.P., 398
Springboard-Harper Investment Pte. Ltd., 938
Sprout Group, 578
Sputnik Technology Ventures, 938
SRK Management Co., 578
SsangYong Cement (Singapore) Ltd, 939
SSM Ventures, 653
St. Paul Venture Capital, Inc., 471
Staenberg Private Capital, LLC, 713
Stamford Financial, 579
Star Capital Group, Inc., 939
Star-Ventures Management GMBH (SVM), 940
Starter Fluid, 250
State Street Bank & Trust Co., 338
Sterling Grace Capital Management, L.P., 579
Sterling Venture Partners, 398
Sterling/Carl Marks Capital {FKA - Sterling Commercial, 580
Still River Fund, The, 450
Stolberg Partners, 580
StoneGate Partners, L.L.C., 450
Stonepath Europe, 941
Strategic Capital Management, 941
Strategic Investments & Holdings, Inc., 581
Stratford Equity Partners, L.P., 679
Strathdon Investments Ltd, 942
Sucsy, Fischer & Co., 370
SudKB & SudVC, 942
Suez Asia Holdings Pte Ltd., 943
Summit Capital Associates, Inc., 581
Summit Group Ltd, The, 943
Summit Partners, 451
Sun Hung Kai Properties Limited, 943
SUNeVision Holdings Ltd, 944
Sunsino Development Associate Inc., 944
Sunwestern Investment Group, 680
Sutter Hill Ventures, 251
Swedestart Management AB, 944
Sweeney & Co., Inc., 308
Sycamore Ventures, 494
Synerfi S.A., 945
T. Rowe Price Threshold Partnerships, 399
TA Associates, Inc., 451
Tailink Venture Partners, 946
Taiwan United Venture Management Corporation, 946
Tamir Fishman Ventures, 946

Tappan Zee Capital Corp., 495
Target Partners, 947
Taylor & Turner, 253
tbg Technologie-Beteiligungsgesellschaft mbH, 947
TCR Europe SA, 947
TDH, 639
Techno Nord VC GmbH, 948
Techno-Venture Co. (Japan), 949
TechnoCap Inc, 949
Technologieholding VC GmbH, 950
Technology Associates Management Corporation, 950
Technology Crossover Ventures, 254
Technology Funding, 254
Technology Partners, 255
Technology Venture Partners Pty Ltd, 950
TechnoPlus Ventures, 951
Technostart GmbH, 951
Techxas Ventures, LLC, 681
TecVenture Partners GmbH, 952
Teknoinvest Management As, 952
Telecom Italia Ventures, 255
Telecom Partners (FKA:Telecom Management, LLC), 285
Telecom Venture Group Ltd. (TVG), 953
Telecommunications Development Fund (TDF), 316
TeleSoft Partners, 256
Telia Business Innovation AB, 953
Telos Venture Partners, 256
Texas Growth Fund Management, 681
THCG Inc., 582
Third Coast Capital, 370
Thoma Cressey Equity Partners, 371
Thompson Clive & Partners Limited, 955
Thompson Clive, Inc., 257
Throunarfelag Islands Plc(AKA:The Icelandic Finance&Invest.), 955
Ticonderoga Capital, Inc. (FKA: Dillon Read Venture Capital), 452
TL Ventures, 640
Tokyo Small & Medium Business Investment & Consultation Co., 956
Toll Technologies, 957
Top Technology Limited (AKA:Hambros-Advanced Technology Tru), 957
Toucan Capital Corp., 399
Transamerica Mezzanine Financing, 645
Transamerica Technology Finance, 309
Transcap Associates, Inc., 371
Trellis Partners, 682
Triad Investors Corp, 319
Tribune Ventures, 372
Trident Capital, 259
Trinity Ventures, 260
TriNova, 959
Triton Ventures, 682
Triune Capital, 260
TrustCapital Partners NV, 959
TSG Capital Group, L.L.C., 309
TTP Venture Managers (FKA: The Technology Partnership), 960
TVM Techno Venture Management, 961
Twinning Ventures, 961
U.S. Venture Partners, 261
UBS Capital, 962
UBS Capital (AKA Phildrew Ventures), 963
UNC Ventures, 453
Union Street Capital Corp., 713
Union Venture Corp., 262
Unit Trust of India (UTI), 964
UOB Venture Management Pte Ltd., 964
Updata Venture Partners, 700
UPS Strategic Enterprise Fund, 339
US Trust Private Equity, 584
Utah Ventures II, L.P. (A.K.A. Union Ventures), 687
Valley Capital Corp., 654
Valley Ventures (FKA: Arizona Growth Partners, L.P.), 136
Value Management & Research AG (VMR), 965
Vanguard Venture Partners, 262
VantagePoint Venture Partners, 263
VCF Partners, 965
Vega Capital Corp., 584
Vencap Equities Alberta, Ltd., 966
Vencon Management, Inc., 585
VenGlobal Capital, 264
Venrock Associates, 586
Ventana Financial Resources, Inc., 372
Ventana Global, 264
Ventex Management, Inc., 683
Venture Associates, Ltd., 285
Venture Capital Fund Managers (Pty), Ltd., The , 967
Venture Capital Fund of New England, The, 454
Venture Capital Management Corp., 328
Venture First Associates, 328
Venture Funding Group International, 587
Venture Growth Associates, 265
Venture Investment Management Company LLC (AKA: VIMAC), 454
Venture Management Services Inc. (FKA: AT&T Ventures), 496
Venture Opportunities Corp., 588
Venture Partners AG, 968
Venture Select, 968
VentureCap Management GmbH (AKA VCH Equity Group AG), 969
Venturepark Incubator (FKA grizzlyfarm AG), 969
Ventures West Management, Inc., 970
Veritas Venture Capital Management, Ltd., 970
Vero Group PLC, 684
Vertex Management, 971
Vertex Management Israel (AKA: Vertex Management III Ltd.), 971
Vesta Capital Partners (AKA: Vesta Group, The), 971
Victory Ventures L.L.C., 588
Vision Capital Management (FKA Glenwood Capital), 267
Vista Capital de Expansion S.A., 972
Vitesse Semiconductor Corporation, 268
VIV NV (AKA Vlaamse Investeringvennootschap NV), 973
Viventures Inc., 973
VK Ventures, 268
Voyager Capital, 714
VS&A Communications Partners, L.P., 588
Wachovia, 340
Wachtel & Co., Inc., 317
Wakefield Group, 607
Walden Capital Management Corporation, 589
Walden International Investment Group (AKA: Walden Group), 269
Walden Israel, 975

WaldenVC, 270
Walnut Capital Corp., 701
Warburg, Pincus & Co., LLC. (FKA: E.M. Warburg, Pincus & Co), 590
Wasatch Venture Fund (FKA: Wasatch Venture Corporation), 687
wellington partners venture capital GmbH, 975
Welsh, Carson, Anderson & Stowe, 591
West Midlands Enterprise Ltd, 976
Westar Capital, 271
WestBridge Capital Advisors (India) Pvt. Ltd., 976
Westbury Partners, 592
Western States Investment Group, 272
Western Technology Investment, 272
Westford Technology Ventures, L.P., 497
Weston Presidio Capital Management, 455
White Pines Management, L.L.C., 462
Whitney & Co. (FKA: J.H. Whitney & Co.), 310
WI Harper Group, 273
William A.M. Burden & Co., 593
William E. Simon & Sons (Asia) LDC, 977
Willis Stein & Partners, 374
Wind Point Partners, 462
Windward Ventures (FKA: Coronado Capital), 274
Winslow Partners LLC, 317
Winthrop Ventures, 593
WK Associates, 977
Wolf Ventures (AKA:Wolf Asset Management Corp.), 286
WomenAngles.net, 318
Woodside Fund, 274
Wooshin Development Finance Corp, 978
Working Ventures Canadian Fund, Inc., 978
Worldview Technology Partners, 275
Worms Capital Management, 594
WSI Holding Corporation, 595
YankeeTek Ventures, 456
Yasuda Enterprise Development Co., Ltd.(FKA: Nippon Ent.Dev), 275
Yorkshire Fund Managers Ltd., 979
Young Associates Limited, 980
Yozma Venture Capital Ltd, 980
Zero Stage Capital Co., Inc., 456
Zodiac Venture Capital KB, 980
Zone Ventures, 276
ZS Fund, L.P., 595

Computer Hardware

1st Source Capital Corp., 375
21st Century Internet Management Partners,LLC, 138
2M Invest, Inc., 138
3i Finland Oy (FKA SFK Finance), 725
ABS Ventures, 390
Academy Funds (FKA: Longleaf Venture Fund LLC), 597
Access Venture Partners, 277
Acer Technology Ventures(FKA:Acer Soft Capital Inc.), 141
ACF Equity Atlantic, Inc, 731
Adams Capital Management, Inc., 622
Adams Street Partners, LLC (FKA: Brinson Private Equity), 343
Adler & Co., 502
Advanced Materials Partners, Inc., 287
Advanta Partners, L.P., 622
Advent-Morro Equity Partners, 734
Allen & Buckeridge Pty Ltd, 737
Allsop Venture Partners, 380
Allstate Private Equity, 344
Alpha Capital Partners, Inc., 344
Alta Partners, 144
Amadeus Capital Partners, 740
American Research & Development Corp., 404
American Securities, L.P., 505
Amerimark Capital Group, 656
Amerindo Investment Advisors, Inc., 505
Ameritech Development Corp., 345
Antares Capital Corp. (FKA: Antares Leveraged Capital Corp), 345
Antares Capital Corporation (FKA: Harbor Ventures Corp.), 320
Anthem Capital, L.P., 391
Apex Venture Partners, 346
Applied Technology, 405
Argentum Group, The , 507
Arkoma Venture Partners, 657
Arthur P. Gould & Co., 507
ASC Group, 746
Ascent Venture Partners, 406
Asset Management Company Venture Capital, 147
Atlantic Capital, 407
Atlantic Coastal Ventures, L.P.(AKA:Multimedia Broadcast In), 312
Atlas Venture, 407
August Capital Management, 148
Austin Ventures, L.P., 657
Bachow & Associates, Inc., 623
Banc One Capital Partners, 608
BancAmerica Capital Investors (FKA:NationsBanc Capital Corp), 598
BANEXI Corp., 753
Bangert Dawes Reade Davis & Thom, 151
Bank One Equity Investors, Inc., 386
Batterson Venture Partners(AKA:BVP), 348
Battery Ventures, L.P., 409
Bay Partners, 153
BCE Capital, 758
Beacon Partners, Inc., 289
Behrman Capital, 512
Benchmark Capital, 154
Berkeley International Capital Corp., 154
Bessemer Venture Partners, 410
Blue Water Capital, LLC, 690
BOME Investors, Inc., 473
Boston University Community Technology Fund , 413
BrainWorks Ventures, 330
Broadmark Capital Corp., 702
Bruce F. Glaspell & Associates, 498
Burr, Egan, Deleage & Co., 414
Business Link Doncaster, 765
C3 Holdings, LLC, 474
Cairnsford Associates Ltd., 766
Cambridge Research & Innovation Ltd (AKA CRIL), 767
Camelot Ventures, 457
Capital Investments, Inc., 717
Capital Strategy Management Co., The, 349
Carillon Capital, Inc., 610
CD Technicom S.A., 774

CE Unterberg Towbin (FKA:Unterberg Harris Capital Partners), 515
CEI Ventures/Coastal Ventures LP, 388
CEO Advisors, 321
CEO Venture Fund, 625
Cerulean Fund/WGC Enterprises, 350
Chanen, Painter & Co., Ltd., 703
Chartwell Capital Management Co., Inc., 321
Cherry Tree Investments, Inc., 464
China Venture Management, Inc., 777
Chisholm Private Capital Partners, 618
CIBC Capital Partners (FKA: CIBC Wood Gundy Capital), 516
CID Equity Partners, 376
Citicorp Venture Capital, Ltd., 517
Citizens Capital and Citizens Ventures, 418
Claflin Capital Management, Inc., 418
Clairvest Group, Inc., 780
Clarion Capital Corp., 610
Colorado Venture Management, 278
Columbine Venture Funds, The , 279
Comdisco Ventures, 162
Commonwealth Capital Ventures L.P., 419
Compass Technology Partners, 163
Concord Venture Management (FKA:Nitzanim), 784
Copernicus Capital Management Ltd, 785
Core Capital Partners, 313
Cornerstone Equity Investors, LLC, 519
Coronado Venture Fund, 133
Corporate Venture Partners, L.P., 519
Crescendo Venture Management LLC (FKA:IAI Ventures), 466
Crest Communications Holdings LLC, 520
Crestview Financial Group, The , 292
CS Capital Partners, LLC, 486
Cullinane & Donnelly Venture Partners, L.P., 293
Cureton & Co., Inc., 662
Cygnus Venture Partners, 791
D.H. Blair Investment Banking Corp., 521
Daewoo Venture Capital Co Ltd, 792
Daimler Chrysler Venture Gmbh (AKA DCV), 792
Danish Development Finance Corp., 793
Davis, Tuttle Venture Partners, L.P.(FKA:Davis Venture), 618
De Vries & Co., Inc., 476
Defta Partners, 167
Delta Partners, 795
Development Corp. of Austin, 467
DFW Capital Partners (AKA:DeMuth, Folger & Wetherill), 486
Divine interVentures (FKA: Platinum Venture Partners), 351
DN Partners, 352
Dongbu Venture Capital Co Ltd, 797
Dow Chemical Co., 458
Downer & Co., 420
Dresdner Kleinwort Capital , 524
Dresner Capital Resources, Inc., 352
Drysdale Enterprises, 173
Duchossois TECnology Partners, LLC, 353
East River Ventures, L.P., 524
Edelson Technology Partners, 487
EDF Ventures (F.K.A. Enterprise Development Fund), 458
Edge Capital Investment Co., LLC, 175
Egan-Managed Capital, 421
EGL Holdings, Inc./Nat West Ventures USA, L.P., 332
EnerTech Capital Partners, L.P., 626
Enterprise Investors, 526
Eos Partners, L.P., 527
EuclidSR Partners , 527
Euroc Venture Capital Corporation, 809
Evanston Business Investment Corp, 354
Evergreen Canada Israel Investments Ltd, 812
Evergreen Ventures, 686
Exeter Capital, L.P., 528
Far East Capital Corp., 179
Fidelity Ventures (FKA: Fidelity Venture Associates), 421
FINOVA Mezzanine Capital, Inc. (FKA: Sirrom Capital Corp), 650
Finovelec, 817
Firemark Advisors, Inc., 488
First Princeton Capital Corp., 489
First Security Business Investment Corp., 686
Fonds D'Investissements R.T.V.L., 819
Foundation Capital, 181
Fowler, Anthony & Co., 422
Frontenac Co., 355
Frontline Capital, Inc., 334
Gateway Associates, L.P., 476
GATX Ventures (FKA: Meier Mitchell & Co.), 183
GATX/MM Venture Partners, 183
GCI, 718
Gemini Capital Fund Management Ltd, 825
Genesee Funding, Inc., 532
Genesis Capital, Inc., 533
Gilde Investment Management, 827
GKM Venture Partners, LP, 184
Glynn Ventures, 186
Granville Baird Capital Partners (FKA:Granville Pr Eq Mngrs), 830
Grayson & Associates, 280
Greater Philadelphia Venture Capital Corp., 627
Greylock, 424
Grotech Capital Group, 394
Grove Street Advisors, LLC, 425
Gujarat Venture Finance Limited, 834
Hanbyuck Investment Co Ltd, 836
Hanover Capital Corp., 535
Harbour Financial Co., 426
HarbourVest Partners, LLC., 426
Health Capital Group, 188
Herbert Young Securities, Inc., 536
Hickory Venture Capital Corporation, 130
HillStreet Capital, Inc., 612
HMS Hawaii Management Partners, 341
Hoak Capital Corp., 666
Hoebich Venture Management, Inc., 190
Horizon Ventures (F.K.A. Technology Investments), 190
Houston Venture Partners (AKA: Houston Partners), 666
HSBC Private Equity (Asia), Ltd. (FKA: HSBC PE Management), 841
Hudson Venture Partners, 538
Hungarian-American Enterprise Fund, The (HAEF), 842
IBB Beteiligungsgesellschaft mbH, 844
IBK Capital Corporation, 844
ICC Venture Capital, 845
IEG Venture Management, Inc., 357
IFCI Venture Cap. Funds (Formerly Risk Capital & Tech.), 847
Impex Venture Management Co., 540

Incorporated Investors, 193
Indekon Management Oy, 849
Industrial Technology Securities Ltd, 851
Information Technology Ventures, 195
Inman & Bowman, 195
Innovation Works, Inc., 628
Innovest Group, Inc., 629
Innvotec Ltd, 854
InterEquity Capital Partners, L.P., 541
IPS Industrial Promotion Services, Ltd., 859
ISEP NV, 860
IT Provider Advisor, 861
J.E. Mann & Co., 542
J.L. Albright Venture Partners, 861
J.P. Morgan Capital Corp., 542
JAFCO Investment (FKA:Nomura/JAFCO Investment (Asia) Limited, 862
Josephberg Grosz & Co., Inc., 545
Justsystem, Inc., 629
Kaiser Permanente (AKA: National Venture Development), 200
KB Partners, LLC, 359
Kemper Ventures, 491
Key Equity Capital Corp.(AKA:Key Community Development Corp), 613
Kinship Partners, 280
Kirlan Venture Capital, Inc., 707
Kitty Hawk Capital, 602
KLB Investment Co., Ltd., 866
Kleiner Perkins Caufield & Byers, 200
Kookmin Venture Capital Co Ltd, 867
Korea Technology Finance Corp., 869
Kyocera International, Inc., 202
Lake Shore Capital Partners, Inc., 360
Lambda Funds, The, 546
Las Americas Administradora, 871
Lazard Technology Partners, 547
Leonard Mautner Associates, 203
Lepercq Capital Management, Inc.(AKA:Lepercq,de Neuflize In), 548
Lighthouse Capital Partners, 205
LM Capital Corp., 324
LTI Ventures Leasing Corp., 298
Lubar & Co., 718
Macquarie Direct Investment Limited, 876
Malmohus Invest AB, 877
Manchester Humphreys, Inc., 642
Maristeth Ventures, L.L.C., 707
Marleau, Lemire, Inc., 878
Massey Burch Capital Corp., 650
Matrix Partners, 433
Mayfield Fund, 210
MC Capital, Inc., 551
McKee & Co., 134
Media Venture Partners, 211
MedTech International, Inc., 670
Menlo Ventures, 212
Meridian Venture Partners (MVP), 633
Merita Capital Limited, 134
Merrill, Pickard, Anderson & Eyre, 213
MESBIC Ventures Holding Co. (AKA Pacesetter Growth Fund, L.P, 671
Meyer, Duffy & Associates, 553
Microtechnology Investments, Ltd., 213
Middlefield Capital Fund, 885
Miller Capital Corp, 135
Miralta Capital, Inc., 887
Mitsui & Co., Ltd., 553
MMG Ventures, L.P., 396
Mohr, Davidow Ventures, 214
Morgan Stanley Venture Partners (AKA: MSDW), 554
MTI Partners Ltd, 890
MWV Capital Partners (FKA:Middlewest Ventures, L.P.), 378
Nanyang Ventures Pty Ltd (AKA: Nanyang Management Pty Ltd), 892
Nassau Capital, L.L.C., 492
National Corporate Finance, Inc., 217
Nazem & Co., 556
Nesbitt Burns, 363
New Business Capital Fund Ltd., 499
New York Life Venture Capital Group, 557
Newbury Ventures, 220
Newtek Ventures, 220
NextGen Capital LLC, 697
NIB Capital Private Equity N.V. (FKA: Parnib Holding NV) , 898
Nikko Capital Co Ltd, 899
Nippon Technology Venture Partners Ltd., 899
Nomura/JAFCO Investment (HK) Limited, 901
North Bridge Venture Partners, 438
North Carolina Technological Development Authority, Inc., 603
NorthEast Ventures, 301
Northwest Venture Associates, Inc.(FKA:Spokane Capital Mgmt), 709
Noveltek Venture Corp., 560
Novus Ventures, 223
NPM Capital (AKA Nederlandse Participatie MIJ NV), 903
Nth Power Technologies, Inc, 224
Oak Investment Partners, 302
Oem Capital, 302
Onondaga Venture Capital Fund, Inc., 562
Open Prairie Ventures, 365
Oregon Resource and Technology Development Fund, 620
Orion Partners, L.P., 439
Oxford Financial Services Corp., 698
Pacific Northwest Partners SBIC, L.P., 710
Palomar Ventures, 228
Pappajohn Capital Resources, 381
Pathfinder Investment Co Pvt Ltd, 910
Pathfinder Venture Capital Funds, 470
Pauli & Co., Inc., 477
Penfund Partners, Inc., 911
PENMAN Partners (FKA PENMAN Asset Management LP), 365
Penn-Janney Fund, Inc., The, 635
Penny Lane Partners, 493
Pequot Capital Management Inc., 564
Perennial Ventures (FKA: Tredegar Investments), 711
Philadelphia Ventures, Inc., 636
Phoenix Partners, The , 711
Pierce Financial Corporation(FKA:Pierce Investment Banking), 698
Platinum Group, Inc., The , 565
Point Venture Partners, 636
Poly Ventures, 566
Pomona Capital, 566
Prelude Technology Investments Ltd, 915

Prescient Capital, 232
Prime Capital Management Co., Inc., 304
Prism Capital, 367
Private Capital Corp., 131
Productivity Fund I & II, The, 367
Prospect Street Ventures (FKA:Prospect Street Invest. Mgmt), 567
Quaestus & Co. Inc. (FKA: Quaestus Management Corp..), 719
Quest Ventures, 233
Red River Ventures, 675
Renaissance Capital Corp., 337
Richard Jaffe & Co., Inc., 676
Roanoke Capital, Ltd., 712
Roser Ventures LLC, 283
Royal Bank Private Equity (FKA: Royal Bank Development Cap), 922
Royalty Capital Fund, L.P. I/Royalty Capital Management, Inc, 443
RRE Ventures LLC, 571
SAE Ventures, 306
Sage Management Group, 444
Sandler Capital Management, 571
Sandlot Capital LLC, 283
SBCA/A.G. Bartholomew & Associates, 131
SBV Venture Partners (AKA:Sigefi, Burnette & Vallee), 240
Seacoast Capital, 446
Seed Capital Ltd, 928
Sequoia Capital, 241
Shannon Development Company, 929
Shattan Group, The, 574
Shaw Venture Partners (FKA: Shaw Glasgow Partners), 621
Shepherd Group LLC, The, 447
Sienna Ventures (FKA: Sienna Holdings Inc.), 242
Sierra Ventures, 243
Sigma Capital Corp., 327
Siguler Guff & Company, LLC, 575
Silicon Valley Bank, 244
Sitra (AKA Finnish National Fund for Research and Dev.), 932
Smart Technology Ventures, 246
Societe Regionale d'Investissement de Bruxelles (SRIB/GIMB), 933
Sofinnova Ventures, 246
SoundView Financial Group, Inc., 307
Southport Partners, 307
Southwest Venture Group, 678
Southwest Venture Partnerships, The, 678
Spencer Trask Ventures, Inc. (FKA: Spencer Trask Securities), 576
Sprout Group, 578
SsangYong Cement (Singapore) Ltd, 939
Sucsy, Fischer & Co., 370
Sunwestern Investment Group, 680
Sutter Hill Ventures, 251
Sweeney & Co., Inc., 308
Tailink Venture Partners, 946
Taylor & Turner, 253
TDH, 639
Techno-Venture Co. (Japan), 949
TechnoCap Inc, 949
Technologieholding VC GmbH, 950
Technology Crossover Ventures, 254
Technology Funding, 254
Telos Venture Partners, 256
Texas Growth Fund Management, 681
Thompson Clive, Inc., 257
Throunarfelag Islands Plc(AKA:The Icelandic Finance&Invest.), 955
Tokyo Small & Medium Business Investment & Consultation Co., 956
Transamerica Technology Finance, 309
Transcap Associates, Inc., 371
Triune Capital, 260
Tvi Investments Bv, 960
UPS Strategic Enterprise Fund, 339
Utah Ventures II, L.P. (A.K.A. Union Ventures), 687
Vanguard Venture Partners, 262
VantagePoint Venture Partners, 263
Vega Capital Corp., 584
Venrock Associates, 586
Ventana Financial Resources, Inc., 372
Ventana Global, 264
Ventex Management, Inc., 683
Venture Capital Fund Managers (Pty), Ltd., The , 967
Venture Capital Fund of New England, The, 454
Venture Capital Management Corp., 328
Venture Growth Associates, 265
Venture Investment Management Company LLC (AKA: VIMAC), 454
Venture Investors Management LLC, 720
Venture Management Services Inc. (FKA: AT&T Ventures), 496
Venture Strategy Partners, 266
Ventures West Management, Inc., 970
Wachtel & Co., Inc., 317
Walden International Investment Group (AKA: Walden Group), 269
WaldenVC, 270
Walnut Capital Corp., 701
Warburg, Pincus & Co., LLC. (FKA: E.M. Warburg, Pincus & Co), 590
Wasatch Venture Fund (FKA: Wasatch Venture Corporation), 687
Wedbush Capital Partners, 271
West Midlands Enterprise Ltd, 976
Westbury Partners, 592
Westford Technology Ventures, L.P., 497
Weston Presidio Capital Management, 455
William E. Simon & Sons (Asia) LDC, 977
Winthrop Ventures, 593
Worldview Technology Partners, 275
Yasuda Enterprise Development Co., Ltd.(FKA: Nippon Ent.Dev), 275
Yorkshire Fund Managers Ltd., 979
Zero Stage Capital Co., Inc., 456
Zone Ventures, 276

Computer Other

3i Austria (FKA Bank Austria TFV High Tech -UB GmbH), 725
3i Finland Oy (FKA SFK Finance), 725
4C Ventures (FKA: Olivetti Holding, N.V.), 501
ABN-AMRO Corporate Investments, 729
Accelerator Media (UK), Ltd, 730
ACT Venture Capital Ltd., 732
Adams, Harkness & Hill, Inc., 401
Advent International Corp., 402
Advent Venture Partners (FKA Advent Limited), 733
Alan I. Goldman & Associates, 483

Alchemy Partners, 736
Alimansky Capital Group, Inc., 504
Alliance Technology Ventures, 330
Alpine Technology Ventures, 144
Alta Berkeley Venture Partners, 739
Alta Partners, 144
Amadeus Capital Partners, 740
American Securities, L.P., 505
Amphion Ventures L.P.(FKA: Wolfensohn Associates, L.P.), 506
Apax Partners & Cie (AKA: Apax France), 742
Apax Partners & Co.Beteiligungsberatung AG, 742
Apex Ventures BV, 743
APIDC-Venture Capital Limited, 743
Ardsheil, Inc., 506
Armada Asset Management, 746
Arthur Rock & Co., 146
August Partners, 508
Australian Technology Group Ltd, 750
AVI Capital, L.P., 149
b-business partners, 752
Bancorp Hawaii SBIC, Inc., 341
BCR Asset Management Pty Ltd., 758
Berlin Capital Fund (FKA LBB Beteiligungsgesellschaft GmbH), 759
Betwin Investments, Inc., 760
Blue Rock Capital, 319
bmp Aktiengesellschaft AG, 761
Boston Financial & Equity Corp., 412
Brantley Venture Partners, 609
Bristol Capital Management, 513
Bulldog Partners Limited, 764
Butler Capital Partners France, 765
Cambridge Research & Innovation Ltd (AKA CRIL), 767
Candover Investments PLC, 768
Capital Network, The (AKA: Texas Capital Network), 659
Capital Services & Resources, Inc., 648
Capman Management GmbH, 770
CastleHill Ventures , 772
CCFL Mezzanine Partners of Canada , 774
CD Technicom S.A., 774
CEI Ventures/Coastal Ventures LP, 388
Charter Ventures, 160
Chase H&Q (FKA Hambrecht & Quist), 160
Citicorp Capital Asia (AKA: CITIC Pacific Ltd.), 780
Classic Fund Management, Ltd., 781
CM Equity Partners, 517
Commerz Beteiligungsgesellschaft mbH (CBG), 783
Compass Technology Partners, 163
Cowen & Co., 520
CR&T Ventures AB, 787
Crescent Capital NI Ltd (FKA Hambro Northern Ireland), 788
Crown Advisors International, Ltd., 521
CSK Venture Capital Co., Ltd., 789
Dali, Hook Partners (FKA: Hook Partners), 662
DANSK Udviklingsfinansiering A/S, 793
Dassault Developpment, 794
Delta Partners, 795
Dougery Ventures, 171
Draper Fisher Jurvetson (FKA: Draper Associates), 172
Easton Hunt Capital Partners, 525
ECICS Ventures Pte Ltd., 801
EDB Investments Pte Ltd., 802
Edge Capital Investment Co., LLC, 175
Elderstreet Investments Ltd, 803
Electra Partners Asia [FKA: JF Electra Limited], 803
EnCompass Ventures, 704
Epicea, 805
Equinox Investment Partners, 294
Equity Partners Management Pty Ltd, 807
Equity Ventures, Ltd, 807
Eqvitec Partners Oy, 807
Evergreen Capital Partners Inc, 528
Federal Business Development Bank, 815
Financial Technology Research Corp., 529
First New England Capital, L.P., 295
Florida Capital Ventures, Ltd., 323
FLV Fund (AKA Flanders Language Valley Fund), 818
Foundation Capital Limited, 822
Friends Ivory & Sime Private Equity (Ivory &Sime Baronsmead), 823
Genevest Consulting Group, S.A., 827
Global Partner Ventures, 694
Go Equity GmbH, 829
Granite Ventures LLC (FKA: H & Q Venture Associates), 186
Graystone Venture Partners, LLC(AKA:Portage Venture Partners, 356
Grotech Capital Group, 394
GrowthWorks Capital, 834
HMS Holtron Management Services, Ltd, 838
Holland Venture B.V. (FKA: Holland Venture Holding C.V.), 839
Horizonte Venture Management GmbH, 840
HPI Holding SA, 841
HSBC Private Equity (Asia), Ltd. (FKA: HSBC PE Management), 841
Hunt Capital Group, 667
ICICI Venture Funds Mngt. Co. Ltd., 846
IDG Technology Venture Investment Inc. (FKA: PTV-China), 846
IDG Ventures, 192
IMH Industrie Management Holding GmbH, 848
IndAsia Fund Advisors Private Limited, 849
Index Ventures, 850
Indosuez Ventures, 194
Indus Venture Management Ltd., 851
Innovationsagentur Gesmbh, 854
InnovationsKapital Management Goteborg AB , 854
Internet Incubator PLC, 856
InvestAmerica Venture Group, Inc., 380
Investissement Desjardins, 857
Invision AG (FKA Aureus Private Equity AG), 858
Ireka Venture Capital Limited, 860
J.P. Morgan Partners (FKA: Chase Capital Partners), 543
James A. Matzdorff & Co., 199
Jerusalem Global Ventures, 864
Kankaku Investment Co Ltd, 865
Kansas City Equity Partners, 477
Kansas Technology Enterprise Corporation, 382
Kansas Venture Capital, Inc., 383
KB Partners, LLC, 359
Kennet Capital Ltd, 866
Keystone Minority Capital Fund, L.P., 630
Korea Development Investment Corp., 868
Lawrence Financial Group, 202
Legal & General Ventures Ltd, 872
Lighthouse Capital Partners, 205

LINC Capital Partners, Inc., 361
LJH Global Investments , 324
London Ventures (Fund Managers) Ltd., 875
LTI Ventures Leasing Corp., 298
Manhattan Venture Co., Inc., 550
Matrix Private Equity, 879
MAVA Investment Management kft (AKA: Hungarian-American Ent), 879
Mayfield Fund, 210
MBA Venture Group, 669
McLean Watson Capital Inc., 880
MDT Advisers, Inc., 433
Mezzanine Management UK Limited, 885
Mid-Atlantic Venture Funds (FKA: NEPA Management Corp.), 634
Midlands Venture Fund Managers Ltd. (AKA: Midven Ltd), 886
Miller Capital Corp, 135
MMC adVentures Ltd, 888
MTI Partners Ltd, 890
Multiventure Investment, Inc., 890
MVP Ventures (AKA: Milk Street Ventures), 436
Nelson Capital Corp., 651
NetSpark Ventures N.V., 895
New Venture Resources, 282
New York State Science & Technology Foundation, 558
Newbury, Piret & Co., Inc., 437
NextPoint Partners L.P.(FKA: Plaza Street), 315
NIF Ventures USA, Inc.(Nippon Investment & Finance Co., Ltd), 222
North Atlantic Capital Corp., 389
North Bridge Venture Partners, 438
Northern Venture Managers Limited, 902
Northwest Ohio Venture Fund, 615
Noveltek Venture Corp., 560
Novus Ventures, 223
Open Prairie Ventures, 365
Oxford Financial Services Corp., 698
Palmer Partners, L.P., 441
Pathfinder Investment Co Pvt Ltd, 910
Patricof & Co. Ventures, Inc., 563
Peninsula Capital Partners, L.L.C, 460
Phoenix Equity Partners (FKA: DLJ European Private Equity), 911
Phoenix Growth Capital Corp., 231
PME Capital, 912
Polestar Capital, Inc., 366
PolyTechnos Venture Partners GmbH, 913
Prime Technology Ventures NV, 916
Quest Ventures, 233
Quester Capital Management Ltd, 920
R-H Capital Partners, 337
Recovery Equity Investors, L.P., 234
Reiten & Co Strategic Investments AS, 921
Rothschild Ventures, Inc., 570
SBC Equity Partners, Inc., 369
SBC Ventures, 499
SEB Foretagsinvest, 927
Seed Capital Ltd, 928
Sigma Partners, 243
Silver Creek Technology Investors (FKA: O'Donnell & Masur), 677
SISIR International Pte Ltd., 932
Sopartec SA, 936
Sorrento Associates, Inc., 247
Southport Partners, 307
Sovereign Capital (FKA:Nash, Sells & Partners Limited), 936
Spring Capital Partners, L.P., 398
State Street Bank & Trust Co., 338
Strathdon Investments Ltd, 942
Summit Capital Associates, Inc., 581
Summit Group Ltd, The, 943
Summit Partners, 451
Sutter Hill Ventures, 251
Swedestart Management AB, 944
Sycamore Ventures, 494
TA Associates, Inc., 451
Techno Nord VC GmbH, 948
Techno-Venture Co. (Japan), 949
TechnoCap Inc, 949
Technologieholding VC GmbH, 950
Technology Venture Partners Pty Ltd, 950
Teknoinvest Management As, 952
TeleSoft Partners, 256
Tera Capital Corporation, 954
TG Asia Ventures Limited, 954
Third Millennium Venture Capital, Ltd., 256
Thompson Clive & Partners Limited, 955
Top Technology Limited (AKA:Hambros-Advanced Technology Tru), 957
Trellis Partners, 682
Triad Investors Corp, 319
TTP Venture Managers (FKA: The Technology Partnership), 960
UBS Capital (AKA Phildrew Ventures), 963
UOB Venture Management Pte Ltd., 964
VCF Partners, 965
Vencap Equities Alberta, Ltd., 966
Venture Associates, Ltd., 285
Venture Funding Group International, 587
Venture Opportunities Corp., 588
Venture Partners AG, 968
Venture TDF Pte Ltd., 968
VentureCap Management GmbH (AKA VCH Equity Group AG), 969
Vero Group PLC, 684
Vertex Management, 971
Walden Israel, 975
WaldenVC, 270
wellington partners venture capital GmbH, 975
West Midlands Enterprise Ltd, 976
Westar Capital, 271
Western States Investment Group, 272
White Pines Management, L.L.C., 462
Wit Capital Corporation, 594
WomenAngles.net, 318
Woodside Fund, 274
Wooshin Development Finance Corp, 978
Worms Capital Management, 594
Zero Stage Capital Co., Inc., 456

Computer Software

1st Source Capital Corp., 375
21st Century Internet Management Partners,LLC, 138
2M Invest, Inc., 138
3i Austria (FKA Bank Austria TFV High Tech -UB GmbH), 725

3i Finland Oy (FKA SFK Finance), 725
3TS Venture Partners AG, 727
Abell Venture Fund, 390
Aberdare Ventures, 138
Aberdeen Asset Managers, 728
Aberlyn Capital Management Co., Inc., 501
ABN AMRO Private Equity (AKA: ABN AMRO Capital (USA) Inc.) , 343
ABS Ventures, 390
Academy Funds (FKA: Longleaf Venture Fund LLC), 597
Accenture Technology Ventures (FKA: AC Ventures), 140
Access Venture Partners, 277
Acer Technology Ventures(FKA:Acer Soft Capital Inc.), 141
ACF Equity Atlantic, Inc, 731
Adams Capital Management, Inc., 622
Adams Street Partners, LLC (FKA: Brinson Private Equity), 343
Adams, Harkness & Hill, Inc., 401
Adler & Co., 502
Advanced Technology Ventures, 401
Advanta Partners, L.P., 622
Advantage Capital Partners, 386
Advent Venture Partners (FKA Advent Limited), 733
Advent-Morro Equity Partners, 734
Akin Gump Investment Partners 2000, LP, 655
Albemarle Private Equity Ltd, 735
Alcatel Ventures, 142
Alexander Hutton, Inc., 702
Alignment Capital Partners, LLC, 655
All Asia Partners, 737
Allegis Capital (AKA:Allegis Media Technology Ventures), 143
Allegra Partners (FKA: Lawrence, Smith & Horey), 504
Alliance Venture Capital Advisors Limited, 738
Allsop Venture Partners, 380
Allstate Private Equity, 344
Alpha Capital Partners, Inc., 344
Alta Berkeley Venture Partners, 739
Altos Ventures, 144
American Capital Strategies, 391
American Research & Development Corp., 404
American Securities, L.P., 505
Amerindo Investment Advisors, Inc., 505
Ameritech Development Corp., 345
Annapolis Ventures LLC, 391
Antares Capital Corp. (FKA: Antares Leveraged Capital Corp), 345
Antares Capital Corporation (FKA: Harbor Ventures Corp.), 320
antfactory, 741
Anthem Capital, L.P., 391
Apax Globis Partners & Co. (APAX Japan), 741
Apax Partners & Cie (AKA: Apax France), 742
Apex Ventures BV, 743
Applied Genomic Technology Capital Funds (AGTC), 405
Applied Technology, 405
APV Technology Partners, 146
Arbor Partners LLC, 457
ARCH Venture Partners, 346
Argentum Group, The , 507
Aria Ventures Ltd., 745
Arthur P. Gould & Co., 507
ASC Group, 746
Ascent Venture Partners, 406
Aspen Ventures (formerly 3i Ventures), 147
Asset Management Company Venture Capital, 147
Atlantic Capital, 407
Atlas Venture, 407
August Capital Management, 148
AUGUSTA Venture GmbH, 749
Aurora Funds, Inc., 598
Austin Ventures, L.P., 657
Authosis, 149
AV Labs, 658
Avery Business Development Services, 320
Aweida Ventures, 277
AxaVision, Inc., 509
Axiom Venture Partners, L.P., 288
Ayala Internet Venture Partners, 751
b-business partners, 752
Baccharis Capital, Inc., 150
Bachow & Associates, Inc., 623
Baird Capital Partners, 347
Banc One Capital Partners, 608
BancAmerica Capital Investors (FKA:NationsBanc Capital Corp), 598
BancBoston Capital/BancBoston Ventures, 408
BANEXI Corp., 753
Bangert Dawes Reade Davis & Thom, 151
Bank One Equity Investors, Inc., 386
Bankers Trust New York Corp./Deutsche Banc Alex Brown, 510
BankInvest Group AS, 754
Baring Private Equity Partners (FKA:Baring Venture Partners), 755
Batavia Investment Management Ltd, 756
Batterson Venture Partners(AKA:BVP), 348
Battery Ventures, L.P., 409
Baxter Associates, Inc., 289
Bay Partners, 153
BCE Capital, 758
BCR Asset Management Pty Ltd., 758
Beacon Partners, Inc., 289
Behrman Capital, 512
Benchmark Capital, 154
Benefit Capital Companies, Inc., The, 480
Berkeley International Capital Corp., 154
Bessemer Venture Partners, 410
Birchmere Ventures, Inc.(FKA:Birchmere Investments), 624
Blue Chip Venture Company, 609
Blue Ribbon AG, 760
Blue Water Capital, LLC, 690
Blueshift Internet Ventures, 761
BlueStar Ventures, 348
Blumberg Capital Ventures, 155
BOME Investors, Inc., 473
Boston Capital Ventures, 411
Boston University Community Technology Fund , 413
Botts & Co., 762
Boulder Ventures, Ltd., 392
BrainHeart Capital AB, 762
Broadmark Capital Corp., 702
Brook Venture Management, L.L.C., 414
Bruce F. Glaspell & Associates, 498
Buena Venture Associates, 659
Burr, Egan, Deleage & Co., 414
Business Link Doncaster, 765
C3 Holdings, LLC, 474
Cairnsford Associates Ltd., 766

Caltech Capital Partners Ltd., 766
Cambridge Technology Capital, 415
Camelot Ventures, 457
Canaan Partners, 290
Canbank Venture Capital Fund Ltd, 767
Capital Development & Investment Co. Ltd., 768
Capital Investments, Inc., 717
Capital Investors, 690
Capital Resource Partners, 415
Capstone Ventures SBIC, L.P., 158
CapVis Equity Partners AG, 771
Carillon Capital, Inc., 610
Carmel Ventures, 772
Castle Harlan Australian Mezzanine Partners Pty. Ltd. , 772
Catalyst Venture Capital Firm, 773
CD Technicom S.A., 774
CE Unterberg Towbin (FKA:Unterberg Harris Capital Partners), 515
CEI Ventures/Coastal Ventures LP, 388
CenterPoint Venture Partners, 661
CEO Advisors, 321
CEO Venture Fund, 625
Cerulean Fund/WGC Enterprises, 350
Champion Consulting Group, Incorporated, 776
Chanen, Painter & Co., Ltd., 703
Charles River Ventures, 417
Charter Growth Capital, 160
Chartwell Capital Management Co., Inc., 321
Cherry Tree Investments, Inc., 464
Chestnut Street Partners, Inc., 417
China Venture Management, Inc., 777
Chisholm Private Capital Partners, 618
Chrysalis Ventures, 384
CIBC Capital Partners (FKA: CIBC Wood Gundy Capital), 516
CID Equity Partners, 376
Circle Ventures, Inc., 376
Citadel Pooled Development Ltd. , 779
Citizens Capital and Citizens Ventures, 418
CIVC Partners (FKA:Continental Illinois Venture Corp.), 350
Claflin Capital Management, Inc., 418
Clairvest Group, Inc., 780
Clal Venture Capital Management Ltd (AKA CVC Management), 781
Clarion Capital Corp., 610
Classic Fund Management, Ltd., 781
Clearstone Venture Partners (FKA: idealab! Capital Partners), 161
CMEA Ventures (FKA:Chemicals & Materials Enterprise Associa), 161
Cohen & Co., L.L.C., 517
Colorado Venture Management, 278
Columbia Capital Group, Inc., 313
Columbine Venture Funds, The , 279
Comdisco Ventures, 162
Commonwealth Capital Ventures L.P., 419
CommTech International, 163
Concord Venture Management (FKA:Nitzanim), 784
Connecticut Innovations, Inc., 291
Continental S.B.I.C., 691
Convergence Partners L.P., 164
Copernicus Capital Management Ltd, 785
CORAL Ventures, 465
Cordova Ventures (FKA:Cordova Capital), 331
Core Capital Partners, 313
Core Pacific Consulting Company, 786
Cornerstone Equity Investors, LLC, 519
Coronado Venture Fund, 133
Corporate Growth Assistance, Ltd., 786
Corporate Venture Partners, L.P., 519
CR&T Ventures AB, 787
Creafund CVBA, 788
Crestview Financial Group, The , 292
Crosbie & Co Inc, 789
Cross Atlantic Capital Partners, 625
Crosslink Capital (FKA: Omega Venture Partners), 165
Crown Capital Corp, 475
Crystal Internet Venture Fund, L.P., 611
Cullinane & Donnelly Venture Partners, L.P., 293
Cureton & Co., Inc., 662
CW Group, Inc., 521
Cygnus Venture Partners, 791
D.H. Blair Investment Banking Corp., 521
Daimler Chrysler Venture Gmbh (AKA DCV), 792
Dakota Group, The , 166
Dali, Hook Partners (FKA: Hook Partners), 662
Danish Development Finance Corp., 793
DANSK Udviklingsfinansiering A/S, 793
Danske eVentures, 794
Dassault Developpment, 794
Davis Group, 166
Davis, Tuttle Venture Partners, L.P.(FKA:Davis Venture), 618
De Vries & Co., Inc., 476
Defta Partners, 167
Delmag Ventures, 394
Delphi Ventures, 167
Delta Ventures, 795
Deucalion Venture Partners, 168
Deutsche Venture Capital GmbH (DVCG), 796
Development Corp. of Austin, 467
DFW Capital Partners (AKA:DeMuth, Folger & Wetherill), 486
Digital Partners, 704
Direct Capital Private Equity, 797
Divine interVentures (FKA: Platinum Venture Partners), 351
Dominion Ventures, Inc., 170
Dongbu Venture Capital Co Ltd, 797
Dow Chemical Co., 458
Downer & Co., 420
Draper Fisher Jurvetson Gotham Venture Partners, 523
Draper Triangle Ventures LP, 626
Dresdner Kleinwort Capital , 524
Dresner Capital Resources, Inc., 352
Drysdale Enterprises, 173
Duchossois TECnology Partners, LLC, 353
DynaFund Ventures, L.L.C., 174
Early Stage Enterprises, L.P., 487
East River Ventures, L.P., 524
eBlast Ventures, LLC, 353
ECI Ventures Ltd, 801
Edelson Technology Partners, 487
EDF Ventures (F.K.A. Enterprise Development Fund), 458
Edge Capital Investment Co., LLC, 175
Edison Venture Fund, 488
Egan-Managed Capital, 421
EGL Holdings, Inc./Nat West Ventures USA, L.P., 332
El Dorado Ventures, 176

Elderstreet Investments Ltd, 803
Electra Partners Asia [FKA: JF Electra Limited], 803
Endeavor Capital Management, 294
EnerTech Capital Partners, L.P., 626
Enterprise Equity (NI) Limited, 805
Enterprise Investors, 526
Enterprise Partners, 178
Eos Partners, L.P., 527
Epicea, 805
EquiNet Venture Partners AG, 806
Equity-South (FKA:Grubb & Williams Ltd.), 333
EuclidSR Partners , 527
Evanston Business Investment Corp, 354
Evergreen Canada Israel Investments Ltd, 812
Evergreen Ventures, 686
Exeter Capital, L.P., 528
eXseed, 813
Fairfax Partners, 693
Far East Capital Corp., 179
Fidelity Ventures (FKA: Fidelity Venture Associates), 421
Financial Technology Ventures, 179
FINOVA Mezzanine Capital, Inc. (FKA: Sirrom Capital Corp), 650
Finovelec, 817
Firemark Advisors, Inc., 488
First Analysis Venture Capital (FKA:First Analysis Corp), 354
First Gen-e Investments, 817
First Union Capital Partners, 600
Flatiron Partners, 530
Flinders Capital Limited, 818
Fluke Venture Partners., 705
ForetagsByggarna AB, 821
Forrest Binkley & Brown, 180
Fort Washington Capital Partners, LLC, 611
FORTKNOX-VENTURE AG, 821
Fortune Consulting Group Incorporated, 821
Fortune Venture Capital Incorporated, 822
Fortune Venture Management Pte Ltd., 822
Foundation Capital, 181
Foundation Capital Limited, 822
Fowler, Anthony & Co., 422
Friends Ivory & Sime Private Equity (Ivory &Sime Baronsmead), 823
Friulia SpA Fin.Reg.Friuli-Venezia, 824
Frontenac Co., 355
Frontier Capital, LLC, 600
Frost Capital Partners, 182
G-51 Capital LLC, 665
Gabriel Venture Partners, 182
Gateway Associates, L.P., 476
GATX Ventures (FKA: Meier Mitchell & Co.), 183
GATX/MM Venture Partners, 183
GCI, 718
GCI Venture Partners, 314
Gemini Capital Fund Management Ltd, 825
Generation Capital Partners, 532
Genesis Capital, Inc., 533
Genesis Partners, 826
Geneva Venture Partners, 184
Genevest Consulting Group, S.A., 827
Geocapital Partners, L.L.C., 489
Gideon Hixon Fund, 467
Gilde Investment Management, 827
Giza Venture Capital (FKA Giza Investment Management), 828
GKM Venture Partners, LP, 184
Global Internet Ventures (GIV), 693
Glynn Ventures, 186
GO Capital, 829
Granite Ventures LLC (FKA: H & Q Venture Associates), 186
Granville Baird Capital Partners (FKA:Granville Pr Eq Mngrs), 830
Gray Ventures, 335
Grayson & Associates, 280
Greater Philadelphia Venture Capital Corp., 627
Greylock, 424
Grieve, Horner, Brown & Asculai, 833
Grotech Capital Group, 394
Grove Street Advisors, LLC, 425
Growth Factory, The, 833
GTCR Golder Rauner, LLC, 356
Guide Ventures, 706
Gujarat Venture Finance Limited, 834
H&Q Asia Pacific, Ltd., 187
Hallador Venture Partners, 188
Hanbyuck Investment Co Ltd, 836
Hanover Capital Corp., 535
Harbour Financial Co., 426
HarbourVest Partners, LLC., 426
Health Capital Group, 188
Heartland Capital Fund, Ltd., 479
Herbert Young Securities, Inc., 536
Hickory Venture Capital Corporation, 130
High Street Capital, LLC, 357
Highland Capital Partners, 427
HillStreet Capital, Inc., 612
HMS Hawaii Management Partners, 341
HMS Holtron Management Services, Ltd, 838
HO2 Partners LLC, 665
Hoak Capital Corp., 666
Hoebich Venture Management, Inc., 190
Hollinger Capital (FKA: Hollinger Ventures), 537
Honho Consulting Company Limited, 839
Horizon Ventures (F.K.A. Technology Investments), 190
Horizonte Venture Management GmbH, 840
Houston Venture Partners (AKA: Houston Partners), 666
HPI Holding SA, 841
HSBC Private Equity (Asia), Ltd. (FKA: HSBC PE Management), 841
HT Capital Advisors, LLC, 538
Hudson Venture Partners, 538
Hummer Winblad Venture Partners, 191
Hungarian-American Enterprise Fund, The (HAEF), 842
iAsia Alliance Capital, 844
IBK Capital Corporation, 844
ICC Venture Capital, 845
Idanta Partners, Ltd., 191
IDG Technology Venture Investment Inc. (FKA: PTV-China), 846
IDG Ventures, 192
IEG Venture Management, Inc., 357
IFCI Venture Cap. Funds (Formerly Risk Capital & Tech.), 847
iMinds (FKA: Interactive Minds), 193
Incorporated Investors, 193
Indekon Management Oy, 849
Index Ventures, 850

Indian Direct Equity Advisors Pvt. Ltd, 850
Indocean Chase Capital Advisors, 850
Industrial Technology Securities Ltd, 851
Industry Ventures , 428
Infinity Capital LLC, 194
Information Technology Ventures, 195
Inman & Bowman, 195
InnoCal, L.P., 196
Innovacom, 853
Innovation Works, Inc., 628
InnovationsKapital Management Goteborg AB , 854
Innovest Group, Inc., 629
Innvotec Ltd, 854
InterEquity Capital Partners, L.P., 541
Interregnum, 856
Intersouth Partners, 601
InterWest Partners, 197
InveStar Capital, Inc., 857
Investissements Novacap (AKA:Novacap Investments, Inc.), 858
ISEP NV, 860
Israel Seed Partners, 860
IT Provider Advisor, 861
J.E. Mann & Co., 542
J.L. Albright Venture Partners, 861
J.P. Morgan Capital Corp., 542
JAFCO Co. Ltd., 862
JAFCO Investment (FKA:Nomura/JAFCO Investment (Asia) Limited, 862
Jefferson Partners , 863
Jerusalem Global Ventures, 864
JK&B Capital, 358
Josephberg Grosz & Co., Inc., 545
JT Venture Partners, LLC, 491
JumpStartUp Fund Advisors Pvt. Ltd., 864
Justsystem, Inc., 629
Kaiser Permanente (AKA: National Venture Development), 200
Kankaku Investment Co Ltd, 865
Kansas City Equity Partners, 477
KB Partners, LLC, 359
Kemper Ventures, 491
Kettle Partners, L.P., 359
Key Equity Capital Corp.(AKA:Key Community Development Corp), 613
Keystone Venture Capital Management Co., 630
Kinship Partners, 280
Kirlan Venture Capital, Inc., 707
Kitty Hawk Capital, 602
KLB Investment Co., Ltd., 866
Kleiner Perkins Caufield & Byers, 200
Kline Hawkes & Co., 201
Korea Technology Finance Corp., 869
KTB Ventures (FKA: KTB Venture Capital), 202
Lake Shore Capital Partners, Inc., 360
Lambda Funds, The, 546
Las Americas Administradora, 871
Lazard Technology Partners, 547
Lee Munder Venture Partners, 430
Leonard Mautner Associates, 203
Lepercq Capital Management, Inc.(AKA:Lepercq,de Neuflize In), 548
Levine Leichtman Capital Partners, Inc., 204
Libon Capital Management Limited, 873
Lightspeed Venture Partners (FKA: Weiss, Peck & Greer), 206
LLR Equity Partners, 631
London Merchant Security (AKA LMS), 874
LTI Ventures Leasing Corp., 298
Lubar & Co., 718
Lucent Venture Partners, Inc., 207
Malmohus Invest AB, 877
Manchester Humphreys, Inc., 642
Marconi Ventures, 431
Maristeth Ventures, L.L.C., 707
MarketCorp Ventures L.P., 299
Marleau, Lemire, Inc., 878
Marquette Venture Partners, 362
Marwit Capital LLC, 209
Maryland Venture Capital Trust, 395
Massachusetts Technology Development Corp. (MTDC), 432
Massey Burch Capital Corp., 650
Maton Venture, 209
Matrix Partners, 433
McGraw-Hill Ventures, 552
McKee & Co., 134
MDT Advisers, Inc., 433
Media Venture Partners, 211
MedTech International, Inc., 670
Mellon Ventures (AKA: Mellon Bank), 632
Menlo Ventures, 212
Mentor Capital Partners, 633
Meridian Venture Partners (MVP), 633
Merita Capital Limited, 134
Meritage Private Equity Fund, 281
Merrill Lynch Investment Managers FKA Mercury Asset Mgmt, 884
Merrill, Pickard, Anderson & Eyre, 213
MESBIC Ventures Holding Co. (AKA Pacesetter Growth Fund, L.P, 671
Metropolitan Venture Partners (MetVP), 553
meVC.com, 213
Meyer, Duffy & Associates, 553
Microtechnology Investments, Ltd., 213
Miralta Capital, Inc., 887
Mission Ventures, 214
Mitsui & Co., Ltd., 553
MMG Ventures, L.P., 396
Mohr, Davidow Ventures, 214
Montgomerie, Huck & Co., 888
Montreux Equity Partners, 216
Morgan Stanley Venture Partners (AKA: MSDW), 554
Morgenthaler Ventures, 614
Motorola Inc., 315
MSC Venture Corporation Sdn. Bhd., 890
MTI Partners Ltd, 890
Murphree Venture Partners, 671
MWV Capital Partners (FKA:Middlewest Ventures, L.P.), 378
Nassau Capital, L.L.C., 492
National Bank Of Kuwait, 555
National City Equity Partners, Inc, 614
Navis Partners (FKA:Fleet Equity Partners), 643
Nazem & Co., 556
Needham & Company, Inc., 556
Nesbitt Burns, 363
Net Partners, 895
NetworkAsia, 896

New England Partners, 437
New Vista Capital, LLC, 218
New York Life Venture Capital Group, 557
Newbridge Capital Limited, 219
Newbury Ventures, 220
Newport Capital Group Pty Ltd, 897
NewSpring Ventures, 634
Newtek Ventures, 220
NextGen Capital LLC, 697
NIB Capital Private Equity N.V. (FKA: Parnib Holding NV) , 898
Nikko Capital Co Ltd, 899
Nomura International, Plc., 900
Nomura/JAFCO Investment (HK) Limited, 901
North Bridge Venture Partners, 438
North Carolina Technological Development Authority, Inc., 603
North Hill Ventures, 438
NorthEast Ventures, 301
Northwest Venture Associates, Inc.(FKA:Spokane Capital Mgmt), 709
Northzone Ventures (FKA Venture Partners AS), 902
Norwest Equity Partners, 223
Novak Biddle Venture Partners, L.P., 697
Novell Ventures, 686
NPM Capital (AKA Nederlandse Participatie MIJ NV), 903
NPV Capital Partners, LLC, 560
Nth Power Technologies, Inc, 224
Oak Investment Partners, 302
Obelisk Capital Pty Ltd, 904
Ohana Ventures, LLC, 615
Ohio Partners, 615
OneLiberty Ventures (FKA: Morgan, Holland Ventures Corp.), 439
Onondaga Venture Capital Fund, Inc., 562
Onset Ventures, 225
Open Prairie Ventures, 365
Oregon Resource and Technology Development Fund, 620
Orien Ventures, 303
Orion Partners, L.P., 439
OVP Venture Partners (FKA: Olympic Venture Partners), 709
PA Early Stage (AKA:Pennsylvania Early Stage Partners), 635
Pac-Link Management Corporation, 906
Pacific Capital Partners, 907
Pacific Northwest Partners SBIC, L.P., 710
PacRim Venture Management , 228
Paladin Partners, 711
Palomar Ventures, 228
Pappajohn Capital Resources, 381
Paradigm Capital Partners LLC, 651
Parcom Ventures BV, 909
Pari Capital AG, 909
Paribas Principal, Inc., 563
Partech International, 229
Pathfinder Investment Co Pvt Ltd, 910
Pathfinder Venture Capital Funds, 470
Pauli & Co., Inc., 477
Penfund Partners, Inc., 911
Penn-Janney Fund, Inc., The, 635
Pennsylvania Growth Fund, 636
Penny Lane Partners, 493
Perennial Ventures (FKA: Tredegar Investments), 711
Philadelphia Ventures, Inc., 636
Phoenix Equity Partners (FKA: DLJ European Private Equity), 911
Phoenix Partners, The , 711
Pierce Financial Corporation(FKA:Pierce Investment Banking), 698
Pittsford Group, Inc., The , 565
Platinum Group, Inc., The , 565
Poalim Capital Markets Technologies, Ltd., 913
Point Venture Partners, 636
Polaris Venture Capital, 913
Polaris Venture Partners, 441
Polestar Capital, Inc., 366
Poly Ventures, 566
Pomona Capital, 566
PowerWord Capital Management, Inc., 914
pre-IPO Aktiengesellschaft, 915
Prelude Technology Investments Ltd, 915
Prescient Capital, 232
Prime Capital Management Co., Inc., 304
Primedia Ventures, 567
Prism Capital, 367
Prism Venture Partners, 441
Private Capital Corp., 131
Productivity Fund I & II, The, 367
Prospect Street Ventures (FKA:Prospect Street Invest. Mgmt), 567
Putnam Lovell Capital Partners, L.P., 232
Pythagoras NV, 919
Quaestus & Co. Inc. (FKA: Quaestus Management Corp..), 719
RAF Ventures, 637
Ralph Wilson Equity Fund, L.L.C., 460
Rand Capital Corporation, 568
Raza Foundries, 233
Red Hat Ventures, 604
Red River Ventures, 675
Regulus International Capital Co., Inc., 304
Renaissance Capital Corp., 337
Richard Jaffe & Co., Inc., 676
Richland Ventures, 652
Ridgewood Capital Management LLC, 494
Riordan, Lewis & Haden, 236
Roanoke Capital, Ltd., 712
Robertson Stephens & Company, LLC, 236
Rocket Ventures, 237
RockMountain Ventures, 282
Rosecliff, 237
Roser Ventures LLC, 283
Rothschild Ventures Asia Pte Ltd., 922
Royal Bank Private Equity (FKA: Royal Bank Development Cap), 922
Royalty Capital Fund, L.P. I/Royalty Capital Management, Inc, 443
RRE Ventures LLC, 571
Rutledge & Co., Inc., 305
RWI Group, LP, 239
SAE Ventures, 306
Sage Management Group, 444
Sandler Capital Management, 571
Sandlot Capital LLC, 283
Sanpaolo IMI Private Equity S.p.A., 925
SBCA/A.G. Bartholomew & Associates, 131
SBV Venture Partners (AKA:Sigefi, Burnette & Vallee), 240
Schooner Capital International, L.P., 444
Scottish Equity Partners Limited, 927
Seacoast Capital, 446
Seed Company Partners, 676

Selby Venture Partners, 241
Sequel Venture Partners, 284
Sequoia Capital, 241
Sevin Rosen Management Co., 677
Shannon Development Company, 929
Shattan Group, The, 574
Shaw Venture Partners (FKA: Shaw Glasgow Partners), 621
Shepherd Group LLC, The, 447
Sherpa Partners, LLC, 471
SI Ventures, 326
Sienna Ventures (FKA: Sienna Holdings Inc.), 242
Sierra Ventures, 243
Sigma Capital Corp., 327
Siguler Guff & Company, LLC, 575
Silicon Valley Bank, 244
Sippl Macdonald Ventures I, L.P., 245
SISIR International Pte Ltd., 932
Sitra (AKA Finnish National Fund for Research and Dev.), 932
Small Industries Development Bank of India (SIDBI), The, 933
Smart Technology Ventures, 246
SMIFS Venture Capital Limited, 933
Societe Regionale d'Investissement de Bruxelles (SRIB/GIMB), 933
Sofinnova Partners, 934
Sofinnova Ventures, 246
SOFTBANK Venture Capital (FKA: SOFTBANK Technology Ventures), 247
Solstice Capital LLC, 449
SoundView Financial Group, Inc., 307
South Atlantic Venture Funds, L.P., 327
Southwest Venture Group, 678
Southwest Venture Partnerships, The, 678
Sovereign Capital (FKA:Nash, Sells & Partners Limited), 936
SpaceVest, 699
Sparkventures, LLC, 449
Spectrum Equity Investors, L.P., 248
Spencer Trask Ventures, Inc. (FKA: Spencer Trask Securities), 576
Spinnaker Ventures, 249
Spire Capital (FKA: Waller Capital Corp.), 577
Sprout Group, 578
SsangYong Cement (Singapore) Ltd, 939
SSM Ventures, 653
Staenberg Private Capital, LLC, 713
Star-Ventures Management GMBH (SVM), 940
STARTech, 679
Starter Fluid, 250
Sterling Grace Capital Management, L.P., 579
Sterling Venture Partners, 398
Still River Fund, The, 450
Stolberg Partners, 580
Stonepath Europe, 941
Sucsy, Fischer & Co., 370
Sun Valley Ventures, 250
SUNeVision Holdings Ltd, 944
Sunsino Development Associate Inc., 944
Sunwestern Investment Group, 680
Sweeney & Co., Inc., 308
Sybase, Inc., 252
Synerfi S.A., 945
Synopsys, Inc., 253
T. Rowe Price Threshold Partnerships, 399
Tailink Venture Partners, 946
Tamir Fishman Ventures, 946
Target Partners, 947
Taylor & Turner, 253
tbg Technologie-Beteiligungsgesellschaft mbH, 947
TDH, 639
Technology Associates Management Corporation, 950
Technology Crossover Ventures, 254
Technology Funding, 254
Technology Partners, 255
Technology Venture Partners Pty Ltd, 950
Technology Ventures, L.L.C., 339
Techxas Ventures, LLC, 681
TecVenture Partners GmbH, 952
Telecom Italia Ventures, 255
Telos Venture Partners, 256
Telsoft Ventures, 953
Texas Growth Fund Management, 681
Thompson Clive & Partners Limited, 955
Thompson Clive, Inc., 257
Thorner Ventures, 258
Throunarfelag Islands Plc(AKA:The Icelandic Finance&Invest.), 955
Tokyo Small & Medium Business Investment & Consultation Co., 956
Toll Technologies, 957
Transamerica Mezzanine Financing, 645
Transamerica Technology Finance, 309
Triad Media Ventures, 309
Trinity Ventures, 260
TriNova, 959
Triune Capital, 260
TTC Ventures, 453
Tvi Investments Bv, 960
U.S. Bancorp Piper Jaffray Ventures, Inc., 472
Union Street Capital Corp., 713
UOB Venture Management Pte Ltd., 964
Updata Venture Partners, 700
UPS Strategic Enterprise Fund, 339
US Trust Private Equity, 584
Utah Ventures II, L.P. (A.K.A. Union Ventures), 687
Value Management & Research AG (VMR), 965
Vanguard Venture Partners, 262
VantagePoint Venture Partners, 263
VCF Partners, 965
Vencon Management, Inc., 585
VenGlobal Capital, 264
Venrock Associates, 586
Ventana Financial Resources, Inc., 372
Ventex Management, Inc., 683
Venture Capital Fund Managers (Pty), Ltd., The , 967
Venture Capital Fund of New England, The, 454
Venture Growth Associates, 265
Venture Investment Management Company LLC (AKA: VIMAC), 454
Venture Investors Management LLC, 720
Venture Management Services Inc. (FKA: AT&T Ventures), 496
Venture Partners AG, 968
Venture Select, 968
Venture Strategy Partners, 266
VentureCap Management GmbH (AKA VCH Equity Group AG), 969
Ventures West Management, Inc., 970

Veritas Venture Capital Management, Ltd., 970
Vertex Management, 971
Victory Ventures L.L.C., 588
Vision Capital Management (FKA Glenwood Capital), 267
Viventures Inc., 973
VK Ventures, 268
Voyager Capital, 714
VTC Partners GmbH, 974
Wachtel & Co., Inc., 317
Wakefield Group, 607
Walden Capital Management Corporation, 589
Walden International Investment Group (AKA: Walden Group), 269
Walden Israel, 975
WaldenVC, 270
Walnut Capital Corp., 701
Warburg, Pincus & Co., LLC. (FKA: E.M. Warburg, Pincus & Co), 590
Wasatch Venture Fund (FKA: Wasatch Venture Corporation), 687
Wasserstein, Perella & Co., Inc., 591
Wedbush Capital Partners, 271
West Midlands Enterprise Ltd, 976
WestBridge Capital Advisors (India) Pvt. Ltd., 976
Westbury Partners, 592
Westford Technology Ventures, L.P., 497
Weston Presidio Capital Management, 455
WestSphere Equity Investors, LP, 592
WI Harper Group, 273
William Blair Capital Partners, 373
William E. Simon & Sons (Asia) LDC, 977
Willis Stein & Partners, 374
Windward Ventures (FKA: Coronado Capital), 274
Winthrop Ventures, 593
Wolf Ventures (AKA:Wolf Asset Management Corp.), 286
WomenAngles.net, 318
Working Ventures Canadian Fund, Inc., 978
Worldview Technology Partners, 275
YankeeTek Ventures, 456
Yasuda Enterprise Development Co., Ltd.(FKA: Nippon Ent.Dev), 275
Yorkshire Fund Managers Ltd., 979
Zone Ventures, 276

Consumer Related

1st Source Capital Corp., 375
21st Century Internet Management Partners,LLC, 138
2nd Generation Capital Corp, 648
550 Digital Media Ventures , 501
Aberdeen Asset Managers, 728
Aberlyn Capital Management Co., Inc., 501
ABN AMRO Private Equity (AKA: ABN AMRO Capital (USA) Inc.) , 343
ABN-AMRO Corporate Investments, 729
ABP Acquisition Corp, 287
Academy Funds (FKA: Longleaf Venture Fund LLC), 597
Accenture Technology Ventures (FKA: AC Ventures), 140
Access Venture Partners, 277
Acer Technology Ventures(FKA:Acer Soft Capital Inc.), 141
ACF Equity Atlantic, Inc, 731
ACT Venture Capital Ltd., 732
Adams Street Partners, LLC (FKA: Brinson Private Equity), 343
Adams, Harkness & Hill, Inc., 401
Adler & Co., 502
Advanced Materials Partners, Inc., 287
Advanta Partners, L.P., 622
Advent International Corp., 402
Advent-Morro Equity Partners, 734
Agio Capital Partners I, L.P., 463
Agribusiness Partners International Partners, 479
Alan I. Goldman & Associates, 483
Albemarle Private Equity Ltd, 735
Alchemy Partners, 736
Alimansky Capital Group, Inc., 504
Allegis Capital (AKA:Allegis Media Technology Ventures), 143
Alliance Venture Capital Advisors Limited, 738
Allied Capital Corporation, 312
Allsop Venture Partners, 380
Allstate Private Equity, 344
Alpha Capital Partners, Inc., 344
Alta Partners, 144
American Acquisition Partners, 483
American Capital Strategies, 391
American Securities, L.P., 505
Amerimark Capital Group, 656
AMP Asset Management Limited - Development Capital, 740
Ampersand Ventures, 404
Amphion Ventures L.P.(FKA: Wolfensohn Associates, L.P.), 506
Annapolis Ventures LLC, 391
Antares Capital Corp. (FKA: Antares Leveraged Capital Corp), 345
Antares Capital Corporation (FKA: Harbor Ventures Corp.), 320
antfactory, 741
Anthem Capital, L.P., 391
Apax Partners & Cie (AKA: Apax France), 742
Apax Partners & Co. Ventures Ltd (AKA: Apax UK), 742
Apax Partners & Co.Beteiligungsberatung AG, 742
Applied Technology, 405
Ardsheil, Inc., 506
Argos Soditic SA, 744
Armada Asset Management, 746
Arthur P. Gould & Co., 507
ASC Group, 746
Ascent Venture Partners, 406
Asian Direct Capital Management, 747
AsiaTech Internet Group (ATIG) (FKA: AsiaTech Ventures), 748
Atlantic Capital, 407
August Capital Management, 148
August Partners, 508
Austin Ventures, L.P., 657
Avery Business Development Services, 320
AVI Capital, L.P., 149
Baccharis Capital, Inc., 150
Baird Capital Partners, 347
Banc One Capital Partners, 608
BancAmerica Capital Investors (FKA:NationsBanc Capital Corp), 598
BancBoston Capital/BancBoston Ventures, 408
Bancorp Hawaii SBIC, Inc., 341
BANEXI Corp., 753
Bangert Dawes Reade Davis & Thom, 151
Bank One Equity Investors, Inc., 386
Bankers Capital Corp., 473
Bankers Trust New York Corp./Deutsche Banc Alex Brown, 510

Banque De Vizille, 754
Baring Private Equity Partners (FKA:Baring Venture Partners), 755
Bastion Capital Corp., 152
Batavia Group, Ltd., The , 511
Batavia Investment Management Ltd, 756
Bausch & Lomb, Inc., 511
Baxter Associates, Inc., 289
BayBG Bayerische Beteiligungsgesellschaft mbH, 757
BCI Partners, 484
BCR Asset Management Pty Ltd., 758
Beacon Partners, Inc., 289
Bedford Capital Corp., 512
Benefit Capital Companies, Inc., The, 480
Berkeley International Capital Corp., 154
Berkshire Partners, 410
Berlin Capital Fund (FKA LBB Beteiligungsgesellschaft GmbH), 759
Berwind Financial Group, L.P., 623
Bessemer Venture Partners, 410
Betwin Investments, Inc., 760
Blue Chip Venture Company, 609
Blue Rock Capital, 319
Blue Water Capital, LLC, 690
BORANCO Management, L.L.C., 277
Boston Capital Ventures, 411
Boston Financial & Equity Corp., 412
Boston Ventures Management, Inc., 413
Botts & Co., 762
Bradford Equities Fund, LLC, 513
Brait Capital Partners, 762
Brand Equity Ventures, 289
Brantley Venture Partners, 609
Bristol Capital Management, 513
Bristol Investment Trust, 413
Broadmark Capital Corp., 702
Bruce F. Glaspell & Associates, 498
Bulldog Partners Limited, 764
Bure Equity, 765
Burr, Egan, Deleage & Co., 414
Business Link Doncaster, 765
Butler Capital Partners France, 765
C3 Holdings, LLC, 474
Calvert Social Venture Partners, L.P., 690
Cambria Group, The, 157
Cambridge Research & Innovation Ltd (AKA CRIL), 767
Camelot Ventures, 457
Canbank Venture Capital Fund Ltd, 767
Candover Investments PLC, 768
Canterbury Capital L.L.C.(AKA: Canterbury Detroit Partners), 514
Capital Development & Investment Co. Ltd., 768
Capital Express, L.L.C., 484
Capital Insights, L.L.C., 645
Capital Investments, Inc., 717
Capital Network, The (AKA: Texas Capital Network), 659
Capital Resource Partners, 415
Capital Services & Resources, Inc., 648
Capital Southwest Corporation, 660
Capital Strategy Management Co., The, 349
Capital Z Asia, 770
Capstone Ventures SBIC, L.P., 158
CapVis Equity Partners AG, 771
Cardinal Ventures, L.L.C., 375
Carillon Capital, Inc., 610
Carousel Capital Partners, 599
Cascade Communications Ventures, LLC, 159
Castle Harlan Australian Mezzanine Partners Pty. Ltd. , 772
Catalyst Group, The , 660
Catterton Partners, 290
CCFL Mezzanine Partners of Canada , 774
Cedar Creek Partners, LLC, 717
CEI Ventures/Coastal Ventures LP, 388
CEO Advisors, 321
Cerulean Fund/WGC Enterprises, 350
CGW Southeast Partners (AKA: Cravey, Green, & Wahlen), 331
Chanen, Painter & Co., Ltd., 703
Charter Ventures, 160
Chartwell Capital Management Co., Inc., 321
Cherry Tree Investments, Inc., 464
Chestnut Street Partners, Inc., 417
China Venture Management, Inc., 777
Chisholm Private Capital Partners, 618
Chrysalis Ventures, 384
Churchill Capital, Inc., 465
CIBC Capital Partners (FKA: CIBC Wood Gundy Capital), 516
CID Equity Partners, 376
Circle Ventures, Inc., 376
CIT Group/Venture Capital, Inc., The, 485
Citadel Pooled Development Ltd. , 779
Citicorp Capital Asia (AKA: CITIC Pacific Ltd.), 780
Citicorp Venture Capital, Ltd., 517
Citizens Capital and Citizens Ventures, 418
Clairvest Group, Inc., 780
Clarion Capital Corp., 610
Clemente Capital (Asia) Ltd., 781
Close Brothers Private Equity, 782
CM Equity Partners, 517
Code, Hennessy & Simmons, LLC., 351
Cohen & Co., L.L.C., 517
Coleman Venture Group, 518
Colonial First State Private Equity Ltd (FKA: Hambro-G Mgmt), 782
Colonnade Capital L.L.C., 691
Colorado Venture Management, 278
Columbia Capital Group, Inc., 313
Comdisco Ventures, 162
Commerz Beteiligungsgesellschaft mbH (CBG), 783
Commonwealth Capital Ventures L.P., 419
Compass Investment Management Ltd., 783
Consumer Venture Partners, 292
Continental S.B.I.C., 691
Continental Venture Capital , 784
Copernicus Capital Management Ltd, 785
Cornerstone Equity Investors, LLC, 519
Coronado Venture Fund, 133
Corpfin Capital S.A., 786
Corporate Growth Assistance, Ltd., 786
Corporate Venture Partners, L.P., 519
Crestview Financial Group, The , 292
Crocker Capital/Crocker Assoc., 164
Crosbie & Co Inc, 789
Crosslink Capital (FKA: Omega Venture Partners), 165
Crown Advisors International, Ltd., 521
Crown Capital Corp, 475
CSK Venture Capital Co., Ltd., 789

Cullinane & Donnelly Venture Partners, L.P., 293
Cureton & Co., Inc., 662
CVC Capital Partners, 790
D.H. Blair Investment Banking Corp., 521
Daewoo Venture Capital Co Ltd, 792
Dakota Group, The , 166
Danish Development Finance Corp., 793
Dauphin Capital Partners, 522
Davis Group, 166
Davis, Tuttle Venture Partners, L.P.(FKA:Davis Venture), 618
De Vries & Co., Inc., 476
Defta Partners, 167
Delta Partners, 795
Desai Capital Management Inc., 522
Deucalion Venture Partners, 168
Development Corp. of Austin, 467
DFW Capital Partners (AKA:DeMuth, Folger & Wetherill), 486
Digital Media Campus, 169
Direct Capital Private Equity, 797
Divine interVentures (FKA: Platinum Venture Partners), 351
DN Partners, 352
Dongbu Venture Capital Co Ltd, 797
Dorset Capital, 170
Dougery Ventures, 171
Dow Chemical Co., 458
Downer & Co., 420
Dresdner Kleinwort Capital , 524
Dresner Capital Resources, Inc., 352
Drysdale Enterprises, 173
DSE Investment Services Limited, 799
Duchossois TECnology Partners, LLC, 353
Dunedin Capital Partners Ltd (FKA:Dunedin Ventures Limited), 799
East River Ventures, L.P., 524
Easton Hunt Capital Partners, 525
eBlast Ventures, LLC, 353
ECI Ventures Ltd, 801
ECICS Ventures Pte Ltd., 801
EDB Investments Pte Ltd., 802
Edelson Technology Partners, 487
Edge Capital Investment Co., LLC, 175
Edison Venture Fund, 488
EGL Holdings, Inc./Nat West Ventures USA, L.P., 332
Electra Fleming Limited, 525
Electra Partners Asia [FKA: JF Electra Limited], 803
Elk Associates Funding Corp., 526
Endeavor Capital Management, 294
Endeavour Capital Pty Ltd, 804
EnerTech Capital Partners, L.P., 626
Enterprise Equity (NI) Limited, 805
Enterprise Investors, 526
Eos Partners, L.P., 527
Equinox Investment Partners, 294
Equitas, L.P., 649
Equity Partners Management Pty Ltd, 807
Equity Ventures, Ltd, 807
Equity-South (FKA:Grubb & Williams Ltd.), 333
Equus Capital Corp., 663
Espirito Santo Development, 808
EURAZEO (FKA Gaz-et-Eaux & AZEO), 809
European Acquisition Capital Ltd., 810
Evanston Business Investment Corp, 354
Evergreen Canada Israel Investments Ltd, 812
Evergreen Capital Partners Inc, 528
Evergreen Ventures, 686
Exeter Capital, L.P., 528
F. Turismo-Capital De Risco SA, 814
Federal Business Development Bank, 815
Fidelity Ventures (FKA: Fidelity Venture Associates), 421
Financial Technology Research Corp., 529
Finansa Capital Limited, 816
FINORPA, 816
FINOVA Mezzanine Capital, Inc. (FKA: Sirrom Capital Corp), 650
First Analysis Venture Capital (FKA:First Analysis Corp), 354
First Atlantic Capital, Ltd., 530
First Charter Partners, Inc., 664
First New England Capital, L.P., 295
First Princeton Capital Corp., 489
First Security Business Investment Corp., 686
First Union Capital Partners, 600
FJC Growth Capital Corp., 129
Flinders Capital Limited, 818
Florida Capital Partners, 322
Florida Capital Ventures, Ltd., 323
Fluke Venture Partners., 705
FLV Fund (AKA Flanders Language Valley Fund), 818
Fonds D'Investissements R.T.V.L., 819
Fonds de Solidarité des Travailleurs du Québec (F.T.Q.), 820
Food Fund Ltd. Partnership, The, 467
Fort Washington Capital Partners, LLC, 611
Fortune International Limited, 821
Founders Equity, Inc., 530
Fountainhead Capital Ltd., 823
Fowler, Anthony & Co., 422
Frederic H. Mayerson Group, The, 612
Fremont Partners, 181
Friends Ivory & Sime Private Equity (Ivory &Sime Baronsmead), 823
Friulia SpA Fin.Reg.Friuli-Venezia, 824
Frontenac Co., 355
Frontline Capital, Inc., 334
Fusient Ventures, 531
GCI, 718
Generation Capital Partners, 532
Genesee Funding, Inc., 532
Genesis Capital, Inc., 533
Geneva Merchant Banking Partners, 601
Gideon Hixon Fund, 467
Glencoe Capital, LLC (FKA: Glencoe Investment Corporation), 356
Global Retail Partners (A.K.A. GRP), 185
Glynn Ventures, 186
Go Equity GmbH, 829
Goldner Hawn Johnson & Morrison Incorporated, 468
Golub Associates, 534
Granite Ventures LLC (FKA: H & Q Venture Associates), 186
Granville Baird Capital Partners (FKA:Granville Pr Eq Mngrs), 830
Graystone Venture Partners, LLC(AKA:Portage Venture Partners, 356
Greater Philadelphia Venture Capital Corp., 627
Gresham Rabo Management Limited, 832
Grieve, Horner, Brown & Asculai, 833

Grotech Capital Group, 394
Grove Street Advisors, LLC, 425
Growth Venture Group Pty Ltd., 833
GrowthWorks Capital, 834
GTCR Golder Rauner, LLC, 356
Gujarat Venture Finance Limited, 834
H&Q Asia Pacific, Ltd., 187
Halder Holdings B.V., 835
Halpern, Denny & Co., 425
Hambro European Ventures (Hambros PLC), 835
Hamilton Robinson & Co., Inc., 296
Hanbyuck Investment Co Ltd, 836
HarbourVest Partners, LLC., 426
Harvest Partners, Inc., 536
Health Capital Group, 188
Heartland Capital Partners, L.P., 665
Herbert Young Securities, Inc., 536
Heritage Partners, 427
HFS Capital (AKA: Hoffman, Fitzgerald & Snyder), 694
Hibernia Capital Partners, 837
High Street Capital, LLC, 357
HillStreet Capital, Inc., 612
Hoebich Venture Management, Inc., 190
Horizon Ventures (F.K.A. Technology Investments), 190
Hotung International Company, Ltd., 840
Howard, Lawson & Co., 628
HSBC Private Equity (Asia), Ltd. (FKA: HSBC PE Management), 841
HT Capital Advisors, LLC, 538
Hudson Venture Partners, 538
Hungarian-American Enterprise Fund, The (HAEF), 842
Hunt Capital Group, 667
IBJS Capital Corp., 539
IBK Capital Corporation, 844
ICC Venture Capital, 845
ICICI Venture Funds Mngt. Co. Ltd., 846
Idanta Partners, Ltd., 191
IFCI Venture Cap. Funds (Formerly Risk Capital & Tech.), 847
IL&FS Venture Corporation (FKA. CreditCapital Venture Fund), 848
Impex Venture Management Co., 540
Incorporated Investors, 193
IndAsia Fund Advisors Private Limited, 849
Indian Direct Equity Advisors Pvt. Ltd, 850
Indocean Chase Capital Advisors, 850
Industry Ventures , 428
Information Technology Ventures, 195
Innova Capital (FKA: Poland Partners Management Company), 853
InnovationsKapital Management Goteborg AB , 854
Innovest Group, Inc., 629
Innvotec Ltd, 854
Integrated Consortium, Inc., 197
InterEquity Capital Partners, L.P., 541
InvestAmerica Venture Group, Inc., 380
Investissement Desjardins, 857
Investissements Novacap (AKA:Novacap Investments, Inc.), 858
IPE Capital-Soc.De Cap.De Risoc SA, 859
IPS Industrial Promotion Services, Ltd., 859
Ireka Venture Capital Limited, 860
ISEP NV, 860
Itochu Technology, 542
J.L. Albright Venture Partners, 861
J.P. Morgan Capital Corp., 542
J.P. Morgan Partners (FKA: Chase Capital Partners), 543
JAFCO Investment (FKA:Nomura/JAFCO Investment (Asia) Limited, 862
James A. Matzdorff & Co., 199
Jefferson Capital Fund, Ltd., 130
Josephberg Grosz & Co., Inc., 545
Kahala Investments, Inc., 668
Kaiser Permanente (AKA: National Venture Development), 200
Kankaku Investment Co Ltd, 865
Kansas City Equity Partners, 477
Kansas Venture Capital, Inc., 383
KB Partners, LLC, 359
Kettle Partners, L.P., 359
Key Equity Capital Corp.(AKA:Key Community Development Corp), 613
Keystone Minority Capital Fund, L.P., 630
Kingsbury Associates, 200
Kitty Hawk Capital, 602
KLB Investment Co., Ltd., 866
Kookmin Venture Capital Co Ltd, 867
Korea Development Investment Corp., 868
Korea Technology Finance Corp., 869
KPMG Advent Management Group (FKA:Advent Western Pacific), 870
Kyoritsu Capital Company, Ltd., 870
Lake Shore Capital Partners, Inc., 360
Lambda Funds, The, 546
Las Americas Administradora, 871
LaSalle Capital Group, Inc., 360
Lawrence Financial Group, 202
Legal & General Ventures Ltd, 872
Leonard Green & Partners, 203
Lepercq Capital Management, Inc.(AKA:Lepercq,de Neuflize In), 548
Levine Leichtman Capital Partners, Inc., 204
LF International, Inc., 204
Liberty Environmental Partners, 205
Lincoln Investment Management Inc., 378
LLR Equity Partners, 631
LM Capital Corp., 324
Lombard Investments, Inc., 206
London Ventures (Fund Managers) Ltd., 875
LTI Ventures Leasing Corp., 298
Lubar & Co., 718
Madison Dearborn Partners, LLC, 361
Madison Investment Partners, Inc., 550
Management Resource Partners, 208
Manchester Humphreys, Inc., 642
Manhattan Venture Co., Inc., 550
MarketCorp Ventures L.P., 299
Marlborough Capital Advisors, 431
Marleau, Lemire, Inc., 878
Marquette Venture Partners, 362
Maryland Venture Capital Trust, 395
Matrix Capital, 695
MAVA Investment Management kft (AKA: Hungarian-American Ent), 879
Mayfair Capital Partners, Inc., 551
MBA Venture Group, 669
MC Capital Asia Private Limited, 880

McCown De Leeuw & Co., 210
McGuire Capital Corp., 670
McKee & Co., 134
MDT Advisers, Inc., 433
Media Venture Partners, 211
MediaVenture Capital AG & Co. KGaA, 882
MedTech International, Inc., 670
Mellon Ventures (AKA: Mellon Bank), 632
Mentor Capital Partners, 633
Meridian Venture Partners (MVP), 633
Merita Capital Limited, 134
Merrill Lynch Investment Managers FKA Mercury Asset Mgmt, 884
Mezzanine Management UK Limited, 885
Mid-Atlantic Venture Funds (FKA: NEPA Management Corp.), 634
Middlefield Capital Fund, 885
Midlands Venture Fund Managers Ltd. (AKA: Midven Ltd), 886
Miller Capital Corp, 135
Miller/Zell Venture Group, 335
Miralta Capital, Inc., 887
Mitiska NV, 887
Mitsui & Co., Ltd., 553
MMG Ventures, L.P., 396
Montgomery Associates, Inc., 215
Moore & Associates, 619
Morgan Grenfell Private Equity Limited, 889
Mountaineer Capital LP, 716
Mutual Fund Public Company Ltd., 891
Nanyang Ventures Pty Ltd (AKA: Nanyang Management Pty Ltd), 892
Nassau Capital, L.L.C., 492
National City Equity Partners, Inc, 614
National Corporate Finance, Inc., 217
National Financial Cos. LLC, 556
National Investment Management, Inc., 217
Navis Partners (FKA:Fleet Equity Partners), 643
Nazem & Co., 556
NCP Advisors Philippines, Inc., 894
Nelson Capital Corp., 651
Nesbitt Burns, 363
New Business Capital Fund Ltd., 499
New Venture Resources, 282
New World Infrastructure Limited, 896
New York State Science & Technology Foundation, 558
Newbridge Capital Limited, 219
Newbury, Piret & Co., Inc., 437
Newtek Ventures, 220
NIF Ventures USA, Inc.(Nippon Investment & Finance Co., Ltd), 222
Nikko Capital Co Ltd, 899
Nomura/JAFCO Investment (HK) Limited, 901
North America Investment Corp., 902
North Atlantic Capital Corp., 389
North Hill Ventures, 438
North Texas MESBIC, Inc., 672
NorthEast Ventures, 301
Northern Venture Managers Limited, 902
Northwest Ohio Venture Fund, 615
Northwest Venture Associates, Inc.(FKA:Spokane Capital Mgmt), 709
Northwood Ventures, 559
Noveltek Venture Corp., 560
NPM Capital (AKA Nederlandse Participatie MIJ NV), 903
Nth Power Technologies, Inc, 224
NTUC Club Investments Pte Ltd (NCI), 904
Nu Capital Access Group, Ltd., 224
Oak Hill Capital Management, Inc., 561
Oak Investment Partners, 302
Onondaga Venture Capital Fund, Inc., 562
Opportunity Capital Partners {FKA: Thompson Capital Mgt), 225
Oregon Resource and Technology Development Fund, 620
Oresa Ventures, S.A., 906
Orion Partners, L.P., 439
Oxford Bioscience Partners, 440
Oxford Financial Services Corp., 698
PA Early Stage (AKA:Pennsylvania Early Stage Partners), 635
Pacific Corporate Group, Inc., 227
Pacific Northwest Partners SBIC, L.P., 710
Palmer Partners, L.P., 441
Paradigm Capital Partners LLC, 651
Parcom Ventures BV, 909
Paribas Principal, Inc., 563
Partners Group, 910
Pathfinder Investment Co Pvt Ltd, 910
Patricof & Co. Ventures, Inc., 563
Pauli & Co., Inc., 477
Penfund Partners, Inc., 911
Peninsula Capital Partners, L.L.C, 460
PENMAN Partners (FKA PENMAN Asset Management LP), 365
Penn-Janney Fund, Inc., The, 635
Pennsylvania Growth Fund, 636
Penny Lane Partners, 493
Penta Capital Partners Ltd, 911
Perennial Ventures (FKA: Tredegar Investments), 711
Pfingsten Partners, L.P., 366
Phillips-Smith Specialty Retail Group, 673
Phoenix Equity Partners (FKA: DLJ European Private Equity), 911
Phoenix Growth Capital Corp., 231
Pierce Financial Corporation(FKA:Pierce Investment Banking), 698
Pittsford Group, Inc., The , 565
Platinum Group, Inc., The , 565
Point Venture Partners, 636
Pomona Capital, 566
PPM Ventures Ltd (FKA: Prudential Venture Managers Ltd), 914
pre-IPO Aktiengesellschaft, 915
Prescient Capital, 232
Prime Capital Management Co., Inc., 304
PrimePartners Asset Management Pte. Ltd., 916
Prism Capital, 367
Private Capital Corp., 131
Priveq Capital Funds, 917
Productivity Fund I & II, The, 367
Prospect Partners LLC (FKA:Kenter, Glatris & Tuttle, LLC, 368
Prospect Street Ventures (FKA:Prospect Street Invest. Mgmt), 567
Provco Group, The , 637
ProVen Private Equity (FKA:Guinness Mahon Development Cap.), 918
Quantum Capital Partners, 325
Quest Ventures, 233
Quester Capital Management Ltd, 920
QuestMark Partners, L.P., 397
R-H Capital Partners, 337

RAF Ventures, 637
Ralph Wilson Equity Fund, L.L.C., 460
Rand Capital Corporation, 568
Recovery Equity Investors, L.P., 234
Red River Ventures, 675
Redwood Capital Corp., 235
Regent Capital Management, 569
Reiten & Co Strategic Investments AS, 921
Renaissance Capital Corp., 337
Reprise Capital Corp., 569
RFE Investment Partners, 305
Richard Jaffe & Co., Inc., 676
Richland Ventures, 652
Ridge Capital Partners, L.L.C., 368
Riordan, Lewis & Haden, 236
River Associates, LLC, 653
River Capital, 338
Roanoke Capital, Ltd., 712
Robertson Stephens & Company, LLC, 236
Rocky Mountain Capital Partners (FKA:Hanifen Imhoff Capital), 283
Rosecliff, 237
Rosenfeld & Co., 620
Roser Ventures LLC, 283
Rosewood Capital, L.P., 237
Rothschild Ventures Asia Pte Ltd., 922
Rothschild Ventures, Inc., 570
Royal Bank Private Equity (FKA: Royal Bank Development Cap), 922
Royalty Capital Fund, L.P. I/Royalty Capital Management, Inc, 443
RRE Ventures LLC, 571
Rutledge & Co., Inc., 305
Sandhurst Venture Fund, L.P., The , 639
Sandler Capital Management, 571
Sanpaolo IMI Private Equity S.p.A., 925
Saugatuck Capital Company, 306
SBC Equity Partners, Inc., 369
SBC Ventures, 499
SBCA/A.G. Bartholomew & Associates, 131
Schooner Capital International, L.P., 444
Schroder Capital Partners (Asia) Pte Ltd, 926
Scripps Ventures, 572
Seacoast Capital, 446
Seed Capital Investments, 928
Sentinel Capital Partners, 573
Sequoia Capital, 241
Shad Run Investments, Inc., 242
Shalor Ventures, Inc., 446
Shannon Development Company, 929
Shansby Group/TSG2, L.P., The , 242
Shared Ventures, Inc., 470
Shattan Group, The, 574
Shaw Venture Partners (FKA: Shaw Glasgow Partners), 621
Shelton Companies, Inc., The , 604
Shepherd Group LLC, The, 447
Sherbrooke Capital Partners, 448
Sienna Ventures (FKA: Sienna Holdings Inc.), 242
Sierra Ventures, 243
Sigma Capital Corp., 327
Siguler Guff & Company, LLC, 575
SISIR International Pte Ltd., 932
SMIFS Venture Capital Limited, 933
Societe Regionale d'Investissement de Bruxelles (SRIB/GIMB), 933
Solstice Capital LLC, 449
Sorrento Associates, Inc., 247
South Atlantic Venture Funds, L.P., 327
Southport Partners, 307
Southwest Venture Group, 678
Sovereign Capital (FKA:Nash, Sells & Partners Limited), 936
SPEF Banques Populaires, 937
Spencer Trask Ventures, Inc. (FKA: Spencer Trask Securities), 576
Sponsored Consulting Services, 249
Sports Capital Partners, 577
Spring Capital Partners, L.P., 398
Sprout Group, 578
SRK Management Co., 578
SsangYong Cement (Singapore) Ltd, 939
Stamford Financial, 579
Start-up Australia Pty Limited, 940
State Street Bank & Trust Co., 338
Stephens Group, Inc., 137
Sterling Grace Capital Management, L.P., 579
Sterling Venture Partners, 398
Sterling/Carl Marks Capital {FKA - Sterling Commercial, 580
Still River Fund, The, 450
Stolberg Partners, 580
Stonebridge Partners, 580
Strategic Capital Management, 941
Strategic Investments & Holdings, Inc., 581
Stratford Equity Partners, L.P., 679
Sucsy, Fischer & Co., 370
Suez Asia Holdings Pte Ltd., 943
Summit Capital Associates, Inc., 581
Summit Partners, 451
Sun Hung Kai Properties Limited, 943
Sun Valley Ventures, 250
Swander Pace Capital, 252
Sweeney & Co., Inc., 308
Sycamore Ventures, 494
Synerfi S.A., 945
T. Rowe Price Threshold Partnerships, 399
TA Associates, Inc., 451
Tailink Venture Partners, 946
Tappan Zee Capital Corp., 495
Taylor & Turner, 253
tbg Technologie-Beteiligungsgesellschaft mbH, 947
TCR Europe SA, 947
TDH, 639
Teak Investment Partners I Limited, 948
Techno-Venture Co. (Japan), 949
TechnoCap Inc, 949
Technology Funding, 254
Texas Growth Fund Management, 681
TG Asia Ventures Limited, 954
Thoma Cressey Equity Partners, 371
Thompson Clive, Inc., 257
Three Cities Research, Inc., 583
Throunarfelag Islands Plc(AKA:The Icelandic Finance&Invest.), 955
Ticonderoga Capital, Inc. (FKA: Dillon Read Venture Capital), 452

Tokyo Small & Medium Business Investment & Consultation Co., 956
Transcap Associates, Inc., 371
Triad Media Ventures, 309
Tribune Ventures, 372
Triune Capital, 260
TSG Capital Group, L.L.C., 309
TTC Ventures, 453
Tvi Investments Bv, 960
TVS Finance Ltd., 961
UBS Capital (AKA Phildrew Ventures), 963
Ulin & Holland, Inc., 453
Ulster Development Capital, Ltd., 963
Union Street Capital Corp., 713
Unit Trust of India (UTI), 964
UOB Venture Management Pte Ltd., 964
US Trust Private Equity, 584
Valley Capital Corp., 654
Vanguard Venture Partners, 262
VantagePoint Venture Partners, 263
Vega Capital Corp., 584
Vencap Equities Alberta, Ltd., 966
Venrock Associates, 586
Ventana Financial Resources, Inc., 372
Ventana Global, 264
Ventex Management, Inc., 683
Venture Associates, Ltd., 285
Venture Capital Fund Managers (Pty), Ltd., The , 967
Venture Capital Management Corp., 328
Venture Funding Group International, 587
Venture Funding, Ltd., 461
Venture Growth Associates, 265
Venture Investment Management Company LLC (AKA: VIMAC), 454
Venture Investors Management LLC, 720
Venture Management Services Inc. (FKA: AT&T Ventures), 496
Venture Opportunities Corp., 588
Venture Strategy Partners, 266
Ventures West Management, Inc., 970
Vero Group PLC, 684
Vertex Management, 971
Victory Ventures L.L.C., 588
Virginia Capital , 701
Vista Capital de Expansion S.A., 972
VK Ventures, 268
Wachovia, 340
Wachtel & Co., Inc., 317
Walden Capital Management Corporation, 589
Walden International Investment Group (AKA: Walden Group), 269
Walden Israel, 975
WaldenVC, 270
Walnut Capital Corp., 701
Wand Partners, 589
Warburg, Pincus & Co., LLC. (FKA: E.M. Warburg, Pincus & Co), 590
Wasserstein, Perella & Co., Inc., 591
Wedbush Capital Partners, 271
Wellmax, Inc., 461
West Central Capital Corp., 684
West Midlands Enterprise Ltd, 976
Westar Capital, 271
Westbury Partners, 592
Weston Presidio Capital Management, 455
WestSphere Equity Investors, LP, 592
White Pines Management, L.L.C., 462
Whitney & Co. (FKA: J.H. Whitney & Co.), 310
William A.M. Burden & Co., 593
William Blair Capital Partners, 373
William E. Simon & Sons (Asia) LDC, 977
Willis Stein & Partners, 374
Wind Point Partners, 462
Windjammer Capital Investors (FKA:Pacific Mezzanine Inv.), 273
Windward Holdings, 311
Wingate Partners, L.P., 685
Winslow Partners LLC, 317
Winthrop Ventures, 593
Wit Capital Corporation, 594
WomenAngles.net, 318
Wooshin Development Finance Corp, 978
Working Ventures Canadian Fund, Inc., 978
Worms Capital Management, 594
Yablon Enterprises, Inc., 641
Yorkshire Fund Managers Ltd., 979
Zero Stage Capital Co., Inc., 456
Zone Ventures, 276
ZS Fund, L.P., 595

Financial Services

2nd Generation Capital Corp, 648
Aberdeen Asset Managers, 728
ABN-AMRO Corporate Investments, 729
ABP Acquisition Corp, 287
Accenture Technology Ventures (FKA: AC Ventures), 140
ACT Venture Capital Ltd., 732
Adams Street Partners, LLC (FKA: Brinson Private Equity), 343
AdCapital AG (FKA Berliner Elektro Holding AG), 732
Advanta Partners, L.P., 622
Advent International Corp., 402
Advent-Morro Equity Partners, 734
Agio Capital Partners I, L.P., 463
Alan I. Goldman & Associates, 483
Albemarle Private Equity Ltd, 735
Alimansky Capital Group, Inc., 504
Allsop Venture Partners, 380
Allstate Private Equity, 344
Alpha Capital Partners, Inc., 344
American Century Ventures, 473
Amerimark Capital Group, 656
Annapolis Ventures LLC, 391
Antares Capital Corp. (FKA: Antares Leveraged Capital Corp), 345
AO Capital Corp, 287
Apax Partners & Co. Ventures Ltd (AKA: Apax UK), 742
Apax Partners & Co.Beteiligungsberatung AG, 742
Ardsheil, Inc., 506
Argos Soditic SA, 744
Arthur P. Gould & Co., 507
ASC Group, 746
AsiaTech Internet Group (ATIG) (FKA: AsiaTech Ventures), 748
Atlantic Capital, 407
August Partners, 508
AxaVision, Inc., 509

B2B-Hive, LLC, 509
Bachow & Associates, Inc., 623
Banc One Capital Partners, 608
BancBoston Capital/BancBoston Ventures, 408
BanChem Financial Services, Inc., 658
Bank Funds, The, 347
Bankers Trust New York Corp./Deutsche Banc Alex Brown, 510
Banque De Vizille, 754
Baring Private Equity Partners (FKA:Baring Venture Partners), 755
Bastion Capital Corp., 152
Batavia Investment Management Ltd, 756
BCR Asset Management Pty Ltd., 758
Bedford Capital Corp., 512
Benefit Capital Companies, Inc., The, 480
Berkshire Partners, 410
Berwind Financial Group, L.P., 623
Betwin Investments, Inc., 760
Boston Capital Ventures, 411
Boston Financial & Equity Corp., 412
Botts & Co., 762
Brantley Venture Partners, 609
Bristol Investment Trust, 413
Brook Venture Management, L.L.C., 414
Bruce F. Glaspell & Associates, 498
Butler Capital Partners France, 765
Camelot Ventures, 457
Canaan Partners, 290
Candover Investments PLC, 768
Capital Network, The (AKA: Texas Capital Network), 659
Capital Partners LLC, 769
Capital Resource Partners, 415
Capital Z Asia, 770
Cardinal Ventures, L.L.C., 375
Carillon Capital, Inc., 610
Carousel Capital Partners, 599
Castle Harlan Australian Mezzanine Partners Pty. Ltd. , 772
CEI Ventures/Coastal Ventures LP, 388
Cerulean Fund/WGC Enterprises, 350
Chanen, Painter & Co., Ltd., 703
Chartwell Capital Management Co., Inc., 321
Cherry Tree Investments, Inc., 464
Chisholm Private Capital Partners, 618
Chrysalis Ventures, 384
CIBC Capital Partners (FKA: CIBC Wood Gundy Capital), 516
CID Equity Partners, 376
Citadel Pooled Development Ltd. , 779
Citicorp Capital Asia (AKA: CITIC Pacific Ltd.), 780
Conning Capital Partners, 292
Continental S.B.I.C., 691
Continental Venture Capital , 784
Cornerstone Equity Investors, LLC, 519
Covent Industrial Capital Investment Co Ltd, 787
Crestview Financial Group, The , 292
Crown Capital Corp, 475
CS Capital Partners, LLC, 486
CSK Venture Capital Co., Ltd., 789
Cullinane & Donnelly Venture Partners, L.P., 293
Cureton & Co., Inc., 662
CyberStarts, 332
D.H. Blair Investment Banking Corp., 521
Davis Group, 166
Desai Capital Management Inc., 522
Deucalion Venture Partners, 168
Deutsche Bank eVentures (AKA DB eVentures), 795
Developers Equity Corp., 169
DN Partners, 352
Draper International, 172
Dresner Capital Resources, Inc., 352
Drysdale Enterprises, 173
DSE Investment Services Limited, 799
Early Stage Enterprises, L.P., 487
eBlast Ventures, LLC, 353
ECICS Ventures Pte Ltd., 801
EDB Investments Pte Ltd., 802
EDF Ventures (F.K.A. Enterprise Development Fund), 458
Edge Capital Investment Co., LLC, 175
Edison Venture Fund, 488
Electra Fleming Limited, 525
Electra Partners Asia [FKA: JF Electra Limited], 803
Enterprise Investors, 526
Eos Partners, L.P., 527
Equinox Investment Partners, 294
Equity Partners Management Pty Ltd, 807
ETF Group, 808
European Acquisition Capital Ltd., 810
European Equity Partners , 810
Evergreen Capital Partners Inc, 528
Evergreen Ventures, 686
Fidelity Ventures (FKA: Fidelity Venture Associates), 421
Financial Technology Research Corp., 529
Financial Technology Ventures, 179
Finansa Capital Limited, 816
FINOVA Mezzanine Capital, Inc. (FKA: Sirrom Capital Corp), 650
Firemark Advisors, Inc., 488
First Charter Partners, Inc., 664
First Princeton Capital Corp., 489
First Union Capital Partners, 600
Flinders Capital Limited, 818
Fonds de Solidarité des Travailleurs du Québec (F.T.Q.), 820
Foundation Capital Limited, 822
Founders Equity, Inc., 530
Fowler, Anthony & Co., 422
Frederic H. Mayerson Group, The, 612
Fremont Partners, 181
Friends Ivory & Sime Private Equity (Ivory &Sime Baronsmead), 823
Frontenac Co., 355
Frontline Capital, Inc., 334
GATX/MM Venture Partners, 183
Genesis Capital, Inc., 533
Gideon Hixon Fund, 467
Gimvindus NV, 828
Glencoe Capital, LLC (FKA: Glencoe Investment Corporation), 356
Global Partner Ventures, 694
Grotech Capital Group, 394
Hamilton Robinson & Co., Inc., 296
Hanbyuck Investment Co Ltd, 836
Hanover Capital Corp., 535
HarbourVest Partners, LLC., 426
Harvest Partners, Inc., 536
Health Capital Group, 188
Hellman & Friedman, 189

Herbert Young Securities, Inc., 536
HillStreet Capital, Inc., 612
Hodgson Martin, Ltd., 839
Horizon Ventures (F.K.A. Technology Investments), 190
Housatonic Partners, 190
HSBC Private Equity (Asia), Ltd. (FKA: HSBC PE Management), 841
HT Capital Advisors, LLC, 538
Hunt Ventures, LP, 667
Impex Venture Management Co., 540
IndAsia Fund Advisors Private Limited, 849
Indocean Chase Capital Advisors, 850
Innovest Group, Inc., 629
Insurance Venture Partners, Inc., 297
IPE Capital-Soc.De Cap.De Risoc SA, 859
Irwin Ventures LLC (FKA: Irwin Ventures Incorporated), 377
J.P. Morgan Capital Corp., 542
J.P. Morgan Partners (FKA: Chase Capital Partners), 543
James A. Matzdorff & Co., 199
Kankaku Investment Co Ltd, 865
Kemper Ventures, 491
Korea Technology Finance Corp., 869
Lake Shore Capital Partners, Inc., 360
Lambda Funds, The, 546
Las Americas Administradora, 871
Lawrence Financial Group, 202
Legal & General Ventures Ltd, 872
Levine Leichtman Capital Partners, Inc., 204
LJH Global Investments , 324
LM Capital Corp., 324
LN Mittal, 874
Lombard Investments, Inc., 206
Lubar & Co., 718
M31 Ventures, LLC, 550
Madison Dearborn Partners, LLC, 361
Madison Investment Partners, Inc., 550
Manhattan Venture Co., Inc., 550
Maristeth Ventures, L.L.C., 707
Matrix Private Equity, 879
McCown De Leeuw & Co., 210
McKee & Co., 134
MDT Advisers, Inc., 433
MedTech International, Inc., 670
Mellon Ventures (AKA: Mellon Bank), 632
Memhard Investment Bankers, Inc., 300
Mentor Capital Partners, 633
Merita Capital Limited, 134
Meyer, Duffy & Associates, 553
Middlefield Capital Fund, 885
Miller Capital Corp, 135
Montgomery Associates, Inc., 215
Moore & Associates, 619
Morgan Grenfell Private Equity Limited, 889
Morgenthaler Ventures, 614
MVC AG (AKA Mitteldeutsche Venture Capital AG), 891
MWV Capital Partners (FKA:Middlewest Ventures, L.P.), 378
Nassau Capital, L.L.C., 492
National Australia Investment Capital Limited, 892
National City Equity Partners, Inc, 614
National Corporate Finance, Inc., 217
National Financial Cos. LLC, 556
Nelson Capital Corp., 651
New World Infrastructure Limited, 896
Newbridge Capital Limited, 219
Newbury, Piret & Co., Inc., 437
Nippon Technology Venture Partners Ltd., 899
North America Investment Corp., 902
North Hill Ventures, 438
Northington Partners, 301
Northwest Ohio Venture Fund, 615
Northwood Ventures, 559
NPM Capital (AKA Nederlandse Participatie MIJ NV), 903
Oak Hill Capital Management, Inc., 561
Obelisk Capital Pty Ltd, 904
Odin Capital Group, 479
Oresa Ventures, S.A., 906
Orion Partners, L.P., 439
PA Early Stage (AKA:Pennsylvania Early Stage Partners), 635
Pacific Corporate Group, Inc., 227
Palmer Partners, L.P., 441
Palomar Ventures, 228
Pathfinder Investment Co Pvt Ltd, 910
Patricof & Co. Ventures, Inc., 563
Penfund Partners, Inc., 911
Peninsula Capital Partners, L.L.C, 460
Pennsylvania Growth Fund, 636
Phoenix Equity Partners (FKA: DLJ European Private Equity), 911
Pierce Financial Corporation(FKA:Pierce Investment Banking), 698
Point Venture Partners, 636
Pomona Capital, 566
Prime Capital Management Co., Inc., 304
Private Capital Corp., 131
Provco Group, The , 637
Putnam Lovell Capital Partners, L.P., 232
Quantum Capital Partners, 325
Quest Ventures, 233
Quester Capital Management Ltd, 920
R-H Capital Partners, 337
Recovery Equity Investors, L.P., 234
Red River Ventures, 675
Reiten & Co Strategic Investments AS, 921
Renaissance Capital Corp., 337
Reprise Capital Corp., 569
RFE Investment Partners, 305
Richard Jaffe & Co., Inc., 676
Richland Ventures, 652
Ridge Capital Partners, L.L.C., 368
Roanoke Capital, Ltd., 712
Rock Creek Partners, L.P., 326
Rosenfeld & Co., 620
Royal Bank Private Equity (FKA: Royal Bank Development Cap), 922
RRE Ventures LLC, 571
Russel Miller Advisors Asia, LLC, 238
Saugatuck Capital Company, 306
SBC Ventures, 499
SBCA/A.G. Bartholomew & Associates, 131
Schooner Capital International, L.P., 444
Sentinel Capital Partners, 573
Shad Run Investments, Inc., 242
Shattan Group, The, 574
Shaw Venture Partners (FKA: Shaw Glasgow Partners), 621
Shawmut Capital Partners, 447

Shelton Companies, Inc., The , 604
Sierra Ventures, 243
Sigma Capital Corp., 327
Siguler Guff & Company, LLC, 575
Societe Regionale d'Investissement de Bruxelles (SRIB/GIMB), 933
South Atlantic Venture Funds, L.P., 327
Southwest Venture Group, 678
Sovereign Capital (FKA:Nash, Sells & Partners Limited), 936
Spencer Trask Ventures, Inc. (FKA: Spencer Trask Securities), 576
Sponsored Consulting Services, 249
Stamford Financial, 579
Sterling Grace Capital Management, L.P., 579
Stolberg Partners, 580
Strategic Capital Management, 941
Strathdon Investments Ltd, 942
Sucsy, Fischer & Co., 370
Summit Group Ltd, The, 943
Summit Partners, 451
Sun Hung Kai Properties Limited, 943
Sun Valley Ventures, 250
Sweeney & Co., Inc., 308
TA Associates, Inc., 451
TDH, 639
Teak Investment Partners I Limited, 948
Techno-Venture Co. (Japan), 949
Thoma Cressey Equity Partners, 371
Thorner Ventures, 258
Throunarfelag Islands Plc(AKA:The Icelandic Finance&Invest.), 955
Ticonderoga Capital, Inc. (FKA: Dillon Read Venture Capital), 452
Tokyo Small & Medium Business Investment & Consultation Co., 956
Trident Capital, 259
TSG Capital Group, L.L.C., 309
TTC Ventures, 453
UNC Ventures, 453
UPS Strategic Enterprise Fund, 339
VantagePoint Venture Partners, 263
Vega Capital Corp., 584
Venture Associates, Ltd., 285
Venture Capital Fund Managers (Pty), Ltd., The , 967
Venture Capital Management Corp., 328
Venture Funding Group International, 587
Venture Growth Associates, 265
Venture Investment Management Company LLC (AKA: VIMAC), 454
Venture Investors Management LLC, 720
Venture Strategy Partners, 266
Virginia Capital , 701
Wachovia, 340
Wachtel & Co., Inc., 317
Walnut Capital Corp., 701
Wand Partners, 589
Warburg, Pincus & Co., LLC. (FKA: E.M. Warburg, Pincus & Co), 590
West Central Capital Corp., 684
West Midlands Enterprise Ltd, 976
Westar Capital, 271
Westbury Partners, 592
Weston Presidio Capital Management, 455
WestSphere Equity Investors, LP, 592
Whitney & Co. (FKA: J.H. Whitney & Co.), 310
William A.M. Burden & Co., 593
William E. Simon & Sons (Asia) LDC, 977
Willis Stein & Partners, 374
Winslow Partners LLC, 317
Winthrop Ventures, 593
WomenAngles.net, 318
Working Ventures Canadian Fund, Inc., 978
Worms Capital Management, 594
Yablon Enterprises, Inc., 641
Zone Ventures, 276

Industrial/Energy

1st Source Capital Corp., 375
21st Century Internet Management Partners,LLC, 138
2nd Generation Capital Corp, 648
3i Finland Oy (FKA SFK Finance), 725
Aberdeen Asset Managers, 728
ABN AMRO Private Equity (AKA: ABN AMRO Capital (USA) Inc.) , 343
ABN-AMRO Corporate Investments, 729
ABP Acquisition Corp, 287
Academy Funds (FKA: Longleaf Venture Fund LLC), 597
Accenture Technology Ventures (FKA: AC Ventures), 140
ACF Equity Atlantic, Inc, 731
ACT Venture Capital Ltd., 732
Adams Capital Management, Inc., 622
Adams Street Partners, LLC (FKA: Brinson Private Equity), 343
Adams, Harkness & Hill, Inc., 401
Adler & Co., 502
Advanced Materials Partners, Inc., 287
Advantage Capital Partners, 386
Advent International Corp., 402
Advent Venture Partners (FKA Advent Limited), 733
Agio Capital Partners I, L.P., 463
Alan I. Goldman & Associates, 483
Albemarle Private Equity Ltd, 735
Alchemy Partners, 736
Alimansky Capital Group, Inc., 504
All Asia Partners, 737
Allied Capital Corporation, 312
Allsop Venture Partners, 380
Allstate Private Equity, 344
Alpha Capital Partners, Inc., 344
Alpine Technology Ventures, 144
Alta Partners, 144
American Acquisition Partners, 483
American Capital Strategies, 391
American Securities, L.P., 505
Amerimark Capital Group, 656
AMP Asset Management Limited - Development Capital, 740
Ampersand Ventures, 404
Amphion Ventures L.P.(FKA: Wolfensohn Associates, L.P.), 506
AMT Capital Ltd. (AKA: AMT Venture Partners, Ltd.), 656
AMWIN Management Pty Ltd, 741
Antares Capital Corp. (FKA: Antares Leveraged Capital Corp), 345
Antares Capital Corporation (FKA: Harbor Ventures Corp.), 320
Anthem Capital, L.P., 391
AO Capital Corp, 287
APIDC-Venture Capital Limited, 743

Applied Technology, 405
Ardsheil, Inc., 506
Arete Corporation, 482
Argentum Group, The , 507
Argos Soditic SA, 744
Artesian Capital, 464
Arthur P. Gould & Co., 507
ASC Group, 746
Ascent Venture Partners, 406
Asian Infrastructure Fund Advisers Limited, 748
Asset Management Company Venture Capital, 147
Atlantic Capital, 407
Australian Technology Group Ltd, 750
Avery Business Development Services, 320
AVI Capital, L.P., 149
Baccharis Capital, Inc., 150
Bachow & Associates, Inc., 623
Bailey & Co. Inc., 752
Baird Capital Partners, 347
Banc One Capital Partners, 608
BancAmerica Capital Investors (FKA:NationsBanc Capital Corp), 598
BancBoston Capital/BancBoston Ventures, 408
BanChem Financial Services, Inc., 658
Bancorp Hawaii SBIC, Inc., 341
BANEXI Corp., 753
Bangert Dawes Reade Davis & Thom, 151
Bank One Equity Investors, Inc., 386
Bankers Capital Corp., 473
Bankers Trust New York Corp./Deutsche Banc Alex Brown, 510
Banque De Vizille, 754
Baring Private Equity Partners (FKA:Baring Venture Partners), 755
Bastion Capital Corp., 152
Batavia Group, Ltd., The , 511
Batavia Investment Management Ltd, 756
Battelle Venture Partners (Scientific Advances), 608
Baxter Associates, Inc., 289
Bayern Kapital Risikokapitalbeteiligungs GmbH, 757
BCR Asset Management Pty Ltd., 758
Beacon Partners, Inc., 289
Bedford Capital Corp., 512
Benefit Capital Companies, Inc., The, 480
Berkeley International Capital Corp., 154
Berkshire Partners, 410
Berlin Capital Fund (FKA LBB Beteiligungsgesellschaft GmbH), 759
Berwind Financial Group, L.P., 623
Betwin Investments, Inc., 760
BOME Investors, Inc., 473
Boston Financial & Equity Corp., 412
Botts & Co., 762
Boulder Ventures, Ltd., 392
Bradford Equities Fund, LLC, 513
Brantley Venture Partners, 609
Bristol Capital Management, 513
Broadmark Capital Corp., 702
Brook Venture Management, L.L.C., 414
Bruce F. Glaspell & Associates, 498
Bulldog Partners Limited, 764
Burr, Egan, Deleage & Co., 414
Burrill & Company, 156
Business Link Doncaster, 765
C3 Holdings, LLC, 474
Caltech Capital Partners Ltd., 766
Calvert Social Venture Partners, L.P., 690
Cambria Group, The, 157
Cambridge Research & Innovation Ltd (AKA CRIL), 767
Cambridge Technology Capital, 415
Canaan Partners, 290
Canbank Venture Capital Fund Ltd, 767
Candover Investments PLC, 768
Canterbury Capital L.L.C.(AKA: Canterbury Detroit Partners), 514
Capital Development & Investment Co. Ltd., 768
Capital For Business, Inc., 474
Capital Investments, Inc., 717
Capital Network, The (AKA: Texas Capital Network), 659
Capital Resource Partners, 415
Capital Services & Resources, Inc., 648
Capital Southwest Corporation, 660
Capital Strategy Management Co., The, 349
CapVis Equity Partners AG, 771
Cardinal Ventures, L.L.C., 375
Cariad Capital, Inc., 642
Carillon Capital, Inc., 610
Castle Harlan Australian Mezzanine Partners Pty. Ltd. , 772
Catalyst Group, The , 660
CCFL Mezzanine Partners of Canada , 774
CDC Services Industries Gestion (CDC IXIS Private Equity), 775
CE Unterberg Towbin (FKA:Unterberg Harris Capital Partners), 515
Cedar Creek Partners, LLC, 717
CEI Ventures/Coastal Ventures LP, 388
CEO Advisors, 321
CEO Venture Fund, 625
Cerulean Fund/WGC Enterprises, 350
CGW Southeast Partners (AKA: Cravey, Green, & Wahlen), 331
Chanen, Painter & Co., Ltd., 703
Chartwell Capital Management Co., Inc., 321
Chase H&Q (FKA Hambrecht & Quist), 160
Chestnut Street Partners, Inc., 417
Chiao Tung Bank, 776
China Venture Management, Inc., 777
Chisholm Private Capital Partners, 618
Churchill Capital, Inc., 465
CIBC Capital Partners (FKA: CIBC Wood Gundy Capital), 516
CID Equity Partners, 376
Circle Ventures, Inc., 376
CIT Group/Venture Capital, Inc., The, 485
Citicorp Capital Asia (AKA: CITIC Pacific Ltd.), 780
Citicorp Venture Capital, Ltd., 517
Citizens Capital and Citizens Ventures, 418
Claflin Capital Management, Inc., 418
Clairvest Group, Inc., 780
Clarion Capital Corp., 610
Close Brothers Private Equity, 782
CM Equity Partners, 517
Code, Hennessy & Simmons, LLC., 351
Cohen & Co., L.L.C., 517
Coleman Venture Group, 518
Colonnade Capital L.L.C., 691
Colorado Venture Management, 278
Columbia Capital Group, Inc., 313
Columbine Venture Funds, The , 279
Commerz Beteiligungsgesellschaft mbH (CBG), 783

Commonwealth Capital Ventures L.P., 419
Compass Investment Management Ltd., 783
Compass Technology Partners, 163
Concord Venture Management (FKA:Nitzanim), 784
Connecticut Innovations, Inc., 291
Continental S.B.I.C., 691
Continental Venture Capital , 784
Core Capital Partners, 313
Core Pacific Consulting Company, 786
Cornerstone Equity Investors, LLC, 519
Coronado Venture Fund, 133
Corpfin Capital S.A., 786
Corporate Growth Assistance, Ltd., 786
Corporate Venture Partners, L.P., 519
Crescent Capital NI Ltd (FKA Hambro Northern Ireland), 788
Crestview Financial Group, The , 292
Crocker Capital/Crocker Assoc., 164
Crosbie & Co Inc, 789
Crown Advisors International, Ltd., 521
Crown Capital Corp, 475
CS Capital Partners, LLC, 486
CSK Venture Capital Co., Ltd., 789
Cureton & Co., Inc., 662
CVC Capital Partners, 790
CW Group, Inc., 521
Cygnus Venture Partners, 791
D.H. Blair Investment Banking Corp., 521
Daewoo Venture Capital Co Ltd, 792
Daimler Chrysler Venture Gmbh (AKA DCV), 792
Danish Development Finance Corp., 793
Davis Group, 166
Davis, Tuttle Venture Partners, L.P.(FKA:Davis Venture), 618
De Vries & Co., Inc., 476
Defta Partners, 167
Delta Partners, 795
Desai Capital Management Inc., 522
Deucalion Venture Partners, 168
Deutsche Asset Management (Australia) Limited, 795
Deutsche Venture Capital GmbH (DVCG), 796
Developers Equity Corp., 169
Development Corp. of Austin, 467
DFW Capital Partners (AKA:DeMuth, Folger & Wetherill), 486
Divine interVentures (FKA: Platinum Venture Partners), 351
DN Partners, 352
Dongbu Venture Capital Co Ltd, 797
Dougery Ventures, 171
Dow Chemical Co., 458
Downer & Co., 420
Draper Fisher Jurvetson (FKA: Draper Associates), 172
Draper Triangle Ventures LP, 626
Dresdner Kleinwort Capital , 524
Dresner Capital Resources, Inc., 352
Drysdale Enterprises, 173
DSE Investment Services Limited, 799
Dunedin Capital Partners Ltd (FKA:Dunedin Ventures Limited), 799
Early Stage Enterprises, L.P., 487
eBlast Ventures, LLC, 353
ECI Ventures Ltd, 801
EDB Investments Pte Ltd., 802
Edelson Technology Partners, 487
EDF Ventures (F.K.A. Enterprise Development Fund), 458
Edge Capital Investment Co., LLC, 175
Edison Venture Fund, 488
EGL Holdings, Inc./Nat West Ventures USA, L.P., 332
Electra Fleming Limited, 525
Electra Partners Asia [FKA: JF Electra Limited], 803
EnerTech Capital Partners, L.P., 626
Enterprise Equity (NI) Limited, 805
Enterprise Investors, 526
Enterprise Partners, 178
Eos Partners, L.P., 527
Epicea, 805
Equinox Investment Partners, 294
Equitas, L.P., 649
Equity Partners Management Pty Ltd, 807
Equity Ventures, Ltd, 807
Equity-South (FKA:Grubb & Williams Ltd.), 333
Equus Capital Corp., 663
Eqvitec Partners Oy, 807
Espirito Santo Development, 808
EURAZEO (FKA Gaz-et-Eaux & AZEO), 809
Euroc Venture Capital Corporation, 809
European Acquisition Capital Ltd., 810
Euroventures Management AB , 811
Evanston Business Investment Corp, 354
Evergreen Capital Partners Inc, 528
Evergreen Ventures, 686
Exeter Capital, L.P., 528
Expanso Capital, 813
Federal Business Development Bank, 815
Fidelity Ventures (FKA: Fidelity Venture Associates), 421
FINADVANCE S.A., 815
Financial Capital Resources, Inc., 333
Financial Technology Research Corp., 529
Finansa Capital Limited, 816
FINORPA, 816
FINOVA Mezzanine Capital, Inc. (FKA: Sirrom Capital Corp), 650
Finovelec, 817
First Analysis Venture Capital (FKA:First Analysis Corp), 354
First Atlantic Capital, Ltd., 530
First Charter Partners, Inc., 664
First Princeton Capital Corp., 489
First Security Business Investment Corp., 686
First Union Capital Partners, 600
Florida Capital Partners, 322
Florida Capital Ventures, Ltd., 323
Fluke Venture Partners., 705
Fonds D'Investissements R.T.V.L., 819
Fonds de Solidarité des Travailleurs du Québec (F.T.Q.), 820
Fort Washington Capital Partners, LLC, 611
FORTKNOX-VENTURE AG, 821
Foundation Capital, 181
Foundation Capital Limited, 822
Founders Equity, Inc., 530
Fowler, Anthony & Co., 422
Fremont Partners, 181
Friends Ivory & Sime Private Equity (Ivory &Sime Baronsmead), 823
Friulia SpA Fin.Reg.Friuli-Venezia, 824
Frontenac Co., 355
Frontier Capital, LLC, 600
Frontline Capital, Inc., 334

GATX Ventures (FKA: Meier Mitchell & Co.), 183
GATX/MM Venture Partners, 183
GCI, 718
Generation Capital Partners, 532
GENES GmbH Venture Services, 826
Genesee Funding, Inc., 532
Genesis Capital, Inc., 533
Geneva Merchant Banking Partners, 601
Gimvindus NV, 828
Glencoe Capital, LLC (FKA: Glencoe Investment Corporation), 356
Global Partner Ventures, 694
Goldner Hawn Johnson & Morrison Incorporated, 468
Golub Associates, 534
Granite Ventures LLC (FKA: H & Q Venture Associates), 186
Granville Baird Capital Partners (FKA:Granville Pr Eq Mngrs), 830
Graystone Venture Partners, LLC(AKA:Portage Venture Partners, 356
Greenwich Venture Partners, Inc., 296
Grotech Capital Group, 394
Grove Street Advisors, LLC, 425
Growth Venture Group Pty Ltd., 833
GrowthWorks Capital, 834
Gryphon Ventures, 425
Gujarat Venture Finance Limited, 834
H&Q Asia Pacific, Ltd., 187
Halder Holdings B.V., 835
Halpern, Denny & Co., 425
Hambro America Biosciences, Inc., 535
Hambro European Ventures (Hambros PLC), 835
Hamilton Robinson & Co., Inc., 296
Hanbyuck Investment Co Ltd, 836
Hanover Capital Corp., 535
Harbour Financial Co., 426
HarbourVest Partners, LLC., 426
Harvest Partners, Inc., 536
Health Capital Group, 188
Heartland Capital Partners, L.P., 665
Herbert Young Securities, Inc., 536
Heritage Partners, 427
Hibernia Capital Partners, 837
Hickory Venture Capital Corporation, 130
High Street Capital, LLC, 357
HillStreet Capital, Inc., 612
HMS Hawaii Management Partners, 341
Horizon Ventures (F.K.A. Technology Investments), 190
Horizonte Venture Management GmbH, 840
Hotung International Company, Ltd., 840
Howard, Lawson & Co., 628
HSBC Private Equity (Asia), Ltd. (FKA: HSBC PE Management), 841
HSBC Private Equity Ltd (FKA Montagu Private Equity Ltd), 841
HT Capital Advisors, LLC, 538
Hungarian-American Enterprise Fund, The (HAEF), 842
Hunt Ventures, LP, 667
Hydro-Quebec CapiTech Inc., 843
IBB Beteiligungsgesellschaft mbH, 844
IBJS Capital Corp., 539
IBK Capital Corporation, 844
ICC Venture Capital, 845
IEG Venture Management, Inc., 357
IFCI Venture Cap. Funds (Formerly Risk Capital & Tech.), 847
Impex Venture Management Co., 540
Incorporated Investors, 193
Indekon Management Oy, 849
Indosuez Ventures, 194
Indus Venture Management Ltd., 851
Information Technology Ventures, 195
InnoCal, L.P., 196
Innovation Works, Inc., 628
Innovationsagentur Gesmbh, 854
InnovationsKapital Management Goteborg AB , 854
Innovest Group, Inc., 629
Innvotec Ltd, 854
Integrated Consortium, Inc., 197
InterEquity Capital Partners, L.P., 541
InvestAmerica Venture Group, Inc., 380
Investissement Desjardins, 857
Investissements Novacap (AKA:Novacap Investments, Inc.), 858
IPS Industrial Promotion Services, Ltd., 859
ISEP NV, 860
Itochu Technology, 542
J.E. Mann & Co., 542
J.P. Morgan Capital Corp., 542
J.P. Morgan Partners (FKA: Chase Capital Partners), 543
James A. Matzdorff & Co., 199
Jefferson Capital Fund, Ltd., 130
Jerusalem Global Ventures, 864
Josephberg Grosz & Co., Inc., 545
Kahala Investments, Inc., 668
Kaiser Permanente (AKA: National Venture Development), 200
Kankaku Investment Co Ltd, 865
Kansas City Equity Partners, 477
Kansas Technology Enterprise Corporation, 382
Kansas Venture Capital, Inc., 383
KB Partners, LLC, 359
Kemper Ventures, 491
Key Equity Capital Corp.(AKA:Key Community Development Corp), 613
Keystone Minority Capital Fund, L.P., 630
Kitty Hawk Capital, 602
KLB Investment Co., Ltd., 866
Kookmin Venture Capital Co Ltd, 867
Korea Development Investment Corp., 868
Korea Technology Finance Corp., 869
Lake Shore Capital Partners, Inc., 360
Lambda Funds, The, 546
Las Americas Administradora, 871
LaSalle Capital Group, Inc., 360
Lawrence Financial Group, 202
Legal & General Ventures Ltd, 872
Leonard Green & Partners, 203
LeVenture Kapitalbeteiligungsgesellschaft mbH & Co.KG, 872
Levine Leichtman Capital Partners, Inc., 204
Liberty BIDCO Investment Corporation, 459
Liberty Environmental Partners, 205
Lighthouse Capital Partners, 205
LINC Capital Partners, Inc., 361
Lincoln Investment Management Inc., 378
Lincolnshire Management Inc., 548
LM Capital Corp., 324
Loeb Partners Corp., 549
Lombard Investments, Inc., 206

London Ventures (Fund Managers) Ltd., 875
LTI Ventures Leasing Corp., 298
Lubar & Co., 718
Madison Dearborn Partners, LLC, 361
Madison Investment Partners, Inc., 550
Malmohus Invest AB, 877
Management Resource Partners, 208
Manchester Humphreys, Inc., 642
Manhattan Venture Co., Inc., 550
Maristeth Ventures, L.L.C., 707
Marlborough Capital Advisors, 431
Marleau, Lemire, Inc., 878
Maryland Venture Capital Trust, 395
Massachusetts Technology Development Corp. (MTDC), 432
Matrix Capital, 695
Matrix Group, 209
Matrix Private Equity, 879
MAVA Investment Management kft (AKA: Hungarian-American Ent), 879
Mayfair Capital Partners, Inc., 551
Mayfield Fund, 210
MBA Venture Group, 669
McCown De Leeuw & Co., 210
McKee & Co., 134
MDT Advisers, Inc., 433
MedTech International, Inc., 670
Mellon Ventures (AKA: Mellon Bank), 632
Memhard Investment Bankers, Inc., 300
Mentor Capital Partners, 633
Meridian Venture Partners (MVP), 633
Merita Capital Limited, 134
Merrill Lynch Investment Managers FKA Mercury Asset Mgmt, 884
Merrill, Pickard, Anderson & Eyre, 213
MESBIC Ventures Holding Co. (AKA Pacesetter Growth Fund, L.P, 671
Metapoint Partners, 435
Mezzanine Management UK Limited, 885
Microtechnology Investments, Ltd., 213
Mid-Atlantic Venture Funds (FKA: NEPA Management Corp.), 634
Middlefield Capital Fund, 885
Midlands Venture Fund Managers Ltd. (AKA: Midven Ltd), 886
Miralta Capital, Inc., 887
Mohr, Davidow Ventures, 214
Montgomerie, Huck & Co., 888
Montgomery Associates, Inc., 215
Moore & Associates, 619
Morgan Grenfell Private Equity Limited, 889
Mountaineer Capital LP, 716
MST Partners, 555
MTI Partners Ltd, 890
MWV Capital Partners (FKA:Middlewest Ventures, L.P.), 378
Nassau Capital, L.L.C., 492
National Australia Investment Capital Limited, 892
National Bank Of Kuwait, 555
National City Equity Partners, Inc, 614
National Corporate Finance, Inc., 217
National Financial Cos. LLC, 556
National Investment Management, Inc., 217
Natural Gas Partners, 300
Navis Partners (FKA:Fleet Equity Partners), 643
Nazem & Co., 556
Needham & Company, Inc., 556
Nelson Capital Corp., 651
Nesbitt Burns, 363
New Business Capital Fund Ltd., 499
New Venture Resources, 282
New York State Science & Technology Foundation, 558
Newbury, Piret & Co., Inc., 437
NewSpring Ventures, 634
Newtek Ventures, 220
NextGen Partners LLC, 221
NIB Capital Private Equity N.V. (FKA: Parnib Holding NV) , 898
NIF Ventures USA, Inc.(Nippon Investment & Finance Co., Ltd), 222
Nikko Capital Co Ltd, 899
Nmas1 Electra Capital Privado , S.G.E.C.R., S.A., 900
Nomura/JAFCO Investment (HK) Limited, 901
North Atlantic Capital Corp., 389
North Carolina Technological Development Authority, Inc., 603
NorthEast Ventures, 301
Northern Venture Managers Limited, 902
Northwest Ohio Venture Fund, 615
Northwest Venture Associates, Inc.(FKA:Spokane Capital Mgmt), 709
Northwood Ventures, 559
Novartis AG, 903
Noveltek Venture Corp., 560
NPM Capital (AKA Nederlandse Participatie MIJ NV), 903
NTC Group, The , 301
Nth Power Technologies, Inc, 224
Nu Capital Access Group, Ltd., 224
Oak Hill Capital Management, Inc., 561
Obelisk Capital Pty Ltd, 904
Onondaga Venture Capital Fund, Inc., 562
Open Prairie Ventures, 365
Opportunity Capital Partners {FKA: Thompson Capital Mgt), 225
Oregon Resource and Technology Development Fund, 620
Orion Partners, L.P., 439
Oxford Financial Services Corp., 698
Pac-Link Management Corporation, 906
Pacific Capital Partners, 907
Pacific Corporate Group, Inc., 227
Pacific Venture Partners, 907
Palmer Partners, L.P., 441
Paradigm Capital Partners LLC, 651
Parcom Ventures BV, 909
Paribas Principal, Inc., 563
Partners Group, 910
Pathfinder Investment Co Pvt Ltd, 910
Pathfinder Venture Capital Funds, 470
Patricof & Co. Ventures, Inc., 563
Pauli & Co., Inc., 477
Penfund Partners, Inc., 911
Peninsula Capital Partners, L.L.C, 460
PENMAN Partners (FKA PENMAN Asset Management LP), 365
Penn-Janney Fund, Inc., The, 635
Pennsylvania Growth Fund, 636
Penny Lane Partners, 493
Perennial Ventures (FKA: Tredegar Investments), 711
Pfingsten Partners, L.P., 366
Philadelphia Ventures, Inc., 636
Phoenix Equity Partners (FKA: DLJ European Private Equity), 911

Phoenix Partners, The , 711
Pierce Financial Corporation(FKA:Pierce Investment Banking), 698
Pittsford Group, Inc., The , 565
Platinum Group, Inc., The , 565
PME Capital, 912
Point Venture Partners, 636
Polaris Venture Partners, 441
Poly Ventures, 566
PolyTechnos Venture Partners GmbH, 913
Pomona Capital, 566
PPM Ventures Ltd (FKA: Prudential Venture Managers Ltd), 914
Prelude Technology Investments Ltd, 915
Prime Capital Management Co., Inc., 304
Prism Capital, 367
Private Capital Corp., 131
Priveq Capital Funds, 917
Productivity Fund I & II, The, 367
Prospect Partners LLC (FKA:Kenter, Glatris & Tuttle, LLC, 368
Proximitas AG Venture Capital, 918
Quantum Capital Partners, 325
Quest Ventures, 233
Quester Capital Management Ltd, 920
R-H Capital Partners, 337
R. Chaney & Co., Inc., 674
RAF Ventures, 637
Ralph Wilson Equity Fund, L.L.C., 460
Rand Capital Corporation, 568
RCT BioVentures NE (Research Corporation Technologies), 442
Red River Ventures, 675
Regulus International Capital Co., Inc., 304
Reiten & Co Strategic Investments AS, 921
Renaissance Capital Corp., 337
Reprise Capital Corp., 569
RFE Investment Partners, 305
Richard Jaffe & Co., Inc., 676
Ridge Capital Partners, L.L.C., 368
Riordan, Lewis & Haden, 236
River Associates, LLC, 653
River Capital, 338
Roanoke Capital, Ltd., 712
Rocky Mountain Capital Partners (FKA:Hanifen Imhoff Capital), 283
Rosecliff, 237
Rosenfeld & Co., 620
Roser Ventures LLC, 283
Rothschild Bioscience Unit, 922
Rothschild Ventures, Inc., 570
Royal Bank Private Equity (FKA: Royal Bank Development Cap), 922
Royalty Capital Fund, L.P. I/Royalty Capital Management, Inc, 443
RRE Ventures LLC, 571
Rutledge & Co., Inc., 305
Saarlandische Wagnisfinanzierungsgesellschaft mbh (AKA SWG), 924
Sage Management Group, 444
Sandhurst Venture Fund, L.P., The , 639
Sanpaolo IMI Private Equity S.p.A., 925
Saugatuck Capital Company, 306
SBC Equity Partners, Inc., 369
SBC Ventures, 499
SBCA/A.G. Bartholomew & Associates, 131
Schneider Electric Ventures, 926
Schooner Capital International, L.P., 444
Schroder Ventures, 445
Seacoast Capital, 446
Seaflower Ventures, 446
SEB Foretagsinvest, 927
Seed Capital Investments, 928
Seed Capital Ltd, 928
Sequoia Capital, 241
SGI Capital L.L.C, 573
Shansby Group/TSG2, L.P., The , 242
Shared Ventures, Inc., 470
Shattan Group, The, 574
Shaw Venture Partners (FKA: Shaw Glasgow Partners), 621
Shelton Companies, Inc., The , 604
Shepherd Group LLC, The, 447
Siemens Venture Capital GmbH, 930
Sienna Ventures (FKA: Sienna Holdings Inc.), 242
Sigma Capital Corp., 327
Siguler Guff & Company, LLC, 575
Silicon Valley Bank, 244
SISIR International Pte Ltd., 932
Sitra (AKA Finnish National Fund for Research and Dev.), 932
Societe Regionale d'Investissement de Bruxelles (SRIB/GIMB), 933
Sofinov (AKA:Caisse de depot et placement du Quebec), 934
Solstice Capital LLC, 449
Sopartec SA, 936
Sorrento Associates, Inc., 247
Southport Partners, 307
Southwest Venture Group, 678
Southwest Venture Partnerships, The, 678
Sovereign Capital (FKA:Nash, Sells & Partners Limited), 936
SPEF Banques Populaires, 937
Spencer Trask Ventures, Inc. (FKA: Spencer Trask Securities), 576
Sponsored Consulting Services, 249
Spring Capital Partners, L.P., 398
SRK Management Co., 578
Stamford Financial, 579
State Street Bank & Trust Co., 338
Stephens Group, Inc., 137
Sterling Grace Capital Management, L.P., 579
Sterling/Carl Marks Capital {FKA - Sterling Commercial, 580
Stolberg Partners, 580
Stonebridge Partners, 580
Strategic Capital Management, 941
Strategic Investments & Holdings, Inc., 581
Stratford Equity Partners, L.P., 679
Strathdon Investments Ltd, 942
Sucsy, Fischer & Co., 370
SudKB & SudVC, 942
Suez Asia Holdings Pte Ltd., 943
Summit Capital Associates, Inc., 581
Summit Group Ltd, The, 943
Summit Partners, 451
Sun Valley Ventures, 250
Sunsino Development Associate Inc., 944
Sutter Hill Ventures, 251
Swedish Industrial Development Fund (AKA Industrifonden), 945
Sweeney & Co., Inc., 308
Sycamore Ventures, 494

Synerfi S.A., 945
T. Rowe Price Threshold Partnerships, 399
TA Associates, Inc., 451
Tailink Venture Partners, 946
Taiwan United Venture Management Corporation, 946
Tappan Zee Capital Corp., 495
tbg Technologie-Beteiligungsgesellschaft mbH, 947
TCR Europe SA, 947
TDH, 639
Teak Investment Partners I Limited, 948
Techno-Venture Co. (Japan), 949
Technologieholding VC GmbH, 950
Technology Associates Management Corporation, 950
Technology Funding, 254
Technostart GmbH, 951
TecVenture Partners GmbH, 952
Texas Growth Fund Management, 681
Third Millennium Venture Capital, Ltd., 256
Thompson Clive & Partners Limited, 955
Thompson Clive, Inc., 257
Three Cities Research, Inc., 583
Throunarfelag Islands Plc(AKA:The Icelandic Finance&Invest.), 955
Tianguis Ltd, 956
Ticonderoga Capital, Inc. (FKA: Dillon Read Venture Capital), 452
Tokyo Small & Medium Business Investment & Consultation Co., 956
Top Taiwan Venture Capital Company, Ltd., 957
Top Technology Limited (AKA:Hambros-Advanced Technology Tru), 957
Transamerica Mezzanine Financing, 645
Transamerica Technology Finance, 309
Transatlantic Capital Ltd., 958
Transcap Associates, Inc., 371
Triune Capital, 260
TSG Capital Group, L.L.C., 309
TTP Venture Managers (FKA: The Technology Partnership), 960
Tvi Investments Bv, 960
UBS Capital (AKA Phildrew Ventures), 963
Ulster Development Capital, Ltd., 963
UNC Ventures, 453
Union Street Capital Corp., 713
UPS Strategic Enterprise Fund, 339
Valley Capital Corp., 654
Valley Ventures (FKA: Arizona Growth Partners, L.P.), 136
VantagePoint Venture Partners, 263
VCF Partners, 965
Vega Capital Corp., 584
Vencap Equities Alberta, Ltd., 966
Venrock Associates, 586
Ventana Financial Resources, Inc., 372
Ventana Global, 264
Ventex Management, Inc., 683
Venture Associates Partners, LLC, 654
Venture Associates, Ltd., 285
Venture Capital Fund of New England, The, 454
Venture Capital Management Corp., 328
Venture Funding Group International, 587
Venture Growth Associates, 265
Venture Investment Management Company LLC (AKA: VIMAC), 454
Venture Investors Management LLC, 720
Venture Opportunities Corp., 588
Venture Strategy Partners, 266
VentureCap Management GmbH (AKA VCH Equity Group AG), 969
Ventures West Management, Inc., 970
Vero Group PLC, 684
Vertex Management, 971
Vista Capital de Expansion S.A., 972
VK Ventures, 268
Wachovia, 340
Wachtel & Co., Inc., 317
Walden International Investment Group (AKA: Walden Group), 269
Walden Israel, 975
WaldenVC, 270
Walnut Capital Corp., 701
Wand Partners, 589
Warburg, Pincus & Co., LLC. (FKA: E.M. Warburg, Pincus & Co), 590
Wellmax, Inc., 461
West Central Capital Corp., 684
West Midlands Enterprise Ltd, 976
Westar Capital, 271
Westbury Partners, 592
Western States Investment Group, 272
Westford Technology Ventures, L.P., 497
Weston Presidio Capital Management, 455
WestSphere Equity Investors, LP, 592
White Pines Management, L.L.C., 462
William A.M. Burden & Co., 593
William E. Simon & Sons (Asia) LDC, 977
Willis Stein & Partners, 374
Wind Point Partners, 462
Windjammer Capital Investors (FKA:Pacific Mezzanine Inv.), 273
Windward Holdings, 311
Wingate Partners, L.P., 685
Winslow Partners LLC, 317
Winthrop Ventures, 593
Wooshin Development Finance Corp, 978
Working Ventures Canadian Fund, Inc., 978
Worldview Technology Partners, 275
Worms Capital Management, 594
Yorkshire Fund Managers Ltd., 979
Zero Stage Capital Co., Inc., 456
Zone Ventures, 276
ZS Fund, L.P., 595

Internet Specific

100 X, 401
21st Century Internet Management Partners,LLC, 138
2M Invest, Inc., 138
3i Finland Oy (FKA SFK Finance), 725
3i Group plc, 726
3K Digital, 727
3TS Venture Partners AG, 727
Aberdare Ventures, 138
ABN-AMRO Corporate Investments, 729
ABS Ventures, 390
Academy Funds (FKA: Longleaf Venture Fund LLC), 597
Accel Partners, 139
Accelerator Media (UK), Ltd, 730

Accenture Technology Ventures (FKA: AC Ventures), 140
Access Venture Partners, 277
Access2Net, 731
ACE Management, 731
Acer Technology Ventures(FKA:Acer Soft Capital Inc.), 141
ACF Equity Atlantic, Inc, 731
Adams Capital Management, Inc., 622
AdCapital AG (FKA Berliner Elektro Holding AG), 732
Adler & Shaykin, 502
Advanced Technology Ventures, 401
Advanta Partners, L.P., 622
Advantage Capital Partners, 386
Advent-Morro Equity Partners, 734
Akin Gump Investment Partners 2000, LP, 655
Alcatel Ventures, 142
Alexander Hutton, Inc., 702
Alice Ventures, 736
Allegis Capital (AKA:Allegis Media Technology Ventures), 143
Allegra Partners (FKA: Lawrence, Smith & Horey), 504
Allen & Buckeridge Pty Ltd, 737
Alpha Capital Partners, Inc., 344
Amadeus Capital Partners, 740
American Research & Development Corp., 404
Amerimark Capital Group, 656
AMWIN Management Pty Ltd, 741
Angel Investors, LP, 145
Angel-Invest, 741
Anila Fund (AKA: Anila.org, LLC), 145
Annapolis Ventures LLC, 391
Antares Capital Corp. (FKA: Antares Leveraged Capital Corp), 345
Antares Capital Corporation (FKA: Harbor Ventures Corp.), 320
antfactory, 741
Apax Partners & Cie (AKA: Apax France), 742
Apax Partners & Co. Ventures Ltd (AKA: Apax UK), 742
Apex Ventures BV, 743
Apollo Invest , 744
Applied Technology, 405
Arbor Partners LLC, 457
ARCH Venture Partners, 346
Argentum Group, The , 507
Argo Global Capital, Inc., 406
Artemis Ventures, 146
Artisan Digital Media, 147
Arts Alliance, 746
AS Venture GmbH, 746
Ascent Venture Partners, 406
AsiaTech Internet Group (ATIG) (FKA: AsiaTech Ventures), 748
Aspen Ventures (formerly 3i Ventures), 147
Aspiro Ventures, 748
Atlas Venture, 407
August Capital Management, 148
August Partners, 508
Auric Asset Management Pte. Ltd., 750
Aurora Funds, Inc., 598
Austin Ventures, L.P., 657
Aweida Ventures, 277
AxaVision, Inc., 509
Axiom Venture Partners, L.P., 288
Axiomlab PLC, 751
b-business partners, 752
bainlab, 752
BancAmerica Capital Investors (FKA:NationsBanc Capital Corp), 598
BancBoston Capital/BancBoston Ventures, 408
BANEXI Corp., 753
Bank One Equity Investors, Inc., 386
BankInvest Group AS, 754
Barnard & Company, 511
Batavia Investment Management Ltd, 756
Battery Ventures, L.P., 409
Bay Partners, 153
BCE Capital, 758
BCI Partners, 484
BCR Asset Management Pty Ltd., 758
Bedford Capital Corp., 512
Behrman Capital, 512
Benchmark Capital, 154
Berkeley International Capital Corp., 154
Bessemer Venture Partners, 410
Big Bang Ventures, 760
Birchmere Ventures, Inc.(FKA:Birchmere Investments), 624
Blue Chip Venture Company, 609
Blue Ribbon AG, 760
Blue Water Capital, LLC, 690
Blueprint Ventures, LLC, 155
Blueshift Internet Ventures, 761
BlueStar Ventures, 348
Blumberg Capital Ventures, 155
bmp Aktiengesellschaft AG, 761
BOME Investors, Inc., 473
Boston Capital Ventures, 411
Boston University Community Technology Fund , 413
Botticelli Venture Funds (AKA: Botticelli Investments), 761
Botts & Co., 762
Boulder Ventures, Ltd., 392
Brad Peery Capital, 156
BrainHeart Capital AB, 762
Brand Equity Ventures, 289
Brightstar, 763
Brook Venture Management, L.L.C., 414
Bruce F. Glaspell & Associates, 498
Buena Venture Associates, 659
Bure Equity, 765
Burr, Egan, Deleage & Co., 414
BV Capital (FKA Bertelsmann Ventures LP), 157
C3 Holdings, LLC, 474
C3 Investments, Inc., 157
Caltech Capital Partners Ltd., 766
Cambrian Ventures, 158
Cambridge Research & Innovation Ltd (AKA CRIL), 767
Cambridge Technology Capital, 415
Camelot Ventures, 457
Canaan Partners, 290
Capital Development & Investment Co. Ltd., 768
Capital Express, L.L.C., 484
Capital Investments, Inc., 717
Capital Investors, 690
Capital Riesgo Internet SCR SA (BSCH), 770
Capital Technology Group, LLC, 610
Capman Management GmbH, 770
Capstone Ventures SBIC, L.P., 158
Carillon Capital, Inc., 610
Carlin Ventures LLC, 514

Carmel Ventures, 772
Castile Ventures, 416
Castle Harlan Australian Mezzanine Partners Pty. Ltd. , 772
Catalyst Fund Management & Research Ltd, 773
Catella IT AB, 773
Cazenove Private Equity, 773
CD Technicom S.A., 774
CDC Innovation Partners, 775
CE Unterberg Towbin (FKA:Unterberg Harris Capital Partners), 515
CEI Ventures/Coastal Ventures LP, 388
Celtic House International, 775
Centennial Ventures, 278
CEO Advisors, 321
CEO Venture Fund, 625
Chanen, Painter & Co., Ltd., 703
Charles River Ventures, 417
Chartwell Capital Management Co., Inc., 321
Cherry Tree Investments, Inc., 464
Chestnut Street Partners, Inc., 417
China Venture Management, Inc., 777
Chisholm Private Capital Partners, 618
Chrysalead, 778
Chrysalis Capital, 778
Chrysalis Ventures, 384
CIBC Capital Partners (FKA: CIBC Wood Gundy Capital), 516
CID Equity Partners, 376
Circle Ventures, Inc., 376
cirlab!, 779
Citadel Pooled Development Ltd. , 779
Citizens Capital and Citizens Ventures, 418
CIVC Partners (FKA:Continental Illinois Venture Corp.), 350
Claflin Capital Management, Inc., 418
Classic Fund Management, Ltd., 781
Clearstone Venture Partners (FKA: idealab! Capital Partners), 161
CMB Capital, LLC (CMBC), 322
CMEA Ventures (FKA:Chemicals & Materials Enterprise Associa), 161
Colorado Venture Management, 278
Commerce One Ventures, 162
Commonwealth Capital Ventures L.P., 419
CommTech International, 163
ComVentures (AKA: Communications Ventures), 163
Concord Venture Management (FKA:Nitzanim), 784
Connecticut Innovations, Inc., 291
Conning Capital Partners, 292
Consumer Venture Partners, 292
Continental S.B.I.C., 691
Continuum Group Limited, 785
Convergence Partners L.P., 164
Copernicus Capital Management Ltd, 785
CORAL Ventures, 465
Cordova Ventures (FKA:Cordova Capital), 331
Core Capital Partners, 313
Corning Capital (AKA: Corning Technology Ventures), 420
CR&T Ventures AB, 787
Crest Communications Holdings LLC, 520
Crestview Financial Group, The , 292
Cross Atlantic Capital Partners, 625
CrossBow Ventures, 322
Crystal Internet Venture Fund, L.P., 611
CSK Venture Capital Co., Ltd., 789
CT Holdings, 661
Cureton & Co., Inc., 662
CVC Capital Partners, 790
CW Group, Inc., 521
CyberStarts, 332
CyberWorks Ventures , 790
Cygnus Venture Partners, 791
Daewoo Venture Capital Co Ltd, 792
Daimler Chrysler Venture Gmbh (AKA DCV), 792
Danish Development Finance Corp., 793
Danske eVentures, 794
Dassault Developpment, 794
Dauphin Capital Partners, 522
Davis Group, 166
DB Venture Partners, 794
De Vries & Co., Inc., 476
Dean & Associates, 279
Defta Partners, 167
Delmag Ventures, 394
Delphi Ventures, 167
Delta Ventures, 795
Diamondhead Ventures, L.P., 169
Digital Partners, 704
Discovery Capital, 797
Divine interVentures (FKA: Platinum Venture Partners), 351
DN Partners, 352
Doll Capital Management, 169
Dominion Ventures, Inc., 170
Dot Edu Ventures, 171
DotCom Ventures L.P., 171
Dow Chemical Co., 458
Draper Fisher Jurvetson Gotham Venture Partners, 523
Draper Richards, 173
Draper Triangle Ventures LP, 626
Dresner Capital Resources, Inc., 352
Duchossois TECnology Partners, LLC, 353
Durlacher Limited, 799
DynaFund Ventures, L.L.C., 174
E-MERGE, 800
e4e Inc., 174
Early Stage Enterprises, L.P., 487
Earlybird Venture Capital, 800
EarlyBirdCapital.com Inc., 524
East River Ventures, L.P., 524
East/West Venture Group FKA:East/West Capital Associates, 175
Easton Hunt Capital Partners, 525
eBlast Ventures, LLC, 353
ECI Ventures Ltd, 801
ECICS Ventures Pte Ltd., 801
eCompanies-Evercore Venture Partners (E2VP), 175
EDB Investments Pte Ltd., 802
Edelson Technology Partners, 487
EDF Ventures (F.K.A. Enterprise Development Fund), 458
Edge Capital Investment Co., LLC, 175
Edison Venture Fund, 488
Eficor Oyj, 803
eFund, LLC, 704
Egan-Managed Capital, 421
EGL Holdings, Inc./Nat West Ventures USA, L.P., 332
El Dorado Ventures, 176
Elderstreet Investments Ltd, 803
Electra Partners Asia [FKA: JF Electra Limited], 803

Emerging Technologies , 804
Endeavor Capital Management, 294
Enterprise Equity (NI) Limited, 805
Enterprise Investors, 526
Enterprise Partners, 178
Eos Partners, L.P., 527
Episode-1 Partners, 806
EquiNet Venture Partners AG, 806
Equity Partners Management Pty Ltd, 807
ETF Group, 808
EuclidSR Partners , 527
EURAZEO (FKA Gaz-et-Eaux & AZEO), 809
Eurofund LP, 810
European Equity Partners , 810
European Webgroup, 811
Evanston Business Investment Corp, 354
EVC Christows PLC (FKA: eVestment Company PLC), 812
eVerger Associates, 812
Evergreen Canada Israel Investments Ltd, 812
Evergreen Ventures, 686
eVolution Global Partners, 813
eXseed, 813
Fairfax Partners, 693
Far East Capital Corp., 179
FastVentures, 814
FBR CoMotion Venture Capital, 705
FBR Technology Venture Partners,L.P.(AKA:Friedman,Billings), 693
FEO Ventures Pte. Ltd., 815
Fidelity Ventures (FKA: Fidelity Venture Associates), 421
Financial Technology Ventures, 179
FINOVA Mezzanine Capital, Inc. (FKA: Sirrom Capital Corp), 650
Firemark Advisors, Inc., 488
First Analysis Venture Capital (FKA:First Analysis Corp), 354
First Union Capital Partners, 600
Flatiron Partners, 530
Flinders Capital Limited, 818
Fluke Venture Partners., 705
FLV Fund (AKA Flanders Language Valley Fund), 818
Fonds de Solidarité des Travailleurs du Québec (F.T.Q.), 820
Foresight, 820
Forrest Binkley & Brown, 180
Fort Washington Capital Partners, LLC, 611
FORTKNOX-VENTURE AG, 821
Fortune Consulting Group Incorporated, 821
Fortune International Limited, 821
Fortune Venture Management Pte Ltd., 822
Foundation Capital, 181
Fowler, Anthony & Co., 422
Fremont Partners, 181
Friends Ivory & Sime Private Equity (Ivory &Sime Baronsmead), 823
Frontenac Co., 355
Frost Capital Partners, 182
Fusient Ventures, 531
G-51 Capital LLC, 665
Gabriel Venture Partners, 182
Galileo Partners, 824
Gamma Investors LLC, 627
Gateway Associates, L.P., 476
GATX/MM Venture Partners, 183
GCI Venture Partners, 314
Gemini Capital Fund Management Ltd, 825
Generation Capital Partners, 532
GENES GmbH Venture Services, 826
Genesis Partners, 826
Genesys Partners, 533
Geneva Venture Partners, 184
Geocapital Partners, L.L.C., 489
Gideon Hixon Fund, 467
Gilde Investment Management, 827
Giza Venture Capital (FKA Giza Investment Management), 828
GKM Venture Partners, LP, 184
Gleacher & Co., 534
Global Crossing Ventures (FKA: Frontier Ventures), 185
Global Internet Ventures (GIV), 693
Global Retail Partners (A.K.A. GRP), 185
GMS Capital, 534
GorillaPark, 830
Granite Ventures LLC (FKA: H & Q Venture Associates), 186
Granville Baird Capital Partners (FKA:Granville Pr Eq Mngrs), 830
Gray Ventures, 335
Greylock, 424
Grieve, Horner, Brown & Asculai, 833
Grosvenor Funds, The, 315
Grotech Capital Group, 394
Grove Street Advisors, LLC, 425
Growth Factory, The, 833
GrowthWorks Capital, 834
GTCR Golder Rauner, LLC, 356
Guide Ventures, 706
Hallador Venture Partners, 188
Hanbyuck Investment Co Ltd, 836
HarbourVest Partners, LLC., 426
Heartland Capital Fund, Ltd., 479
Herbert Young Securities, Inc., 536
Hickory Venture Capital Corporation, 130
High Street Capital, LLC, 357
Highland Capital Partners, 427
Higin Venture Capital Co., Ltd., 838
Hikari Tsushin Capital, Inc., 838
HillStreet Capital, Inc., 612
Hitachi America, Ltd., 189
HMS Holtron Management Services, Ltd, 838
HO2 Partners LLC, 665
Holland Venture B.V. (FKA: Holland Venture Holding C.V.), 839
Hollinger Capital (FKA: Hollinger Ventures), 537
Horizon Ventures (F.K.A. Technology Investments), 190
HSBC Private Equity (Asia), Ltd. (FKA: HSBC PE Management), 841
HT Capital Advisors, LLC, 538
Hudson Venture Partners, 538
Hummer Winblad Venture Partners, 191
Hydro-Quebec CapiTech Inc., 843
i-Hatch Ventures, LLC, 539
i2i Venture, 843
i2s PLC (FKA: Tarpan PLC), 843
iAsia Alliance Capital, 844
IBK Capital Corporation, 844
ICC Venture Capital, 845
IDG Technology Venture Investment Inc. (FKA: PTV-China), 846
IDG Ventures, 192

IEG Venture Management, Inc., 357
iFormation Group, 296
iGlobe Partners Limited, 847
Ignition Corporation, 706
iMinds (FKA: Interactive Minds), 193
Impact Venture Partners, 539
Impex Venture Management Co., 540
Indekon Management Oy, 849
Industrial Technology Securities Ltd, 851
Industry Ventures , 428
Infineon Ventures, 852
Infinity Capital LLC, 194
Inflexion plc, 852
Information Technology Ventures, 195
InnoCal, L.P., 196
Innova Capital (FKA: Poland Partners Management Company), 853
Innovacom, 853
Innovation Works, Inc., 628
InnovationsKapital Management Goteborg AB , 854
Innvotec Ltd, 854
Inova Capital SCR, 855
Interfase Capital Partners LP, 667
Internet Healthcare Group, 297
Internet Incubator PLC, 856
Internet Ventures Scandinavia A/S, 856
Interprise Technology Partners, L.P., 323
Interregnum, 856
Intersouth Partners, 601
InterWest Partners, 197
inVentures Management Ltd, 857
Investissements Novacap (AKA:Novacap Investments, Inc.), 858
Invision AG (FKA Aureus Private Equity AG), 858
Ireka Venture Capital Limited, 860
Ironside Ventures, LLC (FKA: MF Private Capital), 429
Irwin Ventures LLC (FKA: Irwin Ventures Incorporated), 377
ISEP NV, 860
Israel Seed Partners, 860
J.L. Albright Venture Partners, 861
J.P. Morgan Capital Corp., 542
J.P. Morgan Partners (FKA: Chase Capital Partners), 543
JAFCO Co. Ltd., 862
JAFCO Ventures, Inc., 198
JatoTech Management LLC, 668
Jefferson Partners , 863
Jerusalem Global Ventures, 864
Jerusalem Venture Partners (AKA: JVP), 864
JK&B Capital, 358
Josephberg Grosz & Co., Inc., 545
JT Venture Partners, LLC, 491
Jump.Net Ventures, 668
JumpStartUp Fund Advisors Pvt. Ltd., 864
Justsystem, Inc., 629
Kaiser Permanente (AKA: National Venture Development), 200
Kangaroo Village, 865
Kankaku Investment Co Ltd, 865
Kansas City Equity Partners, 477
Kappa-IT Ventures, 865
KB Partners, LLC, 359
Kemper Ventures, 491
Kettle Partners, L.P., 359
Kirlan Venture Capital, Inc., 707
Kitty Hawk Capital, 602
KLB Investment Co., Ltd., 866
Kleiner Perkins Caufield & Byers, 200
Kline Hawkes & Co., 201
Kookmin Venture Capital Co Ltd, 867
Koor Corporate Venture Capital, 868
Korea Technology Finance Corp., 869
KPMG Advent Management Group (FKA:Advent Western Pacific), 870
Kyocera International, Inc., 202
Ladybird Technologies, Ltd., 870
Lake Shore Capital Partners, Inc., 360
Launch Center 39, 547
Lazard Technology Partners, 547
Lee Munder Venture Partners, 430
Legendary Investments PLC, 872
Lepercq Capital Management, Inc.(AKA:Lepercq,de Neuflize In), 548
LG Venture Investment Inc., 873
Liberty Venture Partners, Inc., 631
Lightspeed Venture Partners (FKA: Weiss, Peck & Greer), 206
LLR Equity Partners, 631
LN Mittal, 874
London Merchant Security (AKA LMS), 874
Lost Boys Incubator, 875
LTI Ventures Leasing Corp., 298
Lucent Venture Partners, Inc., 207
Lycos Ventures, 632
M31 Ventures, LLC, 550
Macromedia Ventures, 208
Madrona Venture Group, 707
Magnum Communications (AKA: MCF Advisory Services Ltd), 877
Malmohus Invest AB, 877
Manchester Humphreys, Inc., 642
Mangrove Capital Partners SA, 878
march.fifteen AG (FKA Peterp@n), 878
Marconi Ventures, 431
Maristeth Ventures, L.L.C., 707
Marks and Spencer Ventures Ltd, 878
Marleau, Lemire, Inc., 878
Marquette Venture Partners, 362
Maryland Venture Capital Trust, 395
Massachusetts Technology Development Corp. (MTDC), 432
Massey Burch Capital Corp., 650
Maton Venture, 209
Matrix Partners, 433
Matrix Private Equity, 879
McGraw-Hill Ventures, 552
McKee & Co., 134
MDT Advisers, Inc., 433
Medicis AG, 882
Medicus Venture Partners, 211
Mediphase Venture Partners (FKA: EHealth Technology Fund), 434
Mees Pierson Investeringsmaat. B.V., 435
Mellon Ventures (AKA: Mellon Bank), 632
Menlo Ventures, 212
Mentor Capital Partners, 633
Mercator Broadband Partners, L.P., 696
Meridian Venture Partners (MVP), 633
Merita Capital Limited, 134

Meritage Private Equity Fund, 281
Metropolitan Venture Partners (MetVP), 553
meVC.com, 213
Meyer, Duffy & Associates, 553
Mid-Atlantic Venture Funds (FKA: NEPA Management Corp.), 634
Milestone Venture Partners, 553
Mission Ventures, 214
Mitiska NV, 887
Mitsui & Co., Ltd., 553
MMG Ventures, L.P., 396
Mofet Venture Capital , 888
Mohr, Davidow Ventures, 214
Montreux Equity Partners, 216
Monumental Venture Partners, LLC, 696
Morgan Stanley Venture Partners (AKA: MSDW), 554
Morgenthaler Ventures, 614
Mosaic Venture Partners, 889
Mountaineer Capital LP, 716
MSC Venture Corporation Sdn. Bhd., 890
MTI Partners Ltd, 890
Murphree Venture Partners, 671
Mustang Ventures (FKA Siemens Mustang Ventures), 216
MWV Capital Partners (FKA:Middlewest Ventures, L.P.), 378
Nanyang Ventures Pty Ltd (AKA: Nanyang Management Pty Ltd), 892
Nassau Capital, L.L.C., 492
National Bank Of Kuwait, 555
Navis Partners (FKA:Fleet Equity Partners), 643
nCoTec Ventures Ltd, 893
Needham & Company, Inc., 556
Nesbitt Burns, 363
Net Partners, 895
Netalone.com Ltd, 895
NetCatalyst , 218
NetFuel Ventures, 364
Netjuice, 895
NetSpark Ventures N.V., 895
NetworkAsia, 896
Neurone Venture Capital, 896
New England Partners, 437
New Vista Capital, LLC, 218
Newbridge Capital Limited, 219
Newbury Ventures, 220
Newport Capital Group Pty Ltd, 897
Newtek Capital, 558
Nexit Ventures Oy, 897
Next Ventures Limited, 897
NextGen Capital LLC, 697
NIB Capital Private Equity N.V. (FKA: Parnib Holding NV) , 898
NIIT Ventures, 898
Nikko Capital Co Ltd, 899
Nippon Technology Venture Partners Ltd., 899
Nokia Venture Partners (AKA: Nokia Oy), 222
Nomura International, Plc., 900
Nomura/JAFCO Investment (HK) Limited, 901
Nord Innovation, 901
North Bridge Venture Partners, 438
North Carolina Technological Development Authority, Inc., 603
North Hill Ventures, 438
Northern Stream Capital, 709
Northwest Venture Associates, Inc.(FKA:Spokane Capital Mgmt), 709
Northwood Ventures, 559
Northzone Ventures (FKA Venture Partners AS), 902
Norwest Equity Partners, 223
Novak Biddle Venture Partners, L.P., 697
NPV Capital Partners, LLC, 560
Oak Investment Partners, 302
Odin Capital Group, 479
Ohana Ventures, LLC, 615
OneLiberty Ventures (FKA: Morgan, Holland Ventures Corp.), 439
Onondaga Venture Capital Fund, Inc., 562
Onset Ventures, 225
Open Prairie Ventures, 365
Optical Capital Group , 397
Oracle Corporation, 226
Oregon Resource and Technology Development Fund, 620
Orien Ventures, 303
Origin Ventures LLC, 365
Ovation Capital Partners (FKA:iCentennial Ventures LLC), 562
OVP Venture Partners (FKA: Olympic Venture Partners), 709
PA Early Stage (AKA:Pennsylvania Early Stage Partners), 635
Pacific Venture Partners, 907
Pacifica Fund , 228
PacRim Venture Management , 228
Paladin Partners, 711
Palomar Ventures, 228
Pappajohn Capital Resources, 381
Paradigm Capital Partners LLC, 651
Pari Capital AG, 909
Part'com, 909
Partech International, 229
Partners Group, 910
Pathfinder Venture Capital Funds, 470
PENMAN Partners (FKA PENMAN Asset Management LP), 365
Pequot Capital Management Inc., 564
Perennial Ventures (FKA: Tredegar Investments), 711
Phoenix Partners, The , 711
Piedmont Venture Partners, 604
Pierce Financial Corporation(FKA:Pierce Investment Banking), 698
Pittsford Group, Inc., The , 565
Platinum Group, Inc., The , 565
PME Capital, 912
Poalim Capital Markets Technologies, Ltd., 913
Polaris Venture Capital, 913
Polaris Venture Partners, 441
Poly Ventures, 566
Potomac Ventures, 397
pre-IPO Aktiengesellschaft, 915
Prescient Capital, 232
Primedia Ventures, 567
Primus Venture Partners, Inc., 616
Prism Capital, 367
Prism Venture Partners, 441
Private Capital Corp., 131
ProSeed Capital Holdings CVA, 917
Prospect Street Ventures (FKA:Prospect Street Invest. Mgmt), 567
Ptek Ventures , 336
Q Ventures, 674
Quaestus & Co. Inc. (FKA: Quaestus Management Corp..), 719

Quantum Capital Partners, 325
RAF Ventures, 637
Ralph Wilson Equity Fund, L.L.C., 460
Rand Capital Corporation, 568
Red Hat Ventures, 604
Red River Ventures, 675
red-stars.com, 920
Redleaf Venture Management, 234
Redpoint Ventures, 235
Renaissance Capital Corp., 337
Richland Ventures, 652
Ridge Capital Partners, L.L.C., 368
Ridgewood Capital Management LLC, 494
Robertson Stephens & Company, LLC, 236
Rocket Ventures, 237
RockMountain Ventures, 282
Roser Ventures LLC, 283
Rosewood Capital, L.P., 237
Royal Bank Private Equity (FKA: Royal Bank Development Cap), 922
Royalty Capital Fund, L.P. I/Royalty Capital Management, Inc, 443
RRE Ventures LLC, 571
RSA Ventures, 443
SAE Ventures, 306
Saffron Hill Ventures (FKA LootLab Ltd.), 924
Sage Management Group, 444
Sanderling Ventures, 239
Sandler Capital Management, 571
Sandlot Capital LLC, 283
Sanpaolo IMI Private Equity S.p.A., 925
SBV Venture Partners (AKA:Sigefi, Burnette & Vallee), 240
Schneider Electric Ventures, 926
Schoffstall Ventures , 639
Scoot.com PLC, 926
Scottish Equity Partners Limited, 927
Scripps Ventures, 572
Seacoast Capital, 446
Seapoint Ventures, 712
Seed Capital Partners, 573
Seed Company Partners, 676
Selby Venture Partners, 241
Sequel Venture Partners, 284
Sevin Rosen Management Co., 677
Shad Run Investments, Inc., 242
Shannon Development Company, 929
Shattan Group, The, 574
Shaw Venture Partners (FKA: Shaw Glasgow Partners), 621
Shepherd Group LLC, The, 447
Sherpa Partners, LLC, 471
Shrem Fudim Kelner Technologies Ltd. , 930
SI Ventures, 326
Sienna Ventures (FKA: Sienna Holdings Inc.), 242
Sierra Ventures, 243
Signal Lake Venture Fund, LP, 307
Signia Ventures, 244
Siguler Guff & Company, LLC, 575
Silicon Alley Venture Partners LLC (AKA SAVP) , 576
SilkRoute Capital Limited, 930
Singapore Technologies Telemedia (AKA: ST Telemedia), 931
Sitra (AKA Finnish National Fund for Research and Dev.), 932
Sofinnova Partners, 934
Sofinnova Ventures, 246
SOFTBANK Capital Partners, 448
Softbank Corp., 935
SOFTBANK Venture Capital (FKA: SOFTBANK Technology Ventures), 247
Solstice Capital LLC, 449
Southwest Venture Group, 678
Sovereign Capital (FKA:Nash, Sells & Partners Limited), 936
SpaceVest, 699
Sparkventures, LLC, 449
Spectrum Equity Investors, L.P., 248
Spectrum Venture Management, 937
Speed Ventures, 937
Spencer Trask Ventures, Inc. (FKA: Spencer Trask Securities), 576
Spire Capital (FKA: Waller Capital Corp.), 577
Sponsored Consulting Services, 249
Sports Capital Partners, 577
Sprout Group, 578
Sputnik Technology Ventures, 938
Square One Ventures (AKA: Smaby Group), 471
SsangYong Cement (Singapore) Ltd, 939
SSM Ventures, 653
St. Paul Venture Capital, Inc., 471
Staenberg Private Capital, LLC, 713
Star-Ventures Management GMBH (SVM), 940
STARTech, 679
Starter Fluid, 250
Sterling Grace Capital Management, L.P., 579
Still River Fund, The, 450
Stolberg Partners, 580
Stonepath Europe, 941
Sucsy, Fischer & Co., 370
Sun Valley Ventures, 250
SUNeVision Holdings Ltd, 944
Sybase, Inc., 252
Synergy Ventures, 582
Syntel Inc. Web Incubator Program, 461
T. Rowe Price Threshold Partnerships, 399
Tamir Fishman Ventures, 946
Target Partners, 947
tbg Technologie-Beteiligungsgesellschaft mbH, 947
Technology Crossover Ventures, 254
Technology Partners, 255
Technology Venture Partners Pty Ltd, 950
Technology Ventures, L.L.C., 339
TechSpace Xchange LLC (TSX), 582
Techxas Ventures, LLC, 681
TecVenture Partners GmbH, 952
Telecom Italia Ventures, 255
Telecom Partners (FKA:Telecom Management, LLC), 285
Telia Business Innovation AB, 953
Telos Venture Partners, 256
TG Asia Ventures Limited, 954
ThinkVentures.com Ltd, 954
Thoma Cressey Equity Partners, 371
Thompson Clive & Partners Limited, 955
Thompson Clive, Inc., 257
Thorner Ventures, 258
Throunarfelag Islands Plc(AKA:The Icelandic Finance&Invest.), 955
TI Capital (AKA: Technology & Internet Capital), 259

Tokyo Small & Medium Business Investment & Consultation Co., 956
Toll Technologies, 957
Toucan Capital Corp., 399
Transamerica Technology Finance, 309
Triad Media Ventures, 309
Tribune Ventures, 372
Trident Capital, 259
Trinity Ventures, 260
TriNova, 959
Triton Ventures, 682
Triune Capital, 260
True North Partners LLC, 583
TruePilot, LLC, 606
TrustCapital Partners NV, 959
TTC Ventures, 453
Tvi Investments Bv, 960
TVM Techno Venture Management, 961
U.S. Bancorp Piper Jaffray Ventures, Inc., 472
Union Street Capital Corp., 713
Unit Trust of India (UTI), 964
UOB Venture Management Pte Ltd., 964
Updata Venture Partners, 700
UPS Strategic Enterprise Fund, 339
US Trust Private Equity, 584
Utah Ventures II, L.P. (A.K.A. Union Ventures), 687
Value Management & Research AG (VMR), 965
Vanguard Venture Partners, 262
VantagePoint Venture Partners, 263
VCF Partners, 965
Vencon Management, Inc., 585
Venrock Associates, 586
Ventana Global, 264
Venture Associates, Ltd., 285
Venture Capital Fund of New England, The, 454
Venture Catalyst, 265
Venture Investment Management Company LLC (AKA: VIMAC), 454
Venture Investors Management LLC, 720
Venture Partners AG, 968
Venture Select, 968
Venture Strategy Partners, 266
Venture TDF Pte Ltd., 968
VentureCap Management GmbH (AKA VCH Equity Group AG), 969
VentureLink Holdings, 683
Venturepark Incubator (FKA grizzlyfarm AG), 969
Ventures West Management, Inc., 970
Veritas Venture Capital Management, Ltd., 970
Vertex Management, 971
Vertex Management Israel (AKA: Vertex Management III Ltd.), 971
Vesta Capital Partners (AKA: Vesta Group, The), 971
Victory Ventures L.L.C., 588
VigEcom Limited, 972
Viridian Capital Partners (FKA: Aurora Venture Partners), 607
Vision Capital Management (FKA Glenwood Capital), 267
VIV NV (AKA Vlaamse Investeringvennootschap NV), 973
Viventures Inc., 973
Voyager Capital, 714
VTC Partners GmbH, 974
W.R. Hambrecht & Co., LLC, 269
Wakefield Group, 607
Walden Capital Management Corporation, 589
Walden International Investment Group (AKA: Walden Group), 269
Walden Israel, 975
WaldenVC, 270
Warburg, Pincus & Co., LLC. (FKA: E.M. Warburg, Pincus & Co), 590
Wasatch Venture Fund (FKA: Wasatch Venture Corporation), 687
Wasserstein, Perella & Co., Inc., 591
Watermill eVentures , 455
Wedbush Capital Partners, 271
wellington partners venture capital GmbH, 975
WestBridge Capital Advisors (India) Pvt. Ltd., 976
Weston Presidio Capital Management, 455
Whitney & Co. (FKA: J.H. Whitney & Co.), 310
William E. Simon & Sons (Asia) LDC, 977
Windamere Venture Partners, LLC, 273
Windward Ventures (FKA: Coronado Capital), 274
Wit Japan Investment, Inc., 977
Wolf Ventures (AKA:Wolf Asset Management Corp.), 286
WomenAngles.net, 318
Woodside Fund, 274
Working Ventures Canadian Fund, Inc., 978
Worldview Technology Partners, 275
WSI Holding Corporation, 595
YankeeTek Ventures, 456
Yasuda Enterprise Development Co., Ltd.(FKA: Nippon Ent.Dev), 275
Yorkshire Fund Managers Ltd., 979
Zephyr Internet Partners, 595
Zero Gravity Internet Group, Inc. , 276
Zero Stage Capital Co., Inc., 456
Zone Ventures, 276
Zouk Ventures, 980

Manufacturing

21st Century Internet Management Partners,LLC, 138
2M Invest, Inc., 138
2nd Generation Capital Corp, 648
Aberdeen Asset Managers, 728
Abingworth Venture Management Limited, 729
ABN AMRO Private Equity (AKA: ABN AMRO Capital (USA) Inc.) , 343
ABN-AMRO Corporate Investments, 729
ABP Acquisition Corp, 287
Access Venture Partners, 277
ACT Venture Capital Ltd., 732
Adams Capital Management, Inc., 622
Adams Street Partners, LLC (FKA: Brinson Private Equity), 343
Adams, Harkness & Hill, Inc., 401
Advent International Corp., 402
Advent-Morro Equity Partners, 734
AIG Investment Corporation (Asia) Limited, 735
Alan I. Goldman & Associates, 483
Albemarle Private Equity Ltd, 735
Alimansky Capital Group, Inc., 504
Allegra Partners (FKA: Lawrence, Smith & Horey), 504
Alliance Investment Capital, 737
Alliance Venture Capital Advisors Limited, 738
Allied Capital Corporation, 312

Allsop Venture Partners, 380
Allstate Private Equity, 344
Alpha Capital Partners, Inc., 344
American Capital Strategies, 391
American Securities, L.P., 505
Amerindo Investment Advisors, Inc., 505
AMP Asset Management Limited - Development Capital, 740
Amphion Ventures L.P.(FKA: Wolfensohn Associates, L.P.), 506
Antares Capital Corp. (FKA: Antares Leveraged Capital Corp), 345
Antares Capital Corporation (FKA: Harbor Ventures Corp.), 320
Anthem Capital, L.P., 391
AO Capital Corp, 287
Applied Technology, 405
Ardsheil, Inc., 506
Argentum Group, The , 507
Argos Soditic SA, 744
Argosy Partners, 623
Arthur P. Gould & Co., 507
Ascent Venture Partners, 406
Asian Direct Capital Management, 747
Asset Management Company Venture Capital, 147
Atlantic Capital, 407
August Capital Management, 148
August Partners, 508
Austin Ventures, L.P., 657
Baccharis Capital, Inc., 150
Bachow & Associates, Inc., 623
Baird Capital Partners, 347
Banc One Capital Partners, 608
BancAmerica Capital Investors (FKA:NationsBanc Capital Corp), 598
BancBoston Capital/BancBoston Ventures, 408
BANEXI Corp., 753
Bangert Dawes Reade Davis & Thom, 151
Bank One Equity Investors, Inc., 386
Bastion Capital Corp., 152
BayBG Bayerische Beteiligungsgesellschaft mbH, 757
BCR Asset Management Pty Ltd., 758
Beacon Partners, Inc., 289
Bedford Capital Corp., 512
Benchmark Capital, 154
Berkeley International Capital Corp., 154
Berwind Financial Group, L.P., 623
Bessemer Venture Partners, 410
Boston Capital Ventures, 411
Boston Financial & Equity Corp., 412
Boston Ventures Management, Inc., 413
Botts & Co., 762
Bradford Equities Fund, LLC, 513
Brait Capital Partners, 762
Brand Equity Ventures, 289
Brantley Venture Partners, 609
Bristol Capital Management, 513
Broadmark Capital Corp., 702
Bruce F. Glaspell & Associates, 498
Bulldog Partners Limited, 764
Business Link Doncaster, 765
Butler Capital Partners France, 765
C3 Holdings, LLC, 474
Cairnsford Associates Ltd., 766
Cambria Group, The, 157
Cambridge Research & Innovation Ltd (AKA CRIL), 767
Canbank Venture Capital Fund Ltd, 767
Candover Investments PLC, 768
Canterbury Capital L.L.C.(AKA: Canterbury Detroit Partners), 514
Capital Development & Investment Co. Ltd., 768
Capital Express, L.L.C., 484
Capital For Business, Inc., 474
Capital Investments, Inc., 717
Capital Network, The (AKA: Texas Capital Network), 659
Capital Resource Partners, 415
Capital Services & Resources, Inc., 648
Capital Southwest Corporation, 660
Capital Strategy Management Co., The, 349
CapVis Equity Partners AG, 771
Carillon Capital, Inc., 610
Castle Harlan Australian Mezzanine Partners Pty. Ltd. , 772
CDC Services Industries Gestion (CDC IXIS Private Equity), 775
Cedar Creek Partners, LLC, 717
CEI Ventures/Coastal Ventures LP, 388
CEO Venture Fund, 625
Cerulean Fund/WGC Enterprises, 350
CGW Southeast Partners (AKA: Cravey, Green, & Wahlen), 331
Chartwell Capital Management Co., Inc., 321
Cherry Tree Investments, Inc., 464
Chrysalis Ventures, 384
Churchill Capital, Inc., 465
CIBC Capital Partners (FKA: CIBC Wood Gundy Capital), 516
CID Equity Partners, 376
Citicorp Capital Asia (AKA: CITIC Pacific Ltd.), 780
Citicorp Venture Capital, Ltd., 517
Citizens Capital and Citizens Ventures, 418
Claflin Capital Management, Inc., 418
Clarion Capital Corp., 610
Clemente Capital (Asia) Ltd., 781
Close Brothers Private Equity, 782
CM Equity Partners, 517
Colonnade Capital L.L.C., 691
Columbia Capital Group, Inc., 313
Columbine Venture Funds, The , 279
Comdisco Ventures, 162
Commonwealth Capital Ventures L.P., 419
Consumer Venture Partners, 292
Continental Venture Capital , 784
Copernicus Capital Management Ltd, 785
Cornerstone Equity Investors, LLC, 519
Corpfin Capital S.A., 786
Corporate Growth Assistance, Ltd., 786
Corporate Venture Partners, L.P., 519
Creafund CVBA, 788
Crescent Capital NI Ltd (FKA Hambro Northern Ireland), 788
Crestview Financial Group, The , 292
Crocker Capital/Crocker Assoc., 164
Crosbie & Co Inc, 789
Crown Capital Corp, 475
CS Capital Partners, LLC, 486
CVC Capital Partners, 790
Cygnus Venture Partners, 791
D.H. Blair Investment Banking Corp., 521
Daewoo Venture Capital Co Ltd, 792
Daimler Chrysler Venture Gmbh (AKA DCV), 792
Dakota Group, The , 166
Davis Group, 166
Davis, Tuttle Venture Partners, L.P.(FKA:Davis Venture), 618

De Vries & Co., Inc., 476
Defta Partners, 167
Deucalion Venture Partners, 168
DFW Capital Partners (AKA:DeMuth, Folger & Wetherill), 486
Direct Capital Private Equity, 797
Divine interVentures (FKA: Platinum Venture Partners), 351
DN Partners, 352
Downer & Co., 420
Draper Fisher Jurvetson (FKA: Draper Associates), 172
Dresner Capital Resources, Inc., 352
Drysdale Enterprises, 173
East River Ventures, L.P., 524
Easton Hunt Capital Partners, 525
ECI Ventures Ltd, 801
Edelson Technology Partners, 487
EGL Holdings, Inc./Nat West Ventures USA, L.P., 332
Electra Fleming Limited, 525
Electra Partners Asia [FKA: JF Electra Limited], 803
Endeavor Capital Management, 294
Enterprise Equity (NI) Limited, 805
Enterprise Investors, 526
Eos Partners, L.P., 527
Equinox Investment Partners, 294
Equity Ventures, Ltd, 807
Equity-South (FKA:Grubb & Williams Ltd.), 333
EuclidSR Partners , 527
Euroc Venture Capital Corporation, 809
European Acquisition Capital Ltd., 810
Evanston Business Investment Corp, 354
Evergreen Capital Partners Inc, 528
Evergreen Ventures, 686
Exeter Capital, L.P., 528
Fairgill Investments Property Limited, 814
Financial Technology Research Corp., 529
Finansa Capital Limited, 816
FINORPA, 816
FINOVA Mezzanine Capital, Inc. (FKA: Sirrom Capital Corp), 650
First Charter Partners, Inc., 664
First Princeton Capital Corp., 489
First Union Capital Partners, 600
Florida Capital Partners, 322
Florida Capital Ventures, Ltd., 323
Fluke Venture Partners., 705
Fonds de Solidarité des Travailleurs du Québec (F.T.Q.), 820
Foundation Capital, 181
Foundation Capital Limited, 822
Founders Equity, Inc., 530
Fowler, Anthony & Co., 422
Frederic H. Mayerson Group, The, 612
Friends Ivory & Sime Private Equity (Ivory &Sime Baronsmead), 823
Frontline Capital, Inc., 334
Gateway Associates, L.P., 476
GATX Ventures (FKA: Meier Mitchell & Co.), 183
Genesee Funding, Inc., 532
Genesis Capital, Inc., 533
Geneva Merchant Banking Partners, 601
Gideon Hixon Fund, 467
Gilde Investment Management, 827
Glencoe Capital, LLC (FKA: Glencoe Investment Corporation), 356
Goldner Hawn Johnson & Morrison Incorporated, 468
Golub Associates, 534
Granville Baird Capital Partners (FKA:Granville Pr Eq Mngrs), 830
Graystone Venture Partners, LLC(AKA:Portage Venture Partners, 356
Grieve, Horner, Brown & Asculai, 833
Grotech Capital Group, 394
Growth Venture Group Pty Ltd., 833
GrowthWorks Capital, 834
Gujarat Venture Finance Limited, 834
Halder Holdings B.V., 835
Halpern, Denny & Co., 425
Hambro European Ventures (Hambros PLC), 835
Hamilton Robinson & Co., Inc., 296
Hanbyuck Investment Co Ltd, 836
Hanover Capital Corp., 535
Harbour Financial Co., 426
HarbourVest Partners, LLC., 426
Harvest Partners, Inc., 536
Health Capital Group, 188
Heartland Capital Partners, L.P., 665
Herbert Young Securities, Inc., 536
Heritage Partners, 427
Hibernia Capital Partners, 837
High Street Capital, LLC, 357
HillStreet Capital, Inc., 612
HMS Hawaii Management Partners, 341
Hoak Capital Corp., 666
Hoebich Venture Management, Inc., 190
Howard, Lawson & Co., 628
HT Capital Advisors, LLC, 538
Hudson Venture Partners, 538
Hungarian-American Enterprise Fund, The (HAEF), 842
ICC Venture Capital, 845
ICICI Venture Funds Mngt. Co. Ltd., 846
IDG Technology Venture Investment Inc. (FKA: PTV-China), 846
IEG Venture Management, Inc., 357
Incorporated Investors, 193
IndAsia Fund Advisors Private Limited, 849
Industrial Technology Securities Ltd, 851
Information Technology Ventures, 195
Innovacom, 853
Innovest Group, Inc., 629
InterEquity Capital Partners, L.P., 541
InvestAmerica Venture Group, Inc., 380
Investissements Novacap (AKA:Novacap Investments, Inc.), 858
Itochu Technology, 542
J.E. Mann & Co., 542
J.L. Albright Venture Partners, 861
J.P. Morgan Partners (FKA: Chase Capital Partners), 543
James A. Matzdorff & Co., 199
James B. Kobak & Co., 297
Jefferson Capital Fund, Ltd., 130
Jerusalem Global Ventures, 864
Jordan, Edmiston Group, Inc., The , 545
Josephberg Grosz & Co., Inc., 545
Justsystem, Inc., 629
Kankaku Investment Co Ltd, 865
KB Partners, LLC, 359
Kemper Ventures, 491
Kentucky Highlands Investment Corporation, 384

Key Equity Capital Corp.(AKA:Key Community Development Corp), 613
Keystone Minority Capital Fund, L.P., 630
Kitty Hawk Capital, 602
KLB Investment Co., Ltd., 866
Kleiner Perkins Caufield & Byers, 200
Kyocera International, Inc., 202
Lake Shore Capital Partners, Inc., 360
Lambda Funds, The, 546
Las Americas Administradora, 871
Legal & General Ventures Ltd, 872
Leonard Green & Partners, 203
Lincolnshire Management Inc., 548
LLR Equity Partners, 631
Loeb Partners Corp., 549
Lombard Investments, Inc., 206
London Ventures (Fund Managers) Ltd., 875
Lubar & Co., 718
Madison Dearborn Partners, LLC, 361
Madison Investment Partners, Inc., 550
Manchester Humphreys, Inc., 642
Manhattan Venture Co., Inc., 550
Marleau, Lemire, Inc., 878
Marwit Capital LLC, 209
Matrix Group, 209
Matrix Partners, 433
MAVA Investment Management kft (AKA: Hungarian-American Ent), 879
MBA Venture Group, 669
McCown De Leeuw & Co., 210
MDT Advisers, Inc., 433
Media Venture Partners, 211
MedTech International, Inc., 670
Mellon Ventures (AKA: Mellon Bank), 632
Memhard Investment Bankers, Inc., 300
Mentor Capital Partners, 633
Meridian Venture Partners (MVP), 633
Merita Capital Limited, 134
Merrill Lynch Investment Managers FKA Mercury Asset Mgmt, 884
Merrill, Pickard, Anderson & Eyre, 213
Mesirow Private Equity Investments, Inc., 362
Mezzanine Management UK Limited, 885
Microtechnology Investments, Ltd., 213
Midlands Venture Fund Managers Ltd. (AKA: Midven Ltd), 886
Miralta Capital, Inc., 887
Mitsui & Co., Ltd., 553
Mohr, Davidow Ventures, 214
Monument Advisors, Inc, 378
Moore & Associates, 619
Morgan Grenfell Private Equity Limited, 889
Morgan Stanley Venture Partners (AKA: MSDW), 554
Mountaineer Capital LP, 716
MWV Capital Partners (FKA:Middlewest Ventures, L.P.), 378
Nanyang Ventures Pty Ltd (AKA: Nanyang Management Pty Ltd), 892
Nassau Capital, L.L.C., 492
National Australia Investment Capital Limited, 892
National City Equity Partners, Inc, 614
National Investment Management, Inc., 217
Navis Partners (FKA:Fleet Equity Partners), 643
Nazem & Co., 556
NCP Advisors Philippines, Inc., 894
Nelson Capital Corp., 651
Nesbitt Burns, 363
New Business Capital Fund Ltd., 499
New Vista Capital, LLC, 218
Newbridge Capital Limited, 219
Newbury, Piret & Co., Inc., 437
Newport Capital Group Pty Ltd, 897
Newtek Ventures, 220
NIB Capital Private Equity N.V. (FKA: Parnib Holding NV) , 898
Nomura/JAFCO Investment (HK) Limited, 901
North Atlantic Capital Corp., 389
North Bridge Venture Partners, 438
Northwest Ohio Venture Fund, 615
Northwest Venture Associates, Inc.(FKA:Spokane Capital Mgmt), 709
Northwood Ventures, 559
Norwest Equity Partners, 223
NPM Capital (AKA Nederlandse Participatie MIJ NV), 903
Nth Power Technologies, Inc, 224
Nu Capital Access Group, Ltd., 224
Oak Hill Capital Management, Inc., 561
Onondaga Venture Capital Fund, Inc., 562
Orion Partners, L.P., 439
Pacific Northwest Partners SBIC, L.P., 710
Pacific Venture Partners, 907
Palmer Partners, L.P., 441
Paradigm Capital Partners LLC, 651
Paribas Principal, Inc., 563
Pathfinder Investment Co Pvt Ltd, 910
Pathfinder Venture Capital Funds, 470
Patricof & Co. Ventures, Inc., 563
Pauli & Co., Inc., 477
Penfund Partners, Inc., 911
Peninsula Capital Partners, L.L.C, 460
PENMAN Partners (FKA PENMAN Asset Management LP), 365
Penn-Janney Fund, Inc., The, 635
Penny Lane Partners, 493
Perennial Ventures (FKA: Tredegar Investments), 711
Pfingsten Partners, L.P., 366
Philadelphia Ventures, Inc., 636
Phoenix Equity Partners (FKA: DLJ European Private Equity), 911
Phoenix Growth Capital Corp., 231
Phoenix Partners, The , 711
Pierce Financial Corporation(FKA:Pierce Investment Banking), 698
Platinum Group, Inc., The , 565
Point Venture Partners, 636
Polaris Venture Partners, 441
Polestar Capital, Inc., 366
Poly Ventures, 566
Pomona Capital, 566
PPM Ventures Ltd (FKA: Prudential Venture Managers Ltd), 914
Prelude Technology Investments Ltd, 915
Primaxis Technology Ventures Inc. , 916
Prime Capital Management Co., Inc., 304
Prism Capital, 367
Private Capital Corp., 131
Priveq Capital Funds, 917
Productivity Fund I & II, The, 367
ProVen Private Equity (FKA:Guinness Mahon Development Cap.), 918

Quantum Capital Partners, 325
Quest Ventures, 233
Quester Capital Management Ltd, 920
Recovery Equity Investors, L.P., 234
Red River Ventures, 675
Regulus International Capital Co., Inc., 304
Renaissance Capital Corp., 337
Reprise Capital Corp., 569
RFE Investment Partners, 305
Richard Jaffe & Co., Inc., 676
Ridge Capital Partners, L.L.C., 368
Riordan, Lewis & Haden, 236
River Associates, LLC, 653
River Capital, 338
Roanoke Capital, Ltd., 712
Robertson Stephens & Company, LLC, 236
Rosecliff, 237
Rosenfeld & Co., 620
Royalty Capital Fund, L.P. I/Royalty Capital Management, Inc, 443
RRE Ventures LLC, 571
Rutledge & Co., Inc., 305
Sage Management Group, 444
Sandler Capital Management, 571
Sanpaolo IMI Private Equity S.p.A., 925
Saugatuck Capital Company, 306
SBC Equity Partners, Inc., 369
SBC Ventures, 499
SBCA/A.G. Bartholomew & Associates, 131
Schroder Capital Partners (Asia) Pte Ltd, 926
Scripps Ventures, 572
Seacoast Capital, 446
Sentinel Capital Partners, 573
Sequoia Capital, 241
SGI Capital L.L.C, 573
Shad Run Investments, Inc., 242
Shattan Group, The, 574
Shaw Venture Partners (FKA: Shaw Glasgow Partners), 621
Shelton Companies, Inc., The , 604
Shepherd Group LLC, The, 447
Sienna Ventures (FKA: Sienna Holdings Inc.), 242
Sierra Ventures, 243
Sigma Capital Corp., 327
Siguler Guff & Company, LLC, 575
Silicon Valley Bank, 244
SK Global Co., Ltd., 932
Sofinnova Ventures, 246
SoundView Financial Group, Inc., 307
Southport Partners, 307
Spencer Trask Ventures, Inc. (FKA: Spencer Trask Securities), 576
Spire Capital (FKA: Waller Capital Corp.), 577
Sponsored Consulting Services, 249
Spring Capital Partners, L.P., 398
SsangYong Cement (Singapore) Ltd, 939
Stamford Financial, 579
State Street Bank & Trust Co., 338
Sterling Venture Partners, 398
Stolberg Partners, 580
Strategic Capital Management, 941
Strategic Investments & Holdings, Inc., 581
Stratford Equity Partners, L.P., 679
Sucsy, Fischer & Co., 370
Suez Asia Holdings Pte Ltd., 943
Summit Partners, 451
Sun Valley Ventures, 250
Sustainable Jobs Fund (SJF), The , 606
Swedish Industrial Development Fund (AKA Industrifonden), 945
Sweeney & Co., Inc., 308
Synerfi S.A., 945
T. Rowe Price Threshold Partnerships, 399
TA Associates, Inc., 451
TDH, 639
Technology Crossover Ventures, 254
Texas Growth Fund Management, 681
Thompson Clive, Inc., 257
Throunarfelag Islands Plc(AKA:The Icelandic Finance&Invest.), 955
Tokyo Small & Medium Business Investment & Consultation Co., 956
Top Technology Limited (AKA:Hambros-Advanced Technology Tru), 957
Triune Capital, 260
TSG Capital Group, L.L.C., 309
TTC Ventures, 453
UBS Capital (AKA Phildrew Ventures), 963
Ulster Development Capital, Ltd., 963
Union Street Capital Corp., 713
UOB Venture Management Pte Ltd., 964
UPS Strategic Enterprise Fund, 339
Valeo Ventures, 964
Vega Capital Corp., 584
Vencap Equities Alberta, Ltd., 966
Ventana Financial Resources, Inc., 372
Ventana Global, 264
Ventex Management, Inc., 683
Venture Associates Partners, LLC, 654
Venture Associates, Ltd., 285
Venture Capital Management Corp., 328
Venture Funding Group International, 587
Venture Investment Management Company LLC (AKA: VIMAC), 454
Venture Investors Management LLC, 720
Venture Management Services Inc. (FKA: AT&T Ventures), 496
Venture Opportunities Corp., 588
Venture Strategy Partners, 266
Ventures West Management, Inc., 970
Vertex Management, 971
Victory Ventures L.L.C., 588
VIV NV (AKA Vlaamse Investeringvennootschap NV), 973
Wachovia, 340
Wachtel & Co., Inc., 317
Walden Capital Management Corporation, 589
Walden International Investment Group (AKA: Walden Group), 269
Walnut Capital Corp., 701
Warburg, Pincus & Co., LLC. (FKA: E.M. Warburg, Pincus & Co), 590
Wasatch Venture Fund (FKA: Wasatch Venture Corporation), 687
West Midlands Enterprise Ltd, 976
Westar Capital, 271
Westbury Partners, 592
Westford Technology Ventures, L.P., 497
Weston Presidio Capital Management, 455
WestSphere Equity Investors, LP, 592

White Pines Management, L.L.C., 462
William A.M. Burden & Co., 593
William E. Simon & Sons (Asia) LDC, 977
Willis Stein & Partners, 374
Wind Point Partners, 462
Winslow Partners LLC, 317
Winthrop Ventures, 593
WomenAngles.net, 318
Working Ventures Canadian Fund, Inc., 978
Worldview Technology Partners, 275
Worms Capital Management, 594
ZS Fund, L.P., 595

Medical/Health

1st Source Capital Corp., 375
21st Century Health Ventures, 129
21st Century Internet Management Partners,LLC, 138
2nd Generation Capital Corp, 648
3i Austria (FKA Bank Austria TFV High Tech -UB GmbH), 725
3i Finland Oy (FKA SFK Finance), 725
A.M. Pappas & Associates, 597
Aberdare Ventures, 138
Aberdeen Asset Managers, 728
Aberlyn Capital Management Co., Inc., 501
Abingworth Venture Management Limited, 729
ABN AMRO Private Equity (AKA: ABN AMRO Capital (USA) Inc.) , 343
ABN-AMRO Corporate Investments, 729
ABS Ventures, 390
Acacia Venture Partners, 139
Academy Funds (FKA: Longleaf Venture Fund LLC), 597
Accenture Technology Ventures (FKA: AC Ventures), 140
ACF Equity Atlantic, Inc, 731
ACT Venture Capital Ltd., 732
Adams Capital Management, Inc., 622
Adams Street Partners, LLC (FKA: Brinson Private Equity), 343
Adams, Harkness & Hill, Inc., 401
Adler & Co., 502
Adler & Shaykin, 502
Advanced Materials Partners, Inc., 287
Advanced Technology Ventures, 401
Advantage Capital Partners, 386
Advent International Corp., 402
Advent Venture Partners (FKA Advent Limited), 733
Advent-Morro Equity Partners, 734
Affinity Capital Management(FKA:Peterson-Spencer-Fansler Co), 463
Agio Capital Partners I, L.P., 463
Alan I. Goldman & Associates, 483
Albemarle Private Equity Ltd, 735
Alchemy Partners, 736
Alignment Capital Partners, LLC, 655
Alimansky Capital Group, Inc., 504
Allegra Partners (FKA: Lawrence, Smith & Horey), 504
Alliance Technology Ventures, 330
Alliance Venture Capital Advisors Limited, 738
Allied Capital Corporation, 312
Allsop Venture Partners, 380
Allstate Private Equity, 344
Alpha Capital Partners, Inc., 344
Alta Berkeley Venture Partners, 739
Alta Partners, 144
Amadeus Capital Partners, 740
American Healthcare Fund, 345
American Securities, L.P., 505
Ampersand Ventures, 404
Amphion Ventures L.P.(FKA: Wolfensohn Associates, L.P.), 506
Annapolis Ventures LLC, 391
Antares Capital Corp. (FKA: Antares Leveraged Capital Corp), 345
Antares Capital Corporation (FKA: Harbor Ventures Corp.), 320
Anthem Capital, L.P., 391
Apax Partners & Cie (AKA: Apax France), 742
Apax Partners & Co. Ventures Ltd (AKA: Apax UK), 742
Apax Partners & Co.Beteiligungsberatung AG, 742
APIDC-Venture Capital Limited, 743
Applied Genomic Technology Capital Funds (AGTC), 405
ARCH Venture Partners, 346
Ardsheil, Inc., 506
Argentum Group, The , 507
Argos Soditic SA, 744
Artesian Capital, 464
Arthur P. Gould & Co., 507
Arthur Rock & Co., 146
ASC Group, 746
Ascend Technology Ventures, 747
Ascent Venture Partners, 406
AsiaTech Internet Group (ATIG) (FKA: AsiaTech Ventures), 748
Asset Management Company Venture Capital, 147
Atlantic Capital, 407
Atlantic Medical Management, LLC, 508
Atlas Venture, 407
August Partners, 508
Aurora Funds, Inc., 598
Austin Ventures, L.P., 657
Australian Technology Group Ltd, 750
Avery Business Development Services, 320
Aweida Ventures, 277
Axiom Venture Partners, L.P., 288
BA Venture Partners (AKA: BankAmerica Ventures), 150
Bailey & Co. Inc., 752
Baird Capital Partners, 347
Banc One Capital Partners, 608
BancAmerica Capital Investors (FKA:NationsBanc Capital Corp), 598
BancBoston Capital/BancBoston Ventures, 408
Bancorp Hawaii SBIC, Inc., 341
BANEXI Corp., 753
Bangert Dawes Reade Davis & Thom, 151
Bank One Equity Investors, Inc., 386
BankInvest Group AS, 754
Banque De Vizille, 754
Baring Private Equity Partners (FKA:Baring Venture Partners), 755
Bastion Capital Corp., 152
Batavia Investment Management Ltd, 756
Batterson Venture Partners(AKA:BVP), 348
Bausch & Lomb, Inc., 511
Baxter Associates, Inc., 289
BCM Technologies, Inc., 658
BCR Asset Management Pty Ltd., 758
Beacon Partners, Inc., 289
Bedford Capital Corp., 512

Bedrock Capital Partners, 409
Beecken, Petty & Co. LLC, 348
Behrman Capital, 512
Berkeley International Capital Corp., 154
Berkshire Partners, 410
Berlin Capital Fund (FKA LBB Beteiligungsgesellschaft GmbH), 759
Berwind Financial Group, L.P., 623
Betwin Investments, Inc., 760
BioVentures Investors, LLC, 411
Blue Chip Venture Company, 609
bmp Aktiengesellschaft AG, 761
BOME Investors, Inc., 473
Boston Financial & Equity Corp., 412
Boston Millennia Partners, 412
Boston University Community Technology Fund , 413
Boulder Ventures, Ltd., 392
Brait Capital Partners, 762
Brantley Venture Partners, 609
Bristol Capital Management, 513
Bristol Investment Trust, 413
Broadmark Capital Corp., 702
Brook Venture Management, L.L.C., 414
Bruce F. Glaspell & Associates, 498
Buena Venture Associates, 659
Bulldog Partners Limited, 764
Bure Equity, 765
Burr, Egan, Deleage & Co., 414
Burrill & Company, 156
Business Link Doncaster, 765
C3 Holdings, LLC, 474
Calvert Social Venture Partners, L.P., 690
Cambria Group, The, 157
Cambridge Research & Innovation Ltd (AKA CRIL), 767
Canaan Partners, 290
Canbank Venture Capital Fund Ltd, 767
Candover Investments PLC, 768
Canterbury Capital L.L.C.(AKA: Canterbury Detroit Partners), 514
Capital Development & Investment Co. Ltd., 768
Capital Investments, Inc., 717
Capital Network, The (AKA: Texas Capital Network), 659
Capital Partners LLC, 769
Capital Resource Partners, 415
Capital Services & Resources, Inc., 648
Capital Strategy Management Co., The, 349
Capman Management GmbH, 770
Capstone Ventures SBIC, L.P., 158
CapVis Equity Partners AG, 771
Cardinal Partners (FKA: Cardinal Health Partners), 485
Cardinal Ventures, L.L.C., 375
Carillon Capital, Inc., 610
Carousel Capital Partners, 599
Castle Group, Ltd., The , 515
Castle Harlan Australian Mezzanine Partners Pty. Ltd. , 772
Catalyst Group, The , 660
Catalyst Venture Capital Firm, 773
Catalyst Ventures, 393
CB Health Ventures LLC, 416
CCFL Mezzanine Partners of Canada , 774
CE Unterberg Towbin (FKA:Unterberg Harris Capital Partners), 515
Cedar Creek Partners, LLC, 717
CEI Ventures/Coastal Ventures LP, 388
CEO Advisors, 321
CEO Venture Fund, 625
Cerulean Fund/WGC Enterprises, 350
Chanen, Painter & Co., Ltd., 703
Charter Ventures, 160
Chartwell Capital Management Co., Inc., 321
Chase H&Q (FKA Hambrecht & Quist), 160
Chestnut Street Partners, Inc., 417
Child Health Investment Corporation, 382
China Venture Management, Inc., 777
Chisholm Private Capital Partners, 618
Chrysalis Ventures, 384
Churchill Capital, Inc., 465
CIBC Capital Partners (FKA: CIBC Wood Gundy Capital), 516
CID Equity Partners, 376
Circle Ventures, Inc., 376
Citicorp Capital Asia (AKA: CITIC Pacific Ltd.), 780
Citicorp Venture Capital, Ltd., 517
Citizens Capital and Citizens Ventures, 418
Claflin Capital Management, Inc., 418
Clairvest Group, Inc., 780
Clal Venture Capital Management Ltd (AKA CVC Management), 781
Clarion Capital Corp., 610
Clemente Capital (Asia) Ltd., 781
CM Equity Partners, 517
CMEA Ventures (FKA:Chemicals & Materials Enterprise Associa), 161
Cohen & Co., L.L.C., 517
Coleman Swenson Booth Inc.(FKA:Coleman Swenson Hoffman Booth, 649
Collinson, Howe & Lennox, LLC, 291
Colonial First State Private Equity Ltd (FKA: Hambro-G Mgmt), 782
Colonnade Capital L.L.C., 691
Colorado Venture Management, 278
Columbine Venture Funds, The , 279
Comdisco Ventures, 162
Commerz Beteiligungsgesellschaft mbH (CBG), 783
Commonwealth BioVentures Inc. (CBI), 389
Commonwealth Capital Ventures L.P., 419
CommTech International, 163
Compass Investment Management Ltd., 783
Compass Technology Partners, 163
Concord Venture Management (FKA:Nitzanim), 784
Connecticut Innovations, Inc., 291
Continental S.B.I.C., 691
Continental Venture Capital , 784
CORAL Ventures, 465
Cordova Ventures (FKA:Cordova Capital), 331
Cornerstone Equity Investors, LLC, 519
Coronado Venture Fund, 133
Corpfin Capital S.A., 786
Corporate Growth Assistance, Ltd., 786
Corporate Venture Partners, L.P., 519
Cowen & Co., 520
Crescent Capital NI Ltd (FKA Hambro Northern Ireland), 788
Crestview Financial Group, The , 292
Crocker Capital/Crocker Assoc., 164
Crosbie & Co Inc, 789
CrossBow Ventures, 322

Crosslink Capital (FKA: Omega Venture Partners), 165
Crown Advisors International, Ltd., 521
Crown Capital Corp, 475
CS Capital Partners, LLC, 486
CSK Venture Capital Co., Ltd., 789
Cullinane & Donnelly Venture Partners, L.P., 293
Cureton & Co., Inc., 662
CVC Capital Partners, 790
CW Group, Inc., 521
Cygnus Venture Partners, 791
D.H. Blair Investment Banking Corp., 521
Daewoo Venture Capital Co Ltd, 792
Danish Development Finance Corp., 793
DANSK Udviklingsfinansiering A/S, 793
Dauphin Capital Partners, 522
Davis Group, 166
Davis, Tuttle Venture Partners, L.P.(FKA:Davis Venture), 618
De Vries & Co., Inc., 476
Delphi Ventures, 167
Delta Partners, 795
Denali Venture Capital, 168
Desai Capital Management Inc., 522
Deucalion Venture Partners, 168
Deutsche Venture Capital GmbH (DVCG), 796
Development Corp. of Austin, 467
DFW Capital Partners (AKA:DeMuth, Folger & Wetherill), 486
Direct Capital Private Equity, 797
DN Partners, 352
Domain Associates, L.L.C., 486
Dominion Ventures, Inc., 170
Dongbu Venture Capital Co Ltd, 797
Dougery Ventures, 171
Dow Chemical Co., 458
Downer & Co., 420
Draper Triangle Ventures LP, 626
Dresdner Kleinwort Capital , 524
Dresner Capital Resources, Inc., 352
Drug Royalty Corp., Inc., 798
Drysdale Enterprises, 173
DSE Investment Services Limited, 799
Durlacher Limited, 799
Early Stage Enterprises, L.P., 487
Earlybird Venture Capital, 800
EarlyBirdCapital.com Inc., 524
East River Ventures, L.P., 524
Easton Hunt Capital Partners, 525
eBlast Ventures, LLC, 353
ECI Ventures Ltd, 801
ECICS Ventures Pte Ltd., 801
Edelson Technology Partners, 487
EDF Ventures (F.K.A. Enterprise Development Fund), 458
Edge Capital Investment Co., LLC, 175
EGL Holdings, Inc./Nat West Ventures USA, L.P., 332
Electra Fleming Limited, 525
Electra Partners Asia [FKA: JF Electra Limited], 803
EnCompass Ventures, 704
Enterprise Equity (NI) Limited, 805
Enterprise Investors, 526
Enterprise Partners, 178
Eos Partners, L.P., 527
Epicea, 805
EquiNet Venture Partners AG, 806
Equinox Investment Partners, 294
Equitas, L.P., 649
Equity Partners Management Pty Ltd, 807
Equity Ventures, Ltd, 807
Equity-South (FKA:Grubb & Williams Ltd.), 333
equity4life AG, 807
Equus Capital Corp., 663
Espirito Santo Development, 808
Essex Woodlands Health Ventures (FKA:Woodlands Venture Partn, 354
EuclidSR Partners , 527
Euroc Venture Capital Corporation, 809
Euroventures Benelux Team B.V., 811
Euroventures Management AB , 811
Evanston Business Investment Corp, 354
Evergreen Canada Israel Investments Ltd, 812
Evergreen Capital Partners Inc, 528
Evergreen Ventures, 686
Exeter Capital, L.P., 528
Fairfax Partners, 693
far blue, 814
Far East Capital Corp., 179
Federal Business Development Bank, 815
Ferrer Freeman Thompson & Co, 295
Fidelity Ventures (FKA: Fidelity Venture Associates), 421
Financial Technology Research Corp., 529
Finansa Capital Limited, 816
FINOVA Mezzanine Capital, Inc. (FKA: Sirrom Capital Corp), 650
Finovelec, 817
Firemark Advisors, Inc., 488
First Capital Management Co., 664
First Charter Partners, Inc., 664
First New England Capital, L.P., 295
First Princeton Capital Corp., 489
First Security Business Investment Corp., 686
First Union Capital Partners, 600
Flinders Capital Limited, 818
Florida Capital Partners, 322
Florida Capital Ventures, Ltd., 323
Fluke Venture Partners., 705
Fonds D'Investissements R.T.V.L., 819
Fonds de Solidarité des Travailleurs du Québec (F.T.Q.), 820
ForetagsByggarna AB, 821
Fort Washington Capital Partners, LLC, 611
FORTKNOX-VENTURE AG, 821
Fortune International Limited, 821
Forward Ventures, 180
Foundation Capital, 181
Founders Equity, Inc., 530
Fowler, Anthony & Co., 422
Frazier & Company, 705
Fremont Partners, 181
Friends Ivory & Sime Private Equity (Ivory &Sime Baronsmead), 823
Friulia SpA Fin.Reg.Friuli-Venezia, 824
Frontenac Co., 355
Frontline Capital, Inc., 334
Fuqua Ventures, LLC, 334
Galen Associates (FKA:Galen Partners), 531
Gaon Asset Management, 825
Gateway Associates, L.P., 476

GATX Ventures (FKA: Meier Mitchell & Co.), 183
GATX/MM Venture Partners, 183
GCI Venture Partners, 314
Genesee Funding, Inc., 532
Genesis Capital, Inc., 533
Genesis Partners, 826
Gideon Hixon Fund, 467
Giza Venture Capital (FKA Giza Investment Management), 828
Gleacher & Co., 534
Global Partner Ventures, 694
Glynn Ventures, 186
Go Equity GmbH, 829
Golub Associates, 534
Grand Pacific Venture Capital Company Ltd., 830
Granite Ventures LLC (FKA: H & Q Venture Associates), 186
Granville Baird Capital Partners (FKA:Granville Pr Eq Mngrs), 830
Grayson & Associates, 280
Graystone Venture Partners, LLC(AKA:Portage Venture Partners, 356
Greater Philadelphia Venture Capital Corp., 627
Grieve, Horner, Brown & Asculai, 833
Grotech Capital Group, 394
GrowthWorks Capital, 834
GTCR Golder Rauner, LLC, 356
Gujarat Venture Finance Limited, 834
H&Q Asia Pacific, Ltd., 187
Halpern, Denny & Co., 425
Hambro America Biosciences, Inc., 535
Hamilton Robinson & Co., Inc., 296
Hanbyuck Investment Co Ltd, 836
Hanover Capital Corp., 535
Harbour Financial Co., 426
HarbourVest Partners, LLC., 426
Health Capital Group, 188
Heartland Capital Fund, Ltd., 479
Heartland Capital Partners, L.P., 665
Heidelberg Innovation GmbH, 837
Henry & Co., 323
Herbert Young Securities, Inc., 536
Heritage Partners, 427
HFS Capital (AKA: Hoffman, Fitzgerald & Snyder), 694
Hibernia Capital Partners, 837
Hickory Venture Capital Corporation, 130
High Street Capital, LLC, 357
Highland Capital Partners, 427
HillStreet Capital, Inc., 612
Horizonte Venture Management GmbH, 840
Hotung International Company, Ltd., 840
Houston Venture Partners (AKA: Houston Partners), 666
Howard, Lawson & Co., 628
HSBC Private Equity (Asia), Ltd. (FKA: HSBC PE Management), 841
HSBC Private Equity Ltd (FKA Montagu Private Equity Ltd), 841
HT Capital Advisors, LLC, 538
Hudson Venture Partners, 538
IBK Capital Corporation, 844
ICC Venture Capital, 845
ICF Ventures Private Ltd., 845
ICICI Venture Funds Mngt. Co. Ltd., 846
Idanta Partners, Ltd., 191
IDG Technology Venture Investment Inc. (FKA: PTV-China), 846
IEG Venture Management, Inc., 357
IFCI Venture Cap. Funds (Formerly Risk Capital & Tech.), 847
IMH Industrie Management Holding GmbH, 848
IndAsia Fund Advisors Private Limited, 849
Indekon Management Oy, 849
Index Ventures, 850
Indocean Chase Capital Advisors, 850
Indosuez Ventures, 194
Inman & Bowman, 195
InnoCal, L.P., 196
Innovation Works, Inc., 628
Innovationsagentur Gesmbh, 854
InnovationsKapital Management Goteborg AB , 854
Innovest Group, Inc., 629
Innvotec Ltd, 854
Integra Ventures (F.K.A. Integra Bio-Health Inc.), 706
InterEquity Capital Partners, L.P., 541
Internet Healthcare Group, 297
Intersouth Partners, 601
InterWest Partners, 197
Invesco Private Capital (FKA: Chancellor), 541
InvestAmerica Venture Group, Inc., 380
Investissement Desjardins, 857
Investissements Novacap (AKA:Novacap Investments, Inc.), 858
Investment Securities of Colorado, Inc., 280
IPS Industrial Promotion Services, Ltd., 859
Ironside Ventures, LLC (FKA: MF Private Capital), 429
ISEP NV, 860
Itochu Technology, 542
J.L. Albright Venture Partners, 861
J.P. Morgan Capital Corp., 542
J.P. Morgan Partners (FKA: Chase Capital Partners), 543
JAFCO Co. Ltd., 862
James A. Matzdorff & Co., 199
Jefferson Capital Fund, Ltd., 130
Jerusalem Global Ventures, 864
Johnston Associates, Inc., 490
Josephberg Grosz & Co., Inc., 545
Kaiser Permanente (AKA: National Venture Development), 200
Kansas City Equity Partners, 477
Kansas Technology Enterprise Corporation, 382
Kansas Venture Capital, Inc., 383
KB Partners, LLC, 359
KBL Healthcare Ventures, 546
Kemper Ventures, 491
Key Equity Capital Corp.(AKA:Key Community Development Corp), 613
Keystone Minority Capital Fund, L.P., 630
Kingsbury Associates, 200
Kinship Partners, 280
Kirlan Venture Capital, Inc., 707
Kitty Hawk Capital, 602
KLB Investment Co., Ltd., 866
Kleiner Perkins Caufield & Byers, 200
Kookmin Venture Capital Co Ltd, 867
Korea Development Investment Corp., 868
Korea Technology Finance Corp., 869
Lake Shore Capital Partners, Inc., 360
Lambda Funds, The, 546
Lancet Capital Partner(FKA:Caduceus Capital Partners), 429
Las Americas Administradora, 871
Lawrence Financial Group, 202

Legal & General Ventures Ltd, 872
Leonard Mautner Associates, 203
Levine Leichtman Capital Partners, Inc., 204
Liberty Venture Partners, Inc., 631
Life Science Ventures, 873
Life Sciences Partners BV, 874
Lighthouse Capital Partners, 205
LINC Capital Partners, Inc., 361
Lincolnshire Management Inc., 548
LiveOak Equity Partners, 335
LLR Equity Partners, 631
LM Capital Corp., 324
Loeb Partners Corp., 549
London Ventures (Fund Managers) Ltd., 875
LTI Ventures Leasing Corp., 298
Lubar & Co., 718
M&F Associates, L.P., 549
Macquarie Direct Investment Limited, 876
Madison Dearborn Partners, LLC, 361
Madison Investment Partners, Inc., 550
Magic Venture Capital, LLC, 208
Malmohus Invest AB, 877
Management Resource Partners, 208
Manchester Humphreys, Inc., 642
Manhattan Venture Co., Inc., 550
Marconi Ventures, 431
Marlborough Capital Advisors, 431
Marleau, Lemire, Inc., 878
Marquette Venture Partners, 362
Maryland Venture Capital Trust, 395
Massachusetts Technology Development Corp. (MTDC), 432
Massey Burch Capital Corp., 650
Matrix Capital, 695
Matrix Group, 209
Mayfair Capital Partners, Inc., 551
Mayfield Fund, 210
Mayo Medical Ventures, 468
MBA Venture Group, 669
MC Capital, Inc., 551
McCown De Leeuw & Co., 210
McKee & Co., 134
MDS Discovery Venture Management, Inc., 881
MDS Health Ventures, Inc. (AKA: MDS Capital Corp.), 881
MDT Advisers, Inc., 433
Med-Tech Ventures, Inc., 492
Medical Innovation Partners, 469
Medical Science Partners, 434
Medical Venture Holdings, Inc., 552
Medicis AG, 882
Medicon Valley Capital, 882
Medicus Venture Partners, 211
Mediphase Venture Partners (FKA: EHealth Technology Fund), 434
Medmax Ventures, L.P., 299
MedTech International, Inc., 670
MedVenture Associates, 212
Mellon Ventures (AKA: Mellon Bank), 632
Memhard Investment Bankers, Inc., 300
Mentor Capital Partners, 633
Mercury Private Equity, 883
Meridian Venture Partners (MVP), 633
Merita Capital Limited, 134
Merrill Lynch Investment Managers FKA Mercury Asset Mgmt, 884
Merrill, Pickard, Anderson & Eyre, 213
Mezzanine Management UK Limited, 885
Mid-Atlantic Venture Funds (FKA: NEPA Management Corp.), 634
Middlefield Capital Fund, 885
Midlands Venture Fund Managers Ltd. (AKA: Midven Ltd), 886
Mission Ventures, 214
Mitsui & Co., Ltd., 553
MMG Ventures, L.P., 396
Mofet Venture Capital , 888
Montgomery Associates, Inc., 215
Montgomery Medical Ventures, L.P., 215
Montreux Equity Partners, 216
Moore & Associates, 619
Morgan Grenfell Private Equity Limited, 889
Morgan Stanley Venture Partners (AKA: MSDW), 554
Morgenthaler Ventures, 614
Mosaix Ventures, LLC , 363
Mountaineer Capital LP, 716
MPM Capital (FKA - MPM Asset Management LLC), 436
MST Partners, 555
MTI Partners Ltd, 890
Murphree Venture Partners, 671
Mutual Fund Public Company Ltd., 891
MWV Capital Partners (FKA:Middlewest Ventures, L.P.), 378
Nassau Capital, L.L.C., 492
National City Equity Partners, Inc, 614
National Corporate Finance, Inc., 217
National Financial Cos. LLC, 556
National Investment Management, Inc., 217
Navis Partners (FKA:Fleet Equity Partners), 643
Nazem & Co., 556
NCP Advisors Philippines, Inc., 894
Needham & Company, Inc., 556
Nelson Capital Corp., 651
NeoMed Management AS (FKA Medical Venture Management), 894
Nesbitt Burns, 363
New Business Capital Fund Ltd., 499
New England Partners, 437
New Enterprise Associates, 396
New Venture Resources, 282
New York Life Venture Capital Group, 557
New York State Science & Technology Foundation, 558
Newbury Ventures, 220
Newbury, Piret & Co., Inc., 437
NewMargin Venture Capital, 897
Newport Capital Group Pty Ltd, 897
NewSpring Ventures, 634
Newtek Ventures, 220
NIF Ventures USA, Inc.(Nippon Investment & Finance Co., Ltd), 222
Nikko Capital Co Ltd, 899
NMT New Medical Technologies, 900
Nomura International, Plc., 900
Nomura/JAFCO Investment (HK) Limited, 901
North Atlantic Capital Corp., 389
North Carolina Enterprise Fund, L.P., The, 602
North Carolina Technological Development Authority, Inc., 603
NorthEast Ventures, 301

Northern Venture Managers Limited, 902
Northwest Ohio Venture Fund, 615
Northwest Venture Associates, Inc.(FKA:Spokane Capital Mgmt), 709
Northwood Ventures, 559
Noveltek Venture Corp., 560
NPM Capital (AKA Nederlandse Participatie MIJ NV), 903
NPV Capital Partners, LLC, 560
Oak Hill Capital Management, Inc., 561
Oak Investment Partners, 302
Obelisk Capital Pty Ltd, 904
OmniMed Corp., 673
OneLiberty Ventures (FKA: Morgan, Holland Ventures Corp.), 439
Onondaga Venture Capital Fund, Inc., 562
Onset Ventures, 225
Open Prairie Ventures, 365
Opportunity Capital Partners {FKA: Thompson Capital Mgt), 225
Oregon Resource and Technology Development Fund, 620
Oresa Ventures, S.A., 906
Orien Ventures, 303
Orion Partners, L.P., 439
Oxford Bioscience Partners, 440
Oxford Financial Services Corp., 698
PA Early Stage (AKA:Pennsylvania Early Stage Partners), 635
Pacific Corporate Group, Inc., 227
Pacific Horizon Ventures LLC, 710
Pacific Northwest Partners SBIC, L.P., 710
Pacific Venture Group, 227
Pappajohn Capital Resources, 381
Paribas Principal, Inc., 563
Partech International, 229
Pathfinder Investment Co Pvt Ltd, 910
Pathfinder Venture Capital Funds, 470
Patricof & Co. Ventures, Inc., 563
Pauli & Co., Inc., 477
Penfund Partners, Inc., 911
Peninsula Capital Partners, L.L.C, 460
PENMAN Partners (FKA PENMAN Asset Management LP), 365
Penn-Janney Fund, Inc., The, 635
Pennsylvania Growth Fund, 636
Penny Lane Partners, 493
Pequot Capital Management Inc., 564
Perennial Ventures (FKA: Tredegar Investments), 711
Petra Capital Partners LLC, 652
Philadelphia Ventures, Inc., 636
Phoenix Equity Partners (FKA: DLJ European Private Equity), 911
Phoenix Growth Capital Corp., 231
Phoenix Partners, The , 711
Piedmont Venture Partners, 604
Pierce Financial Corporation(FKA:Pierce Investment Banking), 698
Platinum Group, Inc., The , 565
Point Venture Partners, 636
Polaris Venture Capital, 913
Polaris Venture Partners, 441
Poly Ventures, 566
PolyTechnos Venture Partners GmbH, 913
Pomona Capital, 566
PPM Ventures Ltd (FKA: Prudential Venture Managers Ltd), 914
pre-IPO Aktiengesellschaft, 915
Prelude Technology Investments Ltd, 915
Premier Medical Partner Fund L.P., 231
Prime Capital Management Co., Inc., 304
Prime Technology Ventures NV, 916
Prince Ventures, 367
Prism Venture Partners, 441
Private Capital Corp., 131
Priveq Capital Funds, 917
ProQuest Investments, L.P., 493
Prospect Partners LLC (FKA:Kenter, Glatris & Tuttle, LLC, 368
Provco Group, The , 637
ProVen Private Equity (FKA:Guinness Mahon Development Cap.), 918
Quantum Capital Partners, 325
Quest Ventures, 233
Quester Capital Management Ltd, 920
QuestMark Partners, L.P., 397
R-H Capital Partners, 337
RAF Ventures, 637
Ralph Wilson Equity Fund, L.L.C., 460
Rand Capital Corporation, 568
RCT BioVentures NE (Research Corporation Technologies), 442
Recovery Equity Investors, L.P., 234
Red River Ventures, 675
Reiten & Co Strategic Investments AS, 921
Renaissance Capital Corp., 337
Reprise Capital Corp., 569
RFE Investment Partners, 305
Richard Jaffe & Co., Inc., 676
Richland Ventures, 652
Ridge Capital Partners, L.L.C., 368
Riordan, Lewis & Haden, 236
River Capital, 338
RiverVest Venture Partners , 478
Roanoke Capital, Ltd., 712
Robertson Stephens & Company, LLC, 236
Rock Hill Ventures Inc.(FKA:Hillman Medical Ventures,Inc.), 638
Rosecliff, 237
Rosenfeld & Co., 620
Roser Ventures LLC, 283
Rothschild Bioscience Unit, 922
Rothschild Ventures Asia Pte Ltd., 922
Rothschild Ventures, Inc., 570
Royal Bank Private Equity (FKA: Royal Bank Development Cap), 922
Royalty Capital Fund, L.P. I/Royalty Capital Management, Inc, 443
Rutledge & Co., Inc., 305
S.R. One, Limited, 638
Saarlandische Wagnisfinanzierungsgesellschaft mbh (AKA SWG), 924
SAE Ventures, 306
Sage Management Group, 444
Salix Ventures, L.P., 653
Sanderling Ventures, 239
Sandhurst Venture Fund, L.P., The , 639
Sanpaolo IMI Private Equity S.p.A., 925
Sapient Capital, 721
Saugatuck Capital Company, 306
SBC Equity Partners, Inc., 369
SBC Ventures, 499
SBCA/A.G. Bartholomew & Associates, 131
SBV Venture Partners (AKA:Sigefi, Burnette & Vallee), 240
Schooner Capital International, L.P., 444

Schroder Capital Partners (Asia) Pte Ltd, 926
Schroder Ventures, 445
Scottish Equity Partners Limited, 927
Seacoast Capital, 446
Seaflower Ventures, 446
SEB Foretagsinvest, 927
Seed Capital Investments, 928
Seed Capital Ltd, 928
SENMED Medical Ventures, 616
Sentinel Capital Partners, 573
Sequel Venture Partners, 284
Sequoia Capital, 241
Shad Run Investments, Inc., 242
Shannon Development Company, 929
Shared Ventures, Inc., 470
Shattan Group, The, 574
Shaw Venture Partners (FKA: Shaw Glasgow Partners), 621
Shelton Companies, Inc., The , 604
Shepherd Group LLC, The, 447
Sherbrooke Capital Partners, 448
Siemens Venture Capital GmbH, 930
Sigma Capital Corp., 327
Sigma Partners, 243
Siguler Guff & Company, LLC, 575
Silicon Valley Bank, 244
Sitra (AKA Finnish National Fund for Research and Dev.), 932
Skyline Ventures, 245
Societe Regionale d'Investissement de Bruxelles (SRIB/GIMB), 933
Sofinnova Partners, 934
Sofinnova Ventures, 246
Solstice Capital LLC, 449
Sopartec SA, 936
Sorrento Associates, Inc., 247
South Atlantic Venture Funds, L.P., 327
Southeastern Technology Fund, 132
Southern California Ventures, 247
Southwest Venture Group, 678
Southwest Venture Partnerships, The, 678
Sovereign Capital (FKA:Nash, Sells & Partners Limited), 936
Spencer Trask Ventures, Inc. (FKA: Spencer Trask Securities), 576
Sponsored Consulting Services, 249
Spray Venture Partners, 450
Spring Capital Partners, L.P., 398
Sprout Group, 578
SRK Management Co., 578
St. Paul Venture Capital, Inc., 471
Star-Ventures Management GMBH (SVM), 940
Start-up Australia Pty Limited, 940
State Street Bank & Trust Co., 338
Sterling Venture Partners, 398
Still River Fund, The, 450
Stolberg Partners, 580
Stonebridge Partners, 580
StoneGate Partners, L.L.C., 450
Strategic Capital Management, 941
Strategic Investments & Holdings, Inc., 581
Stratford Equity Partners, L.P., 679
Strathdon Investments Ltd, 942
Sucsy, Fischer & Co., 370
SudKB & SudVC, 942
Suez Asia Holdings Pte Ltd., 943
Summit Capital Associates, Inc., 581
Summit Group Ltd, The, 943
Summit Partners, 451
Sun Valley Ventures, 250
Sunsino Development Associate Inc., 944
Sunwestern Investment Group, 680
Sutter Hill Ventures, 251
Swedestart Management AB, 944
Swedish Industrial Development Fund (AKA Industrifonden), 945
Sweeney & Co., Inc., 308
Sycamore Ventures, 494
Synerfi S.A., 945
Synergy Partners, 252
TA Associates, Inc., 451
Taylor & Turner, 253
tbg Technologie-Beteiligungsgesellschaft mbH, 947
TCR Europe SA, 947
TDH, 639
Teak Investment Partners I Limited, 948
Techno-Venture Co. (Japan), 949
Technologieholding VC GmbH, 950
Technology Funding, 254
Technology Partners, 255
TechnoPlus Ventures, 951
TecVenture Partners GmbH, 952
Teknoinvest Management As, 952
Texas Growth Fund Management, 681
Thoma Cressey Equity Partners, 371
Thompson Clive & Partners Limited, 955
Thompson Clive, Inc., 257
Thorner Ventures, 258
Three Arch Partners, 258
Throunarfelag Islands Plc(AKA:The Icelandic Finance&Invest.), 955
Ticonderoga Capital, Inc. (FKA: Dillon Read Venture Capital), 452
Tokyo Small & Medium Business Investment & Consultation Co., 956
Top Technology Limited (AKA:Hambros-Advanced Technology Tru), 957
Transamerica Mezzanine Financing, 645
Transamerica Technology Finance, 309
Transatlantic Capital Ltd., 958
Transcap Associates, Inc., 371
Triad Investors Corp, 319
Triune Capital, 260
True North Partners LLC, 583
TSG Capital Group, L.L.C., 309
TTP Venture Managers (FKA: The Technology Partnership), 960
TVM Techno Venture Management, 961
TVS Finance Ltd., 961
U.S. Bancorp Piper Jaffray Ventures, Inc., 472
U.S. Medical Resources Corp., 616
U.S. Venture Partners, 261
UBS Capital (AKA Phildrew Ventures), 963
Ulin & Holland, Inc., 453
Ulster Development Capital, Ltd., 963
Union Street Capital Corp., 713
Union Venture Capital Corporation, 963
Unit Trust of India (UTI), 964
UOB Venture Management Pte Ltd., 964
US Trust Private Equity, 584

Utah Ventures II, L.P. (A.K.A. Union Ventures), 687
Valley Capital Corp., 654
Valley Ventures (FKA: Arizona Growth Partners, L.P.), 136
Vanguard Venture Partners, 262
VantagePoint Venture Partners, 263
Vector Fund Management, L.P. (FKA: Vector Securities), 372
Vega Capital Corp., 584
Venca Management, 263
Vencap Equities Alberta, Ltd., 966
Vencon Management, Inc., 585
Venrock Associates, 586
Ventana Financial Resources, Inc., 372
Ventana Global, 264
Ventex Management, Inc., 683
Venture Capital Fund Managers (Pty), Ltd., The , 967
Venture Capital Management Corp., 328
Venture Funding Group International, 587
Venture Funding, Ltd., 461
Venture Growth Associates, 265
Venture Investment Management Company LLC (AKA: VIMAC), 454
Venture Investors Management LLC, 720
Venture Opportunities Corp., 588
Venture Select, 968
Venture Strategy Partners, 266
Venture TDF Pte Ltd., 968
VentureCap Management GmbH (AKA VCH Equity Group AG), 969
Ventures Medical Associates, 683
Ventures West Management, Inc., 970
Veritas Venture Capital Management, Ltd., 970
Vero Group PLC, 684
Versant Ventures (FKA: Palladium Capital), 266
Vertex Management, 971
Victory Ventures L.L.C., 588
Virginia Capital , 701
VK Ventures, 268
Wachtel & Co., Inc., 317
Wakefield Group, 607
Walden Capital Management Corporation, 589
Walden International Investment Group (AKA: Walden Group), 269
Walden Israel, 975
WaldenVC, 270
Walnut Capital Corp., 701
Warburg, Pincus & Co., LLC. (FKA: E.M. Warburg, Pincus & Co), 590
Wasatch Venture Fund (FKA: Wasatch Venture Corporation), 687
Wasserstein, Perella & Co., Inc., 591
Wedbush Capital Partners, 271
Wellmax, Inc., 461
Welsh, Carson, Anderson & Stowe, 591
West Central Capital Corp., 684
West Midlands Enterprise Ltd, 976
Westar Capital, 271
Westbury Partners, 592
Western States Investment Group, 272
Western Technology Investment, 272
Weston Presidio Capital Management, 455
WestSphere Equity Investors, LP, 592
White Pines Management, L.L.C., 462
Whitney & Co. (FKA: J.H. Whitney & Co.), 310
William A.M. Burden & Co., 593
William Blair Capital Partners, 373
Willis Stein & Partners, 374
Wind Point Partners, 462
Windamere Venture Partners, LLC, 273
Windjammer Capital Investors (FKA:Pacific Mezzanine Inv.), 273
Windward Ventures (FKA: Coronado Capital), 274
Wingate Partners, L.P., 685
Winslow Partners LLC, 317
Winthrop Ventures, 593
Wolf Ventures (AKA:Wolf Asset Management Corp.), 286
WomenAngles.net, 318
Wooshin Development Finance Corp, 978
Working Ventures Canadian Fund, Inc., 978
Worms Capital Management, 594
Yasuda Enterprise Development Co., Ltd.(FKA: Nippon Ent.Dev), 275
Yorkshire Fund Managers Ltd., 979
Zero Stage Capital Co., Inc., 456
ZS Fund, L.P., 595
Zurich Scudder Investments (FKA: Scudder Kemper Investments), 596

Other

3i Finland Oy (FKA SFK Finance), 725
Advent International Corp., 402
Axxon Capital, Inc., 408
BancBoston Capital/BancBoston Ventures, 408
Bayern Kapital Risikokapitalbeteiligungs GmbH, 757
BCR Asset Management Pty Ltd., 758
Bruce F. Glaspell & Associates, 498
Capital Across America, L.P., 648
CEI Ventures/Coastal Ventures LP, 388
Citadel Pooled Development Ltd. , 779
Continental Venture Capital , 784
Crocker Capital/Crocker Assoc., 164
CSK Venture Capital Co., Ltd., 789
EPS Finanz AG, 806
Equinox Investment Partners, 294
Equity Partners Management Pty Ltd, 807
Finansa Capital Limited, 816
First Analysis Venture Capital (FKA:First Analysis Corp), 354
Fonds de Solidarité des Travailleurs du Québec (F.T.Q.), 820
GrowthWorks Capital, 834
H&Q Asia Pacific, Ltd., 187
Horizonte Venture Management GmbH, 840
J.P. Morgan Partners (FKA: Chase Capital Partners), 543
JAFCO Co. Ltd., 862
Kansas City Equity Partners, 477
Madison Dearborn Partners, LLC, 361
Massachusetts Technology Development Corp. (MTDC), 432
Medicis AG, 882
MWV Capital Partners (FKA:Middlewest Ventures, L.P.), 378
Navis Partners (FKA:Fleet Equity Partners), 643
NewMargin Venture Capital, 897
NextGen Partners LLC, 221
North Texas Opportunity Fund , 672
Northwood Ventures, 559
Obelisk Capital Pty Ltd, 904
Orix Capital Corporation, 906
Shattan Group, The, 574

SISIR International Pte Ltd., 932
Solstice Capital LLC, 449
Sovereign Capital (FKA:Nash, Sells & Partners Limited), 936
SPEF Banques Populaires, 937
Start-up Australia Pty Limited, 940
Sustainable Jobs Fund (SJF), The , 606
Technostart GmbH, 951
Tokyo Small & Medium Business Investment & Consultation Co., 956
Utah Ventures II, L.P. (A.K.A. Union Ventures), 687
WomenAngles.net, 318
WSI Holding Corporation, 595

Semiconductors/Other Elect.

1st Source Capital Corp., 375
21st Century Internet Management Partners,LLC, 138
2M Invest, Inc., 138
3i Austria (FKA Bank Austria TFV High Tech -UB GmbH), 725
3i Finland Oy (FKA SFK Finance), 725
3TS Venture Partners AG, 727
4C Ventures (FKA: Olivetti Holding, N.V.), 501
Abell Venture Fund, 390
Aberlyn Capital Management Co., Inc., 501
Abingworth Venture Management Limited, 729
ABN-AMRO Corporate Investments, 729
ABP Acquisition Corp, 287
ABS Ventures, 390
Academy Funds (FKA: Longleaf Venture Fund LLC), 597
Accelerator Media (UK), Ltd, 730
Access Venture Partners, 277
ACE Management, 731
Acer Technology Ventures(FKA:Acer Soft Capital Inc.), 141
ACF Equity Atlantic, Inc, 731
ACT Venture Capital Ltd., 732
Adams Capital Management, Inc., 622
Adams Street Partners, LLC (FKA: Brinson Private Equity), 343
Adams, Harkness & Hill, Inc., 401
AdCapital AG (FKA Berliner Elektro Holding AG), 732
Adler & Co., 502
Advanced Materials Partners, Inc., 287
Advanced Technology Ventures, 401
Advantage Capital Partners, 386
Advent International Corp., 402
Advent Venture Partners (FKA Advent Limited), 733
Agilent Ventures, 142
Agio Capital Partners I, L.P., 463
Alan I. Goldman & Associates, 483
Albemarle Private Equity Ltd, 735
Alchemy Partners, 736
Alimansky Capital Group, Inc., 504
All Asia Partners, 737
Alliance Technology Ventures, 330
Allsop Venture Partners, 380
Allstate Private Equity, 344
Alpha Capital Partners, Inc., 344
Alpine Technology Ventures, 144
Alta Partners, 144
Altos Ventures, 144
Amadeus Capital Partners, 740
American Research & Development Corp., 404
American Securities, L.P., 505
Ameritech Development Corp., 345
AMP Asset Management Limited - Development Capital, 740
Ampersand Ventures, 404
Amphion Ventures L.P.(FKA: Wolfensohn Associates, L.P.), 506
AMT Capital Ltd. (AKA: AMT Venture Partners, Ltd.), 656
Antares Capital Corp. (FKA: Antares Leveraged Capital Corp), 345
Antares Capital Corporation (FKA: Harbor Ventures Corp.), 320
Anthem Capital, L.P., 391
Apax Globis Partners & Co. (APAX Japan), 741
Apex Venture Partners, 346
APIDC-Venture Capital Limited, 743
Applied Technology, 405
ARCH Venture Partners, 346
Ardsheil, Inc., 506
Argentum Group, The , 507
Arkoma Venture Partners, 657
Arthur P. Gould & Co., 507
Arthur Rock & Co., 146
ASC Group, 746
Ascent Venture Partners, 406
Aspen Ventures (formerly 3i Ventures), 147
Asset Management Company Venture Capital, 147
Athena Technology Ventures, 148
Atlantic Capital, 407
Atlantic Coastal Ventures, L.P.(AKA:Multimedia Broadcast In), 312
August Capital Management, 148
AUGUSTA Venture GmbH, 749
Auric Asset Management Pte. Ltd., 750
Aurora Funds, Inc., 598
Austin Ventures, L.P., 657
Australian Technology Group Ltd, 750
AVI Capital, L.P., 149
Bachow & Associates, Inc., 623
Bailey & Co. Inc., 752
Baird Capital Partners, 347
Banc One Capital Partners, 608
BancAmerica Capital Investors (FKA:NationsBanc Capital Corp), 598
BancBoston Capital/BancBoston Ventures, 408
BanChem Financial Services, Inc., 658
Bancorp Hawaii SBIC, Inc., 341
BANEXI Corp., 753
Bangert Dawes Reade Davis & Thom, 151
Bank One Equity Investors, Inc., 386
Bankers Capital Corp., 473
Bankers Trust New York Corp./Deutsche Banc Alex Brown, 510
Bastion Capital Corp., 152
Batavia Group, Ltd., The , 511
Battelle Venture Partners (Scientific Advances), 608
Batterson Venture Partners(AKA:BVP), 348
Bay Partners, 153
Bayern Kapital Risikokapitalbeteiligungs GmbH, 757
BCE Capital, 758
BCR Asset Management Pty Ltd., 758
Beacon Partners, Inc., 289
Behrman Capital, 512
Benchmark Capital, 154
Benefit Capital Companies, Inc., The, 480
Berkeley International Capital Corp., 154
Berkshire Partners, 410

Berwind Financial Group, L.P., 623
Bessemer Venture Partners, 410
Betwin Investments, Inc., 760
Blue Chip Venture Company, 609
Blue Rock Capital, 319
Blumberg Capital Ventures, 155
BOME Investors, Inc., 473
Boston Capital Ventures, 411
Boston Financial & Equity Corp., 412
Boston University Community Technology Fund , 413
Boulder Ventures, Ltd., 392
Brait Capital Partners, 762
Brantley Venture Partners, 609
Bristol Capital Management, 513
Broadmark Capital Corp., 702
Brook Venture Management, L.L.C., 414
Bruce F. Glaspell & Associates, 498
Bulldog Partners Limited, 764
Burr, Egan, Deleage & Co., 414
Business Link Doncaster, 765
C3 Holdings, LLC, 474
Caltech Capital Partners Ltd., 766
Calvert Social Venture Partners, L.P., 690
Cambria Group, The, 157
Cambridge Research & Innovation Ltd (AKA CRIL), 767
Camelot Ventures, 457
Canaan Partners, 290
Canbank Venture Capital Fund Ltd, 767
Candover Investments PLC, 768
Canterbury Capital L.L.C.(AKA: Canterbury Detroit Partners), 514
Capital Development & Investment Co. Ltd., 768
Capital Insights, L.L.C., 645
Capital Investments, Inc., 717
Capital Network, The (AKA: Texas Capital Network), 659
Capital Services & Resources, Inc., 648
Capital Southwest Corporation, 660
Capital Strategy Management Co., The, 349
CapVis Equity Partners AG, 771
Cardinal Ventures, L.L.C., 375
Cariad Capital, Inc., 642
Carillon Capital, Inc., 610
Carolinas Capital Investment Corp., 599
Castle Harlan Australian Mezzanine Partners Pty. Ltd. , 772
Catalyst Group, The , 660
Catalyst Venture Capital Firm, 773
CCFL Mezzanine Partners of Canada , 774
CD Technicom S.A., 774
CDC Innovation Partners, 775
CE Unterberg Towbin (FKA:Unterberg Harris Capital Partners), 515
Cedar Creek Partners, LLC, 717
CEI Ventures/Coastal Ventures LP, 388
CenterPoint Venture Partners, 661
CEO Advisors, 321
CEO Venture Fund, 625
Cerulean Fund/WGC Enterprises, 350
Champion Consulting Group, Incorporated, 776
Chanen, Painter & Co., Ltd., 703
Charter Ventures, 160
Chase H&Q (FKA Hambrecht & Quist), 160
Chestnut Street Partners, Inc., 417
Chiao Tung Bank, 776
China Venture Management, Inc., 777
Chisholm Private Capital Partners, 618
Churchill Capital, Inc., 465
CIBC Capital Partners (FKA: CIBC Wood Gundy Capital), 516
CID Equity Partners, 376
Circle Ventures, Inc., 376
Citicorp Capital Asia (AKA: CITIC Pacific Ltd.), 780
Citicorp Venture Capital, Ltd., 517
Citizens Capital and Citizens Ventures, 418
CIVC Partners (FKA:Continental Illinois Venture Corp.), 350
Claflin Capital Management, Inc., 418
Clairvest Group, Inc., 780
Clarion Capital Corp., 610
Clearstone Venture Partners (FKA: idealab! Capital Partners), 161
CM Equity Partners, 517
CMEA Ventures (FKA:Chemicals & Materials Enterprise Associa), 161
Cohen & Co., L.L.C., 517
Coleman Venture Group, 518
Colonnade Capital L.L.C., 691
Colorado Venture Management, 278
Columbine Venture Funds, The , 279
Comdisco Ventures, 162
Commerz Beteiligungsgesellschaft mbH (CBG), 783
Commonwealth Capital Ventures L.P., 419
CommTech International, 163
Compass Investment Management Ltd., 783
Compass Technology Partners, 163
Concord Venture Management (FKA:Nitzanim), 784
Connecticut Innovations, Inc., 291
Continental S.B.I.C., 691
Continental Venture Capital , 784
Convergence Partners L.P., 164
CORAL Ventures, 465
Core Capital Partners, 313
Core Pacific Consulting Company, 786
Cornerstone Equity Investors, LLC, 519
Coronado Venture Fund, 133
Corpfin Capital S.A., 786
Corporate Growth Assistance, Ltd., 786
Corporate Venture Partners, L.P., 519
Cowen & Co., 520
CR&T Ventures AB, 787
Crescent Capital NI Ltd (FKA Hambro Northern Ireland), 788
Crest Communications Holdings LLC, 520
Crestview Financial Group, The , 292
Crocker Capital/Crocker Assoc., 164
Crosbie & Co Inc, 789
Crown Advisors International, Ltd., 521
Crown Capital Corp, 475
Crystal Internet Venture Fund, L.P., 611
CS Capital Partners, LLC, 486
CSK Venture Capital Co., Ltd., 789
Cullinane & Donnelly Venture Partners, L.P., 293
Cureton & Co., Inc., 662
Cygnus Venture Partners, 791
D.H. Blair Investment Banking Corp., 521
Daewoo Venture Capital Co Ltd, 792
Daimler Chrysler Venture Gmbh (AKA DCV), 792
Dali, Hook Partners (FKA: Hook Partners), 662
Danish Development Finance Corp., 793
DANSK Udviklingsfinansiering A/S, 793

Davis, Tuttle Venture Partners, L.P.(FKA:Davis Venture), 618
De Vries & Co., Inc., 476
Defta Partners, 167
Delmag Ventures, 394
Delta Partners, 795
Delta Ventures, 795
Desai Capital Management Inc., 522
Deutsche Effecten und Wechsel-Beteiligungsgesellschaft AG, 796
Deutsche Venture Capital GmbH (DVCG), 796
Development Corp. of Austin, 467
DFW Capital Partners (AKA:DeMuth, Folger & Wetherill), 486
Direct Capital Private Equity, 797
Divine interVentures (FKA: Platinum Venture Partners), 351
DN Partners, 352
Dongbu Venture Capital Co Ltd, 797
Dougery Ventures, 171
Dow Chemical Co., 458
Downer & Co., 420
Draper Fisher Jurvetson (FKA: Draper Associates), 172
Draper International, 172
Dresdner Kleinwort Capital , 524
Dresner Capital Resources, Inc., 352
Drysdale Enterprises, 173
DSE Investment Services Limited, 799
Duchossois TECnology Partners, LLC, 353
Dunedin Capital Partners Ltd (FKA:Dunedin Ventures Limited), 799
DynaFund Ventures, L.L.C., 174
Early Stage Enterprises, L.P., 487
Easton Hunt Capital Partners, 525
ECI Ventures Ltd, 801
ECICS Ventures Pte Ltd., 801
EDB Investments Pte Ltd., 802
EDF Ventures (F.K.A. Enterprise Development Fund), 458
Edge Capital Investment Co., LLC, 175
Edison Venture Fund, 488
EGL Holdings, Inc./Nat West Ventures USA, L.P., 332
El Dorado Ventures, 176
Electra Partners Asia [FKA: JF Electra Limited], 803
EnerTech Capital Partners, L.P., 626
Enterprise Equity (NI) Limited, 805
Enterprise Investors, 526
Enterprise Partners, 178
Eos Partners, L.P., 527
Epicea, 805
Equinox Investment Partners, 294
Equity Ventures, Ltd, 807
Equity-South (FKA:Grubb & Williams Ltd.), 333
Equus Capital Corp., 663
Eqvitec Partners Oy, 807
EURAZEO (FKA Gaz-et-Eaux & AZEO), 809
Euroc Venture Capital Corporation, 809
European Acquisition Capital Ltd., 810
Euroventures Management AB , 811
Evanston Business Investment Corp, 354
Evergreen Canada Israel Investments Ltd, 812
Evergreen Capital Partners Inc, 528
Evergreen Ventures, 686
Exeter Capital, L.P., 528
Far East Capital Corp., 179
FBR Technology Venture Partners,L.P.(AKA:Friedman,Billings), 693
Federal Business Development Bank, 815
Financial Technology Research Corp., 529
Financial Technology Ventures, 179
Finansa Capital Limited, 816
FINORPA, 816
FINOVA Mezzanine Capital, Inc. (FKA: Sirrom Capital Corp), 650
Finovelec, 817
First Analysis Venture Capital (FKA:First Analysis Corp), 354
First Charter Partners, Inc., 664
First Gen-e Investments, 817
First New England Capital, L.P., 295
First Security Business Investment Corp., 686
First Union Capital Partners, 600
FJC Growth Capital Corp., 129
Florida Capital Partners, 322
Florida Capital Ventures, Ltd., 323
Fluke Venture Partners., 705
Fonds de Solidarité des Travailleurs du Québec (F.T.Q.), 820
Forrest Binkley & Brown, 180
Fort Washington Capital Partners, LLC, 611
FORTKNOX-VENTURE AG, 821
Fortune Consulting Group Incorporated, 821
Fortune Venture Capital Incorporated, 822
Fortune Venture Management Pte Ltd., 822
Foundation Capital, 181
Foundation Capital Limited, 822
Fowler, Anthony & Co., 422
Friends Ivory & Sime Private Equity (Ivory &Sime Baronsmead), 823
Frontier Capital, LLC, 600
Frontline Capital, Inc., 334
Gabriel Venture Partners, 182
GATX Ventures (FKA: Meier Mitchell & Co.), 183
GATX/MM Venture Partners, 183
GCI, 718
GCI Venture Partners, 314
Gemini Capital Fund Management Ltd, 825
Generation Capital Partners, 532
Genesee Funding, Inc., 532
Genesis Capital, Inc., 533
Genevest Consulting Group, S.A., 827
Geocapital Partners, L.L.C., 489
Gideon Hixon Fund, 467
GKM Venture Partners, LP, 184
Glencoe Capital, LLC (FKA: Glencoe Investment Corporation), 356
Global Partner Ventures, 694
Glynn Ventures, 186
Go Equity GmbH, 829
Goldner Hawn Johnson & Morrison Incorporated, 468
Golub Associates, 534
Grand Pacific Venture Capital Company Ltd., 830
Granite Ventures LLC (FKA: H & Q Venture Associates), 186
Granville Baird Capital Partners (FKA:Granville Pr Eq Mngrs), 830
Graystone Venture Partners, LLC(AKA:Portage Venture Partners, 356
Grosvenor Funds, The, 315
Grotech Capital Group, 394
Grove Street Advisors, LLC, 425
GrowthWorks Capital, 834

Gujarat Venture Finance Limited, 834
H&Q Asia Pacific, Ltd., 187
Hallador Venture Partners, 188
Hambro European Ventures (Hambros PLC), 835
Hamilton Robinson & Co., Inc., 296
Hanbyuck Investment Co Ltd, 836
Harbour Financial Co., 426
HarbourVest Partners, LLC., 426
Health Capital Group, 188
Herbert Young Securities, Inc., 536
Heritage Partners, 427
Hickory Venture Capital Corporation, 130
High Street Capital, LLC, 357
Highland Capital Partners, 427
Higin Venture Capital Co., Ltd., 838
HillStreet Capital, Inc., 612
HMS Hawaii Management Partners, 341
Hoak Capital Corp., 666
Honho Consulting Company Limited, 839
Horizon Ventures (F.K.A. Technology Investments), 190
Horizonte Venture Management GmbH, 840
Hotung International Company, Ltd., 840
Houston Venture Partners (AKA: Houston Partners), 666
Howard, Lawson & Co., 628
HSBC Private Equity (Asia), Ltd. (FKA: HSBC PE Management), 841
HSBC Private Equity Ltd (FKA Montagu Private Equity Ltd), 841
HT Capital Advisors, LLC, 538
Hungarian-American Enterprise Fund, The (HAEF), 842
Hunt Capital Group, 667
Hydro-Quebec CapiTech Inc., 843
IBB Beteiligungsgesellschaft mbH, 844
IBJS Capital Corp., 539
IBK Capital Corporation, 844
ICC Venture Capital, 845
ICICI Venture Funds Mngt. Co. Ltd., 846
Idanta Partners, Ltd., 191
IEG Venture Management, Inc., 357
IFCI Venture Cap. Funds (Formerly Risk Capital & Tech.), 847
IKB Venture Capital GmbH (AKA IKB Beteiligungsgesellschaft , 848
IMH Industrie Management Holding GmbH, 848
Impex Venture Management Co., 540
Incorporated Investors, 193
IndAsia Fund Advisors Private Limited, 849
Indekon Management Oy, 849
Index Ventures, 850
Indosuez Ventures, 194
Indus Venture Management Ltd., 851
Industrial Technology Securities Ltd, 851
Infinity Capital LLC, 194
Information Technology Ventures, 195
Inman & Bowman, 195
InnoCal, L.P., 196
Innovacom, 853
Innovation Works, Inc., 628
Innovationsagentur Gesmbh, 854
InnovationsKapital Management Goteborg AB , 854
Innovest Group, Inc., 629
Innvotec Ltd, 854
InterEquity Capital Partners, L.P., 541
Internet Incubator PLC, 856
Intersouth Partners, 601
InvestAmerica Venture Group, Inc., 380
InveStar Capital, Inc., 857
Investissement Desjardins, 857
Investissements Novacap (AKA:Novacap Investments, Inc.), 858
Investment Securities of Colorado, Inc., 280
IPS Industrial Promotion Services, Ltd., 859
ISEP NV, 860
Israel Seed Partners, 860
J.E. Mann & Co., 542
J.L. Albright Venture Partners, 861
J.P. Morgan Capital Corp., 542
J.P. Morgan Partners (FKA: Chase Capital Partners), 543
JAFCO Co. Ltd., 862
JAFCO Investment (FKA:Nomura/JAFCO Investment (Asia) Limited, 862
James A. Matzdorff & Co., 199
Jefferson Capital Fund, Ltd., 130
Jerusalem Global Ventures, 864
JK&B Capital, 358
Josephberg Grosz & Co., Inc., 545
JumpStartUp Fund Advisors Pvt. Ltd., 864
Kaiser Permanente (AKA: National Venture Development), 200
Kankaku Investment Co Ltd, 865
Kansas City Equity Partners, 477
Kansas Technology Enterprise Corporation, 382
Kansas Venture Capital, Inc., 383
KB Partners, LLC, 359
Kennet Capital Ltd, 866
Kettle Partners, L.P., 359
Key Equity Capital Corp.(AKA:Key Community Development Corp), 613
Keystone Minority Capital Fund, L.P., 630
Kitty Hawk Capital, 602
KLB Investment Co., Ltd., 866
Kleiner Perkins Caufield & Byers, 200
Kline Hawkes & Co., 201
KLM Capital Group, 201
Kookmin Venture Capital Co Ltd, 867
Korea Development Investment Corp., 868
Korea Technology Finance Corp., 869
KTB Ventures (FKA: KTB Venture Capital), 202
Kyocera International, Inc., 202
Lake Shore Capital Partners, Inc., 360
Lambda Funds, The, 546
Las Americas Administradora, 871
Lawrence Financial Group, 202
Lee Munder Venture Partners, 430
Legal & General Ventures Ltd, 872
Leonard Mautner Associates, 203
LG Venture Investment Inc., 873
Liberty BIDCO Investment Corporation, 459
Liberty Environmental Partners, 205
Libon Capital Management Limited, 873
Lighthouse Capital Partners, 205
LINC Capital Partners, Inc., 361
Lincoln Investment Management Inc., 378
Lincolnshire Management Inc., 548
LJH Global Investments , 324
LM Capital Corp., 324
Loeb Partners Corp., 549
LTI Ventures Leasing Corp., 298

Lubar & Co., 718
Lucent Venture Partners, Inc., 207
Macquarie Direct Investment Limited, 876
Madison Dearborn Partners, LLC, 361
Madison Investment Partners, Inc., 550
Madrona Venture Group, 707
Malmohus Invest AB, 877
Management Resource Partners, 208
Manchester Humphreys, Inc., 642
Manhattan Venture Co., Inc., 550
Marconi Ventures, 431
Maristeth Ventures, L.L.C., 707
Marleau, Lemire, Inc., 878
Marquette Venture Partners, 362
Massachusetts Technology Development Corp. (MTDC), 432
Maton Venture, 209
Matrix Capital, 695
Matrix Group, 209
Matrix Partners, 433
Matrix Private Equity, 879
Mayfair Capital Partners, Inc., 551
Mayfield Fund, 210
MBA Venture Group, 669
MC Capital, Inc., 551
McCown De Leeuw & Co., 210
McKee & Co., 134
McLean Watson Capital Inc., 880
MDT Advisers, Inc., 433
MedTech International, Inc., 670
Mees Pierson Investeringsmaat. B.V., 435
Mellon Ventures (AKA: Mellon Bank), 632
Memhard Investment Bankers, Inc., 300
Menlo Ventures, 212
Mentor Capital Partners, 633
Mercury Private Equity, 883
Meridian Venture Partners (MVP), 633
Merita Capital Limited, 134
Merrill Lynch Investment Managers FKA Mercury Asset Mgmt, 884
Merrill, Pickard, Anderson & Eyre, 213
MESBIC Ventures Holding Co. (AKA Pacesetter Growth Fund, L.P, 671
Metapoint Partners, 435
Mezzanine Management UK Limited, 885
Mid-Atlantic Venture Funds (FKA: NEPA Management Corp.), 634
Middlefield Capital Fund, 885
Miller Capital Corp, 135
Miralta Capital, Inc., 887
Mission Ventures, 214
Mitsui & Co., Ltd., 553
MMG Ventures, L.P., 396
Mohr, Davidow Ventures, 214
Montgomery Associates, Inc., 215
Montreux Equity Partners, 216
Moore & Associates, 619
Morel Ventures Limited, 888
Morgan Grenfell Private Equity Limited, 889
Morgan Stanley Venture Partners (AKA: MSDW), 554
Morgenthaler Ventures, 614
Motorola Inc., 315
Mountaineer Capital LP, 716
MST Partners, 555
MTI Partners Ltd, 890
Multiventure Investment, Inc., 890
Murphree Venture Partners, 671
Mustang Ventures (FKA Siemens Mustang Ventures), 216
MVC AG (AKA Mitteldeutsche Venture Capital AG), 891
MVP Ventures (AKA: Milk Street Ventures), 436
MWV Capital Partners (FKA:Middlewest Ventures, L.P.), 378
Nanyang Ventures Pty Ltd (AKA: Nanyang Management Pty Ltd), 892
National Bank Of Kuwait, 555
National City Equity Partners, Inc, 614
National Corporate Finance, Inc., 217
National Financial Cos. LLC, 556
National Investment Management, Inc., 217
Navis Partners (FKA:Fleet Equity Partners), 643
Nazem & Co., 556
NCP Advisors Philippines, Inc., 894
Needham & Company, Inc., 556
Nesbitt Burns, 363
New Business Capital Fund Ltd., 499
New England Partners, 437
New Venture Resources, 282
New York Life Venture Capital Group, 557
New York State Science & Technology Foundation, 558
Newbridge Capital Limited, 219
Newbury Ventures, 220
Newbury, Piret & Co., Inc., 437
Newtek Ventures, 220
NextGen Capital LLC, 697
NextGen Partners LLC, 221
NextPoint Partners L.P.(FKA: Plaza Street), 315
NIB Capital Private Equity N.V. (FKA: Parnib Holding NV) , 898
NIF Ventures Co., Ltd., 898
NIF Ventures USA, Inc.(Nippon Investment & Finance Co., Ltd), 222
Nikko Capital Co Ltd, 899
Nippon Technology Venture Partners Ltd., 899
Nomura International, Plc., 900
Nomura/JAFCO Investment (HK) Limited, 901
North Atlantic Capital Corp., 389
North Bridge Venture Partners, 438
North Carolina Technological Development Authority, Inc., 603
NorthEast Ventures, 301
Northern Venture Managers Limited, 902
Northwest Ohio Venture Fund, 615
Northwest Venture Associates, Inc.(FKA:Spokane Capital Mgmt), 709
Novak Biddle Venture Partners, L.P., 697
Noveltek Venture Corp., 560
Novus Ventures, 223
NPM Capital (AKA Nederlandse Participatie MIJ NV), 903
NPV Capital Partners, LLC, 560
NTC Group, The , 301
Nth Power Technologies, Inc, 224
Oak Investment Partners, 302
Oem Capital, 302
Ohana Ventures, LLC, 615
Onondaga Venture Capital Fund, Inc., 562
Onset Ventures, 225
Open Prairie Ventures, 365
Opportunity Capital Partners {FKA: Thompson Capital Mgt), 225

Oregon Resource and Technology Development Fund, 620
Orien Ventures, 303
Orion Partners, L.P., 439
Orix Capital Corporation, 906
Oxford Financial Services Corp., 698
PA Early Stage (AKA:Pennsylvania Early Stage Partners), 635
Pac-Link Management Corporation, 906
Pacific Capital Partners, 907
Pacific Corporate Group, Inc., 227
Pacific Northwest Partners SBIC, L.P., 710
Pacific Venture Partners, 907
PacRim Venture Management , 228
Palomar Ventures, 228
Pappajohn Capital Resources, 381
Paradigm Capital Partners LLC, 651
Paribas Principal, Inc., 563
Pathfinder Investment Co Pvt Ltd, 910
Pathfinder Venture Capital Funds, 470
Patricof & Co. Ventures, Inc., 563
Pauli & Co., Inc., 477
Peninsula Capital Partners, L.L.C, 460
Penn-Janney Fund, Inc., The, 635
Pennsylvania Growth Fund, 636
Penny Lane Partners, 493
Pequot Capital Management Inc., 564
Perennial Ventures (FKA: Tredegar Investments), 711
Pfingsten Partners, L.P., 366
Philadelphia Ventures, Inc., 636
Phoenix Equity Partners (FKA: DLJ European Private Equity), 911
Phoenix Growth Capital Corp., 231
Phoenix Partners, The , 711
Pierce Financial Corporation(FKA:Pierce Investment Banking), 698
Pittsford Group, Inc., The , 565
Platinum Group, Inc., The , 565
PME Capital, 912
Point Venture Partners, 636
Polaris Venture Partners, 441
Poly Ventures, 566
PolyTechnos Venture Partners GmbH, 913
PowerWord Capital Management, Inc., 914
Prelude Technology Investments Ltd, 915
Primaxis Technology Ventures Inc. , 916
Prime Capital Management Co., Inc., 304
Prime Technology Ventures NV, 916
PrimePartners Asset Management Pte. Ltd., 916
Private Capital Corp., 131
Priveq Capital Funds, 917
Productivity Fund I & II, The, 367
Prospect Street Ventures (FKA:Prospect Street Invest. Mgmt), 567
Provco Group, The , 637
Proximitas AG Venture Capital, 918
Quantum Capital Partners, 325
Quest Ventures, 233
Quester Capital Management Ltd, 920
R-H Capital Partners, 337
RAF Ventures, 637
Ralph Wilson Equity Fund, L.L.C., 460
Rand Capital Corporation, 568
Raza Foundries, 233
Recovery Equity Investors, L.P., 234
Red River Ventures, 675
Renaissance Capital Corp., 337
Reprise Capital Corp., 569
RFE Investment Partners, 305
Richard Jaffe & Co., Inc., 676
Ridge Capital Partners, L.L.C., 368
Ridgewood Capital Management LLC, 494
River Capital, 338
Roanoke Capital, Ltd., 712
Robertson Stephens & Company, LLC, 236
RockMountain Ventures, 282
Rocky Mountain Capital Partners (FKA:Hanifen Imhoff Capital), 283
Rosecliff, 237
Rosenfeld & Co., 620
Roser Ventures LLC, 283
Rothschild Ventures Asia Pte Ltd., 922
Rothschild Ventures, Inc., 570
Royal Bank Private Equity (FKA: Royal Bank Development Cap), 922
Royalty Capital Fund, L.P. I/Royalty Capital Management, Inc, 443
RRE Ventures LLC, 571
Rutledge & Co., Inc., 305
RWI Group, LP, 239
SAE Ventures, 306
Sage Management Group, 444
Sandhurst Venture Fund, L.P., The , 639
Sanpaolo IMI Private Equity S.p.A., 925
Saugatuck Capital Company, 306
SBC Equity Partners, Inc., 369
SBC Ventures, 499
SBCA/A.G. Bartholomew & Associates, 131
SBV Venture Partners (AKA:Sigefi, Burnette & Vallee), 240
Schneider Electric Ventures, 926
Scottish Equity Partners Limited, 927
Seacoast Capital, 446
Seaflower Ventures, 446
SEB Foretagsinvest, 927
Seed Capital Ltd, 928
Selby Venture Partners, 241
Sequel Venture Partners, 284
Sequoia Capital, 241
Shannon Development Company, 929
Shared Ventures, Inc., 470
Shattan Group, The, 574
Shaw Venture Partners (FKA: Shaw Glasgow Partners), 621
Shelton Companies, Inc., The , 604
Shepherd Group LLC, The, 447
Siemens Venture Capital GmbH, 930
Sienna Ventures (FKA: Sienna Holdings Inc.), 242
Sierra Ventures, 243
Sigma Capital Corp., 327
Sigma Partners, 243
Siguler Guff & Company, LLC, 575
Silicon Valley Bank, 244
Silver Creek Technology Investors (FKA: O'Donnell & Masur), 677
SISIR International Pte Ltd., 932
Sitra (AKA Finnish National Fund for Research and Dev.), 932
SK Global Co., Ltd., 932
Smart Technology Ventures, 246

Societe Regionale d'Investissement de Bruxelles (SRIB/GIMB), 933
Sofinnova Ventures, 246
SOFTBANK Venture Capital (FKA: SOFTBANK Technology Ventures), 247
Sorrento Associates, Inc., 247
SoundView Financial Group, Inc., 307
South Atlantic Venture Funds, L.P., 327
Southport Partners, 307
Southwest Venture Group, 678
Sovereign Capital (FKA:Nash, Sells & Partners Limited), 936
SpaceVest, 699
Spectrum Equity Investors, L.P., 248
Spencer Trask Ventures, Inc. (FKA: Spencer Trask Securities), 576
Spire Capital (FKA: Waller Capital Corp.), 577
Spring Capital Partners, L.P., 398
Springboard-Harper Investment Pte. Ltd., 938
Sprout Group, 578
SRK Management Co., 578
SsangYong Cement (Singapore) Ltd, 939
Stamford Financial, 579
Star Capital Group, Inc., 939
State Street Bank & Trust Co., 338
Sterling/Carl Marks Capital {FKA - Sterling Commercial, 580
Still River Fund, The, 450
Stolberg Partners, 580
Stonebridge Partners, 580
Strategic Capital Management, 941
Strategic Investments & Holdings, Inc., 581
Stratford Equity Partners, L.P., 679
Strathdon Investments Ltd, 942
Sucsy, Fischer & Co., 370
Suez Asia Holdings Pte Ltd., 943
Summit Capital Associates, Inc., 581
Summit Partners, 451
Sun Valley Ventures, 250
Sunsino Development Associate Inc., 944
Sunwestern Investment Group, 680
Sutter Hill Ventures, 251
Swedestart Management AB, 944
Swedish Industrial Development Fund (AKA Industrifonden), 945
Sweeney & Co., Inc., 308
Sycamore Ventures, 494
Synerfi S.A., 945
Synopsys, Inc., 253
T. Rowe Price Threshold Partnerships, 399
TA Associates, Inc., 451
Tailink Venture Partners, 946
Tappan Zee Capital Corp., 495
tbg Technologie-Beteiligungsgesellschaft mbH, 947
TCR Europe SA, 947
TDH, 639
Techno Nord VC GmbH, 948
Techno-Venture Co. (Japan), 949
TechnoCap Inc, 949
Technologieholding VC GmbH, 950
Technology Associates Management Corporation, 950
Technology Funding, 254
Technology Venture Partners Pty Ltd, 950
Technostart GmbH, 951
Techxas Ventures, LLC, 681
Teknoinvest Management As, 952
Telos Venture Partners, 256
Texas Growth Fund Management, 681
THCG Inc., 582
Third Coast Capital, 370
Thompson Clive, Inc., 257
Thorner Ventures, 258
Throunarfelag Islands Plc(AKA:The Icelandic Finance&Invest.), 955
Tokyo Small & Medium Business Investment & Consultation Co., 956
Top Taiwan Venture Capital Company, Ltd., 957
Top Technology Limited (AKA:Hambros-Advanced Technology Tru), 957
Transamerica Mezzanine Financing, 645
Transamerica Technology Finance, 309
Transcap Associates, Inc., 371
Trellis Partners, 682
Triad Investors Corp, 319
TriNova, 959
Triune Capital, 260
TSG Capital Group, L.L.C., 309
TTP Venture Managers (FKA: The Technology Partnership), 960
U.S. Venture Partners, 261
UBS Capital (AKA Phildrew Ventures), 963
Ulster Development Capital, Ltd., 963
Union Street Capital Corp., 713
Union Venture Capital Corporation, 963
UOB Venture Management Pte Ltd., 964
UPS Strategic Enterprise Fund, 339
US Trust Private Equity, 584
Utah Ventures II, L.P. (A.K.A. Union Ventures), 687
Valley Capital Corp., 654
Valley Ventures (FKA: Arizona Growth Partners, L.P.), 136
Vanguard Venture Partners, 262
VantagePoint Venture Partners, 263
VCF Partners, 965
Vega Capital Corp., 584
Vencap Equities Alberta, Ltd., 966
Vencon Management, Inc., 585
VenGlobal Capital, 264
Venrock Associates, 586
Ventana Financial Resources, Inc., 372
Ventana Global, 264
Ventex Management, Inc., 683
Venture Associates Partners, LLC, 654
Venture Associates, Ltd., 285
Venture Capital Fund Managers (Pty), Ltd., The , 967
Venture Capital Fund of New England, The, 454
Venture Capital Management Corp., 328
Venture First Associates, 328
Venture Funding Group International, 587
Venture Growth Associates, 265
Venture Investment Management Company LLC (AKA: VIMAC), 454
Venture Investors Management LLC, 720
Venture Management Services Inc. (FKA: AT&T Ventures), 496
Venture Opportunities Corp., 588
Venture Partners AG, 968
Venture TDF Pte Ltd., 968
VentureCap Management GmbH (AKA VCH Equity Group AG), 969
Ventures West Management, Inc., 970

Veritas Venture Capital Management, Ltd., 970
Vero Group PLC, 684
Vertex Management, 971
Vision Capital Management (FKA Glenwood Capital), 267
VK Ventures, 268
Voyager Capital, 714
Wachtel & Co., Inc., 317
Walden International Investment Group (AKA: Walden Group), 269
Walden Israel, 975
WaldenVC, 270
Walnut Capital Corp., 701
Warburg, Pincus & Co., LLC. (FKA: E.M. Warburg, Pincus & Co), 590
Wasatch Venture Fund (FKA: Wasatch Venture Corporation), 687
Wellmax, Inc., 461
West Midlands Enterprise Ltd, 976
Westar Capital, 271
Western States Investment Group, 272
Westford Technology Ventures, L.P., 497
Weston Presidio Capital Management, 455
WestSphere Equity Investors, LP, 592
White Pines Management, L.L.C., 462
William A.M. Burden & Co., 593
Willis Stein & Partners, 374
Wind Point Partners, 462
Windjammer Capital Investors (FKA:Pacific Mezzanine Inv.), 273
Windward Holdings, 311
Windward Ventures (FKA: Coronado Capital), 274
Wingate Partners, L.P., 685
Winslow Partners LLC, 317
Winthrop Ventures, 593
WK Associates, 977
Wolf Ventures (AKA:Wolf Asset Management Corp.), 286
Woodside Fund, 274
Wooshin Development Finance Corp, 978
Working Ventures Canadian Fund, Inc., 978
Worldview Technology Partners, 275
Worms Capital Management, 594
YankeeTek Ventures, 456
Yasuda Enterprise Development Co., Ltd.(FKA: Nippon Ent.Dev), 275
Yorkshire Fund Managers Ltd., 979
Zero Stage Capital Co., Inc., 456
Zone Ventures, 276
ZS Fund, L.P., 595

Transportation

1st Source Capital Corp., 375
3i Finland Oy (FKA SFK Finance), 725
ABP Acquisition Corp, 287
Academy Funds (FKA: Longleaf Venture Fund LLC), 597
ACT Venture Capital Ltd., 732
Adams Street Partners, LLC (FKA: Brinson Private Equity), 343
AIG Investment Corporation (Asia) Limited, 735
Alan I. Goldman & Associates, 483
Albemarle Private Equity Ltd, 735
Alimansky Capital Group, Inc., 504
Allegra Partners (FKA: Lawrence, Smith & Horey), 504
Allsop Venture Partners, 380
American Securities, L.P., 505
AMP Asset Management Limited - Development Capital, 740
Amphion Ventures L.P.(FKA: Wolfensohn Associates, L.P.), 506
APIDC-Venture Capital Limited, 743
Ardsheil, Inc., 506
Argentum Group, The , 507
Argos Soditic SA, 744
Arthur P. Gould & Co., 507
ASC Group, 746
Asian Infrastructure Fund Advisers Limited, 748
August Partners, 508
Baird Capital Partners, 347
BancAmerica Capital Investors (FKA:NationsBanc Capital Corp), 598
BancBoston Capital/BancBoston Ventures, 408
Bank One Equity Investors, Inc., 386
Bankers Trust New York Corp./Deutsche Banc Alex Brown, 510
Banque De Vizille, 754
Bastion Capital Corp., 152
Batavia Investment Management Ltd, 756
BBS Finance, 757
BCR Asset Management Pty Ltd., 758
Beacon Partners, Inc., 289
Benefit Capital Companies, Inc., The, 480
Berkshire Partners, 410
Berwind Financial Group, L.P., 623
Brait Capital Partners, 762
Brantley Venture Partners, 609
Bruce F. Glaspell & Associates, 498
Bulldog Partners Limited, 764
Cambria Group, The, 157
Candover Investments PLC, 768
Capital Services & Resources, Inc., 648
Capital Strategy Management Co., The, 349
Carillon Capital, Inc., 610
Castle Harlan Australian Mezzanine Partners Pty. Ltd. , 772
CCFL Mezzanine Partners of Canada , 774
Cedar Creek Partners, LLC, 717
CEI Ventures/Coastal Ventures LP, 388
Churchill Capital, Inc., 465
CID Equity Partners, 376
Citicorp Capital Asia (AKA: CITIC Pacific Ltd.), 780
Citicorp Venture Capital, Ltd., 517
Citizens Capital and Citizens Ventures, 418
Clairvest Group, Inc., 780
Close Brothers Private Equity, 782
Continental S.B.I.C., 691
Continental Venture Capital , 784
Cornerstone Equity Investors, LLC, 519
Corpfin Capital S.A., 786
Creafund CVBA, 788
Crown Capital Corp, 475
CS Capital Partners, LLC, 486
CVC Capital Partners, 790
Cycle & Carriage Industries Pte Ltd, 791
Davis Group, 166
Davis, Tuttle Venture Partners, L.P.(FKA:Davis Venture), 618
Deucalion Venture Partners, 168
Developers Equity Corp., 169
Direct Capital Private Equity, 797
DN Partners, 352
Dresdner Kleinwort Capital , 524
Drysdale Enterprises, 173

ECICS Ventures Pte Ltd., 801
Edge Capital Investment Co., LLC, 175
Electra Fleming Limited, 525
Electra Partners Asia [FKA: JF Electra Limited], 803
Elk Associates Funding Corp., 526
Enterprise Investors, 526
Eos Partners, L.P., 527
Equinox Investment Partners, 294
Equity Ventures, Ltd, 807
Equus Capital Corp., 663
European Acquisition Capital Ltd., 810
Evergreen Capital Partners Inc, 528
Evergreen Ventures, 686
Exeter Capital, L.P., 528
Federal Business Development Bank, 815
Financial Technology Research Corp., 529
First Capital Management Co., 664
First Union Capital Partners, 600
Florida Capital Ventures, Ltd., 323
Fonds de Solidarité des Travailleurs du Québec (F.T.Q.), 820
Foundation Capital Limited, 822
Fowler, Anthony & Co., 422
Frontline Capital, Inc., 334
GATX/MM Venture Partners, 183
Generation Capital Partners, 532
Geneva Merchant Banking Partners, 601
Glencoe Capital, LLC (FKA: Glencoe Investment Corporation), 356
Granville Baird Capital Partners (FKA:Granville Pr Eq Mngrs), 830
Grotech Capital Group, 394
GrowthWorks Capital, 834
H&Q Asia Pacific, Ltd., 187
Halder Holdings B.V., 835
Hamilton Robinson & Co., Inc., 296
Hanbyuck Investment Co Ltd, 836
Hanover Capital Corp., 535
Harvest Partners, Inc., 536
Heartland Capital Partners, L.P., 665
Heritage Partners, 427
Hickory Venture Capital Corporation, 130
HSBC Private Equity (Asia), Ltd. (FKA: HSBC PE Management), 841
HSBC Private Equity Ltd (FKA Montagu Private Equity Ltd), 841
HT Capital Advisors, LLC, 538
ICC Venture Capital, 845
IEG Venture Management, Inc., 357
IL&FS Venture Corporation (FKA. CreditCapital Venture Fund), 848
Indekon Management Oy, 849
Innovest Group, Inc., 629
InterEquity Capital Partners, L.P., 541
Investissements Novacap (AKA:Novacap Investments, Inc.), 858
IPS Industrial Promotion Services, Ltd., 859
J.L. Albright Venture Partners, 861
J.P. Morgan Capital Corp., 542
J.P. Morgan Partners (FKA: Chase Capital Partners), 543
James A. Matzdorff & Co., 199
Kankaku Investment Co Ltd, 865
Kansas City Equity Partners, 477
Kitty Hawk Capital, 602
Kookmin Venture Capital Co Ltd, 867
Lake Shore Capital Partners, Inc., 360
Las Americas Administradora, 871
Legal & General Ventures Ltd, 872
Levine Leichtman Capital Partners, Inc., 204
Lombard Investments, Inc., 206
Lubar & Co., 718
Madison Dearborn Partners, LLC, 361
Marlborough Capital Advisors, 431
Marwit Capital LLC, 209
Matrix Group, 209
MBA Venture Group, 669
McCown De Leeuw & Co., 210
McGuire Capital Corp., 670
McKee & Co., 134
Mellon Ventures (AKA: Mellon Bank), 632
Memhard Investment Bankers, Inc., 300
Mentor Capital Partners, 633
Meridian Venture Partners (MVP), 633
Merrill Lynch Investment Managers FKA Mercury Asset Mgmt, 884
Mezzanine Management UK Limited, 885
Mid-Atlantic Venture Funds (FKA: NEPA Management Corp.), 634
Middlefield Capital Fund, 885
Midlands Venture Fund Managers Ltd. (AKA: Midven Ltd), 886
Montgomery Associates, Inc., 215
Moore & Associates, 619
Morgan Grenfell Private Equity Limited, 889
Mountaineer Capital LP, 716
MWV Capital Partners (FKA:Middlewest Ventures, L.P.), 378
National Australia Investment Capital Limited, 892
National City Equity Partners, Inc, 614
Navis Partners (FKA:Fleet Equity Partners), 643
Newbridge Capital Limited, 219
NextGen Partners LLC, 221
NIB Capital Private Equity N.V. (FKA: Parnib Holding NV) , 898
Nomura/JAFCO Investment (HK) Limited, 901
North Atlantic Capital Corp., 389
Northwest Ohio Venture Fund, 615
Northwest Venture Associates, Inc.(FKA:Spokane Capital Mgmt), 709
Northwood Ventures, 559
NPM Capital (AKA Nederlandse Participatie MIJ NV), 903
Nth Power Technologies, Inc, 224
Opportunity Capital Partners {FKA: Thompson Capital Mgt), 225
Oxford Financial Services Corp., 698
PA Early Stage (AKA:Pennsylvania Early Stage Partners), 635
Paribas Principal, Inc., 563
Patricof & Co. Ventures, Inc., 563
Penfund Partners, Inc., 911
PENMAN Partners (FKA PENMAN Asset Management LP), 365
Phoenix Equity Partners (FKA: DLJ European Private Equity), 911
Phoenix Growth Capital Corp., 231
Pierce Financial Corporation(FKA:Pierce Investment Banking), 698
Point Venture Partners, 636
PPM Ventures Ltd (FKA: Prudential Venture Managers Ltd), 914
RBC Ventures, Inc., 619
Recovery Equity Investors, L.P., 234
Red River Ventures, 675
Reprise Capital Corp., 569
Ridge Capital Partners, L.L.C., 368

Riordan, Lewis & Haden, 236
River Capital, 338
Rosenfeld & Co., 620
Rothschild Ventures Asia Pte Ltd., 922
SBC Equity Partners, Inc., 369
SBC Ventures, 499
SBCA/A.G. Bartholomew & Associates, 131
Seacoast Capital, 446
Shannon Development Company, 929
Shattan Group, The, 574
Shaw Venture Partners (FKA: Shaw Glasgow Partners), 621
Shelton Companies, Inc., The , 604
Siguler Guff & Company, LLC, 575
Sofinov (AKA:Caisse de depot et placement du Quebec), 934
Sovereign Capital (FKA:Nash, Sells & Partners Limited), 936
SpaceVest, 699
Spring Capital Partners, L.P., 398
Stolberg Partners, 580
Strategic Capital Management, 941
Suez Asia Holdings Pte Ltd., 943
TCR Europe SA, 947
TDH, 639
Texas Growth Fund Management, 681
Ticonderoga Capital, Inc. (FKA: Dillon Read Venture Capital), 452
Tokyo Small & Medium Business Investment & Consultation Co., 956
UBS Capital (AKA Phildrew Ventures), 963
UOB Venture Management Pte Ltd., 964
UPS Strategic Enterprise Fund, 339
Valeo Ventures, 964
Valley Capital Corp., 654
Vega Capital Corp., 584
Vencap Equities Alberta, Ltd., 966
Ventex Management, Inc., 683
Venture Associates Partners, LLC, 654
Venture Capital Management Corp., 328
Venture Funding Group International, 587
Venture Opportunities Corp., 588
Vertex Management, 971
Walnut Capital Corp., 701
West Midlands Enterprise Ltd, 976
Westar Capital, 271
Westbury Partners, 592
Weston Presidio Capital Management, 455
White Pines Management, L.L.C., 462
William E. Simon & Sons (Asia) LDC, 977
Wind Point Partners, 462
Winslow Partners LLC, 317
Winthrop Ventures, 593
Worms Capital Management, 594
Zero Stage Capital Co., Inc., 456

Utilities

ABP Acquisition Corp, 287
Accenture Technology Ventures (FKA: AC Ventures), 140
Capital Strategy Management Co., The, 349
CEI Ventures/Coastal Ventures LP, 388
Connecticut Innovations, Inc., 291
Continental S.B.I.C., 691
Core Capital Partners, 313
Fort Washington Capital Partners, LLC, 611
Hunt Capital Group, 667
Hydro-Quebec CapiTech Inc., 843
Kansas City Equity Partners, 477
Kinetic Ventures, Inc., 395
Maristeth Ventures, L.L.C., 707
MWV Capital Partners (FKA:Middlewest Ventures, L.P.), 378
National City Equity Partners, Inc, 614
Pacific Corporate Group, Inc., 227
Penfund Partners, Inc., 911
Shattan Group, The, 574
Warburg, Pincus & Co., LLC. (FKA: E.M. Warburg, Pincus & Co), 590

Stage Preference Index

Acquisition

Aberdeen Murray Johnstone Private Equity, 728
ABP Acquisition Corp, 287
Advent-Morro Equity Partners, 734
Allied Capital Corporation, 312
Alta Communications, 403
American Capital Strategies, 391
Ampersand Ventures, 404
AO Capital Corp, 287
Ascent Venture Partners, 406
aventic Partners AG, 750
Baird Capital Partners, 347
BancBoston Capital/BancBoston Ventures, 408
BCR Asset Management Pty Ltd., 758
Botts & Co., 762
Bradford Equities Fund, LLC, 513
C3 Holdings, LLC, 474
Calgary Enterprises, Inc., 514
Capital Prive (FKA NatWest Equity Partners, France), 769
Capital Resource Partners, 415
Capital Southwest Corporation, 660
Capital Strategy Management Co., The, 349
Cascade Communications Ventures, LLC, 159
CEI Ventures/Coastal Ventures LP, 388
Churchill Capital, Inc., 465
Cinven Ltd, 779
Citizens Capital and Citizens Ventures, 418
CIVC Partners (FKA:Continental Illinois Venture Corp.), 350
Continental Venture Capital , 784
Copernicus Capital Management Ltd, 785
Crosbie & Co Inc, 789
De Vries & Co., Inc., 476
DFW Capital Partners (AKA:DeMuth, Folger & Wetherill), 486
Direct Capital Private Equity, 797
Electra Partners Asia [FKA: JF Electra Limited], 803
Equinox Investment Partners, 294
Evergreen Capital Partners Inc, 528
FINADVANCE S.A., 815
Finansa Capital Limited, 816
First Union Capital Partners, 600
Fonds de Solidarité des Travailleurs du Québec (F.T.Q.), 820
Fowler, Anthony & Co., 422
Gresham Rabo Management Limited, 832
Growth Venture Group Pty Ltd., 833
GTCR Golder Rauner, LLC, 356
H&Q Asia Pacific, Ltd., 187
HarbourVest Partners, LLC., 426
Harvest Partners, Inc., 536
High Street Capital, LLC, 357
HSBC Private Equity Ltd (FKA Montagu Private Equity Ltd), 841
HT Capital Advisors, LLC, 538
Hunt Capital Group, 667
Incorporated Investors, 193
Indocean Chase Capital Advisors, 850
J.P. Morgan Partners (FKA: Chase Capital Partners), 543
Josephberg Grosz & Co., Inc., 545
Lincolnshire Management Inc., 548
Loeb Partners Corp., 549
Lombard Investments, Inc., 206
M&F Associates, L.P., 549
Madison Dearborn Partners, LLC, 361
Marwit Capital LLC, 209

Matrix Group, 209
MC Capital, Inc., 551
Mentor Capital Partners, 633
Morgenthaler Ventures, 614
National City Equity Partners, Inc, 614
Navis Partners (FKA:Fleet Equity Partners), 643
Newbridge Capital Limited, 219
Northwood Ventures, 559
Oem Capital, 302
Pacific Corporate Group, Inc., 227
PAMA Group Inc. (FKA:Prudential Asset Management Asia), 908
Perseus LLC, 316
Putnam Lovell Capital Partners, L.P., 232
Quaestus & Co. Inc. (FKA: Quaestus Management Corp..), 719
River Associates, LLC, 653
Saugatuck Capital Company, 306
Seaport Capital, 572
Spring Capital Partners, L.P., 398
Strategic Capital Management, 941
Stratford Equity Partners, L.P., 679
Suez Asia Holdings Pte Ltd., 943
Teak Investment Partners II Limited, 948
Texas Growth Fund Management, 681
Tianguis Ltd, 956
Trident Capital, 259
Venture Associates Partners, LLC, 654
Venture Capital Partners Pty Limited, 967
Virginia Capital , 701
Walden Capital Management Corporation, 589
Warburg, Pincus & Co., LLC. (FKA: E.M. Warburg, Pincus & Co), 590
William Blair Capital Partners, 373
Wind Point Partners, 462
Winslow Partners LLC, 317
Working Ventures Canadian Fund, Inc., 978

Balanced

3I Capital Corporation (US), 401
3i Gestion SA, 725
A.M. Pappas & Associates, 597
Aberdeen Murray Johnstone Private Equity, 728
ABN-AMRO Corporate Investments, 729
Accenture Technology Ventures (FKA: AC Ventures), 140
ACF Equity Atlantic, Inc, 731
ACR Venture Management AB (AKA: ACR Capital AB), 732
Adams, Harkness & Hill, Inc., 401
AdCapital AG (FKA Berliner Elektro Holding AG), 732
Advanced Technology Ventures, 401
Aether Systems Capital, 390
AGF Private Equity, 735
AIG Capital Partners Inc., 503
Alpha Group (FKA:Alpha Associates Management, Ltd.), 738
American Capital Strategies, 391
American Healthcare Fund, 345
Ampersand Ventures, 404
Apax Globis Partners & Co. (APAX Japan), 741
Apax Partners & Co. Ventures Ltd (AKA: Apax UK), 742
Argo Global Capital, Inc., 406
Asian Direct Capital Management, 747
Aspiro Ventures, 748
At India Management Services Pvt. Ltd., 749
Atlas Venture, 407
Axiom Venture Partners, L.P., 288
Axxon Capital, Inc., 408
Ballentine Capital Management , 288
Battery Ventures, L.P., 409
BCR Asset Management Pty Ltd., 758
BioVentures Investors, LLC, 411
Boston Venture Partners, Ltd., 761
BrainWorks Ventures, 330
Bridgepoint Capital Ltd (FKA: NWEP & NatWest Ventures Ltd), 763
Bure Equity, 765
Burrill & Company, 156
Camelot Enterprises Private Limited, 767
Camelot Ventures, 457
Capital Across America, L.P., 648
Carmel Ventures, 772
Castle Harlan Australian Mezzanine Partners Pty. Ltd. , 772
CDC Advisors Private Ltd., 775
CEI Ventures/Coastal Ventures LP, 388
CenturyTel Inc, 387
Champion Consulting Group, Incorporated, 776
Cherry Tree Investments, Inc., 464
Child Health Investment Corporation, 382
Chrysalis Capital, 778
Citizens Capital and Citizens Ventures, 418
Clairvest Group, Inc., 780
Clemente Capital (Asia) Ltd., 781
Close Brothers Investment Limited, 782
CMEA Ventures (FKA:Chemicals & Materials Enterprise Associa), 161
Cordova Ventures (FKA:Cordova Capital), 331
Core Pacific Consulting Company, 786
CPH Investment Corp., 787
Crescent Capital NI Ltd (FKA Hambro Northern Ireland), 788
Crest Communications Holdings LLC, 520
Cross Atlantic Capital Partners, 625
Crosslink Capital (FKA: Omega Venture Partners), 165
Crown Advisors International, Ltd., 521
Crystal Internet Venture Fund, L.P., 611
Cycle & Carriage Industries Pte Ltd, 791
D. Brain Capital Company, Ltd., 791
Dali, Hook Partners (FKA: Hook Partners), 662
Danske eVentures, 794
Dauphin Capital Partners, 522
DB Venture Partners, 794
Deutsche Beteiligungs AG, 796
Domain Associates, L.L.C., 486
Dominion Ventures, Inc., 170
DSE Investment Services Limited, 799
Durlacher Limited, 799
ECICS Ventures Pte Ltd., 801
Edmond de Rothschild Venture Capital Management, 802
Empire Ventures, 620
Enron Broadband Ventures, 663
EPS Finanz AG, 806
Equinox Investment Partners, 294
equity4life AG, 807
EuclidSR Partners , 527
Evergreen Capital Partners Inc, 528
Fidelity Ventures (FKA: Fidelity Venture Associates), 421
Finansa Capital Limited, 816

Finovelec, 817
Five Paces Ventures, 334
FJ Benjamin Holdings Pte Ltd, 818
Forrest Binkley & Brown, 180
Fortune International Limited, 821
Fortune Venture Capital Incorporated, 822
Foster Management Company, 627
Foundation Capital, 181
Fraser & Neave Limited, 823
Friends Ivory & Sime Private Equity (Ivory &Sime Baronsmead), 823
Future Venture Capital Co., Ltd., 824
Gaon Asset Management, 825
General Catalyst Group LLC, 423
Genesis Partners, 826
Geneva Merchant Banking Partners, 601
Gleacher & Co., 534
Glynn Capital Management, 186
Goodwill Communication, Inc., 830
Grotech Capital Group, 394
GrowthWorks Capital, 834
H&Q Asia Pacific, Ltd., 187
Hansol Investment Inc., 837
HarbourVest Partners, LLC., 426
Higin Venture Capital Co., Ltd., 838
Hikari Tsushin Capital, Inc., 838
HomeSeekers.com, 480
Honho Consulting Company Limited, 839
Horizonte Venture Management GmbH, 840
HSBC Private Equity Ltd (FKA Montagu Private Equity Ltd), 841
Hummer Winblad Venture Partners, 191
Hydro-Quebec CapiTech Inc., 843
Hyundai Venture Capital Co., Ltd., 843
IBK Capital Corporation, 844
IDG Technology Venture Investment Inc. (FKA: PTV-China), 846
imGO (AKA: Investor Mobile GO; FKA: Guoco Land Ltd.), 848
Index Ventures, 850
Infineon Ventures, 852
Innvotec Ltd, 854
Ireka Venture Capital Limited, 860
Ironside Ventures, LLC (FKA: MF Private Capital), 429
J.F. Shea & Company, 198
JAFCO Ventures, Inc., 198
Japan Asia Investment Co Ltd, 863
Japan/America Ventures, Inc., 544
Javva Partners LLC, 544
Josephberg Grosz & Co., Inc., 545
JT Venture Partners, LLC, 491
Kaiser Permanente (AKA: National Venture Development), 200
Kaufmann Fund, Inc., The, 546
Keystone Venture Capital Management Co., 630
KLM Capital Group, 201
Kokusai Finance Co., Ltd., 867
Kyoritsu Capital Company, Ltd., 870
Lazard Asia Investment Management (Private) Limited, 871
Legal & General Ventures Ltd, 872
Libon Capital Management Limited, 873
Lightspeed Venture Partners (FKA: Weiss, Peck & Greer), 206
Lippo Group, 874
LLR Equity Partners, 631
LN Mittal, 874
LoneTree Capital Partners, 281
LRM Investeringsmaatschappij Voor Limburg, 875
M&F Associates, L.P., 549
Mapleleaf Capital Corp., 669
Marconi Ventures, 431
MDS Health Ventures, Inc. (AKA: MDS Capital Corp.), 881
Mellon Ventures (AKA: Mellon Bank), 632
Mentor Capital Partners, 633
Mercator Broadband Partners, L.P., 696
Meritage Private Equity Fund, 281
Mitsui Marine Capital Co., Ltd., 887
Montreux Equity Partners, 216
Monument Advisors, Inc, 378
Morel Ventures Limited, 888
Morningside Group, 363
Mountaineer Capital LP, 716
Murphree Venture Partners, 671
MWV Capital Partners (FKA:Middlewest Ventures, L.P.), 378
National Enterprise Company, Ltd., 892
NCB Ventures Limited, 893
NCP Advisors Philippines, Inc., 894
Net Partners, 895
NetworkAsia, 896
New England Partners, 437
New World Infrastructure Limited, 896
Newbridge Capital Limited, 219
NIF Ventures Co., Ltd., 898
Nippon Venture Capital Co., Ltd., 899
North Hill Ventures, 438
North Texas Opportunity Fund , 672
Northington Partners, 301
Northwest Venture Associates, Inc.(FKA:Spokane Capital Mgmt), 709
Northwood Ventures, 559
Norwood Venture Corp., 559
NTUC Club Investments Pte Ltd (NCI), 904
Oak Investment Partners, 302
Oberlin Capital, L.P., 603
OCBC, Wearnes & Walden Investments (s), Ltd., 904
Olympus Capital Holdings Asia, 905
Orange Ventures, 905
Oxford Partners, 303
Pac-Link Management Corporation, 906
Pacifica Fund , 228
PacRim Venture Management , 228
Perennial Ventures (FKA: Tredegar Investments), 711
Perseus LLC, 316
Polaris Venture Capital, 913
Pomona Capital, 566
Portview Communications Partners, 914
PowerWord Capital Management, Inc., 914
Primus Venture Partners, Inc., 616
ProQuest Investments, L.P., 493
Psilos Group Managers LLC, 568
Putnam Lovell Capital Partners, L.P., 232
Pyramid Technology Ventures, 919
Ralph Wilson Equity Fund, L.L.C., 460
Renaissance Partners, 921
Royal Bank Private Equity (FKA: Royal Bank Development Cap), 922
RSA Ventures, 443
Russel Miller Advisors Asia, LLC, 238
Sanpaolo IMI Private Equity S.p.A., 925

Savoy/Socios Fondos de Financiacon Management, 925
Schroder Ventures, 445
Scoot.com PLC, 926
Shanghai Information Investment (SII), 928
Shaw Venture Partners (FKA: Shaw Glasgow Partners), 621
Sherbrooke Capital Partners, 448
Shigagin Capital Co., Ltd., 930
SI Ventures, 326
Siguler Guff & Company, LLC, 575
Singapore Technologies Telemedia (AKA: ST Telemedia), 931
Skyline Ventures, 245
Small Industries Development Bank of India (SIDBI), The, 933
SMIFS Venture Capital Limited, 933
Sofinov (AKA:Caisse de depot et placement du Quebec), 934
Softbank China Venture Capital, 935
Softbank Corp., 935
Softcapital, Inc., 935
Southern Capitol Ventures, 605
Spectrum Equity Investors, L.P., 248
Spencer Trask Ventures, Inc. (FKA: Spencer Trask Securities), 576
Spring Capital Partners, L.P., 398
Sputnik Technology Ventures, 938
Staenberg Private Capital, LLC, 713
Strategic Capital Group Hong Kong Limited, 941
Stratford Equity Partners, L.P., 679
Sun Hung Kai Properties Limited, 943
Sybase, Inc., 252
Sycamore Ventures, 494
Synergy Partners, 252
Teak Investment Partners II Limited, 948
Teak Investment Partners III Ltd., 948
Techxas Ventures, LLC, 681
Telecom Italia Ventures, 255
Tera Capital Corporation, 954
Third Coast Capital, 370
Tokyo Marine Capital Company, 956
Toshiba Corporation, 958
Triangle Venture Capital Group, 959
Trident Capital, 259
True North Partners LLC, 583
TrustCapital Partners NV, 959
TVS Finance Ltd., 961
Twinwood Engineering Ltd, 962
Union Venture Capital Corporation, 963
Updata Venture Partners, 700
Venture Investment Management Company LLC (AKA: VIMAC), 454
VentureLink Holdings, 683
Vertex Management Israel (AKA: Vertex Management III Ltd.), 971
Vickers Ballas Asset Management Pte Ltd., 972
Virginia Capital , 701
Visa International, 267
VLink Global Limited, 974
Walden Capital Management Corporation, 589
Walden International Investment Group (AKA: Walden Group), 269
WaldenVC, 270
Walnut Group, The, 617
Warburg, Pincus & Co., LLC. (FKA: E.M. Warburg, Pincus & Co), 590
WE Simon & Sons, 496
Weston Presidio Capital Management, 455
Whitney & Co. (FKA: J.H. Whitney & Co.), 310
WI Harper Group, 273
Wind Point Partners, 462
Wit Japan Investment, Inc., 977
WomenAngles.net, 318
Working Ventures Canadian Fund, Inc., 978
Worldview Technology Partners, 275
Yorkshire Fund Managers Ltd., 979
Zero Gravity Internet Group, Inc. , 276
Zouk Ventures, 980

Control-block Purchases

Adler & Co., 502
Advent International Corp., 402
Advent Management N.V., 733
Alan I. Goldman & Associates, 483
American Capital Strategies, 391
American Securities, L.P., 505
Ardsheil, Inc., 506
Atlantic Medical Management, LLC, 508
Baccharis Capital, Inc., 150
Bachow & Associates, Inc., 623
Bank Funds, The, 347
Bastion Capital Corp., 152
Bausch & Lomb, Inc., 511
Berwind Financial Group, L.P., 623
Bloom & Co., 512
Boston Ventures Management, Inc., 413
Burr, Egan, Deleage & Co., 414
Cambria Group, The, 157
Capital Strategy Management Co., The, 349
Cardinal Ventures, L.L.C., 375
Cariad Capital, Inc., 642
Carillon Capital, Inc., 610
Castle Group, Ltd., The , 515
Catalyst Group, The , 660
Cerulean Fund/WGC Enterprises, 350
Chase H&Q (FKA Hambrecht & Quist), 160
Clairvest Group, Inc., 780
Cohen & Co., L.L.C., 517
Crown Capital Corp, 475
CW Group, Inc., 521
Defta Partners, 167
DFW Capital Partners (AKA:DeMuth, Folger & Wetherill), 486
ECI Ventures Ltd, 801
Equity-South (FKA:Grubb & Williams Ltd.), 333
Espirito Santo Development, 808
First Princeton Capital Corp., 489
Fonds de Solidarité des Travailleurs du Québec (F.T.Q.), 820
Fowler, Anthony & Co., 422
Frazier & Company, 705
Gateway Associates, L.P., 476
Glencoe Capital, LLC (FKA: Glencoe Investment Corporation), 356
Granite Ventures LLC (FKA: H & Q Venture Associates), 186
Halpern, Denny & Co., 425
Harbison Corporation, 477
High Street Capital, LLC, 357
Hoak Capital Corp., 666

HSBC Private Equity (Asia), Ltd. (FKA: HSBC PE Management), 841
HT Capital Advisors, LLC, 538
Hungarian-American Enterprise Fund, The (HAEF), 842
Innova Capital (FKA: Poland Partners Management Company), 853
Integrated Consortium, Inc., 197
Investissement Desjardins, 857
Investissements Novacap (AKA:Novacap Investments, Inc.), 858
IPS Industrial Promotion Services, Ltd., 859
Jefferson Capital Fund, Ltd., 130
Josephberg Grosz & Co., Inc., 545
Kahala Investments, Inc., 668
Lepercq Capital Management, Inc.(AKA:Lepercq,de Neuflize In), 548
LF International, Inc., 204
Lincoln Investment Management Inc., 378
Lubar & Co., 718
M&F Associates, L.P., 549
Marwit Capital LLC, 209
Media Venture Partners, 211
Memhard Investment Bankers, Inc., 300
Merifin Capital Group, 883
Middlefield Capital Fund, 885
National Corporate Finance, Inc., 217
Nesbitt Burns, 363
Newbridge Capital Limited, 219
Noro-Moseley Partners, 336
North American Business Development Co., L.L.C., 364
Noveltek Venture Corp., 560
NTC Group, The , 301
Oak Hill Capital Management, Inc., 561
Oak Investment Partners, 302
Oem Capital, 302
Onex Corp., 905
PAMA Group Inc. (FKA:Prudential Asset Management Asia), 908
Paribas Principal, Inc., 563
Pauli & Co., Inc., 477
Phoenix Home Life Mutual Insurance Co., 303
Pittsford Group, Inc., The , 565
Prospect Street Ventures (FKA:Prospect Street Invest. Mgmt), 567
RBC Ventures, Inc., 619
Rosewood Capital, L.P., 237
Rutledge & Co., Inc., 305
SAE Ventures, 306
Sandler Capital Management, 571
Saugatuck Capital Company, 306
Schooner Capital International, L.P., 444
Sentinel Capital Partners, 573
Shared Ventures, Inc., 470
Shawmut Capital Partners, 447
Shelton Companies, Inc., The , 604
Sigma Partners, 243
Siguler Guff & Company, LLC, 575
Sorrento Associates, Inc., 247
South Atlantic Venture Funds, L.P., 327
Southport Partners, 307
Southwest Venture Group, 678
Speirs Consultants, Inc., 938
Stephens Group, Inc., 137
Sterling Grace Capital Management, L.P., 579
Stolberg Partners, 580
Summit Capital Group, 680
Summit Partners, 451
Sun Valley Ventures, 250
Sycamore Ventures, 494
TA Associates, Inc., 451
Taylor & Turner, 253
Triune Capital, 260
Tvi Investments Bv, 960
VantagePoint Venture Partners, 263
Vencap Equities Alberta, Ltd., 966
Vero Group PLC, 684
Vertical Group, The, 496
Vista Capital Corp., 268
Westar Capital, 271
William A.M. Burden & Co., 593
Willis Stein & Partners, 374
Wingate Partners, L.P., 685
Winslow Partners LLC, 317
Worms Capital Management, 594

Distressed Debt

Ampersand Ventures, 404
Continental Venture Capital , 784
Crosbie & Co Inc, 789
CS Capital Partners, LLC, 486
Electra Partners Asia [FKA: JF Electra Limited], 803
Finansa Capital Limited, 816
First Floor Capital Sdn. Bhd., 817
Fonds de Solidarité des Travailleurs du Québec (F.T.Q.), 820
Geneva Merchant Banking Partners, 601
Pacific Corporate Group, Inc., 227
Venture Capital Partners Pty Limited, 967

Early Stage

100 X, 401
3i Austria (FKA Bank Austria TFV High Tech -UB GmbH), 725
3K Digital, 727
3TS Venture Partners AG, 727
550 Digital Media Ventures , 501
A.M. Pappas & Associates, 597
Abell Venture Fund, 390
Aberdeen Murray Johnstone Private Equity, 728
ABN AMRO Private Equity (AKA: ABN AMRO Capital (USA) Inc.) , 343
ABN-AMRO Corporate Investments, 729
Academy Funds (FKA: Longleaf Venture Fund LLC), 597
Accel Partners, 139
Accelerator Media (UK), Ltd, 730
Accenture Technology Ventures (FKA: AC Ventures), 140
Access Capital Partners, 730
Access2Net, 731
Acer Technology Ventures(FKA:Acer Soft Capital Inc.), 141
ACT Venture Capital Ltd., 732
Adams Capital Management, Inc., 622
Adams Street Partners, LLC (FKA: Brinson Private Equity), 343
AdCapital AG (FKA Berliner Elektro Holding AG), 732
ADD Partners , 733
Advanced Technology Ventures, 401
Advantage Capital Partners, 386
Advent Venture Partners (FKA Advent Limited), 733

Advent-Morro Equity Partners, 734
Adveq Management AG (FKA Advisers on Private Equity AG), 734
Affinity Capital Management(FKA:Peterson-Spencer-Fansler Co), 463
Agilent Ventures, 142
AIG Capital Partners Inc., 503
Akin Gump Investment Partners 2000, LP, 655
Al Shugart International (ASI), 142
Alcatel Ventures, 142
Alexander Hutton, Inc., 702
Alice Ventures, 736
Allegis Capital (AKA:Allegis Media Technology Ventures), 143
Allen & Buckeridge Pty Ltd, 737
Alta Berkeley Venture Partners, 739
Alta Communications, 403
American Century Ventures, 473
Ampersand Ventures, 404
AMT Capital Ltd. (AKA: AMT Venture Partners, Ltd.), 656
AMWIN Management Pty Ltd, 741
Angel Investors, LP, 145
Angel-Invest, 741
Anila Fund (AKA: Anila.org, LLC), 145
Apax Partners & Cie (AKA: Apax France), 742
Apax Partners & Co. Ventures Ltd (AKA: Apax UK), 742
Apax Partners & Co.Beteiligungsberatung AG, 742
Apex Venture Partners, 346
Apex Ventures BV, 743
APIDC-Venture Capital Limited, 743
Apollo Invest , 744
Applied Genomic Technology Capital Funds (AGTC), 405
APV Technology Partners, 146
Arbor Partners LLC, 457
ARCH Venture Partners, 346
ArgNor Wireless Ventures, 744
Argos Soditic SA, 744
Aria Ventures Ltd., 745
Arkoma Venture Partners, 657
Armada Asset Management, 746
Arts Alliance, 746
ASC Group, 746
Ascend Technology Ventures, 747
Asian Direct Capital Management, 747
Asian Infrastructure Fund Advisers Limited, 748
AsiaTech Internet Group (ATIG) (FKA: AsiaTech Ventures), 748
Aspen Ventures (formerly 3i Ventures), 147
Athena Technology Ventures, 148
Atila Venture Partners Ltd., 749
Atle Ventures (FKA Teknologiparkernas Utveckling AB), 749
Aurora Funds, Inc., 598
Austin Ventures, L.P., 657
AV Labs, 658
aventic Partners AG, 750
Axiom Venture Partners, L.P., 288
Axiomlab PLC, 751
Ayala Internet Venture Partners, 751
b-business partners, 752
B2B-Hive, LLC, 509
bainlab, 752
Baker Capital Corp., 510
BaltCap Management, Ltd, 753
Bamboo Investments Plc (FKA Railike Limited), 753
BancBoston Capital/BancBoston Ventures, 408
BankInvest Group AS, 754
Baring Communications Equity, 755
Batterson Venture Partners(AKA:BVP), 348
Bayern Kapital Risikokapitalbeteiligungs GmbH, 757
BBS Finance, 757
BCE Capital, 758
BCR Asset Management Pty Ltd., 758
Becton, Dickinson & Co. (AKA: BD Ventures), 484
Bedrock Capital Partners, 409
Beecken, Petty & Co. LLC, 348
Benchmark Capital, 154
Berkshires Capital Investors, 410
Berlin Capital Fund (FKA LBB Beteiligungsgesellschaft GmbH), 759
Bessemer Venture Partners, 410
Big Bang Ventures, 760
BioVentures Investors, LLC, 411
Birchmere Ventures, Inc.(FKA:Birchmere Investments), 624
Blue Chip Venture Company, 609
Blue Ribbon AG, 760
Blueprint Ventures, LLC, 155
BlueStar Ventures, 348
Blumberg Capital Ventures, 155
bmp Aktiengesellschaft AG, 761
Boston University Community Technology Fund , 413
Boulder Ventures, Ltd., 392
BrainHeart Capital AB, 762
BrainWorks Ventures, 330
Brait Capital Partners, 762
Bridge Partners, LLC, 393
Brook Venture Management, L.L.C., 414
Bruce F. Glaspell & Associates, 498
Buena Venture Associates, 659
Bulldog Partners Limited, 764
Burrill & Company, 156
BV Capital (FKA Bertelsmann Ventures LP), 157
Calgary Enterprises, Inc., 514
Caltech Capital Partners Ltd., 766
Cambrian Ventures, 158
Cambridge Technology Capital, 415
Camelot Ventures, 457
Canaan Partners, 290
Capital for Companies (CfC), 769
Capital Investors, 690
Capital Riesgo Internet SCR SA (BSCH), 770
Capital Southwest Corporation, 660
Capital Strategy Management Co., The, 349
Capital Technology Group, LLC, 610
Capman Management GmbH, 770
Capricorn Ventures International, 770
Capstone Ventures SBIC, L.P., 158
Cardinal Partners (FKA: Cardinal Health Partners), 485
Carlin Ventures LLC, 514
Castile Ventures, 416
Catalyst Fund Management & Research Ltd, 773
CDC Innovation Partners, 775
CEI Ventures/Coastal Ventures LP, 388
Celtic House International, 775
Centennial Ventures, 278
CenterPoint Venture Partners, 661
Challenger International Ltd., 776

Charles River Ventures, 417
Cheng Xin Technology Development Corp. (FKA:Fidelity VC Corp, 776
Cherry Tree Investments, Inc., 464
Child Health Investment Corporation, 382
Chrysalead, 778
CID Equity Partners, 376
Citizens Capital and Citizens Ventures, 418
Clal Venture Capital Management Ltd (AKA CVC Management), 781
Clarion Capital Corp., 610
Clarity Capital, 419
Classic Fund Management, Ltd., 781
Clearstone Venture Partners (FKA: idealab! Capital Partners), 161
CMB Capital, LLC (CMBC), 322
CMEA Ventures (FKA:Chemicals & Materials Enterprise Associa), 161
Collinson, Howe & Lennox, LLC, 291
Colonial First State Private Equity Ltd (FKA: Hambro-G Mgmt), 782
Colorado Venture Management, 278
Commerz Beteiligungsgesellschaft mbH (CBG), 783
Compass Investment Management Ltd., 783
ComVentures (AKA: Communications Ventures), 163
Concord Venture Management (FKA:Nitzanim), 784
Constellation Ventures, 518
Continental S.B.I.C., 691
Continental Venture Capital , 784
Continuum Group Limited, 785
Convergence Partners L.P., 164
Copernicus Capital Management Ltd, 785
CORAL Ventures, 465
Cordova Ventures (FKA:Cordova Capital), 331
Core Capital Partners, 313
Corning Capital (AKA: Corning Technology Ventures), 420
CR&T Ventures AB, 787
Creafund CVBA, 788
Crescendo Venture Management LLC (FKA:IAI Ventures), 466
Crest Communications Holdings LLC, 520
Cross Atlantic Capital Partners, 625
Crystal Internet Venture Fund, L.P., 611
CS Capital Partners, LLC, 486
CSK Venture Capital Co., Ltd., 789
CT Holdings, 661
CyberWorks Ventures , 790
DANSK Udviklingsfinansiering A/S, 793
Dassault Developpment, 794
Dauphin Capital Partners, 522
DB Venture Partners, 794
Delmag Ventures, 394
Delta Ventures, 795
Denali Venture Capital, 168
Deutsche Venture Capital GmbH (DVCG), 796
Diamondhead Ventures, L.P., 169
Digital Media Campus, 169
Digital Partners, 704
Dinner Club, LLC, The, 692
Discovery Capital, 797
Domain Associates, L.L.C., 486
Dominion Ventures, Inc., 170
DOR Ventures, 798
Dot Edu Ventures, 171
DotCom Ventures L.P., 171
Draper Fisher Jurvetson (FKA: Draper Associates), 172
Draper Fisher Jurvetson Gotham Venture Partners, 523
Draper International, 172
Draper Richards, 173
Draper Triangle Ventures LP, 626
DSE Investment Services Limited, 799
Duchossois TECnology Partners, LLC, 353
Durlacher Limited, 799
DynaFund Ventures, L.L.C., 174
E*Capital Corporation , 174
E-MERGE, 800
e4e Inc., 174
Early Stage Enterprises, L.P., 487
Earlybird Venture Capital, 800
EarlyBirdCapital.com Inc., 524
East/West Venture Group FKA:East/West Capital Associates, 175
eBlast Ventures, LLC, 353
eCompanies-Evercore Venture Partners (E2VP), 175
EDB Investments Pte Ltd., 802
EDF Ventures (F.K.A. Enterprise Development Fund), 458
Edison Venture Fund, 488
eFund, LLC, 704
Egan-Managed Capital, 421
Eircom Enterprise Fund Ltd., 803
El Dorado Ventures, 176
Elderstreet Investments Ltd, 803
Electronics For Imaging (AKA: EFI), 177
Emerging Technologies , 804
Encore Venture Partners, LP, 177
Endeavor Capital Management, 294
Endeavour Capital Pty Ltd, 804
EnerTech Capital Partners, L.P., 626
Enterprise Partners, 178
EnterpriseAsia.com, 805
Epicea, 805
Episode-1 Partners, 806
EquiNet Venture Partners AG, 806
equity4life AG, 807
Eqvitec Partners Oy, 807
Essex Woodlands Health Ventures (FKA:Woodlands Venture Partn, 354
ETF Group, 808
Eurofund LP, 810
European Equity Partners , 810
European Webgroup, 811
Euroventures Management AB , 811
EVC Christows PLC (FKA: eVestment Company PLC), 812
eVerger Associates, 812
eVolution Global Partners, 813
Exponential Business Development Co., 529
F. Turismo-Capital De Risco SA, 814
Fairgill Investments Property Limited, 814
far blue, 814
FBR CoMotion Venture Capital, 705
FBR Technology Venture Partners,L.P.(AKA:Friedman,Billings), 693
First Analysis Venture Capital (FKA:First Analysis Corp), 354
First Floor Capital Sdn. Bhd., 817
First Gen-e Investments, 817
First Union Capital Partners, 600
Flatiron Partners, 530

Fluke Venture Partners., 705
FLV Fund (AKA Flanders Language Valley Fund), 818
Flynn Venture, LLC, 180
Fond Riziveho Kapitalu SRO, 819
Fonds de Solidarité des Travailleurs du Québec (F.T.Q.), 820
Foresight, 820
Forrest Binkley & Brown, 180
Fortune Consulting Group Incorporated, 821
Fortune Venture Management Pte Ltd., 822
Forward Ventures, 180
Foundation Capital Limited, 822
Fowler, Anthony & Co., 422
Friedli Corporate Finance AG, 823
Friulia SpA Fin.Reg.Friuli-Venezia, 824
Frontier Capital, LLC, 600
Fuqua Ventures, LLC, 334
Fusient Ventures, 531
Future Venture Capital Co., Ltd., 824
G-51 Capital LLC, 665
Gabriel Venture Partners, 182
Gamma Investors LLC, 627
Gap Fund Managers Ltd, 825
Gazelle TechVentures, 377
GCI Venture Partners, 314
Gemini Capital Fund Management Ltd, 825
GENES GmbH Venture Services, 826
Genesis Partners, 826
Genesys Partners, 533
Geneva Venture Partners, 184
Genevest Consulting Group, S.A., 827
Geocapital Partners, L.L.C., 489
GKM Venture Partners, LP, 184
Global Crossing Ventures (FKA: Frontier Ventures), 185
Global Internet Ventures (GIV), 693
Global Retail Partners (A.K.A. GRP), 185
Global Technology Ventures (GTV), 829
Global Venture Capital Corporation, 829
GMS Capital, 534
GO Capital, 829
Go Equity GmbH, 829
GorillaPark, 830
Granite Ventures LLC (FKA: H & Q Venture Associates), 186
Gray Ventures, 335
Graystone Venture Partners, LLC(AKA:Portage Venture Partners, 356
Gresham CEA Management Limited, 832
Greylock, 424
Grosvenor Funds, The, 315
GrowthWorks Capital, 834
Guide Ventures, 706
Gujarat Venture Finance Limited, 834
H&Q Asia Pacific, Ltd., 187
HarbourVest Partners, LLC., 426
Healthcare Ventures LLC (FKA: Healthcare Investments), 490
Heidelberg Innovation GmbH, 837
HFS Capital (AKA: Hoffman, Fitzgerald & Snyder), 694
Highland Capital Partners, 427
Hitachi America, Ltd., 189
HMS Holtron Management Services, Ltd, 838
Holland Venture B.V. (FKA: Holland Venture Holding C.V.), 839
Hollinger Capital (FKA: Hollinger Ventures), 537
Horizonte Venture Management GmbH, 840
HSBC Private Equity (Asia), Ltd. (FKA: HSBC PE Management), 841
HT Capital Advisors, LLC, 538
Hudson Venture Partners, 538
Hummer Winblad Venture Partners, 191
Hunt Capital Group, 667
Hunt Ventures, LP, 667
Hydro-Quebec CapiTech Inc., 843
i-Hatch Ventures, LLC, 539
i2b Ventures, 667
i2i Venture, 843
iAsia Alliance Capital, 844
IBB Beteiligungsgesellschaft mbH, 844
ICF Ventures Private Ltd., 845
IDI-Kairos, 847
IFCI Venture Cap. Funds (Formerly Risk Capital & Tech.), 847
iGlobe Partners Limited, 847
Ignite Associates, LLC, 192
IKB Venture Capital GmbH (AKA IKB Beteiligungsgesellschaft , 848
IL&FS Venture Corporation (FKA. CreditCapital Venture Fund), 848
IMH Industrie Management Holding GmbH, 848
iMinds (FKA: Interactive Minds), 193
Impact Venture Partners, 539
Incepta LLC, 706
Index Ventures, 850
Indus Venture Management Ltd., 851
Industry Ventures , 428
Infinity Capital LLC, 194
Infinity Technology Investments Pvt. Ltd., 852
InnoCal, L.P., 196
Innovation Capital Associates Ltd, 853
Innovation Works, Inc., 628
Inova Capital SCR, 855
Institutional Venture Partners, 196
Integra Ventures (F.K.A. Integra Bio-Health Inc.), 706
Interfase Capital Partners LP, 667
Internet Healthcare Group, 297
Internet Ventures Scandinavia A/S, 856
internet.com, 297
Interregnum, 856
Intersouth Partners, 601
InterWest Partners, 197
Investissements Novacap (AKA:Novacap Investments, Inc.), 858
Invision AG (FKA Aureus Private Equity AG), 858
IPE Capital-Soc.De Cap.De Risoc SA, 859
Irwin Ventures LLC (FKA: Irwin Ventures Incorporated), 377
Israel Seed Partners, 860
IT Provider Advisor, 861
ITACT, 861
ITP-Management N.V., 861
J.P. Morgan Partners (FKA: Chase Capital Partners), 543
JAFCO Co. Ltd., 862
JAFCO Investment (FKA:Nomura/JAFCO Investment (Asia) Limited, 862
JatoTech Management LLC, 668
Jerusalem Venture Partners (AKA: JVP), 864
JK&B Capital, 358
Johnston Associates, Inc., 490
Josephberg Grosz & Co., Inc., 545
JT Venture Partners, LLC, 491

JumpStartUp Fund Advisors Pvt. Ltd., 864
Kansas City Equity Partners, 477
Kappa-IT Ventures, 865
KB Partners, LLC, 359
KBL Healthcare Ventures, 546
Kennet Capital Ltd, 866
Kestrel Venture Management (FKA:Corning Venture Management), 429
Kettle Partners, L.P., 359
Kick-Start Ventures, 866
Kitty Hawk Capital, 602
KLM Capital Group, 201
Koch Ventures, 133
Koor Corporate Venture Capital, 868
KTB Ventures (FKA: KTB Venture Capital), 202
Ladybird Technologies, Ltd., 870
Lambda Funds, The, 546
Lancet Capital Partner(FKA:Caduceus Capital Partners), 429
Launch Center 39, 547
Lazard Technology Partners, 547
Lee Munder Venture Partners, 430
Legal & General Ventures Ltd, 872
LF International, Inc., 204
LG Venture Investment Inc., 873
Liberty Venture Partners, Inc., 631
Life Science Ventures, 873
Life Sciences Partners BV, 874
Lightspeed Venture Partners (FKA: Weiss, Peck & Greer), 206
Loeb Partners Corp., 549
Lombard Investments, Inc., 206
London Merchant Security (AKA LMS), 874
London Ventures (Fund Managers) Ltd., 875
Lovett Miller & Co. Incorporated, 325
LTI Ventures Leasing Corp., 298
Lucent Venture Partners, Inc., 207
Lycos Ventures, 632
M&F Associates, L.P., 549
M/C Venture Partners, 431
M31 Ventures, LLC, 550
Macromedia Ventures, 208
Madison Dearborn Partners, LLC, 361
Madrona Venture Group, 707
Magnum Communications (AKA: MCF Advisory Services Ltd), 877
Mangrove Capital Partners SA, 878
march.fifteen AG (FKA Peterp@n), 878
Maristeth Ventures, L.L.C., 707
Massachusetts Technology Development Corp. (MTDC), 432
Massey Burch Capital Corp., 650
Maton Venture, 209
Matrix Partners, 433
Matrix Private Equity, 879
Mayo Medical Ventures, 468
MC Capital Asia Private Limited, 880
McGraw-Hill Ventures, 552
MDS Health Ventures, Inc. (AKA: MDS Capital Corp.), 881
MDT Advisers, Inc., 433
Medicis AG, 882
Medicus Venture Partners, 211
Mediphase Venture Partners (FKA: EHealth Technology Fund), 434
MedVenture Associates, 212
Megunticook Management, 435
Menlo Ventures, 212
Merifin Capital Group, 883
Meritage Private Equity Fund, 281
Merlin Biosciences (AKA Merlin Ventures), 884
Metropolitan Venture Partners (MetVP), 553
meVC.com, 213
Midlands Venture Fund Managers Ltd. (AKA: Midven Ltd), 886
Milestone Venture Partners, 553
Millennium Three Venture Group, L.L.C., 480
Mitiska NV, 887
MMC adVentures Ltd, 888
Mofet Venture Capital , 888
Mohr, Davidow Ventures, 214
Monarch Capital Partners, LLC, 336
Montreux Equity Partners, 216
Monumental Venture Partners, LLC, 696
Morgenthaler Ventures, 614
Mosaic Venture Partners, 889
Mosaix Ventures, LLC , 363
Mountaineer Capital LP, 716
MPM Capital (FKA - MPM Asset Management LLC), 436
MSC Venture Corporation Sdn. Bhd., 890
MTI Partners Ltd, 890
Multiventure Investment, Inc., 890
Murphree Venture Partners, 671
MVM Ltd, 891
National Bank Of Kuwait, 555
Navis Partners (FKA:Fleet Equity Partners), 643
nCoTec Ventures Ltd, 893
NeoMed Management AS (FKA Medical Venture Management), 894
Net Partners, 895
NetCatalyst , 218
Netjuice, 895
New England Partners, 437
New Enterprise Associates, 396
New Jersey Technology Council (AKA:NJTC), 493
New South Ventures, 325
New Things, LLC, 557
New World Venture Advisors, 364
Newbury Ventures, 220
NewMargin Venture Capital, 897
NewSpring Ventures, 634
Newtek Capital, 558
Nexit Ventures Oy, 897
Next Ventures Limited, 897
NextGen Partners LLC, 221
Nextreme Ventures, 221
Nippon Technology Venture Partners Ltd., 899
NMT New Medical Technologies, 900
Nomura/JAFCO Investment (HK) Limited, 901
North America Investment Corp., 902
Northern Stream Capital, 709
Northern Venture Managers Limited, 902
Northwood Ventures, 559
Norwest Equity Partners, 223
Novak Biddle Venture Partners, L.P., 697
Novartis AG, 903
Novell Ventures, 686
Novus Ventures, 223
Oak Investment Partners, 302

Obelisk Capital Pty Ltd, 904
Odin Capital Group, 479
Odlander Fredrikson & Co, 904
Ohana Ventures, LLC, 615
Olympus Capital Holdings Asia, 905
OneLiberty Ventures (FKA: Morgan, Holland Ventures Corp.), 439
Onset Ventures, 225
Open Prairie Ventures, 365
Oracle Corporation, 226
Orien Ventures, 303
Ovation Capital Partners (FKA:iCentennial Ventures LLC), 562
OVP Venture Partners (FKA: Olympic Venture Partners), 709
Oxford Bioscience Partners, 440
PA Early Stage (AKA:Pennsylvania Early Stage Partners), 635
Pacific Capital Partners, 907
Pacific Corporate Group, Inc., 227
Pacific Horizon Ventures LLC, 710
Pacific Northwest Partners SBIC, L.P., 710
Paladin Partners, 711
Palomar Ventures, 228
PAMA Group Inc. (FKA:Prudential Asset Management Asia), 908
Pantheon Ventures Limited, 908
Pari Capital AG, 909
Part'com, 909
Partech International, 229
Partners Group, 910
Pequot Capital Management Inc., 564
Piedmont Venture Partners, 604
Pilotbird, 912
Pino Venture Partners, 912
Polaris Venture Capital, 913
Polaris Venture Partners, 441
PolyTechnos Venture Partners GmbH, 913
Potomac Ventures, 397
pre-IPO Aktiengesellschaft, 915
Prelude Technology Investments Ltd, 915
Prescient Capital, 232
Primaxis Technology Ventures Inc. , 916
Prime Technology Ventures NV, 916
Primedia Ventures, 567
Primus Venture Partners, Inc., 616
Prism Venture Partners, 441
ProQuest Investments, L.P., 493
ProSeed Capital Holdings CVA, 917
ProVen Private Equity (FKA:Guinness Mahon Development Cap.), 918
Proximitas AG Venture Capital, 918
Ptek Ventures , 336
Putnam Lovell Capital Partners, L.P., 232
Pythagoras NV, 919
Q Ventures, 674
Quest Ventures, 233
Ralph Wilson Equity Fund, L.L.C., 460
Reach Incubator, 442
RHO Management, 570
Ridgewood Capital Management LLC, 494
RiverVest Venture Partners , 478
Rocket Ventures, 237
Roser Ventures LLC, 283
Royal Bank Private Equity (FKA: Royal Bank Development Cap), 922
RoyNat Ventures, 923
RSA Ventures, 443
RWI Group, LP, 239
S.R. One, Limited, 638
Saarlandische Wagnisfinanzierungsgesellschaft mbh (AKA SWG), 924
Sadot Venture Capital Management (1992) Ltd, 924
Saffron Hill Ventures (FKA LootLab Ltd.), 924
Salix Ventures, L.P., 653
Sanderling Ventures, 239
Sandlot Capital LLC, 283
Sandton Financial Group, 240
Sanpaolo IMI Private Equity S.p.A., 925
Sapient Capital, 721
SBV Venture Partners (AKA:Sigefi, Burnette & Vallee), 240
Schoffstall Ventures , 639
Scottish Equity Partners Limited, 927
Seapoint Ventures, 712
Seaport Capital, 572
SEB e-invest, 927
SEB Foretagsinvest, 927
Seed Capital Ltd, 928
Seed Capital Partners, 573
Selby Venture Partners, 241
Sequel Venture Partners, 284
Sequoia Capital, 241
Sevin Rosen Management Co., 677
Shaw, Kwei & Partners Limited, 929
Sherpa Partners, LLC, 471
Siemens Venture Capital GmbH, 930
Sienna Ventures (FKA: Sienna Holdings Inc.), 242
Sierra Ventures, 243
Signal Lake Venture Fund, LP, 307
Signia Ventures, 244
Silicon Alley Venture Partners LLC (AKA SAVP) , 576
SilkRoute Capital Limited, 930
SingTel Ventures, 931
Siparex Group (FKA:Siparex Provinces de France), 931
Sitra (AKA Finnish National Fund for Research and Dev.), 932
Skyline Ventures, 245
Small Industries Development Bank of India (SIDBI), The, 933
Smart Technology Ventures, 246
Societe Generale- Private Equity Activity, 933
Sofinnova Partners, 934
Sofinnova Ventures, 246
Softbank China Venture Capital, 935
Softbank Corp., 935
SOFTBANK Venture Capital (FKA: SOFTBANK Technology Ventures), 247
Solstice Capital LLC, 449
Sonera Corporation Corporate Venture Capital, 935
Sopartec SA, 936
Southeastern Technology Fund, 132
Southern Capitol Ventures, 605
Sovereign Capital (FKA:Nash, Sells & Partners Limited), 936
Sparkventures, LLC, 449
Speed Ventures, 937
SPEF Banques Populaires, 937
Spencer Trask Ventures, Inc. (FKA: Spencer Trask Securities), 576
Springboard-Harper Investment Pte. Ltd., 938
Sprout Group, 578
St. Paul Venture Capital, Inc., 471
Star-Ventures Management GMBH (SVM), 940

Starting Point Partners, 250
Sterling Venture Partners, 398
Still River Fund, The, 450
Stonepath Europe, 941
Strathdon Investments Ltd, 942
SudKB & SudVC, 942
Summit Group Ltd, The, 943
Summit Partners, 451
SUNeVision Holdings Ltd, 944
Sustainable Jobs Fund (SJF), The , 606
Swedestart Management AB, 944
Swedish Industrial Development Fund (AKA Industrifonden), 945
Sybase, Inc., 252
Synopsys, Inc., 253
Syntel Inc. Web Incubator Program, 461
Tamir Fishman Ventures, 946
Target Partners, 947
tbg Technologie-Beteiligungsgesellschaft mbH, 947
TechFarm (AKA:TechFund Capital), 254
Techno Nord VC GmbH, 948
TechnoCap Inc, 949
Technologieholding VC GmbH, 950
Technology Associates Management Corporation, 950
Technology Partners, 255
Technology Venture Partners Pty Ltd, 950
Technology Ventures, L.L.C., 339
Technostart GmbH, 951
Techpacific.com Ltd., 951
Techxas Ventures, LLC, 681
TecVenture Partners GmbH, 952
Telecom Partners (FKA:Telecom Management, LLC), 285
Telecom Venture Group Ltd. (TVG), 953
Telecommunications Development Fund (TDF), 316
TeleSoft Partners, 256
Telia Business Innovation AB, 953
Temasek Capital, 954
TG Asia Ventures Limited, 954
ThinkVentures.com Ltd, 954
Thoma Cressey Equity Partners, 371
Thompson Clive & Partners Limited, 955
TL Ventures, 640
Top Technology Limited (AKA:Hambros-Advanced Technology Tru), 957
Toucan Capital Corp., 399
Transpac Capital Pte, Ltd., 958
Trellis Partners, 682
Triad Media Ventures, 309
Tribune Ventures, 372
Trident Capital, 259
Trinity Ventures, 260
TriNova, 959
Triton Ventures, 682
TruePilot, LLC, 606
TTP Venture Managers (FKA: The Technology Partnership), 960
TVM Techno Venture Management, 961
Twinning Ventures, 961
U.S. Bancorp Piper Jaffray Ventures, Inc., 472
U.S. Venture Partners, 261
UBS Capital, 962
UBS Capital (AKA Phildrew Ventures), 963
UOB Venture Management Pte Ltd., 964
Updata Venture Partners, 700
US Trust Private Equity, 584
Utah Ventures II, L.P. (A.K.A. Union Ventures), 687
Value Management & Research AG (VMR), 965
Vault Capital, 714
VCF Partners, 965
VennWorks (FKA: IncuVest LLC) , 586
Venture Associates, Ltd., 285
Venture Catalyst, 265
Venture Investment Management Company LLC (AKA: VIMAC), 454
Venture Management Associates, Inc., 329
Venture Partners AG, 968
Venture Select, 968
Venture TDF Pte Ltd., 968
VentureCap Management GmbH (AKA VCH Equity Group AG), 969
Venturepark Incubator (FKA grizzlyfarm AG), 969
Ventures Medical Associates, 683
Veritas Venture Capital Management, Ltd., 970
Versant Ventures (FKA: Palladium Capital), 266
Vertex Management, 971
Vertex Management Israel (AKA: Vertex Management III Ltd.), 971
Vitesse Semiconductor Corporation, 268
VIV NV (AKA Vlaamse Investeringvennootschap NV), 973
Viventures Inc., 973
Voyager Capital, 714
VTC Partners GmbH, 974
Wakefield Group, 607
Walden Capital Management Corporation, 589
Walden International Investment Group (AKA: Walden Group), 269
Walden Israel, 975
WaldenVC, 270
Warburg, Pincus & Co., LLC. (FKA: E.M. Warburg, Pincus & Co), 590
Wasatch Venture Fund (FKA: Wasatch Venture Corporation), 687
wellington partners venture capital GmbH, 975
WestBridge Capital Advisors (India) Pvt. Ltd., 976
Weston Presidio Capital Management, 455
William Blair Capital Partners, 373
Windamere Venture Partners, LLC, 273
Windward Ventures (FKA: Coronado Capital), 274
WL Ventures (FKA:Lothian Enterprise Ltd.), 978
Wolf Ventures (AKA:Wolf Asset Management Corp.), 286
Wooshin Development Finance Corp, 978
Working Ventures Canadian Fund, Inc., 978
YankeeTek Ventures, 456
Yasuda Enterprise Development Co., Ltd.(FKA: Nippon Ent.Dev), 275
Yorkshire Fund Managers Ltd., 979
Young Associates Limited, 980
Yozma Venture Capital Ltd, 980
Zero Gravity Internet Group, Inc. , 276
Zero Stage Capital Co., Inc., 456
Zone Ventures, 276

Expansion

3i Finland Oy (FKA SFK Finance), 725
3i Group plc, 726
3TS Venture Partners AG, 727

A.M. Pappas & Associates, 597
Abell Venture Fund, 390
Aberdeen Asset Managers, 728
Aberdeen Murray Johnstone Private Equity, 728
ABN AMRO Private Equity (AKA: ABN AMRO Capital (USA) Inc.) , 343
ABN-AMRO Corporate Investments, 729
Accenture Technology Ventures (FKA: AC Ventures), 140
Access Capital Partners, 730
ACE Management, 731
ACT Venture Capital Ltd., 732
Adams Street Partners, LLC (FKA: Brinson Private Equity), 343
Advent Venture Partners (FKA Advent Limited), 733
Advent-Morro Equity Partners, 734
Adveq Management AG (FKA Advisers on Private Equity AG), 734
AIB WBK Fund Management Sp.zoo, 735
AIG Capital Partners Inc., 503
AIG Investment Corporation (Asia) Limited, 735
All Asia Partners, 737
Alliance Venture Capital Advisors Limited, 738
Alpha Group (FKA:Alpha Associates Management, Ltd.), 738
Alta Berkeley Venture Partners, 739
Alta Communications, 403
AMP Asset Management Limited - Development Capital, 740
Ampersand Ventures, 404
AMT Capital Ltd. (AKA: AMT Venture Partners, Ltd.), 656
Antares Capital Corporation (FKA: Harbor Ventures Corp.), 320
Apax Partners & Cie (AKA: Apax France), 742
Apax Partners & Co. Ventures Ltd (AKA: Apax UK), 742
Apax Partners & Co.Beteiligungsberatung AG, 742
APC Asset Management, 743
APIDC-Venture Capital Limited, 743
Arbor Partners LLC, 457
Argo Global Capital, Inc., 406
Argos Soditic SA, 744
Argosy Partners, Inc., 745
Argus Capital Group, 745
Arkansas Capital Corporation, 137
Arkoma Venture Partners, 657
Armada Asset Management, 746
AS Venture GmbH, 746
ASC Group, 746
Asian Direct Capital Management, 747
Atila Venture Partners Ltd., 749
Auric Asset Management Pte. Ltd., 750
aventic Partners AG, 750
AXA Investment Managers Private Equity Europe, 751
Axiom Venture Partners, L.P., 288
Baker Capital Corp., 510
BaltCap Management, Ltd, 753
BancBoston Capital/BancBoston Ventures, 408
BankInvest Group AS, 754
Banque Bruxelles Lambert (ING Group), 754
Barclays Ventures, 755
Baring Private Equity Partners (FKA:Baring Venture Partners), 755
BayBG Bayerische Beteiligungsgesellschaft mbH, 757
BBS Finance, 757
BCE Capital, 758
BCI Partners, 484
BCR Asset Management Pty Ltd., 758
Beecken, Petty & Co. LLC, 348
Berenberg Private Equity GmbH, 759
Berlin Capital Fund (FKA LBB Beteiligungsgesellschaft GmbH), 759
Bessemer Venture Partners, 410
Birchmere Ventures, Inc.(FKA:Birchmere Investments), 624
Blue Chip Venture Company, 609
Blue Water Capital, LLC, 690
Blumberg Capital Ventures, 155
bmp Aktiengesellschaft AG, 761
Botts & Co., 762
Boulder Ventures, Ltd., 392
BrainHeart Capital AB, 762
Bridgepoint Capital Ltd (FKA: NWEP & NatWest Ventures Ltd), 763
Bruce F. Glaspell & Associates, 498
Bulldog Partners Limited, 764
Burrill & Company, 156
C3 Holdings, LLC, 474
Cairnsford Associates Ltd., 766
Calgary Enterprises, Inc., 514
Caltech Capital Partners Ltd., 766
Camelot Ventures, 457
Canaan Partners, 290
Capital For Business, Inc., 474
Capital Prive (FKA NatWest Equity Partners, France), 769
Capital Resource Partners, 415
Capital Southwest Corporation, 660
Capital Strategy Management Co., The, 349
Capital Z Asia, 770
Capman Management GmbH, 770
Capricorn Ventures International, 770
Capstone Ventures SBIC, L.P., 158
CapVest Management, Ltd, 771
CapVis Equity Partners AG, 771
Carousel Capital Partners, 599
Castle Harlan Australian Mezzanine Partners Pty. Ltd. , 772
Catalyst Fund Management & Research Ltd, 773
Catalyst Venture Capital Firm, 773
Catella IT AB, 773
Cazenove Private Equity, 773
CD Technicom S.A., 774
CDC Innovation Partners, 775
CDC Services Industries Gestion (CDC IXIS Private Equity), 775
CEI Ventures/Coastal Ventures LP, 388
Challenger International Ltd., 776
Champion Consulting Group, Incorporated, 776
Chiao Tung Bank, 776
Citadel Pooled Development Ltd. , 779
Citicorp Capital Asia (AKA: CITIC Pacific Ltd.), 780
Citizens Capital and Citizens Ventures, 418
Clal Venture Capital Management Ltd (AKA CVC Management), 781
Classic Fund Management, Ltd., 781
Clemente Capital (Asia) Ltd., 781
Close Brothers Private Equity, 782
CMB Capital, LLC (CMBC), 322
Coates Myer & Co. Pty Ltd. (AKA: CM Capital Investments), 782
Colonial First State Private Equity Ltd (FKA: Hambro-G Mgmt), 782
Commerce One Ventures, 162
Commerz Beteiligungsgesellschaft mbH (CBG), 783
Compass Investment Management Ltd., 783

Concordia Capital, 784
Conning Capital Partners, 292
Constellation Ventures, 518
Continental S.B.I.C., 691
Continental Venture Capital , 784
Copernicus Capital Management Ltd, 785
Cordova Ventures (FKA:Cordova Capital), 331
Core Capital Partners, 313
Covent Industrial Capital Investment Co Ltd, 787
Crest Communications Holdings LLC, 520
Crosbie & Co Inc, 789
Cross Atlantic Capital Partners, 625
CS Capital Partners, LLC, 486
Daimler Chrysler Venture Gmbh (AKA DCV), 792
Dassault Developpment, 794
De Vries & Co., Inc., 476
Deutsche Asset Management (Australia) Limited, 795
Deutsche Beteiligungs AG, 796
Deutsche Effecten und Wechsel-Beteiligungsgesellschaft AG, 796
Deutsche Venture Capital GmbH (DVCG), 796
Direct Capital Private Equity, 797
Dolphin Communications, 523
Domain Associates, L.L.C., 486
Dominion Ventures, Inc., 170
Dorset Capital, 170
Draper International, 172
Dresdner Kleinwort Capital , 524
DSE Investment Services Limited, 799
Earlybird Venture Capital, 800
ECI Ventures Ltd, 801
ECM Equity Capital Management GmbH, 802
EDB Investments Pte Ltd., 802
EDF Ventures (F.K.A. Enterprise Development Fund), 458
Edison Venture Fund, 488
Elderstreet Investments Ltd, 803
Emerging Technologies , 804
Endeavor Capital Management, 294
Endeavour Capital Pty Ltd, 804
Epicea, 805
EquiNet Venture Partners AG, 806
Equity Partners Management Pty Ltd, 807
Eqvitec Partners Oy, 807
ETF Group, 808
EURAZEO (FKA Gaz-et-Eaux & AZEO), 809
Euroventures Benelux Team B.V., 811
Euroventures Management AB , 811
Expanso Capital, 813
F. Turismo-Capital De Risco SA, 814
Fairgill Investments Property Limited, 814
FEO Ventures Pte. Ltd., 815
FINADVANCE S.A., 815
FINORPA, 816
First Analysis Venture Capital (FKA:First Analysis Corp), 354
First Gen-e Investments, 817
First New England Capital, L.P., 295
First Union Capital Partners, 600
Flinders Capital Limited, 818
Fluke Venture Partners., 705
FLV Fund (AKA Flanders Language Valley Fund), 818
Fonds de Solidarité des Travailleurs du Québec (F.T.Q.), 820
Forrest Binkley & Brown, 180
FORTKNOX-VENTURE AG, 821
Fortune Consulting Group Incorporated, 821
Fortune Venture Capital Incorporated, 822
Fortune Venture Management Pte Ltd., 822
Foundation Capital Limited, 822
Fowler, Anthony & Co., 422
Friends Ivory & Sime Private Equity (Ivory &Sime Baronsmead), 823
Friulia SpA Fin.Reg.Friuli-Venezia, 824
Frontier Capital, LLC, 600
Gap Fund Managers Ltd, 825
GATX/MM Venture Partners, 183
Gemini Capital Fund Management Ltd, 825
GENES GmbH Venture Services, 826
Genesis Partners, 826
Geneva Merchant Banking Partners, 601
Genevest Consulting Group, S.A., 827
Gimvindus NV, 828
GKM Venture Partners, LP, 184
Go Equity GmbH, 829
Grand Pacific Venture Capital Company Ltd., 830
Granville Baird Capital Partners (FKA:Granville Pr Eq Mngrs), 830
Green Mountain Advisors, Inc., 689
Gresham CEA Management Limited, 832
Gresham Rabo Management Limited, 832
Greylock, 424
Growth Venture Group Pty Ltd., 833
GTCR Golder Rauner, LLC, 356
Gujarat Venture Finance Limited, 834
H&Q Asia Pacific, Ltd., 187
Halder Holdings B.V., 835
HANNOVER Finanz GmbH, 837
HarbourVest Partners, LLC., 426
Healthcare Ventures LLC (FKA: Healthcare Investments), 490
Heartland Capital Fund, Ltd., 479
Heidelberg Innovation GmbH, 837
Hibernia Capital Partners, 837
High Street Capital, LLC, 357
Holland Venture B.V. (FKA: Holland Venture Holding C.V.), 839
Hollinger Capital (FKA: Hollinger Ventures), 537
Horizonte Venture Management GmbH, 840
Hotung International Company, Ltd., 840
Houston Venture Partners (AKA: Houston Partners), 666
HPI Holding SA, 841
HSBC Private Equity Ltd (FKA Montagu Private Equity Ltd), 841
HSBC Ventures (UK) Ltd, 842
Hudson Venture Partners, 538
Hummer Winblad Venture Partners, 191
Hunt Capital Group, 667
Hydro-Quebec CapiTech Inc., 843
ICC Venture Capital, 845
ICF Ventures Private Ltd., 845
ICICI Venture Funds Mngt. Co. Ltd., 846
IFCI Venture Cap. Funds (Formerly Risk Capital & Tech.), 847
iFormation Group, 296
IKB Venture Capital GmbH (AKA IKB Beteiligungsgesellschaft , 848
IL&FS Venture Corporation (FKA. CreditCapital Venture Fund), 848
IMH Industrie Management Holding GmbH, 848
IndAsia Fund Advisors Private Limited, 849
Index Ventures, 850

Indocean Chase Capital Advisors, 850
Indus Venture Management Ltd., 851
Inflexion plc, 852
Infocomm Investments Pte Ltd (IIPL), 852
InnoCal, L.P., 196
Inroads Capital Partners, L.P., 358
Intermediate Capital Group PLC, 855
Interpacific Venture Group Incorporated, 856
InterWest Partners, 197
InveStar Capital, Inc., 857
Investissements Novacap (AKA:Novacap Investments, Inc.), 858
Invision AG (FKA Aureus Private Equity AG), 858
IPE Capital-Soc.De Cap.De Risoc SA, 859
IT Provider Advisor, 861
J.P. Morgan Partners (FKA: Chase Capital Partners), 543
JAFCO Investment (FKA:Nomura/JAFCO Investment (Asia) Limited, 862
Jefferson Partners , 863
JK&B Capital, 358
Josephberg Grosz & Co., Inc., 545
JT Venture Partners, LLC, 491
Kaiser Permanente (AKA: National Venture Development), 200
Kansas City Equity Partners, 477
Kappa-IT Ventures, 865
KBL Healthcare Ventures, 546
Kennet Capital Ltd, 866
Key Equity Capital Corp.(AKA:Key Community Development Corp), 613
Keystone Venture Capital Management Co., 630
Kick-Start Ventures, 866
Kitty Hawk Capital, 602
Kline Hawkes & Co., 201
Koch Ventures, 133
KPMG Advent Management Group (FKA:Advent Western Pacific), 870
Lambda Funds, The, 546
Lee Munder Venture Partners, 430
Legal & General Ventures Ltd, 872
LF International, Inc., 204
Liberty Venture Partners, Inc., 631
Libon Capital Management Limited, 873
Life Science Ventures, 873
Life Sciences Partners BV, 874
Lightspeed Venture Partners (FKA: Weiss, Peck & Greer), 206
LLR Equity Partners, 631
Loeb Partners Corp., 549
Lombard Investments, Inc., 206
London Ventures (Fund Managers) Ltd., 875
LRM Investeringsmaatschappij Voor Limburg, 875
M&F Associates, L.P., 549
M31 Ventures, LLC, 550
Macquarie Direct Investment Limited, 876
Macquarie Technology Funds Management, 876
Madison Dearborn Partners, LLC, 361
Malmohus Invest AB, 877
Maristeth Ventures, L.L.C., 707
Marks and Spencer Ventures Ltd, 878
Marlborough Capital Advisors, 431
Matrix Group, 209
Matrix Private Equity, 879
MAVA Investment Management kft (AKA: Hungarian-American Ent), 879
MC Capital Asia Private Limited, 880
MC Capital, Inc., 551
McGraw-Hill Ventures, 552
MDS Health Ventures, Inc. (AKA: MDS Capital Corp.), 881
MDT Advisers, Inc., 433
MediaVenture Capital AG & Co. KGaA, 882
Medicis AG, 882
Medicon Valley Capital, 882
Menlo Ventures, 212
Mentor Capital Partners, 633
Merifin Capital Group, 883
Merita Capital Ltd, 884
Meritage Private Equity Fund, 281
Merlin Biosciences (AKA Merlin Ventures), 884
Mezzanine Management UK Limited, 885
Midinvest Oy, 886
Midlands Venture Fund Managers Ltd. (AKA: Midven Ltd), 886
Millennium Three Venture Group, L.L.C., 480
Mitiska NV, 887
Mofet Venture Capital , 888
Morgenthaler Ventures, 614
Mosaix Ventures, LLC , 363
Mountaineer Capital LP, 716
MSC Venture Corporation Sdn. Bhd., 890
MTI Partners Ltd, 890
Multiventure Investment, Inc., 890
Mustang Ventures (FKA Siemens Mustang Ventures), 216
Mutual Fund Public Company Ltd., 891
MVC AG (AKA Mitteldeutsche Venture Capital AG), 891
MVI Sverige AB, 891
Nanyang Ventures Pty Ltd (AKA: Nanyang Management Pty Ltd), 892
National Australia Investment Capital Limited, 892
National Bank Of Kuwait, 555
National City Equity Partners, Inc, 614
Navis Investment Partners (Asia) Limited, 893
Navis Partners (FKA:Fleet Equity Partners), 643
nCoTec Ventures Ltd, 893
Needham & Company, Inc., 556
NeoMed Management AS (FKA Medical Venture Management), 894
Netjuice, 895
NetSpark Ventures N.V., 895
Newbridge Capital Limited, 219
NewMargin Venture Capital, 897
NewSpring Ventures, 634
NextGen Partners LLC, 221
Nmas1 Electra Capital Privado , S.G.E.C.R., S.A., 900
NMT New Medical Technologies, 900
Nomura/JAFCO Investment (HK) Limited, 901
North America Investment Corp., 902
North Hill Ventures, 438
Northwest Venture Associates, Inc.(FKA:Spokane Capital Mgmt), 709
Northwood Ventures, 559
Norwest Equity Partners, 223
Novus Ventures, 223
NPE Investment Advisors (AKA:Nordic Private Equity Partners), 903
NPM Capital (AKA Nederlandse Participatie MIJ NV), 903
Obelisk Capital Pty Ltd, 904
Oberlin Capital, L.P., 603

Odin Capital Group, 479
Ohana Ventures, LLC, 615
Olympus Capital Holdings Asia, 905
Onondaga Venture Capital Fund, Inc., 562
Osprey Capital, LLC, 325
Pac-Link Management Corporation, 906
Pacific Capital Partners, 907
Pacific Corporate Group, Inc., 227
Pacific Equity Partners, 907
Pacific Venture Partners, 907
Palomar Ventures, 228
PAMA Group Inc. (FKA:Prudential Asset Management Asia), 908
Pantheon Ventures Limited, 908
Parcom Ventures BV, 909
Part'com, 909
Partners Group, 910
Pathfinder Investment Co Pvt Ltd, 910
Penta Capital Partners Ltd, 911
Pequot Capital Management Inc., 564
Petra Capital Partners LLC, 652
PME Capital, 912
PolyTechnos Venture Partners GmbH, 913
PowerWord Capital Management, Inc., 914
PPM Ventures Ltd (FKA: Prudential Venture Managers Ltd), 914
pre-IPO Aktiengesellschaft, 915
Prime Technology Ventures NV, 916
PrimePartners Asset Management Pte. Ltd., 916
Primus Venture Partners, Inc., 616
ProQuest Investments, L.P., 493
ProVen Private Equity (FKA:Guinness Mahon Development Cap.), 918
Proximitas AG Venture Capital, 918
Putnam Lovell Capital Partners, L.P., 232
Quadriga Capital Management GMBH, 919
Quantum Capital Partners, 325
Ralph Wilson Equity Fund, L.L.C., 460
Red River Ventures, 675
Reiten & Co Strategic Investments AS, 921
Richland Ventures, 652
RMB Ventures Limited, 921
Royal Bank Private Equity (FKA: Royal Bank Development Cap), 922
RoyNat Ventures, 923
S-Refit GmbH & Co KG , 923
Saarlandische Wagnisfinanzierungsgesellschaft mbh (AKA SWG), 924
Sand Aire Private Equity Ltd, 924
Sandton Financial Group, 240
Sanpaolo IMI Private Equity S.p.A., 925
Saugatuck Capital Company, 306
Schoffstall Ventures , 639
Schroder Capital Partners (Asia) Pte Ltd, 926
Scoot.com PLC, 926
Scottish Development Finance (SDF), 927
Scottish Equity Partners Limited, 927
Seaport Capital, 572
SEB e-invest, 927
SEB Foretagsinvest, 927
Shattan Group, The, 574
Shaw, Kwei & Partners Limited, 929
SI Ventures, 326
Siparex Group (FKA:Siparex Provinces de France), 931
SISIR International Pte Ltd., 932
Small Industries Development Bank of India (SIDBI), The, 933
Societe Generale- Private Equity Activity, 933
Societe Regionale d'Investissement de Bruxelles (SRIB/GIMB), 933
Sonera Corporation Corporate Venture Capital, 935
Sopartec SA, 936
South Atlantic Venture Funds, L.P., 327
Southeastern Technology Fund, 132
Southern Capitol Ventures, 605
Sovereign Capital (FKA:Nash, Sells & Partners Limited), 936
SpaceVest, 699
SPEF Banques Populaires, 937
Spinnaker Ventures, 249
Sprout Group, 578
SsangYong Cement (Singapore) Ltd, 939
SSM Ventures, 653
Stamford Financial, 579
Standard Life Investments (Private Equity) Ltd, 939
Star Capital Group, Inc., 939
Start-up Australia Pty Limited, 940
Sterling/Carl Marks Capital {FKA - Sterling Commercial, 580
Still River Fund, The, 450
StoneGate Partners, L.L.C., 450
Stratford Equity Partners, L.P., 679
Strathdon Investments Ltd, 942
Stratos Ventures Ltd Oy, 942
SudKB & SudVC, 942
Summit Capital Group, 680
Summit Group Ltd, The, 943
Sunsino Development Associate Inc., 944
Sustainable Jobs Fund (SJF), The , 606
Swedish Industrial Development Fund (AKA Industrifonden), 945
Sybase, Inc., 252
Sycamore Ventures, 494
Synergy Partners, 252
Synopsys, Inc., 253
Syntel Inc. Web Incubator Program, 461
Tailink Venture Partners, 946
Taiwan United Venture Management Corporation, 946
Taiwan W&S Financial Management Incorporated, 946
tbg Technologie-Beteiligungsgesellschaft mbH, 947
Teak Investment Partners I Limited, 948
Teak Investment Partners II Limited, 948
Techno Nord VC GmbH, 948
TechnoCap Inc, 949
Technology Associates Management Corporation, 950
Technology Venture Partners Pty Ltd, 950
Techpacific.com Ltd., 951
TecVenture Partners GmbH, 952
Teknia Invest Oy, 952
Telecom Venture Group Ltd. (TVG), 953
Telecommunications Development Fund (TDF), 316
TeleSoft Partners, 256
Telia Business Innovation AB, 953
Temasek Capital, 954
TG Asia Ventures Limited, 954
Thompson Clive & Partners Limited, 955
Toll Technologies, 957
Top Taiwan Venture Capital Company, Ltd., 957
Transpac Capital Pte, Ltd., 958
Tribune Ventures, 372

Trident Capital, 259
TTP Venture Managers (FKA: The Technology Partnership), 960
Twinning Ventures, 961
U.S. Bancorp Piper Jaffray Ventures, Inc., 472
UBF Mittelstandsfunanzierungs AG, 962
UBS Capital, 962
UBS Capital (AKA Phildrew Ventures), 963
Union Venture Capital Corporation, 963
UOB Venture Management Pte Ltd., 964
Value Management & Research AG (VMR), 965
VCF Partners, 965
Veneto Sviluppo S.p.a, 966
Venture Associates, Ltd., 285
Venture Capital Partners Pty Limited, 967
Venture Partners AG, 968
Venture Select, 968
VentureCap Management GmbH (AKA VCH Equity Group AG), 969
Virginia Capital , 701
Vision Capital Management (FKA Glenwood Capital), 267
Vital Capital Limited, 973
VIV NV (AKA Vlaamse Investeringvennootschap NV), 973
Viventures Inc., 973
Wachovia, 340
Walden Capital Management Corporation, 589
Walden Israel, 975
WaldenVC, 270
Warburg, Pincus & Co., LLC. (FKA: E.M. Warburg, Pincus & Co), 590
wellington partners venture capital GmbH, 975
West Midlands Enterprise Ltd, 976
WestBridge Capital Advisors (India) Pvt. Ltd., 976
White Pines Management, L.L.C., 462
Whitney & Co. (FKA: J.H. Whitney & Co.), 310
WI Harper Group, 273
Wind Point Partners, 462
Winslow Partners LLC, 317
WK Associates, 977
WL Ventures (FKA:Lothian Enterprise Ltd.), 978
Wolf Ventures (AKA:Wolf Asset Management Corp.), 286
Wooshin Development Finance Corp, 978
Working Ventures Canadian Fund, Inc., 978
Yasuda Enterprise Development Co., Ltd.(FKA: Nippon Ent.Dev), 275
Zero Gravity Internet Group, Inc. , 276
Zodiac Venture Capital KB, 980

First Stage Financing

21st Century Health Ventures, 129
21st Century Internet Management Partners,LLC, 138
2nd Generation Capital Corp, 648
3i Finland Oy (FKA SFK Finance), 725
3i Group plc, 726
3K Digital, 727
4C Ventures (FKA: Olivetti Holding, N.V.), 501
A.M. Pappas & Associates, 597
Abell Venture Fund, 390
Aberdare Ventures, 138
Aberlyn Capital Management Co., Inc., 501
Abingworth Venture Management Limited, 729
ABS Ventures, 390
Acacia Venture Partners, 139
Academy Funds (FKA: Longleaf Venture Fund LLC), 597
Access Venture Partners, 277
Acer Technology Ventures(FKA:Acer Soft Capital Inc.), 141
ACF Equity Atlantic, Inc, 731
Acorn Ventures, Inc., 141
Adams Capital Management, Inc., 622
Adler & Co., 502
Adler & Shaykin, 502
Advanced Materials Partners, Inc., 287
Advanced Technology Development Fund, 330
Advanced Technology Ventures, 401
Advantage Capital Partners, 386
Advent International Corp., 402
Advent-Morro Equity Partners, 734
Affinity Capital Management(FKA:Peterson-Spencer-Fansler Co), 463
Agribusiness Partners International Partners, 479
Alexander Hutton, Inc., 702
Alignment Capital Partners, LLC, 655
Alimansky Capital Group, Inc., 504
Allegra Partners (FKA: Lawrence, Smith & Horey), 504
Alliance Financial of Houston, 655
Alliance Technology Ventures, 330
Allsop Venture Partners, 380
Allstate Private Equity, 344
Alpha Capital Partners, Inc., 344
Alpine Technology Ventures, 144
Alta Communications, 403
Alta Partners, 144
Altamira Capital Corp., 739
Altos Ventures, 144
Amadeus Capital Partners, 740
American Research & Development Corp., 404
Ameritech Development Corp., 345
Ampersand Ventures, 404
Amphion Ventures L.P.(FKA: Wolfensohn Associates, L.P.), 506
AMT Capital Ltd. (AKA: AMT Venture Partners, Ltd.), 656
Antares Capital Corp. (FKA: Antares Leveraged Capital Corp), 345
Anthem Capital, L.P., 391
APIDC-Venture Capital Limited, 743
Applied Technology, 405
Arete Corporation, 482
Arkoma Venture Partners, 657
Artemis Ventures, 146
Arthur P. Gould & Co., 507
Arthur Rock & Co., 146
Ascent Venture Partners, 406
Asset Management Company Venture Capital, 147
Atlantic Capital, 407
Atlas Venture, 407
August Capital Management, 148
Aurora Funds, Inc., 598
Austin Ventures, L.P., 657
Australian Technology Group Ltd, 750
Authosis, 149
AV Labs, 658
Avery Business Development Services, 320
AVI Capital, L.P., 149
Aweida Ventures, 277
Ayala Internet Venture Partners, 751

BA Venture Partners (AKA: BankAmerica Ventures), 150
Baccharis Capital, Inc., 150
Bailey & Co. Inc., 752
BANEXI Corp., 753
Bank One Equity Investors, Inc., 386
Baring Private Equity Partners (FKA:Baring Venture Partners), 755
Battelle Venture Partners (Scientific Advances), 608
Batterson Venture Partners(AKA:BVP), 348
Battery Ventures, L.P., 409
Baxter Associates, Inc., 289
BCR Asset Management Pty Ltd., 758
Beacon Partners, Inc., 289
Bedford Capital Corp., 512
Beecken, Petty & Co. LLC, 348
Benchmark Capital, 154
Berwind Financial Group, L.P., 623
Bessemer Venture Partners, 410
Birchmere Ventures, Inc.(FKA:Birchmere Investments), 624
Bloom & Co., 512
Blue Chip Venture Company, 609
Blue Rock Capital, 319
BlueStar Ventures, 348
Blumberg Capital Ventures, 155
BOME Investors, Inc., 473
BORANCO Management, L.L.C., 277
Boston Capital Ventures, 411
Boston Financial & Equity Corp., 412
Boston Millennia Partners, 412
Boston University Community Technology Fund , 413
Botts & Co., 762
Boulder Ventures, Ltd., 392
Brand Equity Ventures, 289
Brantley Venture Partners, 609
Bristol Investment Trust, 413
British Steel Ltd., 764
Broadmark Capital Corp., 702
Brook Venture Management, L.L.C., 414
Bruce F. Glaspell & Associates, 498
Buena Venture Associates, 659
Burr, Egan, Deleage & Co., 414
Burrill & Company, 156
Business Link Doncaster, 765
Cable & Howse Ventures, 703
Calgary Enterprises, Inc., 514
Calvert Social Venture Partners, L.P., 690
Cambridge Samsung Partners, 415
Cambridge Technology Capital, 415
Canaan Partners, 290
Canbank Venture Capital Fund Ltd, 767
Capital Development & Investment Co. Ltd., 768
Capital Express, L.L.C., 484
Capital Insights, L.L.C., 645
Capital Investors, 690
Capital Network, The (AKA: Texas Capital Network), 659
Capital Southwest Corporation, 660
Capital Strategy Management Co., The, 349
Capstone Ventures SBIC, L.P., 158
Cardinal Partners (FKA: Cardinal Health Partners), 485
Cardinal Ventures, L.L.C., 375
Carolinas Capital Investment Corp., 599
Castile Ventures, 416
Castle Group, Ltd., The , 515
Catterton Partners, 290
CB Health Ventures LLC, 416
CD Technicom S.A., 774
CEI Ventures/Coastal Ventures LP, 388
CEO Advisors, 321
CEO Venture Fund, 625
Chanen, Painter & Co., Ltd., 703
Charles River Ventures, 417
Charter Ventures, 160
Chartwell Capital Management Co., Inc., 321
Chase H&Q (FKA Hambrecht & Quist), 160
Chestnut Street Partners, Inc., 417
Child Health Investment Corporation, 382
China Venture Management, Inc., 777
Chisholm Private Capital Partners, 618
Chrysalis Ventures, 384
CIBC Oppenheimer & Co., Inc., 516
CID Equity Partners, 376
CIT Group/Venture Capital, Inc., The, 485
Citizens Capital and Citizens Ventures, 418
Claflin Capital Management, Inc., 418
Clarion Capital Corp., 610
CM Equity Partners, 517
CMEA Ventures (FKA:Chemicals & Materials Enterprise Associa), 161
Cohen & Co., L.L.C., 517
Coleman Swenson Booth Inc.(FKA:Coleman Swenson Hoffman Booth, 649
Coleman Venture Group, 518
Collinson, Howe & Lennox, LLC, 291
Colorado Venture Management, 278
Columbia Capital Group, Inc., 313
Columbine Venture Funds, The , 279
Comdisco Ventures, 162
Commonwealth Capital Ventures L.P., 419
ComVentures (AKA: Communications Ventures), 163
Concord Venture Management (FKA:Nitzanim), 784
Connecticut Innovations, Inc., 291
Consumer Venture Partners, 292
Continental S.B.I.C., 691
Continental Venture Capital , 784
Convergence Partners L.P., 164
Copley Venture Partners, 420
Core Capital Partners, 313
Coronado Venture Fund, 133
Corporate Venture Partners, L.P., 519
Crescendo Venture Management LLC (FKA:IAI Ventures), 466
Crest Communications Holdings LLC, 520
Crestview Financial Group, The , 292
CrossBow Ventures, 322
Crown Capital Corp, 475
CS Capital Partners, LLC, 486
CSK Venture Capital Co., Ltd., 789
Cullinane & Donnelly Venture Partners, L.P., 293
Cureton & Co., Inc., 662
CW Group, Inc., 521
Cygnus Venture Partners, 791
Czech Venture Partners Sro, 791
D.H. Blair Investment Banking Corp., 521
Daewoo Venture Capital Co Ltd, 792
Daimler Chrysler Venture Gmbh (AKA DCV), 792
Dakota Group, The , 166

Dali, Hook Partners (FKA: Hook Partners), 662
Danish Development Finance Corp., 793
Dauphin Capital Partners, 522
Davis Group, 166
Davis, Tuttle Venture Partners, L.P.(FKA:Davis Venture), 618
Dean & Associates, 279
Defta Partners, 167
Delphi Ventures, 167
Deucalion Venture Partners, 168
Deutsche Bank eVentures (AKA DB eVentures), 795
Development Corp. of Austin, 467
Digital Partners, 704
Divine interVentures (FKA: Platinum Venture Partners), 351
Doll Capital Management, 169
Domain Associates, L.L.C., 486
Dongbu Venture Capital Co Ltd, 797
DotCom Ventures L.P., 171
Dougery Ventures, 171
Dow Chemical Co., 458
Downer & Co., 420
Draper Fisher Jurvetson (FKA: Draper Associates), 172
Draper Richards, 173
Drysdale Enterprises, 173
Duchossois TECnology Partners, LLC, 353
East River Ventures, L.P., 524
Easton Hunt Capital Partners, 525
ECICS Ventures Pte Ltd., 801
Edelson Technology Partners, 487
EDF Ventures (F.K.A. Enterprise Development Fund), 458
Edge Capital Investment Co., LLC, 175
El Dorado Ventures, 176
Emerald Venture Group, 177
EnCompass Ventures, 704
EnerTech Capital Partners, L.P., 626
Enterprise Equity (NI) Limited, 805
Enterprise Investors, 526
Equity Partners Management Pty Ltd, 807
Equity Ventures, Ltd, 807
Essex Woodlands Health Ventures (FKA:Woodlands Venture Partn, 354
ETCapital Ltd (AKA: Egan & Talbot Capital Ltd), 808
EuclidSR Partners , 527
European Acquisition Capital Ltd., 810
Evanston Business Investment Corp, 354
eVerger Associates, 812
Evergreen Canada Israel Investments Ltd, 812
Evergreen Capital Partners Inc, 528
Exponential Business Development Co., 529
Fairfax Partners, 693
Far East Capital Corp., 179
FBR CoMotion Venture Capital, 705
FBR Technology Venture Partners,L.P.(AKA:Friedman,Billings), 693
Federal Business Development Bank, 815
Fidelity Ventures (FKA: Fidelity Venture Associates), 421
Financial Technology Research Corp., 529
Firemark Advisors, Inc., 488
First Capital Management Co., 664
First Princeton Capital Corp., 489
First Union Capital Partners, 600
Florida Capital Ventures, Ltd., 323
Fluke Venture Partners., 705
Fond Riziveho Kapitalu SRO, 819
Fonds D'Investissements R.T.V.L., 819
Fonds de Solidarité des Travailleurs du Québec (F.T.Q.), 820
Food Fund Ltd. Partnership, The, 467
ForetagsByggarna AB, 821
Forrest Binkley & Brown, 180
Forward Ventures, 180
Foundation Capital, 181
Foundation Capital Limited, 822
Fowler, Anthony & Co., 422
Frazier & Company, 705
Frederic H. Mayerson Group, The, 612
Friulia SpA Fin.Reg.Friuli-Venezia, 824
Frontenac Co., 355
Frontline Capital, Inc., 334
Fusient Ventures, 531
Future Value Ventures, Inc., 717
G-51 Capital LLC, 665
Gabelli Multimedia Partners, 531
Gabriel Venture Partners, 182
Gamma Investors LLC, 627
Gateway Associates, L.P., 476
GATX Ventures (FKA: Meier Mitchell & Co.), 183
GATX/MM Venture Partners, 183
GCI, 718
GCI Venture Partners, 314
Generation Capital Partners, 532
GENES GmbH Venture Services, 826
Geocapital Partners, L.L.C., 489
Gideon Hixon Fund, 467
Gilde Investment Management, 827
Giza Venture Capital (FKA Giza Investment Management), 828
Global Crossing Ventures (FKA: Frontier Ventures), 185
Global Partner Ventures, 694
Global Retail Partners (A.K.A. GRP), 185
Glynn Ventures, 186
Granite Ventures LLC (FKA: H & Q Venture Associates), 186
Grayson & Associates, 280
Greater Philadelphia Venture Capital Corp., 627
Greenwich Venture Partners, Inc., 296
Gresham Rabo Management Limited, 832
Greylock, 424
Grieve, Horner, Brown & Asculai, 833
Grotech Capital Group, 394
Grove Street Advisors, LLC, 425
GrowthWorks Capital, 834
Gryphon Ventures, 425
H&Q Asia Pacific, Ltd., 187
Hallador Venture Partners, 188
Halpern, Denny & Co., 425
Hambro America Biosciences, Inc., 535
Hanbyuck Investment Co Ltd, 836
Harbour Financial Co., 426
HarbourVest Partners, LLC., 426
Health Capital Group, 188
Healthcare Ventures LLC (FKA: Healthcare Investments), 490
Heartland Capital Fund, Ltd., 479
Henry & Co., 323
Herbert Young Securities, Inc., 536
Hickory Venture Capital Corporation, 130
Highland Capital Partners, 427
HillStreet Capital, Inc., 612

HMS Hawaii Management Partners, 341
HO2 Partners LLC, 665
Hodgson Martin, Ltd., 839
Hollinger Capital (FKA: Hollinger Ventures), 537
Horizon Ventures (F.K.A. Technology Investments), 190
Houston Venture Partners (AKA: Houston Partners), 666
HT Capital Advisors, LLC, 538
Hudson Venture Partners, 538
Humana Venture Capital, 384
Hummer Winblad Venture Partners, 191
Hunt Capital Group, 667
Hydro-Quebec CapiTech Inc., 843
Idanta Partners, Ltd., 191
IDG Ventures, 192
IEG Venture Management, Inc., 357
IFCI Venture Cap. Funds (Formerly Risk Capital & Tech.), 847
Impex Venture Management Co., 540
Incorporated Investors, 193
Indekon Management Oy, 849
Indian Direct Equity Advisors Pvt. Ltd, 850
Indosuez Ventures, 194
Industrial Technology Securities Ltd, 851
Industry Ventures , 428
Inman & Bowman, 195
InnoCal, L.P., 196
Innova Capital (FKA: Poland Partners Management Company), 853
Innovacom, 853
Innovation Works, Inc., 628
Innovationsagentur Gesmbh, 854
InnovationsKapital Management Goteborg AB , 854
Innovest Group, Inc., 629
Innvotec Ltd, 854
Institutional Venture Partners, 196
Insurance Venture Partners, Inc., 297
Integrated Consortium, Inc., 197
InterEquity Capital Partners, L.P., 541
Intersouth Partners, 601
InterWest Partners, 197
InvestAmerica Venture Group, Inc., 380
Investissement Desjardins, 857
Investissements Novacap (AKA:Novacap Investments, Inc.), 858
Irwin Ventures LLC (FKA: Irwin Ventures Incorporated), 377
ISEP NV, 860
J.E. Mann & Co., 542
J.L. Albright Venture Partners, 861
JAFCO Ventures, Inc., 198
James B. Kobak & Co., 297
JK&B Capital, 358
Josephberg Grosz & Co., Inc., 545
Justsystem, Inc., 629
Kaiser Permanente (AKA: National Venture Development), 200
Kankaku Investment Co Ltd, 865
Kansas Venture Capital, Inc., 383
KB Partners, LLC, 359
KBL Healthcare Ventures, 546
Kemper Ventures, 491
Kettle Partners, L.P., 359
Keystone Minority Capital Fund, L.P., 630
Keystone Venture Capital Management Co., 630
Kidd, Kamm & Company, 298
Kinetic Ventures, Inc., 395
Kingsbury Associates, 200
Kinship Partners, 280
Kirlan Venture Capital, Inc., 707
Kitty Hawk Capital, 602
Kleiner Perkins Caufield & Byers, 200
Korda & Co., 868
Korea Development Investment Corp., 868
KTB Ventures (FKA: KTB Venture Capital), 202
Lake Shore Capital Partners, Inc., 360
Lambda Funds, The, 546
Landmark Partners, Inc., 298
Las Americas Administradora, 871
Lazard Technology Partners, 547
Lee Munder Venture Partners, 430
Leonard Mautner Associates, 203
LF International, Inc., 204
Liberty Environmental Partners, 205
Lighthouse Capital Partners, 205
LINC Capital Partners, Inc., 361
LiveOak Equity Partners, 335
Livingston Capital, Ltd., 281
LJH Global Investments , 324
Loyalhanna Venture Fund, 631
LTI Ventures Leasing Corp., 298
Lucent Venture Partners, Inc., 207
Lycos Ventures, 632
M&F Associates, L.P., 549
Magic Venture Capital, LLC, 208
Malmohus Invest AB, 877
Manhattan Venture Co., Inc., 550
Marconi Ventures, 431
Maristeth Ventures, L.L.C., 707
MarketCorp Ventures L.P., 299
Marquette Venture Partners, 362
Maryland Venture Capital Trust, 395
Massey Burch Capital Corp., 650
Materia Ventures Associates,L.P. (FKA:Pierce Nordquist Asso), 708
Maton Venture, 209
Matrix Capital, 695
Matrix Partners, 433
Mayfield Fund, 210
MBA Venture Group, 669
MBW Management, Inc., 492
MC Capital, Inc., 551
McLean Watson Capital Inc., 880
MDS Discovery Venture Management, Inc., 881
Med-Tech Ventures, Inc., 492
Media Venture Partners, 211
Medical Innovation Partners, 469
Medical Science Partners, 434
Medical Venture Holdings, Inc., 552
Medmax Ventures, L.P., 299
MedTech International, Inc., 670
MedVenture Associates, 212
Mees Pierson Investeringsmaat. B.V., 435
Menlo Ventures, 212
Merita Capital Limited, 134
Meritage Private Equity Fund, 281
Merrill, Pickard, Anderson & Eyre, 213
Meyer, Duffy & Associates, 553
Microtechnology Investments, Ltd., 213

Mid-Atlantic Venture Funds (FKA: NEPA Management Corp.), 634
Millennium Three Venture Group, L.L.C., 480
Miller Capital Corp, 135
Miralta Capital, Inc., 887
Mission Ventures, 214
Mitsui & Co., Ltd., 553
MK Global Ventures, 214
Montgomerie, Huck & Co., 888
Montgomery Associates, Inc., 215
Montgomery Medical Ventures, L.P., 215
Montreux Equity Partners, 216
Moore & Associates, 619
Moore Capital Management Inc., 554
Morgenthaler Ventures, 614
Motorola Inc., 315
Mountaineer Capital LP, 716
MPM Capital (FKA - MPM Asset Management LLC), 436
MTI Partners Ltd, 890
Murphree Venture Partners, 671
Mustang Ventures (FKA Siemens Mustang Ventures), 216
MVP Ventures (AKA: Milk Street Ventures), 436
National Bank Of Kuwait, 555
Native Venture Capital Co., Ltd., 893
Natural Gas Partners, 300
Nazem & Co., 556
Nelson Capital Corp., 651
New Business Capital Fund Ltd., 499
New England Partners, 437
New Enterprise Associates, 396
New Things, LLC, 557
New Vista Capital, LLC, 218
New York Life Venture Capital Group, 557
New York State Science & Technology Foundation, 558
Newbury Ventures, 220
Newtek Ventures, 220
NextGen Capital LLC, 697
NextGen Partners LLC, 221
NextPoint Partners L.P.(FKA: Plaza Street), 315
NIF Ventures USA, Inc.(Nippon Investment & Finance Co., Ltd), 222
Nikko Capital Co Ltd, 899
Nokia Venture Partners (AKA: Nokia Oy), 222
Nomura/JAFCO Investment (HK) Limited, 901
Noro-Moseley Partners, 336
North Atlantic Capital Corp., 389
North Bridge Venture Partners, 438
North Carolina Enterprise Fund, L.P., The, 602
North Carolina Technological Development Authority, Inc., 603
Northeast Ventures Corp., 469
Northern Venture Managers Limited, 902
Northwest Ohio Venture Fund, 615
Northwest Venture Associates, Inc.(FKA:Spokane Capital Mgmt), 709
Northwood Ventures, 559
Noveltek Venture Corp., 560
Novus Ventures, 223
NPV Capital Partners, LLC, 560
NTC Group, The , 301
Nth Power Technologies, Inc, 224
Nu Capital Access Group, Ltd., 224
Oak Investment Partners, 302
Odin Capital Group, 479
Ohana Ventures, LLC, 615
Ohio Partners, 615
OmniMed Corp., 673
Oresa Ventures, S.A., 906
Orien Ventures, 303
Orion Partners, L.P., 439
Oxford Bioscience Partners, 440
Oxford Financial Services Corp., 698
PA Early Stage (AKA:Pennsylvania Early Stage Partners), 635
Pacific Northwest Partners SBIC, L.P., 710
Pacific Venture Group, 227
Pacifica Fund , 228
Paladin Partners, 711
Palmer Partners, L.P., 441
Palmetto Seed Capital Corp., 645
Palomar Ventures, 228
Pappajohn Capital Resources, 381
Paradigm Capital Partners LLC, 651
Paragon Venture Partners, 229
Partech International, 229
Pathfinder Venture Capital Funds, 470
Patricof & Co. Ventures, Inc., 563
Pequot Capital Management Inc., 564
Perennial Ventures (FKA: Tredegar Investments), 711
Philadelphia Ventures, Inc., 636
Phillips-Smith Specialty Retail Group, 673
Phoenix Growth Capital Corp., 231
Phoenix Home Life Mutual Insurance Co., 303
Phoenix Partners, The , 711
Pittsford Group, Inc., The , 565
Platinum Group, Inc., The , 565
Point Venture Partners, 636
Polaris Venture Partners, 441
Polestar Capital, Inc., 366
Poly Ventures, 566
Prelude Technology Investments Ltd, 915
Premier Medical Partner Fund L.P., 231
Prime Capital Management Co., Inc., 304
Primedia Ventures, 567
Prince Ventures, 367
Prism Capital, 367
Private Capital Corp., 131
Productivity Fund I & II, The, 367
ProQuest Investments, L.P., 493
Prospect Street Ventures (FKA:Prospect Street Invest. Mgmt), 567
Provco Group, The , 637
Putnam Lovell Capital Partners, L.P., 232
Pythagoras NV, 919
Quest Ventures, 233
Quester Capital Management Ltd, 920
RAF Ventures, 637
Ralph Wilson Equity Fund, L.L.C., 460
Raza Foundries, 233
Redleaf Venture Management, 234
Redwood Capital Corp., 235
Richard Jaffe & Co., Inc., 676
Richland Ventures, 652
Ridgewood Capital Management LLC, 494
Riordan, Lewis & Haden, 236
Robertson Stephens & Company, LLC, 236
Rock Hill Ventures Inc.(FKA:Hillman Medical Ventures,Inc.), 638

Rothschild Bioscience Unit, 922
Rothschild Ventures Asia Pte Ltd., 922
Rothschild Ventures, Inc., 570
Royalty Capital Fund, L.P. I/Royalty Capital Management, Inc, 443
RRE Ventures LLC, 571
Ruddick Investment Co., 604
RWI Group, LP, 239
S.R. One, Limited, 638
SAE Ventures, 306
Saffron Hill Ventures (FKA LootLab Ltd.), 924
Sage Management Group, 444
Sandler Capital Management, 571
Sandlot Capital LLC, 283
Sandton Financial Group, 240
Sapient Capital, 721
Saskatchewan Government Growth Fund, 925
SBC Ventures, 499
SBCA/A.G. Bartholomew & Associates, 131
SBV Venture Partners (AKA:Sigefi, Burnette & Vallee), 240
Schneider Electric Ventures, 926
Schooner Capital International, L.P., 444
Schroder Ventures, 445
Scripps Ventures, 572
Seaflower Ventures, 446
Seed Company Partners, 676
Selby Venture Partners, 241
Sequoia Capital, 241
Sevin Rosen Management Co., 677
Shad Run Investments, Inc., 242
Shalor Ventures, Inc., 446
Shannon Development Company, 929
Shared Ventures, Inc., 470
Shaw Venture Partners (FKA: Shaw Glasgow Partners), 621
Shawmut Capital Partners, 447
Shepherd Group LLC, The, 447
Sherbrooke Capital Partners, 448
Shott Capital Management, 574
Sienna Ventures (FKA: Sienna Holdings Inc.), 242
Sierra Ventures, 243
Sigma Partners, 243
Siguler Guff & Company, LLC, 575
Silicon Valley Bank, 244
Silver Creek Technology Investors (FKA: O'Donnell & Masur), 677
Sitra (AKA Finnish National Fund for Research and Dev.), 932
Societe Regionale d'Investissement de Bruxelles (SRIB/GIMB), 933
Sofinnova Ventures, 246
SOFTBANK Capital Partners, 448
SOFTBANK Venture Capital (FKA: SOFTBANK Technology Ventures), 247
Sorrento Associates, Inc., 247
South Atlantic Venture Funds, L.P., 327
Southeast Interactive Technology Funds, 605
Southeastern Technology Fund, 132
Southern California Ventures, 247
Southwest Venture Group, 678
Southwest Venture Partnerships, The, 678
Sovereign Capital (FKA:Nash, Sells & Partners Limited), 936
SpaceVest, 699
Speirs Consultants, Inc., 938
Spencer Trask Ventures, Inc. (FKA: Spencer Trask Securities), 576
Spire Capital (FKA: Waller Capital Corp.), 577
Sponsored Consulting Services, 249
Spray Venture Partners, 450
SRK Management Co., 578
SsangYong Cement (Singapore) Ltd, 939
Sterling Grace Capital Management, L.P., 579
Still River Fund, The, 450
Suez Asia Holdings Pte Ltd., 943
Summit Capital Associates, Inc., 581
Summit Partners, 451
Sundance Venture Partners, L.P., 251
Sutter Hill Ventures, 251
Sweeney & Co., Inc., 308
Sybase, Inc., 252
Sycamore Ventures, 494
Synopsys, Inc., 253
Tailink Venture Partners, 946
Taylor & Turner, 253
TDH, 639
Techno-Venture Co. (Japan), 949
Technologieholding VC GmbH, 950
Technology Crossover Ventures, 254
Technology Funding, 254
Technology Partners, 255
Technology Venture Partners Pty Ltd, 950
Technology Ventures Corp., 500
Techxas Ventures, LLC, 681
Teknoinvest Management As, 952
Telos Venture Partners, 256
Telsoft Ventures, 953
THCG Inc., 582
Third Millennium Venture Capital, Ltd., 256
Thompson Clive, Inc., 257
Thorner Ventures, 258
Three Arch Partners, 258
Tianguis Ltd, 956
Tokyo Small & Medium Business Investment & Consultation Co., 956
Transamerica Mezzanine Financing, 645
Transamerica Technology Finance, 309
Transatlantic Capital Ltd., 958
Trellis Partners, 682
Triad Investors Corp, 319
Triad Ventures, Ltd., 682
Tribune Ventures, 372
Trident Capital, 259
Triune Capital, 260
TTC Ventures, 453
TVM Techno Venture Management, 961
U.S. Medical Resources Corp., 616
U.S. Venture Partners, 261
UPS Strategic Enterprise Fund, 339
US Trust Private Equity, 584
UST Capital Corp., 454
Vanguard Venture Partners, 262
VantagePoint Venture Partners, 263
VCM Venture Capital Management, 965
Venca Management, 263
Vencap Equities Alberta, Ltd., 966
Vencon Management, Inc., 585
VenGlobal Capital, 264

Venrock Associates, 586
Ventana Financial Resources, Inc., 372
Ventana Global, 264
Venture Associates, Ltd., 285
Venture Capital Fund of New England, The, 454
Venture Capital Management Corp., 328
Venture Capital Partners Pty Limited, 967
Venture First Associates, 328
Venture Funding Group International, 587
Venture Growth Associates, 265
Venture Investment Management Company LLC (AKA: VIMAC), 454
Venture Investors Management LLC, 720
Venture Management Services Inc. (FKA: AT&T Ventures), 496
Venture Opportunities Corp., 588
Venture Partners, 310
Venture Select, 968
Venture Strategy Partners, 266
Ventures West Management, Inc., 970
Vertex Management, 971
Vertical Group, The, 496
Victory Ventures L.L.C., 588
Vision Capital Management (FKA Glenwood Capital), 267
Vista Capital Corp., 268
Vlaamse Investeringvennootschap NV, 974
Voyager Capital, 714
Wachtel & Co., Inc., 317
Walden International Investment Group (AKA: Walden Group), 269
Walden Israel, 975
Walnut Capital Corp., 701
Warburg, Pincus & Co., LLC. (FKA: E.M. Warburg, Pincus & Co), 590
Wasserstein, Perella & Co., Inc., 591
Wellmax, Inc., 461
Western States Investment Group, 272
Western Technology Investment, 272
Westford Technology Ventures, L.P., 497
William Blair Capital Partners, 373
Winthrop Ventures, 593
Wolf Ventures (AKA:Wolf Asset Management Corp.), 286
Women's Growth Capital Fund, 318
Woodside Fund, 274
Working Ventures Canadian Fund, Inc., 978
Worldview Technology Partners, 275
YankeeTek Ventures, 456
Yasuda Enterprise Development Co., Ltd.(FKA: Nippon Ent.Dev), 275
Zero Stage Capital Co., Inc., 456

Fund of Funds

Abbott Capital Management, 501
Aberdeen Murray Johnstone Private Equity, 728
ABN AMRO Private Equity (AKA: ABN AMRO Capital (USA) Inc.) , 343
Access Capital Partners, 730
Adams Street Partners, LLC (FKA: Brinson Private Equity), 343
Adveq Management AG (FKA Advisers on Private Equity AG), 734
AIG Capital Partners Inc., 503
Alignment Capital Partners, LLC, 655
AXA Investment Managers, 509
Champion Ventures, 159
CIBC Oppenheimer & Co., Inc., 516
Commerz Beteiligungsgesellschaft mbH (CBG), 783
Continental S.B.I.C., 691
Creafund CVBA, 788
Fondinvest (Grp. Caisse de Depots), 819
Fort Washington Capital Partners, LLC, 611
GENES GmbH Venture Services, 826
Gimvindus NV, 828
HarbourVest Partners, LLC., 426
Koor Corporate Venture Capital, 868
Kreditanstalt fur Wiederaufbau (KfW), 870
Landmark Partners, Inc., 298
Macquarie Investment Management Ltd (MIML), 876
MC Capital, Inc., 551
Mercantile Mutual Investment Management Limited, 883
Mesirow Private Equity Investments, Inc., 362
Nantucket Capital Management, 459
National Bank Of Kuwait, 555
Nomura International, Plc., 900
Pacific Corporate Group, Inc., 227
Pantheon Ventures Limited, 908
Parcom Ventures BV, 909
Partners Group, 910
Poalim Capital Markets Technologies, Ltd., 913
Pomona Capital, 566
Quaestus & Co. Inc. (FKA: Quaestus Management Corp..), 719
Salomon Smith Barney Venture Services LLC, 571
Sonera Corporation Corporate Venture Capital, 935
Strategic Investment Management, 700
Venture Investment Associates, 495
VIV NV (AKA Vlaamse Investeringvennootschap NV), 973
Zurich Scudder Investments (FKA: Scudder Kemper Investments), 596

Fund of Funds of Second

Fondinvest (Grp. Caisse de Depots), 819
Glenmede Trust Company, 490

Generalist PE

Abbott Capital Management, 501
Aberdeen Murray Johnstone Private Equity, 728
Advent-Morro Equity Partners, 734
AIG Capital Partners Inc., 503
Apax Partners & Co. Ventures Ltd (AKA: Apax UK), 742
Baird Capital Partners, 347
BancAmerica Capital Investors (FKA:NationsBanc Capital Corp), 598
BancBoston Capital/BancBoston Ventures, 408
Berenberg Private Equity GmbH, 759
Bridgepoint Capital Ltd (FKA: NWEP & NatWest Ventures Ltd), 763
C3 Holdings, LLC, 474
Camelot Ventures, 457
Capital Resource Partners, 415
Capital Strategy Management Co., The, 349
CCFL Mezzanine Partners of Canada , 774
CEI Ventures/Coastal Ventures LP, 388
CIVC Partners (FKA:Continental Illinois Venture Corp.), 350

Continental Venture Capital , 784
Crosbie & Co Inc, 789
Desai Capital Management Inc., 522
Dorset Capital, 170
Evergreen Capital Partners Inc, 528
Financial Technology Ventures, 179
Fonds de Solidarité des Travailleurs du Québec (F.T.Q.), 820
Forrest Binkley & Brown, 180
Fowler, Anthony & Co., 422
Harbert Management Corp., 130
HarbourVest Partners, LLC., 426
High Street Capital, LLC, 357
Hunt Capital Group, 667
Invision AG (FKA Aureus Private Equity AG), 858
Josephberg Grosz & Co., Inc., 545
Madison Dearborn Partners, LLC, 361
MC Capital, Inc., 551
MCH Private Equity SA, 880
Mentor Capital Partners, 633
Merifin Capital Group, 883
Merita Capital Ltd, 884
National Bank Of Kuwait, 555
National City Equity Partners, Inc, 614
Nmas1 Electra Capital Privado , S.G.E.C.R., S.A., 900
Northwood Ventures, 559
Oak Investment Partners, 302
PAMA Group Inc. (FKA:Prudential Asset Management Asia), 908
Paul Capital Partners, 230
Penfund Partners, Inc., 911
Providence Equity Partners, Inc.(FKA: Providence Ventures), 643
Quadriga Capital Management GMBH, 919
River Associates, LLC, 653
Sanpaolo IMI Private Equity S.p.A., 925
SEB Foretagsinvest, 927
Sports Capital Partners, 577
Summit Capital Group, 680
Walden Capital Management Corporation, 589
Warburg, Pincus & Co., LLC. (FKA: E.M. Warburg, Pincus & Co), 590
Wind Point Partners, 462

Industry Rollups

2nd Generation Capital Corp, 648
Advent International Corp., 402
Agio Capital Partners I, L.P., 463
Allsop Venture Partners, 380
American Capital Strategies, 391
American Securities, L.P., 505
Ardsheil, Inc., 506
Argus Capital Group, 745
August Partners, 508
Banc One Capital Partners, 608
Bedford Capital Corp., 512
Berwind Financial Group, L.P., 623
Brantley Venture Partners, 609
Candover Investments PLC, 768
Cedar Creek Partners, LLC, 717
CID Equity Partners, 376
CM Equity Partners, 517
Crest Communications Holdings LLC, 520
Crown Advisors International, Ltd., 521
ECI Ventures Ltd, 801
EGL Holdings, Inc./Nat West Ventures USA, L.P., 332
Electra Fleming Limited, 525
Eos Partners, L.P., 527
Fairfax Partners, 693
Ferrer Freeman Thompson & Co, 295
Frazier & Company, 705
Frontenac Co., 355
Gemini Investors LLC (AKA: GMN Investors), 423
Heritage Partners, 427
Hoak Capital Corp., 666
Incorporated Investors, 193
Innova Capital (FKA: Poland Partners Management Company), 853
Integrated Consortium, Inc., 197
Interregnum, 856
Kahala Investments, Inc., 668
Key Equity Capital Corp.(AKA:Key Community Development Corp), 613
Levine Leichtman Capital Partners, Inc., 204
LF International, Inc., 204
Livingston Capital, Ltd., 281
Lombard Investments, Inc., 206
Madison Investment Partners, Inc., 550
Management Resource Partners, 208
Mezzanine Management UK Limited, 885
Middlefield Capital Fund, 885
Morgan Grenfell Private Equity Limited, 889
Morgan Stanley Venture Partners (AKA: MSDW), 554
Newbury, Piret & Co., Inc., 437
North American Business Development Co., L.L.C., 364
Nu Capital Access Group, Ltd., 224
Opportunity Capital Partners {FKA: Thompson Capital Mgt), 225
Peninsula Capital Partners, L.L.C, 460
Pfingsten Partners, L.P., 366
Phillips-Smith Specialty Retail Group, 673
Private Equity Partners, 674
Priveq Capital Funds, 917
Prospect Partners LLC (FKA:Kenter, Glatris & Tuttle, LLC, 368
R-H Capital Partners, 337
RFE Investment Partners, 305
Rice, Sangalis, Toole & Wilson (FKA: Rice Capital Partners), 675
Rosenfeld & Co., 620
Rutledge & Co., Inc., 305
Seacoast Capital, 446
Sentinel Capital Partners, 573
SGI Capital L.L.C, 573
Shawmut Capital Partners, 447
Sherbrooke Capital Partners, 448
Speirs Consultants, Inc., 938
Spencer Trask Ventures, Inc. (FKA: Spencer Trask Securities), 576
Spring Capital Partners, L.P., 398
Stephens Group, Inc., 137
Summit Capital Associates, Inc., 581
Sycamore Ventures, 494
UniRock Management Corp., 285
Venture Funding Group International, 587
VTC Partners GmbH, 974
Westar Capital, 271
Willis Stein & Partners, 374

Joint Ventures
Ampersand Ventures, 404
antfactory, 741
Argus Capital Group, 745
Capital Strategy Management Co., The, 349
Connecticut Innovations, Inc., 291
Continental S.B.I.C., 691
Fonds de Solidarité des Travailleurs du Québec (F.T.Q.), 820
GrowthWorks Capital, 834
HarbourVest Partners, LLC., 426
Josephberg Grosz & Co., Inc., 545
Kaiser Permanente (AKA: National Venture Development), 200
Kansas City Equity Partners, 477
MC Capital, Inc., 551
Newbridge Capital Limited, 219
Pacific Corporate Group, Inc., 227
Quaestus & Co. Inc. (FKA: Quaestus Management Corp..), 719
Sonera Corporation Corporate Venture Capital, 935
Technology Partners, 255
Techxas Ventures, LLC, 681

Later Stage
A.M. Pappas & Associates, 597
Accenture Technology Ventures (FKA: AC Ventures), 140
Access Capital Partners, 730
Adams Street Partners, LLC (FKA: Brinson Private Equity), 343
ADD Partners , 733
Advent-Morro Equity Partners, 734
Alliance Investment Capital, 737
Alta Communications, 403
Altos Ventures, 144
Ampersand Ventures, 404
Annapolis Ventures LLC, 391
Antares Capital Corporation (FKA: Harbor Ventures Corp.), 320
APC Asset Management, 743
Argos Soditic SA, 744
Argosy Partners, 623
Atila Venture Partners Ltd., 749
Axiom Venture Partners, L.P., 288
Ayala Internet Venture Partners, 751
Baird Capital Partners, 347
BaltCap Management, Ltd, 753
BancBoston Capital/BancBoston Ventures, 408
Bank Funds, The, 347
BCR Asset Management Pty Ltd., 758
Beecken, Petty & Co. LLC, 348
Berthel Fisher & Company Planning, Inc., 380
Birchmere Ventures, Inc.(FKA:Birchmere Investments), 624
BrainWorks Ventures, 330
Brait Capital Partners, 762
British Steel Ltd., 764
Bruce F. Glaspell & Associates, 498
C3 Holdings, LLC, 474
C3 Investments, Inc., 157
Calgary Enterprises, Inc., 514
Cambridge Technology Capital, 415
Camden Partners, Inc. (FKA: Cahill, Warnock & Co., L.L.C.), 393
Camelot Ventures, 457
Canbank Venture Capital Fund Ltd, 767
Capital For Business, Inc., 474
Capital for Companies (CfC), 769
Capital Resource Partners, 415
Capital Southwest Corporation, 660
Capital Strategy Management Co., The, 349
Capital Z Asia, 770
Capricorn Ventures International, 770
CapVest Management, Ltd, 771
Carousel Capital Partners, 599
Catalyst Fund Management & Research Ltd, 773
Cazenove Private Equity, 773
CEI Ventures/Coastal Ventures LP, 388
Charter Growth Capital, 160
Citizens Capital and Citizens Ventures, 418
CIVC Partners (FKA:Continental Illinois Venture Corp.), 350
Clairvest Group, Inc., 780
Classic Fund Management, Ltd., 781
Clearstone Venture Partners (FKA: idealab! Capital Partners), 161
Close Brothers Private Equity, 782
CMB Capital, LLC (CMBC), 322
CMEA Ventures (FKA:Chemicals & Materials Enterprise Associa), 161
Conning Capital Partners, 292
Continental Venture Capital , 784
CORAL Ventures, 465
Cordova Ventures (FKA:Cordova Capital), 331
Core Capital Partners, 313
Crest Communications Holdings LLC, 520
Crosbie & Co Inc, 789
Crosslink Capital (FKA: Omega Venture Partners), 165
Dauphin Capital Partners, 522
De Vries & Co., Inc., 476
DFW Capital Partners (AKA:DeMuth, Folger & Wetherill), 486
Dolphin Communications, 523
Domain Associates, L.L.C., 486
Dorset Capital, 170
DSE Investment Services Limited, 799
Earlybird Venture Capital, 800
EDF Ventures (F.K.A. Enterprise Development Fund), 458
Edge Capital Investment Co., LLC, 175
Edison Venture Fund, 488
Eficor Oyj, 803
EnerTech Capital Partners, L.P., 626
Equinox Investment Partners, 294
European Equity Partners , 810
Evergreen Capital Partners Inc, 528
Ferrer Freeman Thompson & Co, 295
Financial Technology Ventures, 179
First Analysis Venture Capital (FKA:First Analysis Corp), 354
First Union Capital Partners, 600
Flinders Capital Limited, 818
Fluke Venture Partners., 705
Fonds de Solidarité des Travailleurs du Québec (F.T.Q.), 820
Fortune Consulting Group Incorporated, 821
Fortune Venture Management Pte Ltd., 822
Forward Ventures, 180
Fowler, Anthony & Co., 422
Gazelle TechVentures, 377
GENES GmbH Venture Services, 826
Genesis Partners, 826
GKM Venture Partners, LP, 184
Global Technology Ventures (GTV), 829
Grosvenor Funds, The, 315
GrowthWorks Capital, 834

H&Q Asia Pacific, Ltd., 187
Hamilton Portfolio, Ltd., 836
HarbourVest Partners, LLC., 426
Healthcare Ventures LLC (FKA: Healthcare Investments), 490
Hickory Venture Capital Corporation, 130
Hollinger Capital (FKA: Hollinger Ventures), 537
Housatonic Partners, 190
Hunt Capital Group, 667
i2s PLC (FKA: Tarpan PLC), 843
IDG Ventures, 192
Ignite Associates, LLC, 192
Index Ventures, 850
Inroads Capital Partners, L.P., 358
InterWest Partners, 197
J.P. Morgan Partners (FKA: Chase Capital Partners), 543
JK&B Capital, 358
Josephberg Grosz & Co., Inc., 545
KBL Healthcare Ventures, 546
Kline Hawkes & Co., 201
KLM Capital Group, 201
Lee Munder Venture Partners, 430
Life Sciences Partners BV, 874
Lightspeed Venture Partners (FKA: Weiss, Peck & Greer), 206
Lovett Miller & Co. Incorporated, 325
LTI Ventures Leasing Corp., 298
M31 Ventures, LLC, 550
Macquarie Direct Investment Limited, 876
Madison Dearborn Partners, LLC, 361
Magnum Communications (AKA: MCF Advisory Services Ltd), 877
Marconi Ventures, 431
MC Capital, Inc., 551
McGraw-Hill Ventures, 552
MDS Health Ventures, Inc. (AKA: MDS Capital Corp.), 881
Medicon Valley Capital, 882
Menlo Ventures, 212
Mentor Capital Partners, 633
Meritage Private Equity Fund, 281
Mission Ventures, 214
Mosaix Ventures, LLC , 363
Mountaineer Capital LP, 716
Mustang Ventures (FKA Siemens Mustang Ventures), 216
MWV Capital Partners (FKA:Middlewest Ventures, L.P.), 378
National Bank Of Kuwait, 555
National City Equity Partners, Inc, 614
Navis Partners (FKA:Fleet Equity Partners), 643
Needham & Company, Inc., 556
Newbridge Capital Limited, 219
Newport Capital Group Pty Ltd, 897
Nomura International, Plc., 900
North Hill Ventures, 438
Northern Stream Capital, 709
Northwood Ventures, 559
Norwest Equity Partners, 223
Oak Investment Partners, 302
Oberlin Capital, L.P., 603
Odlander Fredrikson & Co, 904
Onondaga Venture Capital Fund, Inc., 562
Opportunity Capital Partners {FKA: Thompson Capital Mgt), 225
Oracle Corporation, 226
Pacific Asset Partners, 226
Pacific Corporate Group, Inc., 227
Pacific Equity Partners, 907
PAMA Group Inc. (FKA:Prudential Asset Management Asia), 908
Partech International, 229
Penta Capital Partners Ltd, 911
Pequot Capital Management Inc., 564
Petra Capital Partners LLC, 652
Polaris Venture Capital, 913
Pomona Capital, 566
pre-IPO Aktiengesellschaft, 915
ProQuest Investments, L.P., 493
Putnam Lovell Capital Partners, L.P., 232
Quantum Capital Partners, 325
QuestMark Partners, L.P., 397
Raza Foundries, 233
RHO Management, 570
Rock Creek Partners, L.P., 326
Royal Bank Private Equity (FKA: Royal Bank Development Cap), 922
S.R. One, Limited, 638
Saugatuck Capital Company, 306
Seaport Capital, 572
Seidman, Jackson, Fisher & Co., 369
Shaw, Kwei & Partners Limited, 929
Solera Capital LLC, 576
Southern Capitol Ventures, 605
Sovereign Capital (FKA:Nash, Sells & Partners Limited), 936
SpaceVest, 699
Spring Capital Partners, L.P., 398
Sprout Group, 578
Star-Ventures Management GMBH (SVM), 940
Strategic Capital Management, 941
Stratford Equity Partners, L.P., 679
SudKB & SudVC, 942
Synopsys, Inc., 253
Tamir Fishman Ventures, 946
Technology Partners, 255
Texas Growth Fund Management, 681
Thoma Cressey Equity Partners, 371
Ticonderoga Capital, Inc. (FKA: Dillon Read Venture Capital), 452
Trident Capital, 259
TrustCapital Partners NV, 959
U.S. Bancorp Piper Jaffray Ventures, Inc., 472
U.S. Venture Partners, 261
UBF Mittelstandsfunanzierungs AG, 962
UBS Capital, 962
Venture Select, 968
Vertex Management, 971
Wachovia, 340
WaldenVC, 270
Warburg, Pincus & Co., LLC. (FKA: E.M. Warburg, Pincus & Co), 590
WestBridge Capital Advisors (India) Pvt. Ltd., 976
Weston Presidio Capital Management, 455
Wind Point Partners, 462
Winslow Partners LLC, 317
WK Associates, 977
Wolf Ventures (AKA:Wolf Asset Management Corp.), 286
Women's Growth Capital Fund, 318
Working Ventures Canadian Fund, Inc., 978
Yasuda Enterprise Development Co., Ltd.(FKA: Nippon Ent.Dev), 275

Yorkshire Fund Managers Ltd., 979
Yozma Venture Capital Ltd, 980
Zurich Scudder Investments (FKA: Scudder Kemper Investments), 596

Leveraged Buyout

1st Source Capital Corp., 375
21st Century Health Ventures, 129
21st Century Internet Management Partners,LLC, 138
2nd Generation Capital Corp, 648
3i Gestion SA, 725
3i Group plc, 726
A.M. Pappas & Associates, 597
Aberdeen Asset Managers, 728
Aberdeen Murray Johnstone Private Equity, 728
Aberlyn Capital Management Co., Inc., 501
ABN-AMRO Corporate Investments, 729
ABP Acquisition Corp, 287
Acacia Venture Partners, 139
Access Capital Partners, 730
ACF Equity Atlantic, Inc, 731
Acorn Ventures, Inc., 141
ACT Venture Capital Ltd., 732
Adams Street Partners, LLC (FKA: Brinson Private Equity), 343
Adler & Co., 502
Adler & Shaykin, 502
Advanced Materials Partners, Inc., 287
Advanced Technology Development Fund, 330
Advanta Partners, L.P., 622
Advent International Corp., 402
Advent Management N.V., 733
Advent-Morro Equity Partners, 734
Agio Capital Partners I, L.P., 463
Alan I. Goldman & Associates, 483
Albemarle Private Equity Ltd, 735
Alchemy Partners, 736
Alimansky Capital Group, Inc., 504
Allegra Partners (FKA: Lawrence, Smith & Horey), 504
Alliance Financial of Houston, 655
Allied Capital Corporation, 312
Allsop Venture Partners, 380
Allstate Private Equity, 344
Alpha Capital Partners, Inc., 344
Alpha Group (FKA:Alpha Associates Management, Ltd.), 738
Alpinvest Holding NV (AKA NIB Capital Private Equity NV), 739
Alta Communications, 403
American Acquisition Partners, 483
American Capital Strategies, 391
American Securities, L.P., 505
Amerimark Capital Group, 656
Ampersand Ventures, 404
Antares Capital Corp. (FKA: Antares Leveraged Capital Corp), 345
AO Capital Corp, 287
Apax Partners & Cie (AKA: Apax France), 742
Apax Partners & Co. Ventures Ltd (AKA: Apax UK), 742
Applied Technology, 405
Ardsheil, Inc., 506
Argentum Group, The , 507
Argos Soditic SA, 744
Argosy Partners, 623
Argosy Partners, Inc., 745
Argus Capital Group, 745
Artesian Capital, 464
Arthur P. Gould & Co., 507
Arthur Rock & Co., 146
Atlantic Coastal Ventures, L.P.(AKA:Multimedia Broadcast In), 312
Atlantic Medical Management, LLC, 508
Atle Foretagskapital AB (FKA Foretagskapital AB), 749
August Partners, 508
Austin Ventures, L.P., 657
Avery Business Development Services, 320
AXA Investment Managers Private Equity Europe, 751
Baccharis Capital, Inc., 150
Bachow & Associates, Inc., 623
Banc One Capital Partners, 608
BancAmerica Capital Investors (FKA:NationsBanc Capital Corp), 598
BanChem Financial Services, Inc., 658
Bancorp Hawaii SBIC, Inc., 341
BANEXI Corp., 753
Bangert Dawes Reade Davis & Thom, 151
Bank Funds, The, 347
Bank One Equity Investors, Inc., 386
Bankers Capital Corp., 473
Bankers Trust New York Corp./Deutsche Banc Alex Brown, 510
Banque De Vizille, 754
Bastion Capital Corp., 152
Batavia Group, Ltd., The , 511
Battery Ventures, L.P., 409
Baxter Associates, Inc., 289
BBS Finance, 757
BC Partners, 757
BCR Asset Management Pty Ltd., 758
Beacon Partners, Inc., 289
Bedford Capital Corp., 512
Behrman Capital, 512
Benefit Capital Companies, Inc., The, 480
Berenberg Private Equity GmbH, 759
Berkeley International Capital Corp., 154
Berkshire Partners, 410
Berwind Financial Group, L.P., 623
Bloom & Co., 512
Boston Capital Ventures, 411
Boston Financial & Equity Corp., 412
Boston Millennia Partners, 412
Boston Ventures Management, Inc., 413
Botts & Co., 762
BrainHeart Capital AB, 762
Brand Equity Ventures, 289
Bridgepoint Capital Ltd (FKA: NWEP & NatWest Ventures Ltd), 763
Bristol Capital Management, 513
British Steel Ltd., 764
Broadmark Capital Corp., 702
Burr, Egan, Deleage & Co., 414
Butler Capital Partners France, 765
C3 Holdings, LLC, 474
Cairnsford Associates Ltd., 766
Calgary Enterprises, Inc., 514
Cambria Group, The, 157
Cambridge Venture Partners, 375
Camden Partners, Inc. (FKA: Cahill, Warnock & Co., L.L.C.), 393

Candover Investments PLC, 768
Canterbury Capital L.L.C.(AKA: Canterbury Detroit Partners), 514
Capital For Business, Inc., 474
Capital for Companies (CfC), 769
Capital Investments, Inc., 717
Capital Network, The (AKA: Texas Capital Network), 659
Capital Partners LLC, 769
Capital Prive (FKA NatWest Equity Partners, France), 769
Capital Resource Partners, 415
Capital Services & Resources, Inc., 648
Capital Southwest Corporation, 660
Capital Strategy Management Co., The, 349
CapVis Equity Partners AG, 771
Cardinal Ventures, L.L.C., 375
Cariad Capital, Inc., 642
Carillon Capital, Inc., 610
Carolinas Capital Investment Corp., 599
Carousel Capital Partners, 599
Cascade Communications Ventures, LLC, 159
Castle Harlan Australian Mezzanine Partners Pty. Ltd. , 772
Catalyst Group, The , 660
Catterton Partners, 290
CB Health Ventures LLC, 416
Cedar Creek Partners, LLC, 717
CEI Ventures/Coastal Ventures LP, 388
CEO Venture Fund, 625
Cerulean Fund/WGC Enterprises, 350
Chanen, Painter & Co., Ltd., 703
Charles Street Securities, Inc., 515
Charter Ventures, 160
Chartwell Capital Management Co., Inc., 321
Chase H&Q (FKA Hambrecht & Quist), 160
China Venture Management, Inc., 777
Churchill Capital, Inc., 465
CIBC Capital Partners (FKA: CIBC Wood Gundy Capital), 516
CIBC Oppenheimer & Co., Inc., 516
CICLAD, 778
CID Equity Partners, 376
Cinven Ltd, 779
Circle Ventures, Inc., 376
CIT Group/Venture Capital, Inc., The, 485
Citadel Pooled Development Ltd. , 779
Citicorp Capital Asia (AKA: CITIC Pacific Ltd.), 780
Citicorp Venture Capital, Ltd., 517
Citizens Capital and Citizens Ventures, 418
CIVC Partners (FKA:Continental Illinois Venture Corp.), 350
Clairvest Group, Inc., 780
CM Equity Partners, 517
Code, Hennessy & Simmons, LLC., 351
Cohen & Co., L.L.C., 517
Colonnade Capital L.L.C., 691
Commonwealth Capital Ventures L.P., 419
Compass Investment Management Ltd., 783
Compass Technology Partners, 163
Concord Venture Management (FKA:Nitzanim), 784
Consumer Venture Partners, 292
Continental S.B.I.C., 691
Continental Venture Capital , 784
Copernicus Capital Management Ltd, 785
Cornerstone Equity Investors, LLC, 519
Corpfin Capital S.A., 786
Corporate Growth Assistance, Ltd., 786
Crest Communications Holdings LLC, 520
Crocker Capital/Crocker Assoc., 164
Crosbie & Co Inc, 789
Crown Advisors International, Ltd., 521
Crown Capital Corp, 475
Cureton & Co., Inc., 662
CVC Capital Partners, 790
CW Group, Inc., 521
Czech Venture Partners Sro, 791
D.H. Blair Investment Banking Corp., 521
Daewoo Venture Capital Co Ltd, 792
Davis Group, 166
Davis, Tuttle Venture Partners, L.P.(FKA:Davis Venture), 618
De Vries & Co., Inc., 476
Deutsche Beteiligungs AG, 796
Developers Equity Corp., 169
DFW Capital Partners (AKA:DeMuth, Folger & Wetherill), 486
DN Partners, 352
Dorset Capital, 170
Dougery Ventures, 171
Dow Chemical Co., 458
Dresdner Kleinwort Capital , 524
Dresner Capital Resources, Inc., 352
Drysdale Enterprises, 173
Dunedin Capital Partners Ltd (FKA:Dunedin Ventures Limited), 799
ECI Ventures Ltd, 801
Edelson Technology Partners, 487
Edge Capital Investment Co., LLC, 175
EGL Holdings, Inc./Nat West Ventures USA, L.P., 332
Electra Fleming Limited, 525
Electra Partners Asia [FKA: JF Electra Limited], 803
Elk Associates Funding Corp., 526
Emerald Venture Group, 177
Enterprise Equity (NI) Limited, 805
Enterprise Investors, 526
Enterprise Merchant Bank, 382
Eos Partners, L.P., 527
Epicea, 805
Equinox Investment Partners, 294
Equitas, L.P., 649
Equity Ventures, Ltd, 807
Equity-South (FKA:Grubb & Williams Ltd.), 333
Equus Capital Corp., 663
Eqvitec Partners Oy, 807
Espirito Santo Development, 808
EURAZEO (FKA Gaz-et-Eaux & AZEO), 809
European Acquisition Capital Ltd., 810
Euroventures Management AB , 811
Evergreen Canada Israel Investments Ltd, 812
Evergreen Capital Partners Inc, 528
Evergreen Ventures, 686
Exeter Capital, L.P., 528
Expanso Capital, 813
Fairfax Partners, 693
Federal Business Development Bank, 815
Ferrer Freeman Thompson & Co, 295
FHL Capital Corp., 129
Fidelity Ventures (FKA: Fidelity Venture Associates), 421
FINADVANCE S.A., 815
Financial Capital Resources, Inc., 333

FINOVA Mezzanine Capital, Inc. (FKA: Sirrom Capital Corp), 650
First Atlantic Capital, Ltd., 530
First Capital Management Co., 664
First Charter Partners, Inc., 664
First Princeton Capital Corp., 489
First Security Business Investment Corp., 686
First Union Capital Partners, 600
Florida Capital Partners, 322
Florida Capital Ventures, Ltd., 323
Fonds de Solidarité des Travailleurs du Québec (F.T.Q.), 820
Food Fund Ltd. Partnership, The, 467
Founders Equity, Inc., 530
Frazier & Company, 705
Frederic H. Mayerson Group, The, 612
Fremont Partners, 181
Friends Ivory & Sime Private Equity (Ivory &Sime Baronsmead), 823
Friulia SpA Fin.Reg.Friuli-Venezia, 824
Frontenac Co., 355
Gateway Associates, L.P., 476
GATX/MM Venture Partners, 183
GCI, 718
Gemini Investors LLC (AKA: GMN Investors), 423
Generation Capital Partners, 532
GENES GmbH Venture Services, 826
Genesee Funding, Inc., 532
Genesis Capital, Inc., 533
Geneva Merchant Banking Partners, 601
Gilde Investment Management, 827
Gimvindus NV, 828
Glencoe Capital, LLC (FKA: Glencoe Investment Corporation), 356
Global Finance SA, 828
Glynn Ventures, 186
Goldner Hawn Johnson & Morrison Incorporated, 468
Golub Associates, 534
Granite Ventures LLC (FKA: H & Q Venture Associates), 186
Granville Baird Capital Partners (FKA:Granville Pr Eq Mngrs), 830
Graphite Capital (FKA: F&C Ventures Ltd), 831
Grayson & Associates, 280
Greater Philadelphia Venture Capital Corp., 627
Greenwich Venture Partners, Inc., 296
Gresham Rabo Management Limited, 832
Grotech Capital Group, 394
Growth Venture Group Pty Ltd., 833
GTCR Golder Rauner, LLC, 356
H&Q Asia Pacific, Ltd., 187
Halder Holdings B.V., 835
Halpern, Denny & Co., 425
Hambro European Ventures (Hambros PLC), 835
Hamilton Robinson & Co., Inc., 296
Hanbyuck Investment Co Ltd, 836
Hanover Capital Corp., 535
Harbison Corporation, 477
Harbour Financial Co., 426
HarbourVest Partners, LLC., 426
Harvest Partners, Inc., 536
Health Capital Group, 188
Hellman & Friedman, 189
Herbert Young Securities, Inc., 536
Heritage Partners, 427
Hibernia Capital Partners, 837
Hickory Venture Capital Corporation, 130
High Street Capital, LLC, 357
HillStreet Capital, Inc., 612
HMS Hawaii Management Partners, 341
Hoak Capital Corp., 666
Holding Capital Group, Inc., 537
Howard, Lawson & Co., 628
HSBC Private Equity (Asia), Ltd. (FKA: HSBC PE Management), 841
HSBC Private Equity Ltd (FKA Montagu Private Equity Ltd), 841
HSBC Ventures (UK) Ltd, 842
HT Capital Advisors, LLC, 538
Humana Venture Capital, 384
Hungarian-American Enterprise Fund, The (HAEF), 842
IBJS Capital Corp., 539
IBK Capital Corporation, 844
ICC Venture Capital, 845
ICICI Venture Funds Mngt. Co. Ltd., 846
Imperial Ventures, Inc., 193
Impex Venture Management Co., 540
Incorporated Investors, 193
Inman & Bowman, 195
Innova Capital (FKA: Poland Partners Management Company), 853
Innovest Group, Inc., 629
Innvotec Ltd, 854
Insurance Venture Partners, Inc., 297
Integrated Consortium, Inc., 197
InterEquity Capital Partners, L.P., 541
Intermediate Capital Group PLC, 855
InvestAmerica Venture Group, Inc., 380
Investissement Desjardins, 857
Investissements Novacap (AKA:Novacap Investments, Inc.), 858
IPE Capital-Soc.De Cap.De Risoc SA, 859
IPS Industrial Promotion Services, Ltd., 859
ISEP NV, 860
J.P. Morgan Partners (FKA: Chase Capital Partners), 543
James A. Matzdorff & Co., 199
Jefferson Capital Fund, Ltd., 130
Jordan, Edmiston Group, Inc., The , 545
Josephberg Grosz & Co., Inc., 545
Kahala Investments, Inc., 668
Kansas Venture Capital, Inc., 383
Key Equity Capital Corp.(AKA:Key Community Development Corp), 613
Keystone Minority Capital Fund, L.P., 630
Kidd, Kamm & Company, 298
Kinetic Ventures, Inc., 395
KLB Investment Co., Ltd., 866
Lake Shore Capital Partners, Inc., 360
LaSalle Capital Group, Inc., 360
Legal & General Ventures Ltd, 872
Leonard Green & Partners, 203
Lepercq Capital Management, Inc.(AKA:Lepercq,de Neuflize In), 548
Levine Leichtman Capital Partners, Inc., 204
Liberty BIDCO Investment Corporation, 459
LINC Capital Partners, Inc., 361
Lincoln Investment Management Inc., 378
Livingston Capital, Ltd., 281

LM Capital Corp., 324
Loeb Partners Corp., 549
Lombard Investments, Inc., 206
Lovett Miller & Co. Incorporated, 325
Loyalhanna Venture Fund, 631
LRM Investeringsmaatschappij Voor Limburg, 875
Lubar & Co., 718
M&F Associates, L.P., 549
Madison Dearborn Partners, LLC, 361
Madison Investment Partners, Inc., 550
Management Resource Partners, 208
Manchester Humphreys, Inc., 642
Manhattan Venture Co., Inc., 550
MarketCorp Ventures L.P., 299
Marlborough Capital Advisors, 431
Marleau, Lemire, Inc., 878
Marwit Capital LLC, 209
Massachusetts Capital Resource Co., 432
Matrix Capital, 695
Matrix Partners, 433
Mayfair Capital Partners, Inc., 551
MBA Venture Group, 669
MBW Management, Inc., 492
MC Capital, Inc., 551
McCown De Leeuw & Co., 210
McGuire Capital Corp., 670
MCH Private Equity SA, 880
McKee & Co., 134
Media Venture Partners, 211
MedTech International, Inc., 670
Mellon Ventures (AKA: Mellon Bank), 632
Memhard Investment Bankers, Inc., 300
Mentor Capital Partners, 633
Mercury Private Equity, 883
Meridian Venture Partners (MVP), 633
Merifin Capital Group, 883
Merrill Lynch Investment Managers FKA Mercury Asset Mgmt, 884
MESBIC Ventures Holding Co. (AKA Pacesetter Growth Fund, L.P, 671
Mesirow Private Equity Investments, Inc., 362
Metapoint Partners, 435
Mezzanine Management UK Limited, 885
Microtechnology Investments, Ltd., 213
Mid-Atlantic Venture Funds (FKA: NEPA Management Corp.), 634
Middlefield Capital Fund, 885
Midlands Venture Fund Managers Ltd. (AKA: Midven Ltd), 886
Miller/Zell Venture Group, 335
Miralta Capital, Inc., 887
Montgomerie, Huck & Co., 888
Montgomery Associates, Inc., 215
Monument Advisors, Inc, 378
Moore & Associates, 619
Moore Capital Management Inc., 554
Morgan Grenfell Private Equity Limited, 889
Morgan Stanley Venture Partners (AKA: MSDW), 554
Morgenthaler Ventures, 614
MST Partners, 555
Nassau Capital, L.L.C., 492
National Bank Of Kuwait, 555
National City Equity Partners, Inc, 614
National Corporate Finance, Inc., 217
National Financial Cos. LLC, 556
National Investment Management, Inc., 217
Native Venture Capital Co., Ltd., 893
Natural Gas Partners, 300
Navis Partners (FKA:Fleet Equity Partners), 643
Nazem & Co., 556
Needham & Company, Inc., 556
Nelson Capital Corp., 651
Nesbitt Burns, 363
Newbridge Capital Limited, 219
Newbury Ventures, 220
Newbury, Piret & Co., Inc., 437
NIB Capital Private Equity N.V. (FKA: Parnib Holding NV) , 898
Nmas1 Electra Capital Privado , S.G.E.C.R., S.A., 900
Noro-Moseley Partners, 336
North American Business Development Co., L.L.C., 364
North American Capital Corp., 559
North Atlantic Capital Corp., 389
North Texas MESBIC, Inc., 672
Northeast Ventures Corp., 469
Northern Venture Managers Limited, 902
Northwest Ohio Venture Fund, 615
Northwood Ventures, 559
Norwood Venture Corp., 559
NPE Investment Advisors (AKA:Nordic Private Equity Partners), 903
NPM Capital (AKA Nederlandse Participatie MIJ NV), 903
NTC Group, The , 301
Nu Capital Access Group, Ltd., 224
Oak Hill Capital Management, Inc., 561
Oak Investment Partners, 302
Oberlin Capital, L.P., 603
Oem Capital, 302
Onex Corp., 905
Opportunity Capital Partners {FKA: Thompson Capital Mgt), 225
Orion Partners, L.P., 439
Pacific Asset Partners, 226
Pacific Corporate Group, Inc., 227
Pacific Venture Group, 227
PAMA Group Inc. (FKA:Prudential Asset Management Asia), 908
Pantheon Ventures Limited, 908
Pappajohn Capital Resources, 381
Parcom Ventures BV, 909
Paribas Principal, Inc., 563
Partners Group, 910
Pathfinder Venture Capital Funds, 470
Patricof & Co. Ventures, Inc., 563
Pauli & Co., Inc., 477
Penfund Partners, Inc., 911
Peninsula Capital Partners, L.L.C, 460
PENMAN Partners (FKA PENMAN Asset Management LP), 365
Penn-Janney Fund, Inc., The, 635
Pennsylvania Growth Fund, 636
Penny Lane Partners, 493
Penta Capital Partners Ltd, 911
Pfingsten Partners, L.P., 366
Philadelphia Ventures, Inc., 636
Phillips-Smith Specialty Retail Group, 673
Phoenix Equity Partners (FKA: DLJ European Private Equity), 911
Phoenix Home Life Mutual Insurance Co., 303

Pierce Financial Corporation(FKA:Pierce Investment Banking), 698
Platinum Group, Inc., The , 565
PME Capital, 912
Point Venture Partners, 636
Pomona Capital, 566
PPM Ventures Ltd (FKA: Prudential Venture Managers Ltd), 914
Prince Ventures, 367
Prism Capital, 367
Private Capital Corp., 131
Private Equity Investors, Inc., 567
Private Equity Partners, 674
Priveq Capital Funds, 917
Prospect Partners LLC (FKA:Kenter, Glatris & Tuttle, LLC, 368
Providence Equity Partners, Inc.(FKA: Providence Ventures), 643
Putnam Lovell Capital Partners, L.P., 232
Quadriga Capital Management GMBH, 919
Quester Capital Management Ltd, 920
R-H Capital Partners, 337
RAF Ventures, 637
RBC Ventures, Inc., 619
Recovery Equity Investors, L.P., 234
Redwood Capital Corp., 235
Regent Capital Management, 569
Renaissance Capital Corp., 337
RFE Investment Partners, 305
Rice, Sangalis, Toole & Wilson (FKA: Rice Capital Partners), 675
Richard Jaffe & Co., Inc., 676
Ridge Capital Partners, L.L.C., 368
Riordan, Lewis & Haden, 236
River Associates, LLC, 653
River Capital, 338
Roanoke Capital, Ltd., 712
Robertson Stephens & Company, LLC, 236
Rock Hill Ventures Inc.(FKA:Hillman Medical Ventures,Inc.), 638
Rosecliff, 237
Rosenfeld & Co., 620
Rosewood Capital, L.P., 237
Rothschild Ventures Asia Pte Ltd., 922
Rothschild Ventures, Inc., 570
Royal Bank Private Equity (FKA: Royal Bank Development Cap), 922
Royalty Capital Fund, L.P. I/Royalty Capital Management, Inc, 443
Rutledge & Co., Inc., 305
S-Refit GmbH & Co KG , 923
SAE Ventures, 306
Sage Management Group, 444
Sand Aire Private Equity Ltd, 924
Sandhurst Venture Fund, L.P., The , 639
Sandler Capital Management, 571
Sanpaolo IMI Private Equity S.p.A., 925
Saugatuck Capital Company, 306
SBC Equity Partners, Inc., 369
SBCA/A.G. Bartholomew & Associates, 131
Schroder Capital Partners (Asia) Pte Ltd, 926
Schroder Ventures, 445
Seacoast Capital, 446
Seaport Capital, 572
SEB Foretagsinvest, 927
Seidman, Jackson, Fisher & Co., 369
Sentinel Capital Partners, 573
SGI Capital L.L.C, 573
Shad Run Investments, Inc., 242
Shalor Ventures, Inc., 446
Shansby Group/TSG2, L.P., The , 242
Shared Ventures, Inc., 470
Shattan Group, The, 574
Shaw Venture Partners (FKA: Shaw Glasgow Partners), 621
Shawmut Capital Partners, 447
Shelton Companies, Inc., The , 604
Shepherd Group LLC, The, 447
Sherbrooke Capital Partners, 448
Shott Capital Management, 574
Sierra Ventures, 243
Sigma Partners, 243
Siguler Guff & Company, LLC, 575
Siparex Group (FKA:Siparex Provinces de France), 931
Societe Generale- Private Equity Activity, 933
Societe Regionale d'Investissement de Bruxelles (SRIB/GIMB), 933
SOFTBANK Capital Partners, 448
Sorrento Associates, Inc., 247
Southport Partners, 307
Southwest Venture Group, 678
Southwest Venture Partnerships, The, 678
Sovereign Capital (FKA:Nash, Sells & Partners Limited), 936
SPEF Banques Populaires, 937
Speirs Consultants, Inc., 938
Spire Capital (FKA: Waller Capital Corp.), 577
Sponsored Consulting Services, 249
Sports Capital Partners, 577
Spring Capital Partners, L.P., 398
Sprout Group, 578
SSM Ventures, 653
Standard Life Investments (Private Equity) Ltd, 939
State Street Bank & Trust Co., 338
Stephens Group, Inc., 137
Sterling Grace Capital Management, L.P., 579
Sterling Venture Partners, 398
Stolberg Partners, 580
Stonebridge Partners, 580
Strategic Investments & Holdings, Inc., 581
Stratford Equity Partners, L.P., 679
Sucsy, Fischer & Co., 370
Summit Capital Associates, Inc., 581
Summit Capital Group, 680
Summit Partners, 451
Sun Valley Ventures, 250
Sundance Venture Partners, L.P., 251
Sunwestern Investment Group, 680
Swander Pace Capital, 252
Sweeney & Co., Inc., 308
Sycamore Ventures, 494
Synerfi S.A., 945
TA Associates, Inc., 451
Tappan Zee Capital Corp., 495
Taylor & Turner, 253
TCR Europe SA, 947
TDH, 639
Teknia Invest Oy, 952
Texas Growth Fund Management, 681
Thoma Cressey Equity Partners, 371
Thompson Clive, Inc., 257

Three Cities Research, Inc., 583
Throunarfelag Islands Plc(AKA:The Icelandic Finance&Invest.), 955
Tianguis Ltd, 956
Trident Capital, 259
TSG Capital Group, L.L.C., 309
Tvi Investments Bv, 960
U.S. Medical Resources Corp., 616
UBS Capital (AKA Phildrew Ventures), 963
Ulin & Holland, Inc., 453
Ulster Development Capital, Ltd., 963
UNC Ventures, 453
Union Street Capital Corp., 713
Union Venture Corp., 262
UniRock Management Corp., 285
Valley Capital Corp., 654
Valley Ventures (FKA: Arizona Growth Partners, L.P.), 136
VCM Venture Capital Management, 965
Vega Capital Corp., 584
Vencap Equities Alberta, Ltd., 966
Vencon Management, Inc., 585
Ventana Financial Resources, Inc., 372
Ventex Management, Inc., 683
Venture Associates Partners, LLC, 654
Venture Associates, Ltd., 285
Venture Capital Management Corp., 328
Venture Funding Group International, 587
Venture Funding, Ltd., 461
Venture Growth Associates, 265
Venture Opportunities Corp., 588
Vero Group PLC, 684
Vertical Group, The, 496
Virginia Capital , 701
Vista Capital de Expansion S.A., 972
VIV NV (AKA Vlaamse Investeringvennootschap NV), 973
VK Ventures, 268
Vlaamse Investeringvennootschap NV, 974
VS&A Communications Partners, L.P., 588
Walnut Capital Corp., 701
Wand Partners, 589
Warburg, Pincus & Co., LLC. (FKA: E.M. Warburg, Pincus & Co), 590
Wedbush Capital Partners, 271
Wellmax, Inc., 461
Welsh, Carson, Anderson & Stowe, 591
Westar Capital, 271
Westbury Partners, 592
Western States Investment Group, 272
Western Technology Investment, 272
Weston Presidio Capital Management, 455
WestSphere Equity Investors, LP, 592
Whitney & Co. (FKA: J.H. Whitney & Co.), 310
William A.M. Burden & Co., 593
William Blair Capital Partners, 373
William E. Simon & Sons (Asia) LDC, 977
Willis Stein & Partners, 374
Wind Point Partners, 462
Windjammer Capital Investors (FKA:Pacific Mezzanine Inv.), 273
Windward Holdings, 311
Wingate Partners, L.P., 685
Winslow Partners LLC, 317
Winthrop Ventures, 593
Working Ventures Canadian Fund, Inc., 978
Worms Capital Management, 594
Yablon Enterprises, Inc., 641
Yorkshire Fund Managers Ltd., 979
ZS Fund, L.P., 595

Management Buyouts

3i Finland Oy (FKA SFK Finance), 725
3i Group plc, 726
Aberdeen Murray Johnstone Private Equity, 728
ABN-AMRO Corporate Investments, 729
AdCapital AG (FKA Berliner Elektro Holding AG), 732
Advent Venture Partners (FKA Advent Limited), 733
Advent-Morro Equity Partners, 734
Adveq Management AG (FKA Advisers on Private Equity AG), 734
AIG Capital Partners Inc., 503
Allied Capital Corporation, 312
AMP Asset Management Limited - Development Capital, 740
Ampersand Ventures, 404
Antares Capital Corporation (FKA: Harbor Ventures Corp.), 320
AO Capital Corp, 287
Apax Partners & Co.Beteiligungsberatung AG, 742
Argos Soditic SA, 744
Argosy Partners, 623
Argus Capital Group, 745
Asian Direct Capital Management, 747
Baird Capital Partners, 347
BancBoston Capital/BancBoston Ventures, 408
Barclays Ventures, 755
BayBG Bayerische Beteiligungsgesellschaft mbH, 757
BCR Asset Management Pty Ltd., 758
Beecken, Petty & Co. LLC, 348
Berlin Capital Fund (FKA LBB Beteiligungsgesellschaft GmbH), 759
Bulldog Partners Limited, 764
C3 Holdings, LLC, 474
Cairnsford Associates Ltd., 766
Calgary Enterprises, Inc., 514
Capital For Business, Inc., 474
Capital Prive (FKA NatWest Equity Partners, France), 769
Capital Resource Partners, 415
Capital Southwest Corporation, 660
Capital Strategy Management Co., The, 349
CapVis Equity Partners AG, 771
CEI Ventures/Coastal Ventures LP, 388
CGW Southeast Partners (AKA: Cravey, Green, & Wahlen), 331
Churchill Capital, Inc., 465
CICLAD, 778
Cinven Ltd, 779
Citadel Pooled Development Ltd. , 779
Citizens Capital and Citizens Ventures, 418
CIVC Partners (FKA:Continental Illinois Venture Corp.), 350
Close Brothers Private Equity, 782
Colonial First State Private Equity Ltd (FKA: Hambro-G Mgmt), 782
Commerz Beteiligungsgesellschaft mbH (CBG), 783
Continental S.B.I.C., 691
Continental Venture Capital , 784
Crosbie & Co Inc, 789
Daimler Chrysler Venture Gmbh (AKA DCV), 792

De Vries & Co., Inc., 476
Deutsche Asset Management (Australia) Limited, 795
Deutsche Beteiligungs AG, 796
DFW Capital Partners (AKA:DeMuth, Folger & Wetherill), 486
Direct Capital Private Equity, 797
Dorset Capital, 170
ECI Ventures Ltd, 801
ECM Equity Capital Management GmbH, 802
Edison Venture Fund, 488
Elderstreet Investments Ltd, 803
Electra Partners Asia [FKA: JF Electra Limited], 803
Endeavour Capital Pty Ltd, 804
Equity Partners Management Pty Ltd, 807
Euroventures Benelux Team B.V., 811
Evergreen Capital Partners Inc, 528
Expanso Capital, 813
Fairgill Investments Property Limited, 814
FINADVANCE S.A., 815
Finansa Capital Limited, 816
FINORPA, 816
First New England Capital, L.P., 295
Flinders Capital Limited, 818
Fonds de Solidarité des Travailleurs du Québec (F.T.Q.), 820
Fowler, Anthony & Co., 422
GENES GmbH Venture Services, 826
Geneva Merchant Banking Partners, 601
Gilde Investment Management, 827
Gimvindus NV, 828
Go Equity GmbH, 829
Granville Baird Capital Partners (FKA:Granville Pr Eq Mngrs), 830
Gresham Rabo Management Limited, 832
Growth Venture Group Pty Ltd., 833
GrowthWorks Capital, 834
GTCR Golder Rauner, LLC, 356
H&Q Asia Pacific, Ltd., 187
Halder Holdings B.V., 835
HANNOVER Finanz GmbH, 837
HarbourVest Partners, LLC., 426
Harvest Partners, Inc., 536
High Street Capital, LLC, 357
HT Capital Advisors, LLC, 538
Hunt Capital Group, 667
IKB Venture Capital GmbH (AKA IKB Beteiligungsgesellschaft , 848
Incorporated Investors, 193
Intermediate Capital Group PLC, 855
Investissements Novacap (AKA:Novacap Investments, Inc.), 858
J.P. Morgan Partners (FKA: Chase Capital Partners), 543
JAFCO Co. Ltd., 862
Josephberg Grosz & Co., Inc., 545
KPMG Advent Management Group (FKA:Advent Western Pacific), 870
Lambda Funds, The, 546
Legal & General Ventures Ltd, 872
LF International, Inc., 204
Life Science Ventures, 873
Life Sciences Partners BV, 874
Lincolnshire Management Inc., 548
Loeb Partners Corp., 549
Lombard Investments, Inc., 206
London Ventures (Fund Managers) Ltd., 875
M&F Associates, L.P., 549
Macquarie Direct Investment Limited, 876
Madison Dearborn Partners, LLC, 361
Manchester Humphreys, Inc., 642
Matrix Group, 209
Mentor Capital Partners, 633
Merifin Capital Group, 883
Merita Capital Ltd, 884
Midinvest Oy, 886
Monument Advisors, Inc, 378
Morgenthaler Ventures, 614
Mountaineer Capital LP, 716
MVC AG (AKA Mitteldeutsche Venture Capital AG), 891
MVI Sverige AB, 891
National Australia Investment Capital Limited, 892
National Bank Of Kuwait, 555
National City Equity Partners, Inc, 614
Navis Partners (FKA:Fleet Equity Partners), 643
Needham & Company, Inc., 556
Newbridge Capital Limited, 219
Northwood Ventures, 559
Novus Ventures, 223
NPM Capital (AKA Nederlandse Participatie MIJ NV), 903
Oberlin Capital, L.P., 603
Oem Capital, 302
Olympus Capital Holdings Asia, 905
Pacific Corporate Group, Inc., 227
Pacific Equity Partners, 907
PAMA Group Inc. (FKA:Prudential Asset Management Asia), 908
Parcom Ventures BV, 909
Partners Group, 910
Penfund Partners, Inc., 911
Penta Capital Partners Ltd, 911
PPM Ventures Ltd (FKA: Prudential Venture Managers Ltd), 914
Procuritas Partners KB, 917
ProVen Private Equity (FKA:Guinness Mahon Development Cap.), 918
Putnam Lovell Capital Partners, L.P., 232
Quadriga Capital Management GMBH, 919
Red River Ventures, 675
Reiten & Co Strategic Investments AS, 921
River Associates, LLC, 653
RMB Ventures Limited, 921
Rocky Mountain Capital Partners (FKA:Hanifen Imhoff Capital), 283
Royal Bank Private Equity (FKA: Royal Bank Development Cap), 922
Sanpaolo IMI Private Equity S.p.A., 925
Saugatuck Capital Company, 306
Seaport Capital, 572
Shattan Group, The, 574
Shaw, Kwei & Partners Limited, 929
Sprout Group, 578
Sterling/Carl Marks Capital {FKA - Sterling Commercial, 580
Strategic Capital Management, 941
Strategic Investments & Holdings, Inc., 581
Stratford Equity Partners, L.P., 679
SudKB & SudVC, 942
Suez Asia Holdings Pte Ltd., 943
Summit Capital Group, 680
tbg Technologie-Beteiligungsgesellschaft mbH, 947
Temasek Capital, 954

Texas Growth Fund Management, 681
Thompson Clive & Partners Limited, 955
Tianguis Ltd, 956
Transpac Capital Pte, Ltd., 958
UBF Mittelstandsfunanzierungs AG, 962
UBS Capital, 962
UBS Capital (AKA Phildrew Ventures), 963
VCF Partners, 965
Venture Capital Partners Pty Limited, 967
Virginia Capital , 701
VIV NV (AKA Vlaamse Investeringvennootschap NV), 973
Wachovia, 340
Walden Capital Management Corporation, 589
Warburg, Pincus & Co., LLC. (FKA: E.M. Warburg, Pincus & Co), 590
West Midlands Enterprise Ltd, 976
Wind Point Partners, 462
Winslow Partners LLC, 317
WL Ventures (FKA:Lothian Enterprise Ltd.), 978
Wolf Ventures (AKA:Wolf Asset Management Corp.), 286
Working Ventures Canadian Fund, Inc., 978

Mezzanine

1st Source Capital Corp., 375
21st Century Internet Management Partners,LLC, 138
3i Finland Oy (FKA SFK Finance), 725
A.M. Pappas & Associates, 597
ABN-AMRO Corporate Investments, 729
ABS Ventures, 390
Acacia Venture Partners, 139
Accenture Technology Ventures (FKA: AC Ventures), 140
ACF Equity Atlantic, Inc, 731
Adams, Harkness & Hill, Inc., 401
Advanta Partners, L.P., 622
Advantage Capital Partners, 386
Advent International Corp., 402
Agribusiness Partners International Partners, 479
AIG Capital Partners Inc., 503
Alan I. Goldman & Associates, 483
Alimansky Capital Group, Inc., 504
All Asia Partners, 737
Alliance Financial of Houston, 655
Allied Capital Corporation, 312
Allsop Venture Partners, 380
Allstate Private Equity, 344
Alpinvest Holding NV (AKA NIB Capital Private Equity NV), 739
Alta Communications, 403
Alta Partners, 144
Amerimark Capital Group, 656
Amerindo Investment Advisors, Inc., 505
Antares Capital Corp. (FKA: Antares Leveraged Capital Corp), 345
Anthem Capital, L.P., 391
Argentum Group, The , 507
Argosy Partners, Inc., 745
Armada Asset Management, 746
Arthur P. Gould & Co., 507
ASC Group, 746
Atila Venture Partners Ltd., 749
Atlantic Coastal Ventures, L.P.(AKA:Multimedia Broadcast In), 312
Atlas Venture, 407
Auric Asset Management Pte. Ltd., 750
aventic Partners AG, 750
Baccharis Capital, Inc., 150
Bailey & Co. Inc., 752
Banc One Capital Partners, 608
BancAmerica Capital Investors (FKA:NationsBanc Capital Corp), 598
BancBoston Capital/BancBoston Ventures, 408
BanChem Financial Services, Inc., 658
Bancorp Hawaii SBIC, Inc., 341
BANEXI Corp., 753
Bangert Dawes Reade Davis & Thom, 151
Bank One Equity Investors, Inc., 386
Bankers Trust New York Corp./Deutsche Banc Alex Brown, 510
Baring Private Equity Partners (FKA:Baring Venture Partners), 755
Batavia Investment Management Ltd, 756
Battery Ventures, L.P., 409
BayBG Bayerische Beteiligungsgesellschaft mbH, 757
BCR Asset Management Pty Ltd., 758
Beacon Partners, Inc., 289
Benefit Capital Companies, Inc., The, 480
Berkeley International Capital Corp., 154
Berlin Capital Fund (FKA LBB Beteiligungsgesellschaft GmbH), 759
Berwind Financial Group, L.P., 623
Bloom & Co., 512
Boston Financial & Equity Corp., 412
Boston Millennia Partners, 412
Botts & Co., 762
Brand Equity Ventures, 289
Bristol Capital Management, 513
Bristol Investment Trust, 413
Broadmark Capital Corp., 702
Bulldog Partners Limited, 764
Burr, Egan, Deleage & Co., 414
Burrill & Company, 156
Business Link Doncaster, 765
C3 Investments, Inc., 157
Cairnsford Associates Ltd., 766
Calgary Enterprises, Inc., 514
Cambria Group, The, 157
Cambridge Venture Partners, 375
Camelot Ventures, 457
Canbank Venture Capital Fund Ltd, 767
Canterbury Capital L.L.C.(AKA: Canterbury Detroit Partners), 514
Capital Development & Investment Co. Ltd., 768
Capital Investments, Inc., 717
Capital Network, The (AKA: Texas Capital Network), 659
Capital Partners LLC, 769
Capital Resource Partners, 415
Capital Southwest Corporation, 660
Capital Strategy Management Co., The, 349
CapVest Management, Ltd, 771
Carillon Capital, Inc., 610
Cascade Communications Ventures, LLC, 159
Castle Harlan Australian Mezzanine Partners Pty. Ltd. , 772
Catalyst Group, The , 660
Catalyst Venture Capital Firm, 773
CB Health Ventures LLC, 416
CE Unterberg Towbin (FKA:Unterberg Harris Capital Partners), 515

CEI Ventures/Coastal Ventures LP, 388
Challenger International Ltd., 776
Champion Consulting Group, Incorporated, 776
Chanen, Painter & Co., Ltd., 703
Charter Ventures, 160
Chase H&Q (FKA Hambrecht & Quist), 160
Chiao Tung Bank, 776
China Venture Management, Inc., 777
Churchill Capital, Inc., 465
CIBC Capital Partners (FKA: CIBC Wood Gundy Capital), 516
CID Equity Partners, 376
CIT Group/Venture Capital, Inc., The, 485
Citicorp Capital Asia (AKA: CITIC Pacific Ltd.), 780
Citizens Capital and Citizens Ventures, 418
Clemente Capital (Asia) Ltd., 781
CM Equity Partners, 517
CMEA Ventures (FKA:Chemicals & Materials Enterprise Associa), 161
Cohen & Co., L.L.C., 517
Coleman Swenson Booth Inc.(FKA:Coleman Swenson Hoffman Booth, 649
Columbia Capital Group, Inc., 313
Commerz Beteiligungsgesellschaft mbH (CBG), 783
Commonwealth Capital Ventures L.P., 419
Compass Technology Partners, 163
Connecticut Innovations, Inc., 291
Continental S.B.I.C., 691
Continental Venture Capital , 784
Core Pacific Consulting Company, 786
Corporate Growth Assistance, Ltd., 786
Crestview Financial Group, The , 292
Crosbie & Co Inc, 789
CrossBow Ventures, 322
Crown Advisors International, Ltd., 521
Crown Capital Corp, 475
Daewoo Venture Capital Co Ltd, 792
Daiwa Business Investment Co Ltd, The, 793
Davis, Tuttle Venture Partners, L.P.(FKA:Davis Venture), 618
De Vries & Co., Inc., 476
Dean & Associates, 279
Defta Partners, 167
Deutsche Asset Management (Australia) Limited, 795
Deutsche Bank eVentures (AKA DB eVentures), 795
Domain Associates, L.L.C., 486
Dominion Ventures, Inc., 170
Dow Chemical Co., 458
Downer & Co., 420
Dresdner Kleinwort Capital , 524
Dresner Capital Resources, Inc., 352
Drysdale Enterprises, 173
DSE Investment Services Limited, 799
East River Ventures, L.P., 524
Easton Hunt Capital Partners, 525
ECAT Development Capital Limited, 801
ECICS Ventures Pte Ltd., 801
ECM Equity Capital Management GmbH, 802
Edelson Technology Partners, 487
Edge Capital Investment Co., LLC, 175
EGL Holdings, Inc./Nat West Ventures USA, L.P., 332
Electra Fleming Limited, 525
Electra Partners Asia [FKA: JF Electra Limited], 803
Emerald Venture Group, 177
Enterprise Investors, 526
Enterprise Merchant Bank, 382
Eos Partners, L.P., 527
EquiNet Venture Partners AG, 806
Equinox Investment Partners, 294
Equitas, L.P., 649
Equity-South (FKA:Grubb & Williams Ltd.), 333
Eqvitec Partners Oy, 807
Essex Woodlands Health Ventures (FKA:Woodlands Venture Partn, 354
Evergreen Canada Israel Investments Ltd, 812
Evergreen Ventures, 686
Exeter Capital, L.P., 528
Far East Capital Corp., 179
Federal Business Development Bank, 815
FHL Capital Corp., 129
Financial Technology Ventures, 179
FINOVA Mezzanine Capital, Inc. (FKA: Sirrom Capital Corp), 650
First Capital Management Co., 664
First New England Capital, L.P., 295
First Princeton Capital Corp., 489
First Security Business Investment Corp., 686
First Union Capital Partners, 600
FJC Growth Capital Corp., 129
Flinders Capital Limited, 818
Fonds de Solidarité des Travailleurs du Québec (F.T.Q.), 820
FORTKNOX-VENTURE AG, 821
Fortune Consulting Group Incorporated, 821
Forward Ventures, 180
Foundation Capital Limited, 822
Fountainhead Capital Ltd., 823
Fowler, Anthony & Co., 422
Frazier & Company, 705
Frederic H. Mayerson Group, The, 612
Friulia SpA Fin.Reg.Friuli-Venezia, 824
Frost Capital Partners, 182
Future Value Ventures, Inc., 717
G-51 Capital LLC, 665
Gateway Associates, L.P., 476
GATX Ventures (FKA: Meier Mitchell & Co.), 183
GATX/MM Venture Partners, 183
Gemini Investors LLC (AKA: GMN Investors), 423
Genesee Funding, Inc., 532
Geneva Merchant Banking Partners, 601
Glencoe Capital, LLC (FKA: Glencoe Investment Corporation), 356
Global Finance SA, 828
Glynn Ventures, 186
Go Equity GmbH, 829
Golub Associates, 534
Grand Pacific Venture Capital Company Ltd., 830
Granite Ventures LLC (FKA: H & Q Venture Associates), 186
Grayson & Associates, 280
Greater Philadelphia Venture Capital Corp., 627
Green Mountain Advisors, Inc., 689
Greenwich Venture Partners, Inc., 296
Grotech Capital Group, 394
Grove Street Advisors, LLC, 425
GrowthWorks Capital, 834
H&Q Asia Pacific, Ltd., 187
HANNOVER Finanz GmbH, 837

Hanover Capital Corp., 535
Harbour Financial Co., 426
HarbourVest Partners, LLC., 426
Health Capital Group, 188
Healthcare Ventures LLC (FKA: Healthcare Investments), 490
Heidelberg Innovation GmbH, 837
Hellman & Friedman, 189
Herbert Young Securities, Inc., 536
Horizonte Venture Management GmbH, 840
Hotung International Company, Ltd., 840
Howard, Lawson & Co., 628
HPI Holding SA, 841
HSBC Private Equity (Asia), Ltd. (FKA: HSBC PE Management), 841
HSBC Private Equity Ltd (FKA Montagu Private Equity Ltd), 841
Humana Venture Capital, 384
Hummer Winblad Venture Partners, 191
Hydro-Quebec CapiTech Inc., 843
IBJS Capital Corp., 539
IBK Capital Corporation, 844
ICC Venture Capital, 845
ICICI Venture Funds Mngt. Co. Ltd., 846
IFCI Venture Cap. Funds (Formerly Risk Capital & Tech.), 847
iGlobe Partners Limited, 847
IKB Venture Capital GmbH (AKA IKB Beteiligungsgesellschaft , 848
Indosuez Ventures, 194
Industrial Technology Securities Ltd, 851
Innova Capital (FKA: Poland Partners Management Company), 853
Integrated Consortium, Inc., 197
InterEquity Capital Partners, L.P., 541
Intermediate Capital Group PLC, 855
Interpacific Venture Group Incorporated, 856
InveStar Capital, Inc., 857
Investissement Desjardins, 857
IPE Capital-Soc.De Cap.De Risoc SA, 859
J.P. Morgan Partners (FKA: Chase Capital Partners), 543
JAFCO Co. Ltd., 862
JAFCO Ventures, Inc., 198
James A. Matzdorff & Co., 199
Jordan, Edmiston Group, Inc., The , 545
Kahala Investments, Inc., 668
Kankaku Investment Co Ltd, 865
Kansas Venture Capital, Inc., 383
KBL Healthcare Ventures, 546
Keystone Minority Capital Fund, L.P., 630
Kidd, Kamm & Company, 298
Kirlan Venture Capital, Inc., 707
KLB Investment Co., Ltd., 866
Korea Development Investment Corp., 868
Korea Technology Finance Corp., 869
KPMG Advent Management Group (FKA:Advent Western Pacific), 870
Lake Shore Capital Partners, Inc., 360
Lee Munder Venture Partners, 430
Legal & General Ventures Ltd, 872
Liberty BIDCO Investment Corporation, 459
Libon Capital Management Limited, 873
LINC Capital Partners, Inc., 361
Lincoln Investment Management Inc., 378
Lovett Miller & Co. Incorporated, 325
LRM Investeringsmaatschappij Voor Limburg, 875
LTI Ventures Leasing Corp., 298
Macquarie Direct Investment Limited, 876
Malmohus Invest AB, 877
MarketCorp Ventures L.P., 299
Marlborough Capital Advisors, 431
Marleau, Lemire, Inc., 878
Marwit Capital LLC, 209
Massachusetts Capital Resource Co., 432
Materia Ventures Associates,L.P. (FKA:Pierce Nordquist Asso), 708
Matrix Capital, 695
Matrix Group, 209
Mayfair Capital Partners, Inc., 551
MBA Venture Group, 669
McGuire Capital Corp., 670
McKee & Co., 134
MDS Health Ventures, Inc. (AKA: MDS Capital Corp.), 881
Medical Venture Holdings, Inc., 552
MedTech International, Inc., 670
Mellon Ventures (AKA: Mellon Bank), 632
Mentor Capital Partners, 633
Merifin Capital Group, 883
Merita Capital Limited, 134
MESBIC Ventures Holding Co. (AKA Pacesetter Growth Fund, L.P, 671
Mezzanine Management UK Limited, 885
Middlefield Capital Fund, 885
Millennium Three Venture Group, L.L.C., 480
MMG Ventures, L.P., 396
Montgomerie, Huck & Co., 888
Monument Advisors, Inc, 378
Moore & Associates, 619
Morgan Stanley Venture Partners (AKA: MSDW), 554
MSC Venture Corporation Sdn. Bhd., 890
Mustang Ventures (FKA Siemens Mustang Ventures), 216
MVC AG (AKA Mitteldeutsche Venture Capital AG), 891
MVP Ventures (AKA: Milk Street Ventures), 436
National Bank Of Kuwait, 555
National City Equity Partners, Inc, 614
Nazem & Co., 556
Needham & Company, Inc., 556
Nelson Capital Corp., 651
NeoMed Management AS (FKA Medical Venture Management), 894
New Enterprise Associates, 396
Newbury Ventures, 220
Newbury, Piret & Co., Inc., 437
Newport Capital Group Pty Ltd, 897
NIB Capital Private Equity N.V. (FKA: Parnib Holding NV) , 898
NIF Ventures USA, Inc.(Nippon Investment & Finance Co., Ltd), 222
Nikko Capital Co Ltd, 899
Nomura/JAFCO Investment (HK) Limited, 901
Noro-Moseley Partners, 336
North American Capital Corp., 559
North Atlantic Capital Corp., 389
North Carolina Enterprise Fund, L.P., The, 602
North Texas MESBIC, Inc., 672
Northeast Ventures Corp., 469
Northwest Ohio Venture Fund, 615

Northwest Venture Associates, Inc.(FKA:Spokane Capital Mgmt), 709
Norwood Venture Corp., 559
Noveltek Venture Corp., 560
NPE Investment Advisors (AKA:Nordic Private Equity Partners), 903
NPM Capital (AKA Nederlandse Participatie MIJ NV), 903
Nth Power Technologies, Inc, 224
Olympus Capital Holdings Asia, 905
Onondaga Venture Capital Fund, Inc., 562
Opportunity Capital Partners {FKA: Thompson Capital Mgt), 225
Orix Capital Corporation, 906
Oxford Financial Services Corp., 698
Pac-Link Management Corporation, 906
Pacific Capital Partners, 907
Pacific Corporate Group, Inc., 227
Pacific Venture Group, 227
Pacific Venture Partners, 907
Partech International, 229
Pathfinder Investment Co Pvt Ltd, 910
Pathfinder Venture Capital Funds, 470
Pauli & Co., Inc., 477
Pecks Management Partners, Ltd., 564
Penfund Partners, Inc., 911
Peninsula Capital Partners, L.L.C, 460
Penn-Janney Fund, Inc., The, 635
Pennsylvania Growth Fund, 636
Penta Capital Partners Ltd, 911
Pequot Capital Management Inc., 564
Petra Capital Partners LLC, 652
Philadelphia Ventures, Inc., 636
Phillips-Smith Specialty Retail Group, 673
Phoenix Equity Partners (FKA: DLJ European Private Equity), 911
Phoenix Growth Capital Corp., 231
Phoenix Home Life Mutual Insurance Co., 303
Phoenix Partners, The , 711
Pierce Financial Corporation(FKA:Pierce Investment Banking), 698
Point Venture Partners, 636
Pomona Capital, 566
PowerWord Capital Management, Inc., 914
Premier Medical Partner Fund L.P., 231
Prism Capital, 367
Private Capital Corp., 131
Private Equity Investors, Inc., 567
Priveq Capital Funds, 917
ProQuest Investments, L.P., 493
Quantum Capital Partners, 325
R-H Capital Partners, 337
R. Chaney & Co., Inc., 674
RBC Ventures, Inc., 619
Regent Capital Management, 569
Renaissance Capital Corp., 337
RFE Investment Partners, 305
Rice, Sangalis, Toole & Wilson (FKA: Rice Capital Partners), 675
River Capital, 338
Roanoke Capital, Ltd., 712
Robertson Stephens & Company, LLC, 236
Rocky Mountain Capital Partners (FKA:Hanifen Imhoff Capital), 283
Rosenfeld & Co., 620
Rosewood Capital, L.P., 237
Rothschild Ventures Asia Pte Ltd., 922
Rothschild Ventures, Inc., 570
RRE Ventures LLC, 571
Ruddick Investment Co., 604
SAE Ventures, 306
Sage Management Group, 444
Sand Aire Private Equity Ltd, 924
Sanderling Ventures, 239
Sandler Capital Management, 571
Sandton Financial Group, 240
Saskatchewan Government Growth Fund, 925
SBC Equity Partners, Inc., 369
Schroder Ventures, 445
Seacoast Capital, 446
SENMED Medical Ventures, 616
Sentinel Capital Partners, 573
SGI Capital L.L.C, 573
Shalor Ventures, Inc., 446
Shattan Group, The, 574
Shaw, Kwei & Partners Limited, 929
Shawmut Capital Partners, 447
Shott Capital Management, 574
Siemens Venture Capital GmbH, 930
Siguler Guff & Company, LLC, 575
Silicon Valley Bank, 244
Societe Regionale d'Investissement de Bruxelles (SRIB/GIMB), 933
Sofinnova Ventures, 246
SOFTBANK Capital Partners, 448
Solera Capital LLC, 576
Sorrento Associates, Inc., 247
SoundView Financial Group, Inc., 307
Southport Partners, 307
Southwest Venture Group, 678
SpaceVest, 699
Speirs Consultants, Inc., 938
Sponsored Consulting Services, 249
Spring Capital Partners, L.P., 398
Springboard-Harper Investment Pte. Ltd., 938
Stamford Financial, 579
Stephens Group, Inc., 137
Sterling Grace Capital Management, L.P., 579
Sterling/Carl Marks Capital {FKA - Sterling Commercial, 580
Strategic Capital Management, 941
Stratford Equity Partners, L.P., 679
Sucsy, Fischer & Co., 370
Suez Asia Holdings Pte Ltd., 943
Summit Capital Associates, Inc., 581
Summit Partners, 451
Sundance Venture Partners, L.P., 251
Sunsino Development Associate Inc., 944
Sweeney & Co., Inc., 308
Sycamore Ventures, 494
Synerfi S.A., 945
T. Rowe Price Threshold Partnerships, 399
Tailink Venture Partners, 946
Taiwan United Venture Management Corporation, 946
Taiwan W&S Financial Management Incorporated, 946
tbg Technologie-Beteiligungsgesellschaft mbH, 947
TDH, 639
Teak Investment Partners I Limited, 948
Techno-Venture Co. (Japan), 949

Technology Associates Management Corporation, 950
Technology Crossover Ventures, 254
Technology Funding, 254
Technology Partners, 255
Telsoft Ventures, 953
Temasek Capital, 954
Texas Growth Fund Management, 681
Thompson Clive, Inc., 257
Thorner Ventures, 258
Tokyo Small & Medium Business Investment & Consultation Co., 956
Toll Technologies, 957
Top Taiwan Venture Capital Company, Ltd., 957
Transamerica Mezzanine Financing, 645
Transamerica Technology Finance, 309
Transcap Associates, Inc., 371
Transpac Capital Pte, Ltd., 958
Triad Ventures, Ltd., 682
Triune Capital, 260
TTC Ventures, 453
Ulin & Holland, Inc., 453
Ulster Development Capital, Ltd., 963
UNC Ventures, 453
Union Venture Capital Corporation, 963
Union Venture Corp., 262
UniRock Management Corp., 285
UOB Venture Management Pte Ltd., 964
UST Capital Corp., 454
Valley Capital Corp., 654
Valley Ventures (FKA: Arizona Growth Partners, L.P.), 136
VantagePoint Venture Partners, 263
VCM Venture Capital Management, 965
Vector Fund Management, L.P. (FKA: Vector Securities), 372
Vega Capital Corp., 584
Vencap Equities Alberta, Ltd., 966
Ventana Financial Resources, Inc., 372
Ventana Global, 264
Ventex Management, Inc., 683
Venture Funding Group International, 587
Venture Growth Associates, 265
Venture Investors Management LLC, 720
Venture Management Services Inc. (FKA: AT&T Ventures), 496
Venture Opportunities Corp., 588
Venture Partners, 310
VentureCap Management GmbH (AKA VCH Equity Group AG), 969
Vero Group PLC, 684
Vertex Management, 971
Vertical Group, The, 496
Victory Ventures L.L.C., 588
Viventures Inc., 973
VK Ventures, 268
Vlaamse Investeringvennootschap NV, 974
Wachovia, 340
Walden International Investment Group (AKA: Walden Group), 269
Walden Israel, 975
WaldenVC, 270
Walnut Capital Corp., 701
Warburg, Pincus & Co., LLC. (FKA: E.M. Warburg, Pincus & Co), 590
Wedbush Capital Partners, 271
WestBridge Capital Advisors (India) Pvt. Ltd., 976
Westbury Partners, 592
Western Technology Investment, 272
White Pines Management, L.L.C., 462
WI Harper Group, 273
William A.M. Burden & Co., 593
William E. Simon & Sons (Asia) LDC, 977
Windjammer Capital Investors (FKA:Pacific Mezzanine Inv.), 273
Windward Holdings, 311
WK Associates, 977
Working Ventures Canadian Fund, Inc., 978
Worldview Technology Partners, 275
Worms Capital Management, 594
Yasuda Enterprise Development Co., Ltd.(FKA: Nippon Ent.Dev), 275

Open Market

A.M. Pappas & Associates, 597
Fonds de Solidarité des Travailleurs du Québec (F.T.Q.), 820
Healthcare Ventures LLC (FKA: Healthcare Investments), 490
Josephberg Grosz & Co., Inc., 545
NeoMed Management AS (FKA Medical Venture Management), 894
Oak Investment Partners, 302
Pequot Capital Management Inc., 564

Other

Adams Street Partners, LLC (FKA: Brinson Private Equity), 343
Apax Partners & Cie (AKA: Apax France), 742
CIBC Capital Partners (FKA: CIBC Wood Gundy Capital), 516
Pomona Capital, 566
Venture Capital Fund of America, Inc., 587
Vista Capital Corp., 268

Private Placement

Abell Venture Fund, 390
Beecken, Petty & Co. LLC, 348
Bruce F. Glaspell & Associates, 498
Calgary Enterprises, Inc., 514
Camelot Ventures, 457
CEI Ventures/Coastal Ventures LP, 388
Concord Venture Management (FKA:Nitzanim), 784
Continental S.B.I.C., 691
Continental Venture Capital , 784
Crosbie & Co Inc, 789
De Vries & Co., Inc., 476
Domain Associates, L.L.C., 486
Equinox Investment Partners, 294
Essex Woodlands Health Ventures (FKA:Woodlands Venture Partn, 354
Evergreen Capital Partners Inc, 528
Fonds de Solidarité des Travailleurs du Québec (F.T.Q.), 820
Forward Ventures, 180
Fowler, Anthony & Co., 422
Geocapital Partners, L.L.C., 489
GrowthWorks Capital, 834
Harvest Partners, Inc., 536
Healthcare Ventures LLC (FKA: Healthcare Investments), 490
HT Capital Advisors, LLC, 538
Josephberg Grosz & Co., Inc., 545

Kaiser Permanente (AKA: National Venture Development), 200
Kline Hawkes & Co., 201
M&F Associates, L.P., 549
Marlborough Capital Advisors, 431
MC Capital, Inc., 551
Merifin Capital Group, 883
National Bank Of Kuwait, 555
NeoMed Management AS (FKA Medical Venture Management), 894
Newbridge Capital Limited, 219
Northwood Ventures, 559
Oem Capital, 302
Pacific Corporate Group, Inc., 227
PAMA Group Inc. (FKA:Prudential Asset Management Asia), 908
Pequot Capital Management Inc., 564
ProQuest Investments, L.P., 493
Sandton Financial Group, 240
Shattan Group, The, 574
Venture Associates, Ltd., 285
Wachovia, 340
Warburg, Pincus & Co., LLC. (FKA: E.M. Warburg, Pincus & Co), 590
Working Ventures Canadian Fund, Inc., 978

Public Companies

Citicorp Capital Asia (AKA: CITIC Pacific Ltd.), 780
Essex Woodlands Health Ventures (FKA:Woodlands Venture Partn, 354
Intermediate Capital Group PLC, 855

Recapitalizations

3i Group plc, 726
Aberdeen Murray Johnstone Private Equity, 728
ABN-AMRO Corporate Investments, 729
ACT Venture Capital Ltd., 732
AdCapital AG (FKA Berliner Elektro Holding AG), 732
Advent-Morro Equity Partners, 734
AIG Capital Partners Inc., 503
Allegra Partners (FKA: Lawrence, Smith & Horey), 504
Allied Capital Corporation, 312
Alta Communications, 403
American Acquisition Partners, 483
American Capital Strategies, 391
Ampersand Ventures, 404
Argos Soditic SA, 744
Argosy Partners, 623
Argus Capital Group, 745
Asian Direct Capital Management, 747
AXA Investment Managers Private Equity Europe, 751
Bachow & Associates, Inc., 623
Baird Capital Partners, 347
BancAmerica Capital Investors (FKA:NationsBanc Capital Corp), 598
BancBoston Capital/BancBoston Ventures, 408
Barclays Ventures, 755
Batavia Group, Ltd., The , 511
BayBG Bayerische Beteiligungsgesellschaft mbH, 757
Bedford Capital Corp., 512
Beecken, Petty & Co. LLC, 348
Berlin Capital Fund (FKA LBB Beteiligungsgesellschaft GmbH), 759
Berwind Financial Group, L.P., 623
Boston Capital Ventures, 411
Bridgepoint Capital Ltd (FKA: NWEP & NatWest Ventures Ltd), 763
Bulldog Partners Limited, 764
C3 Holdings, LLC, 474
Cairnsford Associates Ltd., 766
Calgary Enterprises, Inc., 514
Capital Express, L.L.C., 484
Capital Resource Partners, 415
Capital Strategy Management Co., The, 349
CapVis Equity Partners AG, 771
Cariad Capital, Inc., 642
Cascade Communications Ventures, LLC, 159
CEI Ventures/Coastal Ventures LP, 388
Churchill Capital, Inc., 465
Citizens Capital and Citizens Ventures, 418
CIVC Partners (FKA:Continental Illinois Venture Corp.), 350
Coleman Venture Group, 518
Commerz Beteiligungsgesellschaft mbH (CBG), 783
Compass Investment Management Ltd., 783
Continental Venture Capital , 784
Corporate Growth Assistance, Ltd., 786
Crosbie & Co Inc, 789
Cullinane & Donnelly Venture Partners, L.P., 293
Dakota Group, The , 166
De Vries & Co., Inc., 476
Deutsche Beteiligungs AG, 796
DFW Capital Partners (AKA:DeMuth, Folger & Wetherill), 486
Doll Capital Management, 169
ECI Ventures Ltd, 801
EGL Holdings, Inc./Nat West Ventures USA, L.P., 332
Elderstreet Investments Ltd, 803
Electra Partners Asia [FKA: JF Electra Limited], 803
Equinox Investment Partners, 294
Equitas, L.P., 649
Equity Partners Management Pty Ltd, 807
Equity-South (FKA:Grubb & Williams Ltd.), 333
Evergreen Capital Partners Inc, 528
F. Turismo-Capital De Risco SA, 814
Finansa Capital Limited, 816
First Princeton Capital Corp., 489
First Union Capital Partners, 600
Fonds de Solidarité des Travailleurs du Québec (F.T.Q.), 820
Fowler, Anthony & Co., 422
Golub Associates, 534
Granville Baird Capital Partners (FKA:Granville Pr Eq Mngrs), 830
Gresham Rabo Management Limited, 832
GTCR Golder Rauner, LLC, 356
H&Q Asia Pacific, Ltd., 187
Halder Holdings B.V., 835
HANNOVER Finanz GmbH, 837
HarbourVest Partners, LLC., 426
Hibernia Capital Partners, 837
High Street Capital, LLC, 357
Howard, Lawson & Co., 628
HSBC Private Equity Ltd (FKA Montagu Private Equity Ltd), 841
ICC Venture Capital, 845

IKB Venture Capital GmbH (AKA IKB Beteiligungsgesellschaft , 848
Incorporated Investors, 193
Innovest Group, Inc., 629
Intermediate Capital Group PLC, 855
J.P. Morgan Partners (FKA: Chase Capital Partners), 543
Josephberg Grosz & Co., Inc., 545
Life Science Ventures, 873
Lincolnshire Management Inc., 548
Lombard Investments, Inc., 206
LRM Investeringsmaatschappij Voor Limburg, 875
Macquarie Direct Investment Limited, 876
MAVA Investment Management kft (AKA: Hungarian-American Ent), 879
Mayfield Fund, 210
Memhard Investment Bankers, Inc., 300
Mentor Capital Partners, 633
Metapoint Partners, 435
Mezzanine Management UK Limited, 885
Midlands Venture Fund Managers Ltd. (AKA: Midven Ltd), 886
Miller Capital Corp, 135
MVC AG (AKA Mitteldeutsche Venture Capital AG), 891
National City Equity Partners, Inc, 614
Navis Partners (FKA:Fleet Equity Partners), 643
Newbridge Capital Limited, 219
Northwood Ventures, 559
NPE Investment Advisors (AKA:Nordic Private Equity Partners), 903
NPM Capital (AKA Nederlandse Participatie MIJ NV), 903
Oem Capital, 302
Palmer Partners, L.P., 441
PAMA Group Inc. (FKA:Prudential Asset Management Asia), 908
Pantheon Ventures Limited, 908
Penny Lane Partners, 493
Penta Capital Partners Ltd, 911
Pequot Capital Management Inc., 564
Perseus LLC, 316
Pierce Financial Corporation(FKA:Pierce Investment Banking), 698
Point Venture Partners, 636
Prime Capital Management Co., Inc., 304
Priveq Capital Funds, 917
Prospect Street Ventures (FKA:Prospect Street Invest. Mgmt), 567
Quaestus & Co. Inc. (FKA: Quaestus Management Corp..), 719
River Associates, LLC, 653
River Capital, 338
Rock Hill Ventures Inc.(FKA:Hillman Medical Ventures,Inc.), 638
Royal Bank Private Equity (FKA: Royal Bank Development Cap), 922
Sandhurst Venture Fund, L.P., The , 639
Saugatuck Capital Company, 306
Seaflower Ventures, 446
Seaport Capital, 572
Shalor Ventures, Inc., 446
Shelton Companies, Inc., The , 604
Shepherd Group LLC, The, 447
Sierra Ventures, 243
Sigma Partners, 243
Siparex Group (FKA:Siparex Provinces de France), 931
Societe Generale- Private Equity Activity, 933
Sovereign Capital (FKA:Nash, Sells & Partners Limited), 936
Stratford Equity Partners, L.P., 679
SudKB & SudVC, 942
Suez Asia Holdings Pte Ltd., 943
Synerfi S.A., 945
TDH, 639
Texas Growth Fund Management, 681
Thoma Cressey Equity Partners, 371
Thompson Clive & Partners Limited, 955
Tianguis Ltd, 956
UBF Mittelstandsfunanzierungs AG, 962
UBS Capital (AKA Phildrew Ventures), 963
Ulin & Holland, Inc., 453
Venca Management, 263
Venture Capital Partners Pty Limited, 967
Venture Partners, 310
VIV NV (AKA Vlaamse Investeringvennootschap NV), 973
Wachovia, 340
Wachtel & Co., Inc., 317
Warburg, Pincus & Co., LLC. (FKA: E.M. Warburg, Pincus & Co), 590
West Midlands Enterprise Ltd, 976
Wind Point Partners, 462
Windward Holdings, 311
WomenAngles.net, 318
Working Ventures Canadian Fund, Inc., 978

Research and Development

21st Century Internet Management Partners,LLC, 138
2nd Generation Capital Corp, 648
4C Ventures (FKA: Olivetti Holding, N.V.), 501
Academy Funds (FKA: Longleaf Venture Fund LLC), 597
Advanced Materials Partners, Inc., 287
Advent International Corp., 402
Alpine Technology Ventures, 144
Amadeus Capital Partners, 740
Ampersand Ventures, 404
Amphion Ventures L.P.(FKA: Wolfensohn Associates, L.P.), 506
Applied Technology, 405
Arete Corporation, 482
Artesian Capital, 464
Arthur P. Gould & Co., 507
Atlas Venture, 407
Avery Business Development Services, 320
Bailey & Co. Inc., 752
Bausch & Lomb, Inc., 511
Baxter Associates, Inc., 289
BCE Capital, 758
Benchmark Capital, 154
Berwind Financial Group, L.P., 623
BORANCO Management, L.L.C., 277
Boston Financial & Equity Corp., 412
Business Link Doncaster, 765
Capital Network, The (AKA: Texas Capital Network), 659
Carolinas Capital Investment Corp., 599
Castle Group, Ltd., The , 515
Catalyst Ventures, 393
CEI Ventures/Coastal Ventures LP, 388
CEO Advisors, 321
Cerulean Fund/WGC Enterprises, 350
Chase H&Q (FKA Hambrecht & Quist), 160
Chestnut Street Partners, Inc., 417
China Venture Management, Inc., 777

Collinson, Howe & Lennox, LLC, 291
Columbine Venture Funds, The , 279
Crestview Financial Group, The , 292
CW Group, Inc., 521
Cygnus Venture Partners, 791
D.H. Blair Investment Banking Corp., 521
Danish Development Finance Corp., 793
Defta Partners, 167
Doll Capital Management, 169
Domain Associates, L.L.C., 486
Dongbu Venture Capital Co Ltd, 797
Drug Royalty Corp., Inc., 798
ECICS Ventures Pte Ltd., 801
EDF Ventures (F.K.A. Enterprise Development Fund), 458
Emerald Venture Group, 177
EnCompass Ventures, 704
Evergreen Canada Israel Investments Ltd, 812
Federal Business Development Bank, 815
Financial Technology Research Corp., 529
Fonds de Solidarité des Travailleurs du Québec (F.T.Q.), 820
Foundation Capital, 181
Frazier & Company, 705
GATX Ventures (FKA: Meier Mitchell & Co.), 183
GCI Venture Partners, 314
Global Partner Ventures, 694
Granite Ventures LLC (FKA: H & Q Venture Associates), 186
GrowthWorks Capital, 834
H&Q Asia Pacific, Ltd., 187
Hallador Venture Partners, 188
Humana Venture Capital, 384
Hummer Winblad Venture Partners, 191
IBK Capital Corporation, 844
Industrial Technology Securities Ltd, 851
InnovationsKapital Management Goteborg AB , 854
ISEP NV, 860
Josephberg Grosz & Co., Inc., 545
Kansas Technology Enterprise Corporation, 382
Kemper Ventures, 491
Korda & Co., 868
Korea Technology Finance Corp., 869
Lighthouse Capital Partners, 205
LINC Capital Partners, Inc., 361
Matrix Capital, 695
MBA Venture Group, 669
MDS Discovery Venture Management, Inc., 881
Med-Tech Ventures, Inc., 492
Medmax Ventures, L.P., 299
MedTech International, Inc., 670
Menlo Ventures, 212
Mid-Atlantic Venture Funds (FKA: NEPA Management Corp.), 634
Mitsui & Co., Ltd., 553
Montgomery Associates, Inc., 215
Moore Capital Management Inc., 554
Multiventure Investment, Inc., 890
NextGen Partners LLC, 221
North Bridge Venture Partners, 438
North Carolina Technological Development Authority, Inc., 603
Northeast Ventures Corp., 469
Northwest Ohio Venture Fund, 615
Northwest Venture Associates, Inc.(FKA:Spokane Capital Mgmt), 709
NPV Capital Partners, LLC, 560
Obelisk Capital Pty Ltd, 904
Oregon Resource and Technology Development Fund, 620
Oxford Bioscience Partners, 440
Oxford Financial Services Corp., 698
Pacific Venture Group, 227
Palmetto Seed Capital Corp., 645
Perennial Ventures (FKA: Tredegar Investments), 711
Phoenix Home Life Mutual Insurance Co., 303
Phoenix Partners, The , 711
ProQuest Investments, L.P., 493
RCT BioVentures NE (Research Corporation Technologies), 442
Regulus International Capital Co., Inc., 304
Rock Hill Ventures Inc.(FKA:Hillman Medical Ventures,Inc.), 638
Rothschild Ventures, Inc., 570
SAE Ventures, 306
Sandler Capital Management, 571
Sapient Capital, 721
SBC Ventures, 499
SBV Venture Partners (AKA:Sigefi, Burnette & Vallee), 240
Seaflower Ventures, 446
Shott Capital Management, 574
Sitra (AKA Finnish National Fund for Research and Dev.), 932
Southwest Venture Group, 678
Speirs Consultants, Inc., 938
Spray Venture Partners, 450
Sweeney & Co., Inc., 308
Telos Venture Partners, 256
Third Millennium Venture Capital, Ltd., 256
Transamerica Technology Finance, 309
Triad Investors Corp, 319
Venrock Associates, 586
Ventana Financial Resources, Inc., 372
Venture Funding Group International, 587
Venture Funding, Ltd., 461
Ventures West Management, Inc., 970
Vertical Group, The, 496
Walden Israel, 975
Western States Investment Group, 272
Western Technology Investment, 272
Working Ventures Canadian Fund, Inc., 978
Worldview Technology Partners, 275
YankeeTek Ventures, 456
Yasuda Enterprise Development Co., Ltd.(FKA: Nippon Ent.Dev), 275

Second Stage Financing

1st Source Capital Corp., 375
21st Century Health Ventures, 129
21st Century Internet Management Partners,LLC, 138
2nd Generation Capital Corp, 648
3i Finland Oy (FKA SFK Finance), 725
3i Group plc, 726
4C Ventures (FKA: Olivetti Holding, N.V.), 501
A.M. Pappas & Associates, 597
Abell Venture Fund, 390
Aberdare Ventures, 138
Aberdeen Asset Managers, 728
Aberdeen Murray Johnstone Private Equity, 728
Aberlyn Capital Management Co., Inc., 501
Abingworth Venture Management Limited, 729

ABS Ventures, 390
Acacia Venture Partners, 139
Acer Technology Ventures(FKA:Acer Soft Capital Inc.), 141
ACF Equity Atlantic, Inc, 731
Acorn Ventures, Inc., 141
ACT Venture Capital Ltd., 732
Adams, Harkness & Hill, Inc., 401
Adler & Co., 502
Adler & Shaykin, 502
Advanced Materials Partners, Inc., 287
Advanced Technology Development Fund, 330
Advanced Technology Ventures, 401
Advanta Partners, L.P., 622
Advantage Capital Partners, 386
Advent International Corp., 402
Advent-Morro Equity Partners, 734
Affinity Capital Management(FKA:Peterson-Spencer-Fansler Co), 463
Agilent Ventures, 142
Agio Capital Partners I, L.P., 463
Agribusiness Partners International Partners, 479
Alan I. Goldman & Associates, 483
Albemarle Private Equity Ltd, 735
Alchemy Partners, 736
Alexander Hutton, Inc., 702
Alignment Capital Partners, LLC, 655
Alimansky Capital Group, Inc., 504
Allegra Partners (FKA: Lawrence, Smith & Horey), 504
Alliance Financial of Houston, 655
Alliance Technology Ventures, 330
Allsop Venture Partners, 380
Allstate Private Equity, 344
Alpha Capital Partners, Inc., 344
Alpine Technology Ventures, 144
Alpinvest Holding NV (AKA NIB Capital Private Equity NV), 739
Alta Communications, 403
Alta Partners, 144
Altos Ventures, 144
Amadeus Capital Partners, 740
American Research & Development Corp., 404
American Securities, L.P., 505
Amerimark Capital Group, 656
Amerindo Investment Advisors, Inc., 505
Ameritech Development Corp., 345
Ampersand Ventures, 404
Amphion Ventures L.P.(FKA: Wolfensohn Associates, L.P.), 506
AMT Capital Ltd. (AKA: AMT Venture Partners, Ltd.), 656
Antares Capital Corp. (FKA: Antares Leveraged Capital Corp), 345
Antares Capital Corporation (FKA: Harbor Ventures Corp.), 320
Anthem Capital, L.P., 391
APIDC-Venture Capital Limited, 743
Applied Technology, 405
Ardsheil, Inc., 506
Argentum Group, The , 507
Argos Soditic SA, 744
Arkoma Venture Partners, 657
Artemis Ventures, 146
Artesian Capital, 464
Arthur P. Gould & Co., 507
ASC Group, 746
Atlantic Medical Management, LLC, 508
Atlas Venture, 407
Atle Foretagskapital AB (FKA Foretagskapital AB), 749
Austin Ventures, L.P., 657
Australian Technology Group Ltd, 750
Authosis, 149
AVI Capital, L.P., 149
Aweida Ventures, 277
Ayala Internet Venture Partners, 751
BA Venture Partners (AKA: BankAmerica Ventures), 150
Baccharis Capital, Inc., 150
Bachow & Associates, Inc., 623
Banc One Capital Partners, 608
BancAmerica Capital Investors (FKA:NationsBanc Capital Corp), 598
Bancorp Hawaii SBIC, Inc., 341
BANEXI Corp., 753
Bangert Dawes Reade Davis & Thom, 151
Bank Funds, The, 347
Bank One Equity Investors, Inc., 386
Bankers Trust New York Corp./Deutsche Banc Alex Brown, 510
Banque De Vizille, 754
Baring Private Equity Partners (FKA:Baring Venture Partners), 755
Batavia Group, Ltd., The , 511
Batavia Investment Management Ltd, 756
Battelle Venture Partners (Scientific Advances), 608
Batterson Venture Partners(AKA:BVP), 348
BCR Asset Management Pty Ltd., 758
Beacon Partners, Inc., 289
Bedford Capital Corp., 512
Beecken, Petty & Co. LLC, 348
Behrman Capital, 512
Benchmark Capital, 154
Berkeley International Capital Corp., 154
Berwind Financial Group, L.P., 623
Bessemer Venture Partners, 410
Betwin Investments, Inc., 760
Birchmere Ventures, Inc.(FKA:Birchmere Investments), 624
Bloom & Co., 512
Blue Chip Venture Company, 609
BlueStar Ventures, 348
BOME Investors, Inc., 473
BORANCO Management, L.L.C., 277
Boston Capital Ventures, 411
Boston Financial & Equity Corp., 412
Boston Millennia Partners, 412
Boston University Community Technology Fund , 413
Boston Ventures Management, Inc., 413
Botts & Co., 762
Brad Peery Capital, 156
Brand Equity Ventures, 289
Bridgepoint Capital Ltd (FKA: NWEP & NatWest Ventures Ltd), 763
Bristol Capital Management, 513
Bristol Investment Trust, 413
British Steel Ltd., 764
Broadmark Capital Corp., 702
Bruce F. Glaspell & Associates, 498
Buena Venture Associates, 659
Burr, Egan, Deleage & Co., 414
Burrill & Company, 156
Business Link Doncaster, 765
Butler Capital Partners France, 765

Cable & Howse Ventures, 703
Calgary Enterprises, Inc., 514
Cambria Group, The, 157
Cambridge Technology Capital, 415
Cambridge Venture Partners, 375
Camelot Ventures, 457
Canaan Partners, 290
Canbank Venture Capital Fund Ltd, 767
Capital Development & Investment Co. Ltd., 768
Capital Express, L.L.C., 484
Capital Insights, L.L.C., 645
Capital Investments, Inc., 717
Capital Investors, 690
Capital Network, The (AKA: Texas Capital Network), 659
Capital Prive (FKA NatWest Equity Partners, France), 769
Capital Resource Partners, 415
Capital Services & Resources, Inc., 648
Capital Southwest Corporation, 660
Capital Strategy Management Co., The, 349
Capstone Ventures SBIC, L.P., 158
Cardinal Partners (FKA: Cardinal Health Partners), 485
Cardinal Ventures, L.L.C., 375
Carillon Capital, Inc., 610
Carolinas Capital Investment Corp., 599
Castile Ventures, 416
Castle Group, Ltd., The , 515
Catalyst Group, The , 660
Catterton Partners, 290
Cazenove Private Equity, 773
CB Health Ventures LLC, 416
CD Technicom S.A., 774
CE Unterberg Towbin (FKA:Unterberg Harris Capital Partners), 515
CEI Ventures/Coastal Ventures LP, 388
CEO Venture Fund, 625
Chanen, Painter & Co., Ltd., 703
Charter Ventures, 160
Chartwell Capital Management Co., Inc., 321
Chase H&Q (FKA Hambrecht & Quist), 160
China Venture Management, Inc., 777
Chisholm Private Capital Partners, 618
Chrysalis Ventures, 384
CIBC Capital Partners (FKA: CIBC Wood Gundy Capital), 516
CID Equity Partners, 376
Circle Ventures, Inc., 376
CIT Group/Venture Capital, Inc., The, 485
Citicorp Venture Capital, Ltd., 517
Citizens Capital and Citizens Ventures, 418
Clarion Capital Corp., 610
CM Equity Partners, 517
CMEA Ventures (FKA:Chemicals & Materials Enterprise Associa), 161
Cohen & Co., L.L.C., 517
Coleman Swenson Booth Inc.(FKA:Coleman Swenson Hoffman Booth, 649
Colorado Venture Management, 278
Columbia Capital Group, Inc., 313
Comdisco Ventures, 162
Compass Investment Management Ltd., 783
ComVentures (AKA: Communications Ventures), 163
Concord Venture Management (FKA:Nitzanim), 784
Connecticut Innovations, Inc., 291
Conning Capital Partners, 292
Consumer Venture Partners, 292
Continental S.B.I.C., 691
Continental Venture Capital , 784
Copley Venture Partners, 420
Core Capital Partners, 313
Coronado Venture Fund, 133
Corporate Growth Assistance, Ltd., 786
Cowen & Co., 520
Crescendo Venture Management LLC (FKA:IAI Ventures), 466
Crest Communications Holdings LLC, 520
Crestview Financial Group, The , 292
Crocker Capital/Crocker Assoc., 164
CrossBow Ventures, 322
Crown Advisors International, Ltd., 521
Crown Capital Corp, 475
CS Capital Partners, LLC, 486
CSK Venture Capital Co., Ltd., 789
Cullinane & Donnelly Venture Partners, L.P., 293
Cureton & Co., Inc., 662
CW Group, Inc., 521
Cygnus Venture Partners, 791
Czech Venture Partners Sro, 791
Daimler Chrysler Venture Gmbh (AKA DCV), 792
Daiwa Business Investment Co Ltd, The, 793
Dakota Group, The , 166
Dali, Hook Partners (FKA: Hook Partners), 662
Dauphin Capital Partners, 522
Davis, Tuttle Venture Partners, L.P.(FKA:Davis Venture), 618
De Vries & Co., Inc., 476
Dean & Associates, 279
Defta Partners, 167
Delphi Ventures, 167
Delta Partners, 795
Deucalion Venture Partners, 168
Deutsche Bank eVentures (AKA DB eVentures), 795
Digital Partners, 704
Divine interVentures (FKA: Platinum Venture Partners), 351
Domain Associates, L.L.C., 486
Dongbu Venture Capital Co Ltd, 797
Dorset Capital, 170
Dougery Ventures, 171
Dow Chemical Co., 458
Downer & Co., 420
Draper International, 172
Draper Richards, 173
Dresdner Kleinwort Capital , 524
Dresner Capital Resources, Inc., 352
Drysdale Enterprises, 173
Duchossois TECnology Partners, LLC, 353
East River Ventures, L.P., 524
ECI Ventures Ltd, 801
ECICS Ventures Pte Ltd., 801
Edelson Technology Partners, 487
EDF Ventures (F.K.A. Enterprise Development Fund), 458
Edge Capital Investment Co., LLC, 175
EGL Holdings, Inc./Nat West Ventures USA, L.P., 332
Electra Partners Asia [FKA: JF Electra Limited], 803
Elk Associates Funding Corp., 526
Emerald Venture Group, 177
EnCompass Ventures, 704
EnerTech Capital Partners, L.P., 626

Enterprise Equity (NI) Limited, 805
Enterprise Investors, 526
Enterprise Merchant Bank, 382
Eos Partners, L.P., 527
Equitas, L.P., 649
Equity Partners Management Pty Ltd, 807
Equity Ventures, Ltd, 807
Essex Woodlands Health Ventures (FKA:Woodlands Venture Partn, 354
ETCapital Ltd (AKA: Egan & Talbot Capital Ltd), 808
EuclidSR Partners , 527
Euroc Venture Capital Corporation, 809
European Acquisition Capital Ltd., 810
eVerger Associates, 812
Evergreen Canada Israel Investments Ltd, 812
Evergreen Capital Partners Inc, 528
Evergreen Ventures, 686
Exeter Capital, L.P., 528
Fairfax Partners, 693
Far East Capital Corp., 179
Federal Business Development Bank, 815
Ferrer Freeman Thompson & Co, 295
Fidelity Ventures (FKA: Fidelity Venture Associates), 421
Financial Technology Research Corp., 529
Financial Technology Ventures, 179
Firemark Advisors, Inc., 488
First Capital Management Co., 664
First Charter Partners, Inc., 664
First Growth Capital, Inc., 333
First Princeton Capital Corp., 489
First Security Business Investment Corp., 686
First Union Capital Partners, 600
FJC Growth Capital Corp., 129
Florida Capital Ventures, Ltd., 323
Fluke Venture Partners., 705
Fond Riziveho Kapitalu SRO, 819
Fonds D'Investissements R.T.V.L., 819
Fonds de Solidarité des Travailleurs du Québec (F.T.Q.), 820
Food Fund Ltd. Partnership, The, 467
Forrest Binkley & Brown, 180
Forward Ventures, 180
Foundation Capital, 181
Foundation Capital Limited, 822
Fowler, Anthony & Co., 422
Frazier & Company, 705
Frederic H. Mayerson Group, The, 612
Friulia SpA Fin.Reg.Friuli-Venezia, 824
Frontenac Co., 355
Frost Capital Partners, 182
Future Value Ventures, Inc., 717
G-51 Capital LLC, 665
Gabelli Multimedia Partners, 531
Galen Associates (FKA:Galen Partners), 531
Gamma Investors LLC, 627
Gateway Associates, L.P., 476
GATX Ventures (FKA: Meier Mitchell & Co.), 183
GATX/MM Venture Partners, 183
GCI, 718
Gemini Investors LLC (AKA: GMN Investors), 423
Generation Capital Partners, 532
GENES GmbH Venture Services, 826
Genesee Funding, Inc., 532
Genesis Capital, Inc., 533
Geneva Merchant Banking Partners, 601
Gideon Hixon Fund, 467
Gilde Investment Management, 827
Giza Venture Capital (FKA Giza Investment Management), 828
Global Crossing Ventures (FKA: Frontier Ventures), 185
Global Partner Ventures, 694
Global Retail Partners (A.K.A. GRP), 185
Glynn Ventures, 186
Golub Associates, 534
Graphite Capital (FKA: F&C Ventures Ltd), 831
Grayson & Associates, 280
Greater Philadelphia Venture Capital Corp., 627
Green Mountain Advisors, Inc., 689
Greenwich Venture Partners, Inc., 296
Gresham Rabo Management Limited, 832
Grieve, Horner, Brown & Asculai, 833
Grotech Capital Group, 394
Grove Street Advisors, LLC, 425
GrowthWorks Capital, 834
Gryphon Ventures, 425
Hallador Venture Partners, 188
Halpern, Denny & Co., 425
Hambro America Biosciences, Inc., 535
Hanbyuck Investment Co Ltd, 836
Hanover Capital Corp., 535
Harbour Financial Co., 426
HarbourVest Partners, LLC., 426
Health Capital Group, 188
Healthcare Ventures LLC (FKA: Healthcare Investments), 490
Heartland Capital Fund, Ltd., 479
Heartland Capital Partners, L.P., 665
Hellman & Friedman, 189
Henry & Co., 323
Herbert Young Securities, Inc., 536
Highland Capital Partners, 427
HillStreet Capital, Inc., 612
Hodgson Martin, Ltd., 839
Hollinger Capital (FKA: Hollinger Ventures), 537
Horizon Ventures (F.K.A. Technology Investments), 190
Hotung International Company, Ltd., 840
Houston Venture Partners (AKA: Houston Partners), 666
Howard, Lawson & Co., 628
HSBC Private Equity (Asia), Ltd. (FKA: HSBC PE Management), 841
HT Capital Advisors, LLC, 538
Humana Venture Capital, 384
Hummer Winblad Venture Partners, 191
Hungarian-American Enterprise Fund, The (HAEF), 842
Hunt Capital Group, 667
Hydro-Quebec CapiTech Inc., 843
IBK Capital Corporation, 844
ICC Venture Capital, 845
Idanta Partners, Ltd., 191
IEG Venture Management, Inc., 357
Imperial Ventures, Inc., 193
Impex Venture Management Co., 540
Incorporated Investors, 193
Indekon Management Oy, 849
Indian Direct Equity Advisors Pvt. Ltd, 850
Indosuez Ventures, 194
Industrial Technology Securities Ltd, 851

Industry Ventures , 428
Inman & Bowman, 195
InnoCal, L.P., 196
Innova Capital (FKA: Poland Partners Management Company), 853
Innovacom, 853
Innovationsagentur Gesmbh, 854
InnovationsKapital Management Goteborg AB , 854
Innovest Group, Inc., 629
Innvotec Ltd, 854
Institutional Venture Partners, 196
Insurance Venture Partners, Inc., 297
Integrated Consortium, Inc., 197
InterEquity Capital Partners, L.P., 541
InterWest Partners, 197
InvestAmerica Venture Group, Inc., 380
Investissement Desjardins, 857
IPS Industrial Promotion Services, Ltd., 859
ISEP NV, 860
Itochu Technology, 542
J.L. Albright Venture Partners, 861
J.P. Morgan Capital Corp., 542
J.P. Morgan Partners (FKA: Chase Capital Partners), 543
JAFCO Ventures, Inc., 198
James A. Matzdorff & Co., 199
JK&B Capital, 358
Jordan, Edmiston Group, Inc., The , 545
Josephberg Grosz & Co., Inc., 545
Justsystem, Inc., 629
Kaiser Permanente (AKA: National Venture Development), 200
Kankaku Investment Co Ltd, 865
Kansas Venture Capital, Inc., 383
KB Partners, LLC, 359
KBL Healthcare Ventures, 546
Kemper Ventures, 491
Kentucky Highlands Investment Corporation, 384
Kettle Partners, L.P., 359
Key Equity Capital Corp.(AKA:Key Community Development Corp), 613
Keystone Minority Capital Fund, L.P., 630
Keystone Venture Capital Management Co., 630
Kidd, Kamm & Company, 298
Kinetic Ventures, Inc., 395
Kingsbury Associates, 200
Kirlan Venture Capital, Inc., 707
KLB Investment Co., Ltd., 866
Kleiner Perkins Caufield & Byers, 200
Kline Hawkes & Co., 201
Kookmin Venture Capital Co Ltd, 867
Korea Development Investment Corp., 868
Kyocera International, Inc., 202
Lake Shore Capital Partners, Inc., 360
Lambda Funds, The, 546
Landmark Partners, Inc., 298
Las Americas Administradora, 871
Lawrence Financial Group, 202
Lazard Technology Partners, 547
Lee Munder Venture Partners, 430
Lepercq Capital Management, Inc.(AKA:Lepercq,de Neuflize In), 548
LF International, Inc., 204
Liberty BIDCO Investment Corporation, 459
Liberty Environmental Partners, 205
Lighthouse Capital Partners, 205
Lightspeed Venture Partners (FKA: Weiss, Peck & Greer), 206
LINC Capital Partners, Inc., 361
Lincoln Investment Management Inc., 378
LiveOak Equity Partners, 335
Livingston Capital, Ltd., 281
LJH Global Investments , 324
Loyalhanna Venture Fund, 631
LTI Ventures Leasing Corp., 298
Lubar & Co., 718
Lucent Venture Partners, Inc., 207
Lycos Ventures, 632
M&F Associates, L.P., 549
Madison Investment Partners, Inc., 550
Malmohus Invest AB, 877
Manhattan Venture Co., Inc., 550
Marconi Ventures, 431
Maristeth Ventures, L.L.C., 707
MarketCorp Ventures L.P., 299
Marleau, Lemire, Inc., 878
Marquette Venture Partners, 362
Maryland Venture Capital Trust, 395
Massachusetts Capital Resource Co., 432
Materia Ventures Associates,L.P. (FKA:Pierce Nordquist Asso), 708
Maton Venture, 209
Matrix Capital, 695
Matrix Partners, 433
Mayfield Fund, 210
MBA Venture Group, 669
MBW Management, Inc., 492
MC Capital, Inc., 551
McGraw-Hill Ventures, 552
McGuire Capital Corp., 670
McKee & Co., 134
McLean Watson Capital Inc., 880
MDS Discovery Venture Management, Inc., 881
Med-Tech Ventures, Inc., 492
Media Venture Partners, 211
Medical Science Partners, 434
Medical Venture Holdings, Inc., 552
Medmax Ventures, L.P., 299
MedTech International, Inc., 670
Mees Pierson Investeringsmaat. B.V., 435
Memhard Investment Bankers, Inc., 300
Menlo Ventures, 212
Mercury Private Equity, 883
Meridian Venture Partners (MVP), 633
Merifin Capital Group, 883
Merita Capital Limited, 134
Merrill Lynch Investment Managers FKA Mercury Asset Mgmt, 884
Merrill, Pickard, Anderson & Eyre, 213
MESBIC Ventures Holding Co. (AKA Pacesetter Growth Fund, L.P, 671
Mesirow Private Equity Investments, Inc., 362
Meyer, Duffy & Associates, 553
Mid-Atlantic Venture Funds (FKA: NEPA Management Corp.), 634
Middlefield Capital Fund, 885
Midlands Venture Fund Managers Ltd. (AKA: Midven Ltd), 886

Millennium Three Venture Group, L.L.C., 480
Miller Capital Corp, 135
Miralta Capital, Inc., 887
Mitsui & Co., Ltd., 553
MK Global Ventures, 214
Montgomerie, Huck & Co., 888
Montgomery Associates, Inc., 215
Montreux Equity Partners, 216
Moore & Associates, 619
Moore Capital Management Inc., 554
Morgan Grenfell Private Equity Limited, 889
Morgan Stanley Venture Partners (AKA: MSDW), 554
Morgenthaler Ventures, 614
Motorola Inc., 315
Mountaineer Capital LP, 716
MTI Partners Ltd, 890
Murphree Venture Partners, 671
Mustang Ventures (FKA Siemens Mustang Ventures), 216
MVP Ventures (AKA: Milk Street Ventures), 436
MWV Capital Partners (FKA:Middlewest Ventures, L.P.), 378
Nassau Capital, L.L.C., 492
National Bank Of Kuwait, 555
National City Equity Partners, Inc, 614
Native Venture Capital Co., Ltd., 893
Natural Gas Partners, 300
Navis Partners (FKA:Fleet Equity Partners), 643
Nazem & Co., 556
Nelson Capital Corp., 651
NeoMed Management AS (FKA Medical Venture Management), 894
New England Partners, 437
New Enterprise Associates, 396
New Vista Capital, LLC, 218
New York Life Venture Capital Group, 557
New York State Science & Technology Foundation, 558
Newbury Ventures, 220
Newbury, Piret & Co., Inc., 437
Newtek Ventures, 220
NextGen Capital LLC, 697
NextGen Partners LLC, 221
NextPoint Partners L.P.(FKA: Plaza Street), 315
NIB Capital Private Equity N.V. (FKA: Parnib Holding NV) , 898
NIF Ventures USA, Inc.(Nippon Investment & Finance Co., Ltd), 222
Nikko Capital Co Ltd, 899
Nokia Venture Partners (AKA: Nokia Oy), 222
Nomura/JAFCO Investment (HK) Limited, 901
Noro-Moseley Partners, 336
North American Capital Corp., 559
North Atlantic Capital Corp., 389
North Bridge Venture Partners, 438
North Carolina Technological Development Authority, Inc., 603
North Hill Ventures, 438
North Texas MESBIC, Inc., 672
Northeast Ventures Corp., 469
Northern Venture Managers Limited, 902
Northwest Ohio Venture Fund, 615
Northwest Venture Associates, Inc.(FKA:Spokane Capital Mgmt), 709
Northwood Ventures, 559
Noveltek Venture Corp., 560
Nth Power Technologies, Inc, 224
Nu Capital Access Group, Ltd., 224
Oak Investment Partners, 302
Odin Capital Group, 479
Ohana Ventures, LLC, 615
Ohio Partners, 615
OmniMed Corp., 673
Opportunity Capital Partners {FKA: Thompson Capital Mgt), 225
Oresa Ventures, S.A., 906
Orion Partners, L.P., 439
Oxford Financial Services Corp., 698
PA Early Stage (AKA:Pennsylvania Early Stage Partners), 635
Pacific Venture Group, 227
Pacifica Fund , 228
Palmer Partners, L.P., 441
Pappajohn Capital Resources, 381
Paradigm Capital Partners LLC, 651
Paragon Venture Partners, 229
Partech International, 229
Pathfinder Investment Co Pvt Ltd, 910
Pathfinder Venture Capital Funds, 470
Patricof & Co. Ventures, Inc., 563
Pauli & Co., Inc., 477
Peninsula Capital Partners, L.L.C, 460
Penn-Janney Fund, Inc., The, 635
Pennsylvania Growth Fund, 636
Penny Lane Partners, 493
Pequot Capital Management Inc., 564
Perennial Ventures (FKA: Tredegar Investments), 711
Philadelphia Ventures, Inc., 636
Phillips-Smith Specialty Retail Group, 673
Phoenix Equity Partners (FKA: DLJ European Private Equity), 911
Phoenix Growth Capital Corp., 231
Phoenix Home Life Mutual Insurance Co., 303
Phoenix Partners, The , 711
Pierce Financial Corporation(FKA:Pierce Investment Banking), 698
Pittsford Group, Inc., The , 565
Platinum Group, Inc., The , 565
Point Venture Partners, 636
Polaris Venture Partners, 441
Polestar Capital, Inc., 366
Poly Ventures, 566
Pomona Capital, 566
Premier Medical Partner Fund L.P., 231
Prime Capital Management Co., Inc., 304
Prince Ventures, 367
Prism Capital, 367
Private Capital Corp., 131
Private Equity Investors, Inc., 567
Private Equity Partners, 674
Priveq Capital Funds, 917
Productivity Fund I & II, The, 367
ProQuest Investments, L.P., 493
Prospect Street Ventures (FKA:Prospect Street Invest. Mgmt), 567
Provco Group, The , 637
ProVen Private Equity (FKA:Guinness Mahon Development Cap.), 918
Putnam Lovell Capital Partners, L.P., 232
Pythagoras NV, 919
Quest Ventures, 233
Quester Capital Management Ltd, 920
QuestMark Partners, L.P., 397

R-H Capital Partners, 337
R. Chaney & Co., Inc., 674
RAF Ventures, 637
Ralph Wilson Equity Fund, L.L.C., 460
Rand Capital Corporation, 568
Raza Foundries, 233
RBC Ventures, Inc., 619
Red River Ventures, 675
Redleaf Venture Management, 234
Redwood Capital Corp., 235
Regent Capital Management, 569
Renaissance Capital Corp., 337
RFE Investment Partners, 305
Richland Ventures, 652
Riordan, Lewis & Haden, 236
Roanoke Capital, Ltd., 712
Robertson Stephens & Company, LLC, 236
Rock Hill Ventures Inc.(FKA:Hillman Medical Ventures,Inc.), 638
Rosecliff, 237
Rosenfeld & Co., 620
Rosewood Capital, L.P., 237
Rothschild Bioscience Unit, 922
Rothschild Ventures, Inc., 570
Royal Bank Private Equity (FKA: Royal Bank Development Cap), 922
Royalty Capital Fund, L.P. I/Royalty Capital Management, Inc, 443
RRE Ventures LLC, 571
Ruddick Investment Co., 604
RWI Group, LP, 239
S.R. One, Limited, 638
SAE Ventures, 306
Sagaponack Partners LLC, 239
Sage Management Group, 444
Sandhurst Venture Fund, L.P., The , 639
Sandler Capital Management, 571
Saskatchewan Government Growth Fund, 925
SBC Equity Partners, Inc., 369
SBCA/A.G. Bartholomew & Associates, 131
SBV Venture Partners (AKA:Sigefi, Burnette & Vallee), 240
Schneider Electric Ventures, 926
Schooner Capital International, L.P., 444
Schroder Ventures, 445
Scripps Ventures, 572
Seacoast Capital, 446
Seaflower Ventures, 446
Seaport Capital, 572
Selby Venture Partners, 241
SENMED Medical Ventures, 616
Sequoia Capital, 241
SGI Capital L.L.C, 573
Shad Run Investments, Inc., 242
Shalor Ventures, Inc., 446
Shannon Development Company, 929
Shared Ventures, Inc., 470
Shattan Group, The, 574
Shaw Venture Partners (FKA: Shaw Glasgow Partners), 621
Shawmut Capital Partners, 447
Shelton Companies, Inc., The , 604
Shepherd Group LLC, The, 447
Sherbrooke Capital Partners, 448
Shott Capital Management, 574
SI Ventures, 326
Sienna Ventures (FKA: Sienna Holdings Inc.), 242
Sierra Ventures, 243
Sigma Capital Corp., 327
Sigma Partners, 243
Siguler Guff & Company, LLC, 575
Silicon Valley Bank, 244
Silver Creek Technology Investors (FKA: O'Donnell & Masur), 677
Societe Regionale d'Investissement de Bruxelles (SRIB/GIMB), 933
Sofinnova Ventures, 246
SOFTBANK Capital Partners, 448
Sorrento Associates, Inc., 247
SoundView Financial Group, Inc., 307
South Atlantic Venture Funds, L.P., 327
Southeastern Technology Fund, 132
Southport Partners, 307
Southwest Venture Group, 678
Southwest Venture Partnerships, The, 678
Sovereign Capital (FKA:Nash, Sells & Partners Limited), 936
SpaceVest, 699
Speirs Consultants, Inc., 938
Spencer Trask Ventures, Inc. (FKA: Spencer Trask Securities), 576
Spire Capital (FKA: Waller Capital Corp.), 577
Sponsored Consulting Services, 249
Spray Venture Partners, 450
Spring Capital Partners, L.P., 398
SRK Management Co., 578
SsangYong Cement (Singapore) Ltd, 939
Standard Life Investments (Private Equity) Ltd, 939
Stephens Group, Inc., 137
Sterling Grace Capital Management, L.P., 579
Sterling/Carl Marks Capital {FKA - Sterling Commercial, 580
Still River Fund, The, 450
Stolberg Partners, 580
Strategic Capital Management, 941
Sucsy, Fischer & Co., 370
Suez Asia Holdings Pte Ltd., 943
Summit Capital Associates, Inc., 581
Summit Partners, 451
Sun Valley Ventures, 250
Sundance Venture Partners, L.P., 251
Sunwestern Investment Group, 680
Sutter Hill Ventures, 251
Swander Pace Capital, 252
Sweeney & Co., Inc., 308
Sybase, Inc., 252
Sycamore Ventures, 494
Synerfi S.A., 945
Synopsys, Inc., 253
Tailink Venture Partners, 946
TCR Europe SA, 947
TDH, 639
Teak Investment Partners I Limited, 948
Techno-Venture Co. (Japan), 949
Technologieholding VC GmbH, 950
Technology Crossover Ventures, 254
Technology Funding, 254
Technology Partners, 255
Technology Venture Partners Pty Ltd, 950
Technology Ventures Corp., 500

Techxas Ventures, LLC, 681
Teknoinvest Management As, 952
Telos Venture Partners, 256
Telsoft Ventures, 953
Texas Growth Fund Management, 681
THCG Inc., 582
Third Millennium Venture Capital, Ltd., 256
Thompson Clive, Inc., 257
Thorner Ventures, 258
Throunarfelag Islands Plc(AKA:The Icelandic Finance&Invest.), 955
Tianguis Ltd, 956
Tokyo Small & Medium Business Investment & Consultation Co., 956
Transamerica Mezzanine Financing, 645
Transamerica Technology Finance, 309
Transatlantic Capital Ltd., 958
Transcap Associates, Inc., 371
Trellis Partners, 682
Triad Investors Corp, 319
Triad Ventures, Ltd., 682
Tribune Ventures, 372
Trident Capital, 259
Triune Capital, 260
TSG Capital Group, L.L.C., 309
TTC Ventures, 453
U.S. Medical Resources Corp., 616
U.S. Venture Partners, 261
UBS Capital, 962
UBS Capital (AKA Phildrew Ventures), 963
Ulin & Holland, Inc., 453
Ulster Development Capital, Ltd., 963
UNC Ventures, 453
Union Street Capital Corp., 713
Union Venture Corp., 262
UniRock Management Corp., 285
UPS Strategic Enterprise Fund, 339
US Trust Private Equity, 584
Valley Capital Corp., 654
Valley Ventures (FKA: Arizona Growth Partners, L.P.), 136
VantagePoint Venture Partners, 263
VCM Venture Capital Management, 965
Vega Capital Corp., 584
Venca Management, 263
Vencap Equities Alberta, Ltd., 966
Vencon Management, Inc., 585
VenGlobal Capital, 264
Venrock Associates, 586
Ventana Financial Resources, Inc., 372
Ventana Global, 264
Ventex Management, Inc., 683
Venture Associates, Ltd., 285
Venture Capital Fund Managers (Pty), Ltd., The , 967
Venture Capital Fund of New England, The, 454
Venture Capital Management Corp., 328
Venture Capital Partners Pty Limited, 967
Venture First Associates, 328
Venture Funding Group International, 587
Venture Growth Associates, 265
Venture Investment Management Company LLC (AKA: VIMAC), 454
Venture Investors Management LLC, 720
Venture Management Services Inc. (FKA: AT&T Ventures), 496
Venture Opportunities Corp., 588
Venture Select, 968
Ventures West Management, Inc., 970
Vero Group PLC, 684
Vertex Management, 971
Vertical Group, The, 496
Victory Ventures L.L.C., 588
Vision Capital Management (FKA Glenwood Capital), 267
Vista Capital de Expansion S.A., 972
VK Ventures, 268
Vlaamse Investeringvennootschap NV, 974
Voyager Capital, 714
Wachtel & Co., Inc., 317
Walden International Investment Group (AKA: Walden Group), 269
Walden Israel, 975
Walnut Capital Corp., 701
Warburg, Pincus & Co., LLC. (FKA: E.M. Warburg, Pincus & Co), 590
Wasserstein, Perella & Co., Inc., 591
Wedbush Capital Partners, 271
Wellmax, Inc., 461
West Central Capital Corp., 684
Westbury Partners, 592
Western Technology Investment, 272
Westford Technology Ventures, L.P., 497
White Pines Management, L.L.C., 462
William E. Simon & Sons (Asia) LDC, 977
Winthrop Ventures, 593
Wit Capital Corporation, 594
Wolf Ventures (AKA:Wolf Asset Management Corp.), 286
Women's Growth Capital Fund, 318
WomenAngles.net, 318
Woodside Fund, 274
Working Ventures Canadian Fund, Inc., 978
Worldview Technology Partners, 275
Worms Capital Management, 594
Yablon Enterprises, Inc., 641
Yasuda Enterprise Development Co., Ltd.(FKA: Nippon Ent.Dev), 275
Yorkshire Fund Managers Ltd., 979
Zero Stage Capital Co., Inc., 456

Seed

100 X, 401
21st Century Internet Management Partners,LLC, 138
2nd Generation Capital Corp, 648
3i Austria (FKA Bank Austria TFV High Tech -UB GmbH), 725
3i Finland Oy (FKA SFK Finance), 725
3K Digital, 727
4C Ventures (FKA: Olivetti Holding, N.V.), 501
A.M. Pappas & Associates, 597
Abingworth Venture Management Limited, 729
Acacia Venture Partners, 139
Academy Funds (FKA: Longleaf Venture Fund LLC), 597
Accel Partners, 139
Access Venture Partners, 277
Acer Technology Ventures(FKA:Acer Soft Capital Inc.), 141
ACF Equity Atlantic, Inc, 731
Acorn Ventures, Inc., 141

Advanced Materials Partners, Inc., 287
Advanced Technology Development Fund, 330
Advantage Capital Partners, 386
Advent International Corp., 402
Affinity Capital Management(FKA:Peterson-Spencer-Fansler Co), 463
Al Shugart International (ASI), 142
Alcatel Ventures, 142
Alice Ventures, 736
Allegis Capital (AKA:Allegis Media Technology Ventures), 143
Alliance Technology Ventures, 330
Alpine Technology Ventures, 144
Alta Berkeley Venture Partners, 739
Alta Communications, 403
Alta Partners, 144
Altos Ventures, 144
Amadeus Capital Partners, 740
American Research & Development Corp., 404
Ampersand Ventures, 404
Amphion Ventures L.P.(FKA: Wolfensohn Associates, L.P.), 506
AMWIN Management Pty Ltd, 741
Apax Partners & Co.Beteiligungsberatung AG, 742
Apex Ventures BV, 743
APIDC-Venture Capital Limited, 743
Applied Technology, 405
ARCH Venture Partners, 346
Arete Corporation, 482
Aria Ventures Ltd., 745
Arkoma Venture Partners, 657
Artemis Ventures, 146
Artesian Capital, 464
Arthur P. Gould & Co., 507
Arthur Rock & Co., 146
Ascend Technology Ventures, 747
Asian Direct Capital Management, 747
AsiaTech Internet Group (ATIG) (FKA: AsiaTech Ventures), 748
Aspen Ventures (formerly 3i Ventures), 147
Asset Management Company Venture Capital, 147
Athena Technology Ventures, 148
Atlantis Group LLC, 598
Atlas Venture, 407
Auric Asset Management Pte. Ltd., 750
Aurora Funds, Inc., 598
Austin Ventures, L.P., 657
Australian Technology Group Ltd, 750
Authosis, 149
AV Labs, 658
Avery Business Development Services, 320
AVI Capital, L.P., 149
Aweida Ventures, 277
AxaVision, Inc., 509
Axiom Venture Partners, L.P., 288
B2B-Hive, LLC, 509
bainlab, 752
Bamboo Investments Plc (FKA Railike Limited), 753
BancBoston Capital/BancBoston Ventures, 408
Baring Private Equity Partners (FKA:Baring Venture Partners), 755
Barrington Partners, 152
Batterson Venture Partners(AKA:BVP), 348
Battery Ventures, L.P., 409
Baxter Associates, Inc., 289
Bay Partners, 153
Bayern Kapital Risikokapitalbeteiligungs GmbH, 757
BCE Capital, 758
BCM Technologies, Inc., 658
Bedrock Capital Partners, 409
Benchmark Capital, 154
Bessemer Venture Partners, 410
Big Bang Ventures, 760
Bloom & Co., 512
Blue Ribbon AG, 760
Blue Rock Capital, 319
Blueshift Internet Ventures, 761
Blumberg Capital Ventures, 155
bmp Aktiengesellschaft AG, 761
BORANCO Management, L.L.C., 277
Boston Financial & Equity Corp., 412
BrainHeart Capital AB, 762
Brantley Venture Partners, 609
Bruce F. Glaspell & Associates, 498
Buena Venture Associates, 659
Burr, Egan, Deleage & Co., 414
Burrill & Company, 156
Business Link Doncaster, 765
BV Capital (FKA Bertelsmann Ventures LP), 157
Cable & Howse Ventures, 703
Cambrian Ventures, 158
Cambridge Research & Innovation Ltd (AKA CRIL), 767
Capital Investors, 690
Capital Network, The (AKA: Texas Capital Network), 659
Capital Strategy Management Co., The, 349
Capital Technology Group, LLC, 610
Capman Management GmbH, 770
Cardinal Partners (FKA: Cardinal Health Partners), 485
Carolinas Capital Investment Corp., 599
Castile Ventures, 416
Castle Group, Ltd., The , 515
Catalyst Fund Management & Research Ltd, 773
Catalyst Ventures, 393
CD Technicom S.A., 774
CDC Innovation Partners, 775
CEI Ventures/Coastal Ventures LP, 388
Centennial Ventures, 278
CEO Advisors, 321
Cerulean Fund/WGC Enterprises, 350
Champion Consulting Group, Incorporated, 776
Charles River Ventures, 417
Charter Ventures, 160
Chestnut Street Partners, Inc., 417
Chiao Tung Bank, 776
Child Health Investment Corporation, 382
China Venture Management, Inc., 777
Chisholm Private Capital Partners, 618
Citizens Capital and Citizens Ventures, 418
Claflin Capital Management, Inc., 418
Classic Fund Management, Ltd., 781
Coates Myer & Co. Pty Ltd. (AKA: CM Capital Investments), 782
Cohen & Co., L.L.C., 517
Coleman Swenson Booth Inc.(FKA:Coleman Swenson Hoffman Booth, 649
Coleman Venture Group, 518
Collinson, Howe & Lennox, LLC, 291
Colorado Venture Management, 278
Columbine Venture Funds, The , 279

Commonwealth BioVentures Inc. (CBI), 389
Commonwealth Capital Ventures L.P., 419
CommTech International, 163
ComVentures (AKA: Communications Ventures), 163
Concord Venture Management (FKA:Nitzanim), 784
Continental S.B.I.C., 691
Continental Venture Capital , 784
Convergence Partners L.P., 164
CORAL Ventures, 465
Core Pacific Consulting Company, 786
Coronado Venture Fund, 133
CR&T Ventures AB, 787
Creafund CVBA, 788
Crescendo Venture Management LLC (FKA:IAI Ventures), 466
Crestview Financial Group, The , 292
Cross Atlantic Capital Partners, 625
CSK Venture Capital Co., Ltd., 789
Cullinane & Donnelly Venture Partners, L.P., 293
CW Group, Inc., 521
CyberStarts, 332
Cygnus Venture Partners, 791
Daimler Chrysler Venture Gmbh (AKA DCV), 792
Dakota Group, The , 166
Danish Development Finance Corp., 793
DANSK Udviklingsfinansiering A/S, 793
Defta Partners, 167
Delmag Ventures, 394
Delphi Ventures, 167
Delta Ventures, 795
Deucalion Venture Partners, 168
Deutsche Effecten und Wechsel-Beteiligungsgesellschaft AG, 796
Deutsche Venture Capital GmbH (DVCG), 796
Developers Equity Corp., 169
Development Corp. of Austin, 467
Digital Media Campus, 169
Digital Partners, 704
Doll Capital Management, 169
Domain Associates, L.L.C., 486
Dot Edu Ventures, 171
DotCom Ventures L.P., 171
Dougery Ventures, 171
Draper Fisher Jurvetson (FKA: Draper Associates), 172
Draper International, 172
e4e Inc., 174
Early Stage Enterprises, L.P., 487
Earlybird Venture Capital, 800
eBlast Ventures, LLC, 353
ECAT Development Capital Limited, 801
ECICS Ventures Pte Ltd., 801
EDB Investments Pte Ltd., 802
Edelson Technology Partners, 487
EDF Ventures (F.K.A. Enterprise Development Fund), 458
Edge Capital Investment Co., LLC, 175
Eircom Enterprise Fund Ltd., 803
El Dorado Ventures, 176
Emerald Venture Group, 177
Emerging Technologies , 804
EnerTech Capital Partners, L.P., 626
Episode-1 Partners, 806
EquiNet Venture Partners AG, 806
Evanston Business Investment Corp, 354
eVerger Associates, 812
Evergreen Canada Israel Investments Ltd, 812
eXseed, 813
Fairgill Investments Property Limited, 814
far blue, 814
FBR CoMotion Venture Capital, 705
Federal Business Development Bank, 815
Financial Technology Research Corp., 529
First Gen-e Investments, 817
First Union Capital Partners, 600
Fluke Venture Partners., 705
FLV Fund (AKA Flanders Language Valley Fund), 818
Fonds de Solidarité des Travailleurs du Québec (F.T.Q.), 820
Foresight, 820
FORTKNOX-VENTURE AG, 821
Fortune Consulting Group Incorporated, 821
Fortune Venture Capital Incorporated, 822
Forward Ventures, 180
Foundation Capital, 181
Frazier & Company, 705
Fusient Ventures, 531
G-51 Capital LLC, 665
Gabelli Multimedia Partners, 531
Gabriel Venture Partners, 182
GATX Ventures (FKA: Meier Mitchell & Co.), 183
GCI Venture Partners, 314
Gemini Capital Fund Management Ltd, 825
Genesis Partners, 826
Geneva Venture Partners, 184
Geocapital Partners, L.L.C., 489
Gideon Hixon Fund, 467
Global Partner Ventures, 694
Global Venture Capital Corporation, 829
Grand Pacific Venture Capital Company Ltd., 830
Greylock, 424
Grosvenor Funds, The, 315
Growth Factory, The, 833
GrowthWorks Capital, 834
Hallador Venture Partners, 188
Hanbyuck Investment Co Ltd, 836
Healthcare Ventures LLC (FKA: Healthcare Investments), 490
Heidelberg Innovation GmbH, 837
Highland Capital Partners, 427
HMS Hawaii Management Partners, 341
HMS Holtron Management Services, Ltd, 838
HO2 Partners LLC, 665
Hoebich Venture Management, Inc., 190
Hotung International Company, Ltd., 840
Hudson Venture Partners, 538
Humana Venture Capital, 384
Hummer Winblad Venture Partners, 191
Hydro-Quebec CapiTech Inc., 843
iAsia Alliance Capital, 844
Idanta Partners, Ltd., 191
IDG Ventures, 192
IEG Venture Management, Inc., 357
iEmerge Ventures, 477
IKB Venture Capital GmbH (AKA IKB Beteiligungsgesellschaft , 848
iMinds (FKA: Interactive Minds), 193
Industrial Technology Investment Corporation, 851
Industrial Technology Securities Ltd, 851
Industry Ventures , 428

Infineon Ventures, 852
InnoFinance Oy (FKA Culminatum Oy), 852
Innovacom, 853
Innovation Works, Inc., 628
Innovationsagentur Gesmbh, 854
InnovationsKapital Management Goteborg AB , 854
Innvotec Ltd, 854
Institutional Venture Partners, 196
Internet Healthcare Group, 297
Interpacific Venture Group Incorporated, 856
Interregnum, 856
Intersouth Partners, 601
InterWest Partners, 197
inVentures Management Ltd, 857
InveStar Capital, Inc., 857
Investment Securities of Colorado, Inc., 280
Invision AG (FKA Aureus Private Equity AG), 858
ISEP NV, 860
Israel Seed Partners, 860
IT Provider Advisor, 861
Jefferson Partners , 863
Jerusalem Global Ventures, 864
Jump.Net Ventures, 668
JumpStartUp Fund Advisors Pvt. Ltd., 864
Kangaroo Village, 865
Kansas Technology Enterprise Corporation, 382
Kappa-IT Ventures, 865
KB Partners, LLC, 359
KBL Healthcare Ventures, 546
Kemper Ventures, 491
Kettle Partners, L.P., 359
Kinship Partners, 280
Kleiner Perkins Caufield & Byers, 200
Korda & Co., 868
Ladybird Technologies, Ltd., 870
Lancet Capital Partner(FKA:Caduceus Capital Partners), 429
Landmark Partners, Inc., 298
Lazard Technology Partners, 547
Lee Munder Venture Partners, 430
Leonard Mautner Associates, 203
LeVenture Kapitalbeteiligungsgesellschaft mbH & Co.KG, 872
Libon Capital Management Limited, 873
Life Science Ventures, 873
Life Sciences Partners BV, 874
Lighthouse Capital Partners, 205
Lightspeed Venture Partners (FKA: Weiss, Peck & Greer), 206
LINC Capital Partners, Inc., 361
London Ventures (Fund Managers) Ltd., 875
Lost Boys Incubator, 875
Lovett Miller & Co. Incorporated, 325
Lucent Venture Partners, Inc., 207
Macromedia Ventures, 208
Magic Venture Capital, LLC, 208
Malmohus Invest AB, 877
Mangrove Capital Partners SA, 878
march.fifteen AG (FKA Peterp@n), 878
Maristeth Ventures, L.L.C., 707
Maryland Venture Capital Trust, 395
Massachusetts Technology Development Corp. (MTDC), 432
Massey Burch Capital Corp., 650
Maton Venture, 209
Mayfield Fund, 210
MBA Venture Group, 669
MCH Private Equity SA, 880
MDS Discovery Venture Management, Inc., 881
MDS Health Ventures, Inc. (AKA: MDS Capital Corp.), 881
Media Venture Partners, 211
MediaVenture Capital AG & Co. KGaA, 882
Medical Innovation Partners, 469
Medical Science Partners, 434
Medical Venture Holdings, Inc., 552
Medicis AG, 882
Medmax Ventures, L.P., 299
MedTech International, Inc., 670
MedVenture Associates, 212
Menlo Ventures, 212
Meritage Private Equity Fund, 281
Merlin Biosciences (AKA Merlin Ventures), 884
Merrill, Pickard, Anderson & Eyre, 213
Mid-Atlantic Venture Funds (FKA: NEPA Management Corp.), 634
Midlands Venture Fund Managers Ltd. (AKA: Midven Ltd), 886
Millennium Three Venture Group, L.L.C., 480
Mission Ventures, 214
Mitiska NV, 887
Mitsui & Co., Ltd., 553
MK Global Ventures, 214
MMC adVentures Ltd, 888
Montgomery Associates, Inc., 215
Montgomery Medical Ventures, L.P., 215
Montreux Equity Partners, 216
Monumental Venture Partners, LLC, 696
Multiventure Investment, Inc., 890
Murphree Venture Partners, 671
MVC AG (AKA Mitteldeutsche Venture Capital AG), 891
MVM Ltd, 891
Native Venture Capital Co., Ltd., 893
Nazem & Co., 556
nCoTec Ventures Ltd, 893
NeoMed Management AS (FKA Medical Venture Management), 894
Net Partners, 895
NetFuel Ventures, 364
Netjuice, 895
Neurone Venture Capital, 896
New Business Capital Fund Ltd., 499
New Enterprise Associates, 396
New South Ventures, 325
New Venture Resources, 282
New Vista Capital, LLC, 218
New York State Science & Technology Foundation, 558
Newbury Ventures, 220
Newtek Ventures, 220
NextGen Partners LLC, 221
Nokia Venture Partners (AKA: Nokia Oy), 222
Nomura/JAFCO Investment (HK) Limited, 901
Nord Innovation, 901
North Bridge Venture Partners, 438
North Carolina Technological Development Authority, Inc., 603
Northeast Ventures Corp., 469
Northwest Ohio Venture Fund, 615
Northwest Venture Associates, Inc.(FKA:Spokane Capital Mgmt), 709
Northzone Ventures (FKA Venture Partners AS), 902

Norwest Equity Partners, 223
Novak Biddle Venture Partners, L.P., 697
NPV Capital Partners, LLC, 560
NTC Group, The , 301
Obelisk Capital Pty Ltd, 904
Olympus Capital Holdings Asia, 905
Oregon Resource and Technology Development Fund, 620
Orien Ventures, 303
Origin Ventures LLC, 365
Osborn Capital LLC, 440
OVP Venture Partners (FKA: Olympic Venture Partners), 709
Oxford Financial Services Corp., 698
PA Early Stage (AKA:Pennsylvania Early Stage Partners), 635
Pac-Link Management Corporation, 906
Pacific Capital Partners, 907
Pacific Northwest Partners SBIC, L.P., 710
Pacific Venture Group, 227
Pacific Venture Partners, 907
Paladin Partners, 711
Palmetto Seed Capital Corp., 645
Palomar Ventures, 228
Pappajohn Capital Resources, 381
Paradigm Capital Partners LLC, 651
Paragon Venture Partners, 229
Pari Capital AG, 909
Partech International, 229
Pathfinder Venture Capital Funds, 470
Patricof & Co. Ventures, Inc., 563
Pequot Capital Management Inc., 564
Perennial Ventures (FKA: Tredegar Investments), 711
Phillips-Smith Specialty Retail Group, 673
Phoenix Home Life Mutual Insurance Co., 303
Phoenix Partners, The , 711
Pilotbird, 912
Pino Venture Partners, 912
PME Capital, 912
Polaris Venture Capital, 913
Polaris Venture Partners, 441
Poly Ventures, 566
PowerWord Capital Management, Inc., 914
Prelude Technology Investments Ltd, 915
Primaxis Technology Ventures Inc. , 916
Prime Technology Ventures NV, 916
Primedia Ventures, 567
Prince Ventures, 367
ProQuest Investments, L.P., 493
ProSeed Capital Holdings CVA, 917
Proximitas AG Venture Capital, 918
Putnam Lovell Capital Partners, L.P., 232
Pythagoras NV, 919
Quaestus & Co. Inc. (FKA: Quaestus Management Corp..), 719
Quantum Fund, Ltd., 920
Quest Ventures, 233
RAF Ventures, 637
RCT BioVentures NE (Research Corporation Technologies), 442
Red Rock Ventures, 234
Redleaf Venture Management, 234
Redwood Capital Corp., 235
Regulus International Capital Co., Inc., 304
RHO Management, 570
Robertson Stephens & Company, LLC, 236
Rock Hill Ventures Inc.(FKA:Hillman Medical Ventures,Inc.), 638
Rocket Ventures, 237
Rothschild Bioscience Unit, 922
Rothschild Ventures Asia Pte Ltd., 922
Rothschild Ventures, Inc., 570
Royalty Capital Fund, L.P. I/Royalty Capital Management, Inc, 443
RWI Group, LP, 239
S-Refit GmbH & Co KG , 923
Saffron Hill Ventures (FKA LootLab Ltd.), 924
Sanderling Ventures, 239
Sandler Capital Management, 571
Sandlot Capital LLC, 283
Sandton Financial Group, 240
Sapient Capital, 721
SBC Ventures, 499
SBV Venture Partners (AKA:Sigefi, Burnette & Vallee), 240
Scottish Equity Partners Limited, 927
Seaflower Ventures, 446
Seed Capital Investments, 928
Seed Capital Ltd, 928
Seed Company Partners, 676
Selby Venture Partners, 241
Sequoia Capital, 241
Shannon Development Company, 929
Shaw Venture Partners (FKA: Shaw Glasgow Partners), 621
Shott Capital Management, 574
Shrem Fudim Kelner Technologies Ltd. , 930
Siemens Venture Capital GmbH, 930
Sierra Ventures, 243
Sigma Partners, 243
Silicon Alley Venture Partners LLC (AKA SAVP) , 576
SingTel Ventures, 931
Sitra (AKA Finnish National Fund for Research and Dev.), 932
Smart Technology Ventures, 246
Sofinnova Ventures, 246
SOFTBANK Capital Partners, 448
SOFTBANK Venture Capital (FKA: SOFTBANK Technology Ventures), 247
Solstice Capital LLC, 449
Sopartec SA, 936
Southeast Interactive Technology Funds, 605
Southern California Ventures, 247
Southwest Venture Group, 678
Speirs Consultants, Inc., 938
Spray Venture Partners, 450
Square One Ventures (AKA: Smaby Group), 471
SRK Management Co., 578
SsangYong Cement (Singapore) Ltd, 939
Start-up Australia Pty Limited, 940
STARTech, 679
StarTech Partners, Ltd., 941
Starter Fluid, 250
Still River Fund, The, 450
Strathdon Investments Ltd, 942
Stratos Ventures Ltd Oy, 942
SudKB & SudVC, 942
Summit Group Ltd, The, 943
Sustainable Jobs Fund (SJF), The , 606
Sutter Hill Ventures, 251
Swedestart Management AB, 944
Sweeney & Co., Inc., 308
Synopsys, Inc., 253

Tailink Venture Partners, 946
Tamir Fishman Ventures, 946
Taylor & Turner, 253
tbg Technologie-Beteiligungsgesellschaft mbH, 947
TechFarm (AKA:TechFund Capital), 254
Techno Nord VC GmbH, 948
Technologieholding VC GmbH, 950
Technology Associates Management Corporation, 950
Technology Venture Partners Pty Ltd, 950
Technology Ventures Corp., 500
Technology Ventures, L.L.C., 339
TechnoPlus Ventures, 951
Technostart GmbH, 951
Techxas Ventures, LLC, 681
Teknia Invest Oy, 952
Telecom Partners (FKA:Telecom Management, LLC), 285
Telecommunications Development Fund (TDF), 316
Telia Business Innovation AB, 953
Temasek Capital, 954
Third Millennium Venture Capital, Ltd., 256
Thorner Ventures, 258
Three Arch Partners, 258
TL Ventures, 640
Toll Technologies, 957
Toucan Capital Corp., 399
Transamerica Mezzanine Financing, 645
Transpac Capital Pte, Ltd., 958
Trellis Partners, 682
Triad Investors Corp, 319
Tribune Ventures, 372
TrustCapital Partners NV, 959
TTC Ventures, 453
TTP Venture Managers (FKA: The Technology Partnership), 960
TVM Techno Venture Management, 961
Twinning Ventures, 961
U.S. Venture Partners, 261
UBS Capital, 962
Union Venture Capital Corporation, 963
UniversityAngels.com, 584
UST Capital Corp., 454
Vanguard Venture Partners, 262
Vencon Management, Inc., 585
VenGlobal Capital, 264
Venrock Associates, 586
Ventana Financial Resources, Inc., 372
Ventana Global, 264
Venture Associates, Ltd., 285
Venture First Associates, 328
Venture Funding Group International, 587
Venture Funding, Ltd., 461
Venture Investment Management Company LLC (AKA: VIMAC), 454
Venture Investors Management LLC, 720
Venture Management Services Inc. (FKA: AT&T Ventures), 496
Venture Partners, 310
Venture Partners AG, 968
Venture Select, 968
Venture Strategy Partners, 266
Venture TDF Pte Ltd., 968
Ventures West Management, Inc., 970
Veritas Venture Capital Management, Ltd., 970
Vertex Management, 971
Vertex Management Israel (AKA: Vertex Management III Ltd.), 971
Vertical Group, The, 496
Viventures Inc., 973
Voyager Capital, 714
VTC Partners GmbH, 974
Walden International Investment Group (AKA: Walden Group), 269
Walden Israel, 975
Warburg, Pincus & Co., LLC. (FKA: E.M. Warburg, Pincus & Co), 590
Watermill eVentures , 455
wellington partners venture capital GmbH, 975
Western States Investment Group, 272
Western Technology Investment, 272
WI Harper Group, 273
WL Ventures (FKA:Lothian Enterprise Ltd.), 978
Woodside Fund, 274
Working Ventures Canadian Fund, Inc., 978
Worldview Technology Partners, 275
WSI Holding Corporation, 595
YankeeTek Ventures, 456
Yasuda Enterprise Development Co., Ltd.(FKA: Nippon Ent.Dev), 275
Zephyr Internet Partners, 595
Zero Stage Capital Co., Inc., 456

Special Situation

1st Source Capital Corp., 375
21st Century Internet Management Partners,LLC, 138
Aberlyn Capital Management Co., Inc., 501
Abingworth Venture Management Limited, 729
Adams, Harkness & Hill, Inc., 401
Adler & Shaykin, 502
Advanced Materials Partners, Inc., 287
Advanta Partners, L.P., 622
Advent International Corp., 402
Advent Management N.V., 733
Alan I. Goldman & Associates, 483
Alchemy Partners, 736
Alimansky Capital Group, Inc., 504
Allegra Partners (FKA: Lawrence, Smith & Horey), 504
Alliance Financial of Houston, 655
Allsop Venture Partners, 380
Allstate Private Equity, 344
Alpha Capital Partners, Inc., 344
Alta Communications, 403
American Capital Strategies, 391
American Securities, L.P., 505
Amphion Ventures L.P.(FKA: Wolfensohn Associates, L.P.), 506
Antares Capital Corp. (FKA: Antares Leveraged Capital Corp), 345
Antares Capital Corporation (FKA: Harbor Ventures Corp.), 320
Anthem Capital, L.P., 391
Argentum Group, The , 507
Argos Soditic SA, 744
ASC Group, 746
Atila Venture Partners Ltd., 749
Atlantic Coastal Ventures, L.P.(AKA:Multimedia Broadcast In), 312
Atlantic Medical Management, LLC, 508

Atle Foretagskapital AB (FKA Foretagskapital AB), 749
August Capital Management, 148
August Partners, 508
Austin Ventures, L.P., 657
Avery Business Development Services, 320
AVI Capital, L.P., 149
Baccharis Capital, Inc., 150
Bachow & Associates, Inc., 623
Bailey & Co. Inc., 752
Banc One Capital Partners, 608
BancAmerica Capital Investors (FKA:NationsBanc Capital Corp), 598
Bancorp Hawaii SBIC, Inc., 341
Bangert Dawes Reade Davis & Thom, 151
Bank Funds, The, 347
Bank One Equity Investors, Inc., 386
Bankers Trust New York Corp./Deutsche Banc Alex Brown, 510
Bastion Capital Corp., 152
Batavia Group, Ltd., The , 511
Batavia Investment Management Ltd, 756
Baxter Associates, Inc., 289
Benchmark Capital, 154
Berkeley International Capital Corp., 154
Berkshire Partners, 410
Berwind Financial Group, L.P., 623
Bloom & Co., 512
Boston Financial & Equity Corp., 412
Boston Ventures Management, Inc., 413
Bristol Capital Management, 513
Burr, Egan, Deleage & Co., 414
Butler Capital Partners France, 765
Cable & Howse Ventures, 703
Calgary Enterprises, Inc., 514
Cambria Group, The, 157
Capital Network, The (AKA: Texas Capital Network), 659
Capital Prive (FKA NatWest Equity Partners, France), 769
Capital Services & Resources, Inc., 648
Capital Strategy Management Co., The, 349
Cardinal Ventures, L.L.C., 375
Carillon Capital, Inc., 610
Castle Harlan Australian Mezzanine Partners Pty. Ltd. , 772
Catterton Partners, 290
CEI Ventures/Coastal Ventures LP, 388
CEO Venture Fund, 625
Cerulean Fund/WGC Enterprises, 350
Chanen, Painter & Co., Ltd., 703
Charter Ventures, 160
Chase H&Q (FKA Hambrecht & Quist), 160
CIBC Capital Partners (FKA: CIBC Wood Gundy Capital), 516
CICLAD, 778
CID Equity Partners, 376
Circle Ventures, Inc., 376
Citicorp Venture Capital, Ltd., 517
Clairvest Group, Inc., 780
CM Equity Partners, 517
Cohen & Co., L.L.C., 517
Coleman Swenson Booth Inc.(FKA:Coleman Swenson Hoffman Booth, 649
Coleman Venture Group, 518
Commonwealth Capital Ventures L.P., 419
Compass Investment Management Ltd., 783
Compass Technology Partners, 163
Continental S.B.I.C., 691
Continental Venture Capital , 784
Cornerstone Equity Investors, LLC, 519
Crest Communications Holdings LLC, 520
Crosbie & Co Inc, 789
Crown Advisors International, Ltd., 521
Crown Capital Corp, 475
Cureton & Co., Inc., 662
CW Group, Inc., 521
Dakota Group, The , 166
Davis Group, 166
Defta Partners, 167
DFW Capital Partners (AKA:DeMuth, Folger & Wetherill), 486
Drug Royalty Corp., Inc., 798
Drysdale Enterprises, 173
Easton Hunt Capital Partners, 525
ECI Ventures Ltd, 801
ECICS Ventures Pte Ltd., 801
Edge Capital Investment Co., LLC, 175
Electra Fleming Limited, 525
Electra Partners Asia [FKA: JF Electra Limited], 803
Enterprise Investors, 526
Enterprise Merchant Bank, 382
Eos Partners, L.P., 527
Equinox Investment Partners, 294
Equitas, L.P., 649
Equity Partners Management Pty Ltd, 807
Equus Capital Corp., 663
Espirito Santo Development, 808
Evergreen Capital Partners Inc, 528
Exeter Capital, L.P., 528
Far East Capital Corp., 179
Ferrer Freeman Thompson & Co, 295
FHL Capital Corp., 129
Fidelity Ventures (FKA: Fidelity Venture Associates), 421
Financial Technology Research Corp., 529
Finansa Capital Limited, 816
First Atlantic Capital, Ltd., 530
First Capital Management Co., 664
First Charter Partners, Inc., 664
First Growth Capital, Inc., 333
First Union Capital Partners, 600
Florida Capital Ventures, Ltd., 323
Fonds de Solidarité des Travailleurs du Québec (F.T.Q.), 820
Food Fund Ltd. Partnership, The, 467
Founders Equity, Inc., 530
Fowler, Anthony & Co., 422
Frazier & Company, 705
Frederic H. Mayerson Group, The, 612
Frontenac Co., 355
Gateway Associates, L.P., 476
Gemini Investors LLC (AKA: GMN Investors), 423
GENES GmbH Venture Services, 826
Genesis Capital, Inc., 533
Geneva Merchant Banking Partners, 601
Golub Associates, 534
Granite Ventures LLC (FKA: H & Q Venture Associates), 186
Graphite Capital (FKA: F&C Ventures Ltd), 831
Greater Philadelphia Venture Capital Corp., 627
Greenwich Venture Partners, Inc., 296
Gresham Rabo Management Limited, 832
Grotech Capital Group, 394

Grove Street Advisors, LLC, 425
H&Q Asia Pacific, Ltd., 187
Hambro America Biosciences, Inc., 535
Hambro European Ventures (Hambros PLC), 835
Harbison Corporation, 477
Harbour Financial Co., 426
HarbourVest Partners, LLC., 426
Harvest Partners, Inc., 536
Hellman & Friedman, 189
Herbert Young Securities, Inc., 536
High Street Capital, LLC, 357
Hoak Capital Corp., 666
HSBC Private Equity (Asia), Ltd. (FKA: HSBC PE Management), 841
HSBC Private Equity Ltd (FKA Montagu Private Equity Ltd), 841
IBJS Capital Corp., 539
Impex Venture Management Co., 540
Incorporated Investors, 193
Indekon Management Oy, 849
Inman & Bowman, 195
Innova Capital (FKA: Poland Partners Management Company), 853
Innovest Group, Inc., 629
Institutional Venture Partners, 196
InterEquity Capital Partners, L.P., 541
InvestAmerica Venture Group, Inc., 380
IPS Industrial Promotion Services, Ltd., 859
J.P. Morgan Capital Corp., 542
James A. Matzdorff & Co., 199
Jefferson Capital Fund, Ltd., 130
Jordan, Edmiston Group, Inc., The , 545
Josephberg Grosz & Co., Inc., 545
Kahala Investments, Inc., 668
Kentucky Highlands Investment Corporation, 384
Key Equity Capital Corp.(AKA:Key Community Development Corp), 613
Landmark Partners, Inc., 298
Las Americas Administradora, 871
LaSalle Capital Group, Inc., 360
Lee Munder Venture Partners, 430
Leonard Mautner Associates, 203
Levine Leichtman Capital Partners, Inc., 204
LF International, Inc., 204
Liberty BIDCO Investment Corporation, 459
LINC Capital Partners, Inc., 361
Lincoln Investment Management Inc., 378
Livingston Capital, Ltd., 281
LJH Global Investments , 324
LTI Ventures Leasing Corp., 298
Lubar & Co., 718
Madison Dearborn Partners, LLC, 361
Malmohus Invest AB, 877
Management Resource Partners, 208
Maristeth Ventures, L.L.C., 707
Marleau, Lemire, Inc., 878
Matrix Private Equity, 879
Mayfair Capital Partners, Inc., 551
MBW Management, Inc., 492
MC Capital, Inc., 551
McCown De Leeuw & Co., 210
Media Venture Partners, 211
MedTech International, Inc., 670
Mellon Ventures (AKA: Mellon Bank), 632
Memhard Investment Bankers, Inc., 300
Mentor Capital Partners, 633
Mercury Private Equity, 883
Meridian Venture Partners (MVP), 633
Merifin Capital Group, 883
Merita Capital Limited, 134
Merrill Lynch Investment Managers FKA Mercury Asset Mgmt, 884
Mesirow Private Equity Investments, Inc., 362
Mezzanine Management UK Limited, 885
Miller/Zell Venture Group, 335
Montgomerie, Huck & Co., 888
Montgomery Associates, Inc., 215
Mountaineer Capital LP, 716
MST Partners, 555
Nassau Capital, L.L.C., 492
National Corporate Finance, Inc., 217
National Financial Cos. LLC, 556
Natural Gas Partners, 300
Nazem & Co., 556
Nesbitt Burns, 363
Newbridge Capital Limited, 219
Newbury Ventures, 220
Newbury, Piret & Co., Inc., 437
NIB Capital Private Equity N.V. (FKA: Parnib Holding NV) , 898
Noro-Moseley Partners, 336
North American Business Development Co., L.L.C., 364
Northwood Ventures, 559
Norwood Venture Corp., 559
Noveltek Venture Corp., 560
NPM Capital (AKA Nederlandse Participatie MIJ NV), 903
Nu Capital Access Group, Ltd., 224
Oak Hill Capital Management, Inc., 561
Oak Investment Partners, 302
Oem Capital, 302
Onex Corp., 905
Orion Partners, L.P., 439
Pacific Corporate Group, Inc., 227
Pacific Venture Group, 227
Palmer Partners, L.P., 441
PAMA Group Inc. (FKA:Prudential Asset Management Asia), 908
Pappajohn Capital Resources, 381
Paragon Venture Partners, 229
Paribas Principal, Inc., 563
Pathfinder Investment Co Pvt Ltd, 910
Pathfinder Venture Capital Funds, 470
Pauli & Co., Inc., 477
Pecks Management Partners, Ltd., 564
Peninsula Capital Partners, L.L.C, 460
Penn-Janney Fund, Inc., The, 635
Pennsylvania Growth Fund, 636
Phoenix Equity Partners (FKA: DLJ European Private Equity), 911
Phoenix Home Life Mutual Insurance Co., 303
Pomona Capital, 566
PPM Ventures Ltd (FKA: Prudential Venture Managers Ltd), 914
Prism Capital, 367
Private Capital Corp., 131
Private Equity Investors, Inc., 567
Priveq Capital Funds, 917
Prospect Partners LLC (FKA:Kenter, Glatris & Tuttle, LLC, 368
Prospect Street Ventures (FKA:Prospect Street Invest. Mgmt), 567

Putnam Lovell Capital Partners, L.P., 232
Quadriga Capital Management GMBH, 919
Quest Ventures, 233
Quester Capital Management Ltd, 920
RBC Ventures, Inc., 619
Recovery Equity Investors, L.P., 234
RFE Investment Partners, 305
Richard Jaffe & Co., Inc., 676
Ridge Capital Partners, L.L.C., 368
Riordan, Lewis & Haden, 236
Rosenfeld & Co., 620
Rosewood Capital, L.P., 237
Rothschild Ventures Asia Pte Ltd., 922
Royalty Capital Fund, L.P. I/Royalty Capital Management, Inc, 443
Rutledge & Co., Inc., 305
SAE Ventures, 306
Sagaponack Partners LLC, 239
Sage Management Group, 444
Sandler Capital Management, 571
Sandlot Capital LLC, 283
Sandton Financial Group, 240
SBC Equity Partners, Inc., 369
SBCA/A.G. Bartholomew & Associates, 131
Schooner Capital International, L.P., 444
Schroder Ventures, 445
Seacoast Capital, 446
Sentinel Capital Partners, 573
SGI Capital L.L.C, 573
Shared Ventures, Inc., 470
Shattan Group, The, 574
Shaw Venture Partners (FKA: Shaw Glasgow Partners), 621
Shawmut Capital Partners, 447
Shepherd Group LLC, The, 447
Sigma Partners, 243
Siguler Guff & Company, LLC, 575
SOFTBANK Capital Partners, 448
Sorrento Associates, Inc., 247
South Atlantic Venture Funds, L.P., 327
Southport Partners, 307
Southwest Venture Group, 678
Speirs Consultants, Inc., 938
Spencer Trask Ventures, Inc. (FKA: Spencer Trask Securities), 576
Sponsored Consulting Services, 249
State Street Bank & Trust Co., 338
Stephens Group, Inc., 137
Sterling Grace Capital Management, L.P., 579
Stolberg Partners, 580
Strategic Capital Management, 941
Sucsy, Fischer & Co., 370
Suez Asia Holdings Pte Ltd., 943
Summit Partners, 451
Sun Valley Ventures, 250
Sundance Venture Partners, L.P., 251
Sunwestern Investment Group, 680
Sycamore Ventures, 494
T. Rowe Price Threshold Partnerships, 399
TA Associates, Inc., 451
Taylor & Turner, 253
Thompson Clive, Inc., 257
Thorner Ventures, 258
Three Cities Research, Inc., 583
Transcap Associates, Inc., 371
Triune Capital, 260
U.S. Medical Resources Corp., 616
Union Venture Corp., 262
VantagePoint Venture Partners, 263
VCM Venture Capital Management, 965
Vector Fund Management, L.P. (FKA: Vector Securities), 372
Vega Capital Corp., 584
Vencon Management, Inc., 585
Ventana Global, 264
Ventex Management, Inc., 683
Venture Capital Fund Managers (Pty), Ltd., The , 967
Venture Capital Partners Pty Limited, 967
Venture Funding Group International, 587
Venture Funding, Ltd., 461
Venture Investors Management LLC, 720
Venture Opportunities Corp., 588
Venture Partners, 310
Vero Group PLC, 684
Vertical Group, The, 496
Victory Ventures L.L.C., 588
Vista Capital Corp., 268
VS&A Communications Partners, L.P., 588
Walden International Investment Group (AKA: Walden Group), 269
Warburg, Pincus & Co., LLC. (FKA: E.M. Warburg, Pincus & Co), 590
Wellmax, Inc., 461
Welsh, Carson, Anderson & Stowe, 591
Westar Capital, 271
Westbury Partners, 592
Western Technology Investment, 272
White Pines Management, L.L.C., 462
William A.M. Burden & Co., 593
Willis Stein & Partners, 374
Windward Holdings, 311
Woodside Fund, 274
Working Ventures Canadian Fund, Inc., 978
Worms Capital Management, 594
Yablon Enterprises, Inc., 641
Yorkshire Fund Managers Ltd., 979

Startup

100 X, 401
21st Century Internet Management Partners,LLC, 138
2M Invest, Inc., 138
3i Austria (FKA Bank Austria TFV High Tech -UB GmbH), 725
3i Finland Oy (FKA SFK Finance), 725
3i Group plc, 726
3K Digital, 727
3TS Venture Partners AG, 727
4C Ventures (FKA: Olivetti Holding, N.V.), 501
A.M. Pappas & Associates, 597
Aberdare Ventures, 138
Aberdeen Murray Johnstone Private Equity, 728
Aberlyn Capital Management Co., Inc., 501
Abingworth Venture Management Limited, 729
ABS Ventures, 390
Acacia Venture Partners, 139
Academy Funds (FKA: Longleaf Venture Fund LLC), 597
Accel Partners, 139

Accenture Technology Ventures (FKA: AC Ventures), 140
Access Venture Partners, 277
ACE Management, 731
Acer Technology Ventures(FKA:Acer Soft Capital Inc.), 141
ACF Equity Atlantic, Inc, 731
ADD Partners , 733
Adler & Co., 502
Adler & Shaykin, 502
Advanced Materials Partners, Inc., 287
Advanced Technology Development Fund, 330
Advanced Technology Ventures, 401
Advantage Capital Partners, 386
Advent Venture Partners (FKA Advent Limited), 733
Adveq Management AG (FKA Advisers on Private Equity AG), 734
Affinity Capital Management(FKA:Peterson-Spencer-Fansler Co), 463
Al Shugart International (ASI), 142
Alice Ventures, 736
All Asia Partners, 737
Alliance Technology Ventures, 330
Alliance Venture Capital Advisors Limited, 738
Allstate Private Equity, 344
Alpine Technology Ventures, 144
Alta Berkeley Venture Partners, 739
Alta Communications, 403
Alta Partners, 144
Altos Ventures, 144
Amadeus Capital Partners, 740
American Research & Development Corp., 404
Ameritech Development Corp., 345
Ampersand Ventures, 404
Amphion Ventures L.P.(FKA: Wolfensohn Associates, L.P.), 506
antfactory, 741
Anthem Capital, L.P., 391
Apax Partners & Cie (AKA: Apax France), 742
Apax Partners & Co. Ventures Ltd (AKA: Apax UK), 742
Apax Partners & Co.Beteiligungsberatung AG, 742
Apex Ventures BV, 743
APIDC-Venture Capital Limited, 743
Applied Genomic Technology Capital Funds (AGTC), 405
Applied Technology, 405
ARCH Venture Partners, 346
Arete Corporation, 482
Arkoma Venture Partners, 657
Artesian Capital, 464
Arthur P. Gould & Co., 507
Arthur Rock & Co., 146
AS Venture GmbH, 746
Ascend Technology Ventures, 747
Asian Direct Capital Management, 747
Asset Management Company Venture Capital, 147
Atlantic Capital, 407
Atlas Venture, 407
Atle Ventures (FKA Teknologiparkernas Utveckling AB), 749
August Capital Management, 148
AUGUSTA Venture GmbH, 749
Auric Asset Management Pte. Ltd., 750
Aurora Funds, Inc., 598
Austin Ventures, L.P., 657
Avery Business Development Services, 320
AVI Capital, L.P., 149
AXA Investment Managers Private Equity Europe, 751
AxaVision, Inc., 509
b-business partners, 752
B2B-Hive, LLC, 509
BA Venture Partners (AKA: BankAmerica Ventures), 150
Baccharis Capital, Inc., 150
bainlab, 752
BANEXI Corp., 753
Baring Communications Equity, 755
Baring Private Equity Partners (FKA:Baring Venture Partners), 755
Battelle Venture Partners (Scientific Advances), 608
Batterson Venture Partners(AKA:BVP), 348
Battery Ventures, L.P., 409
Baxter Associates, Inc., 289
Bay Partners, 153
BayBG Bayerische Beteiligungsgesellschaft mbH, 757
Bayern Kapital Risikokapitalbeteiligungs GmbH, 757
BCE Capital, 758
BCR Asset Management Pty Ltd., 758
Benchmark Capital, 154
Berwind Financial Group, L.P., 623
Bessemer Venture Partners, 410
Big Bang Ventures, 760
Birchmere Ventures, Inc.(FKA:Birchmere Investments), 624
Bloom & Co., 512
Blue Chip Venture Company, 609
Blue Ribbon AG, 760
Blue Rock Capital, 319
Blumberg Capital Ventures, 155
bmp Aktiengesellschaft AG, 761
BOME Investors, Inc., 473
BORANCO Management, L.L.C., 277
Boston Capital Ventures, 411
Boston Financial & Equity Corp., 412
Boston Millennia Partners, 412
Boston University Community Technology Fund , 413
Botticelli Venture Funds (AKA: Botticelli Investments), 761
Boulder Ventures, Ltd., 392
BrainHeart Capital AB, 762
Brait Capital Partners, 762
Brand Equity Ventures, 289
Brantley Venture Partners, 609
Brightstar, 763
British Steel Ltd., 764
Bruce F. Glaspell & Associates, 498
Buena Venture Associates, 659
Bulldog Partners Limited, 764
Burr, Egan, Deleage & Co., 414
Burrill & Company, 156
Business Link Doncaster, 765
Butler Capital Partners France, 765
Cable & Howse Ventures, 703
Cairnsford Associates Ltd., 766
Calgary Enterprises, Inc., 514
Caltech Capital Partners Ltd., 766
Cambridge Research & Innovation Ltd (AKA CRIL), 767
Canbank Venture Capital Fund Ltd, 767
Capital Development & Investment Co. Ltd., 768
Capital Express, L.L.C., 484
Capital Network, The (AKA: Texas Capital Network), 659
Capital Strategy Management Co., The, 349

Capital Technology Group, LLC, 610
Capman Management GmbH, 770
Cardinal Partners (FKA: Cardinal Health Partners), 485
Cardinal Ventures, L.L.C., 375
Carolinas Capital Investment Corp., 599
Castile Ventures, 416
Castle Group, Ltd., The , 515
CastleHill Ventures , 772
Catalyst Fund Management & Research Ltd, 773
Catalyst Venture Capital Firm, 773
Catalyst Ventures, 393
Catella IT AB, 773
CDC Innovation Partners, 775
CEI Ventures/Coastal Ventures LP, 388
Centennial Ventures, 278
CEO Advisors, 321
CEO Venture Fund, 625
Cerulean Fund/WGC Enterprises, 350
Champion Consulting Group, Incorporated, 776
Charles River Ventures, 417
Charter Ventures, 160
Chase H&Q (FKA Hambrecht & Quist), 160
Chestnut Street Partners, Inc., 417
Child Health Investment Corporation, 382
China Venture Management, Inc., 777
Chrysalis Ventures, 384
CID Equity Partners, 376
cirlab!, 779
Citizens Capital and Citizens Ventures, 418
Claflin Capital Management, Inc., 418
Clal Venture Capital Management Ltd (AKA CVC Management), 781
Classic Fund Management, Ltd., 781
CM Equity Partners, 517
CMEA Ventures (FKA:Chemicals & Materials Enterprise Associa), 161
Coates Myer & Co. Pty Ltd. (AKA: CM Capital Investments), 782
Cohen & Co., L.L.C., 517
Coleman Swenson Booth Inc.(FKA:Coleman Swenson Hoffman Booth, 649
Coleman Venture Group, 518
Collinson, Howe & Lennox, LLC, 291
Colorado Venture Management, 278
Columbine Venture Funds, The , 279
Comdisco Ventures, 162
Commerz Beteiligungsgesellschaft mbH (CBG), 783
Commonwealth Capital Ventures L.P., 419
CommTech International, 163
ComVentures (AKA: Communications Ventures), 163
Concord Venture Management (FKA:Nitzanim), 784
Connecticut Innovations, Inc., 291
Consumer Venture Partners, 292
Continental S.B.I.C., 691
Continental Venture Capital , 784
Copley Venture Partners, 420
CORAL Ventures, 465
Cordova Ventures (FKA:Cordova Capital), 331
Core Capital Partners, 313
Core Pacific Consulting Company, 786
Coronado Venture Fund, 133
Covent Industrial Capital Investment Co Ltd, 787
CR&T Ventures AB, 787
Crescendo Venture Management LLC (FKA:IAI Ventures), 466
Crest Communications Holdings LLC, 520
Crocker Capital/Crocker Assoc., 164
Cross Atlantic Capital Partners, 625
CSK Venture Capital Co., Ltd., 789
CW Group, Inc., 521
CyberStarts, 332
Cygnus Venture Partners, 791
D.H. Blair Investment Banking Corp., 521
Daimler Chrysler Venture Gmbh (AKA DCV), 792
Dakota Group, The , 166
Danish Development Finance Corp., 793
DANSK Udviklingsfinansiering A/S, 793
Dassault Developpment, 794
Davis Group, 166
DB Venture Partners, 794
Defta Partners, 167
Delphi Ventures, 167
Deucalion Venture Partners, 168
Deutsche Effecten und Wechsel-Beteiligungsgesellschaft AG, 796
Deutsche Venture Capital GmbH (DVCG), 796
Developers Equity Corp., 169
Development Corp. of Austin, 467
Discovery Capital, 797
Divine interVentures (FKA: Platinum Venture Partners), 351
Doll Capital Management, 169
Domain Associates, L.L.C., 486
Dougery Ventures, 171
Dow Chemical Co., 458
Downer & Co., 420
Draper Atlantic Management Co., LLC, 692
Draper Fisher Jurvetson (FKA: Draper Associates), 172
Durlacher Limited, 799
DynaFund Ventures, L.L.C., 174
E-MERGE, 800
e4e Inc., 174
Early Stage Enterprises, L.P., 487
Earlybird Venture Capital, 800
eBlast Ventures, LLC, 353
ECICS Ventures Pte Ltd., 801
EDB Investments Pte Ltd., 802
Edelson Technology Partners, 487
EDF Ventures (F.K.A. Enterprise Development Fund), 458
Edge Capital Investment Co., LLC, 175
Eficor Oyj, 803
Eircom Enterprise Fund Ltd., 803
El Dorado Ventures, 176
Emerald Venture Group, 177
Emerging Technologies , 804
EnCompass Ventures, 704
Enterprise Equity (NI) Limited, 805
Epicea, 805
Episode-1 Partners, 806
EquiNet Venture Partners AG, 806
Equity Partners Management Pty Ltd, 807
Eqvitec Partners Oy, 807
Essex Woodlands Health Ventures (FKA:Woodlands Venture Partn, 354
ETCapital Ltd (AKA: Egan & Talbot Capital Ltd), 808
ETF Group, 808
EuclidSR Partners , 527
Euroc Venture Capital Corporation, 809

Euroventures Benelux Team B.V., 811
Evanston Business Investment Corp, 354
EVC Christows PLC (FKA: eVestment Company PLC), 812
Evergreen Canada Israel Investments Ltd, 812
Expanso Capital, 813
eXseed, 813
Fairfax Partners, 693
Fairgill Investments Property Limited, 814
FastVentures, 814
Federal Business Development Bank, 815
FEO Ventures Pte. Ltd., 815
Fidelity Ventures (FKA: Fidelity Venture Associates), 421
Financial Technology Research Corp., 529
FINORPA, 816
Finovelec, 817
First Gen-e Investments, 817
First Union Capital Partners, 600
Florida Capital Ventures, Ltd., 323
Fluke Venture Partners., 705
FLV Fund (AKA Flanders Language Valley Fund), 818
Fond Riziveho Kapitalu SRO, 819
Fonds D'Investissements R.T.V.L., 819
Fonds de Solidarité des Travailleurs du Québec (F.T.Q.), 820
Food Fund Ltd. Partnership, The, 467
Foresight, 820
ForetagsByggarna AB, 821
FORTKNOX-VENTURE AG, 821
Fortune Venture Capital Incorporated, 822
Forward Ventures, 180
Foundation Capital, 181
Foundation Capital Limited, 822
Frazier & Company, 705
Friedli Corporate Finance AG, 823
Frontenac Co., 355
Future Value Ventures, Inc., 717
G-51 Capital LLC, 665
Gabelli Multimedia Partners, 531
Gap Fund Managers Ltd, 825
Gateway Associates, L.P., 476
GATX Ventures (FKA: Meier Mitchell & Co.), 183
GCI Venture Partners, 314
Gemini Capital Fund Management Ltd, 825
Generation Capital Partners, 532
GENES GmbH Venture Services, 826
Genesis Partners, 826
Genevest Consulting Group, S.A., 827
Gideon Hixon Fund, 467
Giza Venture Capital (FKA Giza Investment Management), 828
Global Partner Ventures, 694
Global Technology Ventures (GTV), 829
Glynn Ventures, 186
GO Capital, 829
Go Equity GmbH, 829
Grand Pacific Venture Capital Company Ltd., 830
Granite Ventures LLC (FKA: H & Q Venture Associates), 186
Gresham Rabo Management Limited, 832
Greylock, 424
Grieve, Horner, Brown & Asculai, 833
Grotech Capital Group, 394
Grove Street Advisors, LLC, 425
Growth Factory, The, 833
GrowthWorks Capital, 834
Gryphon Ventures, 425
Gujarat Venture Finance Limited, 834
H&Q Asia Pacific, Ltd., 187
Hallador Venture Partners, 188
Halpern, Denny & Co., 425
Hanbyuck Investment Co Ltd, 836
HANNOVER Finanz GmbH, 837
Harbour Financial Co., 426
HarbourVest Partners, LLC., 426
Health Capital Group, 188
Healthcare Ventures LLC (FKA: Healthcare Investments), 490
Heidelberg Innovation GmbH, 837
Highland Capital Partners, 427
HMS Hawaii Management Partners, 341
HMS Holtron Management Services, Ltd, 838
HO2 Partners LLC, 665
Hoebich Venture Management, Inc., 190
Holland Venture B.V. (FKA: Holland Venture Holding C.V.), 839
Horizon Ventures (F.K.A. Technology Investments), 190
Horizonte Venture Management GmbH, 840
Hotung International Company, Ltd., 840
Houston Venture Partners (AKA: Houston Partners), 666
HPI Holding SA, 841
Hudson Venture Partners, 538
Humana Venture Capital, 384
Hummer Winblad Venture Partners, 191
Hydro-Quebec CapiTech Inc., 843
i2i Venture, 843
iAsia Alliance Capital, 844
IBB Beteiligungsgesellschaft mbH, 844
ICF Ventures Private Ltd., 845
ICICI Venture Funds Mngt. Co. Ltd., 846
Idanta Partners, Ltd., 191
IDG Ventures, 192
IEG Venture Management, Inc., 357
IFCI Venture Cap. Funds (Formerly Risk Capital & Tech.), 847
iFormation Group, 296
IKB Venture Capital GmbH (AKA IKB Beteiligungsgesellschaft , 848
IMH Industrie Management Holding GmbH, 848
iMinds (FKA: Interactive Minds), 193
Impex Venture Management Co., 540
Indekon Management Oy, 849
Indosuez Ventures, 194
Indus Venture Management Ltd., 851
Industrial Technology Investment Corporation, 851
Industrial Technology Securities Ltd, 851
Industry Ventures , 428
Infineon Ventures, 852
Information Technology Ventures, 195
Inman & Bowman, 195
InnoFinance Oy (FKA Culminatum Oy), 852
Innovacom, 853
Innovation Works, Inc., 628
Innovationsagentur Gesmbh, 854
InnovationsKapital Management Goteborg AB , 854
Innovest Group, Inc., 629
Innvotec Ltd, 854
Institutional Venture Partners, 196
Internet Healthcare Group, 297
Internet Incubator PLC, 856
Interregnum, 856

Intersouth Partners, 601
InterWest Partners, 197
inVentures Management Ltd, 857
InveStar Capital, Inc., 857
Investissement Desjardins, 857
Investment Securities of Colorado, Inc., 280
Invision AG (FKA Aureus Private Equity AG), 858
IPE Capital-Soc.De Cap.De Risoc SA, 859
ISEP NV, 860
IT Provider Advisor, 861
ITACT, 861
JAFCO Co. Ltd., 862
JAFCO Investment (FKA:Nomura/JAFCO Investment (Asia) Limited, 862
Jerusalem Global Ventures, 864
Johnston Associates, Inc., 490
JT Venture Partners, LLC, 491
Jump.Net Ventures, 668
Kangaroo Village, 865
Kansas City Equity Partners, 477
Kansas Technology Enterprise Corporation, 382
Kappa-IT Ventures, 865
KB Partners, LLC, 359
KBL Healthcare Ventures, 546
Kemper Ventures, 491
Kennet Capital Ltd, 866
Kentucky Highlands Investment Corporation, 384
Kettle Partners, L.P., 359
Keystone Minority Capital Fund, L.P., 630
Kick-Start Ventures, 866
Kinetic Ventures, Inc., 395
Kingsbury Associates, 200
Kinship Partners, 280
Kleiner Perkins Caufield & Byers, 200
Koor Corporate Venture Capital, 868
Korda & Co., 868
Ladybird Technologies, Ltd., 870
Landmark Partners, Inc., 298
Las Americas Administradora, 871
Launchworks Inc., 871
Lazard Technology Partners, 547
Lee Munder Venture Partners, 430
Leonard Mautner Associates, 203
LeVenture Kapitalbeteiligungsgesellschaft mbH & Co.KG, 872
Liberty Environmental Partners, 205
Libon Capital Management Limited, 873
Life Science Ventures, 873
Life Sciences Partners BV, 874
Lighthouse Capital Partners, 205
LINC Capital Partners, Inc., 361
Livingston Capital, Ltd., 281
London Ventures (Fund Managers) Ltd., 875
Lost Boys Incubator, 875
Lovett Miller & Co. Incorporated, 325
LRM Investeringsmaatschappij Voor Limburg, 875
Lucent Venture Partners, Inc., 207
M&F Associates, L.P., 549
Macquarie Technology Funds Management, 876
Macromedia Ventures, 208
Madison Dearborn Partners, LLC, 361
Magic Venture Capital, LLC, 208
Malmohus Invest AB, 877
Mangrove Capital Partners SA, 878
Manhattan Venture Co., Inc., 550
march.fifteen AG (FKA Peterp@n), 878
Marconi Ventures, 431
Maristeth Ventures, L.L.C., 707
Marquette Venture Partners, 362
Maryland Venture Capital Trust, 395
Massachusetts Technology Development Corp. (MTDC), 432
Massey Burch Capital Corp., 650
Materia Ventures Associates,L.P. (FKA:Pierce Nordquist Asso), 708
Matrix Capital, 695
Matrix Partners, 433
Matrix Private Equity, 879
Mayfield Fund, 210
MBA Venture Group, 669
MBW Management, Inc., 492
MDS Discovery Venture Management, Inc., 881
MDS Health Ventures, Inc. (AKA: MDS Capital Corp.), 881
Med-Tech Ventures, Inc., 492
Media Venture Partners, 211
MediaVenture Capital AG & Co. KGaA, 882
Medical Innovation Partners, 469
Medical Science Partners, 434
Medical Venture Holdings, Inc., 552
Medicis AG, 882
Medmax Ventures, L.P., 299
MedTech International, Inc., 670
MedVenture Associates, 212
Mees Pierson Investeringsmaat. B.V., 435
Menlo Ventures, 212
Meritage Private Equity Fund, 281
Merlin Biosciences (AKA Merlin Ventures), 884
Merrill, Pickard, Anderson & Eyre, 213
Midinvest Oy, 886
Midlands Venture Fund Managers Ltd. (AKA: Midven Ltd), 886
Mitiska NV, 887
Mitsui & Co., Ltd., 553
MK Global Ventures, 214
MMC adVentures Ltd, 888
Montgomery Associates, Inc., 215
Montgomery Medical Ventures, L.P., 215
Moore & Associates, 619
Moore Capital Management Inc., 554
Morel Ventures Limited, 888
Motorola Inc., 315
Mountaineer Capital LP, 716
MSC Venture Corporation Sdn. Bhd., 890
MTI Partners Ltd, 890
Multiventure Investment, Inc., 890
Murphree Venture Partners, 671
Mustang Ventures (FKA Siemens Mustang Ventures), 216
MVC AG (AKA Mitteldeutsche Venture Capital AG), 891
MVP Ventures (AKA: Milk Street Ventures), 436
Native Venture Capital Co., Ltd., 893
Natural Gas Partners, 300
Nazem & Co., 556
nCoTec Ventures Ltd, 893
NCP Advisors Philippines, Inc., 894
Netalone.com Ltd, 895
NetFuel Ventures, 364
Netjuice, 895

NetSpark Ventures N.V., 895
New Business Capital Fund Ltd., 499
New Enterprise Associates, 396
New Jersey Technology Council (AKA:NJTC), 493
New Venture Resources, 282
New Vista Capital, LLC, 218
New York Life Venture Capital Group, 557
New York State Science & Technology Foundation, 558
Newbury Ventures, 220
Newtek Ventures, 220
Nexit Ventures Oy, 897
NextGen Capital LLC, 697
NextGen Partners LLC, 221
NIF Ventures USA, Inc.(Nippon Investment & Finance Co., Ltd), 222
NIIT Ventures, 898
Nikko Capital Co Ltd, 899
NMT New Medical Technologies, 900
Nokia Venture Partners (AKA: Nokia Oy), 222
Nomura/JAFCO Investment (HK) Limited, 901
Noro-Moseley Partners, 336
North Bridge Venture Partners, 438
North Carolina Enterprise Fund, L.P., The, 602
North Carolina Technological Development Authority, Inc., 603
Northeast Ventures Corp., 469
Northern Venture Managers Limited, 902
Northwest Ohio Venture Fund, 615
Northwest Venture Associates, Inc.(FKA:Spokane Capital Mgmt), 709
Northzone Ventures (FKA Venture Partners AS), 902
Novartis AG, 903
Noveltek Venture Corp., 560
Novus Ventures, 223
NPV Capital Partners, LLC, 560
Nth Power Technologies, Inc, 224
Oak Investment Partners, 302
Obelisk Capital Pty Ltd, 904
Ohio Partners, 615
Olympus Capital Holdings Asia, 905
OmniMed Corp., 673
Oregon Resource and Technology Development Fund, 620
Oresa Ventures, S.A., 906
Orien Ventures, 303
Osborn Capital LLC, 440
OVP Venture Partners (FKA: Olympic Venture Partners), 709
Oxford Financial Services Corp., 698
PA Early Stage (AKA:Pennsylvania Early Stage Partners), 635
Pac-Link Management Corporation, 906
Pacific Capital Partners, 907
Pacific Northwest Partners SBIC, L.P., 710
Pacific Venture Group, 227
Paladin Partners, 711
Palmer Partners, L.P., 441
Palmetto Seed Capital Corp., 645
Palomar Ventures, 228
Pappajohn Capital Resources, 381
Paragon Venture Partners, 229
Pari Capital AG, 909
Part'com, 909
Partech International, 229
Pathfinder Venture Capital Funds, 470
Patricof & Co. Ventures, Inc., 563
Pequot Capital Management Inc., 564
Perennial Ventures (FKA: Tredegar Investments), 711
Philadelphia Ventures, Inc., 636
Phillips-Smith Specialty Retail Group, 673
Phoenix Home Life Mutual Insurance Co., 303
Phoenix Partners, The , 711
Pilotbird, 912
Pinô Venture Partners, 912
Pittsford Group, Inc., The , 565
Platinum Group, Inc., The , 565
PME Capital, 912
Point Venture Partners, 636
Polaris Venture Capital, 913
Polaris Venture Partners, 441
Polestar Capital, Inc., 366
Poly Ventures, 566
PolyTechnos Venture Partners GmbH, 913
PowerWord Capital Management, Inc., 914
Prelude Technology Investments Ltd, 915
Prime Technology Ventures NV, 916
Primedia Ventures, 567
Primus Venture Partners, Inc., 616
Prince Ventures, 367
Private Capital Corp., 131
ProQuest Investments, L.P., 493
ProSeed Capital Holdings CVA, 917
Prospect Street Ventures (FKA:Prospect Street Invest. Mgmt), 567
ProVen Private Equity (FKA:Guinness Mahon Development Cap.), 918
Proximitas AG Venture Capital, 918
Putnam Lovell Capital Partners, L.P., 232
Quaestus & Co. Inc. (FKA: Quaestus Management Corp..), 719
Quest Ventures, 233
Quester Capital Management Ltd, 920
RAF Ventures, 637
RCT BioVentures NE (Research Corporation Technologies), 442
red-stars.com, 920
Redleaf Venture Management, 234
Redwood Capital Corp., 235
Regulus International Capital Co., Inc., 304
Richard Jaffe & Co., Inc., 676
Ridgewood Capital Management LLC, 494
Riordan, Lewis & Haden, 236
Robertson Stephens & Company, LLC, 236
Rock Hill Ventures Inc.(FKA:Hillman Medical Ventures,Inc.), 638
Rocket Ventures, 237
RockMountain Ventures, 282
Rothschild Bioscience Unit, 922
Rothschild Ventures Asia Pte Ltd., 922
Rothschild Ventures, Inc., 570
Royalty Capital Fund, L.P. I/Royalty Capital Management, Inc, 443
RWI Group, LP, 239
S-Refit GmbH & Co KG , 923
S.R. One, Limited, 638
Saarlandische Wagnisfinanzierungsgesellschaft mbh (AKA SWG), 924
Sadot Venture Capital Management (1992) Ltd, 924
SAE Ventures, 306
Saffron Hill Ventures (FKA LootLab Ltd.), 924
Sanderling Ventures, 239
Sandler Capital Management, 571

Sandlot Capital LLC, 283
Sandton Financial Group, 240
Sapient Capital, 721
Saskatchewan Government Growth Fund, 925
SBC Ventures, 499
SBCA/A.G. Bartholomew & Associates, 131
SBV Venture Partners (AKA:Sigefi, Burnette & Vallee), 240
Schneider Electric Ventures, 926
Schooner Capital International, L.P., 444
Schroder Ventures, 445
Scottish Development Finance (SDF), 927
Scottish Equity Partners Limited, 927
Seaflower Ventures, 446
Seed Capital Ltd, 928
Seed Company Partners, 676
Sequoia Capital, 241
Sevin Rosen Management Co., 677
Shannon Development Company, 929
Shared Ventures, Inc., 470
Shaw Venture Partners (FKA: Shaw Glasgow Partners), 621
Shawmut Capital Partners, 447
Shott Capital Management, 574
Siemens Venture Capital GmbH, 930
Sienna Ventures (FKA: Sienna Holdings Inc.), 242
Sierra Ventures, 243
Sigma Partners, 243
Siguler Guff & Company, LLC, 575
Silicon Alley Venture Partners LLC (AKA SAVP) , 576
Silicon Valley Bank, 244
SilkRoute Capital Limited, 930
SingTel Ventures, 931
Siparex Group (FKA:Siparex Provinces de France), 931
Sitra (AKA Finnish National Fund for Research and Dev.), 932
SK Global Co., Ltd., 932
Societe Regionale d'Investissement de Bruxelles (SRIB/GIMB), 933
Sofinnova Partners, 934
Sofinnova Ventures, 246
SOFTBANK Capital Partners, 448
Softbank Corp., 935
SOFTBANK Venture Capital (FKA: SOFTBANK Technology Ventures), 247
Sonera Corporation Corporate Venture Capital, 935
Sopartec SA, 936
Sorrento Associates, Inc., 247
Southern California Ventures, 247
Southwest Venture Group, 678
Southwest Venture Partnerships, The, 678
Sovereign Capital (FKA:Nash, Sells & Partners Limited), 936
Spectrum Venture Management, 937
Speed Ventures, 937
Speirs Consultants, Inc., 938
Spencer Trask Ventures, Inc. (FKA: Spencer Trask Securities), 576
Spire Capital (FKA: Waller Capital Corp.), 577
Spray Venture Partners, 450
Sprout Group, 578
Square One Ventures (AKA: Smaby Group), 471
SRK Management Co., 578
SsangYong Cement (Singapore) Ltd, 939
SSM Ventures, 653
Star Capital Group, Inc., 939
Start-up Australia Pty Limited, 940
STARTech, 679
Starter Fluid, 250
Still River Fund, The, 450
Stonepath Europe, 941
Strathdon Investments Ltd, 942
Stratos Ventures Ltd Oy, 942
SudKB & SudVC, 942
Summit Group Ltd, The, 943
Sunsino Development Associate Inc., 944
Sutter Hill Ventures, 251
Swedestart Management AB, 944
Sweeney & Co., Inc., 308
Synopsys, Inc., 253
Syntel Inc. Web Incubator Program, 461
Tailink Venture Partners, 946
Taiwan United Venture Management Corporation, 946
Taiwan W&S Financial Management Incorporated, 946
Taylor & Turner, 253
tbg Technologie-Beteiligungsgesellschaft mbH, 947
TDH, 639
Techno Nord VC GmbH, 948
Techno-Venture Co. (Japan), 949
Technologieholding VC GmbH, 950
Technology Associates Management Corporation, 950
Technology Crossover Ventures, 254
Technology Partners, 255
Technology Venture Partners Pty Ltd, 950
Technology Ventures Corp., 500
Technology Ventures, L.L.C., 339
TechnoPlus Ventures, 951
Technostart GmbH, 951
Techpacific.com Ltd., 951
Techxas Ventures, LLC, 681
TecVenture Partners GmbH, 952
Teknia Invest Oy, 952
Teknoinvest Management As, 952
TeleSoft Partners, 256
Telia Business Innovation AB, 953
Telos Venture Partners, 256
Temasek Capital, 954
ThinkVentures.com Ltd, 954
Third Millennium Venture Capital, Ltd., 256
Thompson Clive, Inc., 257
Thorner Ventures, 258
Three Arch Partners, 258
Tokyo Small & Medium Business Investment & Consultation Co., 956
Toll Technologies, 957
Top Taiwan Venture Capital Company, Ltd., 957
Toucan Capital Corp., 399
Transamerica Mezzanine Financing, 645
Transpac Capital Pte, Ltd., 958
Trellis Partners, 682
Triad Investors Corp, 319
Tribune Ventures, 372
Trident Capital, 259
Triune Capital, 260
TTC Ventures, 453
TTP Venture Managers (FKA: The Technology Partnership), 960
TVM Techno Venture Management, 961
Twinning Ventures, 961
U.S. Medical Resources Corp., 616

U.S. Venture Partners, 261
UBS Capital (AKA Phildrew Ventures), 963
Union Venture Capital Corporation, 963
Unit Trust of India (UTI), 964
UniversityAngels.com, 584
UOB Venture Management Pte Ltd., 964
UST Capital Corp., 454
Valeo Ventures, 964
Vanenburg Group, 965
Vanguard Venture Partners, 262
VantagePoint Venture Partners, 263
VCM Venture Capital Management, 965
Venca Management, 263
Vencap Equities Alberta, Ltd., 966
Vencon Management, Inc., 585
Venrock Associates, 586
Ventana Financial Resources, Inc., 372
Ventana Global, 264
Venture Associates, Ltd., 285
Venture Capital Fund of New England, The, 454
Venture First Associates, 328
Venture Funding Group International, 587
Venture Funding, Ltd., 461
Venture Investment Management Company LLC (AKA: VIMAC), 454
Venture Investors Management LLC, 720
Venture Management Services Inc. (FKA: AT&T Ventures), 496
Venture Opportunities Corp., 588
Venture Partners, 310
Venture Partners AG, 968
Venture Select, 968
Venture Strategy Partners, 266
Venture TDF Pte Ltd., 968
VentureCap Management GmbH (AKA VCH Equity Group AG), 969
Venturepark Incubator (FKA grizzlyfarm AG), 969
Ventures Medical Associates, 683
Ventures West Management, Inc., 970
Veritas Venture Capital Management, Ltd., 970
Vertical Group, The, 496
Vesta Capital Partners (AKA: Vesta Group, The), 971
VigEcom Limited, 972
Vitesse Semiconductor Corporation, 268
Viventures Inc., 973
VTC Partners GmbH, 974
Wachtel & Co., Inc., 317
Walden International Investment Group (AKA: Walden Group), 269
Walden Israel, 975
Walnut Capital Corp., 701
Warburg, Pincus & Co., LLC. (FKA: E.M. Warburg, Pincus & Co), 590
Wasserstein, Perella & Co., Inc., 591
wellington partners venture capital GmbH, 975
Wellmax, Inc., 461
Western States Investment Group, 272
Western Technology Investment, 272
Westford Technology Ventures, L.P., 497
WI Harper Group, 273
Windamere Venture Partners, LLC, 273
Winthrop Ventures, 593
WL Ventures (FKA:Lothian Enterprise Ltd.), 978
Woodside Fund, 274
Working Ventures Canadian Fund, Inc., 978
Worldview Technology Partners, 275
WSI Holding Corporation, 595
YankeeTek Ventures, 456
Yasuda Enterprise Development Co., Ltd.(FKA: Nippon Ent.Dev), 275
Yorkshire Fund Managers Ltd., 979
Zero Stage Capital Co., Inc., 456
Zodiac Venture Capital KB, 980

Strategic Alliances

Cairnsford Associates Ltd., 766
Seaflower Ventures, 446

Turnaround

3i Group plc, 726
Aberdeen Murray Johnstone Private Equity, 728
Advent-Morro Equity Partners, 734
AIB WBK Fund Management Sp.zoo, 735
Alchemy Partners, 736
Alta Communications, 403
Ampersand Ventures, 404
AO Capital Corp, 287
Apax Partners & Cie (AKA: Apax France), 742
Apax Partners & Co. Ventures Ltd (AKA: Apax UK), 742
Argos Soditic SA, 744
Argus Capital Group, 745
Armada Asset Management, 746
Asian Direct Capital Management, 747
aventic Partners AG, 750
AXA Investment Managers Private Equity Europe, 751
Baring Private Equity Partners (FKA:Baring Venture Partners), 755
BayBG Bayerische Beteiligungsgesellschaft mbH, 757
BCR Asset Management Pty Ltd., 758
Berlin Capital Fund (FKA LBB Beteiligungsgesellschaft GmbH), 759
Bridgepoint Capital Ltd (FKA: NWEP & NatWest Ventures Ltd), 763
Bulldog Partners Limited, 764
Cairnsford Associates Ltd., 766
Calgary Enterprises, Inc., 514
Capital for Companies (CfC), 769
Capital Strategy Management Co., The, 349
Cascade Communications Ventures, LLC, 159
CDC Services Industries Gestion (CDC IXIS Private Equity), 775
CEI Ventures/Coastal Ventures LP, 388
Close Brothers Private Equity, 782
Continental Venture Capital , 784
Covent Industrial Capital Investment Co Ltd, 787
Crosbie & Co Inc, 789
CS Capital Partners, LLC, 486
DSE Investment Services Limited, 799
eBlast Ventures, LLC, 353
ECM Equity Capital Management GmbH, 802
Elderstreet Investments Ltd, 803
Equinox Investment Partners, 294
Euroventures Management AB , 811
Evergreen Capital Partners Inc, 528

F. Turismo-Capital De Risco SA, 814
Finansa Capital Limited, 816
FINORPA, 816
Fonds de Solidarité des Travailleurs du Québec (F.T.Q.), 820
Fortune Venture Capital Incorporated, 822
Fowler, Anthony & Co., 422
Gimvindus NV, 828
Granville Baird Capital Partners (FKA:Granville Pr Eq Mngrs), 830
Gresham Rabo Management Limited, 832
Growth Venture Group Pty Ltd., 833
H&Q Asia Pacific, Ltd., 187
HANNOVER Finanz GmbH, 837
Harvest Partners, Inc., 536
Hibernia Capital Partners, 837
ICICI Venture Funds Mngt. Co. Ltd., 846
IL&FS Venture Corporation (FKA. CreditCapital Venture Fund), 848
IMH Industrie Management Holding GmbH, 848
Incorporated Investors, 193
IndAsia Fund Advisors Private Limited, 849
Interregnum, 856
Investissements Novacap (AKA:Novacap Investments, Inc.), 858
Josephberg Grosz & Co., Inc., 545
KPMG Advent Management Group (FKA:Advent Western Pacific), 870
Lombard Investments, Inc., 206
MC Capital, Inc., 551
Merifin Capital Group, 883
Midlands Venture Fund Managers Ltd. (AKA: Midven Ltd), 886
Newbridge Capital Limited, 219
Northern Venture Managers Limited, 902
Olympus Capital Holdings Asia, 905
Pacific Corporate Group, Inc., 227
PAMA Group Inc. (FKA:Prudential Asset Management Asia), 908
Pantheon Ventures Limited, 908
Phoenix Equity Partners (FKA: DLJ European Private Equity), 911
PowerWord Capital Management, Inc., 914
PPM Ventures Ltd (FKA: Prudential Venture Managers Ltd), 914
Quaestus & Co. Inc. (FKA: Quaestus Management Corp..), 719
Royal Bank Private Equity (FKA: Royal Bank Development Cap), 922
Sand Aire Private Equity Ltd, 924
Sandton Financial Group, 240
Standard Life Investments (Private Equity) Ltd, 939
Star Capital Group, Inc., 939
Strathdon Investments Ltd, 942
SudKB & SudVC, 942
Synerfi S.A., 945
Teak Investment Partners II Limited, 948
Technology Associates Management Corporation, 950
Teknia Invest Oy, 952
Telecom Venture Group Ltd. (TVG), 953
Thompson Clive & Partners Limited, 955
Tianguis Ltd, 956
Transpac Capital Pte, Ltd., 958
Tvi Investments Bv, 960
UBF Mittelstandsfunanzierungs AG, 962
UBS Capital, 962
UBS Capital (AKA Phildrew Ventures), 963
Venture Associates Partners, LLC, 654

Company Index

1
100 X, 401
1st Source Capital Corp., 375

2
21st Century Health Ventures, 129
21st Century Internet Management Partners,LLC, 138
2M Invest, Inc., 138
2nd Generation Capital Corp, 648

3
3i Austria (FKA Bank Austria TFV High Tech -UB GmbH), 725
3I Capital Corporation (US), 401
3i Finland Oy (FKA SFK Finance), 725
3i Gestion SA, 725
3i Group plc, 726
3K Digital, 727
3TS Venture Partners AG, 727

4
4C Ventures (FKA: Olivetti Holding, N.V.), 501

5
550 Digital Media Ventures, 501

A
A.G. Edwards Capital Inc, 473
A.M. Pappas & Associates, 597
Abbott Capital Management, 501
Abell Venture Fund, 390
Aberdare Ventures, 138
Aberdeen Asset Managers, 728
Aberdeen Murray Johnstone Private Equity, 728
Aberlyn Capital Management Co., Inc., 501
Abingworth Venture Management Limited, 729
ABN AMRO Private Equity (AKA: ABN AMRO Capital (USA) Inc.), 343
ABN-AMRO Corporate Investments, 729
ABP Acquisition Corp, 287
ABS Ventures, 390
Acacia Venture Partners, 139
Academy Funds (FKA: Longleaf Venture Fund LLC), 597
Accel Partners, 139
Accel-KKR Internet Corp., 483
Accelerator Media (UK), Ltd, 730
Accenture Technology Ventures (FKA: AC Ventures), 140
Access Capital Partners, 730
Access Venture Partners, 277
Access2Net, 731
ACE Management, 731
Acer Technology Ventures(FKA:Acer Soft Capital Inc.), 141
ACF Equity Atlantic, Inc, 731
Acorn Ventures, Inc., 141
ACR Venture Management AB (AKA: ACR Capital AB), 732
ACT Venture Capital Ltd., 732
Adams Capital Management, Inc., 622
Adams Street Partners, LLC (FKA: Brinson Private Equity), 343
Adams, Harkness & Hill, Inc., 401
ADC Ventures, 463

AdCapital AG (FKA Berliner Elektro Holding AG), 732
ADD Partners, 733
Adler & Co., 502
Adler & Shaykin, 502
Advanced Materials Partners, Inc., 287
Advanced Technology Development Fund, 330
Advanced Technology Ventures, 401
Advanta Partners, L.P., 622
Advantage Capital Partners, 386
Advent International Corp., 402
Advent Management N.V., 733
Advent Venture Partners (FKA Advent Limited), 733
Advent-Morro Equity Partners, 734
Adveq Management AG (FKA Advisers on Private Equity AG), 734
Aether Systems Capital, 390
Affinity Capital Management(FKA:Peterson-Spencer-Fansler Co), 463
AGF Private Equity, 735
Agilent Ventures, 142
Agio Capital Partners I, L.P., 463
Agribusiness Partners International Partners, 479
AIB WBK Fund Management Sp.zoo, 735
AIG Capital Partners Inc., 503
AIG Investment Corporation (Asia) Limited, 735
Akin Gump Investment Partners 2000, LP, 655
Al Shugart International (ASI), 142
Alan I. Goldman & Associates, 483
Albemarle Private Equity Ltd, 735
Alcatel Ventures, 142
Alce Partners, L.P., 143
Alchemy Partners, 736
Alexander Hutton, Inc., 702
Alice Ventures, 736
Alignment Capital Partners, LLC, 655
Alimansky Capital Group, Inc., 504
All Asia Partners, 737
Allegis Capital (AKA:Allegis Media Technology Ventures), 143
Allegra Partners (FKA: Lawrence, Smith & Horey), 504
Allen & Buckeridge Pty Ltd, 737
Allen & Co., Inc., 504
Alliance Financial of Houston, 655
Alliance Investment Capital, 737
Alliance Technology Ventures, 330
Alliance Venture Capital Advisors Limited, 738
Allied Capital Corporation, 312
Alloy Ventures, 143
Allsop Venture Partners, 380
Allstate Private Equity, 344
ALLTEL Ventures, 137
Alpha Capital Corporation, L.L.C., 622
Alpha Capital Partners, Inc., 344
Alpha Group (FKA:Alpha Associates Management, Ltd.), 738
Alpha Ventures SA, 738
Alpine Technology Ventures, 144
Alpinvest Holding NV (AKA NIB Capital Private Equity NV), 739
Alta Berkeley Venture Partners, 739
Alta Communications, 403
Alta Partners, 144
Altamira Capital Corp., 739
Altira Group LLC, 277
Altos Ventures, 144
Amadeus Capital Partners, 740
American Acquisition Partners, 483
American Capital Strategies, 391
American Century Ventures, 473
American Healthcare Fund, 345
American Research & Development Corp., 404
American Securities, L.P., 505
Amerimark Capital Group, 656
Amerindo Investment Advisors, Inc., 505
Ameritech Development Corp., 345
AMP Asset Management Limited - Development Capital, 740
Ampersand Ventures, 404
Amphion Ventures L.P.(FKA: Wolfensohn Associates, L.P.), 506
AMT Capital Ltd. (AKA: AMT Venture Partners, Ltd.), 656
AMWIN Management Pty Ltd, 741
Angel Investors, LP, 145
Angel-Invest, 741
Angels Forum Management Company, 145
Anila Fund (AKA: Anila.org, LLC), 145
Annapolis Ventures LLC, 391
Antares Capital Corp. (FKA: Antares Leveraged Capital Corp), 345
Antares Capital Corporation (FKA: Harbor Ventures Corp.), 320
antfactory, 741
Anthem Capital, L.P., 391
AO Capital Corp, 287
Apax Globis Partners & Co. (APAX Japan), 741
Apax Partners & Cie (AKA: Apax France), 742
Apax Partners & Co. Ventures Ltd (AKA: Apax UK), 742
Apax Partners & Co.Beteiligungsberatung AG, 742
APC Asset Management, 743
Apex Venture Partners, 346
Apex Ventures BV, 743
APIDC-Venture Capital Limited, 743
Apollo Invest, 744
Applied Genomic Technology Capital Funds (AGTC), 405
Applied Technology, 405
APV Technology Partners, 146
Arbor Partners LLC, 457
ARCH Venture Partners, 346
Ardsheil, Inc., 506
Arena Capital Partners, 507
Arete Corporation, 482
Argentum Group, The, 507
ArgNor Wireless Ventures, 744
Argo Global Capital, Inc., 406
Argos Soditic SA, 744
Argosy Partners, 623
Argosy Partners, Inc., 745
Argus Capital Group, 745
Aria Ventures Ltd., 745
Arkansas Capital Corporation, 137
Arkoma Venture Partners, 657
Armada Asset Management, 746
Artemis Ventures, 146
Artesian Capital, 464
Arthur Andersen Ventures LLC, 657
Arthur P. Gould & Co., 507
Arthur Rock & Co., 146
Artisan Digital Media, 147
Arts Alliance, 746
AS Venture GmbH, 746

ASC Group, 746
Ascend Technology Ventures, 747
Ascent Venture Partners, 406
Asian Direct Capital Management, 747
Asian Infrastructure Fund Advisers Limited, 748
AsiaTech Internet Group (ATIG) (FKA: AsiaTech Ventures), 748
Aspen Ventures (formerly 3i Ventures), 147
Aspiro Ventures, 748
Asset Management Company Venture Capital, 147
At India Management Services Pvt. Ltd., 749
Athena Technology Ventures, 148
Athenian Ventures (FKA: Ohio Valley Venture Fund), 608
Atila Venture Partners Ltd., 749
Atlantic Capital, 407
Atlantic Coastal Ventures, L.P.(AKA:Multimedia Broadcast In), 312
Atlantic Medical Management, LLC, 508
Atlantis Group LLC, 598
Atlas Venture, 407
Atle Foretagskapital AB (FKA Foretagskapital AB), 749
Atle Ventures (FKA Teknologiparkernas Utveckling AB), 749
Attractor Investment Management, 148
August Capital Management, 148
August Partners, 508
AUGUSTA Venture GmbH, 749
Auric Asset Management Pte. Ltd., 750
Aurora Funds, Inc., 598
Austin Ventures, L.P., 657
Australian Technology Group Ltd, 750
Authosis, 149
AV Labs, 658
Avalon Investments Inc., 457
aventic Partners AG, 750
Avery Business Development Services, 320
AVI Capital, L.P., 149
Aweida Ventures, 277
AXA Investment Managers, 509
AXA Investment Managers Private Equity Europe, 751
AxaVision, Inc., 509
Axiom Venture Partners, L.P., 288
Axiomlab PLC, 751
Axxon Capital, Inc., 408
Ayala Internet Venture Partners, 751
Azure Capital Partners, 149

B

b-business partners, 752
B2B-Hive, LLC, 509
BA Venture Partners (AKA: BankAmerica Ventures), 150
Baccharis Capital, Inc., 150
Bachow & Associates, Inc., 623
Bailey & Co. Inc., 752
bainlab, 752
Baird Capital Partners, 347
Baker Capital Corp., 510
Ballentine Capital Management, 288
BaltCap Management, Ltd, 753
Bamboo Investments Plc (FKA Railike Limited), 753
Banc One Capital Partners, 608
BancAmerica Capital Investors (FKA:NationsBanc Capital Corp), 598
BancAmerica Equity Partners (Asia), 753
BancBoston Capital/BancBoston Ventures, 408
BancBoston/Robertson Stephens, 151
BanChem Financial Services, Inc., 658
Bancorp Hawaii SBIC, Inc., 341
Band of Angels, 151
BANEXI Corp., 753
Bangert Dawes Reade Davis & Thom, 151
Bank Funds, The, 347
Bank One Equity Investors, Inc., 386
Bankers Capital Corp., 473
Bankers Trust (AKA:BT Technology Partners), 510
Bankers Trust New York Corp./Deutsche Banc Alex Brown, 510
BankInvest Group AS, 754
Banque Bruxelles Lambert (ING Group), 754
Banque De Vizille, 754
Barclays Ventures, 755
Baring Communications Equity, 755
Baring Private Equity Partners (FKA:Baring Venture Partners), 755
Barksdale Group, 152
Barnard & Company, 511
Barrington Partners, 152
Bastion Capital Corp., 152
Batavia Group, Ltd., The, 511
Batavia Investment Management Ltd, 756
Battelle Venture Partners (Scientific Advances), 608
Batterson Venture Partners(AKA:BVP), 348
Battery Ventures, L.P., 409
Bausch & Lomb, Inc., 511
Baxter Associates, Inc., 289
Bay City Capital LLC, 153
Bay Partners, 153
BayBG Bayerische Beteiligungsgesellschaft mbH, 757
Bayern Kapital Risikokapitalbeteiligungs GmbH, 757
BBS Finance, 757
BC Partners, 757
BCE Capital, 758
BCI Partners, 484
BCM Technologies, Inc., 658
BCR Asset Management Pty Ltd., 758
Beacon Partners, Inc., 289
Bear Ventures, 511
Becton, Dickinson & Co. (AKA: BD Ventures), 484
Bedford Capital Corp., 512
Bedrock Capital Partners, 409
Beecken, Petty & Co. LLC, 348
Behrman Capital, 512
Ben Franklin Technology Center, The, 623
Benchmark Capital, 154
Benefit Capital Companies, Inc., The, 480
Berenberg Private Equity GmbH, 759
Berkeley International Capital Corp., 154
Berkshire Partners, 410
Berkshires Capital Investors, 410
Berlin Capital Fund (FKA LBB Beteiligungsgesellschaft GmbH), 759
Berthel Fisher & Company Planning, Inc., 380
Berwind Financial Group, L.P., 623
Bessemer Venture Partners, 410
Betwin Investments, Inc., 760
Big Bang Ventures, 760

BioAsia Investments, LLC, 155
BioVentures Investors, LLC, 411
Birchmere Ventures, Inc.(FKA:Birchmere Investments), 624
Bloom & Co., 512
Blue Chip Venture Company, 609
Blue Ribbon AG, 760
Blue Rock Capital, 319
Blue Water Capital, LLC, 690
Blueprint Ventures, LLC, 155
Blueshift Internet Ventures, 761
BlueStar Ventures, 348
Bluestem Capital Partners, 647
BlueStream Ventures, 464
Blumberg Capital Ventures, 155
bmp Aktiengesellschaft AG, 761
BOME Investors, Inc., 473
BORANCO Management, L.L.C., 277
Boston Capital Ventures, 411
Boston Financial & Equity Corp., 412
Boston Millennia Partners, 412
Boston University Community Technology Fund, 413
Boston Venture Partners, Ltd., 761
Boston Ventures Management, Inc., 413
Botticelli Venture Funds (AKA: Botticelli Investments), 761
Botts & Co., 762
Boulder Ventures, Ltd., 392
Bowman Capital, 156
Brad Peery Capital, 156
Bradford Equities Fund, LLC, 513
BrainHeart Capital AB, 762
BrainWorks Ventures, 330
Brait Capital Partners, 762
Brand Equity Ventures, 289
Brantley Venture Partners, 609
Bridge Partners, LLC, 393
Bridgepoint Capital Ltd (FKA: NWEP & NatWest Ventures Ltd), 763
Brightstar, 763
Bristol Capital Management, 513
Bristol Investment Trust, 413
British Steel Ltd., 764
Broadmark Capital Corp., 702
Brook Venture Management, L.L.C., 414
Bruce F. Glaspell & Associates, 498
Buena Venture Associates, 659
Bulldog Partners Limited, 764
Bure Equity, 765
Burr, Egan, Deleage & Co., 414
Burrill & Company, 156
Business Link Doncaster, 765
Butler Capital Partners France, 765
BV Capital (FKA Bertelsmann Ventures LP), 157

C

C3 Holdings, LLC, 474
C3 Investments, Inc., 157
Cable & Howse Ventures, 703
Cairnsford Associates Ltd., 766
Calgary Enterprises, Inc., 514
Caltech Capital Partners Ltd., 766
Calvert Social Venture Partners, L.P., 690
Cambria Group, The, 157
Cambrian Ventures, 158
Cambridge Innovations (FKA: Cambridge Incubator), 415
Cambridge Research & Innovation Ltd (AKA CRIL), 767
Cambridge Samsung Partners, 415
Cambridge Technology Capital, 415
Cambridge Venture Partners, 375
Camden Partners, Inc. (FKA: Cahill, Warnock & Co., L.L.C.), 393
Camelot Enterprises Private Limited, 767
Camelot Ventures, 457
Canaan Partners, 290
Canbank Venture Capital Fund Ltd, 767
Candover Investments PLC, 768
Canterbury Capital L.L.C.(AKA: Canterbury Detroit Partners), 514
Capital Across America, L.P., 648
Capital Development & Investment Co. Ltd., 768
Capital Express, L.L.C., 484
Capital For Business, Inc., 474
Capital for Companies (CfC), 769
Capital Insights, L.L.C., 645
Capital Investments, Inc., 717
Capital Investors, 690
Capital Network, The (AKA: Texas Capital Network), 659
Capital Partners LLC, 769
Capital Prive (FKA NatWest Equity Partners, France), 769
Capital Resource Partners, 415
Capital Riesgo Internet SCR SA (BSCH), 770
Capital Services & Resources, Inc., 648
Capital Southwest Corporation, 660
Capital Strategy Management Co., The, 349
Capital Technology Group, LLC, 610
Capital Z Asia, 770
CapitalSouth Partners, L.L.C., 599
Capman Management GmbH, 770
Capricorn Ventures International, 770
Capstone Ventures SBIC, L.P., 158
CapVest Management, Ltd, 771
CapVis Equity Partners AG, 771
Cardinal Investment Company, Inc., 660
Cardinal Partners (FKA: Cardinal Health Partners), 485
Cardinal Ventures, L.L.C., 375
Cariad Capital, Inc., 642
Carillon Capital, Inc., 610
Carlin Ventures LLC, 514
Carmel Ventures, 772
Carolinas Capital Investment Corp., 599
Carousel Capital Partners, 599
Cascade Communications Ventures, LLC, 159
Castile Ventures, 416
Castle Group, Ltd., The, 515
Castle Harlan Australian Mezzanine Partners Pty. Ltd., 772
CastleHill Ventures, 772
Catalyst Fund Management & Research Ltd, 773
Catalyst Group, The, 660
Catalyst Partners Inc., 278
Catalyst Venture Capital Firm, 773
Catalyst Ventures, 393
Catella IT AB, 773
Catterton Partners, 290
Cazenove Private Equity, 773
CB Capital Investors, L.P., 515
CB Health Ventures LLC, 416

CCFL Mezzanine Partners of Canada, 774
CCG Venture Partners, LLC, 661
CD Technicom S.A., 774
CDC Advisors Private Ltd., 775
CDC Innovation Partners, 775
CDC Services Industries Gestion (CDC IXIS Private Equity), 775
CE Unterberg Towbin (FKA:Unterberg Harris Capital Partners), 515
Cedar Creek Partners, LLC, 717
CEI Ventures/Coastal Ventures LP, 388
Celtic House International, 775
Centennial Ventures, 278
CenterPoint Venture Partners, 661
Central America Investment Managers, 776
Century Capital Management, Inc., 417
CenturyTel Inc, 387
CEO Advisors, 321
CEO Venture Fund, 625
Cerulean Fund/WGC Enterprises, 350
CGW Southeast Partners (AKA: Cravey, Green, & Wahlen), 331
Challenger International Ltd., 776
Champion Consulting Group, Incorporated, 776
Champion Ventures, 159
Chancellor Fund, 649
Chanen, Painter & Co., Ltd., 703
Charles River Ventures, 417
Charles Street Securities, Inc., 515
Charter Growth Capital, 160
Charter Ventures, 160
Chartwell Capital Management Co., Inc., 321
Chase H&Q (FKA Hambrecht & Quist), 160
CHB Capital Partners, 278
Cheng Xin Technology Development Corp. (FKA:Fidelity VC Corp, 776
Cherry Tree Investments, Inc., 464
Chestnut Street Partners, Inc., 417
Chiao Tung Bank, 776
Child Health Investment Corporation, 382
China Development Corp., 777
China Enterprise Investment Management Limited, 777
China Venture Management, Inc., 777
ChinaVest, 778
Chisholm Private Capital Partners, 618
Chrysalead, 778
Chrysalis Capital, 778
Chrysalis Ventures, 384
Churchill Capital, Inc., 465
CIBC Capital Partners (FKA: CIBC Wood Gundy Capital), 516
CIBC Oppenheimer & Co., Inc., 516
CICLAD, 778
CID Equity Partners, 376
Cinven Ltd, 779
Circle Ventures, Inc., 376
cirlab!, 779
CIT Group/Venture Capital, Inc., The, 485
Citadel Pooled Development Ltd., 779
Citibank Global Asset Management, 517
Citicorp Capital Asia (AKA: CITIC Pacific Ltd.), 780
Citicorp Venture Capital, Ltd., 517
Citizens Capital and Citizens Ventures, 418
CIVC Partners (FKA:Continental Illinois Venture Corp.), 350
Claflin Capital Management, Inc., 418
Clairvest Group, Inc., 780
Clal Venture Capital Management Ltd (AKA CVC Management), 781
Clarion Capital Corp., 610
Clarity Capital, 419
Classic Fund Management, Ltd., 781
Clearstone Venture Partners (FKA: idealab! Capital Partners), 161
Clemente Capital (Asia) Ltd., 781
Close Brothers Investment Limited, 782
Close Brothers Private Equity, 782
CM Equity Partners, 517
CMB Capital, LLC (CMBC), 322
CMEA Ventures (FKA:Chemicals & Materials Enterprise Associa), 161
CNI Ventures, 133
Coates Myer & Co. Pty Ltd. (AKA: CM Capital Investments), 782
Code, Hennessy & Simmons, LLC., 351
Cohen & Co., L.L.C., 517
Coleman Swenson Booth Inc.(FKA:Coleman Swenson Hoffman Booth, 649
Coleman Venture Group, 518
Collinson, Howe & Lennox, LLC, 291
Colonial First State Private Equity Ltd (FKA: Hambro-G Mgmt), 782
Colonnade Capital L.L.C., 691
Colorado Venture Management, 278
Columbia Capital Group, Inc., 313
Columbine Venture Funds, The, 279
Comdisco Ventures, 162
Commerce One Ventures, 162
Commerz Beteiligungsgesellschaft mbH (CBG), 783
Commonwealth BioVentures Inc. (CBI), 389
Commonwealth Capital Ventures L.P., 419
CommTech International, 163
Compass Investment Management Ltd., 783
Compass Technology Partners, 163
ComVentures (AKA: Communications Ventures), 163
Concord Venture Management (FKA:Nitzanim), 784
Concordia Capital, 784
Connecticut Innovations, Inc., 291
Connecticut-Greene Ventures, L.P., 291
Conning Capital Partners, 292
Constellation Ventures, 518
Consumer Venture Partners, 292
Continental S.B.I.C., 691
Continental Venture Capital, 784
Continuum Group Limited, 785
Convergence Partners L.P., 164
Copernicus Capital Management Ltd, 785
Copley Venture Partners, 420
CORAL Ventures, 465
Cordova Ventures (FKA:Cordova Capital), 331
Core Capital Partners, 313
Core Pacific Consulting Company, 786
Cornerstone Equity Investors, LLC, 519
Corning Capital (AKA: Corning Technology Ventures), 420
Coronado Venture Fund, 133
Corpfin Capital S.A., 786
Corporate Growth Assistance, Ltd., 786
Corporate Venture Partners, L.P., 519
Covent Industrial Capital Investment Co Ltd, 787
Cowen & Co., 520

CPH Investment Corp., 787
CR&T Ventures AB, 787
Cramer Rosenthal McGlynn, LLC, 520
Creafund CVBA, 788
Credit Lyonnais Securities Asia Pvt Equity Limited (CLSA), 788
Crescendo Venture Management LLC (FKA:IAI Ventures), 466
Crescent Capital NI Ltd (FKA Hambro Northern Ireland), 788
Crest Communications Holdings LLC, 520
Crestview Financial Group, The, 292
Crocker Capital/Crocker Assoc., 164
Crosbie & Co Inc, 789
Cross Atlantic Capital Partners, 625
CrossBow Ventures, 322
Crosslink Capital (FKA: Omega Venture Partners), 165
Crossroads Capital Partners, LLC, 165
Crown Advisors International, Ltd., 521
Crown Capital Corp, 475
Crystal Internet Venture Fund, L.P., 611
CS Capital Partners, LLC, 486
CSK Venture Capital Co., Ltd., 789
CT Holdings, 661
Cullinane & Donnelly Venture Partners, L.P., 293
Cupertino Ventures Partnership, L.P., 165
Cureton & Co., Inc., 662
CVC Capital Partners, 790
CW Group, Inc., 521
CyberStarts, 332
CyberWorks Ventures, 790
Cycle & Carriage Industries Pte Ltd, 791
Cygnus Venture Partners, 791
Czech Venture Partners Sro, 791

D
D. Brain Capital Company, Ltd., 791
D.H. Blair Investment Banking Corp., 521
Daewoo Venture Capital Co Ltd, 792
Daimler Chrysler Venture Gmbh (AKA DCV), 792
Dain Raucher Wessels, 466
Daiwa Business Investment Co Ltd, The, 793
Dakota Group, The, 166
Dali, Hook Partners (FKA: Hook Partners), 662
Danish Development Finance Corp., 793
DANSK Udviklingsfinansiering A/S, 793
Danske eVentures, 794
Dassault Developpment, 794
Dauphin Capital Partners, 522
Davis Group, 166
Davis, Tuttle Venture Partners, L.P.(FKA:Davis Venture), 618
Dawes Investment Partners, L.P., 167
DB Venture Partners, 794
De Vries & Co., Inc., 476
Dean & Associates, 279
Defta Partners, 167
Delaware Valley Community Reinvestment Fund (DVCRF), 626
Delmag Ventures, 394
Delphi Ventures, 167
Delta Partners, 795
Delta Ventures, 795
Denali Venture Capital, 168
Desai Capital Management Inc., 522
Deucalion Venture Partners, 168
Deutsche Asset Management (Australia) Limited, 795
Deutsche Bank eVentures (AKA DB eVentures), 795
Deutsche Beteiligungs AG, 796
Deutsche Effecten und Wechsel-Beteiligungsgesellschaft AG, 796
Deutsche Venture Capital GmbH (DVCG), 796
Developers Equity Corp., 169
Development Corp. of Austin, 467
DFW Capital Partners (AKA:DeMuth, Folger & Wetherill), 486
Diamondhead Ventures, L.P., 169
Digital Media Campus, 169
Digital Partners, 704
Digital Ventures (FKA Digital Technology Partners, LLC), 169
Dillon Read & Co., 523
Dinner Club, LLC, The, 692
Direct Capital Private Equity, 797
Discovery Capital, 797
Divine interVentures (FKA: Platinum Venture Partners), 351
DN Partners, 352
Doll Capital Management, 169
Dolphin Communications, 523
Domain Associates, L.L.C., 486
Dominion Ventures, Inc., 170
Dongbu Venture Capital Co Ltd, 797
DOR Ventures, 798
Dorset Capital, 170
Dot Edu Ventures, 171
DotCom Ventures L.P., 171
Dougery Ventures, 171
Dow Chemical Co., 458
Downer & Co., 420
Draper Atlantic Management Co., LLC, 692
Draper Fisher Jurvetson (FKA: Draper Associates), 172
Draper Fisher Jurvetson ePlanet Ventures, LP, 172
Draper Fisher Jurvetson Gotham Venture Partners, 523
Draper International, 172
Draper Richards, 173
Draper Triangle Ventures LP, 626
Dresdner Kleinwort Capital, 524
Dresner Capital Resources, Inc., 352
Drug Royalty Corp., Inc., 798
Drysdale Enterprises, 173
DSE Investment Services Limited, 799
Duchossois TECnology Partners, LLC, 353
Dunedin Capital Partners Ltd (FKA:Dunedin Ventures Limited), 799
Durlacher Limited, 799
DynaFund Ventures, L.L.C., 174

E
E*Capital Corporation, 174
E-MERGE, 800
e4e Inc., 174
Early Stage Enterprises, L.P., 487
Earlybird Venture Capital, 800
EarlyBirdCapital.com Inc., 524
East River Ventures, L.P., 524
East West Venture Investors, L.P., 175
East/West Venture Group FKA:East/West Capital Associates, 175
Easton Hunt Capital Partners, 525
eBlast Ventures, LLC, 353
EBM Sociedad Gestora de Entidades de Capital Riesgo SA, 800

ECAT Development Capital Limited, 801
ECI Ventures Ltd, 801
ECICS Ventures Pte Ltd., 801
ECM Equity Capital Management GmbH, 802
eCOM Partners LLC, 293
eCompanies-Evercore Venture Partners (E2VP), 175
EDB Investments Pte Ltd., 802
Edelson Technology Partners, 487
EDF Ventures (F.K.A. Enterprise Development Fund), 458
Edge Capital Investment Co., LLC, 175
Edison Venture Fund, 488
Edmond de Rothschild Venture Capital Management, 802
Eficor Oyj, 803
eFund, LLC, 704
Egan-Managed Capital, 421
EGL Holdings, Inc./Nat West Ventures USA, L.P., 332
Eircom Enterprise Fund Ltd., 803
El Dorado Ventures, 176
Elderstreet Investments Ltd, 803
Eldon Capital, Inc, 525
Electra Fleming Limited, 525
Electra Partners Asia [FKA: JF Electra Limited], 803
Electronics For Imaging (AKA: EFI), 177
Elk Associates Funding Corp., 526
Embryon Capital, 394
Emerald Venture Group, 177
Emerging Markets Partnership, 314
Emerging Technologies, 804
Empire Ventures, 620
EnCompass Ventures, 704
Encore Venture Partners, LP, 177
Endeavor Capital Management, 294
Endeavour Capital Pty Ltd, 804
EnerTech Capital Partners, L.P., 626
Eno River Capital, 600
Enron Broadband Ventures, 663
Enterprise Equity (NI) Limited, 805
Enterprise Investors, 526
Enterprise Merchant Bank, 382
Enterprise Partners, 178
EnterpriseAsia.com, 805
Eos Partners, L.P., 527
Epicea, 805
Episode-1 Partners, 806
EPS Finanz AG, 806
EquiNet Venture Partners AG, 806
Equinox Investment Partners, 294
Equitas, L.P., 649
Equity Partners Management Pty Ltd, 807
Equity Ventures, Ltd, 807
Equity-South (FKA:Grubb & Williams Ltd.), 333
equity4life AG, 807
Equus Capital Corp., 663
Eqvitec Partners Oy, 807
Espirito Santo Development, 808
Essex Investment Management, 421
Essex Woodlands Health Ventures (FKA:Woodlands Venture Partn, 354
eStreetCapital.com, 133
ETCapital Ltd (AKA: Egan & Talbot Capital Ltd), 808
ETF Group, 808
EuclidSR Partners, 527
EURAZEO (FKA Gaz-et-Eaux & AZEO), 809
Euroc Venture Capital Corporation, 809
Eurofund LP, 810
Eurolink International, 178
European Acquisition Capital Ltd., 810
European Equity Partners, 810
European Investment Bank, The, 811
European Webgroup, 811
Euroventures Benelux Team B.V., 811
Euroventures Management AB, 811
Evanston Business Investment Corp, 354
EVC Christows PLC (FKA: eVestment Company PLC), 812
eVerger Associates, 812
Evergreen Canada Israel Investments Ltd, 812
Evergreen Capital Partners Inc, 528
Evergreen Ventures, 686
eVolution Global Partners, 813
Excel Communications, 663
Exelon Capital Partners, 627
Exeter Capital, L.P., 528
Expanso Capital, 813
Exponential Business Development Co., 529
eXseed, 813

F

F. Turismo-Capital De Risco SA, 814
Fairfax Partners, 693
Fairgill Investments Property Limited, 814
far blue, 814
Far East Capital Corp., 179
FastVentures, 814
FBR CoMotion Venture Capital, 705
FBR Technology Venture Partners,L.P.(AKA:Friedman,Billings), 693
Federal Business Development Bank, 815
FEO Ventures Pte. Ltd., 815
Ferrer Freeman Thompson & Co, 295
FHL Capital Corp., 129
Fidelity Ventures (FKA: Fidelity Venture Associates), 421
FINADVANCE S.A., 815
Financial Capital Resources, Inc., 333
Financial Technology Research Corp., 529
Financial Technology Ventures, 179
Finansa Capital Limited, 816
FINORPA, 816
FINOVA Mezzanine Capital, Inc. (FKA: Sirrom Capital Corp), 650
Finovelec, 817
Firemark Advisors, Inc., 488
First Analysis Venture Capital (FKA:First Analysis Corp), 354
First Atlantic Capital, Ltd., 530
First Avenue Partners, 650
First Capital Management Co., 664
First Charter Partners, Inc., 664
First Floor Capital Sdn. Bhd., 817
First Gen-e Investments, 817
First Growth Capital, Inc., 333
First New England Capital, L.P., 295
First Princeton Capital Corp., 489
First Security Business Investment Corp., 686
First Union Capital Partners, 600

Five Paces Ventures, 334
FJ Benjamin Holdings Pte Ltd, 818
FJC Growth Capital Corp., 129
FLAG Venture Partners (FKA Fox Venture Partners), 295
Flatiron Partners, 530
Flinders Capital Limited, 818
Florida Capital Partners, 322
Florida Capital Ventures, Ltd., 323
Fluke Venture Partners., 705
FLV Fund (AKA Flanders Language Valley Fund), 818
Flynn Venture, LLC, 180
Fond Riziveho Kapitalu SRO, 819
Fondinvest (Grp. Caisse de Depots), 819
Fonds D'Investissements R.T.V.L., 819
Fonds de Solidarité des Travailleurs du Québec (F.T.Q.), 820
Food Fund Ltd. Partnership, The, 467
Forefront Capital, 279
Foresight, 820
ForetagsByggarna AB, 821
Forrest Binkley & Brown, 180
Fort Washington Capital Partners, LLC, 611
FORTKNOX-VENTURE AG, 821
Fortune Consulting Group Incorporated, 821
Fortune International Limited, 821
Fortune Venture Capital Incorporated, 822
Fortune Venture Management Pte Ltd., 822
Forward Ventures, 180
Foster Management Company, 627
Foundation Capital, 181
Foundation Capital Limited, 822
Founders Equity, Inc., 530
Fountainhead Capital Ltd., 823
Fowler, Anthony & Co., 422
Fraser & Neave Limited, 823
Frazier & Company, 705
Frederic H. Mayerson Group, The, 612
Fremont Partners, 181
Friedli Corporate Finance AG, 823
Friends Ivory & Sime Private Equity (Ivory &Sime Baronsmead), 823
Friulia SpA Fin.Reg.Friuli-Venezia, 824
Frontenac Co., 355
Frontier Capital, LLC, 600
Frontline Capital Group, Inc., 531
Frontline Capital, Inc., 334
Frost Capital Partners, 182
Fuqua Ventures, LLC, 334
Fusient Ventures, 531
Fusion Ventures, 601
Future Fund, The, 627
Future Value Ventures, Inc., 717
Future Venture Capital Co., Ltd., 824

G

G-51 Capital LLC, 665
Gabelli Multimedia Partners, 531
Gabelli Securities Inc., 531
Gabriel Venture Partners, 182
Galen Associates (FKA:Galen Partners), 531
Galileo Partners, 824
Gamma Investors LLC, 627
Gaon Asset Management, 825
Gap Fund Managers Ltd, 825
Gateway Associates, L.P., 476
GATX Ventures (FKA: Meier Mitchell & Co.), 183
GATX/MM Venture Partners, 183
Gazelle TechVentures, 377
GCI, 718
GCI Venture Partners, 314
Gemini Capital Fund Management Ltd, 825
Gemini Investors LLC (AKA: GMN Investors), 423
General Catalyst Group LLC, 423
General Enterprise Management Services Ltd (AKA: GEMS), 825
Generation Capital Partners, 532
GENES GmbH Venture Services, 826
Genesee Funding, Inc., 532
Genesis Capital, Inc., 533
Genesis Partners, 826
Genesys Partners, 533
Geneva Merchant Banking Partners, 601
Geneva Venture Partners, 184
Genevest Consulting Group, S.A., 827
Geocapital Partners, L.L.C., 489
Gideon Hixon Fund, 467
Gilde Investment Management, 827
Gimvindus NV, 828
Giza Venture Capital (FKA Giza Investment Management), 828
GKM Venture Partners, LP, 184
Gleacher & Co., 534
Glencoe Capital, LLC (FKA: Glencoe Investment Corporation), 356
Glenmede Trust Company, 490
Global Crossing Ventures (FKA: Frontier Ventures), 185
Global Finance SA, 828
Global Internet Ventures (GIV), 693
Global Partner Ventures, 694
Global Retail Partners (A.K.A. GRP), 185
Global Technology Ventures (GTV), 829
Global Venture Capital Corporation, 829
Glynn Capital Management, 186
Glynn Ventures, 186
GMA Capital LLC (AKA: InvestCare Partners, L.P.), 459
GMAC-Residential Funding, 468
GMS Capital, 534
GO Capital, 829
Go Equity GmbH, 829
Goldner Hawn Johnson & Morrison Incorporated, 468
Golub Associates, 534
Goodwill Communication, Inc., 830
GorillaPark, 830
Grace Venture Capital (AKA: Grace Internet Capital), 424
Grand Central Holdings, 535
Grand Pacific Venture Capital Company Ltd., 830
Granite Ventures LLC (FKA: H & Q Venture Associates), 186
Granville Baird Capital Partners (FKA:Granville Pr Eq Mngrs), 830
Granville Private Equity Spain, 831
Graphite Capital (FKA: F&C Ventures Ltd), 831
Gray Ventures, 335
Grayson & Associates, 280
Graystone Venture Partners, LLC(AKA:Portage Venture Partners, 356
Great Hill Equity Partners, LLC, 424

Greater Philadelphia Venture Capital Corp., 627
Green Mountain Advisors, Inc., 689
Greenfield Technology Ventures, 187
Greenstone Venture Partners, 832
Greenwich Venture Partners, Inc., 296
Gresham CEA Management Limited, 832
Gresham Rabo Management Limited, 832
Greylock, 424
Grieve, Horner, Brown & Asculai, 833
Grosvenor Funds, The, 315
Grotech Capital Group, 394
Grove Street Advisors, LLC, 425
Growth Factory, The, 833
Growth Venture Group Pty Ltd., 833
GrowthWorks Capital, 834
Gryphon Ventures, 425
GTCR Golder Rauner, LLC, 356
Guide Ventures, 706
Gujarat Venture Finance Limited, 834

H

H&Q Asia Pacific, Ltd., 187
Halder Holdings B.V., 835
Hallador Venture Partners, 188
Halpern, Denny & Co., 425
Hambro America Biosciences, Inc., 535
Hambro European Ventures (Hambros PLC), 835
Hambros Bank, 535
Hamilton Portfolio, Ltd., 836
Hamilton Robinson & Co., Inc., 296
Hamon Investment Corporation, 836
Hanbyuck Investment Co Ltd, 836
HANNOVER Finanz GmbH, 837
Hanover Capital Corp., 535
Hansol Investment Inc., 837
Harbert Management Corp., 130
Harbison Corporation, 477
Harbour Financial Co., 426
HarbourVest Partners, LLC., 426
Harvest Partners, Inc., 536
Health Capital Group, 188
Healthcare Ventures LLC (FKA: Healthcare Investments), 490
Heartland Capital Fund, Ltd., 479
Heartland Capital Partners, L.P., 665
Heidelberg Innovation GmbH, 837
Hellman & Friedman, 189
Henry & Co., 323
Herbert Young Securities, Inc., 536
Heritage Partners, 427
HFS Capital (AKA: Hoffman, Fitzgerald & Snyder), 694
HFTP Investment LLC, 537
Hibernia Capital Partners, 837
Hickory Venture Capital Corporation, 130
High Desert Ventures Inc, 499
High Street Capital, LLC, 357
Highland Capital Partners, 427
Higin Venture Capital Co., Ltd., 838
Hikari Tsushin Capital, Inc., 838
HillStreet Capital, Inc., 612
Hitachi America, Ltd., 189
HMS Group, 189
HMS Hawaii Management Partners, 341
HMS Holtron Management Services, Ltd, 838
HO2 Partners LLC, 665
Hoak Capital Corp., 666
Hodgson Martin, Ltd., 839
Hoebich Venture Management, Inc., 190
Holding Capital Group, Inc., 537
Holland Venture B.V. (FKA: Holland Venture Holding C.V.), 839
Hollinger Capital (FKA: Hollinger Ventures), 537
HomeSeekers.com, 480
Honho Consulting Company Limited, 839
Horizon Ventures (F.K.A. Technology Investments), 190
Horizonte Venture Management GmbH, 840
Hotung International Company, Ltd., 840
Housatonic Partners, 190
Houston Venture Partners (AKA: Houston Partners), 666
Howard, Lawson & Co., 628
HPI Holding SA, 841
HRLD Venture Partners, 395
HSBC Private Equity (Asia), Ltd. (FKA: HSBC PE Management), 841
HSBC Private Equity Ltd (FKA Montagu Private Equity Ltd), 841
HSBC Ventures (UK) Ltd, 842
HT Capital Advisors, LLC, 538
Hudson Venture Partners, 538
Humana Venture Capital, 384
Hummer Winblad Venture Partners, 191
Hungarian-American Enterprise Fund, The (HAEF), 842
Hunt Capital Group, 667
Hunt Ventures, LP, 667
Hydro-Quebec CapiTech Inc., 843
Hyundai Venture Capital Co., Ltd., 843

I

i-Hatch Ventures, LLC, 539
i2b Ventures, 667
i2i Venture, 843
i2s PLC (FKA: Tarpan PLC), 843
IAI Ventures, Inc.(AKA: Investment Advisors), 468
iAsia Alliance Capital, 844
IBB Beteiligungsgesellschaft mbH, 844
IBJS Capital Corp., 539
IBK Capital Corporation, 844
ICC Venture Capital, 845
ICF Ventures Private Ltd., 845
ICICI Venture Funds Mngt. Co. Ltd., 846
Idanta Partners, Ltd., 191
IDG Technology Venture Investment Inc. (FKA: PTV-China), 846
IDG Ventures, 192
IDI-Kairos, 847
IEG Venture Management, Inc., 357
iEmerge Ventures, 477
IFCI Venture Cap. Funds (Formerly Risk Capital & Tech.), 847
iFormation Group, 296
iGlobe Partners Limited, 847
Ignite Associates, LLC, 192
Ignition Corporation, 706
IKB Venture Capital GmbH (AKA IKB Beteiligungsgesellschaft, 848
IL&FS Venture Corporation (FKA. CreditCapital Venture Fund), 848

imGO (AKA: Investor Mobile GO; FKA: Guoco Land Ltd.), 848
IMH Industrie Management Holding GmbH, 848
iMinds (FKA: Interactive Minds), 193
Imlay Investments, 335
Impact Venture Partners, 539
Imperial Ventures, Inc., 193
Impex Venture Management Co., 540
Incepta LLC, 706
Incorporated Investors, 193
IndAsia Fund Advisors Private Limited, 849
Indekon Management Oy, 849
Index Ventures, 850
Indian Direct Equity Advisors Pvt. Ltd, 850
Indocean Chase Capital Advisors, 850
Indosuez Ventures, 194
Indus Venture Management Ltd., 851
Industrial Technology Investment Corporation, 851
Industrial Technology Securities Ltd, 851
Industry Ventures, 428
Infineon Ventures, 852
Infinity Capital LLC, 194
Infinity Technology Investments Pvt. Ltd., 852
Inflexion plc, 852
Infocomm Investments Pte Ltd (IIPL), 852
Information Technology Ventures, 195
IngleWood Ventures, 195
Inman & Bowman, 195
InnoCal, L.P., 196
InnoFinance Oy (FKA Culminatum Oy), 852
Innova Capital (FKA: Poland Partners Management Company), 853
Innovacom, 853
Innovation Capital Associates Ltd, 853
Innovation Works, Inc., 628
Innovationsagentur Gesmbh, 854
InnovationsKapital Management Goteborg AB, 854
Innovest Group, Inc., 629
Innvotec Ltd, 854
Inova Capital SCR, 855
Inroads Capital Partners, L.P., 358
Insight Capital Partners LLC, 540
Institutional Venture Partners, 196
Insurance Venture Partners, Inc., 297
Integra Ventures (F.K.A. Integra Bio-Health Inc.), 706
Integrated Consortium, Inc., 197
InterEquity Capital Partners, L.P., 541
Interfase Capital Partners LP, 667
Intermediate Capital Group PLC, 855
Internet Healthcare Group, 297
Internet Incubator PLC, 856
Internet Ventures Scandinavia A/S, 856
internet.com, 297
Interpacific Venture Group Incorporated, 856
Interprise Technology Partners, L.P., 323
Interregnum, 856
Intersouth Partners, 601
InterWest Partners, 197
Invencor, Inc., 198
inVentures Management Ltd, 857
Invesco Private Capital (FKA: Chancellor), 541
InvestAmerica Venture Group, Inc., 380
InveStar Capital, Inc., 857
Investissement Desjardins, 857
Investissements Novacap (AKA:Novacap Investments, Inc.), 858
Investment Securities of Colorado, Inc., 280
Invision AG (FKA Aureus Private Equity AG), 858
IPE Capital-Soc.De Cap.De Risoc SA, 859
IPS Industrial Promotion Services, Ltd., 859
Ireka Venture Capital Limited, 860
Ironside Ventures, LLC (FKA: MF Private Capital), 429
Irwin Ventures LLC (FKA: Irwin Ventures Incorporated), 377
Isabella Capital LLC, 613
ISEP NV, 860
Israel Seed Partners, 860
IT Provider Advisor, 861
ITACT, 861
Itochu Technology, 542
ITP-Management N.V., 861

J

J&W Seligman & Company, 542
J.E. Mann & Co., 542
J.F. Shea & Company, 198
J.L. Albright Venture Partners, 861
J.P. Morgan Capital Corp., 542
J.P. Morgan Partners (FKA: Chase Capital Partners), 543
JAFCO Co. Ltd., 862
JAFCO Investment (FKA:Nomura/JAFCO Investment (Asia) Limited, 862
JAFCO Ventures, Inc., 198
James A. Matzdorff & Co., 199
James B. Kobak & Co., 297
Japan Asia Investment Co Ltd, 863
Japan/America Ventures, Inc., 544
JatoTech Management LLC, 668
Javva Partners LLC, 544
Jefferson Capital Fund, Ltd., 130
Jefferson Capital Partners, Ltd., 695
Jefferson Partners, 863
Jerusalem Global Ventures, 864
Jerusalem Venture Partners (AKA: JVP), 864
JK&B Capital, 358
JNet Ventures, 545
Johnston Associates, Inc., 490
Jordan, Edmiston Group, Inc., The, 545
Josephberg Grosz & Co., Inc., 545
JT Venture Partners, LLC, 491
Jump.Net Ventures, 668
JumpStartUp Fund Advisors Pvt. Ltd., 864
Juniper Networks, 199
Justsystem, Inc., 629

K

Kahala Investments, Inc., 668
Kaiser Permanente (AKA: National Venture Development), 200
Kangaroo Village, 865
Kankaku Investment Co Ltd, 865
Kansas City Equity Partners, 477
Kansas Technology Enterprise Corporation, 382
Kansas Venture Capital, Inc., 383
Kappa-IT Ventures, 865
Katalyst LLC, 630

Kaufmann Fund, Inc., The, 546
KB Partners, LLC, 359
KBL Healthcare Ventures, 546
Kemper Ventures, 491
Kennet Capital Ltd, 866
Kentucky Highlands Investment Corporation, 384
Kestrel Venture Management (FKA:Corning Venture Management), 429
Kettle Partners, L.P., 359
Key Equity Capital Corp.(AKA:Key Community Development Corp), 613
Keystone Minority Capital Fund, L.P., 630
Keystone Venture Capital Management Co., 630
Kick-Start Ventures, 866
Kidd, Kamm & Company, 298
Kinetic Ventures, Inc., 395
Kingsbury Associates, 200
Kinship Partners, 280
Kirlan Venture Capital, Inc., 707
Kitty Hawk Capital, 602
KLB Investment Co., Ltd., 866
Kleiner Perkins Caufield & Byers, 200
Kline Hawkes & Co., 201
KLM Capital Group, 201
Koch Ventures, 133
Kokusai Finance Co., Ltd., 867
Komatsu America International Company (KAIC), 360
Kookmin Venture Capital Co Ltd, 867
Koor Corporate Venture Capital, 868
Korda & Co., 868
Korea Development Investment Corp., 868
Korea Technology Finance Corp., 869
kpe Ventures, 546
KPMG Advent Management Group (FKA:Advent Western Pacific), 870
Kreditanstalt fur Wiederaufbau (KfW), 870
KTB Ventures (FKA: KTB Venture Capital), 202
Kyocera International, Inc., 202
Kyoritsu Capital Company, Ltd., 870

L

Ladybird Technologies, Ltd., 870
Lake Shore Capital Partners, Inc., 360
Lambda Funds, The, 546
Lancet Capital Partner(FKA:Caduceus Capital Partners), 429
Landmark Partners, Inc., 298
Las Americas Administradora, 871
LaSalle Capital Group, Inc., 360
Launch Center 39, 547
Launchworks Inc., 871
Lawrence Financial Group, 202
Lazard Asia Investment Management (Private) Limited, 871
Lazard Technology Partners, 547
Leachman Steinberg Venture Partners, 695
Lee Munder Venture Partners, 430
Legal & General Ventures Ltd, 872
Legendary Investments PLC, 872
Leonard Green & Partners, 203
Leonard Mautner Associates, 203
Lepercq Capital Management, Inc.(AKA:Lepercq,de Neuflize In), 548
Levensohn Capital Management L.L.C, 204
LeVenture Kapitalbeteiligungsgesellschaft mbH & Co.KG, 872
Levine Leichtman Capital Partners, Inc., 204
Lewis Hollingsworth, 669
Lexington Partners, Inc. (FKA: LPNY Advisors, Inc.), 548
LF International, Inc., 204
LG Venture Investment Inc., 873
Liberty BIDCO Investment Corporation, 459
Liberty Environmental Partners, 205
Liberty Venture Partners, Inc., 631
Libon Capital Management Limited, 873
Life Science Ventures, 873
Life Sciences Partners BV, 874
Lighthouse Capital Partners, 205
Lightspeed Venture Partners (FKA: Weiss, Peck & Greer), 206
LINC Capital Partners, Inc., 361
Lincoln Investment Management Inc., 378
Lincolnshire Management Inc., 548
Lippo Group, 874
LiveOak Equity Partners, 335
Livingston Capital, Ltd., 281
LJH Global Investments, 324
LLR Equity Partners, 631
LM Capital Corp., 324
LN Mittal, 874
Loeb Partners Corp., 549
Lombard Investments, Inc., 206
London Merchant Security (AKA LMS), 874
London Ventures (Fund Managers) Ltd., 875
LoneTree Capital Partners, 281
Long Island Venture Fund L.P., 549
Long-Term Partners Limited, 875
Longworth Venture Partners, L.P., 430
Lost Boys Incubator, 875
Lovett Miller & Co. Incorporated, 325
Loyalhanna Venture Fund, 631
LRM Investeringsmaatschappij Voor Limburg, 875
LTI Ventures Leasing Corp., 298
Lubar & Co., 718
Lucent Venture Partners, Inc., 207
LV Capital (AKA LVMH/Group Arnault), 876
Lycos Ventures, 632

M

M&A West Incorporated, 207
M&F Associates, L.P., 549
M/C Venture Partners, 431
M31 Ventures, LLC, 550
Macquarie Direct Investment Limited, 876
Macquarie Investment Management Ltd (MIML), 876
Macquarie Technology Funds Management, 876
Macromedia Ventures, 208
Madison Dearborn Partners, LLC, 361
Madison Investment Partners, Inc., 550
Madrona Venture Group, 707
Magic Venture Capital, LLC, 208
Magnum Communications (AKA: MCF Advisory Services Ltd), 877
Main Street Equity Advisors, LLC, 669
Malmohus Invest AB, 877
Management Resource Partners, 208

Manchester Humphreys, Inc., 642
Mangrove Capital Partners SA, 878
Manhattan Venture Co., Inc., 550
Mapleleaf Capital Corp., 669
march.fifteen AG (FKA Peterp@n), 878
Marconi Ventures, 431
Maristeth Ventures, L.L.C., 707
MarketCorp Ventures L.P., 299
Marks and Spencer Ventures Ltd, 878
Marlborough Capital Advisors, 431
Marleau, Lemire, Inc., 878
Marquette Venture Partners, 362
Marwit Capital LLC, 209
Maryland Venture Capital Trust, 395
Massachusetts Capital Resource Co., 432
Massachusetts Institute of Technology, 432
Massachusetts Technology Development Corp. (MTDC), 432
Massey Burch Capital Corp., 650
Materia Ventures Associates,L.P. (FKA:Pierce Nordquist Asso), 708
Maton Venture, 209
Matrix Capital, 695
Matrix Group, 209
Matrix Partners, 433
Matrix Private Equity, 879
MAVA Investment Management kft (AKA: Hungarian-American Ent), 879
Maveron LLC., 708
Mayfair Capital Partners, Inc., 551
Mayfield Fund, 210
Mayo Medical Ventures, 468
MBA Venture Group, 669
MBW Management, Inc., 492
MC Capital Asia Private Limited, 880
MC Capital, Inc., 551
McCown De Leeuw & Co., 210
MCG Ventures, 696
McGraw-Hill Ventures, 552
McGuire Capital Corp., 670
MCH Private Equity SA, 880
McKee & Co., 134
McLean Watson Capital Inc., 880
MDS Discovery Venture Management, Inc., 881
MDS Health Ventures, Inc. (AKA: MDS Capital Corp.), 881
MDT Advisers, Inc., 433
Med-Tech Ventures, Inc., 492
MedEquity Investors LLC, 434
Media Venture Partners, 211
MediaVenture Capital AG & Co. KGaA, 882
Medical Imaging Innovation & Investments, L.P (AKA: Mi3), 434
Medical Innovation Partners, 469
Medical Science Partners, 434
Medical Venture Holdings, Inc., 552
Medicis AG, 882
Medicon Valley Capital, 882
Medicus Venture Partners, 211
Mediphase Venture Partners (FKA: EHealth Technology Fund), 434
Medmax Ventures, L.P., 299
MedTech International, Inc., 670
MedVenture Associates, 212
Mees Pierson Investeringsmaat. B.V., 435
Megunticook Management, 435
Mellon Ventures (AKA: Mellon Bank), 632
Memhard Investment Bankers, Inc., 300
Menlo Ventures, 212
Mentor Capital Partners, 633
Mercantile Mutual Investment Management Limited, 883
Mercator Broadband Partners, L.P., 696
Mercury Private Equity, 883
Mercury Ventures Ltd., 670
Meridian Venture Partners (MVP), 633
Merifin Capital Group, 883
Merita Capital Limited, 134
Merita Capital Ltd, 884
Meritage Private Equity Fund, 281
Meritech Capital Partners, 212
Merlin Biosciences (AKA Merlin Ventures), 884
Merrill Lynch Investment Managers FKA Mercury Asset Mgmt, 884
Merrill, Pickard, Anderson & Eyre, 213
MESBIC Ventures Holding Co. (AKA Pacesetter Growth Fund, L.P, 671
Mesirow Private Equity Investments, Inc., 362
Metapoint Partners, 435
Metropolitan Venture Partners (MetVP), 553
meVC.com, 213
Meyer, Duffy & Associates, 553
Mezzanine Management UK Limited, 885
Microtechnology Investments, Ltd., 213
Mid-Atlantic Venture Funds (FKA: NEPA Management Corp.), 634
Middlefield Capital Fund, 885
Midinvest Oy, 886
Midlands Venture Fund Managers Ltd. (AKA: Midven Ltd), 886
Milestone Venture Partners, 553
Millennium Three Venture Group, L.L.C., 480
Miller Capital Corp, 135
Miller/Zell Venture Group, 335
Minnesota Management Partners, 469
Minotaur Capital Management, 363
Miralta Capital, Inc., 887
Mission Ventures, 214
Mitiska NV, 887
Mitsui & Co., Ltd., 553
Mitsui Marine Capital Co., Ltd., 887
MK Global Ventures, 214
MMC adVentures Ltd, 888
MMG Ventures, L.P., 396
Mofet Venture Capital, 888
Mohr, Davidow Ventures, 214
Monarch Capital Partners, LLC, 336
Montgomerie, Huck & Co., 888
Montgomery Associates, Inc., 215
Montgomery Medical Ventures, L.P., 215
Montreux Equity Partners, 216
Monument Advisors, Inc, 378
Monumental Venture Partners, LLC, 696
Moore & Associates, 619
Moore Capital Management Inc., 554
Morel Ventures Limited, 888
Morgan Grenfell Private Equity Limited, 889
Morgan Stanley Venture Partners (AKA: MSDW), 554
Morgenthaler Ventures, 614

Morningside Group, 363
Mosaic Venture Partners, 889
Mosaix Ventures, LLC, 363
Motorola Inc., 315
Mountaineer Capital LP, 716
MPM Capital (FKA - MPM Asset Management LLC), 436
MSC Venture Corporation Sdn. Bhd., 890
MST Partners, 555
MTI Partners Ltd, 890
Multiventure Investment, Inc., 890
Murphree Venture Partners, 671
Mustang Ventures (FKA Siemens Mustang Ventures), 216
Mutual Fund Public Company Ltd., 891
MVC AG (AKA Mitteldeutsche Venture Capital AG), 891
MVI Sverige AB, 891
MVM Ltd, 891
MVP Ventures (AKA: Milk Street Ventures), 436
MWV Capital Partners (FKA:Middlewest Ventures, L.P.), 378

N

Nantucket Capital Management, 459
Nanyang Ventures Pty Ltd (AKA: Nanyang Management Pty Ltd), 892
Nassau Capital, L.L.C., 492
National Australia Investment Capital Limited, 892
National Bank Of Kuwait, 555
National City Equity Partners, Inc, 614
National Corporate Finance, Inc., 217
National Enterprise Company, Ltd., 892
National Financial Cos. LLC, 556
National Investment Management, Inc., 217
Native Venture Capital Co., Ltd., 893
Natural Gas Partners, 300
Navis Investment Partners (Asia) Limited, 893
Navis Partners (FKA:Fleet Equity Partners), 643
Nazem & Co., 556
NCB Ventures Limited, 893
nCoTec Ventures Ltd, 893
NCP Advisors Philippines, Inc., 894
Needham & Company, Inc., 556
Nelson Capital Corp., 651
NeoCarta Ventures, 437
NeoMed Management AS (FKA Medical Venture Management), 894
Nesbitt Burns, 363
Net Partners, 895
Netalone.com Ltd, 895
NetCatalyst, 218
NetFuel Ventures, 364
Netjuice, 895
Netscape Communications, 218
NetSpark Ventures N.V., 895
NetworkAsia, 896
Networks Associates, Inc., 218
Neurone Venture Capital, 896
New Business Capital Fund Ltd., 499
New England Partners, 437
New Enterprise Associates, 396
New Horizons Venture Capital, 697
New Jersey Technology Council (AKA:NJTC), 493
New Millennium Partners, LLC, 218
New South Ventures, 325
New Things, LLC, 557
New Venture Resources, 282
New Vista Capital, LLC, 218
New World Infrastructure Limited, 896
New World Venture Advisors, 364
New York Life Venture Capital Group, 557
New York State Science & Technology Foundation, 558
Newbridge Capital Limited, 219
Newbury Ventures, 220
Newbury, Piret & Co., Inc., 437
NewMargin Venture Capital, 897
Newport Capital Group Pty Ltd, 897
NewSpring Ventures, 634
Newtek Capital, 558
Newtek Ventures, 220
Nexit Ventures Oy, 897
Next Ventures Limited, 897
NextGen Capital LLC, 697
NextGen Partners LLC, 221
NextPoint Partners L.P.(FKA: Plaza Street), 315
Nextreme Ventures, 221
Nexus Group LLC, 221
NIB Capital Private Equity N.V. (FKA: Parnib Holding NV), 898
NIF Ventures Co., Ltd., 898
NIF Ventures USA, Inc.(Nippon Investment & Finance Co., Ltd), 222
NIIT Ventures, 898
Nikko Capital Co Ltd, 899
Nippon Technology Venture Partners Ltd., 899
Nippon Venture Capital Co., Ltd., 899
Nmas1 Electra Capital Privado , S.G.E.C.R., S.A., 900
NMT New Medical Technologies, 900
Nokia Venture Partners (AKA: Nokia Oy), 222
Nomura International, Plc., 900
Nomura/JAFCO Investment (HK) Limited, 901
Nord Innovation, 901
Noro-Moseley Partners, 336
North America Investment Corp., 902
North American Business Development Co., L.L.C., 364
North American Capital Corp., 559
North Atlantic Capital Corp., 389
North Bridge Venture Partners, 438
North Carolina Enterprise Fund, L.P., The, 602
North Carolina Technological Development Authority, Inc., 603
North Coast Technology Investors, L.P., 460
North Hill Ventures, 438
North Texas MESBIC, Inc., 672
North Texas Opportunity Fund, 672
NorthEast Ventures, 301
Northeast Ventures Corp., 469
Northern Stream Capital, 709
Northern Venture Managers Limited, 902
Northington Partners, 301
Northwest Ohio Venture Fund, 615
Northwest Venture Associates, Inc.(FKA:Spokane Capital Mgmt), 709
Northwood Ventures, 559
Northzone Ventures (FKA Venture Partners AS), 902
Norwest Equity Partners, 223
Norwood Venture Corp., 559
Notre Capital Ventures, 672

Novak Biddle Venture Partners, L.P., 697
Novartis AG, 903
Novell Ventures, 686
Noveltek Venture Corp., 560
Novo Networks (FKA: eVentures Group, Inc.), 672
Novus Ventures, 223
NPE Investment Advisors (AKA:Nordic Private Equity Partners), 903
NPM Capital (AKA Nederlandse Participatie MIJ NV), 903
NPV Capital Partners, LLC, 560
NTC Group, The, 301
Nth Power Technologies, Inc, 224
NTUC Club Investments Pte Ltd (NCI), 904
Nu Capital Access Group, Ltd., 224
Nucon Capital Corp., 439

O

Oak Hill Capital Management, Inc., 561
Oak Investment Partners, 302
Obelisk Capital Pty Ltd, 904
Oberlin Capital, L.P., 603
OCBC, Wearnes & Walden Investments (s), Ltd., 904
Odeon Capital Partners, L.P., 561
Odin Capital Group, 479
Odlander Fredrikson & Co, 904
Oem Capital, 302
Ohana Ventures, LLC, 615
Ohio Partners, 615
Olympus Capital Holdings Asia, 905
Omega Partners L.P., 493
OmniMed Corp., 673
OneLiberty Ventures (FKA: Morgan, Holland Ventures Corp.), 439
Onex Corp., 905
Onondaga Venture Capital Fund, Inc., 562
Onset Ventures, 225
Open Prairie Ventures, 365
Opportunity Capital Partners {FKA: Thompson Capital Mgt), 225
Optical Capital Group, 397
Oracle Corporation, 226
Orange Ventures, 905
Orchid Asia Holdings, 226
Oregon Resource and Technology Development Fund, 620
Oresa Ventures, S.A., 906
Orien Ventures, 303
Origin Ventures LLC, 365
Orion Partners, L.P., 439
Orix Capital Corporation, 906
Osborn Capital LLC, 440
Osprey Capital, LLC, 325
Osprey Ventures, L.P., 226
Ovation Capital Partners (FKA:iCentennial Ventures LLC), 562
OVP Venture Partners (FKA: Olympic Venture Partners), 709
Oxford Bioscience Partners, 440
Oxford Financial Services Corp., 698
Oxford Partners, 303

P

PA Early Stage (AKA:Pennsylvania Early Stage Partners), 635
Pac-Link Management Corporation, 906
Pacific Asset Partners, 226
Pacific Capital Partners, 907
Pacific Century Group Ventures Ltd., 907
Pacific Corporate Group, Inc., 227
Pacific Equity Partners, 907
Pacific Horizon Ventures LLC, 710
Pacific Northwest Partners SBIC, L.P., 710
Pacific Venture Group, 227
Pacific Venture Partners, 907
Pacifica Fund, 228
PacRim Venture Management, 228
Paladin Partners, 711
Palmer Partners, L.P., 441
Palmetto Seed Capital Corp., 645
Palomar Ventures, 228
PAMA Group Inc. (FKA:Prudential Asset Management Asia), 908
Pangaea Partners, 719
Pantheon Ventures Limited, 908
Pappajohn Capital Resources, 381
Paradigm Capital Partners LLC, 651
Paradigm Venture Partners I(FKA:Emerging Technology Partners, 131
Paragon Venture Partners, 229
Parcom Ventures BV, 909
Pari Capital AG, 909
Paribas Principal, Inc., 563
Part'com, 909
Partech International, 229
Partners Group, 910
Pathfinder Investment Co Pvt Ltd, 910
Pathfinder Venture Capital Funds, 470
Patricof & Co. Ventures, Inc., 563
Paul Capital Partners, 230
Pauli & Co., Inc., 477
Pecks Management Partners, Ltd., 564
Penfund Partners, Inc., 911
Peninsula Capital Partners, L.L.C, 460
PENMAN Partners (FKA PENMAN Asset Management LP), 365
Penn-Janney Fund, Inc., The, 635
Pennell Venture Partners, 564
Pennsylvania Growth Fund, 636
Penny Lane Partners, 493
Penta Capital Partners Ltd, 911
Pequot Capital Management Inc., 564
Perennial Ventures (FKA: Tredegar Investments), 711
Perseus LLC, 316
Petra Capital Partners LLC, 652
Pfingsten Partners, L.P., 366
Philadelphia Ventures, Inc., 636
Phillips-Smith Specialty Retail Group, 673
Phoenix Equity Partners (FKA: DLJ European Private Equity), 911
Phoenix Growth Capital Corp., 231
Phoenix Home Life Mutual Insurance Co., 303
Phoenix Partners, The, 711
Piedmont Venture Partners, 604
Pierce Financial Corporation(FKA:Pierce Investment Banking), 698
Pilotbird, 912
Pino Venture Partners, 912
Pittsford Group, Inc., The, 565
Platinum Group, Inc., The, 565
PME Capital, 912
Poalim Capital Markets Technologies, Ltd., 913

Point Venture Partners, 636
Point West Ventures (FKA: Fourteen Hill Capital, L.P., 231
Polaris Venture Capital, 913
Polaris Venture Partners, 441
Polestar Capital, Inc., 366
Poly Ventures, 566
PolyTechnos Venture Partners GmbH, 913
Pomona Capital, 566
Portview Communications Partners, 914
Potomac Ventures, 397
Powershift Group, 674
PowerWord Capital Management, Inc., 914
PPM Ventures Ltd (FKA: Prudential Venture Managers Ltd), 914
pre-IPO Aktiengesellschaft, 915
Prelude Technology Investments Ltd, 915
Premier Medical Partner Fund L.P., 231
Prescient Capital, 232
Primaxis Technology Ventures Inc., 916
Prime Capital Management Co., Inc., 304
Prime New Ventures, 674
Prime Technology Ventures NV, 916
Primedia Ventures, 567
PrimePartners Asset Management Pte. Ltd., 916
Primus Venture Partners, Inc., 616
Prince Ventures, 367
Prism Capital, 367
Prism Venture Partners, 441
Private Capital Corp., 131
Private Equity Investors, Inc., 567
Private Equity Partners, 674
Priveq Capital Funds, 917
Procuritas Partners KB, 917
Productivity Fund I & II, The, 367
ProQuest Investments, L.P., 493
ProSeed Capital Holdings CVA, 917
Prospect Partners LLC (FKA:Kenter, Glatris & Tuttle, LLC, 368
Prospect Street Ventures (FKA:Prospect Street Invest. Mgmt), 567
Prospect Venture Partners (FKA: Prospect Management, LLC), 232
Provco Group, The, 637
ProVen Private Equity (FKA:Guinness Mahon Development Cap.), 918
Providence Equity Partners, Inc.(FKA: Providence Ventures), 643
Proximitas AG Venture Capital, 918
Psilos Group Managers LLC, 568
PSINet Ventures, 699
Ptek Ventures, 336
Putnam Lovell Capital Partners, L.P., 232
Pyramid Technology Ventures, 919
Pythagoras NV, 919

Q
Q Ventures, 674
Quadriga Capital Management GMBH, 919
Quaestus & Co. Inc. (FKA: Quaestus Management Corp..), 719
Quantum Capital Partners, 325
Quantum Fund, Ltd., 920
Quest Ventures, 233
Quester Capital Management Ltd, 920
QuestMark Partners, L.P., 397

R
R-H Capital Partners, 337
R. Chaney & Co., Inc., 674
RAF Ventures, 637
Ralph Wilson Equity Fund, L.L.C., 460
Rand Capital Corporation, 568
Rare Ventures, 569
Raza Foundries, 233
RBC Dominion Securities Corporation, 569
RBC Ventures, Inc., 619
RCT BioVentures NE (Research Corporation Technologies), 442
Reach Incubator, 442
Recovery Equity Investors, L.P., 234
Red Hat Ventures, 604
Red River Ventures, 675
Red Rock Capital, 687
Red Rock Ventures, 234
red-stars.com, 920
Redleaf Venture Management, 234
Redpoint Ventures, 235
Redwood Capital Corp., 235
Redwood Venture Partners, LLC., 235
Regent Capital Management, 569
Regent Pacific Private Equity, 920
Regulus International Capital Co., Inc., 304
Rein Capital, 494
Reiten & Co Strategic Investments AS, 921
Renaissance Capital Corp., 337
Renaissance Partners, 921
Renaissance Ventures, 699
Reprise Capital Corp., 569
RFE Investment Partners, 305
RHO Management, 570
Rice, Sangalis, Toole & Wilson (FKA: Rice Capital Partners), 675
Richard Jaffe & Co., Inc., 676
Richland Ventures, 652
Ridge Capital Partners, L.L.C., 368
Ridgewood Capital Management LLC, 494
Riggs Capital Partners, 316
Riordan, Lewis & Haden, 236
River Associates, LLC, 653
River Capital, 338
Riverside Management Group, 570
RiverVest Venture Partners, 478
RMB Ventures Limited, 921
Roanoke Capital, Ltd., 712
Robertson Stephens & Company, LLC, 236
Rock Creek Partners, L.P., 326
Rock Hill Ventures Inc.(FKA:Hillman Medical Ventures,Inc.), 638
Rocket Ventures, 237
RockMountain Ventures, 282
Rocky Mountain Capital Partners (FKA:Hanifen Imhoff Capital), 283
Rosecliff, 237
Rosenfeld & Co., 620
Roser Ventures LLC, 283
Rosewood Capital, L.P., 237
Rosewood Stone Group, 238
Rothschild Bioscience Unit, 922
Rothschild Ventures Asia Pte Ltd., 922
Rothschild Ventures, Inc., 570

Royal Bank Private Equity (FKA: Royal Bank Development Cap), 922
Royalty Capital Fund, L.P. I/Royalty Capital Management, Inc, 443
RoyNat Ventures, 923
RRE Ventures LLC, 571
RRZ Capital, 638
RSA Ventures, 443
Ruddick Investment Co., 604
Russel Miller Advisors Asia, LLC, 238
Rustic Canyon Ventures (FKA: TMCT Ventures, L.P.), 238
Rutledge & Co., Inc., 305
RWI Group, LP, 239

S

S-Refit GmbH & Co KG, 923
S.R. One, Limited, 638
Saarlandische Wagnisfinanzierungsgesellschaft mbh (AKA SWG), 924
Sadot Venture Capital Management (1992) Ltd, 924
SAE Ventures, 306
Saffron Hill Ventures (FKA LootLab Ltd.), 924
Sagaponack Partners LLC, 239
Sage Management Group, 444
Sagebrook Technology, 676
Salix Ventures, L.P., 653
Salomon Smith Barney Venture Services LLC, 571
San Francisco Sentry Investment Group(AKA: Storie Partners), 239
Sand Aire Private Equity Ltd, 924
Sanderling Ventures, 239
Sandhurst Venture Fund, L.P., The, 639
Sandler Capital Management, 571
Sandlot Capital LLC, 283
Sandton Financial Group, 240
Sanpaolo IMI Private Equity S.p.A., 925
Sapient Capital, 721
Saskatchewan Government Growth Fund, 925
Saugatuck Capital Company, 306
Savoy/Socios Fondos de Financiacon Management, 925
SBC Communications, 676
SBC Equity Partners, Inc., 369
SBC Ventures, 499
SBCA/A.G. Bartholomew & Associates, 131
SBV Venture Partners (AKA:Sigefi, Burnette & Vallee), 240
Scheer & Company, 306
Schneider Electric Ventures, 926
Schoffstall Ventures, 639
Schooner Capital International, L.P., 444
Schroder Capital Partners (Asia) Pte Ltd, 926
Schroder Ventures, 445
Schroder Ventures International Life Sciences, 445
Scientific-Atlanta, 338
Scoot.com PLC, 926
Scottish Development Finance (SDF), 927
Scottish Equity Partners Limited, 927
Scripps Ventures, 572
Seacoast Capital, 446
Seaflower Ventures, 446
Seapoint Ventures, 712
Seaport Capital, 572
SEB e-invest, 927
SEB Foretagsinvest, 927
Seed Capital Investments, 928
Seed Capital Ltd, 928
Seed Capital Partners, 573
Seed Company Partners, 676
Seidman, Jackson, Fisher & Co., 369
Selby Venture Partners, 241
SENMED Medical Ventures, 616
Sentinel Capital Partners, 573
Sequel Venture Partners, 284
Sequoia Capital, 241
ServiceMaster Venture Fund,LLC(FKA:ServiceMaster Co.Ltd Par), 369
Sevin Rosen Management Co., 677
SGI Capital L.L.C, 573
Shad Run Investments, Inc., 242
Shalor Ventures, Inc., 446
Shanghai Information Investment (SII), 928
Shanghai International Asset Management (HK) Company Ltd, 929
Shannon Development Company, 929
Shansby Group/TSG2, L.P., The, 242
Shared Ventures, Inc., 470
Shattan Group, The, 574
Shaw Venture Partners (FKA: Shaw Glasgow Partners), 621
Shaw, Kwei & Partners Limited, 929
Shawmut Capital Partners, 447
Shelton Companies, Inc., The, 604
Shepherd Group LLC, The, 447
Sherbrooke Capital Partners, 448
Sherpa Partners, LLC, 471
Shigagin Capital Co., Ltd., 930
Shott Capital Management, 574
Shrem Fudim Kelner Technologies Ltd., 930
SI Ventures, 326
Siemens Venture Capital GmbH, 930
Sienna Ventures (FKA: Sienna Holdings Inc.), 242
Sierra Ventures, 243
Sigma Capital Corp., 327
Sigma Partners, 243
Signal Lake Venture Fund, LP, 307
Signature Capital, LLC., 575
Signia Ventures, 244
Siguler Guff & Company, LLC, 575
Silicon Alley Venture Partners LLC (AKA SAVP), 576
Silicon Valley Bank, 244
SilkRoute Capital Limited, 930
Silver Creek Technology Investors (FKA: O'Donnell & Masur), 677
Singapore Technologies Telemedia (AKA: ST Telemedia), 931
SingTel Ventures, 931
Siparex Group (FKA:Siparex Provinces de France), 931
Sippl Macdonald Ventures I, L.P., 245
SISIR International Pte Ltd., 932
Sitra (AKA Finnish National Fund for Research and Dev.), 932
Sixty Wall Street SBIC Fund, 576
SK Global Co., Ltd., 932
Skyline Ventures, 245
Skywood Ventures, 246
Small Industries Development Bank of India (SIDBI), The, 933
Smart Technology Ventures, 246

SMIFS Venture Capital Limited, 933
Societe Generale- Private Equity Activity, 933
Societe Regionale d'Investissement de Bruxelles (SRIB/GIMB), 933
Sofinnova Partners, 934
Sofinnova Ventures, 246
Sofinov (AKA:Caisse de depot et placement du Quebec), 934
SOFTBANK Capital Partners, 448
Softbank China Venture Capital, 935
Softbank Corp., 935
SOFTBANK Venture Capital (FKA: SOFTBANK Technology Ventures), 247
Softcapital, Inc., 935
Solera Capital LLC, 576
Solstice Capital LLC, 449
Sonera Corporation Corporate Venture Capital, 935
Sopartec SA, 936
Sorrento Associates, Inc., 247
SoundView Financial Group, Inc., 307
South Atlantic Venture Funds, L.P., 327
Southeast Interactive Technology Funds, 605
Southeastern Technology Fund, 132
Southern California Ventures, 247
Southern Capitol Ventures, 605
Southport Partners, 307
Southwest Venture Group, 678
Southwest Venture Partnerships, The, 678
Sovereign Capital (FKA:Nash, Sells & Partners Limited), 936
SpaceVest, 699
Sparkventures, LLC, 449
Spectrum Equity Investors, L.P., 248
Spectrum Venture Management, 937
Speed Ventures, 937
SPEF Banques Populaires, 937
Speirs Consultants, Inc., 938
Spencer Trask Ventures, Inc. (FKA: Spencer Trask Securities), 576
Spinnaker Ventures, 249
Spire Capital (FKA: Waller Capital Corp.), 577
Sponsored Consulting Services, 249
Sports Capital Partners, 577
Spray Venture Partners, 450
Spring Capital Partners, L.P., 398
Springboard Venture Managers PLC, 938
Springboard-Harper Investment Pte. Ltd., 938
Sprout Group, 578
Sputnik Technology Ventures, 938
Square One Ventures (AKA: Smaby Group), 471
SRK Management Co., 578
SsangYong Cement (Singapore) Ltd, 939
SSM Ventures, 653
St. Paul Venture Capital, Inc., 471
Staenberg Private Capital, LLC, 713
Stamford Financial, 579
Standard Life Investments (Private Equity) Ltd, 939
Stanford Keene, 606
Star Capital Group, Inc., 939
Star-Ventures Management GMBH (SVM), 940
Start-up Australia Pty Limited, 940
STARTech, 679
StarTech Partners, Ltd., 941
Starter Fluid, 250
Starting Point Partners, 250
State Street Bank & Trust Co., 338
Stephens Group, Inc., 137
Sterling Grace Capital Management, L.P., 579
Sterling Venture Partners, 398
Sterling/Carl Marks Capital {FKA - Sterling Commercial, 580
Sternhill Partners, 679
Steve Walker & Associates, LLC, 399
Still River Fund, The, 450
Stolberg Partners, 580
Stonebridge Partners, 580
StoneGate Partners, L.L.C., 450
Stonepath Europe, 941
Strategic Capital Group Hong Kong Limited, 941
Strategic Capital Management, 941
Strategic Investment Management, 700
Strategic Investments & Holdings, Inc., 581
Stratford Equity Partners, L.P., 679
Strathdon Investments Ltd, 942
Stratos Ventures Ltd Oy, 942
Sucsy, Fischer & Co., 370
SudKB & SudVC, 942
Suez Asia Holdings Pte Ltd., 943
Summit Capital Associates, Inc., 581
Summit Capital Group, 680
Summit Group Ltd, The, 943
Summit Partners, 451
Sun Hung Kai Properties Limited, 943
Sun Valley Ventures, 250
Sundance Venture Partners, L.P., 251
SUNeVision Holdings Ltd, 944
Sunrise Capital Partners, 582
Sunsino Development Associate Inc., 944
Sunwestern Investment Group, 680
Sustainable Jobs Fund (SJF), The, 606
Sutter Hill Ventures, 251
Swander Pace Capital, 252
Swedestart Management AB, 944
Swedish Industrial Development Fund (AKA Industrifonden), 945
Sweeney & Co., Inc., 308
Sybase, Inc., 252
Sycamore Ventures, 494
Synerfi S.A., 945
Synergy Partners, 252
Synergy Ventures, 582
Synopsys, Inc., 253
Syntel Inc. Web Incubator Program, 461

T

T. Rowe Price Threshold Partnerships, 399
TA Associates, Inc., 451
Tailink Venture Partners, 946
Taiwan United Venture Management Corporation, 946
Taiwan W&S Financial Management Incorporated, 946
Tamir Fishman Ventures, 946
Tappan Zee Capital Corp., 495
Target Partners, 947
Taylor & Turner, 253
tbg Technologie-Beteiligungsgesellschaft mbH, 947
TCR Europe SA, 947
TDH, 639
TDH Capital, 640

Teak Investment Partners I Limited, 948
Teak Investment Partners II Limited, 948
Teak Investment Partners III Ltd., 948
TechFarm (AKA:TechFund Capital), 254
Techno Nord VC GmbH, 948
Techno-Venture Co. (Japan), 949
TechnoCap Inc, 949
Technologieholding VC GmbH, 950
Technology Associates Management Corporation, 950
Technology Crossover Ventures, 254
Technology Funding, 254
Technology Partners, 255
Technology Venture Partners Pty Ltd, 950
Technology Ventures Corp., 500
Technology Ventures, L.L.C., 339
TechnoPlus Ventures, 951
Technostart GmbH, 951
Techpacific.com Ltd., 951
TechSpace Xchange LLC (TSX), 582
Techxas Ventures, LLC, 681
TecVenture Partners GmbH, 952
Teknia Invest Oy, 952
Teknoinvest Management As, 952
Telecom Italia Ventures, 255
Telecom Partners (FKA:Telecom Management, LLC), 285
Telecom Venture Group Ltd. (TVG), 953
Telecommunications Development Fund (TDF), 316
TeleSoft Partners, 256
Telia Business Innovation AB, 953
Telos Venture Partners, 256
Telsoft Ventures, 953
Temasek Capital, 954
Tera Capital Corporation, 954
Texas Growth Fund Management, 681
TG Asia Ventures Limited, 954
THCG Inc., 582
ThinkVentures.com Ltd, 954
Third Coast Capital, 370
Third Millennium Venture Capital, Ltd., 256
Thoma Cressey Equity Partners, 371
Thomas Weisel Partners, LLC, 257
Thompson Clive & Partners Limited, 955
Thompson Clive, Inc., 257
Thorner Ventures, 258
Three Arch Partners, 258
Three Cities Research, Inc., 583
Throunarfelag Islands Plc(AKA:The Icelandic Finance&Invest.), 955
TI Capital (AKA: Technology & Internet Capital), 259
Tianguis Ltd, 956
Ticonderoga Capital, Inc. (FKA: Dillon Read Venture Capital), 452
Timberline Venture Partners, 713
TL Ventures, 640
Tokyo Marine Capital Company, 956
Tokyo Small & Medium Business Investment & Consultation Co., 956
Tokyo Venture Capital Co., Ltd., 957
Toll Technologies, 957
Top Taiwan Venture Capital Company, Ltd., 957
Top Technology Limited (AKA:Hambros-Advanced Technology Tru), 957
Toshiba Corporation, 958
Toucan Capital Corp., 399
Transamerica Mezzanine Financing, 645
Transamerica Technology Finance, 309
Transatlantic Capital Ltd., 958
Transcap Associates, Inc., 371
Transpac Capital Pte, Ltd., 958
Trellis Health Ventures, L.P., 259
Trellis Partners, 682
Triad Investors Corp, 319
Triad Media Ventures, 309
Triad Ventures, Ltd., 682
Triangle Venture Capital Group, 959
Tribune Ventures, 372
Trident Capital, 259
Trinity Ventures, 260
TriNova, 959
Triton Ventures, 682
Triune Capital, 260
True North Partners LLC, 583
TruePilot, LLC, 606
TrustCapital Partners NV, 959
TSG Capital Group, L.L.C., 309
TTC Ventures, 453
TTP Venture Managers (FKA: The Technology Partnership), 960
Tudor Investment Corporation, 583
Tvi Investments Bv, 960
TVM Techno Venture Management, 961
TVS Finance Ltd., 961
Twinning Ventures, 961
Twinwood Engineering Ltd, 962
Tyco Ventures, 261

U

U.S. Bancorp Capital Corporation, 472
U.S. Bancorp Piper Jaffray Ventures, Inc., 472
U.S. Medical Resources Corp., 616
U.S. Venture Partners, 261
UBF Mittelstandsfunanzierungs AG, 962
UBS Capital, 962
UBS Capital (AKA Phildrew Ventures), 963
Ulin & Holland, Inc., 453
Ulster Development Capital, Ltd., 963
UNC Ventures, 453
Union Street Capital Corp., 713
Union Venture Capital Corporation, 963
Union Venture Corp., 262
UniRock Management Corp., 285
Unit Trust of India (UTI), 964
UniversityAngels.com, 584
UOB Venture Management Pte Ltd., 964
Updata Venture Partners, 700
Upper Lake Growth Capital, 472
UPS Strategic Enterprise Fund, 339
US Trust Private Equity, 584
UST Capital Corp., 454
Utah Ventures II, L.P. (A.K.A. Union Ventures), 687

V

Valeo Ventures, 964
Valley Capital Corp., 654

Valley Ventures (FKA: Arizona Growth Partners, L.P.), 136
Value Management & Research AG (VMR), 965
Van Wagoner Capital Management, 262
Vanenburg Group, 965
Vanguard Venture Partners, 262
Vantage Partners L.L.C, 584
VantagePoint Venture Partners, 263
Vault Capital, 714
VCF Partners, 965
VCM Venture Capital Management, 965
Vector Capital, 263
Vector Fund Management, L.P. (FKA: Vector Securities), 372
Vega Capital Corp., 584
Venca Management, 263
Vencap Equities Alberta, Ltd., 966
Vencon Management, Inc., 585
Veneto Sviluppo S.p.a, 966
VenGlobal Capital, 264
Venkol Ventures, 586
VennWorks (FKA: IncuVest LLC), 586
Venrock Associates, 586
Ventana Financial Resources, Inc., 372
Ventana Global, 264
Ventech, 967
Ventex Management, Inc., 683
Venture Associates Partners, LLC, 654
Venture Associates, Ltd., 285
Venture Capital Fund Managers (Pty), Ltd., The, 967
Venture Capital Fund of America, Inc., 587
Venture Capital Fund of New England, The, 454
Venture Capital Management Corp., 328
Venture Capital Partners Pty Limited, 967
Venture Catalyst, 265
Venture First Associates, 328
Venture Frogs, LLC, 265
Venture Funding Group International, 587
Venture Funding, Ltd., 461
Venture Growth Associates, 265
Venture Investment Associates, 495
Venture Investment Management Company LLC (AKA: VIMAC), 454
Venture Investors Management LLC, 720
Venture Law Group, 266
Venture Management Associates, Inc., 329
Venture Management Services Inc. (FKA: AT&T Ventures), 496
Venture Opportunities Corp., 588
Venture Partners, 310
Venture Partners AG, 968
Venture Select, 968
Venture Strategy Partners, 266
Venture TDF Pte Ltd., 968
VentureCap Management GmbH (AKA VCH Equity Group AG), 969
VentureLink Holdings, 683
Venturepark Incubator (FKA grizzlyfarm AG), 969
Ventures Medical Associates, 683
Ventures West Management, Inc., 970
Veritas Venture Capital Management, Ltd., 970
Vero Group PLC, 684
Versant Ventures (FKA: Palladium Capital), 266
Vertex Management, 971
Vertex Management Israel (AKA: Vertex Management III Ltd.), 971
Vertical Group, The, 496
Vesta Capital Partners (AKA: Vesta Group, The), 971
Vickers Ballas Asset Management Pte Ltd., 972
Victory Ventures L.L.C., 588
VigEcom Limited, 972
Virginia Capital, 701
Viridian Capital LLC, 606
Viridian Capital Partners (FKA: Aurora Venture Partners), 607
Visa International, 267
Vision Capital Management (FKA Glenwood Capital), 267
Vista Capital Corp., 268
Vista Capital de Expansion S.A., 972
Vital Capital Limited, 973
Vitesse Semiconductor Corporation, 268
VIV NV (AKA Vlaamse Investeringvennootschap NV), 973
Viventures Inc., 973
VK Ventures, 268
Vlaamse Investeringvennootschap NV, 974
VLink Global Limited, 974
Volendam Capital Advisors,Inc., 269
Voyager Capital, 714
VP Private Equity Limited, 974
VS&A Communications Partners, L.P., 588
VTC Partners GmbH, 974
Vulcan Ventures, Inc., 714

W

W.R. Hambrecht & Co., LLC, 269
Wachovia, 340
Wachtel & Co., Inc., 317
Wakefield Group, 607
Walden Capital Management Corporation, 589
Walden International Investment Group (AKA: Walden Group), 269
Walden Israel, 975
WaldenVC, 270
Walnut Capital Corp., 701
Walnut Group, The, 617
Wand Partners, 589
Warburg, Pincus & Co., LLC. (FKA: E.M. Warburg, Pincus & Co), 590
Wasatch Venture Fund (FKA: Wasatch Venture Corporation), 687
Wasserstein, Perella & Co., Inc., 591
Watermill eVentures, 455
WE Simon & Sons, 496
Wedbush Capital Partners, 271
wellington partners venture capital GmbH, 975
Wellmax, Inc., 461
Welsh, Carson, Anderson & Stowe, 591
West Central Capital Corp., 684
West Midlands Enterprise Ltd, 976
Westar Capital, 271
WestBridge Capital Advisors (India) Pvt. Ltd., 976
Westbury Partners, 592
Western States Investment Group, 272
Western Technology Investment, 272
Westford Technology Ventures, L.P., 497
Weston Presidio Capital Management, 455
WestSphere Equity Investors, LP, 592

Wheatley Partners, 592
White Pines Management, L.L.C., 462
Whitney & Co. (FKA: J.H. Whitney & Co.), 310
WI Harper Group, 273
William A.M. Burden & Co., 593
William Blair Capital Partners, 373
William E. Simon & Sons (Asia) LDC, 977
Willis Stein & Partners, 374
Wind Point Partners, 462
Windamere Venture Partners, LLC, 273
Windjammer Capital Investors (FKA:Pacific Mezzanine Inv.), 273
Windward Holdings, 311
Windward Ventures (FKA: Coronado Capital), 274
Wingate Partners, L.P., 685
Winslow Partners LLC, 317
Winthrop Ventures, 593
Wit Capital Corporation, 594
Wit Japan Investment, Inc., 977
WITSoundview Ventures- Dawntreader Funds, 594
WK Associates, 977
WL Ventures (FKA:Lothian Enterprise Ltd.), 978
Wolf Ventures (AKA:Wolf Asset Management Corp.), 286
Women's Growth Capital Fund, 318
WomenAngles.net, 318
Woodside Fund, 274
Wooshin Development Finance Corp, 978
Working Ventures Canadian Fund, Inc., 978
Worldview Technology Partners, 275
Worms Capital Management, 594
WRF Capital, 715
WSI Holding Corporation, 595

X
XDL Intervest Capital Corp. (FKA: XDL Capital Corporation), 979
XL Vision Inc, 329

Y
Yablon Enterprises, Inc., 641
YankeeTek Ventures, 456
Yasuda Enterprise Development Co., Ltd.(FKA: Nippon Ent.Dev), 275
Yorkshire Fund Managers Ltd., 979
Young Associates Limited, 980
Yozma Venture Capital Ltd, 980

Z
Zephyr Internet Partners, 595
Zero Gravity Internet Group, Inc., 276
Zero Stage Capital Co., Inc., 456
Zodiac Venture Capital KB, 980
Zone Ventures, 276
Zouk Ventures, 980
ZS Fund, L.P., 595
Zurich Scudder Investments (FKA: Scudder Kemper Investments), 596